UNDER THE GENERAL EDITORSHIP OF

Robert Morss Lovett

PROFESSOR EMERITUS OF ENGLISH, THE UNIVERSITY OF CHICAGO

Writers

Edited by

SECOND EDITION

1967 Impression

OF THE WESTERN WORLD

Addison Hibbard, LATE DEAN OF THE

COLLEGE OF LIBERAL ARTS, NORTHWESTERN UNIVERSITY

BY Horst Frenz, PROFESSOR OF ENGLISH AND

COMPARATIVE LITERATURE, INDIANA UNIVERSITY

HOUGHTON MIFFLIN COMPANY *Boston*

NEW YORK · ATLANTA · GENEVA, ILL. · DALLAS · PALO ALTO

GENERAL EDITOR'S NOTE

TO THE FIRST EDITION

FOR MANY YEARS there has been a difference of opinion among teachers of literature as to the most fruitful approach to its study, whether by the historical method with emphasis on the social background, or by the æsthetic device of presenting certain standard types and forms. The preoccupation of the nineteenth century with history and social studies gave to the former a natural appeal to students of that period. Of late years there has been a definite reaction in favor of the latter method. Innumerable anthologies have been gathered from one or the other point of view, both of which have frequently been presented with an emphasis verging on intolerance. It is the obvious merit of Mr. Hibbard's anthology that it combines both methods of approach. The literary temper of a time is the result of historical development and social conditions. The classical temper was inevitable in Greece and Rome, as was its return with the Renaissance. The romantic reaction against it was equally inevitable in the Middle Ages and the early nineteenth century, as was the triumph of realism in the late nineteenth century, owing largely to the influence of science and journalism. The recent schools of naturalism, impressionism, expressionism, and so forth are the result of that absence of any dominant temper or direction which is characteristic of a period of decadence. At the same time these tempers devised specific literary types for their expression, the epic, drama, and formal lyric for the classical, free developments of these types for the romantic, supplemented by the short story and the novel, which became the natural forms of literature in the age of realism. But Mr. Hibbard is careful to point out and illustrate the fact that these tempers are not confined to the ages in which they were dominant, but are permanent elements in the human nature which seeks expression in literature.

Besides the historical and the æsthetic aspects of literature there is the biographical, which recognizes that every work of art is in some sort a record of human experience. That experience is conditioned by the social forces and by the æsthetic interests of the time in which it was recorded; but in the case of a great writer, his impact upon history and art —

making the world a different place to live in by virtue of influencing men's hopes and fears, and contributing to the authority or changing the direction of æsthetic doctrines — must be reckoned as the measure of his greatness. It is impossible in a single volume to represent at great length any one writer, but Mr. Hibbard has presented in his biographical introductions a sketch of the writer in his personality and experience, and placed the specimen chosen in relation to his whole work, in regard to which sufficient data are given for further study.

Not the least valuable aspect of Mr. Hibbard's approach is that it lends itself to a consideration of the whole culture of a period, of which literature is one expression. The integration of literature with sculpture and architecture in Greece, and with these supplemented by painting in the Middle Ages and the Renaissance, and finally reinforced by music in the later Renaissance and modern age, is suggested as an opportunity for further investigation, to give the student a comprehensive view of the culture of each period.

I believe that Mr. Hibbard's book will command attention by the novelty of its approach, and win approval by the catholicity of its selections. It has been his object to include nothing that is not essentially important, indeed necessary, to a well-read student, and to give a fresh and stimulating outlook upon this study of masterpieces by relating them to the deeper forces of humanity as revealed in history and artistic forms. It is clear that he offers a challenge to the teacher to emphasize throughout the study of the book the unity of the process which has made the literature of the Western world a great human document, a bible as Carlyle called it, extending from the primitive epics of Greece to the sophisticated and experimental prose of James Joyce or poetry of T. S. Eliot.

ROBERT MORSS LOVETT

PREFACE

TO THE SECOND EDITION

THERE ARE MANY possible ways of introducing the student to the large body of world literature. The late Dean Hibbard in *Writers of the Western World* looked upon literature as an expression of various tempers which throughout the centuries have influenced man's creative work. Following this idea rather than a more conventional arrangement according to periods or genres, he divided the literature of the Western world into three major categories, according to its dominant classical, romantic, or realistic bent. This approach seems to me to be basically sound. I have therefore been happy to undertake the revision of this anthology, which in its more than twelve years of existence has made innumerable friends among teachers and students alike.

In the process of revision, I have not altered the basic structure of the anthology. The material of the first two sections, The Temper of Classicism and The Romantic Mood, has remained the same, except that the selections from Homer, Chaucer, Voltaire, Heine, and Whitman have been enlarged, and a substantial number of John Donne's poems have been added. All introductions, bibliographies, and general references have been revised and brought up to date.

Major changes have been made in the third section, The Realistic Temper, so that it might represent more fully the literature of the whole Western world. Some writers have been dropped, partly because — as in the case of John Galsworthy and Theodore Dreiser — their place as world writers has become somewhat dubious, and partly because in some instances — as in Flaubert and Hardy — short selections from novels are not very satisfactory. I have added *The Jar*, a play by Luigi Pirandello, two stories, "A Hunger Artist" and "First Sorrow," by Franz Kafka, and *The Cherry Orchard* as well as the short story, "The Schoolmistress," by Anton Chekhov. I am particularly happy to have been able to include Irina Skariatina's version of *The Cherry Orchard* which was translated for Eva LeGallienne's National Theater production of Chekhov's play in 1944. The material on Thomas Mann has been enlarged by the addition of the short story, "The Infant Prodigy."

Paul Claudel, though relatively little known in the United States, is an important literary figure in Europe, belonging to the generation of André Gide and Paul Valéry. For this reason I have included seven scenes from his play, *The Satin Slipper*, which is an excellent example of impressionism in modern literature and deserves a place in an anthology which deals with the varied tempers of writers in the Western tradition.   William Faulkner, a recent Nobel prize winner in literature, has also been added and is represented by a story, "A Name for the City," which has not before been reprinted in a college textbook. The introductions in this third section have undergone major revisions, and an attempt has been made to fit the new material into the over-all plan of the book. Here, too, the bibliographies and the references to the other arts have been completely reworked.

I have had the advice of several colleagues, among them Professor Merritt E. Lawlis, Professor H. H. Remak, and Dr. Mary Gaither, all of Indiana University. Mr. Ulrich Weisstein deserves special credit for helping with the revision and arranging the art material, and Miss Arlene Ahlgrim for typing the manuscript. Mr. Richard N. Clark, Jr., has again been responsible for the references to and comments on music, and the editorial staff of Houghton Mifflin Company has given advice and encouragement, and has seen to it that the revised manuscript was completed within a reasonable period of time.

HORST FRENZ

A Note on the 1967 Impression

In this new printing of *Writers of the Western World*, three recent translations have been included: the *Iliad* (books 1 and 18) by Richmond Lattimore; the *Odyssey* (books VI, IX, and XXI) by Albert Cook; and the *Nibelungenlied* (adventures 7 and 16) by Frank Ryder. All bibliographies and general references have been revised and brought up to date. Wherever necessary, corrections have been made in the introductory material and errors eliminated. I am grateful to Professors Martha Waller of Indiana Central College and Norman Carson of Geneva College for a number of suggestions to improve the anthology, and to my students, Mr. Jeffrey Roth and Mr. Klaus-Gerhard Tröller, for assisting me with this revision.

H.F.

PREFACE

TO THE FIRST EDITION

WHEN THERE ARE ALREADY eight or ten collections of world-literature available to the student, the temerity which adds yet another volume to the publishers' lists demands something more adequate than rationalization if the new volume is to be justified. I state my intentions bluntly:

To offer a different and simple classification of literature, and through this arrangement to relate writing to other arts.

To include, so far as possible, those masterpieces of the Western world which time has established as closest to our cultural and intellectual heritage.

To place before the student a more generous selection from these masterpieces than is usual in such collections.

To give more than the usual emphasis to contemporary literature of Europe and America.

The first of these objectives must be explained at some length; the other three may be dismissed briefly.

Although in the main serious literature in all ages and in all countries has been directed toward similar ends, the presentation of truth and beauty and the understanding of human character, these ends have, nevertheless, been sought in different manners and with varying emphases. Obviously this is because writers in different periods have regarded life from different points of view. Conventionally, English literature has been explained chronologically — The Age of Chaucer, The Renaissance, The Period of Anne — convenient blocks hewn from the marble mountain and shaped into chaste but not always convincing images. Perhaps somewhat less commonly, the long record of literature has been compartmentalized by types — possibly some fifty of them altogether, beginning with *academic drama* and ending with *virelay*.

This book has no quarrel with those categories. But it does propose an approach to literature which may be both more convenient and more convincing. If it is true that writing has taken on new attitudes and forms with different writers in varying periods, it is also true that attitudes and forms in different chronological periods have much in common. The mere matter of *time* does not explain enough. The literary *form* a writer elects to use does not explain enough. Instead, then, of thinking of literature as an expression changing with period and type, why not seek to understand the separate *tempers* which prompt these changes? Surely the romantic mood is different from that of the naturalist, and the temper which makes a man a classicist is far removed from that which makes an impressionist or an expressionist. And the romantic temper is much the same whether it be traced in the poetry of Ovid in the first century B.C. or in that of Keats of the nineteenth century, in a story by Boccaccio or in one by Stevenson.

The effort to understand literature by interpreting writing according to its artistic temper has certain advantages over the present artificial classifications in that these tempers are universal; they are as appropriate to the study of Chinese literature as to English and as successfully applied to Russian writing as to French. Furthermore, they avoid the erroneous implication of a judgment based on chronology or type that every piece of writing of the eighteenth century is necessarily different from everything written in the sixteenth or that the spirit obtaining in any given drama is necessarily different from that in any novel. Again, present modes of classification result in certain embarrassments. Creative writers do not, unfortunately, keep one eye on the critics and professors when they are writing. They seldom write pure sixteenth-century prose or pure Victorianism, and they are given to writing drama — Shakespeare is an obvious example — which is at times lyrical, at times dramatic. The present divisions demand too much explanation, too frequent apology. Too often they do violence to writing by forcing it into too rigid, too narrow, categories. I should like to see all this simplified and made less arbitrary.

If critics and academicians must classify — and it is evident that we must — why should we not seek to find a scheme which is applicable to any chronological period, to any geographical section, and to any type of writing?

The working basis for this simpler method of classification may be found, I think, in what we may call the *temper* of literature. I would suggest that when writing is calm, restrained, when it subordinates content to form, it is likely that it is controlled by a temper essentially classical, and that when it is exuberant, idealistic, when content dictates form, the temper is essentially romantic. When I come upon writing which, though romantic in spirit, is based essentially on symbols, which is mystically concerned with what it regards as "essences" and lays emphasis on musical effects, tones, and colors, in the manner of Rimbaud or Mallarmé, Poe or Baudelaire, I should think of it as by temper symbolistic. On the other hand, when the writer is determined to seek out truth, when he is dominated by a desire faithfully to portray character, when his whole manner is objective and he is more concerned with interpreting life through actuality than with telling a story of action, he is realistic. And I should accept as naturalistic that realism which goes beyond realism, which is deterministic and mechanistic in tone, and which tries to understand humanity by the methods of scientific analysis, particularly of man's environment and his heredity. And when I find a literary manner giving great emphasis to atmosphere, to the transcribing of the quality of an experience as it impresses itself on the emotions of the author under the spell of a momentary revelation, the manner of some of Conrad for instance, I should give it the name of impressionism. And then, when I find impressionism in reverse, the objective stated in terms of the subjective, the associated substituted for the actual, I think of it as expressionistic. Before this proposal is charged with being too complicated, I should indicate that the seven manners here suggested are essentially but three: the classical, the romantic, and the realistic. Symbolism is essentially a phase of romanticism; naturalism, impressionism, and expressionism are but variations within the realistic temper.

Of course such a classification is still nothing more than a convenience. Fortunately literature itself is more important than any categories for it which we may devise. But since these tempers or moods are common to individuals as well as to groups, are present in the disposition of readers as well as of writers, the arrangement suggested has the advantage of being natural to all of us. If we must classify, we may as well look in our hearts as go to a textbook in literary history. And somehow, I believe, a mood with which I am personally familiar, which I feel prompting my own actions and thought, offers a more real understanding, a deeper appreciation of literature than a scheme devised for me by some professor, a scheme which classifies a poem according to the number of lines it contains or the year in which it was written. Such an organization as this helps, too, to explain contemporary literature which often reflects a confused blending of two or more of these moods. It is easier to understand Joyce if we know the temper of the symbolist and the expressionist than it is to explain *Ulysses* by reference to the nineteenth century or to the history of the novel as a literary type. It is my hope that the arrangement of this book will throw light down the whole long road to literary modernism.

The contents of this volume are drawn from writers within the tradition of the Western world. It would be great fun, and certainly instructive as well, to incorporate here the writing of Persia, of India, of China, and of Japan. We of the Western world are, perhaps, just a bit too arrogant toward Eastern literatures. And it looks as though the turn of history may force us to pay more intelligent consideration to the culture and thought of the Orient. But that is another volume. Clearly it is the *first* responsibility of the student of the Occident to know something of those great books and poems which, consciously or unconsciously, mould his way of thinking, his everyday life. Where, then, there has been a choice between two great pieces of writing, one within our tradition, one without, it has been my effort to select the first. This working principle, however, has been perforce somewhat modified by the fact that our high schools today have taken all knowledge to be their province and young students are made to "burn over" even the most complex writing. Some few selections, commonly studied in high school, have therefore been passed over in favor of less frequently studied passages.

It is, I have said, my desire to place before the student sufficient material really to represent the work of the author whose writing is to be included in this book. Such an ambition, of course, can be only relative. One cannot know Milton without having read most of Milton; Henry James is not completely introduced to the student in one short story of thirty pages. But, and this is my point here, most of my predecessors in this field seem to have set for themselves the task of including as many writers as possible, some proving themselves so catholic as to present selections from one hundred and fifty or even two hundred authors. But a generosity in the inclusion of great *names* necessarily results in a skimping of the *writing* of these literary figures with the result that it is fairly usual to find an average of five or six pages devoted to each of the authors included. This constitutes what I think of as The Tidbit School of Anthologists. The present volume reduces the number of authors whose work is represented and, consequently, is able to double or even triple the number of pages devoted to each writer in most of the other collections.

This same desire to place before the student good writing within his tradition and experience results, admittedly, in what would be from any purely critical point of view an undue emphasis on English and American and contemporary work. Obviously Katherine Mansfield, Thomas Mann, and T. S. Eliot have not yet won places beside such world figures as Shakespeare or Goethe or Dante. But equally obvious is the fact that the proximity of these and other modern authors to the student of today, the manner of their writing and the stuff of their thought, give them a particular significance which a collection for the modern student should recognize. We live in the past, it is true, but we live also in the present.

Only one further word of explanation need be offered. The editor hopes that his inclusion of illustrations from the realm of various arts, his references to great painting and to records of great music, his citation of books which will develop the student's understanding of these various "tempers," will prove practical to both the teacher and the student. After all, these tempers underlie man's creative moods in all the arts. The references and pictures will, I hope, serve to remove literature from the vacuum in which it is often taught and to relate it, as it should be related, to that great urge, common to all artists, which has made the art of the ages and helped to raise man above the level of the purely practical, the strictly materialistic.

In preparing a manuscript as extensive as this one, I have necessarily had to seek the advice and help of others. It is a very real pleasure to acknowledge here the assistance of Mr. Richard N. Clark, Jr., of Houghton Mifflin Company, in preparing the list of musical compositions, and of Mr. David T. Cook, of the University Prints, for his cooperation in supplying illustrations and the list of paintings, sculpture, and architecture printed at the close of each section. I acknowledge, too, the courteous cooperation of the various publishers owning the copyright for much of the material used here, debts specifically itemized elsewhere. Further help, graciously and efficiently accorded, was secured from Miss Eleanor Lewis and Miss Dorothy Hutchison of the Reference Department of the Charles Deering Library at Northwestern University. To Mrs. Donald F. Cameron I am indebted for aid of a secretarial nature, help which went far beyond that in its intelligence and accuracy. And finally I acknowledge gratefully the scholarly and generous advice I was fortunate enough to receive from Professor Robert Morss Lovett. To all of these people, as well as to others who cannot be specifically named here, I am most grateful. To them may be credited such virtues as the volume has, but beyond this they should be held in no sense responsible.

ADDISON HIBBARD

Contents

THE TEMPER OF CLASSICISM

Introduction   3

HOMER (c. ninth century B.C.)   11
  The *Iliad*, Books I, XVIII   12
  The *Odyssey*, Books, VI, IX, XXI   33

THE BIBLE   54
  The Creation of the World (*Genesis*)   55
  The Story of Joseph and His Brethren (*Genesis*)   56
  The Giving of the Law (*Exodus*)   61
  The Story of Samson (*Judges*)   61
  Ruth (*Ruth*)   64
  The Sermon on the Mount (*Matthew*)   67

ÆSCHYLUS (525–456 B.C.)   70
  Agamemnon   71

SOPHOCLES (496–406 B.C.)   92
  Antigone   93

EURIPIDES (484–406 B.C.)   110
  Medea   111

ARISTOPHANES (445–385 B.C.)   130
  The Frogs   131

PLATO (427–347 B.C.)   156
  Dialogues:
  The Apology   157

ARISTOTLE (384–322 B.C.)   169
  The Nature of Tragedy   169

THEOCRITUS (c. 270 B.C.)   175
  Epigrams:
  For a Herdsman's Offering   175
  For a Picture   175

Daphnis and Menalcas   175
At the Festival of Adonis   177
The Cyclops in Love   178

LUCRETIUS (98–55 B.C.)   180
  On the Nature of Things:
  Proem   181
  Substance is Eternal   183
  The Soul is Mortal   184
  Folly of the Fear of Death   185
  The Origin of Life   187
  Origin of Mankind   188
  Beginnings of Civilization   189

VIRGIL (70–19 B.C.)   191
  The *Æneid*, Books II, IV, VI   191

HORACE (65–8 B.C.)   224
  Alphius   225
  To Lycè   226
  The Reconciliation   226
  Contentment   227
  The Bore   229
  My Prayers With This I Used to Charge   231

MARCUS AURELIUS (121–180 A.D.)   233
  Meditations   234

LUCIAN (c. 120–c. 180)   240
  Dialogues of the Dead:
  Dialogue X — Charon and Hermes   240
  Dialogues of the Gods:
  Dialogue XX — The Judgment of Paris   242
  Sale of Creeds   245

MICHAEL EYQUEM DE MONTAIGNE
   (1533–1592)   250
   The Author to the Reader   251
   That We Taste Nothing Pure   252
   Of Commerce With Books   253
   Of the Inconvenience of Greatness   255

BEN JONSON (1573–1637)   257
   Hymn to Diana   258
   Song: To Celia   258
   To Celia   258
   To the Memory of My Beloved Master,
     William Shakespeare   258
   A Song   259
   Her Triumph   259

JOHN MILTON (1608–1674)   260
   L'Allegro   261
   Il Penseroso   263
   Lycidas   265
   Sonnets:
     On His Being Arrived to the Age of
      Twenty-Three   267

   On His Blindness   267
   On Shakespeare   267
   Paradise Lost (Books I and II)   268

MOLIÈRE (1622–1673)   287
   The Misanthrope   288

JEAN RACINE (1639–1699)   309
   Phædra   310

JONATHAN SWIFT (1667–1745)   328
   From Gulliver's Travels:
     A Voyage to Laputa   329

ALEXANDER POPE (1688–1744)   349
   An Essay on Criticism   350
   The Rape of the Lock   357

VOLTAIRE (1694–1778)   366
   Selections from Candide   367

References:
   LITERATURE   385
   ART   386
   MUSIC   386

THE ROMANTIC MOOD

The Romantics

Introduction   391

OVID (43 B.C.–A.D. 17)   404
   Metamorphoses:
     Apollo and Daphne   404
     Alpheus and Arethusa   406
     Orpheus and Eurydice   407
     Narcissus   408
     The Rape of Proserpine   409
   Heroides:
     Dido to Æneas   410

APULEIUS (c. 160)   413
   From The Golden Ass:
     The Robbers   413
     Cupid and Psyche   419

FROM THE Beowulf (seventh century)   427

FROM The Nibelungenlied (c. 1200)   442
   How Gunther Won Brunhild   443
   How Sigfrid Was Slain   448

AUCASSIN AND NICOLETE (twelfth century)   453

ENGLISH POPULAR BALLADS   466

Edward   466
Lord Thomas and Fair Annet   467
Lamkin   468
The Twa Corbies   470
Sir Patrick Spence   470
The Dæmon Lover   470
Robin Hood's Death and Burial   471
Bonny Barbara Allan   472

DANTE ALIGHIERI (1265-1321)   473

From The Divine Comedy:

Hell (Cantos I–II–III–IV–V)   474
Purgatory (Cantos I–II–III–IV)   482
Paradise (Cantos XXXI–XXXII–
XXXIII)   488

GIOVANNI BOCCACCIO (1313-1375)   493

From The Decameron:

Introduction   494
Simona and Pasquino   502
Federigo's Falcon   503
Patient Griselda   506

FRANÇOIS RABELAIS (1494-1553)   511

From Gargantua:

The Author's Prologue   511
The Study of Gargantua — Old
Plan   513
The Study of Gargantua — New
Plan   514
Great Strife and Debate   517
How a Monk of Sevillé Saved the
Abbey   518
How Pantagruel Persuadeth Panurge
to Take Counsel of a Fool   520

CERVANTES (MIGUEL DE CERVANTES
SAAVEDRA) (1547-1616)   522

From Don Quixote:

The Quality and Way of Living of
Don Quixote   523

Of Don Quixote's First Sally   525
Don Quixote Is Dubbed a Knight   528
The Adventure of the Windmills   531

EDMUND SPENSER (1554-1599)   534

A Letter of the Authors   535
From The Faerie Queene:

Legend of the Knight of the Red
Crosse   537

WILLIAM SHAKESPEARE (1564-1616)   549

Songs from the Plays:

When icicles hang by the wall   551
Who is Silvia?   551
Under the greenwood tree   551
Blow, blow, thou winter wind!   551
O Mistress mine, where are you
roaming?   551
Take, O, take those lips away   551
Hark, hark! the lark   551
Fear no more the heat o' the sun   552
Full fathom five thy father lies   552

Sonnets:

When I consider everything that
grows   552
Shall I compare thee to a summer's
day?   552
As an unperfect actor on the stage   552
When, in disgrace with fortune and
men's eyes   553
When to the sessions of sweet silent
thought   553
If thou survive my well-contented
day   553
O. how much more doth beauty
beauteous seem   553
Not marble, nor the gilded monuments   553
When I have seen by Time's fell hand
defaced   553
Since brass, nor stone, nor earth, nor
boundless sea   554

That time of year thou mayst in me
    behold   554
How like a winter hath my absence
    been   554
To me, fair friend, you never can be
    old   554
When in the chronicle of wasted
    time   554
Not mine own fears, nor the pro-
    phetic soul   554
O, never say that I was false of heart 554
Let me not to the marriage of true
    minds   555
My mistress' eyes are nothing like
    the sun   555
King Lear   555

JEAN JACQUES ROUSSEAU (1712–1778) 596
A Discourse on the Origin of In-
    equality   597
From Confessions:
    The Stolen Ribbon   604
    A Day's Excursion   606
    Life at Les Charmettes   608
    Rousseau's Opera Is Presented   610

JOHANN WOLFGANG VON GOETHE
    (1749–1832)   613
From Faust:
    Prologue in Heaven   614
    Faust — Part I   615

ROBERT BURNS (1759–1796)   643
To a Mouse   644
Tam o' Shanter   645
Green Grow the Rashes, O   647
Of A' the Airts   648
Auld Lang Syne   648
John Anderson My Jo   649
Willie Brewed a Peck o' Maut   649
Ye Flowery Banks   649
A Red, Red Rose   649

Scots, Wha Hae   650
Highland Mary   650
Is There for Honest Poverty   650
O, Wert Thou in the Cauld Blast   651
Mary Morison   651

WILLIAM WORDSWORTH (1770–1850) 652
Expostulation and Reply   653
The Tables Turned   653
Lines Composed Above Tintern Abbey 654
My Heart Leaps Up   656
To the Cuckoo   656

Sonnets:
    Composed Upon Westminster Bridge 656
    It Is a Beauteous Evening, Calm and
        Free   656
    London, 1802   656
    The World Is Too Much With Us   657
    The Solitary Reaper   657
    I Wandered Lonely as a Cloud   657
    Ode to Duty   657
    Ode on Intimations of Immortality 658
    Preface to Lyrical Ballads   660

SAMUEL TAYLOR COLERIDGE (1772–
    1834)   670
Kubla Khan   671
Christabel   672
From Biographia Literaria:
    Chapters XVII and XVIII   679

LORD (GEORGE GORDON) BYRON
    (1788–1824)   685
Maid of Athens, Ere We Part   686
Sonnet on Chillon   686
She Walks in Beauty   687
When We Two Parted   687
From Childe Harold:
    Solitude   687
    Rome — and the Vanity of Human
        Wishes   690

So We'll Go No More A-Roving   696
From *Don Juan:*
   The Lake Poets — and Others   696
   The Isles of Greece   698

PERCY BYSSHE SHELLEY (1792–1822)   700
Hymn to Intellectual Beauty   701
Ode to the West Wind   702
To a Skylark   703
Ozymandias   704
Mutability   705
Adonais   705
To ——   712
From *Prometheus Unbound:*
   The Future of Society   712
   The Ability of Man   713
   The Goal Reached   714

JOHN KEATS (1795–1821)   714
On First Looking into Chapman's
   Homer   715
Proem (from *Endymion*)   715
When I Have Fears That I May Cease
   to Be   716
Robin Hood   716
Lines on the Mermaid Tavern   717
The Eve of St. Agnes   717
Ode on a Grecian Urn   722
Ode to a Nightingale   723
La Belle Dame Sans Merci   724
Fame   724
Lamia   724
Sonnet   732

HEINRICH HEINE (1797–1856)   732
The Mountain Echo   733
The Grenadiers   733
Whene'er I Look Into Thine Eyes   733
A Pine Tree Stands So Lonely   733
I Do Not Know Why This Confronts
   Me   734

Oh Lovely Fishermaiden   734
The Yellow Moon Has Risen   734
Child, You Are Like a Flower   734
Life in This World   734
Where Is Now Your Precious Darling? 734
Doctrine   735
Night Has Come   735

VICTOR HUGO (1802–1885)   735
From *Les Misérables:*
   The Escape Through the Sewers   736

RALPH WALDO EMERSON (1803–1882)   750
Written in Naples   752
Written at Rome   752
The Rhodora   752
Each and All   753
The Sphinx   753
Musketaquid   755
Days   755
Brahma   756
The American Scholar   756

NATHANIEL HAWTHORNE (1804–1864)   764
Young Goodman Brown   765
Ethan Brand   771

ALFRED, LORD TENNYSON (1809–
   1892)   778
Morte d'Arthur   780
Ulysses   782
Break, Break, Break   783
Songs (from *The Princess*)   783
From *In Memoriam A.H.H.*   785
The Brook   789
The Higher Pantheism   790
The Revenge, A Ballad of the Fleet   790
Crossing the Bar   792

ROBERT BROWNING (1812–1889)   793
A Grammarian's Funeral   794

Pippa's Song   796
My Last Duchess   796
Soliloquy of the Spanish Cloister   796
The Lost Leader   797
Meeting at Night   798
Parting at Morning   798
Home-Thoughts, from Abroad   798
Home-Thoughts, from the Sea   798
The Bishop Orders His Tomb at Saint
  Praxed's Church   798
Evelyn Hope   800
Love Among the Ruins   800
Fra Lippo Lippi   801
Andrea Del Sarto   805
Prospice   808
Epilogue to *Asolando*   808

The Symbolists

Introduction   811

THE BIBLE   816

  The Lord Is My Shepherd (Psalm
    xxiii)   816
  God Is Our Refuge (Psalm xlvi)   816

JOHN DONNE (1572–1631)   817

  The Anniversary   817
  The Good-Morrow   818
  Song   818
  The Sun Rising   818
  Woman's Constancy   819
  The Undertaking   819
  The Canonization   819
  The Legacy   820
  A Valediction: Forbidding
    Mourning   820

EDGAR ALLAN POE (1809–1849)   820

  The City in the Sea   822
  The Valley of Unrest   822

The Haunted Palace   823
The Conqueror Worm   823
The Raven   824
Ulalume   826
The Bells   827
Eldorado   828
The Masque of the Red Death   828
Eleonora   831

CHARLES BAUDELAIRE (1821–1867)   833

  L'Invitation au Voyage   834
  Anywhere Out of the World   835
  The Clock   836
  The Plaything of the Poor   836
  Every Man His Chimæra   836
  The Sadness of the Moon   837
  Correspondences   837
  The Flask   837
  The Seven Old Men   837
  The Death of the Poor   838
  A Landscape   838
  Exotic Fragrance   839
  Music   839
  The Flawed Bell   839

HENRIK IBSEN (1828–1906)   839

  The Master Builder   840

"LES SYMBOLISTES"   874

  Paul Verlaine, Il Pleut Doucement sur
    la Ville   874
  Paul Verlaine, À Clymène   874
  Henri de Régnier, The Vase   874
  Arthur Rimbaud, The Frenzied Ship 875
  Stéphane Mallarmé, The Windows 877
  Stéphane Mallarmé, Sea-Wind   877
  Stéphane Mallarmé, L'Après-Midi d'un
    Faune   877
  Henri Bataille, Memories   879
  Villiers de l'Isle-Adam, Vox Populi 879

Joris-Karl Huysmans, Camaïeu in Red   880
Stéphane Mallarmé, In Autumn   881
Henri de Régnier, The Stairway   881
Saint-Pol-Roux, Butterflies   882

References:
   LITERATURE   883
   ART   883
   MUSIC   884

THE REALISTIC TEMPER

The Realists

Introduction   889

GEOFFREY CHAUCER (c. 1340–1400)   895
  From *The Canterbury Tales:*   896
    The Prologue   897
    The Nun's Priest's Tale   906
    The Pardoner's Tale   912
    The Complaint of Chaucer to His Purse   919

DANIEL DEFOE (1660–1731)   920
  A True Relation of the Apparition of Mrs. Veal   921

HONORÉ DE BALZAC (1799–1850)   925
  Selection from *Old Goriot*   926

NICOLAI GOGOL (1809–1852)   937
  The Cloak   938

IVAN TURGENEV (1818–1883)   951
  Mumu   951

WALT WHITMAN (1819–1892)   964
  One's-self I Sing   966
  On Journeys Through the States   966
  The Song of the Open Road   966
  Crossing Brooklyn Ferry   970
  I Hear America Singing   973
  Pioneers! O Pioneers!   974
  O Captain! My Captain!   976

  When Lilacs Last in the Dooryard Bloom'd   976
  Come Up from the Fields Father   980
  To a Locomotive in Winter   980

FYODOR DOSTOEVSKY (1821–1881)   981
  From *Crime and Punishment:*
    The Crime   982

LEO TOLSTOY (1828–1910)   989
  From *Anna Karenina:*
    Farming in Old Russia   990
    The Steeplechase   994
    Anna Visits Her Son   997
    Levin Finds His Faith   1001

ANTON CHEKHOV (1860–1904)   1008
  The Schoolmistress   1009
  The Cherry Orchard   1013

LUIGI PIRANDELLO (1867–1936)   1034
  The Jar   1036

THOMAS MANN (1875–1955)   1045
  The Infant Prodigy   1046
  From *The Magic Mountain:*
    Snow   1050

ERNEST HEMINGWAY (1899–1961)   1061
  The Undefeated   1062

WILLIAM FAULKNER (1897–1962)   1076
  A Name for the City   1078

The Naturalists

Introduction   1087

ÉMILE ZOLA (1840–1902)   1091
  From L'Assommoir:
    The Fight in the Laundry   1092

MAXIM GORKI (1868–1936)   1099
  Chums   1100

The Impressionists

Introduction   1109

THE BIBLE   1112
  What Is Man? (Psalm viii)   1112
  The Voice of the Lord (Psalm xxix)   1113
  How Amiable Are Thy Tabernacles
    (Psalm lxxxiv)   1113

HENRY JAMES (1843–1916)   1113
  The Liar   1114

JOSEPH CONRAD (1857–1924)   1138
  The Lagoon   1139

PAUL CLAUDEL (1868–1955)   1145
  Selections from The Satin Slipper   1146

KATHERINE MANSFIELD (1888–1923)   1162
  The Voyage   1162

The Expressionists

Introduction   1167

JAMES JOYCE (1882–1941)   1171
  From Ulysses:
    The Interment of Patrick Dignam   1172

FRANZ KAFKA (1883–1924)   1186
  First Sorrow   1187
  A Hunger Artist   1188

EUGENE O'NEILL (1888–1953)   1192
  The Hairy Ape   1193

T. S. ELIOT (1888–1965)   1212
  Sweeney Among the Nightingales   1213
  Rhapsody on a Windy Night   1213
  The Hollow Men   1214

References:
  LITERATURE   1216
  ART   1216
  MUSIC   1218

SUPPLEMENTARY BIBLIOGRAPHY   1221
CHRONOLOGICAL TABLE OF AUTHORS   1223
GUIDE TO THE TYPES OF LITERATURE   1229
INDEX OF AUTHORS, TITLES, AND FIRST LINES OF POETRY   1235

Illustrations

Plates 1–15 · CLASSICISM

Delphic Sibyl	*Michelangelo*	
St. John and St. Peter	*Dürer*	
The Dispute of the Sacrament	*Raphael*	
The Death of St. Francis	*Giotto*	
Madonna Della Sedia	*Raphael*	
Œdipus and the Sphinx	*Ingres*	*between*
The Annunciation	*Fra Angelico*	10–11
Parthenon from the Northwest		
Mount Vernon		
Gattamelata	*Donatello*	
Pauline Borghese as Venus	*Canova*	
Greek Slave	*Powers*	
East Frieze of Parthenon (detail)		
Boy Chasing Hare	*Panaitios Painter*	
Apollo Belvedere		

Plates 16–30 · ROMANTICISM

Edmund and Crawford Antrobus	*Lawrence*	
The Bark of Dante	*Delacroix*	
The Lion Hunt	*Rubens*	
Souvenir of Italy. Castel Gandolfo	*Corot*	
The Hay Wain	*Constable*	
Apollo and the Hours	*Reni*	*between*
Peace and Plenty	*Inness*	394–395
W. K. Vanderbilt Mansion	*Hunt*	
Fonthill Abbey	*Wyatt*	
Hymn of Departure for War	*Rude*	
The Nymph of Fontainebleau	*Cellini*	
The Cup of Death	*Vedder*	
Flight of Night	*Hunt*	
Hope	*Watts*	
Toilers of the Sea	*Ryder*	

Plates 31–44 · REALISM (FIRST GROUP)

Portrait of Georg Gisze	*Holbein*	
The Escaped Cow	*Dupre*	
Man with the Hoe	*Millet*	
Æsop	*Velasquez*	
Dr. Tulp's Anatomy Lesson	*Rembrandt*	
The Fog Warning	*Homer*	
Jean Arnolfini and His Wife	*Van Eyck*	*between*
Las Meniñas	*Velasquez*	1066–1067
Turning the Stake Boat	*Eakins*	
The Stag's Thicket	*Courbet*	
The Haymakers	*Bastien-Lepage*	
Los Borrachos (The Topers)	*Velasquez*	
Niccolò da Uzzano	*Donatello*	
Age of Bronze	*Rodin*	

Plates 45–60 · REALISM (SECOND GROUP)

The Poplars	*Monet*	
Le Moulin de la Galette	*Renoir*	
The Dancer	*Degas*	
Boulevard des Italiens at Night	*Pissarro*	
La Grande Jatte	*Seurat*	
The Danaïd	*Rodin*	
Landscape with Cypresses	*Van Gogh*	*between*
La Cascade	*Rousseau*	1130–1131
Mahana no Atua	*Gauguin*	
Landscape	*Cezanne*	
The Green	*Chagall*	
Twittering	*Klee*	
Guernica	*Picasso*	
Scene from "The Hairy Ape"	*Throckmorton*	
Blossoming	*Lipchitz*	
Reclining Figure, 1936	*Moore*	

For permission to use certain illustrations in this book acknowledgment is made to the following: to The Mount Vernon Ladies' Association of the Union, Mount Vernon, Virginia, for *Mount Vernon;* to The Pennsylvania Academy of the Fine Arts, Philadelphia, for *Flight of Night* by Hunt; to the Collection of The Addison Gallery of American Art, Phillips Academy, Andover, for *Toilers of the Sea* by Ryder; to The Museum of Fine Arts, Boston, for *The Fog Warning* by Homer; to The Cleveland Museum of Art for *Turning the Stake Boat* by Eakins; to The Art Institute of Chicago for *La Grande Jatte* by Seurat, and for *Mahana No Atua* by Gauguin; to The Solomon R. Guggenheim Museum for *The Green Violinist* by Chagall; to collection The Museum of Modern Art for *Twittering Machine* by Klee; to The Museum of Modern Art, on extended loan from the artist, for *Guernica* by Picasso; to collection The Museum of Modern Art for *Blossoming*, by Lipchitz; to The Theatre Collection, New York Public Library, for the scene from *The Hairy Ape* by Throckmorton; to the Albright Art Gallery, Room of Contemporary Art Collection, Buffalo, New York, for *Reclining Figure, 1936*, by Moore.

THE

Temper of Classicism

THE

TEMPER OF CLASSICISM

... to think clearly, to feel nobly, and to delineate firmly.

MATTHEW ARNOLD

FOR MORE THAN two thousand years the classical temper, while undergoing minor changes, has remained essentially the temper of writers who, because of inherent disposition or from conviction or custom, have sought to express noble ideas in dignified language and have believed firmly in the power of restraint, the need for decorum, and the value of lucid simplicity. In the history of European literature, however, two epochs have been pre-eminently classical. There was, first, the pre-Christian era, when in Greece such writers as Homer, Sophocles, Æschylus, and Euripides, and in Rome such figures as Cicero, Virgil, and Horace were fixing the mould to shape many a future writer. And, later, in the seventeenth and eighteenth centuries, came the neo-classic period of France and England when Racine and La Fontaine in the one country and Swift and Pope in the other were following the precepts of the ancient Greeks and Romans and setting up new standards of their own.

This introduction, concerned as it is with the broad stream of classicism, must leave to the literary historian the careful recording in chronological sequence of the various tenets of the school. Here it is only necessary to recall that the Greeks and Romans, expressing themselves according to the spirit of their contemporary civilizations, held literature, and

3

more particularly dramatic literature, to be a record of great moments in the lives of mythical heroes, a chronicling of the noble actions of noble people, all to be expressed with simplicity and in a dignified language. Universal qualities, they felt, were the proper themes for presentation and these qualities must, in turn, be presented objectively. With the rediscovery of classical literature that came with the Renaissance, a revival of the classical temper set in. In France, seventeenth-century dramatists adhered carefully to the unities of time and place and action, used the Alexandrine couplet, observed the proprieties, and presented the necessary exposition in the first act. It was their constant purpose to avoid excessive display of physical action, as it was their constant effort to analyze the motives of their leading characters and to preserve decorum. In England the authors of the eighteenth century, while keeping many of the practices they found in the work of Greek and Roman and French writers, added emphasis to certain other conventions such as their insistence on a moral and philosophic tone for literature and their presentation of a mannered society. Besides, they held a high regard for an artificial and set poetic diction.

Critics and literary historians have made much of the impossibility of characterizing a literary manner which extended over many centuries, into many countries, and which underwent many climatic and temporal changes. And if it is one's purpose to find a definition which will fit all times and all peoples, the difficulty is, certainly, insurmountable. However, we are concerned here primarily with the mood of classicism; our effort is to characterize a temper, not to define a movement. Our problem resolves itself into two aspects — form and content.

The truly classical writer exalts the importance of form. In fact he is classical in temper largely because for him form controls his emotions and holds them in constant check. Enthusiasm or exuberance, if not entirely foreign to his nature, is certainly always on leash, and a short leash at that. Classical tragedy has its own rules: balance must be respected, proportion is of great importance, design must keep pace with purpose, the action must move through certain prescribed structural stages. Story and idea must dominate external decorations, and language must be subordinate to the action.

This is not to say that language was insignificant. Indeed, as will be pointed out later on, language became very important, but its importance to the classicist was that it might fit certain conventions and the conventions were designed to formalize language in such a way as to keep it always from detracting from the action which is the movement of drama. Some writers, particularly toward the close of the neo-classical period, looked upon literature as an exercise of rules. But no trend, literary or other, is so wisely judged by its excesses as by its normal practices. The term classical is normally applied to a work of art in which details are subordinated to the central design, emphasis is placed on structure and organization rather than on decoration, expression is held in rein by the central action, and an inherent sense of form guides the author.

This persistent feeling for form manifests itself, in the words of Matthew Arnold, in "clearness of arrangement," "rigor of development," and "simplicity of style." It is, he tells us elsewhere, further distinguished by its quality of being "particular, precise, and firm" as opposed to "general, indeterminate, and faint." For Arnold, in fact, classicism is "the grand style" and arises in poetry "when a noble nature, poetically gifted, treats with simplicity or with severity a serious subject." Another critic tells us that one of the elements of the grand style is "fine line rather than rich color," that it implies a quality of "sculpture rather than of painting," that it is "quiet, austere," that in it there is "nothing voluptuous or even overflowing." All this, then, points the way to classicism and away from romanticism. Where a rigorous emphasis is placed on firmness, on line and contour, there is no room for fancy, and lyric enthusiasm is banned.

The student who would see at a glance just what this difference in emphasis on form and on language can mean to literature will do well to turn to Milton's *Lycidas,* as an instance of emphasis on form, and then read, say Rimbaud's *Drunken Boat* as an example of emphasis on language.

This respect for form carries with it a demand for restraint. Ancient literature believed in the all-importance of the action selected for the story, whereas recent literature often places an equal or a greater emphasis on the manner in which the action is expressed. Language and imagery are for the modern almost as significant as the thought itself. The classical writer held that the language used to express an action was less important than the pattern into which that action was fitted.

This need to keep the story in hand demanded restraint. The dramatist or the poet could not depart from his action to indulge expression for its own sake. But the classical author was restricted by another consideration — he must not let his personal emotion run away with him. This is an important distinction between the classical and the romantic outlook: the one emphasized reason, the other emotion. Restraint was good taste, exuberance was not. Self-control was a virtue, exaggeration was a vice. Moderation was sanity, enthusiasm was weakness. This difference between the classical and the more modern point of view is the difference we find between Plato calmly discoursing on the nature of the soul and Burns giving rein to his emotions as he breaks up a mouse-nest with his plow.

Yet all that has been said about control and restraint does not imply suppression. Classicism has always been free to write of those actions and phases of life to which a Victorian age denied existence. But no puritanical reformer could cavil at the Œdipus complex as treated by Sophocles or call Dido "a loose woman." Stories in the classical manner were robbed of such pruriences as cause the evil-minded to chortle.

Nowhere was this classical idea of restraint and compression so manifest as in the matter of the unities. The theories regarding the three unities have a long record, too long and too complicated to summarize here. We must be content with understanding that these three — the unities of "action," "time," and "place" — serve the purpose of compression by asserting that the action (plot) be definitely restricted in scope, that no more time be used than is absolutely essential to the progress of the action, and that the place of the action be confined within as narrow limits as possible. At different times different critics have placed varying limits on all three. Aristotle, in his *Poetics,* decreed that a tragedy was "an imitation of an action that is complete, and whole, and of a certain magnitude" and pointed out that it must have a beginning, a middle, and an end. From this conviction of Aristotle's arose the doctrine of unity of action, a principle which really says only that the dramatist should not divert his audience with incidents not directly related to his main plot. From a further pronouncement of Aristotle's that "Tragedy endeavors, as far as possible, to confine itself to a single revolution of the sun" grew up, later on, a doctrine which restricted the dramatic time to one day of twenty-four hours, of twelve hours, or even of the few hours actually employed in the presentation on the stage. When action and time had been thus restricted, it was only natural that other critics, particularly the Italian and French dogmatists of the Renaissance, should formulate the doctrine that the action on the stage should be limited to one place.

This compressive function of the three unities will be at once obvious if we see how they are worked out in one of the Greek plays, in the *Agamemnon* of Æschylus, for example. The action of this play is unified by being limited to one major event, the murder of Agamemnon by his wife Clytæmnestra; the time is unified by having all of the action take place within a few hours of one day; and the place employed in the action is restricted to the yard immediately before the palace in the city of Argos. And this restraint, this compression, is a characteristic of the classical temper whether it be in Greek tragedy before the time of Christ or in the neo-classicism of the seventeenth and eighteenth centuries in France and England. What Æschylus had done and Aristotle had taught, Racine, Corneille, Dryden, and Addison carried in practice even further.

The diction of classicism was formal. The same discipline which demanded restricted action and the unities, which forbade exuberance and spontaneity on the part of the author, naturally prescribed a rather formal and conventionalized language. The informal and colloquial were excluded. It is true that Homer gave us his rich epithets — "bright-eyed" Athena, "wine-dark" sea, "rosy-fingered" dawn. But these were essentially dignified, so dignified in fact that Milton and others adopted the formal epithet as part of their poetic manner. Some hint of this dignity and formality of classical diction may be suggested by quoting a few lines from the speech (in the *Agamemnon* of Æschylus) in which Clytæmnestra reports how signal fires have brought the news of the fall of Troy. The chorus asked "what stalwart herald ran so fleetly?" and the queen replies:

> Hephæstus. He from Ida shot the spark;
> And flaming straightway leapt the courier fire
> From height to height; to the Hermæan rock
> Of Lemnos, first from Ida; from the isle
> The Athóan steep of mighty Jove received
> The beaming beacon; then the forward strength
> Of the far-travelling lamp strode gallantly
> Athwart the broad sea's back. The flaming pine
> Rayed out a golden glory like the sun,
> And winged the message to Macistus' watchtower.

By the eighteenth century in England this formality had become a rigid convention. Neo-classical writers were too often content to use stereotyped expressions, too fond of formal diction. What for the ancient Greeks had been a sense of proportion, a respect for unity, an interest in the whole rather than its parts, an ardent effort to find accurate and symmetrical expression for thought, developed, as the classical conventions became fixed through the years, into the worship of refinement and polish. In the neo-classical emphasis on finish, content or idea became subordinate to etiquette and form. Rules dominated and controlled inspiration.

Up to this point we have been thinking of classicism as it found expression in form. Next we shall consider classicism as related to content. But before passing on to the examination of this aspect a word of warning may be necessary. Form and content in truly classical writing are not so easily separated as the divisions of this essay might suggest. In any style of composition form and content are essentially one. That is, form is adapted to content and content dictates form. The two are wedded — more happily wedded in the really classical, perhaps, than in any of the other literary manners.

Classicism is concerned with the intellectual. It elevates reason. Consider simply a list of a few classical and neo-classical authors: Æschylus, Sophocles, Aristophanes, Plato, and Aristotle; Pascal, Racine, La Fontaine, and Molière; Addison, Pope, Swift, and Dr. Johnson. And consider what the names bring to mind: odes and fables, tragedy and comedy, philosophy and criticism, essays and satire. The periods in which these men wrote, whether in Greece, France, or England, were all periods of a highly developed civilization — the Periclean age (490–429 B.C.), the reign of Louis XIV (1638–1715), and the Restoration and reign of Queen Anne (1664–1714). They were periods of a highly cultivated society, of learning and refinement. They were periods when literature and scholarship were esteemed, when those living felt that civilization had reached its apex, that little or nothing remained to be done to bring about perfection. Perfection had, indeed, arrived. Nitze and Dargan, in their *History of French Literature*, write of this time in France:

> The important point, however, is that classicism conceives of man's nature as "complete."
> The gestation of centuries is achieved: man has become conscious of himself, of his position
> in the universe, of his functions, of what he can and cannot do in life.

The world was for these writers a "closed universe." Nobility and intellectual aristocracy were achieved accomplishments. It remained only to write noble thoughts on noble subjects in noble language. Logic and intelligence were in the saddle. Order and good sense must prevail. Feeling must be held in balance by reason. A standard of values was available for all. A philosophic tone pervaded all writing. "Classicism is health," said Goethe thinking of these attitudes, "romanticism is disease." Not one extreme or the other but a middle ground indicated by intelligence was the accepted position of these people. "Mens sana in corpore sano" ("a sound mind in a sound body"), wrote Juvenal, properly enough placing first the healthy mind. Adventure and romance: exotic symbolism, psychological spewings forth; low realism, impressionistic revelations of the moment — these things the classicists either did not know or spurned. Their trust of reason and of the intellect turned them in other directions.

Classicism seeks out universal rather than individual qualities. A classical work of art is objective rather than subjective. Its author does not express his personal moods and fancies but human nature in general. Who, from a reading of the *Alcestis* of Euripides, learns anything about the dramatist's personal grief? And Racine's *Phèdre* — is it the story of Phèdre and Aricia, Hippolytus and Theseus, or is it rather a presentation of the tragedy which results when star-crossed lovers give way to the universal passion of love? Modern authors write of grief, or justice, or the passion of love, but when they do it is with this difference: they are more interested in the individual character and in his particular attitudes of mind than in the universality of the problem confronting the character.

This interest in universal rather than individual qualities reflects itself, as well, in the treatment classicism accorded to nature. In general, nature to the classicist was a philosophical concept; it meant order and the universal. To the romantic, however, nature was largely a matter of landscape, grottoes, valleys, hills, in a confused and wild arrangement. Mere copying of nature, the classicist held, would waste time on insignificant details, would reproduce the flaws as well as the perfections. Classicism corrects the flaws, it draws forth like the bee "from the best and choicest flowers and turns all into honey." It is the normal which attracts the interest:

> "The business of a poet," said Imlac [a character in Dr. Johnson's *Rasselas*], "is to examine, not the individual, but the species; to remark general properties and large appearances; he does not number the streaks of the tulip, or describe the different shades in the verdure of the forest. He is to exhibit in his portraits of nature such prominent and striking features as recall the original to every mind; and must neglect the minuter discriminations, which one may have remarked, and another have neglected, for those characteristics which are alike obvious to vigilance and carelessness."

Or, to quote from *An Essay on Criticism* by Alexander Pope, another neo-classical writer:

> Unerring Nature, still divinely bright,
> One clear, unchanged, and universal light;
> Life, force, and beauty, must to all impart,
> At once the source, and end, and test of Art.

Before such a conception the low and commonplace and the supernatural and extravagant give way to a formal interpretation of nature. The individual and the unusual make place for the universal and the conventional.

The tone of classical writing is edifying. Austere, decorous, dignified, proper, never squalid, with a great repugnance for all that is "low" and a conscious purpose to improve society and mankind, the classical writers gave an æsthetic significance, a nobility of manner, a moral purpose, to their work. They interested themselves characteristically in actions which were excellent. They identified the good and the beautiful. If, toward the close of neo-classicism in the eighteenth century, British authors became "prim, moderate, Whiggish and priggish" it was not the fault of the temper itself, it was simply that the manner had been allowed to lose its flower and go to seed. The classical writers had, at their best, selected for presentation those actions which were most excellent, "those, certainly," as Matthew Arnold has said, "which most powerfully appeal to the great primary human affections: to those elementary feelings which subsist permanently in the race, and which are independent of time." If the eighteenth century was didactic and satiric it was with the worthy aim of correcting society. "If," the neo-classicists seemed to argue, "the aim of literature is to edify, then writing must correct the weaknesses of society, and what better way to indicate the weaknesses of society than to treat them satirically?"

Classicism reflects the spirit of its times. In pre-Christian Greece, in seventeenth- and eighteenth-century France and England — periods when the national feeling was strong, when national civilizations developed — we encounter a classical literature, interestingly enough, growing out of single cities such as Athens, Rome, Paris, and London. The writers of these cities became the spokesmen for a time and a civilization. Brunetière, a French critic of the last century, recognized this *national spirit* (along with beauty of form, an expression of the edifying, a presentation of the natural) as one of the essential qualities of classicism. "Classicism," says H. J. C. Grierson,[1] "is the product of a nation and a generation which has consciously achieved a definite advance, moral, political, intellectual; and is filled with the belief that its view of life is more natural, human, universal and wise than that from which it has escaped. It has effected a synthesis which enables it to look round on life with a sense of its wholeness, its unity in variety; and the work of the artist is to give expression to that consciousness, hence the solidity of his work and hence too its definiteness, and in the hands of great artists its beauty."

If, then, we find the classical temper essentially one which emphasizes proportion, the importance of order, a logical beauty, and the completeness of man's nature, it is because the times which fostered the development of this spirit were themselves ordered, complete. In this sense the classical manner is at odds with the temper of modern literature which often views man as an infinitesimal atom in a disordered universe.

[1] From Grierson, *Classical and Romantic* (1923). By permission of The Macmillan Company, publishers, and the Cambridge University Press.

ILLUSTRATIONS

The Temper of Classicism

THE FIFTEEN illustrations which follow show the classical spirit at work in the realm of art. A study of the reproductions — whether drawn from painting, architecture, sculpture, or ceramics — will disclose a respect for form and an insistence on symmetry and proportion and unity which are characteristically classical. If we consider content, apart from form, we find the same tone reflected in the serious subjects treated by the artists, in the prevailing sense of decorum and dignity, and in the concern for the universal and the general as opposed to the individual and the specific.

For the moment we may consider simply the question of form. Is not the *Delphic Sibyl* carefully unified, with detail subordinated to the central figure? Is not the whole thoughtfully balanced and set forth with a fine sense of line and proportion? In Raphael's *The Dispute of the Sacrament* the space-composition, based on the use of semicircles, results in a harmony of line distinctly classical. A happy respect for form appears again in the *Madonna della Sedia* where the framing circle of the painting is repeated in the curves of the figures of the woman and the children. And, turning to architecture (the *Parthenon* and *Mount Vernon*), we find again this same harmony between individual lines and the whole, the parts contributing effectively to the whole. The classical form of the sculpture is more familiar to us, perhaps because the subjects, as well as the form, are those we associate with Greece; but here, too, line and symmetry and proportion are given emphasis which later schools do not always feel called upon to respect.

If we shift our attention from form to content, this same classical spirit reveals itself. Here are serious subjects portrayed with dignity and serenity. The specific gives way to the general, the individual to the universal. Study the faces of the figures in the reproductions. Are they conventionalized or individualized? How many of the people portrayed could we recognize were we to see them in the street? The cold and impersonal countenances in most of the figures in *The Death of St. Francis, The Annunciation, The Greek Slave,* the *Apollo Belvedere,* are typical rather than individual.

At least two of the illustrations which follow present interesting combinations of two moods — the classical and the realistic. The *St. John and St. Peter* has a fairly strong realistic strain in the character indicated in the two faces, a quality which contrasts with the classical serenity, dignity, and general restraint employed by Dürer elsewhere in the painting. In *The Annunciation* (Fra Angelico) the student in search of classical elements may well hesitate at the fence and the flowering grass — two qualities which approach the realistic.

The exceptions, however, do not overshadow the fact that in these illustrations, as a whole, we find the classical spirit at work — restraint, symmetry and simplicity in form; the noble, decorous, serious, and universal in content. And these features characterize the classical temper whether we are considering literature or painting, music or architecture. They are, in fact, the qualities which make the classical temper.

Plate 1   DELPHIC SIBYL   *Michelangelo*

Plate 2 ST. JOHN AND ST. PETER *Dürer*

Plate 3 THE DISPUTE OF THE SACRAMENT *Raphael*

Plate 4   THE DEATH OF ST. FRANCIS   *Giotto*

Plate 5   MADONNA DELLA SEDIA   *Raphael*

Plate 6   ŒDIPUS AND THE SPHINX   *Ingres*

Plate 7   THE ANNUNCIATION   *Fra Angelico*

Plate 8   PARTHENON FROM THE NORTHWEST

Plate 9   MOUNT VERNON

Plate 10   GATTAMELATA   *Donatello*

Plate 11   PAULINE BORGHESE AS VENUS   *Canova*

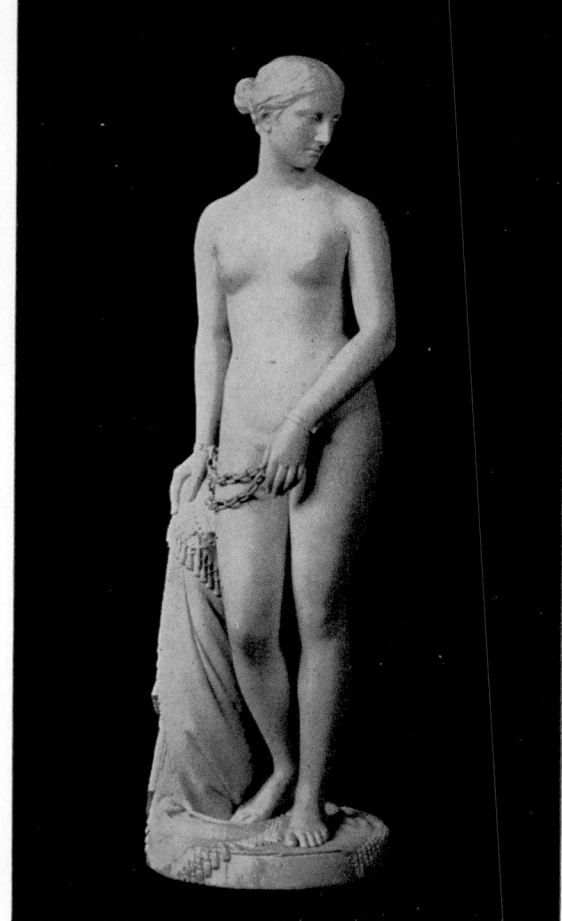

Plate 12   GREEK SLAVE   *Powers*

Plate 13   EAST FRIEZE OF PARTHENON (DETAIL)

Plate 14   BOY CHASING HARE   *Panaitios Painter*

Plate 15   APOLLO BELVEDERE

Homer

The origin of two of the greatest pieces of literature in the European tradition, the *Iliad* and the *Odyssey*, poems which present man of the legendary-historical epoch, is shrouded in a mist of uncertainty. Where Homer was born, when he lived, indeed that he even lived at all, have been matters of speculation among classical scholars. The great difficulty is that the *Iliad* and the *Odyssey* relate events which occurred in a period prior to recorded literary history. "The poems are facts," says Gilbert Murray, "and Homer a hypothesis to account for them."

Between 1800 and 1200 B.C. the Ægean civilization, which had developed at the eastern end of the Mediterranean, was overrun by invaders and penetrated by civilizations from without. These two epics, it seems likely, present a working over of the accounts of these early conflicts made by a single poet, Homer, some hundreds of years later when the accounts themselves had become legendary and the conflicts had been transmuted into myths.

But it is appropriate to leave to the scholars the various problems of historicity and texts. Important for us is that the literature of the Western World starts with these two great epics. Homer has made literature the richer for his Achilles and his Hector, his Odysseus and his Penelope. He has set before us for all time the example of brave men playing out their roles before Fate and yet making their own fate as they acted out their lives. And he has, too, given us interesting stories with organized and unified plots.

The *Iliad* has for a background the wedding of Peleus, the grandson of Zeus, and the goddess Thetis and the fact that Eris, the goddess of discord, had not been invited. Offended by the oversight, Eris proceeded to the ceremony and, to make trouble, tossed into the party a golden apple inscribed "for the fairest." Hera, the wife of Zeus and goddess of womanly virtues, Athene, goddess of wisdom, and Aphrodite, goddess of love, all claimed the prize. In his delightful *Dialogues of the Gods*, Lucian has dramatized this scene. He has Paris, who was asked by Hermes to choose among the three goddesses, answer:

> . . . how shall a mortal and a rustic like myself be judge of such unparalleled beauty? . . . here where all are beautiful alike, I know not how a man may leave looking at one, to look upon another. Where my eyes fall, there they fasten, — for there is beauty: I move them, and what do I find? more loveliness! I am fixed again, yet distracted by neighboring charms. I bathe in beauty: I am enthralled: ah, why am I not all eyes like Argus? Methinks it were a fair award, to give the apple to all three. Then again: one is the wife and sister of Zeus; the others are his daughters. Take it where you will, 'tis a hard matter to judge.

Ultimately Paris awards the apple to Aphrodite upon her promise to see that he meet Helen, the wife of Menelaus, king of Sparta. The meeting led to an elopement and to the ten-year siege of Troy. The actual account in the *Iliad* begins with the quarrel between Achilles and Agamemnon in the ninth year of the war. The settlement of this quarrel leaves Achilles sulking and gives, for a time, the advantage to the Trojans; but when Hector kills Achilles' friend, Patroclus, the Greek warrior forgets his private grievance against Agamemnon and, in personal conflict, revenges the loss of Patroclus by killing Hector. The *Iliad* ends with the funeral of Patroclus and the claiming of Hector's body by Priam, king of Troy and father of Hector. Homer does not recount all of the events of the ten years' siege; he focuses his narrative particularly on the episodes of the last fifty days of the tenth year. Further unity is secured through the poet's centering his story on Achilles, the son of Peleus and Thetis, and a few other heroes of the struggle.

The *Odyssey* takes up the account after Troy has fallen and presents the adventures and wanderings of Odysseus in the ten years which intervene between the victory at Troy and his return home. Homer begins his narration — and here we see the poet's artistic skill at work — with a statement of affairs at the home of Odysseus during the years of his absence, then presents somewhat cursorily the early episodes of Odysseus' travels, finally concentrating his attention on the events of the last forty-two days of his wandering.

The Homeric poems, in the words of Professor T. B. L. Webster, "have in common a central thread into which relevant digressions are inserted, symmetrical composition of scenes, divine machinery, clear characterization of individuals, particularly Achilles, Hector, Andromache, Odysseus, Penelope, similes from animals and everyday life to illustrate behaviour, extensive use of formulae for stock scenes and of stock phrases for people and objects, ready-made to fit different places in the hexameter line, which nevertheless never detract from the swift brilliant immediacy of the narrative."

SUGGESTED REFERENCES: C. M. Bowra, *Tradition and Design in the Iliad* (rev. ed., 1958); Gabriel Germain, *Homer* (1960); G. Steiner and R. Fagles, eds., *Homer. A Collection of Critical Essays* (1962); C. H. Taylor, ed., *Essays on the Odyssey* (1963).

The Iliad[1]

BOOK I

Sing, goddess, the anger of Peleus' son Achilleus
and its devastation, which put pains thousandfold
    upon the Achaians,
hurled in their multitudes to the house of Hades
    strong souls
of heroes, but gave their bodies to be the delicate
    feasting
of dogs, of all birds, and the will of Zeus was
    accomplished 5
since that time when first there stood in division of
    conflict
Atreus' son the lord of men and brilliant Achilleus.
What god was it then set them together in bitter
    collision?
Zeus' son and Leto's, Apollo, who in anger at the
    king drove
the foul pestilence along the host, and the people
    perished, 10
since Atreus' son had dishonoured Chryses, priest
    of Apollo,
when he came beside the fast ships of the Achaians
    to ransom
back his daughter, carrying gifts beyond count and
    holding
in his hands wound on a staff of gold the ribbons
    of Apollo
who strikes from afar, and supplicated all the
    Achaians, 15
but above all Atreus' two sons, the marshals of the
    people:

[1] Reprinted from *The Iliad of Homer* translated by Richmond Lattimore by permission of The University of Chicago Press. Copyright © 1951 by The University of Chicago.

'Sons of Atreus and you other strong-greaved
    Achaians,
to you may the gods grant who have their homes
    on Olympos
Priam's city to be plundered and a fair home-
    coming thereafter,
but may you give me back my own daughter and
    take the ransom, 20
giving honour to Zeus' son who strikes from afar,
    Apollo.'
Then all the rest of the Achaians cried out in
    favour
that the priest be respected and the shining ransom
    be taken;
yet this pleased not the heart of Atreus' son
    Agamemnon,
but harshly he drove him away with a strong order
    upon him: 25
'Never let me find you again, old sir, near our
    hollow
ships, neither lingering now nor coming again
    hereafter,
for fear your staff and the god's ribbons help you
    no longer.
The girl I will not give back; sooner will old age
    come upon her
in my own house, in Argos, far from her own land,
    going 30
up and down by the loom and being in my bed
    as my companion.
So go now, do not make me angry; so you will be
    safer.'
So he spoke, and the old man in terror obeyed him
and went silently away beside the murmuring sea
    beach.
Over and over the old man prayed as he walked in
    solitude 35
to King Apollo, whom Leto of the lovely hair bore:
    'Hear me,
lord of the silver bow who set your power about
    Chryse

and Killa the sacrosanct, who are lord in strength over Tenedos,

Smintheus, if ever it pleased your heart that I built your temple,

if ever it pleased you that I burned all the rich thigh pieces 40

of bulls, of goats, then bring to pass this wish I pray for:

let your arrows make the Danaans pay for my tears shed.'

So he spoke in prayer, and Phoibos Apollo heard him,

and strode down along the pinnacles of Olympos, angered

in his heart, carrying across his shoulders the bow and the hooded 45

quiver; and the shafts clashed on the shoulders of the god walking

angrily. He came as night comes down and knelt then

apart and opposite the ships and let go an arrow.

Terrible was the clash that rose from the bow of silver.

First he went after the mules and the circling hounds, then let go 50

a tearing arrow against the men themselves and struck them.

The corpse fires burned everywhere and did not stop burning.

Nine days up and down the host ranged the god's arrows,

but on the tenth Achilleus called the people to assembly;

a thing put into his mind by the goddess of the white arms, Hera, 55

who had pity upon the Danaans when she saw them dying.

Now when they were all assembled in one place together,

Achilleus of the swift feet stood up among them and spoke forth:

'Son of Atreus, I believe now that straggling backwards

we must make our way home if we can even escape death, 60

if fighting now must crush the Achaians and the plague likewise.

No, come, let us ask some holy man, some prophet,

even an interpreter of dreams, since a dream also

comes from Zeus, who can tell why Phoibos Apollo is so angry,

if for the sake of some vow, some hecatomb he blames us, 65

if given the fragrant smoke of lambs, of he goats, somehow

he can be made willing to beat the bane aside from us.'

He spoke thus and sat down again, and among them stood up

Kalchas, Thestor's son, far the best of the bird interpreters,

who knew all things that were, the things to come and the things past, 70

who guided into the land of Ilion the ships of the Achaians

through that seercraft of his own that Phoibos Apollo gave him.

He in kind intention toward all stood forth and addressed them:

'You have bidden me, Achilleus beloved of Zeus, to explain to

you this anger of Apollo the lord who strikes from afar. Then 75

I will speak; yet make me a promise and swear before me

readily by word and work of your hands to defend me,

since I believe I shall make a man angry who holds great kingship

over the men of Argos, and all the Achaians obey him.

For a king when he is angry with a man beneath him is too strong, 80

and suppose even for the day itself he swallow down his anger,

he still keeps bitterness that remains until its fulfilment

deep in his chest. Speak forth then, tell me if you will protect me.'

Then in answer again spoke Achilleus of the swift feet:

'Speak, interpreting whatever you know, and fear nothing. 85

In the name of Apollo beloved of Zeus to whom you, Kalchas,

make your prayers when you interpret the gods' will to the Danaans,

no man so long as I am alive above earth and see daylight

shall lay the weight of his hands on you beside the hollow ships,

not one of all the Danaans, even if you mean Agamemnon, 90

who now claims to be far the greatest of all the Achaians.'

At this the blameless seer took courage again and spoke forth:

'No, it is not for the sake of some vow or hecatomb he blames us,

but for the sake of his priest whom Agamemnon dishonoured

and would not give him back his daughter nor accept the ransom. 95

Therefore the archer sent griefs against us and
will send them

still, nor sooner thrust back the shameful plague
from the Danaans

until we give the glancing-eyed girl back to her
father

without price, without ransom, and lead also a
blessed hecatomb

to Chryse; thus we might propitiate and persuade
him.'   100

He spoke thus and sat down again, and among
them stood up

Atreus' son the hero wide-ruling Agamemnon

raging, the heart within filled black to the brim
with anger

from beneath, but his two eyes showed like fire in
their blazing.

First of all he eyed Kalchas bitterly and spoke to
him: 105

'Seer of evil: never yet have you told me a good
thing.

Always the evil things are dear to your heart to
prophesy,

but nothing excellent have you said nor ever
accomplished.

Now once more you make divination to the
Danaans, argue

forth your reason why he who strikes from afar
afflicts them,   110

because I for the sake of the girl Chryseis would
not take

the shining ransom; and indeed I wish greatly to
have her

in my own house; since I like her better than
Klytaimestra

my own wife, for in truth she is no way inferior,

neither in build nor stature nor wit, not in accomplishment.   115

Still I am willing to give her back, if such is the
best way.

I myself desire that my people be safe, not perish.

Find me then some prize that shall be my own, lest
I only

among the Argives go without, since that were
unfitting;

you are all witnesses to this thing, that my prize
goes elsewhere.'   120

Then in answer again spoke brilliant swift-footed
Achilleus:

'Son of Atreus, most lordly, greediest for gain of
all men,

how shall the great-hearted Achaians give you a
prize now?

There is no great store of things lying about I
know of.

But what we took from the cities by storm has
been distributed;   125

it is unbecoming for the people to call back things
once given.

No, for the present give the girl back to the god;
we Achaians

thrice and four times over will repay you, if ever
Zeus gives

into our hands the strong-walled citadel of Troy
to be plundered.'

Then in answer again spoke powerful Agamemnon:

'Not that way, good fighter though you be, godlike
Achilleus,   131

strive to cheat, for you will not deceive, you will
not persuade me.

What do you want? To keep your own prize and
have me sit here

lacking one? Are you ordering me to give this
girl back?

Either the great-hearted Achaians shall give me a
new prize   135

chosen according to my desire to atone for the
girl lost,

or else if they will not give me one I myself shall
take her,

your own prize, or that of Aias, or that of Odysseus,

going myself in person; and he whom I visit will
be bitter.

Still, these are things we shall deliberate again
hereafter.   140

Come, now, we must haul a black ship down to the
bright sea,

and assemble rowers enough for it, and put on
board it

the hecatomb, and the girl herself, Chryseis of the
fair cheeks,

and let there be one responsible man in charge of
her,

either Aias or Idomeneus or brilliant Odysseus, 145

or you yourself, son of Peleus, most terrifying of
all men,

to reconcile by accomplishing sacrifice the archer.'

Then looking darkly at him Achilleus of the swift
feet spoke:

'O wrapped in shamelessness, with your mind
forever on profit,

how shall any one of the Achaians readily obey
you   150

either to go on a journey or to fight men strongly
in battle?

I for my part did not come here for the sake of the
Trojan

spearmen to fight against them, since to me they
have done nothing.

Never yet have they driven away my cattle or
my horses,

never in Phthia where the soil is rich and men grow great did they   155
spoil my harvest, since indeed there is much that lies between us,
the shadowy mountains and the echoing sea; but for your sake,
o great shamelessness, we followed, to do you favour,
you with the dog's eyes, to win your honour and Menelaos'
from the Trojans. You forget all this or else you care nothing.   160
And now my prize you threaten in person to strip from me,
for whom I laboured much, the gift of the sons of the Achaians.
Never, when the Achaians sack some well-founded citadel
of the Trojans, do I have a prize that is equal to your prize.
Always the greater part of the painful fighting is the work of   165
my hands; but when the time comes to distribute the booty
yours is far the greater reward, and I with some small thing
yet dear to me go back to my ships when I am weary with fighting.
Now I am returning to Phthia, since it is much better
to go home again with my curved ships, and I am minded no longer   170
to stay here dishonoured and pile up your wealth and your luxury.'
Then answered him in turn the lord of men Agamemnon:
'Run away by all means if your heart drives you. I will not
entreat you to stay here for my sake. There are others with me
who will do me honour, and above all Zeus of the counsels.   175
To me you are the most hateful of all the kings whom the gods love.
Forever quarrelling is dear to your heart, and wars and battles;
and if you are very strong indeed, that is a god's gift.
Go home then with your own ships and your own companions,
be king over the Myrmidons. I care nothing about you.   180
I take no account of your anger. But here is my threat to you.
Even as Phoibos Apollo is taking away my Chryseis.

I shall convey her back in my own ship, with my own
followers; but I shall take the fair-cheeked Briseis,
your prize, I myself going to your shelter, that you may learn well   185
how much greater I am than you, and another man may shrink back
from likening himself to me and contending against me.'
So he spoke. And the anger came on Peleus' son, and within
his shaggy breast the heart was divided two ways, pondering
whether to draw from beside his thigh the sharp sword, driving   190
away all those who stood between and kill the son of Atreus,
or else to check the spleen within and keep down his anger.
Now as he weighed in mind and spirit these two courses
and was drawing from its scabbard the great sword, Athene descended
from the sky. For Hera the goddess of the white arms sent her,   195
who loved both men equally in her heart and cared for them.
The goddess standing behind Peleus' son caught him by the fair hair,
appearing to him only, for no man of the others saw her.
Achilleus in amazement turned about, and straightway
knew Pallas Athene and the terrible eyes shining.
He uttered winged words and addressed her: 'Why have you come now,   201
o child of Zeus of the aegis, once more? Is it that you may see
the outrageousness of the son of Atreus Agamemnon?
Yet will I tell you this thing, and I think it shall be accomplished.
By such acts of arrogance he may even lose his own life.'   205
Then in answer the goddess grey-eyed Athene spoke to him:
'I have come down to stay your anger—but will you obey me?—
from the sky; and the goddess of the white arms Hera sent me,
who loves both of you equally in her heart and cares for you.
Come then, do not take your sword in your hand, keep clear of fighting,   210
though indeed with words you may abuse him, and it will be that way.

And this also will I tell you and it will be a thing
  accomplished.
Some day three times over such shining gifts shall
  be given you
by reason of this outrage. Hold your hand then,
  and obey us.'
Then in answer again spoke Achilleus of the swift
  feet: 215
'Goddess, it is necessary that I obey the word of
  you two,
angry though I am in my heart. So it will be
  better.
If any man obeys the gods, they listen to him
  also.'
He spoke, and laid his heavy hand on the silver
  sword hilt
and thrust the great blade back into the scabbard
  nor disobeyed   220
the word of Athene. And she went back again
  to Olympos
to the house of Zeus of the aegis with the other
  divinities.
But Peleus' son once again in words of derision
spoke to Atreides, and did not yet let go of his
  anger:
'You wine sack, with a dog's eyes, with a deer's
  heart. Never   225
once have you taken courage in your heart to arm
  with your people
for battle, or go into ambuscade with the best of
  the Achaians.
No, for in such things you see death. Far better
  to your mind
is it, all along the widespread host of the Achaians
to take away the gifts of any man who speaks up
  against you.   230
King who feed on your people, since you rule
  nonentities;
otherwise, son of Atreus, this were your last
  outrage.
But I will tell you this and swear a great oath upon
  it:
in the name of this sceptre, which never again will
  bear leaf nor
branch, now that it has left behind the cut stump
  in the mountains,   235
nor shall it ever blossom again, since the bronze
  blade stripped
bark and leafage, and now at last the sons of the
  Achaians
carry it in their hands in state when they administer
the justice of Zeus. And this shall be a great oath
  before you:
some day longing for Achilleus will come to the
  sons of the Achaians,   240

all of them. Then stricken at heart though you
  be, you will be able
to do nothing, when in their numbers before man-
  slaughtering Hektor
they drop and die. And then you will eat out the
  heart within you
in sorrow, that you did no honour to the best of
  the Achaians.'
Thus spoke Peleus' son and dashed to the ground
  the sceptre   245
studded with golden nails, and sat down again.
  But Atreides
raged still on the other side, and between them
  Nestor
the fair-spoken rose up, the lucid speaker of
  Pylos,
from whose lips the streams of words ran sweeter
  than honey.
In his time two generations of mortal men had
  perished,   250
those who had grown up with him and they who
  had been born to
these in sacred Pylos, and he was king in the third
  age.
He in kind intention toward both stood forth and
  addressed them:
'Oh, for shame. Great sorrow comes on the land
  of Achaia.
Now might Priam and the sons of Priam in truth
  be happy,   255
and all the rest of the Trojans be visited in their
  hearts with gladness,
were they to hear all this wherein you two are
  quarrelling,
you, who surpass all Danaans in council, in
  fighting.
Yet be persuaded. Both of you are younger than
  I am.
Yes, and in my time I have dealt with better
  men than   260
you are, and never once did they disregard me.
  Never
yet have I seen nor shall see again such men as
  these were,
men like Peirithoös, and Dryas, shepherd of the
  people,
Kaineus and Exadios, godlike Polyphemos,
or Theseus, Aigeus' son, in the likeness of the
  immortals.   265
These were the strongest generation of earth-born
  mortals,
the strongest, and they fought against the strongest, the beast men
living within the mountains, and terribly they
  destroyed them.

I was of the company of these men, coming from Pylos,

a long way from a distant land, since they had summoned me. 270

And I fought single-handed, yet against such men no one

of the mortals now alive upon earth could do battle. And also

these listened to the counsels I gave and heeded my bidding.

Do you also obey, since to be persuaded is better.

You, great man that you are, yet do not take the girl away 275

but let her be, a prize as the sons of the Achaians gave her

first. Nor, son of Peleus, think to match your strength with

the king, since never equal with the rest is the portion of honour

of the sceptred king to whom Zeus gives magnificence. Even

though you are the stronger man, and the mother who bore you was immortal, 280

yet is this man greater who is lord over more than you rule.

Son of Atreus, give up your anger; even I entreat you

to give over your bitterness against Achilleus, he who

stands as a great bulwark of battle over all the Achaians.'

Then in answer again spoke powerful Agamemnon:

'Yes, old sir, all this you have said is fair and orderly. 286

Yet here is a man who wishes to be above all others,

who wishes to hold power over all, and to be lord of

all, and give them their orders, yet I think one will not obey him.

And if the everlasting gods have made him a spearman, 290

yet they have not given him the right to speak abusively.'

Then looking at him darkly brilliant Achilleus answered him:

'So must I be called of no account and a coward

if I must carry out every order you may happen to give me.

Tell other men to do these things, but give me no more 295

commands, since I for my part have no intention to obey you.

And put away in your thoughts this other thing I tell you.

With my hands I will not fight for the girl's sake, neither

with you nor any other man, since you take her away who gave her.

But of all the other things that are mine beside my fast black 300

ship, you shall take nothing away against my pleasure.

Come, then, only try it, that these others may see also;

instantly your own black blood will stain my spearpoint.'

So these two after battling in words of contention

stood up, and broke the assembly beside the ships of the Achaians. 305

Peleus' son went back to his balanced ships and his shelter

with Patroklos, Menoitios' son, and his own companions.

But the son of Atreus drew a fast ship down to the water

and allotted into it twenty rowers and put on board it

the hecatomb for the god and Chryseis of the fair cheeks 310

leading her by the hand. And in charge went crafty Odysseus.

These then putting out went over the ways of the water

while Atreus' son told his people to wash off their defilement.

And they washed it away and threw the washings into the salt sea.

Then they accomplished perfect hecatombs to Apollo, 315

of bulls and goats along the beach of the barren salt sea.

The savour of the burning swept in circles up to the bright sky.

Thus these were busy about the army. But Agamemnon

did not give up his anger and the first threat he made to Achilleus,

but to Talthybios he gave his orders and Eurybates

who were heralds and hard-working henchmen to him: 'Go now 321

to the shelter of Peleus' son Achilleus, to bring back

Briseis of the fair cheeks leading her by the hand. And if he

will not give her, I must come in person to take her

with many men behind me, and it will be the worse for him.' 325

He spoke and sent them forth with this strong order upon them.

They went against their will beside the beach of the barren

salt sea, and came to the shelters and the ships of the Myrmidons.

The man himself they found beside his shelter and his black ship

sitting. And Achilleus took no joy at all when he saw them. 330

These two terrified and in awe of the king stood waiting

quietly, and did not speak a word at all nor question him.

But he knew the whole matter in his own heart, and spoke first:

'Welcome, heralds, messengers of Zeus and of mortals.

Draw near. You are not to blame in my sight, but Agamemnon 335

who sent the two of you here for the sake of the girl Briseis.

Go then, illustrious Patroklos, and bring the girl forth

and give her to these to be taken away. Yet let them be witnesses

in the sight of the blessed gods, in the sight of mortal

men, and of this cruel king, if ever hereafter 340

there shall be need of me to beat back the shameful destruction

from the rest. For surely in ruinous heart he makes sacrifice

and has not wit enough to look behind and before him

that the Achaians fighting beside their ships shall not perish.'

So he spoke, and Patroklos obeyed his beloved companion. 345

He led forth from the hut Briseis of the fair cheeks and gave her

to be taken away; and they walked back beside the ships of the Achaians,

and the woman all unwilling went with them still. But Achilleus

weeping went and sat in sorrow apart from his companions

beside the beach of the grey sea looking out on the infinite water. 350

Many times stretching forth his hands he called on his mother:

'Since, my mother, you bore me to be a man with a short life,

therefore Zeus of the loud thunder on Olympos should grant me

honour at least. But now he has given me not even a little.

Now the son of Atreus, powerful Agamemnon, 355

has dishonoured me, since he has taken away my prize and keeps it.'

So he spoke in tears and the lady his mother heard him

as she sat in the depths of the sea at the side of her aged father,

and lightly she emerged like a mist from the grey water.

She came and sat beside him as he wept, and stroked him 360

with her hand and called him by name and spoke to him: 'Why then,

child, do you lament? What sorrow has come to your heart now?

Tell me, do not hide it in your mind, and thus we shall both know.'

Sighing heavily Achilleus of the swift feet answered her:

'You know; since you know why must I tell you all this? 365

We went against Thebe, the sacred city of Eëtion,

and the city we sacked, and carried everything back to this place,

and the sons of the Achaians made a fair distribution

and for Atreus' son they chose out Chryseis of the fair cheeks.

Then Chryses, priest of him who strikes from afar, Apollo, 370

came beside the fast ships of the bronze-armoured Achaians to ransom

back his daughter, carrying gifts beyond count and holding

in his hands wound on a staff of gold the ribbons of Apollo

who strikes from afar, and supplicated all the Achaians,

but above all Atreus' two sons, the marshals of the people. 375

Then all the rest of the Achaians cried out in favour

that the priest be respected and the shining ransom be taken;

yet this pleased not the heart of Atreus' son Agamemnon,

but harshly he sent him away with a strong order upon him.

The old man went back again in anger, but Apollo 380

listened to his prayer, since he was very dear to him, and let go

the wicked arrow against the Argives. And now the people

were dying one after another while the god's shafts ranged

everywhere along the wide host of the Achaians, till the seer
knowing well the truth interpreted the designs of the archer.   385
It was I first of all urged then the god's appeasement;
and the anger took hold of Atreus' son, and in speed standing
he uttered his threat against me, and now it is a thing accomplished.
For the girl the glancing-eyed Achaians are taking to Chryse
in a fast ship, also carrying to the king presents. But even   390
now the heralds went away from my shelter leading
Briseus' daughter, whom the sons of the Achaians gave me.
You then, if you have power to, protect your own son, going
to Olympos and supplicating Zeus, if ever before now
either by word you comforted Zeus' heart or by action.   395
Since it is many times in my father's halls I have heard you
making claims, when you said you only among the immortals
beat aside shameful destruction from Kronos' son the dark-misted,
that time when all the other Olympians sought to bind him,
Hera and Poseidon and Pallas Athene. Then you, goddess, went and set him free from his shackles, summoning   401
in speed the creature of the hundred hands to tall Olympos,
that creature the gods name Briareus, but all men
Aigaios' son, but he is far greater in strength than his father.
He rejoicing in the glory of it sat down by Kronion,   405
and the rest of the blessed gods were frightened and gave up binding him.
Sit beside him and take his knees and remind him of these things
now, if perhaps he might be willing to help the Trojans,
and pin the Achaians back against the ships and the water,
dying, so that thus they may all have profit of their own king,   410
that Atreus' son wide-ruling Agamemnon may recognize
his madness, that he did no honour to the best of the Achaians.'

Thetis answered him then letting the tears fall: 'Ah me,
my child. Your birth was bitterness. Why did I raise you?
If only you could sit by your ships untroubled, not weeping,   415
since indeed your lifetime is to be short, of no length.
Now it has befallen that your life must be brief and bitter
beyond all men's. To a bad destiny I bore you in my chambers.
But I will go to cloud-dark Olympos and ask this thing of Zeus who delights in the thunder. Perhaps he will do it.   420
Do you therefore continuing to sit by your swift ships
be angry at the Achaians and stay away from all fighting.
For Zeus went to the blameless Aithiopians at the Ocean
yesterday to feast, and the rest of the gods went with him.
On the twelfth day he will be coming back to Olympos,   425
and then I will go for your sake to the house of Zeus, bronze-founded,
and take him by the knees and I think I can persuade him.'
So speaking she went away from that place and left him
sorrowing in his heart for the sake of the fair-girdled woman
whom they were taking by force against his will. But Odysseus   430
meanwhile drew near to Chryse conveying the sacred hecatomb.
These when they were inside the many-hollowed harbour
took down and gathered together the sails and stowed them in the black ship,
let down mast by the forestays, and settled it into the mast crutch
easily, and rowed her in with oars to the mooring.
They threw over the anchor stones and made fast the stern cables   436
and themselves stepped out on to the break of the sea beach,
and led forth the hecatomb to the archer Apollo,
and Chryseis herself stepped forth from the sea-going vessel.
Odysseus of the many designs guided her to the altar   440
and left her in her father's arms and spoke a word to him:

'Chryses, I was sent here by the lord of men
    Agamemnon
to lead back your daughter and accomplish a
    sacred hecatomb
to Apollo on behalf of the Danaans, that we may
    propitiate
the lord who has heaped unhappiness and tears
    on the Argives.'   445
He spoke, and left her in his arms. And he received
    gladly
his beloved child. And the men arranged the
    sacred hecatomb
for the god in orderly fashion around the strong-
    founded altar.
Next they washed their hands and took up the
    scattering barley.
Standing among them with lifted arms Chryses
    prayed in a great voice: 450
'Hear me, lord of the silver bow, who set your
    power about
Chryse and Killa the sacrosanct, who are lord in
    strength over
Tenedos; if once before you listened to my prayers
and did me honour and smote strongly the host
    of the Achaians,
so one more time bring to pass the wish that I
    pray for.   455
Beat aside at last the shameful plague from the
    Danaans.'
So he spoke in prayer, and Phoibos Apollo heard
    him.
And when all had made prayer and flung down
    the scattering barley
first they drew back the victims' heads and
    slaughtered them and skinned them,
and cut away the meat from the thighs and wrap-
    ped them in fat,   460
making a double fold, and laid shreds of flesh
    upon them.
The old man burned these on a cleft stick and
    poured the gleaming
wine over, while the young men with forks in their
    hands stood about him.
But when they had burned the thigh pieces and
    tasted the vitals,
they cut all the remainder into pieces and spitted
    them   465
and roasted all carefully and took off the pieces.
Then after they had finished the work and got
    the feast ready
they feasted, nor was any man's hunger denied a
    fair portion.
But when they had put away their desire for
    eating and drinking,
the young men filled the mixing bowls with pure
    wine, passing   470

a portion to all, when they had offered drink in the
    goblets.
All day long they propitiated the god with singing,
chanting a splendid hymn to Apollo, these young
    Achaians,
singing to the one who works from afar, who
    listened in gladness.
Afterwards when the sun went down and darkness
    came onward   475
they lay down and slept beside the ship's stern
    cables.
But when the young Dawn showed again with her
    rosy fingers,
they put forth to sea toward the wide camp of the
    Achaians.
And Apollo who works from afar sent them a
    favouring stern wind.
They set up the mast again and spread on it the
    white sails,   480
and the wind blew into the middle of the sail, and
    at the cutwater
a blue wave rose and sang strongly as the ship
    went onward.
She ran swiftly cutting across the swell her
    pathway.
But when they had come back to the wide camp
    of the Achaians
they hauled the black ship up on the mainland,
    high up   485
on the sand, and underneath her they fixed the
    long props.
Afterwards they scattered to their own ships and
    their shelters.
But that other still sat in anger beside his swift
    ships,
Peleus' son divinely born, Achilleus of the swift
    feet.
Never now would he go to assemblies where men
    win glory,   490
never more into battle, but continued to waste
    his heart out
sitting there, though he longed always for the
    clamour and fighting.
But when the twelfth dawn after this day appeared,
    the gods who
live forever came back to Olympos all in a body
and Zeus led them; nor did Thetis forget the
    entreaties   495
of her son, but she emerged from the sea's waves
    early
in the morning and went up to the tall sky and
    Olympos.
She found Kronos' broad-browed son apart from
    the others
sitting upon the highest peak of rugged Olympos.
She came and sat beside him with her left hand
    embracing   500

his knees, but took him underneath the chin with
her right hand
and spoke in supplication to lord Zeus son of
Kronos:
'Father Zeus, if ever before in word or action
I did you favour among the immortals, now grant
what I ask for.
Now give honour to my son short-lived beyond all
other 505
mortals. Since even now the lord of men
Agamemnon
dishonours him, who has taken away his prize
and keeps it.
Zeus of the counsels, lord of Olympos, now do him
honour.
So long put strength into the Trojans, until the
Achaians
give my son his rights, and his honour is increased
among them.' 510
She spoke thus. But Zeus who gathers the clouds
made no answer
but sat in silence a long time. And Thetis, as she
had taken
his knees, clung fast to them and urged once more
her question:
'Bend your head and promise me to accomplish
this thing,
or else refuse it, you have nothing to fear, that I
may know 515
by how much I am the most dishonoured of all
gods.'
Deeply disturbed Zeus who gathers the clouds
answered her:
'This is a disastrous matter when you set me in
conflict
with Hera, and she troubles me with recriminations.
Since even as things are, forever among the
immortals 520
she is at me and speaks of how I help the Trojans
in battle.
Even so, go back again now, go away, for fear she
see us. I will look to these things that they be
accomplished.
See then, I will bend my head that you may
believe me.
For this among the immortal gods is the mightiest
witness 525
I can give, and nothing I do shall be vain nor
revocable
nor a thing unfulfilled when I bend my head in
assent to it.'
He spoke, the son of Kronos, and nodded his head
with the dark brows,
and the immortally anointed hair of the great
god
swept from his divine head, and all Olympos was
shaken. 530

So these two who had made their plans separated,
and Thetis
leapt down again from shining Olympos into the
sea's depth,
but Zeus went back to his own house, and all the
gods rose up
from their chairs to greet the coming of their
father, not one had courage
to keep his place as the father advanced, but stood
up to greet him. 535
Thus he took his place on the throne; yet Hera
was not
ignorant, having seen how he had been plotting
counsels
with Thetis the silver-footed, the daughter of the
sea's ancient,
and at once she spoke revilingly to Zeus son of
Kronos:
'Treacherous one, what god has been plotting
counsels with you? 540
Always it is dear to your heart in my absence to
think of
secret things and decide upon them. Never have
you patience
frankly to speak forth to me the things that you
purpose.'
Then to her the father of gods and men made
answer:
'Hera, do not go on hoping that you will hear all
my 545
thoughts, since these will be too hard for you,
though you are my wife.
Any thought that it is right for you to listen to,
no one
neither man nor any immortal shall hear it before
you.
But anything that apart from the rest of the gods
I wish to
plan, do not always question each detail nor
probe me.' 550
Then the goddess the ox-eyed lady Hera answered:
'Majesty, son of Kronos, what sort of thing have
you spoken?
Truly too much in time past I have not questioned
nor probed you,
but you are entirely free to think out whatever
pleases you.
Now, though, I am terrible afraid you were won
over 555
by Thetis the silver-footed, the daughter of the
sea's ancient.
For early in the morning she sat beside you and
took your
knees, and I think you bowed your head in assent
to do honour
to Achilleus, and to destroy many beside the ships
of the Achaians.'

Then in return Zeus who gathers the clouds made
    answer: 560
'Dear lady, I never escape you, you are always full
    of suspicion.
Yet thus you can accomplish nothing surely, but
    be more
distant from my heart than ever, and it will be
    the worse for you.
If what you say is true, then that is the way I
    wish it.
But go then, sit down in silence, and do as I tell
    you.   565
for fear all the gods, as many as are on Olympos,
    can do nothing
if I come close and lay my unconquerable hands
    upon you.'
He spoke, and the goddess the ox-eyed lady Hera
    was frightened
and went and sat down in silence wrenching her
    heart to obedience,
and all the Uranian gods in the house of Zeus were
    troubled.   570
Hephaistos the renowned smith rose up to speak
    among them,
to bring comfort to his beloved mother, Hera of
    the white arms:
'This will be a disastrous matter and not endurable
if you two are to quarrel thus for the sake of
    mortals
and bring brawling among the gods. There will
    be no pleasure   575
in the stately feast at all, since vile things will be
    uppermost.
And I entreat my mother, though she herself
    understands it,
to be ingratiating toward our father Zeus, that no
    longer
our father may scold her and break up the quiet
    of our feasting.
For if the Olympian who handles the lightning
    should be minded   580
to hurl us out of our places, he is far too strong for
    any.
Do you therefore approach him again with words
    made gentle,
and at once the Olympian will be gracious again
    to us.'
He spoke, and springing to his feet put a two-
    handled goblet
into his mother's hands and spoke again to her
    once more: 585
'Have patience, my mother, and endure it, though
    you be saddened,
for fear that, dear as you are, I see you before my
    own eyes
struck down, and then sorry though I be I shall
    not be able

to do anything. It is too hard to fight against the
    Olympian.
There was a time once before now I was minded
    to help you,   590
and he caught me by the foot and threw me from
    the magic threshold,
and all day long I dropped helpless, and about
    sunset
I landed in Lemnos, and there was not much life
    left in me.
After that fall it was the Sintian men who took
    care of me.'
He spoke, and the goddess of the white arms Hera
    smiled at him,   595
and smiling she accepted the goblet out of her
    son's hand.
Thereafter beginning from the left he poured
    drinks for the other
gods, dipping up from the mixing bowl the sweet
    nectar.
But among the blessed immortals uncontrollable
    laughter
went up as they saw Hephaistos bustling about the
    palace.   600
Thus thereafter the whole day long until the sun
    went under
they feasted, nor was anyone's hunger denied a
    fair portion,
nor denied the beautifully wrought lyre in the
    hands of Apollo
nor the antiphonal sweet sound of the Muses
    singing.
Afterwards when the light of the flaming sun went
    under   605
they went away each one to sleep in his home
    where
for each one the far-renowned strong-handed
    Hephaistos
had built a house by means of his craftsmanship
    and cunning.
Zeus the Olympian and lord of the lightning went
    to
his own bed, where always he lay when sweet
    sleep came on him.   610
Going up to the bed he slept and Hera of the gold
    throne beside him.

BOOK XVIII

So these fought on in the likeness of blazing fire.
    Meanwhile,
Antilochos came, a swift-footed messenger, to
    Achilleus,
and found him sitting in front of the steep-horned
    ships, thinking

over in his heart of things which had now been
    accomplished.
Disturbed, Achilleus spoke to the spirit in his own
    great heart: 5
'Ah me, how is it that once again the flowing-
    haired Achaians
are driven out of the plain on their ships in fear
    and confusion?
May the gods not accomplish vile sorrows upon
    the heart in me
in the way my mother once made it clear to me,
    when she told me
how while I yet lived the bravest of all the
    Myrmidons   10
must leave the light of the sun beneath the hands
    of the Trojans.
Surely, then, the strong son of Menoitios has
    perished.
Unhappy! and yet I told him, once he had beaten
    the fierce fire
off, to come back to the ships, not fight in strength
    against Hektor.'
Now as he was pondering this in his heart and his
    spirit,   15
meanwhile the son of stately Nestor was drawing
    near him
and wept warm tears, and gave Achilleus his sor-
    rowful message:
'Ah me, son of valiant Peleus; you must hear from
    me
the ghastly message of a thing I wish never had
    happened.
Patroklos has fallen, and now they are fighting
    over his body   20
which is naked. Hektor of the shining helm has
    taken his armour.'
He spoke, and the black cloud of sorrow closed
    on Achilleus.
In both hands he caught up the grimy dust, and
    poured it
over his head and face, and fouled his handsome
    countenance,
and the black ashes were scattered over his
    immortal tunic.   25
And he himself, mightily in his might, in the dust
    lay
at length, and took and tore at his hair with his
    hands, and defiled it.
And the handmaidens Achilleus and Patroklos had
    taken
captive, stricken at heart cried out aloud, and
    came running
out of doors about valiant Achilleus, and all of
    them   30
beat their breasts with their hands, and the limbs
    went slack in each of them.

On the other side Antilochos mourned with him,
    letting the tears fall,
and held the hands of Achilleus as he grieved in
    his proud heart,
fearing Achilleus might cut his throat with the
    iron. He cried out
terribly, aloud, and the lady his mother heard
    him   35
as she sat in the depths of the sea at the side of
    her aged father,
and she cried shrill in turn, and the goddesses
    gathered about her,
all who along the depth of the sea were daughters
    of Nereus.
For Glauke was there, Kymodoke and Thaleia,
Nesaie and Speio and Thoë, and ox-eyed Halia; 40
Kymothoë was there, Aktaia and Limnoreia,
Melite and Iaira, Amphithoë and Agauë,
Doto and Proto, Dynamene and Pherousa,
Dexamene and Amphinome and Kallianeira;
Doris and Panope and glorious Galateia,   45
Nemertes and Apseudes and Kallianassa;
Klymene was there, Ianeira and Ianassa,
Maira and Oreithyia and lovely-haired Amatheia,
and the rest who along the depth of the sea were
    daughters of Nereus.
The silvery cave was filled with these, and together
    all of them   50
beat their breasts, and among them Thetis led
    out the threnody:
'Hear me, Nereids, my sisters; so you may all
    know
well all the sorrows that are in my heart, when
    you hear of them from me.
Ah me, my sorrow, the bitterness in this best of
    child-bearing,
since I gave birth to a son who was without fault
    and powerful,   55
conspicuous among heroes; and he shot up like a
    young tree,
and I nurtured him, like a tree grown in the pride
    of the orchard.
I sent him away with the curved ships into the
    land of Ilion
to fight with the Trojans; but I shall never again
    receive him
won home again to his country and into the house
    of Peleus.   60
Yet while I see him live and he looks on the
    sunlight, he has
sorrows, and though I go to him I can do nothing
    to help him.
Yet I shall go, to look on my dear son, and to listen
to the sorrow that has come to him as he stays
    back from the fighting.'
So she spoke, and left the cave, and the others
    together   65

went with her in tears, and about them the wave of the water

was broken. Now these, when they came to the generous Troad,

followed each other out on the sea-shore, where close together

the ships of the Myrmidons were hauled up about swift Achilleus.

There as he sighed heavily the lady his mother stood by him   70

and cried out shrill and aloud, and took her son's head in her arms, then

sorrowing for him she spoke to him in winged words: 'Why then,

child, do you lament? What sorrow has come to your heart now?

Speak out, do not hide it. These things are brought to accomplishment

through Zeus: in the way that you lifted your hands and prayed for,   75

that all the sons of the Achaians be pinned on their grounded vessels

by reason of your loss, and suffer things that are shameful.'

Then sighing heavily Achilleus of the swift feet answered her:

'My mother, all these things the Olympian brought to accomplishment.

But what pleasure is this to me, since my dear companion has perished,   80

Patroklos, whom I loved beyond all other companions,

as well as my own life. I have lost him, and Hektor, who killed him,

has stripped away that gigantic armour, a wonder to look on

and splendid, which the gods gave Peleus, a glorious present,

on that day they drove you to the marriage bed of a mortal.   85

I wish you had gone on living then with the other goddesses

of the sea, and that Peleus had married some mortal woman.

As it is, there must be on your heart a numberless sorrow

for your son's death, since you can never again receive him

won home again to his country; since the spirit within does not drive me   90

to go on living and be among men, except on condition

that Hektor first be beaten down under my spear, lose his life

and pay the price for stripping Patroklos, the son of Menoitios.'

Then in turn Thetis spoke to him, letting the tears fall:

'Then I must lose you soon, my child, by what you are saying,   95

since it is decreed your death must come soon after Hektor's.'

Then deeply disturbed Achilleus of the swift feet answered her:

'I must die soon, then; since I was not to stand by my companion

when he was killed. And now, far away from the land of his fathers,

he has perished, and lacked my fighting strength to defend him.   100

Now, since I am not going back to the beloved land of my fathers,

since I was no light of safety to Patroklos, nor to my other

companions, who in their numbers went down before glorious Hektor,

but sit here beside my ships, a useless weight on the good land,

I, who am such as no other of the bronze-armoured Achaians   105

in battle, though there are others also better in council—

why, I wish that strife would vanish away from among gods and mortals,

and gall, which makes a man grow angry for all his great mind,

that gall of anger that swarms like smoke inside of a man's heart

and becomes a thing sweeter to him by far than the dripping of honey.   110

So it was here that the lord of men Agamemnon angered me.

Still, we will let all this be a thing of the past, and for all our

sorrow beat down by force the anger deeply within us.

Now I shall go, to overtake that killer of a dear life,

Hektor; then I will accept my own death, at whatever   115

time Zeus wishes to bring it about, and the other immortals.

For not even the strength of Herakles fled away from destruction,

although he was dearest of all to lord Zeus, son of Kronos,

but his fate beat him under, and the wearisome anger of Hera.

So I likewise, if such is the fate which has been wrought for me,   120

shall lie still, when I am dead. Now I must win excellent glory, and drive some one of the women of Troy, or some deep-girdled

Dardanian woman, lifting up to her soft cheeks both hands

to wipe away the close bursts of tears in her lamentation,

and learn that I stayed too long out of the fighting. Do not 125

hold me back from the fight, though you love me. You will not persuade me.'

In turn the goddess Thetis of the silver feet answered him:

'Yes, it is true, my child, this is no cowardly action,

to beat aside sudden death from your afflicted companions.

Yet, see now, your splendid armour, glaring and brazen, 130

is held among the Trojans, and Hektor of the shining helmet

wears it on his own shoulders, and glories in it. Yet I think

he will not glory for long, since his death stands very close to him.

Therefore do not yet go into the grind of the war god,

not before with your own eyes you see me come back to you. 135

For I am coming to you at dawn and as the sun rises

bringing splendid armour to you from the lord Hephaistos.'

So she spoke, and turned, and went away from her son,

and turning now to her sisters of the sea she spoke to them:

'Do you now go back into the wide fold of the water 140

to visit the ancient of the sea and the house of our father,

and tell him everything. I am going to tall Olympos

and to Hephaistos, the glorious smith, if he might be willing

to give me for my son renowned and radiant armour.'

She spoke, and they plunged back beneath the wave of the water, 145

while she the goddess Thetis of the silver feet went onward

to Olympos, to bring back to her son the glorious armour.

So her feet carried her to Olympos; meanwhile the Achaians

with inhuman clamour before the attack of man-slaughtering Hektor

fled until they were making for their own ships and the Hellespont; 150

nor could the strong-greaved Achaians have dragged the body

of Patroklos, henchman of Achilleus, from under the missiles,

for once again the men and the horses came over upon him,

and Hektor, Priam's son, who fought like a flame in his fury.

Three times from behind glorious Hektor caught him 155

by the feet, trying to drag him, and called aloud on the Trojans.

Three times the two Aiantes with their battle-fury upon them

beat him from the corpse, but he, steady in the confidence of his great strength,

kept making, now a rush into the crowd, or again at another time

stood fast, with his great cry, but gave not a bit of ground backward. 160

And as herdsmen who dwell in the fields are not able to frighten

a tawny lion in his great hunger away from a carcass,

so the two Aiantes, marshals of men, were not able

to scare Hektor, Priam's son, away from the body.

And now he would have dragged it away and won glory forever 165

had not swift wind-footed Iris come running from Olympos

with a message for Peleus' son to arm. She came secretly

from Zeus and the other gods, since it was Hera who sent her.

She came and stood close to him and addressed him in winged words:

'Rise up, son of Peleus, most terrifying of all men.

Defend Patroklos, for whose sake the terrible fighting 171

stands now in front of the ships. They are destroying each other;

the Achaians fight in defence over the fallen body

while the others, the Trojans, are rushing to drag the corpse off

to windy Ilion, and beyond all glorious Hektor 175

rages to haul it away, since the anger within him is urgent

to cut the head from the soft neck and set it on sharp stakes.

Up, then, lie here no longer; let shame come into your heart, lest

Patroklos become sport for the dogs of Troy to worry,

your shame, if the body goes from here with
    defilement upon it.'   180
Then in turn Achilleus of the swift feet answered
    her:
'Divine Iris, what god sent you to me with a
    message?'
Then in turn swift wind-footed Iris spoke to him:
'Hera sent me, the honoured wife of Zeus; but
    the son of
Kronos, who sits on high, does not know this, nor
    any other   185
immortal, of all those who dwell by the snows of
    Olympos.'
Then in answer to her spoke Achilleus of the
    swift feet:
'How shall I go into the fighting? They have my
    armour.
And my beloved mother told me I must not be
    armoured,
not before with my own eyes I see her come back
    to me.   190
She promised she would bring magnificent arms
    from Hephaistos.
Nor do I know of another whose glorious armour
    I could wear
unless it were the great shield of Telamonian Aias.
But he himself wears it, I think, and goes in the
    foremost
of the spear-fight over the body of fallen Patroklos.'
Then in turn swift wind-footed Iris spoke to
    him: 196
'Yes, we also know well how they hold your
    glorious armour.
But go to the ditch, and show yourself as you are
    to the Trojans,
if perhaps the Trojans might be frightened, and
    give way
from their attack, and the fighting sons of the
    Achaians get wind   200
again after hard work. There is little breathing
    space in the fighting.'
So speaking Iris of the swift feet went away from
    him;
but Achilleus, the beloved of Zeus, rose up, and
    Athene
swept about his powerful shoulders the fluttering
    aegis;
and she, the divine among goddesses, about his
    head circled   205
a golden cloud, and kindled from it a flame far-
    shining.
As when a flare goes up into the high air from a
    city
from an island far away, with enemies fighting
    about it

who all day long are in the hateful division of
    Ares
fighting from their own city, but as the sun goes
    down signal   210
fires blaze out one after another, so that the glare
    goes
pulsing high for men of the neighbouring islands
    to see it,
in case they might come over in ships to beat off
    the enemy;
so from the head of Achilleus the blaze shot into
    the bright air.
He went from the wall and stood by the ditch, nor
    mixed with the other   215
Achaians, since he followed the close command of
    his mother.
There he stood, and shouted, and from her place
    Pallas Athene
gave cry, and drove an endless terror upon the
    Trojans.
As loud as comes the voice that is screamed out
    by a trumpet
by murderous attackers who beleaguer a city, 220
so then high and clear went up the voice of
    Aiakides.
But the Trojans, when they heard the brazen
    voice of Aiakides,
the heart was shaken in all, and the very floating-
    maned horses
turned their chariots about, since their hearts saw
    the coming afflictions.
The charioteers were dumbfounded as they saw
    the unwearied dangerous   225
fire that played above the head of great-hearted
    Peleion
blazing, and kindled by the goddess grey-eyed
    Athene.
Three times across the ditch brilliant Achilleus
    gave his great cry,
and three times the Trojans and their renowned
    companions were routed.
There at that time twelve of the best men among
    them perished   230
upon their own chariots and spears. Meanwhile
    the Achaians
gladly pulled Patroklos out from under the missiles
and set him upon a litter, and his own com-
    panions about him
stood mourning, and along with them swift-footed
    Achilleus
went, letting fall warm tears as he saw his steadfast
    companion   235
lying there on a carried litter and torn with the
    sharp bronze,
the man he had sent off before with horses and
    chariot

into the fighting; who never again came home to
be welcomed.
Now the lady Hera of the ox eyes drove the
unwilling
weariless sun god to sink in the depth of the
Ocean, 240
and the sun went down, and the brilliant Achaians
gave over
their strong fighting, and the doubtful collision
of battle.
The Trojans on the other side moved from the
strong encounter
in their turn, and unyoked their running horses
from under the chariots,
and gathered into assembly before taking thought
for their supper. 245
They stood on their feet in assembly, nor did any
man have the patience
to sit down, but the terror was on them all, seeing
that Achilleus
had appeared, after he had stayed so long from the
difficult fighting.
First to speak among them was the careful
Poulydamas,
Panthöos' son, who alone of them looked before
and behind him. 250
He was companion to Hektor, and born on the
same night with him,
but he was better in words, the other with the
spear far better.
He in kind intention toward all stood forth and
addressed them:
'Now take careful thought, dear friends; for I
myself urge you
to go back into the city and not wait for the divine
dawn 255
in the plain beside the ships. We are too far from
the wall now.
While this man was still angry with great
Agamemnon,
for all that time the Achaians were easier men to
fight with.
For I also used then to be one who was glad to
sleep out
near their ships, and I hoped to capture the
oarswept vessels. 260
But now I terribly dread the swift-footed son of
Peleus.
So violent is the valour in him, he will not be
willing
to stay here in the plain, where now Achaians and
Trojans
from either side sunder between them the wrath of
the war god.
With him, the fight will be for the sake of our
city and women. 265

Let us go into the town; believe me; thus it will
happen.
For this present, immortal night has stopped the
swift-footed
son of Peleus, but if he catches us still in this
place
tomorrow, and drives upon us in arms, a man will
be well
aware of him, be glad to get back into sacred
Ilion, 270
the man who escapes; there will be many Trojans
the vultures
and dogs will feed on. But let such a word be out
of my hearing!
If all of us will do as I say, though it hurts us to do
it,
this night we will hold our strength in the market
place, and the great walls
and the gateways, and the long, smooth-planed,
close-joined gate timbers 275
that close to fit them shall defend our city. Then,
early
in the morning, under dawn, we shall arm ourselves in our war gear
and take stations along the walls. The worse for
him, if he endeavours
to come away from the ships and fight us here for
our city.
Back he must go to his ships again, when he wears
out the strong necks 280
of his horses, driving them at a gallop everywhere
by the city.
His valour will not give him leave to burst in upon
us
nor sack our town. Sooner the circling dogs will
feed on him.'
Then looking darkly at him Hektor of the shining
helm spoke:
'Poulydamas, these things that you argue please
me no longer 285
when you tell us to go back again and be cooped
in our city.
Have you not all had your glut of being fenced in
our outworks?
There was a time when mortal men would speak
of the city
of Priam as a place with much gold and much
bronze. But now
the lovely treasures that lay away in our houses
have vanished, 290
and many possessions have been sold and gone into
Phrygia
and into Maionia the lovely, when great Zeus was
angry.
But now, when the son of devious-devising Kronos
has given

me the winning of glory by the ships, to pin the
    Achaians
on the sea, why, fool, no longer show these
    thoughts to our people.   295
Not one of the Trojans will obey you. I shall not
    allow it.
Come, then, do as I say and let us all be persuaded.
Now, take your supper by positions along the
    encampment,
and do not forget your watch, and let every man
    be wakeful.
And if any Trojan is strongly concerned about his
    possessions,   300
let him gather them and give them to the people,
    to use them in common.
It is better for one of us to enjoy them than for
    the Achaians.
In the morning, under dawn, we shall arm our-
    selves in our war gear
and waken the bitter god of war by the hollow
    vessels.
If it is true that brilliant Achilleus is risen beside
    their   305
ships, then the worse for him if he tries it, since
    I for my part
will not run from him out of the sorrowful battle,
    but rather
stand fast, to see if he wins the great glory, or if I
    can win it.
The war god is impartial. Before now he has
    killed the killer.'
So spoke Hektor, and the Trojans thundered to
    hear him;   310
fools, since Pallas Athene had taken away the wits
    from them.
They gave their applause to Hektor in his counsel
    of evil,
but none to Poulydamas, who had spoken good
    sense before them.
They took their supper along the encampment.
    Meanwhile the Achaians
mourned all night in lamentation over Patroklos.
Peleus' son led the thronging chant of their lamen-
    tation,   316
and laid his manslaughtering hands over the chest
    of his dear friend
with outbursts of incessant grief. As some great
    bearded lion
when some man, a deer hunter, has stolen his cubs
    away from him
out of the close wood; the lion comes back too late,
    and is anguished,   320
and turns into many valleys quartering after the
    man's trail
on the chance of finding him, and taken with
    bitter anger;

so he, groaning heavily, spoke out to the
    Myrmidons:
'Ah me. It was an empty word I cast forth on that
    day
when in his halls I tried to comfort the hero
    Menoitios.   325
I told him I would bring back his son in glory to
    Opous
with Ilion sacked, and bringing his share of war
    spoils allotted.
But Zeus does not bring to accomplishment all
    thoughts in men's minds.
Thus it is destiny for us both to stain the same soil
here in Troy; since I shall never come home, and
    my father,   330
Peleus the aged rider, will not welcome me in his
    great house,
nor Thetis my mother, but in this place the earth
    will receive me.
But seeing that it is I, Patroklos, who follow you
    underground,
I will not bury you till I bring to this place the
    armour
and the head of Hektor, since he was your great-
    hearted murderer.   335
Before your burning pyre I shall behead twelve
    glorious
children of the Trojans, for my anger over your
    slaying.
Until then, you shall lie where you are in front of
    my curved ships
and beside you women of Troy and deep-girdled
    Dardanian women
shall sorrow for you night and day and shed tears
    for you, those whom   340
you and I worked hard to capture by force and the
    long spear
in days when we were storming the rich cities of
    mortals.'
So speaking brilliant Achilleus gave orders to his
    companions
to set a great cauldron across the fire, so that with
    all speed
they could wash away the clotted blood from
    Patroklos.   345
They set up over the blaze of the fire a bath-water
    cauldron
and poured water into it and put logs underneath
    and kindled them.
The fire worked on the swell of the cauldron, and
    the water heated.
But when the water had come to a boil in the
    shining bronze, then
they washed the body and anointed it softly with
    olive oil   350

and stopped the gashes in his body with stored-up
  unguents

and laid him on a bed, and shrouded him in a thin
  sheet

from head to foot, and covered that over with a
  white mantle.

Then all night long, gathered about Achilleus of
  the swift feet,

the Myrmidons mourned for Patroklos and
  lamented over him.   355

But Zeus spoke to Hera, who was his wife and his
  sister:

'So you have acted, then, lady Hera of the ox
  eyes.

You have roused up Achilleus of the swift feet.
  It must be then

that the flowing-haired Achaians are born of your
  own generation.'

Then the goddess the ox-eyed lady Hera answered
  him: 360

'Majesty, son of Kronos, what sort of thing have
  you spoken?

Even one who is mortal will try to accomplish his
  purpose

for another, though he be a man and knows not
  such wisdom as we do.

As for me then, who claim I am highest of all the
  goddesses,

both ways, since I am eldest born and am called
  your consort,   365

yours, and you in turn are lord over all the
  immortals,

how could I not weave sorrows for the men of
  Troy, when I hate them?'

Now as these two were saying things like this to
  each other,

Thetis of the silver feet came to the house of
  Hephaistos,

imperishable, starry, and shining among the immortals,   370

built in bronze for himself by the god of the
  dragging footsteps.

She found him sweating as he turned here and
  there to his bellows

busily, since he was working on twenty tripods

which were to stand against the wall of his strong-
  founded dwelling.

And he had set golden wheels underneath the base
  of each one   375

so that of their own motion they could wheel into
  the immortal

gathering, and return to his house: a wonder to
  look at.

These were so far finished, but the elaborate ear
  handles

were not yet on. He was forging these, and
  beating the chains out.

As he was at work on this in his craftsmanship
  and his cunning   380

meanwhile the goddess Thetis the silver-footed
  drew near him.

Charis of the shining veil saw her as she came
  forward,

she, the lovely goddess the renowned strong-
  armed one had married.

She came, and caught her hand and called her by
  name and spoke to her:

'Why is it, Thetis of the light robes, you have come
  to our house now?   385

We honour you and love you; but you have not
  come much before this.

But come in with me, so I may put entertainment before you.'

She spoke, and, shining among divinities, led the
  way forward

and made Thetis sit down in a chair that was
  wrought elaborately

and splendid with silver nails, and under it was a
  footstool.   390

She called to Hephaistos the renowned smith and
  spoke a word to him:

'Hephaistos, come this way; here is Thetis, who
  has need of you.'

Hearing her the renowned smith of the strong arms
  answered her:

'Then there is a goddess we honour and respect
  in our house.

She save me when I suffered much at the time of
  my great fall   395

through the will of my own brazen-faced mother
  who wanted

to hide me, for being lame. Then my soul would
  have taken much suffering

had not Eurynome and Thetis caught me and held
  me,

Eurynome, daughter of Ocean, whose stream bends
  back in a circle.

With them I worked nine years as a smith, and
  wrought many intricate   400

things; pins that bend back, curved clasps, cups,
  necklaces, working

there in the hollow of the cave, and the stream of
  Ocean around us

went on forever with its foam and its murmur.
  No other

among the gods or among mortal men knew about
  us

except Eurynome and Thetis. They knew, since
  they saved me.   405

Now she has come into our house; so I must by
  all means

do everything to give recompense to lovely-haired
    Thetis
for my life. Therefore set out before her fair
    entertainment
while I am putting away my bellows and all my
    instruments.'
He spoke, and took the huge blower off from the
    block of the anvil   410
limping; and yet his shrunken legs moved lightly
    beneath him.
He set the bellows away from the fire, and gathered
    and put away
all the tools with which he worked in a silver
    strongbox.
Then with a sponge he wiped clean his forehead,
    and both hands,
and his massive neck and hairy chest, and put on
    a tunic,   415
and took up a heavy stick in his hand, and went
    to the doorway
limping. And in support of their master moved his
    attendants.
These are golden, and in appearance like living
    young women.
There is intelligence in their hearts, and there is
    speech in them
and strength, and from the immortal gods they
    have learned how to do things.   420
These stirred nimbly in support of their master,
    and moving
near to where Thetis sat in her shining chair,
    Hephaistos
caught her by the hand and called her by name and
    spoke a word to her:
'Why is it, Thetis of the light robes, you have
    come to our house now?
We honour you and love you; but you have not
    come much before this.   425
Speak forth what is in your mind. My heart is
    urgent to do it
if I can, and if it is a thing that can be accom-
    plished.'
Then in turn Thetis answered him, letting the
    tears fall:
'Hephaistos, is there among all the goddesses on
    Olympos
one who in her heart has endured so many grim
    sorrows   430
as the griefs Zeus, son of Kronos, has given me
    beyond others?
Of all the other sisters of the sea he gave me to a
    mortal,
to Peleus, Aiakos' son, and I had to endure mortal
    marriage
though much against my will. And now he,
    broken by mournful

old age, lies away in his halls. Yet I have other
    troubles.   435
For since he has given me a son to bear and to
    raise up
conspicuous among heroes, and he shot up like a
    young tree,
I nurtured him, like a tree gown in the pride of
    the orchard.
I sent him away in the curved ships to the land
    of Ilion
to fight with the Trojans; but I shall never again
    receive him   440
won home again to his country and into the house
    of Peleus.
Yet while I see him live and he looks on the sun-
    light, he has
sorrows, and though I go to him I can do nothing
    to help him.
And the girl the sons of the Achaians chose out for
    his honour
powerful Agamemnon took her away again out of
    his hands.   445
For her his heart has been wasting in sorrow; but
    meanwhile the Trojans
pinned the Achaians against their grounded ships,
    and would not
let them win outside, and the elders of the Argives
    entreated
my son, and named the many glorious gifts they
    would give him.
But at that time he refused himself to fight the
    death from them;   450
nevertheless he put his own armour upon
    Patroklos
and sent him into the fighting, and gave many men
    to go with him.
All day they fought about the Skaian Gates, and
    on that day
they would have stormed the city, if only Phoibos
    Apollo
had not killed the fighting son of Menoitios there
    in the first ranks   455
after he had wrought much damage, and given
    the glory to Hektor.
Therefore now I come to your knees; so might you
    be willing
to give me for my short-lived son a shield and a
    helmet
and two beautiful greaves fitted with clasps for
    the ankles
and a corselet. What he had was lost with his
    steadfast companion   460
when the Trojans killed him. Now my son lies
    on the ground, heart sorrowing.'
Hearing her the renowned smith of the strong
    arms answered her:

'Do not fear. Let not these things be a thought in
  your mind.
And I wish that I could hide him away from
  death and its sorrow
at that time when his hard fate comes upon him,
  as surely 465
as there shall be fine armour for him, such as
  another
man out of many men shall wonder at, when he
  looks on it.'
So he spoke, and left her there, and went to his
  bellows.
He turned these toward the fire and gave them
  their orders for working.
And the bellows, all twenty of them, blew on the
  crucibles, 470
from all directions blasting forth wind to blow the
  flames high
now as he hurried to be at this place and now at
  another,
wherever Hephaistos might wish them to blow,
  and the work went forward.
He cast on the fire bronze which is weariless, and
  tin with it
and valuable gold, and silver, and thereafter set
  forth 475
upon its standard the great anvil, and gripped in
  one hand
the ponderous hammer, while in the other he
  grasped the pincers.
First of all he forged a shield that was huge and
  heavy,
elaborating it about, and threw around it a shining
triple rim that glittered, and the shield strap was
  cast of silver. 480
There were five folds composing the shield itself,
  and upon it
he elaborated many things in his skill and craftsmanship.
He made the earth upon it, and the sky, and the
  sea's water,
and the tireless sun, and the moon waxing into
  her fullness,
and on it all the constellations that festoon the
  heavens, 485
the Pleiades and the Hyades and the strength
  of Orion
and the Bear, whom men give also the name of
  the Wagon,
who turns about in a fixed place and looks at
  Orion
and she alone is never plunged in the wash of the
  Ocean.
On it he wrought in all their beauty two cities of
  mortal 490

men. And there were marriages in one, and
  festivals.
They were leading the brides along the city from
  their maiden chambers
under the flaring of torches, and the loud bride
  song was arising.
The young men followed the circles of the dance,
  and among them
the flutes and lyres kept up their clamour as in the
  meantime 495
the women standing each at the door of her court
  admired them.
The people were assembled in the market place,
  where a quarrel
had arisen, and two men were disputing over the
  blood price
for a man who had been killed. One man promised
  full restitution
in a public statement, but the other refused and
  would accept nothing. 500
Both then made for an arbitrator, to have a
  decision;
and people were speaking up on either side, to
  help both men.
But the heralds kept the people in hand, as meanwhile the elders
were in session on benches of polished stone in the
  sacred circle
and held in their hands the staves of the heralds
  who lift their voices. 505
The two men rushed before these, and took turns
  speaking their cases,
and between them lay on the ground two talents
  of gold, to be given
to that judge who in this case spoke the straightest
  opinion.
But around the other city were lying two forces
  of armed men
shining in their war gear. For one side counsel
  was divided 510
whether to storm and sack, or share between both
  sides the property
and all the possessions the lovely citadel held hard
  within it.
But the city's people were not giving way, and
  armed for an ambush.
Their beloved wives and their little children stood
  on the rampart
to hold it, and with them the men with age upon
  them, but meanwhile 515
the others went out. And Ares led them, and
  Pallas Athene.
These were gold, both, and golden raiment upon
  them, and they were
beautiful and huge in their armour, being divinities,

and conspicuous from afar, but the people around
  them were smaller.
These, when they were come to the place that was
  set for their ambush,   520
in a river, where there was a watering place for
  all animals,
there they sat down in place shrouding themselves
  in the bright bronze.
But apart from these were sitting two men to
  watch for the rest of them
and waiting until they could see the sheep and the
  shambling cattle,
who appeared presently, and two herdsmen went
  along with them   525
playing happily on pipes, and took no thought of
  the treachery.
Those others saw them, and made a rush, and
  quickly thereafter
cut off on both sides the herds of cattle and the
  beautiful
flocks of shining sheep, and killed the shepherds
  upon them.
But the other army, as soon as they heard the
  uproar arising   530
from the cattle, as they sat in their councils,
  suddenly mounted
behind their light-foot horses, and went after, and
  soon overtook them.
These stood their ground and fought a battle by
  the banks of the river,
and they were making casts at each other with
  their spears bronze-headed;
and Hate was there with Confusion among them,
  and Death the destructive;   535
she was holding a live man with a new wound, and
  another
one unhurt, and dragged a dead man by the feet
  through the carnage.
The clothing upon her shoulders showed strong
  red with the men's blood.
All closed together like living men and fought with
  each other
and dragged away from each other the corpses of
  those who had fallen.   540
He made upon it a soft field, the pride of the
  tilled land,
wide and triple-ploughed, with many ploughmen
  upon it
who wheeled their teams at the turn and drove
  them in either direction.
And as these making their turn would reach the
  end-strip of the field,
a man would come up to them at this point and
  hand them a flagon   545
of honey-sweet wine, and they would turn again
  to the furrows

in their haste to come again to the end-strip of
  the deep field.
The earth darkened behind them and looked like
  earth that has been ploughed
though it was gold. Such was the wonder of the
  shield's forging.
He made on it the precinct of a king, where the
  labourers   550
were reaping, with the sharp reaping hooks in their
  hands. Of the cut swathes
some fell along the lines of reaping, one after
  another,
while the sheaf-binders caught up others and tied
  them with bind-ropes.
There were three sheaf-binders who stood by, and
  behind them
were children picking up the cut swathes, and
  filled their arms with them   555
and carried and gave them always; and by them
  the king in silence
and holding his staff stood near the line of the
  reapers, happily.
And apart and under a tree the heralds made a
  feast ready
and trimmed a great ox they had slaughtered.
  Meanwhile the women
scattered, for the workmen to eat, abundant
  white barley.   560
He made on it a great vineyard heavy with
  clusters,
lovely and in gold, but the grapes upon it were
  darkened
and the vines themselves stood out through poles
  of silver. About them
he made a field-ditch of dark metal, and drove all
  around this
a fence of tin; and there was only one path to the
  vineyard,   565
and along it ran the grape-bearers for the vineyard's stripping.
Young girls and young men, in all their light-
  hearted innocence,
carried the kind, sweet fruit away in their woven
  baskets,
and in their midst a youth with a singing lyre
  played charmingly
upon it for them, and sang the beautiful song for
  Linos   570
in a light voice, and they followed him, and with
  singing and whistling
and light dance-steps of their feet kept time to
  the music.
He made upon it a herd of horn-straight oxen.
  The cattle
were wrought of gold and of tin, and thronged in
  speed and with lowing

out of the dung of the farmyard to a pasturing
    place by a sounding   575
river, and beside the moving field of a reed bed.
The herdsmen were of gold who went along with
    the cattle,
four of them, and nine dogs shifting their feet
    followed them.
But among the foremost of the cattle two formid-
    able lions
had caught hold of a bellowing bull, and he with
    loud lowings   580
was dragged away, as the dogs and the young men
    went in pursuit of him.
But the two lions, breaking open the hide of the
    great ox,
gulped the black blood and the inward guts, as
    meanwhile the herdsmen
were in the act of setting and urging the quick
    dogs on them.
But they, before they could get their teeth in,
    turned back from the lions,   585
but would come and take their stand very close,
    and bayed, and kept clear.
And the renowned smith of the strong arms made
    on it a meadow
large and in a lovely valley for the glimmering
    sheepflocks,
with dwelling places upon it, and covered shelters,
    and sheepfolds.
And the renowned smith of the strong arms made
    elaborate on it   590
a dancing floor, like that which once in the wide
    spaces of Knosos
Daidalos built for Ariadne of the lovely tresses.
And there were young men on it and young girls,
    sought for their beauty
with gifts of oxen, dancing, and holding hands at
    the wrist. These
wore, the maidens long light robes, but the men
    wore tunics   595
of finespun work and shining softly, touched with
    olive oil.
And the girls wore fair garlands on their heads,
    while the young men
carried golden knives that hung from sword-belts
    of silver.
At whiles on their understanding feet they would
    run very lightly,
as when a potter crouching makes trial of his
    wheel, holding   600
it close in his hands, to see if it will run smooth.
    At another
time they would form rows, and run, rows crossing
    each other.
And around the lovely chorus of dancers stood a
    great multitude

happily watching, while among the dancers two
    acrobats
led the measures of song and dance revolving
    among them.   605
He made on it the great strength of the Ocean
    River
which ran around the uttermost rim of the shield's
    strong structure.
Then after he had wrought this shield, which was
    huge and heavy,
he wrought for him a corselet brighter than fire in
    its shining,
and wrought him a helmet, massive and fitting
    close to his temples,   610
lovely and intricate work, and laid a gold top-ridge
    along it,
and out of pliable tin wrought him leg-armour.
    Thereafter
when the renowned smith of the strong arms had
    finished the armour
he lifted it and laid it before the mother of
    Achilleus.
And she like a hawk came sweeping down from
    the snows of Olympos   615
and carried with her the shining armour, the gift
    of Hephaistos.

The Odyssey[1]

BOOK VI

And so godly Odysseus, who had suffered much,
    slept there,
Worn out with fatigue and sleepiness. Yet
    Athene
Went on to the district and city of the Phæacians
Who at one time dwelt in Hyperia of the broad
    dancing place
Close to the Cyclopes, presumptuous men   5
Who used to injure them, and were more powerful
    in strength.
Then godlike Nausithoos rose up and led them off
And settled them in Scheria, far from bread-
    earning men.
He set a wall around the city, built houses,
Made temples to the gods, and divided up the
    fields.   10
But already he had succumbed to his fate and gone
    to Hades.
Alcinoos ruled at the time, who has his thoughts
    from the gods.

[1] Reprinted from *Translation of the Odyssey* by
Albert Cook. By permission of W. W. Norton &
Company, Inc. Copyright © 1967 by Albert Cook.

The bright-eyed goddess Athene went to his home
Devising a return for great-hearted Odysseus.
She entered the highly wrought bedroom where
    there was sleeping   15
A girl like the immortals in shape and in form,
Nausicaa, daughter of great-hearted Alcinoos,
And beside her two servants, who had beauty
    from the Graces,
On either side of the doorposts. The bright doors
    were shut.
She rushed to the girl's bed like a blast of the
    wind,   20
Stood over her head and spoke a word to her,
Likening herself to the daughter of Dumas, famous
    for ships:
Who was the girl's own age and delighted her heart.
In the likeness of her, bright-eyed Athene spoke
    out:
"Nausicaa, how did your mother have such a
    careless child?   25
Your shining garments are lying uncared for
And your wedding is near, when you yourself will
    need
Lovely clothes to put on, and to give to the men
    who will lead you;
Through them does a noble reputation arise
Among men, and a father and queenly mother
    rejoice.   30
But let us go washing as soon as dawn appears.
I will follow as a helper so you may deck yourself
Very soon, since you will not be a maiden much
    longer.
Already in the district, the best men of all the
    Phæacians,
Where your own family is too, are wooing you.   35
But come, and urge your illustrious father at dawn
To harness up mules and a wagon to carry you
And the girdles and the gowns and the shining
    mantles.
It is much better for you to go that way yourself
Than by foot. For the place of washing is far from
    the city."   40
When she had said this, the bright-eyed Athene
    went off
To Olympus, where they say the gods' seat is
    forever
Secure. It is not shaken with winds and is never
    wet
With rain, nor does snow fall there, but a cloudless
    clarity
Spreads far upon it, and a white gleam runs over
    it.   45
In that place the blest gods enjoy themselves day
    after day.
The bright-eyed one went off there when she had
    briefed the girl.

And right away the well-throned Dawn came and
    awakened
The well-gowned Nausicaa. At once she wondered
    at her dream,
And went through the halls to announce it to her
    parents,   50
Her dear father and mother. She found them
    within.
Her mother sat at the hearth with her serving
    women
Turning sea-purple on the distaff. She came on
    her father
At the door as he was going with his illustrious
    kings
To council, where the noble Phæacians were
    summoning him.   55
She stood very close to her dear father and
    addressed him:
"Papa dear, won't you have a chariot harnessed
    for me,
A high one with good wheels, so I may take the
    splendid clothes
And wash them at the river, the ones I have lying
    dirty?
Yes, and it is fitting for you to be with the chief
    men   60
And hold council, wearing clothes on your skin
    that are clean.
And five dear sons have been born to you in the
    halls,
Two of them are married; three are blooming
    youths
Who are always wanting to wear freshly washed
    garments
To go dancing; all these cares are on my mind."   65
So she said. But she was ashamed to speak of
    lusty marriage
To her dear father. He saw all, and replied with
    a word:
"I do not begrudge you mules or anything else,
    child —
Come, the servants will harness you a chariot
A high one, with good wheels, fitted with a
    hood."   70
When he had said this, he bade the servants, and
    they obeyed.
Outside they set up a well-running wagon for
    mules.
They brought up mules and yoked them to the
    chariot.
The girl brought the shining garments from the
    bedroom
And she put them upon the well-polished chariot.
Her mother put all sorts of satisfying food   76
In a chest, and put in dainties, and poured wine

In a goatskin bag. Her daughter got up on the
        chariot.
And she gave her moist olive oil in a golden flask
So she and her serving women might anoint
        themselves.   80
And she took hold of the whip and the glistening
        reins
And whipped them to go; there was clatter of the
        two mules,
They drew it strenuously and bore the clothes and
        the girl,
Not alone: along with her other serving women
        went also.
And when they came to the beautiful stream of
        the river   85
Where there were plentiful places to wash and
        much
Lovely water flowed forth to clean what had got
        very dirty,
There they unharnessed the mules from the
        chariot
And shooed them out along the eddying river
To graze on honey-sweet dog-grass. From the
        chariot   90
They took the clothes in their hands, carried them
        to the black water,
And trod them in pits, swiftly vying with one
        another.
But when they had washed and cleaned all the
        dirty clothes,
They spread them in a row on the strand where
        especially
The ocean washed pebbles up along the shore.   95
They bathed and anointed themselves smooth with
        olive oil.
Then they had their dinner along the banks of the
        river
And waited for the clothes to dry in the beams of
        the sun.
When she herself and the serving maids had
        enjoyed the food,
They played with a ball, having taken off their
        shawls.   100
White-armed Nausicaa began the sport with them.
Just as arrow-shooting Artemis goes along moun-
        tains
Along the lofty Taygetus[1] or Erimanthus[2],
Delighting in the boars and in the swift deer;
And field-haunting nymphs, daughters of aegis-
        bearing Zeus,   105
Play with her, and Leto rejoices in her mind;
She holds her head and her forehead higher than
        all

[1] Mountain range in Laconia (S. Peloponnesus).
[2] A mountain in Arcadia (N. Peloponnesus).

And is easily outstanding, but all are lovely: —
So the unwed girl stood out among her serving
        maids.
But when she was ready to go back home again 110
And had hitched up the mules and folded the
        lovely clothes,
Then the bright-eyed goddess Athene had another
        thought:
Odysseus would wake up, he would see the fair-
        faced girl,
And she would conduct him to the city of the
        Phæacians.
Then the princess threw the ball to a serving
        maid;   115
She missed the maid and shot it into a deep eddy.
They gave a long shout. And godly Odysseus
        woke up.
He sat there and deliberated in his mind and heart:
"Ah me, to what land of mortals have I come
        this time?
Are these men proud and wild and without justice,
Or are they friendly to strangers and have a god-
        fearing mind?   121
How the sound of girls' voices has surrounded me,
Of nymphs, who hold the lofty peaks of mountains,
And the sources of rivers and the grassy meadows!
Or am I somewhere near men who are of clear
        speech?   125
Well, come, I shall make a trial myself and see."
When he had said this, godly Odysseus came from
        under the bushes.
From the thick wood he broke off in his stout hand
        a branch
With leaves, that it might cover the skin round a
        man's loins,
And he went like a mountain-bred lion, who,
        relying   130
On his strength, goes rained on and blown on, but
        his eyes within
Are burning, and he chases after oxen or sheep
Or after the wild deer, and his belly bids him
To try for sheep and to go into their thick fold —
So was Odysseus about to mingle with the fair-
        braided girls   135
Although he was naked. For need had come upon
        him.
Frightfully begrimed with brine did he appear to
        them.
One ran one way, one another, on the jutting
        shores.
The daughter of Alcinoos alone stayed; Athene
Had put courage in her mind and taken fear from
        her limbs.   140
She stood in one place facing him. Odysseus
        wondered

Whether he should grasp the fair-faced girl's knees
    in prayer
Or supplicate where he was at a distance, with
    honeyed words,
To show him the city and also to give him clothes.
As he thought it over, it seemed better to him 145
To supplicate her at a distance with honeyed words,
Lest if he grasped her knees the girl's mind be
    angered.
Right at once he made a honeyed and cunning
    speech:
"I am at your knees, mistress. Are you some god
    or a mortal?
If you are one of the gods who possess broad
    heaven 150
I myself would liken you in look and size and
    form
Most closely to Artemis, the daughter of great
    Zeus.
And if you are one of the mortals who dwells on
    the land,
Three times blest are your father and your
    queenly mother,
And three times blest your kinsmen. Surely their
    hearts 155
Must be warmed forever with happiness on your
    account,
Beholding so fine a shoot stepping into the dance.
Blest above all others within his heart is the man
Who, laden down with bride-gifts, may lead you
    home.
Never before have I seen with my eyes such a
    person, 160
Either man or woman. Awe holds me as I look,
On Delos[1] once by the altar of Apollo I caught
    sight
Of such a one, the sapling of a date palm coming
    up.
For I went there also, and a large company
    followed me
On that journey whereon evil cares lay in store
    for me. 165
When I saw that, I was stunned in spirit a long
    time, lady,
Since such a shaft never rose from the ground; the
    same way
That I wonder at you, and am stunned, and
    dreadfully fear
To touch your knees. And a hard sorrow comes
    upon me.
Yesterday, on the twentieth day, I fled the wine-
    faced ocean, 170

[1] A small island in the Cyclades, southeast of Attica,
sacred to Apollo.

All during that time did the waves and rapid
    storms carry me
From the island of Ogygia. Now a god has cast
    me here
To suffer some evil in this place. I do not think
It will stop, but the gods will perform many
    things yet first.
Do have pity, mistress. As one who has endured
    many evils 175
I come to you first. I know not one of the others,
Of the men who possess this city and this land.
Point the town out to me. Give me a rag to throw
    on,
If perhaps when you came here you had some
    wrapper for the clothing.
May the gods grant you as much as you wish in
    your mind. 180
May they provide you a husband and also a home,
And noble sympathy. Nothing is better or higher
    than that
When a man and wife have a home who are
    sympathetic
In their thoughts. It gives many pains to their
    enemies
And joys to their friends. And they know it best
    themselves." 185
Then white-armed Nausicaa spoke to him in
    answer:
"Stranger, since you seem like a man neither evil
    nor senseless,
And Olympian Zeus himself controls bliss for men,
For the noble and the evil, as he wishes for each,
So perhaps he gave you this, and still you have to
    bear it. 190
And now, since you have come to our city and
    our land,
You will not want for clothing, or for anything
    else
That befits a long-suffering suppliant who en-
    counters us.
I will show you the town and tell you the name of
    the people.
The Phæacians possess this city and this land. 195
I am the daughter of great-hearted Alcinoos
On whom the strength and might of the Phæacians
    depend."
So she said, and she called out to her fair-braided
    servants,
"Come here to me, servants. Where do you flee
    when you see a man?
Surely you don't think him to be one of our
    enemies? 200
There is no man so vigorous and no mortal born
Who would come to the land of the Phæacian
    men

Bringing hostility. For they are very dear to the
   gods.
And we dwell far away in the much-surging ocean,
The remotest of men. And no other mortal has
   congress with us. 205
Now this man, a wretched wanderer, has come
   here,
Whom we must look after, for all strangers and
   beggars
Are in the care of Zeus, and a gift, even small, is
   precious.
Come, maidens, give food and drink to the
   stranger.
Wash him in the river where there is shelter against
   the wind." 210
So she said, but they stood and urged one another
And they took Odysseus down to a shelter, as
   Nausicaa,
Daughter of great-hearted Alcinoos, had ordered.
They put down a mantle and a tunic and clothes
   for him,
And gave him liquid olive oil in a golden flask, 215
And bade him to wash himself in the streams of
   the river.
Then godly Odysseus addressed the servant maids:
"Maidens, stand off where you are, so that I
   myself
May wash the brine from my shoulders and with
   olive oil
May anoint me all over. Oil has been long from
   my skin; 220
I do not want to wash in front of you. I am
   ashamed
To come out naked in the midst of fair-braided
   girls."
So he said, and they went apart and spoke to the
   girl.
But Odysseus in the river washed off of his skin
The brine that he had on his back and his broad
   shoulders, 225
And he wiped from his head the scurf of barren salt
   water.
When he had fully washed and had rubbed himself
   smoothly,
He put on the clothes that the unwed girl had
   provided,
And Athene, she who was born from Zeus, made
   him
Bigger to look at and stouter, and on his head 230
Made his hair flow in curls, like the hyacinth
   flower.
As when some man overlays silver upon gold,
A skilled man whom Hephaestus and Pallas Athene
   have taught
Art of all kinds, and he turns out pleasing products;

So she poured grace upon his head and his
   shoulders. 235
Then he sat off apart, when he had gone along the
   beach of the sea,
Gleaming with beauty and graces. And the girl
   marvelled.
And then she spoke out to her fair-braided serving
   maids:
"Listen to me, white-armed servants, in what I
   say.
Not against the will of all the gods who hold
   Olympus 240
Does this man mix with the Phæacians, who are
   equal to gods.
Beforehand he appeared to me to be unseemly,
And now he seems like the gods who possess
   broad heaven.
Would that a man of this sort might be called my
   husband
And be dwelling here, and it might please him to
   stay 245
In this place. But, maidens, give the stranger
   food and drink."
So she said, and they listened closely and obeyed
   her.
They set out before Odysseus food and drink.
Godly Odysseus, who had suffered much, ate and
   drank
Greedily, for he had been a long time without
   eating. 250
But white-armed Nausicaa had another thought.
She folded up the clothes, put them on the lovely
   chariot
Harnessed the stout-hooved mules, got in herself,
And urged Odysseus on, speaking out to him
   directly:
"Rise up now, stranger, to go to the city, so I
   may 255
Convey you to my skillful father's home, where I
   think
You may get to know all the noblest of the
   Phæacians.
Well, this is what you should do: — you do not
   seem to me to be foolish. —
As long as we are passing the fields and the farms
   of men,
Come speedily along with the serving maids
   behind the mules 260
And the chariot. And I myself shall lead the way.
But when we walk into the city — about which
   there is
A high tower, and a lovely harbor on either side
   of the city
And a narrow entrance, and bobbing ships from
   the voyage

Are pulled in there — it is a slip for one and all. 265
There is the assembly, round a fine temple to
    Poseidon
Fashioned from deep bedded stones that have
    been quarried.
And there they take care of the tackle of the
    black ships,
Cables and sails, and they sharpen oars off to a
    point.
For the Phæacians the bow and the quiver are of
    no concern, 270
But sails and the oars of ships and the balanced
    ships;
Delighting in these, they traverse the hoary sea.
I shun an unseemly repute among them, lest one
Rebuke me hereafter. For there are presumptuous
    men in the district,
And some meaner one, if he met us, might speak
    thus: 275
'Who is this great and handsome stranger that
    follows
Nausicaa? Where did she find him? He will be
    her husband.
From his own ship she brought him wandering
    somewhere
From distant men, since there are not any near
    at hand.
Or has some much-invoked god come at her prayer,
Descending from the sky and will have her all her
    days? 281
Better so, if she went herself and found a husband
From elsewhere. For she despises these men in
    the district,
The Phæacians, though many men who are noble
    woo her.'
So they will say. And these reproaches will come
    against me. 285
I myself would blame anyone else who should do
    such things,
Who against the will of a father and mother dear
    to her
Should mingle with men before coming to open
    marriage.
Stranger, understand quickly what I say, so you
    may
Very soon get an escort and a return from my
    father. 290
Near the road you will find a glorious grove of
    Athene,
One of poplars; a spring flows in it, a meadow is
    about it.
There is my father's preserve and his fruitful
    vineyard,
The same distance from the city that a shout would
    carry,
Sit there a while and wait till the time that we 295

Come to the town and arrive at the house of my
    father.
But when you consider that we have arrived at
    the house,
Then go to the city of the Phæacians and ask
For the house of my father, great-hearted Alcinoos.
It is easy to recognize; even a foolish child 300
Could lead you. There is none of the Phæacians'
    houses
Made to resemble the home of Alcinoos,
Who is a hero. But when the house and courtyard
    enclose you,
Go very swiftly through the hall until you reach
My mother. She sits on the threshold in the fire's
    gleam, 305
And turns sea-purple on the distaff, a wonder to
    see,
Propped against a pillar. And serving maids sit
    behind her.
And there the chair of my father is propped up
    against hers,
Where, seated like an immortal, he drinks his wine.
Pass him by and throw your hands around the
    knees 310
Of my mother, so you may speedily rejoice and
    see
The day of your return, even if you are from very
    far away.
And if that woman thinks kindly of you in her
    heart,
Then there is hope for you of seeing your dear
    ones and reaching
Your well-established home and your own father-
    land." 315
When she had said this, she lashed with her shiny
    whip
At the mules, and they quickly left the streams of
    the river.
They ran along well and nimbly bent their legs.
She managed the reins so that the servants and
    Odysseus
Might follow on foot. And she skillfully applied
    the lash. 320
The sun went down and they came to the famous
    grove
Sacred to Athene, and there godly Odysseus sat
    down.
Then at once he prayed to the daughter of great
    Zeus:
"Hear me, unwearied one, child of aegis-bearing
    Zeus,
Hear me now, since you did not hear me before 325
When I was smitten and the famous earth-shaker
    smote me.
Grant that I come to the Phæacians as a pitied
    man and a friend."

So he said in prayer; and Pallas Athene heard
    him,
But she did not yet appear to him face to face.
    For she feared
Her father's brother. He was contending vehe-
    mently   330
Against godly Odysseus before he reached his own
    land.

BOOK IX

Odysseus of many devices addressed him in answer:
"Lordly Alcinoos, exalted among all your people,
Indeed it is pleasant to listen to such a singer
As this one is, who resembles the gods in his voice.
I would say myself there is no more delightful
    result   5
Than when happiness so prevails through a whole
    district
And when diners seated in order through the halls
Listen to a singer, and the tables nearby are full
Of bread and meat, and the wine-pourer draws
    wine off
From the bowl, carries it around, and pours it in
    the cups.   10
To my mind this seems to be the loveliest thing.
But your heart turns toward me to ask of my
    woeful cares,
So that I may grieve still further as I lament.
What then shall I tell you first, what tell last,
Since the heavenly gods bestowed many cares
    upon me?   15
Well now, I shall tell you my name first, so that you
    too
May know it, and then, when I have escaped the
    pitiless day
I may be your guest-friend, though I dwell far
    off in my halls.
I am Odysseus, son of Laertes, who for my wiles
Am of note among all men, and my fame reaches
    heaven.   20
I dwell in sunny Ithaca. A mountain is on it,
Neriton, with trembling leaves, conspicuous.
Many islands lie about it quite close to one
    another,
Dulichium and Same and wooded Zacynthus;
She herself sits low-lying, farthest out to sea   25
Toward dusk, and they are apart toward dawn and
    the sun;
Rugged but good for bringing up young men.
    And I
Can look upon nothing sweeter than a man's own
    land.
Well, Calypso, the divine goddess, kept me in one
    place

In a hollow cave, desiring that I be her huband.   30
The same way in her halls would the wily Aeaean
Circe have held me back, desiring that I be her
    husband.
But they never persuaded the heart within my
    breast.
So nothing grows sweeter than a man's own
    fatherland
And his parents, even if he dwell in a fertile home
Far off in a foreign land apart from his parents.   36
But come, let me tell you of the much troubled
    return
That Zeus put upon me when I went away from
    Troy.
The wind bearing me from Ilium brought me near
    the Cicones,
To Ismarus. There I sacked the city and killed
    its men.   40
From the city we took the wives and many
    possessions
And divided them so none for my sake would lack
    an equal share.
Then I gave the order for us to take rapid flight,
But the men, great fools as they were, did not
    obey;
They had drunk much wine there and slain many
    sheep   45
Along the strand, many shamble-footed, crumple-
    horned cattle.
Meanwhile the Cicones went and called other
    Cicones
Who were their neighbors, at once more numerous
    and brave,
Who dwelt on the mainland, skilled in fighting
    with men,
From horses, and, when necessary, on foot.   50
As thick as leaves and flowers grow in their
    season,
They came, in early morning. Then an evil fate
    of Zeus was with us
In our dread destinies, so we might suffer many
    pains.
They took their stand and fought a battle by the
    swift ships,
And they threw bronze-tipped spears at one
    another.   55
So long as it was morning and the sacred day
    increased,
We stayed and warded them off, many as there
    were.
But when the sun declined to the time of ox-
    loosing,
Then the Cicones turned and routed the Achaians.
Six from each ship of my well-greaved companions
Perished. The rest of us escaped death and
    destiny.   61

Then we sailed on further, grieving in our hearts,
Glad to escape death, having lost our dear companions.
My bobbing ships, however, did not proceed further
Till someone had thrice called for each of our wretched companions   65
Who had died on the plain slaughtered by the Cicones.
Cloud-gathering Zeus raised a North Wind against the ships
In an immense storm, and covered land and ocean alike
Over with clouds. And night rose up out of heaven.
The ships were borne headlong, and the force of the wind   70
Ripped the sails up into three fragments and four.
We lowered them onto the ships, fearing destruction,
And rowed the ships forward to the mainland hastily.
There for two whole nights and two days continually
We lay, eating our hearts with pain and fatigue alike.   75
But when fair-braided Dawn had brought the third day to the full,
We set up our masts and hoisted the white sails
And took our seats. The wind and the pilots steered them,
And I would have arrived unscathed at my fatherland,
But as I rounded Malea a rushing wave   80
And a North Wind pushed me off and drove me past Cythera.[1]
Thence for nine days I was borne by destructive winds
On the fish-laden ocean. But the tenth day I set foot
On the land of the Lotus-eaters, who eat a flowery food.
Then we went onto the mainland and drew off water,   85
And at once my companions took dinner beside the swift ships.
But when we had partaken of food and of drink,
I sent my companions forth to go and find out
What men they were who ate bread upon the land.
I picked out two men and sent on a third as a herald.   90
They went off at once and mingled with the Lotus-eaters.
And the Lotus-eaters did not plot destruction

[1] An island near Cape Malea off the S. Peloponnesus.

For our companions, but gave them the lotus to taste of.
Whoever among them ate the honey-sweet fruit of the lotus
Wished no longer to bring word back again or return,   95
But wanted to remain there with the Lotus-eaters
To devour the lotus and forget about a return.
Back weeping to the ships I led them, by compulsion,
Dragged them and bound them in the hollow ships under the benches,
And I called all my other trusty companions   100
To hasten and to get on board the rapid ships,
Lest someone perchance eat the lotus and forget a return.
They got in at once and took their seats at the oarlocks.
Seated in order, they beat the hoary sea with their oars.
Then we sailed further on, grieved in our hearts,
To the land of the Cyclopes, an overweening   106
And lawless people, who, trusting in the immortal gods,
Do not sow plants with their hands and do not plough,
But everything grows for them unplowed and unsown,
Wheat and barley and vines that produce a wine-grape   110
Of large clusters, and a rain from Zeus makes them grow.
They have neither assemblies for holding council nor laws,
But they inhabit the crests of the lofty mountains,
In hollow caves, and each one dispenses the laws
For his children and his wives, and is not concerned for the others.   115
A fertile island stretches there from the harbor
Of the land of the Cyclopes, not near and not far away,
A wooded one. And on it numberless wild goats flourish,
For there is no beaten path of men to keep them away.
Nor do hunters land upon it, who in the woods   120
Undergo pains and chase them over the mountain peaks.
And it is not held, either, with flocks or with ploughed lands,
But it lies unsown and unplowed day after day
Bereft of men, and it nourishes bleating goats.
There are no vermilion-prowed ships for the Cyclopes,   125
As there are no shipwrights among them who might work

At good timbered ships to bring it about for them
To visit separate cities among men, as frequently
Men do cross the sea in ships toward one another;
And these would have worked to make the island
    well-settled for them,   130
As it is not really bad, and would bear all things in
    season.
There are meadows in it along the banks of the
    hoary sea,
Soft, moist ones. And there would be fine, un-
    withering vines
And smooth plowing, and they would mow the
    deep-standing grain
In season, as it is very rich beneath the surface. 135
There a sheltered harbor is, where there is no
    need of a rope
Or of throwing out anchor-stones or fastening
    cables,
But they could put in and stay a time till the spirits
Of the sailors urged them on and breezes should be
    blowing.
And glistening water flows down from the head of
    the harbor,   140
A spring under a cave. Poplars grow about it.
There we sailed on in. And some god guided us
Through the murky night. There was not light
    enough to see.
Dark air was deep about the ships, nor did the
    moon
Show forth from heaven, but it was contained in
    clouds.   145
There no one looked upon the island with his
    eyes,
And we did not behold the great waves rolling up
On the mainland, before we beached our well-
    timbered ships.
When the ships had been beached, we took down
    all the sails,
And then we went off ourselves to the surf of the
    sea.   150
We fell asleep there and awaited the godly Dawn.
And when the early-born, rosy-fingered Dawn
    appeared,
We wondered at the island and travelled all
    around it.
The nymphs, daughters of aegis-bearing Zeus,
    roused up
Mountain goats, so that my companions might
    have dinner.   155
At once we took curved bows and long-socketed
    goat spears
Out of the ships. We divided into three groups
And went shooting. At once the god gave us
    satisfying game.
The men of twelve ships followed along with me.
    Nine goats

Fell the lot of each ship. They picked ten out
    just for me.   160
So then for the whole day till the setting of the
    sun,
We sat dining on the endless meat and sweet
    wine,
For the red wine from the ships had not yet been
    exhausted,
But was still there. Each group had drawn off
    much in jars
When we sacked the holy citadel of the Cicones.
We were looking over to the land of the Cyclopes
    nearby,   166
To their smoke, to their sound and that of their
    sheep and goats.
But when the sun went down and the darkness
    came on,
We lay down to sleep beside the surf of the sea.
And when the early-born, rosy-fingered Dawn
    appeared,   170
I called an assembly and spoke to all of them:
'Stay here now, the rest of you, my trusty com-
    panions;
But I will go myself with my ship and companions
To inquire about these men, whoever they may be,
Whether they are overweening and savage and
    unjust   175
Or friendly to strangers, and have a god-fearing
    mind.''
When I had said this, I went on the ship and
    called my companions
To go on board themselves and to undo the cables.
They went on board right away and sat down at
    the oarlocks
Seated in order, they beat the hoary sea with their
    oars.   180
And when we had arrived at the place that was
    nearby,
There we saw a cave on the verge, close to the sea
High up, overhung with laurel. Many animals
Usually slept there, sheep and goats; a courtyard
Was built high around it out of deep-bedded
    stones   185
And tall pines and oak trees with lofty foliage.
There a monstrous man usually slept, who alone
And aloof tended the animals. He did not consort
With the others, but stayed apart and had a
    lawless mind.
And indeed he was formed as a monstrous wonder.
    He looked   190
Not like a grain-eating man but a wooded crest
On lofty mountains that appears singled out from
    the others.
And then I ordered the rest of my trusty com-
    panions

To remain there beside the ship and to guard the
    ship.
But I myself picked out twelve of my best com-
    panions   195
To go on.   Now I held a goatskin flask of black
    wine,
A sweet wine that Maron[1] gave me, Euanthes'
    son —
The priest of Apollo, who watches over Ismarus, —
Because we protected him along with his wife and
    son,
And reverenced him.   He dwelt in the tree-filled
    grove   200
Of Phoebus Apollo.   And he gave me glorious
    gifts:
He gave me seven talents of well-fashioned gold,
And he gave me a mixing bowl all of silver, and
    then
Into two-handled jars, twelve in all, he drew off
    wine
Sweet and unmixed, a godly drink, nor was any 205
Maidservant or serving man in the house aware
    of it,
But himself and his wife and one single house-
    keeper.
And whenever they drank that honey-sweet red
    wine,
He would fill one cup and pour it into twenty
    measures
Of water, and a sweet aroma came from the bowl
Of marvelous fragrance: to abstain then would not
    have been easy.   211
I filled a great skin with it and brought it, and
    also I put
Provisions in a bag.   At once my bold spirit
Sensed that the man would approach, clad in his
    great strength,
The wild man who had clear in his mind neither
    justice nor laws.   215
Speedily we came to the cave and did not find him
Within.   But he was tending rich flocks in a
    pasture.
We entered the cave and gazed at each separate
    thing.
Baskets were weighed down with cheeses, and the
    folds were thronged
With lambs and kids.   All were divided in groups,
And confined; here the first born, there the
    middlers,   221
The dew-fleeced apart too.   All the pails flowed
    with whey,
The vessels and the pans, well-wrought, in which
    he milked them.

[1] A local hero of a town in Thrace.

Then at first my companions besought me with
    speeches
When we had picked some cheeses to go back
    again, and then   225
When we had hastily driven the kids and lambs
    out of the pens
Onto the swift ship, to set sail upon the salt water.
But I did not listen — that would have been far
    better —
So I might see the man and he give me the gifts
    of a guest.
But when he appeared, he was not to be joyful to
    my companions.   230
We kindled a fire there, sacrificed, and ourselves
Also picked out some cheeses and ate, and awaited,
    him
Seated inside, till he did come driving sheep.   He
    carried
A stout burden of dry wood to make his dinner.
Throwing it down inside the cave, he made a
    rumbling noise;   235
And we drew back in fear into a nook of the cave.
But into the broad cavern he drove his fat flocks,
All those that he usually milked, and he left the
    males
By the entrance, rams and he-goats, in the deep
    yard outside.
Then he put a great door-stone on, raising it
    aloft,   240
A mighty one.   And twenty-two excellent wagons
With four wheels could not pry it up from the
    ground,
So great was the towering rock he set on the
    entrance.
He sat down and milked the sheep and the bleating
    goats,
All in due order, and set each young one to his
    mother;   245
And at once when he had curdled half the white
    milk,
He skimmed it off and put it up in wicker baskets,
And half of it he stood in pails so he would have
    it
To drink when he reached for it, to have it for
    supper.
And when he had hurried at attending to all his
    tasks,   250
He kindled a fire, and looked at us, and spoke to
    us:
'Strangers, who are you?   Whence have you sailed
    the watery ways?
For some sort of gain, or do you wander at hazard
The way pirates do who wander over the sea
Risking their lives, bearing evil to foreigners?' 255
So he said, and our own hearts were shattered
    within us,

In terror at his deep voice and the monster himself.
Yet I answered him with a speech and addressed
    him thus:
'We are Achaians coming from Troy, driven off
    course
By all kinds of winds over the great gulf of the
    sea;   260
Wanting to go homeward, we came by other
    passages,
By another way. So Zeus perhaps wished to devise
    it.
We declare we are the men of Agamemnon, son of
    Atreus,
The glory of whom is now the most under heaven,
So great a city did he sack, and he destroyed many
People. And so we have arrived here and come
    up to your knees   266
To see if you may provide some guest-gift or
    otherwise
Give a present, such as is the custom among guest-
    friends.
Mighty one, revere the gods. We are your
    suppliants.
Zeus is the protector of suppliants and guest
    friends,   270
The god of guests, who accompanies respectful
    guests.'
So I said, and he answered me at once in his
    pitiless spirit:
'You are a fool, stranger, or have come from afar,
To bid me to be afraid or to shrink from the gods.
Cyclopes have no regard for aegis-bearing Zeus, 275
Or the blessed gods, since we are mightier by far.
Nor to shrink from something hateful to Zeus,
    would I spare
You or your companions, unless the spirit moved
    me.
But tell me where you have come and put your
    well-made ships,
Whether on the mainland or nearby, so I may
    know.'   280
So he said, testing us; I who knew much was not
    deceived.
I addressed him in return with guileful words:
'The earth-shaker Poseidon has shattered my
    ship
Throwing it on the rocks at the borders of your
    land,
Driving it on the cape, but a wind bore it from the
    ocean.   285
And I escaped with these men from sheer destruc-
    tion.'
So I said; in his pitiless spirit he answered nothing,
But he leapt up, stretched his hands to my
    companions,

Snatched up two together, and dashed them like
    whelps to the earth.
Their brains flowed out onto the ground and wet
    the earth.   290
Then he tore them limb from limb and made them
    his meal.
He ate like a mountain-reared lion, and did not
    leave off,
Their entrails and their flesh and their marrowed
    bones.
We wailed and held our hands out to Zeus when we
Had seen the cruel deeds. Helplessness held our
    hearts.   295
And when the Cyclops had filled up his great belly
By eating human flesh and then drinking unmixed
    milk,
He lay down in the cave, stretched full length
    through the sheep.
And I myself in my great-hearted spirit I made a
    plan
To go closer to him, draw the sharp sword from my
    thigh,   300
And wound him in the chest where the midriff
    holds the liver,
Striking with my hand. But another spirit
    restrained me;
For there we, too, would have perished in sheer
    destruction,
Since from the lofty entrance we could not push
    away
The mighty rock with our hands that he had set
    upon it.   305
And so we lamented then and awaited the godly
    Dawn.
And when the early-born, rosy-fingered Dawn
    appeared,
He kindled a fire and milked his glorious flocks,
All in due order, and set each young one to his
    mother.
And when he had hurried at tending to all his
    tasks,   310
He snatched two more together and made them
    his meal.
When he had finished, he drove the rich flock from
    the cave,
Taking the great door-block off easily. And then
He put it back, as one would put the lid on a
    quiver.
With a great whistling, Cyclops turned his fat
    flock   315
To the mountain. I was left to ponder evils deeply,
If I might somehow avenge me and Athene give
    me glory.
And this seemed to me in my heart to be the
    best plan.
In the fold a great club of the Cyclops was lying,

A green one of olive wood. He had cut it to carry
When it was dry. As we beheld it, we thought
   it   321
To be as large as the mast of a black, twenty-
   oared ship,
A wide freighter that traverses the great gulf:
So great was its length, so great its breadth to
   behold.
I stood by and cut off a piece the size of a cubit, 325
Gave it to my companions and told them to plane
   it;
They made it smooth, and I stood by and sharpened
   it to a point.
I took it at once and brought it to a glow in the
   blazing fire;
Then I hid it well, spacing it under the dung
Which was strewn through the cave in great
   abundant heaps.   330
Then I ordered the others to cast lots for a choice
Of the one who would dare to raise the pole along
   with me
And bore it in his eye when sweet sleep had come
   upon him.
The lots fell to those I would have wished to
   choose myself,
Four men, and I picked myself as the fifth among
   them.   335
He came at evening driving the flocks with their
   lovely fleece.
At once he drove the fat flocks into the broad cave,
All, and did not leave any outside in the deep yard;
Either he suspected something or a god bade him
   so.
Then he put the great doorstone on, raising it
   aloft,   340
And he sat down and milked the sheep and the
   bleating goats,
All in due order and set each young one to his
   mother.
And when he had hurried at attending to all his
   tasks,
He snatched two more together and made them
   his meal.
Then I addressed the Cyclops, standing close to
   him,   345
Holding in my hands an ivy bowl of black wine:
'Here, Cyclops, drink wine, now you have eaten
   human flesh,
So you may see what sort of wine this is that our
   ship contained.
I brought it for libation to you that you might
   pity me
And send me home. Your rage may be borne no
   longer;   350
Cruel wretch, how could anyone else come to you
   later on

Of the number of mankind, since you have not
   acted properly.'
So I said. He took and drank it. He was fearfully
   pleased
As he drank the sweet wine, and he asked me for a
   second.
'Kindly grant me something more and tell me your
   name.   355
At once now, so I may give you a guest gift to
   delight you.
Yes, indeed, for the Cyclopes the grain-giving land
   bears
Large-clustered wine grapes, and a rain of Zeus
   makes them grow,
But this is a runnel of nectar and ambrosia.'
So he said. And I gave him more of the sparkling
   wine.   360
Thrice I brought it and gave it, thrice he thought-
   lessly drank.
And when the wine had overcome the mind of the
   Cyclops,
At that point I addressed him with honeyed words:
'Cyclops, do you ask me my famous name? Well, I
Will tell you. Then give me the guest gift you
   promised.   365
Noman is my own name. Noman do they call me,
My mother and my father and all my other
   companions.'
So I said, and he answered at once in his pitiless
   spirit:
'Noman I shall eat last among his companions
And the others first. This will be my guest gift
   to you.'   370
With that he leaned over and fell down on his
   back. And then
He lay with his massive neck twisted. All-subduing
Sleep seized him. Wine poured out of his gullet,
And chunks of human flesh. He belched out
   drunkenly.
And then I drove the pole up under a mass of
   ashes   375
Until it should heat. And I encouraged all my
   companions
With speeches, lest one of them should draw back
   from me in fear.
But just when the olive pole was ready to catch
   fire
Green as it was, and was glowing dreadfully,
Then I came closer and took it out of the fire. My
   companions   380
Stood about. And some god breathed great
   courage into them.
They lifted the olive pole that was sharp at its
   tip
And thrust it in his eye; I myself, leaning on it
   from above

Twirled it around as a man would drill the wood
  of a ship
With an auger, and others would keep spinning
  with a strap beneath   385
Holding it at either end. And it keeps on going.
So we held the fire-sharpened pole in his eye
And twirled it. The blood flowed around it, hot as
  it was.
The fire singed his eyebrows and eyelids all around
From the burning eye. Its roots swelled in the
  fire to bursting.   390
As when a smith plunges a great axe or an adze
Into cold water and the tempering makes it hiss
Loudly, and just that gives the strength to the
  iron;
So did his eye sizzle around the olive pole.
He wailed a great terrible wail; the rock re-
  sounded,   395
And we were afraid and rushed back, while he drew
The pole out of his eye spattered with much blood;
Then he threw it from him with his hands, mad-
  dened by pain,
And let out a great roar for the Cyclopes, who
  dwelt
All around him in caves throughout the windy
  peaks.   400
When they heard the shout they trailed in from
  every side;
They stood around the cave and asked what
  bothered him:
'Polyphemus, how is it you are hurt so much as
  to shout so
Through the ambrosial night and to make us
  sleepless?
No mortal drives your flocks against your will,
  does he?   405
And no one is murdering you by craft or by force?'
Mighty Polyphemus addressed them from the
  cavern:
'Friends, Noman is murdering me by craft, not by
  force.'
And they answered him and addressed him with
  winged words:
'If no one is compelling you when you are alone,
There is no way to escape a sickness from great
  Zeus.   411
Come now and pray to our father Lord Poseidon.'
So they said and went away; and my own heart
  laughed
At how my name had deceived him, and my
  faultless device.
Cyclops, though, was in pain as he groaned, and
  felt pangs.   415
Groping with his hands, he took the stone from
  the entrance

And sat in the entrance himself, stretching out his
  hands
To see if he could catch someone going outdoors
  with the sheep;
So foolish did he in his mind think me to be.
And I myself kept planning what way might be
  far the best   420
If I could find some release from death for my
  companions,
And for myself. I wove all sorts of wiles and
  deceit
As for very life, since a great ill was near at hand.
This seemed to me in my heart to be the best plan:
The males of the sheep were well-nourished and
  shaggy-coated,   425
Handsome and large, with a fleece of dark violet.
These I joined fast in silence with easily twisted
  twigs
On which the monster Cyclops slept, lawless in
  his mind.
I bound them in threes, and the middle one would
  carry a man.
The other two went on either side, protecting my
  companions.   430
So three sheep bore each mortal man. As for
  myself,
There was a lead ram, far the finest of all the
  sheep,
Whose back I grasped and lay under his shaggy
  belly
Curled up. And with my hand twisted in his
  marvelous wool
I held on relentlessly with an enduring heart. 435
So then, lamenting, we awaited the godly Dawn.
And when the early-born, rosy-fingered Dawn
  appeared,
At that moment he drove the male flocks to
  pasture,
And the females were bleating unmilked around
  the pens.
Their udders were swollen. And then the master,
  afflicted   440
By bad pains, felt over the backs of all the sheep
As they stood erect. And the fool did not perceive
How the men were bound under the breasts of the
  thick-fleeced sheep.
Last of all the lead ram of the flock went outdoors
Encumbered by his wool and by me with my
  rapid thoughts.   445
The mighty Polyphemus felt him over and
  addressed him:
'Friend ram, why of all the sheep do you move
  this way as the last
Out of the cave? You were not left behind by the
  sheep before;

You were much the first to pasture on the tender
  flowers of grass
With your long strides, and you came first to the
  rivers' streams,   450
And you were the first to desire to return to the
  fold
At evening. You are last of all now. Ah, you
  long
For the eye of your master that an evil man put
  out
With his woeful companions, overcoming his mind
  by wine,
Noman, who I say has not yet escaped destruction,
And if only you could sympathize and become able
  to speak   456
To say in what place that man is evading my rage,
Then once he were struck, his brains should be
  dashed through the cave
In all directions on the threshold. And then my
  heart
Should be relieved of the ills worthless Noman
  brought me.'   460
When he had said this, he sent the ram from him
  out the entrance.
When I had gone a short way away from the cave
  and the yard,
I first got loose from the ram and then freed my
  companions.
Speedily we drove the long-legged sheep, rich in
  fat,
Rounding the many of them up, until we came 465
To the ship. We were welcome to our dear
  companions,
We who escaped death. The others they would
  have lamented, wailing,
But I did not allow it and nodded with my eye-
  brows to each
Not to weep. I ordered them to put the many
  sheep
With lovely fleece quickly on the ship and sail the
  salt water.   470
They got on board at once and took their seats at
  the oarlocks;
Seated in order, they beat the hoary sea with their
  oars.
And when I was as far off as a man's shout would
  carry,
I addressed the Cyclops myself with taunting
  speeches:
'Cyclops, you were not destined to eat in your
  hollow cave,   475
For your powerful might, the companions of a
  strengthless man.
And truly it was destined for your evil deeds to
  find you out,

Cruel wretch, since you did not shrink from
  eating the guests
In your house. Zeus and the other gods have paid
  you for that.'
So I said. Then he got very angry in his
  heart.   480
He broke off the crest of a great mountain and
  threw it,
And it fell down in front of the dark blue-prowed
  ship,
Just short, and it missed hitting the end of the
  rudder.
The sea was heaved up by the rock as it descended,
And a great backwashing wave bore the ship at
  once to land,   485
As it swelled from the ocean, and drove it to hit the
  mainland.
And I took hold of a very long pole in my hands
And pushed on out. I called to urge on my com-
  panions,
Nodding with my head, to throw themselves on
  the oars,
So we could flee misfortune. They rowed
  impetuously.   490
When we had crossed twice as much water and
  were far away,
Then I would have shouted to the Cyclops, but
  my companions around me
From all sides tried to restrain me with honeyed
  speeches:
'You wretch, why did you want to provoke the
  wild man,
Who, even now, when he threw his missile into
  the ocean,   495
Has brought the ship back to land? And we
  thought we would die there.
And if he had heard anyone speaking or shouting
  out
He would have broken our brains and our ship
  timbers
Casting a jagged piece of sparkling rock. He
  throws that powerfully.'
So they said, but they did not sway my great-
  hearted spirit.   500
But in my angry spirit I answered him back:
'Cyclops, if someone among mortal men should
  inquire
Of you about the unseemly blindness in your eye,
Say that Odysseus, sacker of cities, blinded it,
The son of Laertes, whose home is in Ithaca.' 505
So I said. He moaned and answered me with a
  tale:
'Well then, the decrees uttered of old have come
  upon me.
Once there was a prophet here, a man fine and
  great,

Telemos, Eurymus' son, who excelled in prophecy,
And grew old prophesying among the Cyclopes,
Who said all these things in the future would come
    to pass,   511
That I would be deprived of my sight at Odysseus'
    hands.
But I always expected some mortal great and
    handsome
To arrive in this place decked out in great strength.
And now, a man small and worthless and feeble 515
Has blinded my eye when he overcame me with
    wine.
Come here now, Odysseus, so I may present you
    with gifts,
And urge the famed earth-shaker to give you an
    escort,
For I am his son, and he declares he is my father,
He himself, if he wishes, will heal me. No one
    else   520
Can do it, of the blessed gods or of mortal men.'
So he said, and I myself addressed him in answer:
'Would I might as surely be able to make you
    devoid
Of breath and life and send you to the hall of
    Hades,
As I am sure not even the earth-shaker will heal
    your eye.'   525
So I said, and then he prayed to Lord Poseidon,
Stretching his hand up to the heaven filled with
    stars:
'Hear me, earth-girdling Poseidon of the dark-blue
    locks,
If truly I am yours, and you declare you are my
    father,
Grant that the city-sacker Odysseus not go home-
    ward,   530
The son of Laertes whose home is in Ithaca.
But if it is his fate to see his dear ones and arrive
At his well-established home and his fatherland,
May he come late and ill, having lost all his
    companions,
On some one else's ship, and find troubles at home.'
So he said in prayer. The god with the dark blue
    locks heard him.   536
And then once more he lifted up a far bigger stone.
Whirling it, he shot it and thrust it with boundless
    strength
And threw it down behind the dark blue-prowed
    ship,
Just short, and it missed hitting the end of the
    rudder.   540
The sea was heaved up by the rock as it descended.
A wave bore the ship forward and drove it to hit
    land.
And when we arrived at the island, where the
    other

Well-timbered ships were waiting, gathered, and
    our companions
Sat lamenting all around, forever awaiting us, 545
As we came there, we beached our ship up on the
    sand
And got out ourselves beside the surf of the sea.
Taking the flocks of Cyclops out of the hollow
    ship,
We divided them so none for my sake would lack
    an equal share.
But my well-greaved companions chose the ram
    especially   550
For me alone, when the flocks were divided. On
    the strand
We slew it and burned the thighs to black-clouded
    Zeus,
The son of Cronos, who rules all. He received
    not the rites,
But he kept on plotting how all the well-timbered
    ships
And the companions faithful to me might be
    destroyed.   555
So then the whole day till the setting of the sun
We sat dining on endless meat and sweet wine.
But when the sun went down and darkness came
    on,
We lay down to sleep beside the surf of the sea.
And when the early-born, rosy-fingered Dawn
    appeared,   560
I myself called to my companions and bade them
To get on board and to loose the cables of the
    stern;
At once they got on and took their seats at the
    oarlocks,
And sitting in order, they beat the hoary deep
    with their oars.
Then we sailed further on, grieved in our hearts,
Glad to escape death, having lost our dear com-
    panions.   566

BOOK XXI

Now the bright-eyed goddess Athene put it into
    the mind
Of Ikarios' daughter, the prudent Penelope,
To set the bow before the suitors and the gray
    iron
In Odysseus' halls, as a contest and a start for
    slaughter.
She stepped upon the high stairway of her quarters
And in her stout hand took hold of the well-curved
    key,   6
A lovely one of bronze. And an ivory handle was
    on it.
And she went on with her serving women into a
    chamber,

The last room, where the treasures of her lord were
    lying,
Bronze and gold and iron that was highly wrought.
There a springy bow was lying, and also a quiver 11
For arrows, and in it were many arrows, that bring
    grief;
These gifts a friend had given him who met him in
    Lacedemon,
Iphitos, son of Eurytos, who was like the im-
    mortals.
The two of them came in Messene upon each
    other   15
In the house of skillful Ortilochus. Odysseus
Had gone there after a debt that the whole
    district owed him.
Messenian men had picked up three hundred
    sheep,
And the shepherds, out of Ithaca, in many-oared
    ships.
For their sake Odysseus had gone a long way
    on embassy   20
While a boy. His father and the other elders had
    sent him out.
And Iphitos came after horses, twelve females of
    his
That had died, along with unweaned, work-
    enduring mules.
Then these brought upon him murder and destiny,
When he went in the presence of the mighty son
    of Zeus   25
The mortal Heracles, who was experienced in huge
    deeds,
Who slaughtered the man as a guest in his own
    house,
A wretch, as he did not respect the gods' wrath
    or the table
That he had set before him. And then he killed the
    very man.
He himself kept the mares with the powerful
    hooves in his halls.   30
Asking for these, the man met Odysseus and gave
    him the bow,
Which great Eurytos had carried before.
He left it when he died to his son in the lofty house.
Odysseus gave him a sharp sword and a mighty
    spear,
The start of a close-binding friendship; but they
    did not know   35
One another at the table, since before that Zeus's
    son slew
Iphitos, son of Eurytos, who was like the im-
    mortals,
Who gave him the bow. And never would godly
    Odysseus
Take it when he went off on the black ships to
    war.

But he left it lying there in the halls as a reminder
Of his dear friend. And he did carry it in his own
    land.   41
And when the divine woman had arrived at her
    chamber
And had gone over the oak threshold that a crafts-
    man once
Skillfully planed for her and straightened with a
    line —
He fitted doorposts up, and set shining doors on
    them —   45
Right away she quickly took the thong from the
    hook,
Inserted the key and shot back the bolts of the
    door,
Aiming them straight, and they groaned like a bull
Feeding in a meadow; so loud did the lovely door
    sound
As it was struck by the key and was quickly
    opened wide.   50
She stood upon the lofty planking. And there
    chests
Were standing, inside of which clothing was stored.
From there she stretched herself up and reached
    the bow from its peg,
Along with the bowcase that surrounded it
    handsomely.
She sat down right there, putting it on her own
    knees   55
And wept aloud as she took down her husband's
    bow.
And when she had her fill of tearful lamentation,
She went on into the hall among the noble suitors
Holding in her hand the springy bow and the
    quiver
For arrows. In it were many arrows that bring
    grief.   60
Her servants brought her a case in which iron lay
In plenty, and so did bronze, the prizes of her lord.
And when the divine woman had come to the
    suitors,
She stood beside the pillar of the stoutly fashioned
    roof
Holding the glistening head-bands before her
    cheeks.   65
A devoted servant stood there on either side of her.
At once she spoke out to the suitors and addressed
    a speech to them:
"Listen to me now, bold suitors, you who have
    always
Beset this house, perpetually eating and drinking
While my husband has been gone away for a long
    time.   70
You could make up no other story as an excuse
Than that you wanted to marry me and make your
    wife.

Well, come now, suitors, since this appears as your
　　prize.
I shall set up the great bow of godly Odysseus.
The one who most nimbly strings the bow in his
　　hands   75
And shoots an arrow through all twelve of the
　　axes,
Him shall I follow, departing from this very lovely
Home of my marriage that is full of the goods of
　　life,
Which I think I shall ever remember, even in a
　　dream."
So she said, and she called to Eumaeus, the godly
　　swineherd,   80
To set up for the suitors the bow and the grey
　　iron.
Eumaeus took them weeping, and he set them out.
The herdsman for his part wailed when he saw his
　　master's bow.
Then Antinoös rebuked them and spoke out to
　　them directly:
"Foolish yokels, who consider only the things of
　　the day.   85
You wretches, why are you dripping tears? Why
　　arouse
The heart in the breast of a woman whose heart
　　lies in pain
In any case, since she has lost her dear husband?
But sit down and eat in silence, or else go on
And wail outdoors, leaving the bow behind right
　　here,   90
An inviolable contest for the suitors. So I think
This polished bow is not to be strung easily,
And there is no man present among all of you
Of the kind Odysseus was. I saw him my own self,
And I do remember him, though I was still a
　　foolish child."   95
So he said, but even so the heart in his breast hoped
To string the bowstring and shoot an arrow through
　　the iron.
Yet he was destined to be the first to taste an
　　arrow
From the hands of blameless Odysseus, whom he
　　dishonored then
As he sat in the halls. And he roused all his
　　companions.   100
Telemachus spoke out to them in his sacred might:
"Well, Zeus, son of Cronos, has made me lacking
　　in sense.
My dear mother says, even though she is prudent,
That she will follow another and leave this house
　　behind.
Yet I am laughing and am pleased in my senseless
　　heart.   105
Come now, you suitors, since this appears as the
　　prize.

A woman whose like now exists not in the Achaian
　　land,
Not in sacred Pylos or in Argos or Mycenae,
Or in Ithaca herself, or upon the black mainland.
You know it yourselves. Why need I praise my
　　mother?   110
Come, do not put it off with excuses or turn away
From stringing the bow any more, so we may see.
And I my very own self would make a try at the
　　bow.
If I do string it and shoot an arrow through the
　　iron,
My lady mother should not leave me in any
　　grief   115
If she went off with another, since I should be left
　　behind
As one able to take up my father's fine weapons."
He spoke, and put the purple tunic off his shoulders,
Sprang upright, and took the sharp sword off his
　　shoulders.
First he stood up the axes, digging one long
　　trench through   120
For all of them, and he straightened it with a line,
And stamped earth down about them. Awe seized
　　all who saw
How neatly he stood them, yet he had never looked
　　at them before.
He went and stood on the threshold and tested
　　the bow.
Three times he made it quiver, striving to draw it,
And three times he slackened his strength, hoping
　　in his heart   126
To string the bowstring and shoot an arrow through
　　the iron.
And he would have drawn it the fourth time,
　　bending it with his strength.
But Odysseus nodded and checked him, impelled
　　as he was.
Then Telemachus spoke out to them in his sacred
　　might: 130
"Well, how weak and cowardly I shall be even in
　　the future,
Or else I am too young and cannot yet rely on my
　　hands
For warding some man off if he gets angry first.
Come now, you who are superior to me in strength,
Try the bow out and let us conclude the contest."
When he had said this, he put the bow away from
　　him on the ground,   136
Leaning it against the tight-fitted, well-made
　　doors.
And then he leaned a swift dart against its fine
　　tip.
Then he sat back down on the chair from which
　　he had stood.

Antinoös, the son of Eupeithes, spoke out to
   them: 140
"Rise, all my companions, in order, from left to
   right,
Beginning at the place from which the wine is
   poured."
So Antinoös said, and his speech was pleasing to
   them.
Leodes, son of Oinops, was the first to stand up.
He was their soothsayer, and he always sat   145
Furthest in by the lovely mixing bowl. To him
   alone
Were reckless things hateful; he resented all the
   suitors.
He was the first then to take the bow and the
   swift dart.
He went and stood on the threshold and tried out
   the bow.
He did not string it. Before that, drawing it up,
He tired his soft, unworn hands. And he spoke
   to the suitors: 151
"My friends, I cannot string it. Let another take
   it.
Many excellent men shall this bow have bereaved
Of life and spirit, since it is better by far
To die than to live and miss what perpetually 155
We are gathered for here, expectant day after day,
And even now someone hopes in his mind and
   desires
To marry Penelope, the wife of Odysseus.
But when he has seen the bow and tested it out
Let him then woo some other of the well-gowned
   Achaian women   160
And seek her in marriage with gifts. She then
   may wed
Whoever gives the most and comes as the destined
   man."
When he had said this, he put the bow away from
   him,
Leaning it against the tight-fitted, well-made
   doors.
Then he leaned the swift dart against its fine
   tip,   165
And then sat back down on the chair from which
   he had stood.
But Antinoös rebuked him and spoke out to him
   directly:
"Leodes, what sort of speech has got past the
   bar of your teeth?
A wretched and grievous one. I am angered as
   I hear it,
If this bow indeed shall deprive excellent men 170
Of spirit and life, when you cannot string it
   yourself.
Your queenly mother did not bear you as the sort
   of man

Who could be capable of drawing a bow and
   arrows,
But other noble suitors shall quickly string it."
So he said, and he called to Melanthios, the
   goatherd.   175
"Come, Melanthios, and kindle a fire in the halls.
Put a large stool down alongside and a fleece
   upon it,
And bring in a great round piece of the fat from
   inside,
So we young men, when we have warmed it and
   rubbed it with grease,
May try the bow out and may conclude the
   contest."   180
So he said. Melanthios at once kindled a quench-
   less fire,
Brought in a stool, put it down and set a fleece
   upon it.
Then he carried in a great round piece of the fat
   from inside.
So the young men tried, when they had warmed
   it. They were not
Able to string it: they were far too lacking in
   strength.   185
Antinoös and godlike Eurymachus, chief of the
   suitors,
Still held back. They were by far the best in
   excellence.
Accompanying each other, the oxherd and the
   swineherd
Of godly Odysseus had both gone out of the
   house.
Divine Odysseus came after them from the house
   himself.   190
And when they were outside of the doors and the
   courtyard,
He raised his voice and addressed them with
   honeyed speeches:
"Oxherd, and you, swineherd, shall I tell you
   something
Or keep it to myself? My heart bids me to speak.
How would you fend for Odysseus if he came from
   somewhere   195
Very suddenly this way and some god had brought
   him in?
Would you fend for the suitors or fend for
   Odysseus?
Speak the way your heart and your spirit command
   you to."
Then the man who was in charge of the oxen
   addressed him:
"Father Zeus, would that you might fulfill this
   wish,   200
That the man himself might come, and a god
   might bring him.

You should learn what my strength is, and how my
    hands go with it."
And so Eumaeus prayed the same way to all the
    gods,
For many-minded Odysseus to return to his own
    home.
And when he had recognized their unerring intent,
He answered them right away and addressed them
    with a speech: 206
"Here I am, home, myself, having suffered many
    pains;
I have come in the twentieth year to my fatherland.
I realize that you alone of the servants I come to
Are longing for me. I have heard none of the
    others   210
Praying for me to reach home again on my return,
And I shall speak the truth to you both as it shall
    be.
If a god indeed subdues the noble suitors beneath
    me,
I shall give you both wives and provide you with
    property
And houses built close to my own. Then you shall
    be   215
Companions and kinsmen of Telemachus and
    myself.
Come now, I shall show you another manifest
    sign
So you may know me well and trust me in your
    hearts:
A scar a boar once inflicted on me with his shining
    tusk
When I went to Parnassus with the sons of
    Autolycus."   220
When he had said this, he moved his rags away
    from the great scar.
Both, when they had seen and well marked the
    particulars,
Wept and threw their arms around skillful
    Odysseus,
And they kept kissing him, embracing his head
    and shoulders.
Odysseus kept kissing their heads and hands the
    same way.   225
The light of the sun would have gone down on them
    as they moaned,
If Odysseus himself had not checked them and
    spoken out:
"Stop wailing and lamenting, lest someone come
    out
Of the hall, see us, and then tell it within too,
But go inside, each in turn and not all together,
I first, and you afterwards. And let this be made
    a sign.   231
That is, when all the others, the whole number of
    noble suitors,

Will not allow the bow and quiver to be given to
    me.
But you, godly Eumaeus, carry the bow through
    the house,
Place it in my hands, and then tell the women 235
To lock up the closely fitted portals of the hall,
And if anyone inside hears in our enclosures
A groaning and beating of men, let her not go
    forth
Out the door at all, but be there in silence at the
    task.
And you, godly Philoitios, I order to bolt the
    gates   240
Of the courtyard with a bolt, and put a cord on
    as well."
When he had said this, he entered the well-
    inhabited halls.
Then he went and sat down on the stool from
    which he had stood,
And the two servants of godly Odysseus also
    went in.
Eurymachus was already turning the bow in his
    hands,   245
Warming it here and there in the fire's flame. But
    he could not
String it even so; his mighty heart swelled heavily.
Angered, he uttered a speech and spoke out
    directly:
"Well now, there is grief for myself and for every-
    one.
Not for the marriage do I moan so greatly, dis-
    tressed as I am   250
There are many other Achaian women, some in
    this very
Sea-circled Ithaca; and some in other cities.
But if we are to such a degree lacking in the force
Of godlike Odysseus that we cannot string his
    bow,
It is a disgrace even for men in the future to hear
    of."   255
Then Antinoös, son of Eupeithes, spoke to him:
"Eurymachus, it will not be so. And you know
    it yourself.
For now through the district the feast day of
    that god
Is sacred. And who would bend the bow? Put it
    down
Quietly. But as for the axes, suppose we let
    them   260
All stand. For I think no one will come into the
    hall
Of Odysseus, son of Laertes, and carry them off.
Come now, let the wine-pourer begin putting drops
    in the cups,
So we may pour libation and lay down the curved
    bow.

And at dawn call Melanthios, the herd of the
goats,   265
To bring the goats that are far outstanding in all
the herds,
So that, setting out thighs to Apollo, famed for
the bow,
We may try the bow out and conclude the
contest."
So Antinoös said, and his speech was pleasing to
them.
Heralds poured water for them over their hands,
And youths filled mixing bowls to the brim for
drinking   271
And served round to all, putting the first drops in
the cups.
When they had poured libation and drunk what
their hearts wished,
Odysseus of many wiles spoke to them with a
trick in mind:
"Listen to me, suitors of the illustrious queen, 275
So I may tell you what the heart in my breast bids
me to.
Eurymachus especially and godly Antinoös
Do I beseech, since he said his speech properly:
Let the bow go now, and turn it over to the gods,
And at dawn the god will give the strength to the
one he wishes.   280
Come then, give me the polished bow, so that
among you
I may test out my strength and hands, whether
the force
Is in me still that was in my supple limbs before,
Or wandering and lack of care have ruined me
already."
So he said, and they all grew insolently angry, 285
Fearing that he might put the string on the
polished bow.
Antinoös rebuked him and spoke out to him
directly:
"Wretched stranger, you have no sense, none in
the least.
Are you not content to dine among us exalted
men,
Secure, not to be deprived of food at all, to hear 290
Our speeches and our discourse? Nor does any
other
Stranger or any beggar listen to our speeches.
Honey-sweet wine besets you, that also harms
other men,
Whoever takes it down in gulps and drinks to
excess.
Wine blinded the Centaur too, illustrious Eury-
tion,   295
In the hall of great-spirited Perithoüs,
When he came to the Lapiths. After he was
blinded with wine,

He went mad and did evils in the home of
Perithoüs.
Distress seized the heroes. They leapt up and
dragged him outdoors
Through the forecourt, and sheared his ears and
nostrils off   300
With the pitiless bronze. Then he grew reckless in
his mind,
And went on, bearing madness in his impetuous
heart.
From that a quarrel grew up between Centaurs
and men.
Being heavy with wine, he found evil first for
himself.
And so I declare great trouble for you, if you
should string   305
This bow. You would not encounter any gentle
use
In our district. We should send you speedily
To King Echetos, the destroyer of all mortal men,
In a black ship. And you would not be saved
there. But drink
Quietly, and do not wrangle with men younger
than you."   310
And then the prudent Penelope answered him:
"Antinoös, it is not fine or just to slight
The guests of Telemachus, whoever comes to this
house.
Do you think, if this stranger does bend the great
bow
Of Odysseus, relying on his hands and his mighty
force,   315
That he will lead me to his home and make me
his wife?
He himself has never yet thought this in his
breast.
Let no one of you dine here grieving in his heart
On that account, since it is not seemly at all."
Eurymachus, son of Polybus, answered her: 320
"Daughter of Ikarios, prudent Penelope,
We do not think this man will lead you home. It is
not seemly,
But we are ashamed at the rumor among men and
women,
Lest sometime some other foul person of the
Achaians may say:
'Yes, far inferior men are wooing the wife   325
Of an excellent man, and cannot string his polished
bow.
But someone else, a beggar, who came on his
wanderings,
Easily strung the bow and shot through the iron.'
So they would say, and this would be a reproach
to us."
Then the prudent Penelope spoke to him: 330

"Eurymachus, there is no way that good reports may exist
In the district, for those who dishonor and devour
A noble man's home. And why make a reproach of this?
The stranger here is very large and of a well-knit frame.
He declares that he is by descent a good father's son. 335
Come now, give him the polished bow, so we may see.
I shall say it out so, and it shall be brought to pass.
If he does string it and Apollo gives him the praise,
I shall clothe him in a mantle and a tunic, lovely clothes.
I shall give him a sharp javelin, a defense against dogs and men, 340
And a two-edged sword. I shall give him sandals for his feet
And send him wherever his heart and spirit bid."
Then sound-minded Telemachus addressed her in answer:
"My mother, no one of the Achaians has more power than I
To give or refuse the bow to whomever he wishes.
Not any of those who rule in craggy Ithaca 346
Or who rule over the islands towards horse-pasturing Elis.
None of them will compel me against my will from giving
This bow to the stranger to take off once for all, if I wish.
But go into the house and attend to your own tasks, 350
The loom and the distaff, and give orders to your servants
To busy themselves with work. The bow shall concern all the men
But me especially. For the strength in the house is mine."
She was amazed at him, and back into the house she went.
The sound-minded speech of her son she took to heart 355
She went into the upper chamber with her serving women,
And then wept for Odysseus, her dear husband, until
Bright-eyed Athene cast sweet sleep upon her eyelids.
Then the divine swineherd took the curved bow, and carried it,
And all the suitors made an outcry in the halls.

One of those overbearing young men would say this: 361
"Where are you carrying the curved bow, miserable swineherd,
You vagabond? Soon the swift dogs you reared yourself,
Shall eat you amid the swine, apart from men, alone,
If Apollo is gracious to us and the other immortal gods." 365
So they said; he carried it and put it in that very place,
Afraid because many made an outcry in the halls.
But Telemachus from the other side voiced a threat:
"Uncle, bring the bow forth. That you heed all will soon not be good.
Lest, though younger than you, I drive you to the fields 370
And throw stones at you. I am mightier than you in strength.
Would I were that much mightier in strength and with my hands
Than all of the suitors who are inside the halls.
Then I should soon send one of them grimly on his way
Out of our house, since they are devising evils." 375
So he said, and all of the suitors sweetly laughed
At him, and they relaxed their difficult anger
Toward Telemachus. The swineherd carried the bow through the house,
Stood beside skillful Odysseus, and put it in his hands.
Then he called forth the nurse Eurycleia and addressed her: 380
"Prudent Eurycleia, Telemachus orders you
To lock up the closely fitted portals of the hall.
And if anyone inside hears in our enclosures
A groaning and a beating of men, let her not go forth
Out the door at all, but be there in silence at the task." 385
So he said, and for her the word was without a wing.
She locked up the doors of the well-inhabited halls.
Philoitios sprang in silence out of the house,
Outdoors, and locked up the gates of the well-fenced court.
Under the portico lay the papyrus-fibre cable 390
Of a bobbing ship. With it he tied the gates, went in,
And then went and sat down on the stool from which he had stood,
And looked at Odysseus. He was already handling the bow,

Turning it in all directions, testing it this way and
  that,
For fear worms had eaten the horns while the
  master was away. 395
So one of them would say, looking at his neighbor:
"This is some fancier and an expert with bows,
And perhaps such as these are lying in his home
  too,
Or else he wants to make one, he handles it so
This way and that in his hands, the beggar skilled
  in evils." 400
And another of the overbearing young men might
  say:
"Would that he might encounter profit to the
  degree
That he shall ever be able to string this bow
  himself."
So the suitors said. But Odysseus of many wiles,
At once when he raised the great bow and viewed
  it on all sides; 405
As when a man skilled at the lyre and at singing
Easily stretches a string over a new peg,
Tying at both ends the flexible gut of the sheep;
So without effort did Odysseus string the great
  bow.
He took it in his right hand and tested the cord.
It sang sweetly beneath like a swallow in its
  sound. 411
Great distress came upon the suitors, and the skin
  of all
Turned color. Zeus thundered greatly, showing
  signs.
Then godly Odysseus, who had endured much,
  rejoiced

That the son of crooked-counseling Cronos sent
  him a portent. 415
He took a swift arrow that lay by him on the table
Bare. The others were lying within the hollow
  quiver,
The ones the Achaians were soon to experience
He put it to the bridge, drew the string and the
  notches,
And shot the arrow right from there, sitting on the
  stool, 420
Aiming it straight, and he did not miss one handle-
  tip
Of all of the axes. The arrow heavy with bronze
Went straight on out the end. He spoke to
  Telemachus:
"Telemachus, the stranger seated in the halls
Does not discredit you. I did not miss my aim 425
Nor did I toil to string the bow. My strength is
  steadfast still;
And is not the way the suitors dishonor me and
  scorn me.
And now it is time for the Achaians to have a meal
  prepared
In the light, and then to make sport in other ways
With singing and the lyre; they are the ornaments
  of a feast." 430
So he said, and nodded with his eyebrows.
  Telemachus,
The dear son of godlike Odysseus, girded on his
  sharp sword,
Put his own hand round his spear and stood close
  to him
Beside his chair, fitted out with glittering bronze.

The Bible

The inclusion of excerpts from the Bible, a book largely written in Hebrew and dominantly Oriental in tone and coloring, in a collection devoted to literature of the Western World is easily justified. The thought and language of the Bible have woven themselves into the very texture of Western literature. More common in our heritage even than the Greek of Homer and the Latin of Virgil are the stories of Ruth and of Joseph, the teaching of the Ten Commandments and of the Sermon on the Mount, the magical imagery and rhythm of the Psalms. From the *Beowulf* of the seventh century to the writings of contemporary authors of the twentieth, our literature draws upon the Bible not only for inspiration but also for patterns of style, figures of speech and diction.

The word *bible* means, literally, a collection of books. As we know it today the Bible consists of two sections, the Old and the New Testaments. The Old Testament, written in Hebrew, presents the sacred writings of the Jews; the New Testament, written in Greek, presents the record of the early Christians. In the different "books" of the Old and the New Testaments, written variously in prose and poetry, may be found many of the literary types known today. Here are sections which are biographical, passages which are lyrical, verses which are elegiac. Here, too, are dramas, essays, letters, parables, short stories. English readers are particulary fortunate in possessing the fine King James Version, a translation published in 1611 at a time when the English idiom was especially rich.

Distinct literary qualities for which the student should be on the watch, particularly in reading the Old Testament, are the use of balanced lines, a frequent parallelism of structure, a melodic rhythm, and a fairly common use of the refrain. There is, however, no uniform meter, no rime.

The very nature of the Bible, the long period in which its parts were composed (from perhaps 1000 B.C. to 200 A.D.), the variety of literary types, the large number of authors included — all these give a range and scope to the Bible which no single book of Western literature can equal. In such a volume practically all of the literary "tempers" manifest themselves in one section or another. The story of Samson is told with classic simplicity. The Psalms are rich in symbolism. The triangular relationship of David, Uriah, and Bath-sheba is related with a realism suggestive of modern writing.

The passages which follow evidence the classical spirit in their simplicity of narrative (Joseph and his Brethren), their concern with the intellectual and moral (The Sermon on the Mount), their formal diction (Ruth), their edifying tone (The Ten Commandments), their interest in the universal (The Creation).

These selections, as well as those in other sections of this volume, are reprinted from *The Pocket Bible*, an arrangement of the King James Version made by Wallace Brockway.

SUGGESTED REFERENCE: H. H. Watts, *The Modern Reader's Guide to the Bible* (2nd ed., 1959).

The Creation of the World

In the beginning God created the heaven and the earth. And the earth was without form, and void; and darkness was upon the face of the deep. And the Spirit of God moved upon the face of the waters. And God said, "Let there be light": and there was light. And God saw the light, that it was good: and God divided the light from the darkness. And God called the light Day, and the darkness he called Night. And the evening and the morning were the first day.

And God said, "Let there be a firmament in the midst of the waters, and let it divide the waters from the waters." And God made the firmament, and divided the waters which were under the firmament from the waters which were above the firmament: and it was so. And God called the firmament Heaven. And the evening and the morning were the second day.

And God said, "Let the waters under the heaven be gathered together unto one place, and let the dry land appear": and it was so. And God called the dry land Earth; and the gathering together of the waters called he Seas: and God saw that it was good. And God said, "Let the earth bring forth grass, the herb yielding seed, and the fruit tree yielding fruit after his kind, whose seed is in itself, upon the earth": and it was so. And the earth brought forth grass, and herb yielding seed after his kind, and the tree yielding fruit, whose seed was in itself, after his kind: and God saw that it

was good. And the evening and the morning were the third day.

And God said, "Let there be lights in the firmament of the heaven to divide the day from the night; and let them be for signs, and for seasons, and for days, and years; and let them be for lights in the firmament of the heaven to give light upon the earth."

And it was so. And God made two great lights; the greater light to rule the day, and the lesser light to rule the night: he made the stars also. And God set them in the firmament of the heaven to give light upon the earth. And to rule over the day and over the night, and to divide the light from the darkness: and God saw that it was good. And the evening and the morning were the fourth day.

And God said, "Let the waters bring forth abundantly the moving creature that hath life, and fowl that may fly above the earth in the open firmament of heaven." And God created great whales, and every living creature that moveth, which the waters brought forth abundantly, after their kind, and every winged fowl after his kind: and God saw that it was good. And God blessed them, saying, "Be fruitful, and multiply, and fill the waters in the seas, and let fowl multiply in the earth." And the evening and the morning were the fifth day.

And God said, "Let the earth bring forth the living creature after his kind, cattle, and creeping thing, and beast of the earth after his kind": and it was so. And God made the beast of the earth after his kind, and cattle after their kind, and every thing that creepeth upon the earth after his kind: and God saw that it was good.

And God said, "Let us make man in our image, after our likeness: and let them have dominion over the fish of the sea, and over the fowl of the air, and over the cattle, and over all the earth, and over every creeping thing that creepeth upon the earth." So God created man in his own image, in the image of God created he him; male and female created he them. And God blessed them, and God said unto them, "Be fruitful, and multiply, and replenish the earth, and subdue it: and have dominion over the fish of the sea, and over the fowl of the air, and over every living thing that moveth upon the earth." And God said, "Behold, I have given you every herb bearing seed, which is upon the face of all the earth, and every tree, in the which is the fruit of a tree yielding seed; to you it shall be for meat. And to every beast of the earth, and to every fowl of the air, and to every thing that creepeth upon the earth, wherein there is life, I have given every green herb for meat." And it was so. And God saw every thing that he had made, and, behold, it was very good. And the evening and the morning were the sixth day.

Thus the heavens and the earth were finished, and all the host of them. And on the seventh day God ended his work which he had made; and he rested on the seventh day from all his work which he had made. And God blessed the seventh day, and sanctified it: because that in it he had rested from all his work which God created and made.

(Genesis.)

The Story of Joseph and His Brethren

Joseph, being seventeen years old, was feeding the flock with his brethren; and the lad was with the sons of Bilhah, and with the sons of Zilpah, his father's wives: and Joseph brought unto his father their evil report. Now Israel loved Joseph more than all his children, because he was the son of his old age: and he made him a coat of many colors. And when his brethren saw that their father loved him more than all his brethren, they hated him, and could not speak peaceably unto him. And Joseph dreamed a dream, and he told it his brethren: and they hated him yet the more. And he said unto them,

"Hear, I pray you, this dream which I have dreamed: for, behold, we were binding sheaves in the field, and, lo, my sheaf arose, and also stood upright; and, behold, your sheaves stood round about, and made obeisance to my sheaf."

And his brethren said to him, "Shalt thou indeed reign over us? or shalt thou indeed have dominion over us?"

And they conspired against him to slay him. And they said one to another, "Behold, this dreamer cometh. Come now therefore, and let us slay him, and cast him into some pit, and we will say, 'Some evil beast hath devoured him': and we shall see what will become of his dreams."

And Reuben heard it, and he delivered him out of their hands; and said, "Let us not kill him."

And it came to pass, when Joseph was come unto his brethren, that they stripped Joseph out of his coat, his coat of many colors that was on him; and they took him, and cast him into a pit: and the pit was empty, there was no water in it. And they sat down to eat bread: and they lifted up their eyes and looked, and, behold, a company of Ishmaelites came from Gilead with their camels bearing spicery and balm and myrrh, going to carry it down to Egypt. And Judah said unto his brethren,

"What profit is it if we slay our brother, and conceal his blood? Come and let us sell him to the Ishmaelites, and let not our hand be upon him; for he is our brother and our flesh."

And his brethren were content. Then there passed by Midianites merchantmen; and they drew and lifted up Joseph out of the pit, and sold Joseph to the Ishmaelites for twenty pieces of silver: and they brought Joseph into Egypt.

And Reuben returned unto the pit; and, behold, Joseph was not in the pit; and he rent his clothes. And he returned unto his brethren, and said, "The child is not; and I, whither shall I go?"

And they took Joseph's coat, and killed a kid of the goats, and dipped the coat in the blood; and they sent the coat of many colors, and they brought it to their father; and said, "This have we found: know now whether it be thy son's coat or no."

And he knew it, and said, "It is my son's coat; an evil beast hath devoured him; Joseph is without doubt rent in pieces."

And Jacob rent his clothes, and put sackcloth upon his loins, and mourned for his son many days.

And Joseph was brought down to Egypt; and Potiphar, an officer of Pharaoh, captain of the guard, an Egyptian, bought him of the hands of the Ishmaelites, which had brought him down thither. And the Lord was with Joseph, and he was a prosperous man; and he was in the house of his master the Egyptian. And his master saw that the Lord was with him, and that the Lord made all that he did to prosper in his hand. And Joseph found grace in his sight, and he served him: and he made him overseer over his house, and all that he had he put into his hand. And it came to pass from the time that he had made him overseer in his house, and over all that he had, that the Lord blessed the Egyptian's house for Joseph's sake; and the blessing of the Lord was upon all that he had in the house, and in the field. And he left all that he had in Joseph's hand; and he knew not ought he had, save the bread which he did eat. And Joseph was a goodly person, and well favored.

And it came to pass after these things, that his master's wife cast her eyes upon Joseph; and she said, "Lie with me." But he refused, and said unto his master's wife, "Behold, my master wotteth [1] not what is with me in the house, and he hath committed all that he hath to my hand! There is none greater in this house than I; neither hath he kept back any thing from me but thee, because thou art his wife: how then can I do this great wickedness, and sin against God?"

And it came to pass, as she spoke to Joseph day by day, that he hearkened not unto her, to lie by her, or to be with her.

And it came to pass about this time, that Joseph went into the house to do his business; and there was none of the men of the house there within. And she caught him by his garment, saying, "Lie with me": and he left his garment in her hand, and fled, and got him out.

And it came to pass, when she saw that he had left his garment in her hand, and was fled forth, that she called unto the men of her house, and spoke unto them, saying, "See, he hath brought in a Hebrew unto us to mock us; he came in unto me to lie with me, and I cried with a loud voice; and it came to pass, when he heard that I lifted up my voice and cried, that he left his garment with me, and fled, and got him out."

And it came to pass, when his master heard the words of his wife, which she spoke unto him, saying, "After this manner did thy servant to me"; that his wrath was kindled. And Joseph's master took him, and put him into the prison, a place where the king's prisoners were bound: and he was there in the prison.

But the Lord was with Joseph, and showed him mercy, and gave him favor in the sight of the keeper of the prison. And the keeper of the prison committed to Joseph's hand all the prisoners that were in the prison; and whatsoever they did there, he was the doer of it. The keeper of the prison looked not to any thing that was under his hand;

[1] knoweth.

because the Lord was with him, and that which he did, the Lord made it to prosper.

And it came to pass at the end of two full years that Pharaoh dreamed: and, behold, he stood by the river. And, behold, there came up out of the river seven well favored kine and fatfleshed; and they fed in a meadow. And, behold, seven other kine came up after them out of the river, ill favored and leanfleshed; and stood by the other kine upon the brink of the river. And the ill favored and leanfleshed kine did eat up the seven well favored and fat kine. So Pharaoh awoke.

And he slept and dreamed the second time: and, behold, seven ears of corn came up upon one stalk, rank and good. And, behold, seven thin ears and blasted with the east wind sprung up after them. And the seven thin ears devoured the seven rank and full ears. And Pharaoh awoke, and, behold, it was a dream.

And it came to pass in the morning that his spirit was troubled; and he sent and called for all the magicians of Egypt, and all the wise men thereof: and Pharaoh told them his dream; but there was none that could interpret them unto Pharaoh.

Then spoke the chief butler unto Pharaoh, saying, "I do remember my faults this day. Pharaoh was wroth with his servants, and put me in ward in the captain of the guard's house, both me and the chief baker: and we dreamed a dream in one night, I and he; we dreamed each man according to the interpretation of his dream. And there was there with us a young man, a Hebrew, servant to the captain of the guard; and we told him, and he interpreted to us our dreams; to each man according to his dream he did interpret. And it came to pass, as he interpreted to us, so it was; me he restored unto mine office, and him he hanged."

Then Pharaoh sent and called Joseph, and they brought him hastily out of the dungeon: and he shaved himself, and changed his raiment, and came in unto Pharaoh. And Pharaoh said unto Joseph, "I have dreamed a dream, and there is none that can interpret it: and I have heard say of thee that thou canst understand a dream to interpret it."

And Joseph said unto Pharaoh, "The dream of Pharaoh is one. God hath showed Pharaoh what he is about to do. The seven good kine are seven years; and the seven good ears are seven years: the dream is one. And the seven thin and ill favored kine that came up after them are seven years; and the seven empty ears blasted with the east wind shall be seven years of famine. This is the thing which I have spoken unto Pharaoh. What God is about to do he showeth unto Pharaoh. Behold, there come seven years of great plenty throughout all the land of Egypt, and there shall arise after them seven years of famine; and all the plenty shall be forgotten in the land of Egypt; and the famine shall consume the land. And the plenty shall not be known in the land by reason of that famine following; for it shall be very grievous. And for that the dream was doubled unto Pharaoh twice; it is because the thing is established by God, and God will shortly bring it to pass. Now therefore let Pharaoh look out a man discreet and wise, and set him over the land of Egypt. Let Pharaoh do this, and let him appoint officers over the land, and take up the fifth part of the land of Egypt in the seven plenteous years. And let them gather all the food of those good years that come, and lay up corn under the hand of Pharaoh, and let them keep food in the cities. And that food shall be for store to the land against the seven years of famine, which shall be in the land of Egypt; that the land perish not through the famine."

And the thing was good in the eyes of Pharaoh, and in the eyes of all his servants. And Pharaoh said unto his servants, "Can we find such a one as this is, a man in whom the Spirit of God is?"

And Pharaoh said unto Joseph, "Forasmuch as God hath showed thee all this, there is none so discreet and wise as thou art. Thou shalt be over my house, and according unto thy word shall all my people be ruled: only in the throne will I be greater than thou." And Pharaoh said unto Joseph, "See, I have set thee over all the land of Egypt."

And Joseph was thirty years old when he stood before Pharaoh king of Egypt. And Joseph went out from the presence of Pharaoh, and went throughout all the land of Egypt. And in the seven plenteous years the earth brought forth by handfuls. And he gathered up all the food of the seven years, which were in the land of Egypt, and laid up the food in the cities: the food of the field, which was round about every city, laid he up in the same. And Joseph gathered corn as the sand of the sea, very much, until he left numbering; for it was without number.

Now when Jacob saw that there was corn in Egypt, Jacob said unto his sons, "Why do ye look one upon another?" And he said, "Behold, I have heard that there is corn in Egypt: get you down thither, and buy for us from thence; that we may live, and not die."

And Joseph's ten brethren went down to buy corn in Egypt. But Benjamin, Joseph's brother, Jacob sent not with his brethren; for he said, "Lest peradventure mischief befall him." And the sons of Israel came to buy corn among those that came: for the famine was in the land of Canaan. And Joseph was the governor over the land, and he it was that sold to all the people of the land: and Joseph's brethren came, and bowed down themselves before him with their faces to the earth.

And Joseph saw his brethren, and he knew them, but made himself strange unto them, and spoke roughly unto them; and he said unto them, "Whence come ye?" And they said, "From the land of Canaan to buy food."

And Joseph knew his brethren, but they knew not him. And Joseph remembered the dreams which he dreamed of them, and said unto them, "Ye are spies; to see the nakedness of the land ye are come."

And they said unto him, "Nay, my lord, but to buy food are thy servants come. Thy servants are twelve brethren, the sons of one man in the land of Canaan; and, behold, the youngest is this day with our father, and one is not."

And Joseph said unto them, "That is it that I spoke unto you, saying 'Ye are spies.' Hereby ye shall be proved: by the life of Pharaoh ye shall not go forth hence, except your youngest brother come hither. Send one of you, and let him fetch your brother, and ye shall be kept in prison, that your words may be proved, whether there be any truth in you: or else by the life of Pharaoh surely ye are spies." And he put them all together into ward three days.

And Joseph said unto them the third day, "This do, and live; for I fear God. If ye be true men, let one of your brethren be bound in the house of your prison: go ye, carry corn for the famine of your houses: but bring your youngest brother unto me; so shall your words be verified, and ye shall not die."

And he turned himself about from them, and wept; and returned to them again, and communed with them, and took from them Simeon, and bound him before their eyes.

Then Joseph commanded to fill their sacks with corn, and to restore every man's money into his sack, and to give them provision for the way: and thus did he unto them. And they laded their asses with the corn, and departed thence. And as one of them opened his sack to give his ass provender in the inn, he espied his money; for, behold, it was in his sack's mouth. And he said unto his brethren, "My money is restored; and, lo, it is even in my sack": and their heart failed them, and they were afraid, saying one to another, "What is this that God hath done unto us?"

And they came unto Jacob their father unto the land of Canaan, and told him all that befell unto them.

And their father Israel said unto them, "If it must be so now, do this; take of the best fruits in the land of your vessels, and carry down the man a present, a little balm, and a littly honey, spices, and myrrh, nuts, and almonds. And take double money in your hand; and the money that was brought again in the mouth of your sacks, carry it again in your hand; peradventure it was an oversight. Take also your brother, and arise, go again unto the man. And God Almighty give you mercy before the man, that he may send away your other brother, and Benjamin. If I be bereaved of my children, I am bereaved."

And the men took that present, and they took double money in their hand, and Benjamin; and rose up, and went down to Egypt, and stood before Joseph. And when Joseph saw Benjamin with them, he said to the ruler of his house,

"Bring these men home, and slay, and make ready; for these men shall dine with me at noon."

And the man brought the men into Joseph's house, and gave them water, and they washed their feet; and he gave their asses provender. And they made ready the present against Joseph came at noon: for they heard that they should eat bread there. And when Joseph came home, they brought him the present which was in their hand into the house, and bowed themselves to him to the earth.

And he lifted up his eyes, and saw his brother Benjamin, his mother's son, and said, "Is this your younger brother, of whom ye spoke unto me?" And he said, "God be gracious unto thee, my son."

And Joseph made haste; for his bowels did yearn[1] upon his brother: and he sought where to weep; and he entered into his chamber, and wept there. And he washed his face, and went out, and refrained himself and said, "Set on bread." And he took and sent messes unto them from before him: but Benjamin's mess was five times so much as any of theirs. And they drank, and were merry with him.

And he commanded the steward of his house, saying, "Fill the men's sacks with food, as much as they can carry, and put every man's money in his sack's mouth. And put my cup, the silver cup, in the sack's mouth of the youngest, and his corn money." And he did according to the word that Joseph had spoken.

Then Joseph could not refrain himself before all them that stood by him; and he cried, "Cause every man to go out from me." And there stood no man with him, while Joseph made himself known unto his brethren. And he wept aloud: and the Egyptians and the house of Pharaoh heard. And Joseph said unto his brethren,

"I am Joseph; doth my father yet live?"

And his brethren could not answer him; for they were troubled at his presence. And Joseph said unto his brethren,

"Come near to me, I pray you." And they came near. And he said,

"I am Joseph your brother, whom ye sold into Egypt. Now therefore be not grieved, nor angry with yourselves, that ye sold me hither: for God did send me before you to preserve life. For these two years hath the famine been in the land: and yet there are five years, in the which there shall neither be earing nor harvest. And God sent me before you to preserve you a posterity in the earth, and to save your lives by a great deliverance. So now it was not you that sent me hither, but God: and he hath made me a father to Pharaoh, and lord of all his house, and a ruler throughout all the land of Egypt."

And he fell upon his brother Benjamin's neck, and wept; and Benjamin wept upon his neck. Moreover he kissed all his brethren, and wept upon them: and after that his brethren talked with him. To all of them he gave each man changes of raiment; but to Benjamin he gave three hundred pieces of silver, and five changes of raiment. And to his father he sent after this manner; ten asses laden with the good things of Egypt, and ten she-asses laden with corn and bread and meat for his father by the way. So he sent his brethren away, and they departed: and he said unto them,

"See that ye fall not out by the way."

And they went up out of Egypt, and came into the land of Canaan unto Jacob their father, and told him, saying,

"Joseph is yet alive, and he is governor over all the land of Egypt."

And Jacob's heart fainted, for he believed them not. And they told him all the words of Joseph, which he had said unto them: and when he saw the wagons which Joseph had sent to carry him, the spirit of Jacob their father revived. And Israel said,

"It is enough; Joseph my son is yet alive: I will go and see him before I die."

And they took their cattle, and their goods, which they had gotten in the land of Canaan, and came into Egypt, Jacob, and all his seed with him: his sons, and his sons' sons with him, his daughters, and his sons' daughters, and all his seed brought he with him into Egypt.

And he sent Judah before him unto Joseph, to direct his face unto Goshen; and they came into the land of Goshen. And Joseph made ready his chariot, and went up to meet Israel his father, to Goshen, and presented himself unto him; and he fell on his neck, and wept on his neck a good while.

[1] i.e., he was moved with sympathy.

And Israel said unto Joseph, "Now let me die, since I have seen thy face, because thou art yet alive."

And Israel dwelt in the land of Egypt, in the country of Goshen; and they had possessions therein, and grew, and multiplied exceedingly. And Jacob lived in the land of Egypt seventeen years: so the whole age of Jacob was a hundred forty and seven years. And the time drew nigh that Israel must die: and he called his son Joseph, and said unto him, "If now I have found grace in thy sight, put, I pray thee, thy hand under my thigh, and deal kindly and truly with me; bury me not, I pray thee, in Egypt. But I will lie with my fathers, and thou shalt carry me out of Egypt, and bury me in their burying place."

And he said, "I will do as thou hast said." And he said, "Swear unto me." And he swore unto him.

And Jacob called unto his sons, and said, "Gather yourselves together, that I may tell you that which shall befall you in the last days.

"Gather yourselves together, and hear, ye sons of
    Jacob;
And hearken unto Israel your father.

Reuben, thou art my firstborn,
My might, and the beginning of my strength,
The excellency of dignity, and the excellency of
    power:
Unstable as water, thou shalt not excel;
Because thou wentest up to thy father's bed;
Then defiledst thou it: he went up to my couch.

Simeon and Levi are brethren;
Instruments of cruelty are in their habitations.
O my soul, come not thou into their secret;
Unto their assembly, mine honor, be not thou
    united:
For in their anger they slew a man,
And in their selfwill they digged down a wall.
Cursed be their anger, for it was fierce;
And their wrath, for it was cruel:
I will divide them in Jacob,
And scatter them in Israel.

Judah, thou art he whom thy brethren shall
    praise:
Thy hand shall be in the neck of thine enemies;
Thy father's children shall bow down before thee.
Judah is a lion's whelp:
From the prey, my son, thou art gone up:
He stooped down, he couched as a lion,
And as an old lion; who shall rouse him up?
The sceptre shall not depart from Judah,

Nor a lawgiver from between his feet,
Until Shiloh come; and unto him shall the gather-
    ing of the people be.

Binding his foal unto the vine,
And his ass's colt unto the choice vine;
He washed his garments in wine,
And his clothes in the blood of grapes:
His eyes shall be red with wine,
And his teeth white with milk.

Zebulun shall dwell at the haven of the sea;
And he shall be for a haven of ships;
And his border shall be unto Zidon.

Issachar is a strong ass
Couching down between two burdens:
And he saw that rest was good,
And the land that it was pleasant;
And bowed his shoulder to bear,
And became a servant unto tribute.

Dan shall judge his people,
As one of the tribes of Israel.
Dan shall be a serpent by the way,
An adder in the path,
That biteth the horse's heels,
So that his rider shall fall backward.

Gad, a troop shall overcome him:
But he shall overcome at the last.

Out of Asher his bread shall be fat,
And he shall yield royal dainties.

Naphtali is a hind let loose:
He giveth goodly words.

Joseph is a fruitful bough,
Even a fruitful bough by a well;
Whose branches run over the wall:
The archers have sorely grieved him,
And shot at him, and hated him:
But his bow abode in strength,
And the arms of his hands were made strong
By the hands of the mighty God of Jacob
(From thence is the shepherd, the stone of Israel).
Even by the God of thy father, who shall help thee;
And by the Almighty, who shall bless thee
With blessings of heaven above,
Blessings of the deep that lieth under,
Blessings of the breasts, and of the womb:
The blessings of thy father have prevailed
Above the blessings of my progenitors
Unto the utmost bound of the everlasting hills:

They shall be on the head of Joseph,
And on the crown of the head of him that was
    separate from his brethren.

Benjamin shall ravin as a wolf:
In the morning he shall devour the prey,
And at night he shall divide the spoil."

And when Jacob had made an end of commanding his sons, he gathered up his feet into the bed, and yielded up the ghost, and was gathered unto his people.

(Genesis.)

The Giving of the Law

And the Lord said unto Moses, "Go unto the people, and sanctify them to-day and to-morrow, and let them wash their clothes, and be ready against the third day: for the third day the Lord will come down in the sight of all the people upon Mount Sinai. And thou shalt set bounds unto the people round about, saying, 'Take heed to yourselves, that ye go not up into the mount, or touch the border of it: whosoever toucheth the mount shall be surely put to death.' There shall not a hand touch it, but he shall surely be stoned, or shot through; whether it be beast or man, it shall not live: when the trumpet soundeth long, they shall come up to the mount."

And Moses went down from the mount unto the people, and sanctified the people; and they washed their clothes. And he said unto the people, "Be ready against the third day: come not at your wives."

And it came to pass on the third day in the morning, that there were thunders and lightnings, and a thick cloud upon the mount, and the voice of the trumpet exceeding loud; so that all the people that was in the camp trembled. And Moses brought forth the people out of the camp to meet with God; and they stood at the nether part of the mount. And Mount Sinai was altogether on a smoke, because the Lord descended upon it in fire; and the smoke thereof ascended as the smoke of a furnace, and the whole mount quaked greatly. And when the voice of the trumpet sounded long, and waxed louder and louder, Moses spoke, and God answered him by a voice. And the Lord came down upon Mount Sinai, on the top of the mount: and the Lord called Moses up to the top of the mount; and Moses went up.

And God spoke all these words, saying, "I am the Lord thy God, which have brought thee out of the land of Egypt, out of the house of bondage.

"Thou shalt have no other gods before me.

"Thou shalt not make unto thee any graven image, or any likeness of any thing that is in heaven above, or that is in the earth beneath, or that is in the water under the earth: thou shalt not bow down thyself to them, nor serve them: for I the Lord thy God am a jealous God, visiting the iniquity of the fathers upon the children unto the third and fourth generation of them that hate me; and showing mercy unto thousands of them that love me, and keep my commandments.

"Thou shalt not take the name of the Lord thy God in vain; for the Lord will not hold him guiltless that taketh his name in vain.

"Remember the sabbath day, to keep it holy. Six days shalt thou labor, and do all thy work: but the seventh day is the sabbath of the Lord thy God: in it thou shalt not do any work, thou, nor thy son, nor thy daughter, thy manservant, nor thy maidservant, nor thy cattle, nor thy stranger that is within thy gates: for in six days the Lord made heaven and earth, the sea, and all that in them is, and rested the seventh day: wherefore the Lord blessed the sabbath day, and hallowed it.

"Honor thy father and thy mother: that thy days may be long upon the land which the Lord thy God giveth thee.

"Thou shalt not kill.

"Thou shalt not commit adultery.

"Thou shalt not steal.

"Thou shalt not bear false witness against thy neighbor.

"Thou shalt not covet thy neighbor's house, thou shalt not covet thy neighbor's wife, nor his manservant, nor his maidservant, nor his ox, nor his ass, nor any thing that is thy neighbor's."

And he gave unto Moses, when he had made an end of communing with him upon Mount Sinai, two tables of testimony, tables of stone, written with the finger of God.

(Exodus.)

The Story of Samson

And the children of Israel did evil again in the sight of the Lord; and the Lord delivered them into the hand of the Philistines forty years.

And there was a certain man of Zorah, of the family of the Danites, whose name was Manoah; and his wife was barren, and bore not. And the angel of the Lord appeared unto the woman, and said unto her,

"Behold now, thou art barren, and bearest not:

but thou shalt conceive, and bear a son. Now therefore beware, I pray thee, and drink not wine nor strong drink, and eat not any unclean thing: for, lo, thou shalt conceive, and bear a son; and no razor shall come on his head: for the child shall be a Nazarite unto God from the womb: and he shall begin to deliver Israel out of the hand of the Philistines."

So Manoah took a kid with a meat offering, and offered it upon a rock unto the Lord: and the angel did wonderously; and Manoah and his wife looked on. For it came to pass, when the flame went up toward heaven from off the altar, that the angel of the Lord ascended in the flame of the altar. And Manoah and his wife looked on it, and fell on their faces to the ground. But the angel of the Lord did no more appear to Manoah and to his wife. Then Manoah knew that he was an angel of the Lord.

And Manoah said unto his wife, "We shall surely die, because we have seen God."

But his wife said unto him, "If the Lord were pleased to kill us, he would not have received a burnt offering and a meat offering at our hands, neither would he have showed us all these things, nor would as at this time have told us such things as these."

And the woman bore a son, and called his name Samson: and the child grew, and the Lord blessed him. And the Spirit of the Lord began to move him at times in the camp of Dan between Zorah and Eshtaol.

And Samson went down to Timnath, and saw a woman in Timnath of the daughters of the Philistines. And he came up, and told his father and his mother, and said, "I have seen a woman in Timnath of the daughters of the Philistines: now therefore get her for me to wife."

Then his father and his mother said unto him, "Is there never a woman among the daughters of thy brethren, or among all my people, that thou goest to take a wife of the uncircumcised Philistines?"

And Samson said unto his father, "Get her for me; for she pleaseth me well."

But his father and his mother knew not that it was of the Lord, that he sought an occasion against the Philistines: for at that time the Philistines had dominion over Israel.

Then went Samson down, and his father and his mother, to Timnath, and came to the vineyards of Timnath: and, behold, a young lion roared against him. And the Spirit of the Lord came mightily upon him, and he rent him as he would have rent a kid, and he had nothing in his hand: but he told not his father or his mother what he

had done. And he went down, and talked with the woman; and she pleased Samson well.

And after a time he returned to take her, and he turned aside to see the carcase of the lion: and behold, there was a swarm of bees and honey in the carcase of the lion. And he took thereof in his hands, and went on eating, and came to his father and mother, and he gave them, and they did eat: but he told not them that he had taken the honey out of the carcase of the lion.

So his father went down unto the woman: and Samson made there a feast; for so used the young men to do. And it came to pass, when they saw him, that they brought thirty companions to be with him. And Samson said unto them,

"I will now put forth a riddle unto you: if ye can certainly declare it me within the seven days of the feast, and find it out, then I will give you thirty sheets and thirty changes of garments: but if ye cannot declare it me, then shall ye give me thirty sheets and thirty changes of garments."

And they said unto him, "Put forth thy riddle, that we may hear it."

And he said unto them,

"Out of the eater came forth meat,
And out of the strong came forth sweetness."

And they could not in three days expound the riddle. And it came to pass on the seventh day that they said unto Samson's wife, "Entice thy husband, that he may declare unto us the riddle, lest we burn thee and thy father's house with fire: have ye called us to take that we have? is it not so?"

And Samson's wife wept before him, and said, "Thou dost but hate me, and lovest me not: thou has put forth a riddle unto the children of my people, and hast not told it me."

And he said unto her, "Behold, I have not told it my father nor my mother, and shall I tell it thee?"

And she wept before him the seven days, while their feast lasted: and it came to pass on the seventh day that he told her, because she lay sore upon him: and she told the riddle to the children of her people. And the men of the city said unto him on the seventh day before the sun went down,

"What is sweeter than honey?
And what is stronger than a lion?"

And he said unto them,

"If ye had not plowed with my heifer,
Ye had not found out my riddle."

And the Spirit of the Lord came upon him, and he went down to Ashkelon, and slew thirty men of them, and took their spoil. and gave change of garments unto them which expounded the riddle. And his anger was kindled, and he went up to his father's house. But Samson's wife was given to his companion, whom he had used as his friend. But it came to pass within a while after, in the time of wheat harvest, that Samson visited his wife with a kid; and he said, "I will go in to my wife into the chamber." But her father would not suffer him to go in. And her father said,

"I verily thought that thou hadst utterly hated her; therefore I gave her to thy companion: is not her younger sister fairer than she? take her, I pray thee, instead of her."

And Samson said concerning them, "Now shall I be more blameless than the Philistines, though I do them a displeasure?"

And Samson went and caught three hundred foxes, and took firebrands, and turned tail to tail, and put a firebrand in the midst between two tails. And when he had set the brands on fire, he let them go into the standing corn of the Philistines, and burnt up both the shocks, and also the standing corn, with the vineyards and olives.

Then the Philistines said, "Who hath done this?"

And they answered, "Samson, the son-in-law of the Timnite, because he had taken his wife, and given her to his companion."

And the Philistines came up, and burnt her and her father with fire.

And Samson said unto them, "Though ye have done this, yet will I be avenged of you, and after that I will cease."

And he smote them hip and thigh with a great slaughter: and he went down and dwelt in the top of the rock Etam.

Then the Philistines went up, and pitched in Judah, and spread themselves in Lehi. And the men of Judah said, "Why are ye come up against us?"

And they answered, "To bind Samson are we come up, to do to him as he hath done to us."

Then three thousand men of Judah went to the top of the rock Etam, and said to Samson, "Knowest thou not that the Philistines are rulers over us? what is this that thou hast done unto us?"

And he said unto them, "As they did unto me, so have I done unto them."

And they said unto him, "We are come down to bind thee, that we may deliver thee into the hand of the Philistines."

And Samson said unto them, "Swear unto me that ye will not fall upon me yourselves."

And they spoke unto him, saying, "No; but we will bind thee fast, and deliver thee into their hand: but surely we will not kill thee."

And they bound him with two new cords, and

brought him up from the rock. And when he came unto Lehi, the Philistines shouted against him: and the Spirit of the Lord came mightily upon him, and the cords that were upon his arms became as flax that was burnt with fire, and his bands loosed from off his hands. And he found a new jawbone of an ass, and put forth his hand, and took it, and slew a thousand men therewith. And Samson said,

"With the jawbone of an ass, heaps upon heaps,
With the jaw of an ass have I slain a thousand men."

And it came to pass, when he had made an end of speaking, that he cast away the jawbone out of his hand, and called that place Ramath-lehi. And he was sore athirst, and called on the Lord, and said,

"Thou hast given this great deliverance into the hand of thy servant: and now shall I die for thirst, and fall into the hand of the uncircumcised?"

But God clove a hollow place that was in the jaw, and there came water thereout; and when he had drunk, his spirit came again, and he revived: wherefore he called the name thereof Enhakkore, which is in Lehi unto this day. And he judged Israel in the days of the Philistines twenty years.

Then went Samson to Gaza, and saw there a harlot, and went in unto her. And it was told the Gazites, saying, "Samson is come hither." And they compassed him in, and laid wait for him all night in the gate of the city, and were quiet all the night, saying, "In the morning, when it is day, we shall kill him."

And Samson lay till midnight, and arose at midnight, and took the doors of the gate of the city, and the two posts, and went away with them, bar and all, and put them upon his shoulders, and carried them up to the top of a hill that is before Hebron.

And it came to pass afterward that he loved a woman in the valley of Sorek, whose name was Delilah. And the lords of the Philistines came up unto her, and said unto her,

"Entice him, and see wherein his great strength lieth, and by what means we may prevail against him, that we may bind him to afflict him: and we will give thee every one of us eleven hundred pieces of silver."

And Delilah said to Samson, "Tell me, I pray thee, wherein thy great strength lieth, and wherewith thou mightest be bound to afflict thee."

And Samson said unto her, "If they bind me with seven green withes that were never dried, then shall I be weak, and be as another man."

Then the lords of the Philistines brought up to her seven green withes which had not been dried, and she bound him with them. Now there were men lying in wait, abiding with her in the chamber. And she said unto him,

"The Philistines be upon thee, Samson." And he broke the withes, as a thread of tow is broken when it toucheth the fire. So his strength was not known. And Delilah said unto Samson, "Behold, thou hast mocked me, and told me lies: now tell me, I pray thee, wherewith thou mightest be bound."

And he said unto her, "If they bind me fast with new ropes that never were occupied, then shall I be weak, and be as another man."

Delilah therefore took new ropes, and bound him therewith, and said unto him, "The Philistines be upon thee, Samson." And there were liers in wait abiding in the chamber. And he brake them from off his arms like a thread.

And Delilah said unto Samson, "Hitherto thou hast mocked me, and told me lies: tell me wherewith thou mightest be bound."

And he said unto her, "If thou weavest the seven locks of my head with the web."

And she fastened it with the pin, and said unto him, "The Philistines be upon thee, Samson."

And he awaked out of his sleep, and went away with the pin of the beam, and with the web. And she said unto him,

"How canst thou say, 'I love thee,' when thine heart is not with me? thou hast mocked me these three times, and hast not told me wherein thy great strength lieth."

And it came to pass, when she pressed him daily with her words, and urged him, so that his soul was vexed unto death, that he told her all his heart, and said unto her, "There hath not come a razor upon mine head; for I have been a Nazarite unto God from my mother's womb: if I be shaven, then my strength will go from me, and I shall become weak, and be like any other man."

And when Delilah saw that he had told her all his heart, she sent and called for the lords of the Philistines, saying, "Come up this once, for he hath showed me all his heart."

Then the lords of the Philistines came up unto her, and brought money in their hand. And she made him sleep upon her knees; and she called for a man, and she caused him to shave off the seven locks of his head; and she began to afflict him, and his strength went from him. And she said,

"The Philistines be upon thee, Samson." And he awoke out of his sleep, and said, "I will go out as at other times before, and shake myself." And he wist not that the Lord was departed from him.

But the Philistines took him, and put out his eyes, and brought him down to Gaza, and bound him with fetters of brass; and he did grind in the prison house. Howbeit the hair of his head began to grow again after he was shaven.

Then the lords of the Philistines gathered them together for to offer a great sacrifice unto Dagon their god, and to rejoice: for they said, "Our God hath delivered Samson our enemy into our hand."

And when the people saw him, they praised their god: for they said, "Our god hath delivered into our hands our enemy, and the destroyer of our country, which slew many of us."

And it came to pass, when their hearts were merry, that they said, "Call for Samson, that he may make us sport."

And they called for Samson out of the prison house; and he made them sport: and they set him between the pillars. And Samson said unto the lad that held him by the hand, "Suffer me that I may feel the pillars whereupon the house standeth, that I may lean upon them."

Now the house was full of men and women; and all the lords of the Philistines were there; and there were upon the roof about three thousand men and women that beheld while Samson made sport. And Samson called unto the Lord, and said, "O Lord God, remember me, I pray thee, and strengthen me, I pray thee, only this once, O God, that I may be at once avenged of the Philistines for my two eyes."

And Samson took hold of the two middle pillars upon which the house stood, and on which it was borne up, of the one with his right hand, and of the other with his left. And Samson said, "Let me die with the Philistines."

And he bowed himself with all his might; and the house fell upon the lords, and upon all the people that were therein. So the dead which he slew at his death were more than they which he slew in his life. Then his brethren and all the house of his father came down, and took him, and brought him up, and buried him between Zorah and Eshtaol in the burying place of Manoah his father. And he judged Israel twenty years.

(Judges.)

Ruth

A TALE

Now it came to pass in the days when the judges ruled, that there was a famine in the land. And a certain man of Beth-lehem-judah went to sojourn in the country of Moab, he, and his wife, and his two sons. And the name of the man was Elimelech, and the name of his wife Naomi, and the name of his two sons Mahlon and Chilion, Ephrathites of Beth-lehem-judah. And they came into the country of Moab, and continued there. And Elimelech Naomi's husband died; and she was left, and her two sons. And they took them wives of the women of Moab; the name of the one was Orpah, and the name of the other Ruth: and they dwelled there about ten years. And Mahlon and Chilion died also both of them; and the woman 10 was left of her two sons and her husband.

Then she arose with her daughters-in-law, that she might return from the country of Moab: for she had heard in the country of Moab how that the Lord had visited his people in giving them 15 bread. Wherefore she went forth out of the place where she was, and her two daughters-in-law with her; and they went on the way to return unto the land of Judah.

And Naomi said unto her two daughters-in-law, 20 "Go, return each to her mother's house: the Lord deal kindly with you, as ye have dealt with the dead, and with me. The Lord grant you that ye may find rest, each of you in the house of her husband." 25

Then she kissed them; and they lifted up their voice, and wept. And they said unto her, "Surely we will return with thee unto thy people."

And Naomi said, "Turn again, my daughters: why will ye go with me? are there yet any more 30 sons in my womb, that they may be your husbands? Turn again, my daughters, go your way; for I am too old to have a husband. If I should say, I have hope, if I should have a husband also to-night, and should also bear sons; would ye tarry for them till 35 they were grown? would ye stay for them from having husbands? nay, my daughters; for it grieveth me much for your sakes that the hand of the Lord is gone out against me."

And they lifted up their voice, and wept again: 40 and Orpah kissed her mother-in-law; but Ruth cleaved unto her. And she said, "Behold, thy sister-in-law is gone back unto her people, and unto her gods: return thou after thy sister-in-law."

And Ruth said, "Intreat me not to leave thee, or 45 to return from following after thee: for whither thou goest, I will go; and where thou lodgest, I will lodge: thy people shall be my people, and thy God my God: where thou diest, will I die, and there will I be buried: the Lord do so to me, and more also, if 50 ought but death part thee and me."

When she saw that she was steadfastly minded to go with her, then she left speaking unto her.

So Naomi returned, and Ruth the Moabitess, her daughter-in-law, with her, which returned out 55 of the country of Moab: and they came to Beth-

lehem in the beginning of barley harvest. And Naomi had a kinsman of her husband's, a mighty man of wealth, of the family of Elimelech; and his name was Boaz. And Ruth the Moabitess said 5 unto Naomi, "Let me now go to the field, and glean ears of corn after him in whose sight I shall find grace." And she said unto her, "Go, my daughter." And she went, and came, and gleaned in the field after the reapers: and her hap was to 10 light on a part of the field belonging unto Boaz, who was of the kindred of Elimelech.

And, behold, Boaz came from Beth-lehem, and said unto the reapers, "The Lord be with you." And they answered him, "The Lord bless thee."

Then said Boaz unto his servant that was set over the reapers, "Whose damsel is this?"

And the servant that was set over the reapers answered and said, "It is the Moabitish damsel that came back with Naomi out of the country of 20 Moab: and she said, 'I pray you, let me glean and gather after the reapers among the sheaves': so she came, and hath continued even from the morning until now, that she tarried a little in the house."

Then said Boaz unto Ruth, "Hearest thou not, my daughter? Go not to glean in another field, neither go from hence, but abide here fast by my maidens: let thine eyes be on the field that they do reap, and go thou after them: have I not charged 30 the young men that they shall not touch thee? and when thou art athirst, go unto the vessels, and drink of that which the young men have drawn."

Then she fell on her face, and bowed herself to the ground, and said unto him, "Why have I 35 found grace in thine eyes, that thou shouldest take knowledge of me, seeing I am a stranger?"

And Boaz answered and said unto her, "It hath fully been showed me all that thou hast done unto thy mother-in-law since the death of thine hus-40 band: and how thou hast left thy father and thy mother, and the land of thy nativity, and art come unto a people which thou knewest not heretofore. The Lord recompense thy work, and a full reward be given thee of the Lord God of Israel, under 45 whose wings thou art come to trust."

Then she said, "Let me find favor in thy sight, my lord; for that thou hast comforted me, and for that thou hast spoken friendly unto thine hand-maid, though I be not like unto one of thine hand-50 maidens."

And Boaz said unto her, "At mealtime come thou thither, and eat of the bread, and dip thy morsel in the vinegar."

And she sat beside the reapers: and he reached 55 her parched corn, and she did eat, and was sufficed, and left. And when she was risen up to glean,

Boaz commanded his young men, saying, "Let her glean even among the sheaves, and reproach her not: and let fall also some of the handfuls of purpose for her, and leave them, that she may glean them, and rebuke her not."

So she gleaned in the field until even, and beat out that she had gleaned: and it was about an ephah [1] of barley. And she took it up, and went into the city: and her mother-in-law saw what she had gleaned: and she brought forth, and gave to 10 her that she had reserved after she was sufficed.

And her mother-in-law said unto her, "Where hast thou gleaned to-day? and where wroughtest thou? blessed be he that did take knowledge of thee."

And she showed her mother-in-law with whom she had wrought, and said, "The man's name with whom I wrought to-day is Boaz."

And Naomi said unto her daughter-in-law, "Blessed be he of the Lord, who hath not left off 20 his kindness to the living and to the dead." And Naomi said unto her, "The man is near of kin unto us, one of our next kinsmen."

And Ruth the Moabitess said, "He said unto me also, 'Thou shalt keep fast by my young men, until 25 they have ended all my harvest.'"

And Naomi said unto Ruth her daughter-in-law, "It is good, my daughter, that thou go out with his maidens, that they meet thee not in any other field."

So she kept fast by the maidens of Boaz to glean unto the end of barley harvest and of wheat harvest; and dwelt with her mother-in-law.

Then Naomi her mother-in-law said unto her, "My daughter, shall I not seek rest for thee, that 35 it may be well with thee? And now is not Boaz of our kindred, with whose maidens thou wast? Behold, he winnoweth barley to-night in the threshingfloor. Wash thyself therefore, and anoint thee, and put thy raiment upon thee, and get 40 thee down to the floor: but make not thyself known unto the man, until he shall have done eating and drinking. And it shall be, when he lieth down, that thou shalt mark the place where he shall lie, and thou shalt go in, and uncover his 45 feet, and lay thee down; and he will tell thee what thou shalt do."

And she said unto her, "All that thou sayest unto me I will do."

And she went down unto the floor, and did according to all that her mother-in-law bade her. And when Boaz had eaten and drunk, and his heart was merry, he went to lie down at the end of the heap of corn: and she came softly, and uncovered his feet, and laid her down. And it came to pass 55

[1] Somewhat more than a bushel.

at midnight, that the man was afraid, and turned himself: and, behold, a woman lay at his feet.

And he said, "Who art thou?"

And she answered, "I am Ruth thine handmaid: 5 spread therefore thy skirt over thine handmaid; for thou art a near kinsman."

And he said, "Blessed be thou of the Lord, my daughter: for thou hast showed more kindness in the latter end than at the beginning, inasmuch as 10 thou followedst not young men, whether poor or rich. And now, my daughter, fear not; I will do to thee all that thou requirest: for all the city of my people doth know that thou art a virtuous woman. And now it is true that I am thy near kinsman: 15 howbeit there is a kinsman nearer than I. Tarry this night, and it shall be in the morning, that if he will perform unto thee the part of a kinsman, well; let him do the kinsman's part: but if he will not do the part of a kinsman to thee, then will I do the 20 part of a kinsman to thee, as the Lord liveth: lie down until the morning."

And she lay at his feet until the morning: and she rose up before one could know another.

And he said, "Let it not be known that a woman 25 came into the floor." Also he said, "Bring the veil that thou hast upon thee, and hold it."

And when she held it, he measured six measures of barley, and laid it on her: and she went into the city. And when she came to her mother-in-law, 30 she said, "Who art thou, my daughter?"

And she told her all that the man had done to her. And she said, "These six measures of barley gave he me; for he said to me, 'Go not empty unto thy mother-in-law.'"

35 Then said she, "Sit still, my daughter, until thou know how the matter will fall: for the man will not be in rest, until he have finished the thing this day."

Then went Boaz up to the gate, and sat him 40 down there: and, behold, the kinsman of whom Boaz spoke came by; unto whom he said, "Ho, such a one! turn aside, sit down here."

And he turned aside, and sat down. And he took ten men of the elders of the city, and said, 45 "Sit ye down here." And they sat down.

And he said unto the kinsman, "Naomi, that is come again out of the country of Moab, selleth a parcel of land, which was our brother Elimelech's: and I thought to advertise thee, saying, 'Buy it 50 before the inhabitants, and before the elders of my people. If thou wilt redeem it, redeem it': but if thou wilt not redeem it, then tell me, that I may know: for there is none to redeem it beside thee; and I am after thee."

55 And he said, "I will redeem it."

Then said Boaz, "What day thou buyest the

field of the hand of Naomi, thou must buy it also of Ruth the Moabitess, the wife of the dead, to raise up the name of the dead upon his inheritance."

And the kinsman said, "I cannot redeem it for myself, lest I mar mine own inheritance: redeem thou my right to thyself; for I cannot redeem it."

And Boaz said unto the elders, and unto all the people, "Ye are witnesses this day, that I have bought all that was Elimelech's, and all that was Chilion's and Mahlon's, of the hand of Naomi. Moreover Ruth the Moabitess, the wife of Mahlon, have I purchased to be my wife, to raise up the name of the dead upon his inheritance, that the name of the dead be not cut off from among his brethren, and from the gate of his place: ye are witnesses this day."

So Boaz took Ruth, and she was his wife: and when he went in unto her, the Lord gave her conception, and she bore a son.

And the women said unto Naomi, "Blessed be the Lord, which hath not left thee this day without a kinsman, that his name may be famous in Israel. And he shall be unto thee a restorer of thy life, and a nourisher of thine old age: for thy daughter-in-law which loveth thee, which is better to thee than seven sons, hath borne him."

And Naomi took the child, and laid it in her bosom, and became nurse unto it. And the women her neighbours gave it a name, saying, "There is a son born to Naomi; and they called his name Obed: he is the father of Jesse, the father of David." (Ruth.)

The Sermon on the Mount

And seeing the multitudes, he went up into a mountain: and when he was set, his disciples came unto him: and he opened his mouth, and taught them, saying,

" *Blessed are the poor in spirit:*
For theirs is the kingdom of heaven.

Blessed are they that mourn:
For they shall be comforted.

Blessed are the meek:
For they shall inherit the earth.

Blessed are they which do hunger and thirst after
righteousness:
For they shall be filled.

Blessed are the merciful:
For they shall obtain mercy.

Blessed are the pure in heart:
For they shall see God.

Blessed are the peacemakers:
For they shall be called the children of God.

Blessed are they which are persecuted for righteousness' sake:
For theirs is the kingdom of heaven.

Blessed are ye, when men shall revile you, and persecute you, and shall say all manner of evil against you falsely, for my sake.
Rejoice, and be exceeding glad: for great is your reward in heaven: for so persecuted they the prophets which were before you.

"Ye are the salt of the earth: but if the salt have lost his savor, wherewith shall it be salted? it is thenceforth good for nothing, but to be cast out, and to be trodden under foot of men.

"Ye are the light of the world. A city that is set on a hill cannot be hid. Neither do men light a candle, and put it under a bushel, but on a candlestick; and it giveth light unto all that are in the house. Let your light so shine before men, that they may see your good works, and glorify your Father which is in heaven.

"Think not that I am come to destroy the law, or the prophets: I am not come to destroy, but to fulfil. For verily I say unto you, 'Till heaven and earth pass, one jot or one tittle shall in no wise pass from the law, till all be fulfilled.' Whosoever therefore shall break one of these least commandments, and shall teach men so, he shall be called the least in the kingdom of heaven: but whosoever shall do and teach them, the same shall be called great in the kingdom of heaven. For I say unto you, 'Except your righteousness shall exceed the righteousness of the scribes and Pharisees, ye shall in no case enter into the kingdom of heaven.'

"Ye have heard that it was said by them of old time, 'Thou shalt not kill'; and whosoever shall kill shall be in danger of the judgment. But I say unto you, 'Whosoever is angry with his brother without a cause shall be in danger of the judgment: and whosoever shall say to his brother, "Raca," [1] shall be in danger of the council: but whosoever shall say, "Thou fool," shall be in danger of hell fire.' Therefore if thou bring thy gift to the altar, and there rememberest that thy brother hath

[1] "vain fellow."

ought against thee; leave there thy gift before the altar, and go thy way; first be reconciled to thy brother, and then come and offer thy gift. Agree with thine adversary quickly, while thou art in the way with him; lest at any time the adversary deliver thee to the judge, and the judge deliver thee to the officer, and thou be cast into prison. Verily I say unto thee, 'Thou shalt by no means come out thence, till thou hast paid the uttermost farthing.'

"Ye have heard that it was said by them of old time, 'Thou shalt not commit adultery.' But I say unto you, 'Whosoever looketh on a woman to lust after her hath committed adultery with her already in his heart. And if thy right eye offendeth thee, pluck it out, and cast it from thee: for it is profitable for thee that one of thy members should perish, and not that thy whole body should be cast into hell. And if thy right hand offend thee, cut it off, and cast it from thee: for it is profitable for thee that one of thy members should perish, and not that thy whole body should be cast into hell.' It hath been said, 'Whosoever shall put away his wife, let him give her a writing of divorcement.' But I say unto you, 'Whosoever shall put away his wife, saving for the cause of fornication, causeth her to commit adultery: and whosoever shall marry her that is divorced committeth adultery.'

"Again, ye have heard that it hath been said by them of old time, 'Thou shalt not forswear thyself, but shalt perform unto the Lord thine oaths.' But I say unto you, 'Swear not at all; neither by heaven; for it is God's throne: nor by the earth; for it is his footstool: neither by Jerusalem; for it is the city of the great King. Neither shalt thou swear by thy head, because thou canst not make one hair white or black. But let your communication be, "Yea, yea"; "Nay, nay": for whatsoever is more than these cometh of evil.'

"Ye have heard that it hath been said, 'An eye for an eye, and a tooth for a tooth.' But I say unto you, 'Resist not evil: but whosoever shall smite thee on thy right cheek, turn to him the other also. And if any man will sue thee at the law, and take away thy coat, let him have thy cloak also. And whosoever shall compel thee to go a mile, go with him twain. Give to him that asketh thee, and from him that would borrow of thee turn not thou away.'

"Ye have heard that it hath been said, 'Thou shalt love thy neighbor, and hate thine enemy.' But I say unto you, 'Love your enemies, bless them that curse you, do good to them that hate you, and pray for them which despitefully use you, and persecute you; that ye may be the children of your Father which is in heaven: for he maketh his sun to rise on the evil and on the good, and sendeth rain on the just and on the unjust.' For if ye love them which love you, what reward have ye? do not even the publicans the same? And if ye salute your brethren only, what do ye more than others? do not even the publicans[1] so? Be ye therefore perfect, even as your Father which is in heaven is perfect.

"Take heed that ye do not your alms before men, to be seen of them: otherwise ye have no reward of your Father which is in heaven. Therefore when thou doest thine alms, do not sound a trumpet before thee, as the hypocrites do in the synagogues and in the streets, that they may have glory of men. Verily I say unto you, 'They have their reward.' But when thou doest alms, let not thy left hand know what thy right hand doeth: that thine alms may be in secret: and thy Father which seeth in secret himself shall reward thee openly.

"And when thou prayest, thou shalt not be as the hypocrites are: for they love to pray standing in the synagogues and in the corners of the streets, that they may be seen of men. Verily I say unto you, 'They have their reward.' But thou, when thou prayest, enter into thy closet, and when thou hast shut thy door, pray to thy Father which is in secret; and thy Father which seeth in secret shall reward thee openly. But when ye pray, use not vain repetitions, as the heathen do: for they think that they shall be heard for their much speaking. Be not ye therefore like unto them: for your Father knoweth what things ye have need of, before ye ask him. After this manner therefore pray ye:

"'*Our Father which art in heaven,*
Hallowed be thy name,
Thy kingdom come.
Thy will be done
In earth, as it is in heaven.

Give us this day
Our daily bread.
And forgive us our debts,
As we forgive our debtors.
And lead us not into temptation,
But deliver us from evil
For thine is the kingdom,
And the power,
And the glory,
For ever. Amen.'

"For if ye forgive men their trespasses, your heavenly Father will also forgive you: but if ye

[1] Tax collectors.

forgive not men their trespasses, neither will your Father forgive your trespasses.

"Moreover when ye fast, be not, as the hypocrites, of a sad countenance: for they disfigure their faces, that they may appear unto men to fast. Verily I say unto you, 'They have their reward.' But thou, when thou fastest, anoint thine head, and wash thy face; that thou appear not unto men to fast, but unto thy Father which is in secret: and thy Father, which seeth in secret shall reward thee openly.

"Lay not up for yourselves treasures upon earth,
Where moth and rust doth corrupt,
And where thieves break through and steal:

But lay up for yourselves treasures in heaven,
Where neither moth nor rust doth corrupt,
And where thieves do not break through nor steal.

For where your treasure is, there will your heart be also.

"The light of the body is the eye: if therefore thine eye be single, thy whole body shall be full of light. But if thine eye be evil, thy whole body shall be full of darkness. If therefore the light that is in thee be darkness, how great is that darkness!

"No man can serve two masters: for either he will hate the one, and love the other; or else he will hold to the one, and despise the other. Ye cannot serve God and Mammon.

"Therefore I say unto you, 'Take no thought for your life, what ye shall eat, or what ye shall drink: nor yet for your body, what ye shall put on.' Is not the life more than meat, and the body than raiment? Behold the fowls of the air: for they sow not, neither do they reap, nor gather into barns; yet your heavenly Father feedeth them. Are ye not much better than they? Which of you by taking thought can add one cubit [1] unto his stature? And why take ye thought for raiment? Consider the lilies of the field, how they grow; they toil not, neither do they spin: and yet I say unto you that even Solomon in all his glory was not arrayed like one of these.

"Wherefore, if God so clothe the grass of the field, which to-day is, and to-morrow is cast into the oven, shall he not much more clothe you, O ye of little faith? Therefore take no thought, saying, 'What shall we eat?' or, 'What shall we drink?' or, 'Wherewithal shall we be clothed?' (For after all these things do the Gentiles seek): for your heavenly Father knoweth that ye have need of all these things. But seek ye first the kingdom of God,

[1] About twenty inches.

and his righteousness; and all these things shall be added unto you. Take therefore no thought for the morrow: for the morrow shall take thought for the things of itself. Sufficient unto the day is the evil thereof.

"Judge not, that ye be not judged. For with what judgment ye judge, ye shall be judged: and with what measure ye mete,[1] it shall be measured to you again. And why beholdest thou the mote that is in thy brother's eye, but considerest not the beam that is in thine own eye? Or how wilt thou say to thy brother, 'Let me pull out the mote out of thine eye'; and, behold, a beam is in thine own eye? Thou hypocrite, first cast out the beam out of thine own eye; and then shalt thou see clearly to cast out the mote out of thy brother's eye.

"Give not that which is holy unto the dogs,
Neither cast ye your pearls before swine,
Lest they trample them under their feet,
And turn again and rend you.

Ask, and it shall be given you;
Seek, and ye shall find;
Knock, and it shall be opened unto you:

For every one that asketh receiveth;
And he that seeketh findeth;
And to him that knocketh it shall be opened.

Of what man is there of you, whom if his son ask bread, will he give him a stone? Or if he ask a fish, will he give him a serpent? If ye then, being evil, know how to give good gifts unto your children, how much more shall your Father which is in heaven give good things to them that ask him? Therefore all things whatsoever ye would that men should do to you, do ye even so to them: for this is the law and the prophets.

"Enter ye in at the strait [2] gate: for wide is the gate, and broad is the way, that leadeth to destruction, and many there be which go in thereat: because strait is the gate, and narrow is the way, which leadeth unto life, and few there be that find it.

"Beware of false prophets, which come to you in sheep's clothing, but inwardly they are ravening wolves. Ye shall know them by their fruits. Do men gather grapes of thorns, or figs of thistles? Even so every good tree bringeth forth good fruit; but a corrupt tree bringeth forth evil fruit. A good tree cannot bring forth evil fruit, neither can a corrupt tree bring forth good fruit. Every tree that bringeth not forth good fruit is hewn down,

[1] Measure.

[2] Narrow.

and cast into the fire. Whereof by their fruits ye shall know them.

"Not every one that saith unto me, 'Lord, Lord,' shall enter into the kingdom of heaven; but he that doeth the will of my Father which is in heaven. Many will say to me in that day, 'Lord, Lord, have we not prophesied in thy name? and in thy name have cast out devils? and in thy name done many wonderful works?' And then will I profess unto them, 'I never knew you: depart from me, ye that work iniquity.'

"Therefore whosoever heareth these sayings of mine, and doeth them, I will liken him unto a wise man, which built his house upon a rock: and the rain descended, and the floods came and the winds blew, and beat upon that house; and it fell not: for it was founded upon a rock. And every one that heareth these sayings of mine, and doeth them not, shall be likened unto a foolish man, which built his house upon the sand: and the rain descended, and the floods came, and the winds blew, and beat upon that house; and it fell: and great was the fall of it."

(Matthew.)

Æschylus · 525-456 B.C.

Few details of the life of Æschylus are known, and the facts we have are not always clearly established. He was born at Eleusis, a city near Athens, in 525 B.C., into a family of the Athenian nobility and, as a young man, served for a time in the Greek army as a soldier fighting the Persians, acquitting himself creditably in the important battles of Marathon and Salamis. Eleusis, his birthplace, was the center of the worship of Demeter (Ceres), the goddess of the harvest and of fruitfulness. It has been suggested that the birth of Æschylus in this city of Demeter may have influenced his writing and have endowed him with his concern for the human soul so manifest in his dramas. It is believed, too, that he was once charged with having revealed some of the mysteries of Eleusis while acting on the stage, a serious charge, but was forgiven because of his fine record at the battle of Marathon. We know, too, that Æschylus visited Sicily where he was the guest of Hieron the First of Syracuse. For this visit the dramatist wrote a play in honor of Hieron and a new city which the tyrant had built. Æschylus was buried at Gela, 456 B.C., in a tomb bearing the epitaph:

> Beneath this stone lies Æschylus, son of Euphorion, the Athenian, who perished in the wheat-bearing land of Gela; of his noble prowess the grove of Marathon can speak, or the long-haired Persian who knows it well.

It is, however, as a dramatist that Æschylus particularly interests us. Living in the Athens of Pericles, the playwright knew Greece at the height of her excellence. Athens was extending her control into something like a world power. The drama was popular and at certain festival seasons of the year the populace crowded into public theatres where plays written by contemporary dramatists were entered in a contest and acted. This festival, which was almost a "tournament" for dramatists, attracted as competitors the best tragic writers of the time. It was held in the theatre of Dionysus (Bacchus) at Athens. Æschylus first appeared before this audience of Athens in 499 B.C. In subsequent years he came off the winner on more than a dozen occasions. So successful was Æschylus that he has sometimes been referred to as the father of Greek tragedy; his contribution to drama helped greatly in its development. For instance, he introduced a second actor where formerly only one had appeared, a fact which gave dramatic life to a form which had been chiefly lyrical. Only seven of the eighty or ninety plays we know Æschylus to have written are now extant: *Prometheus, The Suppliants, The Persians, Seven Against Thebes, Agamemnon, The Choephori,* and *The Eumenides,* the last three constituting the *Oresteia.* The dramas of

Æschylus are noted for their complete unity of action, their high poetic quality, and sublimity of expression and force of diction.

SUGGESTED REFERENCES: E. T. Owen, *The Harmony of Æschylus* (1952); Gilbert Murray, *Æschylus, the Creator of Tragedy* (4th ed., 1964).

Agamemnon [1]

Agamemnon is one of three related plays — the other two are *The Choephori* (*The Libation-Bearers*) and *The Eumenides* (*The Furies*) — giving the record and fate of the ancient house of Atreus. The transition from Homer to this Greek tragedy is a natural one since the play concerns itself with one phase of the aftermath of the fall of Troy — the return of Agamemnon to his city of Argos and his murder by his wife, Clytæmnestra.

In the *Oresteia*, the only complete trilogy in Greek literature to survive to modern times, Æschylus presents a study of evil as it repeats itself in different genera-tions: "Woe springs from wrong, the plant is like the seed," chants the chorus in *The Eumenides*. However, Æschylus does not just write a series of revenge tragedies motivated by relentless fate. His trilogy reveals the workings of a moral force which springs from human nature itself. This interweaving of divine fate and individual guilt together with the expression of a philosophy that "man must learn through suffering" makes *Agamemnon* one of the great tragedies of Western literature.

Dramatis Personæ

WATCHMAN
CLYTÆMNESTRA
CHORUS OF ARGIVE ELDERS
AGAMEMNON
(HERALD TALTHYBIOS)
CASSANDRA
ÆGISTHOS

ARGUMENT

Ten years had passed since Agamemnon, son of Atreus, king of Mykenæ, had led the Hellenes to Troïa to take vengeance on Alexandros (also known as Paris), son of Priam. For Paris had basely wronged Menelaos, king of Sparta, Agamemnon's brother, in that, being received by him as a guest, he enticed his wife Helena to leave her lord and go with him to Troïa. And now the tenth year had come, and Paris was slain, and the city of the Trojans was taken and destroyed, and Agamemnon and the Hellenes were on their way homeward with the spoil and prisoners they had taken. But meanwhile Clytæmnestra too, Agamemnon's queen, had been unfaithful, and had taken as her paramour Ægisthos, son of that Thyestes whom Atreus, his brother, had made to eat, unknowing, of the flesh of his own children. And now, partly led by her adulterer, and partly seeking to avenge the death of her daughter Iphigenea, whom Agamemnon had sacrificed to appease the wrath of Artemis, and partly also jealous because he was bringing back Cassandra, the daughter of Priam, as his concubine, she plotted with Ægisthos against her husband's life. But this was done secretly, and she stationed a guard on the roof of the royal palace to give note when he saw the beacon-fires, by which Agamemnon had promised that he would send tidings that Troïa was taken.

[1] Translation by E. H. Plumptre, *The Tragedies.* D. C. Heath and Company.

SCENE: *Argos.*[1] *The Palace of* AGAMEMNON; *statues of the Gods in front. Watchman on the roof. Time, night.*

Watchman. I ask the Gods a respite from these toils,
This keeping at my post the whole year round,
Wherein, upon the Atreidæ's [2] roof reclined,
Like dog, upon my elbow, I have learnt
To know night's goodly company of stars,   5
And those bright lords that deck the firmament,
And winter bring to men, and harvest-tide;
[The rising and the setting of the stars.]
And now I watch for sign of beacon-torch,
The flash of fire that bringeth news from Troïa,   10
And tidings of its capture. So prevails
A woman's manly-purposed, hoping heart;
And when I keep my bed of little ease,
Drenched with the dew, unvisited by dreams,
(For fear, instead of sleep, my comrade is,   15
So that in sound sleep ne'er I close mine eyes,)
And when I think to sing a tune, or hum,
(My medicine of song to ward off sleep,)
Then weep I, wailing for this house's chance,
No more, as erst, right well administered.   20
Well! may I now find blest release from toils,
When fire from out the dark brings tidings good.
(*Pauses, then springs up suddenly, seeing a light in the distance.*)
Hail! thou torch-bearer of the night, that shedd'st
Light as of morn, and bringest full array

[1] A provincial capital in the Peloponnesus.
[2] The son of Atreus, i.e. Agamemnon.

Of many choral bands in Argos met,   25
Because of this success.   Hurrah! hurrah!
So clearly tell I Agamemnon's queen,
With all speed rising from her couch to raise
Shrill cry of triumph o'er this beacon-fire
Throughout the house, since Ilion's [1] citadel   30
Is taken, as full well that bright blaze shows.
I, for my part, will dance my prelude now;
                            (*Leaps and dances.*)
For I shall score my lord's new turn of luck,
This beacon-blaze may throw of triple six.   34
Well, would that I with this mine hand may touch
The dear hand of our king when he comes home!
As to all else, the word is "Hush!"   An ox
Rests on my tongue; had the house a voice
'Twould tell too clear a tale.   I'm fain to speak
To those who know, forget with those who know
                    not.   (*Exit.*) 40

(*Enter Chorus of twelve Argive elders, chanting as
    they march to take up their position in the centre of
    the stage.   A procession of women bearing torches
    is seen in the distance.*)

Lo! the tenth year now is passing
Since, of Priam great avengers,
Menelaos, Agamemnon,
Double-throned and doubled-sceptred,
Power from sovran Zeus deriving —   45
Mighty pair of the Atreidæ —
Raised a fleet of thousand vessels
Of the Argives from our country,
Potent helpers in their warfare,
Shouting cry of Ares [2] fiercely;   50
E'en as vultures shriek who hover,
Wheeling, whirling o'er their eyrie,
In wild sorrow for their nestlings,
With their oars of stout wings rowing,
Having lost the toil that bound them   55
To their callow fledgings' couches.
But on high One, — or Apollo,
Zeus, or Pan, — the shrill cry hearing,
Cry of birds that are his clients,
Sendeth forth on men transgressing,   60
Erinnys,[3] slow but sure avenger;
So against young Alexandros
Atreus' sons the great King sendeth,
Zeus, of host and guest protector:
He, for bride with many a lover,   65
Will to Danai give and Troïans
Many conflicts, men's limbs straining,
When the knee in dust is crouching,
And the spear-shaft in the onset
Of the battle snaps asunder.   70
But as things are now, so are they,

¹ Ilion or Ilium — Troy.   ² Mars — god of war.
³ The Furies.

So, as destined, shall the end be.
Nor by tears, nor yet libations
Shall he soothe the wrath unbending
Caused by sacred rites left fireless.   75
We, with old frame little honored,
Left behind that host are staying,
Resting strength that equals childhood's
On our staff: for in the bosom
Of the boy, life's young sap rushing,   80
Is of old age but the equal;
Ares not as yet is found there:
And the man in age exceeding,
When the leaf is sere and withered,
Goes with three feet on his journey;   85
Not more Ares-like than boyhood,
Like a day-seen dream he wanders.

(*Enter* CLYTÆMNESTRA, *followed by the
        procession of torch-bearers.*)

Thou, of Tyndareus the daughter,
Queen of Argos, Clytæmnestra,
What has happened? what news cometh?   90
What perceiving, on what tidings
Leaning, dost thou put in motion
All this solemn, great procession?
Of the Gods who guard the city,
Those above and those beneath us,   95
Of the heaven, and of the market,
Lo! with thy gifts blaze the altars;
And through all the expanse of Heaven,
Here and there, the torch-fire rises,
With the flowing, pure persuasion   100
Of the holy unguent nourished,
And the chrism [1] rich and kingly
From the treasure-store's recesses,
Telling what of this thou canst tell,
What is right for thee to utter,   105
Be a healer of my trouble,
Trouble now my soul disturbing,
While anon fond hope displaying
Sacrificial signs propitious,
Wards off care that no rest knoweth,   110
Sorrow mind and heart corroding.

(*The* CHORUS, *taking their places round the central
        thymele, begin their song.*)

STROPHE

Able am I to utter, setting forth
    The might from omens sprung
What met the heroes as they journeyed on,
    (For still, by God's great gift,   115
    My age, yet linked with strength,
    Breathes suasive power of song,)
How the Achæans' [2] twin-throned majesty,

¹ An ointment used in ceremonial rites.
² The Greeks.

Accordant rulers of the youth of Hellas,
  With spear and vengeful hand,   120
Were sent by fierce, strong bird 'gainst Teucrian [1]
    shore,
Kings of the birds to kings of ships appearing,
  One black, with white tail one,
Near to the palace, on the spear-hand side,
  On station seen of all,   125
A pregnant hare devouring with her young,
  Robbed of all runs to come:
Wail as for Linos,[2] wail, wail bitterly,
  And yet may good prevail!

ANTISTROPHE

And the wise prophet of the army seeing 130
  The brave Atreidæ twain
Of diverse mood, knew those that tore the hare,
  And those that led the host;
  And thus divining spake:
  "One day this armament   135
Shall Priam's city [3] sack, and all the herds
Owned by the people, countless, by the towers,
  Fate shall with force lay low.
Only take heed lest any wrath of Gods
Blunt the great curb of Troïa yet encamped,
  Struck down before its time;   141
For Artemis [4] the chaste that house doth hate,
  Her father's wingèd hounds,
Who slay the mother with her unborn young,
  And loathes the eagles' feast.   145
Wail as for Linos, wail, wail bitterly;
  And yet may good prevail!

EPODE

"For she, the fair One, though so kind of heart
To fresh-dropt dew from mighty lion's womb,
  And young that suck the teats   150
  Of all that roam the fields,
  Yet prays Him bring to pass
  The portents of those birds,
The omens good yet also full of dread.
  And Pæan [5] I invoke   155
As Healer, lest she on the Danai [6] send
  Delays that keep the ships
Long time with hostile blasts,
So urging on a new, strange sacrifice,
  Unblest, unfestivalled,   160
By natural growth artificer of strife,
Bearing far other fruit than wife's true fear,
  For there abideth yet,
  Fearful, recurring still,

Ruling the house, full subtle, unforgetting, 165
  Vengeance for children slain."
Such things, with great good mingled, Calchas [1]
    spake,
  In voice that pierced the air,
As destined by the birds that crossed our path
  To this our kingly house: 170
  And in accord with them,
Wail as for Linos, wail, wail bitterly;
  And yet may good prevail.

STROPHE I

O Zeus — whate'er He be,
  If that Name please Him well,   175
  By that on Him I call:
Weighing all other names I fail to guess
Aught else but Zeus, if I would cast aside,
  Clearly, in every deed,
From off my soul this idle weight of care. 180

ANTISTROPHE I

Nor He who erst was great,
  Full of the might to war,
  Avails now; He is gone·
And He who next came hath departed too,
  His victor meeting; but if one to Zeus,   185
  High triumph-praise should sing,
His shall be all the wisdom of the wise;

STROPHE II

Yea, Zeus, who leadeth men in wisdom's way,
  And fixeth fast the law,
  That pain is gain;   190
And slowly dropping on the heart in sleep
  Comes woe-recording care,
And makes the unwilling yield to wiser thoughts:
And doubtless this too comes from grace of Gods,
Seated in might upon their awful thrones. 195

ANTISTROPHE II

And then of those Achæan ships the chief,
  The elder, blaming not
  Or seer or priest;
But tempered to the fate that on him smote....
  When that Achæan host   200
Were vexed with adverse winds and failing stores,
Still kept where Chalkis in the distance lies,
And the vexed waves in Aulis [2] ebb and flow;

STROPHE III

And breezes from the Strymon [3] sweeping down,

---

[1] The Trojan.   [2] Son of Apollo, killed by dogs.
[3] Troy; Priam was king.
[4] Diana, the moon goddess.
[5] God of healing.   [6] Greeks.

[1] A soothsayer with the Greek forces at Troy.
[2] A port in Bœotia.
[3] A river; it was on the banks of this stream that
Orpheus mourned, for seven months, the loss of Eurydice.

Breeding delays and hunger, driving forth   205
  Our men in wandering course,
  On seas without a port.
Sparing nor ships, nor rope, nor sailing gear,
With doubled months wore down the Argive host;
  And when, for that wild storm,   210
Of one more charm far harder for our chiefs
The prophet told, and spake of Artemis,
  In tone so piercing shrill,
The Atreidæ smote their staves upon the ground,
  And could not stay their tears.   215

ANTISTROPHE III

And then the old king lifted up his voice,
And spake, "Great woe it is to disobey;
  Great too to slay my child,
  The pride and joy of home,
Polluting with the streams of maiden's blood   220
Her father's hands upon the altar steps.
  What course is free from ill?
How lose my ships and fail of mine allies?
'Tis meet that they with strong desire should seek
  A rite the winds to soothe,   225
E'en though it be with blood of maiden pure;
  May all end well at last!"

STROPHE IV

So when he himself had harnessed
To the yoke of Fate unbending,
With a blast of strange, new feeling,   230
Sweeping o'er his heart and spirit,
Aweless, godless, and unholy,
He his thoughts and purpose altered
To full measure of all daring,
(Still base counsel's fatal frenzy,   235
Wretched primal source of evils,
Gives to mortal hearts strange boldness.)
And at last his heart he hardened
His own child to slay as victim,
Help in war that they were waging,   240
To avenge a woman's frailty,
Victim for the good ship's safety.

ANTISTROPHE IV

All her prayers and eager callings,
On the tender name of Father,
All her young and maiden freshness,   245
They but set at nought, those rulers,
In their passion for the battle.
And her father gave commandment
To the servants of the Goddess,
When the prayer was o'er, to lift her,   250
Like a kid, above the altar,
In her garments wrapt, face downwards, —
Yea, to seize with all their courage,
And that o'er her lips of beauty

Should be set a watch to hinder   255
Words of curse against the houses,
With the gag's strength silence-working.

STROPHE V

And she upon the ground
Pouring rich folds of veil in saffron dyed,
Cast at each one of those who sacrificed   260
  A piteous glance that pierced,
  Fair as a pictured form;
  And wishing, — all in vain, —
  To speak; for oftentimes
In those her father's hospitable halls   265
She sang, a maiden pure with chastest song,
  And her dear father's life
That poured its threefold cup of praise to God,
  Crowned with all choicest good,
  She with a daughter's love   270
Was wont to celebrate.[1]

ANTISTROPHE V

What then ensued mine eyes
Saw not, nor may I tell, but Calchas' arts
Were found not fruitless.   Justice turns the scale
  For those to whom through pain   275
  At last comes wisdom's gain.
  But for our future fate,
  Since help for it is none,
Good-bye to it before it comes, and this
Has the same end as wailing premature;   280
  For with to-morrow's dawn
It will come clear; may good luck crown our fate!
  So prays the one true guard,
  Nearest and dearest found,
  Of this our Apian land.   285

(*The Chief of the* CHORUS *turns to* CLYTÆMNESTRA,
*and her train of handmaids, who are seen ap-
proaching.*)

Chorus.   I come, O Clytæmnestra, honoring
Thy majesty: 'tis meet to pay respect
To a chief's wife, the man's throne empty left:
But whether thou hast heard good news, or else
In hopes of tidings glad dost sacrifice,   290
I fain would hear, yet will not silence blame.
  Clytæm.   May Morning, as the proverb runs.
    appear
Bearing glad tidings from his mother Night!
Joy thou shalt learn beyond thy hope to hear;
For Argives now have taken Priam's city.   295
  Chorus.   What?   Thy words sound so strange
    they flit by me.

[1] The events here narrated by the Chorus are the
basis for Euripides' *Iphigenia in Aulis*, a play which
might well be read in connection with the *Agamemnon*.

Clytæm. The Archæans hold Troïa. Speak I clear enough?

Chorus. Joy creeps upon me, drawing forth my tears.

Clytæm. Of loyal heart thine eyes give token true.

Chorus. What witness sure hast thou of these events? 300

Clytæm. Full clear (how else?) unless the God deceive.

Chorus. Reliest thou on dreams or visions seen?

Clytæm. I place no trust in mind weighed down with sleep.

Chorus. Hath then some wingless omen charmed thy soul?

Clytæm. My mind thou scorn'st, as though 'twere but a girl's. 305

Chorus. What time has passed since they the city sacked?

Clytæm. This very night, the mother of this morn.

Chorus. What herald could arrive with speed like this?

Clytæm. Hephæstos [1] flashing forth bright flames from Ida:

Beacon to beacon from that courier-fire [2] 310
Sent on its tidings; Ida to the rock
Hermæan named, in Lemnos: from the isle
The height of Athos, dear to Zeus, received
A third great torch of flame, and lifted up,
So as on high to skim the broad sea's back, 315
The stalwart fire rejoicing went its way;
The pine-wood, like a sun, sent forth its light
Of golden radiance to Makistos' watch;
And he, with no delay, nor unawares
Conquered by sleep, performed his courier's part:
Far off the torch-light to Eurîpos' straits 321
Advancing, tells it to Messapion's guards:
They, in their turn, lit up and passed it on,
Kindling a pile of dry and aged heath.
Still strong and fresh the torch, not yet grown dim, 325
Leaping across Asôpos' plain in guise
Like a bright moon, towards Kithæron's rock,
Roused the next station of the courier flame.
And that far-travelled light the sentries there
Refused not, burning more than all yet named: 330
And then the light swooped o'er Gorgôpis' lake,
And passing on to Ægiplanctos' mount,
Bade the bright fire's due order tarry not;
And they, enkindling boundless store, send on
A mighty beard of flame, and then it passed 335

[1] God of fire — Vulcan.
[2] The comparison is to the relay race in which the runners carry a torch. The news has come to Argos by fires lit on hill tops.

The headland e'en that looks on Saron's gulf,
Still blazing. On it swept, until it came
To Arachnæan heights, the watch-tower near;
Then here on the Atreidæ's roof it swoops,
This light, of Ida's fire no doubtful heir. 340
Such is the order of my torch-race games;
One from another taking up the course,
But here the winner is both first and last;
And this sure proof and token now I tell thee,
Seeing that my lord hath sent it me from Troïa. 345

Chorus. I to the Gods, O Queen, will pray hereafter,
But fain would I hear all thy tale again,
E'en as thou tell'st, and satiate my wonder.

Clytæm. This very day the Achæans Troïa hold.
I trow full diverse cry pervades the town: 350
Pour in the same vase vinegar and oil,
And you would call them enemies, not friends;
And so from conquerors and from captives now
The cries of varied fortune one may hear.
For these, low-fallen on the carcases 355
Of husbands and of brothers, children too
By aged fathers, mourn their dear ones' death
And that with throats that are no longer free.
And those the hungry toil of sleepless guard,
After the battle, at their breakfast sets; 360
Not billeted in order fixed and clear,
But just as each his own chance fortune grasps,
They in the captive houses of the Troïans
Dwell, freed at last from all the night's chill frosts,
And dews of heaven, for now, poor wretches, they
Will sleep all night without the sentry's watch; 366
And if they reverence well the guardian Gods
Of that new-conquered country, and their shrines,
Then they, the captors, will not captured be.
Ah! let no evil lust attack the host 370
Conquered by greed, to plunder what they ought not:
For yet they need return in safety home,
Doubling the goal to run their backward race.
But should the host come sinning 'gainst the Gods,
Then would the curse of those that perishèd 375
Be watchful, e'en though no quick ill might fall.
Such thoughts are mine, mere woman though I be.
May good prevail beyond all doubtful chance!
For I have got the blessing of great joy.

Chorus. Thou, lady, kindly, like a sage, dost speak, 380
And I, on hearing thy sure evidence,
Prepare myself to give the Gods due thanks;
For they have wrought full meed for all our toil.

(*Exit* CLYTÆMNESTRA *with her train.*)

O Zeus our King! O Night beloved,
Mighty winner of great glories, 385
Who upon the towers of Troïa

Casted'st snare of closest meshes,
So that none full-grown or youthful
Could o'erleap the net of bondage,
Woe of universal capture; —— 390
Zeus, of host and guest protector,
Who hath brought these things, I worship;
He long since on Alexandros
Stretched his bow that so his arrow
Might not sweep at random, missing, 395
Or beyond the stars shoot idly.

STROPHE I

Yes, one may say, 'tis Zeus, whose blow they feel;
  This one may clearly trace:
    They fared as He decreed:
    Yea, one there was who said, 400
"The Gods deign not to care for mortal men
By whom the grace of things inviolable
    Is trampled under foot."
    No fear of God had he:
Now is it to the children manifest 405
  Of those who, overbold,
Breathed rebel War beyond the bounds of Right,
Their houses overfilled with precious store
  Above the golden mean.
Ah! let our life be free from all that hurts, 410
  So that for one who gains
    Wisdom in heart and soul,
    That lot may be enough.
Since still there is no bulwark strong in wealth
  Against destruction's doom, 415
For one who in the pride of wantonness
Spurns the great altar of the Right and Just.

ANTISTROPHE I

Him woeful, subtle Impulse urges on,
  Resistless in her might,
    Atè's [1] far-scheming child: 420
    All remedy is vain.
It is not hidden, but is manifest,
That mischief with its horrid gleaming light;
  And, like to worthless bronze,
    By friction tried and tests, 425
It turns to tarnished blackness in its hue.
  Since, boy-like, he pursues
A bird upon its flight, and so doth bring
Upon his city shame intolerable:
  And no God hears his prayer, 430
    But bringeth low the unjust,
    Who deals with deeds like this.
Thus Paris came to the Atreidæ's home,
  And stole its queen away,
And so left brand of shame indelible 435
Upon the board where host and guest had sat.

[1] Goddess of infatuation.

STROPHE II

She, leaving to her countrymen at home
Wild din of spear and shield and ships of war,
  And bringing, as her dower,
    To Ilion doom of death,
Passed very swiftly through the palace gates, 440
  Daring what none should dare;
    And many a wailing cry
They raised, the minstrel prophets of the house,
    "Woe for that kingly home! 445
Woe for that kingly home and for its chiefs!
Woe for the marriage-bed and traces left
  Of wife who loved her lord!"
There stands he silent; foully wronged and yet
  Uttering no word of scorn, 450
In deepest woe perceiving she is gone;
  And in his yearning love
For one beyond the sea,
A ghost shall seem to queen it o'er the house;
  The grace of sculptured forms 455
    Is loathèd by her lord,
And in the penury of life's bright eyes
    All Aphroditè's charm
    To utter wreck has gone.

ANTISTROPHE II

And phantom shades that hover round in dreams
Come full of sorrow, bringing vain delight; 461
  For vain it is, when one
    Sees seeming shows of good,
And gliding through his hands the dream is gone,
  After a moment's space, 465
    On wings that follow still
Upon the path where sleep goes to and fro.
  Such are the woes at home
Upon the altar hearth, and worse than these.
But on a wider scale for those who went 470
  From Hellas' [1] ancient shore,
A sore distress that causeth pain of heart
  Is seen in every house.
Yea, many things there are that touch the quick:
  For those whom each did send 475
    He knoweth; but, instead
Of living men, there come to each man's home
    Funeral urns alone,
    And ashes of the dead.

STROPHE III

For Ares,[2] trafficking for golden coin 480
  The lifeless shapes of men,
And in the rush of battle holding scales,
  Sends now from Ilion
    Dust from the funeral pyre,
A burden sore to loving friends at home, 495
  And bitterly bewailed,

[1] Greece.   [2] Mars, god of war.

Filling the brazen urn
With well-smoothed ashes in the place of men;
    And with high praise they mourn
This hero skilled and valiant in the fight,   490
And that who in the battle nobly fell,
    All for another's wife: [1]
And other words some murmur secretly;
    And jealous discontent
Against the Atreidæ, champions in the suit,   495
    Creeps on all stealthily;
    And some around the wall,
In full and goodly form have sepulture
    There upon Ilion's soil,
And their foes' land inters its conquerors.   500

ANTISTROPHE III

And so the murmurs of their subjects rise
    With sullen discontent,
And do the dread work of a people's curse;
    And now my boding fear
    Awaits some news of ill,   505
As yet enwrapt in blackness of the night.
    Not heedless are the Gods
    Of shedders of much blood,
And the dark-robed Erinnyes in due time,
    By adverse chance of life,   510
Place him who prospers in unrighteousness
In gloom obscure; and once among the unseen,
    There is no help for him;
Fame in excess is but a perilous thing;
    For on men's quivering eyes   515
Is hurled by Zeus the blinding thunder-bolt.
    I praise the good success
    That rouses not God's wrath;
Ne'er be it mine a city to lay waste.
    Nor, as a prisoner, see   520
My life wear on beneath another's power!

EPODE

And now at bidding of the courier flame,
    The herald of good news,
A rumor swift spreads through the city streets,
But who knows clearly whether it be true,   525
Or whether God has mingled lies with it?
Who is so childish or so reft of sense,
    As with his heart a-glow
At that fresh uttered message of the flame,
Then to wax sad at changing rumor's sound?   530
It suits the mood that sways a woman's mind
To pour thanksgiving ere the truth is seen:
Quickly, with rapid steps, too credulous,
The limit which a woman sets to trust
    Advances evermore;   535

---

[1] Helen, the wife of Menelaus. Her elopement with
Paris brought on the Trojan War.

And with swift doom of death
A rumor spread by woman perishes.
    (As the CHORUS ends, a HERALD is seen
    approaching, his head wreathed with
    olive.)

Soon we shall know the sequence of the torches
Light-giving, and of all the beacon-fires,
If they be true; or if, as 'twere a dream,   540
This sweet light coming hath beguiled our minds.
I see a herald coming from the shore,
With olive boughs o'ershadowed, and the dust,
Dry sister-twin of mire, announces this,
That neither without voice, nor kindling blaze   545
Of wood upon the mountains, he will signal
With smoke from fire, but either he will come,
With clear speech bidding us rejoice, or else . . .
                                    (Pauses)
The word opposed to this I much mislike.
Nay, may good issue good beginnings crown!   550
Who for our city utters other prayers,
May he himself his soul's great error reap!
    Herald. Hail, soil of this my Argive fatherland.
Now in the light of the tenth year I reach thee,
Though many hopes are shattered, gaining one.
For never did I think in Argive land   556
To die, and share the tomb that most I craved.
Now hail! thou land; and hail! thou light of day:
Zeus our great ruler, and thou Pythian [1] king,
No longer darting arrows from thy bow.   560
Full hostile wast thou by Scamandros' banks,
Now be thou Saviour, yea, and Healer found,
O king Apollo! and the Gods of war,
These I invoke; my patron Hermes [2] too,
Dear herald, whom all heralds reverence, —   565
Those heroes, too, that sent us, — graciously
To welcome back the host that war has spared.
Hail, O ye royal dwellings, home beloved!
Ye solemn thrones, and Gods who face the sun!
If e'er of old, with cheerful glances now   570
After long time receive our king's array.
For he is come, in darkness bringing light
To you and all, our monarch, Agamemnon.
Salute him with all grace; for so 'tis meet,
Since he hath dug up Troïa with the spade   575
Of Zeus the Avenger, and the plain laid waste;
Fallen their altars and the shrines of Gods;
The seed of all the land is rooted out,
This yoke of bondage casting over Troïa,
Our chief, the elder of the Atreidæ, comes,   580
A man full blest, and worthiest of high honor
Of all that are.   For neither Paris' self,
Nor his accomplice city now can boast
Their deed exceeds its punishment.   For he,

---

[1] Apollo.

[2] Hermes — Mercury, herald of the gods.

Found guilty on the charge of rape and theft, 585
Hath lost his prize and brought his father's house,
With lands and all, to waste and utter wreck;
And Priam's sons have double forfeit paid.

Chorus. Joy, joy, thou herald of the Achæan
    host!
Herald. All joy is mine: I shrink from death no
    more.   590
Chorus. Did love for this thy fatherland so try
    thee?
Herald. So that mine eyes weep tears for very
    joy,
Chorus. Disease full sweet then this ye suffered
    from ...
Herald. How so? When taught, I shall thy
    meaning master.
Chorus. Ye longed for us who yearned for you in
    turn.   595
Herald. Say'st thou this land its yearning host
    yearned o'er?
Chorus. Yea, so that oft I groaned in gloom of
    heart.
Herald. Whence came these bodings that an
    army hates?
Chorus. Silence I've held long since a charm for
    ill.
Herald. How, when your lords were absent,
    feared ye any?   600
Chorus. To use thy words, death now would
    welcome be.
Herald. Good is the issue; but in so long time
Some things, one well might say, have prospered
    well,
And some give cause for murmurs. Save the
    Gods,
Who free from sorrow lives out all his life? 605
For should I tell of toils, and how we lodged
Full hardly, seldom putting in to shore,
And then with couch full hard. . . . What gave us
    not
Good cause for mourning? What ill had we not
As daily portion? And what passed on land, 610
That brought yet greater hardship: for our beds
Were under our foes' walls, and meadow mists
From heaven and earth still left us wringing wet,
A constant mischief to our garments, making
Our hair as shaggy as the beasts'. And if 615
One spoke of winter frosts that killed the birds,
By Ida's snow-storms made intolerable,
Or heat, when Ocean in its noontide couch
Windless reclined and slept without a wave. . . .
But why lament o'er this? Our toil is past; 620
Past too is theirs who in the warfare fell,
So that no care have they to rise again.
Why should I count the number of the dead,
Or he that lives mourn o'er a past mischance?

To change and chance I bid a long Farewell: 625
With us, the remnant of the Argive host,
Good fortune wins, no ills as counterpoise.
So it is meet to this bright sun we boast,
Who travel homeward over land and sea;
"The Argive host who now have captured Troïa,
These spoils of battle to the Gods of Hellas 631
Hang on their pegs, enduring prize and joy."
Hearing these things we ought to bless our country
And our commanders; and the grace of Zeus
That wrought this shall be honored. My tale's
    told.   635

Chorus. Thy words o'ercome me, and I say not
    nay;
To learn good keeps youth's freshness with the old.
'Tis meet these things should be a special care
To Clytæmnestra and the house, and yet
That they should make me sharer in their joy. 640

(*Enter* CLYTÆMNESTRA.)

Clytæm. I long ago for gladness raised my cry,
When the first fiery courier came by night,
Telling of Troïa taken and laid waste:
And then one girding at me spake, "Dost think,
Trusting in beacons, Troïa is laid waste? 645
This heart elate is just a woman's way."
In words like these they made me out distraught;
Yet still I sacrificed, and with a strain
Shrill as a woman's, they, now here, now there,
Throughout the city hymns of blessing raised 650
In shrines of Gods, and lulled to gentle sleep
The fragrant flame that on the incense fed.
And now why need'st thou lengthen out thy words?
I from the king himself the tale shall learn;
And that I show all zeal to welcome back 655
My honored lord on his return (for what
Is brighter joy for wife to see than this,
When God has brought her husband back from war,
To open wide her gates?) tell my lord this,
"To come with all his speed, the city's idol;" 660
And "may he find a faithful wife at home,
Such as he left her, noble watch-dog still
For him, and hostile to his enemies;
And like in all things else, who has not broken
One seal of his in all this length of time." 665
No pleasure have I known, nor scandal ill
With any other more than . . . stains on bronze.
Such is my vaunt, and being full of truth,
Not shameful for a noble wife to speak.[1]

(*Exit.*)

Chorus (*to* HERALD). She hath thus spoken in
    thy hearing now.   670
A goodly word for good interpreters.
But tell me, herald, tell of Menelaos,

---

[1] Clytæmnestra has been compared to Lady Macbeth. Does this speech justify the comparison?

If, coming home again in safety he
Is with you, the dear strength of this our land.
   Herald. I cannot make report of false good news,
So that my friends should long rejoice in it.   676
   Chorus. Ah! could'st thou good news speak, and
      also true!
These things asunder are not well concealed.
   Herald. The chief has vanished from the Achæan
     host,
He and his ship. I speak no falsehood here.   680
   Chorus. In sight of all when he from Ilion sailed?
Or did a storm's wide evil part him from you?
   Herald. Like skilful archer thou hast hit the
     mark,
And in few words has told of evil long.
   Chorus. And was it of him as alive or dead   685
The whisper of the other sailors ran?
   Herald. None to that question answer clear can
     give,
Save the Sun-God who feeds the life of earth.
   Chorus. How say'st thou? Did a storm come
     on our fleet,
And do its work through anger of the Gods?   690
   Herald. It is not meet a day of tidings good
To mar with evil news. Apart for each
Is special worship. But when courier brings
With louring face the ills men pray against,
And tells a city that its host has fallen,   695
That for the State there is a general wound,
That many a man from many a home is driven,
As banned by double scourge that Ares loves,
Woe doubly-barbed, Death's two-horsed chariot
   this . . .
When with such griefs as freight a herald comes,
'Tis meet to chant the Erinnyes' dolorous song;   701
But for glad messenger of good deeds wrought
That bring deliverance, coming to a town
Rejoicing in its triumph, . . . how shall I
Blend good with evil, telling of a storm   705
That smote the Achæans, not without God's
   wrath?
For they a compact swore who erst were foes,
Ocean and Fire, and their pledges gave,
Wrecking the ill-starred army of the Argives;
And in the night rose ill of raging storm: 710
For Thrakian tempests shattered all the ships,
Each on the other. Some thus crashed and
   bruised,
By the storm stricken and the surging foam
Of wind-tost waves, soon vanished out of sight,
Whirled by an evil pilot. And when rose   715
The sun's bright orb, behold, the Ægæan sea
Blossomed with wrecks of ships and dead Achæans.
And as for us and our uninjured ship,
Surely 'twas some one stole or begged us off,
Some God, not man, presiding at the helm;   720

And on our ship with good will Fortune sat,
Giver of safety, so that nor in haven
Felt we the breakers, nor on rough rock-beach
Ran we aground. But when we had escaped
The hell of waters, then in clear, bright day,   725
Not trusting in our fortune, we in thought
O'er new ills brooded of our host destroyed,
And eke most roughly handled. And if still
Breathe any of them they report of us
As having perished. How else should they speak?
And we in our turn deem that they are so.   731
God send good ending! Look you, first and chief,
For Menelaos' coming; and indeed,
If any sunbeam know of him alive
And well, by help of Zeus who has not willed   735
As yet to blot out all the regal race,
Some hope there is that he'll come back again.
Know, hearing this, that thou the truth hast heard.
                  (*Exit* HERALD.)

STROPHE I

   Chorus. Who was it named her with such won-
     drous truth?
   (Could it be One unseen,   740
In strange prevision of her destined work,
   Guiding the tongue through chance?)
Who gave that war-wed, strife-upstirring one
The name of Helen, ominous of ill?
   For all too plainly she   745
   Hath been to men, and ships,
   And towers, as doom of Hell.
From bower of gorgeous curtains forth she sailed
With breeze of Zephyr Titan-born and strong;
   And hosts of many men,   750
   Hunters that bore the shield,
Went on the track of those who steered their boat
Unseen to leafy banks of Simois,
   On her account who came,
Dire cause of strife with bloodshed in her train.   755

ANTISTROPHE I

And so the wrath which works its vengeance out
   Dear bride to Ilion brought,
(Ah, all too truly named!) exacting still
   After long lapse of time
The penalty of foul dishonor done   760
To friendship's board and Zeus, of host and guest
   The God, from those who paid
   Their loud-voiced honor then
   Unto that bridal strain,
That hymeneal chorus which to chant   765
Fell to the lot of all the bridegroom's kin.
   But learning other song,
   Priam's ancient city now
Bewaileth sore, and calls on Paris' name.

Wedded in fatal wedlock; all the time   770
  Enduring tear-fraught life
For all the blood its citizens had lost.

STROPHE II

So once a lion's cub,
A mischief in his house,
As foster child one reared,   775
While still it loved the teats;
In life's preluding dawn
Tame, by the children loved,
And fondled by the old,
Oft in his arms 'twas held,   780
Like infant newly born,
With eyes that brightened to the hand that
    stroked,
And fawning at the hest of hunger keen.

ANTISTROPHE II

But when full-grown, it showed
The nature of its sires;   785
For it unbidden made
A feast in recompense
Of all their fostering care,
By banquet of slain sheep;
With blood the house was stained,   790
A curse no slaves could check,
Great mischief murderous:
By God's decree a priest of Atè thus
Was reared, and grew within the man's own house.

STROPHE III

So I would tell that thus to Ilion came   795
Mood as of calm when all the air is still,
The gentle pride and joy of kingly state,
A tender glance of eye,
The full-blown blossom of a passionate love,
  Thrilling the very soul;   800
  And yet she turned aside,
And wrought a bitter end of marriage feast,
  Coming to Priam's race,
  Ill sojourner, ill friend,
Sent by great Zeus, the God of host and guest   805
Erinnys, for whom wives weep many tears.

ANTISTROPHE III

There lives an old saw, framed in ancient days,
In memories of men, that high estate
Full-grown brings forth its young, nor childless
    dies,
But that from good success   810
Springs to the race a woe insatiable.
  But I, apart from all,
  Hold this my creed alone:
For impious act it is that offspring breeds,
  Like to their parent stock: 815

For still in every house
That loves the right their fate for evermore
Rejoiceth in an issue fair and good.

STROPHE IV

But Recklessness of old
Is wont to breed another Recklessness,   820
  Sporting its youth in human miseries,
Or now, or then, whene'er the fixed hour comes:
  That in its youth, in turn,
  Doth full-flushed Lust beget,
And that dread demon-power unconquerable,   825
  Daring that fears not God, —
Two curses black within the homes of men,
  Like those that gendered them.

ANTISTROPHE IV

But Justice shineth bright
In dwellings that are dark and dim with smoke,   830
  And honors life law-ruled,
While gold-decked homes conjoined with hands
    defiled
  She with averted eyes
  Hath left, and draweth near
To holier things, nor worships might of wealth,
  If counterfeit its praise;   836
But still directeth all the course of things
  Towards its destined goal.

(AGAMEMNON *is seen approaching in his chariot,*
followed by another chariot, in which CASSANDRA
is standing, carrying her prophet's wand in her
hand, and wearing fillets round her temples, and
by a great train of soldiers bearing trophies. As
they come on the stage the CHORUS *sings its wel-*
come.)

Come then, king, thou son of Atreus,
  Waster of the towers of Troïa,   840
What of greeting and of homage
Shall I give, nor overshooting,
Nor due need of honor missing?
Men there are who, right transgressing,
Honor semblance more than being.   845
  O'er the sufferer all are ready
  Wail of bitter grief to utter,
Though the biting pang of sorrow
Never to their heart approaches;
So with counterfeit rejoicing   850
Men strain faces that are smileless;
But when one his own sheep knoweth,
The men's eyes cannot deceive him,
When they deem with kindly purpose,
And with fondness weak to flatter.   855
Thou, when thou did'st lead thine army
For Helen's sake — (I will not hide it) —
Wast to me as one whose features

Have been limned by unskilled artist,
Guiding ill the helm of reason,   860
Giving men to death's doom sentenced
Courage which their will rejected.
Now nor from the spirit's surface,
Nor with touch of thought unfriendly,
All the toil, I say, is welcome,   865
If men bring it to good issue.
And thou soon shalt know, enquiring,
Him who rightly, him who wrongly
Of thy citizens fulfilleth
Task of office for the city.   870
　　Agam. First Argos, and the Gods who guard
　　　　the land,
'Tis right to greet; to them in part I owe
This my return, and vengeance that I took
On Priam's city. Not on hearsay proof
Judging the cause, with one consent the Gods 875
Cast in their votes into the urn of blood
For Ilion's ruin and her people's death;
I' the other urn Hope touched the rim alone,
Still far from being filled full. And even yet
The captured city by its smoke is seen,   880
The incense clouds of Atè live on still;
And, in the act of dying with its prey,
From richest store the dust sends savors sweet.
For these things it is meet to give the Gods
Thank-offerings long-enduring; for our nets 885
Of vengeance we set close, and for a woman
Our Argive monster laid the city low,
Foaled by the mare, a people bearing shield,
Taking its leap when set the Pleiades;
And, bounding o'er the tower, that ravenous lion
Lapped up its fill of blood of kingly race.   891
This prelude to the Gods I lengthen out;
And as concerns thy feeling (this I well
Remember hearing) I with thee agree,
And thou in me may'st find an advocate.   895
With but few men is it their natural bent
To honor without grudging prosperous friend:
For ill-souled envy the heart besets,
Doubles his woe who suffers that disease:
He by his own griefs first is overwhelmed,   900
And groans at sight of others' happier lot.
And I with good cause say, (for well I know,)
They are but friendship's mirror, phantom shade,
Who seemed to be my most devoted friends.
Odysseus only, who against his will   905
Sailed with us, still was found true trace-fellow:
And this I say of him or dead or living.
But as for all that touches on the State,
Or on the Gods, in full assembly we,
Calling our council, will deliberate: 910
For what goes well we should with care provide
How longest it may last; and where there needs
A healing charm, there we with all good-will,

By surgery or cautery [1] will try
To turn away the mischief of disease.   915
And now will I to home and household hearth
Move on, and first give thanks unto the Gods
Who led me forth, and brought me back again.
Since Victory follows, long may she remain!

(*Enter* CLYTÆMNESTRA, *followed by female
attendants carrying purple tapestry.*)

　　Clytæm. Ye citizens, ye Argive senators,   920
I will not shrink from telling you the tale
Of wife's true love. As time wears on one drops
All over-shyness. Not learning it from others,
I will narrate my own unhappy life,
The whole long time my lord at Ilion stayed.   925
For first, that wife should sit at home alone
Without her husband is a monstrous grief,
Hearing full many an ill report of him,
Now one and now another coming still,
Bringing news home, worse trouble upon bad.   930
Yea, if my lord had met as many wounds
As rumor told of, floating to our house,
He had been riddled more than any net;
And had he died, as tidings still poured in,
Then he, a second Geryon [2] with three lives, 935
Had boasted of a threefold coverlet
Of earth above, (I will not say below him,)
Dying one death for each of those his forms;
And so, because of all these ill reports,
Full many a noose around my neck have others 940
Loosed by main force, when I had hung myself.
And for this cause no son is with me now,
Holding in trust the pledges of our love,
As he should be, Orestes. Wonder not;
For now a kind ally doth nurture him,   945
Strophios the Phokian,[3] telling me of woes
Of twofold aspect, danger on thy side
At Ilion, and lest loud-voiced anarchy
Should overthrow thy council, since 'tis still
The wont of men to kick at those who fall.   950
No trace of guile bears this excuse of mine;
As for myself, the fountains of my tears
Have flowed till they are dry, no drop remains,
And mine eyes suffer from o'er-late repose,
Watching with tears the beacons set for thee, 955
Left still unheeded. And in dreams full oft
I from my sleep was startled by the gnat
With thin wings buzzing, seeing in the night

---

[1] Healing by searing the flesh.

[2] A giant with three bodies, three heads, six arms and
six legs. Hercules killed him in connection with his
tenth "labor."

[3] Uncle of Orestes to whose home the lad Orestes had
been sent that he might escape the conspiracy against
Agamemnon. For the story of Orestes see the *Chœ-
phorœ* (Æschylus) and the *Electra* (Euripides).

Ills that stretched far beyond the time of sleep.
Now, having borne all this, with mind at ease,   960
I hail my lord as watch-dog of the fold,
The stay that saves the ship, of lofty roof
Main column-prop, a father's only child,
Land that beyond all hope the sailor sees,
Morn of great brightness following after storm,
Clear-flowing fount to thirsty traveller.   966
Yes, it is pleasant to escape all straits:
With words of welcome such as these I greet thee;
May jealous Heaven forgive them! for we bore
Full many an evil in the past; and now,   970
Dear husband, leave thy car,[1] nor on the ground,
O King, set thou the foot that Ilion trampled.
Why linger ye (*turning to her attendants*), ye maids,
  whose task it was
To strew the pathway with your tapestries?
Let the whole road be straightway purple-strown,
That Justice lead to home he looked not for.   976
All else my care, by slumber not subdued,
Will with God's help work out what fate decrees.

    (*The handmaids advance, and are about to
    lay the purple carpets on the ground.*)

    Agam. O child of Leda,[2] guardian of my home,
Thy speech hath with my absence well agreed —
For long indeed thou mad'st it — but fit praise   981
Is boon that I must seek at other hands.
I pray thee, do not in thy woman's fashion
Pamper my pride, nor in barbaric guise
Prostrate on earth raise full-mouthed cries to me;
Make not my path offensive to the Gods   986
By spreading it with carpets. They alone
May claim that honor; but for mortal men
To walk on fair embroidery, to me
Seems nowise without peril. So I bid you   990
To honor me as man, and not as God.
Apart from all foot-mats and tapestry
My fame speaks loudly; and God's greatest gift
Is not to err from wisdom. We must bless
Him only who ends life in fair estate.   995
Should I thus act throughout, good hope were mine.

    Clytæm. Nay, say not this my purposes to
  thwart.

    Agam. Know I change not for the worse my
  purpose.

    Clytæm. In fear, perchance, thou vowèd'st thus
  to act.

    Agam. If any, I, with good ground spoke my
  will.   1000

    Clytæm. What think'st thou Priam, had he
  wrought such deeds . . . ?

    Agam. Full gladly he, I trow, had trod on
  carpets.

  [1] Chariot.
  [2] Both Clytæmnestra and Helen (of Troy) were
daughters of Leda.

    Clytæm. Then shrink not thou through fear of
  men's dispraise.

    Agam. And yet a people's whisper hath great
  might.

    Clytæm. Who is not envied is not enviable.   1005

    Agam. 'Tis not a woman's part to crave for
  strife.

    Clytæm. True, yet the prosperous e'en should
  sometimes yield.

    Agam. Dost thou then prize that victory in the
  strife?

    Clytæm. Nay, list; with all good-will yield me
  this boon.

    Agam. Well, then, if thou wilt have it so, with
  speed   1010
Let some one loose my buskins [1] (servants they
Doing the foot's true work), and as I tread
Upon these robes sea-purpled, may no wrath
From glance of Gods smite on me from afar!
Great shame I feel to trample with my foot   1015
This wealth of carpets, costliest work of looms;
So far for this. This stranger (*pointing to* CAS-
  SANDRA [2]) lead thou in
With kindliness. On him who gently wields
His power God's eye looks kindly from afar.
None of their own will choose a bondslave's life;
And she, the chosen flower of many spoils,   1021
Has followed with me as the army's gift.
But since I turn, obeying thee in this,
I'll to my palace go, on purple treading.

    Clytæm. There is a sea, — and who shall drain
  it dry?   1025
Producing still new store of purple juice,[3]
Precious as silver, staining many a robe.
And in our house, with God's help, O my king,
'Tis ours to boast our palace knows no stint.
Trampling of many robes would I have vowed,
Had that been ordered me in oracles,   1031
When for my lord's return I then did plan
My votive gifts. For while the root lives on,
The foliage stretches even to the house,
And spreads its shade against the dog-star's rage;
So when thou comest to thy hearth and home,   1036
Thou show'st that warmth hath come in winter
  time;
And when from unripe clusters Zeus matures
The wine, then is there coolness in the house,
If the true master dwelleth in his home.   1040
Ah, Zeus! the All-worker, Zeus, work out for me

  [1] Half-boots.
  [2] A captive Agamemnon brought from Troy. Apollo
had given her the gift of prophecy but later, when displeased with her, had provided that no one should
believe her. See ll. 1307–1317.
  [3] The "purple juice" is dye secured from the shell-
fish.

All that I pray for; let it be thy care
To look to what Thou purposest to work.
(*Exeunt* AGAMEMNON, *walking on the tapes-
try,* CLYTÆMNESTRA, *and her attendants.*)

STROPHE I

Chorus. Why thus continually
Do haunting phantoms hover at the gate   1045
    Of my foreboding heart?
Why floats prophetic song, unbought, unbidden?
    Why doth no steadfast trust
    Sit on my mind's dear throne,
To fling it from me as a vision dim?   1050
Long time hath passed since stern-ropes of our ships
Were fastened on the sand, when our great host
    Of those that sailed in ships
    Had come to Ilion's towers:

ANTISTROPHE I

    And now from these mine eyes   1055
I learn, myself reporting to myself,
    Their safe return; and yet
My mind within itself, taught by itself,
    Chanteth Erinnys' dirge,
    The lyreless melody,   1060
And hath no strength of wonted confidence.
Not vain these inner pulses, as my heart
Whirls eddying in breast oracular.
    I, against hope, will pray
    It prove false oracle.   1065

STROPHE II

Of high, o'erflowing health
There is no bound that stays the wish for more,
For evermore disease, as neighbor close
    Whom but a wall divides,
Upon it presses; and man's prosperous state   1070
    Moves on its course, and strikes
    Upon an unseen rock;
But if his fear for safety of his freight,
A part, from well-poised sling, shall sacrifice,
    Then the whole house sinks not,   1075
    O'er filled with wretchedness,
    Nor does he swamp his boat:
    So, too, abundant gift
From Zeus in bounteous fulness, and the fruit
    Of glebe [1] at harvest tide   1080
Have caused to cease sore hunger's pestilence;

ANTISTROPHE II

But blood that once hath flowed
In purple stains of death upon the ground
At a man's feet, who then can bid it back
    By any charm of song?   1085

[1] Soil.

Else him who knew to call the dead to life
    Zeus had not sternly checked,
    As warning unto all;
But unless Fate, firm-fixed, had barred our fate
From any chance of succor from the Gods,   1090
    Then had my heart poured forth
    Its thoughts, outstripping speech.
    But now in gloom it wails
    Sore vexed, with little hope
At any time hereafter fitting end   1095
    To find, unravelling,
My soul within me burning with hot thoughts.

(*Re-enter* CLYTÆMNESTRA.)

Clytæm. (*to* CASSANDRA, *who has remained in the
    chariot during the choral ode*).   Thou too —
    I mean Cassandra — go within;
Since Zeus hath made it thine, and not in wrath,
To share the lustral waters [1] in our house,   1100
Standing with many a slave the altar nigh
Of Zeus, who guards our goods.   Now get thee
    down
From out this car, nor look so over proud.
They say that e'en Alcmena's son [2] endured
Being sold a slave, constrained to bear the yoke:
And if the doom of this ill chance should come,   1106
Great boon it is to meet with lords who own
Ancestral wealth.   But whoso reap full crops
They never dared to hope for, these in all,
And beyond measure, to their slaves are harsh: 1110
From us thou hast what usage doth prescribe.

Chorus. So ends she, speaking words full clear
    to thee:
And seeing thou art in the toils of fate,
If thou obey, thou wilt obey; and yet,
Perchance, obey thou wilt not.   1115

Clytæm. Nay, but unless she, like a swallow,
    speaks
A barbarous tongue unknown, I speaking now
Within her apprehension, bid obey.

Chorus (*to* CASSANDRA, *still standing motionless*).
    Go with her.   What she bids is now the
    best;
Obey her: leave thy seat upon this car.   1120

Clytæm. I have no leisure here to stay without:
For as regards our central altar, there
The sheep stand by as victims for the fire;
For never had we hoped such thanks to give:
If thou wilt do this, make no more delay;   1125
But if thou understandest not my words,
Then wave thy foreign hand in lieu of speech.
    (CASSANDRA *shudders as in horror, but
    makes no sign.*)

Chorus. The stranger seems a clear interpreter
To need.   Her look is like a captured deer's.

[1] Used in purification.   [2] Hercules.

Clytæm. Nay, she is mad, and follows evil
thoughts,   1130
Since, leaving now her city, newly-captured,
She comes, and knows not how to take the curb,
Ere she foam out her passion in her blood.
I will not bear the shame of uttering more. (*Exit.*)
Chorus. And I — I pity her, and will not rage:
Come, thou poor sufferer, empty leave thy car; 1136
Yield to thy doom, and handsel [1] now the yoke.
(CASSANDRA *leaves the chariot, and bursts
into a cry of wailing.*)

STROPHE I

Cass. Woe! woe, and well-a-day! [2]
Apollo! O Apollo!
Chorus. Why criest thou so loud on Loxias? 1140
The wailing cry of mourner suits not him.

ANTISTROPHE I

Cass. Woe! woe and well-a-day!
Apollo! O Apollo!
Chorus. Again with boding words she calls the
God,
Though all unmeet as helper to men's groans. 1145

STROPHE II

Cass. Apollo! O Apollo!
God of all paths, Apollo true to me;
For still thou dost appal me and destroy.
Chorus. She seems her own ills like to prophesy:
The God's great gift is in the slave's mind yet. 1150

ANTISTROPHE II

Cass. Apollo! O Apollo!
God of all paths, Apollo true to me;
What path hast led me? To what roof hast
brought?
Chorus. To that of the Atreidæ. This I tell,
If thou know'st not. Thou wilt not find it false.

STROPHE III

Cass. Ah! Ah! Ah me!   1156
Say rather to a house God hates — that knows
Murder, self-slaughter, rapes,
A human shamble, staining earth with blood.[3]
Chorus. Keen scented seems this stranger,
like a hound,   1160
And sniffs to see whose murder she may find.

ANTISTROPHE III

Cass. Ah! Ah! Ah me!

[1] To try, or use for the first time.
[2] Cassandra is in the throes of prophecy.
[3] Cassandra sees the past as well as the future in this passage.

Lo! (*looking wildly, and pointing to the house*) there
the witnesses whose word I trust, —
Those babes who wail their death
The roasted flesh that made a father's meal.[1] 1165
Chorus. We of a truth had heard thy seeress
fame,
But prophets now are not the race we seek.

STROPHE IV

Cass. Ah me! O horror! What ill schemes
she now?
What is this new great woe?
Great evil plots she in this very house,   1170
Hard for its friends to bear, immedicable;
And help stands far aloof.
Chorus. These oracles of thine surpass my ken;
Those I know well. The whole town rings with
them.

ANTISTROPHE IV

Cass. Ah me! O daring one! what work'st
thou here,   1175
Who having in his bath
Tended thy spouse, thy lord, then . . . How tell the
rest?
For quick it comes, and hand is following hand,
Stretched out to strike the blow.
Chorus. Still I discern not; after words so dark
I am perplexed with thy dim oracles.   1181

STROPHE V

Cass. Ah, horror, horror! What is this I see?
Is it a snare of Hell?
Nay, the true net is she who shares his bed,
Who shares in working death.   1185
Ha! let the Band insatiable in hate
Howl for the race its wild exulting cry
O'er sacrifice that calls
For death by storm of stones.

STROPHE VI

Chorus. What dire Erinnys bidd'st thou o'er
our house   1190
To raise shrill cry? Thy speech but little cheers;
And to my heart there rush
Blood-drops of saffron hue,
Which, when from deadly wound
They fall, together with life's setting rays   1195
End, as it fails, their own appointed course:
And mischief comes apace.

ANTISTROPHE V

Cass. See, see, I say, from that fell heifer there
Keep thou the bull: in robes

[1] Atreus, father of Agamemnon, had caused his
brother, Thyestes, to eat the flesh of his two children.

Entangling him, she with her weapon gores   1200
 Him with the swarthy horns;
Lo! in that bath with water filled he falls,
Smitten to death, and I to thee set forth
 Crime of a bath of blood,
 By murderous guile devised.[1]   1205

ANTISTROPHE VI

Chorus. I may not boast that I keen insight have
In words oracular; yet bode I ill.
 What tidings good are brought
 By any oracles
 To mortal men?   These arts,   1210
In days of evil sore, with many words,
Do still but bring a vague, portentous fear
 For men to learn and know.

STROPHE VII

Cass. Woe, woe! for all sore ills that fall on me!
It is my grief thou speak'st of, blending it   1215
With his. (*Pausing, and then crying out:*)
 Ah! wherefore then
 Hast thou thus brought me here,
 Only to die with thee?
 What other doom is mine?   1220

STROPHE VIII

Chorus. Frenzied art thou, and by some God's
    might swayed,
 And utterest for thyself
 A melody which is no melody,
 Like to that tawny one,
 Insatiate in her wail,   1225
The nightingale, who still with sorrowing soul,
 And "Itys, Itys,"[2] cry,
Bemoans a life o'erflourishing in ills.

ANTISTROPHE VII

Cass. Ah, for the doom of clear-voiced nightin-
    gale!
The Gods gave her a body bearing wings,   1230
 And life of pleasant days
 With no fresh cause to weep:
 But for me waiteth still
 Stroke from the two-edged sword.

[1] The actual murder takes place off stage; we are
told it as Cassandra sees it.

[2] Tereus, king of Thrace, had a son, Itys, by Procne.
When he tired of her he cut out her tongue, and married her sister, Philomela. Procne wove a web which
told Philomela her story, and the two sisters killed Itys,
giving the child to his father as food. The gods punished the two sisters by changing Procne into a swallow
and Philomela into a nightingale.

ANTISTROPHE VIII

Chorus. From what source hast thou these
    dread agonies   1235
 Sent on thee by thy God,
Yet vague and little meaning; and thy cries
 Dire with ill-omened shrieks
 Dost utter as a chant,
And blendest with them strains of shrillest grief?
 Whence treadest thou this track   1241
Of evil-boding path of prophecy?

STROPHE IX

Cass. Woe for the marriage-ties, the marriage-
    ties
Of Paris that brought ruin on his friends!
 Woe for my native stream,   1245
 Scamandros, that I loved!
Once on thy banks my maiden youth was reared,
 (Ah, miserable me!)
Now by Cokytos and by Acheron's[1] shores
 I seem too likely soon to utter song   1250
 Of wild, prophetic speech.

STROPHE X

Chorus. What hast thou spoken now
 With utterance all too clear?
Even a boy its gist might understand;
 I to the quick am pierced   1255
 With throe of deadly pain,
Whilst thou thy moaning cries art uttering
 Over thy sore mischance,
 Wondrous for me to hear.

ANTISTROPHE IX

Cass. Woe for the toil and trouble, toil and
    trouble   1260
Of city that is utterly destroyed!
 Woe for the victims slain
 Of herds that roamed the fields,
My father's sacrifice to save his towers!
 No healing charm they brought   1265
To save the city from its present doom:
And I with hot thoughts wild myself shall cast
 Full soon upon the ground.

ANTISTROPHE X

Chorus. This that thou utterest now
 With all before agrees.   1270
Some Power above dooms thee with purpose ill,
 Down-swooping heavily,
 To utter with thy voice
Sorrows of deepest woe, and bringing death.
 And what the end shall be   1275
 Perplexes in the extreme.

[1] Rivers of Hades.

Cass. Nay, now no more from out of maiden
    veils
My oracle shall glance, like bride fresh wed;
But seems as though 'twould rush with speedy gales
In full, clear brightness to the morning dawn;   1280
So that a greater war than this shall surge
Like wave against the sunlight. Now I'll teach
No more in parables. Bear witness ye,
As running with me, that I scent the track
Of evil deeds that long ago were wrought: 1285
For never are they absent from this house,
That choral band which chants in full accord,
Yet no good music; good is not their theme.
And now, as having drunk men's blood, and so
Grown wilder, bolder, see, the revelling band,   1290
Erinnyes of the race, still haunt the halls,
Not easy to dismiss. And so they sing,
Close cleaving to the house, its primal woe,
And vent their loathing in alternate strains
On marriage-bed of brother ruthless found   1295
To that defiler. Miss I now, or hit,
Like archer skilled? or am I seeress false,
A babbler vain that knocks at every door?
Yea, swear beforehand, ere I die, I know
(And not by rumor only) all the sins   1300
Of ancient days that haunt and vex this house.
  Chorus. How could an oath, how firm soe'er
    confirmed,
Bring aught of healing? Lo, I marvel at thee,
That thou, though born far off beyond the sea,
Should'st tell an alien city's tale as clear   1305
As though thyself had stood by all the while.
  Cass. The seer Apollo set me to this task.
  Chorus. Was he a God, so smitten with desire?
  Cass. There was a time when shame restrained
    my speech.
  Chorus. True; they who prosper still are shy
    and coy.   1310
  Cass. He wrestled hard, breathing hot love on
    me.
  Chorus. And were ye one in act whence children
    spring?
  Cass. I promised Loxias, then I broke my vow.
  Chorus. Wast thou e'en then possessed with
    arts divine?
  Cass. E'en then my country's woes I prophesied.
  Chorus. How wast thou then unscathed by
    Loxias' wrath?   1316
  Cass. I for that fault with no man gained belief.
  Chorus. To us, at least, thou seem'st to speak
    the truth.
  Cass. (*again speaking wildly, as in an ecstasy*).
    Ah, woe is me! Woe's me! Oh, ills on ills!
Again the dread pang of true prophet's gift   1320
With preludes of great evil dizzies me.
See ye those children sitting on the house

In fashion like to phantom forms of dreams?
Infants who perished at their own kin's hands,
Their palms filled full with meat of their own
    flesh,   1325
Loom on my sight, the heart and entrails bearing,
(A sorry burden that!) on which of old
Their father fed. And in revenge for this,
I say a lion, dwelling in his lair,
With not a spark of courage, stay-at-home,   1330
Plots 'gainst my master, now he's home returned,
(Yes mine — for still I must the slave's yoke bear;)
And the ship's ruler, Ilion's conqueror,[1]
Knows not what things the tongue of that lewd
    bitch [2]
Has spoken and spun out in welcome smooth,   1335
And, like a secret Atè, will work out
With dire success: thus 'tis she plans: the man
Is murdered by the woman. By what name
Shall I that loathèd monster rightly call?
An Amphisbæna?[3] or a Skylla[4] dwelling   1340
Among the rocks, the sailors' enemy?
Hades' fierce raging mother, breathing out
Against her friends a curse implacable?
Ah, how she raised her cry, (oh, daring one!)
As for the rout of battle, and she feigns   1345
To hail with joy her husband's safe return!
And if thou dost not credit this, what then?
What will be will. Soon, present, pitying me
Thou'lt own I am too true a prophetess.
  Chorus. Thyestes' banquet on his children's
    flesh   1350
I know and shudder at, and fear o'ercomes me,
Hearing not counterfeits of fact, but truths;
Yet in the rest I hear and miss my path.
  Cass. I say thou'lt witness Agamemnon's death.
  Chorus. Hush, wretched woman, close those
    lips of thine!   1355
  Cass. For this my speech no healing God's at
    hand.
  Chorus. True, if it must be; but may God
    avert it!
  Cass. Thou utterest prayers, but others murder
    plot.
  Chorus. And by what man is this dire evil
    wrought?
  Cass. Sure, thou hast seen my bodings all
    amiss.   1360
  Chorus. I see not his device who works the deed.
  Cass. And yet I speak the Hellenic tongue right
    well.

[1] Agamemnon.
[2] Clytæmnestra. Her conduct during Agamemnon's
absence was clear to Cassandra.
[3] A serpent which moved freely either forward or
backward.
[4] A six-headed monster.

Chorus. So does the Pythian, yet her words are
hard.

Cass. (*in another access of frenzy*). Ah me, this
fire!
It comes upon me now!   1365
Ah me, Apollo, wolf-slayer! woe is me!
This biped lioness [1] who takes to bed
A wolf [2] in absence of the noble lion,[3]
Will slay me, wretched me. And, as one
Mixing a poisoned draught, she boasts that she
Will put my price into her cup of wrath,   1371
Sharpening her sword to smite her spouse with
death,
So paying him for bringing me. Oh, why
Do I still wear what all men flout and scorn,
My wand and seeress wreaths around my neck?
Thee, ere myself I die I will destroy: 1376
                    (*Breaks her wand.*)
Perish ye thus (*casting off her wreaths*): I soon
shall follow you:
Make rich another Atè in my place;
Behold Apollo's self is stripping me
Of my divining garments, and that too,   1380
When he has seen me even in this garb
Scorned without cause among my friends and kin,
By foes, with no diversity of mood.
Reviled as vagrant, wandering prophetess,
Poor, wretched, famished, I endured to live: 1385
And now the Seer who me a seeress made
Hath brought me to this lot of deadly doom.
Now for my father's altar there awaits me
A butcher's block, where I am smitten down
By slaughtering stroke, and with hot gush of
blood.   1390
But the Gods will not slight us when we're dead;
Another yet shall come as champion for us,
A son who slays his mother, to avenge
His father; and the exiled wanderer
Far from his home, shall one day come again, 1395
Upon these woes to set the coping-stone:
For the high Gods have sworn a mighty oath,
His father's fall, laid low, shall bring him back.
Why then do I thus groan in this new home,
When, to begin with, Ilion's town I saw   1400
Faring as it did fare, and they who held
That town are gone by judgment of the Gods?
I too will fare as they, and venture death:
So I these gates of Hades now address,
And pray for blow that bringeth death at once,
That so with no fierce spasm, while the blood 1406
Flows in calm death, I then may close mine eyes.
          (*Goes toward the door of the palace.*)
Chorus. O thou most wretched, yet again most
wise:
Long hast thou spoken, lady, but if well

[1] Clytæmnestra. [2] Ægisthos. [3] Agamemnon.

Thou know'st thy doom, why to the altar go'st
thou,   1410
Like heifer driven of God, so confidently?
Cass. For me, my friends, there is no time to
'scape.
Chorus. Yea; but he gains in time who comes
the last.
Cass. The day is come: small gain for me in
flight.
Chorus. Know then thou sufferest with a heart
full brave.   1415
Cass. Such words as these the happy never hear.
Chorus. Yet mortal man may welcome noble
death.
Cass. (*shrinking back from opening the door*).
Woe's me for thee and thy brave sons, my
father!
Chorus. What cometh now? What fear op-
presseth thee?
Cass. (*again going to the door and then shuddering
in another burst of frenzy*). Fie on't, fie!
Chorus. Whence comes this "Fie?" unless from
mind that loathes?   1421
Cass. The house is tainted with the scent of death.
Chorus. How so? This smells of victims on the
hearth.
Cass. Nay, it is like the blast from out a grave.
Chorus. No Syrian [1] ritual tell'st thou for our
house.   1425
Cass. Well then I go, and e'en within will wail
My fate and Agamemnon's. And for me,
Enough of life. Ah, friends! Ah! not for nought
I shrink in fear, as bird shrinks from the brake.
When I am dead do ye this witness bear,   1430
When in revenge for me, a woman, Death
A woman smites, and man shall fall for man
In evil wedlock wed. This friendly office,
As one about to die, I pray you do me.
Chorus. Thy doom foretold, poor sufferer,
moves my pity.   1435
Cass. I fain would speak once more, yet not to
wail
Mine own death-song; but to the Sun I pray,
To his last rays, that my avengers wreak
Upon my hated murderers judgment due
For me, who die a slave's death, easy prey   1440
Ah, life of man! when most it prospereth,
It is but limned in outline; and when brought
To low estate, then doth the sponge, full soaked,
Wipe out the picture with its frequent touch:
And this I count more piteous e'en than that. 1445
          (*Passes through the door into the palace.*)
Chorus. 'Tis true of all men that they never set
A limit to good fortune; none doth say,
     As bidding it depart,

[1] Attractive or luxurious.

And warding it from palaces of pride,
  "Enter thou here no more."   1450
To this our lord the Blest Ones gave to take
  Priam's city; and he comes
Safe to his home and honored by the Gods;
  But if he now shall pay
The forfeit of blood-guiltiness of old,   1455
And, dying, so work out for those who died,
By his own death another penalty,
  Who then of mortal men,
  Hearing such things as this,
  Can boast that he was born   1460
With fate from evil free?
    Agam. (*from within*). Ah, me! I am struck
        down with deadly stroke.
    Chorus. Hush! who cries out with deadly stroke
        sore smitten?
    Agam. Ah me, again! struck down a second
        time!
                                    (*Dies.*)
    Chorus. By the king's groans I judge the deed
        is done;   1465
But let us now confer for counsels safe.
    Chorus a. I give you my advice to summon here,
Here to the palace, all the citizens.
    Chorus b. I think it best to rush at once on
        them,
And take them in the act with sword yet wet.   1470
    Chorus c. And I too give like counsel, and I vote
For deed of some kind. 'Tis no time to pause.
    Chorus d. Who will see, may. — They but the
        prelude work
Of tyranny usurped o'er all the State.
    Chorus e. Yes, we are slow, but they who
        trample down   1475
The thought of hesitation slumber not.
    Chorus f. I know not what advice to find or
        speak:
He who can act knows how to counsel too.
    Chorus g. I too think with thee; for I have no
        hope
With words to raise the dead again to life.   1480
    Chorus h. What! Shall we drag our life on and
        submit
To these usurpers that defile the house?
    Chorus i. Nay, that we cannot bear: To die
        were better;
For death is gentler far than tyranny.
    Chorus k. Shall we upon this evidence of groans
Guess, as divining that our lord is dead?   1486
    Chorus l. When we know clearly, then should we
        discuss:
To guess is one thing, and to know another.
    Chorus. So vote I too, and on the winning side,
Taking the votes all round that we should learn
How he, the son of Atreus, fareth now.   1491

(*Enter* CLYTÆMNESTRA *from the palace, in robes
  with stains of blood, followed by soldiers and at-
  tendants. The open doors show the corpses of*
  AGAMEMNON *and* CASSANDRA, *the former lying
  in a silvered bath.*)
    CLYTÆM. Though many words before to suit
        the time
Were spoken, now I shall not be ashamed
The contrary to utter: How could one
By open show of enmity to foes   1495
Who seemed as friends, fence in the snares of death
Too high to be o'erleapt? But as for me,
Not without forethought for this long time past,
This conflict comes to me from triumph old
Of his, though slowly wrought. I stand where I
Did smite him down, with all my task well done.
So did I it, (the deed deny I not,)   1502
That he could nor avert his doom nor flee:
I cast around him drag-net as for fish,
With not one outlet, evil wealth of robe: 1505
And twice I smote him, and with two deep groans
He dropped his limbs: And when he thus fell down
I gave him yet a third, thank-offering true
To Hades of the dark, who guards the dead.
So fallen, he gasps out his struggling soul,   1510
And breathing forth a sharp, quick gush of blood,
He showers dark drops of gory rain on me,
Who no less joy felt in them than the corn,
When the blade bears, in glad shower given of God.
Since this is so, ye Argive elders here,   1515
Ye, as ye will, may hail the deed, but I
Boast of it. And were't fitting now to pour
Libation o'er the dead, 'twere justly done,
Yea more than justly; such a goblet full
Of ills hath he filled up with curses dire   1520
At home, and now has come to drain it off.
    Chorus. We marvel at the boldness of thy tongue
Who o'er thy husband's corpse speak'st vaunt
    like this.
    Clytæm. Ye test me as a woman weak of mind;
But I with dauntless heart to you that know 1525
Say, and whether thou dost praise or blame,
Is all alike: — here Agamemnon lies,
My husband, now a corpse, of this right hand,
As artist just, the handiwork: so stands it.

STROPHE

    Chorus. What evil thing, O Queen, or reared
        on earth,   1530
Or draught from salt sea-wave
Hast thou fed on, to bring
Such incense on thyself,
A people's loud-voiced curse?
'Twas thou did'st sentence him,   1535
'Twas thou did'st strike him down;

But thou shalt exiled be,
Hated with strong hate of the citizens.
   Clytæm. Ha! now on me thou lay'st the exile's
     doom.
My subjects' hate, and people's loud-voiced curse,
Though ne'er did'st thou oppose my husband
     there,   1541
Who, with no more regard than had been due
To a brute's death, although he called his own
Full many a fleecy sheep in pastures bred,
Yet sacrificed his child,[1] the dear-loved fruit   1545
Of all my travail-pangs, to be a charm
Against the winds of Thrakia. Shouldst thou not
Have banished him from out this land of ours,
As meed for all his crimes? Yet hearing now
My deeds, thou art a judge full stern. But I   1550
Tell thee to speak thy threats, as knowing well
I am prepared that thou on equal terms
Should'st rule, if thou dost conquer. But if God
Should otherwise decree, then thou shalt learn,
Late though it be, the lesson to be wise.   1555

ANTISTROPHE

   Chorus. Yea, thou art stout of heart, and
     speak'st big words;
And maddened is thy soul
As by a murderous hate;
And still upon thy brow
Is seen, not yet avenged,   1560
The stain of blood-spot foul;
And yet it needs must be,
One day thou, reft of friends,
Shalt pay the penalty of blow for blow.
   Clytæm. Now hear thou too my oaths of solemn
     dread: 1565
By my accomplished vengeance for my child,
By Atè and Erinnys, unto whom
I slew him as a victim, I look not
That fear should come beneath this roof of mine,
So long as on my hearth Ægisthos kindles   1570
The flaming fire, as well disposed to me
As he hath been aforetime. He to us
Is no slight shield of stoutest confidence.
There lies he (*pointing to the corpse of* AGAMEMNON),
     one who foully wronged his wife,
The darling of the Chryseïds[2] at Troïa;   1575
And there (*pointing to* CASSANDRA) this captive
     slave, this auguress,

[1] Iphigenia. See Euripides, *Iphigenia Among the Tauri.*
[2] Chryseïs, a captive taken by the Greeks, had fallen
to the lot of Agamemnon, but Apollo caused her to be
returned to her father. Agamemnon then demanded
Briseïs, a maiden who had been awarded to Achilles.
Clytæmnestra recalls this episode, and the bringing
home of Cassandra as justification for her act of murder.

His concubine, this seeress trustworthy,
Who shared his bed, and yet was as well known
To the sailors as their benches! . . . They have fared
Not otherwise than they deserved: for he   1580
Lies as you see. And she who, like a swan,
Has chanted out her last and dying song,
Lies close to him she loved, and so has brought
The zest of a new pleasure to my bed.

STROPHE I

   Chorus. Ah me, would death might come   1585
Quickly, with no sharp throe of agony,
   Nor long bed-ridden pain,
   Bringing the endless sleep;
Since he, the watchman most benign of all,
   Hath now been smitten low,   1590
And by a woman's means hath much endured,
And at a woman's hand hath lost his life!

STROPHE II

Alas! alas! O Helen, evil-souled,
   Who, though but one, hast slain
Many, yea, very many lives at Troïa.   1595

. . . .

STROPHE III

But now for blood that may not be washed out
   Thou hast to full bloom brought
A deed of guilt for every memorable,
   For strife was in the house,
   Wrought out in fullest strength,   1600
Woe for a husband's life.

STROPHE IV

   Clytæm. Nay, pray not thou for destiny of death,
   Oppressed with what thou see'st;
Nor turn thou against Helena thy wrath,
   As though she murderess were,   1605
And, though but one, had many Danaï's souls
Brought low in death, and wrought o'erwhelming
     woe.

ANTISTROPHE I

   Chorus. O Power that dost attack
Our palace and the two Tantalidæ,[1]
   And dost through women wield   1610
   A might that grieves my heart!
And o'er the body, like a raven foul,
   Against all laws of right,
Standing, she boasteth in her pride of heart
That she can chant her pæan hymn of praise.   1615

ANTISTROPHE IV

   Clytæm. Now thou dost guide aright thy speech
     and thought,
[1] Agamemnon was the grandson of Tantalus.

Invoking that dread Power,
The thrice-gorged evil genius of this house;
  For he it is who feeds
In the heart's depth the raging lust of blood: 1620
Ere the old wound is healed, new bloodshed comes.

STROPHE V

Chorus. Yes, of a Power thou tell'st
Mighty and very wrathful to this house;
Ah me! ah me! an evil tale enough
    Of baleful chance of doom,   1625
    Insatiable of ill:
Yet, ah! it is through Zeus,
The all-appointing and all-working One;
    For what with mortal men
    Is wrought apart from Zeus?   1630
What of all this is not by God decreed?

STROPHE VI

Ah me! ah me!
My king, my king, how shall I weep for thee?
What shall I speak from heart that truly loves?
And now thou liest there, breathing out thy life,
    In impious deed of death,
    In this fell spider's web, —   1636

STROPHE VII

(Yes, woe is me! woe, woe!
Woe for this couch of thine dishonorable!) —
    Slain by a subtle death,   1640
With sword two-edged which her right hand did
    wield.

STROPHE VIII

Clytæm. Thou speak'st big words, as if the deed
    were mine;
    Yet think thou not of me,
    As Agamemnon's spouse;
But in the semblance of this dead man's wife, 1645
The old and keen Avenger of the house
Of Atreus, that cruel banqueter of old,
    Hath wrought out vengeance full
    On him who lieth here,
    And full-grown victim slain   1650
Over the younger victims of the past.

ANTISTROPHE V

Chorus. That thou art guiltless found
Of this foul murder who will witness bear?
How can it be so, how?   And yet, perchance,
    As helper to the deed,   1655
    Might come the avenging Fiend
    Of that ancestral time;
And in this rush of murders of near kin
    Dark Ares presses on,
    Where he will vengeance work   1660
For clotted gore of children slain as food.

ANTISTROPHE VI

Ah me! ah me!
My king, my king, how shall I weep for thee?
What shall I speak from heart that truly loves?
And now thou liest there, breathing out thy life,
    In impious deed of death,   1666
    In this fell spider's web, —

ANTISTROPHE VII

(Yes, woe is me! woe, woe!
Woe for this couch of thine dishonorable!) —
    Slain by a subtle death,   1670
With sword two-edged which her right hand did
    wield.

ANTISTROPHE VIII

Clytæm. Nay, not dishonorable
    His death doth seem to me:
    Did he not work a doom,
    In this our house with guile?   1675
Mine own dear child, begotten of this man,
Iphigeneia, wept with many a tear,
He slew; now slain himself in recompense,
    Let him not boast in Hell,
    Since he the forfeit pays,   1680
    Pierced by the sword in death,
For all the evil that his hand began.

STROPHE IX

Chorus. I stand perplexed in soul, deprived of
    power
    Of quick and ready thought,
    Where now to turn, since thus   1685
    Our home is falling low.
I shrink in fear from the fierce pelting storm
Of blood that shakes the basement of the house:
    No more it rains in drops:
And for another deed of mischief dire,   1690
    Fate whets the righteous doom
    On other whetstones still.

ANTISTROPHE IX

O Earth! O Earth! Oh, would thou had'st re-
    ceived me,
    Ere I saw him on couch
Of bath with silvered walls thus stretched in death!
Who now will bury him, who wail? Wilt thou, 1696
When thou hast slain thy husband, have the heart
To mourn his death, and for thy monstrous deeds
Do graceless grace?   And who will chant the dirge
    With tears in truth of heart,   1700
    Over our godlike chief?

STROPHE X

Clytæm. It is not thine to speak;
    'Twas at our hands he fell,

Yea, he fell low in death,
And we will bury him, 1705
Not with the bitter tears of those who weep
As inmates of the house;
But she, his child, Iphigeneia, there
Shall meet her father, and with greeting kind,
E'en as is fit, by that swift-flowing ford, 1710
Dark stream of bitter woes,
Shall clasp him in her arms,
And give a daughter's kiss.

ANTISTROPHE X

Chorus. Lo! still reproach upon reproach doth
come;
Hard are these things to judge: 1715
The spoiler still is spoiled,
The slayer pays his debt;
Yea, while Zeus liveth through the ages, this
Lives also, that the doer dree his weird; [1]
For this is law fast fixed. 1720
Who now can drive from out the kingly house
The brood of curses dark?
The race to Atè cleaves.

ANTISTROPHE XI

Clytæm. Yes, thou hast touched with truth
That word oracular; 1725
But I for my part wish,
(Binding with strongest oath
The evil dæmon of the Pleisthenids,) [2]
Though hard it be to bear,
To rest content with this our present lot; 1730
And, for the future, that he go to vex
Another race with homicidal deaths.
Lo! 'tis enough for me,
Though small my share of wealth,
At last to have freed my house 1735
From madness that sets each man's hand 'gainst
each.

(*Enter* ÆGISTHOS)

Ægisth. Hail, kindly light of day that vengeance
brings!
Now I can say the Gods on high look down,
Avenging men, upon the woes of earth,
Since lying in the robes the Erinnyes wove 1740
I see this man, right welcome sight to me,
Paying for deeds his father's hand had wrought.
Atreus, our country's ruler, this man's father
Drove out my sire Thyestes, his own brother,
(To tell the whole truth,) quarrelling for rule, 1745
An exile from his country and his home.
And coming back a suppliant on the hearth,
The poor Thyestes found a lot secure,

[1] Suffer his fate.
[2] Pleisthenes, an ancestor of the race.

Nor did he, dying, stain the soil with blood,
There in his home. But this man's godless sire, 1750
Atreus, more prompt than kindly in his deeds,
On plea of keeping festal day with cheer,
To my sire banquet gave of children's flesh,
His own. The feet and finger-tips of hands
He, sitting at the top, apart concealed; 1755
And straight the other, in his blindness taking
The parts that could not be discerned, did eat
A meal which, as thou see'st, perdition works
For all his kin. And learning afterwards
The deed of dread, he groaned and backward fell,
Vomits the feast of blood, and imprecates 1761
On Pelop's sons a doom intolerable,
And makes the o'erturning of the festive board,
With fullest justice, as a general curse,
That so might fall the race of Pleisthenes. 1765
And now thou see'st how here accordingly
This man lies fallen; I, of fullest right,
The weaver of the plot of murderous doom.
For me, a babe in swaddling-clothes, he banished
With my poor father me, his thirteenth child; 1770
And Vengeance brought me back, of full age grown:
And e'en far off I wrought against this man,
And planned the whole scheme of this dark device.
And so e'en death were now right good for me,
Seeing him into the nets of Vengeance fallen. 1775
Chorus. I honor not this arrogance in guilt,
Ægisthos. Thou confessest thou hast slain
Of thy free will our chieftain here, — that thou
Alone did'st plot this murder lamentable;
Be sure, I say, thy head shall not escape 1780
The righteous curse a people hurls with stones.
Ægisth. Dost thou say this, though seated on
the bench
Of lowest oarsmen, while the upper row
Commands the ship? But thou shalt find, though
old,
How hard it is at such an age to learn, 1785
When the word is, "keep temper." But a prison
And fasting pains are admirably apt,
As prophet-healers even for old age.
Dost see, and not see this? Against the pricks
Kick not, lest thou perchance should'st smart for
it.
Chorus. Thou, thou, O Queen, when thy lord
came from war, 1791
While keeping house, thy husband's bed defiling,
Did'st scheme this death for this our hero-chief.
Ægisth. These words of thine shall parents
prove of tears:
But this thy tongue is Orpheus' opposite; 1795
He with his voice led all things on for joy,
But thou, provoking with thy childish cries,
Shalt now be led; and then, being kept in check,
Thou shalt appear in somewhat gentler mood.

Chorus. As though thou should'st o'er Argives
          ruler be,   1800
Who even when thou plotted'st this man's death
Did'st lack good heart to do the deed thyself?

Ægisth. E'en so; to work this fraud was clearly
          part
Fit for a woman. I was foe, of old
Suspected. But now will I with his wealth   1805
See whether I his subjects may command,
And him who will not hearken I will yoke
In heavy harness as a full-fed colt,
Nowise as trace-horse; but sharp hunger joined
With darksome dungeon shall behold him tamed.

Chorus. Why did'st not thou then, coward as
          thou art,   1811
Thyself destroy him? but a woman with thee,
Pollution to our land and our land's Gods,
She slew him. Does Orestes see the light,
Perchance, that he, brought back by Fortune's
          grace,   1815
May for both these prove slayer strong to smite?

Ægisth. Well, since thou think'st to act, not
          merely talk,
Thou shalt know clearly....

          (*Calling his Guards from the palace*)
On then, my troops, the time for deeds is come.

Chorus. On then, let each man grasp his sword
          in hand.   1820

Ægisth. With sword in hand, I too shrink not
          from death.

Chorus. Thou talkest of thy death; we hail the
          word;
And make our own the fortune it implies.

Clytæm. Nay, let us not do other evil deeds,
Thou dearest of all friends. An ill-starred harvest
It is to have reaped so many. Enough of woe: 1826
Let no more blood be shed: Go thou — (*to the
          Chorus*) — go ye,
Ye aged sires, to your allotted homes,
Ere ye do aught amiss and dree your weird:
This that we have done ought to have sufficed;
But should it prove we've had enough of ills, 1831
We will accept it gladly, stricken low
In evil doom by heavy hand of God.
This is a woman's counsel, if there be
That deigns to hear it.   1835

Ægisth.   But that these should fling
The blossoms of their idle speech at me,
And utter words like these, so tempting Fate,
And fail of counsel wise, and flout their master....!

Chorus. It suits not Argives on the vile to
          fawn.   1840

Ægisth. Be sure, hereafter I will hunt thee down.

Chorus. Not so, if God should guide Orestes
          back.

Ægisth. Right well I know how exiles feed on
          hopes.

Chorus. Prosper, wax fat, do foul wrong — 'tis
          thy day.

Ægisth. Know thou shalt pay full price for this
          thy folly.   1845

Chorus. Be bold, and boast, like cock beside
          his mate.

Clytæm. Nay, care not thou for these vain
          howlings; I
And thou together, ruling o'er the house,
Will settle all things rightly.   (*Exeunt.*)

Sophocles · 496–406 B.C.

Born in 496 B.C., Sophocles was a boy fifteen or sixteen years old when the army returned in
triumph to Athens after the battle of Salamis. He is said to have been chosen leader of the chorus
of boys that went out of the city, chanting a hymn to welcome the returning soldiers. Sophocles
himself became a soldier and at fifty-six served as a general under Pericles in the Samian War,
an honor bestowed only on distinguished citizens of Athens. The fifth century B.C. was for the city-
state a time of growth, of imperialistic expansion of power throughout Greece and in Sicily and
Asia. It was also a time when Pericles, the dominant spirit of the century, fostered self-government,
improved the laws, and cultivated the various arts. When Sophocles was in his late forties, the
Parthenon was started and Phidias, the famous sculptor, was called upon to decorate it. Other
great men of the century, in addition to the dramatists, were Anaxagoras the philosopher and
Thucydides the statesman and historian.

Of over a hundred plays Sophocles is known to have written, only seven are now extant; of these seven the three best known are *Antigone, Electra*, and *Œdipus the King*. Two advances in dramatic technique are credited to Sophocles: the addition of a third actor (Æschylus had added the second) and the introduction of certain improvements in the decoration and arrangement of the stage itself. Among the qualities which made Sophocles a great tragic poet were his high idealism, his understanding and presentation of human nature, his ability to seize upon the essential tragic situation, and his skillful handling of plot.

SUGGESTED REFERENCES: F. J. H. Letters, *The Life and Work of Sophocles* (1953); H. D. F. Kitto, *Sophocles, Dramatist and Philosopher* (1958); C. M. Bowra, *Sophoclean Tragedy* (2nd ed., 1964).

Antigone

The play which follows is one of several presenting a chronicle of traditions centering on the house of Thebes. Œdipus, King of Thebes, has died at Colonus, but his two daughters and his son, Eteocles, continued to live in the palace of their father. However, when a second son, Polyneices, made war against Thebes to regain the kingdom, both Eteocles and Polyneices were killed, each by the other. Creon, an uncle, became king and insisted that Polyneices, who was regarded as the trouble-maker, should, contrary both to custom and divine law, be left unburied. Antigone, a sister, flouted the order of Creon and gave Polyneices hurried burial, an act which affords the play its tragic theme.

Creon. And thou did'st dare to disobey these laws?
Antigone. Yes, for it was not Zeus who gave them forth,
Nor justice, dwelling with the gods below,
Who traced these laws for all the sons of men;
Nor did I deem thy edicts strong enough,
That thou, a mortal man, should'st overpass
The unwritten laws of God that know not change.
They are not of to-day nor yesterday,
But live forever, nor can man assign
When first they sprang to being.

The play is remarkable for its concern for the laws of nature, of man, of divinity.

Some of the qualities which reveal Sophocles as a writer of classical temper are his compression, his restraint, his dignified language, his highly unified plot structure. The *Antigone* is typical in its presentation of character in a moment of great crisis dictated by destiny. The precision and polish of language, the restrained emotions of Antigone when she tries to make Creon realize her sense of loss at her brother's death are unmistakably classical:

I answer, had I lost a husband dear,
I might have had another; other sons
By other spouse, if one were lost to me;
But when my father and my mother sleep
In Hades, then no brother more can come.

A romantic would have run riot in presenting this emotion; a realist would have analyzed Antigone's mood and set it down more coldly, perhaps even skeptically.

The translation by E. H. Plumptre is reproduced through the courtesy of G. P. Putnam's Sons.

Dramatis Personæ

CREON, *king of Thebes.*
HÆMON, *son of Creon.*
TEIRESIAS, *a seer.*
GUARD.
FIRST MESSENGER.
SECOND MESSENGER.
EURYDICE, *wife of Creon.*
ANTIGONE, } *daughters of Œdipus.*
ISMENE, }
CHORUS OF THEBAN ELDERS.

SCENE: *Thebes, in front of the Palace. Early morning. Hills in the distance on the left; on the right the city.*

(*Enter* ANTIGONE *and* ISMENE.)

Antig. Ismene, mine own sister, darling one!
Is there, of ills that sprang from Œdipus,
One left that Zeus will fail to bring on us,
The two who yet remain? Nought is there sad,
Nought full of sorrow, steeped in sin or shame, 5
But I have seen it in thy woes and mine.
And now, what new decree is this they tell,
Our captain has enjoined on all the State?
Know'st thou? Hast heard? Or are they hid from thee,
The ills that come from foes upon our friends? 10
Isme. No tidings of our friends, Antigone,
Pleasant or painful, since that hour have come,
When we, two sisters, lost our brothers twain,

In one day dying by a twofold blow.
And since in this last night the Argive[1] host   15
Has left the field, I nothing further know,
Nor brightening fortune, nor increasing gloom.
    Antig. That knew I well, and therefore sent for
      thee
Beyond the gates, that thou may'st hear alone.
    Isme. What meanest thou? It is but all too
      clear   20
Thou broodest darkly o'er some tale of woe.
    Antig. And does not Creon treat our brothers
      twain
One with the rites of burial, one with shame?
Eteocles, so say they, he interred
Fitly, with wonted rites, as one held meet   25
To pass with honor to the dead below.
But for the corpse of Polyneices, slain
So piteously, they say, he has proclaimed
To all the citizens, that none should give
His body burial, or bewail his fate,   30
But leave it still unwept, unsepulchered,
A prize full rich for birds that scent afar
Their sweet repast. So Creon bids, they say,
Creon the good, commanding thee and me, —
Yes, me, I say, — and now is coming here,   35
To make it clear to those who know it not,
And counts the matter not a trivial thing;
But whoso does the things that he forbids,
For him there waits within the city's walls
The death of stoning. Thus, then, stands thy
    case;   40
And quickly thou wilt show, if thou art born
Of noble nature, or degenerate liv'st,
Base child of honored parents.
    Isme.   How could I,
O daring in thy mood, in this our plight,
Or breaking law or keeping, aught avail?   45
    Antig. Wilt thou with me share risk and toil?
      Look to it.
    Isme. What risk is this? What purpose fills thy
      mind?
    Antig. Wilt thou help this my hand to list the
      dead?
    Isme. Mean'st thou to bury him, when law for-
      bids?
    Antig. He is my brother; yes, and thine, though
      thou   50
Would'st fain he were not. I desert him not.
    Isme. O daring one, when Creon bids thee not?
    Antig. He has no right to keep me from mine
      own.
    Isme. Ah me! remember, sister, how our sire
Perished, with hate o'erwhelmed and infamy,   55
From evils that himself did bring to light,

[1] With Polyneices, in the attack against Thebes,
were forces from the city of Argos.

With his own hand himself of eyes bereaving,
And how his wife and mother, both in one,
With twisted cordage, cast away her life;
And thirdly, how our brothers in one day   60
In suicidal conflict wrought the doom,
Each of the other. And we twain are left;
And think, how much more wretchedly than all
We twain shall perish, if, against the law,
We brave our sovereign's edict and his power.   65
This first we need remember, we were born
Women; as such, not made to strive with men.
And next, that they who reign surpass in strength,
And we must bow to this, and worse than this.
I then, entreating those that dwell below,   70
To judge me leniently, as forced to yield,
Will hearken to our rulers. Over-zeal
That still will meddle, little wisdom shows.
    Antig. I will not ask thee, r r though thou
      should'st wish
To do it, should'st thou join with my consent.   75
Do what thou wilt, I go to bury him;
And good it were, in doing this, to die.
Loved I shall be with him whom I have loved,
Guilty of holiest crime. More time is mine
In which to share the favor of the dead,   80
Than that of those who live; for I shall rest
For ever there. But thou, if thus thou please,
Count as dishonored what the Gods approve.
    Isme. I do them no dishonor, but I find
Myself too weak to war against the State.   85
    Antig. Make what excuse thou wilt, I go to rear
A grave above the brother whom I love.
    Isme. Ah, wretched me! how much I fear for
      thee!
    Antig. Fear not for me. Thine own fate raise
      to safety.
    Isme. At any rate, disclose this deed to none;   90
Keep it close hidden: I will hide it too.
    Antig. Speak out! I bid thee. Silent, thou wilt be
More hateful to me, if thou fail to tell
My deed to all men.
    Isme.   Fiery is thy mood,   94
Although thy deeds the very blood might chill.
    Antig. I know I please the souls I ought to
      please.
    Isme. Yes, if thou canst; thou seek'st the im-
      possible.
    Antig. When strength shall fail me, then I'll
      cease to strive.
    Isme. We should not hunt the impossible at all.
    Antig. If thou speak thus, my hatred wilt thou
      gain,   100
And rightly wilt be hated of the dead.
Leave me and my ill counsel to endure
This dreadful doom. I shall not suffer aught
So evil as a death dishonorable.   104

Isme. Go then, if so thou wilt. Of this be sure,
Wild as thou art, thy friends must love thee still.
(Exeunt.)

(*Enter* CHORUS OF THEBAN ELDERS.)

STROPHE I

Chorus. O light of yon bright sun,[1]
Fairest of all that ever shone on Thebes,
Thebes with her seven high gates,
Thou didst appear that day,   110
Eye of the golden dawn,
O'er Dircé's[2] streams advancing,
Driving with quickened curb,
In haste of headlong flight,
The warrior who, in panoply of proof,   115
From Argos came, with shield of glittering white;
Whom Polyneices brought,
Roused by the strife of tongues
Against our fatherland,
As eagle shrieking shrill,   120
He hovered o'er our land,
With snow-white wing bedecked,
Begirt with myriad arms,
And flowing horsehair crests.

ANTISTROPHE I

He stood above our towers,   125
Encircling, with his spears all blood-bestained,
The portals of our gates;
He went, before he filled
His jaws with blood of men,
Ere the pine-fed Hephæstus[3]   130
Had seized our crown of towers.
So loud the battle din
That Ares[4] loves was raised around his rear,
A conflict hard e'en for his dragon foe.
For breath of haughty speech   135
Zeus hateth evermore;
And seeing them advance,
With mighty rushing stream,
And clang of golden arms,
With brandished fire he hurls   140
One who rushed eagerly
From topmost battlement
To shout out, "Victory!"

STROPHE II

Crashing to earth he fell,
Down-smitten, with his torch,   145
Who came, with madman's haste,

[1] According to the convention of the time, the play
begins in the early morning. This chorus, then, appropriately heralds the rising sun.
[2] "Dircé's streams," near Thebes.
[3] Or Vulcan, the god of fire.
[4] Mars, god of war.

Drunken, with frenzied soul,
And swept o'er us with blasts,
The whirlwind blasts of hate.
Thus on one side they fare,   150
And Ares great, like war-horse in his strength,
Smiting now here, now there,
Brought each his several fate.
For seven chief warriors at the seven gates met,
Equals with equals matched,   155
To Zeus, the Lord of War,
Left tribute, arms of bronze;
All but the hateful ones,
Who, from one father and mother sprung,
Stood wielding, hand to hand,   160
Their two victorious spears,
And had their doom of death as common lot.

ANTISTROPHE II

But now, since Victory,
Of mightiest name, hath come
To Thebes, of chariots proud,   165
Joying and giving joy,
After these wars just past,
Learn ye forgetfulness,
And all night long, with dance and voice of hymns,
Let us go round in state   170
To all the shrines of Gods,
While Bacchus, making Thebes resound with
    dance,
Begins the strain of joy.
But, lo! our country's king,
Creon, Menœkeus' son,   175
New ruler, by new change,
And providence of God,
Comes to us steering on some new device;
For, lo! he hath convened,
By herald's loud command,   180
This council of the elders of our land.

(*Enter* CREON.)

Creon. My friends, for what concerns our com-
    monwealth,
The Gods who vexed it with the billowing storms
Have righted it again; and I have sent,
By special summons, calling you to come   185
Apart from all the others. This, in part,
As knowing ye did all along uphold
The might of Laius'[1] throne, in part again,
Because when Œdipus our country ruled,
And, when he perished, then towards his sons   190
Ye still were faithful in your steadfast mind.
And since they fell, as by a double death,
Both on the selfsame day with murderous blow,
Smiting and being smitten, now I hold
Their thrones and all their power of sov'reignty
    [1] Father of Œdipus.

By nearness of my kindred to the dead. 196
And hard it is to learn what each man is,
In heart and mind and judgment, till he gain
Experience in princedom and in laws.
For me, whoe'er is called to guide a State, 200
And does not catch at counsels wise and good,
But holds his peace through any fear of man,
I deem him basest of all men that are,
And so have deemed long since; and whosoe'er
As worthier than his country counts his friend,
I utterly despise him. I myself, 206
Zeus be my witness, who beholdeth all,
Would not keep silence, seeing danger come,
Instead of safety, to my subjects true.
Nor could I take as friend my country's foe; 210
For this I know, that there our safety lies,
And sailing while the good ship holds her course,
We gather friends around us. By these rules
And such as these do I maintain the State.
And now I come, with edicts, close allied 215
To these in spirit, for my citizens,
Concerning those two sons of Œdipus.
Eteocles, who died in deeds of might
Illustrious, fighting for our fatherland,
To honor him with sepulture, all rites 220
Duly performed that to the noblest dead
Of right belong. Not so his brother; him
I speak of, Polyneices, who, returned
From exile, sought with fire to desolate
His father's city and the shrines of Gods, 225
Yes, sought to glut his rage with blood of men,
And lead them captives to the bondslave's doom;
Him I decree that none shall dare entomb,
That none shall utter wail or loud lament,
But leave his corpse unburied, by the dogs 230
And vultures mangled, foul to look upon.
Such is my purpose. Ne'er, if I can help,
Shall the vile have more honor than the just;
But whoso shows himself my country's friend,
Living or dead, from me shall honor gain. 235
Chorus. This is thy pleasure, O Menœkeus' son,
For him who hated, him who loved our State;
And thou hast power to make what laws thou wilt,
Both for the dead and all for us who live.
Creon. Be ye then guardians of the things I
speak. 240
Chorus. Commit this task to one of younger
years.
Creon. Nay, watchmen are appointed for the
corpse.
Chorus. What other task then dost thou lay on
us?
Creon. Not to consent with those that disobey.
Chorus. None are so foolish as to seek for death.
Creon. Yet that shall be the doom; but love of
gain 246

Hath oft with false hopes lured men to their
death.

(Enter GUARD.)

Guard. I will not say, O king, that I have come
Panting with speed, and plying nimble feet,
For I had many halting-points of thought, 250
Backwards and forwards turning, round and round:
For now my mind would give me sage advice;
"Poor wretch, why go where thou must bear the
blame?
Or wilt thou tarry, fool? Shall Creon know
These things from others? How wilt thou 'scape
grief?" 255
Revolving thus, I came in haste, yet slow,
And thus a short way finds itself prolonged;
But, last of all, to come to thee prevailed.
And though I tell of nought, yet I will speak;
For this one hope I cling to, might and main, 260
That I shall suffer nought but destiny.
Creon. What is it then that causes such dismay?
Guard. First, for mine own share in it, this I say,
The deed I did not, do not know who did,
Nor should I rightly come to ill for it. 265
Creon. Thou feel'st thy way and fencest up thy
deed
All round and round. 'Twould seem thou hast
some news.
Guard. Yea, news of fear engenders long delay.
Creon. Wilt thou not speak, and then depart in
peace?
Guard. Well, speak I will. The corpse ... Some
one has been 270
But now and buried it, a little dust
O'er the skin scattering, with the wonted rites.
Creon. What say'st thou? What man dared
this deed of guilt?
Guard. I know not. Neither was there stroke
of axe,
Nor earth cast up by mattock. All the soil 275
Was dry and hard, no track of chariot wheel;
But he who did it went and left no sign.
And when the first day-watchman showed it us,
The sight caused wonder and sore grief to all;
For he had disappeared: no tomb indeed 280
Was over him, but dust all lightly strown,
As by some hand that shunned defiling guilt;
And no sign was there of wild beast or dog
Having come and torn him. Evil words arose
Among us, guard to guard imputing blame, 285
Which might have come to blows, and none was
there
To check its course, for each to each appeared
The man whose hand had done it. Yet not one
Had it brought home, but each disclaimed all
knowledge;

And we were ready in our hands to take 290
Bars of hot iron, and to walk through fire,
And call the Gods to witness none of us
Were privy to his schemes who planned the deed,
Nor his who wrought it. Then at last, when
  nought
Was gained by all our searching, some one speaks,
Who made us bend our gaze upon the ground 296
In fear and trembling: for we neither saw
How to oppose it, nor, accepting it,
How we might prosper in it. And his speech
Was this, that all our tale should go to thee, 300
Not hushed up anywise. This gained the day;
And me, ill-starred, the lot condemns to win
This precious prize. So here I come to thee
Against my will; and surely do I trow
Thou dost not wish to see me. Still 'tis true 305
That no man loves the messenger of ill.
  Chorus. For me, my prince, my mind some time
    has thought
If this perchance has some divine intent.
  Creon. Cease then, before thou fillest me with
    wrath,
Lest thou be found, though full of years, a fool.
For what thou say'st is most intolerable, 311
That for this corpse the providence of Gods
Has any care. What! have they buried him,
As to their patron paying honors high,
Who came to waste their columned shrines with
  fire, 315
To desecrate their offerings and their lands,
And all their wonted customs? Dost thou see
The Gods approving men of evil deeds?
It is not so; but men of rebel mood,
Lifting their head in secret long ago, 320
Still murmured thus against me. Never yet
Had they their neck beneath the yoke, content
To bear it with submission. They, I know,
Have bribed these men to let the deed be done.
No thing in use by man, for power of ill, 325
Can equal money. This lays cities low,
This drives men forth from quiet dwelling-place,
This warps and changes minds of worthiest stamp,
To turn to deeds of baseness, teaching men
All shifts of cunning, and to know the guilt 330
Of every impious deed. But they who, hired,
Have wrought this crime, have labored to their
  cost,
Or soon or late to pay the penalty.
But if Zeus still claims any awe from me,
Know this, and with an oath I tell it thee, 335
Unless ye find the very man whose hand
Has wrought this burial, and before mine eyes
Present him captive, death shall not suffice,
Till first, hung up still living, ye shall show
The story of this outrage, that henceforth, 340

Knowing what gain is lawful, ye may grasp
At that, and learn it is not meet to love
Gain from all quarters. By base profit won
You will see more destroyed than prospering.
  Guard. May I then speak? Or shall I turn and
    go? 345
  Creon. See'st not e'en yet how vexing are thy
    words?
  Guard. Is it thine ears they trouble, or thy soul?
  Creon. Why dost thou gauge my trouble where
    it is?
  Guard. The doer grieves thy heart, but I thine
    ears.
  Creon. Pshaw! what a babbler, born to prate art
    thou! 350
  Guard. May be; yet I this deed, at least, did not.
  Creon. Yes, and for money; selling e'en thy
    soul.
  Guard.   Ah me!
How dire it is, in thinking, false to think!
  Creon. Prate about thinking: but unless ye show
To me the doers, ye shall say ere long 355
That scoundrel gains still work their punishment.
                                    (*Exit.*)

  Guard. God send we find him! Should we find
    him not,
As well may be, (for this must chance decide,)
You will not see me coming here again;
For now, being safe beyond all hope of mine, 360
Beyond all thought, I owe the Gods much thanks.
                                    (*Exit.*)

STROPHE I

Chorus. Many the forms of life,
Wondrous and strange to see,
But nought than man appears
More wondrous and more strange. 365
He, with the wintry gales,
O'er the white foaming sea,
'Mid wild waves surging round,
Wendeth his way across:
Earth, of all Gods, from ancient days the first, 370
  Unworn and undecayed,
He, with his ploughs that travel o'er and o'er,
  Furrowing with horse and mule,
  Wears ever year by year.

ANTISTROPHE I

The thoughtless tribe of birds, 375
The beasts that roam the fields,
The brood in sea-depths born,
He takes them all in nets
Knotted in snaring mesh,
Man, wonderful in skill. 380
And by his subtle arts
He holds in sway the beasts

That roam the fields, or tread the mountain's
    height;
  And brings the binding yoke
Upon the neck of horse with shaggy mane,   385
  Or bull on mountain crest,
  Untamable in strength.

STROPHE II

And speech, and thought as swift as wind,
And tempered mood for higher life of states,
  These he has learnt, and how to flee   390
  Or the clear cold of frost unkind,
  Or darts of storm and shower,
Man all-providing. Unprovided, he
Meeteth no chance the coming days may bring;
  Only from Hades, still   395
  He fails to find escape,
Though skill of art may teach him how to flee
From depths of fell disease incurable.

ANTISTROPHE II

So, gifted with a wondrous might,
Above all fancy's dreams, with skill to plan,   400
  Now unto evil, now to good,
  He turns. While holding fast the laws,
  His country's sacred rights,
That rest upon the oath of Gods on high,
High in the State: an outlaw from the State,   405
  When loving, in his pride,
  The thing that is not good;
Ne'er may he share my hearth, nor yet my
    thoughts,
Who worketh deeds of evil like to this.

(*Enter* GUARDS, *bringing in* ANTIGONE.)

As to this portent which the Gods have sent,   410
I stand in doubt. Can I, who know her, say
That this is not the maid Antigone?
O wretched one of wretched father born,
Thou child of Œdipus,
What means this? Surely 'tis not that they
    bring   415
Thee as a rebel 'gainst the king's decree,
And taken in the folly of thine act?
  Guard. Yes! She it was by whom the deed was
    done.
We found her burying. Where is Creon, pray?
  Chorus. Back from his palace comes he just in
    time.   420

(*Enter* CREON.)

  Creon. What chance is this, with which my
    coming fits?
  Guard. Men, O my king, should pledge them-
    selves to nought;
For cool reflection makes their purpose void.

I surely thought I should be slow to come here,
Cowed by thy threats, which then fell thick on
    me;   425
But now persuaded by the sweet delight
Which comes unlooked for, and beyond our hopes,
I come, although I swore the contrary,
Bringing this maiden, whom in act we found
Decking the grave. No need for lots was now;
The prize was mine, and not another man's.   431
And now, O king, take her, and as thou wilt,
Judge and convict her. I can claim a right
To wash my hands of all this troublous coil.
  Creon. How and where was it that ye seized and
    brought her?   435
  Guard. She was in act of burying. Thou know-
    est all.
  Creon. Dost know and rightly speak the tale
    thou tell'st?
  Guard. I saw her burying that self-same corpse
Thou bad'st us not to bury. Speak I clear?
  Creon. How was she seen, and taken in the
    act?   440
  Guard. The matter passed as follows: — When
    we came,
With all those dreadful threats of thine upon us,
Sweeping away the dust which, lightly spread,
Covered the corpse, and laying stript and bare
The tainted carcase, on the hill we sat   445
To windward, shunning the infected air,
Each stirring up his fellow with strong words,
If any shirked his duty. This went on
Some time, until the glowing orb of day
Stood in mid heaven, and the scorching heat   450
Fell on us. Then a sudden whirlwind rose,
A scourge from heaven, raising squalls on earth,
And filled the plain, the leafage stripping bare
Of all the forest, and the air's vast space
Was thick and troubled, and we closed our eyes,
Until the plague the Gods had sent was past; 456
And when it ceased, a weary time being gone,
The girl is seen, and with a bitter cry,
Shrill as a bird's, when it beholds its nest
All emptied of its infant brood, she wails;   460
Thus she, when she beholds the corpse all stript,
Groaned loud with many moanings, and she
    called
Fierce curses down on those who did the deed.
And in her hand she brings some fine, dry dust,
And from a vase of bronze, well wrought, up-
    raised,   465
She pours the three libations [1] o'er the dead.

---

[1] A ceremonial rite performed out of respect for the dead or in honor of the gods. From the Latin *libare*, to taste or to pour out. The rite consisted in pouring out, three separate times, small quantities of wine or milk or other drink.

And we, beholding, give her chase forthwith,
And run her down, nought terrified at us.
And then we charged her with the former deed,
As well as this. And nothing she denied. 470
But this to me both bitter is and sweet,
For to escape one's-self from ill is sweet,
But to bring friends to trouble, this is hard
And painful. Yet my nature bids me count
Above all these things safety for myself. 475

Creon (*to* ANTIGONE). Thou, then — yes, thou,
  who bend'st thy face to earth —
Confessest thou, or dost deny the deed?

Antig. I own I did it, and will not deny.

Creon (*to* GUARD). Go thou thy way, where'er
  thy will may choose, 479
Freed from a weighty charge. (*Exit* GUARD.)
(*To* ANTIGONE.) And now for thee.
Say in few words, not lengthening out thy speech,
Knew'st thou the edicts which forbade these
  things?

Antig. I knew them. Could I fail? Full clear
  were they.

Creon. And thou did'st dare to disobey these
  laws?

Antig. Yes, for it was not Zeus who gave them
  forth, 485
Nor Justice, dwelling with the Gods below,
Who traced these laws for all the sons of men;
Nor did I deem thy edicts strong enough,
That thou, a mortal man, should'st overpass
The unwritten laws of God that know not change.
They are not of to-day nor yesterday, 491
But live for ever, nor can man assign
When first they sprang to being. Not through fear
Of any man's resolve was I prepared
Before the Gods to bear the penalty 495
Of sinning against these. That I should die
I knew (how should I not?) though thy decree
Had never spoken. And, before my time
If I shall die, I reckon this a gain;
For whoso lives, as I, in many woes, 500
How can it be but he shall gain by death?
And so for me to bear this doom of thine
Has nothing painful. But, if I had left
My mother's son unburied on his death,
In that I should have suffered; but in this 505
I suffer not. And should I seem to thee
To do a foolish deed, 'tis simply this, —
I bear the charge of folly from a fool.

Chorus. The maiden's stubborn will, of stubborn
  sire
The offspring shows itself. She knows not yet 510
To yield to evils.

Creon. Know then, minds too stiff
Most often stumble, and the rigid steel
Baked in the furnace, made exceeding hard,

Thou see'st most often split and shivered lie;
And I have known the steeds of fiery mood 515
With a small curb subdued. It is not meet
That one who lives in bondage to his neighbors
Should think too proudly. Wanton outrage then
This girl first learnt, transgressing these my laws;
But this, when she has done it, is again 520
A second outrage, over it to boast,
And laugh as having done it. Surely, then,
She is the man, not I, if, all unscathed,
Such deeds of might are hers. But be she child
Of mine own sister, or of one more near 525
Than all the kith and kin of Household Zeus,
She and her sister shall not 'scape a doom
Most foul and shameful; for I charge her, too,
With having planned this deed of sepulture.
Go ye and call her. 'Twas but now within 530
I saw her raving, losing self-command.
And still the mind of those who in the dark
Plan deeds of evil is the first to fail,
And so convicts itself of secret guilt.
But most I hate when one found out in guilt 535
Will seek to gloze and brave it to the end.

Antig. And dost thou seek aught else beyond
  my death?

Creon. Nought else for me. That gaining, I
  gain all.

Antig. Why then delay? Of all thy words not
  one
Pleases me now (and may it never please!), 540
And so all mine must grate upon thine ears.
And yet how could I higher glory gain
Than placing my true brother in his tomb?
There is not one of these but would confess
It pleases them, did fear not seal their lips. 545
The tyrant's might in much besides excels,
And it may do and say whate'er it will.

Creon. Of all the race of Cadmos[1] thou alone
Look'st thus upon the deed.

Antig.   They see it too
As I do, but their tongue is tied for thee. 550

Creon. Art not ashamed against their thoughts
  to think?

Antig. There is nought base in honoring our
  own blood.

Creon. And was he not thy kin who fought
  against him?

Antig. Yea, brother, of one father and one
  mother.

Creon. Why then give honor which dishonors
  him? 555

Antig. The dead below will not repeat thy
  words.

Creon. Yes, if thou give like honor to the godless.

[1] Founder of Thebes.

Antig. It was his brother, not his slave that
 died.

Creon. Wasting this land, while *he* died fighting
 for it.

Antig. Yet Hades still craves equal rites for
 all.   560

Creon. The good craves not the portion of the
 bad.

Antig. Who knows if this be holy deemed below?

Creon. Not even when he dies can foe be friend.

Antig. My nature leads to sharing love, not hate.

Creon. Go then below; and if thou must have
 love,   565
Love them.   While I live, women shall not rule.

(Enter Ismene, *led in by Attendants.)*

Chorus. And, lo! Ismene at the gate
Comes shedding tears of sisterly regard,
And o'er her brow a gathering cloud
   Mars the deep roseate blush,   570
   Bedewing her fair cheek.

Creon (*to* Ismene). And thou who, creeping as a
 viper creeps,
Did'st drain my life in secret, and I knew not
That I was rearing two accursèd ones,   574
Subverters of my throne, — come, tell me, then,
Wilt thou confess thou took'st thy part in this,
Or wilt thou swear thou did'st not know of it?

Isme. I did the deed, if she did, go with her;
Yes, share the guilt, and bear an equal blame.

Antig. Nay, justice will not suffer this, for thou
Did'st not consent, nor did I let thee join.   581

Isme. Nay, in thy troubles, I am not ashamed
In the same boat with thee to share thy fate.

Antig. Who did it, Hades knows, and those
 below:
I do not love a friend who loves in words.   585

Isme. Do not, my sister, put me to such shame,
As not to let me join in death with thee,
And so to pay due reverence to the dead.

Antig. Share not my death, nor make thine own
 this deed
   Thou had'st no hand in.   My death shall suffice.   590

Isme. What life to me is sweet, bereaved of thee?

Antig. Ask Creon there, since thou o'er him dost
 watch.

Isme. Why vex me so, in nothing bettered by it?

Antig. 'Tis pain indeed, to laugh my laugh at
 thee.

Isme. But now, at least, how may I profit thee?

Antig. Save thou thyself.   I grudge not thy
 escape.   596

Isme. Ah, woe is me! and must I miss thy fate?

Antig. Thou mad'st thy choice to live, and I to
 die.

Isme. 'Twas not because I failed to speak my
 thoughts.

Antig. To these did'st thou, to those did I seem
 wise.   600

Isme. And yet the offense is equal in us both.

Antig. Take courage.   Thou dost live.   My
 soul long since
Hath died to render service to the dead.

Creon. Of these two girls, the one goes mad but
 now,
The other ever since her life began.   605

Isme. E'en so, O king; no mind that ever lived
Stands firm in evil days, but goes astray.

Creon. Thine did, when, with the vile, vile deeds
 thou choosest.

Isme. How could I live without her presence
 here?

Creon. Speak not of presence.   She is here no
 more.   610

Isme. And wilt thou slay thy son's betrothèd
 bride?

Creon. Full many a field there is which he may
 plough.

Isme. None like that plighted troth 'twixt him
 and her.

Creon. Wives that are vile I love not for my
 sons.

Isme. Ah, dearest Hæmon, how thy father
 shames thee!   615

Creon. Thou with that marriage dost but vex
 my soul.

Chorus. And wilt thou rob thy son of her he
 loved?

Creon. 'Tis Death, not I, shall break the marriage off.

Chorus. Her doom is fixed, it seems, then.   She
 must die.

Creon. Fixed, yes, by me and thee.   No more
 delay,   620
Lead them within, ye slaves.   These must be kept
Henceforth as women, suffered not to roam;
For even boldest natures shrink in fear
When they see Hades overshadowing life.

(Exeunt Guards *with* Antigone *and* Ismene.)

STROPHE I

Chorus. Blessed are those whose life no woe doth
 taste!   625
   For unto those whose house
The Gods have shaken, nothing fails of curse
Or woe, that creeps to generations far.
   E'en thus a wave, (when spreads,
   With blasts from Thracian coasts,   630
   The darkness of the deep.)
   Up from the sea's abyss
Hither and thither rolls the black sand on,

And every jutting peak,
  Swept by the storm-wind's strength,   635
  Lashed by the fierce wild waves,
Re-echoes with the far-resounding roar.

ANTISTROPHE I

1 see the woes that smote, in ancient days,
  The seed of Labdacus,[1]
Who perished long ago, with grief on grief   640
Still falling, nor does this age rescue that;
  Some God still smites it down,
  Nor have they any end:
  For now there rose a gleam,
  Over the last weak shoots,   645
That sprang from out the race of Œdipus;
  Yet this the blood-stained scythe
  Of those that reign below
  Cuts off relentlessly,   649
And maddened speech, and frenzied rage of heart.

STROPHE II

Thy power, O Zeus, what haughtiness of man,
  Yea, what can hold in check?
Which neither sleep, that maketh all things old,
Nor the long months of Gods that never fail,
  Can for a moment seize.   655
  But still as Lord supreme,
  Waxing not old with time,
Thou dwellest in Thy sheen of radiancy
  On far Olympus' height.
Through future near or far as through the past,   660
  One law holds ever good,
Nought comes to life of man unscathed throughout
  by woe.

ANTISTROPHE II

For hope to many comes in wanderings wild,
  A solace and support;
To many as a cheat of fond desires,   665
And creepeth still on him who knows it not,
  Until he burn his foot
  Within the scorching flame.
  Full well spake one of old,
That evil ever seems to be as good   670
  To those whose thoughts of heart
  God leadeth unto woe,
And without woe, he spends but shortest space of
  time.

And here comes Hæmon, last of all thy sons:
  Comes he bewailing sore   675
The fate of her who should have been his bride,
  The maid Antigone,
  Grieving o'er vanished joys?

[1] Grandfather of Œdipus.

(*Enter* HÆMON.)

Creon. Soon we shall know much more than
  seers can tell.
Surely thou dost not come, my son, to rage   680
Against thy father, hearing his decree,
Fixing her doom who should have been thy bride;
Or dost thou love us still, whate'er we do?
  Hæmon. My father, I am thine; and thou dost
  guide
With thy wise counsels, which I gladly follow.   685
No marriage weighs one moment in the scales
With me, while thou dost guide my steps aright.
  Creon. This thought, my son, should dwell
  within thy breast,
That all things stand below a father's will;
For so men pray that they may rear and keep   690
Obedient offspring by their hearths and homes,
That they may both requite their father's foes,
And pay with him like honors to his friend.
But he who reareth sons that profit not,
What could one say of him but this, that he   695
Breeds his own sorrow, laughter to his foes?
Lose not thy reason, then, my son, o'ercome
By pleasure, for a woman's sake, but know,
A cold embrace is that to have at home
A worthless wife, the partner of thy bed.   700
What ulcerous sore is worse than one we love
Who proves all worthless? No! with loathing
  scorn,
As hateful to thee, let that girl go wed
A spouse in Hades.   Taken in the act
I found her, her alone of all the State,   705
Rebellious.   And I will not make myself
False to the State.   She dies.   So let her call
On Zeus, the lord of kindred.   If I rear
Of mine own stock things foul and orderless,
I shall have work enough with those without.   710
For he who in the life of home is good
Will still be seen as just in things of state;
I should be sure that man would govern well,
And know well to be governed, and would stand
In war's wild storm, on his appointed post,   715
A just and good defender.   But the man
Who by transgressions violates the laws,
Or thinks to bid the powers that be obey,
He must not hope to gather praise from me.
No! we must follow whom the State appoints,   720
In things or just and trivial, or, may be,
The opposite of these.   For anarchy
Is our worst evil, brings our commonwealth
To utter ruin, lays whole houses low,
In battle strife hurls firm allies in flight;   725
But they who yield to guidance — these shall find
Obedience saves most men.   Thus health should
  come
To what our rulers order; least of all

Ought men to bow before a woman's sway.
Far better, if it must be so, to fall   730
By a man's hand, than thus to bear reproach,
By woman conquered.
    Chorus.   Unto us, O king.
Unless our years have robbed us of our wit,
Thou seemest to say wisely what thou say'st.
    Hæmon. The Gods, my father, have bestowed
        on man   735
His reason, noblest of all earthly gifts;
And that thou speakest wrongly these thy words
I cannot say, (God grant I ne'er know how
Such things to utter!) yet another's thoughts
May have some reason. 'Tis my lot to watch   740
What each man says or does, or blames in thee,
For dread thy face to one of low estate,
Who speaks what thou wilt not rejoice to hear.
But I can hear the things in darkness said,
How the whole city wails this maiden's fate,   745
As one "who of all women most unjustly,
For noblest deed must die the foulest death,
Who her own brother, fallen in the fray,
Would neither leave unburied, nor expose
To carrion dogs, or any bird of prey,   750
May she not claim the meed of golden praise?"
Such is the whisper that in secret runs
All darkling. And for me, my father, nought
Is dearer than thy welfare. What can be
A nobler prize of honor for the son   755
Than a sire's glory, or for sire than son's?
I pray thee, then, wear not one mood alone,
That what thou say'st is right, and nought but
    that;
For he who thinks that he alone is wise,
His mind and speech above what others have,   760
Such men when searched are mostly empty found.
But for a man to learn, though he be wise,
Yea to learn much, and know the time to yield,
Brings no disgrace. When winter floods the
    streams,
Thou see'st the trees that bend before the storm,
Save their last twigs, while those that will not
    yield   766
Perish with root and branch. And when one hauls
Too tight the mainsail rope, and will not slack,
He has to end his voyage with deck o'erturned.
Do thou then yield; permit thyself to change.   770
Young though I be, if any prudent thought
Be with me, I at least will dare assert
The higher worth of one, who, come what will,
Is full of knowledge. If that may not be
(For nature is not wont to take that bent,)   775
'Tis good to learn from those who counsel well.
    Chorus. My king! 'tis fit that thou should'st
        learn from him,
If he speaks words in season; and, in turn,

That thou [*to* Hæmon] should'st learn of him, for
    both speak well.
    Creon. Shall we at our age stoop to learn from
    him,   780
Young as he is, the lesson to be wise?
    Hæmon. Learn nought thou should'st not learn.
        And if I'm young,
Thou should'st my deeds and not my years con-
    sider.
    Creon. Is that thy deed to reverence rebel souls?
    Hæmon. I would bid none waste reverence on
    the base.   785
    Creon. Has not that girl been seized with that
    disease?
    Hæmon. The men of Thebes with one accord
    say, No.
    Creon. And will my subjects tell us how to rule?
    Hæmon. Dost thou not see thou speakest like a
    boy?
    Creon. Must I then rule for others than myself?
    Hæmon. That is no State which hangs on one
    man's will.   791
    Creon. Is not the State deemed his who governs
    it?
    Hæmon. Brave rule! Alone, and o'er an empty
    land!
    Creon. This boy, it seems, will be his bride's ally.
    Hæmon. If thou art she, for thou art all my
    care.   795
    Creon. Basest of base, against thy father plead-
    ing!
    Hæmon. Yea, for I see thee sin a grievous sin.
    Creon. And do I sin revering mine own sway?
    Hæmon. Thou show'st no reverence, trampling
    on God's laws.
    Creon. O guilty soul, by woman's craft beguiled!
    Hæmon. Thou wilt not find me slave unto the
    base.   801
    Creon. Thy every word is still on her behalf.
    Hæmon. Yea, and on thine and mine, and theirs
    below.
    Creon. Be sure thou shalt not wed her while she
    lives.
    Hæmon. Then she must die, and, dying, others
    slay.   805
    Creon. And dost thou dare to come to me with
    threats?
    Hæmon. Is it a threat against vain thoughts to
    speak?
    Creon. Thou to thy cost shalt teach me wisdom's
    ways,
Thyself in wisdom wanting.
    Hæmon.   I would say
Thou wast unwise, if thou wert not my father.   810
    Creon. Thou woman's slave, I say, prate on no
    more.

Hæmon. Wilt thou then speak, and, speaking, listen not?

Creon. Nay, by Olympus! Thou shalt not go free

To flout me with reproaches   Lead her out   814
Whom my soul hates, that she may die forthwith
Before mine eyes, and near her bridegroom here.

Hæmon. No! Think it not! Near me she shall not die,

And thou shalt never see my face alive,
That thou may'st storm at those who like to yield.
(*Exit.*)

Chorus. The man has gone, O king, in hasty mood.   820
A mind distressed in youth is hard to bear.

Creon. Let him do what he will, and bear himself
As more than man, he shall not save those girls.

Chorus. What! Doest thou mean to slay them both alike?

Creon. Not her who touched it not; there thou say'st well.   825

Chorus. What form of death mean'st thou to slay her with?

Creon. Leading her on to where the desert path
Is loneliest, there alive, in rocky cave
Will I immure her, just so much of food
Before her set as may avert pollution,   830
And save the city from the guilt of blood;
And there, invoking Hades, whom alone
Of all the Gods she worships, she, perchance,
Shall gain escape from death, or then shall know
That Hades-worship is but labor lost. (*Exit.*)   835

STROPHE

Chorus. O Love, in every battle victor owned;
Love, rushing on thy prey,
Now on a maiden's soft and blooming cheek,
In secret ambush hid;
Now o'er the broad sea wandering at will,   840
And now in shepherd's folds;
Of all the Undying Ones none 'scape from thee,
Nor yet of mortal men
Whose lives are measured as a fleeting day;
And who has thee is frenzied in his soul.   845

ANTISTROPHE

Thou makest vile the purpose of the just,
To his own fatal harm;
Thou hast stirred up this fierce and deadly strife,
Of men of nearest kin;
The charm of eyes of bride beloved and fair   850
Is crowned with victory,
And dwells on high among the powers that rule.
Equal with holiest laws;
For Aphrodite, she whom none subdues,
Sports in her might and majesty divine.   855

I, even I, am borne
Beyond the appointed laws;
I look on this, and cannot stay
The fountain of my tears.
For, lo! I see her, see Antigone   860
Wend her sad, lonely way
To that bride-chamber where we all must lie.

(*Enter* ANTIGONE)

Antig. Behold, O men of this my fatherland,
I wend my last lone way,
Seeing the last sunbeam, now and nevermore;   865
He leads me yet alive,
Hades that welcomes all,
To Acheron's [1] dark shore,
With neither part nor lot
In marriage festival,   870
Nor hath the marriage hymn
Been sung for me as bride,
But I shall be the bride of Acheron.

Chorus. And hast thou not all honor, worthiest praise,
Who goest to the home that hides the dead,   875
Not smitten by the sickness that decays,
Nor by the sharp sword's meed,
But of thy own free will, in fullest life,
Alone of mortals, thus
To Hades tak'st thy way?   880

Antig. I heard of old her pitiable end,
On Sipylos' high crag,
The Phrygian stranger [2] from a far land come,
Whom Tantalus begat;
Whom growth of rugged rock,   885
Clinging as ivy clings,
Subdued, and made its own:
And now, so runs the tale,
There, as she melts in shower,
The snow abideth aye,   890
And still bedews yon cliffs that lie below
Those brows that ever weep.
With fate like hers God brings me to my rest.

Chorus. A Goddess she, and of the high Gods born;
And we are mortals, born of mortal seed.   895
And lo! for one who liveth but to die,

---

[1] The river Acheron, together with the Styx, the Phlegethon, and the Cocytus, formed the boundaries of Hades, an underground darkness ruled over by Pluto and his queen, Proserpina.

[2] Niobe. Because she had boasted beyond reason of her children, and had ridiculed the celebration in honor of the goddess Latona, Niobe incurred the wrath of Apollo and Diana who caused the seven sons of Niobe to be killed and the seven daughters to be pierced with arrows even while they mourned the death of their brothers. Niobe herself was turned to "rugged rock."

To gain like doom with those of heavenly race,
  Is great and strange to hear.
  Antig. Ye mock me then.   Alas! Why wait ye
    not,
By all our fathers' Gods, I ask of you,   900
  Till I have passed away,
  But flout me while I live?
  O city that I love,
  O men that claim as yours
  That city stored with wealth,   905
  O Dirkè, fairest fount,
O grove of Thebes, that boasts her chariot host,
  I bid you witness all,
  How, with no friends to weep,
  By what stern laws condemned,   910
I go to that strong dungeon of the tomb,
  For burial strange, ah me!
Nor dwelling with the living, nor the dead.
  Chorus. Forward and forward still to farthest
    verge
Of daring hast thou gone,   915
And now, O child, thou hast rushed violently
  Where Right erects her throne;
Surely thou payest to the uttermost
  Thy father's debt of guilt.
  Antig. Ah! Thou hast touched the quick of all
    my grief,   920
The thrice-told tale of all my father's woe,
  The fate which dogs us all,
The old Labdakid race of ancient fame.
  Woe for the curses dire
  Of that defilèd bed,   925
  With foulest incest stained,
  My mother's with my sire,
Whence I myself have sprung, most miserable.
  And now, I go to them,
  To sojourn in the grave,   930
  Accursèd, and unwed;
  Ah, brother, thou didst find
  Thy marriage fraught with ill,
And thou, though dead, hast smitten down my
    life.
  Chorus. Acts reverent and devout   935
  May claim devotion's name,
But power, in one to whom power comes as trust,
  May never be defied;
  And thee, thy stubborn mood,
  Self-chosen, layeth low.   940
  Antig. Unwept, without a friend,
  Unwed, and whelmed in woe,
I journey on this road that open lies.
No more shall it be mine (O misery!)
To look upon yon daylight's holy eye;   945
  And yet, of all my friends,
  Not one bewails my fate,
  No kindly tear is shed.

(*Enter* CREON.)

  Creon. And know ye not, if men have leave to
    speak
Their songs and wailings thus to stave off death,
That they will never stop? Lead, lead her on,   951
Without delay, and, as I said, immure
In yon cavernous tomb, and then depart.
Leave her to choose, or drear and lonely death,
Or, living, in the tomb to find her home.   955
Our hands are clean in all that touches her;
But she no more shall dwell on earth with us.
  Antig. (*turning towards the cavern*). O tomb,
    my bridal chamber, vaulted home.
Guarded right well for ever, where I go
To join mine own, of whom the greater part   960
Among the dead doth Persephassa [1] hold;
And I, of all the last and saddest, wend
My way below, life's little span unfilled.
And yet I go, and feed myself with hopes
That I shall meet them, by my father loved,   965
Dear to my mother, well-beloved of thee,
Thou darling brother: I, with these my hands,
Washed each dear corpse, arrayed you, poured
    libations,
In rites or burial; and in care for thee,
Thy body, Polyneices, honoring,   970
I gain this recompense.   (And yet in sight
Of all that rightly judge the deed was good;
I had not done it had I come to be
A mother with her children, — had not dared,
Though 'twere a husband dead that moldered
    there,   975
Against my country's will to bear this toil.
And am I asked what law constrained me thus?
I answer, had I lost a husband dear,
I might have had another; other sons
By other spouse, if one were lost to me;   980
But when my father and my mother sleep
In Hades, then no brother more can come.
And therefore, giving thee the foremost place,
I seemed in Creon's eyes, O brother dear,
To sin in boldest daring.   Therefore now   985
He leads me, having taken me by force,
Cut off from marriage bed and marriage song,
Untasting wife's true joy, or mother's bliss,
With infant at her breast, but all forlorn,
Bereaved of friends, in utter misery,   990
Alive, I tread the chambers of the dead.)
What law of Heaven have I transgressed against?
What use for me, ill-starred one, still to look
To any God for succor, or to call
On any friend for aid?   For holiest deed   995
I bear this charge of rank unholiness.
If acts like these the Gods on high approve,

---

[1] Proserpina, queen of the underworld.

We, taught by pain, shall own that we have sinned;
But if these sin [*looking at* CREON] I pray they
    suffer not
Worse evils than the wrongs they do to me. 1000
  Chorus. Still do the same wild blasts
  Vex her who standeth there.
  Creon. Therefore shall these her guards
  Weep sore for this delay.
  Chorus. Ah me! this word of thine 1005
  Tells of death drawing nigh.
  Creon. I cannot bid thee hope
  For other end than this.
  Antig. O citadel of Thebes, my native land,
  Ye Gods of ancient days, 1010
  I go, and linger not.
Behold me, O ye senators of Thebes,
The last, lone scion of the kingly race,
What things I suffer, and from whom they come,
Revering still the laws of reverence. 1015

      (GUARDS *lead* ANTIGONE *away.*)

STROPHE I

  Chorus. So did the form of Danaë [1] bear of old,
  In brazen palace hid,
  To lose the light of heaven,
And in her tomb-like chamber was enclosed:
Yet she, O child, was noble in her race, 1020
And well she stored the golden shower of Zeus.
But great and dread the might of Destiny:
  Nor kingly wealth, nor war,
  Nor tower, nor dark-hulled ships
Beaten by waves, escape. 1025

ANTISTROPHE I

So too was shut, enclosed in dungeon cave,
  Bitter and fierce in mood,
  The son of Dryas,[2] king
Of yon Edonian tribes, for vile reproach,
By Dionysos' hands, and so his strength 1030
And soul o'ermad wastes drop by drop away,
And so he learnt that he, against the God,
  Spake his mad words of scorn;
  For he the Mænad throng
  And bright fire fain had stopped, 1035
And roused the Muses' wrath.

STROPHE II

And by the double sea of those Dark Rocks
  Are shores of Bosporos,
And Thracian isle, as Salmydessos known,

---

[1] Danaë, though secluded by her father, was visited
by Zeus who took the form of a golden shower. She
became the mother of Perseus.
[2] Because Lycurgus, the son of Dryas, had been
critical of the worship of Dionysus, he was made blind
by Zeus and "enclosed in dungeon cave."

  Where Ares, whom they serve, 1040
  God of the region round,
  Saw the dire, blinding wound,
  That smote the twin-born sons
Of Phineus by relentless step-dame's hand,—
  Dark wound, on dark-doomed eyes, 1045
  Not with the stroke of sword,
But blood-stained hands, and point of spindle
  sharp.

ANTISTROPHE II

And they in misery, miserable fate,
  Wasting away, wept sore,
Born of a mother wedded with a curse. 1050
  And she who claimed descent
  From men of ancient fame,
  The old Erechtheid [1] race,
  Amid her father's winds,
Daughter of Boreas,[2] in far distant caves 1055
  Was reared, a child of Gods,
  Swift moving as the steed
  O'er lofty crag, and yet
The ever-living Fates bore hard on her.

    (*Enter* TEIRESIAS, *guided by a Boy.*)

  Teir. Princes of Thebes, we come as travellers
    joined, 1060
One seeing for both, for still the blind must use
A guide's assistance to direct his steps.
  Creon. And what new thing, Teiresias, brings
    thee here?
  Teir. I'll tell thee, and do thou the seer obey.
  Creon. Of old I was not wont to slight thy
    thoughts. 1065
  Teir. So did'st thou steer our city's course full
    well.
  Creon. I bear my witness from good profit gained.
  Teir. Know then, thou walk'st on fortune's
    razor-edge.
  Creon. What means this? How I shudder at
    thy speech!
  Teir. Soon shalt thou know, as thou dost hear
    the signs 1070
Of my dread art. For sitting, as of old,
Upon my ancient seat of augury,
Where every bird finds haven, lo! I hear
Strange cry of wingèd creatures, shouting shrill,
With inarticulate passion, and I knew 1075
That they were tearing each the other's flesh
With bloody talons, for their whirring wings
Made that quite clear: and straightway I, in fear,
Made trial of the sacrifice that lay

---

[1] Erechtheus, a snake-formed spirit, who was suc
cessor to Cecrops, the founder of Athens.
[2] The North Wind.

On fiery altar.   And Hephæstos' flame   1080
Shone not from out the offering; but there oozed
Upon the ashes, trickling from the bones,
A moisture, and it smouldered, and it spat,
And, lo! the gall was scattered to the air,
And forth from out the fat that wrapped them
    round   1085
The thigh-bones fell.   Such omens of decay
From holy sacrifice I learnt from him,
This boy, who now stands here, for he is still
A guide to me, as I to others am.
And all this evil falls upon the State,   1090
From out thy counsels; for our altars all,
Our sacred hearths are full of food for dogs
And birds unclean, the flesh of that poor wretch
Who fell, the son of Œdipus.   And so
The Gods no more hear prayers of sacrifice,   1095
Nor own the flame that burns the victim's limbs;
Nor do the birds give cry of omen good,
But feed on carrion of a slaughtered corpse.
Think thou on this, my son: to err, indeed,
Is common unto all, but having erred,   1100
He is no longer reckless or unblest,
Who, having fallen into evil, seeks
For healing, nor continues still unmoved.
Self-will must bear the charge of stubbornness:
Yield to the dead, and outrage not a corpse.   1105
What prowess is it fallen foes to slay?
Good counsel give I, planning good for thee,
And of all joys the sweetest is to learn
From one who speaketh well, should that bring
    gain.
    Creon.   Old man, as archers aiming at their
      mark,   1110
So ye shoot forth your venomed darts at me;
I know your augur's tricks, and by your tribe
Long since am tricked and sold.   Yes, gain your
    gains,
Get Sardis' amber metal, Indian gold;
That corpse ye shall not hide in any tomb.   1115
Not though the eagles, birds of Zeus, should bear
Their carrion morsels to the throne of God,
Not even fearing this pollution dire,
Will I consent to burial.   Well I know
That man is powerless to pollute the Gods.   1120
But many fall, Teiresias, dotard old,
A shameful fall, who gloze their shameful words
For lucre's sake, with surface show of good.
    Teir.   Ah me!   Does no man know, does none
      consider . . . ?
    Creon.   Consider what?   What trite poor saw
      comes now?   1125
    Teir.   How far good counsel is of all things best?
    Creon.   So far, I trow, as folly is worst ill.
    Teir.   Of that disease thy soul, alas! is full.
    Creon.   I will not meet a seer with evil words.

    Teir.   Thou dost so, saying I divine with
      lies.   1130
    Creon.   The race of seers is ever fond of gold.
    Teir.   And that of tyrants still loves lucre foul.
    Creon.   Dost know thou speak'st thy words of
      those that rule?
    Teir.   I know.   Through me thou rul'st a city
      saved.
    Creon.   Wise seer art thou, yet given o'ermuch
      to wrong.   1135
    Teir.   Thou'lt stir me to speak out my soul's
      dread secrets.
    Creon.   Out with them; only speak them not for
      gain.
    Teir.   So is 't, I trow, in all that touches thee.
    Creon.   Know that thou shalt not bargain with
      my will.
    Teir.   Know, then, and know it well, that thou
      shalt see   1140
Not many winding circuits of the sun,
Before thou giv'st as quittance for the dead,
A corpse by thee begotten; for that thou
Hast to the ground cast one that walked on earth,
And foully placed within a sepulchre   1145
A living soul; and now thou keep'st from them,
The Gods below, the corpse of one unblest,
Unwept, unhallowed, and in these things thou
Canst claim no part, nor yet the Gods above;
But they by thee are outraged; and they wait,   1150
The sure though slow avengers of the grave,
The dread Erinnyes [1] of the mighty Gods,
For thee in these same evils to be snared.
Search well if I say this as one who sells
His soul for money.   Yet a little while,   1155
And in thy house the wail of men and women
Shall make it plain.   And every city stirs
Itself in arms against thee, owning those
Whose limbs the dogs have buried, or fierce wolves,
Or wingèd birds have brought the accursèd taint
To region consecrate.   Doom like to this,   1161
Sure darting as an arrow to its mark,
I launch at thee, (for thou dost vex me sore,)
An archer aiming at the very heart,
And thou shalt not escape its fiery sting.   1165
And now, O boy, lead thou me home again,
That he may vent his spleen on younger men,
And learn to keep his tongue more orderly,
With better thoughts than this his present mood.
                       (*Exit.*)
    Chorus.   The man has gone, O king, predicting
      woe,   1170
And well we know, since first our raven hair
Was mixed with gray, that never yet his words
Were uttered to our State and failed of truth.

   [1] The Furies, who punish those not responsive to
filial duties.

Creon. I know it too, 'tis that that troubles me.
To yield is hard, but, holding out, to smite   1175
One's soul with sorrow, **this** is harder still.

Chorus. We need wise counsel, O Menœkeus'
    son.

Creon. What shall I do? Speak thou, and I'll
    obey.

Chorus. Go then, and free the maiden from her
    tomb,
And give a grave to him who lies exposed.   1180

Creon. Is this thy counsel? Dost thou bid me
    yield?

Chorus. Without delay, O king, for lo! they
    come,
The Gods' swift-footed ministers of ill,
And in an instant lay the self-willed low.

Creon. Ah me! 'tis hard; and yet I bend my will
To do thy bidding. With necessity   1186
We must not fight at such o'erwhelming odds.

Chorus. Go then and act! Commit it not to
    others.

Creon. E'en as I am I'll go. Come, come my
    men,
Present or absent, come, and in your hands   1190
Bring axes: come to yonder eminence.
And I, since now my judgment leans that way,
Who myself bound her, now myself will loose,
Too much I fear lest it should wisest prove
Maintaining ancient laws to end my life.   1195

STROPHE I

Chorus. O Thou of many names,
Of that Cadmeian maid [1]
The glory and the joy,
Whom Zeus as offspring owns,
Zeus, thundering deep and loud,   1200
Who watchest over famed Italia,
And reign'st o'er all the bays that Deo claims
    On fair Eleusis' coast.
Bacchos, who dwell'st in Thebes, the mother-town
    Of all thy Bacchant train,   1205
    Along Ismenus' stream,
    And with the dragon's brood ; [2]

ANTISTROPHE I

Thee, o'er the double peak
Of yonder height the blaze
Of flashing fire beholds,   1210
    Where nymphs of Corycos
    Go forth in Bacchic dance,
And by the flowery stream of Castaly,
And Thee, the ivied slopes of Nysa's hills,
    And vine-clad promontory,   1215

[1] Semele, daughter of Cadmus and mother of Dionysus by Zeus.   [2] Descendants of those born
of the serpent's teeth scattered by Cadmus.

(While words of more than mortal melody
    Shout out the well-known name,)
    Send forth, the guardian lord
    Of the wide streets of Thebes.

STROPHE II

Above all cities Thou,   1220
With her, thy mother whom the thunder slew,
    Dost look on it with love;
And now, since all the city bendeth low
    Beneath the sullen plague,
    Come Thou with cleansing tread   1225
    O'er the Parnassian slopes,
    Or o'er the moaning straits.

ANTISTROPHE II

O Thou, who lead'st the band,
The choral band of stars still breathing fire,
    Lord of the hymns of night,   1230
The child of highest Zeus; appear, O king,
    With Thyian maidens wild,
    Who all night long in dance,
    With frenzied chorus sing
    Thy praise, their lord, Iacchos.   1235

(*Enter* MESSENGER.)

Mess. Ye men of Cadmos and Amphion's house,
I know no life of mortal man which I
Would either praise or blame. 'Tis Fortune's
    chance
That raiseth up, and Fortune bringeth low,
The man who lives in good or evil plight;   1240
And prophet of men's future there is none.
For Creon, so I deemed, deserved to be
At once admired and envied, having saved
This land of Cadmos from the hands of foes;
And, having ruled with fullest sovereignty,   1245
He lived and prospered, joyous in a race
Of goodly offspring. Now, all this is gone;
For when men lose the joys that sweeten life,
I cannot deem they live, but rather count
As if a breathing corpse. His heaped-up stores
Of wealth are large, so be it, and he lives   1251
With all a sovereign's state; and yet, if joy
Be absent, all the rest I count as nought,
And would not weigh them against pleasure's
    charm,
More than a vapor's shadow.

Chorus.   What is this? 1255
What new disaster tell'st thou of our chiefs?

Mess. Dead are they, and the living cause their
    death.

Chorus. Who slays, and who is slaughtered?
    Tell thy tale

Mess. Hæmon is dead, slain, weltering in his
    blood.

Chorus. By his own act, or by his father's hand?   1260

Mess. His own, in wrath against his father's crime.

Chorus. O prophet! true, most true, those words of thine.

Mess. Since things stand thus, we well may counsel take.

Chorus. Lo! Creon's wife comes, sad Eurydice.
She from the house approaches, hearing speech
About her son, or else by accident.   1266

(*Enter* EURYDICE.)

Euryd. I on my way, my friends, as suppliant bound,
To pay my vows at Pallas' shrine, have heard
Your words, and so I chanced to draw the bolt
Of the half-opened door, when lo! a sound   1270
Falls on my ears, of evil striking home,
And terror-struck I fall in deadly swoon
Back in my handmaids' arms; yet tell it me,
Tell the tale once again, for I shall hear,
By long experience disciplined to grief.   1275

Mess. Dear lady, I will tell thee: I was by,
And will not leave one word of truth untold.
Why should we smooth and gloze, where all too soon
We should be found as liars? Truth is still
The only safety. Lo! I went with him,   1280
Thy husband, in attendance, to the edge
Of yonder plain, where still all ruthlessly
The corpse of Polyneices lay exposed,
Mangled by dogs. And, having prayed to her,
The Goddess of all pathways, and to Pluto,   1285
To temper wrath with pity, him they washed
With holy washing; and what yet was left
We burnt in branches freshly cut, and heaped
A high-raised grave from out his native soil,
And then we entered on the stone-paved home,   1290
Death's marriage-chamber for the ill-starred maid.
And some one hears, while standing yet afar,
Shrill voice of wailing near the bridal bower,
By funeral rites unhallowed, and he comes
And tells my master, Creon. On his ears,   1295
Advancing nearer, falls a shriek confused
Of bitter sorrow, and with groaning loud,
He utters one sad cry, "Me miserable!
And am I then a prophet? Do I wend
This day the dreariest way of all my life?   1300
My son's voice greets me. Go, my servants, go,
Quickly draw near, and standing by the tomb,
Search ye and see; and where the stone torn out
Shall make an opening, look ye in, and say
If I hear Haemon's voice, or if my soul   1305
Is cheated by the Gods." And then we searched,
As he, our master, in his frenzy bade us;

And, in the furthest corner of the vault,
We saw her hanging by her neck, with cord   1309
Of linen threads entwined, and him we found
Clasping her form in passionate embrace,
And mourning o'er the doom that robbed him of her,
His father's deed, and that his marriage bed,
So full of woe. When Creon saw him there,
Groaning aloud in bitterness of heart,   1315
He goes to him, and calls in wailing voice,
"Poor boy! what hast thou done? Hast thou then lost
Thy reason? In what evil sinkest thou?
Come forth, my child, on bended knee I ask thee."
And then the boy, with fierce, wild-gleaming eyes,
Glared at him, spat upon his face, and draws,   1321
Still answering nought, the sharp two-handled sword.
Missing his aim (his father from the blow
Turning aside,) in anger with himself,
The poor ill-doomed one, even as he was,   1325
Fell on his sword, and drove it through his breast,
Full half its length, and clasping, yet alive,
The maiden's arm, still soft, he there breathes out
In broken gasps, upon her fair white cheek,
Swift stream of bloody shower. So they lie,   1330
Dead bridegroom with dead bride, and he has gained,
Poor boy, his marriage rites in Hades home,
And left to all men witness terrible,
That man's worst ill is want of counsel wise.

(*Exit* EURYDICE.)

Chorus. What dost thou make of this?   She turneth back,   1335
Before one word, or good or ill, she speaks.

Mess. I too am full of wonder. Yet with hopes
I feed myself, she will not think it meet,
Hearing her son's woes, openly to wail
Out in the town, but to her handmaids there   1340
Will give command to wail her woe at home.
Too trained a judgment has she so to err.

Chorus. I know not. To my mind, or silence hard,
Or vain wild cries, are signs of bitter woe.

Mess. Soon we shall know, within the house advancing,   1345
If, in the passion of her heart, she hides
A secret purpose. Truly dost thou speak;
There is a terror in that silence hard.

Chorus (*seeing* CREON *approaching with the corpse of* HÆMON *in his arms*).

And lo! the king himself is drawing nigh,
And in his hands he bears a record clear,   1350
No woe (if I may speak) by others caused,
Himself the great offender.

(*Enter* CREON, *bearing* HÆMON's *body*.)

Creon. Woe! for the sins of souls of evil mood,
Stern, mighty to destroy!
O ye who look on those of kindred race, 1355
  The slayers and the slain,
Woe for mine own rash plans that prosper not!
Woe for thee, son; but new in life's career,
  And by a new fate dying!
        Woe! woe! 1360
Thou diest, thou art gone,
Not by thine evil counsel, but by mine.
  Chorus. Ah me! Too late thou seem'st to see
    the right.
  Creon.   Ah me!
I learn the grievous lesson. On my head, 1364
God, pressing sore, hath smitten me and vexed,
In ways most rough and terrible (Ah me!),
Shattering my joy, as trampled under foot.
Woe! woe! Man's labors are but labor lost

(*Enter* SECOND MESSENGER.)

  Sec. Mess. My master! thou, as one who hast full
    store,
One source of sorrow bearest in thine arms, 1370
And others in thy house, too soon, it seems,
Thou need'st must come and see.
  Creon.   And what remains
Worse evil than the evils that we bear?
  Sec. Mess. Thy wife is dead, that corpse's mother
    true,
Ill starred one, smitten with a blow just dealt. 1375
  Creon. O agony!
Haven of Death, that none may pacify,
  Why dost thou thus destroy me?
(*Turning to* MESSENGER.) O thou who comest,
    bringing in thy train
  Woes horrible to tell, 1380
Thou tramplest on a man already slain.
What say'st thou? What new tidings bring'st to
    me?
        Ah me! ah me!
Is it that now there waits in store for me
My own wife's death to crown my misery? 1385
  Chorus. Full clearly thou may'st see. No
    longer now
Does yon recess conceal her.
        (*The gates open and show the dead body of*
        EURYDICE.)
  Creon.   Woe is me!
This second ill I gaze on, miserable,
What fate, yea, what still lies in wait for me?
Here in my arms I bear what was my son; 1390
And there, O misery! look upon the dead.
Ah, wretched mother! ah, my son! my son!
  Sec. Mess. In frenzy wild she round the altar
    clung,

And closed her darkening eyelids, and bewailed
The noble fate of Megareus, who died 1395
Long since, and then again that corpse thou hast;
And last of all she cried a bitter cry
Against thy deeds, the murderer of thy sons.
  Creon. Woe! woe! alas!
I shudder in my fear. Will no one strike 1400
A deadly blow with sharp two-edgèd sword?
  Fearful my fate, alas!
And with a fearful woe full sore beset.
  Sec. Mess. She in her death charged thee with
    being the cause
Of all their sorrows, these and those of old. 1405
  Creon. And in what way struck she the murder-
    ous blow?
  Sec. Mess. With her own hand below her heart
    she stabbed,
Hearing her son's most pitiable fate.
  Creon. Ah me! The fault is mine. On no one
    else,
Of all that live, the fearful guilt can come; 1410
I, even I, did slay thee, woe is me!
I, yes, I speak the truth. Lead me, ye guards,
Lead me forth quickly; lead me out of sight,
More crushed to nothing than is nothing's self.
  Chorus. Thou counsellest gain, if gain there be in
    ills, 1415
For present ills when shortest then are best.
  Creon. Oh, come thou then, come thou,
The last of all my dooms, that brings to me
Best boon, my life's last day. Come then, oh
    come,
That never more I look upon the light. 1420
  Chorus. These things are in the future. What
    is near,
That we must do. O'er what is yet to come
They watch, to Whom that work of right belongs.
  Creon. I did but pray for what I most desire.
  Chorus. Pray thou for nothing then: for mortal
    man 1425
There is no issue from a doom decreed.
  Creon (*looking at the two corpses*). Lead me then
    forth, vain shadow that I am,
Who slew thee, O my son, unwillingly,
And thee too — (O my sorrow!) — and I know not
Which way to look or turn. All near at hand 1430
Is turned to evil; and upon my head
There falls a doom far worse than I can bear.
  Chorus. Man's highest blessedness,
    In wisdom chiefly stands;
And in the things that touch upon the Gods, 1435
    'Tis best in word or deed
    To shun unholy pride;
Great words of boasting bring great punishments,
    And so to gray-haired age
    Teach wisdom at the last. 1440

Euripides · 484–406 B.C.

The youngest of the three great writers of Greek tragedy, Euripides was born about 484 B.C. in Pella, a village in central Attica, and died, after some years of voluntary exile from Athens, in Amphipolis about 406 B.C. This span of life covers what is probably the richest period which tragedy, as a form of literature, has enjoyed in the history of the world. During these years Æschylus and Sophocles, as well as Euripides, were among the contestants for honors at the annual Dionysian festival. Unlike his older rivals, Æschylus and Sophocles, Euripides was born into humble social and financial circumstances.

Beyond his career as a dramatist little is known of the life of Euripides. He apparently began service in the army in 466 B.C.; he produced his first play, not now extant, in 455; he first won the Dionysian contest in 422. The *Medea*, reprinted below, won only third prize when it was produced in 431. Euripides wrote ninety or more plays (eighteen of which have survived), entered twenty-two of them in the contests, and was declared winner only four times. It seems likely that his failure to win more frequently is traceable to the fact that the dramatist introduced manner and thought and action which were frequently unconventional and that the populace then, as now, was skeptical of innovations. A combination of circumstances — his distaste for the political turmoil of the time, his view of life and the world and of the traditional gods, the dislike of the Athenians for him or his dislike for them — led him, when in his seventies, to leave Athens first for Magnesia and later for Macedonia. He died during this period of self-imposed exile.

Of the eighteen plays now in existence, those most widely read are perhaps: *Alcestis, Medea, Andromache, Trojan Women, Hippolytus,* and *Iphigenia in Aulis.* Possibly the single most impressive quality in Euripides is the vigor of his thought. His range of subjects was wide, and he introduced a variety of scenic effects. Again and again, he sought to discover the psychological reasons for human actions. Many of his plays are studies of women, their passions, moods, and actions. He goes beyond the conventional attitudes of his time on moral, theological, and social questions. Euripides' presentation of legendary heroes and gods as people is, perhaps, a romantic element; he is, however, essentially classical in his handling of structure and form and language.

Evidence of this classicism is found in the *Medea* selected for study. The adventurous career of Jason in search of the golden fleece, Jason's relations with Medea, the barbaric princess, — these are the stuff of the romantic. On the other hand, the murder of the children of Medea is an episode which the naturalist Zola might have liked to treat. Yet Euripides walks deftly between these two extremes; he gives himself over neither to the extravagances of romance nor to the horror of the murders. Rather, he subordinates both of these and lights unerringly on the tragedy of a woman scorned — and the vengeance which she seeks. The whole is the method of classicism, as is the restriction of the time of action to a single day and of the setting to a place outside Medea's house in Corinth. According to Gilbert Murray, "In speculation he [Euripides] is a critic and a free lance; in artistic form he is intensely traditional. He seems to have loved the very stiffnesses of the form in which he worked. He developed its inherent powers in ways undreamed of, but never broke the mould or strayed away into shapelessness or mere realism."

SUGGESTED REFERENCES: L. H. G. Greenwood, *Aspects of Euripidean Tragedy* (1953); Gilbert Norwood, *Essays on Euripidean Drama* (1954); Gilbert Murray, *Euripides and His Age* (2nd ed., 1955); G. M. A. Grube, *The Drama of Euripides* (2nd ed., 1961).

Medea

According to the old story of Jason and the Golden Fleece the Argonauts, once arrived in the land of Colchis, found the treasure guarded by magical monsters, bulls and a dragon, which they had little hope of overcoming. However, the gods decreed that Medea, a sorceress and daughter of the ruler of the land, should fall in love with Jason and help him secure the Fleece. In return for this assistance Jason promised to marry Medea. After further misadventures, Jason and Medea arrived in Corinth. When they had lived in this city for ten years, Creon, the king of Corinth, offered Jason his daughter in marriage and Jason deserted his barbaric Medea, the mother of his children, for this improved social position. The tragedy by Euripides tells us the result of this faithlessness on the part of Jason.

The *Medea* is characteristic of the work of Euripides in that in the play he presents a theme familiar to his readers, a woman who has been wronged, and treats the theme with profound psychological interest in the display of passion. It is a study in vengeance. The *Medea* has been called a "tragedy of the struggle of jealousy against love, of woman against man, of East against West." A reading of the play makes the unpopularity of Euripides in contemporary Athens somewhat understandable, for in it he scorns the "respectability" of Athens in the fifth century before Christ even as other poets have scorned conventional standards of action in the twentieth century. *Medea* (1946) by the American poet, Robinson Jeffers, is an interesting modern version of the Greek theme.

The translation below is by Wodhull, taken from *The Plays of Euripides*, in Everyman's Library, published by E. P. Dutton & Co., Inc., New York.

Persons of the Drama

NURSE OF MEDEA.
ATTENDANT OF THE CHILDREN.
MEDEA.
CHORUS OF CORINTHIAN WOMEN.
CREON.
JASON.
ÆGEUS.
MESSENGER.
THE TWO SONS OF JASON AND MEDEA.

SCENE: *In front of Medea's house in Corinth.*

NURSE

Ah! would to heaven the Argo [1] ne'er had urged
Its rapid voyage to the Colchian strand
'Twixt the Cyanean rocks, [2] nor had the pine
Been fell in Pelion's forests, nor the hands
Of those illustrious chiefs, who that famed bark   5
Ascended to obtain, the golden fleece
For royal Pelias, plied the stubborn oar;
So to Iolchos' turrets had my Queen
Medea never sailed, her soul with love
For Jason smitten, nor, as since her arts   10
Prevailed on Pelias' daughters to destroy
Their father, in this realm of Corinth dwelt
An exile with her husband and her sons;
Thus to the citizens whose land received her
Had she grown pleasing, and in all his schemes   15
Assisted Jason: to the wedded pair,
Hence bliss supreme arises, when the bond

[1] The ship in which Jason sought the Golden Fleece.
[2] Where the Bosphorus opens into the Black Sea.

Of concord joins them: now their souls are filled
With ruthless hate, and all affection's lost:
For false to his own sons, and her I serve,   20
With a new consort of imperial birth
Sleeps the perfidious Jason, to the daughter
Of Creon wedded, lord of these domains.
The wretched scorned Medea oft exclaims,   24
"O by those oaths, by that right hand thou gav'st
The pledge of faith!" She then invokes the gods
To witness what requital she hath found
From Jason. On a couch she lies, no food
Receiving, her whole frame subdued by grief;
And since she marked the treachery of her lord   30
Melts into tears incessant, from the ground
Her eyes she never raises, never turns
Her face aside, but steadfast as a rock,
Or as the ocean's rising billows, hears
The counsels of her friends, save when she weeps
In silent anguish, with her snowy neck   36
Averted, for her sire, her native land,
And home, which she forsaking hither came
With him who scorns her now. She from her woes
Too late hath learnt how enviable the lot   40
Of those who leave not their paternal roof.
She even hates her children, nor with joy
Beholds them: much I dread lest she contrive
Some enterprise unheard of, for her soul
Is vehement, nor will she tamely brook   45
Injurious treatment; well, full well I know
Her temper, which alarms me, lest she steal
Into their chamber, where the genial couch
Is spread, and with the sword their vitals pierce,
Or to the slaughter of the bridegroom add   50

That of the monarch, and in some mischance,
Yet more severe than death, herself involve:
For dreadful is her wrath, nor will the object
Of her aversion gain an easy triumph.
But lo, returning from the race, her sons   55
Draw near: they think not of their mother's woes,
For youthful souls are strangers to affliction.

ATTENDANT, *with the* SONS *of* JASON
and MEDEA, NURSE

Attend. O thou, who for a length of time hast
   dwelt
Beneath the roofs of that illustrious dame
I serve, why stand'st thou at these gates alone   60
Repeating to thyself a doleful tale:
Or wherefore by Medea from her presence
Art thou dismissed?
   Nurse.   Old man, O you who tend
On Jason's sons, to faithful servants aught
Of evil fortune that befalls their lords   65
Is a calamity: but such a pitch
Of grief am I arrived at, that I felt
An impulse which constrained me to come forth
From these abodes, and to the conscious earth
And heaven proclaim the lost Medea's fate.   70
   Attend. Cease not the plaints of that unhappy
      dame?
   Nurse. Your ignorance I envy: for her woes
Are but beginning, nor have yet attained
Their mid career.
   Attend.   O how devoid of reason,
If we with terms thus harsh may brand our lords,
Of ills more recent nothing yet she knows.   76
   Nurse. Old man, what mean you? Scruple not
      to speak.
   Attend. Nought. What I have already said re-
      pents me.
   Nurse. I by that beard conjure you not to hide
The secret from your faithful fellow-servant.   80
For I the strictest silence will observe
If it be needful.
   Attend.   Some one I o'erheard
(Appearing not to listen, as I came
Where aged men sit near Pirene's [1] fount
And hurl their dice) say that from Corinth's land
Creon, the lord of these domains, will banish   86
The children with their mother; but I know not
Whether th' intelligence be true, and wish
It may prove otherwise.
   Nurse.   Will Jason brook
Such an injurious treatment of his sons,   90
Although he be at variance with their mother?

---

[1] The fountain derived its name from a nymph who,
at the loss of her son, dissolved in tears and became a
spring.

Attend. By new connections are all former ties
Dissolved, and he no longer is a friend
To this neglected race.
   Nurse.   We shall be plunged   95
In utter ruin, if to our old woes,
Yet unexhausted, any fresh we add.
   Attend. Be silent, and suppress the dismal tale,
For 'tis unfit our royal mistress know.
   Nurse. Hear, O ye children, how your father's
      soul
Is turned against you: still, that he may perish 100
I do not pray, because he is my lord;
Yet treacherous to his friends hath he been found.
   Attend. Who is not treacherous? Hast thou
      lived so long
Without discerning how self-love prevails
O'er social? Some by glory, some by gain,   105
Are prompted. Then what wonder, for the sake
Of a new consort, if the father slight
These children?
   Nurse.   Go, all will be well, go in.
Keep them as far as possible away,
Nor suffer them to come into the presence   110
Of their afflicted mother; for her eyes
Have I just seen with wild distraction fired,
As if some horrid purpose against them
She meant to execute; her wrath I know
Will not be pacified, till on some victim   115
It like a thunderbolt from Heaven descends;
May she assail her foes alone, nor aim
The stroke at those she ought to hold most dear.
   Medea (within). Ah me! how grievous are my
      woes! What means
Can I devise to end this hated life?   120
   Nurse. 'Tis as I said: strong agitations seize
Your mother's heart, her choler's raised. Dear
      children,
Beneath these roofs hie instantly, nor come
Into her sight, accost her not, beware
Of these ferocious manners and the rage   125
Which boils in that ungovernable spirit.
Go with the utmost speed, for I perceive
Too clearly that her plaints, which in thick clouds
Arise at first, will kindle ere 'tis long
With tenfold violence. What deeds of horror   130
From that high-soaring, that remorseless soul,
May we expect, when goaded by despair!
                    (*Exeunt* ATTENDANT *and* SONS.)
   Medea (within). I have endured, alas! I have
      endured —
Wretch that I am! — such agonies as call
For loudest plaints. Ye execrable sons   135
Of a devoted mother, perish ye
With your false sire, and perish his whole house!
   Nurse. Why should the sons — ah, wretched
      me! — partake

Their father's guilt? Why hat'st thou them? Ah
    me!
How greatly, O ye children, do I fear   140
Lest mischief should befall you: for the souls
Of kings are prone to cruelty, so seldom
Subdued, and over others wont to rule,
That it is difficult for such to change
Their angry purpose. Happier I esteem   145
The lot of those who still are wont to live
Among their equals. May I thus grow old,
If not in splendor, yet with safety blest!
For first of all, renown attends the name
Of mediocrity, and to mankind   150
Such station is more useful: but not long
Can the extremes of grandeur ever last;
And heavier are the curses which it brings
When Fortune visits us in all her wrath.

CHORUS, NURSE

Chorus. The voice of Colchos' hapless dame I
    heard —   155
A clamorous voice, nor yet is she appeased.
Speak, O thou aged matron, for her cries
I from the innermost apartment heard;
Nor can I triumph in the woes with which
This house is visited; for to my soul   160
Dear are its interests.
Nurse.   This whole house is plunged
In ruin, and its interests are no more.
While Corinth's palace to our lord affords
A residence, within her chamber pines
My mistress, and the counsels of her friends   165
Afford no comfort to her tortured soul.
Medea (*within*). O that a flaming thunderbolt
    from Heaven
Would pierce this brain! for what can longer life
To me avail? Fain would I seek repose
In death, and cast away this hated being.   170
Chorus. Heard'st thou, all-righteous Jove, thou
    fostering earth,
And thou, O radiant lamp of day, what plaints,
What clamorous plaints this miserable wife
Hath uttered? Through insatiable desire,
Ah why would you precipitate your death?   175
O most unwise! These imprecations spare.
What if your lord's affections are engaged
By a new bride, reproach him not, for Jove
Will be the dread avenger of your wrongs;
Nor melt away with unavailing grief,   180
Weeping for the lost partner of your bed.
Medea (*within*). Great Themis[1] and Diana,
    awful queen,
Do ye behold the insults I endure,
Though by each oath most holy I have bound

[1] Goddess of Justice.

That execrable husband. May I see   185
Him and his bride, torn limb from limb, bestrew
The palace; me have they presumed to wrong,
Although I ne'er provoked them. O my sire,
And thou my native land, whence I with shame
Departed when my brother I had slain.   190
Nurse. Heard ye not all she said, with a loud
    voice
Invoking Themis, who fulfils the vow,
And Jove, to whom the tribes of men look up
As guardian of their oaths. Medea's rage
Can by no trivial vengeance be appeased.   195
Chorus. Could we but draw her hither, and
    prevail
On her to hear the counsels we suggest,
Then haply might she check that bitter wrath,
That vehemence of temper; for my zeal
Shall not be spared to aid my friends. But go, 200
And say, "O hasten, ere to those within
Thou do some mischief, for these sorrows rush
With an impetuous tempest on thy soul."
Nurse. This will I do; though there is cause to
    fear
That on my mistress I shall ne'er prevail: 205
Yet I my labor gladly will bestow.
Though such a look she on her servants casts
As the ferocious lioness who guards
Her tender young, when anyone draws near
To speak to her. Thou wouldst not judge amiss,
In charging folly and a total want   211
Of wisdom on the men of ancient days,
Who for their festivals invented hymns,
And to the banquet and the genial board
Confined those actions which o'er human life   215
Diffuse ecstatic pleasures: but no artist
Hath yet discovered, by the tuneful song,
And varied modulations of the lyre,
How we those piercing sorrows may assuage   219
Whence slaughters and such horrid mischief spring
As many a prosperous mansion have o'erthrown.
Could music interpose her healing aid
In these inveterate maladies, such gift
Had been the first of blessings to mankind:
But, 'midst choice viands and the circling bowl, 225
Why should those minstrels strain their useless
    throat?
To cheer the drooping heart, convivial joys
Are in themselves sufficient. (*Exit* NURSE.)
Chorus.   Mingled groans
And lamentations burst upon mine ear:
She in the bitterness of soul exclaims   230
Against her impious husband, who betrayed
His plighted faith. By grievous wrongs opprest,
She the vindictive gods invokes, and Themis,
Jove's daughter, guardian of the sacred oath,
Who o'er the waves to Greece benignly steered 235

Their bark adventurous, launched in midnight
    gloom,
Through ocean's gates which never can be closed!

MEDEA, CHORUS

Medea. From my apartment, ye Corinthian
    dames,
Lest ye my conduct censure, I come forth:
For I have known full many who obtained   240
Fame and high rank; some to the public gaze
Stood ever forth, while others, in a sphere
More distant, chose their merits to display:
Nor yet a few, who, studious of repose,
Have with malignant obloquy been called   245
Devoid of spirit: for no human eyes
Can form a just discernment; at one glance,
Before the inmost secrets of the heart
Are clearly known, a bitter hate 'gainst him
Who never wronged us they too oft inspire.   250
But 'tis a stranger's duty to adopt
The manners of the land in which he dwells;
Nor can I praise that native, led astray
By mere perverseness and o'erweening folly,
Who bitter enmity incurs from those   255
Of his own city. But, alas! my friends,
This unforeseen calamity hath withered
The vigor of my soul. I am undone,
Bereft of every joy that life can yield,
And therefore wish to die. For as to him,   260
My husband, whom it did import me most
To have a thorough knowledge of, he proves
The worst of men. But sure among all those
Who have with breath and reason been endued,
We women are the most unhappy race.   265
First, with abundant gold are we constrained
To buy a husband, and in him receive
A haughty master. Still doth there remain
One mischief than this mischief yet more grievous,
The hazard whether we procure a mate   270
Worthless or virtuous: for divorces bring
Reproach to woman, nor must she renounce
The man she wedded; as for her who comes
Where usages and edicts, which at home
She learnt not, are established, she the gift   275
Of divination needs to teach her how
A husband must be chosen: if aright
These duties we perform, and he the yoke
Of wedlock with complacency sustains,
Ours is a happy life; but if we fail   280
In this great object, better 'twere to die.
For, when afflicted by domestic ills,
A man goes forth, his choler to appease,
And to some friend or comrade can reveal
What he endures; but we to him alone   285
For succor must look up. They still contend
That we, at home remaining, lead a life

Exempt from danger, while they launch the spear:
False are these judgments; rather would I thrice,
Armed with a target, in th' embattled field   290
Maintain my stand, than suffer once the throes
Of childbirth. But this language suits not you:
This is your native city, the abode
Of your loved parents, every comfort life
Can furnish is at hand, and with your friends   295
You here converse: but I, forlorn, and left
Without a home, am by that husband scorned
Who carried me from a Barbarian realm.
Nor mother, brother, or relation now
Have I, to whom I 'midst these storms of woe,
Like an auspicious haven, can repair.   301
Thus far I therefore crave ye will espouse
My interests, as if haply any means
Or any stratagem can be devised
For me with justice to avenge these wrongs   305
On my perfidious husband, on the king
Who to that husband's arms his daughter gave,
And the new-wedded princess; to observe
Strict silence. For although at other times
A woman, filled with terror, is unfit   310
For battle, or to face the lifted sword,
She when her soul by marriage wrongs is fired,
Thirsts with a rage unparalleled for blood.[1]
Chorus. The silence you request I will observe,
For justly on your lord may you inflict   315
Severest vengeance: still I wonder not
If your disastrous fortunes you bewail:
But Creon I behold who wields the sceptre
Of these domains; the monarch hither comes
His fresh resolves in person to declare.   320

CREON, MEDEA, CHORUS

Creon. Thee, O Medea, who, beneath those
    looks
Stern and forbidding, harbor'st 'gainst thy lord
Resentment, I command to leave these realms
An exile; for companions of thy flight
Take both thy children with thee, nor delay.   325
Myself pronounce this edict: I my home
Will not revisit, from the utmost bounds
Of this domain, till I have cast thee forth.
Medea. Ah, wretched me! I utterly am ruined:
For in the swift pursuit, my ruthless foes,   330
Each cable loosing, have unfurled their sails,
Nor can I land on any friendly shore
To save myself, yet am resolved to speak,
Though punishment impend. What cause, O
    Creon
Have you for banishing me?

[1] Women of the higher class in Greece were expected
to lead a secluded life. The tortoise, which kept close
to home, became a symbol for the proper career of a
married woman.

Creon.   Thee I dread   335
(No longer is it needful to disguise
My thoughts) lest 'gainst my daughter thou con-
    trive
Some evil such as medicine cannot reach.[1]
Full many incidents conspire to raise
This apprehension: with a deep-laid craft   340
Art thou endued, expert in the device
Of mischiefs numberless, thou also griev'st
Since thou art severed from thy husband's bed.
I am informed, too, thou hast menaced vengeance
'Gainst me, because my daughter I bestowed   345
In marriage, and the bridegroom, and his bride.
Against these threats I therefore ought to guard
Before they take effect; and better far
Is it for me, O woman, to incur
Thy hatred now, than, soothed by thy mild words,
Hereafter my forbearance to bewail.   351
  Medea. Not now, alas! for the first time, but oft
To me, O Creon, hath opinion proved
Most baleful, and the source of grievous woes.
Nor ever ought the man, who is possest   355
Of a sound judgment, to train up his children
To be too wise: for they who live exempt
From war and all its toils, the odious name
Among their fellow-citizens acquire
Of abject sluggards. If to the unwise   360
You some fresh doctrine broach, you are esteemed
Not sapient, but a trifler: when to those
Who in their own conceit possess each branch
Of knowledge, you in state affairs obtain
Superior fame, to them you grow obnoxious.[2]   365
I also feel the grievance I lament;
Some envy my attainments, others think
My temper uncomplying, though my wisdom
Is not transcendent. But from me it seems
You apprehend some violence; dismiss   370
Those fears; my situation now is such,
O Creon, that to monarchs I can give
No umbrage: and in what respect have you
Treated me with injustice? You bestowed
Your daughter where your inclination led.   375
Though I abhor my husband, I suppose
That you have acted wisely, nor repine
At your prosperity. Conclude the match;
Be happy: but allow me in this land
Yet to reside; for I my wrongs will bear   380
In silence, and to my superiors yield.
  Creon. Soft is the sound of thy persuasive words,
But in my soul I feel the strongest dread

  [1] Medea's past record was that of a sorceress.
  [2] This ironic discussion of education may reflect
Euripides' criticism of the current distrust Athenians
held for philosophy. Athens had just exiled a philosopher friend of the dramatist and some years later was
to kill Socrates.

Lest thou devise some mischief, and now less
Than ever can I trust thee; for 'gainst those   385
Of hasty tempers with more ease we guard,
Or men or women, than the silent foe
Who acts with prudence. Therefore be thou gone
With speed, no answer make: it is decreed,
Nor hast thou art sufficient to avert   390
Thy doom of banishment; for well aware
Am I thou hat'st me.
  Medea.   Spare me, by those knees
And your new-wedded daughter, I implore.
  Creon. Lavish of words, thou never shalt per-
    suade me.
  Medea. Will you then drive me hence, and to
my prayers   395
No reverence yield?
  Creon.   I do not love thee more
Than those of my own house.
  Medea.   With what regret
Do I remember thee, my native land.
  Creon. Except my children, I hold nought so
    dear.
  Medea. To mortals what a dreadful scourge is
    love.   400
  Creon. As fortune dictates, love becomes, I
    ween,
Either a curse or blessing.
  Medea.   Righteous Jove,
Let not the author of my woes escape thee.
  Creon. Away vain woman, free me from my
    cares.
  Medea. No lack of cares have I.
  Creon.   Thou from this spot   405
Shalt by my servants' hands ere long be torn.
  Medea. Not thus, O Creon, I your mercy crave.
  Creon. To trouble me, it seems, thou art re-
    solved.
  Medea. I will depart, nor urge this fond request.
  Creon. Why dost thou struggle then, nor from
our realm   410
Withdraw thyself?
  Medea.   Allow me this one day
Here to remain, till my maturer thoughts
Instruct me to what region I can fly,
Where for my sons find shelter, since their sire
Attends not to the welfare of his race.   415
Take pity on them, for you also know
What 'tis to be a parent, and must feel
Parental love: as for myself, I heed not
The being doomed to exile, but lament
Their hapless fortunes.
  Creon.   No tyrannic rage   420
Within this bosom dwells, but pity oft
Hath warped my better judgment, and though
    now
My error I perceive, shall thy request

Be granted.   Yet of this must I forewarn thee:
If when to-morrow with his orient beams 425
Phœbus the world revisits, he shall view
Thee and thy children still within the bounds
Of these domains, thou certainly shalt die —
Th' irrevocable sentence is pronounced.
But if thou needs must tarry, tarry here 430
This single day, for in so short a space
Thou canst not execute the ills I dread.

                                        (*Exit* CREON.)

Chorus. Alas! thou wretched woman, overpow-
      ered
By thy afflictions, whither wilt thou turn?
What hospitable board, what mansion, find, 435
Or country to protect thee from these ills?
Into what storms of misery have the gods
Caused thee to rush!

      Medea.   On every side distress
Assails me: who can contradict this truth?
Yet think not that my sorrows thus shall end. 440
By yon new-wedded pair must be sustained
Dire conflicts, and no light or trivial woes
By them who in affinity are joined
With this devoted house.   Can ye suppose
That I would e'er have soothed him, had no gain
Or stratagem induced me?   Else to him 446
Never would I have spoken, nor once raised
My suppliant hands.   But now is he so lost
In folly, that, when all my schemes with ease
He might have baffled, if he from this land 450
Had cast me forth, he grants me to remain
For this one day, and ere the setting sun
Three of my foes will I destroy — the sire,
The daughter, and my husband: various means
Have I of slaying them, and, O my friends, 455
Am at a loss to fix on which I first
Shall undertake, or to consume with flames
The bridal mansion, or a dagger plunge
Into their bosoms, entering unperceived
The chamber where they sleep.   But there re-
      mains 460
One danger to obstruct my path: if caught
Stealing into the palace, and intent
On such emprise, in death shall I afford
A subject of derision to my foes,
This obvious method were the best, in which 465
I am most skilled, to take their lives away
By sorceries.   Be it so; suppose them dead.
What city will receive me as its guest,
What hospitable foreigner afford
A shelter in his land, or to his hearth 470
Admit, or snatch me from impending fate?
Alas!   I have no friend.   I will delay
A little longer therefore; if perchance,
To screen me from destruction, I can find
Some fortress, then I in this deed of blood 475

With artifice and silence will engage;
But, if by woes inextricable urged
Too closely, snatching up the dagger them
Am I resolved to slay, although myself
Must perish too; for courage unappalled 480
This bosom animates.   By that dread queen,
By her whom first of all th' immortal powers
I worship, and to aid my bold emprise
Have chosen, the thrice awful Hecaté,[1]
Who in my innermost apartment dwells, 485
Not one of them shall triumph in the pangs
With which they wound my heart; for I will render
This spousal rite to them a plenteous source
Of bitterness and mourning — they shall rue
Their union, rue my exile from this land. 490
But now come on, nor, O Medea, spare
Thy utmost science to devise and frame
Deep stratagems, with swift career advance
To deeds of horror.   Such a strife demands
Thy utmost courage.   Hast thou any sense 495
Of these indignities?   Nor is it fit
That thou, who spring'st from an illustrious sire,
And from that great progenitor the sun,[2]
Shouldst be derided by the impious brood
Of Sisyphus,[3] at Jason's nuptial feast 500
Exposed to scorn: for thou hast ample skill
To right thyself.   Although by Nature formed
Without a genius apt for virtuous deeds,
We women are in mischiefs most expert.

CHORUS

ODE

I. 1

Now upward to their source the rivers flow, 505
   And in a retrograde career
Justice and all the baffled virtues go.
      The views of man are insincere,
      Nor to the gods though he appeal,
      And with an oath each promise seal, 510
Can he be trusted.   Yet doth veering fame
      Loudly assert the female claim,
      Causing our sex to be renowned,
      And our whole lives with glory crowned.
No longer shall we mourn the wrongs 515
Of slanderous and inhuman tongues.

I. 2

Nor shall the Muses, as in ancient days,
   Make the deceit of womankind
The constant theme of their malignant lays.
      For ne'er on our uncultured mind 520

---

[1] A goddess of witchcraft.   Medea kept an image of
Hecate by her hearth.
[2] Medea was a descendant of the Sun god.
[3] Founder of Corinth.

Hath Phœbus, god of verse, bestowed
Genius to frame the lofty ode;
Else had we waked the lyre, and in reply
With descants on man's infamy
Oft lengthened out th' opprobrious page. 525
Yet may we from each distant age
Collect such records as disgrace
Both us and man's imperious race.

II. 1

By love distracted, from thy native strand,
Thou 'twixt the ocean's clashing rocks didst
  sail 530
But now, loathed inmate of a foreign land,
Thy treacherous husband's loss art doomed to
  wail.
O hapless matron, overwhelmed with woe,
From this unpitying realm dishonored must thou
  go.

II. 2

No longer sacred oaths their credit bear, 535
And virtuous shame hath left the Grecian plain,
She mounts to Heaven, and breathes a purer air.
For thee doth no paternal house remain
The sheltering haven from affliction's tides; 539
Over these hostile roofs a mightier queen presides.

JASON, MEDEA, CHORUS

Jason. Not now for the first time, but oft, full oft
Have I observed that anger is a pest
The most unruly. For when in this land,
These mansions, you in peace might have abode,
By patiently submitting to the will 545
Of your superiors, you, for empty words,
Are doomed to exile. Not that I regard
Your calling Jason with incessant rage
The worst of men; but for those bitter taunts
With which you have reviled a mighty king, 550
Too mild a penalty may you esteem
Such banishment. I still have soothed the wrath
Of the offended monarch, still have wished
That you might here continue; but no bounds
Your folly knows, nor can that tongue e'er cease
To utter menaces against your lords; 556
Hence from these regions justly are you doomed
To be cast forth. But with unwearied love
Attentive to your interest am I come,
Lest with your children you by cruel want 560
Should be encompassed; exile with it brings
Full many evils. Me, though you abhor,
To you I harbor no unfriendly thought.

Medea. Thou worst of villains (for this bitter
  charge
Against thy abject cowardice my tongue 565
May justly urge), com'st thou to me, O wretch,

Who to the gods art odious, and to me
And all the human race? It is no proof
Of courage, or of steadfastness, to face
Thy injured friends, but impudence, the worst 570
Of all diseases. Yet hast thou done well
In coming: I by uttering the reproaches
Which thou deservest shall ease my burdened soul,
And thou wilt grieve to hear them. With th'
  events
Which happened first will I begin my charge. 575
Each Grecian chief who in the Argo sailed
Knows how from death I saved thee, when to yoke
The raging bulls whose nostrils poured forth
  flames,
And sow the baleful harvest, thou wert sent:
Then having slain the dragon, who preserved 580
With many a scaly fold the golden fleece,
Nor ever closed in sleep his watchful eyes,
I caused the morn with its auspicious beams
To shine on thy deliverance; but, my sire
And native land betraying, came with thee 585
To Pelion, and Iolchos' gates: for love
Prevailed o'er reason. Pelias next I slew —
Most wretched death — by his own daughters'
  hands
And thus delivered thee from all thy fears.
Yet though to me, O most ungrateful man, 590
Thus much indebted, hast thou proved a traitor,
And to the arms of this new consort fled,
Although a rising progeny is thine.
Hadst thou been childless, 'twere a venial fault
In thee to court another for thy bride. 595
But vanished is the faith which oaths erst bore,
Nor can I judge whether thou think'st the gods
Who ruled the world have lost their ancient power
Or that fresh laws at present are in force
Among mankind, because thou to thyself 600
Art conscious, thou thy plighted faith has broken.
O my right hand, which thou didst oft embrace,
Oft to these knees a suppliant cling! How vainly
Did I my virgin purity yield up
To a perfidious husband, led astray 605
By flattering hopes! Yet I to thee will speak
As if thou wert a friend, and I expected
From thee some mighty favor to obtain:
Yet thou, if strictly questioned, must appear
More odious. Whither shall I turn me now? 610
To those deserted mansions of my father,
Which, with my country, I to thee betrayed,
And hither came; or to the wretched daughters
Of Pelias? They forsooth, whose sire I slew,
Beneath their roofs with kindness would receive me.
'Tis even thus: by those of my own house 616
Am I detested, and, to serve thy cause,
Those very friends, whom least of all I ought
To have unkindly treated, have I made

My enemies. But eager to repay   620
Such favors, 'mongst unnumbered Grecian dames
On me superior bliss hast thou bestowed,
And I, unhappy woman, find in thee
A husband who deserves to be admired
For his fidelity. But from this realm   625
When I am exiled, and by every friend
Deserted, with my children left forlorn,
A glorious triumph, in thy bridal hour,
To thee will it afford, if those thy sons,   629
And I who saved thee, should like vagrants roam.
Wherefore, O Jove, didst thou instruct mankind
How to distinguish by undoubted marks
Counterfeit gold, yet in the front of vice
Impress no brand to show the tainted heart?
   Chorus. How sharp their wrath, how hard to be
      appeased,   635
When friends with friends begin the cruel strife.
   Jason. I ought not to be rash, it seems, in
      speech,
But like the skilful pilot, who, with sails
Scarce half unfurled, his bark more surely guides,
Escape, O woman, your ungoverned tongue.   640
Since you the benefits on me conferred
Exaggerate in so proud a strain, I deem
That I to Venus only, and no god
Or man beside, my prosperous voyage owe.
Although a wondrous subtlety of soul   645
To you belong, 'twere an invidious speech
For me to make should I relate how Love
By his inevitable shafts constrained you
To save my life. I will not therefore state
This argument too nicely, but allow,   650
As you did aid me, it was kindly done.
But by preserving me have you gained more
Than you bestowed, as I shall prove: and first,
Transplanted from barbaric shores, you dwell
In Grecian regions, and have here been taught   655
To act as justice and the laws ordain,
Nor follow the caprice of brutal strength.
By all the Greeks your wisdom is perceived,
And you acquire renown; but had you still
Inhabited that distant spot of earth,   660
You never had been named. I would not wish
For mansions heaped with gold, or to exceed
The sweetest notes of Orpheus' magic lyre,
Were those unfading wreaths which fame bestows
From me withheld by fortune. I thus far   665
On my own labors only have discoursed.
For you this odious strife of words began.
But in espousing Creon's royal daughter,
With which you have reproached me, I will prove
That I in acting thus am wise and chaste,   670
That I to you have been the best of friends,
And to our children. But make no reply.
Since hither from Iolchos' land I came,

Accompanied by many woes, and such
As could not be avoided, what device   675
More advantageous could an exile frame
Than wedding the king's daughter? Not through
      hate
To you, which you reproach me with, not smitten
With love for a new consort, or a wish
The number of my children to augment: 680
For those we have already might suffice,
And I complain not. But to me it seemed
Of great importance that we both might live
As suits our rank, nor suffer abject need,
Well knowing that each friend avoids the poor.
I also wished to educate our sons   686
In such a manner as befits my race
And with their noble brothers yet unborn,
Make them one family, that thus, my house
Cementing, I might prosper. In some measure
Is it your interest too that by my bride   691
I should have sons, and me it much imports,
By future children, to provide for those
Who are in being. Have I judged amiss?
You would not censure me, unless your soul   695
Were by a rival stung.[1] But your whole sex
Hath these ideas; if in marriage blest
Ye deem nought wanting, but if some reverse
Of fortune e'er betide the nuptial couch,
All that was good and lovely ye abhor.   700
Far better were it for the human race
Had children been produced by other means,
No females e'er existing: hence might man
Exempt from every evil have remained.
   Chorus. Thy words hast thou with specious art
      adorned,   705
Yet thou to me (it is against my will
That I such language hold), O Jason, seem'st
Not to have acted justly in betraying
Thy consort.
   Medea.   From the many I dissent
In many points: for, in my judgment, he   710
Who tramples on the laws, but can express
His thoughts with plausibility, deserves
Severest punishment: for that injustice
On which he glories, with his artful tongue,
That he a fair appearance can bestow,   715
He dares to practise, nor is truly wise.
No longer then this specious language hold
To me, who by one word can strike thee dumb.
Hadst thou not acted with a base design,
It was thy duty first to have prevailed   720
On me to give consent, ere these espousals
Thou hadst contracted, nor kept such design
A secret from thy friends.
   Jason.   You would have served

[1] Throughout this speech Jason, in defending himself,
voices his own condemnation.

My cause most gloriously, had I disclosed
To you my purposed nuptials, when the rage   725
Of that proud heart still unsubdued remains.
Medea. Thy real motive was not what thou sayst,
But a Barbarian wife, in thy old age,
Might have appeared to tarnish thy renown.
Jason. Be well assured, love urged me not to
take   730
The daughter of the monarch to my bed.
But 'twas my wish to save you from distress,
As I already have declared, and raise
Some royal brothers to our former sons,
Strengthening with fresh supports our shattered
house.   735
Medea. May that prosperity which brings re-
morse
Be never mine, nor riches such as sting
The soul with anguish.
Jason.   Are you not aware
You soon will change your mind and grow more
wise?
Forbear to spurn the blessings you possess,   740
Nor droop beneath imaginary woes,
When you are happy.
Medea.   Scoff at my distress,
For thou hast an asylum to receive thee:
But from this land am I constrained to roam
A lonely exile.
Jason.   This was your own choice: 745
Accuse none else.
Medea.   What have I done — betrayed
My plighted faith and sought a foreign bed?
Jason. You uttered impious curses 'gainst the
king.
Medea. I also in thy mansions am accursed.
Jason. With you I on these subjects will con-
tend   750
No longer.   But speak freely, what relief,
Or for the children or your exiled state,
You from my prosperous fortunes would receive:
For with a liberal hand am I inclined
My bounties to confer, and hence despatch   755
Such tokens, as to hospitable kindness
Will recommend you.   Woman, to refuse
These offers were mere folly; from your soul
Banish resentment, and no trifling gain
Will hence ensue.
Medea.   No use I of thy friends   760
Will make, nor aught accept; thy presents spare,
For nothing which the wicked man can give
Proves beneficial.
Jason.   I invoke the gods
To witness that I gladly would supply
You and your children with whate'er ye need: 765
But you these favors loathe, and with disdain
Repel your friends: hence an increase of woe

Shall be your lot.
Medea.   Be gone; for thou, with love
For thy young bride inflamed, too long remain'st
Without the palace.   Wed her; though perhaps 770
(Yet with submission to the righteous gods,
This I announce) such marriage thou mayst rue.
                                    (*Exit* JASON.)

CHORUS

ODE

I.   I

Th' immoderate loves in their career,
Nor glory nor esteem attends,
But when the Cyprian queen descends   775
Benignant from her starry sphere,
No goddess can more justly claim
From man the grateful prayer.
Thy wrath, O Venus, still forbear,
Nor at my tender bosom aim   780
That venomed arrow, ever wont t' inspire
Winged from thy golden bow, the pangs of keen
desire.

I.   2

May I in modesty delight,
Best present which the gods can give,
Nor torn by jaring passions live   785
A prey to wrath and cankered spite,
Still envious of a rival's charms,
Nor rouse the endless strife
While on my soul another wife
Impresses vehement alarms: 790
On us, dread queen, thy mildest influence shed
Thou who discern'st each crime that stains the
nuptial bed.

II.   I

My native land, and dearest home!
May I ne'er know an exiled state,
Nor be it ever my sad fate   795
While from thy well-known bourn I roam,
My hopeless anguish to bemoan.
Rather let death, let death
Take at that hour my forfeit breath,
For surely never was there known   800
On earth a curse so great as to exceed,
From his loved country torn, the wretched exile's
need.

II.   2

These eyes attest thy piteous tale,
Which not from fame alone we know;
But, O thou royal dame, thy woe   805
No generous city doth bewail,
Nor one among thy former friends.

Abhorred by Heaven and earth,
Perish the wretch devoid of worth,
Engrossed by mean and selfish ends,   810
Whose heart expands not those he loved to aid;
Never may I lament attachments thus repaid.

ÆGEUS, MEDEA, CHORUS

Ægeus. Medea, hail! for no man can devise
Terms more auspicious to accost his friends.

Medea. And you, O son of wise Pandion, hail
Illustrious Ægeus.   But to these domains   816
Whence came you?

Ægeus.   From Apollo's ancient shrine.

Medea. But to that centre of the world,[1] whence
sounds
Prophetic issue, why did you repair?   819

Ægeus. To question by what means I may obtain
A race of children.

Medea.   By the gods, inform me,
Are you still doomed to drag a childless life?

Ægeus. Such is the influence of some adverse
demon.

Medea. Have you a wife, or did you never try
The nuptial yoke?

Ægeus.   With wedlock's sacred bonds
I am not unacquainted.

Medea.   On the subject   826
Of children, what did Phœbus say?

Ægeus.   His words
Were such as mortals cannot comprehend.

Medea. Am I allowed to know the god's reply?

Ægeus. Thou surely art: such mystery to expound   830
There needs the help of thy sagacious soul.

Medea. Inform me what the oracle pronounced,
If I may hear it.

Ægeus.   "The projecting foot,
Thou, of the vessel must not dare to loose" —

Medea. Till you do what, or to what region
come?   835

Ægeus. "Till thou return to thy paternal lares."

Medea. But what are you in need of, that you
steer
Your bark to Corinth's shores?

Ægeus.   A king, whose name
Is Pittheus, o'er Trœzene's realm presides.

Medea. That most religious man, they say, is
son   840
Of Pelops.

Ægeus. I with him would fain discuss
The god's prophetic voice.

Medea.   For he is wise,
And in this science long hath been expert.

[1] The oracle of Apollo was at Delphi on the slopes of
Parnassus, a spot then thought to be the center of the
earth.

Ægeus. Dearest to me of those with whom I
formed
A league of friendship in the embattled field.   845

Medea. But, O may you be happy, and obtain
All that you wish for.

Ægeus.   Why those downcast eyes,
That wasted form?

Medea.   O Ægeus, he I wedded
To me hath proved of all mankind most base.

Ægeus. What mean'st thou?   In plain terms
thy grief declare.   850

Medea. Jason hath wronged me, though without
a cause.

Ægeus. Be more explicit, what injurious treatment
Complain'st thou of?

Medea.   To me hath he preferred
Another wife, the mistress of this house.

Ægeus. Dared he to act so basely?

Medea.   Be assured   855
That I, whom erst he loved, am now forsaken.

Ægeus. What amorous passion triumphs o'er his
soul?
Or doth he loathe thy bed?

Medea.   'Tis mighty love,
That to his first attachment makes him false.   859

Ægeus. Let him depart then, if he be so void
Of honor as thou sayst.

Medea.   He sought to form
Alliance with a monarch.

Ægeus.   Who bestows
On him a royal bride?   Conclude thy tale.

Medea. Creon, the ruler of this land.

Ægeus.   Thy sorrows
Are then excusable.

Medea.   I am undone,   865
And banished hence.

Ægeus.   By whom?   There's not a word
Thou utter'st but unfolds fresh scenes of woe.

Medea. Me from this realm to exile Creon drives.

Ægeus. Doth Jason suffer this?   I cannot
praise   869
Such conduct.

Medea.   Not in words: though he submits
Without reluctance.   But I by that beard,
And by those knees, a wretched suppliant, crave
Your pity; see me not cast forth forlorn,
But to your realms and to your social hearth
Receive me as a guest; so may your desire   875
For children be accomplished by the gods,
And happiness your close of life attend.
But how important a discovery Fortune
To you here makes you are not yet apprised:
For destitute of heirs will I permit you   880
No longer to remain, but through my aid
Shall you have sons, such potent drugs I know.

Ægeus. Various inducements urge me to comply
With this request, O woman; first an awe
For the immortal gods, and then the hope   885
That I the promised issue shall obtain.
On what my senses scarce can comprehend
I will rely. O that thy arts may prove
Effectual! Thee, if haply thou arriv'st
In my domain, with hospitable rites   890
Shall it be my endeavor to receive,
As justice dictates: but to thee, thus much
It previously behoves me to announce:
I will not take thee with me from this realm,
But to my house if of thyself thou come   895
Thou a secure asylum there shalt find,
Nor will I yield thee up to any foe.
But hence without my aid must thou depart,
For I, from those who in this neighboring land
Of Corinth entertain me as their guest,   900
Wish to incur no censure.

Medea.   Your commands
Shall be obeyed: but would you plight your faith
That you this promise will to me perform,
A noble friend in you I shall have found.

Ægeus. Believ'st thou not? Whence rise these
    anxious doubts?   905

Medea. In you I trust; though Pelias'[1] hostile
    race
And Creon's hate pursue me: but, if bound
By the firm sanction of a solemn oath,
You will not suffer them with brutal force   909
To drag me from your realm, but having entered
Into such compact, and by every god
Sworn to protect me, still remain a friend,
Nor hearken to their embassies. My fortune
Is in its wane, but wealth to them belongs,
And an imperial mansion.

Ægeus.   In these words   915
Hast thou expressed great forethought: but if thus
Thou art disposed to act, I my consent
Will not refuse; for I shall be more safe
If to thy foes some plausible excuse
I can allege, and thee more firmly stablish.   920
But say thou first what gods I shall invoke.

Medea. Swear by the earth on which we tread,
    the sun
My grandsire, and by all the race of gods.

Ægeus. What action, or to do or to forbear?

Medea. That from your land you never will ex-
    pel,   925
Nor while you live consent that any foe
Shall tear me thence.

Ægeus.   By earth, the radiant sun,

[1] Pelias had ruled the kingdom which rightfully
belonged to Jason. Medea, by sorcery, had persuaded
the daughters of Pelias to kill him. Naturally she was
not welcome there.

And every god I swear, I to the terms
Thou hast proposed will steadfastly adhere.

Medea. This may suffice. But what if you in-
    fringe   930
Your oath, what punishment will you endure?

Ægeus. Each curse that can befall the impious
    man.

Medea. Depart, and prosper: all things now ad-
    vance
In their right track, and with the utmost speed
I to your city will direct my course,   935
When I have executed those designs
I meditate, and compassed what I wish.

           (*Exit* ÆGEUS.)

Chorus. But thee, O king, may Maia's wingéd
    son[1]
Lead to thy Athens; there mayst thou attain
All that thy soul desires, for thou to me,   940
O Ægeus, seem'st most generous.

Medea.   Awful Jove,
Thou too, O Justice, who art ever joined
With thundering Jove, and bright Hyperion's
    beams,
You I invoke. Now, O my friends, o'er those
I hate shall we prevail: 'tis the career   945
Of victory that we tread, and I at length
Have hopes the strictest vengeance on my foes
To execute: for where we most in need
Of a protector stood, appeared this stranger,
The haven of my counsels: we shall fix   950
Our cables to this poop, soon as we reach
That hallowed city where Minerva reigns.
But now to you the whole of my designs
Will I relate; look not for such a tale
As yields delight: some servant will I send   955
An interview with Jason to request,
And on his coming, in the softest words
Address him; say these matters are well pleasing
To me, and in the strongest terms applaud
That marriage with the daughter of the king,   960
Which now the traitor celebrates; then add,
"'Tis for our mutual good, 'tis rightly done."
But the request which I intend to make
Is that he here will let my children stay;
Not that I mean to leave them thus behind,   965
Exposed to insults in a hostile realm
From those I hate; but that my arts may slay
The royal maid: with presents in their hands,
A vesture finely wrought and golden crown,
Will I despatch them; these they to the bride   970
Shall bear, that she their exile may reverse:
If these destructive ornaments she take
And put them on, both she, and every one
Who touches her, shall miserably perish—
My presents with such drugs I will anoint.   975

[1] Hermes.

Far as to this relates, here ends my speech.
But I with anguish think upon a deed
Of more than common horror, which remains
By me to be accomplished: for my sons
Am I resolved to slay, them from this arm   980
Shall no man rescue.   When I thus have filled
With dire confusion Jason's wretched house,
I, from this land, yet reeking with the gore
Of my dear sons, will fly, and having dared   984
A deed most impious.   For the scornful taunts
Of those we hate are not to be endured,
Happen what may. Can life be any gain
To me who have no country left, no home,
No place of refuge?   Greatly did I err
When I forsook the mansions of my sire,   990
Persuaded by the flattery of that Greek
Whom I will punish, if just Heaven permit.
For he shall not again behold the children
I bore him while yet living.   From his bride
Nor shall there issue any second race,   995
Since that vile woman by my baleful drugs
Vilely to perish have the Fates ordained.
None shall think lightly of me, as if weak,
Of courage void, or with a soul too tame,
But formed by Heaven in a far different mould,
The terror of my foes, and to my friends   1001
Benignant: for most glorious are the lives
Of those who act with such determined zeal.
   Chorus. Since thy design thus freely thou to us
Communicat'st, I, through a wish to serve   1005
Thy interests, and a reverence for those laws
Which all mankind hold sacred, from thy purpose
Exhort thee to desist.
   Medea.   This cannot be:
Yet I from you, because ye have not felt
Distress like mine, such language can excuse.   1010
   Chorus. Thy guiltless children wilt thou dare to
      slay?
   Medea. My husband hence more deeply shall I
      wound.
   Chorus. But thou wilt of all women be most
      wretched.
   Medea. No matter: all the counsels ye can give
Are now superfluous.   But this instant go   1015
And Jason hither bring; for on your faith,
In all things I depend; nor these resolves
Will you divulge if you your mistress love,
And feel a woman's interest in my wrongs.

CHORUS

ODE

I.   1

Heroes of Erectheus'[1] race   1020
   To the gods who owe your birth,

[1] An early founder of Athens.

And in a long succession trace
Your sacred origin from earth,
Who on wisdom's fruit regale,
Purest breezes still inhale,   1025
And behold skies ever bright,
Wandering through those haunted glades
Where fame relates that the Pierian maids,[1]
Soothing the soul of man with chaste delight,
Taught Harmony to breathe her first enchanting
   tale.   1030

I.   2

   From Cephisus' amber tide,
   At the Cyprian queen's command,
   As sing the Muses, are supplied
   To refresh the thirsty land,
   Fragrant gales of temperate air;   1035
   While around her auburn hair,
   In a vivid chaplet twined
   Never-fading roses bloom
And scent the champaign with their rich per-
   fume,
Love comes in unison with wisdom joined,   1040
Each virtue thrives if Beauty lend her fostering
   care.

II.   1

For its holy streams renowned
   Can that city, can that state
Where friendship's generous train are found
   Shelter thee from public hate,   1045
When, defiled with horrid guilt,
Thou thy children's blood hast spilt?
Think on this atrocious deed
Ere the dagger aim the blow: 1049
Around thy knees our suppliant arms we throw,
   O doom not, doom them not to bleed.

II.   2

How can thy relentless heart
   All humanity disclaim,
Thy lifted arm perform its part?
   Lost to a sense of honest shame,   1055
Canst thou take their lives away
And these guiltless children slay?
Soon as thou thy sons shalt view,
How wilt thou the tear restrain,   1059
Or with their blood thy ruthless hands distain,
   When prostrate they for mercy sue?

JASON, MEDEA, CHORUS

Jason. I at your call am come; for though such
      hate
To me you bear, you shall not be denied
In this request; but let me hear what else

[1] The nine muses.

You would solicit.

Medea.   Jason, I of thee   1065
Crave pardon for the hasty words I spoke;
Since just it were that thou shouldst bear my
    wrath,
When by such mutual proofs of love our union
Hath been cemented. For I reasoned thus, 1069
And in these terms reproached myself: "O wretch,
Wretch that I am, what madness fires my breast?
Or why 'gainst those who counsel me aright
Such fierce resentment harbor? What just cause
Have I to hate the rulers of this land,
My husband too, who acts but for my good   1075
In his espousals with the royal maid,
That to my sons he hence may add a race
Of noble brothers? Shall not I appease
The tempest of my soul? Why, when the gods
Confer their choicest blessings, should I grieve?
Have not I helpless children? Well I know   1081
That we are banished from Thessalia's realm
And left without a friend." When I these thoughts
Maturely had revolved, I saw how great
My folly and how groundless was my wrath. 1085
Now therefore I commend, now deem thee wise
In forming this connection for my sake:
But I was void of wisdom, or had borne
A part in these designs, the genial bed
Obsequiously attended, and with joy   1090
Performed each menial office for the bride.
I will not speak in too reproachful terms
Of my own sex; but we, weak women, are
What nature formed us; therefore our defects
Thou must not imitate, nor yet return   1095
Folly for folly. I submit and own
My judgment was erroneous, but at length
Have I formed better counsels. O my sons,
Come hither, leave the palace, from those doors
Advance, and in a soft persuasive strain   1100
With me unite your father to accost,
Forget past enmity, and to your friends
Be reconciled, for 'twixt us is a league
Of peace established, and my wrath subsides. 1104

(The SONS *of* JASON *and* MEDEA *enter.)*

Take hold of his right hand. Ah me, how great
Are my afflictions oft as I revolve
A deed of darkness in my laboring soul!
How long, alas! my sons, are ye ordained
To live, how long to stretch forth those dear arms?
Wretch that I am! how much am I disposed   1110
To weep! how subject to each fresh alarm!
For I at length desisting from that strife,
Which with your sire I rashly did maintain,
Feel gushing tears bedew my tender cheek.

Chorus. Fresh tears too from these eyes have
    forced their way;   1115

And may no greater ill than that which now
We suffer, overtake us!

Jason.   I applaud
Your present conduct, and your former rage
Condemn not; for 'tis natural that the race
Of women should be angry when their lord   1120
For a new consort trucks them. But your heart
Is for the better changed, and you, though late,
At length acknowledge the resistless power
Of reason; this is acting like a dame
Endued with prudence. But for you, my sons,
Abundant safety your considerate sire   1126
Hath with the favor of the gods procured,
For ye, I trust, shall with my future race
Bear the first rank in this Corinthian realm,
Advance to full maturity; the rest,   1130
Aided by each benignant god, your father
Shall soon accomplish. Virtuously trained up
May I behold you at a riper age
Obtain pre-eminence o'er those I hate.   1134
But, ha! Why with fresh tears do you thus keep
Those eyelids moist? From your averted cheeks
Why is the color fled, or why these words
Receive you not with a complacent ear?

Medea. Nothing: my thoughts were busied for
    these children.   1139

Jason. Be of good courage, and for them depend
On my protecting care.

Medea.   I will obey,
Nor disbelieve the promise thou hast made:
But woman, ever frail, is prone to shed
Involuntary tears.

Jason.   But why bewail   1144
With such deep groans these children?

Medea.   Them I bore;
And that our sons might live, while to the gods
Thou didst address thy vows, a pitying thought
Entered my soul; 'twas whether this could be.
But of th' affairs on which thou com'st to hold
This conference with me, have I told a part   1150
Already, and to thee will now disclose
The sequel: since the rulers of this land
Resolve to banish me, as well I know
That it were best for me to give no umbrage,
Or to the king of Corinth, or to thee,   1155
By dwelling here: because I to this house
Seem to bear enmity, from these domains
Will I depart: but urge thy suit to Creon,
That under thy paternal care our sons   1159
May be trained up, nor from this realm expelled.

Jason. Though doubtful of success, I yet am
    bound
To make th' attempt.

Medea.   Thou rather shouldst enjoin
Thy bride her royal father to entreat,
That he these children's exile may reverse.

Jason. With pleasure; and I doubt not but on
  her,   1165
If like her sex humane, I shall prevail.

    Medea. To aid thee in this difficult emprise
Shall be my care, for I to her will send
Gifts that I know in beauty far exceed
The gorgeous works of man; a tissued vest   1170
And golden crown the children shall present,
But with the utmost speed these ornaments
One of thy menial train must hither bring,
For not with one, but with ten thousand blessings
Shall she be gratified; thee, best of men,   1175
Obtaining for the partner of her bed,
And in possession of those splendid robes
Which erst the sun my grandsire did bestow
On his descendants: take them in your hands,
My children, to the happy royal bride   1180
Instantly bear them, and in dower bestow,
For such a gift as ought not to be scorned
Shall she receive.

    Jason.   Why rashly part with these?
Of tissued robes or gold can you suppose
The palace destitute? These trappings keep,   1185
Nor to another give: for if the dame
On me place real value, well I know
My love she to all treasures will prefer.

    Medea. Speak not so hastily: the gods them-
    selves   1189
By gifts are swayed, as fame relates; and gold
Hath a far greater influence o'er the souls
Of mortals than the most persuasive words:
With fortune, the propitious heavens conspire
To add fresh glories to thy youthful bride,
All here submits to her despotic sway.   1195
But I my children's exile would redeem,
Though at the cost of life, not gold alone.
But these adjacent mansions of the king
Soon as ye enter, O ye little ones,
Your sire's new consort and my queen entreat   1200
That ye may not be banished from this land:
At the same time these ornaments present,
For most important is it that these gifts
With her own hands the royal dame receive.
Go forth, delay not, and, if ye succeed,   1205
Your mother with the welcome tidings greet.

                   (*Exeunt* JASON *and* SONS.)

CHORUS

ODE

I. 1

Now from my soul each hope is fled,
I deem those hapless children dead,
    They rush to meet the wound:
Mistrustful of no latent pest   1210
Th' exulting bride will seize the gorgeous vest,

Her auburn tresses crowned
By baleful Pluto,[1] shall she stand,
And take the presents with an eager hand.

I. 2

The splendid robe of thousand dyes   1215
Will fascinate her raptured eyes,
    And tempt her till she wear
    The golden diadem, arrayed
To meet her bridegroom in th' infernal shade
    She thus into the snare   1220
Of death shall be surprised by fate,
Nor 'scape remorseless Atè's [2] direful hate.

II. 1

But as for thee whose nuptials bring
The proud alliance of a king,
    'Midst dangers unespied   1225
Thou madly rushing, aid'st the blow
Ordained by Heaven to lay thy children low,
    And thy lamented bride:
O man, how little dost thou know
That o'er thy head impends severest woe!   1230

II. 2

Thy anguish I no less bemoan,
No less for thee, O mother, groan,
    Bent on a horrid deed,
Thy children who resolv'st to slay,
Nor fear'st to take their guiltless lives away.   1235
    Those innocents must bleed,
    Because, disdainful of thy charms,
The husband flies to a new consort's arms.

ATTENDANT, SONS, MEDEA, CHORUS

    Attend. Your sons, my honored mistress, are
    set free   1239
From banishment; in her own hands [3] those gifts
With courtesy the royal bride received;
Hence have your sons obtained their peace.

    Medea.   No matter.
    Attend. Why stand you in confusion, when be-
    friended
By prosperous fortune?

    Medea.   Ah!
    Attend.   This harsh reception
Accords not with the tidings which I bring.   1245

    Medea. Alas! and yet again I say, alas!

    Attend. Have I related with unconscious tongue
Some great calamity, by the fond hope
Of bearing glad intelligence misled?

---

[1] Ruler of the underworld.

[2] A trouble-making goddess.

[3] As the poisoned robe took effect as soon as it came
in contact with the warmth of the body, it was essential
that the princess receive it directly.

Medea. For having told what thou hast told,
  no blame 1250
To thee do I impute.

Attend. But on the ground
Why fix those eyes, and shed abundant tears?

Medea. Necessity constrains me: for the gods
Of Erebus and I in evil hour
Our baleful machinations have devised. 1255

Attend. Be of good cheer; for in your children
  still
Are you successful.

Medea. 'Midst the realms of night
Others I first will plunge. Ah, wretched me!

Attend. Not you alone are from your children
  torn,
Mortal you are, and therefore must endure 1260
Calamity with patience.

Medea. I these counsels
Will practise: but go thou into the palace,
And for the children whatsoe'er to-day
Is requisite, make ready. (*Exit* ATTENDANT.)
O my sons!
My sons! ye have a city and a house 1265
Where, leaving hapless me behind, without
A mother ye for ever shall reside.
But I to other realms an exile go,
Ere any help from you I could derive,
Or see you blest; the hymeneal pomp, 1270
The bride, the genial couch, for you adorn,
And in these hands the kindled torch sustain.
How wretched am I through my own perverseness!
You, O my sons, I then in vain have nurtured,
In vain have toiled, and, wasted with fatigue, 1275
Suffered the pregnant matron's grievous throes.
On you, in my afflictions, many hopes
I founded erst: that ye with pious care
Would foster my old age, and on the bier
Extend me after death — much envied lot 1280
Of mortals; but these pleasing anxious thoughts
Are vanished now; for, losing you, a life
Of bitterness and anguish shall I lead.
But as for you, my sons, with those dear eyes
Fated no more your mother to behold, 1285
Hence are ye hastening to a world unknown.
Why do ye gaze on me with such a look
Of tenderness, or wherefore smile? for these
Are your last smiles. Ah wretched, wretched me!
What shall I do? My resolution fails. 1290
Sparkling with joy now I their looks have seen,
My friends, I can no more. To those past schemes
I bid adieu, and with me from this land
My children will convey. Why should I cause
A twofold portion of distress to fall 1295
On my own head, that I may grieve the sire
By punishing his sons? This shall not be:
Such counsels I dismiss. But in my purpose

What means this change? Can I prefer derision,
And with impunity permit the foe 1300
To 'scape? My utmost courage I must rouse:
For the suggestion of these tender thoughts
Proceeds from an enervate heart. My sons,
Enter the regal mansion. (*Exeunt* SONS.)
As for those
Who deem that to be present were unholy 1305
While I the destined victims offer up,
Let them see to it. This uplifted arm
Shall never shrink. Alas! alas! my soul
Commit not such a deed. Unhappy woman,
Desist and spare thy children; we will live 1310
Together, they in foreign realms shall cheer
Thy exile. No, by those avenging fiends
Who dwell with Pluto in the realms beneath,
This shall not be, nor will I ever leave
My sons to be insulted by their foes. 1315
They certainly must die; since then they must,
I bore and I will slay them: 'tis a deed
Resolved on, nor my purpose will I change.
Full well I know that now the royal bride
Wears on her head the magic diadem, 1320
And in the variegated robe expires:
But, hurried on by fate, I tread a path
Of utter wretchedness, and them will plunge
Into one yet more wretched. To my sons 1324
Fain would I say: "O stretch forth your right hands
Ye children, for your mother to embrace.
O dearest hands, ye lips to me most dear,
Engaging features and ingenuous looks,
May ye be blest, but in another world;
For by the treacherous conduct of your sire 1330
Are ye bereft of all this earth bestowed.
Farewell, sweet kisses — tender limbs, farewell!
And fragrant breath! I never more can bear
To look on you, my children." My afflictions
Have conquered me; I now am well aware 1335
What crimes I venture on: but rage, the cause
Of woes most grievous to the human race,
Over my better reason hath prevailed.

Chorus. In subtle questions I full many a time
Have heretofore engaged, and this great point 1340
Debated, whether woman should extend
Her search into abstruse and hidden truths.
But we too have a Muse, who with our sex
Associates to expound the mystic lore
Of wisdom, though she dwell not with us all. 1345
Yet haply a small number may be found,
Among the multitude of females, dear
To the celestial Muses. I maintain,
They who in total inexperience live,
Nor ever have been parents, are more happy 1350
Than they to whom much progeny belongs.
Because the childless, having never tried
Whether more pain or pleasure from their offspring

To mortals rises, 'scape unnumbered toils.
But I observe that they, whose fruitful house   1355
Is with a lovely race of infants filled,
Are harassed with perpetual cares; how first
To train them up in virtue, and whence leave
Fit portions for their sons; but on the good
Or worthless, whether they these toils bestow   1360
Remains involved in doubt.   I yet must name
One evil the most grievous, to which all
The human race is subject; some there are
Who for their sons have gained sufficient wealth,
Seen them to full maturity advance,   1365
And decked with every virtue, when, by fate
If thus it be ordained, comes death unseen
And hurries them to Pluto's gloomy realm.
Can it be any profit to the gods
To heap the loss of children, that one ill   1370
Than all the rest more bitter, on mankind?
   Medea. My friends, with anxious expectation
      long
Here have I waited, from within to learn
How fortune will dispose the dread event.
But one of Jason's servants I behold   1375
With breathless speed advancing: his looks show
That he some recent mischief would relate.

MESSENGER, MEDEA, CHORUS

   Mess. O thou, who impiously hast wrought a
      deed
Of horror, fly, Medea, from this land,
Fly with such haste as not to leave the bark   1380
Or from the car alight.
   Medea.   What crime, to merit
A banishment like this, have I committed?
   Mess. By thy enchantments is the royal maid
This instant dead, and Creon, too, her sire.   1384
   Medea. Most glorious are the tidings you relate:
Henceforth shall you be numbered with my friends
And benefactors.
   Mess.   Ha! what words are these?
Dost thou preserve thy senses yet entire?
O woman, hath not madness fired thy brain?   1389
The wrongs thou to the royal house hast done
Hear'st thou with joy, nor shudder'st at the tale?
   Medea. Somewhat I have in answer to your
      speech:
But be not too precipitate, my friend;
Inform me how they died, for twofold joy
Wilt thou afford, if wretchedly they perished.   1395
   Mess. When with their father thy two sons
      arrived
And went into the mansion of the bride,
We servants, who had shared thy griefs, rejoiced;
For a loud rumor instantly prevailed
That all past strife betwixt thy lord and thee   1400
Was reconciled.   Some kissed the children's hands,

And some their auburn tresses.   I with joy
To those apartments where the women dwell
Attended them.   Our mistress, the new object
Of homage such as erst to thee was paid,   1405
Ere she beheld thy sons on Jason cast
A look of fond desire: but then she veiled
Her eyes, and turned her pallid cheeks away
Disgusted at their coming, till his voice
Appeased her anger with these gentle words: 1410
"O be not thou inveterate 'gainst thy friends,
But lay aside disdain, thy beauteous face
Turn hither, and let amity for those
Thy husband loves still warm that generous breast.
Accept these gifts, and to thy father sue,   1415
That, for my sake, the exile of my sons
He will remit."   Soon as the princess saw
Thy glittering ornaments, she could resist
No longer, but to all her lord's requests
Assented, and before thy sons were gone   1420
Far from the regal mansion with their sire,
The vest, resplendent with a thousand dyes,
Put on, and o'er her loosely floating hair
Placing the golden crown, before the mirror
Her tresses braided, and with smiles surveyed   1425
Th' inanimated semblance of her charms:
Then rising from her seat across the palace
Walked with a delicate and graceful step,
In the rich gifts exulting, and oft turned
Enraptured eyes on her own stately neck,   1430
Reflected to her view: but now a scene
Of horror followed; her complexion changed,
And she reeled backward, trembling every limb;
Scarce did her chair receive her as she sunk
In time to save her falling to the ground.   1435
One of her menial train, an aged dame,
Possest with an idea that the wrath
Either of Pan [1] or of some god unknown
Her mistress had invaded, in shrill tone   1439
Poured forth a vow to Heaven, till from her mouth
She saw foam issue, in their sockets roll
Her wildly glaring eyeballs, and the blood
Leave her whole frame; a shriek, that differed far
From her first plaints, then gave she.   In an in-
      stant
This to her father's house, and that to tell   1445
The bridegroom the mischance which had befallen
His consort, rushed impetuous; through the dome
The frequent steps of those who to and fro
Ran in confusion did resound.   But soon
As the fleet courser at the goal arrives,   1450
She who was silent, and had closed her eyes,
Roused from her swoon, and burst forth into groans

[1] God of woods and fields and flocks. A lover of
music, Pan was, nevertheless, not attractive to the
Dryads because of his horns and hooves. The fright he
often gave people survives in our word *panic*.

Most dreadful, for 'gainst her two evils warred:
Placed on her head the golden crown poured forth
A wondrous torrent of devouring flames,   1455
And the embroidered robes, thy children's gifts,
Preyed on the hapless virgin's tender flesh;
Covered with fire she started from her seat
Shaking her hair, and from her head the crown
With violence attempting to remove,   1460
But still more firmly did the heated gold
Adhere, and the fanned blaze with double lustre
Burst forth as she her streaming tresses shook:
Subdued by fate, at length she to the ground
Fell prostrate: scarce could anyone have known
        her   1465
Except her father; for those radiant eyes
Dropped from their sockets, that majestic face
Its wonted features lost, and blood with fire
Ran down her head in intermingled streams,   1469
While from her bones the flesh, like weeping pitch,
Melted away, through the consuming power
Of those unseen enchantments; 'twas a sight
Most horrible: all feared to touch the corpse,
For her disastrous end had taught us caution.   1474
Meanwhile her hapless sire, who knew not aught
Of this calamity, as he with haste
Entered the palace, stumbled o'er her body;
Instantly shrieking out, then with his arms
Infolded, kissed it oft, and, "O my child,
My wretched child," exclaimed; "what envious
        god,   1480
Author of thy dishonorable fall,
Of thee bereaves an old decrepit man
Whom the grave claims? With thee I wish to die,
My daughter." Scarcely had the hoary father
These lamentations ended; to uplift   1485
His feeble body striving, he adhered
(As ivy with its pliant tendrils clings
Around the laurel) to the tissued vest.
Dire was the conflict; he to raise his knee   1489
From earth attempted, but his daughter's corse
Still held him down, or if with greater force
He dragged it onward, from his bones he tore
The aged flesh: at length he sunk, and breathed
In agonizing pangs his soul away:
For he against such evil could bear up   1495
No longer. To each other close in death
The daughter and her father lie: their fate
Demands our tears. Warned by my words, with
        haste
From this domain convey thyself, or vengeance
Will overtake thee for this impious deed.   1500
Not now for the first time do I esteem
Human affairs a shadow. Without fear
Can I pronounce, they who appear endued
With wisdom, and most plausibly trick out
Specious harangues, deserve to be accounted   1505

The worst of fools. The man completely blest
Exists not. Some in overflowing wealth
May be more fortunate, but none are happy.
    Chorus. Heaven its collected store of evil seems
This day resolved with justice to pour down   1510
On perjured Jason. Thy untimely fate
How do we pity, O thou wretched daughter
Of Creon, who in Pluto's mansions go'st
To celebrate thy nuptial feast.
    Medea.   My friends,
I am resolved, as soon as I have slain   1515
My children, from these regions to depart,
Nor through inglorious sloth will I abandon
My sons to perish by detested hands;
They certainly must die: since then they must,
I bore and I will slay them. O my heart!   1520
Be armed with tenfold firmness. What avails it
To loiter, when inevitable ills
Remain to be accomplished? Take the sword,
And, O my hand, on to the goal that ends
Their life, nor let one intervening thought   1525
Of pity or maternal tenderness
Suspend thy purpose: for this one short day
Forget how fondly thou didst love thy sons,
How bring them forth, and after that lament
Their cruel fate: although thou art resolved   1530
To slay, yet hast thou ever held them dear.
But I am of all women the most wretched.
                                    (*Exit* MEDEA.)

CHORUS

ODE

I

Earth, and thou sun, whose fervid blaze
From pole to pole illumes each distant land,
View this abandoned woman, ere she raise   1535
Against her children's lives a ruthless hand;
    For from thy race, divinely bright,[1]
They spring, and should the sons of gods be
        slain
    By man, 'twere dreadful. O restrain
Her fury, thou celestial source of light,   1540
Ere she with blood pollute your regal dome,
Chased by the demons hence let this Erinnys roam.

II

The pregnant matron's throes in vain
Hast thou endured, and borne a lovely race,
    O thou, who o'er th' inhospitable main,   1545
Where the Cyanean rocks scarce leave a space,
    Thy daring voyage didst pursue.
    Why, O thou wretch, thy soul doth anger rend,
    Such as in murder soon must end?

[1] A reference to Medea's descent from the Sun.

They who with kindred gore are stained shall
    rue   1550
Their guilt inexpiable: full well I know
The gods will on this house inflict severest woe.
    1st Son (within). Ah me! what can I do, or
        whither fly
To 'scape a mother's arm?
    2nd Son (within).   I cannot tell:
For, O my dearest brother, we are lost.   1555
    Chorus. Heard you the children's shrieks? I
        (O thou dame,
Whom woes and evil fortune still attend)
Will rush into the regal dome, from death
Resolved to snatch thy sons.
    1st Son (within).   We by the gods
Conjure you to protect us in this hour   1560
Of utmost peril, for the treacherous snare
Hath caught us, and we perish by the sword.
    Chorus. Art thou a rock, O wretch, or steel, to
        slay
With thine own hand that generous race of sons
Whom thou didst bear? I hitherto have heard
But of one woman, who in ancient days   1566
Smote her dear children, Ino,[1] by the gods
With frenzy stung, when Jove's malignant queen
Distracted from her mansion drove her forth.
But she, yet reeking with the impious gore   1570
Of her own progeny, into the waves
Plunged headlong from the ocean's craggy beach,
And shared with her two sons one common fate.
Can there be deeds more horrible than these
Left for succeeding ages to produce?   1575
Disastrous union with the female sex,
How great a source of woes art thou to man!

JASON, CHORUS

    Jason. Ye dames who near the portals stand, is
        she
Who hath committed these atrocious crimes,
Medea, in the palace, or by flight   1580
Hath she retreated? For beneath the ground
Must she conceal herself, or, borne on wings,
Ascend the heights of Ether, to avoid
The vengeance due for Corinth's royal house.
Having destroyed the rulers of the land,   1585
Can she presume she shall escape unhurt
From these abodes? But less am I concerned
On her account, than for my sons; since they
Whom she hath injured will on her inflict

[1] Ino, a queen in Bœotia, planned to kill her step-
children who were, however, saved by the ram of the
Golden Fleece. King Athamas, their father, became
mad, took Ino and her two children to be a lioness and
cubs, and killed one before Ino, holding the other,
jumped into the sea. Euripides follows a slightly different version of this old story.

Due punishment: but hither am I come   1590
To save my children's lives, lest on their heads
The noble Creon's kindred should retaliate
That impious murder by their mother wrought.
    Chorus. Thou know'st not yet, O thou unhapppy
        man,
What ills thou art involved in, or these words 1595
Had not escaped thee.
    Jason.   Ha, what ills are these
Thou speak'st of? Would she also murder me?
    Chorus. By their own mother's hand thy sons
        are slain.
    Jason. What can you mean? How utterly, O
        woman,
Have you undone me!
    Chorus.   Be assured thy children 1600
Are now no more.
    Jason.   Where was it, or within
Those mansions or without, that she destroyed
Our progeny?
    Chorus.   As soon as thou these doors
Hast oped, their weltering corses wilt thou view.
    Jason. Loose the firm bars and bolts of yonder
        gates   1605
With speed, ye servants, that I may behold
This scene of twofold misery, the remains
Of the deceased, and punish her who slew them.

  MEDEA, *in a chariot drawn by dragons*,[1] JASON,
               CHORUS

    Medea. With levers wherefore dost thou shake
        those doors
In quest of them who are no more, and me   1610
Who dared to perpetrate the bloody deed?
Desist from such unprofitable toil:
But if there yet be aught that thou with me
Canst want, speak freely whatsoe'er thou wilt:
For with that hand me never shalt thou reach, 1615
Such steeds the sun my grandsire gives to whirl
This chariot and protect me from my foes.
    Jason. O most abandoned woman, by the gods,
By me and all the human race abhorred,
Who with the sword could pierce the sons you bore,
And ruin me, a childless wretched man,   1621
Yet after you this impious deed have dared
To perpetrate, still view the radiant sun
And fostering earth; may vengeance overtake you!
For I that reason have regained which erst   1625
Forsook me, when to the abodes of Greece
I from your home, from a barbarian realm,
Conveyed you, to your sire a grievous bane,
And the corrupt betrayer of that land

[1] The familiar *deus ex machina* (god from the machine) of classical tragedy. In this case the rescue is
not performed by a deity outside the action but by
Medea herself in her own dragon-drawn chariot.

Which nurtured you. Some envious god first
    roused   1630
Your evil genius from the shades of hell
For my undoing: after you had slain
Your brother at the altar, you embarked
In the famed Argo. Deeds like these a life   1634
Of guilt commenced; with me in wedlock joined,
You bore those sons, whom you have now destroyed
Because I left your bed. No Grecian dame
Would e'er have ventured on a deed so impious;
Yet I to them preferred you for my bride:
This was a hostile union, and to me   1640
The most destructive; for my arms received
No woman, but a lioness more fell
Than Tuscan Scylla.¹ Vainly should I strive
To wound you with reproaches numberless,
For you are grown insensible of shame!   1645
Vile sorceress, and polluted with the blood
Of your own children, perish — my hard fate
While I lament, for I shall ne'er enjoy
My lovely bride, nor with those sons, who owe
To me their birth and nurture, ever hold   1650
Sweet converse. They, alas! can live no more,
Utterly lost to their desponding sire.

    Medea. Much could I say in answer to this
    charge,
Were not the benefits from me received,
And thy abhorred ingratitude, well known   1655
To Jove, dread sire. Yet was it not ordained,
Scorning my bed, that thou shouldst lead a life
Of fond delight, and ridicule my griefs;
Nor that the royal virgin thou didst wed,
Or Creon, who to thee his daughter gave,   1660
Should drive me from these regions unavenged.
A lioness then call me if thou wilt,
Or by the name of Scylla, whose abode
Was in Etrurian caverns. For thy heart,
As justice prompted, in my turn I wounded. 1665

    Jason. You grieve, and are the partner of my
    woes.

    Medea. Be well assured I am: but what assuages
My grief is this, that thou no more canst scoff.

    Jason. How vile a mother, O my sons, was yours!

    Medea. How did ye perish through your father's
    lust!   1670

    Jason. But my right hand was guiltless of their
    death.

    Medea. Not so thy cruel taunts, and that new
    marriage.

    Jason. Was my new marriage a sufficient cause
For thee to murder them?

¹ Scylla and Charybdis, a rock and a whirlpool in
the Strait of Messina, between Sicily and Italy, were
thought to be monstrous sea creatures. They are
mentioned by Homer, *Odyssey*, Book XII.

    Medea.   Canst thou suppose
Such wrongs sit light upon the female breast?

    Jason. On a chaste woman's; but your soul
    abounds   1676
With wickedness.

    Medea.   Thy sons are now no more,
This will afflict thee.

    Jason.   O'er your head, alas!
They now two evil geniuses impend.

    Medea. The gods know who these ruthless deeds
    began.   1680

    Jason. They know the hateful temper of your
    soul.

    Medea. In detestation thee I hold, and loathe
Thy conversation.

    Jason.   Yours too I abhor;
But we with ease may settle on what terms
To part for ever.

    Medea.   Name those terms. Say how
Shall I proceed? For such my ardent wish. 1686

    Jason. Let me inter the dead, and o'er them
    weep.

    Medea. Thou shalt not. For their corses with
    this hand
Am I resolved to bury in the grove
Sacred to awful Juno,¹ who protects   1690
The citadel of Corinth, lest their foes
Insult them, and with impious rage pluck up
The monumental stone. I in this realm
Of Sisyphus moreover will ordain
A solemn festival and mystic rites,   1695
To make a due atonement for my guilt
In having slain them. To Erectheus' land
I now am on my road, where I shall dwell
With Ægeus, great Pandion's son; but thou
Shalt vilely perish as thy crimes deserve,   1700
Beneath the shattered relics of thy bark,
The Argo, crushed;² such is the bitter end
Of our espousals and thy faith betrayed.

    Jason. May the Erinnys³ of our slaughtered sons
And justice, who requites each murderous deed,
Destroy you utterly!

    Medea.   Will any god   1706
Or demon hear thy curses, O thou wretch,
False to thy oath, and to the sacred laws
Of hospitality?

    Jason.   Most impious woman,
Those hands yet reeking with your children's
    gore —   1710

    Medea. Go to the palace, and inter thy bride.

    Jason. Bereft of both my sons, I thither go.

¹ Juno, wife of Jupiter. There was a temple dedicated to her near Corinth.

² Jason was found dead under the stern of the Argo
where it had been drawn up on the shore.

³ The Furies.

Medea. Not yet enough lament'st thou: to increase
Thy sorrows, mayst thou live till thou art old!
Jason. Ye dearest children.
Medea.   To their mother dear,   1715
But not to thee.
Jason.   Yet them have you destroyed.
Medea. That I might punish thee.
Jason.   One more fond kiss
On their loved lips, ah me! would I imprint.
Medea. Now wouldst thou speak to them, and
    in thine arms   1719
Clasp those whom living thou didst banish hence.
Jason. Allow me, I conjure you by the gods,
My children's tender bodies to embrace.
Medea. Thou shalt not: these presumptuous
    words in vain
By thee were hazarded.
Jason.   Jove, hear'st thou this,

How I with scorn am driven away, how wronged
By that detested lioness, whose fangs   1726
Have slain her children?   Yet shall my loud
    plaints,
While here I fix my seat, if 'tis allowed,
And this be possible, call down the gods
To witness that you hinder me from touching 1730
My murdered sons, and paying the deceased
Funereal honors.   Would to Heaven I ne'er
Had seen them born to perish by your hand!
    Chorus.   Throned on Olympus, with his sovereign
        nod,
Jove unexpectedly performs the schemes   1735
Divine foreknowledge planned; our firmest hopes
Oft fail us: but the god still finds the means
Of compassing what man could ne'er have looked
    for;
And thus doth this important business end.

Aristophanes · 445-385 B.C.

The son of a landowner in Ægina, an island near Athens, Aristophanes was born about 445 B.C. He wrote some forty or fifty comedies (the first in 427) of which eleven have been preserved. His comedy is marked by a strong satirical bent, the point of his attack being contemporary Athenian life, morals, and literature. Aristophanes died about 385 B.C.

Athens, during the life of the dramatist, was in political turmoil. The Peloponnesian War was not long in the past. Sparta and Athens were sparring for the leadership of Greece. Democracy and Empire were being weighed in the balances. In *The Frogs* Aristophanes makes references to a contemporary conspiracy and to the Battle of Arginusæ (406 B.C.), the last victory of the Athenians in the Peloponnesian War.

The period in which he lived was one in which a bewildered conservative such as Aristophanes could only stand by and satirize events he was powerless to prevent. He disliked the changing ideals in education, he distrusted mob rule, he wanted peace for Athens. Indeed that the purpose of the dramatist's writing is satirical criticism of personalities and issues in political and public life is obvious to anyone reading the comedies. *The Wasps*, for instance, ridicules those people who are fond of litigation, *The Peace* and *Lysistrata* bespeak the need for peace, *The Knights* supports democracy and attacks the demagoguery of Cleon; *The Clouds* points out the frailties of all philosophers and rhetoricians in general and of Socrates in particular, and *The Ecclesiazusæ* satirizes conditions in public life.

This satirical treatment of contemporary life is a characteristic classical element. As has been said in the essay on "The Temper of Classicism," the classical outlook on life is essentially a fixed one; it develops at a time when society is stable, when its ideals are established. Furthermore, classicism as a temper seeks to correct nature, to improve society, and resents changes from the prevailing order. What more likely, then, than that a conservative, resentful of threatening changes, should turn to satire as a means of resisting all departures from the established order? This is the underlying motive of Aristophanes' play as well as of the satire of Voltaire, Pope, and Swift later on in the neo-classical eighteenth century.

SUGGESTED REFERENCES: Victor Ehrenberg, *The People of Aristophanes: A Sociology of Attic Comedy* (3rd ed., 1962); Gilbert Murray, *Aristophanes, A Study* (2nd ed., 1964); C. H. Whitman, *Aristophanes and the Comic Hero* (1964).

The Frogs

The Frogs appeared in 405 B.C. when it was given first prize at the Lenæan festival. In this play Æschylus and Euripides, two playwrights then only recently dead, receive the brunt of Aristophanes' attack. Tragedy, Aristophanes holds, is at a low ebb in Athens. Dionysus, in whose honor the dramatic festival is held, finds it necessary to import new — or old — blood and starts off to Hades to bring back a real dramatist. The question is which of two, Æschylus or Euripides, shall be asked to return. And the question provides opportunity for much criticism, serious and frivolous, of the two men, the vote finally going to Æschylus.

Euripides is left in Hades because, to the conservative mind of Aristophanes, he had been a dangerous radical and had promulgated doctrines in his dramas which had helped to foster the new learning and morality that had brought disaster to Athens. But the play is not all satire and burlesque. In some of the lyrical passages of the chorus, Aristophanes proves a great poet.

The translation which follows is that of J. H. Frere, taken from *Comedies of Aristophanes*, in Everyman's Library, published by E. P. Dutton & Co.

Dramatis Personæ

BACCHUS.
XANTHIAS, *servant of Bacchus.*
HERCULES.
CHARON.
ÆACUS.
EURIPIDES.
ÆSCHYLUS.

PLUTO.
DEAD MAN.
PROSERPINE'S SERVANT
MAID.
TWO WOMEN SUTLERS.
MUTES.
CHORUS OF VOTARIES,
and FROGS.

BACCHUS, XANTHIAS

Xan. Master, shall I begin with the usual jokes
That the audience always laugh at?
    Bac.   If you please;
Any joke you please except "being overburthen'd."
— Don't use it yet — We've time enough before us.
    Xan. Well, something else that's comical and clever?   5
    Bac. I forbid being "overpress'd and overburthen'd."
    Xan. Well, but the drollest joke of all — ?
    Bac.   Remember
There's one thing I protest against —
    Xan.   What's that?
    Bac. Why, shifting off your load to the other shoulder,
And fidgeting and complaining of the gripes.   10
    Xan. What then do you mean to say, that I must not say
That I'm ready to befoul myself?
    Bac. (*peremptorily*).   By no means

Except when I take an emetic.
    Xan. (*in a sullen, muttering tone, as if resentful of hard usage*).   What's the use, then,
Of my being burthen'd here with all these bundles.
If I'm to be deprived of the common jokes   15
That Phrynichus, and Lycis, and Ameipsias [1]
Allow the servants always in their comedies,
Without exception, when they carry bundles?
    Bac. Pray, leave them off — for those ingenious sallies
Have such an effect upon my health and spirits   20
That I feel grown old and dull when I get home.
    Xan. (*as before, or with a sort of half-mutinous whine*). It's hard for me to suffer in my limbs,
To be overburthen'd and debarr'd from joking.
    Bac. Well, this is monstrous, quite, and insupportable!
Such insolence in a servant! When your master   25
Is going afoot and has provided you
With a beast to carry ye.
    Xan.   What! do I carry nothing?
    Bac. You're carried yourself.
    Xan.   But I carry bundles, don't I?
    Bac. But the beast bears all the burdens that you carry.
    Xan. Not those that I carry myself — 'tis I that carry 'em.   30
    Bac. You're carried yourself, I tell ye.
    Xan.   I can't explain it,
But I feel it in my shoulders plainly enough.

[1] Writers of comedies. The first won second place in the contest in which *The Frogs* placed first.

Bac. Well, if the beast don't help you, take and try;
Change places with the ass and carry him.
    Xan. (*in a tone of mere disgust*). Oh, dear! I wish I had gone for a volunteer,   35
And left you to yourself. I wish I had.
    Bac. Dismount, you rascal! Here, we're at the house
Where Hercules lives. — Holloh! there! who's within there?
        (BACCHUS *kicks outrageously at the door.*)

HERCULES, BACCHUS, XANTHIAS

    Her. Who's there? (He has bang'd at the door, whoever he is,
With the kick of a centaur.[1]) What's the matter, there?   40
    Bac. (*aside*). Ha! Xanthias!
    Xan.   What?
    Bac. (*aside*).   Did ye mind how he was frighten'd?
    Xan. I suppose he was afraid you were going mad.
    Her. (*aside*). By Jove! I shall laugh outright; I'm ready to burst.
I shall laugh, in spite of myself, upon my life.
    (HERCULES *shifts about, and turns aside to disguise his laughter: this apparent shyness confirms* BACCHUS *in the opinion of his own ascendancy, which he manifests accordingly.*)
    Bac. (*with a tone of protection*). Come hither, friend. — What ails ye? Step this way;   45
I want to speak to ye.
    Her. (*with a good-humored, but unsuccessful endeavor to suppress laughter, or to conceal it. Suppose him, for instance, speaking with his hand before his mouth*). But I can't help laughing,
To see the lion's skin with a saffron robe,
And the club [2] with the women's sandals — altogether —
What's the meaning of it all? Have you been abroad?
    Bac. I've been abroad — in the Fleet — with Cleisthenes.[3]   50
    Her. (*sharply and ironically*). You fought — ?

---

[1] A race of fabulous creatures born from the union of Ixion with a cloud. They combined the body, head, and arms of a man with the body and legs of a horse. Presumably, then, a centaur could kick!
[2] Skin, robe, and club were items commonly worn — or carried — by Hercules.
[3] In the *Clouds* Aristophanes ridicules Cleisthenes as a disreputable fop of the time.

    Bac. (*briskly and sillily*). Yes, that we did — we gain'd a victory;
And we sunk the enemies' ships — thirteen of 'em.
    Her. "So you woke at last and found it was a dream?"
    Bac. But aboard the fleet, as I pursued my studies,
I read the tragedy of Andromeda;[1]   55
And then such a vehement passion struck my heart,
You can't imagine.
    Her.   A small one, I suppose,
My little fellow — a moderate little passion?
    Bac. (*ironically: the irony of imbecility*). It's just as small as Molon [2] is — that's all —
Molon the wrestler, I mean — as small as he is —
    Her. Well, what was it like? what kind of a thing? what was it?   61
    Bac. (*meaning to be very serious and interesting*). No, friend, you must not laugh; it's past a joke;
It's quite a serious feeling — quite distressing;
I suffer from it —
    Her. (*bluntly*). Well, explain. What was it?
    Bac. I can't declare it at once; but I'll explain it
Theatrically and enigmatically: 66
    (*With a buffoonish assumption of tragic gesture and emphasis.*)
Were you ever seized with a sudden passionate longing
For a mess of porridge?
    Her.   Often enough, if that's all.
    Bac. Shall I state the matter to you plainly at once;
Or put it circumlocutorily?[3]   70
    Her. Not about the porridge. I understand your instance.
    Bac. Such is the passion that possesses me
For poor Euripides, that's dead and gone;
And it's all in vain people trying to persuade me
From going after him.
    Her.   What, to the shades below?
    Bac. Yes, to the shades below, or the shades beneath 'em.   76
To the undermost shades of all. I'm quite determined.
    Her. But what's your object?
    Bac. (*with a ridiculous imitation of tragical action and emphasis*). Why, my object is
That I want a clever poet — "for the good,
The gracious and the good, are dead and gone; 80
The worthless and the weak are left alive." [4]

---

[1] By Euripides.
[2] An actor in the plays of Euripides — very tall.
[3] In a roundabout manner.
[4] A quotation from Euripides.

Her. Is not Iophon [1] a good one? — He's alive
  sure?

Bac. If he's a good one, he's our only good one;
But it's a question; I'm in doubt about him.

Her. There's Sophocles; he's older than Euripi-
  ides —   85
If you go so far for 'em, you'd best bring him.

Bac. No; first I'll try what Iophon can do,
Without his father, Sophocles, to assist him.
— Besides, Euripides is a clever rascal;   89
A sharp, contriving rogue that will make a shift
To desert and steal away with me; the other
Is an easy-minded soul, and always was.

Her. Where's Agathon? [1]

Bac.   He's gone and left me too,
Regretted by his friends; a worthy poet —   94

Her. Gone! Where, poor soul?

Bac.   To the banquets of the blest!

Her. But then you've Xenocles [1] —

Bac.   Yes! a plague upon him!

Her. Pythangelus [1] too —

Xan.   But nobody thinks of me;
Standing all this while with the bundles on my
  shoulder.

Her. But have not you other young ingenious
  youths   99
That are fit to out-talk Euripides ten times over;
To the amount of a thousand, at least, all writing
  tragedy — ?

Bac. They're good for nothing — "Warblers of
  the Grove" —
— "Little, foolish, fluttering things" — poor puny
  wretches,
That dawdle and dangle about with the tragic
  muse;
Incapable of any serious meaning —   105
— There's not one hearty poet amongst them all
That's fit to risk an adventurous valiant phrase.

Her. How — "hearty?" What do you mean
  by "valiant phrases?"

Bac. (*the puzzle of a person who is called upon for
  a definition*). I mean a . . . kind . . . of a . . .
  doubtful, bold expression   109
To talk about . . . "*The viewless foot of Time*" —
      (*Tragic emphasis in the quotations.*)
And . . . "*Jupiter's Secret Chamber in the Skies*" —
And about . . . A person's soul . . . not being perjured
When . . . the tongue . . . forswears itself . . . in spite
  of the soul.[2]

[1] Contemporary or near-contemporaries of Aristophanes. Tragic poets. Xenocles once won over Euripides in a dramatic contest. Iophon was the son of
Sophocles.

[2] Bacchus confuses quotations from Æschylus,
Sophocles, and Euripides.

Her. Do you like that kind of stuff?

Bac.   I'm crazy after it.

Her. Why, sure, it's trash and rubbish — Don't
  you think so?   115

Bac. "Men's fancies are their own — Let mine
  alone" —

Her. But, in fact, it seems to me quite bad —
  rank nonsense.

Bac. You'll tell me next what I ought to like for
  supper.

Xan. But nobody thinks of me here, with the
  bundles.

Bac. (*with a careless, easy, voluble, dégagé style*).
    — But now to the business that I came
    upon —   120
      (*Upon a footing of equality. — The tone
      of a person who is dispatching business
      off-hand, with readiness and unconcern.*)
(With the apparel that you see — the same as
  yours)
To obtain a direction from you to your friends,
(To apply to them — in case of anything —
If anything should occur) the acquaintances
That received you there — (the time you went
  before   125
— For the business about Cerberus) [1] — if you'd
  give me
Their names and their directions, and communicate
Any information relative to the country,
The roads — the streets — the bridges, and the
  brothels.
The wharfs — the public walks — the public
  houses,   130
The fountains — aqueducts — and inns, and tav-
  erns,
And lodgings — free from bugs and fleas, if pos-
  sible.
If you know any such —

Xan.   But nobody thinks of me.

Her. What a notion! You! will you risk it?
  are you mad?

Bac. (*meaning to be very serious and manly*). I
  beseech you say no more — no more of that,
But inform me briefly and plainly about my journey: 136
The shortest road and the most convenient one.

Her. (*with a tone of easy, indolent, deliberate ban-
  ter*). Well, — which shall I tell ye first,
  now? — Let me see now —
There's a good convenient road by the Rope and
  Noose;

[1] The twelfth "labor" which Eurystheus set Hercules was that of bringing to him on earth the three-
headed dog, Cerberus, on guard in the Underworld.
Hercules carried the dog to Eurystheus and then took
him back to Pluto's realm.

The Hanging Road.

Bac.   No; that's too close and stifling.

Her. Then, there's an easy, fair, well-beaten
        track,   141

As you go by the Pestle and Mortar —

Bac.   What, the Hemlock?[1]

Her. To be sure —

Bac.   That's much too cold — it will
        never do.

They tell me it strikes a chill to the legs and feet.

Her. Should you like a speedy, rapid, downhill
        road?   145

Bac. Indeed I should, for I'm a sorry traveller.

Her. Go to the Keramicus then.

Bac.   What then?

Her. Get up to the very top of the tower.

Bac.   What then?

Her. Stand there and watch when the Race of
        the Torch[2] begins;

And mind when you hear the people cry "*Start!
        start!*"   150

Then start at once with 'em.

Bac.   Me? Start? Where from?

Her. From the top of the tower to the bottom.

Bac.   No, not I.

It's enough to dash my brains out! I'll not go

Such a road upon any account.

Her.   Well, which way then?

Bac. The way you went yourself.

Her.   But it's a long one,   155

For first you come to a monstrous bottomless lake.

Bac. And what must I do to pass?

Her.   You'll find a boat there;

A little tiny boat, as big as that,

And an old man[3] that ferries you over in it,

Receiving twopence as the usual fee.   160

Bac. Ah! that same twopence governs every-
        thing

Wherever it goes. — I wonder how it managed

To find its way there?

Her.   Theseus[4] introduced it.

— Next you'll meet serpents, and wild beasts, and
        monsters   164

        (*Suddenly and with a shout in* BACCHUS'S *ear.*)

Horrific to behold!

---

[1] A poisonous herb of the parsley family. This was
the drink administered to Socrates in 399 B.C. — a few
years after this play was performed.

[2] A sort of relay race in which the runners carried a
lighted torch. The modern Olympic Games are cere-
monially opened upon the arrival of an athlete carrying a lighted torch.

[3] Charon — the ferryman in Hades. (See Lucian,
Charon and Hermes, p. 240.)

[4] A Hercules-like hero who performed many feats of
strength and bravery.

Bac. (*starting a little*). Don't try to fright me;

You'll not succeed, I promise you. — I'm deter-
        mined.

Her. Then there's an abyss of mire and floating
        filth,

In which the damn'd lie wallowing and over-
        whelm'd;

The unjust, the cruel, and the inhospitable;   169

And the barbarous bilking Cullies[1] that withhold

The price of intercourse with fraud and wrong;

The incestuous, and the parricides, and the rob-
        bers;

The perjurers, and assassins, and the wretches

That wilfully and presumptuously transcribe

Extracts and trash from Morsimus's plays.   175

Bac. And, by Jove! Cinesias with his Pyrrhic
        dancers[2]

Ought to be there — they're worse, or quite as
        bad.

Her. But after this your sense will be saluted

With a gentle breathing sound of flutes and voices,

And a beautiful spreading light like ours on earth,

And myrtle glades and happy quires among,   181

Of women and men with rapid applause and mirth.

Bac. And who are all those folks?

Her.   The initiated.

Xan. (*gives indications of restiveness, as if ready
        to throw down his bundles*). I won't stand
        here like a mule in a procession

Any longer, with these packages and bundles. 185

Her. (*hastily, in a civil hurry, as when you shake
        a man by the hand, and shove him out of the
        room, and give him your best wishes and ad-
        vice all at once*). They'll tell you everything
        you want to know,

For they're established close upon the road,

By the corner of Pluto's house — so fare you
        well;

Farewell, my little fellow.   (*Exit.*)

Bac. (*pettishly*).   I wish you better.

(*To* XANTHIAS) You, sirrah, take your bundles up
        again.   190

Xan. What, before I put them down?

Bac.   Yes! now, this moment.

Xan. Nah! don't insist; there's plenty of people
        going

As corpses with the convenience of a carriage;

They'd take it for a trifle gladly enough.

Bac. But if we meet with nobody?

Xan.   Then I'll take 'em.

Bac. Come, come, that's fairly spoken, and in
        good time: 196

---

[1] Cheating rascals.

[2] The Pyrrhic dance was a war dance imitating the
movements of attack and defence in battle.

For there they're carrying a corpse out to be buried.

(*A funeral, with a corpse on an open bier, crosses the stage.*)

— Holloh! you there — you Deadman — can't you hear?

Would you take any bundles to hell with ye, my good fellow?   199

Deadman. What are they?

Bac.   These.

Deadman.   Then I must have two drachmas.

Bac. I can't — you must take less.

Deadman (peremptorily).   Bearers, move on.

Bac. No, stop! we shall settle between us — you're so hasty.

Deadman. It's no use arguing; I must have two drachmas.

Bac. (emphatically and significantly). Ninepence!

Deadman. I'd best be alive again at that rate.
(*Exit.*)

Bac. Fine airs the fellow gives himself — a rascal!   205

I'll have him punish'd, I vow, for overcharging.

Xan. Best give him a good beating: give me the bundles,

I'll carry 'em.

Bac.   You're a good, true-hearted fellow;

And a willing servant. — Let's move on to the ferry.

CHARON, BACCHUS, XANTHIAS

Char. Hoy!   Bear a hand, there — Heave ashore.

Bac.   What's this?   210

Xan. The lake it is — the place he told us of.

By Jove! and there's the boat — and here's old Charon.

Bac. Well, Charon! — Welcome, Charon! — Welcome kindly!

Char. Who wants the ferryman?   Anybody waiting

To remove from the sorrows of life?   A passage anybody?   215

To Lethe's [1] wharf? — to Cerberus's Reach?

To Tartarus? [2] — to Tænarus? [3] — to Perdition?

---

[1] The river of forgetfulness, situated near the Elysian Fields that the souls of the sinless, who are to be born into the world again, may drink of its waters and thus forget their existence in the world of souls before going back to the Earth to live.

[2] A yawning gulf or cave, a place of punishment in Hades.   Sometimes placed as far below Hades as Hades itself is below the Earth.

[3] One of the avenues of descent into the Underworld — in Laconia a district of which Sparta was the principal city.

Bac. Yes, I.

Char.   Get in then.

Bac. (hesitatingly). Tell me, where are you going? To Perdition really — ?

Char. (not sarcastically, but civilly in the way of business).   Yes, to oblige you, I will

With all my heart — Step in there.

Bac.   Have a care!   220

Take care, good Charon! — Charon, have a care!
(BACCHUS *gets into the boat.*)

Come, Xanthias, come!

Char.   I take no slaves aboard

Except they've volunteer'd for the naval victory. [1]

Xan. I could not — I was suffering with sore eyes.

Char. You must trudge away then, round by the end of the lake there.   225

Xan. And whereabouts shall I wait?

Char.   At the Stone of Repentance,

By the Slough of Despond beyond the Tribulations;

You understand me?

Xan.   Yes, I understand you;

A lucky, promising direction, truly.

Char. (to BACCHUS). Sit down at the oar — Come quick, if there's more coming!   230

(*To* BACCHUS *again*).   Holloh! what's that you're doing?

(BACCHUS *is seated in a buffoonish attitude on the side of the boat where the oar was fastened.*)

Bac.   What you told me.

I'm sitting at the oar.

Char.   Sit there, I tell you,

You Fatguts; that's your place.

Bac. (changes his place).   Well, so I do.

Char. Now ply your hands and arms.

Bac. (makes a silly motion with his arms). Well, so I do.

Char. You'd best leave off your fooling.   Take to the oar,   235

And pull away.

Bac.   But how shall I contrive?

I've never served on board — I'm only a landsman;

I'm quite unused to it —

Char.   We can manage it.

As soon as you begin you shall have some music

That will teach you to keep time.

Bac.   What music's that?

Char. A chorus of Frogs — uncommon musical Frogs.   241

---

[1] Athens has raised a navy by promising slaves certain privileges of free men if they volunteered for the service.   The victory was that at Arginusæ.

Bac. Well, give me the word and the time.
Char.　　　Whooh up, up; whooh up, up.
Chorus. Brekekekex-koax-koax,
Shall the Choral Quiristers [1] of the Marsh
Be censured and rejected as hoarse and harsh;　245
　And their Chromatic essays
　Deprived of praise?
No, let us raise afresh
Our obstreperous Brekekekex;
The customary croak and cry　　　250
　Of the creatures
　At the theatres,
In their yearly revelry,
Brekekekex-koax-koax.
　Bac. (rowing in great misery).
How I'm maul'd,　　　255
How I'm gall'd;
Worn and mangled to a mash —
There they go! "*Koax-koax!*" —
　Frogs. Brekekekex-koax-koax.
　Bac.　Oh, beshrew,　　　260
　　All your crew;
You don't consider how I smart.
　Frogs. Now for a sample of the Art!
　　Brekekekex-koax-koax.　264
　Bac.　I wish you hang'd, with all my heart.
— Have you nothing else to say?
"*Brekekekex-koax-koax*" all day!
　Frogs. We've a right,
　　We've a right;
　And we croak at ye for spite.　270
　　We've a right,
　　We've a right;
　　Day and night,
　　Day and night;
　　Night and day,　275
　Still to creak and croak away.
Phœbus and every Grace
Admire and approve of the croaking race;
And the egregious guttural notes
That are gargled and warbled in their lyrical
　　throats.　280
　　　In reproof
　　　Of your scorn
　　　Mighty Pan
　　　Nods his horn;
　　　Beating time　285
　　　To the rhyme
　　　With his hoof,
　　　With his hoof.
　　Persisting in our plan,
　　We proceed as we began,　290
　　Brekekekex-brekekekex,
　　Kooax, kooax.

Bac.　Oh, the Frogs, consume and rot 'em,
　I've a blister on my bottom.　294
　Hold your tongues, you tuneful creatures.
Frogs. Cease with your profane entreaties.
　All in vain for ever striving:
　　Silence is against our natures.
　With the vernal heat reviving,
　　Our aquatic crew repair　300
　From their periodic sleep,
　In the dark and chilly deep,
　To the cheerful upper air;
　Then we frolic here and there
　All amidst the meadows fair;　305
　Shady plants of asphodel,
　Are the lodges where we dwell;
　Chaunting in the leafy bowers
　All the livelong summer hours,
　Till the sudden gusty showers　310
　Send us headlong, helter, skelter,
　To the pool to seek for shelter;
　Meagre, eager, leaping, lunging,
　From the sedgy wharfage plunging
　To the tranquil depth below,　315
　There we muster all a-row;
　Where, secure from toil and trouble,
　With a tuneful hubble-bubble,
　Our symphonious accents flow.
　　Brekekekex-koax-koax.　320
Bac.　I forbid you to proceed.
Frogs. That would be severe indeed;
　Arbitrary, bold, and rash —
　　Brekekekex-koax-koax.
Bac.　I command you to desist —　325
　— Oh, my back, there! oh, my wrist!
　What a twist!
　What a sprain!
Frogs. Once again —
　We renew the tuneful strain,　330
　　Brekekekex-koax-koax.
Bac.　I disdain — (Hang the pain!)
　All your nonsense, noise, and trash.
　Oh, my blister! Oh, my sprain!
Frogs. Brekekekex-koax-koax.　335
　Friends and Frogs, we must display
　All our powers of voice to-day;
　Suffer not this stranger here,
　With fastidious foreign ear,
　To confound us and abash.　340
　　Brekekex-koax-koax.
Bac.　Well, my spirit is not broke,
　If it's only for the joke,
　I'll outdo you with a croak.
　Here it goes — (*very loud*) "Koax-koax."
Frogs. Now for a glorious croaking crash,　346
　　　　　　(*Still louder.*)
　Brekekekex-koax-koax.

Bac. (*splashing with his oar*).
　　I'll disperse you with a splash.
Frogs. Brekekekex-koax-koax.
Bac.　　　　　I'll subdue
　　Your rebellious, noisy crew —　　　　350
　　— Have amongst you there, slap-dash.
　　　　　　　　　　(*Strikes at them.*)
Frogs. Brekekekex-koax-koax.
　　We defy your oar and you.
Char. Hold! We're ashore just — shift your oar.
　　Get out.
— Now pay for your fare.
Bac.　　　　　There — there it is — the twopence.
　　　(CHARON *returns.* BACCHUS, *finding him-
　　　self alone and in a strange place, begins to
　　　call out.*)
Bac. Hoh, Xanthias! Xanthias, I say!
　　Where's Xanthias?　　　　　　　　356
Xan. A-hoy!
Bac.　　　　Come here.
Xan.　　　　　　I'm glad to see you, master.
Bac. What's that before us there?
Xan.　　　　　　The mire and darkness.
Bac. Do you see the villains and the perjurers
That he told us of?
Xan.　　　　Yes, plain enough, don't you?
Bac. Ah! now I see them, indeed, quite plain —
　　and now too.[1]　　　　　　　　　361
　　　　(*Turning to the audience.*)
Well, what shall we do next?
Xan.　　　　　We'd best move forward;
For here's the place that Hercules there inform'd us
Was haunted by those monsters.
Bac.　　　　　Oh, confound him!
He vapor'd and talk'd at random to deter me　365
From venturing. He's amazingly conceited
And jealous of other people, is Hercules;
He reckon'd I should rival him, and, in fact
(Since I've come here so far), I should rather like
To meet with an adventure in some shape.　　370
Xan. By Jove! and I think I hear a kind of a
　　noise.
Bac. Where? where?
Xan.　　　　　　There, just behind us.
Bac.　　　　　　　　Go behind, then.
Xan. There! — it's before us now. — There!
Bac.　　　　　　　　Go before, then.
Xan. Ah! now I see it — a monstrous beast in-
　　deed!
Bac. What kind?
Xan.　　　A dreadful kind — all kinds at once.
It changes and transforms itself about　　376
To a mule and an ox, — and now to a beautiful
　　creature;

[1] Thus making "villains and perjurers" of the
audience.

A woman!
Bac.　　Where? where is she? Let me seize her.
Xan. But now she's turned to a mastiff all of a
　　sudden.
Bac. It's the Weird hag! the Vampyre![1]
Xan. (*collectedly*).　　　　Like enough.
She's all of a blaze of fire about the mouth.　381
Bac. (*with great trepidation*). Has she got the
　　brazen foot?
Xan. (*with cool despair*).　　Yes, there it is —
By Jove! — and the cloven hoof to the other leg.
Distinct enough — that's she!
Bac.　　　　　　But what shall I do?
Xan. And I, too?
　　　(BACCHUS *runs to the front of the stage, where
　　　there was a seat of honor appropriated to
　　　the priest of* BACCHUS.)
Bac.　　　Save me, Priest, protect and save me,
That we may drink and be jolly together here-
　　after.　　　　　　　　　　　386
Xan. We're ruin'd, Master Hercules.
Bac.　　　　　Don't call me so, I beg.
Don't mention my name, good friend, upon any
　　account.
Xan. Well, BACCHUS, then!
Bac.　　　That's worse, ten thousand times.
　　　(BACCHUS *remains hiding his face before
　　　the seat of the priest — in the meantime
　　　affairs take a more favorable turn.*)
Xan. (*cheerfully*). Come, master, move along —
　　Come, come this way.　　　　　390
Bac. (*without looking round*). What's happened?
Xan.　　Why we're prosperous and victorious:
The storm of fear and danger has subsided,
And (as the actor said the other day)
"Has only left a gentle *qualm* behind."
The Vampyre's vanish'd.
Bac.　　　　Has she? upon your oath?
Xan. By Jove! she has.
Bac.　　　　　No, swear again.
Xan.　　　　　　By Jove!　396
Bac. Is she, by Jupiter?
Xan.　　　　　By Jupiter!
Bac. Oh dear; what a fright I was in with the
　　very sight of her:
It turn'd me sick and pale — but see, the priest
　　here!
He has color'd up quite with the same alarm.　400
— What has brought me to this pass? — It must be
　　Jupiter
With his "*Chamber in the Skies*," and the "*Foot of
　　Time.*"
　　　(*A flute sounds.* BACCHUS *remains ab-
　　　sorbed and inattentive to the objects about
　　　him.*)

[1] The "Empusa," a weird creature in local mythology.

Xan. Holloh, you!

Bac.   What?

Xan.   Why, did you not hear?

Bac.   Why, what?

Xan. The sound of a flute.

Bac. (*recollecting himself*). Indeed! And there's
a smell too;
A pretty mystical ceremonious smell   405
Of torches. We'll watch here, and keep quite quiet.

Chorus of Votaries, Bacchus, Xanthias

Chorus (*shouting and singing*).
              Iacchus! Iaachus! Ho!
              Iacchus! Iacchus! Ho!
Xan. There, Master. there they are, the initia-
ted;
All sporting about as he told us we should find 'em.
They're singing in praise of Bacchus like Diag-
oras.[1]   411
Bac. Indeed, and so they are; but we'll keep
quiet
Till we make them out a little more distinctly.
Chorus: Song
        Mighty Bacchus! Holy Power!
        Hither at the wonted hour   415
            Come away,
            Come away,
        With the wanton holiday,
        Where the revel uproar leads
        To the mystic holy meads,   420
        Where the frolic votaries fly, ⎤
        With a tipsy shout and cry;   ⎬
        Flourishing the Thyrsus [2] high, ⎦
        Flinging forth, alert and airy,
        To the sacred old vagary,   425
        The tumultuous dance and song,
        Sacred from the vulgar throng;
        Mystic orgies, that are known
        To the votaries alone —
        To the mystic chorus solely —   430
        Secret — unreveal'd — and holy.
Xan. Oh glorious virgin, daughter of the god-
dess!
What a scent of roasted griskin [3] reach'd my
senses.
Bac. Keep quiet — and watch for a chance of a
piece of the haslets.[4]
Chorus: Song
        Raise the fiery torches high!   435
        Bacchus is approaching nigh,
        Like the planet of the morn,

[1] A contemporary philosopher and poet.
[2] The staff of Bacchus, around which were twined ivy
and vine leaves.
[3] The spine of a hog.
[4] Heart, liver, and lights of a hog.

        Breaking with the hoary dawn,
          On the dark solemnity —
        There they flash upon the sight; ⎤   440
        All the plain is blazing bright, ⎬
        Flush'd and overflown with light: ⎦
        Age has cast his years away,   ⎤
        And the cares of many a day,   ⎬
        Sporting to the lively lay —   ⎦   445
        Mighty Bacchus! march and lead
        (Torch in hand toward the mead)
        Thy devoted humble Chorus,
        Mighty Bacchus — move before us!
Semichorus. Keep silence — keep peace — and
        let all the profane   450
From our holy solemnity duly refrain;
Whose souls unenlightened by taste, are obscure;
Whose poetical notions are dark and impure;
        Whose theatrical conscience
        Is sullied by nonsense;   455
Who never were train'd by the mighty Cratinus [1]
In mystical orgies poetic and vinous;
Who delight in buffooning and jests out of season;
Who promote the designs of oppression and treason;
Who foster sedition, and strife, and debate;   460
All traitors, in short, to the stage and the state;
Who surrender a fort, or in private, export
To places and harbors of hostile resort,
Clandestine consignments of cables and pitch;
In the way that Thorycion grew to be rich   465
From a scoundrelly dirty collector of tribute;
All such we reject and severely prohibit:
All statesmen retrenching the fees and the salaries
Of theatrical bards, in revenge for the railleries,
And jests, and lampoons, of this holy solemnity,
Profanely pursuing their personal enmity,   471
For having been flouted, and scoff'd, and scorn'd,
All such are admonish'd and heartily warn'd;
        We warn them once,
        We warn them twice,   475
        We warn and admonish — we warn them thrice,
To conform to the law,   ⎤
To retire and withdraw;   ⎬
While the Chorus again with the formal saw   ⎦
(Fixt and assign'd to the festive day)   480
Move to the measure and march away.
Semichorus. March! march! lead forth,
        Lead forth manfully,
        March in order all;
        Bustling, hustling, justling,   485
            As it may befall;
          Flocking, shouting, laughing,
        Mocking, flouting, quaffing,
            One and all;
        All have had a belly-full   490

[1] A dramatist of Athens who once won a contest
against Aristophanes.

Of breakfast brave and plentiful;
  Therefore
  Evermore
With your voices and your bodies
Serve the goddess,   495
  And raise
  Songs of praise;
She shall save the country still,
And save it against the traitor's will;
  So she says.   500
Semichorus. Now let us raise, in a different strain,
The praise of the goddess to giver of grain;
Imploring her favor
With other behavior,   504
In measures more sober, submissive, and graver.
  Semichorus. Ceres,[1] holy patroness,
    Condescend to mark and bless
    With benevolent regard,
    Both the Chorus and the Bard;
    Grant them for the present day   510
    Many things to sing and say,
    Follies intermix'd with sense;
    Folly, but without offence.
    Grant them with the present play
    To bear the prize of verse away.   515
  Semichorus. Now call again, and with a different
    measure,
  The power of mirth and pleasure;
The florid, active Bacchus, bright and gay,
  To journey forth and join us on the way.
  Semichorus. O Bacchus, attend! the customary
    patron   520
  Of every lively lay;
  Go forth without delay
  Thy wonted annual way,
To meet the ceremonious holy matron:
  Her grave procession gracing,   525
  Thine airy footsteps tracing
With unlaborious, light, celestial motion;
And here at thy devotion
  Behold thy faithful quire
  In pitiful attire;   530
All overworn and ragged,
This jerkin old and jagged,
These buskins torn and burst,
  Though sufferers in the fray,
May serve us at the worst   535
  To sport throughout the day;
And there within the shades,
I spy some lovely maids;
With whom we romp'd and revell'd,
Dismantled and dishevell'd;   540
With their bosoms open,
With whom we might be coping.
  Xan. Well, I was always hearty,

[1] Goddess of sowing, reaping, and harvesting.

Disposed to mirth and ease,
I'm ready to join the party.   545
  Bac. (*with a tone of imbecility, like Sir Andrew
    Aguecheek's "Yes, and I too" — "Ay or I
    either"*). And I will, if you please.
  Bacchus (*to the* CHORUS). Prithee, my good
    fellows,
    Would you please to tell us
      Which is Pluto's door,
    I'm an utter stranger,   550
      Never here before.
  Chorus. Friend, you're out of danger,
      You need not seek it far;
    There it stands before ye,
      Before ye, where you are.   555
  Bac. Take up your bundles, Xanthias.
  Xan.   Hang all bundles;
A bundle has no end, and these have none.
    (*Exeunt* BACCHUS *and* XANTHIAS.)
  Semichorus. Now we go to dance and sing
    In the consecrated shades;
    Round the secret holy ring,   560
    With the matrons and the maids.
  Thither I must haste to bring
    The mysterious early light;
    Which must witness every rite
    Of the joyous happy night.   565
  Semichorus. Let us hasten — let us fly —
  Where the lovely meadows lie;
    Where the living waters flow;
    Where the roses bloom and blow.
    — Heirs of Immortality,   570
  Segregated, safe and pure,
  Easy, sorrowless, secure;
  Since our earthly course is run,
  We behold a brighter sun.
  Holy lives — a holy vow —   575
  Such rewards await them now.

SCENE: *The Gate of Pluto's Palace.*

(*Enter* BACCHUS *and* XANTHIAS)

  Bac. (*going up to the door with considerable hesi-
    tation*). Well, how must I knock at the door
    now? Can't ye tell me?
How do the native inhabitants knock at doors?
  Xan. Pah; don't stand fooling there; but smite
    it smartly,
With the very spirit and air of Hercules.   580
  Bac. Holloh!
  Æacus (*from within, with the voice of a royal and
    infernal porter*). Who's there?
  Bac. (*with a forced voice*). 'Tis I, the valiant
    Hercules!
  Æacus. (*coming out*). Thou brutal, abominable,
    detestable,

Vile, villainous, infamous, nefarious scoundrel!
— How durst thou, villain as thou wert, to seize
Our watch-dog, Cerberus, whom I kept and
    tended   585
Hurrying him off, half-strangled in your grasp?
— But now, be sure we have you safe and fast,
Miscreant and villain! — Thee, the Stygian cliffs,
With stern adamantine durance, and the rocks
Of inaccessible Acheron, red with gore,   590
Environ and beleaguer; and the watch,
And swift pursuit of the hideous hounds of hell;
And the horrible Hydra,[1] with her hundred heads,
Whose furious ravening fangs shall rend and tear
    thee;
Wrenching thy vitals forth, with the heart and
    midriff;   595
While inexpressible Tartesian monsters,
And grim Tithrasian Gorgons [2] toss and scatter
With clattering claws, thine intertwined intestines.
To them, with instant summons, I repair,
Moving in hasty march with steps of speed.   600
    (ÆACUS *departs with a tremendous tragical
    exit, and* BACCHUS *falls to the ground in
    a fright.*)
Xan. Holloh, you! What's the matter there —?
Bac.   Oh dear,
I've had an accident.
Xan.   Poh! poh! jump up!
Come! you ridiculous simpleton! don't lie there,
The people will see you.
Bac.   Indeed I'm sick at heart; lah!
    (*Here a few lines are omitted.*)
Xan. Was there ever in heaven or earth such a
    coward?
Bac.   Me?   605
A coward! Did not I show my presence of mind —
And call for a sponge and water in a moment?
Would a coward have done that?
Xan.   What else would he do?
Bac. He'd have lain there stinking like a nasty
    coward;
But I jump'd up at once, like a lusty wrestler,
And look'd about, and wiped myself, withal.   611
Xan. Most manfully done!
Bac.   By Jove, and I think it was;
But tell me, wer'n't you frighten'd with that
    speech?
— Such horrible expressions!
Xan. (*coolly, but with conscious and intentional
    coolness*).   No, not I;
I took no notice —

[1] One of the monsters in Hades assigned to the task
of torturing the evil-doers.

[2] Lesser water divinities; they turned to stone those
upon whom they looked. The adventure of Perseus
with the Gorgon Medusa is perhaps best known.

Bac.   Well, I'll tell you what,   615
Since you're such a valiant-spirited kind of fellow,
Do you be *Me* — with the club and the lion-skin,
Now you're in this courageous temper of mind;
And I'll go take my turn and carry the bundles.
Xan. Well — give us hold — I must humor
    you, forsooth;   620
Make haste (*he changes his dress*), and now behold
    the Xanthian Hercules,
And mind if I don't display more heart and spirit.
Bac. Indeed, and you look the character, com-
    pletely,
Like that heroic Melitensian hangdog —
Come, now for my bundles. I must mind my
    bundles.   625

(*Enter* PROSERPINE'S SERVANT MAID (*a kind of
Dame Quickly*), *who immediately addresses*
XANTHIAS.)

Serv. Maid. Dear Hercules. Well, you're come
    at last. Come in,
For the goddess, as soon as she heard of it, set to
    work
Baking peck loaves and frying stacks of pancakes,
And making messes of furmety; there's an ox
Besides, she has roasted whole, with a relishing
    stuffing,   630
If you'll only just step in this way.
Xan. (*with dignity and reserve*). I thank you,
I'm equally obliged.
Serv. Maid.   No, no, by Jupiter!
We must not let you off, indeed. There's wild
    fowl
And sweetmeats for the desert, and the best of
    wine;
Only walk in.
Xan. (*as before*). I thank you. You'll excuse
    me.   635
Serv. Maid. No, no, we can't excuse you, indeed
    we can't;
There are dancing and singing girls besides.
Xan. (*with dissembled emotion*). What! dancers?
Serv. Maid. Yes, that there are; the sweetest,
    charmingest things
That you ever saw — and there's the cook this
    moment
Is dishing up the dinner.
Xan. (*with an air of lofty condescension*). Go
    before then,   640
And tell the girls — those singing girls you men-
    tioned —
To prepare for my approach in person presently.
(*To* BACCHUS.) You, sirrah! follow behind me
    with the bundles.
Bac. Holloh, you! what, do you take the thing
    in earnest,

Because, for a joke, I drest you up like Hercules?
    (XANTHIAS *continues to gesticulate as*
        HERCULES.)
Come, don't stand fooling, Xanthias.   You'll pro-
    voke me.   646
There, carry the bundles, Sirrah, when I bid
    you.
  Xan. (*relapsing at once into his natural air*).
    Why, sure? do you mean to take the things
    away
That you gave me yourself of your own accord this
    instant?
  Bac. I never mean a thing; I do it at once.   650
Let go of the lion's skin directly, I tell you.
  Xan. (*resigning his heroical insignia with a
    tragical air and tone*). To you, just Gods, I
    make my last appeal,
Bear witness!
  Bac.   What! the Gods? — do you think
    they mind you?
How could you take it in your head, I wonder;
Such a foolish fancy for a fellow like you,   655
A mortal and a slave, to pass for Hercules?
  Xan. There.   Take them. — There — you may
    have them — but, please God,
You may come to want my help some time or
    other.
  Chorus. Dexterous and wily wits,
    Find their own advantage ever;   660
  For the wind where'er it sits,
    Leaves a berth secure and clever
  To the ready navigator;
  That foresees and knows the nature,
  Of the wind can turn and shift   665
  To the sheltered easy side;
  'Tis a practice proved and tried,
  Not to wear a formal face; ⎫
  Fixt in attitude and place, ⎬
  Like an image on its base; ⎭   670
  'Tis the custom of the seas, ⎫
  Which, as all the world agrees, ⎬
  Justifies Theramenes.[1] ⎭
  Bacchus. How ridiculous and strange;
    What a monstrous proposition,   675
  That I should condescend to change
  My dress, my name, and my condition,
  To follow Xanthias, and behave
  Like a mortal and a slave;
  To be set to watch the door   680
  While he wallow'd with his whore,
  Tumbling on a purple bed;
  While I waited with submission,

[1] An Athenian statesman and politician of the day.
He was reputed to be a double-dealer and, later
accused of treason, was forced to drink poison.

  To receive a broken head;
  Or be kick'd upon suspicion   685
  Of impertinence and peeping
  At the joys that he was reaping.

(*Enter Two* WOMEN, *Sutlers or Keepers of an Eating
         House.*)

  1st Woman. What, Platana!   Goody Platana!
    there! that's he,
The fellow that robs and cheats poor victuallers;
That came to our house and eat those nineteen
    loaves.   690
  2nd Woman. Ay, sure enough that's he, the very
    man.
  Xan. (*tauntingly to* BACCHUS). There's mischief
    in the wind for somebody!
  1st Woman. — And a dozen and a half of cutlets
    and fried chops,
At a penny halfpenny a piece —
  Xan. (*significantly*).   There are pains and
    penalties
Impending —
  1st Woman. — And all the garlic: such a quantity
As he swallowed —
  Bac. (*delivers this speech with Herculean dignity,
    after his fashion; having hitherto remained
    silent upon the same principle*). Woman,
    you're beside yourself;   696
You talk you know not what —
  2nd Woman.   No, no! you reckoned
I should not know you again with them there
    buskins.[1]
  1st Woman. — Good lack! and there was all that
    fish besides.
Indeed — with the pickle, and all — and the good
    green cheese   700
That he gorged at once, with the rind, and the rush-
    baskets;
And then, when I called for payment, he looked
    fierce,
And stared at me in the face, and grinned, and
    roared —
  Xan. Just like him!   That's the way wherever
    he goes.
  1st Woman. — And snatched his sword out, and
    behaved like mad.   705
  Xan. Poor souls! you suffered sadly!
  1st Woman.   Yes, indeed;
And then we both ran off with the fright and
    terror,
And scrambled into the loft beneath the roof;
And he took up two rugs and stole them off.
  Xan. Just like him again — but something
    must be done.   710

[1] A boot worn by Greek and Roman tragic actors.

Go call me Cleon,[1] he's my advocate.
   2nd Woman. And Hyperbolus,[1] if you meet him
     send him here.
He's mine; and we'll demolish him, I warrant.
   1st Woman (*going close up to* BACCHUS *in the
    true termagant attitude of rage and defiance,
    with the arms akimbo, and a neck and chin
    thrust out*). How I should like to strike
    those ugly teeth out
With a good big stone, you ravenous greedy vil-
    lain!   715
You gormandising villain! that I should —
Yes, that I should; your wicked ugly fangs
That have eaten up my substance, and devoured
    me.
   Bac. And I could toss you into the public pit
With the malefactors' carcasses; that I could, 720
With pleasure and satisfaction; that I could.
   1st Woman. And I should like to rip that gullet
    out
With a reaping hook that swallowed all my tripe,
And liver and lights — but I'll fetch Cleon here,
And he shall summon him. He shall settle him,
And have it out of him this very day.   726
            (*Exeunt 1st and 2nd* WOMAN.)
   Bac. (*in a pretended soliloquy*). I love poor
    Xanthias dearly, that I do;
I wish I might be hanged else.
   Xan.   Yes, I know —
I know your meaning — No; no more of that,
I won't act Hercules —
   Bac.   Now pray don't say so, 730
My little Xanthias.
   Xan.   How should I be Hercules?
A mortal and a slave, a fellow like me? —
   Bac. I know you're angry, and you've a right to
    be angry;
And if you beat me for it I'd not complain;
But if ever I strip you again, from this time for-
    ward,   735
I wish I may be utterly confounded,
With my wife, my children, and my family,
And the blear-eyed Archedemus into the bargain.
   Xan. I agree then, on that oath, and those con-
    ditions.
       (XANTHIAS *equips himself with the club
        and lion's skin, and* BACCHUS *resumes
        his bundles.*)
   Chorus (*addressing* XANTHIAS)
     Now that you revive and flourish   740
       In your old attire again,
     You must rouse afresh and nourish
       Thoughts of an heroic strain;
       That exalt and raise the figure,

[1] Orators of the time, who had died recently and
were, therefore, close at hand in Hades.

     And assume a fire and vigor;   745
       And an attitude and air
     Suited to the garb you wear;
       With a brow severely bent,
       Like the god you represent.
        But beware,   750
        Have a care!
     If you blunder, or betray
     Any weakness any way;
     Weakness of the heart or brain,
     We shall see you once again   755
     Trudging in the former track,
     With the bundles at your back.

   Xan. (*in reply to the* CHORUS)
     Friends, I thank you for your care;
     Your advice was good and fair;
     Corresponding in its tone   760
     With reflections of my own.
     — Though I clearly comprehend
     All the upshot and the end
     (That if any good comes of it,
     Any pleasure any profit —   765
     He, my master, vill recede
     From the terms that were agreed),
     You shall see me, notwithstanding,
     Stern, intrepid, and commanding.
     Now's the time; for there's a noise!   770
     Now for figure, look, and voice!

(ÆACUS *enters again as a vulgar executioner of the
   law, with suitable understrappers in attendance.*)
   Æacus. Arrest me there that fellow that stole
    the dog.
There! — Pinion him! — Quick!
   Bac. (*tauntingly to* XANTHIAS). There's some-
    body in a scrape.
   Xan. (*in a menacing attitude*). Keep off, and be
    hanged.
   Æacus.   Oh, hoh! do you mean to fight for it?
Here! Pardokas, and Skeblias, and the rest of
    ye,   775
Make up to the rogue, and settle him. Come, be
    quick.
       (*A scuffle ensues, in which* XANTHIAS
        succeeds in obliging* ÆACUS'S *runners
        to keep their distance.*)
   Bac. (*mortified at* XANTHIAS'S *prowess*). Well, is
    not this quite monstrous and outrageous,
To steal the dog, and then to make an assault
In justification of it.
   Xan. (*triumphantly and ironically*). Quite out-
    rageous!
   Æacus (*gravely, and dissembling his mortifica-
    tion*). An aggravated case!

Xan. (*with candor and gallantry*). Well, now —
  by Jupiter,   780
May I die; but I never saw this place before —
Nor ever stole the amount of a farthing from you:
Nor a hair of your dog's tail — But you shall see
  now,
I'll settle all this business nobly and fairly.
— This slave of mine — you may take and torture
  him;   785
And if you make out anything against me,
You may take and put me to death for aught I
  care.

Æacus (*in an obliging tone, softened into deference
  and civility by the liberality of* XANTHIAS's
  proposal). But which way would you please
  to have him tortured?

Xan. (*with a gentlemanly spirit of accommoda-
  tion*). In your own way — with ... the lash
  — with ... knots and screws,
With ... the common usual customary tortures.
With the rack — with ... the water-torture —
  anyway —   791
With fire and vinegar — all sorts of ways.
(*After a very slight pause.*) There's only one thing
  I should warn you of:
I must not have him treated like a child,
To be whipt with fennel, or with lettuce leaves.

Æacus. That's fair — and if so be ... he's
  maim'd or crippled   796
In any respect — the valy [1] shall be paid you.

Xan. Oh no! — by no means! not to me! — by
  no means!
You must not mention it! — Take him to the torture.

Æacus. It had better be here, and under your
  own eye.   800
(*To* BACCHUS.) Come you — put down your
  bundles and make ready.
And mind — Let me hear no lies

Bac.   I'll tell you what:
I'd advise people not to torture me;
I give you notice — I'm a deity.
So mind now — you'll have nobody to blame   805
But your own self —

Æacus.   What's that you're saying there?

Bac. Why that I'm Bacchus, Jupiter's own
  son:
That fellow there's a slave. (*Pointing to* XANTHIAS.)

Æacus (*to* XANTHIAS).   Do ye hear?

Xan.   I hear him —
A reason the more to give him a good beating;
If he's immortal he need never mind it.   810

Bac. Why should not you be beat as well as I
  then,
If you're immortal, as you say you are?

[1] Value.

Xan. Agreed — and him, the first that you see
  flinching,
Or seeming to mind it at all, you may set him down
For an impostor and no real deity.   815

Æacus (*to* XANTHIAS *with warmth and cordiality*).
  Ah, you're a worthy gentleman I'll be bound
  for't;
You're all for the truth and the proof.   Come —
  Strip there both o' ye.

Xan. But how can ye put us to the question
  fairly,
Upon equal terms?

Æacus (*in the tone of a person proposing a convenient, agreeable arrangement*). Oh, easily
  enough,
Conveniently enough — a lash apiece,   820
Each in your turn; you can have 'em one by one.

Xan. That's right. (*Putting himself in an attitude to receive the blow.*) Now mind if ye see
  me flinch or swerve.

Æacus (*striking* XANTHIAS). I've struck you.

Xan. No, by Zeus! I never felt it.

Æacus. Well, then I'll beat this other fellow.
                              (*Striking* BACCHUS.)

Bac. When?   826

Æacus. I've struck already.

Bac. And I didn't even sneeze?

Æacus. No answer there.   I'll try the other
  again.   (*Striking* XANTHIAS.)

Xan. Won't you ever stop? Oh, woe!   830

Æacus. What! Woe?
Were you hurt then?

Xan. No, by Zeus, I was only thinking
Of my feast of Hercules in Diomea.

Æacus. Holy man. I must go back to the other
  one again.   835

Bac. Ho! Ho!

Æacus. What's that?

Bac. I saw some horsemen.

Æacus. But what are you weeping for?

Bac. I'm smelling onions.   840

Æacus. And you don't mind the blows at all?

Bac. Oh, not at all.

Æacus. Well, here we go, back to the other one.

Xan. Oh, ouch!

Æacus. What's that?   845

Xan. (*lifting his foot*). Pull out this thorn.

Æacus. What a job this is! I'll try the other
  again.

Bac. Apollo! [1] (*a cry which he continues as if it
  were a quotation*) thou of Delos and of Pytho.

Xan. He's hurt. Didn't you hear him?

Bac. Me? Not I!   850
I just remembered a verse from Hipponax. [2]

[1] God of music and song, gifted with oracular powers.
[2] Satiric poet.

Xan. (to ÆACUS). You're getting nowhere.
   Beat him on the flanks.

Æacus. No, by Zeus, here's better. Turn up
   your belly.

Bac. Poseidon!   854

Xan. There, he's flinching. Did you hear him?

Bac. (continuing the quotation from Sophocles).
   Who rulest the Ægean peaks and streams
And over the depths of the sea.

   Æacus. Well, after all my pains, I'm quite at a
      loss
To discover which is the true, real deity.
By the Holy Goddess — I'm completely puzzled;
I must take you before Proserpine and Pluto,   861
Being gods themselves they're likeliest to know.

   Bac. Why, that's a lucky thought. I only wish
It had happen'd to occur before you beat us.

   Chorus. Muse, attend our solemn summons   865
      And survey the assembled commons,
      Congregated as they sit,
      An enormous mass of wit,
      — Full of genius, taste, and fire,
      Jealous pride, and critic ire —   870
      Cleophon [1] among the rest
      (Like the swallow from her nest,
      A familiar foreign bird),
      Chatters loud and will be heard,
      (With the accent and the grace   875
      Which he brought with him from Thrace);
      But we fear the tuneful strain
      Will be turn'd to grief and pain;
      He must sing a dirge perforce
      When his trial takes its course;   880
      We shall hear him moan and wail,
      Like the plaintive nightingale.

EPIRREMA [2]

It behooves the sacred Chorus, and of right to
   them belongs,
To suggest the best advice in their addresses and
   their songs,
In performance of our office, we present with all
   humility   885
A proposal for removing groundless fears and dis-
   ability.
First that all that were inveigled into Phrynichus's treason,
Should be suffer'd and received by rules of evidence and reason
To clear their conduct — Secondly, that none of
   our Athenian race

[1] An unprincipled popular leader of the time.

[2] The "after-speech" — a part of Greek comedy in
which the chorus addresses the audience directly,
speaking either in its own right or for the poet. Here
the concern is with public affairs of the time.

Should live suspected and subjected to loss of
   franchise and disgrace,   890
Feeling it a grievous scandal when a single naval
   fight
Renders foreigners and slaves partakers of the
   city's right:
— Not that we condemn the measure; we conceived it wisely done,
As a just and timely measure, and the first and
   only one:
— But your kinsmen and your comrades, those
   with whom you fought and bore   895
Danger, hardship, and fatigue, or with their
   fathers long before,
Struggling on the land and ocean, laboring with
   the spear and oar
— These we think, as they profess repentance for
   their past behavior,
Might, by your exalted wisdom, be received to
   grace and favor.
Better it would be, believe us, casting off revenge
   and pride,   900
To receive as friends and kinsmen all that combat
   on our side
Into full and equal franchise: on the other hand
   we fear,
If your hearts are fill'd with fancies, haughty,
   captious, and severe;
While the shock of instant danger threatens shipwreck to the state,
Such resolves will be lamented and repented of
   too late.   905
      If the Muse foresees at all
      What in future will befall
      Dirty Cleigenes [1] the small —
      He, the sovereign of the bath,
      Will not long escape from scath;   910
      But must perish by and by,
      With his potash and his lye;
      With his realm and dynasty,
      His terraqueous [2] scouring ball,
      And his washes, one and all;   915
      Therefore he can never cease
      To declaim against a peace.

ANTEPIRREMA

Often times have we reflected on a similar abuse,
In the choice of men for office, and of coins for
   common use;
For your old and standard pieces, valued, and
   approved, and tried,   920
Here among the Grecian nations, and in all the
   world beside;

[1] Probably another of the contemporary dema-
gogues.

[2] Containing both water and soil.

Recognised in every realm for trusty stamp and
    pure assay,
Are rejected and abandon'd for the trash of yes-
    terday; [1]
For a vile, adulterate issue, drossy, counterfeit,
    and base,
Which the traffic of the city passes current in their
    place!   925
And the men that stood for office, noted for ac-
    knowledged worth,
And for manly deeds of honor, and for honorable
    birth;
Train'd in exercise and art, in sacred dances and in
    song,
All are ousted and supplanted by a base ignoble
    throng;
Paltry stamp and vulgar mettle raise them to
    command and place,   930
Brazen counterfeit pretenders, scoundrels of a
    scoundrel race;
Whom the state in former ages scarce would have
    allow'd to stand,
At the sacrifice of outcasts, as the scapegoats of
    the land.
— Time it is — and long has been, renouncing all
    your follies past,
To recur to sterling merit and intrinsic worth at
    last.   935
— If we rise, we rise with honor; if we fall, it must
    be so!
— But there was an ancient saying, which we all
    have heard and know,
That the wise, in dangerous cases, have esteem'd
    it safe and good
To receive a slight chastisement from *a wand of
noble* [2] *wood.*

SCENE: XANTHIAS *and* ÆACUS

Æacus. By Jupiter; but he's a gentleman, 940
That master of yours.
    Xan.   A gentleman! To be sure he is;
Why, he does nothing else but wench and drink.
    Æacus. His never striking you when you took
    his name —
Outfacing him and contradicting him! —
    Xan. It might have been worse for him if he had.
    Æacus. Well, that's well spoken, like a true-
    bred slave.   946
It's just the sort of language I delight in.
    Xan. You love excuses?
    Æacus.   Yes; but I prefer
Cursing my master quietly in private.

[1] Bad money drove out good — even in 400 B.C.
[2] If we must be punished, let it be with good or worthy
wood.

Xan. Mischief you're fond of?
    Æacus.   Very fond indeed.
    Xan. What think ye of muttering as you leave
    the room   951
After a beating?
    Æacus.   Why, that's pleasant too.
    Xan. By Jove, is it! But listening at the door
To hear their secrets?
    Æacus.   Oh, there's nothing like it.
    Xan. And then the reporting them in the neigh-
    borhood.   955
    Æacus. That's beyond everything. — That's
    quite ecstatic.
    Xan. Well, give me your hand. And, there,
    take mine — and buss me.
And there again — and now for Jupiter's sake! —
(For he's the patron of our cuffs and beatings)
Do tell me what's that noise of people quarrelling
And abusing one another there within?   961
    Æacus. Æschylus and Euripides, only!
    Xan.   Heh? — ? — ?
    Æacus. Why, there's a desperate business has
    broke out
Among these here dead people; — quite a tumult.
    Xan. As how?
    Æacus.   First, there's a custom we have
    establish'd   965
In favor of professors of the arts.
When any one, the first in his own line,
Comes down amongst us here, he stands entitled
To privilege and precedence, with a seat
At Pluto's royal board.
    Xan.   I understand you. 970
    Æacus. So he maintains it, till there comes a
    better
Of the same sort, and then resigns it up.
    Xan. But why should Æschylus be disturb'd at
    this?
    Æacus. He held the seat for tragedy, as the
    master   974
In that profession.
    Xan.   Well, and who's there now?
    Æacus. He kept it till Euripides appeared;
But he collected audiences about him,
And flourish'd, and exhibited, and harangued
Before the thieves, and housebreakers, and rogues,
Cut-purses, cheats, and vagabonds, and villains,
That make the mass of population here;   981
        (*Pointing to the audience.*)
And they — being quite transported, and de-
    lighted
With his equivocations and evasions,
His subtleties and niceties and quibbles —
In short — they raised an uproar, and declared
    him   985
Archpoet, by a general acclamation.

And he with this grew proud and confident,
And laid a claim to the seat where Æschylus sat.
   Xan. And did not he get pelted for his pains?
   Æacus (with the dry concise importance of superior local information). Why, no — The
      mob call'd out, and it was carried,   990
To have a public trial of skill between them.
   Xan. You mean the mob of scoundrels that you
      mention'd?
   Æacus. Scoundrels indeed! Ay, scoundrels
without number.
   Xan. But Æschylus must have had good friends
      and hearty?
   Æacus. Yes; but good men are scarce both here
      and elsewhere.   995
   Xan. Well, what has Pluto settled to be done?
   Æacus. To have an examination and a trial
In public.
   Xan.   But how comes it? — Sophocles? —
Why does he not put forth his claim amongst them?
   Æacus. No, no! — He's not the kind of man —
      not he!   1000
I tell ye; the first moment that he came,
He went up to Æschylus and saluted him
And kiss'd his cheek and took his hand quite
      kindly;
And Æschylus edged a little from his seat
To give him room; so now the story goes,   1005
(At least I had it from Cleidemides; [1])
He means to attend there as a stander-by,
Proposing to take up the conqueror;
If Æschylus gets the better, well and good,
He gives up his pretensions — but if not,   1010
He'll stand a trial, he says, against Euripides.
   Xan. There'll be strange doings.
   Æacus.   That there will — and shortly
— Here — in this place — strange things, I prom-
      ise you;
A kind of thing that no man could have thought of;
Why, you'll see poetry weigh'd out and measured.
   Xan. What, will they bring their tragedies to
      the steel-yards? [2]   1016
   Æacus. Yes, will they — with their rules and
      compasses
They'll measure, and examine, and compare,
And bring their plummets, and their lines and
      levels,
To take the bearings — for Euripides   1020
Says that he'll make a survey, word by word.
   Xan. Æschylus takes the thing to heart, I
      doubt.
   Æacus. He bent his brows and pored upon the
      ground;
I saw him.
   Xan.   Well, but who decides the business?

[1] An actor.   [2] Scales.

   Æacus. Why, there the difficulty lies — for
      judges,   1025
True learned judges, are grown scarce, and Æschy-
lus
Objected to the Athenians absolutely.
   Xan. Considering them as rogues and villains
      mostly.
   Æacus. As being ignorant and empty generally:
And in their judgment of the stage particularly.
In fine, they've fix'd upon that master of yours,
As having had some practice in the business.   1032
But we must wait within — for when our masters
Are warm and eager, stripes and blows ensue.
   Chorus.. The full-mouth'd master of the tragic
      quire,   1035
We shall behold him foam with rage and ire;
— Confronting in the list
His eager, shrewd, sharp-tooth'd antagonist.
Then will his visual orbs be wildly whirl'd
And huge invectives will be hurl'd   1040
   Superb and supercilious,
   Atrocious, atrabilious,
With furious gesture and with lips of foam,
And lion crest unconscious of the comb;   1044
Erect with rage — his brow's impending gloom
O'ershadowing his dark eyes' terrific blaze.
   The opponent, dexterous and wary,
   Will fend and parry:
While masses of conglomerated phrase,
   Enormous, ponderous, and pedantic,   1050
   With indignation frantic,
     And strength and force gigantic,
     Are desperately sped
     At his devoted head —
Then in different style   1055
The touchstone and the file,
And subtleties of art
In turn will play their part;
Analysis and rule,
And every modern tool;   1060
With critic scratch and scribble,
And nice invidious nibble;
Contending for the important choice,
A vast expenditure of human voice!

SCENE: EURIPIDES, BACCHUS, ÆSCHYLUS

   Eur. Don't give me your advice, I claim the seat
As being a better and superior artist.   1066
   Bac. What, Æschylus, don't you speak? you
      hear his language.
   Eur. He's mustering up a grand commanding
      visage
— A silent attitude — the common trick
That he begins with in his tragedies.   1070
   Bac. Come, have a care, my friend — You'll
      say too much.

Eur. I know the man of old — I've scrutinised
And shown him long ago for what he is,
A rude unbridled tongue, a haughty spirit;
Proud, arrogant, and insolently pompous; 1075
Rough, clownish, boisterous, and overbearing.

Æs. Say'st thou me so? Thou bastard of the earth,
With thy patch'd robes and rags of sentiment
Raked from the streets and stitch'd and tack'd together
Thou mumping, whining, beggarly hypocrite! 1080
But you shall pay for it.

Bac. (*in addressing* ÆSCHYLUS *attempts to speak in more elevated style*). There now, Æschylus,
You grow too warm. Restrain your ireful mood.

Æs. Yes; but I'll seize that sturdy beggar first,
And search and strip him bare of his pretensions.

Bac Quick! Quick! A sacrifice to the winds
— Make ready; 1085
The storm of rage is gathering. Bring a victim.

Æs. — A wretch that has corrupted everything;
Our music with his melodies from Crete;
Our morals with incestuous tragedies.[1]

Bac. Dear, worthy Æschylus, contain yourself,
And as for you, Euripides, move off 1091
This instant, if you're wise; I give you warning.
Or else, with one of his big thumping phrases,
You'll get your brains dash'd out, and all your notions
And sentiments and matter mash'd to pieces. 1095
— And thee, most noble Æschylus (*as above*), I beseech
With mild demeanor calm and affable
To hear and answer. — For it ill beseems
Illustrious bards to scold like market-women.
But you roar out and bellow like a furnace. 1100

Eur. (*in the tone of a town blackguard working himself up for a quarrel*). I'm up to it. —
I'm resolved, and here I stand
Ready and steady — take what course you will;
Let him be first to speak, or else let me.
I'll match my plots and characters against him;
My sentiments and language, and what not: 1105
Ay! and my music too, my Meleager,
My Æolus and my Telephus [2] and all.

Bac. Well, Æschylus, — determine. What say you?

Æs. (*speaks in a tone of grave manly despondency*).
I wish the place of trial had been elsewhere,
I stand at disadvantage here.

Bac. As how? 1110

Æs. Because my poems live on earth above,

[1] In *Hippolytus*, by Euripides, for instance.
[2] Euripides names some of his plays by which he is ready to be judged.

And his died with him, and descended here,
And are at hand as ready witnesses;
But you decide the matter: I submit.

Bac. (*with official pertness and importance*).
Come — let them bring me fire and frankincense, 1115
That I may offer vows and make oblations
For any ingenious critical conclusion
To this same elegant and clever trial —
(*To the* CHORUS.) And you too, — sing me a hymn there. — To the Muses.

Chorus. To the Heavenly Nine [1] we petition, 1120
Ye, that on earth or in air are for ever kindly protecting the vagaries of learned ambition,
And at your ease from above our sense and folly directing (or poetical contests inspecting,
Deign to behold for a while as a scene of amusing attention, all the struggles of style and invention),
Aid, and assist, and attend, and afford to the furious authors your refined and enlighten'd suggestions;
Grant them ability — force and agility, quick recollections, and address in their answers and questions, 1125
Pithy replies, with a word to the wise, and pulling and hauling, with inordinate uproar and bawling,
Driving and drawing, like carpenters sawing, their dramas asunder:
With suspended sense and wonder,
All are waiting and attending
On the conflict now depending! 1130

Bac. Come, say your prayers, you two before the trial. (ÆSCHYLUS *offers incense.*)

Æs. O Ceres, nourisher of my soul, maintain me
A worthy follower of thy mysteries.[2]

Bac. (*to* EURIPIDES). There, you there, make your offering.

Eur. Well, I will;
But I direct myself to other deities. 1135

Bac. Hey, what? Your own? some new ones?

Eur. Most assuredly!

Bac. Well! Pray away, then — to your own new deities. (EURIPIDES *offers incense.*)

Eur. Thou foodful Air, the nurse of all notions;
And ye, the organic powers of sense and speech,
And keen refined olfactory discernment, 1140
Assist my present search for faults and errors.

Chorus. Here beside you, here are we,
Eager all to hear and see

[1] The nine muses.
[2] Greek tragedy developed from some of the ritualistic forms in the Eleusinian mysteries much as European drama developed from the ecclesiastical plays of the middle ages.

This abstruse and mighty battle
Of profound and learned prattle.   1145
— But, as it appears to me,
Thus the course of it will be;
He, the junior and appellant,
Will advance as the assailant.
Aiming shrewd satyric darts   1150
At his rival's noble parts;
And with sallies sharp and keen
Try to wound him in the spleen,
While the veteran rends and raises
Rifted, rough, uprooted phrases,   1155
Wielded like a threshing staff
Scattering the dust and chaff.

Bac. Come, now begin, dispute away, but first
I give you notice
That every phrase in your discourse must be re-
fined, avoiding
Vulgar absurd comparisons, and awkward silly
joking.   1160
Eur. At the first outset, I forbear to state my
own pretensions;
Hereafter I shall mention them, when his have
been refuted;
After I shall have fairly shown how he befool'd
and cheated
The rustic audience that he found, which Phry-
nichus [1] bequeathed him.
He planted first upon the stage a figure veil'd and
muffled,   1165
An Achilles or a Niobe, that never show'd their
faces;
But kept a tragic attitude, without a word to
utter.
Bac. No more they did: 'tis very true.
Eur.   — In the meanwhile the Chorus
Strung on ten strophes right-an-end, but they
remain'd in silence.
Bac. I liked that silence well enough, as well,
perhaps, or better   1170
Than those new talking characters —
Eur. That's from your want of judgment,
Believe me.
Bac. Why, perhaps it is; but what was his
intention?
Eur. Why, mere conceit and insolence; to keep
the people waiting
Till Niobe should deign to speak, to drive his drama
forward.
Bac. O what a rascal. Now I see the tricks he
used to play me.   1175
(*To* Æschylus, *who is showing signs of
indignation by various contortions.*)
— What makes you writhe and winch about? —

[1] An early tragic poet writing a few years before
Æschylus.

Eur.   Because he feels my censures.
— Then having dragg'd and drawl'd along, half-
way to the conclusion,
He foisted in a dozen words of noisy boisterous
accent,
With lofty plumes and shaggy brows, mere bug-
bears of the language.
That no man ever heard before. —
Æs.   Alas! alas!
Bac. (*to* Æschylus).   Have done there!
Eur. He never used a simple word.
Bac. (*to* Æschylus). Don't grind your teeth so
strangely.   1181
Eur. But "Bulwarks and Scamanders" and
"Hippogrifs and Gorgons."
"On burnish'd shields emboss'd in brass"; bloody
remorseless phrases
Which nobody could understand.
Bac.   Well, I confess, for my part,
I used to keep awake at night, with guesses and
conjectures   1185
To think what kind of foreign bird he meant by
griffinhorses.
Æs. A figure on the heads of ships; you goose,
you must have seen them.
Bac. Well, from the likeness, I declare, I took it
for Eruxis. [1]
Eur. So! Figures from the heads of ships art
fit for tragic diction.
Æs. Well then — thou paltry wretch, explain.
What were your own devices?   1190
Eur. Not stories about flying-stags, like yours,
and griffinhorses;
Nor terms nor images derived from tapestry
Persian hangings.
When I received the Muse from you I found her
puff'd and pamper'd
With pompous sentences and terms, a cumbrous
huge virago. [2]
My first attention was applied to make her look
genteelly;   1195
And bring her to a slighter shape by dint of lighter
diet:
I fed her with plain household phrase, and cool
familiar salad,
With water-gruel episode, with sentimental jelly,
With moral mincemeat; till at length I brought her
into compass;
Cephisophon, who was my cook, contrived to make
them relish.   1200
I kept my plots distinct and clear, and, to prevent
confusion,
My leading characters rehearsed their pedigrees
for prologues.

[1] A particularly ugly man.
[2] Impudent, scolding woman.

Æs. 'Twas well, at least, that you forbore to quote your own extraction.

Eur. From the first opening of the scene, all persons were in action;
The master spoke, the slave replied, the women, young and old ones, 1205
All had their equal share of talk —

Æs. Come, then, stand forth and tell us,
What forfeit less than death is due for such an innovation?

Eur. I did it upon principle, from democratic motives.

Bac. Take care, my friend — upon that ground your footing is but ticklish.

Eur. I taught these youths to speechify.

Æs. I say so too. — Moreover 1210
I say that — for the public good — you ought to have been hang'd first.

Eur. The rules and forms of rhetoric, — the laws of composition,
To prate — to state — and in debate to meet a question fairly:
At a dead lift to turn and shift — to make a nice distinction.

Æs. I grant it all — I make it all — my ground of accusation. 1215

Eur. The whole in cases and concerns occurring and recurring
At every turn and every day domestic and familiar,
So that the audience, one and all, from personal experience,
Were competent to judge the piece, and form a fair opinion
Whether my scenes and sentiments agreed with truth and nature. 1220
I never took them by surprise to storm their understandings,
With Memnons[1] and Tydides's[2] and idle rattle-trappings
Of battle-steeds and clattering shields to scare them from their senses;
But for a test (perhaps the best) our pupils and adherents
May be distinguish'd instantly by person and behavior; 1225
His are Phormisius[3] the rough, Meganetes[4] the gloomy,
Hobgoblin-headed, trumpet-mouth'd, grim-visaged, ugly-bearded;
But mine are Cleitophon[5] the smooth, — Theramenes[6] the gentle.

[1] An Ethiopian knight.
[2] Diomede, son of Tydeus, and a chieftain among the Greeks. He wounded Mars in a battle before Troy.
[3] A bearded, rough man.   [4] A soldier.
[5] A conspirator with Theramenes.
[6] See note on page 141.

Bac. Theramenes — a clever hand, a universal genius,
I never found him at a loss in all the turns of party
To change his watchword at a word or at a moment's warning. 1231

Eur. Thus it was that I began,
With a nicer, neater plan;
Teaching men to look about,
Both within doors and without; 1235
To direct their own affairs,
And their house and household wares;
Marking everything amiss —
"Where is that? and — What is this?"
"This is broken — that is gone." 1240
'Tis the modern style and tone.

Bac. Yes, by Jove — and at their homes
Nowadays each master comes,
Of a sudden bolting in
With an uproar and a din; 1245
Rating all the servants round,
"If it's lost, it must be found.
Why was all the garlic wasted?
There, that honey has been tasted:
And these olives pilfer'd here. 1250
Where's the pot we bought last year?
What's become of all the fish?
Which of you has broke the dish?"
Thus it is, but heretofore,
The moment that they cross'd the door, 1255
They sat them down to doze and snore.

Chorus

"Noble Achilles! you see the disaster,
   The shame and affront, and an enemy nigh!"[1]
Oh! bethink thee, mighty master,
   Think betimes of your reply; 1260
Yet beware, lest anger force
Your hasty chariot from the course;
Grievous charges have been heard,
With many a sharp and bitter word,
Notwithstanding, mighty chief, 1265
Let Prudence fold her cautious reef
In your anger's swelling sail;
By degrees you may prevail,
But beware of your behavior
Till the wind is in your favor; 1270
   Now for your answer, illustrious architect,
      Founder of lofty theatrical lays!
   Patron in chief of our tragical trumperies!
   Open the floodgate of figure and phrase!

Æs. My spirit is kindled with anger and shame,
To so base a competitor forced to reply, 1276
But I needs must retort, or the wretch will report
That he left me refuted and foil'd in debate;

[1] From the *Myrmidons*, a tragedy by Æschylus.

Tell me then, What are the principal merits
Entitling a poet to praise and renown?   1280
   Eur. The improvement of morals, the progress
    of mind,
When a poet, by skill and invention,
Can render his audience virtuous and wise.
   Æs. But if you, by neglect or intention,
Have done the reverse, and from brave honest
    spirits   1285
Depraved, and have left them degraded and base,
Tell me, what punishment ought you to suffer?
   Bac. Death, to be sure! — Take that answer
    from me.
   Æs. Observe then, and mark, what our citizens
    were,
When first from my care they were trusted to you;
Not scoundrel informers, or paltry buffoons,   1291
Evading the services due to the state;
But with hearts all on fire, for adventure and war,
Distinguished for hardiness, stature, and strength,
Breathing forth nothing but lances and darts,   1295
Arms, and equipment, and battle array,
Bucklers, and shields, and habergeons, and hau-
    berks,[1]
Helmets, and plumes, and heroic attire.
   Bac. There he goes, hammering on with his
    helmets,
He'll be the death of me one of these days.   1300
   Eur. But how did you manage to make 'em so
    manly,
What was the method, the means that you took?
   Bac. Speak, Æschylus, speak, and behave your-
    self better,
And don't in your rage stand so silent and stern.
   Æs. A drama, brimful with heroical spirit. 1305
   Eur. What did you call it?
   Æs.   "The Chiefs against Thebes." [2]
That inspired each spectator with martial ambi-
    tion,
Courage, and ardor, and prowess, and pride.
   Bac. But you did very wrong to encourage the
    Thebans.
Indeed, you deserve to be punish'd, you do,   1310
For the Thebans are grown to be capital soldiers,
You've done us a mischief by that very thing.
   Æs. The fault was your own, if you took other
    courses;
The lesson I taught was directed to you:
Then I gave you the glorious theme of "the Per-
    sians,"   1315
Replete with sublime patriotical strains,
The record and example of noble achievement,
The delight of the city, the pride of the stage.

   [1] Both the habergeon and the hauberk were coats of
mail, the first shorter and lighter than the second.
   [2] Tragedies by Æschylus.

   Bac. I rejoiced, I confess, when the tidings were
    carried
To old King Darius,[1] so long dead and buried,
And the chorus in concert kept wringing their
    hands,   1321
Weeping and wailing, and crying, Alas!
   Æs. Such is the duty, the task of a poet,
Fulfilling in honor his office and trust.
Look to traditional history — look   1325
To antiquity, primitive, early, remote:
See there, what a blessing illustrious poets
Conferred on mankind, in the centuries past,
Orpheus instructed mankind in religion,
Reclaim'd them from bloodshed and barbarous
    rites: 1330
Musæus [2] deliver'd the doctrine of medicine,
And warnings prophetic for ages to come:
Next came old Hesiod,[3] teaching us husbandry,
Ploughing, and sowing, and rural affairs,
Rural economy, rural astronomy,   1335
Homely morality, labor, and thrift:
Homer himself, our adorable Homer,
What was his title to praise and renown?
What, but the worth of the lessons he taught us,
Discipline, arms, and equipment of war?   1340
   Bac. Yes, but Pantacles was never the wiser;
For in the procession he ought to have led,
When his helmet was tied, he kept puzzling, and
    tried
To fasten the crest on the crown of his head.
   Æs. But other brave warriors and noble com-
    manders   1345
Were train'd in his lessons to valor and skill;
Such was the noble heroical Lamachus; [4]
Others besides were instructed by him;
And I, from his fragments ordaining a banquet,
Furnish'd and deck'd with majestical phrase, 1350
Brought forward the models of ancient achieve-
    ment,
Teucer, Patroclus, and chiefs of antiquity;
Raising and rousing Athenian hearts,
When the signal of onset was blown in their ear,
With a similar ardor to dare and to do;   1355
But I never allow'd of your lewd Sthenobœas,[5]
Or filthy, detestable Phædras [6] — not I —
Indeed, I should doubt if my drama throughout
Exhibit an instance of woman in love.   1359
   Eur. No, you were too stern for an amorous turn,

   [1] In "the Persians."
   [2] Greek poet of the fifth century B.C.
   [3] Greek didactic poet of the eighth century B.C.
   [4] A military leader against Syracuse.
   [5] In a lost Euripidean tragedy Sthenebœa takes her
life because of love for Bellerophon.
   [6] In *Hippolytus* by Euripides, Phædra, the wife of
Theseus, falls in love with Hippolytus.

For Venus and Cupid too stern and too stupid.

Æs. May they leave me at rest, and with peace in my breast,
And infest and pursue your kindred and you,
With the very same blow that despatch'd you below.

Bac. That was well enough said; with the life that he led,   1365
He himself in the end got a wound from a friend.

Eur. But what, after all, is the horrible mischief?
My poor Sthenobœas, what harm have they done?

Æs. The example is followed, the practice has gain'd,
And women of family, fortune, and worth,   1370
Bewilder'd with shame in a passionate fury,
Have poison'd themselves for Bellerophon's sake.

Eur. But at least you'll allow that I never invented it,
Phædra's affair was a matter of fact.   1374

Æs. A fact, with a vengeance! but horrible facts
Should be buried in silence, not bruited abroad,
Nor brought forth on the stage, nor emblazon'd in poetry
Children and boys have a teacher assign'd them —
The bard is a master for manhood and youth,
Bound to instruct them in virtue and truth, 1380
Beholden and bound.[1]

Eur.   But is virtue a sound?
Can any mysterious virtue be found
In bombastical, huge, hyperbolical phrase?

Æs. Thou dirty, calamitous wretch, recollect
That exalted ideas of fancy require   1385
To be clothed in a suitable vesture of phrase;
And that heroes and gods may be fairly supposed
Discoursing in words of a mightier import,
More lofty by far than the children of man; 1389
As the pomp of apparel assign'd to their persons,
Produced on the stage and presented to view,
Surpasses in dignity, splendor, and lustre
Our popular garb and domestic attire,
A practice which nature and reason allow,
But which you disannull'd and rejected.

Eur.   As how?   1395

Æs. When you brought forth your kings, in a villainous fashion,
In patches and rags, as a claim for compassion.

Eur. And this is a grave misdemeanor, forsooth!

Æs. It has taught an example of sordid untruth;
For the rich of the city, that ought to equip, 1400
And to serve with, a ship, are appealing to pity,
Pretending distress — with an overworn dress.

Bac. By Jove, so they do; with a waistcoat brand new,

[1] An early expression of anti-naturalism conviction as the next speech by Æschylus is an expression of the classical attitude.

Worn closely within, warm and new for the skin;
And if they escape in this beggarly shape,   1405
You'll meet 'em at market, I warrant 'em all,
Buying the best at the fishmonger's stall.

Æs. He has taught every soul to sophisticate truth;
And debauch'd all the bodies and minds of the youth;
Leaving them morbid, and pallid, and spare;   1410
And the places of exercise vacant and bare: —
The disorder has spread to the fleet and the crew;
The service is ruin'd, and ruin'd by you —
With prate and debate in a mutinous state;
Whereas, in my day, 'twas a different way;   1415
Nothing they said, nor knew nothing to say,
But to call for their porridge, and cry, "Pull away."

Bac. Yes — yes, they knew this,
How to f . . . in the teeth
Of the rower beneath;   1420
And befoul their own comrades,
And pillage ashore;
But now they forget the command of the oar: —
Prating and splashing,
Discussing and dashing,   1425
They steer here and there,
With their eyes in the air,
Hither and thither,
Nobody knows whither.

Æs. Can the reprobate mark in the course he has run,   1430
One crime unattempted, a mischief undone?
With his horrible passions, of sisters and brothers,
And sons-in-laws, tempted by villainous mothers,
And temples defiled with a bastardly birth,
And women, divested of honor or worth,   1435
That talk about life "as a death upon earth;"
And sophistical frauds and rhetorical bawds;
Till now the whole state is infested with tribes
Of scriveners and scribblers, and rascally scribes —
All practice of masculine vigor and pride,   1440
Our wrestling and running, are all laid aside,
And we see that the city can hardly provide
For the Feast of the Founders, a racer of force
To carry the torch and accomplish a course.

Bac. Well, I laugh'd till I cried   1445
The last festival tide,
At the fellow that ran, —
'Twas a heavy fat man,
And he panted and hobbled,
And stumbled and wabbled,   1450
And the pottery people about the gate,
Seeing him hurried, and tired, and late,
Stood to receive him in open rank,
Helping him on with a hearty spank
Over the shoulder and over the flank,   1455
The flank, the loin, the back, the shoulders,

With shouts of applause from all beholders;
While he ran on with a filthy fright,
Puffing his link to keep it alight.

   Chorus. Ere the prize is lost and won   1460
   Mighty doings will be done.
   Now then — (though to judge aright
   Is difficult, when force and might
   Are opposed with ready slight,
   When the Champion that is cast   1465
   Tumbles uppermost at last)
   — Since you meet in equal match,
   Argue, contradict and scratch,
   Scuffle, and abuse and bite,
   Tear and fight,   1470
   With all your wits and all your might.
   — Fear not for a want of sense
   Or judgment in your audience,
   That defect has been removed;
   They're prodigiously improved,   1475
   Disciplined, alert and smart,
   Drill'd and exercised in art:
   Each has got a little book,
   In the which they read and look,
   Doing all their best endeavor   1480
   To be critical and clever;
   Thus their own ingenious natures,
    Aided and improved by learning,
   Will provide you with spectators
    Shrewd, attentive, and discerning.   1485

Terrestrial Hermes with supreme espial,
Inspector of that old paternal realm,
Aid and assist me now, you suppliant,
Revisiting and returning to my country!

Eur. It is not justly express'd, since he return'd
Clandestinely without authority.   1491
   Bac. That's well remark'd; but I don't compre-
   hend it.
   Eur. (*tauntingly and coolly*). Proceed — Con-
   tinue!
   Bac. (*jealous of his authority*). Yes, you must
   continue.
Æschylus, I command you to continue.
(*To* EURIPIDES.) And you, keep a look-out and
   mark his blunders.   1495
   Æs. "From his sepulchral mound I call my
   father
"To listen and hear —"
   Eur.   There's a tautology!
"To listen and hear —"
   Bac.   Why, don't you see, you ruffian!
It's a dead man he's calling to — Three times   1499
We call to 'em, but they can't be made to hear.
   Æs. And you: your prologues, of what kind
   were they?

   Eur. I'll show ye: and if you'll point out a
   tautology,
Or a single word clapt in to botch a verse —
That's all! — I'll give you leave to spit upon me.
   Bac. (*with an absurd air of patience and resigna-
   tion*). Well, I can't help myself; I'm bound
   to attend.   1505
Begin then with these same fine-spoken prologues.
   Eur. "Œdipus was at first a happy man." ...
   Æs. Not he, by Jove! — but born to misery;
Predicted and predestined by an oracle
Before his birth to murder his own father!   1510
— Could he have been "at first a happy man?"
   Eur. ... "But afterwards became a wretched
   mortal."
   Æs. By no means! he continued to be wretched,
— Born wretched, and exposed as soon as born
Upon a potsherd in a winter's night;   1515
Brought up a foundling with disabled feet;
Then married — a young man to an aged woman,
That proved to be his mother — whereupon
He tore his eyes out.
   Bac.   To complete his happiness,
He ought to have served at sea with Erasinides.[1]
There! — that's enough — now come to music,
   can't ye?   1521
   Eur. I mean it; I shall now proceed to expose
   him
As a bad composer, awkward, uninventive,
Repeating the same strain perpetually. —
   Chorus. I stand in wonder and perplext   1525
   To think of what will follow next.
   Will he dare to criticise
   The noble bard, that did devise
   Our oldest, boldest harmonies,
   Whose mighty music we revere?   1530
   Much I marvel, much I fear. —
   Eur. Mighty fine music, truly! I'll give ye a
   sample;
It's every inch cut out to the same pattern.
   Bac. I'll mark — I've pick'd these pebbles up
   for counters.
   Eur. Noble Achilles! Forth to the rescue!
Forth to the rescue with ready support!   1536
Hasten and go,
There is havoc and woe,
Hasty defeat,
And a bloody retreat,   1540
Confusion and rout,
And the terrible shout
Of a conquering foe,
Tribulation and woe!
   Bac. Whoh hoh there! we've had woes enough,
   I reckon;   1545

[1] An officer in the battle of Arginusæ.

Therefore I'll go to wash away my woe
In a warm bath.

Eur. No, do pray wait an instant,
And let me give you first another strain,
Transferr'd to the stage from music to the lyre.

Bac. Proceed then — only give us no more woes.

Eur. The supremacy sceptre and haughty command 1551
Of the Grecian land — with a flatto-flatto-flatto-thrat —
And the ravenous sphinx, with her horrible brood,
Thirsting for blood — with a flatto-flatto-flatto-thrat,
And armies equipt for a vengeful assault, 1555
For Paris's fault — with a flatto-flatto-flatto-thrat.

Bac. What herb is that same flatto-thrat? some simple,
I guess, you met with in the field of Marathon:
— But such a tune as this! you must have learnt it
From fellows hauling buckets at the well. 1560

Æs. Such were the strains I purified and brought
To just perfection — taught by Phrynichus,
Not copying him, but culling other flowers
From those fair meadows which the Muses love —
— But he filches and begs, adapts and borrows
Snatches of tunes from minstrels in the street,
Strumpets and vagabonds — the lullabys 1567
Of nurses and old women — jigs and ballads —
I'll give ye a proof — Bring me a lyre here, somebody.
What signifies a lyre? the castanets 1570
Will suit him better — Bring the castanets,
With Euripides's Muse to snap her fingers
In cadence to her master's compositions.

Bac. This Muse, I take it, is a Lesbian Muse.[1]

Æs. Gentle halcyons,[2] ye that lave 1575
Your snowy plume,
Sporting on the summer wave;
Ye too that around the room,
On the rafters of the roofs
Strain aloft your airy woof; 1580
Ye spiders, spiders ever spinning,
Never ending, still beginning —
Where the dolphin loves to follow,
Weltering in the surge's hollow,
Dear to Neptune and Apollo; 1585
By the seamen understood
Ominous of harm or good;
In capricious, eager sallies,
Chasing, racing round the galleys.
Well now. Do you see this? 1590

Bac. I see it —

(*After which* ÆSCHYLUS *turns to his antagonist:*)

[1] The women of Lesbos were popularly considered a debauched lot.
[2] The kingfisher.

Such is your music. I shall now proceed
To give a specimen of your monodies [1] —
O dreary shades of night!
What phantoms of affright 1595
Have scared my troubled sense
With saucer eyes immense;
And huge horrific paws
With bloody claws!
Ye maidens haste, and bring 1600
From the fair spring
A bucket of fresh water; whose clear stream
May purify me from this dreadful dream:
But oh! my dream is out!
Ye maidens search about! 1605
O mighty powers of mercy, can it be;
That Glyke, Glyke, she
(My friend and civil neighbor heretofore),
Has robb'd my henroost of its feather'd store?
With the dawn I was beginning, 1610
Spinning, spinning, spinning, spinning,
Unconscious of the meditated crime;
Meaning to sell my yarn at market-time.
Now tears alone are left me,
My neighbor hath bereft me, 1615
Of all — of all — of all — all but a tear!
Since he, my faithful trusty chanticleer
Is flown — is flown! — Is gone — is gone!
— But, O ye nymphs of sacred Ida, bring
Torches and bows, with arrows on the string;
And search around 1621
All the suspected ground:
And thou, fair huntress of the sky;
Deign to attend, descending from on high —
— While Hecate, with her tremendous torch,
Even from the topmost garret to the porch 1626
Explores the premises with search exact,
To find the thief and ascertain the fact —

Bac. Come, no more songs!

Æs. I've had enough of 'em;
For my part, I shall bring him to the balance,
As a true test of our poetic merit, 1631
To prove the weight of our respective verses.

Bac. Well then, so be it — if it must be so,
That I'm to stand here like a cheesemonger
Retailing poetry with a pair of scales. 1635

(*A huge pair of scales are here discovered on the stage.*)

Chorus. Curious eager wits pursue
Strange devices quaint and new,
Like the scene you witness here,
Unaccountable and queer;
I myself, if merely told it, 1640
If I did not here behold it,
Should have deem'd it utter folly,
Craziness and nonsense wholly.

[1] A dirge or lament uttered by a single actor.

Bac. Move up; stand close to the balance!

Eur.   Here are we —

Bac. Take hold now, and each of you repeat a
verse,   1645
And don't leave go before I call to you!

Eur. We're ready.

Bac.   Now, then, each repeat a verse,

Eur. "I wish that Argo with her woven wings."[1]

Æs. "O streams of Sperchius, and ye pastured
plains."[1]

Bac. Let go! — See now — this scale outweighs
that other.   1650
Very considerably —

Eur.   How did it happen?

Bac. He slipp'd a river in, like the wool-jobbers,
To moisten his metre — but your line was light,
A thing with wings — ready to fly away.   1654

Eur. Let him try once again then, and take hold.

Bac. Take hold once more.

Eur.   We're ready.

Bac.   Now repeat.

Eur. "Speech is the temple and altar of persuasion."[1]

Æs. "Death is a God that loves no sacrifice."[1]

Bac. Let go! — See there again! This scale
sinks down;   1659
No wonder that it should, with Death put into it,
The heaviest of all calamities.

Eur. But I put in persuasion finely express'd
In the best terms.

Bac.   Perhaps so; but persuasion
Is soft and light and silly — Think of something
That's heavy and huge, to outweigh him, some-
thing solid.   1665

Eur. Let's see — Where have I got it? Something solid?

Bac. "Achilles[2] has thrown twice — Twice a
deuce ace!"
Come now, one trial more; this is the last.

Eur. "He grasp'd a mighty mace of massy
weight."

Æs. "Cars upon cars, and corpses heap'd pell
mell."   1670

Bac. He has nick'd you again —

Eur.   Why so? What has he done?

Bac. He had heap'd ye up cars and corpses, such
a load
As twenty Egyptian laborers could not carry —

Æs. Come, no more single lines — let him bring
all,
His wife, his children, his Cephisophon,[3]   1675
His books and everything, himself to boot —

[1] Each quotes lines from his own plays.
[2] Euripides is called Achilles because in one of his
plays he represents Achilles as playing at dice.
[3] An actor in the plays of Euripides.

I'll counterpoise them with a couple of lines.

Bac. Well, they're both friends of mine — I
shan't decide
To get myself ill-will from either party;
One of them seems extraordinary clever,   1680
And the other suits my taste particularly.

Pluto. Won't you decide then, and conclude the
business?

Bac. Suppose then I decide; what then?

Pluto.   Then take him
Away with you, whichever you prefer,   1684
As a present for your pains in coming down here.

Bac. Heaven bless ye — Well — let's see now —
Can't ye advise me?
This is the case — I'm come in search of a poet —

Pluto. With what design?

Bac.   With this design; to see
The City again restored to peace and wealth,
Exhibiting tragedies in a proper style.   1690
— Therefore whichever gives the best advice
On public matters I shall take him with me.
— First then of Alcibiades,[1] what think ye?
The City is in hard labor with the question.   1694

Eur. What are her sentiments towards him?

Bac.   What?
"She loves and she detests and longs to have him."
But tell me, both of you, your own opinions.

Eur. (EURIPIDES *and* ÆSCHYLUS *speak each in his
own tragical style*). I hate the man, that in
his country's service
Is slow, but ready and quick to work her harm;
Unserviceable except to serve himself.   1700

Bac. Well said, by Jove! — Now you — Give us
a sentence.

Æs. 'Tis rash and idle policy to foster
A lion's whelp within the city walls,
But when he's rear'd and grown you must indulge
him.

Bac. By Jove then I'm quite puzzled; one of
them   1705
Has answer'd clearly, and the other sensibly:
But give us both of ye one more opinion;
— What means are left of safety for the state?

Eur. To tack Cinesias[2] like a pair of wings
To Cleocritus'[3] shoulders, and dispatch them   1710
From a precipice to sail across the seas.

Bac. It seems a joke; but there's some sense in it.

Eur. ... Then being both equipp'd with little
cruets
They might co-operate in a naval action,
By sprinkling vinegar in the enemies' eyes.   1715
— But I can tell you and will.

Bac.   Speak, and explain then —

[1] An Athenian commander in exile at the time.
[2] Poet and musician.
[3] A contemporary political figure.

Eur. If we mistrust where present trust is placed,
Trusting in what was heretofore mistrusted —
   Bac. How! What? I'm at a loss — Speak it
      again   1719
Not quite so learnedly — more plainly and simply.
   Eur. If we withdraw the confidence we placed
In these our present statesmen, and transfer it
To those whom we mistrusted heretofore,
This seems I think our fairest chance for safety:
   If with our present counsellors we fail,   1725
Then with their opposites we might succeed.
   Bac. That's capitally said, my Palamedes! [1]
My politician! was it all your own?
Your own invention?
   Eur.   All except the cruets;
That was a notion of Cephisophon's.   1730
   Bac. (*to* Æschylus). Now you — what say you?
   Æs.   Inform me about the city —
What kind of persons has she placed in office?
Does she promote the worthiest?
   Bac.   No, not she,
She can't abide 'em.
   Æs.   Rogues then she prefers?
   Bac. Not altogether, she makes use of 'em. 1735
Perforce as it were.
   Æs.   Then who can hope to save
A state so wayward and perverse, that finds
No sort of habit fitted for her wear?
Drugget [2] or superfine, nothing will suit her! 1739
   Bac. Do think a little how she can be saved.
   Æs. Not here; when I return there, I shall speak.
   Bac. No, do pray send some good advice before
     you.
   Æs. When they regard their lands as enemy's
     ground,
Their enemy's possessions as their own,   1744
Their seamen and the fleet their only safeguard,
Their sole resource hardship and poverty,
And resolute endurance in distress —
   Bac. That's well, — but juries eat up everything,
And we shall lose our supper if we stay.   1749
   Pluto. Decide then —
   Bac.   You'll decide for your own selves,
I'll make a choice according to my fancy.
   Eur. Remember, then, your oath to your poor
     friend;
And, as you swore and promised, rescue me.
   Bac. "It was my tongue that swore" [3] — I fix
     on Æschylus.   1754

[1] The subject of a tragedy by Euripides in which he
is presented as a wise and able politician.
[2] A coarse fabric sometimes used for rugs.
[3] "It was my tongue that swore it, not my heart" —
a line from *Hippolytus* which had caused much criticism
of the poet, as though the words a poet put into the
mouth of a character necessarily expressed his own
sentiment or practice.

   Eur. O wretch! what have you done?
   Bac.   Me? done? What should I?
Voted for Æschylus to be sure — Why not?
   Eur. And after such a villainous act, you dare
To view me face to face — Art not ashamed?
   Bac. Why shame, in point of fact, is nothing real:
Shame is the apprehension of a vision   1760
Reflected from the surface of opinion —
— The opinion of the public — they must judge.
   Eur. O cruel! — Will you abandon me to death?
   Bac. Why, perhaps death is life, and life is
     death,   1764
And victuals and drink an illusion of the senses;
For what is Death but an eternal sleep?
And does not Life consist in sleeping and eating?
   Pluto. Now, Bacchus, you'll come here with us
     within.
   Bac. (*a little startled and alarmed*). What for?
   Pluto.   To be received and entertain'd 1769
With a feast before you go.
   Bac.   That's well imagined,
With all my heart — I've not the least objection.
   Chorus. Happy is the man possessing
      The superior holy blessing
      Of a judgment and a taste
      Accurate, refined, and chaste;   1775
      As it plainly doth appear
      In the scene presented here;
      Where the noble worthy Bard
      Meets with a deserved reward,
      Suffer'd to depart in peace   1780
      Freely with a full release,
      To revisit once again
      His kindred and his countrymen —
        Hence moreover
        You discover,   1785
      That to sit with Socrates,
      In a dream of learned ease;
      Quibbling, counter-quibbling, prating,
      Argufying and debating
      With the metaphysic sect,   1790
      Daily sinking in neglect,
      Growing careless, incorrect,
      While the practice and the rules
      Of the true poetic Schools
      Are renounced or slighted wholly,   1795
      Is a madness and a folly.
   Pluto. Go forth with good wishes and hearty
     good-will,
And salute the good people on Pallas's [1] hill;
Let them hear and admire father Æschylus still
In his office of old which again he must fill: 1800
— You must guide and direct them,
Instruct and correct them,
With a lesson in verse,

   [1] Pallas — Athene, goddess of wisdom.

For you'll find them much worse;
Greater fools than before, and their folly much
    more.   1805
And more numerous far than the blockheads of
    yore —
— And give Cleophon this,
And bid him not miss,
But be sure to attend
To the summons I send: 1810
To Nicomachus [1] too,
And the rest of the crew
That devise and invent
  New taxes and tribute,
Are summonses sent,   1815
  Which you'll mind to distribute.
Bid them come to their graves,
Or, like runaway slaves,
If they linger and fail,
We shall drag them to jail;   1820
Down here in the dark
With a brand and a mark.
    Æs. I shall do as you say;
But the while I'm away,
Let the seat that I held   1825
Be by Sophocles fill'd,
As deservedly reckon'd
My pupil and second

    [1] A legal official.

In learning and merit
And tragical spirit —   1830
And take special care;
Keep that reprobate there
Far aloof from the Chair;
Let him never sit in it
An hour or a minute,   1835
By chance or design
To profane what was mine.
    Pluto. Bring forward the torches! — The
      Chorus shall wait
And attend on the Poet in triumph and state
With a thundering chaunt of majestical tone 1840
To wish him farewell, with a tune of his own.
    Chorus. Now may the powers of the earth give
      a safe and speedy departure
To the Bard at his second birth, with a prosperous
    happy revival,
And may the city, fatigued with wars and long
    revolution,
At length be brought to return to just and wise
    resolutions;   1845
Long in peace to remain — Let restless Cleophon
    hasten
Far from amongst us here — since wars are his
    only diversion,
Thrace his native land will afford him wars in
    abundance.

Plato · 427–347 B.C.

    Most of the glory that was Greece is associated with Athens, and much of the renown that belongs to Athens springs from the fact that it was here that three of the world's greatest philosophers — Socrates, Plato, and Aristotle — lived and taught.

    Born on an island not far from Athens (427 B.C.), Plato, as a young man, was both a friend and student of Socrates whose teachings he perpetuated in many of the *Dialogues*. In fact it is urged that so strongly did he esteem the older philosopher that when the city put Socrates to death, by making him drink the hemlock on the charge that he was a corruptor of youth, Plato found the atmosphere of Athens so abhorrent that he left the city.

    For a while Plato stayed at Megara, only a few miles away, where he studied with the great mathematician Euclid. Later he extended his journey to other parts of Greece, to Egypt, and to Italy. His restless, eager mind sought out the thought of his world. In Italy he familiarized himself with the doctrines of Pythagoras, a philosopher of the sixth century B.C. who had found a rational order in the universe and had taught that number is the essence of all things. Through his travels about the Mediterranean, through his life in Athens, Plato grounded himself in the philosophies of his time and of the past. Athens itself was alive with ideas that came from the colonies and the countries with which the city maintained relations. At a time when philosophic debate flourished, Plato founded his famous Academy at Athens in 387 B.C. and taught for forty years until his death in 347 B.C.

Plato's *Dialogues* are books of philosophic discourse concerned with the qualities of Truth and Goodness, the question of immortality of the soul, and the nature of law and justice, the government and organization of the ideal state, the need of man for an ethical code, and problems of religion, science, and education. While on these and other questions Plato left opinions and judgments which constitute a body of classical thought, he was probably just as important as a stimulator of thought as he was as a promulgator of a formal philosophic system.

To present his ideas, Plato employed dialogues in which several of his actual acquaintances participate. By this method he advanced the argument — step by step — sometimes stopping for what appears to be a digression, and finally brought all of the thoughts together into a synthesis, unified, clear, forceful, which, however, did not always, even to Plato's mind, permanently settle the question under debate. His dialogues are explorations into the realm of thought, a searching after an often evasive Truth.

SUGGESTED REFERENCES: A. E. Taylor, *Plato. The Man and His Work* (1957) and *The Mind of Plato* (1960); E. A. Havelock, *Preface to Plato* (1963).

The Apology

In the *Apology* given below, Socrates is responding to two accusations brought against him: that he did not believe in the accepted gods of the state and that he had in turn undermined the faith of the youth of Athens. He ultimately drank the hemlock the Athenian fathers decreed for him.

The translation of the *Apology* is by Miss F. M. Stawell and is reprinted from the Everyman's Library through the courtesy of E. P. Dutton and Company.

PART I

Before the Verdict

I. I do not know, men of Athens, what you have felt in listening to my accusers, but they almost made even me forget myself, they spoke so plausibly. And yet, I may say, they have not spoken one word of truth. And of all the lies they told, I wondered most at their saying that you ought to be on your guard against being misled by me, as I was a great speaker. To feel no shame when they knew that they would be refuted immediately by my own action, when I show you that I am not a great speaker at all, — that did seem to me the height of their audacity; unless perhaps they mean by a great speaker a man who speaks the truth. If that is their meaning, I should agree that I am an orator, though not like them. For they, as I have told you, have said little or nothing that is true; from me you will hear the whole truth. Not, I assure you, that you will get fine arguments like theirs, men of Athens, decked out in splendid phrases, no, but plain speech set forth in any words that come to hand. I believe what I have to say is true, and I ask that none of you should look for anything else. Indeed, gentlemen, it would hardly

suit my age to come before you like a boy, with a made-up speech. And yet, I do ask one thing of you, and I ask it very earnestly: if you find I speak in my defence just as I have been accustomed to speak over the bankers' tables in the market-place, — as many of you have heard me, there and elsewhere — do not be surprised at it, and do not interrupt. For this is how the matter stands. This is the first time I have ever been in a lawsuit, and I am seventy years old, — so I am really an entire stranger to the language of this place. Now, just as you would have forgiven me, I am sure, had I been actually a foreigner, if I had spoken in the tongue and manner to which I had been born, so I think I have a right to ask you now to let my way of speaking pass — be it good or bad — and to give your minds to this question and this only, whether what I say is right or not. That is the virtue of the judge, as truth is the virtue of the orator.

II. Now in making my defence, men of Athens, it will be well for me to deal first with the first false accusations and my first accusers, and afterwards with those that followed. For I have had many accusers who have come before you now for many years, and have not said one word of truth, and I fear them more than Anytus and his supporters, though they are formidable too. But the others, gentlemen, are still more to be feared, I mean the men who took most of you in hand when you were boys, and have gone on persuading you ever since, and accusing me — quite falsely — telling you that there is a man called Socrates, a philosopher, who speculates about the things in the sky, and has searched into the secrets of the earth, and makes the worse appear the better reason. These men, Athenians, the men who have spread this tale abroad, they are the accusers that I fear: for the listeners think that those who study such matters must be atheists as well. Besides, these accusers of mine are many, and they have been at this work for many years, and that, too, when you were at an age at which you would be most ready to believe them, for you were young, some of you mere striplings, and judgment has really gone by default, since there was no one to make the defence. And what is most troublesome of all, it is impossible even to find out their names, unless there be a comedian [1] among them. As for those who have tried to persuade you through envy and prejudice, some, it is true, convincing others because they were convinced themselves, — these are the hardest to deal with of all. It is not possible to call up any of them here and cross-examine them: one is compelled, as it were, to fight with shadows in making one's defence, and hold an inquiry where there is nobody to reply. So I would have you understand with me that my accusers have been, as I say, of two kinds: those who have just brought this charge against me, and others of longer standing, of whom I am speaking now; and I ask you to realise that I must defend myself against the latter first of all, for they were the first whom you heard attack me, and at much greater length than these who followed them. And now, I presume, I must make my defence, men of Athens, and try in the short time I have before me to remove from your minds this calumny which has had so long to grow. I could wish for that result, and for some success in my defence, if it would be good for you and me. But I think it a difficult task, and I am not unaware of its nature. However, let the result be what God wills; I must obey the law, and make my defence.

III. Let us begin from the beginning and see what the accusation is that gave birth to the prejudice on which Meletus [2] relied when he brought this charge. Now, what did they say to raise this prejudice? I must treat them as though they were prosecutors and read their affidavit: "Socrates, we say, is a trouble to the State. He is guilty of inquiring into the things beneath the earth, and the things of the firmament, he makes the worse appear the better reason, and he teaches others so." That is the sort of thing they say: you saw it yourselves in the comedy [3] of Aristophanes — a character called Socrates carried about in a basket, saying that he walked on air, and talking a great deal more nonsense about matters of which I do not understand one word, great or small. And I do

[1] Aristophanes.
[2] A principal among the accusors. He was present as Socrates spoke.   [3] Aristophanes' *Clouds*.

not say this in contempt of such knowledge, if any one is clever at those things. May Meletus never bring so grave a charge against me! But in truth, gentlemen, I have nothing to do with these subjects. I call you yourselves — most of you — to witness: I ask you to instruct and tell each other — those of you who have ever heard me speak, and many of you have — tell each other, I say, if any of you have ever heard one word from me, small or great, upon such themes; and you will realise from this that the other tales people tell about me are of the same character.

IV. There is, in fact, no truth in them at all, nor yet in what you may have heard from others, that I try to make money by my teaching. Now here again, I think it would be a great thing if one could teach men as Gorgias of Leontini can, and Prodicus of Keos, and Hippias of Elis. They can all go to every one of our cities, and take hold of the young men — who are able, as it is, to associate free of charge with any of their fellow-citizens they may choose — and they can persuade them to leave this society for theirs and pay them money and be very grateful to them too. Why, there is another philosopher here from Paros; he is in town, I know: for I happened to meet a friend of mine who has spent more money on sophists than all the rest put together — Callias the son of Hipponicus. Now I put a question to him — he has two sons of his own, — "Callias," I said, "if your two sons were only colts or bullocks we could have hired a trainer for them to make them beautiful and good, and all that they should be; and our trainer would have been, I take it, a horseman or a farmer. But now that they are human beings, have you any trainer in your mind for them? Is there any one who understands what a man and a citizen ought to be? I am sure you have thought of it, because you have sons of your own. Is there any one," I said, "or not?" "Oh yes," said he, "certainly there is." "Who is he?" I asked, "and where does he come from and how much does he charge?" "Euenus," he answered, "from Paros; five minas a head." And I thought Euenus the happiest of men if he really has that power and can teach for such a moderate fee. Now I should have been set up and given myself great airs if I had possessed that knowledge; but I do not possess it, Athenians.

V. Some of you will say perhaps: "But, Socrates, what can your calling be? What has given rise to these calumnies? Surely, if you had done nothing more than any other man, there would not have been all this talk, had you never acted differently from other people. You must tell us what it is, that we may not be left to make our own theories about you."

That seems to me a fair question, and I will try to show you myself what it can be that has given me my name and produced the calumny. Listen to me then. Some of you may think I am in jest, but I assure you I will only tell the truth. The truth is, men of Athens, that I have won my name because of a kind of wisdom, nothing more nor less. What can this wisdom be? The wisdom, perhaps, that is proper to man. It may really be that I am wise in that wisdom: the men I have just named may have a wisdom greater than man's, — or else I know not what to call it. Certainly I do not possess it myself; whoever says I do lies, and speaks to calumniate me. And pray, gentlemen, do not interrupt me: not even if you think I boast. The words that I say will not be my own; I will refer you to a speaker whom you must respect. The witness I will bring you of my wisdom — if such it really is — and of its nature, is the god whose dwelling is at Delphi. Now you knew Chairephon, I think. He was my friend from boyhood, and the friend of your democracy; he went with you into exile, and came back with you.[1] And you know, I think, the kind of man Chairephon was — how eager in everything he undertook. Well, he made a pilgrimage to Delphi, and had the audacity to ask this question from the oracle: and now I beg you, gentlemen, do not interrupt me in what I am about to say. He actually asked if there was any man wiser than I. And the priestess answered, No. I have his brother here to give evidence of this, for Chairephon himself is dead.

VI. Now see why I tell you this. I am going to show you how the calumny arose. When I heard the answer, I asked myself: What can the god mean? What can he be hinting? For certainly I have never thought myself wise in anything, great or small. What can he mean then, when he asserts that I am the wisest of men? He cannot lie of course: that would be impossible for him. And for a long while I was at a loss to think what he could mean. At last, after much thought, I started on some such course of search as this. I betook myself to one of the men who seemed wise, thinking that there, if anywhere, I should refute the utterance, and could say to the oracle: "This man is wiser than I, and you said I was the wisest." Now when I looked into the man — there is no need to give his name — it was one of our citizens, men of Athens, with whom I had an experience of this kind — when we talked together I thought, "This man seems wise to many men, and above all to himself, but he is not so;" and then I tried to show him that he thought he was wise, but he was not. Then he got angry with me, and so did many who

[1] Apollo.

heard us, but I went away and thought to myself, "Well, at any rate I am wiser than this man: probably neither of us knows anything of beauty or of good, but he thinks he knows something when he knows nothing, and I, if I know nothing, at least never suppose that I do. So it looks as though I really were a little wiser than he, just in so far as I do not imagine myself to know things about which I know nothing at all." After that I went to another man who seemed to be wiser still, and I had exactly the same experience: and then he got angry with me too, and so did many more.

VII. Thus I went round them all, one after the other, aware of what was happening and sorry for it, and afraid that they were getting to hate me: but still I felt I must put the word of the god first and foremost, and that I must go through all who seemed to have any knowledge in order to find out what the oracle meant. And by the Dog, men of Athens, — for I must tell you the truth, — this was what I experienced. As I went on with the quest the god had imposed on me, it seemed to me that those who had the highest reputation were very nearly the most deficient of all, and that others who were thought inferior came nearer being men of understanding. I must show you, you see, that my wanderings were a kind of labor of Hercules to prove to myself that the oracle was right. After I had tried the statesmen I went to the poets, — tragedians, writers of lyrics, and all, — thinking that there I should take myself in the act and find I really was more ignorant than they. So I took up the poems of theirs on which they seemed to have spent most pains, and asked them what they meant, hoping to learn something from them too. Now I am really ashamed to tell you the truth; but tell it I must. On the whole, almost all the bystanders could have spoken better about the poems than the men who made them. So here again I soon perceived that what the poets make is not made by wisdom, but by a kind of gift and inspiration, as with the prophets and the seers: they, too, utter many glorious sayings, but they understand nothing of what they say. The poets seemed to me in much the same state; and besides, I noticed that on account of their poetry they thought themselves the wisest of men in other matters too, which they were not. So I left them also, thinking that I had just the same advantage over them as over the politicians.

VIII. Finally I turned to the men who work with their hands. I was conscious I knew nothing that could be called anything; and I was quite sure I should find that they knew a great many wonderful things. And in this I was not disappointed; they did know things that I did not, and in this they were wiser than I. But then, gentlemen, the skilled artisans in their turn seemed to me to have just the same failing as the poets. Because of his skill in his own craft every one of them thought that he was the wisest of men in the highest matters too, and this error of theirs obscured the wisdom they possessed. So that I asked myself, on behalf of the oracle, whether I would rather be as I am, without their wisdom and without their ignorance, or like them in both. And I answered for myself and for the oracle that it was better for me to be as I am.

IX. It was this inquiry, men of Athens, that gave rise to so much enmity against me, and that of the worst and bitterest kind: a succession of calumnies followed, and I received the surname of the Wise. For those who meet me think me wise wherever I refute others; but, sirs, the truth may be that God alone has wisdom, and by that oracle he may have meant just this, that human wisdom is of little or no account. It seems as though he had not been speaking of Socrates the individual; but had merely used my name for an illustration, as if to say: "He, O men, is the wisest of you all, who has learnt, like Socrates, that his wisdom is worth nothing." Such has been my search and my inquiry ever since up to this day, in obedience to the god, whenever I found any one — fellow-citizen or foreigner — who might be considered wise: and if he did not seem so to me I have borne God witness, and pointed out to him that he was not wise at all. And through this incessant work I have had no leisure for any public action worth mentioning, nor yet for my private affairs, but I live in extreme poverty because of this service of mine to God.

X. And besides this, the young men who follow me, those who have most leisure, — sons of our wealthiest citizens, — they take a keen delight themselves in hearing people questioned, and they often copy me and try their hand at examining others on their own account; and, I imagine, they find no lack of men who think they know something but know little or nothing at all. Now those whom they examine get angry — not with themselves, but with me — and say that there is a man called Socrates, an utter scoundrel, who is ruining the young. And when any one asks them what he does or what he teaches, they have really nothing whatever to say, but so as not to seem at a loss they take up the accusations that lie ready to hand against all philosophers, and say that he speaks of the things in the heavens and beneath the earth and teaches men not to believe in the gods and to make the worse appear the better reason. The truth, I imagine, they would not care

to say, namely, that they have been convicted of claiming knowledge when they have none to claim. And being, as I think they are, ambitious, energetic, and numerous, well-organised and using great powers of persuasion, they have gone on calumniating me with singular persistence and vigor till your ears are full of it all. After them Meletus attacked me and Anytus and Lycon, — Meletus on behalf of the poets, Anytus for the artisans and the statesmen, Lycon for the orators, — so that, as I said at first, I should be greatly surprised if in the short time before me I could remove the prejudice that has grown to be so great. There, men of Athens, that is the truth; — I have not hidden one thing from you, great or small; I have not kept back one word. Yet I am fairly sure that I have roused hostility by so doing, which is in itself a proof that what I say is true, and that the calumnies against me are of this nature, and the reasons those I have given. And if you look into the matter, — now or afterwards, — you will find it to be so.

XI. Well, that is a sufficient defence in answer to my first accusers. Now I must try to defend myself against Meletus, — the good man and the patriot, as he calls himself, — and the rest who followed. These are my second accusers, and let us take up their affidavit in its turn. It runs somewhat as follows: Meletus asserts that Socrates is guilty of corrupting the young and not believing in the gods in whom the city believes, but in some strange divinities. That is the sort of charge, and let us take it point by point. He does really say that I am guilty of corrupting the young. But I answer, men of Athens, that Meletus is guilty of an unseemly jest, bringing men to trial on a frivolous charge, pretending that he cares intensely about matters on which he has never spent a thought. That this is so I will try to prove.

XII. Come here, Meletus, and tell me: you really think it of importance that our young men should be as good as possible? "I do indeed." Well, will you tell the court who it is that makes them better? It is plain that you must know since you have given the matter thought. You have found, so you say, the man who corrupts them in me; you have accused me and brought me to trial before these judges: go on and point out to them who it is that makes them better. See, Meletus, you are silent and have not a word to say: and now, are you not ashamed? Is not this proof enough of what I say, that you have never thought of it at all? Yet once more, my friend, I ask you, who is it makes them better? "The laws." No, my good fellow, that is not what I ask: I ask what *man* makes them better, and he, of course must know the laws already. "Well, then, Socrates, I say these judges are the men." Really, Meletus, can these men really teach our youth and make them better? "Most certainly they can." All of them do you mean, or only some? "All of them." Splendid! Splendid! What a wealth of benefactors! And what of the audience? Can they do so or not? "Yes, they can do so too." And what about the Councillors? "Yes, the Councillors too." Well, Meletus, what of the Assembly and those who sit there? They do not corrupt our young men, I suppose? All of them too, you would say, make them better? "Yes, all of them too." Then it really seems that all the Athenians except me can make men good, and that I alone corrupt them. Is that what you mean? "That is exactly what I mean." What a dreadful fate to be cursed with! But answer me: have you the same opinion in the case of horses? Do you think that those who make them better consist of all mankind, with the exception of one single individual who ruins them? Or, on the contrary, that there is only one man who can do them good, or very, very few, the men, namely, who understand them? And that most people, if they use horses and have to do with them, ruin them? Is it not so, Meletus, with horses and all other animals too? Of course it is, whether you and Anytus admit it or not. It would be well, and more than well, with our youth if there was only one man to corrupt them and all the others did them good. However, Meletus, you show us clearly enough that you have never considered our young men: you have made it quite plain that you care nothing about them, that you have never given a thought to the cause for which you have brought me here.

XIII. But tell us now, Meletus, I entreat you, is it better to live in an evil city or a good? Answer us, my friend: it is not a hard question after all. Do not bad men do evil to their nearest neighbours and good men good? "Yes, of course." Well, is there any man who would rather be injured than aided by his fellows? Answer me, my good man. Indeed the law says you must. Is there any one who wishes to be harmed? "Certainly not." Well, you accuse me, we know, of corrupting the youth and making them worse: do you suppose that I do it intentionally or unintentionally? "Intentionally, I have no doubt." Really and truly, Meletus? Is a man of your years so much wiser than a man of mine that you can understand that bad men always do some evil, and good men some good to those who come nearest to them, while I have sunk to such a depth of folly that I am ignorant of it and do not know that if I make one of my fellows wicked I run the risk of getting harm from

him,—and I bring about this terrible state of things intentionally, so you say? I do not believe you, Meletus, nor can any one else, I think. Either I do not corrupt them at all, or if I do, it is done unintentionally, so that in either case you are wrong. And if I do it unintentionally, it is not legal to bring me here for such involuntary errors; you ought to have taken me apart and taught me and reproved me in private; for it is evident that when I learn the truth I shall cease to do what I have done in ignorance. But you shrank from meeting me and teaching me,—you did not choose to do that: you brought me here where those should be brought who need punishment, not those who need instruction.

XIV. Well, men of Athens, it has been plain for some time that Meletus, as I say, has never spent a thought on these matters,—not one, great or small. Nevertheless, you must tell us, Meletus, how you think I corrupt the youth. No doubt, as you say in the indictment, by teaching them not to believe in the gods in whom our city believes but in some new divinities. Is not that how you say I ruin them? "Certainly, I do say so, as strongly as I can." Then, in the name of those gods of whom we speak, explain yourself more clearly to me and to the court. I have not been able to discover whether you say I teach belief in divinities of some kind, in which case I do after all believe in gods, and am not an utter atheist, and so far I am not guilty; only they are not the gods in which the city believes, they are quite different, and that is your charge against me. Or perhaps you mean to say that I do not believe in gods of any kind, and that I teach others so. "Yes, that is what I say; you do not believe in them at all." Meletus, Meletus, you astound me. What makes you say so? Then I do not even believe that the sun and the moon are gods as other men believe? "Most certainly, gentlemen of the court, most certainly; for he says the sun is stone and the moon earth." My dear Meletus, do you imagine you are attacking Anaxagoras?[1] Or do you think so little of the jury, do you fancy them so illiterate as not to know that the books of Anaxagoras, the philosopher of Clazomenæ, are full of all these theories? The young men, we are to suppose, learn them all from me, when they can buy them in the theatre for tenpence at the most and laugh at Socrates if he should pretend that they were his, especially when they are so extraordinary. Now tell me in heaven's name, is this really what you think?— that I believe in no god at all? "In none at all." I cannot believe you, Meletus, I cannot think you

[1] An early Greek philosopher much concerned with the problems of science.

can believe yourself. Men of Athens, I think this man an audacious scoundrel, I consider he has framed this indictment in a spirit of sheer insolence, aggression, and arrogance. One would think he was speaking in riddles, to try "whether the wise Socrates will discover that I am jesting and con-tradicting myself, or whether I shall deceive him and all who hear me." For he surely contradicts himself in his own indictment, almost as if he said: "Socrates is guilty of not believing in gods but believing in them." Such words can only be in jest.

XV. Look at the matter with me, gentlemen of the court, and see how it appears to me. And you must answer us, Meletus, and you sirs, I ask you, as I asked you at first, not to interrupt me if I put the questions in my usual way. Now is there any man, Meletus, who believes that human things exist, but not human beings? Let him answer, sirs, but do not allow him only to interrupt. Is there any one who does not believe in horses but does believe in their trappings? Or who does not believe in flute-players but does believe in flutes? There cannot be, my worthy man; for if you will not answer, I must tell you myself and tell the court as well. But answer this at least: is there any one who believes in things divine and disbelieves in divinities? "No, there is not." How kind of you to answer at last, under pressure from the court! Well, you admit that I believe in things divine, and that I teach others so. They may be new or they may be old, but at the least, according to your own admission, I do believe in things that are divine, and you have sworn to this in your deposition. And if I believe in things divine I must believe in divinities as well. Is that not so? Indeed it is; for since you will not answer I must assume that you assent. And do we not believe that divinities are gods, or the sons of gods? You admit this? "Yes, certainly." Well, now if I believe in divinities, as you grant I do, and if divinities are gods of some kind, then this is what I meant when I said you were speaking in riddles and jesting with us, saying that I do not believe in gods and yet again that I do, since I believe in divinities. Again if these divinities are the bastards of the gods, with nymphs and other women for their mothers, as people say they are, — what man is there who could believe in sons of gods and not in gods? It would be as absurd as to believe in the offspring of horses and of asses, and not believe in horses and asses too. No, Meletus, it can only be that you were testing me when you drew up that charge, or else it was because you could find nothing to accuse me of with any truth. There is no possible way by which you could persuade any man of the least

intelligence to doubt that he who believes in things divine and godlike must believe in divinities and gods, while he who disbelieves the one must disbelieve the other.

XVI. However, men of Athens, I do not think much defence is needed to show that I am innocent of the charge Meletus has made; I think I have now said enough; but what I told you before, namely, that there is deep and widespread enmity against me, that, you must remember, is perfectly true. And this is what will overthrow me, if I am overthrown, not Meletus nor yet Anytus, but the prejudices and envy of the majority, forces that have overthrown many a good man ere now, and will, I imagine, overthrow many more; there is little fear that it will end with me. But maybe some of you will say to me: "And are you not ashamed of a practice that has brought you to the verge of death?" But I have a good answer to give him. "You are not right, my friend," so I would say, "if you think that a man of any worth at all, however slight, ought to reckon up the chances of life and death, and not consider one thing and one alone, and that is whether what he does is right or wrong, a good man's deed or a craven's." According to you, the sons of the gods who died at Troy would have been foolish creatures, and the son of Thetis [1] above all, who thought so lightly of danger compared with the least disgrace, that, when he was resolved to kill Hector and when his mother, goddess as she was, spoke to him, to this effect, if I remember right: "My son, if you avenge the slaughter of your friend Patroclus, and kill Hector, you will die yourself: —

'After the fall of Hector, death is waiting
        for you;' " —

those were her words. But he, when he heard, thought scorn of death and danger: he was far more afraid to live a coward's life and leave his friend unavenged. "Come death then!" he answered, "when I have punished the murderer, that I may not live on here in shame, —

'Here by my longships lying, a burden for
        earth to bear!' "

Do you think that that man cared for death or danger? Hear the truth, men of Athens! The post that a man has taken up because he thought it right himself or because his captain put him there, that post, I believe, he ought to hold in face of every danger, caring no whit for death or any other peril in comparison with disgrace.

XVII. So it would be a strange part for me to
    [1] Achilles.

have played, men of Athens, if I had done as I did under the leaders you chose for me, at Potidæa and Amphipolis and Delium,[1] standing my ground like any one else where they had posted me and facing death, and yet, when God, as I thought and believed, had set me to live the life of philosophy, making inquiry into myself and into others, I were to fear death now, or anything else whatever, and desert my post. It would be very strange; and then, in truth, one would have reason to bring me before the court, because I did not believe in the gods, since I disobeyed the oracle and was afraid of death, and thought I was wise where I was not. For to fear death, sirs, is simply to think we are wise when we are not so: it is to think we know what we know not. No one knows whether death is not the greatest of all goods that can come to man; and yet men fear it as though they knew it was the greatest of all ills. And is not this the folly that should be blamed, the folly of thinking we know what we do not know? Here, again, sirs, it may be that I am different from other men, and if I could call myself wiser than any one in any point, it would be for this, that as I have no real knowledge about the world of Death, so I never fancy that I have. But I do know that it is evil and base to do wrong and disobey the higher will, be it God's or man's. And so for the sake of evils, which I know right well are evils, I will never fear and never fly from things which are, it may be, good. Therefore, though you should acquit me now and refuse to listen to Anytus when he says that either I ought never to have been brought here at all, or else, now that I have been, it is impossible not to sentence me to death, assuring you that if I am set at liberty, your sons will at once put into practice all that I have taught them, and all become entirely corrupt — if, in face of this, you should say to me, "Socrates, for this once we will not listen to Anytus; we will set you free, but on this condition, that you spend your time no longer in this search, and follow wisdom no more. If you are found doing it again you will be put to death." If, I repeat, you were to set me free on that condition, I would answer you: Men of Athens, I thank you and I am grateful to you, but I must obey God rather than you, and, while I have life and strength, I will never cease to follow wisdom, and urge you forward, explaining to every man of you I meet, speaking as I have always spoken, saying, "See here, my friend, you are an Athenian, a citizen of the greatest city in the world, the most famous for wisdom and for power; and are you not ashamed to care for money and money-making and

[1] Three engagements in the Peloponnesian war between Athens and Sparta.

fame and reputation, and not care at all, not make one effort, for truth and understanding and the welfare of your soul?" And should he protest, and assert he cares, I will not let him go at once and send him away free: no! I will question him and examine him, and put him to the proof, and if it seems to me that he has not attained to virtue, and yet asserts he has, I will reproach him for holding cheapest what is worth most, and dearer what is worth less. This I will do for old and young, — for every man I meet, — foreigner and citizen, — but most for my citizens, since you are nearer to me by blood. It is God's bidding, you must understand that; and I myself believe no greater blessing has ever come to you or to your city than this service of mine to God. I have gone about doing one thing and one thing only, — exhorting all of you, young and old, not to care for your bodies or for money above or beyond your souls and their welfare, telling you that virtue does not come from wealth, but wealth from virtue, even as all other goods, public or private, that man can need. If it is by these words that I corrupt our youth, then these words do harm; but if any one asserts that I say anything else, there is nothing in what he says. In face of this I would say, "Men of Athens, listen to Anytus or not, acquit me or acquit me not, but remember that I will do nothing else, not if I were to die a hundred deaths."

XVIII. No! do not interrupt me, Athenians; keep the promise I asked you to give, — not to interrupt what I had to say, but to hear it to the end. I believe it will do you good. I am about to say something else for which you might shout me down, only I beg you not to do so. You must understand that if you put me to death when I am the kind of man I say I am, you will not injure me so much as your own selves. Meletus or Anytus could not injure me; they have not the power. I do not believe it is permitted that a good man should be injured by a bad. He could be put to death, perhaps, or exiled, or disfranchised, and it may be Meletus thinks, and others think, that these are terrible evils, but I do not believe they are. I think it far worse to do what he is doing now, — trying to put a man to death without a cause. So it comes about, men of Athens, that I am far from making my defence for my own sake, as might be thought: I make it for yours, that you may not lose God's gift by condemning me. For if you put me to death you will not easily find another of my like; one, I might say, — even if it sounds a little absurd, — who clings to the city at God's command, as a gadfly clings to a horse; and the horse is tall and thorough-bred, but lazy from his growth, and he needs to be stirred up. And

God, I think, has set me here as something of the kind, — to stir you up and urge you, and prick each one of you and never cease, sitting close to you all day long. You will not easily find another man like that; and, sirs, if you listen to me you will not take my life. But probably you have been annoyed, as drowsy sleepers are when suddenly awakened, and you will turn on me and listen to Anytus, and be glad to put me to death; and then you will spend the rest of your life in sleep, unless God, in his goodness, sends you another man like me. That I am what I say I am, given by God to the city, you may realize from this: it is not the way of a mere man to leave all his own affairs uncared for and all his property neglected during so many years, and go about your business all his life, coming to each individual man, as I have come, as though I were his father or his elder brother, and bidding him think of righteousness. If I had got any profit by this, if I had taken payment for these words, there would have been some explanation for what I did; but you can see for yourselves that my accusers — audacious in everything else — have yet not had the audacity to bring witnesses to assert that I have ever taken payment from any man, or ever asked for it. The witness I could bring myself in my own poverty, would be enough, I think, to prove I speak the truth.

XIX. It may perhaps seem strange that while I have gone about in private to give this counsel, and have been so busy over it, yet I have not found it in my heart to come forward publicly before your democracy and advise the State. The reason is one you have heard me give before, at many times and in many places; and it is this: I have a divine and supernatural sign that comes to me. Meletus referred to it scoffingly in his indictment, but, in truth, it has been with me from boyhood, a kind of voice that comes to me; and, when it comes, it always holds me back from what I may intend to do; it never urges me forward. It is this which has stopped me from taking part in public affairs; and it did well, I think, to stop me. For you may be sure, men of Athens, if I had attempted to enter public life, I should have perished long ago, without any good to you or to myself. Do not be angry with me if I tell you the truth. No man will ever be safe who stands up boldly against you, or against any other democracy, and forbids the many sins and crimes that are committed in the State; the man who is to fight for justice — if he is to keep his life at all — must work in private, not in public.

XX. I will give you a remarkable proof of this, a proof not in words, but in what you value — deeds. Listen, and I will tell you something that happened to me, and you may realise from it that I will never consent to injustice at any man's command for fear of death, but would die on the spot rather than give way. What I have to tell you may seem an arrogant tale and a commonplace of the courts, but it is true.

You know, men of Athens, that I have never held any other office in the State, but I did serve on the Council. And it happened that my tribe, Antiochis, had the Presidency at the time you decided to try the ten generals who had not taken up the dead after the fight at sea.[1] You decided to try them in one body, contrary to law, as you all felt afterwards. On that occasion I was the only one of the Presidents who opposed you, and told you not to break the law; and I gave my vote against it; and when the orators were ready to impeach and arrest me, and you encouraged them and hooted me, I thought then that I ought to take all risks on the side of law and justice, rather than side with you, when your decisions were unjust, through fear of imprisonment or death. That while the city was still under the democracy. When the oligarchy came into power, the Thirty, in their turn, summoned me with four others to the Rotunda, and commanded us to fetch Leon of Salamis from that island, in order to put him to death: the sort of commands they often gave to many others, anxious as they were to incriminate all they could. And on that occasion I showed, not by words only, that for death, to put it bluntly, I did not care one straw, — but I did care, and to the full, about doing what was wicked and unjust. I was not terrified then into doing wrong by that government in all its power: when we left the Rotunda, the other four went off to Salamis and brought Leon back, but I went home. And probably I should have been put to death for it if the government had not been overthrown soon afterwards. Many people will confirm me in what I say.

XXI. Do you believe now that I should have lived so long as this, if I had taken part in public affairs and done what I could for justice like an upright man, putting it, as I was bound to put it, first and foremost? Far from it, men of Athens. Not I, nor any other man on earth. And all through my life you will find that this has been my character, — in public, if ever I had any public work to do, and the same in private, — never yielding to any man against right and justice, though he were one of those whom my calumniators call

[1] The Athenians won the naval battle of Arginusæ in 406 B.C. However, many lives were lost and several generals were sentenced to death for not having tried to recover the bodies of the men killed in the battle.

my scholars. But I have never been any one's teacher. Only, if any man, young or old, has ever heard me at my work and wished to listen, I have never grudged him my permission; I have not talked with him if he would pay me, and refused him if he would not; I am ready for questions from rich and poor alike, and equally ready to question them should they care to answer me and hear what I have to say. And for that, if any one is the better or any one the worse, I ought not to be held responsible; I never promised instruction, I never taught, and if any man says he has ever learnt or heard one word from me in private other than all the world could hear, I tell you he does not speak the truth.

XXII. What then can it be that makes some men delight in my company? You have heard my answer, sirs. I told you the whole truth when I said their delight lay in hearing men examined who thought that they were wise but were not so; and certainly it is not unpleasant. And I, as I believe, have been commanded to do this by God, speaking in oracles and in dreams, in every way by which divine grace has ever spoken to man at all and told him what to do. That, men of Athens, is the truth, and easy to verify. For if it were really the case that I corrupt our young men and have corrupted them, then surely, now that they are older, if they have come to understand that I ever meant to do them harm when they were young, some of them ought to come forward here and now, to accuse and punish me, or if they did not care to come themselves, some who are near to them — their fathers, or their brothers, or others of their kin, — ought to remember and punish it now, if it be true that those who are dear to them have suffered any harm from me. In fact, there are many of them here at this very moment; I can see them for myself; there is Crito, my contemporary, who belongs to the same deme[1] as I, the father of Critobulus there; and here is Lusanias of Sphettos, the father of Æschines, who is beside him; and Antiphon of Kephisia, the father of Epigenes; and others too whose brothers have spent their time with me, Nicostratus, the son of Theozotides, brother of Theodotus. Theodotus is dead; so it cannot be his entreaty that has stopped his brother. And Paralus is here, the son of Demodocus, whose brother Theages was; and Adeimantus, the son of Ariston, whose brother Plato I see, and Aiantodorus with his brother Apollodorus too. And I could tell you of many more, one of whom at least Meletus should have called as a witness in his attack; or, if he forgot then, let him call one now, and I will stand aside, and he can speak if he has anything to say. But, gentlemen, you will find precisely the reverse; you will find them all prepared to stand by me, the man who has done the harm, the man who has injured their nearest and dearest, as Meletus and Anytus say. Those, perhaps, who are ruined themselves might have some reason for supporting me, but those who are uncorrupted, — men of advancing years, their relatives, — what other reason could they have for their support except the right and worthy reason that they know Meletus is lying and I am speaking the truth?

XXIII. There, gentlemen, that is on the whole what I had to say in my defence, with something more, perhaps, to the same effect. Now there may be a man among you who will feel annoyed if he remembers his own conduct when undergoing a trial far less serious than this of mine; how he prayed and supplicated the judges with floods of tears, and brought his little children into court to rouse as much pity as possible, and others of his family and many of his friends; but I, it would appear, will not do anything of the kind, and that in the face, as it might seem, of the utmost danger. Such a man, it may be, observing this, will harden himself against me; this one fact will enrage him and he will give his vote in anger. If this is so with any of you, — I do not say it is, but if it is, — I think it would be reasonable for me to say, "I too, my good man, have kindred of my own, I too was not born, as Homer says, 'from stock or stone,' but from men, so that I have kinsfolk and sons also, three sons, — the eldest of them is already a stripling, the other two are children. And yet I do not intend to bring one of them here, or entreat you to acquit me." And why is it that I will not do anything of the kind? Not from pride, men of Athens, nor from disrespect for you: nor is it because I am at peace about death; it is for the sake of my honor and yours and the honor of the city. I do not think it fitting that I should do such things, a man of my years, and with the name I bear; it may be true or false, but at any rate it is believed that Socrates is in some way different from most other men. And if those among you who bear a name for wisdom or courage or any other virtue were to act like this, it would be disgraceful. I have seen it often in others, when they came under trial, men of some repute, but who behaved in a most extraordinary way, thinking, apparently, that it would be a fearful thing for them to die; as though they would be immortal if you did not put them to death. Such men, I think, bring disgrace upon the city, and any stranger might suppose that the Athenians who bore the highest name for virtue, who had been chosen out expressly for office and

[1] township or ward.

reward, were no whit better than women. We must not behave so, men of Athens, those of us who are thought to be of any worth at all, and you must not allow it, should we try: you must make it plain, and quite plain, that you will be more ready to condemn the man who acts these pitiful scenes before you and makes the city absurd, than him who holds his peace.

XXIV. Even putting honor aside, gentlemen, it does not seem to me right to supplicate a judge and gain acquittal so: we ought rather to instruct him and convince him. The judge does not sit here to grant justice as a favor, but to try the case; he has sworn, not that he will favor those he chooses, but that he will judge according to the law. So we should not teach you to break your oath, and you should not let yourselves be taught. Neither of us would reverence the gods if we did that. Therefore you must not expect me, men of Athens, to act towards you in a way which I do not think seemly or right or reverent — more especially when I am under trial for impiety, and have Meletus here to face. For plainly, were I to win you over by my entreaties, and have you do violence to your oath, plainly I should be teaching you not to believe in the gods, and my own speech would accuse me unmistakably of unbelief. But it is far from being so; for I believe, men of Athens, as not one of my accusers believes, and I leave it to you and to God to decide my case as may be best for me and you.

PART II

After the Verdict and Before the Sentence

XXV. There are many reasons, men of Athens, why I feel no distress at what has now occurred, I mean your condemnation of me. It is not unexpected; on the contrary, I am surprised at the number of votes on either side. I did not think it would be so close. I thought the majority would be great; but in fact, so it appears, if only thirty votes had gone otherwise, I should have been acquitted. Against Meletus, as it is, I appear to have won, and not only so, but it is clear to every one that if Anytus and Lycon had not come forward to accuse me, he would have been fined a thousand drachmas, for he would not have obtained a fifth part of the votes.

XXVI. The penalty he fixes for me is, I understand, death. Very good. And what am I going to fix in my turn, men of Athens? It must be, must it not, what I deserve? Well, then, what do I deserve to receive or pay because I chose not to sit quiet all my life, and turned aside from what most men care for, — money-making and household affairs, leadership in war and public speaking, and all the offices and associations and factions of the State, — thinking myself, as a matter of fact, too upright to be safe if I went into that life? So I held aloof from it all; I should have been of no use there to you or to myself, but I set about going in private to each individual man and doing him the greatest of all services — as I assert — trying to persuade every one of you not to think of what he had but rather of what he was, and how he might grow wise and good, nor consider what the city had, but what the city was, and so with everything else in the world. What, then, do I deserve for this? A reward, men of Athens, if I am really to consider my deserts, and a reward, moreover, that would suit me. And what reward would suit a poor man who has been a public benefactor, and who is bound to refrain from work because of his services in exhorting you? There could be nothing so suitable, men of Athens, as a place at the table in the Presidents' Hall; far more suitable than if any of you had won a horse-race at Olympia or a chariot race. The Olympian victor brings you fancied happiness, but I bring you real: he does not need maintenance, but I do. If I am to fix what I deserve in all fairness, then this is what I fix: — a place at the table in the Presidents' Hall.

XXVII. Perhaps when I say this you will feel that I am speaking much as I spoke about entreaties for pity, that is to say, in a spirit of pride; but it is not so, Athenians. This is how it is: I am convinced that I have never done wrong to any man intentionally, but I cannot convince you; we have only had a little time to talk together. Had it been the custom with you, as with other nations, to spend not one day but many on a trial for life and death, I believe you would have been convinced; but as matters are, it is not easy to remove a great prejudice in a little time.

Well, with this conviction of mine that I have never wronged any man, I am far from meaning to wrong myself by saying that I deserve any harm, or assigning myself anything whatever of the kind. What should I be afraid of? Of suffering what Meletus has assigned, when I say that I do not know, after all, whether it is not good? And to escape it I am to choose what I know quite well is bad? And what punishment should I fix? Imprisonment? Why should I live in prison, slave to the Eleven [1] of the day? Or should I say a fine, with imprisonment until I pay it? But then there is just the difficulty I mentioned a moment ago: I have no money to pay a fine. Or am I to say

[1] A committee or board in charge of prisons, executions, etc. It consisted of one member from each of the ten tribes to which number was added a secretary.

exile? You might, I know, choose that for my punishment. My love of life would indeed be great if I were so blind as not to see that you, my own fellow-citizens, have not been able to endure my ways and words, you have found them too trying and too heavy to bear, so that you want to get rid of them now. And if that is so, will strangers put up with them? Far from it, men of Athens. And it would be a grand life for a man of my years to go into exile and wander about from one city to another. For well I know that wherever I went the young men would listen to my talk as they listen here; and if I drove them away, they would drive me out themselves and persuade their elders to side with them, and if I let them come, their fathers and kindred would banish me on their account.

XXVIII. Perhaps some one will say: "But, Socrates, cannot you leave us and live in peace and quietness?" Now that is just what it is hardest to make you, some of you, believe. If I were to say that this would be to disobey God, and therefore I cannot hold my peace, you would not believe me; you would say I was using my irony. And if I say again that it is in fact the greatest of all goods for a man to talk about virtue every day, and the other matters on which you have heard me speaking and making inquiry into myself and others: if I say that the life without inquiry is no life for man — you would believe that even less. Yet it is so, even as I tell you — only it is not easy to get it believed. Moreover, I am not accustomed to think myself deserving of punishment. However, if I had had any money I should have fixed a price that I could pay, for that would not have harmed me at all; but as it is, since I have no money — unless perhaps you would consent to fix only so much as I could afford to pay? Perhaps I might be able to pay one mina [1] silver; and I will fix the fine at that. But Plato here, gentlemen, and Crito, and Critobulus, and Apollodorus, beg me to say thirty minas, and they tell me they will guarantee it. So I will fix it at this sum, and these men, on whom you can rely, will be sureties for the amount.

PART III

After the Sentence of Death

XXIX. You have hastened matters a little, men of Athens, but for that little gain you will be called the murderers of Socrates the Wise by all who want to find fault with the city. For those who wish to reproach you will insist that I am wise, though I may not be so. Had you but waited a

little longer, you would have found this happen of itself: for you can see how old I am, far on in life, with death at hand. In this I am not speaking to all of you, but only to those who have sentenced me to death. And to them I will say one thing more. It may be, gentlemen, that you imagine I have been convicted for lack of arguments by which I could have convinced you, had I thought it right to say and do anything in order to escape punishment. Far from it. No; convicted I have been, for lack of — not arguments, but audacity and impudence, and readiness to say what would have been a delight for you to hear, lamenting and bewailing my position, saying and doing all kinds of things unworthy of myself, as I consider, but such as you have grown accustomed to hear from others. I did not think it right then to behave through fear unlike a free-born man, and I do not repent now of my defence; I would far rather die after that defence than live upon your terms. As in war, so in a court of justice, not I nor any man should scheme to escape death by any and every means. Many a time in battle it is plain the soldier could avoid death if he flung away his arms and turned to supplicate his pursuers, and there are many such devices in every hour of danger for escaping death, if we are prepared to say and do anything whatever. But, sirs, it may be that the difficulty is not to flee from death, but from guilt. Guilt is swifter than death. And so it is that I, who am slow and old, have been caught by the slower-paced, and my accusers, who are clever and quick, by the quick-footed, by wickedness. And now I am to go away, under sentence of death from you: but on them truth has passed sentence of unrighteousness and injustice. I abide by the decision, and so must they. Perhaps indeed, it had to be just so: and I think it is very well.

XXX. And now that that is over I desire to prophesy to you, you who have condemned me. For now I have come to the time when men can prophesy — when they are to die. I say to you, you who have killed me, punishment will fall on you immediately after my death, far heavier for you to bear — I call God to witness! — than your punishment of me. For you have done this thinking to escape the need of giving any account of your lives: but exactly the contrary will come to pass, and so I tell you. Those who will call you to account will be more numerous, — I have kept them back till now, and you have not noticed them, — and they will be the harder to bear inasmuch as they are younger, and you will be troubled all the more. For if you think that by putting men to death you can stop every one from blaming you for living as

[1] Approximately twenty dollars.

you should not live, I tell you you are mistaken; that way of escape is neither feasible nor noble; the noblest way, and the easiest, is not to maim others, but to fit ourselves for righteousness. That is the prophecy I give to you who have condemned me, and so I leave you.

XXXI. But with those who have acquitted me I should be glad to talk about this matter, until the Archons are at leisure and I go to the place where I am to die. So I will ask you, gentlemen, to stay with me for the time. There is no reason why we should not talk together while we can, and tell each other our dreams. I would like to show you, as my friends, what can be the meaning of this that has befallen me. A wonderful thing, my judges, — for I may call you judges, and not call you amiss, — a wonderful thing has happened to me. The warning that comes to me, my spiritual sign, has always in all my former life been most incessant, and has opposed me in most trifling matters, whenever I was about to act amiss; and now there has befallen me, as you see yourselves, what might really be thought, as it is thought, the greatest of all evils. And yet, when I left my home in the morning, the signal from God was not against me, nor when I came up here into the court, nor in my speech, whatever I was about to say; and yet at other times it has often stopped me in the very middle of what I was saying; but never once in this matter has it opposed me in any word or deed. What do I suppose to be the reason? I will tell you. This that has befallen me is surely good, and it cannot possibly be that we are right in our opinion, those of us who hold that death is an evil. A great proof of this has come to me: it cannot but be that the well-known signal would have stopped me, unless what I was going to meet was good.

XXXII. Let us look at it in this way too, and we shall find much hope that it is so. Death must be one of two things: either it is to have no consciousness at all of anything whatever, or else, as some say, it is a kind of change and migration of the soul from this world to another. Now if there is no consciousness at all, and it is like sleep when the sleeper does not dream, I say there would be a wonderful gain in death. For I am sure if any man were to take that night in which he slept so deeply that he saw no dreams, and put beside it all the other nights and days of his whole life, and compare them, and say how many of them all were better spent or happier than that one night, — I am sure that not the ordinary man alone, but the King of Persia himself, would find them few to count. If death is of this nature I would consider it a gain; for the whole of time would seem no longer than one single night. But if it is a journey

to another land, if what some say is true and all the dead are really there, if this is so, my judges, what greater good could there be? If a man were to go to the House of Death, and leave all these self-styled judges to find the true judges there, who, so it is said, give justice in that world, — Minos and Rhadamanthus, Æacus and Triptolemus, and all the sons of the gods who have done justly in this life, — would that journey be ill to take? Or to meet Orpheus and Musæus, Hesiod and Homer, what would you give for that, any of you? I would give a hundred deaths if it is true. And for me especially it would be a wonderful life there, if I met Palamedes, and Ajax, the son of Telamon, or any of the men of old who died by an unjust decree: to compare my experience with theirs would be full of pleasure, surely. And best of all, to go on still with the men of that world as with the men of this, inquiring and questioning and learning who is wise among them, and who may think he is, but is not. How much would one give, my judges, to question the hero who led the host at Troy, or Odysseus, or Sisyphus, or any of the countless men and women I could name? To talk with them there, and live with them, and question them, would be happiness unspeakable. Certainly there they will not put one to death for that; they are far happier in all things than we of this world, and they are immortal for evermore, — if what some say is true.

XXXIII. And you too, my judges, must think of death with hope, and remember this at least is true, that no evil can come to a good man in life or death, and that he is not forgotten of God; what has come to me now has not come by chance, but it is clear to me that it was better for me to die and be quit of trouble. That is why the signal never came to turn me back, and I cannot say that I am altogether angry with my accusers and those who have condemned me. Yet it was not with that intention that they condemned and accused me; they meant to do me harm, and they are to be blamed for that. This much, however, I will ask of them. When my sons come of age, sirs, will you reprove them and trouble them as I troubled you, if you think they care for money or anything else more than righteousness? And if they seem to be something when they are really nothing, reproach them as I reproached you for not seeking what they need, and for thinking they are somewhat when they are worth nothing. And if you do this, we shall have received justice at your hands, my sons and I.

But now it is time for us to go, I to death, and you to life; and which of us goes to the better state is known to none but God.

Aristotle · 384–322 B.C.

By the time of Aristotle the rich Periclean Age in Athens had passed. The great fifth century before Christ when Æschylus, Sophocles, Euripides, and Aristophanes wrote tragedy and comedy gave way to a decline in the city-states of Greece. Corruption and decay were weakening Athens and Sparta. Macedonia, a region stretching away to the North and East of Greece, rose to great power under Philip and Philip's renowned son, Alexander the Great.

It was in Stagira, a town in Macedonia, that Aristotle was born in 384 B.C. His father was a doctor attached to the court of Macedon. At the age of seventeen, the young Aristotle began his study of philosophy under Plato at Athens, staying on at Plato's Academy, as pupil and as friend, for twenty years. He then left Athens to return to Macedonia where he spent the next twelve years, part of the time as tutor to the young Alexander. At forty-nine Aristotle returned to Athens and founded his academy, a school which he called the Lyceum but which others called the Peripatetic School because of the custom of the young men of walking about as they listened to their lectures. Here for twelve years Aristotle taught philosophy and science. After the death of Alexander, political disturbances made Athens an uncomfortable place for him and his work and he went again to Macedonia, this time to his mother's home in Chalcis, where he soon died (322 B.C.).

Aristotle is a whole university in himself. Like Leonardo da Vinci he manifested a boundless curiosity. Like Bacon he took all knowledge to be his province. His study, writing, and teaching rapidly passed from one phase of thought, one interest, into another: politics, astronomy, psychology, ethics, biology, logic, philosophy, rhetoric, and literature. Without question, his was one of the most fertile minds the world has known, as his *Poetics* (*c.* 350 B.C.) is one of the greatest single pieces of literary criticism.

Selections from the *Poetics* (VI–XV), in the translation of S. H. Butcher, are reprinted by permission of The Macmillan Company.

SUGGESTED REFERENCES: J. H. Randall, *Aristotle* (1960); Lane Cooper, *The Poetics of Aristotle, Its Meaning and Influence* (3rd ed., 1963).

The Nature of Tragedy

Tragedy, then, is an imitation of an action that is serious, complete, and of a certain magnitude; in language embellished with each kind of artistic ornament, the several kinds being found in sepa- 5 rate parts of the play; in the form of action, not of narrative; through pity and fear effecting the proper purgation [1] of these emotions. By "language embellished," I mean language into which rhythm, "harmony," and song enter. By "the several kinds in separate parts," I mean, that some parts are rendered through the medium of verse alone, others again with the aid of song.

Now as tragic imitation implies persons acting, it necessarily follows, in the first place, that Spectacular equipment will be a part of Tragedy. Next, Song and Diction, for these are the medium of imitation. By "Diction" I mean the mere metrical arrangement of the words: as for "Song," it is a term whose sense every one understands.

Again, Tragedy is the imitation of an action; and an action implies personal agents, who necessarily possess certain distinctive qualities both of character and thought; for it is by these that we qualify actions themselves, and these — thought and character — are the two natural causes from which actions spring, and on actions again all success or failure depends. Hence, the Plot is the

[1] Much has been written on the psychological and philosophical significance of this term. Butcher, following Bernays, points out that "purgation" (katharsis) is a medical metaphor "and denotes a pathological effect on the soul analogous to the effect of medicine on the body.... Tragedy excites the emotions of pity and fear — kindred emotions that are in the hearts of all men — and by the act of excitation affords a pleasurable relief." In other words the spectator at a 15 tragedy, following the tribulations of the tragic hero, himself suffers vicariously, is emotionally moved, and, as a result of the experience, finds pleasurable relief. He undergoes a sort of emotional ecstasy, which leaves him, at least for a time, "clean" in soul since through 20 pity and fear his base and selfish passions have been eliminated.

imitation of the action: for by plot I here mean the arrangement of the incidents. By Character I mean that in virtue of which we ascribe certain qualities to the agents. Thought is required wherever a statement is proved, or, it may be, a general truth is enunciated. Every Tragedy, therefore, must have six parts, which parts determine its quality — namely, Plot, Character, Diction, Thought, Spectacle, Song. Two of the parts constitute the medium of imitation, one the manner, and three the objects of imitation. And these complete the list. These elements have been employed, we may say, by the poets to a man; in fact, every play contains Spectacular elements as well as Character, Plot, Diction, Song, and Thought.

But most important of all is the structure of the incidents. For Tragedy is an imitation, not of men, but of an action and of life, and life consists in action, and its end is a mode of action, not a quality. Now character determines men's qualities, but it is by their actions that they are happy or the reverse. Dramatic action, therefore, is not with a view to the representation of character: character comes in as subsidiary to the actions. Hence the incidents and the plot are the end of a tragedy; and the end is the chief thing of all. Again, without action there cannot be a tragedy; there may be without character. The tragedies of most of our modern poets fail in the rendering of character; and of poets in general this is often true. It is the same in painting; and here lies the difference between Zeuxis and Polygnotus. Polygnotus delineates character well: the style of Zeuxis is devoid of ethical quality. Again, if you string together a set of speeches expressive of character, and well finished in point of diction and thought, you will not produce the essential tragic effect nearly so well as with a play which, however deficient in these respects, yet has a plot and artistically constructed incidents. Besides which, the most powerful elements of emotional interest in Tragedy — Peripeteia[1] or Reversal of the Situation, and Recognition scenes — are parts of the plot. A further proof is, that novices in the art attain to finish of diction and precision of portraiture before they can construct the plot. It is the same with almost all the early poets.

The Plot, then, is the first principle, and, as it

[1] Another critical term on which considerable controversy has centered. It was once understood to mean only the "Reversal of Fortune" by which a king is deprived of his throne, a princess buried alive, etc. Later it has been thought of as a "complete change of situation in the course of a single scene" or as "a series of incidents or a train of action tending to bring about a certain end but resulting in something wholly different."

were, the soul of a tragedy: Character holds the second place. A similar fact is seen in painting. The most beautiful colors, laid on confusedly, will not give as much pleasure as the chalk outline of a portrait. Thus Tragedy is the imitation of an action, and of the agents mainly with a view to the action.

Third in order is Thought, — that is, the faculty of saying what is possible and pertinent in given circumstances. In the case of oratory, this is the function of the political art and of the art of rhetoric: and so indeed the older poets make their characters speak the language of civic life; the poets of our time, the language of the rhetoricians. Character is that which reveals moral purpose, showing what kinds of things a man chooses or avoids. Speeches, therefore, which do not make this manifest, or in which the speaker does not choose or avoid anything whatever, are not expressive of character. Thought, on the other hand, is found where something is proved to be or not to be, or a general maxim is enunciated.

Fourth among the elements enumerated comes Diction; by which I mean, as has been already said, the expression of the meaning in words; and its essence is the same both in verse and prose.

Of the remaining elements Song holds the chief place among the embellishments.

The Spectacle has, indeed, an emotional attraction of its own, but, of all the parts, it is the least artistic, and connected least with the art of poetry. For the power of Tragedy, we may be sure, is felt even apart from representation and actors. Besides, the production of spectacular effects depends more on the art of the stage machinist than on that of the poet.

These principles being established, let us now discuss the proper structure of the Plot, since this is the first and most important thing in Tragedy.

Now, according to our definition, Tragedy is an imitation of an action that is complete, and whole, and of a certain magnitude; for there may be a whole that is wanting in magnitude. A whole is that which has a beginning, a middle, and an end. A beginning is that which does not itself follow anything by causal necessity, but after which something naturally is or comes to be. An end, on the contrary, is that which itself naturally follows some other thing, either by necessity, or as a rule, but has nothing following it. A middle is that which follows something as some other thing follows it. A well constructed plot, therefore, must neither begin nor end at haphazard, but conform to these principles.

Again, a beautiful object, whether it be a living organism or any whole composed of parts, must not only have an orderly arrangement of parts, but must also be of a certain magnitude; for beauty depends on magnitude and order. Hence a very small animal organism cannot be beautiful; for the view of it is confused, the object being seen in an almost imperceptible moment of time. Nor, again, can one of vast size be beautiful; for as the eye cannot take it all in at once, the unity and sense of the whole is lost for the spectator; as for instance if there were one a thousand miles long. As, therefore, in the case of animate bodies and organisms a certain magnitude is necessary, and a magnitude which may be easily embraced in one view; so in the plot, a certain length is necessary, and a length which can be easily embraced by the memory. The limit of length in relation to dramatic competition and sensuous presentment, is no part of artistic theory. For had it been the rule for a hundred tragedies to compete together, the performance would have been regulated by the water-clock,[1] — as indeed we are told was formerly done. But the limit as fixed by the nature of the drama itself is this: — the greater the length, the more beautiful will the piece be by reason of its size, provided that the whole be perspicuous. And to define the matter roughly, we may say that the proper magnitude is comprised within such limits, that the sequence of events, according to the law of probability or necessity, will admit of a change from bad fortune to good, or from good fortune to bad.

Unity of plot does not, as some persons think, consist in the unity of the hero. For infinitely various are the incidents in one man's life which cannot be reduced to unity; and so, too, there are many actions of one man out of which we cannot make one action. Hence the error, as it appears, of all poets who have composed a Heracleid, a Theseid,[2] or other poems of the kind. They imagine that as Heracles was one man, the story of Heracles must also be a unity. But Homer, as in all else he is of surpassing merit, here too — whether from art or natural genius — seems to have happily discerned the truth. In composing the *Odyssey* he did not include all the adventures of Odysseus — such as his wound on Parnassus, or his feigned madness at the mustering of the host — incidents between which there was no necessary or probable connexion: but he made the *Odyssey*, and likewise the *Iliad*, to centre round an action that in our sense of the word is one. As therefore,

[1] A clock into which a regulated stream of water pours, the time being determined by the height of the water in a basin.

[2] Poems celebrating the exploits of Hercules or Theseus.

in the other imitative arts, the imitation is one when the object imitated is one, so the plot, being an imitation of an action, must imitate one action and that a whole, the structural union of the parts being such that, if any one of them is displaced or removed, the whole will be disjointed and disturbed. For a thing whose presence or absence makes no visible difference, is not an organic part of the whole.

It is, moreover, evident from what has been said, that it is not the function of the poet to relate what has happened, but what may happen, — what is possible according to the law of probability or necessity. The poet and the historian differ not by writing in verse or prose. The work of Herodotus[1] might be put into verse, and it would still be a species of history, with metre no less than without it. The true difference is that one relates what has happened, the other what may happen. Poetry, therefore, is a more philosophical and a higher thing than history: for poetry tends to express the universal, history the particular. By the universal I mean how a person of a certain type will on occasion speak or act, according to the law of probability or necessity; and it is this universality at which poetry aims in the names she attaches to the personages. The particular is — for example — what Alcibiades[2] did or suffered. In Comedy this is already apparent: for here the poet first constructs the plots on the lines of probability, and then inserts characteristic names; — unlike the lampooners who write about particular individuals. But tragedians still keep to real names, the reason being that what is possible is credible: what has not happened we do not at once feel sure to be possible: but what has happened is manifestly possible: otherwise it would not have happened. Still there are even some tragedies in which there are only one or two well known names, the rest being fictitious. In others, none are well known, — as in Agathon's *Antheus*, where incidents and names alike are fictitious, and yet they give none the less pleasure. We must not, therefore, at all costs keep to the received legends, which are the usual subjects of Tragedy. Indeed, it would be absurd to attempt it; for even subjects that are known are known only to a few, and yet give pleasure to all. It clearly follows that the poet or "maker" should be the maker of plots rather than of verses; since he is a poet because he imitates, and what he imitates are actions. And even if he chances to take an historical subject, he is none the less a poet; for there is no reason why some events that have actually happened should not conform to the law of the probable and possible,

[1] A Greek historian.   [2] An Athenian general.

and in virtue of that quality in them he is their poet or maker.

Of all plots and actions the epeisodic are the worst. I call a plot "epeisodic" in which the episodes or acts succeed one another without probable or necessary sequence. Bad poets compose such pieces by their own fault, good poets, to please the players; for, as they write show pieces for competition, they stretch the plot beyond its capacity, and are often forced to break the natural continuity.

But again, Tragedy is an imitation not only of a complete action, but of events inspiring fear or pity. Such an effect is best produced when the events come on us by surprise; and the effect is heightened when, at the same time, they follow as cause and effect. The tragic wonder will then be greater than if they happened of themselves or by accident; for even coincidences are most striking when they have an air of design. We may instance the statue of Mitys at Argos, which fell upon his murderer while he was a spectator at a festival, and killed him. Such events seem not to be due to mere chance. Plots, therefore, constructed on these principles are necessarily the best.

Plots are either Simple or Complex, for the actions in real life, of which the plots are an imitation, obviously show a similar distinction. An action which is one and continuous in the sense above defined, I call Simple, when the change of fortune takes place without Reversal of the Situation and without Recognition.

A Complex action is one in which the change is accompanied by such Reversal, or by Recognition, or by both. These last should arise from the internal structure of the plot, so that what follows should be the necessary or probable result of the preceding action. It makes all the difference whether any given event is a case of *propter hoc* or *post hoc*.

Reversal of the Situation is a change by which the action veers round to its opposite, subject always to our rule of probability or necessity. Thus in the *Œdipus*,[1] the messenger comes to cheer Œdipus and free him from his alarms about his mother, but by revealing who he is, he produces the opposite effect. Again in the *Lynceus*,[2]

[1] A tragedy by Sophocles.
[2] A tragedy by Theodectes, a pupil of Aristotle. The story of Lynceus is mentioned in Euripides' *Hecuba*. Danaus had fifty daughters; his twin brother, Aegyptus, had fifty sons. Danaus under compulsion agrees that his daughters shall marry the sons of Aegyptus, but gives each daughter a knife with which to kill her husband. The daughter marrying Lynceus, however, spares him. According to one version Lynceus killed Danaus.

Lynceus is being led away to his death, aud Danaus goes with him, meaning to slay him; but the outcome of the preceding incidents is that Danaus is killed and Lynceus saved.

Recognition, as the name indicates, is a change from ignorance to knowledge, producing love or hate between the persons destined by the poet for good or bad fortune. The best form of recognition is coincident with a Reversal of the Situation, as in the *Œdipus*. There are indeed other forms. Even inanimate things of the most trivial kind may in a sense be objects of recognition. Again, we may recognise or discover whether a person has done a thing or not. But the recognition which is most intimately connected with the plot and action is, as we have said, the recognition of persons. This recognition, combined with Reversal, will produce either pity or fear; and actions producing these effects are those which, by our definition, Tragedy represents. Moreover, it is upon such situations that the issues of good or bad fortune will depend. Recognition, then, being between persons, it may happen that one person only is recognised by the other — when the latter is already known — or it may be necessary that the recognition should be on both sides. Thus Iphigenia is revealed to Orestes[1] by the sending of the letter; but another act of recognition is required to make Orestes known to Iphigenia.

Two parts, then, of the plot — Reversal of Situation and Recognition — turn upon surprises. A third part is the Scene of Suffering. The Scene of Suffering is a destructive or painful action, such as death on the stage, bodily agony, wounds and the like.

(The parts of Tragedy which must be treated as elements of the whole have been already mentioned. We now come to the quantitative parts — the separate parts into which Tragedy is divided — namely, Prologue, Episode, Exode, Choric song; this last being divided into Parode and Stasimon. These are common to all plays: peculiar to some are the songs of actors from the stage and the Commos.

The Prologue is that entire part of a tragedy which precedes the Parode of the Chorus. The Episode is that entire part of a tragedy which is between complete choric songs. The Exode is that entire part of a tragedy which has no choric song after it. Of the Choric part the Parode is the first undivided utterance of the Chorus: the Stasimon is a Choric ode without anapæsts or trochaic tetrameters: the Commos is a joint lamentation of Chorus and actors. The parts of Tragedy which must be treated as elements of the whole have

[1] In Euripides' *Iphigenia in Tauris*.

been already mentioned. The quantitative parts
— the separate parts into which it is divided —
are here enumerated.)

As the sequel to what has already been said, we
must proceed to consider what the poet should aim
at, and what he should avoid, in constructing his
plots; and by what means the specific effect of
Tragedy will be produced.

A perfect tragedy should, as we have seen, be
arranged not on the simple but on the complex
plan. It should, moreover, imitate actions which
excite pity or fear, this being the distinctive mark of
tragic imitation. It follows plainly, in the first
place, that the change of fortune presented must
not be the spectacle of a virtuous man brought
from prosperity to adversity: for this moves
neither pity nor fear; it merely shocks us. Nor,
again, that of a bad man passing from adversity
to prosperity: for nothing can be more alien to the
spirit of Tragedy; it possesses no single tragic
quality; it neither satisfies the moral sense nor
calls forth pity or fear. Nor, again, should the
downfall of the utter villain be exhibited. A plot
of this kind would, doubtless, satisfy the moral
sense, but it would inspire neither pity nor fear;
for pity is aroused by unmerited misfortune, fear
by the misfortune of a man like ourselves. Such
an event, therefore, will be neither pitiful nor terrible. There remains, then, the character between
these two extremes, — that of a man who is not
eminently good and just, yet whose misfortune is
brought about not by vice or depravity, but by
some error or frailty. He must be one who is
highly renowned and prosperous, — a personage
like Œdipus, Thyestes,¹ or other illustrious men of
such families.

A well constructed plot should, therefore, be
single in its issue, rather than double as some
maintain. The change of fortune should be not
from bad to good, but, reversely, from good to
bad. It should come about as the result not of
vice, but of some great error or frailty, in a character such as we have described, or better rather than
worse. The practice of the stage bears out our
view. At first the poets recounted any legend that
came in their way. Now, the best tragedies are
founded on the stories of a few houses, — on the
fortunes of Alcmæon, Œdipus, Meleager, Thyestes,
Telephus, and those others who have done or suffered something terrible. A tragedy, then, to be
perfect according to the rules of art should be of
this construction. Hence they are in error who
censure Euripides just because he follows this

¹ Both have been used by various dramatists.
Sophocles' *Œdipus Rex* and Carcinus's *Thyestes* are
examples.

principle in his plays, many of which end unhappily. It is, as we have said, the right ending.
The best proof is that on the stage and in dramatic
competition, such plays, if well worked out, are the
most tragic in effect; and Euripides, faulty though
he may be in the general management of his subject, yet is felt to be the most tragic of the poets.

In the second rank comes the kind of tragedy
which some place first. Like the *Odyssey*, it has a
double thread of plot, and also an opposite catastrophe for the good and for the bad. It is accounted the best because of the weakness of the
spectators; for the poet is guided in what he writes
by the wishes of his audience. The pleasure, however, thence derived is not the true tragic pleasure.
It is proper rather to Comedy, where those who,
in the piece, are the deadliest enemies — like
Orestes and Ægisthus ¹ — quit the stage as friends
at the close, and no one slays or is slain.

Fear and pity may be aroused by spectacular
means; but they may also result from the inner
structure of the piece, which is the better way,
and indicates a superior poet. For the plot
ought to be so constructed that, even without the
aid of the eye, he who hears the tale told will thrill
with horror and melt to pity at what takes place.
This is the impression we should receive from
hearing the story of the Œdipus.² But to produce
this effect by the mere spectacle is a less artistic
method, and dependent on extraneous aids. Those
who employ spectacular means to create a sense
not of the terrible but only of the monstrous, are
strangers to the purpose of Tragedy; for we must not
demand of Tragedy any and every kind of pleasure,
but only that which is proper to it. And since the
pleasure which the poet should afford is that which
comes from pity and fear through imitation, it is
evident that this quality must be impressed upon
the incidents.

Let us then determine what are the circumstances which strike us as terrible or pitiful.

Actions capable of this effect must happen between persons who are either friends or enemies or
indifferent to one another. If an enemy kills an
enemy, there is nothing to excite pity either in the

¹ Orestes was the "deadly enemy" of Ægisthus because the latter was the paramour of his mother,
Clytemnestra, and had plotted the murder of Orestes'
father, Agamemnon. See Æschylus' *Agamemnon* for
a part of this story.
² The son of Laius, King of Thebes. According to
the usual story an oracle had decreed that he should
kill his father; consequently as a child he was exposed
on a mountainside. However he was saved from that
fate only in manhood to kill his father, unrecognized
by him, in a quarrel. See Sophocles' *Œdipus Coloneus.*

act or the intention, — except so far as the suffering in itself is pitiful. So again with indifferent persons. But when the tragic incident occurs between those who are near or dear to one another — if, for example, a brother kills, or intends to kill, a brother, a son his father, a mother her son, a son his mother, or any other deed of the kind is done — these are the situations to be looked for by the poet. He may not indeed destroy the framework of the received legends — the fact, for instance, that Clytemnestra was slain by Orestes and Eriphyle by Alcmæon [1] — but he ought to show invention of his own, and skilfully handle the traditional material. Let us explain more clearly what is meant by skilful handling.

The action may be done consciously and with knowledge of the persons, in the manner of the older poets. It is thus too that Euripides makes Medea [2] slay her children. Or, again, the deed of horror may be done, but done in ignorance, and the tie of kinship or friendship discovered afterwards. The *Œdipus* of Sophocles is an example. Here, indeed, the incident is outside the drama proper; but cases occur where it falls within the action of the play: one may cite the *Alcmæon* of Astydamas, or Telegonus in the *Wounded Odysseus*. Again, there is a third case, — to be about to act with knowledge of the persons and then not to act. The fourth case is when some one is about to do an irreparable deed through ignorance, and makes the discovery before it is done. These are the only possible ways. For the deed must either be done or not done, — and that wittingly or unwittingly. But of all these ways, to be about to act knowing the persons, and then not to act, is the worst. It is shocking without being tragic, for no disaster follows. It is, therefore, never, or very rarely, found in poetry. One instance, however, is in the *Antigone*,[3] where Hæmon threatens to kill Creon. The next and better way is that the deed shall be perpetrated. Still better, that it should be perpetrated in ignorance, and the discovery made afterwards. There is then nothing to shock us, while the discovery produces a startling effect. The last case is the best, as when in the *Cresphontes* Merope [4] is about to slay her son, but recognising who he is, spares his life. So in the *Iphigenia*,[5] the sister recognises the brother just in time. Again in the *Helle*, the son recognises the mother when on the point of giving her up. This, then, is why a few families only, as has been already observed, furnish the subjects of tragedy. It was not art, but happy chance, that led the poets in search of subjects to impress the tragic quality upon their plots. They are compelled, therefore, to have recourse to those houses whose history contains moving incidents like these.

Enough has now been said concerning the structure of the incidents, and the right kind of plot.

In respect of character there are four things to be aimed at. First, and most important, it must be good. Now any speech or action that manifests moral purpose of any kind will be expressive of character: the character will be good if the purpose is good. This rule is relative to each class. Even a woman may be good, and also a slave; though the woman may be said to be an inferior being, and the slave quite worthless. The second thing to aim at is propriety. There is a type of manly valor; but valor in a woman, or unscrupulous cleverness, is inappropriate. Thirdly, the character must be true to life: for this is a distinct thing from goodness and propriety, as here described. The fourth point is consistency: for though the subject of the imitation, who suggested the type, be inconsistent, still he must be consistently inconsistent. As an example of motiveless degradation of character, we have Menelaus in the *Orestes*:[1] of character indecorous and inappropriate, the lament of Odysseus in the Scylla, and the speech of Melanippe: of inconsistency, the *Iphigenia at Aulis*[1] — for Iphigenia the suppliant in no way resembles her later self.

As in the structure of the plot, so too in the portraiture of character, the poet should always aim either at the necessary or the probable. Thus a person of a given character should speak or act in a given way, by the rule either of necessity or of probability; just as this event should follow that by necessary or probable sequence. It is therefore evident that the unravelling of the plot, no less than the complication, must arise out of the plot itself, it must not be brought about by the *Deus ex Machina* — as in the *Medea*, or in the Return of the Greeks in the *Iliad*. The *Deus ex Machina* should be employed only for events external to the drama, — for antecedent or subsequent events, which lie beyond the range of human knowledge, and which require to be reported or foretold; for to the gods we ascribe the power of seeing all things. Within the action there must be nothing irrational. If the irrational cannot be excluded, it should be

---

[1] Alcmæon killed his mother Eriphyle because of her treachery toward his father.

[2] See the *Medea* by Euripides.

[3] A tragedy by Sophocles.

[4] Merope, widow of King Cresphontes of Messina, nearly killed her third son, Æpytus while, disguised, he was attempting to revenge himself on his father's murderer.   [5] A play by Euripides.

[1] A play by Euripides.

outside the scope of the tragedy. Such is the irrational element in the *Œdipus* of Sophocles.

Again, since Tragedy is an imitation of persons who are above the common level, the example of good portrait-painters should be followed. They, while reproducing the distinctive form of the original, make a likeness which is true to life and yet more beautiful. So too the poet, in representing men who are irascible or indolent, or have other defects of character, should preserve the type and yet ennoble it. In this way Achilles is portrayed by Agathon and Homer.

Theocritus · c. 270 B.C.

Very few facts in the life of Theocritus are clearly established. Born in Syracuse, in Sicily, he arrived at distinction as a poet while resident in Alexandria on the banks of the Nile (*c.* 270 B.C.) where he lived for some time under the patronage of King Ptolemy Philadelphus.

The author of many poems which idealized the simple life of the countryside, Theocritus is often called the father of pastoral poetry, his pleasant sketches of rural life being variously termed "bucolics," "pastorals," "idylls." Many of these pastorals present vignettes of rural life in Sicily, poems which are clearly tempered by the idealization with which residents of cities are likely to endow country life. They are often marked by a strong pictorial quality. Frequent subjects are the loves of shepherds and shepherdesses, gods and goddesses, and the joys of nature.

The pastoral form used successfully by Theocritus and later by Virgil and others eventually became conventionalized, particularly during the Renaissance. Of many imitators few were able to mould the form to their own uses as was Spenser in the *Shepherd's Calendar* or Milton in *Lycidas*. In the pastorals may be found both romantic and realistic qualities, the romantic idealization, for instance, of *Daphnis and Menalcas* below, or the realistic detail of the two women at the festival of Adonis, but the pastoral as a type gradually assumed a conventional pattern as to language and subject matter, and became so formal, so polished, that writers essentially classical in temper used it as a medium of expression.

The following selections from *Theocritus, Bion, and Moschus*, are translated by A. Lang and reprinted by permission of The Macmillan Company.

SUGGESTED REFERENCE: A. S. Gow, *The Greek Bucolic Poets* (1953).

Epigrams

FOR A HERDSMAN'S OFFERING

Daphnis, the white-limbed Daphnis, that pipes on his fair flute the pastoral strains offered to Pan these gifts, — his pierced reed-pipes, his crook, a javelin keen, a fawn-skin, and the scrip wherein he was wont, on a time, to carry the apples of Love.

FOR A PICTURE

Thou sleepest on the leaf-strewn ground, oh Daphnis, resting thy weary limbs, and the stakes of thy nets are newly fastened on the hills. But Pan is on thy track, and Priapus, with the golden ivy wreath twined round his winsome head, — both are leaping at one bound into thy cavern. Nay, flee them, flee, shake off thy slumber, shake off the heavy sleep that is falling upon thee.

Daphnis and Menalcas

The scene is among the high mountain pastures of Sicily: "On the sward, at the cliff top lie strewn the white flocks"; and far below shines and murmurs the Sicilian sea. Here Daphnis and Menalcas, two herdsmen of the golden age, meet, while still in their earliest youth, and contend for the prize of pastoral. Their songs, in elegiac measure, are variations on the themes of love and friendship (for Menalcas sings of Milon, Daphnis of Nais), and of nature. Daphnis is the winner; it is his earliest victory, and the prelude to his great renown. . . .

As beautiful Daphnis was following his kine, and Menalcas shepherding his flock, they met, as men tell, on the long ranges of the hills. The beards of both had still the first golden bloom, both were in their earliest youth, both were pipe-players skilled, both skilled in song. Then first Menalcas, looking at Daphnis, thus bespoke him.

"Daphnis, thou herdsman of the lowing kine, art thou minded to sing a match with me? Methinks I shall vanquish thee, when I sing in turn, as readily as I please."

Then Daphnis answered him again in this wise, "Thou shepherd of the fleecy sheep, Menalcas, the pipe-player, never wilt thou vanquish me in song, not thou, if thou shouldst sing till some evil thing befall thee!"

Menalcas. Dost thou care then, to try this and see, dost thou care to risk a stake?

Daphnis. I do care to try this and see, a stake I am ready to risk.

Menalcas. But what shall we stake, what pledge shall we find equal and sufficient?

Daphnis. I will pledge a calf, and do thou put down a lamb, one that has grown to his mother's height.

Menalcas. Nay, never will I stake a lamb, for stern is my father, and stern my mother, and they number all the sheep at evening.

Daphnis. But what, then, wilt thou lay, and where is to be the victor's gain?

Menalcas. The pipe, the fair pipe with nine stops, that I made myself, fitted with white wax, and smoothed evenly, above as below. This would I readily wager, but never will I stake aught that is my father's.

Daphnis. See then, I too, in truth, have a pipe with nine stops, fitted with white wax, and smoothed evenly, above as below. But lately I put it together, and this finger still aches, where the reed split, and cut it deeply.

Menalcas. But who is to judge between us, who will listen to our singing?

Daphnis. That goatherd yonder, he will do, if we call him hither, the man for whom that dog, a black hound with a white patch, is barking among the kids.

Then the boys called aloud, and the goatherd gave ear, and came, and the boys began to sing, and the goatherd was willing to be their umpire. And first Menalcas sang (for he drew the lot), the sweet-voiced Menalcas, and Daphnis took up the answering strain of pastoral song — and 'twas thus Menalcas began:

Menalcas. Ye glades, ye rivers, issue of the Gods, if ever Menalcas the flute-player sang a song ye loved, to please him, feed his lambs; and if ever Daphnis come hither with his calves, may he have no less a boon.

Daphnis. Ye wells and pastures, sweet growth o' the world, if Daphnis sings like the nightingales, do ye fatten this herd of his, and if Menalcas hither lead a flock, may he too have pasture ungrudging to his full desire!

Menalcas. There doth the ewe bear twins, and there the goats; there the bees fill the hives, and there oaks grow loftier than common, wheresoever beautiful Milon's feet walk wandering; ah, if he depart, then withered and lean is the shepherd, and lean the pastures!

Daphnis. Everywhere is spring, and pastures everywhere, and everywhere the cows' udders are swollen with milk, and the younglings are fostered, wheresoever fair Nais roams; ah, if she depart, then parched are the kine, and he that feeds them!

Menalcas. O bearded goat, thou mate of the white herd, and O ye blunt-faced kids, where are the manifold deeps of the forest, thither get ye to the water, for thereby is Milon; go, thou hornless goat, and say to him, "Milon, Proteus[1] was a herdsman, and that of seals, though he was a god."

Daphnis. . . . .

Menalcas. Not mine be the land of Pelops, not mine to own talents of gold, nay, nor mine to outrun the speed of the winds! Nay, but beneath this rock will I sing, with thee in mine arms, and watch our flocks feeding together, and, before us, the Sicilian sea.

Daphnis. . . . .

Menalcas. . . . .

Daphnis. Tempest is the dread pest of the trees, drought of the waters, snares of the birds, and the hunter's net of the wild beasts, but ruinous to man is the love of a delicate maiden. O father, O Zeus, I have not been the only lover, thou too hast longed for a mortal woman.

Thus the boys sang in verses amœbæan,[2] and thus Menalcas began the crowning lay:

Menalcas. Wolf, spare the kids, spare the mothers of my herd, and harm not me, so young as I am to tend so great a flock. Ah, Lampurus, my dog, dost thou then sleep so soundly? A dog should not sleep so sound, that helps a boyish shepherd. Ewes of mine, spare ye not to take your fill of the tender herb, ye shall not weary, 'ere all this grass grows again. Hist, feed on, feed on, fill, all of you, your udders, that there may be milk for the lambs, and somewhat for me to store away in the cheese-crates.

Then Daphnis followed again, and sweetly preluded to his singing:

Daphnis. Me, even me, from the cave, the girl with meeting eyebrows spied yesterday as I was

[1] An attendant of Neptune, god of the sea.
[2] A class of odes characterized by the presence of dialogue; from the Greek word meaning "to exchange." See Horace, *The Reconciliation* for an example.

driving past my calves, and she cried, "How fair, how fair he is!" But I answered her never the word of railing, but cast down my eyes, and plodded on my way.

Sweet is the voice of the heifer, sweet her breath, sweet to lie beneath the sky in summer, by running water.

Acorns are the pride of the oak, apples of the apple tree, the calf of the heifer, and the neatherd glories in his kine.

So sang the lads, and the goatherd thus bespoke them, "Sweet is thy mouth, O Daphnis, and delectable thy song! Better is it to listen to thy singing, than to taste the honeycomb. Take thou the pipe, for thou hast conquered in the singing match. Ah, if thou wilt but teach some lay, even to me, as I tend the goats beside thee, this blunt-horned she-goat will I give thee, for the price of thy teaching, this she-goat that ever fills the milking pail above the brim."

Then was the boy as glad,— and leaped high, and clapped his hands over his victory,— as a young fawn leaps about his mother. But the heart of the other was wasted with grief, and desolate, even as a maiden sorrows that is newly wed.

From this time Daphnis became the foremost among the shepherds, and while yet in his earliest youth, he wedded the nymph Nais.

At the Festival of Adonis

This famous idyl should rather, perhaps, be called a mimus. *It describes the visit paid by two Syracusan women residing in Alexandria, to the festival of the resurrection of Adonis. The festival is given by Arsinoë, wife and sister of Ptolemy Philadelphus, and the poem cannot have been written earlier than his marriage, in 266* B.C.? *Nothing can be more gay and natural than the chatter of the women, which has changed no more in two thousand years than the song of the birds. . . .*

Gorgo. Is Praxinoë at home?

Praxinoë. Dear Gorgo, how long it is since you have been here! She *is* at home. The wonder is that you have got here at last! Eunoë, see that she has a chair. Throw a cushion on it too.

Gorgo. It does most charmingly as it is.

Praxinoë. Do sit down.

Gorgo. Oh, what a thing spirit is! I have scarcely got to you alive, Praxinoë! What a huge crowd, what hosts of four-in-hands! Everywhere cavalry boots, everywhere men in uniform! And the road is endless: yes, you really live *too* far away!

Praxinoë. It is all the fault of that madman of mine. Here he came to the ends of the earth and took — a hole, not a house, and all that we might not be neighbors. The jealous wretch, always the same, ever for spite!

Gorgo. Don't talk of your husband, Dinon, like that, my dear girl, before the little boy, — look how he is staring at you! Never mind, Zopyrion, sweet child, she is not speaking about papa.

Praxinoë. Our Lady! the child takes notice.

Gorgo. Nice papa!

Praxinoë. That papa of his the other day — we call every day "the other day" — went to get soap and rouge at the shop, and back he came to me with salt — the great big endless fellow!

Gorgo. Mine has the same trick, too, a perfect spendthrift — Diocleides! Yesterday he got what he meant for five fleeces, and paid seven shillings a piece for — what do you suppose? — dog-skins, shreds of old leather wallets, mere trash — trouble on trouble. But come, take your cloak and shawl. Let us be off to the rich Ptolemy, the King, to see the Adonis; I hear the Queen has provided something splendid!

Praxinoë. Fine folks do everything finely.

Gorgo. What a tale you will have to tell about the things you have seen, to anyone who has not seen them! It seems nearly time to go.

Praxinoë. Idlers have always holiday. Eunoë, bring the water and put it down in the middle of the room, lazy creature that you are. Cats like always to sleep soft! Come, bustle, bring the water; quicker. I want water first, and how she carries it! give it me all the same; don't pour out so much, you extravagant thing. Stupid girl! Why are you wetting my dress? There, stop, I have washed my hands, as heaven would have it. Where is the key of the big chest? Bring it here.

Gorgo. Praxinoë, that full body becomes you wonderfully. Tell me how much did the stuff cost you just off the loom?

Praxinoë. Don't speak of it, Gorgo! More than eight pounds in good silver money, — and the work on it! I nearly slaved my soul out over it!

Gorgo. Well, it is *most* successful; all you could wish.

Praxinoë. Thanks for the pretty speech! Bring my shawl, and set my hat on my head, the fashionable way. No, child, I don't mean to bite. Boo! Bogies! There's a horse that bites! Cry as much as you please, but I cannot have you lamed. Let us be moving. Phrygia, take the child, and keep him amused, call in the dog, and shut the street door. *(They go into the street.)*

Ye gods, what a crowd! How on earth are we

ever to get through this coil? They are like ants that no one can measure or number. Many a good deed have you done, Ptolemy; since your father joined the immortals, there's never a male-factor to spoil the passer-by, creeping on him in Egyptian fashion — oh! the tricks those perfect rascals used to play. Birds of a feather, ill jesters, scoundrels all! Dear Gorgo, what will become of us? Here come the King's war-horses! My dear man, don't trample on me. Look, the bay's rear-ing, see, what temper! Eunoë, you foolhardy girl, will you never keep out of the way? The beast will kill the man that's leading him. What a good thing it is for me that my brat stays safe at home.

Gorgo. Courage, Praxinoë. We are safe behind them, now, and they have gone to their station.

Praxinoë. There! I begin to be myself again. Ever since I was a child I have feared nothing so much as horses and the chilly snake. Come along, the huge mob is overflowing us.

Gorgo (to an Old Woman). Are you from the Court, mother?

Old Woman. I am, my child.

Praxinoë. Is it easy to get there?

Old Woman. The Achæans got into Troy by trying, my prettiest of ladies. Trying will do everything in the long run.

Gorgo. The old wife has spoken her oracles, and off she goes.

Praxinoë. Women know everything, yes, and how Zeus married Hera!

Gorgo. See, Praxinoë, what a crowd there is about the doors.

Praxinoë. Monstrous, Gorgo! Give me your hand, and you, Eunoë, catch hold of Eutychis; never lose hold of her, for fear lest you get lost. Let us all go in together; Eunoë, clutch tight to me. Oh, how tiresome, Gorgo, my muslin skirt is torn in two already! For heaven's sake, sir, if you ever wish to take care of my shawl!

Stranger. I can hardly help myself, but for all that I will be as careful as I can.

Praxinoë. How close-packed the mob is, they hustle like a herd of swine!

Stranger. Courage, lady, all is well with us now.

Praxinoë. Both this year and for ever may all be well with you, my dear sir, for your care of us. A good kind man! We're letting Eunoë get squeezed — come, wretched girl, push your way through. That is the way. We are all on the right side of the door, quoth the bridegroom, when he shut himself in with his bride.

Gorgo. Do come here, Praxinoë. Look first at these embroideries. How light and how lovely! You will call them the garments of the gods.

Praxinoë. Lady Athene, what spinning women wrought them, what painters designed these draw-ings, so true they are? How naturally they stand and move, like living creatures, not patterns woven. What a clever thing is man! Ah, and himself — Adonis [1] — how beautiful to behold he lies on his silver couch, with the first down on his cheeks, the thrice-beloved Adonis, — Adonis beloved even among the dead.

A Stranger. You weariful women, do cease your endless cooing talk! They bore one to death with their eternal broad vowels!

Gorgo. Indeed! And where may this person come from? What is it to you if we *are* chatter-boxes! Give orders to your own servants, sir. Do you pretend to command ladies of Syracuse? If you must know, we are Corinthians by descent, like Bellerophon [2] himself, and we speak Pelopon-nesian. Dorian women may lawfully speak Doric, I presume?

Praxinoë. Lady Persephone, never may we have more than one master. I am not afraid of *your* putting me on short commons.

Gorgo. Hush, hush, Praxinoë — the Argive woman's daughter, the great singer, is beginning the *Adonis;* she that won the prize last year for dirge-singing. I am sure she will give us some-thing lovely; see, she is (preluding) commencing with her airs and graces.

The Cyclops in Love

Nicias, the physician and poet, being in love, Theo-critus reminds him that in song lies the only remedy. It was by song, he says, that the Cy-clops, Polyphemus, got him some ease, when he was in love with Galatea, the sea-nymph.

The idyl displays, in the most graceful manner, the Alexandrian taste for turning Greek mythology into love stories. No creature could be more remote from love than the original Polyphemus, the cannibal giant of the Odyssey.

There is none other medicine, Nicias, against Love, neither unguent, methinks, nor salve to sprinkle — none, save the Muses of Pieria! [3] Now

[1] A young and attractive shepherd beloved by Venus. After his death he lived half the year on earth and the other half-year Venus was permitted to visit him in the Underworld where he was, thus, "beloved even among the dead."

[2] A hero who rode Pegasus in a fight against Chimæra, a monster. Like Hercules, he performed a series of heroic acts.

[3] The nine muses were born on the Pierian mountains in Macedonia.

a delicate thing is their minstrelsy in man's life, and a sweet, but hard to procure. Methinks thou know'st this well, who art thyself a leech, and beyond all men art plainly dear to the Muses nine.

'Twas surely thus the Cyclops fleeted his life most easily, he that dwelt among us — Polyphemus[1] of old time — when the beard was yet young on his cheek and chin; and he loved Galatea[2] He loved, not with apples, not roses, nor locks of hair, but with fatal frenzy, and all things else he held but trifles by the way. Many a time from the green pastures would his ewes stray back, self-shepherded, to the fold. But he was singing of Galatea, and pining in his place he sat by the seaweed of the beach, from the dawn of day, with the direst hurt beneath his breast of mighty Cypris's[3] sending — the wound of her arrow in his heart!

Yet this remedy he found, and sitting on the crest of the tall cliff, and looking to the deep, 'twas thus he would sing:

Song of the Cyclops

O milk-white Galatea, why cast off him that loves thee? More white than is pressed milk to look upon, more delicate than the lamb art thou, than the young calf wantoner, more sleek than the unripened grape! Here dost thou resort, even so, when sweet sleep possesses me, and home straightway dost thou depart when sweet sleep lets me go, fleeing me like an ewe that has seen the grey wolf.

I fell in love with thee, maiden, I, on the day when first thou camest, with my mother, and didst wish to pluck the hyacinths from the hill, and I was thy guide on the way. But to leave loving thee, when once I had seen thee, neither afterward, nor now at all, have I the strength, even from that hour. But to thee all this is as nothing, by Zeus, nay, nothing at all!

I know, thou gracious maiden, why it is that thou dost shun me. It is all for the shaggy brow that spans all my forehead, from this to the other ear, one long unbroken eyebrow. And but one eye is on my forehead, and broad is the nose that overhangs my lip. Yet I (even such as thou seest me) feed a thousand cattle, and from these I draw and drink the best milk in the world. And cheese I never lack, in summer time or autumn,

nay, nor in the dead of winter, but my baskets are always overladen.

Also I am skilled in piping, as none other of the Cyclopes here, and of thee, my love, my sweet-apple, and of myself too I sing, many a time, deep in the night. And for thee I tend eleven fawns, all crescent-browed, and four young whelps of the bear.

Nay, come thou to me, and thou shalt lack nothing that now thou hast. Leave the grey sea to roll against the land; more sweetly, in this cavern, shalt thou fleet the night with me! Thereby the laurels grow, and there the slender cypresses, there is the ivy dun, and the sweet clustered grapes; there is chill water, that for me deep-wooded Ætna[1] sends down from the white snow, a draught divine! Ah who, in place of these, would choose the sea to dwell in, or the waves of the sea?

But if thou dost refuse because my body seems shaggy and rough, well, I have faggots of oakwood, and beneath the ashes is fire unwearied, and I would endure to let thee burn my very soul, and this my one eye, the dearest thing that is mine.

Ah me, that my mother bore me not a finny thing, so would I have gone down to thee, and kissed thy hand, if thy lips thou would not suffer me to kiss! And I would have brought thee either white lilies, or the soft poppy with its scarlet petals. Nay, these are summer's flowers, and those are flowers of winter, so I could not have brought thee them all at one time.

Now, verily, maiden, now and here will I learn to swim, if perchance some stranger come hither, sailing with his ship, that I may see why it is so dear to thee, to have thy dwelling in the deep.

Come forth, Galatea, and forget as thou comest, even as I that sit here have forgotten, the homeward way! Nay, choose with me to go shepherding, with me to milk the flocks, and to pour the sharp rennet[2] in, and to fix the cheeses.

There is none that wrongs me but that mother of mine, and her do I blame. Never, nay, never once has she spoken a kind word for me to thee, and that though day by day she beholds me wasting. I will tell her that my head, and both my feet are throbbing, that she may somewhat suffer, since I too am suffering.

O Cyclops, Cyclops, whither are thy wits wandering? Ah that thou wouldst go, and weave thy wicker-work, and gather broken boughs to carry to thy lambs: in faith, if thou didst this, far wiser wouldst thou be!

---

[1] Son of Neptune, a one-eyed giant later blinded by Ulysses. See Homer, Odyssey, Book ix.

[2] One of the fifty fair daughters of Nereus, a sea-deity. Her love for Acis was ruined by the unwelcome attention of the Cyclops Polyphemus.

[3] Aphrodite or Venus, goddess of love.

[1] In Sicily.

[2] Dried stomach of such animals as calf or sheep used to curdle milk.

Milk the ewe that thou hast, why pursue the thing that shuns thee? Thou wilt find, perchance, another, and a fairer Galatea. Many be the girls that bid me play with them through the night, and softly they all laugh, if perchance I answer them.

On land it is plain that I too seem to be somebody!

Lo, thus Polyphemus still shepherded his love with song, and lived lighter than if he had given 5 gold for ease.

Lucretius · 98–55 B.C.

Lucretius (Titus Lucretius Carus) was born in Rome about 98 B.C. According to a contemporary, though now generally discredited account, he died (in 55 B.C.) in a fit of madness brought on by a love potion administered by his wife. The fame of Lucretius — a fame which in the minds of some classical scholars ranks him second only to Virgil among the Latin poets — rests on his long work, *De Rerum Natura* (*On the Nature of Things*), a poem divided into six books setting forth the Epicurean doctrine of creation and man's place in nature. He was one of the first of great poets to turn to the problems of science.

Lucretius wrote according to classical conventions in that he respected form and balance, was restrained rather than emotional in his expression, and sought to edify his reader. However, his outlook on life was, at least partially, that of the scientist. In this sense it may be said that his writing is analytic, a quality which we associate with the realistic temper. In justification for his inclusion among the classicists it may be said that he was a classicist reaching out toward science but dominated by the conventions and attitudes of his time. The first line of the proem, which presents the invocation of the muse, is evidence enough that the classical pattern dominated this presentation of scientific thought in the first century B.C.

Lucretius lived and wrote at a time in Roman history which for a poet must have been both exciting and discouraging; exciting because the old Roman Republic was breaking down and the people were in the turmoil which resulted in the Civil Wars; and discouraging because old traditions were disappearing, society was in a state of unusual flux, the old religion was falling into disrepute, and it was a time of political action rather than of philosophic reflection. The years in which Lucretius lived were those which knew the marching and countermarching of Pompey and Crassus, Roman generals who, with Cæsar, formed the first triumvirate; his contemporaries included Cicero the orator and Cato the Younger, patriot and Stoic philosopher; and in 55 B.C., the year of Lucretius' death, Cæsar invaded England.

The period was one of skepticism; Lucretius wrote to give it confidence, particularly such confidence as might be secured from the Epicurean philosophy. When death came so quickly to many people, Lucretius would teach them that death was nothing more than a passing of atoms from one form into another and really need not be taken as a matter of concern, since

"no man wakes up
On whom falls the icy pause of life."

The major points in the Epicureanism he taught included belief that "from nothing nothing can be created" or, stated positively, that all nature consists of atoms and vacuum and that creation is simply a change from one form to another, that atomically nature does not change at all. The soul, too, he believed made up of atoms which are distributed throughout the human body and it is they which afford us our awareness. But there is another quality in our make-up, the mind, which he thought to be located in the breast of man. These atoms in our physical make-up — our "soul" as we please to call it — are sensitive receiving-agents constantly susceptible to the fine films which material objects are constantly giving off, films which are of the same nature as the solid objects themselves. We must, because our own atomic particles are of a piece with those external atoms, trust our senses implicitly. Even the gods, who lived apart from man, however, and showed no concern for human welfare, differed from man only in that they were composed of finer atoms. Lucretius believed, too, in an evolving society which, independent of divine help, has advanced from prehistoric times to higher levels of civilization.

One might think that poetry dedicated to the promulgation of scientific theories would be extremely dull, but Lucretius, because of his intense sympathy with man and his keen feeling for the tragedy of life and the beauties of nature, often raises philosophical ideas to the level of highest poetry.

Probably the most effective translation into English is that by William Ellery Leonard in the *Everyman's Library*. This version is used through the courtesy of the E. P. Dutton Company.

SUGGESTED REFERENCES: E. E. Sikes, *Lucretius, Poet and Philosopher* (1936); Henri Bergson, *The Philosophy of Poetry: The Genius of Lucretius* (1959).

On the Nature of Things

PROEM

(From Book I)

Mother of Rome,[1] delight of Gods and men,
Dear Venus that beneath the gliding stars
Makest to teem the many-voyagèd main
And fruitful lands — for all of living things
Through thee alone are evermore conceived,   5
Through thee are risen to visit the great sun —
Before thee, Goddess, and thy coming on,
Flee stormy wind and massy cloud away,
For thee the dædal [2] Earth bears scented flowers,
For thee the waters of the unvexèd deep   10
Smile, and the hollows of the sérene sky
Glow with diffusèd radiance for thee!
For soon as comes the springtime face of day,
And procreant [3] gales blow from the West unbarred,
First fowls of air, smit to the heart by thee,   15
Foretoken thy approach, O thou Divine,
And leap the wild herds round the happy fields
Or swim the bounding torrents. Thus amain,
Seized with the spell, all creatures follow thee
Whithersoever thou walkest forth to lead,   20
And thence through seas and mountains and swift
      streams,

Through leafy homes of birds and greening plains,
Kindling the lure of love in every breast,
Thou bringest the eternal generations forth,
Kind after kind. And since 'tis thou alone   25
Guidest the Cosmos,[1] and without thee naught
Is risen to reach the shining shores of light,
Nor aught of joyful or of lovely born,
Thee do I crave co-partner in that verse
Which I presume on Nature to compose   30
For Memmius mine,[2] whom thou hast willed to be
Peerless in every grace at every hour —
Wherefore indeed, Divine one, give my words
Immortal charm. Lull to a timely rest
O'er sea and land the savage works of war,   35
For thou alone hast power with public peace
To aid mortality; since he who rules
The savage works of battle, puissant Mars,[3]
How often to thy bosom flings his strength
O'ermastered by the eternal wound of love —   40
And there, with eyes and full throat backward
      thrown,
Gazing, my Goddess, open-mouthed at thee,
Pastures on love his greedy sight, his breath
Hanging upon thy lips. Him thus reclined
Fill with thy holy body, round, above!   45
Pour from those lips soft syllables to win
Peace for the Romans, glorious Lady, peace!
For in a season troublous to the state [4]
Neither may I attend this task of mine
With thought untroubled, nor mid such events   50
The illustrious scion of the Memmian house

[1] Despite his conviction that the gods were indifferent to the welfare of mortals, Lucretius here invokes the aid of Venus as "co-partner" in his verse. This may be because the classical convention of bespeaking the aid of the gods is stronger than his personal philosophic conviction. By referring to Venus as the "Mother of Rome" Lucretius, like Virgil and Ovid later on, credits the founding of Rome to Æneas, the son of Venus by Anchises.

[2] Ingeniously wrought, intricately planned. Dædalus constructed the labyrinth for King Minos of Crete.

[3] Generating, fruitful.

[1] The ordered universe.

[2] The poem is addressed to C. Memmius, a Roman aristocrat, a learned but rather ineffective contemporary of the poet.

[3] God of war.

[4] A reference to the troublous state of Rome. The Republic was failing and the Civil Wars about to begin.

Neglect the civic cause.
                    Whilst human kind
Throughout the lands lay miserably crushed
Before all eyes beneath Religion [1] — who
Would show her head along the region skies,   55
Glowering on mortals with her hideous face —
A Greek it was who first opposing dared
Raise mortal eyes that terror to withstand,
Whom nor the fame of Gods nor lightning's stroke
Nor threatening thunder of the ominous sky   60
Abashed; but rather chafed to angry zest
His dauntless heart to be the first to rend
The crossbars at the gates of Nature old.
And thus his will and hardy wisdom won;
And forward thus he fared afar, beyond   65
The flaming ramparts of the world, until
He wandered the unmeasurable All.[2]
Whence he to us, a conqueror, reports
What things can rise to being,[3] what cannot,
And by what law to each its scope prescribed,   70
Its boundary stone that clings so deep in Time.
Wherefore religion now is under foot,
And us his victory now exalts to heaven.

I know how hard it is in Latian verse
To tell the dark discoveries of the Greeks,[4]   75
Chiefly because our pauper-speech [5] must find
Strange terms to fit the strangeness of the thing;
Yet worth of thine [6] and the expected joy
Of thy sweet friendship do persuade me on   79
To bear all toil and wake the clear nights through,
Seeking with what of words and what of song
I may at last most gloriously uncloud
For thee the light beyond, wherewith to view
The core of being at the centre hid.
And for the rest, summon to judgments true.   85
Unbusied ears and singleness of mind
Withdrawn from cares; lest these my gifts, ar-
        ranged

[1] Lucretius here sees religion as the enemy of science. This passage is a tribute to "A Greek" — Epicurus — who dared to study nature even though his study made him discard the old gods as explanations of nature.
[2] This could be translated the "boundless whole." The reference is to the universe, without limits, not to be measured.
[3] Come into existence. The Epicurean doctrine taught that things could be created only from atoms in which were inherent the qualities of the thing itself. The spontaneous springing up of new forms was, thus, an impossibility.
[4] Greek learning and philosophy was comparatively new in Rome and the New Thought was, at the time Lucretius wrote, creating considerable furor.
[5] Impoverished language. The Roman language lacked scientific terms for the poet to use; he frequently created his own terminology.
[6] Memmius.

For thee with eager service, thou disdain
Before thou comprehendest: since for thee
I prove the súpreme law of Gods and sky,   90
And the primordial [1] germs of things unfold,
Whence Nature all creates, and multiplies
And fosters all, and whither she resolves
Each in the end when each is overthrown.
This ultimate stock we have devised to name   95
Procreant atoms, matter, seeds of things,
Or primal bodies,[2] as primal to the world.

I fear perhaps thou deemest that we fare
An impious road to realms of thought profane;
But 'tis that same religion oftener far   100
Hath bred the foul impieties of men:
As once at Aulis, the elected chiefs,
Foremost of heroes, Danaan counsellors,
Defiled Diana's altar, virgin queen,
With Agamemnon's daughter,[3] foully slain.   105
She felt the chaplet round her maiden locks
And fillets, fluttering down on either cheek,
And at the altar marked her grieving sire,
The priests beside him who concealed the knife,
And all the folk in tears at sight of her.   110
With a dumb terror and a sinking knee
She dropped; nor might avail her now that first
'Twas she who gave the king a father's name.
They raised her up, they bore the trembling girl
On to the altar — hither led not now   115
With solemn rites and hymeneal choir,
But sinless woman, sinfully foredone,
A parent felled her on her bridal day,
Making his child a sacrificial beast
To give the ships auspicious winds for Troy: 120
Such are the crimes to which religion leads.

And there shall come the time when even thou,[4]
Forced by the soothsayer's terror-tales, shalt
        seek
To break from us.   Ah, many a dream even now
Can they concoct to rout thy plans of life,   125
And trouble all thy fortunes with base fears.
I own with reason: for, if men but knew
Some fixèd end to ills, they would be strong
By some device unconquered to withstand
Religions and the menacings of seers.   130

[1] Original.
[2] The Epicurean doctrine assumes created matter and endows this matter with varying "seed" or "primal" qualities.   (See note 3 preceding.)
[3] This passage refers to the sacrifice Agamemnon made at Aulis when, upon the insistence of his Greek (Danaan) counsellors, he offered his daughter Iphigenia on Diana's altar as a sacrifice to propitiate the gods and bring favorable winds that the Greek fleet might sail for Troy.   See Euripides' *Iphigenia in Aulis* and Homer's *Iliad*.   This sort of cruelty in the old religion made Lucretius rebel.
[4] Lucretius continues to address Memmius.

But now nor skill nor instrument is theirs,
Since men must dread eternal pains in death.
For what the soul may be they do not know,
Whether 'tis born, or enter in at birth,
And whether, snatched by death, it die with us,
Or visit the shadows and the vasty caves   136
Of Orcus,[1] or by some divine decree
Enter the brute herds, as our Ennius[2] sang,
Who first from lovely Helicon[3] brought down
A laurel wreath of bright perennial leaves,   140
Renowned forever among the Italian clans.
Yet Ennius too in everlasting verse
Proclaims those vaults of Acheron[4] to be,
Though thence, he said, nor souls nor bodies fare,
But only phantom figures, strangely wan,   145
And tells how once from out those regions rose
Old Homer's[5] ghost to him and shed salt tears
And with his words unfolded Nature's source.
Then be it ours with steady mind to clasp
The purport of the skies — the law behind   150
The wandering courses of the sun and moon;
To scan the powers that speed all life below;
But most to see with reasonable eyes
Of what the mind, of what the soul is made,
And what it is so terrible that breaks   155
On us asleep, or waking in disease,
Until we seem to mark and hear at hand
Dead men whose bones earth bosomed long ago.

SUBSTANCE IS ETERNAL

(From Book I)

This terror, then, this darkness of the mind,
Not sunrise with its flaring spokes of light,
Nor glittering arrows of morning can disperse,
But only Nature's aspect and her law,
Which, teaching us, hath this exordium: 5
Nothing from nothing ever yet was born.[6]

[1] Another name for Pluto, ruler of the Underworld.
[2] Ennius, an early Latin poet of genius, lived about
one hundred years before Lucretius.
[3] The mountain of the Nine Muses.
[4] Acheron, the river of woe, was one of the boundaries
of Hades.
[5] Ennius was a Pythagorean and believed in the
transmigration of souls. He thought he was a reincar-
nation of Homer.
[6] A basic thesis in Epicurean doctrine. The poet goes
on to develop the idea in subsequent lines. (See fifth
paragraph in biographical statement, pages 180–181.)
The first beginning of nature is matter; this matter has
different qualities; all subsequent objects and life
spring from this source without the possibility of divine
or spontaneous creation. Everything in nature comes
from a "seed" inherent in the original supply of matter.
The idea is related to our "cause and effect" and "conservation of energy."

Fear holds dominion over mortality
Only because, seeing in land and sky
So much the cause whereof no wise they know,
Men think Divinities are working there.   10
Meantime, when once we know from nothing still
Nothing can be create, we shall divine
More clearly what we seek: those elements[1]
From which alone all things created are,
And how accomplished by no tool of Gods.   15
Suppose all sprang from all things: any kind
Might take its origin from any thing,
No fixèd seed required.   Men from the sea
Might rise,[2] and from the land the scaly breed,
And, fowl full fledged come bursting from the sky;
The hornèd cattle, the herds and all the wild   21
Would haunt with varying offspring tilth[3] and
        waste;
Nor would the same fruits keep their olden trees,
But each might grow from any stock or limb
By chance and change.   Indeed, and were there not
For each its procreant atoms, could things have   26
Each its unalterable mother old?
But, since produced from fixèd seeds are all,
Each birth goes forth upon the shores of light
From its own stuff, from its own primal bodies.   30
And all from all cannot become, because
In each resides a secret power its own.
Again, why see we lavished o'er the lands
At spring the rose, at summer heat the corn,
The vines that mellow when the autumn lures,   35
If not because the fixèd seeds of things
At their own season must together stream,
And new creations only be revealed
When the due times arrive and pregnant earth
Safely may give unto the shores of light   40
Her tender progenies?   But if from naught
Were their becoming, they would spring abroad
Suddenly, unforeseen, in alien months,
With no primordial germs, to be preserved
From procreant unions at an adverse hour.   45
Nor on the mingling of the living seeds
Would space be needed for the growth of things
Were life an increment of nothing: then
The tiny babe forthwith would walk a man,
And from the turf would leap a branching tree —
Wonders unheard of; for, by Nature, each   51
Slowly increases from its lawful seed,
And through that increase shall conserve its kind.
Whence take the proof that things enlarge and feed
From out their proper matter.   Thus it comes   55
That earth, without her seasons of fixed rains,
Could bear no produce such as makes us glad,

[1] Atoms, particles, "seed" — the idea is not entirely
foreign to the "elements" of the chemist.
[2] Modern science argues that just this happened.
[3] Cultivated land.

And whatsoever lives, if shut from food,
Prolongs its kind and guards its life no more.
Thus easier 'tis to hold that many things   60
Have primal bodies in common (as we see
The single letters common to many words)
Than aught exists without its origins.
Moreover, why should Nature not prepare
Men of a bulk to ford the seas afoot,   65
Or rend the mighty mountains with their hands,
Or conquer Time with length of days, if not
Because for all begotten things abides
The changeless stuff, and what from that may spring
Is fixed forevermore?   Lastly we see   70
How far the tilled surpass the fields untilled
And to the labor of our hands return
Their more abounding crops; there are indeed
Within the earth primordial germs of things,
Which, as the ploughshare turns the fruitful clods
And kneads the mould, we quicken into birth.   76
Else would ye mark, without all toil of ours,
Spontaneous generations, fairer forms.
Confess then, naught from nothing can become,
Since all must have their seeds, wherefrom to
              grow,   80
Wherefrom to reach the gentle fields of air.
    Hence too it comes that Nature all dissolves
Into their primal bodies again, and naught
Perishes ever to annihilation.[1]
For, were aught mortal in its every part,   85
Before our eyes it might be snatched away
Unto destruction; since no force were needed
To sunder its members and undo its bands.
Whereas, of truth, because all things exist,
With seed imperishable, Nature allows   90
Destruction nor collapse of aught, until
Some outward force may shatter by a blow,
Or inward craft, entering its hollow cells,
Dissolve it down.   And more than this, if Time,
That wastes with eld the works along the world,
Destroy entire, consuming matter all,   96
Whence then may Venus back to light of life
Restore the generations kind by kind?
Or how, when thus restored, may dædal Earth
Foster and plenish with her ancient food,   100
Which, kind by kind, she offers unto each?
Whence may the water-springs, beneath the sea,
Or inland rivers, far and wide away,
Keep the unfathomable ocean full?
And out of what does Ether[2] feed the stars?   105
For lapsèd years and infinite age must else

Have eat all shapes of mortal stock away:
But be it the Long Ago contained those germs,
By which this sum of things recruited lives,
Those same infallibly can never die,   110
Nor nothing to nothing evermore return.
And, too, the selfsame power might end alike
All things, were they not still together held
By matter eternal, shackled through its parts,
Now more, now less. A touch might be enough   115
To cause destruction.   For the slightest force
Would loose the weft[1] of things wherein no part
Were of imperishable stock.   But now
Because the fastenings of primordial parts
Are put together diversly and stuff   120
Is everlasting, things abide the same
Unhurt and sure, until some power comes on
Strong to destroy the warp and woof of each:
Nothing returns to naught; but all return
At their collapse to primal forms of stuff.[2]   125
Lo, the rains perish which Ether-father throws
Down to the bosom of Earth-mother; but then
Upsprings the shining grain, and boughs are green
Amid the trees, and trees themselves wax big
And lade[3] themselves with fruits; and hence in
              turn   130
The race of man and all the wild are fed;
Hence joyful cities thrive with boys and girls;
And leafy woodlands echo with new birds;
Hence cattle, fat and drowsy, lay their bulk
Along the joyous pastures whilst the drops   135
Of white ooze trickle from distended bags;
Hence the young scamper on their weakling joints
Along the tender herbs, fresh hearts afrisk
With warm new milk.   Thus naught of what so
              seems
Perishes utterly, since Nature ever   140
Upbuilds one thing from other, suffering naught
To come to birth but through some other's death.

THE SOUL IS MORTAL
(From Book III)

Now come: that thou mayst able be to know
That minds and the light souls of all that live
Have mortal birth and death, I will go on
Verses to build meet for thy rule of life,
Sought after long, discovered with sweet toil.   5
But under one name I'd have thee yoke them both;
And when, for instance, I shall speak of soul,
Teaching the same to be but mortal, think
Thereby I'm speaking also of the mind —

[1] As matter cannot be brought into being by spontaneous creation so, too, matter cannot be destroyed: it simply changes its outward form.

[2] Light.   Ancient mythology used Æther in the sense of light or sky.   This is not a foreknowledge of "ether."

[1] The woof — threads thrown through the warp in weaving.

[2] To their original atomic form.

[3] load.

Since both are one, a substance inter-joined.[1] 10
First, then, since I have taught how soul exists
A subtle fabric, of particles minute,
Made up from atoms smaller much than those
Of water's liquid damp, or fog, or smoke,
So in mobility it far excels,   15
More prone to move, though strook by lighter
        cause,
Even moved by images of smoke or fog —
As where we view, when in our sleeps we're lulled,
The altars exhaling steam and smoke aloft —
For, beyond doubt, these apparitions come   20
To us from outward. Now, then, since thou seest,
Their liquids depart, their waters flow away,
When jars are shivered, and since fog and smoke
Depart into the winds away, believe
The soul no less is shed abroad and dies   25
More quickly far, more quickly is dissolved
Back to its primal bodies, when withdrawn
From out man's members it has gone away.
For, sure, if body (container of the same
Like as a jar), when shivered from some cause, 30
And rarefied by loss of blood from veins,
Cannot for longer hold the soul, how then
Thinkst thou it can be held by any air —
A stuff much rarer than our bodies be?

Besides we feel that mind to being comes   35
Along with body, with body grows and ages.
For just as children totter round about
With frames infirm and tender, so there follows
A weakling wisdom in their minds; and then,
Where years have ripened into robust powers,   40
Counsel is also greater, more increased
The power of mind; thereafter, where already
The body's shattered by master-powers of eld,
And fallen the frame with its enfeebled powers,
Thought hobbles, tongue wanders, and the mind
        gives way;   45
All fails, all's lacking at the selfsame time.
Therefore it suits that even the soul's dissolved,
Like smoke, into the lofty winds of air;
Since we behold the same to being come
Along with body and grow, and, as I've taught, 50
Crumble and crack, therewith outworn by eld.

FOLLY OF THE FEAR OF DEATH
(From Book III)

                    Therefore death to us
Is nothing, nor concerns us in the least,
Since nature of mind is mortal evermore.
And just as in the ages gone before
We felt no touch of ill, when all sides round   5

[1] See fifth paragraph in biographical statement.

To battle came the Carthaginian [1] host,
And the times, shaken by tumultuous war,
Under the aery coasts of arching heaven
Shuddered and trembled, and all humankind
Doubted to which the empery [2] should fall   10
By land and sea, thus when we are no more,
When comes that sundering of our body and soul
Through which we're fashioned to a single state,
Verily naught to us, us then no more,
Can come to pass, naught move our senses then —
No, not if earth confounded were with sea,   16
And sea with heaven. But if indeed do feel
The nature of mind and energy of soul,
After their severance from this body of ours,
Yet nothing 'tis to us who in the bonds   20
And wedlock of the soul and body live,
Through which we're fashioned to a single state.
And, even if time collected after death
The matter of our frames and set it all
Again in place as now, and if again   25
To us the light of life were given, O yet
That process too would not concern us aught,
When once the self-succession of our sense
Has been asunder broken. And now and here,
Little enough we're busied with the selves   30
We were aforetime, nor, concerning them,
Suffer a sore distress. For shouldst thou gaze
Backwards across all yesterdays of time
The immeasurable, thinking how manifold
The motions of matter are, then couldst thou well
Credit this too: often these very seeds   36
(From which we are to-day) of old were set
In the same order as they are to-day —
Yet this we can't to consciousness recall
Through the remembering mind. For there hath
        been   40
An interposèd pause of life, and wide
Have all the motions wandered everywhere
From these our senses. For if woe and ail
Perchance are toward,[3] then the man to whom
The bane can happen must himself be there —   45
At that same time. But death precluded this,
Forbidding life to him on whom might crowd
Such irk and care; and granted 'tis to know:
Nothing for us there is to dread in death,
No wretchedness for him who is no more,   50
The same estate as if ne'er born before,
When death immortal hath ta'en the mortal life.
Hence, where thou seest a man to grieve because
When dead he rots with body laid away,

[1] A reference to the three "Punic Wars" in which
Rome and Carthage had engaged between 265 and
146 B.C. In 146 the city of Carthage was razed by the
Roman forces.
[2] authority, sovereignty.
[3] near, at hand.

Or perishes in flames or jaws of beasts,   55
Know well: he rings not true, and that beneath
Still works an unseen sting upon his heart,
However he deny that he believes
His shall be aught of feeling after death.
For he, I fancy, grants not what he says,   60
Nor what that presupposes, and he fails
To pluck himself with all his roots from life
And cast that self away, quite unawares
Feigning that some remainder's left behind.
For when in life one pictures to oneself   65
His body dead by beasts and vultures torn,
He pities his state, dividing not himself
Therefrom, removing not the self enough
From the body flung away, imagining
Himself that body, and projecting there   70
His own sense, as he stands beside it: hence
He grieves that he is mortal born, nor marks
That in true death there is no second self
Alive and able to sorrow for self destroyed,
Or stand lamenting that the self lies there   75
Mangled or burning.   For if it an evil is
Dead to be jerked about by jaw and fang
Of the wild brutes, I see not why 'twere not
Bitter to lie on fires and roast in flames,
Or suffocate in honey, and, reclined   80
On the smooth oblong of an icy slab,
Grow stiff in cold, or sink with load of earth
Down-crushing from above.
                         "Thee now no more
The joyful house and best of wives shall welcome,
Nor little sons run up to snatch their kisses   85
And touch with silent happiness thy heart.
Thou shalt not speed in undertakings more,
Nor be the warder of thine own no more.
Poor wretch," they say, "one hostile hour hath
          ta'en
Wretchedly from thee all life's many guerdons,"   90
But add not, "yet no longer unto thee
Remains a remnant of desire for them."
If this they only well perceived with mind
And followed up with maxims, they would free
Their state of man from anguish and from fear.   95
"O even as here thou art, aslumber in death,
So shalt thou slumber down the rest of time,
Released from every harrying pang.   But we,
We have bewept thee with insatiate woe,
Standing beside whilst on the awful pyre   100
Thou wert made ashes; and no day shall take
For us the eternal sorrow from the breast."
But ask the mourner what's the bitterness
That man should waste in an eternal grief,
If, after all, the thing's but sleep and rest?   105
For when the soul and frame together are sunk
In slumber, no one then demands his self
Or being.   Well, this sleep may be forever,

Without desire of any selfhood more,
For all it matters unto us asleep.   110
Yet not at all do those primordial germs [1]
Roam round our members, at that time, afar
From their own motions that produce our senses —
Since, when he's startled from his sleep, a man
Collects his senses.   Death is, then, to us   115
Much less — if there can be a less than that
Which is itself a nothing: for there comes
Hard upon death a scattering more great
Of the throng of matter, and no man wakes up
On whom once falls the icy pause of life.   120
    This too, O often from the soul men say,
Along their couches holding of the cups,
With faces shaded by fresh wreaths awry:
"Brief is this fruit of joy to paltry man,
Soon, soon departed, and thereafter, no,   125
It may not be recalled." — As if, forsooth,
It were their prime of evils in great death
To parch, poor tongues, with thirst and arid
          drought,
Or chafe for any lack.
                              Once more, if Nature
Should of a sudden send a voice abroad,   130
And her own self inveigh against us so:
"Mortal, what hast thou of such grave concern
That thou indulgest in too sickly plaints?
Why this bemoaning and beweeping death?
For if thy life aforetime and behind   135
To thee was grateful, and not all thy good
Was heaped as in sieve to flow away
And perish unavailingly, why not,
Even like a banqueter, depart the halls,
Laden with life?   why not with mind content 140
Take now, thou fool, thy unafflicted rest?
But if whatever thou enjoyed hath been
Lavished and lost, and life is now offence,
Why seekest more to add — which in its turn
Will perish foully and fall out in vain?   145
O why not rather make an end of life,
Of labor?   For all I may devise or find
To pleasure thee is nothing: all things are
The same forever.   Though not yet thy body
Wrinkles with years, nor yet the frame exhausts
Outworn, still things abide the same, even if   151
Thou goest on to conquer all of time
With length of days, yea, if thou never diest" —
What were our answer, but that Nature here
Urges just suit and in her words lays down   155
True cause of action?   Yet should one complain.
Riper in years and elder, and lament,
Poor devil, his death more sorely than is fit,
Then would she not, with greater right, on him
Cry out, inveighing with a voice more shrill: 160
"Off with thy tears, and choke thy whines, buffoon!
    [1] The original atoms.

Thou wrinklest — after thou hast had the sum
Of the guerdons [1] of life; yet, since thou cravest
ever
What's not at hand, contemning present good,
That life has slipped away, unperfected   165
And unavailing unto thee. And now,
Or ere thou guessed it, death beside thy head
Stands — and before thou canst be going home
Sated and laden with the goodly feast.
But now yield all that's alien to thine age, —   170
Up, with good grace! make room for sons: thou
must."
Justly, I fancy, would she reason thus,
Justly inveigh and gird: since ever the old
Outcrowded by the new gives way, and ever
The one thing from the others is repaired.   175
Nor no man is consigned to the abyss
Of Tartarus,[2] the black. For stuff must be,
That thus the after-generations grow, —
Though these, their life completed, follow thee;
And thus like thee are generations all —   180
Already fallen, or some time to fall.
So one thing from another rises ever;
And in fee-simple life is given to none,
But unto all mere usufruct.[3]
                                    Look back:
Nothing to us was all fore-passèd eld   185
Of time the eternal, ere we had a birth.
And nature holds this like a mirror up
Of time-to-be when we are dead and gone.
And what is there so horrible appears?
Now what is there so sad about it all?   190
Is't not serener far than any sleep?

THE ORIGIN OF LIFE
(From Book V)

In the beginning, earth gave forth, around
The hills and over all the length of plains,
The race of grasses and the shining green;
The flowery meadows sparkled all aglow
With greening color, and thereafter, lo,   5
Unto the divers kinds of trees was given
An emulous [4] impulse mightily to shoot,
With a free rein, aloft into the air.
As feathers and hairs and bristles are begot
The first on members of the four-foot breeds   10

[1] Rewards or recompense.
[2] Gulf of Tartarus — in Hades. The spirits of evil-
doers were kept in Tartarus; those of the guiltless passed
on to the Elysian Fields. Lucretius is here telling us
there can be no Hades of temporary domicile for the
spirit since the atoms in our make-up are needed that
future generations may grow and flourish.
[3] The right to use temporarily.   [4] Eager in rivalry.

And on the bodies of the strong-y-winged,
Thus then the new Earth first of all put forth
Grasses and shrubs, and afterward begat
The mortal generations, there upsprung —
Innumerable in modes innumerable —   15
After diverging fashions. For from sky
These breathing-creatures never can have dropped,
Nor the land-dwellers ever have come up
Out of sea-pools of salt.[1] How true remains,
How merited is that adopted name   20
Of earth — "The Mother!" — since from out the
earth
Are all begotten. And even now arise
From out the loams how many living things —
Concreted by the rains and heat of the sun.
Wherefore 'tis less a marvel, if they sprang   25
In Long Ago more many, and more big,
Matured of those days in the fresh young years
Of earth and ether. First of all, the race
Of the wingèd ones and parti-colored birds,
Hatched out in spring-time, left their eggs behind;
As now-a-days in summer tree-crickets   31
Do leave their shiny husks of own accord,
Seeking their food and living. Then it was
This earth of thine first gave unto the day
The mortal generations; for prevailed   35
Among the fields abounding hot and wet.
And hence, where any fitting spot was given,
There 'gan to grow womb-cavities, by roots
Affixed to earth. And when in ripened time
The age of the young within (that sought the air
And fled earth's damps) had burst these wombs,
O then   41
Would Nature thither turn the pores of earth
And make her spurt from open veins a juice
Like unto milk; even as a woman now
Is filled, at child-bearing, with the sweet milk, 45
Because all that swift stream of aliment
Is thither turned unto the mother-breasts.
There earth would furnish to the children food;
Warmth was their swaddling cloth, the grass their
bed
Abounding in soft down. Earth's newness then   50
Would rouse no dour spells of the bitter cold,
Nor éxtreme heats nor winds of mighty powers [2] —
For all things grow and gather strength through
time

[1] Lucretius goes far afield from present day science
here. He is trying to account for animal life on earth
but all he can do is devise — some twenty lines farther
down — "womb-cavities" to account for this life.
These simply "'gan to grow"; how, why, when, he does
not say. But he does tell us where: "by roots affixed
to earth."
[2] This passage invites comparison with, say, Milton's
description of the Garden of Eden.

In like proportions; and then earth was young.
    Wherefore, again, again, how merited   55
Is that adopted name of Earth — the Mother! —
Since she herself begat the human race,
And at one well-nigh fixèd time brought forth
Each beast that ranges raving round about
Upon the mighty mountains and all birds   60
Aerial with many a varied shape.
But, lo, because her bearing years must end,
She ceased, like to a woman worn by eld.
For lapsing æons [1] change the nature of
The whole wide world, and all things needs must
    take   65
One status after other, nor aught persists
Forever like itself. All things depart;
Nature she changeth all, compelleth all
To transformation. Lo, *this* moulders down,
A-slack with weary eld, and *that*, again,   70
Prospers in glory, issuing from contempt.
In suchwise, then, the lapsing æons change [2]
The nature of the whole wide world, and earth
Taketh one status after other. And what
She bore of old, she now can bear no longer,   75
And what she never bore, she can to-day.

ORIGIN OF MANKIND

(From Book V)

                 But mortal man
Was then far hardier in the old champaign, [3]
As well he should be, since a hardier earth
Had him begotten; builded too was he
Of bigger and more solid bones within,   5
And knit with stalwart sinews through the flesh,
Nor easily seized by either heat or cold,
Or alien food or any ail or irk.
And whilst so many lustrums [4] of the sun
Rolled on across the sky, men led a life   10
After the roving habit of wild beasts.
Not then were sturdy guiders of curved ploughs,
And none knew then to work the fields with iron,
Or plant young shoots in holes of delvèd loam,
Or lop with hookèd knives from off high trees   15
The boughs of yester-year. What sun and rains
To them had given, what earth of own accord
Created then, was boon enough to glad
Their simple hearts. Mid acorn-laden oaks
Would they refresh their bodies for the nonce;   20
And the wild berries of the arbute-tree,
Which now thou seest to ripen purple-red
In winter time, the old telluric [5] soil

[1] A long period of time; a cosmic or geologic cycle.
[2] The principle of natural selection is clearly suggested.
[3] Field or earth.   [4] Period of five years.
[5] Pertaining to the earth.

Would bear then more abundant and more big.
And many coarse foods, too, in long ago   25
The blooming freshness of the rank young world
Produced, enough for those poor wretches there.
And rivers and springs would summon them of old
To slake the thirst, as now from the great hills
The water's down-rush calls aloud and far   30
The thirsty generations of the wild.
So, too, they sought the grottos of the Nymphs [1] —
The woodland haunts discovered as they ranged —
From forth of which they knew that gliding rills
With gush and splash abounding laved the rocks,
The dripping rocks, and trickled from above   36
Over the verdant moss; and here and there
Welled up and burst across the open flats.
As yet they knew not to enkindle fire
Against the cold, nor hairy pelts to use   40
And clothe their bodies with the spoils of beasts;
But huddled in groves, and mountain-caves, and
    woods,
And 'mongst the thickets hid their squalid backs,
When driven to flee the lashings of the winds
And the big rains. Nor could they then regard
The general good, nor did they know to use   46
In common any customs, any laws:
Whatever of booty fortune unto each
Had proffered, each alone would bear away,
By instinct trained for self to thrive and live.   50
And Venus in the forests then would link
The lovers' bodies; for the woman yielded
Either from mutual flame, or from the man's
Impetuous fury and insatiate lust,
Or from a bribe — as acorn-nuts, choice pears,   55
Or the wild berries of the arbute-tree.
And trusting wondrous strength of hands and legs,
They'd chase the forest-wanderers, the beasts;
And many they'd conquer, but some few they fled,
A-skulk into their hiding-places . . . [2]   60

With the flung stones and with the ponderous heft
Of gnarlèd branch. And by the time of night
O'ertaken, they would throw, like bristly boars,
Their wildman's limbs naked upon the earth,
Rolling themselves in leaves and fronded boughs.
Nor would they call with lamentations loud   66
Around the fields for daylight and the sun,
Quaking and wand'ring in shadows of the night;
But, silent and buried in a sleep, they'd wait
Until the sun with rosy flambeau brought   70
The glory to the sky. From childhood wont
Ever to see the dark and day begot

[1] Lesser female divinities living in groves, forests, fountains, or mountains. Among them were the Dryads, Hamadryads, Naiads, Nereids, and Oreads.
[2] Dots denote a break in the Latin, not an editor's or translator's expurgation. (Leonard.)

In times alternate, never might they be
Wildered by wild misgiving, lest a night
Eternal should possess the lands, with light   75
Of sun withdrawn forever. But their care
Was rather that the clans of savage beasts
Would often make their sleep-time horrible
For those poor wretches; and, from home y-driven,
They'd flee their rocky shelters at approach   80
Of boar, the spumy-lipped, or lion strong,
And in the midnight yield with terror up
To those fierce guests their beds of out-spread
          leaves.
   And yet in those days not much more than now
Would generations of mortality   85
Leave the sweet light of fading life behind.
Indeed, in those days here and there a man,
More oftener snatched upon, and gulped by fangs,
Afforded the beasts a food that roared alive,
Echoing through groves and hills and forest-trees,
Even as he viewed his living flesh entombed   91
Within a living grave; whilst those whom flight
Had saved, with bone and body bitten, shrieked,
Pressing their quivering palms to loathsome sores,
With horrible voices for eternal death —   95
Until, forlorn of help, and witless what
Might medicine their wounds, the writhing pangs
Took them from life. But not in those far times
Would one lone day give over unto doom
A soldiery in thousands marching on   100
Beneath the battle-banners, nor would then
The ramping breakers of the main seas dash
Whole argosies and crews upon the rocks.
But ocean uprisen would often rave in vain,
Without all end or outcome, and give up   105
Its empty menacings as lightly too;
Nor soft seductions of a sérene sea
Could lure by laughing billows any man
Out to disaster: for the science bold
Of ship-sailing lay dark in those far times.   110
Again, 'twas *then* that lack of food gave o'er
Men's fainting limbs to dissolution: now
'Tis plenty overwhelms. Unwary, they
Oft for themselves themselves would then outpour
The poison; now, with nicer art, themselves   115
They give the drafts to others.

BEGINNINGS OF CIVILIZATION
(From Book V)

                           And now what cause
Hath spread divinities of gods abroad
Through mighty nations, and filled the cities full
Of the high altars, and led to practices
Of solemn rites in season — rites which still   5
Flourish in midst of great affairs of state
And midst great centres of man's civic life,

The rites whence still in poor mortality
Is grafted that quaking awe which rears aloft
Still the new temples of gods from land to land 10
And drives mankind to visit them in throngs
On holy days — 'tis not so hard to give
Reason thereof in speech. Because, in sooth,
Even in those days would the race of man
Be seeing excelling visages of gods   15
With mind awake; and in his sleeps, yet more, —
Bodies of wondrous growth.[1] And, thus, to these
Would men attribute sense, because they seemed
To move their limbs and speak pronouncements
          high,
Befitting glorious visage and vast powers.   20
And men would give them an eternal life,
Because their visages forevermore
Were there before them, and their shapes remained,
And chiefly, however, because men would not
          think
Beings augmented with such mighty powers   25
Could well by any force o'ermastered be.
And men would think them in their happiness
Excelling far, because the fear of death
Vexèd no one of them at all, and since
At same time in men's sleeps men saw them do   30
So many wonders, and yet feel therefrom
Themselves no weariness. Besides, men marked
How in a fixèd order rolled around
The systems of the sky, and changèd times
Of annual seasons, nor were able then   35
To know thereof the causes. Therefore 'twas
Men would take refuge in consigning all
Unto divinities,[2] and in feigning all
Was guided by their nod. And in the sky
They set the seats and vaults of gods, because   40
Across the sky night and the moon are seen
To roll along — moon, day, and night, and night's
Old awesome constellations evermore,
And the night-wandering fireballs of the sky,
And flying flames, clouds, and the sun, the rains, 45
Snow and the winds, the lightnings, and the hail,
And the swift rumblings, and the hollow roar
Of mighty menacings forevermore.
   O humankind unhappy! — when it ascribed
Unto divinities such awesome deeds,   50
And coupled thereto rigors of fierce wrath!
What groans did men on that sad day beget
Even for themselves, and O what wounds for us,
What tears for our children's children! Nor, O man,

[1] This explanation of man's perception of the gods
makes divinity and supernatural power pretty largely
figments of fancy and dreams.

[2] Those things which man cannot understand or
himself perform are attributed to divinity. Thus the
gods were a creation of man's ignorance rather than
of his wisdom.

Is thy true piety in this: with head   55
Under the veil, still to be seen to turn
Fronting a stone, and ever to approach
Unto all altars; nor so prone on earth
Forward to fall, to spread upturnèd palms
Before the shrines of gods, nor yet to dew   60
Altars with prófuse blood of four-foot beasts,
Nor vows with vows to link.   But rather this:
To look on all things with a master eye
And mind at peace.   For when we gaze aloft
Upon the skiey vaults of yon great world   65
And ether, fixèd high o'er twinkling stars,
And into our thought there come the journeyings
Of sun and moon, O then into our breasts,
O'erburdened already with their other ills,
Begins forthwith to rear its sudden head   70
One more misgiving: lest o'er us, percase,[1]
It be the gods' immeasurable power
That rolls, with varied motion, round and round
The far white constellations.   For the lack
Of aught of reasons tries the puzzled mind: 75
Whether was ever a birth-time of the world,
And whether, likewise, any end shall be
How far the ramparts of the world can still
Outstand this strain of ever-rousèd motion,
Or whether, divinely with eternal weal   80
Endowed, they can through endless tracts of age
Glide on, defying the o'er-mighty powers
Of the immeasurable ages.   Lo,
What man is there whose mind with dread of gods
Cringes not close, whose limbs with terror-spell   85
Crouch not together, when the parchèd earth
Quakes with the horrible thunderbolt amain,
And across the mighty sky the rumblings run?
Do not the peoples and the nations shake,
And haughty kings do they not hug their limbs,   90
Strook through with fear of the divinities,
Lest for aught foully done or madly said
The heavy time be now at hand to pay?
When, too, fierce force of fury-winds at sea
Sweepeth a navy's admiral down the main   95
With his stout legions and his elephants,
Doth he not seek the peace of gods with vows,
And beg in prayer, a-tremble, lullèd winds
And friendly gales? — in vain, since, often up-caught
In fury-cyclones, is he borne along,   100
For all his mouthings, to the shoals of doom.
Ah, so irrevocably some hidden power
Betramples forevermore affairs of men,
And visibly grindeth with its heel in mire
The lictors'[2] glorious rods and axes dire,   105

[1] Perchance.   [2] Roman officers of petty rank.   One
of their duties was to carry the fasces, a bundle of
birch rods and an axe, a symbol of power of those they
served — kings, emperors, magistrats, consuls.   The
term "fascism" comes from this word.

Having them in derision!   Again, when earth
From end to end is rocking under foot,
And shaken cities ruin down, or threaten
Upon the verge, what wonder is it then
That mortal generations abase themselves,   110
And unto gods in all affairs of earth
Assign as last resort almighty powers
And wondrous energies to govern all?

.   .   .   .

                                        And thus
Began the loathing of the acorn; thus   115
Abandoned were those beds with grasses strewn
And with the leaves beladen.   Thus, again,
Fell into new contempt the pelts of beasts —
Erstwhile a robe of honor, which, I guess,
Aroused in those days envy so malign   120
That the first wearer went to woeful death
By ambuscades, — and yet that hairy prize,
Rent into rags by greedy foemen there
And splashed by blood, was ruined utterly
Beyond all use or vantage.   Thus of old   125
'Twas pelts, and of to-day 'tis purple and gold
That cark[1] men's lives with cares and weary with
     war.
Wherefore, methinks, resides the greater blame
With us vain men to-day: for cold would rack,
Without their pelts, the naked sons of earth;   130
But us it nothing hurts to do without
The purple vestment, broiderèd with gold
And with imposing figures, if we still
Make shift with some mean garment of the Plebs.[2]
So man in vain futilities toils on   135
Forever and wastes in idle cares his years —
Because, of very truth, he hath not learnt
What the true end of getting is, nor yet
At all how far true pleasure may increase.
And 'tis desire for better and for more   140
Hath carried by degrees mortality
Out onward to the deep, and roused up
From the far bottom mighty waves of war.
   But sun and moon, those watchmen of the
     world,
With their own lanterns traversing around   145
The mighty, the revolving vault, have taught
Unto mankind that seasons of the years
Return again, and that the Thing takes place
After a fixèd plan and order fixed.
   Already would they pass their life, hedged round
By the strong towers; and cultivate an earth   151
All portioned out and boundaried; already
Would the sea flower with sail-wingèd ships;
Already men had, under treaty pacts,

[1] Load.
[2] Plebeian.   The common people of ancient Rome,
the populace as opposed to the patricians.

Confederates and allies, when poets began   155
To hand heroic actions down in verse;
Nor long ere this had letters been devised —
Hence is our age unable to look back
On what has gone before, except where reason
Shows us a footprint.
                              Sailings on the seas,   160
Tillings of fields, walls, laws, and arms, and roads,
Dress and the like, all prizes, all delights
Of finer life, poems, pictures, chiselled shapes

Of polished sculptures — all these arts were learned
By practice and the mind's experience,   165
As men walked forward step by eager step.
Thus time draws forward each and everything
Little by little into the midst of men,
And reason uplifts it to the shores of light.
For one thing after other did men see   170
Grow clear by intellect, till with their arts
They've now achieved the súpreme pinnacle.[1]

[1] An early statement of the theory of progress.

Virgil · 70-19 B.C.

Virgil — Publius Vergilius Maro, sometimes called "the Mantuan" — was born on a small farm near Mantua, a city in northern Italy, in 70 B.C. He died at Brindisi in 19 B.C. Educated at home, and in Cremona, Milan, and Rome, he attained a distinction which brought him to the attention of Mæcenas, the same patron of letters who helped Horace. Indeed, it was Virgil who introduced Horace to the wealthy Roman. It is commonly thought that Virgil's farm was part of the region turned over by the Emperor Augustus to his victorious soldiers after the Battle of Philippi (42 B.C.) and that the family property was returned to Virgil later through the intervention of friends, of whom Mæcenas may well have been one.

Virgil's earlier writing was connected with various phases of rural life. The *Eclogues*, completed in 37 B.C., describe, in the manner of Theocritus, the pleasures of the countryside and the joys of friendship. The *Georgics*, 30 B.C., is more didactic in quality, Virgil's purpose being to set forth the aspects and satisfactions of nature as well as to present an exposition of the year's round of labor on the small Italian farm. The *Georgics* includes four books: the first concerned with work in the fields and the calendar and stars which govern the labor; the second, the husbandry of trees and vines; the third, grazing and the rearing of cattle and horses; the fourth, the care of bees.

The poet's friendship with the Emperor Augustus led to the suggestion, perhaps urged by the emperor himself, that Virgil write a long poem which would glorify the history of Rome and the ancestry of Augustus. Virgil was to compose an epic in the manner of Homer, on the grand scale, presenting the Italy of the heroic period. He spent eleven years writing the *Æneid* and, before death intervened, planned to give it three years more of revision and polish. It is commonly said that Virgil had, before his death, forbidden the publication of the *Æneid* and that Augustus prevented the burning of the manuscript.

SUGGESTED REFERENCES: W. F. J. Knight, *Roman Vergil* (2nd ed., 1953); C. M. Bowra, *From Virgil to Milton* (2nd ed., 1963).

The Æneid[1]

The *Æneid* is the story of Æneas and his adventures after the fall of Troy. At the same time, it is the epic of the Roman people.

[1] Translation by Theodore C. Williams in the *Riverside Literature Series*, published by Houghton Mifflin Company.

In many ways the narrative follows the steps and parallels the events Homer described in the *Iliad* and the *Odyssey*. It presents a series of adventures which finally took Æneas to Italy, where he and his company establish a civilization which leads to the founding of Rome. And, since Æneas was a son of Aphrodite, and Augustus was presented as a descendant of Æneas, the direct descent of Augustus from the gods is satisfactorily established.

The *Æneid* is thus a national epic chronicling the record of a people through vicissitudes of warfare and conquest until that people became moulded into a nation. Through the epic Virgil gave Italy a tradition and a purpose which helped to shape its actual history. But the *Æneid*, unlike the epics of Homer, is a "literary" epic, deliberately building a tradition, self-conscious, decorative, and artistic. In this sense it bears a closer relationship to Milton's *Paradise Lost* than to either the *Iliad* or the *Odyssey*.

In form and manner, the *Æneid* fixed the convention for later epics to follow: it invokes the muse and states its epic purpose in the opening pages; it also incorporates descriptions of great battles, employs the epic simile, and relates its story in language both dignified and majestic. Virgil is careful to hold the structure of the whole poem always in line with his epic purpose and to keep his action moving within the pattern fixed by Homer. Individual stories, such for instance as the love of Dido for Æneas, are certainly romantic in tone; but, and this is the point, they are presented with the restraint of the classic tradition. And here are heroic people with noble natures. Characterization is slighted. In short, the poem is classical in spirit rather than romantic or realistic.

BOOK II

A general silence fell; and all gave ear,
While, from his lofty station at the feast,
Father Æneas with these words began:

A grief unspeakable thy gracious word,
O sovereign lady, bids my heart live o'er: 5
How Asia's glory and afflicted throne
The Greek flung down; which woeful scene I saw
And bore great part in each event I tell.
But O! in telling, what Dolopian [1] churl,
Or Myrmidon,[1] or gory follower   10
Of grim Ulysses [2] could the tears restrain?
'Tis evening; lo! the dews of night begin
To fall from heaven, and yonder sinking stars
Invite to slumber. But if thy heart yearn
To hear in brief of all our evil days   15
And Troy's last throes, although the memory
Makes my soul shudder and recoil in pain,
I will essay it.   Wearied of the war,
And by ill-fortune crushed, year after year,
The kings of Greece, by Pallas' skill divine,   20
Build a huge horse, a thing of mountain size,
With timbered ribs of fir. They falsely say
It has been vowed to Heaven for safe return,
And spread this lie abroad. Then they conceal
Choice bands of warriors in the deep, dark side,

[1] Soldiers of Achilles.
[2] As a background for this passage see the selections from the *Iliad* and *Odyssey* of Homer.

And fill the caverns of that monstrous womb   26
With arms and soldiery. In sight of Troy
Lies Tenedos, an island widely famed
And opulent, ere Priam's kingdom fell,
But a poor haven now, with anchorage   30
Not half secure; 'twas thitherward they sailed,
And lurked unseen by that abandoned shore.
We deemed them launched away and sailing far,
Bound homeward for Mycenæ. Teucria [1] then
Threw off her grief inveterate; all her gates   35
Swung wide; exultant went we forth, and saw
The Dorian camp untenanted, the siege
Abandoned, and the shore without a keel.
"Here!" cried we, "the Dolopian pitched; the host
Of fierce Achilles here; here lay the fleet;   40
And here the battling lines to conflict ran."
Others, all wonder, scan the gift of doom
By virgin Pallas given, and view with awe
That horse which loomed so large. Thymœtes [2]
    then
Bade lead it through the gates, and set on high
Within our citadel — or traitor he,   46
Or tool of fate in Troy's predestined fall.
But Capys, as did all of wiser heart,
Bade hurl into the sea the false Greek gift,
Or underneath it thrust a kindling flame,   50
Or pierce the hollow ambush of its womb
With probing spear. Yet did the multitude
Veer round from voice to voice and doubt of all.
Then from the citadel, conspicuous,
Laocoön,[3] with all his following choir,   55
Hurried indignant down; and from afar
Thus hailed the people: "O unhappy men!
What madness this? Who deems our foemen
    fled?
Think ye the gifts of Greece can lack for guile?
Have ye not known Ulysses? The Achæan   60
Hides, caged in yonder beams; or this is reared
For engin'ry on our proud battlements,
To spy upon our roof-tops, or descend
In ruin on the city. 'Tis a snare.
Trust not this horse, O Troy, whate'er it bode!   65
I fear the Greeks, though gift on gift they bear."

So saying, he whirled with ponderous javelin
A sturdy stroke straight at the rounded side
Of the great, jointed beast. A tremor struck
Its towering form, and through the cavernous
    womb   70
Rolled loud, reverberate rumbling, deep and long.
If heaven's decree, if our own wills, that hour,
Had not been fixed on woe, his spear had brought

[1] Troy.
[2] The Trojan who persuaded his people to take the wooden horse into their city.
[3] Son of Priam and Hecuba, a priest of Apollo.

A bloody slaughter on our ambushed foe,
And Troy were standing on the earth this day! 75
O Priam's towers, ye were unfallen still!

But, lo! with hands fast bound behind, a youth
By clamorous Dardan shepherds haled along,
Was brought before our King, — to this sole end
A self-surrendered captive, that he might, 80
Although a nameless stranger, cunningly
Deliver to the Greek the gates of Troy.
His firm-set mind flinched not from either goal, —
Success in crime, or on swift death to fall.
The thronging Trojan youth made haste his way
From every side, all eager to see close 86
Their captive's face, and flout with emulous scorn.
Hear now what Greek deception is, and learn
From one dark wickedness the whole. For he,
A mark for every eye, defenceless, dazed, 90
Stood staring at our Phrygian hosts, and cried:
"Woe worth the day! What ocean or what shore
Will have me now? What desperate path remains
For miserable me? Now have I lost
All foothold with the Greeks, and o'er my head 95
Troy's furious sons call bloody vengeance down."
Such groans and anguish turned all rage away
And stayed our lifted hands. We bade him tell
His birth, his errand, and from whence might be
Such hope of mercy for a foe in chains. 100
Then fearing us no more, this speech he dared:
"O King! I will confess, whate'er befall,
The whole unvarnished truth. I will not hide
My Grecian birth. Yea, thus will I begin.
For Fortune has brought wretched Sinon [1] low; 105
But never shall her cruelty impair
His honor and his truth. Perchance the name
Of Palamedes, Belus' glorious son,
Has come by rumor to your listening ears;
Whom by false witness and conspiracy, 110
Because his counsel was not for this war,
The Greeks condemned, though guiltless, to his
death,
And now make much lament for him they slew.
I, his companion, of his kith and kin,
Sent hither by my humble sire's command, 115
Followed his arms and fortunes from my youth.
Long as his throne endured, and while he throve
In conclave with his kingly peers, we twain
Some name and lustre bore; but afterward,
Because that cheat Ulysses envied him 120
(Ye know the deed), he from this world withdrew,
And I in gloom and tribulation sore
Lived miserably on, lamenting loud
My lost friend's blameless fall. A fool was I
That kept not these lips closed; but I had vowed

[1] The Greek who talked the Trojans into taking the wooden horse into Troy.

That if a conqueror home to Greece I came, 126
I would avenge. Such words moved wrath, and
were
The first shock of my ruin; from that hour,
Ulysses whispered slander and alarm;
Breathed doubt and malice into all men's ears,
And darkly plotted how to strike his blow. 131
Nor rest had he, till Calchas,[1] as his tool, —
But why unfold this useless, cruel story?
Why make delay? Ye count all sons of Greece
Arrayed as one; and to have heard thus far 135
Suffices you. Take now your ripe revenge!
Ulysses smiles and Atreus' royal sons [2]
With liberal price your deed of blood repay."

We ply him then with passionate appeal
And question all his cause: of guilt so dire 140
Or such Greek guile we harbored not the thought.
So on he prates, with well-feigned grief and fear,
And from his lying heart thus told his tale:
"Full oft the Greeks had fain achieved their flight,
And raised the Trojan siege, and sailed away 145
War-wearied quite. O, would it had been so!
Full oft the wintry tumult of the seas
Did wall them round, and many a swollen storm
Their embarcation stayed. But chiefly when,
All fitly built of beams of maple fair, 150
This horse stood forth, — what thunders filled the
skies!
With anxious fears we sent Eurypylus [3]
To ask Apollo's word; and from the shrine
He brings the sorrowful commandment home:
'By flowing blood and by a virgin slain [4] 155
The wild winds were appeased, when first ye came,
Ye sons of Greece, to Ilium's distant shore.
Through blood ye must return. Let some Greek
life
Your expiation be.'
　　　　　The popular ear 159
The saying caught, all spirits were dimmed o'er;
Cold doubt and horror through each bosom ran,
Asking what fate would do, and on what wretch
Apollo's choice would fall. Ulysses, then,
Amid the people's tumult and acclaim,
Thrust Calchas forth, some prophecy to tell 165
To all the throng: he asked him o'er and o'er
What Heaven desired. Already not a few
Foretold the murderous plot, and silently
Watched the dark doom upon my life impend.
Twice five long days the seer his lips did seal,
And hid himself, refusing to bring forth 171

[1] The soothsayer who accompanied the Greeks against Troy.
[2] Agamemnon was of the family of Atreus.
[3] Another Greek soothsayer.
[4] Iphigenia.

His word of guile, and name what wretch should
    die.
At last, reluctant, and all loudly urged
By false Ulysses, he fulfils their plot,
And, lifting up his voice oracular,   175
Points out myself the victim to be slain.
Nor did one voice oppose. The mortal stroke
Horribly hanging o'er each coward head
Was changed to one man's ruin, and their hearts
Endured it well. Soon rose th' accursèd morn;
The bloody ritual was ready; salt   181
Was sprinkled on the sacred loaf; my brows
Were bound with fillets for the offering.
But I escaped that death — yes! I deny not!
I cast my fetters off, and darkling lay   185
Concealed all night in lake-side sedge and mire,
Awaiting their departure, if perchance
They should in truth set sail. But nevermore
Shall my dear, native country greet these eyes.
No more my father or my tender babes   190
Shall I behold. Nay, haply their own lives
Are forfeit, when my foemen take revenge
For my escape, and slay those helpless ones,
In expiation of my guilty deed.
O, by yon powers in heaven which witness truth,
By aught in this dark world remaining now   196
Of spotless human faith and innocence,
I do implore thee look with pitying eye
On these long sufferings my heart hath borne.
O, pity! I deserve not what I bear."   200

Pity and pardon to his tears we gave,
And spared his life. King Priam bade unbind
The fettered hands and loose those heavy chains
That pressed him sore; then with benignant mien
Addressed him thus: "Whate'er thy place or name,
Forget the people thou hast lost, and be   206
Henceforth our countryman. But tell me true!
What means the monstrous fabric of this horse?
Who made it? Why? What offering to Heaven,
Or engin'ry of conquest may it be?"   210
He spake; and in reply, with skilful guile,
Greek that he was! the other lifted up
His hands, now freed and chainless, to the skies:
"O ever-burning and inviolate fires,
Witness my word! O altars and sharp steel, 215
Whose curse I fled, O fillets of the gods,
Which bound a victim's helpless forehead, hear!
'Tis lawful now to break the oath that gave
My troth to Greece. To execrate her kings
Is now my solemn duty. Their whole plot 220
I publish to the world. No fatherland
And no allegiance binds me any more.
O Troy, whom I have saved, I bid thee keep
The pledge of safety by good Priam given,
For my true tale shall my rich ransom be. 225

The Greeks' one hope, since first they opened war
Was Pallas' grace and power. But from the day
When Diomed, bold scorner of the gods,
And false Ulysses, author of all guile,
Rose up and violently bore away   230
Palladium, her holy shrine, hewed down
The sentinels of her acropolis,
And with polluted, gory hands dared touch
The goddess' virgin fillets, white and pure, —
Thenceforth, I say, the courage of the Greeks 235
Ebbed utterly away; their strength was lost,
And favoring Pallas all her grace withdrew.
No dubious sign she gave. Scarce had they set
Her statue in our camp, when glittering flame 239
Flashed from the staring eyes; from all its limbs
Salt sweat ran forth; three times (O wondrous tale!)
It gave a sudden skyward leap, and made
Prodigious trembling of her lance and shield.
The prophet Calchas bade us straightway take
Swift flight across the sea; for fate had willed 245
The Trojan citadel should never fall
By Grecian arm, till once more they obtain
New oracles at Argos, and restore
That god the round ships hurried o'er the sea.
Now in Mycenæ, whither they are fled,   250
New help of heaven they find, and forge anew
The means of war. Back hither o'er the waves
They suddenly will come. So Calchas gave
The meaning of the god. Warned thus, they
    reared
In place of Pallas' desecrated shrine   255
Yon image of the horse, to expiate
The woeful sacrilege. Calchas ordained
That they should build a thing of monstrous size
Of jointed beams, and rear it heavenward,
So might it never pass your gates, nor come 260
Inside your walls, nor anywise restore
Unto the Trojans their lost help divine.
For had your hands Minerva's gift profaned,
A ruin horrible — O, may the gods   264
Bring it on Calchas rather! — would have come
On Priam's throne and all the Phrygian power.
But if your hands should lift the holy thing
To your own citadel, then Asia's host
Would hurl aggression upon Pelops' land,
And all that curse on our own nation fall." 270

Thus Sinon's guile and practised perjury
Our doubt dispelled. His stratagems and tears
Wrought victory where neither Tydeus' son,[1]
Nor mountain-bred Achilles could prevail,
Nor ten years' war, nor fleets a thousand strong.
But now a vaster spectacle of fear   276
Burst over us, to vex our startled souls.
Laocoön, that day by cast of lot

[1] Diomede.

Priest unto Neptune, was in act to slay
A huge bull at the god's appointed fane.   280
Lo! o'er the tranquil deep from Tenedos
Appeared a pair (I shudder as I tell)
Of vastly coiling serpents, side by side,
Stretching along the waves, and to the shore
Taking swift course; their necks were lifted high,
Their gory dragon-crests o'ertopped the waves;   286
All else, half seen, trailed low along the sea;
While with loud cleavage of the foaming brine
Their monstrous backs wound forward fold on fold.
Soon they made land; the furious bright eyes   290
Glowed with ensanguined fire; their quivering
      tongues
Lapped hungrily the hissing, gruesome jaws.
All terror-pale we fled.   Unswerving then
The monsters to Laocoön made way.
First round the tender limbs of his two sons   295
Each dragon coiled, and on the shrinking flesh
Fixed fast and fed.   Then seized they on the sire,
Who flew to aid, a javelin in his hand,
Embracing close in bondage serpentine
Twice round the waist; and twice in scaly grasp
Around his neck, and o'er him grimly peered   301
With lifted head and crest; he, all the while,
His holy fillet fouled with venomous blood,
Tore at his fetters with a desperate hand,
And lifted up such agonizing voice,   305
As when a bull, death-wounded, seeks to flee
The sacrificial altar, and thrusts back
From his doomed head the ill-aimed, glancing
      blade
Then swiftly writhed the dragon-pair away
Unto the templed height, and in the shrine   310
Of cruel Pallas sure asylum found
Beneath the goddess' feet and orbèd shield.

Such trembling horror as we ne'er had known
Seized now on every heart.   "Of his vast guilt
Laocoön," they say, "receives reward;   315
For he with most abominable spear
Did strike and violate that blessèd wood.
Yon statue to the temple!   Ask the grace
Of glorious Pallas!"   So the people cried
In general acclaim.   Ourselves did make   320
A breach within our walls and opened wide
The ramparts of our city.   One and all
Were girded for the task.   Smooth-gliding wheels
Were 'neath its feet; great ropes stretched round its
      neck,
Till o'er our walls the fatal engine climbed,   325
Pregnant with men-at-arms.   On every side
Fair youths and maidens made a festal song,
And hauled the ropes with merry heart and gay.
So on and up it rolled, a tower of doom,
And in proud menace through our Forum moved.

O Ilium, my country, where abode   331
The gods of all my sires!   O glorious walls
Of Dardan's sons! before your gates it passed,
Four times it stopped and dreadful clash of arms
Four times from its vast concave loudly rang.   335
Yet frantic pressed we on, our hearts all blind,
And in the consecrated citadel
Set up the hateful thing.   Cassandra [1] then
From heaven-instructed heart our doom foretold;
But doomed to unbelief were Ilium's sons.   340
Our hapless nation on its dying day
Flung free o'er streets and shrines the votive
      flowers.

The skies rolled on; and o'er the ocean fell
The veil of night, till utmost earth and heaven
And all their Myrmidonian stratagems   345
Were mantled darkly o'er.   In silent sleep
The Trojan city lay; dull slumber chained
Its weary life.   But now the Greek array
Of ordered ships moved on from Tenedos,
Their only light the silent, favoring moon,   350
On to the well-known strand.   The King displayed
A torch from his own ship, and Sinon then,
Whom wrathful Heaven defended in that hour,
Let the imprisoned band of Greeks go free
From that huge womb of wood; the open horse   355
Restored them to the light; and joyfully
Emerging from the darkness, one by one,
Princely Thessander, Sthenelus, and dire
Ulysses glided down the swinging cord.
Closely upon them Neoptolemus,   360
The son of Peleus, came, and Acamas,
King Menelaus, Thoas and Machaon,
And last, Epeüs, who the fabric wrought.
Upon the town they fell, for deep in sleep
And drowsed with wine it lay; the sentinels   365
They slaughtered, and through gates now opened
      wide
Let in their fellows, and arrayed for war
Th' auxiliar legions of the dark design.

That hour it was when heaven's first gift of sleep
On weary hearts of men most sweetly steals.   370
O, then my slumbering senses seemed to see
Hector, with woeful face and streaming eyes;
I seemed to see him from the chariot trailing,
Foul with dark dust and gore, his swollen feet
Pierced with a cruel thong.   Ah me! what change
From glorious Hector when he homeward bore   376
The spoils of fierce Achilles; or hurled far
That shower of torches on the ships of Greece!
Unkempt his beard, his tresses thick with blood,
And all those wounds in sight which he did take

[1] A Trojan prophetess, whom no one believed.
Daughter of Priam.

Defending Troy. Then, weeping as I spoke, 381
I seemed on that heroic shape to call
With mournful utterance: "O star of Troy!
O surest hope and stay of all her sons!
Why tarriest thou so long? What region sends
The long-expected Hector home once more? 386
These weary eyes that look on thee have seen
Hosts of thy kindred die, and fateful change
Upon thy people and thy city fall.
O, say what dire occasion has defiled 390
Thy tranquil brows? What mean those bleeding
        wounds?"

Silent he stood, nor anywise would stay
My vain lament; but groaned, and answered thus:
"Haste, goddess-born, and out of yonder flames
Achieve thy flight. Our foes have scaled the wall;
Exalted Troy is falling. Fatherland 396
And Priam ask no more. If human arm
Could profit Troy, my own had kept her free.
Her Lares and her people to thy hands
Troy here commends. Companions let them be
Of all thy fortunes. Let them share thy quest 401
Of that wide realm, which, after wandering far,
Thou shalt achieve, at last, beyond the sea."
He spoke: and from our holy hearth brought forth
The solemn fillet, the ancestral shrines, 405
And Vesta's [1] ever-bright, inviolate fire.

Now shrieks and loud confusion swept the town;
And though my father's dwelling stood apart
Embowered deep in trees, th' increasing din
Drew nearer, and the battle-thunder swelled. 410
I woke on sudden, and up-starting scaled
The roof, the tower, then stood with listening ear:
'Twas like an harvest burning, when wild winds
Uprouse the flames; 'twas like a mountain stream
That bursts in flood and ruinously whelms 415
Sweet fields and farms and all the ploughman's
        toil,
Whirling whole groves along; while dumb with
        fear,
From some far cliff the shepherd hears the sound.
Now their Greek plot was plain, the stratagem
At last laid bare. Deiphobus' [2] great house 420
Sank vanquished in the fire. Ucalegon's [3]
Hard by was blazing, while the waters wide
Around Sigeum [4] gave an answering glow.
Shrill trumpets rang; loud shouting voices roared;
Wildly I armed me (when the battle calls, 425
How dimly reason shines!); I burned to join
The rally of my peers, and to the heights

[1] Goddess of the hearth and the home.
[2] A son of Priam.
[3] A councillor of Troy.
[4] A promontory at entrance of the Hellespont.

Defensive gather. Frenzy and vast rage
Seized on my soul. I only sought what way
With sword in hand some noble death to die. 430

When Panthus [1] met me, who had scarce escaped
The Grecian spears, — Panthus of Othrys' line,
Apollo's priest within our citadel;
His holy emblems, his defeated gods,
And his small grandson in his arms he bore, 435
While toward the gates with wild, swift steps he
        flew.
"How fares the kingdom, Panthus? What strong
        place
Is still our own?" But scarcely could I ask
When thus, with many a groan, he made reply:
"Dardania's death and doom are come to-day, 440
Implacable. There is no Ilium now;
Our Trojan name is gone, the Teucrian throne
Quite fallen. For the wrathful power of Jove
Has given to Argos all our boast and pride.
The Greek is lord of all yon blazing towers. 445
Yon horse uplifted on our city's heart
Disgorges men-at-arms. False Sinon now,
With scorn exultant, heaps up flame on flame.
Others throw wide the gates. The whole vast
        horde
That out of proud Mycenæ hither sailed 450
Is at us. With confronting spears they throng
Each narrow passage. Every steel-bright blade
Is flashing naked, making haste for blood.
Our sentries helpless meet the invading shock
And give back blind and unavailing war." 455

By Panthus' word and by some god impelled,
I flew to battle, where the flames leaped high,
Where grim Bellona [2] called, and all the air
Resounded high as heaven with shouts of war.
Rhipeus and Epytus of doughty arm 460
Were at my side, Dymas and Hypanis,
Seen by a pale moon, join our little band;
And young Corœbus, Mygdon's princely son,
Who was in Troy that hour because he loved
Cassandra madly, and had made a league 465
As Priam's kinsman with our Phrygian arms:
Ill-starred, to heed not what the virgin [3] raved!
When these I saw close-gathered for the fight,
I thus addressed them: "Warriors, vainly brave,
If ye indeed desire to follow one 470
Who dares the uttermost brave men may do,
Our evil plight ye see: the gods are fled
From every altar and protecting fire,
Which were the kingdom's stay. Ye offer aid
Unto your country's ashes. Let us fight 475

[1] Another Trojan councillor.
[2] A goddess of war.
[3] Cassandra had advised him to retire from the war.

Unto the death!   To arms, my men, to arms!
The single hope and stay of desperate men
Is their despair."   Thus did I rouse their souls.
Then like the ravening wolves, some night of cloud,
When cruel hunger in an empty maw   480
Drives them forth furious, and their whelps behind
Wait famine-throated; so through foemen's steel
We flew to surest death, and kept our way
Straight through the midmost town.   The wings
        of night
Brooded above us in vast vault of shade.   485
But who the bloodshed of that night can tell?
What tongue its deaths shall number, or what eyes
Find meed of tears to equal all its woe?
The ancient City fell, whose throne had stood
Age after age.   Along her streets were strewn   490
The unresisting dead; at household shrines
And by the temples of the gods they lay.
Yet not alone was Teucrian blood required:
Oft out of vanquished hearts fresh valor flamed,
And the Greek victor fell.   Anguish and woe   495
Were everywhere; pale terrors ranged abroad,
And multitudinous death met every eye.

Androgeos, followed by a thronging band
Of Greeks, first met us on our desperate way;
But heedless, and confounding friend with foe,   500
Thus, all unchallenged, hailed us as his own:
"Haste, heroes!   Are ye laggards at this hour?
Others bear off the captives and the spoil
Of burning Troy.   Just from the galleys ye?"
He spoke; but straightway, when no safe reply   505
Returned, he knew himself entrapped, and fallen
Into a foeman's snare; struck dumb was he
And stopped both word and motion; as one steps,
When blindly treading a thick path of thorns,
Upon a snake, and sick with fear would flee   510
That lifted wrath and swollen gorge of green:
So trembling did Androgeos backward fall.
At them we flew and closed them round with war;
And since they could not know the ground, and
        fear   514
Had whelmed them quite, we swiftly laid them low.
Thus Fortune on our first achievement smiled;
And, flushed with victory, Corœbus cried:
"Come, friends, and follow Fortune's finger, where
She beckons us what path deliverance lies.
Change we our shields, and these Greek emblems
        wear.   520
'Twixt guile and valor who will nicely weigh
When foes are met?   These dead shall find us
        arms."
With this, he dons Androgeos' crested helm
And beauteous, blazoned shield; and to his side
Girds, on a Grecian blade.   Young Rhipeus next,
With Dymas and the other soldiery,   526

Repeat the deed, exulting, and array
Their valor in fresh trophies from the slain.
Now intermingled with our foes we moved,
And alien emblems wore; the long, black night   530
Brought many a grapple, and a host of Greeks
Down to the dark we hurled.   Some fled away,
Seeking their safe ships and the friendly shore.
Some cowards foul went clambering back again
To that vast horse and hid them in its maw.   535
But woe is me!   If gods their help withhold,
'Tis impious to be brave.   That very hour
The fair Cassandra passed us, bound in chains,
King Priam's virgin daughter, from the shrine
And altars of Minerva; her loose hair   540
Had lost its fillet; her impassioned eyes
Were lifted in vain prayer, — her eyes alone!
For chains of steel her frail, soft hands confined.
Corœbus' eyes this horror not endured,
And, sorrow-crazed, he plunged him headlong in
The midmost fray, self-offered to be slain,   546
While in close mass our troop behind him poured.
But, at this point, the overwhelming spears
Of our own kinsmen rained resistless down
From a high temple-tower; and carnage wild   550
Ensued, because of the Greek arms we bore
And our false crests.   The howling Grecian band,
Crazed by Cassandra's rescue, charged at us
From every side; Ajax of savage soul,
The sons of Atreus, and that whole wild horde   555
Achilles from Dolopian deserts drew.
'Twas like the bursting storm, when gales contend
West wind and South, and jocund wind of morn
Upon his orient steeds — while forests roar,
And foam-flecked Nereus [1] with fierce trident stirs
The dark deep of the sea.
                    All who did hide   561
In shadows of the night, by our assault
Surprised, and driven in tumultuous flight,
Now start to view.   Full well they now can see
Our shields and borrowed arms, and clearly note
Our speech of alien sound; their multitude   566
O'erwhelms us utterly.   Corœbus first
At mailed Minerva's altar prostrate lay,
Pierced by Peneleus' blade; then Rhipeus fell;
We deemed him of all Trojans the most just,   570
Most scrupulously righteous; but the gods
Gave judgment otherwise.   There Dymas died,
And Hypanis, by their compatriots slain;
Nor thee, O Panthus, in that mortal hour,
Could thy clean hands or Phœbus' priesthood save.
O ashes of my country! funeral pyre   576
Of all my kin! bear witness that my breast
Shrank not from any sword the Grecian drew,
And that my deeds the night my country died
Deserved a warrior's death, had Fate ordained.   580

        [1] An old man of the sea.

But soon our ranks were broken; at my side
Stayed Iphitus and Pelias; one with age
Was long since wearied, and the other bore
The burden of Ulysses' crippling wound.
Straightway the roar and tumult summoned us
To Priam's palace, where a battle raged   586
As if save this no conflict else were known,
And all Troy's dying brave were mustered there.
There we beheld the war-god unconfined;
The Greek besiegers to the roof-tops fled;   590
Or, with shields tortoise-back, the gates assailed.
Ladders were on the walls; and round by round,
Up the huge bulwark as they fight their way,
The shielded left-hand thwarts the falling spears,
The right to every vantage closely clings.   595
The Trojans hurl whole towers and roof-tops down
Upon the mounting foe; for well they see
That the last hour is come, and with what arms
The dying must resist.   Rich gilded beams,
With many a beauteous blazon of old time,   600
Go crashing down.   Men armed with naked swords
Defend the inner doors in close array.
Thus were our hearts inflamed to stand and strike
For the king's house, and to his body-guard
Bring succor, and renew their vanquished powers.
A certain gate I knew, a secret way,   606
Which gave free passage between Priam's halls,
And exit rearward; hither, in the days
Before our fall, the lone Andromache [1]
Was wont with young Astyanax to pass   610
In quest of Priam and her husband's kin.
This way to climb the palace roof I flew,
Where, desperate, the Trojans with vain skill
Hurled forth repellent arms.   A tower was there,
Reared skyward from the roof-top, giving view   615
Of Troy's wide walls and full reconnaissance
Of all Achæa's fleets and tented field;
This, with strong steel, our gathered strength assailed,
And as the loosened courses offered us
Great threatening fissures, we uprooted it   620
From its aerial throne and thrust it down:
It fell with instantaneous crash of thunder
Along the Danaan host in ruin wide.
But fresh ranks soon arrive; thick showers of stone
Rain down, with every missile rage can find.   625

Now at the threshold of the outer court
Pyrrhus [2] triumphant stood, with glittering arms
And helm of burnished brass.   He glittered like
Some swollen viper, fed on poison-leaves,
Whom chilling winter shelters underground,   630
Till, fresh and strong, he sheds his annual scales
And, crawling forth rejuvenate, uncoils

[1] The wife of Hector and mother of Astyanax.
[2] Son of Achilles.

His slimy length; his lifted gorge insults
The sunbeam with three-forked and quivering
    tongue.
Huge Periphas was there; Automedon,   635
Who drove Achilles' steeds, and bore his arms.
Then Scyros' island-warriors assault
The palaces, and hurl reiterate fire
At wall and tower.   Pyrrhus led the van;
Seizing an axe he clove the ponderous doors   640
And rent the hinges from their posts of bronze;
He cut the beams, and through the solid mass
Burrowed his way, till like a window huge
The breach yawned wide, and opened to his gaze
A vista of long courts and corridors,   645
The hearth and home of many an ancient king,
And Priam's own; upon its sacred bourne
The sentry, all in arms, kept watch and ward.
Confusion, groans, and piteous turmoil
Were in that dwelling; women shrieked and wailed
From many a dark retreat, and their loud cry   651
Rang to the golden stars.   Through those vast halls
The panic-stricken mothers wildly roved,
And clung with frantic kisses and embrace
Unto the columns cold.   Fierce as his sire,   655
Pyrrhus moves on; nor bar nor sentinel
May stop his way; down tumbles the great door
Beneath the battering beam, and with it fall
Hinges and framework violently torn.
Force bursts all bars; th' assailing Greeks break in,
Do butchery, and with men-at-arms possess   661
What place they will.   Scarce with an equal rage
A foaming river, when its dykes are down,
O'erwhelms its mounded shores, and through the
    plain   664
Rolls mountain-high, while from the ravaged farms
Its fierce flood sweeps along both flock and fold.

My own eyes looked on Neoptolemus [1]
Frenzied with slaughter, and both Atreus' sons
Upon the threshold frowning; I beheld
Her hundred daughters with old Hecuba;   670
And Priam, whose own bleeding wounds defiled
The altars where himself had blessed the fires;
There fifty nuptial beds gave promise proud
Of princely heirs; but all their brightness now,
Of broidered cunning and barbaric gold,   675
Lay strewn and trampled on.   The Danaan foe
Stood victor, where the raging flame had failed.
But would ye haply know what stroke of doom
On Priam fell?   Now when his anguish saw
His kingdom lost and fallen, his abode   680
Shattered, and in his very hearth and home
Th' exulting foe, the aged King did bind
His rusted armor to his trembling thews —
All vainly — and a useless blade of steel

[1] Another name for Pyrrhus.

He girded on; then charged, resolved to die   685
Encircled by the foe.   Within his walls
There stood, beneath the wide and open sky,
A lofty altar; an old laurel-tree
Leaned o'er it, and enclasped in holy shade
The statues of the tutelary powers.   690
Here Hecuba and all the princesses
Took refuge vain within the place of prayer.
Like panic-stricken doves in some dark storm,
Close-gathering they sate, and in despair
Embraced their graven gods.   But when the Queen
Saw Priam with his youthful harness on,   696
"What frenzy, O my wretched lord," she cried,
"Arrayed thee in such arms?   O, whither now?
Not such defences, nor such arm as thine,
The time requires, though thy companion were   700
Our Hector's self.   O, yield thee, I implore!
This altar now shall save us one and all,
Or we must die together."   With these words
She drew him to her side, and near the shrine
Made for her aged spouse a place to cling.   705

But, lo! just 'scaped of Pyrrhus' murderous hand,
Polites, one of Priam's sons, fled fast
Along the corridors, through thronging foes
And a thick rain of spears.   Wildly he gazed
Across the desolate halls, wounded to death.   710
Fierce Pyrrhus followed after, pressing hard
With mortal stroke, and now his hand and spear
Were close upon: — when the lost youth leaped
        forth
Into his father's sight, and prostrate there
Lay dying, while his life-blood ebbed away.   715
Then Priam, though on all sides death was nigh,
Quit not the strife, nor from loud wrath refrained:
"Thy crime and impious outrage, may the gods
(If Heaven to mortals render debt and due)
Justly reward and worthy honors pay!   720
My own son's murder thou hast made me see,
Blood and pollution impiously throwing
Upon a father's head.   Not such was he,
Not such, Achilles, thy pretended sire,
When Priam was his foe.   With flush of shame 725
He nobly listened to a suppliant's plea
In honor made.   He rendered to the tomb
My Hector's body pale, and me did send
Back to my throne a king."

                              With this proud word
The aged warrior hurled with nerveless arm   730
His ineffectual spear, which hoarsely rang
Rebounding on the brazen shield, and hung
Piercing the midmost boss, — but all in vain.
Then Pyrrhus: "Take these tidings, and convey
A message to my father, Peleus' son!   735
Tell him my naughty deeds!   Be sure and say
How Neoptolemus hath shamed his sires.

Now die!"
                       With this, he trailed before the shrines
The trembling King, whose feet slipped in the
        stream
Of his son's blood.   Then Pyrrhus' left hand
        clutched   740
The tresses old and gray; a glittering sword
His right hand lifted high, and buried it
Far as the hilt in that defenceless heart.
So Priam's story ceased.   Such final doom
Fell on him, while his dying eyes surveyed   745
Troy burning, and her altars overthrown,
Though once of many an orient land and tribe
The boasted lord.   In huge dismemberment
His severed trunk lies tombless on the shore,
The head from shoulder torn, the corpse unknown.

Then first wild horror on my spirit fell   751
And dazed me utterly.   A vision rose
Of my own cherished father, as I saw
The King, his aged peer, sore wounded lying
In mortal agony; a vision too   755
Of lost Creüsa [1] at my ravaged hearth,
And young Iulus' peril.   Then my eyes
Looked round me seeking aid.   But all were fled,
War-wearied and undone; some earthward leaped
From battlement or tower; some in despair   760
Yielded their suffering bodies to the flame.
I stood there sole surviving; when, behold,
To Vesta's altar clinging in dumb fear,
Hiding and crouching in the hallowed shade,
Tyndarus' daughter! [2] — 'twas the burning town
Lighted full well my roving steps and eyes.   766
In fear was she both of some Trojan's rage
For Troy o'erthrown, and of some Greek revenge,
Or her wronged husband's long indignant ire.
So hid she at that shrine her hateful brow,   770
Being of Greece and Troy, full well she knew,
The common curse.   Then in my bosom rose
A blaze of wrath; methought I should avenge
My dying country, and with horrid deed
Pay crime for crime.   "Shall she return unscathed
To Sparta, to Mycenæ's golden pride,   776
And have a royal triumph?   Shall her eyes
Her sire and sons, her hearth and husband see,
While Phrygian captives follow in her train?
Is Priam murdered?   Have the flames swept o'er
My native Troy? and doth our Dardan strand   781
Sweat o'er and o'er with sanguinary dew?
O, not thus unavenged!   For though there be
No glory if I smite a woman's crime,
Nor conqueror's fame for such a victory won,   785
Yet if I blot this monster out, and wring
Full punishment from guilt, the time to come

[1] Wife of Æneas.
[2] Helen.

Will praise me, and sweet pleasure it will be
To glut my soul with vengeance and appease
The ashes of my kindred."
        So I raved,   790
And to such frenzied purpose gave my soul.
Then with clear vision (never had I seen
Her presence so unclouded) I beheld,
In golden beams that pierced the midnight gloom,
My gracious mother, visibly divine,   795
And with that mien of majesty she wears
When seen in heaven; she stayed me with her hand,
And from her lips of rose this counsel gave:
"O son, what sorrow stirs thy boundless rage?
What madness this? Or whither vanisheth   800
Thy love of me? Wilt thou not seek to know
Where bides Anchises, thy abandoned sire,
Now weak with age? or if Creüsa lives
And young Ascanius, who are ringed about   804
With ranks of Grecian foes, and long ere this —
Save that my love can shield them and defend —
Had fallen on flame or fed some hungry sword?
Not Helen's hated beauty works thee woe;
Nor Paris, oft-accused. The cruelty
Of gods, of gods unaided, overwhelms   810
Thy country's power, and from its lofty height
Casts Ilium down. Behold, I take away
The barrier-cloud that dims thy mortal eye,
With murk and mist o'er-veiling. Fear not thou
To heed thy mother's word, nor let thy heart 815
Refuse obedience to her counsel given.
'Mid yonder trembling ruins, where thou see'st
Stone torn from stone, with dust and smoke up-
    rolling,
'Tis Neptune strikes the wall; his trident vast
Makes her foundation tremble, and unseats 820
The city from her throne. Fierce Juno leads
Resistless onset at the Scæan gate,[1]
And summons from the ships the league of powers,
Wearing her wrathful sword. On yonder height
Behold Tritonia [2] in the citadel 825
Clothed with the lightning and her Gorgon-shield!
Unto the Greeks great Jove himself renews
Their courage and their power; 'tis he thrusts on
The gods themselves against the Trojan arms.
Fly, O my son! The war's wild work give o'er!
I will be always nigh and set thee safe 831
Upon thy father's threshold." Having said,
She fled upon the viewless night away.

Then loomed o'er Troy the apparition vast
Of her dread foes divine; I seemed to see 835
All Ilium sink in fire, and sacred Troy,
Of Neptune's building, utterly o'erthrown.
So some huge ash-tree on the mountain's brow
(When rival woodmen, heaving stroke on stroke

[1] A gate of Troy.   [2] Pallas, Minerva.

Of two-edged axes, haste to cast her down) 840
Sways ominously her trembling, leafy top,
And drops her smitten head; till by her wounds
Vanquished at last, she makes her dying groan,
And falls in loud wreck from the cliffs uptorn.

I left the citadel; and, led by Heaven, 845
Threaded the maze of deadly foes and fires,
Through spears that glanced aside and flames that
    fell.
Soon came I to my father's ancient seat,
Our home and heritage. But lo! my sire
(Whom first of all I sought, and first would bear
To safe asylum in the distant hills) 851
Vowed he could never, after fallen Troy,
Live longer on, or bear an exile's woe.
"O you," he cried, "whose blood not yet betrays
The cruel taint of time, whose powers be still 855
Unpropped and undecayed, go, take your flight.
If heavenly wrath had willed my life to spare,
This dwelling had been safe. It is too much
That I have watched one wreck, and for too long
Outlived my vanquished country. Thus, O, thus!
Compose these limbs for death, and say farewell.
My own hand will procure it; or my foe 862
Will end me of mere pity, and for spoil
Will strip me bare. It is an easy loss
To have no grave. For many a year gone by, 865
Accursed of Heaven, I tarry in this world
A useless burden, since that fatal hour
When Jove, of gods the Sire and men the King,
His lightnings o'er me breathed and blasting fire."

Such fixed resolve he uttered o'er and o'er, 870
And would not yield, though with my tears did join
My spouse Creüsa, fair Ascanius,
And our whole house, imploring the gray sire
Not with himself to ruin all, nor add
Yet heavier burdens to our crushing doom. 875
He still cried, "No!" and clung to where he sate
And to the same dread purpose. I once more
Back to the fight would speed. For death alone
I made my wretched prayer. What space was left
For wisdom now? What chance or hope was
    given? 880
"Didst thou, dear father, dream that I could fly
Sundered from thee? Did such an infamy
Fall from a father's lips? If Heaven's decree
Will of this mighty nation not let live
A single soul, if thine own purpose be 885
To cast thyself and thy posterity
Into thy country's grave, behold, the door
Is open to thy death! Lo, Pyrrhus comes
Red-handed from King Priam! He has slain
A son before a father's eyes, and spilt 890
A father's blood upon his own hearthstone.

Was it for this, O heavenly mother mine,
That thou hast brought me safe through sword and
            fire?
That I might see these altars desecrate
By their worst foes? that I might look upon   895
My sire, my wife, and sweet Ascanius
Dead at my feet in one another's blood?
To arms, my men, to arms!   The hour of death
Now beckons to the vanquished.   Let me go
Whither the Greeks are gathered; let me stand   900
Where oft revives the flagging stroke of war:
Not all of us die unavenged this day!"

I clasped my sword-belt round me once again,
Fitted my left arm to my shield, and turned
To fly the house; but at the threshold clung   905
Creüsa to my knees, and lifted up
Iulus to his father's arms.   "If thou
Wouldst rush on death," she cried, "O, suffer us
To share thy perils with thee to the end.
But if this day's work bid thee trust a sword,   910
Defend thy hearthstone first.   Who else shall guard
Thy babe Iulus, or thy reverend sire?
Or me, thy wife that was — what help have I?"

So rang the roof-top with her piteous cries:
But lo! a portent wonderful to see   915
On sudden rose; for while his parents' grief
Held the boy close in arm and full in view,
There seemed upon Iulus' head to glow
A flickering peak of fire; the tongue of flame
Innocuous o'er his clustering tresses played,   920
And hovered round his brows.
                                We, horror-struck,
Grasped at his burning hair, and sprinkled him,
To quench that holy and auspicious fire.
Then sire Anchises with exultant eyes
Looked heavenward, and lifted to the stars   925
His voice and outstretched hands.   "Almighty
            Jove,
If aught of prayer may move thee, let thy grace
Now visit us!   O, hear this holy vow!
And if for service at thine altars done,
We aught can claim, O Father, lend us aid.   930
And ratify the omen thou hast given!"

Scarce ceased his aged voice, when suddenly
From leftward, with a deafening thunder-peal,
Cleaving the blackness of the vaulted sky,
A meteor-star in trailing splendor ran,   935
Exceeding bright.   We watched it glide sublime
O'er tower and town, until its radiant beam
In forest-mantled Ida died away;
But left a furrow on its track in air,
A glittering, long line, while far and wide   940
The sulphurous fume and exhalation flowed.

My father strove not now; but lifted him
In prayer to all the gods, in holy awe
Of that auspicious star, and thus exclaimed:
"Tarry no moment more!   Behold, I come!   945
Whithersoe'er ye lead, my steps obey.
Gods of my fathers, O, preserve our name!
Preserve my son, and his!   This augury
Is yours; and Troy on your sole strength relies.
I yield, dear son; I journey at thy side."   950

He spoke; and higher o'er the blazing walls
Leaped the loud fire, while ever nearer drew
The rolling surges of tumultuous flame.
"Haste, father, on these bending shoulders climb
This back is ready, and the burden light;   955
One peril smites us both, whate'er befall;
One rescue both shall find.   Close at my side
Let young Iulus run, while, not too nigh,
My wife Creüsa heeds what way we go.
Ye servants of our house, give ear, I pray,   960
To my command.   Outside the city's gates
Lies a low mound and long since ruined fane
To Ceres vowed; a cypress' ancient shade
O'erhangs it, which our fathers' pious care
Protected year by year; by various paths   965
Be that our meeting-place.
                              But in thy hands
Bring, sire, our household gods, and sanctities:
For me to touch, who come this very hour
From battle and the fresh blood of the slain,
Were but abomination, till what time   970
In living waters I shall make me clean."

So saying, I bowed my neck and shoulders broad,
O'erspread me with a lion's tawny skin,
And lifted up my load.   Close at my side
Little Iulus twined his hand in mine   975
And followed, with unequal step, his sire.
My wife at distance came.   We hastened on,
Creeping through shadows; I, who once had viewed
Undaunted every instrument of war
And all the gathered Greeks in grim array,   980
Now shook at every gust, and heard all sounds
With fevered trepidation, fearing both
For him I bore and him who clasped my hand.

Now near the gates I drew, and deemed our flight
Safely at end, when suddenly I heard   985
The sounding tread of many warriors
That seemed hard-by, while through the murky
            night
My father peered, and shouted, "O my son,
Away, away! for surely all our foes
Are here upon us, and my eyes behold   990
The glance of glittering shields and flash of arms."
O, then some evil-working, nameless god

Clouded my senses quite: for while I sped
Along our pathless way, and left behind
All paths and regions known — O wretched me! —
Creüsa on some dark disaster fell;   996
She stopped, or wandered, or sank down undone,
I never knew what way, — and nevermore
I looked on her alive.   Yet knew I not
My loss, nor backward turned a look or thought,
Till by that hallowed hill to Ceres vowed   1001
We gathered all, — and she alone came not,
While husband, friends, and son made search in
          vain.
What god, what man, did not my grief accuse
In frenzied word?   In all the ruined land   1005
What worse woe had I seen?   Entrusting then
My sire, my son, and all the Teucrian gods
To the deep shadows of a slanting vale
Where my allies kept guard, I hied me back
To that doomed town, re-girt in glittering arms.
Resolved was I all hazards to renew,   1011
All Troy to re-explore, and once again
Offer my life to perils without end.
The walls and gloomy gates whence forth I came
I first revisit, and retrace my way,   1015
Searching the night once more.   On all sides round
Horror spread wide; the very silence breathed
A terror on my soul.   I hastened then
Back to my fallen home, if haply there
Her feet had strayed; but the invading Greeks   1020
Were its possessors, though the hungry fire
Was blown along the roof-tree, and the flames
Rolled raging upward on the fitful gale.
To Priam's house I haste, and climb once more
The citadel; in Juno's temple there,   1025
The chosen guardians of her wasted halls,
Phœnix and dread Ulysses watched the spoil.
Here, snatched away from many a burning fane,
Troy's treasures lay, — rich tables for the gods,
Thick bowls of massy gold, and vestures rare,   1030
Confusedly heaped up, while round the pile
Fair youths and trembling virgins stood forlorn.

Yet oft my voice rang dauntless through the gloom,
From street to street I cried with anguish vain;
And on Creüsa piteously calling,   1035
Woke the lamenting echoes o'er and o'er.
While on this quest I roamed the city through,
Of reason reft, there rose upon my sight —
O shape of sorrow! — my Creüsa's ghost,
Hers truly, though a loftier port it wore.   1040
I quailed, my hair rose, and I gasped for fear;
But thus she spoke, and soothed my grief away:
"Why to these frenzied sorrows bend thy soul,
O husband ever dear!   The will of Heaven
Hath brought all this to pass.   Fate doth not
          send   1045

Creüsa the long journeys thou shalt take,
Nor hath th' Olympian King so given decree.
Long is thy banishment; thy ship must plough
The vast, far-spreading sea.   Then shalt thou
          come
Unto Hesperia,[1] whose fruitful plains   1050
Are watered by the Tiber, Lydian stream,
Of smooth, benignant flow.   Thou shalt obtain
Fair fortunes, and a throne and royal bride.
For thy beloved Creüsa weep no more!
No Myrmidon's proud palace waits me now;   1055
Dolopian shall not scorn, nor Argive dames
Command a slave of Dardan's royal stem
And wife to Venus's son.   On these loved shores
The Mother of the Gods compels my stay.
Farewell! farewell!   O, cherish evermore   1060
Thy son and mine!"
                    Her utterance scarce had ceased,
When, as I strove through tears to make reply,
She left me, and dissolved in empty air.
Thrice would my frustrate arms her form enfold;
Thrice from the clasp of hand that vision fled,   1065
Like wafted winds and like a fleeting dream.

The night had passed, and to my friends once more
I made my way, much wondering to find
A mighty multitude assembled there
Of friends new-come, — matrons and men-at-
          arms,   1070
And youth for exile bound, — a doleful throng.
From far and near they drew, their hearts prepared
And their possessions gathered, to sail forth
To lands unknown, wherever o'er the wave
I bade them follow.
                    Now above the crest   1075
Of loftiest Ida rose the morning-star,
Chief in the front of day.   The Greeks held fast
The captive gates of Troy.   No help or hope
Was ours any more.   Then, yielding all,
And lifting once again my aged sire,   1080
For refuge to the distant hills I fled.

BOOK IV [2]

Now felt the Queen the sharp, slow-gathering pangs
Of love; and out of every pulsing vein
Nourished the wound and fed its viewless fire.
Her hero's virtues and his lordly line
Keep calling to her soul; his words, his glance,   5
Cling to her heart like lingering, barbèd steel,
And rest and peace from her vexed body fly.

---

[1] The present Italy.
[2] Æneas has started on his voyage which culminates
in his founding of Italy.   Here is told his adventure with
Dido.

A new day's dawn with Phœbus' lamp divine
Lit up all lands, and from the vaulted heaven
Aurora had dispelled the dark and dew;   10
When thus unto the ever-answering heart
Of her dear sister spoke the stricken Queen:
"Anna, my sister, what disturbing dreams
Perplex me and alarm?   What guest is this
New-welcomed to our house?   How proud his mien!
What dauntless courage and exploits of war!   16
Sooth, I receive it for no idle tale
That of the gods he sprang.   'Tis cowardice
Betrays the base-born soul.   Ah me!   How fate
Has smitten him with storms!   What dire extremes
Of war and horror in his tale he told!   21
O, were it not immutably resolved
In my fixed heart, that to no shape of man
I would be wed again (since my first love
Left me by death abandoned and betrayed);   25
Loathed I not so the marriage torch and train,
I could,—who knows?—to this one weakness yield.
Anna, I hide it not!   But since the doom
Of my ill-starred Sichæus,[1] when our shrines
Were by a brother's murder dabbled o'er,   30
This man alone has moved me; he alone
Has shaken my weak will.   I seem to feel
The motions of love's lost, familiar fire.
But may the earth gape open where I tread,
And may almighty Jove with thunder-scourge   35
Hurl me to Erebus'[2] abysmal shade,
To pallid ghosts and midnight fathomless,
Before, O Chastity!   I shall offend
Thy holy power, or cast thy bonds away!
He who first mingled his dear life with mine   40
Took with him all my heart.   'Tis his alone —
O, let it rest beside him in the grave!"
She spoke: the bursting tears her breast o'erflowed:

"O dearer to thy sister than her life,"
Anna replied, "wouldst thou in sorrow's weed   45
Waste thy long youth alone, nor ever know
Sweet babes at thine own breast, nor gifts of love?
Will dust and ashes, or a buried ghost,
Reck what we do?   'Tis true thy grieving heart
Was cold to earlier wooers, Libya's now,   50
And long ago in Tyre.   Iarbas[3] knew
Thy scorn, and many a prince and captain bred
In Afric's land of glory.   Why resist
A love that makes thee glad?   Hast thou no care
What alien lands are these where thou dost reign?
Here are Gætulia's[4] cities and her tribes   56
Unconquered ever; on thy borders rove

[1] Her husband.
[2] A place of darkness between Earth and Hades,
sometimes used to name the place of the dead.
[3] A king and suitor of Dido.
[4] Country in northern Africa.

Numidia's[1] uncurbed cavalry; here too
Lies Syrtis'[1] cruel shore, and regions wide
Of thirsty desert, menaced everywhere   60
By the wild hordes of Barca.[1]   Shall I tell
Of Tyre's hostilities, the threats and rage
Of our own brother?   Friendly gods, I trow,
Wafted the Teucrian ships, with Juno's aid,
To these our shores.   O sister, what a throne,   65
And what imperial city shall be thine,
If thus espoused!   With Trojan arms allied
How far may not our Punic fame extend
In deeds of power?   Call therefore on the gods
To favor thee; and, after omens fair,   70
Give queenly welcome, and contrive excuse
To make him tarry, while yon wintry seas
Are loud beneath Orion's stormful star,
And on his battered ships the season frowns."

So saying, she stirred a passion-burning breast   75
To love more madly still; her words infused
A doubting mind with hope, and bade the blush
Of shame begone.   First to the shrines they went
And sued for grace; performing sacrifice,
Choosing an offering of unblemished ewes,   80
To law-bestowing Ceres, to the god
Of light, to sire Lyæus, lord of wine;
But chiefly into Juno, patroness
Of nuptial vows.   There Dido, beauteous Queen,
Held forth in her right hand the sacred bowl,   85
And poured it full between the lifted horns
Of the white heifer; or on temple floors
She strode among the richly laden shrines,
The eyes of gods upon her, worshipping
With many a votive gift; or, peering deep   90
Into the victims' cloven sides, she read
The fate-revealing tokens trembling there.
How blind the hearts of prophets be!   Alas!
Of what avail be temples and fond prayers
To change a frenzied mind?   Devouring ever,   95
Love's fire burns inward to her bones; she feels
Quick in her breast the viewless, voiceless wound.
Ill-fated Dido ranges up and down
The spaces of her city, desperate,
Her life one flame — like arrow-striken doe,   100
Through Cretan forest rashly wandering,
Pierced by a far-off shepherd, who pursues
With shafts, and leaves behind his light-winged
     steel,
Not knowing; while she scours the dark ravines
Of Dicte and its woodlands; at her heart   105
The mortal barb irrevocably clings.
Around her city's battlements she guides
Æneas, to make show of Sidon's gold,
And what her realm can boast; full oft her voice
Essays to speak and trembling dies away: 110
[1] Countries in northern Africa.

Or, when the daylight fades, she spreads anew
A royal banquet, and once more will plead,
Mad that she is, to hear the Trojan sorrow;
And with oblivious ravishment once more
Hangs on his lips who tells; or when her guests   115
Are scattered, and the wan moon's fading horn
Bedims its ray, while many a sinking star
Invites to slumber, there she weeps alone
In the deserted hall, and casts her down
On the cold couch he pressed. Her love from far
Behold her vanished hero and receives   121
His voice upon her ears; or to her breast,
Moved by a father's image in his child,
She clasps Ascanius,[1] seeking to deceive
Her unblest passion so. Her enterprise   125
Of tower and rampart stops: her martial host
No longer she reviews, nor fashions now
Defensive haven and defiant wall;
But idly all her half-built bastions frown,
And enginery of sieges, high as heaven.   130

But soon the chosen spouse of Jove perceived
The Queen's infection; and because the voice
Of honor to such frenzy spoke not, she,
Daughter of Saturn, unto Venus turned
And counselled thus: "How noble is the praise,   135
How glorious the spoils of victory,
For thee and for thy boy! Your names should be
In lasting, vast renown — that by the snare
Of two great gods in league one woman fell!
It 'scapes me not that my protected realms   140
Have ever been thy fear, and the proud halls
Of Carthage thy vexation and annoy.
Why further go? Prithee, what useful end
Has our long war? Why not from this day forth
Perpetual peace and nuptial amity?   145
Hast thou not worked thy will? Behold and see
How love-sick Dido burns, and all her flesh
The madness feels! So let our common grace
Smile on a mingled people! Let her serve
A Phrygian husband, while thy hands receive   150
Her Tyrian subjects for the bridal dower!"

In answer (reading the dissembler's mind
Which unto Libyan shores were fain to shift
Italia's future throne) thus Venus spoke:
"'Twere mad to spurn such favor, or by choice   155
Be numbered with thy foes. But can it be
That fortune on thy noble counsel smiles?
To me Fate shows but dimly whether Jove
Unto the Trojan wanderers ordains
A common city with the sons of Tyre,   160
With mingling blood and sworn, perpetual peace.
His wife thou art; it is thy rightful due
To plead to know his mind. Go, ask him, then!"

    [1] Son of Æneas.

For humbly I obey!"
            With instant word
Juno the Queen replied: "Leave that to me!   165
But in what wise our urgent task and grave
May soon be sped, I will in brief unfold
To thine attending ear. A royal hunt
In sylvan shades unhappy Dido gives
For her Æneas, when to-morrow's dawn   170
Uplifts its earliest ray and Titan's beam
Shall first unveil the world. But I will pour
Black storm-clouds with a burst of heavy hail
Along their way; and as the huntsmen speed
To hem the wood with snares, I will arouse   175
All heaven with thunder. The attending train
Shall scatter and be veiled in blinding dark,
While Dido and her hero out of Troy
To the same cavern fly. My auspices
I will declare — if thou alike wilt bless;   180
And yield her in true wedlock for his bride.
Such shall their spousal be!" To Juno's will
Cythéra's Queen inclined assenting brow:
And laughed such guile to see.
                    Aurora rose,
And left the ocean's rim. The city's gates   185
Pour forth to greet the morn a gallant train
Of huntsmen, bearing many a woven snare
And steel-tipped javelin; while to and fro
Run the keen-scented dogs and Libyan squires.
The Queen still keeps her chamber; at her doors   190
The Punic lords await; her palfrey, brave
In gold and purple housing, paws the ground
And fiercely champs the foam-flecked bridle-rein.
At last, with numerous escort, forth she shines:
Her Tyrian pall is bordered in bright hues,   195
Her quiver, gold; her tresses are confined
Only with gold; her robes of purple rare
Meet in a golden clasp. To greet her come
The noble Phrygian guests; among them smiles
The boy Iulus; and in fair array   200
Æneas, goodliest of all his train.
In such a guise Apollo (when he leaves
Cold Lycian hills and Xanthus' frosty stream
To visit Delos to Latona dear)
Ordains the song, while round his altars cry   205
The choirs of many islands, with the pied,
Fantastic Agathyrsi;[1] soon the god
Moves o'er the Cynthian steep; his flowing hair
He binds with laurel garland and bright gold;
Upon his shining shoulder as he goes   210
The arrows ring: — not less uplifted mien
Æneas wore; from his illustrious brow
Such beauty shone.
                Soon to the mountains tall
The cavalcade comes nigh, to pathless haunts
Of woodland creatures; the wild goats are seen,   215

    [1] A people of Scythia, noted for their effeminacy.

From pointed crag descending leap by leap
Down the steep ridges; in the vales below
Are routed deer, that scour [1] the spreading plain,
And mass their dust-blown squadrons in wild flight,
Far from the mountain's bound.   Ascanius,   220
Flushed with the sport, spurs on a mettled steed
From vale to vale, and many a flying herd
His chase outspeeds; but in his heart he prays
Among these tame things suddenly to see
A tusky boar, or, leaping from the hills,   225
A growling mountain-lion, golden-maned.

Meanwhile low thunders in the distant sky
Mutter confusedly; soon bursts in full
The storm-cloud and the hail.   The Tyrian troop
Is scattered wide; the chivalry of Troy,   230
With the young heir of Dardan's kingly line,
Of Venus sprung, seek shelter where they may,
With sudden terror; down the deep ravines
The swollen torrents roar.   In that same hour
Queen Dido and her hero out of Troy   235
To the same cavern fly.   Old Mother-Earth
And wedlock-keeping Juno gave the sign;
The flash of lightnings on the conscious air
Were torches to the bridal; from the hills   239
The wailing wood-nymphs sobbed a wedding song.
Such was that day of death, the source and spring
Of many a woe.   For Dido took no heed
Of honor and good-name; nor did she mean
Her loves to hide; but called the lawlessness
A marriage, and with phrases veiled her shame.   245

Swift through the Libyan cities Rumor sped.
Rumor!   What evil can surpass her speed?
In movement she grows mighty, and achieves
Strength and dominion as she swifter flies.
Small first, because afraid, she soon exalts   250
Her stature skyward, stalking through the lands
And mantling in the clouds her baleful brow.
The womb of Earth, in anger at high Heaven,
Bore her, they say, last of the Titan spawn,
Sister to Cœus and Enceladus.   255
Feet swift to run and pinions like the wind
The dreadful monster wears; her carcase huge
Is feathered, and at root of every plume
A peering eye abides; and, strange to tell,
An equal number of vociferous tongues,   260
Foul, whispering lips, and ears, that catch at all.
At night she spreads midway 'twixt earth and
        heaven
Her pinions in the darkness, hissing loud,
Nor e'er to happy slumber gives her eyes:
But with the morn she takes her watchful throne
High on the housetops or on lofty towers,   266
To terrify the nations.   She can cling

[1] Race over.

To vile invention and malignant wrong,
Or mingle with her word some tidings true.

She now with changeful story filled men's ears, 270
Exultant, whether false or true she sung:
How, Trojan-born Æneas having come,
Dido, the lovely widow, looked his way,
Deigning to wed; how all the winter long
They passed in revel and voluptuous ease,   275
To dalliance given o'er; naught heeding now
Of crown or kingdom — shameless! lust-enslaved!
Such tidings broadcast on the lips of men
The filthy goddess spread; and soon she hied
To King Iarbas, where her hateful song   280
To newly-swollen wrath his heart inflamed.
Him the god Ammon got by forced embrace
Upon a Libyan nymph; his kingdoms wide
Possessed a hundred ample shrines to Jove,
A hundred altars whence ascended ever   285
The fires of sacrifice, perpetual seats
For a great god's abode, where flowing blood
Enriched the ground, and on the portals hung
Garlands of every flower.   The angered King,
Half-maddened by malignant Rumor's voice,   290
Unto his favored altars came, and there,
Surrounded by the effluence divine,
Upraised in prayer to Jove his suppliant hands.
"Almighty Jupiter, to whom each day,
At banquet on the painted couch reclined,   295
Numidia pours libation!   Do thine eyes
Behold us?   Or when out of yonder heaven,
O sire, thou launchest the swift thunderbolt,
Is it for naught we fear thee?   Do the clouds
Shoot forth blind fire to terrify the soul   300
With wild, unmeaning roar?   O, look upon
That woman, who was homeless in our realm,
And bargained where to build her paltry town,
Receiving fertile coastland for her farms,
By hospitable grant!   She dares disdain   305
Our proffered nuptial vow.   She has proclaimed
Æneas partner of her bed and throne.
And now that Paris,[1] with his eunuch crew,
Beneath his chin and fragrant, oozy hair
Ties the soft Lydian bonnet,[2] boasting well   310
His stolen prize.   But we to all these fanes,
Though they be thine, a fruitless offering bring,
And feed on empty tales our trust in thee."

As thus he prayed and to the altars clung,
Th' Omnipotent gave ear, and turned his gaze   315
Upon the royal dwelling, where for love
The amorous pair forgot their place and name.

[1] Æneas is likened to Paris, who also stole and
ravished a princess.
[2] To show how effeminate he thinks Æneas, Iarbus
accuses him of wearing a woman's bonnet.

Then thus to Mercury he gave command:
"Haste thee, my son, upon the Zephyrs call,
And take thy wingèd way! My mandate bear 320
Unto that prince of Troy who tarries now
In Tyrian Carthage, heedless utterly
Of empire Heaven-bestowed. On wingèd winds
Hasten with my decrees. Not such the man
His beauteous mother promised; not for this 325
Twice did she shield him from the Greeks in arms:
But that he might rule Italy, a land
Pregnant with thrones and echoing with war;
That he of Teucer's [1] seed a race should sire,
And bring beneath its law the whole wide world.
If such a glory and event supreme 331
Enkindle not his bosom; if such task
To his own honor speak not; can the sire
Begrudge Ascanius the heritage
Of the proud name of Rome? What plans he now?
What mad hope bids him linger in the lap 336
Of enemies, considering no more
The land Lavinian and Ausonia's sons.
Let him to sea! Be this our final word:
This message let our herald faithful bear." 340
He spoke. The god a prompt obedience gave
To his great sire's command. He fastened first
Those sandals of bright gold, which carry him
Aloft o'er land or sea, with airy wings
That race the fleeting wind; then lifted he 345
His wand, wherewith he summons from the grave
Pale-featured ghosts, or, if he will, consigns
To doleful Tartarus; [2] or by its power
Gives slumber or dispels; or quite unseals
The eyelids of the dead: on this relying, 350
He routs the winds or cleaves th' obscurity
Of stormful clouds. Soon from his flight he spied
The summit and the sides precipitous
Of stubborn Atlas, whose star-pointing peak
Props heaven; of Atlas, whose pine-wreathèd brow
Is girdled evermore with misty gloom 356
And lashed of wind and rain; a cloak of snow
Melts on his shoulder; from his aged chin
Drop rivers, and ensheathed in stiffening ice
Glitters his great grim beard.
                    Here first was stayed 360
The speed of Mercury's well-poising wing;
Here making pause, from hence he headlong flung
His body to the sea; in motion like
Some sea-bird's, which along the levelled shore
Or round tall crags where rove the swarming fish,
Flies low along the waves: o'er-hovering so 366
Between the earth and skies, Cyllene's god
Flew downward from his mother's mountain-sire,
Parted the winds and skimmed the sandy marge
Of Libya. When first his wingèd feet 370

[1] First king of Troy.
[2] A dark abysm of the lower world.

Came nigh the clay-built Punic huts, he saw
Æneas building at a citadel,
And founding walls and towers; at his side
Was girt a blade with yellow jaspers starred,
His mantle with the stain of Tyrian shell 375
Flowed purple from his shoulder, broidered fair
By opulent Dido with fine threads of gold,
Her gift of love; straightway the god began:
"Dost thou for lofty Carthage toil, to build
Foundations strong? Dost thou, a wife's weak
        thrall, 380
Build her proud city? Hast thou, shameful loss!
Forgot thy kingdom and thy task sublime?
From bright Olympus, I. He who commands
All gods, and by his sovran deity
Moves earth and heaven — he it was who bade 385
Me bear on wingèd winds his high decree.
What plan is thine? By what mad hope dost thou
Linger so long in lap of Libyan land?
If the proud guerdon of thy destined way
Move not thy heart, if all the arduous toil 390
To thine own honor speak not, look upon
Iulus in his bloom, thy hope and heir
Ascanius. It is his rightful due
In Italy o'er Roman lands to reign."
After such word Cyllene's wingèd god 395
Vanished, and e'er his accents died away,
Dissolved in air before the mortal's eyes.

Æneas at the sight stood terror-dumb
With choking voice and horror-rising hair.
He fain would fly at once and get him gone 400
From that voluptuous land, much wondering
At Heaven's wrathful word. Alas! how stir?
What cunning argument can plead his cause
Before th' infuriate Queen? How break such
        news?
Flashing this way and that, his startled mind 405
Makes many a project and surveys them all.
But, pondering well, his final counsel stopped
At this resolve: he summoned to his side
Mnestheus, Sergestus, and Serestus bold,
And bade them fit the fleet, all silently 410
Gathering the sailors and collecting gear,
But carefully dissembling what emprise
Such novel stir intends: himself the while
(Since high-born Dido dreamed not love so fond
Could have an end) would seek an audience, 415
At some indulgent time, and try what shift
Such matters may require. With joy they heard,
And wrought, assiduous, at their prince's plan.

But what can cheat true love? The Queen fore-
        knew
His stratagem, and all the coming change 420
Perceived ere it began. Her jealous fear

Counted no hour secure. That unclean tongue
Of Rumor told her fevered heart the fleet
Was fitting forth, and hastening to be gone.
Distractedly she raved, and passion-tossed   425
Roamed through her city, like a Mænad [1] roused
By the wild rout of Bacchus, when are heard
The third year's orgies, and the midnight scream
To cold Cithæron calls the frenzied crew.
Finding Æneas, thus her plaint she poured: 430
"Didst hope to hide it, false one, that such crime
Was in thy heart, — to steal without farewell
Out of my kingdom? Did our mutual joy
Not move thee; nor thine own true promise given
Once on a time? Nor Dido, who will die   435
A death of sorrow? Why compel thy ships
To brave the winter stars? Why off to sea
So fast through stormy skies? O, cruelty!
If Troy still stood, and if thou wert not bound   439
For alien shore unknown, wouldst steer for Troy
Through yonder waste of waves? Is it from me
Thou takest flight? O, by these flowing tears,
By thine own plighted word (for nothing more
My weakness left to miserable me),
By our poor marriage of imperfect vow,   445
If aught to me thou owest, if aught in me
Ever have pleased thee — O, be merciful
To my low-fallen fortunes! I implore,
If place be left for prayer, thy purpose change!
Because of thee yon Libyan savages   450
And nomad chiefs are grown implacable,
And my own Tyrians hate me. Yes, for thee
My chastity was slain and honor fair,
By which alone to glory I aspired,
In former days. To whom dost thou in death   455
Abandon me? my guest! — since but this name
Is left me of a husband! Shall I wait
Till fell Pygmalion, my brother, raze
My city walls? Or the Gætulian king,
Iarbas, chain me captive to his car?   460
O, if, ere thou hadst fled, I might but bear
Some pledge of love to thee, and in these halls
Watch some sweet babe Æneas at his play,
Whose face should be the memory of thine own —
I were not so forsaken, lost, undone!"   465

She said. But he, obeying Jove's decree,
Gazed steadfastly away; and in his heart
With strong repression crushed his cruel pain;
Then thus the silence broke: "O Queen, not one
Of my unnumbered debts so strongly urged   470
Would I gainsay. Elissa's [2] memory
Will be my treasure long as memory holds,
Or breath of life is mine. Hear my brief plea!
'Twas not my hope to hide this flight I take,

[1] Maid, attendant upon Bacchus.
[2] Another name for Dido.

As thou hast dreamed. Nay, I did never light   475
A bridegroom's torch, nor gave I thee the vow
Of marriage. Had my destiny decreed,
That I should shape life to my heart's desire,
And at my own will put away the weight
Of toil and pain, my place would now be found   480
In Troy, among the cherished sepulchres
Of my own kin, and Priam's mansion proud
Were standing still; or these my loyal hands
Had rebuilt Ilium for her vanquished sons.
But now to Italy Apollo's power   485
Commands me forth; his Lycian oracles
Are loud for Italy. My heart is there,
And there my fatherland. If now the towers
Of Carthage and thy Libyan colony
Delight thy Tyrian eyes, wilt thou refuse   490
To Trojan exiles their Ausonian shore?
I too by Fate was driven, not less than thou,
To wander far a foreign throne to find.
Oft when in dewy dark night hides the world,
And flaming stars arise, Anchises' shade   495
Looks on me in my dreams with angered brow.
I think of my Ascanius, and the wrong
To that dear heart, from whom I steal away
Hesperia, his destined home and throne.
But now the wingèd messenger of Heaven,   500
Sent down by Jove (I swear by thee and me!),
Has brought on wingèd winds his sire's command.
My own eyes with unclouded vision saw
The god within these walls; I have received
With my own ears his word. No more inflame   505
With lamentation fond thy heart and mine.
'Tis not my own free act seeks Italy."

She with averted eyes and glance that rolled
Speechless this way and that, had listened long
To his reply, till thus her rage broke forth: 510
"No goddess gave thee birth. No Dardanus
Begot thy sires. But on its breast of stone
Caucasus bore thee, and the tigresses
Of fell Hyrcania to thy baby lip
Their udders gave. Why should I longer show   515
A lying smile? What worse can I endure?
Did my tears draw one sigh? Did he once drop
His stony stare? or did he yield a tear
To my lament, or pity this fond heart?
Why set my wrongs in order? Juno, now,   520
And Jove, the son of Saturn, heed no more
Where justice lies. No trusting heart is safe
In all this world. That waif and castaway
I found in beggary and gave him share —
Fool that I was! — in my own royal glory.   525
His lost fleet and his sorry crews I steered
From death away. O, how my fevered soul
Unceasing raves! Forsooth Apollo speaks!
His Lycian oracles! and sent by Jove

The messenger of Heaven on fleeting air   530
The ruthless bidding brings! Proud business
For gods, I trow, that such a task disturbs
Their still abodes! I hold thee back no more,
Nor to thy cunning speeches give the lie.
Begone! Sail on to Italy, thy throne,   535
Through wind and wave! I pray that, if there be
Any just gods of power, thou mayest drink down
Death on the mid-sea rocks, and often call
With dying gasps on Dido's name — while I
Pursue with vengeful fire. When cold death rends
The body from the breath, my ghost shall sit   541
Forever in thy path. Full penalties
Thy stubborn heart shall pay. They'll bring me
          news
In yon deep gulf of death of all thy woe."

Abrupt her utterance ceased; and sick at heart   545
She fled the light of day, as if to shrink
From human eyes, and left Æneas there
Irresolute with horror, while his soul
Framed many a vain reply. Her swooning shape
Her maidens to a marble chamber bore   550
And on her couch the helpless limbs reposed.

Æneas, faithful to a task divine,
Though yearning sore to remedy and soothe
Such misery, and with the timely word
Her grief assuage, and though his burdened heart
Was weak because of love, while many a groan   556
Rose from his bosom, yet no whit did fail
To do the will of Heaven, but of his fleet
Resumed command. The Trojans on the shore
Ply well their task and push into the sea   560
The lofty ships. Now floats the shining keel,
And oars they bring all leafy from the grove,
With oak half-hewn, so hurried was the flight.
Behold them how they haste — from every gate
Forth-streaming! — just as when a heap of corn 565
Is thronged with ants, who, knowing winter nigh,
Refill their granaries; the long black line
Runs o'er the levels, and conveys the spoil
In narrow pathway through the grass; a part
With straining and assiduous shoulder push   570
The kernels huge; a part array the file,
And whip the laggards on; their busy track
Swarms quick and eager with unceasing toil.

O Dido, how thy suffering heart was wrung,
That spectacle to see! What sore lament   575
Was thine, when from the towering citadel
The whole shore seemed alive, the sea itself
In turmoil with loud cries! Relentless Love,
To what mad courses may not mortal hearts
By thee be driven? Again her sorrow flies   580
To doleful plaint and supplication vain;

Again her pride to tyrant Love bows down,
Lest, though resolved to die, she fail to prove
Each hope of living: "O Anna, dost thou see
Yon busy shore? From every side they come. 585
Their canvas woos the winds, and o'er each prow
The merry seamen hang their votive flowers.
Dear sister, since I did forebode this grief,
I shall be strong to bear it. One sole boon
My sorrow asks thee, Anna! Since of thee,   590
Thee only, did that traitor make a friend,
And trusted thee with what he hid so deep —
The feelings of his heart; since thou alone
Hast known what way, what hour the man would
          yield
To soft persuasion — therefore, sister, haste, 595
And humbly thus implore our haughty foe:
'I was not with the Greeks what time they swore
At Aulis to cut off the seed of Troy;
I sent no ships to Ilium. Pray, have I
Profaned Anchises' tomb, or vexed his shade?' 600
Why should his ear be deaf and obdurate
To all I say? What haste? May he not make
One last poor offering to her whose love
Is only pain? O, bid him but delay
Till flight be easy and the winds blow fair. 605
I plead no more that bygone marriage-vow
By him forsworn, nor ask that he should lose
His beauteous Latium and his realm to be.
Nothing but time I crave! to give repose
And more room to this fever, till my fate   610
Teach a crushed heart to sorrow. I implore
This last grace. (To thy sister's grief be kind!)
I will requite with increase, till I die."

Such plaints, such prayers, again and yet again,
Betwixt the twain the sorrowing sister bore. 615
But no words move, no lamentations bring
Persuasion to his soul; decrees of Fate
Oppose, and some wise god obstructs the way
That finds the hero's ear. Oft-times around
The aged strength of some stupendous oak   620
The rival blasts of wintry Alpine winds
Smite with alternate wrath: loud is the roar,
And from its rocking top the broken boughs
Are strewn along the ground; but to the crag
Steadfast it ever clings; far as toward heaven 625
Its giant crest uprears, so deep below
Its roots reach down to Tartarus: — not less
The hero by unceasing wail and cry
Is smitten sore, and in his mighty heart
Has many a pang, while his serene intent   630
Abides unmoved, and tears gush forth in vain.

Then wretched Dido, by her doom appalled,
Asks only death. It wearies her to see
The sun in heaven. Yet that she might hold fast

Her dread resolve to quit the light of day,   635
Behold, when on an incense-breathing shrine
Her offering was laid — O fearful tale! —
The pure libation blackened, and the wine
Flowed like polluting gore.   She told the sight
To none, not even to her sister's ear.   640
A second sign was given: for in her house
A marble altar to her husband's shade,
With garlands bright and snowy fleeces dressed,
Had fervent worship; here strange cries were heard
As if her dead spouse called while midnight reigned,
And round her towers its inhuman song   646
The lone owl sang, complaining o'er and o'er
With lamentation and long shriek of woe.
Forgotten oracles by wizards told
Whisper old omens dire.   In dreams she feels   650
Cruel Æneas goad her madness on,
And ever seems she, friendless and alone,
Some lengthening path to travel, or to seek
Her Tyrians through wide wastes of barren lands.
Thus frantic Pentheus [1] flees the stern array   655
Of the Eumenides,[2] and thinks to see
Two noonday lights blaze o'er his doubled Thebes;
Or murdered Agamemnon's haunted son,
Orestes, flees his mother's phantom scourge
Of flames and serpents foul, while at his door   660
Avenging horrors wait.

                Now sorrow-crazed
And by her grief undone, resolved on death,
The manner and the time her secret soul
Prepares, and, speaking to her sister sad,
She masks in cheerful calm her fatal will: 665
"I know a way — O, wish thy sister joy! —
To bring him back to love, or set me free.
On Ocean's bound and next the setting sun
Lies the last Æthiop land, where Atlas tall
Lifts on his shoulder the wide wheel of heaven,   670
Studded with burning stars.   From thence is come
A witch, a priestess, a Numidian crone,
Who guards the shrine of the Hesperides
And feeds the dragon; she protects the fruit
Of that enchanting tree, and scatters there   675
Her slumb'rous poppies mixed with honey-dew.
Her spells and magic promise to set free
What hearts she will, or visit cruel woes
On men afar.   She stops the downward flow
Of rivers, and turns back the rolling stars;   680
On midnight ghosts she calls: her vot'ries hear
Earth bellowing loud below, while from the hills
The ash-trees travel down.   But, sister mine,
Thou knowest, and the gods their witness give,
How little mind have I to don the garb   685
Of sorcery.   Depart in secret, thou,

[1] Pentheus, King of Thebes, was torn to pieces by the bacchanals.

[2] The furies.

And bid them build a lofty funeral pyre
Inside our palace-wall, and heap thereon
The hero's arms, which that blasphemer hung
Within my chamber; every relic bring,   690
And chiefly that ill-omened nuptial bed,
My death and ruin!   For I must blot out
All sight and token of this husband vile.
'Tis what the witch commands."   She spoke no
     more,
And pallid was her brow.   Yet Anna's mind   695
Knew not what web of death her sister wove
By these strange rites, nor what such frenzy dares;
Nor feared she worse than when Sichæus died,
But hied her forth the errand to fulfil.

Soon as the funeral pyre was builded high   700
In a sequestered garden, looming huge
With boughs of pine and faggots of cleft oak,
The queen herself enwreathed it with sad flowers
And boughs of mournful shade; and crowning all
She laid on nuptial bed the robes and sword   705
By him abandoned; and stretched out thereon
A mock Æneas; — but her doom she knew.
Altars were there; and with loose locks unbound
The priestess with a voice of thunder called
Three hundred gods, Hell, Chaos, the three shapes
Of triple Hecate,[1] the faces three   711
Of virgin Dian.   She aspersed a stream
From dark Avernus [2] drawn, she said; soft herbs
Were cut by moonlight with a blade of bronze,
Oozing black poison-sap; and she had plucked   715
That philter from the forehead of new foal
Before its dam devours.   Dido herself,
Sprinkling the salt meal, at the altar stands;
One foot unsandalled, and with cincture free,
On all the gods and fate-instructed stars,   720
Foreseeing death, she calls.   But if there be
Some just and not oblivious power on high,
Who heeds when lovers plight unequal vow,
To that god first her supplications rise.

Soon fell the night, and peaceful slumbers breathed
On all earth's weary creatures; the loud seas   726
And babbling forests entered on repose;
Now midway in their heavenly course the stars
Wheeled silent on; the outspread lands below
Lay voiceless; all the birds of tinted wing,   730
And flocks that haunt the marge of waters wide
Or keep the thorny wold, oblivious lay
Beneath the night so still; the stings of care
Ceased troubling, and no heart its burden knew.
Not so the Tyrian Queen's deep-grieving soul!   735
To sleep she could not yield; her eyes and heart

[1] Called Luna in heaven, Diana on earth, and Hecate in hell.

[2] A lake, one of the entrances to Hades.

Refused the gift of night; her suffering
Redoubled, and in full returning tide
Her love rebelled, while on wild waves of rage
She drifted to and fro. So, ceasing not   740
From sorrow, thus she brooded on her wrongs:
"What refuge now? Shall I invite the scorn
Of my rejected wooers, or entreat
Of some disdainful, nomad blackamoor
To take me to his bed — though many a time   745
Such husbands I made mock of? Shall I sail
On Ilian ships away, and sink to be
The Trojans' humble thrall? Do they rejoice
That once I gave them bread? Lives gratitude
In hearts like theirs for bygone kindnesses?   750
O, who, if so I stooped, would deign to bear
On yon proud ships the scorned and fallen Queen?
Lost creature! Woe betide thee! Knowest thou
not
The perjured children of Laomedon? [1]
What way is left? Should I take flight alone 755
And join the revelling sailors? Or depart
With Tyrians, the whole attending train
Of my own people? Hard the task to force
Their hearts from Sidon's towers; how once more
Compel to sea, and bid them spread the sail?   760
Nay, perish! Thou hast earned it. Let the sword
From sorrow save thee! Sister of my blood —
Who else but thee, — by my own tears borne down,
Didst heap disaster on my frantic soul,
And fling me to this foe? Why could I not   765
Pass wedlock by, and live a blameless life
As wild things do, nor taste of passion's pain?
But I broke faith! I cast the vows away
Made at Sichæus' grave." Such loud lament
Burst from her breaking heart with doleful sound.

Meanwhile Æneas on his lofty ship,   771
Having made ready all, and fixed his mind
To launch away, upon brief slumber fell.
But the god came; and in the self-same guise
Once more in monitory vision spoke, —   775
All guised as Mercury, — his voice, his hue,
His golden locks, and young limbs strong and fair.
"Hail, goddess-born! Wouldst linger on in sleep
At such an hour? Nor seest thou the snares
That hem thee round? Nor hearest thou the voice
Of friendly zephyrs calling? Senseless man! 781
That woman's breast contrives some treachery
And horrid stroke; for, resolute to die,
She drifts on swollen floods of wrath and scorn.
Wilt thou not fly before the hastening hour 785
Of flight is gone? To-morrow thou wilt see
Yon waters thronged with ships, the cruel glare
Of fire-brands, and yonder shore all flame,
If but the light of morn again surprise

[1] A name for the Trojans.

Thee loitering in this land. Away! Away!   790
Stay not! A mutable and shifting thing
Is woman ever."
                    Such command he spoke,
Then melted in the midnight dark away.
Æneas, by that fleeting vision struck   794
With an exceeding awe, straightway leaped forth
From slumber's power, and to his followers cried:
"Awake, my men! Away! Each to his place
Upon the thwarts! Unfurl at once the sails!
A god from heaven a second time sent down
Urges our instant flight, and bids us cut   800
The twisted cores. Whatever be thy name,
Behold, we come, O venerated Power!
Again with joy we follow! Let thy grace
Assist us as we go! And may thy power
Bring none but stars benign across our sky." 805
So saying, from its scabbard forth he flashed
The lightning of his sword, with naked blade
Striking the hawsers free. Like ardor seized
On all his willing men, who raced and ran;
And, while their galleys shadowed all the sea, 810
Clean from the shore they scudded, with strong
strokes
Sweeping the purple waves and crested foam.

Aurora's first young beams to earth were pouring
As from Tithonus' saffron bed she sprang;
While from her battlements the wakeful Queen 815
Watched the sky brighten, saw the mated sails
Push forth to sea, till all her port and strand
Held not an oar or keel. Thrice and four times
She smote her lovely breast with wrathful hand,
And tore her golden hair. "Great Jove," she
cries,   820
"Shall that departing fugitive make mock
Of me, a queen? Will not my men-at-arms
Draw sword, give chase, from all my city throng-
ing?
Down from the docks, my ships! Out, out! Be-
gone!   824
Take fire and sword! Bend to your oars, ye
slaves!
What have I said? Where am I? What mad
thoughts
Delude this ruined mind? Woe unto thee,
Thou wretched Dido, now thy impious deeds
Strike back upon thee. Wherefore struck they not,
As was most fit, when thou didst fling away   830
Thy sceptre from thy hand? O lying oaths!
O faith forsworn! of him who brings, they boast,
His father's gods along, and bowed his back
To lift an age-worn sire! Why dared I not
Seize on him, rend his body limb from limb,   835
And hurl him piecemeal on the rolling sea?
Or put his troop of followers to the sword,

Ascanius too, and set his flesh before
That father for a feast?   Such fearful war
Had been of doubtful issue.   Be it so!   840
What fears a woman dying?   Would I had
Attacked their camp with torches, kindled flame
From ship to ship, until that son and sire,
With that whole tribe, were unto ashes burned
In one huge holocaust — myself its crown!   845
Great orb of light whose holy beam surveys
All earthly deeds!   Great Juno, patroness
Of conjugal distress, who knowest all!
Pale Hecate, whose name the witches cry
At midnight crossways!   O avenging furies!   850
O gods that guard Queen Dido's dying breath!
Give ear, and to my guiltless misery
Extend your power.   Hear me what I pray!
If it be fated that yon creature curst
Drift to the shore and happy haven find,   855
If Father Jove's irrevocable word
Such goal decree — there may he be assailed
By peoples fierce and bold.   A banished man,
From his Iulus' kisses sundered far,
May his own eyes see miserably slain   860
His kin and kind, and sue for alien arms.
Nor when he basely bows him to receive
Terms of unequal peace, shall he be blest
With sceptre or with life; but perish there
Before his time, and lie without a grave   865
Upon the barren sand.   For this I pray.
This dying word is flowing from my heart
With my spilt blood.   And — O ye Tyrians!
Sting with your hatred all his seed and tribe
Forevermore.   This is the offering   870
My ashes ask.   Betwixt our nations twain,
No love!   No truce or amity!   Arise,
Out of my dust, unknown Avenger, rise!
To harry and lay waste with sword and flame
Those Dardan settlers, and to vex them sore,   375
To-day, to-morrow, and as long as power
Is thine to use!   My dying curse arrays
Shore against shore and the opposing seas
In shock of arms with arms.   May living foes
Pass down from sire to son insatiate war!"   880

She said.   From point to point her purpose flew,
Seeking without delay to quench the flame
Of her loathed life.   Brief bidding she addressed
To Barce then, Sichæus' nurse (her own
Lay dust and ashes in a lonely grave   885
Beside the Tyrian shore), "Go, nurse, and call
My sister Anna!   Bid her quickly bathe
Her limbs in living water, and procure
Due victims for our expiating fires.
Bid her make haste.   Go, bind on thy own brow
The sacred fillet.   For to Stygian Jove   891
It is my purpose now to consummate

The sacrifice ordained, ending my woe,
And touch with flame the Trojan's funeral pyre."

The aged crone to do her bidding ran   895
With trembling zeal.   But Dido (horror-struck
At her own dread design, unstrung with fear,
Her bloodshot eyes wide-rolling, and her cheek
Twitching and fever-spotted, her cold brow
Blanched with approaching death) sped past the
        doors   900
Into the palace garden; there she leaped,
A frenzied creature, on the lofty pyre
And drew the Trojan's sword; a gift not asked
For use like this!   When now she saw the garb
Of Ilian fashion, and the nuptial couch   905
She knew too well, she lingered yet awhile
For memory and tears, and, falling prone
On that cold bed, outpoured a last farewell:
"Sweet relics!   Ever dear when Fate and Heaven
Upon me smiled, receive my parting breath,   910
And from my woe set free!   My life is done.
I have accomplished what my lot allowed;
And now my spirit to the world of death
In royal honor goes.   The founder I
Of yonder noble city, I have seen   915
Walls at my bidding rise.   I was avenged
For my slain husband: I chastised the crimes
Of our injurious brother.   Woe is me!
Blest had I been, beyond deserving blest,
If but the Trojan galleys ne'er had moored   920
Upon my kingdom's bound!"   So saying she
        pressed
One last kiss on the couch.   "Though for my death
No vengeance fall, O, give me death!" she cried.
O thus!   O thus! it is my will to take
The journey to the dark.   From yonder sea   925
May his cold Trojan eyes discern the flames
That make me ashes!   Be this cruel death
His omen as he sails!"
                                She spoke no more.
But almost ere she ceased, her maidens all
Thronged to obey her cry, and found their Queen
Prone fallen on the sword, the reeking steel   931
Still in her bloody hands.   Shrill clamor flew
Along the lofty halls; wild rumor spread
Through the whole smitten city; loud lament,
Groans and the wail of women echoed on   935
From roof to roof, and to the dome of air
The noise of mourning rose.   Such were the cry
If a besieging host should break the walls
Of Carthage or old Tyre, and wrathful flames
O'er towers of kings and worshipped altars roll. 940
Her sister heard.   Half in a swoon, she ran
With trembling steps, where thickest was the
        throng,
Beating her breast, while with a desperate hand

She tore at her own face, and called aloud
Upon the dying Queen. "Was it for this   945
My own true sister used me with such guile?
O, was this horrid deed the dire intent
Of altars, lofty couch, and funeral fires?
What shall I tell for chiefest of my woes?
Lost that I am! Why, though in death, cast off 950
Thy sister from thy heart? Why not invite
One mortal stroke for both, a single sword,
One agony together? But these hands
Built up thy pyre; and my voice implored
The blessing of our gods, who granted me   955
That thou shouldst perish thus — and I not know!
In thy self-slaughter, sister, thou hast slain
Myself, thy people, the grave counsellors
Of Sidon, and yon city thou didst build
To be thy throne! — Go, fetch me water, there! 960
That I may bathe those gashes! If there be
One hovering breath that stays, let my fond lips
Discover and receive!"
                              So saying, she sprang up
From stair to stair, and, clasping to her breast
Her sister's dying form, moaned grievously,   965
And staunched the dark blood with her garment's
      fold.
Vainly would Dido lift her sinking eyes,
But backward fell, while at her heart the wound
Opened afresh; three times with straining arm
She rose; three times dropped helpless, her dimmed
      eyes   970
Turned skyward, seeking the sweet light of day, —
Which when she saw, she groaned.
                              Great Juno then
Looked down in mercy on that lingering pain
And labor to depart: from realms divine
She sent the goddess of the rainbow wing,   975
Iris, to set the struggling spirit free
And loose its fleshly coil. For since the end
Came not by destiny, nor was the doom
Of guilty deed, but of a hapless wight
To sudden madness stung, ere ripe to die,   980
Therefore the Queen of Hades had not shorn
The fair tress from her forehead, nor assigned
That soul to Stygian dark. So Iris came
On dewy, saffron pinions down from heaven,
A thousand colors on her radiant way,   985
From the opposing sun. She stayed her flight
Above that pallid brow: "I come with power
To make this gift to Death. I set thee free
From thy frail body's bound." With her right hand
She cut the tress: then through its every limb 990
The sinking form grew cold; the vital breath
Fled forth, departing on the viewless air.

BOOK VI [1]

After such words and tears, he flung free rein
To the swift fleet, which sped along the wave
To old Eubœan Cumæ's [2] sacred shore.
They veer all prows to sea; the anchor fluke
Makes each ship sure, and shading the long strand
The rounded sterns jut o'er. Impetuously   6
The eager warriors leap forth to land
Upon Hesperian soil. One strikes the flint
To find the seed-spark hidden in its veins;
One breaks the thick-branched trees, and steals
      away   10
The shelter where the woodland creatures bide;
One leads his mates where living waters flow.[3]

Æneas, servant of the gods, ascends
The templed hill where lofty Phœbus reigns,
And that far-off, inviolable shrine   15
Of dread Sibylla, in stupendous cave,
O'er whose deep soul the god of Delos breathes
Prophetic gifts, unfolding things to come.
Here are pale Trivia's golden house and grove.
Here Dædalus, the ancient story tells,   20
Escaping Minos' power, and having made
Hazard of heaven on far-mounting wings,
Floated to northward, a cold, trackless way,
And lightly poised, at last, o'er Cumæ's towers.
Here first to earth come down, he gave to thee
His gear of wings, Apollo! and ordained   26
Vast temples to thy name and altars fair.
On huge bronze doors Androgeos' [4] death was
      done;
And Cecrops' children paid their debt of woe,
Where, seven and seven, — O pitiable sight! — 30
The youths and maidens wait the annual doom,
Drawn out by lot from yonder marble urn.
Beyond, above a sea, lay carven Crete:
The bull was there; the passion, the strange guile;
And Queen Pasiphaë's [5] brute-human son,   35
The Minotaur — of monstrous loves the sign.
Here was the toilsome, labyrinthine maze,
Where, pitying love-lorn Ariadne's tears,
The crafty Dædalus himself betrayed

[1] In Book V, Æneas, after sailing from Carthage, is
driven from his course by a storm and forced to land in
Sicily. Here certain games are held. His fleet is set
afire, but Jupiter steps in to save all but four ships.
Æneas starts again for Italy.
[2] In Italy.
[3] They get wood and fresh water.
[4] A famous wrestler who was executed by the King of
Athens. His father, King Minos, made war on Athens
and, upon winning, demanded seven youths and seven
maidens each year to feed the Minotaur.
[5] The Minotaur, half bull, half man, was the son of
this queen. Cf. l. 577.

The secret of his work; and gave the clue   40
To guide the path of Theseus through the gloom.
O Icarus, in such well-graven scene
How proud thy place should be! but grief forbade
Twice in pure gold a father's fingers strove
To shape thy fall, and twice they strove in vain.

Æneas long the various work would scan;   46
But now Achates comes, and by his side
Deïphobe, the Sibyl, Glaucus' child.
Thus to the prince she spoke:
                          "Is this thine hour
To stand and wonder?   Rather go obtain   50
From young unbroken herd the bullocks seven,
And seven yearling ewes, our wonted way."
Thus to Æneas; his attendants haste
To work her will; the priestess, calling loud,
Gathers the Trojans to her mountain-shrine.   55

Deep in the face of that Eubœan crag
A cavern vast is hollowed out amain,
With hundred openings, a hundred mouths,
Whence voices flow, the Sibyl's answering songs.
While at the door they paused, the virgin cried: 60
"Ask now thy doom! — the god! the god is nigh!"
So saying, from her face its color flew,
Her twisted locks flowed free, the heaving breast
Swelled with her heart's wild blood; her stature
      seemed
Vaster, her accent more than mortal man,   65
As all th' oncoming god around her breathed:
"On with thy vows and prayers, O Trojan, on!
For only unto prayer this haunted cave
May its vast lips unclose."   She spake no more.
An icy shudder through the marrow ran   70
Of the bold Trojans; while their sacred King
Poured from his inmost soul this plaint and prayer:
"Phœbus, who ever for the woes of Troy
Hadst pitying eyes! who gavest deadly aim
To Paris when his Dardan shaft he hurled   75
On great Achilles!   Thou hast guided me
Through many an unknown water, where the seas
Break upon kingdoms vast, and to the tribes
Of the remote Massyli, whose wild land
To Syrtes spreads.   But now, because at last   80
I touch Hesperia's ever-fleeting bound,
May Troy's ill fate forsake me from this day!
O gods and goddesses, beneath whose wrath
Dardania's glory and great Ilium stood,
Spare, for ye may, the remnant of my race!   85
And thou, most holy prophetess, whose soul
Foreknows events to come, grant to my prayer
(Which asks no kingdom save what Fate decrees)
That I may stablish in the Latin land
My Trojans, my far-wandering household-gods,   90
And storm-tossed deities of fallen Troy.

Then unto Phœbus and his sister pale
A temple all of marble shall be given,
And festal days to Phœbus evermore.
Thee also in my realms a spacious shrine   95
Shall honor; thy dark books and holy songs
I there will keep, to be my people's law;
And thee, benignant Sibyl, for all time
A company of chosen priests shall serve.
O, not on leaves, light leaves, inscribe thy songs?
Lest, playthings of each breeze, they fly afar   101
In swift confusion!   Sing thyself, I pray."

So ceased his voice; the virgin through the cave,
Scarce bridled yet by Phœbus' hand divine,
Ecstatic swept along, and vainly strove   105
To fling its potent master from her breast;
But he more strongly plied his rein and curb
Upon her frenzied lips, and soon subdued
Her spirit fierce, and swayed her at his will.
Free and self-moved the cavern's hundred doors 110
Swung open wide, and uttered to the air
The oracles the virgin-priestess sung:
"Thy long sea-perils thou hast safely passed;
But heavier woes await thee on the land.
Truly thy Trojans to Lavinian shore   115
Shall come — vex not thyself thereon — but, oh!
Shall rue their coming thither! war, red war!
And Tiber stained with bloody foam I see.
Simois, Xanthus,[1] and the Dorian horde
Thou shalt behold; a new Achilles now   120
In Latium breathes, — he, too, of goddess born;
And Juno, burden of the sons of Troy,
Will vex them ever; while thyself shalt sue
In dire distress to many a town and tribe
Through Italy; the cause of so much ill   125
Again shall be a hostess-queen, again
A marriage-chamber for an alien bride.
Oh! yield not to thy woe, but front it ever,
And follow boldly whither Fortune calls.
Thy way of safety, as thou least couldst dream,
Lies through a city of the Greeks, thy foes."   131

Thus from her shrine Cumæa's prophetess
Chanted the dark decrees; the dreadful sound
Reverberated through the bellowing cave,
Commingling truth with ecstasies obscure.   135
Apollo, as she raged, flung loosened rein,
And thrust beneath her heart a quickening spur.
When first her madness ceased, and her wild lips
Were still at last, the hero thus began:
"No tribulations new, O Sibyl blest,   140
Can now confront me; every future pain
I have foretasted; my prophetic soul
Endured each stroke of fate before it fell.

[1] Rivers of Troy.   The meaning is that Æneas will
find difficulties in Italy even as he did in Troy.

One boon I ask.   If of th' infernal King
This be the portal where the murky wave   145
Of swollen Acheron o'erflows its bound,
Here let me enter and behold the face
Of my loved sire.   Thy hand may point the way;
Thy word will open wide yon holy doors.
My father through the flames and falling spears,
Straight through the centre of our foes, I bore   151
Upon these shoulders.   My long flight he shared
From sea to sea, and suffered at my side
The anger of rude waters and dark skies, —
Though weak — O task too great for old and
          gray!   155
Thus as a suppliant at thy door to stand,
Was his behest and prayer.   On son and sire,
O gracious one, have pity, — for thy rule
Is over all; no vain authority   159
Hadst thou from Trivia o'er th' Avernian groves.
If Orpheus could call back his loved one's shade,[1]
Emboldened by the lyre's melodious string:
If Pollux [2] by the interchange of death
Redeemed his twin, and oft repassed the way:
If Theseus [3] — but why name him? why recall   165
Alcides' [4] task?   I, too, am sprung from Jove."

Thus, to the altar clinging, did he pray:
The Sibyl thus replied: "Offspring of Heaven,
Anchises' son, the downward path to death
Is easy; all the livelong night and day   170
Dark Pluto's door stands open for a guest.
But O! remounting to the world of light,
This is a task indeed, a strife supreme.
Few, very few, whom righteous Jove did bless,
Or quenchless virtue carried to the stars,   175
Children of gods, have such a victory won.
Grim forests stop the way, and, gliding slow,
Cocytus [5] circles through the sightless gloom.
But if it be thy dream and fond desire
Twice o'er the Stygian gulf to travel, twice   180
On glooms of Tartarus to set thine eyes,
If such mad quest be now thy pleasure — hear
What must be first fulfilled.   A certain tree
Hides in obscurest shade a golden bough,
Of pliant stems and many a leaf of gold,   185
Sacred to Proserpine, infernal [6] Queen
Far in the grove it hides; in sunless vale
Deep shadows keep it in captivity.
No pilgrim to that underworld can pass
But he who plucks this burgeoned, leafy gold;   190

[1] Eurydice.
[2] Twin brothers, Castor and Pollux were granted immortality between them, one to live one day and die the next, thus alternately living forever.
[3] Like Hercules, a hero of many conquests.
[4] Hercules.   [5] A river in Hades.
[6] "Infernal" in that she is queen of the Underworld.

For this hath beauteous Proserpine ordained
Her chosen gift to be.   Whene'er 'tis culled,
A branch out-leafing in like golden gleam,
A second wonder-stem, fails not to spring.
Therefore go seek it with uplifted eyes!   195
And when by will of Heaven thou findest it,
Reach forth and pluck; for at a touch it yields,
A free and willing gift, if Fate ordain;
But otherwise no mortal strength avails,
Nor strong, sharp steel, to rend it from the tree.   200
Another task awaits; thy friend's cold clay
Lies unentombed.   Alas! thou art not aware
(While in my house thou lingerest, seeking light)
That all thy ships are by his death defiled.
Unto his resting-place and sepulchre   205
Go, carry him!   And sable victims bring,
In expiation, to his mournful shade.
So at the last on yonder Stygian groves,
And realms to things that breathe impassable,
Thine eye shall gaze."   So closed her lips inspired.
Æneas then drew forth, with downcast eyes,   211
From that dark cavern, pondering in his heart
The riddle of his fate.   His faithful friend
Achates at his side, with paces slow,
Companioned all his care, while their sad souls   215
Made mutual and oft-renewed surmise
What comrade dead, what cold and tombless clay,
The Sibyl's word would show.
                              But as they mused,
Behold Misenus [1] on the dry sea-sands,
By hasty hand of death struck guiltless down!   220
A son of Æolus, none better knew
To waken heroes by the clarion's call,
With war-enkindling sound.   Great Hector's
          friend
In happier days, he oft at Hector's side
Strode to the fight with glittering lance and horn.
But when Achilles stripped his fallen foe,   226
This dauntless hero to Æneas gave
Allegiance true, in not less noble cause.
But, on a day, he chanced beside the sea
To blow his shell-shaped horn, and wildly dared   230
Challenge the gods themselves to rival song;
Till jealous Triton, if the tale be true,
Grasped the rash mortal, and out-flung him far
'Mid surf-beat rocks and waves of whirling foam.
Now from all sides, with tumult and loud cry,   235
The Trojans came, — Æneas leading all
In faithful grief; they hasten to fulfil
The Sibyl's mandate, and with many a tear
Build, altar-wise, a pyre, of tree on tree
Heaped high as heaven: then they penetrate   240
The tall, old forest, where wild creatures bide,
And fell pitch-pines, or with resounding blows
Of axe and wedge, cleave oak and ash-tree through

[1] The trumpeter of Hector.

Or logs of rowan down the mountains roll.
Æneas oversees and shares the toil, 245
Cheers on his mates, and swings a woodman's steel
But, sad at heart with many a doubt and care,
O'erlooks the forest wide; then prays aloud:
"O, that the Golden Bough from this vast grove
Might o'er me shine! For, O Æolides, 250
The oracle foretold thy fate, too well!"
Scarce had he spoken, when a pair of doves
Before his very eyes flew down from heaven
To the green turf below; the prince of Troy
Knew them his mother's birds, and joyful cried,
"O, guide me on, whatever path there be! 256
In airy travel through the woodland fly,
To where yon rare branch shades the blessed
    ground.
Fail thou not me, in this my doubtful hour,
O heavenly mother!" So saying, his steps he
    stayed, 260
Close watching whither they should signal give;
The lightly-feeding doves flit on and on,
Ever in easy ken of following eyes,
Till over foul Avernus' sulphurous throat
Swiftly they lift them through the liquid air, 265
In silent flight, and find a wished-for rest
On a twy-natured tree,[1] where through green
    boughs
Flames forth the glowing gold's contrasted hue.
As in the wintry woodland bare and chill,
Fresh-budded shines the clinging mistletoe, 270
Whose seed is never from the parent tree
O'er whose round limbs its tawny tendrils twine, —
So shone th' out-leafing gold within the shade
Of dark holm-oak, and so its tinsel-bract[2]
Rustled in each light breeze. Æneas grasped 275
The lingering bough, broke it in eager haste,
And bore it straightway to the Sibyl's shrine.

Meanwhile the Trojans on the doleful shore
Bewailed Misenus, and brought tribute there
Of grief's last gift to his unheeding clay. 280
First, of the full-sapped pine and well-hewn oak
A lofty pyre they build; then sombre boughs
Around it wreathe, and in fair order range
Funereal cypress; glittering arms are piled
High over all; on blazing coals they lift 285
Cauldrons of brass brimmed o'er with waters pure
And that cold, lifeless clay lave and anoint
With many a moan and cry; on their last couch
The poor, dead limbs they lay, and mantle o'er
With purple vesture and familiar pall. 290
Then in sad ministry the chosen few.
With eyes averted, as our sires did use,

[1] Two-natured because it has two kinds of leaves,
natural and gold.
[2] Tinsel-leaves.

Holding the enkindling torch beneath the pyre:
They gather up and burn the gifts of myrrh,
The sacred bread and bowls of flowing oil; 295
And when in flame the dying embers fall,
On thirsty ash they pour the streams of wine.
Good Corynæus, in an urn of brass
The gathered relics hides; and three times round
With blessed olive branch and sprinkling dew, 300
Purges the people with ablution cold
In lustral rite; oft chanting, "Hail! Farewell!"
Faithful Æneas for his comrade built
A mighty tomb, and dedicated there
Trophy of arms, with trumpet and with oar, 305
Beneath a windy hill, which now is called
"Misenus," — for all time the name to bear.

After these toils, they hasten to fulfil
What else the Sibyl said. Straightway they find
A cave profound, of entrance gaping wide, 310
O'erhung with rock, in gloom of sheltering grove,
Near the dark waters of a lake, whereby
No bird might ever pass with scathless wing,
So dire an exhalation is breathed out
From that dark deep of death to upper air: — 315
Hence, in the Grecian tongue, Aornos called.
Here first four youthful bulls of swarthy hide
Were led for sacrifice; on each broad brow
The priestess sprinkled wine; 'twixt the two horns
Outplucked the lifted hair, and cast it forth 320
Upon the holy flames, beginning so
Her offerings; then loudly sued the power
Of Hecate, a Queen in heaven and hell.
Some struck with knives, and caught in shallow
    bowls
The smoking blood. Æneas' lifted hand 325
Smote with a sword a sable-fleecèd ewe
To Night, the mother of th' Eumenides,
And Earth, her sister dread; next unto thee,
O Proserpine, a curst and barren cow;
Then unto Pluto Stygian King he built 330
An altar dark, and piled upon the flames
The ponderous entrails of the bulls, and poured
Free o'er the burning flesh the goodly oil.
Then lo! at dawn's dim, earliest beam began
Beneath their feet a groaning of the ground: 335
The wooded hill-tops shook, and, as it seemed,
She-hounds of hell howled viewless through the
    shade,
To hail their Queen. "Away, O souls profane!
Stand far away!" the priestess shrieked, "nor dare
Unto this grove come near! Æneas, on! 340
Begin thy journey! Draw thy sheathèd blade!
Now, all thy courage! now, th' unshaken soul!"
She spoke, and burst into the yawning cave
With frenzied step; he follows where she leads,
And strides with feet unfaltering at her side. 345

Ye gods! who rule the spirits of the dead!
Ye voiceless shades and silent lands of night!
O Phlegethon![1]   O Chaos! let my song,
If it be lawful, in fit words declare
What I have heard; and by your help divine   350
Unfold what hidden things enshrouded lie
In that dark underworld of sightless gloom.

They walked exploring the unpeopled night,
Through Pluto's vacuous realms, and regions void,
As when one's path in dreary woodlands winds
Beneath a misty moon's deceiving ray,   356
When Jove has mantled all his heaven in shade,
And night seals up the beauty of the world.
In the first courts and entrances of Hell
Sorrows and vengeful Cares on couches lie: 360
There sad Old Age abides, Diseases pale,
And Fear, and Hunger, temptress to all crime;
Want, base and vile, and, two dread shapes to see,
Bondage and Death: then Sleep, Death's next of
    kin:
And dreams of guilty joy.   Death-dealing War   365
Is ever at the doors, and hard thereby
The Furies' beds of steel, where wild-eyed Strife
Her snaky hair with blood-stained fillet binds.
There in the middle court a shadowy elm
Its ancient branches spreads, and in its leaves   370
Deluding visions ever haunt and cling.
Then come strange prodigies of bestial kind:
Centaurs are stabled there, and double shapes
Like Scylla, or the dragon Lerna bred,
With hideous scream; Briareus clutching far   375
His hundred hands, Chimæra girt with flame,
A crowd of Gorgons, Harpies of foul wing,
And giant Geryon's triple-monstered shade.
Æneas, shuddering with sudden fear,
Drew sword and fronted them with naked steel;
And, save his sage conductress bade him know   381
These were but shapes and shadows sweeping by,
His stroke had cloven in vain the vacant air.
Hence the way leads to that Tartarean stream
Of Acheron, whose torrent fierce and foul   385
Disgorges in Cocytus all its sands.
A ferryman of gruesome guise keeps ward
Upon these waters, — Charon, foully garbed,
With unkempt, thick gray beard upon his chin,
And staring eyes of flame; a mantle coarse,   390
All stained and knotted, from his shoulder falls,
As with a pole he guides his craft, tends sail,
And in the black boat ferries o'er his dead; —
Old, but a god's old age looks fresh and strong.   394

To those dim shores the multitude streams on —
Husbands and wives, and pale, unbreathing forms
Of high-souled heroes, boys and virgins fair,

[1] River of fire in Hades.

And strong youth at whose graves fond parents
    mourned.
As numberless the throng as leaves that fall
When autumn's early frost is on the grove;   400
Or like vast flocks of birds by winter's chill
Sent flying o'er wide seas to lands of flowers.
All stood beseeching to begin their voyage
Across that river, and reached out pale hands,
In passionate yearning for its distant shore.   405
But the grim boatman takes now these, now those,
Or thrusts unpitying from the stream away.

Æneas, moved to wonder and deep awe,
Beheld the tumult; "Virgin seer!" he cried,
"Why move the thronging ghosts toward yonder
    stream?   410
What seek they there?   Or what election holds
That these unwilling linger, while their peers
Sweep forward yonder o'er the leaden waves?"
To him, in few, the aged Sibyl spoke:
"Son of Anchises, offspring of the gods,   415
Yon are Cocytus and the Stygian stream,
By whose dread power the gods themselves do fear
To take an oath in vain.   Here far and wide
Thou seest the hapless throng that hath no grave.
That boatman Charon bears across the deep   420
Such as be sepulchred with holy care.
But over that loud flood and dreadful shore
No trav'ler may be borne, until in peace
His gathered ashes rest.   A hundred years   424
Round this dark borderland some haunt and roam,
Then win late passage o'er the longed-for wave."

Æneas lingered for a little space,
Revolving in his soul with pitying prayer
Fate's partial way.   But presently he sees
Leucaspis and the Lycian navy's lord,   430
Orontes; both of melancholy brow,
Both hapless and unhonored after death,
Whom, while from Troy they crossed the wind-
    swept seas,
A whirling tempest wrecked with ship and crew.
There, too, the helmsman Palinurus strayed: 435
Who, as he whilom watched the Libyan stars,
Had fallen, plunging from his lofty seat
Into the billowy deep.   Æneas now
Discerned his sad face through the blinding gloom,
And hailed him thus: "O Palinurus, tell   440
What god was he who ravished thee away
From me and mine, beneath the o'erwhelming
    wave?
Speak on! for he who ne'er had spoke untrue,
Apollo's self, did mock my listening mind,
And chanted me a faithful oracle   445
That thou shouldst ride the seas unharmed, and
    touch

Ausonian shores. Is this the pledge divine?"
Then he, "O chieftain of Anchises' race,
Apollo's tripod told thee not untrue.
No god did thrust me down beneath the wave,
For that strong rudder unto which I clung,   451
My charge and duty, and my ship's sole guide,
Wrenched from its place, dropped with me as I fell.
Not for myself — by the rude seas I swear —
Did I have terror, but lest thy good ship,   455
Stripped of her gear, and her poor pilot lost,
Should fail and founder in that rising flood.
Three wintry nights across the boundless main
The south wind buffeted and bore me on;
At the fourth daybreak, lifted from the surge,   460
I looked at last on Italy, and swam
With weary stroke on stroke unto the land.
Safe was I then. Alas! but as I climbed
With garments wet and heavy, my clenched hand
Grasping the steep rock, came a cruel horde   465
Upon me with drawn blades, accounting me —
So blind they were! — a wrecker's prize and spoil.
Now are the waves my tomb, and wandering winds
Toss me along the coast. O, I implore,
By heaven's sweet light, by yonder upper air,   470
By thy lost father, by Iulus dear,
Thy rising hope and joy, that from these woes,
Unconquered chieftain, thou wilt set me free!
Give me a grave where Velia's haven lies,
For thou hast power! Or if some path there be,
If thy celestial mother guide thee here   476
(For not, I ween, without the grace of gods
Wilt cross yon rivers vast, yon Stygian pool)
Reach me a hand! and bear with thee along!
Until (least gift!) death bring me peace and calm."

Such words he spoke: the priestess thus replied: 481
"Why, Palinurus, these unblest desires?
Wouldst thou, unsepulchred, behold the wave
Of Styx, stern river of th' Eumenides?   484
Wouldst thou, unbidden, tread its fearful stand?
Hope not by prayer to change the laws of Heaven!
But heed my words, and in thy memory
Cherish and keep, to cheer this evil time.
Lo, far and wide, led on by signs from Heaven,
Thy countrymen from many a templed town   490
Shall consecrate thy dust, and build thy tomb,
A tomb with annual feasts and votive flowers,
To Palinurus a perpetual fame!"
Thus was his anguish stayed, from his sad heart
Grief ebbed awhile, and even to this day,   495
Our land is glad such noble name to wear.

The twain continue now their destined way
Unto the river's edge. The Ferryman,
Who watched them through still groves approach
    his shore,

Hailed them, at distance, from the Stygian wave,
And with reproachful summons thus began: 501
"Whoe'er thou art that in this warrior guise
Unto my river comest — quickly tell
Thine errand! Stay thee where thou standest now!
This is ghosts' land, for sleep and slumbrous dark.
That flesh and blood my Stygian ship should bear
Were lawless wrong. Unwillingly I took   507
Alcides, Theseus, and Pirithous,
Though sons of gods, too mighty to be quelled.
One bound in chains yon warder of Hell's door,
And dragged him trembling from our monarch's
    throne: 511
The others, impious, would steal away
Out of her bride-bed Pluto's ravished Queen."

Briefly th' Amphrysian priestess made reply:
"Not ours, such guile! Fear not! This warrior's
    arms   515
Are innocent. Let Cerberus from his cave
Bay ceaselessly, the bloodless shades to scare;
Let Proserpine immaculately keep
The house and honor of her kinsman King.
Trojan Æneas, famed for faithful prayer   520
And victory in arms, descends to seek
His father in this gloomy deep of death.
If loyal goodness move not such as thee,
This branch at least" (she drew it from her breast)
"Thou knowest well."
               Then cooled his wrathful heart;
With silent lips he looked and wondering eyes   526
Upon that fateful, venerable wand,
Seen only once an age. Shoreward he turned,
And pushed their way his boat of leaden hue.
The rows of crouching ghosts along the thwarts   530
He scattered, cleared a passage, and gave room
To great Æneas. The light shallop groaned
Beneath his weight, and, straining at each seam,
Took in the foul flood with unstinted flow.

At last the hero and his priestess-guide   535
Came safe across the river, and were moored
'Mid sea-green sedges in the formless mire.
Here Cerberus,[1] with triple-throated roar,
Made all the region ring, as there he lay
At vast length in his cave. The Sibyl then,   540
Seeing the serpents writhe around his neck,
Threw down a loaf with honeyed herbs imbued
And drowsy essences: he, ravenous,
Gaped wide his three fierce mouths and snatched
    the bait,
Crouched with his large backs loose upon the
    ground   545
And filled his cavern floor from end to end.
Æneas through hell's portal moved, while sleep

---

[1] A guardian dog with three heads and a serpent's tail.

Its warder buried; then he fled that shore
Of Stygian stream, whence travellers ne'er return.
Now hears he sobs, and piteous, lisping cries   550
Of souls of babes upon the threshold plaining;
Whom, ere they took their portion of sweet life,
Dark Fate from nursing bosoms tore, and plunged
In bitterness of death.   Nor far from these,
The throng of dead by unjust judgment slain. 555
Not without judge or law these realms abide.
Wise Minos [1] there the urn of justice moves,
And holds assembly of the silent shades,
Hearing the stories of their lives and deeds.
Close on this place those doleful ghosts abide, 560
Who, not for crime, but loathing life and light
With their own hands took death, and cast away
The vital essence.   Willingly, alas!
They now would suffer need, or burdens bear,
If only life were given! But Fate forbids.   565
Around them winds the sad, unlovely wave
Of Styx: nine times it coils and interflows.
Not far from hence, on every side outspread,
The Fields of Sorrow lie, — such name they bear;
Here all whom ruthless love did waste away   570
Wander in paths unseen, or in the gloom
Of a dark myrtle grove: not even in death
Have they forgot their griefs of long ago.
Here impious Phædra and poor Procris bide;
Lorn Eriphyle bares the vengeful wounds   575
Her own son's dagger made; Evadne here,
And foul Pasiphaë are seen; hard by,
Laodamia,[2] nobly fond and fair;
And Cæneus,[3] not a boy, but maiden now,
By Fate remoulded to her native seeming.   580
Here Tyrian Dido, too, her wound unhealed,
Roamed through a mighty wood. The Trojan's eyes
Beheld her near him through the murky gloom,
As when, in her young month and crescent pale,
One sees th' o'er-clouded moon, or thinks he sees.
Down dropped his tears, and thus he fondly
      spoke: 586
"O suffering Dido! Were those tidings true
That thou didst fling thee on the fatal steel?
Thy death, ah me! I dealt it. But I swear
By stars above us, by powers in Heaven,   590
Or whatsoever oath ye dead believe,
That not by choice I fled thy shores, O Queen!
Divine decrees compelled me, even as now
Among these ghosts I pass, and thread my way
Along this gulf of night and loathsome land. 595
How could I deem my cruel taking leave
Would bring thee at the last to all this woe?

[1] Judge in Hades.
[2] She and the five women mentioned in the preceding
lines met sad or sudden deaths.
[3] He was originally a girl, Cænis, loved by the god
Poseidon who changed her sex.

O, stay! Why shun me? Wherefore haste away?
Our last farewell! Our doom! I speak it now!"
Thus, though she glared with fierce, relentless gaze,
Æneas, with fond words and tearful plea,   601
Would soothe her angry soul. But on the ground
She fixed averted eyes. For all he spoke
Moved her no more than if her frowning brow
Were changeless flint or carved in Parian stone. 605
Then, after pause, away in wrath she fled,
And refuge took within the cool, dark grove,
Where her first spouse, Sichæus, with her tears
Mingled his own in mutual love and true.
Æneas, none the less, her guiltless woe   610
With anguish knew, watched with dimmed eyes her
      way,
And pitied from afar the fallen Queen.
But now his destined way he must be gone;
Now the last regions round the travellers lie,
Where famous warriors in the darkness dwell: 615
Here Tydeus comes in view, with far-renowned
Parthenopæus [1] and Adrastus pale;
Here mourned in upper air with many a moan,
In battle fallen, the Dardanidæ,
Whose long defile Æneas groans to see: 620
Glaucus and Medon and Thersilochus,
Antenor's children three, and Ceres' priest,
That Polypœtes, and Idæus still
Keeping the kingly chariot and spear.
Around him left and right the crowding shades 625
Not only once would see, but clutch and cling
Obstructive, asking on what quest he goes.
Soon as the princes of Argolic blood,
With line on line of Agamemnon's men,
Beheld the hero and his glittering arms   630
Flash through the dark, they trembled with amaze,
Or turned in flight, as if once more they fled
To shelter of the ships; some raised aloft
A feeble shout, or vainly opened wide
Their gaping lips in mockery of sound.   635

Here Priam's son, with body rent and torn,
Deïphobus, is seen, — his mangled face,
His face and bloody hands, his wounded head
Of ears and nostrils infamously shorn.
Scarce could Æneas know the shuddering shade 640
That strove to hide its face and shameful scar;
But, speaking first, he said, in their own tongue:
"Deïphobus, strong warrior, nobly born
Of Teucer's royal stem, what ruthless foe
Could wish to wreak on thee this dire revenge?
Who ventured, unopposed, so vast a wrong?   646
The rumor reached me how, that deadly night,
Wearied with slaying Greeks, thyself didst fall
Prone on a mingled heap of friends and foes.

[1] In this passage the names are those of Greek heroes
who died in one exploit or another.

Then my own hands did for thy honor build   650
An empty tomb upon the Trojan shore,
And thrice with echoing voice I called thy shade.
Thy name and arms are there.   But, O my friend,
Thee could I nowhere find, but launched away,
Nor o'er thy bones their native earth could fling."

To him the son of Priam thus replied: 656
"Nay, friend, no hallowed rite was left undone,
But every debt to death and pity due
The shades of thy Deïphobus received.
My fate it was, and Helen's murderous wrong,   660
Wrought me this woe; of her these tokens tell.
For how that last night in false hope we passed,
Thou knowest, — ah, too well we both recall!
When up the steep of Troy the fateful horse   664
Came climbing, pregnant with fierce men-at-arms,
'Twas she, accurst, who led the Phrygian dames
In choric dance and false bacchantic song,
And, waving from the midst a lofty brand,
Signalled the Greeks from Ilium's central tower.
In that same hour on my sad couch I lay,   670
Exhausted by long care and sunk in sleep,
That sweet, deep sleep, so close to tranquil death.
But my illustrious bride from all the house
Had stolen all arms; from 'neath my pillowed head
She stealthily bore off my trusty sword;   675
Then loud on Menelaus [1] did she call,
And with her own false hand unbarred the door;
Such gift to her fond lord she fain would send
To blot the memory of his ancient wrong!   679
Why tell the tale, how on my couch they broke,
While their accomplice, vile Æolides,[2]
Counselled to many a crime.   O heavenly Powers!
Reward these Greeks their deeds of wickedness,
If with clean lips upon your wrath I call!   684
But, friend, what fortunes have thy life befallen?
Tell point by point.   Did waves of wandering seas
Drive thee this way, or some divine command?
What chastisement of fortune thrusts thee on
Toward this forlorn abode of night and cloud?"

While thus they talked, the crimsoned car of Morn
Had wheeled beyond the midmost point of heaven,
On her ethereal road.   The princely pair   692
Had wasted thus the whole brief gift of hours;
But Sibyl spoke the warning: "Night speeds by,
And we, Æneas, lose it in lamenting.   695
Here comes the place where cleaves our way in
          twain
Thy road, the right, toward Pluto's dwelling goes,
And leads us to Elysium.   But the left
Speeds sinful souls to doom, and is their path
To Tartarus th' accurst."   Deïphobus   700

[1] The husband of Helen before she had been carried
away to Troy by Paris.   [2] Ulysses.

Cried out: "O priestess, be not wroth with us!
Back to the ranks with yonder ghosts I go.
O glory of my race, pass on!   Thy lot
Be happier than mine!"   He spoke, and fled.

Æneas straightway by the leftward cliff   705
Beheld a spreading rampart, high begirt
With triple wall, and circling round it ran
A raging river of swift floods of flame,
Infernal Phlegethon, which whirls along
Loud-thundering rocks.   A mighty gate is there
Columned in adamant; no human power,   711
Nor even the gods, against this gate prevail.
Tall tower of steel it has; and seated there
Tisiphone, in blood-flecked pall arrayed,
Sleepless forever, guards the entering way.   715
Hence groans are heard, fierce cracks of lash and
          scourge,
Loud-clanking iron links and trailing chains.
Æneas motionless with horror stood
O'erwhelmed at such uproar.   "O virgin, say
What shapes of guilt are these?   What penal woe
Harries them thus?   What wailing smites the
          air?"   721
To whom the Sibyl, "Far-famed prince of Troy,
The feet of innocence may never pass
Into this house of sin.   But Hecate,
When o'er th' Avernian groves she gave me power,
Taught me what penalties the gods decree,   726
And showed me all.   There Cretan Rhadamanth [1]
His kingdom keeps, and from unpitying throne
Chastises and lays bare the secret sins
Of mortals who, exulting in vain guile,   730
Elude, till death, their expiation due.
There, armed forever with her vengeful scourge,
Tisiphone, with menace and affront,
The guilty swarm pursues; in her left hand
She lifts her angered serpents, while she calls   735
A troop of sister-furies fierce as she.
Then, grating loud on hinge of sickening sound,
Hell's portals open wide.   O, dost thou see
What sentinel upon that threshold sits,
What shapes of fear keep guard upon that gloom?
Far, far within the dragon Hydra broods   741
With half a hundred mouths, gaping and black;
And Tartarus slopes downward to the dark
Twice the whole space that in the realms of light
Th' Olympian heaven above our earth aspires.   745
Here Earth's first offspring, the Titanic brood,
Roll lightning-blasted in the gulf profound;
The twin Aloïdæ,[2] colossal shades,

[1] A son of Jupiter and ruler of many Greek cities in
Asia.   Because of his ability and justice he was made
a judge in Hades.
[2] Giants who warred against the gods and were slain
by Apollo and Diana.

Came on my view; their hands made stroke at
    Heaven
And strove to thrust Jove from his seat on high.
I saw Salmoneus his dread stripes endure,   751
Who dared to counterfeit Olympian thunder
And Jove's own fire. In chariot of four steeds,
Brandishing torches, he triumphant rode
Through throngs of Greeks, o'er Elis' sacred way,
Demanding worship as a god. O fool!   756
To mock the storm's inimitable flash
With crash of hoofs and roll of brazen wheel!
But mightiest Jove from rampart of thick cloud
Hurled his own shaft, no flickering, mortal flame,
And in vast whirl of tempest laid him low.   761
Next unto these, on Tityos I looked,
Child of old Earth, whose womb all creatures bears:
Stretched o'er nine roods he lies; a vulture huge
Tears with hooked beak at his immortal side,   765
Or deep in entrails ever rife with pain
Gropes for a feast, making his haunt and home
In the great Titan bosom; nor will give
To ever new-born flesh surcease of woe.
Why name Ixion and Pirithous,   770
The Lapithæ, above whose impious brows
A crag of flint hangs quaking to its fall,
As if just toppling down, while couches proud,
Propped upon golden pillars, bid them feast
In royal glory: but beside them lies   775
The eldest of the Furies, whose dread hands
Thrust from the feast away, and wave aloft
A flashing firebrand, with shrieks of woe.
Here in a prison-house awaiting doom
Are men who hated, long as life endured,   780
Their brothers, or maltreated their gray sires,
Or tricked a humble friend; the men who grasped
At hoarded riches, with their kith and kin
Not sharing ever — an unnumbered throng;
Here slain adulterers be; and men who dared   785
To fight in unjust cause, and break all faith
With their own lawful lords. Seek not to know
What forms of woe they feel, what fateful shape
Of retribution hath o'erwhelmed them there.
Some roll huge boulders up; some hang on wheels,
Lashed to the whirling spokes; in his sad seat   791
Theseus is sitting, nevermore to rise;
Unhappy Phlegyas [1] uplifts his voice
In warning through the darkness, calling loud,
'O, ere too late, learn justice and fear God!'   795
Yon traitor sold his country, and for gold
Enchained her to a tyrant, trafficking
In laws, for bribes enacted or made void;
Another did incestuously take
His daughter for a wife in lawless bonds.   800
All ventured some unclean, prodigious crime;

[1] He burnt the temple of Apollo and was punished in
Hades.

And what they dared, achieved. I could not tell,
Not with a hundred mouths, a hundred tongues,
Or iron voice, their divers shapes of sin,
Nor call by name the myriad pangs they bear."

So spake Apollo's aged prophetess.   806
"Now up and on!" she cried. "Thy task fulfil!
We must make speed. Behold yon arching doors,
Yon walls in furnace of the Cyclops forged!
'Tis there we are commanded to lay down   810
Th' appointed offering." So, side by side,
Swift through the intervening dark they strode,
And, drawing near the portal-arch, made pause.
Æneas, taking station at the door,
Pure, lustral waters o'er his body threw,   815
And hung for garland there the Golden Bough.
Now, every rite fulfilled, and tribute due
Paid to the sovereign power of Proserpine,
At last within a land delectable
Their journey lay, through pleasurable bowers
Of groves where all is joy, — a blest abode!   821
An ampler sky its roseate light bestows
On that bright land, which sees the cloudless beam
Of suns and planets to our earth unknown.
On smooth green lawns, contending limb with limb,
Immortal athletes play, and wrestle long   826
'Gainst mate or rival on the tawny sand;
With sounding footsteps and ecstatic song,
Some thread the dance divine: among them moves
The bard of Thrace,[1] in flowing vesture clad,   830
Discoursing seven-noted melody,
Who sweeps the numbered strings with changeful
    hand,
Or smites with ivory point his golden lyre.
Here Trojans be of eldest, noblest race,
Great-hearted heroes, born in happier times,   835
Ilus, Assaracus, and Dardanus,
Illustrious builders of the Trojan town.
Their arms and shadowy chariots he views,
And lances fixed in earth, while through the fields
Their steeds without a bridle graze at will.   840
For if in life their darling passion ran
To chariots, arms, or glossy-coated steeds,
The self-same joy, though in their graves, they feel.
Lo! on the left and right at feast reclined
Are other blessed souls, whose chorus sings   845
Victorious pæans on the fragrant air
Of laurel groves; and hence to earth outpours
Eridanus,[2] through forests rolling free.
Here dwell the brave who for their native land
Fell wounded on the field; here holy priests   850
Who kept them undefiled their mortal day;
And poets, of whom the true-inspired song
Deserved Apollo's name; and all who found

[1] Orpheus.
[2] A river.

New arts, to make man's life more blest or fair;
Yea! here dwell all those dead whose deeds be-
    queath   855
Deserved and grateful memory to their kind.
And each bright brow a snow-white fillet wears.
Unto this host the Sibyl turned, and hailed
Musæus, midmost of a numerous throng,
Who towered o'er his peers a shoulder higher: 860
"O spirits blest! O venerable bard!
Declare what dwelling or what region holds
Anchises,[1] for whose sake we twain essayed
Yon passage over the wide streams of hell."
And briefly thus the hero made reply: 865
"No fixed abode is ours. In shadowy groves
We make our home, or meadows fresh and fair,
With streams whose flowery banks our couches be.
But you, if thitherward your wishes turn,
Climb yonder hill, where I your path may show."

So saying, he strode forth and led them on,   871
Till from that vantage they had prospect fair
Of a wide, shining land; thence wending down,
They left the height they trod; for far below
Father Anchises in a pleasant vale   875
Stood pondering, while his eyes and thought sur-
    veyed
A host of prisoned spirits, who there abode
Awaiting entrance to terrestrial air.
And musing he reviewed the legions bright
Of his own progeny and offspring proud —   880
Their fates and fortunes, virtues and great deeds.
Soon he discerned Æneas drawing nigh
O'er the green slope, and, lifting both his hands
In eager welcome, spread them swiftly forth.
Tears from his eyelids rained, and thus he spoke:
"Art here at last? Hath thy well-proven love 886
Of me thy sire achieved yon arduous way?
Will Heaven, belovèd son, once more allow
That eye to eye we look? and shall I hear
Thy kindred accent mingling with my own?   890
I cherished long this hope. My prophet-soul
Numbered the lapse of days, nor did my thought
Deceive. O, o'er what lands and seas wast driven
To this embrace! What perils manifold
Assailed thee, O my son, on every side!   895
How long I trembled, lest that Libyan throne
Should work thee woe!"
          Æneas thus replied:
"Thine image, sire, thy melancholy shade,
Came oft upon my vision, and impelled
My journey hitherward. Our fleet of ships   900
Lies safe at anchor in the Tuscan seas.
Come, clasp my hand! Come, father, I implore,
And heart to heart this fond embrace receive!"
So speaking, all his eyes suffused with tears;

[1] The father of Æneas, whom he is seeking.

Thrice would his arms in vain that shape enfold.
Thrice from the touch of hand the vision fled, 906
Like wafted winds or likest hovering dreams.

After these things Æneas was aware
Of solemn groves in one deep, distant vale,
Where trees were whispering, and forever flowed
The river Lethe, through its land of calm.   911
Nations unnumbered roved and haunted there:
As when, upon a windless summer morn,
The bees afield among the rainbow flowers
Alight and sip, or round the lilies pure   915
Pour forth in busy swarm, while far diffused
Their murmured songs from all the meadows rise
Æneas in amaze the wonder views,
And fearfully inquires of whence and why;
What yonder rivers be; what people press,   920
Line after line, on those dim shores along.
Said Sire Anchises: "Yonder thronging souls
To reincarnate shape predestined move.
Here, at the river Lethe's wave, they quaff
Care-quelling floods, and long oblivion.   925
Of these I shall discourse, and to thy soul
Make visible the number and array
Of my posterity; so shall thy heart
In Italy, thy new-found home, rejoice."
"O father," said Æneas, "must I deem   930
That from this region souls exalted rise
To upper air, and shall once more return
To cumbering flesh? O, wherefore do they feel,
Unhappy ones, such fatal lust to live?"
"I speak, my son, nor make thee longer doubt,"
Anchises said, and thus the truth set forth,   936
In ordered words from point to point unfolding:

"Know first that heaven and earth and ocean's
    plain,
The moon's bright orb, and stars of Titan birth
Are nourished by one Life; one primal Mind,   940
Immingled with the vast and general frame,
Fills every part and stirs the mighty whole.
Thence man and beast, thence creatures of the air,
And all the swarming monsters that be found
Beneath the level of the marbled sea;   945
A fiery virtue, a celestial power,
Their native seeds retain; but bodies vile,
With limbs of clay and members born to die,
Encumber and o'ercloud; whence also spring
Terrors and passions, suffering and joy;   950
For from deep darkness and captivity
All gaze but blindly on the radiant world.
Nor when to life's last beam they bid farewell
May sufferers cease from pain, nor quite be freed
From all their fleshly plagues; but by fixed law, 955
The strange, inveterate taint works deeply in.
For this, the chastisement of evils past

Is suffered here, and full requital paid.
Some hang on high, outstretched to viewless winds;
For some their sin's contagion must be purged   960
In vast ablution of deep-rolling seas,
Or burned away in fire.   Each man receives
His ghostly portion in the world of dark;
But thence to realms Elysian we go free,
Where for a few these seats of bliss abide,   965
Till time's long lapse a perfect orb fulfils,
And takes all taint away, restoring so
The pure, ethereal soul's first virgin fire.
At last, when the millennial æon strikes,
God calls them forth to yon Lethæan stream,   970
In numerous host, that thence, oblivious all,
They may behold once more the vaulted sky,
And willingly to shapes of flesh return."

So spoke Anchises; then led forth his son,
The Sibyl with him, to the assembled shades   975
(A voiceful throng), and on a lofty mound
His station took, whence plainly could be seen
The long procession, and each face descried.
"Hark now! for of the glories I will tell
That wait our Dardan blood; of our sons' sons   980
Begot upon the old Italian breed,
Who shall be mighty spirits, and prolong
Our names, their heritage.   I will unfold
The story, and reveal the destined years.
Yon princeling, thou beholdest leaning there   985
Upon a royal lance, shall next emerge
Into the realms of day.   He is the first
Of half-Italian strain, the last-born heir
To thine old age by fair Lavinia given,
Called Silvius,[1] a royal Alban name   990
(Of sylvan birth and sylvan nurture he),
A king himself and sire of kings to come,
By whom our race in Alba Longa reign.
Next Procas stands, our Trojan people's boast;
Capys and Numitor, and, named like thee,   995
Æneas Sylvius, like thee renowned
For faithful honor and for deeds of war,
When he ascends at last his Alban throne.
Behold what warrior youth they be!   How strong
Their goodly limbs!   Above their shaded brows
The civic oak they wear!   For thee they build   1001
Nomentum,[2] and the walls of Gabii,
Fidena too, and on the mountains pile
Collatia's citadels, Pometii,
Bola and Cora, Castrum-Inui —   1005
Such be the names the nameless lands shall bear.
See, in that line of sires the son of Mars,
Great Romulus, of Ilian mother born,

[1] Æneas is, then, looking at the spirit of his yet unborn son.   Silvius is to become the progenitor of the
Kings of Alba in Italy.
[2] Italian cities yet to be built.

From far-descended line of Trojan kings!
See from his helm the double crest uprear,   1010
While his celestial father in his mien
Shows forth his birth divine!   Of him, my son,
Great Rome shall rise, and, favored of his star,
Have power world-wide, and men of godlike mind.
She clasps her seven hills in single wall,   1015
Proud mother of the brave!   So Cybele,
The Berecynthian goddess, castle-crowned,
On through the Phrygian kingdoms speeds her car,
Exulting in her hundred sons divine,
All numbered with the gods, all throned on high.

Let now thy visionary glance look long   1021
On this thy race, these Romans that be thine.
Here Cæsar, of Iulus' glorious seed,
Behold ascending to the world of light!
Behold, at last, that man, for this is he,   1025
So oft unto thy listening ears foretold,
Augustus Cæsar, kindred unto Jove.
He brings a golden age; he shall restore
Old Saturn's sceptre to our Latin land,
And o'er remotest Garamant and Ind   1030
His sway extend; the fair dominion
Outruns th' horizon planets, yea, beyond
The sun's bright path, where Atlas' shoulder bears
Yon dome of heaven set thick with burning stars.
Against his coming the far Caspian shores   1035
Break forth in oracles; the Mæotian land
Trembles, and all the seven-fold mouths of Nile.
Not o'er domain so wide Alcides passed,
Although the brazen-footed doe he slew
And stilled the groves of Erymanth, and bade   1040
The beast of Lerna at his arrows quail.
Nor half so far triumphant Bacchus drove,
With vine-entwisted reins, his frolic team
Of tigers from the tall-topped Indian hill.

Still do we doubt if heroes' deeds can fill   1045
A realm so wide?   Shall craven fear constrain
Thee or thy people from Ausonia's shore?
Look, who is he I may discern from far
By olive-branch and holy emblems known?
His flowing locks and hoary beard, behold!   1050
Fit for a Roman king!   By hallowed laws
He shall found Rome anew — from mean estate
In lowly Cures[1] led to mightier sway
But after him arises one whose reign
Shall wake the land from slumber: Tullus then   1055
Shall stir slack chiefs to battle, rallying
His hosts which had forgot what triumphs be.
Him boastful Ancus follows hard upon,
O'erflushed with his light people's windy praise.
Wilt thou see Tarquins now?   And haughty hand

[1] A town of the Sabines where the second king of
Rome, Numa Pompilius, was born.

Of vengeful Brutus seize the signs of power? 1061
He first the consul's name shall take; he first
Th' inexorable fasces [1] sternly bear.
When his own sons in rash rebellion join,
The father and the judge shall sentence give 1065
In beauteous freedom's cause — unhappy he!
Howe'er the age to come the story tell,
'Twill bless such love of honor and of Rome.
'Tis Decius, sire and son, the Drusi, see!
Behold Torquatus with his axe! Look where
Camillus brings the Gallic standards home! 1071

But who are these in glorious armor clad
And equal power? In this dark world of cloud
Their souls in concord move; — but woe is me!
What duel [2] 'twixt them breaks, when by and by
The light of life is theirs, and forth they call 1076
Their long-embattled lines to carnage dire!
Allied by nuptial truce, the sire descends
From Alpine rampart and that castled cliff,
Monœcus by the sea; the son arrays 1080
His hostile legions in the lands of morn.
Forbear, my children! School not your great souls
In such vast wars, nor turn your giant strength
Against the bowels of your native land!
But be thou first, O first in mercy! thou 1085
Who art of birth Olympian! Fling away
Thy glorious sword, mine offspring and mine heir!

Yonder is one whose chariot shall ascend
The laurelled Capitolian steep; he rides
In glory o'er Achæa's hosts laid low, 1090
And Corinth overthrown. There, too, is he
Who shall uproot proud Argos and the towers
Of Agamemnon; vanquishing the heir
Even of Æacus, the warrior seed
Of Peleus' son; such vengeance shall be wrought
For Troy's slain sires, and violated shrines! 1096
Or who could fail great Cato's name to tell?
Or, Cossus, thine? or in oblivion leave
The sons of Gracchus? or the Scipios,
Twin thunderbolts of war, and Libya's bane? 1100
Or, more than kingly in his mean abode,
Fabricius? or Serranus at the plough?
Ye Fabii, how far would ye prolong
My weary praise? But see! 'tis Maximus,
Who by wise waiting saves his native land. 1105

Let others melt and mould the breathing bronze
To forms more fair, — aye! out of marble bring
Features that live; let them plead causes well;
Or trace with pointed wand the cycled heaven,
And hail the constellations as they rise; 1110

[1] Symbol of authority.
[2] The two friends, later to wage war against each other, are Julius Cæsar and Pompey.

But thou, O Roman, learn with sovereign sway
To rule the nations. Thy great art shall be
To keep the world in lasting peace, to spare
The humbled foe, and crush to earth the proud."

So did Anchises speak, then, after pause, 1115
Thus to their wondering ears his word prolonged:
"Behold Marcellus, bright with glorious spoil,
In lifted triumph through his warriors move!
The Roman power in tumultuous days
He shall establish; he rides forth to quell 1120
Afric and rebel Gaul; and to the shrine
Of Romulus the third-won trophy brings."
Then spoke Æneas, for he now could see
A beauteous youth in glittering dress of war,
Though of sad forehead and down-dropping eyes:
"Say, father, who attends the prince? a son? 1126
Or of his greatness some remoter heir?
How his friends praise him, and how matchless he!
But mournful night rests darkly o'er his brow."
With brimming eyes Anchises answer gave: 1130
"Ask not, O son, what heavy weight of woe
Thy race shall bear, when fate shall just reveal
This vision to the world, then yield no more.
O gods above, too glorious did ye deem
The seed of Rome, had this one gift been sure?
The lamentation of a multitude 1136
Arises from the field of Mars, and strikes
The city's heart. O Father Tiber, see
What pomp of sorrow near the new-made tomb
Beside thy fleeting stream! What Ilian [1] youth
Shall e'er his Latin kindred so advance 1141
In hope of glory? When shall the proud land
Of Romulus of such a nursling boast?
Ah, woe is me! O loyal heart and true!
O brave right arm invincible! What foe 1145
Had 'scaped his onset in the shock of arms,
Whether on foot he strode, or if he spurred
The hot flanks of his war-horse flecked with foam?
O lost, lamented child! If thou evade
Thy evil star, Marcellus thou shalt be. 1150
O bring me lilies! Bring with liberal hand!
Sad purple blossoms let me throw — the shade
Of my own kin to honor, heaping high
My gifts upon his grave! So let me pay
An unavailing vow!"
                      Then, far and wide 1155
Through spacious fields of air, they wander free,
Witnessing all; Anchises guides his son
From point to point, and quickens in his mind
Hunger for future fame. Of wars he tells
Soon imminent; of fair Laurentum's tribes; 1160
Of King Latinus' town; [2] and shows what way
Each task and hardship to prevent, or bear.

[1] Trojan.
[2] Laurentum.

Now Sleep has portals twain, whereof the one
Is horn, they say, and easy exit gives
To visions true; the other, gleaming white   1165
With polished ivory, the dead employ
To people night with unsubstantial dreams
Here now Anchises bids his son farewell;
And with Sibylla, his companion sage,

Up through that ivory portal lets him rise.   1170
Back to his fleet and his dear comrades all
Æneas hastes.   Then hold they their straight
    course
Into Caieta's bay.[1]   An anchor holds
Each lofty prow; the sterns stand firm on shore.
    [1] A seaport in Italy.

Horace · 65-8 B.C.

Horace — Quintus Horatius Flaccus — was born in Venusia, an ancient city in southern Italy, 65 B.C. A former slave who had earned his freedom, Horace's father gave his son a surprisingly adequate education, first in Venusia, later in Rome and Athens. As a young man the poet served as a junior officer under Brutus, fighting in the Battle of Philippi (42 B.C.) in the army which lost to the forces of Octavius and Antony. Through the interest of Virgil, Horace, upon his return to Rome, met Mæcenas, a rich patron of the arts, who presented the young man with the Sabine farm, located in central Italy, which he was to make famous in his verse. Even the Emperor Augustus, against whose interests Horace had fought at Philippi, proved magnanimous and befriended the poet in ways gratefully recognized in the *Odes* and other poems. Horace wrote the *Epodes* (one book), two books of satires, the *Odes* (four books), and the *Epistles* including *Ars Poetica*, a discussion of the art of poetry.

Few poets have left so intimate a chronicle of their thought and life. From his satires and odes, the student can reconstruct much of the poet's daily life as well as gain a knowledge of his friends and of the events in which he participated. Kindly, witty, ironical, skeptical, no reformer, Horace was an observer of the world about him rather than an active participant. He is the poet of good fellowship; he wrote much of the joys of wine, women, and song. Many are the verses he dedicated to the Lydias and Phyllises of his acquaintance. Nature inspired his happiest expression; he is the poet of the countryside as well as of the city. Contentment with little — such little as he knew at his Sabine farm — was a constant theme; yet, if we are to believe the words he makes his servant, Davus, utter about his habits, we must believe that he preached restraint, but did not always practice it.

Technically, Horace was a skillful poet. His lines flow with ease and are generally highly polished. The classical temper manifests itself in the forms Horace borrowed so freely from Greece, his use of epithet, his good sense, the grace and beauty of his lines which give constant evidence of his seeking polish and perfection in expression. With Horace, as with other classical writers, the style was as important as thought; indeed the thing said and the manner of saying were, at their best, one.

The translations which follow are by Sir Theodore Martin and are reprinted with the permission of Wm. Blackwood and Sons.

SUGGESTED REFERENCES: L. P. Wilkinson, *Horace and His Lyric Poetry* (2nd ed., 1951); Eduard Fraenkel, *Horace* (1957); Steele Commager, *The Odes of Horace, A Critical Study* (1962); Jacques Perret, *Horace* (1964).

Alphius

(From the *Epodes* — Epode II)

This poem is characteristically Horatian, both in the enthusiasm with which it sings of the simple joys of rusticity, an enthusiasm which leaves us with a taste of grapes and honey and good Lucrine oysters, and in the witty, satirical twist of the last stanza.

Happy the man, in busy schemes unskilled,
  Who, living simply, like our sires of old,
Tills the few acres which his father tilled,
  Vexed by no thoughts of usury or gold;

The shrilling clarion ne'er his slumber mars,   5
  Nor quails he at the howl of angry seas;
He shuns the forum with its wordy jars,
  Nor at a great man's door consents to freeze.

The tender vine-shoots, budding into life,
  He with the stately poplar-tree doth wed,   10
Lopping the fruitless branches with his knife,
  And grafting shoots of promise in their stead;

Or in some valley, up among the hills,
  Watches his wandering herds of lowing kine,
Or fragrant jars with liquid honey fills,   15
  Or shears his silly sheep in sunny shine;

Or when Autumnus o'er the smiling land
  Lifts up his head with rosy apples crowned,
Joyful he plucks the pears, which erst his hand
  Graffed on the stem they're weighing to the
      ground;   20

Plucks grapes in noble clusters purple-dyed,
  A gift for thee, Priapus,[1] and for thee,
Father Sylvanus,[2] where thou dost preside,
  Warding his bounds beneath thy sacred tree.

Now he may stretch his careless limbs to rest,   25
  Where some old ilex[3] spreads its sacred roof;
Now in the sunshine lie, as likes him best,
  On grassy turf of close elastic woof.

And streams the while glide on with murmurs low,
  And birds are singing 'mong the thickets deep,   30
And fountains babble, sparkling as they flow,
  And with their noise invite to gentle sleep.

But when grim winter comes, and o'er his grounds
  Scatters its biting snows with angry roar,

[1] Roman god of fertility.
[2] An old Italian god of the woods, protector of the fields.   [3] The holly.

He takes the field, and with a cry of hounds   35
  Hunts down into the toils the foaming boar;

Or seeks the thrush, poor starveling, to ensnare,
  In filmy net with bait delusive stored,
Entraps the travelled crane, and timorous hare,
  Rare dainties these to glad his frugal board.   40

Who amid joys like these would not forget
  The pangs which love to all its victims bears,
The fever of the brain, the ceaseless fret,
  And all the heart's lamentings and despairs?

But if a chaste and blooming wife, beside,   45
  His cheerful home with sweet young blossoms fills,
Like some stout Sabine,[1] or the sunburnt bride
  Of the lithe peasant of the Apulian[2] hills,

Who piles the hearth with logs well dried and old
  Against the coming of her wearied lord,   50
And, when at eve the cattle seek the fold,
  Drains their full udders of the milky hoard;

And bringing forth from her well-tended store
  A jar of wine, the vintage of the year,
Spreads an unpurchased feast, — oh then, not
    more   55
  Could choicest Lucrine[3] oysters give me cheer,

Or the rich turbot,[4] or the dainty char,[4]
  If ever to our bays the winter's blast
Should drive them in its fury from afar;
  Nor were to me a welcomer repast   60

The Afric hen or the Ionic snipe,
  Than olives newly gathered from the tree,
That hangs abroad its clusters rich and ripe,
  Or sorrel, that doth love the pleasant lea,

Or mallows wholesome for the body's need,   65
  Or lamb foredoomed upon some festal day
In offering to the guardian gods to bleed,
  Or kidling which the wolf hath marked for prey.

What joy, amidst such feasts, to see the sheep,
  Full of the pasture, hurrying homewards come,
To see the wearied oxen, as they creep,   71
  Dragging the upturned ploughshare slowly
    home!

[1] An early Italian people whom Horace, and others, believed to represent the strongest qualities of early Roman character.
[2] Apulia — a province of southern Italy.
[3] The Lucrine Lake was believed to supply the best oysters.
[4] A fish highly esteemed as food.

Or, ranged around the bright and blazing hearth,
　　To see the hinds, a house's surest wealth,
Beguile the evening with their simple mirth,　　75
　　And all the cheerfulness of rosy health!

Thus spake the miser Alphius;[1] and, bent
　　Upon a country life, called in amain
The money he at usury had lent;
　　But ere the month was out, 'twas lent again.　80

To Lycè

(Ode X — From Book III, *Odes*)

Horace never married. This does not mean, as the
two poems which follow will show, that he escaped the
worries and perplexities of love. Indeed for one who
avowedly sought peace and quiet, Horace was strangely
stubborn in his persistent affairs with women.

Though your drink were the Tanais,[2] chillest of
　　　　rivers,
　　And your lot with some conjugal savage were
　　　　cast,
You would pity, sweet Lycè, the poor soul that
　　　　shivers
　　Out here at your door in the merciless blast.

Only hark how the doorway goes straining and
　　　　creaking,　　　5
　　And the piercing wind pipes through the trees
　　　　that surround
The court of your villa, while black frost is streak-
　　　　ing
　　With ice the crisp snow that lies thick on the
　　　　ground!

In your pride — Venus hates it — no longer en-
　　　　velop ye,
　　Or haply you'll find yourself laid on the shelf;　10
You never were made for a prudish Penelope,[3]
　　'Tis not in the blood of your sires or yourself.

Though nor gifts nor entreaties can win a soft
　　　　answer,
　　Nor the violet pale of my love-ravaged cheek,

[1] The ironic twist in this last stanza is characteristically Horatian in spirit. Alphius, a famous money-
lender of the day, sings of the joys of rural life, calls in
his money that he may retire to the country and —
lends it out again.
[2] A river in Scythia, a remote, barbaric region north
of the Black Sea.
[3] Wife of Ulysses. See Homer, *Odyssey*, Books XXI
and XXII. She faithfully waited many years for the
return of her husband.

Though your husband be false with a Greek ballet-
　　　　dancer,　　　15
　　And you still are true, and forgiving, and meek,

Yet be not as cruel — forgive my upbraiding —
　　As snakes, nor as hard as the toughest of oak;
Think, to stand out here, drenched to the skin,
　　　　serenading
　　All night may in time prove too much of a joke.　20

The Reconciliation [1]

(Ode IX — From Book III, *Odes*)

HORACE

Whilst I was dear and thou were kind,
　　And I, and I alone might lie
Upon thy snowy breast reclined,
　　Not Persia's king so blest as I.

LYDIA

Whilst I to thee was all in all,　　　5
　　Nor Chloë might with Lydia vie,
Renowned in ode or madrigal,
　　Not Roman Ilia[2] famed as I.

HORACE

I now am Thracian Chloë's slave,
　　With hand and voice that charms the air,　　10
For whom even death itself I'd brave,
　　So fate the darling girl would spare!

LYDIA

I dote on Calaïs — and I
　　Am all his passion, all his care,
For whom a double death I'd die,　　　15
　　So fate the darling boy would spare!

HORACE

What, if our ancient love return,
　　And bind us with a closer tie,
If I the fair-haired Chloë spurn,
　　And as of old for Lydia sigh?　　　20

LYDIA

Though lovelier than yon star is he,
　　Thou fickle as an April sky,
More churlish, too, than Adria's sea,
　　With thee I'd live, with thee I'd die!

[1] This type of ode, characterized by dialogue, is
given the name Amœbæan, from the Greek word
meaning *to exchange*.
[2] The mother of Romulus and Remus, founders of
Rome.

Contentment

(Satire I — From Book I, *Satires*)

The student may read Horace with assurance that
the poet will not preach or try to elevate his social or
moral standards. Rather, Horace glorified the simple
life and contentment with one's lot

> Like one who has no higher views
> Than with quaint fancies to amuse.

He teaches, if he teaches at all, the importance of little
things, the joy to be found in intelligent, natural living
by one who knows that

> Extremes in either way are bad.

Tell me, Mæcenas,[1] if you can,
How comes it, that no mortal man
Is with his lot in life content,
Whether he owes it to the bent
Of his free choice, or fortune's whim?   5
And why is there such charm for him
In the pursuit his neighbor plies?
"O happy, happy merchants!" cries
The soldier crippled with the banes
Of age, and many hard campaigns.   10
"A soldier's is the life for me!"
The merchant shouts, whilst on the sea
His argosies are tossing far;
"For, mark ye, comes the tug of war,
Host grapples host, and in a breath   15
'Tis glorious victory or death!"
The lawyer deems the farmer blest,
When roused at cock-crow from his rest
By clients — those prodigious bores —
Thundering reveille on his doors;   20
Whilst he, by business dragged to town
From farmy field and breezy down,
Vows happiness is only theirs,
Who dwell in crowded streets and squares.
The cases of this kind we see,   25
So multitudinous they be,
Would tire e'en Fabius'[2] self, that fount
Of endless babble, to recount.
But to my point at once I'll come,
Lest you should think me wearisome.   30
    Suppose some god to say, "For you
What you're so eager for I'll do.
Be you a merchant, man of war!
You for the farm renounce the bar!
Change places! To your clients you,   35
You to your fields! What's here to do?
Not stir? 'Tis yours, and yet you scorn
The bliss you pined for night and morn."

[1] A wealthy Roman; see biographical note.
[2] Some unknown gossip and chatterbox.

Heavens! Were it not most fitting, now,
That Jove[1] at this should fume, and vow   40
He never, never would again
Give credence to the prayers of men?
    But to proceed, and not to seem
To skim the surface of my theme,
Like one who has no higher views   45
Than with quaint fancies to amuse: —
Yet why should truth not be impressed
Beneath the cover of a jest,
As teachers, gentlest of their tribe,
Their pupils now and then will bribe   50
With cakes and sugar-plums to look
With favor on their spelling-book?
Still, be this as it may, let us
Treat a grave subject gravely — thus
    The man who turns from day to day   55
With weary plough the stubborn clay,
Yon vintner — an exceeding knave,
The soldier, sailor rashly brave,
Who sweeps the seas from pole to pole,
All, to a man, protest their sole   60
Incentive thus to toil and sweat
Is a bare competence to get,
On which to some calm nook they may
Retire, and dream old age away.
Just as the tiny ant — for this   65
Their favorite illustration is —
Whate'er it can, away will sweep,
And add to its still growing heap,
Sagacious duly to foresee,
And cater for the time to be.   70
True sage, for when Aquarius[2] drear
Enshrouds in gloom the inverted year,
She keeps her nest, and on the hoard
Subsists, her prudent care has stored;
Whilst you nor summer's fervent heat   75
From the pursuit of wealth can beat,
Nor fire, nor winter, sword, nor wrack;
Nothing can daunt, or hold you back,
As long as lives the creature, who
Can brag he's wealthier than you.   80
    Where is the pleasure, pray unfold,
Of burying your heaps of gold
And silver in some darkling hole,
With trepidation in your soul?
Diminish them, you say, and down   85
They'll dwindle to a paltry crown.
But say you don't what beauty lies
In heaps, however huge their size?
Suppose your granaries contain
Measures ten thousandfold of grain,   90

[1] Jove or Jupiter — Greek, Zeus. The supreme ruler
of the universe.
[2] The Water-Bearer, eleventh sign of the zodiac.
Here it means January or winter.

Your stomach will not, when you dine,
Hold one iota more than mine.
Like the poor slave, that bears the sack
Of loaves upon his aching back,
You'll get no more, no, not one jot,   95
Than does his mate, who carries nought.
Or say, what boots it to the man,
Who lives within boon Nature's plan,
Whether he drive his ploughshare o'er
A thousand acres or five score?   100
    But then, you urge, the joy is deep
Of taking from a bulky heap.
Still, if we're free to pick out all
Our needs require from one that's small,
What better with your barns are you,   105
Than we with our poor sack or two?
Let us imagine, you desire
Some water, and no more require
Than might be in a jar ta'en up,
Or ev'n in, shall we say, a cup?   110
"I will not touch this trickling spring,
But from yon rolling river bring
What store I want," you proudly cry.
Well, be it so! But by-and-by
Those who still strive and strain, like you,   115
For something more than is their due,
By surly Aufidus[1] will be
Swept with its banks into the sea;
Whilst he, who all-abundant thinks
What for his wants suffices, drinks   120
His water undefiled with mud,
Nor sinks unpitied in the flood.
    But most men, blinded and controlled
By the delusive lust of gold,
Say that they never can obtain   125
Enough; because a man, they're fain
To think, is prized, and prized alone
For just so much as he may own.
What's to be done with fools like these?
Let them be wretched, if they please!   130
They have their comforts, it appears,
Like that rich knave, who met the jeers
Of the Athenian mob with this:
"The people hoot at me, and hiss,
But I at home applaud myself,   135
When in my chest I view my pelf."
    See Tantalus,[2] parched sinner, gasp
To catch the stream that slips his grasp!
Nay, smile not! change the name; of you
The story will be quite as true.   140
With panting breath and sleepless eye,

[1] A stream Horace knew well.
[2] A king of Phrygia who, having offended the gods, was forced to stand in water up to his chin and, while suffering from great thirst, was still unable to reach the water about him to drink it.

Upon your hoarded bags you lie,
And can no more their stores abridge,
Than if to touch were sacrilege,
But gaze and gloat on them, as though   145
They were mere pictures. Would you know,
What money can avail, and what
The uses may from it be got?
Buy bread, some herbs, a flask of wine,
To these add whatsoe'er, in fine,   150
Our human nature, if denied,
Feels pinched for and unsatisfied.
That's common-sense. But, day and night,
To watch and ward, half dead with fright,
To live in dread of thieves and fire,   155
Nay, let your very servants tire
Your soul with panic, lest they strip
Your house, and give yourself the slip,
If these the joys that riches give,
Heaven keep me beggared while I live!   160
    But if, you say, you catch a cold,
Or any other illness hold
You fast in bed, you can provide
Some one to sit by your bedside,
To nurse and tend you, and beseech   165
The doctor with caressing speech,
To cure your ailments, and restore you
To kith and kindred, that adore you.
'Tis all delusion! Neither wife
Nor son prays heaven to spare your life: 170
Neighbors, acquaintance, boy and girl,
All, all detest you for a churl.
And can you wonder, you who deem
Mere wealth above all things supreme,
If none vouchsafe that loving thought,   175
For which your life has never wrought?
No! In the chariot-race to train
A jackass to obey the rein
Were just as hopeless, as to win
Or keep the fond regards of kin   180
However near, or yet of friend,
Without some labor to that end.
    Then let this lust of hoarding cease;
And, if your riches shall increase,
Stand less in dread of being poor,   185
And, having managed to secure
All that was once your aim, begin
To round your term of toiling in;
Nor act like that Ummidius, who
(Brief is the tale) was such a screw —   190
Although so rich, he did not count
His wealth, but measured its amount —
That any slave went better dressed,
And to the last he was possessed
By dread that he should die of sheer   195
Starvation. Well, the sequel hear!
His housekeeper, tried past all bearing,

With more than Clytemnestra's [1] daring
Resolved to cure him of his pain,
So cleft him with an axe in twain.   200
   "What is the counsel, then, you give?
That I like Mænius [2] should live,
Or Nomenthanus?" [2]   Are you mad?
Extremes in either way are bad.
When I dissuade you from the vice   205
Of grasping, sordid avarice,
I do not counsel you to be
A spendthrift and a debauchee.
A line there is, not hard to draw,
'Twixt Tanaïs and the sire-in-law   210
Of young Visellius.[3]   Yes, there is
A mean in all such things as this:
Certain fixed bounds, which either way
O'erstep, and you must go astray.
   And so this brings me round again   215
To what I started from, that men
Are like the miser, all, in this:
They ever think their state amiss,
And only those men happy, who
A different career pursue;   220
Pine, if their neighbor's she-goat bears
An ampler store of milk than theirs;
Ne'er think how many myriads are
Still poorer than themselves by far,
And with unceasing effort labor   225
To get a point beyond their neighbor.
So does some wight, more rich than they
For ever bar their onward way;
Just as, when launched in full career,
On, onwards strains the charioteer   230
To outstrip the steeds that head the pace,
And scorns the laggards in the race.
And thus it happens, that we can
So rarely light upon a man
Who may with perfect truth confess   235
His life was one of happiness;
And, when its destined term is spent,
Can from its way retire content,
And like a well-replenished guest.
   But now I've prosed enough; and lest   240
You think I have purloined the olio,[4]
That crams Crispinus's [5] portfolio,
That pink of pendants most absurd,
I will not add one other word.

[1] Agamemnon's wife. She slew her husband with
an axe upon his return from Troy. See Æschylus'
Agamemnon.
[2] Possibly contemporary spendthrifts.
[3] These two names are largely subjects for speculation.
Fairclough suggests that Tanaïs was a freedman of
Mæcenas.   [4] A miscellaneous collection.
[5] A versifier whom Horace satirizes on several occasions.

The Bore

(Satire IX — From Book I, *Satires*)

Here Horace selects for his characterization a social
type common to all ages — the persistent bore. In
Roman classical literature, particularly in the writing of such men as Horace and Juvenal, Petronius
and Apuleius, the satire is a popular medium of expression.

It chanced that I, the other day,
Was sauntering up the Sacred Way,[1]
And musing, as my habit is,
Some trivial random fantasies,
That for the time absorbed me quite,   5
When there comes running up a wight,
Whom only by his name I knew;
"Ha, my dear fellow, how d'ye do?"
Grasping my hand, he shouted. "Why,
As times go, pretty well," said I;   10
"And you, I trust, can say the same."
But after me as still he came,
"Sir, is there anything," I cried,
"You want of me?"   "Oh," he replied,
"I'm just the man you ought to know; —   15
A scholar, author!" "Is it so?
For this I'll like you all the more!"
Then, writhing to evade the bore,
I quicken now my pace, now stop,
And in my servant's ear let drop   20
Some words, and all the while I feel
Bathed in cold sweat from head to heel.
   "Oh, for a touch," I moaned in pain,
"Bolanus,[2] of thy slapdash vein,
To put this incubus [3] to rout!"   25
As he went chattering on about
Whatever he descries or meets,
The crowds, the beauty of the streets,
The city's growth, its splendor, size.
"You're dying to be off," he cries: 30
For all the while I'd been struck dumb.
"I've noticed it some time. But come,
Let's clearly understand each other;
It's no use making all this pother.
My mind's made up to stick by you;   35
So where you go, there I go too."
   "Don't put yourself," I answered, "pray,
So very far out of your way.

[1] A famous street in old Rome.
[2] "Bolanus was apparently some person well known
in Rome as a man who would stand no nonsense, and
who could cut short a bore without ceremony..."
(Martin).
[3] A burden or weight.

I'm on the road to see a friend,
Whom you don't know, that's near his end,   40
Away beyond the Tiber far,
Close by where Cæsar's gardens [1] are."
    "I've nothing in the world to do,
And what's a paltry mile or two?
I like it, so I'll follow you!"   45
    Down dropped my ears on hearing this,
Just like a vicious jackass's
That's loaded heavier than he likes;
But off anew my torment strikes,
"If well I know myself, you'll end   50
With making of me more a friend
Than Viscus,[2] ay, or Varius;[2] for
Of verses who can run off more,
Or run them off at such a pace?
Who danced with such distinguished grace?   55
And as for singing, zounds!" said he,
"Hermogenes[2] might envy me!"
    Here was an opening to break in.
"Have you a mother, father, kin,
To whom your life is precious?" "None; —   60
I've closed the eyes of every one."
Oh happy they, I inly groan.
Now I am left, and I alone.
Quick, quick, despatch me where I stand!
Now is the direful doom at hand   65
Which erst the Sabine beldam old,
Shaking her magic urn, foretold
In days when I was yet a boy: —
"Him shall no poisons fell destroy,
Nor hostile sword in shock of war,   70
Nor gout, nor colic, nor catarrh.
In fulness of the time his thread
Shall by a prate-apace [3] be shred;
So let him, when he's twenty-one,
If he be wise, all babblers shun."   75
    Now we were close to Vesta's [4] fane.
'Twas hard on ten, and he, my bane,[5]
Was bound to answer to his bail,
Or lose his cause, if he should fail.
"Do, if you love me, step aside   80
One moment with me here," he cried.
"Upon my life, indeed, I can't;
Of law I'm wholly ignorant;
And you know where I'm hurrying to."

    [1] Julius Cæsar built the gardens, on the bank of the river Tiber, for the citizens of Rome.
    [2] The first two by inference and Hermogenes by fact were contemporary poets.
    [3] Chatterbox.
    [4] Goddess of the hearth, the home. In this temple at Rome a sacred fire, cared for by six virgin priestesses ("Vestals"), was kept burning. In case the fire went out, it was lighted again by the sun's rays.
    [5] A scourge, disease, poison.

"I'm fairly puzzled what to do.   85
Give you up, or my cause?" "Oh, me,
Me, by all means!" "I won't," quoth he;
And stalks on, holding by me tight.
As with your conqueror to fight
Is hard, I follow. "How," anon   90
He rambles off — "how get you on,
You and Mæcenas? To so few
He keeps himself. So clever, too!
No man more dexterous to seize
And use his opportunities.   95
Just introduce me, and you'll see,
We'll pull together famously;
And hang me, then, if with my backing,
You don't send all your rivals packing!"
    "Things in that quarter, sir, proceed   100
In very different style indeed.
No house more free from all that's base,
In none cabals [1] more out of place.
It hurts me not, if there I see
Men richer, better read than me.   105
Each has his place!" "Amazing tact!
Scarce credible!" "But 'tis the fact."
"You quicken my desire to get
An introduction to his set."
    "With merit such as yours, you need   110
But wish it, and you must succeed.
He's to be won, and that is why
Of strangers he's so very shy."
    "I'll spare no pains, no arts, no shifts!
His servants I'll corrupt with gifts.   115
To-day though driven from his gate,
What matter? I will lie in wait,
To catch some lucky chance; I'll meet,
Or overtake him in the street;
I'll haunt him like his shadow! Nought   120
In life without much toil is bought."
    Just at this moment who but my
Dear friend Aristius [2] should come by?
My rattle-brain right well he knew.
We stop. "Whence, friends, and whither to?"
He asks and answers. Whilst we ran   126
The usual courtesies, I began
To pluck him by the sleeve, to pinch
His arms, that feel but will not flinch,
By nods and winks most plain to see   130
Imploring him to rescue me:
He, wickedly obtuse the while,
Meets all my signals with a smile.

    [1] Schemes or intrigues.
    [2] Aristius Fuscus. "Fuscus, who knew into what hands Horace had fallen, enjoys the joke, and is obdurate to every hint to come to his rescue. His pretext that the day is too sacred for business, being the Jew's Thirtieth Sabbath, is a mere piece of roguishness..." (Martin.)

I, choked with rage, said, "Was there not
Some business, I've forgotten what,   135
You mentioned, that you wished with me
To talk about, and privately?"

"Oh, I remember! Never mind.
Some more convenient time I'll find.
The Thirtieth Sabbath this! Would you   140
Offend the circumcisèd Jew?"

"Religious scruples I have none."
"Ah! But I have. I am but one
Of the *canaille* ¹ — a feeble brother.
Your pardon! Some fine day or other   145
I'll tell you what it was." Oh, day
Of woful doom to me! Away
The rascal bolted like an arrow,
And left me underneath the harrow;
When by the rarest luck, we ran   150
At the next turn against the man
Who had the lawsuit with my bore.
"Ha, knave!" he cried with loud uproar,
"Where are you off to? Will you here
Stand witness?" I present my ear.²   155
To court he hustles him along;
High words are bandied, high and strong,
A mob collects, the fray to see:
So did Apollo ³ rescue me.

My Prayers with This I Used to Charge

(Satire VI — From Book II, *Satires*)

Of this satire Keightley writes: "In this, perhaps
the most pleasing of all Horace's Satires, we have more
clearly than elsewhere a picture of the poet's heart and
mind. We see his grateful and contented spirit, his
genuine love of Nature and rural life, in which no
ancient poet seems to have equalled him, his aversion
to the noise and bustle of a town life, and to the excitement of the luxurious dinner-parties of the capital.
His object seems to have been to let the world and
Mæcenas himself see his gratitude to that friend, who
had gratified the first and chief of his wishes. By way
of contrast, he enumerates some of his annoyances when
in town, and he concludes with an Æsopic fable, illus-
trative of the advantages of the still quiet country life,
over the fears and anxieties of one spent in cities. It
was evidently written at his Sabinum, of which he appears to have been now some time in possession, and
probably in the year (of Rome) 723-724, when Mæcenas

¹ Rabble, mob.
² It was an old custom to ask a bystander to witness
that a summons had been served and for the bystander,
to acknowledge that he had witnessed the act, to allow
his ear to be touched.
³ Apollo was a friend of poets.

during the absence of Cæsar, after the battle of Actium,
had the charge of the city."

My prayers with this I used to charge, —
A piece of land not over large,
Wherein there should a garden be,
A clear spring flowing ceaselessly,
And where, to crown the whole, there should   5
A patch be found of growing wood.
All this, and more, the gods have sent,
And I am heartily content.
    O son of Maia,¹ that I may
These bounties keep is all I pray.   10
If ne'er by craft or base design
I've swelled what little store is mine,
Nor mean it ever shall be wrecked
By profligacy or neglect;
If never from my lips a word   15
Shall drop of wishes so absurd
As, "Had I but that little nook,
Next to my land, that spoils its look!"
Or, "Would some lucky chance unfold
A crock to me of hidden gold,   20
As to the man, whom Hercules
Enriched and settled at his ease,
Who, with the treasure he had found,
Bought for himself the very ground
Which he before for hire had tilled!"   25
If I with gratitude am filled
For what I have — by this I dare
Adjure you to fulfil my prayer,
That you with fatness will endow
My little herd of cattle now,   30
And all things else their lord may own,
Except what wits he has alone,
And be, as heretofore, my chief
Protector, guardian, and relief!
So, when from town and all its ills   35
I to my perch among the hills
Retreat, what better theme to choose
Than satire for my homely Muse?
No fell ambition wastes me there,
No, nor the south wind's leaden air,   40
Nor Autumn's pestilential breath,
With victims feeding hungry death.
Sire of the morn, or if more dear
The name of Janus ² to thine ear,
Through whom whate'er by man is done,   45
From life's first dawning, is begun,
(So willed the gods for man's estate,)
Do thou my verse initiate!
At Rome ³ you hurry me away

¹ Mercury (Hermes) was god of luck and of gain.
² Janus was "sire of the dawn."
³ Horace here begins to recite what morning means in
Rome.

To bail my friend; "Quick, no delay,   50
Or some one — could worse luck befall you? —
Will in the kindly task forestall you."
So go I must, although the wind
Is north and killingly unkind,
Or snow, in thickly-falling flakes,   55
The wintry day more wintry makes.
And when, articulate and clear,
I've spoken what may cost me dear,
Elbowing the crowd that round me close,
I'm sure to crush somebody's toes.   60
"I say, where are you pushing to?
What would you have, you madman, you?"
So flies he at poor me, 'tis odds,
And curses me by all his gods.
"You think that you, now, I daresay,   65
May push whatever stops your way,
When you are to Mæcenas bound!"
Sweet, sweet as honey is the sound,
I won't deny, of that last speech,
But then no sooner do I reach   70
The gloomy Esquiline,[1] than straight
Buzz, buzz around me runs the prate
Of people pestering me with cares,
All about other men's affairs.
"To-morrow, Roscius bade me state,   75
He trusts you'll be in court by eight!"
"The scriveners, worthy Quintus, pray,
You'll not forget they meet to-day,
Upon a point both grave and new,
One touching the whole body, too."   80
"Do get Mæcenas, do, to sign
This application here of mine!"
"Well, well, I'll try." "You can with ease
Arrange it, if you only please."
    Close on eight years it now must be,   85
Since first Mæcenas numbered me
Among his friends, as one to take
Out driving with him, and to make
The confidant of trifles, say,
Like this, "What is the time of day?"   90
"The Thracian Bantam,[2] would you bet
On him, or on the Syrian Pet?"[2]
"These chilly mornings will do harm,
If one don't mind to wrap up warm;"
Such nothings as without a fear   95
One drops into the chinkiest ear.
Yet all this time hath envy's glance
On me looked more and more askance.
From mouth to mouth such comments run;
"Our friend indeed is Fortune's son.   100
Why, there he was, the other day,
Beside Mæcenas at the play;

[1] Here was a cemetery.
[2] Terms designating gladiators — much as we use
similar terms today, i.e. "The Brown Bomber."

And at the Campus, just before,
They had a bout at battledore."
    Some chilling news through lane and street   105
Spreads from the Forum. All I meet
Accost me thus — "Dear friend, you're so
Close to the gods, that you must know:
About the Dacians,[1] have you heard
Any fresh tidings? Not a word!"   110
"You're always jesting!" "Now may all
The gods confound me, great and small,
If I have heard one word!" "Well, well,
But you at any rate can tell
If Cæsar means the lands, which he   115
Has promised to his troops, shall be
Selected from Italian ground,
Or in Trinacria[2] be found?"
And when I swear, as well I can,
That I know nothing, for a man   120
Of silence rare and most discreet
They cry me up to all the street.
    Thus do my wasted days slip by,
Not without many a wish and sigh,
Oh, when shall I the country see,[3]   125
Its woodlands green? Oh, when be free,
With books of great old men, and sleep,
And hours of dreamy ease, to creep
Into oblivion sweet of life,
Its agitations and its strife?   130
When on my table shall be seen
Pythagoras's kinsman bean,[4]
And bacon, not too fat, embellish
My dish of greens, and give it relish?
Oh happy nights, oh feasts divine,   135
When, with the friends I love, I dine
At mine own hearth-fire, and the meat
We leave gives my bluff hinds a treat!
No stupid laws our feasts control,
But each guest drains or leaves the bowl,   140
Precisely as he feels inclined.
If he be strong, and have a mind
For bumpers, good! if not, he's free
To sip his liquor leisurely.
And then the talk our banquet rouses!   145
Not gossip 'bout our neighbors' houses,
Or if 'tis generally thought
That Lepos[5] dances well or not?

[1] Residents of the Roman province of Dacia between
the lower Danube and the Carpathian mountains.
[2] Sicily.
[3] Horace now turns from Rome to listing the delights
of life at his Sabine Farm.
[4] Believing in the transmigration of souls, good
Pythagoreans would not eat beans so that they might
not run the risk of eating the soul of a philosopher.
[5] An actor-dancer.

But what concerns us nearer, and
Is harmful not to understand,　　　　150
Whether by wealth or worth, 'tis plain,
That men to happiness attain?
By what we're led to choose our friends, —
Regard for them, or our own ends?
In what does good consist, and what　　155
Is the supremest form of that?
　　And then friend Cervius will strike in
With some old grandam's tale, akin
To what we are discussing.　Thus,
If some one have cried up to us　　　160
Arellius' wealth, forgetting how
Much care it costs him, "Look you now,
Once on a time," he will begin,
"A country mouse received within
His rugged cave a city brother,　　　165
As one old comrade would another.
'A frugal mouse upon the whole,
But loved his friend, and had a soul,'
And could be free and open-handed,
When hospitality demanded.　　　　170
In brief, he did not spare his hoard
Of corn and pease, long coyly stored;
Raisins he brought, and scraps, to boot,
Half-gnawed, of bacon, which he put
With his own mouth before his guest,　175
In hopes, by offering his best
In such variety, he might
Persuade him to an appetite.
But still the cit, with languid eye,
Just picked a bit, then put it by;　　180
Which with dismay the rustic saw,
As, stretched upon some stubbly straw,
He munched at bran and common grits,
Not venturing on the dainty bits.
At length the town mouse; 'What,' says he,　185
'My good friend, can the pleasure be,
Of grubbing here, on the backbone
Of a great crag, with trees o'ergrown?
Who'd not to these wild woods prefer
The city, with its crowds and stir?　　190

Then come with me to town; you'll ne'er
Regret the hour that took you there.
All earthly things draw mortal breath;
Nor great nor little can from death
Escape, and therefore, friend, be gay,　195
Enjoy life's good things while you may,
Remembering how brief the space
Allowed to you in any case.'
　　His words strike home; and, light of heart,
Behold with him our rustic start,　　200
Timing their journey so, they might
Reach town beneath the cloud of night,
Which was at its high noon, when they
To a rich mansion found their way,
Where shining ivory couches vied　　205
With coverlets in purple dyed,
And where in baskets were amassed
The wrecks of a superb repast,
Which some few hours before had closed.
There, having first his friend disposed　210
Upon a purple tissue, straight
The city mouse begins to wait
With scraps upon his country brother,
Each scrap more dainty than another,
And all a servant's duty proffers,　　215
First tasting everything he offers.
　　The guest, reclining there in state,
Rejoices in his altered fate,
O'er each fresh tidbit smacks his lips,
And breaks into the merriest quips,　220
When suddenly a banging door
Shakes host and guest into the floor.
From room to room they rush aghast,
And almost drop down dead at last,
When loud through all the house resounds　225
The deep bay of Molossian hounds.
　　'Ho!' cries the country mouse.　'This kind
Of life is not for me, I find.
Give me my woods and cavern.　There
At least I'm safe!　And though both spare　230
And poor my food may be, rebel
I never will; so, fare ye well!'"

Marcus Aurelius (Antoninus) · 121–180

　　One of the few great rulers who has left a body of writing worthy the attention of twentieth-century students, Marcus Aurelius (121–180 A.D.) proved himself a notable leader both in war and in peace.　The son of Annius Verus, a civilian who had held high office in Rome, Marcus Aurelius was not born to inherit the empire.　His father died when Marcus was an infant and, as a result of an early adoption, Marcus became emperor of Rome at the age of forty.　He was ruler at a time when the empire was busy with many wars and, consequently, spent much of his time with his army at one or another of the frontiers.　In 168 he conquered the Marcomanni, a Germanic tribe which gave the Romans long and persistent trouble even after they were "subdued." Other years found Marcus Aurelius in the Rhine-Danube region, or suppressing the Quadi, or in Syria. On his return from Syria, the emperor stopped at Athens, taking advantage of his visit in Greece to be initiated into the Eleusinian mysteries, the same sacred rites which Æschylus was accused of having violated by disclosing their secrets. Marcus Aurelius was an able and generous ruler — though hostile to the development of the growing Christianity — and because of his interest in learning endowed various chairs for the teaching of philosophy and rhetoric. He died, in 180 A.D., while engaged in a military expedition against certain Germanic tribes.

The doctrine of Marcus Aurelius is basically the materialism of Stoic thought which would reduce philosophy primarily to a study of natural laws, but the emperor-philosopher did not hesitate to modify the conventional attitudes of Stoicism when he found them inconsistent with his own experience. To Aurelius the object of the good life was tranquillity. The classical calm, which comes with an active life held rigidly between extremes, was most likely to be secured by one who lives "conformably to nature." The four virtues he most emphasizes are wisdom, fortitude, justice, and moderation. The best guide in conduct, he thought, is reason, and he interpreted reason in such a way as to incorporate with it the conscience. Though as emperor and one who believed in the state religion Aurelius was an enemy of Christianity and persecuted the early Christians, a reader of the *Meditations* is frequently impressed by the similarity between the doctrines he taught and some of the major tenets of the Christian faith.

SUGGESTED REFERENCE: A. S. L. Farquharson, *Marcus Aurelius, His Life and His World* (1951).

Meditations

The place of Marcus Aurelius in literature is secured through one book, a sort of diary generally called *The Meditations* but which he appears to have entitled *To Himself*, a name which reflects the personal quality of the work and which modestly suggests that he was writing for personal satisfaction rather than for posterity. *The Meditations* consists of short notes in Greek, often made in military camp while he was with his army at a frontier outpost, summing up his convictions towards such philosophic concepts as duty, the soul, death, the moral code of the individual, and mastery of one's self. Throughout the book he manifests a defiant disregard for all the transitory aspects of life. The translation which follows is from *The Thoughts of the Emperor Marcus Aurelius Antoninus*, translated by George Long. (Little, Brown and Company.)

Begin the morning by saying to thyself, I shall meet with the busybody, the ungrateful, arrogant, 20 deceitful, envious, unsocial. All these things happen to them by reason of their ignorance of what is good and evil. But I who have seen the nature of the good that it is beautiful and of the bad that it is ugly, and the nature of him who does 25 wrong, that it is akin to me, not [only] of the same blood or seed, but that it participates in [the same] intelligence and [the same] portion of the divinity, I can neither be injured by any of them, for no one can fix on me what is ugly, nor can I be angry with 30 my kinsman, nor hate him. For we are made for co-operation, like feet, like hands, like eyelids,

like the rows of the upper and lower teeth. To act against one another then is contrary to nature; and it is acting against one another to be vexed and to turn away.

5 Whatever this is that I am, it is a little flesh and breath, and the ruling part. Throw away thy books; no longer distract thyself: it is not allowed; but as if thou wast now dying, despise the flesh, it is blood and bones and a network, a contexture of 10 nerves, veins and arteries. See the breath also, what kind of a thing it is; air, and not always the same, but every moment sent out and again sucked in. The third then is the ruling part: consider thus: Thou art an old man; no longer let this be a 15 slave, no longer be pulled by the strings like a puppet to unsocial movements, no longer be either dissatisfied with thy present lot, or shrink from the future.

All that is from the gods is full of providence. 20 That which is from fortune is not separated from nature or without an interweaving and involution with the things which are ordered by Providence. From thence all things flow; and there is besides necessity, and that which is for the advantage of 25 the whole universe, of which thou art a part. But that is good for every part of nature which the nature of the whole brings, and what serves to maintain this nature. Now the universe is preserved, as by the changes of the elements so by the 30 changes of things compounded of the elements. Let these principles be enough for thee; let them always be fixed opinions. But cast away the thirst after books, that thou mayest not die murmuring, but cheerfully, truly and from thy heart thankful to the gods.

Remember how long thou hast been putting off these things, and how often thou hast received an opportunity from the gods, and yet dost not use it. Thou must now at last perceive of what universe thou art a part, and of what administrator of the universe thy existence is an efflux,[1] and that a limit of time is fixed for thee, which if thou dost not use for clearing away the clouds from thy mind, it will go and thou wilt go, and it will never return.

Every moment think steadily as a Roman and a man to do what thou hast in hand with perfect and simply dignity, and feeling of affection, and freedom, and justice; and to give thyself relief from all other thoughts. And thou wilt give thyself relief, if thou doest every act of thy life as if it were the last, laying aside all carelessness and passionate aversion from the commands of reason, and all hypocrisy, and self-love, and discontent with the portion which has been given to thee. Thou seest how few the things are, the which if a man lays hold of, he is able to live a life which flows in quiet, and is like the existence of the gods; for the gods on their part will require nothing more from him who observes these things.

Do wrong to thyself, do wrong to thyself, my soul; but thou wilt no longer have the opportunity of honoring thyself. Every man's life is sufficient. But thine is nearly finished, though thy soul reverences not itself, but places thy felicity in the souls of others.

Do the things external which fall upon thee distract thee? Give thyself time to learn something new and good, and cease to be whirled around. But then thou must also avoid being carried about the other way. For those too are triflers who have wearied themselves in life by their activity, and yet have no object to which to direct every movement, and, in a word, all their thoughts.

Through not observing what is in the mind of another a man has seldom been seen to be unhappy; but those who do not observe the movements of their own minds must of necessity be unhappy.

This thou must always bear in mind, what is the nature of the whole, and what is my nature, and how this is related to that, and what kind of a part it is of what kind of a whole; and that there is no one who hinders thee from always doing and saying the things which are according to the nature of which thou art a part.

Theophrastus,[2] in his comparison of bad acts —

[1] Emanation, a flowing out.
[2] A Greek philosopher.

such a comparison as one would make in accordance with the common notions of mankind — says, like a true philosopher, that the offenses which are committed through desire are more blamable than those which are committed through anger. For he who is excited by anger seems to turn away from reason with a certain pain and unconscious contraction; but he who offends through desire, being overpowered by pleasure, seems to be in a manner more intemperate and more womanish in his offenses. Rightly then, and in a way worthy of philosophy, he said that the offense which is committed with pleasure is more blamable than that which is committed with pain; and on the whole the one is more like a person who has been first wronged and through pain is compelled to be angry; but the other is moved by his own impulse to do wrong, being carried toward doing something by desire.

Since it is possible that thou mayest depart from life this very moment, regulate every act and thought accordingly. But to go away from among men, if there are gods, is not a thing to be afraid of, for the gods will not involve thee in evil; but if indeed they do not exist, or if they have no concern about human affairs, what is it to me to live in a universe devoid of gods or devoid of providence? But in truth they do exist, and they do care for human things, and they have put all the means in man's power to enable him not to fall into real evils. And as to the rest, if there was anything evil, they would have provided for this also, that it should be altogether in a man's power not to fall into it. Now, that which does not make a man worse, how can it make a man's life worse? But neither through ignorance, nor having the knowledge, but not the power to guard against or correct these things, is it possible that the nature of the universe has overlooked them; nor is it possible that it has made so great a mistake, either through want of power or want of skill, that good and evil should happen indiscriminately to the good and the bad. But death certainly, and life, honor and dishonor, pain and pleasure, all these things equally happen to good men and bad, being things which make us neither better nor worse. Therefore they are neither good nor evil.

How quickly all these things disappear, in the universe the bodies themselves, but in time the remembrance of them; what is the nature of all sensible things, and particularly whose which attract with the bait of pleasure or terrify by pain, or are noised about by vapory fame; how worthless, and contemptible, and sordid and perishable, and dead they are — all this it is the part of the intellectual faculty to observe. To observe too

who these are whose opinions and voices give reputation; what death is, and the fact that, if a man
looks at it in itself, and by the abstractive power of
reflection resolves into their parts all the things
which present themselves to the imagination in it,
he will then consider it to be nothing else than an
operation of nature; and if anyone is afraid of an
operation of nature he is a child. This, however, is
not only an operation of nature, but it is also a
thing which conduces to the purposes of nature.
To observe, too, how man comes near to the Deity,
and by what part of him, and when this part of
man is so disposed.

Nothing is more wretched than a man who traverses everything in a round, and pries into things
beneath the earth, as the poet says, and seeks by
conjecture what is in the minds of his neighbors,
without perceiving that it is sufficient to attend
to the dæmon [1] within him, and to reverence it sincerely. And reverence of the dæmon consists in
keeping it pure from passion and thoughtlessness,
and dissatisfaction with what comes from gods
and men. For the things from the gods merit
veneration for their excellence; and the things from
men should be dear to us by reason of kinship; and
sometimes even, in a manner, they move our pity
by reason of men's ignorance of good and bad; this
defect being not less than that which deprives us of
the power of distinguishing things that are white
and black.

Though thou shouldest be going to live three
thousand years, and as many times ten thousand
years, still remember that no man loses any other
life than this which he now lives, nor lives any
other than this which he now loses. The longest
and shortest are thus brought to the same. For
the present is the same to all, though that which
perishes is not the same; and so that which is lost
appears to be a mere moment. For a man cannot
lose either the past or the future: for what a man
has not, how can anyone take this from him? These
two things then thou must bear in mind: the one,
that all things from eternity are of like forms and
come round in a circle, and that it makes no difference whether a man shall see the same things
during a hundred years or two hundred, or an infinite time; and the second, that the longest liver
and he who will die soonest lose just the same. For
the present is the only thing of which a man can be
deprived, if it is true that this is the only thing
which he has, and that a man cannot lose a thing
if he has it not.

Remember that all is opinion. For what was
said by the Cynic Monimus is manifest: and manifest too is the use of what was said, if a man re-

[1] Spirit.

ceives what may be got out of it as far as it is true.

The soul of man does violence to itself, first of
all when it becomes an abscess and, as it were, a
tumor on the universe, so far as it can. For to be
vexed at anything which happens is a separation of
ourselves from nature, in some part of which the
natures of all other things are contained. In the
next place, the soul does violence to itself when it
turns away from any man, or even moves towards
him with the intention of injuring, such as are the
souls of those who are angry. In the third place,
the soul does violence to itself when it is overpowered by pleasure or by pain. Fourthly, when
it plays a part, and does or says anything insin-
cerely and untruly. Fifthly, when it allows any
act of its own and any movement to be without an
aim, and does anything thoughtlessly and without considering what it is, it being right that even
the smallest things be done with reference to an
end; and the end of rational animals is to follow
the reason and the law of the most ancient city
and polity.

Of the human life the time is a point, and the
substance is in a flux, and the perception dull, and
the composition of the whole body subject to putre-
faction, and the soul of a whirl, and fortune hard
to divine, and fame a thing devoid of judgment.
And, to say all in a word, everything which belongs
to the body is a stream, and what belongs to the
soul is a dream and vapor, and life is a warfare
and a stranger's sojourn, and after-fame is oblivion. What, then, is that which is able to conduct a man? One thing, and only one — philosophy. But this consists in keeping the dæmon
within a man free from violence and unharmed,
superior to pains and pleasures, doing nothing
without a purpose, nor yet falsely and with hypocrisy, not feeling the need of another man's doing
or not doing anything; and besides, accepting all
that happens, and all that is allotted, as coming
from thence, wherever it is, from whence he himself came; and, finally, waiting for death with a
cheerful mind, as being nothing else than a dissolution of the elements of which every living being
is compounded. But if there is no harm to the elements themselves in each continually changing into
another, why should a man have any apprehension
about the change and dissolution of all the elements? For it is according to nature, and nothing
is evil which is according to nature.

We ought to consider not only that our life is
daily wasting away and a smaller part of it is left,
but another thing also must be taken into the account, that if a man should live longer it is quite
uncertain whether the understanding will still continue sufficient for the comprehension of things, and

retain the power of contemplation which strives to acquire the knowledge of the divine and the human. For if he shall begin to fall into dotage, perspiration and nutrition and imagination and appetite, and whatever else there is of the kind, will not fail; but the power of making use of ourselves, and filling up the measure of our duty, and clearly separating all appearances, and considering whether a man should now depart from life, and whatever else of the kind absolutely requires a disciplined reason, all this is already extinguished. We must make haste then, not only because we are daily nearer to death, but also because the conception of things and the understanding of them cease first.

We ought to observe also that even the things which follow after the things which are produced according to nature contain something pleasing and attractive. For instance, when bread is baked some parts are split at the surface, and these parts which thus open, and have a certain fashion contrary to the purpose of the baker's art, are beautiful in a manner, and in a peculiar way excite a desire for eating. And again, figs, when they are quite ripe, gape open, and in the ripe olives the very circumstance of their being near to rottenness adds a peculiar beauty to the fruit. And the ears of corn bending down, and the lion's eyebrows, and the foam which flows from the mouth of wild boars, and many other things — though they are far from being beautiful, if a man should examine them severally — still, because they are consequent upon the things which are formed by nature, help to adorn them, and they please the mind; so that if a man should have a feeling and deeper insight with respect to the things which are produced in the universe, there is hardly one of those which follow by way of consequence which will not seem to him to be in a manner disposed so as to give pleasure. And so he will see even the real gaping jaws of wild beasts with no less pleasure than those which painters and sculptors show by imitation; and in an old woman and an old man he will be able to see a certain maturity and comeliness; and the attractive loveliness of young persons he will be able to look on with chaste eyes; and many such things will present themselves, not pleasing to every man, but to him only who has become truly familiar with nature and her works.

Hippocrates [1] after curing many diseases himself fell sick and died. The Chaldæi [2] foretold the deaths of many, and then fate caught them too. Alexander, and Pompeius, and Caius Cæsar, after

so often completely destroying whole cities, and in battle cutting to pieces many ten thousands of cavalry and infantry, themselves too at last departed from life. Heraclitus,[1] after so many speculations on the conflagration of the universe, was filled with water internally, and died smeared all over with mud. And lice destroyed Democritus; [2] and other lice killed Socrates. What means all this? Thou hast embarked, thou hast made the voyage, thou art come to shore; get out. If indeed to another life, there is no want of gods, not even there. But if to a state without sensation, thou wilt cease to be held by pains and pleasures, and to be a slave to the vessel, which is as much inferior as that which serves it is superior; for the one is intelligence and deity; the other is earth and corruption.

Do not waste the remainder of thy life in thoughts about others, when thou dost not refer thy thoughts to some object of common utility. For thou losest the opportunity of doing something else when thou hast such thoughts as these, What is such a person doing, and why, and what is he saying, and what is he thinking of, and what is he contriving, and whatever else of the kind makes us wander away from the observation of our own ruling power. We ought then to check in the series of our thoughts everything that is without a purpose and useless, but most of all the overcurious feeling and the malignant; and a man should use himself to think of those things only about which if one should suddenly ask, What hast thou now in thy thoughts? with perfect openness thou mightest immediately answer, This or That; so that from thy words it should be plain that everything in thee is simple and benevolent, and such as befits a social animal, one that cares not for thoughts about pleasure or sensual enjoyments at all, nor has any rivalry or envy and suspicion, or anything else for which thou wouldest blush if thou shouldst say that thou hadst it in thy mind. For the man who is such and no longer delays being among the number of the best, is like a priest and minister of the gods, using too the [deity] which is planted within him, which makes the man uncontaminated by pleasure, unharmed by any pain, untouched by any insult, feeling no wrong, a fighter in the noblest fight, one who cannot be overpowered by any passion, dyed deep with justice, accepting with all his soul everything which happens and is assigned to him as his portion; and not often, nor yet without great necessity and for the general interest, imagining what another says, or does, or thinks. For it is only what belongs to himself that he

[1] A famous Greek physician of ancient times. Sometimes called "The Father of Medicine."
[2] Noted as soothsayers and astrologers.

[1] Philosopher and natural scientist.
[2] Called "the laughing philosopher."

makes the matter for his activity; and he constantly thinks of that which is allotted to himself out of the sum total of things, and he makes his own acts fair, and he is persuaded that his own portion is good. For the lot which is assigned to each man is carried along with him and carries him along with it. And he remembers also that every rational animal is his kinsman, and that to care for all men is according to man's nature; and a man should hold on to the opinion not of all but of those only who confessedly live according to nature. But as to those who live not so, he always bears in mind what kind of men they are both at home and from home, both by night and by day, and what they are, and with what men they live an impure life. Accordingly, he does not value at all the praise which comes from such men, since they are not even satisfied with themselves.

Labor not unwillingly, nor without regard to the common interest, nor without due consideration, nor with distraction; nor let studied ornament set off thy thoughts, and be not either a man of many words, or busy about too many things. And further, let the deity which is in thee be the guardian of a living being, manly and of ripe age, and engaged in matter political, and a Roman, and a ruler, who has taken his post like a man waiting for the signal which summons him from life, and ready to go, having need neither of oath nor of any man's testimony. Be cheerful also, and seek not external help nor the tranquillity which others give. A man then must stand erect, not be kept erect by others.

If thou findest in human life anything better than justice, truth, temperance, fortitude, and, in a word, anything better than thy own mind's self-satisfaction in the things which it enables thee to do according to right reason, and in the condition that is assigned to thee without thy own choice; if, I say, thou seest anything better than this, turn to it with all thy soul, and enjoy that which thou hast found to be the best. But if nothing appears to be better than the deity which is planted in thee, which has subjected to itself all thy appetites, and carefully examines all the impressions, and as Socrates said, has detached itself from the persuasions of sense, and has submitted itself to the gods, and cares for mankind; if thou findest everything else smaller and of less value than this, give place to nothing else, for if thou dost once diverge and incline to it, thou wilt no longer without distraction be able to give the preference to that good thing which is thy proper possession and thy own; for it is not right that anything of any other kind, such as praise from the many, or power, or enjoyment of pleasure, should come into competition with that which is rationally and politically [or, practically]

good. All these things, even though they may seem to adapt themselves [to the better things] in a small degree, obtain the superiority all at once, and carry us away. But do thou, I say, simply and freely choose the better, and hold to it. — But that which is useful is the better. — Well, then, if it is only useful to thee as a rational being, keep to it; but if it is only useful to thee as an animal, say so, and maintain thy judgment without arrogance; only take care that thou makest the inquiry by a sure method.

Never value anything as profitable to thyself which shall compel thee to break thy promise, to lose thy self-respect, to hate any man, to suspect, to curse, to act the hypocrite, to desire anything which needs walls and curtains: for he who has preferred to everything else his own intelligence and dæmon and the worship of its excellence, acts no tragic part, does not groan, will not need either solitude or much company; and, what is chief of all, he will live without either pursuing or flying from [death]; but whether for a longer or a shorter time he shall have the soul inclosed in the body, he cares not at all; for even if he must depart immediately, he will go as readily as if he were going to do anything else which can be done with decency and order; taking care of this only all through life, that his thoughts turn not away from anything which belongs to an intelligent animal and a member of a civil community.

In the mind of one who is chastened and purified thou wilt find no corrupt matter, nor impurity, nor any sore skinned over. Nor is his life incomplete when fate overtakes him, as one may say of an actor who leaves the stage before ending and finishing the play. Besides, there is in him nothing servile, nor affected, nor too closely bound [to other things], nor yet detached [from other things], nothing worthy of blame, nothing which seeks a hiding-place.

Reverence the faculty which produces opinion. On this faculty it entirely depends whether there shall exist in thy ruling part any opinion inconsistent with nature and the constitution of the rational animal. And this faculty promises freedom from hasty judgment, and friendship towards men, and obedience to the gods.

Throwing away, then, all things, hold to these only which are few; and besides bear in mind that every man lives only this present time, which is an indivisible point, and that all the rest of his life is either past or it is uncertain. Short then is the time which every man lives, and small the nook of the earth where he lives; and short too the longest posthumous fame, and even this only continued by a succession of poor human beings, who will very soon die, and who know not even themselves, much less him who died long ago.

To the aids which have been mentioned let this one still be added: — Make for thyself a definition or description of the thing which is presented to thee, so as to see distinctly what kind of a thing it is in its substance, in its nudity, in its complete entirety, and tell thyself its proper name, and the names of the things of which it has been compounded, and into which it will be resolved. For nothing is so productive of elevation of mind as to be able to examine methodically and truly every object which is presented to thee in life, and always to look at things so as to see at the same time what kind of universe this is, and what kind of use everything performs in it, and what value everything has with reference to the whole, and what with reference to man, who is a citizen of the highest city, of which all other cities are like families; what each thing is, and of what it is composed, and how long it is the nature of this thing to endure which now makes an impression on me, and what virtue I have need of with respect to it, such as gentleness, manliness, truth, fidelity, simplicity, contentment, and the rest. Wherefore, on every occasion a man should say: This comes from God; and this is according to the apportionment and spinning of the thread of destiny, and such-like coincidence and chance; and this is from one of the same stock and a kinsman and partner, one who knows not however what is according to his nature. But I know; for this reason I behave towards him according to the natural law of fellowship with benevolence and justice. At the same time however in things indifferent I attempt to ascertain the value of each.

If thou workest at that which is before thee, following right reason seriously, vigorously, calmly, without allowing anything else to distract thee, but keeping thy divine part pure, as if thou shouldst be bound to give it back immediately; if thou holdest to this, expecting nothing, fearing nothing, but satisfied with thy present activity according to nature, and with heroic truth in every word and sound which thou utterest, thou wilt live happy. And there is no man who is able to prevent this.

As physicians have always their instruments and knives ready for cases which suddenly require their skill, so do thou have principles ready for the understanding of things divine and human, and doing everything, even the smallest, with a recollection of the bond which unites the divine and human to one another. For neither wilt thou do anything well which pertains to man without at the same time having a reference to things divine; nor the contrary.

No longer wander at hazard; for neither wilt thou read thy own memoirs, nor the acts of the ancient Romans and Hellenes,[1] and the selections from books which thou wast reserving for thy old age. Hasten then to the end which thou hast before thee, and, throwing away idle hopes, come to thy own aid, if thou carest at all for thyself, while it is in thy power.

They know not how many things are signified by the words stealing, sowing, buying, keeping quiet, seeing what ought to be done; for this is not effected by the eyes, but by another kind of vision.

Body, soul, intelligence: to the body belong sensations, to the soul appetites, to the intelligence principles. To receive the impressions of forms by means of appearances belongs even to animals; to be pulled by the strings of desire belongs both to wild beasts and to men who have made themselves into women, and to a Phalaris and a Nero:[2] and to have the intelligence that guides to the things which appear suitable belongs also to those who do not believe in the gods, and who betray their country, and do their impure deeds when they have shut the doors. If then everything else is common to all that I have mentioned, there remains that which is peculiar to the good man, to be pleased and content with what happens, and with the thread which is spun for him; and not to defile the divinity which is planted in his breast, nor disturb it by a crowd of images, but to preserve it tranquil, following it obediently as a god, neither saying anything contrary to the truth, nor doing anything contrary to justice. And if all men refuse to believe that he lives a simple, modest, and contented life, he is neither angry with any of them, nor does he deviate from the way which leads to the end of life, to which a man ought to come pure, tranquil, ready to depart, and without any compulsion perfectly reconciled to his lot.

[1] The Greeks.
[2] Tyrants in Sicily and Rome respectively.

Lucian · c. 120–c. 180

Though it seems to have been established that Lucian was born in Samosata, an ancient city on the bank of the Euphrates in Syria, the dates of his birth and death can only be approximated. His life span covered approximately sixty years, from about 120 to 180 A.D. Like most young men, Lucian ventured upon various careers before he found his particular interest and capacity; he tried sculpture, the law, and then the life of a professional rhetorician, lecturing in many cities in different lands as well as preparing lectures — an early ghost-writer — for others. Eventually he settled down in Athens where he lived some twenty years, a writer of satire. Before his death, Lucian took a government appointment in Egypt where he is believed to have died.

Lucian's best known works are the *Dialogues of the Gods, Dialogues of the Dead, A True Story*, and the *Life of Peregrinus*. His work is characterized by a keen wit and sprightly manner, is conspicuously satirical; in *A True Story* he turns to caricature by ridiculing current travelers' tales of wonders said to have been found in out-of-the-way places. In style, Lucian is clear, simple, often colloquial. He laughs at the foibles and insincerity of man and society and, even, of the gods. His delight is to prick the bubble of pretension. Particularly did he enjoy deflating philosophers and their philosophies. His lack of concern for conventional attitudes towards the gods and the contemporary great earned for him in some quarters the name of Lucian the Blasphemer. Lucian's literary manner places him with Aristophanes and Horace among the early ranks of the world's great satirists — a roll which also includes such later writers as Ben Jonson, Swift, Addison, and Sheridan in English literature and Rabelais and Voltaire in French.

SUGGESTED REFERENCE: F. G. Allinson, *Lucian, Satirist and Artist* (2nd ed., 1963).

Selections from *Lucian*

Except for the *Frogs* of Aristophanes and some of the broader satire of Horace (*The Bore*), we have so far met little that represented the humorous writing in the classical literature of Greece and Rome. Lucian fills this gap. His humor contains the elements of both satire and parody. In the selections which follow, Lucian pays his disrespectful respects first to the lesser gods and later to the various philosophies of the time. He is at his best when laughing at the superstitions and hypocrisies of people. One notes, too, that by the second century after Christ it is safer than formerly to laugh at deities once held in great respect — the old pagan faith is departing.

This, and the following selections from Lucian, are from *The Works of Lucian*, translated by H. W. and F. G. Fowler. Used by permission of The Clarendon Press, Oxford.

Dialogues of the Dead

X

CHARON, HERMES, *Various Shades*

Ch. I'll tell you how things stand. Our craft, as you see, is small, and leaky, and three-parts rotten; a single lurch, and she will capsize without more ado. And here are all you passengers, each with his luggage. If you come on board like that, I am afraid you may have cause to repent it; especially those who have not learnt to swim.

Her. Then how are we to make a trip of it?

Ch. I'll tell you. They must leave all this nonsense behind them on shore, and come aboard in their skins. As it is, there will be no room to spare. And in future, Hermes, mind you admit no one till he has cleared himself of encumbrances, as I say. Stand by the gangway, and keep an eye on them, and make them strip before you let them pass.

Her. Very good. Well, Number One, who are you?

Men. Menippus. Here are my wallet and staff; overboard with them. I had the sense not to bring my cloak.

Her. Pass on, Menippus; you're a good fellow; you shall have the seat of honor, up by the pilot, where you can see everyone. — Here is a handsome person; who is he?

Char. Charmoleos of Megara; the irresistible whose kiss was worth a thousand pounds.

Her. That beauty must come off — lips, kisses, and all; the flowing locks, the blushing cheeks, the skin entire. That's right. Now we're in better trim; — you may pass on. — And who is the stunning gentleman in the purple and the diadem?

Lam. I am Lampichus, tyrant of Gela.

Her. And what is all this splendor doing here, Lampichus?

Lam. How! would you have a tyrant come hither stripped?

Her. A tyrant! That would be too much to expect. But with a *shade* we must insist. Off with these things.

Lam. There, then: away goes my wealth.

Her. Pomp must go too, and pride; we shall be overfreighted else.

Lam. At least let me keep my diadem and robes.

Her. No, no; off they come!

Lam. Well? That is all, as you see for yourself.

Her. There is something more yet: cruelty, folly, insolence, hatred.

Lam. There, then: I am bare.

Her. Pass on. — And who may you be, my bulky friend?

Dam. Damasias the athlete.

Her. To be sure; many is the time I have seen you in the gymnasium.

Dam. You have. Well, I have peeled; let me pass.

Her. Peeled! my dear sir, what, with all this fleshy encumbrance? Come, off with it; we should go to the bottom if you put one foot aboard. And those crowns, those victories, remove them.

Dam. There; no mistake about it this time; I am as light as any shade among them.

Her. That's more the kind of thing. On with you. — Crato, you can take off that wealth and luxury and effeminacy; and we can't have that funeral pomp here, nor those ancestral glories either; down with your rank and reputation, and any votes of thanks or inscriptions you have about you; and you need not tell us what size your tomb was; remarks of that kind come heavy.

Cra. Well, if I must, I must; there's no help for it.

Her. Hullo! in full armor! What does this mean? and why this trophy?

A General. I am a great conqueror; a valiant warrior; my country's pride.

Her. The trophy may stop behind; we are at peace; there is no demand for arms. — Whom have we here? Whose is this knitted brow, this flowing beard? 'Tis some reverend sage, if outside goes for anything; he mutters; he is wrapped in meditation.

Men. That's a philosopher, Hermes; and an impudent quack into the bargain. Have him out of that cloak; you will find something to amuse you underneath it.

Her. Off with your clothes first; and then we will see to the rest. My goodness, what a bundle: quackery, ignorance, quarrelsomeness, vainglory; idle questionings, prickly arguments, intricate conceptions; humbug and gammon and wishy-washy hair-splittings without end; and hullo! why, here's avarice, and self-indulgence, and impudence! luxury, effeminacy and peevishness! — Yes, I see them all; you need not try to hide them. Away with falsehood and swagger and superciliousness; why, the three-decker is not built that would hold you with all this luggage.

A Philosopher. I resign them all, since such is your bidding.

Men. Have his beard off too, Hermes; only look what a ponderous bush of a thing! There's a good five pounds' weight there.

Her. Yes; the beard must go.

Phil. And who shall shave me?

Her. Menippus here shall take it off with the carpenter's ax; the gangway will serve for a block.

Men. Oh, can't I have a saw, Hermes? It would be much better fun.

Her. The ax must serve. — Shrewdly chopped! — why, you look more like a man and less like a goat already.

Men. A little off the eyebrows?

Her. Why, certainly; he has trained them up all over his forehead, for reasons best known to himself. — Worm! what, sniveling? afraid of death? Oh, get on board with you.

Men. He has still got the biggest thumper of all under his arm.

Her. What's that?

Men. Flattery; many is the good turn that has done him.

Phil. Oh, all right, Menippus; suppose you leave your independence behind you, and your plain-speaking, and your indifference, and your high spirit, and your jests! — No one else here has a jest about him.

Her. Don't you, Menippus! you stick to them; useful commodities, these, on shipboard; light and handy. — You rhetorician there, with your verbosities and your barbarisms, your antitheses and balances and periods, off with the whole pack of them.

Rhet. Away they go.

Her. All's ready. Loose the cable, and pull in the gangway; haul up the anchor; spread all sail; and, pilot, look to your helm. Good luck to our voyage! — What are you all whining about, you fools? You philosopher, late of the beard, — you're as bad as any of them.

Phil. Ah, Hermes: I had thought that the soul was immortal.

Men. He lies: that is not the cause of his distress.

Her. What is it, then?

Men. He knows that he will never have a good dinner again; never sneak about at night with his cloak over his head, going the round of the brothels; never spend his mornings in fooling boys out of their money, under the pretext of teaching them wisdom.

Phil. And pray are *you* content to be dead?

Men. It may be presumed so, as I sought death of my own accord. — By the way, I surely heard a noise, as if people were shouting on the earth?

Her. You did; and from more than one quarter. — There are people running in a body to the Townhall, exulting over the death of Lampichus; the women have got hold of his wife; his infant children fare no better, — the boys are giving them a handsome pelting. Then again you hear the applause that greets the orator Diophantus, as he pronounces the funeral oration of our friend Crato. Ah yes, and that's Damasias's mother, with her women, striking up a dirge. No one has a tear for you, Menippus; your remains are left in peace. Privileged person!

Men. Wait a bit: before long you will hear the mournful howl of dogs, and the beating of crows' wings, as they gather to perform my funeral rites.

Her. I like your spirit. — However, here we are in port. Away with you all to the judgment-seat; it is straight ahead. The ferryman and I must go back for a fresh load.

Men. Good voyage to you, Hermes. — Let us be getting on; what are you all waiting for? We have got to face the judge, sooner or later; and by all accounts his sentences are no joke; wheels, rocks, vultures are mentioned. Every detail of our lives will now come to light!

Dialogues of the Gods

XX. THE JUDGMENT OF PARIS

ZEUS	ATHENE
HERMES	APHRODITE
HERA	PARIS

Zeus. Hermes, take this apple, and go with it to Phrygia; on the Gargaran peak of Ida you will find Priam's son, the herdsman. Give him this message: "Paris, because you are handsome, and wise in the things of love, Zeus commands you to judge between the Goddesses, and say which is the most beautiful. And the prize shall be this apple." — Now, you three, there is no time to be lost: away with you to your judge. I will have nothing to do with the matter: I love you all exactly alike, and I only wish you could all three win. If I were to give the prize to one of you, the other two would hate me, of course. In these circumstances, I am ill qualified to be your judge. But this young Phrygian to whom you are going is of the royal blood — a relation of Ganymede's, — and at the same time a simple countryman; so that we need have no hesitation in trusting his eyes.

Aph. As far as I am concerned, Zeus, Momus [1] himself might be our judge; *I* should not be afraid to show myself. What fault could he find with *me?* But the others must agree too.

Hera. Oh, we are under no alarm, thank you, — though your admirer Ares should be appointed. But Paris will do; whoever Paris is.

Zeus. And my little Athene; have we her approval? Nay, never blush, nor hide your face. Well, well, maidens will be coy; 'tis a delicate subject. But there, she nods consent. Now, off with you; and mind, the beaten ones must not be cross with the judge; I will not have the poor lad harmed. The prize of beauty can be but one.

Herm. Now for Phrygia. I will show the way; keep close behind me, ladies, and don't be nervous. I know Paris well: he is a charming young man; a great gallant, and an admirable judge of beauty. Depend on it, he will make a good award.

Aph. I am glad to hear that; I ask for nothing better than a just judge. — Has he a wife, Hermes, or is he a bachelor?

Herm. Not exactly a bachelor.

Aph. What do you mean?

Herm. I believe there is wife, as it were; a good enough sort of girl — a native of those parts — but sadly countrified! I fancy he does not care very much about her. — Why do you ask?

Aph. I just wanted to know.

Ath. Now, Hermes, that is not fair. No whispering with Aphrodite.

Herm. It was nothing, Athene; nothing about you. She only asked me whether Paris was a bachelor.

Ath. What business is that of hers?

Herm. None that I know of. She meant nothing by the question; she just wanted to know.

Ath. Well, and is he?

Herm. Why, no.

Ath. And does he care for military glory? has he ambition? or is he a *mere* neatherd?

Herm. I couldn't say for certain. But he is a young man, so it is to be presumed that distinction on the field of battle is among his desires.

[1] God of ridicule and adverse criticism.

Aph. There, you see; *I* don't complain; I say nothing when you whisper with *her.* Aphrodite is not so particular as some people.

Herm. Athene asked me almost exactly the same as you did; so don't be cross. It will do you no harm, my answering a plain question. — Meanwhile, we have left the stars far behind us, and are almost over Phrygia. There is Ida: I can make out the peak of Gargarum quite plainly; and if I am not mistaken, there is Paris himself.

Hera. Where is he? I don't see him.

Herm. Look over there to the left, Hera: not on the top, but down the side, by that cave where you see the herd.

Hera. But I *don't* see the herd.

Herm. What, don't you see them coming out from between the rocks, — where I am pointing, look — and the man running down from the crag, and keeping them together with his staff?

Hera. I see him now; if he it is.

Herm. Oh, that is Paris. But we are getting near; it is time to alight and walk. He might be frightened, if we were to descend upon him so suddenly.

Hera. Yes; very well. And now that we are on the earth, you might go on ahead, Aphrodite, and show us the way. You know the country, of course, having been here so often to see Anchises; or so I have heard.

Aph. Your sneers are thrown away on me, Hera.

Herm. Come; I'll lead the way myself. I spent some time on Ida, while Zeus was courting Ganymede. Many is the time that I have been sent here to keep watch over the boy; and when at last the eagle came, I flew by his side, and helped him with his lovely burden. This is the very rock, if I remember; yes, Ganymede was piping to his sheep, when down swooped the eagle behind him, and tenderly, oh, so tenderly, caught him up in those talons, and with the turban in his beak bore him off, the frightened boy straining his neck the while to see his captor. I picked up his pipes — he had dropped them in his fright — and — ah! here is our umpire, close at hand. Let us accost him. — Good-morrow, herdsman!

Par. Good-morrow, youngster. And who may you be, who come thus far afield? And these dames? They are over comely, to be wandering on the mountain-side.

Herm. "These dames," good Paris, are Hera, Athene, and Aphrodite; and I am Hermes, with a message from Zeus. Why so pale and tremulous? Compose yourself; there is nothing the matter. Zeus appoints you the judge of their beauty. "Because you are handsome, and wise in the things of love" (so runs the message), "I leave the decision to you; and for the prize, — read the inscription on the apple."

Par. Let me see what it is about. *For the Fair,* it says. But, my lord Hermes, how shall a mortal and a rustic like myself be judge of such unparalleled beauty? This is no sight for a herdsman's eyes; let the fine city folk decide on such matters. As for me, I can tell you which of two goats is the fairer beast; or I can judge betwixt heifer and heifer; — 'tis my trade. But here, where all are beautiful alike, I know not how a man may leave looking at one, to look upon another. Where my eyes fall, there they fasten, — for there is beauty: I move them, and what do I find? more loveliness! I am fixed again, yet distracted by neighboring charms. I bathe in beauty: I am enthralled: ah, why am I not *all* eyes like Argus? Methinks it were a fair award, to give the apple to all three. Then again: one is the wife and sister of Zeus; the others are his daughters. Take it where you will, 'tis a hard matter to judge.

Herm. So it is, Paris. At the same time — Zeus's orders. There is no way out of it.

Par. Well, please point out to them, Hermes, that the losers must not be angry with me; the fault will be in my eyes only.

Herm. That is quite understood. And now to work.

Par. I must do what I can; there is no help for it. But first let me ask, — am I just to look at them as they are, or must I go into the matter thoroughly?

Herm. That is for you to decide, in virtue of your office. You have only to give your orders; it is as you think best.

Par. As I think best? Then I will be thorough.

Herm. Get ready, ladies. Now, Mr. Umpire. — I will look the other way.

Hera. I approve your decision, Paris. I will be the first to submit myself to your inspection. You shall see that I have more to boast of than white arms and large eyes: nought of me but is beautiful.

Par. Aphrodite, will you also prepare?

Ath. Oh, Paris, — make her take off that girdle, first; there is magic in it; she will bewitch you. For that matter, she has no right to come thus tricked out and painted, — just like a courtesan! She ought to show herself unadorned.

Par. They are right about the girdle, madam; it must go.

Aph. Oh, very well, Athene: then take off that helmet, and show your head bare, instead of trying to intimidate the judge with that waving plume. I suppose you are afraid the color of your eyes may be noticed, without their formidable surroundings.

Ath. Oh, here is my helmet.

Aph. And here is my girdle.

Hera. Now then.

Par. God of wonders! What loveliness is here! Oh, rapture! How exquisite these maiden charms! How dazzling the majesty of Heaven's true queen! And oh, how sweet, how enthralling is Aphrodite's smile! 'Tis too much, too much of happiness. — But perhaps it would be well for me to view each in detail; for as yet I doubt, and know not where to look; my eyes are drawn all ways at once.

Aph. Yes, that will be best.

Par. Withdraw then, you and Athene; and let Hera remain.

Hera. So be it; and when you have finished your scrutiny, you have next to consider, how you would like the present which I offer you. Paris, give me the prize of beauty, and you shall be lord of all Asia.

Par. I will take no presents. Withdraw. I shall judge as I think right. Approach, Athene.

Ath. Behold. And, Paris, if you will say that I am the fairest, I will make you a great warrior and conqueror, and you shall always win, in every one of your battles.

Par. But I have nothing to do with fighting, Athene. As you see, there is peace throughout all Lydia and Phrygia, and my father's dominion is uncontested. But never mind: I am not going to take your present, but you shall have fair play. You can robe again and put on your helmet; I have seen. And now for Aphrodite.

Aph. Here I am; take your time, and examine carefully; let nothing escape your vigilance. And I have something else to say to you, handsome Paris. Yes, you handsome boy, I have long had an eye on you; I think you must be the handsomest young fellow in all Phrygia. But it is such a pity that you don't leave these rocks and crags, and live in a town: you will lose all your beauty in this desert. What have you to do with mountains? What satisfaction can your beauty give to a lot of cows? You ought to have been married long ago; not to any of these dowdy women hereabouts, but to some Greek girl; an Argive, perhaps, or a Corinthian, or a Spartan; Helen, now, is a Spartan, and such a pretty girl — quite as pretty as I am — and so susceptible! Why, if she once caught sight of *you*, she would give up everything, I am sure, to go with you, and a most devoted wife she would be. But you have heard of Helen, of course?

Par. No, ma'am; but I should like to hear all about her now.

Aph. Well, she is the daughter of Leda, the beautiful woman, you know, whom Zeus visited in the disguise of a swan.

Par. And what is she like?

Aph. She is fair, as might be expected from the swan, soft as down (she was hatched from an egg, you know), and such a lithe, graceful figure; and only think, she is so much admired, that there was a war because Theseus ran away with her; and she was a mere child then. And when she grew up, the very first men in Greece were suitors for her hand, and she was given to Menelaus, who is descended from Pelops. — Now, if you like, she shall be your wife.

Par. What, when she is married already?

Aph. Tut, child, you are a simpleton: *I* understand these things.

Par. I should like to understand them too.

Aph. You will set out for Greece on a tour of inspection: and when you get to Sparta, Helen will see you; and for the rest — her falling in love, and going back with you — that will be my affair.

Par. But that is what I cannot believe, — that she will forsake her husband to cross the seas with a stranger, a barbarian.

Aph. Trust me for that. I have two beautiful children, Love and Desire. They shall be your guides. Love will assail her in all his might, and compel her to love you: Desire will encompass you about, and make you desirable and lovely as himself; and I will be there to help. I can get the Graces to come too, and between us we shall prevail.

Par. How this will end, I know not. All I do know is, that I am in love with Helen already. I see her before me — I sail for Greece — I am in Sparta — I am on my homeward journey, with her at my side! Ah, why is none of it true?

Aph. Wait. Do not fall in love yet. You have first to secure my interest with the bride, by your award. The union must be graced with my victorious presence: your marriage-feast shall be my feast of victory. Love, beauty, wedlock; all these you may purchase at the price of yonder apple.

Par. But perhaps after the award you will forget all about *me?*

Aph. Shall I swear?

Par. No; but promise once more.

Aph. I promise that you shall have Helen to wife; that she shall follow you, and make Troy her home; and I will be present with you, and help you in all.

Par. And bring Love, and Desire, and the Graces?

Aph. Assuredly; and Passion and Hymen as well.

Par. Take the apple: it is yours.

Sale of Creeds

Zeus, Hermes, *Several Dealers, Creeds*

Zeus. Now get those benches straight there, and make the place fit to be seen. Bring up the lots, one of you, and put them in line. Give them a rub up first, though; we must have them looking their best, to attract bidders. Hermes, you can declare the sale-room open, and a welcome to all comers. — *For Sale! A varied assortment of Live Creeds. Tenets of every description. — Cash on delivery; or credit allowed on suitable security.*

Hermes. Here they come, swarming in. No time to lose; we must not keep them waiting.

Zeus. Well, let us begin.

Her. What are we to put up first?

Zeus. The Ionic fellow, with the long hair. He seems a showy piece of goods.

Her. Step up, Pythagoreanism, and show yourself.

Zeus. Go ahead.

Her. Now here is a creed of the first water. Who bids for this handsome article? What gentleman says Superhumanity? Harmony of the Universe! Transmigration of souls! Who bids?

First Dealer. He looks all right. And what can he do?

Her. Magic, music, arithmetic, geometry, astronomy, jugglery. Prophecy in all its branches.

First D. Can I ask him some questions?

Her. Ask away, and welcome.

First D. Where do you come from?

Py. Samos.

First D. Where did you get your schooling?

Py. From the sophists in Egypt.

First D. If I buy you, what will you teach me?

Py. Nothing. I will remind you.

First D. Remind me?

Py. But first I shall have to cleanse your soul of its filth.

First D. Well, suppose the cleansing process complete. How is the reminding done?

Py. We shall begin with a long course of silent contemplation. Not a word to be spoken for five years.

First D. You would have been just the creed for Crœsus's son! But *I* have a tongue in my head; I have no ambition to be a statue. And after the five years' silence?

Py. You will study music and geometry.

First D. A charming recipe! The way to be wise: learn the guitar.

Py. Next you will learn to count.

First D. I can do that already.

Py. Let me hear you.

First D. One, two, three, four, —

Py. There you are, you see. *Four* (as you call it) is *ten.* Four the perfect triangle. Four the oath of our school.

First D. Now by Four, most potent Four! — higher and holier mysteries than these I never heard.

Py. Then you will learn of Earth, Air, Fire and Water; their action, their movement, their shapes.

First D. Have Fire and Air and Water *shapes?*

Py. Clearly. That cannot move which lacks shape and form. You will also find that God is a number; an intelligence; a harmony.

First D. You surprise me.

Py. More than this, you have to learn that you yourself are not the person you appear to be.

First D. What, I am some one else, not the I who am speaking to you?

Py. You are that you now: but you have formerly inhabited another body, and borne another name. And in course of time you will change once more.

First D. Why then I shall be immortal, and take one shape after another? But enough of this. And now what is your diet?

Py. Of living things I eat none. All else I eat, except beans.

First D. And why no beans? Do you dislike them?

Py. No. But they are sacred things. Their nature is a mystery. Consider them first in their generative aspect; take a green one and peel it, and you will see what I mean. Again, boil one and expose it to moonlight for a proper number of nights, and you have — blood. What is more, the Athenians use beans to vote with.

First D. Admirable! A very feast of reason. Now just strip, and let me see what you are like. Bless me, here is a creed with a golden thigh! He is no mortal, he is a God. I must have him at any price. What do you start him at?

Her. Forty pounds.

First D. He is mine for forty pounds.

Zeus. Take the gentleman's name and address.

Her. He must come from Italy, I should think; Croton or Tarentum, or one of the Greek towns in those parts. But he is not the only buyer. Some three hundred of them have clubbed together.

Zeus. They are welcome to him. Now up with the next.

Her. What about yonder grubby Pontian?

Zeus. Yes, he will do.

Her. You there with the wallet and cloak; come along, walk round the room. Lot No. 2. A most sturdy and valiant creed, free-born. What offers?

Second D. Hullo, Mr. Auctioneer, are you going to sell a free man?

Her. That was the idea.

Second D. Take care, he may have you up for kidnapping. This might be matter for the Areopagus![1]

Her. Oh, he would as soon be sold as not. He feels just as free as ever.

Second D. But what is one to do with such a dirty fellow? He is a pitiable sight. One might put him to dig perhaps, or to carry water.

Her. That he can do and more. Set him to guard your house, and you will find him better than any watch-dog. — They call him Dog for short.

Second D. Where does he come from? and what is his method?

Her. He can best tell you that himself.

Second D. I don't like his looks. He will probably snarl if I go near him, or take a snap at me, for all I know. See how he lifts his stick, and scowls; an awkward-looking customer!

Her. Don't be afraid. He is quite tame.

Second D. Tell me, good fellow, where do you come from?

Dio. Everywhere.

Second D. What does that mean?

Dio. It means that I am a citizen of the world.

Second D. And your model?

Dio. Heracles.

Second D. Then why no lion's-skin? You have the orthodox club.

Dio. My cloak is my lion's-skin. Like Heracles, I live in a state of warfare, and my enemy is Pleasure; but unlike him I am a volunteer. My purpose is to purify humanity.

Second D. A noble purpose. Now what do I understand to be your strong subject? What is your profession?

Dio. The liberation of humanity, and the treatment of the passions. In short, I am the prophet of Truth and Candor.

Second D. Well, prophet; and if I buy you, how shall you handle my case?

Dio. I shall commence operations by stripping off your superfluities, putting you into fustian, and leaving you closeted with Necessity. Then I shall give you a course of hard labor. You will sleep on the ground, drink water, and fill your belly as best you can. Have you money? Take my advice and throw it into the sea. With wife and children and country you will not concern yourself; there will be no more of that nonsense. You will exchange your present home for a sepulchre, a ruin, or a tub. What with lupines and close-written tomes, your knapsack will never be empty; and you will vote yourself happier than any king. Nor will

[1] The seat of the highest tribunal in Athens.

you esteem it any inconvenience, if a flogging or a turn of the rack should fall to your lot.

Second D. How! Am I a tortoise, a lobster, that I should be flogged and feel it not?

Dio. You will take your cue from Hippolytus; *mutatis mutandis.*

Second D. How so?

Dio. "The heart may burn, the tongue knows nought thereof." Above all, be bold, be impudent; distribute your abuse impartially to king and commoner. They will admire your spirit. You will talk the Cynic jargon with the true Cynic snarl, scowling as you walk, and walking as one should who scowls; an epitome of brutality. Away with modesty, good-nature, and forbearance. Wipe the blush from your cheek for ever. Your hunting-ground will be the crowded city. You will live alone in its midst, holding communion with none, admitting neither friend nor guest; for such would undermine your power. Scruple not to perform the deeds of darkness in broad daylight: select your love-adventures with a view to the public entertainment: and finally, when the fancy takes you, swallow a raw cuttle-fish, and die. Such are the delights of Cynicism.

Second D. Oh, vile creed! Monstrous creed! Avaunt!

Dio. But look you, it is all so easy; it is within every man's reach. No education is necessary, no nonsensical argumentation. I offer you a short cut to Glory. You may be the merest clown — cobbler, fish-monger, carpenter, money-changer; yet there is nothing to prevent your becoming famous. Given brass and boldness, you have only to learn to wag your tongue with dexterity.

Second D. All this is of no use to me. But I might make a sailor or a gardener of you at a pinch; that is, if you are to be had cheap. Three-pence is the most I can give.

Her. He is yours, to have and to hold. And good riddance to the brawling foul-mouthed bully. He is a slanderer by wholesale.

Zeus. Now for the Cyrenaic,[1] the crowned and purple-robed.

Her. Attend please, gentlemen all. A most valuable article, this, and calls for a long purse. Look at him. A sweet thing in creeds. A creed for a king. Has any gentleman a use for the Lap of Luxury? Who bids?

Third D. Come and tell me what you know. If you are a practical creed, I will have you.

Her. Please not to worry him with questions, sir.

[1] A school of philosophy which set up pleasure as the goal of living; founded by Aristippus, who was born at Cyrene.

He is drunk, and cannot answer; his tongue plays him tricks, as you see.

Third D. And who in his senses would buy such an abandoned reprobate? How he smells of scent! And how he slips and staggers about! Well, you must speak for him, Hermes. What can he do? What is his line?

Her. Well, for any gentleman who is not strait-laced, who loves a pretty girl, a bottle, and a jolly companion, he is the very thing. He is also a past master in gastronomy, and a connoisseur in volup-tuousness generally. He was educated at Athens, and has served royalty in Sicily, where he had a very good character. Here are his principles in a nutshell: Think the worst of things: make the most of things: get all possible pleasure out of things.

Third D. You must look for wealthier purchasers. My purse is not equal to such a festive creed.

Her. Zeus, this lot seems likely to remain on our hands.

Zeus. Put it aside, and up with another. Stay, take the pair from Abdera and Ephesus; the creeds of Smiles and Tears. They shall make one lot.

Her. Come forward, you two. Lot No. 4. A superlative pair. The smartest brace of creeds on our catalogue.

Fourth D. Zeus! What a difference is here! One of them does nothing but laugh, and the other might be at a funeral; he is all tears.[1] — You there! what is the joke?

Democr. It is. There is no taking it seriously. All is vanity. Mere interchange of atoms in an in-finite void.

Fourth D. *Your* vanity is infinite, if you like. Stop that laughing, you rascal. — And you, my poor fellow, what are you crying for? I must see what I can make of you.

Heracl. I am thinking, friend, upon human af-fairs; and well may I weep and lament, for the doom of all is sealed. Hence my compassion and my sorrow. For the present, I think not of it; but the future! — the future is all bitterness. Con-flagration and destruction of the world. I weep to think that nothing abides. All things are whirled together in confusion. Pleasure and pain, knowl-edge and ignorance, great and small; up and down they go, the playthings of Time.

Fourth D. And what is Time?

Heracl. A child; and plays at draughts and blind-man's-buff.

Fourth D. And men?

Heracl. Are mortal Gods.

Fourth D. And Gods?

Heracl. Immortal men.

[1] The laughing philosopher is Democritus, the weep-ing philosopher, Heraclitus.

Fourth D. So! Conundrums, fellow? Nuts to crack? You are a very oracle for obscurity.

Heracl. Your affairs do not interest me.

Fourth D. No one will be fool enough to bid for you at that rate.

Heracl. Young and old, him that bids and him that bids not, a murrain seize you all!

Fourth D. A sad case. He will be melancholy mad before long. Neither of these is the creed for my money.

Her. No one bids.

Zeus. Next lot.

Her. The Athenian there? Old Chatterbox?

Zeus. By all means.

Her. Come forward! — A good sensible creed this. Who buys Holiness?

Fifth D. Let me see. What are you good for?

Soc. I teach the art of love.

Fifth D. A likely bargain for me! I want a tutor for my young Adonis.

Soc. And could he have a better? The love I teach is of the spirit, not of the flesh. Under my roof, be sure, a boy will come to no harm.

Fifth D. Very unconvincing that. A teacher of the art of love, and never meddle with anything but the spirit? Never use the opportunities your office gives you?

Soc. Now by Dog and Plane-tree, it is as I say!

Fifth D. Heracles! What strange Gods are these?

Soc. Why, the Dog is a God, I suppose? Is not Anubis[1] made much of in Egypt? Is there not a Dog-star in Heaven, and a Cerberus in the lower world?

Fifth D. Quite so. My mistake. Now what is your manner of life?

Soc. I live in a city of my own building; I make my own laws, and have a novel constitution of my own.

Fifth D. I should like to hear some of your statutes.

Soc. You shall hear the greatest of them all. No woman shall be restricted to one husband. Every man who likes is her husband.

Fifth D. What! Then the laws of adultery are clean swept away?

Soc. I should think they were! and a world of hair-splitting with them.

Fifth D. And what do you do with the handsome boys?

Soc. Their kisses are the reward of merit, of noble and spirited actions.

Fifth D. Unparalleled generosity! — And now, what are the main features of your philosophy?

Soc. Ideas and types of things. All things that

[1] Son of Osiris, a guide of ghosts (Egyptian).

you see, the earth and all that is upon it, the sea, the sky — each has its counterpart in the invisible world.

Fifth D. And where are they?

Soc. Nowhere. Were they anywhere, they were not what they are.

Fifth D. I see no signs of these "types" of yours.

Soc. Of course not; because you are spiritually blind. I see the counterparts of all things; an invisible you, an invisible me; everything is in duplicate.

Fifth D. Come, such a shrewd and lynx-eye creed is worth a bid. Let me see. What do you want for him?

Her. Five hundred.

Fifth D. Done with you. Only I must settle the bill another day.

Her. What name?

Fifth D. Dion; of Syracuse.

Her. Take him, and much good may he do you. Now I want Epicureanism. Who offers for Epicureanism? He is a disciple of the laughing creed and the drunken creed, whom we were offering just now. But he has one extra accomplishment — impiety. For the rest, a dainty, lickerish creed.

Sixth D. What price?

Her. Eight pounds.

Sixth D. Here you are. By the way, you might let me know what he likes to eat.

Her. Anything sweet. Anything with honey in it. Dried figs are his favorite dish.

Sixth D. That is all right. We will get in a supply of Carian fig-cakes.

Zeus. Call the next lot. Stoicism; the creed of the sorrowful countenance, the close-cropped creed.

Her. Ah yes, several customers, I fancy, are on the look-out for him. Virtue incarnate! The very quintessence of creeds! Who is for universal monopoly?

Seventh D. How are we to understand that?

Her. Why, here is monopoly of wisdom, monopoly of beauty, monopoly of courage, monopoly of justice. Sole king, sole orator, sole legislator, sole millionaire.

Seventh D. And I suppose sole cook, sole tanner, sole carpenter, and all that?

Her. Presumably.

Seventh D. Regard me as your purchaser, good fellow, and tell me all about yourself. I dare say you think it rather hard to be sold for a slave?

Chrys. Not at all. These things are beyond our control. And what is beyond our control is indifferent.

Seventh D. I don't see how you make that out.

Chrys. What! Have you yet to learn that of

indifferentia some are *præposita* and others *rejecta*?

Seventh D. Still I don't quite see.

Chrys. No; how should you? You are not familiar with our terms. You lack the *comprehensio visi.* The earnest student of logic knows this and more than this. He understands the nature of subject, predicate, and contingent, and the distinctions between them.

Seventh D. Now in Wisdom's name, tell me, pray, what is a predicate? what is a contingent? There is a ring about those words that takes my fancy.

Chrys. With all my heart. A man lame in one foot knocks that foot accidentally against a stone, and gets a cut. Now the man is *subject* to lameness; which is the *predicate.* And the cut is a *contingency.*

Seventh D. Oh, subtle! What else can you tell me?

Chrys. I have verbal involutions, for the better hampering, crippling, and muzzling of my antagonists. This is performed by the use of the far-famed syllogism.

Seventh D. Syllogism! I warrant him a tough customer.

Chrys. Take a case. You have a child?

Seventh D. Well, and what if I have?

Chrys. A crocodile catches him as he wanders along the bank of a river, and promises to restore him to you, if you will first guess correctly whether he means to restore him or not. Which are you going to say?

Seventh D. A difficult question. I don't know which way I should get him back soonest. In Heaven's name, answer for me, and save the child before he is eaten up.

Chrys. Ha, ha. I will teach you far other things than that.

Seventh D. For instance?

Chrys. There is the "Reaper." There is the "Rightful Owner." Better still, there is the "Electra" and the "Man in the Hood."

Seventh D. Who was he? and who was Electra?

Chrys. She was the Electra, the daughter of Agamemnon, to whom the same thing was known and unknown at the same time. She knew that Orestes was her brother: yet when he stood before her she did not know (until he revealed himself) that her brother was Orestes. As to the Man in the Hood, he will surprise you considerably. Answer me now: do you know your own father?

Seventh D. Yes.

Chrys. Well now, if I present to you a man in a hood, shall you know him? eh?

Seventh D. Of course not.

Chrys. Well, but the Man in the Hood is your

father. You don't know the Man in the Hood. Therefore you don't know your own father.

Seventh D. Why, no. But if I take his hood off, I shall get at the facts. Now tell me, what is the end of your philosophy? What happens when you reach the goal of virtue?

Chrys. In regard to things external, health, wealth, and the like, I am then all that Nature intended me to be. But there is much previous toil to be undergone. You will first sharpen your eyes on minute manuscripts, amass commentaries, and get your bellyful of outlandish terms. Last but not least, it is forbidden to be wise without repeated doses of hellebore.

Seventh D. All this is exalted and magnanimous to a degree. But what am I to think when I find that you are also the creed of cent-per-cent, the creed of the usurer? Has *he* swallowed his hellebore? is *he* made perfect in virtue?

Chrys. Assuredly. On none but the wise man does usury sit well. Consider. His is the art of putting two and two together, and usury is the art of putting interest together. The two are evidently connected, and one as much as the other is the prerogative of the true believer; who, not content, like common men, with simple interest, will also take interest *upon* interest. For interest, as you are probably aware, is of two kinds. There is simple interest, and there is its offspring, compound interest. Hear Syllogism on the subject. "If I take simple interest, I shall also take compound. But I *shall* take simple interest: therefore I shall take compound."

Seventh D. And the same applies to the fees you take from your youthful pupils? None but the true believer sells virtue for a fee?

Chrys. Quite right. I take the fee in my pupil's interest, not because I want it. The world is made up of diffusion and accumulation. I accordingly practise my pupil in the former, and myself in the latter.

Seventh D. But it ought to be the other way. The pupil ought to accumulate, and you, "sole millionaire," ought to diffuse.

Chrys. Ha! you jest with me? Beware of the shaft of insoluble syllogism.

Seventh D. What harm can that do?

Chrys. It cripples; it ties the tongue, and turns the brain. Nay, I have but to will it, and you are stone this instant.

Seventh D. Stone! You are no Perseus, friend?

Chrys. See here. A stone is a body?

Seventh D. Yes.

Chrys. Well, and an animal is a body?

Seventh D. Yes.

Chrys. And you are an animal?

Seventh D. I suppose I am.

Chrys. Therefore you are a body. Therefore a stone.

Seventh D. Mercy, in Heaven's name! Unstone me, and let me be flesh as heretofore.

Chrys. That is soon done. Back with you into flesh! Thus: Is every body animate?

Seventh D. No.

Chrys. Is a stone animate?

Seventh D. No.

Chrys. Now, you are a body?

Seventh D. Yes.

Chrys. And an animate body?

Seventh D. Yes.

Chrys. Then being animate, you cannot be a stone.

Seventh D. Ah! thank you, thank you. I was beginning to feel my limbs growing numb and solidifying like Niobe's. Oh, I must have you, What's to pay?

Her. Fifty pounds.

Seventh D. Here it is.

Her. Are you sole purchaser?

Seventh D. Not I. All these gentlemen here are going shares.

Her. A fine strapping lot of fellows, and will do the "Reaper" credit.

Zeus. Don't waste time. Next lot, — the Peripatetic!

Her. Now, my beauty, now Affluence! Gentlemen, if you want Wisdom for your money, here is a creed that comprises all knowledge.

Eighth D. What is he like?

Her. He is temperate, good-natured, easy to get on with; and his strong point is, that he is twins.

Eighth D. How can that be?

Her. Why, he is one creed outside, and another inside. So remember, if you buy him, one of him is called Esoteric, and the other Exoteric.

Eighth D. And what has he to say for himself?

Her. He has to say that there are three kinds of good: spiritual, corporeal, circumstantial.

Eighth D. *There's* something a man can understand. How much is he?

Her. Eighty pounds.

Eighth D. Eighty pounds is a long price.

Her. Not at all, my dear sir, not at all. You see, there is some money with him, to all appearance. Snap him up before it is too late. Why, from him you will find out in no time how long a gnat lives, to how many fathoms' depth the sunlight penetrates the sea, and what an oyster's soul is like.

Eighth D. Heracles! Nothing escapes him.

Her. Ah, these are trifles. You should hear some of his more abstruse speculations, concerning generation and birth and the development of the embryo; and his distinction between man, the laughing creature, and the ass, which is neither a laughing nor a carpentering nor a shipping creature.

Eighth D. Such knowledge is as useful as it is ornamental. Eighty pounds be it, then.

Her. He is yours.

Zeus. What have we left?

Her. There is Scepticism. Come along, Pyrrhias, and be put up. Quick's the work. The attendance is dwindling; there will be small competition. Well, who buys Lot 9?

Ninth D. I. Tell me first, though, what do you know?

Sc. Nothing.

Ninth D. But how's that?

Sc. There does not appear to me to *be* anything.

Ninth D. Are not *we* something?

Sc. How do I know that?

Ninth D. And you yourself?

Sc. Of that I am still more doubtful.

Ninth D. Well, you *are* in a fix! And what have you got those scales for?

Sc. I use them to weigh arguments in, and get them evenly balanced. They must be absolutely equal — not a feather-weight to choose between them; then, and not till then, can I make uncertain which is right.

Ninth D. What else can you turn your hand to?

Sc. Anything; except catching a runaway.

Ninth D. And why not that?

Sc. Because, friend, everything eludes my grasp.

Ninth D. I believe you. A slow, lumpish fellow you seem to be. And what is the end of your knowledge?

Sc. Ignorance. Deafness. Blindness.

Ninth D. What! sight and hearing both gone?

Sc. And with them judgment and perception, and all, in short, that distinguishes man from a worm.

Ninth D. You are worth money! — What shall we say for him?

Her. Four pounds.

Ninth D. Here it is. Well, fellow; so you are mine?

Sc. I doubt it.

Ninth D. Nay, doubt it not! You are bought and paid for.

Sc. It is a difficult case.... I reserve my decision.

Ninth D. Now, come along with me, like a good slave.

Sc. But how am I to know whether what you say is true?

Ninth D. Ask the auctioneer. Ask my money. Ask the spectators.

Sc. Spectators? But can we be sure there are any?

Ninth D. Oh, I'll send you to the treadmill. That will convince you with a vengeance that I am your master.

Sc. Reserve your decision.

Ninth D. Too late. It is given.

Her. Stop that wrangling and go with your purchaser. Gentlemen, we hope to see you here again to-morrow, when we shall be offering some lots suitable for plain man, artisans, and shopkeepers.

Michael Eyquem de Montaigne · 1533-1592

Between the death of Lucian about 180 A.D. and the birth of Montaigne in 1533 lie thirteen centuries of literary history which cannot be ignored. This span of time included the centuries sometimes rather inappropriately called the Dark Ages and the centuries of medievalism. In general it may be argued that, in comparison with the heyday of classical literature in Greece and Rome or of the eighteenth-century writing in England and the continent, these were dim days for world literature, but the stream of literature by no means ran out; at most it may be thought of as passing underground, reappearing at times during these centuries in such works as the *Beowulf*, the poetry of Chrétien de Troyes, the *Nibelungenlied*, the *Roman de la Rose*, Dante's *Divine Comedy*, Petrarch's *Sonnets to Laura*, Boccaccio's *Decameron*, Chaucer's *Canterbury Tales*, and the popular ballads. No period which brought forth such works as these may fairly be thought of as completely "dark" or barren.

When Montaigne was writing his essays a new spirit — that of the Renaissance — was beginning to dominate Europe. With the capitulation of the Eastern Roman Empire at Constantinople in 1453 to the Turks, scholarship and culture — such as it then was — returned to the West. The impact of this change brought to life a new learning and a fresh vitality. The last of the fifteenth century and the first of the sixteenth saw a rapid development of the arts and sciences. Religious reformation followed; the Church lost much of its former glory and political power. Inventions — paper, printing, gunpowder — developed new resources. The grip of the feudal system weakened. Nationalities and languages became more fixed. Geographical horizons widened. And with this revival of learning came a "humanism" and a new interest in the thought and literature of the classics, a fact testified to by every page of the essays of Montaigne.

Rarely can the creation of a new literary type be credited to one man. The short story, the novel, the drama — these and other forms are, as we know them today, the result of a gradual evolution. Yet to Montaigne (and to Francis Bacon) belongs most of the credit of establishing the familiar essay in the form we know it in the twentieth century. True, even Montaigne built upon the work of his predecessors, for the collecting of proverbs, quotations, adages, and anecdotes — largely from the classics — was a polite literary occupation of the time, and the bringing together of such miscellanea bearing upon a single subject constituted what was known as the *leçon morale*. To these collections of "sayings" Montaigne added personal comment, intimate admissions to the reader, and, further, conceiving of himself as somehow speaking for mankind in general, evolved what is now known as the personal or familiar essay. In 1580 he published two volumes of *Essais;* a third volume appeared eight years later. Montaigne took his title from the French word meaning "attempts," doubtless with the purpose of indicating the exploratory, tentative nature of his writing as compared with more philosophical work. Thus toward the close of the sixteenth century was created the literary form which, to mention only three names from English literature, brought fame later on to Lamb and Hazlitt and Stevenson.

Michael Eyquem de Montaigne was born on the family estate near Bordeaux, France, in 1533. His father, holding somewhat unconventional ideas of education, turned the child over to others to rear in simple surroundings and employed servants who spoke no French to teach him Latin. Later he attended the *collège* of Guyenne in Bordeaux; he began the study of law at thirteen years of age. In 1571, Montaigne withdrew to his country estate to devote his time to reading, study, and meditation. Nine years afterwards the first edition of the *Essais* was issued. Later in life Montaigne was elected mayor of Bordeaux for two terms, traveled extensively in Europe, finally attaining a reputation which brought him invitations to share in the life at court, invitations which he refused, perhaps because of a distaste he held for such a life, perhaps because of a need constantly to watch his health.

SUGGESTED REFERENCES: André Gide, *The Living Thoughts of Montaigne* (1939); D. M. Frame, *Montaigne's Discovery of Man: The Humanization of a Humanist* (1955).

Essays of *Montaigne*

Montaigne's essays present nothing so formal as a philosophical system. "It is myself I paint," he declared in his note to the reader. His papers consist of personal observations revealing his skepticism and giving rise to solemn reflections and garrulous admissions of likes and dislikes. He writes on almost all 5 phases of life, and his work gives the impression of a tolerant, almost classical serenity. Balzac is quoted as having said that Montaigne "carried human reason as far and as high as it could go."

The notes as well as the text which follows are from Montaigne's *Essays* as translated by Charles Cotton 10 and revised by W. Carew Hazlitt (G. Bell and Sons).

The Author to the Reader

Reader thou hast here an honest book; it doth at the outset forewarn thee that, in contriving the same, I have proposed to myself no other than a domestic and private end. I have had no consideration at all either to thy service or to my glory. My powers are not capable of any such design. I have dedicated it to the particular commodity of my kinsfolk and friends, so that, having lost me (which they must do shortly), they may therein recover some traits of my conditions and humors, and by that means preserve more whole, and more life-like, the knowledge they had of me. Had my intention been to seek the world's favor, I should surely have adorned myself with borrowed beauties: I desire therein to be viewed as I appear in mine own genuine, simple, and ordinary manner, without study and artifice; for it is myself I paint. My defects are therein to be read to the life, and my imperfections and my natural form, so far as public reverence hath permitted me. If I had lived among those nations which (they say) yet dwell under the sweet liberty of nature's primitive laws, I assure thee I would most willingly have painted myself quite fully and quite naked. Thus, reader, myself am the matter of my book; there's no reason thou shouldst employ thy leisure about so frivolous and vain a subject. Therefore, farewell.

That We Taste Nothing Pure

The imbecility of our condition is such that things cannot, in their natural simplicity and purity, fall into our use; the elements that we enjoy are changed, and so 'tis with metals; and gold must be debased with some other matter to fit it for our service. Neither has virtue, so simple as that which Aristo, Pyrrho, and also the Stoics, made the End of life; nor the Cyrenaic and Aristippic pleasure, been without mixture useful to it. Of the pleasure and goods that we enjoy, there is not one exempt from some mixture of ill and inconvenience:

"Medio de fonte leporum,
Surgit amari aliquid, quod in ipsis floribus angat." [1]

Our extremest pleasure has some air of groaning and complaining in it; would you not say that it is dying of pain? Nay, when we frame the image of it in its full excellence, we stuff it with sickly and painful epithets and qualities, languor, softness, feebleness, faintness, *morbidezza*: a great testimony of their consanguinity and consubstantiality. The most profound joy has more of severity than gaiety in it. The highest and fullest contentment offers more of the grave than of the merry; "Ipsa felicitas, se nisi temperat, premit." [2] Pleasure chews and grinds us; according to the old Greek verse,[3] which says that the gods sell us

all the goods they give us; that is to say, that they give us nothing pure and perfect, and that we do not purchase but at the price of some evil.

Labor and pleasure, very unlike in nature, associate, nevertheless, by I know not what natural conjunction. Socrates says,[1] that some god tried to mix in one mass and to confound pain and pleasure, but not being able to do it, he bethought him at least, to couple them by the tail. Metrodorus [2] said, that in sorrow there is some mixture of pleasure. I know not whether or no he intended anything else by that saying; but for my part, I am of opinion that there is design, consent, and complacency in giving a man's self up to melancholy. I say, that besides ambition, which may also have a stroke in the business, there is some shadow of delight and delicacy which smiles upon and flatters us even in the very lap of melancholy. Are there not some constitutions that feed upon it?

"Est quædam flere voluptas:" [3]

and one Attalus in Seneca [4] says, that the memory of our lost friends is as grateful to us, as bitterness in wine, when too old, is to the palate —

"Minister vetuli, puer, Falerni
Inger' mi calices amariores" [5] —

and as apples that have a sweet tartness.

Nature discovers this confusion to us; painters hold that the same motions and screwings of the face that serve for weeping, serve for laughter too; and indeed, before the one or the other be finished, do but observe the painter's manner of handling, and you will be in doubt to which of the two the design tends; and the extreme of laughter does, at last bring tears. "Nullum sine auctoramento malum est." [6]

When I imagine man abounding with all the conveniences that are to be desired (let us put the case that all his members were always seized with a pleasure like that of generation, in its most excessive height) I feel him melting under the weight of his delight, and see him utterly unable to support so pure, so continual, and so universal a pleasure. Indeed, he is running away whilst he is there, and naturally makes haste to escape, as from a place where he cannot stand firm, and where he is afraid of sinking.

[1] In *Phædo*, ii. 1, 20.   [2] Seneca, *Ep.* 99.
[3] "'Tis a certain kind of pleasure to weep." — Ovid, *Trist.*, iv. 3, 27.
[4] *Ep.* 70.
[5] "Boy, when you pour out old Falernian wine, the bitterest put into my bowl." — Catullus, xxvii. 1.
[6] "No evil is without its compensation." — Seneca, *Ep.* 69.

[1] "In the very source of our pleasure, there is something that is bitter, and that vexes even the flowers." — Lucretius, iv. 1130.
[2] "Even felicity, unless it moderate itself, oppresses." — Seneca, *Ep.* 74.
[3] Epicharmus, in Xenophon, *Mem. of Socrates*, ii. 1, 20.

When I religiously confess myself to myself, I find that the best virtue I have has in it some tincture of vice; and I am afraid that Plato, in his purest virtue (I, who am as sincere and loyal a lover of virtue of that stamp, as any other whatever) if he had listened and laid his ear close to himself, and he did so no doubt, would have heard some jarring sound of human mixture, but faint and only perceptible to himself. Man is wholly and throughout but patch and motley. Even the laws of justice themselves cannot subsist without mixture of injustice; insomuch that Plato says,[1] they undertake to cut off the hydra's head, who pretend to clear the law of all inconveniences. "Omne magnum exemplum habet aliquid ex iniquo, quod contra singulos utilitate publica rependitur," [2] says Tacitus.

It is likewise true, that for the use of life and the service of public commerce, there may be some excesses in the purity and perspicacity of our minds; that penetrating light has in it too much of subtlety and curiosity: we must a little stupefy and blunt them to render them more obedient to example and practice, and a little veil and obscure them, the better to proportion them to this dark and earthy life. And therefore common and less speculative souls are found to be more proper for and more successful in the management of affairs; and the elevated and exquisite opinions of philosophy unfit for business. This sharp vivacity of soul, and the supple and restless volubility attending it, disturb our negotiations. We are to manage human enterprises more superficially and roughly, and leave a great part to fortune; it is not necessary to examine affairs with so much subtlety and so deep: a man loses himself in the consideration of so many contrary lustres, and so many various forms; "Volutantibus res inter se pugnantes, obtorpuerant . . . animi." [3]

'Tis what the ancients say of Simonides, that by reason his imagination suggested to him, upon the question King Hiero had put to him [4] (to answer which he had had many days to meditate in), several sharp and subtle considerations, whilst he doubted which was the most likely, he totally despaired of the truth.

He who dives into and in his inquisition comprehends all circumstances and consequences, hinders his election: a little engine well-handled is sufficient for executions, whether of less or greater weight. The best managers are those who can worst give account how they are so; while the greatest talkers, for the most part, do nothing to purpose: I know one of this sort of men, and a most excellent discourser upon all sorts of good husbandry, who has miserably let a hundred thousand livres yearly revenue slip through his hands; I know another who talks, who better advises than any man of his counsel, and there is not in the world a fairer show of soul and understanding than he has; nevertheless, when he comes to the test, his servants find him quite another thing; not to make any mention of his misfortunes.

Of Commerce with Books [1]

These two commerces are fortuitous, and depending upon others: the one is troublesome by its rarity, the other withers with age, so that they could never have been sufficient for the business of my life. That of books, which is the third, is much more certain, and much more our own. It yields all other advantages to the two first; but has the constancy and facility of its service for its own share. It goes side by side with me in my whole course, and everywhere is assisting me: it comforts me in my old age and solitude; it eases me of a troublesome weight of idleness, and delivers me at all hours from company that I dislike: it blunts the point of griefs, if they are not extreme, and have not got an entire possession of my soul. To divert myself from a troublesome fancy, 'tis but to run to my books; they presently fix me to them and drive the other out of my thoughts; and do not mutiny at seeing that I have only recourse to them for want of other more real, natural, and lively commodities; they always receive me with the same kindness. He may well go afoot, they say, who leads his horse in his hand; and our James, king of Naples and Sicily, who, handsome, young and healthful, caused himself to be carried about on a barrow, extended upon a pitiful mattress in a poor robe of grey cloth, and a cap of the same, but attended withal by a royal train of litters, led horses of all sorts, gentlemen and officers, did yet herein represent a tender and unsteady authority: "The sick man is not to be pitied, who has his cure in his sleeve." In the experience and practice of this maxim, which is a very true one, consists all the benefit I reap from books; and yet

[1] *Republic*, iv. 5.

[2] "Every great example has in it some mixture of injustice, which recompenses the wrong done to particular men by the public utility." — Tacitus, *Annals*, xiv. 44.

[3] "Whilst they considered of things so indifferent in themselves, they were astonished, and knew not what to do." — Livy, xxxii. 20.

[4] What God was. — Cicero, *De Nat. Deor.*, i. 22.

[1] This is the third part of Montaigne's *Of Three Commerces*, Book III, Chapter III.

I make as little use of them, almost, as those who know them not: I enjoy them as a miser doth his money, in knowing that I may enjoy them when I please: my mind is satisfied with this right of possession. I never travel without books, either in peace or war; and yet sometimes I pass over several days, and sometimes months, without looking on them: I will read by-and-by, say I to myself, or to-morrow, or when I please; and in the interim, time steals away without any inconvenience. For it is not to be imagined to what degree I please myself and rest content in this consideration, that I have them by me to divert myself with them when I am so disposed, and to call to mind what a refreshment they are to my life. 'Tis the best viaticum I have found out for this human journey, and I very much pity those men of understanding who are unprovided of it. I the rather accept of any other sort of diversion, how light soever, because this can never fail me.

When at home, I a little more frequent my library, whence I overlook at once all the concerns of my family. 'Tis situated at the entrance into my house, and I thence see under me my garden, court, and base-court, and almost all parts of the building. There I turn over now one book, and then another, on various subjects without method or design. One while I meditate, another I record and dictate, as I walk to and fro, such whimsies as these I present to you here. 'Tis in the third story of a tower, of which the ground room is my chapel, the second storey a chamber with a withdrawing-room and closet, where I often lie, to be more retired; and above is a great wardrobe. This formerly was the most useless part of the house. I there pass away both most of the days of my life and most of the hours of those days. In the night I am never there. There is by the side of it a cabinet handsome enough, with a fireplace very commodiously contrived, and plenty of light: and were I not more afraid of the trouble than the expense — the trouble that frights me from all business, I could very easily adjoin on either side, and on the same floor, a gallery of an hundred paces long, and twelve broad, having found walls already raised for some other design, to the requisite height. Every place of retirement requires a walk: my thoughts sleep if I sit still; my fancy does not go by itself, as when my legs move it: and all those who study without a book are in the same condition. The figure of my study is round, and there is no more open wall than what is taken up by my table and my chair, so that the remaining parts of the circle present me a view of all my books at once, ranged upon five rows of shelves round about me. It has three noble and free prospects, and is sixteen

paces in diameter. I am not so continually there in winter; for my house is built upon an eminence, as its name imports, and no part of it is so much exposed to the wind and weather as this, which pleases me the better, as being of more difficult access and a little remote, as well upon the account of exercise, as also being there more retired from the crowd. 'Tis there that I am in my kingdom, and there I endeavor to make myself an absolute monarch, and to sequester this one corner from all society, conjugal, filial, and civil; elsewhere I have but verbal authority only, and of a confused essence. That man, in my opinion, is very miserable, who has not at home where to be by himself, where to entertain himself alone, or to conceal himself from others. Ambition sufficiently plagues her proselytes, by keeping them always in show, like the statue of a public square: "Magna servitus est magna fortuna."[1] They cannot so much as be private in the water-closet.[2] I have thought nothing so severe in the austerity of life that our monks affect, as what I have observed in some of their communities; namely, by rule to have a perpetual society of place, and numerous persons present in every action whatever; and think it much more supportable to be always alone, than never to be so.

If any one shall tell me that it is to undervalue the muses, to make use of them only for sport and to pass away the time, I shall tell him, that he does not know, so well as I, the value of the sport, the pleasure, and the pastime; I can hardly forbear to add that all other end is ridiculous. I live from hand to mouth, and, with reverence be it spoken, I only live for myself; there all my designs terminate. I studied, when young, for ostentation; since, to make myself a little wiser; and now for my diversion, but never for any profit. A vain and prodigal humor I had after this sort of furniture, not only for the supplying my own need, but, moreover, for ornament and outward show, I have since quite cured myself of.

Books have many charming qualities to such as know how to choose them; but every good has its ill; 'tis a pleasure that is not pure and clean, no more than others: it has its inconveniences, and great ones too. The soul indeed is exercised therein; but the body, the care of which I must withal never neglect, remains in the meantime without action, and grows heavy and sombre. I know no excess more prejudicial to me, nor more to be avoided in this my declining age.

These have been my three favorite and particular

[1] "A great fortune is a great slavery." — Seneca, *De Consol. ad Polyb.*, c. 26.

[2] "Ils n'ont pas seulement leur retraict pour retraicte."

occupations; I speak not of those I owe to the world by civil obligation.

Of the Inconvenience of Greatness

Since we cannot attain unto it, let us revenge ourselves by railing at it; and yet it is not absolutely railing against anything, to proclaim its defects, because they are in all things to be found, how beautiful or how much to be coveted soever. Greatness has, in general, this manifest advantage, that it can lower itself when it pleases, and has, very near, the choice of both the one and the other condition; for a man does not fall from all heights; there are several from which one may descend without falling down. It does, indeed, appear to me that we value it at too high a rate, and also overvalue the resolution of those whom we have either seen, or heard, have contemned it, or displaced themselves of their own accord: its essence is not so evidently commodious that a man may not, without a miracle, refuse it. I find it a very hard thing to undergo misfortunes, but to be content with a moderate measure of fortune, and to avoid greatness I think a very easy matter. 'Tis, methinks, a virtue to which I, who am no conjuror, could without any great endeavor arrive. What, then, is to be expected from them that would yet put into consideration the glory attending this refusal, wherein there may lurk worse ambition than even in the desire itself, and fruition of greatness? Forasmuch as ambition never comports itself better, according to itself, than when it proceeds by obscure and unfrequented ways.

I incite my courage to patience, but I rein it as much as I can towards desire. I have as much to wish for as another, and allow my wishes as much liberty and indiscretion; but, yet it never befel me to wish for either empire or royalty, or the eminency of those high and commanding fortunes: I do not aim that way; I love myself too well. When I think to grow greater 'tis but very moderately, and by a compelled and timorous advancement, such as is proper for me in resolution, in prudence, in health, in beauty, and even in riches too; but this supreme reputation, this mighty authority, oppress my imagination; and, quite contrary to that other,[1] I should, peradventure, rather choose to be the second or third in Perigord, than the first at Paris: at least, without lying, rather the third at Paris than the first. I would neither dispute, a miserable unknown, with a nobleman's porter, nor make crowds open in adoration as I

[1] Julius Cæsar.

pass. I am trained up to a moderate condition, as well by my choice as fortune; and have made it appear, in the whole conduct of my life and enterprises, that I have rather avoided than otherwise the climbing above the degree of fortune wherein God has placed me by my birth: all natural constitution is equally just and easy. My soul is so sneaking that I measure not good fortune by the height, but by the facility.

But if my heart be not great enough, 'tis open enough to make amends, at any one's request, freely to lay open its weakness. Should any one put me upon comparing the life of L. Thorius Balbus, a brave man, handsome, learned, healthful, understanding, and abounding in all sorts of conveniences and pleasures, leading a quiet life, and all his own, his mind well prepared against death, superstition, pain, and other incumbrances of human necessity, dying, at last, in battle, with his sword in his hand, for the defence of his country, on the one part; and on the other part, the life of M. Regulus, so great and high as is known to every one, and his end admirable; the one without name and without dignity, the other exemplary, and glorious to wonder, I should doubtless say as Cicero did, could I speak as well as he.[1] But if I was to compare them with my own,[2] I should then also say that the first is as much according to my capacity, and from desire, which I conform to my capacity, as the second is far beyond it; that I could not approach the last but with veneration, the other I could readily attain by use.

But let us return to our temporal greatness, from which we are digressed. I disrelish all dominion, whether active or passive. Otanes,[3] one of the seven who had right to pretend to the kingdom of Persia, did, as I should willingly have done, which was, that he gave up to his concurrents his right of being promoted to it, either by election or by lot, provided that he and his might live in the empire out of all authority and subjection, those of the ancient laws excepted, and might enjoy all liberty that was not prejudicial to these, being as impatient of commanding as of being commanded.

The most painful and difficult employment in the world, in my opinion, is worthily to discharge the office of a king. I excuse more of their mistakes than men commonly do, in consideration of the intolerable weight of their function, which astounds me. 'Tis hard to keep measure in so

[1] Cicero, *De Finibus*, ii. 20, gives the preference to Regulus, and proclaims him the happier man.
[2] "Touch it in my own phrase," says Cotton.
[3] Herodotus, iii. 83.

immeasurable a power; yet so it is, that it is, even to those who are not of the best nature, a singular incitement to virtue, to be seated in a place where you cannot do the least good that shall not be put upon record; and where the least benefit redounds to so many men, and where your talent of administration, like that of preachers, principally addresses itself to the people, no very exact judge, easy to deceive, and easily content. There are few things wherein we can give a sincere judgment, by reason that there are few wherein we have not, in some sort, a private interest. Superiority and inferiority, dominion and subjection, are bound to a natural envy and contest, and must of necessity perpetually intrench upon one another. I believe neither the one nor the other touching the rights of the other party; let reason therefore, which is inflexible and without passion, determine when we can avail ourselves of it. 'Tis not above a month ago that I read over two Scotch authors contending upon this subject, of whom he who stands for the people makes kings to be in a worse condition than a carter; and he who writes for monarchy places them some degrees above God Almighty in power and sovereignty.

Now, the inconveniency of greatness that I have made choice of to consider in this place, upon some occasion that has lately put it into my head, is this: there is not, peradventure, anything more pleasant in the commerce of men than the trials that we make against one another, out of emulation of honor and worth, whether in the exercises of the body or in those of the mind, wherein sovereign greatness can have no true part. And, in earnest, I have often thought that by force of respect itself men use princes disdainfully and injuriously in that particular; for the thing I was infinitely offended at in my childhood, that they who exercised with me forbore to do their best because they found me unworthy of their utmost endeavor, is what we see happen to them daily, every one finding himself unworthy to contend with them. If we discover that they have the least desire to get the better of us, there is no one who will not make it his business to give it them, and who will not rather betray his own glory than offend theirs; and will, therein, employ so much force only as is necessary to save their honor. What share have they, then, in the engagement, where every one is on their side? Methinks I see those Paladins of ancient times presenting themselves to jousts and battle with enchanted arms and bodies. Brisson,[1] running against Alexander,

purposely missed his blow, and made a fault in his career; Alexander chid him for it, but he ought to have had him whipped. Upon this consideration Carneades said,[1] that "the sons of princes learned nothing right but to ride; by reason that, in all their other exercises, every one bends and yields to them; but a horse, that is neither a flatterer nor a courtier, throws the son of a king with no more ceremony than he would throw that of a porter."

Homer was fain to consent that Venus, so sweet and delicate a goddess as she was, should be wounded at the battle of Troy, thereby to ascribe courage and boldness to her; qualities that cannot possibly be in those who are exempt from danger. The gods are made to be angry, to fear, to run away, to be jealous, to grieve, to be transported with passions, to honor them with the virtues that, amongst us, are built upon these imperfections. Who does not participate in the hazard and difficulty can claim no interest in the honor and pleasure that are the consequents of hazardous actions. 'Tis pity a man should be so potent that all things must give way to him; fortune therein sets you too remote from society, and places you in too great a solitude. This easiness and mean facility of making all things bow under you is an enemy to all sorts of pleasure: 'tis to slide, not to go; 'tis to sleep, and not to live. Conceive man accompanied with omnipotence: you overwhelm him; he must beg disturbance and opposition as an alms: his being and his good are in indigence.[2]

Their good qualities are dead and lost; for they can only be perceived by comparison, and we put them out of this: they have little knowledge of true praise, having their ears deafened with so continual and uniform an approbation. Have they to do with the stupidest of all their subjects? they have no means to take any advantage of him; if he but say: "'Tis because he is my king," he thinks he has said enough to express, that he, therefore, suffered himself to be overcome. This quality stifles and consumes the other true and essential qualities: they are sunk in the royalty; and leave them nothing to recommend themselves with but actions that directly concern and serve the function of their place; 'tis so much to be a king, that this alone remains to them. The outer glare that environs him conceals and shrouds him from us; our sight is there repelled and dissipated, being filled and stopped by this prevailing light. The

[1] Plutarch, *On Satisfaction or Tranquillity of the Mind.* But in his essay, *How a Man may Distinguish a Flatterer from a Friend,* he calls him Chriso.

[1] Plutarch, *How a Man,* &c., *ubi supra.*

[2] In the Bordeaux copy, Montaigne here adds, "Evil to man is, in its turn, good; and good, evil. Neither is pain always to be shunned, nor pleasure always to be pursued."

senate awarded the prize of eloquence to Tiberius; he refused it, esteeming that though it had been just, he could derive no advantage from a judgment so partial, and that was so little free to judge.

As we give them all advantages of honor, so do we soothe and authorize all their vices and defects, not only by approbation, but by imitation also. Every one of Alexander's followers carried his head on one side, as he did;[1] and the flatterers of Dionysius ran against one another in his presence, and stumbled at and overturned whatever was under foot, to show they were as purblind as he.[2] Hernia itself has also served to recommend a man to favor; I have seen deafness affected; and because the master hated his wife, Plutarch[3] has seen his courtiers repudiate theirs, whom they loved: and, which is yet more, uncleanliness and all manner of dissolution have so been in fashion; as also disloyalty, blasphemy, cruelty, heresy, superstition, irreligion, effeminacy, and worse, if worse there be; and by an example yet more dangerous than that of

[1] Plutarch, *On the Difference*, &c., *ubi supra*.
[2] *Idem, ibid.*, who, however, only gives one instance, and in this he tells us that the man visited his wife privately.
[3] *Ubi supra.*

Mithridates'[1] flatterers who, as their master pretended to the honor of a good physician, came to him to have incisions and cauteries made in their limbs; for these others suffered the soul, a more delicate and noble part, to be cauterised.

But to end where I began: the Emperor Adrian, disputing with the philosopher Favorinus about the interpretation of some word, Favorinus soon yielded him the victory; for which his friends rebuking him; "You talk simply," said he, "would you not have him wiser than I, who commands thirty legions?"[2] Augustus wrote verses against Asinius Pollio, and "I," said Pollio, "say nothing, for it is not prudence to write in contest with him who has power to prescribe;"[3] and he had reason; for Dionysius, because he could not equal Philoxenus in poesy and Plato in discourse, condemned the one to the quarries, and sent the other to be sold for a slave into the island of Ægina.[4]

[1] *Idem, ibid.*
[2] Spartian, *Life of Adrian*, c. 15.
[3] Macrobus, *Saturn*, ii. 4.
[4] Plutarch, On Satisfaction of Mind, c. 10. Diogenes Laertius, however, in his *Life of Plato*, iii. 18, says that Plato's offence was speaking too freely to the tyrant.

Ben Jonson · 1573-1637

When Ben Jonson was born in Westminster, England, in 1573, Montaigne was a young man of forty in France. But the two had been born into different social worlds as well as different countries. Montaigne was reared in luxury, with special tutors, and every advantage; Jonson's family was comparatively poor. Jonson's father had died some weeks before Ben was born; his mother was soon to marry a bricklayer. The boy was educated through the generosity of an acquaintance at the local Westminster School.

It was a spirited England into which young Ben was born and in which he spent his boyhood. Sir Francis Drake was circumnavigating the globe; the Spanish Armada was decisively defeated; the Globe theatre was being built in a London to which young William Shakespeare had just come up from Stratford. The literary figures in the England of Jonson's youth were such men as Kyd and Lyly, Greene and Spenser; Sidney and Marlowe. The Puritans were attacking the art of poetry; Francis Bacon was writing his essays.

Whether or not Jonson actually attended Cambridge University for a period is a question open to dispute, but it is known that as a young man he served as a soldier in Flanders fighting against the Spanish. By 1598, however, when he was only twenty-five years old, he had made a name for himself as a playwright and actor in London.

At the height of his success, Jonson was the chief literary arbiter of the city. He was in favor at the court of James, his plays brought him wealth, his learning respect. But this Horatio Alger-like record is somewhat marred by two periods in prison, the first for killing a fellow-actor in a duel, the second because of unpopular ideas expressed in his writing. Jonson was a prolific and versatile author; he gained reputation as a writer of comedy, tragedy, masques, and lyrics, and upon his death in 1637, was buried in Westminster Abbey. Among his most important comedies are *Every Man in His Humour* (1598), *Every Man Out of His Humour* (1599), *Volpone* (1606), *The Alchemist* (1610), and *Bartholomew Fair* (1614). His two tragedies are *Sejanus* (1603) and *Catiline* (1611).

Although in his comedies Jonson's manner was often realistic, the tragedies and the lyrics reflect the dignified, classical temper. If Jonson's tragedies are less read today than the comedies it is probably because the former are overburdened with his learning. The lyrics here printed are only a few among many which survive because of their finish and grace, qualities which made many poets, among them Lovelace and Suckling, emulate Jonson's manner. The lines to Shakespeare are both a fine tribute to Jonson's rival in drama and a conclusive rejoinder to those who argue that someone other than Shakespeare wrote the Shakespearean plays.

SUGGESTED REFERENCES: J. B. Bamborough, *Ben Jonson* (1959); J. A. Barish, ed., *Ben Jonson: A Collection of Critical Essays* (1963).

Hymn to Diana

Queen and Huntress, chaste and fair,
  Now the sun is laid to sleep,
Seated in thy silver chair
  State in wonted manner keep:
    Hesperus entreats thy light,   5
    Goddess excellently bright.

Earth, let not thy envious shade
  Dare itself to interpose;
Cynthia's shining orb was made
  Heaven to clear when day did close: 10
    Bless us then with wishéd sight,
    Goddess excellently bright.

Lay thy bow of pearl apart
  And thy crystal-shining quiver;
Give unto the flying hart   15
  Space to breathe, how short soever:
    Thou that mak'st a day of night,
    Goddess excellently bright.

Song: to Celia

Come, my Celia, let us prove,
While we can, the sports of love.
Time will not be ours for ever;
He, at length, our good will sever;
Spend not then his gifts in vain.   5
Suns that set may rise again;
But if once we lose this light,
'Tis with us perpetual night.
Why should we defer our joys?
Fame and rumor are but toys.   10
Cannot we delude the eyes
Of a few poor household spies?

Or his easier ears beguile,
Thus removéd by our wile?
'Tis no sin love's fruits to steal;   15
But the sweet theft to reveal,
To be taken, to be seen,
These have crimes accounted been.

To Celia

Drink to me only with thine eyes,
  And I will pledge with mine;
Or leave a kiss but in the cup,
  And I'll not look for wine.
The thirst that from the soul doth rise   5
  Doth ask a drink divine;
But might I of Jove's nectar sup,
  I would not change for thine.

I sent thee late a rosy wreath,
  Not so much honoring thee   10
As giving it a hope, that there
  It could not withered be.
But thou thereon didst only breathe,
  And sent'st it back to me;
Since when it grows, and smells, I swear, 15
  Not of itself, but thee.

To the Memory of My Beloved Master, William Shakespeare

To draw no envy, Shakespeare, on thy name,
Am I thus ample to thy book and fame;
While I confess thy writings to be such
As neither man, nor muse, can praise too much.
'Tis true, and all men's suffrage. But these ways
Were not the paths I meant unto thy praise;   6

For silliest ignorance on these may light,
Which, when it sounds at best, but echoes right;
Or blind affection, which doth ne'er advance
The truth, but gropes, and urgeth all by chance; 10
Or crafty malice might pretend this praise,
And think to ruin, where it seemed to raise.
These are, as [1] some infamous bawd or whore
Should praise a matron.   What could hurt her
      more?
But thou art proof against them, and, indeed, 15
Above the ill fortune of them, or the need.
I therefore will begin.   Soul of the age!
The applause, delight, the wonder of our stage!
My Shakespeare, rise!   I will not lodge thee by
Chaucer, or Spenser, or bid Beaumont lie 20
A little farther off, to make thee a room:
Thou art a monument without a tomb,
And art alive still while thy book doth live
And we have wits to read and praise to give.
That I not mix thee so, my brain excuses, 25
I mean with great, but disproportioned Muses;
For if I thought my judgment were of years,
I should commit thee surely with thy peers,
And tell how far thou didst our Lyly outshine,
Or sporting Kyd, or Marlowe's mighty line. 30
And though thou hadst small Latin and less Greek,
From thence to honor thee, I would not seek
For names; but call forth thundering Æschylus,
Euripides, and Sophocles to us;
Pacuvius,[2] Accius,[2] him of Cordova [3] dead, 35
To life again, to hear thy buskin tread,
And shake a stage; or, when thy socks were on,
Leave thee alone for the comparison
Of all that insolent Greece or haughty Rome
Sent forth, or since did from their ashes come. 40
Triumph, my Britain, thou hast one to show
To whom all scenes of Europe homage owe.
He was not of an age, but for all time!
And all the Muses still were in their prime,
When, like Apollo, he came forth to warm 45
Our ears, or like a Mercury to charm!
Nature herself was proud of his designs,
And joyed to wear the dressing of his lines!
Which were so richly spun, and woven so fit,
As, since, she will vouchsafe no other wit. 50
The merry Greek, tart Aristophanes,
Neat Terence,[4] witty Plautus,[4] now not please;
But antiquated and deserted lie,
As they were not of Nature's family.
Yet must I not give Nature all; thy art, 55
My gentle Shakespeare, must enjoy a part.
For though the poet's matter nature be,
His art doth give the fashion; and, that he

Who casts to write a living line, must sweat
(Such as thine are) and strike the second heat 60
Upon the Muses' anvil; turn the same
(And himself with it) that he thinks to frame,
Or, for the laurel, he may gain a scorn;
For a good poet's made, as well as born.
And such wert thou!   Look how the father's face
Lives in his issue, even so the race 66
Of Shakespeare's mind and manners brightly
      shines
In his well turned, and true filed lines;
In each of which he seems to shake a lance,
As brandished at the eyes of ignorance. 70
Sweet Swan of Avon! what a sight it were
To see thee in our water yet appear,
And make those flights upon the banks of Thames,
That so did take Eliza,[1] and our James!
But stay, I see thee in the hemisphere 75
Advanced, and made a constellation there!
Shine forth, thou star of poets, and with rage
Or influence, chide or cheer the drooping stage,
Which, since thy flight from hence, hath mourned
      like night,
And despairs day, but for thy volume's light. 80

A Song

O do not wanton with those eyes,
   Lest I be sick with seeing;
Nor cast them down, but let them rise,
   Lest shame destroy their being.

O be not angry with those fires, 5
   For then their threats will kill me;
Nor look too kind on my desires,
   For then my hopes will spill me.

O do not steep them in thy tears,
   For so will sorrow slay me; 10
Nor spread them as distract with fears;
   Mine own enough betray me.

Her Triumph

See the chariot at hand here of Love,
   Wherein my lady rideth!
Each that draws is a swan or a dove,
   And well the car Love guideth.
As she goes all hearts do duty 5
      Unto her beauty,
And enamored do wish so they might
      But enjoy such a sight,

---

[1] As though.   [2] Roman tragic poets.
[3] Seneca was born in Spain.
[4] Roman writers of comedy.

[1] Queen Elizabeth.

That they still were to run by her side,
Through swords, through seas, whither she would
    ride.   10

Do but look on her eyes; they do light
    All that Love's world compriseth!
Do but look on her hair; it is bright
    As Love's star when it riseth!
Do but mark, her forehead's smoother   15
    Than words that soothe her;
And from her arched brows, such a grace
    Sheds itself through the face,
As alone there triumphs to the life

All the gain, all the good, of the elements'
    strife.   20

Have you seen but a bright lily grow
    Before rude hands have touched it?
Have you marked but the fall of the snow
    Before the soil hath smutched it?
Have you felt the wool of the beaver   25
    Or swan's down ever?
Or have smelt o' the bud o' the briar?
    Or the nard in the fire?
Or have tasted the bag of the bee?
O so white! O so soft! O so sweet is she!   30

John Milton · 1608-1674

Asked to name the half-dozen great figures in world literature, any reader reared in the American or English tradition will list Milton, along with Chaucer and Shakespeare, in close association with such masters as Homer and Virgil and Dante. Milton combined great scholarship, a significant philosophy, a vital interest in political affairs, and high poetic skill. His has been called "the organ voice of England" and he used it courageously to serve intellectual honesty and to preserve and foster individual liberty of thought and action as well as to justify the ways of God to man.

John Milton was born in Cheapside, London, December 9, 1608, a year in which both Ben Jonson and Shakespeare were popular dramatists for the London stage. Milton's father, a scrivener or sort of notary solicitor, had renounced the Catholic Church and adopted the reformed faith, an act which brought about a break with his family and cost him his inheritance. Whatever one's religious attitudes, one recognizes in this step the same sort of moral conviction which motivated the career of the son. Milton entered Christ's College, Cambridge, in 1625 and, taking a master's degree, remained there most of the time until 1632. There is record to indicate that, like some modern students, he rebelled at the routine of education. But, even so, he did not leave Christ's without having established for himself a reputation as a student of the classics and as a writer of promise. While there he gave up an earlier plan to enter the church and decided to become a poet.

The next five years, from 1632 to 1638, were the most formative period of Milton's life. His father had retired to Horton, in Buckinghamshire, and there Milton settled down to quiet study and dedicated himself to the cause of poetry. He read widely in the Greek and Latin classics, he studied mathematics and music. Here it was that he wrote *L'Allegro*, *Il Penseroso*, *Comus* (a masque), *Lycidas*, and many of his so-called minor poems.

Milton left Horton in 1638 for travel on the Continent but, after a year spent mostly in Italy, returned to England where he believed growing political disturbance demanded his residence. By 1642 Civil War broke out between Parliament and King and, a few years later, Charles had surrendered to the Scots, and was, in 1649, executed. Even before the open break between Puritans and Loyalists, Milton had allied himself firmly with the Puritan party by a series of pamphlets attacking Archbishop Laud and the abuses he found in the established church. The attention of the Puritans having been called to his work by pamphlets he had written in defense of the new régime, particularly one called *Tenure of Kings and Magistrates* justifying the execution of Charles, he was made Latin Secretary to the Council of State after the Puritans took over the government.

During the two decades between 1640 and the Restoration of Charles II in 1660, Milton's literary work was largely polemical. He wrote in defense of divorce; in what is undoubtedly his greatest piece of prose, the *Areopagitica*, he attacked a licensing act which provided a literary censorship; he defended the execution of Charles; and in his *Defense of the People of England* he justified Puritan acts and objectives. By 1652, so intensively had he given himself to his work, he went blind and was forced, for the rest of his life, to dictate to secretaries and to his daughters.

With his retirement from the Latin secretaryship in 1658, Milton entered another phase of his writing. Blind, wedded to a third wife in the hope that she would regulate his household and hold his daughters in check, Milton was able to turn to the particular project he had so long planned. Even as early as the Horton period Milton appears to have contemplated the writing of a long poem. For a while he had considered shaping the Arthurian material into an epic. To the same end he made plans to use various Biblical stories. "He who would not be frustrate of his hope to write well hereafter on laudable things ought himself to be a true poem," he wrote in explanation of his life-long intent. But it was not until 1667, nine years after his retirement, that *Paradise Lost* was published. *Paradise Regained* and *Samson Agonistes*, a tragedy in the Greek manner, followed four years later. On November 8, 1674, Milton died and was buried at St. Giles's Church in London.

A full study of the three rather distinct periods — the early poems written at Horton, the prose polemics in defense of Puritanism, the poetry of the last years which manifested his genius — demands separate and detailed presentation. Here one can only point out that Milton combined in his writing elements that were clearly classical with those that were distinctly Elizabethan, and these in turn with still others which were prompted by the spirit of the Reformation. His early style was influenced by Ovid and Virgil, by Spenser and Donne and Jonson. In his nature were brought together qualities which were notably practical, strongly intellectual, and Puritanically religious. But he was, except for some of the earlier verse, always serious, dignified, thoughtful. He wrote of high themes severely. His close reliance on unity of purpose, even the poetic genres he employed — ode, pastoral elegy, sonnet, tragedy, and epic — declare this classical temper. The very title of his most significant prose work, the *Areopagitica*, reflects a classical training and interest. And *Paradise Lost* weds Christian doctrine to a form predominantly classical. It would be strange indeed if, respecting Spenser as he did, and incorporating so much that was Elizabethan in his point of view, Milton should have kept his work wholly free from Romantic coloring and have rigorously excluded from all of his poetry certain emotional moments which an Æschylus might have presented in a somewhat more restrained manner. To Matthew Arnold the grand style in poetry arose "when a noble nature, poetically gifted, treats with simplicity or with severity a serious subject." Surely on this basis Milton was characteristically classical in temper.

SUGGESTED REFERENCES: J. H. Hanford, *A Milton Handbook* (5th ed., 1961); W. R. Parker, *Milton, A Biography* (1966).

The Poetry of *John Milton*

The selections which follow include from the Horton period *L'Allegro*, *Il Penseroso*, and *Lycidas*. The first two are companion-pieces presenting pictures of landscape and life as they appear, respectively, to a person in a gay and in a pensive mood — or perhaps to different people in these same moods. *Lycidas* is a pastoral elegy, influenced by Theocritus, commemorating the death of Edward King, a classmate at Cambridge. The years Milton devoted to the Commonwealth are represented here only by a sonnet or two. From the third period, that of Milton's poetic maturity, the first two books of *Paradise Lost* are printed in their entirety.

L'Allegro

Hence, loathèd Melancholy,
  Of Cerberus and blackest Midnight born,
In Stygian cave forlorn,
  'Mongst horrid shapes, and shrieks, and sights
    unholy,   5
Find out some uncouth [1] cell,
  Where brooding Darkness spreads his jealous
    wings,
And the night-raven sings;
  There under ebon [2] shades, and low-browed
    rocks,

[1] Unknown.   [2] Black.

As ragged as thy locks,
   In dark Cimmerian desert [1] ever dwell.   10
But come, thou Goddess fair and free,
In heaven ycleped [2] Euphrosyne,[3]
And by men, heart-easing Mirth,
Whom lovely Venus at a birth
With two sister Graces more   15
To ivy-crownèd Bacchus bore;
Or whether (as some sager sing)
The frolic Wind that breathes the spring,
Zephyr with Aurora playing,
As he met her once a-Maying,   20
There on beds of violets blue,
And fresh-blown roses washed in dew,
Filled her with thee, a daughter fair,
So buxom, blithe, and debonair.
   Haste thee, Nymph, and bring with thee   25
Jest and youthful Jollity,
Quips, and Cranks, and wanton Wiles,
Nods, and Becks, and wreathèd Smiles,
Such as hang on Hebe's [4] cheek,
And love to live in dimple sleek;   30
Sport that wrinkled Care derides,
And Laughter holding both his sides.
Come, and trip it as ye go,
On the light fantastic toe;
And in thy right hand lead with thee   35
The mountain Nymph, sweet Liberty;
And, if I give thee honor due,
Mirth, admit me of thy crew,
To live with her, and live with thee,
In unreproved [5] pleasures free;   40
To hear the lark begin his flight,
And singing startle the dull night,
From his watch-tower in the skies,
Till the dappled Dawn doth rise;
Then to come, in spite of sorrow,   45
And at my window bid good-morrow,
Through the sweet-briar or the vine,
Or the twisted eglantine;
While the cock with lively din
Scatters the rear of Darkness thin;   50
And to the stack, or the barn-door,
Stoutly struts his dames before:
Oft listening how the hounds and horn
Cheerly rouse the slumbering Morn,
From the side of some hoar [6] hill,   55
Through the high wood echoing shrill:

Sometime walking, not unseen,
By hedgerow elms, on hillocks green,
Right against the eastern gate,
Where the great Sun begins his state,   60
Robed in flames and amber light,
The clouds in thousand liveries dight; [1]
While the ploughman, near at hand,
Whistles o'er the furrowed land,
And the milkmaid singeth blithe,   65
And the mower whets his scythe,
And every shepherd tells his tale [2]
Under the hawthorn in the dale.
   Straight mine eye hath caught new pleasures,
Whilst the landscape round it measures: 70
Russet lawns, and fallows gray,
Where the nibbling flocks do stray;
Mountains on whose barren breast
The laboring clouds do often rest;
Meadows trim with daisies pied;   75
Shallow brooks, and rivers wide.
Towers and battlements it sees
Bosomed high in tufted trees,
Where perhaps some Beauty lies,
The Cynosure [3] of neighboring eyes.   80
Hard by, a cottage chimney smokes
From betwixt two aged oaks,
Where Corydon and Thyrsis [4] met
Are at their savory dinner set
Of herbs and other country messes,   85
Which the neat-handed Phillis dresses;
And then in haste her bower she leaves,
With Thestylis to bind the sheaves;
Or, if the earlier season lead,
To the tanned haycock in the mead.   90
   Sometimes with secure [5] delight
The upland hamlets will invite,
When the merry bells ring round,
And the jocund rebecks [6] sound
To many a youth and many a maid   95
Dancing in the chequered shade;
And young and old come forth to play
On a sunshine holiday,
Till the livelong daylight fail;
Then to the spicy nut-brown ale,   100
With stories told of many a feat,
How fairy Mab [7] the junkets eat:

---

[1] Homer uses the term to characterize a region perpetually dark and enshrouded in mist.
[2] Called.
[3] One of the three graces presiding over the banquet and dance and all social pleasures.
[4] Daughter of Jupiter and Juno and cup-bearer to the gods.
[5] Innocent or simple.   [6] White with frost.

[1] Dressed, adorned.
[2] Counts his sheep.
[3] Center of attention.
[4] The names in this passage are frequently used in classical pastoral poetry.
[5] Carefree.   [6] Fiddle.
[7] A mischief-loving fairy, popularly supposed to control dreams. A poetic description of the havoc she wrought is given by Shakespeare in *Romeo and Juliet*, I, 4, 53 ff.

She[1] was pinched and pulled, she said;
And he, by Friar's[2] lantern led,
Tells how the drudging Goblin sweat   105
To earn his cream-bowl duly set,
When in one night, ere glimpse of morn,
His shadowy flail hath threshed the corn
That ten day-laborers could not end;
Then lies him down, the lubber[3] fiend,   110
And, stretched out all the chimney's length,
Basks at the fire his hairy strength,
And crop-full out of doors he flings,
Ere the first cock his matin rings.
Thus done the tales, to bed they creep,   115
By whispering winds soon lulled asleep.
Towered cities please us then,
And the busy hum of men,
Where throngs of Knights and Barons bold,
In weeds of peace, high triumphs hold,   120
With store of Ladies, whose bright eyes
Rain influence, and judge the prize
Of wit or arms, while both contend
To win her grace whom all commend.
There let Hymen[4] oft appear   125
In saffron robe, with taper clear,
And pomp, and feast, and revelry,
With mask and antique pageantry;
Such sights as youthful Poets dream
On summer eves by haunted stream.   130
Then to the well-trod stage anon,
If Jonson's learned sock[5] be on,
Or sweetest Shakespeare, Fancy's child,
Warble his native wood-notes wild.
And ever, against eating cares,   135
Lap me in soft Lydian[6] airs,
Married to immortal verse,
Such as the meeting soul may pierce,
In notes with many a winding bout[7]
Of linkèd sweetness long drawn out   140
With wanton heed and giddy cunning,
The melting voice through mazes running,
Untwisting all the chains that tie
The hidden soul of harmony;
That Orpheus'[8] self may heave his head   145
From golden slumber on a bed
Of heapèd Elysian[9] flowers, and hear
Such strains as would have won the ear

[1] One of those telling stories.
[2] Friar Rush or Jack-o'-Lantern or Will-o'-the-wisp.
[3] Clumsy.   [4] God of marriage.
[5] Comedy. The *soccus* was a light shoe worn by actors in classical comedy.
[6] One of the three moods in the music of ancient Greece.   [7] Turn.
[8] Orpheus was so skillful a musician that even the trees and stones were affected by his notes.
[9] Elysium, a land to which heroes went without dying — the Blessed Isles.

Of Pluto to have quite set free
His half-regained Eurydice.[1]   150
These delights if thou canst give.
Mirth, with thee I mean to live.

Il Penseroso

Hence, vain deluding Joys,
    The brood of Folly without father bred!
How little you bested,[2]
    Or fill the fixèd mind with all your toys!
Dwell in some idle brain,   5
    And fancies fond with gaudy shapes possess,
As thick and numberless
    As the gay motes that people the sunbeams,
Or likest hovering dreams,
    The fickle pensioners of Morpheus' train. 10
But, hail! thou Goddess sage and holy!
Hail, divinest Melancholy!
Whose saintly visage is too bright
To hit the sense of human sight,
And therefore to our weaker view   15
O'erlaid with black, staid Wisdom's hue;
Black, but such as in esteem
Prince Memnon's[3] sister might beseem,
Or that starred Ethiop Queen[4] that strove
To set her beauty's praise above   20
The Sea-Nymphs, and their powers offended.
Yet thou art higher far descended:
Thee bright-haired Vesta[5] long of yore
To solitary Saturn bore;
His daughter she; in Saturn's reign   25
Such mixture was not held a stain.
Oft in glimmering bowers and glades
He met her, and in secret shades
Of woody Ida's[6] inmost grove,
Whilst yet there was no fear of Jove.   30
Come, pensive Nun, devout and pure,
Sober, steadfast, and demure,
All in a robe of darkest grain,
Flowing with majestic train,
And sable stole of cypress lawn   35
Over thy decent[7] shoulders drawn.
Come; but keep thy wonted state,
With even step, and musing gait,
And looks commercing with the skies,
Thy rapt soul sitting in thine eyes: 40

[1] See Ovid's *Orpheus and Eurydice* for this story.
[2] Profit.
[3] King of Ethiopia at time of Trojan War. Noted for his physical beauty.
[4] Cassiopeia became a constellation after Perseus carried her to heaven.
[5] Goddess of the hearth and fire.
[6] Mount Ida in Crete.   [7] Modest or comely.

There, held in holy passion still,
Forget thyself to marble, till
With a sad leaden downward cast
Thou fix them on the earth as fast.
And join with thee calm Peace and Quiet,   45
Spare Fast, that oft with gods doth diet,
And hears the Muses in a ring
Aye round about Jove's altar sing;
And add to these retirèd Leisure,
That in trim gardens takes his pleasure;   50
But, first and chiefest, with thee bring
Him that yon soars on golden wing,
Guiding the fiery-wheelèd throne,
The Cherub Contemplation;
And the mute Silence hist along,   55
'Less Philomel ¹ will deign a song,
In her sweetest saddest plight,
Smoothing the rugged brow of Night,
While Cynthia checks her dragon yoke ²
Gently o'er the accustomed oak.   60
Sweet bird, that shunn'st the noise of folly,
Most musical, most melancholy!
Thee, Chauntress, oft the woods among
I woo, to hear thy even-song;
And, missing thee, I walk unseen   65
On the dry smooth-shaven green,
To behold the wandering Moon,
Riding near her highest noon,
Like one that had been led astray
Through the heaven's wide pathless way,   70
And oft, as if her head she bowed,
Stooping through a fleecy cloud.
Oft, on a plat of rising ground,
I hear the far-off curfew sound,
Over some wide-watered shore,   75
Swinging slow with sullen roar;
Or, if the air will not permit,
Some still removèd place will fit,
Where glowing embers through the room
Teach light to counterfeit a gloom,   80
Far from all resort of mirth,
Save the cricket on the hearth,
Or the Bellman's drowsy charm
To bless the doors from nightly harm.
Or let my lamp, at midnight hour,   85
Be seen in some high lonely tower,
Where I may oft outwatch the Bear,³
With thrice-great Hermes,⁴ or unsphere

¹ The nightingale.
² Milton sometimes creates his own mythology.
It was Ceres and not Diana (Cynthia) who drove the
winged-dragon team.
³ The constellation of the Great Bear. To "outwatch" it would be to stay up until dawn.
⁴ Hermes Trismegistus, a fabled magician and philosopher; many books on mysticism were credited to him.

The spirit of Plato, to unfold
What worlds or what vast regions hold   90
The immortal mind that hath forsook
Her mansion in this fleshly nook;
And of those demons that are found
In fire, air, flood, or underground,
Whose power hath a true consent   95
With planet or with element.
Sometime let gorgeous Tragedy
In sceptred pall come sweeping by,
Presenting Thebes, or Pelops' line,
Or the tale of Troy divine,   100
Or what (though rare) of later age
Ennobled hath the buskined ¹ stage.
But, O sad Virgin! that thy power
Might raise Musæus ² from his bower;
Or bid the soul of Orpheus sing   105
Such notes as, warbled to the string,
Drew iron tears down Pluto's cheek,
And made Hell grant what Love did seek;
Or call up him that left half-told
The story of Cambuscan bold,³   110
Of Camball, and of Algarsife,
And who had Canace to wife,
That owned the virtuous ⁴ ring and glass,
And of the wondrous horse of brass
On which the Tartar King did ride;   115
And if aught else great Bards beside
In sage and solemn tunes have sung,
Of turneys, and of trophies hung,
Of forests, and enchantments drear,
Where more is meant than meets the ear.   120
Thus, Night, oft see me in thy pale career,
Till civil-suited Morn appear,
Not tricked and frounced, as she was wont
With the Attic boy ⁵ to hunt,
But kerchieft in a comely cloud,   125
While rocking winds are piping loud,
Or ushered with a shower still,
When the gust hath blown his fill,
Ending on the rustling leaves,
With minute-drops from off the eaves.   130
And, when the sun begins to fling
His flaring beams, me, Goddess, bring
To archèd walks of twilight groves,
And shadows brown, that Sylvan ⁶ loves,
Of pine, or monumental oak,   135
Where the rude axe with heavèd stroke

¹ The buskin, or heavy boot, was worn by actors in
classical tragedy.
² Son of Orpheus and a poet.
³ The names in these lines are references to characters
in the *Squire's Tale* by Chaucer.
⁴ Powerful because of its magic qualities.
⁵ Cephalus, who was loved by Aurora, the dawn.
⁶ Sylvanus, a god of the forest.

Was never heard the Nymphs to daunt,
Or fright them from their hallowed haunt.
There, in close covert, by some brook,
Where no profaner eye may look,   140
Hide me from Day's garish eye,
While the bee with honeyed thigh,
That at her flowery work doth sing,
And the waters murmuring,
With such consort as they keep,   145
Entice the dewy-feathered Sleep.
And let some strange mysterious dream
Wave at his wings, in airy stream
Of lively portraiture displayed,
Softly on my eyelids laid.   150
And as I wake, sweet music breathe
Above, about, or underneath,
Sent by some Spirit to mortals good,
Or the unseen Genius of the wood.
But let my due feet never fail   155
To walk the studious cloister's pale,[1]
And love the high embowèd roof,
With antique pillars massy proof,
And storied windows richly dight,
Casting a dim religious light.   160
There let the pealing organ blow,
To the full voiced Quire below,
In service high and anthems clear,
As may with sweetness, through mine ear,
Dissolve me into ecstasies,   165
And bring all Heaven before mine eyes.
And may at last my weary age
Find out the peaceful hermitage,
The hairy gown and mossy cell,
Where I may sit and rightly spell   170
Of every star that Heaven doth shew,
And every herb that sips the dew;
Till old experience do attain
To something like prophetic strain.
These pleasures, Melancholy, give,   175
And I with thee will choose to live.

Lycidas

Yet once more, O ye Laurels, and once more,
Ye Myrtles brown, with ivy never sere,
I come to pluck your berries harsh and crude,
And with forced fingers rude ,
Shatter your leaves before the mellowing year.   5
Bitter constraint and sad occasion dear
Compels me to disturb your season due;
For Lycidas [2] is dead, dead ere his prime,

[1] Limits.
[2] A name borrowed from Theocritus and pastoral
elegy. Milton here mourns the loss of Edward King, a
fellow student at Cambridge, who had been drowned

Young Lycidas, and hath not left his peer.
Who would not sing for Lycidas? he knew   10
Himself to sing, and build the lofty rhyme.
He must not float upon his watery bier
Unwept, and welter to the parching wind,
Without the meed of some melodious tear.
Begin, then, Sisters of the sacred well [1]   1[5]
That from beneath the seat of Jove doth spring;
Begin, and somewhat loudly sweep the string.
Hence with denial vain and coy excuse:
So may some gentle Muse [2]
With lucky [3] words favor *my* destined urn,   2[0]
And as he passes turn,
And bid fair peace be to my sable shroud!
    For we were nursed upon the self-same hill,
Fed the same flock, by fountain, shade, and rill;
Together both, ere the high lawns appeared   25
Under the opening eyelids of the Morn,
We drove a-field, and both together heard
What time the grey-fly winds her sultry horn,
Battening [4] our flocks with the fresh dews of night,
Oft till the star that rose at evening bright   30
Toward heaven's descent had sloped his westering
        wheel.
Meanwhile the rural ditties were not mute;
Tempered to the oaten flute
Rough Satyrs danced, and Fauns with cloven heel
From the glad sound would not be absent long;   35
And old Damœtas [5] loved to hear our song.
    But, oh! the heavy change, now thou art gone,
Now thou art gone and never must return!
Thee, Shepherd, thee the woods and desert caves
With wild thyme and the gadding vine o'er-
        grown,   40
And all their echoes, mourn.
The willows, and the hazel copses green,
Shall now no more be seen
Fanning their joyous leaves to thy soft lays
As killing as the canker to the rose,   45
Or taint-worm to the weanling herds that graze,
Or frost to flowers, that their gay wardrobe wear,
When first the white-thorn blows;
Such, Lycidas, thy loss to shepherd's ear.
    Where were ye, Nymphs, when the remorseless
        deep   50
Closed o'er the head of your loved Lycidas?
For neither were ye playing on the steep

in the Irish Sea. King had studied for a career in the
Church, and the year of composition of *Lycidas*, 1637,
preceded by only a few years the open break between
Parliament and King Charles.
[1] The nine muses.
[2] Poet.
[3] Favorable.   [4] Feeding.
[5] A pastoral name probably representing some
Cambridge tutor.

Where your old Bards, the famous Druids, lie,
Nor on the shaggy top of Mona [1] high,
Nor yet where Deva [2] spreads her wizard stream.
Ay me! I fondly dream   56
"Had ye been there," . . . for what could that have
        done?
What could the Muse [3] herself that Orpheus bore,
The Muse herself, for her enchanting son,
Whom universal nature did lament,   60
When, by the rout that made the hideous roar,
His gory visage down the stream was sent,
Down the swift Hebrus to the Lesbian shore?
    Alas! what boots it with uncessant care
To tend the homely slighted Shepherd's trade,   65
And strictly meditate the thankless Muse?
Were it not better done, as others use,
To sport with Amaryllis in the shade,
Or with the tangles of Neæra's hair?
Fame is the spur that the clear spirit doth raise   70
(That last infirmity of noble mind)
To scorn delights and live laborious days;
But the fair guerdon when we hope to find,
And think to burst out into sudden blaze,   74
Comes the blind Fury [4] with the abhorrèd shears,
And slits the thin-spun life. "But not the praise,"
Phœbus replied, and touched my trembling ears:
"Fame is no plant that grows on mortal soil,
Nor in the glistering foil [5]
Set off to the world, nor in broad rumor lies,   80
But lives and spreads aloft by those pure eyes
And perfect witness of all-judging Jove;
As he pronounces lastly on each deed,
Of so much fame in heaven expect thy meed."
    O fountain Arethuse, [6] and thou honored flood,
Smooth-sliding Mincius, [6] crowned with vocal
        reeds,   86
That strain I heard was of a higher mood.
But now my oat proceeds,
And listens to the Herald of the Sea, [7]
That came in Neptune's plea.   90
He asked the waves, and asked the felon winds,
What hard mishap hath doomed this gentle swain?
And questioned every gust of rugged wings
That blows from off each beakèd promontory.
They knew not of his story;   95
And sage Hippotades [8] their answer brings,

    [1] Anglesey, an island county of Wales which had
been a seat of the Druids.
    [2] The river Dee.   [3] Calliope.
    [4] Atropos, the one of the three Fates who cuts the
thread of life.   [5] Tinsel.
    [6] See Ovid's *Alpheus and Arethusa.* Theocritus sang
of the fountain Arethusa and Virgil of the river Mincius;
thus both allusions refer to pastoral poetry.
    [7] Triton.
    [8] Æolus, the god of the winds and son of Hippotes.

That not a blast was from his dungeon strayed:
The air was calm, and on the level brine
Sleek Panope [1] with all her sisters played.
It was that fatal and perfidious bark,   100
Built in the eclipse, and rigged with curses dark,
That sunk so low that sacred head of thine.
    Next, Camus, [2] reverend Sire, went footing slow,
His mantle hairy and his bonnet sedge,
Inwrought with figures dim, and on the edge   105
Like to that sanguine flower [3] inscribed with woe.
"Ah! who hath reft," quoth he, "my dearest
        pledge?"
Last came, and last did go,
The Pilot of the Galilean Lake; [4]
Two massy keys he bore of metals twain   110
(The golden opes, the iron shuts amain).
He shook his mitred locks, and stern bespake: —
"How well could I have spared for thee, young
        swain,
Enow of such as, for their bellies' sake,
Creep, and intrude, and climb into the fold!   115
Of other care they little reckoning make
Than how to scramble at the shearers' feast,
And shove away the worthy bidden guest.
Blind mouths! that scarce themselves know how to
        hold
A sheep-hook, or have learnt aught else the least
That to the faithful Herdman's art belongs!   121
What recks it them? What need they? They are
        sped;
And, when they list, their lean and flashy songs
Grate on their scrannel [5] pipes of wretched straw;
The hungry sheep look up, and are not fed,   125
But, swoln with wind and the rank mist they
        draw,
Rot inwardly, and foul contagion spread;
Besides what the grim Wolf [6] with privy paw
Daily devours apace, and nothing said.
But that two-handed engine [7] at the door   130
Stands ready to smite once, and smite no more."
    Return, Alpheus; the dread voice is past
That shrunk thy streams; return, Sicilian Muse,
And call the vales, and bid them hither cast
Their bells and flowerets of a thousand hues.   135
Ye valleys low, where the mild whispers use [8]
Of shades, and wanton winds, and gushing brooks,
On whose fresh lap the swart star sparely looks,

    [1] One of the Nereids, a sea-nymph.
    [2] The river Cam at Cambridge.
    [3] The hyacinth which was supposed to have bloomed
from the blood of Hyacinthus.
    [4] St. Peter.   [5] Thin.   [6] The Roman Church
    [7] Milton's meaning here is not clear; it has been sug-
gested that the reference is to the two houses of Parliament.
    [8] Dwell or frequent.

Throw hither all your quaint enamelled eyes,
That on the green turf suck the honeyed showers,
And purple all the ground with vernal flowers. 141
Bring the rathe [1] primrose that forsaken dies,
The tufted crow-toe, and pale jessamine,
The white pink, and the pansy freaked with jet,
The glowing violet.   145
The musk-rose, and the well-attired woodbine,
With cowslips wan that hang the pensive head,
And every flower that sad embroidery wears;
Bid amaranthus all his beauty shed,
And daffadillies fill their cups with tears,   150
To strew the laureate hearse where Lycid lies.
For so, to interpose a little ease,
Let our frail thoughts dally with false surmise.
Ay me! whilst thee the shores and sounding seas
Wash far away, where'er thy bones are hurled;
Whether beyond the stormy Hebrides,   156
Where thou perhaps under the whelming tide
Visit'st the bottom of the monstrous world;
Or whether thou, to our moist vows denied,
Sleep'st by the fable of Bellerus [2] old,   160
Where the great Vision of the guarded mount
Looks toward Namancos and Bayona's hold.[3]
Look homeward, Angel, now, and melt with ruth:
And, O ye dolphins, waft the hapless youth.
  Weep no more, woeful shepherds, weep no more,
For Lycidas, your sorrow, is not dead,   166
Sunk though he be beneath the watery floor.
So sinks the day-star in the ocean bed,
And yet anon repairs his drooping head,
And tricks his beams, and with new-spangled ore
Flames in the forehead of the morning sky: 171
So Lycidas sunk low, but mounted high,
Through the dear might of Him that walked the
        waves,
Where, other groves and other streams along,
With nectar pure his oozy locks he laves,   175
And hears the unexpressive [4] nuptial song,
In the blest kingdoms meek of joy and love.
There entertain him all the Saints above,
In solemn troops, and sweet societies,
That sing, and singing in their glory move,   180
And wipe the tears for ever from his eyes.
Now, Lycidas, the Shepherds weep no more;
Henceforth thou art the Genius of the shore,
In thy large recompense, and shalt be good
To all that wander in that perilous flood.   185

  Thus sang the uncouth Swain to the oaks and
        rills,
While the still Morn went out with sandals grey:
He touched the tender stops of various quills,[5]
With eager thought warbling his Doric [6] lay:

[1] Early.   [2] Land's End.   [3] In Spain.
[4] Inexpressible.   [5] Reeds or pipes.   [6] Pastoral.

And now the sun had stretched out all the hills,
And now was dropt into the western bay.   191
At last he rose, and twitched [1] his mantle blue:
To-morrow to fresh woods, and pastures new.

On His Being Arrived to the Age of Twenty-Three

How soon hath Time, the subtle thief of youth,
Stolen on his wing my three and twentieth year!
My hasting days fly on with full career,
But my late spring no bud or blossom shew'th.

Perhaps my semblance might deceive the truth, 5
  That I to manhood am arrived so near,
  And inward ripeness doth much less appear,
  That some more timely-happy spirits endu'th.
Yet be it less or more, or soon or slow,
  It shall be still in strictest measure even   10
  To that same lot, however mean or high,
Toward which Time leads me, and the will of
        Heaven.
  All is, if I have grace to use it so,
  As ever in my great Task-master's eye.

On His Blindness

When I consider how my light is spent
  Ere half my days in this dark world and wide,
  And that one Talent which is death to hide
  Lodged with me useless, though my soul more
        bent
To serve therewith my Maker, and present   5
  My true account, lest He returning chide;
  "Doth God exact day-labor, light denied?"
  I fondly ask. But Patience, to prevent
That murmur, soon replies, "God doth not need
  Either man's work or his own gifts. Who best
  Bear his mild yoke, they serve him best. His
        state   11
Is kingly: thousands at his bidding speed,
  And post o'er land and ocean without rest;
  They also serve who only stand and wait."

On Shakespeare

What needs my Shakespeare for his honored bones
The labor of an age in pilèd stones?
Or that his hallowed relics should be hid
Under a star-ypointing pyramid?
Dear son of memory, great heir of fame,   5
What need'st thou such weak witness of thy name?

[1] Gathered.

Thou in our wonder and astonishment
Hast built thyself a livelong monument.
For whilst, to the shame of slow-endeavoring art,
Thy easy numbers flow, and that each heart   10
Hath from the leaves of thy unvalued [1] book
Those Delphic [2] lines with deep impression took,
Then thou, our fancy of itself bereaving,
Dost make *us* marble with too much conceiving,
And so sepulchred in such pomp dost lie   15
That kings for such a tomb would wish to die.

Paradise Lost

BOOK I

The Argument

This First Book proposes, first in brief, the whole
subject — Man's disobedience, and the loss thereupon
of Paradise, wherein he was placed: then touches the
prime cause of his fall — the Serpent, or rather Satan
in the Serpent; who, revolting from God, and drawing
to his side many legions of Angels, was, by the command
of God, driven out of Heaven, with all his crew, into
the great Deep. Which action passed over, the Poem
hastes into the midst of things; presenting Satan, with
his Angels, now fallen into Hell — described here not
in the Centre (for heaven and earth may be supposed
as yet not made, certainly not yet accursed), but in a
place of utter darkness, fitliest called Chaos. Here
Satan, with his Angels lying on the burning lake,
thunderstruck and astonished, after a certain space
recovers, as from confusion; calls up him who, next in
order and dignity, lay by him: they confer of their
miserable fall. Satan awakens all his legions, who lay
till then in the same manner confounded. They rise:
their numbers; array of battle; their chief leaders
named, according to the idols known afterwards in
Canaan and the countries adjoining. To these Satan
directs his speech; comforts them with hope yet of
regaining Heaven; but tells them, lastly, of a new world
and new kind of creature to be created, according to
an ancient prophecy, or report, in Heaven — for that
Angels were long before this visible creation was the
opinion of many ancient Fathers. To find out the
truth of this prophecy, and what to determine thereon,
he refers to a full council. What his associates thence
attempt. Pandemonium, the palace of Satan, rises,
suddenly built out of the Deep: the infernal Peers
there sit in council.

Of Man's first disobedience, and the fruit
Of that forbidden tree whose mortal taste
Brought death into the World, and all our woe,
With loss of Eden, till one greater Man
Restore us, and regain the blissful Seat,   5

[1] Invaluable.
[2] The Delphic oracle; i.e., inspired.

Sing, Heavenly Muse,[1] that, on the secret top
Of Oreb, or of Sinai, didst inspire
That Shepherd who first taught the chosen seed
In the beginning how the heavens and earth
Rose out of Chaos: or, if Sion hill   10
Delight thee more, and Siloa's brook that flowed
Fast by the oracle of God,[2] I thence
Invoke thy aid to my adventrous song,
That with no middle flight intends to soar
Above the Aonian mount,[3] while it pursues   15
Things unattempted yet in prose or rhyme.
And chiefly Thou, O Spirit, that dost prefer
Before all temples the upright heart and pure,
Instruct me, for Thou know'st; Thou from the first
Wast present, and, with mighty wings outspread,
Dove-like sat'st brooding on the vast Abyss,   21
And mad'st it pregnant: what in me is dark
Illumine, what is low raise and support;
That, to the highth of this great argument,[4]
I may assert [5] Eternal Providence,   25
And justify the ways of God to men.

Say first — for Heaven hides nothing from thy
        view,
Nor the deep tract of Hell — say first what cause
Moved our grand [6] Parents, in that happy state,
Favored of Heaven so highly, to fall off   30
From their Creator, and transgress his will
For one restraint, lords of the World besides.
Who first seduced them to that foul revolt?
   The infernal Serpent; he it was whose guile,
Stirred up with envy and revenge, deceived   35
The mother of mankind, what time his pride
Had cast him out from Heaven, with all his host
Of rebel Angels, by whose aid, aspiring
To set himself in glory above his peers,
He trusted to have equalled the Most High,   40
If he opposed, and, with ambitious aim
Against the throne and monarchy of God,
Raised impious war in Heaven and battle proud,
With vain attempt. Him the Almighty Power
Hurled headlong flaming from the ethereal sky, 45
With hideous ruin and combustion, down
To bottomless perdition, there to dwell
In adamantine chains and penal fire,
Who durst defy the Omnipotent to arms.
   Nine times the space that measures day and
        night   50

[1] Milton follows the classical convention by invoking the muse, but departs from it to the extent of
calling upon the "heavenly muse" that inspired Moses
and David rather than any of the "sacred nine"
traditionally invoked in epic poetry.
[2] The temple of Jerusalem was on Mt. Moriah at the
foot of which flowed "Siloa's brook."
[3] Mt. Helicon, sacred as the home of the Muses.
[4] Theme.   [5] Vindicate.   [6] First.

To mortal men, he, with his horrid crew,
Lay vanquished, rolling in the fiery gulf,
Confounded, though immortal. But his doom
Reserved him to more wrath; for now the thought
Both of lost happiness and lasting pain   55
Torments him: round he throws his baleful eyes,
That witnessed huge affliction and dismay,
Mixed with obdúrate pride and steadfast hate.
At once, as far as Angels ken, he views
The dismal situation waste and wild.   60
A dungeon horrible, on all sides round,
As one great furnace flamed; yet from those flames
No light; but rather darkness visible
Served only to discover sights of woe,
Regions of sorrow, doleful shades, where peace   65
And rest can never dwell, hope never comes
That comes to all, but torture without end
Still urges, and a fiery deluge, fed
With ever-burning sulphur unconsumed.
Such place Eternal Justice had prepared   70
For those rebellious; here their prison ordained
In utter darkness, and their portion set,
As far removed from God and light of Heaven
As from the centre thrice to the utmost pole.[1]
Oh how unlike the place from whence they fell!   75
There the companions of his fall, o'erwhelmed
With floods and whirlwinds of tempestuous fire,
He soon discerns; and, weltering by his side,
One next himself in power, and next in crime,
Long after known in Palestine, and named   80
BEELZEBUB. To whom the Arch-Enemy,
And thence in Heaven called SATAN, with bold
          words
Breaking the horrid silence, thus began: —
"If thou beest he — but Oh how fallen! how
          changed
From him! — who, in the happy realms of light,
Clothed with transcendent brightness, didst out-
          shine   86
Myriads, though bright — if he whom mutual
          league,
United thoughts and counsels, equal hope
And hazard in the glorious enterprise,
Joined with me once, now misery hath joined   90
In equal ruin; into what pit thou seest
From what highth fallen: so much the stronger
          proved
He with his thunder: and till then who knew
The force of those dire arms? Yet not for those,
Nor what the potent Victor in his rage   95

[1] Milton's conception of the universe is, in general,
that of the Ptolemaic system. For him, too, the earth
is surrounded by ten hollow spheres. The starry universe hangs from heaven above it by a golden chain and
outside the universe is chaos. At the bottom of chaos
is hell.

Can else inflict, do I repent, or change,
Though changed in outward lustre, that fixed mind,
And high disdain from sense of injured merit,
That with the Mightiest raised me to contend,
And to the fierce contention brought along   100
Innumerable force of Spirits armed,
That durst dislike his reign, and, me preferring,
His utmost power with adverse power opposed
In dubious battle on the plains of Heaven,
And shook his throne. What though the field be
          lost?   105
All is not lost — the unconquerable will,
And study of revenge, immortal hate,
And courage never to submit or yield:
And what is else not to be overcome;
That glory never shall his wrath or might   110
Extort from me. To bow and sue for grace
With suppliant knee, and deify his power
Who, from the terror of this arm, so late
Doubted his empire — that were low indeed;
That were an ignominy and shame beneath   115
This downfall; since, by fate, the strength of Gods,
And this empyreal substance, cannot fail;
Since, through experience of this great event,
In arms not worse, in foresight much advanced,
We may with more successful hope resolve   120
To wage by force or guile eternal war,
Irreconcilable to our grand Foe,
Who now triumphs, and in the excess of joy
Sole reigning holds the tyranny of Heaven."
     So spake the apostate Angel, though in pain, 125
Vaunting aloud, but racked with deep despair;
And him thus answered soon his bold Compeer: —
"O Prince, O Chief of many thronèd Powers
That led the embattled Seraphim to war
Under thy conduct, and, in dreadful deeds   130
Fearless, endangered Heaven's perpetual King,
And put to proof his high supremacy,
Whether upheld by strength, or chance, or fate!
Too well I see and rue the dire event
That, with sad overthrow and foul defeat,   135
Hath lost us Heaven, and all this mighty host
In horrible destruction laid thus low,
As far as Gods and Heavenly Essences
Can perish: for the mind and spirit remains
Invincible, and vigor soon returns,   140
Though all our glory extinct, and happy state
Here swallowed up in endless misery.
But what if He our Conqueror (whom I now
Of force believe almighty, since no less
Than such could have o'erpowered such force as
          ours)   145
Have left us this our spirit and strength entire,
Strongly to suffer and support our pains,
That we may so suffice[1] his vengeful ire,
          [1] Satisfy.

Or do him mightier service as his thralls
By right of war, whate'er his business be,   150
Here in the heart of Hell to work in fire,
Or do his errands in the gloomy Deep?
What can it then avail though yet we feel
Strength undiminished, or eternal being
To undergo eternal punishment?"   155
    Whereto with speedy words the Arch-Fiend re-
plied: —
"Fallen Cherub, to be weak is miserable,
Doing or suffering: but of this be sure —
To do aught good never will be our task,
But ever to do ill our sole delight,   160
As being the contrary to His high will
Whom we resist. If then his providence
Out of our evil seek to bring forth good,
Our labor must be to pervert that end,
And out of good still to find means of evil;   165
Which ofttimes may succeed so as perhaps
Shall grieve him, if I fail [1] not, and disturb
His inmost counsels from their destined aim.
But see! the angry Victor hath recalled
His ministers of vengeance and pursuit   170
Back to the gates of Heaven: the sulphurous hail,
Shot after us in storm, o'erblown hath laid
The fiery surge that from the precipice
Of Heaven received us falling; and the thunder,
Winged with red lightning and impetuous rage,   175
Perhaps hath spent his shafts, and ceases now
To bellow through the vast and boundless Deep.
Let us not slip the occasion, whether scorn
Or satiate fury yield it from our Foe.
Seest thou yon dreary plain, forlorn and wild,   180
The seat of desolation, void of light,
Save what the glimmering of these livid flames
Casts pale and dreadful? Thither let us tend
From off the tossing of these fiery waves;
There rest, if any rest can harbor there;   185
And, re-assembling our afflicted powers,
Consult how we may henceforth most offend
Our Enemy, our own loss how repair,
How overcome this dire calamity,
What reinforcement we may gain from hope,   190
If not what resolution from despair."
    Thus Satan, talking to his nearest Mate,
With head uplift above the wave, and eyes
That sparkling blazed; his other parts besides
Prone on the flood, extended long and large,   195
Lay floating many a rood, in bulk as huge
As whom the fables name of monstrous size,
Titanian or Earth-born, that warred on Jove,
Briareos or Typhon,[2] whom the den

By ancient Tarsus [1] held, or that sea-beast   200
Leviathan,[2] which God of all his works
Created hugest that swim the ocean-stream.
Him, haply slumbering on the Norway foam,
The pilot of some small night-foundered skiff,
Deeming some island, oft, as seamen tell,   205
With fixèd anchor in his scaly rind,
Moors by his side under the lee, while night
Invests the sea, and wishèd morn delays.
So stretched out huge in length the Arch-Fiend lay,
Chained on the burning lake; nor ever thence   210
Had risen, or heaved his head, but that the will
And high permission of all-ruling Heaven
Left him at large to his own dark designs,
That with reiterated crimes he might
Heap on himself damnation, while he sought   215
Evil to others, and enraged might see
How all his malice served but to bring forth
Infinite goodness, grace, and mercy, shewn
On Man by him seduced, but on himself   219
Treble confusion, wrath, and vengeance poured.
    Forthwith upright he rears from off the pool
His mighty stature; on each hand the flames
Driven backward slope their pointing spires, and,
        rolled
In billows, leave i' the midst a horrid vale.
Then with expanded wings he steers his flight   225
Aloft, incumbent on the dusky air,
That felt unusual weight; till on dry land
He lights — if it were land that ever burned
With solid, as the lake with liquid fire,
And such appeared in hue as when the force   230
Of subterranean wind transports a hill
Torn from Pelorus,[3] or the shattered side
Of thundering Ætna, whose combustible
And fuelled entrails, thence conceiving fire,
Sublimed [4] with mineral fury, aid the winds,   235
And leave a singèd bottom all involved
With stench and smoke. Such resting found the
        sole
Of unblest feet. Him followed his next Mate;
Both glorying to have scaped the Stygian flood
As gods, and by their own recovered strength,   240
Not by the sufferance of supernal power.
    "Is this the region, this the soil, the clime,"
Said then the lost Archangel, "this the seat
That we must change for Heaven? — this mournful
        gloom
For that celestial light? Be it so, since He   245
Who now is sovran can dispose and bid
What shall be right: farthest from Him is best,

[1] Mistake.
[2] The Titans and the giants were both "Earth-born"
in that they were the offspring of Uranus and Ge
(Earth). Briareos was a Titan, Typhon a giant.

[1] Typhon is said to have lived in a den in Tarsus. the
capital of Cilicia.
[2] See *Psalms* civ, 26.
[3] A cape in Sicily.
[4] Changed to a gas.

Whom reason hath equalled, force hath made
    supreme
Above his equals. Farewell, happy fields,
Where joy for ever dwells! Hail, horrors! hail,
Infernal World! and thou, profoundest Hell,   251
Receive thy new possessor — one who brings
A mind not to be changed by place or time.
The mind is its own place, and in itself
Can make a Heaven of Hell, a Hell of Heaven.
What matter where, if I be still the same,   256
And what I should be, all but [1] less than he
Whom thunder hath made greater? Here at least
We shall be free; the Almighty hath not built
Here for his envy, will not drive us hence: 260
Here we may reign secure; and, in my choice,
To reign is worth ambition, though in Hell:
Better to reign in Hell than serve in Heaven.
But wherefore let we then our faithful friends,
The associates and co-partners of our loss,   265
Lie thus astonished on the oblivious pool,
And call them not to share with us their part
In this unhappy mansion, or once more
With rallied arms to try what may be yet
Regained in Heaven, or what more lost in Hell?"
    So Satan spake; and him Beëlzebub   271
Thus answered: — "Leader of those armies bright
Which, but the Omnipotent, none could have
    foiled!
If once they hear that voice, their liveliest pledge
Of hope in fears and dangers — heard so oft   275
In worst extremes, and on the perilous edge
Of battle, when it raged, in all assaults
Their surest signal — they will soon resume
New courage and revive, though now they lie
Grovelling and prostrate on yon lake of fire,   280
As we erewhile, astounded and amazed;
No wonder, fallen such a pernicious highth!"
    He scarce had ceased when the superior Fiend
Was moving toward the shore; his ponderous
    shield,
Ethereal temper, massy, large, and round,   285
Behind him cast. The broad circumference
Hung on his shoulders like the moon, whose orb
Through optic glass the Tuscan artist [2] views
At evening, from the top of Fesolè,[3]
Or in Valdarno,[4] to descry new lands,   290
Rivers, or mountains, in her spotty globe.
His spear — to equal which the tallest pine
Hewn on Norwegian hills, to be the mast
Of some great Ammiral,[5] were but a wand —

He walked with, to support uneasy steps   295
Over the burning marle, not like those steps
On Heaven's azure; and the torrid clime
Smote on him sore besides, vaulted with fire.
Nathless [1] he so endured, till on the beach
Of that inflamèd sea he stood, and called   300
His legions — Angel Forms, who lay entranced
Thick as autumnal leaves that strow the brooks
In Vallombrosa, where the Etrurian shades
High over-arched embower; or scattered sedge
Afloat, when with fierce winds Orion [2] armed   305
Hath vexed the Red-Sea coast, whose waves o'er-
    threw
Busiris [3] and his Memphian chivalry,
While with perfidious hatred they pursued
The sojourners of Goshen,[4] who beheld
From the safe shore their floating carcases   310
And broken chariot-wheels. So thick bestrown,
Abject and lost, lay these, covering the flood,
Under amazement of their hideous change.
He called so loud that all the hollow deep
Of Hell resounded: — "Princes, Potentates,   315
Warriors, the Flower of Heaven — once yours;
    now lost,
If such astonishment as this can seize
Eternal Spirits! Or have ye chosen this place
After the toil of battle to repose
Your wearied virtue, for the ease you find   320
To slumber here, as in the vales of Heaven?
Or in this abject posture have ye sworn
To adore the Conqueror, who now beholds
Cherub and Seraph rolling in the flood
With scattered arms and ensigns, till anon   325
His swift pursuers from Heaven-gates discern
The advantage, and, descending, tread us down
Thus drooping, or with linkèd thunderbolts
Transfix us to the bottom of this gulf? —
Awake, arise, or be for ever fallen!"   330
    They heard, and were abashed, and up they
    sprung
Upon the wing, as when men wont to watch,
On duty sleeping found by whom they dread,
Rouse and bestir themselves ere well awake.
Nor did they not perceive the evil plight   335
In which they were, or the fierce pains not feel;
Yet to their General's voice they soon obeyed
Innumerable. As when the potent rod
Of Amram's son,[5] in Egypt's evil day,
Waved round the coast, up-called a pitchy cloud
Of locusts, warping on the eastern wind,   341

---

[1] All but — only.
[2] Galileo. Milton knew him and of his work on the
telescope.
[3] A hill near Florence.
[4] Florence is in this valley of the Arno.
[5] Admiral or, as here used, the flagship of the admiral.

[1] Nevertheless.
[2] The name of a constellation supposed to bring
storms.
[3] A Pharaoh.
[4] See Exodus xiv, 21–31.
[5] Moses.

That o'er the realm of impious Pharaoh hung
Like Night, and darkened all the land of Nile;
So numberless were those bad Angels seen
Hovering on wing under the cope of Hell,   345
'Twixt upper, nether, and surrounding fires;
Till, as a signal given, the uplifted spear
Of their great Sultan waving to direct
Their course, in even balance down they light
On the firm brimstone, and fill all the plain: 350
A multitude like which the populous North
Poured never from her frozen loins to pass
Rhene [1] or the Danaw,[2] when her barbarous sons
Came like a deluge on the South, and spread
Beneath Gibraltar to the Libyan sands.   355
Forthwith, from every squadron and each band,
The heads and leaders thither haste where stood
Their great Commander — godlike Shapes, and
        Forms
Excelling human; princely Dignities;
And Powers that erst in Heaven sat on thrones, 360
Though of their names in Heavenly records now
Be no memorial, blotted out and rased
By their rebellion from the Books of Life.
Nor had they yet among the sons of Eve
Got them new names, till, wandering o'er the
        earth,   365
Through God's high sufferance for the trial of man,
By falsities and lies the greatest part
Of mankind they corrupted to forsake
God their Creator, and the invisible
Glory of Him that made them to transform   370
Oft to the image of a brute, adorned
With gay religions full of pomp and gold,
And devils to adore for deities:
Then were they known to men by various names,
And various idols through the heathen world.   375
    Say, Muse, their names then known, who first,
        who last,
Roused from the slumber on that fiery couch,
At their great Emperor's call, as next in worth
Came singly where he stood on the bare strand,
While the promiscuous crowd stood yet aloof.   380
    The chief were those who, from the pit of Hell
Roaming to seek their prey on Earth, durst fix
Their seats, long after, next the seat of God,
Their altars by His altar, gods adored
Among the nations round, and durst abide   385
Jehovah thundering out of Sion, throned
Between the Cherubim; yea, often placed
Within His sanctuary itself their shrines,
Abominations: and with cursèd things
His holy rites and solemn feasts profaned,   390
And with their darkness durst affront His light.
First, *Moloch*, horrid King, besmeared with blood
Of human sacrifice, and parents' tears;

[1] Rhine.   [2] Danube.

Though, for the noise of drums and timbrels loud,
Their children's cries unheard that passed through
        fire   395
To his grim idol. Him the Ammonite
Worshiped in Rabba and her watery plain
In Argob and in Basan, to the stream
Of utmost Arnon.[1] Nor content with such
Audacious neighborhood, the wisest heart   400
Of Solomon he led by fraud to build
His temple right against the temple of God
On that opprobrious hill, and made his grove
The pleasant valley of Hinnom, Tophet thence
And black Gehenna called, the type of Hell.   405
Next *Chemos*, the obscene dread of Moab's sons,
From Aroar to Nebo and the wild
Of southmost Abarim; in Hesebon
And Horonaim, Seon's realm, beyond
The flowery dale of Sibma clad with vines,   410
And Elealè to the Asphaltic Pool:[2]
Peor his other name, when he enticed
Israel in Sittim, on their march from Nile,
To do him wanton rites, which cost them woe.
Yet thence his lustful orgies he enlarged   415
Even to that hill of scandal, by the grove
Of Moloch homicide, lust hard by hate,
Till good Josiah drove them thence to Hell.
With these came they who, from the bordering
        flood
Of old Euphrates to the brook that parts   420
Egypt from Syrian ground, had general names
Of *Baalim* and *Ashtaroth* — those male,
These feminine. For Spirits, when they please,
Can either sex assume, or both; so soft
And uncompounded is their essence pure,   425
Not tied or manacled with joint or limb,
Nor founded on the brittle strength of bones,
Like cumbrous flesh; but, in what shape they
        choose,
Dilated or condensed, bright or obscure,
Can execute their aery purposes,   430
And works of love or enmity fulfil.
For those the race of Israel oft forsook
Their Living Strength, and unfrequented left
His righteous altar, bowing lowly down
To bestial gods; for which their heads, as low   435
Bowed down in battle, sunk before the spear
Of despicable foes. With these in troop
Came *Astoreth*, whom the Phœnicians called
Astarte, queen of heaven, with crescent horns;
To whose bright image nightly by the moon   440

[1] The student who so desires can trace most of the
names in these lines with the aid of a good Biblical
concordance, but the geographical location is less important than the poetical effect Milton gains through
sound and suggestion.
[2] Dead Sea.

Sidonian virgins paid their vows and songs;
In Sion also not unsung, where stood
Her temple on the offensive mountain, built
By that uxorious king [1] whose heart, though large,
Beguiled by fair idolatresses, fell   445
To idols foul.   *Thammuz* [2] came next behind,
Whose annual wound in Lebanon allured
The Syrian damsels to lament his fate
In amorous ditties all a summer's day,
While smooth Adonis from his native rock   450
Ran purple to the sea, supposed with blood
Of Thammuz yearly wounded: the love-tale
Infected Sion's daughters with like heat,
Whose wanton passions in the sacred porch
Ezekiel saw, when, by the vision led,   455
His eye surveyed the dark idolatries
Of alienated Judah.   Next came one
Who mourned in earnest, when the captive Ark
Maimed his brute image, head and hands lopt off,
In his own temple, on the grunsel-edge,[3]   460
Where he fell flat and shamed his worshipers:
Dagon [4] his name, sea-monster, upward man
And downward fish; yet had his temple high
Reared in Azotus, dreaded through the coast
Of Palestine, in Gath and Ascalon,   465
And Accaron and Gaza's frontier bounds.
Him followed *Rimmon*, whose delightful seat
Was fair Damascus, on the fertile banks
Of Abbana and Pharphar, lucid streams.
He also against the house of God was bold: 470
A leper once he lost, and gained a king [5] —
Ahaz, his sottish conqueror, whom he drew
God's altar to disparage and displace
For one of Syrian mode, whereon to burn
His odious offerings, and adore the gods   475
Whom he had vanquished.   After these appeared
A crew who, under names of old renown —
Osiris, Isis, Orus, and their train —
With monstrous shapes and sorceries abused
Fanatic Egypt and her priests to seek   480
Their wandering gods disguised in brutish forms
Rather than human.   Nor did Israel scape
The infection, when their borrowed gold composed
The calf in Oreb, and the rebel king
Doubled that sin in Bethel and in Dan,   485
Likening his Maker to the grazèd ox —
Jehovah, who, in one night, when he passed
From Egypt marching, equalled [6] with one stroke

[1] Solomon.
[2] According to Phœnician legendry the wounds of
Thammuz, who had been killed by a boar, bled afresh
each year and stained red the water in the river Adonis.
[3] Ground-sill.
[4] A god of the Philistines.   See I Samuel v, 4–7.
[5] II Kings v.
[6] Laid low.   See Exodus xii, 29.

Both her first-born and all her bleating gods.
Belial came last; than whom a Spirit more lewd 490
Fell not from Heaven, or more gross to love
Vice for itself.   To him no temple stood
Or altar smoked; yet who more oft than he
In temples and at altars, when the priest
Turns atheist, as did Eli's sons,[1] who filled 495
With lust and violence the house of God?
In courts and palaces he also reigns,
And in luxurious cities, where the noise
Of riot ascends above their loftiest towers,
And injury and outrage; and, when night   500
Darkens the streets, then wander forth the sons
Of Belial,[2] flown with insolence and wine.
Witness the streets of Sodom, and that night
In Gibeah, when the hospitable door
Exposed a matron, to avoid worse rape.[3]   505
     These were the prime in order and in might:
The rest were long to tell; though far renowned
The Ionian gods — of Javan's issue held
Gods, yet confessed later than Heaven and Earth,
Their boasted parents; — *Titan*, Heaven's first-
     born,   510
With his enormous brood, and birthright seized
By younger *Saturn*: he from mightier Jove,
His own and Rhea's son, like measure found;
So *Jove* usurping reigned.   These, first in Crete
And Ida known, thence on the snowy top   515
Of cold Olympus ruled the middle air,
Their highest heaven; or on the Delphian cliff,
Or in Dodona, and through all the bounds
Of Doric land; or who with Saturn old
Fled over Adria to the Hesperian fields,   520
And o'er the Celtic roamed the utmost Isles.
     All these and more came flocking; but with looks
Downcast and damp; yet such wherein appeared
Obscure some glimpse of joy to have found their
     Chief
Not in despair, to have found themselves not lost
In loss itself; which on his countenance cast 526
Like doubtful hue.   But he, his wonted pride
Soon recollecting, with high words, that bore
Semblance of worth, not substance, gently raised
Their fainting courage, and dispelled their fears: 530
Then straight commands that, at the warlike sound
Of trumpets loud and clarions, be upreared
His mighty standard.   That proud honor claimed
Azazel as his right, a Cherub tall;
Who forthwith from the glittering staff unfurled 535
The imperial ensign; which, full high advanced,
Shone like a meteor streaming to the wind,
With gems and golden lustre rich emblazed,
Seraphic arms and trophies; all the while
Sonorous metal blowing martial sounds: 540

[1] I Samuel ii, 12–17.   [2] Tipsy.
[3] See Judges xix.

At which the universal host up-sent
A shout that tore Hell's concave, and beyond
Frighted the reign of Chaos and old Night.
All in a moment through the gloom were seen
Ten thousand banners rise into the air,   545
With orient [1] colors waving: with them rose
A forest huge of spears; and thronging helms
Appeared, and serried shields in thick array
Of depth immeasurable.   Anon they move
In perfect phalanx to the Dorian [2] mood   550
Of flutes and soft recorders [3] — such as raised
To highth of noblest temper heroes old
Arming to battle, and instead of rage
Deliberate valor breathed, firm, and unmoved
With dread of death to flight or foul retreat;   555
Nor wanting power to mitigate and swage
With solemn touches troubled thoughts, and chase
Anguish and doubt and fear and sorrow and pain
From mortal or immortal minds.   Thus they,
Breathing united force with fixèd thought,   560
Moved on in silence to soft pipes that charmed
Their painful steps o'er the burnt soil.   And now
Advanced in view they stand — a horrid front
Of dreadful length and dazzling arms, in guise
Of warriors old, with ordered spear and shield,   565
Awaiting what command their mighty Chief
Had to impose.   He through the armèd files
Darts his experienced eye, and soon traverse [4]
The whole battalion views — their order due,
Their visages and stature as of Gods;   570
Their number last he sums.   And now his heart
Distends with pride, and, hardening in his strength,
Glories: for never, since created Man,
Met such embodied force as, named with these,
Could merit more than that small infantry   575
Warred on by cranes [5] — though all the giant
          brood
Of Phlegra with the heroic race were joined
That fought at Thebes and Ilium, on each side
Mixed with auxiliar gods; and what resounds
In fable or romance of Uther's son,[6]   580
Begirt with British and Armoric knights; [7]
And all who since, baptized or infidel,
Jousted in Aspramont,[8] or Montalban,[8]
Damasco,[8] or Marocco,[8] or Trebisond,[8]
Or whom Biserta sent from Afric shore   585
When Charlemain with all his peerage fell
By Fontarabbia.[9]   Thus far these beyond

---

[1] Bright.   [2] Grave.   [3] Flageolets.   [4] Across.
[5] An allusion to the supposed warfare between cranes
and pygmies in Ethiopia.
   [6] King Arthur.   [7] Knights of Brittany.
   [8] Places celebrated in medieval romance as scenes of
chivalric battle.
   [9] Legend has it that Charlemagne's rear guard was
annihilated at Roncevalles.

Compare of mortal prowess, yet observed
Their dread Commander.   He, above the rest
In shape and gesture proudly eminent,   590
Stood like a tower.   His form had yet not lost
All her original brightness, nor appeared
Less than Archangel ruined, and the excess
Of glory obscured: as when the sun new-risen
Looks through the horizontal misty air   595
Shorn of his beams, or, from behind the moon,
In dim eclipse, disastrous twilight sheds
On half the nations, and with fear of change
Perplexes monarchs.   Darkened so, yet shone
Above them all the Archangel: but his face   600
Deep scars of thunder had intrenched, and care
Sat on his faded cheek, but under brows
Of dauntless courage, and considerate pride
Waiting revenge.   Cruel his eye, but cast
Signs of remorse and passion, to behold   605
The fellows of his crime, the followers rather
(Far other once beheld in bliss), condemned
For ever now to have their lot in pain —
Millions of Spirits for his fault amerced [1]
Of Heaven, and from eternal splendors flung   610
For his revolt — yet faithful how they stood,
Their glory withered; as, when heaven's fire
Hath scathed the forest oaks or mountain pines,
With singèd top their stately growth, though bare,
Stands on the blasted heath.   He now prepared 615
To speak; whereat their doubled ranks they bend
From wing to wing, and half enclose him round
With all his peers: Attention held them mute.
Thrice he assayed, and thrice, in spite of scorn,
Tears, such as Angels weep, burst forth: at last 620
Words interwove with sighs found out their way: —
   "O myriads of immortal Spirits!   O Powers
Matchless, but with the Almighty! — and that
          strife
Was not inglorious, though the event was dire,
As this place testifies, and this dire change,   625
Hateful to utter.   But what power of mind,
Foreseeing or presaging, from the depth
Of knowledge past or present, could have feared
How such united force of gods, how such
As stood like these, could ever know repulse?   630
For who can yet believe, though after loss,
That all these puissant legions, whose exile
Hath emptied Heaven, shall fail to reascend,
Self-raised, and re-possess their native seat?
For me, be witness all the host of Heaven,   635
If counsels different, or danger shunned
By me, have lost our hopes.   But he who reigns
Monarch in Heaven till then as one secure
Sat on his throne, upheld by old repute,
Consent or custom, and his regal state   640
Put forth at full, but still his strength concealed —
   [1] Deprived.

Which tempted our attempt, and wrought our fall.
Henceforth his might we know, and know our own,
So as not either to provoke, or dread
New war provoked: our better part remains   645
To work in close design, by fraud or guile,
What force effected not; that he no less
At length from us may find, Who overcomes
By force hath overcome but half his foe.
Space may produce new Worlds; whereof so rife 650
There went a fame in Heaven that He ere long
Intended to create, and therein plant
A generation whom his choice regard
Should favor equal to the Sons of Heaven.
Thither, if but to pry, shall be perhaps   655
Our first eruption — thither, or elsewhere;
For this infernal pit shall never hold
Celestial Spirits in bondage, nor the Abyss
Long under darkness cover.   But these thoughts
Full counsel must mature.   Peace is despaired; 660
For who can think submission?   War, then, war
Open or understood, must be resolved."

    He spake; and, to confirm his words, outflew
Millions of flaming swords, drawn from the thighs
Of mighty Cherubim; the sudden blaze   665
Far round illumined Hell.   Highly they raged
Against the Highest and fierce with graspèd arms
Clashed on their sounding shields the din of war,
Hurling defiance toward the vault of Heaven.

    There stood a hill not far, whose grisly top   670
Belched fire and rolling smoke; the rest entire
Shone with a glossy scurf — undoubted sign
That in his womb was hid metallic ore,
The work of sulphur.[1]   Thither, winged with
        speed,
A numerous brigad hastened: as when bands   675
Of pioneers, with spade and pickaxe armed,
Forerun the royal camp, to trench a field,
Or cast a rampart.   Mammon led them on —
Mammon, the least erected Spirit that fell
From Heaven; for even in Heaven his looks and
        thoughts   680
Were always downward bent, admiring more
The riches of Heaven's pavement, trodden gold,
Than aught divine or holy else enjoyed
In vision beatific.   By him first
Men also, and by his suggestion taught,   685
Ransacked the Centre,[2] and with impious hands
Rifled the bowels of their mother Earth
For treasures better hid.   Soon had his crew
Opened into the hill a spacious wound,
And digged out ribs of gold.   Let none admire 690
That riches grow in Hell; that soil may best

[1] According to an early principle of chemistry sulphur was the basic element of metals.
[2] The earth according to Ptolemaic doctrine was the center of the universe.

Deserve the precious bane.   And here let those
Who boast in mortal things, and wondering tell
Of Babel, and the works of Memphian kings,[1]
Learn how their greatest monuments of fame,   695
And strength, and art, are easily outdone
By Spirits reprobate, and in an hour
What in an age they, with incessant toil
And hands innumerable, scarce perform.
Nigh on the plain, in many cells prepared,   700
That underneath had veins of liquid fire
Sluiced from the lake, a second multitude
With wondrous art founded the massy ore,
Severing each kind, and scummed the bullion-dross.
A third as soon had formed within the ground   705
A various mould, and from the boiling cells
By strange conveyance filled each hollow nook;
As in an organ, from one blast of wind,
To many a row of pipes the sound-board breathes.
Anon out of the earth a fabric huge   710
Rose like an exhalation, with the sound
Of dulcet symphonies and voices sweet —
Built like a temple, where pilasters round
Were set, and Doric pillars overlaid
With golden architrave; nor did there want   715
Cornice or frieze, with bossy sculptures graven:
The roof was fretted gold.   Not Babylon
Nor great Alcairo such magnificence
Equalled in all their glories, to enshrine
Belus or Serapis their gods, or seat   720
Their kings, when Egypt with Assyria strove
In wealth and luxury.   The ascending pile
Stood fixed her stately highth; and straight the
        doors,
Opening their brazen folds, discover, wide
Within, her ample spaces o'er the smooth   725
And level pavement: from the archèd roof,
Pendent by subtle magic, many a row
Of starry lamps and blazing cressets, fed
With naphtha and asphaltus, yielded light
As from a sky.   The hasty multitude   730
Admiring entered; and the work some praise,
And some the Architect.   His hand was known
In Heaven by many a towered structure high,
Where sceptred Angels held their residence,
And sat as Princes, whom the supreme King   735
Exalted to such power, and gave to rule,
Each in his hierarchy, the Orders bright.
Nor was his name unheard or unadored
In ancient Greece; and in Ausonian land[2]
Men called him Mulciber;[3] and how he fell   740
From Heaven they fabled, thrown by angry Jove
Sheer o'er the crystal battlements: from morn
To noon he fell, from noon to dewy eve,
A summer's day, and with the setting sun
Dropt from the zenith, like a falling star,   745

[1] The Pyramids.   [2] Italy.   [3] Vulcan.

On Lemnos, the Ægæan isle. Thus they relate,
Erring; for he with this rebellious rout
Fell long before; nor aught availed him now
To have built in Heaven high towers; nor did he
    scape
By all his engines, but was headlong sent,   750
With his industrious crew, to build in Hell.
    Meanwhile the wingèd Haralds, by command
Of sovran power, with awful ceremony
And trumpet's sound, throughout the host proclaim
A solemn council forthwith to be held   755
At Pandæmonium, the high capital
Of Satan and his peers. Their summons called
From every band and squarèd regiment
By place or choice the worthiest: they anon
With hundreds and with thousands trooping came
Attended. All access was thronged; the gates   761
And porches wide, but chief the spacious hall
(Though like a covered field, where champions boid
Wont ride in armed, and at the Soldan's [1] chair
Defied the best of Panim chivalry   765
To mortal combat, or career with lance),
Thick swarmed, both on the ground and in the air,
Brushed with the hiss of rustling wings. As bees
In spring-time, when the Sun with Taurus rides,
Pour forth their populous youth about the hive 770
In clusters; they among fresh dews and flowers
Fly to and fro, or on the smoothèd plank,
The suburb of their straw-built citadel,
New rubbed with balm, expatiate, and confer
Their state-affairs: so thick the aerie crowd 775
Swarmed and were straitened; till, the signal given,
Behold a wonder! They but now who seemed
In bigness to surpass Earth's giant sons,
Now less than smallest dwarfs, in narrow room
Throng numberless — like that pygmean race 780
Beyond the Indian mount; or faery elves,
Whose midnight revels, by a forest-side
Or fountain, some belated peasant sees,
Or dreams he sees, while overhead the moon
Sits arbitress and nearer to the Earth 785
Wheels her pale course: they, on their mirth and
    dance
Intent, with jocund music charm his ear;
At once with joy and fear his heart rebounds.
Thus incorporeal Spirits to smallest forms
Reduced their shapes immense, and were at large,
Though without number still, amidst the hall 791
Of that infernal court. But far within,
And in their own dimensions like themselves,
The great Seraphic Lords and Cherubim
In close recess [2] and secret conclave sat, 795
A thousand demi-gods on golden seats,
Frequent [3] and full. After short silence then,
And summons read, the great consult began.

   [1] Sultan's.   [2] retirement.   [3] packed or crowded.

BOOK II

The Argument

   The consultation begun, Satan debates whether another battle be to be hazarded for the recovery of
Heaven: some advise it, others dissuade. A third proposal is preferred, mentioned before by Satan — to
search the truth of that prophecy or tradition in Heaven
concerning another world, and another kind of creature,
equal, or not much inferior, to themselves, about this
time to be created. Their doubt who shall be sent on
this difficult search: Satan, their chief, undertakes alone
the voyage; is honored and applauded. The council
thus ended, the rest betake them several ways and to
several employments, as their inclinations lead them, to
entertain the time till Satan return. He passes on his
journey to Hell-gates; finds them shut, and who sat
there to guard them; by whom at length they are opened,
and discover to him the great gulf between Hell and
Heaven. With what difficulty he passes through,
directed by Chaos, the Power of that place, to the sight
of this new World which he sought.

High on a throne of royal state, which far
Outshone the wealth of Ormus [1] and of Ind,
Or where the gorgeous East with richest hand
Showers on her kings barbaric pearl and gold,
Satan exalted sat, by merit raised   5
To that bad eminence; and, from despair
Thus high uplifted beyond hope, aspires
Beyond thus high, insatiate to pursue
Vain war with Heaven; and, by success untaught,
His proud imaginations thus displayed: —   10
   "Powers and Dominions, Deities of Heaven! —
For, since no deep within her gulf can hold
Immortal vigor, though oppressed and fallen,
I give not Heaven for lost: from this descent
Celestial Virtues rising will appear   15
More glorious and more dread than from no fall,
And trust themselves to fear no second fate! —
Me though just right, and the fixed laws of Heaven,
Did first create your leader — next, free choice,
With what besides in council or in fight   20
Hath been achieved of merit — yet this loss,
Thus far at least recovered, hath much more
Established in a safe, unenvied throne,
Yielded with full consent. The happier state
In Heaven, which follows dignity, might draw 25
Envy from each inferior; but who here
Will envy whom the highest place exposes
Foremost to stand against the Thunderer's aim
Your bulwark, and condemns to greatest share
Of endless pain? Where there is, then, no good 30
For which to strive, no strife can grow up there
From faction: for none sure will claim in Hell
Precedence; none whose portion is so small

   [1] An island in the Persian Gulf formerly famed as a
diamond market.

Of present pain that with ambitious mind
Will covet more! With this advantage, then, 35
To union, and firm faith, and firm accord,
More than can be in Heaven, we now return
To claim our just inheritance of old,
Surer to prosper than prosperity
Could have assured us; and by what best way,
Whether of open war or covert guile, 41
We now debate. Who can advise may speak."

He ceased; and next him Moloch, sceptred king,
Stood up — the strongest and the fiercest Spirit
That fought in Heaven, now fiercer by despair. 45
His trust was with the Eternal to be deemed
Equal in strength, and rather than be less
Cared not to be at all; with that care lost
Went all his fear: of God, or Hell, or worse,
He recked not, and these words thereafter spake: —
"My sentence is for open war. Of wiles, 51
More unexpert, I boast not: them let those
Contrive who need, or when they need; not now.
For, while they sit contriving, shall the rest —
Millions that stand in arms, and longing wait 55
The signal to ascend — sit lingering here,
Heaven's fugitives, and for their dwelling-place
Accept this dark opprobrious den of shame,
The prison of His tyranny who reigns
By our delay? No! let us rather choose, 60
Armed with Hell-flames and fury, all at once
O'er Heaven's high towers to force resistless way,
Turning our tortures into horrid arms
Against the Torturer; when, to meet the noise
Of his almighty engine, he shall hear 65
Infernal thunder, and, for lightning, see
Black fire and horror shot with equal rage
Among his Angels, and his throne itself
Mixed with Tartarean sulphur and strange fire,
His own invented torments. But perhaps 70
The way seems difficult, and steep to scale
With upright wing against a higher foe!
Let such bethink them, if the sleepy drench
Of that forgetful lake benumb not still,
That in our proper motion [1] we ascend 75
Up to our native seat; descent and fall
To us is adverse. Who but felt of late,
When the fierce foe hung on our broken rear
Insulting, and pursued us through the Deep,
With what compulsion and laborious flight 80
We sunk thus low? The ascent is easy, then;
The event is feared! Should we again provoke
Our stronger, some worse way his wrath may find
To our destruction, if there be in Hell
Fear to be worse destroyed! What can be worse 85
Than to dwell here, driven out from bliss, con-
demned

[1] As creatures of the ethereal composition of angels
their "proper motion" was upward.

In this abhorrèd deep to utter woe;
Where pain of unextinguishable fire
Must exercise us without hope of end
The vassals of his anger, when the scourge 90
Inexorably, and the torturing hour,
Calls us to penance? More destroyed than thus,
We should be quite abolished, and expire.
What fear we then? what doubt we to incense
His utmost ire? which, to the highth enraged, 95
Will either quite consume us, and reduce
To nothing this essential — happier far
Than miserable to have eternal being! —
Or, if our substance be indeed divine,
And cannot cease to be, we are at worst 100
On this side nothing; and by proof we feel
Our power sufficient to disturb his Heaven,
And with perpetual inroads to alarm,
Though inaccessible, his fatal Throne:
Which, if not victory, is yet revenge." 105

He ended frowning, and his look denounced [1]
Desperate revenge, and battle dangerous
To less than gods. On the other side up rose
Belial, in act more graceful and humane.
A fairer person lost not heaven; he seemed 110
For dignity composed, and high exploit.
But all was false and hollow; though his tongue
Dropt manna, and could make the worse appear
The better reason, to perplex and dash
Maturest counsels: for his thoughts were low —
To vice industrious, but to nobler deeds 116
Timorous and slothful. Yet he pleased the ear,
And with persuasive accent thus began: —
"I should be much for open war, O Peers,
As not behind in hate, if what was urged 120
Main reason to persuade immediate war
Did not dissuade me most, and seem to cast
Ominous conjecture on the whole success;
When he who most excels in fact of arms,
In what he counsels and in what excels 125
Mistrustful, grounds his courage on despair
And utter dissolution, as the scope
Of all his aim, after some dire revenge.
First, what revenge? The towers of Heaven are
filled
With armèd watch, that render all access 130
Impregnable: oft on the bordering Deep
Encamp their legions, or with obscure wing
Scout far and wide into the realm of Night,
Scorning surprise. Or, could we break our way
By force, and at our heels all Hell should rise 135
With blackest insurrection to confound
Heaven's purest light, yet our great Enemy,
All incorruptible, would on his throne
Sit unpolluted, and the ethereal mould,
Incapable of stain, would soon expel 140

[1] promised.

Her mischief, and purge off the baser fire,
Victorious.   Thus repulsed, our final hope
Is flat despair: we must exasperate
The Almighty Victor to spend all his rage;
And that must end us; that must be our cure   145
To be no more.   Sad cure! for who would lose,
Though full of pain, this intellectual being,
Those thoughts that wander through eternity,
To perish rather, swallowed up and lost
In the wide womb of uncreated Night,   150
Devoid of sense and motion?   And who knows,
Let this be good,[1] whether our angry Foe
Can give it, or will ever?   How he can
Is doubtful; that he never will is sure.
Will He, so wise, let loose at once his ire,   155
Belike through impotence or unaware,
To give his enemies their wish, and end
Them in his anger whom his anger saves
To punish endless?   'Wherefore cease we, then?'
Say they who counsel war; 'we are decreed,   160
Reserved, and destined to eternal woe;
Whatever doing, what can we suffer more,
What can we suffer worse?'   Is this, then, worst —
Thus sitting, thus consulting, thus in arms?
What when we fled amain, pursued and strook   165
With Heaven's afflicting thunder, and besought
The Deep to shelter us?   This Hell then seemed
A refuge from those wounds.   Or when we lay
Chained on the burning lake?   That sure was
          worse.
What if the breath that kindled those grim fires,
Awaked, should blow them into sevenfold rage,   171
And plunge us in the flames; or from above
Should intermitted vengeance arm again
His red right hand to plague us?   What if all
Her stores were opened, and this firmament   175
Of Hell should spout her cataracts of fire,
Impendent horrors, threatening hideous fall
One day upon our heads; while we perhaps,
Designing or exhorting glorious war,
Caught in a fiery tempest, shall be hurled,   180
Each on his rock transfixed, the sport and prey
Of racking whirlwinds, or for ever sunk
Under yon boiling ocean, wrapt in chains,
There to converse with everlasting groans,
Unrespited, unpitied, unreprieved,   185
Ages of hopeless end?   This would be worse.
War, therefore, open or concealed, alike
My voice dissuades; for what can force or guile
With Him, or who deceive His mind, whose eye
Views all things at one view?   He from Heaven's
          highth   190
All these our motions vain sees and derides,
Not more almighty to resist our might
Than wise to frustrate all our plots and wiles.

[1] Even if death be advantageous.

Shall we, then, live thus vile — the race of Heaven
Thus trampled, thus expelled, to suffer here   195
Chains and these torments?   Better these than
          worse,
By my advice; since fate inevitable
Subdues us, and omnipotent decree,
The Victor's will.   To suffer, as to do,
Our strength is equal; nor the law unjust   200
That so ordains.   This was at first resolved,
If we were wise, against so great a foe
Contending, and so doubtful what might fall.
I laugh when those who at the spear are bold
And venturous, if that fail them, shrink, and fear
What yet they know must follow — to endure   206
Exile, or ignominy, or bonds, or pain,
The sentence of their conqueror.   This is now
Our doom; which if we can sustain and bear,
Our Supreme Foe in time may much remit   210
His anger, and perhaps, thus far removed,
Not mind us not offending, satisfied
With what is punished; whence these raging fires
Will slacken, if his breath stir not their flames.
Our purer essence then will overcome   215
Their noxious vapor; or, inured, not feel;
Or, changed at length, and to the place conformed
In temper and in nature, will receive
Familiar the fierce heat; and, void of pain,
This horror will grow mild, this darkness light;   220
Besides what hope the never-ending flight
Of future days may bring, what chance, what
          change
Worth waiting — since our present lot appears
For happy though but ill, for ill not worst,
If we procure not to ourselves more woe."   225
     Thus Belial, with words clothed in reason's garb,
Counselled ignoble ease and peaceful sloth,
Not peace; and after him thus Mammon spake: —
     "Either to disenthrone the King of Heaven
We war, if war be best, or to regain   230
Our own right lost.   Him to unthrone we then
May hope, when everlasting Fate shall yield
To fickle Chance, and Chaos judge the strife.
The former, vain to hope, argues as vain
The latter; for what place can be for us   235
Within Heaven's bound, unless Heaven's Lord
          Supreme
We overpower?   Suppose he should relent,
And publish grace to all, on promise made
Of new subjection; with what eyes could we
Stand in his presence humble, and receive   240
Strict laws imposed, to celebrate his throne
With warbled hymns, and to his Godhead sing
Forced Halleluiahs, while he lordly sits
Our envied sovran, and his altar breathes
Ambrosial odors and ambrosial flowers,   245
Our servile offerings?   This must be our task

In Heaven, this our delight.   How wearisome
Eternity so spent in worship paid
To whom we hate!   Let us not then pursue,
By force impossible, by leave obtained   250
Unacceptáble, though in Heaven, our state
Of splendid vassalage; but rather seek
Our own good from ourselves, and from our own
Live to ourselves, though in this vast recess,
Free and to none accountable, preferring   255
Hard liberty before the easy yoke
Of servile pomp.   Our greatness will appear
Then most conspicuous when great things of small,
Useful of hurtful, prosperous of adverse,
We can create, and in what place soe'er   260
Thrive under evil, and work ease out of pain
Through labor and endurance.   This deep world
Of darkness do we dread?   How oft amidst
Thick clouds and dark doth Heaven's all-ruling Sire
Choose to reside, his glory unobscured,   265
And with the majesty of darkness round
Covers his throne, from whence deep thunders roar,
Mustering their rage, and Heaven resembles Hell!
As He our darkness, cannot we His light
Imitate when we please?   This desert soil   270
Wants not her hidden lustre, gems and gold;
Nor want we skill or art from whence to raise
Magnificence; and what can Heaven shew more?
Our torments also may, in length of time,
Become our elements, these piercing fires   275
As soft as now severe, our temper changed
Into their temper; which must needs remove
The sensible [1] of pain.   All things invite
To peaceful counsels, and the settled state
Of order, how in safety best we may   280
Compose our present evils, with regard
Of what we are and where, dismissing quite
All thoughts of war.   Ye have what I advise."
　　He scarce had finished, when such murmur filled
The assembly as when hollow rocks retain   285
The sound of blustering winds, which all night long
Had roused the sea, now with hoarse cadence lull
Seafaring men o'erwatched, whose bark by chance,
Or pinnace, anchors in a craggy bay
After the tempest.   Such applause was heard   290
As Mammon ended, and his sentence pleased,
Advising peace: for such another field
They dreaded worse than Hell; so much the fear
Of thunder and the sword of Michaël
Wrought still within them; and no less desire   295
To found this nether empire, which might rise
By policy and long process' of time,
In emulation opposite to Heaven.
Which when Beëlzebub perceived — than whom,
Satan except, none higher sat — with grave   300
Aspect he rose, and in his rising seemed
　　[1] sense.

A pillar of state.   Deep on his front engraven
Deliberation sat, and public care;
And princely counsel in his face yet shone,
Majestic, though in ruin.   Sage he stood,   305
With Atlantean [1] shoulders, fit to bear
The weight of mightiest monarchies; his look
Drew audience and attention still as night
Or summer's noontide air, while thus he spake: —
　　"Thrones and Imperial Powers, Offspring of
　　　　Heaven,   310
Ethereal Virtues! or these titles now
Must we renounce, and, changing style, be called
Princes of Hell? for so the popular vote
Inclines — here to continue, and build up here
A growing empire; doubtless! while we dream,   315
And know not that the King of Heaven hath
　　doomed
This place our dungeon — not our safe retreat
Beyond his potent arm, to live exempt
From Heaven's high jurisdiction, in new league
Banded against his throne, but to remain   320
In strictest bondage, though thus far removed,
Under the inevitable curb, reserved
His captive multitude.   For He, be sure,
In highth or depth, still first and last will reign
Sole king, and of his kingdom lose no part   325
By our revolt, but over Hell extend
His empire, and with iron sceptre rule
Us here, as with his golden those in Heaven.
What [2] sit we then projecting peace and war?
War hath determined [3] us and foiled with loss
Irreparable; terms of peace yet none   331
Vouchsafed or sought; for what peace will be given
To us enslaved, but custody severe,
And stripes and arbitrary punishment
Inflicted? and what peace can we return,   335
But, to our power, hostility and hate,
Untamed reluctance, and revenge, though slow,
Yet ever plotting how the Conquerer least
May reap his conquest, and may least rejoice
In doing what we most in suffering feel?   340
Nor will occasion want, nor shall we need
With dangerous expedition to invade
Heaven, whose high walls fear no assault or siege,
Or ambush from the Deep.   What if we find
Some easier enterprise?   There is a place   345
(If ancient and prophetic fame in Heaven
Err not) — another World, the happy seat
Of some new race, called Man, about this time
To be created like to us, though less
In power and excellence, but favored more   350
Of Him who rules above; so was His will

　　[1] Giant-like.   Atlas was charged with the responsibility of supporting the heavens on his shoulders.
　　[2] why, wherefore.
　　[3] "Determined" our present fate.

Pronounced among the gods, and by an oath
That shook Heaven's whole circumference confirmed.
Thither let us bend all our thoughts, to learn
What creatures there inhabit, of what mould   355
Or substance, how endued, and what their power
And where their weakness: how attempted best,
By force or subtlety.   Though Heaven be shut,
And Heaven's high Arbitrator sit secure
In his own strength, this place may lie exposed,   360
The utmost border of his kingdom, left
To their defence who hold it: here, perhaps,
Some advantageous act may be achieved
By sudden onset — either with Hell-fire
To waste his whole creation, or possess   365
All as our own, and drive, as we are driven,
The puny habitants; or, if not drive,
Seduce them to our party, that their God
May prove their foe, and with repenting hand
Abolish his own works.   This would surpass   370
Common revenge, and interrupt His joy
In our confusion, and our joy upraise
In His disturbance; when his darling sons,
Hurled headlong to partake with us, shall curse
Their frail original, and faded bliss —   375
Faded so soon!   Advise if this be worth
Attempting, or to sit in darkness here
Hatching vain empires."   Thus Beëlzebub
Pleaded his devilish counsel — first devised
By Satan, and in part proposed: for whence,   380
But from the author of all ill, could spring
So deep a malice, to confound the race
Of mankind in one root, and Earth with Hell
To mingle and involve, done all to spite
The great Creator?   But their spite still serves   385
His glory to augment.   The bold design
Pleased highly those Infernal States, and joy
Sparkled in all their eyes: with full assent
They vote: whereat his speech he thus renews: —
"Well have ye judged, well ended long debate,   390
Synod of Gods, and, like to what ye are,
Great things resolved, which from the lowest deep
Will once more lift us up, in spite of fate,
Nearer our ancient Seat — perhaps in view
Of those bright confines, whence, with neighboring arms,   395
And opportune excursion, we may chance
Re-enter Heaven; or else in some mild zone
Dwell, not unvisited of Heaven's fair light,
Secure, and at the brightening orient beam
Purge off this gloom: the soft delicious air,   400
To heal the scar of these corrosive fires,
Shall breathe her balm.   But, first, whom shall we send
In search of this new World? whom shall we find
Sufficient? who shall tempt with wandering feet

The dark, unbottomed, infinite Abyss,   405
And through the palpable obscure find out
His uncouth way, or spread his aerie flight,
Upborne with indefatigable wings
Over the vast Abrupt,[1] ere he arrive
The happy Isle?   What strength, what art can then   410
Suffice, or what evasion bear him safe
Through the strict senteries and stations thick
Of angels watching round?   Here he had need
All circumspection: and we now no less
Choice in our suffrage; for on whom we send   415
The weight of all, and our last hope, relies."
   This said, he sat; and expectation held
His look suspense, awaiting who appeared
To second, or oppose, or undertake
The perilous attempt.   But all sat mute,   420
Pondering the danger with deep thoughts; and each
In other's countenance read his own dismay,
Astonished.   None among the choice and prime
Of those Heaven-warring champions could be found
So hardy as to proffer or accept,   425
Alone, the dreadful voyage; till, at last,
Satan, whom now transcendent glory raised
Above his fellows, with monarchal pride
Conscious of highest worth, unmoved thus spake: —
"O Progeny of Heaven!   Empyreal Thrones!
With reason hath deep silence and demur   431
Seized us, though undismayed.   Long is the way
And hard, that out of Hell leads up to Light.
Our prison strong, this huge convex of fire,
Outrageous to devour, immures us round   435
Ninefold; and gates of burning adamant,
Barred over us, prohibit all egress.
These passed, if any pass, the void profound
Of unessential Night receives him next,
Wide-gaping, and with utter loss of being   440
Threatens him, plunged in that abortive gulf.
If thence he scape, into whatever world,
Or unknown region, what remains him less
Than unknown dangers, and as hard escape?
But I should ill become this throne, O Peers,   445
And this imperial sovranty, adorned
With splendor, armed with power, if aught proposed
And judged of public moment in the shape
Of difficulty or danger, could deter
Me from attempting.   Wherefore do I assume   450
These royalties, and not refuse to reign,
Refusing to accept as great a share
Of hazard as of honor, due alike
To him who reigns, and so much to him due
Of hazard more as he above the rest   455
High honored sits?   Go, therefore, mighty Powers,

[1] "Abrupt" place or barrier.

Terror of Heaven, though fallen; intend [1] at home,
While here shall be our home, what best may ease
The present misery, and render Hell
More tolerable; if there be cure or charm   460
To respite, or deceive, or slack the pain
Of this ill mansion: intermit no watch
Against a wakeful Foe, while I abroad
Through all the coasts of dark destruction seek
Deliverance for us all.   This enterprise   465
None shall partake with me."   Thus saying, rose
The Monarch, and prevented all reply;
Prudent lest, from his resolution raised,[2]
Others among the chief might offer now,
Certain to be refused, what erst they feared,   470
And, so refused, might in opinion stand
His rivals, winning cheap the high repute
Which he through hazard huge must earn.   But
          they
Dreaded not more the adventure than his voice
Forbidding; and at once with him they rose.   475
Their rising all at once was as the sound
Of thunder heard remote.   Towards him they bend
With awful reverence prone, and as a God
Extol him equal to the Highest in Heaven.
Nor failed they to express how much they praised
That for the general safety he despised   481
His own: for neither do the Spirits damned
Lose all their virtue; lest bad men should boast
Their specious deeds on earth, which glory excites,
Or close ambition varnished o'er with zeal.   485
    Thus they their doubtful consultations dark
Ended, rejoicing in their matchless Chief:
As, when from mountain-tops the dusky clouds
Ascending, while the North-wind sleeps, o'er-
          spread
Heaven's cheerful face, the louring element   490
Scowls o'er the darkened landscape snow or shower,
If chance the radiant sun, with farewell sweet,
Extend his evening beam, the fields revive,
The birds their notes renew, and bleating herds
Attest their joy, that hill and valley rings.   495
O shame to men!   Devil with devil damned
Firm concord holds; men only disagree
Of creatures rational, though under hope
Of heavenly grace, and, God proclaiming peace,
Yet live in hatred, enmity, and strife   500
Among themselves, and levy cruel wars
Wasting the earth, each other to destroy:
As if (which might induce us to accord)
Man had not hellish foes enow besides,
That day and night for his destruction wait!   505
    The Stygian council thus dissolved; and forth
In order came the grand Infernal Peers:
Midst came their mighty Paramount,[3] and seemed
Alone the Antagonist of Heaven, nor less

Than Hell's dread Emperor, with pomp supreme,
And god-like imitated state: him round   511
A globe of fiery Seraphim inclosed
With bright emblazonry, and horrent [1] arms.
Then of their session ended they bid cry
With trumpet's regal sound the great result: 515
Toward the four winds four speedy Cherubim
Put to their mouths the sounding alchymy,
By harald's voice explained; the hollow Abyss
Heard far and wide, and all the host of Hell
With deafening shout returned them loud acclaim.
Thence more at ease their minds, and somewhat
          raised   521
By false presumptuous hope, the rangèd Powers
Disband; and, wandering, each his several way
Pursues, as inclination or sad choice
Leads him perplexed, where he may likeliest find
Truce to his restless thoughts, and entertain   526
The irksome hours, till his great Chief return.
Part on the plain, or in the air sublime,
Upon the wing or in swift race contend,
As at the Olympian games or Pythian fields;   530
Part curb their fiery steeds, or shun the goal
With rapid wheels, or fronted brigads form:
As when, to warn proud cities, war appears
Waged in the troubled sky, and armies rush
To battle in the clouds; before each van   535
Prick [2] forth the ærie knights, and couch their
          spears,
Till thickest legions close; with feats of arms
From either end of heaven the welkin burns.
Others, with vast Typhœan [3] rage, more fell,
Rend up both rocks and hills, and ride the air 540
In whirlwind; Hell scarce holds the wild up-
          roar: —
As when Alcides,[4] from Œchalia crowned
With conquest, felt the envenomed robe, and tore
Through pain up by the roots Thessalian pines,
And Lichas from the top of Œta threw   545
Into the Euboic sea.   Others, more mild,
Retreated in a silent valley, sing
With notes angelical to many a harp
Their own heroic deeds, and hapless fall
By doom of battle, and complain that Fate   550
Free Virtue should enthrall to Force or Chance.
Their song was partial, but the harmony
(What could it less when Spirits immortal sing?)
Suspended Hell, and took with ravishment   554
The thronging audience.   In discourse more sweet
(For Eloquence the Soul, Song charms the Sense)
Others apart sat on a hill retired,

[1] Bristling.   [2] Ride.
[3] Resembling Typhœus, a fabled creature with a
hundred snake heads, father of Cerberus. He fought
with Zeus for supremacy of the Underworld.
[4] Hercules.

[1] ponder.   [2] encouraged.   [3] leader.

In thoughts more elevate, and reasoned high
Of Providence, Foreknowledge, Will, and Fate —
Fixed fate, free will, foreknowledge absolute —   560
And found no end, in wandering mazes lost.
Of good and evil much they argued then,
Of happiness and final misery,
Passion and apathy, and glory and shame:
Vain wisdom all, and false philosophy! —   565
Yet, with a pleasing sorcery, could charm
Pain for a while or anguish, and excite
Fallacious hope, or arm the obdurèd breast
With stubborn patience as with triple steel.
Another part, in squadrons and gross bands,   570
On bold adventure to discover wide
That dismal world, if any clime perhaps
Might yield them easier habitation, bend
Four ways their flying march, along the banks
Of four infernal rivers, that disgorge   575
Into the burning lake their baleful streams —
Abhorrèd Styx, the flood of deadly hate;
Sad Acheron of sorrow, black and deep;
Cocytus, named of lamentation loud
Heard on the rueful stream; fierce Phlegeton,   580
Whose waves of torrent fire inflame with rage.
Far off from these, a slow and silent stream,
Lethe, the river of oblivion, rolls
Her watery labyrinth, whereof who drinks   584
Forthwith his former state and being forgets —
Forgets both joy and grief, pleasure and pain.
Beyond this flood a frozen continent
Lies dark and wild, beat with perpetual storms
Of whirlwind and dire hail, which on firm land
Thaws not, but gathers heap, and ruin seems   590
Of ancient pile; all else deep snow and ice,
A gulf profound as that Serbonian[1] bog
Betwixt Damiata and Mount Casius old,
Where armies whole have sunk: the parching air
Burns frore, and cold performs the effect of fire.
Thither, by harpy-footed Furies haled,   596
At certain revolutions all the damned
Are brought; and feel by turns the bitter change
Of fierce extremes, extremes by change more fierce,
From beds of raging fire to starve in ice   600
Their soft ethereal warmth, and there to pine
Immovable, infixed, and frozen round
Periods of time, — thence hurried back to fire.
They ferry over this Lethean sound
Both to and fro, their sorrow to augment,   605
And wish and struggle, as they pass, to reach
The tempting stream, with one small drop to lose
In sweet forgetfulness all pain and woe,
All in one moment, and so near the brink;
But Fate withstands, and, to oppose the attempt,

[1] Lake Serbonis (now extinct) in Egypt was surrounded with shifting sands which swallowed those
who ventured near it.

Medusa with Gorgonian terror guards   611
The ford, and of itself the water flies
All taste of living wight, as once it fled
The lip of Tantalus.   Thus roving on
In confused march forlorn, the adventrous bands,
With shuddering horror pale, and eyes aghast,   616
Viewed first their lamentable lot, and found
No rest.   Through many a dark and dreary vale
They passed, and many a region dolorous,
O'er many a frozen, many a fiery Alp,   620
Rocks, caves, lakes, fens, bogs, dens, and shades of
     death —
A universe of death, which God by curse
Created evil, for evil only good;
Where all life dies, death lives, and Nature breeds,
Perverse, all monstrous, all prodigious things,   625
Abominable, inutterable, and worse
Than fables yet have feigned or fear conceived,
Gorgons, and Hydras, and Chimæras dire.
     Meanwhile the Adversary of God and Man,   629
Satan, with thoughts inflamed of highest design,
Puts on swift wings, and toward the gates of Hell
Explores his solitary flight: sometimes
He scours the right hand coast, sometimes the left;
Now shaves with level wing the Deep, then soars
Up to the fiery concave towering high.   635
As when far off at sea a fleet descried
Hangs in the clouds, by equinoctial winds
Close sailing from Bengala, or the isles
Of Ternate and Tidore, whence merchants bring
Their spicy drugs; they on the trading flood,   640
Through the wide Ethiopian[1] to the Cape,
Ply stemming nightly toward the pole: so seemed
Far off the flying Fiend.   At last appear
Hell-bounds, high reaching to the horrid roof,
And thrice threefold the gates; three folds were
     brass,   645
Three iron, three of adamantine rock,
Impenetrable, impaled with circling fire,
Yet unconsumed.   Before the gates there sat
On either side a formidable Shape.
The one seemed woman to the waist, and fair,   650
But ended foul in many a scaly fold,
Voluminous and vast — a serpent armed
With mortal sting.   About her middle round
A cry of Hell-hounds never-ceasing barked   654
With wide Cerberean mouths full loud, and rung
A hideous peal; yet, when they list, would creep,
If aught disturbed their noise, into her womb,
And kennel there; yet there still barked and
     howled
Within unseen.   Far less abhorred than these
Vexed Scylla, bathing in the sea that parts   660
Calabria from the hoarse Trinacrian shore;
Nor uglier follow the night-hag, when, called
     [1] The Indian Ocean.

In secret, riding through the air she comes,
Lured with the smell of infant blood, to dance
With Lapland witches, while the laboring moon
Eclipses at their charms.   The other Shape —   666
If shape it might be called that shape had none
Distinguishable in member, joint, or limb;
Or substance might be called that shadow seemed,
For each seemed either — black it stood as Night
Fierce as ten Furies, terrible as Hell,   671
And shook a dreadful dart: what seemed his head
The likeness of a kingly crown had on.
Satan was now at hand, and from his seat
The monster moving onward came as fast   675
With horrid strides; Hell trembled as he strode.
The undaunted Fiend what this might be ad-
      mired —
Admired, not feared (God and his Son except,
Created thing naught valued he nor shunned),
And with disdainful look thus first began: —   680
   "Whence and what art thou, execrable Shape,
That dar'st, though grim and terrible, advance
Thy miscreated front athwart my way
To yonder gates?   Through them I mean to pass,
That be assured, without leave asked of thee.   685
Retire; or taste thy folly, and learn by proof,
Hell-born, not to contend with Spirits of Heaven."
   To whom the Goblin, full of wrath, replied: —
"Art thou that Traitor-Angel, art thou he,
Who first broke peace in Heaven and faith, till
      then   690
Unbroken, and in proud rebellious arms
Drew after him the third part of Heaven's sons,
Conjured [1] against the Highest — for which both
      thou
And they, outcast from God, are here condemned
To waste eternal days in woe and pain?   695
And reckon'st thou thyself with Spirits of Heaven,
Hell-doomed, and breath'st defiance here and
      scorn,
Where I reign king, and, to enrage thee more,
Thy king and lord?   Back to thy punishment,
False fugitive; and to thy speed add wings,   700
Lest with a whip of scorpions I pursue
Thy lingering, or with one stroke of this dart
Strange horror seize thee, and pangs unfelt before."
   So spake the grisly Terror, and in shape,
So speaking and so threatening, grew tenfold   705
More dreadful and deform.   On the other side,
Incensed with indignation, Satan stood
Unterrified, and like a comet burned,
That fires the length of Ophiuchus [2] huge
In the arctic sky, and from his horrid hair   710
Shakes pestilence and war.   Each at the head
Levelled his deadly aim; their fatal hands
No second stroke intend; and such a frown

   [1] Sworn by oath.   [2] A northern constellation.

Each cast at the other as when two black clouds,
With heaven's artillery fraught, come rattling on
Over the Caspian, — then stand front to front   716
Hovering a space, till winds the signal blow
To join their dark encounter in mid-air.
So frowned the mighty combatants that Hell
Grew darker at their frown; so matched they
      stood;   720
For never but once more was either like
To meet so great a foe.   And now great deeds
Had been achieved, whereof all Hell had rung,
Had not the snaky Sorceress, that sat
Fast by Hell-gate and kept the fatal key,   725
Risen, and with hideous outcry rushed between.
   "O father, what intends thy hand," she cried,
"Against thy only son?   What fury, O son,
Possesses thee to bend that mortal dart
Against thy father's head?   And know'st for
      whom?   730
For Him who sits above, and laughs the while
At thee, ordained his drudge to execute
Whate'er his wrath, which He calls justice, bids —
His wrath, which one day will destroy ye both!"
   She spake, and at her words the hellish Pest   735
Forbore: then these to her Satan returned: —
   "So strange thy outcry, and thy words so
      strange
Thou interposest, that my sudden hand,
Prevented, spares to tell thee yet by deeds
What it intends, till first I know of thee   740
What thing thou art, thus double-formed, and
      why,
In this infernal vale first met, thou call'st
Me father, and that phantasm call'st my son.
I know thee not, nor ever saw till now
Sight more detestable than him and thee."   745
To whom thus the Portress of Hell-gate replied: —
"Hast thou forgot me, then; and do I seem
Now in thine eye so foul? — once deemed so fair
In Heaven, when at the assembly, and in sight
Of all the Seraphim with thee combined   750
In bold conspiracy against Heaven's King,
All on a sudden miserable pain
Surprised thee, dim thine eyes, and dizzy swum
In darkness, while thy head flames thick and fast
Threw forth, till on the left side opening wide, 755
Likest to thee in shape and countenance bright,
Then shining heavenly fair, a goddess armed,
Out of thy head I sprung.   Amazement seized
All the host of Heaven; back they recoiled afraid
At first, and called me *Sin*, and for a sign   760
Portentous held me; but, familiar grown,
I pleased, and with attractive graces won
The most averse — thee chiefly, who, full oft
Thyself in me thy perfect image viewing,
Becam'st enamored; and such joy thou took'st   765

With me in secret that my womb conceived
A growing burden.   Meanwhile war arose,
And fields were fought in Heaven: wherein re-
          mained
(For what could else?) to our Almighty Foe
Clear victory; to our part loss and rout   770
Through all the Empyrean.   Down they fell,
Driven headlong from the pitch of Heaven, down
Into this Deep; and in the general fall
I also: at which time this powerful Key
Into my hands was given, with charge to keep   775
These gates for ever shut, which none can pass
Without my opening.   Pensive here I sat
Alone; but long I sat not, till my womb,
Pregnant by thee, and now excessive grown,
Prodigious motion felt and rueful throes.   780
At last this odious offspring whom thou seest,
Thine own begotten, breaking violent way,
Tore through my entrails, that, with fear and pain
Distorted, all my nether shape thus grew
Transformed: but he my inbred enemy   785
Forth issued, brandishing his fatal dart,
Made to destroy.   I fled, and cried out *Death!*
Hell trembled at the hideous name, and sighed
From all her caves, and back resounded *Death!*
I fled; but he pursued (though more, it seems,   790
Inflamed with lust than rage), and, swifter far,
Me overtook, his mother, all dismayed,
And, in embraces forcible and foul
Engendering with me, of that rape begot
These yelling monsters, that with ceaseless cry   795
Surround me, as thou saw'st — hourly conceived
And hourly born, with sorrow infinite
To me: for, when they list, into the womb
That bred them they return, and howl, and gnaw
My bowels, their repast; then, bursting forth   800
Afresh, with conscious terrors vex me round,
That rest or intermission none I find.
Before mine eyes in opposition sits
Grim Death, my son and foe, who sets them on,
And me, his parent, would full soon devour   805
For want of other prey, but that he knows
His end with mine involved, and knows that I
Should prove a bitter morsel, and his bane,
Whenever that shall be: so Fate pronounced.
But thou, O father, I forewarn thee, shun   810
His deadly arrow; neither vainly hope
To be invulnerable in those bright arms,
Though tempered heavenly; for that mortal dint,
Save He who reigns above, none can resist."
     She finished; and the subtle Fiend his lore   815
Soon learned, now milder, and thus answered
          smooth: —
     "Dear daughter — since thou claim'st me for
          thy sire,
And my fair son here show'st me, the dear pledge

Of dalliance had with thee in Heaven, and joys
Then sweet, now sad to mention, through dire
          change   820
Befallen us unforeseen, unthought-of — know,
I come no enemy, but to set free
From out this dark and dismal house of pain
Both him and thee, and all the Heavenly host
Of Spirits that, in our just pretences armed,   825
Fell with us from on high.   From them I go
This uncouth errand sole, and one for all
Myself expose, with lonely steps to tread
The unfounded Deep, and through the void im-
          mense
To search, with wandering quest, a place foretold
Should be — and, by concurring signs, ere now   831
Created vast and round — a place of bliss
In the purlieues of Heaven; and therein placed
A race of upstart creatures, to supply   834
Perhaps our vacant room, though more removed,
Lest Heaven, surcharged with potent multitude,
Might hap to move new broils.   Be this, or aught
Than this more secret, now designed, I haste
To know; and, this once known, shall soon return,
And bring ye to the place where thou and Death
Shall dwell at ease, and up and down unseen   841
Wing silently the buxom [1] air, imbalmed
With odors.   There ye shall be fed and filled
Immeasurably; all things shall be your prey."
     He ceased; for both seemed highly pleased, and
          Death   845
Grinned horrible a ghastly smile, to hear
His famine should be filled, and blessed his maw
Destined to that good hour.   No less rejoiced
His mother bad, and thus bespake her Sire: —
     "The key of this infernal Pit, by due   850
And by command of Heaven's all-powerful King,
I keep, by Him forbidden to unlock
These adamantine gates; against all force
Death ready stands to interpose his dart,
Fearless to be o'ermatched by living might.   855
But what owe I to His commands above,
Who hates me, and hath hither thrust me down
Into this gloom of Tartarus profound,
To sit in hateful office here confined,
Inhabitant of Heaven and heavenly-born   860
Here in perpetual agony and pain,
With terrors and with clamors compassed round
Of mine own brood, that on my bowels feed?
Thou art my father, thou my author, thou
My being gav'st me; whom should I obey   865
But thee? whom follow?   Thou wilt bring me soon
To that new world of light and bliss, among
The gods who live at ease, where I shall reign
At thy right hand voluptuous, as beseems
Thy daughter and thy darling, without end."   870
     [1] Yielding.

Thus saying, from her side the fatal key,
Sad instrument of all our woe, she took;
And, toward the gate rolling her bestial train,
Forthwith the huge porcullis high up-drew,
Which, but herself, not all the Stygian Powers   875
Could once have moved; then in the keyhole turns
The intricate wards, and every bolt and bar
Of massy iron or solid rock with ease
Unfastens   On a sudden open fly,
With impetuous recoil and jarring sound,   880
The infernal doors, and on their hinges grate
Harsh thunder, that the lowest bottom shook
Of Erebus.[1] She opened; but to shut
Excelled her power: the gates wide open stood,
That with extended wings a bannered host,   885
Under spread ensigns marching, might pass
    through
With horse and chariots ranked in loose array;
So wide they stood, and like a furnace-mouth
Cast forth redounding smoke and ruddy flame.
Before their eyes in sudden view appear   890
The secrets of the hoary Deep — a dark
Illimitable ocean, without bound,
Without dimension; where length, breadth, and
    highth,
And time, and place, are lost; where eldest Night
And Chaos, ancestors of Nature, hold   895
Eternal anarchy, amidst the noise
Of endless wars, and by confusion stand.
For Hot, Cold, Moist, and Dry, four champions
    fierce,
Strive here for mastery, and to battle bring
Their embryon atoms: they around the flag   900
Of each his faction, in their several clans,
Light-armed or heavy, sharp, smooth, swift, or
    slow,
Swarm populous, unnumbered as the sands
Of Barca or Cyrene's [2] torrid soil,
Levied to side with warring winds, and poise   905
Their lighter wings.   To whom these most adhere
He rules a moment: Chaos umpire sits,
And by decision more imbroils the fray
By which he reigns: next him, high arbiter,
Chance governs all.   Into this wild Abyss,   910
The womb of Nature, and perhaps her grave,
Of neither Sea, nor Shore, nor Air, nor Fire,
But all these in their pregnant causes mixed
Confusedly, and which thus must ever fight,
Unless the Almighty Maker them ordain   915
His dark materials to create more worlds —
Into this wild Abyss the wary Fiend
Stood on the brink of Hell and looked a while,
Pondering his voyage; for no narrow frith

[1] Darkness, daughter of Chaos. Virgil used the
name for Hell itself.
[2] Cities in northern Africa.

He had to cross.   Nor was his ear less pealed   920
With noises loud and ruinous (to compare
Great things with small) than when Bellona storms
With all her battering engines, bent to rase
Some capital city; or less than if this frame
Of heaven were falling, and these elements   925
In mutiny had from her axle torn
The steadfast Earth.   At last his sail-broad vans [1]
He spreads for flight, and, in the surging smoke
Uplifted, spurns the ground; thence many a league,
As in a cloudy chair, ascending rides   930
Audacious; but, that seat soon failing, meets
A vast vacuity.   All unawares,
Fluttering his pennons vain, plumb-down he drops
Ten thousand fadom deep, and to this hour
Down had been falling, had not, by ill chance,   935
The strong rebuff of some tumultuous cloud,
Instinct with fire and nitre, hurried him
As many miles aloft.   That fury stayed —
Quenched in a boggy Syrtis,[2] neither sea,
Nor good dry land — nigh foundered, on he fares,
Treading the crude consistence, half on foot,   941
Half flying; behoves him now both oar and sail.
As when a gryphon through the wilderness
With wingèd course, o'er hill or moory dale,
Pursues the Arimaspian,[3] who by stealth   945
Had from his wakeful custody purloined
The guarded gold; so eagerly the Fiend
O'er bog or steep, through strait, rough, dense, or
    rare,
With head, hands, wings, or feet, pursues his way,
And swims, or sinks, or wades, or creeps, or flies.
At length a universal hubbub wild   951
Of stunning sounds, and voices all confused,
Borne through the hollow dark, assaults his ear
With loudest vehemence.   Thither he plies
Undaunted, to meet there whatever Power   955
Or Spirit of the nethermost Abyss
Might in that noise reside, of whom to ask
Which way the nearest coast of darkness lies
Bordering on light; when straight behold the
    throne
Of *Chaos*, and his dark pavilion spread   960
Wide on the wasteful Deep!   With him enthroned
Sat sable-vested *Night*, eldest of things,
The consort of his reign; and by them stood
Orcus and Ades, and the dreaded name
Of Demogorgon; Rumor next, and Chance,   965
And Tumult, and Confusion, all embroiled,
And Discord with a thousand various mouths.
    To whom Satan, turning boldly, thus: — "Ye
    Powers

[1] wings.
[2] A place of quicksands — off northern Africa.
[3] Herodotus wrote of this one-eyed tribe that stole
gold from the griffins.

And Spirits of this nethermost Abyss,
Chaos and ancient Night, I come no spy   970
With purpose to explore or to disturb
The secrets of your realm; but, by constraint
Wandering this darksome desert, as my way
Lies through your spacious empire up to light,
Alone and without guide, half lost, I seek,   975
What readiest path leads where your gloomy
          bounds
Confine with Heaven; or, if some other place,
From your dominion won, the Ethereal King
Possesses lately, thither to arrive
I travel this profound.   Direct my course: 980
Directed, no mean recompense it brings
To your behoof, if I that region lost,
All usurpation thence expelled, reduce
To her original darkness and your sway
(Which is my present journey), and once more 985
Erect the standard there of ancient Night.
Yours be the advantage all, mine the revenge!"

     Thus Satan; and him thus the Anarch old,
With faltering speech and visage incomposed,
Answered: — "I know thee, stranger, who thou
          art —   990
That mighty leading Angel, who of late
Made head against Heaven's King, though over-
          thrown.
I saw and heard; for such a numerous host
Fled not in silence through the frighted Deep,
With ruin upon ruin, rout on rout,   995
Confusion worse confounded; and Heaven-gates
Poured out by millions her victorious bands,
Pursuing.   I upon my frontiers here
Keep residence; if all I can will serve
That little which is left so to defend,   1000
Encroached on still through our intestine broils
Weakening the sceptre of old Night: first, Hell,
Your dungeon, stretching far and wide beneath;
Now lately Heaven and Earth, another world
Hung o'er my realm, linked in a golden chain 1005
To that side Heaven from whence your legions fell!
If that way be your walk, you have not far;
So much the nearer danger.   Go, and speed;
Havoc, and spoil, and ruin, are my gain."

     He ceased; and Satan staid not to reply,   1010
But, glad that now his sea should find a shore,
With fresh alacrity and force renewed

Springs upward, like a pyramid of fire,
Into the wild expanse, and through the shock
Of fighting elements, on all sides round   1015
Environed, wins his way; harder beset
And more endangered than when Argo passed [1]
Through Bosporus betwixt the justling rocks,
Or when Ulysses on the larboard shunned
Charybdis, and by the other Whirlpool steered.
So he with difficulty and labor hard   1021
Moved on.   With difficulty and labor he;
But, he once passed, soon after, when Man fell,
Strange alteration!   Sin and Death amain,
Following his track (such was the will of Heaven)
Paved after him a broad and beaten way   1026
Over the dark Abyss, whose boiling gulf
Tamely endured a bridge of wondrous length,
From Hell continued, reaching the utmost Orb [2]
Of this frail World; by which the Spirits perverse
With easy intercourse pass to and fro   1031
To tempt or punish mortals, except whom
God and good Angels guard by special grace.

     But now at last the sacred influence
Of light appears, and from the walls of Heaven
Shoots far into the bosom of dim Night   1036
A glimmering dawn.   Here Nature first begins
Her farthest verge, and Chaos to retire,
As from her outmost works, a broken foe,
With tumult less and with less hostile din;   1040
That Satan with less toil, and now with ease,
Wafts on the calmer wave by dubious light,
And, like a weather-beaten vessel, holds
Gladly the port, though shrouds and tackle torn;
Or in the emptier waste, resembling air,   1045
Weighs his spread wings, at leisure to behold
Far off the empyreal Heaven, extended wide
In circuit, undetermined square or round,
With opal towers and battlements adorned
Of living sapphire, once his native seat,   1050
And, fast by, hanging in a golden chain,
This pendent World, in bigness as a star
Of smallest magnitude close by the moon.
Thither, full fraught with mischievous revenge,
Accursed, and in a cursèd hour, he hies.   1055

[1] The reference is to Jason and his search, aboard the
Argo, for the golden fleece.
[2] The last of the ten spheres surrounding the earth.

Molière · 1622-1673

Molière was born Jean Baptiste Poquelin in 1622. His father was an able and prosperous uphol-sterer who held a commission for this work at the royal court. Young Jean was reared to the same trade, but his education at a Jesuit college and his enthusiasm for the theatre made the work repug-nant to him. When, as a young man, he met Madeleine Béjart, an actress, his career was fixed. With her and a group of her relatives and friends he organized a stock company which, however, soon failed. Long years of work in the provinces followed, years which gave him experience as an actor and increased his knowledge of the stage, which made possible his success as a playwright. Returning to Paris in 1658, he soon made a reputation, was favored by the king with command performances, and was entertained at court. In 1662 the dramatist married Armande Béjart, who may or may not have been the daughter of his old friend Madeleine, but who made Molière's future years none too calm. It has been suggested that the relations between Alceste and Célimène in *The Misanthrope* find their parallel in the relations between Molière and his young and coquettish wife.

France in Molière's day, like the England of his contemporary Milton, was exciting. The country passed from the rule of Louis XIII into the hands of ministers only finally to come under the firm and autocratic rule of Louis XIV. With Louis XIV came the prominence of the court at Versailles, the formal rule of an absolute monarch. And Molière was constantly stimulated by the competition with his two rivals, Racine and Corneille.

More closely than any other writer who has earned a place in the literature of the Western World, Molière identified himself with the theatre. When the time came for him to make his final exit his career took on the form of a tragedy. Racked with illness during those last weeks, he never-theless wrote one of his great plays, *Le Malade Imaginaire*, the story of a man sick only in his imag-ination. The curtain for the fifth, and last, act came (1673) at the Palais Royal where he was taking the lead in this same comedy. Gripped by a convulsion, Molière passed it off with a laugh, finished the play, went home and died. But even with death Molière was not to know peace. Because the acting profession was in disrepute with the church, and because he had not formally recanted to a priest, burial in holy ground was refused. Through the intervention of Louis XIV, interment in the cemetery of St. Eustache was finally granted by the archbishop, but a formal ceremony was denied and the burial was not to take place until after sunset.

Some of Molière's better known plays are *Les Précieuses Ridicules, L'École des Maris, L'École des Femmes, Tartuffe, Le Misanthrope, Le Médecin Malgré Lui,* and *Le Malade Imaginaire.* He was most successful in comedy and as a comic actor; in tragedy, with a few exceptions, he was a failure. The plays are notable for their farcical arraignment of society in the comedy of manners and of character which they present, for their satire, and for a style which was exuberant and sprightly as well as lucid. He held always for the control of conduct by the intellect but preached no particular doctrine other than that of sanity in social relations. He deplored formality and artificiality in behavior, condemned all excesses — even those of the neo-classical playwrights who sometimes held too rigidly to the formalism of the theatre — and was the enemy of all pretense and bigotry. His rule for both life and the theatre was the classical one of the golden mean.

SUGGESTED REFERENCES: D. B. W. Lewis, *Molière, The Comic Mask* (1959); J. D. Hubert, *Molière and the Comedy of Intellect* (1962); Lionel Gossman, *Men and Masks: A Study of Molière* (1963); Jacques Guicharnaud, ed., *Molière: A Collection of Critical Essays* (1964).

The Misanthrope[1]

The Misanthrope was first acted on June 4, 1666, at the theatre of the Palais Royal. It enjoyed at that time no great success, running only for twenty-one performances. It grew in popularity, however, with the passing years to become today probably Molière's most respected play. The reader will note the scarcity of incident and the fact that the play is composed largely of a series of conversations. It is the comedy of Alceste, of the love affair of a man who hates mankind and believes only in speaking the truth.

The play manifests the classical temper in its simplicity of subject and thought and the fixed qualities of its characters. The classical unities restrict its action to one room on one day. The misanthrope was a subject familiar to classical writers — to Plutarch, to Lucian — as well as to Shakespeare (in *Timon of Athens*). In Act II, Scene V, when the dramatist is discussing the capacity for self-deception of one in love, Molière is quoting almost directly from *On the Nature of Things* by Lucretius. But perhaps the strongest classical quality which the play manifests is the degree to which Molière succeeds in portraying the universal in the particular where more modern writers would seek the particular for the sake of its particularity.

Dramatis Personæ

ALCESTE, *in love with Célimène*
PHILINTE, *his friend*
ORONTE, *in love with Célimène*
CÉLIMÈNE, *beloved by Alceste*
ÉLIANTE, *her cousin*
ARSINOÉ, *Célimène's friend*
ACASTE ⎫
　　　　⎬ *marquises*
CLITANDRE ⎭
BASQUE, *servant to Célimène*
DUBOIS, *servant to Alceste*
AN OFFICER OF THE MARÉCHAUSSÉE

SCENE: *At Paris, in* CÉLIMÈNE'S *house.*

ACT I

SCENE I.   PHILINTE, ALCESTE

Philinte. What is the matter? What ails you?
Alceste (seated). Leave me, I pray.
Philinte. But, once more, tell me what strange whim . . .
Alceste. Leave me, I tell you, and get out of my sight.
Philinte. But you might at least listen to people, without getting angry.
Alceste. I choose to get angry, and I do not choose to listen.
Philinte. I do not understand you in these abrupt moods, and although we are friends, I am the first . . .
Alceste (rising quickly). I, your friend? Lay not that flattering unction to your soul. I have until now professed to be so; but after what I have just seen of you, I tell you candidly that I am such no longer; I have no wish to occupy a place in a corrupt heart.
Philinte. I am then very much to be blamed from your point of view, Alceste?

Alceste. To be blamed? You ought to die from very shame; there is no excuse for such behavior, and every man of honor must be disgusted at it. I see you almost stifle a man with caresses, show him the most ardent affection, and overwhelm him with protestations, offers, and vows of friendship. Your ebullitions of tenderness know no bounds; and when I ask you who that man is, you can scarcely tell me his name; your feelings for him, the moment you have turned your back, suddenly cool; you speak of him most indifferently to me. Zounds! I call it unworthy, base, and infamous, so far to lower one's self as to act contrary to one's own feelings, and if, by some mischance, I had done such a thing, I should hang myself at once out of sheer vexation.
Philinte. I do not see that it is a hanging matter at all; and I beg of you not to think it amiss if I ask you to show me some mercy, for I shall not hang myself, if it be all the same to you.
Alceste. That is a sorry joke.
Philinte. But, seriously, what would you have people do?
Alceste. I would have people be sincere, and that, like men of honor, no word be spoken that comes not from the heart.
Philinte. When a man comes and embraces you warmly, you must pay him back in his own coin, respond as best you can to his show of feeling, and return offer for offer, and vow for vow.
Alceste. Not so. I cannot bear so base a method, which your fashionable people generally affect; there is nothing I detest so much as the contortions of these great time-and-lip servers, these affable dispensers of meaningless embraces, these obliging utterers of empty words, who view every one in civilities, and treat the man of worth and the fop alike. What good does it do if a man heaps endearments on you, vows that he is your friend, that he believes in you, is full of zeal for you, esteems

[1] Translated by Henri Van Laun.

and loves you, and lauds you to the skies, when he rushes to do the same to the first rapscallion he meets? No, no, no heart with the least self-respect cares for esteem so prostituted; he will hardly relish it, even when openly expressed, when he finds that he shares it with the whole universe. Preference must be based on esteem, and to esteem every one is to esteem no one. Since you abandon yourself to the vices of the times, Zounds! you are not the man for me. I decline this over-complaisant kindness, which uses no discrimination. I like to be distinguished; and, to cut the matter short, the friend of all mankind is no friend of mine.

Philinte. But when we are of the world, we must conform to the outward civilities which custom demands.

Alceste. I deny it. We ought to punish pitilessly that shameful pretense of friendly intercourse. I like a man to be a man, and to show on all occasions the bottom of his heart in his discourse. Let that be the thing to speak, and never let our feelings be hidden beneath vain compliments.

Philinte. There are many cases in which plain speaking would become ridiculous, and could hardly be tolerated. And, with all due allowance for your unbending honesty, it is as well to conceal your feelings sometimes. Would it be right or decent to tell thousands of people what we think of them? And when we meet with some one whom we hate or who displeases us, must we tell him so openly?

Alceste. Yes.

Philinte. What! Would you tell old Emilia, that it ill becomes her to set up for a beauty at her age, and that the paint she uses disgusts every one?

Alceste. Undoubtedly.

Philinte. Or Dorilas, that he is a bore, and that there is no one at court who is not sick of hearing him boast of his courage, and the luster of his house?

Alceste. Decidedly so.

Philinte. You are jesting.

Alceste. I am not jesting at all; and I would not spare any one in that respect. It offends my eyes too much; and whether at Court or in town, I behold nothing but what provokes my spleen. I become quite melancholy and deeply grieved to see men behave to each other as they do. Everywhere I find nothing but base flattery, injustice, self-interest, deceit, roguery. I cannot bear it any longer; I am furious; and my intention is to break with all mankind.

Philinte. This philosophical spleen is somewhat too savage. I cannot but laugh to see you in these gloomy fits, and fancy that I perceive in us two,

brought up together, the two brothers described in *The School for Husbands,*[1] who ...

Alceste. Good Heavens! drop your insipid comparisons.

Philinte. Nay, seriously, leave off these vagaries. The world will not alter for all your meddling. And as plain speaking has such charms for you, I shall tell you frankly that this complaint of yours is as good as a play, wherever you go, and that all those invectives against the manners of the age, make you a laughing stock to many people.

Alceste. So much the better, Zounds! so much the better. That is just what I want. It is a very good sign, and I rejoice at it. All men are so odious to me, that I should be sorry to appear rational in their eyes.

Philinte. But do you wish harm to all mankind?

Alceste. Yes; I have conceived a terrible hatred for them.

Philinte. Shall all poor mortals, without exception, be included in this aversion? There are some, even in the age in which we live ...

Alceste. No, they are all alike; and I hate all men: some, because they are wicked and mischievous; others because they lend themselves to the wicked, and have not that healthy contempt with which vice ought to inspire all virtuous minds. You can see how unjustly and excessively complacent people are to that bare-faced scoundrel with whom I am at law. You may plainly perceive the traitor through his mask; he is well known everywhere in his true colors; his rolling eyes and his honeyed tones impose only on those who do not know him. People are aware that this low-bred fellow, who deserves to be pilloried, has, by the dirtiest jobs, made his way in the world; and that the splendid position he has acquired makes merit repine and virtue blush. Yet whatever dishonorable epithets may be launched against him everywhere, nobody defends his wretched honor. Call him a rogue, an infamous wretch, a confounded scoundrel if you like, all the world will say "yea," and no one contradicts you. But for all that, his bowing and scraping are welcome everywhere; he is received, smiled upon, and wriggles himself into all kinds of society; and, if any appointment is to be secured by intriguing, he will carry the day over a man of the greatest worth. Zounds! these are mortal stabs to me, to see vice parleyed with; and sometimes I feel suddenly inclined to fly into a wilderness far from the approach of men.

Philinte. Great Heaven! let us torment ourselves a little less about the vices of our age, and be a little more lenient to human nature. Let us

[1] *L'École des Maris,* a play by Molière first produced June 24, 1661.

not scrutinize it with the utmost severity, but look with some indulgence at its failings. In society, we need virtue to be more pliable. If we are too wise, we may be equally to blame. Good sense avoids all extremes, and requires us to be soberly rational. This unbending and virtuous stiffness of ancient times shocks too much the ordinary customs of our own; it requires too great perfection from us mortals; we must yield to the times without being too stubborn; it is the height of folly to busy ourselves in correcting the world. I, as well as yourself, notice a hundred things every day which might be better managed, differently enacted; but whatever I may discover at any moment, people do not see me in a rage like you. I take men quietly just as they are; I accustom my mind to bear with what they do; and I believe that at Court, as well as in the city, my phlegm is as philosophical as your bile.

Alceste. But this phlegm, good sir, you who reason so well, could it not be disturbed by anything? And if perchance a friend should betray you; if he forms a subtle plot to get hold of what is yours; if people should try to spread evil reports about you, would you tamely submit to all this without flying into a rage?

Philinte. Ay, I look upon all these faults of which you complain as vices inseparably connected with human nature; in short, my mind is no more shocked at seeing a man a rogue, unjust, or selfish, than at seeing vultures, eager for prey, mischievous apes, or fury-lashed wolves.

Alceste. What! I should see myself deceived, torn to pieces, robbed, without being ... Zounds! I shall say no more about it; all this reasoning is beside the point!

Philinte. Upon my word, you would do well to keep silence. Rail a little less at your opponent, and attend a little more to your suit.

Alceste. That I shall not do; that is settled long ago.

Philinte. But whom then do you expect to solicit for you?

Alceste. Whom? Reason, my just right, equity.

Philinte. Shall you not pay a visit to any of the judges?

Alceste. No. Is my cause unjust or dubious?

Philinte. I am agreed on that; but you know what harm intrigues do, and ...

Alceste. No. I am resolved not to stir a step. I am either right or wrong.

Philinte. Do not trust to that.

Alceste. I shall not budge an inch.

Philinte. Your opponent is powerful, and by his underhand work, may induce ...

Alceste. It does not matter.

Philinte. You will make a mistake.

Alceste. Be it so. I wish to see the end of it.

Philinte. But ...

Alceste. I shall have the satisfaction of losing my suit.

Philinte. But after all ...

Alceste. I shall see by this trial whether men have sufficient impudence, are wicked, villainous, and perverse enough to do me this injustice in the face of the whole world.

Philinte. What a strange fellow!

Alceste. I could wish, were it to cost me ever so much, that, for the fun of the thing, I lost my case.

Philinte. But people will really laugh at you, Alceste, if they hear you go on in this fashion.

Alceste. So much the worse for those who will.

Philinte. But this rectitude, which you exact so carefully in every case, this absolute integrity in which you intrench yourself, do you perceive it in the lady you love? As for me, I am astonished that, appearing to be at war with the whole human race, you yet, notwithstanding everything that can render it odious to you, have found aught to charm your eyes. And what surprises me still more, is the strange choice your heart has made. The sincere Éliante has a liking for you, the prude Arsinoé looks with favor upon you, yet your heart does not respond to their passion; whilst you wear the chains of Célimène, who sports with you, and whose coquettish humor and malicious wit seems to accord so well with the manner of the times. How comes it that, hating these things as mortally as you do, you endure so much of them in that lady? Are they no longer faults in so sweet a charmer? Do not you perceive them, or if you do, do you excuse them?

Alceste. Not so. The love I feel for this young widow does not make me blind to her faults, and, notwithstanding the great passion with which she has inspired me, I am the first to see, as well as to condemn, them. But for all this, do what I will, I confess my weakness, she has the art of pleasing me. In vain I see her faults; I may even blame them; in spite of all, she makes me love her. Her charms conquer everything, and, no doubt, my sincere love will purify her heart from the vices of our times.

Philinte. If you accomplish this, it will be no small task. Do you believe yourself beloved by her?

Alceste. Yes, certainly! I should not love her at all, did I not think so.

Philinte. But if her love for you is so apparent, how comes it that your rivals cause you so much uneasiness?

Alceste. It is because a heart, deeply smitten,

claims all to itself; I come here only with the intention of telling her what, on this subject, my feelings dictate.

Philinte. Had I but to choose, her cousin Éliante would have all my love. Her heart, which values yours, is stable and sincere; and this more compatible choice would have suited you better.

Alceste. It is true; my good sense tells me so every day; but good sense does not always rule love.

Philinte. Well, I fear much for your affections; and the hope which you cherish may perhaps...

SCENE II: ORONTE, ALCESTE, PHILINTE

Oronte (*to* ALCESTE). I have been informed yonder, that Éliante and Célimène have gone out to make some purchases. But as I heard that you were here, I came to tell you, most sincerely, that I have conceived the greatest regard for you, and that, for a long time, this regard has inspired me with the most ardent wish to be reckoned among your friends. Yes; I like to do homage to merit; and I am most anxious that a bond of friendship should unite us. I suppose that a zealous friend, and of my standing, is not altogether to be rejected. (*All this time* ALCESTE *has been musing, and seems not to be aware that* ORONTE *is addressing him. He looks up only when* ORONTE *says to him*) — It is to you, if you please, that this speech is addressed.

Alceste. To me, sir?

Oronte. To you. Is it in any way offensive to you?

Alceste. Not in the least. But my surprise is very great; and I did not expect that honor.

Oronte. The regard in which I hold you ought not to astonish you, and you can claim it from the whole world.

Alceste. Sir...

Oronte. Our whole kingdom contains nothing above the dazzling merit which people discover in you.

Alceste. Sir...

Oronte. Yes; for my part, I prefer you to the most important in it.

Alceste. Sir...

Oronte. May Heaven strike me dead, if I lie! And, to convince you, on this very spot, of my feelings, allow me, sir, to embrace you with all my heart, and to solicit a place in your friendship. Your hand, if you please. Will you promise me your friendship?

Alceste. Sir...

Oronte. What! you refuse me?

Alceste. Sir, you do me too much honor; but friendship is a sacred thing, and to lavish it on every occasion is surely to profane it. Judgment and choice should preside at such a compact; we ought to know more of each other before engaging ourselves; and it may happen that our dispositions are such that we may both of us repent of our bargain.

Oronte. Upon my word! that is wisely said; and I esteem you all the more for it. Let us therefore leave it to time to form such a pleasing bond; but, meanwhile I am entirely at your disposal. If you have any business at Court, every one knows how well I stand with the King; I have his private ear; and, upon my word, he treats me in everything with the utmost intimacy. In short, I am yours in every emergency; and, as you are a man of brilliant parts, and to inaugurate our charming amity, I come to read you a sonnet which I made a little while ago, and to find out whether it be good enough for publicity.

Alceste. I am not fit, sir, to decide such a matter. You will therefore excuse me.

Oronte. Why so?

Alceste. I have the failing of being a little more sincere in those things than is necessary.

Oronte. The very thing I ask; and I should have reason to complain, if, in laying myself open to you that you might give me your frank opinion, you should deceive me, and disguise anything from me.

Alceste. If that be the case, sir, I am perfectly willing.

Oronte. *Sonnet*... It is a sonnet... *Hope*... It is to a lady who flattered my passion with some hope. *Hope*... They are not long, pompous verses, but mild, tender and melting little lines.

(*At every one of these interruptions he looks at* ALCESTE.)

Alceste. We shall see.

Oronte. Hope... I do not know whether the style will strike you as sufficiently clear and easy, and whether you will approve of my choice of words.

Alceste. We shall soon see, sir.

Oronte. Besides, you must know that I was only a quarter of an hour in composing it.

Alceste. Let us hear, sir; the time signifies nothing.

Oronte (*reads*).

> Hope, it is true, oft gives relief,
> Rocks for a while our tedious pain,
> But what a poor advantage, Phillis,
> When nought remains, and all is gone!

Philinte. I am already charmed with this little bit.

Alceste (*softly to* PHILINTE). What! do you mean to tell me that you like this stuff?

Oronte.

> You once showed some complaisance,
> But less would have sufficed,
> You should not take that trouble
> To give me nought but hope.

Philinte. In what pretty terms these thoughts are put!

Alceste. How now! you vile flatterer, you praise this rubbish!

Oronte.

> If I must wait eternally,
> My passion, driven to extremes,
> Will fly to death.
> Your tender cares cannot prevent this,
> Fair Phillis, aye we're in despair,
> When we must hope for ever.

Philinte. The conclusion is pretty, amorous, admirable.

Alceste (softly, and aside to PHILINTE). A plague on the conclusion! I wish you had concluded to break your nose, you poisoner to the devil!

Philinte. I never heard verses more skilfully turned.

Alceste (softly, and aside). Zounds! . . .

Oronte (to PHILINTE). You flatter me; and you are under the impression perhaps . . .

Philinte. No, I am not flattering at all.

Alceste (softly, and aside). What else are you doing, you wretch?

Oronte (to ALCESTE). But for you, you know our agreement. Speak to me, I pray, in all sincerity.

Alceste. These matters, sir, are always more or less delicate, and every one is fond of being praised for his wit. But I was saying one day to a certain person, who shall be nameless, when he showed me some of his verses, that a gentleman ought at all times to exercise a great control over that itch for writing which sometimes attacks us, and should keep a tight rein over the strong propensity which one has to display such amusements; and that, in the frequent anxiety to show their productions, people are frequently exposed to act a very foolish part.

Oronte. Do you wish to convey to me by this that I am wrong in desiring . . .

Alceste. I do not say that exactly. But I told him that writing without warmth becomes a bore; that there needs no other weakness to disgrace a man; that even if people, on the other hand, had a hundred good qualities, we view them from their worst sides.

Oronte. Do you find anything to object to in my sonnet?

Alceste. I do not say that. But, to keep him from writing, I set before his eyes how, in our days, that desire had spoiled a great many very worthy people.

Oronte. Do I write badly? Am I like them in any way?

Alceste. I do not say that. But, in short, I said to him, What pressing need is there for you to rhyme, and what the deuce drives you into print? If we can pardon the sending into the world of a badly-written book, it will only be in those unfortunate men who write for their livelihood. Believe me, resist your temptations, keep these effusions from the public, and do not, how much soever you may be asked, forfeit the reputation which you enjoy at Court of being a man of sense and a gentleman, to take, from the hands of a greedy printer, that of a ridiculous and wretched author. That is what I tried to make him understand.

Oronte. This is all well and good, and I seem to understand you. But I should like to know what there is in my sonnet to . . .

Alceste. Candidly, you had better put it in your closet. You have been following bad models, and your expressions are not at all natural. Pray what is — *Rocks for a while our tedious pain?* And what, *When nought remains, and all is gone?* What, *You should not take that trouble to give me nought but hope?* And what, *Phillis, aye we're in despair when we must hope for ever?* This figurative style, that people are so vain of, is beside all good taste and truth; it is only a play upon words, sheer affectation, and it is not thus that nature speaks. The wretched taste of the age is what I dislike in this. Our forefathers, unpolished as they were, had a much better one; and I value all that is admired now-a-days far less than an old song which I am going to repeat to you:

> Had our great monarch granted me
> His Paris large and fair;
> And I straightway must quit for aye
> The love of my true dear;
> Then would I say, King Hal, I pray,
> Take back your Paris fair,
> I love much mo my dear, I trow,
> I love much mo my dear.

This versification is not rich, and the style is antiquated; but do you not see that it is far better than all those trumpery trifles against which good sense revolts, and that in this, passion speaks from the heart?

> Had our great monarch granted me
> His Paris large and fair;
> And I straightway must quit for aye
> The love of my true dear;

Then would I say, King Hal, I pray,
Take back your Paris fair,
I love much mo my dear, I trow,
I love much mo my dear.

This is what a really loving heart would say.
(*To* PHILINTE, *who is laughing*) Yes, master wag,
in spite of all your wit, I care more for this than for
all the florid pomp and the tinsel which everybody
is admiring now-a-days.

Oronte. And I, I maintain that my verses are
very good.

Alceste. Doubtless you have your reasons for
thinking them so; but you will allow me to have
mine, which, with your permission, will remain
independent.

Oronte. It is enough for me that others prize
them.

Alceste. That is because they know how to dissemble, which I do not.

Oronte. Do you really believe that you have
such a great share of wit?

Alceste. If I praised your verses, I should have
more.

Oronte. I shall do very well without your approbation.

Alceste. You will have to do without it, if it be
all the same.

Oronte. I should like much to see you compose
some on the same subject, just to have a sample
of your style.

Alceste. I might, perchance, make some as bad;
but I should take good care not to show them to
any one.

Oronte. You are mighty positive; and this great
sufficiency...

Alceste. Pray, seek some one else to flatter you,
and not me.

Oronte. But, my little sir, drop this haughty
tone.

Alceste. In truth, my big sir, I shall do as I like.

Philinte (coming between them). Stop, gentlemen!
that is carrying the matter too far. Cease, I pray.

Oronte. Ah! I am wrong, I confess; and I leave
the field to you. I am your servant, sir, most
heartily.

Alceste. And I, sir, am your most humble
servant.

SCENE III: PHILINTE, ALCESTE

Philinte. Well! you see. By being too sincere,
you have got a nice affair on your hands; I saw
that Oronte, in order to be flattered...

Alceste. Do not talk to me.

Philinte. But...

Alceste. No more society for me.

Philinte. Is it too much...

Alceste. Leave me alone.

Philinte. If I...

Alceste. Not another word.

Philinte. But what...

Alceste. I will hear no more.

Philinte. But...

Alceste. Again?

Philinte. People insult...

Alceste. Ah! Zounds! this is too much. Do not
dog my steps.

Philinte. You are making fun of me; I shall not
leave you.

ACT II

SCENE I: ALCESTE, CÉLIMÈNE

Alceste. Will you have me speak candidly to
you, madam? Well, then, I am very much dissatisfied with your behavior. I am very angry
when I think of it; and I perceive that we shall
have to break with each other. Yes; I should only
deceive you were I to speak otherwise. Sooner or
later a rupture is unavoidable; and if I were to
promise the contrary a thousand times, I should
not be able to bear this any longer.

Célimène. Oh, I see! it is to quarrel with me, that
you wished to conduct me home?

Alceste. I do not quarrel. But your disposition,
madam, is too ready to give any first comer an
entrance into your heart. Too many admirers
beset you; and my temper cannot put up with that.

Célimène. Am I to blame for having too many
admirers? Can I prevent people from thinking me
amiable? and am I to take a stick to drive them
away, when they endeavor by tender means to
visit me?

Alceste. No, madam, there is no need for a stick,
but only a heart less yielding and less melting at
their love-tales. I am aware that your good looks
accompany you, go where you will; but your reception retains those whom your eyes attract; and
that gentleness, accorded to those who surrender
their arms, finishes on their hearts the sway which
your charms began. The too agreeable expectation which you offer them increases their assiduities towards you; and your complacency, a little
less extended, would drive away the great crowd
of so many admirers. But, tell me, at least,
madam, by what good fortune Clitandre has the
happiness of pleasing you so mightily? Upon
what basis of merit and sublime virtue do you
ground the honor of your regard for him? Is it
by the long nail on his little finger that he has acquired the esteem which you display for him?

Are you, like all the rest of the fashionable world, fascinated by the dazzling merit of his fair wig? Do his great rolls make you love him? Do his many ribbons charm you? Is it by the attraction of his large *rhingrave* [1] that he has conquered your heart, whilst at the same time he pretended to be your slave? Or have his manner of smiling, and his falsetto voice,[2] found out the secret of moving your feelings?

Célimène. How unjustly you take umbrage at him! Do not you know why I countenance him; and that he has promised to interest all his friends in my lawsuit?

Alceste. Lose your lawsuit, madam, with patience, and do not countenance a rival whom I detest.

Célimène. But you are getting jealous of the whole world.

Alceste. It is because the whole world is so kindly received by you.

Célimène. That is the very thing to calm your frightened mind, because my good will is diffused over all: you would have more reason to be offended if you saw me entirely occupied with one.

Alceste. But as for me, whom you accuse of too much jealousy, what have I more than any of them, madam, pray?

Célimène. The happiness of knowing that you are beloved.

Alceste. And what grounds has my lovesick heart for believing it?

Célimène. I think that, as I have taken the trouble to tell you so, such an avowal ought to satisfy you.

Alceste. But who will assure me that you may not, at the same time, say as much to everybody else perhaps?

Célimène. Certainly, for a lover, this is a pretty amorous speech, and you make me out a very nice lady. Well! to remove such a suspicion, I retract this moment everything I have said; and no one but yourself shall for the future impose upon you. Will that satisfy you?

Alceste. Zounds! why do I love you so! Ah! if ever I get heart-whole out of your hands, I shall bless Heaven for this rare good fortune. I make no secret of it; I do all that is possible to tear this unfortunate attachment from my heart; but hitherto my greatest efforts have been of no avail; and it is for my sins that I love you thus.

Célimène. It is very true that your affection for me is unequalled.

[1] Large German breeches introduced into France about this time.

[2] An artificial, mincing manner of speech affected by some nobles as proof of their gentility.

Alceste. As for that, I can challenge the whole world. My love for you cannot be conceived; and never, madam, has any man loved as I do.

Célimène. Your method, however, is entirely new, for you love people only to quarrel with them; it is in peevish expression alone that your feelings vent themselves; no one ever saw such a grumbling swain.

Alceste. But it lies with you alone to dissipate this ill-humor. For mercy's sake let us make an end of all these bickerings; deal openly with each other, and try to put a stop . . .

SCENE II: CÉLIMÈNE, ALCESTE, BASQUE

Célimène. What is the matter?
Basque. Acaste is below.
Célimène. Very well! bid him come up.

SCENE III: CÉLIMÈNE, ALCESTE

Alceste. What! can one never have a little private conversation with you? You are always ready to receive company; and you cannot, for a single instant, make up your mind to be "not at home."
Célimène. Do you wish me to quarrel with Acaste?
Alceste. You have such regard for people, which I by no means like.
Célimène. He is a man never to forgive me, if he knew that his presence could annoy me.
Alceste. And what is that to you, to inconvenience yourself so . . .
Célimène. But, good Heaven! the amity of such as he is of importance; they are a kind of people who, I do not know how, have acquired the right to be heard at Court. They take their part in every conversation; they can do you no good, but they may do you harm; and, whatever support one may find elsewhere, it will never do to be on bad terms with these very noisy gentry.
Alceste. In short, whatever people may say or do, you always find reasons to bear with every one; and your very careful judgment . . .

SCENE IV: ALCESTE, CÉLIMÈNE, BASQUE

Basque. Clitandre is here too, madam.
Alceste. Exactly so. (*Wishes to go.*)
Célimène. Where are you running to?
Alceste. I am going.
Célimène. Stay.
Alceste. For what?
Célimène. Stay.
Alceste. I cannot.
Célimène. I wish it.

Alceste. I will not. These conversations only weary me; and it is too bad of you to wish me to endure them.

Célimène. I wish it, I wish it.

Alceste. No, it is impossible.

Célimène. Very well, then; go, begone; you can do as you like.

SCENE V: ÉLIANTE, PHILINTE, ACASTE, CLITANDRE, ALCESTE, CÉLIMÈNE, BASQUE

Éliante (*to* CÉLIMÈNE). Here are the two marquises coming up with us. Has any one told you?

Célimène. Yes. (*To* BASQUE) Place chairs for everyone. (BASQUE *places chairs, and goes out.*) (*To* ALCESTE) You are not gone?

Alceste. No; but I am determined, madam, to have you make up your mind either for them or for me.

Célimène. Hold your tongue.

Alceste. This very day you shall explain yourself.

Célimène. You are losing your senses.

Alceste. Not at all. You shall declare yourself.

Célimène. Indeed!

Alceste. You must take your stand.

Célimène. You are jesting, I believe.

Alceste. Not so. But you must choose. I have been too patient.

Clitandre. Egad! I have just come from the Louvre, where Cléonte, at the levee, made himself very ridiculous. Has he not some friend who could charitably enlighten him upon his manners?

Célimène. Truth to say, he compromises himself very much in society; everywhere he carries himself with an air that is noticed at first sight, and when after a short absence you meet him again, he is still more absurd than ever.

Acaste. Egad! Talk of absurd people, just now, one of the most tedious ones was annoying me. That reasoner, Damon, kept me, if you please, for a full hour in the broiling sun, away from my Sedan chair.

Célimène. He is a strange talker, and one who always finds the means of telling you nothing with a great flow of words. There is no sense at all in his tittle-tattle, and all that we hear is but noise.

Éliante (*to* PHILINTE). This beginning is not bad; and the conversation takes a sufficiently agreeable turn against our neighbors.

Clitandre. Timante, too, madam, is another original.

Célimène. He is a complete mystery from top to toe, who throws upon you, in passing, a bewildered glance, and who, without having anything to do, is always busy. Whatever he utters is accompanied with grimaces; he quite oppresses people by his ceremonies. To interrupt a conversation, he has always a secret to whisper to you, and that secret turns out to be nothing. Of the merest molehill he makes a mountain, and whispers everything in your ear, even to a "good-day."

Acaste. And Geralde, madam?

Célimène. That tiresome story-teller! He never comes down from his nobleman's pedestal; he continually mixes with the best society, and never quotes any one of minor rank than a Duke, Prince, or Princess. Rank is his hobby, and his conversation is of nothing but horses, carriages, and dogs. He *thee's* and *thou's* persons of the highest standing, and the word *Sir* is quite obsolete with him.

Clitandre. It is said that he is on the best of terms with Bélise.

Célimène. Poor silly woman, and the dreariest company! When she comes to visit me, I suffer from martyrdom; one has to rack one's brain perpetually to find out what to say to her; and the impossibility of her expressing her thoughts allows the conversation to drop every minute. In vain you try to overcome her stupid silence by the assistance of the most commonplace topics; even the fine weather, the rain, the heat and the cold are subjects, which, with her, are soon exhausted. Yet for all that, her calls, unbearable enough, are prolonged to an insufferable length; and you may consult the clock, or yawn twenty times, but she stirs no more than a log of wood.

Acaste. What think you of Adraste?

Célimène. Oh! What excessive pride! He is a man positively puffed out with conceit. His self-importance is never satisfied with the Court, against which he inveighs daily; and whenever an office, a place, or a living is bestowed on another, he is sure to think himself unjustly treated.

Clitandre. But young Cléon, whom the most respectable people go to see, what say you of him?

Célimène. That it is to his cook he owes his distinction, and to his table that people pay visits.

Éliante. He takes pains to provide the most dainty dishes.

Célimène. True; but I should be very glad if he would not dish up himself. His foolish person is a very bad dish, which, to my thinking, spoils every entertainment which he gives.

Philinte. His uncle Damis is very much esteemed; what say you to him, madam?

Célimène. He is one of my friends.

Philinte. I think him a perfect gentleman, and sensible enough.

Célimène. True; but he pretends to too much wit, which annoys me. He is always upon stilts, and, in all his conversations, one sees him laboring to say smart things. Since he took it into his head to be clever, he is so difficult to please that nothing suits his taste. He must needs find mistakes in everything that one writes, and thinks that to bestow praise does not become a wit, that to find fault shows learning, that only fools admire and laugh, and that, by not approving of anything in the works of our time, he is superior to all other people. Even in conversations he finds something to cavil at, the subjects are too trivial for his condescension; and, with arms crossed on his breast, he looks down from the height of his intellect with pity on what every one says.

Acaste. Drat it! his very picture.

Clitandre (*to* CÉLIMÈNE). You have an admirable knack of portraying people to the life.

Alceste. Capital, go on, my fine courtly friends. You spare no one, and every one will have his turn. Nevertheless, let but any one of those persons appear, and we shall see you rush to meet him, offer him your hand, and, with a flattering kiss, give weight to your protestations of being his servant.

Clitandre. Why this to us? If what is said offends you, the reproach must be addressed to this lady.

Alceste. No, gadzooks! it concerns you; for your assenting smiles draw from her wit all these slanderous remarks. Her satirical vein is incessantly recruited by the culpable incense of your flattery; and her mind would find fewer charms in raillery, if she discovered that no one applauded her. Thus it is that to flatterers we ought everywhere to impute the vices which are sown among mankind.

Philinte. But why do you take so great an interest in those people, for you would condemn the very things that are blamed in them?

Célimène. And is not this gentleman bound to contradict? Would you have him subscribe to the general opinion; and must he not everywhere display the spirit of contradiction with which Heaven has endowed him? Other people's sentiments can never please him. He always supports a contrary idea, and he would think himself too much of the common herd, were he observed to be of any one's opinion but his own. The honor of gainsaying has so many charms for him, that he very often takes up the cudgels against himself; he combats his own sentiments as soon as he hears them from other folks' lips.

Alceste. In short, madam, the laughters are on your side; and you may launch your satire against me.

Philinte. But it is very true, too, that you always take up arms against everything that is said; and, that your avowed spleen cannot bear people to be praised or blamed.

Alceste. 'Sdeath! spleen against mankind is always seasonable, because they are never in the right, and I see that, in all their dealings, they either praise impertinently, or censure rashly.

Célimène. But ...

Alceste. No, madam, no, though I were to die for it, you have pastimes which I cannot tolerate; and people are very wrong to nourish in your heart this great attachment to the very faults which they blame in you.

Clitandre. As for myself, I do not know; but I openly acknowledge that hitherto I have thought this lady faultless.

Acaste. I see that she is endowed with charms and attractions; but the faults which she has have not struck me.

Alceste. So much the more have they struck me; and far from appearing blind, she knows that I take care to reproach her with them. The more we love any one, the less we ought to flatter her. True love shows itself by overlooking nothing; and, were I a lady, I would banish all those meanspirited lovers who submit to all my sentiments, and whose mild complacencies every moment offer up incense to my vagaries.

Célimène. In short, if hearts were ruled by you we ought, to love well, to relinquish all tenderness, and make it the highest aim of perfect attachment to rail heartily at the persons we love.

Éliante. Love, generally speaking, is little apt to put up with these decrees, and lovers are always observed to extol their choice. Their passion never sees aught to blame in it, and in the beloved all things become lovable. They think their faults perfections, and invent sweet terms to call them by. The pale one vies with the jessamine in fairness; another, dark enough to frighten people, becomes an adorable brunette; the lean one has a good shape and is lithe; the stout one has a portly and majestic bearing; the slattern, who has few charms, passes under the name of a careless beauty; the giantess seems a very goddess in their sight; the dwarf is an epitome of all the wonders of Heaven; the proud one has a soul worthy of a diadem; the artful brims with wit; the silly one is very good-natured; the chatterbox is good-tempered; and the silent one modest and reticent. Thus a passionate swain loves even the very faults of those of whom he is enamored.

Alceste. And I maintain that ...

Célimène. Let us drop the subject, and take a turn or two in the gallery. What! are you going, gentlemen?

Clitandre and Acaste. No, no, madam.

Alceste. The fear of their departure troubles you very much. Go when you like, gentlemen; but I

MOLIÈRE

297

tell you beforehand that I shall not leave until you leave.

Acaste. Unless it inconveniences this lady, I have nothing to call me elsewhere the whole day.

Clitandre. I, provided I am present when the King retires, I have no other matter to call me away.

Célimène (to ALCESTE). You only joke, I fancy.

Alceste. Not at all. We shall soon see whether it is me of whom you wish to get rid.

SCENE VI: ALCESTE, CÉLIMÈNE, ÉLIANTE, ACASTE, PHILINTE, CLITANDRE, BASQUE

Basque (to ALCESTE). There is a man downstairs, sir, who wishes to speak to you on business which cannot be postponed.

Alceste. Tell him that I have no such urgent business.

Basque. He wears a jacket with large plaited skirts embroidered with gold.

Célimène (to ALCESTE). Go and see who it is, or else let him come in.

SCENE VII: ALCESTE, CÉLIMÈNE, ÉLIANTE, ACASTE, PHILINTE, CLITANDRE, A GUARD OF THE MARÉCHAUSSÉE

Alceste (going to meet the GUARD). What may be your pleasure? Come in, sir.

Guard. I would have a few words privately with you, sir.

Alceste. You may speak aloud, sir, so as to let me know.

Guard. The Marshals of France, whose commands I bear, hereby summon you to appear before them immediately, sir.

Alceste. Whom? Me, sir?

Guard. Yourself.

Alceste. And for what?

Philinte (to ALCESTE). It is this ridiculous affair between you and Oronte.

Célimène (to PHILINTE). What do you mean?

Philinte. Oronte and he have been insulting each other just now about some trifling verses which he did not like; and the Marshals wish to nip the affair in the bud.

Alceste. Well, I shall never basely submit.

Philinte. But you must obey the summons: come, get ready.

Alceste. How will they settle this between us? Will the edict of these gentlemen oblige me to approve of the verses which are the cause of our quarrel? I will not retract what I have said; I think them abominable.

Philinte. But with a little milder tone...

Alceste. I will not abate one jot; the verses are execrable.

Philinte. You ought to show a more accommodating spirit. Come along.

Alceste. I shall go, but nothing shall induce me to retract.

Philinte. Go and show yourself.

Alceste. Unless an express order from the King himself commands me to approve of the verses which cause all this trouble, I shall ever maintain, egad, that they are bad, and that a fellow deserves hanging for making them. (*To* CLITANDRE *and* ACASTE *who are laughing*) Hang it! gentlemen, I did not think I was so amusing.

Célimène. Go quickly whither you are wanted.

Alceste. I am going, madam; but shall come back here to finish our discussion.

ACT III

SCENE I: CLITANDRE, ACASTE

Clitandre. My dear marquis, you appear mightily pleased with yourself; everything amuses you, and nothing discomposes you. But really and truly, think you, without flattering yourself, that you have good reasons for appearing so joyful?

Acaste. Egad, I do not find, on looking at myself, any matter to be sorrowful about. I am wealthy, I am young, and am descended from a family which, with some appearance of truth, may be called noble; and I think that, by the rank which my lineage confers upon me, there are very few offices to which I might not aspire. As for courage, which we ought especially to value, it is well known — this without vanity — that I do not lack it; and people have seen me carry on an affair of honor in a manner sufficiently vigorous and brisk. As for wit, I have some, no doubt; and as for good taste, to judge and reason upon everything without study; at "first nights," of which I am very fond, to take my place as a critic upon the stage, to give my opinion as a judge, to applaud, and point out the best passages by repeated bravoes, I am sufficiently adroit; I carry myself well, and am good-looking, have particularly fine teeth, and a good figure. I believe, without flattering myself, that, as for dressing in good taste, very few will dispute the palm with me. I find myself treated with every possible consideration, very much beloved by the fair sex; and I stand very well with the King. With all that, I think, dear marquis, that one might be satisfied with one's self anywhere.

Clitandre. True. But, finding so many easy conquests elsewhere, why come you here to utter fruitless sighs?

Acaste. I? Zounds! I have neither the wish nor the disposition to put up with the indifference of any woman. I leave it to awkward and ordinary people to burn constantly for cruel fair maidens, to languish at their feet, and to bear with their severities, to invoke the aid of sighs and tears, and to endeavor, by long and persistent assiduities, to obtain what is denied to their little merit. But men of my stamp, marquis, are not made to love on trust, and be at all the expenses themselves. Be the merit of the fair ever so great, I think, thank Heaven, that we have our value as well as they; that it is not reasonable to enthrall a heart like mine without its costing them anything; and that, to weigh everything in a just scale, the advances should be, at least, reciprocal.

Clitandre. Then you think that you are right enough here, marquis?

Acaste. I have some reason, marquis, to think so.

Clitandre. Believe me, divest yourself of this great mistake: you flatter yourself, dear friend, and are altogether self-deceived.

Acaste. It is true. I flatter myself, and am, in fact, altogether, self-deceived.

Clitandre. But what causes you to judge your happiness to be complete?

Acaste. I flatter myself.

Clitandre. Upon what do you ground your belief?

Acaste. I am altogether self-deceived.

Clitandre. Have you any sure proofs?

Acaste. I am mistaken, I tell you.

Clitandre. Has Célimène made you any secret avowal of her inclinations?

Acaste. No, I am very badly treated by her.

Clitandre. Answer me, I pray.

Acaste. I meet with nothing but rebuffs.

Clitandre. A truce to your raillery; and tell me what hope she has held out to you.

Acaste. I am the rejected, and you are the lucky one. She has a great aversion to me, and one of these days I shall have to hang myself.

Clitandre. Nonsense. Shall we two, marquis, to adjust our love affairs, make a compact together? Whenever one of us shall be able to show a certain proof of having the greater share in Célimène's heart, the other shall leave the field free to the supposed conqueror, and by that means rid him of an obstinate rival.

Acaste. Egad! you please me with these words, and I agree to that from the bottom of my heart. But, hush.

SCENE II: Célimène, Acaste, Clitandre

Célimène. What! here still?

Clitandre. Love, madam, detains us.

Célimène. I hear a carriage below. Do you know whose it is?

Clitandre. No.

SCENE III: Célimène, Acaste, Clitandre, Basque

Basque. Arsinoé, madam, is coming up to see you.

Célimène. What does the woman want with me?

Basque. Éliante is down stairs talking to her.

Célimène. What is she thinking about, and what brings her here?

Acaste. She has everywhere the reputation of being a consummate prude, and her fervent zeal…

Célimène. Psha, downright humbug. In her inmost soul she is as worldly as any; and her every nerve is strained to hook some one, without being successful, however. She can only look with envious eyes on the accepted lovers of others; and in her wretched condition, forsaken by all, she is for ever railing against the blindness of the age. She endeavors to hide the dreadful isolation of her home under a false cloak of prudishness; and to save the credit of her feeble charms, she brands as criminal the power which they lack. Yet a swain would not come at all amiss to the lady; and she has even a tender hankering after Alceste. Every attention that he pays me, she looks upon as a theft committed by me, and as an insult to her attractions; and her jealous spite, which she can hardly hide, breaks out against me at every opportunity, and in an underhand manner. In short, I never saw anything, to my fancy, so stupid. She is impertinent to the last degree…

SCENE IV: Arsinoé, Célimène, Clitandre, Acaste

Célimène. Ah! what happy chance brings you here, madam? I was really getting uneasy about you.

Arsinoé. I have come to give you some advice as a matter of duty.

Célimène. How very glad I am to see you! (*Exeunt* Clitandre *and* Acaste, *laughing*.)

SCENE V: Arsinoé, Célimène

Arsinoé. They could not have left at a more convenient opportunity.

Célimène. Shall we sit down?

Arsinoé. It is not necessary. Friendship, madam, must especially show itself in matters which may be of consequence to us; and as there are none of greater importance than honor and decorum, I come to prove to you, by an advice which closely touches your reputation, the friendship which I feel for you. Yesterday I was with some people of rare virtue, where the conversation turned upon you; and there, your conduct, which is causing some stir, was unfortunately, madam, far from being commended. That crowd of people, whose visits you permit, your gallantry and the noise it makes, were criticized rather more freely and more severely than I could have wished. You can easily imagine whose part I took. I did all I could to defend you. I exonerated you, and vouched for the purity of your heart, and the honesty of your intentions. But you know there are things in life, which one cannot well defend, although one may have the greatest wish to do so; and I was at last obliged to confess that the way in which you lived did you some harm; that, in the eyes of the world, it had a doubtful look; that there was no story so ill-natured as not to be everywhere told about it; and that, if you liked, your behavior might give less cause for censure. Not that I believe that decency is in any way outraged. Heaven forbid that I should harbor such a thought! But the world is so ready to give credit to the faintest shadow of a crime, and it is not enough to live blameless one's self. Madam, I believe you to be too sensible not to take in good part this useful counsel, and to ascribe it only to the inner promptings of an affection that feels an interest in your welfare.

Célimène. Madam, I have a great many thanks to return you. Such counsel lays me under an obligation; and, far from taking it amiss, I intend this very moment to repay the favor, by giving you an advice which also touches your reputation closely; and as I see you prove yourself my friend by acquainting me with the stories that are current of me, I shall follow so nice an example, by informing you what is said of you. In a house the other day, where I paid a visit, I met some people of exemplary merit, who, while talking of the proper duties of a well spent life, turned the topic of the conversation upon you, madam. There your prudishness and your too fervent zeal were not at all cited as a good example. This affectation of a grave demeanor, your eternal conversations on wisdom and honor, your mincings and mouthings at the slightest shadows of indecency, which an innocent though ambiguous word may convey, that lofty esteem in which you hold yourself, and those pitying glances which you cast upon all, your frequent lectures and your acrid censures on things which are pure and harmless; all this, if I may speak frankly to you, madam, was blamed unanimously. What is the good, said they, of this

modest mien and this prudent exterior, which is belied by all the rest? She says her prayers with the utmost exactness; but she beats her servants and pays them no wages. She displays great fervor in every place of devotion; but she paints and wishes to appear handsome. She covers the nudities in her pictures; but loves the reality. As for me, I undertook your defense against every one, and positively assured them that it was nothing but scandal; but the general opinion went against me, as they came to the conclusion that you would do well to concern yourself less about the actions of others, and take a little more pains with your own; that one ought to look a long time at one's self before thinking of condemning other people; that when we wish to correct others, we ought to add the weight of a blameless life; and that even then, it would be better to leave it to those whom Heaven has ordained for the task. Madam, I also believe you to be too sensible not to take in good part this useful counsel, and to ascribe it only to the inner promptings of an affection that feels an interest in your welfare.

Arsinoé. To whatever we may be exposed when we reprove, I did not expect this retort, madam, and, by its very sting, I see how my sincere advice has hurt your feelings.

Célimène. On the contrary, madam; and, if we were reasonable, these mutual counsels would become customary. If honestly made use of, they would to a great extent destroy the excellent opinion people have of themselves. It depends entirely on you whether we shall continue this trustworthy practice with equal zeal, and whether we shall take great care to tell each other, between ourselves, what we hear, you of me, I of you.

Arsinoé. Ah! madam, I can hear nothing said of you. It is in me that people find so much to reprove.

Célimène. Madam, it is easy, I believe, to blame or praise everything; and every one may be right, according to his age and taste. There is a time for gallantry, there is one also for prudishness. One may out of policy take to it, when youthful attractions have faded away. It sometimes serves to hide vexatious ravages of time. I do not say that I shall not follow your example, one of these days. Those things come with old age; but twenty, as every one well knows, is not an age to play the prude.

Arsinoé. You certainly pride yourself upon a very small advantage, and you boast terribly of your age. Whatever difference there may be between your years and mine, there is no occasion to make such a tremendous fuss about it; and I am at a loss to know, madam, why you would get so angry, and what makes you goad me in this manner.

Célimène. And I, madam, am at an equal loss to know why one hears you inveigh so bitterly against me everywhere. Must I always suffer for your vexations? Can I help it, if people refuse to pay you any attentions? If men will fall in love with me, and will persist in offering me each day those attentions of which your heart would wish to see me deprived, I cannot alter it, and it is not my fault. I leave you the field free, and do not prevent you from having charms to attract people.

Arsinoë. Alas! and do you think that I would trouble myself about this crowd of lovers of which you are so vain, and that it is not very easy to judge at what price they may be attracted now-a-days? Do you wish to make it be believed, that, judging by what is going on, your merit alone attracts this crowd; that their affection for you is strictly honest, and that it is for nothing but your virtue that they all pay you their court? People are not blinded by those empty pretenses; the world is not duped in that way; and I see many ladies who are capable of inspiring a tender feeling, yet who do not succeed in attracting a crowd of beaux; and from that fact we may draw our conclusion that those conquests are not altogether made without some great advances; that no one cares to sigh for us, for our handsome looks only; and that the attentions bestowed on us are generally dearly bought. Do not therefore pull yourself up with vain-glory about the trifling advantages of a poor victory; and moderate slightly the pride on your good looks, instead of looking down upon people on account of them. If I were at all envious about your conquests, I dare say, that I might manage like other people; be under no restraint, and thus show plainly that one may have lovers, when one wishes for them.

Célimène. Do have some then, madam, and let us see you try it; endeavor to please by this extraordinary secret; and without ...

Arsinoë. Let us break off this conversation, madam, it might excite too much both your temper and mine; and I would have already taken my leave, had I not been obliged to wait for my carriage.

Célimène. Please stay as long as you like, and do not hurry yourself on that account, madam. But instead of wearying you any longer with my presence, I am going to give you some more pleasant company. This gentleman, who comes very opportunely, will better supply my place in entertaining you.

SCENE VI: ALCESTE, CÉLIMÈNE, ARSINOÉ

Célimène. Alceste, I have to write a few lines, which I cannot well delay. Please to stay with this lady; she will all the more easily excuse my rudeness.

SCENE VII: ALCESTE, ARSINOÉ

Arsinoë. You see, I am left here to entertain you, until my coach comes round. She could have devised no more charming treat for me, than such a conversation. Indeed, people of exceptional merit attract the esteem and love of every one; and yours has undoubtedly some secret charm, which makes me feel interested in all your doings. I could wish that the Court, with a real regard to your merits would do more justice to your deserts. You have reason to complain; and it vexes me to see that day by day nothing is done for you.

Alceste. For me, madam? And by what right could I pretend to anything? What service have I rendered to the State? Pray, what have I done, so brilliant in itself, to complain of the Court doing nothing for me?

Arsinoë. Not every one whom the State delights to honor, has rendered signal services; there must be an opportunity as well as the power; and the abilities which you allow us to perceive, ought ...

Alceste. For Heaven's sake, let us have no more of my abilities, I pray. What would you have the Court to do? It would have enough to do, and have its hands full, to discover the merits of people.

Arsinoë. Sterling merit discovers itself. A great deal is made of yours in certain places; and let me tell you that, not later than yesterday, you were highly spoken of in two distinguished circles, by people of very great standing.

Alceste. As for that, madam, every one is praised now-a-days, and very little discrimination is shown in our times. Everything is equally endowed with great merit, so that it is no longer an honor to be lauded. Praises abound, they throw them at one's head, and even my valet is put in the gazette.

Arsinoë. As for me, I could wish that, to bring yourself into greater notice, some place at Court might tempt you. If you will only give me a hint that you seriously think about it, a great many engines might be set in motion to serve you; and I know some people whom I could employ for you, and who would manage the matter smoothly enough.

Alceste. And what should I do when I got there, madam? My disposition rather prompts me to keep away from it. Heaven, when ushering me into the world, did not give me a mind suited for the atmosphere of a Court. I have not the qualifications necessary for success, nor for making my fortune there. To be open and candid is my chief talent; I possess not the art of deceiving people in conversation; and he who has not the gift of concealing his thoughts, ought not to stay long in those places. When not at Court, one has not, doubtless, that standing, and the advantage of those honorable titles which it bestows now-a-days; but, on the other hand, one has not the vexation of playing the silly fool. One has not to bear a thousand galling rebuffs; one is not, as it were, forced to praise the verses of mister so-and-so, to laud madam such and such, and to put up with the whims of some ingenious marquis.

Arsinoé. Since you wish it, let us drop the subject of the Court: but I cannot help grieving for your amours; and, to tell you my opinions candidly on that head, I could heartily wish your affections better bestowed. You certainly deserve a much happier fate, and she who has fascinated you is unworthy of you.

Alceste. But in saying so, madam, remember, I pray, that this lady is your friend.

Arsinoé. True. But really my conscience revolts at the thought of suffering any longer the wrong that is done to you. The position in which I see you afflicts my very soul, and I caution you that your affections are betrayed.

Alceste. This is certainly showing me a deal of good feeling, madam, and such information is very welcome to a lover.

Arsinoé. Yes, for all Célimène is my friend, I do not hesitate to call her unworthy of possessing the heart of a man of honor; and hers only pretends to respond to yours.

Alceste. That is very possible, madam, one cannot look into the heart; but your charitable feelings might well have refrained from awakening such a suspicion as mine.

Arsinoé. Nothing is easier than to say no more about it, if you do not wish to be undeceived.

Alceste. Just so. But whatever may be openly said on this subject is not half so annoying as hints thrown out; and I for one would prefer to be plainly told that only which could be clearly proved.

Arsinoé. Very well! and that is sufficient; I can fully enlighten you upon this subject. I will have you believe nothing but what your own eyes see. Only have the kindness to escort me as far as my house; and I will give you undeniable proof of the faithlessness of your fair one's heart; and if, after that, you can find charms in any one else, we will perhaps find you some consolation.

ACT IV

SCENE I: ÉLIANTE, PHILINTE

Philinte. No, never have I seen so obstinate a mind, nor a reconciliation more difficult to effect.

In vain was Alceste tried on all sides; he would still maintain his opinion; and never, I believe, has a more curious dispute engaged the attention of those gentlemen. "No, gentlemen," exclaimed he, "I will not retract, and I shall agree with you on every point, except on this one. At what is Oronte offended? and with what does he reproach me? Does it reflect upon his honor that he cannot write well? What is my opinion to him, which he has altogether wrongly construed? One may be a perfect gentleman, and write bad verses; those things have nothing to do with honor. I take him to be a gallant man in every way; a man of standing, of merit, and courage, anything you like, but he is a wretched author. I shall praise, if you wish, his mode of living, his lavishness, his skill in riding, in fencing, in dancing; but as to praising his verses, I am his humble servant; and if one has not the gift of composing better, one ought to leave off rhyming altogether, unless condemned to it on forfeit of one's life." In short, all the modification they could with difficulty obtain from him, was to say, in what he thought a much gentler tone — "I am sorry, sir, to be so difficult to please; and out of regard to you, I could wish, with all my heart, to have found your sonnet a little better." And they compelled them to settle this dispute quickly with an embrace.

Éliante. He is very eccentric in his doings; but I must confess that I think a great deal of him; and the candor upon which he prides himself has something noble and heroic in it. It is a rare virtue now-a-days, and I, for one, should not be sorry to meet with it everywhere.

Philinte. As for me, the more I see of him, the more I am amazed at that passion to which his whole heart is given up. I cannot conceive how, with a disposition like his, he has taken it into his head to love at all; and still less can I understand how your cousin happens to be the person to whom his feelings are inclined.

Éliante. That shows that love is not always produced by compatibility of temper; and in this case, all the pretty theories of gentle sympathies are belied.

Philinte. But do you think him beloved in return, to judge from what we see?

Éliante. That is a point not easily decided. How can we judge whether it be true she loves? Her own heart is not so very sure of what it feels. It sometimes loves, without being quite aware of it, and at other times thinks it does, without the least grounds.

Philinte. I think that our friend will have more trouble with this cousin of yours than he imagines; and to tell you the truth, if he were of my mind, he would bestow his affections elsewhere; and by a better choice, we should see him, madam, profit by the kind feelings which your heart evinces for him.

Éliante. As for me, I do not mince matters, and I think that in such cases we ought to act with sincerity. I do not run counter to his tender feelings; on the contrary, I feel interested in them; and, if it depended only on me, I would unite him to the object of his love. But if, as it may happen in love affairs, his affections should receive a check, and if Célimène should respond to the love of any one else, I could easily be prevailed upon to listen to his addresses, and I should have no repugnance whatever to them on account of their rebuff elsewhere.

Philinte. Nor do I, from my side, oppose myself, madam, to the tender feelings which you entertain for him; and he himself, if he wished, could inform you what I have taken care to say to him on that score. But if, by the union of those two, you should be prevented from accepting his attentions, all mine would endeavor to gain that great favor which your kind feelings offer to him; only too happy, madam, to have them transferred to myself, if his heart could not respond to yours.

Éliante. You are in the humor to jest, Philinte.

Philinte. Not so, madam, I am speaking my inmost feelings. I only wait the opportune moment to offer myself openly, and am wishing most anxiously to hurry its advent.

Scene II: Alceste, Éliante, Philinte

Alceste. Ah, madam! obtain me justice, for an offense which triumphs over all my constancy.

Éliante. What ails you? What disturbs you?

Alceste. This much ails me, that it is death to me to think of it; and the upheaving of all creation would less overwhelm me than this accident. It is all over with me... My love... I cannot speak.

Éliante. Just endeavor to be composed.

Alceste. Oh, just Heaven; can the odious vices of the basest minds be joined to such beauty?

Éliante. But, once more, what can have...

Alceste. Alas! All is ruined! I am! I am betrayed! I am stricken to death. Célimène... would you credit it! Célimène deceives me and is faithless.

Éliante. Have you just grounds for believing so?

Philinte. Perhaps it is a suspicion, rashly conceived; and your jealous temper often harbors fancies...

Alceste. Ah! 'Sdeath, please to mind your own business, sir. (*To* Éliante) Her treachery is but too certain, for I have in my pocket a letter in her own handwriting. Yes, madam, a letter, intended

for Oronte, has placed before my eyes my disgrace and her shame; Oronte, whose addresses I believed she avoided, and whom, of all my rivals, I feared the least.

Philinte. A letter may deceive by appearances, and is sometimes not so culpable as may be thought.

Alceste. Once more, sir, leave me alone, if you please, and trouble yourself only about your own concerns.

Éliante. You should moderate your passion; and the insult...

Alceste. You must be left to do that, madam; it is to you that my heart has recourse today to free itself from this goading pain. Avenge me on an ungrateful and perfidious relative who basely deceives such constant tenderness. Avenge me for an act that ought to fill you with horror.

Éliante. I avenge you? How?

Alceste. By accepting my heart. Take it, madam, instead of the false one; it is in this way that I can avenge myself upon her; and I shall punish her by the sincere attachment, and the profound love, the respectful cares, the eager devotions, the ceaseless attentions which this heart will henceforth offer up at your shrine.

Éliante. I certainly sympathize with you in your sufferings, and do not despise your proffered heart; but the wrong done may not be so great as you think, and you might wish to forego this desire for revenge. When the injury proceeds from a beloved object, we form many designs which we never execute; we may find as powerful a reason as we like to break off the connection, the guilty charmer is soon again innocent; all the harm we wish her quickly vanishes, and we know what a lover's anger means.

Alceste. No, no, madam, no. The offense is too cruel; there will be no relenting, and I have done with her. Nothing shall change the resolution I have taken, and I should hate myself for ever loving her again. Here she comes. My anger increases at her approach. I shall taunt her with her black guilt, completely put her to the blush, and, after that, bring you a heart wholly freed from her deceitful attractions.

Scene III: Célimène, Alceste

Alceste (*aside*). Grant, Heaven, that I may control my temper.

Célimène (*aside*). Ah! (*To* Alceste) What is all this trouble that I see you in, and what means those long-drawn sighs, and those black looks which you cast at me?

Alceste. That all the wickedness of which a heart is capable is not to be compared to your perfidy;

that neither fate, hell, nor Heaven in its wrath, ever produced anything so wicked as you are.

Célimène. These are certainly pretty compliments, which I admire very much.

Alceste. Do not jest. This is no time for laughing. Blush rather, you have cause to do so; and I have undeniable proofs of your treachery. This is what the agitations of my mind prognosticated; it was not without cause that my love took alarm; by these frequent suspicions, which were hateful to you, I was trying to discover the misfortune which my eyes have beheld; and in spite of all your care and your skill in dissembling, my star foretold me what I had to fear. But do not imagine that I will bear unavenged this slight of being insulted. I know that we have no command over our inclinations, that love will everywhere spring up spontaneously, that there is no entering a heart by force, and that every soul is free to name its conqueror: I should thus have no reason to complain if you had spoken to me without dissembling, and rejected my advances from the very beginning; my heart would then have been justified in blaming fortune alone. But to see my love encouraged by a deceitful avowal on your part, is an action so treacherous and perfidious, that it cannot meet with too great a punishment; and I can allow my resentment to do anything. Yes, yes; after such an outrage, fear everything; I am no longer myself, I am mad with rage. My senses, struck by the deadly blow with which you kill me, are no longer governed by reason; I give way to the outbursts of a just wrath, and am no longer responsible for what I may do.

Célimène. Whence comes, I pray, such a passion? Speak! Have you lost your senses?

Alceste. Yes, yes, I lost them when, to my misfortune, I beheld you, and thus took the poison which kills me, and when I thought to meet with some sincerity in those treacherous charms that bewitched me.

Célimène. Of what treachery have you to complain?

Alceste. Ah! how double-faced she is! how well she knows how to dissemble! But I am fully prepared with the means of driving her to extremities. Cast your eyes here and recognize your writing. This picked-up note is sufficient to confound you, and such proof cannot easily be refuted.

Célimène. And this is the cause of your perturbation of spirits?

Alceste. You do not blush on beholding this writing!

Célimène. And why should I blush?

Alceste. What! You add boldness to craft! Will you disown this note because it bears no name?

Célimène. Why should I disown it, since I wrote it.

Alceste. And you can look at it without becoming confused at the crime of which its style accuses you!

Célimène. You are, in truth, a very eccentric man.

Alceste. What! you thus out-brave this convincing proof! And the contents so full of tenderness for Oronte, need have nothing in them to outrage me, or to shame you?

Célimène. Oronte! Who told you that this letter is for him?

Alceste. The people who put it into my hands this day. But I will even suppose that it is for some one else. Has my heart any less cause to complain of yours? Will you, in fact, be less guilty toward me?

Célimène. But if it is a woman to whom this letter is addressed, how can it hurt you, or what is there culpable in it?

Alceste. Hem! The prevarication is ingenious, and the excuse excellent. I must own that I did not expect this turn; and nothing but that was wanting to convince me. Do you dare to have recourse to such palpable tricks? Do you think people entirely destitute of common sense? Come, let us see a little by what subterfuge, with what air, you will support so palpable a falsehood; and how you can apply to a woman every word of this note which evinces so much tenderness! Reconcile, if you can, to hide your deceit, what I am about to read....

Célimène. It does not suit me to do so. I think it ridiculous that you should take so much upon yourself, and tell me to my face what you have the daring to say to me!

Alceste. No, no, without flying into a rage, take a little trouble to explain these terms.

Célimène. No, I shall do nothing of the kind, and it matters very little to me what you think upon the subject.

Alceste. I pray you, show me, and I shall be satisfied, if this letter can be explained as meant for a woman.

Célimène. Not at all. It is for Oronte; and I will have you believe it. I accept all his attentions gladly; I admire what he says, I like him, and I shall agree to whatever you please. Do as you like, and act as you think proper; let nothing hinder you and do not harass me any longer.

Alceste (*aside*). Heavens! can anything more cruel be conceived, and was ever heart treated like mine? What! I am justly angry with her, I come to complain, and I am quarrelled with instead! My grief and my suspicions are excited to the utmost,

I am allowed to believe everything, she boasts of everything; and yet, my heart is still sufficiently mean not to be able to break the bonds that hold it fast, and not to arm itself with a generous contempt for the ungrateful object of which it is too much enamored. (*To* Célimène) Perfidious woman, you know well how to take advantage of my great weakness, and to employ for your own purpose that excessive, astonishing, and fatal love which your treacherous looks have inspired! Defend yourself at least from this crime that overwhelms me, and stop pretending to be guilty. Show me, if you can, that this letter is innocent; my affection will even consent to assist you. At any rate, endeavor to appear faithful, and I shall strive to believe you such.

Célimène. Bah, you are mad with your jealous frenzies, and do not deserve the love which I have for you. I should much like to know what could compel me to stoop for you to the baseness of dissembling; and why, if my heart were disposed towards another, I should not say so candidly. What! does the kind assurance of my sentiments towards you not defend me sufficiently against all your suspicions? Ought they to possess any weight at all with such a guarantee? Is it not insulting me even to listen to them? And since it is with the utmost difficulty that we can resolve to confess our love, since the strict honor of our sex, hostile to our passion, strongly opposes such a confession, ought a lover who sees such an obstacle overcome for his sake, doubt with impunity our avowal? And is he not greatly to blame in not assuring himself of the truth of that which is never said but after a severe struggle with one's self? Begone, such suspicions deserve my anger, and you are not worthy of being cared for. I am silly, and am vexed at my own simplicity in still preserving the least kindness for you. I ought to place my affections elsewhere, and give you a just cause for complaint.

Alceste. Ah! you traitress! mine is a strange infatuation for you; those tender expressions are, no doubt, meant only to deceive me. But it matters little, I must submit to my fate; my very soul is wrapt up in you; I will see to the bitter end how your heart will act towards me, and whether it will be black enough to deceive me.

Célimène. No, you do not love me as you ought to love.

Alceste. Indeed! Nothing is to be compared to my exceeding love; and, in its eagerness to show itself to the whole world, it goes even so far as to form wishes against you. Yes, I could wish that no one thought you handsome, that you were reduced to a miserable existence; that Heaven, at

your birth, had bestowed upon you nothing; that you had no rank, no nobility, no wealth, so that I might openly proffer my heart, and thus make amends to you for the injustice of such a lot; and that, this very day, I might have the joy and the glory of seeing you owe everything to my love.

Célimène. This is wishing me well in a strange way. Heaven grant that you may never have occasion... But here comes Monsieur Dubois curiously decked out.

SCENE IV: Célimène, Alceste, Dubois

Alceste. What means this strange attire, and that frightened look? What ails you?

Dubois. Sir ...

Alceste. Well?

Dubois. The most mysterious event.

Alceste. What is it?

Dubois. Our affairs are turning out badly, sir.

Alceste. What?

Dubois. Shall I speak out?

Alceste. Yes, do, and quickly.

Dubois. Is there no one there?

Alceste. Curse your trifling! Will you speak?

Dubois. Sir, we must beat a retreat.

Alceste. What do you mean?

Dubois. We must steal away from this quietly.

Alceste. And why?

Dubois. I tell you that we must leave this place.

Alceste. The reason?

Dubois. You must go, sir, without staying to take leave.

Alceste. But what is the meaning of this strain?

Dubois. The meaning is, sir, that you must make yourself scarce.

Alceste. I shall knock you on the head to a certainty, booby, if you do not explain yourself more clearly.

Dubois. A fellow, sir, with a black dress, and as black a look, got as far as the kitchen to leave a paper with us, scribbled over in such a fashion that old Nick himself could not have read it. It is about your lawsuit, I make no doubt; but the very devil, I believe, could not make head nor tail of it.

Alceste. Well! what then? What has the paper to do with the going away of which you speak, you scoundrel?

Dubois. I must tell you, sir, that, about an hour afterwards, a gentleman who often calls, came to ask for you quite eagerly, and not finding you at home, quietly told me, knowing how attached I am to you, to let you know... Stop a moment, what the deuce is his name?

Alceste. Never mind his name, you scoundrel, and tell me what he told you.

Dubois. He is one of your friends, in short, that is sufficient. He told me that for your very life you must get away from this, and that you are threatened with arrest.

Alceste. But how! has he not specified anything?

Dubois. No. He asked me for ink and paper, and has sent you a line from which you can, I think, fathom the mystery!

Alceste. Hand it over then.

Célimène. What can all this mean?

Alceste. I do not know, but I am anxious to be informed. Have you almost done, devil take you?

Dubois (*after having fumbled for some time for the note*). After all, sir, I have left it on your table.

Alceste. I do not know what keeps me from ...

Célimène. Do not put yourself in a passion, but go and unravel this perplexing business.

Alceste. It seems that fate, whatever I may do has sworn to prevent my having a conversation with you. But, to get the better of her, allow me to see you again, madam, before the end of the day.

ACT V

SCENE I: ALCESTE, PHILINTE

Alceste. I tell you, my mind is made up about it.

Philinte. But, whatever this blow may be, does it compel you ...

Alceste. You may talk and argue till doomsday if you like, nothing can avert me from what I have said. The age we live in is too perverse, and I am determined to withdraw altogether from intercourse with the world. What! when honor, probity, decency, and the laws, are all against my adversary; when the equity of my claim is everywhere cried up; when my mind is at rest as to the justice of my cause, I meanwhile see myself betrayed by its issue! What! I have got justice on my side, and I lose my case! A wretch, whose scandalous history is well known, comes off triumphant by the blackest falsehood! All good faith yields to his treachery! He finds the means of being in the right, whilst cutting my throat! The weight of his dissimulation, so full of cunning, overthrows the right and turns the scales of justice! He obtains even a decree of courts to crown his villainy. And, not content with the wrong he is doing me, there is abroad in society an abominable book, of which the very reading is to be condemned, a book that deserves the utmost severity, and of which the scoundrel has the impudence to proclaim me the author. Upon this, Oronte is observed to mutter, and tries wickedly to support the imposture! He, who holds

an honorable position at Court, to whom I have done nothing except having been sincere and candid, who came to ask me in spite of myself of my opinion of some of his verses; and because I treat him honestly, and will not betray either him or truth, he assists in overwhelming me with a trumped-up crime! Behold him now my greatest enemy! And I shall never obtain his sincere forgiveness, because I did not think that his sonnet was good! 'Sdeath! to think that mankind is made thus! The thirst for fame induces them to do such things! This is the good faith, the virtuous zeal, the justice and the honor to be found amongst them! Let us begone; it is too much to endure the vexations they are devising; let us get out of this wood, this cut-throat hole; and since men behave towards each other like real wolves, wretches, you shall never see me again as long as I live.

Philinte. I think you are acting somewhat hastily; and the harm done is not so great as you would make it out. Whatever your adversary dares to impute to you has not had the effect of causing you to be arrested. We see his false reports defeating themselves, and this action is likely to hurt him much more than you.

Alceste. Him? he does not mind the scandal of such tricks as these. He has a license to be an arrant knave; and this event, far from damaging his position, will obtain him a still better standing tomorrow.

Philinte. In short, it is certain that little notice has been taken of the report which his malice spread against you; from that side you have already nothing to fear; and as for your lawsuit, of which you certainly have reason to complain, it is easy for you to bring the trial on afresh, and against this decision ...

Alceste. No, I shall leave it as it is. Whatever cruel wrong this verdict may inflict, I shall take particular care not to have it set aside. We see too plainly how right is maltreated in it, and I wish to go down to posterity as a signal proof, as a notorious testimony of the wickedness of the men of our age. It may indeed cost me twenty thousand francs, but at the cost of twenty thousand francs I shall have the right of railing against the iniquity of human nature, and of nourishing an undying hatred of it.

Philinte. But after all ...

Alceste. But after all, your pains are thrown away. What can you, sir, say upon this head? Would you have the assurance to wish, to my face, to excuse the villainy of all that is happening?

Philinte. No, I agree with you in all that you say. Everything goes by intrigue, and by pure influence. It is only trickery which carries the day in our time, and men ought to act differently. But is their want of equity a reason for wishing to withdraw from their society? All human failings give us, in life, the means of exercising our philosophy. It is the best employment for virtue; and if probity reigned everywhere, if all hearts were candid, just, and tractable, most of our virtues would be useless to us, inasmuch as their functions are to bear, without annoyance, the injustice of others in our good cause; and just in the same way as a heart full of virtue ...

Alceste. I know that you are a most fluent speaker, sir; that you always abound in fine arguments; but you are wasting your time, and all your fine speeches. Reason tells me to retire for my own good. I cannot command my tongue sufficiently; I cannot answer for what I might say, and should very probably get myself into a hundred scrapes. Allow me, without any more words, to wait for Célimène. She must consent to the plan that brings me here. I shall see whether her heart has any love for me; and this very hour will prove it to me.

Philinte. Let us go upstairs to Éliante, and wait her coming.

Alceste. No, my mind is too harassed. You go and see her, and leave me in this little dark corner with my black care.

Philinte. That is strange company to leave you in; I will induce Éliante to come down.

Scene II: Célimène, Oronte, Alceste

Oronte. Yes, madam, it remains for you to consider whether, by ties so dear, you will make me wholly yours, I must be absolutely certain of your affection: a lover dislikes to be held in suspense upon such a subject. If the ardor of my affection has been able to move your feelings, you ought not to hesitate to let me see it; and the proof, after all, which I ask of you, is not to allow Alceste to wait upon you any longer; to sacrifice him to my love, and, in short, to banish him from your house this very day.

Célimène. But why are you so incensed against him; you, whom I have so often heard speak of his merits?

Oronte. There is no need, madam, of these explanations; the question is, what are your feelings? Please to choose between the one or the other; my resolution depends entirely upon yours.

Alceste (coming out of his corner). Yes, this gentleman is right, madam, you must make a choice; and his request agrees perfectly with mine. I am equally eager, and the same anxiety brings me here. My love requires a sure proof. Things cannot go on any longer in this way, and the moment has arrived for explaining your feelings.

Oronte. I have no wish, sir, in any way to disturb, by an untimely affection, your good fortune.

Alceste. And I have no wish, sir, jealous or not jealous, to share aught in her heart with you.

Oronte. If she prefers your affection to mine ...

Alceste. If she has the slightest inclination towards you ...

Oronte. I swear henceforth not to pretend to it again.

Alceste. I peremptorily swear never to see her again.

Oronte. Madam, it remains with you now to speak openly.

Alceste. Madam, you can explain yourself fearlessly.

Oronte. You have simply to tell us where your feelings are engaged.

Alceste. You may simply finish the matter, by choosing between us two.

Oronte. What! you seem to be at a loss to make such a choice.

Alceste. What! your heart still wavers, and appears uncertain!

Célimène. Good Heavens, how out of place is this persistence, and how very unreasonable you both show yourselves! It is not that I do not know whom to prefer, nor is it my heart that wavers. It is not at all in doubt between you two; and nothing could be more quickly accomplished than the choice of my affections. But to tell the truth, I feel too confused to pronounce such an avowal before you; I think that disobliging words ought not to be spoken in people's presence; that a heart can give sufficient proof of its attachment without going so far as to break with every one; and gentler intimations suffice to inform a lover of the ill success of his suit.

Oronte. No, no, I do not fear a frank avowal; for my part I consent to it.

Alceste. And I demand it; it is just its very publicity that I claim, and I do not wish you to spare my feelings in the least. Your great study has always been to keep friends with every one; but no more trifling, no more uncertainty. You must explain yourself clearly, or I shall take your refusal as a verdict; I shall know, for my part, how to interpret your silence, and shall consider it as a confirmation of the worst.

Oronte. I owe you many thanks, sir, for this wrath, and I say in every respect as you do.

Célimène. How you weary me with such a whim! Is there any justice in what you ask? And have I not told you what motive prevents me? I will be judged by Éliante, who is just coming.

SCENE III: ÉLIANTE, PHILINTE, CÉLIMÈNE, ORONTE, ALCESTE

Célimène. Good cousin, I am being persecuted here by people who have concerted to do so. They both demand, with the same warmth, that I should declare whom my heart has chosen, and that, by a decision which I must give before their very faces, I should forbid one of them to tease me any more with his attentions. Say, has ever such a thing been done?

Éliante. Pray, do not consult me upon such a matter. You may perhaps address yourself to the wrong person, for I am decidedly for people who speak their mind.

Oronte. Madam, it is useless for you to decline.

Alceste. All your evasions here will be badly supported.

Oronte. You must speak, you must, and no longer waver.

Alceste. You need do no more than remain silent.

Oronte. I desire but one word to end our discussions.

Alceste. To me your silence will convey as much as speech.

SCENE IV: ARSINOÉ, CÉLIMÈNE, ÉLIANTE, ALCESTE, PHILINTE, ACASTE, CLITANDRE, ORONTE

Acaste (*to* CÉLIMÈNE). We have both come, by your leave, madam, to clear up a certain little matter with you.

Clitandre (*to* ORONTE *and* ALCESTE). Your presence happens fortunately, gentlemen; for this affair concerns you also.

Arsinoé (*to* CÉLIMÈNE). No doubt you are surprised at seeing me here, madam; but these gentlemen are the cause of my intrusion. They both came to see me, and complained of a proceeding which I could not have credited. I have too high an opinion of your kindness of heart ever to believe you capable of such a crime; my eyes even have refused to give credence to their strongest proofs, and in my friendship, forgetting trivial disagreements, I have been induced to accompany them here, to hear you refute this slander.

Acaste. Yes, madam, let us see, with composure, how you will manage to bear this out. This letter has been written by you, to Clitandre.

Clitandre. And this tender epistle you have addressed to Acaste.

Acaste (*to* ORONTE *and* ALCESTE). This writing is not altogether unknown to you, gentlemen, and I have no doubt that her kindness has before now made you familiar with her hand. But this is well worth the trouble of reading.

"*You are a strange man to condemn my liveliness of spirits, and to reproach me that I am never so merry as when I am not with you. Nothing could be more unjust; and if you do not come very soon to ask my pardon for this offense, I shall never forgive you as long as I live. Our great hulking booby of a Viscount.*" He ought to have been here. "*Our great hulking booby of a Viscount, with whom you begin your complaints, is a man who would not at all suit me; and ever since I watched him for full three-quarters of an hour spitting in a well to make circles in the water, I never could have a good opinion of him. As for the little Marquis . . .*" that is myself, ladies and gentlemen, be it said without the slightest vanity, . . . "*as for the little Marquis, who held my hand yesterday for a long while, I think that there is nothing so diminutive as his whole person, and his sole merit consists in his cloak and sword. As to the man with the green shoulder knot.*" (*To* ALCESTE) It is your turn now, sir. "*As to the man with the green shoulder knot, he amuses me sometimes with his bluntness and his splenetic behavior; but there are hundreds of times when I think him the greatest bore in the world. Respecting the man with the big waistcoat . . .*" (*To* ORONTE) This is your share. "*Respecting the man with the big waistcoat, who has thought fit to set up as a wit, and wishes to be an author in spite of every one, I cannot even take the trouble to listen to what he says; and his prose bores me just as much as his poetry. Take it for granted that I do not always enjoy myself so much as you think; and that I wish for you, more than I care to say, amongst all the entertainments to which I am dragged; and that the presence of those we love is an excellent relish to our pleasures.*"

Clitandre. Now for myself.

"*Your Clitandre, whom you mention to me, and who has always such a quantity of soft expressions at his command, is the last man for whom I could feel any affection. He must be crazed in persuading himself that I love him; and you are so too in believing that I do not love you. You had better change your fancies for his, and come and see me as often as you can, to help me in bearing the annoyance of being pestered by him.*" This shows the model of a lovely character, madam; and I need not tell you what to call it. It is enough. We shall, both of us, show this admirable sketch of your heart everywhere and to everybody.

Acaste. I might also say something, and the subject is tempting; but I deem you beneath my anger; and I will show you that little marquises can find worthier hearts than yours to console themselves.

SCENE V: CÉLIMÈNE, ÉLIANTE, ARSINOÉ,
ALCESTE, ORONTE, PHILINTE

Oronte. What! Am I to be pulled to pieces in this fashion, after all that you have written to me? And does your heart, with all its semblance of love, plight its faith to all mankind by turns! Bah, I have been too great a dupe, but I shall be so no longer. You have done me a service, in showing yourself in your true colors to me. I am the richer by a heart which you thus restore to me, and find my revenge in your loss. (*To* ALCESTE) Sir, I shall no longer be an obstacle to your flame, and you may settle matters with this lady as soon as you please.

SCENE VI: CÉLIMÈNE, ÉLIANTE, ARSINOÉ,
ALCESTE, PHILINTE

Arsinoé (*to* CÉLIMÈNE). This is certainly one of the basest actions which I have ever seen; I can no longer be silent, and feel quite upset. Has any one ever seen the like of it? I do not concern myself much in the affairs of other people, but this gentleman (*pointing to* ALCESTE), who has staked the whole of his happiness on you, an honorable and deserving man like this, and who worshipped you to madness, ought he to have been ...

Alceste. Leave me, I pray you, madam, to manage my own affairs; and do not trouble yourself unnecessarily. In vain do I see you espouse my quarrel. I am unable to repay you for this great zeal; and if ever I intended to avenge myself by choosing some one else, it would not be you whom I would select.

Arsinoé. And do you imagine, sir, that I ever harbored such a thought, and that I am so very anxious to secure you? You must be very vain, indeed, to flatter yourself with such an idea. Célimène's leavings are a commodity, of which no one needs be so very much enamored. Pray, undeceive yourself, and do not carry matters with so high a hand. People like me are not for such as you. You will do much better to remain dangling after her skirts, and I long to see so beautiful a match.

SCENE VII: CÉLIMÈNE, ÉLIANTE, ALCESTE,
PHILINTE

Alceste (*to* CÉLIMÈNE). Well! I have held my tongue, notwithstanding all I have seen, and I have let every one have his say before me. Have I controlled myself long enough? and will you now allow me ...

Célimène. Yes, you may say what you like; you

are justified when you complain, and you may reproach me with anything you please. I confess that I am in the wrong; and overwhelmed by confusion I do not seek by any idle excuse to palliate my fault. The anger of the others I have despised; but I admit my guilt towards you. No doubt, your resentment is just; I know how culpable I must appear to you; that everything speaks of my treachery to you, and that, in short, you have cause to hate me. Do so, I consent to it.

Alceste. But can I do so, you traitress? Can I thus get the better of all my tenderness for you? And although I wish to hate you with all my soul, shall I find a heart quite ready to obey me. (*To* ÉLIANTE *and* PHILINTE) You see what an unworthy passion can do, and I call you both as witnesses of my infatuation. Nor, truth to say, is this all, and you will see me carry it out to the bitter end, to show you that it is wrong to call us wise, and that in all hearts there remains still something of the man. (*To* CÉLIMÈNE) Yes, perfidious creature, I am willing to forget your crimes. I can find, in my own heart, an excuse for all your doings, and hide them under the name of a weakness into which the vices of the age betrayed your youth, provided your heart will second the design which I have formed of avoiding all human creatures, and that you are determined to follow me without delay into the solitude in which I have made a vow to pass my days. It is by that only, that, in every one's opinion, you can repair the harm done by your letters, and that, after the scandal which every noble heart must abhor, it may still be possible for me to love you.

Célimène. What! I renounce the world before I grow old, and bury myself in your wilderness!

Alceste. If your affection responds to mine what need the rest of the world signify to you? Am I not sufficient for you?

Célimène. Solitude is frightful to a widow of twenty. I do not feel my mind sufficiently grand and strong to resolve to adopt such a plan. If the gift of my hand can satisfy your wishes, I might be induced to tie such bonds; and marriage ...

Alceste. No. My heart loathes you now, and this refusal alone effects more than all the rest. As you are not disposed, in those sweet ties, to find all in all in me, as I would find all in all in you, begone, I refuse your offer, and this much-felt outrage frees me for ever from your unworthy toils.

SCENE VIII: ÉLIANTE, ALCESTE, PHILINTE

Alceste (*to* ÉLIANTE). Madam, your beauty is adorned by a hundred virtues; and I never saw anything in you but what was sincere. For a long while I thought very highly of you; but allow me to esteem you thus for ever, and suffer my heart in its various troubles not to offer itself for the honor of your acceptance. I feel too unworthy, and begin to perceive that Heaven did not intend me for the marriage bond; that the homage of only the remainder of a heart unworthy of you, would be below your merit, and that in short . . .

Éliante. You may pursue this thought. I am not at all embarrassed with my hand; and here is your friend, who, without giving me much trouble, might possibly accept it if I asked him.

Philinte. Ah! madam, I ask for nothing better

than that honor, and I could sacrifice my life and soul for it.

Alceste. May you, to taste true contentment, preserve for ever these feelings towards each other! Deceived on all sides, overwhelmed with injustice, I will fly from an abyss where vice is triumphant, and seek out some small secluded nook on earth, where one may enjoy the freedom of being an honest man.

Philinte. Come, madam, let us leave nothing untried to deter him from the design on which his heart is set.

Jean Racine · 1639-1699

Jean Racine's life belongs to turbulent and brilliant seventeenth-century France. The span of his years, between 1639 and 1699, was lived out under the reigns of Louis XIII and Louis XIV and during the days of Marie de Medici, of Richelieu, and Mazarin. He saw the government in turmoil, nobles quarreling with nobles, the pomp of court life, a discontented populace, the oppression of the Huguenots and Jansenists for religious reasons, and lived, for almost forty years, under the spectacular and artificial society of Louis XIV, Grand Monarque and "lieutenant de Dieu," who, in unifying France, at the same time planted the roots of discord which ultimately led to revolution.

Racine was born in Ferté-Milon, educated at Beauvais, Port-Royal, and at the Collège d'Harcourt. As both his mother and father — the latter a solicitor — had died when Racine was only a few years old, the boy was reared by his Jansenist grandparents. A contemporary of Corneille, LaFontaine, Molière, Boileau, he held aloof during most of his life from literary cliques. The decade between 1667 and 1677 saw the production of *Andromaque, Britannicus, Bérénice, Bajazet, Mithridate, Iphigénie, Phèdre.* When Racine began his career as a dramatist, Corneille was already a success and inevitable comparisons of the work of the two men brought on a rivalry. Within a few days after *Phèdre* was produced, a rival dramatist, urged on by enemies of Racine, produced a second *Phèdre* which temporarily overshadowed Racine's masterpiece. Following this unpleasant episode, though not necessarily because of it, Racine all but retired from the theatre. He returned to the piety of his Jansenist upbringing, married, and settled into a quiet domestic life during which he held a government post or two and, in the subsequent twenty-odd years, he wrote only two plays, *Esther* and *Athalie,* both based on Biblical narratives.

With Corneille and Racine neo-classicism probably rose to its greatest height in modern literature. They not only set standards in France but influenced writers in England as well. The sixty years of Racine's life were years which, across the channel, brought the publication of work by Milton, Dryden, Addison, and Defoe. And, a few years later, Pope did for the neo-classical movement in England what Corneille and Racine had done in France.

Racine wrote decorous tragedy. He carefully respected the unities of time and place and action. His concern is not so much with unfolding character as with character in moments of deep passion, with the mind wrought upon by emotion. He evolved a form fairly rigid and, in many ways, marked by simplicity.

SUGGESTED REFERENCES: J. C. Lapp, *Aspects of Racinian Tragedy* (1955); Bernard Weinberg, *The Art of Jean Racine* (1963); Roland Barthes, *On Racine* (1964).

Phædra[1]

In *Phèdre* — or *Phædra* — we see the above noted qualities of Racine clearly manifested. Here is a heroine driven by great passion, the dramatic action springing from the fact that this passion is illicit. Here, too, are compression and unity. The reader who desires to bring to a focus the difference between classical and romantic treatment of tragedy need only compare and contrast Shakespeare's Juliet and Racine's Phèdre.

Characters

THESEUS, *son of Ægeus and King of Athens*
PHÆDRA, *wife of Theseus and daughter of Minos and Pasiphaë*
HIPPOLYTUS, *son of Theseus and Antiope, Queen of the Amazons*
ARICIA, *princess of the blood royal of Athens*
ŒNONE, *nurse of Phædra*
THERAMENES, *tutor of Hippolytus*
ISMENE, *friend of Aricia*
PANOPE, *waiting-woman of Phædra*
GUARDS

The scene is laid in Trœzen, a town of the Peloponnesus.

ACT I

(*Enter* HIPPOLYTUS *and* THERAMENES.)

Hipp. My mind is settled, dear Theramenes,
And I must stay no more in lovely Trœzen,
Racking my soul in doubt and mortal anguish.
I am ashamed of my long idleness.
Look you, my father gone six months and more —
One so dear gone — and to what fate befallen   6
I do not know, nor do I know what corner
Of all the wide earth hides him!
    Thera.   Ah, my prince, —
And where, then, would you seek him? I have sailed
Over the seas on either side of Corinth.   10
Where Acheron is lost among the Shades
I asked, indeed, if aught were known of Theseus!
And to content you, I have gone to Elis,
Rounded Tœnarus, sailed to the far waters
Where Icarus[2] once fell. What newer hope . . . ?
Under what favored sky would you think now   16
To trace his footsteps? Who knows if your father
Wishes the secret of his absence known?
Perhaps while we are trembling for his life
The hero calmly plots a fresh intrigue,   20
And only waits till the deluded lady —

[1] Racine, *Phædra.* Translated by Robert Henderson.
[2] Icarus, provided with wings fastened to his body with wax, flew so high that the heat of the sun melted the wax and he was plunged into the sea.

Hipp. Peace, good Theramenes! Respect his name.
The waywardness of youth is his no longer,
And nothing so unworthy should detain him.
Now for a long time, Phædra has held that heart
Inconstant once, and she need fear no rival.   26
And if I seek him, it is but my duty.
I leave a place I dare no longer see!
    Thera. Indeed! When, prince, did you begin to dread
These peaceful haunts, so dear to happy childhood,   30
Where I have often known you rather stay
Than face the tumult and the pomp of Athens?
What danger do you shun? Or is it grief?
    Hipp. All things are changed. That happy past is gone.
Since then, the gods sent Phædra!
    Thera.   Now I see!   35
It is the queen whose sight offends you. Yes, —
For with a step-dame's spite she schemed your exile
At her first sight of you. But then, her hatred
Is somewhat milder, if not wholly vanished.
A dying woman — one who longs for death!   40
What danger can she bring upon your head?
Weary of life, and weary of herself, —
Sick with some ill she will not ever speak of, —
Can Phædra then lay plots? —
    Hipp.   I do not fear
The hatred of the queen. There is another   45
From whom I fly, and that is young Aricia,
The sole survivor of an impious race.
    Thera. What! You become her persecutor, too?
The gentle sister of the cruel sons
Of Pallas, did not share their perfidy.   50
Why should you hate such charming innocence?
    Hipp. If it were hate, I should not need to fly.
    Thera. Then will you tell me what your flying means?
Is this the proud Hippolytus I see?
Love's fiercest foe alive? — the fiercest hater   55
Of Theseus' well-worn yoke? — Now can it be
That Venus, scorned, will justify your father?
And is Hippolytus, like other mortals,
To bow, perforce, and offer incense to her? —

And can he love? . . .

Hipp.   *My* friend, you must not ask me.
You who have known my heart through all my
          life,   61
And known it to be proud and most disdainful,—
You will not ask that I should shame myself
By now disowning all that I professed.
My mother was an Amazon, — my wildness,   65
Which you think strange, I suckled at her breast,
And as I grew, why, Reason did approve
What Nature planted in me.   Then you told me
The story of my father,[1] and you know
How, often, when I listened to your voice   70
I kindled, hearing of his noble acts, —
And you would tell how he brought consolation
To mortals for the absence of Alcides,
And how he cleared the roads of monsters, — rob-
          bers, —
Procrustes, Cercyron, Sciro, Sinnis slain,   75
Scattered the Epidaurian giant's bones,
And how Crete ran with blood of the Minotaur!
But when you told me of less glorious deeds, —
Troth plighted here and there and everywhere,
Young Helen stolen from her home at Sparta,   80
And Peribœa's tears in Salamis,
And many other trusting ones deceived,
Whose very names he cannot now remember, —
Lone Ariadne, crying to the rocks, —
And last of all this Phædra, bound to him   85
By better ties, — You know that with regret
I heard, and urged that you cut short the tale.
I had been happier, could I erase
This one unworthy part of his bright story
Out of my memory.   Must I in turn   90
Be made love's slave, and brought to bend so low?
It is the more contemptible in me,
For no such brilliance clings about my name
As to the name of Theseus, — no monsters quelled
Have given me the right to share his weakness. 95
And if I must be humbled for my pride,
Aricia should have been the last to tame me!
Was I not mad that I should have forgotten
Those barriers which must keep us far apart
Eternally?   For by my father's order   100
Her brothers' blood must never flow again
In a child of hers.   He dreads a single shoot
From any stock so guilty, and would bury
Their name with her; so even to the tomb
No torch of Hymen may be lit for her.   105
Shall I espouse her rights against my father,
Provoke his wrath, launch on a mad career? —

Thera. But if your time has come, dear prince,
          the gods

[1] Theseus was a Hercules-like hero who had many
adventures and killed many monsters as suggested in
the following lines.

Will care but little for your guiding reason.
Theseus would shut your eyes; — he but unseals
          them.   110
His hatred kindles you to burn, rebellious,
And only lends his enemy new charms.
Then, too, why should you fear a guiltless passion?
Do you not dare this once to try its sweetness, 114
Rather than follow such a hair-drawn scruple? —
Afraid to stray where Hercules has wandered? —
What heart so stout that Venus has not won it?
And you, so long her foe, where would you be
Had your own mother, always scorning love,
Never been moved with tenderness for Theseus?
What good to act a pride you do not feel?   121
If you are changed, confess it!   For some time
You have been seldom seen urging the car
With wild delight, rapid, along the shore,
Or, skillful in the art that Neptune taught,   125
Making th' unbroken steed obey the bit.
The forest has flung back our shouts less often.
A secret burden, cast upon your spirits,
Has dimmed your eye. — Can I then doubt your
          love?
It is in vain that you conceal your hurt.   130
Tell me, has not Aricia touched your heart?

Hipp. Theramenes, I go to find my father.

Thera. Will you not see the queen before you
          leave?

Hipp. So I intend.   And you may tell her so.
Yes, I will see her, since it is my duty.   135
But what new ill vexes her dear Œnone?

(*Enter* ŒNONE.)

Œnone. Alas, my lord, what grief was e'er like
          mine?
The queen has almost touched the gates of death.
It is in vain I watch her night and day,
In my very arms this secret malady   140
Is killing her — her mind is all disordered.
She rises from her bed, weary yet restless,
Pants for the outer air, yet she commands me
That none should see her in her misery.
She comes!   145
Hipp. That is enough.   I shall not vex her
Nor make her see the face of one she hates.

(*Exeunt* HIPPOLYTUS *and* THERAMENES.)

(*Enter* PHÆDRA.)

Phædra. Yes, this is far enough.   Stay here,
Œnone.
My strength is failing.   I must rest a little.
I am dazzled with the light; it has been long   150
Since I have seen it.   Ah, and my trembling knees
Are failing me —
Œnone. Dear Heaven, I would our tears
Might bring relief.

Phædra. And how these clumsy trinkets,   155
These veils oppress me! Whose officious hand
Tied up these knots, and gathered all these coils
Over my brow? All things conspire against me
And would distress me more!

Œnone. That which you wish   160
This moment, frets you next! Did you not ask
A minute past, that we should deck you out,
Saying you felt your energy return,
Saying you sickened of your idleness,
And wished to go and see the light of day?   165
You sought the sun, and now you see it here, —
And now you would be hidden from its shining!

Phædra. O splendid author of a hapless race, —
You whom my mother boasted as her father, —
Well may you blush to see me in such plight.   170
For the last time I look on thee, O Sun!

Œnone. So! And are you still in love with
death?
Will you not ever make your peace with life,
And leave these cruel accents of despair?

Phædra. I wish that I were seated in the forest.
When may I follow with delighted eye,   176
Through glorious dust, flying in full career, —
A chariot? —

Œnone. Madam?

Phædra. Have I lost my wits?   180
What did I say? Where am I? Ah, and where
Do my vain wishes wander? For the gods
Have made me mad! And now I blush, Œnone,
I hide my face, for you have seen too clearly
The grief and shame, that, quite in spite of me,
Will overflow my eyes.   186

Œnone. If you must blush,
Blush at the silence that inflames your grief.
Deaf to my voice, you will not have my care.
Then will you have no pity on yourself,   190
But let your life be ended in mid-course?
What evil spell has drained its fountains dry?
Night-shadows thrice have darkened all the
heavens
Since sleep came to your eyes, and now three times
The dawn has chased the darkness back again
Since your pale lips knew food. You faint, are lan-
guid, —   196
What awful purpose have you in your heart?
How do you dare attempt to lose your life
And so offend the gods who gave it you, —
And so prove false to Theseus and your mar-
riage? —   200
Yes, and betray your most unhappy children,
Bending their necks yourself, beneath the yoke?
That day, be sure, which robs them of their mother
Will give his high hopes back to the stranger's
son, —
To that proud enemy of you and yours,   205

Born of an Amazon, — Hippolytus! —

Phædra. You gods!

Œnone. Ah, this is a reproach to move you!

Phædra. Unhappy one, what name have your
lips spoken?   209

Œnone. Your anger is most just, and it is well
That hated name can rouse such rage! Then live,
And hear again the claims of love and duty!
Live, then, — and stop this son of Scythia
From crushing down your children by his sway,
Ruling the noblest offspring of the gods, —   215
The purest blood of Greece! Never delay!
Death threatens every moment! Now restore
Your shattered strength, while the dim torch of
life
Burns, and can yet be fanned into a flame.

Phædra. I have endured its guilt and shame too
long.   220

Œnone. Why? What remorse is gnawing at
your heart?
What crime can have disturbed you so? Your
hands
Have not been stained with the blood of innocence.

Phædra. No, I thank Heaven my hands are free
from stain, —
I would my soul were innocent as they!   225

Œnone. Why then, what awful plan have you
been scheming,
At which your conscience still should be afraid?

Phædra. Have I not said enough? Spare me
the rest!
I die to save myself a full confession.

Œnone. Die, then, — and keep a silence more
than human! —   230
But seek some other hand to close your eyes,
For I will go before you to the Shades.
There are a thousand highways always open,
And since you have so little faith in me,
I'll go the shortest! When has my love failed you?
Remember, in my arms you lay, new-born.   236
For you I left my country and my children, —
And is this payment for my service to you?

Phædra. What will you gain from words that are
so bitter?   239
Were I to speak, horror would freeze your blood.

Œnone. What can you say more terrible to me
Than to behold you die before my eyes?

Phædra. If you should know my sin, I still
should die,
But with guilt added —

Œnone. Oh, my dearest lady,   245
By all the tears that I have wept for you,
By these poor knees I clasp, now ease my mind
From doubt and torture!

Phædra. As you wish. Then rise.

Œnone. I hear you. Speak.   250

Phædra. Ah, how shall I begin?

Œnone. Leave off your fears, — you hurt me
with distrust.

Phædra. O malice of great Venus! Into what
madness,

What wild distractions, did she cast my mother!

Œnone. Let them be blotted from all memory,
Buried in silence, for all times to come.   256

Phædra. My sister, Ariadne,[1] what was the love
Which brought you death, forsaken on lone shores?

Œnone. Madam, what deep pain is it prompts
reproaches

Thus against all your kin — ?   260

Phædra. It is her will —

It is the will of Venus, and I perish,
Last and least happy of a family
Where all were wretched!

Œnone. Do you love?   265

Phædra. I feel.

All of its fever —

Œnone. Ah! For whom?

Phædra. Now hear

The final horror. Yes, I love. My lips   270
Tremble to name him.

Œnone. Whom?

Phædra. And do you know him? —

He whom I tortured long, — the Amazon's son!

Œnone. Hippolytus! Great gods!   275

Phædra. Yes, you have named him.

Œnone. Blood freezes in my veins! O cursed
race!

Ill-omened journey! Land of misery,
Why did we ever reach these dangerous shores?

Phædra. My wound is not a new one. Scarcely
had I   280

Been bound to Theseus by our marriage tie,
With peace and happiness seeming so well secured,
Until at Athens I saw my enemy.
I looked, I first turned pale, then blushed to see
him,

And all my soul was in the greatest turmoil;   285
A mist made dim my sight, and my voice faltered,
And now my blood ran cold, then burned like fire.
In all my fevered body I could feel
Venus, whose fury had pursued so many
Of my sad race. I sought to shun her torments
With fervent vows. I built a shrine for her,   291
And there, 'mid many victims did I seek
The reason I had lost; but all for nothing.
I found no remedy for pain of love!
I offered incense vainly on her altars,   295
I called upon her name, and while I called her,
I loved Hippolytus, always before me!
And when I made her altars smoke with victims,

[1] Theseus had deserted Ariadne and married her
sister, Phædra.

'Twas for a god whose name I dared not utter, —
And still I fled his presence, only to find him — 300
(The worst of horrors) — in his father's features!
At last I raised revolt against myself,
And stirred my courage up to persecute
The enemy I loved. To banish him
I wore a harsh and jealous step-dame's manner,
And ceaselessly I clamored for his exile,   306
Till I had torn him from his father's arms!
I breathed once more, Œnone. In his absence
The days passed by less troubled than before —
Innocent days! I hid my bitter grief,   310
Submitted to my husband, cherished the fruits
Of our most fatal marriage, — and in vain!
Again I saw the one whom I had banished,
Brought here by my own husband, and again
The old wound bled. And now it is not love   315
Hid in my heart, but Venus in her might
Seizing her prey. Justly I fear my sin!
I hate my life, and hold my love in horror.
I die: — I would have kept my name unsullied,
Burying guilty passion in the grave;   320
But I have not been able to refuse you;
You weep and pray, and so I tell you all,
And I shall be content, if as I perish,
You do not vex me with unjust reproaches,
Nor vainly try to snatch away from death   325
The last faint sparks of life, yet lingering!

(*Enter* PANOPE.)

Panope. I wish that I might hide sad tidings
from you,

But 'tis my duty, madam, to reveal them.
The hand of death has seized your peerless husband.

You are the last to hear it.   330

Œnone. What is this?

Panope. The queen begs Heaven for the safe
return

Of Theseus, but she trusts, indeed, in vain —
She is deceived. Hippolytus, his son,
Has learned from vessels newly come to port   335
That Theseus is dead.

Phædra. Oh, gods!

Panope. At Athens

Opinions are divided; some would have it
Your child should rule, and some, despite the law,
Are bold, and dare support the stranger's son, 341
While one presuming faction, it is said,
Would crown Aricia, and the house of Pallas.
I thought it well to warn you of this danger.
Hippolytus is ready, now, to start,   345
And if he chance to show himself in Athens,
The crowd, I fear, will follow in his lead.

Œnone. It is enough. The queen has heard
your message,

And she will not neglect your timely warning.
(Exit Panope.)
Dear lady, I had almost ceased from urging   350
That you should wish to live.   I thought to follow
My mistress to that tomb from which my pleading
Had failed to turn her, — but this new misfortune
Changes the aspect of affairs, and prompts us
To take fresh measures.   Madam, Theseus is
gone,   355
And you must fill his place.   He leaves a son, —
Slave if you die, but if you live, a king!
Upon whom can he lean, but you, his mother?
There is no hand but yours to dry his tears.   359
Live then, for him, or else his guiltless weeping
Will move the gods to wrath against his mother.
Live, for no blame is in your passion now.
The king is dead, you bear the bonds no longer
Which made your love a thing of crime and horror.
You need no longer dread Hippolytus,   365
For you may see him, now, without reproach.
Perhaps, if he is certain of your hatred,
He means to lead the rebels.   Undeceive him!
Soften his callous heart, and bend his pride!
King of this fertile land, his portion lies   370
Here in his Trœzen, yet he knows the laws, —
They give your son these walls Minerva built,
Aye, and protects, — but if a common foe
Threatens you both, you had best be united.
For you must thwart Aricia!   375
  Phædra. I consent.
Yes, I will live, if life can yet be mine, —
If my affection for a son has power
To rouse my sinking heart, at such a dangerous
hour!   (Exeunt.)

ACT II

(Enter Aricia and Ismene.)

  Aricia. Hippolytus has asked to see me here?
Hippolytus has asked to bid farewell?   381
'Tis true, Ismene?   You are not deceived?
  Ismene. This is the first result of Theseus' death,
And you may look to see from every side
Hearts that he kept away, now turning to you.
Aricia soon shall find all Greece low-bending   386
To do her homage.
  Aricia. Then it is not only
An idle tale?   Am I a slave no longer?
Have I no enemies?   390
  Ismene. The gods, Aricia,
Trouble your peace no more, for Theseus' soul
Is with your brothers, now.
  Aricia. Does rumor tell
How Theseus died?   395
  Ismene. Tales most incredible
Are spread.   Some say, that, seizing a new bride,

The faithless man was swallowed by the waves.
Others have said, and this report prevails,
That he, together with Pirithous,   400
Went to the world below, seeking the shores
Of Cocytus, showing his living self
To the pale ghosts, but could not leave the gloom,
For they who enter there abide forever.
  Aricia. Can I believe a mortal may descend
Into that gulf before his destined hour?   406
What lure could ever overcome its terrors?
  Ismene. Nay, he is dead; 'tis only you who
doubt it.
The men of Athens all bewail his loss.
Trœzen already hails Hippolytus,   410
And Phædra, fearing for her children's rights,
Asks counsel of such friends as share her troubles,
Here in this palace!
  Aricia. Will Hippolytus
Prove kinder than his father, make my chains
light,   415
And pity my misfortunes?
  Ismene. Yes, I think so.
  Aricia. Indeed, I think you do not know him
well,
Or you would not believe a heart so hard
Could ever pity, or could look on me   420
As one not sharing in the scorn he feels
For all our sex.   Does he not still avoid
Whatever place we go?
  Ismene. I know the stories
Of proud Hippolytus, but I have seen him   425
When he was near to you, and watched to see
How one supposed so cold would bear himself.
I found his manners not at all like those
Which I had looked to see, for in his face
Was great confusion, at your slightest glance.   430
He could not turn his languid eyes away,
But still looked back again to gaze at you.
Love is a word that may offend his pride,
But though the tongue deny it, looks betray!
  Aricia. How eagerly my heart hears what you
say,   435
Though it may be delusion, dear Ismene!
Did it seem possible to you, who know me,
That I, poor toy of unrelenting fate,
Fed upon bitter tears by night and day,
Could ever taste the maddening draught of love?
I am the last frail offspring of my race —   441
My royal race, the Children of the Earth,
And of them, I alone survive war's fury.
Yes, I have lost six brothers, in their youth, —
Mown by the sword, cut off in their first flower!
They were the hope of an illustrious house.   446
Earth drank their blood with sorrow; it was kin
To his whom she brought forth.   And well you
know,

Since then, no heart in Greece could sigh for me,
Lest, by a sister's flame, her brothers' ashes   450
Might chance to blaze again.   And, too, you know
How I disdained the cautions of my captor,
His care, and his suspicion, and you know
How often I have thanked the king's injustice,
Since I had never loved the thought of love.   455
He happily confirmed my inclinations, —
But then, I never yet had seen his son!
It is not merely that my eye is caught,
And that I love him for his grace and beauty, —
Charms which he does not know, or seems to
          scorn, —   460
I love him for a kind of wealth that's rarer.
He has his father's virtues, not his faults.
I love, and I must grant it, that high pride
Which never stooped beneath the yoke of love.
Phædra gains little glory from a lover   465
Free of his sighs; I am too proud, I think,
To share devotion with a thousand others,
Or enter in a door that's never shut.
But to make one who never stooped before   469
Bend his proud neck, — to pierce a heart of stone,
And bind one captive, whom his chains astonish,
Who struggles vainly in his pleasant bonds, —
That takes my fancy, and I long for it.
The god of strength was easier disarmed
Than this Hippolytus, for Hercules   475
Yielded so often to the eyes of beauty
That he made triumph cheap.   But, dear Ismene,
I take too little heed of a resistance
Which I may never quell.   If I am humbled,
And if I find defeat, then you will hear me   480
Speak ill of that same pride I so admire!
What! can he love?   And have I been so happy
That I have bent — ?

Ismene. He comes, — and you shall hear him.

(*Enter* HIPPOLYTUS.)

Hipp. Lady, before you go, it is my duty   485
To tell you of the changes of your fortune.
What I have feared is true; my sire is dead.
Yes, his long stay was what I had supposed it.
For only death, which came to end his labors,
Could keep him hidden from the world so long.   490
The gods at last have doomed Alcides' friend —
His friend, and his successor.   Since your hatred
I think will grant his virtues, it can hear
Some praise for him, without resenting it,
Knowing that it is due.   I have one hope   495
To soothe me in my sorrow.   I can free you.
Now I revoke the laws, whose strictness moved me
To pity for you; you are your own mistress
Of heart and hand.   Here in my heritage,
In Trœzen, here where Pittheus once reigned,   500
And where I now am king, by my own right,

I leave you free, free as myself, — and more.

Aricia. Your kindness is too great; it overcomes
          me.
A goodness which will pay disgrace with honor
Can give a greater force than you would think   505
To the harsh laws from which you would release
          me.

Hipp. Athens, not knowing how to fill the throne
Left empty, speaks of you, and then of me,
And then of Phædra's son.

Aricia.   Of me, my lord?

Hipp. I know that by the law it is not mine,
For Greece reproaches me my foreign mother.   511
But if my brother were my only rival,
My rights are clearly truer ones than his,
So that I should not care for twists of the law.
There is a juster claim to check my boldness.   515
I yield my place to you, or rather, grant
That you should have it, — you should hold the
          scepter,
Bequeathed to you from Earth's great son, Erec-
          theus.[1]
It came, then, to Ægeus,[1] and the city
Which was protected and increased by him   520
Was glad to welcome such a king as Theseus,
Leaving your luckless brothers out of mind.
Now Athens calls you back within her walls.
Long strife has cost her groans enough already,
Her fields are glutted with your kinsmen's blood,
Fattening those same furrows whence it sprang.
I will rule here in Trœzen; Phædra's son   527
Has his rich kingdom waiting him in Crete.
Athens is yours, and I will do my best
To bring to you the votes which are divided   530
Between us two.

Aricia.   I fear a dream deceives me.
For I am stunned, my lord, at what I hear.
Am I, indeed, awake?   Can I believe
Such generosity as this?   What god
Has put it in your heart?   Well you deserve   535
That fame you have, yet it falls short of you.
For me, you will be traitor to yourself!
Was it not grace enough never to hate me,
To have been free so long from enmity,
Which some have harbored —

Hipp.   Hate you?   I to hate you?
However darkly you have seen my pride,   541
Did you suppose a monster gave me birth?
What savagery, what hatred, full of venom
Would not become less evil, seeing you?
Could I resist this charm which caught my soul —

Aricia. Why, what is this, sir?   546

Hipp. I have said too much
Not to say more.   No prudence can resist
The violence of passion.   Now, at last,

          [1] Ancestors of Theseus.

Silence is broken. I must tell you now   550
The secret that my heart can hold no longer.
You see before you an unhappy victim
Of hasty pride, — a prince who begs compassion.
For I was long the enemy of love.
I mocked his fetters, I despised his captives,   555
And while I pitied these poor, shipwrecked mortals,
I watched the storms, and seemed quite safe on
    land.
And now I find that I have such a fate,
And must be tossed upon a sea of troubles!
My boldness is defeated in a moment,   560
And all my boasted pride is humbleness.
For nearly six months past, ashamed, despairing,
Carrying with me always that sharp arrow
Which tears my heart, I struggle quite in vain
To free me, both from you and from myself. 565
I leave your presence; — leaving, I find you near,
And in the forest's darkness see your form.
Black night, no less than daylight brings the vision
Of charms that I avoid. All things conspire
To make Hippolytus your slave. The fruit 570
Of all my sighs is only that I cannot
Find my own self again. My bow, my spear,
Please me no longer. I have quite forgotten
My chariot, and the teaching of the Sea God.
The woods can only echo back my groans, 575
Instead of flinging back those joyous shouts
With which I urged my horses. Hearing this,
A tale of passion so uncouth, you blush
At your own handiwork. These are wild words
With which I offer you my heart, a captive 580
Held, strangely, by a silken jess.[1] And yet
The off'ring should be dearer to your eyes,
Since such words come as strangers to my lips.
Nor do not scorn my vows, so poorly spoken 584
Since, but for you, they never had been formed.

(*Enter* THERAMENES.)

Thera. My lord, I came to tell you of the queen.
She comes to seek you.
    Hipp. Me?
    Thera. And what she wishes
I do not know. I speak at her request, 590
For she would talk with you before you go.
    Hipp. What shall I say to her? Can she ex-
    pect — ?
    Aricia. You cannot, noble prince, refuse to hear
    her,
Though you are sure she is your enemy.
There is a shade of pity due her tears. 595
    Hipp. Shall we part so? And will you let me
    leave you
Not knowing if I have offended you, —
The goddess I adore, — with all this boldness?

[1] ribbon.

Or if this heart, which I now leave with you —
    Aricia. Go now, my prince, and do whatever
    deeds 600
Your generosity would have you do.
Make Athens own my scepter. All these gifts
I will accept. But the high throne of Empire
Is not the thing most precious to my eyes!
        (*Exeunt* ARICIA *and* ISMENE.)
    Hipp. Friend, are we ready? — But the queen is
    coming. 605
See that the ship is trimmed and fit to sail.
Hurry, gather the crew, and hoist the signal,
And then return, the sooner to release me
From a most irksome meeting.
        (*Exit* THERAMENES.)

(*Enter* PHÆDRA *and* ŒNONE)

    Phædra (*to* ŒNONE). Look, I see him! 610
My blood forgets to flow, — tongue will not speak
What I have come to say!
    Œnone. Think of your son.
And think that all his hopes depend on you.
    Phædra. They tell me that you leave us, hastily.
I come to add my own tears to your sorrow, 616
And I would plead my fears for my young son.
He has no father, now; 'twill not be long
Until the day that he will see my death,
And even now, his youth is much imperiled 620
By a thousand foes. You only can defend him.
And in my inmost heart, remorse is stirring, —
Yes, and fear, too, lest I have shut your ears
Against his cries; I fear that your just anger
May, before long, visit on him that hatred 625
His mother earned.
    Hipp. Madam, you need not fear.
Such malice is not mine.
    Phædra. I should not blame you
If you should hate me; I have injured you. 630
So much you know; — you could not read my
    heart.
Yes, I have tried to be your enemy,
For the same land could never hold us both.
In private and abroad I have declared it; —
I was your enemy! I found no peace 635
Till seas had parted us; and I forbade
Even your name to be pronounced to me.
And yet, if punishment be meted out
Justly, by the offense; — if only hatred
Deserves a hate, then never was there woman 640
Deserved more pity, and less enmity.
    Hipp. A mother who is jealous for her children
Will seldom love the children of a mother
Who came before her. Torments of suspicion
Will often follow on a second marriage. 645
Another would have felt that jealousy
No less than you; perhaps more violently.

Phædra. Ah, prince, but Heaven made me quite
    exempt
From what is usual, and I can call
That Heaven as my witness! 'Tis not this — 650
No, quite another ill devours my heart!
    Hipp. This is no time for self-reproaching,
    madam.
Perhaps your husband still beholds the light,
Perhaps he may be granted safe return
In answer to our prayers; his guarding god   655
Is Neptune, whom he never called in vain.
    Phædra. He who has seen the mansions of the
    dead
Returns not thence. Since Theseus has gone
Once to those gloomy shores, we need not hope,
For Heaven will not send him back again.   660
Prince, there is no release from Acheron; —
It is a greedy maw, — and yet I think
He lives and breathes in you, — and still I see him
Before me here; I seem to speak to him —
My heart — ! Oh, I am mad! Do what I will,
I cannot hide my passion.   666
    Hipp. Yes, I see
What strange things love will do, for Theseus, dead,
Seems present to your eyes, and in your soul
A constant flame is burning.   670
    Phædra. Ah, for Theseus
I languish and I long, but not, indeed,
As the Shades have seen him, as the fickle lover
Of a thousand forms, the one who fain would ravish
The bride of Pluto; — but one faithful, proud, 675
Even to slight disdain, — the charm of youth
That draws all hearts, even as the gods are
    painted, —
Or as yourself. He had your eyes, your manner, —
He spoke like you, and he could blush like you,
And when he came across the waves to Crete, 680
My childhood home, worthy to win the love
Of Minos' daughters, — what were you doing then?
Why did my father gather all these men,
The flower of Greece, and leave Hippolytus? 684
Oh, why were you too young to have embarked
On board the ship that brought your father there?
The monster would have perished at your hands,
Despite the windings of his vast retreat.[1]
My sister would have armed you with the clue 689
To guide your steps, doubtful within the maze. —
But no — for Phædra would have come before her,
And love would first have given me the thought,
And I it would have been, whose timely aid
Had taught you all the labyrinthine ways!
The care that such a dear life would have cost me!
No thread could satisfy my lover's fears. 696
I would have wished to lead the way myself,

[1] The reference is to Theseus' killing of the Minotaur
who lived in the labyrinth of Crete.

And share the peril you were sure to face.
Yes, Phædra would have walked the maze with
    you, —
With you come out in safety, or have perished!
    Hipp. Gods! What is this I hear? Have you
    forgotten   701
That Theseus is my father and your husband?
    Phædra. Why should you fancy I have lost re-
    membrance
And that I am regardless of my honor?
    Hipp. Forgive me, madam! With a blush I own
That I mistook your words, quite innocent. 706
For very shame I cannot see you longer —
Now I will go —
    Phædra. Ah, prince, you understood me,
Too well, indeed! For I had said enough. 710
You could not well mistake. But do not think
That in those moments when I love you most
I do not feel my guilt. No easy yielding
Has helped the poison that infects my mind.
The sorry object of divine revenge, 715
I am not half so hateful to your sight
As to myself. The gods will bear me witness, —
They who have lit this fire within my veins, —
The gods who take their barbarous delight
In leading some poor mortal heart astray! 720
Nay, do you not remember, in the past,
How I was not content to fly? — I drove you
Out of the land, so that I might appear
Most odious — and to resist you better
I tried to make you hate me — and in vain! 725
You hated more, and I loved not the less,
While your misfortunes lent you newer charms.
I have been drowned in tears and scorched by fire!
Your own eyes might convince you of the truth
If you could look at me, but for a moment! 730
What do I say? You think this vile confession
That I have made, is what I meant to say?
I did not dare betray my son. For him
I feared, — and came to beg you not to hate him.
This was the purpose of a heart too full 735
Of love for you to speak of aught besides.
Take your revenge, and punish me my passion!
Prove yourself worthy of your valiant father,
And rid the world of an offensive monster!
Does Theseus' widow dare to love his son? 740
Monster indeed! Nay, let her not escape you!
Here is my heart! Here is the place to strike!
It is most eager to absolve itself!
It leaps impatiently to meet your blow! — 744
Strike deep! Or if, indeed, you find it shameful
To drench your hand in such polluted blood, —
If that be punishment too mild for you, —
Too easy for your hate, — if not your arm,
Then lend your sword to me. — Come! Give it
    now! —

Œnone. What would you do, my lady? Oh,
    just gods!   750
But someone comes; — go quickly. Run from
    shame.
You cannot fly, if they should find you thus.
          (*Exeunt* PHÆDRA *and* ŒNONE.)

(*Enter* THERAMENES.)

Thera. Is that the form of Phædra that I see
Go hurrying? What are these signs of sorrow?
Where is your sword? Why are you pale and
    shaken?   755
Hipp. Friend, let us fly. Indeed, I am confused
With greatest horror and astonishment.
Phædra — but no; gods, let this dreadful secret
Remain forever buried and unknown.
Thera. The ship is ready if you wish to sail,   760
But Athens has already cast her vote.
Their leaders have consulted all the tribes.
Your brother is elected; — Phædra wins!
Hipp. Phædra?
Thera. A herald bringing a commission   765
Has come from Athens, placing the reins of power
In Phædra's hands. Her son is king. —
Hipp. O gods, —
O ye who know her, is it thus, indeed,
That ye reward her virtue?   770
Thera. Meanwhile rumor
Is whispering that Theseus is not dead, —
That there are those who saw him in Epirus, —
But I have searched, and I know all too well —
Hipp. No matter. Let no chances be neglected.
This rumor must be hunted to its source,   776
And if it be not worthy of belief
Let us then sail, and at whatever cost,
We'll trust the scepter to deserving hands.
          (*Exeunt.*)

ACT III

(*Enter* PHÆDRA *and* ŒNONE.)

Phædra. Ah, let them take away the worthless
    honors   780
They bring to me; — why urge that I should see
    them?
What flattery can soothe my wounded heart?
Far rather hide me. I have said too much.
My madness bursting like a stream in flood,   784
I spoke what never should have reached his ears.
Oh, gods! The way he heard me! How reluctant
To take my meaning, — dull and cold as marble,
And only eager for a quick retreat!
And how his blushes made my shame the deeper!
Why did you turn me from the death I sought? 790
Ah, when his sword was pointed at my breast,
Did he grow pale? — or try to snatch it from me?

That I had touched it was enough for him
To make it seem forever horrible,
And to defile whatever hand should hold it.   795
Œnone. When you will brood upon your bitter
    grief,
You only fan a fire that must be quenched.
Would it not more become the blood of Minos [1]
To find you peace in cares that are more noble? —
And in defiance of this wretch, who flies   800
From what he hates, reign on the throne you're
    offered?
Phædra. I reign? — And shall I hold the rod of
    empire,
When reason can no longer reign in me?
When I have lost control of mine own senses?
When I do gasp beneath a shameful yoke?   805
When I am dying? —
Œnone. Fly!
Phædra. I cannot leave him.
Œnone. You dare not fly from one you dared to
    banish?
Phædra. That time is past. He knows how I
    am frenzied,   810
For I have overstepped my modesty,
And blazoned out my shame before his eyes.
Against my will, hope crept into my heart.
Did you not call my failing powers to me?
Was it not you, yourself, called back my soul 815
Which fluttered on my lips, and with your counsel
Lent me new life? Who told me I might love
    him?
Œnone. Blame me or blame me not for your
    misfortunes, —
What could I not have done if it would save you?
But if your anger ever was aroused   820
By insult, can you pardon him his scorn?
How cruel were his eyes, severe and fixed,
Surveying you, half prostrate at his feet!
How hateful, then, his savage pride appeared!
Why did not Phædra see as I saw then?   825
Phædra. This pride that you detest may yield to
    time.
The rudeness of the forest clings about him,
For he was bred there by the strictest laws.
Love is a word he never knew before.
Perhaps it was surprise that stunned him so; —
There was much vehemence in all I said.   831
Œnone. Remember that his mother was bar-
    baric —
Phædra. She was a Scythian, but she learned to
    love.
Œnone. He has a bitter hate for all our sex.
Phædra. Well, then no rival ever rules his heart.
Your counsel comes a little late, Œnone.   836

[1] Minos was king of Crete and father of Ariadne and
Phædra.

Now you must serve my madness, not my reason.
Love cannot find a way into his heart,
So let us take him where he has more feeling.   839
The lure of power seemed somewhat to touch him.
He could not hide that he was drawn to Athens, —
His vessels' prows were pointed there already,
With sails all set to run before the breeze.
Go, and on my behalf, touch his ambition, —
Dazzle his eyes with prospects of the crown.   845
The sacred diadem shall grace his brow, —
My highest honor is to set it there,
And he shall have the power I cannot keep.
He'll teach my son how men are ruled. — It may be
That he will deign to be a father to him.   850
He shall control both son and mother; — try him, —
Try every means to move him, for your words
Should meet more favor than my own could find.
Urge him with groans and tears, — say Phædra's
        dying,
Nor blush to speak in pleading terms with him.
My last hope is in you, — do what you will,   856
I'll sanction it, — the issue is my fate!
                                (*Exit* ŒNONE.)
Phædra (alone). Venus implacable, thou seest
        me shamed,
And I am sore confounded.   Have I not
Been humbled yet enough?   Can cruelty   860
Stretch farther still?   Thine arrows have struck
        home!
It is thy victory!   Wouldst gain new triumphs? —
Then seek an enemy more obdurate, —
Hippolytus neglects thee, braves thine anger.
He never bows his knee before thine altars.   865
Thy name offends his proud, disdainful hearing.
Our interests are alike, — avenge thyself,
Force him to love — But what is this, Œnone?
Already back?   Then it must be he hates me,
And will not hear you speak —   870

                (*Enter* ŒNONE.)

Œnone. Yes, you must stifle
A love that's vain, and best call back your virtue.
The king we thought was dead will soon appear
Here to your eyes.   Yes, Theseus will be here,
For he has come again.   The eager people   875
Are hastening to see him.   I had gone
As you commanded, seeking for the prince,
When all the air was torn, — a thousand shouts —
Phædra. My husband living!   'Tis enough,
        Œnone.
I owned a passion that dishonors him.   880
He is alive.   I wish to know no more.
Œnone. What is it?
Phædra. What I prophesied to you, —
What you refused to hear, while with your weeping
You overcame repentance.   Had I died   885

I had deserved some pity, earlier.
I took your counsel, and I die dishonored.
    Œnone. You die?
    Phædra. Just Heavens!   What I have done to-
        day!
My husband comes, and with him comes his son,
And I shall see the witness of my passion,   891
The object of my most adulterous flame
Watch with what face I make his father welcome,
Knowing my heart is big with sighs he scorned,
And my eyes wet with tears that could not move
        him.   895
Will his respect for Theseus make him hide it? —
Conceal my madness? — not disgrace his father?
And do you think he can repress the horror
Which he must have for me?   A fruitless silence!
I know my treason, and I lack the boldness   900
Of those abandoned women, who can feel
Tranquillity in crime, — can show a forehead
All unashamed.   I know my madness well,
Recall it all.   I think that these high roofs
And all these walls can speak.   They will accuse
        me.   905
They only wait until my husband comes,
And then they will reveal my perfidy.
'Tis death alone can take away this horror.
Is it so great an ill to cease to live?
Death holds no fear for those in misery.   910
I tremble only for the name I leave, —
My son's sad heritage.   The blood of Jove
Might justly swell the pride of those who boast it,
But what a heavy weight a mother's guilt
Leaves for her children!   Yes, I dread that scorn
For my disgrace, which will be cast on them   916
With too much truth.   I tremble when I think
How they will never dare to raise their heads,
Crushed with that curse. —
    Œnone. Nay, do not doubt my pity.   920
There never was a juster fear than yours.
Then why do you expose them to this shame?
And why must you accuse yourself, destroying
The one hope left?   It will be said of Phædra
That she well knows of her own perfidy,   925
That she has fled from out her husband's sight, —
And proud Hippolytus may well rejoice
That, dying, you should lend his tale belief.
What answer can I make him?   It will be
For him, a story easy to deny,   930
And I shall hear him, while triumphantly
He tells your shame to every open ear.
Why, I had sooner Heaven's fire consumed me!
Deceive me not!   And do you love him still?   934
What think you now of this contemptuous prince?
    Phædra. As of a monster fearful to mine eyes!
    Œnone. Why do you give him easy victory?
You are afraid!   Dare to accuse him first!

Say he is guilty of the charge he brings
This day against you. Who shall say it's false?
All things conspire against him. In your hands 941
His sword, which he most happily forgot, —
Your present trouble, and your past distress, —
Your warnings to his father, — and his exile
Which you accomplished with your earnest pray-
    ers — 945
    Phædra. So! You would have me slander inno-
    cence!
    Œnone. My zeal asks nothing from you but your
    silence.
I also tremble. I am loath to do it.
I'd face a thousand deaths more willingly.
But since, without this bitter deed, I lose you, 950
And since, for me, your life outweighs all else,
Why, I will speak. Theseus, however angry,
Will do no worse than banish him again.
A father, punishing, remains a father.
His anger will be soothed with easy penance. 955
But even if some guitless blood be spilt,
Is not your honor of a greater worth, —
A treasure far too precious to be risked?
You must submit, no matter what is needful,
For when your reputation is at stake, 960
Then you must sacrifice your very conscience.
But someone comes. 'Tis Theseus —
    Phædra. Look, I see
Hippolytus most stern, and in his eyes
There is my ruin written. I am helpless. 965
My fate is yours. Do with it as you will.

(Enter THESEUS, HIPPOLYTUS, *and* THERAMENES.*)*

    Theseus. Fortune will fight no longer with my
    wishes,
But to your arms it brings me back —
    Phædra. Wait, Theseus.
Nay, do not hurry to profane caresses 970
One time so sweet, which I am now not worthy
Even to taste of, for you have been wronged.
Fortune has proved most spiteful. In your ab-
    sence
It has not spared your wife. I am not fit
To meet you tenderly, and from this time 975
I only care how I shall bear my shame.
    (Exeunt PHÆDRA *and* ŒNONE.*)*
    Theseus. Strange welcome for your father, is it
    not?
What does it mean, my son?
    Hipp. Why, only Phædra
Can solve that mystery. If I can move you 980
By any wish, then let me never see her.
Hippolytus begs leave to disappear, —
To leave the home that holds your wife, forever.
    Theseus. You, my son! Leave me?

    Hipp. 'Twas not I who sought her 985
You were the one to lead her to these shores!
My lord, at your departure you thought fit
To leave Aricia and the queen in Trœzen,
And I, myself, was charged with their protection.
But now, what cares will need to keep me here?
My idle youth has shown what skill it has 991
Over such petty foes as roam the woods.
May I not leave this life of little glory, —
Of ease — and dip my spear in nobler blood?
Before you reached my age, more than one tyrant,
More than one monster had already felt 996
The force of your good arm. You had succeeded
In whipping insolence; you had removed
All of the dangers lurking on our coasts.
The traveler no longer feared for outrage, 1000
And Hercules, himself, who knew your deeds,
Relied on you, and rested from his labors.
But I — the son of such a noble father, —
I am unknown, and I am far behind 1004
Even my mother's footsteps. Let my courage
Have scope to act. If there is yet some monster
Escaped from you, then let me seek for glory,
Bringing the spoils to you; or let it be
That memory of death well met with courage
Shall keep my name a living one, — shall prove
To all the world I am my father's son. 1011
    Theseus. Why, what is this? What terror can
    have seized you?
What makes my kindred fly before my face?
If I return to find myself so feared,
To find so little welcome in my home, 1015
Then why did Heaven free me from my prison?
My only friend, misled by his own passion
Set out to rob the tyrant of Epirus, —
To rob him of his wife! Regretfully
I gave the lover aid. Fate blinded us, — 1020
Myself as well as him. The tyrant seized me,
Defenseless and unarmed. With tears I saw
Pirithous cast forth to be devoured
By savage beasts, that lapped the blood of men.
He shut me in a gloomy cave, far down, 1025
Deep in the earth, near to the realm of Pluto.
I lay six months, before the gods had pity,
Then I escaped the eyes that guarded me.
I purged the world of this, its enemy,
And he, himself has fed his monsters' hunger. 1030
But when I come, with an expectant joy,
When I draw close to all that is most precious
Of what the gods have left me, — when my soul
Looks for its happiness in these dear places,
Then I am welcome only with a shudder, 1035
With turning from me, and with hasty flight.
And since it seems that I inspire such terror,
Would I were still imprisoned in Epirus! 1038
Phædra complains that I have suffered outrage.

Who has betrayed me? Speak! Was I avenged?
Why was I not? Has Greece, to whom mine arm
Has often brought good help, sheltered my foe?
You do not answer. Is it that my son, —
My own son — has he joined mine enemies?
I'll enter, for I cannot bear to wonder.   1045
I'll learn at once the culprit and the crime,
And Phædra must explain her trouble to me.

(*Exit.*)

Hipp. What mean these words? They freeze
    my very blood!   1048
Will Phædra, in her frenzy, blame herself, —
Make sure of her destruction? And the king, —
What will he say? O gods! The fatal poison
That love has spread through all my father's house!
I burn with fires his hatred disapproves.
How changed he finds me from the son he knew!
My mind is much alarmed with dark forebodings,
But surely innocence need never fear.   1056
Come, let us go, and in some other place
Consider how I best may move my father
To make him tender, and to tell a love   1059
Troubled, but never vanquished, by his frown.

(*Exeunt.*)

ACT IV

(*Enter* THESEUS *and* ŒNONE.)

Theseus. Ah, what is this I hear? Presump-
    tuous traitor!
And would he have disgraced his father's honor?
With what relentless footsteps Fate pursues me!
I know not where I go, nor where I am!
My kindest love, how very ill repaid!   1065
Bold scheme! Oh, most abominable thought!
A wretch who did not shrink from violence
To reach the object of his evil passion!
I know this sword, — it served to arm his fury, —
The sword I gave him for a nobler use!   1070
And could the sacred ties of blood not stop him?
And Phædra, — was she loath to have him pun-
    ished?
She held her silence. Was it to spare his guilt?
Œnone. Only to spare a most unhappy father.
She knew it shameful that her eyes had kindled
So infamous a love, — had prompted him   1076
To such a crime, — and Phædra would have died.
I saw her raise her arm, and ran to save her.
To me alone you owe it that she lives.
And since I pity her, and pity you   1080
I came, unwilling, to explain her tears.
Theseus. The traitor! Well indeed might he
    turn pale!
It was for fear he trembled when he saw me!
I was amazed that he should show no gladness.
The coldness of his greeting chilled my love. 1085

But was this guilty passion that consumes him
Declared before I banished him from Athens?
    Œnone. Remember, sire, how Phædra urged it
    on you.
It was illicit love that caused her hatred.
    Theseus. And then this flame burst out again at
    Trœzen?   1090
    Œnone. Sire, I have told you all there is. The
    queen
Is left to bear her grief alone too long.
Let me now leave you. I will wait on her. (*Exit.*)

(*Enter* HIPPOLYTUS.)

    Theseus. Ah, there he is! Great gods! That
    noble manner
Might well deceive an eye less fond than mine!
Why should the sacred mark of virtue shine   1096
Bright on the forehead of an evil wretch?
Why should the blackness of a traitor's heart
Not show itself by sure and certain signs?
    Hipp. My father, may I ask what fatal cloud
Has troubled so the face of majesty?   1101
Dare you not trust this secret to your son?
    Theseus. Traitor, how dare you show yourself
    before me?
Monster, whom Heaven's bolts have spared too
    long!
A last survivor of that robber band   1105
Whereof I cleansed the earth, your brutal lust
Scorned to respect even my marriage bed!
And now you dare, — my hated foe, — to come
Here to my presence, here where all things are
    filled
And foul with infamy, instead of seeking   1110
Some unknown land, that never heard my name.
Fly, traitor, fly! Stay not to tempt my wrath!
I scarce restrain it. Do not brave my hatred.
I have been shamed forever; 'tis enough
To be the father of so vile a son,   1115
Without your death, to stain indelibly
The splendid record of my noble deeds.
Fly! And unless you yearn for punishment
To make you yet another villain slain,
Take heed that this sun, shining on us now   1120
Shall see your foot no more upon this soil.
I say it once again, — fly! — and in haste!
Rid all my realms of your detested person.
On thee, — on thee, great Neptune, do I call!
If once I cleared thy shores of murderers,   1125
Remember, then, thy promise to reward me
For these good deeds, by granting my first prayer.
I was held long in close captivity.
I did not then demand thy mighty aid,
For I have saved so great a privilege   1130
To use in greatest need. That time is come.
And now I ask, — avenge a wretched father!

I leave this traitor subject to thy wrath.
I ask that thou shouldst quench his fires in blood,
And by thy fury, I will judge thy favor!   1135
    Hipp. Phædra accuses me of wanton passion!
A final horror to confuse my soul!
Such blows, unlooked for, falling all at once,
Have crushed me, choked me, struck me into
    silence!
    Theseus. Traitor, you thought that in a timid
    silence   1140
Phædra would cover your brutality.
But, though you fled, you still should not have left
    her
Holding the sword that seals your condemnation.
Or rather, to complete your perfidy,
You should have robbed her both of speech and
    life!   1145
    Hipp. Most justly angered at so black a lie,
I might be pardoned, should I speak the truth.
But it concerns your honor to conceal it.
Welcome that reverence which stops my tongue,
And, without seeking to increase your troubles,
Look closely at my life, as it has been.   1151
Great crimes come never singly; they are linked
To sins that went before. Who once has sinned,
May, at the last, do greater violence
To all that men hold sacred. Vice, like virtue,
Grows in small steps, and no true innocence   1156
Can ever fall at once to deepest guilt.
No man of virtue, in a single day,
Can turn himself to treason, murder, incest!
I am the son of one both chaste and brave.   1160
I have not proved unworthy of my birth.
Pittheus,[1] one by all men reckoned wise,
Deigned to instruct me, when I left her keeping.
I do not wish to boast upon my merits,
But if I may lay claim to any virtue,   1165
I think I have displayed, beyond all else,
That I abhor those sins with which you charge me.
Look you, Hippolytus is known in Greece
As one so continent he's thought austere,
And all men know how I abstain, unbending.   1170
The daylight is not purer than my heart.
Then how could I, if burning so profanely, —
    Theseus. Villain, it is that very pride condemns
    you!
I see the hateful reason for your coldness,
For only Phædra charmed your shameless eyes.
Your heart, quite cold to other witcheries,   1176
Refused the pure flame of a lawful love.
    Hipp. No, father, I have hidden it too long.
This heart has not disdained its sacred flame.
Here, at your feet, I'll tell my real offense.   1180
I love, and love, indeed, where you forbid it.

    [1] Former king of Trœzen where Theseus had been
reared.

My heart's devotion binds me to Aricia, —
The child of Pallas has subdued your son!
Her I adore, rebellious to your laws.
For her alone I breathe my ardent sighs.   1185
    Theseus. You love her? Gods! But no, — I
    see the truth.
You play this crime to justify yourself.
    Hipp. Sir, for six months I kept me from her
    presence,
And still I love her. I have come to tell it, —
Trembling I come — ! Can nothing free your
    mind   1190
Of such an error? Can my oaths not soothe you?
By Heaven — Earth, — by all the powers of
    Nature —
    Theseus. The wicked will not ever shrink from
    lying.
Be still, and spare me tiresome vows and pleadings,
Since your false virtue knows no other way.   1195
    Hipp. Although you think it false and insincere,
Phædra has cause enough to know it true.
    Theseus. Ah, how your boldness rouses all my
    anger!
    Hipp. What is my term and place of banish-
    ment?
    Theseus. Were you beyond the Pillars of Al-
    cides,   1200
Your perjured presence still were far too near me!
    Hipp. What friends will pity me, if you forsake
    me
And think me guilty of so vile a crime?
    Theseus. Go seek for friends who praise adultery,
And look for those who clap their hands at in-
    cest! —   1205
Low traitors, lawless, — steeped in infamy, —
Fit comforters for such an one as you!
    Hipp. Are incest and adultery the words
Which you will cast at me? I hold my peace.   1209
Yet think what mother Phædra had — remember
Her blood, not mine, is tainted with these horrors!
    Theseus. So then! Before my eyes your rage
    bursts out,
And loses all restraint. Go from my sight! —
This last time I will say it, — traitor, go!
And do not wait until a father's anger   1215
Drives you away in public execration!
                      (*Exit* HIPPOLYTUS.)
    Theseus (*alone*). Wretch! Thou must meet in-
    evitable ruin!
Neptune has sworn by Styx, — an oath most
    dreadful
Even to gods, — and he will keep his promise.
Thou canst not ever flee from his revenge.   1220
I loved thee, and in spite of this offense
My heart is moved by what I see for thee.
Nay, but thy doom is but too fully earned.

Had father ever better cause for rage?
O you just gods, who see my crushing grief, 1225
Why was I cursed with such an evil son?

(*Enter* PHÆDRA.)

Phædra. I come to you, my lord, in proper dread,
For I have heard your voice raised high in anger,
And much I fear that deeds have followed threats.
Oh, spare your child, if there is still some time! 1230
Respect your race, your blood, I do beseech you.
I would not hear that blood cry from the earth!
Save me the horror and the lasting shame
Of having caused his father's hand to shed it!
Theseus. No, madam, I am free from such a
    stain. 1235
But still the wretch has not escaped my vengeance.
The hand of an Immortal holds his doom,
And pledges his destruction. 'Tis a debt
That Neptune owes me. You shall be avenged.
Phædra. A debt to you? Prayers made in
    anger — 1240
Theseus. Fear not.
They will not fail. But join your prayers to mine,
And paint his crimes for me in all their blackness,
To fan my sluggish wrath to whitest heat.
You do not know of all his villainy. 1245
His rage against you feeds itself on slanders.
Your words, he says, are full of all deceit.
He says Aricia has his heart and soul,
That he loves only her —
Phædra. Aricia? —
Theseus. Yes. 1250
He said it to my face: — an idle pretext!
A trick I am not caught by. Let us hope
That Neptune does swift justice. I am going
Now to his altars, urging he keep his oath. 1255
              (*Exit* THESEUS.)
Phædra (*alone*). So he is gone! What words
have struck mine ears?
What smothered fires are burning in my heart?
What fatal stroke falls like a thunder-bolt?
Stung with remorse that would not give me peace,
I tore myself from out Œnone's arms 1260
And hurried here to help Hippolytus,
With all my soul and strength. Who knows, in-
    deed,
But that new-found repentance might have moved
    me
To speak in accusation of myself? —
And if my voice had not been choked with shame,
Perhaps I might have told the frightful truth. 1266
Hippolytus can feel — but not for me!
Aricia has his heart, his plighted word!
You gods! I thought his heart could not be
    touched
By any love, when, deaf to all my tears, 1270

He armed his eye with scorn, his brow with threats.
I thought him strong against all other women,
And yet another has prevailed upon him!
She tamed his pride, and she has gained his
    favor!
Perhaps he has a heart that's quick to melt, 1275
And I alone am she he cannot bear!
Then shall I charge myself with his protection?

(*Enter* ŒNONE.)

Phædra. Dear nurse, and do you know what I
    have learned?
Œnone. No, but in truth I come with trembling
    limbs.
I dreaded what you planned when you went out,
And fear of fatal madness turned me pale. 1281
Phædra. Who would have thought it, nurse? I
    had a rival.
Œnone. A rival?
Phædra. Yes, he loves. I cannot doubt it.
This wild Hippolytus I could not tame, — 1285
Who scorned to be admired, and who was wearied
With lovers' sighs, — this tiger whom I dreaded
Fawns on the hand of one who broke his pride.
Aricia found the entrance to his heart!
Œnone. Aricia? 1290
Phædra. 'Tis a torture yet untried!
Now for what other pains am I reserved?
All I have suffered, — ecstasies of passion,
Longings and fears, the horrors of remorse,
The shame of being spurned with contumely, 1295
Were feeble tastes of what is now my torment.
They love each other! By what secret charm
Have they deceived me? When and where and
    how
Did they contrive to meet? You knew it all, —
And why, then, was I kept from knowing of it?
You never told me of their stolen hours 1301
Of love and of delight. Have they been seen
Talking together often? — did they seek
The forest shadows? Ah, they had full freedom
To be together. Heaven watched their sighs. 1305
They loved, — and never felt that they were guilty.
The morning sun shone always clear for them,
While I, — an outcast from the face of Nature,
Shunned the bright day, and would have hid my-
    self, —
Death the one god whom I dared ask for aid! 1310
I waited for the freedom of the grave.
My woe was fed with bitterness, and watered
With many tears. It was too closely watched.
I did not dare to weep without restraint,
And knowing it a solace perilous, 1315
I feared it, and I hid my mortal terror
Beneath a face most tranquil. Oftentimes
I stopped my tears, and made myself to smile —

Œnone. What fruit can they desire from fruitless
    love?
For they can meet no more.   1320
    Phædra. That love will stay,
And it will stay forever.   While I speak —
O dreadful thought — they laugh and scorn my
    madness
And my distracted heart.   In spite of exile,
In spite of that which soon must come to part
    them,   1325
They make a thousand oaths to bind their union.
Œnone, can I bear this happiness
Which so insults me?   I would have your pity.
Yes, she must be destroyed.   My husband's fury
Against her hated race shall be renewed.   1330
The punishment must be a heavy one.
Her guilt outruns the guilt of all her brothers.
I'll plead with Theseus, in my jealousy, —
What do I say?   Oh, have I lost my senses?
Is Phædra jealous? will she, then, go begging   1335
For Theseus' help?   He lives, — and yet I burn.
For whom?   Whose heart is this I claim as mine?
My hair stands up with horror at my words,
And from this time, my guilt has passed all bounds!
Hypocrisy and incest breathe at once   1340
Through all I do.   My hands are ripe for murder,
To spill the guiltless blood of innocence.
Do I still live, a wretch, and dare to face
The holy Sun, from whom I have my being?
My father's father was the king of gods;   1345
My race is spread through all the universe. —
Where can I hide?   In the dark realms of Pluto?
But there my father holds the fatal urn.
His hands award the doom irrevocable. —
Minos is judge of all the ghosts in hell.   1350
And how his awful shade will start and shudder
When he shall see his daughter brought before him,
And made confess such many-colored sins,
Such crimes, perhaps, as hell itself knows not!
O father, what will be thy words at seeing   1355
So dire a sight?   I see thee drop the urn,
Turning to seek some punishment unheard of, —
To be, thyself, mine executioner!
O spare me!   For a cruel deity
Destroys thy race.   O look upon my madness,
And in it see her wrath.   This aching heart   1361
Gathers no fruit of pleasure from its crime.
It is a shame which hounds me to the grave,
And ends a life of misery in torment.
    Œnone. Ah, madam, drive away this groundless
    fear.   1365
Look not so hard upon a little sin.
You love.   We cannot conquer destiny.
Why, you were drawn as by a fatal charm; —
Is that a marvel we have never seen?
Has love, then, come to triumph over you,   1370

And no one else?   By nature man is weak.
You are a mortal, — bow to mortal fortune.
You chafe against a yoke that many others
Have borne before you.   They upon Olympus, —
The very gods themselves, who make us tremble
For our poor sins, have burned with lawless pas-
    sions.   1376
    Phædra. What words are these?   What counsels
    do you give me?
Why will you still pour poison in mine ears?
You have destroyed me.   You have brought me
    back
When I should else have left the light of day. 1380
You made me to forget my solemn duty,
And see Hippolytus, whom I had shunned.
What have you done?   Why did those wicked lips
Slander his faultless life with blackest lies?
It may be you have murdered him.   By now   1385
The prayer unholy of a heartless father
May have been granted.   I will have no words!
Go, monster!   Leave me to my sorry fate.
May the just gods repay you properly,
And may your punishment remain forever   1390
To strike with fear, all such as you, who strive
To feed the frailty of the great with cunning,
To push them to the very brink of ruin
To which their feet incline, — to smooth the path
Of guilt.   Such flatterers the gods, in anger, 1395
Bestow on kings as their most fatal gift!
                  (*Exit* Phædra.)
    Œnone (*alone*). O gods!   What is there I've not
    done to serve her?
And this is the reward that I have won!   (*Exit.*)

ACT V

(*Enter* Hippolytus *and* Aricia.)

    Aricia. Can you keep silent in this mortal dan-
    ger?   1399
Your father loves you.   Will you leave him so —
When he is thus deceived?   If you are cruel, —
If, in your heart, you will not see my tears,
Why then, content, — and do not ever see me.
Abandon poor Aricia, — but at least
If you must go, make sure your life is safe.   1405
Defend your honor from a shameful stain,
And force your father to recall his prayers.
There still is time.   Why, for a mere caprice,
Should you leave open way for Phædra's slanders?
Let Theseus know the truth.   1410
    Hipp. Could I say more
And not expose him to a great disgrace?
How should I dare, by speaking what I know,
To make my father's brow blush red with shame?
You only know the hateful mystery.   1415
I have not showed my heart to any other

But you and Heaven. Judge, then, if I love you,
Since you have seen I could not hide from you
All I would fain have hidden from myself!
Remember under what a seal I spoke.   1420
Forget what I have said, if that may be,
And never let so pure a mouth give voice
To such a secret. Let us trust to Heaven
To give me justice, for the gods are just.   1424
For their own honor they will clear the guiltless.
The time will come for Phædra to be punished.
She cannot always flee the shame she merits.
I ask no other favor than your silence.
In all besides, I give my wrath free scope.
Make your escape from this captivity,   1430
Be bold, and come with me upon my flight.
Oh, do not stay on this accursèd soil
Where virtue breathes the air of pestilence.
To hide your leaving, take the good advantage
Of all this turmoil, roused by my disgrace.   1435
I promise you the means of flight are ready.
You have, as yet, no other guards than mine.
Defenders of great strength will fight our quarrel.
Argos has open arms, and Sparta calls us.
Let us appeal for justice to our friends,   1440
And let us not stand by while Phædra joins us
Together in one ruin, driving us
Down from the throne, — and swells her son's pos-
        sessions
By robbing us. Come, take this happy chance.
What fear can hold you back? You seem to pause.
Only your better fortune makes me urge   1446
That we be bold. When I am all a-fire,
Why are you ice? Are you afraid to follow
One who is banished?

    Aricia. Ah, but such an exile   1450
Would be most dear to me. For with what joy
I'd live, if I could link my fate to yours,
And be forgot by all the world. But still
We are not bound by that sweet tie together.
Then how am I to steal away with you?   1455
I know the strictest honor need not stop me
From seeking freedom from your father's hands,
For this, indeed, is not my parents' home,
And flight is lawful, when one flies from tyrants.
But you, sir, love me, and my virtue shrinks —

    Hipp. No, no! To me your honor is as dear
As it is to yourself. A nobler purpose   1462
Brings me to you. I ask you leave your foes
And follow with your husband. That same Heaven
Which sends these woes, sets free the pledge be-
        tween us   1465
From human hands. There are not always torches
To light the face of Hymen. Come with me —
Beside the gates of Trœzen is a temple,
Amid the ancient tombs of princes, buried.
They who are false can never enter there,   1470

And there no mortal dares make perjured oaths,
For instant punishment will come on guilt.
There is not any stronger check to falsehood
Than what is present there, — fear of a death
That cannot be escaped. There we shall go,   1475
If you consent, and swear eternal love,
And call the god who watches there to witness
Our solemn vows, and ask his guarding care.
I will invoke the holiest of powers —   1479
The chaste Diana and the Queen of Heaven, —
Yes, all the gods, who know my inmost heart,
Will answer for my sacred promises.

    Aricia. Here is the king. Away — make no
        delay.
I linger yet a while to hide my flight.
Go you, and leave me with some trusted one   1485
To lead my timid footsteps to your side.

                 (*Exit* HIPPOLYTUS.)

        (*Enter* THESEUS *and* ISMENE.)

    Theseus. O gods, throw light upon my troubled
        mind!
Show me the truth which I am seeking here.

    Aricia (*to* ISMENE). Be ready, dear Ismene, for
        our flight.   (*Exit* ISMENE.)

    Theseus. Your color changes, and you seem con-
        fused.   1490
Madam, — what dealing had my son with you?

    Aricia. Sire, he was bidding me his last farewell.

    Theseus. It seems your eyes can tame that stub-
        born pride,
And the first sighs he breathes are paid to you.

    Aricia. I cannot well deny the truth; he has not
Inherited your hatred and injustice, —   1496
He does not treat me as a criminal.

    Theseus. That is to say, — he swore eternal love.
Do not depend on such a fickle heart.
He swore as much to others, long before.   1500

    Aricia. He, Sire?

    Theseus. You stop the roving of his taste.
How should you bear so vile a partnership?

    Aricia. And how can you endure that wicked
        slanders
Should make so pure a life seem black as pitch?
How do you know so little of his heart?   1506
Do you so ill distinguish innocence
From the worst guilt? What mist before your
        eyes
Can make them blind to such an open virtue?
Ah! 'Tis too much to let false tongues defame
        him!   1510
Repent! Call back again your fatal prayers.
Oh, be afraid, lest Heaven in its justice
Hate you enough to hear your wish and grant it!
The gods, in anger, often take our victims, —

And oftentimes they punish us with gifts!   1515
    Theseus. No, it is vain to seek to hide his guilt
Your love is blind to his depravity.
But I have witnesses beyond reproach, —
Tears I have seen, — true tears, that may be
    trusted.
    Aricia. Take heed, my lord.   Although your
    mighty hand   1520
Has rid the world of many beasts and monsters,
You have not slain them all, — there's one alive! —
Your son, himself, forbids that I say more,
And since I know how much he still reveres you,
I know that I should cause him much distress
If I should dare to finish.   I shall act   1526
Like reverence, — and to be silent, — leave you.
                  (*Exit* ARICIA.)
    Theseus (*alone*). What is there in her mind?
    What hidden meaning
Lurks in a speech begun, then broken short?
Would both deceive me with a vain pretense? 1530
Have they conspired to put me to this torture?
And yet, for all that I am most severe,
What plaintive voice is crying in my heart?
I have a secret pity that disturbs me.
Œnone must be questioned, once again,   1535
For I must see this crime in clearer light.
Guards, bid Œnone come to me, — alone.

(*Enter* PANOPE.)

    Panope. I do not know the purpose of the queen,
Yet, seeing her distress, I fear the worst; —
Despair most fatal, painted on her features, —
Death's pallor is already in her face.   1541
Œnone, shamed and driven from her sight,
Has thrown herself into the ocean's depths.
What moved her to so rash a deed, none knows,
And now the waves forever hide her from us.   1545
    Theseus. What is it that you say?
    Panope. Her sad fate adds
New trouble to the queen's tempestuous soul.
Sometimes, to soothe her secret pain, she clasps
Her children to her, bathes them with her tears, —
Then suddenly forgets her mother's love,   1551
And thrusts them from her with a look of horror.
She wanders back and forth with doubtful steps,
Her eye looks vacantly, and will not know us.
She wrote three times, and thrice she changed her
    mind,   1555
And tore the letter when it scarce was started.
Be willing then to see her, Sire, — to help her.
                  (*Exit* PANOPE.)
   Theseus. Œnone dead, and Phædra bent on
    dying?
Oh, call my son to me again, great Heaven!
Let him defend himself, for I am ready   1560
To hear him, now.   Oh, haste not to bestow

Thy fatal bounty, Neptune.   Rather my prayers
Should stay unheard forever.   Far too soon
I raised too cruel hands, and I believed
Lips that may well have lied!   Ah, what may fol-
    low?   1565

(*Enter* THERAMENES.)

    Theseus. 'Tis you, Theramenes?   Where is my
    son?
I gave him to your keeping in his childhood, —
But why should tears be flowing from thine eyes?
How is it with my son — ?
    Thera. You worry late.   1570
It is a vain affection.   He is dead.
    Theseus. O gods!
    Thera. Yes, I have seen the very flower
Of all mankind cut down; and I am bold
To say that never man deserved it less.   1575
    Theseus. My son!   My son is dead!   When I
    was reaching
My arms to him again, then why should Heaven
Hasten his doom?   What sudden blow was this?
    Thera. When we had scarcely passed the gates
    of Trœzen, —
He, silent in his chariot, his guards   1580
Downcast and silent, too, all ranged around him, —
He turned his steeds to the Mycenian road,
And, lost in thought, allowed the reins to lie
Loose on their backs, and his high-mettled charg-
    ers,
One time so eager to obey his voice,   1585
Now seemed to know his sadness and to share it.
Then, coming from the sea, a frightful cry
Shatters the troubled air with sudden discord;
And groaning from the bosom of the earth
Answers the crying of that fearful voice.   1590
It froze the blood within our very hearts!
Our horses hear, and stand with bristling manes.
Meanwhile there rises on the watery plain
A mountain wave, mighty, with foaming crest.
It rolls upon the shore, and as it breaks   1595
It throws before our eyes a raging monster.
Its brow is armed with terrifying horns
And all its body clothed with yellow scales.
In front it is a bull, behind, a dragon,
Turning and twisting in impatient fury.   1600
It bellows till the very shores do tremble.
The sky is struck with horror at the sight.
The earth in terror quakes; breath of the beast
Poisons the air.   The very wave that brought it
Runs back in fear.   All fly, forgetting courage 1605
Which cannot help, — and in a nearby temple
Take refuge, — all but brave Hippolytus.
A hero's worthy son, he stays his horses.
Seizes his darts, and rushing forward, hurls
A missle with sure aim, and wounds the beast   1610

Deep in the flank. It springs, raging with pain,
Right to the horses' feet, and roaring, falls,
Writhes in the dust, shows them his fiery throat,
And covers them with flame and smoke and blood.
Fear lends them wings; deaf to his voice for once,
Heeding no curb, the horses race away.   1616
Their master tires himself in futile efforts.
Each courser's bit is red with blood and foam.
Some say a god, in all this wild disorder,   1619
Is seen, pricking their dusty flanks with goads.
They rush to jagged rocks, urged by this terror.
The axle crashes, and the hardy youth
Sees his car broken, shattered into bits.
He himself falls, entangled in the reins. —
Forgive my grief. That cruel sight will be   1625
For me, the source of never-ending tears.
I saw thy luckless son, — I saw him, Sire,
Dragged by those horses that his hands had fed.
He could not stop their fierce career, — his cries
But added to their terror. All his body   1630
Was soon a mass of wounds. Our anguished cries
Filled the whole plain. At length the horses slack-
    ened.
They stopped close by the ancient tombs which
    mark
The place where lie the ashes of his fathers.
I ran there panting, and behind me came   1635
His guard, along a track fresh-stained with blood,
Reddening all the rocks; locks of his hair
Hung dripping in the briers, — gory triumphs!
I came and called him. Stretching out his hand,
He opened dying eyes, soon to be closed.   1640
"The gods have robbed me of a guiltless life."
I heard him say, "Take care of sad Aricia,
When I am dead. Friend, if my father mourn
When he shall know his son's unhappy fate, —
One accused falsely, — then, to give me peace,
Tell him to treat his captive tenderly,   1646
And to restore —" The hero's breath had failed,
And in my arms there lay a mangled body, —
A thing most piteous, the bleeding spoil
Of Heaven's wrath, — his father could not know
    him.   1650
Theseus. Alas, my son: — my hope, now lost for-
    ever!
The gods are ruthless. They have served me well,
And I am left to live a life of anguish
And of a great remorse.
    Thera. And then Aricia,   1655
Flying from you, came timidly to take him
To be her husband, there, before the gods.
And coming close, she saw the grass, all reeking,
All bloody red, and (sad for a lover's eyes!)
She saw him, lying there, disfigured, pale, —   1660
And for a time she knew not her misfortune.
She did not know the hero she adores.

She looked and asked, "Where is Hippolytus?"
Only too sure, at last, that he was lying
Before her there, with sad eyes, silently   1665
Reproaching Heaven, she groaned, and shuddering
Fell fainting, all but lifeless, at his feet.
Ismene, all in tears, knelt down beside her,
And called her back to life, a life of nothing
But sense of pain. And I to whom the light   1670
Is only darkness, now, come to discharge
The duty he imposed on me: to tell you
His last desire, — a melancholy task. —
But here his mortal enemy is coming.

(Enter PHÆDRA *and Guards.)*

    Theseus. Madam, you've triumphed, and my
        son is killed!   1675
Ah, but what room have I for fear! How justly
Suspicion racks me that in blaming him
I erred! But he is dead; accept your victim,
Rightly or wrongly slain. Your heart may leap.
For me, my eyes shall be forever blind.   1680
Since you have said it, I'll believe him guilty.
His death is cause enough for me to weep.
It would be folly, should I seek a light
Which could not bring him back to soothe my grief,
And which might only make me more unhappy.
I will go far from you and from this shore,   1686
For here the vision of my mangled son
Would haunt my memory, and drive me mad.
I wish I might be banished from the world,
For all the world must rise in judgment on me.
Even my glory weights my punishment,   1691
For if I bore a name less known to men,
'Twere easier to hide me. Ah, I mourn
And hate all prayers the gods have granted me.
Nor will I ever go to them again   1695
With useless pleadings. All that they can give
Is far outweighed by what they took from me.
    Phædra. My lord, I cannot hear you and be
        silent.
I must undo the wrong that he has suffered, —
Your son was innocent.   1700
    Theseus. Unhappy father!
And I condemned him for a word of yours!
You think I can forgive such cruelty — ?
    Phædra. Moments are precious to me; let me
        speak.
'Twas I who cast an eye of lawless passion   1705
On chaste and dutiful Hippolytus.
The gods had lit a baleful fire in me,
And vile Œnone's cunning did the rest.
She feared Hippolytus, — who knew my mad-
        ness, —
Would tell you of that passion which he hated.   1711
And so she took advantage of my weakness
And hastened, that she might accuse him first.

She has been punished now, but all too lightly.
She sought to flee my anger, — cast herself
Into the waves. The sword had long since cut
My thread of life, but still I heard the cry   1716
Of slandered innocence, and I determined
To die a slower way, and first confess
My penitence to you. There is a poison
Medea brought to Athens, in my veins.   1720
The venom works already in my heart.
A strange and fatal chill is spreading there.
I see already, through a gathering mist,
The husband whom I outrage with my presence.
Death veils the light of Heaven from mine eyes,

And gives it back its purity, defiled.   1726
    Panope. She dies, my lord.
    Theseus. I would the memory.
Of her disgraceful deed might perish with her!
Ah! I have learned too late! Come, let us go,
And with the blood of mine unhappy son   1731
Mingle our tears, — embrace his dear remains,
Repenting deeply for a hated prayer.
Let him have honor such as he deserves,
And, to appease his sore-offended spirit,   1735
No matter what her brothers' guilt has been,
From this day forth, Aricia is my daughter.
    (Exeunt.)

Jonathan Swift · 1667–1745

Swift's place in literature is essentially that of a critic of society.   He wrote at a time in England when social conditions were relatively stable.   A hundred years earlier there had been the excitement of the Renaissance and the impetus of the new learning; a hundred years later there was to be the turmoil resulting from developing industry and new inventions.   But the first few decades of the eighteenth century, when Swift was most productive as a writer, were the days of the coffee house, of Queen Anne, of the sort of social aristocracy portrayed satirically in Pope's *Rape of the Lock*. This is not to say, however, that the political scene was calm.   The Whigs and the Tories were battling, somewhat more venomously than usual, for supremacy.   Swift sided first with one, then with the other.   Walpole became prime minister.   Wesley and Methodism rose to prominence. The South Sea Bubble — a scheme for making money rapidly — swelled and burst.   And among Swift's contemporaries and friends were Pope, Steele, Addison, Prior, and Gay — the first three, with Swift, bringing luster to the writing and pamphleteering of a time when journalism was rising into prominence.

Jonathan Swift was born in Dublin, November 30, 1667, the son of English parents who had removed to Ireland only some few years before his birth.   Swift's father, a lawyer of no great success, died before Jonathan was born.   His mother returned shortly after to England.   Young Swift was left to the mercies and care of an uncle who saw that the lad was educated at Kilkenny School and was later sent to Trinity College, Dublin.   In his college studies Swift appears to have given little evidence of his later brilliance.

In 1689, when Swift was twenty-two years old, he went to England and took up his residence with a distinguished relative, Sir William Temple, at the Temple estate, Moor Park, near Farnham. Most of the next ten years were spent at Moor Park where Swift served as a secretary to Sir William. During these years, however, Swift went to Ireland where he entered the Church of Ireland and served for a while as vicar at Kilroot near Belfast.   Later on he held similar posts in the country near Dublin.   For several years Swift expected recognition and preferment — either in government or the Church.   Finally despairing of a position of responsibility in the government, Swift was obliged to content himself with an appointment as Dean of St. Patrick's at Dublin, a post made available to him by Queen Anne.   Though he disliked Ireland intensely as a place of residence for a man of his talents, Swift eventually found himself in sympathy with the people sufficiently to write various pamphlets and tracts attacking one form or another of England's misrule of that country.

Writing, politics, the church — these did not bring Swift trouble enough.   Further complications developed because of his relations with two women — "Stella" and "Vanessa."   Stella (Esther Johnson) was, like himself, a distant relative or beneficiary of Sir William Temple, and Swift had known her during his days at Moor Park.   Left with a small income, hardly sufficient to keep her in England, Stella moved to Dublin and took up her residence near Swift.   At a later time Esther Vanhomrigh, the daughter of a Dublin merchant whom Swift had met in England, followed the churchman to Ireland.   For reasons not known Swift married neither Stella nor Vanessa.   However, the two names play important parts in Swift's writing.   The last years of Dean Swift's life — he lived well into his seventy-eighth year — were clouded by dementia.   His powers failed to the extent that it was necessary to appoint guardians.   He died in Dublin on October 19, 1745, and was buried at St. Patrick's where he shared the coffin of Stella.

Swift's social criticism was expressed through satire.   His wit was mordant, his humor marked by exaggeration.   Leaving behind him numerous pamphlets and much verse, Swift is remembered today largely for four titles: *The Tale of a Tub* (1704); *The Battle of the Books* (1704), a volume setting forth the controversy as to the values of ancient and modern learning; *Gulliver's Travels* (1726); a *Modest Proposal for Preventing the Children of Poor People from being a Burden to their Parents or the Country* (1729), which proposed that the desired result be attained through fattening the children and eating them.   Of these four the one most widely read is *Gulliver's Travels*, a serious book of bitter criticism which, because of the narrative mould in which it was cast, has somehow lived on to earn the reputation of being a book for children — a last ironic tribute to the master of irony.

SUGGESTED REFERENCES: Ricardo Quintana, *Swift, An Introduction* (1955); Irvin Ehrenpreis, *Swift: The Man, His Works, and the Age* (1962); E. L. Tuveson, ed., *Swift: A Collection of Critical Essays* (1965).

Gulliver's Travels

First published in 1726, *Gulliver's Travels* is a satire on the vices, foibles, and frailties of mankind.   The scheme of organization sends a certain Lemuel Gulliver, "first a surgeon, and then a captain of several ships," on four major journeys to fabulous lands: the first to Lilliput, a land of small people and considerable chicanery; the second to Brobdingnag, a country inhabited by giants, a minor Utopia; the third to Laputa and adjacent countries where live impracticable peoples much bent on foolish researches; the fourth to Houyhnhnmland, a region where horses are endowed with intelligence and man is a filthy slave.   After each of these four journeys Gulliver returns, but always the call to adventure takes him away again to the ends of the earth.   The attacks on mankind and the details of the adventures of Gulliver are, of course, Swift's own, but as predecessors in this field of marvelous adventure to unreal lands, Swift had plenty of models.   The three most often mentioned are Lucian's *True Story*, Rabelais' *Gargantua*, and Cyrano de Bergerac's *Voyage to the Moon*.   While Swift gives every evidence of having held man and particularly man's intelligence in contempt, it need not be assumed that he was a hater of all humanity.   He contemned the race, but exempted individuals.   He once wrote to Pope: "When you think of the world give it one lash the more at my request."   In the selections which follow from Part III — The Voyage to Laputa — Swift attacks impractical scholarship and absurd scientific projects.

PART III

A Voyage to Laputa, Balnibarbi, Glubbdubdrib, Luggnagg, and Japan

The Author sets out on his third voyage, is taken by pirates.   The malice of a Dutchman.   His arrival at an island.   He is received into Laputa.

I had not been at home above ten days, when Captain William Robinson, a Cornish man, Commander of the *Hope-well*, a stout ship of three hundred tons, came to my house.   I had formerly been surgeon of another ship where he was master, and a fourth part owner, in a voyage to the Levant; he had always treated me more like a brother than an inferior officer, and hearing of my arrival made me a visit, as I apprehended only out of friendship, for nothing passed more than what is usual after long absences.   But repeating his visits often, expressing his joy to find me in good health, asking whether I were now settled for life, adding that he intended a voyage to the East Indies in two months; at last he plainly invited me, though with some apologies, to be surgeon of the ship; that I should have another surgeon under me besides our two mates; that my salary should be double to the

usual pay; and that having experienced my knowledge in sea-affairs to be at least equal to his, he
would enter into any engagement to follow my
advice, as much as if I had share in the command.

He said so many other obliging things, and I
knew him to be so honest a man, that I could not
reject his proposal; the thirst I had of seeing the
world, notwithstanding my past misfortunes, continuing as violent as ever. The only difficulty
that remained, was to persuade my wife, whose
consent however I at last obtained by the prospect
of advantage she proposed to her children.

We set out the 5th of August, 1706, and arrived
at Fort St. George¹ the 11th of April, 1707. We
stayed there three weeks to refresh our crew, many
of whom were sick. From thence we went to
Tonquin,² where the Captain resolved to continue
some time, because many of the goods he intended
to buy were not ready, nor could he expect to be
dispatched in some months. Therefore in hopes to
defray some of the charges he must be at, he bought
a sloop, loaded it with several sorts of goods, wherewith the Tonquinese usually trade to the neighboring islands, and putting fourteen men on board,
whereof three were of the country, he appointed
me master of the sloop, and gave me power to
traffic for two months, while he transacted his
affairs at Tonquin.

We had not sailed above three days, when a
great storm arising, we were driven five days to
the north-north-east, and then to the east; after
which we had fair weather, but still with a pretty
strong gale from the west. Upon the tenth day
we were chased by two pirates, who soon overtook
us; for my sloop was so deep loaden, that she sailed
very slow, neither were we in a condition to defend
ourselves.

We were boarded about the same time by both
the pirates, who entered furiously at the head of
their men, but finding us all prostrate upon our
faces (for so I gave order) they pinioned us with
strong ropes, and setting a guard upon us, went
to search the sloop.

I observed among them a Dutchman, who
seemed to be of some authority, though he was not
commander of either ship. He knew us by our
countenances to be Englishmen, and jabbering to
us in his own language, swore we should be tied
back to back, and thrown into the sea. I spoke
Dutch tolerably well; I told him who we were, and
begged him in consideration of our being Christians
and Protestants, of neighboring countries, in strict
alliance, that he would move the Captains to take
some pity on us. This inflamed his rage; he re-

¹ Madras.
² A town in French Indo-China.

peated his threatenings, and turning to his companions, spoke with great vehemence, in the
Japanese language, as I suppose, often using the
word *Christianos*.

The largest of the two pirate ships was commanded by a Japanese Captain, who spoke a little
Dutch, but very imperfectly. He came up to me,
and after several questions, which I answered in
great humility, he said we should not die. I made
the Captain a very low bow, and then turning to
the Dutchman, said, I was sorry to find more
mercy in a heathen, than in a brother Christian.
But I had soon reason to repent those foolish
words; for that malicious reprobate, having often
endeavored in vain to persuade both the Captains
that I might be thrown into the sea (which they
would not yield to after the promise made me, that
I should not die), however prevailed so far as to
have a punishment inflicted on me, worse in all
human appearance than death itself. My men
were sent by an equal division into both the pirate
ships, and my sloop new manned. As to myself,
it was determined that I should be set adrift in a
small canoe, with paddles and a sail, and four days'
provisions, which last the Japanese Captain was
so kind to double out of his own stores, and would
permit no man to search me. I got down into the
canoe, while the Dutchman standing upon the
deck, loaded me with all the curses and injurious
terms his language could afford.

About an hour before we saw the pirates, I had
taken an observation, and found we were in the
latitude of 46 N. and of longitude 183. When I
was at some distance from the pirates, I discovered
by my pocket-glass several islands to the southeast. I set up my sail, the wind being fair, with
a design to reach the nearest of those islands, which
I made a shift to do in about three hours. It was
all rocky; however I got many birds' eggs, and
striking fire, I kindled some heath and dry sea-
weed, by which I roasted my eggs. I ate no other
supper, being resolved to spare my provisions as
much as I could. I passed the night under the
shelter of a rock, strowing some heath under me,
and slept pretty well.

The next day I sailed to another island, and
thence to a third and fourth, sometimes using my
sail, and sometimes my paddles. But not to
trouble the reader with a particular account of
my distress, let it suffice that on the fifth day I
arrived at the last island in my sight which lay
south-south-east to the former.

This island was at a greater distance than I expected, and I did not reach it in less than five hours.
I encompassed it almost round before I could find
a convenient place to land in, which was a small

creek about three times the wideness of my canoe. I found the island to be all rocky, only a little intermingled with tufts of grass and sweet smelling herbs. I took out my small provisions, and after having refreshed myself, I secured the remainder in a cave, whereof there were great numbers. I gathered plenty of eggs upon the rocks, and got a quantity of dry sea-weed and parched grass, which I designed to kindle the next day, and roast my eggs as well as I could. (For I had about me my flint, steel, match, and burning-glass.) I lay all night in the cave where I had lodged my provisions. My bed was the same dry grass and sea-weed which I intended for fuel. I slept very little, for the disquiets of my mind prevailed over my weariness, and kept me awake. I considered how impossible it was to preserve my life in so desolate a place, and how miserable my end must be. Yet I found myself so listless and desponding that I had not the heart to rise, and before I could get spirits enough to creep out of my cave the day was far advanced. I walked a while among the rocks; the sky was perfectly clear, and the sun so hot that I was forced to turn my face from it: when all on a sudden it became obscured, as I thought, in a manner very different from what happens by the interposition of a cloud. I turned back, and perceived a vast opaque body between me and the sun, moving forwards towards the island: it seemed to be about two miles high, and hid the sun six or seven minutes, but I did not observe the air to be much colder, or the sky more darkened, than if I had stood under the shade of a mountain. As it approached nearer over the place where I was, it appeared to be a firm substance, the bottom flat, smooth, and shining very bright from the reflection of the sea below. I stood upon a height about two hundred yards from the shore, and saw this vast body descending almost to a parallel with me, at less than an English mile distance. I took out my pocket-perspective, and could plainly discover numbers of people moving up and down the sides of it, which appeared to be sloping, but what those people were doing, I was not able to distinguish.

The natural love of life gave me some inward motions of joy, and I was ready to entertain a hope that this adventure might some way or other help to deliver me from the desolate place and condition I was in. But at the same time the reader can hardly conceive my astonishment, to behold an island in the air, inhabited by men, who were able (as it should seem) to raise or sink, or put it into a progressive motion, as they pleased. But not being at that time in a disposition to philosophise upon this phenomenon, I rather chose to observe what course the island would take, because

it seemed for a while to stand still. Yet soon after it advanced nearer, and I could see the sides of it, encompassed with several gradations of galleries, and stairs at certain intervals, to descend from one to the other. In the lowest gallery I beheld some people fishing with long angling rods, and others looking on. I waved my cap (for my hat was long since worn out) and my handkerchief towards the island; and upon its nearer approach, I called and shouted with the utmost strength of my voice; and then looking circumspectly, I beheld a crowd gather to that side which was most in my view. I found by their pointing towards me and to each other, that they plainly discovered me, although they made no return to my shouting. But I could see four or five men running in great haste up the stairs to the top of the island, who then disappeared. I happened rightly to conjecture, that these were sent for orders to some person in authority upon this occasion.

The number of people increased, and in less than half an hour the island was moved and raised in such a manner, that the lowest gallery appeared in a parallel of less than an hundred yards distance from the height where I stood. I then put myself into the most supplicating postures, and spoke in the humblest accent, but received no answer. Those who stood nearest over against me seemed to be persons of distinction, as I supposed by their habit. They conferred earnestly with each other, looking often upon me. At length one of them called out in a clear, polite, smooth dialect, not unlike in sound to the Italian; and therefore I returned an answer in that language, hoping at least that the cadence might be more agreeable to his ears. Although neither of us understood the other, yet my meaning was easily known, for the people saw the distress I was in.

They made signs for me to come down from the rock, and go towards the shore, which I accordingly did; and the flying island being raised to a convenient height, the verge directly over me, a chain was let down from the lowest gallery, with a seat fastened to the bottom, to which I fixed myself, and was drawn up by pulleys.

The humors and dispositions of the Laputians described. An account of their learning. Of the King and his Court. The Author's reception there. The inhabitants subject to fear and disquietudes. An account of the women.

At my alighting I was surrounded by a crowd of people, but those who stood nearest seemed to be of better quality. They beheld me with all the marks and circumstances of wonder; neither indeed was I much in their debt, having never till then seen a race of mortals so singular in their shapes, habits, and countenances. Their heads were all reclined either to the right or the left; one of their eyes turned inward, and the other directly up to the zenith. Their outward garments were adorned with the figures of suns, moons, and stars, interwoven with those of fiddles, flutes, harps, trumpets, guitars, harpsichords, and many other instruments of music, unknown to us in Europe. I observed here and there many in the habit of servants, with a blown bladder fastened like a flail to the end of a short stick, which they carried in their hands. In each bladder was a small quantity of dried pease, or little pebbles (as I was afterwards informed). With these bladders they now and then flapped the mouths and ears of those who stood near them, of which practice I could not then conceive the meaning; it seems the minds of these people are so taken up with intense speculations, that they neither can speak, nor attend to the discourses of others, without being roused by some external taction upon the organs of speech and hearing; for which reason those persons who are able to afford it always keep a flapper (the original is *climenole*) in their family, as one of their domestics, nor ever walk abroad or make visits without him. And the business of this officer is, when two or more persons are in company, gently to strike with his bladder the mouth of him who is to speak, and the right ear of him or them to whom the speaker addresseth himself. This flapper is likewise employed diligently to attend his master in his walks, and upon occasion to give him a soft flap on his eyes, because he is always so wrapped up in cogitation, that he is in manifest danger of falling down every precipice, and bouncing his head against every post, and in the streets, of justling others, or being justled himself into the kennel.[1]

It was necessary to give the reader this information, without which he would be at the same loss with me, to understand the proceedings of these people, as they conducted me up the stairs, to the top of the island, and from thence to the royal palace. While we were ascending, they forgot several times what they were about, and left me to myself, till their memories were again roused by their flappers; for they appeared altogether unmoved by the sight of my foreign habit and countenance, and by the shouts of the vulgar, whose thoughts and minds were more disengaged.

At last we entered the palace, and proceeded into the chamber of presence, where I saw the King seated on his throne, attended on each side by per-

[1] ditch or gutter..

sons of prime quality. Before the throne was a large table filled with globes and spheres, and mathematical instruments of all kinds. His Majesty took not the least notice of us, although our entrance was not without sufficient noise, by the concourse of all persons belonging to the court. But he was then deep in a problem, and we attended at least an hour, before he could solve it. There stood by him on each side a young page, with flaps in their hands, and when they saw he was at leisure, one of them gently struck his mouth, and the other his right ear; at which he started like one awaked on the sudden, and looking towards me and the company I was in, recollected the occasion of our coming, whereof he had been informed before. He spoke some words, whereupon immediately a young man with a flap came up to my side, and flapped me gently on the right ear; but I made signs, as well as I could, that I had no occasion for such an instrument; which, as I afterwards found, gave his Majesty and the whole court a very mean opinion of my understanding. The King, as far as I could conjecture, asked me several questions, and I addressed myself to him in all the languages I had. When it was found that I could neither understand nor be understood, I was conducted by the King's order to an apartment in his palace (this prince being distinguished above all his predecessors for his hospitality to strangers), where two servants were appointed to attend me. My dinner was brought, and four persons of quality, whom I remembered to have seen very near the King's person, did me the honor to dine with me. We had two courses of three dishes each. In the first course there was a shoulder of mutton, cut into an equilateral triangle, a piece of beef into a rhomboides, and a pudding into a cycloid. The second course was two ducks, trussed up into the form of fiddles; sausages and puddings resembling flutes and hautboys, and a breast of veal in the shape of a harp. The servants cut our bread into cones, cylinders, parallelograms, and several other mathematical figures.

While we were at dinner, I made bold to ask the names of several things in their language; and those noble persons, by the assistance of their flappers, delighted to give me answers, hoping to raise my admiration of their great abilities, if I could be brought to converse with them. I was soon able to call for bread and drink, or whatever else I wanted.

After dinner my company withdrew, and a person was sent to me by the King's order, attended by a flapper. He brought with him pen, ink, and paper, and three or four books, giving me to understand by signs, that he was sent to teach me the language. We sat together four hours, in which time I wrote down a great number of words in columns, with the translations over against them. I likewise made a shift to learn several short sentences. For my tutor would order one of my servants to fetch something, to turn about, to make a bow, to sit, or stand, or walk, and the like. Then I took down the sentence in writing. He showed me also in one of his books the figures of the sun, moon, and stars, the zodiac, the tropics, and polar circles, together with the denominations of many figures of planes and solids. He gave me the names and descriptions of all the musical instruments, and the general terms of art in playing on each of them. After he had left me, I placed all my words with their interpretations in alphabetical order. And thus in a few days, by the help of a very faithful memory, I got some insight into their language.

The word, which I interpret the *Flying* or *Floating Island*, is in the original *Laputa*, whereof I could never learn the true etymology. *Lap* in the old obsolete language signifieth *high*, and *untuh*, a *governor*, from which they say my corruption was derived *Laputa*, from *Lapuntuh*. But I do not approve of this derivation, which seems to be a little strained. I ventured to offer to the learned among them a conjecture of my own, that *Laputa* was *quasi lap outed; lap* signifying properly the dancing of the sunbeams in the sea, and *outed*, a wing, which however I shall not obtrude, but submit to the judicious reader.[1]

Those to whom the King had entrusted me, observing how ill I was clad, ordered a tailor to come next morning, and take my measure for a suit of clothes. This operator did his office after a different manner from those of his trade in Europe. He first took my altitude by a quadrant, and then with a rule and compasses described the dimensions and outlines of my whole body, all which he entered upon paper, and in six days brought my clothes very ill made, and quite out of shape, by happening to mistake a figure in the calculation. But my comfort was, that I observed such accidents very frequent, and little regarded.

During my confinement for want of clothes, and by an indisposition that held me some days longer, I much enlarged my dictionary; and when I went next to court, was able to understand many things the King spoke, and to return him some kind of answers. His Majesty had given orders that the island should move north-east and by east, to the vertical point over Lagado, the metropolis of the whole kingdom below upon the firm earth. It was about ninety leagues distant, and our voyage lasted

[1] Throughout the paragraph Swift is having fun at the expense of the philologists.

four days and an half. I was not in the least sensible of the progressive motion made in the air by the island. On the second morning about eleven o'clock, the King himself in person, attended by his nobility, courtiers, and officers, having prepared all their musical instruments, played on them for three hours without intermission, so that I was quite stunned with the noise; neither could I possibly guess the meaning, till my tutor informed me. He said that the people of their island had their ears adapted to hear the music of the spheres, which always played at certain periods, and the court was now prepared to bear their part in whatever instrument they most excelled.

In our journey towards Lagado, the capital city, his Majesty ordered that the island should stop over certain towns and villages, from whence he might receive the petitions of his subjects. And to this purpose several packthreads were let down with small weights at the bottom. On these packthreads the people strung their petitions, which mounted up directly like the scraps of paper fastened by school-boys at the end of the string that holds their kite. Sometimes we received wine and victuals from below, which were drawn up by pulleys.

The knowledge I had in mathematics gave me great assistance in acquiring their phraseology, which depended much upon that science and music; and in the latter I was not unskilled. Their ideas are perpetually conversant in lines and figures. If they would, for example, praise the beauty of a woman, or any other animal, they describe it by rhombs, circles, parallelograms, ellipses, and other geometrical terms, or by words of art drawn from music, needless here to repeat. I observed in the King's kitchen all sorts of mathematical and musical instruments, after the figures of which they cut up the joints that were served to his Majesty's table.

Their houses are very ill built, the walls bevil, without one right angle in any apartment, and this defect ariseth from the contempt they bear to practical geometry, which they despise as vulgar and mechanic, those instructions they give being too refined for the intellectuals of their workmen, which occasions perpetual mistakes. And although they are dexterous enough upon a piece of paper in the management of the rule, the pencil, and the divider, yet in the common actions and behavior of life, I have not seen a more clumsy, awkward, and unhandy people, nor so slow and perplexed in their conceptions upon all other subjects, except those of mathematics and music. They are very bad reasoners, and vehemently given to opposition, unless when they happen to be of the right opinion, which is seldom their case. Imagination, fancy, and invention, they are wholly strangers to, nor have any words in their language by which those ideas can be expressed; the whole compass of their thoughts and mind being shut up within the two forementioned sciences.

Most of them, and especially those who deal in the astronomical part, have great faith in judicial astrology, although they are ashamed to own it publicly. But what I chiefly admired, and thought altogether unaccountable, was the strong disposition I observed in them towards news and politics, perpetually enquiring into public affairs, giving their judgments in matters of state, and passionately disputing every inch of a party opinion. I have indeed observed the same disposition among most of the mathematicians I have known in Europe, although I could never discover the least analogy between the two sciences; unless those people suppose, that because the smallest circle hath as many degrees as the largest, therefore the regulation and management of the world require no more abilities than the handling and turning of a globe. But I rather take this quality to spring from a very common infirmity of human nature, inclining us to be more curious [1] and conceited in matters where we have least concern, and for which we are least adapted either by study or nature.

These people are under continual disquietudes, never enjoying a minute's peace of mind; and their disturbances proceed from causes which very little affect the rest of mortals. Their apprehensions arise from several changes they dread in the celestial bodies. For instance, that the earth, by the continual approaches of the sun towards it, must in course of time be absorbed or swallowed up. That the face of the sun will by degrees be encrusted with its own effluvia, and give no more light to the world. That the earth very narrowly escaped a brush from the tail of the last comet, which would have infallibly reduced it to ashes; and that the next, which they have calculated for one and thirty years hence, will probably destroy us. For if in its perihelion it should approach within a certain degree of the sun (as by their calculations they have reason to dread) it will conceive a degree of heat ten thousand times more intense than that of red-hot glowing iron; and in its absence from the sun, carry a blazing tail ten hundred thousand and fourteen miles long; through which if the earth should pass at the distance of one hundred thousand miles from the nucleus or main body of the comet, it must in its passage be set on fire, and reduced to ashes. That the sun daily spending its rays without any nutriment to supply them, will

[1] careful.

at last be wholly consumed and annihilated; which must be attended with the destruction of this earth, and of all the planets that receive their light from it.

They are so perpetually alarmed with the apprehensions of these and the like impending dangers, that they can neither sleep quietly in their beds, nor have any relish for the common pleasures or amusements of life. When they meet an acquaintance in the morning, the first question is about the sun's health, how he looked at his setting and rising, and what hopes they have to avoid the stroke of the approaching comet. This conversation they are apt to run into with the same temper that boys discover, in delighting to hear terrible stories of sprites and hobgoblins, which they greedily listen to, and dare not go to bed for fear.

The women of the island have abundance of vivacity: they contemn their husbands, and are exceedingly fond of strangers, whereof there is always a considerable number from the continent below, attending at court, either upon affairs of the several towns and corporations, or their own particular occasions, but are much despised, because they want the same endowments. Among these the ladies choose their gallants: but the vexation is, that they act with too much ease and security, for the husband is always so rapt in speculation, that the mistress and lover may proceed to the greatest familiarities before his face, if he be but provided with paper and implements, and without his flapper at his side.

The wives and daughters lament their confinement to the island, although I think it the most delicious spot of ground in the world; and although they live here in the greatest plenty and magnificence, and are allowed to do whatever they please, they long to see the world, and take the diversions of the metropolis, which they are not allowed to do without a particular licence from the King; and this is not easy to be obtained, because the people of quality have found by frequent experience how hard it is to persuade their women to return from below. I was told that a great court lady,[1] who had several children, is married to the prime minister, the richest subject in the kingdom, a very graceful person, extremely fond of her, and lives in the finest palace of the island, went down to Lagado, on the pretence of health, there hid herself for several months, till the King sent a warrant to search for her, and she was found in an obscure eating-house all in rags, having pawned her clothes to maintain an old deformed footman, who beat

[1] The allusion is to a contemporary scandal in England; as here introduced Swift uses the reference to attack Walpole.

her every day, and in whose company she was taken much against her will. And although her husband received her with all possible kindness, and without the least reproach, she soon after contrived to steal down again with all her jewels, to the same gallant, and hath not been heard of since.

This may perhaps pass with the reader rather for an European or English story, than for one of a country so remote. But he may please to consider, that the caprices of womankind are not limited by any climate or nation, and that they are much more uniform than can be easily imagined.

In about a month's time I had made a tolerable proficiency in their language, and was able to answer most of the King's questions, when I had the honor to attend him. His Majesty discovered not the least curiosity to enquire into the laws, government, history, religion, or manners of the countries where I had been, but confined his questions to the state of mathematics, and received the account I gave him with great contempt and indifference, though often roused by his flapper on each side.

The Author leaves Laputa; is conveyed to Balnibarbi, arrives at the metropolis. A description of the metropolis, and the country adjoining. The Author hospitably received by a great Lord. His conversation with that Lord.

Although I cannot say that I was ill treated in this island, yet I must confess I thought myself too much neglected, not without some degree of contempt. For neither prince nor people appeared to be curious in any part of knowledge, except mathematics and music, wherein I was far their inferior, and upon that account very little regarded.

On the other side, after having seen all the curiosities of the island, I was very desirous to leave it, being heartily weary of those people. They were indeed excellent in two sciences for which I have great esteem, and wherein I am not unversed; but at the same time so abtracted and involved in speculation, that I never met with such disagreeable companions. I conversed only with women, tradesmen, flappers, and court-pages, during two months of my abode there, by which at last I rendered myself extremely contemptible; yet these were the only people from whom I could ever receive a reasonable answer.

I had obtained by hard study a good degree of knowledge in their language; I was weary of being confined to an island where I received so little countenance, and resolved to leave it with the first opportunity.

There was a great lord at court, nearly related to the King, and for that reason alone used with respect. He was universally reckoned the most ignorant and stupid person among them. He had performed many eminent services for the crown, had great natural and acquired parts, adorned with integrity and honor, but so ill an ear for music, that his detractors reported he had been often known to beat time in the wrong place; neither could his tutors without extreme difficulty teach him to demonstrate the most easy proposition in the mathematics. He was pleased to show me many marks of favor, often did me the honor of a visit, desired to be informed in the affairs of Europe, the laws and customs, the manners and learning of the several countries where I had travelled. He listened to me with great attention, and made very wise observations on all I spoke. He had two flappers attending him for state, but never made use of them except at court, and in visits of ceremony, and would always command them to withdraw when we were alone together.

I entreated this illustrious person to intercede in my behalf with his Majesty for leave to depart, which he accordingly did, as he was pleased to tell me, with regret: for indeed he had made me several offers very advantageous, which however I refused with expressions of the highest acknowledgment.

On the 16th day of February I took leave of his Majesty and the court. The King made me a present to the value of about two hundred pounds English, and my protector his kinsman as much more, together with a letter of recommendation to a friend of his in Lagado, the metropolis. The island being then hovering over a mountain about two miles from it, I was let down from the lowest gallery, in the same manner as I had been taken up.

The continent, as far as it is subject to the monarch of the Flying Island, passes under the general name of *Balnibarbi*, and the metropolis, as I said before, is called *Lagado*. I felt some little satisfaction in finding myself on firm ground. I walked to the city without any concern, being clad like one of the natives, and sufficiently instructed to converse with them. I soon found out the person's house to whom I was recommended, presented my letter from his friend the grandee in the island, and was received with much kindness. This great lord, whose name was Munodi, ordered me an apartment in his own house, where I continued during my stay, and was entertained in a most hospitable manner.

The next morning after my arrival, he took me in his chariot to see the town, which is about half the bigness of London, but the houses very strangely built, and most of them out of repair. The people in the streets walked fast, looked wild, their eyes fixed, and were generally in rags. We passed through one of the town gates, and went about three miles into the country, where I saw many laborers working with several sorts of tools in the ground, but was not able to conjecture what they were about; neither did I observe any expectation either of corn or grass, although the soil appeared to be excellent. I could not forbear admiring at these odd appearances both in town and country, and I made bold to desire my conductor, that he would be pleased to explain to me what could be meant by so many busy heads, hands, and faces, both in the streets and the fields, because I did not discover any good effects they produced; but on the contrary, I never knew a soil so unhappily cultivated, houses so ill contrived and so ruinous, or a people whose countenances and habit expressed so much misery and want.[1]

This Lord Munodi was a person of the first rank, and had been some years Governor of Lagado, but by a cabal of ministers was discharged for insufficiency. However, the King treated him with tenderness, as a well-meaning man, but of a low contemptible understanding.

When I gave that free censure of the country and its inhabitants, he made no further answer than by telling me that I had not been long enough among them to form a judgment, and that the different nations of the world had different customs, with other common topics to the same purpose. But when we returned to his palace, he asked me how I liked the building, what absurdities I observed, and what quarrel I had with the dress or looks of his domestics. This he might safely do, because every thing about him was magnificent, regular, and polite. I answered that his Excellency's prudence, quality, and fortune, had exempted him from those defects which folly and beggary had produced in others. He said if I would go with him to his country-house, about twenty miles distant, where his estate lay, there would be more leisure for this kind of conversation. I told his Excellency that I was entirely at his disposal, and accordingly we set out next morning.

During our journey he made me observe the several methods used by farmers in managing their lands, which to me were wholly unaccountable; for except in some very few places I could not discover one ear of corn or blade of grass. But in three hours travelling the scene was wholly altered; we

came into a most beautiful country; farmers' houses at small distances, neatly built; the fields enclosed, containing vineyards, corn-grounds, and meadows. Neither do I remember to have seen a more delightful prospect. His Excellency observed my countenance to clear up; he told me with a sigh that there his estate began, and would continue the same till we should come to his house. That his countrymen ridiculed and despised him for managing his affairs no better, and for setting so ill an example to the kingdom, which however was followed by very few, such as were old, and wilful, and weak like himself.

We came at length to the house, which was indeed a noble structure, built according to the best rules of ancient architecture. The fountains, gardens, walks, avenues, and groves were all disposed with exact judgment and taste. I gave due praises to every thing I saw, whereof his Excellency took not the least notice till after supper, when, there being no third companion, he told me with a very melancholy air that he doubted he must throw down his houses in town and country, to rebuild them after the present mode, destroy all his plantations, and cast others into such a form as modern usage required, and give the same directions to all his tenants, unless he would submit to incur the censure of pride, singularity, affectation, ignorance, caprice, and perhaps increase his Majesty's displeasure.

That the admiration I appeared to be under would cease or diminish when he had informed me of some particulars, which probably I never heard of at court, the people there being too much taken up in their own speculations, to have regard to what passed here below.

The sum of his discourse was to this effect. That about forty years ago certain persons went up to Laputa, either upon business or diversion, and after five months continuance came back with a very little smattering in mathematics, but full of volatile spirits acquired in that airy region. That these persons upon their return began to dislike the management of every thing below, and fell into schemes of putting all arts, sciences, languages, and mechanics upon a new foot. To this end they procured a royal patent for erecting an Academy of Projectors in Lagado;[1] and the humor prevailed so strongly among the people, that there is not a town of any consequence in the kingdom without such an academy. In these colleges the professors contrive new rules and methods of agriculture and building, and new instruments and tools for all trades and manufactures, whereby, as they undertake, one man shall do the work of ten; a palace

[1] Swift's purpose in this paragraph is to condemn the contemporary English enthusiasm for "projects" which threatened, he thought, to leave the necessary work undone in an impractical following of science.

[1] The Royal Society of London.

may be built in a week, of materials so durable as to last for ever without repairing. All the fruits of the earth shall come to maturity at whatever season we think fit to choose, and increase an hundred fold more than they do at present, with innumerable other happy proposals. The only inconvenience is, that none of these projects are yet brought to perfection, and in the mean time, the whole country lies miserably waste, the houses in ruins, and the people without food or clothes. By all which, instead of being discouraged, they are fifty times more violently bent upon prosecuting their schemes, driven equally on by hope and despair; that as for himself, being not of an enterprising spirit, he was content to go on in the old forms, to live in the houses his ancestors had built, and act as they did in every part of life without innovation. That some few other persons of quality and gentry had done the same, but were looked on with an eye of contempt and ill-will, as enemies to art, ignorant, and ill commonwealth's-men, preferring their own ease and sloth before the general improvement of their country.

His Lordship added that he would not by any further particulars prevent the pleasure I should certainly take in viewing the grand Academy, whither he was resolved I should go. He only desired me to observe a ruined building upon the side of a mountain about three miles distant, of which he gave me this account. That he had a very convenient mill within half a mile of his house, turned by a current from a large river, and sufficient for his own family as well as a great number of his tenants. That about seven years ago a club of those projectors came to him with proposals to destroy this mill, and build another on the side of that mountain, on the long ridge whereof a long canal must be cut for a repository of water, to be conveyed up by pipes and engines to supply the mill; because the wind and air upon a height agitated the water, and thereby made it fitter for motion; and because the water descending down a declivity would turn the mill with half the current of a river whose course is more upon a level. He said, that being then not very well with the court, and pressed by many of his friends, he complied with the proposal; and after employing an hundred men for two years, the work miscarried, the projectors went off, laying the blame entirely upon him, railing at him ever since, and putting others upon the same experiment, with equal assurance of success, as well as equal disappointment.

In a few days we came back to town, and his Excellency, considering the bad character he had in the Academy, would not go with me himself, but recommended me to a friend of his to bear me company thither. My lord was pleased to represent me as a great admirer of projects, and a person of much curiosity and easy belief; which indeed was not without truth, for I had myself been a sort of projector in my younger days.

The Author permitted to see the Grand Academy of Lagado. The Academy largely described. The Arts wherein the professors employ themselves.

This Academy is not an entire single building, but a continuation of several houses on both sides of a street, which growing waste was purchased and applied to that use.

I was received very kindly by the Warden, and went for many days to the Academy. Every room hath in it one or more projectors, and I believe I could not be in fewer than five hundred rooms.

The first man I saw was of a meagre aspect, with sooty hands and face, his hair and beard long, ragged and singed in several places. His clothes, shirt, and skin were all of the same color. He had been eight years upon a project for extracting sun-beams out of cucumbers, which were to be put into vials hermetically sealed, and let out to warm the air in raw inclement summers. He told me he did not doubt in eight years more he should be able to supply the Governor's gardens with sunshine at a reasonable rate; but he complained that his stock was low, and entreated me to give him something as an encouragement to ingenuity, especially since this had been a very dear season for cucumbers. I made him a small present, for my lord had furnished me with money on purpose, because he knew their practice of begging from all who go to see them.

I went into another chamber, but was ready to hasten back, being almost overcome with a horrible stink. My conductor pressed me forward, conjuring me in a whisper to give no offence, which would be highly resented, and therefore I durst not so much as stop my nose. The projector of this cell was the most ancient student of the Academy; his face and beard were of a pale yellow; his hands and clothes daubed over with filth. When I was presented to him, he gave me a close embrace (a compliment I could well have excused). His employment from his first coming into the Academy, was an operation to reduce human excrement to its original food, by separating the several parts, removing the tincture which it receives from the gall, making the odor exhale, and scumming off the saliva. He had a weekly allowance from the society, of a vessel filled with human ordure, about the bigness of a Bristol barrel.

I saw another at work to calcine ice into gunpowder, who likewise showed me a treatise he had written concerning the malleability of fire, which he intended to publish.

There was a most ingenious architect who had contrived a new method for building houses, by beginning at the roof, and working downwards to the foundation, which he justified to me by the like practice of those two prudent insects, the bee and the spider.

There was a man born blind, who had several apprentices in his own condition: their employment was to mix colors for painters, which their master taught them to distinguish by feeling and smelling. It was indeed my misfortune to find them at the time not very perfect in their lessons, and the professor himself happened to be generally mistaken: this artist is much encouraged and esteemed by the whole fraternity.

In another apartment I was highly pleased with a projector, who had found a device of ploughing the ground with hogs, to save the charges of ploughs, cattle, and labor. The method is this: in an acre of ground you bury, at six inches distance and eight deep, a quantity of acorns, dates, chestnuts, and other mast or vegetables whereof these animals are fondest; then you drive six hundred or more of them into the field, where in a few days they will root up the whole ground in search of their food, and make it fit for sowing, at the same time manuring it with their dung. It is true, upon experiment they found the charge and trouble very great, and they had little or no crop. However, it is not doubted that this invention may be capable of great improvement.

I went into another room, where the walls and ceiling were all hung round with cobwebs, except a narrow passage for the artist to go in and out. At my entrance he called aloud to me not to disturb his webs. He lamented the fatal mistake the world had been so long in of using silk-worms, while we had such plenty of domestic insects, who infinitely excelled the former, because they understood how to weave as well as spin. And he proposed farther that by employing spiders the charge of dyeing silks should be wholly saved, whereof I was fully convinced when he showed me a vast number of flies most beautifully colored, wherewith he fed his spiders, assuring us that the webs would take a tincture from them; and as he had them of all hues, he hoped to fit everybody's fancy, as soon as he could find proper food for the flies, of certain gums, oils, and other glutinous matter to give a strength and consistence to the threads.

There was an astronomer who had undertaken to place a sun-dial upon the great weathercock on the town-house, by adjusting the annual and diurnal motions of the earth and sun, so as to answer and coincide with all accidental turnings by the wind.

I was complaining of a small fit of the colic, upon which my conductor led me into a room, where a great physician resided, who was famous for curing that disease by contrary operations from the same instrument. He had a large pair of bellows with a long slender muzzle of ivory. This he conveyed eight inches up the anus, and drawing in the wind, he affirmed he could make the guts as lank as a dried bladder. But when the disease was more stubborn and violent, he let in the muzzle while the bellows were full of wind, which he discharged into the body of the patient, then withdrew the instrument to replenish it, clapping his thumb strongly against the orifice of the fundament; and this being repeated three or four times, the adventitious wind would rush out, bringing the noxious along with (it like water put into a pump), and the patient recover. I saw him try both experiments upon a dog, but could not discern any effect from the former. After the latter, the animal was ready to burst, and made so violent a discharge, as was very offensive to me and my companions. The dog died on the spot, and we left the doctor endeavoring to recover him by the same operation.

I visited many other apartments, but shall not trouble my reader with all the curiosities I observed, being studious of brevity.

I had hitherto seen only one side of the Academy, the other being appropriated to the advancers of speculative learning, of whom I shall say something when I have mentioned one illustrious person more, who is called among them *the universal artist*. He told us he had been thirty years employing his thoughts for the improvement of human life. He had two large rooms full of wonderful curiosities, and fifty men at work. Some were condensing air into a dry tangible substance, by extracting the nitre, and letting the aqueous or fluid particles percolate; others softening marble for pillows and pin-cushions; others petrifying the hoofs of a living horse to preserve them from foundering. The artist himself was at that time busy upon two great designs; the first, to sow land with chaff, wherein he affirmed the true seminal virtue to be contained, as he demonstrated by several experiments which I was not skilful enough to comprehend. The other was, by a certain composition of gums, minerals, and vegetables outwardly applied, to prevent the growth of wool upon two young lambs; and he hoped in a reasonable time to propagate the breed of naked sheep all over the kingdom.

We crossed a walk to the other part of the Academy, where, as I have already said, the projectors in speculative learning resided.

The first professor I saw was in a very large room, with forty pupils about him. After salutation, observing me to look earnestly upon a frame, which took up the greatest part of both the length and breadth of the room, he said perhaps I might wonder to see him employed in a project for improving speculative knowledge by practical and mechanical operations. But the world would soon be sensible of its usefulness, and he flattered himself that a more noble exalted thought never sprang in any other man's head. Every one knew how laborious the usual method is of attaining to arts and sciences; whereas by his contrivance the most ignorant person at a reasonable charge, and with a little bodily labor, may write books in philosophy, poetry, politics, law, mathematics, and theology, without the least assistance from genius or study. He then led me to the frame, about the sides whereof all his pupils stood in ranks. It was twenty foot square, placed in the middle of the room. The superficies was composed of several bits of wood, about the bigness of a die, but some larger than others. They were all linked together by slender wires. These bits of wood were covered on every square with paper pasted on them, and on these papers were written all the words of their language, in their several moods, tenses, and declensions, but without any order. The professor then desired me to observe, for he was going to set his engine at work. The pupils at his command took each of them hold of an iron handle, whereof there were forty fixed round the edges of the frame, and giving them a sudden turn, the whole disposition of the words was entirely changed. He then commanded six and thirty of the lads to read the several lines softly as they appeared upon the frame; and where they found three or four words together that might make part of a sentence, they dictated to the four remaining boys who were scribes. This work was repeated three or four times, and at every turn the engine was so contrived that the words shifted into new places, as the square bits of wood moved upside down.

Six hours a day the young students were employed in this labor, and the professor showed me several volumes in large folio already collected, of broken sentences, which he intended to piece together, and out of those rich materials to give the world a complete body of all arts and sciences; which however might be still improved, and much expedited, if the public would raise a fund for making and employing five hundred such frames in Lagado, and oblige the managers to contribute in common their several collections.

He assured me, that this invention had employed all his thoughts from his youth, that he had emptied the whole vocabulary into his frame, and made the strictest computation of the general proportion there is in books between the numbers of particles, nouns, and verbs, and other parts of speech.

I made my humblest acknowledgment to this illustrious person for his great communicativeness, and promised if ever I had the good fortune to return to my native country, that I would do him justice, as the sole inventor of this wonderful machine; the form and contrivance of which I desired leave to delineate upon paper, as in the figure here annexed. I told him, although it were the custom of our learned in Europe to steal inventions from each other, who had thereby at least this advantage, that it became a controversy which was the right owner, yet I would take such caution, that he should have the honor entire without a rival.

We next went to the school of languages, where three professors sat in consultation upon improving that of their own country.

The first project was to shorten discourse by cutting polysyllables into one, and leaving out verbs and participles, because in reality all things imaginable are but nouns.

The other project was a scheme for entirely abolishing all words whatsoever; and this was urged as a great advantage in point of health as well as brevity. For it is plain that every word we speak is in some degree a diminution of our lungs by corrosion, and consequently contributes to the shortening of our lives. An expedient was therefore offered, that since words are only names for *things*, it would be more convenient for all men to carry about them such things as were necessary to express the particular business they are to discourse on. And this invention would certainly have taken place, to the great ease as well as health of the subject, if the women, in conjunction with the vulgar and illiterate, had not threatened to raise a rebellion, unless they might be allowed the liberty to speak with their tongues, after the manner of their ancestors; such constant irreconcilable enemies to science are the common people. However, many of the most learned and wise adhere to the new scheme of expressing themselves by things, which hath only this inconvenience attending it, that if a man's business be very great, and of various kinds, he must be obliged in proportion to carry a greater bundle of things upon his back, unless he can afford one or two strong servants to attend him. I have often beheld two of these sages almost sinking under the weight of their packs, like pedlars among us; who, when they met in the streets, would lay down their loads, open their sacks, and hold conversation for an hour together; then put up their implements, help each other to resume their burthens, and take their leave.

But for short conversations a man may carry implements in his pockets and under his arms, enough to supply him, and in his house he cannot be at a loss. Therefore the room where company meet who practise this art, is full of all things ready at hand, requisite to furnish matter for this kind of artificial converse.

Another great advantage proposed by this invention was that it would serve as an universal language to be understood in all civilised nations, whose goods and utensils are generally of the same kind, or nearly resembling, so that their uses might easily be comprehended. And thus ambassadors would be qualified to treat with foreign princes or ministers of state, to whose tongues they were utter strangers.

I was at the mathematical school, where the master taught his pupils after a method scarce imaginable to us in Europe. The proposition and demonstration were fairly written on a thin wafer, with ink composed of a cephalic tincture. This the student was to swallow upon a fasting stomach, and for three days following eat nothing but bread and water. As the water digested, the tincture mounted to his brain, bearing the proposition along with it. But the success hath not hitherto been answerable, partly by some error in the *quantum* or composition, and partly by the perverseness of lads, to whom this bolus is so nauseous, that they generally steal aside, and discharge it upwards before it can operate; neither have they been yet persuaded to use so long an abstinence as the prescription requires.

A further account of the Academy. The Author proposes some improvements, which are honorably received.

In the school of political projectors I was but ill entertained, the professors appearing in my judgment wholly out of their senses, which is a scene that never fails to make me melancholy. These unhappy people were proposing schemes for persuading monarchs to choose favorites upon the score of their wisdom, capacity, and virtue; of teaching ministers to consult the public good; of rewarding merit, great abilities, eminent services; of instructing princes to know their true interest by placing it on the same foundation with that of their people; of choosing for employments persons qualified to exercise them; with many other wild impossible chimæras, that never entered before into the heart of man to conceive, and confirmed in me the old observation, that there is nothing so extravagant and irrational which some philosophers have not maintained for truth.

But however I shall so far do justice to this part of the Academy, as to acknowledge that all of them were not so visionary. There was a most ingenious doctor who seemed to be perfectly versed in the whole nature and system of government. This illustrious person had very usefully employed his studies in finding out effectual remedies for all diseases and corruptions, to which the several kinds of public administration are subject by the vices or infirmities of those who govern, as well as by the licentiousness of those who are to obey. For instance, whereas all writers and reasoners have agreed, that there is a strict universal resemblance between the natural and the political body; can there be any thing more evident, than that the health of both must be preserved, and the diseases cured by the same prescriptions? It is allowed that senates and great councils are often troubled with redundant, ebullient, and other peccant humors, with many diseases of the head, and more of the heart; with strong convulsions, with grievous contractions of the nerves and sinews in both hands, but especially the right; with spleen, flatus, vertigos, and deliriums; with scrofulous tumors full of foetid virulent matter, with sour frothy ructations, with canine appetites and crudeness of digestion, besides many others needless to mention. This doctor therefore proposed, that upon the meeting of a senate, certain physicians should attend at the three first days of their sitting, and at the close of each day's debate, feel the pulses of every senator; after which, having maturely considered, and consulted upon the nature of the several maladies, and the methods of cure, they should on the fourth day return to the senate house, attended by their apothecaries stored with proper medicines; and before the members sat, administer to each of them lenitives, aperitives, abstersives, corrosives, restringents, palliatives, laxatives, cephalalgics, icterics, apophlegmatics, acoustics, as their several cases required; and according as these medicines should operate, repeat, alter, or omit them at the next meeting.

This project could not be of any great expense to the public, and would, in my poor opinion, be of much use for the dispatch of business in those countries where senates have any share in the legislative power; beget unanimity, shorten debates, open a few mouths which are now closed, and close many more which are now open; curb the petulancy of the young, and correct the positiveness of the old; rouse the stupid, and damp the pert.

Again, because it is a general complaint, that the favorites of princes are troubled with short and weak memories, the same doctor proposed, that whoever attended a first minister, after having told his business with the utmost brevity and in the plainest words, should at his departure give the said minister a tweak by the nose, or a kick in the belly, or tread on his corns, or lug him thrice by both ears, or run a pin into his breech, or pinch his arm black and blue, to prevent forgetfulness; and at every levee day repeat the same operation, till the business were done or absolutely refused.

He likewise directed, that every senator in the great council of a nation, after he had delivered his opinion, and argued in the defence of it, should be obliged to give his vote directly contrary; because if that were done, the result would infallibly terminate in the good of the public.

When parties in a state are violent, he offered a wonderful contrivance to reconcile them. The method is this. You take a hundred leaders of each party, you dispose them into couples of such whose heads are nearest of a size; then let two nice operators saw off the occiput of each couple at the same time, in such a manner that the brain may be equally divided. Let the occiputs thus cut off be interchanged, applying each to the head of his opposite party-man. It seems indeed to be a work that requireth some exactness, but the professor assured us that if it were dexterously performed the cure would be infallible. For he argued thus; that the two half brains being left to debate the matter between themselves within the space of one skull, would soon come to a good understanding, and produce that moderation, as well as regularity of thinking, so much to be wished for in the heads of those who imagine they come into the world only to watch and govern its motion: and as to the difference of brains in quantity or quality among those who are directors in faction, the doctor assured us from his own knowledge that it was a perfect trifle.

I heard a very warm debate between two professors, about the most commodious and effectual ways and means of raising money without grieving the subject. The first affirmed the justest method would be to lay a certain tax upon vices and folly, and the sum fixed upon every man to be rated after the fairest manner by a jury of his neighbors. The second was of an opinion directly contrary, to tax those qualities of body and mind for which men chiefly value themselves, the rate to be more or less according to the degrees of excelling, the decision whereof should be left entirely to their own breast. The highest tax was upon men who are the greatest favorites of the other sex, and the assessments according to the number and natures of the favors they have received; for which they are allowed to be their own vouchers. Wit, valor, and politeness were likewise proposed to be largely taxed, and collected in the same manner, by every person's giving his own word for the quantum of what he possessed. But as to honor, justice, wisdom, and learning, they should not be taxed at all, because they are qualifications of so singular a kind, that no man will either allow them in his neighbor, or value them in himself.

The women were proposed to be taxed according to their beauty and skill in dressing, wherein they had the same privilege with the men, to be determined by their own judgment. But constancy, chastity, good sense, and good nature were not rated, because they would not bear the charge of collecting.

To keep senators in the interest of the crown, it was proposed that the members should raffle for employments, every man first taking an oath, and giving security that he would vote for the court, whether he won or no; after which the losers had in their turn the liberty of raffling upon the next vacancy. Thus hope and expectation would be kept alive, none would complain of broken promises, but impute their disappointments wholly to fortune, whose shoulders are broader and stronger than those of a ministry.

Another professor showed me a large paper of instructions for discovering plots and conspiracies against the government. He advised great statesmen to examine into the diet of all suspected persons; their times of eating; upon which side they lay in bed; with which hand they wiped their posteriors; to take a strict view of their excrements, and, from the color, the odor, the taste, the consistence, the crudeness or maturity of digestion, form a judgment of their thoughts and designs. Because men are never so serious, thoughtful, and intent, as when they are at stool, which he found by frequent experiment; for in such conjunctures, when he used merely as a trial to consider which was the best way of murdering the king, his ordure would have a tincture of green, but quite different when he thought only of raising an insurrection or burning the metropolis.

The whole discourse was written with great acuteness, containing many observations both curious and useful for politicians, but as I conceived not altogether complete. This I ventured to tell the author, and offered if he pleased to supply him with some additions. He received my proposition with more compliance than is usual among writers, especially those of the projecting species, professing he would be glad to receive farther information.

I told him that in the kingdom of Tribnia,[1] by the natives called Langden,[1] where I had sojourned some time in my travels, the bulk of the people consist in a manner wholly of discoverers, witnesses, informers, accusers, prosecutors, evidences, swearers, together with their several subservient and subaltern instruments, all under the colors and conduct of ministers of state and their deputies. The plots in that kingdom are usually the workmanship of those persons who desire to raise their own characters of profound politicians, to restore new vigor to a crazy administration, to stifle or divert general discontents, to fill their pockets with forfeitures, and raise or sink the opinion of public credit, as either shall best answer their private advantage. It is first agreed and settled among them, what suspected persons shall be accused of a plot; then, effectual care is taken to secure all their letters and papers, and put the criminals in chains. These papers are delivered to a set of artists, very dexterous in finding out the mysterious meanings of words, syllables, and letters. For instance, they can discover a close-stool to signify a privy council; a flock of geese, a senate; a lame dog, an invader; a codshead, a ———;[2] the plague, a standing army; a buzzard, a prime minister; the gout, a high priest; a gibbet, a secretary of state; a chamber-pot, a committee of grandees; a sieve, a court lady; a broom, a revolution; a mouse-trap, an employment; a bottomless pit, the treasury; a sink, the court; a cap and bells, a favorite; a broken reed, a court of justice; an empty tun, a general; a running sore, the administration.

When this method fails, they have two others more effectual, which the learned among them call acrostics and anagrams. First they can decipher all initial letters into political meanings. Thus, *N.* shall signify a plot; *B.* a regiment of horse; *L.* a fleet at sea; or secondly by transposing the letters of the alphabet in any suspected paper, they can discover the deepest designs of a discontented party. So for example if I should say in a letter to a friend, *Our brother* Tom *has just got the piles*, a skilful decipherer would discover that the same letters which compose that sentence may be analysed into the following words: *Resist, a plot is brought home; The tour.* And this is the anagrammatic method.

[1] A rearrangement of the letters gives us "Britain" and "England."
[2] Probably "king" has been omitted.

The professor made me great acknowledgments for communicating these observations, and promised to make honorable mention of me in his treatise.

I saw nothing in this country that could invite me to a longer continuance, and began to think of returning home to England.

The Author leaves Lagado, arrives at Maldonada. No ship ready. He takes a short voyage to Glubbdubdrib. His reception by the Governor.

The continent of which this kingdom is a part extends itself, as I have reason to believe, eastward to that unknown tract of America, westward of California, and north of the Pacific Ocean, which is not above a hundred and fifty miles from Lagado, where there is a good port and much commerce with the great island of Luggnagg, situated to the north-west about 29 degrees north latitude, and 140 longitude. This island of Luggnagg stands south-eastwards of Japan, about an hundred leagues distant. There is a strict alliance between the Japanese Emperor and the King of Luggnagg, which affords frequent opportunities of sailing from one island to the other. I determined therefore to direct my course this way, in order to my return to Europe. I hired two mules with a guide to show me the way, and carry my small baggage. I took leave of my noble protector, who had shown me so much favor and made me a generous present at my departure.

My journey was without any accident or adventure worth relating. When I arrived at the port of Maldonada (for so it is called) there was no ship in the harbor bound for Luggnagg, nor likely to be in some time. The town is about as large as Portsmouth. I soon fell into some acquaintance, and was very hospitably received. A gentleman of distinction said to me that since the ships bound for Luggnagg could not be ready in less than a month, it might be no disagreeable amusement for me to take a trip to the little island of Glubbdubdrib, about five leagues off to the south-west. He offered himself and a friend to accompany me, and that I should be provided with a small convenient barque for the voyage.

Glubbdubdrib, as nearly as I can interpret the word, signifies the Island of *Sorcerers* or *Magicians*. It is about one third as large as the Isle of Wight, and extremely fruitful: it is governed by the head of a certain tribe, who are all magicians. This tribe marries only among each other, and the eldest in succession is Prince or Governor. He hath a noble palace, and a park of about three thousand acres, surrounded by a wall of hewn stone twenty foot high. In this park are several small enclosures for cattle, corn, and gardening.

The Governor and his family are served and attended by domestics of a kind somewhat unusual. By his skill in necromancy, he hath a power of calling whom he pleaseth from the dead, and commanding their service for twenty-four hours, but no longer; nor can he call the same persons up again in less than three months, except upon very extraordinary occasions.

When we arrived at the island, which was about eleven in the morning, one of the gentlemen who accompanied me, went to the Governor, and desired admittance for a stranger, who came on purpose to have the honor of attending on his Highness. This was immediately granted, and we all three entered the gate of the palace between two rows of guards, armed and dressed after a very antic[1] manner, and something in their countenances that made my flesh creep with a horror I cannot express. We passed through several apartments, between servants of the same sort, ranked on each side as before, till we came to the chamber of presence, where after three profound obeisances, and a few general questions, we were permitted to sit on three stools near the lowest step of his Highness's throne. He understood the language of Balnibarbi, although it were different from that of his island. He desired me to give him some account of my travels; and to let me see that I should be treated without ceremony, he dismissed all his attendants with a turn of his finger, at which to my great astonishment they vanished in an instant, like visions in a dream, when we awake on a sudden. I could not recover myself in some time, till the Governor assured me that I should receive no hurt; and observing my two companions to be under no concern, who had been often entertained in the same manner, I began to take courage, and related to his Highness a short history of my several adventures, yet not without some hesitation, and frequently looking behind me to the place where I had seen those domestic spectres. I had the honor to dine with the Governor, where a new set of ghosts served up the meat, and waited at table. I now observed myself to be less terrified than I had been in the morning. I stayed till sunset, but humbly desired his Highness to excuse me for not accepting his invitation of lodging in the palace. My two friends and I lay at a private house in the town adjoining, which is the capital of this little island; and the next morning we returned to pay our duty to the Governor, as he was pleased to command us.

After this manner we continued in the island for ten days, most part of every day with the Governor, and at night in our lodging. I soon grew so familiarized to the sight of spirits, that after the third or fourth time they gave me no emotion at all; or if I had any apprehensions left, my curiosity prevailed over them. For his Highness the Governor ordered me to call up whatever persons I would choose to name, and in whatever numbers among all the dead from the beginning of the world to the present time, and command them to answer any questions I should think fit to ask; with this condition, that my questions must be confined within the compass of the times they lived in. And one thing I might depend upon, that they would certainly tell me truth, for lying was a talent of no use in the lower world.

I made my humble acknowledgments to his Highness for so great a favor. We were in a chamber from whence there was a fair prospect into the park. And because my first inclination was to be entertained with scenes of pomp and magnificence, I desired to see Alexander the Great, at the head of his army just after the battle of Arbela; which upon a motion of the Governor's finger immediately appeared in a large field under the window where we stood. Alexander was called up into the room: it was with great difficulty that I understood his Greek, and had but little of my own. He assured me upon his honor that he was not poisoned, but died of a fever by excessive drinking.

Next I saw Hannibal passing the Alps, who told me he had not a drop of vinegar in his camp.

I saw Cæsar and Pompey at the head of their troops, just ready to engage. I saw the former in his last great triumph. I desired that the senate of Rome might appear before me in one large chamber, and an assembly of somewhat a latter age[1] in counterview in another. The first seemed to be an assembly of heroes and demigods; the other a knot of pedlars, pickpockets, highway-men, and bullies.

The Governor at my request gave the sign for Cæsar and Brutus to advance towards us. I was struck with a profound veneration at the sight of Brutus, and could easily discover the most consummate virtue, the greatest intrepidity and firmness of mind, the truest love of his country, and general benevolence for mankind in every lineament of his countenance. I observed with much pleasure that these two persons were on good in-

[1] strange, ludicrous.

[1] Parliament of England.

telligence with each other, and Cæsar freely confessed to me that the greatest actions of his own life were not equal by many degrees to the glory of taking it away. I had the honor to have much conversation with Brutus; and was told, that his ancestor Junius, Socrates, Epaminondas, Cato the younger, Sir Thomas More, and himself were perpetually together: a sextumvirate to which all the ages of the world cannot add a seventh.

It would be tedious to trouble the reader with relating what vast numbers of illustrious persons were called up, to gratify that insatiable desire I had to see the world in every period of antiquity placed before me. I chiefly fed my eyes with beholding the destroyers of tyrants and usurpers, and the restorers of liberty to oppressed and injured nations. But it is impossible to express the satisfaction I received in my own mind, after such a manner as to make it a suitable entertainment to the reader.

The Author returns to Maldonada. Sails to the kingdom of Luggnagg. The Author confined. He is sent for to Court. The manner of his admittance. The King's great lenity to his subjects.

The day of our departure being come, I took leave of his Highness the Governor of Glubbdubdrib, and returned with my two companions to Maldonada, where after a fortnight's waiting, a ship was ready to sail for Luggnagg. The two gentlemen, and some others, were so generous and kind as to furnish me with provisions, and see me on board. I was a month in this voyage. We had one violent storm, and were under a necessity of steering westward to get into the trade wind, which holds for above sixty leagues. On the 21st of April, 1709, we sailed into the river of Clumegnig, which is a seaport town, at the southeast point of Luggnagg. We cast anchor within a league of the town, and made a signal for a pilot. Two of them came on board in less than half an hour, by whom we were guided between certain shoals and rocks, which are very dangerous in the passage, to a large basin, where a fleet may ride in safety within a cable's length of the town wall.

Some of our sailors, whether out of treachery or inadvertence, had informed the pilots that I was a stranger and a great traveller, whereof these gave notice to a custom-house officer, by whom I was examined very strictly upon my landing. This officer spoke to me in the language of Balnibarbi, which by the force of much commerce is generally understood in that town, especially by seamen, and those employed in the customs. I gave him a short account of some particulars, and made my story as plausible and consistent as I could; but I thought it necessary to disguise my country, and call myself an Hollander, because my intentions were for Japan, and I knew the Dutch were the only Europeans permitted to enter into that kingdom. I therefore told the officer, that having been shipwrecked on the coast of Balnibarbi, and cast on a rock, I was received up into Laputa, or the Flying Island (of which he had often heard), and was now endeavoring to get to Japan, from whence I might find a convenience of returning to my own country. The officer said I must be confined till he could receive orders from court, for which he would write immediately, and hoped to receive an answer in a fortnight. I was carried to a convenient lodging, with a sentry placed at the door; however I had the liberty of a large garden, and was treated with humanity enough, being maintained all the time at the King's charge. I was visited by several persons, chiefly out of curiosity, because it was reported that I came from countries very remote of which they had never heard.

I hired a young man who came in the same ship to be an interpreter; he was a native of Luggnagg, but had lived some years at Maldonada, and was a perfect master of both languages. By his assistance I was able to hold a conversation with those who came to visit me; but this consisted only of their questions, and my answers.

The dispatch came from court about the time we expected. It contained a warrant for conducting me and my retinue to Traldragdubh or Trildrogdrib, for it is pronounced both ways as near as I can remember, by a party of ten horse. All my retinue was that poor lad for an interpreter, whom I persuaded into my service, and at my humble request, we had each of us a mule to ride on. A messenger was dispatched half a day's journey before us, to give the King notice of my approach, and to desire that his Majesty would please to appoint a day and hour, when it would be his gracious pleasure that I might have the honor to *lick the dust before his footstool.* This is the court style, and I found it to be more than matter of form. For upon my admittance two days after my arrival, I was commanded to crawl on my belly, and lick the floor as I advanced; but on account of my being a stranger, care was taken to have it made so clean that the dust was not offensive. However, this was a peculiar grace, not allowed to any but persons of the highest rank, when they desire an admittance. Nay, sometimes the floor is strewn with dust on purpose, when the person to be admitted happens to have powerful enemies at court. And I have seen a great lord with his mouth so crammed, that when he had crept to the proper distance from the throne, he was not able to speak a word. Neither is there any remedy, because it is capital for those who receive an audience to spit or wipe their mouths in his Majesty's presence. There is indeed another custom, which I cannot altogether approve of. When the King hath a mind to put any of his nobles to death in a gentle indulgent manner, he commands to have the floor strowed with a certain brown powder, of a deadly composition, which being licked up infallibly kills him in twenty-four hours. But in justice to this prince's great clemency, and the care he hath of his subjects' lives (wherein it were much to be wished that the monarchs of Europe would imitate him), it must be mentioned for his honor, that strict orders are given to have the infected parts of the floor well washed after every such execution; which if his domestics neglect, they are in danger of incurring his royal displeasure. I myself heard him give directions, that one of his pages should be whipped, whose turn it was to give notice about washing the floor after an execution, but maliciously had omitted it; by which neglect a young lord of great hopes coming to an audience, was unfortunately poisoned, although the King at that time had no design against his life. But this good prince was so gracious as to forgive the poor page his whipping, upon promise that he would do so no more, without special orders.

To return from this digression; when I had crept within four yards of the throne, I raised myself gently upon my knees, and then striking my forehead seven times on the ground, I pronounced the following words, as they had been taught me the night before, *Ickpling gloffthrobb squutserumm blhiop mlashnalt zwin tnodbalkguffh slhiophad gurdlubh asht.* This is the compliment established by the laws of the land for all persons admitted to the King's presence. It may be rendered into English thus: *May your Celestial Majesty outlive the sun, eleven moons and a half.* To this the King returned some answer, which although I could not understand, yet I replied as I had been directed: *Fluft drin yalerick dwuldom prastrad mirpush,* which properly signifies, *My tongue is in the mouth of my friend,* and by this expression was meant that I desired leave to bring my interpreter; whereupon the young man already mentioned was accordingly introduced, by whose intervention I answered as many questions as his Majesty could put in above an hour. I spoke in the Balnibarbian tongue, and my interpreter delivered my meaning in that of Luggnagg.

The King was much delighted with my company, and ordered his *Bliffmarklub,* or High Chamberlain, to appoint a lodging in the court for me and my interpreter, with a daily allowance for my table, and a large purse of gold for my common expenses.

I stayed three months in this country out of perfect obedience to his Majesty, who was pleased highly to favor me, and made me very honorable offers. But I thought it more consistent with prudence and justice to pass the remainder of my days with my wife and family.

The Luggnaggians commended. A particular description of the Struldbrugs, with many conversations between the Author and some eminent persons upon that subject.

The Luggnaggians are a polite and generous people, and although they are not without some share of that pride which is peculiar to all Eastern countries, yet they show themselves courteous to strangers, especially such who are countenanced by the court. I had many acquaintance among persons of the best fashion, and being always attended by my interpreter, the conversation we had was not disagreeable.

One day in much good company I was asked by a person of quality, whether I had seen any of their *Struldbrugs,* or *Immortals.* I said I had not, and desired he would explain to me what he meant by such an appellation applied to a mortal creature. He told me, that sometimes, though very rarely, a child happened to be born in a family with a red circular spot in the forehead, directly over the left eyebrow, which was an infallible mark that it should never die. The spot, as he described it, was about the compass of a silver threepence, but in the course of time grew larger, and changed its color; for at twelve years old it became green, so continued till five and twenty, then turned to a deep blue; at five and forty it grew coal black, and as large as an English shilling, but never admitted any further alteration. He said these births were so rare, that he did not believe there could be above eleven hundred *struldbrugs* of both sexes in the whole kingdom, of which he computed about fifty in the metropolis, and among the rest a young girl born about three years ago. That these productions were not peculiar to any family, but a mere effect of chance; and the children of the *struldbrugs* themselves were equally mortal with the rest of the people.

I freely own myself to have been struck with inexpressible delight upon hearing this account, and the person who gave it me happening to understand the Balnibarbian language, which I spoke very well, I could not forbear breaking out into expressions perhaps a little too extravagant. I cried out as in a rapture: Happy nation where every child hath at least a chance for being immortal! Happy people who enjoy so many living examples of ancient virtue, and have masters ready to instruct them in the wisdom of all former ages! but, happiest beyond all comparison are those excellent *struldbrugs*, who being born exempt from that universal calamity of human nature, have their minds free and disengaged, without the weight and depression of spirits caused by the continual apprehension of death. I discovered my admiration that I had not observed any of these illustrious persons at court; the black spot on the forehead being so remarkable a distinction, that I could not have easily overlooked it; and it was impossible that his Majesty, a most judicious prince, should not provide himself with a good number of such wise and able counsellors. Yet perhaps the virtue of those reverend sages was too strict for the corrupt and libertine manners of a court. And we often find by experience that young men are too opinionative and volatile to be guided by the sober dictates of their seniors. However, since the King was pleased to allow me access to his royal person, I was resolved upon the very first occasion to deliver my opinion to him on this matter freely and at large, by the help of my interpreter; and whether he would please to take my advice or no, yet in one thing I was determined, that his Majesty having frequently offered me an establishment in this country, I would with great thankfulness accept the favor, and pass my life here in the conversation of those superior beings the *struldbrugs*, if they would please admit me.

The gentleman to whom I addressed my discourse, because (as I have already observed) he spoke the language of Balnibarbi, said to me with a sort of a smile, which usually ariseth from pity to the ignorant, that he was glad of any occasion to keep me among them, and desired my permission to explain to the company what I had spoke. He did so, and they talked together for some time in their own language, whereof I understood not a syllable, neither could I observe by their countenances what impression my discourse had made on them. After a short silence, the same person told me that his friends and mine (so he thought fit to express himself) were very much pleased with the judicious remarks I had made on the great happiness and advantages of immortal life; and they were desirous to know in a particular

manner, what scheme of living I should have formed to myself, if it had fallen to my lot to have been born a *struldbrug*.

I answered, it was easy to be eloquent on so copious and delightful a subject, especially to me who have been often apt to amuse myself with visions of what I should do if I were a king, a general, or a great lord; and upon this very case I had frequently run over the whole system how I should employ myself and pass the time if I were sure to live for ever.

That if it had been my good fortune to come into the world a *struldbrug*, as soon as I could discover my own happiness by understanding the difference between life and death, I would first resolve by all arts and methods whatsoever to procure myself riches. In the pursuit of which by thrift and management, I might reasonably expect, in about two hundred years to be the wealthiest man in the kingdom. In the second place, I would from my earliest youth apply myself to the study of arts and sciences, by which I should arrive in time to excel all others in learning. Lastly, I would carefully record every action and event of consequence that happened in the public, impartially draw the characters of the several successions of princes and great ministers of state, with my own observations on every point. I would exactly set down the several changes in customs, language, fashions of dress, diet and diversions. By all which acquirements, I should be a living treasury of knowledge and wisdom, and certainly become the oracle of the nation.

I would never marry after threescore, but live in an hospitable manner, yet still on the saving side. I would entertain myself in forming and directing the minds of hopeful young men, by convincing them from my own remembrance, experience and observation, fortified by numerous examples, of the usefulness of virtue in public and private life. But my choice and constant companions should be a set of my own immortal brotherhood, among whom I would elect a dozen from the most ancient down to my own contemporaries. Where any of these wanted fortunes, I would provide them with convenient lodges round my own estate, and have some of them always at my table, only mingling a few of the most valuable among you mortals, whom length of time would harden me to lose with little or no reluctance, and treat your posterity after the same manner; just as a man diverts himself with the annual succession of pinks and tulips in his garden, without regretting the loss of those which withered the preceding year.

These *struldbrugs* and I would mutually communicate our observations and memorials through the course of time, remark the several gradations by which corruption steals into the world, and oppose it in every step, by giving perpetual warning and instruction to mankind; which, added to the strong influence of our own example, would probably prevent that continual degeneracy of human nature so justly complained of in all ages.

Add to all this the pleasure of seeing the various revolutions of states and empires, the changes in the lower and upper world, ancient cities in ruins, and obscure villages become the seats of kings. Famous rivers lessening into shallow brooks, the ocean leaving one coast dry, and overwhelming another; the discovery of many countries yet unknown. Barbarity overrunning the politest nations, and the most barbarous become civilized. I should then see the discovery of the longitude, the perpetual motion, the universal medicine, and many other great inventions brought to the utmost perfection.

What wonderful discoveries should we make in astronomy, by outliving and confirming our own predictions, by observing the progress and returns of comets, with the changes of motion in the sun, moon, and stars.

I enlarged upon many other topics, which the natural desire of endless life and sublunary happiness could easily furnish me with. When I had ended, and the sum of my discourse had been interpreted as before, to the rest of the company, there was a good deal of talk among them in the language of the country, not without some laughter at my expense. At last the same gentleman who had been my interpreter said he was desired by the rest to set me right in a few mistakes, which I had fallen into through the common imbecility of human nature, and upon that allowance was less answerable for them. That this breed of *struldbrugs* was peculiar to their country, for there were no such people either in Balnibarbi or Japan, where he had the honor to be ambassador from his Majesty, and found the natives in both those kingdoms very hard to believe that the fact was possible; and it appeared from my astonishment when he first mentioned the matter to me, that I received it as a thing wholly new, and scarcely to be credited. That in the two kingdoms above mentioned, where during his residence he had conversed very much, he observed long life to be the universal desire and wish of mankind. That whoever had one foot in the grave was sure to hold back the other as strongly as he could. That the oldest had still hopes of living one day longer, and looked on death as the greatest evil, from which nature always prompted him to retreat; only in this island of Luggnagg the appetite for living was not so eager, from the continual example of the *struldbrugs* before their eyes.

That the system of living contrived by me was unreasonable and unjust, because it supposed a perpetuity of youth, health, and vigor, which no man could be so foolish to hope, however extravagant he may be in his wishes. That the question therefore was not whether a man would choose to be always in the prime of youth, attended with prosperity and health, but how he would pass a perpetual life under all the usual disadvantages which old age brings along with it. For although few men will avow their desires of being immortal upon such hard conditions, yet in the two kingdoms before mentioned of Balnibarbi and Japan, he observed that every man desired to put off death for some time longer, let it approach ever so late; and he rarely heard of any man who died willingly, except he were incited by the extremity of grief or torture. And he appealed to me whether in those countries I had travelled as well as my own, I had not observed the same general disposition.

After this preface he gave me a particular account of the *struldbrugs* among them. He said they commonly acted like mortals, till about thirty years old, after which by degrees they grew melancholy and dejected, increasing in both till they came to fourscore. This he learned from their own confession; for otherwise there not being above two or three of that species born in an age, they were too few to form a general observation by. When they came to fourscore years, which is reckoned the extremity of living in this country, they had not only all the follies and infirmities of other old men, but many more which arose from the dreadful prospect of never dying. They were not only opinionative, peevish, covetous, morose, vain, talkative, but uncapable of friendship, and dead to all natural affection, which never descended below their grandchildren. Envy and impotent desires are their prevailing passions. But those objects against which their envy seems principally directed, are the vices of the younger sort, and the deaths of the old. By reflecting on the former, they find themselves cut off from all possibility of pleasure; and whenever they see a funeral, they lament and repine that others have gone to a harbor of rest, to which they themselves never can hope to arrive. They have no remembrance of anything but what they learned and observed in their youth and middle age, and even that is very imperfect. And for the truth or particulars of any fact, it is safer to depend on common traditions than upon their best recollections. The least miserable among them appear to be those who turn to dotage, and entirely lose their memories; these meet with more pity and assistance, because they want many bad qualities which abound in others.

If a *struldbrug* happen to marry one of his own kind, the marriage is dissolved of course by the courtesy of the kingdom, as soon as the younger of the two comes to be fourscore. For the law thinks it a reasonable indulgence, that those who are condemned without any fault of their own to a perpetual continuance in the world, should not have their misery doubled by the load of a wife.

As soon as they have completed the term of eighty years, they are looked on as dead in law; their heirs immediately succeed to their estates, only a small pittance is reserved for their support, and the poor ones are maintained at the public charge. After that period they are held incapable of any employment of trust or profit, they cannot purchase lands or take leases, neither are they allowed to be witnesses in any cause, either civil or criminal, not even for the decision of meers and bounds.

At ninety they lose their teeth and hair, they have at that age no distinction of taste, but eat and drink whatever they can get, without relish or appetite. The diseases they were subject to still continue without increasing or diminishing. In talking they forget the common appellation of things, and the names of persons, even of those who are their nearest friends and relations. For the same reason they never can amuse themselves with reading, because their memory will not serve to carry them from the beginning of a sentence to the end; and by this defect they are deprived of the only entertainment whereof they might otherwise be capable.

The language of this country being always upon the flux, the *struldbrugs* of one age do not understand those of another, neither are they able after two hundred years to hold any conversation (farther than by a few general words) with their neighbors the mortals; and thus they lie under the disadvantage of living like foreigners in their own country.

This was the account given me of the *struldbrugs*, as near as I can remember. I afterwards saw five or six of different ages, the youngest not above two hundred years old, who were brought to me at several times by some of my friends; but although they were told that I was a great traveller, and had seen all the world, they had not the least curiosity

to ask me a question; only desired I would give them *slumskudask*, or a token of remembrance, which is a modest way of begging, to avoid the law that strictly forbids it, because they are provided for by the public, although indeed with a very scanty allowance.

They are despised and hated by all sorts of people; when one of them is born, it is reckoned ominous, and their birth is recorded very particularly; so that you may know their age by consulting the registry, which however hath not been kept above a thousand years past, or at least hath been destroyed by time or public disturbances. But the usual way of computing how old they are, is by asking them what kings or great persons they can remember, and then consulting history, for infallibly the last prince in their mind did not begin his reign after they were fourscore years old.

They were the most mortifying sight I ever beheld, and the women more horrible than the men. Besides the usual deformities in extreme old age, they acquired an additional ghastliness in proportion to their number of years, which is not to be described; and among half a dozen, I soon distinguished which was the eldest, although there was not above a century or two between them.

The reader will easily believe, that from what I had heard and seen, my keen appetite for perpetuity of life was much abated. I grew heartily ashamed of the pleasing visions I had formed, and thought no tyrant could invent a death into which I would not run with pleasure from such a life. The King heard of all that had passed between me and my friends upon this occasion, and rallied me very pleasantly, wishing I would send a couple of *struldbrugs* to my own country, to arm our people against the fear of death; but this it seems is forbidden by the fundamental laws of the kingdom, or else I should have been well content with the trouble and expense of transporting them.

I could not but agree that the laws of this kingdom, relating to the *struldbrugs*, were founded upon the strongest reasons, and such as any other country would be under the necessity of enacting in the like circumstances. Otherwise, as avarice is the necessary consequent of old age, those immortals would in time become proprietors of the whole nation, and engross the civil power, which, for want of abilities to manage, must end in the ruin of the public.

Alexander Pope · 1688-1744

If one knows the times into which Alexander Pope was born and something of his physical weakness, one will understand his frailties. Born in London, May 21, 1688, Pope found himself a Catholic in a society which at the time scorned Catholics. His religion precluded his attending the usual schools and compelled him to study by himself and with tutors. The only child of parents who married late in life, he was sickly, undersized, and misshapen. He grew up too much by himself and developed a highly personal and somewhat unnatural outlook on society and people. The early eighteenth century was a time when literary men lived largely in public life, ardently took sides in politics, frequently wrote journalistic pamphlets, lampooned others and were themselves lampooned, sought patronage at court, sometimes in rather devious ways, and were almost obliged to play the flatterer before wealth and political greatness that they might secure patronage and readers. Pope thrived in this atmosphere. He seemed to delight in public quarrels. At an early age he antagonized Wycherley by carrying out his suggestion that Pope improve some of Wycherley's poems. Later on, in the *Essay on Criticism*, he attacked the critic John Dennis; in the *Epistle to Dr. Arbuthnot* he evened accounts he thought he owed Addison; and in the *Dunciad* he paid his satiric compliments to Lewis Theobald whose chief offense had been that he had published an edition of Shakespeare which was better than Pope's. Yet Pope had a few close friends: Swift, Dr. Arbuthnot, Parnell, Gay, Bolingbroke, and the Earl of Oxford (who with Pope formed the Scriblerus Club). Among these men there was, as Professor George Sherburn has pointed out, a "lasting warmth of friendship and a wealth of intellectual stimulation."

It may be that Pope's literary brilliance was a compensation for his physical and social handicaps. When, at twelve years of age, he moved with his parents to Binfield, near Windsor Forest, he was even then reading Latin and Greek diligently, familiarizing himself with such older English poets as Chaucer and Spenser, and writing imitations of Ovid and Statius, of Chaucer and Waller. Before he was twenty-five, he had published two of his most famous poems: *An Essay on Criticism* and *The Rape of the Lock*. His next great literary activity was that of translating Homer. He gave eleven years to the *Iliad* and the *Odyssey*, translations which proved so popular as to bring him eight thousand pounds in royalties and permit him to retire to a country estate of quiet and beauty. His third phase of activity centered on moral and satiric writing and includes such important contributions as the *Dunciad*, the *Essay on Man*, and the *Epistle to Dr. Arbuthnot*. On May 30, 1744, at the age of fifty-six, Pope died.

SUGGESTED REFERENCES: Geoffrey Tillotson, *On the Poetry of Pope* (3rd ed., 1959); G. W. Sherburn, *The Early Career of Alexander Pope* (1963); Maynard Mack, *Essential Articles for the Study of Alexander Pope* (1964).

The Poetry of *Alexander Pope*

The two selections which follow, *An Essay on Criticism* and *The Rape of the Lock*, evince many of the characteristic qualities of Pope. Both poems show the poet's mastery of the heroic couplet, his epigrammatic manner, and his preciseness of expression. And both poems reflect Pope's classical learning and his neoclassical emphasis on certain of the classical dicta. In both, a wit and humor characteristically eighteenth-century in quality play an important role. And in both we find an enthusiasm for satire such as we met in Horace.

The *Essay on Criticism* is a didactic poem presenting not so much Pope's own ideas as the heritage passed down from Aristotle and Horace and Quintilian modified by the mind of Boileau. In the *Essay* Pope teaches that Art is to be approached seriously and only by one who has at his command real learning and a respect for the dictates of good taste. The first precept for the writer is to follow nature,

"Unerring Nature, still divinely bright,
One clear, unchanged, and universal light,"

but that this is not the same nature followed by the realist or the romantic is made clear by the further injunction that nature must be approached through a careful following of the old rules and then must appear not in her own right and as natural nature but as "Nature methodized."

The Rape of the Lock, while sharing many of the qualities of the *Essay*, shows Pope in a mood lighter than is common in his work. Based on an actual incident, the narrative presents a tid-bit of gossip enlarged, through the method of the mock heroic, to epic stature.

An Essay on Criticism

Contents

PART I

Introduction. That 'tis as great a fault to judge ill, as to write ill, and a more dangerous one to the public, v. 1. That a true Taste is as rare to be found, as a true Genius, v. 9 to 18. That most men are born with some Taste, but spoiled by false Education, v. 19 to 25. The multitude of Critics, and causes of them, v. 26 to 45. That we are to study our own Taste, and know the Limits of it, v. 46 to 67. Nature the best guide of Judgment, v. 68 to 87. Improved by Art and Rules, which are but methodized Nature, 88. Rules derived from the Practice of the Ancient Poets, *v. id.* to 110. That therefore the Ancients are necessary to be studied, by a Critic, particularly Homer and Virgil, v. 120 to 138. Of Licenses, and the use of them by the Ancients, v. 140 to 180. Reverence due to the Ancients, and praise of them, v. 181, *etc.*

'Tis hard to say, if greater want of skill
Appear in writing or in judging ill;
But, of the two, less dang'rous is th' offence
To tire our patience, than mislead our sense.
Some few in that, but numbers err in this,   5
Ten censure wrong for one who writes amiss;
A fool might once himself alone expose,
Now one in verse makes many more in prose.
  'Tis with our judgments as our watches, none
Go just alike, yet each believes his own.   10
In Poets as true genius is but rare,
True Taste as seldom is the Critic's share;
Both must alike from Heav'n derive their light,
These born to judge, as well as those to write.
Let such teach others who themselves excel,   15
And censure freely who have written well.
Authors are partial to their wit, 'tis true,
But are not Critics to their judgment too?
  Yet if we look more closely, we shall find
Most have the seeds of judgment in their mind·

Nature affords at least a glimm'ring light;   21
The lines, tho' touch'd but faintly, are drawn right.
But as the slightest sketch, if justly trac'd,
Is by ill-coloring but the more disgrac'd,
So by false learning is good sense defac'd;   25
Some are bewilder'd in the maze of schools,
And some made coxcombs Nature meant but fools.
In search of wit these lose their common sense,
And then turn Critics in their own defence:
Each burns alike, who can, or cannot write,   30
Or with a Rival's, or an Eunuch's spite.
All fools have still an itching to deride,
And fain would be upon the laughing side.
If Mævius [1] scribble in Apollo's spite,
There are, who judge still worse than he can write.
  Some have at first for Wits, then Poets past,   36
Turn'd Critics next, and proved plain fools at last.
Some neither can for Wits nor Critics pass,
As heavy mules are neither horse nor ass.
Those half-learn'd witlings, num'rous in our isle,
As half-form'd insects on the banks of Nile;   41
Unfinish'd things, one knows not what to call,
Their generation's so equivocal:
To tell 'em would a hundred tongues require,
Or one vain wit's, that might a hundred tire.   45
  But you who seek to give and merit fame,
And justly bear a Critic's noble name,
Be sure yourself and your own reach to know,
How far your genius, taste, and learning go;
Launch not beyond your depth, but be discreet,   50
And mark that point where sense and dullness meet
Nature to all things fix'd the limits fit,
And wisely curb'd proud man's pretending wit.
As on the land while here the ocean gains,
In other parts it leaves wide sandy plains;   55
Thus in the soul while memory prevails,
The solid pow'r of understanding fails;
Where beams of warm imagination play,
The memory's soft figures melt away.
One science only will one genius fit;   60
So vast is art; so narrow human wit:
Not only bounded to peculiar arts,
But oft in those confin'd to single parts.
Like Kings we lose the conquests gain'd before,
By vain ambition still to make them more: 65
Each might his sev'ral province well command,
Would all but stoop to what they understand.
  First follow Nature, and your judgment frame
By her just standard, which is still the same:
Unerring NATURE, still divinely bright,   70
One clear, unchang'd, and universal light,
Life, force, and beauty, must to all impart,
At once the source, and end, and test of Art.

[1] A Roman poet of little ability.

Art from that fund each just supply provides;
Works without show, and without pomp presides:
In some fair body thus th' informing soul　76
With spirits feeds, with vigor fills the whole,
Each motion guides, and ev'ry nerve sustains;
Itself unseen, but in th' effects remains.
Some, to whom Heav'n in wit has been profuse,　80
Want as much more, to turn it to its use;
For wit and judgment often are at strife,
Tho' meant each other's aid, like man and wife.
'Tis more to guide, than spur the Muse's steed;
Restrain his fury, than provoke his speed;　85
The winged courser, like a gen'rous horse,
Shows most true mettle when you check his course.

Those RULES of old discover'd, not devis'd
Are Nature still, but Nature methodiz'd:
Nature, like Liberty, is but restrain'd　90
By the same Laws, which first herself ordain'd.

Hear how learn'd Greece her useful rules indites,
When to repress, and when indulge our flights:
High on Parnassus' top her sons she show'd,
And pointed out those arduous paths they trod;　95
Held from afar, aloft, th' immortal prize,
And urg'd the rest by equal steps to rise.
Just precepts thus from great examples giv'n,
She drew from them what they deriv'd from
　　　Heav'n.
The gen'rous Critic fann'd the Poet's fire,　100
And taught the world with Reason to admire.
Then Criticism the Muse's handmaid prov'd,
To dress her charms, and make her more belov'd:
But following wits from that intention stray'd,
Who could not win the mistress, woo'd the maid;
Against the Poets their own arms they turn'd.　106
Sure to hate most the men from whom they learn'd.
So modern 'Pothecaries, taught the art
By Doctor's bills to play the Doctor's part,
Bold in the practice of mistaken rules,　110
Prescribe, apply, and call their masters fools.
Some on the leaves of ancient authors prey,
Nor time nor moths e'er spoil'd so much as they.
Some drily plain, without invention's aid,
Write dull receipts how poems may be made.　115
These leave the sense, their learning to display,
And those explain the meaning quite away.

You then whose judgment the right course would
　　　steer,
Know well each ANCIENT's proper character;
His Fable, Subject, scope in every page;　120
Religion, Country, genius of his Age:
Without all these at once before your eyes,
Cavil you may, but never criticize.
Be Homer's works your study and delight,
Read them by day, and meditate by night;　125
Thence form your judgment, thence your maxims
　　　bring.

And trace the Muses upward to their spring.
Still with itself compar'd, his text peruse;
And let your comment be the Mantuan Muse.[1]
When first young Maro[1] in his boundless mind
A work t' outlast immortal Rome design'd,　131
Perhaps he seem'd above the critic's law,
And but from Nature's fountains scorn'd to draw;
But when t' examine ev'ry part he came,
Nature and Homer were, he found, the same.　135
Convinced, amazed, he checks the bold design,
And rules as strict his labor'd work confine
As if the Stagyrite[2] o'erlook'd each line.
Learn hence for ancient rules a just esteem;
To copy Nature is to copy them.　140

Some beauties yet no precepts can declare,
For there's a happiness as well as care.
Music resembles poetry; in each
Are nameless graces which no methods teach,
And which a master-hand alone can reach.　145
If, where the rules not far enough extend,
(Since rules were made but to promote their end)
Some lucky license answer to the full
Th' intent proposed, that license is a rule.
Thus Pegasus, a nearer way to take,　150
May boldly deviate from the common track.
Great Wits sometimes may gloriously offend,
And rise to faults true Critics dare not mend;
From vulgar bounds with brave disorder part,
And snatch a grace beyond the reach of Art,　155
Which, without passing thro' the judgment, gains
The heart, and all its end at once attains.
In prospects thus some objects please our eyes,
Which out of Nature's common order rise,
The shapeless rock, or hanging precipice.　160
But tho' the ancients thus their rules invade,
(As Kings dispense with laws themselves have
　　　made)
Moderns, beware! or if you must offend
Against the precept, ne'er transgress its end;
Let it be seldom, and compell'd by need;　165
And have at least their precedent to plead;
The Critic else proceeds without remorse,
Seizes your fame, and puts his laws in force.
I know there are to whose presumptuous
　　　thoughts
Those freer beauties, e'en in them, seem faults.
Some figures monstrous and misshaped appear,　171
Consider'd singly, or beheld too near,
Which, but proportion'd to their light or place,
Due distance reconciles to form and grace.
A prudent chief not always must display　175
His powers in equal ranks and fair array,
But with th' occasion and the place comply,
Conceal his force, nay, seem sometimes to fly.

[1] Virgil.
[2] Aristotle.

Those oft are stratagems which errors seem.
Nor is it Homer nods, but we that dream.   180
    Still green with bays each ancient altar stands
Above the reach of sacrilegious hands,
Secure from flames, from Envy's fiercer rage,
Destructive war, and all-involving Age.
See from each clime the learn'd their incense bring!
Hear in all tongues consenting pæans ring!   186
In praise so just let ev'ry voice be join'd,
And fill the gen'ral chorus of mankind.
Hail, Bards triumphant! born in happier days,
Immortal heirs of universal praise!   190
Whose honors with increase of ages grow,
As streams roll down, enlarging as they flow;
Nations unborn your mighty names shall sound,
And worlds applaud that must not yet be found!
O may some spark of your celestial fire   195
The last, the meanest of your sons inspire,
(That on weak wings, from far, pursues your
      flights,
Glows while he reads, but trembles as he writes)
To teach vain Wits a science little known,   199
T' admire superior sense, and doubt their own.

PART II

Causes hindering a true Judgment. 1. Pride, v.
208. 2. Imperfect Learning, v. 215. 3. Judging by
parts, and not by the whole, v. 233 to 288. Critics in
Wit, Language, Versification, only, v. 288, 305, 399, *etc.*
4. Being too hard to please, or too apt to admire, v. 384.
5. Partiality — too much Love to a Sect — to the
Ancients or Moderns, v. 394. 6. Prejudice or Preven-
tion, v. 408. 7. Singularity, v. 424. 8. Inconstancy,
v. 430. 9. Party Spirit, v. 452, *etc.* 10. Envy, v. 466.
Against Envy, and in praise of Good-nature, v. 508, *etc.*
When Severity is chiefly to be used by Critics, v. 526, *etc.*

Of all the causes which conspire to blind
Man's erring judgment, and misguide the mind,
What the weak head with strongest bias rules,
Is Pride, the never failing vice of fools.
Whatever Nature has in worth denied   205
She gives in large recruits of needful Pride:
For as in bodies, thus in souls, we find
What wants in blood and spirits swell'd with wind:
Pride, where Wit fails, steps in to our defense,
And fills up all the mighty void of Sense: 210
If once right Reason drives that cloud away,
Truth breaks upon us with resistless day.
Trust not yourself; but your defects to know,
Make use of ev'ry friend — and ev'ry foe.
    A little learning is a dangerous thing;   215
Drink deep, or taste not the Pierian spring:[1]

[1] Birthplace of the muses.

There shallow draughts intoxicate the brain,
And drinking largely sobers us again.
Fired at first sight with what the Muse imparts,
In fearless youth we tempt the heights of arts,
While from the bounded level of our mind   221
Short views we take, nor see the lengths behind:
But more advanc'd, behold with strange surprise
New distant scenes of endless science rise!
So pleas'd at first the tow'ring Alps we try,   225
Mount o'er the vales, and seem to tread the sky;
Th' eternal snows appear already past,
And the first clouds and mountains seem the last:
But those attain'd, we tremble to survey
The growing labors of the lengthen'd way;   230
Th' increasing prospect tires our wand'ring eyes,
Hills peep o'er hills, and Alps on Alps arise!
    A perfect judge will read each work of wit
With the same spirit that its author writ;
Survey the Whole, nor seek slight faults to find   235
Where Nature moves, and Rapture warms the
    mind:
Nor lose, for that malignant dull delight,
The gen'rous pleasure to be charm'd with wit.
But in such lays as neither ebb nor flow,
Correctly cold, and regularly low,   240
That shunning faults one quiet tenor keep,
We cannot blame indeed — but we may sleep.
In Wit, as Nature, what affects our hearts
Is not th' exactness of peculiar parts;
'Tis not a lip or eye we beauty call,   245
But the joint force and full result of all.
Thus when we view some well proportion'd dome,
(The world's just wonder, and ev'n thine, O
    Rome!)
No single parts unequally surprise,
All comes united to th' admiring eyes;   250
No monstrous height, or breadth, or length, ap-
    pear;
The Whole at once is bold and regular.
    Whoever thinks a faultless piece to see,
Thinks what ne'er was, nor is, nor e'er shall be.
In every work regard the writer's end,   255
Since none can compass more than they intend;
And if the means be just, the conduct true,
Applause, in spite of trivial faults, is due.
As men of breeding, sometimes men of wit,
T' avoid great errors must the less commit;   260
Neglect the rules each verbal critic lays,
For not to know some trifles is a praise.
Most Critics, fond of some subservient art,
Still make the Whole depend upon a part:
They talk of Principles, but Notions prize,   265
And all to one lov'd Folly sacrifice.
    Once on a time La Mancha's Knight,[1] they say,
A certain bard encount'ring on the way,

[1] Don Quixote.

Discours'd in terms as just, with looks as sage,
As e'er could Dennis,[1] of the Grecian Stage;   270
Concluding all were desp'rate sots and fools
Who durst depart from Aristotle's rules.
Our Author, happy in a judge so nice,
Produc'd his play, and begg'd the Knight's advice;
Made him observe the subject and the plot,   275
The manners, passions, unities; what not?
All which exact to rule were brought about,
Were but a Combat in the lists left out.
"What! leave the Combat out?" exclaims the
    Knight.
"Yes, or we must renounce the Stagyrite."   280
"Not so, by Heav'n!" (he answers in a rage),
"Knights, squires, and steeds must enter on the
    stage."
"So vast a throng the stage can ne'er contain."
"Then build a new, or act it in a plain."
    Thus Critics of less judgment than caprice,   285
Curious, not knowing, not exact, but nice,
Form short Ideas, and offend in arts
(As most in manners), by a love to parts.
    Some to Conceit alone their taste confine,   289
And glitt'ring thoughts struck out at ev'ry line;
Pleas'd with a work where nothing's just or fit,
One glaring Chaos and wild heap of wit.
Poets, like painters, thus unskill'd to trace
The naked nature and the living grace,
With gold and jewels cover ev'ry part,   295
And hide with ornaments their want of art.
True Wit is Nature to advantage dress'd,
What oft was thought, but ne'er so well express'd;
Something whose truth convinc'd at sight we find,
That gives us back the image of our mind.   300
As shades more sweetly recommend the light,
So modest plainness sets off sprightly wit:
For works may have more wit than does 'em good,
As bodies perish thro' excess of blood.
    Others for Language all their care express,   305
And value books, as women men, for Dress:
Their praise is still — the Style is excellent;
The Sense they humbly take upon content.
Words are like leaves; and where they most abound,
Much fruit of sense beneath is rarely found.   310
False Eloquence, like the prismatic glass,
Its gaudy colors spreads on ev'ry place;
The face of Nature we no more survey,
All glares alike, without distinction gay;
But true expression, like th' unchanging Sun,   315
Clears and improves whate'er it shines upon;
It gilds all objects, but it alters none.
Expression is the dress of thought, and still
Appears more decent as more suitable.
A vile conceit in pompous words express'd   320
Is like a clown in regal purple dress'd:

[1] A contemporary playwright and critic.

For diff'rent styles with diff'rent subjects sort,
As sev'ral garbs with country, town, and court.
Some by old words to fame have made pretense,
Ancients in phrase, mere moderns in their sense;
Such labor'd nothings, in so strange a style,   326
Amaze th' unlearn'd, and make the learned smile;
Unlucky as Fungoso[1] in the play,
These sparks with awkward vanity display
What the fine gentleman wore yesterday;   330
And but so mimic ancient wits at best,
As apes our grandsires in their doublets drest.
In words as fashions the same rule will hold,
Alike fantastic if too new or old:
Be not the first by whom the new are tri'd,   335
Nor yet the last to lay the old aside.
    But most by Numbers judge a Poet's song,
And smooth or rough with them is right or wrong.
In the bright Muse though thousand charms con-
    spire,
Her voice is all these tuneful fools admire;   340
Who haunt Parnassus but to please their ear,
Not mend their minds; as some to Church repair,
Not for the doctrine, but the music there.
These equal syllables alone require,
Tho' oft the ear the open vowels tire,   345
While expletives their feeble aid do join,
And ten low words oft creep in one dull line:
While they ring round the same unvaried chimes,
With sure returns of still expected rhymes;
Where'er you find "the cooling western breeze,"
In the next line, it "whispers thro' the trees";   351
If crystal streams "with pleasing murmurs creep,"
The reader's threaten'd (not in vain) with "sleep";
Then, at the last and only couplet, fraught
With some unmeaning thing they call a thought,
A needless Alexandrine ends the song,   356
That, like a wounded snake, drags its slow length
    along.
Leave such to tune their own dull rhymes, and
    know
What's roundly smooth, or languishingly slow;
And praise the easy vigor of a line   360
Where Denham's[2] strength and Waller's[2] sweet-
    ness join.
True ease in writing comes from art, not chance,
As those move easiest who have learn'd to dance.
'Tis not enough no harshness gives offense;
The sound must seem an Echo to the sense.   365
Soft is the strain when Zephyr gently blows,
And the smooth stream in smoother numbers flows;
But when loud surges lash the sounding shore,
The hoarse rough verse should like the torrent roar.

[1] This is a character in Ben Jonson's *Every Man Out of His Humor.*
[2] English poets. The first died in 1668; the second in 1687.

When Ajax strives some rock's vast weight to
    throw,   370
The line, too, labors, and the words move slow:
Not so when swift Camilla scours the plain,
Flies o'er th' unbending corn, and skims along the
    main.
Hear how Timotheus'[1] varied lays surprise,
And bid alternate passions fall and rise!   375
While at each change the son of Libyan Jove
Now burns with glory, and then melts with love;
Now his fierce eyes with sparkling fury glow,
Now sighs steal out, and tears begin to flow: 379
Persians and Greeks like turns of nature found,
And the world's victor stood subdued by Sound!
The pow'r of Music all our hearts allow,
And what Timotheus was is Dryden now.

    Avoid Extremes, and shun the fault of such
Who still are pleas'd too little or too much.   385
At ev'ry trifle scorn to take offense;
That always shows great pride or little sense:
Those heads, as stomachs, are not sure the best
Which nauseate all, and nothing can digest.
Yet let not each gay Turn thy rapture move;   390
For fools admire, but men of sense approve:
As things seem large which we thro' mists descry,
Dullness is ever apt to magnify.

    Some foreign writers, some our own despise;
The Ancients only, or the Moderns prize.   395
Thus Wit, like Faith, by each man is apply'd
To one small sect, and all are damn'd beside.
Meanly they seek the blessing to confine,
And force that sun but on a part to shine,
Which not alone the southern wit sublimes,   400
But ripens spirits in cold northern climes;
Which from the first has shone on ages past,
Enlights the present, and shall warm the last;
Tho' each may feel increases and decays,
And see now clearer and now darker days.   405
Regard not then if Wit be old or new,
But blame the false and value still the true.

    Some ne'er advance a Judgment of their own,
But catch the spreading notion of the Town;
They reason and conclude by precedent,   410
And own stale nonsense which they ne'er invent.
Some judge of authors' names, not works, and then
Nor praise nor blame the writings, but the men.
Of all this servile herd, the worst is he
That in proud dullness joins with Quality;   415
A constant Critic at the great man's board,
To fetch and carry nonsense for my Lord.
What woeful stuff this madrigal would be
In some starv'd hackney sonneteer or me!
But let a Lord once own the happy lines,   420
How the wit brightens! how the style refines!

    [1] The allusions in these lines are to Dryden's *Alexan-
der's Feast.*

Before his sacred name flies ev'ry fault,
And each exalted stanza teems with thought!
    The Vulgar thus through Imitation err,
As oft the Learn'd by being singular;   425
So much they scorn the crowd, that if the throng
By chance go right, they purposely go wrong.
So Schismatics the plain believers quit,
And are but damn'd for having too much wit.
Some praise at morning what they blame at night,
But always think the last opinion right   431
A Muse by these is like a mistress us'd
This hour she's idoliz'd, the next abus'd;
While their weak heads, like towns unfortify'd,   434
'Twixt sense and nonsense daily change their side.
Ask them the cause; they're wiser still they say;
And still tomorrow's wiser than today.
We think our fathers fools, so wise we grow;
Our wiser sons no doubt will think us so.
Once School-divines this zealous isle o'er-spread;
Who knew most Sentences was deepest read.   441
Faith, Gospel, all seem'd made to be disputed,
And none had sense enough to be confuted.
Scotists and Thomists[1] now in peace remain
Amidst their kindred cobwebs in Duck-lane.[2]   445
If Faith itself has diff'rent dresses worn,
What wonder modes in Wit should take their turn?
Oft, leaving what is natural and fit,
The current folly proves the ready wit;
And authors think their reputation safe,   450
Which lives as long as fools are pleas'd to laugh.

    Some, valuing those of their own side or mind,
Still make themselves the measure of mankind:
Fondly we think we honor merit then,
When we but praise ourselves in other men.   455
Parties in Wit attend on those of State,
And public faction doubles private hate.
Pride, Malice, Folly, against Dryden rose,
In various shapes of Parsons, Critics, Beaux:
But sense surviv'd when merry jests were past;
For rising merit will buoy up at last.   461
Might he return and bless once more our eyes,
New Blackmores and new Milbourns[3] must arise.
Nay, should great Homer lift his awful head,
Zoilus[4] again would start up from the dead.   465
Envy will merit as its shade pursue,
But like a shadow proves the substance true;
For envy'd Wit, like Sol eclips'd, makes known
Th' opposing body's grossness, not its own.
When first that sun too pow'rful beams displays,
It draws up vapors which obscure its rays;   471
But ev'n those clouds at last adorn its way,
Reflect new glories, and augment the day.

    [1] Disciples of Duns Scotus and Thomas Aquinas.
    [2] A place where second-hand books were sold.
    [3] Both were severe critics of Dryden.
    [4] A vitriolic critic of Homer.

Be thou the first true merit to befriend;
His praise is lost who stays till all commend. 475
Short is the date, alas, of modern rhymes,
And 'tis but just to let them live betimes.
No longer now that golden age appears,
When Patriarch-wits surviv'd a thousand years:
Now length of Fame (our second life) is lost, 480
And bare threescore is all ev'n that can boast:
Our sons their fathers' failing language see,
And such as Chaucer is shall Dryden be.
So when the faithful pencil has design'd
Some bright Idea of the master's mind, 485
Where a new world leaps out at his command,
And ready Nature waits upon his hand;
When the ripe colors soften and unite,
And sweetly melt into just shade and light;
When mellowing years their full perfection give,
And each bold figure just begins to live, 491
The treach'rous colors the fair art betray,
And all the bright creation fades away!

Unhappy Wit, like most mistaken things,
Atones not for that envy which it brings, 495
In youth alone its empty praise we boast,
But soon the short-liv'd vanity is lost;
Like some fair flow'r the early spring supplies,
That gaily blooms, but ev'n in blooming dies.
What is this Wit, which must our cares employ?
The owner's wife that other men enjoy; 501
Then most our trouble still when most admired,
And still the more we give, the more required;
Whose fame with pains we guard, but lose with
      ease,
Sure some to vex, but never all to please, 505
'Tis what the vicious fear, the virtuous shun;
By fools 'tis hated, and by knaves undone!

If Wit so much from Ign'rance undergo,
Ah, let not Learning too commence its foe!
Of old those met rewards who could excel, 510
And such were prais'd who but endeavor'd well;
Tho' triumphs were to gen'rals only due,
Crowns were reserv'd to grace the soldiers too.
Now they who reach Parnassus' lofty crown 514
Employ their pains to spurn some others down;
And while self-love each jealous writer rules,
Contending wits become the sport of fools;
But still the worst with most regret commend,
For each ill Author is as bad a Friend.
To what base ends, and by what abject ways, 520
Are mortals urg'd thro' sacred lust of praise!
Ah, ne'er so dire a thirst of glory boast,
Nor in the Critic let the Man be lost!
Good nature and good sense must ever join;
To err is human, to forgive divine. 525

But if in noble minds some dregs remain,
Not yet purg'd off, of spleen and sour disdain,
Discharge that rage on more provoking crimes,
Nor fear a dearth in these flagitious times.
No pardon vile Obscenity should find, 530
Tho' wit and art conspire to move your mind;
But Dullness with Obscenity must prove
As shameful sure as Impotence in love.
In the fat age of pleasure, wealth, and ease
Sprung the rank weed, and thriv'd with large in-
      crease: 535
When love was all an easy Monarch's care,
Seldom at council, never in a war;
Jilts rul'd the state, and statesmen farces writ;
Nay wits had pensions, and young Lords had wit:
The Fair sat panting at a Courtier's play, 540
And not a Mask went unimprov'd away;
The modest fan was lifted up no more,
And Virgins smil'd at what they blush'd before.
The following license of a Foreign reign
Did all the dregs of bold Socinus drain; 545
Then unbelieving priests reform'd the nation,
And taught more pleasant methods of salvation;
Where Heav'n's free subjects might their rights
      dispute,
Lest God himself should seem too absolute;
Pulpits their sacred satire learn'd to spare, 550
And Vice admir'd to find a flatt'rer there!
Encourag'd thus, Wit's Titans brav'd the skies,
And the press groan'd with licens'd blasphemies.
These monsters, Critics! with your darts engage,
Here point your thunder, and exhaust your rage!
Yet shun their fault, who, scandalously nice, 556
Will needs mistake an author into vice:
All seems infected that th' infected spy,
As all looks yellow to the jaundic'd eye.

PART III

Rules for the Conduct of Manners in a Critic.
1. Candor, v. 563. Modesty, v. 566. Good-breeding,
v. 572. Sincerity, and Freedom of advice, v. 578.
2. When one's Counsel is to be restrained, v. 584.
Character of an incorrigible Poet, v. 600. And of an
impertinent Critic, v. 610, *etc.* Character of a good
Critic, v. 629. The History of Criticism, and Characters
of the best Critics, Aristotle, v. 645. Horace, v. 653.
Dionysius, v. 665. Petronius, v. 667. Quintilian, v.
670. Longinus, v. 675. Of the Decay of Criticism, and
its Revival. Erasmus, v. 693. Vida, v. 705. Boileau,
v. 714. Lord Roscommon, *etc.*, v. 725. Conclusion.

Learn then what MORALS Critics ought to show,
For 'tis but half a Judge's task, to know. 561
'Tis not enough, taste, judgment, learning, join;
In all you speak, let truth and candor shine:
That not alone what to your sense is due
All may allow; but seek your friendship too. 565

Be silent always, when you doubt your sense;
And speak, tho' sure, with seeming diffidence:
Some positive, persisting fops we know,
Who if once wrong, will needs be always so;
But you, with pleasure own your errors past,   570
And make each day a Critique on the last.

'Tis not enough your counsel still be true;
Blunt truths more mischief than nice falsehoods do;
Men must be taught as if you taught them not,
And things unknown propos'd as things forgot.   575
Without Good Breeding, truth is disapprov'd;
That only makes superior sense belov'd.

Be niggards of advice on no pretence:
For the worst avarice is that of sense.
With mean complaisance ne'er betray your trust,
Nor be so civil as to prove unjust.   581
Fear not the anger of the wise to raise;
Those best can bear reproof, who merit praise.

'Twere well might Critics still this freedom take,
But Appius[1] reddens at each word you speak,   585
And stares, tremendous, with a threat'ning eye,
Like some fierce Tyrant in old tapestry.
Fear most to tax an Honorable fool,
Whose right it is, uncensur'd, to be dull;
Such, without wit, are Poets when they please, 590
As without learning they can take Degrees.
Leave dang'rous truths to unsuccessful Satires,
And flattery to fulsome Dedicators,
Whom, when they praise, the world believes no more,
Than when they promise to give scribbling o'er.
'Tis best sometimes your censure to restrain,   596
And charitably let the dull be vain:
Your silence there is better than your spite,
For who can rail so long as they can write?
Still humming on, their drowsy course they keep,
And lash'd so long, like tops, are lash'd asleep. 601
False steps but help them to renew the race,
As, after stumbling, Jades will mend their pace.
What crowds of these, impenitently bold,
In sounds and jingling syllables grown old,   605
Still run on Poets, in a raging vein,
Ev'n to the dregs and squeezings of the brain,
Strain out the last dull droppings of their sense,
And rhyme with all the rage of Impotence!

Such shameless Bards we have; and yet 'tis true,
There are as mad, abandon'd Critics too.   611
The bookful blockhead, ignorantly read,
With loads of learned lumber in his head,
With his own tongue still edifies his ears,
And always list'ning to himself appears.   615
All books he reads, and all he reads assails,
From Dryden's Fables down to D'Urfey's Tales.[2]

[1] John Dennis, who had written a play called *Appius and Virginia*.
[2] Versified tales by a particularly inept contemporary poet.

With him, most authors steal their works, or buy;
Garth did not write his own Dispensary.
Name a new Play, and he's the Poet's friend,   620
Nay show'd his faults — but when would Poets mend?
No place so sacred from such fops is barr'd,
Nor is Paul's church more safe than Paul's church yard:
Nay, fly to Altars; there they'll talk you dead;
For Fools rush in where Angels fear to tread.   625
Distrustful sense with modest caution speaks,
It still looks home, and short excursions makes;
But rattling nonsense in full volleys breaks,
And never shock'd, and never turn'd aside,
Bursts out, resistless, with a thund'ring tide. 630

But where's the man, who counsel can bestow,
Still pleas'd to teach, and yet not proud to know?
Unbiass'd, or by favor, or by spite;
Not dully prepossess'd, nor blindly right;
Tho' learn'd, well-bred; and tho' well-bred, sincere;
Modestly bold, and humanly severe: 636
Who to a friend his faults can freely show,
And gladly praise the merit of a foe?
Blest with a taste exact, yet unconfin'd;
A knowledge both of books and human kind;   640
Gen'rous converse; a soul exempt from pride;
And love to praise, with reason on his side?

Such once were Critics; such the happy few,
Athens and Rome in better ages knew.
The mighty Stagirite first left the shore,   645
Spread all his sails, and durst the deeps explore;
He steer'd securely, and discover'd far,
Led by the light of the Mæonian Star.
Poets, a race long unconfined, and free,
Still fond and proud of savage liberty,   650
Receiv'd his laws; and stood convinc'd 'twas fit,
Who conquer'd Nature, should preside o'er Wit.

Horace still charms with graceful negligence,
And without method talks us into sense,
Will, like a friend, familiarly convey   655
The truest notions in the easiest way.
He, who supreme in judgment, as in wit,
Might boldly censure, as he boldly writ,
Yet judg'd with coolness, tho' he sung with fire;
His Precepts teach but what his works inspire.   660
Our Critics take a contrary extreme,
They judge with fury, but they write with phlegm:
Nor suffers Horace more in wrong Translations
By Wits, than Critics in as wrong Quotations.

See Dionysius[1] Homer's thoughts refine,   665
And call new beauties forth from ev'ry line!

Fancy and art in gay Petronius[2] please,
The scholar's learning, with the courtier's ease.

[1] Historian and critic of the first century B.C.
[2] A Latin poet, A.D. 65.

In grave Quintilian's [1] copious work, we find
The justest rules, and clearest method join'd: 670
Thus useful arms in magazines we place,
All rang'd in order, and dispos'd with grace,
But less to please the eye, than arm the hand,
Still fit for use, and ready at command.

    Thee, bold Longinus! [2] all the Nine [3] inspire, 675
And bless their Critic with a Poet's fire.
An ardent Judge, who zealous in his trust,
With warmth gives sentence, yet is always just;
Whose own example strengthens all his laws;
And is himself that great Sublime he draws. 680

    Thus long succeeding Critics justly reign'd,
Licence repress'd, and useful laws ordain'd.
Learning and Rome alike in empire grew;
And Arts still follow'd where her Eagles flew; 684
From the same foes, at last, both felt their doom,
And the same age saw Learning fall, and Rome.
With Tyranny, then Superstition join'd,
As that the body, this enslav'd the mind;
Much was believ'd, but little understood,
And to be dull was constru'd to be good; 690
A second deluge Learning thus o'er-run,
And the Monks finish'd what the Goths begun.

    At length Erasmus,[4] that great injur'd name,
(The glory of the Priesthood, and the shame!)
Stemm'd the wild torrent of a barb'rous age, 695
And drove those holy Vandals off the stage.

    But see! each Muse, in Leo's [5] golden days,
Starts from her trance, and trims her wither'd bays;
Rome's ancient Genius, o'er its ruins spread,
Shakes off the dust, and rears his rev'rend head.
Then sculpture and her sister-arts revive; 701
Stones leap'd to form, and rocks began to live;
With sweeter notes each rising Temple rung;
A Raphael painted, and a Vida [6] sung.
Immortal Vida: on whose honor'd brow 705
The Poet's bays and Critic's ivy grow:
Cremona now shall ever boast thy name,
As next in place to Mantua, next in fame!
But soon by impious arms from Latium chas'd,
Their ancient bounds the banish'd Muses pass'd;
Thence Arts o'er all the northern world advance,
But Critic-learning flourish'd most in France; 712
The rules a nation, born to serve, obeys;
And Boileau [7] still in right of Horace sways.
But we, brave Britons, foreign laws despis'd, 715
And kept unconquer'd, and unciviliz'd;

[1] A famous Latin critic, A.D. 60.
[2] Athenian critic and philosopher, A.D. 273.
[3] Muses.
[4] Learned scholar of sixteenth century.
[5] A learned pope — about 1500.
[6] Italian poet — about 1510.
[7] French critic — died 1711.

Fierce for the liberties of wit, and bold,
We still defy'd the Romans, as of old.
Yet some there were, among the sounder few
Of those who less presum'd, and better knew, 720
Who durst assert the juster ancient cause,
And here restor'd Wit's fundamental laws.
Such was the Muse, whose rules and practice tell,
"Nature's chief Masterpiece is writing well."
Such was Roscommon,[1] not more learn'd than good,
With manners gen'rous as his noble blood; 726
To him the wit of Greece and Rome was known,
And ev'ry author's merit, but his own.
Such late was Walsh [2] — the Muse's judge and
    friends,
Who justly knew to blame or to commend; 730
To failings mild, but zealous for desert;
The clearest head, and the sincerest heart.
This humble praise, lamented shade! receive,
This praise at least a grateful Muse may give: 734
The Muse, whose early voice you taught to sing,
Prescrib'd her heights, and prun'd her tender wing,
(Her guide now lost) no more attempts to rise,
But in low numbers short excursions tries:
Content, if hence, th' unlearn'd their wants may
    view,
The learn'd reflect on what before they knew: 740
Careless of censure, nor too fond of fame;
Still pleas'd to praise, yet not afraid to blame;
Averse alike to flatter, or offend;
Not free from faults, nor yet too vain to mend.

The Rape of the Lock

An Heroi-Comical Poem

Nolueram, Belinda, tuos violare capillos;
Sed juvat, hoc precibus me tribuisse tuis.[3]
Mart. Epig., XII, 84

TO MRS.[4] ARABELLA FERMOR

Madam,
    It will be in vain to deny that I have some regard
for this piece, since I dedicate it to You. Yet you may
bear me witness, it was intended only to divert a few
young Ladies, who have good sense and good humor
enough to laugh not only at their sex's little unguarded
follies, but at their own. But as it was communicated

[1] Seventeenth-century English scholar who had a
plan for fixing the English language.
[2] Walsh had helped Pope with advice toward his
writing career.
[3] I did not want, Belinda, to violate your locks, but
it is pleasure to pay this tribute to your entreaties.
[4] "*Mrs.*" in the days of Pope was used to designate
unmarried as well as married women.

with the air of a Secret, it soon found its way into the world. An imperfect copy having been offered to a Bookseller, you had the good nature for my sake to consent to the publication of one more correct: This I was forced to, before I had executed half my design, for the Machinery was entirely wanting to complete it.

The Machinery, Madam, is a term invented by the Critics, to signify that part which the Deities, Angels, or Demons are made to act in a Poem: For the ancient Poets are in one respect like many modern Ladies: let an action be never so trivial in itself, they always make it appear of the utmost importance. These Machines I determined to raise on a very new and odd foundation, the Rosicrucian doctrine of Spirits.

I know how disagreeable it is to make use of hard words before a Lady; but 'tis so much the concern of a Poet to have his works understood, and particularly by your Sex, that you must give me leave to explain two or three difficult terms.

The Rosicrucians are a people I must bring you acquainted with. The best account I know of them is in a French book called *Le Comte de Gabalis*, which both in its title and size is so like a Novel, that many of the Fair Sex have read it for one by mistake. According to these Gentlemen, the four Elements are inhabited by Spirits, which they call Sylphs, Gnomes, Nymphs, and Salamanders. The Gnomes or Demons of Earth delight in mischief; but the Sylphs, whose habitation is in the Air, are the best-conditioned creatures imaginable. For, they say, any mortals may enjoy the most intimate familiarities with these gentle Spirits, upon a condition very easy to all true Adepts, an inviolate preservation of Chastity.

As to the following Cantos, all the passages of them are as fabulous as the Vision at the beginning, or the Transformation at the end (except the loss of your Hair, which I always mention with reverence). The Human persons are as fictitious as the airy ones; and the character of Belinda, as it is now managed, resembles you in nothing but in Beauty.

If this Poem had as many Graces as there are in your Person, or in your Mind, yet I could never hope it should pass through the world half so Uncensured as You have done. But let its fortune be what it will, mine is happy enough, to have given me this occasion of assuring you that I am, with the truest esteem, MADAM,

Your most obedient, Humble Servant,

A. Pope

CANTO I

What dire offence from amorous causes springs,
What mighty contests rise from trivial things,
I sing — This verse to *Caryll*,[1] muse! is due:
This, even Belinda may vouchsafe to view:
Slight is the subject, but not so the praise,   5
If she inspire, and he approve my lays.
  Say what strange motive, Goddess! could compel
A well-bred Lord to assault a gentle Belle?

[1] John Caryll, a friend of Pope.

O say what stranger cause, yet unexplored,
Could make a gentle Belle reject a Lord?   10
In tasks so bold can little men engage,
And in soft bosoms dwells such mighty rage?
  Sol thro' white curtains shot a tim'rous ray,
And oped those eyes that must eclipse the day.
Now lapdogs give themselves the rousing shake,   15
And sleepless lovers just at twelve awake:
Thrice rung the bell, the slipper knocked the
        ground,
And the pressed watch returned a silver sound.
Belinda still her downy pillow prest,
Her guardian Sylph prolonged the balmy rest.   20
'Twas he had summoned to her silent bed
The morning-dream that hovered o'er her head;
A youth more glittering than a Birthnight Beau [1]
(That even in slumber caused her cheek to glow)
Seemed to her ear his winning lips to lay,   25
And thus in whispers said, or seemed to say:
  "Fairest of mortals, thou distinguished care
Of thousand bright Inhabitants of Air!
If e'er one vision touched thy infant thought,
Of all the nurse and all the priest have taught —
Of airy elves by moonlight shadows seen,   31
The silver token, and the circled green,
Or virgins visited by Angel-powers,
With golden crowns and wreaths of heavenly flow-
        ers;
Hear and believe! thy own importance know,   35
Nor bound thy narrow views to things below.
Some secret truths, from learned pride concealed,
To maids alone and children are revealed:
What tho' no credit doubting Wits may give?
The fair and innocent shall still believe.   40
Know, then, unnumbered Spirits round thee fly,
The light militia of the lower sky.
These, tho' unseen, are ever on the wing,
Hang o'er the Box, and hover round the Ring.[2]
Think what an equipage thou hast in air,   45
And view with scorn two pages and a chair.
As now your own, our beings were of old,
And once inclosed in woman's beauteous mold;
Thence, by a soft transition, we repair
From earthly vehicles to these of air.   50
Think not, when woman's transient breath is
        fled,
That all her vanities at once are dead;
Succeeding vanities she still regards,
And, tho' she plays no more, o'erlooks the cards.
Her joy in gilded chariots, when alive,   55
And love of Ombre,[3] after death survive.
For when the Fair in all their pride expire,
To their first elements their souls retire.

[1] A gentleman ready to attend a court celebration.
[2] Hyde Park circus, a riding place.
[3] A card game.

The sprites of fiery termagants in flame
Mount up, and take a Salamander's name. 60
Soft yielding minds to water glide away,
And sip, with Nymphs, their elemental tea.
The graver prude sinks downward to a Gnome
In search of mischief still on earth to roam.
The light coquettes in Sylphs aloft repair, 65
And sport and flutter in the fields of air.
   "Know further yet: whoever fair and chaste
Rejects mankind, is by some Sylph embraced;
For spirits, freed from mortal laws, with ease
Assume what sexes and what shapes they please.
What guards the purity of melting maids, 71
In courtly balls, and midnight masquerades,
Safe from the treacherous friend, the daring spark,
The glance by day, the whisper in the dark;
When kind occasion prompts their warm desires, 75
When music softens, and when dancing fires?
'Tis but their Sylph, the wise Celestials know,
Tho' Honor is the word with men below.
   "Some nymphs there are, too conscious of their
      face,
For life predestined to the Gnome's embrace. 80
These swell their prospects and exalt their pride,
When offers are disdained, and love denied:
Then gay ideas crowd the vacant brain,
While peers, and dukes, and all their sweeping
      train,
And garters, stars, and coronets appear, 85
And in soft sounds, "Your Grace" salutes their
      ear.
'Tis these that early taint the female soul,
Instruct the eyes of young coquettes to roll,
Teach infant cheeks a bidden blush to know,
And little hearts to flutter at a Beau. 90
   "Oft, when the world imagine women stray,
The Sylphs thro' mystic mazes guide their way;
Thro' all the giddy circle they pursue,
And old impertinence expel by new.
What tender maid but must a victim fall 95
To one man's treat, but for another's ball?
When Florio speaks, what virgin could withstand,
If gentle Damon did not squeeze her hand?
With varying vanities, from every part,
They shift the moving toyshop of their heart; 100
Where wigs with wigs, with sword-knots sword-
      knots strive,
Beaux banish beaux, and coaches coaches drive.
This erring mortals levity may call;
Oh blind to truth! the Sylphs contrive it all.
   "Of these am I, who thy protection claim, 105
A watchful sprite, and Ariel is my name.
Late, as I ranged the crystal wilds of air,
In the clear mirror of thy ruling star
I saw, alas! some dread event impend,
Ere to the main this morning sun descend, 110

But Heaven reveals not what, or how or where.
Warned by the Sylph, O pious maid, beware!
This to disclose is all thy guardian can:
Beware of all, but most beware of Man!"
   He said; when Shock,[1] who thought she slept too
      long, 115
Leaped up, and waked his mistress with his tongue.
'Twas then, Belinda, if report say true,
Thy eyes first opened on a billet-doux;
Wounds, charms, and ardors were no sooner read,
But all the vision vanished from thy head. 120
   And now, unveiled, the toilet stands displayed,
Each silver vase in mystic order laid.
First, robed in white, the nymph intent adores,
With head uncovered, the cosmetic powers.
A heavenly image in the glass appears; 125
To that she bends, to that her eyes she rears.
Th' inferior priestess, at her altar's side,
Trembling begins the sacred rites of Pride.
Unnumbered treasures ope at once, and here
The various offerings of the world appear; 130
From each she nicely culls with curious toil,
And decks the Goddess with the glittering spoil.
This casket India's glowing gems unlocks,
And all Arabia breathes from yonder box.
The tortoise here and elephant unite, 135
Transformed to combs, the speckled, and the
      white.
Here files of pins extend their shining rows,
Puffs, powders, patches, bibles, billet-doux.
Now awful beauty puts on all its arms;
The Fair each moment rises in her charms, 140
Repairs her smiles, awakens every grace,
And calls forth all the wonders of her face;
Sees by degrees a purer blush arise,
And keener lightnings quicken in her eyes.
The busy Sylphs surround their darling care, 145
These set the head, and those divide the hair,
Some fold the sleeve, whilst others plait the gown;
And Betty's[2] praised for labors not her own.

CANTO II

Not with more glories, in th' ethereal plain,
The sun first rises o'er the purpled main,
Than, issuing forth, the rival of his beams
Launched on the bosom of the silver Thames.
Fair nymphs, and well-dressed youths around her
      shone, 5
But every eye was fixed on her alone.
On her white breast a sparkling cross she wore,
Which Jews might kiss, and infidels adore.
Her lively looks a sprightly mind disclose,
Quick as her eyes, and as unfixed as those: 10
Favors to none, to all she smiles extends;
Oft she rejects, but never once offends.

   [1] A lap-dog.   [2] Belinda's maid.

Bright as the sun, her eyes the gazers strike,
And, like the sun, they shine on all alike.
Yet graceful ease, and sweetness void of pride,   15
Might hide her faults, if belles had faults to hide;
If to her share some female errors fall,
Look on her face, and you'll forget 'em all.

This nymph, to the destruction of mankind,
Nourished two locks, which graceful hung behind
In equal curls, and well conspired to deck   21
With shining ringlets the smooth ivory neck.
Love in these labyrinths his slaves detains,
And mighty hearts are held in slender chains.
With hairy springes we the birds betray,   25
Slight lines of hair surprise the finny prey,
Fair tresses man's imperial race ensnare,
And beauty draws us with a single hair.

Th' adventurous Baron the bright locks admired;
He saw, he wished, and to the prize aspired.   30
Resolved to win, he meditates the way,
By force to ravish, or by fraud betray;
For when success a lover's toil attends,
Few ask if fraud or force attained his ends.

For this, ere Phœbus rose, he had implored   35
Propitious Heaven, and every Power adored,
But chiefly Love — to Love an altar built
Of twelve vast French romances, neatly gilt.
There lay three garters, half a pair of gloves,
And all the trophies of his former loves;   40
With tender billet-doux he lights the pyre,
And breathes three amorous sighs to raise the fire.
Then prostrate falls, and begs with ardent eyes
Soon to obtain, and long possess the prize:
The Powers gave ear, and granted half his prayer,
The rest the winds dispersed in empty air.   46

But now secure the painted vessel glides,
The sunbeams trembling on the floating tides;
While melting music steals upon the sky,
And softened sounds along the waters die: 50
Smooth flow the waves, the zephyrs gently play,
Belinda smiled, and all the world was gay.
All but the Sylph — with careful thoughts opprest
Th' impending woe sat heavy on his breast.
He summons straight his denizens of air;   55
The lucid squadrons round the sails repair:
Soft o'er the shrouds aërial whispers breathe
That seemed but zephyrs to the train beneath.
Some to the sun their insect-wings unfold,
Waft on the breeze, or sink in clouds of gold;   60
Transparent forms too fine for mortal sight,
Their fluid bodies half dissolved in light,
Loose to the wind their airy garments flew,
Thin glittering textures of the filmy dew,
Dipt in the richest tincture of the skies,   65
Where light disports in ever-mingling dyes,
While every beam new transient colors flings,

Colors that change whene'er they wave their wings.
Amid the circle, on the gilded mast,
Superior by the head was Ariel placed;   70
His purple pinions opening to the sun,
He raised his azure wand, and thus begun:

"Ye Sylphs and Sylphids, to your chief give ear.
Fays, Fairies, Genii, Elves, and Dæmons, hear!
Ye know the spheres and various tasks assigned   75
By laws eternal to th' aërial kind.
Some in the fields of purest ether play,
And bask and whiten in the blaze of day:
Some guide the course of wandering orbs on high,
Or roll the planets thro' the boundless sky: 80
Some, less refined, beneath the moon's pale light
Pursue the stars that shoot athwart the night,
Or suck the mists in grosser air below,
Or dip their pinions in the painted bow,
Or brew fierce tempests on the wintry main,   85
Or o'er the glebe [1] distil the kindly rain.
Others, on earth, o'er human race preside,
Watch all their ways, and all their actions guide:
Of these the chief the care of nations own,
And guard with arms divine the British Throne.   90

"Our humbler province is to tend the Fair,
Not a less pleasing, tho' less glorious care;
To save the Powder from too rude a gale;
Nor let th' imprisoned Essences exhale;
To draw fresh colors from the vernal flowers;   95
To steal from rainbows ere they drop in showers
A brighter Wash; to curl their waving hairs,
Assist their blushes and inspire their airs;
Nay oft, in dreams invention we bestow,
To change a Flounce, or add a Furbelow.   100

"This day black omens threat the brightest Fair,
That e'er deserved a watchful spirit's care;
Some dire disaster, or by force or slight;
But what, or where, the Fates have wrapt in night.
Whether the nymph shall break Diana's law, [2]   105
Or some frail China jar receive a flaw;
Or stain her honor, or her new brocade,
Forget her prayers, or miss a masquerade,
Or lose her heart, or necklace, at a ball;
Or whether Heaven has doomed that Shock must fall.   110
Haste, then, ye Spirits! to your charge repair:
The fluttering fan be Zephyretta's care;
The drops to thee, Brillante, we consign;
And, Momentilla, let the watch be thine;
Do thou, Crispissa, tend her favorite Lock;   115
Ariel himself shall be the guard of Shock.

"To fifty chosen sylphs, of special note,
We trust th' important charge, the petticoat;
Oft have we known that seven-fold fence to fail,
Tho' stiff with hoops, and armed with ribs of whale.   120

[1] land.   [2] Of chastity.

Form a strong line about the silver bound,
And guard the wide circumference around.

"Whatever spirit, careless of his charge,
His post neglects, or leaves the Fair at large,
Shall feel sharp vengeance soon o'ertake his sins:
Be stopped in vials, or transfixed with pins,   126
Or plunged in lakes of bitter washes lie,
Or wedged whole ages in a bodkin's eye;
Gums and pomatums shall his flight restrain,
While clogged he beats his silken wings in vain, 130
Or alum styptics with contracting power
Shrink his thin essence like a rivelled [1] flower:
Or, as Ixion [2] fixed, the wretch shall feel
The giddy motion of the whirling mill,
In fumes of burning chocolate shall glow,   135
And tremble at the sea that froths below!"

He spoke; the spirits from the sails descend;
Some, orb in orb, around the nymph extend;
Some thread the mazy ringlets of her hair;
Some hang upon the pendants of her ear;   140
With beating hearts the dire event they wait,
Anxious, and trembling for the birth of Fate.

CANTO III

Close by those meads, for ever crowned with flow-
     ers,
Where Thames with pride surveys his rising towers
There stands a structure of majestic frame,
Which from the neighboring Hampton takes its
     name.[3]
Here Britain's statesmen oft the fall foredoom   5
Of foreign tyrants, and of nymphs at home;
Here, thou, great ANNA! whom three realms obey,
Dost sometimes counsel take — and sometimes tea.

Hither the Heroes and the Nymphs resort,
To taste awhile the pleasures of a court;   10
In various talk th' instructive hours they past,
Who gave the ball, or paid the visit last;
One speaks the glory of the British Queen,
And one describes a charming Indian screen;
A third interprets motions, looks, and eyes;   15
At every word a reputation dies.
Snuff, or the fan, supply each pause of chat,
With singing, laughing, ogling, *and all that*.

Meanwhile, declining from the noon of day,
The sun obliquely shoots his burning ray;   20
The hungry judges soon the sentence sign,
And wretches hang that jurymen may dine;
The merchant from th' Exchange returns in peace,
And the long labors of the toilet cease.
Belinda now, whom thirst of fame invites,   25
Burns to encounter two adventurous knights,

[1] shriveled.
[2] By way of punishment Ixion was fastened to the
spokes of a constantly revolving wheel.
[3] Hampton Court, a Royal Palace.

At Ombre singly to decide their doom,
And swells her breast with conquests yet to come.
Straight the three bands prepare in arms to join,
Each band the number of the sacred Nine.   30
Soon as she spreads her hand, th' aërial guard
Descend, and sit on each important card:
First Ariel perched upon a Matadore,[1]
Then each according to the rank they bore;
For Sylphs, yet mindful of their ancient race,   35
Are, as when women, wondrous fond of place.

Behold four Kings in majesty revered,
With hoary whiskers and a forky beard;
And four fair Queens, whose hands sustain a flower,
Th' expressive emblem of their softer power;   40
Four Knaves, in garbs succinct,[2] a trusty-band,
Caps on their heads, and halberts in their hand;
And party-colored troops, a shining train,
Draw forth to combat on the velvet plain.

The skilful nymph reviews her force with care;
"Let Spades be trumps!" she said, and trumps
     they were.   46
Now move to war her sable Matadores,
In show like leaders of the swarthy Moors.
Spadillio [3] first, unconquerable lord!
Led off two captive trumps, and swept the board.
As many more Manillio [3] forced to yield,   51
And marched a victor from the verdant field.
Him Basto [3] followed, but his fate more hard
Gained but one trump and one plebeian card.
With his broad sabre next, a chief in years,   55
The hoary Majesty of Spades appears,
Puts forth one manly leg, to sight revealed;
The rest his many colored robe concealed.[4]
The rebel Knave, who dares his prince engage,
Proves the just victim of his royal rage.   60
Even mighty Pam,[5] that kings and queens o'er-
     threw,
And mowed down armies in the fights of Loo,[5]

[1] The three high cards in ombre were given this name.
[2] Neatly fitted.
[3] The names suggest clearly enough that the game of
ombre (from *l'hombre* or "the man") reached London
by way of Spain. Usually played by three people, the
game was one in which each player was dealt nine cards,
the ombre playing against the other two and having
the privilege of declaring the trump. If either of the
two took more tricks than the ombre, "codille" was
called, the winner taking the stake and the ombre being
required to provide the stake for the next deal. The
three "best" cards were the matadores. They were
"Spadillio" (the ace of spades), "Manillio" (the two
of trumps when trump was a black suit or the seven of
trumps when trump was a red suit), and "Basto"
(the ace of clubs).
[4] Cards in Belinda's day portrayed what we now call
the "face cards" at full length.
[5] The knave of clubs was the ranking card in the game
of loo.

Sad chance of war! now destitute of aid,
Falls undistinguished by the victor Spade.
    Thus far both armies to Belinda yield;   65
Now to the Baron Fate inclines the field.
His warlike amazon her host invades,
Th' imperial consort of the crown of Spades.
The Club's black tyrant first her victim died,
Spite of his haughty mien and barbarous pride: 70
What boots the regal circle on his head,
His giant limbs, in state unwieldy spread;
That long behind he trails his pompous robe,
And of all monarchs only grasps the globe?
    The Baron now his Diamonds pours apace; 75
Th' embroidered King who shows but half his face,
And his refulgent Queen, with powers combined,
Of broken troops an easy conquest find.
Clubs, Diamonds, Hearts, in wild disorder seen,
With throngs promiscuous strew the level green. 80
Thus when dispersed a routed army runs,
Of Asia's troops, and Afric's sable sons,
With like confusion different nations fly,
Of various habit, and of various dye;
The pierced battalions disunited fall   85
In heaps on heaps; one fate o'erwhelms them all.
    The Knave of Diamonds tries his wily arts,
And wins (oh shameful chance!) the Queen of
      Hearts.
At this, the blood the virgin's cheek forsook,
A livid paleness spreads o'er all her look; 90
She sees, and trembles at th' approaching ill,
Just in the jaws of ruin, and Codille.
And now (as oft in some distempered state)
On one nice trick depends the general fate!
An Ace of Hearts steps forth: the King unseen 95
Lurked in her hand, and mourned his captive
      Queen.
He springs to vengeance with an eager pace,
And falls like thunder on the prostrate Ace.
The nymph, exulting, fills with shouts the sky;
The walls, the woods, and long canals reply. 100
    Oh thoughtless mortals! ever blind to fate,
Too soon dejected, and too soon elate.
Sudden these honors shall be snatched away.
And cursed for ever this victorious day.
    For lo! the board with cups and spoons is
      crowned,   105
The berries [1] crackle, and the mill turns round;
On shining altars of japan they raise
The silver lamp; the fiery spirits blaze:
From silver spouts the grateful liquors glide,
While China's earth receives the smoking tide. 110
At once they gratify their scent and taste,
And frequent cups prolong the rich repast.

[1] Coffee was ground as well as prepared before the
guests.

Straight hover round the Fair her airy band;
Some, as she sipped, the fuming liquor fanned,
Some o'er her lap their careful plumes displayed,
Trembling, and conscious of the rich brocade. 116
Coffee (which makes the politician wise,
And see thro' all things with his half-shut eyes)
Sent up in vapors to the Baron's brain
New stratagems, the radiant Lock to gain.   120
Ah, cease, rash youth! desist ere 'tis too late,
Fear the just Gods, and think of Scylla's fate!
Changed to a bird, and sent to flit in air,
She dearly pays for Nisus' [1] injured hair!
    But when to mischief mortals bend their will,
How soon they find fit instruments of ill!   126
Just then, Clarissa drew with tempting grace
A two-edged weapon from her shining case:
So ladies in romance assist their knight,
Present the spear, and arm him for the fight. 130
He takes the gift with reverence, and extends
The little engine on his fingers' ends;
This just behind Belinda's neck he spread,
As o'er the fragrant streams she bends her head.
Swift to the Lock a thousand sprites repair; 135
A thousand wings, by turns, blow back the hair;
And thrice they twitched the diamond in her ear;
Thrice she looked back, and thrice the foe drew
      near.
Just in that instant, anxious Ariel sought
The close recesses of the virgin's thought.   140
As on the nosegay in her breast reclined,
He watched th' ideas rising in her mind,
Sudden he viewed, in spite of all her art,
An earthly Lover lurking at her heart.
Amazed, confused, he found his power expired, 145
Resigned to fate, and with a sigh retired.
    The Peer now spreads the glittering forfex wide,
To inclose the Lock; now joins it, to divide.
Even then, before the fatal engine closed,
A wretched Sylph too fondly interposed;   150
Fate urged the shears, and cut the Sylph in twain
(But airy substance soon united again).
The meeting points the sacred hair dissever
From the fair head, for ever, and for ever!
    Then flashed the living lightning from her eyes,
And screams of horror rend th' affrighted skies. 156
Not louder shrieks to pitying Heaven are cast,
When husbands, or when lapdogs breathe their
      last;
Or when rich China vessels, fallen from high,
In glittering dust and painted fragments lie! 160

[1] Scylla cut off a purple lock from the hair of King
Nisus, her father, that King Minos whom she loved
might conquer her father. She was turned into a bird
constantly chased by her father who had taken the
form of a sea-eagle. The story is told in Ovid's *Metamorphosis* viii.

"Let wreaths of triumph now my temples twine,"
The Victor cried, "the glorious prize is mine!
While fish in streams, or birds delight in air,
Or in a coach and six the British Fair,
As long as Atalantis [1] shall be read,   165
Or the small pillow grace a lady's bed,
While visits shall be paid on solemn days,
When numerous wax-lights in bright order blaze:
While nymphs take treats, or assignations give,
So long my honor, name, and praise shall live!   170
What Time would spare, from Steel receives its
     date,
And monuments, like men, submit to Fate!
Steel could the labor of the Gods destroy,
And strike to dust th' imperial towers of Troy;
Steel could the works of mortal pride confound   175
And hew triumphal arches to the ground.
What wonder, then, fair Nymph! thy hairs should
     feel
The conquering force of unresisted steel?"

CANTO IV

But anxious cares the pensive nymph opprest,
And secret passions labored in her breast.
Not youthful kings in battle seized alive,
Not scornful virgins who their charms survive,
Not ardent lovers robbed of all their bliss,   5
Not ancient ladies when refused a kiss,
Not tyrants fierce that unrepenting die,
Not Cynthia when her mantua's pinned awry,
E'er felt such rage, resentment, and despair,
As thou, said Virgin! for thy ravished hair.   10
   For, that sad moment, when the Sylphs with-
        drew,
And Ariel weeping from Belinda flew,
Umbriel, a dusky, melancholy sprite
As ever sullied the fair face of light,
Down to the central earth, his proper scene,   15
Repaired to search the gloomy cave of Spleen.[2]
   Swift on his sooty pinions flits the Gnome,
And in a vapor reached the dismal dome.
No cheerful breeze this sullen region knows,
The dreaded East is all the wind that blows.   20
Here in a grotto sheltered close from air,
And screened in shades from day's detested glare,
She sighs for ever on her pensive bed,
Pain at her side, and Megrim [3] at her head.
Two handmaids wait the throne; alike in place,   25
But differing far in figure and in face.
Here stood Ill-nature, like an ancient maid,
Her wrinkled form in black and white arrayed!

[1] A contemporary volume of scandal widely read.
It was written by a Mrs. Manley and called *The New Atalantis*.
[2] The seat of ill-temper and depression.
[3] Migraine or headache.

With store of prayers for mornings, nights, and
     noons,
Her hand is filled; her bosom with lampoons.   30
There Affectation, with a sickly mien,
Shows in her cheek the roses of eighteen,
Practised to lisp, and hang the head aside,
Faints into airs, and languishes with pride;
On the rich quilt sinks with becoming woe,   35
Wrapt in a gown for sickness and for show.
The fair ones feel such maladies as these,
When each new night-dress gives a new disease.
   A constant vapor o'er the palace flies
Strange phantoms rising as the mists arise;   40
Dreadful as hermits' dreams in haunted shades,
Or bright as visions of expiring maids:
Now glaring fiends, and snakes on rolling spires,
Pale spectres, gaping tombs, and purple fires;
Now lakes of liquid gold, Elysian scenes,   45
And crystal domes, and angels in machines.[1]
   Unnumbered throngs on every side are seen,
Of bodies changed to various forms by Spleen.
Here living Teapots stand, one arm held out,
One bent; the handle this, and that the spout: 50
A Pipkin [2] there, like Homer's Tripod [3] walks;
Here sighs a Jar, and there a Goose-pie talks;
Men prove with child, as powerful fancy works,
And maids turned bottles call aloud for corks.
   Safe passed the Gnome thro' this fantastic band,
A branch of healing spleenwort in his hand.   56
Then thus addressed the Power — "Hail, wayward
     Queen!
Who rule the sex to fifty from fifteen:
Parent of Vapors and of female wit,
Who give th' hysteric or poetic fit,   60
On various tempers act by various ways,
Make some take physic, others scribble plays;
Who cause the proud their visits to delay,
And send the godly in a pet to pray.
A nymph there is that all your power disdains,   65
And thousands more in equal mirth maintains.
But oh! if e'er thy Gnome could spoil a grace,
Or raise a pimple on a beauteous face,
Like citron-waters matrons' cheeks inflame,
Or change complexions at a losing game;   70
If e'er with airy horns I planted heads,
Or rumpled petticoats, or tumbled beds,
Or caused suspicion when no soul was rude,
Or discomposed the head-dress of a prude,
Or e'er to costive lapdog gave disease,   75
Which not the tears of brightest eyes could ease,

[1] Deus ex machina.   [2] Small earthenware jar.
[3] According to Homer's *Iliad*, Vulcan made twenty
tripods which he placed on golden wheels and which
then moved about the hall according to the wish of
the gods — much as a modern machine might progress
under remote control.

Hear me, and touch Belinda with chagrin;
That single act gives half the world the spleen."
   The Goddess, with a discontented air,
Seems to reject him tho' she grants his prayer. 80
A wondrous Bag with both her hands she binds,
Like that where once Ulysses held the winds;
There she collects the force of female lungs,
Sighs, sobs, and passions, and the war of tongues.
A Vial next she fills with fainting fears,   85
Soft sorrows, melting griefs, and flowing tears.
The Gnome rejoicing bears her gifts away,
Spreads his black wings, and slowly mounts to day.
   Sunk in Thalestris'[1] arms the nymph he found,
Her eyes dejected, and her hair unbound.   90
Full o'er their heads the swelling Bag he rent,
And all the Furies issued at the vent.
Belinda burns with more than mortal ire,
And fierce Thalestris fans the rising fire.
"O wretched maid!" she spread her hands, and
     cried,   95
(While Hampton's echoes, "Wretched maid!" re-
     plied),
"Was it for this you took such constant care
The bodkin, comb, and essence to prepare?
For this your locks in paper durance bound?
For this with torturing irons wreathed around? 100
For this with fillets strained your tender head,
And bravely bore the double loads of lead?
Gods! shall the ravisher display your hair,
While the fops envy, and the ladies stare!
Honor forbid! at whose unrivalled shrine   105
Ease, Pleasure, Virtue, all, our sex resign.
Methinks already I your tears survey,
Already hear the horrid things they say,
Already see you a degraded toast,
And all your honor in a whisper lost!   110
How shall I, then, your hapless fame defend?
'Twill then be infamy to seem your friend!
And shall this prize, th' inestimable prize,
Exposed thro' crystal to the gazing eyes,
And heightened by the diamond's circling rays, 115
On that rapacious hand for ever blaze?
Sooner shall grass in Hyde Park Circus grow,
And Wits take lodgings in the sound of Bow,[2]
Sooner let earth, air, sea, to chaos fall,
Men, monkeys, lapdogs, parrots, perish all!" 120
   She said; then raging to Sir Plume repairs,
And bids her Beau demand the precious hairs
(Sir Plume, of amber snuff-box justly vain,
And the nice conduct of a clouded cane):
With earnest eyes, and round unthinking face,
He first the snuff-box opened, then the case, 126

[1] One of the Amazons.
[2] Bow bells, in a quarter of London where no fashionable wit would live.

And thus broke out — "My lord, why, what the
     devil!
Z — ds! damn the Lock! 'fore Gad, you must be
     civil!
Plague on 't! 'tis past a jest — nay, prithee, pox!
Give her the hair." — He spoke, and rapped his
     box.   130
   "It grieves me much," replied the Peer again,
"Who speaks so well should ever speak in vain:
But by this Lock, this sacred Lock, I swear
(Which never more shall join its parted hair;
Which never more its honors shall renew,   135
Clipped from the lovely head where late it grew),
That, while my nostrils draw the vital air,
This hand, which won it, shall for ever wear."
He spoke, and speaking, in proud triumph spread
The long-contended honors of her head.   140
   But Umbriel, hateful Gnome, forbears not so;
He breaks the Vial whence the sorrows flow.
Then see! the nymph in beauteous grief appears,
Her eyes half-languishing, half drowned in tears;
On her heaved bosom hung her drooping head, 145
Which with a sigh she raised, and thus she said:
   "For ever cursed be this detested day,
Which snatched my best, my favorite curl away!
Happy! ah, ten times happy had I been,
If Hampton Court these eyes had never seen! 150
Yet am not I the first mistaken maid,
By love of courts to numerous ills betrayed.
O had I rather unadmired remained
In some lone isle, or distant northern land;
Where the gilt chariot never marks the way, 155
Where none learn Ombre, none e'er taste Bohea!
There kept my charms concealed from mortal
     eye,
Like roses, that in deserts bloom and die.
What moved my mind with youthful lords to
     roam?
O had I stayed, and said my prayers at home; 160
'Twas this the morning omens seemed to tell,
Thrice from my trembling hand the patch-box
     fell;
The tottering china shook without a wind;
Nay, Poll sat mute, and Shock was most unkind!
A Sylph, too, warned me of the threats of fate, 165
In mystic visions, now believed too late!
See the poor remnants of these slighted hairs!
My hands shall rend what even thy rapine spares.
These, in two sable ringlets taught to break,
Once gave new beauties to the snowy neck; 170
The sister-lock now sits uncouth alone,
And in its fellow's fate foresees its own;
Uncurled it hangs, the fatal shears demands,
And tempts once more thy sacrilegious hands.
O hadst thou, cruel! been content to seize 175
Hairs less in sight, or any hairs but these!"

CANTO V

She said: the pitying audience melt in tears;
But Fate and Jove had stopped the Baron's ears.
In vain Thalestris with reproach assails,
For who can move when fair Belinda fails?
Not half so fixed the Trojan [1] could remain,   5
While Anna begged and Dido raged in vain;
Then grave Clarissa graceful waved her fan;
Silence ensued, and thus the nymph began:
    "Say, why are beauties praised and honored
        most,
The wise man's passion, and the vain man's toast?
Why decked with all that land and sea afford,   11
Why angels called, and angel-like adored?
Why round our coaches crowd the white-gloved
        beaux?
Why bows the side-box from its inmost rows?
How vain are all these glories, all our pains,   15
Unless Good Sense preserve what Beauty gains;
That men may say when we the front-box grace,
'Behold the first in virtue as in face!'
Oh! if to dance all night, and dress all day,
Charmed the smallpox, or chased old age away;   20
Who would not scorn what housewife's cares pro-
        duce,
Or who would learn one earthly thing of use?
To patch, nay, ogle, might become a saint,
Nor could it sure be such a sin to paint.
But since, alas! frail beauty must decay,   25
Curled or uncurled, since locks will turn to gray;
Since painted, or not painted, all shall fade,
And she who scorns a man must die a maid;
What then remains, but well our power to use,
And keep good humor still whate'er we lose?   30
And trust me, dear, good humor can prevail,
When airs, and flights, and screams, and scolding
        fail.
Beauties in vain their pretty eyes may roll;
Charms strike the sight, but merit wins the soul."
    So spoke the dame, but no applause ensued;   35
Belinda frowned, Thalestris called her prude.
"To arms, to arms!" the fierce virago cries,
And swift as lightning to the combat flies.
All side in parties, and begin th' attack;
Fans clap, silks rustle, and tough whalebones
        crack;   40
Heroes' and heroines' shouts confusedly rise,
And bass and treble voices strike the skies.
No common weapons in their hands are found,
Like Gods they fight nor dread a mortal wound.
    So when bold Homer makes the Gods engage,   45
And heavenly breasts with human passions rage;
'Gainst Pallas, Mars; Latona, Hermes arms;
And all Olympus rings with loud alarms;

[1] Æneas, who deserted Dido.

Jove's thunder roars, Heaven trembles all around,
Blue Neptune storms, the bellowing deeps re-
        sound: 50
Earth shakes her nodding towers, the ground gives
        way,
And the pale ghosts start at the flash of day!
    Triumphant Umbriel, on a sconce's height,
Clapped his glad wings, and sat to view the fight:
Propped on their bodkin-spears, the sprites sur-
        vey   55
The growing combat, or assist the fray.
    While thro' the press enraged Thalestris flies,
And scatters death around from both her eyes,
A Beau and Witling perished in the throng,
One died in metaphor, and one in song: 60
"O cruel Nymph! a living death I bear,"
Cried Dapperwit, and sunk beside his chair.
A mournful glance Sir Fopling upwards cast,
"Those eyes are made so killing" — was his
        last.
Thus on Mæander's flowery margin lies   65
Th' expiring swan, and as he sings he dies.
    When bold Sir Plume had drawn Clarissa down,
Chloe stepped in, and killed him with a frown;
She smiled to see the doughty hero slain,
But, at her smile, the beau revived again.   70
Now Jove suspends his golden scales in air,
Weighs the men's wits against the lady's hair;
The doubtful beam long nods from side to side;
At length the wits mount up, the hairs subside.
    See fierce Belinda on the Baron flies,   75
With more than usual lightning in her eyes;
Nor feared the chief th' unequal fight to try,
Who sought no more than on his foe to die.
But this bold lord, with manly strength endued,
She with one finger and a thumb subdued: 80
Just where the breath of life his nostrils drew,
A charge of snuff the wily virgin threw;
The Gnomes direct, to every atom just,
The pungent grains of titillating dust.
Sudden, with starting tears each eye o'erflows,   85
And the high dome reëchoes to his nose.
    "Now meet thy fate," incensed Belinda cried,
And drew a deadly bodkin from her side.
(The same, his ancient personage to deck,
Her great-great-grandsire wore about his neck,   90
In three seal-rings; which after, melted down,
Formed a vast buckle for his widow's gown:
Her infant grandame's whistle next it grew,
The bells she jingled, and the whistle blew;
Then in a bodkin graced her mother's hairs,   95
Which long she wore and now Belinda wears.)
    "Boast not my fall," he cried, "insulting foe!
Thou by some other shalt be laid as low;
Nor think to die dejects my lofty mind:
All that I dread is leaving you behind!   100

Rather than so, ah, let me still survive,
And burn in Cupid's flames — but burn alive."
"Restore the Lock!" she cries; and all around
"Restore the Lock!" the vaulted roofs rebound.
Not fierce Othello in so loud a strain   105
Roared for the handkerchief that caused his pain.
But see how oft ambitious aims are crossed,
And chiefs contend till all the prize is lost!
The lock, obtained with guilt, and kept with pain,
In every place is sought, but sought in vain: 110
With such a prize no mortal must be blest.
So Heaven decrees! with Heaven who can contest?
   Some thought it mounted to the lunar sphere,
Since all things lost on earth are treasured there.
There heroes' wits are kept in ponderous vases, 115
And beaux' in snuffboxes and tweezer-cases.
There broken vows, and deathbed alms are found,
And lovers' hearts with ends of riband bound,
The courtier's promises, and sick man's prayers,
The smiles of harlots, and the tears of heirs,   120
Cages for gnats, and chains to yoke a flea,
Dried butterflies, and tomes of casuistry.
   But trust the Muse — she saw it upward rise,
Tho' marked by none but quick poetic eyes:
(So Rome's great founder to the heavens with-
     drew,   125

To Proculus alone confessed in view):
A sudden star, it shot thro' liquid air,
And drew behind a radiant trail of hair.
Not Berenice's locks first rose so bright,
The heavens bespangling with dishevelled light.
The Sylphs behold it kindling as it flies,   131
And pleased pursue its progress thro' the skies.
   This the beau monde shall from the Mall survey,
And hail with music its propitious ray;
This the blest lover shall for Venus take,   135
And send up vows from Rosamonda's lake;
This Partridge soon shall view in cloudless skies,
When next he looks thro' Galileo's eyes;
And hence th' egregious wizard shall foredoom
The fate of Louis, and the fall of Rome.   140
   Then cease, bright Nymph! to mourn thy rav-
     ished hair,
Which adds new glory to the shining sphere!
Not all the tresses that fair head can boast
Shall draw such envy as the Lock you lost.
For after all the murders of your eye,   145
When, after millions slain, yourself shall die;
When those fair suns shall set, as set they must,
And all those tresses shall be laid in dust,
This Lock the Muse shall consecrate to fame,
And 'midst the stars inscribe Belinda's name.   150

Voltaire · 1694–1778

François Marie Arouet, better known as Voltaire — a name he chose during one of his terms of confinement in the Bastille — was born in Paris on November 21, 1694. His father was a notary; his mother, who died when Voltaire was only seven years old, appears to have left the boy opportunity for acquaintance with people of social rank. Sent to a Jesuit school, the Collège Louis-le-Grand, at the age of ten, the young man, at seventeen, left the institution determined to adopt a literary career. In deference to a father who was strongly opposed to writing as a profession, Voltaire for a while made a pretense at following the law, but he could not give up his enthusiasm for literature and it was not long before he was accused of the authorship of one or two libelous poems and found himself in trouble — the sort of trouble with society which was to follow him through most of his life. In May, 1716, he was sent away from Paris, and, upon his return, he was imprisoned in the Bastille for a brief period. Once released, he was soon exiled again. Upon his father's death he came into a small fortune which was soon augmented by a pension. Indeed, Voltaire is a literary figure who seems always to have esteemed money and to have found means, through writing, lotteries, investments, or living with wealthy nobles, to have prospered rather handsomely. A quarrel with one of the nobles of Paris brought further trouble, a threatened duel, the Bastille again, and exile — this time to England.

Voltaire's three years in England were formative years; they brought him acquaintance with the Walpoles, with the dramatist Congreve, with Pope, with new modes of thought. Particularly was he influenced by the freedom of social and political expression which he believed he found in the London of that day.

In 1750 Voltaire went to Potsdam as the guest of the King of Prussia, Frederick the Great. But this three-year sojourn in Prussia, like some of Voltaire's alliances, ended in distrust and suspicion. Eventually he went to Switzerland, took up residence at Les Délices, near Geneva, and then moved on to Ferney, north of Geneva but on French soil. Here he lived perhaps his calmest years and gained his reputation as the friend of those oppressed for social or political reasons.

Among Voltaire's writings are four or five rather separate types: dramas (both comedy and tragedy), of which *Zaïre* and *Mérope* are perhaps best known; epic poems, such as the *Henriade* and *Pucelle;* tales, of which *Candide* is the most famous; history, as exemplified in his *Siècle de Louis XIV;* and personal correspondence.

It is likely that for us today the spirit of Voltaire is a greater heritage than the actual body of his writing. Scheming, vain, financially ambitious, he may not have been a pleasant person with whom to associate. Yet qualities like these must not be allowed to outweigh his masterly intelligence, his long battle for freedom of expression, and his defense of those oppressed for their having given voice to unpopular opinions.

Voltaire was a great writer rather than a great philosopher. His style was characterized by irony and sarcasm, by superficiality, and by pungent phrasing. While he wrote much, his ideas were presented in a highly condensed manner. And most of his work is highly critical whether it be of society, of politics, or of religion. The essentially satirical bent of his work places him among — though well out in front of — such neo-classical writers as Molière and La Fontaine in France, and Swift, Addison, and Pope in England.

SUGGESTED REFERENCES: Alfred Noyes, *Voltaire* (1939); Norman L. Tortey, *The Spirit of Voltaire* (1938); W. H. Barber, *Voltaire: Candide* (1960).

Candide

Candide, reprinted here in part, is a vivid expression of Voltaire's skepticism. In it he finds occasion to pay his disrespectful respects to many of the evils which he spent a lifetime attacking. He had been particularly irritated by a philosophical concept then popular. Leibniz in Germany, Shaftesbury and Bishop Warburton in England, had argued that this is the best of all possible worlds. Pope had phrased the same idea in his "Whatever is, is right." Rousseau had taught a rather careless optimism. Yet, despite the doctrine of these men, the year 1755 had witnessed a terrible earthquake in Portugal and Spain. Fifteen thousand people had been killed. And in this best of all possible worlds, queried Voltaire, these innocent people are killed by an act of God? The Catholics argued that the earthquake was a visitation of God because some Protestants lived in the two countries; the Protestants argued that the earthquake had been sent to punish countries which were dominantly Catholic. Voltaire's satiric mind seized on the occasion to attack the religious optimism then rampant. He decided to treat the question in narrative form and from a specific, rather than from an abstract, point of view. He would send a "candid" young man through the experiences of life and let him make report on this best of all possible worlds! Many of the events presented in the tale had actual parallels as many of the characters portrayed were actual realities. The "Bulgarians," for instance, were the Prussians, the "Abares," the French; and Dr. Pangloss was, perhaps, a fictionized Leibniz and Pope and Shaftesbury

moulded into a single absurdity. *Candide*, then, is an answer to the reigning doctrine of careless optimism. The translation is taken from *Candide and Other Romances*, translated by Richard Aldington in the Broadway Translations, published by E. P. Dutton & Co. Inc., New York.

[*Chapters I–IV relate Candide's life as a youth in a castle in Westphalia, his meeting with the beautiful "Miss Cunegonde," his training by the learned Dr. Pangloss to believe that this is the "best of all possible worlds," his expulsion from the castle because of the love he manifested for the young lady, his experiences among the Bulgarians, and his meeting again with Dr. Pangloss on shipboard.*]

CHAPTER V

Storm, shipwreck, earthquake, and what happened to Dr. Pangloss, to Candide and the Anabaptist Jacques

Half the enfeebled passengers, suffering from that inconceivable anguish which the rolling of a ship causes in the nerves and in all the humors of bodies shaken in contrary directions, did not retain strength enough even to trouble about the danger. The other half screamed and prayed; the sails were torn, the masts broken, the vessel leaking. Those worked who could, no one co-operated, no one commanded. The Anabaptist [1] tried to help the crew a little; he was on the main-deck; a furious sailor struck him violently and stretched him on the deck; but the blow he delivered gave him so violent a shock that he fell head-first out of the ship. He remained hanging and clinging to part of the broken mast. The good Jacques ran to his aid, helped him to climb back, and from the effort he made was flung into the sea in full view of the sailor, who allowed him to drown without condescending even to look at him. Candide came up, saw his benefactor reappear for a moment and then be engulfed for ever. He tried to throw himself after him into the sea; he was prevented by the philosopher Pangloss, who proved to him that the Lisbon roads had been expressly created for the Anabaptist to be drowned in them. While he was proving this *a priori*, the vessel sank, and every one perished except Pangloss, Candide and the brutal sailor who had drowned the virtuous Anabaptist; the blackguard swam successfully to the shore and Pangloss and Candide were carried there on a plank.

When they had recovered a little, they walked toward Lisbon; they had a little money by the help of which they hoped to be saved from hunger after having escaped the storm.

Weeping the death of their benefactor, they had scarcely set foot in the town when they felt the earth tremble under their feet; the sea rose in foaming masses in the port and smashed the ships which rode at anchor. Whirlwinds of flame and ashes covered the streets and squares; the houses collapsed, the roofs were thrown upon the foundations, and the foundations were scattered; thirty thousand inhabitants of every age and both sexes were crushed under the ruins. Whistling and swearing, the sailor said:

"There'll be something to pick up here."

"What can be the sufficient reason for this phenomenon?" said Pangloss.

"It is the last day!" cried Candide.

The sailor immediately ran among the debris, dared death to find money, found it, seized it, got drunk, and having slept off his wine, purchased the favors of the first woman of good-will he met on the ruins of the houses and among the dead and dying. Pangloss, however, pulled him by the sleeve.

"My friend," said he, "this is not well, you are disregarding universal reason, you choose the wrong time."

"Blood and 'ounds!" he retorted, "I am a sailor

[1] A radical and mystical religious sect which arose in Germany in the sixteenth century.

and I was born in Batavia; four times have I stamped on the crucifix during four voyages to Japan; [1] you have found the right man for your universal reason!"

Candide had been hurt by some falling stones; he lay in the street covered with debris. He said to Pangloss:

"Alas! Get me a little wine and oil; I am dying."

"This earthquake is not a new thing," replied Pangloss. "The town of Lima felt the same shocks in America last year; similar causes produce similar effects; there must certainly be a train of sulphur underground from Lima to Lisbon."

"Nothing is more probable," replied Candide; "but, for God's sake, a little oil and wine."

"What do you mean, probable?" replied the philosopher; "I maintain that it is proved."

Candide lost consciousness, and Pangloss brought him a little water from a neighboring fountain.

Next day they found a little food as they wandered among the ruins and regained a little strength. Afterwards they worked like others to help the inhabitants who had escaped death. Some citizens they had assisted gave them as good a dinner as could be expected in such a disaster; true, it was a dreary meal; the hosts watered their bread with their tears, but Pangloss consoled them by assuring them that things could not be otherwise.

"For," said he, "all this is for the best; for, if there is a volcano at Lisbon, it cannot be anywhere else; for it is impossible that things should not be where they are; for all is well."

A little, dark man, a familiar of the Inquisition, who sat beside him, politely took up the conversation, and said:

"Apparently you do not believe in original sin; for, if everything is for the best, there was neither fall nor punishment."

"I most humbly beg your excellency's pardon," replied Pangloss still more politely, "for the fall of man and the curse necessarily entered into the best of all possible worlds."

"Then you do not believe in free-will?" said the familiar.

"Your excellency will pardon me," said Pangloss; "free-will can exist with absolute necessity; for it was necessary that we should be free; for in short, limited will...."

[1] After a conspiracy of Christians in Japan, all foreigners were expelled. The Dutch, who had revealed the plot to the Emperor of Japan, alone were permitted to remain, on condition that they gave up all signs of Christianity and stamped on the crucifix.

Pangloss was in the middle of his phrase when the familiar nodded to his armed attendant who was pouring out port or Oporto wine for him.

CHAPTER VI

How a splendid auto-da-fé was held to prevent earthquakes, and how Candide was flogged

After the earthquake which destroyed three-quarters of Lisbon, the wise men of that country could discover no more efficacious way of preventing a total ruin than by giving the people a splendid auto-da-fé.[1] It was decided by the university of Coimbre that the sight of several persons being slowly burned in great ceremony is an infallible secret for preventing earthquakes.

Consequently they had arrested a Biscayan convicted of having married his fellow-godmother, and two Portuguese who, when eating a chicken, had thrown away the bacon; after dinner they came and bound Dr. Pangloss and his disciple Candide, one because he had spoken and the other because he had listened with an air of approbation; they were both carried separately to extremely cool apartments, where there was never any discomfort from the sun; a week afterwards each was dressed in a sanbenito and their heads were ornamented with paper mitres; Candide's mitre and sanbenito were painted with flames upside down and with devils who had neither tails nor claws; but Pangloss's devils had claws and tails, and his flames were upright.

Dressed in this manner they marched in procession and listened to a most pathetic sermon, followed by lovely plain-song music. Candide was flogged in time to the music, while the singing went on; the Biscayan and the two men who had not wanted to eat bacon were burned, and Pangloss was hanged, although this is not the custom. The very same day, the earth shook again with a terrible clamor.

Candide, terrified, dumbfounded, bewildered, covered with blood, quivering from head to foot, said to himself:

"If this is the best of all possible worlds, what are the others? Let it pass that I was flogged, for I was flogged by the Bulgarians, but, O my dear Pangloss! The greatest of philosophers! Must I

[1] An "act of faith." The public announcement of sentences imposed by the Inquisition together with the ceremony and execution of the sentences. The condemned heretics were frequently burned at the stake.

see you hanged without knowing why! O my dear Anabaptist! The best of men! Was it necessary that you should be drowned in port! O Miss Cunegonde! The pearl of women! Was it necessary that your belly should be slit!"

He was returning, scarcely able to support himself, preached at, flogged, absolved and blessed, when an old woman accosted him and said:

"Courage, my son, follow me."

CHAPTER VII

How an old woman took care of Candide and how he regained that which he loved

Candide did not take courage, but he followed the old woman to a hovel; she gave him a pot of ointment to rub on, and left him food and drink; she pointed out a fairly clean bed; near the bed there was a suit of clothes.

"Eat, drink, sleep," said she, "and may our Lady of Atocha, my Lord Saint Anthony of Padua and my Lord Saint James of Compostella take care of you; I shall come back to-morrow."

Candide, still amazed by all he had seen, by all he had suffered, and still more by the old woman's charity, tried to kiss her hand.

"'Tis not my hand you should kiss," said the old woman. "I shall come back to-morrow. Rub on the ointment, eat and sleep."

In spite of all his misfortune, Candide ate and went to sleep. Next day the old woman brought him breakfast, examined his back and smeared him with another ointment; later she brought him dinner, and returned in the evening with supper. The next day she went through the same ceremony.

"Who are you?" Candide kept asking her. "Who has inspired you with so much kindness? How can I thank you?"

The good woman never made any reply; she returned in the evening without any supper.

"Come with me," said she, "and do not speak a word."

She took him by the arm and walked into the country with him for about a quarter of a mile; they came to an isolated house, surrounded with gardens and canals. The old woman knocked at a little door. It was opened; she led Candide up a back stairway into a gilded apartment, left him on a brocaded sofa, shut the door and went away. Candide thought he was dreaming, and felt that his whole life was a bad dream and the present moment an agreeable dream.

The old woman soon reappeared; she was supporting with some difficulty a trembling woman of majestic stature, glittering with precious stones and covered with a veil.

"Remove the veil," said the old woman to Candide. The young man advanced and lifted the veil with a timid hand. What a moment! What a surprise! He thought he saw Miss Cunegonde, in fact he was looking at her, it was she herself. His strength failed him, he could not utter a word and fell at her feet. Cunegonde fell on the sofa. The old woman dosed them with distilled waters; they recovered their senses and began to speak: at first they uttered only broken words, questions and answers at cross-purposes, sighs, tears, exclamations. The old woman advised them to make less noise and left them alone.

"What! Is it you?" said Candide. "You are alive, and I find you here in Portugal! Then you were not raped? Your belly was not slit, as the philosopher Pangloss assured me?"

"Yes, indeed," said the fair Cunegonde; "but those two accidents are not always fatal."

"But your father and mother were killed?"

"'Tis only too true," said Cunegonde, weeping.

"And your brother?"

"My brother was killed too."

"And why are you in Portugal? And how did you know I was here? And by what strange adventure have you brought me to this house?"

"I will tell you everything," replied the lady, "but first of all you must tell me everything that has happened to you since the innocent kiss you gave me and the kicks you received."

Candide obeyed with profound respect; and, although he was bewildered, although his voice was weak and trembling, although his back was still a little painful, he related in the most natural manner all he had endured since the moment of their separation. Cunegonde raised her eyes to Heaven; she shed tears at the death of the good Anabaptist and Pangloss, after which she spoke as follows to Candide, who did not miss a word and devoured her with his eyes.

[*The intervening chapters recount the experiences of Cunegonde during her separation from Candide, the arrival of the two (with the old woman) at Cadiz in miserable circumstances, the sad personal history of the old woman, the embarking of the three on a ship bound for Paraguay, their arrival at Buenos Ayres, and the forced separation of Candide from the two women.*]

CHAPTER XIV

How Candide and Cacambo were received by the Jesuits in Paraguay

Candide had brought from Cadiz a valet of a sort which is very common on the coasts of Spain and in the colonies. He was one-quarter Spanish, the child of a half-breed in Tucuman; he had been a choir-boy, a sacristan, a sailor, a monk, a postman, a soldier and a lackey. His name was Cacambo and he loved his master because his master was a very good man. He saddled the two Andalusian horses with all speed.

"Come, master, we must follow the old woman's advice; let us be off and ride without looking behind us."

Candide shed tears.

"O my dear Cunegonde! Must I abandon you just when the governor was about to marry us! Cunegonde, brought here from such a distant land, what will become of you?"

"She will become what she can," said Cacambo. "Women never trouble about themselves; God will see to her; let us be off."

"Where are you taking me? Where are we going? What shall we do without Cunegonde?" said Candide.

"By Saint James of Compostella," said Cacambo, "you were going to fight the Jesuits; let us go and fight for them; I know the roads, I will take you to their kingdom, they will be charmed to have a captain who can drill in the Bulgarian fashion; you will make a prodigious fortune; when a man fails in one world, he succeeds in another. 'Tis a very great pleasure to see and do new things."

"Then you have been in Paraguay?" said Candide.

"Yes, indeed," said Cacambo. "I was servitor in the College of the Assumption, and I know the government of *Los Padres* as well as I know the streets of Cadiz. Their government is a most admirable thing. The kingdom is already more than three hundred leagues in diameter and is divided into thirty provinces. *Los Padres* have everything and the people have nothing; 'tis the masterpiece of reason and justice. For my part, I know nothing so divine as *Los Padres* who here make war on the Kings of Spain and Portugal and in Europe act as their confessors; who here kill Spaniards and at Madrid send them to Heaven; all this delights me; come on; you will be the happiest of men. What a pleasure it will be to *Los Padres* when they know there is coming to them a captain who can drill in the Bulgarian manner!"

As soon as they reached the first barrier, Cacambo told the picket that a captain wished to speak to the Commandant. This information was carried to the main guard. A Paraguayan officer ran to the feet of the Commandant to tell him the news. Candide and Cacambo were disarmed and their two Andalusian horses were taken from them. The two strangers were brought in between two ranks of soldiers; the Commandant was at the end, with a three-cornered hat on his head, his gown tucked up, a sword at his side and a spontoon in his hand. He made a sign and immediately the two new-comers were surrounded by twenty-four soldiers. A sergeant told them that they must wait, that the Commandant could not speak to them, that the reverend provincial father did not allow any Spaniard to open his mouth in his presence or to remain more than three hours in the country.

"And where is the reverend provincial father?" said Cacambo.

"He is on parade after having said Mass, and you will have to wait three hours before you will be allowed to kiss his spurs."

"But," said Cacambo, "the captain who is dying of hunger just as I am, is not a Spaniard but a German; can we not break our fast while we are waiting for his reverence?"

The sergeant went at once to inform the Commandant of this.

"Blessed be God!" said that lord. "Since he is a German I can speak to him; bring him to my arbor."

Candide was immediately taken to a leafy summerhouse decorated with a very pretty colonnade of green marble and gold, and lattices enclosing parrots, humming-birds, colibris, guinea-hens and many other rare birds. An excellent breakfast stood ready in gold dishes; and while the Paraguayans were eating maize from wooden bowls, out of doors and in the heat of the sun, the reverend father Commandant entered the arbor.

He was a very handsome young man, with a full face, a fairly white skin, red cheeks, arched eyebrows, keen eyes, red ears, vermilion lips, a haughty air, but a haughtiness which was neither that of a Spaniard nor of a Jesuit. Candide and Cacambo were given back the arms which had been taken from them and their two Andalusian horses; Cacambo fed them with oats near the arbor, and kept his eye on them for fear of a surprise.

Candide first kissed the hem of the Commandant's gown and then they sat down to table.

"So you are a German?" said the Jesuit in that language.

"Yes, reverend father," said Candide.

As they spoke these words they gazed at each other with extreme surprise and an emotion they could not control.

"And what part of Germany do you come from?" said the Jesuit.

"From the filthy province of Westphalia," said Candide; "I was born in the castle of Thunderten-tronckh."

"Heavens! Is it possible!" cried the Commandant.

"What a miracle!" cried Candide.

"Can it be you?" said the Commandant.

"'Tis impossible!" said Candide.

They both fell over backwards, embraced and shed rivers of tears.

"What! Can it be you, reverend father? You, the fair Cunegonde's brother! You, who were killed by the Bulgarians! You, the son of My Lord the Baron! You, a Jesuit in Paraguay! The world is indeed a strange place! O Pangloss! Pangloss! How happy you would have been if you had not been hanged!"

The Commandant sent away the negro slaves and the Paraguayans who were serving wine in goblets of rock-crystal. A thousand times did he thank God and St. Ignatius; he clasped Candide in his arms; their faces were wet with tears.

"You would be still more surprised, more touched, more beside yourself," said Candide, "if I were to tell you that Miss Cunegonde, your sister, whom you thought disembowelled, is in the best of health."

"Where?"

"In your neighborhood, with the governor of Buenos Ayres; and I came to make war on you."

Every word they spoke in this long conversation piled marvel on marvel. Their whole souls flew from their tongues, listened in their ears and sparkled in their eyes. As they were Germans, they sat at table for a long time, waiting for the reverend provincial father; and the Commandant spoke as follows to his dear Candide.

CHAPTER XV

How Candide killed his dear Cunegonde's brother

"I shall remember all my life the horrible day when I saw my father and mother killed and my sister raped. When the Bulgarians had gone, my adorable sister could not be found, and my mother, my father and I, two maid-servants and three little murdered boys were placed in a cart to be buried in a Jesuit chapel two leagues from the castle of my fathers. A Jesuit sprinkled us with holy water; it was horribly salt; a few drops fell in my eyes; the father noticed that my eyelid trembled, he put his hand on my heart and felt that it was still beating; I was attended to and at the end of three weeks was as well as if nothing had happened. You know, my dear Candide, that I was a very pretty youth, and I became still prettier; and so the Reverend Father Croust, the Superior of the house, was inspired with a most tender friendship for me; he gave me the dress of a novice and some time afterwards I was sent to Rome. The Father General wished to recruit some young German Jesuits. The sovereigns of Paraguay take as few Spanish Jesuits as they can; they prefer foreigners, whom they think they can control better. The Reverend Father General thought me apt to labor in his vineyard. I set off with a Pole and a Tyrolese. When I arrived I was honored with a subdeaconship and a lieutenancy; I am now colonel and priest. We shall give the King of Spain's troops a warm reception; I guarantee they will be excommunicated and beaten. Providence has sent you here to help us. But is it really true that my dear sister Cunegonde is in the neighborhood with the governor of Buenos Ayres?"

Candide assured him on oath that nothing could be truer. Their tears began to flow once more.

The Baron seemed never to grow tired of embracing Candide; he called him his brother, his savior.

"Ah! My dear Candide," said he, "perhaps we shall enter the town together as conquerors and regain my sister Cunegonde."

"I desire it above all things," said Candide, "for I meant to marry her and I still hope to do so."

"You, insolent wretch!" replied the Baron. "Would you have the impudence to marry my sister who has seventy-two quarterings! I consider you extremely impudent to dare to speak to me of such a fool-hardy intention!"

Candide, petrified at this speech, replied:

"Reverend Father, all the quarterings in the world are of no importance; I rescued your sister from the arms of a Jew and an Inquisitor; she is under considerable obligation to me and wishes to marry me. Doctor Pangloss always said that men are equal and I shall certainly marry her."

"We shall see about that, scoundrel!" said the Jesuit Baron of Thunder-ten-tronckh, at the same time hitting him violently in the face with the flat of his sword. Candide promptly drew his own and stuck it up to the hilt in the Jesuit Baron's belly; but, as he drew it forth smoking, he began to weep.

"Alas! My God," said he, "I have killed my old master, my friend, my brother-in-law; I am the

mildest man in the world and I have already killed three men, two of them priests."

Cacambo, who was acting as sentry at the door of the arbor, ran in.

"There is nothing left for us but to sell our lives dearly," said his master. "Somebody will certainly come into the arbor and we must die weapon in hand."

Cacambo, who had seen this sort of thing before, did not lose his head; he took off the Baron's Jesuit gown, put it on Candide, gave him the dead man's square bonnet, and made him mount a horse. All this was done in the twinkling of an eye.

"Let us gallop, master; every one will take you for a Jesuit carrying orders and we shall have passed the frontiers before they can pursue us."

As he spoke these words he started off at full speed and shouted in Spanish:

"Way, way for the Reverend Father Colonel...."

CHAPTER XVII

Arrival of Candide and his valet in the country of Eldorado and what they saw there

When they reached the frontiers of the Oreillons, Cacambo said to Candide:

"You see this hemisphere is no better than the other; take my advice, let us go back to Europe by the shortest road."

"How can we go back," said Candide, "and where can we go? If I go to my own country, the Bulgarians and the Abares are murdering everybody; if I return to Portugal I shall be burned; if we stay here, we run the risk of being spitted at any moment. But how can I make up my mind to leave that part of the world where Miss Cunegonde is living?"

"Let us go to Cayenne," said Cacambo, "we shall find Frenchmen there, for they go all over the world; they might help us. Perhaps God will have pity on us."

It was not easy to go to Cayenne. They knew roughly the direction to take, but mountains, rivers, precipices, brigands and savages were everywhere terrible obstacles. Their horses died of fatigue; their provisions were exhausted; for a whole month they lived on wild fruits and at last found themselves near a little river fringed with cocoanut-trees which supported their lives and their hopes.

Cacambo, who always gave advice as prudent as the old woman's, said to Candide:

"We can go no farther, we have walked far enough; I can see an empty canoe in the bank, let us fill it with cocoanuts, get into the little boat and drift with the current; a river always leads to some inhabited place. If we do not find anything pleasant, we shall at least find something new."

"Come on then," said Candide, "and let us trust to Providence."

They drifted for some leagues between banks which were sometimes flowery, sometimes bare, sometimes flat, sometimes steep. The river continually became wider; finally it disappeared under an arch of frightful rocks which towered up to the very sky. The two travellers were bold enough to trust themselves to the current under this arch. The stream, narrowed between walls, carried them with horrible rapidity and noise. After twenty-four hours they saw daylight again; but their canoe was wrecked on reefs; they had to crawl from rock to rock for a whole league and at last they discovered an immense horizon, bordered by inaccessible mountains. The country was cultivated for pleasure as well as for necessity; everywhere the useful was agreeable. The roads were covered or rather ornamented with carriages of brilliant material and shape, carrying men and women of singular beauty, who were rapidly drawn along by large red sheep whose swiftness surpassed that of the finest horses of Andalusia, Tetuan and Mequinez.

"This country," said Candide, "is better than Westphalia."

He landed with Cacambo near the first village he came to. Several children of the village, dressed in torn gold brocade, were playing coits outside the village. Our two men from the other world amused themselves by looking on; their coits were large round pieces, yellow, red and green which shone with peculiar lustre. The travellers were curious enough to pick up some of them; they were of gold, emeralds and rubies, the least of which would have been the greatest ornament in the Mogul's throne.

"No doubt," said Cacambo, "these children are the sons of the King of this country playing at coits."

At that moment the village schoolmaster appeared to call them into school.

"This," said Candide, "is the tutor of the Royal Family."

The little beggars immediately left their game, abandoning their coits and everything with which they had been playing. Candide picked them up, ran to the tutor, and presented them to him humbly, giving him to understand by signs that their Royal Highnesses had forgotten their gold and their precious stones. The village schoolmaster smiled, threw them on the ground, gazed for a moment at Candide's face with much surprise and continued on his way.

The travellers did not fail to pick up the gold, the rubies and the emeralds.

"Where are we?" cried Candide. "The children of the King must be well brought up, since they are taught to despise gold and precious stones."

Cacambo was as much surprised as Candide. At last they reached the first house in the village, which was built like a European palace. There were crowds of people round the door and still more inside; very pleasant music could be heard and there was a delicious smell of cooking. Cacambo went up to the door and heard them speaking Peruvian; it was his maternal tongue, for every one knows that Cacambo was born in a village of Tucuman where nothing else is spoken.

"I will act as your interpreter," he said to Candide. "This is an inn, let us enter."

Immediately two boys and two girls of the inn, dressed in cloth of gold, whose hair was bound up with ribbons, invited them to sit down to the table d'hôte. They served four soups each garnished with two parrots, a boiled condor which weighed two hundred pounds, two roast monkeys of excellent flavor, three hundred colibris in one dish and six hundred humming-birds in another, exquisite ragouts and delicious pastries, all in dishes of a sort of rock-crystal. The boys and girls brought several sorts of drinks made of sugar-cane.

Most of the guests were merchants and coachmen, all extremely polite, who asked Cacambo a few questions with the most delicate discretion and answered his in a satisfactory manner.

When the meal was over, Cacambo, like Candide, thought he could pay the reckoning by throwing on the table two of the large pieces of gold he had picked up; the host and hostess laughed until they had to hold their sides. At last they recovered themselves.

"Gentlemen," said the host, "we perceive you are strangers; we are not accustomed to seeing them. Forgive us if we began to laugh when you offered us in payment the stones from our highways. No doubt you have none of the money of this country, but you do not need any to dine here. All the hotels established for the utility of commerce are paid for by the government. You have been ill-entertained here because this is a poor village; but everywhere else you will be received as you deserve to be."

Cacambo explained to Candide all that the host had said, and Candide listened in the same admiration and disorder with which his friend Cacambo interpreted.

"What can this country be," they said to each other, "which is unknown to the rest of the world and where all nature is so different from ours? Probably it is the country where everything is for the best; for there must be one country of that sort. And, in spite of what Dr. Pangloss said, I often noticed that everything went very ill in Westphalia."

CHAPTER XVIII

What they saw in the land of Eldorado

CACAMBO informed the host of his curiosity, and the host said:

"I am a very ignorant man and am all the better for it; but we have here an old man who has retired from the court and who is the most learned and most communicative man in the kingdom."

And he at once took Cacambo to the old man. Candide now played only the second part and accompanied his valet.

They entered a very simple house, for the door was only of silver and the panelling of the apartments in gold, but so tastefully carved that the richest decorations did not surpass it. The antechamber indeed was only encrusted with rubies and emeralds; but the order with which everything was arranged atoned for the extreme simplicity.

The old man received the two strangers on a sofa padded with colibri feathers, and presented them with drinks in diamond cups; after which he satisfied their curiosity in these words:

"I am a hundred and seventy-two years old and I heard from my late father, the King's equerry, the astonishing revolutions of Peru of which he had been an eye-witness. The kingdom where we now are is the ancient country of the Incas, who most imprudently left it to conquer part of the world and were at last destroyed by the Spaniards.

"The princes of their family who remained in their native country had more wisdom; with the consent of the nation, they ordered that no inhabitants should ever leave our little kingdom, and this it is that has preserved our innocence and our felicity. The Spaniards had some vague knowledge of this country, which they called Eldorado, and about a hundred years ago an Englishman named Raleigh came very near to it; but, since we are surrounded by inaccessible rocks and precipices, we have hitherto been exempt from the rapacity of the nations of Europe who have an inconceivable lust for the pebbles and mud of our land and would kill us to the last man to get possession of them."

The conversation was long; it touched upon the form of the government, manners, women, public spectacles and the arts. Finally Candide, who was always interested in metaphysics, asked through Cacambo whether the country had a religion. The old man blushed a little.

"How can you doubt it?" said he. "Do you think we are ingrates?"

Cacambo humbly asked what was the religion of Eldorado. The old man blushed again.

"Can there be two religions?" said he: "We have, I think, the religion of every one else; we adore God from evening until morning."

"Do you adore only one god?" said Cacambo, who continued to act as the interpreter of Candide's doubts.

"Manifestly," said the old man, "there are not two or three or four. I must confess that the people of your world ask very extraordinary questions."

Candide continued to press the old man with questions; he wished to know how they prayed to God in Eldorado.

"We do not pray," said the good and respectable sage, "we have nothing to ask from him; he has given us everything necessary and we continually give him thanks."

Candide was curious to see the priests; and asked where they were. The good old man smiled.

"My friends," said he, "we are all priests; the King and all the heads of families solemnly sing praises every morning, accompanied by five or six thousand musicians."

"What! Have you no monks to teach, to dispute, to govern, to intrigue and to burn people who do not agree with them?"

"For that, we should have to become fools," said the old man; "here we are all of the same opinion and do not understand what you mean with your monks."

At all this Candide was in an ecstasy and said to himself:

"This is very different from Westphalia and the castle of His Lordship the Baron; if our friend Pangloss had seen Eldorado, he would not have said that the castle of Thunder-ten-tronckh was the best of all that exists on the earth; certainly, a man should travel."

After this long conversation the good old man ordered a carriage to be harnessed with six sheep and gave the two travellers twelve of his servants to take them to court.

"You will excuse me," he said, "if my age deprives me of the honour of accompanying you. The King will receive you in a manner which will not displease you and doubtless you will pardon the customs of the country if any of them disconcert you."

Candide and Cacambo entered the carriage; the six sheep galloped off and in less than four hours they reached the King's palace, which was situated at one end of the capital. The portal was two hundred and twenty feet high and a hundred feet wide; it is impossible to describe its material. Anyone can see the prodigious superiority it must have over the pebbles and sand we call *gold* and *gems*.

Twenty beautiful maidens of the guard received Candide and Cacambo as they alighted from the carriage, conducted them to the baths and dressed them in robes woven from the down of colibris; after which the principal male and female officers of the Crown led them to his Majesty's apartment through two files of a thousand musicians each, according to the usual custom. As they approached the throne-room, Cacambo asked one of the chief officers how they should behave in his Majesty's presence; whether they should fall on their knees or flat on their faces, whether they should put their hands on their heads or on their backsides; whether they should lick the dust of the throne-room; in a word, what was the ceremony? "The custom," said the chief officer, "is to embrace the King and to kiss him on either cheek."

Candide and Cacambo threw their arms round his Majesty's neck; he received them with all imaginable favor and politely asked them to supper.

Meanwhile they were carried to see the town, the public buildings rising to the very skies, the market-places ornamented with thousands of columns, the fountains of rose-water and of liquors distilled from sugar-cane, which played continually in the public squares paved with precious stones which emitted a perfume like that of cloves and cinnamon.

Candide asked to see the law-courts; he was told there were none, and that nobody ever went to law. He asked if there were prisons and was told there were none. He was still more surprised and pleased by the palace of sciences, where he saw a gallery two thousand feet long, filled with instruments of mathematics and physics.

After they had explored all the afternoon about a thousandth part of the town, they were taken back to the King. Candide sat down to table with his Majesty, his valet Cacambo and several ladies. Never was better cheer, and never was anyone wittier at supper than his Majesty. Cacambo explained the King's witty remarks to Candide and even when translated they still appeared witty. Among all the things which amazed Candide, this did not amaze him the least.

They enjoyed this hospitality for a month. Candide repeatedly said to Cacambo:

"Once again, my friend, it is quite true that the castle where I was born cannot be compared with this country; but then Miss Cunegonde is not here and you probably have a mistress in Europe. If we remain here, we shall only be like everyone else; but if we return to our own world with only twelve sheep laden with Eldorado pebbles, we shall be richer than all the kings put together; we shall have no more Inquisitors to fear and we can easily regain Miss Cunegonde."

Cacambo agreed with this; it is so pleasant to be on the move, to show off before friends, to make a parade of the things seen on one's travels, that these two happy men resolved to be so no longer and to ask his Majesty's permission to depart.

"You are doing a very silly thing," said the King. "I know my country is small; but when we are comfortable anywhere we should stay there; I certainly have not the right to detain foreigners, that is a tyranny which does not exist either in our manners or our laws; all men are free, leave when you please, but the way out is very difficult. It is impossible to ascend the rapid river by which you miraculously came here and which flows under arches of rock. The mountains which surround the whole of my kingdom are ten thousand feet high and as perpendicular as rocks; they are more than ten leagues broad, and you can only get down from them by way of precipices. However, since you must go, I will give orders to the directors of machinery to make a machine which will carry you comfortably. When you have been taken to the other side of the mountains, nobody can proceed any farther with you; for my subjects have sworn never to pass this boundary and they are too wise to break their oath. Ask anything else of me you wish."

"We ask nothing of your Majesty," said Cacambo, "except a few sheep laden with provisions, pebbles and the mud of this country."

The King laughed.

"I cannot understand," said he, "the taste you people of Europe have for our yellow mud; but take as much as you wish, and much good may it do you."

He immediately ordered his engineers to make a machine to hoist these two extraordinary men out of his kingdom.

Three thousand learned scientists worked at it; it was ready in a fortnight and only cost about twenty million pounds sterling in the money of that country. Candide and Cacambo were placed on the machine; there were two large red sheep saddled and bridled for them to ride on when they had passed the mountains, twenty sumpter sheep laden with provisions, thirty carrying presents of the most curious productions of the country and fifty

laden with gold, precious stones and diamonds.
The King embraced the two vagabonds tenderly.

Their departure was a splendid sight and so was
the ingenious manner in which they and their sheep
were hoisted on to the top of the mountains.

The scientists took leave of them after having
landed them safely, and Candide's only desire and
object was to go and present Miss Cunegonde with
his sheep.

"We have sufficient to pay the governor of
Buenos Ayres," said he, "if Miss Cunegonde can
be bought. Let us go to Cayenne, and take ship,
and then we will see what kingdom we will buy."

CHAPTER XIX

What happened to them at Surinam and how Candide
made the acquaintance of Martin

Our two travellers' first day was quite pleasant.
They were encouraged by the idea of possessing
more treasures than all Asia, Europe and Africa
could collect. Candide in transport carved the
name of Cunegonde on the trees.

On the second day two of the sheep stuck in a
marsh and were swallowed up with their loads; two
other sheep died of fatigue a few days later; then
seven or eight died of hunger in a desert; several
days afterwards others fell off precipices. Finally,
after they had travelled for a hundred days, they
had only two sheep left. Candide said to Cacambo:

"My friend, you see how perishable are the
riches of this world; nothing is steadfast but virtue
and the happiness of seeing Miss Cunegonde
again."

"I admit it," said Cacambo, "but we still have
two sheep with more treasures than ever the King
of Spain will have, and in the distance I see a town
I suspect is Surinam, which belongs to the Dutch.
We are at the end of our troubles and the beginning
of our happiness."

As they drew near the town they met a negro
lying on the ground wearing only half his clothes,
that is to say, a pair of blue cotton drawers; this
poor man had no left leg and no right hand.

"Good Heavens!" said Candide to him in Dutch,
"what are you doing there, my friend, in this horrible state?"

"I am waiting for my master, the famous merchant Mr Vanderdendur."

"Was it Mr Vanderdendur," said Candide,
"who treated you in this way?"

"Yes, sir," said the negro, "it is the custom. We
are given a pair of cotton drawers twice a year as
clothing. When we work in the sugar-mills and the
grindstone catches our fingers, they cut off the
hand; when we try to run away, they cut off a leg.
Both these things happened to me. This is the
price paid for the sugar you eat in Europe. But
when my mother sold me for ten patagons on the
coast of Guinea, she said to me: 'My dear child,
give thanks to our fetishes, always worship them,
and they will make you happy; you have the honor
to be a slave of our lords the white men and thereby
you have made the fortune of your father and
mother.' Alas! I do not know whether I made
their fortune, but they certainly did not make
mine. Dogs, monkeys and parrots are a thousand
times less miserable than we are; the Dutch fetishes
who converted me tell me that we are all of us,
whites and blacks, the children of Adam. I am not
a genealogist, but if these preachers tell the truth,
we are all second cousins. Now, you will admit
that no one could treat his relatives in a more
horrible way."

"O Pangloss!" cried Candide. "This is an
abomination you had not guessed; this is too much,
in the end I shall have to renounce optimism."

"What is optimism?" said Cacambo.

"Alas!" said Candide, "it is the mania of maintaining that everything is well when we are
wretched."

And he shed tears as he looked at his negro; and
he entered Surinam weeping.

The first thing they inquired was whether there
was any ship in the port which could be sent to
Buenos Ayres. The person they addressed happened to be a Spanish captain, who offered to
strike an honest bargain with them. He arranged
to meet them at an inn. Candide and the faithful
Cacambo went and waited for him with their two
sheep.

Candide, who blurted everything out, told the
Spaniard all his adventures and confessed that he
wanted to elope with Miss Cunegonde.

"I shall certainly not take you to Buenos Ayres,"
said the captain. "I should be hanged and you
would, too. The fair Cunegonde is his Lordship's
favorite mistress."

Candide was thunderstruck; he sobbed for a long
time; then he took Cacambo aside.

"My dear friend," said he, "this is what you
must do. We each have in our pockets five or six
million pounds worth of diamonds; you are more
skilful than I am; go to Buenos Ayres and get Miss
Cunegonde. If the governor makes any difficulties give him a million; if he is still obstinate give
him two; you have not killed an Inquisitor so they

will not suspect you. I will fit out another ship, I will go and wait for you at Venice; it is a free country where there is nothing to fear from Bulgarians, Abares, Jews or Inquisitors."

Cacambo applauded this wise resolution; he was in despair at leaving a good master who had become his intimate friend; but the pleasure of being useful to him overcame the grief of leaving him. They embraced with tears. Candide urged him not to forget the good old woman. Cacambo set off that very same day; he was a very good man, this Cacambo.

Candide remained some time longer at Surinam waiting for another captain to take him to Italy with the two sheep he had left. He engaged servants and bought everything necessary for a long voyage. At last Mr. Vanderdendur, the owner of a large ship, came to see him.

"How much do you want," he asked this man, "to take me straight to Venice with my servants, my baggage and these two sheep?"

The captain asked for ten thousand piastres. Candide did not hesitate.

"Oh! Ho!" said the prudent Vanderdendur to himself, "this foreigner gives ten thousand piastres immediately! He must be very rich."

He returned a moment afterwards and said he could not sail for less than twenty thousand.

"Very well, you shall have them," said Candide.

"Whew!" said the merchant to himself, "this man gives twenty thousand piastres as easily as ten thousand."

He came back again, and said he could not take him to Venice for less than thirty thousand piastres.

"Then you shall have thirty thousand," replied Candide.

"Oho!" said the Dutch merchant to himself again, "thirty thousand piastres is nothing to this man; obviously the two sheep are laden with immense treasures; I will not insist any further; first let me make him pay the thirty thousand piastres, and then we will see."

Candide sold two little diamonds, the smaller of which was worth more than all the money the captain asked. He paid him in advance. The two sheep were taken on board. Candide followed in a little boat to join the ship which rode at anchor; the captain watched his time, set his sails and weighed anchor; the wind was favorable. Candide, bewildered and stupefied, soon lost sight of him.

"Alas!" he cried, "this is a trick worthy of the old world."

He returned to shore, in grief; for he had lost enough to make the fortune of twenty kings.

He went to the Dutch judge; and, as he was rather disturbed, he knocked loudly at the door; he went in, related what had happened and talked a little louder than he ought to have done. The judge began by fining him ten thousand piastres for the noise he had made; he then listened patiently to him, promised to look into his affair as soon as the merchant returned, and charged him another ten thousand piastres for the expenses of the audience.

This behavior reduced Candide to despair; he had indeed endured misfortunes a thousand times more painful; but the calmness of the judge and of the captain who had robbed him, stirred up his bile and plunged him into a black melancholy. The malevolence of men revealed itself to his mind in all its ugliness; he entertained only gloomy ideas. At last a French ship was about to leave for Bordeaux and, since he no longer had any sheep laden with diamonds to put on board, he hired a cabin at a reasonable price and announced throughout the town that he would give the passage, food and two thousand piastres to an honest man who would make the journey with him, on condition that this man was the most unfortunate and the most disgusted with his condition in the whole province.

Such a crowd of applicants arrived that a fleet would not have contained them. Candide, wishing to choose among the most likely, picked out twenty persons who seemed reasonably sociable and who all claimed to deserve his preference. He collected them in a tavern and gave them supper, on condition that each took an oath to relate truthfully the story of his life, promising that he would choose the man who seemed to him the most deserving of pity and to have the most cause for being discontented with his condition, and that he would give the others a little money.

The sitting lasted until four o'clock in the morning. As Candide listened to their adventures he remembered what the old woman had said on the voyage to Buenos Ayres and how she had wagered that there was nobody on the boat who had not experienced very great misfortunes. At each story which was told him, he thought of Pangloss.

"This Pangloss," said he, "would have some difficulty in supporting his system. I wish he were here. Certainly, if everything is well, it is only in Eldorado and not in the rest of the world."

He finally determined in favor of a poor man of letters who had worked ten years for the booksellers at Amsterdam. He judged that there was no occupation in the world which could more disgust a man.

This man of letters, who was also a good man, had been robbed by his wife, beaten by his son, and abandoned by his daughter, who had eloped with a Portuguese. He had just been deprived of a small post on which he depended and the preachers of Surinam were persecuting him because they thought he was a Socinian. It must be admitted that the others were at least as unfortunate as he was; but Candide hoped that this learned man would help to pass the time during the voyage. All his other rivals considered that Candide was doing them a great injustice; but he soothed them down by giving each of them a hundred piastres.

CHAPTER XX

What happened to Candide and Martin at sea

So the old man, who was called Martin, embarked with Candide for Bordeaux. Both had seen and suffered much; and if the ship had been sailing from Surinam to Japan by way of the Cape of Good Hope they would have been able to discuss moral and physical evil during the whole voyage. However, Candide had one great advantage over Martin, because he still hoped to see Mademoiselle Cunegonde again, and Martin had nothing to hope for; moreover, he possessed gold and diamonds; and, although he had lost a hundred large red sheep laden with the greatest treasures on earth, although he was still enraged at being robbed by the Dutch captain, yet when he thought of what he still had left in his pockets and when he talked of Cunegonde, especially at the end of a meal, he still inclined towards the system of Pangloss.

"But what do you think of all this, Martin?" said he to the man of letters. "What is your view of moral and physical evil?"

"Sir," replied Martin, "my priests accused me of being a Socinian; but the truth is I am a Manichean."[1]

"You are poking fun at me," said Candide, "there are no Manicheans left in the world."

"I am one," said Martin. "I don't know what to do about it, but I am unable to think in any other fashion."

"You must be possessed by the devil," said Candide.

"He takes so great a share in the affairs of this world," said Martin, "that he might well be in me, as he is everywhere else; but I confess that when I consider this globe, or rather this globule, I think that God has abandoned it to some evil creature — always excepting Eldorado. I have never seen a town which did not desire the ruin of the next town, never a family which did not wish to exter-

minate some other family. Everywhere the weak loathe the powerful before whom they cower and the powerful treat them like flocks of sheep whose wool and flesh are to be sold. A million drilled assassins go from one end of Europe to the other murdering and robbing with discipline in order to earn their bread, because there is no honester occupation; and in the towns which seem to enjoy peace and where the arts flourish, men are devoured by more envy, troubles and worries than the afflictions of a besieged town. Secret griefs are even more cruel than public miseries. In a word, I have seen so much and endured so much that I have become a Manichean."

"Yet there is some good," replied Candide.

"There may be," said Martin, "but I do not know it."

In the midst of this dispute they heard the sound of cannon. The noise increased every moment. Every one took his telescope. About three miles away they saw two ships engaged in battle; and the wind brought them so near the French ship that they had the pleasure of seeing the fight at their ease. At last one of the two ships fired a broadside so accurately and so low down that the other ship began to sink. Candide and Martin distinctly saw a hundred men on the main deck of the sinking ship; they raised their hands to Heaven and uttered frightful shrieks; in a moment all were engulfed.

"Well!" said Martin, "that is how men treat each other."

"It is certainly true," said Candide, "that there is something diabolical in this affair."

As he was speaking, he saw something of a brilliant red swimming near the ship. They launched a boat to see what it could be; it was one of his sheep. Candide felt more joy at recovering this sheep than grief at losing a hundred all laden with large diamonds from Eldorado. The French captain soon perceived that the captain of the remaining ship was a Spaniard and that the sunken ship was a Dutch pirate; the captain was the very same who had robbed Candide. The immense wealth this scoundrel had stolen was swallowed up with him in the sea and only a sheep was saved.

"You see," said Candide to Martin, "that crime is sometimes punished; this scoundrel of a Dutch captain has met the fate he deserved."

"Yes," said Martin, "but was it necessary that the other passengers on his ship should perish too? God punished the thief, and the devil punished the others."

Meanwhile the French and Spanish ships continued on their way and Candide continued his conversation with Martin. They argued for a fortnight and at the end of the fortnight they had

---

[1] A follower of the Persian teacher Manichæus (third century A.D.) who believed in the inherent evil of matter.

got no further than at the beginning. But after all, they talked, they exchanged ideas, they consoled each other. Candide stroked his sheep. "Since I have found you again," said he, "I may very likely find Cunegonde."

CHAPTER XXI

Candide and Martin approach the coast of France and argue

At last they sighted the coast of France.

"Have you ever been to France, Monsieur Martin?" said Candide.

"Yes," said Martin, "I have traversed several provinces. In some half the inhabitants are crazy, in others they are too artful, in some they are usually quite gentle and stupid, and in others they think they are clever; in all of them the chief occupation is making love, the second scandal-mongering and the third talking nonsense."

"But, Monsieur Martin, have you seen Paris?"

"Yes, I have seen Paris; it is a mixture of all the species; it is a chaos, a throng where everybody hunts for pleasure and hardly anybody finds it, at least so far as I could see. I did not stay there long; when I arrived there I was robbed of everything I had by pickpockets at Saint-Germain's fair; they thought I was a thief and I spent a week in prison; after which I became a printer's reader to earn enough to return to Holland on foot. I met the scribbling rabble, the intriguing rabble and the fanatical rabble. We hear that there are very polite people in the town; I am glad to think so."

"For my part, I have not the least curiosity to see France," said Candide. "You can easily guess that when a man has spent a month in Eldorado he cares to see nothing else in the world but Mademoiselle Cunegonde. I shall go and wait for her at Venice; we will go to Italy by way of France; will you come with me?"

"Willingly," said Martin. "They say that Venice is only for the Venetian nobles but that foreigners are nevertheless well received when they have plenty of money; I have none, you have plenty, I will follow you anywhere."

"Apropos," said Candide, "do you think the earth was originally a sea, as we are assured by that large book belonging to the captain?"

"I don't believe it in the least," said Martin, "any more than all the other whimsies we have been pestered with recently!"

"But to what end was this world formed?" said Candide.

"To infuriate us," replied Martin.

"Are you not very much surprised," continued Candide, "by the love those two girls of the country of the Oreillons had for those two monkeys, whose adventure I told you?"

"Not in the least," said Martin. "I see nothing strange in their passion; I have seen so many extraordinary things that nothing seems extraordinary to me."

"Do you think," said Candide, "that men have always massacred each other, as they do today? Have they always been liars, cheats, traitors, brigands, weak, flighty, cowardly, envious, gluttonous, drunken, grasping, and vicious, bloody, backbiting, debauched, fanatical, hypocritical and silly?"

"Do you think," said Martin, "that sparrow hawks have always eaten the pigeons they came across?"

"Yes, of course," said Candide.

"Well," said Martin, "if sparrow hawks have always possessed the same nature, why should you expect men to change theirs?"

"Oh!" said Candide, "there is a great difference; free will . . ." Arguing thus, they arrived at Bordeaux.

[The omitted chapters tell what happened in France and in England, of a meeting with Paquette the prostitute, of a visit to Venice, and of a strange dinner with six deposed kings.]

CHAPTER XXVII

Candide's voyage to Constantinople

The faithful Cacambo had already spoken to the Turkish captain who was to take Sultan Achmet back to Constantinople and had obtained permission for Candide and Martin to come on board. They both entered this ship after having prostrated themselves before his miserable Highness.

On the way, Candide said to Martin: "So we have just supped with six dethroned kings! And among those six kings there was one to whom I gave charity. Perhaps there are many other princes still more unfortunate. Now, I have only lost a hundred sheep and I am hastening to Cunegonde's arms. My dear Martin, once more, Pangloss was right, all is well."

"I hope so," said Martin.

"But," said Candide, "this is a very singular experience we have just had at Venice. Nobody has ever seen or heard of six dethroned kings supping together in a tavern."

"'Tis no more extraordinary," said Martin, "than most of the things which have happened to us. It is very common for kings to be dethroned; and as to the honor we have had of supping with them, 'tis a trifle not deserving our attention."

Scarcely had Candide entered the ship when he threw his arms round the neck of his old valet, of his friend Cacambo. "Well!" said he, "what is Cunegonde doing? Is she still a marvel of beauty? Does she still love me? How is she? Of course you have bought her a palace in Constantinople?"

"My dear master," replied Cacambo, "Cunegonde is washing dishes on the banks of Propontis [1] for a prince who possesses very few dishes; she is a slave in the house of a former sovereign named Ragotsky, who receives in his refuge three crowns a day from the Grand Turk; but what is even more sad is that she has lost her beauty and has become horribly ugly."

"Ah! beautiful or ugly," said Candide, "I am a man of honor and my duty is to love her always. But how can she be reduced to so abject a condition with the five or six millions you carried off?"

"Ah!" said Cacambo, "did I not have to give two millions to Señor Don Fernando d'Ibaraa y Figueora y Mascarenes y Lampourdos y Souza, Governor of Buenos Ayres, for permission to bring away Mademoiselle Cunegonde? And did not a pirate bravely strip us of all the rest? And did not this pirate take us to Cape Matapan, to Milo, to Nicaria, to Samos, to Petra, to the Dardanelles, to Marmora, to Scutari? Cunegonde and the old woman are servants to the prince I mentioned, and I am slave to the dethroned Sultan."

"What a chain of terrible calamities!" said Candide. "But after all, I still have a few diamonds; I shall easily deliver Cunegonde. What a pity she has become so ugly."

Then, turning to Martin, he said: "Who do you think is the most to be pitied, the Sultan Achmet, the Emperor Ivan, King Charles Edward, or me?"

"I do not know at all," said Martin. "I should have to be in your hearts to know."

"Ah!" said Candide, "if Pangloss were here he would know and would tell us."

"I do not know," said Martin, "what scales your Pangloss would use to weigh the misfortunes of men and to estimate their sufferings. All I presume is is that there are millions of men on the earth a hundred times more to be pitied than King Charles Edward, the Emperor Ivan and the Sultan Achmet."

"That may very well be," said Candide.

In a few days they reached the Black Sea channel. Candide began by paying a high ransom for Cacambo and, without wasting time, he went on board a galley with his companions bound for the shores of Propontis, in order to find Cunegonde however ugly she might be. Among the galley slaves were two convicts who rowed very badly and from time to time the Levantine captain applied several strokes of a bull's pizzle to their naked shoulders. From a natural feeling of pity Candide watched them more attentively than the other galley slaves and went up to them. Some features of their disfigured faces appeared to him to have some resemblance to Pangloss and the wretched Jesuit, the Baron, Mademoiselle Cunegonde's brother. This idea disturbed and saddened him. He looked at them still more carefully. "Truly," said he to Cacambo, "if I had not seen Dr. Pangloss hanged, and if I had not been so unfortunate as to kill the Baron, I should think they were rowing in this galley."

At the words Baron and Pangloss, the two convicts gave a loud cry, stopped on their seats and dropped their oars. The Levantine captain ran up to them and the lashes with the bull's pizzle were redoubled.

"Stop! Stop, sir!" cried Candide. "I will give you as much money as you want."

"What! Is it Candide?" said one of the convicts.

"What! Is it Candide?" said the other.

"Is it a dream?" said Candide. "Am I awake? Am I in this galley? Is that my Lord the Baron whom I killed? Is that Dr. Pangloss whom I saw hanged?"

"It is, it is," they replied.

"What! Is that the great philosopher?" said Martin.

"Ah! sir," said Candide to the Levantine captain, "how much money do you want for My Lord Thunder-ten-tronckh, one of the first Barons of the empire, and for Dr. Pangloss, the most profound metaphysician of Germany?"

"Dog of a Christian," replied the Levantine captain, "since these two dogs of Christian convicts are Barons and metaphysicians, which no doubt is a high rank in their country, you shall pay me fifty thousand sequins."

"You shall have them, sir. Row back to Constantinople like lightning and you shall be paid at once. But, no, take me to Mademoiselle Cunegonde."

The captain, at Candide's first offer had already turned the bow towards the town, and rowed there more swiftly than a bird cleaves the air.

Candide embraced the Baron and Pangloss a hundred times. "How was it I did not kill you, my dear Baron? And, my dear Pangloss, how do you happen to be alive after having been hanged? And why are you both in a Turkish galley?"

"Is it really true that my dear sister is in this country?" said the Baron.

"Yes," replied Cacambo.

"So once more I see my dear Candide!" cried Pangloss.

[1] Ancient name for the Sea of Marmara in Turkey.

Candide introduced Martin and Cacambo. They all embraced and all talked at the same time. The galley flew; already they were in the harbor. They sent for a Jew, and Candide sold him for fifty thousand sequins a diamond worth a hundred thousand, for which he swore by Abraham he could not give any more. The ransom of the Baron and Pangloss was immediately paid. Pangloss threw himself at the feet of his liberator and bathed them with tears; the other thanked him with a nod and promised to repay the money at the first opportunity. "But is it possible that my sister is in Turkey?" said he.

"Nothing is so possible," replied Cacambo, "since she washes up the dishes of a prince of Transylvania."

They immediately sent for two Jews; Candide sold some more diamonds; and they all set out in another galley to rescue Cunegonde.

CHAPTER XXVIII

What happened to Candide, to Cunegonde, to Pangloss, to Martin, etc.

"Pardon once more," said Candide to the Baron, "pardon me, reverend father, for having thrust my sword through your body."

"Let us say no more about it," said the Baron. "I admit I was a little too sharp; but since you wish to know how it was you saw me in a galley, I must tell you that after my wound was healed by the brother apothecary of the college, I was attacked and carried off by a Spanish raiding party; I was imprisoned in Buenos Ayres at the time when my sister had just left. I asked to return to the Vicar-General in Rome. I was ordered to Constantinople to act as almoner to the Ambassador of France. A week after I had taken up my office I met towards evening a very handsome young page of the Sultan. It was very hot; the young man wished to bathe; I took the opportunity to bathe also. I did not know that it was a most serious crime for a Christian to be found naked with a young Mahometan. A cadi sentenced me to a hundred strokes on the soles of my feet and condemned me to the galley. I do not think a more horrible injustice has ever been committed. But I should very much like to know why my sister is in the kitchen of a Translyvanian sovereign living in exile among the Turks."

"But, my dear Pangloss," said Candide, "how does it happen that I see you once more?"

"It is true," said Pangloss, "that you saw me hanged; and in the natural course of events I should have been burned. But you remember, it poured with rain when they were going to roast me; the storm was so violent that they despaired of lighting the fire; I was hanged because they could do nothing better; a surgeon bought my body, carried me home and dissected me. He first made a crucial incision in me from the navel to the collar-bone. Nobody could have been worse hanged than I was. The executioner of the holy Inquisition, who was a sub-deacon, was marvellously skilful in burning people, but he was not accustomed to hang them; the rope was wet and did not slide easily and it was knotted; in short, I still breathed. The crucial incision caused me to utter so loud a scream that the surgeon fell over backwards and, thinking he was dissecting the devil, fled away in terror and fell down the staircase in his flight. His wife ran in at the noise from another room; she saw me stretched out on the table with my crucial incision; she was still more frightened than her husband, fled, and fell on top of him. When they had recovered themselves a little, I heard the surgeon's wife say to the surgeon:

"'My dear, what were you thinking of, to dissect a heretic? Don't you know the devil always possesses them? I will go and get a priest at once to exorcise him.'

"At this I shuddered and collected the little strength I had left to shout

"'Have pity on me!'

"At last the Portuguese barber grew bolder; he sewed up my skin; his wife even took care of me, and at the end of a fortnight I was able to walk again. The barber found me a situation and made me lackey to a Knight of Malta who was going to Venice; but, as my master had no money to pay me wages, I entered the service of a Venetian merchant and followed him to Constantinople.

"One day I took it into my head to enter a mosque; there was nobody there except an old Imam and a very pretty young devotee who was reciting her prayers; her breasts were entirely uncovered; between them she wore a bunch of tulips, roses, anemones, ranunculus, hyacinths and auriculas; she dropped her bunch of flowers; I picked it up and returned it to her with a most respectful alacrity. I was so long putting them back that the Imam grew angry and, seeing I was a Christian, called for help. I was taken to the cadi, who sentenced me to receive a hundred strokes on the soles of my feet and sent me to the galleys. I was chained on the same seat and in the same galley as My Lord the Baron. In this galley there were four young men from Marseilles, five Neapolitan priests and two monks from Corfu, who assured us that similar accidents occurred every day. His Lordship the Baron claimed that he had suffered a greater injustice than I; and I claimed that it was much more permissible to replace a bunch of flowers between a woman's breasts than to be naked with one of the Sultan's pages. We argued continually, and every day received twenty strokes of the bull's pizzle, when the chain of events of this universe led you to our galley and you ransomed us."

"Well! my dear Pangloss," said Candide, "when you were hanged, dissected, stunned with blows and made to row in the galleys, did you always think that everything was for the best in this world?"

"I am still of my first opinion," replied Pangloss, "for after all I am a philosopher; and it would be unbecoming for me to recant, since Leibnitz could not be in the wrong and pre-established harmony is the finest thing imaginable like the plenum [1] and subtle matter."

CHAPTER XXIX

How Candide found Cunegonde and the old woman again

While Candide, the Baron, Pangloss, Martin and Cacambo were relating their adventures, reasoning upon contingent or non-contingent events of the universe, arguing about effects and causes, moral and physical evil, free-will and necessity, and the consolations to be found in the Turkish galleys, they came to the house of the Transylvanian prince on the shores of Propontis.

The first objects which met their sight were Cunegonde and the old woman hanging out towels to dry on the line.

At this sight the Baron grew pale. Candide, that tender lover, seeing his fair Cunegonde sunburned, blear-eyed, flat-breasted, with wrinkles round her eyes and red, chapped arms, recoiled three paces in horror, and then advanced from mere politeness.

She embraced Candide and her brother. They embraced the old woman; Candide bought them both.

In the neighborhood was a little farm; the old woman suggested that Candide should buy it, until some better fate befell the group. Cunegonde did not know that she had become ugly, for nobody had told her so; she reminded Candide of his

[1] Latin — "full." A philosophical conception which holds that all space is fully occupied by matter.

promises in so peremptory a tone that the good Candide dared not refuse her.

He therefore informed the Baron that he was about to marry his sister.

"Never," said the Baron, "will I endure such baseness on her part and such insolence on yours; nobody shall ever reproach me with this infamy; my sister's children could never enter the chapters of Germany. No, my sister shall never marry anyone but a Baron of the Empire."

Cunegonde threw herself at his feet and bathed them in tears; but he was inflexible.

"Madman," said Candide, "I rescued you from the galleys, I paid your ransom and your sister's; she was washing dishes here, she is ugly, I am so kind as to make her my wife, and you pretend to oppose me! I should kill you again if I listened to my anger."

"You may kill me again," said the Baron, "but you shall never marry my sister while I am alive."

CHAPTER XXX

Conclusion

At the bottom of his heart Candide had not the least wish to marry Cunegonde. But the Baron's extreme impertinence determined him to complete the marriage, and Cunegonde urged it so warmly that he could not retract. He consulted Pangloss, Martin and the faithful Cacambo. Pangloss wrote an excellent memorandum by which he proved that the Baron had no rights over his sister and that by all the laws of the empire she could make a left-handed marriage with Candide. Martin advised that the Baron should be thrown into the sea; Cacambo decided that he should be returned to the Levantine captain and sent back to the galleys, after which he would be returned by the first ship to the Vicar-General at Rome. This was thought to be very good advice; the old woman approved it; they said nothing to the sister; the plan was carried out with the aid of a little money and they had the pleasure of duping a Jesuit and punishing the pride of a German Baron.

It would be natural to suppose that when, after so many disasters, Candide was married to his mistress, and living with the philosopher Pangloss, the philosopher Martin, the prudent Cacambo and the old woman, having brought back so many diamonds from the country of the ancient Incas, would lead the most pleasant life imaginable. But he was so cheated by the Jews that he had nothing left but his little farm; his wife, growing uglier every day, became shrewish and unendurable; the old woman was ailing and even more bad-tempered than Cunegonde. Cacambo, who worked in the garden and then went to Constantinople to sell vegetables, was overworked and cursed his fate. Pangloss was in despair because he did not shine in some German university.

As for Martin, he was firmly convinced that people are equally uncomfortable everywhere; he accepted things patiently. Candide, Martin and Pangloss sometimes argued about metaphysics and morals. From the windows of the farm they often watched the ships going by, filled with effendis, pashas, and cadis, who were being exiled to Lemnos, to Mitylene and Erzerum. They saw other cadis, other pashas and other effendis coming back to take the place of the exiles and to be exiled in their turn. They saw the neatly impaled heads which were taken to the Sublime Porte. These sights redoubled their discussions; and when they were not arguing, the boredom was so excessive that one day the old woman dared to say to them:

"I should like to know which is worse, to be raped a hundred times by negro pirates, to have a buttock cut off, to run the gauntlet among the Bulgarians, to be whipped and flogged in an *auto-da-fé*, to be dissected, to row in a galley, in short, to endure all the miseries through which we have passed, or to remain here doing nothing?"

"'Tis a great question," said Candide.

These remarks led to new reflections, and Martin especially concluded that man was born to live in the convulsions of distress or in the lethargy of boredom. Candide did not agree, but he asserted nothing. Pangloss confessed that he had always suffered horribly; but, having once maintained that everything was for the best, he had continued to maintain it without believing it.

One thing confirmed Martin in his detestable principles, made Candide hesitate more than ever, and embarrassed Pangloss. And it was this. One day there came to their farm Paquette and Friar Giroflée, who were in the most extreme misery; they had soon wasted their three thousand piastres, had left each other, made it up, quarrelled again, been put in prison, escaped, and finally Friar Giroflée had turned Turk. Paquette continued her occupation everywhere and now earned nothing by it.

"I foresaw," said Martin to Candide, "that your gifts would soon be wasted and would only make them the more miserable. You and Cacambo were once bloated with millions of piastres and you are no happier than Friar Giroflée and **Paquette.**"

"Ah! Ha!" said Pangloss to Paquette, "so Heaven brings you back to us, my dear child? Do you know that you cost me the end of my nose, an eye and an ear! What a plight you are in! Ah! What a world this is!"

This new occurrence caused them to philosophise more than ever.

In the neighborhood there lived a very famous Dervish, who was supposed to be the best philosopher in Turkey; they went to consult him; Pangloss was the spokesman and said:

"Master, we have come to beg you to tell us why so strange an animal as man was ever created."

"What has it to do with you?" said the Dervish. "Is it your business?"

"But, reverend father," said Candide, "there is a horrible amount of evil in the world."

"What does it matter," said the Dervish, "whether there is evil or good? When his highness sends a ship to Egypt, does he worry about the comfort or discomfort of the rats in the ship?"

"Then what should we do?" said Pangloss.

"Hold your tongue," said the Dervish.

"I flattered myself," said Pangloss, "that I should discuss with you effects and causes, this best of all possible worlds, the origin of evil, the nature of the soul and pre-established harmony."

At these words the Dervish slammed the door in their faces.

During this conversation the news went round that at Constantinople two viziers and the mufti had been strangled and several of their friends impaled. This catastrophe made a prodigious noise everywhere for several hours. As Pangloss, Candide and Martin were returning to their little farm, they came upon an old man who was taking the air under a bower of orange-trees at his door. Pangloss, who was as curious as he was argumentative, asked him what was the name of the mufti who had just been strangled.

"I do not know," replied the old man. "I have never known the name of any mufti or of any vizier. I am entirely ignorant of the occurrence you mention; I presume that in general those who meddle with public affairs sometimes perish miserably and that they deserve it; but I never inquire what is going on in Constantinople; I content myself with sending there for sale the produce of the garden I cultivate."

Having spoken thus, he took the strangers into his house. His two daughters and his two sons presented them with several kinds of sherbet which they made themselves, caymac flavored with candied citron peel, oranges, lemons, limes, pine-apples, dates, pistachios and Mocha coffee which had not been mixed with the bad coffee of

Batavia and the Isles. After which this good Mussulman's two daughters perfumed the beards of Candide, Pangloss and Martin.

"You must have a vast and magnificent estate?" said Candide to the Turk.

"I have only twenty acres," replied the Turk. "I cultivate them with my children; and work keeps at bay three great evils: Boredom, vice and need."

As Candide returned to his farm he reflected deeply on the Turk's remarks. He said to Pangloss and Martin:

"That good old man seems to me to have chosen an existence preferable by far to that of the six kings with whom we had the honor to sup."

"Exalted rank," said Pangloss, "is very dangerous, according to the testimony of all philosophers; for Eglon, King of the Moabites, was murdered by Ehud; Absalom was hanged by the hair and pierced by three darts; King Nadab, son of Jeroboam, was killed by Baasha; King Elah by Zimri; Ahaziah by Jehu; Athaliah by Jehoiada; the Kings Jehoiakim, Jeconiah and Zedekiah were made slaves. You know in what manner died Crœsus, Astyages, Darius, Denys of Syracuse, Pyrrhus, Perseus, Hannibal, Jugurtha, Ariovistus, Cæsar, Pompey, Nero, Otho, Vitellius, Domitian, Richard II of England, Edward II, Henry VI, Richard III, Mary Stuart, Charles I, the three Henrys of France, the Emperor Henry IV. You know . . ."

"I also know," said Candide, "that we should cultivate our gardens."

"You are right," said Pangloss, "for, when man was placed in the Garden of Eden, he was placed there *ut operaratur eum*, to dress it and to keep it; which proves that man was not born for idleness."

"Let us work without arguing," said Martin; "'tis the only way to make life endurable."

The whole small fraternity entered into this praiseworthy plan, and each started to make use of his talents. The little farm yielded well. Cunegonde was indeed very ugly, but she became an excellent pastry-cook; Paquette embroidered; the old woman took care of the linen. Even Friar Giroflée performed some service; he was a very good carpenter and even became a man of honor; and Pangloss sometimes said to Candide:

"All events are linked up in this best of all possible worlds; for, if you had not been expelled from the noble castle, by hard kicks in your backside for love of Miss Cunegonde, if you had not been clapped into the Inquisition, if you had not wandered about America on foot, if you had not stuck your sword in the Baron, if you had not lost all your sheep from the land of Eldorado, you would not be eating candied citrons and pistachios here."

"'Tis well said," replied Candide, "but we must cultivate our gardens."

References for

THE TEMPER OF CLASSICISM

A NOTE ON THE REFERENCES

Following each section of this anthology are three sets of references: (1) a list of books in the field of literature which are thought to be useful to the student who would read further regarding each of the literary "tempers," (2) a list of reproductions (painting, sculpture, architecture) which reflect in the field of art the literary mood which is being considered, and (3) a list of musical recordings which illustrate the same mood in music. Such lists, the student should keep in mind, run the danger of oversimplifying. In all three — literature, art, music — the characteristics of classicism or romanticism or any other temper may appear in fairly pure state or, perhaps as often, two or more tempers may be fused in one poem, one painting, one symphony. In painting, for instance, we may find a classical subject treated in a realistic manner, a romantic subject symbolically presented. The items are classified below according to what seem *dominant* qualities.

LITERATURE

ARISTOTLE (384–322 B.C.)
  Poetics

HORACE (65–8 B.C.)
  The Art of Poetry

LONGINUS (*c.* 213–273)
  On the Sublime

JOHN DRYDEN (1631–1700)
  An Essay of Dramatic Poesy

NICHOLAS BOILEAU-DESPRÉAUX (1636–1711)
  The Art of Poetry

ALEXANDER POPE (1688–1744)
  An Essay on Criticism

MATTHEW ARNOLD (1822–1888)
  Essays in Criticism

IRVING BABBITT
  The New Laokoön (1910)

WALTER JACKSON BATE
  From Classic to Romantic: Premises of Taste in Eighteenth-Century England (new ed., 1961)

E. B. BORGERHOFF
  The Freedom of French Classicism (1950)

C. M. BOWRA
  From Virgil to Milton (new ed., 1961)

THOMAS BULFINCH
  The Age of Fable (rev. by W. H. Klapp, 1961)

JOSEPH CAMPBELL
  The Hero With a Thousand Faces (1949)

H. CAUDWELL
  Introduction to French Classicism (2nd ed., 1954)

T. S. ELIOT
  Classics and the Man of Letters (1942)
  What is a Classic? (1945)

J. G. FRAZER
  The Golden Bough. A Study in Magic and Religion (3rd ed., 1960)

H. J. C. GRIERSON
  The Background of English Literature, Classical and Romantic, and other Collected Essays and Addresses (2nd ed., 1960)

MOSES HADAS
  Ancilla to Classical Reading (1954)

EDITH HAMILTON
  The Great Age of Greek Literature (1942)
  The Roman Way (1932)

PHILIP W. HARSH
  A Handbook of Classical Drama (3rd ed., 1963)

GILBERT HIGHET
  The Classical Tradition; Greek and Roman Influences on Western Literature (2nd ed., 1954)

KAROLY KERENYI
  The Gods of the Greeks and Romans (1962)

HUGH LLOYD-JONES, ed.
  The Greek World (1965)

A. R. MONCRIEFF
  Classic Myth and Legend (1934)

GILBERT MURRAY
  The Classical Tradition in Poetry (2nd ed., 1930)

DAN S. NORTON and PETER RUSHTON
  Classical Myths in English Literature (1952)

W. J. OATES, ed.
  From Sophocles to Picasso: The Present-Day Vitality of the Classical Tradition (1962)

M. R. RIDLEY
  Studies in Three Literatures. English, Latin, Greek. Contrasts and Comparisons (1962)

H. J. ROSE
  Outlines of Classical Literature (1959)

RICHARD HINTON THOMAS
  The Classical Ideal in German Literature 1755–1805 (1939)

J. A. K. THOMSON
  The Classical Background of English Literature (1948)

385

ART

GIOTTO (1266?–1336)
The Presentation of the Virgin
The Death of St. Francis

FRA ANGELICO (1387–1455)
The Annunciation
The Entombment

MANTEGNA (1431–1506)
The Triumph of Cæsar
Judith and Holofernes

LEONARDO DA VINCI (1452–1519)
Mona Lisa
Bacchus

MICHELANGELO (1475–1564)
Detail of Adam in Creation of Man
Libyan Sibyl

RAPHAEL (1483–1520)
School of Athens
Madonna della Sedia
The Alba Madonna

DÜRER (1471–1528)
Knight, Death, and the Devil
Adoration of the Magi

MENGS (1728–1774)
Parnassus

POUSSIN (1594–1665)
Shepherds of Arcadia

DAVID (1748–1825)
Oath of the Horatii
Paris and Helen
Rape of the Sabine Women
Madame Récamier

GÉRARD (1770–1837)
Psyche Receiving the Kiss of Love
Madam Récamier

INGRES (1780–1867)
The Apotheosis of Homer
La Source
The Countess d'Haussonville

BENJAMIN WEST (1738–1820)
Death of Wolfe at Quebec
Colonel Guy Johnson

GILBERT STUART (1755–1828)
Thomas Jefferson
Mrs. Richard Yates
Benjamin West

ALBERTI (1404–1472)
Palazzo Ruccelai, Florence

SAN GALLO and MICHELANGELO (XVI Century)
Palazzo Farnese, Rome

JEFFERSON (1743–1826)
Capitol, Richmond, Virginia
Monticello, Virginia

SOANE (1753–1837)
Bank of England

CHALGRIN (XIX Century)
Arc de Triomphe de l'Étoile

VIGNON (1762–1820)
Church of the Madeleine

GABRIEL (1698–1782)
Petit Trianon

after Myron
Discus Thrower

after Polykleitos
Spearbearer

PRAXITELES
Hermes

DONATELLO (1386–1466)
St. George

VERROCCHIO (1435–1488)
Putto Poised on Globe

MICHELANGELO (1475–1564)
Bust of Brutus

HORATIO GREENOUGH (1805–1852)
George Washington

EUTHYMIDES (VI Century B.C.)
Theseus Carrying off Korone

DOURIS (V Century B.C.)
Voting between Ajax and Odysseus

MUSIC

It was suggested earlier in this text that when literature is calm and restrained, when it subordinates content to form, it is controlled by a temper essentially classical. The same thing can be said about music, although in music, more readily than in literature, one mood flows into another, and the classifications cannot be followed too rigidly.

The qualities of classic music at its best and purest are easily observable. There is a stricter adherence to the rules and models inherited from preceding composers than is apparent in later music. One authority defines classic music as music

> in which a more or less consciously accepted scheme of design is evident, with an emphasis on elements of proportions and of beauty as such — as distinguished from that class in which the main object appears to be the expression of emotion, or even the representation in tone of ideas which usually receive, not a musical, but rather a literary or pictorial expression.[1]

[1] Percy A. Scholes, *The Oxford Companion to Music* (New York: Oxford University Press, 1938), pp. 174–75.

By Mozart's time there were several generally accepted forms which musical composition followed. One of the most important of these forms will be discussed here, the *sonata form*. *Sonata form*, the customary form of first movements — the Rondo, theme and variation, or minuet are other forms found in other movements — should not be confused with the musical composition known as the *sonata*. A sonata commonly is a composition in four movements — an opening allegro, a slow movement, a lively movement (frequently a minuet), and a final movement which is almost always fast. The first movements of sonatas in classical style are written in *sonata form*. Here is a useful description of that form. Sonata form

is an expanded ABA pattern divided into an exposition, a development section, and a recapitulation. . . .

A movement in sonata form . . . will begin with the statement of the principal subject. This subject may be of almost any length and nature, the only real requirement being that it allow ample possibilities for later development. It is followed by a second subject designed as a contrast and written in a different key. If the first subject was strongly rhythmical, the second is likely to be primarily melodic; or if the first was announced by the brass, the second may well be given out by the woodwinds. Once these two themes have been stated, the essential basis of the entire movement is established: one might paraphrase Coleridge by saying that sonata form is devoted to the reconciliation of opposite or discordant themes. The announcement of these two subjects will usually be followed by a brief section devoted to a considerably less important closing subject. . . .

This middle section is . . . freer. . . . It allows for varied treatment in distant keys of any material presented by the exposition, and it may even include new material. There is really no restriction on the composer except that he exploit the possibilities of his themes and that he have a final cadence (usually a brilliant cadenza in the concerto) leading back to the original key of the movement and thus introducing the recapitulation.

This last section is exactly what its name implies — the final A section of the vastly expanded ABA form. It repeats the first, second, and closing subjects, putting them all in the tonic key this time in order to achieve an effect of finality. This repetition, like that of the simple ABA form, does not have to be exact and literal, but it must be unmistakable and must give the effect of repetition rather than of further development. . . . Reducing sonata form to its simplest terms, we may summarily describe it as the statement of a first subject, a contrasting second subject, and a closing subject; the development of this thematic material; and finally its restatement.[1]

[1] Calvin S. Brown, *Music and Literature* (Athens, Georgia: The University of Georgia Press, 1948), pp. 162–63. The reader who is interested in the relation of music and the written word will find this a fascinating book.

Sonata form, then, is one of the patterns which the classical composers followed in composing their symphonies; it is the skeleton which supported their musical creations. When we hear a great classical symphony like the "Haffner" by Mozart several times, we become aware of the genius which fills out the pattern and makes the composition what it is. Mozart had unlimited melodic resources; some of his melodies are the loveliest the world has ever heard. In this symphony he has shaped that material into a magnificent architectural structure. In the "Haffner" we have a combination of lyric melody and mathematical construction which makes it one of the great classic symphonies.

But, we may ask, what is the difference between a classical theme and a romantic theme? A romantic composer could clothe the same form with his musical ideas; the form would be classical; what is there about the classical theme that makes it distinguishable from the romantic?

Classical music is absolute music — music which is complete without words. A classical theme is a theme which in itself is self-sufficient. The author as a composer and we as hearers are interested in *it* and in its elaboration and development in a composition. It may have emotional overtones but we are not primarily interested in these. A romantic theme, on the other hand, is one which is heard more as the expression of an emotion, or a sentiment, than as an element in a musical structure.

Since classical music leans so heavily upon form, the titles generally indicate the technical nature of the composition. Once the listener is familiar with the structure of the various forms, the music will be much more intelligible than it is at first hearing. All of the music listed in this book is serious music; all of it is music which should be heard more than once to be appreciated properly.

R. N. C.

COMPOSITIONS

CARL PHILLIP EMANUEL BACH (1714–1788)
Symphony No. 3 in C Major

This work is classical in form and thematic material; it has three movements, and is performed as a continuous work. It is a forerunner of later compositions more like the symphonies of Haydn and Mozart.

CORELLI (1653–1713)
Concerto Grosso in G Minor ("Christmas Concerto")

A Concerto Grosso in the 18th century was really an orchestral concerto — a succession of movements played by two or more solo instrumentalists, and accompanied by the whole orchestra. This is typical in form, but outstanding for the beauty of its melodies.

HÄNDEL (1685–1759)
Suites for Harpsichord, Book 1: Nos. 4, 5, 6

The suite is an adaptation of the dance music of the period by the classical composers, as contrasted to the Sonata, which grew out of church music. Each suite usually consists of a prelude and several movements written in a dance form. All movements are written in the same key, a fact which created a certain monotony not relieved until composers wrote symphonies, each movement of which might be in a different key. The Händel suites are typical of the classical suite.

HAYDN (1732–1809)
Symphony No. 102 in B Flat Major

A classical symphony, but in the themes of the slow movement may be detected romantic overtones which foreshadow the fully developed romanticism of the 19th century. A good example of Haydn's symphonic style.

BACH (1685–1750)
Suite for Unaccompanied 'Cello, No. 3

A prelude and six dances. This is the work of Johann Sebastian Bach, the father of an illustrious musical family.

Preludes and Fugues from the "Well Tempered Clavichord"

Before hearing these it may be well to study the form of the fugue in a good source book, such as the *Oxford Companion to Music*. Bach's fugues are masterpieces of counterpoint, the art of interweaving melodies into a pattern. This is absolute music at its purest.

MOZART (1756–1791)
Symphony in D Major ("Haffner"), K. 385

A model of a classical symphony as written by Mozart. It includes a brilliant opening movement, a quiet second one, a robust third, and a vigorous finale.

Quintet for Clarinet and Strings, K. 581

Classical in form, with warmly melodic themes. Note especially the theme and variations, and the hints of romanticism in the Romanza.

Sonata in F Major, K. 332

A piano sonata, in which each movement is in sonata form. A good sonata to study for purpose of learning the form; the accompanying folder has a good analysis which is helpful.

An Chloe (A song for Soprano and Piano), K. 524

BEETHOVEN (1770–1827)
Symphony No. 4 in B Flat Major, Op. 60

All movements but the third are in sonata form, and the thematic material is (again in all but the third movement) less subjective than in others of his symphonies.

Symphony No. 8, in F Major, Op. 93

Strict observance of classical form and objective thematic material place this symphony in the classical list.

Concerto No. 4 for Piano and Orchestra, in G Major

The first and last movements are classical in form (first — sonata form; last — Rondo). The content is a blend of classical and romantic material; the second movement is more romantic than any of the others.

TSCHAIKOWSKY (1840–1893)
Serenade in C Major, Op. 48

Tschaikowsky said of his first movement: "It is my homage to Mozart; it is intended to be an imitation of his style." It is sonata form without a development section. All but the third movement are classical in form.

PROKOFIEFF (1891–1953)
Classical Symphony in D Major

A composition which attempts (and succeeds very well) to capture the spirit of Mozart. Prokofieff here wrote music which he believed Mozart might have written were he living today. It is classical in form, Mozartian in spirit, but modern in idiom.

IBERT (1890–   )
Concertino da Camera for Saxophone and Orchestra (1st and 3rd Movements)
These movements use distinctly modern material in a formal pattern which is more like the old *concerto grosso* than is at first apparent.

HINDEMITH (1895–   )
Quartet No. 3, Op. 22
Another modern composer whose material is extremely modern, but who shows a tendency in his compositions to follow classical patterns.

GREGORIAN CHANT
Plainsong (or Gregorian Chant) is pure melody, and needs no accompaniment. It is the music of the Church and belongs to the pre-harmonic age, that is, the age before harmony was used for accompaniment.

BLOCH (1880–   )
Concerto Grosso for Piano and String Orchestra

A modern treatment of the 18th-century form. Compare with the concerto by Corelli.

THE

Romantic Mood

THE ROMANTICS

THE SYMBOLISTS

THE

Romantic Mood

THE ROMANTICS

THE SYMBOLISTS

THE

ROMANTICS

❧

> Will no one tell me what she sings? —
> Perhaps the plaintive numbers flow
> For old, unhappy, far-off things,
> And battles long ago.
>
> WORDSWORTH

WILL THE REGENERATION of society be more readily secured through law and order and a respect for authority, through love and faith and a following of ideals, or through the analysis of a situation, a facing of facts, and the spread of science? It is impossible to give a satisfactory answer to such a question. At times in the history of the world one conviction has dominated, at other times another. And within a given period convincing supporters for each of these attitudes may be found. It is true, too, that any one individual gives different answers at different periods of his life according to the mood which may prevail at a given time.

Through all the vicissitudes of history, through all the years in which man has set down his ideas and his dreams for others to read, the romantic spirit has inspired great literature. It is in the very make-up of man. It is part of his utterance whenever he gives rein to his emotions and his imagination, whenever he imagines in nature a sympathetic response to

391

his inner promptings, whenever he is stirred by unusual wonder and beauty to unrestrained expression of his feelings, whenever, in fact, within him sings

> The self-same song that found a path
> Through the sad heart of Ruth, when sick for home,
> She stood in tears amid the alien corn;
>   The same that oft-times hath
> Charm'd magic casements, opening on the foam
> Of perilous seas, in faery lands forlorn.

The lineage of this romantic temper is both long and honorable, a temper more ancient than our books on the "Romantic Movement" would lead us to suppose. The history of letters teaches us, again and again, that movements do not spring full grown from the rib of literature. Textbooks of literature make much of the "pre-romantics" of the eighteenth century, but even these precursors had their forerunners in Oriental writing, in the early myths of Greece and Rome, in the *Daphnis and Chloë* of Longus and *The Golden Ass* of Apuleius. Just how persistent in the literature of the West this romantic spirit is will be manifest to anyone who recalls the tale of *Cupid and Psyche* presented in the *Golden Ass* of Apuleius, the idyl of youthful love in a setting of sympathetic nature in *Daphnis and Chloë*, the adversities of Siegfried and Brunhild, and the battles with strange monsters of the deep which enliven the *Beowulf*. This romantic temper shows itself again in the Middle Ages in the beast epic of, for instance, the *Roman de Reynard*, a twelfth-century series of picaresque tales as essentially romantic as *Kubla Khan* or the *Waverley* novels. There is, too, the whole series of medieval romances: *Aucassin and Nicolete, Gawain and the Green Knight, Richard Cœur de Lion, Sir Ferumbras, Flore and Blanchefleur* and the rest, — tales of courtly jousting, of ladies generous or parsimonious in the bestowal of their favors, of the crusades filled with adventure. And then the balladry — surely it springs as much as the beast epics and the metrical romances from the very heart of the romantic spirit. *Sir Patrick Spence, Robin Hood's Death and Burial, Lord Thomas and Fair Annet, The Dæmon Lover, Bonny Barbara Allan* — where else is the romantic manner so concentrated? Melancholy, strange beauty, passion, the supernatural, zest and enthusiasm for life, fabulous deeds — all these were qualities of the ballads long before the time of Wordsworth and Coleridge and the beginnings of the so-called "Romantic Movement" in 1798. To confine this romantic temper within a century or two of literary history is to overlook, as well, Spenser's *Faerie Queene* and that greatest of all love stories in English, Shakespeare's *Romeo and Juliet*. Certainly even a sketchy list of this nature testifies to the presence of the romantic spirit long before Young and Thomson and the Wartons, the official "precursors" of romanticism. It might be argued that there was as full a display of romantic qualities in our literature before *The Lyrical Ballads* as in Wordsworth, Coleridge, Keats, Shelley, and Byron — that there was as romantic a literature before Rousseau as after. Indeed, as Professor Bernbaum points out, the distinction of being the "first romantic" has been variously accorded to St. Paul, Christ, Plato, Homer, Milton and, since he incited rebellion, the Serpent in the Garden of Eden.

For decades, critics of literature on the Continent, in England, in America, have attempted to find ready definitions of romanticism. The romantic spirit has been variously characterized as: "the return to nature" (Rousseau), "liberalism in literature" (Hugo), "sentimental melancholy" (Phelps), "imagination as contrasted with reason" (Neilson), "the grotesque" (Hugo), "reawakening of the Middle Ages" (Heine), "the Renascence of wonder" (Watts-Dunton), "a tendency toward individualism" (Brunetière), and "curiosity and the love of beauty" (Pater). Other key ideas which have been suggested rather commonly are "enthusiasm for the wild and irregular," respect for the manner of living of "the noble savage," "emotional psychology," the "democratic attitude," an "attack upon the established order," and "the restoration of passion." And, again, we are told that the romantic manner is made up of ecstasy, is characterized by spontaneity, a zest for living, the excessive, that it is fond of playing upon our senses by a reliance on terror and the supernatural. With still other critics romanticism is revolt, or dreaming, or faith without reason, or a listening to the music of a distant drum.

Rarely do moods exist unmixed. The romantic manner is too complex for such simplification. One cannot characterize Byron, Carlyle, or Coleridge in a single phrase. And yet the romantic manner in literature, as distinguished from the "Romantic Movement" in literary history, is easily recognized. One need glance over only a few familiar verses to see in them many of those qualities known to be romantic:

> The mystery and majesty of Earth.
> The joy, the exultation . . .
>
> *Shelley*

> Then sing, ye Birds, sing, sing a joyous song!
> And let the young lambs bound
> As to the tabor's sound!
>
> *Wordsworth*

> 'Tis the middle of Night by the castle clock.
>
> *Coleridge*

> La Belle Dame sans Merci
> Hath thee in thrall.
>
> *Keats*

> He who, from zone to zone,
> Guides through the boundless sky thy certain flight,
> In the long way that I must tread alone,
> Will lead my steps aright.
>
> *Bryant*

Does any reader take these lines to be by Æschylus or Sophocles or Racine or Pope? Does anyone see in them the doctrines of the classicist or the realist? They are of the very stuff of which romanticism is made.

We must not expect to find all of the qualities mentioned above present in any one piece of writing or in any one romantic writer. What does make us characterize literature as "romantic" is the presence of *enough* of these qualities, and the exclusion of *enough* of those elements which we think of as classical or realistic, to swing the balance in favor of the romantic spirit. In our consideration of this spirit in literature we must avoid the

(continued on page 395)

The Romantic Mood

THE ROMANTIC as contrasted with the classical writer is emotional and passionate. He seeks an escape from the actual world to a world of the past, the remote in time and space; he finds new satisfaction in nature, particularly in a nature informal, wild, and irregular. The romantic is moody; at times exuberant, at times tinged by a deep melancholy. He is likely to live in an imagined rather than a real world. An individualist, he is a democrat believing with Rousseau in the dignity and worth of the elemental man. He seeks adventure and lives by faith rather than by reason. For the romantic in art, form is less important than idea. The key word is *freedom* — freedom to give rein to one's emotions and dreams, to let color and mass dominate line.

Consider, for instance, *The Bark of Dante* and *Fonthill Abbey*. Here surely are feeling and passion and emotion such as did not appear in the illustrations gathered within the classical group. Note the faces of the men in and about Dante's boat, particularly the face of the man trying to climb over the end of the bark. Can the expression in that face be duplicated among all the classical figures? Or note the tall tower and pointed lines of Fonthill Abbey. Would anyone mistake them for the features of the Parthenon? See how nature assumes importance in Corot's *Souvenir of Italy*, Constable's *The Hay Wain*, Inness' *Peace and Plenty*. Man has come outdoors under the sky. He is a creature of his moods and his fancies. *Fonthill Abbey* speaks of his melancholy; *The Lion Hunt* of his delight in action and adventure.

In addition to showing the main characteristics of romanticism, the last six plates in the group are examples of the pictorial use of symbolism. Here the imagination and fancy are still free to roam, but they move with a second significance, an allegorical implication. Rude's *Hymn of Departure for War* gathers all of the action as well as most of the warlike symbols into a single statue. In *Toilers of the Sea*, Ryder conveys the notion of the sea's menacing and primitive wildness by depicting irregular cloud-formations which veil the sun and by emphasizing a disproportion in size of boat and fishermen rather than through a direct representation of the surging waves in a sea-storm. Vedder's *Cup of Death* also bears heavy overtones of the symbolic (here: the allegorical) in the figure of the death-bringing angel. Symbolical in their own way, too, are Hunt's *Flight of Night* and Watts' *Hope*.

In painting or architecture or literature — in all the arts — the romantic temper is exuberant, free. If it is at times given over to melancholy, to a turning back to the past, it is, as well, capable of great action and restless in its search to attain a better world even as the towers of its cathedrals reach to clutch the sky.

Plate 16   EDMUND AND CRAWFORD ANTROBUS   *Lawrence*

Plate 17   THE BARK OF DANTE   *Delacroix*

Plate 18   THE LION HUNT   *Rubens*

Plate 19   SOUVENIR OF ITALY. CASTEL GANDOLFO   *Corot*

Plate 20   THE HAY WAIN   *Constable*

Plate 21   APOLLO AND THE HOURS   *Reni*

Plate 22   PEACE AND PLENTY   *Inness*

Plate 23   W. K. VANDERBILT MANSION   *Hunt*

Plate 24   FONTHILL ABBEY   *Wyatt*

Plate 25   HYMN OF DEPARTURE FOR WAR   *Rude*

Plate 26   THE NYMPH OF FONTAINEBLEAU   *Cellini*

Plate 27

THE CUP OF DEATH

Vedder

Plate 28   FLIGHT OF NIGHT   *Hunt*

Plate 29   HOPE   *Watts*

Plate 30

TOILERS OF

THE SEA

Ryder

danger of setting down a formula which such writing is to follow. Instead, we should look for those features which, more or less regularly, in various combinations and with notable omissions, somehow work together to create the romantic outlook on life.

Among the qualities of the romantic temper, *the presentation of the individual point of view* may be placed first. It is not concerned with portraying a rational or external world; it is very much concerned with portraying the world from the vantage point of the personality of the writer. Irving Babbitt seeking, as he did, for a more precise order in the universe, seems to regret the romantic's "power to enthrall the individual sensibility." Yet it is this "individual sensibility" which makes each romantic writer what he is. If it is to be ruled out, then romanticism itself must go, for it is largely this power to set forth one's individual emotions, personal ideals, one's responses to "moonlight on a midnight stream," which distinguishes this temper from the classical and from the realistic. Indeed, romanticism *is* subjectivism; it springs, as F. L. Lucas has insisted, from the author's capacity to "release the unconscious." "Life in this world," says Lascelles Abercrombie, "is likely to be most satisfactory when the mind withdraws from outer things and turns in upon itself." When the romantic poet looks abroad and finds that

> There is a pleasure in the pathless woods,
> There is a rapture on the lonely shore

it is not the pathless woods and the lonely shore in themselves that he finds valuable, but the internal responses to which they give rise. They stimulate within him a pleasurable freeing of emotion. In the woods and the shore, Narcissus-like, he finds himself reflected. No one has ever insisted that the romantics were better students of nature than the botanists; they care very little if at all for nature as nature. They care very much for nature as a symbol of their own individual life. At its worst such reliance on the emotions brings us to the maudlin sentimentality of, say, a Coleridge when he permitted himself to apostrophize a young ass as

> Innocent Fool! thou poor despised forlorn!
> I hail thee brother — spite of the world's scorn!

At its best this same trusting of the personal emotion, this releasing of the individual imagination, will make us see

> The blue Mediterranean, where he lay,
> Lulled by the coil of his crystalline streams;

or hail a Grecian urn as

> Thou still unravished bride of quietness.

Romanticism, no more than classicism, is to be judged by its weaknesses; emotion and passion — there is room for these in literature.

Nor was this personal emotion by any means restricted to the beauties of rural nature. Charles Lamb, for instance, found the same release in the heart of London that Wordsworth found about Grasmere. He wrote to Wordsworth:

... I have passed all my days in London, until I have formed as many and as intense local attachments as any of you mountaineers can have done with dead Nature. The lighted shops of the Strand and Fleet Street; the innumerable trades, tradesmen and customers, coaches, wagons, playhouses; all the bustle and wickedness round about Covent Garden; the very women of the Town; the watchmen, drunken scenes, rattles; life awake, if you awake, at all hours of the night; the impossibility of being dull in Fleet Street; the crowds, the very dirt and mud, the sun shining upon houses and pavements, the print shops, the old book stalls, parsons cheap'ning books, coffee houses, steams of soups from kitchens, the pantomimes — London itself a pantomime and a masquerade — all these things work themselves into my mind, and feed me, without a power of satiating me. The wonder of these sights impels me into night-walks about her crowded streets, and I often shed tears in the motley Strand from fulness of joy at so much life. All these emotions must be strange to you. So are your rural emotions to me. But consider, what I must have been doing all my life, not to have lent great portions of my heart with usury to such scenes?

The passage shows Lamb as thorough a romantic as Wordsworth: the personal attitude comes to the front, it manifests an aroused emotion. The degree to which a writer allows himself to live in his sensations distinguishes him as romantic or realistic. Paul Elmer More, unsympathetic as he was toward the romantic spirit, held that the romantic attitude is "an expansive conceit of the emotions which goes with the illusion of beholding the infinite within the stream of nature itself instead of apart from the stream." And to the classicist or the realist this reliance on the emotions may well appear as a "conceit"; it is a way of life different from theirs. But it is no more conclusive for More to damn the emotion characteristic of romanticism than, say, for Coleridge to condemn the artificiality of classicism.

The romantic writer often shifts his point of view. Trusting his personal sensations, he finds the world one day "dancing with the daffodils" and another day tells us that "a tear is an intellectual thing." Joy and enthusiasm alternate with melancholy and Byronic pessimism. Even when regarding the same scene, a poet finds it one day the basis for happiness, another day reason for despair, as witness Wordsworth's sonnet *Composed Upon Westminster Bridge* in which London appeared to him a desired city, and yet, in the same month, September, 1802, another sonnet *Written in London* portrays the same city as one which lives by "rapine, avarice, and expense." Could any clearer evidence of the mercurial quality of the romantic, of his persistent trust in his sensations and his moods, be found? And yet were Wordsworth to be confronted by a classicist and told to restrain his personal emotion, or by a realist and told to make up his mind once for all that London might be pictured truthfully, he would have little sympathy or understanding for either. His concern was with himself, not with London, and all he need retort, to justify his inconsistency, would be that one day one mood was uppermost, another day the other, for, as he says in his famous *Preface*, "all good poetry is the spontaneous overflow of powerful feelings." With Wordsworth, as with all romantics, feeling is of more import than action or situation. The poet is, in fact, "a man pleased with his own passions and volitions." Keats knew this when he cried, "O for a life of sensations rather than of thoughts." Baudelaire expressed the same point of view: "One should always be drunk ... It is time to seek intoxication. That you may not be a slave of Time, drink, drink without ceasing.

Of wine, of poetry, of virtue, as you may wish." And something of this intoxication overpowered Shelley:

> Sudden, thy shadow fell on me;
> I shrieked, and clasped my hands in ecstasy!

Illogical as it may seem, it is all logical enough if one will only grant the romantic the right
to view life subjectively and emotionally and not ask him to be consistent with anything
but his own feeling.

*And this subjective, emotional life carries with it, as has been indicated, a spontaneous release
of the unconscious, a firm trust in a personal and unrestrained imagination, an enthusiasm and
a wonder and an ecstasy before life.* It affords what appears either to the classicist or the
realist an *excessive* response. It is likely to be at one extreme or the other — zestful or
melancholy. In a single poet, Shelley, this romantic running of the gamut of the emotions
gives us the line from *Alastor*

> As one that in a silver vision floats

and from the *Hymn to Intellectual Beauty*

> This dim vast vale of tears, vacant and desolate.

Life to the romantic is like that; it is a "silver vision" or a "dim vast vale of tears," it
dances along merrily or plods dejectedly, it is in the valleys or on the mountain tops, it is
gay or sad. It is at its happiest, perhaps, when it can combine both extremes in one situation, when moonlight shines on castle ruins, or when flowers "give thoughts that do often
lie too deep for tears."

The romantic writer is strongly moved by the mystery of existence. Life is often full of
terror; the supernatural is at times uppermost. "Monk" Lewis in *The Monk* with its underground passages and vaults, the awful retribution of the Inquisition; Anne Radcliffe in
The Mysteries of Udolpho with its sentimental landscapes, tumbling waterfalls, and wild
scenery; Horace Walpole in the *Castle of Otranto* with its supernatural warrior and its weird
architecture of the castle — all these are manifestations of one phase of the romantic imagination. Coleridge, too, had this sense of the supernatural:

> A savage place! as holy and enchanted
> As e'er beneath a waning moon was haunted
> By woman wailing for her demon-lover!

Indeed, just how strong an element this was will be obvious to the student who reads the
selections from the *Biographia Literaria* and finds the explanation Coleridge gives concerning the two aspects of the collaboration in the *Lyrical Ballads* — "In the one, the
incidents and agents were to be, in part at least, supernatural. . . ." The romantic poet
is carried away by a sense of wonder — wonder at beauty, at melancholy, at the mystery of
life itself. The world is new, the grass is "dew-pearled"; in ecstasy the poet stands full of
wonder and awe-stricken by the mystery of the morning. Daphnis and Chloë are driving
their flocks afield, Aucassin is searching for his Nicolete in the forest in France while, in
another forest across the channel, Robin Hood blows his horn for Little John.

The search for a better world may be considered the second major characteristic of the romantic temper. Indeed, it is not certain that this desire for escape, for the creation of an idealized world, is entirely distinct from the individual, emotional quality, since the escape to this perfect universe is often sought through these very emotions. When reality dulls, ecstasy and enthusiasm offer surcease. When the life of experience palls, there is still the life of mystery and the supernatural to explore.

A "brave new world" the romantic finds in revolt, in freedom, in aspiration and faith, in a nature which he endows with a spiritual quality, even in the remote past.

The romantic shuns actuality. His desire is to remake the world — or find a new one — nearer to the heart's desire. There is in him nothing of the classicist's respect for convention or the realist's intent to face facts. He cries with Cowper:

> Oh for a lodge in some vast wilderness,
> Some boundless contiguity of shade,
> Where rumor of oppression and deceit,
> Of unsuccessful or successful war,
> Might never reach me more.

With Keats, if seclusion is to be his lot, he wishes to choose a place away from urban conventionalities:

> O Solitude! if I must with thee dwell,
> Let it not be among the jumbled heap
> Of murky buildings; climb with me the steep, —
> Nature's observatory —

It is not mere coincidence that so many of our romantic writers found interest in countries other than those of their birth. Coleridge and Wordsworth once looked to France to show England the way out of her injustices. Thomas Moore wrote of the vale of Cashmere. Byron, Shelley, and Keats found escape in Italy and Greece, Stevenson in the South Seas. Tennyson turned to the romantic past for his *Idylls of the King*. In fact, the romantic has always been in search of a distant goal. Daphnis and Chloë did not play out their story in the streets of Athens. Beowulf's progress has been marked on no maritime chart. Indeed, nobody has been to Xanadu. And no one has walked the forests of Arcadia.

Yet the romantic temper was not naïvely escapist. If the new world sought was not ready-made, then the romantic was intent on making the world anew. It is not by chance that the decades of the great romantic movement in England were the decades as well of the democratic movement and of changes in governments in America, in France, in Europe generally. The romantic mood may express a nostalgic desire for comfort and quiet seclusion, but it was made of sterner stuff than this only. It was Byron who praised the

> Eternal Spirit of the chainless Mind!
> Brightest in dungeons, Liberty;

and who at the time of his death had thrown himself into the cause of freedom for Greece.

The quest for a better world accounts, too, for the preoccupation of the romantic writer with dreams. "If I had to hazard an Aristotelian definition of Romanticism," writes F. L.

Lucas, "it might run — 'Romantic literature is a dream-picture of life; providing sustenance and fulfillment for impulses cramped by society or reality.'"

> A damsel with a dulcimer
> In a vision once I saw:

says Coleridge. To Wordsworth the earth we pace appeared to be

> An unsubstantial, fairy place

fit home for the cuckoo! H. J. C. Grierson recognizes this ethereal quality in medieval romance. "It is," says Grierson, "the conscious contrast with reason that makes modern romance in the full sense. It is not because it reflects the life and serious thought of the age that medieval romance is interesting but because it does not, but represents men's dreams." Whether it be in ancient Greece, in medieval Europe, in nineteenth-century England and France, or in the literature of symbolism, it is the romantic temper which has pressed on from the known world to the terra incognita of dreams.

> Fiction is to the grown man [writes Stevenson] what play is to the child; it is there that he changes the atmosphere and tenor of his life; and when the game so chimes with his fancy that he can join in it with all his heart, when it pleases him with every turn, when he loves to recall it and dwells upon its recollection with entire delight, fiction is called romance.

It is all a part of his desire to seek out a new, a perfect world, to obey "the ideal laws of the day-dream."

"*The great romantic knows that he lives by faith and not by reason,*" Grierson says elsewhere. His is a literature of aspiration, of idealization. His very day-dreams confirm it. The classicist, the romantic thinks, may have the world of reason so long as he leaves man his faith in the spirit.

> One impulse from a vernal wood
> May teach you more of man,
> Of moral evil and of good,
> Than all the sages can,

wrote Wordsworth. And Shelley found that

> The awful shadow of some unseen Power
> Floats though unseen among us —

And Byron tells us that he loves no man the less, but nature more, and that he delights in stealing away from actualities

> To mingle with the Universe, and feel
> What I can ne'er express, yet cannot all conceal.

This belief in the presence of the spiritual in nature is commonly expressed in Greek and classical philosophy, indeed it is in the best tradition of Oriental as well as Occidental thought. The romantics by no means fathered this faith in the spiritual, but finding it ready-made for them they accepted it more eagerly as part of their mental luggage than either the classicist or the realist had been wont to do. The Bible through its romantic stories and parables tells us in countless ways that man cannot live by bread alone; hundreds of medieval legends and romances reiterate the conviction; Christian fathers injected the doctrine of faith into the pagan *Beowulf;* Wordsworth and Shelley, Emerson and Lowell, taught it again to the nineteenth century.   This belief in the spirit was, the romantics maintained, ultimately to bring about the regeneration of mankind.   The revolution, whether it was urged by the Bible or by Shelley, was to be brought about by love.

The romantic set a high value on nature.   It meant for him irregularity and wildness — the lack of order and convention — as for the neo-classicist it had been uniformity and universality.   No reader of the eighteenth-century books on landscape can fail to observe this insistence on the irregular.   "We went," writes Thomas Amory, "over a wilder and more romantic country than any I had before seen."   From this attitude it was not far to a regard for the unconventional, the primitive life.   The sophistication so esteemed by the neo-classicist was discarded.   The open air was discovered again.   Writers in the eighteenth and nineteenth centuries took to describing nature for its own sake.   It was — Charles Lamb's later advocacy of city life notwithstanding — welcomed as an escape from the hum-drum of city life.   But more than for this, nature was esteemed as a reflection of the romantic's personal emotions, as a manifestation of the spiritual, as an expression of the infinite.   "Gie me," says Robert Burns,

> Gie me ae spark o' Nature's fire,
> That's a' the learning I desire.

Wordsworth is, of course, the chief spokesman for the romantics on this score.   To him nature was not only guide, philosopher, and friend, but priest and protector as well.   He was

> . . . well pleased to recognise
> In nature and the language of the sense,
> The anchor of my present thoughts, the nurse,
> The guide, the guardian of my heart, and soul
> Of all my being.

And, at least in theory, many city dwellers, often living comfortably on investments or allowances, held that society had contaminated man — that what he most needed was to live simply and naturally as a "son of nature" close to the soil.   The "noble savage" conception was a part of the romantic attitude.   The vogue for the islands of the South Seas first arose in England in the 1770's.   A decade before, Rousseau had written his *Contrat Social.*   A decade later, Robert Burns published his *Poems* and convinced the world that

> An honest man's the noblest work of God.
> And certes in fair virtue's heavenly road,
> The cottage leaves the palace far behind.

Society in the city, Burns told his readers, was "studied in arts of hell, in wickedness re fined!"

Nature, for these romantics, was a refuge.   The woods offered not only solace but cure. A whole convention in literature and painting grew up around the question of what constituted an "artistic" landscape.

Yet the eighteenth-century romantics did not discover nature. Shakespeare had long before written his "How sweet the moonlight sleeps upon this bank" and before that Edmund Spenser had spoken of a "shadie grove" with "loftie trees yclad with sommers pride" which offered shelter to the Knight of the Red Cross and a "lovely Ladie." And, lest we forget that the romantic temper is a mood and not simply a movement, we should recall the world of nature which the ancient Greeks populated with dryads and centaurs and satyrs — a romantic world made of material not unlike that which Herman Melville, Stevenson, Maugham, and James Norman Hall have woven into our twentieth-century conception of, for example, the Marquesas.

The romantic temper, in its desire to escape the actual world, turned at times to the past. It was part of the same desire to idealize a civilization which was not that in which the romantics themselves moved — whether it were a dream universe, a life of aspiration and faith, the simplicity of the noble savage, or a past epoch. The virtues of honesty and bravery and simplicity are always more obviously the property of other eras than of the one in which we live. Sir Walter Scott's novels popularized the history and political activity of the twelfth century in *The Talisman* and of the fifteenth century in *Quentin Durward*. MacPherson and Chatterton capitalized on this same antiquarian interest. Translations from the Scandinavian literature renewed the enthusiasm for the medieval. Bishop Percy gathered into his *Reliques* the ancient balladry of a people. Horace Walpole, Anne Radcliffe, and William Beckford wrote their Gothic novels. Walpole's story moved mysteriously through a medieval castle, Mrs. Radcliffe's portrayed romantic settings in the mountains of Italy, and Beckford's introduced a magnificence of Oriental background — all influences reflected in the *Kubla Khan* and *Christabel* of Coleridge, Keats's *Eve of St. Agnes*, and Byron's *Giaour*. Often prompted by nostalgia, the romantic writers sighed, with Wordsworth,

> For old, unhappy, far-off things,
> And battles long ago.

Even unhappy things and lost battles — if far enough in the past — became glamorous.

And allied with this enthusiasm for the remote in time is the interest of the romantic writer in things remote in space. The poet, we are told, is "affected more than other men by absent things as if they were present." Thomas Campbell in a famous line summed up the sentiment for all time:

> 'Tis distance lends enchantment to the view.

Or, if we turn from landscape to music, we hear Wordsworth declare that

> . . . sweetest melodies
> Are those that are by distance made more sweet.

"If I had to choose a single characteristic of Romance as the most noteworthy," says Sir Walter Raleigh, "I think I should choose Distance, and should call Romance the magic of Distance." It is not unusual that a traveler returned from far away areas finds a romantic halo about his head. He is one such as Shelley has pictured in *Alastor:*

> His wandering step,
> Obedient to high thoughts, has visited
> The awful ruins of the days of old:
> Athens and Tyre, and Balbec, and the waste
> Where stood Jerusalem, the fallen towers
> Of Babylon, the eternal pyramids,
> Memphis and Thebes.

Still another means of escape for the romantic writer is that of adventure heightened by exaggeration. For him countries are greener, women are fairer, and men are braver than they are in the epoch we know. In romance we are all brave and fair: we all overcome the villains, the repulsive giants, the wicked knights and evil sorceresses.

Lucian who wrote the *True History* knew this. Here is a Baron Munchausen of romance who, writing almost two thousand years ago, sensed well this love the romantic temper has for adventure and out-wrote many of the boldest of our romancers. His whales were as large as countries; his forests were composed of strange, semi-human trees. He wrote, he avowed, "of matters which I neither saw nor suffered, nor heard by report from others, which are in no being, nor possible ever to have a beginning. Let no man therefore in any case give any credit to them." And in so doing he proved himself a true romantic, if not a true historian.

What great hero, what bold adventurer, has not been made the subject of romance? Shall we begin with Hercules and Prometheus, or with Odysseus himself, and call the roll through Alexander the Great and Beowulf and Charlemagne, real or legendary characters of the ancient past? Shall we name Abelard and Guy of Warwick, Roland and Marco Polo, Sir Triamour and King Hal? And what of King Arthur and Lancelot, Robin Hood and Will Scarlet? And then there were those three gentlemen of the Renaissance — Sir Philip Sidney, Sir Francis Drake, and Sir Walter Raleigh. How much poorer would our literature be without these men! And, more recently, we have had such authors as Sir Walter Scott, Stevenson, and Cooper, such romantic characters as D'Artagnan, Cyrano de Bergerac, and Monsieur Beaucaire. Such adventurers as these were predestined to become the heroes of romance.

Before leaving the subject of romanticism, we should, perhaps, turn for a moment to a consideration of literary style. There can be no one definite literary style in romanticism simply because of the very nature of the manner itself. Freedom, the individuality of the writer, spontaneity — such qualities as these comprise the romantic outlook. And when we have freedom and individuality and spontaneity we have, despite certain dicta of Coleridge, not rules for writing, but the *absence* of rules. The romantic temper is the individual poet's way of saying a thing, untempered by tradition, unbound by rules. In classical writing style is the constant concern of the writer; in romantic writing *content* dominates form. In classicism, says F. H. Hedge, the author "stands aloof from his theme, in the other [romanticism] he pervades it."

So it is that no rigid rules for the romantic style can be laid down. Yet, as has been said above, we all recognize this style when we are reading. This is because, in a larger sense, when compared with classicism or realism for instance, there are certain prominent qualities which mark the romantic manner. As compared with classicism, for example, the romantic temper is impassioned, spontaneous, enthusiastic where the earlier manner is staid, dignified, conventional. The classical writer is almost exclusively concerned with the narrative; the romantic colors his story with his own moods and reflections. Romanticism is dominated by spirit; it is sprightly, active, alert. Romance moves where it pleases, while realism is bound to earth by its concern for details and actualities.

Exuberance is a strong characteristic of the romantic style. Such an author often overwrites. Every central idea may be embellished by a host of related and — if they be but interesting — even unrelated ideas. "The temper of the romantic writer," says Sidney Colvin, "is one of excitement, while the temper of the classical writer is one of self-possession." The classical temper simplifies; the romantic temper decorates; the classical temper sees a character from one point of view; the romantic temper recognizes that human nature is complex. The French, and for that matter the English, classicists were constantly railing at Shakespeare for his irrelevancies and inconsistencies, for his departures from decorum. It is through such irrelevancies that Shakespeare proves to be a romantic at heart.

This exuberance and individual freedom untrammeled by rules affected form as well as content. Prose took on new rhythms as well as new ideas. Poetry assumed new colors and tones. Keats was born to replace Pope, Shelley to take the place of Ben Jonson. Characters in fiction were no longer one- but many-sided. Words were used for their suggestive as well as for their obvious meaning. "Rhythm has now become once more an intoxicant," says F. L. Lucas, thus recalling to our minds the injunction of Baudelaire: "One must be always intoxicated." Archaisms in speech became popular for the rich associations of the past they called up.

Whether we approach the romantic temper through content or through form, we come back to the same starting points: freedom, exuberance, individuality, spontaneity. It is, it might be said, the negation of law since, whether in ancient Greece or modern America, it is the voice of man unrestrained, free, crying out for a world which he has not yet found but which he feels to exist, a world where colors are not faded, where life is not confined, and where the spirit is left free to its visions.

Ovid (*Publius Ovidius Naso*) · 43 B.C.–A.D. 17

In beginning the readings in the romantic temper we turn to Ovid and Rome at the time of the birth of Christ. Reared in the same atmosphere as his contemporaries Virgil and Horace, and using many of the same literary conventions, Ovid was essentially romantic in spirit.

The son of a citizen in the landowning class, Ovid was born at Sulmo, a town ninety miles east of Rome in the Abruzzi Mountains, in 43 B.C. At an early age he went to Rome to study under the rhetoricians. In his youth he manifested a genuine interest in poetry, an enthusiasm which his father ineffectively tried to dampen. To improve his education he traveled to Athens, Troy, and the cities of Asia Minor. Indifferent to a public career, Ovid devoted himself to his poetry. Among his early writings are the *Amores*, love poems, and the *Heroides*, a series of love epistles from heroines of Greek story to their absent lovers. His *Ars amatoria* (*The Art of Love*) was in parts so frank and practical in its advice that it brought forth a storm of protest, and the Emperor Augustus — he who befriended Horace — had to banish the poet to a village on the shores of the Black Sea.

SUGGESTED REFERENCES: Wilmon Brewer, *Ovid's Metamorphoses in European Culture* (2nd ed., 1957); L. P. Wilkinson, *Ovid Surveyed* (1962).

The Metamorphoses

The *Metamorphoses*, Ovid's best-known work, is a series of stories drawn from Greek and Roman mythology presenting cases of strange transformations of gods and goddesses who were, for one reason or another, changed into trees, birds, fountains, and other natural objects. Most commonly celebrating love, Ovid's poetry is characterized by a sensuous quality not always restrained in its expression. His work evidences, too, a deep sense for the beauty of nature. Gracious, inventive, sparkling, charged with fancy and imagination, the verse is entertaining rather than deeply philosophical. Beyond great technical skill, Ovid wrote in a style generally felicitous in its vivacity and freshness. He was a romantic living in an age dominantly classical in spirit. Many later writers, among them Boccaccio, Chaucer, and Spenser, have been indebted to Ovid for subject or manner or inspiration. The selections which follow are translated by H. T. Riley and are reprinted from Bohn's Classical Library.

Apollo and Daphne

Daphne, the daughter of Peneus, was the first love of Phœbus; whom, not blind chance, but the vengeful anger of Cupid assigned to him.

The Delian God,[1] proud of having lately subdued the serpent, had seen him bending the bow and drawing the string, and had said, "What hast thou to do, wanton boy, with gallant arms? Such a burden as that better befits my shoulders; I, who

[1] Apollo, who was born on the Island of Delos, in the Ægean.

am able to give unerring wounds to the wild beasts, wounds to the enemy; who lately slew with arrows innumerable the swelling Python, that covered so many acres of land with his pestilential belly. Do thou be contented to excite I know not what flames with thy torch; and do not lay claim to praises properly my own."

To him the son of Venus replies, "Let thy bow shoot all things, Phœbus; my bow shall shoot thee; and as much as all animals fall short of thee, so much is thy glory less than mine." He thus said; and cleaving the air with his beating wings, with activity he stood upon the shady heights of Parnassus, and drew two weapons out of his arrow-bearing quiver, of different workmanship; the one repels, the other excites desire. That which causes love is of gold, and is brilliant, with a sharp point; that which repels it is blunt, and contains lead beneath the reed. This one the God fixed in the Nymph, the daughter of Peneus, but with the other he wounded the very marrow of Apollo, through his bones pierced by the arrow. Immediately the one is in love; the other flies from the very name of a lover, rejoicing in the recesses of the woods, and in the spoils of wild beasts taken in hunting, and becomes a rival of the virgin Phœbe. A fillet tied together her hair, put up without any order. Many a one courted her; she hated all wooers; not able to endure, and quite unacquainted with man, she traverses the solitary parts of the woods, and she cares not what Hymen,[1] what love, or what marriage means. Many a

[1] One of the gods of marriage.

time did her father say, "My daughter, thou owest me a son-in-law;" many a time did her father say, "My daughter, thou owest me grandchildren." She, utterly abhorring the nuptial torch,[1] as though a crime, has her beauteous face covered with the blush of modesty; and clinging to her father's neck, with caressing arms, she says, "Allow me, my dearest father, to enjoy perpetual virginity; her father, in times bygone, granted this to Diana."

He indeed complied. But that very beauty forbids thee to be what thou wishest, and the charms of thy person are an impediment to thy desires. Phœbus falls in love, and he covets an alliance with Daphne, now seen by him, and what he covets he hopes for, and his own oracles deceive him; and as the light stubble is burned, when the ears of corn are taken off, and as hedges are set on fire by the torches, which perchance a traveller has either held too near them, or has left there, now about the break of day, thus did the God burst into a flame; thus did he burn throughout his breast, and cherish a fruitless passion with his hopes. He beholds her hair hanging unadorned upon her neck, and he says, "And what would it be if it were arranged?" He sees her eyes, like stars, sparkling with fire; he sees her lips, which it is not enough to have merely seen; he praises both her fingers and her hands, and her arms and her shoulders naked, from beyond the middle; whatever is hidden from view, he thinks to be still more beauteous. Swifter than the light wind she flies, and she stops not at these words of his, as he calls her back:

"O Nymph, daughter of Peneus, stay, I entreat thee! I am not an enemy following thee. In this way the lamb flies from the wolf; thus the deer flies from the lion; thus the dove flies from the eagle with the trembling wing; in this way each creature flies from its enemy: love is the cause of my following thee. Ah! wretched me! shouldst thou fall on thy face, or should the brambles tear thy legs, that deserve not to be injured, and should I prove the cause of pain to thee. The places are rugged, through which thou art thus hastening; run more leisurely, I entreat thee, and restrain thy flight; I myself will follow more leisurely. And yet, enquire whom thou dost please; I am not an inhabitant of the mountains, I am not a shepherd; I am not here, in rude guise, watching the herds or the flocks. Thou knowest not, rash girl, thou knowest not from whom thou art flying, and therefore it is that thou dost fly. The Delphian land, Claros and Tenedos, and the Pataræan

[1] According to Roman custom, five torches were lighted at the hearth of the bride's home and then carried before her as she went to the home of her husband.

palace pays service to me. Jupiter is my sire; by me, what shall be, what has been, and what is, is disclosed; through me, songs harmonize with the strings. My own arrow, indeed, is unerring; yet one there is still more unerring than my own, which has made this wound in my heart, before unscathed. The healing art is my discovery, and throughout the world I am honored as the bearer of help, and the properties of simples are subjected to me. Ah, wretched me! that love is not to be cured by any herbs; and that those arts which afford relief to all, are of no avail for their master."

The daughter of Peneus flies from him, about to say still more, with timid step, and together with him she leaves his unfinished address. Then, too, she appeared lovely; the winds exposed her form to view, and the gusts meeting her, fluttered about her garments, as they came in contact, and the light breeze spread behind her her careless locks; and thus, by her flight, was her beauty increased. But the youthful God has not patience any longer to waste his blandishments; and as love urges him on, he follows her steps with hastening pace. As when the greyhound has seen the hare in the open field, and the one by the speed of his legs pursues his prey, the other seeks her safety; the one is like as if just about to fasten on the other, and now, even now, hopes to catch her, and with nose outstretched plies upon the footsteps of the hare. The other is in doubt whether she is caught already, and is delivered from his very bite, and leaves behind the mouth just touching her. And so is the God, and so is the virgin; he swift with hopes, she with fear.

Yet he that follows, aided by the wings of love, is the swifter, and denies her any rest; and is now just at her back as she flies, and is breathing upon her hair scattered upon her neck. Her strength being now spent, she grows pale, and being quite faint, with the fatigue of so swift a flight, looking upon the waters of Peneus, she says, "Give me, my father, thy aid, if you rivers have divine power. Oh Earth, either yawn to swallow me, or by changing it, destroy that form, by which I have pleased too much, and which causes me to be injured."

Hardly had she ended her prayer, when a heavy torpor seizes her limbs; and her soft breasts are covered with a thin bark. Her hair grows into green leaves, her arms into branches; her feet, the moment before so swift, adhere by sluggish roots; a leafy canopy overspreads her features; her elegance alone remains in her. This, too, Phœbus admires, and placing his right hand upon the stock, he perceives that the breast still throbs beneath the new bark; and then, embracing the branches as though limbs in his arms, he gives kisses to the wood, and yet the wood shrinks from his kisses. To her the God said: "But since thou canst not be my wife, at least thou shalt be my tree; my hair, my lyre, my quiver shall always have thee, oh laurel! Thou shalt be presented to the Latian chieftains, when the joyous voice of the soldiers shall sing the song of triumph, and the long procession shall resort to the Capitol. Thou, the same, shalt stand as a most faithful guardian at the gate-posts of Augustus before his doors, and shalt protect the oak placed in the centre; and as my head is ever youthful with unshorn locks, do thou, too, always wear the lasting honors of thy foliage."

Pæan had ended his speech; the laurel nodded assent with its new-made boughs, and seemed to shake its top just like a head.

Alpheus and Arethusa

But Jupiter being the mediator between his brother and his disconsolate sister, divides the rolling year equally between them.[1] For now, the Goddess, a common Divinity of two kingdoms, is so many months with her mother, and just as many with her husband. Immediately the appearance of both her mind and her countenance is changed; for the brow of the Goddess, which, of late, might appear sad, even to Pluto himself, is full of gladness; as the Sun, which has lately been covered with watery clouds, when he comes forth from the clouds, now dispersed. The genial Ceres, now at ease on the recovery of her daughter, thus asks, "What was the cause of thy wanderings? Why art thou, Arethusa, a sacred spring?" The waters are silent, and the Goddess raises her head from the deep fountain; and, having dried her green tresses with her hand, she relates the old amours of the stream of Elis.

"I was," says she, "one of the Nymphs which exist in Achaia, nor did any one more eagerly skim along the glades than myself, nor with more industry set the nets. But though the reputation for beauty was never sought by me, although, too, I was of robust make, still I had the name of being beautiful. But my appearance, when so much commended, did not please me; and I, like a country lass, blushed at those endowments of person in which other females are wont to take a pride, and I deemed it a crime to please. I remember, I was returning weary from the Stymphalian wood; the weather was hot, and my toil had redoubled the intense heat. I found a stream gliding on without any eddies, without any noise, and clear to the bottom; through which every pebble, at so great a depth, might be counted, and which you could hardly suppose to be in motion. The hoary willows and poplars, nourished by the water, furnished a shade, spontaneously produced, along the shelving banks. I approached, and, at first, I dipped the soles of my feet, and then, as far as the knee. Not content with that, I undressed, and I laid my soft garments upon a bending willow; and, naked, I plunged into the waters.

"While I was striking them, and drawing them towards me, moving in a thousand ways, and was sending forth my extended arms, I perceived a most unusual murmuring noise beneath the middle of the stream; and, alarmed, I stood on the edge of the nearer bank. 'Whither dost thou hasten, Arethusa?' said Alpheus from his waves. 'Whither dost thou hasten?' again he said to me, in a hollow tone. Just as I was, I fled without my clothes; for the other side had my garments. So much the more swiftly did he pursue, and become inflamed; and, because I was naked, the more tempting to him did I appear. Thus was I running; thus unrelentingly was he pursuing me; as the doves are wont to fly from the hawk with trembling wings, and as the hawk is wont to pursue the trembling doves, I held out in my course even as far as Orchomenus, and Psophis, and Cyllene, and the Mænalian vallies, and cold Erymanthus and Elis. Nor was he swifter than I, but, unequal to him in strength, I was unable, any longer, to keep up the chase; for he was able to endure prolonged fatigue. However, I ran over fields and over mountains covered with trees, rocks too, and crags, and where there was no path. The sun was upon my back; I saw a long shadow advancing before my feet, unless, perhaps, it was my fear that saw it. But, at all events, I was alarmed at the sound of his feet, and his increased hardness of breathing was now fanning the fillets of my hair. Wearied with the exertion of my flight, I said, 'Give aid, Dictynna, to thy armor-bearer, or I am overtaken; I, to whom thou hast so often given thy bow to carry, and thy darts enclosed in the quiver.' The Goddess was moved, and, taking one of the dense clouds, she threw it over me. The river looked about for me, concealed in the darkness, and in his ignorance, sought about the encircling cloud; and twice, unconsciously did he go around the

[1] When Ceres found that Pluto had taken away her daughter, Proserpina, she complained to Jupiter who ruled that the daughter should divide her year, living with Ceres six months and with Pluto six months. Arethusa here tells Ceres of an experience she had while Ceres was away searching for Proserpina.

place where the Goddess had concealed me, and twice did he cry, 'Ho, Arethusa! Ho, Arethusa!' What, then, were my feelings, in my wretchedness? Were they not just those of the lamb, as it hears the wolves howling around the high sheep-folds? Or of the hare, which, lurking in the bush, beholds the hostile noses of the dogs, and dares not make a single movement with her body? Yet he does not depart; for no further does he trace any prints of my feet. He watches the cloud and the spot. A cold perspiration takes possession of my limbs, thus besieged, and azure-colored drops distil from all my body. Wherever I move my foot, there flows a lake; drops trickle from my hair, and, in less time than I take in acquainting thee with my fate, I was changed into a stream. But still the river recognized the waters, the objects of his love; and, having laid aside the shape of a mortal, which he had assumed, he was changed into his own waters, that he might mingle with me. Thereupon, the Delian Goddess cleaved the ground. Sinking, I was carried through dark caverns to Ortygia, which, being dear to me, from the surname of my own Goddess, was the first to introduce me to the upper air."

Orpheus and Eurydice

Thence Hymenæus, clad in a saffron-colored robe, passed through the unmeasured tract of air, and directed his course to the regions of the Ciconians, and, in vain, was invoked by the voice of Orpheus. He presented himself indeed, but he brought with him neither auspicious words, nor joyful looks, nor yet a happy omen. The torch, too, which he held, was hissing with a smoke that brought tears to the eyes, and as it was, it found no flames amid its waving. The issue was more disastrous than the omens; for the newmade bride, while she was strolling along the grass, attended by a train of Naiads, was killed, having received the sting of a serpent on her ancle.

After the Rhodopeian bard had sufficiently bewailed her in the upper realms of air, that he might try the shades below as well, he dared to descend to Styx by the Tænarian gate, and amid the phantom inhabitants and ghosts that had enjoyed the tomb, he went to Persephone, and him that held these unpleasing realms, the Ruler of the shades; and touching his strings in concert with his words, he thus said, "O ye Deities of the world that lies beneath the earth, to which we all come at last, each that is born to mortality; if I may be allowed, and you suffer me to speak the truth, laying aside the artful expressions of a deceitful tongue; I have

not descended hither from curiosity to see dark Tartarus, nor to bind the three-fold throat of the Medusæan monster, bristling with serpents. But my wife was the cause of my coming; into whom a serpent, trodden upon by her, diffused its poison, and cut short her growing years. I was wishful to be able to endure this, and I will not deny that I have endeavored to do so. Love has proved the stronger. That God is well known in the regions above. Whether he be so here, too, I am uncertain; but yet I imagine that even here he is; and if the story of the rape of former days is not untrue, 'twas love that united you two together. By these places filled with horrors, by this vast Chaos, and by the silence of these boundless realms, I entreat you, weave over again the quick-spun thread of the life of Eurydice.

"To you we all belong; and having staid but a little while above, sooner or later we all hasten to one abode. Hither are we all hastening. This is our last home; and you possess the most lasting dominion over the human race. She, too, when, in due season she shall have completed her allotted number of years, will be under your sway. The enjoyment of her I beg as a favor. But if the Fates deny me this privilege in behalf of my wife, I have determined that I will not return. Triumph in the death of us both."

As he said such things, and touched the strings to his words, the bloodless spirits wept. Tantalus did not catch at the retreating water, and the wheel of Ixion stood still, as though in amazement; the birds did not tear the liver of Tityus; and the granddaughters of Belus paused at their urns; thou, too, Sisyphus, didst seat thyself on thy stone. The story is, that then, for the first time, the cheeks of the Eumenides, overcome by his music, were wet with tears; nor could the royal consort, nor he who rules the infernal regions, endure to deny him his request; and they called for Eurydice. She was among the shades newly arrived, and she advanced with a slow pace, by reason of her wound.

The Rhotopeian hero receives her, and, at the same time, this condition, that he turn not back his eyes until he has passed the Avernian vallies, or else that the grant will be revoked. The ascending path is mounted in deep silence, steep, dark, and enveloped in deepening gloom. And now they were not far from the verge of the upper earth. He, enamored, fearing lest she should flag, and impatient to behold her, turned his eyes; and immediately she sank back again. She hapless one! both stretching out her arms, and struggling to be grasped, and to grasp him, caught nothing but the fleeting air. And now, dying a second time, she did not at all complain of her husband; for why should she complain of being beloved? And now she pronounced the last farewell, which scarcely did he catch with his ears; and again was she hurried back to the same place.

Narcissus

Thus had he deceived her, thus, too, other Nymphs that sprung from the water or the mountains, thus the throng of youths before them. Some one, therefore, who had been despised by him, lifting up his hands towards heaven, said, "Thus, though he should love, let him not enjoy what he loves!" Rhamnusia[1] assented to a prayer so reasonable. There was a clear spring, like silver, with its unsullied waters, which neither shepherds, nor she-goats feeding on the mountains, nor any other cattle, had touched; which neither bird nor wild beast had disturbed, nor bough falling from a tree. There was grass around it, which the neighboring water nourished, and a wood, that suffered the stream to become warm with no rays of the sun. Here the youth,[2] fatigued both with the labor of hunting and the heat, lay down, attracted by the appearance of the spot, and the spring; and, while he was endeavoring to quench his thirst, another thirst grew upon him.

While he is drinking, being attracted with the reflection of his own form, seen in the water, he falls in love with a thing that has no substance; and he thinks that to be a body, which is but a shadow. He is astonished at himself, and remains unmoved with the same countenance, like a statue formed of Parian marble. Lying on the ground, he gazes on his eyes like two stars, and fingers worthy of Bacchus,[3] and hair worthy of Apollo, and his youthful cheeks and ivory neck, and the comeliness of his mouth, and his blushing complexion mingled with the whiteness of snow; and everything he admires, for which he himself is worthy to be admired. In his ignorance, he covets himself; and he that approves, is himself the thing approved. While he pursues, he is pursued, and at the same moment he inflames and burns. How often does he give vain kisses to the deceitful spring; how often does he thrust his arms, catching at the neck he sees, into the middle of the water,

[1] Nemesis, goddess of punishment.
[2] Narcissus, the personification of self-conceit. He spurned the nymphs and fell in love with his own image — with the result set down here.
[3] The Greek Dionysus, god of wine and good-fellowship; the sponsor of animal life and vegetation. He stood generally for the advance of civilization.

and yet he does not catch himself in them. He knows not what he sees, but what he sees, by it is he inflamed; and the same mistake that deceives his eyes, provokes them. Why, credulous youth, dost vainly catch at the flying image? What thou art seeking is nowhere; what thou art in love with, turn but away and thou shalt lose it; what thou seest, the same is but the shadow of a reflected form: it has nothing of its own. It comes and stays with thee; with thee it will depart, if thou canst but depart thence.

No regard for food, no regard for repose, can draw him away thence; but, lying alone upon the overshadowed grass, he gazes upon the fallacious image with unsatiated eyes, and by his own sigh he himself is undone. Raising himself a little while, extending his arms to the woods that stand around him, he says, "Was ever, O, ye woods! any one more fatally in love? For this ye know, who have been a convenient shelter for many a one. And do you remember any one, who ever thus pined away, during so long a time, though so many ages of your life have been spent? It both pleases me, and I see it, but what I see, and what pleases me, yet I cannot obtain; so great a mistake possesses one in love; and to make me grieve the more, neither a vast sea separates us, nor a long way, nor mountains, nor a city with its gates closed: we are kept asunder by a little water. He himself wishes to be embraced; for as often as I extend my lips to the limpid stream, so often does he struggle towards me with his face held up; you would think he might be touched. It is a very little that stands in the way of lovers. Whoever thou art, come up hither. Why, dear boy, the choice one, dost thou deceive me? or whither dost thou retire, when pursued? Surely, neither my form nor my age is such as thou shouldst shun; the Nymphs, too, have courted me. Thou encouragest I know not what hopes in me with that friendly look, and when I extend my arms to thee, thou willingly extendest thine; when I smile, thou smilest in return; often, too, have I observed thy tears, when I was weeping; my signs, too, thou returnest by thy nods, and, as I guess by the motion of thy beauteous mouth, thou returnest words that come not to my ears. In thee 'tis I, I now perceive; nor does my form deceive me. I burn with the love of myself, and both raise the flames and endure them. What shall I do? Should I be entreated, or should I entreat? What, then, shall I entreat? What I desire is in my power; plenty has made me poor. Oh! would that I could depart from my own body! a new wish, indeed, in a lover; I could wish that what I am in love with was away. And now grief is taking away my strength, and no long period of my life remains; and in my early days am I cut off: nor is death grievous to me, now about to get rid of my sorrows by death. I wish that he who is beloved could enjoy a longer life. Now we two, of one mind, shall die in the extinction of one life."

Thus he said, and, with his mind but ill at ease, he returned to the same reflection, and disturbed the water with his tears; and the form was rendered defaced by the moving of the stream; when he saw it beginning to disappear, he cried aloud, "Whither dost thou fly? Stay, I beseech thee! and do not in thy cruelty abandon thy lover; let it be allowed me to behold that which I may not touch, and to give nourishment to my wretched frenzy." And, while he was grieving, he tore his garment from the upper border, and beat his naked breast with his palms, white as marble. His breast, when struck, received a little redness, not otherwise than as apples are wont, which are partly white and partly red; or as a grape, not yet ripe, in the parti-colored clusters, is wont to assume a purple tint. Soon as he beheld this again in the water when clear, he could not endure it any longer; but, as yellow wax with the fire, or the hoar frost of the morning, is wont to waste away with the warmth of the sun, so he, consumed by love, pined away, and wasted by degrees with a hidden flame. And now, no longer was his complexion of white mixed with red; neither his vigor nor his strength, nor the points which had charmed when seen so lately, nor even his body, which formerly Echo had been in love with, now remained. Yet, when she saw these things, although angry, and mindful of his usage of her, she was grieved, and, as often as the unhappy youth said, "Alas!" she repeated, "Alas!" with re-echoing voice; and when he struck his arms with his hands, she, too, returned the like sound of a blow.

His last accents as he looked into the water, as usual, were these: "Ah, youth, beloved in vain!" and the spot returned just as many words; and after he had said, "Farewell!" Echo, too, said, "Farewell!" He laid down his wearied head upon the green grass, when night closed the eyes that admired the beauty of their master; and even then, after he had been received into the infernal abodes, he used to look at himself in the Stygian waters. His Naiad sisters lamented him, and laid their hair, cut off, over their brother; the Dryads, too, lamented him, and Echo resounded to their lamentations. And now they were preparing the funeral pile, and the shaken torches, and the bier. The body was nowhere to be found. Instead of his body, they found a yellow flower, with white leaves encompassing it in the middle.

The Rape of Proserpine

Not far from the walls of Henna there is a lake of deep water, Pergus by name; Caÿster [1] does not hear more songs of swans, in his running streams, than that. A wood skirts the lake, surrounding it on every side, and with its foliage, as though with an awning, keeps out the rays of the sun. The boughs produce a coolness, the moist ground flowers of Tyrian hue. There the spring is perpetual. In this grove, while Proserpine is amusing herself, and is plucking either violets or white lilies, and while, with child-like eagerness, she is filling her baskets and her bosom, and is striving to out-do her companions of the same age in gathering, almost at the same instant she is beheld, beloved, and seized by Pluto; in such great haste is love. The Goddess, affrighted, with lamenting lips calls both her mother and her companions, but more frequently her mother; and as she has torn her garment from the upper edge, the collected flowers fall from her loosened robes. So great, too, is the innocence of her childish years, this loss excites the maiden's grief as well. The ravisher drives on his chariot, and encourages his horses, called, each by his name, along whose necks and manes he shakes the reins, dyed with swarthy rust. He is borne through deep lakes, and the pools of the Palici, smelling strong of sulphur, and boiling fresh from out of the burst earth; and where the Bacchiadæ, a race sprung from Corinth, with its two seas, built a city between unequal harbors.

There is a stream in the middle, between Cyane and the Pisæan Arethusa,[2] which is confined within itself, being enclosed by mountain ridges at a short distance from each other. Here was Cyane, the most celebrated among the Sicilian Nymphs, from whose name the pool also was called, who stood up from out of the midst of the water, as far as the higher part of her stomach, and recognized the God, and said, "No further shall you go. Thou mayst not be the son-in-law of Ceres against her will. The girl should have been asked of her mother, not carried away. But if I may be allowed to compare little matters with great ones, Anapis also loved me. Yet I married him, courted, and not frightened into it, like her." She thus said, and stretching her arms on different sides, she stood in his way. The son of Saturn [3] no longer restrained his rage; and encouraging his terrible steeds, he threw his royal scepter, hurled with a strong arm, into the lowest depths of the stream.

[1] A river in Ionia, famous for the melodic song of its swans.

[2] See Ovid's *Alpheus and Arethusa*.

[3] Pluto.

The earth, thus struck, made a way down to Tartarus, and received the descending chariot in the middle of the yawning space. But Cyane, lamenting both the ravished Goddess, and the slighted privileges of her spring, carries in her silent mind an inconsolable wound, and is entirely dissolved into tears, and melts away into those waters, of which she had been but lately the great guardian Divinity. You might see her limbs soften, her bones become subjected to bending, her nails lay aside their hardness: each, too, of the smaller extremities of the whole of her body melts away; both her azure hair, her fingers, her legs, and her feet; for easy is the change of those small members into a cold stream. After that, her back, her shoulders, her side, and her breast dissolve, vanishing into thin rivulets. Lastly, pure water, instead of live blood, enters her corrupted veins, and nothing remains which you can grasp in your hands.

In the meantime, throughout all lands and in every sea, the daughter is sought in vain by her anxious mother. Aurora,[1] coming with her ruddy looks, does not behold her taking any rest, neither does Hesperus.[2] She, with her two hands, sets light to some pines at the flaming Ætna, and giving herself no rest, bears them through the frosty darkness. Again when the genial day has dulled the light of the stars, she seeks her daughter from the rising of the sun to the setting thereof. Fatigued by the labor, she has now contracted thirst, and no streams have washed her mouth, when by chance she beholds a cottage covered with thatch, and knocks at its humble door, upon which an old woman comes out and sees the Goddess, and gives her, asking for water, a sweet drink which she has lately distilled from parched pearled barley. While she is drinking it thus presented, a boy of impudent countenance and bold, stands before the Goddess, and laughs, and calls her greedy. She is offended; and a part being not yet quaffed, the Goddess sprinkles him, as he is thus talking, with the barley mixed with the liquor.

His face contracts the stains, and he bears legs where just now he was bearing arms; a tail is added to his changed limbs; and he is contracted into a diminutive form, that no great power of doing injury may exist; his size is less than that of a small lizard. He flies from the old woman, astounded and weeping, and trying to touch the monstrosity; and he seeks a lurking place, and has a name suited to his color, having his body speckled with various spots.

[1] Dawn.
[2] Evening star.

Heroides
Dido to Æneas

Descendant of Dardanus, receive the lines of Elissa about to die; the words that thou dost read, thou readest as the last words from me.

Thus does the white swan, as he lies on the wet grass, when the fates summon him, sing at the fords of Mæander. Nor do I address thee because I hope that thou canst be moved by my entreaties: for that, against the will of the Deity, have I wished. But since I have unfortunately lost a merited return, and my good name, and my chastity of body and mind, 'tis a trifling thing to lose a few words. Still then art thou determined to go, and to forsake the wretched Dido; and the same winds will bear away thy sails, and thy promises. Thou art determined, Æneas, with thy ships to part with thy vows, and to go after Italian realms, while thou knowst not where they are. Neither rising Carthage, nor its growing walls influence thee; nor the supreme rule conceded to thy sceptre. Thou dost fly from a city built: thou dost seek one to be erected: the one region must be sought throughout the world, the other has been reached by thee.

And yet, shouldst thou find the land, who will give it thee to possess? Who will deliver up his own fields to be occupied by persons whom he knows not? Another love awaits thee to be entertained, and another Dido, and another vow must be plighted for thee once again to break. When will it be that thou shalt found a city equal to Carthage, and aloft from thy citadel look down on thy multitudes? Though all this should come to pass, and thy wishes should meet with no impediment, whence will come thy wife, to love thee as I? I burn, as the waxen torches tipped with sulphur; as the pious frankincense poured on the smoking altars. Æneas is ever placed before my eyes as I watch: both night and day bring back Æneas to my mind. He, indeed, is ungrateful and deaf to my deserts; and one whom I could fain be without, were I not demented.

Still, though he intends what is wrong, I do not hate Æneas: but I complain that he is faithless, and having complained, the more distractedly do I love him. Venus, show mercy to thy daughter-in-law, and do thou, Love, his brother, embrace thy brother; let him fight under thy banners. Or else I will, who have begun to love (and, indeed, I deny it not); only let him afford an object for my passion. I am deceived; and that image is falsely suggested to me. He differs from the disposition of his mother. Stones and mountains, and oaks growing on the lofty rocks, and savage wild beasts have begotten thee; or else the ocean, just as thou seest it now, agitated by the winds; which still thou dost prepare to pass with its hostile billows. Whither dost thou fly? The storm prevents thee; may the favor of the storm be to my advantage. Behold how Eurus [1] is raising the foaming waves. Let me owe that to the tempests, which I had rather owe to thee. The winds and the waves are more righteous than thy feelings. (Although thou dost deserve it, deceiver,) I am not of that value, that thou shouldst perish, while thou art flying from me over the extended main.

Thou dost give way to a costly hatred, and of amount too great; if that, so that thou avoid me, 'tis a trifling thing for thee to die. Soon will the winds be lulled; and the waves, in their stillness, being becalmed, Triton will run amid the seas with his azure steeds. Would that thou, too, couldst be changed, together with the winds! And unless thou dost exceed the oak in hardness, thou wilt be. Just as if thou wast ignorant of what the raging sea can do! How rashly dost thou trust the waves that thou hast so oft experienced? Though, the deep inviting, thou shouldst even weigh thy anchor, still, many a danger does the wide ocean contain. It is not the interest of those who tempt the main, to violate their oath. That place exacts retribution for perfidy. Especially when Love has been injured; because the mother of Love is said to have been born naked in the waves of Cythera.[2]

Lost, I am apprehensive of destroying thee, or of injuring thee who hast injured me; lest my enemy, shipwrecked, may swallow the waves of the deep. Live on, I pray; thus would I rather lose thee, than by thy death. Mayst thou rather be esteemed the cause of my destruction. Come, suppose that thou art overtaken by a fierce hurricane (let there be no meaning in the omen); what then will be thy feelings? At once will recur the perjuries of thy deceiving tongue, and Dido, compelled by Phrygian perfidy to die. The form of thy beguiled wife will be standing before thy eyes, disconsolate and blood-stained, with dishevelled locks. "Depart, whatever it is, I have deserved it all," thou mayst say; and the lightnings that shall fall, thou wilt think to be hurled against thee.

Give a short respite for the madness of the sea and thine own; a safe voyage will be the great reward of thy delaying. Let no regard be had for me; let regard be had for the boy Iülus; 'tis

enough for thee to have the credit of my death. What has the boy Ascanius [1] deserved? What have the Penates, thy household Gods, deserved? The waves will overwhelm the Divinities rescued from the flames. But neither dost thou carry them with thee; nor, what thou dost boast of, perfidious man, to me, have the sacred things, and thy father burdened thy shoulders. All this thou dost invent; nor, indeed, does thy tongue begin to deceive with me, nor am I the first to suffer. If you ask where is the mother of the beauteous Iülus, she has perished, left alone by her cruel husband. This didst thou relate to me; and yet it moved me not; torment me thus grieving; through my own punishment will thy culpability be the less.

But my mind is not in doubt, but that thy own Divinities condemn thee. Over seas, over lands, the seventh winter is buffeting thee. Cast ashore by the waves, I received thee in a harbor of safety, and having hardly heard thy name, I offered thee my realm. Still, with these kind offices do I wish that I had been content; and that the report of our intercourse had been buried in oblivion. That day proved my ruin, on which the lowering storm, by its sudden rain, drove us into the arched cave, I heard a noise; I thought the mountain Nymphs made the outcry; the Furies gave the signal for my doom. Offended Chastity, thus violated, exacts satisfaction for Sichæus, to whom, ah wretched me! filled with shame, I am hastening.

A statue of Sichæus has been consecrated by me in a marble temple, branches, hung up, and white wool conceal it. Four times from that spot did I hear myself called by a well-known voice; in low accents it said — "Elissa, come." There is no delay; I am coming; I am coming, a wife due to thee alone: but still detained by shame at my crime. Grant pardon to my error; an apt contriver of it beguiled me; he diminishes the guiltiness of my fault. His mother a Goddess, and his aged father, the affectionate burden of his son, gave me hopes of a husband that would be firmly attached. If I was to err, my error has a fair excuse; give him but constancy; then, in no respect will it be to be regretted. That course of fatality which existed before, continues to the last, and attends the closing moments of my existence. My slaughtered husband falls at the concealed altars; and my brother has the reward of criminality so great.

An exile am I banished, and I leave both the ashes of my husband and my native land; and, my enemy pursuing me, I am driven into laborious wanderings. I am thrown upon coasts unknown; and escaping both my brother and the ocean, I

[1] The East Wind.
[2] An island near Laconia where Venus was taken after arising from the sea.

[1] Ascanius, also known as Iülus, was the son of Æneas.

purchase that shore, which, perfidious man, I have offered to thee. I build a city, and I erect walls extending far and wide, that raise the envy of neighboring spots. Wars threaten; a stranger and a woman, I am harassed by wars; and with difficulty do I prepare the unfinished gates of my city and my arms. A thousand suitors have I pleased; who have combined, complaining that I have preferred, I know not whom, to their alliance. Why dost thou hesitate to deliver me up in chains to the Gætulian Iarbas? I would yield my arms up to thy criminality. There is my brother, too, whose impious hand, stained with the blood of my husband, may be stained with mine.

Put down thy Gods, and the sacred things, which, by touching them, thou dost pollute; an impious right-hand but ill worships the Gods of heaven. If thou wast about to be their worshipper when they had escaped from the fire, the Gods regret that they did escape. Perhaps, too, perjured man, thou dost leave Dido in a state of pregnancy; and a part of thyself lies concealed in my body. To the destiny of its mother, a wretched infant will be added, and thou wilt be the cause of the death of one not yet born; with its mother will die as well the brother of Iülus, and one doom will carry off the two together. But a God commands you to be gone. I wish he had forbidden you to come, and that the Punic ground had not been trodden by the Trojans. Under this guide (a God forsooth), thou art buffeted by unfavorable winds, and thou dost waste the slowly passing time on the boisterous seas; Pergamus ought hardly to be sought again by thee with labor so great, if it were as great as it was when Hector was alive.

Thou art not seeking thy native Simoïs, but the waves of the Tiber; shouldst thou arrive, forsooth, where thou dost wish, thou wilt be a stranger. And as this region, which thou dost seek, lies concealed, and, hidden, avoids thy ships, it will hardly be met with by thee when an aged man. Receive rather, all wanderings laid aside, this people for my dower, and the wealth of Pygmalion, which I have brought. More propitiously, transfer Ilium to a Tyrian city, and hold both this, the place of thy sovereignty, and the sacred sceptre. If thy mind is greedy for warfare, if Jülus is seeking whence a triumph may be gained, acquired by his warlike skill; that nothing may be wanting we will find here an enemy for him to subdue; this spot is adapted to the regulations of peace, and to arms.

Do thou only, by thy mother, and by the weapons of thy brother, his arrows, and by the Gods,

companions of thy flight, the sacred relics of Troy (then, may they survive, whoever thou art bringing with thee from thy nation, and may that cruel war prove the limit of thy woes, and may Ascanius happily fill up the measure of his years, and in repose may the bones of aged Anchises [1] rest), spare, I pray, that house, which offers itself to be possessed by thee. What crime dost thou lay to my charge, except that I have loved? I am not a woman of Phthia, or one sprung from great Mycenæ, nor have my husband and my father ever been in arms against thee.

If thou art ashamed of me as a wife, I may be called not thy bride, but thy entertainer. So long as Dido is thine, she will endure to anything. The seas that beat against the African shore are known to me; at certain seasons they both give and deny a passage. When the gales shall allow of a passage, thou shalt open thy canvass to the winds. — Now, worthless seaweed surrounds thy ship, cast up. Entrust it to me to watch for the opportunity; with greater safety wilt thou depart; and shouldst thou thyself desire it, I will not allow thee to stay. Thy companions, too, require rest; and thy shattered fleet, only half repaired, requires a little delay. In return for my kindnesses, and if, even beyond that, I should be under any obligation to thee, in place of my hope of thy marriage ties do I implore a little respite; until the waves and my passion are assuaged; until by time and experience I learn to be able with fortitude to endure my sorrows. But if not, I have determined to pour forth my life: to me thou art not able for long to be cruel.

I wish that thou couldst see what is my appearance as I write! I am writing; and in my lap there is the Trojan sword: along my cheeks the tears are falling, too, upon the drawn sword which soon will be bathed in blood, in place of tears. How well do thy gifts agree with my destiny! At small expense dost thou prepare my sepulchre. And not now for the first time is my breast smitten by a weapon: that spot has a wound from cruel Love. Anna, my sister, my sister Anna! unfortunately the confidant of my error, soon wilt thou be presenting thy tears, the last gifts, to my ashes. And, consumed on the pile, I shall not have the inscription, "Elissa, the wife of Sichæus:" but on the marble of my tomb will there be this epitaph — "Æneas afforded both the cause and the instrument of her death. Dido fell, having herself employed her own hand."

[1] Father of Æneas.

Apuleius · c. 160

Lucius Apuleius, an African, was born about A.D. 125 in the town of Madaura in Numidia. He received his education primarily in Carthage and in Athens, in the latter city giving particular attention to the study of Plato's philosophy. But his special interest in the religious practices of different sects led him to travel extensively in various countries, more especially those of the East. After a brief residence in Rome, he returned to Africa, falling ill in Tripoli where he was nursed back to health by a wealthy widow whom he later married. Accused of having resorted to magic to win the widow's favor, Apuleius wrote an *Apology* or defence which, apparently, was effective in securing his freedom. His later years were spent in the activities of a literary man and lecturer in and around Carthage.

An early teller of tales, Apuleius belongs to the tradition which includes Æsop's *Fables*, Longus' *Daphnis and Chloë*, Ovid's *Metamorphoses*. These tales were the forerunners of such later collections as the *Arabian Nights*, the *Decameron*, the *Tales* of Bandello, and the *Canterbury Tales* of Chaucer.

Apuleius is known to readers today largely through one book, the *Metamorphoses* or *Golden Ass*. The volume is a collection of tales, many taken over from contemporary sources, rather loosely strung together as adventures which befell him upon his having rubbed himself with a magic lotion and been turned into an ass. Not until he eats of certain roses can he expect to return to human form. The whole makes an early picaresque novel, a fact which both Cervantes and LeSage must have recognized since they both paid Apuleius the compliment of borrowing from the *Metamorphoses*.

SUGGESTED REFERENCES: J. B. Pike, *Apuleius: His Life and Works* (1918); Elizabeth Hazelton Haight, *Apuleius and His Influences* (2nd ed., 1963).

The Golden Ass

Since Latin was not his native tongue, Apuleius wrote in a style which scholars find unusual and somewhat complex. His use of idiom and his admixture of qualities foreign to classical Latin, particularly his introduction of oriental elements, differentiates him from other Latin writers of the period. His exuberant manner, his interest in magic and the "tall tale," his frequent shift of mood from the serious to the frivolous, from the horrible to the voluptuous, his display of rather artificial emotions, and his whimsical fancy mark him as a romantic writing at a time predominantly classical. The two stories used here, *The Robbers* and *Cupid and Psyche*, distinctly reflect this romantic quality. The translation below is that of W. Adlington as revised by S. Gaselee. Reprinted by permission of the Harvard University Press.

The Robbers

When noon was come, and now the broiling heat of the sun had most power, we turned into a village to certain old men of the thieves' acquaintance and friends, for verily their meeting and embracing together did give me (poor ass) cause to deem the same: and they took the truss from my back, and

gave them part of the treasure that was in it, and they seemed to whisper and tell them that it was stolen goods; and after that we were unladen of our burdens they let us loose into a meadow to 5 pasture, but I would not feed there with my own horse and Milo's ass, for that I was not wont to eat hay, but I must seek my dinner in some other place. Wherefore I leaped into a garden which was behind the stable, and being well-nigh perished 10 with hunger, although I could find nothing there but raw and green salads, yet I filled my hungry guts therewithal abundantly, and, praying unto all the gods, I looked about in every place if I could espy any roses in the gardens nearby, and my being 15 alone did put me in good hope, that if I could find any remedy, being far from the public road and hidden by the bushes, I should presently out of the low gait of a beast be changed out of every one's sight into a man walking upright.

Now while I tossed on the flood of these cogita- 20 tions, I looked about, and behold I saw afar off a shadowed valley adjoining to a wood, where, amongst divers other herbs and pleasant verdures, I thought I saw many flourishing roses of bright damask color. So that I said within my mind, 25 which was not wholly bestial: "Verily the place is the grove of Venus and the Graces, where secretly glittereth the royal hue of so lively and delectable a flower." Then I, desiring the help of the god of good fortune, ran lustily towards the wood, in so much that I felt myself no more an ass but a swift-coursing horse, but my agility and quickness could not prevent the cruelty of my fortune; for, when I came to the place, I perceived that they were no roses neither tender nor pleasant, neither moistened with the heavenly drops of dew nor celestial liquor, which grow out of the rich thicket and thorns. Neither did I perceive that there was any valley at all, but only the bank of the river environed with great thick trees, which had long branches like unto laurel, and bear a flower without any manner of scent but somewhat red of hue, and the common people call them by the name of laurel-roses, which are very poisonous to all manner of beasts. Then was I so entangled with unhappy fortune, that I little esteemed mine own life, and went willingly to eat of those roses, though I knew them to be present poison. But as I drew near very slowly, I saw a young man that seemed to be the gardener come upon me, the same that I had devoured up all his herbs in the garden, and he, knowing now full well his great loss, came swearing with a great staff in his hand, and laid upon me in such sort that I was well nigh dead; but I speedily devised some remedy for myself, for I lifted up my legs and kicked him with my hinder heels, so that I left him lying at the hill foot well nigh slain, and so I ran away: incontinently came out a certain woman, doubtless his wife, who, seeing from above her husband lying half dead, cried and howled in pitiful sort, hasting towards her husband, to the intent that by her loud cries she might purchase to me present destruction; for all the persons of the town, moved and raised by her noise, came forth and cried for dogs, and hied them on madly to tear me down. Out came a great company of bandogs and mastiffs, more fit to pull down bears and lions than me, whom when I beheld I thought verily that I should presently die, so that I took what counsel I might from the occasion, and thought no more of flight, but turned myself about and ran as fast as ever I might to the stable whither we had lodged. Then the men of the town called in their dogs, which they scarce could hold, and took me, and bound me to the staple of a post with a great thong, and scourged me till I was well nigh dead: and they would have undoubtedly have slain me, had it not come to pass that my belly, narrowed with the pain of their beating and reeking with the green herbs that lay therein, caught such a looseness that I all besprinkled the faces of some with my liquid dung, and with the filthy stench thereof enforced the others to leave my sides now well-nigh broken.

Not long after, which was now towards eventide, the thieves loaded us again, and especially me, with the heaviest burden, and brought us forth out of the stable, and when we had gone a good part of our journey, what with the long way, my great burden, the beating of staves, and my worn hooves, lame and tottering, I was so weary that I could scarcely go; then, as I walked by a little river running with fair water, I said to myself: "Behold, now I have found a good occasion. For I will fall down when I come yonder, bending my legs beneath me, and surely I will not rise again for any scourging or beating, and not only will I defy the cudgel, but even be pierced by the sword, if they shall use it upon me." And the cause why I determined so to do was this: I thought that I was so utterly feeble and weak that I deserved my discharge for ill health, and certainly that the robbers (partly for that they would not stay in their journey, partly in haste to flee) would take off the burden from my back, and put it upon my two fellows, and so for my further punishment leave me as a prey to the wolves and ravenous beasts. But evil fortune prevented so good a consideration; for the other ass, being of the same purpose that I was of, and forestalling me, by feigned and colored weariness fell down first with all his burden upon the ground as though he were dead, and he would not rise neither with beating nor pricking, nor stand upon his feet, though they pulled him all about by the tail, by his legs, and by his ears; which when the thieves beheld, as without all hope, they said one to another: "What, should we stand here so long about a dead or rather a stony ass? Let us be gone;" and so they took his burden and divided some to me and some to my horse. And then they drew their swords and cut through all his hamstrings, and dragged him a little from the way, and threw his body while he yet breathed from the point of a hill down into a great valley. Then I, considering with myself of the evil fortune of my poor companion, purposed now to forget all subtlety and deceit and to play the good ass to get my masters' favor, for I perceived by their talk that we were well nigh come home to our journey's end where they lived and had their dwelling. And after that we had passed over a little hill, we came to our appointed place, where when we were unladen of our burdens and all things carried in, I tumbled and wallowed in the dust to refresh myself instead of water.

The thing and the time compel me to make description of the places and especially of the den where the thieves did inhabit: I will prove my wit what I can do, and then consider you whether I was an ass in judgement and sense, or no. First there was an exceeding great hill compassed about with big trees, very high, with many turning bottoms, surrounded by sharp rocks, whereby it was inaccessible; there were many winding and hollow valleys environed with thickets and thorns, and naturally fortressed round about. From the top of the hill ran a spring both leaping and bubbling which poured down the steep slope its silvery waves, and then, scattering abroad into many little brooks, watered all the valleys below, that it seemed like unto a sea enclosed, or a standing flood. Before the den, where was no more hill, stood a high tower, and at the foot thereof, and on either side, were sheep-cots fenced and wattled with clay; before the gate of the house were walls enclosing a narrow path, in such sort that I well warrant you would judge it to be a very den for thieves, and there was nothing else near save a little cot covered roughly with thatch, wherein the thieves did nightly accustom to watch by order, as after I perceived.

And when they were all crept crouching into the house, and we fast tied with strong halters at the door, they began to chide with an old woman there, crooked with age, who had the government and rule of all those young men, and said: "How is it, old witch, old trot, that art the shame of life and rejected of very death, that thou sittest idly all day at home, and (having no regard to our perilous labors) hast provided nothing for our suppers thus late, but sittest doing nought but swilling wine into that greedy belly of thine from morning to night?" Then the old woman trembled and began to say in a terrified and harsh voice: "Behold, my puissant and faithful masters, you shall have meat and pottage enough by and by, cooked with a sweet savor. Here is first store of bread, wine plenty, filled in clean rinsed pots, likewise hot water prepared to bathe you hastily after your wont." Which when she had said, they put off all their garments and refreshed themselves by a great fire, and after that they were washed with the hot water and anointed with oil, they sat down at the table garnished with all kinds of dainty meat.

Now they were no sooner set down, but in came another company of young men, more in number than was before, whom you would judge at once likewise to be thieves; for they also brought in their prey of gold and silver money, and plate, and robes both silken and gold-embroidered, and, when they had likewise washed, they sat amongst the rest, and casting lots they served one another by order. The thieves drank and ate exceedingly, laying out the meat in heaps, the bread in mounds, and the wine-cups like a marching army, crying, laughing, and making such noise, that I thought I was amongst the tyrannous and wild drunken Lapiths and Centaurs.[1] At length one of them, more stout than the rest, spoke in this sort: "We verily have manfully conquered the house of Milo of Hypata, and besides all the riches and treasure which by force we have brought away, we are all come home safe, none being lost, and are increased the more, if it be worthy of mention, by the eight feet of this horse and this ass. But you, that have roved about among the towns of Bœotia,[2] have lost your valiant captain Lamachus, whose loss I more regarded than all this treasure which you have brought. But it is his own bravery that hath destroyed him, and therefore the memory of him shall be renowned forever amongst the most noble kings and valiant captains; but you accustom when you go abroad, like doughty robbers indeed, to creep through every corner and hole for every trifle, doing a paltry business in baths and the huts of aged women."

Then one of them that came last answered: "Why, are you only ignorant, that the greater the house is, the sooner it may be robbed and spoiled? For though the family of servants be great and dispersed in divers lodgings, yet every man had rather defend his life than save at his own hazard the riches of his master; but when the people be few and poor and live alone, then will they hide and protect very fiercely, even at the danger of their lives, their substance, how little or great soever it be. And to the intent you will believe me, I will show you our story as an example. We were scarce come nigh unto seven-gated Thebes, and began at once to enquire of the fortunes of the greatest men thereof, which is the fountain of our art and science, and we learned at length where a rich chuff called Chryseros did dwell, who, for fear of offices and burdens in the public weal, with great pains dissimulated his estate and lived sole and solitary in a small cot (howbeit well fortified) and huddled daily in ragged and torn apparel over his bags of gold. Wherefore we devised with ourselves to go first to his house and spoil him of all his riches, which we thought we should easily do if we had but to fight against him alone. And at once when night came we quickly drew towards his door, which we thought best neither to move it, nor lift it out of the hinges, and we would not break it open lest by

---

[1] Thessaly, a wild rocky region, was the home of the Lapithæ and the Centaurs. At the wedding of Peirithous, prince of the Lapithæ, the Centaurs were invited but, losing their self-control under the influence of wine, attacked the bride. The Lapithæ, in a furious fight, and with the aid of Theseus, drove the Centaurs from the region.

[2] In Greece.

the noise we should raise up (to our harm) the neighbors by. Then our strong and valiant captain Lamachus, trusting his own strength and force, thrust in his hand through a hole of the door, which was made for the key, and thought to pull back the bolt; but the covetous caitiff Chryseros, vilest of all that go on two feet, being awake and seeing all, but making no noise, came softly to the door and caught his hand, and with a great nail nailed it fast to a post of the gate, which when he had done, and had left him thus crucified, he ran up to a high chamber of his hovel, and in a very loud voice called every one of his neighbors by name, desiring them to look to their common safety with all possible speed, for his house was afire. Then every one, for fear of the danger that was nigh him, came running out to aid him; wherewith we (fearing our present peril) knew not what was best to be done, whether we should leave our companion there, or yield ourselves to die with him; but by his consent we devised a better way, for we cut through the joint of this our leader where the arm joins to the shoulder, and so let it hang there, and then bound up his wound with clouts lest we should be traced by the drops of blood, and so we took all that was left of Lamachus and led him away. Now when we hurried along, trembling for our affection to him, and were so nigh pursued that we were in present danger, and Lamachus could not keep our company by reason of faintness (and on the other side it was not for his profit to linger behind) he spoke unto us as a man of singular courage and virtue, desiring us by much entreaty and prayer, and by the puissance of the god Mars and the faith of our confederacy, to deliver our brave comrade from torment and miserable captivity: and further he asked how was it possible that so courageous a captain could live without his hand, wherewith alone he could rob and slay so many people, but he would rather think himself sufficiently happy if he might be slain by the hand of a friend. But when he saw that we all refused to commit any such wicked deed, he drew out his sword with his other hand, and after that he had often kissed it, he thrust it with a strong blow clean through his body. Then we honored the corpse of so puissant a man, and wrapped it in linen clothes and threw it into the sea to hide it: so lieth our master Lamachus buried and hid in the grave of water.

"Now he ended his life worthily of his courage, as I have declared; but Alcimus, though he were a man of great enterprise, yet could he not void himself from evil fortune: for on a day when he had entered into an old woman's hut that slept, to rob her, he went up into the higher chamber, where he should first have strangled her, but he had more

regard to throw down everything out of the window to us that stood under: and when he had cleverly despoiled all, he would leave nothing behind, but went to the old woman's bed where she lay asleep and threw her from it, and would have taken off the coverlet to have thrown down likewise, but the old hag awaked and fell at his knees, and desired him in this manner: 'O sir, I pray you, cast not away such torn and ragged clouts into my neighbors' houses, whither this window looks; for they are rich enough and need no such things.' Then Alcimus (thinking her words to be true) was brought in belief that such things as he had thrown out already, and such things as he should throw out after, were not fallen down to his fellows, but into other men's houses; wherefore he went to the window to see, and especially to behold the places round about, as she had told him, thrusting his body out of the window; but while he strove to do this, strongly indeed but somewhat rashly, the old trot marked him well, and came behind him softly, and although she had but small strength, yet with a sudden force she took him by the heels and thrust him out headlong while his body was balancing and unsure; and beside that the height was very great, he fell upon a marvellous great stone that lay near and burst his ribs, whereby he vomited and spewed flakes of blood, and when he had told us all, he suffered not long torment, but presently died. Then we gave unto him the same burial and sent him a worthy comrade to Lamachus, as we had done before.

"When we had thus lost two of our companions, we liked not Thebes, but marched towards the next city called Platæa,[1] where we found great fame concerning a man named Demochares that purposed to set forth a great game, where should be a trial of all kinds of weapons: he was come of a good house, marvellous rich, liberal, and well deserved that which he had, and had prepared many shews and pleasures for the common people: in so much that there is no man can either by wit or eloquence shew in fit words all the manifold shapes of his preparations, for first he had provided gladiators of a famous band, then all manner of hunters most fleet of foot, then guilty men without hope of reprieve who were judged for their punishment to be food for wild beasts. He had ordained a machine made of beams fixed together, great towers and platforms like a house to move hither and thither, very well painted, to be places to contain all the quarry: he had ready a great number of wild beasts and all sorts of them, especially he had brought from abroad those noble creatures that

[1] In Bœotia.

were soon to be the death of so many condemned persons. But amongst so great preparations of noble price, he bestowed the most part of his patrimony in buying of a vast multitude of great bears, which either by chasing he had caught himself, or which he dearly bought or which were given him by divers of his friends, who strove one with another in making him such gifts: and all these he kept and nourished to his very great cost. Howbeit for all his care of the public pleasure, he could not be free from the malicious eyes of envy: for some of them were well-nigh dead, with too long tying up; some meagre with the broiling heat of the sun; some languished with long lying, but all (having sundry diseases) were so afflicted that they died one after another, and there were well-nigh none left, in such sort that you might see their wrecks piteously lying in the streets and all but dead: and then the common people, having no other meat to feed on, and forced by their rude poverty to find any new meat and cheap feasts, would come forth and fill their bellies with the flesh of the bears.

"Then by and by Babulus and I devised a pretty sport to suit this case; we drew to our lodging one of the bears that was greater of bulk than all the rest, as though we would prepare to eat thereof, where we flayed off his skin and kept his claws whole, but we meddled not with the head, but cut it off by the neck, and so let it hang to the skin. Then we razed off the flesh from the back, and cast dust thereon, and set it in the sun to dry: and while it was drying by the heat of the heavenly fire, we made merry with the flesh, and then we devised with ourselves with an oath that one of us, being more valiant than the rest, not so much in body as in courage (so that he would straightway consent thereto) should put on the skin, and, feigning that he were a bear, should be led to Demochares' house in the night, by which means we thought to be received and easily let in. Many of our brave brotherhood were desirous to play the bear in this subtle sleight, but especially one Thrasyleon of a courageous mind was chosen by all our band to take the risk of this enterprise. Then we put him, very calm in mind and face, into the bear's skin, which was soft and fitted him finely in every point; we buckled fast the edges thereof with fine stitching, and covered the same, though small, with the thick hair growing about it that it might not be seen: we thrust his head into the opening of the bear's throat where his neck had been cut out, and after this we made little holes through his nostrils and eyes for Thrasyleon to see out and take wind at, in such sort that he seemed a very lively and natural beast: when this was done, we brought him into a cage which we hired with a little money for

the purpose, and he crept nimbly in after like a bear with a good courage.

"Thus we began our subtlety, and then we imagined thus: we feigned letters as though they came from one Nicanor which dwelt in the country of Thrace, which was of great acquaintance with this Demochares, wherein we wrote that he had sent him, being his friend, the first-fruits of his coursing and hunting. When night was come, we took cover of the darkness, and brought Thrasyleon's cage and our forged letters, and presented them to Demochares. When Demochares wonderingly beheld this mighty bear, and saw the timely liberality of Nicanor his friend, he was glad, and commanded his servant to deliver unto us that brought him this joy ten gold crowns, as he had great store in his coffers: then (as the novelty of a thing doth accustom to stir men's minds to behold the same) many persons came on every side to see this bear, but Thrasyleon (lest they should by curious viewing and prying perceive the truth) ran often upon them to put them in fear, so that they durst not come nigh. Then the people said with one voice: 'Verily Demochares is right happy, in that, after the death of so many beasts, he hath gotten, in spite of fortune, so goodly a bear to supply him afresh.' He commanded that with great care his servants should put him into the park close by, but I immediately spoke unto him and said: 'Sir, I pray you, take heed how you put a beast tired with the heat of the sun and with long travel amongst others which (as I hear say) have divers maladies and diseases; let him rather lie in some open place of your house, where the breeze blows through, yea nigh to some water, where he may take air and ease himself, for do not you know that such kind of beasts do greatly delight to couch under shadow of trees and dewy caves, nigh unto pleasant wells and waters?' Hereby Demochares, admonished and remembering how many he had before that perished, was contented that we should put the bear's cage where we would. Moreover we said unto him: 'We ourselves are determined to lie all night nigh unto the bear, to look unto him, which is tired with the heat and his long journey, and to give him meat and drink at his due hour.' Then he answered: 'Verily, masters, you need not to put yourselves to such pains: for I have men, yea, almost all my family of servants, that serve for nothing but for this purpose of tending bears.'

"Then we took leave of him and departed, and when we were come without the gates of the town we perceived before us a great sepulchre standing out of the highway, in a privy and secret place. And thither we went and opened there certain coffins, half rotted with age, wherein we found the corruption of man, and the ashes and dust of his long-buried body, which should serve to hold the prey we were very soon to get: and then, according to the custom of our band, having a respect to the dark and moonless time of the night when we thought that every man was sunk in his first and strongest sleep, we went with our weapons and besieged the doors of Demochares round about, in earnest that we were soon to plunder the same. Then Thrasyleon was ready at hand, seizing upon that time of night which is for robbers most fit, and crept out of the cage and went to kill all such of his guards as he found asleep; but when he came to the porter he slew him also and took the key and opened the gates and let us all in: and he shewed us now in the midst of the house a large counter, wherein looking sharply he saw put the night before a great abundance of treasure: which when by violence of us all we had broken open, I bade every one of my fellows take as much gold and silver as they could quickly bear away, and carry it to the sepulchre, and there quickly hide it in the house of those dead who were to us most faithful allies, and then come soon back to take another burden; but I, for our common weal, would stand alone at the gate watching diligently when they would return, and the bear running about the house would make such of the family afraid as fortuned to wake and come out: for who is he that is so puissant and courageous, that at the sight of so great a monster would not quail and flee away and keep his chamber well barred, especially in the night?

"Now when we had brought this matter to so good a point, there chanced a pitiful case; for as I looked for my companions that should come from the sepulchre, behold there was a boy of the house that fortuned to be awaked by the noise, as fate would have it, and look out of a window and espy the bear running freely about the house, and he went back on his steps a-tiptoe and very secretly, and told all the servants, and at once the house was filled with the whole train of them. Incontinently they came forth with torches, lanterns, candles and tapers, and other lights, that they might see all the yard over; they came not unarmed, but with clubs, spears, and naked swords, to guard the entrances, and they set on greyhounds and mastiffs, even those with great ears and shaggy hair, to subdue the poor beast. Then I, during this broil, thought to run away, but because I would see Thrasyleon fighting wonderfully with the dogs, I lay behind the gate to behold him. And although I might perceive that he was at the very term or limit of life, yet remembered he his own faithfulness and

ours, and valiantly resisted the gaping and ravenous mouths of the hound of Hell: for he took well to play the part which he so willingly had taken in hand himself, and with much ado, so long as the breath was in him, now flying and now pursuing, with many twistings and turnings of his body, tumbled at length out of the house; but when he was come to liberty abroad, yet could he not save himself by flight, for all the dogs of the street (which were fierce and many) joined themselves to the greyhounds and mastiffs that had just come out of the house, to chase him like a great host: alas, what a pitiful sight it was when our poor Thrasyleon was thus environed and compassed with so many furious dogs that tore and rent him miserably! Then I, impatient of his so great misery, ran in amongst the press of the people, and aiding my comrade secretly with my words (for no more could I do) exhorted all the leaders of this chase in this manner: 'O great extreme mischance, what a precious and excellent beast do we lose!' but my words did nothing prevail to help the poor wretch. For there came running out a tall man with a spear in his hand, that thrust him clean through, and afterwards many that stood by, released of their fear, drew out their swords, and so they killed him. But verily our brave captain Thrasyleon, the great honor of our band, when his life, (that was worthy never to die), was utterly overcome, but not his fortitude, would not bewray the league between us, either by crying, howling, or any other means, but (being torn with dogs, and wounded with weapons) did still send forth a bellowing cry more like that of a beast than of a man: and taking his present fortune in good part, with courage and glory enough did finish his life with such a terror unto the assembly, that no person was so hardy (until it was morn, nay, until it was high day) as to touch him, though he were a beast stark dead: but at last there came a butcher more valiant than the rest, who (opening the paunch of the beast) slit off the skin from the hardy and venturous thief. In this manner there was lost to us also our captain Thrasyleon, but there was not lost to him his fame and honor. When all this was done, we packed up our treasure which the faithful dead in the sepulchre had kept for us, and we got us out of the bounds of Platæa, thinking always with ourselves that there was no fidelity to be found amongst the living; and no wonder, for that it hath passed over to the ghosts and the dead in hatred of our deceitfulness. And so, being wearied with the weight of our burdens, and very tired with our rough travel, having thus lost three of our soldiers, we are come home with this present prey that you see."

Thus when they had spoken and poured libation

of pure wine from cups of gold in memory of their slain companions, they sung hymns to the god Mars to pacify him withal, and laid them down to sleep. Then the old woman gave us fresh barley in plenty without measure, in so much that my horse, the only lord of all that abundance, might well think he was at some priestly banquet that day. But I, that was accustomed to eat flour finely milled and long cooked with broth, thought that but a sour kind of meat; wherefore espying a corner where lay the loaves of bread left by all the band, I got me thither, and used upon them my jaws which ached with long famine and seemed to be full of cobwebs. Now when the night was come the thieves awaked and rose up: and when they had buckled on their weapons and disguised their faces with vizors, like unto spectres, they departed, and yet for all the great sleep that came upon me, I could in no wise leave eating, and whereas, when I was a man, I could be contented with one or two loaves at the most, now my guts were so greedy that three panniers full would scarcely serve me; and while I labored at this business, the morning came, and, being moved by even an ass's shamefastness, I left my food at last (though well I liked it) and at a stream hard by I quenched my thirst. And suddenly after, the thieves returned home careful and heavy, bringing no burdens with them, no not so much as one poor cloak, but with all their swords and strength, yea even with the might of their whole band, only a maiden that seemed by her habit to be some gentlewoman born, and the daughter of some noble of that country, who was so fair and beautiful, that though I were an ass, yet I swear that I had a great affection to her. The virgin lamented and tore her hair, and spoiled her garments for the great sorrow she was in, but the thieves brought her within the cave, and essayed to comfort her in this sort: "Weep not, fair gentlewoman, we pray you, for be you assured that we will do no outrage or violence to your person, but take patience awhile for our profit; for necessity and poor estate hath compelled us to this enterprise: we warrant you that your parents (although they be covetous) from their great store will be contented to give us money enough to redeem and ransom you, that are their own blood, from our hands."

Cupid and Psyche[1]

In a certain city lived a king and queen who had three daughters exceeding fair. But the beauty of the elder sisters, though pleasant to behold, yet passed not the measure of human praise, while such was the loveliness of the youngest that men's speech was too poor to commend it worthily and could express it not at all. Many of the citizens and of strangers, whom the fame of this excellent vision had gathered thither, confounded by that matchless beauty, could but kiss the finger-tips of their right hands at sight of her, as in adoration to the goddess Venus herself. And soon a rumor passed through the country that she whom the blue deep had borne, forbearing her divine dignity, was even then moving among men, or that by some fresh germination from the stars, not the sea now, but the earth, had put forth a new Venus, endued with the flower of virginity.

This belief, with the fame of the maiden's loveliness, went daily further into distant lands, so that many people were drawn together to behold that glorious model of the age. Men sailed no longer to Paphos, to Cnidos or Cythera,[1] to the presence of the goddess Venus: her sacred rites were neglected, her images stood uncrowned, the cold ashes were left to disfigure her forsaken altars. It was to a maiden that men's prayers were offered, to a human countenance they looked, in propitiating so great a godhead: when the girl went forth in the morning they strewed flowers on her way, and the victims proper to that unseen goddess were presented as she passed along. This conveyance of divine worship to a mortal kindled meantime the anger of the true Venus. "Lo! now, the ancient parent of nature," she cried, "the fountain of all elements! Behold me, Venus, benign mother of the world, sharing my honors with a mortal maiden, while my name, built up in heaven, is profaned by the mean things of earth! Shall a perishable woman bear my image about with her? In vain did the shepherd of Ida[2] prefer me! Yet shall she have little joy, whosoever she be, of her usurped and unlawful loveliness!" Thereupon she called to her that winged, bold boy,[3] of evil ways, who wanders armed by night through men's houses, spoiling their marriages; and stirring yet more by her speech his inborn wantonness, she led him to the city, and showed him Psyche as she walked.

"I pray thee," she said, "give thy mother a full revenge. Let this maid become the slave of an unworthy love." Then, embracing him closely, she departed to the shore and took her throne upon

---

[1] Translated by Walter Pater in *Marius the Epicurean.* By permission of The Macmillan Company, publishers.

[1] The first two were favorite resorts of Venus and it was to the island of Cythera that Venus was wafted after she had been born from the foam of the sea.

[2] It was on Mount Ida that Paris awarded the golden apple to Venus for her beauty.

[3] Cupid.

the crest of the wave. And lo! at her unuttered will, her ocean-servants are in waiting: the daughters of Nereus are there singing their song, and Portunus, and Salacia, and the tiny charioteer of the dolphin, with a host of Tritons leaping through the billows. And one blows softly through his sounding sea-shell, another spreads a silken web against the sun, a third presents the mirror to the eyes of his mistress, while the others swim side by side below, drawing her chariot. Such was the escort of Venus as she went upon the sea.

Psyche meantime, aware of her loveliness, had no fruit thereof. All people regarded and admired, but none sought her in marriage. It was but as on the finished work of the craftsman that they gazed upon that divine likeness. Her sisters, less fair than she, were happily wedded. She, even as a widow, sitting at home, wept over her desolation, hating in her heart the beauty in which all men were pleased.

And the king, supposing the gods were angry, inquired of the oracle of Apollo, and Apollo answered him thus: "Let the damsel be placed on the top of a certain mountain, adorned as for the bed of marriage, and of death. Look not for a son-in-law of mortal birth; but for that evil serpent-thing, by reason of whom even the gods tremble and the shadows of Styx [1] are afraid."

So the king returned home and made known the oracle to his wife. For many days she lamented, but at last the fulfillment of the divine precept is urgent upon her, and the company make ready to conduct the maiden to her deadly bridal. And now the nuptial torch gathers dark smoke and ashes: the pleasant sound of the pipe is changed into a cry: the marriage hymn concludes in a sorrowful wailing: below her yellow wedding-veil the bride shook away her tears; insomuch that the whole city was afflicted together at the ill-luck of the stricken house.

But the mandate of the god impelled the hapless Psyche to her fate, and, these solemnities being ended, the funeral of the living soul goes forth, all the people following. Psyche, bitterly weeping, assists not at her marriage but at her own obsequies, and while the parents hesitate to accomplish a thing so unholy the daughter cries to them: "Wherefore torment your luckless age by long weeping? This was the prize of my extraordinary beauty! When all people celebrated us with divine honors, and in one voice named the New Venus, it was then ye should have wept for me as one dead. Now at last I understand that that one name of Venus has been my ruin. Lead me and set me upon the appointed place. I am in haste to submit

[1] A river — one of the boundaries of the Underworld.

to that well-omened marriage, to behold that goodly spouse. Why delay the coming of him who was born for the destruction of the whole world?"

She was silent, and with firm step went on the way. And they proceeded to the appointed place on a steep mountain, and left there the maiden alone, and took their way homewards dejectedly. The wretched parents, in their close-shut house, yielded themselves to perpetual night; while to Psyche, fearful and trembling and weeping sore upon the mountain-top, comes the gentle Zephyrus.[1] He lifts her mildly, and, with vesture afloat on either side, bears her by his own soft breathing over the windings of the hills, and sets her lightly among the flowers in the bosom of a valley below.

Psyche, in those delicate grassy places, lying sweetly on her dewy bed, rested from the agitation of her soul and arose in peace. And lo! a grove of mighty trees, with a fount of water, clear as glass, in the midst; and hard by the water, a dwelling-place, built not by human hands but by some divine cunning. One recognized, even at the entering, the delightful hostelry of a god. Golden pillars sustained the roof, arched most curiously in cedar-wood and ivory. The walls were hidden under wrought silver, — all tame and woodland creatures leaping forward to the visitor's gaze. Wonderful indeed was the craftsman, divine or half-divine, who by the subtlety of his art had breathed so wild a soul into the silver! The very pavement was distinct with pictures in goodly stones. In the glow of its precious metal the house is its own daylight, having no need of the sun. Well might it seem a place fashioned for the conversation of gods with men!

Psyche, drawn forward by the delight of it, came near, and, her courage growing, stood within the doorway. One by one, she admired the beautiful things she saw; and, most wonderful of all! no lock, no chain, nor living guardian protected that great treasure-house. But as she gazed there came a voice, — a voice, as it were, unclothed by bodily vesture. "Mistress!" it said, "all these things are thine. Lie down, and relieve thy weariness, and rise again for the bath when thou wilt. We thy servants, whose voice thou hearest, will be beforehand with our service, and a royal feast shall be ready."

And Psyche understood that some divine care was providing, and, refreshed with sleep and the bath, sat down to the feast. Still she saw no one: only she heard words falling here and there, and had voices alone to serve her. And the feast being ended, one entered the chamber and sang to her unseen, while another struck the chords of a harp,

[1] The West Wind.

invisible with him who played on it. Afterwards the sound of a company singing together came to her, but still so that none was present to sight, yet it appeared that a great multitude of singers was there.

And the hour of evening inviting her, she climbed into the bed; and as the night was far advanced, behold a sound of a certain clemency approaches her. Then fearing for her maidenhood in so great solitude, she trembled, and more than any evil she knew dreaded that she knew not. And now the husband, that unknown husband, drew near, and ascended the couch, and made her his wife; and lo! before the rise of dawn he had departed hastily. And the attendant voices ministered to the needs of the newly married. And so it happened with her for a long season. And as nature has willed, this new thing, by continual use, became a delight to her: the sound of the voice grew to be her solace in that condition of loneliness and uncertainty.

One night the bridegroom spoke thus to his beloved, "O Psyche, most pleasant bride! Fortune is grown stern with us, and threatens thee with mortal peril. Thy sisters, troubled at the report of thy death and seeking some trace of thee, will come to the mountain's top. But if by chance their cries reach thee, answer not, neither look forth at all, lest thou bring sorrow upon me and destruction upon thyself." Then Psyche promised that she would do according to his will. But the bridegroom was fled away again with the night. And all that day she spent in tears, repeating that she was now dead indeed, shut up in that golden prison, powerless to console her sisters sorrowing after her, or to see their faces; and so went to rest weeping.

And after a while came the bridegroom again, and embracing her as she wept, complained, "Was this thy promise, my Psyche? What have I to hope from thee? Even in the arms of thy husband thou ceasest not from pain. Do now as thou wilt. Indulge thine own desire, though it seeks what will ruin thee. Yet wilt thou remember my warning, repentant too late." Then, protesting that she is like to die, she obtains from him that he suffer her to see her sisters, and present to them moreover what gifts she would of golden ornaments; but therewith he ofttimes advised her never at any time yielding to pernicious counsel, to inquire concerning his bodily form, lest she fall, through unholy curiosity, from so great a height of fortune, nor feel ever his embrace again. "I would die a hundred times," she said, cheerfully at last, "rather than be deprived of thy most sweet usage. I love thee as my own soul, beyond comparison even with Love himself. Only bid thy servant Zephyrus

bring hither my sisters, as he brought me. My honeycomb! My Husband! Thy Psyche's breath of life!" So he promised; and ere the light appeared, vanished from the hands of his bride.

And the sisters, coming to the place where Psyche was abandoned, wept loudly among the rocks, and called upon her by name, so that the sound came down to her, and running out of the palace distraught, she cried, "Wherefore afflict your souls with lamentation? I whom you mourn am here." Then, summoning Zephyrus, she reminded him of her husband's bidding; and he bare them down with a gentle blast. "Enter now," she said, "into my house, and relieve your sorrow in the company of Psyche your sister."

And Psyche displayed to them all the treasures of the golden house, and its great family of ministering voices, nursing in them the malice which was already at their hearts. And at last one of them asks curiously who the lord of that celestial array may be, and what manner of man her husband. And Psyche answered dissemblingly, "A young man, handsome and mannerly, with a goodly beard. For the most part he hunts upon the mountains." And lest the secret should slip from her in the way of further speech, loading her sisters with gold and gems, she commanded Zephyrus to bear them away.

And they returned home, on fire with envy. "See now the injustice of fortune!" cried one. "We, the elder children, are given like servants to be the wives of strangers, while the youngest is possessed of so great riches, who scarcely knows how to use them. You saw, sister! what a hoard of wealth lies in the house; what glittering gowns; what splendor of precious gems, besides all that gold trodden under foot. If she indeed has, as she said, a bridegroom so goodly then no one in all the world is happier. And it may be that this husband, being of divine nature, will make her too a goddess. Nay, so in truth it is. It was even thus she bore herself. Already she looks aloft and breathes divinity, who, though but a woman, has voices for her handmaidens, and can command the winds." "Think," answered the other, "how arrogantly she dealt with us, grudging us these trifling gifts out of all that store, and when our company became a burden, causing us to be hissed and driven away from her through the air! But I am no woman if she keep her hold on this great fortune; and if the insult done us has touched thee too, take we counsel together. Meanwhile let us hold our peace, and know nought of her, alive or dead. For they are not truly happy of whose happiness other folk are unaware."

And the bridegroom, whom still she knows not,

warns her thus a second time, as he talks with her by night: "Seest thou what peril besets thee? Those cunning wolves have made ready for thee their snares, of which the sum is that they persuade thee to search into the fashion of my countenance, the seeing of which, as I have told thee often, will be the seeing of it no more forever. But do thou neither listen nor make answer to ought regarding thy husband. Besides, we have sown also the seed of our race. Even now this bosom grows with a child to be born to us, a child, if thou but keep our secret, of divine quality; if thou profane it, subject to death." And Psyche was glad at the tidings, rejoicing in that solace of a divine seed, and in the glory of that pledge of love to be, and the dignity of the name of mother. Anxiously she notes the increase of the days, the waning months. And again, as he tarries briefly beside her, the bridegroom repeats his warning: "Even now the sword is drawn with which thy sisters seek thy life. Have pity on thyself, sweet wife, and upon our child, and see not those evil women again." But the sisters make their way into the palace once more, crying to her in wily tones, "O Psyche! and thou too wilt be a mother! How great will be the joy at home! Happy indeed shall we be to have the nursing of the golden child. Truly if he be answerable to the beauty of his parents, it will be a birth of Cupid himself."

So, little by little, they stole upon the heart of their sister. She, meanwhile, bids the lyre to sound for their delight, and the playing is heard: she bids the pipes to move, the quire to sing, and the music and the singing come invisibly, soothing the mind of the listener with sweetest modulation. Yet not even thereby was their malice put to sleep: once more they seek to know what manner of husband she has, and whence that seed. And Psyche, simple over-much, forgetful of her first story, answers, "My husband comes from a far country, trading for great sums. He is already of middle age, with whitening locks." And therewith she dismisses them again.

And returning home upon the soft breath of Zephyrus one cried to the other, "What shall be said of so ugly a lie? He who was a young man with goodly beard is now in middle life. It must be that she told a false tale: else is she in very truth ignorant of what manner of man he is. Howsoever it be, let us destroy her quickly. For if she indeed knows not, be sure that her bridegroom is one of the gods: it is a god she bears in her womb. And let that be far from us! If she be called the mother of a god, then will life be more than I can bear."

So, full of rage against her, they returned to Psyche, and said to her craftily, "Thou livest in an ignorant bliss, all incurious of thy real danger. It is a deadly serpent, as we certainly know, that comes to sleep at thy side. Remember the words of the oracle, which declared thee destined to a cruel beast. There are those who have seen it at nightfall, coming back from its feeding. In no long time, they say, it will end its blandishments. It but waits for the babe to be formed in thee, that it may devour thee by so much the richer. If indeed the solitude of this musical place, or it may be the loathsome commerce of a hidden love, delight thee, we at least in sisterly piety have done our part." And at last the unhappy Psyche, simple and frail of soul, carried away by the terror of their words, losing memory of her husband's precepts and her own promise, brought upon herself a great calamity. Trembling and turning pale, she answers them, "And they who tell those things, it may be, speak the truth. For in very deed never have I seen the face of my husband, nor know I at all what manner of man he is. Always he frights me diligently from the sight of him, threatening some great evil should I too curiously look upon his face. Do ye, if ye can help your sister in her great peril, stand by her now."

Her sisters answered her, "The way of safety we have well considered, and will teach thee. Take a sharp knife, and hide it in that part of the couch where thou art wont to lie: take also a lamp filled with oil, and set it privily behind the curtain. And when he shall have drawn up his coils into the accustomed place, and thou hearest him breathe in sleep, slip then from his side and discover the lamp, and, knife in hand, put forth thy strength, and strike off the serpent's head." And so they departed in haste.

And Psyche left alone (alone but for the furies which beset her) is tossed up and down in her distress, like a wave of the sea; and though her will is firm, yet, in the moment of putting hand to the deed, she falters, and is torn asunder by various apprehensions of the great calamity upon her. She hastens and anon delays, now full of distrust, and now of angry courage: under one bodily form she loathes the monster and loves the bridegroom. But twilight ushers in the night; and at length in haste she makes ready for the terrible deed. Darkness came, and the bridegroom; and he first falls into a deep sleep.

And she, erewhile of no strength, the hard purpose of destiny assisting her, is confirmed in force. With lamp plucked forth, knife in hand, she put by her sex; and lo! as the secrets of the bed became manifest, the sweetest and most gentle of all creatures, Love himself, reclined there, in his own proper loveliness! At sight of him the very flame of the lamp kindled more gladly! But Psyche was afraid of the vision, and, faint of soul, trembled back upon her knees, and would have hidden the steel in her own bosom. But the knife slipped from her hand; and now, undone, yet ofttimes looking upon the beauty of that divine countenance, she lives again. She sees the locks of that golden head, pleasant with the unction of the gods, shed down in graceful entanglement behind and before, about the ruddy cheeks and white throat. The pinions of the winged god, yet fresh with the dew, are spotless upon his shoulders, the delicate plumage wavering over them as they lie at rest. Smooth he was, and touched with light, worthy of Venus his mother. At the foot of the couch lay his bow and arrows, the instruments of his power, propitious to men.

And Psyche, gazing hungrily thereon, draws an arrow from the quiver, and trying the point upon the thumb, tremulous still, drave in the barb, so that a drop of blood came forth. Thus fell she, by her own act, and unaware, into the love of Love. Falling upon the bridegroom, with indrawn breath, in a hurry of kisses from eager and open lips, she shuddered as she thought how brief that sleep might be. And it chanced that a drop of burning oil fell from the lamp upon the god's shoulder. Ah! maladroit minister of love, thus to wound him from whom all fire comes; though 'twas a lover, I trow, first devised thee, to have the fruit of his desire even in the darkness! At the touch of the fire the god started up, and beholding the overthrow of her faith, quietly took flight from her embraces.

And Psyche, as he rose upon the wing, laid hold on him with her two hands, hanging upon him in his passage through the air, till she sinks to the earth through weariness. And as she lay there, the divine lover, tarrying still, lighted upon a cypress tree which grew near, and, from the top of it, spake thus to her, in great emotion. "Foolish one! unmindful of the command of Venus, my mother, who had devoted thee to one of base degree, I fled to thee in his stead. Now know I that this was vainly done. Into mine own flesh pierced mine arrow, and I made thee my wife, only that I might seem a monster beside thee — that thou shouldst seek to wound the head wherein lay the eyes so full of love to thee! Again and again, I thought to put thee on thy guard concerning these things, and warned thee in loving-kindness. Now I would but punish thee by my flight hence." And therewith he winged his way into the deep sky.

Psyche, prostrate upon the earth, and following far as sight might reach the flight of the bridegroom, wept and lamented; and when the breadth of space had parted him wholly from her, cast herself down from the bank of a river which was nigh. But the stream, turning gentle in honor of the god, put her forth again unhurt upon its margin. And as it happened, Pan, the rustic god, was sitting just then by the waterside. Hard by, his flock of goats browsed at will. And the shaggy god called her, wounded and outworn, kindly to him and said, "I am but a rustic herdsman, pretty maiden, yet wise, by favor of my great age and long experience; and if I guess truly by those faltering steps, by thy sorrowful eyes and continual sighing, thou laborest with excess of love. Listen then to me, and seek not death again, in the stream or otherwise. Put aside thy woe, and turn thy prayers to Cupid. He is in truth a delicate youth: win him by the delicacy of thy service."

So the shepherd-god spoke, and Psyche, answering nothing, but with a reverence to this serviceable deity, went on her way. And while she, in her search after Cupid, wandered through many lands, he was lying in the chamber of his mother, heart-sick. And the white bird which floats over the waves plunged in haste into the sea, and approaching Venus, as she bathed, made known to her that her son lies afflicted with some grievous hurt, doubtful of life. And Venus cried, angrily, "My son, then, has a mistress! And it is Psyche, who witched away my beauty and was the rival of my godhead, whom he loves!"

Therewith she issued from the sea, and returning to her golden chamber, found there the lad, sick, as she had heard, and cried from the doorway, "Well done, truly! to trample thy mother's precepts under foot, to spare my enemy that cross of an unworthy love; nay, unite her to thyself, child as thou art, that I might have a daughter-in-law who hates me! I will make thee repent of thy sport, and the savor of thy marriage bitter. There is one who shall chasten this body of thine, put out thy torch and unstring thy bow. Not till she has plucked forth that hair, into which so oft these hands have smoothed the golden light, and sheared away thy wings, shall I feel the injury done me avenged." And with this she hastened in anger from the doors.

And Ceres and Juno[1] met her, and sought to know the meaning of her troubled countenance. "Ye come in season," she cried; "I pray you, find for me Psyche. It must needs be that ye have heard the disgrace of my house." And they, ignorant of what was done, would have soothed her anger, saying, "What fault, Mistress, hath thy son committed, that thou wouldst destroy the girl he

[1] Ceres, goddess of sowing and the harvests; Juno, the sister and wife of Jupiter, noted for her matronly qualities.

loves? Knowest thou not that he is now of age? Because he wears his years so lightly must he seem to thee ever but a child? Wilt thou forever thus pry into the pastimes of thy son, always accusing his wantonness, and blaming in him those delicate wiles which are all thine own?" Thus, in secret fear of the boy's bow, did they seek to please him with their gracious patronage. But Venus, angry at their light taking of her wrongs, turned her back upon them, and with hasty steps made her way once more to the sea.

Meanwhile Psyche, tossed in soul, wandering hither and thither, rested not night or day in the pursuit of her husband, desiring, if she might not soothe his anger by the endearments of a wife, at the least to propitiate him with the prayers of a handmaid. And seeing a certain temple on the top of a high mountain, she said, "Who knows whether yonder place be not the abode of my lord?" Thither, therefore, she turned her steps, hastening now the more because desire and hope pressed her on, weary as she was with the labors of the way, and so, painfully measuring out the highest ridges of the mountain, drew near to the sacred couches. She sees ears of wheat, in heaps or twisted into chaplets; ears of barley also, with sickles and all the instruments of harvest, lying there in disorder, thrown at random from the hands of the laborers in the great heat. These she curiously sets apart, one by one, duly ordering them; for she said within herself, "I may not neglect the shrines, nor the holy service, of any god there be, but must rather win by supplication the kindly mercy of them all."

And Ceres found her bending sadly upon her task, and cried aloud, "Alas, Psyche! Venus, in the furiousness of her anger, tracks thy footsteps through the world, seeking for thee to pay her the utmost penalty; and thou, thinking of anything rather than thine own safety, hast taken on thee the care of what belongs to me!" Then Psyche fell down at her feet, and sweeping the floor with her hair, washing the footsteps of the goddess in her tears, besought her mercy, with many prayers: "By the gladdening rites of harvest, by the lighted lamps and mystic marches of the marriage and mysterious invention of thy daughter Proserpine, and by all beside that the holy place of Attica veils in silence, minister, I pray thee, to the sorrowful heart of Psyche! Suffer me to hide myself but for a few days among the heaps of corn, till time have softened the anger of the goddess, and my strength, outworn in my long travail, be recovered by a little rest."

But Ceres answered her, "Truly thy tears move me, and I would fain help thee; only I dare not incur the ill-will of my kinswoman. Depart hence as quickly as may be." And Psyche, repelled against hope, afflicted now with twofold sorrow, making her way back again, beheld among the half-lighted woods of the valley below a sanctuary builded with cunning art. And that she might lose no way of hope, howsoever doubtful, she drew near to the sacred doors. She sees there gifts of price, and garments fixed upon the door-posts and to the branches of the trees, wrought with letters of gold which told the name of the goddess to whom they were dedicated, with thanksgiving for that she had done. So, with bent knee and hands laid about the glowing altar, she prayed, saying, "Sister and spouse of Jupiter! be thou to these my desperate fortunes Juno the Auspicious! I know that thou dost willingly help those in travail with child; deliver me from the peril that is upon me." And as she prayed thus, Juno in the majesty of her godhead was straightway present, and answered, "Would that I might incline favorably to thee: but against the will of Venus, whom I have ever loved as a daughter, I may not, for very shame, grant thy prayer."

And Psyche, dismayed by this new shipwreck of her hope, communed thus with herself, "Whither, from the midst of the snares that beset me, shall I take my way once more? In what dark solitude shall I hide me from the all-seeing eye of Venus? What if I put on at length a man's courage, and yielding myself unto her as my mistress, soften by a humility not yet too late the fierceness of her purpose? Who knows but that I may find him also whom my soul seeketh after, in the abode of his mother?"

And Venus, renouncing all earthly aid in her search, prepared to return to heaven. She ordered the chariot to be made ready, wrought for her by Vulcan as a marriage-gift, with a cunning of hand which had left his work so much the richer by the weight of gold it lost under his tool. From the multitude which housed the bed-chamber of their mistress, white doves came forth, and with joyful motions bent their painted necks beneath the yoke. Behind it, with playful riot, the sparrows sped onward, and other birds sweet of song, making known by their soft notes the approach of the goddess. Eagle and cruel hawk alarmed not the quireful family of Venus. And the clouds broke away, as the uttermost ether opened to receive her, daughter and goddess, with great joy.

And Venus passed straightway to the house of Jupiter to beg from him the service of Mercury, the god of speech. And Jupiter refused not her prayer. And Venus and Mercury descended from heaven together; and as they went, the former said to the latter, "Thou knowest, my brother of Arcady, that never at any time have I done anything without thy help; for how long time, moreover, I have sought a certain maiden in vain. And now nought remains but that by thy heraldry, I proclaim a reward for whomsoever shall find her. Do thou my bidding quickly." And therewith she conveyed to him a little scrip, in the which was written the name of Psyche, with other things; and so returned home.

And Mercury failed not in his office; but departing into all lands, proclaimed that whosoever delivered up to Venus the fugitive girl should receive from herself seven kisses — one thereof full of the inmost honey of her throat. With that the doubt of Psyche was ended. And now, as she came near to the doors of Venus, one of the household, whose name was Use-and-Wont, ran out to her, crying, "Hast thou learned, Wicked Maid! now at last! that thou hast a mistress?" and seizing her roughly by the hair, drew her into the presence of Venus. And when Venus saw her, she cried out, saying, "Thou hast deigned, then, to make thy salutations to thy mother-in-law. Now will I in turn treat thee as becometh a dutiful daughter-in-law."

And she took barley and millet and poppyseed, every kind of grain and seed, and mixed them together, and laughed, and said to her: "Methinks so plain a maiden can earn lovers only by industrious ministry: now will I also make trial of thy service. Sort me this heap of seed, the one kind from the others, grain by grain; and get thy task done before the evening." And Psyche, stunned by the cruelty of her bidding, was silent, and moved not her hand to the inextricable heap. And there came forth a little ant, which had understanding of the difficulty of her task, and took pity upon the consort of the god of Love; and he ran deftly hither and thither, and called together the whole army of his fellows. "Have pity," he cried, "nimble scholars of the Earth, Mother of all things! — have pity upon the wife of Love, and hasten to help her in her perilous effort." Then, one upon the other, the hosts of the insect people hurried together; and they sorted asunder the whole heap of seed, separating every grain after its kind, and so departed quickly out of sight.

And at nightfall Venus returned, and seeing that task finished with so wonderful diligence, she cried, "The work is not thine, thou naughty maid, but his in whose eyes thou hast found favor." And calling her again in the morning, "See now the grove," she said, "beyond yonder torrent. Certain sheep feed there, whose fleeces shine with gold. Fetch me straightway a lock of that precious stuff, having gotten it as thou mayst."

And Psyche went forth willingly, not to obey the command of Venus, but even to seek a rest from her labor in the depths of the river. But from the river, the green reed, lowly mother of music, spake to her: "O Psyche! pollute not these waters by self-destruction, nor approach that terrible flock; for, as the heat groweth, they wax fierce. Lie down under yon planetree, till the quiet of the river's breath have soothed them. Thereafter thou mayst shake down the fleecy gold from the trees of the grove, for it holdeth by the leaves."

And Psyche, instructed thus by the simple reed, in the humanity of its heart, filled her bosom with the soft golden stuff, and returned to Venus. But the goddess smiled bitterly, and said to her, "Well know I who was the author of this thing also. I will make further trial of thy discretion, and the boldness of thy heart. Seest thou the utmost peak of yonder steep mountain? The dark stream which flows down thence waters the Stygian fields, and swells the flood of Cocytus.[1] Bring me now, in this little urn, a draught from its innermost source." And therewith she put into her hands a vessel of wrought crystal.

And Psyche set forth in haste on her way to the mountain, looking there at last to find the end of her hapless life. But when she came to the region which borders on the cliff that was shown to her, she understood the deadly nature of her task. From a great rock, steep and slippery, a horrible river of water poured forth, falling straightway by a channel exceeding narrow into the unseen gulf below. And lo! creeping from the rocks on either hand, angry serpents, with their long necks and sleepless eyes. The very waters found a voice and bade her depart in smothered cries of, "Depart hence!" and, "What doest thou here? Look around thee!" and, "Destruction is upon thee!" And then sense left her, in the immensity of her peril, as one changed to stone.

Yet not even then did the distress of this innocent soul escape the steady eye of a gentle providence. For the bird of Jupiter [2] spread his wings and took flight to her, and asked her, "Didst thou think, simple one, even thou! that thou couldst steal one drop of that relentless stream, the holy river of Styx, terrible even to the gods? But give me thine urn." And the bird took the urn, and filled it at the source, and returned to her quickly from among the teeth of the serpents, bringing with him of the waters, all unwilling — nay! warning him to depart away and not molest them.

And she, receiving the urn with great joy, ran back quickly that she might deliver it to Venus, and yet again satisfied not the angry goddess.

[1] Another river bounding the Underworld.

[2] The eagle was the special messenger of Jupiter.

"My child!" she said, "in this one thing further must thou serve me. Take now this tiny casket, and get thee down even unto hell, and deliver it to Proserpine. Tell her that Venus would have of her beauty so much at least as may suffice for but one day's use, that beauty she possessed erewhile being forworn and spoiled, through her tendance upon the sick-bed of her son; and be not slow in returning."

And Psyche perceived there the last ebbing of her fortune — that she was now thrust openly upon death, who must go down, of her own motion, to Hades and the Shades. And straightway she climbed to the top of an exceeding high tower, thinking within herself, "I will cast myself down thence: so shall I descend most quickly into the kingdom of the dead." And the tower again broke forth into speech: "Wretched Maid! Wretched Maid! Wilt thou destroy thyself? If the breath quit thy body, then wilt thou indeed go down into Hades, but by no means return hither. Listen to me. Among the pathless wilds not far from this place lies a certain mountain, and therein one of hell's vent-holes. Through the breach a rough way lies open, following which thou wilt come, by straight course, to the castle of Orcus.[1] And thou must not go empty-handed. Take in each hand a morsel of barley-bread, soaked in hydromel; and in thy mouth two pieces of money. And when thou shalt be now well onward in the way of death, then wilt thou overtake a lame ass laden with wood, and a lame driver, who will pray thee reach him certain cords to fasten the burden which is falling from the ass; but be thou cautious to pass on in silence. And soon as thou comest to the river of the dead, Charon, in that crazy bark he has, will put thee over upon the further side. There is greed even among the dead; and thou shalt deliver to him, for the ferrying, one of those two pieces of money, in such wise that he take it with his hand from between thy lips. And as thou passest over the stream, a dead old man, rising on the water, will put up to thee his moldering hands, and pray thee draw him into the ferry-boat. But beware thou yield not to unlawful pity.

"When thou shalt be come over, and art upon the causeway, certain aged women, spinning, will cry to thee to lend thy hand to their work; and beware again that thou take no part therein; for this also is the snare of Venus, whereby she would cause thee to cast away one at least of those cakes thou bearest in thy hands. And think not that a slight matter; for the loss of either one of them will be to thee the losing of the light of day. For a watch-dog exceeding fierce lies ever before the

[1] Pluto, god of the Underworld.

threshold of that lonely house of Proserpine. Close his mouth with one of thy cakes; so shalt thou pass by him, and enter straightway into the presence of Proserpine herself. Then do thou deliver thy message, and taking what she shall give thee, return back again; offering the watch-dog the other cake, and to the ferryman that other piece of money thou hast in thy mouth. After this manner mayst thou return again beneath the stars. But withal, I charge thee, think not to look into, nor open, the casket thou bearest, with that treasure of the beauty of the divine countenance hidden therein."

So spake the stones of the tower; and Psyche delayed not, but proceeding diligently after the manner enjoined, entered into the house of Proserpine, at whose feet she sat down humbly, and would have neither the delicate couch nor that divine food the goddess offered her, but did straightway the business of Venus. And Proserpine filled the casket secretly, and shut the lid, and delivered it to Psyche, who fled therewith from Hades with new strength. But coming back into the light of day, even as she hasted now to the ending of her service, she was seized by a rash curiosity. "Lo! now," she said within herself, "my simpleness! who bearing in my hands the divine loveliness, heed not to touch myself with a particle at least therefrom, that I may please the more, by the favor of it, my fair one, my beloved." Even as she spoke, she lifted the lid; and behold! within, neither beauty, nor anything beside, save sleep only, the sleep of the dead, which took hold upon her, filling all her members with its drowsy vapor, so that she lay down in the way and moved not, as in the slumber of death.

And Cupid being healed of his wound, because he would endure no longer the absence of her he loved, gliding through the narrow window of the chamber where he was holden, his pinions being now repaired by a little rest, fled forth swiftly upon them, and coming to the place where Psyche was, shook that sleep away from her, and set him in his prison again, awaking her with the innocent point of his arrow: "Lo! thine old error again," he said, "which had like once more to have destroyed thee! But do thou now what is lacking of the command to my mother: the rest shall be my care." With these words, the lover rose upon the air; and being consumed inwardly with the greatness of his love, penetrated with vehement wing into the highest place of heaven, to lay his cause before the father of the gods. And the father of the gods took his hand in his, and kissed his face, and said to him, "At no time, my son, hast thou regarded me with due honor. Often hast thou vexed my bosom, wherein lies the disposition of the stars, with those busy darts of thine. Nevertheless, because thou hast grown up between these mine hands, I will accomplish thy desire." And straightway he bade Mercury call the gods together; and, the council-chamber being filled, sitting upon a high throne, "Ye gods," he said, "all ye whose names are in the white book of the Muses, ye know yonder lad. It seems good to me that his youthful heats should by some means be restrained. And that all occasion may be taken from him, I would even confine him in the bonds of marriage. He has chosen and embraced a mortal maiden. Let him have fruit of his love, and possess her forever."

Thereupon he bade Mercury produce Psyche in heaven; and holding out to her his ambrosial cup, "Take it," he said, "and live forever; nor shall Cupid ever depart from thee." And the gods sat 5 down together to the marriage-feast. On the first couch lay the bridegroom, and Psyche in his bosom. His rustic serving-boy bare the wine to Jupiter; and Bacchus to the rest. The Seasons crimsoned all things with their roses. Apollo sang 10 to the lyre, while a little Pan prattled on his reeds, and Venus danced very sweetly to the soft music. Thus — with due rites — did Psyche pass into the power of Cupid; and from them was born the daughter whom men call Voluptas.

Beowulf · Seventh Century

In the *Beowulf* the romantic spirit speaks through an Old English poem of the so-called Dark Ages and thus becomes, for readers of this volume, the first evidence of a literary temper later to speak through such voices as those of Wordsworth and Coleridge, Keats and Shelley. Here are enthusiasm and wonder, a sense of the mystery of life, a turning to the past, and bold daring and high adventure. Other early English poems include fragments from *The Fight at Finnsburgh* and from the *Waldere* and such poems as the *Widsith* and the *Seafarer*.

Neither the author nor the date of composition of the *Beowulf* is known. The events narrated in the epic took place on the Continent before the Angles migrated to England (fifth century), but the poem itself took the shape in which we know it after the migration. Scholars generally believe that some individual — an Englishman — during the last half of the seventh century worked over the old legends and chronicles which had been part of the folk heritage when the Angles lived on the Continent, and added the Christian elements. The manuscript of the poem dates from the tenth century. Thus, while the action of the poem took place in Denmark and Sweden, the poem may justifiably be considered an *English* poem because of its authorship and of the fact that it recounts some history and much legendry of a people which migrated from Northern Europe and made England their home. Here, then, is mythology, but supported by a great deal of historical evidence. As Mary E. Waterhouse has pointed out in the introductory essay to her translation of *Beowulf* in blank verse, it is "a tale of mythology drawn in brilliant tones against a much darker canvas of historical fact. It shows the glory of the individual soul moving against the gloomy background of circumstance."

The poem is chiefly concerned with three adventures of a hero named Beowulf. This hero fights with a monster, Grendel, who has been killing the warriors in a neighboring country. In revenge for Beowulf's treatment of Grendel, Grendel's mother attacks the people, and this time Beowulf swims down to the depths of the sea, seeks out the mother-creature, kills her, and cuts off the head from the corpse of Grendel which he finds in the sea-home. The third adventure takes place when Beowulf is an old man. His country is attacked by a fire-spreading dragon, guardian of a great hoard of wealth. Beowulf seeks out the dragon, gives battle, is wounded and, after killing the beast with the help of a comrade, dies of his wounds. Within the framework of these three accounts the poem is fairly well organized; however, interspersed with these adventures are other episodes, such as King Hygelac's foray against the Hetwaras early in the sixth century.

The following selections are from two of the major events. The reader will note the occasional interpolation of Christian doctrine with the pagan story and the vivid descriptive phrases which characterize the style of the poem. Some of these phrases which now strike us as most effective and unusual were, at the time the poem was composed, little more than clichés. Thus we find the king called the "helmet of his people," the sea called the "whale's road," the ship a "ringed prow," and the harp a "glee wood."

The translation is by Clarence Griffin Child, and several of the footnotes are based on those of Professor Child. The selections are printed with the consent of the publishers, Houghton Mifflin Company.

SUGGESTED REFERENCES: Dorothy Whitelock, *The Audience of Beowulf* (2nd ed., 1958); L. E. Nicholson, *An Anthology of Beowulf Criticism* (1963); Kenneth Sisam, *The Structure of Beowulf* (1965).

Beowulf

OF SCYLD SCEFING (FROM WHOM HROTHGAR SPRANG, WHOM BEOWULF BEFRIENDED) AND HIS DEATH

Lo! We have heard tell of the might in days of old of the Spear-Danes' folk-kings, how deeds of prowess were wrought by the athelings.[1] Oft Scyld Scefing reft away their mead-benches from the throngs of his foes, from many a people. Fear came of the earl, after he was found at the first in his need. Redress he won for that, waxed under the clouds, throve in his glories, till of them that dwelt nigh him over the whale-road, each must obey him, and pay him tribute. That was a good king!

To him in after time a son was born, young in his courts, whom God sent for a help to the people, for he saw the dire need they had suffered long time till then through lack of a leader; for this the Lord of Life, the King of Glory, gave him honor in the world. Renowned was Beowulf;[2] the fame of the son of Scyld spread wide in the Scedelands. In such wise worthily among his father's friends by goodly gifts of gold must a man in his youth so prevail that in old age, when war shall come, willing comrades may cleave to their lord and do him service; among every people a man shall thrive by deeds of praise.

Then, at the hour of his fate, in fulness of valor, Scyld went his way. They bare him forth to the sea flood, his own close comrades, as he had himself bidden them, the while he, the Scyldings' friend, the land's dear lord, long time held sway by his word. There at the haven stood the ringed prow, the atheling's ship, gleaming and eager to start. They laid him down then, their lord beloved, the

[1] princes.
[2] Not the hero of the poem, Beowulf the Geat.

ring-giver, in the ship's bosom, placed the mighty one at the mast.

Much treasure was there, trappings of price from far-off lands. Never heard I of keel fitted out more bravely with weapons of war and weeds[1] of battle, with bills and with burnies.[2] A heap of jewels lay in his bosom that must needs fare far with him into the grip of the flood. Truly with no less gift-offerings and folk-treasures did they in this wise dispose him than they that at his birth sent him forth alone on the waves, being but a child. Thereto they set for him a golden standard high overhead, let the wave bear him, gave him to the deep. Sorrow of soul was theirs and mood of mourning. Men dwelling in halls, heroes under heaven, cannot in truth say who came by that lading.

Of Beowulf, Scyld's son (of the same name as Beowulf the Geat, whose deeds are hereafter told), and his succession; of Hrothgar and the building of his hall, Heorot; and of the monster, Grendel, and his wrath at the rejoicing there, and of his descent from the brood of Cain.

For long thereafter in the walled towns was Beowulf, the loved folk-king of the Scyldings, known to fame among the peoples (his father had gone elsewhere, the prince from his own), till in time was born to him the great Healfdene, who, whilst he lived, ruled the Scyldings in kindness, the ancient one, fierce in battle.

To him, leader of battle-hosts, four children were born into the world, which were, told in order, Heorogar, and Hrothgar, and Halga the Brave, while Sigeneow, as I have heard say, was Sæwela's queen, the valorous Scylfing's beloved bed-sharer. Fortune in battle was given then to Hrothgar and fame in war, so that, by the time the youth grew of age, his dear kinsfolk, a great following of young warriors, obeyed him gladly.

[1] clothing or armor (as in widow's weeds).
[2] coat of mail.

It came to his mind to bid men build him a hall-dwelling, a mead-house, greater than children of men had ever heard of, and that there within it he would part to young and old what God had given him, save the people's land and the lives of men. Then, as I heard, on many a kindred far and wide through the mid-earth was the task laid of making fair the folk-hall. Speedily it befell him in time among men that it was in every wise ready, the greatest of hall-houses, and he made for it, who far and wide held sway by his word, the name of Heorot.[1] He belied not his pledge and dealt out rings and treasure at the feast. The hall rose lofty and broad-gabled. Warring surges it awaited of loathly flame, nor was it long before deadly hate must awaken through the murderous strife of son and father-in-law.

Then the demon fell, that dwelt in darkness, scarce for a space endured that he should hear each day rejoicing loud in the hall; there was sound of the harp there and clear song of the gleeman. One spake that knew how to tell of man's first making of old, said that the Almighty framed the world, the plain bright in beauty which the waters encircle, and, glorying in His handiwork, set the sun and moon to lighten the earth-dwellers, and decked the corners of the earth with boughs and leaves, and gave life to every kind of creature that walks alive. So the warriors lived in joy and plenty, till one, a fiend of hell, began to do evil. The grim demon, the fell prowler about the borders of the homes of men, who held the moors, the fens, and the fastnesses, was called Grendel. In the domain of the giant-race, Cain, the man reft of joy, dwelt for a time, after the Creator had doomed him. On his posterity the Eternal Lord took vengeance for the murder, in that he slew Abel. God took no joy in that feud, but banished him, for his deed, far from mankind. By him were the wanton ones all begotten, the eotens[2] and elves and monsters of the deep, the giants also who strove long against God — for that He repaid them in due requital.

How Grendel ravaged Heorot, and caused it to remain unused and desolate at night; of the long continuance of this evil, and how Hrothgar and his people despaired of succor.

Then went Grendel, when night had come, to spy about the high house and see how the Ring-Danes had left it after the beer-drinking. There he found the company of athelings sleeping after the feast; sorrow they knew not, or the evil haps of men. The baneful wight, grim and greedy, fierce and pitiless, was soon alert, and took, where they

[1] Hart (stag) hall, possibly from the fact that its walls were decorated with antlers.

[2] giants.

rested, thirty thanes. Thence fared he back homeward, boastfully exultant over his spoil, and sought his abiding-places with that glut of slaughter.

Thereupon at dawn, with break of day, plain enough to the warriors was Grendel's might in strife. Then was weeping upraised after all their glad feasting, a great cry at dawn. When they had seen the track of the loathly one, the woeful demon, the prince renowned, the atheling passing good, sat joyless, underwent heaviness of grief, suffered sorrow for his thanes; too sore was that trouble, too hateful and lingering. Nor was it longer than after one night that Grendel again wrought murderous destruction still more grievous, nor recked of the violence and evil — too fixed was he in them. It was easy then finding one who sought a place of rest for himself farther away, a bed apart from the buildings, now that the hate of that thane of hell had been shown and truly declared by a clear token; he kept himself farther away from then on, and in some safer place, that might escape the demon.

Thus had Grendel mastery and warred against the right, he alone against all, till the fairest of houses stood idle. A great while it was, twelve winters' season, that the friend of the Scyldings endured this trouble, every woe, the utmost of sorrow. In due course thereafter it became known openly to the children of men through songs sorrowfully, that Grendel had striven for a time against Hrothgar, waged for many half-years a ruthless war, ceaseless strife, evil, and violence, nor would in peaceful wise lift the deadly doom from any man of the might of the Danes, nor durst any even among the worshipful ones look for better fortune at the slayer's hands. The grisly monster, the dark death-shadow, rested not in pursuit of young and old, lay in wait and made ambush. Night after night he held the misty moors; men know not whither the creatures of hell will walk on their rounds.

In this wise, often, the enemy of mankind, the lonely one terrible, wrought many an outrage, deeds that shamed them hard to bear. On dark nights he stayed in Heorot, the hall brave with gold, yet he might not touch the gift-stool — its treasures he scorned — nor knew he desire for it.

That was a great grief and sorrow of heart to the friend of the Scyldings. Many a one strong in council oft sat deliberating; counsel they devised what with bold hearts it were best to do against the terror descending unforeseen. Sometimes they vowed offerings in their temples of idols, besought with words of prayer that the slayer of demons would find relief for the people's sorrow. Such was their custom, the trust of the heathen; the thoughts of their breasts were intent on hell, the Creator they knew not — knew not the judge of men's deeds, the Lord God, nor truly knew they how to praise the Guardian of the Heavens, the King of Glory. Woe shall be his who needs must through his fierce frowardness thrust down his soul into the bosom of the fire, look for no comfort, in no wise return; well shall it be for him that may, after the day of death, seek out the Lord and plead for peace in the Father's bosom.

Of Beowulf the Geat and his coming to rid Hrothgar of Grendel.

Thus then without ceasing the son of Healfdene brooded his season of sorrow. The wise warrior might not amend his woes; too sore was the strife, the dire distress, greatest of evils of the night, that had come on the people, too hateful and lingering. Of this and Grendel's deeds, the thane of Hygelac,[1] of goodly fame among the Geats, heard tell when from home. Strongest in might of manhood was he in this life's day, noble and powerful. He bade be fitted for himself a good sea-goer, said he would seek out the war-king, the mighty prince over the swan-road, seeing he had need of men. Men deemed wise blamed him no whit for that journey, dear though he was to them. They spurred on the valiant-minded hero, and sought signs for casting his fortune.

He, the worthy one, took to himself picked warriors of the Geat-folk, the boldest he might find. One of fifteen, he set out for the sea-wood. A man skilled in the sea pointed out the landmarks. Time went on, the ship was on the wave, the boat beneath the bluff. The warriors ready went up on the prow. The currents of the sea eddied along the shore. The warsmen bare their bright trappings, war-gear splendrous, into the bosom of the vessel. The men shoved out the well-joined wood on its willing journey. Then went over the billowy sea, sped by the wind, the foamy-necked ship, likest to a bird, till next day at the hour awaited the curved prow had gone so far that the seafarers might see the land, the shore-cliffs gleam, the broad sea-nesses.[2] Then was the ocean-farer at end of its voyage.

Thereupon the folk of the Weders [3] stepped up quickly on the plain and tied the sea-wood; their sarks rattled, their weeds of war. God they thanked because the wave-paths had proved easy for them. Then from the steep shore, the warden of the Scyldings, whose duty it was to keep watch of the sea-cliffs, saw them bear over the bulwarks their shining shields and gear ready as for battle. He was fretted in his mind's thought with the wish

[1] The hero of the epic.

[2] capes.   [3] the Geats.

to know what men they were. The thane of Hrothgar went riding, therefore, on his horse to the shore; stoutly he shook the mighty shaft in his hands, asked in words duly considered: "What men are ye having battle-gear, clad in burnies, who thus come leading a deep ship hither over the sea-road, over the waters? I have long been boundary warden, kept watch of the shore, that no foe with a ship's company might work harm in the land of the Danes. No bearers of shields ever undertook to come hither more openly; surely you had not leave from the wagers of war, the consent of the kinsfolk. Never saw I in the world a greater earl or warrior in harness, than is one of you. No lurker at home in the hall is he, with weapons bedight, save his looks and matchless aspect lie. Now must I learn of what blood ye are, ere ye fare further as false spies into the Danes' land. Hear ye now, ye seafaring ones, dwelling afar, my plain thought; it is best most quickly to make known whence ye come."

How Beowulf made known his race and errand to the coast-guard and was bidden go to Hrothgar.

To him the most worshipful one, the leader of the company, spake in answer: "We are of the kin of the Geat-folk and Hygelac's hearth-companions. My father, Ecgtheow by name, the noble high-prince, was known to the peoples. He bided years a many ere he went hoary from his home. Every man of wise mind far and wide remembereth him well. We have come with kind intent to seek thy lord, the son of Healfdene, the people's protector. Be thou good in advising us. We have a weighty errand to the famed lord of the Danes, nor shall any part of it, as I ween, be kept hid. Thou knowest if it be so, as we have truly heard tell, that among the Scyldings a secret foe, I know not what of spoilers, giveth on dark nights proof of hate beyond the knowing through the terror he worketh, through fell deeds and death-fall. I, therefore, out of largeness of soul may counsel Hrothgar, how he, the wise one and good, may master the foe, if that ever the press of his troubles may know change, solace come after, and the waves of care grow cooler, else he shall suffer this season of sorrow forever, stress of need, so long as in its high place shall stand the fairest of houses."

The warden spake, the fearless retainer, where he sat on his horse: "Of each of these, of words and works, must an able warrior who judgeth well know the difference. I gather that this fellowship is of true thought toward the lord of the Scyldings. Bear forth then your weapons and gear. I shall guide you, and likewise bid my war-thanes keep in due charge from any foe your ship, the newly tarred vessel, on the shore, till that the bent-necked wood bear back the hero beloved, over the sea-streams, to the bounds of the Weders. To a wager of war such as he will it be given to come out unhurt from this bout of battle."

Then went they to him. The ship stayed without moving; the broad-beamed craft rested on its cable at anchor. The graven boars [1] shone over their gold-decked cheek-guards, gleaming and tempered in the fire; grimly warlike of temper, the boar kept his watch. The men hastened on; they went together till they might see, splendid and covered with gold, the timbered house where the king dwelt, that was among earth-dwellers famed beyond all others of halls under heaven, — the sheen of it flashed over many lands. Then the bold one in battle showed them the home of brave men where it shone, that they might go to it straightway; he, one from among its warsmen, turned his horse and word spake after: "It is time for me to go. May the Father Almighty through His grace keep you safe in your goings. I will to the sea to keep watch for unfriendly folk."

Of Beowulf's coming to Heorot, and its announcement to Hrothgar.

The street was cobbled; it showed the men the way as they went together. The war-burnie gleamed, hard and hand-linked, the bright-ringed iron sang in their harness, as they then first came faring to the hall in their trappings of terror.

Spent with the sea, they set up their broad shields, their well-hardened bucklers against the wall of the hall, and bowed them to the benches; their burnies and war-gear rang. The spears, the seamen's weapons, stood in one place together with the shafts of ash-wood gray above; the mailed band was well dight with weapons. A proud warrior then asked the warsmen, where they sat, of what kin they were: "Whence bear ye your shields covered with gold, your gray battle-sarks, and helmets grim, your heap of battle-shafts? I am Hrothgar's herald and serving-man. Never saw I, of stranger folk, thus many men of more valiant bearing. I ween in proud daring, not as driven to exile but through greatness of soul, have ye sought Hrothgar."

Him then the proud prince of the Weders, strong in might, answered, and word spake after: "We are Hygelac's table-comrades. Beowulf is my name. I will tell thy lord, the mighty prince, the son of Healfdene, mine errand, if he will grant us, good as he is, to give him greeting."

Wulfgar spake; he was prince of the Wendles; his boldness of heart, his prowess and wisdom were known unto many: "I will ask the mighty prince, the giver of rings, the lord of the Scyldings, friend

[1] crests on their helmets.

of the Danes, as thou desirest, concerning thine errand, and quickly make known to thee the answer he of his goodness thinketh to give me."

He turned him then quickly where Hrothgar sat, old and with hair exceeding white, among his band of earls. The valiant one went till he stood at the shoulder of the lord of the Danes, for he knew the ways of men of gentle birth. Wulfgar spake to his gracious lord: "Hither have fared over the ocean-stretches, come from afar, men of the Geats. The warriors name the foremost man among them Beowulf. They pray, my lord, that they may exchange speech with thee. Make thou not denial, O Hrothgar, to gladden them with thy converse. They seem from their war-gear worthy of the respect of earls; the leader at least, who hath led these warsmen hither, is surely goodly."

How Hrothgar bade the Geats be welcome, and Beowulf told his errand.

Hrothgar, helm of the Scyldings, spake: "I knew him as a child. His father of old was named Ecgtheow; to him Hrethel the Geat at his home gave his only daughter. Boldly now hath his son come hither, and sought out a true friend. The seafaring ones when they carried thither to the Geats costly gifts for friendly remembrance brought word that he, the bold one in war, had in his hand-grip the strength of thirty. Him, I have hope, the Holy God has sent us West-Danes of His grace for aid against dread of Grendel. Gifts must I tender the good youth for his brave spirit. Make haste and bid the band of kinsmen come in together. Say to them also in fitting words they are welcome among the Dane-folk."

Then Wulfgar went to the door of the hall, stood there and spake: "My lord, the victorious prince of the East-Danes bids me tell you he knoweth your high kinship, and that ye in his sight, ye bold in heart, are welcome hither over the sea-waves. Now may ye go in your war-gear, under your battle-masks, to see Hrothgar. Let your war-shields and spears, shafts for the killing, abide here the outcome of your converse."

Then the mighty one arose with many a man about him, a press of doughty thanes. Some remained there, as the brave one bade them, kept watch of the war-gear. Together they went speedily where the hero directed, under Heorot's roof.

The bold one went, stern beneath his helmet, till he stood within. Beowulf spake — the network of the burnie, linked by the smith's craft, gleamed upon him: "Hail to thee, Hrothgar! I am Hygelac's kinsman and war-thane. I have already in my youth essayed many deeds of pro[w]... me openly were Grendel's doings made the land of my people. Seafaring men say that this hall, the fairest of dwellings, stands idle and useless to all, so soon as the evening's light becometh hid 'neath the bright heaven. Then did wise men, Lord Hrothgar, the worthiest of my people, counsel that I seek thee, for they knew the strength of my might, saw it for themselves when I came from battle, blood-stained from the foe, where I bound five of them, overthrew the race of eotens, and slew the nickers [1] by night in the waves — suffered perilous straits, repaid the hate shown the Weders (woes they endured!), put an end to their sorrows. And now I, by my single hand, shall bring Grendel, the demon, the giant one, to judgment. I desire now therefore, prince of the Bright-Danes, to ask thee one boon. Refuse me not, guardian of warriors, loved friend of the people, now I am come from so far, that I alone with my band of earls, my body of brave men, may cleanse Heorot. I have also learned that the monster in his recklessness takes no thought to use weapons: I then, so may my liege-lord, Hygelac, find pleasure in me, shall think scorn to bear sword or the broad shield, yellow-rimmed, to the battle, but with my hand-grip shall I join with the fiend and fight to the death, foe against foe. He must there, whom death taketh, believe it the Lord's award. I ween that Grendel, if he prevail, shall feast undismayed on the Geat-folk in the war-hall, as he hath oft done on the might of the Hrethmen. Thou shalt not need then to hide my head away; for Grendel will have me, stained with blood, if death take me, will bear away the bloody corse and think to devour it; he, the lone-goer, will eat it ungrieving, and smear with my blood his moorlairs; no longer shalt thou need then to care for my body's nurture. Send to Hygelac, if warfare take me, the best of battle-weeds, goodliest of garments, that guards my breast — it was the bequest of Hrethla, and the handwork of Weland.[2] Wyrd [3] goeth ever as she must!"

Of Hrothgar's answer, telling of Grendel, and of the feasting.

Hrothgar, helm of the Scyldings, spake: "To be a bulwark of defence and a prop hast thou sought us, my friend Beowulf. Thy father waged the greatest of feuds; with his own hand he slew Heatholaf among the Wulfings. Then might not the kin of the Weders hold to him for fear of war. Thence sought he the folk of the South-Danes, the Honor-Scyldings, over the moil of the waves, when I first ruled the Dane-folk and held in my youth the treasure-city of heroes; it was when Heorogar, my

elder brother, Healfdene's child, had died and was no more living — a better man was he than I. Afterward, I settled the feud for money, sending ancient treasure to the Wulfings over the back of the waters; oaths your father sware to me.

"Sorrow it is to me in soul to say to any man what despite and instant evil Grendel hath wrought me in Heorot through his malice. My hall-company, my band of warsmen, is minished; Wyrd swept them away into the horror that compasseth Grendel. God may readily stay the mad spoiler in his deeds. Full often boasted my warsmen drunken with beer, over their ale-horns, that they in the beer-hall with their dread blades would await a meeting with Grendel. Then was the mead-hall, this lordly dwelling, at morning-tide, when day grew light, stained with gore, all the bench-boards besprent with blood, the hall with the bloodshed; wherefore I had so many the fewer true thanes, warriors beloved, as death took away. Sit now to the feasting and unfold to my men thy purpose and hope of success, as thy mind may prompt thee."

Then was a bench set for the Geatmen in the hall all together. There the strong-hearted ones went to sit, in excellence of might. A thane looked to the task set him, to bear in his hands the fretted ale-stoup, and poured out the shining mead. Now and again the gleeman sang clear in Heorot. There was joy among the warriors, a worshipful company by no means small of Danes and Weders . . .

How Beowulf kept watch for Grendel.

Then Hrothgar, lord of the Scyldings, went him forth from the hall with his troop of warriors. The warrior-leader would go to his rest with Wealhtheow, his wife. The Kingly Glory had set, as men have heard, a guard against Grendel in the hall. A charge apart he held in respect to the lord of the Danes, kept ward for the giant one.

Truly, the prince of the Geats put ready trust in his bold might and the Lord's grace. He took off him then his iron burnie, his helm from his head, gave his richly-chased sword, choicest of blades, to his serving-thane, and bade the man keep his wargear. Ere he mounted his bed, spake Beowulf, the worthy one of the Geats, a vaunting word: "In no wise count I myself less in battle-crafts and deeds of war than Grendel himself. Therefore I will not with the sword slay him and take his life, though the might is mine wholly. These helps — to strike at me and hew my shield — he knows not, daring though he be in deeds of malice. But we, this night, if he dare seek strife without weapons, shall lay aside the sword. And, at the end, may the wise God, the Holy Lord, award the mastery on either hand as seemeth Him meet."

[1] water-sprites.
[2] A famous smith of Teutonic legend.
[3] Fate, destiny.

Then the brave one in battle laid him down, the head-pillow received the earl's cheek, and about him many a hardy seafarer bowed him to his hall-rest. No one of them thought that he thereafter should ever again seek his loved home, his people, or the free town where he was reared, seeing they had heard tell that, ere then, a murderous death had taken off too many by far of the Dane-folk in the wine-hall. But the Lord gave them the destiny to speed in the strife, help and aid to the people of the Weders, such that they all overcame their foe through one man's strength, the might of himself alone. The truth is made known that the Mighty God ruleth mankind from everlasting.

In the dark night came striding the walker in shadow. Those set to watch, that should guard the gabled hall, slept, all save one. It was known to men the fell spoiler might not, if the Lord willed not, swing them under the shadow. But that single one, watching in flush of wrath with swelling anger, bided the award of battle.

Of the coming of Grendel, and of Beowulf's encounter with him.

Then from the moor, from under the misty fells, came Grendel striding; God's wrath he bare. The fell spoiler planned to trap one of the race of men in the high hall. Under the clouds he went till he might see without trouble the wine-hall, the treasure-house of men, brave with gold. It was not the first time he had sought the home of Hrothgar; never, though, before or since in the days of his life found he hall-thanes more doughty. Came then making his way to the hall the warring one severed from joy. The door, fastened with bands forged in the fire, soon gave way when he laid hold of it with his hands; bent on evil, puffed up with wrath as he was, he brake open the mouth of the hall. Quickly then the fiend trod in on the shining floor, strode on, fierce of mood. And unlovely light, likest to flame, stood in his eyes. He saw in the hall many warriors sleeping, a fellowship of one blood assembled together, the throng of kinsfolk. Then his heart laughed within him. He thought, the grisly monster, ere day came, to sunder life from body of each of them, for hope of a fill of feasting had come to him. But no longer was it fate's decree that he might, after that night, feed on more of the race of men.

The kinsman of Hygelac, strong in might, watched how the fell spoiler was of mind to set about his sudden onslaughts. The monster thought not to be long about it, but for a first start seized quickly on a sleeping thane, tore him taken unawares, bit into his bone-frame, drank the blood from the veins, and swallowed him down piece by piece. Soon he had bolted all the lifeless body, hand and foot. He stepped forward nearer, took next in his hands the hero, bold of heart, on his bed. The fiend reached for him with his claw, but he grasped it with set purpose, and threw his weight on Grendel's arm. Soon found that herder of evils that never in any other man, in any corner of the earth, had he met with mightier hand-grip. He was affrighted mind and heart, yet might he make off none the sooner. His one thought was to get him gone; he was minded to flee into the darkness, to seek the drove of devils. There was then for him no such doings as he before that, in earlier days, had fallen in with.

Remembered then the good kinsman of Hygelac his evening's vaunt; he stood upright and laid fast hold upon him. The fingers of the giant one snapped. He was getting free and the hero stepped forward. The mighty one meant, if so he might, to get at large, and flee away to his fen-lairs. He knew his fingers' strength was in the foeman's close grip. That was an ill journey the doer of mischief had taken to Heorot.

The lordly hall was clamorous with the din. Panic fell on all the Danes that dwelt in the city, on every bold warrior and earl. Maddened were the raging strugglers; the building reëchoed. It was great wonder, then, that the wine-hall held firm against them in their battle-rage, that it did not fall, the fair dwelling of man's making, to the earth, save that shrewd care had bound it so fast with iron bands within and without. Then, as I have heard tell, when they strove in their fury, mead-benches many, decked with gold, fell over from the raised floor. The wise ones among the Scyldings had never thought that any man of men by his might should ever shatter that fabric, passing good and made brave with bones of beasts, or spoil it through cunning, save the fire's embrace might swallow it up in smoke.

An uproar strange enough rose on high. Quaking terror lay upon the North-Danes, upon those who heard the outcry, hearkened God's foe yelling out his stave of terror, his song of defeat, the thrall of hell bewailing his hurt. Much too tightly that one held him, who had of men the strongest might in this life's day.

Of Beowulf's victory and Grendel's flight.

The protector of earls would not in any wise let him that came with murder in his heart go from him alive; he counted not his life's day of price to any. Earls of his a plenty made play with their tried swords, handed down from their fathers, to save their lord's life, if in any wise they might: they knew not, those bold-hearted warsmen, when they went into the fight and thought to hew G every side and find out his soul, that not of blades on earth, none of battle-bills, could touch that fell spoiler, for he had laid his spell on weapons of victory, on every keen edge. Woeful was his last end to be in this life's day, and his outlawed ghost must fare far into the fiend's grip. Then found he, that before in mirth of mood had wrought mankind many evils (he was under God's ban), that his body would avail him not, seeing that the brave kinsman of Hygelac had him by the hand; hateful to each was the other alive. The grisly monster suffered hurt of body. In his shoulder a fearful wound began to show; the sinews sprang apart, the bone-frame cracked asunder. Fame of the battle was given to Beowulf. Grendel must flee away beneath the fen-fells, sick unto death, go seek out his dwelling, reft of his comfort. He knew then the more surely that his life's end was come, his measure of days. The will of all the Danes was fulfilled by that deadly strife. He then, who had come from afar, the wise one and bold of heart, had cleansed Heorot, and saved it from peril. The prince of the Geatmen had made whole his boast to the East-Danes in that he had taken away all their trouble, the burden of spiteful hate they till then had suffered, and in stress of need must suffer, a sorrow by no means small. A manifest token of this it was, when the valorous one laid down the hand, the arm and shoulder — the whole claw of Grendel was there together — beneath the broad roof.

How the Danes rejoiced and followed Grendel's track to his lair; how they raced their horses on the way back and hearkened to songs of Beowulf's deed, and of Sigemund and Heremod.

In the morning, then, as I have heard tell, was there many a warrior about the mead hall; from far and near the leaders of the people fared through the wide ways to see the marvel, the tracks of the foe. Grendel's life-ending seemed no matter for sorrow to any of those that scanned the way he trod after his undoing, how in weariness of heart, worsted in the fight, hunted forth and nigh unto death, he bare himself away then in flight to the mere of the nickers. Its flood there was seething with gore, its dread coil of waters all mingled with hot blood; the deep welled with the blood of slaughter, after that, bereft of joys, he laid down his life, his heathen soul, doomed to death, in his fen-shelter, where hell took him.

Back then from the mere on their joyful way went riding on their steeds the old tried comrades, men of valor, and many a youth likewise, the warriors on their dapple-grays. There was Beowulf's glory remembered. Oft said many a one that south or north, between the seas, over the wide earth, beneath the reach of the sky, no other of shield-bearers was better, or more worthy of a kingdom. No whit though truly did they cast blame on their lord and friend, the kindly Hrothgar, for he was a good king. Whiles, the bold in battle let their yellow steeds leap or race together, where the going seemed good or was known to be best; whiles, a thane of the king, a man laden with proud vaunts, who kept in mind old stories without end, found new words for them, soothly bound together — and afterward began to tell Beowulf's feat with cunning skill and in happy wise to frame well-ordered speech, add word answering to word, and told aught man might choose of what he had heard tell of Sigemund's deeds of prowess, many things not widely known, the strife of the son of Wæls, journeys to far lands, feuds and deeds of violence, that the children of men had not wist of readily, save Fitela were with him when he was minded to tell somewhat of such like, the uncle to his nephew — close comrades ever in every strife....

Of Hrothgar's praise of Beowulf and Beowulf's reply.

Hrothgar spake; he went to the hall, stood beside the pillar, looked on the steep-pitched roof, brave with gold, and Grendel's hand: "For this sight thanks be paid forthwith to the Almighty! Much of evil and harm have I suffered from Grendel. Ever may God, the Lord of Glory, work wonder on wonder. It was not long ago that I thought not forever to look for help in aught of my troubles whilst the fairest of houses stood bloodstained and gory — a woe wide-reaching for each of my wise ones who hoped not to the end of time to guard the people's fastness from foes, from ghosts, and from demons. Now hath a man through the Lord's might done a deed we might none of us compass aforetime for all our wisdom. Behold, truly, this may say even such a one of women, if she yet liveth, that hath brought forth this son among the races of men, that the everlasting God hath been gracious to her in her childbearing. Now will I love thee, Beowulf, best of men, as a son in my heart; hold thou close henceforth this new kinship. No lack shall be thine of things worth having in the world, that I have at my bidding. Full oft for less service have I given award of treasured riches to a warrior not so worthy, one weaker in battle. Thou hast wrought for thyself by thy deeds that thy fame shall live for ever and ever. May the Almighty requite thee with good, as till now He hath done!"

Beowulf spake, the son of Ecgtheow: "Full gladly in thy service have we carried through this mighty task, this fight; boldly we dared the strength of the unknown. I wish mightily thou couldst have seen him, the foe himself in his trappings, bowed to his fall. I thought to bind him full speedily with hard bonds on his death-bed, so that he through the grip of my hands should lie toiling for his life, save his body should slip away. I could not, since the Lord willed it not, cut him off from his going; I held him not fast enough, the deadly foe, — much too strong was the fiend in his footing. Yet for his life's fending he left behind him his claw to mark his path, his arm, and his shoulder; none the less might he buy there, in his need, no comfort, nor shall he, because of it, live the longer, the loathly spoiler, burdened with sins, for his hurt hath straitly clutched him in its close grip with bonds of bale. There the outcast, in the guilt of his sins, shall abide the great judgment, as the Lord in His splendor is minded to mete it unto him."

Then in his vaunting speech was the warrior, the son of Ecglaf, more quiet concerning deeds of war, after that the athelings had seen, each of them there before him above the high roof, through the earl's might, the hand and fingers of the fiend. Most like to steel was each strong nail, the handspurs of the heathen one, the monstrous barbs of the foeman. Each one said that no blade of doughty men, though ever so good, would have so laid hold of him as to shear away the battle-fist, all bloody, of the monster.

How Beowulf was feasted and gifts given him.

Then forthwith was Heorot bidden to be decked inwardly by the hand; many of them there were, of men and of women, that made ready the wine-hall, the guest-house. Gleaming with gold shone the hangings on the wall, wondrous things many to see for any one that looketh at such things. The bright house was much broken, all fastened though it was within with iron bands. The hinges were wrenched away; the roof alone was left all whole, when the monster, guilty of deeds of outrage, hopeless of life, had turned to flee. Not easy is it to flee away, let him do it that will, for each that hath a soul of the children of men dwelling on earth must needs strive toward the place made ready for him, forced on him by fate, where his body shall sleep, fast in its bed of rest, after life's feasting.

Then was it the time and hour that the son of Healfdene should go to the hall; the king himself desired to eat of the feast. Never heard I of a people with a greater host bear themselves more becomingly about their treasure-giver. In the pride of their renown they bowed them to the benches, rejoiced in the plenty. In fair wise their kinsmen, the valorous-hearted Hrothgar and Hrothulf, drank in the high hall many a mead-cup.

Heorot was filled within with friends; in no wise at this time had the Folk-Scyldings wrought wickedness.

Then, in reward for his victory, the son of Healfdene gave to Beowulf a golden standard, a broidered war-banner, a helmet and burnie; a mighty treasure-sword full many saw borne before the warrior. He needed not feel shame before the bowsmen for the gifts given him for his keeping; never heard I of many men that gave to others on the mead-bench four treasures in friendlier wise. About the helmet's crown, a raised ridge without, wound with small rods, maintained a guard for the head, that the file-furnished blades, hard of temper, might not harm it in their boldness, when the warrior with shield must go forth against his foes. Then the safeguard of earls bade eight steeds, their bridles heavy with gold, be led indoors on the floor of the hall; on one of them rested a saddle, fashioned with cunning art and well-dight with treasure, that had been the battle-seat of the high king when the son of Healfdene had will to wage the sword-play; never at the front failed the far-famed one's battle-might, when the slain were falling. And then the prince of the Ingwines gave Beowulf the right over both of these, the steeds and the weapons, bade him have good joy of them. In such wise, manfully, the mighty prince, treasure-warden of heroes, paid for shocks of battle with steeds and treasure, such as none might ever belie that hath will to speak the truth according to the right. . . .

Of the queen's gifts to Beowulf and of the feast and their going to rest when evening came.

A cup was borne to him, and pledges proffered with friendly speech, and twisted gold laid before him in token of gracious regard, with two arm-jewels, a coat of mail, rings, and the fairest of collars I have heard tell of on earth — of none fairer heard I under the sky smong the hoarded treasures of heroes, after that Hama bare off to the bright city the collar of the Brosings,[1] the jewel and coffer, fled the evil wiles of Eormanric,[2] and chose eternal gain. Hygelac the Geat, grandson of Swerting, had this collar on his last foray, when beneath his standard he guarded his treasure, kept ward of his battle-spoil; him Wyrd took away, after that he, for his foolhardiness, had undergone woes and vengeance at the hands of the Frisians. The lord of the realm carried with him at that time this adornment and its precious stones over the cup of the waves. He fell beneath his shield, and the king's body came into the Franks' grasp, and his

[1] The collar, according to the *Edda*, worn by the goddess Freyja.

[2] Hermanric, King of the Goths.

breast-mail and the collar as well. The fighting-men of less degree despoiled the corse after the battle's end. The people of the Geats filled the abode of the dead.

The hall caught up the clamor of the revel. Wealhtheow made discourse, and spake before the company: "Take thy joy in this collar, dear Beowulf, youth blessed of fortune, and use this mail and these treasures of the people, and thrive well. Give proof of thyself by thy might and be friendly in giving counsel to these youths; I shall keep in mind thy due therefor. Thou hast so wrought that far and near, forever henceforth, men shall pay thee honor, even so far as the sea enfoldeth its windy walls. Be, whilst thou livest, an atheling blest with wealth; I heartily wish thee holdings of treasure. Be thou helpful in doing for my son, guarding his welfare. Here is each earl true to the other, mild of mood, loyal to his liege-lord. The thanes are willing, the people in every wise ready at bidding. Ye warriors well-drunken, do ye as I bid."

Then went she to her place. There was the choicest of feasts. The men drank of the wine; of Wyrd they recked not, the grim doom fixed from aforetime, as it had come to many an earl. When that even came and Hrothgar went him, the ruler, to his rest, in his house, unnumbered earls kept ward of the hall, as they oft had done before. They bared the bench-floor and it was spread through its length with beds and pillows. Ready and doomed for death, one of the beer-servers bowed him to his rest in the hall. They set at their heads their battle-targes,[1] the framed wood of their bright shields. There, over each atheling, were plain to see on the bench the helmet lifted in battle, the ringed burnie, the mighty shafts in their strength. It was their rule to be ever and again ready for the fray at home or in wartime, either one, even at what time soever need might befall their liege-lord. That was a good people!

Of the coming of Grendel's dam.

They sank then to sleep. One paid sorely for his evening's rest, even as full often had befallen them after Grendel took the gold-hall for his own, did what was not right till the end came, death following upon his sins. It became plain, and known far and wide of men, that an avenger still lived even yet after him, the loathly one, for a long time following upon that bitter warfare. Grendel's mother kept thought of her sorrow, a she-one, a monster-wife, that was fated to dwell midst the water's terrors, in the cold streams, after Cain had slain by the sword his only brother, his kin by one father — outlawed he went away then, with the

[1] shields.

mark of murder on him, to flee the joys of men, and dwelt in waste places. Of him were born many demons ordained of fate; Grendel was one of them, an outcast filled with hatred, who found at Heorot a man watching, awaiting battle. There the monster came to grips with him, but he was mindful of the strength of his might, the deep-seated gift God had given him, and trusted him for grace in the Almighty, for comfort and aid; hence he overcame the field, felled the demon of hell. Then went he forth, that foe of mankind, abject and reft of joy, to look on the house of death. And, still thereafter, his mother, greedy, and dark of mood, was of mind to go a journey fraught with grief to avenge the death of her son, came therefore to Heorot, where the Ring Danes slept in the hall. Then when Grendel's mother made her way in, was there straightway there for the earls a turning backward to what had been before. The terror was less even by so much as is woman's strength, the fierceness of a woman in fight, beside a weapon-bearer's, when the sword bound with gold, wrought with the hammer, the blade blood-stained, sheareth with its tough edge the swine that standeth above the helmet.

Then in the hall from above the benches was the hard-edged sword taken down, many a broad shield lifted in the hand's grip; they whom the terror seized took no thought of helmet or broad burnie. The monster was in haste, would thence away to save her life, for that she was discovered. Quickly had she one of the athelings fast in her clutch, and went off to the fen. He whom she slew at his rest was a strong shield-warrior, a warsman of enduring fame, of all the men in office of comrade the dearest to Hrothgar between the seas. Beowulf was not there, for before then, after the treasure-giving, another resting-place had been fixed upon for the mighty Geat. There was outcry in Heorot. She had taken in its gore the hand of Grendel that so much had been made of. Sorrow was begun anew, was come again to their homes. The bargain was not good, seeing they must on either hand make purchase with the lives of friends.

Then was the old king, the hoar warrior, stricken in spirit when he knew his chief thane, the one dearest to him, to be lifeless and dead. Beowulf, the warrior crowned with victory, was quickly fetched to the bower. At daybreak, he, together with his earls, the high-born warrior himself with his followers, went where the wise king awaited if so be, after tidings thus grievous, the Almighty might ever will to work a change for him. The hero tried in battle went then with his fellowship over the floor — the timbered hall rang — to give words of greeting to the wise lord of the Ingwines, asked him, as courtesy bade, if his night had been peaceful.

How Hrothgar told Beowulf of the loss of Æschere and of Grendel's dam.

Hrothgar, helm of the Scyldings, spake: "Ask not concerning that which gives joy. Sorrow is renewed among the Dane-folk. Dead is Æschere, Yrmenlaf's elder brother, my counsellor and adviser, the comrade who stood shoulder to shoulder with me when we kept guard of our heads in battle, when the footmen met together, and boar-helms clashed. Such an atheling, passing good, as Æschere was, should an earl be. The murderous demon, the wandering one, with her hand hath slain him in Heorot. I know not what path from here the fell one hath taken, glorying in her carrion food, glad of her fill. She hath avenged thine onslaught, that thou didst kill Grendel yesternight in pitiless wise by thy close grip, for that he long had minished and slain my people. Guilty of death, he fell in battle, and now hath a second come, a spoiler mighty for mischief; she is minded to avenge her kinsman, and hath carried her vengeance so far that it may seem torment of spirit hard to bear to many a thane that sorroweth in his soul for his treasure-giver. Now the hand lieth helpless that was earnest to thee of aught whatsoever that is worth the having.

"I have heard the dwellers in the land, my people, they that hold sway in their halls, say they have seen such twain as these, mighty prowlers along the borders of the homes of men, making the moors their own. One of these was, so far as they might most carefully judge, in form like a woman: the other misbegotten one trod in man's shape the path of exile, save that he was greater in size than any man. Him in days of old the earth-dwellers named Grendel: they knew not his father, or whether any lurking demons were ever born to him. They take as theirs a country hidden away, the wolf-fells and windy nesses, perilous fen-ways, where the flood of the mountain-stream goeth downward under the earth beneath the mists of the forelands. It is not far hence, measured in miles, where the mere standeth. Rime-covered thickets hang over it; a wood fast-rooted shadoweth the waters. There may a fearful marvel be seen each night, a fire in the flood. None liveth ever so wise of the children of men that knoweth the bottom. Though the rover of the heath, the stag, strong with his antlers, may seek, hunted from afar, that thick wood, he will yield up his spirit first, his life on its brink, ere he will hide away his head within it. The place is not goodly. Thence riseth a coil of waters dark to the clouds, when the wind stirreth up foul weather till the air groweth thick and the heavens make outcry.

"Now, again, is help in thee alone. That country thou know'st not yet, the fearsome place, where thou mayest find the much-sinning one. Seek it if thou darest. I shall requite thee for the strife with gifts for the keeping, with old-time treasures and twisted gold, as I did before, shouldst thou come thence away."

How Hrothgar and Beowulf went to the mere in which the monster dwelt.

Beowulf spake, the son of Ecgtheow: "Sorrow not, man of wise mind! It is better one should avenge his friend than mourn for him long. Each of us must abide life's end in this world. Let him that may, win fame ere death; that shall be best thereafter for a warrior, when life is no more.

"Arise, warden of the realm, let us go quickly to look upon the track of Grendel's fellow. I promise thee he shall not flee to shelter, not in earth's bosom, or mountain forest, or ocean's bed, go where he will. For this day have patience in thine every woe, as I ween thou wilt."

Then the old man sprang up and gave thanks to God, the mighty Lord, for that the hero had spoken. A horse then, a steed with plaited mane, was bridled for Hrothgar. The wise king went in state; with him fared forth a foot-band of shield-bearers. The tracks were plain to see far along the forest-ways, the path she hath taken across the levels; straight went she over the murky moor, bare away, with his soul gone from him, the best of Hrothgar's kindred that with him governed the homestead.

Then over the steep stone-fells and narrow tracks, in close by-paths, an unknown way, by beetling cliffs and many a nicker's lair, went the son of athelings. With a few wise-minded men, he went before to see the place, till he found suddenly the mountain trees, the joyless wood, leaning over the hoar rock. The water stood beneath, blood-stained and troubled. It was for all the Danes, for the friends of the Scyldings, a sorrow of soul to bear, grief to many a thane and every earl, when they came upon the head of Æschere on the sea-cliff. The flood boiled, as the people gazed upon it, with blood and hot gore.

The horn at times sang its stirring lay of battle. All the band sat them down. They saw in the water many of the dragon kind, strange sea-drakes making trial of the surge, likewise on the jutting rocks the nickers lying, that oft at hour of dawn make foray grief-giving on the sail-road, and dragons and wild beasts beside. In bitter wrath and swollen with fury, these hasted away; they heard the call, the war-horn singing. The prince of the Geats severed the life from one with a bow, as it strove with the sea, so that the stout battle-shaft went home to its life. Slower was it then in swimming the deep, seeing death had gripped it. Then quickly was it hemmed in closely in the waves with boar-spears keen-barbed, assailed with shrewd thrusts, and drawn on the headland, the wondrous wave-lifter. The men gazed on the fearsome un-friendly thing.

Then Beowulf put on him his earl's armor: in no wise had he misgivings for his life. His war-burnie hand-woven, broad and cunningly adorned, that could well shield his body so battle-grip might not harm his breast or the foe's shrewd clasp his life, must needs make trial of the deeps. But his head the white helmet guarded, that must mingle with the sea-depths, seek the coil of the surges, well-dight as it was with treasure-work, bound with lordly chains, as the weapon-smith wrought it in far-off days, decked it with wonders, set it with swine-shapes, that thereafter brand nor battle blade might bite it. Not least of these great helps was that which Hrothgar's spokesman had loaned him in his need; the hafted sword was named Hrunting. It was one of the chiefest of old-time treasures. Its edge was iron, dyed with poison-twigs, hardened with blood; never in battle did it betray any that clasped it in hand, durst tread the ways of terror, the meeting-place of the foe. That was not the first time it should do a deed of prowess. Surely the son of Ecglaf in the might of his strength kept not thought of what he before spake, drunken with wine, when he lent that weapon to a warrior better with the sword than he. He durst not him-self hazard his life beneath the waves, striving to do a warrior's duty: thereby he forfeited the honor, the acclaims of prowess. Not so was it with the other, after he had arrayed himself for the strife.

How Beowulf sought out and fought with the monster.

Beowulf spake, the son of Ecgtheow: "Keep thou now in mind, great son of Healfdene, wise prince, freehanded friend of men, now I am ready for my venture, that of which we already have spoken, that, should I for thy need be shorn of life, thou wouldst ever be to me, gone hence away, in the place of a father. Be thou a guardian to my thanes, my close comrades, if the strife take me. Likewise send the treasures thou gavest me, dear Hrothgar, to Hygelac; then may the lord of the Geats, the son of Hrethel, know by the gold and see, when he looketh on the treasure, that I found a giver of rings goodly in manly virtues, had joy of him whilst I might. And do thou let Hunferth, warrior famed afar, have his precious war-sword with its tough edge, handed down from old. I

shall win fame for myself with Hrunting or death shall take me."

After these words the prince of the Weder-Geats hasted in his valor, would in no wise await an an-swer; the coil of the waters laid hold of the warrior. It was a day's while ere he might see the bottom-level. Soon she, that, ravenous for food, grim and greedy, had held for half a hundred winters the stretches of the flood, found that some one of men was there from above searching out the home of beings not man-like. She laid hold then upon him, seized him in her terrible claws. His hale body she hurt not thereby: his mail without shielded him round, so she might not, with her loathly fingers, reach through his war-coat, the linked battle-sark. The sea-wolf, when she came to the bottom, bare him then, the ring-giving prince, to her home, in such wise he might not, brave as he was, wield his weapons, though, because of it, many strange be-ings pressed him close in the deep, many a sea-beast with its fighting-tushes brake his battle-sark, har-ried their troubler.

Then the earl was aware he was in one knows not what fearsome hall, where no water might harm him aught, or the quick grip of the flood touch him, because of the roofed hall. He saw the light of fire, a flashing flare brightly shining. The worthy one looked then on the she-wolf of the sea-bottom, the mighty water-wife. The full strength of onset he gave with his battle-axe, his hand held not back from the stroke, so that on her head the ring-decked blade sang out its greedy war-song. The foe found then that the battle-gleamer would not bite, or harm her life, for its edge betrayed the prince in his need. Erstwhile had it gone through many a close encounter, cloven oft the helm and battle-mail of the doomed; for the first time then did the dear treasure lay down its glory. Still was the kinsman of Hygelac, mindful of proud deeds, of one thought, and in no wise lost courage. In wrath the warrior threw aside the chased sword, strong and steel-edged, set with jewels, that it lay on the earth; he trusted to his strength, to the might of his hand-grip. So must a man do when he thinketh to reach in battle enduring fame: he careth naught for his life.

Then the lord of the War-Geats — he shrank not at all from the strife — seized Grendel's mother by the shoulders. Strong in battle he hurled his life's foe, for that he was swollen with wrath, so she fell to the ground. Quickly she paid him back his dues to his hand in savage clinchings, and laid hold upon him. Spent in spirit, the fighter on foot, strongest of warriors, tripped so he fell. Then she threw her-self on the stranger in her hall, and drew her dagger broad and bright-edged — she thought to avenge her son, her only child. His woven breast-mail lay on his shoulder; it shielded his life, withstood the in-thrust of point and blade. Then had the son of Ecgtheow, foremost fighter of the Geats, gone to his death beneath the broad deeps, had not his battle-burnie, the stout battle-mesh, given him help, and Holy God, the Wise Lord, Ruler of the Heavens, held sway over victory in battle, awarded it aright. Readily thereafter he found his feet.

How Beowulf slew the monster, and returned with Grendel's head.

He saw then among the war-gear a blade oft victorious, an old sword of the eotens, doughty of edge, one prized by warriors; it was the choicest of weapons, save that it was greater than any other man might bear out to the battle-play, good and brave to see, the work of giants. The warrior of the Scyldings seized it by its chain-bound hilt. Raging and battle-fierce, he drew the ring-marked blade, and despairing of life smote so wrathfully that the hard edge gripped her by the neck, brake the bone-rings; the sword went clean through her fated body, and she fell to the ground.

The sword was bloody; the hero gloried in his deed. The fire flamed forth; light stood within there, even as when the candle of the sky shineth brightly from heaven. He looked about the dwelling, turned him then to the wall. The thane of Hygelac, wrathful and steadfast of thought, raised the hard weapon by the hilt. The edge was not useless to the warrior, for he was minded to requite Grendel speedily for the many onslaughts he had made on the West-Danes far oftener than a single time, when he slew Hygelac's hearth-com-rades in their sleep, ate fifteen men as they slept of the Dane-folk, and bare off as many more, a loathly spoil. Beowulf, relentless warrior, so far paid Grendel his dues for that, that he now saw him lying on his bed, battle-weary and lifeless, in such wise as the strife in Heorot had scathed him. The corse sprang far when it underwent a blow after death, a hard sword-stroke, and Beowulf cut off the head.

Soon the men of wise thought, who with Hroth-gar looked on the water, saw that the swirl of the wave was all mingled with blood, that the flood was stained with it. The white-haired old men spake together of the goodly atheling, how they looked not he should come again, glorying in victory, to seek their mighty prince, for, because of the blood, it seemed to many that the sea-wolf had slain him. Then came the ninth hour of the day. The brave Scyldings left the cliff; the gold-giving friend of men went him homeward. The strangers sat there, sick at heart, and stared on the mere. They wished and yet trusted not, to see their dear lord's self.

Then the war-brand, the sword, began, because of the monster's blood, to fall away in battle-icicles; a marvel was it how it all melted likest to ice, when the Father, that holdeth sway over times and sea-sons, freeth the bonds of the frost, unwindeth the flood's fetters. He is the true Lord.

The chief of the Weder-Geats took no more of the treasure-holdings in the dwelling, though he saw many there, but only the head, and with it, the sword's hilt, brave with gold; the sword had already melted, its chased blade burned wholly, so hot was the blood, so poisonous the demon of strange kind, that met her death there in the hall.

Soon was he swimming, that had borne erstwhile the battle-shock of the foe. He dove up through the water. The moil of the waves was all cleansed, the wide domains where the strange demon had yielded up her life's day and this world that passeth.

The safeguard of seafarers, the strong of heart, came swimming then to land; he joyed in his sea-spoil, the mighty burden he had with him. Then went they to him, his chosen band of thanes; God they thanked, had joy of their lord, for that it was given them to see him safe. Speedily then the hel-met and burnie of the unfaltering one were loosed. The pool, the water beneath the clouds, stained with the blood of slaughter, grew still.

Forth thence they fared by the foot-paths, joyful of heart. The men measured the earth-way, the well-known road, bold as kings. The head they bare from the sea-cliff with toil that was heavy for any of them, great of courage though they were; four it took to bear Grendel's head with labor on the shaft of death to the gold-hall, till to the hall came faring forthwith the fourteen Geats, picked men brave in battle. Their liege-lord together with them trod boldly in the midst of them the meadow-stretches.

Then the foremost of the thanes, the man brave of deed, exalted in glory, the warrior bold in strife, came in to greet Hrothgar. Grendel's head, grisly to behold, was borne into the hall, where the men were drinking before the earls and the lady as well. The men looked on that sight strange to see.

How Beowulf told of the fight, and was praised and counselled by Hrothgar; of the feasting, and how on the morrow the Geats prepared to leave the land of the Danes.

Beowulf spake, the son of Ecgtheow: "Lo, with joy we have brought thee, son of Healfdene, lord of the Scyldings, in token of glory, the sea-spoil thou here beholdest. Not easily came I forth with my life, hazarded with sore hardship the toils of war beneath the waters. Almost had the strife been ended, save that God shielded me. Naught might

I achieve with Hrunting in the strife, good as that weapon is, but the Ruler of Men vouchsafed it me to see hanging on the wall an old sword, noble and mighty — most oft is He guide to the friendless — so that I drew the weapon. Then I slew in the struggle the guardians of the hall, for the chance was given me. The battle-blade then, the chased sword, was burned to naught, when the blood sprang forth, hottest of battle-gore; I bare away thence the hilt from my foes, avenged in fitting wise their evil deeds and the Danes' death-fall. I promise thee, therefore, thou mayest in Heorot sleep free from care with thy fellowship of warriors, and every thane of thy people likewise, young and old — that thou needest not, lord of the Scyldings, have dread of death-peril for them on this hand, for thine earls, as thou didst ere this." Then the golden hilt, the work of giants long ago, was given into the hand of the old prince, the white-haired battle-leader. After the overthrow of the devilish ones, it fell, the work of marvellous smiths, into the keeping of the Danes' lord; when the grim-hearted one, God's foe, with murder upon him, gave up the world, and his mother also, it fell in this wise into the keeping of the best of world-kings, between the seas, of those that in Scedenig parted gifts of gold.

Hrothgar spake, looked on the hilt, the old heirloom, on which was written the beginning of that far-off strife, when the flood, the streaming ocean, slew the giant kind — they had borne themselves lawlessly. The people were estranged from the Eternal Lord; the Wielder, therefore, gave them their requital through the whelming of the waters. So was it duly lined in rimed staves on the guard of gleaming gold, set down and told for them for whom that sword was wrought, choicest of blades, with twisted hilt and decked with dragon-shapes.

Then the wise one spake, the son of Healfdene; all were silent: "That, lo, may he say that worketh truth and right among the people (the old warden of the realm keepeth all in mind from of old) that this earl was born of a nobler race. Thy fame is exalted, my friend Beowulf, among every people throughout the wide ways. Wholly with quietness dost thou maintain it, thy might with wisdom of heart. I shall fulfil my troth to thee, that we spake of, ere now, together. Thou shalt be in every wise a comfort, long-established, to thy people, a help to the warriors. Heremod was not so to the children of Ecgwela, the Honor-Scyldings. He grew not up to do as they would have him, but to cause death-fall and deadly undoing for the Dane-folk. In the swelling anger of his heart he slew his table-companions, they that stood at his shoulder, till he went alone, the mighty prince, from the joys of men. Though the mighty God raised him up and set him forth in the joys of dominion and gifts of strength above other men, none the less there grew in his mind and soul a blood-greed. He gave out rings to the Danes not at all as befitted his high estate, lived joyless, and so suffered stress for his vengeful doings, a fate long-enduring at the hands of his people. Do thou learn by this. Lay hold upon manly worth. As one wise in years, I have framed thee this discourse.

"A marvel it is how mighty God in the greatness of His soul bestoweth wise judgment on mankind, land holdings and earlship; He hath rule over all. Whiles letteth He the heart's thought of a man of high race turn to having and holding, giveth him the joys of this world in his country, a fastness-city of men to keep, so contriveth for him that he ruleth parts of the earth, a wide realm, such that he may not know the bounds thereof. He dwelleth in fatness; sickness nor age turn him aside no whit; preying sorrow darkeneth not his soul, nor doth strife show itself anywhere, nor warring hate, but all the world wendeth to his will. He knoweth not the worse, till that within him a deal of overweening pride groweth and waxeth, while the warder sleepeth, shepherd of the soul. Too fast is that sleep, bound round with troubles; very nigh is the slayer that in grievous wise shooteth with his bow. Then is he smitten in the breast, with his helmet upon him, by a bitter shaft.

"He cannot guard him from the devious strange biddings of the Accursed Fiend. That seemeth him too little which he hath long held. Perverse of mind, he is greedy, giveth not at all out of pride the rings of plate-gold, and he forgetteth and taketh no heed of the fate to come, because of the deal of blessings God, the King of Glory, hath already given him. Therefore, at the end, it happeneth that the fleeting body sinketh and falleth, marked for death. Another taketh over the earl's former holdings, who dealeth out treasure without repining, and shall take no thought for fear.

"Guard thee from death-dealing malice, dear Beowulf, best of men, and choose the better, the eternal gain. Give not thyself to over-pride, O warrior renowned. Now is the flower of thy strength for one while; soon shall it be hereafter that sickness or the sword's edge, foe's clutch or flood's whelm, the sword's grip or the spear's flight, or grievous old age, shall part thee from thy strength, or the brightness of thine eyes shall fail and grow dark; straightway shall it be, princely one, that death shall overcome thee.

"Half a hundred years beneath the clouds I so ruled the Ring-Danes and warded them in war with spear and sword from many a people through this mid-earth, that I counted myself without a foe 'neath the stretch of the heaven. Behold! a change came to my land, grief after joy, when Grendel, the old-time foe, became my invader; ceaselessly from that troubling I suffered exceeding sorrow of spirit. Thanks be to God, the Eternal Lord, that I have bided in life so long that I may look with mine eyes on this head, gory from the sword.

"Go now to thy mead-bench, honored warrior; taste of the joy of the feast; treasures full many shall be between us twain, when morn shall come."

The Geat was glad at heart and went therewith to find his place, as the wise one had bidden. Then anew, in fair wise, was the feast spread for them, mighty in valor, sitting in the hall. The helm of night darkened down dusky over the bandsmen. The press of warriors all arose; the white-haired prince, the old Scylding, desired to seek his bed. The Great, the valiant shield-warrior, listed well, past the telling, to rest him. Soon the hall-thane, who took care with courteous observance for the hero's every need, such as in that day seafarers should have, led him forth, come from afar, worn with his venture. Then the great-hearted one took his rest.

The hall lifted itself broad and brave with gold. The guest slept within till the black raven, blithe of heart, heralded the joy of heaven. Then the bright sun came gliding over the plain. The wars-men hasted, the athelings were eager to fare again to their people. He who had come to them, the large of heart, would take ship far thence. The brave one bade the son of Ecglaf bear off Hrunting, bade him take his sword, his beloved blade, spake him thanks for its lending, said he accounted it a good war-friend, of might in battle, belied not in words the sword's edge. That was a man great of soul! And when the warriors were in forward-ness for the journey, with their gear made ready, the atheling dear to the Danes, the hero brave in the fight, went to the high-seat, where the other was, and greeted Hrothgar.

How Beowulf took leave of Hrothgar, and was given rich gifts, and departed with his men.

Beowulf spake, the son of Ecgtheow: "We, sea-faring ones, come from afar, wish now to say that we mean now to make our way to Hygelac. We have been well entreated here in all man could wish; thou has dealt well by us. If then on earth, O Lord of Men, I may earn more of thy heart's love by deeds of war than I yet have done, I shall straightway be ready. Should I learn over the stretches of the flood that thy neighbors burden thee with dread, as they that hate thee at times have done, I shall bring a thousand thanes, war-riors, to thine help. I know of Hygelac, Lord of the Geat-folk, the people's herd, that though he be young he will uphold me in word and deed that I may do thee full honor and bear to thine aid the spear's shaft, the stay of his strength, when need of men shall be thine. If, furthermore, Hrethric, son of the king, take service at the court of the Geats, he shall find many friends there; far-off lands are better to seek by him that may trust in him-self."

Hrothgar spake to him in answer: "Now hath the wise Lord sent these sayings into thy soul. Never heard I man so young in years counsel more wisely. Thou art strong in might and safe in thought, and wise in thy sayings. I account it likely that if it hap the spear, the fierce battle-sword, sickness, or the steel, taketh away the son of Hrethel, thy prince, the people's herd, and thou hast thy life, that the Sea-Geats will have no man better to choose for king, for treasure-warden of the war-riors, if thou art willing to rule the realm of thy kinsfolk. Thy brave spirit liketh me, passing well, ever the more, dear Beowulf. Thou hast so wrought that peace shall be between the Geat-folk and the Spear-Danes, and strife be at rest, the guileful onslaughts they have erstwhile undergone. Whilst I rule this wide realm, treasure shall be in common; greeting shall many a one send another by gifts across the gannet's bath; the ringed ship shall bring over the sea offerings and tokens of love. I know the peoples are fast wrought together both toward foe and toward friend, void of reproach in every wise as the way was of old."

Then, thereto, the son of Healfdene, shield of earls, gave him in the hall twelve treasures, bade him make his way with these gifts safe and sound to his dear people, and come again speedily. The king, then, goodly of birth, Lord of the Scyldings, kissed the best of thanes and clasped him about the neck. The tears of the white-haired king fell; old and wise, two things he might look for, but of these the second more eagerly, that they might yet again see one another, mighty in counsel. The man was so dear to him, that he might not bear the tumult of his heart, for in his breast, fast in the bonds of thought, deep-hidden yearning for the dear warrior burned throughout his blood.

Beowulf, gold-proud warrior, trod thence over the grassy earth, rejoicing in his treasure. The sea-goer awaited her master, as she rode at anchor. Oft then, as they went, was the gift of Hrothgar spoken of with praise. That was a king in all things blameless, till old age, that hath scathed many a man, took from him the joys of might.

[*At this point the story continues with an account of Beowulf's return to his country, of his eventual suc-cession to the throne of Hygelac, and of a fierce dragon which guarded a great hoard of wealth. When, in*

*vengeance for a theft from the hoard, the dragon began
to raid the kingdom, killing thanes and burning halls,
Beowulf resolved to seek out the dragon and kill him
in battle. The encounter is told in detail and with
great vividness. Single-handed Beowulf attacked,
but, when his weapons failed him, his friend Wiglaf
joins him and the two overcome the dragon. However
Beowulf has been fatally wounded and dies. The
closing section tells of the honor paid Beowulf in
death.]*

*Of the burning of Beowulf, and the building of Beo-
wulf's Barrow, and of their remembering him with
praise.*

Then the Geat-folk made ready for him a pile, as
he had prayed them, firmly based on the earth and 15
hung with helmets and shields and bright burnies;
with grief the warriors laid in the midst of it their
great prince, their lord beloved. Then began the
warriors to quicken on the cliff the greatest of
death-fires; the wood-smoke rose dark above the 20
pitchy flame, while the fire roared, blent with the
sound of weeping as the turmoil of the wind ebbed,
till, hot in the hero's breast, it had crumbled the
bone-frame. With thoughts left void of gladness
and with sorrow of heart, they made their lament 25
for their liege-lord's death. His wife, likewise, in
deepest grief, her hair close bound, made her song
of mourning again and yet again for Beowulf —
that she foresaw with grievous dread days of evil

for herself, many a death-fall, terror of battle,
shame and captivity.

Heaven swallowed up the smoke. Then the
Weder-folk built a burial-mound on the cliff that
was high and broad, seen afar by the seafarer, and
they made it, the beacon of the one who was mighty
in battle, in ten days. They carried a wall about
the remains of the fire, the goodliest they who were
most wise might contrive. In the barrow they
placed the rings and jewels, all the trappings likewise which the men of bold heart had taken before
from the hoard. They let the earth keep the
treasures of earls and the gold lie in the ground
where it still now abideth, as useless to men as it
was aforetime.

Then about the mound rode the sons of athelings
brave in battle, twelve in all. They were minded
to speak their sorrow, lament their king, frame
sorrow in words and tell of the hero. They praised
his earlship and did honor to his prowess as best
they knew. It is meet that a man thus praise his
liege-lord in words, hold him dear in his heart, when
he must forth from the body to become as a thing
that is naught.

So the Geat-folk, his hearth-comrades, grieved
for their lord, said that he was a king like to none
other in the world, of men the mildest and most
gracious to men, the most friendly to his people and
most eager to win praise.

The Nibelungenlied · c. 1200

In the *Nibelungenlied* we are still concerned with the period of Western Europe which provided
much of the legendary material for the *Beowulf*, but the advance of five centuries in time in this
German poem assures us more historical background for the action. The *Nibelungenlied* is an epic
reflecting the days of chivalry and early German life. In it considerable historical fact is interwoven
against a background of folklore and legendry which had already been used in the *Eddas* of Iceland
and in the Norse *Sagas.*

The poem, which has been called a "German Iliad," is written in Middle High German. The
narrative presents a struggle between the forces of good and evil as set forth by an unknown
poet about the year 1200. Its theme is fidelity. The earlier material of the poem was probably a
personification of nature with Sigfrid representing the dawning day, Brunhild typifying the sun-
maiden, the Nibelungs the power of darkness, and so on, but in its present form most of this allegory
has disappeared and we have a story of revenge and murder resulting from unfaithfulness and
jealousy. The poem is characterized by directness of narrative, a strong awareness of national
pride, and a deep tragic feeling.

The materials of the *Nibelungenlied* are today perhaps best known to the Western world through
the operas of Richard Wagner, who drew on them for his "Ring cycle."

In brief, the *Nibelungenlied* chronicles a period in the early history of the Burgundians, who lived near the Rhine. Sigfrid, a prince of the Netherlands, seeks the hand of Kriemhild, sister to Gunther, Gernot and Giselher, kings of Burgundy. Gunther agrees to give his sister to Sigfrid on the condition that the hero aids him in securing as his queen the beautiful and powerful Brunhild, queen of Iceland. By use of a magic helmet that makes him invisible Sigfrid helps Gunther to overcome Brunhild in three contests. (This strange wooing is recounted in the Seventh Adventure reprinted below.) In the bridal night, however, Brunhild discovers that Gunther actually lacks the strength he seemed to have displayed in wooing her and she ties him up in her girdle. Once more Sigfrid is called to assistance and, in the dark of the next night, he overcomes the queen again. Thinking Gunther had really defeated her, Brunhild submits to the king. Unfortunately, Kriemhild knows that Sigfrid has twice conquered Brunhild and in a quarrel seeks to vanquish her with this charge, producing Brunhild's ring and girdle as proofs. Hagen, Gunther's loyal vassal, takes it upon himself treacherously to slay Sigfrid during a hunt (in the manner related in the Sixteenth Adventure below) in order to restore his lord's honor. For a long time Kriemhild nurses her revenge. Finally she marries Etzel (Attila), the king of the Huns, invites her brothers and the knights of Burgundy to a great festival, and has them killed in a series of combats. Furious that such brave heroes should fall at the hand of a woman, old Hildebrand, the armor bearer of Dietrich of Berne, slays Kriemhild with his sword. Dietrich and Etzel are left mourning over the bodies of the dead.

SUGGESTED REFERENCE: W. A. Mueller, *The Nibelungenlied Today: Its Substance, Essence, and Significance* (1962).

How Gunther Won Brunhild[1]

Meanwhile their ship had come so close to land
The king could see the fairest maidens stand
Far above in the windows of the city —
But none he recognized, which seemed to him a pity.

He turned to question Sigfrid, his companion: 5
"Who might these maidens be, in your opinion,
Looking down at us on the ocean tide?
Whoever their lord may be, there's spirit there and pride."

Noble Sigfrid answered, "Cast a glance,
In secret, among these girls. Given the chance,   10
Now tell me, which would you choose to be your bride?"
"All right, I shall," bold and eager, Gunther cried.

"I see one now, by the window over there,
Dressed in a snow-white dress, of such a rare
And lovely form — my eyes would never err,   15
If they had the chance to choose, and I would marry her."

[1] Reprinted from *The Song of the Nibelungs* by Frank G. Ryder (translator) by permission of the Wayne State University Press. Copyright © 1962 by Wayne State University Press.

"The light of your eyes served you well in the choice,
For that is noble Brunhild, the lovely prize
Toward which your heart and mind and will, unceasing,
Urge you." Her every gesture seemed to Gunther pleasing.   20

The queen soon ordered her maids to stand away
From the window ledge: it was not right to stay
Where strangers could stare at them. And they obeyed her.
But we shall also hear of them what they did later.

With the strangers in mind, they put their finery on,   25
Like lovely women always, and were gone
To the narrow windows where, looking through,
They had seen the heroes stand — all this for a better view.

But they were only four who came to the land.
Sigfrid led Gunther's horse out on the sand —   30
Maidens watched from the window as he did it,
Which seemed to Gunther all to his greater fame and credit.

He led him by the bridle, the graceful steed,
Big and strong and handsome, of perfect breed.
Royal Gunther rose to the saddle then.   35
This was Sigfrid's service, soon forgotten again.

He went to the ship and brought his horse to land.
No common thing was this, that he should stand
Beside the stirrups of another knight,
And from the windows highborn ladies watched
    the sight.   40

In perfect harmony the princely pair:
White as the snow the clothes they brought to
    wear
And of their steeds the same; their shields well
    made,
From which, as they held them high, the bright
    reflection played;

Their saddles studded with jewels; fine and small
The gauge of their martingales. To Brunhild's
    hall   46
They came in splendor. Bells of bright red gold
Hung on their saddles. They rode to this land
    as suits the bold,

With newly whetted spears and well made swords
Broad and sharp, held by the handsome lords 50
So that the point reached down to the very spur.
This fair Brunhild watched, nothing escaping her.

With them came Sir Dankwart, and Hagen came,
Their noble vassals, wearing garments the same,
Richly made, in color black as the raven.   55
Their shields were things of beauty — massive,
    broad, and proven!

From India came the splendid jewels fastened
Upon their clothes, which with their moving
    glistened.
Unguarded they left their craft by the waterside,
And turning toward the castle now, began to
    ride.   60

Eighty-six towers they saw in all,
Three palaces, and a nobly fashioned hall
Of marble green as the grass, and it was here
That with her lords and ladies dwelt Brunhild the
    fair.

The city was open wide, the gates unlocked, 65
Toward them quickly Brunhild's vassals walked,
Eager to welcome guests in their mistress' land.
They took their horses in charge, the shield from
    each one's hand.

A chamberlain said, "Now give your weapons over,
And your suits of mail." Said Hagen, "That's
    one favor   70
We will not do you. We'll keep them close at
    hand."
Sigfrid answered: "Let me explain how matters
    stand.

That is their custom at court. They let no guest
Carry weapons here. So it is best
To let them take our arms and lay them aside." 75
Much against his will, Gunther's man complied.

Wine was poured for them; the guests were made
To feel at home. At court a bold parade
Of warriors dressed to suit their princely station,
Still the strangers got their share of admiration. 80

The news had been conveyed to Brunhild, the
    queen,
That unknown men in elegant clothes were seen
Arriving at court, borne by the ocean tide.
Now the lovely maiden asked of this; she cried:

"These men, these strangers, tell me who they
    are,   85
Coming all unknown and from afar,
To stand so proudly here within my walls —
And to whose honor and credit this heroes' voyage
    falls."

One of her retinue spoke, "This much I can say:
None have I ever seen until this day — 90
Except that one among them I can tell
Looks like Sigfrid. Truly I counsel you: welcome
    him well.

The second is a man of such good breeding
That he would be a king — only needing
Wide lands to rule. Perhaps he really is — 95
To stand among those men with dignity like his!

The third among these men appears so gruff,
And yet in form, my Queen, handsome enough;
Look at those flashing eyes and the angry stare.
I'll wager anything there's a fierce temper there.

The youngest of the group is most refined — 101
His bearing and his breeding seem the kind
We cherish in maidens, such his gentle charm.
Things would go hard with us if he ever came to
    harm.

For all his handsome form and gentle tone, 105
Many a winsome wife would weep alone
If he ever turned to rage. He seems indeed
A bold and dauntless man, a knight of the noble
    breed."

The queen cried out: "My dress, my battle-gear!
If mighty Sigfrid has made this journey here 110
With thought of winning my love, he'll pay with
    his life.
I'm not so afraid of him that I mean to be his
    wife."

Soon the fair Brunhild, in fitting dress,
Came with her beautiful maids, surely no less
Than a hundred in all, fair and handsomely clad.
Here they could see the strangers — at which their
    hearts were glad.   116

As escort for the ladies, Iceland's lords,
Vassals of Brunhild, came, bearing their swords —
Five hundred, and maybe more. Alarmed by that,
The doughty guests arose from the couches where
    they sat.   120

And now would you like to hear the words that
    passed,
When Brunhild saw the prince of the Rhine at
    last?
"Welcome to Iceland, Sigfrid," said the queen,
"And will you tell me, please, what does this
    voyage mean?"

"Your gracious favor, Lady, has reversed   125
The order of your greeting. He is first
Who stands before me here, this noble lord,
My liege — I must decline the honor you accord.

Born to the Rhenish throne — what more to say?
And all for the love of you we are here today.   130
He means to marry you, at any cost.
Reflect on this! My lord will not yield, and you
    are lost!

Gunther is his name, a glorious king.
In all the world he wishes this one thing:
To gain your love. This trip I did not choose,   135
But that was his command and I could not refuse."

"If you are a vassal, and he the one who bears
The crown, the challenge is his. In case he dares
To take it up and wins, I'll be his wife.
But if I vanquish him, all of you lose your life!"   140

Hagen spoke, "Lady, let us see
These mighty contests. Awesome they must be
Before you hear surrender from Gunther, my
    king.
For you are the sort of beauty he thinks of
    marrying."

"He shall throw the stone, and jump, and shoot
    the spear.   145
Before you answer rashly, let this be clear;
Life and honor both you stand to lose,"
The beautiful woman said. "Think before you
    choose."

Sigfrid said to the king, as he stepped up near,
"Say what you feel like saying. Have no fear   150

Because of the queen or the hurt you might incur.
I know some tricks to keep you safe enough from
    her."

Said royal Gunther, "Gracious lady, decree
As suits your pleasure. If more — so let it be!
For I shall brave it all for your sweet sake.   155
I must have you in marriage — for this my life
    is at stake."

Now that Brunhild knew the king's intent,
She told them to hasten the start of the games and
    sent
To get good armor for the battlefield:
Mail of red gold, and a hard-bossed shield.   160

Here was the silken tunic that she wore
In many battles. No weapon ever tore
Its lovely Libyan wool, carefully made
With light designs in shining woven work and
    braid.

During this time, arrogant taunt and threat   165
Were the strangers' lot. Dankwart was much
    upset,
And Hagen worried over Gunther's fate.
They thought: "The good we get from this trip
    will not be great."

Meanwhile crafty Sigfrid walked away,
Unnoticed, back to where their vessel lay,   170
And took the Mantle from its hiding place,
And quickly slipped it on, so none could see his
    face.

Returned, he found a crowd of knights, who came
To hear the queen decree her lofty game.
He wisely came upon them unaware.   175
Not a soul could see him, of all the people there.

The place for the game was set, the ring was drawn,
Ready for the host of lookers-on —
More than seven hundred referees,
For they would say who won; in armor all of these.

Brunhild now had come, weapons in hand,   181
As if she meant to conquer some monarch's land —
In silks with golden brooches fastened in,
Beneath which gleamed the shining whiteness of
    her skin.

Then came her retinue of knights, to hold   185
The mighty breadth of shield, of pure red gold
With heavy straps as hard as steel and bright,
Under the guard of which the lovely maid would
    fight.

The enarmes upon her shield were a noble braid,
With precious stones, green as the grass, inlaid, 190
Their many gleams competing with the gold.
The man who won her love must certainly be bold.

People say that, at the boss, her shield
Was three hands thick, and this the maid could
    wield!
A splendid mass of gold and steel so great,   195
Four of her chamberlains could hardly bear its
    weight.

When mighty Hagen watched them bring the
    shield,
His mood of bitterness was unconcealed:
"What now, King Gunther? A nice farewell to
    life!
This woman you hope to marry is surely the devil's
    wife!"   200

But listen, too, how ample her attire!
A tunic of silk from Azagouc, with the fire
Of many precious stones, whose color shone
From the rich and noble cloth and the queen who
    had it on.

They also brought the maiden a mighty spear, 205
Enormous in size, yet part of the battle gear
She always used. The stock was heavily made,
The point was sharp and true, a fearsome cutting
    blade.

I tell you, amazing tales have made the rounds
About how heavy it was. A hundred pounds 210
Of metal alone, they say, went into the spear;
It was all three men could lift. Great was
    Gunther's fear.

He thought to himself, "Is our whole plan
    amiss?
How could the devil in hell get out of this?
If I were back alive in Burgundy,   215
She'd wait a long, long while for any love from
    me!"

Now Hagen's brother spoke, the brave Dankwart:
"I rue this trip from the bottom of my heart.
They call us knights — is this the way we die,
Here, at the hands of women, under this foreign
    sky?   220

I'm sorry that I ever came to this land!
But if my brother had his weapons in hand,
And I the use of mine, they'd soon dispense,
All these men of Brunhild's, with some of their
    insolence.

They'd learn to watch their step, take that from
    me!   225
This beautiful woman here — before I'd see
My master die, her own life-breath would cease,
Though I had sworn a thousand oaths to keep the
    peace!"

"They'd never stop our getting out of here,"
His brother Hagen said, "if we had the gear   230
We need when the fighting breaks, and swords at
    our side.
We'd teach this mighty woman a humbling of her
    pride!"

The noble lady heard what Hagen said.
With a smile about her lips, she turned her head,
And looking back she spoke, "If he feels so brave,
Give them back the armor, the sharp swords they
    gave."   236

When at the lady's behest they got their swords,
Dankwart flushed with joy. "And now, my lords,
We'll take the game as it comes. Since we are
    armed,"
The valiant warrior cried, "Gunther cannot be
    harmed."   240

But Brunhild's strength was clearly an awesome
    thing.
They brought a heavy stone up to the ring,
A mammoth piece of rock, huge and round.
It took a dozen men to lift it off the ground.

She used to throw it after she threw the spear. 245
The men of Burgundy were filled with fear.
"Great God," said Hagen, "he's chosen his lover
    well!
She ought to be the cursed devil's bride in hell."

Back from her white and gleaming wrist she rolled
Her sleeves, and took her shield in hand to hold,
And lifted up her spear. The games were on. 251
At the thought of Brunhild's wrath, their con-
    fidence was gone.

If Sigfrid had not come to Gunther's aid,
The king would have lost his life to the mighty
    maid.
Now secretly he went and touched his hand.   255
Sigfrid's stratagem left Gunther all unmanned.

"What touched me?" Gunther thought. He
    looked around —
And all about him no one to be found!
"It is I, Sigfrid, your loyal friend.
As for the queen, let all your fears be at an end. 260

Hand over now your shield for me to hold
And make a careful note of what you're told.
You go through the motions, the work is mine."
Gunther knew his man; this was a welcome sign.

"Keep my trick a secret. Tell no one of it. 265
The queen shall not increase her fame nor profit
At your expense — which is what she wants to
     do.
Look how that woman stands undaunted in front
     of you!"

The maiden made her throw, a mighty one,
Against the great new shield that Siglind's son 270
Held in his hands. As if a wind had chanced
To sweep across the steel, the sparks of fire danced.

Clear through the shield the mighty blade-point
     came,
And over the rings of mail there flashed a flame.
Both of the heroes staggered under the blow — 275
But for the Magic Cape it would have laid them
     low.

Blood burst from Sigfrid's mouth, but he was
     swift
In leaping back to the ring, there to lift
The spear she had hurled with force enough to
     cleave
His shield, and send it back at her with a mighty
     heave.   280

"I do not want to kill the girl," he thought.
He turned the blade of the spear around and shot,
Shaft first, and straight at her tunic he aimed the
     throw.
Her coat of mail rang loud with the powerful force
     of the blow.

Out of the rings of mail the fire swirled   285
Like sparks in the wind. The son of Sigmund
     hurled
A mighty spear; her power gone, she fell
Beneath the blow. Never would Gunther have
     done so well.

How quickly the fair Brunhild sprang to her feet!
"My compliments, Gunther! The noble lord I
     greet   290

Who made that throw." (For so she thought
     him to be.
But she was tricked at her game by a mightier
     man than he.)

Straight to her place she went, with an angry
     frown;

High in the air the maiden raised the stone.
She gave it a mighty heave — and how it flew—
Her armor clanging, she jumped after the stone
     she threw.   296

The stone had traveled twenty yards or so,
And still the jump she made surpassed her throw.
Now the hero Sigfrid walked to the stone.
Gunther hefted it, but Sigfrid threw it alone.   300

Sigfrid was tall and powerfully built. He threw,
And the stone went farther. His jump was farther,
     too.
His vast skill and cunning made him so strong
That he could make the leap and carry Gunther
     along.

The jump was over, the stone was on the ground,
And none in sight but Gunther, all around.   306
Beautiful Brunhild flashed an angry red:
Except for Sigfrid's feat, Gunther would be dead.

Now that she saw him standing safe and sound
At the end of the ring, she shouted, "Gather
     'round,   310
Kin of mine, men of my retinue,
You shall be in liege to Gunther, all of you."

And all the warriors laid their weapons down,
And knelt in obeisance to the Burgundian crown
Of Gunther the mighty, thinking the while, of
     course,   315
That he had won the contest by his own sheer
     force.

He greeted her graciously, like a perfect knight.
She placed her hand in his, granting the right
Of command to him and giving him full domain —
Much to the joy of Hagen, his great and valiant
     thane.   320

She asked the noble king to come with her
Into the palace, this time to confer
Upon the warrior services multiplied
(Which Dankwart and Hagen had to accept and
     be satisfied).

Sigfrid was not the least ingenious of men. 325
He took his mantle back to store it again,
And then returned where all the women sat,
And asked the king a question (a wise precaution,
     that):

"What do you wait for, sir? Why do we need
Delay these many games the queen decreed? 330
Let's see what kind they are!" — all this a show
He cunningly put on, as if he didn't know.

The queen inquired, "How could it possibly be,
Sigfrid, my lord, that you should fail to see
The victory which the hand of Gunther gained?"
Hagen of Burgundy it was who thus explained: 336

"True, my lady, by some unhappy slip
Our good companion here was down at the ship
When the lord of all the Rhineland conquered
    you,"
Gunther's man went on, "and so he never knew."

"I'm glad to hear that news," Sigfrid cried. 341
"So now at last someone has leveled your pride;
A mortal man has proved he could best you. Fine!
And now, my noble lady, follow us back to the
    Rhine!"

The fair maid answered, "Not yet! Before I go,
All my kin and all my men must know. 346
I cannot lightly leave my native land;
First I must have my friends and family close at
    hand."

So out on every path her heralds flew
Till all her troops, her kith and kin all knew 350
That they were summoned to court without delay.
For them she ordered splendid clothing given
    away.

And every day they came, from dawn to late,
Down to Brunhild's castle, like streams in spate.
"Hello," said Hagen of Trony, "what have we
    here? 355
This waiting for Brunhild's men is apt to cost us
    dear.

What if they now descend on us in force —
(We don't know what she has in mind, of course.
What if she's mad enough to plot our death?)
Then an evil day for us was the day she first drew
    breath!" 360

Stalwart Sigfrid said, "Leave this to me,
The thing you fear will never come to be,
For I shall bring you help, to Iceland here,
Knights you have never seen, men who have no
    peer.

Now I shall go and do not ask me where. 365
Meanwhile your honor stands in God's good care.
I'll not be long. You'll have a thousand men,
The finest fighters I know, when I come back
    again."

"Just so you aren't too long!" replied the king.
"We're duly grateful for the help you bring." 370
"I shall be back in hardly more than a day,
Tell Brunhild that it was you who sent me away."

How Sigfrid Was Slain

Gunther and Hagen, bold, but with the face
Of false deceit, proposed a forest chase:
To hunt with sharpened spears the wild swine,
The bison and the bear — is there any sport so
    fine?

They took with them supplies of every kind. 5
Sigfrid rode, in grace and noble mind.
Beside a cooling spring he lost his life —
This was the work of Brunhild, royal Gunther's
    wife.

To Kriemhild's side the stalwart knight had gone.
His hunting gear and theirs was loaded on, 10
Ready to cross the Rhine. Never before
In all her days, had Kriemhild cause to suffer more.

He kissed his love upon her lips and cried,
"God grant I see you safe again, my bride,
And may your eyes see me. Now you must find
Diversion with your kin, I cannot stay behind." 16

She thought of the words she spoke in Hagen's
    ear
(And dared not now repeat). In pain and fear
The princess grieved that she was ever born —
Kriemhild wept, her tears unnumbered, all forlorn.

"Give up this hunt!" she cried. "Last night I
    dreamed 21
A painful thing. Two wild boars, it seemed,
Pursued my lord across a field. In sleep,
The flowers all turned red. I have my right to
    weep;

I fear from many hands an evil plot — 25
What if someone here should think he'd got
Ill use from us and turned this thought to hate?
Dear lord, I say, turn back, before it is too late."

"I'll soon return, my dear, I swear I will.
I know no persons here who wish me ill, 30
For all your kin are well disposed to me,
And I have always acted so that this should be."

"Oh no, my lord, I fear it can't go well.
Alas, I dreamed last night two mountains fell
On top of you, and I never saw you again. 35
If you should leave me now, my heart will be
    heavy with pain."

He held his perfect wife in arms' embrace,
With lover's kiss caressed her lovely face.
He took his leave and soon he went away.
Alas, she never saw him safe beyond that day. 40

They rode to a certain heavy wood, in quest
Of hunt and sport, and many of the best
Were they who followed Gunther's party there.
The only ones who stayed were Gernot and Giselher

The horses went ahead, across the Rhine,   45
Full laden with the hunters' bread and wine,
Their fish and meat, and other good supplies
To suit a wealthy king in full and fitting wise.

At the forest edge they had their camp site
    placed.
By this device the haughty hunters faced   50
Where game would run, there on a spacious isle.
They told the king that Sigfrid had ridden up
    meanwhile.

The hunters' stations now were occupied
At every major point. Lord Sigfrid cried,
The stalwart man, "And who shall show the way
To the woods and the waiting game, you lords in
    bold array?"   56

Hagen said, "Before the hunting starts,
Why not split our group in several parts?
Thus my lords and I may recognize
Which hunter masters best our forest enterprise. 60

All the men and hounds we shall divide.
And each one choose the way he wants to ride.
Whoever hunts the best, his be the praise!"
The hunters did not wait, but went their separate
    ways.

"One dog is all I need — more's a waste,"   65
Lord Sigfrid said, "a hound that's had his taste,
To help him hold the scent through all this wood."
Thus said Kriemhild's lord: "This hunting will be
    good."

His ancient huntsman chose a goodly hound
Who soon had led them to a spot of ground   70
Where game in plenty ran. They bagged at will
Whatever rose from cover — experts do it still.

All the hound could flush fell to the hand
Of valiant Sigfrid, prince of Netherland —
So fast his horse that nothing got away.   75
His was the greatest praise for work in the hunt
    that day.

In all respects a skilled and sturdy man!
He made the kill with which the hunt began:
A mighty boar that fell at a single blow.
Shortly then he saw a monstrous lion go.   80

He strung and shot as the dog flushed his prey.
The sharp and pointed arrow sped its way.
The lion sprang three times — then it fell.
His fellow huntsmen praised him, saying he hunted
    well.

He added elk and bison to his bag,   85
Aurochs — four of them — and a giant stag;
His horse was fast, it never fell behind,
And they could not escape — no hope for hart or
    hind.

The hunting dog now found a giant boar.
It fled, the master hunter on the spoor   90
Without a moment's pause, and sticking tight.
The angry pig turned back and rushed the gallant
    knight.

What other hunter could have drawn his sword
To slay as easily as Kriemhild's lord?
After the kill they brought the hound-dog in.   95
Now the Burgundians learned how good his luck
    had been.

His fellow sportsmen said, "If you don't mind,
You might, my lord, just leave a few behind.
You've emptied hill and forest all this while.
Please let something live!" At this he had to
    smile.   100

There still was noise and clamor all around
Of hunters, and hunting dogs, so great a sound
That hill and forest answered. (The men released
A full two dozen packs, to hunt the forest beast.

And many animals would not survive.)   105
The other hunters thought they might contrive
To win the prize — an honor not for earning
With hardy Sigfrid there, where hunting fires were
    burning.

The chase was over now — and yet not quite.
Returning hunters brought to the camping site 110
Hides of many beasts, a host of game.
And ah, what wonderful things for the royal
    kitchen came!

The king was ready now to take repast,
And ordered the hunt informed. A single blast
Upon a horn sufficed to signify: 115
The noble prince had come to the camping site
    nearby.

A hunter of Sigfrid's cried: "My lord, I hear
By the sound of horns they want us all to appear
At camp again. I'll send an answer back."
(They blew for the other hunters, by way of
    keeping track.)   120

"We'd better leave the woods," Sir Sigfrid cried.
They hurried on, his horse at an even ride.
Their noise aroused a savage beast who broke
And ran — an angry bear. The hero, turning,
    spoke:

"I think we'll have some sport for our comrades
    there.   125
Let go the hunting dog, I see a bear.
He'll come to camp with us — as good as done!
He cannot save himself, unless he can really
    run."

The hunting-hound was loosed, the bear took
    flight.
Off to ride him down went Kriemhild's knight. 130
He came where trees lay felled and blocked the
    path.
The mighty beast now felt secure from the hunter's
    wrath.

The haughty warrior leapt at once from his steed
And ran on foot. The bear, forgetting heed
And caution, failed to run and soon was caught 135
And swiftly tied — and not a scratch had Sigfrid
    got!

The captured beast could neither claw nor bite.
He tied him to the saddle, the fearless knight,
And mounting, rode to camp. The feat was done
In a hero's pride of heart and all for the sake of
    fun.   140

He came to camp arrayed in his splendid gear:
Broad-bladed and massive, his mighty spear,
Down to his very spurs a handsome sword,
And a horn of reddish gold in the hand of the
    gallant lord.

Of finer hunting garb I never heard.   145
He wore a black silk cape; his cap was furred
With sable skins and very richly made.
He had a quiver, too, adorned with costly braid,

And covered with panther hide — by purpose so
Because its smell was sweet. He had a bow   150
No man except himself could bend an inch,
If he were asked to draw, without an archer's
    winch.

His suit was made throughout of otter's skin
With patches sewn from head to hem therein.
The gleaning pelts had golden buckles on;   155
At the hunter's right and left the clasps of red
    gold shone.

He carried Balmung, too, his handsome sword,
So broad and sharp as never to fail its lord

In helmet strokes, its edges true and tried.
This was a huntsman great in confidence and
    pride.   160

And since I have the full account to tell:
The choicest arrows filled his quiver well,
Spliced with gold, the blades were a good hand
    wide.
Whatever felt their cut, so stricken, swiftly died.

He rode with spirit, the way of hunting men.   165
Gunther's thanes could see him coming then.
They hurried out to hold his tourney-mare.
There at his saddle, tied, was a big and vicious
    bear!

Jumping down, he loosed the ropes that bound
The bear by foot and maw. The dogs around, 170
As many as saw the beast, gave tongue and bayed.
The bear was all for the woods; the men — a bit
    afraid!

Into the kitchens he went, confused by the noise.
Ho, but that place was not for the kitchen-boys!
Kettles were tumbled, hardly a fire was whole. 175
And oh, what foods were strewn among the ash
    and coal!

Men were leaping up on every hand.
The bear was angry now. At the king's command
The dogs that still were leashed they cut away.
With a better end that would have been a merry
    day.   180

No waiting now, but up with spear and bow
And after the bear, to see where he would go.
They dared not shoot with all the dogs around.
They raised a fearful racket and made the hills
    resound.

The bear, pursued by dogs, began to flee.   185
Kriemhild's lord kept up — and none but he.
He ran him down, with his sword he struck him
    dead;
Later they brought him back to camp and the
    fire-stead.

All that saw it praised a mighty deed.
They bade the noble hunters come and eat.   190
The whole assemblage sat on a pleasant sward.
What marvelous foods were set before each noble
    lord!

The stewards took their time in bringing wine.
Otherwise no service quite so fine
Was ever seen. These men would have no reason
To fear a word of censure, but for their stain of
    treason.   195

Sigfrid said, "It gives me some surprise
When they send us from the kitchen such supplies
Of excellent food, and no one brings the wine.
If they serve their huntsmen thus, the next time
    I'll decline.   200

I think I merit better service," he cried.
Falsely spoke the king, from the tableside:
"We'll make up later what you missed at first.
This is Hagen's fault — he'd let us die of thirst."

Said Hagen of Trony, "Listen, my lord, to me. 205
I thought the hunt today was meant to be
In Spessart and that is where I sent the wine.
We missed our drinks today; I'll not forget next
    time."

"Confound them," answered Sigfrid then,
    declaring:
"They should have brought me seven sumpters
    bearing   210
Spiced wine and mead. And failing that,
Was there no place closer to the Rhine we could
    have sat?"

Said Hagen of Trony, "Noble knights, my king,
Not far from here I know a cooling spring.
Do not be angry now — why not go there?"   215
(Counsel fraught, for many, with sorrow and
    grievous care).

The pang of thirst was all that Sigfrid feared.
He ordered the table that much sooner cleared,
That he might go to the hills and find the spring.
There they worked their plot — a black and
    faithless thing.   220

They placed on carts the game Sigfrid had killed
To have it carried home, and all who beheld
Granted Sigfrid honor in high degree.
(Hagen broke faith with him — and he broke it
    wretchedly).

As they were about to go to the linden tree   225
Lord Hagen said, "They're always telling me
How nothing is fast enough to keep the pace
With Sigfrid running. I wish he'd show us how
    he can race!"

Cried the Prince of the Low Lands, Sigmund's
    son:
"Find out for yourself, my friend! If you want to
    run   230
A race to the spring, all right. Whoever's faster
To the finish we shall all acknowledge master."

"Very well," said Hagen then, "let's try."
Stalwart Sigfrid made a bold reply:

"I'll first lie down in the grass before your feet."
Royal Gunther smiled, the words he heard were
    sweet.   236

Sigfrid had more to say: "I'll tell you what.
I'll carry every bit of clothes I've got,
My spear and shield, and all my hunting gear."
He put his quiver next to his sword and laced it
    there.   240

Gunther and Hagen removed their clothes and
    stood
In their white underwear. It did no good.
Across the clover like two wild panthers burst
The pair of running men, but Sigfrid got there
    first.

(In all, from many men, he won renown!)   245
He loosed his sword, and put his quiver down
And leaned on a linden branch his giant spear.
The splendid stranger stood by the waters flowing
    clear.

With perfect sense of form in everything,
He laid his shield on the ground beside the spring
And would not drink, however great his thirst 251
(Evil thanks he got!) till Gunther drank there first.

The spring was pure and good and cool.
Gunther bent his head above the pool
And after drinking rose and stepped away.   255
Ah, if Sigfrid could have done the same that day!

He paid the price for the courteous thing he did.
His sword and bow Lord Hagen took and hid
And hurried back where the spear had lain before.
He looked for a certain mark on the cape that
    Sigfrid wore.   260

As Sigfrid leaned to drink, he took his aim
And hurled it through the cross. The heart-blood
    came
Welling from the wound, richly to spill
On Hagen's clothes. No knight has ever done so
    ill.

He left the spear embedded by Sigfrid's heart. 265
Never in all this world did Hagen start
And run so fast from any man before.
When good Lord Sigfrid knew the vicious wound
    he bore,

He leapt from the spring like a man out of his
    mind.
Up from his heart and towering out behind   270
Rose the shaft of the spear. His bow and sword
He sought in vain, or Hagen would have his due
    reward.

The wounded man could find no blade to wield,
And nothing left to fight with but his shield.
He snatched it up and after Hagen he ran —
Even thus he still caught up with Gunther's man.

Mortally wounded as he was, he hit   277
So hard with his shield that from the edge of it
The precious jewels spun, and the shield was
          shattered.
For that most splendid knight revenge was all
          that mattered.   280

Hagen stumbled and fell at Sigfrid's blows —
So violent all the island echoes rose!
Had Sigfrid sword in hand, he would have killed
          him.
What rage in the wounded man, as hurt and anger
          filled him!

The color of Sigfrid's skin had turned all pale. 285
He could not stand. His strength was doomed to
          fail;
He bore the mark of death in all his pallor.
Many lovely women later mourned his valor.

So Kriemhild's husband fell where flowers grew.
They saw the blood that left his wound burst
          through,   290
And then from bitter hurt he cursed them all,
Whose faithless plotting first designed his cruel
          fall.

Cried Sigfrid dying, "Cowards, knave on knave!
Is murder your reward for the help I gave?
I kept my faith with you, and so I pay!   295
A shame upon your race, what you have done
          today.

Every child that's born to you will bear
The stain of this forever. Far too unfair
Is this revenge you take for your hate of me!
You should be banned in shame from decent
          company."   300

The other knights ran up where he lay slain.
It was, for many there, a day of pain,
For he was mourned by all that ever served
A loyal cause — no more than a gallant man
          deserved.

Another mourned: the king of Burgundy.   305
The dying man looked up; "What need has he
To weep for hurt who caused it? Scorn of men
Is all it earns," said he. "Why not forget it then?"

Cried Hagen, "I don't know what you're mourning
          for.
Our fears are at an end. How many more   310
Will dare to stand against us? A fortunate hour,
I say, when I destroyed his pride and all his
          power!"

Cried Sigfrid, "Boasting is an easy art.
If I had seen the murder in your heart,
I should have taken care to guard my life.   315
I worry not so much for me as for my wife.

And God have pity that my son was born,
Whom men in later days will heap with scorn
For having kin who bear the murderer's taint.
If only I had strength! — I have a just com-
          plaint."   320

Said the dying man, in anguish: "Noble king,
If you intend to do a loyal thing
In all this world for any man, then take
My wife in your protection, for grace and mercy's
          sake.

And let it profit her that she's your sister,   325
As you are a well-born prince, in faith assist her.
My father and men have a long time to wait.
Never did woman's pleasure end in pain so great."

The flowers all around were wet with blood.
He fought with death but not for long — what
          good?   330
Death has always owned the sharper sword.
He had no longer strength to speak, that gallant
          lord.

Soon, when the warriors saw the knight was dead,
They placed him on a shield all golden red,
And then debated how they might proceed   335
Best to conceal the fact that Hagen did this deed.

And many spoke: "We have seen evil done.
Hide it then, and all shall speak as one
That Kriemhild's husband rode a forest lane
To hunt alone, was met by bandits there, and
          slain."   340

"I'll take him back," said Hagen. "Have no
          doubt:
It's all the same to me if she finds out.
She caused my lady Brunhild misery —
Now let her weep as much as she wants, for all
          of me!"

Aucassin and Nicolete · Twelfth Century

Aucassin and Nicolete belongs to that type of literature known as the medieval romance, a narrative dealing with knights and fair ladies, with an emphasis on the theme of love. As is the case with the *Beowulf* and the *Nibelungenlied* and the popular ballads, authorship is lost in the dark recess of time.

This example of the medieval romance is representative of a whole cult in the literature of the time: the stories of Richard the Lion-Hearted, of Guy of Warwick, of Charlemagne, of Alexander the Great, and of the heroes at Troy. In addition to *Aucassin and Nicolete*, some of the metrical romances most popular today are: *Sir Gawain and the Green Knight, Floris and Blanchefleur, Sir Isumbras,* and the various stories of King Arthur as told by Malory in the *Morte d'Arthur*.

The details of this particular narrative are generally supposed to be of Oriental origin although the manner and form in which the tale has been preserved is that of Provençal romance. The combination of prose and poetry in which the story is presented characterizes it as a "chante-fable." Stories like this in which knights and ladies are involved in adventure and love, which reflect the age of chivalry, were as popular in medieval times as the novel is today. *Aucassin and Nicolete* is an idyl with all the grace and charm and sentiment true romances should employ. The translation is by Arthur Lang.

SUGGESTED REFERENCE: Albert B. Taylor, *An Introduction to Medieval Romance* (1930).

'Tis of Aucassin and Nicolete.
Who would list to the good lay
Gladness of the captive gray?
'Tis how two young lovers met,
Aucassin and Nicolete,
Of the pains the lover bore
And the sorrows he outwore,
For the goodness and the grace,
Of his love, so fair of face.

Sweet the song, the story sweet,
There is no man hearkens it,
No man living 'neath the sun,
So outwearied, so foredone,
Sick and woeful, worn and sad,
But is healed, but is glad,
'Tis so sweet.

So say they, speak they, tell they the Tale:

How the Count Bougars de Valence made war on Count Garin de Biaucaire, war so great, and so marvelous, and so mortal that never a day dawned but always he was there, by the gates and walls, and barriers of the town with a hundred knights, and ten thousand men at arms, horsemen and footmen: so burned he the Count's land, and spoiled his country, and slew his men. Now the Count Garin de Biaucaire was old and frail, and his good days were gone over. No heir had he, neither son nor daughter, save one young man only; such an one as I shall tell you. Aucassin was the name of the damoiseau [1]: fair was he, goodly, and great, and featly [2] fashioned of his body, and limbs. His hair was yellow, in little curls, his eyes blue and laughing, his face beautiful and shapely, his nose high and well set, and so richly seen was he in all things good, that in him was none evil at all. But so suddenly overtaken was he of Love, who is a great master, that he would not, of his will, be dubbed knight, nor take arms, nor follow tourneys, nor do whatsoever him beseemed. Therefore his father and mother said to him:

"Son, go take thine arms, mount thy horse, and hold thy land, and help thy men, for if they see thee among them, more stoutly will they keep in battle their lives, and lands, and thine, and mine."

"Father," said Aucassin, "I marvel that you will be speaking. Never may God give me aught of my desire if I be made knight, or mount my horse, or face stour [3] and battle wherein knights smite and are smitten again, unless thou give me Nicolete, my true love, that I love so well."

"Son," said the father, "this may not be. Let Nicolete go, a slave girl she is, out of a strange

[1] young man. [2] neatly.
[3] battle or conflict.

land, and the captain of this town bought her of the Saracens,[1] and carried her hither, and hath reared her and let christen the maid, and took her for his daughter in God, and one day will find a young man for her, to win her bread honorably. Herein hast thou nought to make or mend, but if a wife thou wilt have, I will give thee the daughter of a King, or a Count. There is no man so rich in France, but if thou desire his daughter, thou shalt have her."

"Faith! my father," said Aucassin, "tell me where is the place so high in all the world, that Nicolete, my sweet lady and love, would not grace it well? If she were Empress of Constantinople or of Germany, or Queen of France or England, it were little enough for her; so gentle is she and courteous, and debonaire, and compact of all good qualities."

Here singeth one:

Aucassin was of Biaucaire
Of a goodly castle there,
But from Nicolete the fair
None might win his heart away
Though his father, many a day,   25
And his mother said him nay,
"Ha! fond child, what wouldest thou?
Nicolete is glad enow!
Was from Carthage cast away,
Paynims [2] sold her on a day!   30
Wouldst thou win a lady fair
Choose a maid of high degree.
Such an one is meet for thee."
"Nay of these I have no care,
Nicolete is debonaire,   35
Her body sweet and the face of her
Take my heart as in a snare,
Loyal love is but her share
     That is so sweet."

Then speak they, say they, tell they the Tale: 40

When the Count Garin de Biaucaire knew that he would avail not to withdraw Aucassin his son from the love of Nicolete, he went to the Captain of the city, who was his man, and spake to him saying: 45
"Sir Count; away with Nicolete thy daughter in God; cursed be the land whence she was brought into this country, for by reason of her do I lose Aucassin, that will neither be dubbed knight, nor do aught of the things that fall to him to be done.   50 And wit ye well," he said, "that if I might have her at my will, I would burn her in a fire, and yourself might well be sore adread."

[1] Mohammedan Arabs against whom the crusaders fought.
   55
[2] infidels.

"Sir," said the Captain, "this is grievous to me that he comes and goes and hath speech with her. I had bought the maiden at mine own charges, and nourished her, and baptized, and made her my daughter in God. Yea, I would have given her to a young man that should win her bread honorably. With this had Aucassin thy son nought to make or mend. But, sith it is thy will and thy pleasure, I will send her into that land and that country where never will he see her with his eyes."   10
"Have a heed to thyself," said the Count Garin, "thence might great evil come on thee."

So parted they from each other. Now the Captain was a right rich man: so had he a rich palace with a garden in face of it; in an upper chamber   15 thereof he let place Nicolete with one old woman to keep her company, and in that chamber put bread and meat and wine and such things as were needful. Then he let seal the door, that none   20 might come in or go forth, save that there was one window, over against the garden, and strait enough, where through came to them a little air.

Here singeth one:

Nicolete as ye heard tell
Prisoned is within a cell
That is painted wondrously
With colors of a far countrie,
And the window of marble wrought.
There the maiden stood in thought,
With straight brows and yellow hair.
Never saw ye fairer fair!
On the wood she gazed below,
And she saw the roses blow,
Heard the birds sing loud and low,
Therefore spoke she woefully:
"Ah me, wherefore do I lie
Here in prison wrongfully:
Aucassin, my love, my knight,
Am I not thy heart's delight,
Thou that lovest me aright!
'Tis for thee that I must dwell
In the vaulted chamber cell,
Hard beset and all alone!
By our Lady Mary's Son
Here no longer will I wonn,[1]
     If I may flee!"

Then speak they, say they, tell they the Tale:

Nicolete was in prison, as ye have heard soothly, in the chamber. And the noise and bruit [2] of it went through all the country and all the land, how that Nicolete was lost. Some said she had fled the country, and some that the Count Garin de Biaucaire had let slay her. Whosoever had joy thereof,

[1] live or dwell.   [2] rumor.

Aucassin had none, so he went to the Captain of the town and spoke to him, saying:

"Sir Captain, what hast thou made of Nicolete, my sweet lady and love, the thing that best I love in all the world? Hast thou carried her off or ravished her away from me? Know well that if I die of it, the price shall be demanded of thee, and that will be well done, for it shall be even as if thou hadst slain me with thy two hands, for thou hast taken from me the thing that in this world I loved the best."

"Fair Sir," said the Captain, "let these things be. Nicolete is a captive that I did bring from a strange country. Yea, I bought her at my own charges of the Saracens, and I bred her up and baptized her, and made her my daughter in God. And I have cherished her, and one of these days I would have given her a young man, to win her bread honorably. With this thou hast naught to make, but do thou take the daughter of a King or a Count. Nay more, what wouldst thou deem thee to have gained, hadst thou made her thy leman, and taken her to thy bed? Plentiful lack of comfort hadst thou got thereby, for in Hell would thy soul have lain while the world endures, and into Paradise wouldst thou have entered never."

"In Paradise what have I to win? Therein I seek not to enter, but only to have Nicolete, my sweet lady that I love so well. For into Paradise go none but such folk as I shall tell thee now. Thither go these same old priests, and halt old men and maimed, who all day and night cower continually before the altars, and in the crypts; and such folk as wear old amices[1] and old clouted frocks, and naked folk and shoeless, and covered with sores, perishing of hunger and thirst, and of cold, and of little ease. These be they that go into Paradise, with them have I naught to make. But into Hell would I fain go; for into Hell fare the goodly clerks, and goodly knights that fall in tourneys and great wars, and stout men at arms, and all men noble. With these would I liefly[2] go. And thither pass the sweet ladies and courteous that have two lovers, or three, and their lords also thereto. Thither goes the gold, and the silver, and cloth of vair,[3] and cloth of gris,[4] and harpers, and makers, and the princes of this world. With these I would gladly go, let me but have with me Nicolete, my sweetest lady."

"Certes," quoth the Captain, "in vain wilt thou speak thereof, for never shalt thou see her; and if thou hadst word with her, and thy father knew it, he would let burn in a fire both her and me, and thyself might well be sore adread."

[1] Hoods worn by monks.
[2] willingly.   [3] fur.   [4] gray fur.

"That is even what irketh me," quoth Aucassin. So he went from the Captain sorrowing.

Here singeth one:

Aucassin did so depart
Much in dole and heavy at heart
For his love so bright and dear,
None might bring him any cheer,
None might give good words to hear.
To the palace doth he fare
Climbeth up the palace-stair,
Passeth to a chamber there,
Thus great sorrow doth he bear,
For his lady and love so fair.
"Nicolete, how fair art thou,
Sweet thy foot-fall, sweet thine eyes,
Sweet the mirth of thy replies,
Sweet thy laughter, sweet thy face,
Sweet thy lips and sweet thy brow,
And the touch of thine embrace,
All for thee I sorrow now,
Captive in an evil place,
Whence I ne'er may go my ways
Sister, sweet friend!"

So say they, speak they, tell they the Tale:

While Aucassin was in the chamber sorrowing for Nicolete his love, even then the Count Bougars de Valence, that had his war to wage, forgat it no wit, but had called up his horsemen and his footmen, so made he for the castle to storm it. And the cry of battle arose, and the din, and knights and men at arms busked[1] them, and ran to walls and gates to hold the keep. And the townsfolk mounted to the battlements, and cast down bolts and pikes. Then while the assault was great and even at its height, the Count Garin de Biaucaire came into the chamber where Aucassin was making lament, sorrowing for Nicolete, his sweet lady that he loved so well.

"Ha! son," quoth he, "how caitiff[2] art thou, and cowardly, that canst see men assail thy goodliest castle and strongest. Know thou that if thou lose it, thou losest all. Son, go to, take arms, and mount thy horse, and defend thy land, and help thy men, and fare into the stour. Thou needst not smite nor be smitten. If they do but see thee among them, better will they guard their substance, and their lives, and thy land and mine. And thou art so great, and hardy of thy hands, that well mightst thou do this thing, and to do it is thy devoir."[3]

"Father," said Aucassin, "what is this thou sayest now? God grant me never aught of my desire,

[1] prepared.   [2] cowardly, base.
[3] duty.

if I be dubbed knight, or mount steed, or go into the stour where knights do smite and are smitten, if thou givest me not Nicolete, my sweet lady, whom I love so well."

"Son," quoth his father, "this may never be: rather would I be quite disinherited and lose all that is mine, than that thou shouldst have her to thy wife, or to love *par amours.*"

So he turned him about. But when Aucassin saw him going he called to him again saying,

"Father, go to now, I will make with thee fair covenant."

"What covenant, fair son?"

"I will take up arms, and go into the stour, on this covenant, that, if God bring me back sound and safe, thou wilt let me see Nicolete my sweet lady, even so long that I may have of her two words or three, and one kiss."

"That will I grant," said his father.

At this was Aucassin glad.

Here one singeth:

Of the kiss heard Aucassin
That returning he shall win.
None so glad would he have been
Of a myriad marks of gold
Of a hundred thousand told.
Called for raiment brave of steel,
Then they clad him, head to heel,
Twyfold hauberk doth he don,
Firmly braced the helmet on.
Girt the sword with hilt of gold,
Horse doth mount, and lance doth wield,
Looks to stirrups and to shield,
Wondrous brave he rode to field.
Dreaming of his lady dear
Setteth spurs to the destrere,[1]
Rideth forward without fear,
Through the gate and forth away
   To the fray.

So speak they, say they, tell they the Tale:

Aucassin was armed and mounted as ye have heard tell. God! how goodly sat the shield on his shoulder, the helm on his head, and the baldric on his left haunch! And the damoiseau was tall, fair, featly fashioned, and hardy of his hands, and the horse whereon he rode swift and keen, and straight had he spurred him forth of the gate. Now believe ye not that his mind was on kine, nor cattle of the booty, nor thought he how he might strike a knight, nor be stricken again: nor no such thing. Nay, no memory had Aucassin of aught of these; rather he so dreamed of Nicolete, his sweet lady, that he dropped his reins, forgetting all there was

[1] war-horse.

to do, and his horse that had felt the spur, bore him into the press and hurled among the foe, and they laid hands on him all about, and took him captive, and seized away his spear and shield, and straightway they led him off a prisoner, and were even now discoursing of what death he should die.

And when Aucassin heard them,

"Ha! God," said he, "sweet Savior. Be these my deadly enemies that have taken me, and will soon cut off my head? And once my head is off, no more shall I speak with Nicolete, my sweet lady, that I love so well. Natheless have I here a good sword, and sit a good horse unwearied. If now I keep not my head for her sake, God help her never, if she love me more!"

The damoiseau was tall and strong, and the horse whereon he sat was right eager. And he laid hand to sword, and fell a-smiting to right and left, and smote through helm and *nasal,*[1] and arm and clenched hand, making a murder about him, like a wild boar when hounds fall on him in the forest, even till he struck down ten knights, and seven he hurt, and straightway he hurled out of the press, and rode back again at full speed, sword in hand. The Count Bougars de Valence heard say they were about hanging Aucassin, his enemy, so he came into that place and Aucassin was aware of him, and gat his sword into his hand, and lashed at his helm with such a stroke that he drave it down on his head, and he being stunned, fell groveling. And Aucassin laid hands on him, and caught him by the *nasal* of his helmet, and gave him to his father.

"Father," quoth Aucassin, "lo here is your mortal foe, who hath so warred on you with all malengin.[2] Full twenty years did this war endure, and might not be ended by man."

"Fair son," said his father, "thy feats of youth shouldst thou do, and not seek after folly."

"Father," said Aucassin, "sermon me no sermons, but fulfill my covenant."

"Ha! what covenant, fair son?"

"What, father, hast thou forgotten it? By mine own head, whosoever forgets, will I not forget it, so much it hath me at heart. Didst thou not covenant with me when I took up arms, and went into the stour, that if God brought me back safe and sound, thou wouldst let me see Nicolete, my sweet lady, even so long that I may have of her two words or three, and one kiss? So didst thou covenant, and my mind is that thou keep thy word."

"I!" quoth the father, "God forsake me when I keep this covenant! Nay, if she were here I would

[1] Part of the helmet.
[2] guile.

let her burn in the fire, and thyself shouldst be sore adread."

"Is this thy last word?" quoth Aucassin.

"So help me God," quoth his father, "yea!"

"Certes," quoth Aucassin, "this is a sorry thing meseems, when a man of thine age lies!"

"Count of Valence," quoth Aucassin, "I took thee?"

"In sooth, Sir, didst thou," said the Count.

"Give me thy hand," saith Aucassin.

"Sir, with good will."

So he set his hand in the other's.

"Now givest thou me thy word," saith Aucassin, "that never whiles thou art living man wilt thou avail to do my father dishonor, or harm him in body, or in goods, but do it thou wilt?"

"Sir, in God's name," saith he, "mock me not, but put me to my ransom; ye cannot ask of me gold nor silver, horses nor palfreys, *vair* nor *gris*, hawks nor hounds, but I will give you them."

"What?" quoth Aucassin. "Ha, knowest thou not it was I that took thee?"

"Yea, sir," quoth the Count Bougars.

"God help me never, but I will make thy head fly from thy shoulders, if thou makest not truth," said Aucassin.

"In God's name," said he, "I make what promise thou wilt."

So they did the oath, and Aucassin let mount him on a horse, and took another and so led him back till he was all in safety.

Here one singeth:

When the Count Garin doth know
That his child would ne'er forego
Love of her that loved him so,
Nicolete, the bright of brow,
In a dungeon deep below
Childe Aucassin did he throw.
Even there the Childe [1] must dwell
In a dun-walled marble cell.
There he waileth in his woe
Crying thus as ye shall know.
"Nicolete, thou lily white,
My sweet lady, bright of brow,
Sweeter than the grape art thou,
Sweeter than sack posset good
In a cup of maple wood!
Was it not but yesterday
That a palmer came this way,
Out of Limousin came he,
And at ease he might not be,
For a passion him possessed
That upon his bed he lay,
Lay, and tossed, and knew not rest

[1] A youth of noble birth.

In his pain discomforted.
But thou camest by the bed,
Where he tossed amid his pain,
Holding high thy sweeping train,
And thy kirtle of ermine,
And thy smock of linen fine,
Then these fair white limbs of thine,
Did he look on, and it fell
That the palmer straight was well,
Straight was hale — and comforted,
And he rose up from his bed,
And went back to his own place,
Sound and strong, and full of face!
My sweet lady, lily white,
Sweet thy footfall, sweet thine eyes,
And the mirth of thy replies,
Sweet thy laughter, sweet thy face,
Sweet thy lips and sweet thy brow,
And the touch of thine embrace.
Who but doth in thee delight?
I for love of thee am bound
In this dungeon underground,
All for loving thee must lie
Here where loud on thee I cry,
Here for loving thee must die
    For thee, my love."

Then say they, speak they, tell they the Tale:

Aucassin was cast into prison as ye have heard tell, and Nicolete, of her part, was in the chamber. Now it was summer time, the month of May, when days are warm, and long, and clear, and the night still and serene. Nicolete lay one night on her bed, and saw the moon shine clear through a window, yea, and heard the nightingale sing in the garden, so she minded her of Aucassin her lover whom she loved so well. Then fell she to thoughts of Count Garin de Biaucaire, that hated her to the death; therefore deemed she that there she would no longer abide, for that, if she were told of, and the Count knew whereas she lay, an ill death would he make her die. Now she knew that the old woman slept who held her company. Then she arose, and clad her in a mantle of silk she had by her, very goodly, and took napkins, and sheets of the bed, and knotted one to the other, and made therewith a cord as long as she might, so knitted it to a pillar in the window, and let herself slip down into the garden, then caught up her raiment in both hands, behind and before, and kilted up her kirtle, because of dew that she saw lying deep on the grass, and so went her way down through the garden.

Her locks were yellow and curled, her eyes blue and smiling, her face feately fashioned, the nose high and fairly set, the lips more red than cherry or rose in time of summer, her teeth white and small; her breasts so firm that they bore up the folds of her bodice as they had been two apples; so slim she was in the waist that your two hands might have clipped her, and the daisy flowers that brake beneath her as she went tip-toe, and that bent above her instep, seemed black against her feet, so white was the maiden. She came to the postern gate, and unbarred it, and went out through the streets of Biaucaire, keeping always on the shadowy side, for the moon was shining right clear, and so wandered she till she came to the tower where her lover lay. The tower was flanked with buttresses, and she cowered under one of them, wrapped in her mantle. Then thrust she her head through a crevice of the tower that was old and worn, and so heard she Aucassin wailing within, and making dole and lament for the sweet lady he loved so well. And when she had listened to him she began to say:

Here one singeth:

Nicolete the bright of brow
On a pillar leanest thou,
All Aucassin's wail dost hear
For his love that is so dear,
Then thou spakest, shrill and clear,
"Gentle knight withouten fear
Little good befalleth thee,
Little help of sigh or tear,
Ne'er shalt thou have joy of me.
Never shalt thou win me; still
Am I held in evil will
Of thy father and thy kin,
Therefore must I cross the sea,
And another land must win."
Then she cut her curls of gold,
Cast them in the dungeon hold,
Aucassin doth clasp them there,
Kissed the curls that were so fair,
Them doth in his bosom bear,
Then he wept, even as of old,
All for his love!

Then say they, speak they, tell they the Tale:

When Aucassin heard Nicolete say that she would pass into a far country, he was all in wrath. "Fair sweet friend," quoth he, "thou shalt not go, for then wouldst thou be my death. And the first man that saw thee and had the might withal, would take thee straightway into his bed to be his leman. And once thou camest into a man's bed and that bed not mine, wit ye well that I would not tarry till I had found a knife to pierce my heart and slay myself. Nay, verily, wait so long I would not; but would hurl myself on it so soon as

I could find a wall, or a black stone, thereon would I dash my head so mightily, that the eyes would start, and my brain burst. Rather would I die even such a death, than know thou hadst lain in a man's bed, and that bed not mine."

"Aucassin," she said, "I trow thou lovest me not as much as thou sayest, but I love thee more than thou lovest me."

"Ah, fair sweet friend," said Aucassin, "it may not be that thou shouldst love me even as I love thee. Woman may not love man as man loves woman, for a woman's love lies in the glance of her eye, and the bud of her breast, and her foot's tip-toe, but the love of man is in his heart planted, whence it can never issue forth and pass away."

Now while Aucassin and Nicolete held this parley together, the town's guards came down a street, with swords drawn beneath their cloaks, for the Count Garin had charged them that if they could take her they should slay her. But the sentinel that was on the tower saw them coming, and heard them speaking of Nicolete as they went, and threatening to slay her.

"God!" quoth he, "this were great pity to slay so fair a maid! Right great charity it were if I could say aught to her, and they perceive it not, and she should be on her guard against them, for if they slay her, then were Aucassin, my damoiseau, dead, and that were great pity."

Here one singeth:

Valiant was the sentinel,
Courteous, kind, and practiced well,
So a song did sing and tell
Of the peril that befell.
"Maiden fair that lingerest here,
Gentle maid of merry cheer,
Hair of gold, and eyes as clear
As the water in a mere,
Thou, meseems, hast spoken word
To thy lover and thy lord,
That would die for thee, his dear;
Now beware the ill accord,
Of the cloaked men of the sword,
These have sworn and keep their word,
They will put thee to the sword
Save thou take heed!"

Then speak they, say they, tell they the Tale:

"Ha!" quoth Nicolete, "be the soul of thy father and the soul of thy mother in the rest of Paradise, so fairly and so courteously hast thou spoken me! Please God, I will be right ware of them, God keep me out of their hands."

So she shrank under her mantle into the shadow of the pillar till they had passed by, and then took she farewell of Aucassin, and so fared till she came unto the castle wall. Now that wall was wasted and broken, and some deal mended, so she clomb thereon till she came between wall and fosse,[1] and so looked down, and saw that the fosse was deep and steep, whereat she was sore adread.

"Ah, God," saith she, "sweet Savior! If I let myself fall hence, I shall break my neck, and if here I abide, tomorrow they will take me and burn me in a fire. Yet liefer would I perish here than that tomorrow the folk should stare on me for a gazing-stock."

Then she crossed herself, and so let herself slip into the fosse, and when she had come to the bottom, her fair feet, and fair hands that had not custom thereof, were bruised and frayed, and the blood springing from a dozen places, yet felt she no pain nor hurt, by reason of the great dread wherein she went. But if she were in cumber[2] to win there, in worse was she to win out. But she deemed that there to abide was of none avail, and she found a pike sharpened, that they of the city had thrown out to keep the hold. Therewith made she one stepping place after another, till, with much travail, she climbed the wall. Now the forest lay within two crossbow shots, and the forest was of thirty leagues this way and that. Therein also were wild beasts, and beasts serpentine, and she feared that if she entered there they would slay her. But anon she deemed that if men found her there they would hale her back into the town to burn her.

Here one singeth:

Nicolete, the fair of face,
Climbed upon the coping stone,
There made she lament and moan
Calling on our Lord alone
For his mercy and his grace.
"Father, king of Majesty,
Listen, for I nothing know
Where to flee or whither go.
If within the wood I fare,
Lo, the wolves will slay me there,
Boars and lions terrible,
Many in the wild wood dwell,
But if I abide the day,
Surely worse will come of it,
Surely will the fire be lit
That shall burn my body away,
Jesus, lord of Majesty,
Better seemeth it to me,
That within the wood I fare,
Though the wolves devour me there

[1] moat.
[2] distress.

Than within the town to go,
Ne'er be it so!"

Then speak they, say they, tell they the Tale:

Nicolete made great moan, as ye have heard; then commended she herself to God, and anon fared till she came unto the forest. But to go deep in it she dared not, by reason of the wild beasts, and beasts serpentine. Anon crept she into a little thicket, where sleep came upon her, and she slept till prime next day, when the shepherds issued forth from the town and drove their bestial between wood and water. Anon came they all into one place by a fair fountain which was on the fringe of the forest, thereby spread they a mantle, and thereon set bread. So while they were eating, Nicolete wakened, with the sound of the singing birds, and the shepherds, and she went unto them, saying, "Fair boys, our Lord keep you!"

"God bless thee," quoth he that had more words to his tongue than the rest.

"Fair boys," quoth she, "know ye Aucassin, the son of Count Garin de Biaucaire?"

"Yea, well we know him."

"So may God help you, fair boys," quoth she, "tell him there is a beast in this forest, and bid him come chase it, and if he can take it, he would not give one limb thereof for a hundred marks of gold, nay, nor for five hundred, nor for any ransom."

Then looked they on her, and saw her so fair that they were all astonished.

"Will I tell him thereof?" quoth he that had more words to his tongue than the rest; "foul fall him who speaks of the thing or tells him the tidings. These are but visions ye tell of, for there is no beast so great in this forest, stag, nor lion, nor boar, that one of his limbs is worth more than two deniers,[1] or three at the most, and ye speak of such great ransom. Foul fall him that believes your word, and him that telleth Aucassin. Ye be a Fairy, and we have none liking for your company, nay, hold on your road."

"Nay, fair boys," quoth she, "nay, ye will do my bidding. For this beast is so mighty of medicine that thereby will Aucassin be healed of his torment. And lo! I have five sols[2] in my purse, take them, and tell him: for within three days must he come hunting it hither, and if within three days he find it not, never will he be healed of his torment."

"My faith," quoth he, "the money will we take, and if he come hither we will tell him, but seek him we will not."

[1] An old French coin of little value, about one-twelfth of a sou.
[2] sous.

"In God's name," quoth she; and so took fare-well of the shepherds, and went her way.

Here one singeth:

Nicolete the bright of brow
From the shepherds doth she pass
All below the blossomed bough
Where an ancient way there was,
Overgrown and choked with grass,   5
Till she found the cross-roads where
Seven paths do all way fare,
Then she deemeth she will try,
Should her lover pass thereby,
If he love her loyally.   10
So she gathered white lilies,
Oak-leaf, that in green wood is,
Leaves of many a branch I wis,
Therewith built a lodge of green,
Goodlier was never seen,   15
Swore by God who may not lie,
"If my love the lodge should spy,
He will rest awhile thereby
If he love me loyally."
Thus his faith she deemed to try,   20
"Or I love him not, not I,
    Nor he loves me!"

Then speak they, say they, tell they the Tale:

Nicolete built her lodge, of boughs, as ye have heard, right fair and featously, and wove it well, within and without, of flowers and leaves. So lay she hard by the lodge in a deep coppice to know what Aucassin will do. And the cry and the bruit went abroad through all the country and all the land, that Nicolete was lost. Some told that she had fled, and some that the Count Garin had let slay her. Whosoever had joy thereof, no joy had Aucassin. And the Count Garin, his father, had taken him out of prison, and had sent for the knights of that land, and the ladies, and let make a right great feast, for the comforting of Aucassin his son. Now at the high time of the feast, was Aucassin leaning from the gallery, all woeful and discomforted. Whatsoever men might devise of mirth, Aucassin had no joy thereof, nor no desire, for he saw not her that he loved. Then a knight looked on him, and came to him, and said:

"Aucassin, of that sickness of thine have I been sick, and good counsel will I give thee, if thou wilt hearken to me —"

"Sir," said Aucassin, "gramercy, good counsel would I fain hear."

"Mount thy horse," quoth he, "and go take thy pastime in yonder forest, there wilt thou see the good flowers and grass, and hear the sweet birds

sing. Perchance thou shalt hear some word, whereby thou shalt be the better."

"Sir," quoth Aucassin, "gramercy, that will I do."

He passed out of the hall, and went down the stairs, and come to the stable where his horse was. He let saddle and bridle him, and mounted, and rode forth from the castle, and wandered till he came to the forest, so rode till he came to the fountain and found the shepherds at point of noon. And they had a mantle stretched on the grass, and were eating bread, and making great joy.

Here singeth one:

There were gathered shepherds all,   15
Martin, Esmeric, and Hal,
Aubrey, Robin, great and small.
Saith the one, "Good fellows all,
God keep Aucassin the fair,
And the maid with yellow hair,   20
Bright of brow and eyes of vair.
She that gave us gold to ware.
Cakes therewith to buy ye know,
Goodly knives and sheaths also.
Flutes to play, and pipes to blow,   25
    May God him heal!"

Here speak they, say they, tell they the Tale:

When Aucassin heard the shepherds, anon he bethought him of Nicolete, his sweet lady he loved so well, and he deemed that she had passed thereby; then set he spurs to his horse, and so came to the shepherds.

"Fair boys, God be with you."

"God bless you," quoth he that had more words to his tongue than the rest.

"Fair boys," quoth Aucassin, "say the song again that anon ye sang."

"Say it we will not," quoth he that had more words to his tongue than the rest, "foul fall him who will sing it again for you, fair sir!"

"Fair boys," quoth Aucassin, "know ye me not?"

"Yea, we know well that you are Aucassin, our damoiseau, natheless we be not your men, but the Count's."

"Fair boys, yet sing it again, I pray you."

"Hearken! by the Holy Heart," quoth he, "wherefore should I sing for you, if it likes me not? Lo, there is no such rich man in this country, saving the body of Garin the Count, that dare drive forth my oxen, or my cows, or my sheep, if he finds them in his fields, or his corn, lest he lose his eyes for it, and wherefore should I sing for you, if it likes me not?"

"God be your aid, fair boys, sing it ye will, and take ye these ten sols I have here in a purse."

"Sir, the money will we take, but never a note will I sing, for I have given my oath, but I will tell thee a plain tale, if thou wilt."

"By God," saith Aucassin, "I love a plain tale better than naught."

"Sir, we were in this place, a little time agone, between prime and tierce,[1] and were eating our bread by this fountain, even as now we do, and a maid came past, the fairest thing in the world, whereby we deemed that she should be a fay, and all the wood shone round about her. Anon she gave us of that she had, whereby we made covenant with her, that if ye came hither we would bid you hunt in this forest, wherein is such a beast that, an ye might take him, ye would not give one limb of him for five hundred marks of silver, nor for no ransom; for this beast is so mighty of medicine, that, an ye could take him, ye should be healed of your torment, and within three days must ye take him, and if ye take him not then, never will ye look on him. So chase ye the beast, and ye will, or an ye will let be, for my promise have I kept with her."

"Fair boys," quoth Aucassin, "ye have said enough. God grant me to find this quarry."

Here singeth one:

Aucassin when he had heard,
Sore within his heart was stirred,
Left the shepherds on that word,
Far into the forest spurred
Rode into the wood; and fleet
Fled his horse through paths of it,
Three words spake he of his sweet,
"Nicolete the fair, the dear,
'Tis for thee I follow here
Track of boar, nor slot of deer,
But thy sweet body and eyes so clear,
All thy mirth and merry cheer,
That my very heart have slain,
So please God to me maintain
I shall see my love again,
        Sweet sister, friend!"

Then speak they, say they, tell they the Tale:

Aucassin fared through the forest from path to path after Nicolete, and his horse bare him furiously. Think ye not that the thorns him spared, nor the briars, nay, not so, but tare his raiment, that scarce a knot might be tied with the soundest part thereof, and the blood sprang from his arms,

and flanks, and legs, in forty places, or thirty, so that behind the Childe men might follow on the track of his blood in the grass. But so much he went in thoughts of Nicolete, his lady sweet, that he felt no pain nor torment, and all the day hurled through the forest in this fashion nor heard no word of her. And when he saw Vespers draw nigh, he began to weep for that he found her not. All down an old road, and grassgrown he fared, when anon, looking along the way before him, he saw such an one as I shall tell you. Tall was he, and great of growth, laidly[1] and marvelous to look upon: his head huge, and black as charcoal, and more than the breadth of a hand between his two eyes, and great cheeks, and a big nose and broad, big nostrils and ugly, and thick lips redder than a collop,[2] and great teeth yellow and ugly, and he was shod with hosen and shoon of bull's hide, bound with cords of bark over the knee, and all about him a great cloak twyfold, and he leaned on a grievous cudgel, and Aucassin came unto him, and was afraid when he beheld him.

"Fair brother, God aid thee."

"God bless you," quoth he.

"As God he helpeth thee, what makest thou here?"

"What is that to thee?"

"Nay, naught, naught," saith Aucassin, "I ask but out of courtesy."

"But for whom weepest thou," quoth he, "and makest such heavy lament? Certes, were I as rich a man as thou, the whole world should not make me weep."

"Ha! know ye me?" saith Aucassin.

"Yea, I know well that ye be Aucassin, the son of the Count, and if ye tell me for why ye weep, then will I tell you what I make here."

"Certes," quoth Aucassin, "I will tell you right gladly. Hither came I this morning to hunt in the forest; and with me a white hound, the fairest in the world; him have I lost, and for him I weep."

"By the Heart our Lord bare in his breast," quoth he, "are ye weeping for a stinking hound? Foul fall him that holds thee high henceforth! for there is no such rich man in the land, but if thy father asked it of him, he would give thee ten, or fifteen, or twenty, and be the gladder for it. But I have cause to weep and make dole."

"Wherefore so, brother?"

"Sir, I will tell thee. I was hireling to a rich villain, and drove his plow; four oxen had he. But three days since came on me great misadventure, whereby I lost the best of mine oxen, Roger, the best of my team. Him go I seeking, and have neither eaten nor drunken these three days, nor may I go to the town, lest they cast me into prison, seeing that I have not wherewithal to pay. Out of all the wealth of the world have I no more than ye see on my body. A poor mother bare me, that had no more but one wretched bed; this have they taken from under her, and she lies in the very straw. This ails me more than mine own case, for wealth comes and goes; if now I have lost, another tide will I gain, and will pay for mine ox whenas I may; never for that will I weep. But you weep for a stinking hound. Foul fall whoso thinks well of thee!"

"Certes thou art a good comforter, brother, blessed be thou! And of what price was thine ox?"

"Sir, they ask me twenty sols for him, whereof I cannot abate one doit."

"Nay, then," quoth Aucassin, "take these twenty sols I have in my purse, and pay for thine ox."

"Sir," saith he, "gramercy. And God give thee to find that thou seekest."

So they parted each from other, and Aucassin rode on: the night was fair and still, and so long he went that he came to the lodge of boughs, that Nicolete had builded and woven within and without, over and under, with flowers, and it was the fairest lodge that might be seen. When Aucassin was ware of it, he stopped suddenly, and the light of the moon fell therein.

"God!" quoth Aucassin, "here was Nicolete, my sweet lady, and this lodge builded she with her fair hands. For the sweetness of it, and for love of her, will I alight, and rest here this night long."

He drew forth his foot from the stirrup to alight, and the steed was great and tall. He dreamed so much on Nicolete his right sweet lady, that he slipped on a stone, and drave his shoulder out of its place. Then knew he that he was hurt sore, natheless he bore him with what force he might, and fastened with the other hand the mare's son to a thorn. Then turned he on his side, and crept backwise into the lodge of boughs. And he looked through a gap in the lodge and saw the stars in heaven, and one that was brighter than the rest; so began he to say:

Here one singeth:

"Star, that I from far behold,
Star, the Moon calls to her fold,
Nicolete with thee doth dwell,
My sweet love with locks of gold,
God would have her dwell afar,
Dwell with him for evening star,
Would to God, whate'er befell,

Would that with her I might dwell.
I would clip [1] her close and strait,
Nay, were I of much estate,
Some king's son desirable,
Worthy she to be my mate,
Me to kiss and clip me well,
 Sister, sweet friend!"

So speak they, say they, tell they the Tale:

When Nicolete heard Aucassin, right so came she unto him, for she was not far away. She passed within the lodge, and threw her arms about his neck, and clipped and kissed him.

"Fair sweet friend, welcome be thou."

"And thou, fair sweet love, be thou welcome."

So either kissed and clipped the other, and fair joy was them between.

"Ha! sweet love," quoth Aucassin, "but now was I sore hurt, and my shoulder wried, but I take no force of it, nor have no hurt therefrom since I have thee."

Right so felt she his shoulder and found it was wried from its place. And she so handled it with her white hands, and so wrought in her surgery, that by God's will who loveth lovers, it went back into its place. Then took she flowers, and fresh grass, and leaves green, and bound these herbs on the hurt with a strip of her smock, and he was all healed.

"Aucassin," saith she, "fair sweet love, take counsel what thou wilt do. If thy father let search this forest tomorrow, and men find me here, they will slay me, come to thee what will."

"Certes, fair sweet love, therefore should I sorrow heavily, but, an if I may, never shall they take thee."

Anon gat he on his horse, and his lady before him, kissing and clipping her, and so rode they at adventure.

Here one singeth:

Aucassin the frank, the fair,
Aucassin of the yellow hair,
Gentle knight, and true lover,
From the forest doth he fare,
Holds his love before him there,
Kissing cheek, and chin, and eyes,
But she spake in sober wise,
"Aucassin, true love and fair,
To what land do we repair?"
Sweet my love, I take no care,
Thou art with me everywhere!
So they pass the woods and downs,
Pass the villages and towns,

[1] embrace.

Hills and dales and open land,
Came at dawn to the sea sand,
Lighted down upon the strand,
Beside the sea.

Then say they, speak they, tell they the Tale:

Aucassin lighted down and his love, as ye have heard sing. He held his horse by the bridle, and his lady by the hands; so went they along the sea shore, and on the sea they saw a ship, and he called unto the sailors, and they came to him. Then held he such speech with them, that he and his lady were brought aboard that ship, and when they were on the high sea, behold a mighty wind and tyrannous arose, marvelous and great, and drave them from land to land, till they came unto a strange country, and won the haven of the castle of Torelore. Then asked they what this land might be, and men told them that it was the country of the King of Torelore. Then he asked what manner of man was he, and was there war afoot, and men said,

"Yea, and mighty!"

Therewith took he farewell of the merchants, and they commended him to God. Anon Aucassin mounted his horse, with his sword girt, and his lady before him, and rode at adventure till he was come to the castle. Then asked he where the King was, and they said that he was in childbed.

"Then where is his wife?"

And they told him she was with the host, and had led with her all the force of that country.

Now when Aucassin heard that saying, he made great marvel, and came into the castle, and lighted down, he and his lady, and his lady held his horse. Right so went he up into the castle, with his sword girt, and fared hither and thither till he came to the chamber where the King was lying.

Here one singeth:

Aucassin the courteous knight
To the chamber went forthright,
To the bed with linen dight
Even where the King was laid.
There he stood by him and said:
"Fool, what makst thou here abed?"
Quoth the King: "I am brought to bed
Of a fair son, and anon
When my month is over and gone,
And my healing fairly done,
To the Minister will I fare
And will do my churching there,
As my father did repair.
Then will sally forth to war,
Then will drive my foes afar
From my countrie!"

Then speak they, say they, tell they the Tale:

When Aucassin heard the King speak on this wise, he took all the sheets that covered him, and threw them all abroad about the chamber. Then saw he behind him a cudgel, and caught it into his hand, and turned, and took the King, and beat him till he was well-nigh dead.

"Ha! fair sir," quoth the King, "what would you with me? Art thou beside thyself, that beatest me in mine own house?"

"By God's heart," quoth Aucassin, "thou ill son of an ill wench, I will slay thee if thou swear not that never shall any man in all thy land lie in of child henceforth for ever."

So he did that oath, and when he had done it,

"Sir," said Aucassin, "bring me now where thy wife is with the host."

"Sir, with good will," quoth the King.

He mounted his horse, and Aucassin gat on his own, and Nicolete abode in the Queen's chamber. Anon rode Aucassin and the King even till they came to that place where the Queen was, and lo! men were warring with baked apples, and with eggs, and with fresh cheeses, and Aucassin began to look on them, and made great marvel.

Here singeth one:

Aucassin his horse doth stay,
From the saddle watched the fray,
All the stour and fierce array;
Right fresh cheeses carried they,
Apples baked, and mushrooms gray,
Whoso splasheth most the ford
He is master called and lord.
Aucassin doth gaze awhile,
Then began to laugh and smile
And made game.

Then speak they, say they, tell they the Tale:

When Aucassin beheld these marvels, he came to the King, and said, "Sir, be these thine enemies?"

"Yea, Sir," quoth the King.

"And will ye that I should avenge you of them?"

"Yea," quoth he, "with all my heart."

Then Aucassin put hand to sword, and hurled among them, and began to smite to the right hand and the left, and slew many of them. And when the King saw that he slew them, he caught at his bridle and said,

"Ha! fair sir, slay them not in such wise."

"How," quoth Aucassin, "will ye not that I should avenge you of them?"

"Sir," quoth the King, "over-much already hast

thou avenged me. It is nowise our custom to slay each other."

Anon turned they and fled. Then the King and Aucassin betook them again to the castle of Torelore, and the folk of that land counseled the King to put Aucassin forth, and keep Nicolete for his son's wife, for that she seemed a lady high of lineage. And Nicolete heard them and had no joy of it, so began to say:

Here singeth one:

Thus she spake the bright of brow:
"Lord of Torelore and king,
Thy folk deem me a light thing,
When my love doth me embrace,　　　15
Fair he finds me, in good case,
Then am I in such derray,
Neither harp, nor lyre, nor lay,
Dance nor game, nor rebeck play
　　Were so sweet."　　　20

Then speak they, say they, tell they the Tale:

Aucassin dwelt in the castle of Torelore, in great ease and great delight, for that he had with him Nicolete his sweet love, whom he loved so well. 25 Now while he was in such pleasure and such delight, came a troop of Saracens by sea, and laid siege to the castle and took it by main strength. Anon took they the substance that was therein and carried off the men and maidens captives. 30 They seized Nicolete and Aucassin, and bound Aucassin hand and foot, and cast him into one ship, and Nicolete into another. Then rose there a mighty wind over sea, and scattered the ships. Now that ship wherein was Aucassin, went wan- 35 dering on the sea, till it came to the castle of Biaucaire, and the folk of the country ran together to wreck her, and there found they Aucassin, and they knew him again. So when they of Biaucaire saw their damoiseau, they made great joy of him, 40 for Aucassin had dwelt full three years in the castle of Torelore, and his father and mother were dead. So the people took him to the castle of Biaucaire, and there were they all his men. And he held the land in peace.　　　45

.　　.　　.　　.　　.　　.　　.　　.

Now leave we Aucassin, and speak we of Nicolete. The ship wherein she was cast pertained to the King of Carthage, and he was her father, and she had twelve brothers, all princes or kings. 50 When they beheld Nicolete, how fair she was, they did her great worship, and made much joy of her, and many times asked her who she was, for surely seemed she a lady of noble line and high parentry. But she might not tell them of her lineage, for she 55 was but a child when men stole her away. So

sailed they till they won the City of Carthage, and when Nicolete saw the walls of the castle, and the country-side, she knew that there had she been nourished and thence stolen away, being but a child. Yet was she not so young a child but that 5 well she knew she had been daughter of the King of Carthage; and of her nurture in that City.

Here one singeth:

Nicolete the good and true　　　10
To the land hath come anew,
Sees the palaces and walls,
And the houses and the halls!
Then she spake and said, "Alas!
That of birth so great I was,　　　15
Cousin of the Amiral
And the very child of him
Carthage counts King of Paynim,
Wild folk hold me here withal;
Nay, Aucassin, love of thee　　　20
Gentle knight, and true, and free,
Burns and wastes the heart of me.
Ah, God grant it of his grace,
That thou hold me, and embrace,
That thou kiss me on the face
　　Love and lord!"

Then speak they, say they, tell they the Tale:

When the King of Carthage heard Nicolete speak in this wise, he cast his arms about her neck. 30
"Fair sweet love," saith he, "tell me who thou art, and be not adread of me."

"Sir," said she, "I am daughter to the King of Carthage, and was taken, being then a little child, it is now fifteen years gone." 35

When all they of the court heard her speak thus, they knew well that she spake sooth: so made they great joy of her, and led her to the castle in great honor, as the King's daughter. And they would have given her to her lord a King of Paynim, but 40 she had no mind to marry. There dwelt she three days or four. And she considered by that means she might seek for Aucassin. Then she got her a viol, and learned to play on it, till they would have married her on a day to a great King of Paynim, 45 and she stole forth by night, and came to the seaport, and dwelt with a poor woman thereby. Then took she a certain herb, and therewith smeared her head and her face, till she was all brown and stained. And she let make coat, and mantle, and 50 smock, and hose, and attired herself as if she had been a harper. So took she the viol and went to a mariner, and so wrought on him that he took her aboard his vessel. Then hoisted they sail, and fared on the high seas even till they came to the 55 land of Provence. And Nicolete went forth and took the viol, and went playing through all that country, even till she came to the castle of Biaucaire, where Aucassin lay.

Here one singeth:

At Biaucaire below the tower
Sat Aucassin, on an hour,
Heard the bird, and watched the flower,
With his barons him beside,
Then came on him in that tide,
The sweet influence of love
And the memory thereof;
Thought of Nicolete the fair,
And the dainty face of her
He had loved so many years,
Then was he in dule [1] and tears!
Even then came Nicolete
On the stair a foot she set,
And she drew the viol bow
Through the strings and chanted so;
"Listen, lords and knights, to me,
Lords of high or low degree,
To my story list will ye
All of Aucassin and her
That was Nicolete the fair?
And their love was long to tell
Deep woods through he sought her well,
Paynims took them on a day
In Torelore and bound they lay.
Of Aucassin naught know we,
But fair Nicolete the free
Now in Carthage doth she dwell,
There her father loves her well,
Who is king of that countrie.
Her a husband hath he found,
Paynim lord that serves Mahound! [2]
Ne'er with him the maid will go,
For she loves a damoiseau,
Aucassin, that ye may know,
Swears to God that never mo
With a lover she will go
Save with him she loveth so
  In long desire."

So speak they, say they, tell they the Tale:

When Aucassin heard Nicolete speak in this wise, he was right joyful, and drew her on one side, and spoke, saying:

"Sweet fair friend, know ye nothing of this Nicolete, of whom ye have thus sung?"

"Yea, Sir, I know her for the noblest creature, and the most gentle, and the best that ever was born on ground. She is daughter to the King of Carthage that took her there where Aucassin was taken, and brought her into the city of Carthage,

[1] doleful.   [2] Satan.

till he knew that verily she was his own daughter, whereon he made right great mirth. Anon wished he to give her for her lord one of the greatest kings of all Spain, but she would rather let herself be hanged or burned, than take any lord, how great soever."

"Ha! fair sweet friend," quoth the Count Aucassin, "if thou wilt go into that land again, and bid her come and speak to me, I will give thee of my substance, more than thou wouldst dare to ask or take. And know ye, that for the sake of her, I have no will to take a wife, howsoever high her lineage. So wait I for her, and never will I have a wife, but her only. And if I knew where to find her, no need would I have to seek her."

"Sir," quoth she, "if ye promise me that, I will go in quest of her for your sake, and for hers, that I love much."

So he sware to her, and anon let give her twenty livres, and she departed from him, and he wept for the sweetness of Nicolete. And when she saw him weeping, she said:

"Sir, trouble not thyself so much withal. For in a little while shall I have brought her into this city, and ye shall see her."

When Aucassin heard that, he was right glad thereof. And she departed from him, and went into the city to the house of the Captain's wife, for the Captain her father in God was dead. So she dwelt there, and told all her tale; and the Captain's wife knew her, and knew well that she was Nicolete that she herself had nourished. Then she let wash and bathe her, and there rested she eight full days. Then took she an herb that was named *Eyebright* and anointed herself therewith, and was as fair as ever she had been all the days of her life. Then she clothed herself in rich robes of silk whereof the lady had great store, and then sat herself in the chamber on a silken coverlet, and called the lady and bade her go and bring Aucassin her love, and she did even so. And when she came to the Palace she found Aucassin weeping, and making lament for Nicolete his love, for that she delayed so long. And the lady spake unto him and said:

"Aucassin, sorrow no more, but come thou on with me, and I will shew thee the thing in the world that thou lovest best; even Nicolete thy dear love, who from far lands hath come to seek of thee." And Aucassin was right glad.

Here singeth one:

When Aucassin heareth now
That his lady bright of brow
Dwelleth in his own countrie,
Never man was glad as he.

To her castle doth he hie
With the lady speedily,
Passeth to the chamber high,
Findeth Nicolete thereby.
Of her true love found again   5
Never maid was half so fain.
Straight she leaped upon her feet;
When his love he saw at last,
Arms about her did he cast,
Kissed her often, kissed her sweet   10
Kissed her lips and brows and eyes.

Thus all night do they devise,
Even till the morning white.
Then Aucassin wedded her,
Made her Lady of Biaucaire.
Many years abode they there,
Many years in shade or sun,
In great gladness and delight.
Ne'er hath Aucassin regret
Nor his lady Nicolete.
Now my story all is done,
    Said and sung!

English Popular Ballads

The very nature of the "popular" or "folk" ballad makes it impossible to assign definite dates or authorship to these early bits of literature. They took form, during the fourteenth century or earlier, among a people unfamiliar with written literature. It is generally believed that these primitive verses were of communal authorship, the product of groups gathering together to dance and sing, and that on such occasions the stories of great adventures, of exciting experiences, were gradually fitted to dance tunes, that verse was added to verse perhaps at different times, until both the narrative and the metrical pattern had become fixed in form. Professor Louise Pound has pointed out that it is somewhat ridiculous to assume that man can compose in groups before he does so as an individual, and she insists that single primitive artists were the ballad creators. Sufficient evidence exists both in England and in America to indicate that for hundreds of years these ballads, no matter how they first came into being, have been kept alive orally by generations who have never seen them in print.

The ballad, then, is verse designed for singing or recitation, usually presenting a dramatic or tragic episode in narrative form. Most frequently it is based on love or some great misfortune, on physical courage and adventure, on some domestic episode. The ballad as a type is likely to manifest several or all of the following qualities: simplicity and economy of narrative, abrupt transitions, slight concern for characterization, the use of dialogue, frequent repetition, freedom from moralizing, an interest in the supernatural.

This love of adventure and concern with the past as well as the primitive language in which the the ballads were told explain their popularity as a form of romantic literature.

The ballad was established as a literary genre through the publication in 1765 of Bishop Percy's *Reliques of Ancient English Poetry*, a book which greatly interested the romantic poets and caused them frequently to imitate the old ballad in form and spirit.

SUGGESTED REFERENCE: F. J. Child, ed., *English and Scottish Popular Ballads* (1962).

Edward

1. "Why dois [1] your brand [2] sae drap wi bluid,
          Edward, Edward,
   Why dois your brand sae drap wi bluid,
       And why sae sad gang yee O?"
   "O I hae killed my hauke [3] sae guid,   5
          Mither, mither,

[1] does.   [2] sword.   [3] hawk.

O I hae killed my hauke sae guid,
    And I had nae mair bot [1] hee O."

2. "Your haukis bluid was nevir sae reid,[2]
          Edward, Edward,   10
   Your haukis bluid was nevir sae reid,
       My deir son I tell thee O."

[1] but.   [2] red.

"O I hae killed my reid-roan steid,
          Mither, mither,
O I hae killed my reid-roan steid,   15
  That erst was sae fair and frie O."

3. "Your steid was auld, and ye hae gat mair,
          Edward, Edward,
Your steid was auld, and ye hae gat mair,
  Sum other dule¹ ye drie² O."   20
"O I hae killed my fadir deir,
          Mither, mither,
O I hae killed my fadir deir,
  Alas, and wae is mee O!"

4. "And whatten penance wul ye drie for that,   25
          Edward, Edward,
And whatten penance wul ye drie for that?
  My deir son, now tell me O."
"Ile set my feit in yonder boat,
          Mither, mither,   30
Ile set my feit in yonder boat,
  And Ile fare ovir the sea O."

5. "And what wul ye doe wi your towirs and your
    ha,
          Edward, Edward?
And what wul ye doe wi your towirs and your
    ha,³   35
  That were sae fair to see O?"
"Ile let thame stand tul they doun fa,
          Mither, mither,
Ile let thame stand tul they doun fa,
  For here nevir mair maun⁴ I bee O."   40

6. "And what wul ye leive to your bairns and
    your wife,
          Edward, Edward?
And what wul ye leive to your bairns and your
    wife,
  Whan ye gang ovir the sea O?"
"The warldis⁵ room, late them beg thrae life,   45
          Mither, mither,
The warldis room, late them beg thrae life,
  For thame nevir mair wul I see O."

7. "And what wul ye leive to your ain mither deir,
          Edward, Edward?   50
And what wul ye leive to your ain mither deir?
  My deir son, now tell me O."
"The curse of hell frae me sall ye beir,
          Mither, mither,
The curse of hell frae me sall ye beir,   55
  Sic counseils ye gave to me O."

¹ grief.   ² suffer.   ³ hall.
⁴ must.   ⁵ world's.

Lord Thomas and Fair Annet

1. Lord Thomas and Fair Annet
  Sate a' day on a hill;
Whan night was cum, and sun was sett,
  They had not talkt their fill.

2. Lord Thomas said a word in jest,   5
  Fair Annet took it ill:
"A, I will nevir wed a wife
  Against my ain friends' will."

3. "Gif ye wull nevir wed a wife,
  A wife wull neir wed yee:"   10
Sae he is hame to tell his mither,
  And knelt upon his knee.

4. "O rede,¹ O rede, mither," he says,
  "A gude rede gie to mee;
O sall I tak the nut-browne bride,   15
  And let Faire Annet bee?"

5. "The nut-browne bride haes gowd and gear,
  Fair Annet she has gat nane;
And the little beauty Fair Annet haes
  O it wull soon be gane."   20

6. And he has till his brother gane:
  "Now, brother, rede ye mee;
A, sall I marrie the nut-browne bride,
  And let Fair Annet bee?"

7. "The nut-browne bride has oxen, brother,   25
  The nut-browne bride has kye;²
I wad hae ye marrie the nut-browne bride,
  And cast Fair Annet bye."

8. "Her oxen may dye i the house, billie,
  And her kye into the byre,³   30
And I sall hae nothing to mysell
  Bot a fat fadge⁴ by the fyre."

9. And he has till his sister gane:
  "Now, sister, rede ye mee;
O sall I marrie the nut-browne bride,   35
  And set Fair Annet free?"

10. "I'se rede ye tak Fair Annet, Thomas,
  And let the browne bride alane;
Lest ye sould sigh, and say, Alace,
  What is this we brought hame!"   40

11. "No, I will tak my mither's counsel,
  And marrie me owt o hand;

¹ advice.   ² cattle.   ³ barn.   ⁴ woman.

And I will tak the nut-browne bride,
Fair Annet may leive the land."

12. Up then rose Fair Annet's father,   45
Twa hours or it wer day,
And he is gane into the bower
Wherein Fair Annet lay.

13. "Rise up, rise up, Fair Annet," he says,
"Put on your silken sheene;[1]   50
Let us gae to St. Marie's kirke,
And see that rich weddeen."

14. "My maides, gae to my dressing-roome,
And dress to me my hair;
Whaireir yee laid a plait before   55
See yee lay ten times mair.

15. "My maids, gae to my dressing-room,
And dress to me my smock;
The one half is o the holland[2] fine,
The other o needle-work."   60

16. The horse Fair Annet rade upon,
He amblit like the wind;
Wi siller he was shod before,
Wi burning gowd[3] behind.

17. Four and twenty siller bells   65
Wer a' tyed till his mane,
And yae tift[4] o the norland wind,
They tinkled ane by ane.

18. Four and twenty gay gude knichts
Rade by Fair Annet's side,   70
And four and twenty fair ladies,
As gin she had bin a bride.

19. And whan she cam to Marie's kirk,
She sat on Marie's stean;[5]
The cleading[6] that Fair Annet had on   75
It skinkled[7] in their een.

20. And whan she cam into the kirk,
She shimmerd like the sun;
The belt that was about her waist
Was a' wi pearles bedone.   80

21. She sat her by the nut-browne bride,
And her een they wer sae clear,
Lord Thomas he clean forgat the bride,
Whan Fair Annet drew near.

22. He had a rose into his hand,   85
He gae it kisses three,

And reaching by the nut-browne bride,
Laid it on Fair Annet's knee.

23. Up than spak the nut-browne bride,
She spak wi meikle[1] spite: 90
"And whair gat ye that rose-water,
That does mak yee sae white?"

24. "O I did get the rose-water
Whair ye wull neir get nane,
For I did get that very rose-water   95
Into my mither's wame."[2]

25. The bride she drew a long bodkin
Frae out her gay head-gear,
And strake Fair Annet unto the heart,
That word spak nevir mair.   100

26. Lord Thomas he saw Fair Annet wex pale,
And marvelit what mote bee;
But whan he saw her dear heart's blude,
A' wood-wroth[3] wexed hee.

27. He drew his dagger, that was sae sharp,   105
That was sae sharp and meet,[4]
And drave it into the nut-browne bride,
That fell deid at his feit.

28. "Now stay for me, dear Annet," he sed,
"Now stay, my dear," he cry'd;   110
Then strake the dagger untill his heart,
And fell deid by her side.

29. Lord Thomas was buried without kirkwa,[5]
Fair Annet within the quiere,
And o the tane thair grew a birk,[6]   115
The other a bonny briere.[7]

30. And ay they grew, and ay they threw,
As they wad faine be neare;
And by this ye may ken right weil
They were twa luvers deare.   120

Lamkin

1. It's Lamkin was a mason good
as ever built wi stane;
He built Lord Wearie's castle,
but payment got he nane.

[1] finery.   [2] a kind of linen.   [3] gold.
[4] a whiff.   [5] stone.   [6] clothing.   [7] sparkled.

[1] much.   [2] womb.
[3] mad, angry.   [4] straight.
[5] outside the walled churchyard; as a suicide he could not be buried within.
[6] birch.   [7] briar.

2. "O pay me, Lord Wearie,   5
      come, pay me my fee:"
   "I canna pay you, Lamkin,
      for I maun gang oer the sea."

3. "O pay me now, Lord Wearie,
      come, pay me out o hand:"   10
   "I canna pay you, Lamkin,
      unless I sell my land."

4. "O gin ye winna pay me,
      I here sall mak a vow,
   Before that ye come hame again,   15
      ye sall hae cause to rue."

5. Lord Wearie got a bonny ship,
      to sail the saut sea faem;
   Bade his lady weel the castle keep,
      ay till he should come hame.   20

6. But the nourice [1] was a fause limmer [2]
      as eer hung on a tree;
   She laid a plot wi Lamkin,
      whan her lord was oer the sea.

7. She laid a plot wi Lamkin,   25
      when the servants were awa,
   Loot [3] him in at a little shot-window,
      and brought him to the ha.

8. "O whare's a' the men o this house,
      that ca me Lamkin?"   30
   "They're at the barn-well thrashing;
      'twill be lang ere they come in."

9. "And whare's the women o this house,
      that ca me Lamkin?"
   "They're at the far well washing;   35
      'twill be lang ere they come in."

10. "And whare's the bairns o this house,
       that ca me Lamkin?"
    "They're at the school reading;
       'twill be night or they come hame." 40

11. "O whare's the lady o this house,
       that ca's me Lamkin?"
    "She's up in her bower sewing,
       but we soon can bring her down."

12. Then Lamkin's tane a sharp knife,   45
       that hang down by his gaire,[4]
    And he has gien the bonny babe
       a deep wound and a sair.

13. Then Lamkin he rocked,
       and the fause nourice sang,   50
    Till frae ilkae bore [1] o the cradle
       the red blood out sprang.

14. Then out it spak the lady,
       as she stood on the stair:
    "What ails my bairn, nourice,   55
       that he's greeting [2] sae sair?

15. O still my bairn nourice,
       O still him with the pap!"
    "He winna still, lady,
       for this nor for that."   60

16. "O still my bairn, nourice,
       O still him wi the wand!"
    "He winna still, lady,
       for a' his father's land."

17. "O still my bairn, nourice,   65
       O still him wi the bell!"
    "He winna still, lady,
       till ye come down yoursel."

18. O the firsten step she steppit,
       she steppit on a stane;   70
    But the neisten [3] step she steppit,
       she met him Lamkin.

19. "O mercy, mercy, Lamkin,
       hae mercy upon me!
    Though you've taen my young son's life, 75
       ye may let mysel be."

20. "O sall I kill her, nourice,
       or sall I lat her be?"
    "O kill her, kill her, Lamkin,
       for she neer was good to me."   80

21. "O scour the bason, nourice,
       and mak it fair and clean,
    For to keep this lady's heart's blood,
       for she's come o noble kin."

22. "There need nae bason, Lamkin,   85
       lat it run through the floor;
    What better is the heart's blood
       o the rich than o the poor?"

23. But ere three months were at an end,
       Lord Wearie came again;   90
    But dowie,[4] dowie was his heart
       when first he came hame.

[1] nurse.   [2] rogue.
[3] let.   [4] gore.

[1] crack.   [2] crying.
[3] next.   [4] sad.

24. "O wha's blood is this," he says,
    "that lies in the chamer?" [1]
    "It is your lady's heart's blood;   95
    'tis as clear as the lamer." [2]

25. "And wha's blood is this," he says,
    "that lies in my ha?"
    "It is your young son's heart's blood;
    'tis the clearest ava." [3]   100

26. O sweetly sang the black-bird
    that sat upon the tree;
    But sairer grat [4] Lamkin,
    when he was condemned to die.

27. And bonny sang the mavis,[5]   105
    out o the thorny brake;
    But sairer grat the nourice,
    when she was tied to the stake.

The Twa Corbies

1. As I was walking all alane,
    I herd twa corbies [6] making amane; [7]
    The tane unto the t' other say,
    "Where sall we gang and dine to-day?"

2. "In behint yon auld fail [8] dyke,   5
    I wot there lies a new slain knight;
    And naebody kens that he lies there,
    But his hawk, his hound, and lady fair.

3. "His hound is to the hunting gane,
    His hawk to fetch the wild-fowl hame,   10
    His lady's ta'en another mate,
    So we may mak our dinner sweet.

4. "Ye'll sit on his white hause-bane,[9]
    And I'll pike out his bonny blue een;
    Wi ae lock o his gowden hair   15
    We'll theek [10] our nest when it grows bare.

5. "Mony a one for him makes mane,
    But nane sall ken where he is gane;
    Oer his white banes when they are bare,
    The wind sall blaw for evermair."   20

Sir Patrick Spence

1. The king sits in Dumferling toune,
    Drinking the blude-reid wine:
    "O whar will I get a guid sailor,
    To sail this schip of mine?"

2. Up and spak an eldern knicht,   5
    Sat at the kings richt kne:
    "Sir Patrick Spence is the best sailor
    That sails upon the se."

3. The king has written a braid [1] letter,
    And signd it wi his hand,   10
    And sent it to Sir Patrick Spence,
    Was walking on the sand.

4. The first line that Sir Patrick red,
    A loud lauch [2] lauched he;
    The next line that Sir Patrick red,   15
    The teir blinded his ee.

5. "O wha is this has don this deid,
    This ill deid don to me,
    To send me out this time o' the yeir,
    To sail upon the se!   20

6. "Mak hast, mak haste, my mirry men all,
    Our guid schip sails the morne:"
    "O say na sae, my master deir,
    For I feir a deadlie storme.

7. "Late late yestreen I saw the new moone,   25
    Wi the auld moone in her arme,
    And I feir, I feir, my deir master,
    That we will cum to harme."

8. O our Scots nobles wer richt laith [3]
    To weet [4] their cork-heild schoone;   30
    Bot lang owre [5] a' the play wer playd,
    Thair hats they swam aboone.[6]

9. O lang, lang may their ladies sit,
    Wi thair fans into their hand,
    Or eir they se Sir Patrick Spence   35
    Cum sailing to the land.

10. O lang, lang may the ladies stand,
    Wi thair gold kems [7] in their hair,
    Waiting for thair ain deir lords,
    For they'll se thame na mair.   40

11. Haf owre, half owre to Aberdour,
    It's fiftie fadom deip,
    And thair lies guid Sir Patrick Spence,
    Wi the Scots lords at his feit.

The Dæmon Lover

1. "O where have you been, my long, long love,
    This long seven years and mair?"
    "O I'm come to seek my former vows
    Ye granted me before."

---

[1] chamber.	[2] amber.	[3] of all.	[4] wept.
[5] thrush.	[6] ravens.	[7] moan.	
[8] turf.	[9] neck-bone.	[10] cover.	

[1] broad.	[2] laugh.	[3] loath.	[4] wet.
[5] before.	[6] above.	[7] combs.	

2. "O hold your tongue of your former vows, 5
   For they will breed sad strife;
   O hold your tongue of your former vows,
   For I am become a wife."

3. He turned him right and round about,
   And the tear blinded his ee: 10
   "I wad never hae trodden on Irish ground,
   If it had not been for thee."

4. "I might hae had a king's daughter,
   Far, far beyond the sea;
   I might have had a king's daughter, 15
   Had it not been for love o thee."

5. "If ye might have had a king's daughter,
   Yersel ye had to blame;
   Ye might have taken the king's daughter,
   For ye kend that I was nane. 20

6. "If I was to leave my husband dear,
   And my two babes also,
   O what have you to take me to,
   If with you I should go?"

7. "I hae seven ships upon the sea — 25
   The eighth brought me to land —
   With four-and-twenty bold mariners,
   And music on every hand."

8. She has taken up her two little babes,
   Kissd them baith cheek and chin: 30
   "O fair ye weel, my ain two babes,
   For I'll never see you again."

9. She set her foot upon the ship,
   No mariners could she behold;
   But the sails were o the taffetie, 35
   And the masts o the beaten gold.

10. She had not saild a league, a league,
    A league but barely three,
    When dismal grew his countenance,
    And drumlie [1] grew his ee. 40

11. They had not saild a league, a league,
    A league but barely three,
    Until she espied his cloven foot,
    And she wept right bitterlie.

12. "O hold your tongue of your weeping," says he,
    "Of your weeping now let me be; 46
    I will shew you how the lilies grow
    On the banks of Italy."

[1] sad.

13. "O what hills are yon, yon pleasant hills,
    That the sun shines sweetly on?" 50
    "O yon are the hills of heaven," he said,
    "Where you will never win."

14. "O whaten a mountain is yon," she said,
    "All so dreary wi frost and snow?"
    "O yon is the mountain of hell," he cried, 55
    "Where you and I will go."

15. He strack the tap-mast wi his hand,
    The fore-mast wi his knee,
    And he brake that gallant ship in twain,
    And sank her in the sea. 60

Robin Hood's Death and Burial

1. When Robin Hood and Little John
   Down a down a down a down
   Went oer yon bank of broom,
   Said Robin Hood bold to Little John,
   "We have shot for many a pound." 5
   Hey down, a down, a down.

2. "But I am not able to shoot one shot more,
   My broad arrows will not flee;
   But I have a cousin lives down below,
   Please God, she will bleed me." 10

3. Now Robin he is to fair Kirkly gone,
   As fast as he can win; [1]
   But before he came there, as we do hear,
   He was taken very ill.

4. And when he came to fair Kirkly hall, 15
   He knockd all at the ring,
   But none was so ready as his cousin herself
   For to let bold Robin in.

5. "Will you please to sit down, cousin Robin,"
   she said,
   "And drink some beer with me?" 20
   "No, I will neither eat nor drink,
   Till I am blooded by thee."

6. "Well, I have a room, cousin Robin," she said,
   "Which you did never see,
   And if you please to walk therein, 25
   You blooded by me shall be."

7. She took him by the lily-white hand,
   And led him to a private room,
   And there she blooded bold Robin Hood,
   While one drop of blood would run down. 30

[1] reach there.

8. She blooded him in a vein of the arm,
    And locked him up in the room;
   Then did he bleed all the live-long day,
    Until the next day at noon.

9. He then bethought him of a casement there, 35
    Thinking for to get down;
   But was so weak he could not leap,
    He could not get him down.

10. He then bethought him of his bugle-horn,
     Which hung low down to his knee;   40
    He set his horn unto his mouth,
     And blew out weak blasts three.

11. Then Little John, when hearing him,
     As he sat under a tree,
    "I fear my master is now near dead,   45
     He blows so wearily."

12. Then Little John to fair Kirkly is gone,
     As fast as he can dree;[1]
    But when he came to Kirkly-hall,
     He broke locks two or three: 50

13. Until he came bold Robin to see,
     Then he fell on his knee;
    "A boon, a boon," cries Little John,
     "Master, I beg of thee."

14. "What is that boon," said Robin Hood,   55
     "Little John, [thou] begs of me?"
    "It is to burn fair Kirkly-hall,
     And all their nunnery."

15. "Now nay, now nay," quoth Robin Hood,
     "That boon I'll not grant thee;   60
    I never hurt woman in all my life,
     Nor men in woman's company.

16. "I never hurt fair maid in all my time,
     Nor at mine end shall it be;
    But give me my bent bow in my hand,   65
     And a broad arrow I'll let flee;
    And where this arrow is taken up,
     There shall my grave digged be.

17. "Lay me a green sod under my head,
     And another at my feet;   70
    And lay my bent bow by my side,
     Which was my music sweet;
    And make my grave of gravel and green,
     Which is most right and meet.

18. "Let me have length and breadth enough,   75
     With a green sod under my head;

[1] manage.

That they may say, when I am dead
Here lies bold Robin Hood."

19. These words they readily granted him,
     Which did bold Robin please: 80
    And there they buried bold Robin Hood,
     Within the fair Kirkleys.

Bonny Barbara Allan

1. It was in and about the Martinmas[1] time,
    When the green leaves were a falling,
   That Sir John Graeme, in the West Country,
    Fell in love with Barbara Allan.

2. He sent his man down through the town   5
    To the place where she was dwelling:
   "O haste and come to my master dear,
    Gin[2] ye be Barbara Allan."

3. O hooly, hooly rose she up,
    To the place where he was lying,   10
   And when she drew the curtain by,
    "Young man, I think you're dying."

4. "O it's I'm sick, and very, very sick,
    And 'tis a' for Barbara Allan";
   "O the better for me ye's never be,   15
    Tho your heart's blood were a spilling.

5. "O dinna ye mind, young man," said she,
    "When ye was in the tavern a drinking,
   That ye made the healths gae round and round,
    And slighted Barbara Allan?"   20

6. He turned his face unto the wall,
    And death was with him dealing:
   "Adieu, adieu, my dear friends all,
    And be kind to Barbara Allan."

7. And slowly, slowly raise she up,   25
    And slowly, slowly left him,
   And sighing said she coud not stay,
    Since death of life had reft him.

8. She had not gane a mile but twa,
    When she heard the dead-bell ringing,   30
   And every jow that the dead-bell geid,
    It cry'd, Woe to Barbara Allan!

9. "Oh mother, mother, make my bed!
    O make it saft and narrow!
   Since my love died for me today,   35
    I'll die for him tomorrow."

[1] A festival honoring St. Martin of France; November 11.
[2] if.

Dante Alighieri · 1265-1321

Dante was born in 1265 into a respectable family of rank residing in the city of Florence. Educated first by Dominican monks and later in a Franciscan school, Dante appears to have made an intensive study of the Provençal and early French poets and as a young man to have written many a line of love poetry. Despite the conventionalized portraits of the poet crowned with a wreath, and the sentimental impression most people have of him mooning his life away in love for a scornful Beatrice, Dante spent much of his career amidst intrigue and warfare and was, for some years at least, a man of action. The long struggle between the papal party (the Guelfs) and the imperial party (the Ghibellines) was nominally over, but Florence in the aftermath of this strife was divided into local factions known as the Whites and the Blacks. As one party gained power and then another, exile and murder claimed many of Dante's friends and acquaintances. In one of the battles, that of Campaldino, Dante took part. This practical side of his nature was recognized by his appointment as a Prior, one of six serving as magistrates for the republic. Moreover he went on ambassadorial missions for his city. While absent on one of these missions in 1302 he was, as a White, exiled from the city and never went back, though thirteen years later he was invited to return if he would subscribe to certain humiliating conditions. Something of the quality of his temper is manifest in his refusal, made on the ground that he preferred to watch the sun and stars and meditate on the truths of philosophy with honor than return under such dishonorable terms to Florence. The rest of his life was spent in various cities of Italy — Verona, Bologna, Padua — and it is possible that he spent some time in Paris. He died in 1321 in Ravenna.

Only a few details of Beatrice's life are known, and those are given by Dante himself. He met her only on rare occasions: once when he was nine years old, once again at eighteen, and once when, in a party of ladies, she ridiculed his affection. What should be understood is that in the Florence of his time the theory of courtly love, transmitted by the poets of France, had built up a strong literary convention which idealized and etherealized woman. Much of Dante's portrayal of Beatrice is but a following of this convention. Thus transformed by the spirit of the times, the Beatrice who scarcely knew Dante, who married a wealthy banker, and who died when the poet was twenty-five, became a creation of Dante's mind, a spiritualized, intellectualized love, which left Dante free to marry (about the time of the death of Beatrice) Gemma Donati, and to rear a family of three or four children.

In addition to numerous love poems, sonnets, and "ballata," Dante is the author of the *Vita Nuova* (*New Life*) which has to do with his life as a young man and his love for Beatrice, the *Convivio* (*Banquet*) which though never finished was planned as a text on universal knowledge, *De Monarchia*, a treatise on politics and government, *De Vulgari Eloquentia*, a defense of the use of Italian as a literary language, and *The Divine Comedy*.

SUGGESTED REFERENCES: Paget Toynbee, *Dante Alighieri, His Life and Works* (5th ed., 1965); John Freccero, ed., *Dante. A Collection of Critical Essays* (1965); Mark Musa, ed., *Essays on Dante* (1965).

The Divine Comedy

Dante called his greatest work simply the *Commedia* or *Comedy*. The qualifying adjective *divine* was added to the title by later admirers. The work is a comedy only in the sense that it ends happily, that is, with Dante's ascent into Paradise and the promise of man's salvation. The shifting scenes of the poem represent the respective states of the human soul after death as they correspond to man's moral attitude in life. The souls our poet meets in the numerous circles of Hell, Purgatory, and Paradise are punished in strict accordance with their transgressions, physical or spiritual, on earth. The arrangement of the circles to which they are assigned is based on Aristotle's scheme of virtues and vices as it is developed in his *Ethics;* to each virtue are opposed two vices, the extremes or excesses, to which that virtue is the mean. In the spiritual realm beyond the grave the sins are reproduced and inflicted upon the sinners themselves. The souls, thus suffering and hoping for expiation, are well informed about the nature of their crimes; theirs is an almost prophetic lucidity, past and future being open to their vision and only the historical present remaining unintelligible. Their curiosity to hear about contemporary Italian life gives rise to a number of topical conversations in the course of which Dante finds occasion to comment upon and to deplore the political and moral state of affairs.

As the miserable souls are consoled and their pain relieved by the conversation with the poet, Dante is instructed in the ways of God and men, in the retribution which God ordains for man's spiritual corruption and in the purgation enacted in the time of suspension between death and the Last Judgment. Through pity and terror — the Aristotelian categories — the poet is purged from his own impure inclinations, and we, suffering and rejoicing with him, are made to experience the religious and moral beauty of a pure and uncorrupted life on earth.

In *The Divine Comedy* we have not only a fictitious narrative, or an action — Dante's journey measured by the encounters or stations on his way — but also an allegorical account of man's spiritual life and a poetic vehicle of moral instruction. "Taken literally," Dante wrote to a contemporary, "the subject (of *The Divine Comedy*) is the state of the soul after death, simply considered. But allegorically taken, its subject is man, according as by his good or ill deserts he renders himself liable to the reward or punishment of Justice." And the full significance of the poem does not begin to show until the reader gets at least a clue to this underlying meaning. Thus in the first few lines of the *Inferno* Dante meets with a leopard, a lion, and a wolf in a wood where he had lost the "right way." The leopard may be understood to represent the temptations of the flesh, cupidity; the lion to stand for pride; the wolf to imply avarice and perhaps lust; while the wood itself may signify worldly cares. Almost every line, every detail which Dante presents thus has a double meaning. Virgil, as guide to Dante, stands for philosophy and natural religion just as Beatrice, taken allegorically,

perhaps represents theology or revealed religion. The poet's skill of organization is nowhere better shown than in this interweaving of narrative and allegory.

The translation by Charles Eliot Norton is reprinted here by permission of Houghton Mifflin Company. Notes marked with an *N* are also Professor Norton's.

Hell

CANTO I

Dante, astray in a wood, reaches the foot of a hill which he begins to ascend; he is hindered by three beasts; he turns back and is met by Virgil, who proposes to guide him into the eternal world.

Midway upon the journey of our life I found myself in a dark wood, where the right way was lost.[1] Ah! how hard a thing it is to tell what this wild and rough and difficult wood was, which in thought renews my fear! So bitter is it that death is little more. But in order to treat of the good that I found in it, I will tell of the other things that I saw there.

I cannot well report how I entered it, so full was I of slumber at that moment when I abandoned the true way. But after I had reached the foot of a hill,[2] where that valley ended which had pierced my heart with fear, I looked upward, and saw its shoulders clothed already with the rays of the planet[3] which leads man aright along every path. Then was the fear a little quieted which had lasted in the lake of my heart through the night that I had passed so piteously. And even as one who with spent breath, issued forth from the sea upon the shore, turns to the perilous water and gazes, so did my mind, which still was flying, turn back to look again upon the pass which never left person alive.[4]

[1] The action of the poem begins on the night before Good Friday of the year 1300, as we learn from Canto xxi. 112–114. Dante was thirty-five years old, midway on the road of life, or, as he says in the *Convito*, iv. 24, 30, at "the summit of the arch of life." The dark wood is the forest of the world of sense, "the erroneous wood of this life," that is, the wood in which man loses his way. *N.*

[2] The hill is the type of the true course of life, opposed to the false course in the wood of the valley. The man conscious of having lost his moral way, alarmed for his soul, seeks to escape from the sin and cares in which he is involved, by ascending the hill of virtue whose summit is "lighted by dayspring from on high." *N.*

[3] According to the Ptolemaic system the sun was a planet. *N.*

[4] The pass is the dangerous road through the dark wood, "the end whereof are the ways of death," for he who walks therein is "dead in trespasses and sins." *N.*

After I had rested a little my weary body, I again took my way along the desert slope,[1] so that the firm foot was always the lower. And lo! almost at the beginning of the steep a she-leopard,[2] light and very nimble, which was covered with a spotted coat. And she did not withdraw from before my face, nay, hindered so my road that I often turned to go back.

The time was the beginning of the morning, and the Sun was mounting up with those stars that were with him when the Love Divine first set in motion those beautiful things;[3] so that the hour of the time and the sweet season were occasion to me of good hope concerning that wild beast with the dappled skin; but not so that the sight which appeared to me of a lion[4] did not give me fear. He appeared to be coming against me, with his head high and with ravening hunger, so that it appeared that the air was affrighted at him; and a she-wolf,[5] which in her leanness seemed laden with all cravings, and ere now had made many folk to live forlorn, — she brought on me so much heaviness, with the fear that came from sight of her, that I lost hope of the height. And such as is he who gains willingly, and the time arrives which makes him lose, so that in all his thoughts he laments and is sad, such did the beast without peace make me, which, coming on against me, was pushing me back, little by little, thither where the Sun is silent.

While I was falling back to the low place, one who appeared faint-voiced through long silence presented himself before my eyes. When I saw him in the great desert, "Have pity on me!" I cried to him, "whatso thou be, whether shade or real man." He answered me: "Not man; man once I was, and my parents were Lombards, and both Mantuans by country. I was born *sub Julio*, though late,[1] and I lived at Rome under the good Augustus, at the time of the false and lying gods. I was a poet, and sang of that just son of Anchises[2] who came from Troy, after proud Ilion had been burned. But thou, why dost thou return to such great annoy? Why dost thou not ascend the delectable mountain which is the source and cause of all joy?" "Art thou then that Virgil and that fount which pours forth so broad a stream of speech?" replied I with bashful front to him: "O honor and light of the other poets! may the long study avail me and the great love, which have made me search thy volume! Thou art my master and my author; thou alone art he from whom I took the fair style that has done me honor. Behold the beast because of which I turned; help me against her, famous sage, for she makes my veins and pulses tremble." "It behoves thee to hold another course," he replied, when he saw me weeping, "if thou wouldst escape from this savage place; for this beast, because of which thou criest out, lets not any one pass along her way, but so hinders him that she kills him; and she has a nature so malign and evil that she never sates her greedy will, and after food has more hunger than before. Many are the animals with which she wives, and there shall be more yet, until the hound[3] shall come that will make her die of grief. He shall not feed on land or pelf, but wisdom and love and valor, and his birthplace shall be between Feltro and Feltro.[4] Of that low Italy shall he be the salvation, for which the virgin Camilla died, and Euryalus, Turnus and Nisus of their wounds.[5] He shall hunt her through every town till he shall have put her back again in Hell, there whence envy first sent her forth. Wherefore I think and deem it for thy best that thou follow me, and I will be thy guide, and will lead thee hence through the eternal place where thou shalt hear the despairing shrieks, shalt see the ancient spirits woeful who each proclaim the second death.[6] And then thou shalt see

---

[1] Desert, because "narrow is the way that leadeth unto life, and few there be that find it." *Matthew* vii. 14. *N.*

[2] The leopard is the type of the temptations of the flesh, the pleasures of sense with their fair, varied outside seeming. *N.*

[3] It was a common belief, which existed from early Christian times, that the Spring was the season of the Creation.... *N.*

[4] The lion is the type of pride, the disposition which is the root of the sins of violence. *N.*

[5] The wolf is the type of avarice, that covetousness of earthly goods which turns the heart from seeking the goods of heaven, and is the main source of sins of fraud.

The imagery of these three beasts seems to have been suggested by *Jeremiah* v. 6. "A lion out of the forest shall slay them, and a wolf of the evenings shall spoil them, a leopard shall watch over their cities." *N.*

[1] Virgil was twenty-five years old at the time of Cæsar's death, B.C. 44. *N.*

[2] "Æneas, than whom none was more just." *Æneid*, 1. 544. *N.*

[3] After centuries of controversy, it is still doubtful of whom the hound is the symbol. *N.*

[4] No satisfactory explanation has been given of the meaning of "between Feltro and Feltro." *N.*

[5] Camilla and Turnus died for Italy fighting against the Trojans, Euryalus and Nisus died on the Trojan side. Virgil commemorates all them in the Æneid. *N.*

[6] That is, who each by their misery proclaim the torments of the second death. The appelation of "the second death," given to the sufferings endured by the sinners in Hell, is derived from *Revelation* xx. 10, 14; xxi. 8. *N.*

those who are contented in the fire,[1] because they hope to come, whenever it may be, to the blessed folk; to whom if thou wouldst then ascend, there shall be a soul [2] more worthy than I for that. With her I will leave thee at my departure; for that Emperor who reigns thereabove wills not, because I was rebellious [3] to His law, that through me any one should come into His city. In all parts He governs and there He reigns: there is His city and His lofty seat. O happy the man whom thereto He elects!" And I to him: "Poet, I beseech thee by that God whom thou didst not know, in order that I may escape this ill and worse, that thou lead me thither where thou now hast said, so that I may see the gate of St. Peter,[4] and those whom thou reportest so afflicted."

Then he moved on, and I held behind him.

CANTO II

Dante, doubtful of his own powers, is discouraged at the outset. — Virgil cheers him by telling him that he has been sent to his aid by a blessed Spirit from Heaven, who revealed herself as Beatrice. — Dante casts off fear, and the poets proceed.

The day was going, and the dusky air was taking the living things that are on earth from their fatigues, and I alone was preparing to sustain the war alike of the journey and of the woe, which my memory that errs not shall retrace.

O Muses, O lofty genius, now assist me! O memory that didst inscribe that which I saw, here shall thy nobility appear!

I began:

"Poet, who guidest me, consider my power, if it be sufficient, before thou trust me to the deep pass. Thou sayest that the parent of Silvius [5] while still corruptible went to the immortal world and was there in the body; and truly if the Adversary of every ill was courteous to him, it seems not unmeet to the man of understanding, thinking on the high effect that should proceed from him, and on the

who and the what [1]; for in the empyrean heaven he was chosen for father of revered Rome and of her empire; both which (would one say truth) were ordained for the holy place [2] where the successor of the greater Peter has his seat. Through this going, whereof thou givest him vaunt, he learned things which were the cause of his victory and of the papal mantle. Afterward the Chosen Vessel [3] went thither to bring thence comfort to that faith which is the beginning of the way of salvation. But I, why go I thither? or who concedes it? I am not Æneas, I am not Paul; neither I nor others believe me worthy of this; wherefore if I yield myself to go, I fear lest the going may be mad. Thou art wise, thou understandest better than I speak."

And as is he who unwills what he willed, and by reason of new thoughts changes his purpose, so that he withdraws wholly from what he had begun, such I became on that dark hillside: because in my thought I abandoned the enterprise which had been so hasty in its beginning.

"If I have rightly understood thy speech," replied that shade of the magnanimous one,[4] "thy soul is hurt by cowardice, which often-times encumbers a man so that it turns him back from honorable enterprise, as false seeing does a beast when it shies. In order that thou loose thee from this fear I will tell thee why I came, and what I heard at the first moment that I grieved for thee. I was among those who are suspended,[5] and a Lady blessed and beautiful called me, such that I besought her to command. Her eyes were more shining than the star, and she began to say to me sweet and clear, with angelic voice, in her speech: 'O courteous Mantuan soul! of whom the fame yet lasts in the world, and shall last so long as motion continues,[6] my friend, and not of fortune, is so hindered on his road upon the desert hillside that he has turned for fear, and I am afraid, through that which I have heard of him in heaven, lest he be already so astray that I may have risen late to his succor. Now do thou move, and with thy ornate speech and with whatever is needful for his deliverance, assist him so that I may be consoled thereby. I am Beatrice who make thee go. I come from a place whither I desire to return. Love moved me, that makes me speak. When I shall be before my

---

[1] "Contented in the fire," that is, contented in the purifying pains of Purgatory, by which they are made fit for Paradise. *N.*

[2] Beatrice.

[3] Not actively rebellious, but "one who did not duly worship God." See Canto iv. 36. *N.*

[4] The gate of St. Peter is the gate of Purgatory, which is unlocked by the keys of the Kingdom of Heaven that Christ gave to Peter.... *N.*

[5] Æneas was the "parent of Silvius." While still living ("corruptible") he visited the Underworld even as Dante is now doing. See the sixth book of Virgil's *Æneid* in this volume.

[1] It is not strange that God was thus gracious to him, since he was the Father of the Roman people (the Who), and founder of the Roman empire (the What). *N.*

[2] Rome as well as Jerusalem was a holy city, the Empire as well as the Church a divine institution.... *N.*

[3] St. Paul.   [4] Virgil.

[5] In Limbo, neither in the proper Hell nor in Heaven. *N.*

[6] That is: so long as time shall last.... *N.*

Lord, I will often praise thee to Him.' Then she was silent, and thereon I began: 'O Lady of Virtue! through whom alone the human race excels all contained within that heaven which has the smallest circles,[1] thy command so pleases me that to obey it, were it already done, were slow to me. There is no need for thee further to open to me thy will; but tell me the reason why thou dost not beware of descending down here into this centre, from the ample place [2] whither thou burnest to return.' 'Since thou wishest to know so inwardly, I will tell thee briefly,' she replied to me, 'wherefore I fear not to come here within. One need be afraid only of those things that have power to do one harm, of others not, for they are not fearful. I am made by God, thanks be to Him, such that your misery touches me not, nor does the flame of this burning assail me. A gentle Lady [3] is in heaven who feels compassion for this hindrance whereto I send thee, so that she breaks stern judgment there above. She summoned Lucia [4] in her request, and said, "Thy faithful one now has need of thee, and I commend him to thee." Lucia, the foe of every cruel one, moved and came to the place where I was, seated with the ancient Rachel.[5] She said, "Beatrice, true praise of God, why dost thou not succor him who so loved thee that for thee he came forth from the vulgar throng? Dost thou not hear the pity of his plaint? Dost thou not see the death that combats him on the stream where the sea has no vaunt?" [6] Never were persons in the world swift to do their good, or to fly their harm, as I, after these words were uttered, came down here from my blessed seat, putting my trust in thy upright speech, which honors thee and them who have heard it.' After she had said this to me, weeping she turned her lucent eyes, whereby she made me more quick to come. And I came to thee

thus as she willed. I withdrew thee from before that wild beast which took from thee the short way on the beautiful mountain. What is it then? Why, why dost thou hold back? why dost thou harbor such cowardice in thy heart? why hast thou not daring and assurance, since three such blessed Ladies care for thee in the court of Heaven, and my speech pledges thee such good?"

As the flowerets, bent and closed by the chill of night, when the sun brightens them erect themselves all open on their stem, so I became with my drooping courage, and such good daring ran to my heart that I began like a person enfreed: "O compassionate she who succored me, and courteous thou who didst speedily obey the true words that she addressed to thee! Thou by thy words hast so disposed my heart with desire of going, that I have returned to my first intent. Now go, for one sole will is in us both: thou leader, thou lord, and thou master." Thus I said to him; and when he moved on, I entered along the deep and savage road.

CANTO III

The gate of Hell. — Virgil leads Dante in. — The punishment of those who had lived without infamy and without praise. — Acheron, and the sinners on its bank. — Charon. — Earthquake. — Dante swoons.

"Through me is the way into the woeful city; through me is the way into the eternal woe; through me is the way among the lost people. Justice moved my lofty maker: the divine Power, the supreme Wisdom and the primal Love made me. Before me were no things created, save eternal, and I eternal last. Leave every hope, ye who enter!"

These words of obscure color I saw written at the top of a gate; whereat I: "Master, their meaning is dire to me."

And he to me, like a person well advised: "Here it behoves to leave every fear; it behoves that all cowardice should here be dead. We have come to the place where I have told thee that thou shalt see the woeful people, who have lost the good of the understanding." [1]

And when he had put his hand cn mine with a cheerful look, wherefrom I took courage, he brought me within to the secret things. Here sighs, laments, and deep wailings were resounding through the starless air; wherefore at first I wept thereat. Strange tongues, horrible utterances,

---

[1] The heaven of the moon, the innermost of the nine revolving heavens, the nearest to the earth. Through Beatrice, as symbol of the knowledge of the things of God revealed to man, and by reason of man's capacity to receive the revelation, the human race is exalted above all other created things save the angels alone. *N.*

[2] The Empyrean.

[3] The Virgin Mary, the fount of mercy, never spoken of by name in Hell. *N.*

[4] Whether any real person is intended by Lucia is doubtful, but as an allegorical figure she is the symbol, as her name indicates, of illuminating Grace. *N.*

[5] Rachel was adopted by the Church, from a very early period, as the type of the contemplative life.... *N.*

[6] Dost thou not see him in danger of death from the sins that assail him in the flood of human life, a flood more stormy with passion and darker with evil than the ocean with its tempests? *N.*

[1] The ultimate end and felicity of human life is to see God and the truth in him (*S. T. Suppl.* xcii. i); this is the supreme good of the understanding. *N.*

words of woe, accents of anger, voices high and faint, and sounds of hands with them, were making a tumult which whirls always in that air forever dark, like the sand when the whirlwind breathes.

And I, who had my head girt with horror, said: "Master, what is that which I hear? and what folk is it that seems so overcome with its woe?"

And he to me: "The wretched souls of those who lived without infamy and without praise maintain this miserable mode. They are mingled with that caitiff [1] choir of the angels, who were not rebels, nor were faithful to God, but were for themselves. The heavens chased them out in order to be not less beautiful, nor does the deep Hell receive them, for the damned would have some boast of them."

And I: "Master, what is so grievous to them, that makes them lament so bitterly?"

He answered: "I will tell thee very briefly. These have not hope of death; and their blind life is so debased, that they are envious of every other lot. Fame of them the world permits not to be; mercy and justice disdain them. Let us not speak of them, but do thou look and pass on."

And I, who was gazing, saw a banner, which, whirling, ran so swiftly that it seemed to me disdainful of any pause, and behind it came so long a train of folk, that I should never have believed death had undone so many. After I had recognized some among them, I saw and knew the shade of him who made, through cowardice, the great refusal.[2] At once I understood and was certain, that this was the sect of the caitiffs displeasing to God and to his enemies. These wretches, who never were alive, were naked, and much stung by gad-flies and by wasps that were there; these streaked their faces with blood, which, mingled with tears, was gathered at their feet by loathsome worms.

And when I gave myself to looking onward, I saw people on the bank of a great river; wherefore I said: "Master, now grant to me that I may know who these are, and what rule makes them appear so ready to pass over, as I discern through the faint light." And he to me: "The things will be clear to thee, when we shall stay our steps on the sad shore of Acheron."[3] Then with eyes ashamed and downcast, fearing lest my speech might be troublesome to him, far as to the river I refrained from speaking.

And behold! coming toward us in a boat, an old man, white with ancient hair, crying: "Woe to you, wicked souls! hope not ever to see the Heavens! I come to carry you to the other bank, into the eternal darkness, into heat and into frost. And thou who art there, living soul, depart from these that are dead." But when he saw that I did not depart, he said: "By another way, by other ports thou shalt come to the shore, not here, for passage; a lighter bark must carry thee."[1]

And my Leader to him: "Charon, vex not thyself; it is thus willed there where is power for that which is willed; and ask no more." Thereon were quiet the fleecy jaws of the ferryman of the livid marsh, who round about his eyes had wheels of flame.

But those souls, who were weary and naked, changed color and gnashed their teeth, soon as they heard his cruel words. They blasphemed God and their parents, the human race, the place, the time and the seed of their sowing and of their birth. Then, all of them bitterly weeping, drew together to the evil bank, which awaits every man who fears not God. Charon the demon, with eyes of glowing coal, beckoning to them, collects them all; he beats with his oar whoever lingers.

As in autumn the leaves depart one after the other, until the bough sees all its spoils upon the earth, in like wise the evil seed of Adam throw themselves from that shore one by one, at signals, as the bird at his recall. Thus they go over the dusky wave, and before they have landed on the farther side, already on this a new throng is assembled.

"My son," said the courteous Master, "those who die in the wrath of God, all come together here from every land; and they are eager to pass over the stream, for the divine justice spurs them so that fear is turned to desire. A good soul never passes this way; and therefore if Charon fret at thee, well mayest thou now know what his speech signifies."

This ended, the gloomy plain trembled so mightily, that the memory of the terror even now bathes me with sweat. The tearful land gave forth a wind that flashed a crimson light which vanquished all sensation in me, and I fell as a man whom slumber seizes.

[1] Base, miserable.

[2] By him "who made the great refusal" is probably intended Pope Celestine V, who, after having held the papacy for five months in 1294, abdicated.... N.

[3] The river of woe — in Hades.

[1] The boat that bears the souls of the redeemed to Purgatory. Charon recognizes that Dante is not among the damned. The gods and other personages of heathen mythology were held by the Church to have been demons who had a real existence; they were adopted into the Christian mythology, and hence appear with entire propriety as characters in Hell. Charon and other beings of this order were familiar to the readers of the sixth book of the Æneid. N.

CANTO IV

The further side of Acheron. — Virgil leads Dante into Limbo, the First Circle of Hell, containing the spirits of those who lived virtuously but without faith in Christ. — Greeting of Virgil by his fellow poets. — They enter a castle, where are the shades of ancient worthies. — After seeing them Virgil and Dante depart.

A heavy thunder broke the deep sleep in my head, so that I started up like a person who is waked by force, and, risen erect, I moved my rested eye round about, and looked fixedly to distinguish the place where I was. True it is, that I found myself on the brink of the woeful valley of the abyss which collects a thunder of infinite wailings. It was so dark, deep, and cloudy, that, though I fixed my sight on the depth, I did not discern anything there.

"Now let us descend here below into the blind world," began the Poet all deadly pale, "I will be first, and thou shalt be second."

And I, who had observed his color, said: "How shall I come, if thou fearest, who art wont to be the comfort to my doubting?" And he to me: "The anguish of the folk who are here below paints on my face that pity which thou takest for fear. Let us go on, for the long way urges us."

Thus he placed himself,[1] and thus he made me enter into the first circle[2] that girds the abyss. Here, as one listened, there was no lamentation but that of sighs which made the eternal air to tremble; this came of the woe without torments felt by the crowds, which were many and great, of infants and of women and of men.

The good Master to me: "Thou dost not ask what spirits are these that thou seest. Now I would have thee know, before thou goest farther, that these did not sin; and though they have merits it suffices not, because they did not have baptism,[3] which is part of the faith that thou believest; and if they were before Christianity, they did not duly worship God: and of such as these am I myself. For such defects, and not for other guilt, are we lost, and only so far harmed that without hope we live in desire."

Great woe seized me at my heart when I heard him, because I knew that people of much worth were suspended in that limbo. "Tell me, my Master, tell me, Lord," I began, with wish to be assured of that faith which vanquishes every error,[1] "did ever any one who afterwards was blessed go forth from here, either by his own or by another's merit?" And he, who understood my covert speech, answered: "I was new in this state[2] when I saw a Mighty One come hither crowned with sign of victory. He drew out hence the shade of the first parent, of Abel his son, and that of Noah, of Moses the law-giver and obedient, Abraham the patriarch, and David the King, Israel with his father and with his offspring, and with Rachel, for whom he did so much, and many others; and He made them blessed: and I would have thee know that before these, human spirits were not saved."

We ceased not going on because he spoke, but all the while were passing through the wood, the wood, I mean, of crowded spirits; nor yet had our way been long from the place of my slumber, when I saw a fire, which overcame a hemisphere of darkness.[3] We were still a little distant from it, yet not so far but that I could in part discern that honorable folk possessed that place. "O thou who honorest both science and art, who are these, who have such honor that it separates them from the manner of the others?" And he to me: "The honorable renown of them which sounds above in thy life wins grace in heaven which thus advances them." At this a voice was heard by me: "Honor the loftiest Poet! his shade returns which had departed." When the voice had stopped and was quiet, I saw four great shades coming to us; they had a semblance neither sad nor glad. The good Master began to say: "Look at him with that sword in hand who comes before the three, even as lord; he is Homer, the sovereign poet; the next who comes is Horace, the satirist; Ovid is the third, and the last is Lucan. Since each shares with me the name which the single voice sounded, they do me honor, and in that do well."

Thus I saw assembled the fair school of that Lord of the loftiest song who soars above the others like an eagle. After they had discoursed somewhat together, they turned to me with sign of salutation; and my Master smiled thereat. And far more of honor yet they did me, for they made me of their band, so that I was the sixth amid so much wisdom. Thus we went on as far as the light, speaking things concerning which

---

[1] In the lead, in front of Dante. *N.*

[2] The Limbo (Lat. *limbus*, edge, hem, border). *N.*

[3] Such merit as they might have could not secure salvation for them, for only he who receives baptism becomes a member of Christ, and through His merits is freed alike from the fault and from the penalty of original sin. *N.*

---

[1] Wishing especially to be assured in regard to the descent of Christ into Hell. *N.*

[2] Virgil died B.C. 19.

[3] The fire may be the symbol of the partial light afforded by philosophy to the virtuous heathen, whose abode the poets are approaching. *N.*

silence is becoming, even as was speech there where I was.

We came to the foot of a noble castle, seven times circled by high walls,[1] defended round about by a fair streamlet. This we passed as if hard ground; through seven gates [2] I entered with these sages; we came to a meadow of fresh verdure. People were there with slow and grave eyes, of great authority in their looks; they spoke seldom, and with soft voices. Thereon we withdrew ourselves upon one side, into an open, luminous, and high place, so that they all could be seen. There before me upon the green enamel were shown to me the great spirits, whom for having seen I inwardly exalt myself.

I saw Electra with many companions, among whom I recognized Hector and Æneas, Cæsar in armor, with his gerfalcon [3] eyes; I saw Camilla and Penthesilea, on the other side I saw the King Latinus, who was sitting with Lavinia his daughter. I saw that Brutus who drove out Tarquin; Lucretia, Julia, Marcia, and Cornelia; and alone, apart, I saw the Saladin. When I raised my brows a little more, I saw the Master of those who know,[4] seated amid the philosophic family; all regard him, all do him honor. Here I saw Socrates and Plato, who in front of the others stand nearest to him; Democritus, who ascribes the world to chance; Diogenes, Anaxagoras, and Thales, Empedocles, Heraclitus, and Zeno; and I saw the good collector of the qualities, Dioscorides, I mean; [5] and I saw Orpheus, Tully, and Linus, and moral Seneca, Euclid the geometer, and Ptolemy, Hippocrates, Avicenna, and Galen, and Averrhoës, who made the great comment.[6] I cannot report of all in full, because the long theme so drives me that many times the speech comes short of the fact.

The company of six is reduced to two. By an-

[1] The castle is the symbol of the abode of Philosophy, or human wisdom unenlightened by revelation; its seven high walls may perhaps signify the four moral and three intellectual virtues, — prudence, temperance, fortitude and justice, understanding, knowledge and wisdom, all which could be attained by the virtuous heathen. (S. T.)

[2] The seven gates may typify the seven liberal arts of the Trivium and the Quadrivium, by which names the courses of instruction in them were known in the schools of the Middle Ages. The Trivium included Grammar, Logic and Rhetoric; the Quadrivium, Music, Arithmetic, Geometry and Astronomy.... N.

[3] A large falcon.

[4] Aristotle.

[5] Dioscorides, a physician in Cilicia, of the first century A.D., who in his treatise de materia medica wrote of the qualities of plants. N.

[6] The great comment on Aristotle. N.

other way the wise guide leads me out from the quiet into the air that trembles, and I come into a region where is nothing that can give light.

CANTO V

The Second Circle, that of Carnal Sinners. — Minos. — Shades renowned of old. — Francesca da Rimini.

Thus I descended from the first circle down into the second, which girdles less space, and so much more woe that it goads to wailing. There stands Minos horribly, and snarls; he examines the transgressions at the entrance; he judges, and he sends according as he entwines himself. I mean, that when the ill born soul comes there before him it confesses itself wholly, and that discerner of the sins sees what place of Hell is for it; he girds himself with his tail so many times as the grades he wills that it be set down. Always many of them stand before him; they go, in turn, each ot the judgment; they speak and hear, and then are whirled below. "O thou that comest to the woeful inn," said Minos to me, when he saw me, leaving the act of so great an office, "beware how thou enterest, and to whom thou trustest thyself; let not the amplitude of the entrance deceive thee." And my Leader to him: "Wherefore dost thou too cry out? [1] Hinder not his fated going, thus is it willed there where is power for that which is willed; and ask no more."

Now the notes of woe begin to make themselves heard by me; now I am come where much wailing smites me. I had come into a place mute of all light, that bellows as the sea does in a tempest, if it be combated by contrary winds. The infernal hurricane which never rests carries along the spirits with its rapine; whirling and smiting it molests them.[2] When they arrive before its rush, here are the shrieks, the complaint, and the lamentation; here they blaspheme the divine power. I understood that to such torment are condemned the carnal sinners who subject the reason to the appetite. And as their wings bear along the starlings in the cold season in a large and full troop, so did that blast the evil spirits; hither, thither, down, up it carries them; no hope ever comforts them, neither of repose, nor of less pain.

And as the cranes go singing their lays, making in air a long line of themselves, so I saw come, uttering wails, shades borne along by the aforesaid strife. Wherefore I said: "Master, who are these folk whom the black air so castigates?" "The first of

[1] As Charon had done. N.

[2] The storm and darkness are symbols of the tempest of the passions.... N.

those of whom thou wishest to have knowledge," said he to me then, "was empress of many tongues. She was so abandoned to the vice of luxury [1] that lust she made licit [2] in her law, to take away the blame into which she had been brought. She is Semiramis, of whom it is read that she succeeded Ninus [3] and had been his wife; she held the land which the Sultan rules. That other is she [4] who, for love, slew herself, and broke faith to the ashes of Sichæus; next is Cleopatra, the luxurious. See Helen, for whom so long a time of ill revolved; and see the great Achilles, who fought to the end with love.[5] See Paris, Tristan, — " and more than a thousand shades whom love had parted from our life he showed me, and, pointing to them, named to me.

After I had heard my Teacher name the dames of eld and the cavaliers, pity overcame me, and I was well nigh bewildered. I began: "Poet, willingly would I speak with those two that go together, and seem to be so light upon the wind." [6] And he to me: "Thou shalt see when they are nearer to us, and do thou then pray them by that love which leads them, and they will come." Soon as the wind sways them toward us, I lifted my voice: "O wearied souls, come to speak with us, if Another [7] deny it not."

As doves, called by desire, with wings open and steady, come through the air borne by their will to their sweet nest, these issued from the troop where Dido is, coming to us through the malign air, so strong was the compassionate cry.

"O living creature, gracious and benign, that goest through the black air visiting us who stained the world blood-red, if the King of the universe were a friend we would pray Him for thy peace, since thou hast pity on our perverse ill. Of what

[1] Luxury in the obsolete, Shakespearean sense of lasciviousness. N.

[2] Lawful.   [3] Founder of Nineveh.   [4] Dido.

[5] According to the post-Homeric account of the death of Achilles, which was current in the Middle Ages, he was slain by Paris in the temple of Apollo in Troy, "whither he had been lured by the promise of a meeting with Polyxena, the daughter of Priam, with whom he was enamored." N.

[6] These two are Francesca da Rimini . . . and her lover, Paolo, the brother of her husband. . . . Their death, at the hands of her husband, took place about 1285. N.

[7] The name of God is never spoken by the spirits in Hell, save once, in blasphemous defiance, by Vanni Fucci (xxv. 3); nor by Dante in addressing them. N.

it pleases thee to hear, and what to speak, we will hear and we will speak to you, while the wind, as now, is hushed for us. The city where I was born sits upon the seashore, where the Po,[1] with his followers, descends to have peace. Love, which quickly lays hold on gentle heart, seized this one for the fair person that was taken from me, and the mode still hurts me. Love, which absolves no loved one from loving, seized me for the pleasing of him so strongly that, as thou seest, it does not even now abandon me. Love brought us to one death. Cain awaits him who quenched our life." These words were borne to us from them.

Soon as I had heard those injured souls I bowed my face, and held it down so long until the Poet said to me: "What art thou thinking?" When I replied, I began: "Alas! how many sweet thoughts, how great desire, led these unto the woeful pass." Then I turned me again to them, and spoke, and began: "Francesca, thy torments make me sad and piteous to weeping. But tell me, at the time of the sweet sighs, by what and how did love concede to thee to know thy dubious desires?" And she to me: "There is no greater woe than the remembering in misery the happy time, and that thy Teacher knows. But if thou hast so great desire to know the first root of our love, I will do like one who weeps and tells.

"We were reading one day, for delight, of Lancelot, how love constrained him. We were alone and without any suspicion. Many times that reading urged our eyes, and took the color from our faces, but only one point was it that overcame us. When we read of the longed-for smile being kissed by such a lover, this one, who never shall be divided from me, kissed my mouth all trembling. Gallehaut was the book, and he who wrote it.[2] That day we read no farther in it."

While the one spirit said this, the other was so weeping that through pity I swooned as if I had been dying, and fell as a dead body falls.

[*Further progress through Hell reveals to Dante other circles and other punishments reserved for those who are carnal sinners, gluttonous, avaricious, heretical; who do violence to themselves, to others, to God, to Nature, and to Art; who are frauds, seducers, flatterers, hypocrites, etc. On Easter morning Dante reaches Purgatory.*]

[1] A river in Italy.

[2] In the Romance, it was Gallehaut that prevailed on Guenever to give a kiss to Lancelot. N.

Purgatory

CANTO I

The new theme. — Invocation of the Muses. — Dawn of Easter on the shore of Purgatory. — The Four Stars. — Cato. — The cleansing of Dante from the stains of Hell.

To run over better waters the little vessel of my genius now hoists her sails, as she leaves behind her a sea so cruel; and I will sing of that second realm where the human spirit is purified, and becomes worthy to ascend to heaven.

But here let dead poesy rise again, O holy Muses, since I am yours, and here let Calliope [1] somewhat mount up, accompanying my song with that sound of which the wretched Picae felt the stroke such that they despaired of pardon.[2]

A sweet color of oriental sapphire, which was gathering in the serene aspect of the mid sky, pure even to the first circle,[3] renewed delight to my eyes, soon as I issued forth from the dead air which had afflicted my eyes and my breast. The fair planet which incites to love was making all the Orient to smile, veiling the Fishes that were in her train.[4] I turned me to the right hand, and gave heed to the other pole, and saw four stars, never seen save by the first people.[5] The heavens appeared to rejoice in their flamelets. O widowed northern region, since thou art deprived of beholding these! [6] When I had withdrawn from regarding them, turning me a little to the other pole,[7] there whence the Wain [8] had already disappeared, I saw close

[1] Muse of epic poetry.
[2] The nine daughters of Pieros, king of Emathia, who, contending in song with the Muses, were for their presumption changed to magpies. *N.*
[3] "The first circle" is the horizon, to which the clear blue sky extended, its color undimmed by earthly vapors. *N.*
[4] At the spring equinox Venus is in the sign of the Pisces, which immediately precedes that of Aries, in which is the Sun. The time indicated is therefore an hour or more before sunrise on Easter morning, April 10. *N.*
[5] Purgatory is in the southern hemisphere, and "the other" is the South pole. The four stars are the symbols of the cardinal virtues, — Prudence, Temperance, Fortitude, and Justice, — the virtues of active life, sufficient to guide men in the right path, but not to bring them to Paradise. These stars had been visible only in the golden age. *N.*
[6] Allegorically interpreted, these words signify that the virtues of which these stars are the symbols are little practised by mankind, whose abode is the northern hemisphere. *N.*
[7] The North pole.
[8] Ursa Major.

to me an old man alone, in aspect worthy of so much reverence that no son owes more to his father.[1] He wore his beard long and mingled with white hair, like his locks, of which a double list fell upon his breast. The rays of the four holy stars so adorned his face with light, that I saw him, as though the sun had been in front.

"Who are ye that, counter to the blind stream, have fled from the eternal prison?" said he, moving those venerable plumes. "Who has guided you? Or who was a lamp to you, issuing forth from the deep night which ever makes the infernal valley black? Are the laws of the abyss thus broken? or is a new design changed in heaven that, being damned, ye come to my rocks?"

My Leader then took hold of me, and with words, and with hands, and with signs, controlled to reverence my knees and brow. Then he answered him: "Of myself I came not; a Lady descended from Heaven, by reason of whose prayers I succored this man with my company. But since it is thy will that more of our condition be unfolded to thee, how it truly is, mine cannot be that this be denied to thee. This man has not yet seen his last evening, but through his folly was so near thereto that there was very little time to turn. Even as I have said, I was sent to him to rescue him, and there was no other way than this, along which I have set myself. I have shown to him all the guilty people; and now I intend to show him those spirits that purge themselves under thy ward. How I have brought him, it would be long to tell thee; from on high descends power which aids me to lead him to see thee and to hear thee. Now may it please thee to look graciously upon his coming. He goes seeking liberty, which is so dear, as he knows who for it renounces life. This thou knowest; for death for its sake was not bitter to thee in Utica, where thou didst leave the vesture which on the great day shall be so bright.[2] The eternal edicts are not violated by us, for this one is alive, and Minos does not bind me; but I am of the circle where are the chaste eyes of thy Marcia,[3] who in her look still prays thee, O holy breast, that for thine own thou hold her. For her love, then, incline thyself to us; allow us to go on through thy seven realms:[4] I will report this grace from thee

[1] This old man, as soon appears, is the younger Cato, and the office here given to him of warden of the souls in the outer region of Purgatory was suggested by the position assigned to him by Virgil in the *Æneid.... N.*
[2] The garment of the body. The words are interesting as indicating Dante's conviction that Cato, a heathen, is at the Last Judgment to be among the blessed. *N.*
[3] Cato's wife.   [4] The seven circles of Purgatory.

to her, if thou deignest to be mentioned there below."

"Marcia so pleased my eyes while I was on earth," said he then, "that whatsoever grace she wished from me, I did; now that she dwells on the other side of the evil stream,[1] she can move me no more, by that law which was made when thence I issued forth.[2] But if a Lady of Heaven move and direct thee, as thou sayest, there is no need of flatteries; it may well suffice thee that thou ask me for her sake. Go then, and see thou gird this one with a smooth rush, and that thou wash his face so that thou cleanse it from all stain, for it were not befitting to go with eye dimmed by any cloud before the first minister that is of those of Paradise.[3] This little island, round about at its very base, down there yonder where the wave beats it, bears rushes upon its soft ooze. No plant of other kind, that puts forth leaf or grows hard, can there have life, because it yields not to the shocks.[4] Thereafter let not your return be this way; the Sun, which now is rising, will show you how to take the mountain by easier ascent."

On this he disappeared, and I rose up, without speaking, and drew me quite close to my Leader, and bent my eyes on him. He began: "Son, follow my steps; let us turn back, for from here this plain slopes to its low bounds."

The dawn was vanquishing the matin hour, which was flying before it, so that from afar I discerned the trembling of the sea. We went along over the solitary plain like a man who turns to the road which he has lost, and, till he find it, seems to himself to go in vain. When we were where the dew contends with the sun, and, through being in a place where there is shade, is little dispersed, my Master softly placed both his hands outspread upon the grass; whereon I, who was aware of his intent, stretched toward him my tearful cheeks: then he wholly uncovered on me that color which hell had concealed.[5]

We came, then, to the desert shore which never saw man navigate its waters who afterwards had experience of return. Here he girt me, even as pleased the other.[6] O marvel! that such as he

[1] The Acheron.
[2] The law that as one of the redeemed he cannot be touched by other than heavenly affections. *N.*
[3] The first of the angels who do service in Purgatory. *N.*
[4] Of the waves beating on the shore. *N.*
[5] Color which Hell had hidden with its smoke and foul exhalations. Allegorically, when the soul enters upon the way of purification, Reason, with the dew of repentance, washes off the stain of sin, and girds the spirit with humility. *N.*
[6] Cato.

culled the humble plant, such it instantly sprang up again there whence he had plucked it. [1]

CANTO II

Sunrise. — The Poets on the shore. — Coming of a boat, guided by an angel, bearing souls to Purgatory. — Their landing. — Casella and his song. — Cato hurries the souls to the mountain.

The sun had now reached the horizon whose meridian circle covers Jerusalem with its highest point; and the night which circles opposite to him was issuing forth from the Ganges with the Scales which fall from her hand when she exceeds; [2] so that where I was the white and red cheeks of the beautiful Aurora were becoming orange through too much age.

We were still alongside the sea, like folk who are thinking of their road, who go in heart and in body linger; and lo! as, at approach of the morning, Mars glows ruddy through the dense vapors, down in the west above the ocean floor, such appeared to me, — so may I again behold it! — a light along the sea coming so swiftly that no flight equals its motion. From which when I had a little withdrawn my eye to ask my Leader, again I saw it, brighter become and larger. Then on each side of it appeared to me a something, I knew not what, white, and beneath, little by little, another came forth from it.[3] My Master still said not a word, until the first white things appeared as wings; then, when he clearly recognized the pilot, he cried out: "Mind, mind thou bend thy knees: Lo! the Angel of God: fold thy hands: henceforth shalt thou see such officials. See how he scorns human instruments, so that he wills not oar, or other sail than his own wings, between such distant shores. See, how he holds them straight toward heaven, stirring the air with his eternal feathers, which are not changed like mortal hair."

Then, as the Bird Divine came more and more toward us, the brighter he appeared; so that my

[1] The goods of the spirit are not diminished by appropriation. *N.*
[2] Purgatory and Jerusalem are antipodal, and the Ganges or India was arbitrarily assumed to be their common horizon, the Western horizon to the one, the Eastern to the other. The night is here taken as the point of the Heavens opposite the sun, and the sun being in Aries, the night is in Libra. When night exceeds, that is, at the autumnal equinox, when the night becomes longer than the day, the sun enters Libra, which may therefore be said to drop from the hand of night. *N.*
[3] This other white thing was the boat on which stood the glowing angel with his white wings. *N.*

eye endured him not near by, but I bent it down: and he came on to the shore with a little vessel, swift and light, so that the water swallowed naught of it. At the stern stood the Celestial Pilot, such that he seemed inscribed among the blest;[1] and more than a hundred spirits sat within. "*In exitu Israel de Egypto*"[2] they all were singing together with one voice, with whatso of that psalm is after written. Then he made them the sign of the Holy Cross; whereon they all threw themselves upon the strand; and he went away swift as he had come.

The crowd which remained there seemed strange to the place, gazing round about, like one who makes essay of new things. The Sun, who with his bright arrows had chased the Capricorn from mid-heaven,[3] was shooting forth the day on every side, when the new people raised their brows toward us, saying to us: "If ye know, show us the way to go to the mountain." And Virgil answered: "Ye perhaps believe that we are experienced of this place, but we are pilgrims, even as ye are. We came just now, a little while before you, by another way, which was so rough and difficult that the ascent henceforth will seem play to us."

The souls, who by my breathing had become aware that I was still alive, marvelling, became deadly pale. And as to hear news the folk press to a messenger who bears an olive branch,[4] and no one shows himself shy of crowding, so all of those fortunate souls fastened themselves on my countenance, as if forgetting to go to make themselves fair.

I saw one of them drawing forward to embrace me with so great affection, that it moved me to do the like. O shades, empty save in aspect! Three times I clasped my hands behind it, and as often returned with them unto my breast. With wonder, I believe, I painted me; whereat the shade smiled and drew back, and I, following it, pressed forward. Gently it said, that I should pause; then I knew who it was, and I prayed it that it would stay to speak with me a little. It replied to me: "Even as

I loved thee in the mortal body, so loosed from it I love thee; therefore I stay; but wherefore art thou going?"

"My Casella,[1] in order to return another time to this place where I am, do I make this journey," said I, "but from thee how has so much time been taken?"[2]

And he to me: "No wrong has been done me if he who[3] takes both when and whom it pleases him has many times denied to me this passage; for of a just will[4] his own is made. For three months, indeed, he has taken with all peace whoso has wished to enter. Wherefore I, who had now turned to the seashore where the water of Tiber becomes salt, was benignantly received by him.[5] To that outlet has he now directed his wing, because always there assemble there who towards Acheron do not descend."

And I: "If a new law take not from thee memory or practice of the song of love which was wont to quiet all my longings, may it please thee therewith somewhat to comfort my soul, which coming hither with its body is so wearied."

"*Love which in my mind discourses with me,*"[6] he then began so sweetly, that the sweetness still within me sounds. My Master, and I, and that folk who were with him, appeared so content as if naught else could touch the mind of any.

We were all fast and attentive to his notes; and lo! the venerable old man crying: "What is this, ye laggard spirits? What negligence, what stay is this? Run to the mountain to strip off the slough which lets not God be manifest to you."

As, when picking up grain or tares, the doves assembled at their feeding, quiet, without display of their wonted pride, if aught appear of which they are afraid, suddenly let the food alone, because they are assailed by a greater care, so I saw that fresh troop leave the song, and go towards the hillside, like one that goes, but knows not where he may come out: nor was our departure less speedy.

---

[1] Literally, "blessed by inscription;" possibly the meaning is, "that blessedness seemed written on his countenance." *N.*

[2] "When Israel went out of Egypt" — the beginning of Psalm cxiv.

[3] When Aries, in which the sun was rising, is on the horizon, Capricorn is at the zenith. *N.*

[4] It was an old custom, which lasted till the sixteenth century, for messengers, bearing news of victory or of peace, to carry an olive-branch in their hand as a sign of good tidings. *N.*

[1] A musical friend of Dante.

[2] "How has thy coming hither been delayed so long since thy death?" *N.*   [3] The Celestial Pilot.

[4] That is, of the Divine Will. . . . *N.*

[5] The Tiber is the local symbol of the Church of Rome, from whose bosom those who die at peace with her pass to Purgatory. The Jubilee, proclaimed by Boniface VIII, had begun at Christmas, 1289, so that for three months now the Celestial Pilot had received graciously all who had taken advantage of it to gain remission of their sins. *N.*

[6] The first verse of a *canzone* by Dante. . . . *N.*

CANTO III

*Ante-Purgatory. — Souls of those who have died in
contumacy of the Church. — Manfred.*

Although the sudden flight had scattered them
over the plain, turned to the mount whereto reason
spurs us, I drew up close to my trusty companion.
And how should I have run without him? Who
would have led me up over the mountain? He
seemed to me of his own self remorseful. O conscience, upright and stainless, how bitter a sting
to thee is little fault!

When his feet left the haste which mars the
dignity of every act, my mind, which at first had
been restrained, let loose its attention, as though
eager, and I set my face against the hill which rises
highest towards heaven from the sea. The sun,
which behind was flaming ruddy, was broken in
front of me by the figure which the staying of its
rays upon me formed. When I saw the ground
darkened only in front of me,[1] I turned me to one
side with fear of having been abandoned: and my
Comfort, turning wholly round to me, began to say:
"Why dost thou still distrust? Dost thou not
believe me with thee, and that I guide thee? It is
already evening there where the body is buried
within which I cast a shadow; Naples holds it, and
from Brundusium it was taken: if in front of me
there is no shadow now, marvel not more than at
the heavens, of which the one obstructs not the
other's radiance.[2] The Power, which wills not
that how it acts be revealed to us, disposes bodies
like this to suffer torments both of heat and cold.
Mad is he who hopes that our reason can traverse
the infinite way which One Substance in Three
Persons holds. Be content, O human race, with
the *quia*;[3] for if ye had been able to see everything,
there had been no need for Mary to bear child: and
ye have seen desiring fruitlessly men such that their
desire would have been quieted,[4] which is given
them eternally for a grief. I speak of Aristotle
and of Plato, and of many others." And here he
bowed his front, and said no more, and remained
disturbed.

[1] Dante till now has not observed that the spirits
cast no shadow. *N.*

[2] The nine concentric heavens are transparent, so
that the radiance from one passes unobstructed through
the others. *N.*

[3] *Quia* is used here, as often in mediæval Latin, for
quod. The meaning is, Be content to know that the
thing is, seek not to know *why* or *how* — *propter quid* —
it is as it is. *N.*

[4] If mere human wisdom sufficed for attaining to the
knowledge of the things of God, the desires of the
heathen sages whom Dante saw in Limbo, would have
been satisfied. *N.*

We had come, meanwhile, to the foot of the
mountain; here we found the cliff so steep, that
the legs would there be nimble in vain. Between
Lerici and Turbìa[1] the most deserted, the most
secluded path is a stairway easy and open, compared with that. "Now who knows on which
hand the hillside slopes," said my Master, staying
his step, "so that one who goes without wings may
ascend?"

And while he was holding his face bent down,
and was questioning his mind about the road, and
I was looking up round about the rock, a company
of souls appeared to me on the left hand, who were
moving their feet towards us, and seemed not doing
so, so slowly were they coming. "Lift," said I,
"Master, thine eyes; behold on this side those who
will give us counsel, if of thyself thou canst not
have it." He looked at them, and with a relieved
air replied: "Let us go thither, for they come
slowly, and do thou confirm thy hope, sweet son."

That people was still as far, — I mean after a
thousand steps of ours, — as a good thrower would
cast with his hand, when they all pressed up to
the hard masses of the high bank, and stood still
and close, as one who goes in doubt stops to look.[2]
"O ye who have made good ends, O spirits already
elect," Virgil began, "by that peace which, I believe, is awaited by you all, tell us, where the mountain lies so that the going up is possible; for to lose
time is most displeasing to him who knows most."

As the sheep come forth from the fold by ones,
and twos, and threes, and the others stand timid,
holding eye and muzzle to the ground; and what
the first does the others also do, huddling themselves to it if it stop, silly and quiet, and wherefore
know not; so I then saw the head of that fortunate
flock moving to approach, modest in countenance
and dignified in gait.

When those in front saw the light broken on the
ground at my right side, so that the shadow was
cast by me on the rock, they stopped, and drew
somewhat back; and all the rest who were coming
behind did the like, not knowing why. "Without
your asking, I confess to you that this is a human
body which ye see, whereby the light of the sun
on the ground is cleft. Marvel not, but believe
that not without power which comes from heaven
does he seek to surmount this wall." Thus the

[1] Lerici, on the Gulf of Spezzia, and Turbìa, just above
Monaco, are at the two ends of the Riviera; between
them the mountains rise steeply from the shore, along
which in Dante's time there was no road. *N.*

[2] They stopped, surprised, at seeing Virgil and Dante
advancing to the left, against the rule in Purgatory,
where the course is always to the right, symbolizing
progress in good. In Hell the contrary rule holds. *N.*

Master: and that worthy people said: "Turn, proceed before us, then;" with the backs of their hands making sign. And one of them began: "Whoever thou art, turn thy face as thou thus goest on; consider whether in the world thou didst ever see me?" I turned me toward him, and looked at him fixedly: blond was he, and beautiful, and of gentle aspect, but a blow had divided one of his eyebrows.

When I had humbly disclaimed having ever seen him, he said: "Now look!" and showed me a wound high upon his breast. Then he said, smiling; "I am Manfred,[1] grandson of the Empress Constance: wherefore I pray thee, that when thou returnest, thou go to my beautiful daughter,[2] mother of the honor of Sicily and of Aragon, and tell to her the truth[3] if aught else be told. After I had my body broken by two mortal stabs, I rendered myself, weeping, to Him who pardons willingly. My sins were horrible, but the Infinite Goodness has such wide arms that it takes whatever turns to it. If the Pastor of Cosenza,[4] who was set on the hunt of me by Clement, had then rightly read this page[5] in God, the bones of my body would still be at the head of the bridge near Benevento, under the protection of the heavy cairn. Now the rain bathes them, and the wind moves them forth from the kingdom, hard by the Verde,[6] whither he transported them with extinguished light.[7] By their malediction[8] one is not

[1] The natural son of the Emperor Frederick II. He was born about 1231; in 1258 he was crowned King of Sicily. The Papacy was hostile to him as it had been to his father, and Pope Urban IV and his successor Clement IV offered the throne of Sicily to Charles of Anjou, the brother of St. Louis. In 1265 Charles came with a large force to Italy. He was crowned King of Sicily at Rome, he then advanced toward Naples, and in February, 1265/6, routed the forces of Manfred at Benevento. Manfred himself was slain in the battle. N.

[2] Constance, the daughter of Manfred, was married in 1262 to Peter III of Aragon.

[3] That, though I died excommunicated, I am not among the lost souls. N.

[4] The Archbishop of Cosenza, at command of the Pope, Clement IV, took the body of Manfred from his grave near Benevento, and threw it unburied, as the corpse of one excommunicated, on the bank of the Verde. N.

[5] Had he so read the word and the works of God which reveal His infinite mercy, as rightly to comprehend them. N.

[6] By the Verde Dante seems to intend the river now known as the Garigliano, which, for part of its course, formed the boundary of the States of the Church and the Kingdom of Naples. N.

[7] Not with candles burning, as in proper funeral rites. N.   [8] That is, of Pope or Bishop.

so lost that the Eternal Love cannot return, while hope has speck of green.[1] True is it, that whoso dies in contumacy of Holy Church, though he repent him at the end, needs must stay outside,[2] upon this bank, thirtyfold the whole time that he has been in his presumption,[3] if such decree become not shortened through good prayers. See if hereafter thou canst make me glad,[4] revealing to my good Constance how thou hast seen me, and also this prohibition;[5] for here by means of those on earth much may be gained."

CANTO IV

Ante-Purgatory. — Ascent to a shelf of the mountain. — The negligent, who postponed repentance to the last hour. — Belacqua.

When by reason of delights, or of pains which any capacity of ours may experience, the soul is wholly engaged by it, to any other faculty it seems no further to give heed: and this is counter to the error which believes that one soul above another is kindled within us. And therefore, when a thing is heard or seen which may hold the soul intently turned to it, the time goes by, and the man perceives it not: for one faculty is that which listens, and another is that which keeps the soul entire; the latter is as it were bound, and the former is loose.

Of this I had true experience, hearing that spirit and wondering: for full fifty degrees had the sun ascended,[6] and I was not aware of it, when we came where those souls with one accord cried out to us: "Here is what you ask."

The man of the farm, when the grape is growing dark,[7] often hedges up a larger opening with a forkful of his thorns, than was the passage from which my Leader and I behind him ascended alone, when the troop departed from us. One goes to Sanleo, and descends to Noli, one mounts up Bismantova[8] to its summit, with only feet; but here it behoves that one fly, I mean with the swift wings

[1] While life lasts and man may hope by repentance, however late, to obtain forgiveness of his sins. N.

[2] Outside the gate of Purgatory.

[3] This notion of a period of exclusion from Purgatory proper for those who have died in contumacy of Holy Church seems to be original with Dante. The power of the prayers of the good on earth to shorten the period of suffering of the souls in Purgatory is, however, the accepted doctrine of the Church. N.

[4] By securing for me the prayers of the good. N.

[5] The prohibition of entering within Purgatory proper. N.

[6] It was now about nine o'clock A.M. N.

[7] At the time of vintage. N.

[8] These all are places difficult of access. N.

and with the feathers of great desire, behind that guide who gave me hope and made a light for me. We ascended through the cleft rock, and on each side the wall pressed close on us, and the ground beneath required both feet and hands.

When we were upon the upper edge of the high bank, on the open hillside: "My Master," said I, "what way shall we take?" And he to me: "Let no step of thine fall back, always win up behind me on the mountain, till some sage guide appear for us."

The summit was so high that it surpassed the sight; and the mountain-side far steeper than a line from the mid quadrant to the centre.[1] I was weary, when I began: "O sweet Father, turn and regard how I remain alone if thou stay not." "My son," said he, "far as here drag thyself on," pointing out to me a ledge a little above, which on that side circles all the hill. His words so spurred me, that I forced myself on, scrambling after him, until the belt[2] was beneath my feet. There we both sat down, turning toward the east, whence we had ascended, for to look back is wont to encourage a man. I first turned my eyes to the low shores, then I raised them to the sun, and wondered that we were struck by it on the left. The Poet well perceived that I was all bewildered at the chariot of the light, where it was entering[3] between us and Aquilo. Wherefore he to me: "If Castor and Pollux[4] were in company with that mirror which sheds its light up and down, thou wouldst see the Zodiac revolving ruddy still closer to the Bears, if it went not out of its old road.[5] How this can be, if thou wishest to be able to conceive, with collected thought imagine Zion and this mountain to stand upon the earth so that both have one sole horizon and different hemispheres; then thou wilt see, if thy intelligence right clearly heed, how the road which Phaëthon, to his harm, knew not how

to drive,[1] must needs pass this mountain on the one side, and that[2] on the other." "Surely, my Master," said I, "I never saw so clearly as I now discern, there where my wit seemed deficient, that the midcircle of the supernal motion, which in a certain art[3] is called Equator, and which always remains between the sun and the winter, is distant, for the reason that thou tellest, as far from here toward the north, as the Hebrews saw it toward the warm region. But, if it please thee, willingly would I know how far we have to go, for the hill rises higher than my eyes are able." And he to me: "This mountain is such, that ever at the beginning below it is hard, and the more one goes up, behold! the less it troubles him; therefore when it shall seem to thee so pleasant, that the going up will be easy to thee as going down the current in a vessel, then wilt thou be at the end of this path; there mayst thou expect repose from toil: more I answer not, and this I know for true."

And as he ended his words, a voice near by sounded: "Perchance before then thou wilt be constrained to sit." At the sound of it each of us turned, and we saw at the left a great stone, of which neither he nor I had taken note before. Thither we drew; and there were persons who were reposing in the shadow behind the rock, as one through indolence sets himself to repose. And one of them, who seemed to me weary, was seated, and was clasping his knees, holding his face down low between them. "O sweet my Lord," said I, "look at him, who shows himself more indolent than if sloth were his sister." Then that one turned to us and gave heed, moving his look only up along his thigh, and said: "Now go thou up, for thou art valiant." I recognized then who he was, and that effort[4] which was still quickening my breath a little, did not hinder my going to him, and after I had reached him, he scarcely raised his head, saying: "Hast thou clearly seen how the sun drives his chariot over thy left shoulder?"

His lazy acts and his short words moved my lips a little to a smile; then I began: "Belacqua,[5] henceforth I grieve not for thee,[6] but tell me why thou

---

[1] A steeper inclination than that of an angle of forty-five degrees. *N.*

[2] The encircling ledge. *N.*

[3] Dante having his face turned toward the East was bewildered at seeing the sun on his left hand. Aquilo, the north wind, is put for the North. *N.*

[4] Twin sons of Leda and Zeus. As the friends of sailors they were supposed to play about the masts of ships in the form of electric flames in a way to foretell weather conditions. The reference here is to their use to represent Gemini, the third sign in the Zodiac.

[5] If the sun were in the sign of the Gemini, —Castor and Pollux, — which is nearer the constellations of the Bears than Aries, in which the sun now is, it would make the Zodiac ruddy still farther to the north. In Purgatory the sun being seen from south of the equator is on the left hand, while at Jerusalem, its antipodes in the northern hemisphere, it is seen on the right. *N.*

[1] This road is the Ecliptic, the great circle of the Heavens round which the sun seems to travel in his annual course. *N.*

[2] Mount Zion.   [3] Astronomy.

[4] The effort of climbing up to the ledge. *N.*

[5] Belacqua, according to Benvenuto da Imola, was a Florentine, a maker of citherns and other musical instruments; he carved with great care the necks and heads of his citherns, and sometimes he played on them. Dante, because of his love of music, had been well acquainted with him. *N.*

[6] A humorous suggestion that he had feared lest Belacqua might be in Hell. *N.*

art seated here? dost thou await a guide, or has
only thy wonted mood recaptured thee?" And he:
"Brother, what avails the going up? For the bird
of God that sits at the gate would not let me go to
the torments.[1] It behoves that heaven first circle
around me outside the gate, as long as it did in life,
because I delayed my good sighs[2] until the end;
unless, before then, the prayer assist me which
rises from a heart that lives in grace: what avails
the other, which is not heard in heaven?"

And already the Poet was mounting up before
me, and was saying: "Come on now: thou seest
that the meridian is touched by the sun, and on
the shore the night now covers Morocco with her
foot."[3]

[*In the twenty-nine following cantos of the* Purgatory *Dante continues his progress and meets with
spirits not yet admitted to Paradise because of such
faults as delayed repentance, great pride, envy, wrath,
avarice, gluttony, and lust. In this book the poet
develops his idea of free will. Toward the end Dante
meets Beatrice who is to be his guide in Paradise.
He drinks of the water of the River Eunoë and is made
fit to ascend to Heaven.*

In the early cantos of Paradise *Dante discusses
with Beatrice such subjects as the possibility of making amends for broken vows and the fall of man; with
St. Thomas Aquinas the vanity of worldly desires
and the wisdom of Solomon. St. Peter examines
Dante as to his faith, St. John as to his conception of
Love. Beatrice then bids Dante farewell and takes
her place among the spirits in Heaven. We are next
introduced to the Rose of Paradise.*]

Paradise

CANTO XXXI

*The Rose of Paradise. — St. Bernard. — Prayer to
Beatrice. — The glory of the Blessed Virgin.*

In form then of a pure white rose the holy host
was shown to me, which, in His own blood, Christ
made His bride. But the other,[4] which, flying, sees
and sings the glory of Him who enamors it, and the

[1] The angel who sits as porter at the gate of Purgatory would not allow him yet to enter to endure the torments by which his sins were to be purged away. *N.*
[2] Sighs of contrition and repentance. *N.*
[3] Morocco is here taken for the western verge of our
hemisphere, ninety degrees from Jerusalem on the one
hand, and from Purgatory on the other. At noon in
Purgatory, it would be nightfall in Morocco. *N.*
[4] The angelic host.

goodness which made it so great, like a swarm of
bees which one while inflower themselves and one
while return to where their work acquires savor,
were descending into the great flower which is
adorned with so many leaves, and thence rising up
again to where their love always abides. They had
their faces all of living flame, and their wings of
gold, and the rest so white that no snow reaches
that limit. When they descended into the flower,
from bench to bench, they imparted of the peace
and of the ardor which they acquired as they
fanned their sides. Nor did the interposing of so
great a flying plenitude, between what was above
and the flower, impede the sight or the splendor;
for the divine light penetrates through the universe, according as it is worthy, so that naught can
be an obstacle to it. This secure and joyous
realm, thronged with ancient and with modern
folk, had its look and love all on one mark.

O Trinal Light, which in a single star, scintillating on their sight, dost so satisfy them, look down
here upon our tempest!

If the Barbarians, coming from a region such
that every day it is covered by Helicé,[1] revolving
with her son of whom she is fond, when they beheld
Rome and her lofty work, — what time Lateran
rose above mortal things,[2] — were wonder-struck,
I, who to the divine from the human, to the eternal
from the temporal, had come, and from Florence to
a people just and sane, with what amazement must
I have been full! Truly what with it and with the
joy I was well pleased not to hear, and to stand
mute. And as a pilgrim who is refreshed within the
temple of his vow as he looks around, and hopes
some day to report how it was, so, journeying
through the living light, I carried my eyes over the
ranks, now up, now down, and now circling about.
I saw faces persuasive to love, beautified by the
light of Another and by their own smile, and actions
graced with every dignity.

My look had now comprehended the general form
of Paradise as a whole, and on no part had my
sight as yet been fixed; and I turned me with rekindled wish to ask my Lady about things as to
which my mind was in suspense. One thing I purposed, and another answered me; I was thinking
to see Beatrice, and I saw an old man, robed like

[1] The nymph Callisto, or Helicé, bore to Zeus a son,
Arcas; she was metamorphosed by Hera into a bear, and
then transferred to Heaven by Jupiter as the constellation of the Great Bear, while her son was changed into
the constellation of Arctophylax or the lesser Bear. In
the far north these constellations are always high in the
heavens. *N.*
[2] When Rome was mistress of the world and the
Lateran the seat of imperial or papal power. *N.*

the people in glory. His eyes and his cheeks were overspread with benignant joy, his mien kindly such as befits a tender father. And: "Where is she?" on a sudden said I. Whereon he: "To terminate thy desire, Beatrice urged me from my place, and if thou lookest up to the third circle from the highest rank, thou wilt again see her upon the throne which her merits have allotted to her." Without answering I lifted up my eyes, and saw her as she made for herself a crown reflecting from herself the eternal rays. From that region which thunders highest up no mortal eye is so far distant, in whatsoever sea it lets itself sink deepest,[1] as there from Beatrice was my sight. But this was naught to me, for her image did not descend to me blurred by aught between.

"O Lady, in whom my hope is strong, and who, for my salvation, didst endure to leave thy footprints in Hell, of all those things which I have seen through thy power and through thy goodness, I recognize the grace and the virtue. Thou hast drawn me from servitude to liberty by all those ways, by all the modes whereby thou hadst the power to do it. Guard thou in me thine own magnificence so that my soul, which thou hast made whole, may, pleasing to thee, be unloosed from the body." Thus I prayed; and she, so distant, as it seemed, smiled and looked at me; then turned to the eternal fountain.

And the holy old man said: "In order that thou mayst complete perfectly thy journey, for which end prayer and holy love sent me, fly with thine eyes through this garden; for seeing it will prepare thy look to mount further through the divine radiance. And the Queen of Heaven, for whom I burn wholly with love, will grant us every grace, because I am her faithful Bernard."[2]

As is he who comes perchance from Croatia to see our Veronica,[3] who by reason of its ancient fame is never sated, but says in thought, so long as it is shown: "My Lord Jesus Christ, true God, was then your semblance like to this?"[4] such was I, gazing

[1] From the highest region of the air to the lowest depth of the sea. *N.*

[2] St. Bernard of Clairvaux, to whom, because of his fervent devotion to her, the Blessed Virgin had deigned to show herself during his life. *N.*

[3] The likeness of the Saviour miraculously impressed upon the kerchief presented to him by a holy woman, on his way to Calvary, wherewith to wipe the sweat and dust from his face, and now religiously preserved at Rome, and shown at St. Peter's, on certain of the chief holydays. *N.*

[4] The pilgrim, who has long heard of the Veronica and desired to see it, cannot sate his desire in gazing at it, and in his thought says: "This, then, Lord Jesus, is your likeness." *N.*

on the living charity of him who, in this world, in contemplation, tasted of that peace.

"Son of Grace, this glad existence," began he, "will not be known to thee holding thine eyes only down here at the base, but look on the circles even to the most remote, until thou seest upon her seat the Queen to whom this realm is subject and devoted." I lifted up my eyes; and as at morning the eastern parts of the horizon surpass that where the sun declines, thus, as if going with my eyes from valley to mountain, I saw a part on the extreme verge vanquishing in light all the rest of the front.[1] And even as there where the pole which Phaëthon guided ill is awaited,[2] the glow is brightest, and on this side and that the light diminishes, so that pacific oriflamme[3] was vivid at the middle, and on each side in equal measure the flame slackened. And at that mid part I saw more than a thousand jubilant Angels with wings outspread, each distinct both in effulgence and in act. I saw there, smiling at their sports and at their songs, a Beauty[4] which was joy in the eyes of all the other saints. And if I had such wealth in speech as in imagining, I should not dare to attempt the least of its delightfulness.

Bernard, when he saw my eyes fixed and intent upon the object of his own burning glow, turned his own with such affection to it, that he made mine more ardent to gaze anew.

CANTO XXXII

St. Bernard describes the order of the Rose, and points out many of the Saints. — The children in Paradise. — The angelic festival. — The patricians of the Court of Heaven.

With affection set on his Delight, that contemplator freely assumed the office of a teacher, and began these holy words: "The wound which Mary closed up and anointed, that one who is so beautiful at her feet is she who opened it and who pierced it. Beneath her, in the order which the third seats make, sits Rachel with Beatrice, as thou seest. Sara, Rebecca, Judith, and she[5] who was great-grandmother of the singer who, through sorrow for

[1] All the rest of the circumference. *N.*

[2] Where the chariot of the sun is about to rise. *N.*

[3] This oriflamme of peace is the part of the rose of Paradise where the Virgin is seated, and its mid point is the Virgin herself. It is called "the pacific" in contrast with the warlike oriflamme, the banner given by the archangel Gabriel to the ancient kings of France, which bore a flame on a field of gold, whence its name, *aurea flamma. N.*

[4] The Blessed Virgin.   [5] Ruth.

his sin, said *Miserere mei*,[1] thou mayst see thus from rank to rank in gradation downward, as with the name of each I go downward through the rose from leaf to leaf. And from the seventh row downwards, even as down to it, Hebrew women follow in succession, dividing all the tresses of the flower; because these are the wall by which the sacred stairs are separated according to the look which faith turned on Christ. On this side, where the flower is mature with all its leaves, are seated those who believed in Christ about to come. On the other side, where the semi-circles are broken by empty spaces, are those who turned their faces on Christ already come.[2] And as on this side the glorious seat of the Lady of Heaven, and the other seats below it, make so great a division, thus, opposite, does the seat of the great John, who, ever holy, endured the desert and martyrdom, and then Hell for two years;[3] and beneath him Francis and Benedict and Augustine and others are allotted thus to divide, far down as here from circle to circle. Now behold the high divine foresight; for one and the other aspect of the faith will fill this garden equally. And know that downwards from the row which midway cleaves[4] the two divisions, they are seated for no merit of their own, but for that of others, under certain conditions; for all these are spirits absolved ere they had true power of choice. Well canst thou perceive it by their faces, and also by their childish voices, if thou lookest well upon them and if thou listenest to them. Now thou art perplexed, and in perplexity art silent; but I will loose for thee the strong bond in which thy subtle thoughts fetter thee.[5] Within

[1] "Have mercy upon me." *Psalm li.* 1.
[2] The circle of the Rose is divided vertically in two equal parts. In the upper tiers of the one half, far as midway down the flower, the saints of the Old Dispensation, who believed in Christ about to come, are seated. These benches are full. On the corresponding benches of the other half, on which are some empty spaces, sit the redeemed of the New Dispensation who have believed in Christ already come. On one side the line of division between the semi-circles is made by the Hebrew women from the Virgin Mary downwards; on the opposite side the line is made by St. John Baptist and other saints who had rendered special service to Christ and his Church. The lower tiers of seats are occupied by innocent children elect to bliss. *N.*
[3] The two years from the death of John to the death of Christ and his descent to Hell, to draw from the *limbus patrum* the souls predestined to salvation. *N.*
[4] Those who are seated below the row which cleaves horizontally the two halves are children too young to have merit of their own. *N.*
[5] The perplexity was, How can there be difference of merit in the innocent, assigning them to different seats in Paradise? *N.*

the amplitude of this realm a casual point can have no place,[1] any more than sadness, or thirst, or hunger; for whatever thou seest is established by eternal law, so that here the ring answers exactly to the finger. And therefore this folk, hastened to true life, is not *sine causa* more and less excellent here among themselves.[2] The King, through whom this realm reposes in such great love and in such great delight that no will dares for more, creating all the minds in His own glad aspect, endows with grace diversely according to His pleasure; and here let the fact suffice.[3] And this is expressly and clearly noted for you in the Holy Scripture in the case of those twins who, within their mother, had their anger stirred.[4] Therefore, according to the color of the hair of such grace,[5] the highest light must needs befittingly crown them. Without, then, merit from their own ways, they are placed in different grades, differing only in their primary keenness of vision.[6] In the early centuries, indeed, the faith of parents alone sufficed, together with innocence, to secure salvation; after the first ages were complete, it was needful for males, through circumcision, to acquire power for their innocent wings. But after the time of grace had come, without perfect baptism in Christ, such innocence was held back there below.[7]

"Look now upon the face which most resembles Christ, for only its brightness can prepare thee to see Christ."

I saw raining down on her such great joy, borne in the holy minds created to fly across through that height, that whatsoever I had seen before held me not suspended in such great wonder, nor showed to me such likeness unto God. And that Love which had before descended to her, in front of her spread wide his wings, singing "*Ave, Maria, gratia plena.*" The blessed Court responded to the divine song from all sides, so that every countenance became thereby the more serene.

"O holy Father, who for me endurest to be here

[1] No least thing can here be matter of chance. *N.*
[2] It is not "without cause" that these children enjoy different measures of bliss. *N.*
[3] Without attempt to account for it or to seek the "wherefore" of the will of God. *N.*
[4] Jacob and Esau.
[5] ... The argument is, that God imparts grace to one or another according to his pleasure; and as the hair of children differs in color without apparent reason, so the endowment of grace differs in measure for each, and in proportion to this diversity, does the light of Heaven crown them. *N.*
[6] In their innate capacity to see God, which is in proportion to the grace vouchsafed to them before birth. *N.*
[7] In the limbo of children.

below, leaving the sweet place in which thou sittest by eternal allotment, who is that Angel who with such joy looks into the eyes of our Queen, so enamored that he seems of fire?" Thus did I again recur to the teaching of him who was deriving beauty from Mary, as the morning star from the sun. And he to me, "Confidence and grace as much as there can be in Angel and in soul, are all in him, and we would have it so, for he it is [1] who bore the palm down to Mary, when the Son of God willed to load Himself with our burden.

"But come now with thine eyes, as I shall proceed speaking, and note the great patricians of this most just and pious empire. Those two who sit there above, most happy through being nearest to the Empress, are, as it were, two roots of this rose. He who on the left is next her is the Father because of whose audacious tasting the human race tastes so much bitterness. On the right see that ancient Father of Holy Church, to whom Christ entrusted the keys of this lovely flower. And he [2] who saw before his death all the grievous times of the fair bride, who was won with the spear and with the nails, sits at his side; and by the other rests that leader, under whom the ingrate, fickle and stubborn people lived on manna. Opposite Peter see Anna sitting, so content to gaze upon her daughter, that she moves not her eyes as she sings Hosannah; and opposite the eldest father of a family sits Lucia,[3] who moved thy Lady, when thou didst bend thy brow to rush downward.[4]

"But because the time flies which holds thee slumbering,[5] here will we make a stop, like a good tailor who makes the gown according as he has cloth, and we will direct our eyes to the First Love, so that, looking towards Him, thou mayst penetrate so far as is possible through His effulgence.

[1] The angel Gabriel.

[2] St. John, the Evangelist, who in his long life witnessed and suffered from the persecutions which the early Church had to endure.

[3] The introduction of Lucia here is not less enigmatic than the choice of her for the functions which she performs in the other parts of the poems, *Hell*, ii. 97–108; *Purgatory*, ix. 55–63. N.

[4] When in despair of reaching the height thou wert speeding down into the low place. See *Hell*, i. 61. N.

[5] Dante has told us at the beginning of his ascent through the Heavens that he knows not whether he was there in body or only in spirit (Cantos i. 73–75; ii. 37–39). The hint of slumber let fall thus *obiter* in this verse affords, perhaps, the clue to his real conception. The body was lying in apparent physical sleep, while the soul, far from the body, was actually visiting the spiritual world. The journey through Paradise is the type of the deliverance of the soul from captivity to the law of sin, and from the body of this death. N.

But, lest perchance, moving thy wings, thou go backward, believing to advance, it is needful that grace be obtained by prayer; grace from her who has the power to aid thee; and do thou follow me with thy affection so that thy heart depart not from my speech."

And he began this holy prayer.

CANTO XXXIII

Prayer to the Virgin. — The Beatific Vision. — The Ultimate Salvation.

"Virgin Mother, daughter of thine own Son, humble and exalted more than any creature, fixed term of the eternal counsel, thou art she who didst so ennoble human nature that its own Maker disdained not to become its creature. Within thy womb was rekindled the Love through whose warmth this flower has thus blossomed in the eternal peace. Here thou art to us the noonday torch of charity, and below, among mortals, thou art the living fount of hope. Lady, thou art so great, and so availest, that whoso would have grace, and has not recourse to thee, would have his desire fly without wings. Thy benignity not only succors him who asks, but oftentimes freely foreruns the asking. In thee mercy, in thee pity, in thee magnificence, in thee whatever of goodness is in any creature, are united. Now doth this man, who, from the lowest abyss of the universe, far even as here, has seen one after one the spiritual lives, supplicate thee of grace, for power such that he may be able with his eyes to uplift himself higher toward the Ultimate Salvation. And I, who never for my own vision burned more than I do for his, proffer to thee all my prayers, and pray that they be not scant, that with thy prayers thou wouldst dispel for him every cloud of his mortality, so that the Supreme Pleasure may be displayed to him. Further I pray thee, Queen, who canst whatso thou wilt, that, after so great a vision, thou wouldst preserve his affections sound. May thy guardianship vanquish human impulses. Behold Beatrice with all the Blessed for my prayers clasp their hands to thee."

The eyes beloved and venerated by God, fixed on the speaker, showed to us how pleasing unto her are devout prayers. Then to the Eternal Light were they directed, to which it may not be believed that eye so clear of any creature enters in.

And I, who to the end of all desires was approaching, even as I ought, ended within myself the ardor of my longing.[1] Bernard made a sign to me, and

[1] The ardor of longing ceased in the consummation and enjoyment of desire. N.

smiled, that I should look upward; but I was already, of myself, such as he wished; for my sight, becoming pure, was entering more and more through the radiance of the lofty Light which in Itself is true.

Thenceforward my vision was greater than our speech, which yields to such a sight, and the memory yields to such excess.

As is he who dreaming sees, and after the dream the passion remains imprinted, and the rest returns not to the mind, such am I; for my vision almost wholly departs, while the sweetness that was born of it yet distils within my heart. Thus the snow is by the sun unsealed; thus by the wind, on the light leaves, was lost the saying of the Sibyl.

O Supreme Light, that so high upliftest Thyself from mortal conceptions, re-lend to my mind a little of what Thou didst appear, and make my tongue so powerful that it may be able to leave one single spark of Thy glory for the folk to come; for, by returning somewhat to my memory and by sounding a little in these verses, more of Thy victory shall be conceived.

I think that by the keenness of the living ray which I endured, I should have been dazed if my eyes had been averted from it; and I remember that on this account I was the more hardy to sustain it till I conjoined my gaze with the Infinite Goodness.

O abundant Grace, whereby I presumed to fix my look through the Eternal Light till that there I consummated the seeing!

I saw that in its depth is enclosed, bound up with love in one volume, that which is dispersed in leaves through the universe; substance and accidents and their modes, fused together, as it were, in such wise, that that of which I speak is one simple Light. The universal form of this knot [1] I believe that I saw, because, in saying this, I feel that I rejoice more spaciously. One single moment only is greater oblivion for me than five and twenty centuries to the emprise [2] which made Neptune wonder at the shadow of Argo. [3]

Thus my mind, wholly rapt, was gazing fixed,

motionless, and intent, and ever with gazing grew enkindled. In that Light one becomes such that it is impossible he should ever consent to turn himself from it for other sight; because the Good which is the object of the will is all collected in it, and outside of it that is defective which is perfect there.

Now will my speech fall more short, even in respect to that which I remember, than that of an infant who still bathes his tongue at the breast. Not because more than one simple semblance was in the Living Light wherein I was gazing, which is always such as it was before; but through my sight, which was growing strong in me as I looked, one sole appearance, as I myself changed, was altering itself to me.

Within the profound and clear subsistence of the lofty Light appeared to me three circles of three colors and of one dimension, and one seemed reflected by the other, as Iris by Iris,[1] and the third seemed fire which from the one and from the other is equally breathed forth.

O how inadequate is speech, and how feeble toward my conception! and this toward what I saw is such that it suffices not to call it little.

O Light Eternal, that sole abidest in Thyself, sole understandest Thyself, and, by Thyself understood and understanding, lovest and smilest on Thyself! That circle, which appeared in Thee generated as a reflected light, being awhile surveyed by my eyes, seemed to me depicted with our effigy within itself, of its own very color; wherefore my sight was wholly set upon it. As is the geometer who wholly applies himself to measure the circle, and finds not by thinking that principle of which he is in need, such was I at that new sight. I wished to see how the image was conformed to the circle, and how it has its place therein; but my own wings were not for this, had it not been that my mind was smitten by a flash in which its wish came.

To the high fantasy here power failed; but now my desire and my will were revolved, like a wheel which is moved evenly, by the Love which moves the sun and the other stars.[2]

---

[1] This union of substance and accident and their modes; the unity of creation in the Creator. *N.*

[2] enterprise.

[3] The larger joy felt in the mention of what he saw, is proof that it was seen, but the vision so surpassed human faculties, though their power was exalted by grace, that they could not retain it in its completeness, but lost more of it in a single moment, than

any loss which long lapse of time may work for past events.

Neptune wondered at the shadow of Argo because it was the first vessel that sailed the sea. *N.*

[1] As one arch of the rainbow by the other. *N.*

[2] By the grace of God Dante's desire was fulfilled in this vision, and his beatitude perfected in the conformity of his will with the Divine.

Giovanni Boccaccio · 1313-1375

Our reading in the romances of the Middle Ages has made us familiar with tales and ballads which came into being anonymously. Boccaccio drew on this and similar material, but in his stories we find the folk element disappearing and the hand of a single artist consciously shaping the old tales into literary form. The fall of Constantinople and the enthusiasm of the Renaissance were still in the future, but even then Italy was developing a culture and a society of her own.

Boccaccio, like Dante, lived in an Italy torn by political intrigue and struggle. Civil war was often rampant. Freebooting was common. The strongest government was growing up in the cities, in Florence, Venice, Milan, and Naples. Robert of Naples, the leader of the Guelphs, was the King Robert whose daughter Boccaccio courted and glorified as Fiammetta.

Boccaccio was born in Paris in 1313, the illegitimate son of an Italian banker temporarily residing in France. Soon after his son's birth, the father returned to Italy, and the boy was established in Florence. Like so many plans made by parents of children born to literary careers, the father's hope that the young Boccaccio would enter into business, or at least become a student of canon law, went agley. The young man would have neither of these prosaic occupations. And when, at the age of twenty-three, Boccaccio met Maria d'Aquino, a natural daughter of King Robert of Naples, any plans that even the young man might have had for himself were interrupted that he might spend his time and his ingenuity in pursuit of her whom, in his many writings, he calls Fiammetta. His suit was, for a time, successful, but ladies like Maria d'Aquino are distinguished for the ephemeral quality of their affection — and all Boccaccio was left was a memory. This memory the young writer turned into literature; he wrote of Fiammetta as he knew her, recounted the story of his meeting with her, even reversed the process and wrote of the affair from the point of view of the lady. After all, it was something for the son of a banker to have made a conquest of a princess — if even for a few weeks or months.

Giovanni Boccaccio is one of the world's great story tellers. His narrative power, however, lay not so much in his creative imagination, or in his capacity for weaving new plots, as in his facility for taking the old stories of Italy, France, Persia, or India and retelling them effectively in a style often witty and ironical. Perhaps the best testimony to the quality of his writing lies in the fact that such figures as Chaucer, Shakespeare, Dryden, and Keats in England, and Molière and LaFontaine in France, paid Boccaccio the compliment of retelling his tales.

The *Filostrato* and the *Teseide* are intimate books, the first a retelling of the old Troilus and Cressida story (which Chaucer used) and the second an epic poem (also borrowed by Chaucer for the *Knight's Tale*) in the manner of Virgil's *Æneid*. The *Decameron*, by far the most vital of Boccaccio's work, was completed about 1353.

By this time he had regretted what he considered the careless frivolity of much of his early writing. Turning to scholarly work, he wrote the earliest life of Dante, lectured on Dante's work, and, through his friendship with Petrarch, met a Greek scholar whom he persuaded to translate Homer. Thus the same man who once wrote of Fiammetta also introduced Homer to modern literature.

Like the *Canterbury Tales* and the *Arabian Nights*, the *Decameron* presents its stories in a "frame." In 1348 the city of Florence, as well as much of the rest of Europe, was visited by a plague, The Black Death. Thousands died in a few weeks. Boccaccio hit upon the device of having seven ladies and three noblemen flee the plague in the city and take up a brief residence in the suburbs near Fiesole. The ten agree that in rotation each shall be king or queen for a day, shall decree the entertainment to be followed, and shall dictate the telling of stories to assure the pleasant passing of the days. Thus the ten people, each telling a tale a day for ten days, relate a hundred stories, ranging in plot, as Joseph Wood Krutch says, "from rude farce to romantic tragedy and ranging in mood from Rabelaisian brutality to tender sentiment." Boccaccio saw, Krutch continues, "in the rough boisterous comedy and the bloody tragedy, as well as in the romance which the popular tales embodied, a crude expression of the Italian temperament, something quite different from the classical modes of feeling . . . and so . . . he devoted himself to the task of making them art by giving them perfect form." The lords and ladies who tell the stories are scantily treated by Boccaccio; they are little more than pegs on which to hang the tales. But the characters in the stories they tell are often clearly and concisely delineated.

Although many of the stories the ten relate have to do with cuckolded husbands and deceived wives, a quick dismissal of Boccaccio as "immoral" is not justified. We must first remember the truth of the old statement "other times, other manners," but more important than the difference between the conventions of the fourteenth and the twentieth centuries is the fact that Boccaccio was much less interested in the behavior of the people in his stories than in the witty turn, the droll trickery. Laughter and comedy dominate episode.

The translation used is that by J. M. Rigg from the *Everyman's Library*, published by E. P. Dutton & Co., Inc., New York.

SUGGESTED REFERENCES: Francis McManus, *Boccaccio* (1947); Joseph Wood Krutch, *Five Masters* (3rd ed., 1961); A. D. Scaglione, *Nature and Love in the Late Middle Ages* (1963).

The Decameron

INTRODUCTION

Beginneth here the first day of the Decameron, in which, when the author has set forth, how it came to pass that the persons, who appear hereafter, met together for interchange of discourse, they, under the rule of Pampinea, discourse of such matters as most commend themselves to each in turn.

As often, most gracious ladies, as I bethink me, how compassionate you are by nature one and all, I do not disguise from myself that the present work must seem to you to have but a heavy and distressful prelude, in that it bears upon its very front what must needs revive the sorrowful memory of the late mortal pestilence, the course whereof was grievous not merely to eye-witnesses but to all who in any other wise had cognisance of it. But I would have you know, that you need not therefore be fearful to read further, as if your reading were ever to be accompanied by sighs and tears. This horrid beginning will be to you even such as to wayfarers is a steep and rugged mountain, beyond which stretches a plain most fair and delectable, which the toil of the ascent and descent does but serve to render more agreeable to them; for, as the last degree of joy brings with it sorrow, so misery has ever its sequel of happiness. To this brief exordium of woe — brief, I say, inasmuch as it can be put within the compass of a few letters — succeed forthwith the sweets and delights which I have promised you, and which, perhaps, had I not done so, were not to have been expected from it. In truth, had it been honestly possible to guide you whither I would bring you by a road less rough than this will be, I would gladly have so done. But, because without this review of the past, it would not be in my power to shew how the matters, of which you will hereafter read, came to pass, I am almost bound of necessity to enter upon it, if I would write of them at all.

I say, then, that the years of the beatific incarnation of the Son of God had reached the tale of one thousand three hundred and forty-eight, when in the illustrious city of Florence, the fairest of all the cities of Italy, there made its appearance that deadly pestilence, which, whether disseminated by the influence of the celestial bodies, or sent upon us mortals by God in His just wrath by way of retribution for our iniquities, had had its origin some years before in the East, whence, after destroying an innumerable multitude of living beings, it had propagated itself without respite from place to place, and so, calamitously, had spread into the West.

In Florence, despite all that human wisdom and forethought could devise to avert it, as the cleansing of the city from many impurities by officials appointed for the purpose, the refusal of entrance to all sick folk, and the adoption of many precautions for the preservation of health; despite also humble supplications addressed to God, and often repeated both in public procession and otherwise, by the devout; towards the beginning of the spring of the said year the doleful effects of the pestilence began to be horribly apparent by symptoms that shewed as if miraculous.

Not such were they as in the East, where an issue of blood from the nose was a manifest sign of inevitable death; but in men and women alike it first betrayed itself by the emergence of certain tumors in the groin or the armpits, some of which grew as large as a common apple, others as an egg, some more, some less, which the common folk called gavoccioli. From the two said parts of the body this deadly gavocciolo soon began to propagate and spread itself in all directions indifferently; after which the form of the malady began to change, black spots or livid making their appearance in many cases on the arm or the thigh or elsewhere, now few and large, now minute and numerous. And as the gavocciolo had been and still was an infallible token of approaching death, such also were these spots on whomsoever they shewed themselves. Which maladies seemed to set entirely at naught both the art of the physician and the virtues of physic; indeed, whether it was that the disorder was of a nature to defy such treatment, or that the physicians were at fault — besides the qualified there was now a multitude both of men and of women who practised without having received the slightest tincture of medical science — and, being in ignorance of its source, failed to apply the proper remedies; in either case, not merely were those that recovered few, but almost all within three days from the appearance of the said symptoms, sooner or later, died, and in most cases without any fever or other attendant malady.

Moreover, the virulence of the pest was the greater by reason that intercourse was apt to convey it from the sick to the whole, just as fire devours things dry or greasy when they are brought close to it. Nay, the evil went yet further, for not merely by speech or association with the sick was the malady communicated to the healthy with consequent peril of common death; but any that touched the clothes of the sick or aught else that had been touched or used by them, seemed thereby to contract the disease.

So marvellous sounds that which I have now to relate, that, had not many, and I among them, observed it with their own eyes, I had hardly dared to credit it, much less to set it down in writing, though I had had it from the lips of a credible witness.

I say, then, that such was the energy of the contagion of the said pestilence, that it was not merely propagated from man to man, but, what is much more startling, it was frequently observed, that things which had belonged to one sick or dead of the disease, if touched by some other living creature, not of the human species, were the occasion, not merely of sickening, but of an almost instantaneous death. Whereof my own eyes (as I said a little before) had cognisance, one day among others, by the following experience. The rags of a poor man who had died of the disease being strewn about the open street, two hogs came thither, and after, as is their wont, no little trifling with their snouts, took the rags between their teeth and tossed them to and fro about their chaps; whereupon, almost immediately, they gave a few turns, and fell down dead, as if by poison, upon the rags which in an evil hour they had disturbed.

In which circumstances, not to speak of many others of a similar or even graver complexion, divers apprehensions and imaginations were engendered in the minds of such as were left alive, inclining almost all of them to the same harsh resolution, to wit, to shun and abhor all contact with the sick and all that belonged to them, thinking thereby to make each his own health secure. Among whom there were those who thought that to live temperately and avoid all excess would count for much as a preservative against seizures of this kind. Wherefore they banded together, and, dissociating themselves from all others, formed communities in houses where there were no sick, and lived a separate and secluded life, which they regulated with the utmost care, avoiding every kind of luxury, but eating and drinking very moderately of the most delicate viands and the finest wines, holding converse with none but one another, lest tidings of sickness or death should reach them, and diverting their minds with music and such other delights as they could devise. Others, the bias of whose minds was in the opposite direction, maintained, that to drink freely, frequent places of public resort, and take their pleasure with song and revel, sparing to satisfy no appetite, and to laugh and mock at no event, was the sovereign remedy for so great an evil: and that which they affirmed they also put in practice, so far as they were able, resorting day and night, now to this tavern, now to that, drinking with an entire disregard of rule or measure, and by preference making the houses of others, as it were, their inns, if they but saw in them aught that was particularly to their taste or liking; which they were readily able to do, because the owners, seeing death imminent, had become as reckless of their property as of their lives; so that most of the houses were open to all comers, and no distinction was observed between the stranger who presented himself and the rightful lord. Thus, adhering ever to their inhuman determination to shun the sick, as far as possible, they ordered their life. In this extremity of our city's suffering and tribulation the venerable authority of laws, human and divine, was abased and all but totally dissolved, for lack of those who should have administered and enforced them, most of whom, like the rest of the citizens, were either dead or sick, or so hard bested for servants that they were unable to execute any office; whereby every man was free to do what was right in his own eyes.

Not a few there were who belonged to neither of the two said parties, but kept a middle course between them, neither laying the same restraint upon their diet as the former, nor allowing themselves the same license in drinking and other dissipations as the latter, but living with a degree of freedom sufficient to satisfy their appetites, and not as recluses. They therefore walked abroad, carrying in their hands flowers or fragrant herbs or divers sorts of spices, which they frequently raised to their noses, deeming it an excellent thing thus to comfort the brain with such perfumes, because the air seemed to be everywhere laden and reeking with the stench emitted by the dead and the dying, and the odors of drugs.

Some again, the most sound, perhaps, in judgment, as they were also the most harsh in temper, of all, affirmed that there was no medicine for the disease superior or equal in efficacy to flight; following which prescription a multitude of men and women, negligent of all but themselves, deserted their city, their houses, their estates, their kinsfolk, their goods, and went into voluntary exile, or migrated to the country parts, as if God in visiting men with this pestilence in requital of their iniquities would not pursue them with His wrath wherever they might be, but intended the destruction of such alone as remained within the circuit of the walls of the city; or deeming, perchance, that it was now time for all to flee from it, and that its last hour was come.

Of the adherents of these divers opinions not all died, neither did all escape; but rather there were, of each sort and in every place, many that sickened, and by those who retained their health were treated after the example which they themselves, while whole, had set, being everywhere left to languish in almost total neglect. Tedious were it to recount, how citizen avoided citizen, how among neighbors was scarce found any that shewed fellow-feeling for another, how kinsfolk held aloof, and never met, or but rarely; enough that this sore affliction entered so deep into the minds of men and women, that in the horror thereof brother was forsaken by brother, nephew by uncle, brother by sister, and oftentimes husband by wife; nay, what is more, and scarcely to be believed, fathers and mothers

were found to abandon their own children, untended, unvisited, to their fate, as if they had been strangers. Wherefore the sick of both sexes, whose number could not be estimated, were left without resource but in the charity of friends (and few such there were), or the interest of servants, who were hardly to be had at high rates and on unseemly terms, and being, moreover, one and all, men and women of gross understanding, and for the most part unused to such offices, concerned themselves no further than to supply the immediate and expressed wants of the sick, and to watch them die; in which service they themselves not seldom perished with their gains. In consequence of which dearth of servants and dereliction of the sick by neighbors, kinsfolk and friends, it came to pass — a thing, perhaps, never before heard of — that no woman, however dainty, fair or well-born she might be, shrank, when stricken with the disease, from the ministrations of a man, no matter whether he were young or no, or scrupled to expose to him every part of her body, with no more shame than if he had been a woman, submitting of necessity to that which her malady required; wherefrom, perchance, there resulted in after time some loss of modesty in such as recovered. Besides which many succumbed who, with proper attendance, would, perhaps, have escaped death; so that, what with the virulence of the plague and the lack of due tendance of the sick, the multitude of the deaths, that daily and nightly took place in the city, was such that those who heard the tale — not to say witnessed the fact — were struck dumb with amazement. Whereby, practices contrary to the former habits of the citizens could hardly fail to grow up among the survivors.

It had been, as to-day it still is, the custom for the women that were neighbors and of kin to the deceased to gather in his house with the women that were most closely connected with him, to wail with them in common, while on the other hand his male kinsfolk and neighbors, with not a few of the other citizens, and a due proportion of the clergy according to his quality, assembled without, in front of the house, to receive the corpse; and so the dead man was born on the shoulders of his peers, with funeral pomp of taper and dirge, to the church selected by him before his death. Which rites, as the pestilence waxed in fury, were either in whole or in great part disused, and gave way to others of a novel order. For not only did no crowd of women surround the bed of the dying, but many passed from this life unregarded, and few indeed were they to whom were accorded the lamentations and bitter tears of sorrowing relations; nay, for the most part, their place was taken by the laugh, the jest, the festal gathering; observances which the women, domestic piety in large measure set aside, had adopted with very great advantage to their health. Few also there were whose bodies were attended to the church by more than ten or twelve of their neighbors, and those not the honorable and respected citizens; but a sort of corpse-carriers drawn from the baser ranks, who called themselves becchini [1] and performed such offices for hire, would shoulder the bier, and with hurried steps carry it, not to the church of the dead man's choice, but to that which was nearest at hand, with four or six priests in front and a candle or two, or, perhaps, none; nor did the priests distress themselves with too long and solemn an office, but with the aid of the becchini hastily consigned the corpse to the first tomb which they found untenanted. The condition of the lower, and, perhaps, in great measure of the middle ranks, of the people shewed even worse and more deplorable; for, deluded by hope or constrained by poverty, they stayed in their quarters, in their houses, where they sickened by thousands a day, and, being without service or help of any kind, were, so to speak, irredeemably devoted to the death which overtook them. Many died daily or nightly in the public streets; of many others, who died at home, the departure was hardly observed by their neighbors, until the stench of their putrefying bodies carried the tidings; and what with their corpses and the corpses of others who died on every hand the whole place was a sepulchre.

It was the common practice of most of the neighbors, moved no less by fear of contamination by the putrefying bodies than by charity towards the deceased, to drag the corpses out of the houses with their own hands, aided, perhaps, by a porter, if a porter was to be had, and to lay them in front of the doors, where any one who made the round might have seen, especially in the morning, more of them than he could count; afterwards they would have biers brought up, or, in default, planks, whereon they laid them. Nor was it once or twice only that one and the same bier carried two or three corpses at once; but quite a considerable number of such cases occurred, one bier sufficing for husband and wife, two or three brothers, father and son, and so forth. And times without number it happened, that, as two priests, bearing the cross, were on their way to perform the last office for some one, three or four biers were brought up by the porters in rear of them, so that, whereas the priests supposed that they had but one corpse to

bury, they discovered that there were six or eight, or sometimes more. Nor, for all their number, were their obsequies honored by either tears or lights or crowds of mourners; rather, it was come to this, that a dead man was then of no more account than a dead goat would be to-day. From all which it is abundantly manifest, that that lesson of patient resignation, which the sages were never able to learn from the slight and infrequent mishaps which occur in the natural course of events, was now brought home even to the minds of the simple by the magnitude of their disasters, so that they became indifferent to them.

As consecrated ground there was not in extent sufficient to provide tombs for the vast multitude of corpses which day and night, and almost every hour, were brought in eager haste to the churches for interment, least of all, if ancient custom were to be observed and a separate resting-place assigned to each, they dug, for each graveyard, as soon as it was full, a huge trench, in which they laid the corpses as they arrived by hundreds at a time, piling them up as merchandise is stowed in the hold of a ship, tier upon tier, each covered with a little earth, until the trench would hold no more. But I spare to rehearse with minute particularity each of the woes that came upon our city, and say in brief, that, harsh as was the tenor of her fortunes, the surrounding country knew no mitigation; for there — not to speak of the castles, each, as it were, a little city in itself — in sequestered village, or on the open champaign, by the wayside, on the farm, in the homestead, the poor hapless husbandmen and their families, forlorn of physicians' care or servants' tendance, perished day and night alike, not as men, but rather as beasts. Wherefore, they too, like the citizens, abandoned all rule of life, all habit of industry, all counsel of prudence; nay, one and all, as if expecting each day to be their last, not merely ceased to aid Nature to yield her fruit in due season of their beasts and their lands and their past labors, but left no means unused, which ingenuity could devise, to waste their accumulated store; denying shelter to their oxen, asses, sheep, goats, pigs, fowls, nay, even to their dogs, man's most faithful companions, and driving them out into the fields to roam at large amid the unsheaved, nay, unreaped corn. Many of which, as if endowed with reason, took their fill during the day, and returned home at night without any guidance of herdsman. But enough of the country! What need we add, but (reverting to the city) that such and so grievous was the harshness of heaven, and perhaps in some degree of man, that, what with the fury of the pestilence, the panic of those whom it spared, and their consequent neglect or

[1] Probably from the name of the pronged or hooked implement with which they dragged the corpses out of the houses.

desertion of not a few of the stricken in their need, it is believed without any manner of doubt, that between March and the ensuing July upwards of a hundred thousand human beings lost their lives within the walls of the city of Florence, which before the deadly visitation would not have been supposed to contain so many people! How many grand palaces, how many stately homes, how many splendid residences, once full of retainers, of lords, of ladies, were now left desolate of all, even to the meanest servant! How many families of historic fame, of vast ancestral domains, and wealth proverbial, found now no scion to continue the succession! How many brave men, how many fair ladies, how many gallant youths, whom any physician, were he Galen, Hippocrates, or Æsculapius himself, would have pronounced in the soundest of health, broke fast with their kinsfolk, comrades and friends in the morning, and when evening came, supped with their forefathers in the other world!

Irksome it is to myself to rehearse in detail so sorrowful a history. Wherefore, being minded to pass over so much thereof as I fairly can, I say, that our city, being thus well-nigh depopulated, it so happened, as I afterwards learned from one worthy of credit, that on a Tuesday morning after Divine Service the venerable church of Santa Maria Novella was almost deserted save for the presence of seven young ladies habited sadly in keeping with the season. All were connected either by blood or at least as friends or neighbors; and fair and of good understanding were they all, as also of noble birth, gentle manners, and a modest sprightliness. In age none exceeded twenty-eight, or fell short of eighteen years. Their names I would set down in due form, had I not good reason to withhold them, being solicitous lest the matters which here ensue, as told and heard by them, should in after time be occasion of reproach to any of them, in view of the ample indulgence which was then, for the reasons heretofore set forth, accorded to the lighter hours of persons of much riper years than they, but which the manners of to-day have somewhat restricted; nor would I furnish material to detractors, ever ready to bestow their bite where praise is due, to cast by invidious speech the least slur upon the honor of these noble ladies. Wherefore, that which each says may be apprehended without confusion, I intend to give them names more or less appropriate to the character of each. The first, then, being the eldest of the seven, we will call Pampinea, the second Fiammetta, the third Filomena, the fourth Emilia, the fifth we will distinguish as Lauretta, the sixth as Neifile, and the last, not without reason, shall be named Elisa.

'Twas not of set purpose but by mere chance that these ladies met in the same part of the church; but at length grouping themselves into a sort of circle, after heaving a few sighs, they gave up saying paternosters, and began to converse (among other topics) on the times.

So they continued for a while, and then Pampinea, the rest listening in silent attention, thus began: — "Dear ladies mine, often have I heard it said, and you doubtless as well as I, that wrong is done to none by whoso but honestly uses his reason. And to fortify, preserve, and defend his life to the utmost of his power is the dictate of natural reason in every one that is born. Which right is accorded in such measure that in defence thereof men have been held blameless in taking life. And if this be allowed by the laws, albeit on their stringency depends the well-being of every mortal, how much more exempt from censure should we, and all other honest folk, be in taking such means as we may for the preservation of our life? As often as I bethink me how we have been occupied this morning, and not this morning only, and what has been the tenor of our conversation, I perceive — and you will readily do the like — that each of us is apprehensive on her own account; nor thereat do I marvel, but at this I do marvel greatly, that, though none of us lacks a woman's wit, yet none of us has recourse to any means to avert that which we all justly fear. Here we tarry, as if, methinks, for no other purpose than to bear witness to the number of the corpses that are brought hither for interment, or to hearken if the brothers there within, whose number is now almost reduced to nought, chant their offices at the canonical hours, or, by our weeds of woe, to obtrude on the attention of every one that enters, the nature and degree of our sufferings.

"And if we quit the church, we see dead or sick folk carried about, or we see those, who for their crimes were of late condemned to exile by the outraged majesty of the public laws, but who now, in contempt of those laws, well knowing that their ministers are a prey to death or disease, have returned, and traverse the city in packs, making it hideous with their riotous antics; or else we see the refuse of the people, fostered on our blood, becchini, as they call themselves, who for our torment go prancing about here and there and everywhere, making mock of our miseries in scurrilous songs. Nor hear we aught but: — Such and such are dead; or, Such and such are dying; and should hear dolorous wailing on every hand, were there but any to wail. Or go we home, what see we there? I know not if you are in like case with me; but there, where once were servants in plenty,

I find none left but my maid, and shudder with terror, and feel the very hairs of my head to stand on end; and turn or tarry where I may, I encounter the ghosts of the departed, not with their wonted mien, but with something horrible in their aspect that appals me.   For which reasons church and street and home are alike distressful to me, and the more so that none, methinks, having means and place of retirement as we have, abides here save only we; or if any such there be, they are of those, as my senses too often have borne witness, who make no distinction between things honorable and their opposites, so they but answer the cravings of appetite, and, alone or in company, do daily and nightly what things soever give promise of most gratification.   Nor are these secular persons alone; but such as live recluse in monasteries break their rule, and give themselves up to carnal pleasures, persuading themselves that they are permissible to them, and only forbidden to others, and, thereby thinking to escape, are become unchaste and dissolute.   If such be our circumstances — and such most manifestly they are — what do we here? what wait we for? what dream we of? why are we less prompt to provide for our own safety than the rest of the citizens?   Is life less dear to us than to all other women? or think we that the bond which unites soul and body is stronger in us than in others, so that there is no blow that may light upon it, of which we need be apprehensive?   If so, we err, we are deceived.   What insensate folly were it in us so to believe!   We have but to call to mind the number and condition of those, young as we, and of both sexes, who have succumbed to this cruel pestilence, to find therein conclusive evidence to the contrary.   And lest from lethargy or indolence we fall into the vain imagination that by some lucky accident we may in some way or another, when we would, escape — I know not if your opinion accord with mine — I should deem it most wise in us, our case being what it is, if, as many others have done before us, and are still doing, we were to quit this place, and, shunning like death the evil example of others, betake ourselves to the country, and there live as honorable women on one of the estates, of which none of us has any lack, with all cheer of festal gathering and other delights, so long as in no particular we overstep the bounds of reason.   There we shall hear the chant of birds, have sight of verdant hills and plains, of cornfields undulating like the sea, of trees of a thousand sorts; there also we shall have a larger view of the heavens, which, however harsh to usward, yet deny not their eternal beauty; things fairer far for eye to rest on than the desolate walls of our city.   Moreover, we shall there breathe a fresher air,

find ampler store of things meet for such as live in these times, have fewer causes of annoy.   For, though the husbandmen die there, even as here the citizens, they are dispersed in scattered homesteads, and 'tis thus less painful to witness.   Nor, so far as I can see, is there a soul here whom we shall desert; rather we may truly say, that we are ourselves deserted; for, our kinsfolk being either dead or fled in fear of death, no more regardful of us than if we were strangers, we are left alone in our great affliction.   No censure, then, can fall on us if we do as I propose; and otherwise grievous suffering, perhaps death, may ensue.   Wherefore, if you agree, 'tis my advice, that, attended by our maids with all things needful, we sojourn, now on this, now on the other estate, and in such way of life continue, until we see — if death should not first overtake us — the end which Heaven reserves for these events.   And I remind you that it will be at least as seemly in us to leave with honor, as in others, of whom there are not a few, to stay with dishonor."

The other ladies praised Pampinea's plan, and indeed were so prompt to follow it, that they had already begun to discuss the manner in some detail, as if they were forthwith to rise from their seats and take the road, when Filomena, whose judgment was excellent, interposed, saying: — "Ladies, though Pampinea has spoken to most excellent effect, yet it were not well to be so precipitate as you seem disposed to be.   Bethink you that we are all women; nor is there any here so young, but she is of years to understand how women are minded towards one another, when they are alone together, and how ill they are able to rule themselves without the guidance of some man.   We are sensitive, perverse, suspicious, pusillanimous and timid; wherefore I much misdoubt, that, if we find no other guidance than our own, this company is like to break up sooner, and with less credit to us, than it should.   Against which it were well to provide at the outset."   Said then Elisa: — "Without doubt man is woman's head, and, without man's governance, it is seldom that aught that we do is brought to a commendable conclusion.   But how are we to come by the men?   Every one of us here knows that her kinsmen are for the most part dead, and that the survivors are dispersed, one here, one there, we know not where, bent each on escaping the same fate as ourselves; nor were it seemly to seek the aid of strangers; for, as we are in quest of health, we must find some means so to order matters that, wherever we seek diversion or repose, trouble and scandal do not follow us."

While the ladies were thus conversing, there came into the church three young men, young, I say, but not so young that the age of the youngest was less than twenty-five years; in whom neither the sinister course of events, nor the loss of friends or kinsfolk, nor fear for their own safety, had availed to quench, or even temper, the ardor of their love. The first was called Pamfilo, the second Filostrato, and the third Dioneo. Very debonair and chivalrous were they all; and in this troublous time they were seeking if haply, to their exceeding great solace, they might have sight of their fair friends, all three of whom chanced to be among the said seven ladies, besides some that were of kin to the young men. At one and the same moment they recognised the ladies and were recognised by them: wherefore, with a gracious smile, Pampinea thus began: — "Lo, fortune is propitious to our enterprise, having vouchsafed us the good offices of these young men, who are as gallant as they are discreet, and will gladly give us their guidance and escort, so we but take them into our service." Whereupon Neifile, crimson from brow to neck with the blush of modesty, being one of those that had a lover among the young men, said: — "For God's sake, Pampinea, have a care what you say. Well assured am I that nought but good can be said of any of them, and I deem them fit for office far more onerous than this which you propose for them, and their good and honorable company worthy of ladies fairer by far and more tenderly to be cherished than such as we. But 'tis no secret that they love some of us here; wherefore I misdoubt that, if we take them with us, we may thereby give occasion for scandal and censure merited neither by us nor by them." "That," said Filomena, "is of no consequence; so I but live honestly, my conscience gives me no disquietude; if others asperse me, God and the truth will take arms in my defence. Now, should they be disposed to attend us, of a truth we might say with Pampinea, that fortune favors our enterprise." The silence which followed betokened consent on the part of the other ladies, who then with one accord resolved to call the young men, and acquaint them with their purpose, and pray them to be of their company. So without further parley Pampinea, who had a kinsman among the young men, rose and approached them where they stood intently regarding them; and greeting them gaily, she opened to them their plan, and besought them on the part of herself and her friends to join their company on terms of honorable and fraternal comradeship. At first the young men thought she did but trifle with them; but when they saw that she was in earnest, they answered with alacrity that they were ready, and promptly, even before they left the church, set matters in train for their de-

parture. So all things meet being first sent forward in due order to their intended place of sojourn, the ladies with some of their maids, and the three young men, each attended by a man-servant, sallied forth of the city on the morrow, being Wednesday, about daybreak, and took the road; nor had they journeyed more than two short miles when they arrived at their destination. The estate [1] lay upon a little hill some distance from the nearest highway, and, embowered in shrubberies of divers hues, and other greenery, afforded the eye a pleasant prospect. On the summit of the hill was a palace with galleries, halls and chambers, disposed around a fair and spacious court, each very fair in itself, and the goodlier to see for the gladsome pictures with which it was adorned; the whole set amidst meads and gardens laid out with marvellous art, wells of the coolest water, and vaults of the finest wines, things more suited to dainty drinkers than to sober and honorable women. On their arrival the company, to their no small delight, found their beds already made, the rooms well swept and garnished with flowers of every sort that the season could afford, and the floors carpeted with rushes. When they were seated, Dioneo, a gallant who had not his match for courtesy and wit, spoke thus: — "My ladies, 'tis not our forethought so much as your own mother-wit that has guided us hither. How you mean to dispose of your cares I know not; mine I left behind me within the city-gate when I issued thence with you a brief while ago. Wherefore, I pray you, either address yourselves to make merry, to laugh and sing with me (so far, I mean, as may consist with your dignity), or give me leave to hie me back to the stricken city, there to abide with my cares." To whom blithely Pampinea replied, as if she too had cast off all her cares: — "Well sayest thou, Dioneo, excellent well; gaily we mean to live; 'twas a refuge from sorrow that here we sought, nor had we other cause to come hither. But, as no anarchy can long endure, I who initiated the deliberations of which this fair company is the fruit, do now, to the end that our joy may be lasting, deem it expedient, that there be one among us in chief authority, honored and obeyed by us as our superior, whose exclusive care it shall be to devise how we may pass our time blithely. And that each in turn may prove the weight of the care, as well as enjoy the pleasure, of sovereignty, and, no distinction being made of sex, envy be felt by none by reason of exclusion from the office; I propose, that the weight and honor be borne by each one for a day; and let the

[1] Identified by tradition with the Villa Palmieri (now Crawford) on the slope of Fiesole.

first to bear sway be chosen by us all, those that follow to be appointed towards the vesper hour by him or her who shall have had the signory for that day; and let each holder of the signory be, for the time, sole arbiter of the place and manner in which we are to pass our time."

Pampinea's speech was received with the utmost applause, and with one accord she was chosen queen for the first day. Whereupon Filomena hied her lightly to a bay-tree, having often heard of the great honor in which its leaves, and such as were deservedly crowned therewith, were worthy to be holden; and having gathered a few sprays, she made thereof a goodly wreath of honor, and set it on Pampinea's head; which wreath was thenceforth, while their company endured, the visible sign of the wearer's sway and sovereignty.

No sooner was Queen Pampinea crowned than she bade all be silent. She then caused summon to her presence their four maids, and the servants of the three young men, and, all keeping silence, said to them: — "That I may shew you all at once, how, well still giving place to better, our company may flourish and endure, as long as it shall pleasure us, with order meet and assured delight and without reproach, I first of all constitute Dioneo's man, Parmeno, my seneschal, and entrust him with the care and control of all our household, and all that belongs to the service of the hall. Pamfilo's man, Sirisco, I appoint treasurer and chancellor of our exchequer; and be he ever answerable to Parmeno. While Parmeno and Sirisco are too busy about their duties to serve their masters, let Filostrato's man, Tindaro, have charge of the chambers of all three. My maid, Misia, and Filomena's maid, Licisca, will keep in the kitchen, and with all due diligence prepare such dishes as Parmeno shall bid them. Lauretta's maid, Chimera, and Fiammetta's maid, Stratilia, we make answerable for the ladies' chambers, and wherever we may take up our quarters, let them see that all is spotless. And now we enjoin you, one and all alike, as you value our favor, that none of you, go where you may, return whence you may, hear or see what you may, bring us any tidings but such as be cheerful." These orders thus succinctly given were received with universal approval. Whereupon Pampinea rose, and said gaily: — "Here are gardens, meads, and other places delightsome enough, where you may wander at will, and take your pleasure; but on the stroke of tierce,[1] let all be here to breakfast in the shade."

Thus dismissed by their new queen the gay company sauntered gently through a garden, the

young men saying sweet things to the fair ladies, who wove fair garlands of divers sorts of leaves and sang love-songs.

Having thus spent the time allowed them by the queen, they returned to the house, where they found that Parmeno had entered on his office with zeal; for in a hall on the ground-floor they saw tables covered with the whitest of cloths, and beakers that shone like silver, and sprays of broom scattered everywhere. So, at the bidding of the queen, they washed their hands, and all took their places as marshalled by Parmeno. Dishes, daintily prepared, were served, and the finest wines were at hand; the three serving-men did their office noiselessly; in a word all was fair and ordered in a seemly manner; whereby the spirits of the company rose, and they seasoned their viands with pleasant jests and sprightly sallies. Breakfast done, the tables were removed, and the queen bade fetch instruments of music; for all, ladies and young men alike, knew how to tread a measure, and some of them played and sang with great skill: so, at her command, Dioneo having taken a lute, and Fiammetta a viol, they struck up a dance in sweet concert; and, the servants being dismissed to their repast, the queen, attended by the other ladies and the two young men, led off a stately carol; which ended they fell to singing ditties dainty and gay. Thus they diverted themselves until the queen, deeming it time to retire to rest, dismissed them all for the night. So the three young men and the ladies withdrew to their several quarters, which were in different parts of the palace. There they found the beds well made, and abundance of flowers, as in the hall; and so they undressed, and went to bed.

Shortly after none[1] the queen rose, and roused the rest of the ladies, as also the young men, averring that it was injurious to the health to sleep long in the daytime. They therefore hied them to a meadow, where the grass grew green and luxuriant, being nowhere scorched by the sun, and a light breeze gently fanned them. So at the queen's command they all ranged themselves in a circle on the grass, and hearkened while she thus spoke:

"You mark that the sun is high, the heat intense, and the silence unbroken save by the cicalas among the olive-trees. It were therefore the height of folly to quit this spot at present. Here the air is cool and the prospect fair, and here, observe, are dice and chess. Take, then, your pleasure as you may be severally minded; but, if you take my advice, you will find pastime for the hot hours before us, not in play, in which the loser must needs

[1] The canonical hour following prime, roughly speaking about 9 A.M.

[1] The canonical hour following sext, i.e. 3 P.M.

be vexed, and neither the winner nor the onlooker much the better pleased, but in telling of stories, in which the invention of one may afford solace to all the company of his hearers. You will not each have told a story before the sun will be low, and the heat abated, so that we shall be able to go and severally take our pleasure where it may seem best to each. Wherefore, if my proposal meet with your approval — for in this I am disposed to consult your pleasure — let us adopt it; if not, divert yourselves as best you may, until the vesper hour."

The queen's proposal being approved by all, ladies and men alike, she added: — "So please you, then, I ordain, that, for this first day, we be free to discourse of such matters as most commend themselves to each in turn."

SIMONA AND PASQUINO

Simona loves Pasquino; they are together in a garden; Pasquino rubs a leaf of sage against his teeth, and dies; Simona is arrested, and, with intent to shew the judge how Pasquino died, rubs one of the leaves of the same plant against her teeth, and likewise dies.

When Pamfilo had done with his story, the king, betraying no compassion for Andreuola, glancing at Emilia, signified to her his desire that she should now continue the sequence of narration. Emilia made no demur, and thus began: —

Dear gossips, Pamfilo's story puts me upon telling you another in no wise like thereto, save in this, that as Andreuola lost her lover in a garden, so also did she of whom I am to speak, and, being arrested like Andreuola, did also deliver herself from the court, albeit 'twas not by any vigor or firmness of mind, but by a sudden death. And, as 'twas said among us a while ago, albeit Love affects the mansions of the noble, he does not, therefore, disdain the dominion of the dwellings of the poor, nay, does there at times give proof of his might no less signal than when he makes him feared of the wealthiest as a most potent lord. Which, though not fully, will in some degree appear in my story, wherewith I am minded to return to our city, from which to-day's discourse, roving from matter to matter, and one part of the world to another, has carried us so far.

Know then that no great while ago there dwelt in Florence a maid most fair, and, for her rank, debonair — she was but a poor man's daughter — whose name was Simona; and though she must needs win with her own hands the bread she ate, and maintain herself by spinning wool; yet was she not, therefore, of so poor a spirit, but that she dared to give harborage in her mind to Love, who for some time had sought to gain entrance there by means of the gracious deeds and words of a young man of her own order that went about distributing wool to spin for his master, a wool-monger. Love being thus, with the pleasant image of her beloved Pasquino, admitted into her soul, mightily did she yearn, albeit she hazarded no advance, and heaved a thousand sighs fiercer than fire with every skein of yarn that she wound upon her spindle, while she called to mind who he was that had given her that wool to spin. Pasquino on his part became, meanwhile, very anxious that his master's wool should be well spun, and most particularly about that which Simona span, as if, indeed, it and it alone was to furnish forth the whole of the cloth. And so, what with the anxiety which the one evinced, and the gratification that it afforded to the other, it befell that, the one waxing unusually bold, and the other casting off not a little of her wonted shyness and reserve, they came to an understanding for their mutual solace; which proved so delightful to both, that neither waited to be bidden by the other, but 'twas rather which should be the first to make the overture.

While thus they sped their days in an even tenor of delight, and ever grew more ardently enamored of one another, Pasquino chanced to say to Simona that he wished of all things she would contrive how she might betake her to a garden, whither he would bring her, that there they might be more at their ease, and in greater security. Simona said that she was agreeable; and, having given her father to understand that she was minded to go to San Gallo for the pardoning, she hied her with one of her gossips, Lagina by name, to the garden of which Pasquino had told her. Here she found Pasquino awaiting her with a friend, one Puccino, otherwise Stramba; and Stramba and Lagina falling at once to love-making, Pasquino and Simona left a part of the garden to them, and withdrew to another part for their own solace.

Now there was in their part of the garden a very fine and lovely sage-bush, at foot of which they sat them down and made merry together a great while, and talked much of a junketing they meant to have in the garden quite at their ease. By and by Pasquino, turning to the great sage-bush, plucked therefrom a leaf, and fell to rubbing his teeth and gums therewith, saying that sage was an excellent detergent of aught that remained upon them after a meal. Having done so, he returned to the topic of the junketing of which he had spoken before. But he had not pursued it far before his countenance entirely changed, and forthwith he lost sight and speech, and shortly after died. Whereupon Simona fell aweeping and shrieking and calling Stramba and Lagina; who, notwithstanding they came up with all speed, found Pasquino not only dead but already swollen from head to foot, and covered with black spots both on the face and on the body; whereupon Stramba broke forth with: — "Ah! wicked woman! thou hast poisoned him;" and made such a din that 'twas heard by not a few that dwelt hard by the garden; who also hasted to the spot, and seeing Pasquino dead and swollen, and hearing Stramba bewail himself and accuse Simona of having maliciously poisoned him, while she, all but beside herself for grief to be thus suddenly bereft of her lover, knew not how to defend herself, did all with one accord surmise that 'twas even as Stramba said. Wherefore they laid hands on her, and brought her, still weeping bitterly, to the palace of the Podestà: where at the instant suit of Stramba, backed by Atticciato and Malagevole, two other newly-arrived friends of Pasquino, a judge forthwith addressed himself to question her of the matter; and being unable to discover that she had used any wicked practice, or was guilty, he resolved to take her with him and go see the corpse, and the place, and the manner of the death, as she had recounted it to him; for by her words he could not well understand it. So, taking care that there should be no disturbance, he had her brought to the place where Pasquino's corpse lay swollen like a tun, whither he himself presently came, and marvelling as he examined the corpse, asked her how the death had come about. Whereupon, standing by the sage-bush, she told him all that had happened, and that he might perfectly apprehend the occasion of the death, she did as Pasquino had done, plucked one of the leaves from the bush, and rubbed her teeth with it. Whereupon Stramba and Atticciato, and the rest of the friends and comrades of Pasquino, making in the presence of the judge open mock of what she did, as an idle and vain thing, and being more than ever instant to affirm her guilt, and to demand the fire as the sole condign penalty, the poor creature, that, between grief for her lost lover and dread of the doom demanded by Stramba, stood mute and helpless, was stricken no less suddenly, and in the same manner, and for the same cause (to wit, that she had rubbed her teeth with the sage leaf) as Pasquino, to the no small amazement of all that were present.

Oh! happy souls for whom one and the same day was the term of ardent love and earthly life! Happier still, if to the same bourn ye fared! Ay, and even yet more happy, if love there be in the other world, and there, even as here, ye love! But happiest above all Simona, so far as we, whom she has left behind, may judge, in that Fortune brooked not that the witness of Stramba, Atticciato and Malagevole, carders, perchance, or yet viler fellows, should bear down her innocence, but found a more seemly issue, and, appointing her a like lot with her lover, gave her at once to clear herself from their foul accusation, and to follow whither the soul, that she so loved, of her Pasquino had preceded her!

The judge, and all else that witnessed the event, remained long time in a sort of stupefaction, knowing not what to say of it; but at length recovering his wits, the judge said: — "'Twould seem that this sage is poisonous, which the sage is not used to be. Let it be cut down to the roots and burned, lest another suffer by it in like sort." Which the gardener proceeding to do in the judge's presence, no sooner had he brought the great bush down, than the cause of the deaths of the two lovers plainly appeared: for underneath it was a toad of prodigious dimensions, from whose venomous breath, as they conjectured, the whole of the bush had contracted a poisonous quality. Around which toad, none venturing to approach it, they set a stout ring-fence of faggots, and burned it together with the sage. So ended Master Judge's inquest on the death of hapless Pasquino, who with his Simona, swollen as they were, were buried by Stramba, Atticciato, Guccio Imbratta, and Malagevole in the church of San Paolo, of which, as it so happened, they were parishioners.

FEDERIGO'S FALCON

Federigo degli Alberighi loves and is not loved in return: he wastes his substance by lavishness until nought is left but a single falcon, which, his lady being come to see him at his house, he gives her to eat: she, knowing his case, changes her mind, takes him to husband and makes him rich.

So ended Filomena; and the queen, being ware that besides herself only Dioneo (by virtue of his privilege) was left to speak, said with gladsome mien: — 'Tis now for me to take up my parable; which, dearest ladies, I will do with a story like in some degree to the foregoing, and that, not only that you may know how potent are your charms to sway the gentle heart, but that you may also learn how upon fitting occasions to make bestowal of your guerdons of your own accord, instead of always waiting for the guidance of Fortune, which most times, not wisely, but without rule or measure, scatters her gifts.

You are then to know, that Coppo di Borghese
Domenichi, a man that in our day was, and perchance still is, had in respect and great reverence
in our city, being not only by reason of his noble
lineage, but, and yet more, for manners and merit
most illustrious and worthy of eternal renown, was
in his old age not seldom wont to amuse himself
by discoursing of things past with his neighbors
and other folk; wherein he had not his match for
accuracy and compass of memory and concinnity
of speech. Among other good stories, he would
tell, how that there was of yore in Florence a
gallant named Federigo di Messer Filippo Alberighi, who for feats of arms and courtesy had not
his peer in Tuscany; who, as is the common lot of
gentlemen, became enamored of a lady named
Monna Giovanna, who in her day held rank among
the fairest and most elegant ladies of Florence; to
gain whose love he jousted, tilted, gave entertainments, scattered largess, and in short set no bounds
to his expenditure. However the lady, no less
virtuous than fair, cared not a jot for what he did
for her sake, nor yet for him.

Spending thus greatly beyond his means, and
making nothing, Federigo could hardly fail to
come to lack, and was at length reduced to such
poverty that he had nothing left but a little estate,
on the rents of which he lived very straitly, and a
single falcon, the best in the world. The estate
was at Campi, and thither, deeming it no longer
possible for him to live in the city as he desired, he
repaired, more in love than ever before; and there,
in complete seclusion, diverting himself with hawking, he bore his poverty as patiently as he might.

Now, Federigo being thus reduced to extreme
poverty, it so happened that one day Monna Giovanna's husband, who was very rich, fell ill, and,
seeing that he was nearing his end, made his will,
whereby he left his estate to his son, who was now
growing up, and in the event of his death without
lawful heir named Monna Giovanna, whom he
dearly loved, heir in his stead; and having made
these dispositions he died.

Monna Giovanna, being thus left a widow, did
as our ladies are wont, and repaired in the summer
to one of her estates in the country which lay very
near to that of Federigo. And so it befell that the
urchin began to make friends with Federigo, and
to shew a fondness for hawks and dogs, and having
seen Federigo's falcon fly not a few times, took a
singular fancy to him, and greatly longed to have
him for his own, but still did not dare to ask him of
Federigo, knowing that Federigo prized him so
much. So the matter stood when by chance the
boy fell sick; whereby the mother was sore distressed, for he was her only son, and she loved him

as much as might be, insomuch that all day long
she was beside him, and ceased not to comfort him,
and again and again asked him if there were aught
that he wished for, imploring him to say the word,
and, if it might by any means be had, she would
assuredly do her utmost to procure it for him.
Thus repeatedly exhorted, the boy said: —
"Mother mine, do but get me Federigo's falcon,
and I doubt not I shall soon be well." Whereupon
the lady was silent a while, bethinking her what
she should do. She knew that Federigo had long
loved her, and had never had so much as a single
kind look from her: wherefore she said to herself: —
How can I send or go to beg of him this falcon,
which by what I hear is the best that ever flew,
and moreover is his sole comfort? And how could
I be so unfeeling as to seek to deprive a gentleman
of the one solace that is now left him? And so,
albeit she very well knew that she might have the
falcon for the asking, she was perplexed, and knew
not what to say, and gave her son no answer. At
length, however, the love she bore the boy carried
the day, and she made up her mind, for his contentment, come what might, not to send, but to go
herself and fetch him the falcon. So: — "Be of
good cheer, my son," she said, "and doubt not
thou wilt soon be well; for I promise thee that the
very first thing that I shall do to-morrow morning
will be to go and fetch thee the falcon." Whereat
the child was so pleased that he began to mend
that very day.

On the morrow the lady, as if for pleasure, hied
her with another lady to Federigo's little house,
and asked to see him. 'Twas still, as for some days
past, no weather for hawking, and Federigo was in
his garden, busy about some small matters which
needed to be set right there. When he heard that
Monna Giovanna was at the door, asking to see
him, he was not a little surprised and pleased, and
hied him to her with all speed. As soon as she
saw him, she came forward to meet him with
womanly grace, and having received his respectful
salutation, said to him: — "Good morrow, Federigo," and continued: — "I am come to requite
thee for what thou hast lost by loving me more
than thou shouldst: which compensation is this,
that I and this lady that accompanies me will
breakfast with thee without ceremony this morning." "Madam," Federigo replied with all humility, "I mind not ever to have lost aught by loving you, but rather to have been so much profited
that, if I ever deserved well in aught, 'twas to
your merit that I owed it, and to the love that I
bore you. And of a surety had I still as much to
spend as I have spent in the past, I should not
prize it so much as this visit you so frankly pay me,

come as you are to one who can afford you but a sorry sort of hospitality." Which said, with some confusion, he bade her welcome to his house, and then led her into his garden, where, having none else to present to her by way of companion, he said: — "Madam, as there is none other here, this good woman, wife of this husbandman, will bear you company, while I go to have the table set." Now, albeit his poverty was extreme, yet he had not known as yet how sore was the need to which his extravagance had reduced him; but this morning 'twas brought home to him, for that he could find nought wherewith to do honor to the lady, for love of whom he had done the honors of his house to men without number: wherefore, distressed beyond measure, and inwardly cursing his evil fortune, he sped hither and thither like one beside himself, but never a coin found he, nor yet aught to pledge. Meanwhile it grew late, and sorely he longed that the lady might not leave his house altogether unhonored, and yet to crave help of his own husbandman was more than his pride could brook. In these desperate straits his glance happened to fall on his brave falcon on his perch in his little parlor. And so, as a last resource, he took him, and finding him plump, deemed that he would make a dish meet for such a lady. Wherefore, without thinking twice about it, he wrung the bird's neck, and caused his maid forthwith pluck him and set him on a spit, and roast him carefully; and having still some spotless table-linen, he had the table laid therewith, and with a cheerful countenance hied him back to his lady in the garden, and told her that such breakfast as he could give her was ready. So the lady and her companion rose and came to table, and there, with Federigo, who waited on them most faithfully, ate the brave falcon, knowing not what they ate.

When they were risen from table, and had dallied a while in gay converse with him, the lady deemed it time to tell the reason of her visit: wherefore, graciously addressing Federigo, thus began she: — "Federigo, by what thou rememberest of thy past life and my virtue, which, perchance, thou hast deemed harshness and cruelty, I doubt not thou must marvel at my presumption, when thou hearest the main purpose of my visit; but if thou hadst sons, or hadst had them, so that thou mightest know the full force of the love that is borne them, I should make no doubt that thou wouldst hold me in part excused. Nor, having a son, may I, for that thou hast none, claim exemption from the laws to which all other mothers are subject, and, being thus bound to own their sway, I must, though fain were I not, and though 'tis neither meet nor right, crave of thee that which I know

thou dost of all things and with justice prize most highly, seeing that this extremity of thy adverse fortune has left thee nought else wherewith to delight, divert and console thee; which gift is no other than thy falcon, on which my boy has so set his heart that, if I bring him it not, I fear lest he grow so much worse of the malady that he has, that thereby it may come to pass that I lose him. And so, not for the love which thou dost bear me, and which may nowise bind thee, but for that nobleness of temper, whereof in courtesy more conspicuously than in aught else thou hast given proof, I implore thee that thou be pleased to give me the bird, that thereby I may say that I have kept my son alive, and thus made him for aye thy debtor."

No sooner had Federigo apprehended what the lady wanted, than, for grief that 'twas not in his power to serve her, because he had given her the falcon to eat, he fell a-weeping in her presence, before he could so much as utter a word. At first the lady supposed that 'twas only because he was loath to part with the brave falcon that he wept, and as good as made up her mind that he would refuse her: however, she awaited with patience Federigo's answer, which was on this wise: — "Madam, since it pleased God that I should set my affections upon you there have been matters not a few, in which to my sorrow I have deemed Fortune adverse to me; but they have all been trifles in comparison of the trick that she now plays me: the which I shall never forgive her, seeing that you are come here to my poor house, where while I was rich, you deigned not to come, and ask a trifling favor of me, which she has put it out of my power to grant: how 'tis so, I will briefly tell you. When I learned that you, of your grace, were minded to breakfast with me, having respect to your high dignity and desert, I deemed it due and seemly that in your honor I should regale you, to the best of my power, with fare of a more excellent quality than is commonly set before others; and, calling to mind the falcon which you now ask of me, and his excellence, I judged him meet food for you, and so you have had him roasted on the trencher this morning; and well indeed I thought I had bestowed him; but, as now I see that you would fain have had him in another guise, so mortified am I that I am not able to serve you, that I doubt I shall never know peace of mind more." In witness whereof he had the feathers and feet and beak of the bird brought in and laid before her.

The first thing the lady did, when she had heard Federigo's story, and seen the relics of the bird, was to chide him that he had killed so fine a falcon to furnish a woman with a breakfast; after which the magnanimity of her host, which poverty had been and was powerless to impair, elicited no small share of inward commendation. Then, frustrate of her hope of possessing the falcon, and doubting of her son's recovery, she took her leave with the heaviest of hearts, and hied her back to the boy: who, whether for fretting, that he might not have the falcon, or by the unaided energy of his disorder, departed this life not many days after, to the exceeding great grief of his mother. For a while she would do nought but weep and bitterly bewail herself; but being still young, and left very wealthy, she was often urged by her brothers to marry again, and though she would rather have not done so, yet being importuned, and remembering Federigo's high desert, and the magnificent generosity with which he had finally killed his falcon to do her honor, she said to her brothers: — "Gladly, with your consent, would I remain a widow, but if you will not be satisfied except I take a husband, rest assured that none other will I ever take save Federigo degli Alberighi." Whereupon her brothers derided her, saying: — "Foolish woman, what is't thou sayst? How shouldst thou want Federigo, who has not a thing in the world?" To whom she answered: — "My brothers, well wot I that 'tis as you say; but I had rather have a man without wealth than wealth without a man." The brothers, perceiving that her mind was made up, and knowing Federigo for a good man and true, poor though he was, gave her to him with all her wealth. And so Federigo, being mated with such a wife, and one that he had so much loved, and being very wealthy to boot, lived happily, keeping more exact accounts, to the end of his days.

PATIENT GRISELDA

The Marquis of Saluzzo, overborne by the entreaties of his vassals, consents to take a wife, but, being minded to please himself in the choice of her, takes a husbandman's daughter. He has two children by her, both of whom he makes her believe that he has put to death. Afterward, feigning to be tired of her, and to have taken another wife, he turns her out of doors in her shift, and brings his daughter into the house in guise of his bride; but, finding her patient under it all, he brings her home again, and shews her her children, now grown up, and honors her, and causes her to be honored, as Marchioness.

Ended the king's long story, with which all seemed to be very well pleased, quoth Dioneo with a laugh: — "The good man that looked that

night to cause the bogey's tail to droop, would scarce have contributed two pennyworth of all the praise you bestow on Messer Torello:" then, witting that it now only remained for him to tell, thus he began: — Gentle my ladies, this day, meseems, is dedicate to Kings and Soldans and folk of the like quality; wherefore, that I stray not too far from you, I am minded to tell you somewhat of a Marquis; certes, nought magnificent, but a piece of mad folly, albeit there came good thereof to him in the end. The which I counsel none to copy, for that great pity 'twas that it turned out well with him.

There was in olden days a certain Marquis of Saluzzo, Gualtieri by name, a young man, but head of the house, who, having neither wife nor child, passed his time in nought else but in hawking and hunting, and of taking a wife and begetting children had no thought; wherein he should have been accounted very wise: but his vassals, brooking it ill, did oftentimes entreat him to take a wife, that he might not die without an heir, and they be left without a lord; offering to find him one of such a pattern, and of such parentage, that he might marry with good hope, and be well content with the sequel. To whom: — "My friends," replied Gualtieri, "you enforce me to that which I had resolved never to do, seeing how hard it is to find a wife, whose ways accord well with one's own, and how plentiful is the supply of such as run counter thereto, and how grievous a life he leads who chances upon a lady that matches ill with him. And to say that you think to know the daughters by the qualities of their fathers and mothers, and thereby — so you would argue — to provide me with a wife to my liking, is but folly; for I wot not how you may penetrate the secrets of their mothers so as to know their fathers; and granted that you do know them, daughters oftentimes resemble neither of their parents. However, as you are minded to rivet these fetters upon me, I am content that so it be; and that I may have no cause to reproach any but myself, should it turn out ill, I am resolved that my wife shall be of my own choosing; but of this rest assured, that, no matter whom I choose, if she receive not from you the honor due to a lady, you shall prove to your great cost, how sorely I resent being thus constrained by your importunity to take a wife against my will."

The worthy men replied that they were well content, so only he would marry without more ado. And Gualtieri, who had long noted with approval the mien of a poor girl that dwelt on a farm hard by his house, and found her fair enough, deemed that with her he might pass a tolerably happy life. Wherefore he sought no further, but forthwith resolved to marry her; and having sent for her father, who was a very poor man, he contracted with him to take her to wife. Which done, Gualtieri assembled all the friends he had in those parts, and: — "My friends," quoth he, "you were and are minded that I should take a wife, and rather to comply with your wishes, than for any desire that I had to marry, I have made up my mind to do so. You remember the promise you gave me, to wit, that, whomsoever I should take, you would pay her the honor due to a lady. Which promise I now require you to keep, the time being come when I am to keep mine. I have found hard by here a maiden after mine own heart, whom I purpose to take to wife, and to bring hither to my house in the course of a few days. Wherefore bethink you, how you may make the nuptial feast splendid, and welcome her with all honor; that I may confess myself satisfied with your observance of your promise, as you will be with my observance of mine." The worthy men, one and all, answered with alacrity that they were well content, and that, whoever she might be, they would entreat her as a lady, and pay her all due honor as such. After which, they all addressed them to make goodly and grand and gladsome celebration of the event, as did also Gualtieri. He arranged for a wedding most stately and fair, and bade thereto a goodly number of his friends and kinsfolk, and great gentlemen, and others, of the neighborhood; and therewithal he caused many a fine and costly robe to be cut and fashioned to the figure of a girl who seemed to him of the like proportions as the girl that he purposed to wed; and laid in store, besides, of girdles and rings, with a costly and beautiful crown, and all the other paraphernalia of a bride.

The day that he had appointed for the wedding being come, about half tierce he got him to horse with as many as had come to do him honor, and having made all needful dispositions: — "Gentlemen," quoth he, "'tis time to go bring home the bride." And so away he rode with his company to the village; where, being come to the house of the girl's father, they found her returning from the spring with a bucket of water, making all the haste she could, that she might afterwards go with the other women to see Gualtieri's bride come by. Whom Gualtieri no sooner saw, than he called her by her name, to wit, Griselda, and asked her where her father was. To whom she modestly made answer: — "My lord, he is in the house." Whereupon Gualtieri dismounted, and having bidden the rest await him without, entered the cottage alone; and meeting her father, whose name was Giannucolo: — "I am come," quoth he, "to wed Griselda, but first of all there are some matters I would learn from her own lips in thy presence." He then asked her, whether, if he took her to wife, she would study to comply with his wishes, and be not wroth, no matter what he might say or do, and be obedient, with not a few other questions of a like sort: to all which she answered, ay. Whereupon Gualtieri took her by the hand, led her forth, and before the eyes of all his company, and as many other folk as were there, caused her to be stript naked, and let bring the garments that he had had fashioned for her, and had her forthwith arrayed therein, and upon her unkempt head let set a crown; and then, while all wondered: — "Gentlemen," quoth he, "this is she whom I purpose to make my wife, so she be minded to have me for husband." Then, she standing abashed and astonied, he turned to her, saying: — "Griselda, wilt thou have me for thy husband?" To whom: — "Ay, my lord," answered she. "And I will have thee to wife," said he, and married her before them all. And having set her upon a palfrey, he brought her home with pomp.

The wedding was fair and stately, and had he married a daughter of the King of France, the feast could not have been more splendid. It seemed as if, with the change of her garb, the bride had acquired a new dignity of mind and mien. She was, as we have said, fair of form and feature; and therewithal she was now grown so engaging and gracious and debonair, that she shewed no longer as the shepherdess, and the daughter of Giannucolo, but as the daughter of some noble lord, insomuch that she caused as many as had known her before to marvel. Moreover, she was so obedient and devoted to her husband, that he deemed himself the happiest and luckiest man in the world. And likewise so gracious and kindly was she to her husband's vassals, that there was none of them but loved her more dearly than himself, and was zealous to do her honor, and prayed for her welfare and prosperity and aggrandisement, and instead of, as erstwhile, saying that Gualtieri had done foolishly to take her to wife, now averred that he had not his like in the world for wisdom and discernment, for that, save to him, her noble qualities would ever have remained hidden under her sorry apparel and the garb of the peasant girl. And in short she so comported herself as in no long time to bring it to pass that, not only in the marquisate, but far and wide besides, her virtues and her admirable conversation were matter of common talk, and, if aught had been said to the disadvantage of her husband, when he married her, the judgment was now altogether to the contrary effect.

She had not been long with Gualtieri before she

conceived; and in due time she was delivered of a girl; whereat Gualtieri made great cheer. But, soon after, a strange humor took possession of him, to wit, to put her patience to the proof by prolonged and intolerable hard usage; wherefore he began by afflicting her with his gibes, putting on a vexed air, and telling her that his vassals were most sorely dissatisfied with her by reason of her base condition, and all the more so since they saw that she was a mother, and that they did nought but most ruefully murmur at the birth of a daughter. Whereto Griselda, without the least change of countenance or sign of discompose, made answer: — "My lord, do with me as thou mayst deem best for thine own honor and comfort, for well I wot that I am of less account than they, and unworthy of this honorable estate to which of thy courtesy thou hast advanced me." By which answer Gualtieri was well pleased, witting that she was in no degree puffed up with pride by his, or any other's, honorable entreatment of her. A while afterwards, having in general terms given his wife to understand that the vassals could not endure her daughter, he sent her a message by a servant. So the servant came, and: — "Madam," quoth he with a most dolorous mien, "so I value my life, I must needs do my lord's bidding. He has bidden me take your daughter and . . ." He said no more, but the lady by what she heard, and read in his face, and remembered of her husband's words, understood that he was bidden to put the child to death. Whereupon she presently took the child from the cradle, and having kissed and blessed her, albeit she was very sore at heart, she changed not countenance, but placed it in the servant's arms, saying: — "See that thou leave nought undone that my lord and thine has charged thee to do, but leave her not so that the beasts and the birds devour her, unless he have so bidden thee." So the servant took the child, and told Gualtieri what the lady had said; and Gualtieri, marvelling at her constancy, sent him with the child to Bologna, to one of his kinswomen, whom he besought to rear and educate the child with all care, but never to let it be known whose child she was.

Soon after it befell that the lady again conceived, and in due time was delivered of a son, whereat Gualtieri was overjoyed. But, not content with what he had done, he now even more poignantly afflicted the lady; and one day with a ruffled mien: — "Wife," quoth he, "since thou gavest birth to this boy, I may on no wise live in peace with my vassals, so bitterly do they reproach me that a grandson of Giannucolo is to succeed me as their lord; and therefore I fear that, so I be not minded

to be sent a-packing hence, I must even do herein as I did before, and in the end put thee away, and take another wife." The lady heard him patiently, and answered only: — "My lord, study how thou mayst content thee and best please thyself, and waste no thought upon me, for there is nought I desire save in so far as I know that 'tis thy pleasure." Not many days after, Gualtieri, in like manner as he had sent for the daughter, sent for the son, and having made a shew of putting him to death, provided for his, as for the girl's, nurture at Bologna. Whereat the lady shewed no more discompose of countenance or speech than at the loss of her daughter: which Gualtieri found passing strange, and inly affirmed that there was never another woman in the world that would have so done. And but that he had marked that she was most tenderly affectionate towards her children, while 'twas well pleasing to him, he had supposed that she was tired of them, whereas he knew that 'twas of her discretion that she so did. His vassals, who believed that he had put the children to death, held him mightily to blame for his cruelty, and felt the utmost compassion for the lady. She, however, said never aught to the ladies that condoled with her on the death of her children, but that the pleasure of him that had begotten them was her pleasure likewise.

Years not a few had passed since the girl's birth, when Gualtieri at length deemed the time come to put his wife's patience to the final proof. Accordingly, in the presence of a great company of his vassals he declared that on no wise might he longer brook to have Griselda to wife, that he confessed that in taking her he had done a sorry thing and the act of a stripling, and that he therefore meant to do what he could to procure the Pope's dispensation to put Griselda away, and take another wife: for which cause being much upbraided by many worthy men, he made no other answer but only that needs must it so be. Whereof the lady being apprised, and now deeming that she must look to go back to her father's house, and perchance tend the sheep, as she had aforetime, and see him, to whom she was utterly devoted, engrossed by another woman, did inly bewail herself right sorely: but still with the same composed mien with which she had borne Fortune's former buffets, she set herself to endure this last outrage. Nor was it long before Gualtieri by counterfeit letters, which he caused to be sent to him from Rome, made his vassals believe that the Pope had thereby given him a dispensation to put Griselda away, and take another wife. Wherefore, having caused her to be brought before him, he said to her in the presence of not a few: — "Wife, by license granted me by the Pope, I am now free to put thee away, and take another wife; and, for that my forbears have always been great gentlemen and lords of these parts, whereas thine have ever been husbandmen, I purpose that thou go back to Giannucolo's house with the dowry that thou broughtest me; whereupon I shall bring home a lady that I have found, and who is meet to be my wife."

'Twas not without travail most grievous that the lady, as she heard this announcement, got the better of her woman's nature, and suppressing her tears, made answer: — "My lord, I ever knew that my low degree was on no wise congruous with your nobility, and acknowledged that the rank I had with you was of your and God's bestowal, nor did I ever make as if it were mine by gift, or so esteem it, but still accounted it as a loan. 'Tis your pleasure to recall it, and therefore it should be, and is, my pleasure to render it up to you. So, here is your ring, with which you espoused me; take it back. You bid me take with me the dowry that I brought you; which to do will require neither paymaster on your part nor purse nor pack-horse on mine; for I am not unmindful that naked was I when you first had me. And if you deem it seemly that that body in which I have borne children, by you begotten, be beheld of all, naked will I depart; but yet, I pray you, be pleased, in guerdon of the virginity that I brought you and take not away, to suffer me to bear hence upon my back a single shift — I crave no more — besides my dowry." There was nought of which Gualtieri was so fain as to weep; but yet, setting his face as a flint, he made answer: — "I allow thee a shift to thy back; so get thee hence." All that stood by besought him to give her a robe, that she, who had been his wife for thirteen years and more, might not be seen to quit his house in so sorry and shameful a plight, having nought on her but a shift. But their entreaties went for nothing: the lady in her shift, and barefoot and bareheaded, having bade them adieu, departed the house, and went back to her father amid the tears and lamentations of all that saw her. Giannucolo, who had ever deemed it a thing incredible that Gualtieri should keep his daughter to wife, and had looked for this to happen every day, and had kept the clothes that she had put off on the morning that Gualtieri had wedded her, now brought them to her; and she, having resumed them, applied herself to the petty drudgery of her father's house, as she had been wont, enduring with fortitude this cruel visitation of adverse Fortune.

Now no sooner had Gualtieri dismissed Griselda, than he gave his vassals to understand that he had taken to wife a daughter of one of the Counts of Panago. He accordingly made great preparations as for the nuptials, during which he sent for Griselda. To whom, being come, quoth he: — "I am bringing hither my new bride, and in this her first home-coming I purpose to shew her honor; and thou knowest that women I have none in the house that know how to set chambers in due order, or attend to the many other matters that so joyful an event requires; wherefore do thou, that understandest these things better than another, see to all that needs be done, and bid hither such ladies as thou mayst see fit, and receive them, as if thou wert the lady of the house, and then, when the nuptials are ended, thou mayst go back to thy cottage." Albeit each of these words pierced Griselda's heart like a knife, for that, in resigning her good fortune, she had not been able to renounce the love she bore Gualtieri, nevertheless: — "My lord," she made answer, "I am ready and prompt to do your pleasure." And so, clad in her sorry garments of coarse romagnole, she entered the house, which, but a little before, she had quitted in her shift, and addressed her to sweep the chambers, and arrange arras and cushions in the halls, and make ready the kitchen, and set her hand to everything, as if she had been a paltry serving-wench: nor did she rest until she had brought all into such meet and seemly trim as the occasion demanded. This done, she invited in Gualtieri's name all the ladies of those parts to be present at his nuptials, and awaited the event. The day being come, still wearing her sorry weeds, but in heart and soul and mien the lady, she received the ladies as they came, and gave each a gladsome greeting.

Now Gualtieri, as we said, had caused his children to be carefully nurtured and brought up by a kinswoman of his at Bologna, which kinswoman was married into the family of the Counts of Panago; and, the girl being now twelve years old, and the loveliest creature that ever was seen, and the boy being about six years old, he had sent word to his kinswoman's husband at Bologna, praying him to be pleased to come with this girl and boy of his to Saluzzo, and to see that he brought a goodly and honorable company with him, and to give all to understand that he brought the girl to him to wife, and on no wise to disclose to any, who she really was. The gentleman did as the Marquis bade him, and within a few days of his setting forth arrived at Saluzzo about breakfast-time with the girl, and her brother, and a noble company, and found all the folk of those parts, and much people besides, gathered there in expectation of Gualtieri's new bride. Who, being received by the ladies, was no sooner come into the hall, where the tables were set, than Griselda advanced to meet her, saying with hearty cheer: — "Welcome, my lady." So the ladies, who had with much instance, but in vain, besought Gualtieri, either to let Griselda keep in another room, or at any rate to furnish her with one of the robes that had been hers, that she might not present herself in such a sorry guise before the strangers, sate down to table; and the service being begun, the eyes of all were set on the girl, and every one said that Gualtieri had made a good exchange, and Griselda joined with the rest in greatly commending her, and also her little brother. And now Gualtieri, sated at last with all that he had seen of his wife's patience, marking that this new and strange turn made not the least alteration in her demeanor, and being well assured that 'twas not due to apathy, for he knew her to be of excellent understanding, deemed it time to relieve her of the suffering which he judged her to dissemble under a resolute front; and so, having called her to him in presence of them all, he said with a smile: — "And what thinkst thou of our bride?" "My lord," replied Griselda, "I think mighty well of her; and if she be but as discreet as she is fair — and so I deem her — I make no doubt but you may reckon to lead with her a life of incomparable felicity; but with all earnestness I entreat you, that you spare her those tribulations which you did once inflict upon another that was yours, for I scarce think she would be able to bear them, as well because she is younger, as for that she has been delicately nurtured, whereas that other had known no respite of hardship since she was but a little child." Marking that she made no doubt but that the girl was to be his wife, and yet spoke never a whit the less sweetly, Gualtieri caused her to sit down beside him, and: — "Griselda," said he, "'tis now time that thou see the reward of thy long patience, and that those, who have deemed me cruel and unjust and insensate, should know that what I did was done of purpose aforethought, for that I was minded to give both thee and them a lesson, that thou mightst learn to be a wife, and they in like manner might learn how to take and keep a wife, and that I might beget me perpetual peace with thee for the rest of my life; whereof being in great fear, when I came to take a wife, lest I should be disappointed, I therefore, to put the matter to the proof, did, and how sorely thou knowest, harass and afflict thee. And since I never knew thee either by deed or by word to deviate from my will, I now, deeming myself to have of thee that assurance of happiness which I desired, am minded to restore

to thee at once all that, step by step, I took from thee, and by extremity of joy to compensate the tribulations that I inflicted on thee. Receive, then, this girl, whom thou supposest to be my bride, and her brother, with glad heart, as thy children and mine. These are they, whom by thee and many another it has long been supposed that I did ruthlessly to death, and I am thy husband, that loves thee more dearly than aught else, deeming that other there is none that has the like good cause to be well content with his wife."

Which said, he embraced and kissed her; and then, while she wept for joy, they rose and hied them there where sate the daughter, all astonied to hear the news, whom, as also her brother, they tenderly embraced, and explained to them, and many others that stood by, the whole mystery. Whereat the ladies, transported with delight, rose from table and betook them with Griselda to a chamber, and, with better omen, divested her of her sorry garb, and arrayed her in one of her own robes of state; and so, in guise of a lady (howbeit in her rags she had shewed as no less) they led her back into the hall. Wondrous was the cheer which there they made with the children; and, all overjoyed at the event, they revelled and made merry amain, and prolonged the festivities for several days; and very discreet they pronounced Gualtieri, albeit they censured as intolerably harsh the probation to which he had subjected Griselda, and most discreet beyond all compare they accounted Griselda.

Some days after, the Count of Panago returned to Bologna, and Gualtieri took Giannucolo from his husbandry, and established him in honor as his father-in-law, wherein to his great solace he lived for the rest of his days. Gualtieri himself, having mated his daughter with a husband of high degree, lived long and happily thereafter with Griselda, to whom he ever paid all honor.

Now what shall we say in this case but that even into the cots of the poor the heavens let fall at times spirits divine, as into the palaces of kings souls that are fitter to tend hogs than to exercise lordship over men? Who but Griselda had been able, with a countenance not only tearless, but cheerful, to endure the hard and unheard-of trials to which Gualtieri subjected her? Who perhaps might have deemed himself to have made no bad investment, had he chanced upon one, who, having been turned out of his house in her shift, had found means so to dust the pelisse of another as to get herself thereby a fine robe.

François Rabelais · 1494-1553

Rabelais combines elements of the old medievalism with elements of the new spirit, the intellectual awakening of Europe; here is the exuberance and enthusiasm of the Renaissance and hearty laughter for the pedantry of the old learning. The author's natural bent for satire suggests the classical temper, but the distortion and the exaggeration, the wild disregard for conventional literary form dominate and account for the romantic elements.

It is the fate of few, and only the most original, writers to have their names pass into common usage as terms in literary criticism. With Rabelais this happened. When today we speak of a passage of literature as "Rabelaisian," we express our conviction that the passage is marked by a strong and somewhat gross humor which moves along on a current of satire and is characterized by exaggeration.

Born about 1495 at Chinon in the province of Touraine, France, Rabelais spent his youth in monastery schools and, as a young man, entered first the order of the Franciscans and later that of the Benedictines. Still unhappy after the change, he began the study of medicine and, rapidly earning his medical degree, practiced his profession in France and Italy. He was a priest who laughed at the foibles of the priestly life, a professor who ridiculed the prevailing forms of education, and a physician who made use of his medical knowledge to secure many of his humorous effects.

Rabelais's literary reputation rests on two books — usually thought of as one — *Pantagruel* (1533) and *Gargantua* (1535). For a complete appreciation of their significance a thorough understanding of the life and thought of the fifteenth and sixteenth centuries is important. One should know that, during the lifetime of Rabelais, France was in social and political turmoil. Charles V of Spain, Henry VIII of England, and Francis I of France kept Europe seething with their ambitions for imperialistic expansion and centralization of power. The Church, as well, was involved in strife. Rabelais was twenty-six years old when Martin Luther appeared before the Diet of Worms and the Reformation was under way. It was from a background of this sort that Rabelais expressed his ideas on war, on education, on monastery life. Without an understanding of the times, much in Rabelais seems pointless and mere buffoonery. The spirit which pervades this work is that which prompted Aristophanes and Lucian, but the Frenchman wrote without the restraint which distinguished the classicists. Rabelais is akin, also, to the English satirist Swift, but different in that Swift was usually more bitter, more trenchant than his French predecessor.

SUGGESTED REFERENCES: S. P. Putnam, ed., *The Portable Rabelais* (1946); M. A. Screech, *The Rabelaisian Marriage; Aspects of Rabelais's Religion, Ethics and Comic Philosophy* (1958).

Gargantua

The style of Rabelais is a strange mixture of coined words, long lists, gross expressions, distortions and exaggerations, medical details, erudition, force, gaiety, classical background and allusions, and over all is thrown the soft mantle of humor and the bright cloak of satire. His criticism is tempered with a broad understanding of, and a sympathy for, humanity. Certain qualities, however, come between this sixteenth-century writer and his twentieth-century reader; the slow pace of the action, a formlessness and disregard for unity, and a coarseness of expression more shocking to today's reader than it was to the author's contemporaries. That,

however, these features which today strike us as weaknesses were sometimes deliberately planned is evident to the student who will read carefully "The Author's Prologue." The translation used here is by Urquhart and Motteux.

THE AUTHOR'S PROLOGUE

Most noble and illustrious drinkers, and you thrice precious pockified blades, (for to you, and none else do I dedicate my writings,) Alcibiades, in that dialogue of Plato's which is entitled, *The Banquet*, whilst he was setting forth the praises of his schoolmaster, Socrates, (without all question the prince of philosophers,) amongst other discourses to that purpose said, that he resembled the Sileni. Sileni of old were little boxes, like those we now may see in the shops of apothecaries, painted on the outside with wanton toyish figures, as harpies, satyrs, bridled geese, horned hares, saddled ducks, flying goats, thiller harts, and other such counterfeited pictures, at pleasure, to excite people unto laughter, as Silenus himself, who was the foster-father of good Bacchus, was wont to do; but within those capricious caskets called Sileni, were carefully preserved and kept many rich and fine drugs, such as balm, ambergreese, amomon,[1] musk, civet, with several kinds of precious stones, and other things of great price. Just such another thing was Socrates: for to have eyed his outside, and esteemed of him by his exterior appearance, you would not have given the peel of an onion for him, so deformed he was in body, and ridiculous in his gesture. He had a sharp pointed nose, with the look of a bull, and countenance of a fool; he was in his carriage simple, boorish in his apparel, in fortune poor, unhappy in his wives, unfit for all offices in the commonwealth, always laughing, tippling, and merry, carousing to every one, with continual gibes and jeers, the better by those means to conceal his divine knowledge. Now, opening this box, you would have found within it a heavenly and inestimable drug, a more than human understanding, an admirable virtue, matchless learning, invincible courage, inimitable sobriety, certain contentment of mind, perfect assurance, and an incredible disregard of all that for which men commonly do so much watch, run, sail, fight, travel, toil, and turmoil themselves.

Whereunto (in your opinion) doth this little flourish of a preamble tend? For so much as you, my good disciples, and some other jolly fools of ease and leisure, reading the pleasant titles of some books, of our invention, as Gargantua, Pantagruel, Whippot, the Dignity of Codpieces, of Pease and Bacon, with a commentary, &c., are too ready to judge, that there is nothing in them but jests, mockeries, lascivious discourse, and recreative lies; because the outside (which is the title) is usually, without any farther inquiry, entertained with scoffing and derision. But truly it is very unbeseeming to make so slight account of the works of men, seeing yourselves avouch that it is not the habit that makes the monk, many being monasterially accoutered, who inwardly are nothing less than monachal; and that there are of those that wear Spanish caps, who have but little of the valor of Spaniards in them. Therefore is it, that you must open the book, and seriously consider of the

[1] An herb of the ginger family.

matter treated in it. Then shall you find that it containeth things of far higher value than the box did promise; that is to say, that the subject thereof is not so foolish, as by the title at the first sight it would appear to be.

And put the case, that in the literal sense you meet with purposes merry and solacious[1] enough, and consequently very correspondent to their inscriptions, yet must not you stop there as at the melody of the charming Sirens, but endeavor to interpret that in a sublimer sense, which possibly you intended to have spoken in the jollity of your heart. Did you ever pick the lock of a cupboard to steal a bottle of wine out of it? Tell me truly, and, if you did, call to mind the countenance which then you had. Or, did you ever see a dog with a marrow-bone in his mouth, — the beast of all others, says Plato, lib. 2, de Republica, the most philosophical? If you have seen him, you might have remarked with what devotion and circumspectness he wards and watcheth it: with what care he keeps it: how fervently he holds it: how prudently he gobbets it: with what affection he breaks it: and with what diligence he sucks it. To what end all this? What moveth him to take all these pains? What are the hopes of his labor? What doth he expect to reap thereby? Nothing but a little marrow. True it is, that this little is more savory and delicious than the great quantities of other sorts of meat, because the marrow, (as Galen testifieth, 3, facult. nat. and 11, de usu partium) is a nourishment most perfectly elabored by nature.

In imitation of this dog, it becomes you to be wise to smell, feel, and have in estimation, these fair, goodly books, stuffed with high conceptions, which though seemingly easy in the pursuit, are in the cope and encounter somewhat difficult. And then, like him, you must, by a sedulous lecture, and frequent meditation, break the bone, and suck out the marrow; that is, my allegorical sense, or the things I to myself propose to be signified by these Pythagorical symbols; with assured hope, that in so doing, you will at last attain to be both well-advised and valiant by the reading of them: for, in the perusal of this treatise, you shall find another kind of taste, and a doctrine of a more profound and abstruse consideration, which will disclose unto you the most glorious doctrines and dreadful mysteries, as well in what concerneth our religion, as matters of the public state and life economical.

Do you believe, upon your conscience, that Homer, whilst he was couching his Iliads and Odysses, had any thought upon those allegories, which Plutarch, Heraclides Ponticus, Eustathius,

[1] entertaining.

Cornutus, squeezed out of him, and which Politian filched again from them? If you trust it, with neither hand nor foot do you come near to my opinion, which judgeth them to have been as little dreamed of by Homer, as the gospel sacraments were by Ovid, in his Metamorphosis; though a certain gulligut [1] friar, and true bacon-picker would have undertaken to prove it, if, perhaps, he had met with as very fools as himself, and as the proverb says, "a lid worthy of such a kettle."

If you give any credit thereto, why do not you the same to these jovial new Chronicles of mine? Albeit, when I did dictate them, I thought thereof no more than you, who possibly were drinking the whilst, as I was. For in the composing of this lordly book, I never lost nor bestowed any more, nor any other time, than what was appointed to serve me for taking of my bodily refection, that is, whilst I was eating and drinking. And, indeed, that is the fittest and most proper hour, wherein to write these high matters and deep sentences: as Homer knew very well, the paragon of all philologues, and Ennius, the father of the Latin poets, as Horace calls him, although a certain sneaking jobbernol [2] alleged that his verses smelled more of the wine than oil.

So saith a Turlupin or a new start-up grub of my books; but a turd for him. The fragrant odor of the wine, oh! how much more dainty, pleasant, laughing, celestial, and delicious it is, than that smell of oil! and I will glory as much when it is said of me, that I have spent more on wine than oil, as did Demosthenes, when it was told him, that his expense on oil was greater than on wine. I truly hold it for an honor and praise to be called and reputed a frolic Gaulter and a Robin Goodfellow; for under this name am I welcome in all choice companies of Pantagruelists. It was upbraided to Demosthenes, by an envious, surly knave, that his Orations did smell like the sarpler, or wrapper of a foul and filthy oil vessel. For this cause interpret you all my deeds and sayings, in the perfectest sense; reverence the cheese-like brain that feeds you with these faire billevezees, and trifling jollities, and do what lies in you to keep me always merry. Be frolic now, my lads, cheer up your hearts, and joyfully read the rest, with all the ease of your body and profit of your reins. But hearken, joltheads, you viedazes, or dickens take ye, remember to drink a health to me for the favor again, and I will pledge you instantly, Tout aresmetys.

[The reader should know how marvelous a child Gargantua was. Suffice it to say here that, according to Rabelais, a special herd of 17,913 cows was set aside that he might be properly supplied with milk and that he was moved about in an ox-cart which served as a bassinet. To make his shirt nine hundred ells of linen were used, with two hundred additional ells called for to make the gussets under the armpits. A pair of breeches took 1105⅓ ells of white broadcloth; his shoes another 406 ells of crimson velvet. And the shoes were soled with the hides of 1100 brown cows. No wonder that when, as a youth, he walked through the streets of Paris he was able to reach over and steal the bells from the tower of the cathedral of Notre Dame!]

THE STUDY OF GARGANTUA — OLD PLAN

The first day being thus spent, and the bells put up again in their own place, the citizens of Paris, in acknowledgment of this courtesy, offered to maintain and feed his mare as long as he pleased, which Gargantua took in good part, and they sent her to graze in the forest of Biere. I think she is not there now. This done, he with all his heart submitted his study to the discretion of Ponocrates; who for the beginning appointed that he should do as he was accustomed, to the end he might understand by what means, in so long time, his old masters had made him so sottish and ignorant. He disposed therefore of his time in such fashion, that ordinarily he did awake betwixt eight and nine o'clock, whether it was day or not, for so had his ancient governors ordained, alleging that which David saith, *Vanum est vobis ante lucem surgere.* [1] Then did he tumble and toss, wag his legs, and wallow in the bed some time, the better to stir up and rouse his vital spirits, and apparelled himself according to the season: but willingly he would wear a great long gown of thick frieze, furred with fox-skins. Afterwards he combed his head with an Almain comb, which is the four fingers and the thumb. For his preceptor said that to comb himself otherwise, to wash and make himself neat, was to lose time in this world. Then he dunged, pissed, spewed, belched, cracked, yawned, spitted, coughed, yexed, sneezed and snotted himself like an archdeacon, and, to suppress the dew and bad air, went to breakfast, having some good fried tripes, fair rashers on the coals, excellent gammons of bacon, store of fine minced meat, and a great deal of sippet brewis, made up of the fat of the beef-pot, laid upon bread, cheese, and chopped parsley strewed together. Ponocrates showed him that he ought not to eat so soon after rising out of his bed, unless he had performed some exercise beforehand. Gargantua answered, What! have not I sufficiently well exercised myself? I have wal-

[1] glutton.　　[2] blockhead.

[1] It is foolish to arise before dawn.

lowed and rolled myself six or seven turns in my bed before I rose. Is not that enough? Pope Alexander did so, by the advice of a Jew his physician, and lived till his dying day in despite of his enemies. My first masters have used me to it, saying that to breakfast made a good memory, and therefore they drank first. I am very well after it, and dine but the better. And Master Tubal, who was the first licenciate at Paris, told me that it was not enough to run apace, but to set forth betimes: so doth not the total welfare of our humanity depend upon perpetual drinking in a ribble rabble, like ducks, but on drinking early in the morning; *unde versus,*

> To rise betimes is no good hour,
> To drink betimes is better sure.

After that he had thoroughly broke his fast, he went to church, and they carried to him, in a great basket, a huge impantoufled or thick-covered breviary, weighing, what in grease, clasps, parchment and cover, little more or less than eleven hundred and six pounds. There he heard six-and-twenty or thirty masses. This while, to the same place came his orison-mutterer impale-tocked, or lapped up about the chin like a tufted whoop, and his breath pretty well antidoted with store of the vine-tree syrup. With him he mumbled all his kiriels and dunsicals breborions, which he so curiously thumbed and fingered, that there fell not so much as one grain to the ground. As he went from the church, they brought him, upon a dray drawn with oxen, a confused heap of paternosters and aves of St. Claude, every one of them being of the bigness of a hat-block; and thus walking through the cloisters, galleries, or garden, he said more in turning them over than sixteen hermits would have done. Then did he study some paltry half-hour with his eyes fixed upon his book; but, as the comic saith, his mind was in the kitchen. Pissing then a full urinal, he sat down at table; and because he was naturally phlegmatic, he began his meal with some dozens of gammons, dried neat's tongues, hard roes of mullet, called botargos, andouilles or sausages, and such other forerunners of wine. In the meanwhile, four of his folks did cast into his mouth one after another continually mustard by whole shovelfuls. Immediately after that, he drank a horrible draught of white wine for the ease of his kidneys. When that was done, he ate according to the season meat agreeable to his appetite, and then left off eating when his belly began to strout, and was like to crack for fullness. As for his drinking, he had in that neither end nor rule. For he was wont to say, That the limits and bounds of drinking were, when the cork of the shoes of him that drinketh swelleth up half a foot high.

THE STUDY OF GARGANTUA — NEW PLAN

When Ponocrates knew Gargantua's vicious manner of living, he resolved to bring him up in another kind; but for a while he bore with him, considering that nature cannot endure such a change, without great violence. Therefore to begin his work the better, he requested a learned physician of that time, called Master Theodorus, seriously to perpend, if it were possible, how to bring Gargantua unto a better course. The said physician purged him canonically with Anticyrian-hellebore, by which medicine he cleansed all the alteration, and perverse habitude of his brain. By this means also Ponocrates made him forget all that he had learned under his ancient preceptors, as Timotheus [1] did to his disciples, who had been instructed under other musicians. To do this better, they brought him into the company of learned men, which were there, in whose imitation he had a great desire and affection to study otherwise, and to improve his parts. Afterwards he put himself into such a road and way of studying that he lost not any one hour in the day, but employed all his time in learning, and honest knowledge. Gargantua awak'd, then about four o'clock in the morning. Whilst they were in rubbing of him, there was read unto him some chapter of the Holy Scripture aloud and clearly, with a pronunciation fit for the matter, and hereunto was appointed a young page born in Basché, named Anagnostes. According to the purpose and argument of that lesson, he oftentimes gave himself to worship, adore, pray, and send up his supplications to that good God, whose word did show his majesty and marvellous judgment. Then went he into the secret places to make excretion of his natural digestions. There his master repeated what had been read, expounding unto him the most obscure and difficult points. In returning, they considered the face of the sky, if it was such as they had observed it the night before, and into what signs the sun was entering, as also the moon for that day. This done, he was appareled, combed, curled, trimmed and perfumed, during which time they repeated to him the lessons of the day before. He himself said them by heart, and upon them would ground some practical cases concerning the estate of man, which he would prosecute sometimes two or three hours, but ordinarily they ceased as soon as he was fully clothed. Then for three good hours he had a lecture read unto him. This done, they went forth, still conferring of the substance of the lecture, either unto a field near the university called the Brack, or unto

[1] Greek poet and musician.

the meadows where they played at the ball, the long-tennis, and at the pile trigone, most gallantly exercising their bodies, as formerly they had done their minds. All their play was but in liberty, for they left off when they pleased, and that was commonly when they did sweat over all their body, or were otherwise weary. Then were they very well wiped and rubbed, shifted their shirts, and walking soberly, went to see if dinner was ready. Whilst they stayed for that, they did clearly and eloquently pronounce some sentences that they had retained of the lecture. In the meantime Master Appetite came, and then very orderly sat they down at table. At the beginning of the meal, there was read some pleasant history of the warlike actions of former times, until he had taken a glass of wine. Then, if they thought good, they continued reading, or began to discourse merrily together; speaking first of the virtue, propriety, efficacy and nature of all that was served in at that table; of bread, of wine, of water, of salt, of fleshes, fishes, fruits, herbs, roots, and of their dressing. By means whereof, he learned in a little time all the passages competent for this, that were to be found in Pliny, Athenæus, Dioscorides, Julius Pollux, Galen, Porphyrius, Oppian, Polybius, Heliodorus, Aristotle, Ælian, and others. Whilst they talked of these things, many times, to be the more certain, they caused the very books to be brought to the table, and so well and perfectly did he in his memory retain the things above said, that in that time there was not a physician that knew half so much as he did. Afterwards they conferred of the lessons read in the morning, and, ending their repast with some conserve or marmalade of quinces, he picked his teeth with mastic tooth-pickers, washed his hands and eyes with fair fresh water, and gave thanks unto God in some fine canticks,[1] made in praise of the divine bounty and munificence. This done, they brought in cards, not to play, but to learn a thousand pretty tricks, and new inventions, which were all grounded upon arithmetic. By this means he fell in love with that numerical science, and every day after dinner and supper he passed his time in it as pleasantly, as he was wont to do at cards and dice: so that at last he understood so well both the theory and practical part thereof, that Tunstal the Englishman, who had written very largely of that purpose, confessed that verily in comparison of him he had no skill at all. And not only in that, but in the other mathematical sciences, as geometry, astronomy, music, &c. For in waiting on the concoction, and attending the digestion of his food, they made a thousand pretty instruments and geometrical figures, and

[1] songs.

did in some measure practice the astronomical canons.

After this they recreated themselves with singing musically, in four or five parts, or upon a set theme or ground at random, as it best pleased them. In matter of musical instruments, he learned to play upon the lute, the virginals, the harp, the Allman flute with nine holes, the violin, and the sackbut. This hour thus spent, and digestion finished, he did purge his body of natural excrements, then betook himself to his principal study for three hours together, or more, as well to repeat his matutinal lectures, as to proceed in the book wherein he was, as also to write handsomely, to draw and form the antique and Roman letters. This being done, they went out of their house, and with them a young gentleman of Touraine, named the Esquire Gymnast, who taught him the art of riding. Changing then his clothes, he rode a Naples courser, Dutch roussin, a Spanish gennet, a barbed or trapped steed, then a light fleet horse, unto whom he gave a hundred carieres, made him go the high saults, bounding in the air, free a ditch with a skip, leap over a stile or pale, turn short in a ring both to the right and left hand. There he broke not his lance; for it is the greatest foolery in the world to say, I have broken ten lances at tilts or in fight. A carpenter can do even as much. But it is a glorious and praiseworthy action, with one lance to break and overthrow ten enemies. Therefore with a sharp, stiff, strong, and well-steeled lance, would he usually force up a door, pierce a harness, beat down a tree, carry away the ring, lift up a cuirassier saddle, with the mail-coat and gauntlet. All this he did in complete arms from head to foot. As for the prancing flourishes, and smacking popisms, for the better cherishing of the horse, commonly used in riding, none did them better than he. The voltiger of Ferrara was but as an ape compared to him. He was singularly skilful in leaping nimbly from one horse to another without putting foot to ground, and these horses were called desultories. He could likewise from either side, with a lance in his hand, leap on horseback without stirrups, and rule the horse at his pleasure without a bridle, for such things are useful in military engagements. Another day he exercised the battle-ax, which he so dexterously wielded, both in the nimble, strong, and smooth management of that weapon, and that in all the feats practiceable by it, that he passed knight of arms in the field, and at all essays.

Then tossed he the pike, played with the two-handed sword, with the back sword, with the Spanish tuck, the dagger, poniard, armed, unarmed, with a buckler, with a cloak, with a target. Then would he hunt the hart, the roebuck, the bear, the fallow deer, the wild boar, the hare, the pheasant, the partridge and the bustard. He played at the balloon, and made it bound in the air, both with fist and foot. He wrestled, ran, jumped, not at three steps and a leap, called the hops, nor at clochepied, called the hare's leap, nor yet at the Almanes; for, said Gymnast, these jumps are for the wars altogether unprofitable, and of no use: but at one leap he would skip over a ditch, spring over a hedge, mount six paces upon a wall, ramp and grapple after this fashion up against a window, of the full height of a lance. He did swim in deep waters on his belly, on his back, sideways, with all his body, with his feet only, with one hand in the air, wherein he held a book, crossing thus the breadth of the River Seine, without wetting, and dragging along his cloak with his teeth, as did Julius Cæsar; then with the help of one hand he entered forcibly into a boat, from whence he cast himself again headlong into the water, sounded the depths, hollowed the rocks, and plunged into the pits and gulfs. Then turned he the boat about, governed it, led it swiftly or slowly with the stream and against the stream, stopped it in his course, guided it with one hand, and with the other laid hard about him with a huge great oar, hoisted the sail, hied up along the mast by the shrouds, ran upon the edge of the decks, set the compass in order, tackled the bowlines, and steered the helm. Coming out of the water, he ran furiously up against a hill, and with the same alacrity and swiftness ran down again. He climbed up trees like a cat, leaped from one to the other like a squirrel. He did pull down the great boughs and branches, like another Milo; then with two sharp well-steeled daggers, and two tried bodkins, would he run up by the wall to the very top of a house like a rat; then suddenly come down from the top to the bottom with such an even composition of members, that by the fall he would catch no harm.

He did cast the dart, throw the bar, put the stone, practice the javelin, the boar spear or partisan, and the halbert. He broke the strongest bows in drawing, bended against his breast the greatest cross-bows of steel, took his aim by the eye with the hand-gun, and shot well, traversed and planted the cannon, shot at but-marks, at the papgay from below upwards, or to a height from above downwards, or to a descent; then before him sidewise, and behind him, like the Parthians. They tied a cable-rope to the top of a high tower, by one end whereof hanging near the ground he wrought himself with his hands to the very top; then upon the same tract came down so sturdily and firm that you could not on a plain meadow

have run with more assurance. They set up a great pole fixed upon two trees. There would he hang by his hands, and with them alone, his feet touching at nothing, would go back and fore along the aforesaid rope with so great swiftness, that hardly could one overtake him with running; and then, to exercise his breast and lungs, he would shout like all the devils in hell. I heard him once call Eudemon from St. Victor's gate to Montmartre. Stentor never had such a voice at the siege of Troy. Then for the strengthening of his nerves or sinews, they made him two great sows of lead, each of them weighing eight thousand and seven hundred quintals, which they called Alteres. Those he took up from the ground, in each hand one, then lifted them up over his head, and held them so without stirring three quarters of an hour or more, which was an inimitable force. He fought at barriers with the stoutest and most vigorous champions; and when it came to the cope, he stood so sturdily on his feet, that he abandoned himself unto the strongest, in case they could remove him from his place, as Milo was wont to do of old. In whose imitation likewise he held a pomegranate in his hand, to give it unto him that could take it from him. The time being thus bestowed, and himself rubbed, cleansed, wiped, and refreshed with other clothes, he returned fair and softly; and passing through certain meadows, or other grassy places, beheld the trees and plants, comparing them with what is written of them in the books of the ancients, such as Theophrast, Dioscorides, Marinus, Pliny, Nicander, Macer, and Galen, and carried home to the house great handfuls of them, whereof a young page called Rizotomos had charge; together with little mattocks, pickaxes, grubbing hooks, cabbies, pruning knives, and other instruments requisite for herborizing. Being come to their lodging, whilst supper was making ready, they repeated certain passages of that which had been read, and then sat down at table. Here remark, that his dinner was sober and thrifty, for he did then eat only to prevent the gnawings of his stomach, but his supper was copious and large; for he took then as much as was fit to maintain and nourish him; which indeed is the true diet prescribed by the art of good and sound physic, although a rabble of logger-headed physicians, muzzled in the brabbling shop of sophisters, counsel the contrary. During that repast was continued the lesson read at dinner as long as they thought good: the rest was spent in good discourse, learned and profitable. After that they had given thanks, he set himself to sing vocally, and play upon harmonious instruments, or otherwise passed his time at some pretty sports, made with cards and dice, or in practicing the feats of legerdemain with cups and balls. There they staid some nights in frolicking thus, and making themselves merry till it was time to go to bed; and on other nights they would go make visits unto learned men, or to such as had been travellers in strange and remote countries. When it was full night before they retired themselves, they went unto the most open place of the house to see the face of the sky, and there beheld the comets, if any were, as likewise the figures, situations, aspects, oppositions and conjunctions of both the fixed stars and planets.

Then with his master did he briefly recapitulate, after the manner of the Pythagoreans, that which he had read, seen, learned, done and understood in the whole course of that day.

Then prayed they unto God the Creator, in falling down before him, and strengthening their faith towards him, and glorifying him for his boundless bounty; and, giving thanks unto him for the time that was past, they recommended themselves to his divine clemency for the future. Which being done, they went to bed, and betook themselves to their repose and rest.

GREAT STRIFE AND DEBATE

At that time, which was the season of vintage, in the beginning of harvest, when the country shepherds were set to keep the vines, and hinder the starlings from eating up the grapes, as some cake-bakers of Lerné happened to pass along in the broad highway, driving into the city ten or twelve horses loaded with cakes, the said shepherds courteously entreated them to give them some for their money, as the price then ruled in the market. For here it is to be remarked, that it is a celestial food to eat for breakfast, hot fresh cakes with grapes, especially the frail clusters, the great red grapes, the muscadine, the verjuice grape, and the luskard, for those that are costive. . . . The bun-sellers or cake-makers were in nothing inclinable to their request; but, (which was worse,) did injure them most outrageously, calling them brattling gabblers, licorous gluttons, freckled bittors, mangy rascals, sleep-a-bed scoundrels, drunken roysters, sly knaves, drowsy loiterers, slapsauce fellows, slabber-degullion druggels, lubbardly louts, cozening foxes, ruffian rogues, paultry customers, sychophant-varlets, drawlatch hoydons, flouting milksops, jeering companions, staring clowns, forlorn snakes, ninny lobcocks, scurvy sneaksbies, fondling fops, base loons, saucy coxcombs, idle lusks, scoffing braggards, noddy meacocks, blockish grutnols, doddipol joltheads, jobbernol goosecaps, foolish

loggerheads, flutch calf-lollies, grouthead gnat-snappers, lobdotterels, gaping changelings, codshead loobies, woodcock slangams, ninnie-hammer flycatchers, noddie-peak simpletons, turdy-guts, lousy shepherds, and other such like defamatory epithets; saying further that it was not for them to eat of these dainty cakes, but might very well content themselves with the coarse unraunged bread, or to eat of the great brown household loaf. To which provoking words, one amongst them, called Forgier, an honest fellow of his person, and a notable springal,[1] made answer very calmly thus. How long is it since you have got horns, that you are become so proud? Indeed formerly you were wont to give us some freely, and will you not now let us have any for our money? This is not the part of good neighbors, neither do we serve you thus, when you come hither to buy our good corn, whereof you make your cakes and buns. Besides that, we would have given you to the bargain some of our grapes, but, by his zounds, you may chance to repent it, and possibly have need of us at another time, when we shall use you after the like manner, and therefore remember it. Then Marquet, a prime man in the confraternity of the cake-bakers, said unto him, Yea, sir, thou art pretty well crest-risen this morning, thou didst eat yesternight too much mullet and bolymong. Come hither, sirrah, come hither, I will give thee some cakes. Whereupon Forgier dreading no harm, in all simplicity went towards him, and drew a sixpence out of his leather satchel, thinking that Marquet would have sold him some of his cakes. But instead of cakes, he gave him with his whip such a rude lash overthwart the legs, the marks of the whipcord knots were apparent in them, then would have fled away; but Forgier cried out as loud as he could, O murder, murder, help, help, help! and in the meantime threw a great cudgel after him, which he carried under his arm, wherewith he hit him in the coronal joint of his head, upon the crotaphic artery of the right side thereof, so forcibly, that Marquet fell down from his mare, more like a dead than a living man. Meanwhile the farmers and country swains that were watching their walnuts near to that place, came running with their great poles and long staves, and laid such load on these cake-bakers, as if they had been to thrash upon green rye. The other shepherds and shepherdesses, hearing the lamentable shout of Forgier, came with their slings and slackies following them, and throwing great stones at them, as thick as if it had been hail. At last they overtook them, and took from them about four or five dozen of their cakes. Nevertheless they paid for them the ordi-

[1] youth, fellow.

nary price, and gave them over and above one hundred eggs, and three baskets full of mulberries. Then did the cake-bakers help to get up to his mare, Marquet, who was most shrewdly wounded, and forthwith returned to Lerné, changing the resolution they had to go to Pareille, threatening very sharp and boisterously the cowherds, shepherds, and farmers, of Seuillé and Sinays. This done, the shepherds and shepherdesses made merry with these cakes and fine grapes, and sported themselves together at the sound of the pretty small pipe, scoffing and laughing at those vainglorious cake-bakers, who had that day met with a mischief for want of crossing themselves with a good hand in the morning. Nor did they forget to apply to Forgier's leg some fair great red medicinal grapes, and so handsomely dressed it and bound it up, that he was quickly cured.

[*This quarrel over the cakes leads to an invasion and to a long, heroic struggle. The following chapter recounts the events of one of the more notable battles.*]

HOW A MONK OF SEUILLÉ SAVED THE ABBEY

So much they did, and so far they went pillaging and stealing, that at last they came to Seuillé, where they robbed both men and women, and took all they could catch: nothing was either too hot or too heavy for them. Although the plague was there in the most part of all the houses, they nevertheless entered everywhere, then plundered and carried away all that was within, and yet for all this not one of them took any hurt, which is a most wonderful case. For the curates, vicars, preachers, physicians, chirurgeons, and apothecaries, who went to visit, to dress, to cure, to heal, to preach unto and admonish those that were sick, were all dead of the infection, and these devilish robbers and murderers caught never any harm at all. Whence comes this to pass, my masters? I beseech you think upon it. The town being thus pillaged, they went unto the abbey with a horrible noise and tumult, but they found it shut and made fast against them. Whereupon the body of the army marched forward towards a pass or ford called the Gué de Véde, except seven companies of foot and two hundred lancers, who, staying there, broke down the walls of the close, to waste, spoil, and make havoc of all the vines and vintage within that place. The monks (poor devils) knew not in that extremity to which of all their sancts they should vow themselves. Nevertheless, at all adventures, they rang the bells *ad capitulum capitulantes.* There it was decreed that they should make a fair

procession, stuffed with good lectures, prayers, and litanies *contra hostium insidias*, and jolly responses *pro pace*.

There was then in the abbey a claustral monk, called Friar John of the funnels and gobbets, in French *des entoumeures*, young, gallant, frisk, lusty, nimble, quick, active, bold, adventurous, resolute, tall, lean, wide-mouthed, long-nosed, a fair despatcher of morning prayers, unbridler of masses, and runner over of vigils; and, to conclude summarily in a word, a right monk, if ever there was any, since the monking world monked a monkery; for the rest, a clerk even to the teeth in matter of breviary. This monk, hearing the noise that the enemy made within the enclosure of the vineyard, went out to see what they were doing; and perceiving that they were cutting and gathering the grapes, whereon was grounded the foundation of all their next year's wine, returned unto the choir of the church where the other monks were, all amazed and astonished like so many bell-melters. Whom when he heard sing, ini, nim, pe, ne, ne, ne, ne, nene, tum ne, num, num, im, i, mi, co, o, no, o, o, neno, ne, no, no, no, rum, nenum, num: It is well ... sung, said he. By the virtue of God, why do not you sing, Panniers, farewell, vintage is done? The devil snatch me, if they be not already within the middle of our close, and cut so well both vines and grapes, that, by Cod's body, there will not be found for these four years to come so much as a gleaning in it. By the belly of Sanct James, what shall we poor devils drink the while? Lord God, *da mihi potum.* Then said the prior of the convent: What should this drunken fellow do here? let him be carried to prison for troubling the divine service. Nay, said the monk, the wine service, let us behave ourselves so that it be not troubled; for you yourself, my lord prior, love to drink of the best, and so doth every honest man. Never yet did a man of worth dislike good wine; it is a monastical apophthegm. But these responses that you chant here, by G—, are not in season. Wherefore is it, that our devotions were instituted to be short in the time of harvest and vintage, and long in the advent, and all the winter? The late friar, Massepelosse, of good memory, a true zealous man, or else I give myself to the devil, of our religion, told me, and I remember it well, how the reason was, that in this season we might press and make the wine, and in winter whiff it up. Hark you, my masters, you that love the wine, Cod's body, follow me; for Sanct Anthony burn me as freely as a faggot, if they get leave to taste one drop of the liquor that will not now come and fight for relief of the wine. Hog's belly, the goods of the church! Ha, no, no. What the devil, Sanct Thomas of England was well content to die for them; if I died in the same cause, should not I be a sanct likewise? Yes. Yet shall not I die there for all this, for it is I that must do it to others and send them a-packing.

As he spake this he threw off his great monk's habit, and laid hold upon the staff of the cross, which was made of the heart of a sorbapple-tree, it being of the length of a lance, round, of a full grip, and a little powdered with lilies called flower de luce, the workmanship whereof was almost all defaced and worn out. Thus went he out in a fair long-skirted jacket, putting his frock scarfwise athwart his breast, and in this equipage, with his staff, shaft or truncheon of the cross, laid on so lustily, brisk, and freely upon his enemies, who, without any order, or ensign, or trumpet, or drum, were busied in gathering the grapes of the vineyard. For the cornets, guidons, and ensign-bearers had laid down their standards, banners, and colors by the wall sides; the drummers had knocked out the heads of their drums on one end to fill them with grapes; the trumpeters were loaded with great bundles of bunches and huge knots of clusters; in sum, everyone of them was out of array, and all in disorder. He hurried therefore, upon them so rudely, without crying gare or beware, that he overthrew them like hogs, tumbled them over like swine, striking athwart and alongst, and by one means or other laid so about him, after the old fashion of fencing, that to some he beat out their brains, to others he crushed their arms, battered their legs, and bethwacked their sides till their ribs cracked with it. To others again he unjointed the spondyles or knuckles of the neck, disfigured their chaps, gashed their faces, made their cheeks hang flapping on their chin, and so swinged and belammed them that they fell down before him like hay before a mower. To some others he spoiled the frame of their kidneys, marred their backs, broke their thigh-bones, pashed in their noses, poached out their eyes, cleft their mandibles, tore their jaws, dung in their teeth into their throat, shook asunder their omoplates or shoulder blades, sphacelated their shins, mortified their shanks, inflamed their ankles, heaved off the hinges their ishies, their sciatica or hip-gout, dislocated the joints of their knees, squattered into pieces the boughts or pestles of their thighs, and so thumped, mauled and belabored them everywhere, that never was corn so thick and threefold threshed upon by ploughmen's flails as were the pitifully disjointed members of their mangled bodies under the merciless baton of the cross. If any offered to hide himself amongst the thickest of the vines, he laid him squat as a flounder, bruised the ridge of his back, and dashed his reins like a dog. If any thought by

flight to escape, he made his head to fly in pieces by the lamdoidal commissure, which is a seam in the hinder part of the skull. If anyone did scramble up into a tree, thinking there to be safe, he rent up his perinee, and impaled him in the fundament. If any of his old acquaintance happened to cry out, Ha, Friar John, my friend Friar John, quarter, quarter, I yield myself to you, to you I render myself! So thou shalt, said he, and must, whether thou wouldst or no, and withal render and yield up thy soul to all the devils in hell; then suddenly gave them dronos, that is, so many knocks, thumps, raps, dints, thwacks, and bangs, as sufficed to warn Pluto of their coming and despatch them a-going. If any was so rash and full of temerity as to resist him to his face, then was it he did show the strength of his muscles, for without more ado he did transpierce him, by running him in at the breast, through the mediastine and the heart. Others, again, he so quashed and bethumped, that, with a sound bounce under the hollow of their short ribs, he overturned their stomachs so that they died immediately. To some, with a smart souse on the epigaster, he would make their midriff swag, then, redoubling the blow, gave them such a homepush on the navel that he made their puddings to gush out. To others through their ballocks he pierced their bumgut, and left not bowel, tripe, nor entrail in their body that had not felt the impetuosity, fierceness, and fury of his violence. Believe, that it was the most horrible spectacle that ever one saw. Some cried unto Sanct Barbe, others to St. George. O the holy Lady Nytouch, said one, the good Sanctess; O our Lady of Succours, said another, help, help! Others cried, Our Lady of Cunaut, of Loretto, of Good Tidings, on the other side of the water St. Mary Over. Some vowed a pilgrimage to St. James, and others to the holy handkerchief of Chamberry, which three months after that burnt so well in the fire that they could not get one thread of it saved. Others sent up their vows to St. Cadouin, others to St. John d'Angely, and to St. Eutropiius of Xaintes. Other again invoked St. Mesmes of Cinon, St. Martin of Candes, St. Cloüaud of Sinays, the holy relics of Laurezay, with a thousand other jolly little sancts and santrels. Some died without speaking, others spoke without dying; some died in speaking, others spoke in dying. Others shouted as loud as they could Confession, Confession, *Confiteor, Miserere, In manus!* So great was the cry of the wounded, that the prior of the abbey with all his monks came forth, who, when they saw these poor wretches so slain amongst the vines, and wounded to death, confessed some of them. But whilst the priests were busied in confessing them, the little monkies ran all to the place where Friar John was, and asked him wherein he would be pleased to require their assistance. To which he answered that they should cut the throats of those he had thrown down upon the ground. They presently, leaving their outer habits and cowls upon the rails, began to throttle and make an end of those whom he had already crushed. Can you tell with what instruments they did it? With fair gullies, which are little hulch-backed demi-knives, the iron tool whereof is two inches long, and the wooden handle one inch thick, and three inches in length, wherewith the little boys in our country cut ripe walnuts in two while they are yet in the shell, and pick out the kernel, and they found them very fit for the expediting of that weasand-slitting exploit. In the meantime Friar John, with his formidable baton of the cross, got to the breach which the enemies had made, and there stood to snatch up those that endeavored to escape. Some of the monkitos carried the standards, banners, ensigns, guidons, and colours into their cells and chambers to make garters of them. But when those that had been shriven would have gone out at the gap of the said breach, the sturdy monk quashed and felled them down with blows, saying, These men have had confession and are penitent souls; they have got their absolution and gained the pardons: they go into paradise as straight as a sickle, or as the way is to Faye (like Crooked-Lane at Eastcheap). Thus by his prowess and valor were discomfited all those of the army that entered into the close of the abbey, unto the number of thirteen thousand, six hundred, twenty and two, besides the women and little children, which is always to be understood. Never did Maugis the Hermit bear himself more valiantly with his bourbon or pilgrim's staff against the Saracens, of whom it is written in the Acts of the four sons of Aymon, than did this monk against his enemies with the staff of the cross.

HOW PANTAGRUEL PERSUADETH PANURGE TO TAKE COUNSEL OF A FOOL

When Pantagruel [1] had withdrawn himself, he, by a little sloping window in one of the galleries, perceived Panurge in a lobby not far from thence, walking alone, with the gesture, carriage, and garb of a fond dotard, raving, wagging, and shaking his hands, dandling, lolling, and nodding with his head, like a cow bellowing for her calf; and, having then called him nearer, spoke unto him thus: You are at this present, as I think not unlike to a mouse entangled in a snare, who the more that she goeth about to rid and unwind herself out of the gin

[1] Pantagruel is the son of Gargantua.

wherein she is caught, by endeavoring to clear and deliver her feet from the pitch whereto they stick, the foulier she is bewrayed with it, and the more strongly pestered therein. Even so is it with you. For the more that you labor, strive, and enforce yourself to disencumber and extricate your thoughts out of the implicating involutions and fetterings of the grievous and lamentable gins and springs of anguish and perplexity, the greater difficulty there is in the relieving of you, and you remain faster bound than ever. Nor do I know for the removal of this inconveniency any remedy but one.

Take heed, I have often heard it said in a vulgar proverb, The wise may be instructed by a fool. Seeing the answers and responses of sage and judicious men have in no manner of way satisfied you, take advice of some fool, and possibly by so doing you may come to get that counsel which will be agreeable to your heart's desire and contentment. You know how by the advice and counsel and prediction of fools, many kings, princes, states, and commonwealths have been preserved, several battles gained and divers doubts of a most perplexed intricacy resolved. I am not so diffident of your memory as to hold it needful to refresh it with a quotation of examples, nor do I so far undervalue your judgment but that I think it will acquiesce in the reason of this my subsequent discourse. As he who narrowly takes heed to what concerns the dexterous management of his private affairs, domestic businesses, and those adoes which are confined within the strait-laced compass of one family, who is attentive, vigilant, and active in the economic rule of his own house, whose frugal spirit never strays from home, who loseth no occasion whereby he may purchase to himself more riches, and build up new heaps of treasure on his former wealth, and who knows warily how to prevent the inconveniences of poverty, is called a worldly wise man, though perhaps in the second judgment of the intelligences which are above he be esteemed a fool, — so, on the contrary, is he most like, even in the thoughts of all celestial spirits, to be not only sage, but to presage events to come by divine inspiration, who laying quite aside those cares which are conducible to his body or his fortunes, and, as it were, departing from himself, rids all his senses of terrene affections, and clears his fancies of those plodding studies which harbor in the minds of thriving men. All which neglects of sublunary things are vulgarly imputed folly. After this manner, the son of Picus, King of the Latins, the great soothsayer Faunus, was called Fatuus by the witless rabble of the common people. The like we daily see practised amongst the comic players, whose dramatic roles, in distribution of the personages, appoint the acting of the fool to him who is the wisest of the troop. In approbation also of this fashion the mathematicians allow the very same horoscope to princes and to sots. Whereof a right pregnant instance by them is given in the nativities of Æneas and Choroebus; the latter of which two is by Euphorion said to have been a fool, and yet had with the former the same aspects and heavenly genethliac influences.

I shall not, I suppose, swerve much from the purpose in hand, if I relate unto you what John Andrew said upon the return of a papal writ, which was directed to the mayor and burgesses of Rochelle, and after him by Panorme, upon the same pontifical canon; Barbatias on the Pandects, and recently by Jason in his Councils, concerning Seyny John, the noted fool of Paris, and Caillet's fore great-grandfather. The case is this.

At Paris, in the roastmeat cookery of the Petit Chastelet, before the cookshop of one of the roast-meat sellers of that lane, a certain hungry porter was eating his bread, after he had by parcels kept it a while above the reek and steam of a fat goose on the spit, turning at a great fire, and found it so besmoked with the vapor, to be savory, which the cook observing, took no notice, till after having ravined his penny loaf, whereof no morsel had been unsmokified, he was about decamping and going away. But, by your leave, as the fellow thought to have departed thence shot-free, the master-cook laid hold upon him by the gorget, and demanded payment for the smoke of his roast meat. The porter answered that he had sustained no loss at all; that by what he had done there was no diminution made of the flesh; that he had taken nothing of his, and that therefore he was not indebted to him in anything. As for the smoke in question, that, although he had not been there, it would howsoever have been evaporated; besides, that before that time it had never been seen nor heard that roastmeat smoke was sold upon the streets of Paris. The cook hereto replied, that he was not obliged nor any way bound to feed and nourish for naught a porter whom he had never seen before with the smoke of his roast meat, and thereupon swore that if he would not forthwith content and satisfy him with present payment for the repast which he had thereby got, that he would take his crooked staves from off his bask; which, instead of having loads thereafter laid upon them, should serve for fuel to his kitchen fires. Whilst he was going about so to do, and to have pulled them to him by one of the bottom rungs which he had caught in his hand, the sturdy porter got out of his grip, drew forth the knotty cudgel, and stood to

his own defence. The altercation waxed hot in words, which moved the gaping hoidens of the sottish Parisians to run from all parts thereabouts, to see what the issue would be of that bubbling strife and contention. In the interim of this dispute, to the very good purpose Seyny John, the fool and citizen of Paris, happened to be there, whom the cook perceiving, said to the porter, Wilt thou refer and submit to the noble Seyny John the decision of the difference and controversy which is betwixt us? Yes, by the blood of a goose, answered the porter, I am content. Seyny John the fool, finding that the cook and porter had compromised the determination of their variance and debate to the discretion of his award and arbitrament, after that the reasons on either side whereupon was grounded the mutual fierceness of their brawling jar had been to the full displayed and laid open before him, commanded the porter to draw out of the fob of his belt a piece of money, if he had it. Whereupon the porter immediately, without delay, in reverence to the authority of such a judicious umpire, put the tenth part of a silver Philip into his hand. This little Philip, Seyny John took; then set it on his left shoulder, to try by feeling if it was of a sufficient weight. After that, laying it on the palm of his hand, he made it ring and tingle, to understand by the ear if it was of a good alloy in the metal whereof it was composed. Thereafter he put it to the ball or apple of his left eye, to explore by the sight if it was well stamped and marked; all which being done, in a profound silence of the whole doltish people who were the spectators of this pageantry, to the great hope of the cook's and despair of the porter's prevalency in the suit that was in agitation, he finally caused the porter to make it sound several times upon the stall of the cook's shop. Then with a presidential majesty holding his bauble sceptre-like in his hand, muffling his head with a hood of marten skins, each side whereof had the resemblance of an ape's face sprucified up with ears of pasted paper, and having about his neck a bucked ruff, raised, furrowed, and ridged with pointing sticks of the shape and fashion of small organ pipes, he first with all the force of his lungs coughed two or three times, and then with an audible voice pronounced this following sentence: The court declareth that the porter who ate his bread at the smoke of the roast, hath civilly paid the cook with the sound of his money. And the said court ordaineth that everyone return to his own home, and attend his proper business, without cost and charges, and for a cause. This verdict, award, and arbitrament of the Parisian fool did appear so equitable, yea, so admirable to the aforesaid doctors, that they very much doubted if the matter had been brought before the sessions for justice of the said place, or that the judges of the Rota at Rome had been umpires therein, or yet that the Areopagites [1] themselves had been the deciders thereof, if by any one part, or all of them together, it had been so judicially sententiated and awarded. Therefore, advise, if you will be counselled by a fool.

[1] Areopagus, the "hill of Ares" (or Mars), was the seat of the highest court in ancient Athens.

Cervantes · 1547-1616

Cervantes in Spain, Ben Jonson, Edmund Spenser, and Shakespeare in England, Montaigne in France — these men were contemporaries. Any period which can claim such names as these is great just as Athens was great when Sophocles, Euripides, and Aristophanes walked her streets. Europe was well into the Renaissance; men were stirred with a new fervor. It was the time of Philip II of Spain, of Queen Elizabeth of England, of the colonization of America, of the defeat of the Spanish Armada, of the incorporation of the East India Company, of the massacre of St. Bartholomew. Proud men inhabited the earth. And, in this new spirit, Cervantes in *Don Quixote* laughed away the last vestiges of feudal chivalry.

Born in Alcalá de Henares in 1547, Miguel de Cervantes Saavedra was the son of an apothecary and surgeon. The first half of the life of Cervantes, though not distinguished by the same eccentricity, was almost as crowded with action and adventure as the life of his most popular hero, Don Quixote. The search of Cervantes' father for a subsistence took the boy first to one locality and then to another, Valladolid, Madrid, and Seville. In 1569 he was in Rome. At twenty-three he entered the Spanish army. At the Battle of Lepanto, in October, 1571, Cervantes was ill with a fever on a Spanish vessel, but arising from his bed insisted on being given a post of responsibility. In this battle he was wounded three times, one of the shots permanently injuring his left hand in such a way as to render it useless. The following year saw him in another engagement off Navarino. Other campaigns followed. Cervantes' military career came to a close when in September, 1575, his ship and all aboard were captured by Barbary pirates. For five years he was held a captive and slave, years during which he engaged in endless schemes for escape. So numerous and so bold were his attempts that the Viceroy of Algiers, Hassan Pasha, is credited with stating that so long as he had "the maimed Spaniard in safe keeping, his Christians, ships, and city were secure."

In 1580 Cervantes was ransomed. During the next five years he turned his hand to many things, failing in most of them. Several times he found himself in prison for debts. Finally, perhaps recalling some modest success at writing in his youth, he turned to literature. He sold his plays for a pittance; poems helped give him a reputation but brought him and his family little to eat. Only two of his books are much read today, the *Exemplary Novels* and *Don Quixote*. The publication of *The Life and Achievements of the Renown'd Don Quixote de la Mancha* (1605) brought him immediate fame and success — though not wealth. Unauthorized editions of the first part sprang up in other parts of Spain and abroad. A rival published an alleged "second part" before Cervantes had completed his own version in 1615. The next year, on the same day that Shakespeare died at Stratford, April 23, 1616, Cervantes died at Madrid.

SUGGESTED REFERENCES: Gary MacEoin, *Cervantes* (1950); S. B. Arbó, *Cervantes, The Man and His Time* (1955); E. C. Riley, *Cervantes's Theory of the Novel* (1962).

Don Quixote

Don Quixote was begun as a satire on the convention-alities of the chivalric romances popular at the time, but evidently Cervantes lost himself in his story and his beloved Don Quixote, for he made much more than that of the book. Like Chaucer, he has given us a picture of contemporary life and manners and, like Chaucer, he incorporated as characters people from the various strata of society. Here are knights and farm-ers, merchants and mule-drivers, ladies of fashion and women of easy virtue. The whole glows with a kindly understanding and tolerance. Even while ridiculing the artificiality of the nobility, Cervantes manifested his own true nobility of spirit. Sainte-Beuve was led to call *Don Quixote* "the Bible of Humanity." It is full of life, of humor, and downright good fun.

Although the satirical intent of Cervantes may sug-gest a classical element, and the simple outspokenness of Sancho Panza is certainly realistic, *Don Quixote* as a whole is obviously romantic in temper. It was, first of all, Cervantes' purpose to show the fallacy of the old chivalric romance by introducing stories more amazing even than the romances they were to displace; the book is full of strange and wild adventures, of extravagant conflicts. Logic is thrown aside and an almost unre-strained imagination given rein. Quixote is sincerely and absurdly bent on making the world a better place in which to live; he is the arch-idealist. And these we have found to be familiar characteristics of the romantic spirit.

The translation is by Peter Motteux as revised by Ozell.

THE QUALITY AND WAY OF LIVING OF THE RENOWN'D DON QUIXOTE DE LA MANCHA

At a certain Village in *La Mancha*,[1] which I shall not name, there liv'd not long ago one of those old-fashion'd Gentlemen who are never without a Lance upon a Rack, an old Target, a lean Horse, and a Greyhound. His Diet consisted more of Beef[2] than Mutton; and with minc'd Meat on most Nights, Lentils on *Fridays*, Eggs and Bacon on *Saturdays*, and a Pigeon extraordinary on *Sun-days*, he consumed three Quarters of his Revenue: The rest was laid out in a Plush-Coat, Velvet-Breeches, with Slippers of the same, for Holidays; and a Suit of the very best home-spun Cloth, which he bestowed on himself for Working-days. His whole Family was a Housekeeper something turn'd of Forty, a Niece not Twenty, and a Man that serv'd him in the House and in the Field, and could saddle a Horse, and handle the Pruning-Hook. The Master himself was nigh fifty Years of

[1] A small Territory partly in the Kingdom of Aragon, and partly in Castile; it is a Liberty within itself, dis-tinct from all the country about.

[2] Beef being cheaper in Spain than Mutton.

Age, of a hale and strong Complexion, lean-body'd, and thin-fac'd, an early Riser, and a Lover of Hunting. Some say his Sirname was Quixada, or Quesada (for Authors differ in this Particular): However, we may reasonably conjecture he was call'd Quixada (i.e. Lanthorn-Jaws) tho' this con-cerns us but little, provided we keep strictly to the Truth in every Point of this History.

You must know then, that when our Gentleman had nothing to do (which was almost all the Year round) he pass'd his Time in reading Books of Knight-Errantry; which he did with that Applica-tion and Delight, that at last he in a manner wholly left off his Country-Sports, and even the Care of his Estate; nay, he grew so strangely besotted with those Amusements, that he sold many Acres of Arable-Land to purchase Books of that kind; by which means he collected as many of them as were to be had: But among them all, none pleas'd him like the Works of the famous Feliciano de Sylva; for the Clearness of his Prose, and those intricate Expressions with which 'tis interlac'd, seem'd to him so many Pearls of Eloquence, especially when he came to read the Challenges, and the amorous Addresses, many of them in this extraordinary Stile. "The Reason of your unreasonable Usage of my Reason, does so enfeeble my Reason, that I have Reason to expostulate with your Beauty": And this, "The sublime Heavens, which with your Divinity divinely fortify you with the Stars, and fix you the Deserver of the Desert that is deserv'd by your Grandeur." These, and such like Ex-pressions, strangely puzzled the poor Gentleman's Understanding, while he was breaking his Brain to unravel their Meaning, which Aristotle himself could never have found, though he should have been rais'd from the Dead for that very Purpose.

He did not so well like those dreadful Wounds which Don Belianis gave and received; for he con-sidered that all the Art of Surgery could never se-cure his Face and Body from being strangely dis-figured with Scars. However, he highly com-mended the Author for concluding his Book with a Promise to finish that unfinishable Adventure; and many times he had a Desire to put Pen to Paper, and faithfully and literally finish it himself; which he had certainly done, and doubtless with good Success, had not his Thoughts been wholly en-grossed in much more important Designs.

He would often dispute with the Curate of the Parish, a Man of Learning, that had taken his Degrees at Ciguenza,[1] who was the better Knight Palmerin of England, or Amadis de Gaul? But Master Nicholas, the Barber of the same Town, would say, that none of 'em could compare with

[1] A university in Spain.

the Knight of the Sun; and that if any one came near him, 'twas certainly Don Galaor, the Brother of Amadis de Gaul; for he was a Man of a most commodious Temper, neither was he so finical, nor such a puling whining Lover as his Brother; and as for Courage, he was not a jot behind him.

In fine, he gave himself up so wholly to the reading of Romances, that a-Nights he would pore on 'till 'twas Day, and a-Days he would read on 'till 'twas Night; and thus by sleeping little, and reading much, the Moisture of his Brain was exhausted to that Degree, that at last he lost the Use of his Reason. A world of disorderly Notions, pick'd out of his Books, crouded into his Imagination; and now his Head was full of nothing but Inchantments, Quarrels, Battles, Challenges, Wounds, Complaints, Amours, Torments, and abundance of Stuff and Impossibilities; insomuch, that all the Fables and fantastical Tales which he read, seem'd to him now as true as the most authentick Histories. He would say, that the Cid Ruydiaz [1] was a very brave Knight, but not worthy to stand in Competition with the Knight of the Burning Sword, who with a single Backstroke had cut in sunder two fierce and mighty Giants. He liked yet better Bernardo del Carpio, who at Roncesvalles depriv'd of Life the inchanted Orlando, having lifted him from the Ground, and choak'd him in the Air, as Hercules did Antœus the Son of the Earth.

As for the Giant Morgante, he always spoke very civil Things of him; for though he was one of that monstrous Brood, who ever were intolerably proud and brutish, he still behav'd himself like a civil and well-bred Person.

But of all Men in the World he admir'd Rinaldo of Montalban, and particularly his sallying out of his Castle to rob all he met; and then again when Abroad he carried away the Idol of Mahomet, which was all massy Gold, as the History says: But he so hated that Traitor Galalon,[2] that for the Pleasure of kicking him handsomely, he would have given up his Housekeeper; nay, and his Niece into the bargain.

Having thus lost his Understanding, he unluckily stumbled upon the oddest Fancy that ever enter'd into a Madman's Brain; for now he thought it convenient and necessary, as well for the Increase of his own Honor, as the Service of the Publick, to turn Knight-Errant, and roam through the whole World arm'd Cap-a-pee, and mounted on his Steed, in quest of Adventures; that thus imitating those Knight-Errants of whom he had read, and following their Course of Life, redressing all manner of Grievances, and exposing himself to Danger on all Occasions, at last, after a happy Conclusion of his Enterprizes, he might purchase everlasting Honor and Renown. Transported with these agreeable Delusions, the poor Gentleman already grasp'd in Imagination the Imperial Sceptre of Trapizonde, and, hurry'd away by his mighty Expectations, he prepares with all Expedition to take the Field.

The first Thing he did was to scour a Suit of Armor that had belong'd to his Great-Grandfather, and had lain Time out of Mind carelessly rusting in a Corner: But when he had clean'd and repair'd it as well as he could, he perceiv'd there was a material Piece wanting; for instead of a complete Helmet, there was only a single Head-piece: However, his Industry supply'd that Defect, for with some Pasteboard he made a kind of Half-Beaver, or Vizor, which being fitted to the Head-piece, made it look like an entire Helmet. Then, to know whether it were Cutlass-Proof, he drew his Sword, and tried its Edge upon the Pasteboard Vizor; but with the very first Stroke he unluckily undid in a Moment what he had been a whole Week a doing. He did not like its being broke with so much Ease, and therefore to secure it from the like Accident, he made it a-new, and fenc'd it with thin Plates of Iron, which he fix'd on the Inside of it so artificially, that at last he had Reason to be satisfy'd with the Solidity of the Work; and so, without any farther Experiment, he resolv'd it should pass to all Intents and Purposes for a full and sufficient Helmet.

The next Moment he went to view his Horse, whose Bones stuck out like the Corners of a Spanish Real, being a worse Jade than Gonela's *qui tantum pellis & ossa fuit*; [1] however, his Master thought, that neither Alexander's Bucephalus, nor the Cid's Babieca could be compared with him. He was four Days considering what Name to give him; for, as he argu'd with himself, there was no Reason that a Horse bestrid by so famous a Knight, and withal so excellent in himself, should not be distinguish'd by a particular Name; and therefore he studied to give him such a one as should demonstrate as well what kind of Horse he had been before his Master was a Knight-Errant, as what he was now; thinking it but just, since the Owner chang'd his Profession, that the Horse should also change his Title, and be dignify'd with another; a good big Word, such a one as should fill the Mouth, and seem consonant with the Quality and Profes-

---

[1] Cid Ruydiaz, a famous Spanish Commander, of whom many Fables are written.

[2] Galalon, the Spaniards say, betray'd the French Army at Roncesvalles.

[1] Which was all skin and bones.

sion of his Master. And thus after many Names which he devis'd, rejected, chang'd, lik'd, dislik'd, and pitch'd upon again, he concluded to call him Rozinante;[1] a Name, in his Opinion, lofty, sounding, and significant of what he had been before, and also of what he was now; in a Word, a Horse before or above all the vulgar Breed of Horses in the World.

When he had thus given his Horse a Name so much to his Satisfaction he thought of chusing one for himself; and having seriously ponder'd on the Matter eight whole Days more, at last he determin'd to call himself Don Quixote. Whence the Author of this most authentick History draws this Inference, That his right Name was Quixada, and not Quesada, as others obstinately pretend. And observing, that the valiant Amadis, not satisfy'd with the bare Appellation of Amadis, added to it the Name of his Country, that it might grow more famous by his Exploits, and so stil'd himself Amadis de Gaul; so he, like a true Lover of his native Soil, resolv'd to call himself Don Quixote de la Mancha; which Addition, to his thinking, denoted very plainly his Parentage and Country, and consequently would fix a lasting Honor on that Part of the World.

And now his Armor being scour'd, his Head-Piece improv'd to a Helmet, his Horse and himself new nam'd, he perceiv'd he wanted nothing but a Lady, on whom he might bestow the Empire of his Heart; for he was sensible that a Knight-Errant without a Mistress, was a Tree without either Fruit or Leaves, and a Body without a Soul. Should I, said he to himself, by good or ill Fortune chance to encounter some Giant, as 'tis common in Knight-Errantry, and happen to lay him prostrate on the Ground, transfix'd with my Lance, or cleft in two, or, in short, overcome him, and have him at my Mercy, would it not be proper to have some Lady, to whom I may send him as a Trophy of my Valor? Then when he comes into her Presence, throwing himself at her Feet, he may thus make his humble Submission: "Lady, I am the Giant Caraculiambro, Lord of the Island of Malindrania, vanquish'd in single Combat by that never-deservedly-enough-extoll'd Knight-Errant Don Quixote de la Mancha, who has commanded me to cast my self most humbly at your Feet, that it may please your Honor to dispose of me according to your "Will." Oh! how elevated was the Knight with the Conceit of this imaginary Submission of the Giant; especially having withal bethought himself of a Person, on whom he might confer the Title of his Mistress! Which, 'tis believ'd

[1] Rozinante means "strong low-class horse."

happen'd thus: Near the Place where he lived, dwelt a good likely Country Lass, for whom he had formerly had a sort of an Inclination, though 'tis believ'd, she never heard of it, nor regarded it in the least. Her Name was Aldonza Lorenzo and this was she whom he thought he might entitle to the Sovereignty of his Heart: Upon which he studied to find her out a new Name, that might have some Affinity with her old one, and yet at the same time sound somewhat like that of a Princess, or Lady of Quality: So at last he resolved to call her Dulcinea, with the Addition of del Toboso, from the Place where she was born; a Name, in his Opinion, sweet, harmonious, extraordinary, and no less significative than the others which he had devis'd.

OF DON QUIXOTE'S FIRST SALLY

These Preparations being made, he found his Designs ripe for Action, and thought it now a Crime to deny himself any longer to the injur'd World, that wanted such a Deliverer; the more when he consider'd what Grievances he was to redress, what Wrongs and Injuries to remove, what Abuses to correct, and what Duties to discharge. So one Morning before Day, in the greatest Heat of July, without acquainting any one with his Design, with all the Secrecy imaginable, he arm'd himself Cap-a-pee, lac'd on his ill-contriv'd Helmet, brac'd on his Target, grasp'd his Lance, mounted Rozinante, and at the private Door of his Back-yard sally'd out into the Fields, wonderfully pleas'd to see with how much Ease he had succeeded in the Beginning of his Enterprise. But he had not gone far e'er a terrible Thought alarm'd him, a Thought that had like to have made him renounce his great Undertaking; for now it came into his Mind, that the Honor of Knighthood had not yet been conferr'd upon him, and therefore, according to the Laws of Chivalry, he neither could nor ought to appear in Arms against any profess'd Knight: Nay, he also consider'd, that tho' he were already knighted, it would become him to wear white Armor, and not to adorn his Shield with any Device, till he had deserved one by some extraordinary Demonstration of his Valor.

These Thoughts stagger'd his Resolution; but his Folly prevailing more than any Reason, he resolv'd to be dubb'd a Knight by the first he should meet, after the Example of several others, who, as his distracting Romances inform'd him, had formerly done the like. As for the other Difficulty about wearing white Armor, he propos'd to overcome it by scouring his own at Leisure 'till it should look whiter than Ermin. And having thus dismiss'd these busy Scruples, he very calmly rode on, leaving it to his Horse's Discretion to go which Way he pleas'd; firmly believing, that in this consisted the very Being of Adventures. And as he thus went on, I cannot but believe, said he to himself, that when the History of my famous Atchievements shall be given to the World, the learned Author will begin it in this very Manner, when he comes to give an Account of this my early setting out: "Scarce had the ruddy-color'd Phœbus begun to spread the golden Tresses of his lovely Hair over the vast Surface of the earthly Globe, and scarce had those feather'd Poets of the Grove, the pretty painted Birds, tun'd their little Pipes, to sing their early Welcomes in soft melodious Strains to the beautiful Aurora, who having left her jealous Husband's Bed, display'd her rosy Graces to mortal Eyes from the Gates and Balconies of the Manchegan Horizon, when the renowned Knight Don Quixote de la Mancha, disdaining soft Repose, forsook the voluptuous Down and mounting his famous Steed Rozinante, enter'd the ancient and celebrated Plains of Montiel." This was indeed the very Road he took; and then proceeding, "O happy Age! O fortunate Times! cry'd he, decreed to usher into the World my famous Atchievements; Atchievements worthy to be engraven on Brass, carv'd in Marble, and delineated in some Masterpiece of Painting, as Monuments of my Glory, and Examples for Posterity! And thou venerable Sage, wise Enchanter, whatever be thy Name; thou whom Fate has ordained to be the Compiler of this rare History, forget not, I beseech thee, my trusty Rozinante, the eternal Companion of all my Adventures." After this, as if he had been really in Love; "O Princess Dulcinea, cry'd he, Lady of this captive Heart, much Sorrow and Woe you have doom'd me to in banishing me thus, and imposing on me your rigorous Commands, never to appear before your beauteous Face! Remember, Lady, that loyal Heart your Slave, who for your Love submits to so many Miseries." To these extravagant Conceits, he added a world of others, all in Imitation, and in the very Stile of those, which the reading of Romances had furnish'd him with; and all this while he rode so softly, and the Sun's Heat increas'd so fast, and was so violent, that it would have been sufficient to have melted his Brains had he had any left.

He travell'd almost all that Day without meeting any Adventure worth the Trouble of relating; which put him into a kind of Despair; for he desir'd nothing more than to encounter immediately some Person on whom he might try the Vigor of his Arm.

Some Authors say, that his first Adventure was that of the Pass called Puerto Lapice; others, that of the Windmills; but all that I could discover of Certainty in this Matter, and that I meet with in the Annals of La Mancha, is, that he travelled all that Day; and towards the Evening, he and his Horse being heartily tir'd, and almost famish'd, Don Quixote looking about him, in hopes to discover some Castle, or at least some Shepherd's Cottage, there to repose and refresh himself, at last, near the Road which he kept, he espy'd an Inn, as welcome a Sight to his longing Eyes as if he had discover'd a Star directing him to the Gate, nay, to the Palace of his Redemption. Thereupon hast'ning towards the Inn with all the speed he could, he got thither just at the close of the Evening. There stood by Chance at the Inn-door two young Female Adventurers, alias Common Wenches, who were going to Sevil with some Carriers, that happen'd to take up their Lodging there that very Evening: And, as whatever our Knight-Errant saw, thought, or imagin'd, was all of a romantick Cast, and appear'd to him altogether after the Manner of the Books that had perverted his Imagination, he no sooner saw the Inn, but he fancy'd it to be a Castle fenc'd with four Towers, and lofty Pinnacles glittering with Silver, together with a deep Moat, Draw-Bridge, and all those other Appurtenances peculiar to such kind of Places.

Therefore when he came near it, he stopp'd awhile at a Distance from the Gate, expecting that some Dwarf wou'd appear on the Battlements, and sound his Trumpet to give notice of the Arrival of a Knight; but finding that no Body came, and that Rozinante was for making the best of his Way to the Stable, he advanc'd to the Inn-door, where spying the two young Doxies, they seem'd to him two beautiful Damsels, or graceful Ladies, taking the Benefit of the fresh Air at the Gate of the Castle. It happen'd also at the very Moment, that a Swineherd getting together his Hogs (for, without begging Pardon, so they are call'd) from the Stubble-field, winded his Horn; and Don Quixote presently imagin'd this was the wish'd-for Signal, which some Dwarf gave to notify his Approach; therefore with the greatest Joy in the World he rode up to the Inn. The Wenches, affrighted at the Approach of a man cas'd in Iron, and arm'd with a Lance and Target,[1] were for running into their Lodging; but Don Quixote perceiving their Fear by their Flight, lifted up the Pasteboard Beaver of his Helmet, and discovering his wither'd dusty Face, with comely Grace and

   [1] shield.

grave Delivery accosted them in this Manner: "I beseech ye, Ladies, do not fly, nor fear the least Offence: The Order of Knighthood, which I profess, does not permit me to countenance or offer Injuries to any one in the Universe, and least of all to Virgins of such high Rank as your Presence denotes." The Wenches look'd earnestly upon him, endeavoring to get a Glimpse of his Face, which his ill-contriv'd Beaver partly hid; but when they heard themselves stiled Virgins, a Thing so out of the Way of their Profession, they could not forbear laughing outright; which Don Quixote resented as a great Affront. "Give me leave to tell ye, Ladies, cry'd he, that Modesty and Civility are very becoming in the Fair Sex; whereas Laughter without Ground is the highest Piece of Indiscretion: However, added he, I do not presume to say this to offend you, or incur your Displeasure; no, Ladies, I assure you I have no other Design but to do you Service." This uncommon Way of Expression, join'd to the Knight's scurvy Figure, increas'd their Mirth; which incens'd him to that Degree, that this might have carry'd Things to an Extremity, had not the Inn-keeper luckily appear'd at that Juncture. He was a Man whose Burden of Fat inclin'd him to Peace and Quietness, yet when he had observ'd such a strange Disguise of human Shape in his odd Armor and Equipage, he could hardly forbear keeping the Wenches Company in their Laughter; but having the Fear of such a warlike Appearance before his Eyes, he resolv'd to give him good Words, and therefore accosted him civilly: Sir Knight, said he, if your Worship be dispos'd to alight, you will fail of nothing here but of a Bed; as for all other Accommodations, you may be supply'd to your Mind. Don Quixote observing the Humility of the Governor of the Castle, (for such the Inn-keeper and Inn seem'd to him) Senior Castellano, said he, the least Thing in the World suffices me; for Arms are the only Things I value, and Combat is my Bed of Repose. The Inn-keeper thought he had call'd him, Castellano,[1] as taking him to be one of the true Castilians, whereas he was indeed of Andalusia, nay, of the Neighborhood of St. Lucar, no less thievish than Cacus, or less mischievous than a Truant-Scholar, or Court-Page, and therefore he made him this Reply; "At this rate, Sir Knight, your Bed might be a Pavement, and your Rest to be still awake; you may then safely alight, and I dare assure you, you can hardly miss being kept awake all the Year long in this House, much less one single Night." With that he went and held

[1] Castellano signifies both a Constable or Governor of a castle, and an inhabitant of the Kingdom of Castile in Spain.

Don Quixote's stirrup, who having not broke his Fast that Day, dismounted with no small Trouble or Difficulty. He immediately desir'd the Governor (that is, the Inn-keeper) to have special Care of his Steed, assuring him, that there was not a better in the Universe; upon which the Inn-keeper view'd him narrowly, but could not think him to be half so good as Don Quixote said: However, having set him up in the Stable, he came back to the Knight to see what he wanted, and found him pulling off his Armor by the Help of the good-natur'd Wenches, who had already reconcil'd themselves to him; but though they had eas'd him of his Corslet and Back-plate, they could by no means undo his Gorget, nor take off his ill-contriv'd Beaver, which he had ty'd so fast with green Ribbons, that 'twas impossible to get it off without cutting them; now he would by no means permit that, and so was forc'd to keep on his Helmet All Night, which was one of the most pleasant Sights in the World: And while his Armor was taking off by the two kind Lasses, imagining them to be Persons of Quality, and Ladies of that Castle, he very gratefully made them the following Compliment, 'in Imitation of an old Romance.'

There never was on Earth a Knight
    So waited on by Ladies fair,
As once was he, Don Quixote hight,
    When first he left his Village dear:
Damsels t'undress him ran with Speed,
And Princesses to dress his Steed.

O Rozinante! for that is my Horse's Name, Ladies, and mine Don Quixote de la Mancha; I never thought to have discover'd it, 'till some Feats of Arms atchiev'd by me in your Service, had made me better known to your Ladyships; but Necessity forcing me to apply to present Purpose that Passage of the ancient Romance of Sir Lancelot, which I now repeat, has extorted the Secret from me before its Time; yet a Day will come, when you shall command, and I obey, and then the Valor of my Arm shall evince the Reality of my Zeal to serve your Ladyships.

The two Females, who were not used to such rhetorical Speeches, could make no Answer to this; they only ask'd him whether he would eat any thing? That I will with all my Heart, cry'd Don Quixote, whatever it be, for I am of Opinion nothing can come to me more seasonably. Now, as Ill-luck would have it, it happen'd to be Friday, and there was nothing to be had at the Inn but some Pieces of Fish, which is called Abadexo in Castile, Bacallao in Andalusia, Curadillo in some Places, and in others Truchuela or Little Trout, though after all 'tis but Poor Jack: So they ask'd him whether he could eat any of that Truchuela, because they had no other Fish to give him. Don Quixote imagining they meant a small Trout, told them, that provided there were more than one 'twas the same Thing to him, they would serve him as well as a great one; for, continued he, 'tis all one to me whether I am paid a Piece of Eight in one single Piece, or in eight small Reals, which are worth as much: Besides, 'tis probable these Small Trouts may be like Veal, which is finer Meat than Beef; or like the Kid, which is better than the Goat. In short, let it be what it will, so it comes quickly, for the Weight of Armor and the Fatigue of Travel are not to be supported without recruiting Food. Thereupon they laid the Cloth at the Inn-door, for the Benefit of the fresh Air, and the Landlord brought him a Piece of that Salt-fish, but ill-water'd, and as ill-dres'd; and as for the Bread, 'twas as mouldy and brown as the Knight's Armor: But 'twould have made one laugh to have seen him eat; for having his Helmet on, with his Beaver lifted up, 'twas impossible for him to feed himself without Help, so that one of those Ladies had that Office; but there was no giving him Drink that Way, and he must have gone without it, had not the Inn-keeper bored a Cane, and setting one End of it to his Mouth, pour'd the Wine in at the other; all which the Knight suffer'd patiently, because he would not cut the Ribbons that fasten'd his Helmet.

While he was at Supper, a Sow-gelder happen'd to sound his Cane-Trumpet, or Whistle of Reeds, four or five times as he came near the Inn; which made Don Quixote the more positive of his being in a famous Castle, where he was entertain'd with Musick at Supper, that the Poor Jack was young Trout, the Bread of the finest Flour, the Wenches Great Ladies, and the Inn-keeper the Governor of the Castle; which made him applaud himself for his Resolution, and his setting out on such an Account. The only Thing that vex'd him was, that he was not yet dubb'd a Knight; for he fansy'd he could not lawfully undertake any Adventure till he had receiv'd the Order of Knighthood.

AN ACCOUNT OF THE PLEASANT METHOD TAKEN BY DON QUIXOTE TO BE DUBB'D A KNIGHT

Don Quixote's Mind being disturb'd with that Thought, he abridg'd even his short Supper: And as soon as he had done, he call'd his Host, then shut him and himself up in the Stable, and falling at his Feet, I will never rise from this Place, cry'd he, most valorous Knight, till you have graciously vouchsafed to grant me a Boon. which I will now beg of you, and which will redound to your Honor and the Good of Mankind. The Inn-keeper, strangely at a Loss to find his Guest at his Feet, and talking at this rate, endeavor'd to make him rise, but all in vain, till he had promis'd to grant him what he ask'd. I expected no less from your great Magnificence, Noble Sir, reply'd Don Quixote, and therefore I make bold to tell you, that the Boon which I beg, and you generously condescend to grant me, is, that To-morrow you will be pleased to bestow the Honor of Knighthood upon me. This Night I will watch my Armor in the Chapel of your Castle, and then in the Morning you shall gratify me, as I passionately desire, that I may be duly qualify'd to seek out Adventures in every Corner of the Universe, to relieve the Distress'd, according to the Laws of Chivalry, and the Inclinations of Knight-Errants like my self. The Inn-keeper, who, as I said, was a sharp Fellow, and had already a shrewd Suspicion of the Disorder in his Guest's Understanding, was fully convinc'd of it when he heard him talk after this manner; and, to make Sport that Night, resolv'd to humor him in his Desires, telling him he was highly to be commended for his Choice of such an Employment, which was altogether worthy a Knight of the first Order, such as his gallant Deportment discover'd him to be: That he himself had in his Youth follow'd that honorable Profession, ranging through many Parts of the World in search of Adventures, without so much as forgetting to visit the Percheles of Malaga,[1] the Isles of Riaran, the Compass of Sevil, the Quick-silver-House of Segovia, the Olive Field of Valencia, the Circle of Granada, the Wharf of St. Lucar, the Potro of Cordova,[2] the Hedge-Taverns of Toledo, and divers other Places, where he had exercised the Nimbleness of his Feet and the Subtility of his Hands, doing Wrongs in Abundance, soliciting many Widows, undoing some Damsels, bubbling young Heirs, and in a Word, making himself famous in most of the Courts of Judicature in Spain, till at length he retired to this Castle, where he liv'd on his own Estate and those of others, entertaining all Knights-Errant of what Quality or Condition soever, purely for the great Affection he bore them, and to partake of what they got in Recompense of his Good-will. He added, That his Castle at present had no Chapel where the Knight might keep the Vigil of his Arms, it being pull'd down in order to be new-built; but

---

[1] These are all Places noted for Rogueries and disorderly Doings.

[2] A Square in the City of Cordova, where a Fountain gushes out from the Mouth of a Horse, near which is also a Whipping-post. The Spanish Word Potro signifies a Colt or young Horse.

that he knew they might lawfully be watch'd in any other Place in a Case of Necessity, and therefore he might do it that Night in the Court-yard of the Castle; and in the Morning (God willing) all the necessary Ceremonies should be perform'd, so that he might assure himself he should be dubb'd a Knight, nay, as much a Knight as any one in the World could be. He then ask'd Don Quixote whether he had any Money? Not a Cross, reply'd the Knight, for I never read in any History of Chivalry that any Knight-Errant ever carry'd Money about him. You are mistaken, cry'd the Inn-keeper; for admit the Histories are silent in this Matter, the Authors thinking it needless to mention Things so evidently necessary as Money and clean Shirts, yet there is no Reason to believe the Knights went without either; and you may rest assur'd, that all the Knight-Errants, of whom so many Histories are full, had their Purses well lin'd to supply themselves with Necessaries, and carry'd also with them some Shirts, and a small Box of Salves to heal their Wounds; for they had not the Conveniency of Surgeons to cure 'em every Time they fought in Fields and Desarts, unless they were so happy as to have some Sage or Magician for their Friend to give them present Assistance, sending them some Damsel or Dwarf through the Air in a Cloud, with a small Bottle of Water of so great a Virtue, that they no sooner tasted a Drop of it, but their Wounds were as perfectly cured as if they had never receiv'd any. But when they wanted such a Friend in former Ages, the Knights thought themselves oblig'd to take care, that their Squires should be provided with Money and other Necessaries, as Lint and Salves to dress their Wounds; and if those Knights ever happen'd to have no Squires, which was but very seldom, then they carry'd those Things behind them in a little Bag, as if it had been something of greater Value, and so neatly fitted to their Saddle, that it was hardly seen; for had it not been upon such an Account, the carrying of Wallets was not much allow'd among Knight-Errants. I must therefore advise you, continu'd he, nay, I might even charge and command you, as you are shortly to be my Son in Chivalry, never from this Time forwards to ride without Money, nor without the other Necessaries of which I spoke to you, which you will find very beneficial when you least expect it. Don Quixote promis'd to perform very punctually all his Injunctions; and so they dispos'd every thing in order to his Watching his Arms in a great Yard that adjoin'd to the Inn. To which Purpose the Knight, having got them all together, laid them in a Horse-trough close by a Well in that Yard; then bracing his Target and grasping his Lance, just as it drew dark, he began to walk about by the Horse-trough with a graceful Deportment. In the mean while the Inn-keeper acquainted all those that were in the House with the Extravagancies of his Guest, his Watching his Arms, and his Hopes of being made a Knight. They all admir'd very much at so strange a kind of Folly, and went on to observe him at a Distance; where they saw him sometimes walk about with a great deal of Gravity, and sometimes lean on his Lance, with his Eyes all the while fix'd upon his Arms. 'Twas now undoubted Night, but yet the Moon did shine with such a Brightness, as might almost have vy'd with that of the Planet which lent it her; so that the Knight was wholly expos'd to the Spectators' View. While he was thus employ'd, one of the Carriers who lodg'd in the Inn came out to water his Mules, which he could not do without removing the Arms out of the Trough. With that Don Quixote, who saw him make towards him, cry'd out to him aloud, O thou, whoe'er thou art, rash Knight, that prepares to lay thy Hands on the Arms of the most valorous Knight-Errant that ever wore a Sword, take heed; do not audaciously attempt to profane them with a Touch, lest instant Death be the too sure Reward of thy Temerity. But the Carrier never regarded these dreadful Threats; and laying hold on the Armor by the Straps, without any more ado threw it a good way from him; though it had been better for him to have let it alone; for Don Quixote no sooner saw this, but lifting up his Eyes to Heaven, and addressing his Thoughts, as it seem'd, to his Lady Dulcinea, Assist me, Lady, cry'd he, in the first Opportunity that offers itself to your faithful Slave; nor let your Favor and Protection be deny'd me in this first Trial of my Valor! Repeating such-like Ejaculations, he let slip his Target, and lifting up his Lance with both his Hands, he gave the Carrier such a terrible Knock on his inconsiderate Head with his Lance, that he laid him at his Feet in a woful Condition; and had he back'd that Blow with another, the Fellow would certainly have had no need of a Surgeon. This done, Don Quixote took up his Armor, laid it again in the Horse-trough, and then walk'd on backwards and forwards with great Unconcern as he did at first.

Soon after another Carrier, not knowing what had happen'd, came also to water his Mules, while the first yet lay on the Ground in a Trance; but as he offer'd to clear the Trough of the Armor, Don Quixote, without speaking a Word, or imploring any one's Assistance, once more dropp'd his Target, lifted up his Lance, and then let it fall so heavily on the Fellow's Pate, that without damaging his

Lance, he broke the Carrier's Head in three or four Places. His Outcry soon alarm'd and brought thither all the People in the Inn, and the Landlord among the rest; which Don Quixote perceiving, Thou Queen of Beauty (cry'd he, bracing on his Shield, and drawing his Sword) thou Courage and Vigor of my weaken'd Heart, now is the Time when thou must enliven thy adventurous Slave with the Beams of thy Greatness, while this Moment he is engaging in so terrible an Adventure! With this, in his Opinion, he found himself supply'd with such an Addition of Courage, that had all the Carriers in the World at once attack'd him, he would undoubtedly have fac'd them all. On the other Side, the Carriers, enrag'd to see their Comrades thus us'd, though they were afraid to come near, gave the Knight such a Volley of Stones, that he was forc'd to shelter himself as well as he could under the Covert of his Target, without daring to go far from the Horse-trough, lest he should seem to abandon his Arms. The Inn-keeper call'd to the Carriers as loud as he could to let him alone; that he had told them already he was mad, and consequently the Law would acquit him, though he should kill 'em. Don Quixote also made yet more Noise, calling 'em false and treacherous Villains, and the Lord of the Castle base and unhospitable, and a discourteous Knight, for suffering a Knight-Errant to be so abus'd. I would make thee know (cry'd he) what a perfidious Wretch thou art, had I but receiv'd the Order of Knighthood; but for you, base ignominious Rabble! fling on, do your worst; come on, draw nearer if you dare, and receive the Reward of your Indiscretion and Insolence. This he spoke with so much Spirit and Undauntedness, that he struck a Terror into all his Assailants; so that partly through Fear, and partly through the Inn-keeper's Perswasions, they gave over flinging Stones at him; and he, on his Side, permitted the Enemy to carry off their Wounded, and then return'd to the Guard of his Arms as calm and compos'd as before.

The Inn-keeper, who began somewhat to disrelish these mad Tricks of his Guest, resolv'd to dispatch him forthwith, and bestow on him that unlucky Knighthood, to prevent farther Mischief: So coming to him, he excus'd himself for the Insolence of those base Scoundrels, as being done without his Privity or Consent; but their Audaciousness, he said, was sufficiently punished. He added, that he had already told him there was no Chapel in his Castle; and that indeed there was no need of one to finish the rest of the Ceremony of Knighthood, which consisted only in the Application of the Sword to the Neck and Shoulders, as he had read in the Register of the Ceremonies of the Order; and that this might be perform'd as well in a Field as anywhere else: That he had already fulfill'd the Obligation of watching his Arms, which requir'd no more than Two Hours Watch, whereas he had been Four Hours upon the Guard. Don Quixote, who easily believ'd him, told him he was ready to obey him, and desir'd him to make an End of the Business as soon as possible, for if he were but Knighted, and should see himself once attack'd, he believ'd he should not leave a Man alive in the Castle, except those whom he should desire him to spare for his Sake.

Upon this the Inn-keeper, lest the Knight should proceed to such Extremities, fetch'd the Book in which he us'd to set down the Carriers Accounts for Straw and Barley; and having brought with him the two kind Females, already mentioned, and a Boy that held a Piece of lighted Candle in his Hand, he order'd Don Quixote to kneel: Then reading in his Manual, as if he had been repeating some pious Oration, in the midst of his Devotion he lifted up his Hand, and gave him a good Blow on the Neck, and then a gentle Slap on the Back with the Flat of his Sword, still mumbling some Words between his Teeth in the Tone of a Prayer. After this he ordered one of the Wenches to gird the Sword about the Knight's Waist; which she did with much Solemnity, and, I may add, Discretion, considering how hard a Thing it was to forbear laughing at every Circumstance of the Ceremony: 'Tis true, the Thoughts of the Knight's late Prowess, did not a little contribute to the Expression of her Mirth. As she girded on his Sword, Heav'n, cry'd the kind Lady, make your Worship a lucky Knight, and prosper you wherever you go. Don Quixote desir'd to know her Name, that he might understand to whom he was indebted for the Favor she had bestow'd upon him, and also make her Partaker of the Honor he was to acquire by the Strength of his Arm. To which the Lady answer'd with all Humility, that her Name was Tolosa, a Cobbler's Daughter, that kept a Stall among the little Shops of Sanchobinaya at Toledo; and that whenever he pleas'd to command her, she would be his humble Servant. Don Quixote begg'd of her to do him the Favor to add hereafter the Title of Lady to her Name, and for his Sake to be call'd from that Time the Lady Tolosa; which she promis'd to do. Her Companion having buckl'd on his Spurs, occasion'd the like Conference between them; and when he had ask'd her Name, she told him she went by the Name of Miller, being the Daughter of an honest Miller of Antequera. Our new Knight intreated her also to stile her self the Lady Miller, making her new Offers of

Service. These extraordinary Ceremonies (the like never seen before) being thus hurried over in a kind of Post-haste, Don Quixote could not rest till he had taken the Field in quest of Adventures; therefore having immediately saddled his Rozinante, and being mounted, he embrac'd the Inn-keeper, and return'd him so many Thanks at so extravagant a rate, for the Obligation he had laid upon him in dubbing him a Knight, that 'tis impossible to give a true Relation of 'em all: To which the Inn-keeper, in haste to get rid of him, return'd as rhetorical, though shorter, Answers; and, without stopping his Horse for the Reckoning, was glad with all his Heart to see him go.

OF THE GOOD SUCCESS WHICH THE VALOROUS DON QUIXOTE HAD IN THE MOST TERRIFYING AND NEVER–TO–BE–IMAGIN'D ADVENTURE OF THE WIND–MILLS, WITH OTHER TRANSACTIONS WORTHY TO BE TRANSMITTED TO POSTERITY

As they were thus discoursing, they discover'd some thirty or forty Wind-mills, that are in that Plain; and as soon as the Knight had spy'd them, Fortune, cry'd he, directs our Affairs better than we our selves could have wish'd: Look yonder, Friend Sancho, there are at least thirty outrageous Giants, whom I intend to encounter; and having depriv'd them of Life, we will begin to enrich our selves with their Spoils: For they are lawful Prize; and the Extirpation of that cursed Brood will be an acceptable Service to Heaven. What Giants, quoth Sancho Pança? Those whom thou see'st yonder, answer'd Don Quixote, with their long-extended Arms; some of that detested Race have Arms of so immense a Size, that sometimes they reach two Leagues in Length. Pray look better, Sir, quoth Sancho; those things yonder are no Giants, but Wind-mills, and the Arms you fancy, are their Sails, which being whirl'd about by the Wind, make the Mill go. 'Tis a Sign, cry'd Don Quixote, thou art but little acquainted with Adventures! I tell thee, they are Giants; and therefore if thou art afraid, go aside and say thy Prayers, for I am resolv'd to engage in a dreadful unequal Combat against them all. This said, he clapp'd Spurs to his Horse Rozinante, without giving Ear to his Squire Sancho, who bawl'd out to him, and assur'd him, that they were Wind-mills, and no Giants. But he was so fully possess'd with a strong Conceit of the contrary, that he did not so much as hear his Squire's Outcry, nor was he sensible of what they were, although he was already very near them: Far from that, Stand, Cowards, cry'd he as loud as he could; stand your Ground, ignoble Creatures, and fly not basely from a single Knight, who dares encounter you all. At the same Time the Wind rising, the Mill-Sails began to move, which, when Don Quixote spy'd, Base Miscreants, cry'd he, though you move more Arms than the Giant Briareus, you shall pay for your Arrogance. He most devoutly recommended himself to his Lady Dulcinea, imploring her Assistance in this perilous Adventure; and so covering himself with his Shield, and couching his Lance, he rush'd with Rozinante's utmost Speed upon the first Wind-mill he could come at, and running his Lance into the Sail, the Wind whirl'd it about with such Swiftness, that the Rapidity of the Motion presently broke the Lance into Shivers, and hurl'd away both Knight and Horse along with it, till down he fell rolling a good Way off in the Field. Sancho Pança ran as fast as his Ass could drive to help his Master, whom he found lying, and not able to stir, such a Blow he and Rozinante had receiv'd. Mercy o' me! cry'd Sancho, did not I give your Worship fair Warning? Did not I tell you they were Wind-mills, and that no Body could think otherwise, unless he had also Wind-mills in his Head? Peace, Friend Sancho, reply'd Don Quixote: There is nothing so subject to the Inconstancy of Fortune as War. I am verily perswaded, that cursed Necromancer Freston, who carry'd away my Study and my Books, has transform'd these Giants into Wind-mills, to deprive me of the Honor of the Victory; such is his inveterate Malice against me: But in the End, all his pernicious Wiles and Stratagems shall prove ineffectual against the prevailing Edge of my Sword. Amen, say I, reply'd Sancho; and so heaving him up again upon his Legs, once more the Knight mounted poor Rozinante, that was half Shoulder-slipp'd with his Fall.

This Adventure was the Subject of their Discourse, as they made the best of their Way towards the Pass of Lapice; for Don Quixote took that Road, believing he could not miss of Adventures in one so mightily frequented. However, the Loss of his Lance was no small Affliction to him; and as he was making his Complaint about it to his Squire, I have read, said he, Friend Sancho, that a certain Spanish Knight, whose Name was Diego Perez de Vargas, having broken his Sword in the Heat of an Engagement, pull'd up by the Roots a huge Oak-Tree, or at least tore down a massy Branch, and did such wonderful Execution, crushing and grinding so many Moors with it that Day, that he won himself and his Posterity the Sirname of The Pounder, or Bruiser. I tell thee this, because I intend to tear up the next Oak, or

Holm-Tree we meet; with the Trunk whereof I hope to perform such wondrous Deeds, that thou wilt esteem thy self particularly happy in having had the Honor to behold them, and been the ocular Witness of Atchievements which Posterity will scarce be able to believe. Heaven grant you may, cry'd Sancho: I believe it all, because your Worship says it. But, an't please you, sit a little more up-right in your Saddle; you ride sideling methinks; but that, I suppose, proceeds from your being bruis'd by the Fall. It does so, reply'd Don Quixote; and if I do not complain of the Pain, 'tis because a Knight-Errant must never complain of his Wounds, though his Bowels were dropping out through 'em. Then I've no more to say, quoth Sancho; and yet, Heaven knows my Heart, I shou'd be glad to hear your Worship hone a little now and then when something ails you: For my Part, I shall not fail to bemoan my self when I suffer the smallest Pain, unless indeed it can be proved, that the Rule of not complaining extends to the Squires as well as Knights. Don Quixote could not forbear smiling at the Simplicity of his Squire; and told him he gave him Leave to complain not only when he pleas'd, but as much as he pleas'd, whether he had any Cause or no; for he had never yet read any thing to the contrary in any Book of Chivalry. Sancho desir'd him, however, to con-sider, that 'twas high Time to go to Dinner; but his Master answer'd him, that he might eat when-ever he pleas'd; as for himself he was not yet dis-pos'd to do it. Sancho having thus obtain'd leave, fix'd himself as orderly as he cou'd upon his Ass; and taking some Victuals out of his Wallet, fell to munching lustily as he rode behind his Master; and ever and anon he lifted his Bottle to his Nose, and fetch'd such hearty Pulls, that it would have made the best pamper'd Vintner in Malaga a-dry to have seen him. While he thus went on stuffing and swilling, he did not think in the least of all his Master's great Promises; and was so far from esteeming it a Trouble to travel in quest of Ad-ventures, that he fancy'd it to be the greatest Pleasure in the World, though they were never so dreadful.

In fine, they pass'd that Night under some Trees; from one of which Don Quixote tore a wither'd Branch, which in some sort was able to serve him for a Lance, and to this he fix'd the Head or Spear of his broken Lance. But he did not sleep all that Night, keeping his Thoughts intent on his dear Dulcinea, in Imitation of what he had read in Books of Chivalry, where the Knights pass that Time, without Sleep, in Forests and Desarts, wholly taken up with the entertaining Thoughts of their absent Mistresses. As for Sancho, he did not spend the Night at that idle Rate; for having his Paunch well stuff'd with something more sub-stantial than Dandelion-Water, he made but one Nap of it; and had not his Master wak'd him, neither the sprightly Beams which the Sun darted on his Face, nor the Melody of the Birds, that chearfully on every Branch welcom'd the smiling Morn, wou'd have been able to have made him stir. As he got up, to clear his Eye-sight, he took two or three long-winded Swigs at his friendly Bottle for a Morning's Draught: But he found it somewhat lighter than it was the Night before; which Misfortune went to his very Heart, for he shrewdly mistrusted that he was not in a way to cure it of that Distemper as soon as he could have wish'd. On the other side, Don Quixote wou'd not break Fast, having been feasting all Night on the more delicate and savory Thoughts of his Mistress; and therefore they went on directly towards the Pass of Lapice, which they discover'd about Three a'Clock. When they came near it, Here it is, Brother Sancho, said Don Quixote, that we may wanton, and as it were, thrust our Arms up to the very Elbows, in that which we call Adventures. But let me give thee one necessary Caution; Know, that tho' thou should'st see me in the greatest Extremity of Danger, thou must not offer to draw thy Sword in my Defence, unless thou findest me assaulted by base Plebeians and vile Scoundrels; for in such a Case thou may'st assist thy Master: But if those with whom I am fighting are Knights, thou must not do it; for the Laws of Chivalry do not allow thee to encounter a Knight, till thou art one thy self. Never fear, quoth Sancho; I'll be sure to obey your Worship in that, I'll warrant you; for I've ever lov'd Peace and Quietness, and never car'd to thrust my self into Frays and Quar-rels: And yet I don't care to take Blows at any one's Hands neither; and shou'd any Knight offer to set upon me first, I fancy I should hardly mind your Laws; for all Laws, whether of God or Man, allow one to stand in his own Defence if any offer to do him a Mischief. I agree to that, reply'd Don Quixote; but as for helping me against any Knights, thou must set Bounds to thy natural Im-pulses. I'll be sure to do it, quoth Sancho; ne'er trust me if I don't keep your Commandment as well as I do the Sabbath.

As they were talking, they spy'd coming towards them two Monks of the Order of St. Benedict mounted on two Dromedaries, for the Mules on which they rode were so high and stately, that they seem'd little less. They wore Riding-Masks, with Glasses at the Eyes, against the Dust, and Um-brellas to shelter them from the Sun. After them came a Coach, with four or five Men on Horseback, and two Muleteers on Foot. There prov'd to be in the Coach a Biscayan Lady, who was going to Seville to meet her Husband, that was there in order to embark for the Indies, to take Possession of a considerable Post. Scarce had Don Quixote perceiv'd the Monks, who were not of the same Company, though they went the same Way, but he cry'd to his Squire, Either I am deceiv'd, or this will prove the most famous Adventure that ever was known; for without all question those two black Things that move towards us must be some Necromancers, that are carrying away by Force some Princess in that Coach; and 'tis my Duty to prevent so great an Injury. I fear me this will prove a worse Job than the Wind-mills, quoth Sancho. 'Slife, Sir, don't you see these are Benedictin Friars, and 'tis likely the Coach belongs to some Travellers that are in't: Therefore once more take Warning, and don't you be led away by the Devil. I have already told thee Sancho, reply'd Don Quixote, thou art miserably ignorant in Matters of Adventures: What I say is true, and thou shalt find it so presently. This said, he spurr'd on his Horse, and posted himself just in the midst of the Road where the Monks were to pass. And when they came within Hearing, Curs'd Implements of Hell, cry'd he in a loud and haughty Tone, immediately release those high-born Princesses whom you are violently conveying away in the Coach, or else prepare to meet with instant Death, as the just Punishment of your pernicious Deeds. The Monks stopp'd their Mules, no less astonish'd at the Figure, than at the Expressions of the Speaker. Sir Knight, cry'd they, we are no such Persons as you are pleas'd to term us, but religious Men, of the Order of St. Benedict, that travel about our Affairs; and are wholly ignorant whether or no there are any Princesses carry'd away by Force in that Coach. I'm not to be deceiv'd with fair Words, reply'd Don Quixote; I know you well enough, perfidious Caitiffs; and immediately, without expecting their Reply, he set Spurs to Rozinante, and ran so furiously, with his Lance couch'd, against the first Monk, that if he had not prudently flung himself off to the Ground, the Knight wou'd certainly have laid him either dead, or grievously wounded. The other observing the discourteous Usage of his Companion, clapp'd his Heels to his over-grown Mule's Flanks, and scour'd o'er the Plain as if he had been running a Race with the Wind. Sancho Pança no sooner saw the Monk fall, but he nimbly skipp'd off his Ass, and running to him, began to strip him immediately. But then the two Muleteers, who waited on the Monks, came up to him, and ask'd why he offer'd to strip him? Sancho told them,

that this belong'd to him as lawful Plunder, being the Spoils won in Battle by his Lord and Master Don Quixote. The Fellows, with whom there was no jesting, not knowing what he meant by his Spoils and Battle, and seeing Don Quixote at a good Distance in deep Discourse by the Side of the Coach, fell both upon poor Sancho, threw him down, tore his Beard from his Chin, trampled on his Guts, thump'd and maul'd him in every Part of his Carcase, and there left him sprawling without Breath or Motion. In the mean while the Monk, fear'd out of his Wits, and as pale as a Ghost, got upon his Mule again as fast as he cou'd, and spurr'd after his Friend, who staid for him at a Distance, expecting the Issue of this strange Adventure; but being unwilling to stay to see the End of it, they made the best of their Way, making more Signs of the Cross than if the Devil had been posting after them.

Don Quixote, as I said, was all that while engaged with the Lady in the Coach. Lady, cry'd he, your Discretion is now at Liberty to dispose of your beautiful self as you please; for the presumptuous Arrogance of those who attempted to enslave your Person lies prostrate in the Dust, overthrown by this my strenuous Arm: And that you may not be at a Loss for the Name of your Deliverer, know I am call'd Don Quixote de la Mancha, by Profession a Knight-Errant and Adventurer, Captive to that peerless Beauty Donna Dulcinea del Toboso: Nor do I desire any other Recompense for the Service I have done you, but that you return to Toboso to present your selves to that Lady, and let her know what I have done to purchase your Deliverance. To this strange Talk, a certain Biscayan, the Lady's Squire, Gentleman-Usher, or what you'll please to call him, who rode along with the Coach, listen'd with great Attention; and perceiving that Don Quixote not only stopp'd the Coach, but would have it presently go back to Toboso, he bore briskly up to him, and laying hold on his Lance, Get gone, cry'd he to him in bad Spanish, and worse Biscayan, Get gone, thou Knight, and Devil go with thou; or by he who me create, if thou do not leave the Coach, me kill thee now so sure as me be a Biscayan. Don Quixote, who made shift to understand him well enough, very calmly made him this Answer: Wert thou a Gentleman, as thou art not, ere this I would have chastis'd thy Insolence and Temerity, thou inconsiderable Mortal. What! me no Gentleman? reply'd the Biscayan; I swear thou be Liar, as me be Christian. If thou throw away Lance and draw Sword, me will make no more of thee than Cat does of Mouse: Me will shew thee me be Biscayan, and Gentleman by Land, Gentleman by

Sea, Gentleman in spite of Devil; and thou lye if thou say contrary. I'll try Titles with you, as the Man said, reply'd Don Quixote; and with that throwing away his Lance, he drew his Sword, grasp'd his Target, and attack'd the Biscayan, fully bent on his Destruction. The Biscayan seeing him come on so furiously, would gladly have alighted, not trusting to his Mule, which was one of those scurvy Jades that are let out to Hire; but all he had Time to do was only to draw his Sword, and snatch a Cushion out of the Coach to serve him instead of a Shield; and immediately they assaulted one another with all the Fury of mortal Enemies. The Bystanders did all they could to prevent their Fighting; but 'twas in vain, for the Biscayan swore in his Gibberish he would kill his very Lady, and all those who presum'd to hinder him, if they would not let him fight. The Lady in the Coach being extremely affrighted at these Passages, made her Coachman drive out of Harm's way, and at a Distance was an Eye-witness of the furious Combat. At the same time the Biscayan let fall such a mighty Blow on Don Quixote's Shoulder over his Target, that had not his Armor been Sword-proof he would have cleft him down to the very Waist. The Knight feeling the Weight of that unmeasurable Blow, cry'd out aloud, Oh! Lady of my Soul, Dulcinea! Flower of all Beauty, vouchsafe to succor your Champion in this dangerous Combat, undertaken to set forth your Worth. The breathing out of this short Prayer, the griping fast of his Sword, the covering of himself with his Shield, and the charging of his Enemy, was but the Work of a Moment; for Don Quixote was resolv'd to venture the Fortune of the Combat all upon one Blow. The Biscayan, who

read his Design in his dreadful Countenance, resolv'd to face him with equal Bravery, and stand the terrible Shock, with uplifted Sword, and cover'd with the Cushion, not being able to manage his jaded Mule, who defying the Spur, and not being cut out for such Pranks, would move neither to the Right nor to the Left. While Don Quixote, with his Sword aloft, was rushing upon the wary Biscayan, with a full Resolution to cleave him asunder, all the Spectators stood trembling with Terror and Amazement, expecting the dreadful Event of those prodigious Blows which threaten'd the two desperate Combatants: The Lady in the Coach, with her Women, were making a thousand Vows and Offerings to all the Images and Places of Devotion in Spain, that Providence might deliver them and the Squire out of the great Danger that threaten'd them.

But here we must deplore the abrupt End of this History, which the Author leaves off just at the very Point when the Fortune of the Battle is going to be decided, pretending that he could find nothing more recorded of Don Quixote's wondrous Atchievements than what he had already related. However, the second Undertaker of this Work could not believe, that so curious a History could lie for ever inevitably buried in Oblivion; or that the Learned of La Mancha were so regardless of their Country's Glory, as not to preserve in their Archives, or at least in their Closets, some Memoirs, as Monuments of this famous Knight; and therefore he wou'd not give over inquiring after the Continuation of this pleasant History, till at last he happily found it, as the next Book will inform the Reader.

Edmund Spenser · 1554–1599

Spenser in England and Cervantes in Spain — they were born within seven years of each other — both grew up in a world which made them familiar with the medieval romances and both wrote largely from this background. Cervantes, however, used the old tales with the intent of satire, whereas Spenser wove these legends skillfully and with imagination into admirable stories which, at the same time, serve as vehicles for allegory.

Rarely is a great poet of the stature of Spenser so infrequently read. And the reason is readily apparent. Allegory, for which Spenser had a great liking, frequently draws a veil between the poet and the general reader, particularly if the allegory is, as it is with Spenser, involved and directed toward the presentation of moral doctrines. When the author of *The Faerie Queene* further elects to clothe his narrative in a language artificial and archaic, the veil becomes almost a curtain. Even if the reader persists until he penetrates these barriers to the poet's meaning, he will usually need a more than normally sensitive ear to catch the full values of euphony and the niceties of sound, a more than normally keen imagination to sense fully the richness of imagery, and a more than normally alert mind to appreciate the combined beauties of the whole. Those readers who themselves bring to a reading of Spenser the attitude of a poet will find that the curtain is really a heavy tapestry, embroidered with scenes from ancient legendry and telling romantic stories of the days of chivalry — of knights and fair ladies, of dragons and necromancers. If few students, even specialists in English literature, have read all six books of *The Faerie Queene*, fewer still have added to this reading a first-hand knowledge of *The Shepherd's Calendar* and the sonnets. But such poets as Milton and Pope, Wordsworth and Keats, have been greatly influenced by Spenser. Byron borrowed the stanza-form of *The Faerie Queene* for his *Childe Harold*. For such reasons as these Spenser has been dubbed "the poets' poet."

Edmund Spenser was born in London about 1552. He was educated at the Merchant Taylors' School and at Cambridge, where he took the bachelor's degree in 1573. Something of the family's financial circumstances is evident in the fact that he was given help at the first institution and was entered as a "sizar" — a "self-help" student — at Cambridge. Two or three years after receiving his master's degree in 1576, Spenser made the acquaintance of Sir Philip Sidney and the Earl of Leicester. These friendships proved important to him in later years. In 1580 Spenser was made secretary to the Lord Deputy of Ireland, taking up in that country a residence which was to continue, except for brief visits to England, almost to the day of his death on January 13, 1599. The secretaryship lost, Spenser occupied himself in one capacity or another with such success that he rose to considerable fame and to the proprietorship of an estate of three thousand acres and an old feudal property known as Kilcolman Castle. When Kilcolman was burned in an Irish rebellion in 1598, he returned with his family to England where he died a few days later. He was buried at Westminster Abbey, near Chaucer, in the South Transept.

Spenser's better known works include *The Shepherd's Calendar* (1579), a collection of twelve pastoral poems, one poem devoted to each month of the year; the collection of sonnets, *Amoretti* (1595), dedicated to Elizabeth Boyle whom he married; and *The Faerie Queene*, the first three books of which were published in 1590 at the prompting of Sir Walter Raleigh. In 1596 three more books appeared in print, but Spenser's early death prevented his carrying the project any further than the beginning of Book VII.

SUGGESTED REFERENCES: Alexander C. Judson, *The Life of Edmund Spenser* (1945); H. S. V. Jones, *A Spenser Handbook* (1947); B. E. C. Davis, *Edmund Spenser* (2nd ed., 1962).

A Letter of the Authors

Expounding his whole intention in the course of this worke: which, for that it giveth great light to the reader, for the better understanding is hereunto annexed.

To the Right Noble and Valorous

SIR WALTER RALEIGH, *Knight*

Lord Wardein of the Stanneryes, and Her Maiesties Liefetenaunt of the County of Cornewayll

Sir, knowing how doubtfully all Allegories may be construed, and this booke of mine, which I have entituled the Faery Queene, being a continued Allegory, or darke conceit, I haue thought good,

as well for avoyding of gealous opinions and misconstructions, as also for your better light in reading thereof, (being so by you commanded,) to discover unto you the general intention and mean-
5 ing, which in the whole course thereof I have fashioned, without expressing of any particular purposes, or by accidents, therein occasioned. The generall end therefore of all the booke is to fashion a gentleman or noble person in vertuous
10 and gentle discipline: Which for that I conceived shoulde be most plausible and pleasing, being colored with an historicall fiction, the which the most part of men delight to read, rather for variety of matter then for profite of the ensample, I chose
15 the historye of King Arthure, as most fitte for the excellency of his person, being made famous by many mens former workes, and also furthest from

the daunger of envy, and suspition of present time. In which I have followed all the antique Poets historicall; first Homere, who in the Persons of Agamemnon and Ulysses hath ensampled a good governor and a vertuous man, the one in his Ilias, the other in his Odysseis: then Virgil, whose like intention was to doe in the person of Æneas: after him Ariosto comprised them both in his Orlando: and lately Tasso disseuered them againe, and formed both parts in two persons, namely that part which they in Philosophy call Ethice, or vertues of a private man, colored in his Rinaldo; the other named Politice in his Godfredo. By ensample of which excellente Poets, I labor to puortraict in Arthure, before he was king, the image of a brave knight, perfected in the twelve private morall vertues, as Aristotle hath devised; the which is the purpose of these first twelve bookes: which if I finde to be well accepted, I may be perhaps encoraged to frame the other part of polliticke vertues in his person, after that hee came to be king.

To some, I know, this Methode will seeme displeasaunt, which had rather have good discipline delivered plainly in way of precepts, or sermoned at large, as they use, then thus clowdily enwrapped in Allegoricall devises. But such, me seeme, should be satisfide with the use of these dayes, seeing all things accounted by their showes, and nothing esteemed of, that is not delightfull and pleasing to commune sence. For this cause is Xenophon preferred before Plato, for that the one, in the exquisite depth of his judgement, formed a Commune welth, such as it should be; but the other in the person of Cyrus, and the Persians, fashioned a governement, such as might best be: So much more profitable and gratious is doctrine by ensample, then by rule. So haue I labored to doe in the person of Arthure: whome I conceive, after his long education by Timon, to whom he was by Merlin delivered to be brought up, so soone as he was borne of the Lady Igrayne, to have seene in a dream or vision the Faery Queen, with whose excellent beauty ravished, he awaking resolved to seeke her out; and so being by Merlin armed, and by Timon throughly instructed, he went to seeke her forth in Faerye land. In that Faery Queene I meane glory in my generall intention, but in my particular I conceive the most excellent and glorious person of our soveraine the Queene, and her kingdome in Faery land. And yet, in some places els, I doe otherwise shadow her. For considering she beareth two persons, the one of a most royall Queene or Empresse, the other of a most vertuous and beautiful Lady, this latter part in some places I doe expresse in Belphœbe, fashioning her name according to your owne excellent conceipt of

Cynthia, (Phœbe and Cynthia being both names of Diana.) So in the person of Prince Arthure I sette forth magnificence in particular; which vertue, for that (according to Aristotle and the rest) it is the perfection of all the rest, and conteineth in it them all, therefore in the whole course I mention the deedes of Arthure applyable to that vertue, which I write of in that booke. But of the xii. other vertues, I make xii. other knights the patrones, for the more variety of the history: Of which these three bookes contayn three.

The first of the knight of the Redcrosse, in whome I expresse Holynes: The seconde of Sir Guyon, in whome I sette forth Temperaunce: The third of Britomartis, a Lady Knight, in whome I picture Chastity. But, because the beginning of the whole worke seemeth abrupte, and as depending upon other antecedents, it needs that ye know the occasion of these three knights seuerall adventures. For the Methode of a Poet historical is not such, as of an Historiographer. For an Historiographer discourseth of affayres orderly as they were donne, accounting as well the times as the actions; but a Poet thrusteth into the middest, even where it most concerneth him, and there recoursing to the thinges forepaste, and divining of thinges to come, maketh a pleasing Analysis of all.

The beginning therefore of my history, if it were to be told by an Historiographer should be the twelfth booke, which is the last; where I devise that the Faery Queene kept her Annuall feaste xii. dayes; uppon which xii. severall dayes, the occasions of the xii. severall adventures hapned, which, being undertaken by xii. severall knights, are in these xii. books severally handled and discoursed. The first was this. In the beginning of the feast, there presented him selfe a tall clownishe younge man, who falling before the Queene of Faries desired a boone (as the manner then was) which during that feast she might not refuse; which was that hee might have the atchievement of any adventure, which during that feaste should happen: that being graunted, he rested him on the floore, unfitte through his rusticity for a better place. Soone after entred a faire Ladye in mourning weedes, riding on a white Asse, with a dwarfe behind her leading a warlike steed, that bore the Armes of a knight, and his speare in the dwarfes hand. Shee, falling before the Queene of Faeries, complayned that her father and mother, an ancient King and Queene, had bene by an huge dragon many years shut up in a brasen Castle, who thence suffred them not to yssew; and therefore besought the Faery Queene to assygne her some one of her knights to take on him that exployt. Presently that clownish person, upstarting, desired that adventure: whereat the Queene much wondering, and the Lady much gainesaying, yet he earnestly importuned his desire. In the end the Lady told him, that unlesse that armor which she brought, would serve him (that is, the armor of a Christian man specified by Saint Paul, vi. Ephes.) that he could not succeed in that enterprise; which being forthwith put upon him, with dewe furnitures thereunto, he seemed the goodliest man in al that company, and was well liked of the Lady. And eftesonnes taking on him knighthood, and mounting on that straunge Courser, he went forth with her on that adventure: where beginneth the first booke, viz.

A gentle knight was pricking on the playne. &c.

The second day ther came in a Palmer, bearing an Infant with bloody hands, whose Parents he complained to have bene slayn by an Enchaunteresse called Acrasia; and therfore craved of the Faery Queene, to appoint him some knight to performe that adventure; which being assigned to Sir Guyon, he presently went forth with that same Palmer: which is the beginning of the second booke, and the whole subject thereof. The third day there came in a Groome, who complained before the Faery Queene, that a vile Enchaunter, called Busirane, had in hand a most faire Lady, called Amoretta, whom he kept in most grievous torment, because she would not yield him the pleasure of her body. Whereupon Sir Scudamour, the lover of that Lady, presently tooke on him that adventure. But being vnable to performe it by reason of the hard Enchauntments, after long sorrow, in the end met with Britomartis, who succored him, and reskewed his loue.

But by occasion hereof many other adventures are intermedled; but rather as Accidents then intendments: As the love of Britomart, the overthrow of Marinell, the misery of Florimell, the vertuousnes of Belphœbe, the lasciviousnes of Hellenora, and many the like.

Thus much, Sir, I have briefly overronne to direct your understanding to the wel-head of the History; that from thence gathering the whole intention of the conceit, ye may as in a handfull gripe al the discourse, which otherwise may happily seeme tedious and confused. So, humbly craving the continuance of your honorable favor towards me, and th' eternall establishment of your happines, I humbly take leave.

23. Ianuary 1589,

Yours most humbly affectionate,

ED. SPENSER.

The First Book of The Faerie Queene

Contayning the Legend of the Knight of the Red Crosse, or of Holinesse

1

Lo! I, the man whose Muse whylome [1] did
  maske,
As time her taught, in lowly Shephards weeds, [2]
Am now enforst, a farre unfitter taske,
For trumpets sterne to chaunge mine Oaten reeds,
And sing of Knights and Ladies gentle deeds; 5
Whose praises having slept in silence long,
Me, all too meane, the sacred Muse areeds [3]
To blazon broade emongst her learned throng:
Fierce warres and faithful loves shall moralize my
  song.

2

Helpe then, O holy virgin! chiefe of nyne, [4] 10
Thy weaker Novice to performe thy will;
Lay forth out of thine everlasting scryne [5]
The antique rolles, which there lye hidden still,
Of Faerie knights, and fayrest Tanaquill, [6]
Whom that most noble Briton Prince [7] so long 15
Sought through the world, and suffered so much ill,
That I must rue his undeserved wrong:
O, helpe thou my weake wit, and sharpen my dull
  tong!

3

And thou, most dreaded impe [8] of highest Jove,
Faire Venus sonne, that with thy cruell dart 20
At that good knight so cunningly didst rove,
That glorious fire it kindled in his hart;
Lay now thy deadly Heben [9] bowe apart,
And with thy mother mylde come to mine ayde;
Come, both; and with you bring triumphant
  Mart, [10] 25
In loves and gentle jollities arraid,
After his murdrous spoyles and bloudie rage allayd.

4

And with them eke, O Goddesse [11] heavenly
  bright!
Mirror of grace and Majestie divine,

[1] formerly.
[2] The reference is to the poet's *Shepherd's Calendar* published in 1579. [3] prompts.
[4] Clio, muse of history. [5] shrine or chest.
[6] A daughter of the king of fairies, Oberon; here the reference is to Gloriana or Queen Elizabeth.
[7] King Arthur.
[8] child; Cupid was the son of Venus.
[9] ebony. [10] Mars. [11] Queen Elizabeth.

Great Ladie of the greatest Isle, whose light   30
Like Phœbus lampe throughout the world doth
    shine,
Shed thy faire beames into my feeble eyne,
And raise my thoughtes, too humble and too vile,
To thinke of that true glorious type of thine,
The argument of mine afflicted stile: [1]   35
The which to heare vouchsafe, O dearest dread,[2]
    a-while!

CANTO I

The Patrone of true Holinesse
Foule Error doth defeate:
Hypocrisie, him to entrappe,
Doth to his home entreate.

1

A gentle Knight was pricking [3] on the plaine,
Ycladd in mightie armes and silver shielde,
Wherein old dints of deepe woundes did remaine,
The cruell markes of many a bloody fielde;
Yet armes till that time did he never wield.   5
His angry steede did chide his foming bitt,
As much disdayning to the curbe to yield:
Full jolly [4] knight he seemd, and faire did sitt,
As one for knightly giusts [5] and fierce encounters
    fitt.

2

And on his brest a bloodie Crosse he bore,   10
The deare remembrance of his dying Lord,
For whose sweete sake that glorious badge he wore,
And dead, as living, ever him ador'd:
Upon his shield the like was also scor'd,
For soveraine hope which in his helpe he had.   15
Right faithfull true he was in deede and word,
But of his cheere [6] did seeme too solemne sad;
Yet nothing did he dread, but ever was ydrad.[7]

3

Upon a great adventure he was bond,
That greatest Gloriana [8] to him gave,   20
(That greatest Glorious Queene of Faery lond)
To winne him worshippe, and her grace to have,
Which of all earthly things he most did crave:
And ever as he rode his hart did earne [9]
To prove his puissance in battell brave   25
Upon his foe, and his new force to learne,
Upon his foe, a Dragon horrible and stearne.

4

A lovely Ladie rode him faire beside,
Upon a lowly Asse more white then snow,

Yet she much whiter; but the same did hide   30
Under a vele, that wimpled [1] was full low;
And over all a blacke stole shee did throw:
As one that inly mournd, so was she sad,
And heavie sate upon her palfrey slow;
Seemed in heart some hidden care she had,   35
And by her, in a line, a milkewhite lambe she lad.

5

So pure and innocent, as that same lambe,
She was in life and every vertuous lore;
And by descent from Royall lynage came
Of ancient Kinges and Queenes, that had of yore
Their scepters stretcht from East to Westerne
    shore,   41
And all the world in their subjection held;
Till that infernall feend with foule uprore
Forewasted [2] all their land, and them expeld;
Whom to avenge she had this Knight from far
    compeld.[3]   45

6

Behind her farre away a Dwarfe did lag,
That lasie seemd, in being ever last,
Or wearied with bearing of her bag
Of needments at his backe.   Thus as they past,
The day with cloudes was suddeine overcast,   50
And angry Jove an hideous storme of raine
Did poure into his Lemans [4] lap [5] so fast
That everie wight [6] to shrowd [7] it did constrain;
And this faire couple eke to shroud themselves were
    fain.

7

Enforst to seeke some covert high at hand,   55
A shadie grove not farr away they spide,
That promist ayde the tempest to withstand;
Whose loftie trees, yclad with sommers pride,
Did spred so broad, that heavens light did hide,
Not perceable with power of any starr: 60
And all within were pathes and alleies wide,
With footing worne, and leading inward farr.
Faire harbor that them seems, so in they entred ar.

8

And foorth they passe, with pleasure forward led,
Joying to heare the birdes sweete harmony,   65
Which, therein shrouded from the tempest dred,
Seemed in their song to scorne the cruell sky.
Much can they praise the trees so straight and hy,
The sayling Pine; [8] the Cedar proud and tall;
The vine-propp Elme; the Poplar never dry;   70

---

[1] lowly style.   [2] object of reverence.
[3] riding or spurring.   [4] handsome.
[5] jousts.   [6] countenance.   [7] dreaded.
[8] Queen Elizabeth.   [9] yearn.

---

[1] folded.   [2] completely laid waste.
[3] summoned.   [4] lovers.
[5] the earth.   [6] person.   [7] shelter.
[8] "sailing" since used for masts.

The builder Oake, sole king of forrests all;
The Aspine good for staves; the Cypresse [1] funerall;

9

The Laurell, meed of mightie Conquerors
And Poets sage; the Firre that weepeth still:
The Willow, worne of forlorne Paramours; 75
The Eugh, obedient to the benders will;
The Birch for shaftes; the Sallow [2] for the mill;
The Mirrhe sweete-bleeding in the bitter wound;
The warlike Beech; the Ash for nothing ill;
The fruitfull Olive; and the Platane [3] round; 80
The carver Holme; [4] the Maple seeldome inward
    sound.

10

Led with delight, they thus beguile the way,
Untill the blustring storme is overblowne;
When, weening [5] to returne whence they did stray,
They cannot finde that path, which first was
    showne, 85
But wander too and fro in waies unknowne,
Furthest from end then, when they neerest weene,
That makes them doubt their wits be not their
    owne:
So many pathes, so many turnings seene,
That which of them to take in diverse doubt they
    been. 90

11

At last resolving forward still to fare,
Till that some end they finde, or in or out,
That path they take that beaten seemed most bare,
And like to lead the labyrinth about; [6]
Which when by tract they hunted had throughout,
At length it brought them to a hollowe cave 96
Amid the thickest woods. The Champion stout
Eftsoones [7] dismounted from his courser brave,
And to the Dwarfe a while his needlesse spere he
    gave. 99

12

"Be well aware," quoth then that Ladie milde,
"Least suddaine mischiefe ye too rash provoke:
The danger hid, the place unknowne and wilde,
Breedes dreadfull doubts. Oft fire is without
    smoke,
And perill without show: therefore your stroke,
Sir Knight, with-hold, till further tryall made."
"Ah Ladie," (sayd he) "shame were to revoke 106
The forward footing for an hidden shade:
Vertue gives her selfe light through darknesse for
    to wade."

13

"Yea but" (quoth she) "the perill of this place
I better wot [1] then you: though nowe too late 110
To wish you backe returne with foule disgrace,
Yet wisedome warnes, whilst foot is in the gate,[2]
To stay the steppe, ere forced to retrate.
This is the wandring wood, this _Errors_ den,
A monster vile, whom God and man does hate: 115
Therefore I read [3] beware." "Fly, fly!" (quoth
    then
The fearfull Dwarfe) "this is no place for living
    men."

14

But, full of fire and greedy hardiment,
The youthfull Knight could not for ought be staide;
But forth unto the darksom hole he went, 120
And looked in: his glistring armoor made
A litle glooming light, much like a shade;
By which he saw the ugly monster plaine,
Halfe like a serpent horribly displaide,
But th' other halfe did womans shape retaine, 125
Most lothsom, filthie, foule, and full of vile dis-
    daine.

15

And, as she lay upon the durtie ground,
Her huge long taile her den all overspred,
Yet was in knots and many boughtes [4] upwound,
Pointed with mortall sting. Of her there bred 130
A thousand yong ones, which she dayly fed,
Sucking upon her poisnous dugs; each one
Of sundrie shapes, yet all ill-favored: [5]
Soone as that uncouth light upon them shone,
Into her mouth they crept, and suddain all were
    gone. 135

16

Their dam upstart out of her den effraide,
And rushed forth, hurling her hideous taile
About her cursed head; whose folds displaid
Were stretcht now forth at length without entraile.[6]
She lookt about, and seeing one in mayle, 140
Armed to point, sought backe to turne againe;
For light she hated as the deadly bale,[7]
Ay wont in desert darknes to remaine,
Where plain none might see her, nor she see any
    plaine.

17

Which when the valiant Elfe [8] perceiv'd, he lept
As Lyon fierce upon the flying pray, 146
And with his trenchand blade her boldly kept

[1] Frequently associated with death.
[2] A variety of willow.   [3] plane-tree.
[4] oak.   [5] thinking.   [6] out of.   [7] directly.

[1] know.   [2] way.   [3] counsel.   [4] coils.
[5] ugly.   [6] twists.   [7] destruction.
[8] fairy knight, i.e. the Knight of the Red Cross.

From turning backe, and forced her to stay:
Therewith enrag'd she loudly gan to bray,
And turning fierce her speckled taile advaunst,   150
Threatning her angrie sting, him to dismay;
Who, nought aghast, his mightie hand enhaunst: [1]
The stroke down from her head unto her shoulder
     glaunst.

18

Much daunted with that dint her sence was
     dazd;
Yet kindling rage her selfe she gathered round,   155
And all attonce her beastly bodie raizd
With doubled forces high above the ground:
Tho, wrapping up her wrethed sterne arownd,
Lept fierce upon his shield, and her huge traine
All suddenly about his body wound,   160
That hand or foot to stirr he strove in vaine.
God helpe the man so wrapt in Errors endlesse
     traine!

19

His Lady, sad to see his sore constraint,
Cride out, "Now, now, Sir knight, shew what ye
     bee:
Add faith unto your force, and be not faint;   165
Strangle her, els she sure will strangle thee."
That when he heard, in great perplexitie,
His gall did grate for griefe [2] and high disdaine;
And, knitting all his force, got one hand free,
Wherewith he grypt her gorge with so great paine,
That soone to loose her wicked bands did her con-
     straine.   171

20

Therewith she spewd out of her filthie maw [3]
A floud of poyson [4] horrible and blacke,
Full of great lumps of flesh and gobbets [5] raw,
Which stunck so vildly, that it forst him slacke   175
His grasping hold, and from her turne him backe.
Her vomit full of bookes and papers [6] was,
With loathly frogs and toades, which eyes did
     lacke,
And creeping sought way in the weedy gras:
Her filthie parbreake [7] all the place defiled has.   180

21

As when old father Nilus gins to swell
With timely pride above the Aegyptian vale
His fattie waves doe fertile slime outwell,
And overflow each plaine and lowly dale:

[1] raised.   [2] His anger rose in the pain.
[3] belly.   [4] poison.   [5] pieces.
[6] An allusion to the attacks the Catholics had made
on Elizabeth and the established Church in England.
[7] vomit.

But, when his later spring gins to avale,[1]   185
Huge heapes of mudd he leaves, wherein there
     breed
Ten thousand kindes of creatures, partly male
And partly femall, of his fruitful seed;
Such ugly monstrous shapes elswher may no man
     reed.[2]

22

The same so sore annoyed has the knight,   190
That, welnigh choked with the deadly stinke,
His forces faile, ne can no lenger fight
Whose corage when the feend perceivd to shrinke,
She poured forth out of her hellish sinke
Her fruitfull cursed spawne of serpents small,   195
Deformed monsters, fowle, and blacke as inke,
Which swarming all about his legs did crall,
And him encombred sore, but could not hurt at all.

23

As gentle shepheard in sweete eventide,
When ruddy Phebus gins to welke [3] in west,   200
High on an hill, his flocke to vewen wide,
Markes which doe byte their hasty supper best;
A cloud of cumbrous gnattes doe him molest,
All striving to infixe their feeble stinges,
That from their noyance he no where can rest;   205
But with his clownish hands their tender wings
He brusheth oft, and oft doth mar their murmur-
     ings.

24

Thus ill bestedd,[4] and fearefull more of shame
Then of the certeine perill he stood in
Halfe furious unto his foe he came,   210
Resolvd in minde all suddenly to win,
Or soone to lose, before he once would lin; [5]
And stroke at her with more than manly force,
That from her body, full of filthie sin,
He raft [6] her hatefull heade without remorse: 215
A streame of cole-black blood forth gushed from
     her corse.

25

Her scattered brood, soone as their Parent deare
They saw so rudely falling to the ground,
Groning full deadly, all with troublous feare
Gathred themselves about her body round,   220
Weening their wonted entrance to have found
At her wide mouth; but being there withstood,
They flocked all about her bleeding wound,
And sucked up their dying mothers bloud,
Making her death their life, and eke her hurt their
     good.   225

[1] recede.   [2] see.   [3] fade.
[4] situated.   [5] stop.   [6] reft, struck off.

26

That detestable sight him much amazde,
To see th' unkindly Impes, of heaven accurst,
Devoure their dam; on whom while so he gazd,
Having all satisfide their bloudy thurst,
Their bellies swolne he saw with fulnesse burst,
And bowels gushing forth: well worthy end   231
Of such as drunke her life the which them nurst!
Now needeth him no lenger labor spend,
His foes have slaine themselves, with whom he
    should contend.

27

His Lady, seeing all that chaunst from farre,
Approcht in hast to greet his victorie;   236
And saide, "Faire knight, borne under happie
    starre,
Who see your vanquisht foes before you lye,
Well worthie be you of that Armory,[1]
Wherein ye have great glory wonne this day,   240
And proov'd your strength on a strong enimie,
Your first adventure: many such I pray,
And henceforth ever wish that like succeed it
    may!"

28

Then mounted he upon his Steede againe,
And with the Lady backward sought to wend.   245
That path he kept which beaten was most plaine,
Ne ever would to any byway bend,
But still did follow one unto the end,
The which at last out of the wood them brought.
So forward on his way (with God to frend)   250
He passed forth, and new adventure sought:
Long way he traveiled before he heard of ought.

29

At length they chaunst to meet upon the way
An aged Sire, in long blacke weedes yclad,
His feete all bare, his beard all hoarie gray,   255
And by his belt his booke he hanging had:
Sober he seemde, and very sagely sad,
And to the ground his eyes were lowly bent,
Simple in shew, and voide of malice bad;
And all the way he prayed as he went,   260
And often knockt his brest, as one that did repent.

30

He faire the knight saluted, louting [2] low,
Who faire him quited, as that courteous was;
And after asked him, if he did know
Of straunge adventures, which abroad did pas,   265
"Ah! my dear sonne," (quoth he) "how should,
    alas!
Silly [3] old man, that lives in hidden cell,

[1] armor.   [2] bowing.   [3] simple.

Bidding [1] his beades all day for his trespas,
Tydings of warre and worldly trouble tell?
With holy father sits not [2] with such thinges to
    mell.[3]   270

31

"But if of daunger, which hereby doth dwell,
And homebredd evil ye desire to heare,
Of a straunge man I can you tidings tell,
That wasteth all this countrie, farre and neare."
"Of such," (saide he,) "I chiefly doe inquere,   275
And shall thee well rewarde to shew the place,
In which that wicked wight his dayes doth weare;
For to all knighthood it is foule disgrace,
That such a cursed creature lives so long a space."

32

"Far hence" (quoth he) "in wastfull wilder
    nesse   280
His dwelling is, by which no living wight
May ever passe, but thorough great distresse."
"Now," (saide the Ladie,) "draweth toward
    night,
And well I wote, that of your later fight
Ye all forwearied be; for what so strong,   285
But, wanting rest, will also want of might?
The Sunne, that measures heaven all day long,
At night doth baite [4] his steedes the Ocean waves
    emong.

33

"Then with the Sunne take, Sir, your timely rest,
And with new day new worke at once begin: 290
Untroubled night, they say, gives counsell best."
"Right well, Sir knight, ye have advised bin,"
Quoth then that aged man: "the way to win
Is wisely to advise; now day is spent:
Therefore with me ye may take up your In   295
For this same night." The knight was well con-
    tent;
So with that godly father to his home they went.

34

A little lowly Hermitage it was,
Downe in a dale, hard by a forests side,
Far from resort of people that did pas   300
In traveill to and froe: a little wyde [5]
There was an holy chappell edifyde,[6]
Wherein the Hermite dewly wont to say
His holy things each morne and eventyde:
Thereby a christall streame did gently play,   305
Which from a sacred fountaine welled forth
    alway.

[1] telling.   [2] befits not.   [3] meddle.
[4] feed.   [5] distant.   [6] built.

35

Arrived there, the little house they fill,
Ne looke for entertainement where none was;
Rest is their feast, and all thinges at their will:
The noblest mind the best contentment has.   310
With faire discourse the evening so they pas;
For that olde man of pleasing wordes had store,
And well could file his tongue as smooth as glas:
He told of Saintes and Popes,[1] and evermore
He strowd an *Ave-Mary* after and before.   315

36

The drouping night thus creepeth on them fast;
And the sad [2] humor [3] loading their eyeliddes,
As messenger of Morpheus on them cast
Sweet slombring deaw, the which to sleep them
    biddes.   319
Unto their lodgings then his guestes he riddes: [4]
Where when all drowned in deadly sleepe he findes,
He to his studie goes; and there amiddes
His magick bookes, and artes of sundrie kindes,
He seeks out mighty charmes to trouble sleepy
    minds.

37

Then choosing out few words most horrible,   325
(Let none them read) thereof did verses frame;
With which, and other spelles like terrible,
He bad awake blacke Plutos griesly Dame; [5]
And cursed heven; and spake reprochful shame
Of highest God, the Lord of life and light: 330
A bold bad man, that dar'd to call by name
Great Gorgon,[6] prince of darknes and dead night:
At which Cocytus [7] quakes, and Styx [7] is put to
    flight.

38

And forth he cald out of deepe darkness dredd
Legions of Sprights, the which, like litle flyes   335
Fluttering about his ever-damned hedd,
Awaite whereto their service he applyes,
To aide his friendes, or fray [8] his enimies.
Of those he chose out two, the falsest twoo,
And fittest for to forge true-seeming lyes: 340
The one of them he gave a message too,
The other by him selfe staide, other worke to doo.

39

He, making speedy way through spersed [9] ayre,
And through the world of waters wide and deepe,
To Morpheus house doth hastily repaire.   345

Amid the bowels of the earth full steepe,
And low, where dawning day doth never peepe,
His dwelling is; there Tethys [1] his wet bed
Doth ever wash, and Cynthia [2] still doth steepe
In silver deaw his ever-drouping hed,   350
Whiles sad Night over him her mantle black doth
    spred.

40

Whose double gates he findeth locked fast,
The one faire fram'd of burnisht Yvory,
The other all with silver overcast;
And wakeful dogges before them farre doe lye,   355
Watching to banish Care their enimy,
Who oft is wont to trouble gentle Sleepe.
By them the Sprite doth passe in quietly,
And unto Morpheus comes, whom drowned deepe
In drowsie fit he findes: of nothing he takes keepe.[3]

41

And more to lulle him in his slumber soft,   361
A trickling streame from high rock tumbling downe,
And ever-drizling raine upon the loft,[4]
Mixt with a murmuring winde, much like the
    sowne
Of swarming Bees, did cast him in a swowne.   365
No other noyse, nor peoples troublous cryes,
As still are wont t' annoy the walled towne,
Might there be heard; but carelesse Quiet lyes
Wrapt in eternall silence farre from enimyes.

42

The Messenger approching to him spake;   370
But his waste wordes retournd to him in vaine:
So sound he slept, that nought mought him awake.
Then rudely he him thrust, and pusht with paine,
Whereat he gan to stretch; but he againe
Shooke him so hard, that forced him to speake.   375
As one then in a dreame, whose dryer [5] braine
Is tost with troubled sights and fancies weake,
He mumbled soft, but would not all his silence
    breake.

43

The Sprite then gan more boldly him to wake,
And threatned unto him the dreaded name   380
Of Hecate: [6] whereat he gan to quake,
And, lifting up his lompish [7] head, with blame
Halfe angrie asked him, for what he came.

---

[1] The old man, a Catholic, represents hypocrisy.
[2] heavy.   [3] moisture.
[4] dismisses or sends.   [5] Proserpine.
[6] A demon and magician of the lower world.
[7] A river in Hades.   [8] scare.   [9] far-flung.

[1] The ocean.   [2] The moon.
[3] care.   [4] upper floor.
[5] A "dry" brain was not believed as keen as a "moist"
one.
[6] A witch of the lower regions.
[7] "lumpish" or heavy.

"Hether" (quoth he,) "me Archimago sent,
He that the stubborne Sprites can wisely tame,
He bids thee to him send for his intent   386
A fit false dreame, that can delude the sleepers
    sent."

44

The God obayde; and, calling forth straight way
A diverse [1] Dreame out of his prison darke,
Delivered it to him, and downe did lay   390
His heavie head, devoide of careful carke; [2]
Whose sences all were straight benumbd and
    starke.
He, backe returning by the Yvorie dore,
Remounted up as light as chearefull Larke;
And on his little winges the dreame he bore   395
In hast unto his Lord, where he him left afore.

45

Who all this while, with charmes and hidden
    artes,
Had made a Lady of that other Spright,
And fram'd of liquid ayre her tender partes,
So lively and so like in all mens sight,   400
That weaker sence it could have ravisht quight:
The maker selfe, for all his wondrous witt,
Was nigh beguiled with so goodly sight.
Her all in white he clad, and over it   404
Cast a black stole, most like to seeme for Una [3] fit.

46

Now, when that ydle dreame was to him brought,
Unto that Elfin knight he bad him fly,
Where he slept soundly void of evil thought,
And with false shewes abuse his fantasy,
In sort as he him schooled privily: 410
And that new creature, borne without her dew, [4]
Full of the makers guyle, with usage sly
He taught to imitate that Lady trew,
Whose semblance she did carrie under feigned hew.

47

Thus well instructed, to their worke they hast,
And comming where the knight in slomber lay,   416
The one upon his hardy head him plast,
And made him dreame of loves and lustfull play,
That nigh his manly hart did melt away,
Bathed in wanton blis and wicked ioy: 420
Then seemed him his Lady by him lay,
And to him playnd, how that false winged boy
Her chast hart had subdewed, to learne Dame
    pleasures toy.

[1] treacherous.
[2] care.
[3] Truth.
[4] Unnaturally, not in the "due" way.

48

And she her selfe of beautie soveraigne Queene,
Faire Venus seemde unto his bed to bring   425
Her, whom he waking evermore did weene
To be the chastest flowre, that ay did spring
On earthly braunch, the daughter of a king,
Now a loose Leman to vile service bound:
And eke the Graces seemed all to sing,   430
Hymen iô Hymen, dauncing all around,
Whilst freshest Flora her with Yvie girlond
    crowned.

49

In this great passion of unwonted lust,
Or wonted feare of doing ought amis,
He started up, as seeming to mistrust   435
Some secret ill, or hidden foe of his:
Lo there before his face his Lady is,
Under blake stole hyding her bayted hooke,
And as halfe blushing offred him to kis,
With gentle blandishment and lovely looke,   440
Most like that virgin true, which for her knight
    him took.

50

All cleane dismayd to see so uncouth sight,
And halfe enraged at her shamelesse guise,
He thought have slaine her in his fierce despight: [1]
But hasty heat tempring with sufferance wise,   445
He stayde his hand, and gan himselfe advise
To prove his sence, and tempt her faigned truth.
Wringing her hands in wemens pitteous wise,
Tho [2] can [3] she weepe, to stirre up gentle ruth, [4]
Both for her noble bloud, and for her tender youth.

51

And said, Ah Sir, my liege Lord and my love,
Shall I accuse the hidden cruell fate,   452
And mightie causes wrought in heaven above,
Or the blind God, that doth me thus amate, [5]
For hoped love to winne me certaine hate?   455
Yet thus perforce he bids me do, or die.
Die is my dew: yet rew my wretched state
You, whom my hard avenging destinie
Hath made iudge of my life or death indifferently.

52

Your owne deare sake forst me at first to leave
My Fathers kingdome, There she stopt with
    teares;   461
Her swollen hart her speach seemd to bereave,
And then againe begun, My weaker yeares
Captiv'd to fortune and frayle worldly feares,
Fly to your faith for succor and sure ayde: 465

[1] anger.   [2] then.   [3] did.
[4] pity.   [5] dishearten.

Let me not dye in languor and long teares.
Why Dame (quoth he) what hath ye thus dis-
    mayd?
What frayes ye, that were wont to comfort me
    affrayd?

53

Love of your selfe, she said, and deare constraint
Lets me not sleepe, but wast the wearie night   470
In secret anguish and unpittied plaint,
Whiles you in carelesse sleepe are drowned quight.
Her doubtfull words made that redouted knight
Suspect her truth: yet since no'untruth he knew,
Her fawning love with foule disdainefull spight   475
He would not shend,[1] but said, Deare dame I rew,
That for my sake unknowne such griefe unto you
    grew.

54

Assure your selfe, it fell not all to ground;
For all so deare as life is to my hart,
I deeme your love, and hold me to you bound;   480
Ne let vaine feares procure your needlesse smart,
Where cause is none, but to your rest depart.
Not all content, yet seemd she to appease[2]
Her mournefull plaintes, beguiled of her art,
And fed with words, that could not chuse but
    please,   485
So slyding softly forth, she turnd as to her ease.

55

Long after lay he musing at her mood,
Much grieu'd to thinke that gentle Dame so light,
For whose defence he was to shed his blood.
At last dull wearinesse of former fight   490
Having yrockt a sleepe his irkesome spright,
That troublous dreame gan freshly tosse his braine
With bowres, and beds, and Ladies deare delight:
But when he saw his labor all was vaine,
With that misformed spright he backe returnd
    againe.   495

CANTO II

The guilefull great Enchanter parts
The Redcrosse Knight from Truth:
Into whose stead faire falshood steps,
And works him woefull ruth.

1

By this the Northerne wagoner[3] had set
His sevenfold teme[4] behind the stedfast starre[5]
That was in Ocean waves yet never wet,

    [1] blame.   [2] stop.
    [3] The constellation in which Arcturus is found.
    [4] The seven stars of the Great Dipper.
    [5] The North Star.

But firme is fixt, and sendeth light from farre
To al that in the wide deepe wandring arre;   5
And chearefull Chaunticlere with his note shrill
Had warned once, that Phœbus fiery carre
In hast was climbing up the Easterne hill,
Full envious that night so long his roome did fill:

2

When those accursed messengers of hell,   10
That feigning dreame, and that faire-forged
    Spright,
Came to their wicked maister, and gan tel
Their bootelesse paines, and ill succeeding night:
Who, in all rage to see his skilfull might
Deluded so, gan threaten hellish paine,   15
And sad Proserpines wrath, them to affright:
But, when he saw his threatning was but vaine,
He cast about, and searcht his baleful bokes againe.

3

Eftsoones[1] he tooke that miscreated faire,
And that false other Spright, on whom he spred   20
A seeming body of the subtile aire,
Like a young Squire, in loves and lusty-hed
His wanton dayes that ever loosely led,
Without regard of armes and dreaded fight:
Those two he tooke, and in a secret bed,   25
Covered with darknesse and misdeeming[2] night,
Them both together laid, to joy in vaine delight.

4

Forthwith he runnes with feigned faithfull hast
Unto his guest, who after troublous sights
And dreames, gan now to take more sound re-
    past,   30
Whom suddenly he wakes with fearefull frights,
As one aghast with feends or damned sprights,
And to him cals, Rise rise unhappy Swaine,
That here wex old in sleepe, whiles wicked wights
Have knit themselves in Venus shamefull chaine;
Come see, where your false Lady doth her honor
    staine.   36

5

All in amaze he suddenly up start
With sword in hand, and with the old man went;
Who soone him brought into a secret part,
Where that false couple were full closely ment[3]   40
In wanton lust and lewd embracement:
Which when he saw, he burnt with gealous fire,
The eye of reason was with rage yblent,[4]
And would have slaine them in his furious ire,
But hardly was restreined of that aged sire.   45

    [1] speedily.   [2] misleading.
    [3] mixed.   [4] blinded.

6

Returning to his bed in torment great,
And bitter anguish of his guiltie sight,
He could not rest, but did his stout heart eat,
And wast his inward gall with deepe despight,
Yrkesome of life, and too long lingring night.   50
At last faire Hesperus [1] in highest skie
Had spent his lampe, and brought forth dawning
    light
Then up he rose, and clad him hastily;
The Dwarfe him brought his steed: so both away
    do fly.

7

Now when the rosy fingred Morning faire,   55
Weary of aged Tithones [2] saffron bed,
Had spred her purple robe through deawy aire,
And the high hils Titan [3] discovered,
The royall virgin shooke off drousy-hed; [4]
And, rising forth out of her baser bowre,   60
Lookt for her knight, who far away was fled,
And for her dwarfe, that wont to wait each howre:
Then gan she wail and weepe to see that woeful
    stowre.[5]

8

And after him she rode with so much speede
As her slowe beast could make; but all in vaine,   65
For him so far had borne his light-foot steede,
Pricked with wrath and fiery fierce disdaine,
That him to follow was but fruitlesse paine:
Yet she her weary limbes would never rest;
But every hil and dale, each wood and plaine,   70
Did search, sore grieved in her gentle brest,
He so ungently left her, whome she loved best.

9

But subtill Archimago, when his guests
He saw divided into double parts,
And Una wandring in woods and forrests,   75
Th' end of his drift, he praisd his divelish arts
That had such might over true meaning harts;
Yet rests not so, but other meanes doth make,
How he may worke unto her further smarts;
For her he hated as the hissing snake,   80
And in her many troubles did most pleasure take.

10

He then devisde himselfe how to disguise;
For by his mighty science he could take

As many formes and shapes in seeming wise,
As ever Proteus [1] to himselfe could make: 85
Sometime a fowle, sometime a fish in lake,
Now like a foxe, now like a dragon fell;
That of himselfe he ofte for feare would quake,
And oft would flie away.   O! who can tell
The hidden powre of herbes, and might of Magick
    spel?   90

11

But now seemde best the person to put on
Of that good knight, his late beguiled guest:
In mighty armes he was yclad anon,
And silver shield; upon his coward brest
A bloody crosse, and on his craven crest   95
A bounch of heares discolored diversly.
Full jolly knight he seemde, and wel addrest;
And when he sate upon his courser free,
Saint George [2] himselfe ye would have deemed him
    to be.

12

But he, the knight whose semblaunt he did
    beare,   100
The true Saint George, was wandred far away,
Still flying from his thoughts and gealous feare:
Will was his guide, and griefe led him astray.
At last him chaunst to meete upon the way
A faithlesse Sarazin,[3] all armde to point,   105
In whose great shield was writ with letters gay
Sans foy;[4] full large of limbe and every joint
He was, and cared not for God or man a point.[5]

13

Hee had a faire companion [6] of his way,
A goodly Lady clad in scarlot red,   110
Purfled [7] with gold and pearle of rich assay;
And like a Persian mitre on her hed
Shee wore, with crowns and owches [8] garnished,
The which her lavish lovers to her gave.
Her wanton palfrey all was overspred   115
With tinsell trappings, woven like a wave,
Whose bridle rung with golden bels and bosses [9]
    brave.

14

With faire disport, and courting dalliaunce
She intertainde her lover all the way;
But, when she saw the knight his speare advaunce,
She soone left off her mirth and wanton play,   121

[1] The evening star.
[2] Tithonus, a Prince of Troy, was loved by Aurora and made immortal, but as he did not have eternal youth he aged so that he became little more than a harsh voice. He was then changed into a grasshopper.
[3] The sun.   [4] drowsiness.   [5] misfortune.

[1] The son of Poseidon, Proteus was a sea-god who could change his shape at pleasure.
[2] The patron saint of England.
[3] A Saracen or pagan.   [4] "Without faith."   [5] bit.
[6] This was Duessa who represented falsehood and the Catholic faith.
[7] bordered.   [8] jewels.   [9] studs.

And bad her knight addresse him to the fray,
His foe was nigh at hand.　He, prickte with pride
And hope to winne his Ladies hearte that day,
Forth spurred fast: adowne his coursers side　125
The red bloud trickling stained the way, as he did
　　ride.

15

The knight of the Redcrosse, when him he spide
Spurring so hote with rage dispiteous,[1]
Gan fairely couch his speare, and towards ride.
Soone meete they both, both fell and furious,　130
That, daunted with theyr forces hideous,
Their steeds doe stagger, and amazed stand;
And eke themselves, too rudely rigorous,
Astonied with the stroke of their owne hand,
Doe backe rebutte,[2] and ech to other yealdeth
　　land.　　　　　　　　　　　　　　　　135

16

As when two rams, stird with ambitious pride,
Fight for the rule of the rich fleeced flocke,
Their horned fronts so fierce on either side
Doe meete, that, with the terror of the shocke,
Astonied, both stand sencelesse as a blocke,　140
Forgetfull of the hanging victory:
So stood these twaine, unmoved as a rocke,
Both staring fierce, and holding idely
The broken reliques of their former cruelty.

17

The Sarazin, sore daunted with the buffe,　145
Snatcheth his sword, and fiercely to him flies;
Who well it wards, and quyteth [3] cuff with cuff:
Each others equall puissaunce envies,
And through their iron sides with cruell spies
Does seeke to perce; repining courage yields　150
No foote to foe: the flashing fier flies,
As from a forge, out of their burning shields;
And streams of purple bloud new die the verdant
　　fields.

18

"Curse on that Cross," (quoth then the Sara-
　　zin,)
"That keepes thy body from the bitter fitt![4]　155
Dead long ygoe, I wote, thou haddest bin,
Had not that charme from thee forwarned itt:
But yet I warne thee now assured sitt,
And hide [5] thy head."　Therewith upon his crest
With rigor so outrageous he smitt,　　　　160
That a large share it hewd out of the rest,
And glauncing downe his shield from blame [6] him
　　fairly blest.[7]

[1] cruel, without pity.　　[2] recoil.　　[3] requites.
[4] death blow.　　[5] protect.　　[6] harm.　　[7] protected.

19

Who, thereat wondrous wroth, the sleeping
　　spark
Of native vertue gan eftsoones revive;
And at his haughty helmet making mark,　165
So hugely stroke, that it the steele did rive.[1]
And cleft his head.　He, tumbling downe alive,
With bloudy mouth his mother earth did kis,
Greeting his grave: his grudging ghost did strive
With the fraile flesh; at last it flitted is,　170
Whither the soules doe fly of men that live amis.

20

The Lady, when she saw her champion fall
Like the old ruines of a broken towre,
Staid not to waile his woefull funerall,
But from him fled away with all her powre;　175
Who after her as hastily gan scowre,[2]
Bidding the dwarfe with him to bring away
The Sarazins shield, signe of the conquerore.
Her soone he overtooke, and bad to stay;
For present cause was none of dread her to dis-
　　may.　　　　　　　　　　　　　　　　180

21

Shee turning backe, with ruefull countenaunce,
Cride, "Mercy, mercy, Sir, vouchsafe to show
On silly Dame, subject to hard mischaunce,
And to your mighty wil!"　Her humblesse low,
In so ritch weedes, and seeming glorious show,　185
Did much emmove his stout heroicke heart;
And said, "Deare dame, your suddein overthrow
Much rueth me; but now put feare apart,
And tel both who ye be, and who that tooke your
　　part."

22

Melting in teares, then gan shee thus lament.
"The wretched woman, whom unhappy howre　191
Hath now made thrall to your commandement,
Before that angry heavens list [3] to lowre,
And fortune false betraide me to thy powre,
Was (O! what now availeth that I was?)　195
Borne the sole daughter of an Emperour,
He that the wide West under his rule has,
And high hath set his throne where Tiberis doth
　　pas.

23

"He, in the first flowre of my freshest age,
Betrothed me unto the onely haire [4]　　　200
Of a most mighty king, most rich and sage:
Was never Prince so faithfull and so faire,
Was never Prince so meeke and debonaire;
But ere my hoped day of spousall shone,

[1] split.　　[2] hurry.　　[3] chose.　　[4] heir.

My dearest Lord fell from high honors staire   205
Into the hands of hys accursed fone,[1]
And cruelly was slaine; that shall I ever mone.

24

"His blessed body, spoild of lively breath,
Was afterward, I know not how, convaid,
And fro me hid: of whose most innocent death   210
When tidings came to mee, unhappy maid,
O, how great sorrow my sad soule assaid![2]
Then forth I went his woefull corse to find,
And many yeares throughout the world I straid,
A virgin widow, whose deepe wounded mind   215
With love long time did languish, as the stricken
     hind.

25

"At last it chaunced this proud Sarazin
To meete me wandring; who perforce me led
With him away, but yet could never win
The fort that ladies hold in soveraigne dread.   220
There lies he now with foule dishonor dead,
Who, whiles he livde, was called proud Sans foy,
The eldest of three brethren; all three bred
Of one bad sire, whose youngest is Sans joy;
And twixt them both was born the bloudy bold
     Sans loy.[3]   225

26

"In this sad plight, friendlesse, unfortunate,
Now miserable I, Fidessa, dwell,
Craving of you, in pitty of my state,
To doe none ill, if please ye not doe well."
He in great passion al this while did dwell,   230
More busying his quicke eies her face to view,
Then his dull eares to heare what shee did tell;
And said, "faire lady, hart of flint would rew
The undeserved woes and sorrowes, which ye shew.

27

"Henceforth in safe assuraunce may ye rest,   235
Having both found a new friend you to aid,
And lost an old foe that did you molest;
Better new friend then an old foe is said."
With chaunge of chear the seeming simple maid
Let fal her eien, as shamefast, to the earth,   240
And yeelding soft, in that she nought gainsaid,
So forth they rode, he feining seemely merth,
And shee coy lookes: so dainty, they say, maketh
     derth.[4]

28

Long time they thus together traveiled;
Til, weary of their way, they came at last   245

Where grew two goodly trees, that faire did spred
Their armes abroad, with gray mosse overcast;
And their greene leaves, trembling with every
     blast,
Made a calme shadowe far in compasse round:
The fearefull shepheard, often there aghast,   250
Under them never sat, ne wont there sound
His mery oaten pipe, but shund th' unlucky
     ground.

29

But this good knight, soone as he them can spie,
For the coole shade him thither hastly got:
For golden Phœbus, now ymounted hie,   255
From fiery wheeles of his faire chariot
Hurled his beame so scorching cruell hot,
That living creature mote it not abide;
And his new Lady it endured not.
There they alight, in hope themselves to hide
From the fierce heat, and rest their weary limbs a
     tide.[1]   261

30

Faire seemly pleasaunce each to other makes,
With goodly purposes, there as they sit;
And in his falsed fancy he her takes
To be the fairest wight that lived yit;   265
Which to expresse he bends his gentle wit:
And, thinking of those braunches greene to frame
A girlond for her dainty forehead fit,
He pluckt a bough; out of whose rifte there came
Smal drops of gory bloud, that trickled down the
     same.   270

31

Therewith a piteous yelling voice was heard,
Crying, "O! spare with guilty hands to teare
My tender sides in this rough rynd embard;[2]
But fly, ah! fly far hence away, for feare
Least to you hap that happened to me heare,   275
And to this wretched Lady, my deare love;
O, too deare love, love bought with death too
     deare!"
Astond he stood, and up his heare did hove;[3]
And with that suddein horror could no member
     move.

32

At last whenas the dreadfull passion   280
Was overpast, and manhood well awake,
Yet musing at the straunge occasion,
And doubting much his sence, he thus bespake:
"What voice of damned Ghost from Limbo [4] lake.
Or guilefull spright wandring in empty aire,   285

[1] foes.   [2] tried.   [3] "Without law."
[4] "So daintiness or scarcity makes valuable."

[1] time.   [2] imprisoned.   [3] rise.
[4] A region bordering hell.

Both which fraile men doe oftentimes mistake,
Sends to my doubtfull eares these speaches rare,
And ruefull plaints, me bidding guiltlesse blood to
    spare?"

33

Then, groning deep; "Nor damned Ghost,"
    (quoth he,)
"Nor guilefull sprite to thee these words doth
    speake;   290
But once a man, Fradubio,[1] now a tree;
Wretched man, wretched tree! whose nature weake
A cruell witch, her cursed will to wreake,
Hath thus transformd, and plast in open plaines,
Where Boreas doth blow full bitter bleake,   295
And scorching Sunne does dry my secret vaines;
For though a tree I seme, yet cold and heat me
    paines."

34

"Say on, Fradubio, then, or man or tree,"
Quoth then the Knight; "by whose mischievous
    arts
Art thou misshaped thus, as now I see?   300
He oft finds med'cine who his griefe imparts,
But double griefs afflict concealing harts,
As raging flames who striveth to suppresse."
"The author then," (said he) "of all my smarts,
Is one Duessa, a false sorceresse,   305
That many errant knights hath broght to wretch-
    ednesse.

35

"In prime of youthly yeares, when corage hott
The fire of love, and joy of chevalree,
First kindled in my brest, it was my lott
To love this gentle Lady, whome ye see   310
Now not a Lady, but a seeming tree;
With whome, as once I rode accompanyde,
Me chaunced of a knight encountred bee,
That had a like faire Lady by his syde;
Lyke a faire Lady, but did fowle Duessa hyde.   315

36

"Whose forged beauty he did take in hand [2]
All other Dames to have exceeded farre:
I in defence of mine did likewise stand,
Mine, that did then shine as the Morning starre.
So both to batteill fierce arraunged arre,   320
In which his harder fortune was to fall
Under my speare: such is the dye of warre.
His Lady, left as a prise martiall,
Did yield her comely person to be at my call.

    [1] Doubt.
    [2] maintain.

37

"So doubly lov'd of ladies, unlike faire,   325
Th' one seeming such, the other such indeede,
One day in doubt I cast for to compare
Whether [1] in beauties glorie did exceede.
A Rosy girlond was the victors meede.
Both seemde to win, and both seemde won to bee,
So hard the discord was to be agreede.   331
Frælissa was as faire as faire mote bee,
And ever false Duessa seemde as faire as shee.

38

"The wicked witch, now seeing all this while
The doubtfull ballaunce equally to sway,   335
What not by right she cast to win by guile:
And by her hellish science raisd streight way
A foggy mist that overcast the day,
And a dull blast, that breathing on her face
Dimmed her former beauties shining ray,   340
And with foule ugly forme did her disgrace:
Then was she fayre alone, when none was faire in
    place.

39

"Then cride she out, 'Fye, fye! deformed wight,
Whose borrowed beautie now appeareth plaine
To have before bewitched all mens sight: 345
O! leave her soone, or let her soone be slaine.'
Her loathly visage viewing with disdaine,
Eftsoones I thought her such as she me told,
And would have kild her; but with faigned paine
The false witch did my wrathfull hand withhold:
So left her, where she now is turnd to treen
    mould.[2]   351

40

"Thensforth I tooke Duessa for my Dame,
And in the witch unweeting joyd long time,
Ne ever wist but that she was the same;
Till on a day (that day is everie Prime,   355
When Witches wont do penance for their crime,)
I chaunst to see her in her proper hew,
Bathing her self in origane [3] and thyme:
A filthy foule old woman I did vew,
That ever to have toucht her I did deadly rew.   360

41

"Her neather partes misshapen, monstruous,
Were hidd in water, that I could not see,
But they did seeme more foule and hideous,
Then womans shape man would believe to bee.
Thensforth from her most beastly companie   365
I gan refraine, in minde to slipp away,
Soone as appeard safe opportunitie:

    [1] which.   [2] form of a tree.
    [3] sweet marjoram.

For danger great, if not assurd decay,
I saw before mine eyes, if I were knowne to stray.

42

"The divelish hag by chaunges of my cheare 370
Perceiv'd my thought; and, drownd in sleepie
    night,
With wicked herbes and oyntments did besmeare
My body all, through charmes and magicke might,
That all my senses were bereaved quight:
Then brought she me into this desert waste, 375
And by my wretched lovers side me pight; [1]
Where now, enclosd in wooden wals full faste,
Banisht from living wights, our wearie daies we
    waste."

43

"But how long time," said then the Elfin knight,
"Are you in this misformed hous to dwell?" 380
"We may not chaunge," (quoth he,) "this evill
    plight,
Till we be bathed in a living [2] well:
That is the terme prescribed by the spell."
"O! how," sayd he, "mote I that well out find,
That may restore you to your wonted well?" 385
"Time and suffised [3] fates to former kynd [4]

[1] placed.   [2] flowing.   [3] satisfied.   [4] nature.

Shall us restore; none else from hence may us un-
    bynd."

44

The false Duessa, now Fidessa hight,
Heard how in vaine Fradubio did lament,
And knew well all was true. But the good knight,
Full of sad feare and ghastly dreriment,[1] 391
When all this speech the living tree had spent,
The bleeding bough did thrust into the ground,
That from the blood he might be innocent,
And with fresh clay did close the wooden wound:
Then, turning to his Lady, dead with feare her
    fownd. 396

45

Her seeming dead he fowned with feigned feare,
As all unweeting of that well she knew;
And paynd himselfe with busie care to reare
Her out of carelesse swowne. Her eyelids blew,
And dimmed sight, with pale and deadly hew, 401
At last she up gan lift: with trembling cheare
Her up he tooke, (too simple and too trew)
And oft her kist. At length, all passed feare,[2]
He set her on her steede, and forward forth did
    beare. 405

[1] sorrow.   [2] all fear passed.

William Shakespeare · 1564-1616

England at the time of Spenser and Shakespeare was Merry England. It was a time of change and action. Queen Elizabeth was expanding the power of the throne. Scotland was joined to England. Conspiracy and struggle clouded the relations of England with France and Spain. But Merry England was also restless England. Shakespeare saw two religions in rivalry for control — Catholicism and Anglicanism — and a third, Puritanism, rising to power. Court life was gay and colorful. Drake and Raleigh and Essex were popular heroes. Even though the social classes of nobles, gentry, yeomen, and commoners were fairly fixed, it was a time when ambitious men changed quickly from one rank into another. Society was in a state of flux. And with all of the action existed a fondness for sports — hunting, dancing, cock-fighting, bull-baiting. The streets were filled with acrobats and strolling players. The two important theaters in existence when Shakespeare went up from Stratford to London, the *Theater* and the *Curtain*, were supplemented in a few years by others — the *Swan*, the *Hope*, the *Rose*, the *Globe*. In all England there were perhaps five million people, in London some two hundred thousand.

Shakespeare was born at Stratford-on-Avon in 1564 and was buried there in 1616. The facts of the poet's life, at least those which have been definitely established, are few. In education he went little beyond a study of Latin grammar and literature; at eighteen or nineteen he married Anne Hathaway, who was several years his senior; he was father of three children, Susanna and the twins Hamnet and Judith; about 1585 he left Stratford for London where, by 1592, he had a growing reputation both as an actor and as a playwright; in 1594 he and his company of actors played before the Queen; in 1597 his financial condition was so advanced as to permit him to purchase the largest house in Stratford and, sometime later, he retired to that Warwickshire town to spend the years remaining before his death on April 23, 1616.

To such barren facts as these may be added many colorful legends and suppositions, legends such as those which state that Shakespeare's father was a butcher and that when the young William slaughtered beef "he would doe it in a high style and make a speech," that he left Stratford for London because of a poaching episode and of the trouble he brought upon himself when he pilloried the irate landowner in a scurrilous ballad. We like, too, to learn that as an actor Shakespeare performed before audiences at such playhouses as the *Theater*, the *Rose*, the *Curtain*, and the *Globe*, and that perhaps, among other roles, he played the parts of the ghost in *Hamlet* and of Adam in *As You Like It*.

The plays of Shakespeare have overshadowed his two long poems, *Venus and Adonis* (1593) and *The Rape of Lucrece* (1594), and even his *Sonnets* (1609). The plays, usually listed as thirty-eight, include several which, it is generally conceded, were written in collaboration with others. Scholars have shown much persistence and ingenuity in arranging the plays in chronological order, but that is a problem which need not concern us here. Of interest, however, is the grouping of the plays into four rather loosely knit periods, an arrangement which reflects the progress of Shakespeare's mind and manner over the two decades from 1592 to 1612. The first period, from the time of his first work until about 1594, was chiefly devoted to dramas of chronicle history — such plays as *Richard III* and *King John;* the second period, from 1594 to perhaps 1601, was a time devoted primarily to comedy — to such plays as *The Merry Wives of Windsor* and *Much Ado about Nothing;* the third period, from 1601 to about 1609, was the epoch of such plays as *Hamlet* and *King Lear;* while to the fourth period, that from 1610 to 1612, belong such romantic comedies as *The Winter's Tale* and *The Tempest.*

But once he had his narrative, he brought to it an understanding of human nature, a rich quality of characterization, a highly imaginative mind which made something strangely new of the old figures and old setting. To them he added a wit which flashed through repartee, a fancy which found its expression in lyrical passages of lasting beauty, a poetical power which gave new coloring and new strength even to familiar events and to historical personages. Shakespeare is a dramatist who writes of the human spirit with an authority and an understanding one rarely encounters. He was, in the estimate of Dryden, "the man who of all Moderns, and perhaps Ancient Poets, had the largest and most comprehensive soul." Shakespeare preached no doctrine; his concern was with life itself. So rich is Shakespeare's mind, so wide his range, that examples of his work might be used to illustrate any of the three major tempers — classical, romantic, or realistic — according to the passage selected. Few philosophers have been so philosophical; few psychologists have presented a truer psychology; and few historians have so caught the spirit of the time. In his many-sidedness he was a son of the Renaissance.

SUGGESTED REFERENCES: Marchette Chute, *Shakespeare of London* (1949); E. K. Chambers, *Shakespeare: A Survey* (1962); Peter Alexander, *Shakespeare* (1964); L. B. Wright, *Shakespeare for Everyman* (1964); Alfred Harbage, ed., *Shakespeare. The Tragedies. A Collection of Critical Essays* (1965).

Songs from the Plays

(From *Love's Labor's Lost*)

When icicles hang by the wall,
    And Dick the shepherd blows his nail,
And Tom bears logs into the hall,
    And milk comes frozen home in pail,
When blood is nipped and ways be foul,   5
Then nightly sings the staring owl,
    Tu-whit, tu-who! a merry note,
While greasy Joan doth keel [1] the pot.

When all aloud the wind doth blow,
    And coughing drowns the parson's saw,[2]   10
And birds sit brooding in the snow,
    And Marian's nose looks red and raw,
When roasted crabs [3] hiss in the bowl,
Then nightly sings the staring owl,
    Tu-whit, tu-who! a merry note,   15
While greasy Joan doth keel the pot.

(From *Two Gentlemen of Verona*)

Who is Silvia? what is she,
    That all our swains commend her?
Holy, fair, and wise is she;
    The heaven such grace did lend her
That she might admiréd be.   5

Is she kind as she is fair?
    For beauty lives with kindness.
Love doth to her eyes repair
    To help him of his blindness,
And, being helped, inhabits there.   10

Then to Silvia let us sing
    That Silvia is excelling;
She excels each mortal thing
    Upon the dull earth dwelling —
To her let us garlands bring.   15

(From *As You Like It*)

Under the greenwood tree
Who loves to lie with me,
And turn his merry note
Unto the sweet bird's throat,
Come hither! come hither! come hither!   5
    Here shall he see
    No enemy
But winter and rough weather.

Who doth ambition shun
And loves to live i' the sun,   10
Seeking the food he eats
And pleased with what he gets,

Come hither! come hither! come hither!
    Here shall he see
    No enemy   15
But winter and rough weather.

(From *As You Like It*)

Blow, blow, thou winter wind!
Thou art not so unkind
As man's ingratitude;
Thy tooth is not so keen,
Because thou art not seen,   5
    Although thy breath be rude.

Heigh ho! sing, heigh ho! unto the green holly;
Most friendship is feigning, most loving mere folly.
    Then, heigh ho, the holly!
    This life is most jolly.   10

Freeze, freeze, thou bitter sky!
That dost not bite so nigh
    As benefits forgot;
Though thou the waters warp,
Thy sting is not so sharp   15
    As friend remembered not.
Heigh ho! sing, heigh ho! etc.

(From *Twelfth Night*)

O Mistress mine, where are you roaming?
Oh, stay and hear; your true love's coming,
    That can sing both high and low.
Trip no further, pretty sweeting,
Journeys end in lovers meeting,   5
    Every wise man's son doth know.

What is Love? 'tis not hereafter;
Present mirth hath present laughter;
    What's to come is still unsure.
In delay there lies no plenty;   10
Then come kiss me, sweet and twenty;
    Youth's a stuff will not endure.

(From *Measure for Measure*)

Take, O, take those lips away
    That so sweetly were forsworn;
And those eyes, the break of day,
    Lights that do mislead the morn.
But my kisses bring again,   5
        Bring again;
Seals of love, but sealed in vain,
        Sealed in vain!

(From *Cymbeline*)

Hark, hark! the lark at heaven's gate sings
    And Phœbus 'gins arise,
His steeds to water at those springs
    On chaliced flowers that lies;

---

[1] cool.   [2] sermon.   [3] crab-apples.

And winking Mary-buds begin   5
   To ope their golden eyes.
With every thing that pretty is,
   My lady sweet, arise!
      Arise, arise!

(From *Cymbeline*)

Fear no more the heat o' the sun,
   Nor the furious winter's rages;
Thou thy worldly task hast done,
   Home art gone, and ta'en thy wages.
Golden lads and girls all must,   5
As chimney-sweepers, come to dust.

Fear no more the frown o' the great;
   Thou art past the tyrant's stroke;
Care no more to clothe and eat;
   To thee the reed is as the oak.   10
The scepter, learning, physic must
All follow this, and come to dust.

Fear no more the lightning-flash,
   Nor th' all-dreaded thunder-stone;
Fear not slander, censure rash;   15
   Thou hast finished joy and moan.
All lovers young, all lovers must
Consign to thee, and come to dust.

No exorciser harm thee!
   Nor no witchcraft charm thee!   20
Ghost unlaid forbear thee!
   Nothing ill come near thee!
Quiet consummation have;
And renownéd be thy grave!

(From *The Tempest*)

Full fathom five thy father lies.
Of his bones are coral made;
Those are pearls that were his eyes;
   Nothing of him that doth fade
But doth suffer a sea change   5
Into something rich and strange.
Sea-nymphs hourly ring his knell:
         Ding-dong!
Hark! now I hear them — Ding-dong, bell!

Sonnets

One who reads the *Sonnets* consecutively — the series includes one hundred and fifty-two sonnets — finds that they, as well as the plays, unfold a story. The first hundred and twenty-six are largely concerned with friendship for a young man and the advice he wants to give this man; the second group, numbers 127 to 152,

narrate a love affair with a dark lady who is unfaithful to both her husband and to Shakespeare because of her infatuation for the young man of the earlier sonnets. The order of the writing of the sonnets, the extent to which they reflect personal experience and emotion, the identity of the people presented — these are all matters for scholarly speculation. The *Sonnets* were entered in the *Register* for publication on May 20, 1609; the time covered by the events narrated would appear to be the years between 1593 and 1596.

15

When I consider everything that grows
Holds in perfection but a little moment,
That this huge stage presenteth nought but shows
Whereon the stars in secret influence comment;
When I perceive that men as plants increase,   5
Cheered and checked even by the self-same sky;
Vaunt in their youthful sap, at height decrease,
And wear their brave state out of memory;
Then the conceit of this inconstant stay
Sets you most rich in youth before my sight,   10
Where wasteful Time debateth with Decay,
To change your day of youth to sullied night;
   And all in war with Time for love of you,
   As he takes from you, I engraft you new.

18

Shall I compare thee to a summer's day?
Thou art more lovely and more temperate:
Rough winds do shake the darling buds of May,
And summer's lease hath all too short a date;
Sometime too hot the eye of heaven shines,   5
And often is his gold complexion dimmed;
And every fair [1] from fair sometime declines,
By chance or nature's changing course untrimmed:
But thy eternal summer shall not fade
Nor lose possession of that fair thou ow'st;   10
Nor shall Death brag thou wand'rest in his shade,
When in eternal lines to time thou grow'st;
   So long as men can breathe or eyes can see,
   So long lives this and this gives life to thee.

23

As an unperfect actor on the stage
Who with his fear is put beside his part,
Or some fierce thing replete with too much rage,
Whose strength's abundance weakens his own heart,
So I, for fear of trust, forget to say   5
The perfect ceremony of love's rite,
And in mine own love's strength seem to decay,
O'ercharged with burden of mine own love's might.

[1] beauty.

O, let my books be then the eloquence
And dumb presagers of my speaking breast,   10
Who plead for love and look for recompense
More than that tongue that more hath more ex-
    pressed.
  O, learn to read what silent love hath writ;
  To hear with eyes belongs to love's fine wit.

29

When, in disgrace with fortune and men's eyes,
I all alone beweep my outcast state,
And trouble deaf heaven with my bootless cries,
And look upon myself, and curse my fate,
Wishing me like to one more rich in hope,   5
Featured like him, like him with friends possessed,
Desiring this man's art and that man's scope,
With what I most enjoy contented least;
Yet in these thoughts myself almost despising,
Haply I think on thee — and then my state,   10
Like to the lark at break of day arising
From sullen earth, sings hymns at heaven's gate;
  For thy sweet love remembered such wealth
    brings
  That then I scorn to change my state with
    kings.

30

When to the sessions of sweet silent thought
I summon up remembrance of things past,
I sigh the lack of many a thing I sought,
And with old woes new wail my dear time's waste.
Then can I drown an eye, unused to flow,   5
For precious friends hid in death's dateless [1]
    night,
And weep afresh love's long since cancelled woe,
And moan the expense [2] of many a vanish'd
    sight.
Then can I grieve at grievances foregone,
And heavily from woe to woe tell o'er   10
The sad account of fore-bemoanèd moan,
Which I new pay as if not paid before.
  But if the while I think on thee, dear friend,
  All losses are restored and sorrows end.

32

If thou survive my well-contented day,
When that churl Death my bones with dust shall
    cover,
And shalt by fortune once more re-survey
These poor rude lines of thy deceasèd lover,
Compare them with the bettering of the time,   5
And though they be outstripped by every pen,
Reserve them for my love, not for their rime,
Exceeded by the height of happier men.

[1] endless.   [2] loss.

O, then vouchsafe me but this loving thought:
"Had my friend's Muse grown with this growing
    age,   10
A dearer birth than this his love had brought,
To march in ranks of better equipage:
  But since he died and poets better prove,
  Theirs for their style I'll read, his for his love."

54

O, how much more doth beauty beauteous seem
By that sweet ornament which truth doth give!
The rose looks fair, but fairer we it deem
For that sweet odor which doth in it live.
The canker-blooms have full as deep a dye   5
As the perfumèd tincture of the roses,
Hang on such thorns, and play as wantonly
When summer's breath their masked buds dis-
    closes;
But, for [1] their virtue only is their show,
They live unwooed and unrespected fade,   10
Die to themselves.   Sweet roses do not so;
Of their sweet deaths are sweetest odors made:
  And so of you, beauteous and lovely youth,
  When that shall fade, my verse distills your
    truth.

55

Not marble, nor the gilded monuments
Of princes, shall outlive this powerful rime;
But you shall shine more bright in these contents
Than unswept stone, besmeared with sluttish
    time.
When wasteful war shall statues overturn,   5
And broils root out the work of masonry,
Nor Mars his sword nor war's quick fire shall
    burn
The living record of your memory.
'Gainst death and all-oblivious enmity
Shall you pace forth; your praise shall still find
    room   10
Even in the eyes of all posterity
That wear this world out to the ending doom.
  So, till the judgment that [2] yourself arise,
  You live in this, and dwell in lovers' eyes.

64

When I have seen by Time's fell hand defaced
The rich-proud cost of outworn buried age;
When sometime lofty towers I see downrazed,
And brass eternal slave to mortal rage;
When I have seen the hungry ocean gain   5
Advantage on the kingdom of the shore,
And the firm soil win of the watery main,
Increasing store with loss, and loss with store:

[1] because.   [2] when.

When I have seen such interchange of state,
Or state itself confounded to decay;   10
Ruin hath taught me thus to ruminate, —
That Time will come and take my love away.
   This thought is as a death, which cannot choose
   But weep to have that which it fears to lose.

65

Since brass, nor stone, nor earth, nor boundless
    sea,
But sad mortality o'er-sways their power,
How with this rage shall beauty hold a plea,
Whose action is no stronger than a flower?
O, how shall summer's honey breath hold out   5
Against the wrackful siege of battering days,
When rocks impregnable are not so stout,
Nor gates of steel so strong, but Time decays?
O fearful meditation! where, alack,   9
Shall Time's best jewel from Time's chest lie hid?
Or what strong hand can hold his swift foot back?
Or who his spoil of beauty can forbid?
   O, none, unless this miracle have might,
   That in black ink my love may still shine bright.

73

That time of year thou mayst in me behold
When yellow leaves, or none, or few, do hang
Upon those boughs which shake against the cold,
Bare ruin'd choirs, where late the sweet birds sang.
In me thou see'st the twilight of such day   5
As after sunset fadeth in the west;
Which by and by black night doth take away,
Death's second self, that seals up all in rest.
In me thou see'st the glowing of such fire
That on the ashes of his youth doth lie,   10
As the death-bed whereon it must expire,
Consum'd with that which it was nourish'd by.
   This thou perceiv'st, which makes thy love more
     strong,
   To love that well which thou must leave ere long.

97

How like a winter hath my absence been
From thee, the pleasure of the fleeting year!
What freezings have I felt, what dark days seen!
What old December's bareness everywhere!
And yet this time remov'd was summer's time; 5
The teeming autumn, big with rich increase,
Bearing the wanton burden of the prime,
Like widowed wombs after their lords' decease:
Yet this abundant issue seem'd to me
But hope of orphans and unfather'd fruit;   10
For summer and his pleasures wait on thee.
And, thou away, the very birds are mute:
   Of, if they sing, 'tis with so dull a cheer,
   That leaves look pale, dreading the winter's near.

104

To me, fair friend, you never can be old,
For as you were when first your eye I eyed,
Such seems your beauty still.   Three winters
    cold
Have from the forests shook three summers' pride,
Three beauteous springs to yellow autumn turned
In process of the seasons have I seen,   6
Three April perfumes in three hot Junes burned
Since first I saw you fresh, which yet are green.
Ah! yet doth beauty, like a dial-hand,
Steal from his figure and no pace perceived; 10
So your sweet hue, which methinks still doth
    stand,
Hath motion and mine eye may be deceived:
   For fear of which, hear this, thou age unbred:
   Ere you were born was beauty's summer dead.

106

When in the chronicle of wasted time
I see descriptions of the fairest wights,
And beauty making beautiful old rime
In praise of ladies dead and lovely knights,
Then, in the blazon of sweet beauty's best, 5
Of hand, of foot, of lip, of eye, of brow,
I see their antique pen would have expressed
Even such a beauty as you master now.
So all their praises are but prophecies
Of this our time, all you prefiguring;   10
And, for they looked but with divining eyes,
They had not skill enough your worth to sing:
   For we, which now behold these present days,
   Have eyes to wonder, but lack tongues to
     praise.

107

Not mine own fears, nor the prophetic soul
Of the wide world dreaming on things to come,
Can yet the lease of my true love control,
Supposed as forfeit to a confined doom.
The mortal moon hath her eclipse endured, 5
And the sad augurs mock their own presage;
Incertainties now crown themselves assured,
And peace proclaims olives of endless age.
Now with the drops of this most balmy time
My love looks fresh, and Death to me subscribes,
Since, spite of him, I'll live in this poor rime, 11
While he insults o'er dull and speechless tribes:
   And thou in this shalt find thy monument,
   When tyrants' crests and tombs of brass are
     spent.

109

O, never say that I was false of heart,
Though absence seemed my flame to qualify.
As easy might I from myself depart

As from my soul, which in thy breast doth lie:
That is my home of love: if I have ranged,   5
Like him that travels I return again,
Just to the time, not with the time exchanged,
So that myself bring water for my stain.
Never believe, though in my nature reigned
All frailties that besiege all kinds of blood,   10
That it could so preposterously be stained,
To leave for nothing all thy sum of good;
    For nothing this wide universe I call,
    Save thou, my rose; in it thou art my all.

Love's not Time's fool, though rosy lips and cheeks
Within his bending sickle's compass come;   10
Love alters not with his brief hours and weeks,
But bears it out even to the edge of doom.
    If this be error and upon me proved,
    I never writ, nor no man ever loved.

116

Let me not to the marriage of true minds
Admit impediments. Love is not love
Which alters when it alteration finds,
Or bends with the remover to remove:
O, no! it is an ever-fixèd mark,   5
That looks on tempests and is never shaken;
It is the star to every wandering bark,
Whose worth's unknown, although his height be
    taken.

130

My mistress' eyes are nothing like the sun;
Coral is far more red than her lips' red:
If snow be white, why then her breasts are dun;
If hairs be wires, black wires grow on her head.
I have seen roses damasked, red and white,   5
But no such roses see I in her cheeks;
And in some perfumes is there more delight
Than in the breath that from my mistress reeks.
I love to hear her speak, yet well I know
That music hath a far more pleasing sound: 10
I grant I never saw a goddess go, —
My mistress, when she walks, treads on the ground:
    And yet, by heaven, I think my love as rare
    As any she belied with false compare.

The Tragedy of King Lear

Shakespeare wrote *King Lear* sometime before Christmas, 1606, at which time the tragedy is known to have been presented at Whitehall. An acceptable date, though one not definitely established, is 1605. The first printed edition, in quarto form, appeared in 1608.

As is customary with Shakespeare's plays, *King Lear* had numerous antecedents. The basic Lear story, of a king and his faithless daughters, is found in the folklore of various countries and the story had been used by at least one playwright before Shakespeare. The sources most directly employed by the dramatist, however, appear to have been the *Mirror for Magistrates*, Holinshed's *Chronicles*, and the old play, *King Leir*. But as is again customary with Shakespeare, this early material was taken and moulded, added to and subtracted from, until a new form emerged. Where the old story had ended happily in the victory of France and the restoration of Lear, Shakespeare's tragedy closed with the defeat of France, the hanging of Cordelia, and the death of Lear. Apparently original elements which the poet grafted on to the early legend include the faithfulness of Kent, the pathos of the fool, the interest of the two unfaithful daughters in Edmund, and the insanity of Lear.

In a great play which is a work of art it seems futile to look for a "theme," but if a concept has to be found here it is that of man's inhumanity:

> "Poor naked wretches, wheresoe'er you are,
>   That bide the pelting of this pitiless storm,
>   How shall your houseless heads and unfed sides,
>   Your loop'd and window'd raggedness, defend you
>   From seasons such as these?"

In the tragic impact of the closing scenes, however, the reader must not forget that there is goodness as well as evil in the play.

Lear is dominantly romantic in temper. The distinctly imaginative quality — as in the storm scenes and in the vivid description of the view from the "cliff" where Gloucester plans to commit suicide — belongs to this romantic spirit as does the interplay between nature and man's thought which persists throughout the tragedy. Other elements which distinguish *Lear* from classical tragedy are found in the plucking out of Gloucester's eyes on the stage (instead of off stage), the piling on of misfortune — in addition to blindness and insanity, there is warfare, intrigue, unfilial conduct — and the use of a major plot (the Lear story) with the minor plots (the Gloucester-sons relationship and the conspiracy of Edmund with Goneril and Regan). And yet it cannot be denied that the structure of *Lear* is unified.

Dramatis Personæ

LEAR, *King of Britain*
KING OF FRANCE
DUKE OF BURGUNDY
DUKE OF CORNWALL
DUKE OF ALBANY
EARL OF KENT
EARL OF GLOUCESTER
EDGAR, *son to Gloucester*
EDMUND, *bastard son to Gloucester*
CURAN, *a courtier*
Old Man, *tenant to Gloucester*

Doctor
Fool
OSWALD, *steward to Goneril*
A Captain employed by Edmund
Gentleman attendant on Cordelia
A Herald
Servants to Cornwall
GONERIL ⎫
REGAN ⎬ *daughters to Lear*
CORDELIA ⎭

Knights of Lear's train, Captains, Messengers, Soldiers, and Attendants

SCENE: *Britain*

ACT I

SCENE I. *King Lear's palace.*

(*Enter* KENT, GLOUCESTER, *and* EDMUND.)

Kent. I thought the King had more affected [1] the Duke of Albany than Cornwall.

Glou. It did always seem so to us; but now, in the division of the kingdom, it appears not which of the Dukes he values most; for qualities are 5 so weigh'd, that curiosity in neither can make choice of either's moiety.[2]

Kent. Is not this your son, my lord?

Glou. His breeding, sir, hath been at my charge. I have so often blush'd to acknowledge him, 10 that now I am braz'd [3] to 't.

Kent. I cannot conceive you.

Glou. Sir, this young fellow's mother could; whereupon she grew round-womb'd, and had, indeed, sir, a son for her cradle ere she had a 15 husband for her bed. Do you smell a fault?

Kent. I cannot wish the fault undone, the issue of it being so proper.[4]

Glou. But I have a son, sir, by order of law, some year elder than this, who yet is no dearer in 20 my account. Though this knave came something saucily into the world before he was sent for, yet was his mother fair; there was good sport at his making, and the whoreson must be acknowledged. Do you know this noble gentleman, Edmund? 25

Edm. No, my lord.

Glou. My Lord of Kent. Remember him hereafter as my honorable friend.

Edm. My services to your lordship.

Kent. I must love you, and sue to know you 30 better.

[1] liked, had more affection for.
[2] half or share.
[3] accustomed, hardened.
[4] handsome, comely.

Edm. Sir, I shall study deserving.

Glou. He hath been out [1] nine years, and away he shall again. The King is coming.

(*Sennet. Enter one bearing a coronet, then* KING LEAR, *then the* DUKES OF ALBANY *and* CORNWALL, *next* GONERIL, REGAN, CORDELIA, *with followers.*)

Lear. Attend the lords of France and Burgundy, Gloucester. 35

Glou. I shall, my lord.

(*Exeunt* GLOUCESTER *and* EDMUND.)

Lear. Meantime we shall express our darker [2] purpose.
Give me the map there. Know that we have divided
In three our kingdom; and 'tis our fast intent
To shake all cares and business from our age, 40
Conferring them on younger strengths, while we
Unburden'd crawl toward death. Our son of Cornwall,
And you, our no less loving son of Albany,
We have this hour a constant will to publish
Our daughters' several dowers, that future strife
May be prevented now. The Princes, France and Burgundy, 46
Great rivals in our youngest daughter's love,
Long in our court have made their amorous sojourn,
And here are to be answer'd. Tell me, my daughters, —
Since now we will divest us both of rule, 50
Interest of territory, cares of state, —
Which of you shall we say doth love us most,
That we our largest bounty may extend
Where nature doth with merit challenge? Goneril,
Our eldest-born, speak first. 55

[1] away from home.
[2] more secret.

Gon. Sir, I love you more than word can wield
    the matter;
Dearer than eye-sight, space, and liberty;
Beyond what can be valued, rich or rare;
No less than life, with grace, health, beauty, honor;
As much as child e'er lov'd, or father found;   60
A love that makes breath poor, and speech unable:
Beyond all manner of so much I love you.
    Cor. (*Aside.*) What shall Cordelia speak? Love
    and be silent.
    Lear. Of all these bounds, even from this line to
    this,
With shadowy forests and with champains rich'd,
With plenteous rivers and wide-skirted meads, 66
We make thee lady. To thine and Albany's issues
Be this perpetual. What says our second daughter,
Our dearest Regan, wife of Cornwall? Speak.
    Reg. I am made of that self metal as my sister,
And prize me at her worth. In my true heart 71
I find she names my very deed of love;
Only she comes too short, that I profess
Myself an enemy to all other joys
Which the most precious square of sense possesses;
And find I am alone felicitate [1]   76
In your dear Highness' love.
    Cor. (*Aside.*)   Then poor Cordelia!
And yet not so; since, I am sure, my love's
More ponderous than my tongue.
    Lear. To thee and thine hereditary ever 80
Remain this ample third of our fair kingdom;
No less in space, validity, and pleasure,
Than that conferr'd on Goneril. Now, our joy,
Although our last and least, to whose young love
The vines of France and milk of Burgundy 85
Strive to be interess'd, [2] what can you say to draw
A third more opulent than your sisters? Speak.
    Cor. Nothing, my lord.
    Lear. Nothing!
    Cor. Nothing.   90
    Lear. Nothing will come of nothing. Speak
    again.
    Cor. Unhappy that I am, I cannot heave
My heart into my mouth. I love your Majesty
According to my bond, [3] no more nor less.
    Lear. How, how, Cordelia! Mend your speech
    a little,   95
Lest you may mar your fortunes.
    Cor.   Good my lord,
You have begot me, bred me, lov'd me: I
Return those duties back as are right fit;
Obey you, love you, and most honor you.
Why have my sisters husbands, if they say 100
They love you all? Haply, when I shall wed,
That lord whose hand must take my plight shall
    carry

[1] made happy.   [2] interested.   [3] obligation.

Half my love with him, half my care and duty.
Sure, I shall never marry like my sisters
To love my father all.   105
    Lear. But goes thy heart with this?
    Cor.   Ay, my good lord.
    Lear. So young, and so untender?
    Cor. So young, my lord, and true.
    Lear. Let it be so; thy truth, then, be thy dower!
For, by the sacred radiance of the sun, 110
The mysteries of Hecate, [1] and the night;
By all the operation of the orbs
From whom we do exist, and cease to be;
Here I disclaim all my paternal care,
Propinquity and property of blood, 115
And as a stranger to my heart and me
Hold thee, from this, for ever. The barbarous
    Scythian, [2]
Or he that makes his generation messes
To gorge his appetite, shall to my bosom
Be as well neighbor'd, piti'd, and reliev'd, 120
As thou my sometime daughter.
    Kent.   Good my liege, —
    Lear. Peace, Kent!
Come not between the dragon and his wrath.
I lov'd her most, and thought to set my rest
On her kind nursery. (*To* Cor.) Hence, and
    avoid my sight! —   125
So be my grave my peace, as here I give
Her father's heart from her! Call France. — Who
    stirs?
Call Burgundy. Cornwall and Albany,
With my two daughters' dowers digest the third;
Let pride, which she calls plainness, marry her. 130
I do invest you jointly with my power,
Pre-eminence, and all the large effects
That troop with majesty. Ourself, by monthly
    course,
With reservation of an hundred knights,
By you to be sustain'd, shall our abode 135
Make with you by due turn. Only we shall retain
The name, and all the addition to a king;
The sway, revenue, execution of the rest,
Beloved sons, be yours; which to confirm,
This coronet part between you.
    Kent.   Royal Lear, 140
Whom I have ever honor'd as my king,
Lov'd as my father, as my master follow'd
As my great patron thought on in my prayers, —
    Lear. The bow is bent and drawn; make from
    the shaft.   144
    Kent. Let it fall rather, though the fork invade

[1] A goddess associated with ghosts and the nether world.

[2] A nomadic people once living along the northern coast of the Black Sea; they were supposed to eat their relatives.

The region of my heart: be Kent unmannerly
When Lear is mad. What wouldst thou do, old
    man?
Thinkst thou that duty shall have dread to speak
When power to flattery bows? To plainness hon-
    or's bound,   149
When majesty falls to folly. Reserve thy state;
And, in thy best consideration, check
This hideous rashness. Answer my life my judg-
    ment,
Thy youngest daughter does not love thee least;
Nor are those empty-hearted whose low sounds
Reverb [1] no hollowness.

    Lear.   Kent, on thy life, no more. 155
    Kent. My life I never held but as a pawn
To wage against thy enemies, ne'er fear to lose it,
Thy safety being motive.
    Lear.   Out of my sight!
    Kent. See better, Lear; and let me still remain
The true blank [2] of thine eye.   160
    Lear. Now, by Apollo, —
    Kent.   Now, by Apollo, king,
Thou swear'st thy gods in vain.
    Lear.   O, vassal! miscreant!
              (*Laying his hand on his sword.*)
    Alb. ⎫
    Corn.⎬ Dear sir, forbear.
    Kent. Kill thy physician, and thy fee bestow
Upon the foul disease. Revoke thy gift;   165
Or, whilst I can vent clamor from my throat,
I'll tell thee thou dost evil.
    Lear.   Hear me, recreant!
On thine allegiance, hear me!
That thou hast sought to make us break our vows
Which we durst never yet, and with strain'd pride
To come betwixt our sentences and our power, 171
Which nor our nature nor our place can bear,
Our potency made good, take thy reward.
Five days we do allot thee, for provision
To shield thee from disasters of the world;   175
And on the sixth to turn thy hated back
Upon our kingdom. If, on the tenth day follow-
    ing,
Thy banish'd trunk be found in our dominions,
The moment is thy death. Away! By Jupiter,
This shall not be revok'd.   180
    Kent. Fare thee well, king! Sith [3] thus thou
    wilt appear,
Freedom lives hence, and banishment is here.
(*To* CORDELIA.) The gods to their dear shelter
    take thee, maid,
That justly think'st, and hast most rightly said!
(*To* REGAN *and* GONERIL.) And your large speeches
    may your deeds approve,   185

    [1] reverberates.
    [2] The blank, or white, center of the target. [3] since.

That good effects may spring from words of love.
Thus Kent, O princes, bids you all adieu;
He'll shape his old course in a country new. (*Exit.*)

    (*Flourish. Re-enter* GLOUCESTER, *with* FRANCE,
        BURGUNDY, *and Attendants.*)

    Glou. Here's France and Burgundy, my noble
    lord.
    Lear. My Lord of Burgundy,   190
We first address toward you, who with this king
Hath rivall'd for our daughter. What, in the least,
Will you require in present dower with her,
Or cease your quest of love?
    Bur.   Most royal Majesty,
I crave no more than what your Highness offer'd,
Nor will you tender less.
    Lear.   Right noble Burgundy, 196
When she was dear to us, we did hold her so;
But now her price is fallen. Sir, there she stands:
If aught within that little-seeming substance,
Or all of it, with our displeasure piec'd,   200
And nothing more, may fitly like your Grace,
She's there, and she is yours.
    Bur.   I know no answer.
    Lear. Will you, with those infirmities she owes,
Unfriended, new-adopted to our hate,
Dower'd with our curse, and stranger'd with our
    oath,   205
Take her, or leave her?
    Bur.   Pardon me, royal sir;
Election makes not up [1] in such conditions.
    Lear. Then leave her, sir; for, by the power that
    made me,
I tell you all her wealth. (*To* FRANCE.) For you,
    great king,
I would not from your love make such a stray, 210
To match you where I hate; therefore beseech you
To avert your liking a more worthier way
Than on a wretch whom Nature is asham'd
Almost to acknowledge hers.
    France.   This is most strange,
That she, whom even but now was your best object,
The argument of your praise, balm of your age, 216
The best, the dearest, should in this trice of time
Commit a thing so monstrous, to dismantle
So many folds of favor. Sure, her offence
Must be of such unnatural degree,   220
That monsters it, or your fore-vouch'd affection
Fallen into taint; which to believe of her,
Must be a faith that reason without miracle
Should never plant in me.
    Cor.   I yet beseech your Majesty, —
If for I want that glib and oily art,   225
To speak and purpose not; since what I well in-
    tend,

    [1] The phrase seems to mean "one cannot elect."

I'll do 't before I speak, — that you make known
It is no vicious blot, murder, or foulness,
No unchaste action, or dishonored step,   229
That hath depriv'd me of your grace and favor;
But even for want of that for which I am richer,
A still-soliciting eye, and such a tongue
That I am glad I have not, though not to have it
Hath lost me in your liking.

Lear.   Better thou
Hadst not been born than not to have pleas'd me
     better.   235

France. Is it but this, — a tardiness in nature
Which often leaves the history unspoke
That it intends to do? My Lord of Burgundy,
What say you to the lady? Love's not love
When it is mingled with regards that stands   240
Aloof from the entire point. Will you have her?
She is herself a dowry.

Bur.   Royal king,
Give but that portion which yourself propos'd,
And here I take Cordelia by the hand,
Duchess of Burgundy.   245

Lear. Nothing. I have sworn; I am firm.

Bur. I am sorry, then, you have so lost a father
That you must lose a husband.

Cor.   Peace be with Burgundy!
Since that respect and fortunes are his love,
I shall not be his wife.   250

France. Fairest Cordelia, that art most rich
     being poor,
Most choice forsaken, and most lov'd despis'd!
Thee and thy virtues here I seize upon,
Be it lawful I take up what's cast away.
Gods, gods! 'tis strange that from their cold'st
     neglect   255
My love should kindle to inflam'd respect.
Thy dowerless daughter, king, thrown to my
     chance,
Is queen of us, of ours, and our fair France.
Not all the dukes of waterish Burgundy
Can buy this unpriz'd precious maid of me.   260
Bid them farewell, Cordelia, though unkind;
Thou losest here, a better where [1] to find.

Lear. Thou hast her, France. Let her be thine;
     for we
Have no such daughter, nor shall ever see
That face of hers again. — (*To* Cor.) Therefore
     be gone   265
Without our grace, our love, our benison. [2] —
Come, noble Burgundy.

     (*Flourish. Exeunt all but* FRANCE, GONE-
     RIL, REGAN, *and* CORDELIA.)

France. Bid farewell to your sisters.

Cor. The jewels of our father, with wash'd eyes
Cordelia leaves you. I know you what you are;

And like a sister am most loath to call   271
Your faults as they are named.   Love well our
     father,
To your professed bosoms I commit him;
But yet, alas, stood I within his grace,
I would prefer him to a better place.   275
So, farewell to you both.

Reg. Prescribe not us our duty.

Gon.   Let your study
Be to content your lord, who hath receiv'd you
At fortune's alms. You have obedience scanted,
And well are worth the want that you have wanted.

Cor. Time shall unfold what plighted cunning
     hides;   281
Who covers faults, at last shame them derides.
Well may you prosper!

France.   Come, my fair Cordelia.
     (*Exeunt* FRANCE *and* CORDELIA.)

Gon. Sister, it is not little I have to say of what
most nearly appertains to us both. I think our
father will hence to-night.   286

Reg. That's most certain, and with you; next
month with us.

Gon. You see how full of changes his age is; the
observation we have made of it hath not been   290
little. He always lov'd our sister most; and with
what poor judgement he hath now cast her off appears too grossly.

Reg. 'Tis the infirmity of his age; yet he hath
ever but slenderly known himself.   295

Gon. The best and soundest of his time hath
been but rash; then must we look from his age to
receive not alone the imperfections of long-en-
graffed condition,[1] but therewithal the unruly waywardness that infirm and choleric years bring 300
with them.

Reg. Such unconstant starts are we like to have
from him as this of Kent's banishment.

Gon. There is further compliment of leavetaking
between France and him. Pray you, let us   305
hit together; if our father carry authority with such
disposition as he bears, this last surrender of his
will but offend us.

Reg. We shall further think of it.   309

Gon. We must do something, and i' the heat.[2]
     (*Exeunt.*

SCENE II. *The Earl of Gloucester's castle.*

(*Enter Bastard* EDMUND *with a letter.*)

Edm. Thou, Nature, art my goddess; to thy law
My services are bound.   Wherefore should I
Stand in the plague of custom, and permit
The curiosity of nations to deprive me,
For that I am some twelve or fourteen moonshines

_____
[1] place.   [2] blessing.
[1] long-established disposition.   [2] immediately.

Lag of [1] a brother? Why bastard? Wherefore
base?   6
When my dimensions are as well compact,
My mind as generous, and my shape as true,
As honest madam's issue? Why brand they us
With base? with baseness? bastardy? base, base?
Who, in the lusty stealth of nature, take   11
More composition and fierce quality
Than doth, within a dull, stale, tired bed,
Go to the creating a whole tribe of fops,
Got 'tween asleep and wake? Well, then,   15
Legitimate Edgar, I must have your land.
Our father's love is to the bastard Edmund
As to the legitimate.   Fine word, "legitimate"!
Well, my legitimate, if this letter speed
And my invention thrive, Edmund the base   20
Shall top the legitimate. I grow; I prosper.
Now, gods, stand up for bastards!

(*Enter* GLOUCESTER.)

Glou. Kent banish'd thus! and France in choler
parted!
And the King gone to-night! subscrib'd his power!
Confin'd to exhibition! All this done   25
Upon the gad! [2] Edmund, how now! what news?
Edm. So please your lordship, none.
                        (*Putting up the letter.*)
Glou. Why so earnestly seek you to put up that
letter?
Edm. I know no news, my lord.
Glou. What paper were you reading?   30
Edm. Nothing, my lord.
Glou. No? What needed, then, that terrible
dispatch of it into your pocket? The quality of
nothing hath not such need to hide itself. Let's
see. Come, if it be nothing, I shall not need   35
spectacles.
Edm. I beseech you, sir, pardon me. It is a
letter from my brother, that I have not all o'er-
read; and for so much as I have perus'd, I find it
not fit for your o'er-looking.   40
Glou. Give me the letter, sir.
Edm. I shall offend, either to detain or give it.
The contents, as in part I understand them, are
to blame.
Glou. Let's see, let's see.   45
Edm. I hope, for my brother's justification, he
wrote this but as an essay or taste of my virtue.
Glou. (*Reads.*) "This policy and reverence of
age makes the world bitter to the best of our times;
keeps our fortunes from us till our oldness can- 50
not relish them. I begin to find an idle and fond
bondage in the oppression of aged tyranny; who

[1] younger than, behind in age.
[2] suddenly, in haste, as one moves when pricked by a
gad.

sways, not as it hath power, but as it is suffer'd.
Come to me, that of this I may speak more. If
our father would sleep till I wak'd him, you   55
should enjoy half his revenue for ever, and live the
beloved of your brother,   EDGAR."
Hum — conspiracy! — "Sleep till I wake him,
you should enjoy half his revenue!" — My son
Edgar! Had he a hand to write this? a heart   60
and brain to breed it in? — When came this to
you? Who brought it?
Edm. It was not brought me, my lord; there's
the cunning of it. I found it thrown in at the
casement of my closet.   65
Glou. You know the character to be your brother's?
Edm. If the matter were good, my lord, I durst
swear it were his; but, in respect of that, I would
fain think it were not.   70
Glou. It is his.
Edm. It is his hand, my lord; but I hope his
heart is not in the contents.
Glou. Has he never before sounded you in this
business?   75
Edm. Never, my lord; but I have heard him
oft maintain it to be fit that, sons at perfect age,
and fathers declin'd, the father should be as ward
to the son, and the son manage his revenue.   79
Glou. O villain, villain! His very opinion in the
letter! Abhorred villain! Unnatural, detested,
brutish villain! worse than brutish! Go, sirrah,
seek him; I'll apprehend him. Abominable villain! Where is he?   84
Edm. I do not well know, my lord. If it shall
please you to suspend your indignation against my
brother till you can derive from him better testimony of his intent, you should run a certain course;
where, if you violently proceed against him, mis-
taking his purpose, it would make a great gap   90
in your own honor, and shake in pieces the heart
of his obedience. I dare pawn down my life for
him, that he hath writ this to feel my affection to
your honor, and to no other pretence of danger.
Glou. Think you so?   95
Edm. If your honor judge it meet, I will place
you where you shall hear us confer of this, and by
an auricular [1] assurance have your satisfaction;
and that without any further delay than this very
evening.   100
Glou. He cannot be such a monster —
Edm. Nor is not, sure.
Glou. To his father, that so tenderly and entirely loves him. Heaven and earth! Edmund,
seek him out; wind me into him, I pray you. 105
Frame the business after your own wisdom. I
would unstate myself, to be in a due resolution.

[1] hearing (by your own ears).

Edm. I will seek him, sir, presently; convey the business as I shall find means, and acquaint you withal. 110

Glou. These late eclipses in the sun and moon portend no good to us. Though the wisdom of nature can reason it thus and thus, yet nature finds itself scourg'd by the sequent effects. Love cools, friendship falls off, brothers divide: in 115 cities, mutinies; in countries, discord; in palaces, treason; and the bond crack'd 'twixt son and father. This villain of mine comes under the prediction; there's son against father: the King falls from bias of nature;[1] there's father against 120 child. We have seen the best of our time; machinations, hollowness, treachery, and all ruinous disorders, follow us disquietly to our graves. Find out this villain, Edmund; it shall lose thee nothing; do it carefully. And the noble and true- 125 hearted Kent banish'd! his offence, honesty! 'Tis strange. (*Exit.*)

Edm. This is the excellent foppery of the world, that, when we are sick in fortune, — often the surfeits of our own behavior, — we make 130 guilty of our disasters the sun, the moon, and the stars, as if we were villains on necessity, fools by heavenly compulsion, knaves, thieves, and treachers by spherical predominance, drunkards, liars, and adulterers by an enforc'd obedience of 135 planetary influence, and all that we are evil in, by a divine thrusting on. An admirable evasion of whoremaster man, to lay his goatish[2] disposition on the charge of a star! My father compounded with my mother under the dragon's tail; and 140 my nativity was under *Ursa major*; so that it follows, I am rough and lecherous. Fut,[3] I should have been that I am, had the maidenliest star in the firmament twinkled on my bastardizing. Edgar — 145

(*Enter* EDGAR.)

and pat he comes like the catastrophe of the old comedy. My cue is villanous melancholy, with a sigh like Tom o' Bedlam[4] — O, these eclipses do portend these divisions! *fa, sol, la, mi.*

Edg. How now, brother Edmund! what serious contemplation are you in? 151

Edm. I am thinking, brother, of a prediction I read this other day, what should follow these eclipses.

Edg. Do you busy yourself with that? 155

Edm. I promise you, the effects he writes of succeed unhappily; as of unnaturalness between the child and the parent; death, dearth, dissolu-

[1] unnatural action.   [2] lewd.
[3] An oath, by God's foot becomes 'Sfoot or *fut*.
[4] A beggarly, insane person.

tions of ancient amities; divisions in state, menaces and maledictions against king and nobles; 160 needless diffidences, banishment of friends, dissipation of cohorts, nuptial breaches, and I know not what.

Edg. How long have you been a sectary astronomical?[1] 165

Edm. Come, come; when saw you my father last?

Edg. Why, the night gone by.

Edm. Spake you with him?

Edg. Ay, two hours together. 170

Edm. Parted you in good terms? Found you no displeasure in him by word nor countenance?

Edg. None at all.

Edm. Bethink yourself wherein you may have offended him; and at my entreaty forbear his 175 presence until some little time hath qualified the heat of his displeasure, which at this instant so rageth in him, that with the mischief of your person it would scarcely allay.

Edg. Some villain hath done me wrong. 180

Edm. That's my fear. I pray you, have a continent forbearance till the speed of his rage goes slower; and, as I say, retire with me to my lodging, from whence I will fitly bring you to hear my lord speak. Pray ye, go; there's my key. If you do stir abroad, go arm'd. 186

Edg. Arm'd, brother!

Edm. Brother, I advise you to the best; I am no honest man if there be any good meaning toward you. I have told you what I have seen and heard; but faintly, nothing like the image and horror of it. Pray you, away. 192

Edg. Shall I hear from you anon?

Edm. I do serve you in this business.

(*Exit* EDGAR.)

A credulous father, and a brother noble, 195
Whose nature is so far from doing harms
That he suspects none; on whose foolish honesty
My practices ride easy. I see the business.
Let me, if not by birth, have lands by wit:
All with me's meet that I can fashion fit. (*Exit.*)

SCENE III. *The Duke of Albany's palace.*

(*Enter* GONERIL *and* OSWALD, *her Steward.*)

Gon. Did my father strike my gentleman for chiding of his Fool?

Osw. Ay, madam.

Gon. By day and night he wrongs me; every hour
He flashes into one gross crime or other
That sets us all at odds. I'll not endure it. 5
His knights grow riotous, and himself upbraids us

[1] A follower of astrology.

On every trifle. When he returns from hunting,
I will not speak with him; say I am sick.
If you come slack [1] of former services,
You shall do well; the fault of it I'll answer. 10
  Osw. He's coming, madam; I hear him.
                    (*Horns within.*)
  Gon. Put on what weary negligence you please,
You and your fellows; I'd have it come to question.
If he distaste it, let him to my sister,
Whose mind and mine, I know, in that are one, 15
Not to be over-rul'd. Idle old man,
That still would manage those authorities
That he hath given away! Now, by my life,
Old fools are babes again, and must be us'd
With checks as flatteries, when they are seen
        abus'd. 20
Remember what I have said.
  Osw.   Well, madam.
  Gon. And let his knights have colder looks
        among you;
What grows of it, no matter. Advise your fellows
        so.
I would breed from hence occasions, and I shall,
That I may speak. I'll write straight to my sister,
To hold my very course. Prepare for dinner. 26
                              (*Exeunt.*)

SCENE IV. *A hall in the same.*
        (*Enter* KENT *disguised.*)

  Kent. If but as well I other accents borrow,
That can my speech defuse, my good intent
May carry through itself to that full issue
For which I raz'd my likeness. Now, banish'd
        Kent,
If thou canst serve where thou dost stand con-
        demn'd, 5
So may it come, thy master, whom thou lov'st,
Shall find thee full of labors.

  (*Horns within. Enter* LEAR, KNIGHTS, *and
        Attendants.*)

  Lear. Let me not stay a jot for dinner; go get
it ready. (*Exit an attendant.*) How now! what
art thou? 10
  Kent. A man, sir.
  Lear. What dost thou profess? What wouldst
thou with us?
  Kent. I do profess to be no less than I seem; to
serve him truly that will put me in trust; to 15
love him that is honest; to converse with him that
is wise and says little; to fear judgment; to fight
when I cannot choose; and to eat no fish.
  Lear. What art thou? 19

[1] lessen your services.

  Kent. A very honest-hearted fellow, and as poor
as the King.
  Lear. If thou be'st as poor for a subject as he's
for a king, thou art poor enough. What wouldst
thou?
  Kent. Service. 25
  Lear. Who wouldst thou serve?
  Kent. You.
  Lear. Dost thou know me, fellow?
  Kent. No, sir; but you have that in your coun-
tenance which I would fain call master. 30
  Lear. What's that?
  Kent. Authority.
  Lear. What services canst thou do? 33
  Kent. I can keep honest counsel, ride, run, mar
a curious tale in telling it, and deliver a plain
message bluntly. That which ordinary men are
fit for, I am qualified in; and the best of me is
diligence.
  Lear. How old art thou? 39
  Kent. Not so young, sir, to love a woman for
singing, nor so old to dote on her for anything. I
have years on my back forty-eight.
  Lear. Follow me; thou shalt serve me. If I
like thee no worse after dinner, I will not part from
thee yet. Dinner, ho, dinner! Where's my 45
knave? my Fool? Go you, and call my Fool
hither. (*Exit an attendant.*)

        (*Enter Steward* OSWALD.)

You, you, sirrah, where's my daughter?
  Osw. So please you, — (*Exit.*) 49
  Lear. What says the fellow there? Call the
clotpoll [1] back. (*Exit a knight.*) Where's my
Fool, ho? I think the world's asleep.

        !(*Re-enter* KNIGHT.)

How now! where's that mongrel?
  Knight. He says, my lord, your daughter is not
well. 55
  Lear. Why came not the slave back to me when
I call'd him?
  Knight. Sir, he answered me in the roundest
manner, he would not.
  Lear. He would not! 60
  Knight. My lord, I know not what the matter
is; but, to my judgment, your Highness is not
entertain'd with that ceremonious affection as
you were wont. There's a great abatement of
kindness appears as well in the general depend-
ants as in the Duke himself also and your daughter.
  Lear. Ha! say'st thou so? 67
  Knight. I beseech you, pardon me, my lord, if
I be mistaken; for my duty cannot be silent when
I think your Highness wrong'd. 70

[1] blockhead, literally "clod-head."

Lear. Thou but rememb'rest [1] me of mine own conception. I have perceived a most faint neglect of late, which I have rather blamed as mine own jealous curiosity than as a very pretence and purpose of unkindness. I will look further into 't. But where's my Fool? I have not seen him this two days. 77

Knight. Since my young lady's going into France, sir, the Fool hath much pined away.

Lear. No more of that; I have noted it well. Go you, and tell my daughter I would speak with her. (*Exit an attendant.*) Go you, call hither my Fool. (*Exit an attendant.*) 83

(Re-enter Steward OSWALD.)

O, you sir, you, come you higher, sir. Who am I, sir? 85

Osw. My lady's father.

Lear. "My lady's father"! My lord's knave! You whoreson dog! you slave! you cur!

Osw. I am none of these, my lord; I beseech your pardon. 90

Lear. Do you bandy looks with me, you rascal? (*Striking him.*)

Osw. I'll not be strucken, my lord.

Kent. Nor tripp'd neither, you base foot-ball player. (*Tripping up his heels.*)

Lear. I thank thee, fellow. Thou serv'st me, and I'll love thee. 96

Kent. Come, sir, arise, away! I'll teach you differences. Away, away! If you will measure your lubber's length again, tarry; but away! go to. Have you wisdom? So. (*Pushes OSWALD out.*)

Lear. Now, my friendly knave, I thank thee. There's earnest of thy service. 102

(*Giving KENT money.*)

(Enter FOOL.)

Fool. Let me hire him too; here's my coxcomb. (*Offering KENT his cap.*)

Lear. How now, my pretty knave! how dost thou? 105

Fool. Sirrah, you were best take my coxcomb.

Kent. Why, Fool?

Fool. Why? For taking one's part that's out of favor. Nay, an thou canst not smile as the wind sits,[2] thou'lt catch cold shortly. There, 110 take my coxcomb. Why, this fellow has banish'd two on 's daughters, and did the third a blessing against his will; if thou follow him, thou must needs wear my coxcomb. — How now, nuncle! [3]

[1] remindest.

[2] in the direction from which the wind comes; *i.e.*, if you can't smile for the right people.

[3] Mine uncle = "nuncle," a form of address often used by court jesters.

Would I had two coxcombs and two daughters!

Lear. Why, my boy? 116

Fool. If I gave them all my living, I'd keep my coxcombs myself. There's mine; beg another of thy daughters.

Lear. Take heed, sirrah; the whip. 120

Fool. Truth's a dog must to kennel; he must be whipp'd out, when Lady the brach [1] may stand by the fire and stink.

Lear. A pestilent gall to me!

Fool. Sirrah, I'll teach thee a speech. 125

Lear. Do.

Fool. Mark it, nuncle:

"Have more than thou showest,
    Speak less than thou knowest,
    Lend less than thou owest, 130
    Ride more than thou goest,
    Learn more than thou trowest,
    Set less than thou throwest;
    Leave thy drink and thy whore,
    And keep in-a-door, 135
    And thou shalt have more
    Than two tens to a score."

Kent. This is nothing, Fool.

Fool. Then 'tis like the breath of an unfee'd lawyer; you gave me nothing for 't. Can you make no use of nothing, nuncle? 141

Lear. Why, no, boy; nothing can be made out of nothing.

Fool. (*To KENT.*) Prithee, tell him so much the rent of his land comes to. He will not believe a Fool. 146

Lear. A bitter fool!

Fool. Dost thou know the difference, my boy, between a bitter fool and a sweet one?

Lear. No, lad; teach me. 150

Fool. "That lord that counsell'd thee
    To give away thy land,
    Come place him here by me,
    Do thou for him stand:
    The sweet and bitter fool 155
    Will presently appear;
    The one in motley here,
    The other found out there."

Lear. Dost thou call me fool, boy?

Fool. All thy other titles thou hast given away; that thou wast born with. 161

Kent. This is not altogether fool, my lord.

Fool. No, faith, lords and great men will not let me; if I had a monopoly out,[2] they would have part on 't. And ladies, too, they will not let me 165 have all the fool to myself; they'll be snatching.

[1] A keen-scented hound.

[2] taken out a monopoly; the reference is to the custom of courtiers' sharing in the profits of a monopoly granted by the king.

Nuncle, give me an egg, and I'll give thee two crowns.

Lear. What two crowns shall they be? 169

Fool. Why, after I have cut the egg i' the middle, and eat up the meat, the two crowns of the egg. When thou clovest thy crown i' the middle, and gav'st away both parts, thou bor'st thine ass on thy back o'er the dirt. Thou hadst little wit in thy bald crown, when thou gav'st thy golden 175 one away. If I speak like myself in this, let him be whipp'd that first finds it so.

"Fools had ne'er less grace in a year;
   For wise men are grown foppish,
And know not how their wits to wear, 180
   Their manners are so apish."

Lear. When were you wont to be so full of songs, sirrah?

Fool. I have used it, nuncle, e'er since thou mad'st thy daughters thy mothers; for when thou gav'st them the rod, and puttest down thine own breeches, 187

"Then they for sudden joy did weep,
   And I for sorrow sung,
That such a king should play bo-peep, 190
   And go the fools among."

Prithee, nuncle, keep a schoolmaster that can teach thy Fool to lie. I would fain learn to lie.

Lear. An you lie, sirrah, we'll have you whipp'd.

Fool. I marvel what kin thou and thy 195 daughters are. They'll have me whipp'd for speaking true, thou'lt have me whipp'd for lying; and sometimes I am whipp'd for holding my peace. I had rather be any kind o' thing than a Fool; and yet I would not be thee, nuncle; 200 thou hast pared thy wit o' both sides, and left nothing i' the middle. Here comes one o' the parings.

(*Enter* GONERIL.)

Lear. How now, daughter! what makes that frontlet [1] on? Methinks you are too much of late i' the frown. 206

Fool. Thou wast a pretty fellow when thou hadst no need to care for her frowning; now thou art an O without a figure. I am better than thou art now; I am a Fool, thou art nothing. (*To* GON.) Yes, forsooth, I will hold my tongue; so your face bids me, though you say nothing. Mum, mum, 212

"He that keeps nor crust nor crumb,
   Weary of all, shall want some."

(*Pointing to* LEAR.) That's a sheal'd peascod.[2] 215

Gon. Not only, sir, this your all-licens'd Fool, But other of your insolent retinue

[1] A band worn on the forehead; here the reference is to her frowns.
[2] A pod from which the peas have been taken.

Do hourly carp and quarrel, breaking forth
In rank and not-to-be-endured riots. Sir,
I had thought, by making this well known unto you, 220
To have found a safe redress; but now grow fearful,
By what yourself, too, late have spoke and done,
That you protect this course, and put it on
By your allowance; which if you should, the fault
Would not scape censure, nor the redresses sleep,
Which, in the tender of a wholesome weal, 226
Might in their working do you that offence,
Which else were shame, that then necessity
Will call discreet proceeding.

Fool. For, you know, nuncle, 230
   "The hedge-sparrow fed the cuckoo so long,
      That it had it head bit off by it young."
So, out went the candle, and we were left darkling.[1]

Lear. Are you our daughter?

Gon. Come, sir, 235
I would you would make use of your good wisdom,
Whereof I know you are fraught, and put away
These dispositions, which of late transport you
From what you rightly are. 239

Fool. May not an ass know when the cart draws the horse? "Whoop, Jug! I love thee."[2]

Lear. Doth any here know me? This is not Lear.
Doth Lear walk thus? speak thus? Where are his eyes?
Either his notion weakens, his discernings
Are lethargied — Ha! waking? 'Tis not so. 245
Who is it that can tell me who I am?

Fool. Lear's shadow.

Lear. I would learn that; for, by the marks of sovereignty, knowledge, and reason, I should be false persuaded I had daughters. 250

Fool. Which they will make an obedient father.

Lear. Your name, fair gentlewoman?

Gon. This admiration, sir, is much o' the savor
Of other your new pranks. I do beseech you
To understand my purposes aright. 255
As you are old and reverend, you should be wise.
Here do you keep a hundred knights and squires;
Men so disorder'd, so debosh'd [3] and bold,
That this our court, infected with their manners,
Shows like a riotous inn. Epicurism and lust 260
Makes it more like a tavern or a brothel
Than a grac'd palace. The shame itself doth speak
For instant remedy. Be then desir'd
By her, that else will take the thing she begs,
A little to disquantity [4] your train; 265

[1] in the dark.
[2] Possibly words of an old song.
[3] debauched.   [4] diminish.

And the remainders, that shall still depend,
To be such men as may besort your age,
Which know themselves and you.

Lear.   Darkness and devils!
Saddle my horses; call my train together!
Degenerate bastard! I'll not trouble thee;   270
Yet have I left a daughter.

Gon. You strike my people; and your disorder'd
    rabble
Make servants of their betters.

(Enter ALBANY.)

Lear. Woe, that too late repents! — O, sir, are
    you come?   274
Is it your will? Speak, sir. — Prepare my horses. —
Ingratitude, thou marble-hearted fiend,
More hideous when thou show'st thee in a child
Than the sea-monster!

Alb.   Pray, sir, be patient.
Lear. (*To* GON.) Detested kite! thou liest.
My train are men of choice and rarest parts,   280
That all particulars of duty know,
And in the most exact regard support
The worships of their name. O most small fault,
How ugly didst thou in Cordelia show!
Which, like an engine, wrench'd my frame of
    nature   285
From the fix'd place; drew from my heart all love,
And added to the gall. O Lear, Lear, Lear!
Beat at this gate, that let thy folly in,

                (*Striking his head.*)

And thy dear judgment out! Go, go, my people.
Alb. My lord, I am guiltless as I am ignorant
Of what hath moved you.

Lear.   It may be so, my lord.   291
Hear, Nature! hear, dear goddess, hear!
Suspend thy purpose, if thou didst intend
To make this creature fruitful!
Into her womb convey sterility!   295
Dry up in her the organs of increase,
And from her derogate [1] body never spring
A babe to honor her! If she must teem,
Create her child of spleen, that it may live
And be a thwart disnatur'd torment to her!   300
Let it stamp wrinkles in her brow of youth,
With cadent [2] tears fret channels in her cheeks,
Turn all her mother's pains and benefits
To laughter and contempt, that she may feel
How sharper than a serpent's tooth it is   305
To have a thankless child! — Away, away! (*Exit.*)
Alb. Now, gods that we adore, whereof comes
    this?
Gon. Never afflict yourself to know more of it;
But let his disposition have that scope
As dotage gives it.   310

  [1] degenerate.   [2] falling.

(Re-enter LEAR.)

Lear. What, fifty of my followers at a clap!
Within a fortnight!
Alb.   What's the matter, sir?
Lear. I'll tell thee. (*To* GON.) Life and death!
    I am asham'd
That thou hast power to shake my manhood thus;
That these hot tears, which break from me per-
    force,   315
Should make thee worth them. Blasts and fogs
    upon thee!
The untented [1] woundings of a father's curse
Pierce every sense about thee! Old fond eyes,
Beweep this cause again, I'll pluck ye out,
And cast you, with the waters that you loose,   320
To temper clay. Ha! is it come to this?
Let it be so: I have another daughter,
Who, I am sure, is kind and comfortable.
When she shall hear this of thee, with her nails
She'll flay thy wolvish visage. Thou shalt find   325
That I'll resume the shape which thou dost think
I have cast off for ever. Thou shalt, I warrant
    thee. (*Exeunt* LEAR, KENT, *and attendants.*)
Gon. Do you mark that?
Alb. I cannot be so partial, Goneril,
To the great love I bear you, —   330
Gon. Pray you, content. — What, Oswald, ho!
(*To the Fool.*) You, sir, more knave than fool, after
    your master.
Fool. Nuncle Lear, nuncle Lear, tarry! Take
the Fool with thee.

    A fox, when one has caught her,   335
    And such a daughter,
    Should sure to the slaughter,
    If my cap would buy a halter.
    So the Fool follows after.   (*Exit.*)

Gon. This man hath had good counsel, — a
    hundred knights!   340
'Tis politic and safe to let him keep
At point a hundred knights; yes, that, on every
    dream,
Each buzz, each fancy, each complaint, dislike,
He may enguard his dotage with their powers,
And hold our lives in mercy. Oswald, I say!   345
Alb. Well, you may fear too far.
Gon.   Safer than trust too far.
Let me still take away the harms I fear,
Not fear still to be taken. I know his heart.
What he hath utter'd I have writ my sister.
If she sustain him and his hundred knights,   350
When I have show'd the unfitness, —

(Re-enter Steward OSWALD.)

                 How now, Oswald!
What, have you writ that letter to my sister?

  [1] uncared for, incurable.

Osw. Ay, madam.

Gon. Take you some company, and away to horse.

Inform her full of my particular fear; 355
And thereto add such reasons of your own
As may compact it more.   Get you gone;
And hasten your return. (*Exit* OSWALD.) No, no, my lord,
This milky gentleness and course of yours
Though I condemn not, yet, under pardon, 360
You are much more at task for want of wisdom
Than prais'd for harmful mildness.

Alb. How far your eyes may pierce I cannot tell.
Striving to better, oft we mar what's well.

Gon. Nay, then — 365
Alb. Well, well; the event.   (*Exeunt.*)

SCENE V. *Court before the same.*

(*Enter* LEAR, KENT, *and* FOOL.)

Lear. Go you before to Gloucester with these letters.   Acquaint my daughter no further with anything you know than comes from her demand out of the letter.   If your diligence be not speedy, I shall be there afore you. 5

Kent. I will not sleep, my lord, till I have delivered your letter.   (*Exit.*)

Fool. If a man's brains were in 's heels, were't not in danger of kibes? [1]

Lear. Ay, boy. 10

Fool. Then, I prithee, be merry; thy wit shall not go slip-shod.

Lear. Ha, ha, ha!

Fool. Shalt see thy other daughter will use thee kindly; for though she's as like this as a crab 's like an apple, yet I can tell what I can tell. 16

Lear. What canst tell, boy?

Fool. She will taste as like this as a crab does to a crab.   Thou canst tell why one's nose stands i' the middle on's face? 20

Lear. No.

Fool. Why, to keep one's eyes of either side's nose, that what a man cannot smell out, he may spy into.

Lear. I did her wrong — 25

Fool. Canst tell how an oyster makes his shell?

Lear. No.

Fool. Nor I neither; but I can tell why a snail has a house.

Lear. Why? 30

Fool. Why, to put's head in; not to give it away to his daughters, and leave his horns without a case.

Lear. I will forget my nature.   So kind a father!
Be my horses ready? 35

[1] chilblains.

Fool. Thy asses are gone about 'em.   The reason why the seven stars [1] are no moe than seven is a pretty reason.

Lear. Because they are not eight?

Fool. Yes, indeed.   Thou wouldst make a good Fool. 41

Lear. To take 't [2] again perforce!   Monster ingratitude!

Fool. If thou wert my Fool, nuncle, I'd have thee beaten for being old before thy time. 45

Lear. How's that?

Fool. Thou shouldst not have been old till thou hadst been wise.

Lear. O, let me not be mad, not mad, sweet heaven!

Keep me in temper; I would not be mad! 50

(*Enter* GENTLEMEN.)

How now! are the horses ready?

Gent. Ready, my lord.

Lear. Come, boy.

Fool. She that's a maid now, and laughs at my departure,

Shall not be a maid long, unless things be cut shorter.   (*Exeunt.*) 55

ACT II

SCENE I. *The Earl of Gloucester's castle.*

(*Enter Bastard* EDMUND *and* CURAN, *severally.*)

Edm. Save thee,[3] Curan.

Cur. And you, sir.   I have been with your father, and given him notice that the Duke of Cornwall and Regan his duchess will be here with him this night.

Edm. How comes that?

Cur. Nay, I know not.   You have heard of the news abroad; I mean the whisper'd ones, for they are yet but ear-kissing arguments? [4]

Edm. Not I.   Pray you, what are they? 10

Cur. Have you heard of no likely wars toward 'twixt the Dukes of Cornwall and Albany?

Edm. Not a word.

Cur. You may do, then, in time.   Fare you well, sir.   (*Exit.*) 15

Edm. The Duke be here to-night?   The better best!

This weaves itself perforce into my business.
My father hath set guard to take my brother;
And I have one thing, of a queasy question,
Which I must act.   Briefness and fortune, work! 20

[1] The Pleiades.
[2] "It" may mean his kingdom which he had divided
[3] God save thee.
[4] Statements only closely whispered.

(*Enter* EDGAR.)

Brother, a word; descend. Brother, I say!
My father watches; O sir, fly this place;
Intelligence is given where you are hid;
You have now the good advantage of the night.
Have you not spoken 'gainst the Duke of Corn-
    wall? 25
He's coming hither, now, i' the night, i' the haste,
And Regan with him. Have you nothing said
Upon his party 'gainst the Duke of Albany?
Advise yourself.
   Edg.   I am sure on 't, not a word.
   Edm. I hear my father coming. Pardon me, 30
In cunning I must draw my sword upon you.
Draw; seem to defend yourself; now quit you well.
Yield! Come before my father. Light, ho,
   here! —
Fly, brother. — Torches, torches! — So, farewell.
                    (*Exit* EDGAR.)
Some blood drawn on me would beget opinion 35
                  (*Wounds his arm.*)
Of my more fierce endeavor. I have seen drunkards
Do more than this in sport. — Father, father! —
Stop, stop! — No help?

(*Enter* GLOUCESTER, *and Servants with torches.*)

   Glou. Now, Edmund, where's the villain?
   Edm. Here stood he in the dark, his sharp sword
   out, 40
Mumbling of wicked charms, conjuring the moon
To stand auspicious mistress, —
   Glou.   But where is he?
   Edm. Look, sir, I bleed.
   Glou.   Where is the villain, Edmund?
   Edm. Fled this way, sir. When by no means
   he could —
   Glou. Pursue him, ho! Go after. (*Exeunt
   some Servants.*) By no means what? 45
   Edm. Persuade me to the murder of your lord-
   ship;
But that I told him, the revenging gods
'Gainst parricides [1] did all the thunder bend;
Spoke, with how manifold and strong a bond
The child was bound to the father; sir, in fine, 50
Seeing how loathly opposite I stood
To his unnatural purpose, in fell motion,
With his prepared sword, he charges home
My unprovided body, latch'd [2] mine arm;
And when he saw my best alarum'd spirits, 55
Bold in the quarrel's right, rous'd to the encounter,
Or whether gasted [3] by the noise I made,
Full suddenly he fled.
   Glou.   Let him fly far.

[1] Those who kill their parents.
[2] lanced.
[3] frightened.

Not in this land shall he remain uncaught;
And found, — dispatch. The noble Duke my
   master, 60
My worthy arch and patron, comes to-night.
By his authority I will proclaim it,
That he which finds him shall deserve our thanks,
Bringing the murderous coward to the stake;
He that conceals him, death. 65
   Edm. When I dissuaded him from his intent,
And found him pight [1] to do it, with curst speech
I threaten'd to discover him; he replied,
"Thou unpossessing bastard! dost thou think,
If I would stand against thee, would the reposal 70
Of any trust, virtue, or worth in thee
Make thy words faith'd? No! what I should
   deny, —
As this I would; ay, though thou didst produce
My very character,[2] — I'd turn it all
To thy suggestion, plot, and damned practice; 75
And thou must make a dullard of the world
If they not thought the profits of my death
Were very pregnant and potential spurs
To make thee seek it."
   Glou.   O strange and fast'ned villain!
Would he deny his letter? (I never got him.) 80
                (*Tucket [3] within.*)
Hark, the Duke's trumpets! I know not why he
   comes.
All ports I'll bar, the villain shall not scape;
The Duke must grant me that. Besides, his pic-
   ture
I will send far and near, that all the kingdom
May have due note of him; and of my land, 85
Loyal and natural boy, I'll work the means
To make thee capable.

(*Enter* CORNWALL, REGAN, *and Attendants.*)

   Corn. How now, my noble friend! since I came
   hither,
Which I can call but now, I have heard strange
   news.
   Reg. If it be true, all vengeance comes too short
Which can pursue the offender. How dost, my
   lord? 91
   Glou. O, madam, my old heart is crack'd, it's
   crack'd!
   Reg. What, did my father's godson seek your
   life?
He whom my father nam'd? your Edgar?
   Glou. O, lady, lady, shame would have it hid! 95
   Reg. Was he not companion with the riotous
   knights
That tended upon my father?

[1] fixed on, determined.
[2] handwriting or signature.
[3] flourish on a trumpet.

Glou. I know not, madam. 'Tis too bad, too bad.

Edm. Yes, madam, he was of that consort.

Reg. No marvel, then, though he were ill af-
fected: 100
'Tis they have put him on the old man's death,
To have the expense and waste of his revenues.
I have this present evening from my sister
Been well inform'd of them; and with such cau-
tions,
That if they come to sojourn at my house, 105
I'll not be there.

Corn.   Nor I, assure thee, Regan.
Edmund, I hear that you have shown your father
A child-like office.[1]

Edm.   'Twas my duty, sir.

Glou. He did bewray his practice; and receiv'd
This hurt you see, striving to apprehend him.

Corn. Is he pursued?

Glou.   Ay, my good lord. 111

Corn. If he be taken, he shall never more
Be fear'd of doing harm. Make your own purpose,
How in my strength you please. For you, Ed-
mund,
Whose virtue and obedience doth this instant 115
So much commend itself, you shall be ours.
Natures of such deep trust we shall much need;
You we first seize on.

Edm.   I shall serve you, sir,
Truly, however else.

Glou.   For him I thank your Grace.

Corn. You know not why we came to visit
you, — 120

Reg. Thus out of season, threading dark-ey'd
night?
Occasions, noble Gloucester, of some poise,
Wherein we must have use of your advice.
Our father he hath writ, so hath our sister,
Of differences, which I best thought it fit 125
To answer from our home; the several messengers
From hence attend dispatch. Our good old friend,
Lay comforts to your bosom; and bestow
Your needful counsel to our businesses,
Which craves the instant use.

Glou.   I serve you, madam.
Your Graces are right welcome. 131

          (*Exeunt. Flourish.*)

SCENE II. *Before Gloucester's castle.*

(*Enter* KENT *and Steward* OSWALD, *severally.*)

Osw. Good dawning to thee, friend. Art of this
house?

Kent. Ay.

Osw. Where may we set our horses?

Kent. I' the mire. 5

[1] filial duty.

Osw. Prithee, if thou lov'st me, tell me.

Kent. I love thee not.

Osw. Why, then, I care not for thee.

Kent. If I had thee in Lipsbury pinfold,[1] I
would make thee care for me. 10

Osw. Why dost thou use me thus? I know
thee not.

Kent. Fellow, I know thee.

Osw. What dost thou know me for? 14

Kent. A knave; a rascal; an eater of broken
meats; a base, proud, shallow, beggarly, three-
suited,[2] hundred-pound, filthy, worsted-stocking
knave; a lily-livered, action-taking, whoreson,
glass-gazing, superserviceable, finical rogue; one-
trunk-inheriting slave; one that wouldst be a 20
bawd, in way of good service, and art nothing but
the composition of a knave, beggar, coward, pan-
dar, and the son and heir of a mongrel bitch; one
whom I will beat into clamorous whining, if thou
deni'st the least syllable of thy addition. 25

Osw. Why, what a monstrous fellow art thou,
thus to rail on one that is neither known of thee
nor knows thee!

Kent. What a brazen-fac'd varlet art thou, to
deny thou knowest me! Is it two days since I 30
tripp'd up thy heels, and beat thee before the
King? Draw, you rogue; for, though it be night,
yet the moon shines. I'll make a sop o' the moonshine of you, you whoreson cullionly[3] barber-
monger! Draw! (*Drawing his sword.*) 35

Osw. Away! I have nothing to do with thee.

Kent. Draw, you rascal! You come with letters
against the King; and take Vanity[4] the puppet's
part against the royalty of her father. Draw,
you rogue, or I'll so carbonado[5] your shanks, —
draw, you rascal! Come your ways. 41

Osw. Help, ho! murder! help!

Kent. Strike, you slave! Stand, rogue, stand!
You neat[6] slave, strike. (*Beating him.*)

Osw. Help, ho! murder! murder! 45

(*Enter Bastard* EDMUND *with his rapier drawn,*
CORNWALL, REGAN, GLOUCESTER, *and Servants.*)

Edm. How now! What's the matter? Part.

Kent. With you, goodman boy, if you please.
Come, I'll flesh ye; come on, young master.

Glou. Weapons! arms! What's the matter here?

Corn. Keep peace, upon your lives! 50
He dies that strikes again. What is the matter?

[1] Possibly a public pound for stray cattle.
[2] with only three suits.
[3] base.
[4] Vanity as acted by a puppet in the old morality
plays.
[5] To prepare meat for cooking.
[6] pure.

Reg. The messengers from our sister and the King.

Corn. What is your difference? Speak.

Osw. I am scarce in breath, my lord. 55

Kent. No marvel, you have so bestirr'd your valor. You cowardly rascal, Nature disclaims in thee. A tailor made thee.

Corn. Thou art a strange fellow. A tailor make a man? 60

Kent. A tailor, sir. A stone-cutter or a painter could not have made him so ill, though they had been but two years o' the trade.

Corn. Speak yet, how grew your quarrel?

Osw. This ancient ruffian, sir, whose life I have spar'd at suit of his gray beard, — 66

Kent. Thou whoreson zed![1] thou unnecessary letter! My lord, if you will give me leave, I will tread this unbolted[2] villain into mortar, and daub the wall of a jakes[3] with him. Spare my gray beard, you wagtail? 71

Corn. Peace, sirrah!
You beastly knave, know you no reverence?

Kent. Yes, sir; but anger hath a privilege.

Corn. Why art thou angry? 75

Kent. That such a slave as this should wear a sword,
Who wears no honesty. Such smiling rogues as these,
Like rats, oft bite the holy cords a-twain
Which are too intrinse[4] to unloose; smooth every passion
That in the natures of their lords rebel; 80
Bring oil to fire, snow to their colder moods;
Renege, affirm, and turn their halcyon beaks
With every gale and vary of their masters,
Knowing nought, like dogs, but following.
A plague upon your epileptic visage! 85
Smile you my speeches, as I were a fool?
Goose, if I had you upon Sarum[5] Plain,
I'd drive ye cackling home to Camelot.

Corn. What, art thou mad, old fellow?

Glou. How fell you out? Say that. 90

Kent. No contraries hold more antipathy
Than I and such a knave.

Corn. Why dost thou call him knave? What is his fault?

Kent. His countenance likes me not.

Corn. No more, perchance, does mine, nor his, nor hers.

Kent. Sir, 'tis my occupation to be plain; 95
I have seen better faces in my time
Than stands on any shoulder that I see

[1] "Z," the last letter in the alphabet; since "s" can be used for it it has been called "the unnecessary letter."
[2] coarse.   [3] a privy.
[4] intricate.   [5] Salisbury.

Before me at this instant.

Corn.   This is some fellow
Who, having been prais'd for bluntness, doth affect
A saucy roughness, and constrains the garb 100
Quite from his nature. He cannot flatter, he;
An honest mind and plain, he must speak truth!
An they will take it, so; if not, he's plain.
These kind of knaves I know, which in this plainness
Harbor more craft and more corrupter ends 105
Than twenty silly ducking observants
That stretch their duties nicely.

Kent. Sir, in good sooth, in sincere verity,
Under the allowance of your great aspect,
Whose influence, like the wreath of radiant fire 110
On flickering Phœbus' front, —

Corn.   What mean'st by this?

Kent. To go out of my dialect, which you discommend so much. I know, sir, I am no flatterer. He that beguil'd you in a plain accent was a plain 114
knave; which for my part I will not be, though I should win your displeasure to entreat me to 't.

Corn. What was the offence you gave him?

Osw. I never gave him any.
It pleas'd the King his master very late
To strike at me, upon his misconstruction; 120
When he, compact, and flattering his displeasure,
Tripp'd me behind; being down, insulted, rail'd,
And put upon him such a deal of man
That 't worthied him, got praises of the King
For him attempting who was self-subdued; 125
And, in the fleshment[1] of this dread exploit,
Drew on me here again.

Kent.   None of these rogues and cowards
But Ajax[2] is their fool.

Corn.   Fetch forth the stocks!
You stubborn ancient knave, you reverend braggart,
We'll teach you —

Kent.   Sir, I am too old to learn. 130
Call not your stocks for me; I serve the King,
On whose employment I was sent to you.
You shall do small respects, show too bold malice
Against the grace and person of my master,
Stocking his messenger. 135

Corn. Fetch forth the stocks! As I have life and honor,
There shall he sit till noon.

Reg. Till noon! Till night, my lord; and all night too.

[1] pride.
[2] Greek hero before Troy. To such boasters as these even Ajax appears a fool.

Kent. Why, madam, if I were your father's dog,
You should not use me so.

Reg. Sir, being his knave, I will.
(*Stocks brought out.*)

Corn. This is a fellow of the self-same color 141
Our sister speaks of. Come, bring away the stocks!

Glou. Let me beseech your Grace not to do so.
His fault is much, and the good King his master
Will check him for 't. Your purpos'd low correction 145
Is such as basest and contemned'st wretches
For pilferings and most common trespasses
Are punish'd with. The King must take it ill
That he's so slightly valued in his messenger, 149
Should have him thus restrained.

Corn. I'll answer that.

Reg. My sister may receive it much more worse
To have her gentleman abus'd, assaulted,
For following her affairs. Put in his legs.
(*Kent is put in the stocks.*)
Come, my good lord, away.
(*Exeunt all but* Gloucester *and* Kent.)

Glou. I am sorry for thee, friend; 'tis the Duke's
pleasure, 155
Whose disposition, all the world well knows,
Will not be rubb'd nor stopp'd. I'll entreat for thee.

Kent. Pray, do not, sir. I have watch'd and
travell'd hard;
Some time I shall sleep out, the rest I'll whistle.
A good man's fortune may grow out at heels. 160
Give you good morrow!

Glou. The Duke's to blame in this; 'twill be ill
taken. (*Exit.*)

Kent. Good King, that must approve the common saw,[1]
Thou out of heaven's benediction com'st
To the warm sun! 165
Approach, thou beacon to this under globe,
That by thy comfortable beams I may
Peruse this letter! Nothing almost sees miracles
But misery. I know 'tis from Cordelia,
Who hath most fortunately been inform'd 170
Of my obscured course; (*reads*) "— and shall find
time
From this enormous[2] state — seeking to give
Losses their remedies." — All weary and o'er-
watch'd,
Take vantage, heavy eyes, not to behold
This shameful lodging. 175
Fortune, good-night! Smile once more; turn thy
wheel! (*Sleeps.*)

[1] confirm the popular saying.
[2] unusual, lawless.

Scene III. *The same.*

(*Enter* Edgar.)

Edg. I heard myself proclaim'd;
And by the happy hollow of a tree
Escap'd the hunt. No port is free; no place
That guard and most unusual vigilance
Does not attend my taking. Whiles I may scape 5
I will preserve myself, and am bethought
To take the basest and most poorest shape
That ever penury, in contempt of man,
Brought near to beast. My face I'll grime with
filth,
Blanket my loins, elf[1] all my hairs in knots, 10
And with presented nakedness out-face
The winds and persecutions of the sky.
The country gives me proof and precedent
Of Bedlam beggars, who, with roaring voices,
Strike in their numb'd and mortified arms 15
Pins, wooden pricks, nails, sprigs of rosemary;
And with this horrible object, from low farms,
Poor pelting villages, sheep-cotes, and mills,
Sometimes with lunatic bans, sometimes with
prayers,
Enforce their charity. Poor Turlygod! poor
Tom! 20
That's something yet. Edgar I nothing am.
(*Exit.*)

Scene IV. *The same.*

(*Enter* Lear, Fool, *and* Gentleman. Kent
in the stocks.)

Lear. 'Tis strange that they should so depart
from home,
And not send back my messengers.

Gent. As I learn'd,
The night before there was no purpose in them
Of this remove.

Kent. Hail to thee, noble master!

Lear. Ha! 5
Mak'st thou this shame thy pastime?

Kent. No, my lord.

Fool. Ha, ha! he wears cruel garters. Horses
are tied by the heads, dogs and bears by the neck,
monkeys by the loins, and men by the legs. When
a man's over-lusty at legs, then he wears wooden
nether-stocks. 11

Lear. What's he that hath so much thy place
mistook
To set thee here?

Kent. It is both he and she;
Your son and daughter.

Lear. No. 15

Kent. Yes.

[1] tangle.

Lear. No, I say.

Kent. I say, yea.

Lear. No, no, they would not.

Kent. Yes, they have.   20

Lear. By Jupiter, I swear, no.

Kent. By Juno, I swear, ay.

Lear.   They durst not do 't;
They could not, would not do 't. 'Tis worse than
        murder,
To do upon respect such violent outrage.
Resolve me, with all modest haste, which way   25
Thou mightst deserve, or they impose, this usage,
Coming from us.

Kent.   My lord, when at their home
I did commend your Highness' letters to them,
Ere I was risen from the place that show'd
My duty kneeling, came there a reeking post,   30
Stew'd in his haste, half breathless, panting forth
From Goneril his mistress salutations;
Deliver'd letters, spite of intermission,
Which presently they read. On those contents,
They summon'd up their meiny,[1] straight took
        horse;   35
Commanded me to follow, and attend
The leisure of their answer; gave me cold looks:
And meeting here the other messenger,
Whose welcome, I perceiv'd, had poison'd mine, —
Being the very fellow which of late   40
Display'd so saucily against your Highness, —
Having more man than wit about me, drew.
He rais'd the house with loud and coward cries.
Your son and daughter found this trespass worth
The shame which here it suffers.   45

Fool. Winter's not gone yet, if the wild geese
fly that way.

        "Fathers that wear rags
                Do make their children blind;
        But fathers that bear bags   50
                Shall see their children kind.
        Fortune, that arrant whore,
                Ne'er turns the key to the poor."

But, for all this, thou shalt have as many dolours[2]
for thy daughters as thou canst tell in a year. 55

Lear. O, how this mother[3] swells up toward my
        heart!
Hysterica passio, down, thou climbing sorrow,
Thy element's below! — Where is this daughter?

Kent. With the Earl, sir, here within.

Lear.   Follow me not;
Stay here.   (*Exit.*)   60

Gent. Made you no more offence but what you
speak of?

Kent. None.

[1] household.
[2] A play on words, dolours (griefs) and dollars.
[3] hysteria, the same as "hysterica passio."

How chance the King comes with so small a number?

Fool. An thou hadst been set i' the stocks for
that question, thou'dst well deserv'd it.   66

Kent. Why, Fool?

Fool. We'll set thee to school to an ant, to
teach thee there's no laboring i' the winter. All
that follow their noses are led by their eyes   70
but blind men; and there's not a nose among
twenty but can smell him that's stinking. Let
go thy hold when a great wheel runs down a hill,
lest it break thy neck with following; but the
great one that goes upward, let him draw   75
thee after. When a wise man gives thee better
counsel, give me mine again; I would have none
but knaves follow it, since a fool gives it.

        "That sir which serves and seeks for gain,
                And follows but for form,   80
        Will pack when it begins to rain,
                And leave thee in the storm.
        But I will tarry; the Fool will stay,
                And let the wise man fly.
        The knave turns fool that runs away;   85
                The Fool no knave, perdy."[1]

(*Re-enter* LEAR *and* GLOUCESTER.)

Kent. Where learn'd you this, Fool?

Fool. Not i' the stocks, fool.

Lear. Deny to speak with me? They are sick?
        They are weary?
They have travell'd all the night? Mere fetches;
The images of revolt and flying off.   91
Fetch me a better answer.

Glou.   My dear lord,
You know the fiery quality of the Duke;
How unremovable and fix'd he is
In his own course.   95

Lear. Vengeance! plague! death! confusion!
"Fiery"? What "quality"? Why, Gloucester,
        Gloucester,
I'd speak with the Duke of Cornwall and his wife.

Glou. Well, my good lord, I have inform'd
        them so.

Lear. "Inform'd" them! Dost thou under-
        stand me, man?   100

Glou. Ay, my good lord.

Lear. The King would speak with Cornwall; the
        dear father
Would with his daughter speak, commands her
        service.
Are they "inform'd" of this? My breath and
        blood!
"Fiery"? The fiery duke? Tell the hot duke
        that —   105
No, but not yet; may be he is not well.

[1] A mild oath, "par Dieu."

Infirmity doth still neglect all office
Whereto our health is bound; we are not ourselves
When nature, being oppress'd, commands the mind
To suffer with the body. I'll forbear,   110
And am fallen out with my more headier will,
To take the indispos'd and sickly fit
For the sound man. — Death on my state! where-
fore   (*Looking on* KENT.)
Should he sit here? This act persuades me
That this remotion [1] of the Duke and her   115
Is practice only. Give me my servant forth.
Go tell the Duke and 's wife I'd speak with them,
Now, presently. Bid them come forth and hear
me,
Or at their chamber-door I'll beat the drum
Till it cry sleep to death.   120
    Glou. I would have all well betwixt you.
                                        (*Exit.*)
    Lear. O me, my heart, my rising heart! But,
down!
    Fool. Cry to it, nuncle, as the cockney did to
the eels when she put 'em i' the paste alive; she
knapp'd 'em o' the coxcombs with a stick,   125
and cried, "Down, wantons, down!" 'Twas her
brother that, in pure kindness to his horse, but-
tered his hay.

(*Enter* CORNWALL, REGAN, GLOUCESTER, *and
Servants.*)

    Lear. Good morrow to you both.
    Corn.   Hail to your Grace!
                        (KENT *is set at liberty.*)
    Reg. I am glad to see your Highness.   130
    Lear. Regan, I think you are; I know what
reason
I have to think so. If thou shouldst not be glad,
I would divorce me from thy mother's tomb,
Sepulchring an adulteress. (*To* KENT.) O, are
you free?
Some other time for that. Beloved Regan,   135
Thy sister's naught. O Regan, she hath tied
Sharp-tooth'd unkindness, like a vulture, here.
                            (*Points to his heart.*)
I can scarce speak to thee; thou 'lt not believe
With how deprav'd a quality — O Regan!
    Reg. I pray you, sir, take patience. I have
hope   140
You less know how to value her desert
Than she to scant her duty.
    Lear.   Say, how is that?
    Reg. I cannot think my sister in the least
Would fail her obligation. If, sir, perchance
She have restrain'd the riots of your followers, 145
'Tis on such ground, and to such wholesome end,
As clears her from all blame.
    [1] removal.

    Lear. My curses on her!
    Reg.   O, sir, you are old;
Nature in you stands on the very verge
Of her confine. You should be rul'd and led 150
By some discretion that discerns your state
Better than you yourself. Therefore, I pray you,
That to our sister you do make return;
Say you have wrong'd her, sir.
    Lear.   Ask her forgiveness?
Do you but mark how this becomes the house: 155
"Dear daughter, I confess that I am old;
                            (*Kneeling.*)
Age is unnecessary. On my knees I beg
That you'll vouchsafe me raiment, bed, and food."
    Reg. Good sir, no more; these are unsightly
tricks.
Return you to my sister.
    Lear. (*Rising.*)   Never, Regan: 160
She hath abated me of half my train;
Look'd black upon me; struck me with her tongue,
Most serpent-like, upon the very heart.
All the stor'd vengeances of heaven fall   164
On her ingrateful top! Strike her young bones,[1]
You taking airs,[2] with lameness!
    Corn.   Fie, sir, fie!
    Lear. You nimble lightnings, dart your blinding
flames
Into her scornful eyes! Infect her beauty,
You fen-suck'd [3] fogs, drawn by the powerful sun,
To fall and blast her pride!   170
    Reg. O the blest gods! so will you wish on me,
When the rash mood is on.
    Lear. No, Regan, thou shalt never have my
curse.
Thy tender-hefted nature shall not give
Thee o'er to harshness. Her eyes are fierce; but
thine   175
Do comfort and not burn. 'Tis not in thee
To grudge my pleasures, to cut off my train,
To bandy hasty words, to scant my sizes,
And in conclusion to oppose the bolt
Against my coming in. Thou better know'st 180
The offices of nature, bond of childhood,
Effects of courtesy, dues of gratitude.
Thy half o' the kingdom hast thou not forgot,
Wherein I thee endow'd.
    Reg.   Good sir, to the purpose.
                            (*Tucket within.*)
    Lear. Who put my man i' the stocks?

(*Enter Steward* OSWALD.)

    Corn.   What trumpet's that?
    Reg. I know 't; my sister's. This approves her
letter,   186

[1] unborn children.   [2] you infectious airs.
[3] nursed in the marshes.

That she would soon be here. (*To* OSWALD.) Is your lady come?

Lear. This is a slave whose easy-borrow'd pride
Dwells in the fickle grace of her he follows.
Out, varlet, from my sight!

Corn. What means your Grace? 190

(*Enter* GONERIL.)

Lear. Who stock'd my servant? Regan, I have good hope
Thou didst not know on 't. Who comes here? O heavens,
If you do love old men, if your sweet sway
Allow obedience, if you yourselves are old,
Make it your cause; send down, and take my part!
(*To* GON.) Art not asham'd to look upon this beard? 196
O Regan, will you take her by the hand?

Gon. Why not by the hand, sir? How have I offended?
All's not offence that indiscretion finds
And dotage terms so.

Lear. O sides, you are too tough;
Will you yet hold? How came my man i' the stocks? 201

Corn. I set him there, sir; but his own disorders
Deserv'd much less advancement.

Lear. You! did you?

Reg. I pray you, father, being weak, seem so.
If, till the expiration of your month, 205
You will return and sojourn with my sister,
Dismissing half your train, come then to me.
I am now from home, and out of that provision
Which shall be needful for your entertainment.

Lear. Return to her, and fifty men dismiss'd!
No, rather I abjure all roofs, and choose 211
To wage against the enmity o' the air;
To be a comrade with the wolf and owl, —
Necessity's sharp pinch. Return with her?
Why, the hot-blooded France, that dowerless took 215
Our youngest born, I could as well be brought
To knee his throne, and, squire-like, pension beg
To keep base life afoot. Return with her?
Persuade me rather to be slave and sumpter [1]
To this detested groom. (*Pointing at* OSWALD.)

Gon. At your choice, sir. 220

Lear. I prithee, daughter, do not make me mad;
I will not trouble thee, my child; farewell!
We'll no more meet, no more see one another.
But yet thou art my flesh, my blood, my daughter;
Or rather a disease that's in my flesh, 225
Which I must needs call mine; thou art a boil,
A plague-sore, an embossed carbuncle,
In my corrupted blood. But I'll not chide thee;

[1] pack-horse.

Let shame come when it will, I do not call it.
I do not bid the thunder-bearer shoot, 230
Nor tell tales of thee to high-judging Jove.
Mend when thou canst; be better at thy leisure.
I can be patient; I can stay with Regan,
I and my hundred knights.

Reg. Not altogether so;
I look'd not for you yet, nor am provided 235
For your fit welcome. Give ear, sir, to my sister;
For those that mingle reason with your passion
Must be content to think you old, and so —
But she knows what she does.

Lear. Is this well spoken?

Reg. I dare avouch it, sir. What, fifty followers! 240
Is it not well? What should you need of more?
Yea, or so many, sith that both charge and danger
Speak 'gainst so great a number? How, in one house,
Should many people, under two commands,
Hold amity? 'Tis hard; almost impossible. 245

Gon. Why might not you, my lord, receive attendance
From those that she calls servants or from mine?

Reg. Why not, my lord? If then they chanc'd to slack ye,
We could control them. If you will come to me, —
For now I spy a danger — I entreat you 250
To bring but five and twenty; to no more
Will I give place or notice.

Lear. I gave you all.

Reg. And in good time you gave it.

Lear. Made you my guardians, my depositaries;
But kept a reservation to be followed 255
With such a number. What, must I come to you
With five and twenty, Regan? Said you so?

Reg. And speak 't again, my lord; no more with me.

Lear. Those wicked creatures yet do look wellfavor'd
When others are more wicked; not being the worst 260
Stands in some rank of praise. (*To* GON.) I'll go with thee.
Thy fifty yet doth double five and twenty,
And thou art twice her love.

Gon. Hear me, my lord:
What need you five and twenty, ten, or five,
To follow in a house where twice so many 265
Have a command to tend you?

Reg. What need one?

Lear. O, reason not the need! Our basest beggars
Are in the poorest thing superfluous.
Allow not nature more than nature needs,

Man's life is cheap as beast's.   Thou art a lady;
If only to go warm were gorgeous,   271
Why, nature needs not what thou gorgeous wear'st,
Which scarcely keeps thee warm.   But, for true
    need, —
You heavens, give me that patience, patience I
    need!
You see me here, you gods, a poor old man,   275
As full of grief as age; wretched in both!
If it be you that stirs these daughters' hearts
Against their father, fool me not so much
To bear it tamely; touch me with noble anger,
And let not women's weapons, water-drops,   280
Stain my man's cheeks!   No, you unnatural hags,
I will have such revenges on you both
That all the world shall — I will do such things, —
What they are, yet I know not; but they shall be
The terrors of the earth.   You think I'll weep: 285
No, I'll not weep.
I have full cause of weeping; but this heart
              (Storm and tempest.)
Shall break into a hundred thousand flaws,
Or ere I'll weep.   O, Fool!   I shall go mad!
   (Exeunt LEAR, GLOUCESTER, KENT, and FOOL.)
Corn. Let us withdraw; 'twill be a storm.   290
Reg. This house is little; the old man and 's
    people
Cannot be well bestow'd.
Gon. 'Tis his own blame; hath put himself from
    rest,
And must needs taste his folly.
Reg. For his particular, I'll receive him gladly,
But not one follower.
Gon.   So am I purpos'd.   296
Where is my Lord of Gloucester?

       (*Re-enter* GLOUCESTER.)

Corn. Followed the old man forth.   He is re-
    turn'd.
Glou. The King is in high rage.
Corn.   Whither is he going?
Glou. He calls to horse; but will I know not
    whither.   300
Corn. 'Tis best to give him way; he leads him-
    self.
Gon. My lord, entreat him by no means to stay.
Glou. Alack, the night comes on, and the high
    winds
Do sorely ruffle; for many miles about
There's scarce a bush.
Reg.   O, sir, to wilful men,   305
The injuries that they themselves procure
Must be their schoolmasters.   Shut up your doors.
He is attended with a desperate train;
And what they may incense him to, being apt
To have his ear abus'd, wisdom bids fear.   310

Corn. Shut up your doors, my lord; 'tis a wild
    night:
My Regan counsels well.   Come out o' the storm.
                    (*Exeunt.*)

ACT III

SCENE I.   *The open country near Gloucester's
castle.*

(*Storm still.   Enter* KENT *and a* GENTLEMAN,
severally.)

Kent. Who's there, besides foul weather?
Gent. One minded like the weather, most un-
    quietly.
Kent. I know you.   Where's the King?
Gent. Contending with the fretful elements;
Bids the wind blow the earth into the sea,   5
Or swell the curled waters 'bove the main,
That things might change or cease; tears his white
    hair,
Which the impetuous blasts, with eyeless rage,
Catch in their fury, and make nothing of;
Strives in his little world of man to out-scorn   10
The to-and-fro-conflicting wind and rain.
This night, wherein the cub-drawn bear would
    couch,
The lion and the belly-pinched wolf
Keep their fur dry, unbonneted he runs,   14
And bids what will take all.
Kent.   But who is with him?
Gent. None but the Fool; who labors to outjest
His heart-struck injuries.
Kent.   Sir, I do know you;
And dare, upon the warrant of my note,
Commend a dear thing to you.   There is division,
Although as yet the face of it is cover'd   20
With mutual cunning, 'twixt Albany and Cornwall;
Who have — as who have not, that their great
    stars
Thron'd and set high? — servants, who seem no
    less,
Which are to France the spies and speculations
Intelligent of our state; what hath been seen,   25
Either in snuffs and packings of the Dukes,
Or the hard rein which both of them have borne
Against the old kind king, or something deeper,
Whereof perchance these are but furnishings;
But, true it is, from France there comes a power   30
Into this scattered kingdom; who already,
Wise in our negligence, have secret feet
In some of our best ports, and are at point
To show their open banner.   Now to you:
If on my credit you dare build so far   35
To make your speed to Dover, you shall find
Some that will thank you, making just report

Of how unnatural and bemadding sorrow
The King hath cause to plain.
I am a gentleman of blood and breeding;   40
And, from some knowledge and assurance, offer
This office to you.

Gent. I will talk further with you.

Kent.   No, do not.
For confirmation that I am much more
Than my out-wall, open this purse, and take   45
What it contains. If you shall see Cordelia, —
As fear not but you shall, — show her this ring;
And she will tell you who that fellow is
That yet you do not know. Fie on this storm!
I will go seek the King.   50

Gent. Give me your hand. Have you no more
    to say?

Kent. Few words, but, to effect, more than all
    yet;
That, when we have found the King, — in which
    your pain
That way, I'll this, — he that first lights on him
Holla the other.   *(Exeunt severally.)*   55

SCENE II. *The same. Storm still.*

(Enter LEAR and FOOL.)

Lear. Blow, winds, and crack your cheeks!
    Rage! Blow!
You cataracts and hurricanoes, spout
Till you have drench'd our steeples, drown'd the
    cocks!
You sulphurous and thought-executing fires,
Vaunt-couriers [1] of oak-cleaving thunderbolts,   5
Singe my white head! And thou, all-shaking
    thunder,
Strike flat the thick rotundity o' the world!
Crack nature's moulds, all germens [2] spill at once,
That makes ingrateful man!   9

Fool. O nuncle, court holy-water in a dry house
is better than this rain-water out o' door. Good
nuncle, in; ask thy daughters' blessing. Here's a
night pities neither wise men nor fools.

Lear. Rumble thy bellyful! Spit, fire! Spout,
    rain!
Nor rain, wind, thunder, fire, are my daughters.   15
I tax not you, you elements, with unkindness;
I never gave you kingdom, call'd you children,
You owe me no subscription. Then let fall
Your horrible pleasure. Here I stand, your slave,
A poor, infirm, weak, and despis'd old man;   20
But yet I call you servile ministers,
That will with two pernicious daughters join
Your high engender'd [3] battles 'gainst a head

[1] heralds.   [2] seeds.

[3] high created (since the storms brewed in the heavens).

So old and white as this. Oh! Oh! 'tis foul!

Fool. He that has a house to put 's head in has a
good head-piece.   26

    "The cod-piece [1] that will house
        Before the head has any,
    The head and he shall louse;
        So beggars marry many.   30
    The man that makes his toe
        What he his heart should make
    Shall of a corn cry woe,
        And turn his sleep to wake."

For there was never yet fair woman but she made
mouths in a glass.   36

(Enter KENT.)

Lear. No, I will be the pattern of all patience;
I will say nothing.

Kent. Who's there?

Fool. Marry, here's grace and a cod-piece; that's
a wise man and a fool.   41

Kent. Alas, sir, are you here? Things that love
    night
Love not such nights as these; the wrathful
    skies
Gallow the very wanderers of the dark,
And make them keep their caves. Since I was
    man,   45
Such sheets of fire, such bursts of horrid thunder,
Such groans of roaring wind and rain, I never
Remember to have heard. Man's nature cannot
    carry
The affliction nor the fear.

Lear.   Let the great gods,
That keep this dreadful pudder o'er our heads,   50
Find out their enemies now. Tremble, thou
    wretch,
That hast within thee undivulged crimes,
Unwhipp'd of justice! Hide thee, thou bloody
    hand;
Thou perjur'd, and thou simular [2] of virtue
That art incestuous! Caitiff, to pieces shake,   55
That under covert and convenient seeming
Has practis'd on man's life! Close pent-up guilts,
Rive your concealing continents, and cry
These dreadful summoners grace. I am a man
More sinn'd against than sinning.

Kent.   Alack, bare-headed!
Gracious my lord, hard by here is a hovel;   61
Some friendship will it lend you 'gainst the tempest.
Repose you there; while I to this hard house —
More harder than the stones whereof 'tis rais'd;
Which even but now, demanding after you,   65

[1] Part of the dress of men; a baggy flap at the front
of close-fitting hose.

[2] simulator.

Deni'd me to come in — return, and force
Their scanted courtesy.

Lear.   My wits begin to turn.
Come on, my boy. How dost, my boy? Art cold?
I am cold myself. Where is this straw, my fellow?
The art of our necessities is strange,   70
And can make vile things precious. Come, your
      hovel.
Poor Fool and knave, I have one part in my heart
That's sorry yet for thee.

Fool. (*Singing.*)
"He that has and a little tiny wit, —
   With heigh-ho, the wind and the rain, —   75
   Must make content with his fortunes fit,
      For the rain it raineth every day."

Lear. True, boy. Come, bring us to this hovel.
            (*Exeunt* LEAR *and* KENT.)

Fool. This is a brave night to cool a courtezan.
I'll speak a prophecy ere I go: 80
   When priests are more in word than matter;
   When brewers mar their malt with water;
   When nobles are their tailors' tutors;
   No heretics burn'd, but wenches' suitors;
   When every case in law is right;   85
   No squire in debt, nor no poor knight;
   When slanders do not live in tongues;
   Nor cutpurses come not to throngs;
   When usurers tell their gold i' the field;
   And bawds and whores do churches build;   90
      Then shall the realm of Albion
      Come to great confusion.
   Then comes the time, who lives to see 't,
   That going shall be us'd with feet.
This prophecy Merlin [1] shall make; for I live before
      his time.   (*Exit.*) 95

SCENE III. *Gloucester's castle.*

(*Enter* GLOUCESTER *and* EDMUND.)

Glou. Alack, alack, Edmund, I like not this
unnatural dealing. When I desired their leave
that I might pity him, they took from me the
use of mine own house; charg'd me, on pain of
perpetual displeasure, neither to speak of him,
entreat for him, or any way sustain him.   6

Edm. Most savage and unnatural!

Glou. Go to; say you nothing. There is division between the Dukes, and a worse matter
than that. I have received a letter this night; 10
'tis dangerous to be spoken; I have lock'd the letter in my closet. These injuries the King now
bears will be revenged home; there is part of a
power already footed. We must incline to the
King. I will look him, and privily relieve him.

[1] A prophet and magician of ancient Britain.

Go you and maintain talk with the Duke, that 16
my charity be not of him perceived. If he ask
for me, I am ill, and gone to bed. If I die for it,
as no less is threat'ned me, the King my old master
must be relieved. There is strange things toward,[1]
Edmund; pray you, be careful.   (*Exit.*) 21

Edm. This courtesy, forbid thee, shall the Duke
Instantly know; and of that letter too.
This seems a fair deserving, and must draw me
That which my father loses; no less than all. 25
The younger rises when the old doth fall. (*Exit.*)

SCENE IV. *The open country. Before a hovel.*

(*Enter* LEAR, KENT, *and* FOOL.)

Kent. Here is the place, my lord; good my lord,
      enter.
The tyranny of the open night's too rough
For nature to endure.   (*Storm still.*)

Lear.   Let me alone.

Kent. Good my lord, enter here.

Lear.   Wilt break my heart?

Kent. I had rather break mine own. Good
      my lord, enter.   5

Lear. Thou think'st 'tis much that this conten-
      tious storm
Invades us to the skin; so 'tis to thee;
But where the greater malady is fix'd,
The lesser is scarce felt. Thou'dst shun a bear;
But if thy flight lay toward the roaring sea, 10
Thou'dst meet the bear i' the mouth. When the
      mind's free,
The body 's delicate; the tempest in my mind
Doth from my senses take all feeling else
Save what beats there. Filial ingratitude!
Is it not as this mouth should tear this hand 15
For lifting food to 't? But I will punish home.
No, I will weep no more. In such a night
To shut me out! Pour on! I will endure.
In such a night as this! O Regan, Goneril!
Your old kind father, whose frank heart gave all, —
O, that way madness lies; let me shun that; 21
No more of that.

Kent.   Good my lord, enter here.

Lear. Prithee, go in thyself; seek thine own ease.
This tempest will not give me leave to ponder
On things would hurt me more. But I'll go in. 25
(*To the* FOOL.) In, boy; go first. You houseless
      poverty, —
Nay, get thee in. I'll pray, and then I'll sleep.
                              (*Exit* FOOL.)
Poor naked wretches, wheresoe'er you are,
That bide the pelting of this pitiless storm,
How shall your houseless heads and unfed sides, 30

[1] about to happen.

Your loop'd [1] and window'd [1] raggedness, defend
you
From seasons such as these? O, I have ta'en
Too little care of this! Take physic, pomp;
Expose thyself to feel what wretches feel,
That thou mayst shake the superflux [2] to them,
And show the heavens more just. 36

Edg. (*Within.*) Fathom and half, fathom and
half! Poor Tom!

(*The* FOOL *runs out from the hovel.*)

Fool. Come not in here, nuncle, here's a spirit.
Help me, help me! 40

Kent. Give me thy hand. Who's there?

Fool. A spirit, a spirit! He says his name's poor
Tom.

Kent. What art thou that dost grumble there
i' the straw? Come forth. 45

(*Enter* EDGAR, *disguised as a madman.*)

Edg. Away! the final fiend follows me!
"Through the sharp hawthorn blow the winds."
Hum! go to thy bed, and warm thee.

Lear. Did'st thou give all to thy daughters, and
art thou come to this? 50

Edg. Who gives anything to poor Tom? whom
the foul fiend hath led through fire and through
flame, and through ford and whirlpool, o'er bog
and quagmire; that hath laid knives under his
pillow, and halters in his pew; set ratsbane by his
porridge; made him proud of heart, to ride 56
on a bay trotting-horse over four-inch'd bridges,
to course his own shadow for a traitor. Bless thy
five wits! Tom's a-cold, — O, do de, do de, do
de. Bless thee from whirlwinds, star-blasting,
and taking! Do poor Tom some charity, 61
whom the foul fiend vexes. There could I have
him now, — and there, — and there again, and
there. (*Storm still.*)

Lear. Has his daughters brought him to this
pass? 65
Couldst thou save nothing? Wouldst thou give
'em all?

Fool. Nay, he reserv'd a blanket, else we had
been all sham'd.

Lear. Now, all the plagues that in the pendulous air
Hang fated o'er men's faults light on thy daughters! 70

Kent. He hath no daughters, sir.

Lear. Death, traitor! nothing could have sub-
du'd nature
To such a lowness but his unkind daughters.
Is it the fashion, that discarded fathers
Should have thus little mercy on their flesh? 75

[1] full of holes.   [2] superfluous amount.

Judicious punishment! 'Twas this flesh begot
Those pelican [1] daughters.

Edg. "Pillicock sat on Pillicock-hill." [2]
Alow, alow, loo, loo!

Fool. This cold night will turn us all to fools
and madmen. 81

Edg. Take heed o' the foul fiend. Obey thy
parents; keep thy word justly; swear not; commit
not with man's sworn spouse; set not thy sweet
heart on proud array. Tom's a-cold. 85

Lear. What hast thou been?

Edg. A serving-man, proud in heart and mind;
that curl'd my hair; wore gloves in my cap;
serv'd the lust of my mistress' heart, and did the
act of darkness with her; swore as many oaths 90
as I spake words, and broke them in the sweet
face of heaven: one that slept in the contriving
of lust, and wak'd to do it. Wine lov'd I dearly,
dice dearly; and in woman out-paramour'd the
Turk: false of heart, light of ear, bloody of 95
hand; hog in sloth, fox in stealth, wolf in greedi-
ness, dog in madness, lion in prey. Let not the
creaking of shoes nor the rustling of silks betray
thy poor heart to woman. Keep thy foot out of
brothels, thy hand out of plackets,[3] thy pen 100
from lenders' books, and defy the foul fiend.
"Still through the hawthorn blows the cold wind."
Says suum, mun, nonny. Dolphin my boy, boy,
sessa! [4] let him trot by. (*Storm still.*)

Lear. Thou wert better in a grave than to 105
answer with thy uncover'd body this extremity
of the skies. Is man no more than this? Consider him well. Thou ow'st the worm no silk,
the beast no hide, the sheep no wool, the cat no
perfume. Ha! here's three on 's are sophisti- 110
cated! Thou art the thing itself; unaccommodated
man [5] is no more but such a poor, bare, forked
animal as thou art. Off, off, you lendings! come,
unbutton here. (*Tearing off his clothes.*) 114

(*Enter* GLOUCESTER, *with a torch.*)

Fool. Prithee, nuncle, be contented; 'tis a
naughty night to swim in. Now a little fire in a
wild field were like an old lecher's heart; a small
spark, all the rest on 's body cold. Look, here
comes a walking fire.

Edg. This is the foul fiend Flibbertigibbet; 120
he begins at curfew, and walks till the first cock;
he gives the web and the pin, squints the eye,

[1] Young pelicans were supposed to live from blood
sucked from their mother.
[2] Words of an old nursery rime.
[3] An opening in a woman's skirt.
[4] Edgar gives way to nonsense.
[5] man without conveniences.

and makes the hare-lip; mildews the white wheat, and hurts the poor creature of earth.

> "St. Withold footed thrice the 'old;   125
>   He met the night-mare, and her ninefold;
>   Bid her alight,
>   And her troth plight,
>   And, aroint thee, witch, aroint thee!" [1]

Kent. How fares your Grace?   130
Lear. What's he?
Kent. Who's there? What is 't you seek?
Glou. What are you there? Your names?
Edg. Poor Tom, that eats the swimming frog, the toad, the tadpole, the wall-newt, [2] and   135 the water; that in the fury of his heart, when the foul fiend rages, eats cow-dung for salads; swallows the old rat and the ditch-dog; drinks the green mantle of the standing pool; who is whipp'd from tithing to tithing, [3] and stock'd, punish'd,   140 and imprison'd; who hath three suits to his back, six shirts to his body,

> Horse to ride, and weapon to wear;
> But mice and rats, and such small deer,
> Have been Tom's food for seven long year.   145

Beware my follower. Peace, Smulkin; [4] peace, thou fiend!
Glou. What, hath your Grace no better company?
Edg. The prince of darkness is a gentleman. Modo [4] he's call'd, and Mahu. [4]
Glou. Our flesh and blood, my lord, is grown so vile   150
That it doth hate what gets it.
Edg. Poor Tom's a-cold.
Glou. Go in with me; my duty cannot suffer To obey in all your daughters' hard commands. Though their injunction be to bar my doors,   155 And let this tyrannous night take hold upon you, Yet have I ventur'd to come seek you out, And bring you where both fire and food is ready.
Lear. First let me talk with this philosopher. What is the cause of thunder?   160
Kent. Good my lord, take his offer; go into the house.
Lear. I'll take a word with this same learned Theban.
What is your study?
Edg. How to prevent the fiend, and to kill vermin.
Lear. Let me ask you one word in private.   165
Kent. Importune him once more to go, my lord; His wits begin to unsettle.
Glou.   Canst thou blame him?
                                    (*Storm still.*)

[1] be gone; get away.
[2] A lizard.   [3] parish to parish.
[4] Evil spirits.

His daughters seek his death. Ah, that good Kent!
He said it would be thus, poor banish'd man!
Thou say'st the King grows mad; I'll tell thee, friend,   170
I am almost mad myself. I had a son,
Now outlaw'd from my blood; he sought my life,
But lately, very late. I lov'd him, friend,
No father his son dearer; true to tell thee,
The grief hath craz'd my wits. What a night 's this!   175
I do beseech your Grace, —
Lear.   O, cry you mercy, sir.
Noble philosopher, your company.
Edg. Tom's a-cold.
Glou. In, fellow, there, into the hovel; keep thee warm.
Lear. Come, let's in all.
Kent.   This way, my lord.
Lear.   With him;
I will keep still with my philosopher.   181
Kent. Good my lord, soothe him; let him take the fellow.
Glou. Take him you on.
Kent. Sirrah, come on; go along with us.
Lear. Come, good Athenian.   185
Glou. No words, no words: hush.
Edg. "Child Rowland to the dark tower came; [1]
    His word was still, 'Fie, foh, and fum,
    I smell the blood of a British man.'"

                                    (*Exeunt*).

SCENE V. *Gloucester's castle.*

(*Enter* CORNWALL *and* EDMUND.)

Corn. I will have my revenge ere I depart his house.
Edm. How, my lord, I may be censured that nature thus gives way to loyalty, something fears me to think of.   5
Corn. I now perceive, it was not altogether your brother's evil disposition made him seek his death; but a provoking merit, set a-work by a reproveable badness in himself.   9
Edm. How malicious is my fortune, that I must repent to be just! This is the letter which he spoke of, which approves him an intelligent party to the advantages of France. O heavens! that this treason were not, or not I the detector!
Corn. Go with me to the Duchess.   15
Edm. If the matter of this paper be certain, you have mighty business in hand.
Corn. True or false, it hath made thee Earl of Gloucester. Seek out where thy father is, that he may be ready for our apprehension.   20

[1] Words of an old ballad.

Edm. (*Aside.*) If I find him comforting the King, it will stuff his suspicion more fully. — I will persevere in my course of loyalty, though the conflict be sore between that and my blood. 24

Corn. I will lay trust upon thee; and thou shalt find a dearer father in my love. (*Exeunt.*)

SCENE VI. *A building attached to Gloucester's castle.*

(*Enter* KENT *and* GLOUCESTER.)

Glou. Here is better than the open air; take it thankfully. I will piece out the comfort with what addition I can. I will not be long from you. (*Exit.*)

Kent. All the power of his wits have given 5 way to his impatience. The gods reward your kindness!

(*Enter* LEAR, EDGAR, *and* FOOL.)

Edg. Fraretto [1] calls me; and tells me Nero is an angler in the lake of darkness. Pray, innocent,[2] and beware the foul fiend. 10

Fool. Prithee, nuncle, tell me whether a madman be a gentleman or a yeoman?

Lear. A king, a king!

Fool. No, he's a yeoman that has a gentleman to his son; for he's a mad yeoman that sees his son a gentleman before him. 16

Lear. To have a thousand with red burning spits
Come hissing in upon 'em, —

Edg. The foul fiend bites my back.

Fool. He's mad that trusts in the tameness of 20 a wolf, a horse's health, a boy's love, or a whore's oath.

Lear. It shall be done; I will arraign them straight.
(*To* EDGAR.) Come, sit thou here, most learned justicer;[3]
(*To the* FOOL.) Thou, sapient sir, sit here. Now, you she foxes! 25

Edg. Look, where he stands and glares!
Wantest thou eyes at trial, madam?
"Come o'er the bourn, Bessy, to me," — [4]

Fool. "Her boat hath a leak,
And she must not speak 30
Why she dares not come over to thee."

Edg. The foul fiend haunts poor Tom in the voice of a nightingale. Hopdance [5] cries in Tom's belly for two white herring. Croak not, black angel; I have no food for thee. 35

[1] Another demon.
[2] The fool. [3] justice.
[4] Line from old ballad.
[5] Another demon.

Kent. How do you, sir? Stand you not so amaz'd:
Will you lie down and rest upon the cushions?

Lear. I'll see their trial first. Bring in their evidence.
(*To* EDGAR.) Thou robed man of justice, take thy place;
(*To the* FOOL.) And thou, his yoke-fellow of equity, 40
Bench by his side. (*To* KENT.) You are o' the commission,
Sit you too.

Edg. Let us deal justly.
"Sleepest or wakest thou, jolly shepherd?
Thy sheep be in the corn; 45
And for one blast of thy minikin [1] mouth,
Thy sheep shall take no harm."
Purr! the cat is gray.

Lear. Arraign her first; 'tis Goneril. I here take my oath before this honorable assembly, she kick'd the poor king her father. 51

Fool. Come hither, mistress. Is your name Goneril?

Lear. She cannot deny it.

Fool. Cry you mercy, I took you for a joint-stool.[2] 56

Lear. And here's another, whose warp'd looks proclaim
What store her heart is made on. Stop her there!
Arms, arms, sword, fire! Corruption in the place!
False justicer, why hast thou let her scape? 60

Edg. Bless thy five wits!

Kent. O pity! Sir, where is the patience now
That you so oft have boasted to retain?

Edg. (*Aside.*) My tears begin to take his part so much,
They mar my counterfeiting. 65

Lear. The little dogs and all,
Tray, Blanch, and Sweetheart, see, they bark at me.

Edg. Tom will throw his head at them. Avaunt, you curs!
Be thy mouth or black or white, 70
Tooth that poisons if it bite;
Mastiff, greyhound, mongrel grim,
Hound or spaniel, brach or lym,
Or bobtail tike or trundle-tail,
Tom will make him weep and wail; 75
For, with throwing thus my head,
Dogs leapt the hatch, and all are fled.
Do de, de, de. Sessa! Come, march to wakes and fairs and market-towns. Poor Tom, thy horn [3] is dry. 80

[1] small, dainty.
[2] a low stool.
[3] A horn in which the beggar stored drink.

Lear. Then let them anatomize Regan; see what breeds about her heart. Is there any cause in nature that make these hard hearts? (*To* EDG.) You, sir, I entertain for one of my hundred; only I do not like the fashion of your garments. You 85 will say they are Persian, but let them be chang'd.

(*Re-enter* GLOUCESTER.)

Kent. Now, good my lord, lie here and rest a while.

Lear. Make no noise, make no noise; draw the curtains; so, so, so. We'll go to supper i' the morning. 91

Fool. And I'll go to bed at noon.

Glou. Come hither, friend; where is the King my master?

Kent. Here, sir; but trouble him not, his wits are gone.

Glou. Good friend, I prithee, take him in thy arms; 95

I have o'erheard a plot of death upon him.
There is a litter ready; lay him in 't,
And drive toward Dover, friend, where thou shalt meet
Both welcome and protection. Take up thy master.
If thou shouldst dally half an hour, his life, 100
With thine, and all that offer to defend him,
Stand in assured loss. Take up, take up;
And follow me, that will to some provision
Give thee quick conduct.

Kent.   Oppressed nature sleeps.
This rest might yet have balm'd thy broken sinews, 105
Which, if convenience will not allow,
Stand in hard cure. (*To the* FOOL.) Come, help to bear thy master;
Thou must not stay behind.

Glou.   Come, come, away.

(*Exeunt all but* EDGAR.)

Edg. When we our betters see bearing our woes,
We scarcely think our miseries our foes. 110
Who alone suffers, suffers most i' the mind,
Leaving free things and happy shows behind;
But then the mind much sufferance doth o'erskip,
When grief hath mates, and bearing fellowship.
How light and portable my pain seems now, 115
When that which makes me bend makes the King bow,
He childed as I fathered! Tom, away!
Mark the high noises; and thyself bewray,
When false opinion, whose wrong thoughts defile thee,
In thy just proof repeals and reconciles thee. 120
What will hap more to-night, safe scape the King!
Lurk, lurk.   (*Exit.*)

SCENE VII. *Gloucester's castle.*

(*Enter* CORNWALL, REGAN, GONERIL, *Bastard* EDMUND, *and Servants.*)

Corn. (*To* GON.) Post speedily to my lord your husband; show him this letter. The army of France is landed. — Seek out the traitor Gloucester. (*Exeunt some of the Servants.*)

Reg. Hang him instantly. 5

Gon. Pluck out his eyes.

Corn. Leave him to my displeasure. — Edmund, keep you our sister company; the revenges we are bound to take upon your traitorous father are not fit for your beholding. Advise the Duke, 10 where you are going, to a most festinate[1] preparation; we are bound to the like. Our posts shall be swift and intelligent betwixt us. Farewell, dear sister; farewell, my lord of Gloucester.

(*Enter Steward* OSWALD.)

How now! where's the King? 15

Osw. My Lord of Gloucester hath convey'd him hence.
Some five or six and thirty of his knights,
Hot questrists[2] after him, met him at gate,
Who, with some other of the lords dependants,
Are gone with him toward Dover, where they boast 20
To have well-armed friends.

Corn.   Get horses for your mistress.

Gon. Farewell, sweet lord, and sister.

Corn. Edmund, farewell.

(*Exeunt* GONERIL, EDMUND, *and* OSWALD.)
                    Go seek the traitor Gloucester,
Pinion him like a thief, bring him before us.

(*Exeunt other Servants.*)

Though well we may not pass upon his life 25
Without the form of justice, yet our power
Shall do a courtesy to our wrath, which men
May blame, but not control.

(*Enter* GLOUCESTER *and* SERVANTS.)
                    Who's there? The traitor?

Reg. Ingrateful fox! 'tis he.

Corn. Bind fast his corky[3] arms. 30

Glou. What means your Graces? Good my friends, consider
You are my guests. Do me no foul play, friends.

Corn. Bind him, I say. (*Servants bind him.*)

Reg.   Hard, hard. O filthy traitor!

Glou. Unmerciful lady as you are, I'm none.

Corn. To this chair bind him. Villain, thou shalt find — (*Regan plucks his beard.*) 35

Glou. By the kind gods, 'tis most ignobly done
To pluck me by the beard.

[1] hasty, speedy.   [2] searchers.   [3] withered.

Reg. So white, and such a traitor!

Glou.   Naughty lady,
These hairs, which thou dost ravish from my
    chin,
Will quicken, and accuse thee.   I am your host:
With robber's hands my hospitable favors [1]   41
You should not ruffle thus.   What will you do?

Corn. Come, sir, what letters had you late from
    France?

Reg. Be simple-answer'd, for we know the
    truth.

Corn. And what confederacy have you with
    the traitors   45
Late footed [2] in the kingdom?

Reg. To whose hands you have sent the lunatic
    king,
Speak.

Glou. I have a letter guessingly set down,
Which came from one that's of a neutral heart,
And not from one oppos'd.

Corn.   Cunning.

Reg.   And false.

Corn. Where has thou sent the King?   51

Glou. To Dover.

Reg. Wherefore to Dover?   Wast thou not
    charg'd at peril —

Corn. Wherefore to Dover?   Let him answer
    that.

Glou. I am tied to the stake, and I must stand
    the course.[3]   55

Reg. Wherefore to Dover?

Glou. Because I would not see thy cruel nails
Pluck out his poor old eyes; nor thy fierce sister
In his anointed flesh stick boarish fangs.
The sea, with such a storm as his bare head   60
In hell-black night endur'd, would have buoy'd
    up
And quench'd the stelled [4] fires;
Yet, poor old heart, he holp [5] the heavens to
    rain.
If wolves had at thy gate howl'd that stern time,
Thou shouldst have said, "Good porter, turn the
    key."   65
All cruels else subscribe; but I shall see
The winged vengeance overtake such children.

Corn. See 't shalt thou never.   Fellows, hold
    the chair.
Upon these eyes of thine I'll set my foot.

Glou. He that will think to live till he be old,
Give me some help! — O cruel!   O you gods!   71

[1] features.
[2] settled.
[3] A reference to bear-baiting.   Gloucester the bear is
tied and is set upon by the dogs.
[4] fixed.
[5] helped.

Reg. One side will mock another; the other too.

Corn. If you see vengeance —

1. Serv.   Hold your hand, my lord!
I have serv'd you ever since I was a child;
But better service have I never done you   75
Than now to bid you hold.

Reg.   How now, you dog!

1. Serv. If you did wear a beard upon your
    chin,
I'd shake it on this quarrel.   What do you mean?

Corn. My villain!   (*They draw and fight.*)

1. Serv. Nay, then, come on, and take the
    chance of anger.   80

Reg. Give me thy sword.   A peasant stand up
    thus?
            (*Takes a sword, and runs at him behind.*)

1. Serv. Oh, I am slain!   My lord, you have
    one eye left
To see some mischief on him.   Oh!   (*Dies.*)

Corn. Lest it see more, prevent it.   Out, vile
    jelly!
Where is thy lustre now?   85

Glou. All dark and comfortless.   Where's my
    son Edmund?
Edmund, enkindle all the sparks of nature,
To quit [1] this horrid act.

Reg.   Out, treacherous villain!
Thou call'st on him that hates thee.   It was he
That made the overture of thy treasons to us,   90
Who is too good to pity thee.

Glou. O my follies! then Edgar was abus'd.
Kind gods, forgive me that, and prosper him!

Reg. Go thrust him out at gates, and let him
    smell
His way to Dover.   (*Exit one with* GLOUCESTER.)
            How is 't, my lord?   How look you?   95

Corn. I have received a hurt; follow me, lady.
Turn out that eyeless villain; throw this slave
Upon the dunghill.   Regan, I bleed apace;
Untimely comes this hurt.   Give me your arm.
            (*Exit* CORNWALL, *led by* REGAN.)

2. Serv. I'll never care what wickedness I do,
If this man come to good.

3. Serv.   If she live long,   101
And in the end meet the old course of death,
Women will all turn monsters.

2. Serv. Let's follow the old earl, and get the
    Bedlam
To lead him where he would: his roguish madness
Allows itself to anything.   106

3. Serv. Go thou: I'll fetch some flax and whites
    of eggs
To apply to his bleeding face.   Now, Heaven help
    him!   (*Exeunt severally.*)

[1] requite.

ACT IV

SCENE I. *The open country near Gloucester's castle.*

(*Enter* EDGAR.)

Edg. Yet better thus, and known to be contemn'd,
Than, still contemn'd and flatter'd, to be worst.
The lowest and most dejected thing of fortune
Stands still in esperance,[1] lives not in fear.
The lamentable change is from the best;   5
The worst returns to laughter. Welcome, then,
Thou unsubstantial air that I embrace!
The wretch that thou hast blown unto the worst
Owes nothing to thy blasts.

(*Enter* GLOUCESTER, *led by an* OLD MAN.)
                    But who comes here?
My father, poorly led? World, world, O world!
But that thy strange mutations make us hate thee,   11
Life would not yield to age.
Old Man. O, my good lord, I have been your tenant, and your father's tenant, these fourscore years.   15
Glou. Away, get thee away! Good friend, be gone;
Thy comforts can do me no good at all;
Thee they may hurt.
Old Man. Alack, sir, you cannot see your way.
Glou. I have no way, and therefore want no eyes;   20
I stumbled when I saw. Full oft 'tis seen,
Our means secure us, and our mere defects
Prove our commodities.[2] O dear son Edgar,
The food of thy abused father's wrath!
Might I but live to see thee in my touch,   25
I'd say I had eyes again!
Old Man.   How now! Who's there?
Edg. (*Aside.*) O gods! Who is't can say, "I am at the worst"?
I am worse than e'er I was.
Old Man.   'Tis poor mad Tom.
Edg. (*Aside.*) And worse I may be yet; the worst is not
So long as we can say, "This is the worst."   30
Old Man. Fellow, where goest?
Glou.   Is it a beggar-man?
Old Man. Madman and beggar too.
Glou. He has some reason, else he could not beg.
I' the last night's storm I such a fellow saw,
Which made me think a man a worm. My son
Came then into my mind, and yet my mind   36

[1] hope.
[2] i.e., our advantages make us careless and our defects bring us advantages.

Was then scarce friends with him. I have heard more since.
As flies to wanton boys, are we to the gods,
They kill us for their sport.
Edg. (*Aside.*)   How should this be?
Bad is the trade that must play fool to sorrow,   40
Ang'ring itself and others. — Bless thee, master!
Glou. Is that the naked fellow?
Old Man.   Ay, my lord.
Glou. Then, prithee, get thee away. If, for my sake,
Thou wilt o'ertake us, hence a mile or twain
I' the way toward Dover, do it for ancient love;   45
And bring some covering for this naked soul,
Which I'll entreat to lead me.
Old Man.   Alack, sir, he is mad.
Glou. 'Tis the time's plague, when madmen lead the blind.
Do as I bid thee, or rather do thy pleasure;
Above the rest, be gone.   50
Old Man. I'll bring him the best 'parel that I have,
Come on 't what will.   (*Exit.*)
Glou. Sirrah, naked fellow —
Edg. Poor Tom's a-cold. (*Aside.*) I cannot daub it further.
Glou. Come hither, fellow.   55
Edg. (*Aside.*) And yet I must. — Bless thy sweet eyes, they bleed.
Glou. Know'st thou the way to Dover?
Edg. Both stile and gate, horse-way and foot-path. Poor Tom hath been scar'd out of his good wits. Bless thee, good man's son, from the   60
foul fiend! Five fiends have been in poor Tom at once; of lust, as Obidicut; Hobbididence, prince of dumbness; Mahu, of stealing; Modo, of murder; Flibbertigibbet, of mopping and mowing, who since possesses chambermaids and waiting-women. So, bless thee, master!   66
Glou. Here, take this purse, thou whom the heavens' plagues
Have humbled to all strokes. That I am wretched
Makes thee the happier; heavens, deal so still!
Let the superfluous[1] and lust-dieted man,   70
That slaves[2] your ordinance, that will not see
Because he does not feel, feel your power quickly;
So distribution should undo excess,
And each man have enough. Dost thou know Dover?
Edg. Aye, master.   75
Glou. There is a cliff, whose high and bending head
Looks fearfully in the confined deep.
Bring me but to the very brim of it,

[1] Having more than enough, in luxury.
[2] enslaves.

And I'll repair the misery thou dost bear
With something rich about me. From that place
I shall no leading need.

Edg. Give me thy arm; 81
Poor Tom shall lead thee. (*Exeunt.*)

SCENE II. *Before the Duke of Albany's palace.*

(*Enter* GONERIL, *Bastard* EDMUND, *and Steward* OSWALD.)

Gon. Welcome, my lord! I marvel our mild
husband
Not met us on the way. — Now, where's your
master?

Osw. Madam, within; but never man so chang'd.
I told him of the army that was landed;
He smil'd at it. I told him you were coming; 5
His answer was, "The worse." Of Gloucester's
treachery,
And of the loyal service of his son,
When I inform'd him, then he call'd me sot,
And told me I had turn'd the wrong side out.
What most he should dislike seems pleasant to
him;
What like, offensive. 10

Gon. (*To* EDM.) Then shall you go no further.
It is the cowish terror of his spirit,
That dares not undertake; he'll not feel wrongs
Which tie him to an answer. Our wishes on the
way
May prove effects. Back, Edmund, to my brother;
Hasten his musters and conduct his powers. 16
I must change names [1] at home, and give the distaff
Into my husband's hands. This trusty servant
Shall pass between us. Ere long you are like to
hear,
If you dare venture in your own behalf, 20
A mistress's command. Wear this; spare speech;
Decline your head. This kiss, if it durst speak,
Would stretch thy spirits up into the air.
Conceive, and fare thee well.

Edm. Yours in the ranks of death. (*Exit.*)
Gon. My most dear Gloucester!
O, the difference of man and man! 26
To thee a woman's services are due;
My Fool usurps my body.

Osw. Madam, here comes my lord.
(*Exit.*)

(*Enter the* DUKE OF ALBANY.)

Gon. I have been worth the whistle.[2]
Alb. O Goneril!
You are not worth the dust which the rude wind

¹ Some texts read "arms."

˙ Even a dog might have been greeted with a whistle.

Blows in your face. I fear your disposition. 31
That nature which contemns its origin
Cannot be bordered certain in itself.
She that herself will sliver and disbranch
From her material sap, perforce must wither 35
And come to deadly use.[1]

Gon. No more; the text is foolish.

Alb. Wisdom and goodness to the vile seem vile;
Filths savor but themselves. What have you
done?
Tigers, not daughters, what have you perform'd?
A father, and a gracious aged man, 41
Whose reverence even the head-lugg'd bear[2]
would lick,
Most barbarous, most degenerate! have you
madded.
Could my good brother suffer you to do it?
A man, a prince, by him so benefited! 45
If that the heavens do not their visible spirits
Send quickly down to tame these vile offences,
It will come,
Humanity must perforce prey on itself,
Like monsters of the deep.

Gon. Milk-liver'd[3] man! 50
That bear'st a cheek for blows, a head for wrongs,
Who hast not in thy brows an eye discerning
Thine honor from thy suffering, that not know'st
Fools do those villains pity who are punish'd
Ere they have done their mischief, where's thy
drum? 55
France spreads his banners in our noiseless land,
With plumed helm thy state begins to threat;
Whiles thou, a moral fool, sits still, and criest,
"Alack, why does he so?"

Alb. See thyself, devil!
Proper deformity seems not in the fiend 60
So horrid as in woman.

Gon. O vain fool!
Alb. Thou changed and self-cover'd thing, for
shame!
Be-monster not thy feature.[4] Were't my fitness
To let these hands obey my blood,
They are apt enough to dislocate and tear 65
Thy flesh and bones. Howe'er thou art a fiend,
A woman's shape doth shield thee.

Gon. Marry, your manhood — Mew!

(*Enter a* MESSENGER.)

Alb. What news?

¹ Freely, the passage may be read: I distrust your
make-up. A nature which forgets its filial duty cannot
be trusted. She who will sever relationships with her
family (Lear) will come to a bad end.

² A bear at the head of which bears are pulling.

³ cowardly.

⁴ Don't turn your features into those of a monster.

Mess. O, my good lord, the Duke of Cornwall's
    dead;   70
Slain by his servant, going to put out
The other eye of Gloucester.
    Alb.   Gloucester's eyes!
    Mess. A servant that he bred, thrill'd with re-
    morse,
Oppos'd against the act, bending his sword
To his great master; who, thereat enrag'd,   75
Flew on him, and amongst them fell'd him dead;
But not without that harmful stroke, which since
Hath pluck'd him after.
    Alb.   This shows you are above,
You justicers, that these our nether crimes
So speedily can venge! But, O poor Gloucester!
Lost he his other eye?
    Mess.   Both, both, my lord.   81
This letter, madam, craves a speedy answer.
'Tis from your sister.
    Gon. (*Aside.*) One way I like this well;
But being widow, and my Gloucester with her,
May all the building in my fancy pluck   85
Upon my hateful life. Another way,
The news is not so tart. — I'll read, and answer.
                                    (*Exit.*)
    Alb. Where was his son when they did take his
    eyes?
    Mess. Come with my lady hither.
    Alb.   He is not here.   89
    Mess. No, my good lord; I met him back again.
    Alb. Knows he the wickedness?
    Mess. Ay, my good lord; 'twas he inform'd
    against him;
And quit the house on purpose, that their punish-
    ment
Might have the freer course.
    Alb.   Gloucester, I live   94
To thank thee for the love thou show'dst the King,
And to revenge thine eyes. Come hither, friend;
Tell me what more thou know'st.   (*Exeunt.*)

SCENE III. *The French camp near Dover.*

(*Enter* KENT *and a* GENTLEMAN.)

    Kent. Why the King of France is so suddenly
gone back, know you no reason?
    Gent. Something he left imperfect in the state,
which since his coming forth is thought of; which
imports to the kingdom so much fear and dan-   5
ger that his personal return was most required and
necessary.
    Kent. Who hath he left behind him General?
    Gent. The Marshal of France, Monsieur La
Far.   10
    Kent. Did your letters pierce the Queen to any
demonstration of grief?

    Gent. Ay, sir; she took them, read them in my
    presence;
And now and then an ample tear trill'd down
Her delicate cheek. It seem'd she was a queen   15
Over her passion, who, most rebel-like,
Sought to be king o'er her.
    Kent.   O, then it mov'd her.
    Gent. Not to a rage; patience and sorrow strove
Who should express her goodliest. You have seen
Sunshine and rain at once: her smiles and tears   20
Were like a better way; those happy smilets
That play'd on her ripe lip seem'd not to know
What guests were in her eyes, which, parted thence,
As pearls from diamonds dropp'd. In brief,
Sorrow would be a rarity most beloved,   25
If all could so become it.
    Kent.   Made she no verbal question?
    Gent. Faith, once or twice she heav'd the name
    of "father"
Pantingly forth, as if it press'd her heart;
Cried, "Sisters! sisters! Shame of ladies! sisters!
Kent! father! sisters! What, i' the storm? i' the
    night?   30
Let pity not be believ'd!" There she shook
The holy water from her heavenly eyes;
And, clamor-moistened, then away she started
To deal with grief alone.
    Kent.   It is the stars,
The stars above us, govern our conditions;   35
Else one self mate and make could not beget
Such different issues. You spoke not with her
    since?
    Gent. No.
    Kent. Was this before the King return'd?
    Gent.   No, since.
    Kent. Well, sir, the poor distressed Lear's i' the
    town;   40
Who sometime, in his better tune, remembers
What we are come about, and by no means
Will yield to see his daughter.
    Gent.   Why, good sir?
    Kent. A sovereign shame so elbows him. His
    own unkindness,
That stripp'd her from his benediction, turn'd her
To foreign casualties, gave her dear rights   46
To his dog-hearted daughters, — these things
    sting
His mind so venomously, that burning shame
Detains him from Cordelia.
    Gent.   Alack, poor gentleman!
    Kent. Of Albany's and Cornwall's powers you
    heard not?   50
    Gent. 'Tis so, they are afoot.
    Kent. Well, sir, I'll bring you to our master
    Lear,
And leave you to attend him. Some dear cause

Will in concealment wrap me up a while;
When I am known aright, you shall not grieve 55
Lending me this acquaintance.   I pray you, go
Along with me.   (*Exeunt.*)

SCENE IV.   *The same.   A tent.*

(*Enter, with drum and colors,* CORDELIA, DOC-
TOR, *and Soldiers.*)

Cor. Alack, 'tis he!   Why, he was met even now
As mad as the vex'd sea, singing aloud,
Crown'd with rank fumiter and furrow-weeds,
With hardocks, hemlock, nettles, cuckoo-flowers,
Darnel, and all the idle weeds that grow 5
In our sustaining corn.   A sentry send forth;
Search every acre in the high-grown field,
And bring him to our eye.   (*Exit an Officer.*)
               What can man's wisdom
In the restoring his bereaved sense?
He that helps him take all my outward worth. 10
   Doct. There is means, madam.
Our foster-nurse of nature is repose,
The which he lacks; that to provoke in him,
Are many simples operative, whose power
Will close the eye of anguish.
   Cor.   All blest secrets, 15
All you unpublish'd virtues of the earth,
Spring with my tears! be aidant and remediate [1]
In the good man's distress!   Seek, seek for him,
Lest his ungovern'd rage dissolve the life
That wants the means to lead it.

(*Enter a* MESSENGER.)

   Mess.   News, madam! 20
The British powers are marching hitherward.
   Cor. 'Tis known before; our preparation stands
In expectation of them.   O dear father,
It is thy business that I go about;
Therefore great France 25
My mourning and importune tears hath pitied.
No blown ambition doth our arms incite,
But love, dear love, and our ag'd father's right.
Soon may I hear and see him!   (*Exeunt.*)

SCENE V.   *Gloucester's castle.*

(*Enter* REGAN *and Steward* OSWALD.)

   Reg. But are my brother's powers set forth?
   Osw.   Ay, madam.
   Reg. Himself in person there?
   Osw.   Madam, with much ado.
Your sister is the better soldier.
   Reg. Lord Edmund spake not with your lord at
home?
   Osw. No, madam. 5

[1] helpful and healing.

   Reg. What might import my sister's letter to
him?
   Osw. I know not, lady.
   Reg. Faith, he is posted hence on serious matter.
It was great ignorance, Gloucester's eyes being out,
To let him live; where he arrives he moves 10
All hearts against us.   Edmund, I think, is gone,
In pity of his misery, to dispatch
His nighted life; moreover, to descry
The strength o' the enemy.
   Osw. I must needs after him, madam, with my
letter. 15
   Reg. Our troops set forth to-morrow, stay with
us;
The ways are dangerous.
   Osw.   I may not, madam:
My lady charg'd my duty in this business.
   Reg. Why should she write to Edmund?   Might
not you
Transport her purposes by word?   Belike 20
Some things — I know not what.   I'll love thee
much,
Let me unseal the letter.
   Osw.   Madam, I had rather ——
   Reg. I know your lady does not love her hus-
band;
I am sure of that; and at her late being here
She gave strange œillades [1] and most speaking
looks
To noble Edmund.   I know you are of her bosom. [2] 25
   Osw. I, madam?
   Reg. I speak in understanding; y' are, I know't.
Therefore I do advise you, take this note: [3]
My lord is dead; Edmund and I have talk'd; 30
And more convenient is he for my hand
Than for your lady's.   You may gather more.
If you do find him, pray you, give him this;
And when your mistress hears thus much from you,
I pray, desire her call her wisdom to her. 35
So, fare you well.
If you do chance to hear of that blind traitor,
Preferment falls on him that cuts him off.
   Osw. Would I could meet him, madam!   I
should show
What party I do follow.
   Reg.   Fare thee well.   (*Exeunt.*) 40

SCENE VI.   *Fields near Dover.*

(*Enter* GLOUCESTER, *and* EDGAR, *dressed like a
peasant.*)

   Glou. When shall I come to the top of that same
hill?

[1] amorous glances.
[2] i.e., "in her confidence."
[3] i.e., "note this well."

Edg. You do climb up it now; look, how we
labor.

Glou. Methinks the ground is even.

Edg. Horrible steep.
Hark, do you hear the sea?

Glou. No, truly.

Edg. Why, then, your other senses grow imperfect 5
By your eyes' anguish.

Glou. So may it be, indeed.
Methinks thy voice is alter'd, and thou speak'st
In better phrase and matter than thou didst.

Edg. You're much deceiv'd. In nothing am I
chang'd
But in my garments.

Glou. Methinks you're better spoken.

Edg. Come on, sir, here's the place; stand still.
How fearful 11
And dizzy 'tis, to cast one's eyes so low!
The crows and choughs [1] that wing the midway
air
Show scarce so gross as beetles. Half way down
Hangs one that gathers samphire,[2] dreadful trade!
Methinks he seems no bigger than his head. 16
The fishermen, that walk upon the beach,
Appear like mice; and yond tall anchoring bark,
Diminish'd to her cock; her cock, a buoy
Almost too small for sight. The murmuring surge,
That on the unnumb'red idle pebbles chafes, 21
Cannot be heard so high. I'll look no more,
Lest my brain turn, and the deficient sight
Topple down headlong.

Glou. Set me where you stand.

Edg. Give me your hand; you are now within a
foot 25
Of the extreme verge. For all beneath the moon
Would I not leap upright.

Glou. Let go my hand.
Here, friend, 's another purse; in it a jewel
Well worth a poor man's taking. Fairies and
gods
Prosper it with thee! Go thou further off; 30
Bid me farewell, and let me hear thee going.

Edg. Now fare ye well, good sir.

Glou. With all my heart.

Edg. Why I do trifle thus with his despair
Is done to cure it.

Glou. (*Kneeling.*) O you mighty gods!
This world I do renounce, and in your sights 35
Shake patiently my great affliction off.
If I could bear it longer, and not fall
To quarrel with your great opposeless wills,
My snuff [3] and loathed part of nature should

[1] jack-daws.
[2] An herb much used in making relish.
[3] base part.

Burn itself out. If Edgar live, O bless him! 40
Now, fellow, fare thee well.

Edg. Gone, sir; farewell!
— And yet I know not how conceit may rob
The treasury of life, when life itself
Yields to the theft. (GLOU. *throws himself for-
ward.*) Had he been where he thought,
By this had thought been past. Alive or dead? —
Ho, you sir! friend! Hear you, sir! speak! — 46
Thus might he pass indeed; yet he revives. —
What are you, sir?

Glou. Away, and let me die.

Edg. Hadst thou been aught but gossamer,
feathers, air,
So many fathom down precipitating, 50
Thou'dst shiver'd like an egg: but thou dost
breathe;
Hast heavy substance; bleed'st not; speak'st; art
sound.
Ten masts at each make not the altitude
Which thou hast perpendicularly fell.
Thy life's a miracle. Speak yet again. 55

Glou. But have I fallen, or no?

Edg. From the dread summit of this chalky
bourn.
Look up a-height; the shrill-gorg'd lark so far
Cannot be seen or heard. Do but look up.

Glou. Alack, I have no eyes. 60
Is wretchedness depriv'd that benefit,
To end itself by death? 'Twas yet some comfort,
When misery could beguile the tyrant's rage,
And frustrate his proud will.

Edg. Give me your arm.
Up: so. How is't? Feel you your legs? You
stand. 65

Glou. Too well, too well.

Edg. This is above all strangeness.
Upon the crown o' the cliff, what thing was that
Which parted from you?

Glou. A poor unfortunate beggar.

Edg. As I stood here below, methought his eyes
Were two full moons; he had a thousand noses, 70
Horns whelk'd [1] and waved like the enridged sea.
It was some fiend; therefore, thou happy father,
Think that the clearest gods, who make them
honors
Of men's impossibilities, have preserv'd thee.

Glou. I do remember now. Henceforth I'll
bear 75
Affliction till it do cry out itself,
"Enough, enough," and die. That thing you
speak of,
I took it for a man; often 'twould say,
"The fiend, the fiend!" He led me to that place.

Edg. Bear free and patient thoughts.

[1] knobby.

(*Enter* LEAR *fantastically dressed with wild flowers.*)

But who comes here? 80
The safer sense will ne'er accommodate
His master thus.

Lear. No, they cannot touch me for coining;
I am the King himself.

Edg. O thou side-piercing sight! 85

Lear. Nature's above art in that respect.
There's your press-money.[1] That fellow handles
his bow like a crow-keeper;[2] draw me a clothier's
yard. Look, look, a mouse! Peace, peace; this
piece of toasted cheese will do 't. There's 90
my gauntlet; I'll prove it on a giant. Bring up
the brown bills.[3] O, well flown, bird! I' the clout,
i' the clout.[4] Hewgh! Give the word.[5]

Edg. Sweet marjoram.

Lear. Pass. 95

Glou. I know that voice.

Lear. Ha! Goneril, with a white beard! They
flatter'd me like a dog, and told me I had the white
hairs in my beard ere the black ones were there.
To say "ay" and "no" to everything that I 100
said! "Ay" and "no" too was no good divinity.
When the rain came to wet me once, and the wind
to make me chatter; when the thunder would not
peace at my bidding; there I found 'em, there I
smelt 'em out. Go to, they are not men o' 105
their words: they told me I was everything; 'tis a
lie, I am not ague-proof.

Glou. The trick of that voice I do well remember.
Is't not the King?

Lear. Ay, every inch a king!
When I do stare, see how the subject quakes. 110
I pardon that man's life. What was thy cause?
Adultery?
Thou shalt not die. Die for adultery! No:
The wren goes to 't, and the small gilded fly
Does lecher in my sight. 115
Let copulation thrive; for Gloucester's bastard son
Was kinder to his father than my daughters
Got 'tween the lawful sheets.
To 't, luxury, pell-mell! for I lack soldiers.
Behold yond simp'ring dame, 120
Whose face between her forks presages snow,
That minces[6] virtue, and does shake the head
To hear of pleasure's name, —
The fitchew,[7] nor the soiled horse,[8] goes to't
With a more riotous appetite. 125
Down from the waist they are Centaurs,

[1] A fee paid soldiers when they are pressed into service.
[2] scarecrow.   [3] pikes.   [4] bull's-eye.
[5] pass-word.   [6] pretends.
[7] pole-cat.   [8] An over-fed horse

Though women all above;
But to the girdle do the gods inherit,
Beneath is all the fiends';
There's hell, there's darkness, there's the sulphurous pit, 130
Burning, scalding, stench, consumption; fie, fie, fie!
pah, pah! Give me an ounce of civet;[1] good
apothecary, sweeten my imagination. There's
money for thee.

Glou. O, let me kiss that hand! 135

Lear. Let me wipe it first; it smells of mortality.

Glou. O ruin'd piece of nature! This great world
Shall so wear out to nought. Dost thou know me?

Lear. I remember thine eyes well enough.
Dost thou squiny[2] at me? No, do thy worst, 140
blind Cupid; I'll not love. Read thou this challenge; mark but the penning of it.

Glou. Were all thy letters suns, I could not see.

Edg. (*Aside.*) I would not take this from report.
It is;
And my heart breaks at it. 145

Lear. Read.

Glou. What, with the case of eyes?

Lear. O, ho, are you there with me? No eyes
in your head, nor no money in your purse? Your
eyes are in a heavy case, your purse in a light; 150
yet you see how this world goes.

Glou. I see it feelingly.

Lear. What, art mad? A man may see how this
world goes with no eyes. Look with thine ears;
see how yond justice rails upon yond simple 155
thief. Hark, in thine ear: change places, and,
handy-dandy, which is the justice, which is the
thief? Thou hast seen a farmer's dog bark at a
beggar?

Glou. Ay, sir. 160

Lear. And the creature run from the cur?
There thou mightst behold the great image of
authority: a dog's obey'd in office.
Thou rascal beadle, hold thy bloody hand!
Why dost thou lash that whore? Strip thy own back; 165
Thou hotly lusts to use her in that kind
For which thou whip'st her. The usurer hangs the cozener.[3]
Through tatter'd clothes great vices do appear;
Robes and furr'd gowns hide all. Plate sins with gold
And the strong lance of justice hurtless breaks;
Arm it in rags, a pigmy's straw does pierce it. 171
None does offend, none, I say, none; I'll able 'em.
Take that of me, my friend, who have the power
To seal the accuser's lips. Get thee glass eyes,
And, like a scurvy politician, seem 175

[1] perfume.   [2] squint.   [3] a cheat.

To see the things thou dost not. Now, now, now,
  now.
Pull off my boots; harder, harder: so.

  Edg. O, matter and impertinency mix'd!
Reason in madness!

  Lear. If thou wilt weep my fortunes, take my
  eyes.   180
I know thee well enough; thy name is Gloucester.
Thou must be patient; we came crying hither.
Thou know'st, the first time that we smell the air,
We wawl and cry. I will preach to thee; mark.

  Glou. Alack, alack the day!   185

  Lear. When we are born, we cry that we are come
To this great stage of fools. — This a good block.[1]
It were a delicate stratagem, to shoe
A troop of horse with felt. I'll put 't in proof;
And when I have stol'n upon these son-in-laws, 190
Then, kill, kill, kill, kill, kill, kill!

      (*Enter a* GENTLEMAN *with Attendants.*)

  Gent. O, here he is! Lay hand upon him. Sir,
Your most dear daughter —

  Lear. No rescue? What, a prisoner? I am even
The natural fool of fortune. Use me well; 195
You shall have ransom. Let me have surgeons;
I am cut to the brains.

  Gent.   You shall have anything.

  Lear. No seconds? All myself?
Why, this would make a man a man of salt,[2]
To use his eyes for garden water-pots, 200
Ay, and laying autumn's dust.

  Gent.   Good sir, —

  Lear. I will die bravely, like a smug bridegroom.
  What!
I will be jovial. Come, come; I am a king,
My masters, know you that?

  Gent. You are a royal one, and we obey you. 205

  Lear. Then there's life in 't. Come, an you get
it, you shall get it by running. Sa, sa, sa, sa.
      (*Exit running; attendants follow.*)

  Gent. A sight most pitiful in the meanest wretch,
Past speaking of in a king! Thou hast one
  daughter
Who redeems Nature from the general curse 210
Which twain have brought her to.

  Edg. Hail, gentle sir.

  Gent.   Sir, speed you: what's your will?

  Edg. Do you hear aught, sir, of a battle toward?

  Gent. Most sure and vulgar; every one hears
  that,
Which can distinguish sound.

  Edg.   But, by your favor, 215
How near's the other army?

---

[1] Probably, *hat*. If it were a felt hat, it would explain his plan for shoeing the troop of horse.

[2] The salt of tears.

  Gent. Near and on speedy foot; the main descry[1]
Stands on the hourly thought.

  Edg.   I thank you, sir; that's all.

  Gent. Though that the Queen on special cause
  is here,
Her army is mov'd on.   (*Exit.*)

  Edg.   I thank you, sir. 220

  Glou. You ever-gentle gods, take my breath
  from me;
Let not my worser spirit tempt me again
To die before you please!

  Edg.   Well pray you, father.

  Glou. Now, good sir, what are you?

  Edg. A most poor man, made tame to fortune's
  blows;   225
Who, by the art of known and feeling sorrows,
Am pregnant to good pity. Give me your hand,
I'll lead you to some biding.

  Glou.   Hearty thanks;
The bounty and the benison of Heaven
To boot, and boot!

      (*Enter Steward* OSWALD.)

  Osw.   A proclaim'd prize! Most happy! 230
That eyeless head of thine was first fram'd flesh
To raise my fortunes. Thou old unhappy traitor,
Briefly thyself remember; the sword is out
That must destroy thee.

  Glou.   Now let thy friendly hand
Put strength enough to 't.   (*Edgar interposes.*)

  Osw.   Wherefore, bold peasant, 235
Dar'st thou support a publish'd traitor? Hence;
Lest that the infection of his fortune take
Like hold on thee. Let go his arm.

  Edg. 'Chill[2] not let go, zir, without vurther
'casion.   240

  Osw. Let go, slave, or thou diest!

  Edg. Good gentleman, go your gait, and let
poor volk pass. An 'chud[3] ha' bin zwagger'd[4]
out of my life, 'twould not ha' bin zo long as 'tis
by a vortnight. Nay, come not near th' old 245
man; keep out, 'che vor ye,[5] or Ise try whether
your costard[6] or my ballow[7] be the harder.
'Chill be plain with you.

  Osw. Out, dunghill!

  Edg. 'Chill pick your teeth, zir. Come, no
matter vor your foins.[8]   251

    (*They fight, and Edgar knocks him down.*)

  Osw. Slave, thou hast slain me. Villain, take
  my purse.
If ever thou wilt thrive, bury my body;
And give the letters which thou find'st about me

---

[1] i.e., the main army will be descried shortly.

[2] I will.   [3] If I could.

[4] swaggered.   [5] I warn you.

[6] head.   [7] cudgel.   [8] thrusts (in fencing).

To Edmund Earl of Gloucester; seek him out 255
Upon the English party. O, untimely death!
Death!   (*Dies.*)

Edg.   I know thee well; a serviceable villain,
As duteous to the vices of thy mistress
As badness would desire.

Glou.   What, is he dead?

Edg. Sit you down, father; rest you.   260
Let's see these pockets; the letters that he speaks
    of
May be my friends. He's dead; I am only sorry
He had no other death's-man. Let us see.
Leave, gentle wax; and, manners, blame us not.
To know our enemies' minds, we rip their hearts;
Their papers, is more lawful.   266

(*Reads the letter.*) "Let our reciprocal vows be
remem'bred. You have many opportunities to
cut him off; if your will want not, time and place
will be fruitfully offer'd. There is nothing 270
done, if he return the conqueror; then am I the
prisoner, and his bed my gaol; from the loathed
warmth whereof deliver me, and supply the place
for your labor.

"Your — wife, so I would say —   275
         "Affectionate servant,
              "GONERIL."

O indistinguish'd space of woman's will!
A plot upon her virtuous husband's life;
And the exchange my brother! Here, in the sands,
Thee I'll rake up, the post unsanctified   281
Of murderous lechers; and in the mature time
With this ungracious paper strike the sight
Of the death-practis'd duke. For him 'tis well
That of thy death and business I can tell. 285

Glou. The King is mad; how stiff is my vile
    sense
That I stand up and have ingenious [1] feeling
Of my huge sorrows! Better I were distract;
So should my thoughts be sever'd from my griefs,
                          (*Drum afar off.*)
And woes by wrong imaginations lose   290
The knowledge of themselves.

Edg.   Give me your hand.
Far off, methinks, I hear the beaten drum.
Come, father, I'll bestow you with a friend.
                              (*Exeunt.*)

SCENE VII. *A tent in the French camp.*

(*Enter* CORDELIA, KENT, *and* DOCTOR.)

Cor. O thou good Kent, how shall I live and
    work
To match thy goodness? My life will be too short,
And every measure fail me.

Kent. To be acknowledg'd, madam, is o'erpaid.

[1] conscious.

All my reports go with the modest truth;   5
Nor more nor clipp'd, but so.

Cor.   Be better suited;
These weeds [1] are memories of those worser hours.
I prithee, put them off.

Kent.   Pardon, dear madam;
Yet to be known shortens my made intent.
My boon I make it, that you know me not   10
Till time and I think meet.

Cor. Then be't so, my good lord. (*To the* DOC-
TOR.) How does the King?

Doct. Madam, sleeps still.

Cor. O you kind gods,
Cure this great breach in his abused nature! 15
The untun'd and jarring senses, O, wind up
Of this child-changed [2] father!

Doct.   So please your Majesty
That we may wake the King? He hath slept long.

Cor. Be govern'd by your knowledge, and pro-
    ceed
I' the sway of your own will.

(*Enter* LEAR *in a chair carried by Servants.*
GENTLEMAN *in attendance.*)

                          Is he array'd? 20

Gent. Ay, madam; in the heaviness of sleep
We put fresh garments on him.

Doct. Be by, good madam, when we do awake
    him;
I doubt not of his temperance.

Cor.   Very well.

Doct. Please you, draw near. — Louder the
    music there!   25

Cor. O my dear father! Restoration hang
Thy medicine on my lips; and let this kiss
Repair those violent harms that my two sisters
Have in thy reverence made!

Kent.   Kind and dear princess!

Cor. Had you not been their father, these white
    flakes
Did challenge pity of them. Was this a face 30
To be oppos'd against the warring winds?
To stand against the deep dread-bolted thunder?
In the most terrible and nimble stroke
Of quick, cross lightning? to watch — poor
    perdu? [3]   35
With this thin helm? Mine enemy's dog,
Though he had bit me, should have stood that
    night
Against my fire; and wast thou fain, poor father,
To hovel thee with swine and rogues forlorn
In short and musty straw? Alack, alack!   40

[1] clothes.
[2] Changed by the action of his children.
[3] A military term denoting a soldier assigned a dangerous post.

'Tis wonder that thy life and wits at once
Had not concluded all. He wakes; speak to him.
   Doct. Madam, do you; 'tis fittest.
   Cor. How does my royal lord? How fares your
      Majesty?
   Lear. You do me wrong to take me out o' the
      grave.   45
Thou art a soul in bliss; but I am bound
Upon a wheel of fire, that mine own tears
Do scald like molten lead.
   Cor.   Sir, do you know me?
   Lear. You are a spirit, I know; when did you die?
   Cor. Still, still, far wide!   50
   Doct. He's scarce awake; let him alone a while.
   Lear. Where have I been? Where am I? Fair
      daylight?
I am mightily abus'd. I should even die with pity,
To see another thus. I know not what to say.
I will not swear these are my hands. Let's see;   55
I feel this pin prick. Would I were assur'd
Of my condition!
   Cor.   O, look upon me, sir,
And hold your hand in benediction o'er me.
No, sir, you must not kneel.
   Lear.   Pray, do not mock me.
I am a very foolish fond old man,   60
Fourscore and upward, not an hour more nor less;
And, to deal plainly,
I fear I am not in my perfect mind.
Methinks I should know you, and know this man;
Yet I am doubtful; for I am mainly ignorant   65
What place this is, and all the skill I have
Remembers not these garments; nor I know not
Where I did lodge last night. Do not laugh at
      me;
For, as I am a man, I think this lady
To be my child Cordelia.
   Cor.   And so I am, I am.   70
   Lear. Be your tears wet? Yes, faith. I pray,
      weep not.
If you have poison for me, I will drink it.
I know you do not love me; for your sisters
Have, as I do remember, done me wrong: 74
You have some cause, they have not.
   Cor.   No cause, no cause.
   Lear. Am I in France?
   Kent.   In your own kingdom, sir.
   Lear. Do not abuse me.
   Doct. Be comforted, good madam; the great
      rage,
You see, is kill'd in him: and yet it is danger
To make him even o'er the time he has lost.   80
Desire him to go in; trouble him no more
Till further settling.
   Cor. Will 't please your Highness walk?
   Lear.   You must bear with me.

Pray you now, forget and forgive; I am old and
      foolish.
        (*Exeunt all but* KENT *and* GENTLEMAN.)
   Gent. Holds it true, sir, that the Duke of Corn-
wall was so slain?   86
   Kent. Most certain, sir.
   Gent. Who is conductor of his people?
   Kent. As 'tis said, the bastard son of Gloucester.
   Gent. They say Edgar, his banish'd son, is with
the Earl of Kent in Germany.   91
   Kent. Report is changeable. 'Tis time to look
about; the powers of the kingdom approach apace.
   Gent. The arbitrement [1] is like to be bloody.
Fare you well, sir.   (*Exit.*)   95
   Kent. My point and period will be thoroughly
      wrought,
Or well or ill, as this day's battle's fought. (*Exit.*)

ACT V

SCENE I. *The British camp, near Dover.*

(*Enter, with drum and colors,* EDMUND, REGAN,
Gentlemen, and Soldiers.)

   Edm. Know of the Duke if his last purpose hold,
Or whether since he is advis'd by aught
To change the course. He's full of alteration
And self-reproving; bring his constant pleasure.
        (*To a Gentleman, who goes out.*)
   Reg. Our sister's man is certainly miscarried. 5
   Edm. 'Tis to be doubted, madam.
   Reg.   Now, sweet lord,
You know the goodness I intend upon you.
Tell me — but truly — but then speak the truth,
Do you not love my sister?
   Edm.   In honor'd love.
   Reg. But have you never found my brother's
      way   10
To the forfended [2] place?
   Edm.   That thought abuses you.
   Reg. I am doubtful that you have been con-
      junct
And bosom'd with her, — as far as we call hers.
   Edm. No, by mine honor, madam.
   Reg. I never shall endure her. Dear my lord,
Be not familiar with her.
   Edm.   Fear me not.   16
She and the Duke her husband!

(*Enter, with drum and colors,* ALBANY, GON-
ERIL, *and Soldiers.*)

   Gon. (*Aside.*) I had rather lose the battle than
      that sister
Should loosen him and me.
   Alb. Our very loving sister, well be-met.   20
   [1] settlement.   [2] forbidden.

Sir, this I heard: the King is come to his daughter,
With others whom the rigor of our state
Forc'd to cry out. Where I could not be honest,
I never yet was valiant. For this business,
It toucheth us, as France invades our land, 25
Not bolds the King, with others, whom, I fear,
Most just and heavy causes make oppose.

Edm. Sir, you speak nobly.

Reg. Why is this reason'd?

Gon. Combine together 'gainst the enemy;
For these domestic and particular broils 30
Are not the question here.

Alb. Let's then determine
With the ancient of war on our proceeding.

Edm. I shall attend you presently at your tent.

Reg. Sister, you'll go with us?

Gon. No. 35

Reg. 'Tis most convenient; pray you, go with us.

Gon. (*Aside.*) O, ho, I know the riddle.¹ — I will
go. (*Exeunt both the armies.*)

(*As they are going out, enter* EDGAR *disguised.*
ALBANY *remains.*)

Edg. If e'er your Grace had speech with man so
poor,
Hear me one word.

Alb. I'll overtake you. — Speak.

Edg. Before you fight the battle, ope this letter.
If you have victory, let the trumpet sound 41
For him that brought it. Wretched though I
seem,
I can produce a champion that will prove
What is avouch'd there. If you miscarry,
Your business of the world hath so an end, 45
And machination ceases. Fortune love you!

Alb. Stay till I have read the letter.

Edg. I was forbid it.
When time shall serve, let but the herald cry,
And I'll appear again. (*Exit.*)

Alb. Why, fare thee well; I will o'erlook thy
paper. 50

(*Re-enter* EDMUND.)

Edm. The enemy's in view; draw up your
powers.
Here is the guess of their true strength and forces
By diligent discovery; but your haste
Is now urg'd on you.

Alb. We will greet the time.
(*Exit.*)

Edm. To both these sisters have I sworn my
love; 55
Each jealous of the other, as the stung
Are of the adder. Which of them shall I take?

¹ i.e., I know you want to watch my conduct with
Edmund.

Both? one? or neither? Neither can be enjoy'd,
If both remain alive. To take the widow
Exasperates, makes mad her sister Goneril; 60
And hardly shall I carry out my side,
Her husband being alive. Now then we'll use
His countenance for the battle; which being done,
Let her who would be rid of him devise
His speedy taking off. As for the mercy 65
Which he intends to Lear and to Cordelia,
The battle done, and they within our power,
Shall never see his pardon; for my state
Stands on me to defend, not to debate. (*Exit.*)

SCENE II. *A field between the two camps.*

(*Alarum within. Enter, with drum and colors,* LEAR,
CORDELIA, *and Soldiers, over the stage; and
exeunt.*)

(*Enter* EDGAR *and* GLOUCESTER.)

Edg. Here, father, take the shadow of this tree
For your good host; pray that the right may thrive.
If ever I return to you again,
I'll bring you comfort.

Glou. Grace go with you, sir!
(*Exit* EDGAR.)

(*Alarum and retreat within. Re-enter* EDGAR.)

Edg. Away, old man; give me thy hand; away!
King Lear hath lost, he and his daughter ta'en. 6
Give me thy hand; come on.

Glou. No further, sir; a man may rot even here.

Edg. What, in ill thoughts again? Men must
endure
Their going hence, even as their coming hither; 10
Ripeness is all. Come on.

Glou. And that's true too.
(*Exeunt.*)

SCENE III. *The British camp near Dover.*

(*Enter, in conquest, with drum and colors,* EDMUND;
LEAR *and* CORDELIA *as prisoners:* CAPTAIN,
Soldiers, etc.)

Edm. Some officers take them away. Good
guard,
Until their greater pleasures first be known
That are to censure them.

Cor. We are not the first
Who, with best meaning, have incurr'd the worst.
For thee, oppressed king, I am cast down; 5
Myself could else out-frown false Fortune's frown.
Shall we not see these daughters and these sisters?

Lear. No, no, no, no! Come, let's away to
prison;
We two alone will sing like birds i' the cage.

When thou dost ask me blessing, I'll kneel down
And ask of thee forgiveness. So we'll live, 11
And pray, and sing, and tell old tales, and laugh
At gilded butterflies, and hear poor rogues
Talk of court news; and we'll talk with them too,
Who loses and who wins; who's in, who's out; 15
And take upon's the mystery of things
As if we were God's spies; and we'll wear out,
In a wall'd prison, packs and sects of great ones,
That ebb and flow by the moon.

    Edm.   Take them away.

    Lear. Upon such sacrifices, my Cordelia, 20
The gods themselves throw incense. Have I
    caught thee?
He that parts us shall bring a brand from heaven,
And fire us hence like foxes. Wipe thine eyes;
The good-years shall devour them, flesh and fell,
Ere they shall make us weep. We'll see 'em
    starv'd first. 25
Come.   (*Exeunt* LEAR *and* CORDELIA, *guarded.*)

    Edm. Come hither, captain; hark.
Take thou this note (*giving a paper*); go follow
    them to prison.
One step I have advanc'd thee; if thou dost
As this instructs thee, thou dost make thy way
To noble fortunes. Know thou this, that men 30
Are as the time is; to be tender-minded
Does not become a sword. Thy great employ-
    ment
Will not bear question; either say thou'lt do 't,
Or thrive by other means.

    Capt.   I'll do 't, my lord.

    Edm. About it; and write happy when thou hast
    done. 35
Mark, I say, instantly; and carry it so
As I have set it down.

    Capt. I cannot draw a cart, nor eat dried oats;
If it be man's work, I'll do 't.   (*Exit.*)

    (*Flourish. Enter* ALBANY, GONERIL, REGAN,
      another CAPTAIN *and Soldiers.*)

    Alb. Sir, you have show'd to-day your valiant
    strain, 40
And fortune led you well. You have the captives
Who were the opposites of this day's strife;
I do require them of you, so to use them
As we shall find their merits and our safety
May equally determine.

    Edm.   Sir, I thought it fit 45
To send the old and miserable king
To some retention and appointed guard;
Whose age had charms in it, whose title more,
To pluck the common bosom on his side,
And turn our impress'd lances in our eyes 50
Which do command them. With him I sent the
    Queen,

My reason all the same; and they are ready
To-morrow, or at further space, to appear
Where you shall hold your session. At this time
We sweat and bleed: the friend hath lost his friend;
And the best quarrels, in the heat, are curs'd 56
By those that feel their sharpness:
The question of Cordelia and her father
Requires a fitter place.

    Alb.   Sir, by your patience,
I hold you but a subject of this war, 60
Not as a brother.

    Reg.   That's as we list to grace him.
Methinks our pleasure might have been demanded,
Ere you had spoke so far. He led our powers,
Bore the commission of my place and person;
The which immediacy may well stand up, 65
And call itself your brother.

    Gon.   Not so hot.
In his own grace he doth exalt himself,
More than in your addition.

    Reg.   In my rights,
By me invested, he compeers the best.

    Alb. That were the most, if he should husband
    you. 70

    Reg. Jesters do oft prove prophets.

    Gon.   Holla, holla!
That eye that told you so look'd but a-squint.

    Reg. Lady, I am not well;[1] else I should answer
From a full-flowing stomach.[2] General,
Take thou my soldiers, prisoners, patrimony; 75
Dispose of them, of me; the walls are thine.
Witness the world, that I create thee here
My lord and master.

    Gon.   Mean you to enjoy him?

    Alb. The let-alone lies not in your good will.

    Edm. Nor in thine, lord.

    Alb.   Half-blooded fellow, yes. 80

    Reg. (*To* EDMUND.) Let the drum strike, and
    prove my title thine.

    Alb. Stay yet; hear reason. Edmund, I arrest
    thee
On capital treason; and, in thy arrest,
This gilded serpent. (*Pointing to* GON.) For
    your claim, fair sister,
I bar it in the interest of my wife. 85
'Tis she is sub-contracted to this lord,
And I, her husband, contradict your bans.
If you will marry, make your loves to me,
My lady is bespoke.

    Gon.   An interlude!

    Alb. Thou art armed, Gloucester; let the trumpet
    sound. 90
If none appear to prove upon thy person
Thy heinous, manifest, and many treasons,

[1] Goneril's poison is taking effect.
[2] i.e, angrily.

There is my pledge (*throwing down a glove*). I'll
    prove it on thy heart,
Ere I taste bread, thou art in nothing less
Than I have here proclaim'd thee.

Reg.   Sick, O, sick! 95

Gon. (*Aside.*) If not, I'll ne'er trust medicine.

Edm. There's my exchange (*throwing down a
    glove*). What in the world he is
That names me traitor, villain-like he lies.
Call by the trumpet; — he that dares approach,
On him, on you, who not? I will maintain 100
My truth and honor firmly.

Alb. A herald, ho!

Edm.   A herald, ho, a herald!

Alb. Trust to thy single virtue; for thy soldiers,
All levied in my name, have in my name 104
Took their discharge.

Reg.   My sickness grows upon me.

Alb. She is not well; convey her to my tent.
                  (*Exit* REGAN, *led.*)

(*Enter a* HERALD.)

Come hither, herald, — Let the trumpet sound —
And read out this. 108

Capt. Sound, trumpet!   (*A trumpet sounds.*)

Her. (*Reads.*) "If any man of quality or degree
within the lists of the army will maintain upon
Edmund, supposed Earl of Gloucester, that he is
a manifold traitor, let him appear by the third
sound of the trumpet. He is bold in his defence."

Edm. Sound!   (*First trumpet.*) 115

Her. Again!   (*Second trumpet.*)

Her. Again!   (*Third trumpet.*)
              (*Trumpet answers within.*)

(*Enter* EDGAR, *at the third sound, armed, with a
trumpet before him.*)

Alb. Ask him his purposes, why he appears
Upon this call o' the trumpet.

Her.   What are you?
Your name, your quality? and why you answer 120
This present summons?

Edg.   Know, my name is lost,
By treason's tooth bare-gnawn and canker-bit;
Yet am I noble as the adversary
I come to cope.

Alb.   Which is that adversary?

Edg. What's he that speaks for Edmund Earl
    of Gloucester? 125

Edm. Himself; what say'st thou to him?

Edg.   Draw thy sword.
That, if my speech offend a noble heart,
Thy arm may do thee justice; here is mine.
Behold, it is the privilege of mine honors,
My oath, and my profession. I protest, 130

Maugre [1] thy strength, place, youth, and eminence,
Despite thy victor-sword and fire-new fortune,
Thy valor, and thy heart, thou art a traitor;
False to thy gods, thy brother, and thy father;
Conspirant 'gainst this high illustrious prince; 135
And, from the extremest upward of thy head
To the descent and dust below thy foot,
A most toad-spotted traitor. Say thou "No,"
This sword, this arm, and my best spirits are bent
To prove upon thy heart, whereto I speak, 140
Thou liest.

Edm.   In wisdom I should ask thy name;
But, since thy outside looks so fair and warlike,
And that thy tongue some 'say of breeding breathes,
What safe and nicely I might well delay,
By rule of knighthood, I disdain and spurn. 145
Back do I toss these treasons to thy head;
With the hell-hated lie o'erwhelm thy heart;
Which, for they yet glance by and scarcely bruise,
This sword of mine shall give them instant way,
Where they shall rest for ever. Trumpets,
    speak! 150
      (*Alarums. They fight.* EDMUND *falls.*)

Alb. Save him, save him!

Gon.   This is mere practice, Gloucester.
By the law of war thou wast not bound to answer
An unknown opposite. Thou art not vanquish'd.
But cozen'd [2] and beguil'd.

Alb.   Shut your mouth, dame,
Or with this paper shall I stop it. Hold, sir. —
Thou worse than any name, read thine own evil. 156
No tearing, lady; I perceive you know it.

Gon. Say, if I do, the laws are mine, not thine.
Who can arraign me for 't?   (*Exit.*)

Alb.   Most monstrous! oh! —
Know'st thou this paper?

Edm.   Ask me not what I know. 160

Alb. Go after her; she's desperate; govern her.

Edm. What you have charg'd me with, that have
    I done;
And more, much more; the time will bring it out.
'Tis past, and so am I. But what art thou 164
That hast this fortune on me? If thou'rt noble,
I do forgive thee.

Edg.   Let's exchange charity.
I am no less in blood than thou art, Edmund;
If more, the more thou'st wrong'd me.
My name is Edgar, and thy father's son.
The gods are just, and of our pleasant vices 170
Make instruments to plague us.
The dark and vicious place where thee he got
Cost him his eyes.

Edm.   Thou'st spoken right, 'tis true
The wheel is come full circle; I am here.

[1] in spite of.
[2] cheated.

Alb. Methought thy very gait did prophesy 175
A royal nobleness. I must embrace thee.
Let sorrow split my heart, if ever I
Did hate thee or thy father!
　　Edg.　　　　　　　　　Worthy prince, I know 't.
Alb. Where have you hid yourself?
How have you known the miseries of your father?
　　Edg. By nursing them, my lord. List a brief
　　　tale;　　　　　　　　　　　　　　　181
And when 'tis told, oh, that my heart would burst!
The bloody proclamation to escape,
That follow'd me so near, — oh, our lives' sweet-
　　ness!
That we the pain of death would hourly die 185
Rather than die at once! — taught me to shift
Into a madman's rags, to assume a semblance
That very dogs disdain'd; and in this habit
Met I my father with his bleeding rings, 189
Their precious stones new lost; became his guide,
Led him, begg'd for him, sav'd him from despair;
Never, — O fault! — reveal'd myself unto him,
Until some half-hour past, when I was arm'd.
Not sure, though hoping, of this good success,
I ask'd his blessing, and from first to last 195
Told him our pilgrimage; but his flaw'd heart,
Alack, too weak the conflict to support!
'Twixt two extremes of passion, joy and grief,
Burst smilingly.
　　Edm.　　　This speech of yours hath mov'd me,
And shall perchance do good. But speak you on;
You look as you had something more to say. 201
　　Alb. If there be more, more woeful, hold it in;
For I am almost ready to dissolve,
Hearing of this.
　　Edg.　　　　　This would have seem'd a period
To such as love not sorrow; but another, 205
To amplify too much, would make much more,
And top extremity.
Whilst I was big in clamor came there in a man,
Who, having seen me in my worst estate,
Shunn'd my abhorr'd society; but then, finding 210
Who 'twas that so endur'd, with his strong arms
He fastened on my neck, and bellowed out
As he'd burst heaven; threw him on my father;
Told the most piteous tale of Lear and him
That ever ear received; which in recounting, 215
His grief grew puissant,[1] and the strings of life
Began to crack. Twice then the trumpets
　　sounded,
And there I left him tranc'd.
　　Alb.　　　　　　　　But who was this?
　　Edg. Kent, sir, the banish'd Kent; who in
　　　disguise
Follow'd his enemy king, and did him service 220
Improper for a slave.
　　[1] powerful.

(*Enter a* GENTLEMAN *with a bloody knife.*)
Gent. Help, help, O, help!
Edg.　　　　　What kind of help?
Alb.　　　　　　　　　　　　　Speak, man.
Edg. What means this bloody knife?
Gent.　　　　　　　　　'Tis hot, it smokes;
It came even from the heart of — O, she's dead!
Alb. Who dead? Speak, man.　　　　　225
Gent. Your lady, sir, your lady; and her sister
By her is poison'd; she confesses it.
Edm. I was contracted to them both. All three
Now marry in an instant.
　　Edg.　　　　　　　Here comes Kent.

(*Enter* KENT.)
Alb. Produce the bodies, be they alive or dead.
This judgment of the heavens, that makes us
　　tremble,　　　　　　　　　　　　231
Touches us not with pity.　(*Exit* GENTLEMAN.)
　　　　　　　　　— O, is this he?
The time will not allow the compliment
Which very manners urges.
　　Kent.　　　　　　　I am come
To bid my king and master aye good-night. 235
Is he not here?
　　Alb.　　　　Great thing of us forgot!
Speak, Edmund, where's the King? and where's
　　Cordelia?
　　(*The bodies of* GONERIL *and* REGAN *are
　　　brought in.*)
See'st thou this object, Kent?
　　Kent. Alack, why thus?
　　Edm.　　　　　　Yet Edmund was belov'd!
The one the other poison'd for my sake, 240
And after slew herself.
　　Alb. Even so. Cover their faces.
　　Edm. I pant for life. Some good I mean to do,
Despite of mine own nature. Quickly send,
Be brief in it, to the castle; for my writ 245
Is on the life of Lear and on Cordelia.
Nay, send in time.
　　Alb.　　　　Run, run, O, run!
　　Edg. To who, my lord? Who has the office?
　　　Send
Thy token of reprieve.
　　Edm. Well thought on. Take my sword, 250
Give it the captain.
　　Edg.　　　　Haste thee, for thy life.
　　　　　　　　　　　　(*Exit* GENTLEMAN.)
　　Edm. He hath commission from thy wife and me
To hang Cordelia in the prison, and
To lay the blame upon her own despair,
That she fordid herself.　　　　　　255
　　Alb. The gods defend her! Bear him hence a
　　　while.　　　　　　　　(EDMUND *is borne off.*)

(*Re-enter* LEAR *with* CORDELIA *in his arms,* GENTLE-
MAN *following.*)

Lear. Howl, howl, howl! O, you are men of
stones!
Had I your tongues and eyes, I'd use them so
That heaven's vault should crack. She's gone
for ever!
I know when one is dead, and when one lives; 260
She's dead as earth. Lend me a looking-glass;
If that her breath will mist or stain the stone,
Why, then she lives.
Kent.   Is this the promis'd end?
Edg. Or image of that horror?
Alb.   Fall, and cease!
Lear. This feather stirs; she lives! If it be so,
It is a chance which does redeem all sorrows 266
That ever I have felt.
Kent. (*Kneeling.*)   O my good master!
Lear. Prithee, away.
Edg.   'Tis noble Kent, your friend.
Lear. A plague upon you, murderers, traitors
all!
I might have sav'd her; now she's gone for ever! 270
Cordelia, Cordelia! stay a little. Ha!
What is 't thou say'st? Her voice was ever soft,
Gentle, and low; an excellent thing in woman.
I kill'd the slave that was a-hanging thee.
Gent. 'Tis true, my lords, he did.
Lear.   Did I not, fellow? 275
I have seen the day, with my good biting falchion [1]
I would have made him skip. I am old now,
And these same crosses spoil me. Who are you?
Mine eyes are not o' the best. I'll tell you straight.
Kent. If Fortune brag of two she lov'd and
hated,   280
One of them we behold.
Lear. This is a dull sight. Are you not Kent?
Kent.   The same,
Your servant Kent. Where is your servant Caius?
Lear. He's a good fellow, I can tell you that;
He'll strike, and quickly too. He's dead and
rotten.   285
Kent. No, my good lord; I am the very man, —
Lear. I'll see that straight.
Kent. — That, from your first of difference and
decay,
Have follow'd your sad steps.
Lear.   You are welcome hither.
Kent. Nor no man else; all's cheerless, dark,
and deadly.   290

[1] sword.

Your eldest daughters have fordone themselves,
And desperately are dead.
Lear.   Ay, so I think.
Alb. He know not what he says; and vain is it
That we present us to him.

(*Enter a* MESSENGER.)

Edg.   Very bootless.
Mess. Edmund is dead, my lord.
Alb.   That's but a trifle here. — 295
You lords and noble friends, know our intent.
What comfort to this great decay may come
Shall be appli'd. For us, we will resign,
During the life of this old majesty,
To him our absolute power; (*to* EDGAR *and* KENT)
you, to your rights,   300
With boot, and such addition as your honors
Have more than merited. All friends shall taste
The wages of their virtue, and all foes
The cup of their deservings. O, see, see!
Lear. And my poor fool [1] is hang'd! No, no,
no life!   305
Why should a dog, a horse, a rat, have life,
And thou no breath at all? Thou'lt come no more,
Never, never, never, never, never!
Pray you, undo this button. Thank you, sir.
Do you see this? Look on her, look, her lips, 310
Look there, look there!   (*Dies.*)
Edg.   He faints! My lord, my lord!
Kent. Break, heart; I prithee, break!
Edg.   Look up, my lord.
Kent. Vex not his ghost; O, let him pass! He
hates him
That would upon the rack of this tough world
Stretch him out longer.
Edg.   He is gone, indeed. 315
Kent. The wonder is he hath endur'd so long;
He but usurp'd his life.
Alb. Bear them from hence. Our present busi-
ness
Is general woe. (*To* KENT *and* EDGAR.) Friends
of my soul, you twain
Rule in this realm, and the gor'd state sustain. 320
Kent. I have a journey, sir, shortly to go.
My master calls me; I must not say no.
Edg. The weight of this sad time we must obey;
Speak what we feel, not what we ought to say.
The oldest hath borne most; we that are young 325
Shall never see so much, nor live so long.
(*Exeunt, with a dead march.*)

[1] A term of endearment for Cordelia.

Jean Jacques Rousseau · 1712-1778

Turning from Shakespeare and Spenser to Rousseau, we leave the "Merry England" of the early seventeenth century for an artificially gay, but oppressed, France of the eighteenth century.

The reign of Louis XIV, which was surely no happy one for the common people of France, gave way to the regency of Louis' nephew, and this in turn to the rule of Louis XV. It was a period in which the government was against the clergy and the people against the state. Wars were almost interminable; the War of the Austrian Succession and the Seven Years' War in Europe and in America devoured the life and the patience of the people. A dissolute court left France too frequently to the rule of a Madame de Pompadour — "a prime minister in petticoats" — and of other royal mistresses. It was a period in which wit was more esteemed than morality. Toward the close of Rousseau's life, however, the people were tiring of a government by mistresses. Ominous rumblings indicated the approaching French Revolution. It was Rousseau's function to express the feeling of unrest.

The inclusion of the work of Jean Jacques Rousseau in a collection of world literature is justified not so much by his contribution to literature through the novel, the essay, poetry, or the drama — though he wrote in all these forms — as by the effect on literature of the doctrines which he advanced. His writing is less important than the influence his writing exercised. The romantic temper had manifested itself in many men before Rousseau — in Apuleius, Ovid, Boccaccio, Spenser, Shakespeare, in all the medieval romancers in fact. But with Rousseau came Romanticism itself. And with Rousseau came two revolutions — the American and the French.

A listing of the major doctrines in Rousseau's writing is almost tantamount to a restatement of the tenets of the Romantic Movement. Nature, Rousseau tells us, is a benevolent and safe guide; the closer both society and individual man approach the simplicity of primitive living, without actually returning to the state of the savage, the nobler and the happier we shall all be. We must, also, learn to trust the human heart as a guide to human action, since emotion and natural instinct prompt wiser conduct than does reason. The hero is the man of feeling, often melancholy, moved by sentiment to unhesitant tears before the ruins of old castles and stand'ng in silent ecstasy before the pathos of the setting sun. Civilization and life in the city cramp the spirit and foster hypocrisy. Real satisfaction comes in rustic simplicity. But Nature is to be respected not only as a picturesque manifestation of that satisfaction; it is as well the source of truly genuine religion. The individual must learn confidence in himself, and society must give the natural abilities of the individual full play. Liberty, in the writing of Rousseau, takes on added significance. Love is emphasized and sex is exalted.

"Man is born free, and everywhere he 's in chains" are the opening words of the *Social Contract*. It was Rousseau's purpose to strike off the shackles of convention which hampered man's freedom, and, interestingly enough, he succeeded in finding an audience in the formal society of the eighteenth century. His novel, *The New Héloïse*, in which these doctrines were most vividly expressed, went through fifty printings in the thirty-nine years between 1761 and 1800. "People had been the children of decorum for a hundred years, children of reason for at least fifty," writes Matthew Josephson, and "now, amid a general effusion of 'natural' sentiment, led by their intuition rather than reason, inspired by hope, and believing willingly the strange new dogma that man was born good, they moved more rapidly through a great transition toward a re-ordering of human society in the sense which the new prophet demanded."

Rousseau's most important works are: *Discourse on the Sciences and Arts* (1750), which first brought him public recognition; *Discourse on the Origin of Inequality among Men* (1755), of which a section is reprinted below; *La Nouvelle Héloïse* (1760), a novel presenting the ideas developed in the former essays and a book which was for many years a Bible to the romantics; the *Social Contract*

(1762), the most closely organized formulation of his theory of government and its relations to man and society; *Émile* (1762), a treatise on education; and the *Confessions* (published posthumously in 1781 and 1788), which constitutes one of the frankest autobiographical statements any writer has left to posterity, but one in which it is sometimes difficult to winnow truth from fancy.

The major facts in the life of Jean Jacques Rousseau may be quickly told. Of French origin, he was born in Geneva, Switzerland, in 1712. His father was a maker of watches who, while Rousseau was very young, found himself entangled with the law and left for France. As his mother had died in childbirth, Rousseau was brought up by relatives and was soon turned over as an apprentice, first to one trade and then to another. Finding these distasteful, he turned to travel and miscellaneous work, serving for a while as a lackey in the home of a man of wealth. Later he took up the teaching of music, at which he failed. Soon he was in Paris copying music for a livelihood. Here he met a domestic in his boarding-house, one Thérèse le Vasseur, who bore him five children, children that he promptly turned over to state foundling institutions to rear. Later in life he married Thérèse. In 1749 he won the prize offered by the Academy of Dijon for an essay on the relationship between civilization and morals. From this time on Rousseau's reputation was great, though it cannot be said that his place was secure. He was constantly in trouble, real or imaginary. His later years were mentally clouded. When he was not actually in difficulty he imagined himself persecuted. After the publication of *Émile* he left France for Switzerland; trouble in Switzerland led him to England; trouble in England led to his return to Paris; and trouble in Paris led to his retirement to a country-seat in France where he died at the home of a patron.

SUGGESTED REFERENCES: F. C. Green, *Jean-Jacques Rousseau. A Critical Study of His Life and Writings* (1955); Frances Winwar, *Jean-Jacques Rousseau. Conscience of an Era* (1961); Ernst Cassirer, *The Question of Jean-Jacques Rousseau* (1963).

A Discourse on the Origin of Inequality

In the essay of which the following pages form a part, Rousseau emphasizes two sorts of inequality: the inequality which springs from *natural* qualities and makes some men stronger, some more intelligent, than others; and, *social* inequality, or differences between people based on such artificial standards as class, fortune, birth, differences which are meaningless and should be discarded. Civilization with its emphasis on social standards, Rousseau holds, is an enemy of mankind. What is needed is a return to primitive values, not of the savage, but of man living naturally, unbiased by these artificial social standards. His essay says in prose what Burns said in verse:

The rank is but the guinea stamp:
The man's the gowd for a' that.

Rousseau would have man reaffirm his original dignity, his former freedom. Americans owe much to Rousseau for ideas promulgated in the following essay and in his *Social Contract*. Without these essays, our Declaration of Independence might have been delayed and would probably have been phrased differently. Rousseau taught a doctrine which was both romantic and democratic.

The translation which follows is that of G. D. H. Cole and is reprinted from *The Social Contract and Discourses of Jean Jacques Rousseau*, in *Everyman's Library*, published by E. P. Dutton & Co., Inc., New York.

5 The first man who, having enclosed a piece of ground, bethought himself of saying *This is mine*, and found people simple enough to believe him, was the real founder of civil society. From how many crimes, wars and murders, from how many 10 horrors and misfortunes might not any one have saved mankind, by pulling up the stakes, or filling up the ditch, and crying to his fellows, "Beware of listening to this impostor; you are undone if you once forget that the fruits of the earth belong to us 15 all, and the earth itself to nobody." But there is great probability that things had then already come to such a pitch, that they could no longer continue as they were; for the idea of property depends on many prior ideas, which could only be acquired 20 successively, and cannot have been formed all at once in the human mind. Mankind must have made very considerable progress, and acquired considerable knowledge and industry which they must also have transmitted and increased from age 25 to age, before they arrived at this last point of the state of nature. Let us then go farther back, and endeavor to unify under a single point of view that

slow succession of events and discoveries in the most natural order.

Man's first feeling was that of his own existence, and his first care that of self-preservation. The produce of the earth furnished him with all he needed, and instinct told him how to use it. Hunger and other appetites made him at various times experience various modes of existence; and among these was one which urged him to propagate his species — a blind propensity that, having nothing to do with the heart, produced a merely animal act. The want once gratified, the two sexes knew each other no more; and even the offspring was nothing to its mother, as soon as it could do without her.

Such was the condition of infant man; the life of an animal limited at first to mere sensations, and hardly profiting by the gifts nature bestowed on him, much less capable of entertaining a thought of forcing anything from her. But difficulties soon presented themselves, and it became necessary to learn how to surmount them: the height of the trees, which prevented him from gathering their fruits, the competition of other animals desirous of the same fruits, and the ferocity of those who needed them for their own preservation, all obliged him to apply himself to bodily exercises. He had to be active, swift of foot, and vigorous in fight. Natural weapons, stones and sticks, were easily found: he learnt to surmount the obstacles of nature, to contend in case of necessity with other animals, and to dispute for the means of subsistence even with other men, or to indemnify himself for what he was forced to give up to a stronger.

In proportion as the human race grew more numerous, men's cares increased. The difference of soils, climates and seasons, must have introduced some differences into their manner of living. Barren years, long and sharp winters, scorching summers which parched the fruits of the earth, must have demanded a new industry. On the seashore and the banks of rivers, they invented the hook and line, and became fishermen and eaters of fish. In the forests they made bows and arrows, and became huntsmen and warriors. In cold countries they clothed themselves with the skins of the beasts they had slain. The lightning, a volcano, or some lucky chance acquainted them with fire, a new resource against the rigors of winter: they next learned how to preserve this element, then how to reproduce it, and finally how to prepare with it the flesh of animals which before they had eaten raw.

This repeated relevance of various beings to himself, and one to another, would naturally give rise in the human mind to the perceptions of certain relations between them. Thus the relations which we denote by the terms, great, small, strong, weak,

swift, slow, fearful, bold, and the like, almost insensibly compared at need, must have at length produced in him a kind of reflection, or rather a mechanical prudence, which would indicate to him the precautions most necessary to his security.

The new intelligence which resulted from this development increased his superiority over other animals, by making him sensible of it. He would now endeavor, therefore, to ensnare them, would play them a thousand tricks, and though many of them might surpass him in swiftness or in strength, would in time become the master of some and the scourge of others. Thus, the first time he looked into himself, he felt the first emotion of pride; and, at a time when he scarce knew how to distinguish the different orders of beings, by looking upon his species as of the highest order, he prepared the way for assuming pre-eminence as an individual.

Other men, it is true, were not then to him what they now are to us, and he had no greater intercourse with them than with other animals; yet they were not neglected in his observations. The conformities, which he would in time discover between them, and between himself and his female, led him to judge of others which were not then perceptible; and finding that they all behaved as he himself would have done in like circumstances, he naturally inferred that their manner of thinking and acting was altogether in conformity with his own. This important truth, once deeply impressed on his mind, must have induced him, from an intuitive feeling more certain and much more rapid than any kind of reasoning, to pursue the rules of conduct, which he had best observe towards them, for his own security and advantage.

Taught by experience that the love of well-being is the sole motive of human actions, he found himself in a position to distinguish the few cases, in which mutual interest might justify him in relying upon the assistance of his fellows; and also the still fewer cases in which a conflict of interests might give cause to suspect them. In the former case, he joined in the same herd with them, or at most in some kind of loose association, that laid no restraint on its members, and lasted no longer than the transitory occasion that formed it. In the latter case, every one sought his own private advantage, either by open force, if he thought himself strong enough, or by address and cunning, if he felt himself the weaker.

In this manner, men may have insensibly acquired some gross ideas of mutual undertakings, and of the advantages of fulfilling them: that is, just so far as their present and apparent interest was concerned: for they were perfect strangers to foresight, and were so far from troubling themselves about the distant future, that they hardly thought of the morrow. If a deer was to be taken, every one saw that, in order to succeed, he must abide faithfully by his post: but if a hare happened to come within the reach of any one of them, it is not to be doubted that he pursued it without scruple, and, having seized his prey, cared very little, if by so doing he caused his companions to miss theirs.

It is easy to understand that such intercourse would not require a language much more refined than that of rooks or monkeys, who associate together for much the same purpose. Inarticulate cries, plenty of gestures and some imitative sounds, must have been for a long time the universal language; and by the addition, in every country, of some conventional articulate sounds (of which, as I have already intimated, the first institution is not too easy to explain) particular languages were produced; but these were rude and imperfect, and nearly such as are now to be found among some savage nations.

Hurried on by the rapidity of time, by the abundance of things I have to say, and by the almost insensible progress of things in their beginnings, I pass over in an instant a multitude of ages; for the slower the events were in their succession, the more rapidly may they be described.

These first advances enabled men to make others with greater rapidity. In proportion as they grew enlightened, they grew industrious. They ceased to fall asleep under the first tree, or in the first cave that afforded them shelter; they invented several kinds of implements of hard and sharp stones, which they used to dig up the earth, and to cut wood; they then made huts out of branches, and afterwards learnt to plaster them over with mud and clay. This was the epoch of a first revolution, which established and distinguished families, and introduced a kind of property, in itself the source of a thousand quarrels and conflicts. As, however, the strongest were probably the first to build themselves huts which they felt themselves able to defend, it may be concluded that the weak found it much easier and safer to imitate, than to attempt to dislodge them: and of those who were once provided with huts, none could have any inducement to appropriate that of his neighbor; not indeed so much because it did not belong to him, as because it could be of no use, and he could not make himself master of it without exposing himself to a desperate battle with the family which occupied it.

The first expansions of the human heart were the effects of a novel situation, which united husbands and wives, fathers and children, under one roof. The habit of living together soon gave rise to the finest feelings known to humanity, conjugal love and paternal affection. Every family became a little society, the more united because liberty and reciprocal attachment were the only bonds of its union. The sexes, whose manner of life had been hitherto the same, began now to adopt different ways of living. The women became more sedentary, and accustomed themselves to mind the hut and their children, while the men went abroad in search of their common subsistence. From living a softer life, both sexes also began to lose something of their strength and ferocity: but, if individuals became to some extent less able to encounter wild beasts separately, they found it, on the other hand, easier to assemble and resist in common.

The simplicity and solitude of man's life in this new condition, the paucity of his wants, and the implements he had invented to satisfy them, left him a great deal of leisure, which he employed to furnish himself with many conveniences unknown to his fathers: and this was the first yoke he inadvertently imposed on himself, and the first source of the evils he prepared for his descendants. For, besides continuing thus to enervate both body and mind, these conveniences lost with use almost all their power to please, and even degenerated into real needs, till the want of them became far more disagreeable than the possession of them had been pleasant. Men would have been unhappy at the loss of them, though the possession did not make them happy.

We can here see a little better how the use of speech became established, and insensibly improved in each family, and we may form a conjecture also concerning the manner in which various causes may have extended and accelerated the progress of language, by making it more and more necessary. Floods or earthquakes surrounded inhabited districts with precipices or waters: revolutions of the globe tore off portions from the continent, and made them islands. It is readily seen that among men thus collected and compelled to live together, a common idiom must have arisen much more easily than among those who still wandered through the forests of the continent. Thus it is very possible that after their first essays in navigation the islanders brought over the use of speech to the continent: and it is at least very probable that communities and languages were first established in islands, and even came to perfection there before they were known on the mainland.

Everything now begins to change its aspect. Men, who have up to now been roving in the woods, by taking to a more settled manner of life, come gradually together, form separate bodies, and at length in every country arises a distinct nation, united in character and manners, not by regulations or laws, but by uniformity of life and food, and the common influence of climate. Permanent neighborhood could not fail to produce, in time, some connection between different families. Among young people of opposite sexes, living in neighboring huts, the transient commerce required by nature soon led, through mutual intercourse, to another kind not less agreeable, and more permanent. Men began now to take the difference between objects into account, and to make comparisons; they acquired imperceptibly the ideas of beauty and merit, which soon gave rise to feelings of preference. In consequence of seeing each other often, they could not do without seeing each other constantly. A tender and pleasant feeling insinuated itself into their souls, and the least opposition turned it into an impetuous fury: with love arose jealousy; discord triumphed, and human blood was sacrificed to the gentlest of all passions.

As ideas and feelings succeeded one another, and heart and head were brought into play, men continued to lay aside their original wildness; their private connections became every day more intimate as their limits extended. They accustomed themselves to assemble before their huts round a large tree; singing and dancing, the true offspring of love and leisure, became the amusement, or rather the occupation, of men and women thus assembled together with nothing else to do. Each one began to consider the rest, and to wish to be considered in turn; and thus a value came to be attached to public esteem. Whoever sang or danced best, whoever was the handsomest, the strongest, the most dexterous, or the most eloquent, came to be of most consideration; and this was the first step towards inequality, and at the same time towards vice. From these first distinctions arose on the one side vanity and contempt and on the other shame and envy: and the fermentation caused by these new leavens ended by producing combinations fatal to innocence and happiness.

As soon as men began to value one another, and the idea of consideration had got a footing in the mind, every one put in his claim to it, and it became impossible to refuse it to any with impunity. Hence arose the first obligations of civility even among savages; and every intended injury became an affront; because, besides the hurt which might result from it, the party injured was certain to find in it a contempt for his person, which was often more insupportable than the hurt itself. Thus, as every man punished the contempt shown him by others, in proportion to his opinion

of himself, revenge became terrible, and men bloody and cruel. This is precisely the state reached by most of the savage nations known to us: and it is for want of having made a proper distinction in our ideas, and seen how very far they already are from the state of nature, that so many writers have hastily concluded that man is naturally cruel, and requires civil institutions to make him more mild; whereas nothing is more gentle than man in his primitive state, as he is placed by nature at an equal distance from the stupidity of brutes, and the fatal ingenuity of civilised man. Equally confined by instinct and reason to the sole care of guarding himself against the mischiefs which threaten him, he is restrained by natural compassion from doing any injury to others, and is not led to do such a thing even in return for injuries received. For, according to the axiom of the wise Locke, *There can be no injury, where there is no property.*

But it must be remarked that the society thus formed, and the relations thus established among men, required of them qualities different from those which they possessed from their primitive constitution. Morality began to appear in human actions, and every one, before the institution of law, was the only judge and avenger of the injuries done him, so that the goodness which was suitable in the pure state of nature was no longer proper in the new-born state of society. Punishments had to be made more severe, as opportunities of offending became more frequent, and the dread of vengeance had to take the place of the rigor of the law. Thus, though men had become less patient, and their natural compassion had already suffered some diminution, this period of expansion of the human faculties, keeping a just mean between the indolence of the primitive state and the petulant activity of our egoism, must have been the happiest and most stable of epochs. The more we reflect on it, the more we shall find that this state was the least subject to revolutions, and altogether the very best man could experience; so that he can have departed from it only through some fatal accident, which, for the public good, should never have happened. The example of savages, most of whom have been found in this state, seems to prove that men were meant to remain in it, that it is the real youth of the world, and that all subsequent advances have been apparently so many steps towards the perfection of the individual, but in reality towards the decrepitude of the species.

So long as men remained content with their rustic huts, so long as they were satisfied with clothes made of the skins of animals and sewn together with thorns and fishbones, adorned themselves only with feathers and shells, and continued to paint their bodies different colors, to improve and beautify their bows and arrows and to make with sharp-edged stones fishing boats or clumsy musical instruments; in a word, so long as they undertook only what a single person could accomplish, and confined themselves to such arts as did not require the joint labor of several hands, they lived free, healthy, honest and happy lives, so long as their nature allowed, and as they continued to enjoy the pleasures of mutual and independent intercourse. But from the moment one man began to stand in need of the help of another; from the moment it appeared advantageous to any one man to have enough provisions for two, equality disappeared, property was introduced, work became indispensable, and vast forests became smiling fields, which man had to water with the sweat of his brow, and where slavery and misery were soon seen to germinate and grow up with the crops.

Metallurgy and agriculture were the two arts which produced this great revolution. The poets tell us it was gold and silver, but, for the philosophers, it was iron and corn, which first civilised men, and ruined humanity. Thus both were unknown to the savages of America, who for that reason are still savage: the other nations also seem to have continued in a state of barbarism while they practised only one of these arts. One of the best reasons, perhaps, why Europe has been, if not longer, at least more constantly and highly civilised than the rest of the world, is that it is at once the most abundant in iron and the most fertile in corn.

It is difficult to conjecture how men first came to know and use iron; for it is impossible to suppose they would of themselves think of digging the ore out of the mine, and preparing it for smelting, before they knew what would be the result. On the other hand, we have the less reason to suppose this discovery the effect of any accidental fire, as mines are only formed in barren places, bare of trees and plants; so that it looks as if nature had taken pains to keep the fatal secret from us. There remains, therefore, only the extraordinary accident of some volcano which, by ejecting metallic substances already in fusion, suggested to the spectators the idea of imitating the natural operation. And we must further conceive them as possessed of uncommon courage and foresight, to undertake so laborious a work, with so distant a prospect of drawing advantage from it; yet these qualities are united only in minds more advanced than we can suppose those of these first discoverers to have been.

With regard to agriculture, the principles of it were known long before they were put in practice; and it is indeed hardly possible that men, constantly employed in drawing their subsistence from plants and trees, should not readily acquire a knowledge of the means made use of by nature for the propagation of vegetables. It was in all probability very long, however, before their industry took that turn, either because trees, which together with hunting and fishing afforded them food, did not require their attention; or because they were ignorant of the use of corn, or without instruments to cultivate it; or because they lacked foresight to future needs; or lastly, because they were without means of preventing others from robbing them of the fruit of their labor.

When they grew more industrious, it is natural to believe that they began, with the help of sharp stones and pointed sticks, to cultivate a few vegetables or roots around their huts; though it was long before they knew how to prepare corn, or were provided with the implements necessary for raising it in any large quantity; not to mention how essential it is, for husbandry, to consent to immediate loss, in order to reap a future gain — a precaution very foreign to the turn of a savage's mind; for, as I have said, he hardly foresees in the morning what he will need at night.

The invention of the other arts must therefore have been necessary to compel mankind to apply themselves to agriculture. No sooner were artificers wanted to smelt and forge iron, than others were required to maintain them; the more hands that were employed in manufactures, the fewer were left to provide for the common subsistence, though the number of mouths to be furnished with food remained the same: and as some required commodities in exchange for their iron, the rest at length discovered the method of making iron serve for the multiplication of commodities. By this means the arts of husbandry and agriculture were established on the one hand, and the art of working metals and multiplying their uses on the other.

The cultivation of the earth necessarily brought about its distribution; and property, once recognised, gave rise to the first rules of justice; for, to secure each man his own, it had to be possible for each to have something. Besides, as men began to look forward to the future, and all had something to lose, every one had reason to apprehend that reprisals would follow any injury he might do to another. This origin is so much the more natural, as it is impossible to conceive how property can come from anything but manual labor: for what else can a man add to things which he does not originally create, so as to make them his own property? It is the husbandman's labor alone that, giving him a title to the produce of the ground he has tilled, gives him a claim also to the land itself, at least till harvest; and so, from year to year, a constant possession which is easily transformed into property. When the ancients, says Grotius, gave to Ceres the title of Legislatrix, and to a festival celebrated in her honor the name of Thesmophoria, they meant by that that the distribution of lands had produced a new kind of right: that is to say, the right of property, which is different from the right deducible from the law of nature.

In this state of affairs, equality might have been sustained, had the talents of individuals been equal, and had, for example, the use of iron and the consumption of commodities always exactly balanced each other; but, as there was nothing to preserve this balance, it was soon disturbed; the strongest did most work; the most skilful turned his labor to best account; the most ingenious devised methods of diminishing his labor: the husbandman wanted more iron, or the smith more corn, and, while both labored equally, the one gained a great deal by his work, while the other could hardly support himself. Thus natural inequality unfolds itself insensibly with that of combination, and the difference between men, developed by their different circumstances, becomes more sensible and permanent in its effects, and begins to have an influence, in the same proportion, over the lot of individuals.

Matters once at this pitch, it is easy to imagine the rest. I shall not detain the reader with a description of the successive invention of other arts, the development of language, the trial and utilisation of talents, the inequality of fortunes, the use and abuse of riches, and all the details connected with them which the reader can easily supply for himself. I shall confine myself to a glance at mankind in this new situation.

Behold then all human faculties developed, memory and imagination in full play, egoism interested, reason active, and the mind almost at the highest point of its perfection. Behold all the natural qualities in action, the rank and condition of every man assigned him; not merely his share of property and his power to serve or injure others, but also his wit, beauty, strength or skill, merit or talents: and these being the only qualities capable of commanding respect, it soon became necessary to possess or to affect them.

It now became the interest of men to appear what they really were not. To be and to seem became two totally different things; and from this distinction sprang insolent pomp and cheating trickery, with all the numerous vices that go in their train. On the other hand, free and independent as men were before, they were now, in consequence of a multiplicity of new wants, brought into subjection, as it were, to all nature, and particularly to one another; and each became in some degree a slave even in becoming the master of other men: if rich, they stood in need of the services of others; if poor, of their assistance; and even a middle condition did not enable them to do without one another. Man must now, therefore, have been perpetually employed in getting others to interest themselves in his lot, and in making them, apparently at least, if not really, find their advantage in promoting his own. Thus he must have been sly and artful in his behavior to some, and imperious and cruel to others; being under a kind of necessity to ill-use all the persons of whom he stood in need, when he could not frighten them into compliance, and did not judge it his interest to be useful to them. Insatiable ambition, the thirst of raising their respective fortunes, not so much from real want as from the desire to surpass others, inspired all men with a vile propensity to injure one another, and with a secret jealousy, which is the more dangerous, as it puts on the mask of benevolence, to carry its point with greater security. In a word, there arose rivalry and competition on the one hand, and conflicting interests on the other, together with a secret desire on both of profiting at the expense of others. All these evils were the first effects of property, and the inseparable attendants of growing inequality.

Before the invention of signs to represent riches, wealth could hardly consist in anything but lands and cattle, the only real possessions men can have. But, when inheritances so increased in number and extent as to occupy the whole of the land, and to border on one another, one man could aggrandise himself only at the expense of another; at the same time the supernumeraries, who had been too weak or too indolent to make such acquisitions, and had grown poor without sustaining any loss, because, while they saw everything change around them, they remained still the same, were obliged to receive their subsistence, or steal it, from the rich; and this soon bred, according to their different characters, dominion and slavery, or violence and rapine. The wealthy, on their part, had no sooner begun to taste the pleasure of command, than they disdained all others, and, using their old slaves to acquire new, thought of nothing but subduing and enslaving their neighbors; like ravenous wolves, which, having once tasted human flesh, despise every other food and thenceforth seek only men to devour.

Thus, as the most powerful or the most miserable considered their might or misery as a kind of right to the possessions of others, equivalent, in their opinion, to that of property, the destruction of equality was attended by the most terrible disorders. Usurpations by the rich, robbery by the poor, and the unbridled passions of both, suppressed the cries of natural compassion and the still feeble voice of justice, and filled men with avarice, ambition and vice. Between the title of the strongest and that of the first occupier, there arose perpetual conflicts, which never ended but in battles and bloodshed. The new-born state of society thus gave rise to a horrible state of war; men thus harassed and depraved were no longer capable of retracing their steps or renouncing the fatal acquisitions they had made, but, laboring by the abuse of the faculties which do them honor, merely to their own confusion, brought themselves to the brink of ruin.

Attonitus novitate mali, divesque miserque,
Effugere optat opes; et quæ modo voverat odit.[1]

It is impossible that men should not at length have reflected on so wretched a situation, and on the calamities that overwhelmed them. The rich, in particular, must have felt how much they suffered by a constant state of war, of which they bore all the expense; and in which, though all risked their lives, they alone risked their property. Besides, however speciously they might disguise their usurpations, they knew that they were founded on precarious and false titles; so that, if others took from them by force what they themselves had gained by force, they would have no reason to complain. Even those who had been enriched by their own industry, could hardly base their proprietorship on better claims. It was in vain to repeat, "I built this well; I gained this spot by my industry." Who gave you your standing, it might be answered, and what right have you to demand payment of us for doing what we never asked you to do? Do you not know that numbers of your fellow-creatures are starving, for want of what you have too much of? You ought to have had the express and universal consent of mankind, before appropriating more of the common subsistence than you needed for your own maintenance. Destitute of valid reasons to justify and sufficient strength to defend himself, able to crush individuals with ease, but easily crushed himself by a troop of bandits, one against all, and incapable, on account of mutual jealousy, of joining with his equals against numerous enemies united by the common hope of plunder, the rich man, thus urged by necessity, conceived at length the profoundest plan that ever entered the mind of man: this was

[1] Ovid, *Metamorphoses*, xi, 127.
Both rich and poor, shocked at their new-found ills,
Would fly from wealth, and lose what they had sought.

to employ in his favor the forces of those who attacked him, to make allies of his adversaries, to inspire them with different maxims, and to give them other institutions as favorable to himself as the law of nature was unfavorable.

With this view, after having represented to his neighbors the horror of a situation which armed every man against the rest, and made their possessions as burdensome to them as their wants, and in which no safety could be expected either in riches or in poverty, he readily devised plausible arguments to make them close with his design. "Let us join," said he, "to guard the weak from oppression, to restrain the ambitious, and secure to every man the possession of what belongs to him: let us institute rules of justice and peace, to which all without exception may be obliged to conform; rules that may in some measure make amends for the caprices of fortune, by subjecting equally the powerful and the weak to the observance of reciprocal obligations. Let us, in a word, instead of turning our forces against ourselves, collect them in a supreme power which may govern us by wise laws, protect and defend all the members of the association, repulse their common enemies, and maintain eternal harmony among us."

Far fewer words to this purpose would have been enough to impose on men so barbarous and easily seduced; especially as they had too many disputes among themselves to do without arbitrators, and too much ambition and avarice to go long without masters. All ran headlong to their chains, in hopes of securing their liberty; for they had just wit enough to perceive the advantages of political institutions, without experience enough to enable them to foresee the dangers. The most capable of foreseeing the dangers were the very persons who expected to benefit by them; and even the most prudent judged it not inexpedient to sacrifice one part of their freedom to ensure the rest; as a wounded man has his arm cut off to save the rest of his body.

Such was, or may well have been, the origin of society and law, which bound new fetters on the poor, and gave new powers to the rich; which irretrievably destroyed natural liberty, eternally fixed the law of property and inequality, converted clever usurpation into unalterable right, and, for the advantage of a few ambitious individuals, subjected all mankind to perpetual labor, slavery and wretchedness. It is easy to see how the establishment of one community made that of all the rest necessary, and how, in order to make head against united forces, the rest of mankind had to unite in turn. Societies soon multiplied and spread over the face of the earth, till hardly a corner of the world was left in which a man could escape the yoke, and withdraw his head from beneath the sword which he saw perpetually hanging over him by a thread. Civil right having thus become the common rule among the members of each community, the law of nature maintained its place only between different communities, where, under the name of the right of nations, it was qualified by certain tacit conventions, in order to make commerce practicable, and serve as a substitute for natural compassion, which lost, when applied to societies, almost all the influence it had over individuals, and survived no longer except in some great cosmopolitan spirits, who, breaking down the imaginary barriers that separate different peoples, follow the example of our Sovereign Creator, and include the whole human race in their benevolence.

But bodies politic, remaining thus in a state of nature among themselves, presently experienced the inconveniences which had obliged individuals to forsake it; for this state became still more fatal to these great bodies than it had been to the individuals of whom they were composed. Hence arose national wars, battles, murders, and reprisals, which shock nature and outrage reason; together with all those horrible prejudices which class among the virtues the honor of shedding human blood. The most distinguished men hence learned to consider cutting each other's throats a duty; at length men massacred their fellow-creatures by thousands without so much as knowing why, and committed more murders in a single day's fighting, and more violent outrages in the sack of a single town, than were committed in the state of nature during whole ages over the whole earth. Such were the first effects which we can see to have followed the division of mankind into different communities....

Confessions[1]

THE STOLEN RIBBON

[*This incident, from Book II, occurred when Rousseau was about twenty years old and serving as a servant-secretary in the establishment of Madame de Vercellis. The mistress had just died.*]

She left a year's wages to her underservants. I received nothing, not having been entered on the list of her establishment. However, the Comte de la Roque ordered thirty *livres* to be given me, and left me the new suit which I was wearing, and

[1] The following selections are from the *Everyman* edition of the *Confessions*, by an unnamed translator.

which M. Lorenzi wanted to take from me. He even promised to try and find a place for me, and gave me leave to go and see him. I went there two or three times without being able to speak to him. Being easily rebuffed, I did not go again. It will soon be seen that I was wrong. Would that I had finished all that I had to say about my stay at Madame de Vercellis's! But, although my condition apparently remained the same, I did not leave the house as I entered it. I carried away from it lasting recollections of crime and the insupportable weight of remorse, which, after forty years, still lies heavy on my conscience; while the bitterness of it, far from growing weaker, makes itself more strongly felt with my advancing years. Who would believe that a childish fault could have such cruel consequences? For these more than probable consequences my heart is inconsolable. I have, perhaps, caused the ruin of an amiable, honest, and estimable girl, who certainly was far more worthy than myself, and doomed her to disgrace and misery.

It is almost unavoidable that the break up of an establishment should cause some confusion in the house, and that several things should get lost; however, the servants were so honest, and the Lorenzis so watchful, that nothing was missing when the inventory was taken. Only Mademoiselle Pontal had lost a piece of old red and silver-colored ribbon. Many other things of greater value were at my disposal; this ribbon alone tempted me; I stole it, and, as I took no trouble to conceal it, it was soon found. They wanted to know how it had come into my possession. I became confused, stammered, blushed, and at last said that Marion had given it to me. Marion was a young girl from Maurienne, whom Madame de Vercellis had taken for her cook, when she left off giving dinners and discharged her own, as she had more need of good soup than of fine stews. Marion was not only pretty but had a fresh color, only found on the mountains, and, above all, there was something about her so gentle and modest, that it was impossible for anyone to see her without loving her; in addition to that, she was a good and virtuous girl, and of unquestionable honesty. All were surprised when I mentioned her name. We were both equally trusted and it was considered important to find out which of us two was really the thief. She was sent for; a number of people were assembled, amongst them the Comte de la Roque. When she came, the ribbon was shown to her. I boldly accused her; she was astounded, and unable to utter a word; looked at me in a manner that would have disarmed the Devil himself, but against which my barbarous heart was proof. At last, she denied the theft firmly, but without anger, addressed herself to me, exhorted me to reflect, and not to disgrace an innocent girl who had never done me any harm; but I, with infernal impudence, persisted in my story, and declared to her face that she had given me the ribbon. The poor girl began to cry, and only said to me: "Ah! Rousseau, I thought you were a good man. You make me very unhappy, but I should not like to be in your place." That was all. She proceeded to defend herself with equal simplicity and firmness, but without allowing herself to utter the slightest reproach against me. This moderation, contrasted with my decided tone, did her harm. It did not seem natural to suppose, on the one side, such devilish impudence, and, on the other, such angelic mildness. Although the matter did not appear to be absolutely settled, they were prepossessed in my favor. In the confusion which prevailed, they did not give themselves time to get to the bottom of the affair; and the Comte de la Roque, in dismissing us both, contented himself with saying that the conscience of the guilty one would amply avenge the innocent. His prediction has been fulfilled; it fulfils itself every day.

I do not know what became of the victim of my false accusation; but it is not likely that she afterwards found it easy to get a good situation. She carried away with her an imputation upon her honesty which was in every way cruel. The theft was only a trifling one, but still it was a theft, and, what is worse, made use of to lead a young man astray; lastly, lying and obstinacy left nothing to be hoped from one in whom so many vices were united. I do not even consider misery and desertion as the greatest danger to which I exposed her. At her age, who knows to what extremes discouragement and the feeling of ill-used innocence may have carried her? Oh, if my remorse at having, perhaps, made her unhappy is unendurable, one may judge what I feel at the thought of having, perhaps, made her worse than myself!

This cruel remembrance at times so sorely troubles and upsets me, that in my sleepless hours I seem to see the poor girl coming to reproach me for my crime, as if it had been committed only yesterday. As long as I have lived quietly, it has tormented me less; but in the midst of a stormy life it robs me of the sweet consolation of persecuted innocence, it makes me feel what I think I have said in one of my books, that "Remorse goes to sleep when our fortunes are prosperous, and makes itself felt more keenly in adversity." However, I have never been able to bring myself to unburden my heart of this confession to a friend. The closest intimacy has never led me so far with anyone, not even with Madame de Warens. All that I have been able to do has been to confess that I had to reproach myself with an atrocious act, but I have never stated wherein it consisted. This burden has remained to this day upon my conscience without alleviation; and I can affirm that the desire of freeing myself from it in some degree, has greatly contributed to the resolution I have taken of writing my Confessions.

I have behaved straightforwardly in the confession which I have just made, and it will assuredly be found that I have not attempted to palliate the blackness of my offense. But I should not fulfil the object of this book, if I did not at the same time set forth my inner feelings, and hesitated to excuse myself by what is strictly true. Wicked intent was never further from me than at that cruel moment; and when I accused the unhappy girl, it is singular, but it is true, that my friendship for her was the cause of it. She was present to my thoughts; I threw the blame on the first object which presented itself. I accused her of having done what I meant to do, and of having given me the ribbon, because my intention was to give it to her. When I afterwards saw her appear, my heart was torn; but the presence of so many people was stronger than repentance. I was not afraid of punishment, I was only afraid of disgrace; and that I feared more than death, more than crime, more than anything else in the world. I should have rejoiced if the earth had suddenly opened, swallowed me up and suffocated me; the unconquerable fear of shame overcame everything, and alone made me impudent. The greater my crime, the more the dread of confessing it made me fearless. I saw nothing but the horror of being recognised and publicly declared, in my own presence, a thief, liar, and slanderer. Complete embarrassment deprived me of every other feeling. If I had been allowed to recover myself I should have assuredly confessed everything. If M. de la Roque had taken me aside and said to me: "Do not ruin this poor girl; if you are guilty, confess it to me," I should have immediately thrown myself at his feet, of that I am perfectly certain. But, when I needed encouragement, they only intimidated me. And yet it is only fair to consider my age. I was little more than a child, or rather, I still was one. In youth real crimes are even more criminal than in riper years; but that which is only weakness is less so, and my offence was at bottom scarcely anything else. Thus the recollection of it afflicts me not so much by reason of the evil in itself as on account of its evil consequences. It has even done me the good of securing me for the rest of my life against every act tending to crime, by the terrible

impression which I have retained of the only offence that I have ever committed; and I believe
that my horror of a lie is due in great measure to
my regret at having been capable myself of telling
one so shameful.   If it is a crime that can be expiated, as I venture to believe, it must be expiated
by all the unhappiness which has overwhelmed the
last years of my life, by forty years of honorable
and upright conduct in difficult circumstances; and
poor Marion finds so many avengers in this world,
that, however great my offence against her may
have been, I have little fear of dying without absolution.   This is what I have to say on this matter: permit me never to speak of it again.

A DAY'S EXCURSION

One morning, the dawn appeared so beautiful
that I threw on my clothes and hurried out into the
country to see the sun rise.   I enjoyed this sight in
all its charm; it was the week after the festival of
St. John.   The earth, decked in its greatest splendor, was covered with verdure and flowers; the
nightingales, nearly at the end of their song, seemed
to delight in singing the louder; all the birds, uniting in their farewell to Spring, were singing in honor
of the birth of a beautiful summer day, one of those
beautiful days which one no longer sees at my age
and which are unknown in the melancholy land [1]
in which I am now living.

Without perceiving it, I had wandered some
distance from the town; the heat increased, and I
walked along under the shady trees of a little valley by the side of a brook.   I heard behind me the
sound of horses' hoofs and the voices of girls, who
seemed in a difficulty, but, nevertheless, were
laughing heartily at it.   I turned round, and heard
myself called by name; when I drew near, I found
two young ladies of my acquaintance, Mademoiselle de Graffenried and Mademoiselle Galley, who
being poor horsewomen, did not know how to make
their horses cross the brook.   Mademoiselle de
Graffenried was an amiable young Bernese, who,
having been driven from her home in consequence
of some youthful folly, had followed the example
of Madame de Warens, at whose house I had sometimes seen her; but, as she had no pension, she had
been only too glad to attach herself to Mademoiselle Galley, who, having conceived a friendship for
her, had persuaded her mother to let her stay with
her as her companion until she could find some
employment.   Mademoiselle Galley was a year
younger than her companion, and better-looking;
there was something about her more delicate and

[1] Rousseau wrote this section of the *Confessions* while
living in a voluntary exile in rural England.

more refined; at the same time, she had a very neat
and well-developed figure, the greatest charm a girl
can possess.   They loved each other tenderly, and
their good nature could not fail to keep up this
intimacy, unless some lover came to disturb it.
They told me that they were on their way to
Toune, an old château belonging to Madame Galley; they begged me to assist them to get their
horses across, which they could not manage by
themselves.   I wanted to whip the horses, but
they were afraid that I might be kicked and they
themselves thrown off.   I accordingly had recourse
to another expedient.   I took Mademoiselle Galley's horse by the bridle, and then, pulling it after
me, crossed the brook with the water up to my
knees; the other horse followed without any hesitation.   After this, I wanted to take leave of the
young ladies and go my way like a fool.   They
whispered a few words to each other, and Mademoiselle de Graffenried, turning to me, said, "No,
no; you shan't escape us like that.   You have got
wet in serving us, and we owe it as a duty to our
conscience to see that you get dry.   You must
come with us, if you please; we make you our
prisoner."   My heart beat; I looked at Mademoiselle Galley.   "Yes, yes," added she, laughing at
my look of affright; "prisoner of war.   Get up behind her; we will give a good account of you."
"But, mademoiselle," I objected, "I have not the
honor of your mother's acquaintance; what will she
say when she sees me?"   "Her mother is not at
Toune," replied Mademoiselle de Graffenried;
"we are alone; we return this evening, and you can
return with us."

The effect of electricity is not more rapid than
was the effect of these words upon me.   Trembling
with joy, I sprang upon Mademoiselle de Graffenried's horse; and, when I was obliged to put my
arm round her waist to support myself, my heart
beat so violently that she noticed it.   She told me
that hers was beating too, since she was afraid of
falling.   In the situation in which I was, this was
almost an invitation to me to verify the truth for
myself; but I had not the courage; and, during the
whole of the ride, my two arms surrounded her like
a belt, which certainly held her tight, but never
shifted its place for a moment.   Many women who
read this would like to box my ears — and they
would not be wrong.

The pleasant excursion and the chatter of the
young ladies made me so talkative that we were
never silent for a moment until evening — in fact,
as long as we were together.   They had put me so
completely at my ease, that my tongue was as
eloquent as my eyes, although not in the same
manner.   For a few moments only, when I found

myself alone with one or the other, the conversation became a little constrained; but the absent one soon returned, and did not allow us time to investigate the reason of our embarrassment.

When we reached Toune, after I had first dried myself, we breakfasted. Next, it was necessary to proceed to the important business of dinner. The young ladies from time to time left off their cooking to kiss the farmer's children, and their poor scullion looked on and smothered his vexation. Provisions had been sent from the town, and all that was requisite for a good dinner, especially in the matter of delicacies; but, unfortunately, the wine had been forgotten. This was no wonder, since the young ladies did not drink it; but I was sorry for it, since I had counted upon its assistance to give me courage. They also were annoyed, possibly for the same reason, although I do not think so. Their lively and charming gaiety was innocence personified; besides, what could the two of them have done with me? They sent all round the neighborhood to try and get some wine, but without success, so abstemious and poor are the peasants of this canton. They expressed their regret to me; I said that they need not be so concerned about it, that they did not require wine in order to intoxicate me. This was the only compliment I ventured to pay them during the day; but I believe that the roguish creatures saw clearly enough that the compliment was sincere.

We dined in the farmer's kitchen, the two friends seated on benches on either side of the long table, and their guest between them on a three-legged stool. What a dinner! what an enchanting remembrance! Why should a man, when he can enjoy pleasures so pure and real at so little cost, try to find new ones? No supper at any of the *petites maisons* of Paris could be compared to this meal, not only for gaiety and cheerfulness, but, I declare, for sensual enjoyment.

After dinner we practised a little economy. Instead of drinking the coffee which remained over from breakfast, we kept it for our tea with the cream and cakes which they had brought with them; and, to keep up our appetites, we went into the orchard to finish our dessert with cherries. I climbed up the tree, and threw down bunches of fruit, while they threw the stones back at me through the branches. Once Mademoiselle Galley, holding out her apron and throwing back her head, presented herself as a mark so prettily, and I took such accurate aim, that I threw a bunch right into her bosom. How we laughed! I said to myself, If my lips were only cherries, how readily would I throw them into the same place!

The day passed in this manner in the most un-restrained enjoyment, which, however, never over-stepped the limits of the strictest decency. No *double-entendre*, no risky jest was uttered; and this decency was by no means forced, it was perfectly natural, and we acted and spoke as our hearts prompted. In short, my modesty — others will call it stupidity — was so great, that the greatest liberty of which I was guilty was once to kiss Mademoiselle Galley's hand. It is true that the circumstances gave special value to this favor. We were alone, I was breathing with difficulty, her eyes were cast down; my mouth, instead of giving utterance to words, fastened upon her hand, which she gently withdrew after I had kissed it, looking at me in a manner that showed no irritation. I do not know what I might have said to her; her friend came into the room, and appeared to me distinctly ugly at that moment.

At last, they remembered that they ought not to wait till night before returning to the town. We only just had time to get back while it was daylight, and we hastened to set out in the same order as we came. If I had dared, I would have changed the order; for Mademoiselle Galley's looks had created a profound impression upon my heart; but I did not venture to say anything, and it was not for her to make the proposal. On the way, we said to ourselves that it was a great pity that the day was over; but, far from complaining that it had been too short, we agreed that we had possessed the secret of lengthening it by the aid of all the amusements with which we had known how to occupy it.

I left them almost at the spot where they had found me. With what regret we separated! with what delight we planned to meet again! Twelve hours spent together were for us as good as centuries of intimacy. The sweet remembrance of that day cost the young girls nothing; the tender union between us three was worth far livelier pleasures, which would not have suffered it to exist; we loved one another openly and without shame, and were ready to love one another always in the same manner. Innocence of character has its enjoyment, which is certainly equal to any other, since it knows no relaxation and never ceases. As for me, I know that the memory of so beautiful a day touches and charms me more, and goes straighter to my heart, than the recollection of any pleasures that I have ever enjoyed. I did not exactly know what I wanted with these two charming persons, but both of them interested me exceedingly. I do not say that, if I had had control of the arrangements, my heart would have been equally shared between them. I had a slight feeling of preference; I should have been quite happy to have Mademoiselle de Graffenried as a mistress; but, if it had depended entirely upon myself, I think I should have preferred her for an intimate friend. Be that as it may, it seemed to me, when I left them, that I could no longer live without them both. Who would have said that I was never to see them in my life again, and that our love of a day was to end there?

My readers will not fail to laugh at my love adventures, and to remark that, after lengthy preliminaries, even those which made greatest progress, end in a kiss of the hand. Oh, my readers, do not be mistaken! I have, perhaps, had greater enjoyment in my amours which have ended in a simple kiss of the hand, than you will ever have in yours, which, at least, have begun with that!

LIFE AT LES CHARMETTES

[*Les Charmettes was the home of Madame de Warens with whom Rousseau lived off and on over a period of ten years, years which were the most happy and peaceful Rousseau knew. This description of the daily life is from Book VI.*]

I got up every day before sunrise; I climbed through a neighboring orchard to a very pretty path above the vineyard which ran along the slope as far as Chambéri. During my walk I offered a prayer, which did not consist merely of idle, stammering words, but of a sincere uplifting of the heart to the Creator of this delightful Nature, whose beauties were spread before my eyes. I never like to pray in a room: it has always seemed to me as if the walls and all the petty handiwork of man interposed between myself and God. I love to contemplate Him in His works, while my heart uplifts itself to Him. My prayers were pure, I venture to say, and for that reason deserved to be heard. I only asked for myself and for her, who was inseparably associated with my wishes, an innocent and peaceful life, free from vice, pain, and distressing needs; the death of the righteous, and their lot in the future. For the rest, this act of worship consisted rather of admiration and contemplation than of requests, for I knew that the best means of obtaining the blessings which are necessary for us from the giver of all true blessings, was to deserve, rather than to ask for, them. My walk consisted of a tolerably long round, during which I contemplated with interest and pleasure the rustic scenery by which I was surrounded, the only thing of which heart and eye never tire. From a distance I looked to see if it was day with mamma.[1] When I saw

[1] Rousseau called Madame de Warens "mamma"; she called him "the little one."

her shutters open, I trembled with joy and ran towards the house; if they were shut, I remained in the garden until she awoke, amusing myself by going over what I had learned the evening before, or by gardening. The shutters opened, I went to embrace her while she was still in bed, often still half asleep; and this embrace, as pure as it was tender, derived from its very innocence a charm which is never combined with sensual pleasure.

We usually took *café au lait* for breakfast. This was the period of the day when we were most undisturbed, and chatted most at our ease. We usually sat a considerable time over our breakfast, and from that time I have always had a great liking for this meal. I infinitely prefer the fashion of the Swiss and English, with whom breakfast is really a meal at which all the family assemble, to that of the French, who breakfast separately in their rooms, or, most commonly, take no breakfast at all. After an hour or two of conversation, I went to my books till dinner. I began with some philosophical treatise, such as the Logic of Port-Royal, Locke's Essay, Malebranche, Leibnitz, Descartes, &c. I soon observed that all these authors nearly always contradicted each other, and I conceived the fanciful idea of reconciling them, which fatigued me greatly, and made me lose considerable time. I muddled my head without making any progress. At last, abandoning this plan, I adopted one that was infinitely better, to which I attribute all the progress which, in spite of my want of talent, I may have made; for it is certain that I never had much capacity for study. As I read each author, I made a practice of adopting and following up all his ideas, without any admixture of my own or of those of anyone else, and without ever attempting to argue with him. I said to myself: "Let me begin by laying up a store of ideas, no matter whether they be true or false, provided only they are definite, until my head is sufficiently equipped with them to be able to select and compare them." I know that this method is not without its inconveniences; but it has answered my purpose of self-instruction. After I had spent some years in thinking exactly as others thought, without, so to speak, reflecting, and almost without reasoning, I found myself in possession of a fund of learning sufficient to satisfy myself, and to enable me to think without the assistance of another. Then, when travelling and business matters deprived me of the opportunity of consulting books, I amused myself by going over and comparing what I had read, by weighing everything in the scale of reason, and, sometimes, by passing judgment upon my masters. I did not find that my critical faculties had lost their vigor owing to my having begun to exercise them late; and, when I published my own ideas, I have never been accused of being a servile disciple, or of swearing *in verba magistri.*[1]

From these studies I proceeded to elementary geometry, beyond which I never advanced, although I persistently attempted, in some degree, to overcome my weakness of memory by dint of retracing my steps hundreds of times, and by incessantly going over the same ground. I did not like Euclid, whose object is rather a chain of proofs than the connection of ideas. I preferred Father Lamy's "Geometry," which from that time became one of my favorite works, and which I am still able to read with pleasure. Next came algebra, in which I still took Father Lamy for my guide. When I was more advanced, I took Father Reynaud's "Science of Calculation"; then his "Analysis Demonstrated," which I merely skimmed. I have never got so far as to understand properly the application of algebra to geometry. I did not like this method of working without knowing what I was doing; and it appeared to me that solving a geometrical problem by means of equations was like playing a tune by simply turning the handle of a barrel-organ. The first time that I found by calculation, that the square of a binomial was composed of the square of each of its parts added to twice the product of those parts, in spite of the correctness of my multiplication, I would not believe it until I had drawn the figure. I had considerable liking for algebra, in so far as it dealt with abstract quantities; but, when it was applied to space and dimensions, I wanted to see the operation explained by lines; otherwise I was entirely unable to comprehend it.

After this came Latin. I found this my most difficult task, and I have never made much progress in it. At first I began with the Port-Royal method, but without result. Its barbarous verses disgusted me, and my ear could never retain them. The mass of rules confused me, and when learning the last, I forgot all that had preceded it. A man who has no memory does not want to study words; and it was just in order to strengthen my memory that I persisted in this study, which I was finally obliged to abandon. I was sufficiently acquainted with the construction to be able to read an easy author with the help of a dictionary. I kept to this plan with tolerable success. I limited myself to translations, not written, but mental, By dint of continual practice, I was able to read the Latin authors with tolerable ease, but I have never been able to speak or write in that language, which

frequently caused me embarrassment, when I found myself, I know not how, enrolled a member of the society of men of letters. Another disadvantage resulting from this method of learning is, that I have never learned prosody, still less the rules of versification. However, in my desire to feel the harmony of the language in verse as well as prose, I made great efforts to succeed in this; but I am convinced that it is impossible without the aid of a master. After I had learned the structure of the easiest of all verses, the hexameter, I had sufficient patience to scan nearly the whole of Virgil, marking the feet and quantities; then, when I afterwards had any doubt whether a syllable was long or short, I referred to my Virgil. It may easily be conceived that this made me commit many errors, in consequence of the license allowed by the rules of versification. But, if there is an advantage in self-instruction, there are also great disadvantages, especially the incredible amount of labor necessary. This I know better than anyone else.

Before noon I left my books, and, if dinner was not ready, I paid a visit to my friends the pigeons, or worked in the garden until it was. When I heard myself called, I was very glad to run to table, provided with an excellent appetite; for it is a remarkable thing that, however ill I may be, my appetite never fails. We dined very pleasantly, talking of our affairs, until mamma was able to eat. Two or three times a week, when it was fine, we took our coffee in a cool and shady arbor behind the house, which I had decorated with hops, which made it very agreeable during the heat. We spent some little time in looking at our vegetables and flowers, and in talking about our mode of life, which heightened the enjoyment of it. I had another little family at the bottom of the garden — some bees. I rarely failed to visit them, and mamma often accompanied me. I took great interest in their work: it amused me immensely to see them returning from their foraging expeditions, their little legs often so loaded that they could scarcely move. At first my curiosity made me too inquisitive, and I was stung two or three times; but at last they got to know me so well, that they let me go as close to them as I pleased; and, however full their hives were, when they were ready to swarm, I had them all round me, on my hands and on my face, without ever getting stung. All animals rightly distrust human beings; but when they once feel sure that they do not mean to hurt them, their confidence becomes so great that a man must be worse than a barbarian to abuse it.

I returned to my books, but my afternoon occupations deserved less to be called work and study than recreation and amusement. I have never

[1] "By the words of a master": an allusion to the disciples of Pythagoras, who slavishly reproduced the ideas of their master. (Translator's note.)

been able to endure close application in my room after dinner, and, generally speaking, any effort during the heat of the day is painful to me. However, I occupied myself with reading without study, without restraint, and almost without any system. My most regular occupations were history and geography; and, as these did not require any great effort of mind, I made as much progress as was possible, considering my weak memory. I tried to study Father Pétau, and plunged into the obscurities of chronology; but I was disgusted by the critical portion of it, which is most intricate, and by preference I took up the study of the exact measurement of time and the course of the heavenly bodies. I should also have become fond of astronomy, if I had had the necessary appliances; but I was obliged to content myself with a few elementary principles, learnt from books, and some crude observations which I made with a telescope, merely to learn the general idea of the situation of the heavenly bodies; for my shortsightedness does not allow me to distinguish the stars clearly with the naked eye. In regard to this, I remember an adventure which has often made me laugh since. I had bought an astronomical chart, in order to study the constellations. I fastened this chart to a frame, and, when the nights were clear, I went into the garden, and placed my frame on four stakes about my own height, with the chart turned downwards. In order to prevent the wind from blowing out my candle, I put it in a pail, which I placed between the four stakes on the ground. Then, looking alternately at the map with my eyes and the stars with my telescope, I practised myself in distinguishing the constellations and the individual stars. I think I have mentioned that M. Noiret's garden was in the form of a terrace, so that everything that took place could be seen from the road. One evening, some peasants, who were passing by at rather a late hour, saw me, most comically attired, busy at my work. The dim light, which fell upon my chart, without their being able to see where it came from, since it was hidden from their eyes by the edges of the pail, the four stakes, the large sheet of paper covered with figures, the frame, and the movements of my telescope, which kept appearing and disappearing, gave an air of witchcraft to the whole proceeding, which terrified them.

My dress was not calculated to reassure them. A broad-brimmed hat over my cap, and a short, wadded night-dress belonging to mamma, which she had forced me to put on, presented to their eyes the appearance of a real sorcerer; and, as it was nearly midnight, they had no doubt that a witches' meeting was going to commence. Feeling

little curiosity to see any more, they ran away in great alarm, woke up their neighbors to tell them of the apparition they had seen, and the story spread so quickly that, on the following day, everyone in the neighborhood knew that a witches' gathering had been held in M. Noiret's garden. I do not know what would have been the result of this rumor, had not one of the peasants, who had been a witness of my incantations, carried a complaint on the same day to two Jesuits, who often came to see us, and who, without knowing what it was all about, in the meantime disabused them of the idea. They told us the story; I told them the origin of it, and we enjoyed a hearty laugh over it. However, it was decided, for fear of its being repeated, that for the future I should take my observations without the assistance of a light, and that I should consult my chart at home. Those who have read, in my "Letters from the Mountain," of my Venetian magic, will, I hope, find that sorcery had long been my vocation.

ROUSSEAU'S OPERA IS PRESENTED AT COURT

[*Rousseau, who always fancied himself a musician, had an opera presented at court. The following selection shows how he conducted himself on the occasion.*]

When everything was ready and the day fixed for the performance, it was proposed to me that I should take a journey to Fontainebleau, to be present at the last rehearsal, at any rate. I went with Mademoiselle Fel, Grimm, and, I think, the Abbé Raynal, in one of the Royal carriages. The rehearsal was tolerable; I was better satisfied with it than I had expected to be. The orchestra was a powerful one, consisting of those of the Opera and the Royal band. Jelyotte played Colin; Mademoiselle Fel, Colette; Cuvitier, the Devin (soothsayer). The choruses were from the Opera. I said little. Jelyotte had arranged everything, and I did not desire to have any control over his arrangements; but, in spite of my Roman air, I was as bashful as a schoolboy amongst all these people.

On the following day, when the rehearsal was to take place, I went to breakfast at the *Café du Grand Commun*, which was full of people, talking about the rehearsal of the previous evening, and the difficulty there had been in getting in. An officer who was present said that he had found no difficulty, gave a long account of the proceedings, described the author, and related what he had said and done; but what astounded me most in his long description, given with equal confidence and simplicity, was that there was not a word of truth in it. It was perfectly clear to me, that the man who spoke so positively about this rehearsal had never been present, since he had before his eyes the author, whom he pretended he had observed so closely, and did not recognise him. The most remarkable thing about this incident was the effect which it produced upon me. This man was somewhat advanced in years; there was nothing of the coxcomb or swaggerer about him, either in his manner or tone; his countenance was intelligent, while his cross of Saint-Louis showed that he was an old officer. In spite of his unblushing effrontery, in spite of myself, he interested me; while he retailed his lies I blushed, cast down my eyes, and was on thorns; I sometimes asked myself whether it might not be possible to think that he was mistaken, and really believed what he said. At last, trembling for fear that someone might recognise me and put him to shame, I hurriedly finished my chocolate without saying a word, and, holding my head down as I passed him, I left the *café* as soon as possible, while the company were discussing his description of what had taken place. In the street, I found that I was bathed in perspiration; and I am certain that, if anyone had recognised and addressed me by name before I left, I should have exhibited all the shame and embarrassment of a guilty person, simply from the feeling of humiliation which the poor fellow would have experienced, if his lies had been detected.

I now come to one of the critical moments of my life, in which it is difficult to confine myself to simple narrative, because it is almost impossible to prevent even the narrative bearing the stamp of censure or apology. However, I will attempt to relate how, and from what motives I acted, without adding an expression of praise or blame.

On that day I was dressed in my usual careless style, with a beard of some days' growth and a badly combed wig. Considering this want of good manners as a proof of courage, I entered the hall where the King, the Queen, the Royal Family, and the whole Court were presently to arrive. I proceeded to take my seat in the box to which M. de Cury conducted me; it was his own — a large stage box, opposite a smaller and higher one, where the King sat with Madame de Pompadour. Surrounded by ladies, and the only man in front of the box, I had no doubt that I had been put there on purpose to be seen. When the theatre was lighted up, and I found myself, dressed in the manner I was, in the midst of people all most elegantly attired, I began to feel ill at ease. I asked myself whether I was in my right place, and whether I was suitably dressed. After a few moments of uneasiness, I answered "Yes," with a boldness which perhaps was due rather to the impossibility of drawing back than to the force of my arguments. I said to myself: I am in my place, since I am going to see my own piece performed; because I have been invited; because I composed it solely for that purpose; because, after all, no one has more right than myself to enjoy the fruit of my labor and talents. I am dressed as usual, neither better nor worse. If I again begin to yield to public opinion in any single thing, I shall soon become its slave again in everything. To be consistent, I must not be ashamed, wherever I may be, to be dressed in accordance with the condition of life which I have chosen for myself. My outward appearance is simple and careless, but not dirty or slovenly. A beard in itself is not so, since it is bestowed upon us by Nature, and, according to times and fashions, is sometimes even an ornament. People will consider me ridiculous, impertinent. Well, what does it matter to me? I must learn how to put up with ridicule and censure, provided they are not deserved. After this little soliloquy, I felt so encouraged that I should have behaved with intrepidity, if it had been necessary. But, whether it was the effect of the presence of the ruler, or the natural disposition of those near me, I saw nothing in the curiosity, of which I was the object, except civility and politeness. This so affected me, that I began to be uneasy again about myself and the fate of my piece, and to fear that I might destroy the favorable impressions which showed only an inclination to applaud me. I was armed against their raillery; but their kindly attitude, which I had not expected, so completely overcame me, that I trembled like a child when the performance began.

I soon found I had no reason for uneasiness. The piece was very badly acted, but the singing was good, and the music well executed. From the first scene, which is really touching in its simplicity, I heard in the boxes a murmur of surprise and applause hitherto unheard of at similar performances. The growing excitement soon reached such a height, that it communicated itself to the whole audience, and, in the words of Montesquieu, "the very effect increased the effect." In the scene between the two good little people, this effect reached its highest point. There is never any clapping when the King is present: this allowed everything to be heard, and the piece and the author were thereby benefited. I heard around me women, who seemed to me as beautiful as angels, whispering and saying to each other in a low tone, "Charming! delightful! every note speaks to the heart!" The pleasure of affecting so many amiable persons moved me to tears, which I was unable to restrain during the first duet, when I observed that I was not the only one who wept. For a moment I felt anxious, when I recalled the concert at M. de Treytorens's. This reminiscence produced upon me the same effect as the slave who held the crown over the head of a Roman general in his triumphal procession, but it did not last long, and I soon abandoned myself, completely and without reserve, to the delight of tasting the sweets of my success. And yet I am sure that at this moment I was much more affected by sensual impulse than by the vanity I felt as an author. If none but men had been present, I am convinced that I should not have been consumed, as I was, by the incessant desire of catching with my lips the delightful tears which I caused to flow. I have seen pieces excite more lively transports of admiration, but never so complete, so delightful, and so moving an intoxication, which completely overcame the audience, especially at a first performance before the Court. Those who saw it on this occasion can never have forgotten it, for the effect was unique.

The same evening, M. le Duc d'Aumont sent word to me to present myself at the château on the following day at eleven o'clock, when he would present me to the King. M. de Cury, who brought me the message, added that he believed that it was a question of a pension, the bestowal of which the King desired to announce to me in person.

Will it be believed, that the night which succeeded so brilliant a day was for me a night of anguish and perplexity? My first thought, after that of this presentation, was a certain necessity, which had greatly troubled me on the evening of the performance, and had frequently obliged me to retire, and might trouble me again on the next day, in the gallery or the King's apartments, amongst all the great people, while waiting for His Majesty to pass. This infirmity was the chief cause which prevented me from going into society, or from staying in a room with ladies when the doors were closed. The mere idea of the situation in which this necessity might place me, was enough to effect me to such an extent, that it made me feel ready to faint, unless I should be willing to create a scandal, to which I should have preferred death. Only those who know what this condition is, can imagine the horror of running the risk of it.

I next pictured myself in the King's presence and presented to His Majesty, who condescended to stop and speak to me. On such an occasion, tact and presence of mind were indispensable in answering. Would my accursed timidity, which embarrasses me in the presence of the most ordinary stranger, abandon me when I found myself in the presence of the King of France? would it suffer me to select, on the spur of the moment, the proper answer? It was my desire, without abandoning the austerity of tone and manner which I had assumed, to show that I was sensible of the honor which so great a monarch bestowed upon me. It was necessary that I should convey some great and useful truth in words of well-selected and well-deserved eulogy. To be able to prepare a happy answer beforehand, it would have been necessary to know exactly what he might say to me; and, even had this been possible, I felt perfectly certain that I should not be able to recollect in his presence a single word of all that I had previously thought over. What would become of me at this moment, before the eyes of all the Court, if, in my embarrassment, some of my usual silly utterances were to escape my lips? This danger alarmed, frightened, and made me tremble so violently, that I resolved, at all hazards, not to expose myself to it.

I lost, it is true, the pension, which was in a manner offered to me; but, at the same time, I escaped the yoke which it would have imposed upon me. Adieu truth, liberty, and courage! How could I, from that time forth, have dared to speak of independence and disinterestedness? I could only flatter or keep my mouth closed if I accepted this pension; and besides, who would guarantee the payment of it? What steps should I have had to take, how many people I should have been obliged to solicit! It would have cost me more trouble and far more unpleasantness to keep it, than to do without it. Consequently, in renouncing all thoughts of it, I believed that I was acting in a manner quite consistent with my principles, and sacrificing the appearance to the reality. I communicated my resolution to Grimm, who had nothing to say against it. To others I alleged my ill-health as an excuse, and I left the same morning.

My departure caused some stir, and was generally censured. My reasons could not be appreciated by everybody; it was much easier to accuse me of a foolish pride, and this more readily allayed the jealousy of all who felt they would not have acted like myself. The following day, Jelyotte wrote me a note, in which he gave me an account of the success of my piece and of the great fancy which the King himself had conceived for it. "All day long," he informed me, "his Majesty is continually singing, with the most execrable voice in his kingdom, and utterly out of tune, *J'ai perdu mon serviteur; j'ai perdu tout mon bonheur.*" He added that, in a fortnight, a second performance of the *Devin* was to be given, which would establish in the eyes of all the public the complete success of the first.

Johann Wolfgang von Goethe · 1749–1832

Rousseau and Goethe both had strong romantic qualities, but while Rousseau was concerned with social and political reforms, Goethe preferred to lead mainly the life of the scholar and literary man.

One may characterize Goethe as a Renaissance figure living in the eighteenth century. His many-sidedness, his varied interests and his desire for knowledge were qualities which we associate with the Renaissance, with Leonardo da Vinci, with Shakespeare, with a period when learning was still so unified that a single rich mind might compass most of its aspects. Goethe studied law and was admitted to practice; he had actual experience in helping to administer the state as a councilor at Weimar; he knew music and practiced painting; he read intensively on the subject of medieval alchemy; he was more than a dabbler in anatomy, botany, and chemistry; he was in charge of the court theatre; he knew philosophy and thought philosophically. But he is known to us today primarily as a writer. Here, too, he was versatile, for his writing includes work in the fields of poetry, the novel, the drama, criticism, and autobiography. He progressed through the "Sturm und Drang" (storm and stress) period of romanticism, as shown in such a play as *Götz von Berlichingen*, to the restraint of the classical attitude evident in such a drama as *Iphigenie auf Tauris*. Goethe was of the Renaissance, too, in his limitless energy and activity. And yet, he was very much a part of his time, just as the heritage he left to literature makes him a man of all ages.

Johann Wolfgang von Goethe was born August 28, 1749, at Frankfort, the son of a rather stern father of good education and of ability and social standing such as to make him an imperial councilor at Frankfort. As a boy Goethe learned Latin, Greek, Italian, and French, adding English and Hebrew somewhat later. At sixteen the young man entered the university at Leipzig, but his education was interrupted by illness and he later finished his law work at the University of Strasbourg. Throughout his university study it was literature and art, however, rather than law, which claimed his first enthusiasm. Like his contemporaries Rousseau and Burns, in France and Scotland, Goethe was much distracted by one love affair after another, experiences testified to in many of his poems. At the age of twenty-seven, the poet went to Weimar as a state councilor and, a few years later, in 1782, he was made a noble. In 1786 he went on a protracted visit of many months to Italy, a visit which proved of great importance to his development as a writer, both as to his thought and his style, since it brought him to an acceptance of classical standards. One of the strongest literary influences on the German poet and dramatist was his long and close friendship with Schiller. Goethe died at Weimar, March 22, 1832, in his eighty-third year.

Among the many writings of Goethe some of the most important in the tracing of his development are perhaps: *Götz von Berlichingen*, a drama (1773); *Sorrows of Young Werther*, a novel (1774); the three dramas, *Iphigenie* (1787), *Egmont* (1788), and *Torquato Tasso* (1790); *Wilhelm Meister's Apprenticeship*, a novel (1796); the autobiographical *Poetry and Truth* (1811–14); and the two parts of *Faust*, a dramatic poem, published in 1808 and 1832 after the writer had worked on them off and on for a period of fifty or sixty years.

SUGGESTED REFERENCES: Karl Vietor, *Goethe. The Poet* (1949) and *Goethe. The Thinker* (1950); Stuart Atkins, *Goethe's Faust. A Literary Analysis* (1958); Henry Hatfield, *Goethe: A Critical Introduction* (1963); Richard Friedenthal, *Goethe. His Life and Times* (1965).

Faust

The story of *Faust* grew from an old legend — Marlowe treated the same theme in 1588 — but Goethe clothed the legend in German thought and in his own ideas and ideals. The selection here printed from the first part of *Faust* should be read for its narrative and poetic values rather than for its allegory and symbolism, special points which may be left for the more advanced student of Goethe. Bayard Taylor, the translator, gives the general reader a workable basis when he points out that "*Faust* is, in the most comprehensive sense, a drama of the life of man."

The early romantic temper of Goethe, before his visit to Italy, manifests itself in Part I of the *Faust* in many ways; perhaps the most obvious is the Gretchen-Faust story. But the general disregard for the unities, the use of the supernatural (as in the Walpurgis Night section), the highly imaginative element, the sympathy for humanity, the Gothic setting, are enough to establish the presence of the romantic manner. The student who desires to see, within the range of the writing of one man, the difference between the romantic and classical mood will do well to continue his reading of *Faust* through Part II.

The translation, by Bayard Taylor, is reprinted here through the courtesy of Houghton Mifflin Company.

PROLOGUE IN HEAVEN

THE LORD. THE HEAVENLY HOSTS. *Afterwards* MEPHISTOPHELES.

(*The* THREE ARCHANGELS *come forward.*)

Raphael. The sun-orb sings, in emulation,
'Mid brother-spheres, his ancient round:
His path predestined through Creation
He ends with step of thunder-sound.
The angels from his visage splendid   5
Draw power, whose measure none can say:
The lofty works, uncomprehended,
Are bright as on the earliest day.
Gabriel. And swift, and swift beyond conceiving,
The splendor of the world goes round,   10
Day's Eden-brightness still relieving
The awful Night's intense profound:
The ocean-tides in foam are breaking,
Against the rocks' deep bases hurled,
And both, the spheric race partaking,   15
Eternal, swift, are onward whirled!
Michael. And rival storms abroad are surging
From sea to land, from land to sea,
A chain of deepest action forging
Round all, in wrathful energy.   20
There flames a desolation, blazing
Before the Thunder's crashing way:
Yet, Lord, Thy messengers are praising
The gentle movement of Thy Day.
The Three. Though still by them uncomprehended,   25
From these the angels draw their power,
And all Thy works, sublime and splendid,
Are bright as in Creation's hour.
Mephistopheles. Since Thou, O Lord, deign'st to approach again
And ask us how we do, in manner kindest,   30
And heretofore to meet myself wert fain,
Among Thy menials, now, my face Thou findest.
Pardon, this troop [1] I cannot follow after
With lofty speech, though by them scorned and spurned:
My pathos certainly would move Thy laughter,   35
If Thou hadst not all merriment unlearned.
Of suns and worlds I've nothing to be quoted;
How men torment themselves, is all I've noted.
The little god o' the world sticks to the same old way,
And is as whimsical as on Creation's day.   40
Life somewhat better might content him,
But for the gleam of heavenly light which Thou hast lent him:
He calls it Reason — thence his power's increased,
To be far beastlier than any beast.
Saving Thy Gracious Presence, he to me   45
A long-legged grasshopper appears to be,
That springing flies, and flying springs,
And in the grass the same old ditty sings.
Would he still lay among the grass he grows in!
Each bit of dung he seeks, to stick his nose in.   50
The Lord. Hast thou, then, nothing more to mention?
Com'st ever, thus, with ill intention?
Find'st nothing right on earth, eternally?
Mephistopheles. No, Lord! I find things, there, still bad as they can be.
Man's misery even to pity moves my nature;   55
I've scarce the heart to plague the wretched creature.
The Lord. Know'st Faust?
Mephistopheles.   The Doctor Faust?
The Lord.   My servant, he!
Mephistopheles. Forsooth! He serves you after strange devices:
No earthly meat or drink the fool suffices:
His spirit's ferment far aspireth;   60
Half conscious of his frenzied, crazed unrest,

[1] The three archangels.

The fairest stars from Heaven he requireth,
From Earth the highest raptures and the best,
And all the Near and Far that he desireth
Fails to subdue the tumult of his breast. 65
   The Lord. Though still confused his service unto Me,
I soon shall lead him to a clearer morning.
Sees not the gardener, even while buds his tree,
Both flower and fruit the future years adorning?
   Mephistopheles. What will you bet? There's still a chance to gain him, 70
If unto me full leave you give,
Gently upon *my* road to train him!
   The Lord. As long as he on earth shall live,
So long I make no prohibition.
While Man's desires and aspirations stir, 75
He cannot choose but err.
   Mephistopheles. My thanks! I find the dead no acquisition,
And never cared to have them in my keeping.
I much prefer the cheeks where ruddy blood is leaping,
And when a corpse approaches, close my house: 80
It goes with me, as with the cat the mouse.
   The Lord. Enough! What thou hast asked is granted.
Turn off this spirit from his fountain-head;
To trap him, let thy snares be planted,
And him, with thee, be downward led; 85
Then stand abashed, when thou art forced to say:
A good man, through obscurest aspiration,
Has still an instinct of the one true way.
   Mephistopheles. Agreed! But 'tis a short probation.
About my bet I feel no trepidation. 90
If I fulfil my expectation,
You'll let me triumph with a swelling breast:
Dust shall he eat, and with a zest,
As did a certain snake, my near relation.
   The Lord. Therein thou'rt free, according to thy merits; 95
The like of thee have never moved My hate.
Of all the bold, denying Spirits,
The waggish knave least trouble doth create.
Man's active nature, flagging, seeks too soon the level;
Unqualified repose he learns to crave; 100
Whence, willingly, the comrade him I gave,
Who works, excites, and must create, as Devil.
But ye,[1] God's sons in love and duty,
Enjoy the rich, the ever-living Beauty!
Creative Power, that works eternal schemes, 105
Clasp you in bonds of love, relaxing never,
And what in wavering apparition gleams

[1] The Lord now addresses the archangels.

Fix in its place with thoughts that stand forever!
     (*Heaven closes: the* ARCHANGELS *separate.*)
   Mephistopheles (*solus*). I like, at times, to hear
    The Ancient's word,
And have a care to be most civil: 110
It's really kind of such a noble Lord
So humanly to gossip with the Devil!

FIRST PART OF THE TRAGEDY

SCENE I. *Night. A lofty-arched, narrow, Gothi chamber.* FAUST, *in a chair at his desk, restless.*

   Faust. I've studied now Philosophy
And Jurisprudence, Medicine, —
And even, alas! Theology, —
From end to end, with labor keen;
And here, poor fool! with all my lore 5
I stand, no wiser than before:
I'm Magister — yea, Doctor — hight,
And straight or cross-wise, wrong or right.
These ten years long, with many woes,
I've led my scholars by the nose, — 10
And see, that nothing can be known!
That knowledge cuts me to the bone.
I'm cleverer, true, than those fops of teachers,
Doctors and Magisters, Scribes and Preachers;
Neither scruples nor doubts come now to smite me,
Nor Hell nor Devil can longer affright me. 16
For this, all pleasure am I foregoing;
I do not pretend to aught worth knowing,
I do not pretend I could be a teacher
To help or convert a fellow-creature. 20
Then, too, I've neither lands nor gold,
Nor the world's least pomp or honor hold —
No dog would endure such a curst existence!
Wherefore, from Magic I seek assistance,
That many a secret perchance I reach 25
Through spirit-power and spirit-speech,
And thus the bitter task forego
Of saying the things I do not know, —
That I may detect the inmost force
Which binds the world, and guides its course; 30
Its germs, productive powers explore,
And rummage in empty words no more!

O full and splendid Moon, whom I
Have, from this desk, seen climb the sky
So many a midnight, — would thy glow 35
For the last time beheld my woe!
Ever thine eye, most mournful friend,
O'er books and papers saw me bend;
But would that I, on mountains grand,
Amid thy blessed light could stand, 40
With spirits through mountain-caverns hover,
Float in thy twilight the meadows over,

And, freed from the fumes of lore that swathe me,
To health in thy dewy fountains bathe me!

Ah, me! this dungeon still I see,   45
This drear, accursed masonry,
Where even the welcome daylight strains
But duskly through the painted panes.
Hemmed in by many a toppling heap
Of books worm-eaten, gray with dust,   50
Which to the vaulted ceiling creep,
Against the smoky paper thrust, —
With glasses, boxes, round me stacked,
And instruments together hurled,
Ancestral lumber, stuffed and packed —   55
Such is my world: and what a world!

And do I ask, wherefore my heart
Falters, oppressed with unknown needs?
Why some inexplicable smart
All movement of my life impedes?   60
Alas! in living Nature's stead,
Where God His human creature set,
In smoke and mould the fleshless dead
And bones of beasts surround me yet!

Fly! Up, and seek the broad, free land!   65
And this one Book of Mystery [1]
From Nostradamus' very hand,
Is 't not sufficient company?
When I the starry courses know,
And Nature's wise instruction seek,   70
With light of power my soul shall glow,
As when to spirits spirits speak.
'Tis vain, this empty brooding here,
Though guessed the holy symbols be:
Ye, Spirits, come — ye hover near —   75
Oh, if you hear me, answer me!
     (*He opens the Book, and perceives the sign
        of the Macrocosm.[2]*)

Ha! what a sudden rapture leaps from this
I view, through all my senses swiftly flowing!
I feel a youthful, holy, vital bliss
In every vein and fibre newly glowing.   80
Was it a God who traced this sign,
With calm across my tumult stealing,
My troubled heart to joy unsealing,
With impulse, mystic and divine,
The powers of Nature here, around my path, re-
     vealing?   85
Am I a God? — so clear mine eyes!
In these pure features I behold
Creative Nature to my soul unfold.

---

[1] The reference is to a book by a French physician of
the early sixteenth century. The author's real name
was Michel de Nôtre-Dame.
[2] Here simply "the universe."

What says the sage, now first I recognize:
"The spirit-world no closures fasten;   90
Thy sense is shut, thy heart is dead:
Disciple, up! untiring, hasten
To bathe thy breast in morning-red!"
     (*He contemplates the sign.*)
How each the Whole its substance gives,
Each in the other works and lives!   95
Like heavenly forces rising and descending,
Their golden urns reciprocally lending,
With wings that winnow blessing
From Heaven through Earth I see them pressing,
Filling the All with harmony unceasing!   100
How grand a show! but, ah! a show alone.
Thee, boundless Nature, how make thee my own?
Where you, ye breasts? Founts of all Being, shin-
     ing,
Whereon hang Heaven's and Earth's desire,
Whereto our withered hearts aspire, —   105
Ye flow, ye feed: and am I vainly pining?
     (*He turns the leaves impatiently, and per-
       ceives the sign of the* EARTH-SPIRIT.)
How otherwise upon me works this sign!
Thou, Spirit of the Earth, art nearer:
Even now my powers are loftier, clearer:
I glow, as drunk with new-made wine: 110
New strength and heart to meet the world incite me,
The woe of earth, the bliss of earth, invite me,
And though the shock of storms may smite me,
No crash of shipwreck shall have power to fright
     me!
Clouds gather over me —   115
The moon conceals her light —
The lamp's extinguished! —
Mists rise, — red, angry rays are darting
Around my head! — There falls
A horror from the vaulted roof,   120
And seizes me!
I feel thy presence, Spirit I invoke!
Reveal thyself!
Ha! in my heart what rending stroke!
With new impulsion   125
My senses heave in this convulsion!
I feel thee draw my heart, absorb, exhaust me:
Thou must! thou must! and though my life it cost
     me!
     (*He seizes the book, and mysteriously pro-
       nounces the sign of the* SPIRIT. *A ruddy
       flame flashes: the* SPIRIT *appears in the
       flame.*)
Spirit. Who calls me?
Faust (*with averted head*). Terrible to see!
Spirit. Me hast thou long with might attracted,
Long from my sphere thy food exacted,   131
And now —
Faust.   Woe! I endure not thee!

Spirit. To view me is thine aspiration,
My voice to hear, my countenance to see;
Thy powerful yearning moveth me,   135
Here am I! — what mean perturbation
Thee, superhuman, shakes? Thy soul's high call-
      ing, where?
Where is the breast, which from itself a world did
      bear,
And shaped and cherished — which with joy ex-
      panded,
To be our peer, with us, the Spirits, banded?   140
Where art thou, Faust, whose voice has pierced to
      me,
Who towards me pressed with all thine energy?
He art thou, who, my presence breathing, seeing,
Trembles through all the depths of being,
A writhing worm, a terror-stricken form?   145
Faust. Thee, form of flame, shall I then fear?
Yes, I am Faust: I am thy peer!
      Spirit. In the tides of Life, in Action's storm,
A fluctuant wave,
A shuttle free,   150
Birth and the Grave,
An eternal sea,
A weaving, flowing
Life, all-glowing,
Thus at Time's humming loom 'tis my hand pre-
      pares   155
The garment of Life which the Deity wears!
Faust. Thou, who around the wide world wend-
      est,
Thou busy Spirit, how near I feel to thee!
      Spirit. Thou'rt like the Spirit which thou com-
      prehendest,
Not me!   (*Disappears.*) 160
Faust (*overwhelmed*). Not thee!
Whom then?
I, image of the Godhead!
Not even like thee!   (*A knock.*)
O Death! — I know it — 'tis my Famulus![1]   165
My fairest luck finds no fruition:
In all the fulness of my vision
The soulless sneak disturbs me thus!

(*Enter* WAGNER, *in dressing-gown and night-cap,
a lamp in his hand.* FAUST *turns impatiently.*)

Wagner. Pardon, I heard your declamation;
'Twas sure an old Greek tragedy you read?   170
In such an art I crave some preparation,
Since now it stands one in good stead.
I've often heard it said, a preacher
Might learn, with a comedian for a teacher.
Faust. Yes, when the priest comedian is by
      nature,   175
As haply now and then the case may be.

[1] A student assistant in the home of a professor.

Wagner. Ah, when one studies thus, a prisoned
      creature,
That scarce the world on holidays can see, —
Scarce through a glass, by rare occasion,
How shall one lead it by persuasion?   180
Faust. You'll ne'er attain it, save you know the
      feeling,
Save from the soul it rises clear,
Serene in primal strength, compelling
The hearts and minds of all who hear.
You sit forever gluing, patching;   185
You cook the scraps from others' fare;
And from your heap of ashes hatching
A starveling flame, ye blow it bare!
Take children's, monkeys' gaze admiring,
If such your taste, and be content;   190
But ne'er from heart to heart you'll speak inspir-
      ing,
Save your own heart is eloquent!
Wagner. Yet through delivery orators succeed;
I feel that I am far behind, indeed.
Faust. Seek thou the honest recompense!   195
Beware, a tinkling fool to be!
With little art, clear wit and sense
Suggest their own delivery;
And if thou'rt moved to speak in earnest,
What need, that after words thou yearnest?   200
Yes, your discourses, with their glittering show,
Where ye for men twist shredded thought like
      paper,
Are unrefreshing as the winds that blow
The rustling leaves through chill autumnal vapor!
Wagner. Ah, God! but Art is long,   205
And Life, alas! is fleeting.
And oft, with zeal my critic-duties meeting,
In head and breast there's something wrong.
How hard it is to compass the assistance
Whereby one rises to the source!   210
And, haply, ere one travels half the course
Must the poor devil quit existence.
Faust. Is parchment, then, the holy fount before
      thee,
A draught wherefrom thy thirst forever slakes?
No true refreshment can restore thee,   215
Save what from thine own soul spontaneous breaks.
Wagner. Pardon! a great delight is granted
When, in the spirit of the ages planted,
We mark how, ere our time, a sage has thought,
And then, how far his work, and grandly, we have
      brought.   220
Faust. O yes, up to the stars at last!
Listen, my friend: the ages that are past
Are now a book with seven seals protected:
What you the Spirit of the Ages call
Is nothing but the spirit of you all,   225
Wherein the Ages are reflected.

So, oftentimes, you miserably mar it!
At the first glance who sees it runs away.
An offal-barrel and a lumber-garret,
Or, at the best, a Punch-and-Judy play,   230
With maxims most pragmatical and hitting,
As in the mouths of puppets are befitting!
  Wagner. But then, the world — the human
      heart and brain!
Of these one covets some slight apprehension.
  Faust. Yes, of the kind which men attain!   235
Who dares the child's true name in public mention?
The few, who thereof something really learned,
Unwisely frank, with hearts that spurned conceal-
      ing,
And to the mob laid bare each thought and feeling,
Have evermore been crucified and burned.   240
I pray you, Friend, 'tis now the dead of night;
Our converse here must be suspended.
  Wagner. I would have shared your watches with
      delight,
That so our learned talk might be extended.
To-morrow, though, I'll ask, in Easter leisure,   245
This and the other question, at your pleasure.
Most zealously I seek for erudition:
Much do I know — but to know all is my ambi-
      tion.   (*Exit.*)
  Faust (solus). That brain, alone, not loses hope,
      whose choice is
To stick in shallow trash forevermore, —   250
Which digs with eager hand for buried ore,
And, when it finds an angle-worm, rejoices!

Dare such a human voice disturb the flow,
Around me here, of spirit-presence fullest?
And yet, this once my thanks I owe   255
To thee, of all earth's sons the poorest, dullest!
For thou hast torn me from that desperate state
Which threatened soon to overwhelm my senses:
The apparition was so giant-great,   259
It dwarfed and withered all my soul's pretences!

I, image of the Godhead, who began —
Deeming Eternal Truth secure in nearness —
To sun myself in heavenly light and clearness,
And laid aside the earthly man; —   264
I, more than Cherub, whose free force had planned
To flow through Nature's veins in glad pulsation,
To reach beyond, enjoying in creation
The life of Gods, behold my expiation!
A thunder-word hath swept me from my stand.

With thee I dare not venture to compare me.   270
Though I possessed the power to draw thee near
      me,
The power to keep thee was denied my hand.
When that ecstatic moment held me,

I felt myself so small, so great;
But thou hast ruthlessly repelled me   275
Back upon Man's uncertain fate.
What shall I shun?   Whose guidance borrow?
Shall I accept that stress and strife?
Ah! every deed of ours, no less than every sorrow,
Impedes the onward march of life.   280

Some alien substance more and more is cleaving
To all the mind conceives of grand and fair;
When this world's Good is won by our achieving,
The Better, then, is named a cheat and snare.
The fine emotions, whence our lives we mould,
Lie in the earthly tumult dumb and cold.   286
If hopeful Fancy once, in daring flight,
Her longings to the Infinite expanded,
Yet now a narrow space contents her quite,
Since Time's wild wave so many a fortune stranded.
Care at the bottom of the heart is lurking: 291
Her secret pangs in silence working,
She, restless, rocks herself, disturbing joy and rest:
In newer masks her face is ever drest,
By turns as house and land, as wife and child, pre-
      sented, —   295
As water, fire, as poison, steel:
We dread the blows we never feel,
And what we never lose is yet by us lamented!
I am not like the Gods!   That truth is felt too
      deep:
The worm am I, that in the dust doth creep, —   300
That, while in dust it lives and seeks its bread,
Is crushed and buried by the wanderer's tread.

Is not this dust, these walls within them hold,
The hundred shelves, which cramp and chain me,
The frippery, the trinkets thousand-fold,   305
That in this mothy den restrain me?
Here shall I find the help I need?
Shall here a thousand volumes teach me only
That men, self-tortured, everywhere must bleed, —
And here and there one happy man sits lonely?
What mean'st thou by that grin, thou hollow
      skull,   311
Save that thy brain, like mine, a cloudy mirror,
Sought once the shining day, and then, in twilight
      dull,
Thirsting for Truth, went wretchedly to Error?
Ye instruments, forsooth, but jeer at me   315
With wheel and cog, and shapes uncouth of won-
      der;
I found the portal, you the keys should be;
Your wards are deftly wrought, but drive no bolts
      asunder!
Mysterious even in open day,
Nature retains her veil, despite our clamors: 320
That which she doth not willingly display

Cannot be wrenched from her with levers, screws,
    and hammers.
Ye ancient tools, whose use I never knew,
Here, since my father used ye, still ye moulder:
Thou, ancient scroll, hast worn thy smoky hue 325
Since at this desk the dim lamp wont to smoulder.
'Twere better far, had I my little idly spent,
Than now to sweat beneath its burden, I confess it!
What from your fathers' heritage is lent,
Earn it anew, to really possess it!   330
What serves not, is a sore impediment:
The Moment's need creates the thing to serve and
    bless it!

Yet, wherefore turns my gaze to yonder point so
    lightly?
Is yonder flask a magnet for mine eyes?
Whence, all around me, glows the air so brightly,
As when in woods at night the mellow moonbeam
    lies?   336

I hail thee, wondrous, rarest vial!
I take thee down devoutly, for the trial:
Man's art and wit I venerate in thee.
Thou summary of gentle slumber-juices,   340
Essence of deadly finest powers and uses,
Unto thy master show thy favor free!
I see thee, and the stings of pain diminish;
I grasp thee, and my struggles slowly finish:
My spirit's flood-tide ebbeth more and more.   345
Out on the open ocean speeds my dreaming,
The glassy flood before my feet is gleaming,
A new day beckons to a newer shore!

A fiery chariot, borne on buoyant pinions,
Sweeps near me now!   I soon shall ready be   350
To pierce the ether's high, unknown dominions,
To reach new spheres of pure activity!
This godlike rapture, this supreme existence,
Do I, but now a worm, deserve to track?
Yes, resolute to reach some brighter distance,   355
On Earth's fair sun I turn my back!
Yes, let me dare those gates to fling asunder,
Which every man would fain go slinking by!
'Tis time, through deeds this word of truth to
    thunder:
That with the height of Gods Man's dignity may
    vie!   360
Nor from that gloomy gulf to shrink affrighted,
Where Fancy doth herself to self-born pangs com-
    pel, —
To struggle toward that pass benighted,
Around whose narrow mouth flame all the fires of
    Hell, —
To take this step with cheerful resolution,   365
Though Nothingness should be the certain, swift
    conclusion!

And now come down, thou cup of crystal clearest!
Fresh from thine ancient cover thou appearest,
So many years forgotten to my thought!
Thou shon'st at old ancestral banquets cheery,
The solemn guests thou madest merry,   371
When one thy wassail to the other brought.
The rich and skilful figures o'er thee wrought,
The drinker's duty, rhyme-wise to explain them,
Or in one breath below the mark to drain them,   375
From many a night of youth my memory caught.
Now to a neighbor shall I pass thee never,
Nor on thy curious art to test my wit endeavor:
Here is a juice whence sleep is swiftly born.
It fills with browner flood thy crystal hollow; 380
I chose, prepared it: thus I follow, —
With all my soul the final drink I swallow,
A solemn festal cup, a greeting to the morn!
             (*He sets the goblet to his mouth.*)

      (*Chime of bells and choral song.*)

Chorus of Angels. Christ is arisen!
      Joy to the Mortal One,   385
      Whom the unmerited,
      Clinging, inherited
      Needs did imprison.
Faust. What hollow humming, what a sharp,
    clear stroke,
Drives from my lip the goblet's, at their meeting?
Announce the booming bells already woke   391
The first glad hour of Easter's festal greeting?
Ye choirs, have ye begun the sweet, consoling chant
Which, through the night of Death, the angels
    ministrant
Sang, God's new Covenant repeating?   395
Chorus of Women. With spices and precious
      Balm, we arrayed him;
      Faithful and gracious,
      We tenderly laid him:
      Linen to bind him   400
      Cleanlily wound we:
      Ah! when we would find him,
      Christ no more found we!
Chorus of Angels. Christ is ascended!
      Bliss hath invested him, —   405
      Woes that molested him,
      Trials that tested him,
      Gloriously ended!
Faust. Why, here in dust, entice me with your
    spell,
Ye gentle, powerful sounds of Heaven?   410
Peal rather there, where tender natures dwell.
Your messages I hear, but faith has not been given:
The dearest child of Faith is Miracle.
I venture not to soar to yonder regions
Whence the glad tidings hither float;   415

And yet, from childhood up familiar with the note,
To Life it now renews the old allegiance.
Once Heavenly Love sent down a burning kiss
Upon my brow, in Sabbath silence holy;
And, filled with mystic presage, chimed the church-
    bell slowly, 420
And prayer dissolved me in a fervent bliss.
A sweet, uncomprehended yearning
Drove forth my feet through woods and meadows
    free,
And while a thousand tears were burning,
I felt a world arise for me. 425
These chants, to youth and all its sports appealing,
Proclaimed the Spring's rejoicing holiday;
And Memory holds me now, with childish feeling,
Back from the last, the solemn way.
Sound on, ye hymns of Heaven, so sweet and
    mild! 430
My tears gush forth: the Earth takes back her
    child!

    Chorus of Disciples. Has He, victoriously,
        Burst from the vaulted
        Grave, and all-gloriously
        Now sits exalted? 435
        Is He, in glow of birth,
        Rapture creative near?
        Ah! to the woe of earth
        Still are we native here.
        We, his aspiring 440
        Followers, Him we miss;
        Weeping, desiring,
        Master, Thy bliss!
    Chorus of Angels. Christ is arisen,
        Out of Corruption's womb: 445
        Burst ye the prison,
        Break from your gloom!
        Praising and pleading him,
        Lovingly needing him,
        Brotherly feeding him, 450
        Preaching and speeding him,
        Blessing, succeeding Him,
        Thus is the Master near, —
        Thus is He here!

[*Scene II, "Before the City-Gate," presents a
motley group of apprentices, servant-girls, students,
peasants, soldiers, etc., bent on enjoying a holiday.
Faust and Wagner join the merrymakers. Faust is
accorded the respect of the populace for the good he
has done, but remains dejected. He tells Wagner
that two souls reside within his breast "and each
withdraws from, and repels, its brother"; one holds
worldly things in high esteem, the other yearns for
"high ancestral spaces." At the close the two are
joined by a black poodle which behaves most strangely.
The events of Scene III take place in Faust's study*

*where the dog reveals himself as Mephistopheles.
Under a spell Faust goes to sleep; Mephistopheles
leaves after having promised to return.*]

SCENE IV. *The Study.* FAUST. MEPHISTOPHELES.

  Faust. A knock? Come in! Again my quiet
    broken?
  Mephistopheles. 'Tis I!
  Faust.   Come in!
  Mephistopheles.   Thrice must
    the words be spoken.
  Faust. Come in, then!
  Mephistopheles.   Thus thou pleasest me.
I hope we'll suit each other well;
For now, thy vapors to dispell, 5
I come, a squire of high degree,
In scarlet coat, with golden trimming,
A cloak in silken lustre swimming,
A tall cock's-feather in my hat,
A long, sharp sword for show or quarrel, — 10
And I advise thee, brief and flat,
To don the self-same gay apparel,
That, from this den released, and free,
Life be at last revealed to thee!
  Faust. This life of earth, whatever my attire, 15
Would pain me in its wonted fashion.
Too old am I to play with passion;
Too young, to be without desire.
What from the world have I to gain?
Thou shalt abstain — renounce — refrain! 20
Such is the everlasting song
That in the ears of all men rings, —
That unrelieved, our whole life long,
Each hour, in passing, hoarsely sings.
In very terror I at morn awake, 25
Upon the verge of bitter weeping,
To see the day of disappointment break,
To no one hope of mine — not one — its promise
    keeping: —
That even each joy's presentiment
With wilful cavil would diminish, 30
With grinning masks of life prevent
My mind its fairest work to finish!
Then, too, when night descends, how anxiously
Upon my couch of sleep I lay me:
There, also, comes no rest to me, 35
But some wild dream is sent to fray me.
The God that in my breast is owned
Can deeply stir the inner sources;
The God, above my powers enthroned,
He cannot change external forces. 40
So, by the burden of my days oppressed,
Death is desired, and Life a thing unblest!
  Mephistopheles. And yet is never Death a wholly
    welcome guest.

Faust. O fortunate, for whom, when victory glances,
The bloody laurels on the brow he bindeth!   45
Whom, after rapid, maddening dances,
In clasping maiden-arms he findeth!
O would that I, before that spirit-power,
Ravished and rapt from life, had sunken!

Mephistopheles. And yet, by some one, in that nightly hour,   50
A certain liquid was not drunken.

Faust. Eavesdropping, ha! thy pleasure seems to be.

Mephistopheles. Omniscient am I not; yet much is known to me.

Faust. Though some familiar tone, retrieving
My thoughts from torment, led me on,   55
And sweet, clear echoes came, deceiving
A faith bequeathed from Childhood's dawn,
Yet now I curse whate'er entices
And snares the soul with visions vain;
With dazzling cheats and dear devices   60
Confines it in this cave of pain!
Cursed be, at once, the high ambition
Wherewith the mind itself deludes!
Cursed be the glare of apparition
That on the finer sense intrudes!   65
Cursed be the lying dream's impression
Of name, and fame, and laurelled brow!
Cursed, all that flatters as possession,
As wife and child, as knave and plow!
Cursed Mammon be, when he with treasures   70
To restless action spurs our fate!
Cursed when, for soft, indulgent leisures,
He lays for us the pillows straight!
Cursed be the vine's transcendent nectar, —
The highest favor Love lets fall!   75
Cursed, also, Hope! — cursed Faith, the spectre!
And cursed be Patience most of all!

Chorus of Spirits (invisible). Woe! woe!
Thou hast it destroyed,
The beautiful world,   80
With powerful fist:
In ruin 'tis hurled,
By the blow of a demigod shattered!
The scattered
Fragments into the Void we carry,   85
Deploring
The beauty perished beyond restoring.
Mightier
For the children of men,
Brightlier   90
Build it again,
In thine own bosom build it anew!
Bid the new career
Commence,
With clearer sense,   95

And the new songs of cheer
Be sung thereto!

Mephistopheles. These are the small dependants
Who give me attendance.
Hear them, to deeds and passion   100
Counsel in shrewd old-fashion!
Into the world of strife,
Out of this lonely life
That of senses and sap has betrayed thee,
They would persuade thee.   105
This nursing of the pain forego thee,
That, like a vulture, feeds upon thy breast!
The worst society thou find'st will show thee
Thou art a man among the rest.
But 'tis not meant to thrust   110
Thee into the mob thou hatest!
I am not one of the greatest,
Yet, wilt thou to me entrust
Thy steps through life, I'll guide thee, —
Will willingly walk beside thee, —   115
Will serve thee at once and forever
With best endeavor,
And, if thou art satisfied,
Will as servant, slave, with thee abide.

Faust. And what shall be my counter-service therefor?   120

Mephistopheles. The time is long: thou need'st not now insist.

Faust. No — no! The Devil is an egotist,
And is not apt, without a why or wherefore,
"For God's sake," others to assist.
Speak thy conditions plain and clear!   125
With such a servant danger comes, I fear.

Mephistopheles. Here, an unwearied slave, I'll wear thy tether,
And to thine every nod obedient be:
When *There* again we come together,
Then shalt thou do the same for me.   130

Faust. The *There* my scruples naught increases
When thou hast dashed this world to pieces,
The other, then, its place may fill.
Here, on this earth, my pleasures have their sources;
Yon sun beholds my sorrows in his courses;   135
And when from these my life itself divorces,
Let happen all that can or will!
I'll hear no more: 'tis vain to ponder
If there we cherish love or hate,
Or, in the spheres we dream of yonder,   140
A High and Low our souls await.

Mephistopheles. In this sense, even, canst thou venture.
Come, bind thyself by prompt indenture,
And thou mine arts with joy shalt see:
What no man ever saw, I'll give to thee.   145

Faust. Canst thou, poor Devil, give me whatso-
ever?
When was a human soul, in its supreme endeavor,
E'er understood by such as thou?
Yet, hast thou food which never satiates, now,—
The restless, ruddy gold hast thou,   150
That runs, quicksilver-like, one's fingers through,—
A game whose winnings no man ever knew, —
A maid, that, even from my breast,
Beckons my neighbor with her wanton glances,
And Honor's godlike zest,   155
The meteor that a moment dances, —
Show me the fruits that, ere they're gathered, rot,
And trees that daily with new leafage ciothe them!
   Mephistopheles. Such a demand alarms me not:
Such treasures have I, and can show them.   160
But still the time may reach us, good my friend,
When peace we crave and more luxurious diet.
   Faust. When on an idler's bed I stretch myself
      in quiet,
There let, at once, my record end!
Canst thou with lying flattery rule me,   165
Until, self-pleased, myself I see, —
Canst thou with rich enjoyment fool me,
Let that day be the last for me!
The bet I offer.
   Mephistopheles. Done!
   Faust.   And heartily!
When thus I hail the Moment flying: 170
"Ah, still delay — thou art so fair!" [1]
Then bind me in thy bonds undying,
My final ruin then declare!
Then let the death-bell chime the token,
Then art thou from thy service free!   175
The clock may stop, the hand be broken,
Then Time be finished unto me!
   Mephistopheles. Consider well: my memory
      good is rated.
   Faust. Thou hast a perfect right thereto.
My powers I have not rashly estimated: 180
A slave am I, whate'er I do —
If thine, or whose? 'tis needless to debate it.
   Mephistopheles. Then at the Doctors'-banquet [2]
      I, to-day,
Will as a servant wait behind thee.
But one thing more! Beyond all risk to bind
      thee,   185
Give me a line or two, I pray.
   Faust. Demand'st thou, Pedant, too, a docu-
      ment?
Hast never known a man, nor proved his word's
      intent?

[1] These lines are the crux of the agreement Faust
makes with Mephistopheles.

[2] Banquet in celebration of receiving a doctor's
degree.

Is't not enough, that what I speak to-day
Shall stand, with all my future days agreeing? 190
In all its tides sweeps not the world away,
And shall a promise bind my being?
Yet this delusion in our hearts we bear:
Who would himself therefrom deliver?
Blest he, whose bosom Truth makes pure and fair!
No sacrifice shall he repent of ever.   196
Nathless a parchment, writ and stamped with care,
A spectre is, which all to shun endeavor.
The word, alas! dies even in the pen,
And wax and leather keep the lordship then.   200
What wilt from me, Base Spirit, say? —
Brass, marble, parchment, paper, clay?
The terms with graver, quill, or chisel, stated?
I freely leave the choice to thee.
   Mephistopheles. Why heat thyself, thus in-
      stantly,   205
With eloquence exaggerated?
Each leaf for such a pact is good;
And to subscribe thy name thou'lt take a drop of
      blood.
   Faust. If thou therewith art fully satisfied,
So let us by the farce abide.   210
   Mephistopheles. Blood is a juice of rarest quality.
   Faust. Fear not that I this pact shall seek to
      sever!
The promise that I make to thee
Is just the sum of my endeavor.
I have myself inflated all too high;   215
My proper place is thy estate:
The Mighty Spirit deigns me no reply,
And Nature shuts on me her gate.
The thread of Thought at last is broken,
And knowledge brings disgust unspoken.   220
Let us the sensual deeps explore,
To quench the fervors of glowing passion!
Let every marvel take form and fashion
Through the impervious veil it wore!
Plunge we in Time's tumultuous dance,   225
In the rush and roll of Circumstance!
Then may delight and distress,
And worry and success,
Alternately follow, as best they can:
Restless activity proves the man!   230
   Mephistopheles. For you no bound, no term is set.
Whether you everywhere be trying,
Or snatch a rapid bliss in flying,
May it agree with you, what you get!
Only fall to, and show no timid balking.   235
   Faust. But thou hast heard, 'tis not of joy we're
      talking.
I take the wildering whirl, enjoyment's keenest
      pain,
Enamored hate, exhilarant disdain.
My bosom, of its thirst for knowledge sated,

Shall not, henceforth, from any pang be wrested,
And all of life for all mankind created   241
Shall be within mine inmost being tested:
The highest, lowest forms my soul shall borrow,
Shall heap upon itself their bliss and sorrow,
And thus, my own sole self to all their selves expanded,   245
I too, at last, shall with them all be stranded!
    Mephistopheles. Believe me, who for many a
        thousand year
The same tough meat have chewed and tested.
That from the cradle to the bier
No man the ancient leaven has digested!   250
Trust one of us, this Whole supernal
Is made but for a God's delight!
He dwells in splendor single and eternal,
But *us* he thrusts in darkness, out of sight,
And *you* he dowers with Day and Night.   255
    Faust. Nay, but I will!
    Mephistopheles.   A good reply!
One only fear still needs repeating:
The art is long, the time is fleeting.
Then let thyself be taught, say I!
Go, league thyself with a poet,   260
Give the rein to his imagination,
Then wear the crown, and show it,
Of the qualities of his creation, —
The courage of the lion's breed,
The wild stag's speed,   265
The Italian's fiery blood,
The North's firm fortitude!
Let him find for thee the secret tether
That binds the Noble and Mean together,
And teach thy pulses of youth and pleasure   270
To love by rule, and hate by measure!
I'd like, myself, such a one to see:
Sir Microcosm his name should be.
    Faust. What am I, then, if 'tis denied my part
The crown of all humanity to win me,   275
Whereto yearns every sense within me?
    Mephistopheles. Why, on the whole, thou'rt —
        what thou art.
Set wigs of million curls upon thy head, to raise
    thee,
Wear shoes an ell in height, — the truth betrays
    thee,
And thou remainest — what thou art.   280
    Faust. I feel, indeed, that I have made the treasure
Of human thought and knowledge mine, in vain;
And if I now sit down in restful leisure,
No fount of newer strength is in my brain:
I am no hair's-breadth more in height,   285
Nor nearer to the Infinite.
    Mephistopheles. Good Sir, you see the facts precisely

As they are seen by each and all.
We must arrange them now, more wisely,
Before the joys of life shall pall.   290
Why, Zounds! Both hands and feet are, truly —
And head and virile forces — thine:
Yet all that I indulge in newly,
Is't thence less wholly mine?
If I've six stallions in my stall,   295
Are not their forces also lent me?
I speed along, completest man of all,
As though my legs were four-and-twenty.
Take hold, then! let reflection rest,
And plunge into the world with zest!   300
I say to thee, a speculative wight
Is like a beast on moorlands lean,
That round and round some fiend misleads to evil
    plight,
While all about lie pastures fresh and green.
    Faust. Then how shall we begin?
    Mephistopheles.   We'll try a wider sphere.
What place of martyrdom is here!   306
Is't life, I ask, is't even prudence,
To bore thyself and bore the students?
Let Neighbor Paunch to that attend!
Why plague thyself with threshing straw forever?
The best thou learnest, in the end   311
Thou dar'st not tell the youngsters — never!
I hear one's footsteps, hither steering.
    Faust. To see him now I have no heart.
    Mephistopheles. So long the poor boy waits a
        hearing,   315
He must not unconsoled depart.
Thy cap and mantle straightway lend me!
I'll play the comedy with art.
                (*He disguises himself.*)
My wits, be certain, will befriend me.
But fifteen minutes' time is all I need;   320
For our fine trip, meanwhile, prepare thyself with
    speed!   (*Exit* FAUST.)
    Mephistopheles (in FAUST's *long mantle*). Reason
        and Knowledge only thou despise,
The highest strength in man that lies!
Let but the Lying Spirit bind thee
With magic works and shows that blind thee,   325
And I shall have thee fast and sure! —
Fate such a bold, untrammelled spirit gave him,
As forwards, onwards, ever must endure;
Whose over-hasty impulse drave him
Past earthly joys he might secure.   330
Dragged through the wildest life, will I enslave
    him,
Through flat and stale indifference;
With struggling, chilling, checking, so deprave him
That, to his hot, insatiate sense,
The dream of drink shall mock, but never lave
    him: 335

Refreshment shall his lips in vain implore —
Had he not made himself the Devil's, naught could
    save him,
Still were he lost forevermore!

(*A Student enters.*)

Student. A short time, only, am I here,
And come, devoted and sincere,   340
To greet and know the man of fame,
Whom men to me with reverence name.

Mephistopheles. Your courtesy doth flatter me:
You see a man, as others be.
Have you, perchance, elsewhere begun?   345

Student. Receive me now, I pray, as one
Who comes to you with courage good,
Somewhat of cash, and healthy blood:
My mother was hardly willing to let me;   349
But knowledge worth having I fain would get me.

Mephistopheles. Then you have reached the
    right place now.

Student. I'd like to leave it, I must avow;
I find these walls, these vaulted spaces
Are anything but pleasant places.
'Tis all so cramped and close and mean;   355
One sees no tree, no glimpse of green,
And when the lecture-halls receive me,
Seeing, hearing, and thinking leave me.

Mephistopheles. All that depends on habitude.
So from its mother's breasts a child   360
At first, reluctant, takes its food,
But soon to seek them is beguiled.
Thus, at the breasts of Wisdom clinging,
Thou'lt find each day a greater rapture bringing.

Student. I'll hang thereon with joy, and freely
    drain them;   365
But tell me, pray, the proper means to gain them.

Mephistopheles. Explain, before you further
    speak,
The special faculty you seek.

Student. I crave the highest erudition;
And fain would make my acquisition   370
All that there is in Earth and Heaven,
In Nature and in Science too.

Mephistopheles. Here is the genuine path for
    you;
Yet strict attention must be given.

Student. Body and soul thereon I'll wreak;   375
Yet, truly, I've some inclination
On summer holidays to seek
A little freedom and recreation.

Mephistopheles. Use well your time! It flies so
    swiftly from us;
But time through order may be won, I promise.   380
So, Friend, (my views to briefly sum,)
First, the *collegium logicum.*[1]

[1] A course in logic.

There will your mind be drilled and braced,
As if in Spanish boots[1] 'twere laced,
And thus, to graver paces brought,   385
'Twill plod along the path of thought,
Instead of shooting here and there,
A will-o'-the-wisp in murky air.
Days will be spent to bid you know,
What once you did at a single blow,   390
Like eating and drinking, free and strong, —
That one, two, three! thereto belong.
Truly the fabric of mental fleece
Resembles a weaver's masterpiece,
Where a thousand threads one treadle throws,   395
Where fly the shuttles hither and thither,
Unseen the threads are knit together,
And an infinite combination grows.
Then, the philosopher steps in
And shows, no otherwise it could have been: 400
The first was so, the second so,
Therefore the third and fourth are so;
Were not the first and second, then
The third and fourth had never been.
The scholars are everywhere believers,   405
But never succeed in being weavers.
He who would study organic existence,
First drives out the soul with rigid persistence;
Then the parts in his hand he may hold and class,
But the spiritual link is lost, alas!   410
Encheiresin naturæ,[2] this Chemistry names,
Nor knows how herself she banters and blames!

Student. I cannot understand you quite.

Mephistopheles. Your mind will shortly be set
    aright,
When you have learned, all things reducing,   415
To classify them for your using.

Student. I feel as stupid, from all you've said,
As if a mill-wheel whirled in my head!

Mephistopheles. And after — first and foremost
    duty —
Of Metaphysics learn the use and beauty!   420
See that you most profoundly gain
What does not suit the human brain!
A splendid word to serve, you'll find
For what goes in — or won't go in — your mind.
But first, at least this half a year,   425
To order rigidly adhere;
Five hours a day, you understand,
And when the clock strikes, be on hand!
Prepare beforehand for your part
With paragraphs all got by heart,   430
So you can better watch, and look
That naught is said but what is in the book:
Yet in thy writing as unwearied be,
As did the Holy Ghost dictate to thee!

[1] An instrument for torturing the foot.

[2] A treatment, or handling, of nature.

Student. No need to tell me twice to do it! 435
I think, how useful 'tis to write;
For what one has, in black and white,
One carries home and then goes through it.
Mephistopheles. Yet choose thyself a faculty!
Student. I cannot reconcile myself to Juris-
  prudence. 440
Mephistopheles. Nor can I therefore greatly
  blame you students:
I know what science this has come to be.
All rights and laws are still transmitted
Like an eternal sickness of the race, —
From generation unto generation fitted, 445
And shifted round from place to place.
Reason becomes a sham, Beneficence a worry:
Thou art a grandchild, therefore woe to thee!
The right born with us, ours in verity,
This to consider, there's, alas! no hurry. 450
  Student. My own disgust is strengthened by
  your speech.
O lucky he, whom you shall teach!
I've almost for Theology decided.
  Mephistopheles. I should not wish to see you
  here misguided:
For, as regards this science, let me hint 455
'Tis very hard to shun the false direction;
There's so much secret poison lurking in 't,
So like the medicine, it baffles your detection.
Hear, therefore, one alone, for that is best, in sooth,
And simply take your master's words for truth. 460
On *words* let your attention centre!
Then through the safest gate you'll enter
The temple-halls of Certainty.
  Student. Yet in the word must some idea be.
  Mephistopheles. Of course! But only shun too
  over-sharp a tension, 465
For just where fails the comprehension,
A word steps promptly in as deputy.
With words 'tis excellent disputing;
Systems to words 'tis easy suiting;
On words 'tis excellent believing; 470
No word can ever lose a jot from thieving.
  Student. Pardon! With many questions I de-
  tain you,
Yet must I trouble you again.
Of Medicine I still would fain
Hear one strong word that might explain you. 475
Three years is but a little space,
And, God! who can the field embrace?
If one some index could be shown,
'Twere easier groping forward, truly.
  Mephistopheles (*aside*). I'm tired enough of this
  dry tone, — 480
Must play the Devil again, and fully.
(*Aloud.*) To grasp the spirit of Medicine is easy:
Learn of the great and little world your fill,

To let it go at last, so please ye,
Just as God will! 485
In vain that through the realms of science you
  may drift;
Each one learns only — just what learn he can:
Yet he who grasps the Moment's gift,
He is the proper man.
Well-made you are, 'tis not to be denied, 490
The rest a bold address will win you;
If you but in yourself confide,
At once confide all others in you.
To lead the women, learn the special feeling!
Their everlasting aches and groans, 495
In thousand tones,
Have all one source, one mode of healing;
And if your acts are half discreet,
You'll always have them at your feet.
A title first must draw and interest them, 500
And show that yours all other arts exceeds;
Then, as a greeting, you are free to touch and test
  them,
While, thus to do, for years another pleads.
You press and count the pulse's dances,
And then, with burning sidelong glances, 505
You clasp the swelling hips, to see
If tightly laced her corsets be.
  Student. That's better, now! The How and
  Where, one sees.
  Mephistopheles. My worthy friend, gray are all
  theories,
And green alone Life's golden tree. 510
  Student. I swear to you, 'tis like a dream to me.
Might I again presume, with trust unbounded,
To hear your wisdom thoroughly expounded?
  Mephistopheles. Most willingly, to what extent
  I may.
  Student. I cannot really go away: 515
Allow me that my album first I reach you, —
Grant me this favor, I beseech you!
  Mephistopheles. Assuredly.
                    (*He writes, and returns the book.*)
  Student (*reads*).   *Eritis sicut Deus, sci-
  entes bonum et malum.*[1]
      (*Closes the book with reverence, and with-
      draws.*)
  Mephistopheles. Follow the ancient text, and
  the snake thou wast ordered to trample!
With all thy likeness to God, thou'lt yet be a sorry
  example! 520

          (FAUST *enters.*)
  Faust. Now, whither shall we go?
  Mephistopheles.   As best it pleases thee.
The little world, and then the great, we'll see.
  [1] Genesis III, 5. — "Ye shall be as God, knowing
good and evil."

With what delight, what profit winning,
Shalt thou sponge through the term beginning!

Faust. Yet with the flowing beard I wear,   525
Both ease and grace will fail me there.
The attempt, indeed, were a futile strife;
I never could learn the ways of life.
I feel so small before others, and thence
Should always find embarrassments.   530

Mephistopheles. My friend, thou soon shalt lose
all such misgiving:
Be thou but self-possessed, thou hast the art of
living!

Faust. How shall we leave the house, and start?
Where hast thou servant, coach and horses?

Mephistopheles. We'll spread this cloak with
proper art,   535
Then through the air direct our courses.
But only, on so bold a flight,
Be sure to have thy luggage light.
A little burning air, which I shall soon prepare us,
Above the earth will nimbly bear us,   540
And, if we're light, we'll travel swift and clear:
I gratulate thee on thy new career!

SCENE V.   AUERBACH'S *Cellar in Leipzig.*
Carousal of jolly companions.

Frosch. Is no one laughing? no one drinking?
I'll teach you how to grin, I'm thinking.
To-day you're like wet straw, so tame;
And usually you're all aflame.

Brander. Now that's your fault; from you we
nothing see,   5
No beastliness and no stupidity.

Frosch (pours a glass of wine over BRANDER'S
head). There's both together!

Brander.   Twice a swine!

Frosch. You wanted them: I've given you mine.

Siebel. Turn out who quarrels — out the door!
With open throat sing chorus, drink and roar!   10
Up! holla! ho!

Altmayer.   Woe's me, the fearful bellow!
Bring cotton, quick! He's split my ears, that
fellow.

Siebel. When the vault echoes to the song,
One first perceives the bass is deep and strong.

Frosch. Well said! and out with him that takes
the least offence!   15
               Ah, tara, lara, da!

Altmayer.   Ah, tara, lara, da!

Frosch. The throats are tuned, commence!
*(Sings.) The dear old holy Roman realm,
How does it hold together?*   20

Brander. A nasty song! Fie! a political song —
A most offensive song! Thank God, each morning,
therefore,

That you have not the Roman realm to care for!
At least, I hold it so much gain for me,
That I nor Chancellor nor Kaiser be.   25
Yet also we must have a ruling head, I hope,
And so we'll choose ourselves a Pope.
You know the quality that can
Decide the choice, and elevate the man.

*Frosch (sings).   Soar up, soar up, Dame Night-
ingale!*   30
Ten thousand times my sweetheart hail!

Siebel. No, greet my sweetheart not! I tell you,
I'll resent it.

Frosch. My sweetheart greet and kiss! I dare
you to prevent it!
*(Sings.)   Draw the latch! the darkness makes:
Draw the latch! the lover wakes.*   35
Shut the latch! the morning breaks.

Siebel. Yes, sing away, sing on, and praise, and
brag of her!
I'll wait my proper time for laughter:
Me by the nose she lead, and now she'll lead you
after.
Her paramour should be an ugly gnome,   40
Where four roads cross, in wanton play to meet her:
An old he-goat, from Blocksberg coming home,
Should his good-night in lustful gallop bleat her!
A fellow made of genuine flesh and blood
Is for the wench a deal too good.   45
Greet her? Not I: unless, when meeting,
To smash her windows be a greeting!

Brander (pounding on the table). Attention!
Hearken now to me!
Confess, Sirs, I know how to live.
Enamored persons here have we,   50
And I, as suits their quality,
Must something fresh for their advantage give.
Take heed! 'Tis of the latest cut, my strain,
And all strike in at each refrain!
(He sings.)   There was a rat in the cellar-nest,   55
Whom fat and butter made smoother:
He had a paunch beneath his vest
Like that of Doctor Luther.
The cook laid poison cunningly,
And then as sore oppressed was he   60
As if he had love in his bosom.

Chorus (shouting). As if he had love in his bosom!

Brander. He ran around, he ran about,
His thirst in puddles laving;
He gnawed and scratched the house throughout,
But nothing cured his raving.   66
He whirled and jumped, with torment mad,
And soon enough the poor beast had,
As if he had love in his bosom.

Chorus. As if he had love in his bosom!   70

Brander.   And driven at last, in open day,
He ran into the kitchen,

Fell on the hearth, and squirming lay,
In the last convulsion twitching.
Then laughed the murderess in her glee: 75
"Ha! ha! he's at his last gasp," said she.
"As if he had love in his bosom!"
   Chorus. As if he had love in his bosom!
   Siebel. How the dull fools enjoy the matter!
To me it is a proper art 80
Poison for such poor rats to scatter.
   Brander. Perhaps you'll warmly take their part?
   Altmayer. The bald-pate pot-belly I have noted:
Misfortune tames him by degrees;
For in the rat by poison bloated 85
His own most natural form he sees.

   (*Enter* FAUST *and* MEPHISTOPHELES.)

   Mephistopheles. ¡Before all else, I bring thee hither
Where boon companions meet together,
To let thee see how smooth life runs away.
Here, for the folk, each day's a holiday: 90
With little wit, and ease to suit them,
They whirl in narrow, circling trails,
Like kittens playing with their tails;
And if no headache persecute them,
So long the host may credit give, 95
They merrily and careless live.
   Brander. The fact is easy to unravel,
Their air's so odd, they've just returned from travel:
A single hour they've not been here.
   Frosch. You've verily hit the truth! Leipzig to me is dear:
Paris in miniature, how it refines its people! 100
   Siebel. Who are the strangers, should you guess?
   Frosch. Let me alone! I'll set them first to drinking,
And then, as one a child's tooth draws, with cleverness,
I'll worm their secret out, I'm thinking. 105
They're of a noble house, that's very clear:
Haughty and discontented they appear.
   Brander. They're mountebanks, upon a revel.
   Altmayer. Perhaps.
   Frosch.   Look out, I'll smoke them now!
   Mephistopheles (*to* FAUST). Not if he had them by the neck, I vow, 110
Would e'er these people scent the Devil!
   Faust. Fair greeting, gentlemen!
   Siebel.   Our thanks: we give the same.
   (*Murmurs, inspecting* MEPHISTOPHELES *from the side.*)
In one foot is the fellow lame?
   Mephistopheles. Is it permitted that we share your leisure?

In place of cheering drink, which one seeks vainly here, 115
Your company shall give us pleasure.
   Altmayer. A most fastidious person you appear.
   Frosch. No doubt 'twas late when you from Rippach [1] started?
And supping there with Hans occasioned your delay?
   Mephistopheles. We passed, without a call, to-day. 120
At our last interview, before we parted
Much of his cousins did he speak, entreating
That we should give to each his kindly greeting.
                  (*He bows to* FROSCH.)
   Altmayer (*aside*). You have it now! he understands.
   Siebel.   A knave sharp-set!
   Frosch. Just wait awhile: I'll have him yet. 125
   Mephistopheles. If I am right, we heard the sound
Of well-trained voices, singing chorus;
And truly, song must here rebound
Superbly from the arches o'er us.
   Frosch. Are you, perhaps, a virtuoso? 130
   Mephistopheles. O no! my wish is great, my power is only so-so.
   Altmayer. Give us a song!
   Mephistopheles.   If you desire, a number.
   Siebel. So that it be a bran-new strain!
   Mephistopheles. We've just retraced our way from Spain,
The lovely land of wine, and song, and slumber. 135
(*Sings.*) There was a king once reigning,
     Who had a big black flea —
   Frosch. Hear, hear! A flea! D'ye rightly take the jest?
I call a flea a tidy guest.
   Mephistopheles (*sings*). There was a king once reigning, 140
     Who had a big black flea,
     And loved him past explaining,
     As his own son were he.
     He called his man of stitches;
     The tailor came straightway: 145
     Here, measure the lad for breeches,
     And measure his coat, I say!
   Brander. But mind, allow the tailor no caprices:
Enjoin upon him, as his head is dear,
To most exactly measure, sew and shear, 150
So that the breeches have no creases!
   Mephistopheles. In silk and velvet gleaming
     He now was wholly drest —
     Had a coat with ribbons streaming,
     A cross upon his breast. 155
     He had the first of stations,

[1] Locality near Leipzig.

A minister's star and name;
And also all his relations
Great lords at court became.

And the lords and ladies of honor   160
Were plagued, awake and in bed;
The queen she got them upon her,
The maids were bitten and bled.
And they did not dare to brush them,
  Or scratch them, day or night: 165
We crack them and we crush them,
  At once, whene'er they bite.
Chorus (*shouting*). We crack them and we crush
  them,
  At once, whene'er they bite!
Frosch. Bravo! bravo! that was fine.   170
Siebel. Every flea may it so befall!
Brander. Point your fingers and nip them all!
Altmayer. Hurrah for Freedom! Hurrah for
  wine!
Mephistopheles. I fain would drink with you,
  my glass to Freedom clinking,   174
If 'twere a better wine that here I see you drinking.
Siebel. Don't let us hear that speech again!
Mephistopheles. Did I not fear the landlord
  might complain,
I'd treat these worthy guests, with pleasure,
To some from out our cellar's treasure.
Siebel. Just treat, and let the landlord me
  arraign!   180
Frosch. And if the wine be good, our praises
  shall be ample.
But do not give too very small a sample;
For, if its quality I decide,
With a good mouthful I must be supplied.
Altmayer (*aside*). They're from the Rhine! I
  guessed as much, before.   185
Mephistopheles. Bring me a gimlet here!
Brander.   What shall therewith be done?
You've not the casks already at the door?
Altmayer. Yonder, within the landlord's box of
  tools, there's one!
Mephistopheles (*takes the gimlet*). (*To* FROSCH.)
Now, give me of your taste some intimation.
Frosch. How do you mean? Have you so many
  kinds?   190
Mephistopheles. The choice is free: make up
  your minds.
Altmayer (*to* FROSCH). Aha! you lick your chops,
  from sheer anticipation.
Frosch. Good! if I have the choice, so let the
  wine be Rhenish!
Our Fatherland can best the sparkling cup re-
  plenish.
Mephistopheles (*boring a hole in the edge of the
  table, at the place where* FROSCH *sits*). Get

me a little wax, to make the stoppers,
  quick!   195
Altmayer. Ah! I perceive a juggler's trick.
Mephistopheles (*to* BRANDER). And you?
Brander.   Champagne shall be my wine,
And let it sparkle fresh and fine!
    (MEPHISTOPHELES *bores: in the mean time
      one has made the wax stoppers, and
      plugged the holes with them.*)
Brander. What's foreign one can't always keep
  quite clear of,
For good things, oft, are not so near;   200
A German can't endure the French to see or hear of,
Yet drinks their wines with hearty cheer.
Siebel (*as* MEPHISTOPHELES *approaches his seat*).
For me, I grant, sour wine is out of place;
Fill up my glass with sweetest, will you?
Mephistopheles (*boring*). Tokay shall flow at
  once, to fill you!   205
Altmayer. No — look me, Sirs, straight in the
  face!
I see you have your fun at our expense.
Mephistopheles. O no! with gentlemen of such
  pretence,
That were to venture far, indeed.
Speak out, and make your choice with speed!   210
With what a vintage can I serve you?
Altmayer. With any — only satisfy our need.
    (*After the holes have been bored and plugged.*)
Mephistopheles (*with singular gestures*). Grapes
  the vine-stem bears,
  Horns the he-goat wears!
The grapes are juicy, the vines are wood,   215
The wooden table gives wine as good!
Into the depths of Nature peer, —
Only believe, there's a miracle here!
Now draw the stoppers, and drink your fill!
All (*as they draw out the stoppers, and the wine
  which has been desired flows into the glass of each*).
O beautiful fountain, that flows at will!   220
Mephistopheles. But have a care, that you
  nothing spill!   (*They drink repeatedly.*)
All (*sing*). As 'twere five hundred hogs, we feel
So cannibalic jolly!
See, now, the race is happy — it is free!
Faust. To leave them is my inclination.   225
Mephistopheles. Take notice, first! their bestial-
  ity
Will make a brilliant demonstration.
Siebel (*drinks carelessly: the wine spills upon the
earth, and turns to flame*). Help! Fire! Help!
Hell-fire is sent!
Mephistopheles (*charming away the flame*). Be
quiet, friendly element!
(*To the revellers.*) A bit of purgatory 'twas for this
  time, merely.   230

Siebel. What mean you? Wait!—you'll pay
  for't dearly!
You'll know us, to your detriment.
  Frosch. Don't try that game a second time upon
  us!
  Altmayer. I think we'd better send him packing
  quietly.
  Siebel. What, Sir! you dare to make so free, 235
And play your hocus-pocus on us!
  Mephistopheles. Be still, old wine-tub.
  Siebel.   Broomstick, you!
You face it out, impertinent and heady?
  Brander. Just wait! a shower of blows is ready.
  Altmayer (*draws a stopper out of the table: fire
  flies in his face*). I burn! I burn!
  Siebel.   'Tis magic! Strike—
The knave is outlawed! Cut him as you like! 241
    (*They draw their knives, and rush upon
    MEPHISTOPHELES.*)
  Mephistopheles (*with solemn gestures*). False
    word and form of air,
    Change place, and sense ensnare!
    Be here—and there! 244
    (*They stand amazed and look at each other.*)
  Altmayer. Where am I? What a lovely land!
  Frosch. Vines? Can I trust my eyes?
  Siebel.   And purple grapes at hand!
  Brander. Here, over this green arbor bending,
See, what a vine! what grapes depending!
    (*He takes* SIEBEL *by the nose: the others do
    the same reciprocally, and raise their
    knives.*)
  Mephistopheles (*as above*). Loose, Error, from
    their eyes the band,
And how the Devil jests, be now enlightened! 250
    (*He disappears with* FAUST: *the revellers
    start and separate.*)
  Siebel. What happened?
  Altmayer.   How?
  Frosch.   Was that your nose I tightened?
  Brander (*to* SIEBEL). And yours that still I have
    in hand?
  Altmayer. It was a blow that went through
    every limb!
Give me a chair! I sink! my senses swim.
  Frosch. But what has happened, tell me
    now? 255
  Siebel. Where is he? If I catch the scoundrel
    hiding,
He shall not leave alive, I vow.
  Altmayer. I saw him with these eyes upon a
    wine-cask riding
Out of the cellar-door, just now.
Still in my feet the fright like lead is weighing. 260
    (*He turns towards the table.*)
Why! If the fount of wine should still be playing?

  Siebel. 'Twas all deceit, and lying, false design!
  Frosch. And yet it seemed as I were drinking
    wine.
  Brander. But with the grapes how was it, pray?
  Altmayer. Shall one believe no miracles, just
    say! 265

[*The events of Scene VI occur in a "Witches'
Kitchen" where Mephistopheles has taken Faust
that he may regain his lost youth. Much mystical
foolishness takes place around a steaming caldron
while they await the return of the old hag who is to
rejuvenate Faust. When the witch appears, she
makes a magic circle and brews a potion which, as
Faust sets it to his lips to drink, shoots forth flame.
The scene closes with Faust looking longingly at the
image of a beautiful woman of which he catches sight
in a mirror, but Mephistopheles assures him that
with this drink in his blood he will find "each woman
beautiful as Helen."*]

SCENE VII. *A street.* FAUST. MARGARET
  (*passing by*).

  Faust. Fair lady, let it not offend you,
That arm and escort I would lend you!
  Margaret. I'm neither lady, neither fair,
And home I can go without your care.
    (*She releases herself, and exit.*)
  Faust. By Heaven, the girl is wondrous fair! 5
Of all I've seen, beyond compare;
So sweetly virtuous and pure,
And yet a little pert, be sure!
The lip so red, the cheek's clear dawn,
I'll not forget while the world rolls on! 10
How she cast down her timid eyes,
Deep in my heart imprinted lies:
How short and sharp of speech was she,
Why, 'twas a real ecstasy!

    (MEPHISTOPHELES *enters.*)

  Faust. Hear, of that girl I'd have possession! 15
  Mephistopheles. Which, then?
  Faust.   The one who just went by.
  Mephistopheles. She, there? She's coming from
    confession,
Of every sin absolved; for I,
Behind her chair, was listening nigh.
So innocent is she, indeed, 20
That to confess she had no need.
I have no power o'er souls so green.
  Faust. And yet, she's older than fourteen.
  Mephistopheles. How now! You're talking like
    Jack Rake,
Who every flower for himself would take, 25

And fancies there are no favors more,
Nor honors, save for him in store;
Yet always doesn't the thing succeed.
    Faust. Most Worthy Pedagogue, take heed!
Let not a word of moral law be spoken!   30
I claim, I tell thee, all my right;
And if that image of delight
Rest not within mine arms to-night,
At midnight is our compact broken.
    Mephistopheles. But think, the chances of the
       case!   35
I need, at least, a fortnight's space,
To find an opportune occasion.
    Faust. Had I but seven hours for all,
I should not on the Devil call,
But win her by my own persuasion.   40
    Mephistopheles. You almost like a Frenchman
       prate!
Yet, pray, don't take it as annoyance!
Why, all at once, exhaust the joyance?
Your bliss is by no means so great
As if you'd use, to get control,   45
All sorts of tender rigmarole,
And knead and shape her to your thought,
As in Italian tales 'tis taught.
    Faust. Without that, I have appetite.
    Mephistopheles. But now, leave jesting out of
       sight!   50
I tell you, once for all, that speed
With this fair girl will not succeed;
By storm she cannot captured be;
We must make use of strategy.
    Faust. Get me something the angel keeps!   55
Lead me thither where she sleeps!
Get me a kerchief from her breast, —
A garter that her knee has pressed!
    Mephistopheles. That you may see how much
       I'd fain
Further and satisfy your pain,   60
We will no longer lose a minute;
I'll find her room to-day, and take you in it.
    Faust. And shall I see — possess her?
    Mephistopheles.   No!
Unto a neighbor she must go,
And meanwhile thou, alone, mayst glow   65
With every hope of future pleasure,
Breathing her atmosphere in fullest measure.
    Faust. Can we go thither?
    Mephistopheles.   'Tis too early yet.
    Faust. A gift for her I bid thee get!   (*Exit.*)
    Mephistopheles. Presents at once? That's good:
       he's certain to get at her!   70
Full many a pleasant place I know,
And treasures, buried long ago:
I must, perforce, look up the matter.   (*Exit.*)

SCENE VIII. *Evening. A small, neatly
       kept chamber.*

    *Margaret (plaiting and binding up the braids of
    her hair).* I'd something give, could I but
    say
Who was that gentleman, to-day.
Surely a gallant man was he,
And of a noble family;
So much could I in his face behold, —   5
And he wouldn't, else, have been so bold!   (*Exit.*)

(MEPHISTOPHELES. FAUST.)

    Mephistopheles. Come in, but gently: follow me!
    Faust (after a moment's silence). Leave me alone,
    I beg of thee!
    Mephistopheles (prying about). Not every girl
    keeps things so neat.
    Faust (looking around). O welcome, twilight
    soft and sweet,   10
That breathes throughout this hallowed shrine!
Sweet pain of love, bind thou with fetters fleet
The heart that on the dew of hope must pine!
How all around a sense impresses
Of quiet, order, and content!   15
This poverty what bounty blesses!
What bliss within this narrow den is pent!
    (*He throws himself into a leathern arm-
    chair near the bed.*)
Receive me, thou, that in thine open arms
Departed joy and pain wert wont to gather!
How oft the children, with their ruddy charms,   20
Hung here, around this throne, where sat the
    father!
Perchance my love, amid the childish band,
Grateful for gifts the Holy Christmas gave her,
Here meekly kissed the grandsire's withered hand.
I feel, O maid! thy very soul   25
Of order and content around me whisper, —
Which leads thee with its motherly control,
The cloth upon thy board bids smoothly thee un-
    roll,
The sand beneath thy feet makes whiter, crisper.
O dearest hand, to thee 'tis given   30
To change this hut into a lower heaven!
And here!   (*He lifts one of the bed-curtains.*)
        What sweetest thrill is in my blood!
Here could I spend whole hours, delaying:
Here Nature shaped, as if in sportive playing,
The angel blossom from the bud.   35
Here lay the child, with Life's warm essence
The tender bosom filled and fair,
And here was wrought, through holier, purer
    presence,
The form diviner beings wear!

And I?   What drew me here with power?   40
How deeply am I moved, this hour!
What seek I?   Why so full my heart, and sore?
Miserable Faust!   I know thee now no more.

Is there a magic vapor here?
I came, with lust of instant pleasure,   45
And lie dissolved in dreams of love's sweet leisure!
Are we the sport of every changeful atmosphere?

And if, this moment, came she in to me,
How would I for the fault atonement render!
How small the giant lout would be,   50
Prone at her feet, relaxed and tender!
   Mephistopheles.   Be quick!   I see her there, re-
turning.
   Faust.   Go! go!   I never will retreat.
   Mephistopheles.   Here is a casket, not unmeet,
Which elsewhere I have just been earning.   55
Here, set it in the press, with haste!
I swear, 'twill turn her head, to spy it:
Some baubles I therein had placed,
That you might win another by it.
True, child is child, and play is play.   60
   Faust.   I know not, should I do it?
   Mephistopheles.   Ask you, pray?
Yourself, perhaps, would keep the bubble?
Then I suggest, 'twere fair and just
To spare the lovely day your lust,
And spare to me the further trouble.   65
You are not miserly, I trust?
I rub my hands, in expectation tender —
     (*He places the casket in the press, and locks
     it again.*)
Now quick, away!
The sweet young maiden to betray,
So that by wish and will you bend her;   70
And you look as though
To the lecture-hall you were forced to go, —
As if stood before you, gray and loath,
Physics and Metaphysics both!
But away!   (*Exeunt.*)   75
   Margaret (*with a lamp*).   It is so close, so sultry,
here!   (*She opens the window.*)
And yet 'tis not so warm outside.
I feel, I know not why, such fear! —
Would mother came! — where can she bide?
My body's chill and shuddering, —   80
I'm but a silly, fearsome thing!
     (*She begins to sing, while undressing.*)
   There was a King in Thule,[1]
   Was faithful till the grave, —
   To whom his mistress, dying,
   A golden goblet gave.   85

[1] Ultima Thule; the term signifies a remote, mysterious land.

   Naught was to him more precious;
   He drained it at every bout:
   His eyes with tears ran over.
   As oft as he drank thereout.

   When came his time of dying,   90
   The towns in his land he told,
   Naught else to his heir denying
   Except the goblet of gold.

   He sat at the royal banquet
   With his knights of high degree,   95
   In the lofty hall of his fathers
   In the Castle by the Sea.

   There stood the old carouser,
   And drank the last life-glow;
   And hurled the hallowed goblet   100
   Into the tide below.

   He saw it plunging and filling,
   And sinking deep in the sea:
   Then fell his eyelids forever,
   And never more drank he!   105
     (*She opens the press in order to arrange
     her clothes, and perceives the casket of
     jewels.*)
How comes that lovely casket here to me?
I locked the press, most certainly.
'Tis truly wonderful!   What can within it be?
Perhaps 'twas brought by some one as a pawn,
And mother gave a loan thereon?   110
And here there hangs a key to fit:
I have a mind to open it.
What is that?   God in Heaven!   Whence came
Such things?   Never beheld I aught so fair!
Rich ornaments, such as a noble dame   115
On highest holidays might wear!
How would the pearl-chain suit my hair?
Ah, who may all this splendor own?
     (*She adorns herself with the jewelry, and
     steps before the mirror.*)
Were but the ear-rings mine, alone!
One has at once another air.   120
What helps one's beauty, youthful blood?
One may possess them, well and good;
But none the more do others care.
They praise us half in pity, sure:
To gold still tends,   125
On gold depends
All, all!   Alas, we poor!

[*In Scene IX Mephistopheles informs Faust that
Margaret's mother has taken the jewels from her and
given them to a priest.   Faust orders Mephistopheles
to find even a more splendid set of jewels to replace*

the first. Scene X presents an episode at the house of Martha, Margaret's friend, to whom the young girl has gone to show her second gift of jewels. As they are talking, Mephistopheles enters, lies to Martha about the death of her husband and tells her that the two witnesses legally necessary to establish the death may be secured. In fact he promises to bring with him, at his next visit, this second witness (who will be Faust). In this way a meeting between Faust and Margaret is arranged for the evening — in Martha's garden. In Scene XI, Faust resents Mephistopheles' easy assumption that he would be a party to the lie, but nevertheless agrees to go since it will afford him an opportunity to see Margaret.]

SCENE XII.   *Garden.*   MARGARET *on* FAUST'S *arm.*   MARTHA *and* MEPHISTOPHELES *walking up and down.*

Margaret. I feel, the gentleman allows for me,
Demeans himself, and shames me by it;
A traveller is so used to be
Kindly content with any diet.
I know too well that my poor gossip can   5
Ne'er entertain such an experienced man.
    Faust. A look from thee, a word, more entertains
Than all the lore of wisest brains.
                    (*He kisses her hand.*)
    Margaret. Don't incommode yourself! How could you ever kiss it!
It is so ugly, rough to see!   10
What work I do, — how hard and steady is it!
Mother is much too close with me.   (*They pass.*)
    Martha. And you, Sir, travel always, do you not?
    Mephistopheles. Alas, that trade and duty us so harry!
With what a pang one leaves so many a spot,   15
And dares not even now and then to tarry!
    Martha. In young, wild years it suits your ways,
This round and round the world in freedom sweeping;
But then come on the evil days,
And so, as bachelor, into his grave a-creeping,   20
None ever found a thing to praise.
    Mephistopheles. I dread to see how such a fate advances.
    Martha. Then, worthy Sir, improve betimes your chances!   (*They pass.*)
    Margaret. Yes, out of sight is out of mind!
Your courtesy an easy grace is;   25
But you have friends in other places,
And sensibler than I, you'll find.
    Faust. Trust me, dear heart! what men call sensible
Is oft mere vanity and narrowness.

                                How so?
    Faust. Ah, that simplicity and innocence ne'er know   30
Themselves, their holy value, and their spell!
That meekness, lowliness, the highest graces
Which Nature portions out so lovingly —
    Margaret. So you but think a moment's space on me,
All times I'll have to think on you, all places!   35
    Faust. No doubt you're much alone?
    Margaret. Yes, for our household small has grown,
Yet must be cared for, you will own.
We have no maid: I do the knitting, sewing, sweeping,
The cooking, early work and late, in fact;   40
And mother, in her notions of housekeeping,
Is so exact!
Not that she needs so much to keep expenses down:
We, more than others, might take comfort, rather:
A nice estate was left us by my father,   45
A house, a little garden near the town.
But now my days have less of noise and hurry;
My brother is a soldier,
My little sister's dead.
True, with the child a troubled life I led,   50
Yet I would take again, and willing, all the worry,
So very dear was she.
    Faust.   An angel, if like thee!
    Margaret. I brought it up, and it was fond of me.
Father had died before it saw the light,
And mother's case seemed hopeless quite,   55
So weak and miserable she lay;
And she recovered, then, so slowly, day by day.
She could not think, herself, of giving
The poor wee thing its natural living;
And so I nursed it all alone   60
With milk and water: 'twas my own.
Lulled in my lap with many a song,
It smiled, and tumbled, and grew strong.
    Faust. The purest bliss was surely then thy dower.
    Margaret. But surely, also, many a weary hour.
I kept the baby's cradle near   66
My bed at night: if't even stirred, I'd guess it,
And waking, hear.
And I must nurse it, warm beside me press it,
And oft, to quiet it, my bed forsake,   70
And dandling back and forth the restless creature take,
Then at the wash-tub stand, at morning's break;
And then the marketing and kitchen-tending,
Day after day, the same thing, never-ending.
One's spirits, Sir, are thus not always good,   75
But then one learns to relish rest and food.
                                (*They pass.*)

Martha. Yes, the poor women are bad off, 'tis true:
A stubborn bachelor there's no converting.

Mephistopheles. It but depends upon the like of you,
And I should turn to better ways than flirting. 80

Martha. Speak plainly, Sir, have you no one detected?
Has not your heart been anywhere subjected?

Mephistopheles. The proverb says: One's own warm hearth
And a good wife, are gold and jewels worth.

Martha. I mean, have you not felt desire, though ne'er so slightly? 85

Mephistopheles. I've everywhere, in fact, been entertained politely.

Martha. I meant to say, were you not touched in earnest, ever?

Mephistopheles. One should allow one's self to jest with ladies never.

Martha. Ah, you don't understand!

Mephistopheles. I'm sorry I'm so blind:
But I am sure — that you are very kind. 90
(They pass.)

Faust. And me, thou angel! didst thou recognize,
As through the garden-gate I came?

Margaret. Did you not see it? I cast down my eyes.

Faust. And thou forgiv'st my freedom, and the blame
To my impertinence befitting,
As the Cathedral thou wert quitting? 95

Margaret. I was confused, the like ne'er happened me;
No one could ever speak to my discredit.
Ah, thought I, in my conduct has he read it —
Something immodest or unseemly free?
He seemed to have the sudden feeling 100
That with this wench 'twere very easy dealing.
I will confess, I knew not what appeal
On your behalf, here, in my bosom grew;
But I was angry with myself, to feel 105
That I could not be angrier with you.

Faust. Sweet darling!

Margaret. Wait a while!
(She plucks a star-flower, and pulls off the leaves, one after the other.)

Faust. Shall that a nosegay be?

Margaret. No, it is just in play.

Faust. How?

Margaret. Go! you'll laugh at me.
(She pulls off the leaves and murmurs.)

Faust. What murmurest thou?

Margaret (half aloud). He loves me — loves me not.

Faust. Thou sweet, angelic soul!

Margaret (continues). Loves me — not — loves me — not — 110
(Plucking the last leaf, she cries with frank delight:)
He loves me!

Faust. Yes, child! and let this blossom-word
For thee be speech divine! He loves thee!
Ah, know'st thou what it means? He loves thee!
(He grasps both her hands.)

Margaret. I'm all a-tremble!

Faust. O tremble not! but let this look,
Let this warm clasp of hands declare thee 115
What is unspeakable!
To yield one wholly, and to feel a rapture
In yielding, that must be eternal!
Eternal! — for the end would be despair.
No, no, — no ending! no ending! 120

Martha (coming forward). The night is falling.

Mephistopheles. Ay! we must away.

Martha. I'd ask you, longer here to tarry,
But evil tongues in this town have full play.
It's as if nobody had nothing to fetch and carry,
Nor other labor, 125
But spying all the doings of one's neighbor:
And one becomes the talk, do whatsoe'er one may.
Where is our couple now?

Mephistopheles. Flown up the alley yonder,
The wilful summer-birds!

Martha. He seems of her still fonder.

Mephistopheles. And she of him. So runs the world away! 130

SCENE XIII. *A Garden-Arbor.* MARGARET *comes in, conceals herself behind the door, puts her finger to her lips, and peeps through the crack.*

Margaret. He comes!

Faust (entering). Ah, rogue! a tease thou art:
I have thee! *(He kisses her.)*

Margaret (clasping him, and returning the kiss). Dearest man! I love thee from my heart. *(MEPHISTOPHELES knocks.)*

Faust (stamping his foot). Who's there?

Mephistopheles. A friend!

Faust. A beast!

Mephistopheles. 'Tis time to separate.

Martha (coming). Yes, Sir, 'tis late.

Faust. May I not, then, upon you wait?

Margaret. My mother would — farewell!

Faust. Ah, can I not remain?
Farewell!

Martha. Adieu!

Margaret. And soon to meet again! 6
(Exeunt FAUST and MEPHISTOPHELES.)

Margaret. Dear God! However is it, such

A man can think and know so much?
I stand ashamed and in amaze,
And answer "Yes" to all he says,   10
A poor, unknowing child! and he —
I can't think what he finds in me!   (*Exit.*)

[*The next setting is a forest and cavern. Faust soliloquizes on his past and reflects upon his relations with Margaret. Mephistopheles enters to chide him about his mood and asserts that, despite his contract with the Devil, "the Doctor's in thy body still." He reproves Faust for remaining so long away from Margaret. Faust is torn between his conscience and his desire for Margaret, and the reader is given reason to believe that Faust is still able to distinguish between good and evil.*]

SCENE XV.   *Margaret's Room*

Margaret (at the spinning-wheel, alone). My peace
  is gone,
    My heart is sore:
    I never shall find it,
    Ah, nevermore!

    Save I have him near,   5
    The grave is here;
    The world is gall
    And bitterness all.

    My poor weak head
    Is racked and crazed;   10
    My thought is lost,
    My senses mazed.

    My peace is gone,
    My heart is sore:
    I never shall find it,   15
    Ah, nevermore!

    To see him, him only,
    At the pane I sit;
    To meet him, him only,
    The house I quit.   20

    His lofty gait,
    His noble size,
    The smile of his mouth,
    The power of his eyes,

    And the magic flow   25
    Of his talk, the bliss
    In the clasp of his hand,
    And, ah! his kiss!

    My peace is gone,
    My heart is sore: 30
    I never shall find it,
    Ah, nevermore!

    My bosom yearns
    For him alone;
    Ah, dared I clasp him,   35
    And hold, and own!

    And kiss his mouth,
    To heart's desire,
    And on his kisses
    At last expire!   40

[*Scene XVI is again Martha's garden. Margaret and Faust are in serious discussion, Margaret having asked Faust as to his religion. Faust replies that it is easy to declare belief in God, but refuses such a glib answer, expressing a faith in a mystic force which pervades nature but to which he does not care to give a name. Margaret next complains of Faust's friend, Mephistopheles, whom she instinctively feels to be a knave. Faust gives Margaret a sleeping potion which she is to administer to her mother that Faust may visit Margaret in her room that night. He assures her the drug will do no permanent injury. As Margaret leaves, Mephistopheles enters, having eavesdropped at the whole conversation. Faust gives way to his repulsion at the conduct of Mephistopheles and calls him an "abortion of filth and fire." Scene XVII reveals that Margaret has given herself to Faust.*]

SCENE XVIII.   *Donjon. In a niche of the wall a shrine, with an image of the Mater Dolorosa. Pots of flowers before it.*

Margaret (putting fresh flowers in the pots). In-
  cline, O Maiden,
Thou sorrow-laden,
Thy gracious countenance upon my pain!

The sword Thy heart in,
With anguish smarting,   5
Thou lookest up to where Thy Son is slain!

Thou seest the Father;
Thy sad sighs gather,
And bear aloft Thy sorrow and His pain!

Ah, past guessing,   10
Beyond expressing,
The pangs that wring my flesh and bone!

Why this anxious heart so burneth,
Why it trembleth, why it yearneth,
Knowest Thou, and Thou alone!   15

Where'er I go, what sorrow,
What woe, what woe and sorrow
Within my bosom aches!
Alone, and ah! unsleeping,
I'm weeping, weeping, weeping,   20
The heart within me breaks.

The pots before my window,
Alas! my tears did wet,
As in the early morning
For thee these flowers I set.   25

Within my lonely chamber
The morning sun shone red:
I sat, in utter sorrow,
Already on my bed.

Help! rescue me from death and stain!   30
O Maiden!
Thou sorrow-laden,
Incline Thy countenance upon my pain!

[*The next scene opens with Margaret's brother,
Valentine, praising the virtue of his sister. Soon
Mephistopheles and Faust appear in the street before
Margaret's window. Valentine does not like the
appearance of Mephistopheles and a quarrel develops
in which Faust kills Valentine.*]

SCENE XX. *Cathedral. Service, organ and
anthem.* MARGARET *among much people: the*
EVIL SPIRIT *behind* MARGARET.

Evil Spirit. How otherwise was it, Margaret,
When thou, still innocent,
Here to the altar cam'st,
And from the worn and fingered book
Thy prayers didst prattle,   5
Half sport of childhood,
Half God within thee!
Margaret!
Where tends thy thought?
Within thy bosom   10
What hidden crime?
Pray'st thou for mercy on thy mother's soul,
That fell asleep to long, long torment, and through
        thee?
Upon thy threshold whose the blood?
And stirreth not and quickens   15
Something beneath thy heart,

Thy life disquieting
With most foreboding presence?
Margaret. Woe! woe!
Would I were free from the thoughts   20
That cross me, drawing hither and thither,
Despite me!
*Chorus. Dies iræ, dies illa,
        Solvet sæclum in favilla!* [1]
                        (*Sound of the organ.*)
Evil Spirit. Wrath takes thee!   25
        The trumpet peals!
        The graves tremble!
        And thy heart
        From ashy rest
        To fiery torments   30
        Now again requickened,
        Throbs to life!
Margaret. Would I were forth!
        I feel as if the organ here
        My breath takes from me,   35
        My very heart
        Dissolved by the anthem!
*Chorus. Judex ergo cum sedebit,
        Quidquid latet, adparebit,
        Nil inultum remanebit.* [2]   40
Margaret. I cannot breathe!
        The massy pillars
        Imprison me!
        The vaulted arches
        Crush me! — Air!   45
Evil Spirit. Hide thyself!   Sin and shame
Stay never hidden.
Air?   Light?
Woe to thee!
*Chorus. Quid sum miser tunc dicturus,   50
        Quem patronum rogaturus,
        Cum vix justus sit securus?* [3]
Evil Spirit. They turn their faces,
The glorified, from thee:
The pure, their hands to offer,   55
Shuddering, refuse thee!
Woe!
Chorus. Quid sum miser tunc dicturus?
Margaret. Neighbor! your cordial!
                        (*She falls in a swoon.*)

[1] These, and the following Latin lines, are from an
old hymn by Thomas of Celano. The words were a
part of the requiem of the Roman Church as early as
the fourteenth century. A modern author has translated the passages as follows: "The day of wrath, that
dreadful day, the world will disintegrate into ashes."
[2] "When the judge has been seated, whatever is hidden will be revealed; nothing will remain unavenged."
[3] "Unhappy then, what can I say? What protector
may I call upon, when even the righteous tremble?"

SCENE XXI.   *Walpurgis-Night.*[1]   *The Hartz Mountains.   District of Schierke and Elend.*
FAUST.   MEPHISTOPHELES.

Mephistopheles. Dost thou not wish a broom-stick-steed's assistance?
The sturdiest he-goat I would gladly see:
The way we take, our goal is yet some distance.
  Faust. So long as in my legs I feel the fresh existence,
This knotted staff suffices me.   5
What need to shorten so the way?
Along this labyrinth of vales to wander,
Then climb the rocky ramparts yonder,
Wherefrom the fountain flings eternal spray,
Is such delight, my steps would fain delay.   10
The spring-time stirs within the fragrant birches,
And even the fir-tree feels it now:
Should then our limbs escape its gentle searches?
  Mephistopheles. I notice no such thing, I vow!
'Tis winter still within my body: 15
Upon my path I wish for frost and snow.
How sadly rises, incomplete and ruddy,
The moon's lone disk, with its belated glow,
And lights so dimly, that, as one advances,
At every step one strikes a rock or tree!   20
Let us, then, use a Jack-o'-lantern's glances:
I see one yonder, burning merrily.
Ho, there! my friend! I'll levy thine attendance:
Why waste so vainly thy resplendence?
Be kind enough to light us up the steep!   25
  Will-o'-the-Wisp. My reverence, I hope, will me enable
To curb my temperament unstable;
For zigzag courses we are wont to keep.
  Mephistopheles. Indeed? he'd like mankind to imitate!
Now, in the Devil's name, go straight,   30
Or I'll blow out his being's flickering spark!
  Will-o'-the-Wisp. You are the master of the house, I mark,
And I shall try to serve you nicely.
But then, reflect: the mountain's magic-mad to-day,
And if a will-o'-the-wisp must guide you on the way,   35
You mustn't take things too precisely.
  Faust, Mephistopheles, Will-o'-the-Wisp (*in alternating song*). We, it seems, have entered newly
In the sphere of dreams enchanted.

[1] A witches-sabbath which, according to tradition, occurred on the night preceding the first day of May and on the top of the Brocken, the highest peak of the Hartz Mountains. The name is derived, by a strange bit of association, from Saint Walpurga, an English nun who died in a convent in Bavaria.

Do thy bidding, guide us truly,
That our feet be forwards planted   40
In the vast, the desert spaces!
See them swiftly changing places,
Trees on trees beside us trooping,
And the crags above us stooping,
And the rocky snouts, outgrowing, —   45
Hear them snoring, hear them blowing!
O'er the stones, the grasses, flowing
Stream and streamlet seek the hollow.
Hear I noises? songs that follow?
Hear I tender love-petitions?   50
Voices of those heavenly visions?
Sounds of hope, of love undying!
And the echoes, like traditions
Of old days, come faint and hollow.

Hoo-hoo! Shoo-hoo! Nearer hover   55
Jay and screech-owl, and the plover, —
Are they all awake and crying?
Is't the salamander pushes,
Bloated-bellied, through the bushes?
And the roots, like serpents twisted,   60
Through the sand and boulders toiling,
Fright us, weirdest links uncoiling
To entrap us, unresisted:
Living knots and gnarls uncanny
Feel with polypus-antennæ   65
For the wanderer. Mice are flying,
Thousand-colored, herd-wise hieing
Through the moss and through the heather!
And the fire-flies wink and darkle,
Crowded swarms that soar and sparkle,   70
And in wildering escort gather!

Tell me, if we still are standing,
Or if further we're ascending?
All is turning, whirling, blending,
Trees and rocks with grinning faces,   75
Wandering lights that spin in mazes,
Still increasing and expanding!
  Mephistopheles. Grasp my skirt with heart undaunted!
Here a middle-peak is planted,
Whence one seëth, with amaze,   80
Mammon in the mountain blaze.
  Faust. How strangely glimmers through the hollows
A dreary light, like that of dawn!
Its exhalation tracks and follows
The deepest gorges, faint and wan.   85
Here steam, there rolling vapor sweepeth;
Here burns the glow through film and haze:
Now like a tender thread it creepeth,
Now like a fountain leaps and plays.
Here winds away, and in a hundred   90

Divided veins the valley braids:
There, in a corner pressed and sundered,
Itself detaches, spreads and fades.
Here gush the sparkles incandescent
Like scattered showers of golden sand; —   95
But, see! in all their height, at present,
The rocky ramparts blazing stand.

Mephistopheles. Has not Sir Mammon grandly
         lighted
His palace for this festal night?
'Tis lucky thou hast seen the sight;   100
The boisterous guests approach that were invited.

Faust. How raves the tempest through the air!
With what fierce blows upon my neck 'tis beating!

Mephistopheles. Under the old ribs of the rock
         retreating,
Hold fast, lest thou be hurled down the abysses
         there!   105
The night with the mist is black;
Hark! how the forests grind and crack!
Frightened, the owlets are scattered:
Hearken! the pillars are shattered,
The evergreen palaces shaking!   110
Boughs are groaning and breaking,
The tree-trunks terribly thunder,
The roots are twisting asunder!
In frightfully intricate crashing
Each on the other is dashing,   115
And over the wreck-strewn gorges
The tempest whistles and surges!
Hear'st thou voices higher ringing?
Far away, or nearer singing?
Yes, the mountain's side along,   120
Sweeps an infuriate glamouring song!

Witches (*in chorus*). The witches ride to the
         Brocken's top,
The stubble is yellow, and green the crop.
There gathers the crowd for carnival:
Sir Urian sits over all.   125
And so they go over stone and stock;
The witch she ——s, and ——s the buck.

A Voice. Alone, old Baubo's[1] coming now;
She rides upon a farrow-sow.

Chorus. Then honor to whom the honor is due!
Dame Baubo first, to lead the crew!   131
A tough old sow and the mother thereon,
Then follow the witches, every one.

A Voice. Which way com'st thou hither?

Voice.   O'er the Ilsen-stone.
I peeped at the owl in her nest alone: 135
How she stared and glared!

---

[1] Here used as a symbol for the obscene and gross.
Baubo, according to Greek mythology, was the nurse
of Ceres who, when Ceres lost her daughter Persephone,
sought to distract the mother with indecent gestures
and tales.

Voice. Betake thee to Hell!
Why so fast and so fell?

Voice. She has scored and has flayed me:
See the wounds she has made me!   140

Witches (*chorus*). The way is wide, the way is
         long:
See, what a wild and crazy throng!
The broom it scratches, the fork it thrusts,
The child is stifled, the mother bursts.

Wizards (*semichorus*). As doth the snail in shell,
         we crawl: 145
Before us go the women all.
When towards the Devil's House we tread,
Woman's a thousand steps ahead.

Other Semichorus. We do not measure with such
         care:
Woman in thousand steps is there,   150
But howsoe'er she hasten may,
Man in one leap has cleared the way.

Voice (*from above*). Come on, come on, from
         Rocky Lake!

Voice (*from below*). Aloft we'd fain ourselves
         betake.
We've washed, and are bright as ever you will,   155
Yet we're eternally sterile still.

Both Choruses. The wind is hushed, the star
         shoots by,
The dreary moon forsakes the sky;
The magic notes, like spark on spark,
Drizzle, whistling through the dark.   160

Voice (*from below*). Halt, there! Ho, there!

Voice (*from above*). Who calls from the rocky
         cleft below there?

Voice (*below*). Take me, too! take me, too!
I'm climbing now three hundred years,
And yet the summit cannot see: 165
Among my equals I would be.

Both Choruses. Bears the broom and bears the
         stock,
Bears the fork and bears the buck:
Who cannot raise himself to-night
Is evermore a ruined wight.   170

Half-Witch (*below*). So long I stumble, ill be-
         stead,
And the others are now so far ahead!
At home I've neither rest nor cheer,
And yet I cannot gain them here.

Chorus of Witches. To cheer the witch will salve
         avail;   175
A rag will answer for a sail;
Each trough a goodly ship supplies;
He ne'er will fly, who now not flies.

Both Choruses. When round the summit whirls
         our flight,
Then lower, and on the ground alight;   180
And far and wide the heather press

With witchhood's swarms of wantonness!
                    (*They settle down.*)
  Mephistopheles. They crowd and push, they roar
      and clatter!
They whirl and whistle, pull and chatter!
They shine, and spirt, and stink, and burn!   185
The true witch-element we learn.
Keep close! or we are parted, in our turn.
Where art thou?
  Faust (*in the distance*). Here!
  Mephistopheles.   What! whirled so far astray?
Then house-right I must use, and clear the way.
Make room! Squire Voland [1] comes! Room,
      gentle rabble, room!   190
Here, Doctor, hold to me: in one jump we'll resume
An easier space, and from the crowd be free:
It's too much, even for the like of me.
Yonder, with special light, there's something shin-
      ing clearer
Within those bushes; I've a mind to see.   195
Come on! we'll slip a little nearer.
  Faust. Spirit of Contradiction! On! I'll follow
      straight.
'Tis planned most wisely, if I judge aright:
We climb the Brocken's top in the Walpurgis-
      Night,
That arbitrarily, here, ourselves we isolate.   200
  Mephistopheles. But see, what motley flames
      among the heather!
There is a lively club together:
In smaller circles one is not alone.
  Faust. Better the summit, I must own:
There fire and whirling smoke I see.   205
They seek the Evil One in wild confusion:
Many enigmas there might find solution.
  Mephistopheles. But there enigmas also knotted
      be.
Leave to the multitude their riot!
Here will we house ourselves in quiet.   210
It is an old, transmitted trade,
That in the greater world the little worlds are made.
I see stark-nude young witches congregate,
And old ones, veiled and hidden shrewdly:
On my account be kind, nor treat them rudely!   215
The trouble's small, the fun is great.
I hear the noise of instruments attuning, —
Vile din! yet one must learn to bear the crooning.
Come, come along! It *must* be, I declare!
I'll go ahead and introduce thee there,   220
Thine obligation newly earning.
That is no little space: what say'st thou, friend?
Look yonder! thou canst scarcely see the end:
A hundred fires along the ranks are burning.
They dance, they chat, they cook, they drink, they
      court: 225

[1] Another name for the Devil.

Now where, just tell me, is there better sport?
  Faust. Wilt thou, to introduce us to the revel,
Assume the part of wizard or of devil?
  Mephistopheles. I'm mostly used, 'tis true, to go
      incognito,
But on a gala-day one may his orders show.   230
The Garter does not deck my suit,
But honored and at home is here the cloven foot.
Perceiv'st thou yonder snail? It cometh, slow and
      steady;
So delicately its feelers pry,
That it hath scented me already: 235
I cannot here disguise me, if I try.
But come! we'll go from this fire to a newer:
I am the go-between, and thou the wooer.
  (*To some, who are sitting around dying embers:*) Old
      gentlemen, why at the outskirts? Enter!
I'd praise you if I found you snugly in the centre,
With youth and revel round you like a zone: 241
You each, at home, are quite enough alone.
  General. Say, who would put his trust in nations,
Howe'er for them one may have worked and
      planned?
For with the people, as with women,   245
Youth always has the upper hand.
  Minister. They're now too far from what is just
      and sage.
I praise the old ones, not unduly;
When we were all-in-all, then, truly,
Then was the real golden age.   250
  Parvenu. We also were not stupid, either,
And what we should not, often did;
But now all things have from their bases slid,
Just as we meant to hold them fast together.
  Author. Who, now, a work of moderate sense
      will read?   255
Such works are held as antique and mossy;
And as regards the younger folk, indeed,
They never yet have been so pert and saucy.
  Mephistopheles (*who all at once appears very old*).
I feel that men are ripe for Judgment-Day,
Now for the last time I've the witches'-hill as-
      cended: 260
Since to the lees *my* cask is drained away,
The world's, as well, must soon be ended.
  Huckster-Witch. Ye gentlemen, don't pass me
      thus!
Let not the chance neglected be!
Behold my wares attentively: 265
The stock is rare and various.
And yet, there's nothing I've collected —
No shop, on earth, like this you'll find! —
Which has not, once, sore hurt inflicted
Upon the world, and on mankind.   270
No dagger's here, that set not blood to flowing;
No cup, that hath not once, within a healthy frame

Poured speedy death, in poison glowing:
No gems, that have not brought a maid to shame;
No sword, but severed ties for the unwary,   275
Or from behind struck down the adversary.

Mephistopheles. Gossip! the times thou badly
    comprehendest:
What's done has happed — what haps, is done!
'Twere better if for novelties thou sendest:
By such alone can we be won.   280

Faust. Let me not lose myself in all this pother!
This is a fair, as never was another!

Mephistopheles. The whirlpool swirls to get
    above:
Thou'rt shoved thyself, imagining to shove.   284

Faust. But who is that?

Mephistopheles.   Note her especially,
'Tis Lilith.

Faust.   Who?

Mephistopheles.   Adam's first wife is she.
Beware the lure within her lovely tresses,
The splendid sole adornment of her hair!
When she succeeds therewith a youth to snare,
Not soon again she frees him from her jesses.   290

Faust. Those two, the old one with the young
    one sitting,
They've danced already more than fitting.

Mephistopheles. No rest to-night for young or
    old!
They start another dance: come now, let us take
    hold!

Faust (dancing with the young witch). A lovely
    dream once came to me;   295
I then beheld an apple-tree,
And there two fairest apples shone:
They lured me so, I climbed thereon.

The Fair One. Apples have been desired by you,
Since first in Paradise they grew;   300
And I am moved with joy, to know
That such within my garden grow.

Mephistopheles (dancing with the old one). A dis-
    solute dream once came to me:
Therein I saw a cloven tree,
Which had a —— —— ——;   305
Yet, —— as 'twas, I fancied it.

The Old One. I offer here my best salute
Unto the knight with cloven foot!
Let him a —— —— prepare,
If him —— —— does not scare.   310

Proktophantasmist.[1] Accursèd folk! How dare
    you venture thus?
Had you not, long since, demonstration
That ghosts can't stand on ordinary foundation?
And now you even dance, like one of us!

[1] The Greek prefix signifies "buttocks" and the
whole is a satirical reference to a Berlin bookseller,
named Nicolai, who pretended to high place as a critic.

The Fair One (dancing). Why does he come, then,
    to our ball?   315
Faust (dancing). O, everywhere on him you fall!
When others dance, he weighs the matter:
If he can't every step bechatter,
Then 'tis the same as were the step not made;
But if you forwards go, his ire is most displayed.   320
If you would whirl in regular gyration
As he does in his dull old mill,
He'd show, at any rate, good-will, —
Especially if you heard and heeded his hortation.

Proktophantasmist. You still are here? Nay, 'tis
    a thing unheard!   325
Vanish, at once! We've said the enlightening
    word.
The pack of devils by no rules is daunted:
We are so wise, and yet is Tegel [1] haunted.
To clear the folly out, how have I swept and
    stirred!
'Twill ne'er be clean: why, 'tis a thing unheard!   330

The Fair One. Then cease to bore us at our ball!

Proktophantasmist. I tell you, spirits, to your
    face,
I give to spirit-despotism no place;
My spirit cannot practise it at all.

                    (The dance continues.)
Naught will succeed, I see, amid such revels;   335
Yet something from a tour I always save,
And hope, before my last step to the grave,
To overcome the poets and the devils.

Mephistopheles. He now will seat him in the
    nearest puddle;
The solace this, whereof he's most assured: 340
And when upon his rump the leeches hang and
    fuddle,
He'll be of spirits and of Spirit cured.

(To Faust, *who has left the dance.)* Wherefore
    forsakest thou the lovely maiden,
That in the dance so sweetly sang?

Faust. Ah! in the midst of it there sprang   345
A red mouse from her mouth — sufficient reason!

Mephistopheles. That's nothing! One must not
    so squeamish be;
So the mouse was not gray, enough for thee.
Who'd think of that in love's selected season?

Faust. Then saw I —

Mephistopheles.   What?

Faust.   Mephisto, seest thou there,
Alone and far, a girl most pale and fair?   351
She falters on, her way scarce knowing,
As if with fettered feet that stay her going.
I must confess, it seems to me
As if my kindly Margaret were she.   355

Mephistopheles. Let the thing be! All thence
    have evil drawn:

[1] A castle near Berlin popularly thought to be haunted.

It is a magic shape, a lifeless eidolon.
Such to encounter is not good:
Their blank, set stare benumbs the human blood,
And one is almost turned to stone.   360
Medusa's tale to thee is known.
   Faust. Forsooth, the eyes they are of one whom,
      dying,
No hand with loving pressure closed;
That is the breast whereon I once was lying, —
The body sweet, beside which I reposed!   365
   Mephistopheles. 'Tis magic all, thou fool, seduced
      so easily!
Unto each man his love she seems to be.
   Faust. The woe, the rapture, so ensnare me,
That from her gaze I cannot tear me!
And, strange! around her fairest throat   370
A single scarlet band is gleaming,
No broader than a knife-blade seeming!
   Mephistopheles. Quite right! The mark I also
     note.
Her head beneath her arm she'll sometimes carry;
'Twas Perseus lopped it, her old adversary.   375
Thou crav'st the same illusion still!
Come, let us mount this little hill;
The Prater [1] shows no livelier stir,
And, if they've not bewitched my sense,
I verily see a theatre.   380
What's going on?
   Servibilis. [2] 'Twill shortly recommence:
A new performance — 'tis the last of seven.
To give that number is the custom here:
'Twas by a Dilettante written,
And Dilettanti in the parts appear.   385
That now I vanish, pardon, I entreat you!
As Dilettante I the curtain raise.
   Mephistopheles. When I upon the Blocksberg
     meet you,
I find it good: for that's your proper place.

[*Scene XXII is called "Walpurgis-Night's
Dream," an "intermezzo," and has no vital relationship to the Faust story.*]

SCENE XXIII. *Dreary Day. A field.* FAUST.
    MEPHISTOPHELES.

   Faust. In misery! In despair! Long wretchedly
astray on the face of the earth, and now imprisoned! That gracious, ill-starred creature shut
in a dungeon as a criminal, and given up to fearful
torments! To this has it come! to this! —   5
Treacherous, contemptible spirit, and thou hast
concealed it from me! — Stand, then, — stand!

  [1] A park in Vienna.
  [2] Here used in sense of "stage-manager" or official of
a theatre.

Roll the devilish eyes wrathfully in thy head!
Stand and defy me with thine intolerable presence!
Imprisoned! In irretrievable misery! De-   10
livered up to evil spirits, and to condemning, unfeeling Man! And thou hast lulled me, meanwhile,
with the most insipid dissipations, hast concealed
from me her increasing wretchedness, and suffered
her to go helplessly to ruin!   15
   Mephistopheles. She is not the first.
   Faust. Dog! Abominable monster! Transform
him, thou Infinite Spirit! transform the reptile
again into his dog-shape, in which it pleased him
often at night to scamper on before me, to roll   20
himself at the feet of the unsuspecting wanderer,
and hang upon his shoulders when he fell! Transform him again into his favorite likeness, that he
may crawl upon his belly in the dust before me, —
that I may trample him, the outlawed, under   25
foot! Not the first! O woe! woe which no human
soul can grasp, that more than one being should
sink into the depths of this misery, — that the
first, in its writhing death-agony under the eyes of
the Eternal Forgiver, did not expiate the guilt   30
of all others! The misery of this single one pierces
to the very marrow of my life; and thou art calmly
grinning at the fate of thousands!
   Mephistopheles. Now we are already again at the
end of our wits, where the understanding of you   35
men runs wild. Why didst thou enter into fellowship with us, if thou canst not carry it out? Wilt
fly, and art not secure against dizziness? Did we
thrust ourselves upon thee, or thou thyself upon us?
   Faust. Gnash not thus thy devouring teeth   40
at me! It fills me with horrible disgust. Mighty,
glorious Spirit, who hast vouchsafed to me Thine
apparition, who knowest my heart and my soul,
why fetter me to the felon-comrade, who feeds on
mischief and gluts himself with ruin?   45
   Mephistopheles. Hast thou done?
   Faust. Rescue her, or woe to thee! The fear-
fulest curse be upon thee for thousands of ages!
   Mephistopheles. I cannot loosen the bonds of the
Avenger, nor undo his bolts. Rescue her?   50
Who was it that plunged her into ruin? I, or thou?
(*Faust looks around wildly.*) Wilt thou grasp the
thunder? Well, that it has not been given to you,
miserable mortals! To crush to pieces the innocent
respondent — that is the tyrant-fashion of re-   55
lieving one's self in embarrassments.
   Faust. Take me thither! She shall be free!
   Mephistopheles. And the danger to which thou
wilt expose thyself? Know that the guilt of blood,
from thy hand, still lies upon the town! Aveng-   60
ing spirits hover over the spot where the victim
fell, and lie in wait for the returning murderer.
   Faust. That, too, from thee? Murder and death

of a world upon thee, monster! Take me thither,
I say, and liberate her! 65

Mephistopheles. I will convey thee there; and
hear, what I can do! Have I all the power in
Heaven and on Earth? I will becloud the jailer's
senses: get possession of the key, and lead her forth
with human hand! I will keep watch: the 70
magic steeds are ready, I will carry you off. So
much is in my power.

Faust. Up and away!

SCENE XXIV. *Night. Open field.* FAUST *and*
MEPHISTOPHELES *speeding onward on black horses.*

Faust. What weave they there round the raven-
stone?

Mephistopheles. I know not what they are brew-
ing and doing.

Faust. Soaring up, sweeping down, bowing and
bending!

Mephistopheles. A witches'-guild.

Faust. They scatter, devote and doom! 5

Mephistopheles. On! on!

SCENE XXV. *Dungeon.*

*Faust (with a bunch of keys and a lamp, before an
iron door).* A shudder, long unfelt, comes
o'er me;
Mankind's collected woe o'erwhelms me, here.
She dwells within the dark, damp walls before me,
And all her crime was a delusion dear!
What! I delay to free her? 5
I dread, once again to see her?
On! my shrinking but lingers Death more near.

*(He grasps the lock: the sound of singing is
heard inside.)*

My mother, the harlot,
Who put me to death;
My father, the varlet, 10
Who eaten me hath!
Little sister, so good,
Laid my bones in the wood,
In the damp moss and clay:
Then was I a beautiful bird o' the wood; 15
Fly away! Fly away!

Faust (unlocking). She does not dream her lover
listens near;
That he the rattling chain, the rustling straw, can
hear.

(He enters.)

Margaret (hiding herself on the pallet). Woe!
woe! They come. O death of bitterness!

Faust (whispering). Hush! hush! The hour is
come that frees thee. 20

Margaret (throwing herself before him). Art thou
a man, then pity my distress!

Faust. Thy cries will wake the guards, and they
will scize thee!

(He takes hold of the fetters to unlock them.)

Margaret (on her knees). Who, headsman! unto
thee such power
Over me could give?
Thou'rt come for me at midnight-hour: 25
Have mercy on me, let me live!
Is't not soon enough when morning chime has rung?

(She rises.)

And I am yet so young, so young!
And now Death comes, and ruin!
I, too, was fair, and that was my undoing. 30
My love was near, but now he's far;
Torn lies the wreath, scattered the blossoms are.
Seize me not thus so violently!
Spare me! What have I done to thee?
Let me not vainly entreat thee! 35
I never chanced, in all my days, to meet thee!

Faust. Shall I outlive this misery?

Margaret. Now am I wholly in thy might.
But let me suckle, first, my baby!
I blissed it all this livelong night; 40
They took't away, to vex me, maybe,
And now they say I killed the child outright.
And never shall I be glad again.
They sing songs about me! 'tis bad of the folk to
do it!
There's an old story has the same refrain; 45
Who bade them so construe it?

Faust (falling upon his knees). Here lieth one
who loves thee ever,
The thraldom of thy woe to sever.

Margaret (flinging herself beside him). O let us
kneel, and call the Saints to hide us!
Under the steps beside us, 50
The threshold under,
Hell heaves in thunder!
The Evil One
With terrible wrath
Seeketh a path 55
His prey to discover!

Faust (aloud). Margaret! Margaret!

Margaret (attentively listening). That was the
voice of my lover!

(She springs to her feet: the fetters fall off.)

Where is he? I heard him call me.
I am free! No one shall enthrall me. 60
To his neck will I fly,
On his bosom lie!
On the threshold he stood, and *Margaret!* calling,
Midst of Hell's howling and noises appalling,
Midst of the wrathful, infernal derision, 65
I knew the sweet sound of the voice of the vision!

Faust. 'Tis I!

Margaret.   'Tis thou! O, say it once again!
(*Clasping him.*) 'Tis he! 'tis he! Where now is all
        my pain?
The anguish of the dungeon, and the chain?
'Tis thou! Thou comest to save me,   70
And I am saved! —
Again the street I see
Where first I looked on thee;
And the garden, brightly blooming,
Where I and Martha wait thy coming.   75
        Faust (*struggling to leave*). Come! Come with
        me!
Margaret.   Delay, now!
So fain I stay, when thou delayest!
                                (*Caressing him.*)
        Faust. Away, now!
If longer here thou stayest,
We shall be made to dearly rue it.   80
        Margaret. Kiss me! — canst no longer do it?
My friend, so short a time thou'rt missing,
And hast unlearned thy kissing?
Why is my heart so anxious, on thy breast?
Where once a heaven thy glances did create me,   85
A heaven thy loving words expressed,
And thou didst kiss, as thou wouldst suffocate me —
Kiss me!
Or I'll kiss thee!   (*She embraces him.*)
Ah, woe! thy lips are chill,   90
And still.
How changed in fashion
Thy passion!
Who has done me this ill?
                        (*She turns away from him.*)
        Faust. Come, follow me! My darling, be more
        bold: 95
I'll clasp thee, soon, with warmth a thousand-fold;
But follow now! 'Tis all I beg of thee.
        Margaret (*turning to him*). And is it thou?
        Thou, surely, certainly?
Faust. 'Tis I! Come on!
Margaret.   Thou wilt unloose my chain,
And in thy lap wilt take me once again.   100
How comes it that thou dost not shrink from me? —
Say, dost thou know, my friend, whom thou mak'st
        free?
        Faust. Come! come! The night already van-
        isheth.
        Margaret. My mother have I put to death;
I've drowned the baby born to thee.   105
Was it not given to thee and me?
Thee, too! — 'Tis thou! It scarcely true doth
        seem —
Give me thy hand! 'Tis not a dream!
Thy dear, dear hand! — But, ah, 'tis wet!
Why, wipe it off! Methinks that yet   110

There's blood thereon.
Ah, God! what hast thou done?
Nay, sheathe thy sword at last!
Do not affray me!
        Faust. O, let the past be past!   115
Thy words will slay me!
        Margaret. No, no! Thou must outlive us.
Now I'll tell thee the graves to give us:
Thou must begin to-morrow
The work of sorrow!   120
The best place give to my mother,
Then close at her side my brother,
And me a little away,
But not too very far, I pray!
And here, on my right breast, my baby lay!   125
Nobody else will lie beside me! —
Ah, within thine arms to hide me,
That was a sweet and a gracious bliss,
But no more, no more can I attain it!
I would force myself on thee and constrain it,   130
And it seems thou repellest my kiss:
And yet 'tis thou, so good, so kind to see!
        Faust. If thou feel'st it is I, then come with me!
Margaret. Out yonder?
Faust.   To freedom.
Margaret.   If the grave is there,
Death lying in wait, then come!   135
From here to eternal rest:
No further step — no, no!
Thou goest away! O Henry, if I could go!
        Faust. Thou canst! Just will it! Open stands
        the door.
        Margaret. I dare not go: there's no hope any
        more.   140
Why should I fly? They'll still my steps waylay!
It is so wretched, forced to beg my living,
And a bad conscience sharper misery giving!
It is so wretched, to be strange, forsaken,
And I'd still be followed and taken!   145
        Faust. I'll stay with thee.
        Margaret. Be quick! Be quick!
Save thy perishing child!
Away! Follow the ridge
Up by the brook,   150
Over the bridge,
Into the wood,
To the left, where the plank is placed
In the pool!
Seize it in haste!   155
'Tis trying to rise,
'Tis struggling still!
Save it! Save it!
        Faust. Recall thy wandering will!
One step, and thou art free at last!   160
        Margaret. If the mountain we had only passed!
There sits my mother upon a stone, —

I feel an icy shiver!
There sits my mother upon a stone,
And her head is wagging ever.   165
She beckons, she nods not, her heavy head falls o'er;
She slept so long that she wakes no more.
She slept, while we were caressing:
Ah, those were the days of blessing!
   Faust. Here words and prayers are nothing
     worth;   170
I'll venture, then, to bear thee forth.
   Margaret. No — let me go! I'll suffer no force!
Grasp me not so murderously!
I've done, else, all things for the love of thee.
   Faust. The day dawns: Dearest! Dearest! 175
   Margaret. Day? Yes, the day comes, — the
     last day breaks for me!
My wedding-day it was to be!
Tell no one thou has been with **Margaret!**
Woe for my garland! The chances
Are over — 'tis all in vain!   180
We shall meet once again,
But not at the dances!
The crowd is thronging, no word is spoken:
The square below
And the streets overflow: 185
The death-bell tolls, the wand is broken.[1]

[1] Margaret here visualizes the usual events of judgment and execution.

I am seized, and bound, and delivered —
Shoved to the block — they give the sign!
Now over each neck has quivered
The blade that is quivering over mine.   190
Dumb lies the world like the grave!
   Faust. O had I ne'er been born!
   Mephistopheles (appears outside). Off! or you're
     lost ere morn.
Useless talking, delaying and praying!
My horses are neighing: 195
The morning twilight is near.
   Margaret. What rises up from the threshold here?
He! he! suffer him not!
What does he want in this holy spot?
He seeks me!
   Faust.   Thou shalt live.   200
   Margaret. Judgment of God! myself to thee I
     give.
   Mephistopheles (to FAUST*).* Come! or I'll leave
     her in the lurch, and thee!
   Margaret. Thine am I, Father! rescue me!
Ye angels, holy cohorts, guard me,
Camp around, and from evil ward me!   205
Henry! I shudder to think of thee.
   Mephistopheles. She is judged!
   Voice (from above).   She is saved!
   Mephistopheles (to FAUST*).*   Hither to me!
     (*He disappears with* FAUST.)
   Voice (from within, dying away). Henry! Henry!

Robert Burns · 1759-1796

Although the curtain for the "official" opening of "the Romantic Movement" in England did not rise until the publication of Wordsworth's *Lyrical Ballads*, in 1798, no poetry was more imbued with the romantic spirit than that of Robert Burns whose first volume, *Poems*, appeared in print twelve years before the *Lyrical Ballads*. The reason for this is not far to seek: Rousseau had already published (1762) his *Social Contract* and his ideas were being widely circulated; the American Revolution with its insistence on the rights of man to govern himself was only recently concluded; the first reverberations of the developing French Revolution were heard across the channel. Old theories of kingship were breaking down. Man as an individual was coming into political rights; democracy was taking shape as a principle of government; the responsibility of the powerful for the less fortunate was gaining recognition.

One of the penalties Burns paid for writing romantic verse was that of having his own life romanticized and misunderstood. Born (1759) in Alloway, near Ayr, on the "bonnie Doon," the oldest of a family of seven children and the son of a hard-working small-farmer, Robert Burns was not ushered into a world of luxury. What education he received, in reading and mathematics, he earned by himself; what livelihood he shared in, he earned behind the plough and in the hard, tedious routine of life on a small Scottish farm. On his father's death, Robert and his brother toiled rigorously and with little success to eke out an existence from the none too kindly soil. Impoverished and overworked, during these years Burns injured his health. And it was much this same sort of life, together with that of the duties of an excise officer, to which Burns returned after his sojourn in Edinburgh in 1786 and 1787. However glamorous Burns' life in certain aspects may appear, this background of struggle and poverty must not be forgotten.

The small Kilmarnock edition of his *Poems*, which he published in 1786 to defray the expenses of a contemplated journey to Jamaica, brought him, in addition to twenty pounds profit, a reputation which took him to Edinburgh and postponed the trip indefinitely. A second edition, published the following year, brought him royalties of four hundred pounds. For a time it seemed that the poet's fortune had greatly improved. But the sum soon disappeared: he helped his brother, travelled about England and Scotland, and in general did not know how to be penurious. He married Jean Armour, returned to farming, was appointed excise officer first at fifty pounds a year and, later on at Dumfries, at seventy pounds a year. He died at Dumfries in 1796 at the age of thirty-seven, the greatest of all Scottish poets and one of the greatest lyricists in world literature.

Burns wrote most frequently of nature, of friendship, of love, and of conviviality, and much of his work carries a deep undertone of seriousness. He knew the world about him, its frivolities and artificialities. Much of his work is satirically critical of this outside world of Calvinistic religion and of politics and social standards.

> I'm truly sorry man's dominion
> Has broken Nature's social union

is good Burns doctrine as well as good Rousseauism. He was sincere and honest. Like Horace, he found contentment in simple things.

The romanticism of Burns finds expression in his strong faith in nature, his sympathy for those who live the modest life of rusticity whether man, as in *The Cotter's Saturday Night*, or beast, as in *To a Mouse*. He is the exponent of spontaneity rather than of restraint. Emotions are the stuff of which many of the poems are made; tears are frequently next to laughter and laughter next to tears. His melancholy, too, is that of the romantic:

> The wan moon is setting beyond the white wave
> And time is setting wi' me, O.

He speaks for the heart of Scotland and, in a slightly lesser degree, for that of all mankind. It is not only *Auld Lang Syne* which is sung around the world!

SUGGESTED REFERENCES: Hans Hecht, *Robert Burns, the Man and His Work* (1950); David Daiches, *Robert Burns* (1950); Thomas Crawford, *Burns. A Study of the Poems and Songs* (1960).

To a Mouse

ON TURNING HER UP IN HER NEST WITH THE PLOUGH,
NOVEMBER, 1785

1

Wee, sleekit,[1] cowrin, tim'rous beastie
O, what a panic's in thy breastie!
Thou need na start awa sae hasty
    Wi' bickering brattle![2]

I wad be laith to rin an' chase thee,
    Wi' murdering pattle![1]   5

2

I'm truly sorry man's dominion
Has broken Nature's social union,
An' justifies that ill opinion
    Which makes thee startle   10
At me, thy poor, earth-born companion
    An' fellow mortal!

[1] sleek.
[2] with hurrying fury.

[1] Small spade for cleaning a plough.

3

I doubt na, whyles, but thou may thieve;
What then? poor beastie, thou maun live!
A daimen icker in a thrave [1]   15
  'S a sma' request;
I'll get a blessin wi' the lave,[2]
  An' never miss 't!

4

Thy wee-bit housie, too, in ruin!
Its silly wa's the win's are strewin!   20
An' naething, now, to big [3] a new ane,
  O' foggage [4] green!
An' bleak December's win's ensuin,
  Baith snell [5] an' keen!

5

Thou saw the fields laid bare an' waste,   25
An' weary winter comin fast,
An' cozie here, beneath the blast,
  Thou thought to dwell,
Till crash! the cruel coulter past
  Out thro' thy cell.   30

6

That wee bit heap o' leaves an' stibble,
Has cost thee monie a weary nibble!
Now thou's turned out, for a' thy trouble,
  But house or hald,[6]
To thole [7] the winter's sleety dribble,   35
  An' cranreuch [8] cauld!

7

But Mousie, thou art no thy lane,
In proving foresight may be vain:
The best-laid schemes o' mice an' men
  Gang aft agley,[9]   40
An' lea'e us nought but grief an' pain,
  For promised joy!

8

Still thou art blest, compared wi' me!
The present only toucheth thee:
But och! I backward cast my e'e,   45
  On prospects drear!
An' forward, tho' I canna see,
  I guess an' fear!

[1] An occasional ear of corn in twenty-four sheaves.
[2] rest or remainder.
[3] build.
[4] coarse grass.
[5] biting.
[6] without house or abode.
[7] endure.
[8] hoar-frost.
[9] awry.

Tam o' Shanter

When chapman billies [1] leave the street,
And drouthy [2] neebors neebors meet;
As market-days are wearing late,
An' folk begin to tak the gate; [3]
While we sit bousing at the nappy,[4]   5
An' getting fou and unco [5] happy,
We think na on the lang Scots miles,
The mosses, waters, slaps,[6] and styles,
That lie between us and our hame,
Whare sits our sulky, sullen dame,   10
Gathering her brows like gathering storm,
Nursing her wrath to keep it warm.

This truth fand honest Tam o' Shanter,
As he frae Ayr ae night did canter:
(Auld Ayr, wham ne'er a town surpasses,   15
For honest men and bonie lasses).

O Tam, had'st thou but been sae wise,
As taen thy ain wife Kate's advice!
She tauld thee weel thou was a skellum,[7]
A blethering, blustering, drunken blellum; [8]   20
That frae November till October,
Ae market-day thou was nae sober;
That ilka [9] melder [10] wi' the miller,
Thou sat as lang as thou had siller;
That ev'ry naig [11] was ca'd [12] a shoe on,   25
The smith and thee gat roaring fou on;
That at the Lord's house, even on Sunday,
Thou drank wi' Kirkton Jean till Monday.
She prophesied, that, late or soon,
Thou would be found deep drowned in Doon,   30
Or catched wi' warlocks [13] in the mirk [14]
By Alloway's auld, haunted kirk.

Ah! gentle dames, it gars me greet,[15]
To think how monie counsels sweet,
How monie lengthened, sage advices   35
The husband frae the wife despises!

But to our tale: Ae market-night,
Tam had got planted unco right,
Fast by an ingle,[16] bleezing finely,
Wi' reaming swats,[17] that drank divinely;   40
And at his elbow, Souter [18] Johnie,
His ancient, trusty, drouthy cronie:
Tam lo'ed him like a very brither;
They had been fou for weeks thegither.

[1] pedlar-fellows.	[2] thirsty.	[3] go home.
[4] ale.	[5] uncommonly.	[6] gaps in fences
[7] rascal.	[8] babbler.	[9] every.
[10] grinding.	[11] nag.	[12] shod.
[13] wizards.	[14] dark.	[15] makes me weep.
[16] fireplace.	[17] foaming ale.	[18] shoemaker.

The night drave on wi' sangs and clatter;   45
And ay the ale was growing better:
The landlady and Tam grew gracious
Wi' secret favors, sweet and precious:
The Souter tauld his queerest stories;
The landlord's laugh was ready chorus: 50
The storm without might rair and rustle,
Tam did na mind the storm a whistle.

Care, mad to see a man sae happy,
E'en drowned himsel amang the nappy.
As bees flee hame wi' lades o' treasure,   55
The minutes winged their way wi' pleasure:
Kings may be blest but Tam was glorious,
O'er a' the ills o' life victorious!

But pleasures are like poppies spread:
You seize the flow'r, its bloom is shed;   60
Or like the snow falls in the river,
A moment white — then melts for ever;
Or like the borealis race,
That flit ere you can point their place;
Or like the rainbow's lovely form   65
Evanishing amid the storm.
Nae man can tether time or tide;
The hour approaches Tam maun ride:
That hour, o' night's black arch the keystane,
That dreary hour Tam mounts his beast in;   70
And sic a night he taks the road in,
As ne'er poor sinner was abroad in.

The wind blew as 'twad blawn its last;
The rattling showers rose on the blast;
The speedy gleams the darkness swallowed;   75
Loud, deep, and lang the thunder bellowed:
That night, a child might understand,
The Deil had business on his hand.

Weel mounted on his gray mare Meg,
A better never lifted leg,   80
Tam skelpit [1] on thro' dub [2] and mire,
Despising wind, and rain, and fire;
Whiles holding fast his guid blue bonnet,
Whiles crooning o'er some auld Scots sonnet,
Whiles glow'ring round wi' prudent cares,   85
Lest bogles [3] catch him unawares:
Kirk-Alloway was drawing nigh,
Whare ghaists and houlets [4] nightly cry.

By this time he was cross the ford,
Where in the snaw the chapman smoor'd; [5]   90
And past the birks [6] and meikle stane,
Whare drunken Charlie brak's neck-bane;
And thro' the whins,[7] and by the cairn,[8]

Whare hunters fand the murdered bairn; [1]
And near the thorn, aboon the well,   95
Whare Mungo's mither hanged hersel.
Before him Doon pours all his floods;
The doubling storm roars thro' the woods;
The lightnings flash from pole to pole;
Near and more near the thunders roll: 100
When, glimmering thro' the groaning trees,
Kirk-Alloway seemed in a bleeze,[2]
Thro' ilka bore [3] the beams were glancing,
And loud resounded mirth and dancing.

Inspiring bold John Barleycorn,   105
What dangers thou canst make us scorn!
Wi' tippenny,[4] we fear nae evil;
Wi' usquabae,[5] we'll face the Devil!
The swats sae reamed in Tammie's noddle,
Fair play, he cared na deils a boddle.[6]   110
But Maggie stood, right sair astonished,
Till, by the heel and hand admonished,
She ventured forward on the light;
And, vow! Tam saw an unco sight!

Warlocks and witches in a dance: 115
Nae cotillion, brent new [7] frae France,
But hornpipes, jigs, strathspeys, and reels,[8]
Put life and mettle in their heels.
A winnock-bunker [9] in the east,
There sat Auld Nick, in shape o' beast;   120
A tousie tyke,[10] black, grim, and large,
To gie them music was his charge:
He screwed the pipes, and gart them skirl,[11]
Till roof and rafters a' did dirl.[12]
Coffins stood round, like open presses,   125
That shawed the dead in their last dresses;
And, by some devilish cantraip [13] sleight,
Each in its cauld hand held a light:
By which heroic Tam was able
To note upon the haly table,   130
A murderer's banes, in gibbet-airns; [14]
Twa span-lang, wee, unchristened bairns;
A thief new-cutted frae a rape [15] —
Wi' his last gasp his gab [16] did gape;
Five tomahawks wi' bluid rep-rusted;   135
Five scymitars wi' murder crusted;
A garter which a babe had strangled;
A knife a father's throat had mangled —
Whom his ain son o' life bereft —
The gray hairs yet stack to the heft;   140
Wi' mair of horrible and awefu,'
Which even to name wad be unlawfu'.

[1] hurried.   [2] mud-puddle.   [3] bogies, hobgoblins.
[4] owls.   [5] smothered.   [6] birches.
[7] furze.   [8] rock-pile.

[1] child.   [2] blaze.   [3] opening.   [4] two-penny ale.
[5] whiskey.   [6] copper-penny.   [7] brand-new.
[8] various Scottish dances.   [9] window-seat.
[10] shaggy cur.   [11] made them shriek.   [12] rattle.
[13] magic.   [14] irons.   [15] rope.   [16] mouth.

As Tammie glowered, amazed, and curious,
The mirth and fun grew fast and furious;
The piper loud and louder blew, 145
The dancers quick and quicker flew,
They reeled, they set, they crossed, they cleekit,[1]
Till ilka carlin [2] swat [3] and reekit,[4]
And coost her duddies [5] to the wark,
And linket [6] at it in her sark! [7] 150

Now Tam, O Tam! had thae been queans,[8]
A' plump and strapping in their teens!
Their sarks, instead o' creeshie [9] flannen,
Been snaw-white seventeen hunder linen! —
Thir [10] breeks o' mine, my only pair, 155
That ance were plush, o' guid blue hair,
I wad hae gi'en them off my hurdies [11]
For ae blink o' the bonie burdies!

But withered beldams, auld and droll,
Rigwoodie [12] hags wad spean [13] a foal, 160
Louping [14] and flinging on a crummock,[15]
I wonder did na turn thy stomach!

But Tam kend what was what fu' brawlie.[16]
There was ae winsome wench and wawlie,[17]
That night enlisted in the core,[18] 165
Lang after kend on Carrick shore
(For monie a beast to dead she shot,
An' perished monie a bonie boat,
And shook baith meikle corn and bear,[19]
And kept the country-side in fear). 170
Her cutty sark,[20] o' Paisley harn,[21]
That while a lassie she had worn,
In longitude tho' sorely scanty,
It was her best, and she was vauntie.[22]

Ah! little kend thy reverend grannie, 175
That sark she coft [23] for her wee Nannie,
Wi' twa pund Scots [24] ('twas a' her riches),
Wad ever graced a dance of witches!

But here my Muse her wing maun cour,[25]
Sic flights are far beyond her power: 180
To sing how Nannie lap and flang
(A souple jad she was and strang),
And how Tam stood like ane bewitched,
And thought his very een enriched;

Even Satan glowered, and fidged [1] fu' fain, 185
And hotched [2] and blew wi' might and main;
Till first ae caper, syne anither,
Tam tint [3] his reason a' thegither,
And roars out: "Weel done, Cutty-sark!"
And in an instant all was dark; 190
And scarcely had he Maggie rallied,
When out the hellish legion sallied.

As bees bizz out wi' angry fyke,[4]
When plundering herds assail their byke; [5]
As open pussie's [6] mortal foes, 195
When, pop! she starts before their nose;
As eager runs the market-crowd,
When "Catch the thief!" resounds aloud:
So Maggie runs, the witches follow,
Wi, monie an eldritch [7] skriech and hollo. 200

Ah, Tam! ah, Tam! thou'll get thy fairin! [8]
In hell they'll roast thee like a herrin!
In vain thy Kate awaits thy comin!
Kate soon will be a woefu' woman!
Now, do thy speedy utmost, Meg, 205
And win the key-stane of the brig;
There, at them thou thy tail may toss,
A running stream they dare na cross!
But ere the key-stane she could make,
The fient [9] a tail she had to shake; 210
For Nannie, far before the rest,
Hard upon noble Maggie prest,
And flew at Tam wi' furious ettle; [10]
But little wist she Maggie's mettle!
Ae spring brought off her master hale, 215
But left behind her ain gray tail:
The carlin [11] claught her by the rump,
And left poor Maggie scarce a stump.

Now, wha this tale o' truth shall read,
Ilk man, and mother's son, take heed: 220
Whene'er to drink you are inclined,
Or cutty sarks run in your mind,
Think! ye may buy the joys o'er dear:
Remember Tam o' Shanter's mare.

Green Grow the Rashes, O

CHORUS

Green grow the rashes,[12] O;
Green grow the rashes, O;
The sweetest hours that e'er I spend,
Are spent among the lasses, O.

[1] clutched. [2] each old hag. [3] sweated.
[4] steamed. [5] threw off her clothes. [6] tripped.
[7] shirt. [8] girls. [9] greasy.
[10] these. [11] buttocks. [12] scrawny.
[13] wean (because of disgust). [14] leaping.
[15] staff. [16] well. [17] goodly.
[18] company. [19] barley. [20] a short shirt.
[21] cloth. [22] proud. [23] bought.
[24] A pound Scots was about forty cents. [25] lower.

[1] fidgeted. [2] squirmed. [3] lost. [4] fuss.
[5] hive. [6] a hare's. [7] ghostly. [8] reward.
[9] devil. [10] intent.
[11] witch. [12] rushes.

1

There's nought but care on ev'ry han', 5
In every hour that passes, O:
What signifies the life o' man,
An' 'twere nae for the lasses, O.

2

The war'ly [1] race may riches chase,
An' riches still may fly them, O; 10
An' tho' at last they catch them fast,
Their hearts can ne'er enjoy them, O.

3

But gie me a cannie [2] hour at e'en,
My arms about my dearie, O,
An' war'ly cares an' war'ly men 15
May a' gae tapsalteerie,[3] O!

4

For you sae douce,[4] ye sneer at this;
Ye're nought but senseless asses, O;
The wisest man the warl' e'er saw,
He dearly loved the lasses, O. 20

5

Auld Nature swears, the lovely dears
Her noblest work she classes, O:
Her prentice han' she tried on man,
An' then she made the lasses, O.

CHORUS

Green grow the rashes, O;
Green grow the rashes, O; 25
The sweetest hours that e'er I spend,
Are spent among the lasses, O.

Of A' the Airts

1

Of a' the airts [5] the wind can blaw
I dearly like the west,
For there the bonie lassie lives,
The lassie I lo'e best.
There wild woods grow, and rivers row,[6] 5
And monie a hill between,
But day and night my fancy's flight
Is ever wi' my Jean.

2

I see her in the dewy flowers —
I see her sweet and fair. 10

I hear her in the tunefu' birds —
I hear her charm the air.
There's not a bonie flower that springs
By fountain, shaw,[1] or green,
There's not a bonie bird that sings, 15
But minds me o' my Jean.

Auld Lang Syne

CHORUS

For auld lang syne, my dear,
For auld lang syne,
We'll tak a cup o' kindness yet
For auld lang syne!

1

Should auld acquaintance be forgot, 5
And never brought to mind?
Should auld acquaintance be forgot,
And auld lang syne!

2

And surely ye'll be your pint-stowp,[2]
And surely I'll be mine, 10
And we'll tak a cup o' kindness yet
For auld lang syne!

3

We two hae run about the braes,[3]
And pou'd the gowans [4] fine,
But we've wandered monie a weary fit [5] 15
Sin' auld lang syne.

4

We twa hae paidled in the burn [6]
Frae morning sun till dine,
But seas between us braid hae roared
Sin' auld lang syne. 20

5

And there's a hand, my trusty fiere,[7]
And gie's a hand o' thine,
And we'll tak a right guid-willie waught [8]
For auld lang syne!

CHORUS

For auld lang syne, my dear, 25
For auld lang syne,
We'll tak a cup o' kindness yet
For auld lang syne!

[1] wood. [2] pint-cup. [3] hillsides.
[4] daisies. [5] foot. [6] brook.
[7] comrade. [8] draught for good will.

[1] worldly. [2] quiet. [3] topsy-turvy.
[4] sedate. [5] directions. [6] roll.

John Anderson My Jo

I

John Anderson my jo,[1] John,
    When we were first acquent,
Your locks were like the raven,
    Your bonie brow was brent;[2]
But now your brow is beld,[3] John,   5
    Your locks are like the snaw,
But blessings on your frosty pow,[4]
    John Anderson my jo!

2

John Anderson my jo, John,
    We clamb the hill thegither,   10
And monie a cantie[5] day, John,
    We've had wi' ane anither:
Now we maun totter down, John,
    And hand in hand we'll go,
And sleep thegither at the foot,   15
    John Anderson my jo!

Willie Brewed a Peck o' Maut

CHORUS

We are na fou,[6] we're nae that fou,
    But just a drappie[7] in our e'e!
The cock may craw, the day may daw,
    And ay we'll taste the barley-bree![8]

I

O, Willie brewed a peck o' maut,
    And Rob and Allan cam to see.   5
Three blyther hearts that lee-lang[9] night
    Ye wad na found in Christendie.

2

Here are we met three merry boys,
    Three merry boys I trow are we;
And monie a night we've merry been,   10
    And monie mae[10] we hope to be!

3

It is the moon, I ken her horn,
    That's blinkin in the lift[11] sae hie:
She shines sae bright to wyle us hame,   15
    But, by my sooth, she'll wait a wee!

4

Wha first shall rise to gang awa,
    A cuckold, coward loun is he!

[1] sweetheart.   [2] smooth.   [3] bald.   [4] head.
[5] happy.   [6] full.   [7] drop.   [8] barley brew.
[9] livelong.   [10] more.   [11] sky.

Wha first beside his chair shall fa',
    He is the King amang us three!   20

CHORUS

We are na fou, we're nae that fou,
    But just a drappie in our e'e!
The cock may craw, the day may daw,
    And ay we'll taste the barley-bree!

Ye Flowery Banks

I

Ye flowery banks o' bonie Doon,
    How can ye blume sae fair?
How can ye chant, ye little birds,
    And I sae fu' o' care?

2

Thou'll break my heart, thou bonie bird,   5
    That sings upon the bough:
Thou minds me o' the happy days
    When my fause Luve was true!

3

Thou'll break my heart, thou bonie bird,
    That sings beside thy mate: 10
For sae I sat, and sae I sang,
    And wist na o' my fate!

4

Aft hae I roved by bonie Doon
    To see the woodbine twine,
And ilka[1] bird sang o' its luve,   15
    And sae did I o' mine.

5

Wi' lightsome heart I pu'd a rose
    Frae aff its thorny tree,
And my fause luver staw[2] my rose,
    But left the thorn wi' me.   20

A Red, Red Rose

I

O, my luve is like a red, red rose,
    That's newly sprung in June.
O, my luve is like the melodie,
    That's sweetly played in tune.

2

As fair art thou, my bonie lass,
    So deep in luve am I,

[1] each.   [2] stole.

And I will luve thee still, my dear,
    Till a' the seas gang dry.

3

Till a' the seas gang dry, my dear,
    And the rocks melt wi' the sun!   10
And I will luve thee still, my dear,
    While the sands o' life shall run.

4

And fare thee weel, my only luve,
    And fare thee weel a while!
And I will come again, my luve,   15
    Tho' it were ten thousand mile!

Scots, Wha Hae

1

Scots, wha hae wi' Wallace bled,
Scots, wham Bruce has aften led,
    Welcome to your gory bed
        Or to victorie!

2

Now's the day, and now's the hour: 5
See the front o' battle lour,
See approach proud Edward's power —
        Chains and slaverie!

3

Wha will be a traitor knave?
Wha can fill a coward's grave?   10
Wha sae base as be a slave? —
        Let him turn, and flee!

4

Wha for Scotland's King and Law
Freedom's sword will strongly draw,
    Freeman stand or freeman fa',   15
        Let him follow me!

5

By Oppression's woes and pains,
By your sons in servile chains,
    We will drain our dearest veins
        But they shall be free!   20

6

Lay the proud usurpers low!
Tyrants fall in every foe!
    Liberty's in every blow!
        Let us do, or die!

Highland Mary

1

Ye banks and braes [1] and streams around
    The castle o' Montgomery,
Green be your woods, and fair your flowers,
    Your waters never drumlie! [2]
There Summer first unfald her robes,   5
    And there the langest tarry!
For there I took the last fareweel
    O' my sweet Highland Mary!

2

How sweetly bloomed the gay, green birk,[3]
    How rich the hawthorn's blossom,   10
As underneath their fragrant shade
    I clasped her to my bosom!
The golden hours on angel wings
    Flew o'er me and my dearie:
For dear to me as light and life   15
    Was my sweet Highland Mary.

3

Wi' monie a vow and locked embrace
    Our parting was fu' tender;
And, pledging aft to meet again,
    We tore oursels asunder.   20
But O, fell Death's untimely frost,
    That nipt my flower sae early!
Now green's the sod, and cauld's the clay,
    That wraps my Highland Mary!

4

O, pale, pale now, those rosy lips   25
    I aft hae kissed sae fondly;
And closed for ay, the sparkling glance
    That dwalt on me sae kindly;
And mouldering now in silent dust
    That heart that lo'ed me dearly!   30
But still within my bosom's core
    Shall live my Highland Mary.

Is There for Honest Poverty

1

Is there for honest poverty
    That hings his head, an' a' that?
The coward slave, we pass him by —
    We dare be poor for a' that!
For a' that, an' a' that,   5
    Our toils obscure, an' a' that,
The rank is but the guinea's stamp,
    The man's the gowd [4] for a' that.

[1] hills.   [2] muddy.   [3] birch.   [4] gold.

2

What though on hamely fare we dine,
  Wear hoddin [1] grey, an' a' that?
Gie fools their silks, and knaves their wine —   10
  A man's a man for a' that.
For a' that, an' a' that,
  Their tinsel show, an' a' that,
The honest man, tho' e'er sae poor,   15
  Is king o' men for a' that.

3

Ye see yon birkie [2] ca'd "a lord,"
  Wha struts, an' stares, an' a' that?
Tho' hundreds worship at his word,
  He's but a cuif [3] for a' that.   20
For a' that, an' a' that,
  His ribband, star, an' a' that,
The man o' independent mind,
  He looks an' laughs at a' that.

4

A prince can mak a belted knight,   25
  A marquis, duke, an' a' that!
But an honest man's aboon [4] his might —
  Guid faith, he mauna fa' [5] that!
For a' that, an' a' that,
  Their dignities, an' a' that,   30
The pith o' sense an' pride o' worth
  Are higher rank than a' that.

5

Then let us pray that come it may
  (As come it will for a' that)
That Sense and Worth o'er a' the earth   35
  Shall bear the gree [6] an' a' that!
For a' that, an' a' that,
  It's comin yet for a' that,
That man to man the world o'er
  Shall brithers be for a' that.   40

O, Wert Thou in the Cauld Blast

1

O, wert thou in the cauld blast
  On yonder lea, on yonder lea,
My plaidie to the angry airt, [7]
  I'd shelter thee, I'd shelter thee.

[1] homespun gray.   [2] young fellow.   [3] fool.
[4] above.   [5] claim.   [6] prize.
[7] quarter from which the wind blows.

Or did Misfortune's bitter storms   5
  Around thee blaw, around thee blaw,
Thy bield [1] should be my bosom,
  To share it a', to share it a'.

2

Or were I in the wildest waste,
  Sae black and bare, sae black and bare,   10
The desert were a Paradise,
  If thou wert there, if thou wert there.
Or were I monarch of the globe,
  Wi' thee to reign, wi' thee to reign,
The brightest jewel in my crown   15
  Wad be my queen, wad be my queen.

Mary Morison

1

O Mary, at thy window be!
  It is the wished, the trysted hour.
Those smiles and glances let me see,
  That make the miser's treasure poor.
How blythely wad I bide the stoure, [2]   5
  A weary slave frae sun to sun,
Could I the rich reward secure —
  The lovely Mary Morison!

2

Yestreen, when to the trembling string
  The dance gaed thro' the lighted ha',   10
To thee my fancy took its wing,
  I sat, but neither heard or saw:
Tho' this was fair, and that was braw,
  And yon the toast of a' the town,
I sighed and said amang them a': —   15
  "Ye are na Mary Morison!"

3

O Mary, canst thou wreck his peace
  Wha for thy sake wad gladly die?
Or canst thou break that heart of his
  Whase only faut is loving thee?
If love for love thou wilt na gie,
  At least be pity to me shown:
A thought ungentle canna be
  The thought o' Mary Morison.

[1] shelter.   [2] conflict.

William Wordsworth · 1770–1850

The first thirty years of the nineteenth century were a Golden Age in English poetry. The days of Elizabeth may be regarded as the first great period in English literature; the beginning nineteenth century as the second. During this period romanticism triumphed and found its expression in the works of Wordsworth, Coleridge, Byron, Shelley, and Keats, the most important poets of their time.

Political conditions were changing rapidly in England and on the Continent. The United States and England fought their second war (1812). France was under the sway of Napoleon who threatened to invade England; the Battle of Waterloo (1815) brought his downfall. Society was restless: there was in England a demand for sweeping suffrage reforms; the common man was rising to greater importance; industry, with the development of science and invention, was creating new power and changing England from an agricultural to a manufacturing country; such cities as Liverpool and Manchester were growing greatly. The progress of the Industrial Revolution was too rapid for necessary social adjustments. Unemployment caused low wages and led to disturbances which had to be settled by a number of social and political reforms.

These developments were accompanied by a new trend in English poetry. Wordsworth presented the experience of the common man and called our attention to the spiritual aspect of nature; Coleridge took as his province the supernatural and popularized transcendental philosophy; Byron delighted to attack conventional society and argued well for the freedom of man and for revolt against oppression; Shelley taught brotherly love and the perfectibility of man; Keats preached beauty and found a romantic interest in classical backgrounds. With these men poetry passed from the city to the Lake Country of England and to the towns of Italy. Mysticism, sentiment, nature worship, interest in the past in time and the remote in distance were the themes common to contemporary poetry.

In America, too, a poetic fervor was in the offing. During these years were born: Poe, Whitman, Emerson, Lowell, Whittier, Hawthorne, Longfellow, Holmes, Thoreau — most of the great poets of the nineteenth century in this country.

Wordsworth was born, April 7, 1770, at Cockermouth in Cumberland, England, in "The Lake Country." His childhood was lived simply, in rustic surroundings. Leaving the Lake District to attend St. John's College, Cambridge (where he was graduated in 1791), to pay various visits to France and Germany, and for temporary residence elsewhere in England, Wordsworth nevertheless returned to this chosen locality to spend his manhood and old age. The Lake District with its sometimes quiet, sometimes wild scenery had a decisive influence on his life and poetry. Here, living with his sister Dorothy or his wife Mary Hutchinson in several different cottages at Hawkshead, at Grasmere, and at Rydal Mount, he passed six of the eight decades of his life. Wordsworth developed an intensive friendship with Coleridge, who lived at times not more than a few miles away. The poet died on April 23, 1850, and was buried in the churchyard at Grasmere.

Another important influence on Wordsworth's work was his travel and his experiences on the European Continent. At first indifferent to the change of thought and government accompanying the French Revolution, Wordsworth soon became an advocate of revolutionary doctrine. Wordsworth had adopted Rousseauism with so much enthusiasm that his relatives at home discontinued his allowance and he was compelled to return to England. Even after his country had declared war on France, Wordsworth retained his loyalty to revolutionary principles for a while, but subsequently his romantic passion for French liberty and ideals diminished. Later a friend left him a small inheritance which allowed Wordsworth to settle down to the writing of poetry.

Wordsworth published three volumes of important verse: the *Lyrical Ballads* (1798) with Coleridge; *Poems* (1807); and *The Excursion* (1814). A collected edition of his poetry was issued in six volumes in 1836. *The Prelude* and *The Recluse* appeared posthumously in 1850 and 1888 respectively. The poems are of a varied nature: reflective and didactic (as in *Tintern Abbey* and *Expostulation and Reply*), pastorals (*Michael*), lyrics (*I Wandered Lonely as a Cloud*), odes (*To Duty*), and sonnets (*It Is a Beauteous Evening*). In *Laodamia* and some few other poems Wordsworth manifested an interest at variance with the romantic temper. He usually wrote of nature, yet frequently presented more or less psychological studies of the life of simple people. His effort was to present the mind of man at a time of stress, whether it be the mind of another or of himself. Wordsworth sought to write convincingly of the dignity of man and of the spiritual and psychical influence of nature. The publication of the *Lyrical Ballads* changed the course of English poetry and at his best Wordsworth is to be considered one of the major English poets.

SELECTED REFERENCES: Arthur Beatty, *William Wordsworth: His Doctrine and Art* (3rd ed., 1960); Helen Dabishire, *The Poet Wordsworth* (3rd ed., 1962); H. G. Hartman, *Wordsworth's Poetry, 1787–1814* (1964); C. R. Woodring, *Wordsworth* (1965).

Expostulation and Reply

"Why, William, on that old gray stone,
Thus for the length of half a day,
Why, William, sit you thus alone,
And dream your time away?

"Where are your books? — that light bequeathed
To beings else forlorn and blind!
Up! up! and drink the spirit breathed
From dead men to their kind.

"You look round on your Mother Earth,
As if she for no purpose bore you;
As if you were her first-born birth,
And none had lived before you!"

One morning thus, by Esthwaite lake,
When life was sweet, I knew not why,
To me my good friend Matthew spake,
And thus I made reply: —

"The eye, — it cannot choose but see;
We cannot bid the ear be still;

Our bodies feel, where'er they be,
Against or with our will.

"Nor less I deem that there are powers
Which of themselves our minds impress;
That we can feed this mind of ours
In a wise passiveness.

"Think you, 'mid all this mighty sum
Of things forever speaking,
That nothing of itself will come
But we must still be seeking?

"Then ask not wherefore, here, alone,
Conversing as I may,
I sit upon this old gray stone,
And dream my time away."

The Tables Turned

Up! up! my friend, and quit your books;
Or surely you'll grow double:
Up! up! my friend, and clear your looks;
Why all this toil and trouble?

The sun, above the mountain's head,   5
A freshening lustre mellow
Through all the long, green fields has spread,
His first sweet evening yellow.

Books! 'tis a dull and endless strife:
Come, hear the woodland linnet,   10
How sweet his music! on my life,
There's more of wisdom in it.

And hark! how blithe the throstle sings!
He, too, is no mean preacher:
Come forth into the light of things,   15
Let Nature be your teacher.

She has a world of ready wealth,
Our minds and hearts to bless, —
Spontaneous wisdom breathed by health,
Truth breathed by cheerfulness.   20

One impulse from a vernal wood
May teach you more of man,
Of moral evil and of good,
Than all the sages can.

Sweet is the lore which Nature brings;   25
Our meddling intellect
Misshapes the beauteous forms of things, —
We murder to dissect.

Enough of Science and of Art;
Close up those barren leaves;   30
Come forth, and bring with you a heart
That watches and receives.

Lines Composed a Few Miles Above Tintern Abbey, on Revisiting the Banks of the Wye During a Tour. July 13, 1798

No poem of mine was composed under circumstances more pleasant for me to remember than this. I began it upon leaving Tintern, after crossing the Wye, and concluded it just as I was entering Bristol in the evening, after a ramble of four or five days, with my Sister. Not a line of it was altered, and not any part of it written down till I reached Bristol. It was published almost immediately after in the little volume of which so much has been said in these Notes. — *Wordsworth.*

Five years have passed; five summers, with the
     length
Of five long winters! and again I hear
These waters, rolling from their mountain-springs

With a soft inland murmur. — Once again
Do I behold these steep and lofty cliffs,   5
That on a wild secluded scene impress
Thoughts of more deep seclusion; and connect
The landscape with the quiet of the sky.
The day is come when I again repose
Here, under this dark sycamore, and view   10
These plots of cottage-ground, these orchard-tufts,
Which at this season, with their unripe fruits,
Are clad in one green hue, and lose themselves
'Mid groves and copses. Once again I see   14
These hedge-rows, hardly hedge-rows, little lines
Of sportive wood run wild: these pastoral farms,
Green to the very door; and wreaths of smoke
Sent up, in silence, from among the trees!
With some uncertain notice, as might seem
Of vagrant dwellers in the houseless woods   20
Or of some Hermit's cave, where by his fire
The hermit sits alone.

           These beauteous forms,
Through a long absence, have not been to me
As is a landscape to a blind man's eye:
But oft, in lonely rooms, and 'mid the din   25
Of towns and cities, I have owed to them
In hours of weariness, sensations sweet,
Felt in the blood, and felt along the heart;
And passing even into my purer mind,
With tranquil restoration: — feelings too   30
Of unremembered pleasure: such, perhaps,
As have no slight or trivial influence
On that best portion of a good man's life,
His little, nameless, unremembered, acts
Of kindness and of love. Nor less, I trust,   35
To them I may have owed another gift,
Of aspect more sublime; that blessed mood,
In which the burthen of the mystery,
In which the heavy and the weary weight
Of all this unintelligible world,   40
Is lightened: — that serene and blessed mood,
In which the affections gently lead us on —
Until, the breath of this corporeal frame
And even the motion of our human blood
Almost suspended, we are laid asleep   45
In body, and become a living soul:
While with an eye made quiet by the power
Of harmony, and the deep power of joy,
We see into the life of things.

               If this
Be but a vain belief, yet, oh! how oft —   50
In darkness and amid the many shapes
Of joyless daylight; when the fretful stir
Unprofitable, and the fever of the world,
Have hung upon the beatings of my heart —
How oft, in spirit, have I turned to thee,   55
O sylvan Wye! thou wanderer through the woods,
How often has my spirit turned to thee!

And now, with gleams of half-extinguished
    thought,
With many recognitions dim and faint,
And somewhat of a sad perplexity,   60
The picture of the mind revives again:
While here I stand, not only with the sense
Of present pleasure, but with pleasing thoughts
That in this moment there is life and food
For future years.   And so I dare to hope,   65
Though changed, no doubt, from what I was when
    first
I came among these hills; when like a roe
I bounded o'er the mountains, by the sides
Of the deep rivers, and the lonely streams,
Wherever nature led: more like a man   70
Flying from something that he dreads, than one
Who sought the thing he loved. For nature
    then
(The coarser pleasures of my boyish days,
And their glad animal movements all gone by)
To me was all in all. — I cannot paint   75
What then I was. The sounding cataract
Haunted me like a passion; the tall rock,
The mountain, and the deep and gloomy wood,
Their colors and their forms, were then to me
An appetite; a feeling and a love,   80
That had no need of a remoter charm,
By thought supplied, nor any interest
Unborrowed from the eye. — That time is past,
And all its aching joys are now no more,
And all its dizzy raptures. Not for this   85
Faint I, nor mourn nor murmur; other gifts
Have followed; for such loss, I would believe,
Abundant recompense. For I have learned
To look on nature, not as in the hour
Of thoughtless youth; but hearing oftentimes   90
The still, sad music of humanity,
Nor harsh nor grating, though of ample power
To chasten and subdue. And I have felt
A presence that disturbs me with the joy
Of elevated thoughts; a sense sublime   95
Of something far more deeply interfused,
Whose dwelling is the light of setting suns,
And the round ocean and the living air,
And the blue sky, and in the mind of man;
A motion and a spirit, that impels   100
All thinking things, all objects of all thought,
And rolls through all things. Therefore am I
    still
A lover of the meadows and the woods,
And mountains; and of all that we behold
From this green earth; of all the mighty world   105
Of eye, and ear, — both what they half create,
And what perceive; well pleased to recognize
In nature and the language of the sense,
The anchor of my purest thoughts, the nurse,

The guide, the guardian of my heart, and soul   110
Of all my moral being.

                  Nor perchance,
If I were not thus taught, should I the more
Suffer my genial spirits to decay:
For thou art with me here upon the banks
Of this fair river; thou my dearest Friend,   115
My dear, dear Friend;[1] and in thy voice I catch
The language of my former heart, and read
My former pleasures in the shooting lights
Of thy wild eyes. Oh! yet a little while
May I behold in thee what I was once,   120
My dear, dear Sister! and this prayer I make,
Knowing that Nature never did betray
The heart that loved her; 'tis her privilege,
Through all the years of this our life, to lead
From joy to joy: for she can so inform   125
The mind that is within us, so impress
With quietness and beauty, and so feed
With lofty thoughts, that neither evil tongues,
Rash judgments, nor the sneers of selfish men,
Nor greetings where no kindness is, nor all   130
The dreary intercourse of daily life,
Shall e'er prevail against us, or disturb
Our cheerful faith, that all which we behold
Is full of blessings. Therefore let the moon
Shine on thee in thy solitary walk;   135
And let the misty mountain-winds be free
To blow against thee: and, in after years,
When these wild ecstasies shall be matured
Into a sober pleasure; when thy mind
Shall be a mansion for all lovely forms,   140
Thy memory be as a dwelling-place
For all sweet sounds and harmonies; oh! then,
If solitude, or fear, or pain, or grief,
Should be thy portion, with what healing
    thoughts
Of tender joy wilt thou remember me,   145
And these my exhortations! Nor, perchance —
If I should be where I no more can hear
Thy voice, nor catch from thy wild eyes these
    gleams
Of past existence — wilt thou then forget
That on the banks of this delightful stream   150
We stood together; and that I, so long
A worshipper of Nature, hither came
Unwearied in that service: rather say
With warmer love — oh! with far deeper zeal
Of holier love. Nor wilt thou then forget,   155
That after many wanderings, many years
Of absence, these steep woods and lofty cliffs,
And this green pastoral landscape, were to me
More dear, both for themselves and for thy sake!

[1] Dorothy Wordsworth, his sister.

My Heart Leaps Up

My heart leaps up when I behold
  A rainbow in the sky:
So was it when my life began;
So is it now I am a man;
So be it when I shall grow old,   5
  Or let me die!
The Child is father of the Man;
And I could wish my days to be
Bound each to each by natural piety.

To the Cuckoo

O blithe New-comer! I have heard,
I hear thee and rejoice.
O Cuckoo! shall I call thee Bird,
Or but a wandering Voice?

While I am lying on the grass   5
Thy twofold shout I hear,
From hill to hill it seems to pass,
At once far off, and near.

Though babbling only to the vale,
Of sunshine and of flowers,   10
Thou bringest unto me a tale
Of visionary hours.

Thrice welcome, darling of the Spring!
Even yet thou art to me
No bird, but an invisible thing,   15
A voice, a mystery;

The same whom in my schoolboy days
I listened to; that cry
Which made me look a thousand ways,
In bush, and tree, and sky.   20

To seek thee did I often rove
Through woods and on the green;
And thou wert still a hope, a love;
Still longed for, never seen.

And I can listen to thee yet;   25
Can lie upon the plain
And listen, till I do beget
That golden time again.

O blessed Bird! the earth we pace
Again appears to be   30
An unsubstantial, faery place,
That is fit home for thee!

Composed Upon Westminster Bridge, September 3, 1802

Earth has not anything to show more fair:
Dull would he be of soul who could pass by
A sight so touching in its majesty:
This City now doth like a garment wear
The beauty of the morning: silent, bare,   5
Ships, towers, domes, theatres, and temples lie
Open unto the fields, and to the sky,—
All bright and glittering in the smokeless air.
Never did sun more beautifully steep
In his first splendor valley, rock, or hill;   10
Ne'er saw I, never felt, a calm so deep!
The river glideth at his own sweet will:
Dear God! the very houses seem asleep;
And all that mighty heart is lying still!

It Is a Beauteous Evening, Calm and Free

It is a beauteous evening, calm and free.
The holy time is quiet as a nun,
Breathless with adoration; the broad sun
Is sinking down in its tranquillity;
The gentleness of heaven broods o'er the sea;   5
Listen! the mighty Being is awake,
And doth with his eternal motion make
A sound like thunder—everlastingly.
Dear Child! dear Girl! that walkest with me here,
If thou appear untouched by solemn thought,   10
Thy nature is not therefore less divine;
Thou liest in Abraham's bosom all the year,
And worship'st at the Temple's inner shrine,
God being with thee when we know it not.

London, 1802

Milton! thou shouldst be living at this hour:
England hath need of thee; she is a fen
Of stagnant waters; altar, sword, and pen,
Fireside, the heroic wealth of hall and bower,
Have forfeited their ancient English dower   5
Of inward happiness. We are selfish men;
Oh! raise us up, return to us again;
And give us manners, virtue, freedom, power.
Thy Soul was like a Star, and dwelt apart;
Thou hadst a voice whose sound was like the sea;
Pure as the naked heavens, majestic, free,   11
So didst thou travel on life's common way,
In cheerful godliness; and yet thy heart
The lowliest duties on herself did lay.

The World Is Too Much With Us

The world is too much with us; late and soon,
Getting and spending, we lay waste our powers:
Little we see in Nature that is ours;
We have given our hearts away, a sordid boon!
The Sea that bares her bosom to the moon;   5
The winds that will be howling at all hours,
And are up-gathered now like sleeping flowers;
For this, for everything, we are out of tune:
It moves us not. — Great God!   I'd rather be
A Pagan suckled in a creed outworn;   10
So might I, standing on this pleasant lea,
Have glimpses that would make me less forlorn;
Have sight of Proteus rising from the sea;
Or hear old Triton blow his wreathèd horn.

The Solitary Reaper

Behold her, single in the field,
Yon solitary Highland Lass!
Reaping and singing by herself;
Stop here, or gently pass!
Alone she cuts and binds the grain,   5
And sings a melancholy strain;
O listen! for the vale profound
Is overflowing with the sound.

No nightingale did ever chaunt
More welcome notes to weary bands   10
Of travellers in some shady haunt,
Among Arabian sands:
A voice so thrilling ne'er was heard
In spring-time from the cuckoo-bird,
Breaking the silence of the seas   15
Among the farthest Hebrides.

Will no one tell me what she sings?
Perhaps the plaintive numbers flow
For old, unhappy, far-off things,
And battles long ago: 20
Or is it some more humble lay,
Familiar matter of to-day?
Some natural sorrow, loss, or pain,
That has been, and may be again!

Whate'er the theme, the maiden sang   25
As if her song could have no ending;
I saw her singing at her work,
And o'er the sickle bending; —
I listened, motionless and still;
And, as I mounted up the hill,   30
The music in my heart I bore
Long after it was heard no more.

I Wandered Lonely as a Cloud

I wandered lonely as a cloud
That floats on high o'er vales and hills,
When all at once I saw a crowd,
A host, of golden daffodils;
Beside the lake, beneath the trees,   5
Fluttering and dancing in the breeze.

Continuous as the stars that shine
And twinkle on the milky way,
They stretched in never-ending line
Along the margin of a bay: 10
Ten thousand saw I at a glance,
Tossing their heads in sprightly dance.

The waves beside them danced; but they
Out-did the sparkling waves in glee:
A poet could not but be gay,   15
In such a jocund company:
I gazed — and gazed — but little thought
What wealth the show to me had brought:

For oft, when on my couch I lie
In vacant or in pensive mood,   20
They flash upon that inward eye
Which is the bliss of solitude;
And then my heart with pleasure fills,
And dances with the daffodils.

Ode to Duty

Stern Daughter of the Voice of God!
O Duty! if that name thou love
Who art a light to guide, a rod
To check the erring, and reprove;
Thou who art victory and law   5
When empty terrors overawe;
From vain temptations dost set free,
And calm'st the weary strife of frail humanity!

There are who ask not if thine eye
Be on them; who, in love and truth   10
Where no misgiving is, rely
Upon the genial sense of youth:
Glad hearts! without reproach or blot,
Who do thy work, and know it not:
Oh! if through confidence misplaced   15
They fail, thy saving arms, dread Power! around
      them cast.

Serene will be our days and bright
And happy will our nature be
When love is an unerring light,
And joy its own security.   20

And they a blissful course may hold
Ev'n now, who, not unwisely bold,
Live in the spirit of this creed;
Yet seek thy firm support, according to their need.

I, loving freedom, and untried,   25
No sport of every random gust,
Yet being to myself a guide,
Too blindly have reposed my trust:
And oft, when in my heart was heard
Thy timely mandate, I deferred   30
The task, in smoother walks to stray;
But thee I now would serve more strictly, if I may.

Through no disturbance of my soul,
Or strong compunction in me wrought,
I supplicate for thy control;   35
But in the quietness of thought:
Me this unchartered freedom tires;
I feel the weight of chance-desires:
My hopes no more must change their name,
I long for a repose that ever is the same.   40

Stern Lawgiver! yet thou dost wear
The Godhead's most benignant grace;
Nor know we anything so fair
As is the smile upon thy face:
Flowers laugh before thee on their beds   45
And fragrance in thy footing treads;
Thou dost preserve the stars from wrong;
And the most ancient heavens, through Thee, are
    fresh and strong.

To humbler functions, awful Power!
I call thee: I myself commend   50
Unto thy guidance from this hour;
Oh, let my weakness have an end!
Give unto me, made lowly wise,
The spirit of self-sacrifice;
The confidence of reason give;   55
And in the light of truth thy Bondman let me live!

Ode on Intimations of Immortality from Recollections of Early Childhood

This was composed during my residence at Town-end, Grasmere. Two years at least passed between the writing of the four stanzas and the remaining part. To the attentive and competent reader the whole sufficiently explains itself; but there may be no harm in adverting here to particular feelings or *experiences* of my own mind on which the structure of the poem partly rests. Nothing was more difficult for me in childhood than to admit the notion of death as a state applicable to my own being. I have said elsewhere —

    "A simple child,
      That lightly draws its breath,
    And feels its life in every limb,
      What should it know of death!" —

But it was not so much from feelings of animal vivacity that *my* difficulty came as from a sense of the indomitableness of the Spirit within me. I used to brood over the stories of Enoch and Elijah, and almost to persuade myself that, whatever might become of others, I should be translated, in something of the same way, to heaven. With a feeling congenial to this, I was often unable to think of external things as having external existence, and I communed with all that I saw as something not apart from, but inherent in, my own immaterial nature. Many times while going to school have I grasped at a wall or tree to recall myself from this abyss of idealism to the reality. At that time I was afraid of such processes. In later periods of life I have deplored, as we have all reason to do, a subjugation of an opposite character, and have rejoiced over the remembrances, as is expressed in the lines —

    "Obstinate questionings
   Of sense and outward things,
    Fallings from us, vanishings"; etc.

To that dream-like vividness and splendor which invest objects of sight in childhood, everyone, I believe, if he would look back, could bear testimony, and I need not dwell upon it here: but having in the poem regarded it as presumptive evidence of a prior state of existence, I think it right to protest against a conclusion, which has given pain to some good and pious persons, that I meant to inculcate such a belief. It is far too shadowy a notion to be recommended to faith, as more than an element in our instincts of immortality.... — *Wordsworth.*

There was a time when meadow, grove, and stream,
The earth, and every common sight
      To me did seem
      Apparelled in celestial light,
The glory and the freshness of a dream.   5
It is not now as it hath been of yore; —
      Turn wheresoe'er I may,
       By night or day,
The things which I have seen I now can see no more.

      The rainbow comes and goes,   10
      And lovely is the rose;
      The moon doth with delight
Look round her when the heavens are bare;
      Waters on a starry night
      Are beautiful and fair;   15
The sunshine is a glorious birth;
But yet I know, where'er I go,
That there hath past away a glory from the earth.

Now, while the birds thus sing a joyous song,
  And while the young lambs bound 20
    As to the tabor's sound,
To me alone there came a thought of grief:
A timely utterance gave that thought relief,
    And I again am strong.
The cataracts blow their trumpets from the steep; — 25
No more shall grief of mine the season wrong:
I hear the echoes through the mountains throng,
The winds come to me from the fields of sleep,
    And all the earth is gay;
      Land and sea 30
  Give themselves up to jollity,
    And with the heart of May
Doth every beast keep holiday; —
    Thou child of joy,
Shout round me, let me hear thy shouts, thou happy 35
    Shepherd-boy!

Ye blessèd Creatures, I have heard the call
  Ye to each other make; I see
The heavens laugh with you in your jubilee;
  My heart is at your festival,
    My head hath its coronal, 40
The fulness of your bliss, I feel — I feel it all.
  Oh evil day! if I were sullen
  While Earth herself is adorning
    This sweet May-morning; 45
  And the children are culling
    On every side
In a thousand valleys far and wide,
Fresh flowers; while the sun shines warm,
And the babe leaps up on his mother's arm: — 50
  I hear, I hear, with joy I hear!
  — But there's a tree, of many, one,
A single field which I have looked upon,
Both of them speak of something that is gone:
    The pansy at my feet 55
    Doth the same tale repeat:
Whither is fled the visionary gleam?
Where is it now, the glory and the dream?

Our birth is but a sleep and a forgetting;
The Soul that rises with us, our life's Star, 60
  Hath had elsewhere its setting,
    And cometh from afar;
  Not in entire forgetfulness,
  And not in utter nakedness,
But trailing clouds of glory do we come 65
    From God, who is our home:
Heaven lies about us in our infancy!
Shades of the prison-house begin to close
    Upon the growing Boy,
But he beholds the light, and whence it flows, 70

He sees it in his joy;
The Youth, who daily farther from the east
  Must travel, still is Nature's priest,
    And by the vision splendid
    Is on his way attended; 75
At length the Man perceives it die away,
And fade into the light of common day.

Earth fills her lap with pleasures of her own;
Yearnings she hath in her own natural kind,
And, even with something of a mother's mind 80
    And no unworthy aim,
  The homely nurse doth all she can
To make her foster-child, her inmate, Man,
    Forget the glories he hath known,
And that imperial palace whence he came. 85
Behold the Child among his new-born blisses,
A six years' darling of a pigmy size!
See, where 'mid work of his own hand he lies,
Fretted by sallies of his mother's kisses,
With light upon him from his father's eyes! 90
See, at his feet, some little plan or chart,
Some fragment from his dream of human life,
Shaped by himself with newly-learnèd art;
    A wedding or a festival,
    A mourning or a funeral; 95
    And this hath now his heart,
    And unto this he frames his song:
    Then will he fit his tongue
To dialogues of business, love, or strife;
    But it will not be long 100
    Ere this be thrown aside,
    And with new joy and pride
The little actor cons another part;
Filling from time to time his "humorous stage"
With all the Persons, down to palsied Age, 105
That life brings with her in her equipage;
    As if his whole vocation
    Were endless imitation.

Thou, whose exterior semblance doth belie
    Thy soul's immensity; 110
Thou best philosopher, who yet dost keep
Thy heritage, thou eye among the blind,
That, deaf and silent, read'st the eternal deep,
Haunted for ever by the eternal Mind, —
    Mighty Prophet! Seer blest! 115
    On whom those truths do rest
Which we are toiling all our lives to find,
In darkness lost, the darkness of the grave;
Thou, over whom thy Immortality
Broods like the day, a master o'er a slave, 120
A Presence which is not to be put by;
Thou little child, yet glorious in the might
Of heaven-born freedom on thy being's height,
Why with such earnest pains dost thou provoke

The years to bring the inevitable yoke,   125
Thus blindly with thy blessedness at strife?
Full soon thy soul shall have her earthly freight,
And custom lie upon thee with a weight
Heavy as frost, and deep almost as life!

        O joy! that in our embers   130
        Is something that doth live,
        That Nature yet remembers
        What was so fugitive!
The thought of our past years in me doth breed
Perpetual benediction: not indeed   135
For that which is most worthy to be blest,
Delight and liberty, the simple creed
Of Childhood, whether busy or at rest,
With new-fledged hope still fluttering in his
        breast: —
        — Not for these I raise   140
        The song of thanks and praise;
        But for those obstinate questions
        Of sense and outward things,
        Fallings from us, vanishings;
        Blank misgivings of a creature   145
Moving about in worlds not realized,
High instincts, before which our mortal nature
Did tremble like a guilty thing surprised:
        But for those first affections,
        Those shadowy recollections,   150
        Which, be they what they may,
Are yet the fountain-light of all our day,
Are yet a master-light of all our seeing;
        Uphold us, cherish, and have power to make
Our noisy years seem moments in the being   155
Of the eternal Silence: truths that wake,
        To perish never;
Which neither listlessness, nor mad endeavor,
        Nor man nor boy,
Nor all that is at enmity with joy,   160
Can utterly abolish or destroy!
        Hence, in a season of calm weather
        Though inland far we be,
Our souls have sight of that immortal sea
        Which brought us hither;   165
        Can in a moment travel thither —
And see the children sport upon the shore,
And hear the mighty waters rolling evermore.

Then, sing, ye birds, sing, sing a joyous song!
        And let the young lambs bound   170
        As to the tabor's sound!
    We, in thought, will join your throng,
        Ye that pipe and ye that play,
        Ye that through your hearts to-day
        Feel the gladness of the May!   175
What though the radiance which was once so
        bright

Be now for ever taken from my sight,
        Though nothing can bring back the hour
Of splendor in the grass, of glory in the flower;
        We will grieve not, rather find   180
        Strength in what remains behind;
        In the primal sympathy
        Which having been must ever be;
        In the soothing thoughts that spring
        Out of human suffering;   185
        In the faith that looks through death,
In years that bring the philosophic mind.

And O, ye Fountains, Meadows, Hills, and Groves,
Forbode not any severing of our loves!
Yet in my heart of hearts I feel your might;   190
I only have relinquished one delight
To live beneath your more habitual sway:
I love the brooks which down their channels fret
Even more than when I tripped lightly as they;
The innocent brightness of a new-born day   195
        Is lovely yet;
The clouds that gather round the setting sun
Do take a sober coloring from an eye
That hath kept watch o'er man's mortality;
Another race hath been, and other palms are won.
Thanks to the human heart by which we live,   201
Thanks to its tenderness, its joys, and fears,
To me the meanest flower that blows can give
Thoughts that do often lie too deep for tears.

Preface to Lyrical Ballads

The first edition of the *Lyrical Ballads* (1798) led to
so much discussion and questioning of the purpose that,
upon the appearance of the second edition in 1800,
Wordsworth added a preface. Particularly questioned
was Wordsworth's desire to write of simple subjects in a
simple language. In the *Preface* Wordsworth condemns the artificiality of neo-classical formalism and
presents his own convictions. The following pages are
significant as a defense of the romantic spirit made by
the high-priest of the romantic movement.

The first Volume of these Poems has already
been submitted to general perusal. It was published as an experiment, which, I hoped, might be
of some use to ascertain how far, by fitting to
metrical arrangement a selection of the real language of men in a state of vivid sensation, that sort
of pleasure and that quantity of pleasure may be
imparted, which a Poet may rationally endeavor
to impart.

I had formed no very inaccurate estimate of the
probable effect of those Poems: I flattered myself
that they who should be pleased with them would
read them with more than common pleasure; and,

on the other hand, I was well aware, that by those who should dislike them they would be read with more than common dislike. The result has differed from my expectation in this only, that a greater number have been pleased than I ventured to hope I should please.

Several of my Friends are anxious for the success of these Poems, from a belief that, if the views with which they were composed were indeed realized, a class of poetry would be produced, well adapted to interest mankind permanently, and not unimportant in the quality and in the multiplicity of its moral relations: and on this account they have advised me to prefix a systematic defence of the theory upon which the Poems were written. But I was unwilling to undertake the task, knowing that on this occasion the Reader would look coldly upon my arguments, since I might be suspected of having been principally influenced by the selfish and foolish hope of *reasoning* him into an approbation of these particular Poems: and I was still more unwilling to undertake the task, because adequately to display the opinions, and fully to enforce the arguments, would require a space wholly disproportionate to a preface. For, to treat the subject with the clearness and coherence of which it is susceptible, it would be necessary to give a full account of the present state of the public taste in this country, and to determine how far this taste is healthy or depraved; which, again, could not be determined without pointing out in what manner language and the human mind act and re-act on each other, and without retracing the revolutions, not of literature alone, but likewise of society itself. I have therefore altogether declined to enter regularly upon this defence; yet I am sensible that there would be some impropriety in abruptly obtruding upon the Public, without a few words of introduction, Poems so materially different from those upon which general approbation is at present bestowed.

It is supposed that by the act of writing in verse an Author makes a formal engagement that he will gratify certain known habits of association; that he not only thus apprises the Reader that certain classes of ideas and expressions will be found in his book, but that others will be carefully excluded. This exponent or symbol held forth by metrical language must in different eras of literature have excited very different expectations: for example, in the age of Catullus, Terence, and Lucretius, and that of Statius or Claudian; and in our own country, in the age of Shakespeare and Beaumont and Fletcher, and that of Donne and Cowley, or Dryden, or Pope. I will not take upon me to determine the exact import of the promise which, by the act of writing in verse, an Author in the present day makes to his reader; but it will undoubtedly appear to many persons that I have not fulfilled the terms of an engagement thus voluntarily contracted. They who have been accustomed to the gaudiness and inane phraseology of many modern writers, if they persist in reading this book to its conclusion, will, no doubt, frequently have to struggle with feelings of strangeness and awkwardness: they will look round for poetry, and will be induced to inquire by what species of courtesy these attempts can be permitted to assume that title. I hope, therefore, the reader will not censure me for attempting to state what I have proposed to myself to perform; and also (as far as the limits of a preface will permit) to explain some of the chief reasons which have determined me in the choice of my purpose: that at least he may be spared any unpleasant feeling of disappointment, and that I myself may be protected from one of the most dishonorable accusations which can be brought against an Author, namely, that of an indolence which prevents him from endeavoring to ascertain what is his duty, or, when his duty is ascertained, prevents him from performing it.

The principal object, then, proposed in these Poems, was to choose incidents and situations from common life, and to relate or describe them throughout, as far as was possible, in a selection of language really used by men, and, at the same time, to throw over them a certain coloring of imagination, whereby ordinary things should be presented to the mind in an unusual aspect, and further, and above all, to make these incidents and situations interesting by tracing in them, truly though not ostentatiously, the primary laws of our nature: chiefly, as far as regards the manner in which we associate ideas in a state of excitement. Humble and rustic life was generally chosen, because in that condition the essential passions of the heart find a better soil in which they can attain their maturity, are less under restraint, and speak a plainer and more emphatic language; because in that condition of life our elementary feelings co-exist in a state of greater simplicity, and, consequently, may be more accurately contemplated, and more forcibly communicated; because the manners of rural life germinate from those elementary feelings; and from the necessary character of rural occupations, are more easily comprehended, and are more durable; and, lastly, because in that condition the passions of men are incorporated with the beautiful and permanent forms of nature. The language, too, of these men is adopted (purified indeed from what appears to be its real defects, from all lasting and rational causes of dislike or disgust), because such men hourly communicate with the best objects from which the best part of language is originally derived; and because, from their rank in society and the sameness and narrow circle of their intercourse, being less under the influence of social vanity, they convey their feelings and notions in simple and unelaborated expressions. Accordingly such a language, arising out of repeated experience and regular feelings, is a more permanent, and a far more philosophical language, than that which is frequently substituted for it by Poets, who think that they are conferring honor upon themselves and their art, in proportion as they separate themselves from the sympathies of men, and indulge in arbitrary and capricious habits of expression, in order to furnish food for fickle tastes and fickle appetites of their own creation.[1]

I cannot, however, be insensible to the present outcry against the triviality and meanness, both of thought and language, which some of my contemporaries have occasionally introduced into their metrical compositions; and I acknowledge that this defect, where it exists, is more dishonorable to the Writer's own character than false refinement or arbitrary innovation, though I should contend at the same time that it is far less pernicious in the sum of its consequences. From such verses the Poems in these volumes will be found distinguished at least by one mark of difference, that each of them has a worthy *purpose*. Not that I always began to write with a distinct purpose formally conceived; but habits of meditation have, I trust, so prompted and regulated my feelings, as that my descriptions of such objects as strongly excite those feelings, will be found to carry along with them a *purpose*. If this opinion be erroneous, I can have little right to the name of a Poet. For all good poetry is the spontaneous overflow of powerful feelings: and though this be true, Poems to which any value can be attached were never produced on any variety of subjects but by a man who, being possessed of more than usual organic sensibility, had also thought long and deeply. For our continued influxes of feeling are modified and directed by our thoughts, which are indeed the representatives of all our past feelings; and as, by contemplating the relation of these general representatives to each other, we discover what is really important to men, so, by the repetition

[1] It is worth while here to observe that the affecting parts of Chaucer are almost always expressed in language pure and universally intelligible even to this day. (Wordsworth.)

and continuance of this act, our feelings will be connected with important subjects, till at length, if we be originally possessed of much sensibility, such habits of mind will be produced that, by obeying blindly and mechanically the impulses of those habits, we shall describe objects, and utter sentiments, of such a nature, and in such connection with each other, that the understanding of the Reader must necessarily be in some degree enlightened, and his affections strengthened and purified.

It has been said that each of these Poems has a purpose. Another circumstance must be mentioned which distinguishes these Poems from the popular Poetry of the day; it is this, that the feeling therein developed gives importance to the action and situation, and not the action and situation to the feeling.

A sense of false modesty shall not prevent me from asserting that the Reader's attention is pointed to this mark of distinction, far less for the sake of these Particular Poems than from the general importance of the subject. The subject is indeed important! For the human mind is capable of being excited without the application of gross and violent stimulants; and he must have a very faint perception of its beauty and dignity who does not know this, and who does not further know, that one being is elevated above another, in proportion as he possesses this capability. It has therefore appeared to me, that to endeavor to produce or enlarge this capability is one of the best services in which, at any period, a Writer can be engaged; but this service, excellent at all times, is especially so at the present day. For a multitude of causes, unknown to former times, are now acting with a combined force to blunt the discriminating powers of the mind, and, unfitting it for all voluntary exertion, to reduce it to a state of almost savage torpor. The most effective of these causes are the great national events which are daily taking place, and the increasing accumulation of men in cities, where the uniformity of their occupations produces a craving for extraordinary incident which the rapid communication of intelligence hourly gratifies. To this tendency of life and manners the literature and theatrical exhibitions of the country have conformed themselves. The invaluable works of our elder writers, I had almost said the works of Shakespeare and Milton, are driven into neglect by frantic novels, sickly and stupid German Tragedies, and deluges of idle and extravagant stories in verse. — When I think upon this degrading thirst after outrageous stimulation, I am almost ashamed to have spoken of the feeble endeavor made in these volumes to counteract it; and, reflecting upon the magnitude of the general evil, I should be oppressed with no dishonorable melancholy, had I not a deep impression of certain inherent and indestructible qualities of the human mind, and likewise of certain powers in the great and permanent objects that act upon it, which are equally inherent and indestructible; and were there not added to this impression a belief that the time is approaching when the evil will be systematically opposed by men of greater powers, and with far more distinguished success.

Having dwelt thus long on the subjects and aim of these Poems, I shall request the Reader's permission to apprise him of a few circumstances relating to their *style*, in order, among other reasons, that he may not censure me for not having performed what I never attempted. The reader will find that personifications of abstract ideas rarely occur in these volumes, and are utterly rejected as an ordinary device to elevate the style and raise it above prose. My purpose was to imitate, and, as far as is possible, to adopt the very language of men; and assuredly such personifications do not make any natural or regular part of that language. They are, indeed, a figure of speech occasionally prompted by passion, and I have made use of them as such; but have endeavored utterly to reject them as a mechanical device of style, or as a family language which Writers in metre seem to lay claim to by prescription. I have wished to keep the Reader in the company of flesh and blood, persuaded that by so doing I shall interest him. Others who pursue a different track will interest him likewise; I do not interfere with their claim, but wish to prefer a claim of my own. There will also be found in these volumes little of what is usually called poetic diction; as much pains has been taken to avoid it as is ordinarily taken to produce it; this has been done for the reason already alleged, to bring my language near to the language of men; and further, because the pleasure which I have proposed to myself to impart is of a kind very different from that which is supposed by many persons to be the proper object of poetry. Without being culpably particular, I do not know how to give my Reader a more exact notion of the style in which it was my wish and intention to write, than by informing him that I have at all times endeavored to look steadily at my subject; consequently there is, I hope, in these Poems little falsehood of description, and my ideas are expressed in language fitted to their respective importance. Something must have been gained by this practice, as it is friendly to one property of all good poetry, namely, good sense; but it has necessarily cut me off from a large portion of phrases and figures of speech which from father to son have long been

regarded as the common inheritance of Poets. I have also thought it expedient to restrict myself still further, having abstained from the use of many expressions, in themselves proper and beautiful, but which have been foolishly repeated by bad Poets, till such feelings of disgust are connected with them as it is scarcely possible by any art of association to overpower.

If in a poem there should be found a series of lines, or even a single line, in which the language, though naturally arranged, and according to the strict laws of metre, does not differ from that of prose, there is a numerous class of critics who, when they stumble upon these prosaisms, as they call them, imagine that they have made a notable discovery, and exult over the Poet as over a man ignorant of his own profession. Now these men would establish a canon of criticism which the Reader will conclude he must utterly reject, if he wishes to be pleased with these volumes. And it would be a most easy task to prove to him that not only the language of a large portion of every good poem, even of the most elevated character, must necessarily, except with reference to the metre, in no respect differ from that of good prose, but likewise that some of the most interesting parts of the best poems will be found to be strictly the language of prose when prose is well written. The truth of this assertion might be demonstrated by innumerable passages from almost all the poetical writings, even of Milton himself. To illustrate the subject in a general manner, I will here adduce a short composition of Gray, who was at the head of those who, by their reasonings, have attempted to widen the space of separation betwixt Prose and Metrical composition, and was more than any other man curiously elaborate in the structure of his own poetic diction.

> In vain to me the smiling mornings shine,
> And reddening Phœbus lifts his golden fire:
> The birds in vain their amorous descant join,
> Or cheerful fields resume their green attire.
> These ears, alas! for other notes repine;
> *A different object do these eyes require;*
> *My lonely anguish melts no heart but mine;*
> *And in my breast the imperfect joys expire:*
> Yet morning smiles the busy race to cheer,
> And new-born pleasure brings to happier men;
> The fields to all their wonted tribute bear;
> To warm their little loves the birds complain.
> *I fruitless mourn to him that cannot hear,*
> *And weep the more because I weep in vain.*

It will easily be perceived, that the only part of this Sonnet which is of any value is the lines printed in Italics; it is equally obvious that, except in the rhyme, and in the use of the single word "fruitless" for fruitlessly, which is so far a defect, the language of these lines does in no respect differ from that of prose.

By the foregoing quotation it has been shown that the language of Prose may yet be well adapted to poetry; and it was previously asserted that a large portion of the language of every good poem can in no respect differ from that of good Prose. We will go further. It may be safely affirmed that there neither is, nor can be, any essential difference between the language of prose and metrical composition. We are fond of tracing the resemblance between Poetry and Painting, and, accordingly, we call them Sisters: but where shall we find bonds of connection sufficiently strict to typify the affinity betwixt metrical and prose composition? They both speak by and to the same organs; the bodies in which both of them are clothed may be said to be of the same substance, their affections are kindred, and almost identical, not necessarily differing in degree; Poetry [1] sheds no tears "such as angels weep," but natural and human tears; she can boast of no celestial ichor that distinguishes her vital juices from those of Prose; the same human blood circulates through the veins of them both.

If it be affirmed that rhyme and metrical arrangement of themselves constitute a distinction which overturns what has just been said on the strict affinity of metrical language with that of Prose, and paves the way for other artificial distinctions which the mind voluntarily admits, I answer that the language of such Poetry as is here recommended is, as far as is possible, a selection of the language really spoken by men; that this selection, wherever it is made with true taste and feeling, will of itself form a distinction far greater than would at first be imagined, and will entirely separate the composition from the vulgarity and meanness of ordinary life; and, if metre be superadded thereto, I believe that a dissimilitude will be produced altogether sufficient for the gratification of a rational mind. What other distinction would we have? Whence is it to come? And where is it to exist? Not, surely, where the Poet

[1] I here use the word "Poetry" (though against my own judgment) as opposed to the word Prose, and synonymous with metrical composition. But much confusion has been introduced into criticism by this contradistinction of Poetry and Prose, instead of the more philosophical one of Poetry and Matter of Fact, or Science. The only strict antithesis to Prose is Metre; nor is this, in truth, a *strict* antithesis; because lines and passages of metre so naturally occur in writing prose, that it would be scarcely possible to avoid them, even were it desirable. (Wordsworth.)

speaks through the mouths of his characters: it cannot be necessary here, either for elevation of style, or any of its supposed ornaments: for, if the Poet's subject be judiciously chosen, it will naturally, and upon fit occasion, lead him to passions, the language of which, if selected truly and judiciously, must necessarily be dignified and variegated, and alive with metaphors and figures. I forbear to speak of an incongruity which would shock the intelligent Reader, should the Poet interweave any foreign splendor of his own with that which the passion naturally suggests: it is sufficient to say that such addition is unnecessary. And, surely, it is more probable that those passages, which with propriety abound with metaphors and figures, will have effect if, upon other occasions where the passions are of a milder character, the style also be subdued and temperate.

But, as the pleasure which I hope to give by the Poems now presented to the reader must depend entirely on just notions upon this subject, and as it is in itself of high importance to our taste and moral feelings, I cannot content myself with these detached remarks. And if, in what I am about to say, it shall appear to some that my labor is unnecessary, and that I am like a man fighting a battle without enemies, such persons may be reminded that, whatever may be the language outwardly holden by men, a practical faith in the opinions which I am wishing to establish is almost unknown. If my conclusions are admitted, and carried as far as they must be carried if admitted at all, our judgments concerning the works of the greatest Poets, both ancient and modern, will be far different from what they are at present, both when we praise and when we censure: and our moral feelings influencing and influenced by these judgments will, I believe, be corrected and purified.

Taking up the subject, then, upon general grounds, let me ask what is meant by the word Poet? What is a Poet? To whom does he address himself? And what language is to be expected from him? — He is a man speaking to men: a man, it is true, endowed with more lively sensibility, more enthusiasm and tenderness, who has a greater knowledge of human nature, and a more comprehensive soul, than are supposed to be common among mankind; a man pleased with his own passions and volitions, and who rejoices more than other men in the spirit of life that is in him; delighting to contemplate similar volitions and passions as manifested in the goings-on of the Universe, and habitually impelled to create them where he does not find them. To these qualities he has added a disposition to be affected more than other men by absent things as if they were present; an ability of conjuring up in himself passions, which are indeed far from being the same as those produced by real events, yet (especially in those parts of the general sympathy which are pleasing and delightful) do more nearly resemble the passions produced by real events than anything which, from the motions of their own minds merely, other men are accustomed to feel in themselves; — whence, and from practice, he has acquired a greater readiness and power in expressing what he thinks and feels, and especially those thoughts and feelings which, by his own choice, or from the structure of his own mind, arise in him without immediate external excitement.

But, whatever portion of this faculty we may suppose even the greatest Poet to possess, there cannot be a doubt that the language which it will suggest to him must often, in liveliness and truth, fall short of that which is uttered by men in real life, under the actual pressure of those passions, certain shadows of which the Poet thus produces, or feels to be produced, in himself.

However exalted a notion we would wish to cherish of the character of a Poet, it is obvious that, while he describes and imitates passions, his employment is in some degree mechanical, compared with the freedom and power of real and substantial action and suffering. So that it will be the wish of the Poet to bring his feelings near to those of the persons whose feelings he describes, nay, for short spaces of time, perhaps, to let himself slip into an entire delusion, and even confound and identify his own feelings with theirs; modifying only the language which is thus suggested to him by a consideration that he describes for a particular purpose, that of giving pleasure. Here, then, he will apply the principle of selection which has been already insisted upon. He will depend upon this for removing what would otherwise be painful or disgusting in the passion; he will feel that there is no necessity to trick out or to elevate nature: and, the more industriously he applies this principle the deeper will be his faith that no words, which *his* fancy or imagination can suggest, will be to be compared with those which are the emanations of reality and truth.

But it may be said by those who do not object to the general spirit of these remarks, that, as it is impossible for the Poet to produce upon all occasions language as exquisitely fitted for the passion as that which the real passion itself suggests, it is proper that he should consider himself as in the situation of a translator, who does not scruple to substitute excellencies of another kind for those which are unattainable by him; and endeavors occasionally to surpass his original, in order to make some amends for the general inferiority to which he feels that he must submit. But this would be to encourage idleness and unmanly despair. Further, it is the language of men who speak of what they do not understand; who talk of Poetry as of a matter of amusement and idle pleasure; who will converse with us as gravely about a *taste* for Poetry, as they express it, as if it were a thing as indifferent as a taste for ropedancing or Frontiniac or Sherry. Aristotle, I have been told, has said, that Poetry is the most philosophic of all writing: it is so: its object is truth, not individual and local, but general, and operative; not standing upon external testimony, but carried alive into the heart by passion; truth which is its own testimony, which gives competence and confidence to the tribunal to which it appeals, and receives them from the same tribunal. Poetry is the image of man and nature. The obstacles which stand in the way of the fidelity of the Biographer and Historian, and of their consequent utility, are incalculably greater than those which are to be encountered by the Poet who comprehends the dignity of his art. The Poet writes under one restriction only, namely, that of the necessity of giving immediate pleasure to a human Being possessed of that information which may be expected from him, not as a lawyer, a physician, a mariner, an astronomer, or a natural philosopher, but as a Man. Except this one restriction, there is no object standing between the Poet and the image of things; between this, and the Biographer and Historian, there are a thousand.

Nor let this necessity of producing immediate pleasure be considered as a degradation of the Poet's art. It is far otherwise. It is an acknowledgment of the beauty of the universe, an acknowledgment the more sincere because not formal, but indirect; it is a task light and easy to him who looks at the world in the spirit of love: further, it is a homage paid to the native and naked dignity of man, to the grand elementary principle of pleasure, by which he knows, and feels, and lives, and moves. We have no sympathy but what is propagated by pleasure: I would not be misunderstood; but wherever we sympathize with pain, it will be found that the sympathy is produced and carried on by subtle combinations with pleasure. We have no knowledge, that is, no general principles drawn from the contemplation of particular facts, but what has been built up by pleasure, and exists in us by pleasure alone. The Man of science, the Chemist and Mathematician, whatever difficulties and disgusts they may have had to struggle with, know and feel this. However painful may be the objects with which the Anatomist's knowledge is connected, he feels that his knowledge is pleasure; and where he has no pleasure he has no knowledge. What then does the Poet? He considers man and the objects that surround him as acting and re-acting upon each other, so as to produce an infinite complexity of pain and pleasure; he considers man in his own nature and in his ordinary life as contemplating this with a certain quantity of immediate knowledge, with certain convictions, intuitions, and deductions, which from habit acquire the quality of intuitions; he considers him as looking upon his complex scene of ideas and sensations, and finding everywhere objects that immediately excite in him sympathies which, from the necessities of his nature, are accompanied by an overbalance of enjoyment.

To this knowledge which all men carry about with them, and to these sympathies in which, without any other discipline than that of our daily life, we are fitted to take delight, the Poet principally directs his attention. He considers man and nature as essentially adapted to each other, and the mind of man as naturally the mirror of the fairest and most interesting qualities of nature. And thus the Poet, prompted by this feeling of pleasure which accompanies him through the whole course of his studies, converses with general nature, with affections akin to those which, through labor and length of time, the Man of science has raised up in himself, by conversing with those particular parts of nature which are the objects of his studies. The knowledge both of the Poet and the Man of science is pleasure; but the knowledge of the one cleaves to us as a necessary part of our existence, our natural and inalienable inheritance; the other is a personal and individual acquisition, slow to come to us, and by no habitual and direct sympathy connecting us with our fellow-beings. The Man of science seeks truth as a remote and unknown benefactor; he cherishes and loves it in his solitude: the Poet, singing a song in which all human beings join with him, rejoices in the presence of truth as our visible friend and hourly companion. Poetry is the breath and finer spirit of all knowledge; it is the impassioned expression which is in the countenance of all Science. Emphatically may it be said of the Poet, as Shakespeare hath said of man, "that he looks before and after." He is the rock of defence for human nature; an upholder and preserver, carrying everywhere with him relationship and love. In spite of difference of soil and climate, of language and manners, of laws and customs, in spite of things silently gone out of mind, and things violently destroyed; the Poet binds together by passion and knowledge the vast empire of human society, as it is spread over the whole earth, and over all time. The objects of the Poet's thoughts are everywhere; though the eyes and senses of man are, it is true, his favorite guides, yet he will follow wheresoever he can find an atmosphere of sensation in which to move his wings. Poetry is the first and last of all knowledge — it is as immortal as the heart of man. If the labors of Men of science should ever create any material revolution, direct or indirect, in our condition, and in the impressions which we habitually receive, the Poet will sleep then no more than at present; he will be ready to follow the steps of the Man of science, not only in those general indirect effects, but he will be at his side, carrying sensation into the midst of the objects of the science itself. The remotest discoveries of the Chemist, the Botanist, or Mineralogist, will be as proper objects of the Poet's art as any upon which it can be employed, if the time should ever come when these things shall be familiar to us, and the relations under which they are contemplated by the followers of these respective sciences shall be manifestly and palpably material to us as enjoying and suffering beings. If the time should ever come when what is now called science, thus familiarized to men, shall be ready to put on, as it were, a form of flesh and blood, the Poet will lend his divine spirit to aid the transfiguration, and will welcome the Being thus produced, as a dear and genuine inmate of the household of man. — It is not, then, to be supposed that any one, who holds that sublime notion of Poetry which I have attempted to convey, will break in upon the sanctity and truth of his pictures by transitory and accidental ornaments, and endeavor to excite admiration of himself by arts, the necessity of which must manifestly depend upon the assumed meanness of his subject.

What I have thus far said applies to Poetry in general; but especially to those parts of composition where the Poet speaks through the mouths of his characters; and upon this point it appears to authorize the conclusion that there are few persons of good sense who would not allow that the dramatic parts of composition are defective in proportion as they deviate from the real language of nature, and are colored by a diction of the Poet's own, either peculiar to him as an individual Poet or belonging simply to Poets in general; to a body of men who, from the circumstance of their compositions being in metre, it is expected will employ a particular language.

It is not, then, in the dramatic parts of composition that we look for this distinction of language; but still it may be proper and necessary where the Poet speaks to us in his own person and character. To this I answer by referring the

Reader to the description which I have before given of a Poet. Among the qualities there enumerated as principally conducing to form a Poet, is implied nothing differing in kind from other men, but only in degree. The sum of what was said is, that the poet is chiefly distinguished from other men by a greater promptness to think and feel without immediate external excitement, and a greater power in expressing such thoughts and feelings as are produced in him in that manner. But these passions and thoughts and feelings are the general passions and thoughts and feelings of men. And with what are they connected? Undoubtedly with our moral sentiments and animal sensations, and with the causes which excite these; with the operations of the elements, and the appearances of the visible universe; with storm and sunshine, with the revolutions of the seasons, with cold and heat, with loss of friends and kindred, with injuries and resentments, gratitude and hope, with fear and sorrow. These, and the like, are the sensations and objects which the Poet describes, as they are the sensations of other men, and the objects which interest them. The Poet thinks and feels in the spirit of human passions. How, then, can his language differ in any material degree from that of all other men who feel vividly and see clearly? It might be *proved* that it is impossible. But supposing that this were not the case, the Poet might then be allowed to use a peculiar language when expressing his feelings for his own gratification, or that of men like himself. But Poets do not write for Poets alone, but for men. Unless, therefore, we are advocates for that admiration which subsists upon ignorance, and that pleasure which arises from hearing what we do not understand, the Poet must descend from this supposed height; and, in order to excite rational sympathy, he must express himself as other men express themselves. To this it may be added, that while he is only selecting from the real language of men, or, which amounts to the same thing, composing accurately in the spirit of such selection, he is treading upon safe ground, and we know what we are to expect from him. Our feelings are the same with respect to metre; for, as it may be proper to remind the Reader, the distinction of metre is regular and uniform, and not, like that which is produced by what is usually called POETIC DICTION, arbitrary, and subject to infinite caprices upon which no calculation whatever can be made. In the one case, the Reader is utterly at the mercy of the Poet respecting what imagery or diction he may choose to connect with the passion; whereas, in the other, the metre obeys certain laws, to which the Poet and Reader both willingly submit because

they are certain, and because no interference is made by them with the passion but such as the concurring testimony of ages has shown to heighten and improve the pleasure which co-exists with it.

It will now be proper to answer an obvious question, namely, Why, professing these opinions, have I written in verse? To this, in addition to such answer as is included in what I have already said, I reply, in the first place, Because, however I may have restricted myself, there is still left open to me what confessedly constitutes the most valuable object of all writing, whether in prose or verse; the great and universal passions of men, the most general and interesting of their occupations, and the entire world of nature before me — to supply endless combinations of forms and imagery. Now, supposing for a moment that whatever is interesting in these objects may be as vividly described in prose, why should I be condemned for attempting to superadd to such description the charm which, by the consent of all nations, is acknowledged to exist in metrical language? To this, by such as are yet unconvinced, it may be answered that a very small part of the pleasure given by Poetry depends upon the metre, and that it is injudicious to write in metre, unless it be accompanied with the other artificial distinctions of style with which metre is usually accompanied, and that, by such deviation, more will be lost from the shock which will thereby be given to the Reader's associations than will be counterbalanced by any pleasure which he can derive from the general power of numbers. In answer to those who still contend for the necessity of accompanying metre with certain appropriate colors of style in order to the accomplishment of its appropriate end, and who also, in my opinion, greatly underrate the power of metre in itself, it might, perhaps, as far as relates to these Volumes, have been almost sufficient to observe, that poems are extant, written upon more humble subjects, and in a more naked and simple style than I have aimed at, which poems have continued to give pleasure from generation to generation. Now, if nakedness and simplicity be a defect, the fact here mentioned affords a strong presumption that poems somewhat less naked and simple are capable of affording pleasure at the present day; and, what I wished *chiefly* to attempt, at present, was to justify myself for having written under the impression of this belief.

But various causes might be pointed out why, when the style is manly, and the subject of some importance, words metrically arranged will long continue to impart such a pleasure to mankind as he who proves the extent of that pleasure will be desirous to impart. The end of poetry is to produce excitement in co-existence with an over-balance of pleasure; but, by the supposition, excitement is an unusual and irregular state of the mind; ideas and feelings do not, in that state, succeed each other in accustomed order. If the words, however, by which this excitement is produced be in themselves powerful, or the images and feelings have an undue proportion of pain connected with them, there is some danger that the excitement may be carried beyond its proper bounds. Now the co-presence of something regular, something to which the mind has been accustomed in various moods and in a less excited state, cannot but have great efficacy in tempering and restraining the passion by an intertexture of ordinary feeling, and of feeling not strictly and necessarily connected with the passion. This is unquestionably true; and hence, though the opinion will at first appear paradoxical, from the tendency of metre to divest language, in a certain degree, of its reality, and thus to throw a sort of half-consciousness of unsubstantial existence over the whole composition, there can be little doubt but that more pathetic situations and sentiments, that is, those which have a greater proportion of pain connected with them, may be endured in metrical composition, especially in rhyme, than in prose. The metre of the old ballads is very artless, yet they contain many passages which would illustrate this opinion; and, I hope, if the following poems be attentively perused, similar instances will be found in them. This opinion may be further illustrated by appealing to the Reader's own experience of the reluctance with which he comes to the reperusal of the distressful parts of *Clarissa Harlowe*, or *The Gamester*; while Shakespeare's writings, in the most pathetic scenes, never act upon us, as pathetic, beyond the bounds of pleasure — an effect which, in a much greater degree than might at first be imagined, is to be ascribed to small, but continual and regular impulses of pleasurable surprise from the metrical arrangement. — On the other hand (what it must be allowed will much more frequently happen), if the Poet's words should be incommensurate with the passion, and inadequate to raise the Reader to a height of desirable excitement, then (unless the Poet's choice of his metre has been grossly injudicious), in the feelings of pleasure which the reader has been accustomed to connect with metre in general, and in the feeling, whether cheerful or melancholy, which he has been accustomed to connect with that particular movement of metre, there will be found something which will greatly contribute to impart passion to the words, and to effect the complex end which the Poet proposes to himself.

If I had undertaken a SYSTEMATIC defence of the theory here maintained, it would have been my duty to develop the various causes upon which the pleasure received from metrical language depends. Among the chief of these causes is to be reckoned a principle which must be well known to those who have made any of the Arts the object of accurate reflection; namely, the pleasure which the mind derives from the perception of similitude in dissimilitude. This principle is the great spring of the acitivity of our minds, and their chief feeder. From this principle the direction of the sexual appetite, and all the passions connected with it, take their origin: it is the life of our ordinary conversation; and upon the accuracy with which similitude in dissimilitude, and dissimilitude in similitude, are perceived, depend our taste and our moral feelings. It would not be a useless employment to apply this principle to the consideration of metre, and to show that metre is hence enabled to afford much pleasure, and to point out in what manner that pleasure is produced. But my limits will not permit me to enter upon this subject, and I must content myself with a general summary.

I have said that poetry is the spontaneous overflow of powerful feelings: it takes its origin from emotion recollected in tranquillity; the emotion is contemplated till, by a species of re-action, the tranquillity gradually disappears, and an emotion, kindred to that which was before the subject of contemplation, is gradually produced, and does itself actually exist in the mind. In this mood successful composition generally begins, and in a mood similar to this it is carried on; but the emotion of whatever kind, and in whatever degree, from various causes, is qualified by various pleasures, so that in describing any passions whatsoever, which are voluntarily described, the mind will, upon the whole, be in a state of enjoyment. If Nature be thus cautious to preserve in a state of enjoyment a being so employed, the Poet ought to profit by the lesson held forth to him, and ought especially to take care, that, whatever passions he communicates to his Reader, those passions, if his Reader's mind be sound and vigorous, should always be accompanied with an overbalance of pleasure. Now the music of harmonious metrical language, the sense of difficulty overcome, and the blind association of pleasure which has been previously received from works of rhyme or metre of the same or similar construction, an indistinct perception perpetually renewed of language closely resembling that of real life, and yet, in the circumstance of metre, differing from it so widely — all these imperceptibly make up a complex feeling of delight, which is of the most important use in tempering the painful feeling always found inter-mingled with powerful descriptions of the deeper passions. This effect is always produced in pathetic and impassioned poetry; while, in lighter compositions, the ease and gracefulness with which the Poet manages his numbers are themselves confessedly a principal source of the gratification of the Reader. All that it is *necessary* to say, however, upon this subject, may be effected by affirming, what few persons will deny, that of two descriptions either of passions, manners, or characters, each of them equally well executed, the one in prose and the other in verse, the verse will be read a hundred times where the prose is read once.

Having thus explained a few of my reasons for writing in verse, and why I have chosen subjects from common life, and endeavored to bring my language near to the real language of men, if I have been too minute in pleading my own cause, I have at the same time been treating a subject of general interest; and for this reason a few words shall be added with reference solely to these particular poems, and to some defects which will probably be found in them. I am sensible that my associations must have sometimes been particular instead of general, and that, consequently, giving to things a false importance, I may have sometimes written upon unworthy subjects; but I am less apprehensive on this account, than that my language may frequently have suffered from those arbitrary connections of feelings and ideas with particular words and phrases from which no man can altogether protect himself. Hence I have no doubt that, in some instances, feelings, even of the ludicrous, may be given to my Readers by expressions which appeared to me tender and pathetic. Such faulty expressions, were I convinced they were faulty at present, and that they must necessarily continue to be so, I would willingly take all reasonable pains to correct. But it is dangerous to make these alterations on the simple authority of a few individuals, or even of certain classes of men; for where the understanding of an author is not convinced, or his feelings altered, this cannot be done without great injury to himself: for his own feelings are his stay and support; and, if he set them aside in one instance, he may be induced to repeat this act till his mind shall lose all confidence in itself, and becomes utterly debilitated. To this it may be added, that the Reader ought never to forget that he is himself exposed to the same errors as the Poet, and, perhaps, in a much greater degree: for there can be no presumption in saying of most readers, that it is not probable they will be so well acquainted with the various stages of meaning through which words have passed, or with the

fickleness or stability of the relations of particular ideas to each other; and, above all, since they are so much less interested in the subject, they may decide lightly and carelessly.

Long as the reader has been detained, I hope he will permit me to caution him against a mode of false criticism which has been applied to poetry, in which the language closely resembles that of life and nature. Such verses have been triumphed over in parodies of which Dr. Johnson's stanza is a fair specimen:

> I put my hat upon my head
> And walked into the Strand,
> And there I met another man
> Whose hat was in his hand.

Immediately under these lines I will place one of the most justly-admired stanzas of the "Babes in the Wood."

> These pretty Babes with hand in hand
> Went wandering up and down;
> But never more they saw the Man
> Approaching from the Town.

In both these stanzas the words, and the order of the words, in no respect differ from the most unimpassioned conversation. There are words in both, for example, "The Strand," and "the Town," connected with none but the most familiar ideas; yet the one stanza we admit as admirable, and the other as a fair example of the superlatively contemptible. Whence arises this difference? Not from the metre, not from the language, not from the order of the words; but the *matter* expressed in Dr. Johnson's stanza is contemptible. The proper method of treating trivial and simple verses, to which Dr. Johnson's stanza would be a fair parallelism, is not to say, this is a bad kind of poetry, or, this is not poetry; but, this wants sense; it is neither interesting in itself, nor can *lead* to anything interesting; the images neither originate in that sane state of feeling which arises out of thought, nor can excite thought or feeling in the Reader. This is the only sensible manner of dealing with such verses. Why trouble yourself about the species till you have previously decided upon the genus? Why take pains to prove that an ape is not a Newton, when it is self-evident that he is not a man?

One request I must make of my Reader, which is, that in judging these Poems he would decide by his own feelings genuinely, and not by reflection upon what will probably be the judgment of others. How common is it to hear a person say, I myself do not object to this style of composition, or this or that expression, but, to such and such classes of people it will appear mean or ludicrous! This mode of criticism, so destructive of all sound unadulterated judgment, is almost universal: let the Reader then abide independently by his own feelings, and, if he finds himself affected, let him not suffer such conjectures to interfere with his pleasure.

If an Author, by any single composition, has impressed us with respect for his talents, it is useful to consider this as affording a presumption, that on other occasions where we have been displeased he, nevertheless, may not have written ill or absurdly; and further, to give him so much credit for this one composition as may induce us to review what has displeased us, with more care than we should otherwise have bestowed upon it. This is not only an act of justice, but, in our decisions upon poetry especially, may conduce, in a high degree, to the improvement of our own taste: for an *accurate* taste in poetry, and in all the other arts, as Sir Joshua Reynolds has observed, is an *acquired* talent, which can only be produced by thought and a long-continued intercourse with the best models of composition. This is mentioned, not with so ridiculous a purpose as to prevent the most inexperienced Reader from judging for himself (I have already said that I wish him to judge for himself), but merely to temper the rashness of decision, and to suggest, that, if Poetry be a subject on which much time has not been bestowed, the judgment may be erroneous; and that, in many cases, it necessarily will be so.

Nothing would, I know, have so effectually contributed to further the end which I have in view, as to have shown of what kind the pleasure is, and how that pleasure is produced, which is confessedly produced by metrical composition essentially different from that which I have here endeavored to recommend: for the Reader will say that he has been pleased by such composition; and what more can be done for him? The power of any art is limited; and he will suspect that, if it be proposed to furnish him with new friends, that can be only upon condition of his abandoning his old friends. Besides, as I have said, the Reader is himself conscious of the pleasure which he has received from such composition, composition to which he has peculiarly attached the endearing name of Poetry; and all men feel an habitual gratitude, and something of an honorable bigotry, for the objects which have long continued to please them; we not only wish to be pleased, but to be pleased in that particular way in which we have been accustomed to be pleased. There is in these feelings enough to resist a host of arguments; and I should be the less able to combat them successfully, as I am willing to allow that, in order entirely to enjoy the Poetry which I am recommending, it would be necessary to give up much of what is ordinarily enjoyed. But would my limits have permitted me to point out how this pleasure is produced, many obstacles might have been removed, and the Reader assisted in perceiving that the powers of language are not so limited as he may suppose; and that it is possible for poetry to give other enjoyments, of a purer, more lasting, and more exquisite nature. This part of the subject has not been altogether neglected, but it has not been so much my present aim to prove, that the interest excited by some other kinds of poetry is less vivid, and less worthy of the nobler powers of the mind, as to offer reasons for presuming that if my purpose were fulfilled, a species of poetry would be produced which is genuine poetry; in its nature well adapted to interest mankind permanently, and likewise important in the multiplicity and quality of its moral relations.

From what has been said, and from a perusal of the Poems, the Reader will be able clearly to perceive the object which I had in view: he will determine how far it has been attained, and, what is a much more important question, whether it be worth attaining; and upon the decision of these two questions will rest my claim to the approbation of the Public.

Samuel Taylor Coleridge · 1772–1834

Coleridge, who collaborated with Wordsworth in the *Lyrical Ballads*, distinguished himself as a poet as well as a critic. A man of great promise and lesser accomplishment, he was constantly planning great things, but failed to bring them to fulfillment. Ill-health, almost from boyhood, was a real handicap, and when for relief from pain he fell to using opium, his power of accomplishment was seriously weakened. One may suspect that Coleridge, though capable, was inefficient. He was a dreamer, a man of intense intellectual and imaginative activity, impractical, a man whose reach exceeded his grasp.

Samuel Taylor Coleridge was born October 21, 1772, at Ottery St. Mary in Devonshire. His father was vicar of the parish there and master in the local grammar school. When his father died, the family's financial situation demanded that Samuel, if he was to get an education, be sent to a charity school in London, Christ's Hospital. The boy early showed great promise in his study of philosophy and the classics. In 1791, Coleridge entered Jesus College, Cambridge, like Spenser before him a "sizar," compelled to work to pay part of his expenses. Before he had completed work for his degree, the young man suddenly left Cambridge (he had become involved in debt or in love — or both), and enlisted in the Fifteenth Light Dragoons where he remained only four months. Returning to Cambridge, he still did not complete the requirements for his degree. The same year he met the poet Southey and became interested in "Pantisocracy," an impracticable scheme for founding a Utopian community on the banks of the Susquehanna in America. Twelve able young men, according to the plan, were to marry twelve robust young women, emigrate to America, and form an ideal commonwealth. In 1795, while this plan was perhaps still in the air, Coleridge married Sara Fricker, but the marriage proved to have its unhappy aspects. Coleridge moved from one venture to another, preached sermons, lectured, projected and started journals, fell in with Wordsworth and settled down for what was to be the beginning of his most fruitful period — the years between 1797 and 1802. In 1798, with Dorothy and William Wordsworth, he went to Germany and there studied philosophy. During 1804–06 he was in Malta as secretary to the governor. But by this time the powers of the poet were dimmed by his addiction to opium. In 1816 he took asylum with a friend, James Gillman, at Highgate, near London. Gillman, until Coleridge's death July 25, 1834, supervised his health and living and gave him the kindly care that preserved such capacities as Coleridge could exercise. Those who knew him well, particularly during these years, testify to his gracious manner and his brilliance as a conversationalist.

The bulk of Coleridge's poetry is by no means large. Yet three or four poems have become a part of the heritage of, at least, the English reader. *The Rime of the Ancient Mariner* and those two marvelously imaginative fragments, *Kubla Khan* and *Christabel*, fill a niche peculiarly their own. Here the romantic temper strikes sparks. These are poems in which Coleridge lets play his almost unrestrained imagination; here are enthusiasm and ecstasy; and here, surely, is a dream-world at once remote in time and space. The poems show Coleridge the master of the supernatural; they present a sense of melody and rhythm which sets them off by themselves. And without that rich account of a poet's mind and thought, the *Biographia Literaria*, English criticism would be much the poorer.

SUGGESTED REFERENCES: E. K. Chambers, *Samuel Taylor Coleridge* (2nd ed., 1950); Humphrey House, *Coleridge* (2nd ed., 1962); Marshall Suther, *Visions of Xanadu* (1965).

Kubla Khan [1]

Concerning the writing of this poem Coleridge tells us: "In the summer of the year 1797, the Author, then in ill health, had retired to a lonely farmhouse between Porlock and Linton, on the Exmoor confines of Somerset and Devonshire. In consequence of a slight indisposi-

[1] A Mongol leader of the thirteenth century. He conquered China, founded the Yüan dynasty, and made Buddhism the state religion.

tion, an anodyne had been prescribed, from the effects of which he fell asleep in his chair at the moment he was reading the following sentence, or words of the same substance, in *Purchas's Pilgrimage*: — "Here the Khan Kubla commanded a palace to be built, and a stately garden thereunto: and thus ten miles of fertile ground were inclosed with a wall." The Author continued for about three hours in a profound sleep, at least of the external senses, during which time he has the most vivid confidence that he could not have composed less than from two to three hundred lines; if that indeed can be called composition in which all the images rose up before him as *things*, with a parallel production of the correspondent expressions, without any sensation or consciousness of effort. On awaking he appeared to himself to have a distinct recollection of the whole, and taking his pen, ink, and paper, instantly and eagerly wrote down the lines that are here preserved. At this moment he was unfortunately called out by a person on business from Porlock, and detained by him above an hour, and on his return to his room, found, to his no small surprise and mortification, that though he still retained some vague and dim recollection of the general purport of the vision, yet, with the exception of some eight or ten scattered lines and images, all the rest had passed away like the images on the surface of a stream into which a stone had been cast, but, alas! without the after restoration of the latter."

> In Xanadu did Kubla Khan
> A stately pleasure-dome decree:
> Where Alph, the sacred river, ran
> Through caverns measureless to man
>   Down to a sunless sea.   5
> So twice five miles of fertile ground
> With walls and towers were girdled round:
> And here were gardens bright with sinuous rills
> Where blossomed many an incense-bearing tree,
> And here were forests ancient as the hills,   10
> Enfolding sunny spots of greenery.
>
> But oh! that deep romantic chasm which slanted
> Down the green hill athwart a cedarn cover!
> A savage place! as holy and enchanted
> As e'er beneath a waning moon was haunted   15
> By woman wailing for her demon-lover!
> And from this chasm, with ceaseless turmoil seeth-
>   ing,
> As if this earth in fast thick pants were breathing,
> A mighty fountain momently was forced,
> Amid whose swift half-intermitted burst   20
> Huge fragments vaulted like rebounding hail,
> Or chaffy grain beneath the thresher's flail:
> And 'mid these dancing rocks at once and ever
> It flung up momently the sacred river.
> Five miles meandering with a mazy motion   25
> Through wood and dale the sacred river ran,
> Then reached the caverns measureless to man,
> And sank in tumult to a lifeless ocean:
> And 'mid this tumult Kubla heard from far
> Ancestral voices prophesying war!   30
>
> The shadow of the dome of pleasure
> Floated midway on the waves;
> Where was heard the mingled measure
> From the fountain and the caves.
> It was a miracle of rare device,   35
> A sunny pleasure-dome with caves of ice!

> A damsel with a dulcimer
> In a vision once I saw:
> It was an Abyssinian maid,
> And on her dulcimer she played,   40
> Singing of Mount Abora.
>
> Could I revive within me
> Her symphony and song,
> To such a deep delight 'twould win me,
> That with music loud and long,   45
> I would build that dome in air,
> That sunny dome! those caves of ice!
> And all who heard should see them there,
> And all should cry, Beware! Beware!
> His flashing eyes, his floating hair!   50
> Weave a circle round him thrice,
> And close your eyes with holy dread,
> For he on honey-dew hath fed,
> And drunk the milk of Paradise.

Christabel [1]

PART I

> 'Tis the middle of night by the castle clock,
> And the owls have awakened the crowing cock,
> Tu — whit! —— Tu — whoo!
> And hark, again! the crowing cock,
> How drowsily it crew.   5
>
> Sir Leoline, the Baron rich,
> Hath a toothless mastiff bitch.
> From her kennel beneath the rock
> She maketh answer to the clock,
> Four for the quarters, and twelve for the   10
>   hour;
> Ever and aye, by shine and shower,
> Sixteen short howls, not over loud;
> Some say, she sees my lady's shroud.
>
> Is the night chilly and dark?
> The night is chilly, but not dark.   15

[1] Writing of this poem, Coleridge has pointed out that:

1. The first part was written in 1797, the second part in 1800, and that he contemplated the composition of "three parts yet to come" (which were, however, never written).

2. The meter of the poem is based on the presence of four accents in each line though the number of syllables may vary from seven to twelve. The variation in syllables was an effort to secure varying effects "in the nature of imagery and passion."

3. The poem was "partly founded on the notion that the virtuous of the world save the wicked."

The thin gray cloud is spread on high,
It covers but not hides the sky.
The moon is behind, and at the full;
And yet she looks both small and dull.
The night is chill, the cloud is gray: 20
'Tis a month before the month of May,
And the Spring comes slowly up this way.

    The lovely lady, Christabel,
Whom her father loves so well,
What makes her in the wood so late,   25
A furlong from the castle gate?
She had dreams all yesternight
Of her own betrothèd knight;
And she in the midnight wood will pray
For the weal of her lover that's far away.   30

    She stole along, she nothing spoke,
The sighs she heaved were soft and low,
And naught was green upon the oak
But moss and rarest mistletoe:
She kneels beneath the huge oak tree   35
And in silence prayeth she.

    The lady sprang up suddenly,
The lovely lady, Christabel!
It moaned as near, as near can be,
But what it is she cannot tell. —   40
On the other side it seems to be,
Of the huge, broad-breasted, old oak tree.

    The night is chill; the forest bare;
Is it the wind that moaneth bleak?
There is not wind enough in the air   45
To move away the ringlet curl
From the lovely lady's cheek —
There is not wind enough to twirl
The one red leaf, the last of its clan,
That dances as often as dance it can,   50
Hanging so light, and hanging so high,
On the topmost twig that looks up at the sky.

    Hush, beating heart of Christabel!
Jesu Maria, shield her well!
She folded her arms beneath her cloak,   55
And stole to the other side of the oak.
      What sees she there?

    There she sees a damsel bright,
Drest in a silken robe of white,
That shadowy in the moonlight shone: 60
The neck that made that white robe wan,
Her stately neck, and arms were bare;
Her blue-veined feet unsandalled were,
And wildly glittered here and there
The gems entangled in her hair.   65

I guess, 'twas frightful there to see
A lady so richly clad as she —
Beautiful exceedingly!

    "Mary mother, save me now!"
(Said Christabel) "And who art thou?"   70

    The lady strange made answer meet,
And her voice was faint and sweet: —
"Have pity on my sore distress,
I scarce can speak for weariness:
Stretch forth thy hand, and have no fear!"   75
Said Christabel, "How camest thou here?"
And the lady, whose voice was faint and sweet,
Did thus pursue her answer meet: —

    "My sire is of a noble line,
And my name is Geraldine: 80
Five warriors seized me yestermorn,
Me, even me, a maid forlorn:
They choked my cries with force and fright,
And tied me on a palfrey white.
The palfrey was as fleet as wind,   85
And they rode furiously behind.
They spurred amain, their steeds were white:
And once we crossed the shade of night.
As sure as Heaven shall rescue me,
I have no thought what men they be;   90
Nor do I know how long it is
(For I have lain entranced, I wis)
Since one, the tallest of the five,
Took me from the palfrey's back,
A weary woman, scarce alive.   95
Some muttered words his comrades spoke:
He placed me underneath this oak;
He swore they would return with haste;
Whither they went I cannot tell —
I thought I heard, some minutes past,   100
Sounds as of a castle bell.
Stretch forth thy hand (thus ended she),
And help a wretched maid to flee."

    Then Christabel stretched forth her hand,
And comforted fair Geraldine: 105
"Oh well, bright dame! may you command
The service of Sir Leoline:
And gladly our stout chivalry
Will he send forth, and friends withal,
To guide and guard you safe and free   110
Home to your noble father's hall."

    She rose: and forth with steps they passed
That strove to be, and were not, fast.
Her gracious stars the lady blest,
And thus spake on sweet Christabel: 115
"All our household are at rest,

The hall as silent as the cell;
Sir Leoline is weak in health,
And may not well awakened be,
But we will move as if in stealth,   120
But I beseech your courtesy,
This night, to share your couch with me."

They crossed the moat, and Christabel
Took the key that fitted well;
A little door she opened straight,   125
All in the middle of the gate;
The gate that was ironed within and without,
Where an army in battle array had marched out.
The lady sank, belike through pain,
And Christabel with might and main   130
Lifted her up, a weary weight,
Over the threshold of the gate: [1]
Then the lady rose again,
And moved, as she were not in pain.

So free from danger, free from fear,   135
They crossed the court: right glad they were.
And Christabel devoutly cried
To the lady by her side:
"Praise we the Virgin all divine
Who hath rescued thee from thy distress!"   140
"Alas, alas!" said Geraldine, [2]
"I cannot speak for weariness."
So free from danger, free from fear,
They crossed the court: right glad they were.

Outside her kennel the mastiff old   145
Lay fast asleep in moonshine cold.
The mastiff old did not awake,
Yet she an angry moan did make!
And what can ail the mastiff bitch?
Never till now she uttered yell   150
Beneath the eye of Christabel.
Perhaps it is the owlet's scritch:
For what can ail the mastiff bitch? [3]

They passed the hall, that echoes still,
Pass as lightly as you will!   155
The brands were flat, the brands were dying,
Amid their own white ashes lying;
But when the lady passed, there came
A tongue of light, a fit of flame; [4]
And Christabel saw the lady's eye,   160

[1] Demons cannot cross thresholds which have been blessed.
[2] As an evil spirit, of course, she will not pray.
[3] The dog, like other animals, is supposed to recognize evil spirits.
[4] Further evidence of her relationship to Satan and evil.

And nothing else saw she thereby,
Save the boss of the shield of Sir Leoline tall,
Which hung in a murky old niche in the wall.
"Oh softly tread," said Christabel,
"My father seldom sleepeth well."   165

Sweet Christabel her feet doth bare,
And jealous of the listening air,
They steal their way from stair to stair,
Now in glimmer, and now in gloom,
And now they pass the Baron's room,   170
As still as death, with stifled breath!
And now have reached her chamber door;
And now doth Geraldine press down
The rushes of the chamber floor.

The moon shines dim in the open air,   175
And not a moon beam enters here.
But they without its light can see
The chamber carved so curiously,
Carved with figures strange and sweet,
All made out of the carver's brain,   180
For a lady's chamber meet:
The lamp with twofold silver chain
Is fastened to an angel's feet.

The silver lamp burns dead and dim;
But Christabel the lamp will trim.   185
She trimmed the lamp, and made it bright,
And left it swinging to and fro,
While Geraldine, in wretched plight,
Sank down upon the floor below.

"O weary lady, Geraldine,   190
I pray you, drink this cordial wine!
It is a wine of virtuous powers;
My mother made it of wild flowers."

"And will your mother pity me,
Who am a maiden most forlorn?"   195
Christabel answered — "Woe is me!
She died the hour that I was born.
I have heard the gray-haired friar tell,
How on her death-bed she did say,
That she should hear the castle-bell   200
Strike twelve upon my wedding-day.
O mother dear! that thou wert here!"
"I would," said Geraldine, "she were!"

But soon with altered voice, said she —
"Off, wandering mother! Peak and pine!   205
I have power to bid thee flee."
Alas! what ails poor Geraldine?
Why stares she with unsettled eye?
Can she the bodiless dead espy?
And why with hollow voice cries she,   210

"Off, woman, off! this hour is mine —
Though thou her guardian spirit be,
Off, woman, off! 'tis given to me."

Then Christabel knelt by the lady's side,
And raised to heaven her eyes so blue —   215
"Alas!" said she, "this ghastly ride —
Dear lady! it hath wildered you!"
The lady wiped her moist cold brow,
And faintly said, "'tis over now!"

Again the wild-flower wine she drank: 220
Her fair large eyes 'gan glitter bright,
And from the floor whereon she sank,
The lofty lady stood upright;
She was most beautiful to see,
Like a lady of a far countrée.   225

And thus the lofty lady spake —
"All they, who live in the upper sky,
Do love you, holy Christabel!
And you love them, and for their sake
And for the good which me befell,   230
Even I in my degree will try,
Fair maiden, to requite you well.
And now unrobe yourself; for I
Must pray, ere yet in bed I lie."

Quoth Christabel, "So let it be!"   235
And as the lady bade, did she.
Her gentle limbs did she undress,
And lay down in her loveliness.

But through her brain of weal and woe
So many thoughts moved to and fro,   240
That vain it were her lids to close:
So half-way from the bed she rose,
And on her elbow did recline
To look at the lady Geraldine.

Beneath the lamp the lady bowed,   245
And slowly rolled her eyes around;
Then drawing in her breath aloud,
Like one that shuddered, she unbound
The cincture from beneath her breast:
Her silken robe, and inner vest,   250
Dropt to her feet, and full in view,
Behold! her bosom and half her side —
A sight to dream of, not to tell!
Oh shield her! shield sweet Christabel!

Yet Geraldine nor speaks nor stirs;   255
Ah! what a stricken look was hers!
Deep from within she seems half-way
To lift some weight with sick assay,
And eyes the maid and seeks delay;

Then suddenly, as one defied,   260
Collects herself in scorn and pride,
And lay down by the maiden's side! —
And in her arms the maid she took,
            Ah well-a-day!
And with low voice and doleful look   265
            These words did say:
"In the touch of this bosom there worketh a spell,
Which is lord of thy utterance, Christabel!
Thou knowest to-night, and wilt know to-morrow,
This mark of my shame, this seal of my sorrow: 270
            But vainly thou warrest,
                  For this is alone in
            Thy power to declare,
                  That in the dim forest
Thou heard'st a low moaning,   275
And found'st a bright lady, surpassingly fair:
And didst bring her home with thee in love and in
            charity,
To shield her and shelter her from the damp air."

THE CONCLUSION TO PART I

It was a lovely sight to see
The lady Christabel, when she   280
Was praying at the old oak tree.
            Amid the jagged shadows
            Of mossy leafless boughs,
            Kneeling in the moonlight,
            To make her gentle vows;   285
Her slender palms together prest,
Heaving sometimes on her breast;
Her face resigned to bliss or bale —
Her face, oh call it fair, not pale,
And both blue eyes more bright than clear,   290
Each about to have a tear.

With open eyes (ah woe is me!)
Asleep, and dreaming fearfully,
Fearfully dreaming, yet, I wis,
Dreaming that alone, which is —   295
O sorrow and shame! Can this be she,
The lady, who knelt at the old oak tree?
And lo! the worker of these harms,
That holds the maiden in her arms,
Seems to slumber still and mild,   300
As a mother with her child.

A star hath set, a star hath risen,
O Geraldine! since arms of thine
Have been the lovely lady's prison.
O Geraldine! one hour was thine —   305
Thou'st had thy will! By tairn and rill,
The night-birds all that hour were still.
But now they are jubilant anew,
From cliff and tower, tu — whoo! tu — whoo!
Tu — whoo! tu — whoo! from wood and fell!   310

And see! the lady Christabel
Gathers herself from out her trance;
Her limbs relax, her countenance
Grows sad and soft; the smooth thin lids
Close o'er her eyes; and tears she sheds —   315
Large tears that leave the lashes bright!
And oft the while she seems to smile
As infants at a sudden light!

Yea, she doth smile, and she doth weep,
Like a youthful hermitess,   320
Beauteous in a wilderness,
Who, praying always, prays in sleep.
And, if she move unquietly,
Perchance, 'tis but the blood so free
Comes back and tingles in her feet.   325
No doubt she hath a vision sweet.
What if her guardian spirit 'twere?
What if she knew her mother near?
But this she knows, in joys and woes,
That saints will aid if men will call: 330
For the blue sky bends over all!

PART II

Each matin bell, the Baron saith,
Knells us back to a world of death.
These words Sir Leoline first said,
When he rose and found his lady dead: 335
These words Sir Leoline will say,
Many a morn to his dying day!

And hence the custom and law began,
That still at dawn the sacristan,
Who duly pulls the heavy bell,   340
Five and forty beads must tell
Between each stroke — a warning knell,
Which not a soul can choose but hear
From Bratha Head to Wyndermere.[1]

Saith Bracy the bard, "So let it knell!   345
And let the drowsy sacristan
Still count as slowly as he can!
There is no lack of such, I ween,
As well fill up the space between."
In Langdale Pike and Witch's lair,   350
And Dungeon-ghyll so foully rent,
With ropes of rock and bells of air
Three sinful sextons' ghosts are pent,
Who all give back, one after t' other,
The death-note to their living brother;   355
And oft too, by the knell offended,
Just as their one! two! three! is ended,

[1] Places named throughout this section are in the
Lake District. The setting as a whole is, of course,
not so specific.

The devil mocks the doleful tale
With a merry peal from Borrowdale.

The air is still! through mist and cloud   360
That merry peal comes ringing loud;
And Geraldine shakes off her dread,
And rises lightly from the bed;
Puts on her silken vestments white,
And tricks her hair in lovely plight,   365
And nothing doubting of her spell
Awakens the lady Christabel.
"Sleep you, sweet lady Christabel?
I trust that you have rested well."

And Christabel awoke and spied   370
The same who lay down by her side —
Oh rather say, the same whom she
Raised up beneath the old oak tree!
Nay, fairer yet; and yet more fair!
For she belike hath drunken deep   375
Of all the blessedness of sleep!
And while she spake, her looks, her air,
Such gentle thankfulness declare,
That (so it seemed) her girded vests
Grew tight beneath her heaving breasts.   380
"Sure I have sinned!" said Christabel,
"Now heaven be praised if all be well!"
And in low faltering tones, yet sweet,
Did she the lofty lady greet,
With such perplexity of mind   385
As dreams too lively leave behind.

So quickly she rose, and quickly arrayed
Her maiden limbs, and having prayed
That He, who on the cross did groan,
Might wash away her sins unknown,   390
She forthwith led fair Geraldine
To meet her sire, Sir Leoline.

The lovely maid and lady tall
Are pacing both into the hall,
And pacing on through page and groom,   395
Enter the Baron's presence-room.

The Baron rose, and while he prest
His gentle daughter to his breast,
With cheerful wonder in his eyes
The lady Geraldine espies,   400
And gave such welcome to the same,
As might beseem so bright a dame!

But when he heard the lady's tale,
And when she told her father's name,
Why waxed Sir Leoline so pale,   405
Murmuring o'er the name again,
Lord Roland de Vaux of Tryermaine?

Alas! they had been friends in youth;
But whispering tongues can poison truth;
And constancy lives in realms above;
And life is thorny; and youth is vain; 410
And to be wroth with one we love
Doth work like madness in the brain.
And thus it chanced, as I divine,
With Roland and Sir Leoline.
Each spake words of high disdain 415
And insult to his heart's best brother:
They parted — ne'er to meet again!
But never either found another
To free the hollow heart from paining —
They stood aloof, the scars remaining, 420
Like cliffs which had been rent asunder;
A dreary sea now flows between: —
But neither heat, nor frost, nor thunder,
Shall wholly do away, I ween,
The marks of that which once hath been. 425

Sir Leoline, a moment's space,
Stood gazing on the damsel's face:
And the youthful Lord of Tryermaine
Came back upon his heart again. 430

Oh then the Baron forgot his age,
His noble heart swelled high with rage;
He swore by the wounds in Jesu's side,
He would proclaim it far and wide,
With trump and solemn heraldry, 435
That they who thus had wronged the dame,
Were base as spotted infamy!
"And if they dare deny the same,
My herald shall appoint a week,
And let the recreant traitors seek 440
My tourney court — that there and then
I may dislodge their reptile souls
From the bodies and forms of men!"
He spake: his eye in lightning rolls!
For the lady was ruthlessly seized; and he kenned
In the beautiful lady the child of his friend! 446

And now the tears were on his face,
And fondly in his arms he took
Fair Geraldine, who met the embrace,
Prolonging it with joyous look. 450
Which when she viewed, a vision fell
Upon the soul of Christabel,
The vision of fear, the touch and pain!
She shrunk and shuddered, and saw again —
(Ah, woe is me! Was it for thee, 455
Thou gentle maid! such sights to see?)

Again she saw that bosom old,
Again she felt that bosom cold,
And drew in her breath with a hissing sound:

Whereat the Knight turned wildly round, 460
And nothing saw but his own sweet maid
With eyes upraised, as one that prayed.

The touch, the sight, had passed away,
And in its stead that vision blest,
Which comforted her after-rest 465
While in the lady's arms she lay,
Had put a rapture in her breast,
And on her lips and o'er her eyes
Spread smiles like light!
                    With new surprise,
"What ails then my beloved child?"
The Baron said — His daughter mild 470
Made answer, "All will yet be well!"
I ween, she had no power to tell
Aught else: so mighty was the spell.

Yet he, who saw this Geraldine, 475
Had deemed her sure a thing divine.
Such sorrow with such grace she blended,
As if she feared she had offended
Sweet Christabel, that gentle maid!
And with such lowly tones she prayed, 480
She might be sent without delay
Home to her father's mansion.

                    "Nay!
Nay, by my soul!" said Leoline.
"Ho! Bracy, the bard, the charge be thine!
Go thou, with music sweet and loud, 485
And take two steeds with trappings proud,
And take the youth whom thou lov'st best
To bear thy harp, and learn thy song,
And clothe you both in solemn vest,
And over the mountains haste along, 490
Lest wandering folk, that are abroad,
Detain you on the valley road.
And when he has crossed the Irthing flood,
My merry bard! he hastes, he hastes
Up Knorren Moor, through Halegarth Wood, 495
And reaches soon that castle good
Which stands and threatens Scotland's wastes.

"Bard Bracy! bard Bracy! your horses are fleet
Ye must ride up the hall, your music so sweet
More loud than your horses' echoing feet! 500
And loud and loud to Lord Roland call,
Thy daughter is safe in Langdale hall!
Thy beautiful daughter is safe and free —
Sir Leoline greets thee thus through me.
He bids thee come without delay 505
With all thy numerous array;
And take thy lovely daughter home:
And he will meet thee on the way
With all his numerous array
White with their panting palfreys' foam: 510

And by mine honor! I will say,
That I repent me of the day
When I spake words of fierce disdain
To Roland de Vaux of Tryermaine! —
— For since that evil hour hath flown, 515
Many a summer's sun hath shone;
Yet ne'er found I a friend again
Like Roland de Vaux of Tryermaine."

The lady fell, and clasped his knees,
Her face upraised, her eyes o'erflowing; 520
And Bracy replied, with faltering voice,
His gracious hail on all bestowing! —
"Thy words, thou sire of Christabel,
Are sweeter than my harp can tell;
Yet might I gain a boon of thee, 525
This day my journey should not be,
So strange a dream hath come to me;
That I had vowed with music loud
To clear yon wood from thing unblest,
Warned by a vision in my rest! 530
For in my sleep I saw that dove,
That gentle bird, whom thou dost love,
And call'st by thy own daughter's name —
Sir Leoline! I saw the same
Fluttering, and uttering fearful moan, 535
Among the green herbs in the forest alone.
Which when I saw and when I heard,
I wondered what might ail the bird;
For nothing near it could I see,
Save the grass and green herbs underneath
        the old tree. 540

"And in my dream methought I went
To search out what might there be found;
And what the sweet bird's trouble meant,
That thus lay fluttering on the ground.
I went and peered, and could descry 545
No cause for her distressful cry;
But yet for her dear lady's sake
I stooped, methought, the dove to take,
When lo! I saw a bright green snake
Coiled around its wings and neck. 550
Green as the herbs on which it couched,
Close by the dove's its head it crouched,
And with the dove it heaves and stirs,
Swelling its neck as she swelled hers!
I woke; it was the midnight hour, 555
The clock was echoing in the tower;
But though my slumber was gone by,
This dream it would not pass away —
It seems to live upon my eye!
And thence I vowed this self-same day, 560
With music strong and saintly song
To wander through the forest bare,
Lest aught unholy loiter there."

Thus Bracy said: the Baron, the while,
Half-listening heard him with a smile; 565
Then turned to Lady Geraldine,
His eyes made up of wonder and love;
And said in courtly accents fine,
"Sweet maid, Lord Roland's beauteous dove,
With arms more strong than harp or song, 570
Thy sire and I will crush the snake!"
He kissed her forehead as he spake,
And Geraldine, in maiden wise,
Casting down her large bright eyes,
With blushing cheek and courtesy fine 575
She turned her from Sir Leoline;
Softly gathering up her train,
That o'er her right arm fell again;
And folded her arms across her chest,
And couched her head upon her breast, 580
And looked askance at Christabel —
Jesu Maria, shield her well!

A snake's small eye blinks dull and shy,
And the lady's eyes they shrunk in her head,
Each shrunk up to a serpent's eye, 585
And with somewhat of malice, and more of dread,
At Christabel she looked askance! —
One moment — and the sight was fled!
But Christabel in dizzy trance
Stumbling on the unsteady ground 590
Shuddered aloud, with a hissing sound;
And Geraldine again turned round,
And like a thing that sought relief,
Full of wonder and full of grief,
She rolled her large bright eyes divine 595
Wildly on Sir Leoline.

The maid, alas! her thoughts are gone,
She nothing sees — no sight but one!
The maid, devoid of guile and sin,
I know not how, in fearful wise 600
So deeply had she drunken in
That look, those shrunken serpent eyes,
That all her features were resigned
To this sole image in her mind;
And passively did imitate 605
That look of dull and treacherous hate!
And thus she stood, in dizzy trance,
Still picturing that look askance
With forced unconscious sympathy
Full before her father's view — 610
As far as such a look could be
In eyes so innocent and blue!

And when the trance was o'er, the maid
Paused awhile, and inly prayed:
Then falling at the Baron's feet, 615
"By my mother's soul do I entreat

That thou this woman send away!"
She said: and more she could not say:
For what she knew she could not tell,
O'ermastered by the mighty spell.   620

Why is thy cheek so wan and wild,
Sir Leoline? Thy only child
Lies at thy feet, thy joy, thy pride,
So fair, so innocent, so mild;
The same, for whom thy lady died!   625
O, by the pangs of her dear mother
Think thou no evil of thy child!
For her, and thee, and for no other,
She prayed the moment ere she died:
Prayed that the babe for whom she died,   630
Might prove her dear lord's joy and pride!
That prayer her deadly pangs beguiled,
   Sir Leoline!
And wouldst thou wrong thy only child,
   Her child and thine?   635

Within the Baron's heart and brain
If thoughts, like these, had any share,
They only swelled his rage and pain,
And did but work confusion there.
His heart was cleft with pain and rage,   640
His cheeks they quivered, his eyes were wild,
Dishonored thus in his old age;
Dishonored by his only child,
And all his hospitality
To the insulted daughter of his friend   645
By more than woman's jealousy
Brought thus to a disgraceful end —
He rolled his eye with stern regard
Upon the gentle minstrel bard,
And said in tones abrupt, austere —   650
"Why, Bracy! dost thou loiter here?
I bade thee hence!" The bard obeyed;
And turning from his own sweet maid,
The aged knight, Sir Leoline,
Led forth the lady Geraldine!   655

THE CONCLUSION TO PART II

A little child, a limber elf,
Singing, dancing to itself,
A fairy thing with red round cheeks,
That always finds, and never seeks,
Makes such a vision to the sight   660
As fills a father's eyes with light;
And pleasures flow in so thick and fast
Upon his heart, that he at last
Must needs express his love's excess
With words of unmeant bitterness.   665
Perhaps 'tis pretty to force together
Thoughts so all unlike each other;
To mutter and mock a broken charm.

To dally with wrong that does no harm.
Perhaps 'tis tender too and pretty   670
At each wild word to feel within
A sweet recoil of love and pity.
And what, if in a world of sin
(O sorrow and shame should this be true!)
Such giddiness of heart and brain   675
Comes seldom save from rage and pain,
So talks as it's most used to do.

Biographia Literaria

In these two chapters Coleridge discusses some of
the principles laid down by Wordsworth in his *Preface*
to the second edition of the *Lyrical Ballads*. Coleridge
quotes from both the *Preface* and various poems of
Wordsworth to illustrate his critical dicta.

CHAPTER XVII

As far then as Mr. Wordsworth in his preface
contended, and most ably contended, for a reformation in our poetic diction, as far as he has evinced
the truth of passion, and the dramatic propriety
of those figures and metaphors in the original poets,
which, stripped of their justifying reasons, and
converted into mere artifices of connection or
ornament, constitute the characteristic falsity in
the poetic style of the moderns; and as far as he
has, with equal acuteness and clearness, pointed
out the process by which this change was effected,
and the resemblances between that state into which
the reader's mind is thrown by the pleasurable confusion of thought from an unaccustomed train of
words and images; and that state which is induced
by the natural language of impassioned feeling; he
undertook a useful task, and deserves all praise,
both for the attempt and for the execution. The
provocations to this remonstrance in behalf of
truth and nature were still of perpetual recurrence
before and after the publication of this preface.
I cannot likewise but add, that the comparison of
such poems of merit, as have been given to the
public within the last ten or twelve years, with the
majority of those produced previously to the appearance of that preface, leave no doubt on my
mind, that Mr. Wordsworth is fully justified in
believing his efforts to have been by no means ineffectual. Not only in the verses of those who have
professed their admiration of his genius, but even
of those who have distinguished themselves by
hostility to his theory, and depreciation of his
writings, are the impressions of his principles
plainly visible. It is possible, that with these
principles others may have been blended, which
are not equally evident; and some which are un-

steady and subvertible from the narrowness or imperfection of their basis. But it is more than possible, that these errors of defect or exaggeration, by kindling and feeding the controversy, may have conduced not only to the wider propagation of the accompanying truths, but that, by their frequent presentation to the mind in an excited state, they may have won for them a more permanent and practical result. A man will borrow a part from his opponent the more easily, if he feels himself justified in continuing to reject a part. While there remain important points in which he can still feel himself in the right, in which he still finds firm footing for continued resistance, he will gradually adopt those opinions, which were the least remote from his own convictions, as not less congruous with his own theory than with that which he reprobates. In like manner with a kind of instinctive prudence, he will abandon by little and little his weakest posts, till at length he seems to forget that they had ever belonged to him, or affects to consider them at most as accidental and "petty annexments," the removal of which leaves the citadel unhurt and unendangered.

My own differences from certain supposed parts of Mr. Wordsworth's theory ground themselves on the assumption, that his words had been rightly interpreted, as purporting that the proper diction for poetry in general consists altogether in a language taken, with due exceptions, from the mouths of men in real life, a language which actually constitutes the natural conversation of men under the influence of natural feelings. My objection is, first, that in any sense this rule is applicable only to certain classes of poetry; secondly, that even to these classes it is not applicable, except in such a sense, as hath never by any one (as far as I know or have read,) been denied or doubted; and lastly, that as far as, and in that degree in which it is practicable, it is yet as a rule useless, if not injurious, and therefore either need not, or ought not to be practised. The poet informs his reader, that he had generally chosen low and rustic life; but not as low and rustic, or in order to repeat that pleasure of doubtful moral effect, which persons of elevated rank and of superior refinement oftentimes derive from a happy imitation of the rude unpolished manners and discourse of their inferiors. For the pleasure so derived may be traced to three exciting causes. The first is the naturalness, in fact, of the things represented. The second is the apparent naturalness of the representation, as raised and qualified by an imperceptible infusion of the author's own knowledge and talent, which infusion does, indeed, constitute it an imitation as distinguished from a mere copy. The third cause

may be found in the reader's conscious feeling of his superiority awakened by the contrast presented to him; even as for the same purpose the kings and great barons of yore retained, sometimes actual clowns and fools, but more frequently shrewd and witty fellows in that character. These, however, were not Mr. Wordsworth's objects. *He* chose low and rustic life, "because in that condition the essential passions of the heart find a better soil, in which they can attain their maturity, are less under restraint, and speak a plainer and more emphatic language; because in that condition of life our elementary feelings coexist in a state of greater simplicity, and consequently may be more accurately contemplated, and more forcibly communicated; because the manners of rural life germinate from those elementary feelings; and from the necessary character of rural occupations are more easily comprehended, and are more durable; and lastly, because in that condition the passions of men are incorporated with the beautiful and permanent forms of nature."

Now it is clear to me, that in the most interesting of the poems, in which the author is more or less dramatic, as *The Brothers, Michael, Ruth, The Mad Mother,* and others, the persons introduced are by no means taken from low or rustic life in the common acceptation of those words; and it is not less clear, that the sentiments and language, as far as they can be conceived to have been really transferred from the minds and conversation of such persons, are attributable to causes and circumstances not necessarily connected with "their occupations and abode." The thoughts, feelings, language, and manners of the shepherd-farmers in the vales of Cumberland and Westmoreland, as far as they are actually adopted in those poems, may be accounted for from causes, which will and do produce the same results in every state of life, whether in town or country. As the two principal I rank that independence, which raises a man above servitude, or daily toil for the profit of others, yet not above the necessity of industry and a frugal simplicity of domestic life; and the accompanying unambitious, but solid and religious, education, which has rendered few books familiar, but the Bible, and the Liturgy or Hymn book. To this latter cause, indeed, which is so far accidental, that it is the blessing of particular countries and a particular age, not the product of particular places or employments, the poet owes the show of probability, that his personages might really feel, think, and talk with any tolerable resemblance to his representation. It is an excellent remark of Dr. Henry More's, that "a man of confined education, but of good parts, by constant reading of the

Bible will naturally form a more winning and commanding rhetoric than those that are learned: the intermixture of tongues, and of artificial phrases debasing *their* style."

It is, moreover, to be considered that to the formation of healthy feelings, and a reflecting mind, negations involve impediments not less formidable than sophistication and vicious intermixture. I am convinced that, for the human soul to prosper in rustic life a certain vantage-ground is prerequisite. It is not every man that is likely to be improved by a country life or by country labors. Education, or original sensibility, or both, must pre-exist, if the changes, forms, and incidents of nature are to prove a sufficient stimulant. And where these are not sufficient, the mind contracts and hardens by want of stimulants: and the man becomes selfish, sensual, gross, and hard-hearted. Let the management of the Poor Laws in Liverpool, Manchester, or Bristol be compared with the ordinary dispensation of the poor rates in agricultural villages, where the farmers are the overseers and guardians of the poor. If my own experience have not been particularly unfortunate, as well as that of the many respectable country clergymen with whom I have conversed on the subject, the result would engender more than scepticism concerning the desirable influences of low and rustic life in and for itself. Whatever may be concluded on the other side, from the stronger local attachments and enterprising spirit of the Swiss, and other mountaineers, applies to a particular mode of pastoral life, under forms of property that permit and beget manners truly republican, not to rustic life in general, or to the absence of artificial cultivation. On the contrary the mountaineers, whose manners have been so often eulogized, are in general better educated and greater readers than men of equal rank elsewhere. But where this is not the case, as among the peasantry of North Wales, the ancient mountains, with all their terrors and all their glories, are pictures to the blind, and music to the deaf.

I should not have entered so much into detail upon this passage, but here seems to be the point, to which all the lines of difference converge as to their source and centre; — I mean, as far as, and in whatever respect, my poetic creed *does* differ from the doctrines promulgated in this preface. I adopt with full faith, the principle of Aristotle, that poetry, as poetry, is essentially ideal, that it avoids and excludes all accident; that its apparent individualities of rank, character, or occupation must be representative of a class; and that the persons of poetry must be clothed with generic attributes, with the common attributes of the class:

not with such as one gifted individual might possibly possess, but such as from his situation it is most probable before-hand that he would possess. If my premises are right and my deductions legitimate, it follows that there can be no poetic medium between the swains of Theocritus and those of an imaginary golden age.

The characters of the vicar and the shepherd-mariner in the poem of *The Brothers*, and that of the shepherd of Green-head Ghyll in the *Michael*, have all the verisimilitude and representative quality, that the purposes of poetry can require. They are persons of a known and abiding class, and their manners and sentiments the natural product of circumstances common to the class. Take Michael, for instance:

An old man stout of heart, and strong of limb.
His bodily frame had been from youth to age
Of an unusual strength: his mind was keen,
Intense, and frugal, apt for all affairs,
And in his shepherd's calling he was prompt
And watchful more than ordinary men.
Hence he had learned the meaning of all winds,
Of blasts of every tone; and oftentimes
When others heeded not, He heard the South
Make subterraneous music, like the noise
Of bagpipers on distant Highland hills.
The Shepherd, at such warning, of his flock
Bethought him, and he to himself would say,
"The winds are now devising work for me!"
And truly, at all times, the storm, that drives
The traveller to a shelter, summoned him
Up to the mountains: he had been alone
Amid the heart of many thousand mists,
That came to him and left him on the heights.
So lived he, until his eightieth year was past.
And grossly that man errs, who should suppose
That the green valleys, and the streams and rocks,
Were things indifferent to the Shepherd's thoughts.
Fields, where with cheerful spirits he had breathed
The common air; the hills, which he so oft
Had climbed with vigorous steps; which had impressed
So many incidents upon his mind
Of hardship, skill or courage, joy or fear;
Which, like a book, preserved the memory
Of the dumb animals, whom he had saved,
Had fed or sheltered, linking to such acts,
So grateful in themselves, the certainty
Of honorable gain; these fields, these hills
Which were his living Being, even more
Than his own blood — what could they less? had laid
Strong hold on his affections, were to him
A pleasurable feeling of blind love,
The pleasure which there is in life itself.

On the other hand, in the poems which are pitched in a lower key, as the *Harry Gill*, and *The Idiot Boy*, the feelings are those of human nature in general; though the poet has judiciously laid the scene in the country, in order to place himself in the vicinity of interesting images, without the necessity of ascribing a sentimental perception of their beauty to the persons of his drama. In *The Idiot Boy*, indeed, the mother's character is not so much the real and native product of a "situation where the essential passions of the heart find a better soil, in which they can attain their maturity and speak a plainer and more emphatic language," as it is an impersonation of an instinct abandoned by judgment. Hence the two following charges seem to me not wholly groundless: at least, they are the only plausible objections, which I have heard to that fine poem. The one is, that the author has not, in the poem itself, taken sufficient care to preclude from the reader's fancy the disgusting images of ordinary morbid idiocy, which yet it was by no means his intention to represent. He was even by the "burr, burr, burr," uncounteracted by any preceding description of the boy's beauty, assisted in recalling them. The other is, that the idiocy of the boy is so evenly balanced by the folly of the mother, as to present to the general reader rather a laughable burlesque on the blindness of anile dotage, than an analytic display of maternal affection in its ordinary workings.

In *The Thorn*, the poet himself acknowledges in a note the necessity of an introductory poem, in which he should have portrayed the character of the person from whom the words of the poem are supposed to proceed: a superstitious man moderately imaginative, of slow faculties and deep feelings, "a captain of a small trading vessel, for example, who, being past the middle age of life, had retired upon an annuity, or small independent income, to some village or country town of which he was not a native, or in which he had not been accustomed to live. Such men having nothing to do become credulous and talkative from indolence." But in a poem, still more in a lyric poem — and the Nurse in *Romeo and Juliet* alone prevents me from extending the remark even to dramatic poetry, if indeed even the Nurse can be deemed altogether a case in point — it is not possible to imitate truly a dull and garrulous discourser, without repeating the effects of dullness and garrulity. However this may be, I dare assert, that the parts — (and these form the far larger portion of the whole) — which might as well or still better have proceeded from the poet's own imagination, and have been spoken in his own character, are those which have given, and which will continue to give, universal delight; and that the passages exclusively appropriate to the supposed narrator, such as the last couplet of the third stanza; [1] the seven last

lines of the tenth; [1] and the five following stanzas, with the exception of the four admirable lines at the commencement of the fourteenth, are felt by many unprejudiced and unsophisticated hearts, as sudden and unpleasant sinkings from the height to which the poet had previously lifted them, and to which he again re-elevates both himself and his reader.

If then I am compelled to doubt the theory, by which the choice of characters was to be directed, not only *a priori*, from grounds of reason, but both from the few instances in which the poet himself need be supposed to have been governed by it, and from the comparative inferiority of those instances; still more must I hesitate in my assent to the sentence which immediately follows the former citation; and which I can neither admit as particular fact, nor as general rule. "The language, too, of these men has been adopted (purified indeed from what appear to be its real defects, from all lasting and rational causes of dislike or disgust) because such men hourly communicate with the best objects from which the best part of language is originally derived; and because, from their rank in society and the sameness and narrow circle of their intercourse, being less under the action of social vanity, they convey their feelings and notions in simple and unelaborated expressions." To this I reply; that a rustic's language, purified from all provincialism and grossness, and so far reconstructed as to be made consistent with the rules of grammar — (which are in essence no other than the laws of universal logic, applied to psychological materials) — will not differ from the language of any other man of common sense, however learned or refined he may be, except as far as the notions, which the rustic has to convey, are fewer and more indiscriminate. This will become still clearer, if we add the consideration — (equally important though less obvious) — that the rustic, from the more imperfect development of his faculties, and from the lower state of their cultivation, aims almost solely to convey insulated facts, either those of his scanty experience or his traditional belief; while the educated man chiefly seeks to discover and express those connections of things, or those relative bearings of fact to fact, from which some more or less general law is deducible. For facts

---

[1] I've measured it from side to side;
'Tis three feet long, and two feet wide.

[1] Nay, rack your brain — 'tis all in vain,
I'll tell you every thing I know;
But to the Thorn, and to the Pond
Which is a little step beyond,
I wish that you would go:
Perhaps, when you are at the place,
You something of her tale may trace.

are valuable to a wise man, chiefly as they lead to the discovery of the indwelling law, which is the true being of things, the sole solution of their modes of existence, and in the knowledge of which consists our dignity and our power.

As little can I agree with the assertion, that from the objects with which the rustic hourly communicates the best part of language is formed. For first, if to communicate with an object implies such an acquaintance with it, as renders it capable of being discriminately reflected on, the distinct knowledge of an uneducated rustic would furnish a very scanty vocabulary. The few things and modes of action requisite for his bodily conveniences would alone be individualized, while all the rest of nature would be expressed by a small number of confused general terms. Secondly, I deny that the words and combinations of words derived from the objects, with which the rustic is familiar, whether with distinct or confused knowledge, can be justly said to form the best part of language. It is more than probable, that many classes of the brute creation possess discriminating sounds, by which they can convey to each other notices of such objects as concern their food, shelter, or safety. Yet we hesitate to call the aggregate of such sounds a language, otherwise than metaphorically. The best part of human language, properly so called, is derived from reflection on the acts of the mind itself. It is formed by a voluntary appropriation of fixed symbols to internal acts, to processes and results of imagination, the greater part of which have no place in the consciousness of uneducated man; though in civilized society, by imitation and passive remembrance of what they hear from their religious instructors and other superiors, the most uneducated share in the harvest which they neither sowed, nor reaped. If the history of the phrases in hourly currency among our peasants were traced, a person not previously aware of the fact would be surprised at finding so large a number, which three or four centuries ago were the exclusive property of the universities and the schools; and, at the commencement of the Reformation, had been transferred from the school to the pulpit, and thus gradually passed into common life. The extreme difficulty, and often the impossibility, of finding words for the simplest moral and intellectual processes of the languages of uncivilized tribes has proved perhaps the weightiest obstacle to the progress of our most zealous and adroit missionaries. Yet these tribes are surrounded by the same nature as our peasants are; but in still more impressive forms; and they are, moreover, obliged to particularize many more of them. When, therefore, Mr. Wordsworth adds, "accordingly, such a language" — (meaning, as before, the language of rustic life purified from provincialism) — "arising out of repeated experience and regular feelings, is a more permanent, and a far more philosophical language, than that which is frequently substituted for it by Poets, who think that they are conferring honor upon themselves and their art in proportion as they indulge in arbitrary and capricious habits of expression;" it may be answered, that the language, which he has in view, can be attributed to rustics with no greater right, than the style of Hooker or Bacon to Tom Brown or Sir Roger L'Estrange.[1] Doubtless, if what is peculiar to each were omitted in each, the result must needs be the same. Further, that the poet, who uses an illogical diction, or a style fitted to excite only the low and changeable pleasure of wonder by means of groundless novelty, substitutes a language of folly and vanity, not for that of the rustic, but for that of good sense and natural feeling.

Here let me be permitted to remind the reader, that the positions, which I controvert, are contained in the sentences — "a selection of the real language of men;" — "the language of these men" (that is, men in low and rustic life) "has been adopted; I have proposed to myself to imitate, and, as far as is possible, to adopt the very language of men."

"Between the language of prose and that of metrical composition, there neither is, nor can be, any *essential difference:*" it is against these exclusively that my opposition is directed.

I object, in the very first instance, to an equivocation in the use of the word "real." Every man's language varies, according to the extent of his knowledge, the activity of his faculties, and the depth or quickness of his feelings. Every man's language has, first, its individualities; secondly, the common properties of the class to which he belongs; and thirdly, words and phrases of universal use. The language of Hooker, Bacon, Bishop Taylor, and Burke differs from the common language of the learned class only by the superior number and novelty of the thoughts and relations which they had to convey. The language of Algernon Sidney differs not at all from that, which every well-educated gentleman would wish to write, and (with due allowances for the undeliberateness, and less connected train, of thinking natural and proper to conversation) such as he would wish to talk. Neither one nor the other differ half as much from the general language of cultivated society, as the language of Mr. Wordsworth's homeliest composition differs from that

[1] Writers of the seventeenth century.

of a common peasant. For "real" therefore, we must substitute ordinary, or *lingua communis*. And this, we have proved, is no more to be found in the phraseology of low and rustic life than in that of any other class. Omit the peculiarities of each and the result of course must be common to all. And assuredly the omissions and changes to be made in the language of rustics, before it could be transferred to any species of poem, except the drama or other professed imitation, are at least as numerous and weighty, as would be required in adapting to the same purpose the ordinary language of tradesmen and manufacturers. Not to mention, that the language so highly extolled by Mr. Wordsworth varies in every county, nay in every village, according to the accidental character of the clergyman, the existence or non-existence of schools; or even, perhaps, as the exciseman, publican, and barber happen to be, or not to be, zealous politicians, and readers of the weekly newspaper *pro bono publico*. Anterior to cultivation the *lingua communis* of every country, as Dante has well observed, exists every where in parts, and no where as a whole.

Neither is the case rendered at all more tenable by the addition of the words, "in a state of excitement." For the nature of a man's words, where he is strongly affected by joy, grief, or anger, must necessarily depend on the number and quality of the general truths, conceptions and images, and of the words expressing them, with which his mind had been previously stored. For the property of passion is not to create; but to set in increased activity. At least, whatever new connections of thoughts or images, or — (which is equally, if not more than equally, the appropriate effect of strong excitement) — whatever generalizations of truth or experience the heat of passion may produce; yet the terms of their conveyance must have preexisted in his former conversations, and are only collected and crowded together by the unusual stimulation. It is indeed very possible to adopt in a poem the unmeaning repetitions, habitual phrases, and other blank counters, which an unfurnished or confused understanding interposes at short intervals, in order to keep hold of his subject, which is still slipping from him, and to give him time for recollection; or, in mere aid of vacancy, as in the scanty companies of a country stage the same player pops backwards and forwards, in order to prevent the appearance of empty spaces, in the procession of Macbeth, or Henry VIII. But what assistance to the poet, or ornament to the poem, these can supply, I am at a loss to conjecture. Nothing assuredly can differ either in origin or in mode more widely from the

apparent tautologies of intense and turbulent feeling, in which the passion is greater and of longer endurance than to be exhausted or satisfied by a single representation of the image or incident exciting it. Such repetitions I admit to be a beauty of the highest kind; as illustrated by Mr. Wordsworth himself from the song of Deborah. *At her feet he bowed, he fell, he lay down: at her feet he bowed, he fell: where he bowed, there he fell down dead.* (Judges v, 27.)

CHAPTER XVIII

I conclude, therefore, that the attempt is impracticable; and that, were it not impracticable, it would still be useless. For the very power of making the selection implies the previous possession of the language selected. Or where can the poet have lived? And by what rules could he direct his choice, which would not have enabled him to select and arrange his words by the light of his own judgment? We do not adopt the language of a class by the mere adoption of such words exclusively, as that class would use, or at least understand; but likewise by following the order, in which the words of such men are wont to succeed each other. Now this order, in the intercourse of uneducated men, is distinguished from the diction of their superiors in knowledge and power, by the greater disjunction and separation in the component parts of that, whatever it be, which they wish to communicate. There is a want of that prospectiveness of mind, that surview, which enables a man to foresee the whole of what he is to convey, appertaining to any one point; and by this means so to subordinate and arrange the different parts according to their relative importance, as to convey it at once, and as an organized whole.

Now I will take the first stanza, on which I have chanced to open, in the *Lyrical Ballads*. It is one of the most simple and the least peculiar in its language.

> In distant countries have I been,
> And yet I have not often seen
> A healthy man, a man full grown,
> Weep in the public roads, alone.
> But such a one, on English ground,
> And in the broad highway, I met;
> Along the broad highway he came,
> His cheeks with tears were wet:
> Sturdy he seemed, though he was sad;
> And in his arms a lamb he had.

The words here are doubtless such as are current in all ranks of life; and of course not less so in the hamlet and cottage than in the shop, manufactory, college, or palace. But is this the *order*, in which the rustic would have placed the words? I am grievously deceived, if the following less compact mode of commencing the same tale be not a far more faithful copy. "I have been in a many parts, far and near, and I don't know that I ever saw before a man crying by himself in the public road; a grown man I mean, that was neither sick nor hurt," etc., etc. But when I turn to the following stanza in *The Thorn*:

> At all times of the day and night
> This wretched woman thither goes;
> And she is known to every star,
> And every wind that blows:
> And there, beside the Thorn, she sits,
> When the blue day-light's in the skies,
> And when the whirlwind's on the hill,
> Or frosty air is keen and still,
> And to herself she cries,

> Oh misery! Oh misery!
> Oh woe is me! Oh misery!

and compare this with the language of ordinary men; or with that which I can conceive at all likely to proceed, in real life, from such a narrator, as is supposed in the note to the poem; compare it either in the succession of the images or of the sentences; I am reminded of the sublime prayer and hymn of praise, which Milton, in opposition to an established liturgy, presents as a fair specimen of common extemporary devotion, and such as we might expect to hear from every self-inspired minister of a conventicle! And I reflect with delight, how little a mere theory, though of his own workmanship, interferes with the processes of genuine imagination in a man of true poetic genius, who possesses, as Mr. Wordsworth, if ever man did, most assuredly does possess,

> The Vision and the Faculty divine.

Lord (George Gordon) Byron · 1788–1824

Byron was born in London, January 22, 1788. His father was Captain John Byron of the Guards and his mother Catherine Gordon, a Scotswoman. Like other men of his class Byron was educated at Harrow and later attended Trinity College, Cambridge. About two years the poet spent traveling in Spain, Portugal, Greece, and the near East. (It was on this journey that he swam the Hellespont.) Upon his return to London and the publication of the first two cantos of *Childe Harold* in 1812, he was suddenly a man of fame and much sought for at the dining tables of society. After three years of London gaiety, Byron was anxious to "settle down" and, eventually successful in his courtship of Miss "Annabella" Milbanke, married on January 2, 1815. In a little more than a year, however, the two were separated and Byron left England for the Continent, never to return. Byron's life from here on is a record of successful publication, of liaisons with various women, of residence in one Italian city or another, and of his efforts to secure political freedom for Venice. He died in Missolonghi, April 19, 1824, while seeking to recruit forces to fight for the freedom of Greece. His remains were buried in the village of Hucknall-Torkard.

So factual an account hardly reveals the dominant element in Byron's life: the spirit of revolt. He rebelled against artificial standards of society, against conventions of religion, against the political attitude of the English aristocrats, against the tyranny which held the Mediterranean peoples in subjection, against whatever was formally accepted and thoughtlessly followed. His first speech in the House of Lords was in defense of labor — and that soon after the turn into the nineteenth century!

George Gordon Noel, Lord Byron came by this pugnacious temperament naturally. He was the descendant of a family of warriors, what he himself called "a line of cut-throat ancestors." Seven Byrons had fought on the side of King Charles. His grandfather was "Foul-Weather Jack,"

Admiral John Byron. His father — "Mad Jack Gordon" — a fiery libertine and captain in the Guards, despite running through the estates of two wives in a few years, was constantly in debt. Born into this family, forced to keep up appearances even when relatively impoverished, lame from birth, reared by a mother who alternately berated and fondled him, Byron was proud and sensitive. Nor is it strange that he was a poet of revolt. Prometheus-like, he reviled and defied the accepted gods.

Byron's period of writing extended barely over ten years, yet during this time he published prolifically. A selective list, including his most representative work of various types and periods, might incorporate: *Hours of Idleness* (1807), a collection of revised juvenile poems; *English Bards and Scotch Reviewers* (1809), in which he pays his ironic and satiric respects to his contemporaries; *Childe Harold* (1812 and 1818), a glorified travel book written in the Spenserian stanza; *Manfred* (1817), a poetic drama; *Don Juan* (1819; 1821–23), a fascinating collection of narratives and reflections, serious, humorous, and satirical; *The Vision of Judgment* (1822), a satirical attack on Southey, the poet laureate; and *Cain* (1821), a drama. In a sense Byron is the arch-romantic. Boldly wayward, sadly melancholic, full of genius and with a thorough contempt for convention and restraint, Byron lived passionately. And his work is shot through with these same qualities, with a regard for nature — as in the majestic apostrophe to the ocean — and with a strong spirit of adventure — as in those narratives of *The Giaour* and the *Bride of Abydos* which stole a reading public from Sir Walter Scott.

SUGGESTED REFERENCES: Andrew Rutherford, *Byron. A Critical Study* (1961); W. H. Marshall, *The Structure of Byron's Major Poems* (1962); Paul West, ed., *Byron. A Collection of Critical Essays* (1963).

Maid of Athens, Ere We Part

Ζώη μοῦ, σᾶς ἀγαπῶ [1]

Maid of Athens, ere we part,
Give, oh give me back my heart!
Or, since that has left my breast,
Keep it now, and take the rest!
Hear my vow before I go,   5
Ζῶη μοῦ, σᾶς ἀγαπῶ.

By those tresses unconfined,
Wooed by each Ægean wind;
By those lids whose jetty fringe
Kiss thy soft cheeks' blooming tinge;   10
By those wild eyes like the roe,
Ζῶη μοῦ, σᾶς ἀγαπῶ.

By that lip I long to taste;
By that zone-encircled waist;
By all the token-flowers that tell   15
What words can never speak so well·
By love's alternate joy and woe,
Ζῶη μοῦ, σᾶς ἀγαπῶ.

Maid of Athens! I am gone:
Think of me, sweet! when alone.   20
Though I fly to Istambol,
Athens holds my heart and soul:
Can I cease to love thee? No!
Ζῶη μοῦ, σᾶς ἀγαπῶ.

[1] "*Ζῶη μοῦ, σᾶς ἀγαπῶ.*" Romaic expression of tenderness: If I translate it, I shall affront the gentlemen, as it may seem that I supposed they could not; and if I do not, I may affront the ladies. For fear of any misconstruction on the part of the latter, I shall do so, begging pardon of the learned. It means, "My life, I love you!" which sounds very prettily in all languages, and is as much in fashion in Greece at this day as, Juvenal tells us, the two first words were amongst the Roman ladies, whose erotic expressions were all Hellenised. (Byron.)

Sonnet on Chillon [1]

Eternal Spirit of the chainless Mind!
Brightest in dungeons, Liberty! thou art,
For there thy habitation is the heart —
The heart which love of thee alone can bind·
And when thy sons to fetters are consigned —   5
To fetters, and the damp vault's dayless gloom,
Their country conquers with their martyrdom,
And Freedom's fame finds wings on every wind.
Chillon! thy prison is a holy place,
And thy sad floor an altar — for 'twas trod,   10
[1] The castle of Chillon is located on Lake Geneva.

Until his very steps have left a trace
Worn, as if thy cold pavement were a sod,
By Bonnivard![1]   May none those marks efface!
For they appeal from tyranny to God.

She Walks in Beauty

She walks in beauty, like the night
Of cloudless climes and starry skies;
And all that's best of dark and bright
   Meet in her aspect and her eyes:
Thus mellow'd to that tender light   5
   Which heaven to gaudy day denies.

One shade the more, one ray the less,
   Had half impair'd the nameless grace
Which waves in every raven tress,
   Or softly lightens o'er her face;   10
Where thoughts serenely sweet express
   How pure, how dear their dwelling-place.

And on that cheek, and o'er that brow,
   So soft, so calm, yet eloquent,
The smiles that win, the tints that glow,   15
   But tell of days in goodness spent,
A mind at peace with all below,
   A heart whose love is innocent!

When We Two Parted

When we two parted
   In silence and tears,
Half broken-hearted
   To sever for years,
Pale grew thy cheek and cold,   5
   Colder thy kiss;
Truly that hour foretold
   Sorrow to this.

The dew of the morning
   Sunk chill on my brow —   10
It felt like the warning
   Of what I feel now.
Thy vows are all broken
   And light is thy fame:
I hear thy name spoken,   15
   And share in its shame.

They name thee before me,
   A knell to mine ear;

[1] François Bonivard, a prior, was imprisoned at
Chillon (1530–1536) for his part in an uprising against
the Duke of Savoy.   The purpose of the insurrection
was to make the city of Geneva a republic.

A shudder comes o'er me —
   Why wert thou so dear?   20
They know not I knew thee,
   Who knew thee too well: —
Long, long shall I rue thee,
   Too deeply to tell.

In secret we met —   25
   In silence I grieve,
That thy heart could forget,
   Thy spirit deceive.
If I should meet thee
   After long years,   30
How should I greet thee? —
   With silence and tears.

Childe Harold

This long poem, consisting of four cantos, has been
called a guide-book.   It is, really, a series of pictures
of scenes visited and of reflections made by the poet
before these scenes.   It contains narrative, descriptive,
and lyrical passages.   The "Childe," a name given in
former days to noble youth preparing for knighthood,
is of course Byron himself.   The poem presents the
poet's record of travel in southern Europe in 1809–1811
and of another trip about Europe and Italy in 1816–18.
The passages which follow are portions of the third and
fourth cantos.

SOLITUDE

Lake Leman [1] woos me with its crystal face,
The mirror where the stars and mountains view
The stillness of their aspect in each trace
Its clear depth yields of their far height and hue:
There is too much of Man here, to look through
With a fit mind the might which I behold;   6
But soon in me shall Loneliness renew
Thoughts hid, but not less cherished than of old,
Ere mingling with the herd had penned me in their
   fold.

To fly from, need not be to hate, mankind: 10
All are not fit with them to stir and toil,
Nor is it discontent to keep the mind
Deep in its fountain, lest it overboil
In the hot throng, where we become the spoil
Of our infection, till too late and long,   15
We may deplore and struggle with the coil,
In wretched interchange of wrong for wrong
Midst a contentious world, striving where none are
   strong.

There, in a moment, we may plunge our years
In fatal penitence, and in the blight   20
[1] Lake Geneva.

Of our own Soul turn all our blood to tears,
And color things to come with hues of Night;
The race of life becomes a hopeless flight
To those that walk in darkness: on the sea
The boldest steer but where their ports invite —
But there are wanderers o'er Eternity,   26
Whose bark drives on and on, and anchored ne'er
        shall be.

Is it not better, then, to be alone,
And love Earth only for its earthly sake?
By the blue rushing of the arrowy Rhone,   30
Or the pure bosom of its nursing Lake,
Which feeds it as a mother who doth make
A fair but froward infant her own care,
Kissing its cries away as these awake; —
Is it not better thus our lives to wear,   35
Than join the crushing crowd, doomed to inflict
        or bear?

I live not in myself, but I become
Portion of that around me; and to me
High mountains are a feeling, but the hum
Of human cities torture: I can see   40
Nothing to loathe in Nature, save to be
A link reluctant in a fleshly chain,
Classed among creatures, when the soul can flee,
And with the sky — the peak — the heaving
        plain
Of ocean, or the stars, mingle — and not in vain. 45

And thus I am absorbed, and this is life:
I look upon the peopled desert past,
As on a place of agony and strife,
Where, for some sin, to Sorrow I was cast,
To act and suffer, but remount at last   50
With a fresh pinion; which I feel to spring,
Though young, yet waxing vigorous as the
        Blast
Which it would cope with, on delighted wing,
Spurning the clay-cold bonds which round our
        being cling.

And when, at length, the mind shall be all free
From what it hates in this degraded form,   56
Reft of its carnal life, save what shall be
Existent happier in the fly and worm, —
When Elements to Elements conform,
And dust is as it should be, shall I not   60
Feel all I see, less dazzling, but more warm?
The bodiless thought? the Spirit of each spot?
Of which, even now, I share at times the immortal
        lot?

Are not the mountains, waves, and skies, a part
Of me and of my Soul, as I of them?   65

Is not the love of these deep in my heart
With a pure passion? should I not contemn
All objects, if compared with these? and stem
A tide of suffering, rather than forgo
Such feelings for the hard and worldly phlegm
Of those whose eyes are only turned below,   71
Gazing upon the ground, with thoughts which
        dare not glow?

.   .   .   .

Clear, placid Leman! thy contrasted lake,
With the wild world I dwelt in, is a thing
Which warns me, with its stillness, to forsake   75
Earth's troubled waters for a purer spring.
This quiet sail is as a noiseless wing
To waft me from distraction; once I loved
Torn Ocean's roar, but thy soft murmuring
Sounds sweet as if a Sister's voice reproved,   80
That I with stern delights should e'er have been
        so moved.

It is the hush of night, and all between
Thy margin and the mountains, dusk, yet clear,
Mellowed and mingling, yet distinctly seen,
Save darkened Jura, whose capped heights ap-
        pear   85
Precipitously steep; and drawing near,
There breathes a living fragrance from the shore,
Of flowers yet fresh with childhood; on the ear
Drops the light drip of the suspended oar,
Or chirps the grasshopper one good-night carol
        more.   90

He is an evening reveler, who makes
His life an infancy, and sings his fill;
At intervals, some bird from out the brakes
Starts into voice a moment, then is still.
There seems a floating whisper on the hill,   95
But that is fancy, for the Starlight dews
All silently their tears of Love instill,
Weeping themselves away, till they infuse
Deep into Nature's breast the spirit of her hues.

Ye Stars! which are the poetry of Heaven!   100
If in your bright leaves we would read the fate
Of men and empires, — 'tis to be forgiven,
That in our aspirations to be great,
Our destinies o'erleap their mortal state,
And claim a kindred with you; for ye are   105
A Beauty and a Mystery, and create
In us such love and reverence from afar,
That Fortune, Fame, Power, Life, have named
        themselves a star.

All Heaven and Earth are still — though not
        in sleep,   109
But breathless, as we grow when feeling most:

And silent, as we stand in thoughts too deep: —
All Heaven and Earth are still: From the high
　host
Of stars, to the lulled lake and mountain-coast,
All is concentered in a life intense,
Where not a beam, nor air, nor leaf is lost, 115
But hath a part of Being, and a sense
Of that which is of all Creator and Defense.

Then stirs the feeling infinite, so felt
In solitude, where we are *least* alone;
A truth, which through our being then doth
　melt, 120
And purifies from self: it is a tone,
The soul and source of Music, which makes
　known
Eternal harmony, and sheds a charm
Like to the fabled Cytherea's zone,[1]
Binding all things with beauty; — 'twould dis-
　arm 125
The specter Death, had he substantial power to
　harm.

Not vainly did the early Persian make
His altar the high places, and the peak
Of earth-o'ergazing mountains, and thus take
A fit and unwalled temple, there to seek 130
The Spirit, in whose honor shrines are weak,
Upreared of human hands. Come, and compare
Columns and idol-dwellings — Goth or Greek —
With Nature's realms of worship, earth and air —
Nor fix on fond abodes to circumscribe thy prayer!

The sky is changed! — and such a change! Oh,
　Night, 136
And Storm, and Darkness, ye are wondrous
　strong,
Yet lovely in your strength, as is the light
Of a dark eye in Woman! Far along,
From peak to peak, the rattling crags among 140
Leaps the live thunder! Not from one lone
　cloud,
But every mountain now hath found a tongue,
And Jura answers, through her misty shroud,
Back to the joyous Alps, who call to her aloud!

And this is in the Night: — Most glorious
　Night! 145
Thou wert not sent for slumber! let me be
A sharer in thy fierce and far delight, —
A portion of the tempest and of thee!
How the lit lake shines, a phosphoric sea,
And the big rain comes dancing to the earth! 150
And now again 'tis black, — and now, the glee

[1] A girdle worn by Cytherea (Venus) and popularly
thought to move one who saw it to love.

Of the loud hills shakes with its mountain-mirth,
As if they did rejoice o'er a young Earthquake's
　birth.

Now, where the swift Rhone cleaves his way
　between
Heights which appear as lovers who have parted
In hate, whose mining depths so intervene, 156
That they can meet no more, though broken-
　hearted:
Though in their souls, which thus each other
　thwarted,
Love was the very root of the fond rage
Which blighted their life's bloom, and then de-
　parted: — 160
Itself expired, but leaving them an age
Of years all winters, — war within themselves to
　wage:

Now, where the quick Rhone thus hath cleft his
　way,
The mightiest of the storms hath ta'en his stand:
For here, not one, but many, make their play,
And fling their thunder-bolts from hand to
　hand, 166
Flashing and cast around: of all the band,
The brightest through these parted hills hath
　forked
His lightnings, — as if he did understand,
That in such gaps as Desolation worked, 170
There the hot shaft should blast whatever therein
　lurked.

Sky, Mountains, River, Winds, Lake, Light-
　nings! ye!
With night, and clouds, and thunder, and a Soul
To make these felt and feeling, well may be
Things that have made me watchful; the far
　roll 175
Of your departing voices, is the knoll [1]
Of what in me is sleepless, — if I rest.
But where of ye, O tempests! is the goal?
Are ye like those within the human breast?
Or do ye find, at length, like eagles, some high
　nest? 180

Could I embody and unbosom now
That which is most within me, — could I wreak
My thoughts upon expression, and thus throw
Soul, heart, mind, passions, feelings, strong or
　weak,
All that I would have sought, and all I seek, 185
Bear, know, feel — and yet breathe — into *one*
　word,
And that one word were Lightning, I would
　speak:

[1] knell.

But as it is, I live and die unheard,
With a most voiceless thought, sheathing it as a
    sword. 189

I have not loved the World, nor the World me;
I have not flattered its rank breath, nor bowed
To its idolatries a patient knee,
Nor coined my cheek to smiles, — nor cried
    aloud
In worship of an echo: in the crowd
They could not deem me one of such — I
    stood 195
Among them, but not of them — in a shroud
Of thoughts which were not their thoughts, and
    still could,
Had I not filed [1] my mind, which thus itself sub-
    dued.

I have not loved the World, nor the World me, —
But let us part fair foes; I do believe, 200
Though I have found them not, that there may
    be
Words which are things, — hopes which will not
    deceive,
And Virtues which are merciful, nor weave
Snares for the failing: I would also deem 204
O'er others' griefs that some sincerely grieve —
That two, or one, are almost what they seem, —
That Goodness is no name — and Happiness no
    dream.

ROME — AND THE VANITY OF HUMAN WISHES

Oh Love! no habitant of earth thou art —
An unseen seraph, we believe in thee, —
A faith whose martyrs are the broken heart, —
But never yet hath seen, nor e'er shall see
The naked eye, thy form, as it should be; 5
The mind hath made thee, as it peopled heaven,
Even with its own desiring phantasy,
And to a thought such shape and image given,
As haunts the unquench'd soul — parch'd, wear-
    ied, wrong, and riven.

Of its own beauty is the mind diseased, 10
And fevers into false creation: — where,
Where are the forms the sculptor's soul hath
    seiz'd?
In him alone. Can Nature show so fair?
Where are the charms and virtues which we dare
Conceive in boyhood and pursue as men, 15
The unreach'd Paradise of our despair,
Which o'er-informs the pencil and the pen,
And overpowers the page where it would bloom
    again?
[1] defiled.

Who loves, raves — 'tis youth's frenzy — but
    the cure
Is bitterer still, as charm by charm unwinds 20
Which robed our idols, and we see too sure
Nor worth nor beauty dwells from out the
    mind's
Ideal shape of such; yet still it binds
The fatal spell, and still it draws us on,
Reaping the whirlwind from the oft-sown winds;
The stubborn heart, its alchemy begun, 26
Seems ever near the prize — wealthiest when most
    undone.

We wither from our youth, we gasp away —
Sick — sick; unfound the boon, unslaked the
    thirst,
Though to the last, in verge of our decay, 30
Some phantom lures, such as we sought at first —
But all too late, — so are we doubly curst.
Love, fame, ambition, avarice — 'tis the same,
Each idle, and all ill, and none the worst —
For all are meteors with a different name, 35
And Death the sable smoke where vanishes the
    flame.

Few — none — find what they love or could
    have loved,
Though accident, blind contact, and the strong
Necessity of loving, have removed
Antipathies — but to recur, ere long, 40
Envenom'd with irrevocable wrong;
And Circumstance, that unspiritual god
And miscreator, makes and helps along
Our coming evils with a crutch-like rod,
Whose touch turns Hope to dust, — the dust we
    all have trod. 45

Our life is a false nature: 'tis not in
The harmony of things, — this hard decree,
This uneradicable taint of sin,
This boundless upas,[1] this all-blasting tree,
Whose root is earth, whose leaves and branches
    be 50
The skies which rain their plagues on men like
    dew —
Disease, death, bondage — all the woes we see,
And worse, the woes we see not — which throb
    through
The immedicable soul, with heart-aches ever new.

Yet let us ponder boldly — 'tis a base 55
Abandonment of reason to resign
Our right of thought — our last and only place

[1] A tree of Java the sap of which is poisonous. The tree was once thought to be so deadly that even birds flying overhead dropped dead.

Of refuge; this, at least, shall still be mine:
Though from our birth the faculty divine
Is chain'd and tortured — cabin'd, cribb'd, con-
fined,   60
And bred in darkness, lest the truth should
shine
Too brightly on the unprepared mind,
The beam pours in, for time and skill will couch
the blind.

Arches on arches! as it were that Rome,
Collecting the chief trophies of her line,   65
Would build up all her triumphs in one dome,
Her Coliseum stands; the moonbeams shine
As 'twere its natural torches, for divine
Should be the light which streams here to illume
This long-explored but still exhaustless mine   70
Of contemplation; and the azure gloom
Of an Italian night, where the deep skies assume

Hues which have words, and speak to ye of
heaven,
Floats o'er this vast and wondrous monument,
And shadows forth its glory. There is given   75
Unto the things of earth, which Time hath bent,
A spirit's feeling, and where he hath leant
His hand, but broke his scythe, there is a power
And magic in the ruin'd battlement,
For which the palace of the present hour   80
Must yield its pomp, and wait till ages are its
dower.

Oh Time! the beautifier of the dead,
Adorner of the ruin, comforter
And only healer when the heart hath bled;
Time! the corrector where our judgments err, 85
The test of truth, love — sole philosopher,
For all beside are sophists — from thy thrift,
Which never loses though it doth defer —
Time, the avenger! unto thee I lift
My hands, and eyes, and heart, and crave of thee
a gift: 90

Amidst this wreck, where thou hast made a
shrine
And temple more divinely desolate,
Among thy mightier offerings here are mine,
Ruins of years, though few, yet full of fate:
If thou hast ever seen me too elate,   95
Hear me not; but if calmly I have borne
Good, and reserved my pride against the hate
Which shall not whelm me, let me not have
worn
This iron in my soul in vain — shall *they* not
mourn?

And thou, who never yet of human wrong   100
Left the unbalanced scale, great Nemesis! [1]
Here, where the ancient paid thee homage long—
Thou who didst call the Furies from the abyss,
And round Orestes bade them howl and hiss
For that unnatural retribution [2] — just,   105
Had it but been from hands less near — in this
Thy former realm, I call thee from the dust!
Dost thou not hear my heart? — Awake! thou
shalt, and must.

It is not that I may not have incurr'd
For my ancestral faults or mine the wound 110
I bleed withal, and, had it been conferr'd
With a just weapon, it had flow'd unbound;
But now my blood shall not sink in the ground;
To thee I do devote it — *thou* shalt take
The vengeance, which shall yet be sought and
found,   115
Which if *I* have not taken for the sake——
But let that pass — I sleep, but thou shalt yet
awake.

And if my voice break forth, 'tis not that now
I shrink from what is suffer'd: let him speak
Who hath beheld decline upon my brow,   120
Or seen my mind's convulsion leave it weak;
But in this page a record will I seek.
Not in the air shall these my words disperse,
Though I be ashes; a far hour shall wreak
The deep prophetic fulness of this verse,   125
And pile on human heads the mountain of my
curse!

That curse shall be Forgiveness. — Have I
not —
Hear me, my mother Earth! behold it, Heaven!
Have I not had to wrestle with my lot?
Have I not suffer'd things to be forgiven?   130
Have I not had my brain sear'd, my heart riven,
Hopes sapp'd, name blighted, Life's life lied
away?
And only not to desperation driven,
Because not altogether of such clay
As rots into the souls of those whom I survey.   135

From mighty wrongs to petty perfidy
Have I not seen what human things could do?
From the loud roar of foaming calumny
To the small whisper of the as paltry few,
And subtler venom of the reptile crew,   140

[1] A goddess of judgment and retribution.
[2] For killing a guilty mother, Orestes was made
frantic by pursuing Furies.

The Janus [1] glance of whose significant eye,
Learning to lie with silence, would *seem* true,
And without utterance, save the shrug or sigh,
Deal round to happy fools its speechless obloquy.

But I have lived, and have not lived in vain: 145
My mind may lose its force, my blood its fire,
And my frame perish even in conquering pain;
But there is that within me which shall tire
Torture and Time, and breathe when I expire;
Something unearthly, which they deem not of,
Like the remember'd tone of a mute lyre,   151
Shall on their soften'd spirits sink, and move
In hearts all rocky now the late remorse of love.

The seal is set. — Now welcome, thou dread
        power!
Nameless, yet thus omnipotent, which here 155
Walk'st in the shadow of the midnight hour
With a deep awe, yet all distinct from fear;
Thy haunts are ever where the dead walls rear
Their ivy mantles, and the solemn scene
Derives from thee a sense so deep and clear 160
That we become a part of what has been,
And grow unto the spot, all-seeing but unseen.

And here [2] the buzz of eager nations ran,
In murmur'd pity, or loud-roar'd applause,
As man was slaughter'd by his fellowman.   165
And wherefore slaughter'd? wherefore, but be-
        cause
Such were the bloody Circus' genial laws,
And the imperial pleasure. — Wherefore not?
What matters where we fall to fill the maws
Of worms — on battle-plains or listed spot? 170
Both are but theatres where the chief actors rot.

I see before me the Gladiator lie:
He leans upon his hand — his manly brow
Consents to death, but conquers agony,
And his droop'd head sinks gradually low — 175
And through his side the last drops, ebbing
        slow
From the red gash, fall heavy, one by one,
Like the first of a thunder-shower; and now
The arena swims around him — he is gone,
Ere ceased the inhuman shout which hail'd the
        wretch who won.   180

He heard it, but he heeded not — his eyes
Were with his heart, and that was far away;
He reck'd not of the life he lost nor prize,
But where his rude hut by the Danube lay,

[1] Janus, porter at gates of Heaven, was given two
faces that he might look both ways at once.
[2] The Coliseum.

There were his young barbarians all at play, 185
There was their Dacian mother — he, their sire,
Butcher'd to make a Roman holiday —
All this rush'd with his blood — Shall he expire
And unavenged? Arise! ye Goths, and glut your
        ire!

But here, where Murder breathed her bloody
        steam;   190
And here, where buzzing nations choked the
        ways,
And roar'd or murmur'd like a mountain stream
Dashing or winding as its torrent strays;
Here, where the Roman million's blame or praise
Was death or life, the playthings of a crowd, 195
My voice sounds much — and fall the stars'
        faint rays
On the arena void — seats crush'd — walls
        bow'd —
And galleries, where my steps seem echoes
        strangely loud.

A ruin — yet what ruin! from its mass
Walls, palaces, half-cities, have been rear'd; 200
Yet oft the enormous skeleton ye pass,
And marvel where the spoil could have appear'd.
Hath it indeed been plunder'd, or but clear'd?
Alas! developed, opens the decay,
When the colossal fabric's form is near'd: 205
It will not bear the brightness of the day,
Which streams too much on all years, man, have
        reft away.

But when the rising moon begins to climb
Its topmost arch, and gently pauses there;
When the stars twinkle through the loops of
        time,   210
And the low night-breeze waves along the air
The garland-forest, which the gray walls wear,
Like laurels on the bald first Cæsar's head;
When the light shines serene but doth not glare,
Then in this magic circle raise the dead: 215
Heroes have trod this spot — 'tis on their dust ye
        tread.

"While stands the Coliseum, Rome shall stand;
When falls the Coliseum, Rome shall fall;
And when Rome falls — the World."   From
        our own land
Thus spake the pilgrims o'er this mighty wall
In Saxon times,[1] which we are wont to call   221
Ancient; and these three mortal things are still
On their foundations, and unalter'd all;

[1] About the beginning of the eighth century. Gibbon
quotes this remark as evidence that the Coliseum was
then intact.

Rome and her Ruin past Redemption's skill,
The World, the same wide den — of thieves, or
  what ye will.   225

Simple, erect, severe, austere, sublime —
Shrine of all saints and temple of all gods,
From Jove to Jesus — spared and blest by time;
Looking tranquillity, while falls or nods
Arch, empire, each thing round thee, and man
  plods   230
His way through thorns to ashes — glorious
  dome!
Shalt thou not last? Time's scythe and tyrants'
  rods
Shiver upon thee — sanctuary and home
Of art and piety — Pantheon! — pride of Rome!

Relic of nobler days, and noblest arts!   235
Despoil'd yet perfect, with thy circle spreads
A holiness appealing to all hearts —
To art a model; and to him who treads
Rome for the sake of ages, Glory sheds
Her light through thy sole aperture; to those   240
Who worship, here are altars for their beads;
And they who feel for genius may repose
Their eyes on honor'd forms, whose busts around
  them close.

There is a dungeon, in whose dim drear light
What do I gaze on? Nothing: Look again!   245
Two forms are slowly shadow'd on my sight —
Two insulated phantoms of the brain:
It is not so; I see them full and plain —
An old man, and a female young and fair,
Fresh as a nursing mother, in whose vein   250
The blood is nectar: — but what doth she there,
With her unmantled neck, and bosom white and
  bare?

Full swells the deep pure fountain of young life,
Where on the heart and from the heart we took
Our first and sweetest nurture, when the wife,
Blest into mother, in the innocent look,   256
Or even the piping cry of lips that brook
No pain and small suspense, a joy perceives
Man knows not, when from out its cradled nook
She sees her little bud put forth its leaves —   260
What may the fruit be yet? I know not — Cain
  was Eve's.

But here youth offers to old age the food,
The milk of his own gift: it is her sire
To whom she renders back the debt of blood
Born with her birth. No; he shall not expire   265
While in those warm and lovely veins the fire
Of health and holy feeling can provide

Great Nature's Nile, whose deep stream rises
  higher
Than Egypt's river: from that gentle side
Drink, drink and live, old man! Heaven's realm
  holds no such tide.   270

The starry fable of the milky way
Has not thy story's purity; it is
A constellation of a sweeter ray,
And sacred Nature triumphs more in this
Reverse of her decree, than in the abyss   275
Where sparkle distant worlds: — Oh, holiest
  nurse!
No drop of that clear stream its way shall miss
To thy sire's heart, replenishing its source
With life, as our freed souls rejoin the universe.

Turn to the mole which Hadrian rear'd on high,[1]
Imperial mimic of old Egypt's piles,   281
Colossal copyist of deformity
Whose travell'd phantasy from the far Nile's
Enormous model, doom'd the artist's toils
To build for giants, and for his vain earth,   285
His shrunken ashes, raise this dome: How smiles
The gazer's eye with philosophic mirth,
To view the huge design which sprung from such a
  birth!

But lo! the dome — the vast and wondrous
  dome,[2]
To which Diana's marvel was a cell —   290
Christ's mighty shrine above his martyr's tomb!
I have beheld the Ephesian's miracle; —
Its columns strew the wilderness, and dwell
The hyæna and the jackal in their shade;
I have beheld Sophia's bright roofs swell   295
Their glittering mass i' the sun, and have sur-
  vey'd
Its sanctuary the while the usurping Moslem
  pray'd;

But thou, of temples old, or altars new,
Standest alone, with nothing like to thee —
Worthiest of God, the holy and the true.   300
Since Zion's desolation, when that He
Forsook his former city, what could be,
Of earthly structures, in his honor piled,
Of a sublimer aspect? Majesty,
Power, Glory, Strength, and Beauty all are
  aisled   305
In this eternal ark of worship undefiled.

Enter: its grandeur overwhelms thee not;
And why? It is not lessen'd; but thy mind,

[1] The castle of St. Angelo.
[2] St. Peter's.

Expanded by the genius of the spot,
Has grown colossal, and can only find   310
A fit abode wherein appear enshrined
Thy hopes of immortality; and thou
Shalt one day, if found worthy, so defined,
See thy God face to face, as thou dost now
His Holy of Holies, nor be blasted by his brow. 315

Thou movest, but increasing with the advance,
Like climbing some great Alp, which still doth
    rise,
Deceived by its gigantic elegance;
Vastness which grows, but grows to harmonise —
All musical in its immensities;   320
Rich marbles, richer painting — shrines where
    flame
The lamps of gold — and haughty dome which
    vies
In air with Earth's chief structures, though their
    frame
Sits on the firm-set ground, and this the clouds
    must claim.

Thou seest not all; but piecemeal thou must
    break,   325
To separate contemplation, the great whole;
And as the ocean many bays will make
That ask the eye — so here condense thy soul
To more immediate objects, and control
Thy thoughts until thy mind hath got by heart
Its eloquent proportions, and unroll   331
In mighty graduations, part by part,
The glory which at once upon thee did not dart,

Not by its fault — but thine: Our outward sense
Is but of gradual grasp — and as it is   335
That what we have of feeling most intense
Outstrips our faint expression; even so this
Outshining and o'erwhelming edifice
Fools our fond gaze, and greatest of the great
Defies at first our Nature's littleness,   340
Till, growing with its growth, we thus dilate
Our spirits to the size of that they contemplate.

Then pause, and be enlighten'd; there is more
In such a survey than the sating gaze
Of wonder pleased, or awe which would adore
The worship of the place, or the mere praise 346
Of art and its great masters, who could raise
What former time, nor skill, nor thought could
    plan;
The fountain of sublimity displays
Its depth, and thence may draw the mind of
    man   350
Its golden sands, and learn what great conceptions
    can.

Or, turning to the Vatican, go see
Laocoön's [1] torture dignifying pain —
A father's love and mortal's agony
With an immortal's patience blending: Vain 355
The struggle; vain, against the coiling strain
And gripe, and deepening of the dragon's grasp,
The old man's clench; the long envenom'd chain
Rivets the living links, — the enormous asp
Enforces pang on pang, and stifles gasp on gasp.

Or view the Lord of the unerring bow,   361
The God of life, and poesy, and light —
The Sun in human limbs array'd, and brow
All radiant from his triumph in the fight;
The shaft hath just been shot — the arrow
    bright   365
With an immortal's vengeance; in his eye
And nostril beautiful disdain, and might
And majesty, flash their full lightnings by,
Developing in that one glance the Deity.

But in his delicate form — a dream of Love, 370
Shaped by some solitary nymph, whose breast
Long'd for a deathless lover from above,
And madden'd in that vision — are exprest
All that ideal beauty ever bless'd
The mind with in its most unearthly mood,   375
When each conception was a heavenly guest —
A ray of immortality — and stood
Starlike, around, until they gather'd to a god!

And if it be Prometheus stole from Heaven
The fire which we endure, it was repaid   380
By him to whom the energy was given
Which this poetic marble hath array'd
With an eternal glory — which, if made
By human hands, is not of human thought;
And Time himself hath hallow'd it, nor laid   385
One ringlet in the dust — nor hath it caught
A tinge of years, but breathes the flame with which
    'twas wrought.

.   .   .   .

But I forget. — My Pilgrim's [2] shrine is won,
And he and I must part, — so let it be, —
His task and mine alike are nearly done;   390
Yet once more let us look upon the sea;
The midland ocean breaks on him and me,
And from the Alban Mount we now behold
Our friend of youth, that Ocean, which when we

[1] A marble statue portraying a Trojan priest and his
two sons being crushed by serpents. The story is told
in the Æneid.
[2] The "pilgrim" is the hero of the poem.

Beheld it last by Calpe's [1] rock unfold   395
Those waves, we follow'd on till the dark Euxine
    roll'd

Upon the blue Symplegades: [2] long years —
Long, though not very many — since have done
Their work on both; some suffering and some
    tears
Have left us nearly where we had begun: 400
Yet not in vain our mortal race hath run;
We have had our reward, and it is here, —
That we can yet feel gladden'd by the sun,
And reap from earth, sea, joy almost as dear
As if there were no man to trouble what is clear.   405

Oh! that the Desert were my dwelling-place,
With one fair Spirit for my minister,
That I might all forget the human race,
And, hating no one, love but only her!
Ye elements! — in whose ennobling stir   410
I feel myself exalted — Can ye not
Accord me such a being? Do I err
In deeming such inhabit many a spot?
Though with them to converse can rarely be our
    lot.

There is a pleasure in the pathless woods,   415
There is a rapture on the lonely shore,
There is society, where none intrudes,
By the deep Sea, and music in its roar:
I love not Man the less, but Nature more,
From these our interviews, in which I steal   420
From all I may be, or have been before,
To mingle with the Universe, and feel
What I can ne'er express, yet cannot all conceal.

Roll on, thou deep and dark blue Ocean — roll!
Ten thousand fleets sweep over thee in vain;   425
Man marks the earth with ruin — his control
Stops with the shore; upon the watery plain
The wrecks are all thy deed, nor doth remain
A shadow of man's ravage, save his own,
When, for a moment, like a drop of rain,   430
He sinks into thy depths with bubbling groan,
Without a grave, unknell'd, uncoffin'd, and un-
    known.

His steps are not upon thy paths, — thy fields
Are not a spoil for him, — thou dost arise

[1] One of the mountains thrown up by Hercules to
mark his progress. It is one of the so-called "Pillars
of Hercules."
[2] The "Clashing Islands" at the entrance to the
Euxine Sea, through which Jason and the Argonauts
had to pass on their quest of the Golden Fleece.

And shake him from thee; the vile strength he
    wields
For earth's destruction thou dost all despise,   435
Spurning him from thy bosom to the skies,
And send'st him, shivering in thy playful spray
And howling, to his Gods, where haply lies
His petty hope in some near port or bay,   440
And dashest him again to earth: — there let him
    lay.

The armaments which thunderstrike the walls
Of rock-built cities, bidding nations quake,
And monarchs tremble in their capitals,
The oak leviathans, whose huge ribs make   445
Their clay creator the vain title take
Of lord of thee, and arbiter of war —
These are thy toys, and, as the snowy flake,
They melt into thy yeast of waves, which mar
Alike the Armada's pride or spoils of Trafalgar.   450

Thy shores are empires, changed in all save
    thee —
Assyria, Greece, Rome, Carthage, what are they?
Thy waters wash'd them power while they were
    free,
And many a tyrant since; their shores obey
The stranger, slave, or savage; their decay   455
Has dried up realms to deserts: — not so
    thou; —
Unchangeable, save to thy wild waves' play,
Time writes no wrinkle on thine azure brow:
Such as creation's dawn beheld, thou rollest now.

Thou glorious mirror, where the Almighty's
    form   460
Glasses itself in tempests; in all time, —
Calm or convulsed, in breeze, or gale, or storm,
Icing the pole, or in the torrid clime
Dark-heaving — boundless, endless, and sub-
    lime,
The image of eternity, the throne   465
Of the Invisible; even from out thy slime
The monsters of the deep are made; each zone
Obeys thee; thou goest forth, dread, fathomless,
    alone.

And I have loved thee, Ocean! and my joy
Of youthful sports was on thy breast to be   470
Borne, like thy bubbles, onward: from a boy
I wanton'd with thy breakers — they to me
Were a delight; and if the freshening sea
Made them a terror — 'twas a pleasing fear,
For I was as it were a child of thee,   475
And trusted to thy billows far and near,
And laid my hand upon thy mane — as I do here.

My task is done, my song hath ceased, my
    theme
Has died into an echo; it is fit   479
The spell should break of this protracted dream.
The torch shall be extinguish'd which hath lit
My midnight lamp — and what is writ, is writ;
Would it were worthier! but I am not now
That which I have been — and my visions flit
Less palpably before me — and the glow   485
Which in my spirit dwelt is fluttering, faint, and
    low.

Farewell! a word that must be, and hath been —
A sound which makes us linger; — yet — fare-
    well!
Ye! who have traced the Pilgrim to the scene
Which is his last, if in your memories dwell 490
A thought which once was his, if on ye swell
A single recollection, not in vain
He wore his sandal-shoon and scallop-shell;
Farewell! with *him* alone may rest the pain,
If such there were — with *you*, the moral of his
    strain.   495

So We'll Go No More A-Roving

So, we'll go no more a-roving
    So late into the night,
Though the heart be still as loving,
    And the moon be still as bright.

For the sword outwears its sheath,   5
    And the soul wears out the breast,
And the heart must pause to breathe,
    And love itself have rest.

Though the night was made for loving,
    And the day returns too soon,   10
Yet we'll go no more a-roving
    By the light of the moon.

Selections from Don Juan

Don Juan — a name borrowed from Don Juan
Tenorio, a libertine in Spanish fiction — is a humorous and satirical arraignment of society, politics, and
literature. In this long poem of sixteen cantos (more
were contemplated) Byron had in mind to compose
"the comic epic of the human race." Angered by the
accusations of immorality hurled at the first five books
of *Don Juan*, he wrote in 1822: "*Don Juan* will be
known by and bye, for what it is intended, a *Satire* on
abuses of the present states of Society, and not an
eulogy of vice." Byron's ability as both story teller
and poet, his highly developed comic sense, and his gay,
flippant asides give the work unusual vividness.

THE LAKE POETS [1] — AND OTHERS

DEDICATION

Bob Southey! You're a poet — Poet-laureate,
    And representative of all the race;
Although 'tis true that you turn'd out a Tory at
    Last, — yours has lately been a common case;
And now, my Epic Renegade! what are ye at?   5
    With all the Lakers, in and out of place?
A nest of tuneful persons, to my eye
Like "four and twenty Blackbirds in a pye;

"Which pye being open'd they began to sing"
    (This old song and new simile holds good),   10
"A dainty dish to set before the King,"
    Or Regent, who admires such kind of food; —
And Coleridge, too, has lately taken wing,
    But like a hawk encumber'd with his hood, —
Explaining metaphysics to the nation —   15
I wish he would explain his Explanation.

You, Bob! are rather insolent, you know,
    At being disappointed in your wish
To supersede all warblers here below,
    And be the only Blackbird in the dish;   20
And then you overstrain yourself, or so,
    And tumble downward like the flying fish
Gasping on deck, because you soar too high, Bob,
And fall, for lack of moisture quite a-dry, Bob!

And Wordsworth, in a rather long "Excursion"   25
    (I think the quarto holds five hundred pages),
Has given a sample from the vasty version
    Of his new system to perplex the sages;
'Tis poetry — at least by his assertion,
    And may appear so when the dog-star rages —
And he who understands it would be able   31
To add a story to the Tower of Babel.

You — Gentlemen! by dint of long seclusion
    From better company, have kept your own
At Keswick, and, through still continued fusion 35
    Of one another's minds, at last have grown
To deem as a most logical conclusion,
    That Poesy has wreaths for you alone:
There is a narrowness in such a notion,
Which makes me wish you'd change your lakes for
    ocean.   40

I would not imitate the petty thought,
    Nor coin my self-love to so base a vice,
For all the glory your conversion brought,
    Since gold alone should not have been its price.

[1] Byron could not forgive the Lake Poets — Southey,
Wordsworth, and Coleridge — for their having turned
from liberal to conservative thought.

You have your salary:[1] was't for that you wrought?
  And Wordsworth has his place in the Excise.[2] 46
You're shabby fellows — true — but poets still,
  And duly seated on the immortal hill.

Your bays may hide the baldness of your brows —
  Perhaps some virtuous blushes; — let them go —
To you I envy neither fruit nor boughs —   51
  And for the fame you would engross below,
The field is universal, and allows
  Scope to all such as feel the inherent glow:
Scott, Rogers, Campbell, Moore, and Crabbe, will try
                          55
'Gainst you the question with posterity.

For me, who, wandering with pedestrian Muses,
  Contend not with you on the winged steed,
I wish your fate may yield ye, when she chooses,
  The fame you envy, and the skill you need; 60
And recollect a poet nothing loses
  In giving to his brethren their full meed
Of merit, and complaint of present days
Is not the certain path to future praise.

He that reserves his laurels for posterity   65
  (Who does not often claim the bright reversion)
Has generally no great crop to spare it, he
  Being only injured by his own assertion;
And although here and there some glorious rarity
  Arises like Titan from the sea's immersion, 70
The major part of such appellants go
To — God knows where — for no one else can know.

If, fallen in evil days on evil tongues,
  Milton appealed to the Avenger, Time,
If Time, the Avenger, execrates his wrongs,   75
  And makes the word "Miltonic" mean "sub-
    lime,"
He deign'd not to belie his soul in songs,
  Nor turn his very talent to a crime;
He did not loathe the Sire to laud the Son,
But closed the tyrant-hater he begun.   80

Think'st thou, could he — the blind Old Man —
    arise,
  Like Samuel from the grave, to freeze once more
The blood of monarchs with his prophecies,
  Or be alive again — again all hoar
With time and trials, and those helpless eyes,   85
  And heartless daughters — worn — and pale —
    and poor;
Would he adore a sultan? he obey
The intellectual eunuch Castlereagh?[3]

[1] As poet laureate.
[2] A government post with salary and little work.
[3] British statesman and at one time foreign secretary.

Cold-blooded, smooth-faced, placid miscreant!
  Dabbling its sleek young hands in Erin's gore, 90
And thus for wider carnage taught to pant,
  Transferr'd to gorge upon a sister shore,
The vulgarest tool that Tyranny could want,
  With just enough of talent, and no more,
To lengthen fetters by another fix'd,   95
And offer poison long already mix'd.

An orator of such set trash of phrase
  Ineffably — legitimately vile,
That even its grossest flatterers dare not praise,
  Nor foes — all nations — condescend to smile;
Not even a sprightly blunder's spark can blaze   101
  From that Ixion grindstone's ceaseless toil,
That turns and turns to give the world a notion
Of endless torments and perpetual motion.

A bungler even in its disgusting trade,   105
  And botching, patching, leaving still behind
Something of which its masters are afraid,
  States to be curb'd, and thoughts to be confined,
Conspiracy or Congress to be made —
  Cobbling at manacles for all mankind —   110
A tinkering slave-maker, who mends old chains,
With God and man's abhorrence for its gains.

If we may judge of matter by the mind,
  Emasculated to the marrow It
Hath but two objects, how to serve, and bind,   115
  Deeming the chain it wears even men may fit,
Eutropius of its many masters, — blind
  To worth as freedom, wisdom as to wit,
Fearless — because no feeling dwells in ice,
Its very courage stagnates to a vice.   120

Where shall I turn me not to view its bonds,
  For I will never feel them; — Italy!
Thy late reviving Roman soul desponds
  Beneath the lie this State-thing breathed o'er
    thee —
Thy clanking chain, and Erin's yet green wounds,
  Have voices — tongues to cry aloud for me. 126
Europe has slaves, allies, kings, armies still,
And Southey lives to sing them very ill.

Meantime, Sir Laureate, I proceed to dedicate,
  In honest simple verse, this song to you.   130
And, if in flattering strains I do not predicate,
  'Tis that I still retain my "buff and blue;"
My politics as yet are all to educate:
  Apostasy's so fashionable, too,
To keep one creed's a task grown quite Hercu-
    lean: 135
Is it not so, my Tory, Ultra-Julian?

THE ISLES OF GREECE

Thus, usually, when *he* [1] was asked to sing,
  He gave the different nations something na-
     tional;
'Twas all the same to him — "God save the king,"
Or "*Ça ira*," [2] according to the fashion all:
His muse made increment of any thing,   5
  From the high lyric down to the low rational:
If Pindar [3] sang horse-races, what should hinder
Himself from being as pliable as Pindar?

In France, for instance, he would write a chanson;
  In England a six canto quarto tale;   10
In Spain, he'd make a ballad or romance on
  The last war — much the same in Portugal;
In Germany, the Pegasus he'd prance on
  Would be old Goethe's (see what says De Staël);
In Italy he'd ape the "Trecentisti;" [4]   15
In Greece, he'd sing some sort of hymn like this
     t' ye:

1

The Isles of Greece, the Isles of Greece!
  Where burning Sappho [5] loved and sung,
Where grew the arts of war and peace,
  Where Delos [6] rose, and Phœbus sprung!   20
Eternal summer gilds them yet,
But all, except their sun, is set.

2

The Scian [7] and the Teian [8] muse,
  The hero's harp, the lover's lute,
Have found the fame your shores refuse;   25
  Their place of birth alone is mute
To sounds which echo further west
Than your sires' "Islands of the Blest." [9]

3

The mountains look on Marathon [10] —
  And Marathon looks on the sea;   30
And musing there an hour alone,
  I dreamed that Greece might still be free;
For standing on the Persians' grave,
I could not deem myself a slave.

[1] Southey.
[2] A song of the French Revolution.
[3] Wrote many odes commemorating victories in the Greek games.
[4] Italian artists of the fourteenth century.
[5] Greek poetess of about 610 B.C.
[6] An island in the Ægean Sea where Phœbus was born.
[7] Homer.
[8] Anacreon.
[9] The Canaries, probably.
[10] The Greeks defeated the Persians here in 490 B.C.

4

A king [1] sate on the rocky brow   35
  Which looks o'er sea-born Salamis;
And ships, by thousands, lay below,
  And men in nations; — all were his!
He counted them at break of day —
And when the sun set where were they?   40

5

And where are they? and where art thou,
  My country?   On thy voiceless shore
The heroic lay is tuneless now —
  The heroic bosom beats no more!
And must thy lyre, so long divine,   45
Degenerate into hands like mine?

6

'Tis something, in the dearth of fame,
  Though linked among a fettered race,
To feel at least a patriot's shame,
  Even as I sing, suffuse my face;   50
For what is left the poet here?
For Greeks a blush — for Greece a tear.

7

Must *we* but weep o'er days more blest?
  Must *we* but blush? — Our fathers bled.
Earth! render back from out thy breast   55
  A remnant of our Spartan dead!
Of the three hundred grant but three,
To make a new Thermopylæ! [2]

8

What, silent still? and silent all?
  Ah! no; — the voices of the dead   60
Sound like a distant torrent's fall,
  And answer, "Let one living head,
But one arise, — we come, we come!"
'Tis but the living who are dumb.

9

In vain — in vain: strike other chords;   65
  Fill high the cup with Samian wine!
Leave battles to the Turkish hordes,
  And shed the blood of Scio's vine!
Hark! rising to the ignoble call —
How answers each bold Bacchanal!   70

10

You have the Pyrrhic dance [3] as yet,
  Where is the Pyrrhic phalanx gone?
Of two such lessons, why forget
  The nobler and the manlier one?

[1] Xerxes, King of Persia.
[2] Where Xerxes defeated the Spartans in 480 B.C.
[3] A war dance.

You have the letters Cadmus [1] gave —   75
Think ye he meant them for a slave?

11

Fill high the bowl with Samian wine!
  We will not think of themes like these!
It made Anacreon's song divine:
  He served — but served Polycrates —   80
A tyrant; but our masters then
Were still, at least, our countrymen.

12

The tyrant of the Chersonese
  Was freedom's best and bravest friend;
That tyrant was Miltiades! [2]   85
Oh! that the present hour would lend
Another despot of the kind!
Such chains as his were sure to bind.

13

Fill high the bowl with Samian wine!
  On Suli's rock, and Parga's shore,   90
Exists the remnant of a line
  Such as the Doric [3] mothers bore;
And there, perhaps, some seed is sown,
The Heracleidan blood [4] might own.

14

Trust not for freedom to the Franks —   95
  They have a king who buys and sells:
In native swords, and native ranks,
  The only hope of courage dwells;
But Turkish force, and Latin fraud,
Would break your shield, however broad.   100

15

Fill high the bowl with Samian wine!
  Our virgins dance beneath the shade —
I see their glorious black eyes shine;
  But gazing on each glowing maid,
My own the burning tear-drop laves,   105
To think such breasts must suckle slaves.

16

Place me on Sunium's [5] marbled steep,
  Where nothing, save the waves and I,
May hear our mutual murmurs sweep;
  There, swan-like, let me sing and die: 110
A land of slaves shall ne'er be mine —
Dash down yon cup of Samian wine!

. . . .

[1] Sometimes credited with inventing the alphabet.
[2] Greek leader at Marathon.   [3] Spartan.
[4] The blood of Hercules.
[5] Southern point of Attica.

Milton's the Prince of Poets — so we say;
  A little heavy, but no less divine:
An independent being in his day —   115
  Learned, pious, temperate in love and wine;
But, his life falling into Johnson's way,
  We're told this great High Priest of all the Nine
Was whipt at college — a harsh sire — odd spouse,
For the first Mrs. Milton left his house.   120

All these are, *certes*, entertaining facts,
  Like Shakespeare's stealing deer, Lord Bacon's
    bribes;
Like Titus' youth, and Cæsar's earliest acts;
  Like Burns (whom Doctor Currie well de-
    scribes);
Like Cromwell's pranks; — but although Truth
  exacts   125
These amiable descriptions from the scribes
As most essential to their hero's story,
They do not much contribute to his glory.

All are not moralists, like Southey, when
  He prated to the world of "Pantisocracy;" [1]
Or Wordsworth unexcised, unhired, who then   131
  Seasoned his pedlar poems with Democracy;
Or Coleridge, long before his flighty pen
  Let to the *Morning Post* its aristocracy;
When he and Southey, following the same path,
Espoused two partners [2] (milliners of Bath).   136

Such names at present cut a convict figure,
  The very Botany Bay [3] in moral geography;
Their loyal treason, renegado rigor,
  Are good manure for their more bare biography.
Wordsworth's last quarto, by the way, is bigger 141
  Than any since the birthday of typography;
A drowsy frowsy poem, called the "*Excursion*,"
Writ in a manner which is my aversion.

He there builds up a formidable dyke   145
  Between his own and others' intellect;
But Wordsworth's poem, and his followers, like
  Joanna Southcote's Shiloh, and her sect,
Are things which in this century don't strike
  The public mind, — so few are the elect;   150
And the new births of both their stale virginities
Have proved but dropsies, taken for divinities.

But let me to my story: I must own,
  If I have any fault, it is digression —
Leaving my people to proceed alone,   155
  While I soliloquize beyond expression;

[1] See biographical note on Coleridge.
[2] They married sisters.
[3] Convict colony in Australia.

But these are my addresses from the throne,
  Which put off business to the ensuing session:
Forgetting each omission is a loss to
The world, not quite so great as Ariosto.[1]   160

I know that what our neighbors call "lon-
  gueurs"[2]
  (We've not so good a *word*, but have the
  thing,
In that complete perfection which insures
  An epic from Bob Southey every spring),
Form not the true temptation which allures   165
  The reader; but 'twould not be hard to bring
Some fine examples of the *epopée*,[3]
To prove its grand ingredient is *ennui*.

We learn from Horace, "Homer sometimes
  sleeps;"
  We feel without him, — Wordsworth sometimes
  wakes, —   170
To show with what complacency he creeps,
  With his dear "*Waggoners*," around his lakes.
He wishes for "a boat" to sail the deeps —
  Of Ocean? — No, of air; and then he makes
Another outcry for "a little boat,"   175
And drivels seas to set it well afloat.

If he must fain sweep o'er the ethereal plain,
  And Pegasus runs restive in his "Waggon,"

[1] Italian poet (1474-1533) who wrote *Orlando Furioso*.
[2] tediousness.
[3] epic.

Could he not beg the loan of Charles's Wain?[1]
  Or pray Medea[2] for a single dragon?   180
Or if, too classic for his vulgar brain,
  He feared his neck to venture such a nag on,
And he must needs mount nearer to the moon,
Could not the blockhead ask for a balloon?

"Pedlars," and "Boats," and "Waggons!" Oh!
  ye shades   185
  Of Pope and Dryden, are we come to this?
That trash of such sort not alone evades
  Contempt, but from the bathos' vast abyss
Floats scumlike uppermost, and these Jack Cades
  Of sense and song above your graves may hiss —
The "little boatman" and his "Peter Bell"   191
Can sneer at him who drew "Achitophel"![3]

T' our tale. — The feast was over, the slaves
  gone,
  The dwarfs and dancing girls had all retired;
The Arab lore and Poet's song were done,   195
  And every sound of revelry expired;
The lady and her lover, left alone,
  The rosy flood of Twilight's sky admired; —
Ave Maria! o'er the earth and sea,
That heavenliest hour of Heaven is worthiest
  thee!   200

. . . .

[1] "Wain" is wagon; the term is given to the Great
Bear or "dipper."
[2] Medea escaped from a burning house in a chariot
drawn by dragons. See the play by Euripides.
[3] Dryden.

Percy Bysshe Shelley · 1792-1822

Percy Bysshe Shelley was born at "Field Place," the estate of his family in Sussex, on August 4, 1792. His father, Timothy Shelley, a Member of Parliament, enjoyed much more than a comfortable living as a country squire. The young Shelley was educated according to the best English standards at a private academy, at Eton, and at Oxford. He had reason to look forward to an income of several thousand pounds a year, to the life of a country gentleman in England.

Yet, before he was twenty, Shelley had been expelled from Oxford because of a two-page pamphlet he had written on *The Necessity of Atheism*, had broken with his father, had married Harriet Westbrook, the beautiful daughter of a retired innkeeper, had publicly flouted the commonly held conventions of marriage and religion, and was traveling about from England to Scotland to Ireland to Wales spreading doctrines of rebellion against the conventions of society. A few years later he deserted Harriet and his two children, lived with, and eventually married, **Mary Godwin**, the daughter of

William Godwin, author of the famous *Enquiry Concerning Political Justice*, became friendly with Byron in Switzerland, moved his new family about from Milan to Leghorn, from Venice to Rome and Naples. And, on July 8, 1822 — not yet thirty years old — he was drowned with his friend Williams when their light sailing craft, returning from Leghorn to the Gulf of Spezia, foundered during a storm. His body, found some days later, was cremated on the shore and the ashes, taken to the Protestant cemetery in Rome, were placed near the grave of Keats whom Shelley had so nobly celebrated in the *Adonais*.

Breaking traditions and flaunting the conventions which were demanded by his position, Shelley acted sincerely on convictions which happened to be at variance with those held by members of his social class. Furthermore, he believed that man is essentially good, that what man needs is a greater willingness to live by his emotions, that a transcendental idealism is a safer guide than custom or law. He was a neo-Platonist in thought, a perfectionist who held the belief that once society trusted its ideals all other reforms would become unnecessary. Truth, he felt convinced, would ultimately win. The brotherhood of man was an attainable reality.

In his poetry, Shelley gave expression to his age, an age of economic and social revolution, of tumult and uncertainty. As Professor Kenneth N. Cameron has pointed out, his poems may be divided into four major groups: The political and social scene is reflected in *Queen Mab* (1813), *The Masque of Anarchy* (1819), *Ode to Liberty* (1820), *Hellas, A Lyrical Drama* (1822), and *Ozymandias* (1818). *Alastor or the Spirit of Solitude* (1816) and *Epipsychidion* (1821) are the poetic expression of a psychological examination of Shelley's own life and mind. The relation of man to the universe is expressed in *Hymn to Intellectual Beauty* (1816), *To a Skylark* (1820), and *Adonais* (1821). The idea of a new world order to arise in the future appears in such works as the drama *Prometheus Unbound* (1820) and the lyrical *Ode to the West Wind* (1819).

Of Shelley's prose writings, *A Philosophical View of Reform* and the unfinished *Defense of Poesy* are important for an understanding of his thoughts on reform and his theories of poetry.

SUGGESTED REFERENCES: N. I. White, *Portrait of Shelley* (1945); Kenneth N. Cameron, *The Young Shelley* (1951); G. M. Ridenour, ed., *Shelley. A Collection of Critical Essays* (1965).

Hymn to Intellectual Beauty

The "spirit of beauty," the "awful loveliness," which Shelley here celebrates is beauty conceived according to Plato. This doctrine holds that material beauty as we know it about us is but a physical reflection of a spiritual essence or pure beauty. Once man — and he must perpetually strive to attain it — gains a sense of this ideal beauty, the world will become a more perfect place in which to live.

The awful shadow of some unseen Power
  Floats though unseen among us — visiting
  This various world with as inconstant wing
As summer winds that creep from flower to flower —
Like moonbeams that behind some piny mountain shower, 5
    It visits with inconstant glance
    Each human heart and countenance;
Like hues and harmonies of evening —
    Like clouds in starlight widely spread —
    Like memory of music fled — 10

Like aught that for its grace may be
Dear, and yet dearer for its mystery.

Spirit of BEAUTY, that dost consecrate
  With thine own hues all thou dost shine upon
  Of human thought or form — where art thou gone? 15
Why dost thou pass away and leave our state,
This dim vast vale of tears, vacant and desolate?
    Ask why the sunlight not for ever
    Weaves rainbows o'er yon mountain-river,
Why aught should fail and fade that once is shown,
    Why fear and dream and death and birth 21
    Cast on the daylight of this earth
    Such gloom — why man has such a scope
For love and hate, despondency and hope?

No voice from some sublimer world hath ever 25
  To sage or poet these responses given —
    Therefore the names of Demon, Ghost, and Heaven,

Remain the records of their vain endeavor,
Frail spells — whose uttered charm might not
    avail to sever,
    From all we hear and all we see,   30
    Doubt, chance, and mutability.
Thy light alone — like mist o'er mountains driven,
    Or music by the night-wind sent
    Through strings of some still instrument,
    Or moonlight on a midnight stream,   35
Gives grace and truth to life's unquiet dream.

Love, Hope, and Self-esteem, like clouds depart
    And come, for some uncertain moments lent.
    Man were immortal, and omnipotent,
Didst thou, unknown and awful as thou art,   40
Keep with thy glorious train firm state within his
    heart.
    Thou messenger of sympathies,
    That wax and wane in lovers' eyes —
Thou — that to human thought art nourishment,
    Like darkness to a dying flame!   45
    Depart not as thy shadows came,
    Depart not — lest the grave should be,
Like life and fear, a dark reality.

While yet a boy I sought for ghosts, and sped
    Through many a listening chamber, cave and
    ruin,   50
    And starlight wood, with fearful steps pursuing
Hopes of high talk with the departed dead.
I called on poisonous names with which our youth
    is fed;
    I was not heard — I saw them not —
    When musing deeply on the lot   55
Of life, at that sweet time when winds are wooing
    All vital things that wake to bring
    News of birds and blossoming —
    Sudden, thy shadow fell on me;
I shrieked, and clasped my hands in ecstasy!   60

I vowed that I would dedicate my powers
    To thee and thine — have I not kept the vow?
    With beating heart and streaming eyes, even now
I call the phantoms of a thousand hours
Each from his voiceless grave: they have in visioned
    bowers   65
    Of studious zeal or love's delight
    Outwatched with me the envious night —
They know that never joy illumed my brow
    Unlinked with hope that thou wouldst free
    This world from its dark slavery,   70
    That thou — O awful LOVELINESS,
Wouldst give whate'er these words cannot express.

The day becomes more solemn and serene
    When noon is past — there is a harmony

In autumn, and a luster in its sky,   75
Which through the summer is not heard or seen,
As if it could not be, as if it had not been!
    Thus let thy power, which like the truth
    Of nature on my passive youth
Descended, to my onward life supply   80
    Its calm — to one who worships thee,
    And every form containing thee,
    Whom, SPIRIT fair, thy spells did bind
To fear himself, and love all human kind.

Ode to the West Wind

I

O wild West Wind, thou breath of Autumn's being,
Thou, from whose unseen presence the leaves dead
Are driven, like ghosts from an enchanter fleeing,

Yellow, and black, and pale, and hectic red,
Pestilence-stricken multitudes!   O thou   5
Who chariotest to their dark wintry bed

The wingèd seeds, where they lie cold and low,
Each like a corpse within its grave, until
Thine azure sister of the Spring shall blow

Her clarion o'er the dreaming earth, and fill   10
(Driving sweet buds like flocks to feed in air)
With living hues and odors plain and hill:

Wild Spirit, which art moving everywhere;
Destroyer and Preserver; hear, oh hear!

2

Thou on whose stream, 'mid the steep sky's com-
    motion,   15
Loose clouds like earth's decaying leaves are shed,
Shook from the tangled boughs of heaven and
    ocean,

Angels of rain and lightning! there are spread
On the blue surface of thine airy surge,
Like the bright hair uplifted from the head   20

Of some fierce Mænad,[1] even from the dim verge
Of the horizon to the zenith's height,
The locks of the approaching storm.   Thou dirge

Of the dying year, to which this closing night
Will be the dome of a vast sepulchre,   25
Vaulted with all thy congregated might

Of vapors, from whose solid atmosphere
Black rain, and fire, and hail, will burst: Oh hear!
_____
[1] The Mænads were followers of Bacchus.

3

Thou who didst waken from his summer-dreams
The blue Mediterranean, where he lay,   30
Lulled by the coil of his crystalline streams,

Beside a pumice isle in Baiae's [1] bay,
And saw in sleep old palaces and towers
Quivering within the wave's intenser day,

All overgrown with azure moss, and flowers   35
So sweet, the sense faints picturing them! Thou
For whose path the Atlantic's level powers

Cleave themselves into chasms, while far below
The sea-blooms and the oozy woods which wear
The sapless foliage of the ocean know   40

Thy voice, and suddenly grow gray with fear
And tremble and despoil themselves: Oh hear!

4

If I were a dead leaf thou mightest bear;
If I were a swift cloud to fly with thee;
A wave to pant beneath thy power, and share   45

The impulse of thy strength, only less free
Than Thou, O uncontrollable! If even
I were as in my boyhood, and could be

The comrade of thy wanderings over heaven,
As then, when to outstrip thy skyey speed   50
Scarce seemed a vision; I would ne'er have striven

As thus with thee in prayer in my sore need.
Oh! lift me as a wave, a leaf, a cloud!
I fall upon the thorns of life! I bleed!

A heavy weight of hours has chained and bowed   55
One too like thee — tameless, and swift, and
proud.

5

Make me thy lyre, ev'n as the forest is:
What if my leaves are falling like its own!
The tumult of thy mighty harmonies

Will take from both a deep, autumnal tone,   60
Sweet though in sadness. Be thou, Spirit fierce,
My spirit! Be thou me, impetuous one!

Drive my dead thoughts over the universe
Like withered leaves to quicken a new birth!
And, by the incantation of this verse,   65

[1] A town near Naples.

Scatter, as from an unextinguished hearth
Ashes and sparks, my words among mankind!
Be through my lips to unawakened earth

The trumpet of a prophecy! O, Wind,
If Winter comes, can Spring be far behind?   70

To a Skylark

Hail to thee, blithe Spirit!
    Bird thou never wert,
That from Heaven, or near it,
    Pourest thy full heart
In profuse strains of unpremeditated art.   5

    Higher still and higher
        From the earth thou springest
    Like a cloud of fire;
        The blue deep thou wingest,
And singing still dost soar, and soaring ever
    singest.   10

    In the golden lightning
        Of the sunken sun,
    O'er which clouds are bright'ning,
        Thou dost float and run;
Like an unbodied joy whose race is just begun.   15

    The pale purple even
        Melts around thy flight;
    Like a star of Heaven,
        In the broad daylight
Thou art unseen, but yet I hear thy shrill delight,

    Keen as are the arrows   21
        Of that silver sphere,
    Whose intense lamp narrows
        In the white dawn clear
Until we hardly see — we feel that it is there.   25

    All the earth and air
        With thy voice is loud,
    As, when night is bare,
        From one lonely cloud
The moon rains out her beams, and Heaven is
    overflowed.   30

    What thou art we know not;
        What is most like thee?
    From rainbow clouds there flow not
        Drops so bright to see
As from thy presence showers a rain of melody.   35

    Like a Poet hidden
        In the light of thought,

Singing hymns unbidden,
   Till the world is wrought
To sympathy with hopes and fears it heeded not: 40

Like a high-born maiden
   In a palace-tower,
Soothing her love-laden
   Soul in secret hour
With music sweet as love, which overflows her
   bower: 45

Like a glow-worm golden
   In a dell of dew,
Scattering unbeholden
   Its aërial hue
Among the flowers and grass, which screen it from
   the view! 50

Like a rose embowered
   In its own green leaves,
By warm winds deflowered,
   Till the scent it gives
Makes faint with too much sweet those heavy-
   wingèd thieves: 55

Sound of vernal showers
   On the twinkling grass,
Rain-awakened flowers,
   All that ever was
Joyous, and clear, and fresh, thy music doth sur-
   pass: 60

Teach us, Sprite or Bird,
   What sweet thoughts are thine:
I have never heard
   Praise of love or wine
That panted forth a flood of rapture so divine. 65

Chorus Hymeneal,
   Or triumphal chant,
Matched with thine would be all
   But an empty vaunt,
A thing wherein we feel there is some hidden
   want. 70

What objects are the fountains
   Of thy happy strain?
What fields, or waves, or mountains?
   What shapes of sky or plain?
What love of thine own kind? what ignorance of
   pain? 75

With thy clear keen joyance
   Languor cannot be:
Shadow of annoyance

Never came near thee:
Thou lovest — but ne'er knew love's sad satiety. 80

Waking or asleep,
   Thou of death must deem
Things more true and deep
   Than we mortals dream,
Or how could thy notes flow in such a crystal
   stream? 85

We look before and after,
   And pine for what is not:
Our sincerest laughter
   With some pain is fraught;
Our sweetest songs are those that tell of saddest
   thought. 90

Yet if we could scorn
   Hate, and pride, and fear;
If we were things born
   Not to shed a tear,
I know not how thy joy we ever should come
   near. 95

Better than all measures
   Of delightful sound,
Better than all treasures
   That in books are found,
Thy skill to poet were, thou scorner of the ground!

Teach me half the gladness 101
   That thy brain must know,
Such harmonious madness
   From my lips would flow
The world should listen then — as I am listening
   now. 105

Ozymandias

I met a traveller from an antique land
Who said: Two vast and trunkless legs of stone
Stand in the desert ... Near them, on the sand,
Half sunk, a shattered visage lies, whose frown,
And wrinkled lip, and sneer of cold command, 5
Tell that its sculptor well those passions read
Which yet survive, stamped on these lifeless things,
The hand that mocked them, and the heart that
   fed:
And on the pedestal these words appear:
"My name is Ozymandias, king of kings: 10
Look on my works, ye Mighty, and despair!"
Nothing beside remains.   Round the decay
Of that colossal wreck, boundless and bare
The lone and level sands stretch far away.

Mutability

The flower that smiles to-day
    To-morrow dies;
All that we wish to stay
    Tempts and then flies.
What is this world's delight?   5
Lightning that mocks the night,
    Brief even as bright.

Virtue, how frail it is!
    Friendship how rare!
Love, how it sells poor bliss   10
    For proud despair!
But we, though soon they fall,
Survive their joy, and all
    Which ours we call.

Whilst skies are blue and bright,   15
    Whilst flowers are gay,
Whilst eyes that change ere night
    Make glad the day;
Whilst yet the calm hours creep,
Dream thou — and from thy sleep   20
    Then wake to weep.

Adonais

AN ELEGY ON THE DEATH OF JOHN KEATS,
AUTHOR OF ENDYMION, HYPERION, ETC.

PREFACE [1]

It is my intention to subjoin to the London edition of this poem a criticism upon the claims of its lamented object to be classed among the writers of the highest genius who have adorned our age. My known repugnance to the narrow principles of taste on which several of his earlier compositions were modeled prove, at least, that I am an impartial judge. I consider the fragment of *Hyperion* as second to nothing that was ever produced by a writer of the same years.

John Keats died at Rome of a consumption, in his twenty-fourth year, on the —— of ——[2] 1821; and was buried in the romantic and lonely cemetery of the Protestants in that city, under the pyramid which is the tomb of Cestius, and the massy walls and towers, now moldering and desolate, which formed the circuit of ancient Rome. The cemetery is an open space

[1] Shelley's preface is complete except for two quotations from the Greek with which he introduces the statement.

[2] The dates were left blank by Shelley who did not know them at the time he wrote.

among the ruins, covered in winter with violets and daisies. It might make one in love with death, to think that one should be buried in so sweet a place.

The genius of the lamented person to whose memory I have dedicated these unworthy verses was not less delicate and fragile than it was beautiful; and where cankerworms abound, what wonder if its young flower was blighted in the bud? The savage criticism on his *Endymion*, which appeared in the *Quarterly Review*, produced the most violent effect on his susceptible mind; the agitation thus originated ended in the rupture of a blood-vessel in the lungs; a rapid consumption ensued, and the succeeding acknowledgments from more candid critics of the true greatness of his powers were ineffectual to heal the wound thus wantonly inflicted.

It may be well said that these wretched men know not what they do. They scatter their insults and their slanders without heed as to whether the poisoned shaft lights on a heart made callous by many blows, or one like Keats's composed of more penetrable stuff. One of their associates is, to my knowledge, a most base and unprincipled calumniator. As to *Endymion*, was it a poem, whatever might be its defects, to be treated contemptuously by those who had celebrated, with various degrees of complacency and panegyric, *Paris* and *Woman* and a *Syrian Tale* and Mrs. Lefanu and Mr. Barrett and Mr. Howard Payne and a long list of the illustrious obscure? Are these the men who in their venal good nature presumed to draw a parallel between the Rev. Mr. Milman and Lord Byron? What gnat did they strain at here, after having swallowed all those camels? Against what woman taken in adultery dares the foremost of these literary prostitutes to cast his opprobrious stone? Miserable man! you, one of the meanest, have wantonly defaced one of the noblest specimens of the workmanship of God. Nor shall it be your excuse, that, murderer as you are, you have spoken daggers, but used none.

The circumstances of the closing scene of poor Keats's life were not made known to me until the *Elegy* was ready for the press. I am given to understand that the wound which his sensitive spirit had received from the criticism of *Endymion* was exasperated by the bitter sense of unrequited benefits; the poor fellow seems to have been hooted from the stage of life, no less by those on whom he had wasted the promise of his genius, than those on whom he had lavished his fortune and his care. He was accompanied to Rome, and attended in his last illness by Mr. Severn, a young artist of the highest promise, who, I have been informed, "almost risked his own life, and sacrificed every prospect to unwearied attendance upon his dying friend." Had I known these circumstances before the completion of my poem, I should have been tempted to add my feeble tribute of applause to the more solid recompense which the virtuous man finds in the recollection of his own motives. Mr. Severn can dispense with a reward from "such stuff as dreams are made of." His conduct is a golden augury of the success of his future career — may the unextinguished Spirit of his illustrious friend animate the creations of his pencil, and plead against Oblivion for his name! — *Shelley.*

1

I weep for Adonais — he is dead!
Oh, weep for Adonais! though our tears
Thaw not the frost which binds so dear a head!
And thou, sad Hour, selected from all years
To mourn our loss, rouse thy obscure compeers,
And teach them thine own sorrow, say: "With
    me   6
Died Adonais; till the Future dares
Forget the Past, his fate and fame shall be
An echo and a light unto eternity!"

2

Where wert thou, mighty Mother, when he lay,
When thy Son lay, pierced by the shaft which
    flies   11
In darkness? where was lorn Urania [1]
When Adonais died?   With veilèd eyes,
'Mid listening Echoes, in her Paradise
She sat, while one, with soft enamored breath, 15
Rekindled all the fading melodies,
With which, like flowers that mock the corse
    beneath,
He had adorned and hid the coming bulk of Death.

3

Oh, weep for Adonais — he is dead!
Wake, melancholy Mother, wake and weep! 20
Yet wherefore?   Quench within their burning
    bed
Thy fiery tears, and let thy loud heart keep
Like his, a mute and uncomplaining sleep;
For he is gone where all things wise and fair
Descend. — Oh, dream not that the amorous
    Deep   25
Will yet restore him to the vital air;
Death feeds on his mute voice, and laughs at our
    despair.

4

Most musical of mourners, weep again!
Lament anew, Urania! — He died,
Who was the sire [2] of an immortal strain, 30
Blind, old, and lonely, when his country's pride,
The priest, the slave, and the liberticide
Trampled and mocked with many a loathèd rite
Of lust and blood; he went, unterrified,
Into the gulf of death; but his clear Sprite 35
Yet reigns o'er earth, the third [3] among the sons
    of light.

5

Most musical of mourners, weep anew!
Not all to that bright station dared to climb;

[1] The Muse of Astronomy.   [2] Milton.
[3] The other two were probably Homer and Dante.

And happier they their happiness who knew,
Whose tapers yet burn through that night of
    time   40
In which suns perished; others more sublime,
Struck by the envious wrath of man or God,
Have sunk, extinct in their refulgent prime;
And some yet live, treading the thorny road,
Which leads, through toil and hate, to Fame's
    serene abode.   45

6

But now, thy youngest, dearest one has perished,
The nursling of thy widowhood, who grew,
Like a pale flower by some sad maiden cherished
And fed with true-love tears, instead of dew;
Most musical of mourners, weep anew! 50
Thy extreme hope, the loveliest and the last,
The bloom, whose petals, nipped before they
    blew,
Died on the promise of the fruit, is waste;
The broken lily lies — the storm is overpast.

7

To that high Capital,[1] where kingly Death 55
Keeps his pale court in beauty and decay,
He came; and bought, with price of purest breath,
A grave among the eternal. — Come away!
Haste, while the vault of blue Italian day
Is yet his fitting charnel-roof! while still 60
He lies, as if in dewy sleep he lay;
Awake him not! surely he takes his fill
Of deep and liquid rest, forgetful of all ill.

8

He will awake no more, oh, never more! —
Within the twilight chamber spreads apace 65
The shadow of white Death, and at the door
Invisible Corruption waits to trace
His extreme way to her dim dwelling-place;
The eternal Hunger sits, but pity and awe
Soothe her pale rage, nor dares she to deface 70
So fair a prey, till darkness and the law
Of change shall o'er his sleep the mortal curtain
    draw.

9

Oh, weep for Adonais! — The quick Dreams,
The passion-wingèd ministers of thought,
Who were his flocks, whom near the living
    streams   75
Of his young spirit he fed, and whom he taught
The love which was its music, wander not, —
Wander no more, from kindling brain to brain,
But droop there, whence they sprung; and mourn
    their lot

[1] Rome.

Round the cold heart, where, after their sweet
  pain,
They ne'er will gather strength, or find a home   80
  again.

10

And one with trembling hands clasps his cold
  head,
And fans him with her moonlight wings, and
  cries;
"Our love, our hope, our sorrow, is not dead;
See, on the silken fringe of his faint eyes,   85
Like dew upon a sleeping flower, there lies
A tear some Dream has loosened from his brain."
Lost Angel of a ruined Paradise!
She knew not 'twas her own; as with no stain
She faded, like a cloud which had outwept its
  rain.   90

11

One from a lucid urn of starry dew
Washed his light limbs, as if embalming them;
Another clipped her profuse locks, and threw
The wreath upon him, like an anadem,[1]
Which frozen tears instead of pearls begem;   95
Another in her willful grief would break
Her bow and wingèd reeds, as if to stem
A greater loss with one which was more weak;
And dull the barbèd fire against his frozen cheek.

12

Another Splendor on his mouth alit,   100
That mouth whence it was wont to draw the
  breath
Which gave it strength to pierce the guarded wit,
And pass into the panting heart beneath
With lightning and with music; the damp death
Quenched its caress upon his icy lips;   105
And, as a dying meteor stains a wreath
Of moonlight vapor, which the cold night clips,
It flushed through his pale limbs, and passed to
  its eclipse.

13

And others came — Desires and Adorations,
Wingèd Persuasions and veiled Destinies,   110
Splendors, and Glooms, and glimmering Incarna-
  tions
Of hopes and fears, and twilight Fantasies;
And Sorrow, with her family of Sighs,
And Pleasure, blind with tears, led by the gleam
Of her own dying smile instead of eyes,   115
Came in slow pomp; — the moving pomp might
  seem
Like pageantry of mist on an autumnal stream.

[1] garland.

14

All he had loved, and molded into thought
From shape, and hue, and odor, and sweet
  sound,
Lamented Adonais.   Morning sought   120
Her eastern watch-tower, and her hair unbound,
Wet with the tears which should adorn the
  ground,
Dimmed the aërial eyes that kindle day;
Afar the melancholy thunder moaned,
Pale Ocean in unquiet slumber lay,   125
And the wild winds flew round, sobbing in their
  dismay.

15

Lost Echo sits amid the voiceless mountains,
And feeds her grief with his remembered lay,
And will no more reply to winds or fountains,
Or amorous birds perched on the young green
  spray,   130
Or herdsman's horn, or bell at closing day;
Since she can mimic not his lips, more dear
Than those[1] for whose disdain she pined away
Into a shadow of all sounds: — a drear
Murmur, between their songs, is all the woodmen
  hear.   135

16

Grief made the young Spring wild, and she threw
  down
Her kindling buds, as if she Autumn were,
Or they dead leaves; since her delight is flown,
For whom should she have waked the sullen
  year?
To Phœbus was not Hyacinth [2] so dear   140
Nor to himself Narcissus,[3] as to both
Thou, Adonais; wan they stand and sere
Amid the faint companions of their youth,
With dew all turned to tears; odor, to sighing ruth.

17

Thy spirit's sister, the lorn nightingale,   145
Mourns not her mate with such melodious pain;
Not so the eagle, who like thee could scale
Heaven, and could nourish in the sun's domain
Her mighty youth with morning, doth complain,
Soaring and screaming round her empty nest, 150
As Albion wails for thee: the curse of Cain

[1] Echo (line 127) was in love with Narcissus.   It is
to his lips that Shelley here refers.
[2] Beloved by Apollo and changed into a flower upon
his death.
[3] A great egotist, Narcissus fell in love with his own
image.

Light on his head [1] who pierced thy innocent
    breast,
And scared the angel soul that was its earthly
    guest!

18

Ah, woe is me!   Winter is come and gone,
But grief returns with the revolving year;   155
The airs and streams renew their joyous tone;
The ants, the bees, the swallows reappear;
Fresh leaves and flowers deck the dead Season's
    bier;
The amorous birds now pair in every brake,
And build their mossy homes in field and
    brere; [2]   160
And the green lizard, and the golden snake,
Like unimprisoned flames, out of their trance
    awake.

19

Through wood and stream and field and hill
    and Ocean
A quickening life from the Earth's heart has
    burst,
As it has ever done, with change and motion, 165
From the great morning of the world when first
God dawned on Chaos; in its stream immersed,
The lamps of Heaven flash with a softer light;
All baser things pant with life's sacred thirst;
Diffuse themselves; and spend in love's delight
The beauty and the joy of their renewèd might. 171

20

The leprous corpse, touched by this spirit tender,
Exhales itself in flowers of gentle breath;
Like incarnations of the stars, when splendor
Is changed to fragrance, they illumine death 175
And mock the merry worm that wakes beneath.
Nought we know, dies.   Shall that alone which
    knows
Be as a sword consumed before the sheath
By sightless lightning? — the intense atom
    glows
A moment, then is quenched in a most cold repose.

21

Alas! that all we loved of him should be,   181
But for our grief, as if it had not been,
And grief itself be mortal!   Woe is me!
Whence are we, and why are we? of what scene
The actors or spectators?   Great and mean 185
Meet massed in death, who lends what life
    must borrow.

[1] The reference is to the unfavorable critic referred
to in Shelley's preface.
[2] brier.

As long as skies are blue and fields are green,
Evening must usher night, night urge the
    morrow,
Month follow month with woe, and year wake year
    to sorrow.

22

He will awake no more, oh, never more!   190
"Wake thou," cried Misery, "childless Mother,
    rise
Out of thy sleep, and slake, in thy heart's core,
A wound more fierce than his with tears and
    sighs."
And all the Dreams that watched Urania's eyes,
And all the Echoes whom their sister's song 195
Had held in holy silence, cried, "Arise!"
Swift as a Thought by the snake Memory stung,
From her ambrosial rest the fading Splendor
    sprung.

23

She rose like an autumnal Night, that springs
Out of the East, and follows wild and drear 200
The golden Day, which, on eternal wings,
Even as a ghost abandoning a bier,
Had left the Earth a corpse.   Sorrow and fear
So struck, so roused, so rapt Urania:
So saddened round her like an atmosphere 205
Of stormy mist; so swept her on her way
Even to the mournful place where Adonais lay.

24

Out of her secret Paradise she sped,
Through camps and cities rough with stone,
    and steel,
And human hearts, which to her airy tread 210
Yielding not, wounded the invisible
Palms of her tender feet where'er they fell;
And barbèd tongues, and thoughts more sharp
    than they,
Rent the soft Form they never could repel,
Whose sacred blood, like the young tears of
    May,   215
Paved with eternal flowers that undeserving way.

25

In the death-chamber for a moment Death,
Shamed by the presence of that living Might,
Blushed to annihilation, and the breath
Revisited those lips, and life's pale light 220
Flashed through those limbs, so late her dear
    delight.
"Leave me not wild and drear and comfortless,
As silent lightning leaves the starless night!
Leave me not!" cried Urania; her distress
Roused Death; Death rose and smiled, and met
    her vain caress.   225

26

"Stay yet awhile! speak to me once again;
Kiss me, so long but as a kiss may live;
And in my heartless breast and burning brain
That word, that kiss, shall all thoughts else
    survive,
With food of saddest memory kept alive,   230
Now thou art dead, as if it were a part
Of thee, my Adonais!   I would give
All that I am to be as thou now art!
But I am chained to Time, and cannot thence
    depart!

27

"O gentle child, beautiful as thou wert,   235
Why didst thou leave the trodden paths of men
Too soon, and with weak hands though mighty
    heart
Dare the unpastured dragon [1] in his den?
Defenceless as thou wert, oh, where was then
Wisdom the mirrored shield, or scorn the spear?
Or hadst thou waited the full cycle, when   241
Thy spirit should have filled its crescent sphere,
The monsters of life's waste had fled from thee
    like deer.

28

"The herded wolves, bold only to pursue;
The obscene ravens, clamorous o'er the dead; 245
The vultures to the conqueror's banner true,
Who feed where Desolation first has fed,
And whose wings rain contagion; — how they
    fled,
When, like Apollo, from his golden bow
The Pythian [2] of the age one arrow sped   250
And smiled! — The spoilers tempt no second
    blow,
They fawn on the proud feet that spurn them lying
    low.

29

"The sun comes forth, and many reptiles spawn;
He sets, and each ephemeral insect then
Is gathered into death without a dawn,   255
And the immortal stars awake again;
So is it in the world of living men:
A godlike mind soars forth, in its delight
Making earth bare and veiling heaven, and when
It sinks, the swarms that dimmed or shared its
    light   260
Leave to its kindred lamps the spirit's awful night."

[1] The world, humanity.
[2] Byron attacked the critics in his *English Bards and
Scotch Reviewers*.   He is here compared to Apollo who
slew the python.

30

Thus ceased she; and the mountain shepherds
    came,
Their garlands sere, their magic mantles rent;
The Pilgrim of Eternity,[1] whose fame
Over his living head like Heaven is bent,   265
An early but enduring monument,
Came, veiling all the lightnings of his song
In sorrow; from her wilds Ierne [2] sent
The sweetest lyrist [3] of her saddest wrong,
And love taught grief to fall like music from his
    tongue.

31

Midst others of less note, came one frail Form,[4]
A phantom among men; companionless
As the last cloud of an expiring storm
Whose thunder is its knell; he, as I guess,
Had gazed on Nature's naked loveliness,   275
Actæon-like,[5] and now he fled astray
With feeble steps o'er the world's wilderness,
And his own thoughts, along that rugged way,
Pursued, like raging hounds, their father and their
    prey.

32

A pardlike [6] Spirit beautiful and swift —   280
A Love in desolation masked; — a Power
Girt round with weakness; — it can scarce uplift
The weight of the superincumbent hour;
It is a dying lamp, a falling shower,
A breaking billow; — even whilst we speak   285
Is it not broken?   On the withering flower
The killing sun smiles brightly: on a cheek
The life can burn in blood, even while the heart
    may break.

33

His head was bound with pansies overblown,
And faded violets, white, and pied, and blue; 290
And a light spear topped with a cypress cone,
Round whose rude shaft dark ivy-tresses grew
Yet dripping with the forest's noonday dew,
Vibrated, as the ever-beating heart
Shook the weak hand that grasped it; of that
    crew   295
He came the last, neglected and apart;
A herd-abandoned deer struck by the hunter's dart.

[1] Byron.
[2] Ireland.
[3] Thomas Moore.
[4] Shelley.
[5] Because he had looked upon Artemis as she bathed,
Actæon, the hunter, was killed by his own dogs.
[6] leopard-like.

34

All stood aloof, and at his partial [1] moan
Smiled through their tears; well knew that gentle
    band
Who in another's fate now wept his own,　300
As in the accents of an unknown land
He sung new sorrow: sad Urania scanned
The Stranger's mien, and murmured: "Who art
    thou?"
He answered not, but with a sudden hand
Made bare his branded and ensanguined brow,
Which was like Cain's or Christ's — oh! that it
    should be so!　306

35

What softer voice is hushed over the dead?
Athwart what brow is that dark mantle thrown?
What form leans sadly o'er the white deathbed,
In mockery of monumental stone,　310
The heavy heart heaving without a moan?
If it be He,[2] who, gentlest of the wise,
Taught, soothed, loved, honored the departed
    one,
Let me not vex, with inharmonious sighs,
The silence of that heart's accepted sacrifice.　315

36

Our Adonais has drunk poison — oh!
What deaf and viperous murderer could crown
Life's early cup with such a draught of woe?
The nameless worm would now itself disown;
It felt, yet could escape, the magic tone　320
Whose prelude held all envy, hate, and wrong,
But what was howling in one breast alone,
Silent with expectation of the song,
Whose master's hand is cold, whose silver lyre
    unstrung.

37

Live thou,[3] whose infamy is not thy fame!　325
Live! fear no heavier chastisement from me,
Thou noteless blot on a remembered name!
But be thyself, and know thyself to be!
And ever at thy season be thou free
To spill the venom when thy fangs o'erflow;　330
Remorse and Self-contempt shall cling to thee;
Hot Shame shall burn upon thy secret brow,
And like a beaten hound tremble thou shalt — as
    now.

38

Nor let us weep that our delight is fled
Far from these carrion kites that scream below;

[1] affectionate.　　　　[2] Leigh Hunt.
[3] The adverse critic of Keats.

He wakes or sleeps with the enduring dead;　336
Thou canst not soar where he is sitting now.
Dust to the dust! but the pure spirit shall flow
Back to the burning fountain whence it came,
A portion of the Eternal, which must glow　340
Through time and change, unquenchably the
    same,
Whilst thy cold embers choke the sordid hearth
    of shame.

39

Peace, peace! he is not dead, he doth not sleep —
He hath awakened from the dream of life —
'Tis we, who, lost in stormy visions, keep　345
With phantoms an unprofitable strife,
And in mad trance strike with our spirit's knife
Invulnerable nothings. — *We* decay
Like corpses in a charnel; fear and grief
Convulse us and consume us day by day,　350
And cold hopes swarm like worms within our living
    clay.

40

He has outsoared the shadow of our night;
Envy and calumny and hate and pain,
And that unrest which men miscall delight,
Can touch him not and torture not again;　355
From the contagion of the world's slow stain
He is secure, and now can never mourn
A heart grown cold, a head grown gray in vain;
Nor, when the spirit's self has ceased to burn,
With sparkless ashes load an unlamented urn.　360

41

He lives, he wakes — 'tis Death is dead, not he;
Mourn not for Adonais. — Thou young Dawn,
Turn all thy dew to splendor, for from thee
The spirit thou lamentest is not gone;
Ye caverns and ye forests, cease to moan!　365
Cease, ye faint flowers and fountains, and thou
    Air,
Which like a mourning veil thy scarf hadst
    thrown
O'er the abandoned Earth, now leave it bare
Even to the joyous stars which smile on its despair!

42

He is made one with Nature: there is heard　370
His voice in all her music, from the moan
Of thunder to the song of night's sweet bird;
He is a presence to be felt and known
In darkness and in light, from herb and stone,
Spreading itself where'er that Power may move　376
Which has withdrawn his being to its own;
Which wields the world with never-wearied love,
Sustains it from beneath, and kindles it above.

43

He is a portion of the loveliness
Which once he made more lovely; he doth bear
His part, while the one Spirit's plastic stress   381
Sweeps through the dull dense world, compelling there
All new successions to the forms they wear;
Torturing the unwilling dross that checks its flight
To its own likeness, as each mass may bear,   385
And bursting in its beauty and its might
From trees and beasts and men into the Heaven's light.

44

The splendors of the firmament of time
May be eclipsed, but are extinguished not:
Like stars to their appointed height they climb,
And death is a low mist which cannot blot   391
The brightness it may veil.   When lofty thought
Lifts a young heart above its mortal lair,
And love and life contend in it for what
Shall be its earthly doom, the dead live there   395
And move like winds of light on dark and stormy air.

45

The inheritors of unfulfilled renown
Rose from their thrones, built beyond mortal thought,
Far in the Unapparent.   Chatterton
Rose pale, — his solemn agony had not   400
Yet faded from him; Sidney, as he fought
And as he fell and as he lived and loved
Sublimely mild, a Spirit without spot,
Arose; and Lucan,[1] by his death approved;
Oblivion as they rose shrank like a thing reproved.

46

And many more, whose names on Earth are dark,
                                    406
But whose transmitted effluence cannot die
So long as fire outlives the parent spark,
Rose, robed in dazzling immortality.
"Thou art become as one of us," they cry;   410
"It was for thee yon kingless sphere has long
Swung blind in unascended majesty,
Silent alone amid an Heaven of song.
Assume thy wingèd throne, thou Vesper of our throng!"

47

Who mourns for Adonais?   Oh, come forth,   415
Fond wretch! and know thyself and him aright.

[1] Chatterton, Sidney, and Lucan were all poets who died young, the first at eighteen, the second at thirty-two, and the third at twenty-six.

Clasp with thy panting soul the pendulous Earth.
As from a center, dart thy spirit's light
Beyond all worlds, until its spacious might
Satiate the void circumference; then shrink   420
Even to a point within our day and night;
And keep thy heart light lest it make thee sink
When hope has kindled hope, and lured thee to the brink.

48

Or go to Rome, which is the sepulchre,
Oh, not of him, but of our joy; 'tis nought   425
That ages, empires, and religions there
Lie buried in the ravage they have wrought;
For such as he can lend, — they borrow not
Glory from those who made the world their prey;
And he is gathered to the kings of thought   430
Who waged contention with their time's decay,
And of the past are all that cannot pass away.

49

Go thou to Rome, — at once the Paradise,
The grave, the city, and the wilderness;
And where its wrecks like shattered mountains rise,
And flowering weeds, and fragrant copses dress   435
The bones of Desolation's nakedness,
Pass, till the Spirit of the spot shall lead
Thy footsteps to a slope of green access,
Where, like an infant's smile, over the dead   440
A light of laughing flowers along the grass is spread:

50

And gray walls moulder round, on which dull Time
Feeds, like slow fire upon a hoary brand;
And one keen pyramid [1] with wedge sublime,
Pavilioning the dust of him who planned   445
This refuge for his memory, doth stand
Like flame transformed to marble; and beneath,
A field is spread, on which a newer band
Have pitched in Heaven's smile their camp of death,
Welcoming him we lose with scarce extinguished breath.   450

51

Here pause: these graves are all too young as yet
To have outgrown the sorrow which consigned
Its charge to each; and if the seal is set,
Here, on one fountain of a mourning mind,
Break it not thou! too surely shalt thou find   455
Thine own well full, if thou returnest home,
Of tears and gall.   From the world's bitter wind
Seek shelter in the shadow of the tomb.
What Adonais is, why fear we to become?

[1] Where Caius Cestius is buried.

52

The One remains, the many change and pass; 460
Heaven's light for ever shines, Earth's shadows
    fly;
Life, like a dome of many-colored glass,
Stains the white radiance of Eternity,
Until Death tramples it to fragments. — Die,
If thou wouldst be with that which thou dost
    seek!   465
Follow where all is fled! — Rome's azure sky,
Flowers, ruins, statues, music, words, are weak
The glory they transfuse with fitting truth to speak.

53

Why linger, why turn back, why shrink, my
    Heart?   469
Thy hopes are gone before; from all things here
They have departed; thou shouldst now depart!
A light is passed from the revolving year,
And man, and woman; and what still is dear
Attracts to crush, repels to make thee wither.
The soft sky smiles, — the low wind whispers
    near;   475
'Tis Adonais calls! oh, hasten thither,
No more let Life divide what Death can join to-
    gether.

54

That Light whose smile kindles the Universe,
That Beauty in which all things work and move,
That Benediction which the eclipsing Curse   480
Of birth can quench not, that sustaining Love
Which through the web of being blindly wove
By man and beast and earth and air and sea,
Burns bright or dim, as each are mirrors of
The fire for which all thirst, now beams on me,
Consuming the last clouds of cold mortality.   486

55

The breath whose might I have invoked in song
Descends on me; my spirit's bark is driven
Far from the shore, far from the trembling throng
Whose sails were never to the tempest given;   490
The massy earth and spherèd skies are riven!
I am borne darkly, fearfully, afar;
Whilst, burning through the inmost veil of
    Heaven,
The soul of Adonais, like a star,
Beacons from the abode where the Eternal are.   495

To ——

1

One word is too often profaned
    For me to profane it,

One feeling too falsely disdained
    For thee to disdain it;
One hope is too like despair   5
    For prudence to smother,
And pity from thee more dear
    Than that from another.

2

I can give not what men call love,
    But wilt thou accept not   10
The worship the heart lifts above
    And the Heavens reject not, —
The desire of the moth for the star,
    Of the night for the morrow,
The devotion to something afar   15
    From the sphere of our sorrow?

Prometheus Unbound

THE FUTURE OF SOCIETY

In the tragedy of *Prometheus Bound* by Æschylus
the Titan Prometheus was, for an offense against Jupiter, bound to the side of a mountain in the Caucasus.
Here he was subjected to fearful tortures, such as that
of having a vulture constantly feeding on his liver. In
Shelley's poem, Prometheus, through the intercession
of Love or the principle of goodness inherent in nature,
is freed and Jupiter relegated to a life of darkness in the
nether world. Prometheus, in the words of Shelley,
is "the type of the highest perfection of moral and intellectual nature, impelled by the purest and truest
motives to the best and noblest ends."

In the selections which follow we catch a glimpse of
Shelley's conception of the ideal man, his power for
good, and the condition of the reborn world once man
fully trusts his ideals.

Prometheus. We feel what thou hast heard and
    seen: yet speak.
Spirit of the Hour.   Soon as the sound had ceased
    whose thunder filled
The abysses of the sky and the wide earth,
There was a change: the impalpable thin air
And the all-circling sunlight were transformed,   5
As if the sense of love dissolved in them
Had folded itself round the spherèd world.
My vision then grew clear, and I could see
Into the mysteries of the universe:
Dizzy as with delight I floated down,   10
Winnowing the lightsome air with languid plumes,
My coursers sought their birthplace in the sun,
Where they henceforth will live exempt from toil,
Pasturing flowers of vegetable fire;
And where my moonlike car will stand within   15
A temple, gazed upon by Phidian forms
Of thee, and Asia, and the Earth, and me,

And you fair nymphs looking the love we feel, —
In memory of the tidings it has borne, —
Beneath a dome fretted with graven flowers, 20
Poised on twelve columns of resplendent stone,
And open to the bright and liquid sky.
Yoked to it by an amphisbænic [1] snake
The likeness of those wingèd steeds will mock
The flight from which they find repose. Alas, 25
Whither has wandered now my partial tongue
When all remains untold which ye would hear?
As I have said, I floated to the earth:
It was, as it is still, the pain of bliss
To move, to breathe, to be; I wandering went 30
Among the haunts and dwellings of mankind,
And first was disappointed not to see
Such mighty change as I had felt within
Expressed in outward things; but soon I looked, 34
And behold, thrones were kingless, and men walked
One with the other even as spirits do,
None fawned, none trampled; hate, disdain, or fear,
Self-love or self-contempt, on human brows
No more inscribed, as o'er the gate of hell,
"All hope abandon ye who enter here"; 40
None frowned, none trembled, none with eager fear
Gazed on another's eye of cold command,
Until the subject of a tyrant's will
Became, worse fate, the abject of his own,
Which spurred him, like an outspent horse, to
    death.
None wrought his lips in truth-entangling lines 45
Which smiled the lie his tongue disdained to speak;
None, with firm sneer, trod out in his own heart
The sparks of love and hope till these remained
Those bitter ashes, a soul self-consumed, 50
And the wretch crept a vampire among men,
Infecting all with his own hideous ill;
None talked that common, false, cold, hollow talk
Which makes the heart deny the *yes* it breathes,
Yet question that unmeant hypocrisy 55
With such a self-mistrust as has no name.
And women, too, frank, beautiful, and kind
As the free heaven which rains fresh light and
    dew
On the wide earth, past; gentle radiant forms,
From custom's evil taint exempt and pure; 60
Speaking the wisdom once they could not think,
Looking emotions once they feared to feel;
And changed to all which once they dared not be,
Yet being now, made earth like heaven; nor
    pride,
Nor jealousy, nor envy, nor ill shame, 65
The bitterest of those drops of treasured gall,
Spoilt the sweet taste of the nepenthe, love.

[1] Two-headed, capable of moving forward or backward.

Thrones, altars, judgment-seats, and prisons;
    wherein,
And beside which, by wretched men were borne
Sceptres, tiaras, swords, and chains, and tomes 70
Of reasoned wrong, glozed on by ignorance,
Were like those monstrous and barbaric shapes,
The ghosts of a no-more-remembered fame,
Which, from their unworn obelisks, look forth
In triumph o'er the palaces and tombs 75
Of those who were their conquerors: mouldering
    round,
These imaged to the pride of kings and priests
A dark yet mighty faith, a power as wide
As is the world it wasted, and are now
But an astonishment; even so the tools 80
And emblems of its last captivity,
Amid the dwellings of the peopled earth,
Stand, not o'erthrown, but unregarded now.
And those foul shapes, abhorred by god and man, —
Which, under many a name and many a form 85
Strange, savage, ghastly, dark and execrable,
Were Jupiter, the tyrant of the world;
And which the nations, panic-stricken, served
With blood, and hearts broken by long hope, and
    love
Dragged to his altars soiled and garlandless, 90
And slain amid men's unreclaiming tears,
Flattering the thing they feared, which fear was
    hate, —
Frown, mouldering fast, o'er their abandoned
    shrines:
The painted veil, by those who were, called life,
Which mimicked, as with colors idly spread, 95
All men believed or hoped, is torn aside;
The loathsome mask has fallen, the man remains
Sceptreless, free, uncircumscribed, but man
Equal, unclassed, tribeless, and nationless,
Exempt from awe, worship, degree, the king 100
Over himself; just, gentle, wise: but man
Passionless? —— no, yet free from guilt or pain,
Which were, for his will made or suffered them,
Nor yet exempt, though ruling them like slaves,
From chance, and death, and mutability, 10
The clogs of that which else might oversoar
The loftiest star of unascended heaven,
Pinnacled dim in the intense inane.

THE ABILITY OF MAN

Man, oh, not men! a chain of linkèd thought,
Of love and might to be divided not,
Compelling the elements with adamantine stress;
As the sun rules, even with a tyrant's gaze,
The unquiet republic of the maze 5
Of planets, struggling fierce towards heaven's free
    wilderness.

Man, one harmonious soul of many a soul,
Whose nature is its own divine control,
Where all things flow to all, as rivers to the sea;
Familiar acts are beautiful through love;   10
Labor, and pain, and grief, in life's green grove
Sport like tame beasts, none knew how gentle
    they could be!

His will, with all mean passions, bad delights,
And selfish cares, its trembling satellites,
A spirit ill to guide, but mighty to obey,   15
Is as a tempest-wingèd ship, whose helm
Love rules, through waves which dare not over-
    whelm,
Forcing life's wildest shores to own its sovereign
    sway.

All things confess his strength. Through the
    cold mass
Of marble and of color his dreams pass;   20
Bright threads whence mothers weave the robes
    their children wear;
Language is a perpetual Orphic song,
Which rules with Dædal [1] harmony a throng
Of thoughts and forms, which else senseless and
    shapeless were.

The lightning is his slave; heaven's utmost deep
Gives up her stars, and like a flock of sheep   26
They pass before his eye, are numbered, and roll
    on!
The tempest is his steed, he strides the air;
And the abyss shouts from her depth laid bare.

[1] Intricately contrived.

Heaven, hast thou secrets? Man unveils me; I
    have none.   30

THE GOAL REACHED

This is the day, which down the void abysm
At the Earth-born's spell yawns for Heaven's
    despotism,
    And Conquest is dragged captive through the
    deep:
Love, from its awful throne of patient power
In the wise heart, from the last giddy hour   5
    Of dread endurance, from the slippery, steep,
And narrow verge of crag-like agony, springs
And folds over the world its healing wings.

Gentleness, Virtue, Wisdom, and Endurance,
These are the seals of that most firm assurance   10
    Which bars the pit over Destruction's strength;
And if, with infirm hand, Eternity,
Mother of many acts and hours, should free
    The serpent that would clasp her with its length:
These are the spells by which to reassume   15
An empire o'er the disentangled doom.

To suffer woes which Hope thinks infinite;
To forgive wrongs darker than death or night;
    To defy Power, which seems omnipotent;
To love, and bear; to hope till Hope creates   20
From its own wreck the thing it contemplates;
    Neither to change, nor falter, nor repent;
This, like thy glory, Titan, is to be
Good, great and joyous, beautiful and free;
This is alone Life, Joy, Empire, and Victory.   25

John Keats · 1795-1821

John Keats was born October 31, 1795, in Finnsbury, London, and died in Rome February 23, 1821, at the age of twenty-five. His active career as a writer was restricted to approximately five years.

Keats' father was the keeper of the stables at the Swan and Hoop Inn, his mother the daughter of the inn-keeper. For a few years the young Keats attended a good private school maintained by a Mr. Clark at Enfield, but when the boy was fifteen his mother's death left him an orphan, and a practical-minded guardian apprenticed him to a surgeon. Keats appears to have taken kindly to the medical profession, although he left the surgeon to whom he had been apprenticed, to study in the London hospitals from 1815 through 1816. He actually performed a few operations and was licensed to practice. Cowden Clark, the son of his former schoolmaster, had read with him frequently, had kept him supplied with books during the period of his study of surgery, and had generally kindled in him a fondness for literature. In May, 1816, Leigh Hunt published Keats' sonnet *On First Looking into Chapman's Homer* and, sometime during the winter of 1816-17, the young man, just turned twenty-one, determined to give up the scalpel for the pen. In 1818 appeared *Endymion*, a poem most scurrilously attacked in the leading reviews of the day. The same year brought two menacing events: Keats was forced to give up a walking trip because of the beginning inroads of tuberculosis, and that December his brother Tom died from the same disease. Keats may well have suspected, particularly since his mother had died from a similar ailment only eight years before, that his own years were to be few.

However, with the turn into the new year, 1819, Keats was to know a few months of delirious happiness. While visiting at the home of Charles Brown, the friend with whom he had been on the walking trip, he met Fanny Brawne and fell in love with her. To this new happiness, Keats found facile expression in poetry. Within a few months he had written *The Eve of St. Agnes*, the odes *On a Grecian Urn*, *To a Nightingale*, and *To Autumn*, the narrative *Lamia*, and collaborated with Brown on a play called *Otho the Great*. But the intense activity of his writing and the passion of his love affair undermined his health. The late winter found Keats in the throes of disease. He was nursed carefully by the Hunts and the Brawnes, but his physician, and his own knowledge, assured him that another winter in the north would prove fatal. In the company of Joseph Severn, a painter friend, he left for Italy. He is reported to have asked his physician, "Doctor, when will this posthumous life of mine come to an end?" It came to an end the next February in Rome. He was buried in the Protestant cemetery there under an epitaph of his own writing: "Here lies one whose name was writ in water."

During his life, Keats published three volumes of poetry: *Poems* (1817), *Endymion* (1818), and *Lamia, Isabella, The Eve of St. Agnes, and Other Poems* (1820). Some few fugitive pieces were published after his death. At its best, the poetry of Keats is distinguished for its high artistry, its sensuous quality, its idealization of life through the imagination. The poet believed strongly in his own conception of truth, a truth found not through examination of scientific data, not through an examination of historical facts, but a higher, perhaps transcendental truth, manifest to one who, in seeing life imaginatively, finds beauty. Romantic qualities are at once obvious in his melancholy, in his interest in the past and in the supernatural.

SUGGESTED REFERENCES: J. M. Murry, *Keats* (new rev. ed., 1955); W. J. Bate, *John Keats* (1963) and ed., *Keats. A Collection of Critical Essays* (1964).

On First Looking into Chapman's *Homer*

This poem was written after a night's reading, with his friend Charles Clark, of Chapman's translation of Homer.

Much have I traveled in the realms of gold,
And many goodly states and kingdoms seen;
Round many western islands have I been
Which bards in fealty to Apollo hold.
Oft of one wide expanse had I been told,   5
That deep-browed Homer ruled as his demesne:
Yet did I never breathe its pure serene
Till I heard Chapman speak out loud and bold:
Then felt I like some watcher of the skies
When a new planet swims into his ken;   10
Or like stout Cortez [1] when with eagle eyes
[1] Keats should have written *Balboa*.

He stared at the Pacific — and all his men
Looked at each other with a wild surmise —
Silent, upon a peak in Darien.

Endymion

BOOK I

PROEM

A thing of beauty is a joy for ever:
Its loveliness increases; it will never
Pass into nothingness; but still will keep
A bower quiet for us, and a sleep
Full of sweet dreams, and health, and quiet breath-
    ing.   5
Therefore, on every morrow, are we wreathing
A flowery band to bind us to the earth.
Spite of despondence, of the inhuman dearth

Of noble natures, of the gloomy days,
Of all the unhealthy and o'er-darkened ways   10
Made for our searching: yes, in spite of all,
Some shape of beauty moves away the pall
From our dark spirits.   Such the sun, the moon,
Trees old and young, sprouting a shady boon
For simple sheep; and such are daffodils   15
With the green world they live in; and clear rills
That for themselves a cooling covert make
'Gainst the hot season; the mid-forest brake,
Rich with a sprinkling of fair musk-rose blooms:
And such too is the grandeur of the dooms   20
We have imagined for the mighty dead;
All lovely tales that we have heard or read:
An endless fountain of immortal drink,
Pouring unto us from the heaven's brink.

Nor do we merely feel these essences   25
For one short hour; no, even as the trees
That whisper round a temple become soon
Dear as the temple's self, so does the moon,
The passion poesy, glories infinite,
Haunt us till they become a cheering light   30
Unto our souls, and bound to us so fast,
That, whether there be shine, or gloom o'ercast,
They always must be with us, or we die.

Therefore, 'tis with full happiness that I
Will trace the story of Endymion.   35
The very music of the name has gone
Into my being, and each pleasant scene
Is growing fresh before me as the green
Of our own valleys: so I will begin
Now while I cannot hear the city's din;   40
Now while the early budders are just new,
And run in mazes of the youngest hue
About old forests; while the willow trails
Its delicate amber; and the dairy pails
Bring home increase of milk.   And, as the year   45
Grows lush in juicy stalks, I'll smoothly steer
My little boat, for many quiet hours,
With streams that deepen freshly into bowers.
Many and many a verse I hope to write,
Before the daisies, vermeil rimm'd and white,   50
Hide in deep herbage; and ere yet the bees
Hum about globes of clover and sweet peas,
I must be near the middle of my story.
O may no wintry season, bare and hoary,
See it half finished: but let Autumn bold,   55
With universal tinge of sober gold,
Be all about me when I make an end.
And now at once, adventuresome, I send
My herald thought into a wilderness:
There let its trumpet blow, and quickly dress   60
My uncertain path with green, that I may speed
Easily onward, thorough flowers and weed.

When I Have Fears That I May Cease to Be

When I have fears that I may cease to be
Before my pen has gleaned my teeming brain,
Before high-piled books, in charactery,
Hold like rich garners the full ripened grain;
When I behold, upon the night's starred face,   5
Huge cloudy symbols of a high romance,
And think that I may never live to trace
Their shadows, with the magic hand of chance;
And when I feel, fair creature of an hour,
That I shall never look upon thee more,   10
Never have relish in the faery power
Of unreflecting love: — then on the shore
Of the wide world I stand alone, and think
Till love and fame to nothingness do sink.

Robin Hood

TO A FRIEND

No! those days are gone away,
And their hours are old and grey,
And their minutes buried all
Under the down-trodden pall
Of the leaves of many years: 5
Many times have winter's shears,
Frozen North, and chilling East,
Sounded tempests to the feast
Of the forest's whispering fleeces,
Since men knew nor rent nor leases.   10

No, the bugle sounds no more;
And the twanging bow no more;
Silent is the ivory shrill
Past the heath and up the hill;
There is no mid-forest laugh,   15
Where lone Echo gives the half
To some wight, amaz'd to hear
Jesting, deep in forest drear.

On the fairest time of June
You may go, with sun or moon,   20
Or the seven stars to light you;
Or the polar ray to right you;
But you never may behold
Little John, or Robin bold;
Never one, of all the clan,   25
Thrumming on an empty can
Some old hunting ditty, while
He doth his green way beguile
To fair hostess Merriment,
Down beside the pasture Trent;   30
For he left the merry tale
Messenger for spicy ale.

Gone, the merry morris din;
Gone, the song of Gamelyn;
Gone, the tough-belted outlaw   35
Idling in the "grenè shawe";
All are gone away and past!
And if Robin should be cast
Sudden from his turfed grave,
And if Marian should have   40
Once again her forest days,
She would weep, and he would craze:
He would swear, for all his oaks,
Fall'n beneath the dockyard strokes,
Have rotted on the briny sea;   45
She would weep that her wild bees
Sang not to her — strange! that honey
Can't be got without hard money!

So it is: yet let us sing,
Honor to the old bow-string!   50
Honor to the bugle-horn!
Honor to the woods unshorn!
Honor to the Lincoln green!
Honor to the archer keen!
Honor to tight little John,   55
And the horse he rode upon!
Honor to bold Robin Hood,
Sleeping in the underwood!
Honor to maid Marian,
And to all the Sherwood-clan!   60
Though their days have hurried by
Let us too a burden try.

Lines on the Mermaid Tavern

Souls of Poets dead and gone,
What Elysium have ye known,
Happy field or mossy cavern,
Choicer than the Mermaid Tavern?
Have ye tippled drink more fine   5
Than mine host's Canary wine?
Or are fruits of Paradise
Sweeter than those dainty pies
Of venison? A generous food!
Drest as though bold Robin Hood   10
Would, with his maid Marian,
Sup and browse from horn and can.

I have heard that on a day
Mine host's sign-board flew away,
Nobody knew whither, till   15
An astrologer's old quill
To a sheepskin gave the story,
Said he saw you in your glory,
Underneath a new old sign
Sipping beverage divine,   20

And pledging with contented smack
The Mermaid in the Zodiac.

Souls of Poets dead and gone,
What Elysium have ye known,
Happy field or mossy cavern,
Choicer than the Mermaid Tavern?   25

The Eve of St. Agnes

The medieval setting of this poem reflects the romantic's turn to the past. The poem is distinctly Keatsian in its rich imagery and color, its presentation of the sensuous. The superstition on which the poem is based holds that a maid, after performing certain rites, will behold her future husband in her dreams.

1

St. Agnes' Eve [1] — Ah, bitter chill it was!
The owl, for all his feathers, was a-cold;
The hare limped trembling through the frozen grass,
And silent was the flock in woolly fold:
Numb were the Beadsman's [2] fingers, while he told   5
His rosary, and while his frosted breath,
Like pious incense from a censer old,
Seemed taking flight for heaven, without a death,
Past the sweet Virgin's picture, while his prayer he saith.

2

His prayer he saith, this patient, holy man;   10
Then takes his lamp, and riseth from his knees,
And back returneth, meagre, barefoot, wan,
Along the chapel aisle by slow degrees:
The sculptured dead, on each side, seem to freeze,
Emprisoned in black, purgatorial rails: 15
Knights, ladies, praying in dumb orat'ries, [3]
He passeth by; and his weak spirit fails
To think how they may ache in icy hoods and mails.

3

Northward he turneth through a little door,
And scarce three steps, ere Music's golden tongue   20
Flattered to tears this aged man and poor;

[1] January 21 is St. Agnes Day.
[2] One who receives alms in exchange for his prayers for the welfare of the founders.
[3] Small chapels used for prayer. They are "dumb" since the worshippers are all sculptured figures.

But no — already had his death-bell rung:
The joys of all his life were said and sung:
His was harsh penance on St. Agnes' Eve:
Another way he went, and soon among   25
Rough ashes sat he for his soul's reprieve,
And all night kept awake, for sinners' sake to
grieve.

4

That ancient Beadsman heard the prelude soft;
And so it chanced, for many a door was wide,
From hurry to and fro.   Soon, up aloft,   30
The silver, snarling trumpets 'gan to chide:
The level chambers, ready with their pride,
Were glowing to receive a thousand guests:
The carved angels, ever eager-eyed,
Stared, where upon their heads the cornice rests,
With hair blown back, and wings put crosswise on
their breasts.   36

5

At length burst in the argent revelry,
With plume, tiara, and all rich array,
Numerous as shadows haunting faerily
The brain, new-stuffed, in youth, with triumphs
gay   40
Of old romance.   These let us wish away,
And turn, sole-thoughted, to one Lady there,
Whose heart had brooded, all that wintry day,
On love, and winged St. Agnes' saintly care,
As she had heard old dames full many times de-
clare.   45

6

They told her how, upon St. Agnes' Eve,
Young virgins might have visions of delight,
And soft adorings from their loves receive
Upon the honeyed middle of the night,
If ceremonies due they did aright;   50
As, supperless to bed they must retire,
And couch supine their beauties, lily white;
Nor look behind, nor sideways, but require
Of Heaven with upward eyes for all that they de-
sire.

7

Full of this whim was thoughtful Madeline: 55
The music, yearning like a God in pain,
She scarcely heard: her maiden eyes divine,
Fixed on the floor, saw many a sweeping train [1]
Pass by — she heeded not at all: in vain
Came many a tiptoe, amorous cavalier,   60
And back retired; not cooled by high disdain,
But she saw not: her heart was otherwhere;
She sighed for Agnes' dreams, the sweetest of the
year.
[1] Skirts sweeping the floor.

8

She danced along with vague, regardless eyes,
Anxious her lips, her breathing quick and short:
The hallowed hour was near at hand: she sighs   66
Amid the timbrels,[1] and the thronged resort
Of whisperers in anger, or in sport;
'Mid looks of love, defiance, hate, and scorn,
Hoodwinked with faery fancy; all amort,[2]   70
Save to St. Agnes and her lambs,[3] unshorn,
And all the bliss to be before to-morrow morn.

9

So, purposing each moment to retire,
She lingered still.   Meantime, across the moors,
Had come young Porphyro, with heart on fire   75
For Madeline.   Beside the portal doors,
Buttressed from moonlight, stands he, and im-
plores
All saints to give him sight of Madeline,
But for one moment in the tedious hours,
That he might gaze and worship all unseen;   80
Perchance speak, kneel, touch, kiss — in sooth
such things have been.

10

He ventures in: let no buzzed whisper tell:
All eyes be muffled, or a hundred swords
Will storm his heart, Love's fev'rous citadel:
For him, those chambers held barbarian hordes,
Hyena foemen, and hot-blooded lords,   86
Whose very dogs would execrations howl
Against his lineage: not one breast affords
Him any mercy, in that mansion foul,
Save one old beldame, weak in body and in soul.   90

11

Ah, happy chance! the aged creature came,
Shuffling along with ivory-headed wand,
To where he stood, hid from the torch's flame,
Behind a broad hall-pillar, far beyond
The sound of merriment and chorus bland: 95
He startled her; but soon she knew his face,
And grasped his fingers in her palsied hand,
Saying, "Mercy, Porphyro! hie thee from this
place;
They are all here to-night, the whole blood-thirsty
race!

12

"Get hence! get hence! there's dwarfish Hildebrand;   100
He had a fever late, and in the fit

[1] A tambourine-like instrument.
[2] dead.
[3] The symbol of St. Agnes was a lamb.   Two unshorn
lambs were annually sacrificed to her in the ceremony.

He cursed thee and thine, both house and land:
Then there's that old Lord Maurice, not a whit
More tame for his gray hairs — Alas me! flit!
Flit like a ghost away." — "Ah, Gossip dear, 105
We're safe enough; here in this armchair sit,
And tell me how" — "Good Saints! not here,
    not here;
Follow me, child, or else these stones will be thy
    bier."

13

He followed through a lowly arched way,
Brushing the cobwebs with his lofty plume; 110
And as she muttered "Well-a — well-a-day!"
He found him in a little moonlight room,
Pale, latticed, chill, and silent as a tomb.
"Now tell me where is Madeline," said he,
"O tell me, Angela, by the holy loom 115
Which none but secret sisterhood may see,
When they St. Agnes' wool are weaving, piously."

14

"St. Agnes! Ah! it is St. Agnes' Eve —
Yet men will murder upon holy days:
Thou must hold water in a witch's sieve, 120
And be liege-lord of all the Elves and Fays,
To venture so: it fills me with amaze
To see thee, Porphyro! — St. Agnes' Eve!
God's help! my lady fair the conjuror plays
This very night: good angels her deceive! 125
But let me laugh awhile, I've mickle[1] time to
    grieve."

15

Feebly she laugheth in the languid moon,
While Porphyro upon her face doth look,
Like puzzled urchin on an aged crone
Who keepeth closed a wond'rous riddlebook, 130
As spectacled she sits in chimney nook.
But soon his eyes grew brilliant, when she told
His lady's purpose; and he scarce could brook
Tears, at the thought of those enchantments
    cold,
And Madeline asleep in lap of legends old. 135

16

Sudden a thought came like a full-blown rose,
Flushing his brow, and in his pained heart
Made purple riot: then doth he propose
A stratagem, that makes the beldame start:
"A cruel man and impious thou art: 140
Sweet lady, let her pray, and sleep, and dream
Alone with her good angels, far apart
From wicked men like thee. Go, go! I deem
Thou canst not surely be the same that thou didst
    seem."

[1] much.

17

"I will not harm her, by all saints I swear," 145
Quoth Porphyro: "O may I ne'er find grace
When my weak voice shall whisper its last prayer,
If one of her soft ringlets I displace,
Or look with ruffian passion in her face:
Good Angela, believe me by these tears; 150
Or I will, even in a moment's space,
Awake, with horrid shout, my foemen's ears,
And beard them, though they be more fanged than
    wolves and bears."

18

"Ah! why wilt thou affright a feeble soul? 154
A poor, weak, palsy-stricken, churchyard thing,
Whose passing-bell may ere the midnight toll;
Whose prayers for thee, each morn and evening,
Were never missed." Thus plaining, doth she
    bring
A gentler speech from burning Porphyro;
So woful, and of such deep sorrowing, 160
That Angela gives promise she will do
Whatever he shall wish, betide her weal or woe.

19

Which was, to lead him, in close secrecy,
Even to Madeline's chamber, and there hide
Him in a closet, of such privacy 165
That he might see her beauty unespied,
And win perhaps that night a peerless bride,
While legioned faeries paced the coverlet,
And pale enchantment held her sleepy-eyed.
Never on such a night have lovers met, 170
Since Merlin paid his Demon[1] all the monstrous
    debt.

20

"It shall be as thou wishest," said the Dame:
"All cates[2] and dainties shall be stored there
Quickly on this feast-night: by the tambor frame[3]
Her own lute thou wilt see: no time to spare, 175
For I am slow and feeble, and scarce dare
On such a catering trust my dizzy head.
Wait here, my child, with patience; kneel in
    prayer
The while: Ah! thou must needs the lady wed,
Or may I never leave my grave among the dead."

21

So saying, she hobbled off with busy fear. 181
The lover's endless minutes slowly passed;

[1] Merlin, a magician, was the son of a demon and
owed, presumably, a debt to the Devil for the gift of
magic granted him. He "paid" the debt when he was
done away with through the magic of Vivien, an en-
chantress, whom he had taught his secret.

[2] provisions.   [3] embroidery frame.

The Dame returned, and whispered in his ear
To follow her; with aged eyes aghast
From fright of dim espial. Safe at last,　185
Through many a dusky gallery, they gain
The maiden's chamber, silken, hushed and
　　chaste;
Where Porphyro took covert, pleased amain.[1]
His poor guide hurried back with agues in her
　　brain.

22

Her faltering hand upon the balustrade,　190
Old Angela was feeling for the stair,
When Madeline, St. Agnes' charmed maid,
Rose, like a missioned spirit, unaware:
With silver taper's light, and pious care,
She turned, and down the aged gossip led　195
To a safe level matting. Now prepare,
Young Porphyro, for gazing on that bed;
She comes, she comes again, like ring-dove frayed[2]
　　and fled.

23

Out went the taper as she hurried in;
Its little smoke, in pallid moonshine, died:　200
She closed the door, she panted, all akin
To spirits of the air, and visions wide:
No uttered syllable, or, woe betide!
But to her heart, her heart was voluble,
Paining with eloquence her balmy side;　205
As though a tongueless nightingale should swell
Her throat in vain, and die, heart-stifled in her
　　dell.

24

A casement high and triple-arched there was,
All garlanded with carven imag'ries
Of fruits, and flowers, and bunches of knot-
　　grass,　210
And diamonded with panes of quaint device,
Innumerable of stains and splendid dyes,
As are the tiger-moth's deep-damasked wings;
And in the mist, 'mong thousand heraldries,
And twilight saints, and dim emblazonings,　215
A shielded scutcheon blushed with blood of queens
　　and kings.

25

Full on this casement shone the wintry moon,
And threw warm gules[3] on Madeline's fair
　　breast,
As down she knelt for heaven's grace and boon;
Rose-bloom fell on her hands, together prest,　220
And on her silver cross soft amethyst,
And on her hair a glory, like a saint:
[1] mightily.　　　[2] frightened.　　　[3] blood-red.

She seem'd a splendid angel, newly drest,
Save wings, for heaven: — Porphyro grew faint:
She knelt, so pure a thing, so free from mortal
　　taint.　225

26

Anon his heart revives: her vespers done,
Of all its wreathed pearls her hair she frees;
Unclasps her warmed jewels one by one;
Loosens her fragrant bodice; by degrees
Her rich attire creeps rustling to her knees:　230
Half-hidden, like a mermaid in sea-weed,
Pensive awhile she dreams awake, and sees,
In fancy, fair St. Agnes in her bed,
But dares not look behind, or all the charm is fled.

27

Soon, trembling in her soft and chilly nest,　235
In sort of wakeful swoon, perplexed she lay,
Until the poppied warmth of sleep oppressed
Her soothed limbs, and soul fatigued away;
Flown, like a thought, until the morrow-day;
Blissfully havened both from joy and pain;　240
Clasped like a missal[1] where swart Paynims[2]
　　pray;
Blinded alike from sunshine and from rain,
As though a rose should shut, and be a bud again.

28

Stol'n to this paradise, and so entranced,
Porphyro gazed upon her empty dress,　245
And listened to her breathing, if it chanced
To wake into a slumberous tenderness;
Which when he heard, that minute did he bless,
And breathed himself: then from the closet crept,
Noiseless as fear in a wide wilderness,　250
And over the hushed carpet, silent, stept,
And 'tween the curtains peeped, where lo! — how
　　fast she slept.

29

Then by the bed-side, where the faded moon
Made a dim, silver twilight, soft he set
A table, and, half anguished, threw thereon　255
A cloth of woven crimson, gold, and jet: —
O for some drowsy Morphean amulet!
The boisterous, midnight, festive clarion,
The kettle-drum, and far-heard clarionet,　259
Affray his ears, though but in dying tone: —
The hall-door shuts again, and all the noise is gone.

30

And still she slept an azure-lidded sleep,
In blanched linen, smooth, and lavendered,
While he from forth the closet brought a heap
[1] prayer-book.　　　[2] Pagans.

Of candied apple, quince, and plum, and gourd;
With jellies soother [1] than the creamy curd, 266
And lucent syrops, tinct with cinnamon;
Manna and dates, in argosy transferred
From Fez; and spiced dainties, every one,
From silken Samarcand [2] to cedared Lebanon.[3]

31

These delicates he heaped with glowing hand
On golden dishes and in baskets bright 272
Of wreathed silver: sumptuous they stand
In the retired quiet of the night,
Filling the chilly room with perfume light. —
"And now, my love, my seraph fair, awake! 276
Thou art my heaven, and I thine eremite: [4]
Open thine eyes, for meek St. Agnes' sake,
Or I shall drowse beside thee, so my soul doth
ache."

32

Thus whispering, his warm, unnerved arm 280
Sank in her pillow. Shaded was her dream
By the dusk curtains: — 'twas a midnight charm
Impossible to melt as iced stream:
The lustrous salvers in the moonlight gleam;
Broad golden fringe upon the carpet lies: 285
It seemed he never, never could redeem
From such a steadfast spell his lady's eyes;
So mused awhile, entoiled in woofed phantasies.

33

Awakening up, he took her hollow lute, —
Tumultuous, — and, in chords that tenderest
be, 290
He played an ancient ditty, long since mute,
In Provence called "La belle dame sans mercy":
Close to her ear touching the melody; —
Wherewith disturbed, she uttered a soft moan:
He ceased — she panted quick — and suddenly
Her blue affrayed eyes wide open shone: 296
Upon his knees he sank, pale as smooth-sculptured
stone.

34

Her eyes were open, but she still beheld,
Now wide awake, the vision of her sleep:
There was a painful change, that nigh expelled
The blisses of her dream so pure and deep 301
At which fair Madeline began to weep,
And moan forth witless words with many a sigh;

[1] smoother.
[2] A city in Turkestan noted for its manufacture of silk.
[3] The timbers for Solomon's Temple came from the cedars of Lebanon in southern Syria.
[4] hermit.

While still her gaze on Porphyro would keep;
Who knelt, with joined hands and piteous eye,
Fearing to move or speak, she looked so dream-
ingly. 306

35

"Ah, Porphyro!" said she, "but even now
Thy voice was at sweet tremble in mine ear,
Made tuneable with every sweetest vow;
And those sad eyes were spiritual and clear: 310
How changed thou art! how pallid, chill, and
drear!
Give me that voice again, my Porphyro,
Those looks immortal, those complainings dear!
Oh leave me not in this eternal woe,
For if thou diest, my Love, I know not where to
go." 315

36

Beyond a mortal man impassioned far
At these voluptuous accents, he arose,
Ethereal, flushed, and like a throbbing star
Seen mid the sapphire heaven's deep repose;
Into her dream he melted, as the rose 320
Blendeth its odor with the violet, —
Solution sweet: meantime the frost-wind blows
Like Love's alarum pattering the sharp sleet
Against the window-panes; St. Agnes' moon hath
set.

37

'Tis dark: quick pattereth the flaw-blown [1]
sleet: 325
"This is no dream, my bride, my Madeline!"
'Tis dark: the iced gusts still rave and beat:
"No dream, alas! alas! and woe is mine!
Porphyro will leave me here to fade and pine. —
Cruel! what traitor could thee hither bring? 330
I curse not, for my heart is lost in thine,
Though thou forsakest a deceived thing; —
A dove forlorn and lost with sick unpruned wing."

38

"My Madeline! sweet dreamer! lovely bride!
Say, may I be for aye thy vassal blest? 335
Thy beauty's shield, heart-shaped and vermeil [2]
dyed?
Ah, silver shrine, here will I take my rest
After so many hours of toil and quest,
A famished pilgrim, — saved by miracle.
Though I have found, I will not rob thy nest 340
Saving of thy sweet self; if thou think'st well
To trust, fair Madeline, to no rude infidel.

[1] wind-blown.
[2] vermilion.

39

"Hark! 'tis an elfin storm from faery land,
Of haggard seeming, but a boon indeed:
Arise — arise! the morning is at hand: —   345
The bloated wassailers will never heed: —
Let us away, my love, with happy speed;
There are no ears to hear, or eyes to see, —
Drowned all in Rhenish and the sleepy mead:
Awake! arise! my love, and fearless be,   350
For o'er the southern moors I have a home for
    thee."

40

She hurried at his words, beset with fears,
For there were sleeping dragons all around,
At glaring watch, perhaps, with ready spears —
Down the wide stairs a darkling way they
    found. —   355
In all the house was heard no human sound.
A chain-drooped lamp was flickering by each
    door;
The arras, rich with horseman, hawk, and
    hound,
Fluttered in the besieging wind's uproar;
And the long carpets rose along the gusty floor.

41

They glide, like phantoms, into the wide hall;   361
Like phantoms to the iron porch they glide,
Where lay the Porter, in uneasy sprawl,
With a huge empty flagon by his side:
The wakeful bloodhound rose, and shook his
    hide,   365
But his sagacious eye an inmate owns:
By one, and one, the bolts full easy slide: —
The chains lie silent on the footworn stones; —
The key turns, and the door upon its hinges groans.

42

And they are gone: ay, ages long ago   370
These lovers fled away into the storm.
That night the Baron dreamt of many a woe,
And all his warrior-guests, with shade and form
Of witch, and demon, and large coffin-worm,
Were long be-nightmared.   Angela the old   375
Died palsy-twitched, with meagre face deform;
The Beadsman, after thousand aves told,
For aye unsought-for slept among his ashes cold.

Ode on a Grecian Urn

1

Thou still unravished bride of quietness,
    Thou foster-child of Silence and slow Time,
Sylvan historian, who canst thus express

A flowery tale more sweetly than our rhyme:
What leaf-fringed legend haunts about thy shape
    Of deities or mortals, or of both,   6
      In Tempe or the dales of Arcady?
What men or gods are these?   What maidens
    loth?
What mad pursuit?   What struggle to escape?
    What pipes and timbrels?   What wild ec-
    stasy?   10

2

Heard melodies are sweet, but those unheard
    Are sweeter; therefore, ye soft pipes, play on;
Not to the sensual [1] ear, but, more endeared,
    Pipe to the spirit ditties of no tone:
Fair youth, beneath the trees, thou canst not
    leave   15
    Thy song, nor ever can those trees be bare;
    Bold Lover, never, never canst thou kiss,
Though winning near the goal — yet, do not
    grieve;
    She cannot fade, though thou hast not thy
    bliss,
    For ever wilt thou love, and she be fair!   20

3

Ah, happy, happy boughs! that cannot shed
    Your leaves, nor ever bid the Spring adieu;
And, happy melodist, unwearied,
    For ever piping songs for ever new.
More happy love! more happy, happy love!   25
    For ever warm and still to be enjoyed,
    For ever panting, and for ever young;
All breathing human passion far above,
    That leaves a heart high-sorrowful and cloyed,
    A burning forehead, and a parching tongue.   30

4

Who are these coming to the sacrifice?
    To what green altar, O mysterious priest,
Lead'st thou that heifer lowing at the skies,
    And all her silken flanks with garlands drest?
What little town by river or sea shore,   35
    Or mountain-built with peaceful citadel,
    Is emptied of this folk, this pious morn?
And, little town, thy streets for evermore
    Will silent be; and not a soul to tell
    Why thou art desolate, can e'er return.   40

5

O Attic [2] shape!   Fair attitude! with brede [3]
Of marble men and maidens overwrought,
With forest branches and the trodden weed;
    Thou, silent form! dost tease us out of thought

---

[1] sensuous.   [2] Attica, ancient Athens.
[3] embroidery.

As doth eternity: Cold Pastoral! 45
  When old age shall this generation waste,
    Thou shalt remain, in midst of other woe
  Than ours, a friend to man, to whom thou say'st,
"Beauty is truth, truth beauty," — that is all
    Ye know on earth, and all ye need to know. 50

Ode to a Nightingale

It is said that Keats composed this noble ode while
seated one morning under a plum tree. In a mood of
depression resulting from the recent death of his brother
Tom, the song of the nightingale moved Keats greatly.

I

My heart aches, and a drowsy numbness pains
  My sense, as though of hemlock [1] I had drunk,
Or emptied some dull opiate to the drains
  One minute past, and Lethe-wards had sunk:
'Tis not through envy of thy happy lot, 5
  But being too happy in thine happiness, —
    That thou, light-winged Dryad of the trees,
      In some melodious plot
Of beechen green, and shadows numberless,
    Singest of summer in full-throated ease. 10

2

O for a draught of vintage! that hath been
  Cooled a long age in the deep-delved earth,
Tasting of Flora and the country green,
  Dance, and Provençal song, and sunburnt mirth!
O for a beaker full of the warm South, 15
  Full of the true, the blushful Hippocrene, [2]
    With beaded bubbles winking at the brim,
      And purple-stained mouth;
That I might drink, and leave the world unseen,
    And with thee fade away into the forest dim: 20

3

Fade far away, dissolve, and quite forget
  What thou among the leaves hast never known,
The weariness, the fever, and the fret
  Here, where men sit and hear each other groan;
Where palsy shakes a few, sad, last gray hairs, 25
  Where youth grows pale, and spectre-thin, and
    dies;
    Where but to think is to be full of sorrow
      And leaden-eyed despairs,
Where Beauty cannot keep her lustrous eyes,
    Or new Love pine at them beyond tomorrow.

[1] poison.
[2] A spring of the muses on Mt. Helicon.

4

Away! away! for I will fly to thee, 31
  Not charioted by Bacchus and his pards,[1]
But on the viewless [2] wings of Poesy,
  Though the dull brain perplexes and retards:
Already with thee! tender is the night, 35
  And haply the Queen-Moon is on her throne,
    Clustered around by all her starry Fays;
      But here there is no light,
Save what from heaven is with the breezes
    blown
    Through verdurous glooms and winding mossy
    ways. 40

5

I cannot see what flowers are at my feet,
  Nor what soft incense hangs upon the boughs,
But, in embalmed darkness, guess each sweet
  Wherewith the seasonable month endows
The grass, the thicket, and the fruit-tree wild; 45
  White hawthorn, and the pastoral eglantine;
    Fast-fading violets covered up in leaves;
      And mid-May's eldest child,
The coming musk-rose, full of dewy wine,
    The murmurous haunt of flies on summer
    eves. 50

6

Darkling I listen; and for many a time
  I have been half in love with easeful Death,
Called him soft names in many a mused rhyme,
  To take into the air my quiet breath;
Now more than ever seems it rich to die, 55
  To cease upon the midnight with no pain,
    While thou art pouring forth thy soul abroad
      In such an ecstasy!
Still wouldst thou sing, and I have ears in vain —
    To thy high requiem become a sod. 60

7

Thou wast not born for death, immortal Bird!
  No hungry generations tread thee down;
The voice I hear this passing night was heard
  In ancient days by emperor and clown:
Perhaps the self-same song that found a path 65
  Through the sad heart of Ruth, when, sick for
    home,
    She stood in tears amid the alien corn; [3]
      The same that oft-times hath
Charmed magic casements, opening on the foam
    Of perilous seas, in faery lands forlorn. 70

8

Forlorn! the very word is like a bell
  To toll me back from thee to my sole self!
[1] leopards.   [2] unseen.   [3] See Ruth, II.

Adieu! the fancy cannot cheat so well
  As she is famed to do, deceiving elf.
Adieu! adieu! thy plaintive anthem fades   75
  Past the near meadows, over the still stream,
    Up the hill-side; and now 'tis buried deep
      In the next valley-glades:
Was it a vision, or a waking dream?
      Fled is that music: — Do I wake or sleep?   80

La Belle Dame Sans Merci

"Ah, what can ail thee, Knight-at-arms,
  Alone and palely loitering?
The sedge has withered from the lake,
  And no birds sing.

"Ah, what can ail thee, Knight-at-arms,   5
  So haggard and so woe-begone?
The squirrel's granary is full,
  And the harvest's done.

"I see a lily on thy brow
  With anguish moist and fever-dew,   10
And on thy cheeks a fading rose
  Fast withereth too."

"I met a lady in the meads,
  Full beautiful — a faery's child;
Her hair was long, her foot was light,   15
  And her eyes were wild.

"I made a garland for her head,
  And bracelets too, and fragrant zone;
She looked at me as she did love,
  And made sweet moan.   20

"I set her on my pacing steed,
  And nothing else saw all day long;
For sidelong would she bend, and sing
  A faery's song.

"She found me roots of relish sweet,   25
  And honey wild and manna-dew;
And sure in language strange she said,
  'I love thee true.'

"She took me to her elfin grot,
  And there she gazed and sighed full sore,   30
And there I shut her wild, wild eyes —
  With kisses four.

"And there she lullèd me asleep,
  And there I dreamed — ah! woe betide! —
The latest dream I ever dreamed   35
  On the cold hill's side.

"I saw pale kings, and princes too,
  Pale warriors, death-pale were they all:
They cried — 'La belle Dame sans Merci
  Hath thee in thrall!'   40

"I saw their starved lips in the gloam
  With horrid warning gapèd wide,
And I awoke, and found me here
  On the cold hill side.

"And this is why I sojourn here   45
  Alone and palely loitering,
Though the sedge is withered from the lake,
  And no birds sing."

Fame

Fame, like a wayward Girl, will still be coy
  To those who woo her with too slavish knees,
But makes surrender to some thoughtless Boy,
  And dotes the more upon a heart at ease;
She is a Gipsy, will not speak to those   5
  Who have not learned to be content without her;
A Jilt, whose ear was never whispered close,
  Who thinks they scandal her who talk about her;
A very Gipsy is she, Nilus-born,[1]
  Sister-in-law to jealous Potiphar;[2]   10
Ye love-sick Bards, repay her scorn for scorn,
  Ye Artists lovelorn, madmen that ye are!
Make your best bow to her and bid adieu,
Then, if she likes it, she will follow you.

Lamia

As a note to the last line of this poem Keats printed the following:

"Philostratus, in his fourth book *de Vita Apollonii*, hath a memorable instance in this kind, which I may not omit, of one Menippus Lycius, a young man twenty-five years of age, that going betwixt Cenchreas and Corinth, met such a phantasm in the habit of a fair gentlewoman, which, taking him by the hand, carried him home to her house, in the suburbs of Corinth, and told him she was a Phœnician by birth, and if he would tarry with her, he should hear her sing and play, and drink such wine as never any drank, and no man should molest him; but she, being fair and lovely, would live and die with him, that was fair and lovely to behold. The young man, a philosopher, otherwise staid and discreet, able to moderate his passions, though not this of love, tarried with her a while to his great content, and at last married her, to whose wedding, amongst other guests, came Apollonius; who, by some probable conjectures, found her out to be a serpent, a lamia; and

---

[1] Gypsies were supposed to come from Egypt.
[2] One of Pharaoh's officers, whose wife loved Joseph.

that all her furniture was, like Tantalus' gold, described by Homer, no substance but mere illusions. When she saw herself descried, she wept, and desired Apollonius to be silent, but he would not be moved, and thereupon she, plate, house, and all that was in it, vanished in an instant: many thousands took notice of this fact, for it was done in the midst of Greece." (Burton's *Anatomy of Melancholy*, Part 3. Sect. 2. Memb. 1. Subs. 1.)

PART I

Upon a time, before the faery broods
Drove Nymph and Satyr from the prosperous
    woods,
Before king Oberon's bright diadem,
Sceptre, and mantle, clasped with dewy gem,
Frighted away the Dryads and the Fauns 5
From rushes green, and brakes, and cow-sliped
    lawns,
The ever-smitten Hermes empty left
His golden throne, bent warm on amorous theft:
From high Olympus had he stolen light,
On this side of Jove's clouds, to escape the sight 10
Of his great summoner, and made retreat
Into a forest on the shores of Crete.
For somewhere in that sacred island dwelt
A nymph, to whom all hoofed Satyrs knelt;
At whose white feet the languid Tritons poured 15
Pearls, while on land they withered and adored.
Fast by the springs where she to bathe was wont,
And in those meads where sometimes she might
    haunt,
Were strewn rich gifts, unknown to any Muse,
Though Fancy's casket were unlocked to choose. 20
Ah, what a world of love was at her feet!
So Hermes thought, and a celestial heat
Burnt from his winged heels to either ear,
That from a whiteness, as the lily clear,
Blushed into roses 'mid his golden hair,
Fallen in jealous curls about his shoulders bare. 25

From vale to vale, from wood to wood, he flew,
Breathing upon the flowers his passion new,
And wound with many a river to its head,
To find where this sweet nymph prepared her secret
    bed: 30
In vain; the sweet nymph might nowhere be found,
And so he rested, on the lonely ground,
Pensive, and full of painful jealousies
Of the Wood-Gods, and even the very trees.
There as he stood, he heard a mournful voice, 35
Such as once heard, in gentle heart, destroys
All pain but pity: thus the lone voice spake:
"When from this wreathed tomb shall I awake!
When move in a sweet body fit for life,
And love, and pleasure, and the ruddy strife 40

Of hearts and lips! Ah, miserable me!"
The God, dove-footed, glided silently
Round bush and tree, soft-brushing, in his speed,
The taller grasses and full-flowering weed,
Until he found a palpitating snake, 45
Bright, and cirque-couchant [1] in a dusky brake.

She was a gordian [2] shape of dazzling hue,
Vermilion-spotted, golden, green, and blue;
Striped like a zebra, freckled like a pard,
Eyed like a peacock, and all crimson barred; 50
And full of silver moons, that, as she breathed,
Dissolved, or brighter shone, or interwreathed
Their lustres with the gloomier tapestries —
So rainbow-sided, touched with miseries,
She seemed, at once, some penanced lady elf, 55
Some demon's mistress, or the demon's self.
Upon her crest she wore a wannish fire
Sprinkled with stars, like Ariadne's tiar: [3]
Her head was serpent, but ah, bitter-sweet!
She had a woman's mouth with all its pearls com-
    plete: 60
And for her eyes: what could such eyes do there
But weep, and weep, that they were born so fair?
As Proserpine still weeps for her Sicilian air.
Her throat was serpent, but the words she spake
Came, as through bubbling honey, for Love's
    sake, 65
And thus; while Hermes on his pinions lay,
Like a stooped falcon ere he takes his prey.

"Fair Hermes, crowned with feathers, fluttering
    light,
I had a splendid dream of thee last night:
I saw thee sitting, on a throne of gold, 70
Among the Gods, upon Olympus old,
The only sad one; for thou didst not hear
The soft, lute-fingered Muses chaunting clear,
Nor even Apollo when he sang alone,
Deaf to his throbbing throat's long, long melodious
    moan. 75
I dreamt I saw thee, robed in purple flakes,
Break amorous through the clouds, as morning
    breaks,
And, swiftly as a bright Phœbean [4] dart,
Strike for the Cretan isle; and here thou art!
Too gentle Hermes, hast thou found the maid?" 80
Whereat the star of Lethe [5] not delayed
His rosy eloquence, and thus inquired:

[1] Lying coiled.   [2] Like the Gordian Knot.
[3] Bacchus in wooing Ariadne gave her a golden crown, or tiara, set with gems. After her death it became a constellation in the heavens.
[4] Derived from Phœbus Apollo.
[5] Hermes as messenger guided souls to Lethe in Hades.

"Thou smooth-lipped serpent, surely high in-
    spired!
Thou beauteous wreath, with melancholy eyes,
Possess whatever bliss thou canst devise,   85
Telling me only where my nymph is fled, —
Where she doth breathe!" "Bright planet, thou
    hast said,"
Returned the snake, "but seal with oaths, fair
    God!"
"I swear," said Hermes, "by my serpent rod,[1]
And by thine eyes, and by thy starry crown!"   90
Light flew his earnest words, among the blossoms
    blown.
Then thus again the brilliance feminine:
"Too frail of heart! for this lost nymph of thine,
Free as the air, invisibly, she strays
About these thornless wilds; her pleasant days   95
She tastes unseen; unseen her nimble feet
Leave traces in the grass and flowers sweet;
From weary tendrils, and bowed branches green,
She plucks the fruit unseen, she bathes unseen:
And by my power is her beauty veiled   100
To keep it unaffronted, unassailed
By the love-glances of unlovely eyes,
Of Satyrs, Fauns, and bleared Silenus'[2] sighs.
Pale grew her immortality, for woe
Of all these lovers, and she grieved so   105
I took compassion on her, bade her steep
Her hair in weird syrops, that would keep
Her loveliness invisible, yet free
To wander as she loves, in liberty.
Thou shalt behold her, Hermes, thou alone,   110
If thou wilt, as thou swearest, grant my boon!"
Then, once again, the charmed God began
An oath, and through the serpent's ears it ran
Warm, tremulous, devout, psalterian.
Ravished, she lifted her Circean head,   115
Blushed a live damask, and swift-lisping said,
"I was a woman, let me have once more
A woman's shape, and charming as before.
I love a youth of Corinth — O the bliss!
Give me my woman's form, and place me where he
    is.   120
Stoop, Hermes, let me breathe upon thy brow,
And thou shalt see thy sweet nymph even now."
The God on half-shut feathers sank serene,
She breathed upon his eyes, and swift was seen
Of both the guarded nymph near-smiling on the
    green.   125
It was no dream; or say a dream it was,
Real are the dreams of Gods, and smoothly pass
Their pleasures in a long immortal dream.
One warm, flushed moment, hovering, it might seem

    [1] Hermes carried a wand, caduceus, twined with
snakes, and topped with wings.
    [2] A pot-bellied, jovial old Satyr.

Dashed by the wood-nymph's beauty, so he
    burned;   130
Then, lighting on the printless verdure, turned
To the swooned serpent, and with languid arm,
Delicate, put to proof the lithe Caducean[1] charm.
So done, upon the nymph his eyes he bent
Full of adoring tears and blandishment,   135
And towards her stept: she, like a moon in wane,
Faded before him, cowered, nor could restrain
Her fearful sobs, self-folding like a flower
That faints into itself at evening hour:
But the God fostering her chilled hand,   140
She felt the warmth, her eyelids opened bland,
And, like new flowers at morning song of bees,
Bloomed, and gave up her honey to the lees.
Into the green-recessed woods they flew;
Nor grew they pale, as mortal lovers do.   145

    Left to herself, the serpent now began
To change; her elfin blood in madness ran,
Her mouth foamed, and the grass, therewith be-
    sprent,[2]
Withered at dew so sweet and virulent;
Her eyes in torture fixed, and anguish drear,   150
Hot, glazed, and wide, with lid-lashes all sear,
Flashed phosphor and sharp sparks, without one
    cooling tear.
The colors all inflamed throughout her train,
She writhed about, convulsed with scarlet pain:
A deep volcanian yellow took the place   155
Of all her milder-mooned body's grace;
And, as the lava ravishes the mead,
Spoilt all her silver mail, and golden brede;
Made gloom of all her frecklings, streaks and bars,
Eclipsed her crescents, and licked up her stars:
So that, in moments few, she was undrest   161
Of all her sapphires, greens, and amethyst,
And rubious-argent: of all these bereft,
Nothing but pain and ugliness were left.
Still shone her crown; that vanished, also she   165
Melted and disappeared as suddenly;
And in the air, her new voice luting soft,
Cried, "Lycius! gentle Lycius!" — Borne aloft
With the bright mists about the mountains hoar
These words dissolved: Crete's forests heard no
    more.   170

    Whither fled Lamia, now a lady bright,
A full-born beauty new and exquisite?
She fled into that valley they pass o'er
Who go to Corinth from Cenchreas' shore;
And rested at the foot of those wild hills,   175
The rugged founts of the Peræan rills,
And of that other ridge whose barren back
Stretches, with all its mist and cloudy rack,

    [1] See note to line 89.   [2] wet.

South-westward to Cleone.   There she stood
About a young bird's flutter from a wood,   180
Fair, on a sloping green of mossy tread,
By a clear pool, wherein she passioned
To see herself escaped from so sore ills,
While her robes flaunted with the daffodils.

Ah, happy Lycius! — for she was a maid   185
More beautiful than ever twisted braid,
Or sighed, or blushed, or on spring-flowered lea
Spread a green kirtle to the minstrelsy:
A virgin purest lipped, yet in the lore
Of love deep learned to the red heart's core: 190
Not one hour old, yet of sciential brain
To unperplex bliss from its neighbor pain;
Define their pettish limits, and estrange
Their points of contact, and swift counterchange;
Intrigue with the specious chaos, and dispart   195
Its most ambiguous atoms with sure art;
As though in Cupid's college she had spent
Sweet days a lovely graduate, still unshent,[1]
And kept his rosy terms in idle languishment.

Why this fair creature chose so faerily   200
By the wayside to linger, we shall see;
But first 'tis fit to tell how she could muse
And dream, when in the serpent prison-house,
Of all she list, strange or magnificent:
How, ever, where she willed, her spirit went;   205
Whether to faint Elysium, or where
Down through tress-lifting waves the Nereids fair
Wind into Thetis' bower by many a pearly stair;
Or where God Bacchus drains his cups divine,
Stretched out, at ease, beneath a glutinous pine;
Or where in Pluto's gardens palatine[2]   211
Mulciber's[3] columns gleam in far piazzian[4] line.
And sometimes into cities she would send
Her dream, with feast and rioting to blend;
And once, while among mortals dreaming thus,
She saw the young Corinthian Lycius   216
Charioting foremost in the envious race,
Like a young Jove with calm uneager face,
And fell into a swooning love of him.
Now on the moth-time of that evening dim   220
He would return that way, as well she knew,
To Corinth from the shore; for freshly blew
The eastern soft wind, and his galley now
Grated the quaystones with her brazen prow
In port Cenchreas, from Egina isle   225
Fresh anchored; whither he had been awhile
To sacrifice to Jove, whose temple there
Waits with high marble doors for blood and incense
        rare.
Jove heard his vows, and bettered his desire;

[1] without reproach.   [2] palatial.
[3] Vulcan's.   [4] Lines to form a square or plaza.

For by some freakful chance he made retire   230
From his companions, and set forth to walk,
Perhaps grown wearied of their Corinth talk:
Over the solitary hills he fared,
Thoughtless at first, but ere eve's star appeared
His phantasy was lost, where reason fades,   235
In the calmed twilight of Platonic shades.
Lamia beheld him coming, near, more near —
Close to her passing, in indifference drear,
Her silent sandals swept the mossy green;
So neighbored to him, and yet so unseen   240
She stood: he passed, shut up in mysteries,
His mind wrapped like his mantle, while her eyes
Followed his steps, and her neck regal white
Turned — syllabling thus, "Ah, Lycius bright,
And will you leave me on the hills alone?   245
Lycius, look back! and be some pity shown."
He did; not with cold wonder fearingly,
But Orpheus-like at an Eurydice;
For so delicious were the words she sung,
It seemed he had loved them a whole summer long:
And soon his eyes had drunk her beauty up,   251
Leaving no drop in the bewildering cup,
And still the cup was full, — while he, afraid
Lest she should vanish ere his lip had paid
Due adoration, thus began to adore;   255
Her soft look growing coy, she saw his chain so
        sure:
"Leave thee alone!   Look back!   Ah, Goddess, see
Whether my eyes can ever turn from thee!
For pity do not this sad heart belie —
Even as thou vanishest so shall I die.   260
Stay! though a Naiad of the rivers, stay!
To thy far wishes will thy streams obey:
Stay! though the greenest woods be thy domain,
Alone they can drink up the morning rain:
Though a descended Pleiad, will not one   265
Of thine harmonious sisters keep in tune
Thy spheres, and as thy silver proxy shine?
So sweetly to these ravished ears of mine
Came thy sweet greeting, that if thou shouldst fade
Thy memory will waste me to a shade: —   270
For pity do not melt!" — "If I should stay,"
Said Lamia, "here, upon this floor of clay,
And pain my steps upon these flowers too rough,
What canst thou say or do of charm enough
To dull the nice remembrance of my home?   275
Thou canst not ask me with thee here to roam
Over these hills and vales, where no joy is, —
Empty of immortality and bliss!
Thou art a scholar, Lycius, and must know
That finer spirits cannot breathe below   280
In human climes, and live: Alas! poor youth,
What taste of purer air hast thou to soothe
My essence?   What serener palaces,
Where I may all my many senses please,

And by mysterious sleights a hundred thirsts ap-
    pease?   285
It cannot be — Adieu!" So said, she rose
Tiptoe with white arms spread. He, sick to lose
The amorous promise of her lone complain,
Swooned, murmuring of love, and pale with pain.
The cruel lady, without any show   290
Of sorrow for her tender favorite's woe,
But rather, if her eyes could brighter be,
With brighter eyes and slow amenity,
Put her new lips to his, and gave afresh
The life she had so tangled in her mesh: 295
And as he from one trance was wakening
Into another, she began to sing,
Happy in beauty, life, and love, and every thing,
A song of love, too sweet for earthly lyres,
While, like held breath, the stars drew in their
    panting fires.   300
And then she whispered in such trembling tone,
As those who, safe together met alone
For the first time through many anguished days,
Use other speech than looks; bidding him raise
His drooping head, and clear his soul of doubt,
For that she was a woman, and without   306
Any more subtle fluid in her veins
Than throbbing blood, and that the self-same pains
Inhabited her frail-strung heart as his.
And next she wondered how his eyes could miss 310
Her face so long in Corinth, where, she said,
She dwelt but half retired, and there had led
Days happy as the gold coin could invent
Without the aid of love; yet in content
Till she saw him, as once she passed him by, 315
Where 'gainst a column he lent thoughtfully
At Venus' temple porch, 'mid baskets heaped
Of amorous herbs and flowers, newly reaped
Late on that eve, as 'twas the night before
The Adonian feast;[1] whereof she saw no more, 320
But wept alone those days, for why should she
    adore?
Lycius from death awoke into amaze,
To see her still, and singing so sweet lays;
Then from amaze into delight he fell
To hear her whisper woman's lore so well; 325
And every word she spake enticed him on
To unperplexed delight and pleasure known.
Let the mad poets say whate'er they please
Of the sweets of Faeries, Peris, Goddesses,
There is not such a treat among them all, 330
Haunters of cavern, lake, and waterfall,
As a real woman, lineal indeed
From Pyrrha's[2] pebbles or old Adam's seed.
Thus gentle Lamia judged, and judged aright,
That Lycius could not love in half a fright, 335
So threw the goddess off, and won his heart
    [1] Feast in honor of Adonis.

More pleasantly by playing woman's part,
With no more awe than what her beauty gave,
That, while it smote, still guaranteed to save.
Lycius to all made eloquent reply,   340
Marrying to every word a twin-born sigh;
And last, pointing to Corinth, asked her sweet,
If 'twas too far that night for her soft feet.
The way was short, for Lamia's eagerness
Made, by a spell, the triple league decrease 345
To a few paces; not at all surmised
By blinded Lycius, so in her comprised.
They passed the city gates, he knew not how,
So noiseless, and he never thought to know.

As men talk in a dream, so Corinth all,   350
Throughout her palaces imperial,
And all her populous streets and temples lewd,
Muttered, like tempest in the distance brewed,
To the wide-spreaded night above her towers.
Men, women, rich and poor, in the cool hours, 355
Shuffled their sandals o'er the pavement white,
Companioned or alone; while many a light
Flared, here and there, from wealthy festivals,
And threw their moving shadows on the walls,
Or found them clustered in the corniced shade 360
Of some arched temple door, or dusky colonnade.

Muffling his face, of greeting friends in fear,
Her fingers he pressed hard, as one came near
With curled gray beard, sharp eyes, and smooth
    bald crown,
Slow-stepped, and robed in philosophic gown: 365
Lycius shrank closer, as they met and past,
Into his mantle, adding wings to haste,
While hurried Lamia trembled: "Ah," said he,
"Why do you shudder, love, so ruefully?
Why does your tender palm dissolve in dew?" 370
"I'm wearied," said fair Lamia: "tell me who
Is that old man? I cannot bring to mind
His features: — Lycius! wherefore did you blind
Yourself from his quick eyes?" Lycius replied,
"'Tis Apollonius sage, my trusty guide 375
And good instructor; but to-night he seems
The ghost of folly haunting my sweet dreams."

While yet he spake they had arrived before
A pillared porch, with lofty portal door,
Where hung a silver lamp, whose phosphor glow
Reflected in the slabbed steps below, 381
Mild as a star in water; for so new,

    [2] According to legend Jupiter caused a great flood to
destroy mankind, except for Deucalion and his wife,
Pyrrha. After the flood the two repeopled the earth
by throwing pebbles behind them, those thrown by
Pyrrha turning into women, those thrown by Deucalion into men.

And so unsullied was the marble's hue,
So through the crystal polish, liquid fine,
Ran the dark veins, that none but feet divine   385
Could e'er have touched there.   Sounds Æolian [1]
Breathed from the hinges, as the ample span
Of the wide doors disclosed a place unknown
Some time to any, but those two alone,
And a few Persian mutes, who that same year   390
Were seen about the markets: none knew where
They could inhabit; the most curious
Were foiled, who watched to trace them to their
      house:
And but the flitter-winged verse must tell,
For truth's sake, what woe afterwards befel,   395
'Twould humor many a heart to leave them thus,
Shut from the busy world of more incredulous.

PART II

Love in a hut, with water and a crust,
Is — Love, forgive us! — cinders, ashes, dust;
Love in a palace is perhaps at last
More grievous torment than a hermit's fast: —
That is a doubtful tale from faery land,   5
Hard for the non-elect to understand.
Had Lycius lived to hand his story down,
He might have given the moral a fresh frown,
Or clenched it quite: but too short was their bliss
To breed distrust and hate, that make the soft
      voice hiss.   10
Besides, there, nightly, with terrific glare,
Love, jealous grown of so complete a pair,
Hovered and buzzed his wings, with fearful roar,
Above the lintel of their chamber door,
And down the passage cast a glow upon the floor.

For all this came a ruin: side by side   16
They were enthroned, in the even tide,
Upon a couch, near to a curtaining
Whose airy texture, from a golden string,
Floated into the room, and let appear   20
Unveiled the summer heaven, blue and clear,
Betwixt two marble shafts: — there they reposed,
Where use had made it sweet, with eyelids closed,
Saving a tithe which love still open kept,
That they might see each other while they almost
      slept;   25
When from the slope side of a suburb hill,
Deafening the swallow's twitter, came a thrill
Of trumpets — Lycius started — the sounds fled,
But left a thought, a buzzing in his head.
For the first time, since first he harbored in   30
That purple-lined palace of sweet sin,

[1] An Æolian harp is so constructed as to give forth
sounds when played upon by the winds.   Æolus was
the god of the winds.

His spirit passed beyond its golden bourn
Into the noisy world almost forsworn.
The lady, ever watchful, penetrant,
Saw this with pain, so arguing a want   35
Of something more, more than her empery
Of joys; and she began to moan and sigh
Because he mused beyond her, knowing well
That but a moment's thought is passion's passing
      bell.
"Why do you sigh, fair creature?" whispered he:
"Why do you think?" returned she tenderly: 41
"You have deserted me; — where am I now?
Not in your heart while care weighs on your brow:
No, no, you have dismissed me; and I go
From your breast houseless: ay, it must be so."   45
He answered, bending to her open eyes,
Where he was mirrored small in paradise,
"My silver planet, both of eve and morn!
Why will you plead yourself so sad forlorn,
While I am striving how to fill my heart   50
With deeper crimson, and a double smart?
How to entangle, trammel up and snare
Your soul in mine, and labyrinth you there
Like the hid scent in an unbudded rose?
Ay, a sweet kiss — you see your mighty woes.   55
My thoughts! shall I unveil them?   Listen then!
What mortal hath a prize, that other men
May be confounded and abashed withal,
But lets it sometimes pace abroad majestical,
And triumph, as in thee I should rejoice   60
Amid the hoarse alarm of Corinth's voice.
Let my foes choke, and my friends shout afar,
While through the thronged streets your bridal
      car
Wheels round its dazzling spokes." — The lady's
      cheek
Trembled; she nothing said, but, pale and meek,   65
Arose and knelt before him, wept a rain
Of sorrows at his words; at last with pain
Beseeching him, the while his hand she wrung,
To change his purpose.   He thereat was stung,
Perverse, with stronger fancy to reclaim   70
Her wild and timid nature to his aim:
Besides, for all his love, in self despite,
Against his better self, he took delight
Luxurious in her sorrows, soft and new.
His passion, cruel grown, took on a hue   75
Fierce and sanguineous as 'twas possible
In one whose brow had no dark veins to swell.
Fine was the mitigated fury, like
Apollo's presence when in act to strike
The serpent — Ha, the serpent! certes, she   80
Was none.   She burnt, she loved the tyranny,
And, all subdued, consented to the hour
When to the bridal he should lead his paramour.
Whispering in midnight silence, said the youth,

"Sure some sweet name thou hast, though, by my
    truth,   85
I have not asked it, ever thinking thee
Not mortal, but of heavenly progeny,
As still I do.   Hast any mortal name,
Fit appellation for this dazzling frame?
Or friends or kinsfolk on the citied earth,   90
To share our marriage feast and nuptial mirth?"
"I have no friends," said Lamia, "no, not one;
My presence in wide Corinth hardly known:
My parents' bones are in their dusty urns
Sepulchred, where no kindled incense burns,   95
Seeing all their luckless race are dead, save me,
And I neglect the holy rite for thee.
Even as you list invite your many guests;
But if, as now it seems, your vision rests
With any pleasure on me, do not bid   100
Old Apollonius — from him keep me hid."
Lycius, perplexed at words so blind and blank,
Made close inquiry; from whose touch she shrank,
Feigning a sleep; and he to the dull shade
Of deep sleep in a moment was betrayed.   105

It was the custom then to bring away
The bride from home at blushing shut of day,
Veiled, in a chariot, heralded along
By strewn flowers, torches, and a marriage song,
With other pageants: but this fair unknown   110
Had not a friend.   So being left alone,
(Lycius was gone to summon all his kin)
And knowing surely she could never win
His foolish heart from its mad pompousness,
She set herself, high-thoughted, how to dress   115
The misery in fit magnificence.
She did so, but 'tis doubtful how and whence
Came, and who were her subtle servitors.
About the halls, and to and from the doors,
There was a noise of wings, till in short space   120
The glowing banquet-room shone with wide-
    arched grace.
A haunting music, sole perhaps and lone
Supportress of the faery-roof, made moan
Throughout, as fearful the whole charm might
    fade.
Fresh carved cedar, mimicking a glade   125
Of palm and plantain, met from either side,
High in the midst, in honor of the bride:
Two palms and then two plantains, and so on,
From either side their stems branched one to one
All down the aisled place; and beneath all   130
There ran a stream of lamps straight on from wall
    to wall,
So canopied, lay an untasted feast
Teeming with odors.   Lamia, regal drest,
Silently paced about, and as she went,
In pale contented sort of discontent,   135

Missioned her viewless servants to enrich
The fretted splendor of each nook and niche.
Between the tree-stems, marbled plain at first,
Came jasper pannels; then, anon, there burst
Forth creeping imagery of slighter trees,   140
And with the larger wove in small intricacies.
Approving all, she faded at self-will,
And shut the chamber up, close, hushed and still,
Complete and ready for the revels rude,
When dreadful guests would come to spoil her
    solitude.   145

The day appeared, and all the gossip rout.
O senseless Lycius!   Madman! wherefore flout
The silent-blessing fate, warm cloistered hours,
And show to common eyes these secret bowers?
The herd approached; each guest, with busy brain,
Arriving at the portal, gazed amain,   151
And entered marveling: for they knew the street,
Remembered it from childhood all complete
Without a gap, yet ne'er before had seen
That royal porch, that high-built fair demesne;   155
So in they hurried all, mazed, curious and keen:
Save one, who looked thereon with eye severe,
And with calm-planted steps walked in austere;
'Twas Apollonius: something too he laughed,
As though some knotty problem, that had daft   160
His patient thought, had now begun to thaw,
And solve and melt: — 'twas just as he foresaw.

He met within the murmurous vestibule
His young disciple.   "'Tis no common rule,
Lycius," said he, "for uninvited guest   165
To force himself upon you, and infest
With an unbidden presence the bright throng
Of younger friends; yet must I do this wrong,
And you forgive me."   Lycius blushed, and led
The old man through the inner doors broadspread;
With reconciling words and courteous mien   171
Turning into sweet milk the sophist's spleen.

Of wealthy lustre was the banquet-room,
Filled with pervading brilliance and perfume:
Before each lucid panel fuming stood   175
A censer fed with myrrh and spiced wood,
Each by a sacred tripod held aloft,
Whose slender feet wide-swerved upon the soft
Wool-woofed carpets: fifty wreaths of smoke
From fifty censers their light voyage took   180
To the high roof, still mimicked as they rose
Along the mirrored walls by twin-clouds odorous.
Twelve sphered tables, by silk seats insphered,
High as the level of a man's breast reared
On libbard's [1] paws, upheld the heavy gold   185
Of cups and goblets, and the store thrice told
    [1] leopard's.

Of Ceres' horn, and, in huge vessels, wine
Come from the gloomy tun with merry shine.
Thus loaded with a feast the tables stood,
Each shrining in the midst the image of a God. 190

When in an antechamber every guest
Had felt the cold full sponge to pleasure pressed,
By minist'ring slaves, upon his hands and feet,
And fragrant oils with ceremony meet
Poured on his hair, they all moved to the feast 195
In white robes, and themselves in order placed
Around the silken couches, wondering
Whence all this mighty cost and blaze of wealth
  could spring.

Soft went the music the soft air along,
While fluent Greek a voweled undersong 200
Kept up among the guests, discoursing low
At first, for scarcely was the wine at flow;
But when the happy vintage touched their brains,
Louder they talk, and louder come the strains
Of powerful instruments: — the gorgeous dyes, 205
The space, the splendor of the draperies,
The roof of awful richness, nectarous cheer,
Beautiful slaves, and Lamia's self, appear,
Now, when the wine has done its rosy deed,
And every soul from human trammels freed, 210
No more so strange; for merry wine, sweet wine,
Will make Elysian shades not too fair, too divine.
Soon was God Bacchus at meridian height;
Flushed were their cheeks, and bright eyes double
  bright:
Garlands of every green, and every scent 215
From vales deflowered, or forest-trees branch-rent,
In baskets of bright osiered gold were brought
High as the handles heaped, to suit the thought
Of every guest; that each, as he did please,
Might fancy-fit his brows, silk-pillowed at his
  ease. 220

What wreath for Lamia? What for Lycius?
What for the sage, old Apollonius?
Upon her aching forehead be there hung
The leaves of willow and of adder's tongue; [1]
And for the youth, quick, let us strip for him 225
The thyrsus, [2] that his watching eyes may swim
Into forgetfulness; and, for the sage,
Let spear-grass and the spiteful thistle wage
War on his temples. Do not all charms fly
At the mere touch of cold philosophy? 230
There was an awful rainbow once in heaven:
We know her woof, her texture; she is given
In the dull catalogue of common things.

[1] A fern.
[2] The staff, entwined with ivy and surmounted by a
pine cone, carried by followers of Bacchus.

Philosophy will clip an Angel's wings,
Conquer all mysteries by rule and line, 235
Empty the haunted air, and gnomed mine —
Unweave a rainbow, as it erewhile made
The tender-personed Lamia melt into a shade.

By her glad Lycius sitting, in chief place,
Scarce saw in all the room another face, 240
Till, checking his love trance, a cup he took
Full brimmed, and opposite sent forth a look
'Cross the broad table, to beseech a glance
From his old teacher's wrinkled countenance,
And pledge him. The bald-head philosopher 245
Had fixed his eye, without a twinkle or stir
Full on the alarmed beauty of the bride,
Brow-beating her fair form, and troubling her
  sweet pride.
Lycius then pressed her hand, with devout touch,
As pale it lay upon the rosy couch: 250
'Twas icy, and the cold ran through his veins,
Then sudden it grew hot, and all the pains
Of an unnatural heat shot to his heart.
"Lamia, what means this? Wherefore dost thou
  start?
Know'st thou that man?" Poor Lamia answered
  not. 255
He gazed into her eyes, and not a jot
Owned they the lovelorn piteous appeal:
More, more he gazed: his human senses reel:
Some hungry spell that loveliness absorbs;
There was no recognition in those orbs. 260
"Lamia!" he cried — and no soft-toned reply.
The many heard, and the loud revelry
Grew hush; the stately music no more breathes;
The myrtle sickened in a thousand wreaths.
By faint degrees, voice, lute, and pleasure ceased;
A deadly silence step by step increased, 266
Until it seemed a horrid presence there,
And not a man but felt the terror in his hair.
"Lamia!" he shrieked; and nothing but the shriek
With its sad echo did the silence break. 270
"Begone, foul dream!" he cried, gazing again
In the bride's face, where now no azure vein
Wandered on fair-spaced temples; no soft bloom
Misted the cheek; no passion to illume
The deep-recessed vision: — all was blight; 275
Lamia, no longer fair, there sat a deadly white.
"Shut, shut those juggling eyes, thou ruthless man!
Turn them aside, wretch! or the righteous ban
Of all the Gods, whose dreadful images
Here represent their shadowy presences, 280
May pierce them on the sudden with the thorn
Of painful blindness; leaving thee forlorn,
In trembling dotage to the feeblest fright
Of conscience, for their long offended might,
For all thine impious proud-heart sophistries, 285

Unlawful magic, and enticing lies.
Corinthians! look upon that grey-beard wretch!
Mark how, possessed, his lashless eyelids stretch
Around his demon eyes!   Corinthians, see!
My sweet bride withers at their potency."   290
"Fool!" said the sophist, in an under-tone
Gruff with contempt; which a death-nighing
        moan
From Lycius answered, as heart-struck and lost,
He sank supine beside the aching ghost.
"Fool! Fool!" repeated he, while his eyes still   295
Relented not, nor moved; "from every ill
Of life have I preserved thee to this day,
And shall I see thee made a serpent's prey?"
Then Lamia breathed death-breath; the sophist's
        eye,
Like a sharp spear, went through her utterly,   300
Keen, cruel, perceant,[1] stinging: she, as well
As her weak hand could any meaning tell,
Motioned him to be silent; vainly so,
He looked and looked again a level — No!
"A serpent!" echoed he; no sooner said,   305
Than with a frightful scream she vanished:
   [1] piercing.

And Lycius' arms were empty of delight,
As were his limbs of life, from that same night.
On the high couch he lay! — his friends came
        round —   309
Supported him — no pulse, or breath they found,
And, in its marriage robe, the heavy body wound.

Sonnet

Bright star, would I were steadfast as thou art —
    Not in lone splendor hung aloft the night
And watching, with eternal lids apart,
    Like Nature's patient, sleepless Eremite,
The moving waters at their priestlike task   5
    Of pure ablution round earth's human shores,
Or gazing on the new soft fallen mask
    Of snow upon the mountains and the moors —
No — yet still steadfast, still unchangeable,
    Pillowed upon my fair love's ripening breast,   10
To feel forever its soft fall and swell,
    Awake forever in a sweet unrest,
Still, still to hear her tender-taken breath,
And so live ever — or else swoon to death.

Heinrich Heine · 1797-1856

Heine, a contemporary of Shelley, Keats, and Byron, lived most of his productive life in Paris.
Born at Düsseldorf, Germany, on December 13, 1797, the son of Jewish parents, he early knew the
unpleasantness imposed upon Jews in the Germany of the time.   After having made an attempt
to enter business, he earned a doctorate in law.   For a while he sought new experiences in England,
later on in Italy.   Finally he settled in Paris where he made a living as a journalist, editor, and
author.   Always in his mind and heart was a deep passion for liberty and democracy; much of his
effort was directed toward the promotion of an understanding between Germany and France.   The
last eight years of his life he spent in bed as an invalid, suffering from a fatal disease of the
spine.

Heine wrote travel sketches, some criticism, two unsuccessful tragedies, and the usual run of
articles, necessary to the career of a journalist, on politics and contemporary events.   He was by
nature a reformer and moved by a great zeal for justice.   A single volume, his *Buch der Lieder*,
published in 1827, was sufficient to give him his place in world literature.   Heine as a poet was brilliant, facile.   His work is distinguished by a strong subjectivism, a reliance on the symbols of
nature, and by a marked ironic quality.   Frequently his emotional lyrics are made to end with a fillip
of satire.

As a voice of German romanticism, Heine spoke for the rebellious spirit of man.   He called himself "a soldier in the wars for liberty."   He evinced a strong interest in nature, particularly nature
associated with the sea, and wrote with zeal and passion of his personal emotions and sentiments.
Romantic qualities, also, were his use of old legends, his enthusiasm for Napoleon, and his persistent
melancholy.

Of the poems that follow, the first three are translated by Sir Theodore Martin, the others by
Louis Untermeyer, from *Heinrich Heine: Poems*, copyright, 1937, by Harcourt, Brace and Company,
Inc.

SUGGESTED REFERENCES: Louis Untermeyer, *Heinrich Heine: Paradox and Poet* (2 vols., 1937);
Antonia Vallentin, *Heine, Poet in Exile* (1956); Laura Hofrichter, *Heinrich Heine* (1963).

The Mountain Echo

At sad slow pace across the vale
  There rode a horseman brave:
"Ah! travel I now to my mistress's arms,
Or but to the darksome grave?"
    The echo answer gave: 5
    "The darksome grave!"

And farther rode the horseman on,
  With sighs his thoughts express'd:
"If I thus early must go to my grave,
Yet in the grave is rest."   10
    The answering voice confess'd:
    "The grave is rest!"

Adown the horseman's furrow'd cheek
  A tear fell on his breast:
"If rest I can only find in the grave,
For me the grave is best."   15
    The hollow voice confess'd:
    "The grave is best!"

The Grenadiers

Two grenadiers travell'd tow'rds France one day,
  On leaving their prison in Russia,
And sadly they hung their heads in dismay
  When they reach'd the frontiers of Prussia.

For there they first heard the story of woe,   5
  That France had utterly perish'd,
The grand army had met with an overthrow,
  They had captured their Emperor cherish'd.

Then both of the grenadiers wept full sore
  At hearing the terrible story;   10
And one of them said: "Alas! once more
  My wounds are bleeding and gory."

The other one said: "The game's at an end,
  With thee I would die right gladly,
But I've wife and child, whom at home I should
  tend,   15
  For without me they'll fare but badly."

"What matters my child, what matters my wife?
  A heavier care has arisen;
Let them beg, if they're hungry, all their life —
  My Emperor sighs in a prison!"   20

"Dear brother, pray grant me this one last prayer·
  If my hours I now must number,
O take my corpse to my country fair,
  That there it may peacefully slumber.

"The legion of honor, with ribbon red,   25
  Upon my bosom place thou,
And put in my hand my musket dread,
  And my sword around me brace thou.

"And so in my grave will I silently lie,
  And watch like a guard o'er the forces,   30
Until the roaring of cannon hear I,
  And the trampling of neighing horses.

"My Emperor then will ride over my grave,
  While the swords glitter brightly and rattle;
Then armed to the teeth will I rise from the
  grave,   35
  For my Emperor hasting to battle!"

Whene'er I Look Into Thine Eyes

Whene'er I look into thine eyes,
Then every fear that haunts me flies;
But when I kiss thy mouth, oh then
I feel a giant's strength again.

When leaning on thy darling breast,   5
I feel with heavenly rapture blest;
But when thou sayest, "I love thee!"
Then must I weep, and bitterly.

A Pine Tree Stands So Lonely

A pine tree stands so lonely
  In the North where the high winds blow,
He sleeps; and the whitest blanket
  Wraps him in ice and snow.

He dreams — dreams of a palm tree   5
   That far in an Orient land,
Languishes, lonely and drooping,
   Upon the burning sand.

I Do Not Know Why This Confronts Me

I do not know why this confronts me,
   This sadness, this echo of pain;
A curious legend still haunts me,
   Still haunts and obsesses my brain:

The air is cool and it darkles,   5
   Softly the Rhine flows by.
The mountain peak still sparkles
   In the fading flush of the sky.

And on one peak, half-dreaming
   She sits, enthroned and fair;   10
Like a goddess, dazzling and gleaming,
   She combs her golden hair.

With a golden comb she is combing
   Her hair as she sings a song —
A song that, heard through the gloaming,   15
   Is magically sweet and strong.

The boatman has heard; it has bound him
   In the throes of a strange, wild love.
He is blind to the reefs that surround him;
   He sees but the vision above.   20

And lo, the wild waters are springing —
   The boat and the boatman are gone . . .
And this, with her poignant singing,
   The Loreley has done.

Oh Lovely Fishermaiden

Oh lovely fishermaiden,
   Come, bring your boat to land;
And we will sit together
   And whisper, hand in hand.

Oh rest upon my bosom,   5
   And fear no harm from me.
You give your body daily,
   Unfearing to the sea . . .

My heart is like the ocean
   With storm and ebb and flow —   10
And many a pearly treasure
   Burns in the depths below.

The Yellow Moon Has Risen

The yellow moon has risen,
   It slants upon the sea;
And in my arms' soft prison
   My love leans close to me.

Warm with her gentle clinging,   5
   I lie on the sands, half awake.
"Oh what do you hear in the swinging
   Of the winds, and why do you shake?"

"That's never the wind that is swinging,
   That murmur that troubles me;   10
It is the mermaidens singing —
   My sisters drowned in the sea."

Child, You Are Like a Flower

Child, you are like a flower,
   So sweet and pure and fair;
I look at you and sadness
   Comes on me, like a prayer.

I must lay my hands on your forehead   5
   And pray God to be sure
To keep you forever and always
   So sweet and fair — and pure.

Life in This World

Life in this world is a muddled existence —
Our German professor will give me assistance.
He knows how to whip the whole thing into order;
He'll make a neat System and keep it in line.
With scraps from his nightcap and dressing-gown's
   border   5
He'd fill all the gaps in Creation's design.

Where Is Now Your Precious Darling?

"Where is now your precious darling,
   That you sang about so sweetly,
When the magic, flaming torrent
   Fired and filled your heart completely?"

Ah, that fire is extinguished,   5
   And my heart no longer flashes;
And this book's an urn containing
   All my love — and all its ashes.

Doctrine

Beat on the drum and blow the fife
  And kiss the *vivandière*, my boy.
Fear nothing — that's the whole of life;
  Its deepest truth, its soundest joy.

Beat reveillé, and with a blast   5
  Arouse all men to valiant strife.
Waken the world; and then, at last,
  March on . . . That is the whole of life.

This is Philosophy; this is Truth;
  This is the burning source of joy!   10
I've borne this wisdom from my youth,
  For I, too, was a drummer-boy.

Night Has Come

Night has come with silent footsteps,
  On the beaches by the ocean;
And the waves, with curious whispers,
  Ask the moon, "Have you a notion

"Who that man is? Is he foolish,   5
  Or with love is he demented?
For he seems so sad and cheerful,
  So cast down yet so contented."

And the moon, with shining laughter,
  Answers them, "If you must know it,   10
He is both in love *and* foolish;
  And, besides that, he's a poet!"

Victor Hugo · 1802–1885

Victor Marie Hugo's father was an officer in the French army. The young Hugo was educated chiefly in Paris and Madrid, but, because of his moving about with his father and an estrangement which developed between his parents, his training was, at best, haphazard. As a schoolboy he was much given to the writing of verses — odes, riddles, satires, epics, and melodrama. The death of his mother, with whom he had lived his later youth, left him separated from his father and, at least for a while, almost impoverished. Once his literary fame had begun to grow, he married Adèle Foucher, to whom he had been attached since boyhood.

Hugo devoted his life to two pursuits — literature and politics. His record in politics is too complicated for a brief summary, but it may be noted that at one time he was the recipient of a pension from Louis XVIII, that he represented Paris in 1848 in the National Assembly, that upon the usurpation of Louis Napoleon (1852) he retired in more or less voluntary exile to the Island of Jersey, and that, upon his return to France in 1870, he was made a member of the National Assembly at Bordeaux and, later, a senator. His literary reputation far exceeded his political success. The last decade or two of his life were years of literary glory, days spent as the idol of literate France. A true romantic even in death, he was buried (May 31, 1885), in accordance with a request he had made, in a simple pauper's coffin. However, a magnificent funeral ceremony took place at the Panthéon. His pauper's coffin was raised on a dais beneath the Arch of Triumph.

In France Hugo is esteemed chiefly as a poet. Most of his best verses are found in the volumes *Songs of the Orient* (1829), *Songs at Twilight* (1835), and *Lights and Shadows* (1840). He made his mark in drama with *Hernani* (1830), *Lucrezia Borgia* (1833), and *Ruy Blas* (1838). But in England and America Hugo is thought of as essentially a novelist. Of the several novels he wrote, *Notre Dame de Paris* (1831), *Les Misérables* (1862), and *Toilers of the Sea* (1866) have established his reputation with English readers.

In all his writing Hugo was an arch-romantic. In verse he revived the meters and cadences of the sixteenth century; in drama — especially in his preface to *Cromwell* — he attacked what he believed to be the outmoded conventions of classicism; and in his novels he wrote of romantic love, of brave heroes who sacrifice all for those who are dear to them. As a poet Hugo discarded classical conventions, permitted himself great freedom as to subject and meter, and made frequent use of local color. He is the greatest literary figure in French romanticism, which included, among others, such poets as de Vigny, Gautier, de Nerval, and Leconte de Lisle.

SUGGESTED REFERENCES: Elliot M. Grant, *The Career of Victor Hugo* (1945); Matthew Josephson, *Victor Hugo* (1942).

Les Misérables

Les Misérables, probably the most important of Hugo's novels, recounts the career of Jean Valjean, a hard-working peasant who is sent to the galleys for the theft of a loaf of bread. The original five-year sentence is extended to a much longer term because of Valjean's various attempts to escape. Made more brute than man by his experience, the hero, in a period of freedom, steals valuable silver from a kindly bishop who had given him shelter. The bishop, when the police capture the thief and return the silver, announces that he had freely given the stolen property to Valjean. This generous act reawakens all the essential good in the hero who spends the rest of his life performing noble acts of sacrifice for fellow outcasts from society. His every move, however, is watched by the police, particularly by Javert, an able and implacable detective. The selection below narrates an episode in which Valjean gives assistance to Marius following street fighting, an incident which ends with the hero's again meeting Javert.

The translation is that of Lascelles Wraxall.

THE ESCAPE THROUGH THE SEWERS

Marius was really a prisoner, prisoner to Jean Valjean; the hand which had clutched him behind at the moment when he was falling, and of which he felt the pressure as he lost his senses, was Jean Valjean's.

Jean Valjean had taken no other part in the struggle than that of exposing himself. Had it not been for him, in the supreme moment of agony no one would have thought of the wounded. Thanks to him, who was everywhere present in the carnage like a Providence, those who fell were picked up, carried to the ground-floor room, and had their wounds dressed, and in the intervals he repaired the barricade. But nothing that could resemble a blow, an attack, or even personal defence, could be seen with him, and he kept quiet and succored. However, he had only a few scratches; and the bullets had no billet for him. If suicide formed part of what he dreamed of when he came to this sepulchre, he had not been successful, but we doubt whether he thought of suicide, which is an irreligious act. Jean Valjean did not appear to see Marius in the thick of the combat, but in truth he did not take his eyes off him. When a bullet laid Marius low Jean Valjean leaped upon him with the agility of a tiger, dashed upon him as on a prey, and carried him off.

The whirlwind of the attack was at this moment so violently concentrated on Enjolras and the door of the wine-shop that no one saw Jean Valjean, supporting the fainting Marius in his arms, cross the unpaved ground of the barricade, and disappear round the corner of Corinth. Our readers will remember this corner, which formed a sort of cape in the street, and protected a few square feet of ground from bullets and grape-shot, and from glances as well. There is thus at times in fires a room which does not burn, and in the most raging seas, beyond a promontory, or at the end of a reef, a little quiet nook. It was in this corner of the inner trapeze of the barricade that Eponine drew her last breath. Here Jean Valjean stopped, let Marius slip to the ground, leant against a wall, and looked around him.

The situation was frightful; for the instant, for two or three minutes perhaps, this piece of wall was a shelter, but how to get out of this massacre? He recalled the agony he had felt in the Rue Polonceau, eight years previously, and in what way he had succeeded in escaping; it was difficult then, but now it was impossible. He had in front of him that implacable and silent six-storied house, which only seemed inhabited by the dead man leaning out of his window; he had on his right the low barricade which closed the Petite Truanderie; to climb over this obstacle appeared easy, but a row of bayonet-points could be seen over the crest of the barricade; they were line troops posted beyond the barricade and on the watch. It was evident that crossing the barricade was seeking a platoon fire, and that any head which appeared above the wall of paving-stones would serve as a mark for sixty muskets. He had on his left the battle-field, and death was behind the corner of the wall.

What was he to do? a bird alone could have escaped from this place. And he must decide at once, find an expedient, and make up his mind. They were fighting a few paces from him, but fortunately all were obstinately engaged at one point, the wine-shop door, but if a single soldier had the idea of turning the house or attacking it on the flank all would be over. Jean Valjean looked at the house opposite to him, he looked at the barricade by his side, and then looked on the ground, with the violence of supreme extremity, wildly, and as if he would have liked to dig a hole with his eyes. By force of looking, something vaguely discernible in such an agony was designed, and assumed a shape at his feet, as if the eyes had the power to produce the thing demanded. He perceived a few paces from him, at the foot of the small barricade so pitilessly guarded and watched from without, and beneath a pile of paving-stones which almost concealed it, an iron grating, laid flat and flush with the ground. This grating made of strong cross bars was about two feet square, and the framework of paving-stones which supported it had been torn out, and it was as it were dismounted. Through the bars a glimpse could be caught of an obscure opening, something like a chimney-pot or the cylinder of a cistern. Jean Valjean dashed up, and his old skill in escapes rose to his brain like a beam of light. To remove the paving-stones, tear up the grating, take Marius, who was inert as a dead body, on his shoulders, descend with this burden on his loins, helping himself with his elbows and knees, into this sort of well which was fortunately of no great depth, to let the grating fall again over his head, to set foot on a paved surface, about ten feet below the earth, all this was executed like something done in delirium, with a giant's strength and the rapidity of an eagle; this occupied but a few minutes. Jean Valjean found himself with the still fainting Marius in a sort of long subterranean corridor, where there was profound peace, absolute silence, and night. The impression which he had formerly felt in falling out of the street into the convent recurred to him, still what he now carried was not Cosette, but Marius.

He had scarce heard above his head like a vague murmur the formidable tumult of the wine-shop being taken by assault....

It was in the sewer of Paris that Jean Valjean found himself. This is a further resemblance of Paris with the sea, as in the ocean the diver can disappear there. It was an extraordinary transition, in the very heart of the city. Jean Valjean had left the city, and in a twinkling, the time required to lift a trap and let it fall again, he had passed from broad daylight to complete darkness, from mid-day to midnight, from noise to silence, from the uproar of thunder to the stagnation of the tomb, and, by an incident far more prodigious even than that of the Rue Polonceau, from the extremest peril to the most absolute security. A sudden fall into a cellar, disappearance in the oubliette [1] of Paris, leaving this street where death was all around for this species of sepulchre in which was life; it was a strange moment. He stood for some minutes as if stunned, listening and amazed. The

[1] A dungeon.

trap-door of safety had suddenly opened beneath him, and the heavenly kindness had to some extent snared him by treachery. Admirable ambuscades of Providence! Still the wounded man did not stir, and Jean Valjean did not know whether what he was carrying in this fosse [1] were alive or dead.

His first sensation was blindness, for he all at once could see nothing. He felt too that in a moment he had become deaf, for he could hear nothing more. The frenzied storm of murder maintained a few yards above him only reached him confusedly and indistinctly, and like a rumor in a deep place. He felt that he had something solid under his feet, but that was all; still it was sufficient. He stretched out one arm, then the other; he touched the wall on both sides and understood that the passage was narrow; his foot slipped, and he understood that the pavement was damp. He advanced one foot cautiously, fearing a hole, a cesspool, or some gulf, and satisfied himself that the pavement went onwards. A fetid gust warned him of the spot where he was. At the expiration of a few minutes he was no longer blind, a little light fell through the trap by which he descended, and his eye grew used to this cellar. He began to distinguish something. The passage in which he had run to earth — no other word expresses the situation better — was walled up behind him; it was one of those blind alleys called in the special language branches. Before him he had another wall, a wall of night. The light of the trap expired ten or twelve feet from the spot where Jean Valjean was, and scarce produced a livid whiteness on a few yards of the damp wall of the sewer. Beyond that the opaqueness was massive, to enter it seemed horrible, and resembled being swallowed up by an earthquake. Yet it was possible to bury oneself in this wall of fog, and it must be done; and must even be done quickly. Jean Valjean thought that the grating which he had noticed in the street might also be noticed by the troops, and that all depended on chance. They might also come down into the well and search, so he had not a minute to lose. He had laid Marius on the ground and now picked him up — that is again the right expression — took him on his shoulders and set out. He resolutely entered the darkness.

The truth is, that they were less saved than Jean Valjean believed; perils of another nature, but equally great, awaited them. After the flashing whirlwind of the combat, came the cavern of miasmas and snares, after the chaos of the cloaca.[2] Jean Valjean had passed from one circle of the Inferno into another. When he had gone fifty yards he was obliged to stop, for a question oc-

[1] A canal or ditch — the sewer.   [2] sewer.

curred to him; the passage ran into another, which it intersected, and two roads offered themselves. Which should he take? ought he to turn to the left or right? how was he to find his way in this black labyrinth? This labyrinth, we have said, has a clue in its slope, and following the slope leads to the river. Jean Valjean understood this immediately: he said to himself that he was probably in the sewer of the Halles, that if he turned to the left and followed the incline he would arrive in a quarter of an hour at some opening on the Seine between the Pont au Change and the Pont Neuf, that is to say, appear in broad daylight in the busiest part of Paris. Perhaps he might come out at some street opening, and passers-by would be stupefied at seeing two blood-stained men emerge from the ground at their feet. The police would come up and they would be carried off to the nearest guard-room; they would be prisoners before they had come out. It would be better, therefore, to bury himself in the labyrinth, confide in the darkness, and leave the issue to Providence.

He went up the incline and turned to the right; when he had gone round the corner of the gallery the distant light from the trap disappeared, the curtain of darkness fell on him again, and he became blind once more. For all that he advanced as rapidly as he could; Marius' arms were passed round his neck, and his feet hung down behind. He held the two arms with one hand and felt the wall with the other. Marius' cheek touched his and was glued to it, as it was bloody, and he felt a warm stream which came from Marius drip on him and penetrate his clothing. Still, a warm breath in his ear, which touched the wounded man's mouth, indicated respiration, and consequently life. The passage in which Jean Valjean was now walking was not so narrow as the former, and he advanced with some difficulty. The rain of the previous night had not yet passed off, and formed a small torrent in the centre, and he was forced to hug the wall in order not to lave his feet in the water. He went on thus darkly, resembling beings of the night groping in the invisible, and subterraneously lost in the veins of gloom. Still, by degrees, either that a distant grating sent a little floating light into this opaque mist, or that his eyes grew accustomed to the obscurity, he regained some vague vision, and began to notice confusedly, at one moment the wall he was touching, at another the vault under which he was passing. The pupil is dilated at night, and eventually finds daylight in it, in the same way as the soul is dilated in misfortune and eventually finds God in it.

To direct himself was difficult, for the sewers represent, so to speak, the outline of the streets standing over them. There were in the Paris of that day two thousand two hundred streets, and imagine beneath them that forest of dark branches called the sewer. The system of drains existing at that day, if placed end on end, would have given a length of eleven leagues. We have already said that the present network, owing to the special activity of the last thirty years, is no less than sixty leagues. Jean Valjean began by deceiving himself; he fancied that he was under the Rue St. Denis, and it was unlucky that he was not so. There is under that street an old stone drain, dating from Louis XIII, which runs straight to the collecting sewer, called the Great Sewer, with only one turn on the right, by the old Court of Miracles, and a single branch, the Saint Martin sewer, whose four arms cut each other at right angles. But the gut of the little Truanderie, whose entrance was near the Corinth wine-shop, never communicated with the sewer of the Rue St. Denis; it falls into the Montmartre drain, and that is where Jean Valjean now was. There opportunities for losing himself were abundant, for the Montmartre drain is one of the most labyrinthine of the old network. Luckily Jean Valjean had left behind him the drain of the Halles, whose geometrical plan represents a number of intertwined topmasts; but he had before him more than one embarrassing encounter, and more than one street corner — for there are streets — offering itself in the obscurity as a note of interrogation. In the first place on his left, the vast Plâtrière drain, a sort of Chinese puzzle, thrusting forth and intermingling its chaos of T's and Z's under the Post Office, and the rotunda of the Halle au blé as far as the Seine, where it terminates in a Y; secondly, on his right the curved passage of the Rue du Cadran, with its three teeth, which are so many blind alleys; thirdly, on his left the Mail branch, complicated almost at the entrance by a species of fork, and running with repeated zigzags to the great cesspool of the Louvre, which ramifies in every direction; and lastly, on his right the blind alley of the Rue du Jeûneurs, without counting other pitfalls, ere he reached the surrounding drain which alone could lead him to some issue sufficiently distant to be safe.

Had Jean Valjean had any notion of all we have just stated he would have quickly perceived, merely by feeling the wall, that he was not in the subterranean gallery of the Rue St. Denis. Instead of the old carved stone, instead of the old architecture, haughty and royal even in the drain, with its timber supports and running courses of granite, which cost eight hundred livres the toise,[1] he would feel under his hand modern cheapness,

[1] Slightly over two yards.

the economic expedient, brickwork supported on a layer of beton, which costs two hundred francs the metre, that bourgeois masonry, known as *à petits matériaux,* but he knew nothing of all this. He advanced anxiously, but calmly, seeing nothing, hearing nothing, plunged into chance, that is to say, swallowed up in Providence. By degrees, however, we are bound to state that a certain amount of horror beset him, and the shadow which enveloped him entered his mind. He was walking in an enigma. This aqueduct of the cloaca is formidable, for it intersects itself in a vertiginous manner, and it is a mournful thing to be caught in this Paris of darkness. Jean Valjean was obliged to find, and almost invent, his road without seeing it. In this unknown region each step that he ventured might be his last. How was he to get out of it? would he find an issue? would he find it in time? could he pierce and penetrate this colossal subterranean sponge with its passages of stone? would he meet there some unexpected knot of darkness? would he arrive at something inextricable and impassable? would Marius die of hemorrhage, and himself of hunger? would they both end by being lost there, and form two skeletons in a corner of this night? He did not know; he asked himself all this and could not find an answer. The intestines of Paris are a precipice, and like the prophet he was in the monster's belly.

He suddenly had a surprise; at the most unexpected moment, and without ceasing to walk in a straight line, he perceived that he was no longer ascending; the water of the gutter plashed against his heels instead of coming to his toes. The sewer was now descending; why? was he about to reach the Seine suddenly? That danger was great, but the peril of turning back was greater still, and he continued to advance. He was not proceeding toward the Seine; the ridge which the soil of Paris makes on the right bank disembogues one of its watersheds into the Seine, and the other in the great sewer. The crest of this ridge, which determines the division of the waters, designs a most capricious line; the highest point is in the St. Avoye sewer, beyond the Rue Michel-le-comte, in the Louvre sewer, near the boulevards, and in the Montmartre drain, near the Halles. This highest point Jean Valjean had reached, and he was proceeding toward the surrounding sewer, or in the right direction, but he knew it not. Each time that he reached a branch he felt the corners, and if he found the opening narrower than the passage in which he was he did not enter, but continued his march, correctly judging that any narrower way must end in a blind alley, and could only take

him from his object, that is to say, an outlet. He thus avoided the fourfold snare laid for him in the darkness by the four labyrinths which we have enumerated. At a certain moment he recognized that he was getting from under that part of Paris petrified by the riot, where the barricades had suppressed circulation, and returning under living and normal Paris. He suddenly heard above his head a sound like thunder, distant but continuous; it was the rolling of vehicles.

He had been walking about half an hour, at least that was the calculation he made, and had not thought of resting; he had merely changed the hand which held Marius up. The darkness was more profound than ever, but this darkness reassured him. All at once he saw his shadow before him; it stood out upon a faint and almost indistinct redness, which vaguely impurpled the roadway at his feet and the vault above his head, and glided along the greasy walls of the passage. He turned his head in stupefaction, and saw behind him at a distance, which appeared immense, a sort of horrible star glistening, which seemed to be looking at him. It was the gloomy police star rising in the sewer. Behind this star there moved confusedly nine or ten black, upright, indistinct, and terrible forms.

The meaning was as follows: on the day of June 6th a battue [1] of the sewers was ordered, for it was feared lest the conquered should fly to them as a refuge, and Prefect Gisquet ordered occult Paris to be searched, while General Bugeaud swept public Paris; a double connected operation, which required a double strategy of the public force, represented above by the army and beneath by the police. Three squads of agents and sewer-men explored the subway of Paris, the first the right bank, the second the left bank, and the third the Cité. The agents were armed with carbines, bludgeons, swords, and daggers, and what was at this moment pointed at Jean Valjean was the lantern of the round of the right bank. This round had just inspected the winding gallery and three blind alleys which are under the Rue du Cadran. While the police were carrying their light about there, Jean Valjean in his progress came to the entrance of the gallery, found it narrower than the main gallery, and had not entered it. The police, on coming out of the Cadran gallery, fancied that they could hear the sound of footsteps in the direction of the outer drain, and they were really Jean Valjean's footsteps. The head sergeant of the round raised his lantern, and the squad began peering into the mist in the direction whence the noise had come.

[1] A hunting method by which beaters drive game ahead of them to a place favorable for shooting.

It was an indescribable moment for Jean Valjean; luckily, if he saw the lantern well the lantern saw him badly, for it was the light and he was the darkness. He was too far off, and blended with the blackness of the spot, so he drew himself up against the wall and stopped. However, he did not explain to himself what was moving behind him; want of sleep and food and emotion had made him to pass into a visionary state. He saw a flash, and round this flash, sprites. What was it? he did not understand. When Jean Valjean stopped the noise ceased; the police listened and heard nothing, they looked and saw nothing, and hence consulted together. There was at that period at that point in the Montmartre drain a sort of square called *de service*, which has since been suppressed, owing to the small internal lake which the torrents of rain formed there, and the squad assembled on this square. Jean Valjean saw them make a sort of circle, and then bull-dog heads came together and whispered. The result of this council held by the watch-dogs was that they were mistaken, that there had been no noise, that there was nobody there, that it was useless to enter the surrounding sewer, that it would be time wasted, but that they must hasten to the St. Merry drain, for if there were any thing to be done and any "boussingot" to track, it would be there. From time to time parties new-sole their old insults. In 1832, the word *boussingot* formed the transition between the word *jacobin*, no longer current, and the word *demagogue*, at that time almost unused, and which has since done such excellent service. The sergeant gave orders to left-wheel toward the watershed of the Seine. Had they thought of dividing into two squads and going in both directions, Jean Valjean would have been caught. It is probable that the instructions of the Prefecteur, fearing the chance of a fight with a large body of insurgents, forbade the round from dividing. The squad set out again, leaving Jean Valjean behind; and in all this movement he perceived nothing except the eclipse of the lantern, which was suddenly turned away.

Before starting, the sergeant, to satisfy his police conscience, discharged his carbine in the direction where Jean Valjean was. The detonation rolled echoing along the crypt, like the rumbling of these Titanic bowels. A piece of plaster which fell into the gutter and plashed up the water a few yards from Jean Valjean warned him that the bullet had struck the vault above his head. Measured and slow steps echoed for some time along the wooden causeway, growing more and more deadened by the growing distance; the group of black forms disappeared; a light oscillated and floated, forming on the vault a ruddy circle, which decreased and disappeared; the silence again became profound, the obscurity again became complete, and blindness and deafness again took possession of the gloom, and Jean Valjean, not daring yet to stir, remained leaning for a long time against the wall, with outstretched ear and dilated eyeballs, watching the evanishment of the patrol of phantoms.

We must do the police of that day the justice of saying that even in the gravest public conjunctures, they imperturbably accomplished their duties as watchmen. A riot was not in their eyes a pretext to leave the bridle to malefactors and to neglect society for the reason that the government was in danger. The ordinary duties were performed correctly in addition to the extraordinary duties, and were in no way disturbed. In the midst of an incalculable political event, under the pressure of a possible revolution, an agent, not allowing himself to be affected by the insurrection and the barricade, would track a robber. Something very like this occurred on the afternoon of June 6, on the right bank of the Seine, a little beyond the Pont des Invalides. There is no bank there at the present day, and the appearance of the spot has been altered. On this slope two men, a certain distance apart, were observing each other; the one in front seemed to be trying to get away, while the one behind wanted to catch him up. It was like a game of chess played at a distance and silently; neither of them seemed to be in a hurry, and both walked slowly, as if they were afraid that increased speed on the part of one would be imitated by the other. It might have been called an appetite following a prey, without appearing to do so purposely; the prey was crafty, and kept on guard.

The proportions required between the tracked ferret and the tracking dog were observed. The one trying to escape was thin and weak; the one trying to catch was a tall fellow, and evidently a rough customer. The first, feeling himself the weaker, avoided the second, but did so in a deeply furious way; any one who could have observed him would have seen in his eyes the gloomy hostility of flight, and all the threat which there is in fear; the slope was deserted, there were no passers-by, not even a boatman or raftsman in the boats moored here and there. They could only be noticed easily from the opposite quay, and any one who had watched them at that distance, would have seen that the man in front appeared a bristling, ragged, and shambling fellow, anxious and shivering under a torn blouse, while the other was a classic and official personage, wearing the frock-coat of authority buttoned up to the chin. The reader would probably recognize these two men, were he to see them more closely. What was the object of the last one? probably he wished to clothe the other man more warmly. When a man dressed by the state pursues a man in rags, it is in order to make of him also a man dressed by the state. The difference of color is the sole question, — to be dressed in blue is glorious, to be dressed in red is disagreeable, for there is a purple of the lower classes. It was probably some disagreeable thing, and some purple of this sort, which the first man desired to avoid.

If the other allowed him to go on ahead, and did not yet arrest him, it was, in all appearance, in the hope of seeing him arrive at some significative rendezvous and some group worth capturing. This delicate operation is called tracking. What renders this conjecture highly probable, is the fact that the buttoned-up man perceiving from the slope an empty fiacre passing, made a sign to the driver; the driver understood, evidently perceived with whom he had to deal, turned round, and began following the two men along the quay. This was not perceived by the ragged, shambling fellow in front. The hackney coach rolled along under the trees of the Champs Elysées, and over the parapet could be seen the bust of the driver, whip in hand. One of the secret instructions of the police to the agents is "always have a hackney coach at hand in case of need." While each of these men manœuvred with irreproachable strategy, they approached an incline in the quay, which allowed drivers coming from Passy to water their horses in the river. This incline has since been suppressed for the sake of symmetry, — horses die of thirst, but the eye is flattered. It was probable that the man in the blouse would ascend by this incline in order to try and escape in the Champs Elysées, a place adorned with trees, but, to make up for that, much frequented by police agents, where the other could easily procure assistance. This point of the quay is a very little distance from the house brought from Moret to Paris in 1824, by Colonel Brack, and called the house of Francis I. A piquet is always stationed there. To the great surprise of his watcher, the tracked man did not turn up the road to the watering-place, but continued to advance along the bank parallel with the quay. His position was evidently becoming critical, for unless he threw himself into the Seine, what could he do?

There were no means now left him of returning to the quay, no incline or no steps, and they were close to the spot marked by the turn in the Seine, near the Pont de Jena, where the bank, gradually contracting, ended in a narrow strip, and was lost in the water. There he must inevitably find himself blockaded between the tall wall on his right, the river on his left and facing him, and authority at his heels. It is true that this termination of the bank was masked from sight by a pile of rubbish seven feet high, the result of some demolition. But did this man hope to conceal himself profitably behind this heap? the expedient would have been puerile. He evidently did not dream of that, for the innocence of robbers does not go so far. The pile of rubbish formed on the water-side a sort of eminence extending in a promontory to the quay wall; the pursued man reached this small mound and went round it, so that he was no longer seen by the other. The latter, not seeing, was not seen, and he took advantage of this to give up all dissimulation and walk very fast. In a few minutes he reached the heap and turned it, but there stood stupefied. The man he was pursuing was not there, it was a total eclipse of the man in the blouse. The bank did not run more than thirty yards beyond the heap, and then plunged under the water which washed the quay wall. The fugitive could not have thrown himself into the Seine, or have climbed up the quay wall, without being seen by his pursuer. What had become of him?

The man in the buttoned-up coat walked to the end of the bank and stood there for a moment, thoughtfully, with clenched fists and scowling eye. All at once he smote his forehead; he had just perceived, at the point where the ground ended and the water began, a wide, low, arched, iron grating, provided with a heavy lock, and three massive hinges. This grating, a sort of gate pierced at the bottom of the quay, opened on the river as much as on the bank, and a black stream poured from under it into the Seine. Beyond the heavy rusty bars could be distinguished a sort of arched and dark passage. The man folded his arms and looked at the grating reproachfully, and this look not being sufficient, he tried to push it open, he shook it, but it offered a sturdy resistance. It was probable that it had just been opened, although no sound had been heard, a singular thing with so rusty a gate, but it was certain that it had been closed again. This indicated that the man who had opened the gate had not a pick-lock but a key. This evidence at once burst on the mind of the man who was trying to open the grating, and drew from him this indignant apostrophe, —

"That is strong! a government key!"

Then, calming himself immediately, he expressed a whole internal world of ideas by this outburst of monosyllables, marked by an almost ironical accent, —

"Stay, stay, stay, stay."

This said, hoping we know not what, either to see the man come out or others enter, he posted himself on the watch behind the heap of rubbish, with the patient rage of a yard-mastiff. On its side, the hackney coach, which regulated itself by all his movements, stopped above him near the parapet. The driver, foreseeing a long halt, put on his horses the nose bag full of damp oats so well known to the Parisians upon whom the government, we may remark parenthetically, places it sometimes. The few passers over the Pont de Jena, before going on, turned their heads to look for a moment at these motionless objects, — the man on the bank and the hackney coach on the quay.

Jean Valjean had resumed his march, and had not stopped again. This march grew more and more laborious; for the level of these passages varies; the average height is about five feet six inches and was calculated for a man's stature. Jean Valjean was compelled to stoop so as not to dash Marius against the roof, and was forced at each moment to bend down, then draw himself up and incessantly feel the wall. The dampness of the stones and of the flooring rendered them bad supports, either for the hand or the foot, and he tottered in the hideous dungheap of the city. The intermittent flashes of the street gratings only appeared at lengthened intervals, and were so faint that the bright sunshine seemed to be moonlight; all the rest was fog, miasma, opaqueness, and blackness. Jean Valjean was hungry and thirsty, the latter most, and it was like the sea, there was water, water everywhere, but not a drop to drink. His strength, which, as we know, was prodigious, and but slightly diminished by age, owing to his chaste and sober life, was, however, beginning to give way; fatigue assailed him, and his decreasing strength increased the weight of his burden. Marius, who was perhaps dead, was heavy, like all inert bodies, but Jean Valjean held him so that his chest was not affected, and he could breathe with pressure. He felt between his legs the rapid gliding of rats, and one was so startled as to bite him. From time to time a gush of fresh air came through the gratings, which revived him.

It might be about three P.M. when he reached the external sewer, and was at first amazed by the sudden widening. He unexpectedly found himself in a gallery whose two walls his outstretched arms did not reach, and under an arch which his head did not touch. The grand sewer, in fact, is eight feet in width by seven high. At the point where the Montmartre drain joins the grand sewer two other subterranean galleries, that of the Rue de Provence and that of the Abattoir, form crossroads. Between these four ways a less sagacious man would have been undecided, but Jean Valjean selected the widest, that is to say, the encircling sewer. But here the question came back again, — Should he ascend or descend? He thought that the situation was pressing, and that he must at all risks now reach the Seine, in other words, descend, so he turned to the left. It was fortunate that he did so, for it would be an error to suppose that the encircling sewer has two issues, one toward Bercy, the other toward Passy, and that it is, as its name indicates, the subterranean belt of Paris on the right bank. The grand sewer, which is nought else, it must be borne in mind, than the old Menilmontant stream, leads, if you ascend it, to a blind alley, that is to say, to its old starting-point, a spring at the foot of the Menilmontant mound. It has no direct communication with the branch which collects the waters of Paris after leaving the Popincourt quarter, and which falls into the Seine by the Amelot sewer above the old isle of Louviers. This branch, which completes the collecting sewer, is separated from it under the Rue Menilmontant by masonry-work, which marks where the waters divide to run up-stream and down-stream. If Jean Valjean had remounted the gallery he would have arrived, exhausted by fatigue and dying, at a wall; he would have been lost.

Strictly speaking, by going back a little way, entering the passage of les Filles du Calvaire, on condition that he did not hesitate at the subterranean dial of the Boucherat crossroads, by taking the St. Louis passage, then on the left the St. Gilles trench, then by turning to the right and avoiding the St. Sebastian gallery, he might have reached the Ameot sewer, and then if he did not lose his way in the species of F which is under the Bastille, he would have reached the issue on the Seine near the arsenal. But for that he must have thoroughly known, in all its ramifications and piercings, the enormous madrepore [1] of the sewer. Now we dwell on the fact that he knew nothing of this frightful labyrinth in which he was marching, and had he been asked where he was he would have replied, — In night. His instinct served him well; going down, in fact, was the only salvation possible. He left on his right the two passages which ramify in the shape of a claw under the Rues Laffitte and St. Georges, and the long bifurcate corridor of the Chaussée d'Antin. A little beyond an affluant, which was probably the Madeleine branch, he stopped, for he was very weary. A large grating, probably the one in the Rue d'Anjou, produced an almost bright light. Jean Valjean, with the gentle movements which a brother would

[1] coral; the sewers had the intricate structure of coral.

bestow on a wounded brother, laid Marius on the *banquette* of the drain, and his white face gleamed under the white light of the trap as from the bottom of a tomb. His eyes were closed, his hair was attached to his forehead like pincers dried in blood, his hands were hanging and dead, his limbs cold, and blood was clotted at the corner of his lips. Coagulated blood had collected in his cravat knot, his shirt entered the wounds, and the cloth of his coat rubbed the gaping edges of the quivering flesh. Jean Valjean, removing the clothes with the tips of his fingers, laid his hand on his chest, — the heart still beat. Jean Valjean tore up his shirt, bandaged the wounds as well as he could, and stopped the blood that was flowing; then stooping down in this half daylight over Marius, who was still unconscious and almost breathless, he looked at him with indescribable hatred. In moving Marius' clothes he had found in his pockets two things, the loaf, which he had forgotten the previous evening, and his pocket-book. He ate the bread and opened the pocket-book. On the first page he read the lines written by Marius, as will be remembered, —

"My name is Marius Pontmercy, carry my body to my grandfather's, M. Gillenormand, No. 6, Rue des Filles du Calvaire, in the Marais."

Jean Valjean read by the light of the grating these lines, and remained for a time as it were absorbed in himself, and repeating in a low voice, M. Gillenormand, No. 6, Rue des Filles du Calvaire. He returned the portfolio to Marius' pocket; he had eaten, and his strength had come back to him. He raised Marius again, carefully laid his head on his right shoulder, and began descending the sewer. The grand sewer, running along the thalweg [1] of the valley of Menilmontant, is nearly two leagues in length, and is paved for a considerable portion of the distance. This nominal torch of the streets of Paris, with which we enlighten for the reader Jean Valjean's subterranean march, he did not possess. Nothing informed him what zone of the city he was traversing, nor what distance he had gone, still the growing paleness of the flakes of light which he met from time to time indicated to him that the sun was retiring from the pavement, and that day would be soon ended, and the rolling of vehicles over his head, which had become intermittent instead of continuous, and then almost ceased, proved to him that he was no longer under central Paris, and was approaching some solitary region, near the external boulevards or most distant quays, where there are fewer houses and streets, and the drain has fewer gratings. The obscurity thickened around Jean Valjean; still he

[1] The course of a stream at the lowest part of a valley.

continued to advance, groping his way in the shadow.

This shadow suddenly became terrible.

He felt that he was entering water, and that he had under his feet no longer stone but mud. It often happens on certain coasts of Brittany or Scotland that a man, whether traveller or fisherman, walking at low water on the sands some distance from the coast suddenly perceives that during the last few minutes he has found some difficulty in walking. The shore beneath his feet is like pitch, his heels are attached to it, it is no longer sand but bird-lime; the sand is perfectly dry, but at every step taken, so soon as the foot is raised the imprint it leaves fills with water. The eye, however, has perceived no change, the immense expanse is smooth and calm, all the sand seems alike, nothing distinguishes the soil which is solid from that which is no longer so, and the little merry swarm of water-fleas continue to leap tumultuously round the feet of the wayfarer. The man follows his road, turns toward the land, and tries to approach the coast, not that he is alarmed at what? Still he feels as if the heaviness of his feet increased at every step that he takes; all at once he sinks in, sinks in two or three inches. He is decidedly not on the right road, and stops to look about him. Suddenly he looks at his feet, but they have disappeared, the sand covers them. He draws his feet out of the sand and tries to turn back, but he sinks in deeper still. The sand comes up to his ankle, he pulls it out and turns to his left, when the sand comes to his knee, he turns to the right, and the sand comes up to his thigh, then he recognizes with indescribable terror that he is caught in a quicksand, and has under him the frightful medium in which a man can no more walk than a fish can swim. He throws away his load, if he have one, and lightens himself like a ship in distress; but it is too late, for the sand is already above his knees. He calls out, waves his hat or handkerchief, but the sand gains on him more and more. If the shore is deserted, if land is too distant, if the quicksand is too ill-famed, if there is no hero in the vicinity, it is all over with him, and he is compelled to be swallowed up. He is condemned to that long, awful, implacable interment, impossible to delay or hasten, which lasts hours, which never ends, which seizes you when erect, free, and in perfect health, which drags you by the feet, which, at every effort you attempt, every cry you utter, drags you a little deeper; which seems to punish you for your resistance by a redoubled clutch, which makes a man slowly enter the ground while allowing him ample time to regard the houses, the trees, the green fields, the smoke from the villages on the plain, the sails of the vessels on the sea, the birds that fly and sing, the sun, and the sky. A quicksand is a sepulchre that converts itself into a tide, and ascends from the bottom of the earth toward a living man. Each minute is an inexorable sexton. The wretch tries to sit, to lie down, to walk, to crawl; all the movements that he makes bury him; he draws himself up, and only sinks deeper; he feels himself being swallowed up; he yells, implores, cries to the clouds, writhes his arms, and grows desperate. Then he is in the sand up to his waist; the sand reaches his chest, he is but a bust. He raises his hands, utters furious groans, digs his nails into the sand, tries to hold by a pebble, raises himself on his elbows to tear up a weak sea-weed, and sobs frenziedly; but the sand mounts. It reaches his shoulders, it reaches his neck, the face alone is visible now. The mouth cries, and the sand fills it, and then there is a silence. The eyes still look, but the sand closes them, and there is night. Then the forehead sinks, and a little hair waves above the sand; a hand emerges, dips up the sand, is waved, and disappears. It is a sinister effacement of a man. At times the rider is swallowed up with his horse, at times the carter with his cart; it is a shipwreck otherwhere than in the water, it is the land drowning man. The land penetrated by the ocean becomes a snare, it offers itself as a plain, and opens like a wave. The abyss has its acts of treachery.

Such a mournful adventure, always possible on some sea-shore, was also possible some thirty years ago in the sewer of Paris. Before the important works began in 1833 the subway of Paris was subject to sudden breakings-in. The water filtered through a subjacent and peculiarly friable soil; and the roadway, if made of paving-stones, as in the old drains, or of concrete upon beton, as in the new galleries, having no support, bent. A bend in a planking of this nature is a crevice, and a crevice is a bursting in. The roadway broke away for a certain length, and such a gap, a gulf of mud, was called in the special language *fontis*. What is a fontis? It is the quicksand of the sea-shore suddenly met with under-ground; it is the quicksand of St. Michel in a sewer. The moistened soil is in a state of fusion, all its particles are held in suspense in a shifting medium; it is not land and it is not water. The depth is at times very great. Nothing can be more formidable than meeting with such a thing; if water predominate death is quick, for a man is drowned; if earth predominate, death is slow, for he is sucked down.

Can our readers imagine such a death? If it be frightful to sink in a quicksand on the sea-shore what is it in a cloaca? instead of fresh air, daylight, a clear horizon, vast sounds, the free clouds from which life rains, the bark perceived in the distance, that hope under every form, of possible passers-by, of possible help up to the last minute, — instead of all this, deafness, blindness, a black archway, the interior of a tomb already made, death in the mud under a tombstone! slow asphyxia by uncleanliness, a sarcophagus where asphyxia opens its claws in the filth, and clutches you by the throat; fetidness mingled with the death-rattle, mud instead of the sand, sulphuretted hydrogen in lieu of the hurricane, ordure instead of the ocean! and to call and gnash the teeth, and writhe and struggle and expire, with this enormous city which knows nothing of it above one's head.

Inexpressible the horror of dying thus! Death sometimes expiates its atrocity by a certain terrible dignity. On the pyre, in shipwreck, a man may be great; in the flames, as in the foam, a superb attitude is possible, and a man transfigures himself. But in this case it is not so; for the death is unclean. It is humiliating to expire in such a way, and the last floating visions are abject. Mud is the synonym of shame, and is little, ugly, and infamous. To die in a butt of Malmsey like Clarence, — very well; but in a sewer like Escoubleau is horrible. To struggle in it is hideous, for at the same time as a man is dying, he is wallowing. There is enough darkness for it to be Hell, and enough mud for it to be merely a slough, and the dying man does not know whether he is about to become a spectre or a frog. Everywhere else the sepulchre is sinister, but here it is deformed.

The depth of the fontis varied, as did their length and density, according to the nature of the subsoil. At times a fontis was three or four feet deep, at times eight or ten, and sometimes it was bottomless. In one the mud was almost solid, in another nearly liquid. In the Lunière fontis, a man would have taken a day in disappearing, while he would have been devoured in five minutes by the Phélippeaux slough. The mud bears more or less well according to its degree of density, and a lad escapes where a man is lost. The first law of safety is to throw away every sort of loading, and every sewerman who felt the ground giving way under him began by getting rid of his basket of tools. The fontis had various causes, friability of soil, some convulsion beyond man's depth, violent summer showers, the incessant winter rain, and long fine rains. At times the weight of the surrounding houses upon a marshy or sandy soil broke the roofs of the subterranean galleries and made them shrink, or else it happened that the road-way broke and slit up under the terrific pressure. The pile of the Pantheon destroyed in this way about a century ago a portion of the cellars in the Montagne Ste. Geneviève. When a sewer gave way under the weight of the houses, the disorder was expressed above in the street by a sort of saw-toothed parting between the paving-stones. This rent was developed in a serpentine line, along the whole length of the injured drain, and in such a case, the evil being visible, the remedy might be prompt. It often happened also that the internal ravage was not revealed by any scar outside, and in that case, woe to the sewer men. Entering the injured drain incautiously, they might be lost in it. The old registers mention several nightmen buried in this manner in the fontis. They mention several names, among others that of the sewer-man swallowed up in a slough under the opening on the Rue Carême-Prenant, of the name of Blaise Poutrain; this Blaise was brother of Nicholas Poutrain, who was the last sexton of the cemetery called the Charnier des Innocents in 1785, when that cemetery expired. There was also the young and charming Vicomte d'Escoubleau, to whom we have alluded, one of the heroes of the siege of Lerida, where the assault was made in silk stockings and with violins at their head. L'Escoubleau, surprised one night with his cousin, the Duchesse de Sourdis, drowned himself in a cesspool of the Beautreillis drain, where he had taken refuge to escape the Duc. Madame de Sourdis, when informed of this death, asked for her smelling-bottle, and forgot to weep through inhaling her salts. In such a case, there is no love that holds out, the cloaca extinguishes it. Hero refuses to wash the corpse of Leander, and Thisbe stops her nose in the presence of Pyramus, saying, Pouah!

Jean Valjean found himself in presence of a fontis: this sort of breaking in was frequent at that day in the subsoil of the Champs Elysées, which was difficult to manage, and most injurious to underground drains owing to its extreme fluidity. This fluidity exceeds even the inconsistency of the sands of St. George's district, which could only be overcome by laying rubble on beton, and of the gas-infected clay strata in the Quartier des Martyrs, which are so liquid, that a passage could only be effected under the Galerie des Martyrs by means of an iron tube. When in 1836 the authorities demolished and rebuilt under the Faubourg St. Honoré the old stone drain in which Jean Valjean is now engaged, the shifting sand which is the subsoil of the Champs Elysées as far as the Seine offered such an obstacle that the operation lasted six months, to the great annoyance of those living on the water-side, especially such as had mansions and coaches. The works were more than difficult, they were dangerous, but we must allow that it rained for four and a half months, and the Seine overflowed thrice. The fontis which Jean Valjean came across was occasioned by the shower of the previous evening. A giving way of the pavement, which was badly supported by the subjacent sand, had produced a deposit of rain water, and when the filtering had taken place the ground broke in, and the road-way, being dislocated, fell into the mud. How far? it was impossible to say, for the darkness was denser there than anywhere else; it was a slough of mud in a cavern of night. Jean Valjean felt the pavement depart from under him as he entered the slough; there was water at top and mud underneath. He must pass it, for it was impossible to turn back: Marius was dying, and Jean Valjean worn out. Where else could he go? Jean Valjean advanced; the slough appeared but of slight depth at the first few steps, but as he advanced his legs sank in. He soon had mud up to the middle of the leg, and water up to the middle of the knee. He walked along, raising Marius with both arms as high as he could above the surface of the water; the mud now came up to his knees and the water to his waist. He could no longer draw back, and he sank in deeper and deeper. This mud, dense enough for the weight of one man, could not evidently bear two; Marius and Jean Valjean might have had a chance of getting out separately, but, for all that, Jean Valjean continued to advance, bearing the dying man, who was perhaps a corpse. The water came up to his armpits, and he felt himself drowning; he could scarce move in the depth of mud in which he was standing, for the density which was the support was also the obstacle. He still kept Marius up, and advanced with an extraordinary expenditure of strength, but he was sinking. He had only his head out of water and his two arms sustaining Marius. In the old paintings of the Deluge there is a mother holding her child in the same way. As he still sank he threw back his face to escape the water and be able to breathe; any one who saw him in this darkness would have fancied he saw a mask floating on the gloomy waters; he vaguely perceived above him Marius's hanging head and livid face; he made a desperate effort, and advanced his foot, which struck against something solid, a resting-place. It was high time.

He drew himself up, and writhed and rooted himself with a species of fury upon this support. It produced on him the effect of the first step of a staircase reascending to life. This support met with in the mud, at the supreme moment, was the beginning of the other side of the roadway, which had fallen in without breaking, and bent under the water like a plank in a single piece. A well-constructed pavement forms a curve, and possesses such firmness. This fragment of roadway, partly submerged, but solid, was a real incline, and once upon it they were saved. Jean Valjean ascended it, and attained the other side of the slough. On leaving the water his foot caught against a stone and he fell on his knees. He found that this was just, and remained on them for some time, with his soul absorbed in words addressed to God. He rose, shivering, chilled, bent beneath the dying man he carried, dripping with filth, but with his soul full of strange brightness.

He set out once again, still, if he had not left his life in the fontis, he seemed to have left his strength there. This supreme effort had exhausted him, and his fatigue was now so great that he was obliged to rest every three or four paces, to take breath, and leant against the wall. Once he was obliged to sit down on the banquette in order to alter Marius's position, and believed that he should remain there. But if his vigor were dead his energy was not so, and he rose again. He walked desperately, almost quickly, went thus one hundred yards without raising his head, almost without breathing, and all at once ran against the wall. He had reached an elbow of the drain, and on arriving head down at the turning came against the wall. He raised his eyes, and at the end of the passage down there, far, very far away, perceived a light. But this time it was no terrible light, but white, fair light. It was daylight. Jean Valjean saw the outlet. A condemned soul that suddenly saw from the middle of the furnace the issue from Gehenna would feel what Jean Valjean felt. It would fly wildly with the stumps of its burnt wings toward the radiant gate. Jean Valjean no longer felt fatigue, he no longer felt Marius' weight, he found again his muscles of steel, and ran rather than walked. As he drew nearer, the outlet became more distinctly designed; it was an arch, not so tall as the roof, which gradually contracted, and not so wide as the gallery, which grew narrower at the same time as the roof became lowered. The tunnel finished inside in the shape of a funnel, a faulty reduction, imitated from the wickets of houses of correction, logical in a prison, but illogical in a drain, and which has since been corrected.

Jean Valjean reached the issue and then stopped; it was certainly the outlet, but they could not get out. The arch was closed by a strong grating, and this grating, which apparently rarely turned on its oxidized hinges, was fastened to the stone wall by a heavy lock, which, red with rust, seemed an enormous brick. The key-hole was visible, as well as the bolt deeply plunged into its iron box. It was one of those Bastile locks of which ancient Paris was so prodigal. Beyond the grating were the open air, the river, daylight, the bank, very narrow, but sufficient to depart, the distant quays, Paris, that gulf in which a man hides himself so easily, the wide horizon, and liberty. On the right could be distinguished, down the river, the Pont de Jena, and up it the Pont des Invalides; the spot would have been a favorable one to await night and escape. It was one of the most solitary points in Paris, the bank facing the Gros-Caillou. The flies went in and out through the grating bars. It might be about half-past eight in the evening, and day was drawing in: Jean Valjean laid Marius along the wall on the dry part of the way, then walked up to the grating and seized the bars with both hands; the shock was frenzied, but the effect *nil*. The grating did not stir. Jean Valjean seized the bars one after the other, hoping he might be able to break out the least substantial one, and employ it as a lever to lift the gate off the hinges, or break the lock, but not a bar stirred. A tiger's teeth are not more solidly set in their jaws. Without a lever it was impossible to open the grating, and the obstacle was invincible.

Must he finish, then, there? what should he do? what would become of him? he had not the strength to turn back and recommence the frightful journey which he had already made. Moreover, how was he to cross again that slough from which he had only escaped by a miracle? And after the slough, was there not the police squad, which he assuredly would not escape twice; and then where should he go, and what direction take? following the slope would not lead to his object, for if he reached another outlet, he would find it obstructed by an iron plate or a grating. All the issues were indubitably closed in that way; accident had left the grating by which they entered open, but it was plain that all the other mouths of the sewer were closed. They had only succeeded in escaping into a prison.

It was all over, and all that Jean Valjean had done was useless: God opposed it. They were both caught in the dark and immense web of death, and Jean Valjean felt the fearful spider already running along the black threads in the darkness. He turned his back to the grating and fell on the pavement near Marius, who was still motionless, and whose head had fallen between his knees. There was no outlet, that was the last drop of agony. Of whom did he think in this profound despondency? Neither of himself nor of Marius! of Cosette. In the midst of his annihilation a hand

was laid on his shoulder, and a low voice said, —
"Half shares."

Some one in this shadow? As nothing so resembles a dream as despair, Jean Valjean fancied
that he was dreaming. He had not heard a footstep. Was it possible? He raised his eyes, and a
man was standing before him. This man was
dressed in a blouse, his feet were naked, and he
held his shoes in his hand; he had evidently taken
them off in order to be able to reach Jean Valjean
without letting his footsteps be heard. Jean Valjean had not a moment's hesitation: however unexpected the meeting might be, the man was known
to him: it was Thénardier.[1] Although, so to speak,
aroused with a start, Jean Valjean, accustomed to
alarms and to unexpected blows, which it is necessary to parry quickly, at once regained possession
of all his presence of mind. Besides, the situation
could not be worse, a certain degree of distress is
not capable of any crescendo, and Thénardier himself could not add any blackness to this night.
There was a moment's expectation. Thénardier,
raising his right hand to the level of his forehead,
made a screen of it; then he drew his eyebrows together with a wink, which, with a slight pinching of
the lips, characterizes the sagacious attention of a
man who is striving to recognize another. He did
not succeed. Jean Valjean, as we said, was turning his back to the light, and was besides so disfigured, so filthy, and blood-stained, that he could
not have been recognized in broad daylight. On
the other hand, Thénardier, with his face lit up by
the light from the grating, a cellar brightness, it is
true, livid but precise in his lividness, leapt at
once into Jean Valjean's eyes, to employ the energetic popular metaphor. This inequality of conditions sufficed to insure some advantage to Jean
Valjean in the mysterious duel which was about to
begin between the two situations and the two men.
The meeting took place between Jean Valjean
masked and Thénardier unmasked. Jean Valjean
at once perceived that Thénardier did not recognize him; and they looked at each other silently in
his gloom, as if taking one another's measure.
Thénardier was the first to break the silence.

"How do you mean to get out?"

Jean Valjean not replying, Thénardier continued, —

"It is impossible to pick the lock; and yet you
must get out of here."

"That is true," said Jean Valjean.

"Well, then, half shares."

"What do you mean?"

"You have killed the man, very good, and I
have the key."

[1] An old enemy.

Thénardier pointed to Marius, and continued,
— "I do not know you, but you must be a friend,
and I wish to help you."

Jean Valjean began to understand. Thénardier
took him for an assassin. The latter continued, —

"Listen, mate, you did not kill this man without
looking to see what he had in his pockets. Give
me my half and I open the gate."

And half drawing a heavy key from under his
ragged blouse, he added, —

"Would you like to see how the key is made?
look here."

Jean Valjean was so astounded that he doubted
whether what he saw was real. It was Providence
appearing in a horrible form, and the good angel
issuing from the ground in the shape of Thénardier. The latter thrust his hand into a wide
pocket hidden under his blouse, drew out a rope,
and handed it to Jean Valjean.

"There," he said, "I give you the rope in the
bargain."

"What am I to do with the rope?"

"You also want a stone, but you will find that
outside, as there is a heap of them."

"What am I to do with a stone?"

"Why, you ass, as you are going to throw the
cove into the river you want a rope and a stone,
or else the body will float on the water."

Jean Valjean took the rope mechanically, and
Thénardier snapped his fingers as if a sudden idea
had occurred to him.

"Hilloh, mate, how did you manage to get
through that slough? I did not dare venture into
it. Peuh! you do not smell pleasant."

After a pause he added, —

"I ask you questions, but you are right not to
answer: it is an apprenticeship for the magistrate's
ugly quarter of an hour. And then, by not speaking at all a man runs no risk of speaking too loud.
No matter, though I cannot see your face and do
not know your name, you would do wrong in supposing that I do not know who you are and what
you want. I know all about it: you have smashed
that swell a little, and now want to get rid of him
somewhere. You prefer the river, that great
nonsense-hider, and I will help you out of the hob-
ble. It is my delight to aid a good fellow when in
trouble."

While commending Jean Valjean for his silence
it was plain that he was trying to make him speak.
He pushed his shoulder, so as to be able to see his
profile, and exclaimed, though without raising the
pitch of his voice, —

"Talking of the slough, you are a precious ass.
Why did you not throw the man into it?"

Jean Valjean preserved silence. Thénardier

continued, raising his rag of a cravat to the Adam's apple, a gesture which completes the capable air of a serious man.

"Really, you may have acted sensibly, for the workmen who went to-morrow to stop up the hole would certainly have found the swell, and your trail would be followed up. Some one has passed through the sewer; who? how did he get out? was he seen to do so? The police are full of sense: the drain is a traitor, and denounces you. Such a find is a rarity, it attracts attention, for few people employ the sewer for their little business, while the river belongs to everybody, and is the real grave. At the end of a month your man is fished up at the nets of St. Cloud: well, who troubles himself about that? it's cold meat, that's all. Who killed the man? Paris, and justice makes no inquiries. You acted wisely."

The more loquacious Thénardier became, the more silent Jean Valjean was. Thénardier shook his shoulder again.

"And now let's settle our business. You have seen my key, so show me your money."

Thénardier was haggard, firm, slightly menacing, but remarkably friendly. There was one strange fact: Thénardier's manner was not simple; he did not appear entirely at his ease: while not affecting any mysterious air, he spoke in a low voice. From time to time he laid his finger on his lip, and muttered "Chut!" it was difficult to guess why, for there were only themselves present. Jean Valjean thought that other bandits were probably hidden in some corner no great distance off, and that Thénardier was not anxious to share with them. The latter continued, —

"Now for a finish. How much had the swell about him?"

Jean Valjean felt in his pockets. It was, as will be remembered, always his rule to have money about him, for the gloomy life of expedients to which he was condemned rendered it a law for him. This time, however, he was unprovided. In putting on upon the previous evening his National Guard uniform, he forgot, mournfully absorbed as he was, to take out his pocket-book, and he had only some change in his waistcoat-pocket. He turned out his pocket, which was saturated with slime, and laid on the banquette a louis d'or, two five-franc pieces, and five or six double sous. Thénardier thrust out his lower lip with a significant twist of the neck.

"You did not kill him for much," he said.

He began most familiarly feeling in Jean Valjean and Marius' pockets, and Jean Valjean, who was most anxious to keep his back to the light, allowed him to do so. While feeling in Marius' coat, Thénardier, with the dexterity of a conjuror, managed to tear off, without Jean Valjean perceiving the fact, a strip, which he concealed under his blouse; probably thinking that this piece of cloth might help him to recognize hereafter the assassinated man and the assassin. However, he found no more than the thirty francs.

"It is true," he said; "one with the other, you have no more than that."

And forgetting his phrase half shares, he took all. He hesitated a little at the double sous, but on reflection he took them too, while grumbling, "I don't care, it is killing people too cheaply."

This done, he again took the key from under his blouse.

"Now, my friend, you must be off. It is here as at the fairs; you pay when you go out. You have paid, so you can go."

And he began laughing. We may be permitted to doubt whether he had the pure and disinterested intention of saving an assassin, when he gave a stranger the help of this key, and allowed any one but himself to pass through this gate. Thénardier helped Jean Valjean to replace Marius on his back, and then proceeded to the grating on the tips of his naked feet. After making Jean Valjean a sign to follow him, he placed his finger on his lip, and remained for some seconds as if in suspense; but when the inspection was over he put the key in the lock. The bolt slid, and the gate turned on its hinges without grinding or creaking. It was plain that this grating and these hinges, carefully oiled, opened more frequently than might be supposed. This gentleness was ill-omened; it spoke of furtive comings and goings, of the mysterious entrances and exits of night-men, and the crafty foot fall of crime. The sewer was evidently an accomplice of some dark band, and this taciturn grating was a receiver. Thénardier held the door ajar, left just room for Jean Valjean to pass, relocked the gate, and plunged back into the darkness, making no more noise than a breath; he seemed to walk with the velvety pads of a tiger. A moment later this hideous providence had disappeared, and Jean Valjean was outside.

He let Marius slip down on to the bank. They were outside; the miasmas, the darkness, the horror, were behind him; the healthy, pure, living, joyous, freely respirable air inundated him. All around him was silence, but it was the charming silence of the sun setting in the full azure. Twilight was passing, and night, the great liberator, the friend of all those who need a cloak of darkness to escape from an agony, was at hand. The sky offered itself on all sides like an enormous calm, and the river rippled up to his feet with the sound of a kiss. The aerial dialogue of the nests bidding each other goodnight in the elms of the Champ Elysées was audible. A few stars, faintly studding the pale blue of the zenith, formed in the immensity little imperceptible flashes. Night unfolded over Jean Valjean's head all the sweetness of infinitude. It was the undecided and exquisite hour which says neither yes nor no. There was already sufficient night for a man to lose himself in it a short distance off, and yet sufficient daylight to recognize any one close by. Jean Valjean was for a few seconds irresistibly overcome by all this august and caressing serenity. There are minutes of oblivion in which suffering gives up harassing the wretch; all is eclipsed in the thought; peace covers the dreamer like a light, and under the gleaming twilight the soul shines in imitation of the sky which is becoming illumined. Jean Valjean could not refrain from contemplating the vast clear obscure which he had above him, and pensively took a bath of ecstasy and prayer in the majestic silence of the eternal heavens. Then, as if the feeling of duty returned to him, he eagerly bent down over Marius, and lifting some water in the hollow of his hand, softly threw a few drops into his face. Marius' eyelids did not move, but he still breathed through his parted lips. Jean Valjean was again about to plunge his hand into the river, when he suddenly felt some annoyance, as when we feel there is some one behind us though we cannot see him. He turned round, and there was really some one behind him, as there had been just before.

A man of tall stature, dressed in a long coat, with folded arms, and carrying in his right hand a cudgel, whose leaden knob could be seen, was standing a few paces behind Jean Valjean, who was leaning over Marius. It was with the help of the darkness a species of apparition; a simple man would have been frightened at it owing to the twilight, and a thoughtful one on account of the bludgeon. Jean Valjean recognized Javert. The reader has doubtless guessed that the tracker of Thénardier was no other than Javert. Javert, after his unhoped-for escape from the barricade, went to the prefecture of police, made a verbal report to the prefect in person in a short audience, and then immediately returned to duty, which implied — the note found on him will be remembered — a certain surveillance of the right bank of the river at the Champs Elysées, which had for some time past attracted the attention of the police. There he perceived Thénardier and followed him. The rest is known.

It will be also understood that the grating so obligingly opened for Jean Valjean was a clever trick on the part of Thénardier. He felt that Javert was still there; the watched man has a scent which never deceives him; and it was necessary to throw a bone to this grayhound. An assassin, what a chance! he could not let it slip. Thénardier, on putting Jean Valjean outside in his place, offered a prey to the policeman, made him loose his hold, caused himself to be forgotten in a greater adventure, recompensed Javert for his loss of time, which always flatters a spy, gained thirty francs, and fully intended for his own part to escape by the help of this diversion.

Jean Valjean had passed from one rock to another; these two meetings one upon the other, falling from Thénardier on Javert, were rude. Javert did not recognize Jean Valjean, who, as we have said, no longer resembled himself. He did not unfold his arms, but secured his grasp of his bludgeon by an imperceptible movement, and said, in a sharp, calm voice, —

"Who are you?"

"Myself."

"What do you mean?"

"I am Jean Valjean."

Javert placed his cudgel between his teeth, bent his knees, bowed his back, laid his two powerful hands on Jean Valjean's shoulders, which they held as in two vices, examined and recognized him. Their faces almost touched, and Javert's glance was terrific. Jean Valjean remained inert under Javert's gripe, like a lion enduring the claw of a lynx.

"Inspector Javert," he said, "you have me. Besides, since this morning I have considered myself your prisoner. I did not give you my address in order to try and escape you. Take me, but grant me one thing."

Javert did not seem to hear, but kept his eyeballs fixed on Jean Valjean. His wrinkled chin thrust up his lips towards his nose, a sign of stern reverie. At length he loosed his hold of Jean Valjean, drew himself up, clutched his cudgel, and, as if in a dream, muttered rather than asked this question, —

"What are you doing here? and who is that man?"

Jean Valjean replied, and the sound of his voice seemed to awaken Javert, —

"It is of him that I wished to speak. Do with me as you please, but help me first to carry him home. I only ask this of you."

Javert's face was contracted in the same way as it always was when any one believed him capable of a concession; still he did not say no. He stooped again, took from his pocket a handkerchief, which he dipped in the water, and wiped Marius' ensanguined forehead.

"This man was at the barricade," he said in a low voice, and as if speaking to himself; "he was the one whom they called Marius."

He was a first-class spy, who had observed everything, listened to everything, heard everything, and picked up everything when he believed himself a dead man; who even spied in his death agony, and, standing on the first step of the sepulchre, took notes. He seized Marius' hand, and felt his pulse.

"He is wounded," said Jean Valjean.

"He is a dead man," said Javert.

Jean Valjean replied, —

"No; not yet."

"Then you brought him from the barricade here?" Javert observed.

His preoccupation must have been great for him not to dwell on this alarming escape through the sewers, and not even remark Jean Valjean's silence after his question. Jean Valjean, on his side, seemed to have a sole thought; he continued, —

"He lives in the Marais, in the Rue des Filles du Calvaire, with his grandfather. I do not know his name."

Jean Valjean felt in Marius' pocket, took out the portfolio, opened it at the page on which Marius had written in pencil, and offered it to Javert. There was still sufficient floating light in the air to be able to read, and Javert, besides, had in his eyes the feline phosphorescence of night birds. He deciphered the few lines written by Marius, and growled, "Gillenormand, No. 6, Rue des Filles du Calvaire." Then he cried, "Driver!"

Our readers will remember the coachman waiting above in case of need. A moment after the hackney, which came down the incline leading to the watering-place, was on the bank. Marius was deposited on the back seat, and Javert sat down by Jean Valjean's side on the front one. When the door was closed the fiacre started off rapidly along the quays in the direction of the Bastile. They quitted the quay and turned into the streets; and the driver, a black outline on his seat, lashed his lean horses. There was an icy silence in the hackney-coach; Marius motionless, with his body reclining in one corner, his head on his chest, his arms pendant, and his legs stiff, appeared to be only waiting for a coffin; Jean Valjean seemed made of gloom, and Javert of stone; and in this fiacre full of night, whose interior, each time that it passed a lamp, seemed to be lividly lit up as if by an intermittent flash, accident united and appeared to confront the three immobilities of tragedy, — the corpse, the spectre, and the statue.

Ralph Waldo Emerson · 1803–1882

Romanticism, transplanted to the United States, allied itself with a movement known as "transcendentalism." In order to understand how the two attitudes are related, we must realize that the American movement was based on doctrines of ancient and modern European philosophers (particularly of the German Kant) after those doctrines had been passed on to them through the romantic writings of Coleridge, Wordsworth, Carlyle, and Goethe. The leading American transcendentalists were Emerson and Thoreau. Other followers included Bronson Alcott, Margaret Fuller, and W. H. Channing. Familiar transcendental convictions were: that one should live close to nature and have faith in his conscience and his ideals; that manual labor is dignified; that one must live spiritually; that man should approach God directly as an individual rather than through an intermediary priest or clergyman; that man is divine in his own right; and that, because all men are divine, mankind is a single great brotherhood. Many of these ideas we recognize from our reading of Wordsworth, Coleridge, and Goethe, as familiar convictions of the European romanticists.

Emerson gave to the literature of this country its most stimulating philosophical writing. He did not introduce a new or logical "system" of philosophy — what he had to say was largely found in Plato as modified by European thinkers — but he spoke with authority in a popular manner which localized and gave body to his ideas, and in a voice which New England and the Middle West could understand.

Ralph Waldo Emerson was born in Boston, May 25, 1803, the son of the pastor of the "First Church" (Unitarian) in Boston. Prepared for college at the Boston Latin School, Emerson entered Harvard as the "President's freshman," a designation which meant that in return for certain modest services a portion of the fees was remitted. The appointment was also, no doubt, a recognition of the fact that Emerson was the son of a widow in rather straitened circumstances as well as a young man of promise. Not an especially brilliant student, Emerson proceeded normally, made friends, and was elected "class poet." For a time he taught school, but as the occupation was most distasteful to him he decided to enter Harvard Theological School. He was licensed to preach in 1826. Three years later he was appointed assistant pastor, and later pastor, of the Second Church (Unitarian) in Boston. That same year he married Ellen Tucker. Before long, however, the young pastor found that even the liberal theology of the Unitarians somewhat confined his freedom of expression and that, for him, some of the forms had become empty rituals. In 1832 he resigned from the church and became the last in a long line of preachers in his immediate family. That December he sailed for Europe, traveling in Italy, France, and England and making the acquaintance of such men as Coleridge, Wordsworth, and Carlyle. Upon his return to America, Emerson settled in Concord, a young man who had found himself and who was ready to set forth his convictions for others through his lectures, his poems, and his essays. His first wife having died before he went to Europe, he married Lydia Jackson in 1835. For the next four decades Emerson resided at Concord, living quietly and simply, taking his part in village responsibilities, lecturing in New England and the Middle West, his popularity at one time calling him as far west as the Pacific coast. His last days were dimmed by fading faculties; he died in his seventy-ninth year, April 27, 1882.

Emerson's most important publications were the long essay, *Nature* (1836), which set forth once and for all most of his doctrine, *Essays* (1841), a second series of *Essays* (1844), *Poems* (1846), *Representative Men* (1850), *English Traits* (1856), and *The Conduct of Life* (1860). His two most famous addresses were *The American Scholar* given as the Phi Beta Kappa oration (1837) and the *Divinity School Address* (1838). Some of the independence of spirit which Emerson brought to Americans was manifest in the first address in which he declared, in opposing European influence, "We will walk on our own feet; we will work with our own hands; we will speak with our own minds . . ." One critic called this address "the American Declaration of Independence in the intellectual life."

Emerson's thought pervades his lectures, essays, and poems evenly and consistently. Indeed the essays were frequently lectures turned into literature. Throughout the whole body of the writing a few leading doctrines stand forth, some few certain attitudes manifest themselves. Emerson is persistently optimistic, frequently mystical, and always the idealist. Nature, we are told, is a harmonious unit anxious to work in co-operation with mankind will man only permit her to do so. God *is* nature; mankind is protected by a great brooding "Over-Soul" which we can hear speak if we will trust our native intuition. The true hero, the true poet, is he who lives thus in accord with nature and the over-soul; and immortality comes only to those who throw themselves trustingly into the arms of this beneficent spirit. All bibles and all creeds are good so far as they are expressions of this world-soul, so long as they are sincere manifestations of the inner heart of man. Consistency in small things is not important, but consistency based on the dictates of this spiritual entity is all-important. We must be self-reliant. Man needs solitude that he may escape the perfunctory conventions of civilization and learn what is true for him.

As a writer, whether of poetry or prose, Emerson had a tendency to deal in abstraction, to ignore the actual, work-a-day world, to write of love, for instance, rather than of lovers. Life, action, passion are wanting; dramatic and epic qualities are not his. The esoteric is sometimes confused with the imaginative. On the other hand, we must not quibble with a philosopher because he does not write romances. What we have in the poems and essays are elevation of thought, inspiration for the individual, a religious doctrine of more than theoretical value, and, often, brilliant passages which stand out in any poetry like flashes of lightning on a dark night:

> Not many men see beauty in the fogs
> Of close low pine-woods in a river town.

Emerson conceived the poet as the interpreter, the articulator of life. His purpose was not so much to be an artist as to enfranchise the human spirit.

The romantic temper finds expression in Emerson in the high regard in which he held nature, his effort to dignify the individual, his resentment of formal restraints (as in church doctrine), his lack of concern for conventional poetic patterns, his insistence that man should live by faith rather than by reason, his emotion before the mystery of existence, and his withdrawing from the active life in an effort to make the world a better place for man to exert his inherent and natural capabilities.

SUGGESTED REFERENCES: F. I. Carpenter, *Emerson Handbook* (1953); M. R. Konvitz and S. E. Whicher, eds., *Emerson. A Collection of Critical Essays* (1962).

Written in Naples

We are what we are made; each following day
Is the Creator of our human mould
Not less than was the first; the all-wise God
Gilds a few points in every several life,
And as each flower upon the fresh hillside,   5
And every colored petal of each flower,
Is sketched and dyed, each with a new design,
Its spot of purple, and its streak of brown,
So each man's life shall have its proper lights,
And a few joys, a few peculiar charms,   10
For him round-in the melancholy hours
And reconcile him to the common days.
Not many men see beauty in the fogs
Of close low pine-woods in a river town;
Yet unto me not morn's magnificence,   15
Nor the red rainbow of a summer eve,
Nor Rome, nor joyful Paris, nor the halls
Of rich men blazing hospitable light,
Nor wit, nor eloquence, — no, nor even the song
Of any woman that is now alive, —   20
Hath such a soul, such divine influence,
Such resurrection of the happy past,
As is to me when I behold the morn
Ope in such low moist roadside, and beneath
Peep the blue violets out of the black loam,   25
Pathetic silent poets that sing to me
Thine elegy, sweet singer, sainted wife.[1]

Written at Rome

Emerson believed that an all-pervading spirit of goodness, which he termed the "Over-Soul," filled the universe and flowed freely through all men. To one who lives in this world-spirit all places — Rome or Concord — are essentially alike.

Alone in Rome. Why, Rome is lonely too; —
Besides, you need not be alone; the soul
Shall have society of its own rank.
Be great, be true, and all the Scipios,

[1] Emerson's first wife, Ellen, died from tuberculosis shortly after their marriage.

The Catos, the wise patriots of Rome,   5
Shall flock to you and tarry by your side,
And comfort you with their high company.
Virtue alone is sweet society,
It keeps the key to all heroic hearts,
And opens you a welcome in them all.   10
You must be like them if you desire them,
Scorn trifles and embrace a better aim
Than wine or sleep or praise;
Hunt knowledge as the lover woos a maid,
And ever in the strife of your own thoughts   15
Obey the nobler impulse; that is Rome:
That shall command a senate to your side;
For there is no might in the universe
That can contend with love. It reigns forever.
Wait then, sad friend, wait in majestic peace   20
The hour of heaven. Generously trust
Thy fortune's web to the beneficent hand
That until now has put his world in fee
To thee. He watches for thee still. His love
Broods over thee, and as God lives in heaven,   25
However long thou walkest solitary,
The hour of heaven shall come, the man appear.

The Rhodora

ON BEING ASKED, WHENCE IS THE FLOWER?

In May, when sea-winds pierced our solitudes,
I found the fresh Rhodora [1] in the woods,
Spreading its leafless blooms in a damp nook,
To please the desert and the sluggish brook.
The purple petals, fallen in the pool,   5
Made the black water with their beauty gay;
Here might the redbird come his plumes to cool,
And court the flower that cheapens his array.
Rhodora! if the sages ask thee why
This charm is wasted on the earth and sky,   10
Tell them, dear, that if eyes were made for seeing,
Then Beauty is its own excuse for being:
Why thou wert there, O rival of the rose!
I never thought to ask, I never knew:

[1] A low shrub bearing purple flowers; common in New England and Canada.

But, in my simple ignorance, suppose 15
The self-same Power that brought me there brought
     you.

Each and All

Here we meet two familiar romantic and transcendental tenets: the divinity of nature and the brotherhood which man shares with man and with nature. Emerson tells us that composition, the relationship of one item in nature to another, is more important than the individual item.

Little thinks, in the field, yon red-cloaked clown
Of thee from the hill-top looking down;
The heifer that lows in the upland farm,
Far-heard, lows not thine ear to charm;
The sexton, tolling his bell at noon,   5
Deems not that great Napoleon
Stops his horse, and lists with delight,
Whilst his files sweep round yon Alpine height;
Nor knowest thou what argument
Thy life to thy neighbor's creed has lent.   10
All are needed by each one;
Nothing is fair or good alone.
I thought the sparrow's note from heaven,
Singing at dawn on the alder bough;
I brought him home, in his nest, at even;   15
He sings the song, but it cheers not now,
For I did not bring home the river and sky; —
He sang to my ear, — they sang to my eye.
The delicate shells lay on the shore;
The bubbles of the latest wave   20
Fresh pearls to their enamel gave,
And the bellowing of the savage sea
Greeted their safe escape to me.
I wiped away the weeds and foam,
I fetched my sea-born treasures home;   25
But the poor, unsightly, noisome things
Had left their beauty on the shore
With the sun and the sand and the wild uproar.
The lover watched his graceful maid,
As 'mid the virgin train she strayed,   30
Nor knew her beauty's best attire
Was woven still by the snow-white choir.
At last she came to his hermitage,
Like the bird from the woodlands to the cage; —
The gay enchantment was undone,   35
A gentle wife, but fairy none.
Then I said, "I covet truth;
Beauty is unripe childhood's cheat;
I leave it behind with the games of youth:" —
As I spoke, beneath my feet   40
The ground-pine curled its pretty wreath,
Running over the club-moss burrs;
I inhaled the violet's breath;

Around me stood the oaks and firs;
Pine-cones and acorns lay on the ground;
Over me soared the eternal sky,   45
Full of light and of deity;
Again I saw, again I heard,
The rolling river, the morning bird; —
Beauty through my senses stole;   50
I yielded myself to the perfect whole.

The Sphinx

Mr. Emerson wrote in his notebook in 1859: "I have often been asked the meaning of the 'Sphinx.' It is this: The perception of identity unites all things and explains one by another, and the most rare and strange is equally facile as the most common. But if the mind live only in particulars, and see only differences (wanting the power to see the whole — all in each), then the world addresses to this mind a question it cannot answer, and each new fact tears it in pieces and it is vanquished by the distracting variety." (E. W. Emerson.)

The Sphinx is drowsy,
    Her wings are furled:
Her ear is heavy,
    She broods on the world.
"Who'll tell me my secret,   5
    The ages have kept? —
I awaited the seer
    While they slumbered and slept: —

"The fate of the man-child,
    The meaning of man;   10
Known fruit of the unknown;
    Dædalian [1] plan;
Out of sleeping a waking,
    Out of waking a sleep;
Life death overtaking;   15
    Deep underneath deep?

"Erect as a sunbeam,
    Upspringeth the palm;
The elephant browses,
    Undaunted and calm;   20
In beautiful motion
    The thrush plies his wings;
Kind leaves of his covert,
    Your silence he sings.

"The waves, unashamèd,   25
    In difference sweet,
Play glad with the breezes,
    Old playfellows meet;
The journeying atoms,

[1] intricate.

Primordial wholes,   30
Firmly draw, firmly drive,
  By their animate poles.

"Sea, earth, air, sound, silence,
  Plant, quadruped, bird,
By one music enchanted,   35
  One deity stirred, —
Each the other adorning,
  Accompany still;
Night veileth the morning,
  The vapor the hill.   40

"The babe by its mother
  Lies bathèd in joy;
Glide its hours uncounted, —
  The sun is its toy;
Shines the peace of all being,   45
  Without cloud, in its eyes;
And the sum of the world
  In soft miniature lies.

"But man crouches and blushes,
  Absconds and conceals;   50
He creepeth and peepeth,
  He palters and steals;
Infirm, melancholy,
  Jealous glancing around,
An oaf, an accomplice,   55
  He poisons the ground.

"Out spoke the great mother,
  Beholding his fear; —
At the sound of her accents
  Cold shuddered the sphere: —   60
'Who has drugged my boy's cup?
Who has mixed my boy's bread?
Who, with sadness and madness,
  Has turned my child's head?'"

I heard a poet answer   65
  Aloud and cheerfully,
"Say on, sweet Sphinx! thy dirges
  Are pleasant songs to me.
Deep love lieth under
  These pictures of time;   70
They fade in the light of
  Their meaning sublime.

"The fiend that man harries
  Is love of the Best;
Yawns the pit of the Dragon,   75
  Lit by rays from the Blest.
The Lethe of Nature
  Can't trance him again,
Whose soul sees the perfect,
  Which his eyes seek in vain.   80

"To vision profounder,
  Man's spirit must dive;
His aye-rolling orb
  At no goal will arrive;
The heavens that now draw him   85
  With sweetness untold,
Once found, — for new heavens
  He spurneth the old.

"Pride ruined the angels,
  Their shame them restores;   90
Lurks the joy that is sweetest
  In stings of remorse.
Have I a lover
  Who is noble and free? —
I would he were nobler   95
  Than to love me.

"Eterne alternation
  Now follows, now flies;
And under pain, pleasure, —
  Under pleasure, pain lies.   100
Love works at the centre,
  Heart-heaving alway;
Forth speed the strong pulses
  To the borders of day.

"Dull Sphinx, Jove keep thy five wits;   105
  Thy sight is growing blear;
Rue, myrrh and cummin [1] for the Sphinx,
  Her muddy eyes to clear!"
The old Sphinx bit her thick lip, —
  Said, "Who taught thee me to name?   110
I am thy spirit, yoke-fellow;
  Of thine eye I am eyebeam.

"Thou art the unanswered question;
  Couldst see thy proper eye,
Alway it asketh, asketh;   115
  And each answer is a lie.
So take thy quest through nature,
  It through thousand natures ply;
Ask on, thou clothed eternity;
  Time is the false reply."   120

Uprose the merry Sphinx,
  And crouched no more in stone;
She melted into purple cloud,
  She silvered in the moon;
She spired into a yellow flame;   125
  She flowered in blossoms red;
She flowed into a foaming wave:
  She stood Monadnoc's [2] head.

[1] A variety of parsley.
[2] A mountain.

Through a thousand voices
    Spoke the universal dame;   130
"Who telleth one of my meanings
    Is master of all I am."

Musketaquid

Because I was content with these poor fields,
Low, open meads, slender and sluggish streams,
And found a home in haunts which others scorned,
The partial wood-gods overpaid my love,
And granted me the freedom of their state,   5
And in their secret senate have prevailed
With the dear, dangerous lords that rule our life,
Made moon and planets parties to their bond,
And through my rock-like, solitary wont
Shot million rays of thought and tenderness.   10
For me, in showers, in sweeping showers, the Spring
Visits the valley; — break away the clouds, —
I bathe in the morn's soft and silvered air,
And loiter willing by yon loitering stream.
Sparrows far off, and nearer, April's bird,   15
Blue-coated, — flying before from tree to tree,
Courageous sing a delicate overture
To lead the tardy concert of the year.
Onward and nearer rides the sun of May;
And wide around, the marriage of the plants   20
Is sweetly solemnized.   Then flows amain
The surge of summer's beauty; dell and crag,
Hollow and lake, hillside and pine arcade,
Are touched with genius.   Yonder ragged cliff
Has thousand faces in a thousand hours.   25
Beneath low hills, in the broad interval
Through which at will our Indian rivulet
Winds mindful still of sannup and of squaw,
Whose pipe and arrow oft the plough unburies,
Here in pine houses built of new-fallen trees,   30
Supplanters of the tribe, the farmers dwell.
Traveller, to thee, perchance, a tedious road,
Or, it may be, a picture; to these men,
The landscape is an armory of powers,
Which, one by one, they know to draw and use.   35
They harness beast, bird, insect, to their work;
They prove the virtues of each bed of rock,
And, like the chemist 'mid his loaded jars,
Draw from each stratum its adapted use
To drug their crops or weapon their arts withal.   40
They turn the frost upon their chemic heap,
They set the wind to winnow pulse and grain,
They thank the spring-flood for its fertile slime,
And, on cheap summit-levels of the snow,
Slide with the sledge to inaccessible woods   45
O'er meadows bottomless.   So, year by year,

They fight the elements with elements
(That one would say, meadow and forest walked,
Transmuted in these men to rule their like),
And by the order in the field disclose   50
The order regnant in the yeoman's brain.

What these strong masters wrote at large in miles,
I followed in small copy in my acre;
For there's no rood has not a star above it;
The cordial quality of pear or plum   55
Ascends as gladly in a single tree
As in broad orchards resonant with bees;
And every atom poises for itself,
And for the whole.   The gentle deities
Showed me the lore of colors and of sounds,   60
The innumerable tenements of beauty,
The miracle of generative force,
Far-reaching concords of astronomy
Felt in the plants and in the punctual birds;
Better, the linkèd purpose of the whole,   65
And, chiefest prize, found I true liberty
In the glad home plain-dealing Nature gave.
The polite found me impolite; the great
Would mortify me, but in vain; for still
I am a willow of the wilderness,   70
Loving the wind that bent me.   All my hurts
My garden spade can heal.   A woodland walk,
A quest of river-grapes, a mocking thrush,
A wild-rose, or rock-loving columbine,
Salve my worst wounds.   75
For thus the wood-gods murmured in my ear:
"Dost love our manners?   Canst thou silent lie?
Canst thou, thy pride forgot, like Nature pass
Into the winter night's extinguished mood?
Canst thou shine now, then darkle,   80
And being latent, feel thyself no less?
As, when the all-worshipped moon attracts the eye,
The river, hill, stems, foliage are obscure,
Yet envies none, none are unenviable."

Days

Daughters of Time, the hypocritic Days,
Muffled and dumb like barefoot dervishes,
And marching single in an endless file,
Bring diadems and fagots in their hands.
To each they offer gifts after his will,   5
Bread, kingdoms, stars, and sky that holds them all.
I, in my pleachèd garden, watched the pomp,
Forgot my morning wishes, hastily
Took a few herbs and apples, and the Day
Turned and departed silent.   I, too late,   10
Under her solemn fillet saw the scorn.

Brahma

Emerson suggested that readers who had difficulty in understanding this poem simply read *Jehovah* for *Brahma* and his meaning would then be clear. The poem is an expression of his thesis that deity pervades all things and that he who lives the good life is leading a religious life. Thought and the object of thought are, he implies, one. The poem reflects Emerson's interest in Oriental thought.

If the red slayer think he slays,
　Or if the slain think he is slain,
They know not well the subtle ways
　I keep, and pass, and turn again.

Far or forgot to me is near;
　Shadow and sunlight are the same;
The vanished gods to me appear;
　And one to me are shame and fame.

They reckon ill who leave me out;
　When me they fly, I am the wings;
I am the doubter and the doubt,
　And I the hymn the Brahmin sings.

The strong gods pine for my abode,
　And pine in vain the sacred Seven;
But thou, meek lover of the good!
　Find me, and turn thy back on heaven.

The American Scholar

AN ORATION DELIVERED BEFORE THE PHI BETA KAPPA
SOCIETY, AT CAMBRIDGE, AUGUST 31, 1837

Mr. President and Gentlemen:

I greet you on the recommencement of our literary year. Our anniversary is one of hope, and, perhaps, not enough of labor. We do not meet for games of strength or skill, for the recitation of histories, tragedies, and odes, like the ancient Greeks; for parliaments of love and poesy, like the Troubadours; nor for the advancement of science, like our contemporaries in the British and European capitals. Thus far, our holiday has been simply a friendly sign of the survival of the love of letters amongst a people too busy to give to letters any more. As such it is precious as the sign of an indestructible instinct. Perhaps the time is already come when it ought to be, and will be, something else; when the sluggard intellect of this continent will look from under its iron lids and fill the postponed expectation of the world with something better than the exertions of mechanical skill. Our day of dependence, our long apprenticeship to the learning of other lands, draws

to a close. The millions that around us are rushing into life, cannot always be fed on the sere remains of foreign harvests. Events, actions arise, that must be sung, that will sing themselves. Who can doubt that poetry will revive and lead in a new age, as the star in the constellation Harp, which now flames in our zenith, astronomers announce, shall one day be the pole-star for a thousand years?

In this hope I accept the topic which not only usage but the nature of our association seem to prescribe to this day, — the AMERICAN SCHOLAR. Year by year we come up hither to read one more chapter of his biography. Let us inquire what light new days and events have thrown on his character and his hopes.

It is one of those fables which out of an unknown antiquity convey an unlooked-for wisdom, that the gods, in the beginning, divided Man into men, that he might be more helpful to himself; just as the hand was divided into fingers, the better to answer its end.

The old fable covers a doctrine ever new and sublime; that there is One Man, — present to all particular men only partially, or through one faculty; and that you must take the whole society to find the whole man. Man is not a farmer, or a professor, or an engineer, but he is all. Man is priest, and scholar, and statesman, and producer, and soldier. In the *divided* or social state these functions are parcelled out to individuals, each of whom aims to do his stint of the joint work, whilst each other performs his. The fable implies that the individual, to possess himself, must sometimes return from his own labor to embrace all the other laborers. But, unfortunately, this original unit, this fountain of power, has been so distributed to multitudes, has been so minutely subdivided and peddled out, that it is spilled into drops, and cannot be gathered. The state of society is one in which the members have suffered amputation from the trunk, and strut about so many walking monsters, — a good finger, a neck, a stomach, an elbow, but never a man.

Man is thus metamorphosed into a thing, into many things. The planter, who is Man sent out into the field to gather food, is seldom cheered by any idea of the true dignity of his ministry. He sees his bushel and his cart, and nothing beyond, and sinks into the farmer, instead of Man on the farm. The tradesman scarcely ever gives an ideal worth to his work, but is ridden by the routine of his craft, and the soul is subject to dollars. The priest becomes a form; the attorney a statute-book; the mechanic a machine; the sailor a rope of the ship.

In this distribution of functions the scholar is the delegated intellect. In the right state he is *Man Thinking*. In the degenerate state, when the victim of society, he tends to become a mere thinker, or still worse, the parrot of other men's thinking.

In this view of him, as Man Thinking, the theory of his office is contained. Him Nature solicits with all her placid, all her monitory pictures; him the past instructs; him the future invites. Is not indeed every man a student, and do not all things exist for the student's behoof? And, finally, is not the true scholar the only true master? But the old oracle said, "All things have two handles: beware of the wrong one." In life, too often, the scholar errs with mankind and forfeits his privilege. Let us see him in his school, and consider him in reference to the main influences he receives.

I. The first in time and the first in importance of the influences upon the mind is that of nature. Every day, the sun; and, after sunset, Night and her stars. Ever the winds blow; ever the grass grows. Every day, men and women, conversing — beholding and beholden. The scholar is he of all men whom this spectacle most engages. He must settle its value in his mind. What is nature to him? There is never a beginning, there is never an end, to the inexplicable continuity of this web of God, but always circular power returning into itself. Therein it resembles his own spirit, whose beginning, whose ending, he never can find, — so entire, so boundless. Far too as her splendors shine, system on system shooting like rays, upward, downward, without centre, without circumference, — in the mass and in the particle, Nature hastens to render account of herself to the mind. Classification begins. To the young mind every thing is individual, stands by itself. By and by, it finds how to join two things and see in them one nature; then three, then three thousand; and so, tyrannized over by its own unifying instinct, it goes on tying things together, diminishing anomalies, discovering roots running under ground whereby contrary and remote things cohere and flower out from one stem. It presently learns that since the dawn of history there has been a constant accumulation and classifying of facts. But what is classification but the perceiving that these objects are not chaotic, and are not foreign, but have a law which is also a law of the human mind? The astronomer discovers that geometry, a pure abstraction of the human mind, is the measure of planetary motion. The chemist finds proportions and intelligible method throughout matter; and science is nothing but the finding of analogy, identity, in the most remote parts. The ambitious soul sits down before each refractory fact; one after another reduces all strange constitutions, all new powers, to their class and their law, and goes on forever to animate the last fibre of organization, the outskirts of nature, by insight.

Thus to him, to this schoolboy under the bending dome of day, is suggested that he and it proceed from one root; one is leaf and one is flower; relation, sympathy, stirring in every vein. And what is that root? Is not that the soul of his soul? A thought too bold; a dream too wild. Yet when this spiritual light shall have revealed the law of more earthly natures, — when he has learned to worship the soul, and to see that the natural philosophy that now is, is only the first gropings of its gigantic hand, he shall look forward to an ever expanding knowledge as to a becoming creator. He shall see that nature is the opposite of the soul, answering to it part for part. One is seal and one is print. Its beauty is the beauty of his own mind. Its laws are the laws of his own mind. Nature then becomes to him the measure of his attainments. So much of nature as he is ignorant of, so much of his own mind does he not yet possess. And, in fine, the ancient precept, "Know thyself," and the modern precept, "Study nature," becomes at last one maxim.

II. The next great influence into the spirit of the scholar is the mind of the Past, — in whatever form, whether of literature, of art, of institutions, that mind is inscribed. Books are the best type of the influence of the past, and perhaps we shall get at the truth, — learn the amount of this influence more conveniently, — by considering their value alone.

The theory of books is noble. The scholar of the first age received into him the world around; brooded thereon; gave it the new arrangement of his own mind, and uttered it again. It came into him life; it went out from him truth. It came to him short-lived actions; it went out from him immortal thoughts. It came to him business; it went from him poetry. It was dead fact; now, it is quick thought. It can stand, and it can go. It now endures, it now flies, it now inspires. Precisely in proportion to the depth of mind from which it issued, so high does it soar, so long does it sing.

Or, I might say, it depends on how far the process had gone, of transmuting life into truth. In proportion to the completeness of the distillation, so will the purity and imperishableness of the product be. But none is quite perfect. As no air-pump can by any means make a perfect vacuum, so neither can any artist entirely exclude the conventional, the local, the perishable from his book, or write a book of pure thought, that shall be as efficient, in all respects, to a remote posterity, as to contemporaries, or rather to the second age. Each age, it is found, must write its own books; or rather, each generation for the next succeeding. The books of an older period will not fit this.

Yet hence arises a grave mischief. The sacredness which attaches to the act of creation, the act of thought, is transferred to the record. The poet chanting was felt to be a divine man: henceforth the chant is divine also. The writer was a just and wise spirit: henceforward it is settled the book is perfect; as love of the hero corrupts into worship of his statue. Instantly the book becomes noxious: the guide is a tyrant. The sluggish and perverted mind of the multitude, slow to open to the incursions of Reason, having once so opened, having once received this book, stands upon it, and makes an outcry if it is disparaged. Colleges are built on it. Books are written on it by thinkers, not by Man Thinking; by men of talent, that is, who start wrong, who set out from accepted dogmas, not from their own sight of principles. Meek young men grow up in libraries, believing it their duty to accept the views which Cicero, which Locke, which Bacon, have given; forgetful that Cicero, Locke, and Bacon were only young men in libraries when they wrote these books.

Hence, instead of Man Thinking, we have the bookworm. Hence the book-learned class, who value books, as such; not as related to nature and the human constitution, but as making a sort of Third Estate with the world and the soul. Hence the restorers of readings, the emendators, the bibliomaniacs of all degrees.

Books are the best of things, well used; abused, among the worst. What is the right use? What is the one end which all means go to effect? They are for nothing but to inspire. I had better never see a book than to be warped by its attraction clean out of my own orbit, and made a satellite instead of a system. The one thing in the world, of value, is the active soul. This every man is entitled to; this every man contains within him, although in almost all men obstructed and as yet unborn. The soul active sees absolute truth and utters truth, or creates. In this action it is genius; not the privilege of here and there a favorite, but the sound estate of every man. In its essence it is progressive. The book, the college, the school of art, the institution of any kind, stop with some past utterance of genius. This is good, say they, — let us hold by this. They pin me down. They look backward and not forward. But genius looks forward: the eyes of man are set in his forehead,

not in his hindhead: man hopes: genius creates. Whatever talents may be, if the man create not, the pure efflux of the Deity is not his; — cinders and smoke there may be, but not yet flame. There are creative manners, there are creative actions, and creative words; manners, actions, words, that is, indicative of no custom or authority, but springing spontaneous from the mind's own sense of good and fair.

On the other part, instead of being its own seer, let it receive from another mind its truth, though it were in torrents of light, without periods of solitude, inquest, and self-recovery, and a fatal disservice is done. Genius is always sufficiently the enemy of genius by over-influence. The literature of every nation bears me witness. The English dramatic poets have Shakespearized now for two hundred years.

Undoubtedly there is a right way of reading, so it be sternly subordinated. Man Thinking must not be subdued by his instruments. Books are for the scholar's idle times. When he can read God directly, the hour is too precious to be wasted in other men's transcripts of their readings. But when the intervals of darkness come, as come they must, — when the sun is hid and the stars withdraw their shining, — we repair to the lamps which were kindled by their ray, to guide our steps to the East again, where the dawn is. We hear, that we may speak. The Arabian proverb says, "A fig tree, looking on a fig tree, becometh fruitful."

It is remarkable, the character of the pleasure we derive from the best books. They impress us with the conviction that one nature wrote and the same reads. We read the verses of one of the great English poets, of Chaucer, of Marvell, of Dryden, with the most modern joy, — with a pleasure, I mean, which is in great part caused by the abstraction of all *time* from their verses. There is some awe mixed with the joy of our surprise, when this poet, who lived in some past world, two or three hundred years ago, says that which lies close to my own soul, that which I also had wellnigh thought and said. But for the evidence thence afforded to the philosophical doctrine of the identity of all minds, we should suppose some pre-established harmony, some foresight of souls that were to be, and some preparation of stores for their future wants, like the fact observed in insects, who lay up food before death for the young grub they shall never see.

I would not be hurried by any love of system, by any exaggeration of instincts, to underrate the Book. We all know, that as the human body can be nourished on any food, though it were boiled grass and the broth of shoes, so the human mind can be fed by any knowledge. And great and heroic men have existed who had almost no other information than by the printed page. I only would say that it needs a strong head to bear that diet. One must be an inventor to read well. As the proverb says, "He that would bring home the wealth of the Indies, must carry out the wealth of the Indies." There is then creative reading as well as creative writing. When the mind is braced by labor and invention, the page of whatever book we read becomes luminous with manifold allusion. Every sentence is doubly significant, and the sense of our author is as broad as the world. We then see, what is always true, that as the seer's hour of vision is short and rare among heavy days and months, so is its record, perchance, the least part of his volume. The discerning will read, in his Plato or Shakespeare, only that least part, — only the authentic utterances of the oracle; — all the rest he rejects, were it never so many times Plato's and Shakespeare's.

Of course there is a portion of reading quite indispensable to a wise man. History and exact science he must learn by laborious reading. Colleges, in like manner, have their indispensable office, — to teach elements. But they can only highly serve us when they aim not to drill, but to create; when they gather from far every ray of various genius to their hospitable halls, and by the concentrated fires, set the hearts of their youth on flame. Thought and knowledge are natures in which apparatus and pretension avail nothing. Gowns and pecuniary foundations, though of towns of gold, can never countervail the least sentence or syllable of wit. Forget this, and our American colleges will recede in their public importance, whilst they grow richer every year.

III. There goes in the world a notion that the scholar should be a recluse, a valetudinarian, — as unfit for any handiwork or public labor as a penknife for an axe. The so-called "practical men" sneer at speculative men, as if, because they speculate or *see*, they could do nothing. I have heard it said that the clergy, — who are always, more universally than any other class, the scholars of their day, — are addressed as women; that the rough spontaneous conversation of men they do not hear, but only a mincing and diluted speech. They are often virtually disfranchised; and indeed there are advocates for their celibacy. As far as this is true of the studious classes, it is not just and wise. Action is with the scholar subordinate, but it is essential. Without it he is not yet man. Without it thought can never ripen into truth. Whilst the world hangs before the eye as a cloud of beauty, we cannot even see its beauty. Inaction is cowardice, but there can be no scholar without the heroic mind. The preamble of thought, the transition through which it passes from the unconscious to the conscious, is action. Only so much do I know, as I have lived. Instantly we know whose words are loaded with life, and whose not.

The world, — this shadow of the soul, or *other me*, — lies wide around. Its attractions are the keys which unlock my thoughts and make me acquainted with myself. I run eagerly into this resounding tumult. I grasp the hands of those next me, and take my place in the ring to suffer and to work, taught by an instinct that so shall the dumb abyss be vocal with speech. I pierce its order; I dissipate its fear; I dispose of it within the circuit of my expanding life. So much only of life as I know by experience, so much of the wilderness have I vanquished and planted, or so far have I extended my being, my dominion. I do not see how any man can afford, for the sake of his nerves and his nap, to spare any action in which he can partake. It is pearls and rubies to his discourse. Drudgery, calamity, exasperation, want, are instructors in eloquence and wisdom. The true scholar grudges every opportunity of action past by, as a loss of power. It is the raw material out of which the intellect moulds her splendid products. A strange process too, this by which experience is converted into thought, as a mulberry leaf is converted into satin. The manufacture goes forward at all hours.

The actions and events of our childhood and youth are now matters of calmest observation. They lie like fair pictures in the air. Not so with our recent actions, — with the business which we now have in hand. On this we are quite unable to speculate. Our affections as yet circulate through it. We no more feel or know it than we feel the feet, or the hand, or the brain of our body. The new deed is yet a part of life, — remains for a time immersed in our unconscious life. In some contemplative hour it detaches itself from the life like a ripe fruit, to become a thought of the mind. Instantly, it is raised, transfigured; the corruptible has put on incorruption. Henceforth it is an object of beauty, however base its origin and neighborhood. Observe too the impossibility of antedating this act. In its grub state, it cannot fly, it cannot shine, it is a dull grub. But suddenly, without observation, the self-same thing unfurls beautiful wings, and is an angel of wisdom. So is there no fact, no event, in our private history, which shall not, sooner or later, lose its adhesive, inert form, and astonish us by soaring from our body into the empyrean. Cradle and infancy, school and playground, the fear of boys, and dogs, and ferules, the love of little maids and berries, and many another fact that once filled the whole sky, are gone already; friend and relative, profession and party, town and country, nation and world, must also soar and sing.

Of course, he who has put forth his total strength in fit actions has the richest return of wisdom. I will not shut myself out of this globe of action, and transplant an oak into a flower-pot, there to hunger and pine; nor trust the revenue of some single faculty, and exhaust one vein of thought, much like those Savoyards, who, getting their livelihood by carving shepherds, shepherdesses, and smoking Dutchmen, for all Europe, went out one day to the mountain to find stock, and discovered that they had whittled up the last of their pine trees. Authors we have, in numbers, who have written out their vein, and who, moved by a commendable prudence, sail for Greece or Palestine, follow the trapper into the prairie, or ramble round Algiers, to replenish their merchantable stock.

If it were only for a vocabulary, the scholar would be covetous of action. Life is our dictionary. Years are well spent in country labors; in town; in the insight into trades and manufactures; in frank intercourse with many men and women; in science; in art; to the one end of mastering in all their facts a language by which to illustrate and embody our perceptions. I learn immediately from any speaker how much he has already lived, through the poverty or the splendor of his speech. Life lies behind us as the quarry from whence we get tiles and copestones for the masonry of to-day. This is the way to learn grammar. Colleges and books only copy the language which the field and the work-yard made.

But the final value of action, like that of books, and better than books, is that it is a resource. That great principle of Undulation in nature, that shows itself in the inspiring and expiring of the breath; in desire and satiety; in the ebb and flow of the sea; in day and night; in heat and cold; and, as yet more deeply ingrained in every atom and every fluid, is known to us under the name of Polarity, — these "fits of easy transmission and reflection," as Newton called them, are the law of nature because they are the law of spirit.

The mind now thinks, now acts, and each fit reproduces the other. When the artist has exhausted his materials, when the fancy no longer paints, when thoughts are no longer apprehended and books are a weariness, — he has always the resource to *live*. Character is higher than intellect. Thinking is the function. Living is the functionary. The stream retreats to its source. A great soul will be strong to live, as well as strong

to think. Does he lack organ or medium to impart his truths? He can still fall back on this elemental force of living them. This is a total act. Thinking is a partial act. Let the grandeur of justice shine in his affairs. Let the beauty of affection cheer his lowly roof. Those "far from fame," who dwell and act with him, will feel the force of his constitution in the doings and passages of the day better than it can be measured by any public and designed display. Time shall teach him that the scholar loses no hour which the man lives. Herein he unfolds the sacred germ of his instinct, screened from influence. What is lost in seemliness is gained in strength. Not out of those on whom systems of education have exhausted their culture, comes the helpful giant to destroy the old or to build the new, but out of unhandselled savage nature; out of terrible Druids and Berserkers come at last Alfred and Shakespeare.

I hear therefore with joy whatever is beginning to be said of the dignity and necessity of labor to every citizen. There is virtue yet in the hoe and the spade, for learned as well as for unlearned hands. And labor is everywhere welcome; always we are invited to work; only be this limitation observed, that a man shall not for the sake of wider activity sacrifice any opinion to the popular judgments and modes of action.

I have now spoken of the education of the scholar by nature, by books, and by action. It remains to say somewhat of his duties.

They are such as become Man Thinking. They may all be comprised in self-trust. The office of the scholar is to cheer, to raise, and to guide men by showing them facts amidst appearances. He plies the slow, unhonored, and unpaid task of observation. Flamsteed and Herschel, in their glazed observatories, may catalogue the stars with the praise of all men, and the results being splendid and useful, honor is sure. But he, in his private observatory, cataloguing obscure and nebulous stars of the human mind, which as yet no man has thought of as such, — watching days and months sometimes for a few facts; correcting still his old records; — must relinquish display and immediate fame. In the long period of his preparation he must betray often an ignorance and shiftlessness in popular arts, incurring the disdain of the able who shoulder him aside. Long he must stammer in his speech; often forgo the living for the dead. Worse yet, he must accept — how often! — poverty and solitude. For the ease and pleasure of treading the old road, accepting the fashions, the education, the religion of society, he takes the cross of making his own, and, of course, the self-accusation, the faint heart, the frequent uncertainty and loss of time, which are the nettles and tangling vines in the way of the self-relying and self-directed; and the state of virtual hostility in which he seems to stand to society, and especially to educated society. For all this loss and scorn, what offset? He is to find consolation in exercising the highest functions of human nature. He is one who raises himself from private considerations and breathes and lives on public and illustrious thoughts. He is the world's eye. He is the world's heart. He is to resist the vulgar prosperity that retrogrades ever to barbarism, by preserving and communicating heroic sentiments, noble biographies, melodious verse, and the conclusions of history. Whatsoever oracles the human heart, in all emergencies, in all solemn hours, has uttered as its commentary on the world of actions, — these he shall receive and impart. And whatsoever new verdict Reason from her inviolable seat pronounces on the passing men and events of to-day, — this he shall hear and promulgate.

These being his functions, it becomes him to feel all confidence in himself, and to defer never to the popular cry. He and he only knows the world. The world of any moment is the merest appearance. Some great decorum, some fetish of a government, some ephemeral trade, or war, or man, is cried up by half mankind and cried down by the other half, as if all depended on this particular up or down. The odds are that the whole question is not worth the poorest thought which the scholar has lost in listening to the controversy. Let him not quit his belief that a popgun is a popgun, though the ancient and honorable of the earth affirm it to be the crack of doom. In silence, in steadiness, in severe abstraction, let him hold by himself; add observation to observation, patient of neglect, patient of reproach, and bide his own time, — happy enough if he can satisfy himself alone that this day he has seen something truly. Success treads on every right step. For the instinct is sure, that prompts him to tell his brother what he thinks. He then learns that in going down into the secrets of his own mind he has descended into the secrets of all minds. He learns that he who has mastered any law in his private thoughts, is master to that extent of all men whose language he speaks, and of all into whose language his own can be translated. The poet, in utter solitude remembering his spontaneous thoughts and recording them, is found to have recorded that which men in crowded cities find true for them also. The orator distrusts at first the fitness of his frank confessions, his want of knowledge of the persons he addresses, until he finds that he is the complement of his hearers;

— that they drink his words because he fulfils for them their own nature; the deeper he dives into his privatest, secretest presentiment, to his wonder he finds this is the most acceptable, most public, and universally true. The people delight in it; the better part of every man feels, This is my music; this is myself.

In self-trust all the virtues are comprehended. Free should the scholar be, — free and brave. Free even to the definition of freedom, "without any hindrance that does not arise out of his own constitution." Brave; for fear is a thing which a scholar by his very function puts behind him. Fear always springs from ignorance. It is a shame to him if his tranquillity, amid dangerous times, arise from the presumption that like children and women his is a protected class; or if he seek a temporary peace by the diversion of his thoughts from politics or vexed questions, hiding his head like an ostrich in the flowering bushes, peeping into microscopes, and turning rhymes, as a boy whistles to keep his courage up. So is the danger a danger still; so is the fear worse. Manlike let him turn and face it. Let him look into its eye and search its nature, inspect its origin, — see the whelping of this lion, — which lies no great way back; he will then find in himself a perfect comprehension of its nature and extent; he will have made his hands meet on the other side, and can henceforth defy it and pass on superior. The world is his who can see through its pretension. What deafness, what stone-blind custom, what overgrown error you behold is there only by sufferance, — by your sufferance. See it to be a lie, and you have already dealt it its mortal blow.

Yes, we are the cowed, — we the trustless. It is a mischievous notion that we are come late into nature; that the world was finished a long time ago. As the world was plastic and fluid in the hands of God, so it is ever to so much of his attributes as we bring to it. To ignorance and sin, it is flint. They adapt themselves to it as they may; but in proportion as a man has any thing in him divine, the firmament flows before him and takes his signet and form. Not he is great who can alter matter, but he who can alter my state of mind. They are the kings of the world who give the color of their present thought to all nature and all art, and persuade men by the cheerful serenity of their carrying the matter, that this thing which they do is the apple which the ages have desired to pluck, now at last ripe, and inviting nations to the harvest. The great man makes the great thing. Wherever Macdonald sits, there is the head of the table. Linnæus makes botany the most alluring of studies, and wins it from the farmer and the herb-woman; Davy, chemistry; and Cuvier, fossils. The day is always his who works in it with serenity and great aims. The unstable estimates of men crowd to him whose mind is filled with a truth, as the heaped waves of the Atlantic follow the moon.

For this self-trust, the reason is deeper than can be fathomed, — darker than can be enlightened. I might not carry with me the feeling of my audience in stating my own belief. But I have already shown the ground of my hope, in adverting to the doctrine that man is one. I believe man has been wronged; he has wronged himself. He has almost lost the light that can lead him back to his prerogatives. Men are become of no account. Men in history, men in the world of to-day, are bugs, are spawn, and are called "the mass" and "the herd." In a century, in a millennium, one or two men; that is to say, one or two approximations to the right state of every man. All the rest behold in the hero or the poet their own green and crude being, — ripened; yes, and are content to be less, so *that* may attain to its full stature. What a testimony, full of grandeur, full of pity, is borne to the demands of his own nature, by the poor clansman, the poor partisan, who rejoices in the glory of his chief. The poor and the low find some amends to their immense moral capacity, for their acquiescence in a political and social inferiority. They are content to be brushed like flies from the path of a great person, so that justice shall be done by him to that common nature which it is the dearest desire of all to see enlarged and glorified. They sun themselves in the great man's light, and feel it to be their own element. They cast the dignity of man from their downtrod selves upon the shoulders of a hero, and will perish to add one drop of blood to make that great heart beat, those giant sinews combat and conquer. He lives for us, and we live in him.

Men, such as they are, very naturally seek money or power; and power because it is as good as money, — the "spoils," so called, "of office." And why not? for they aspire to the highest, and this, in their sleep-walking, they dream is highest. Wake them and they shall quit the false good and leap to the true, and leave governments to clerks and desks. This revolution is to be wrought by the gradual domestication of the idea of Culture. The main enterprise of the world for splendor, for extent, is the upbuilding of a man. Here are the materials strewn along the ground. The private life of one man shall be a more illustrious monarchy, more formidable to its enemy, more sweet and serene in its influence to its friend, than any kingdom in history. For a man, rightly viewed,

comprehendeth the particular natures of all men. Each philosopher, each bard, each actor has only done for me, as by a delegate, what one day I can do for myself. The books which once we valued more than the apple of the eye, we have quite exhausted. What is that but saying that we have come up with the point of view which the universal mind took through the eyes of one scribe; we have been that man, and have passed on. First, one, then another, we drain all cisterns, and waxing greater by all these supplies, we crave a better and more abundant food. The man has never lived that can feed us ever. The human mind cannot be enshrined in a person who shall set a barrier on any one side to this unbounded, unboundable empire. It is one central fire, which, flaming now out of the lips of Etna, lightens the capes of Sicily, and now out of the throat of Vesuvius, illuminates the towers and vineyards of Naples. It is one light which beams out of a thousand stars. It is one soul which animates all men.

But I have dwelt perhaps tediously upon this abstraction of the Scholar. I ought not to delay longer to add what I have to say of nearer reference to the time and to this country.

Historically, there is thought to be a difference in the ideas which predominate over successive epochs, and there are data for marking the genius of the Classic, of the Romantic, and now of the Reflective or Philosophical age. With the views I have intimated of the oneness or the identity of the mind through all individuals, I do not much dwell on these differences. In fact, I believe each individual passes through all three. The boy is a Greek; the youth, romantic; the adult, reflective. I deny not, however, that a revolution in the leading idea may be distinctly enough traced.

Our age is bewailed as the age of Introversion. Must that needs be evil? We, it seems, are critical; we are embarrassed with second thoughts; we cannot enjoy any thing for hankering to know whereof the pleasure consists; we are lined with eyes; we see with our feet; the time is infected with Hamlet's unhappiness, —

"Sicklied o'er with the pale cast of thought."

It is so bad then? Sight is the last thing to be pitied. Would we be blind? Do we fear lest we should outsee nature and God, and drink truth dry? I look upon the discontent of the literary class as a mere announcement of the fact that they find themselves not in the state of mind of their fathers, and regret the coming state as untried; as a boy dreads the water before he has learned that he can swim. If there is any period one would desire to be born in, is it not the age of Revolution; when the old and the new stand side by side and admit of being compared; when the energies of all men are searched by fear and by hope; when the historic glories of the old can be compensated by the rich possibilities of the new era? This time, like all times, is a very good one, if we but know what to do with it.

I read with some joy of the auspicious signs of the coming days, as they glimmer already through poetry and art, through philosophy and science, through church and state.

One of these signs is the fact that the same movement which effected the elevation of what was called the lowest class in the state, assumed in literature a very marked and as benign an aspect. Instead of the sublime and beautiful, the near, the low, the common, was explored and poetized. That which had been negligently trodden under foot by those who were harnessing and provisioning themselves for long journeys into far countries, is suddenly found to be richer than all foreign parts. The literature of the poor, the feelings of the child, the philosophy of the street, the meaning of household life, are the topics of the time. It is a great stride. It is a sign — is it not? — of new vigor when the extremities are made active, when currents of warm life run into the hands and the feet. I ask not for the great, the remote, the romantic; what is doing in Italy or Arabia; what is Greek art, or Provençal minstrelsy; I embrace the common, I explore and sit at the feet of the familiar, the low. Give me insight into to-day, and you may have the antique and future worlds. What would we really know the meaning of? The meal in the firkin; the milk in the pan; the ballad in the street; the news of the boat; the glance of the eye; the form and the gait of the body; — show me the ultimate reason of these matters; show me the sublime presence of the highest spiritual cause lurking, as always it does lurk, in these suburbs and extremities of nature; let me see every trifle bristling with the polarity that ranges it instantly on an eternal law; and the shop, the plough, and the ledger referred to the like cause by which light undulates and poets sing; — and the world lies no longer a dull miscellany and lumber-room, but has form and order; there is no trifle, there is no puzzle, but one design unites and animates the farthest pinnacle and the lowest trench.

This idea has inspired the genius of Goldsmith, Burns, Cowper, and, in a newer time, of Goethe, Wordsworth, and Carlyle. This idea they have differently followed and with various success. In contrast with their writing, the style of Pope, of Johnson, of Gibbon, looks cold and pedantic.

This writing is bloodwarm. Man is surprised to find that things near are not less beautiful and wondrous than things remote. The near explains the far. The drop is a small ocean. A man is related to all nature. This perception of the worth of the vulgar is fruitful in discoveries. Goethe, in this very thing the most modern of the moderns, has shown us, as none ever did, the genius of the ancients.

There is one man of genius who has done much for this philosophy of life, whose literary value has never yet been rightly estimated; — I mean Emanuel Swedenborg. The most imaginative of men, yet writing with the precision of a mathematician, he endeavored to engraft a purely philosophical Ethics on the popular Christianity of his time. Such an attempt of course must have difficulty which no genius could surmount. But he saw and showed the connection between nature and the affections of the soul. He pierced the emblematic or spiritual character of the visible, audible, tangible world. Especially did his shade-loving muse hover over and interpret the lower parts of nature; he showed the mysterious bond that allies moral evil to the foul material forms, and has given in epical parables a theory of insanity, of beasts, of unclean and fearful things.

Another sign of our times, also marked by an analogous political movement, is the new importance given to the single person. Every thing that tends to insulate the individual, — to surround him with barriers of natural respect, so that each man shall feel the world is his, and man shall treat with man as a sovereign state with a sovereign state, — tends to true union as well as greatness. "I learned," said the melancholy Pestalozzi, "that no man in God's wide earth is either willing or able to help any other man." Help must come from the bosom alone. The scholar is that man who must take up into himself all the ability of the time, all the contributions of the past, all the hopes of the future. He must be an university of knowledges. If there be one lesson more than another which should pierce his ear, it is, The world is nothing, the man is all; in yourself is the law of all nature, and you know not yet how a globule of sap ascends; in yourself slumbers the whole of Reason; it is for you to know all; it is for you to dare all. Mr. President and Gentlemen, this confidence in the unsearched might of man belongs, by all motives, by all prophecy, by all preparation, to the American Scholar. We have listened too long to the courtly muses of Europe. The spirit of the American freeman is already suspected to be timid, imitative, tame. Public and private avarice make the air we breathe thick and fat. The scholar is decent, indolent, complaisant. See already the tragic consequence. The mind of this country, taught to aim at low objects, eats upon itself. There is no work for any but the decorous and the complaisant. Young men of the fairest promise, who begin life upon our shores, inflated by the mountain winds, shined upon by all the stars of God, find the earth below not in unison with these, but are hindered from action by the disgust which the principles on which business is managed inspire, and turn drudges, or die of disgust, some of them suicides. What is the remedy? They did not yet see, and thousands of young men as hopeful now crowding to the barriers for the career do not yet see, that if the single man plant himself indomitably on his instincts, and there abide, the huge world will come round to him. Patience, — patience; with the shades of all the good and great for company; and for solace the perspective of your own infinite life; and for work the study

and the communication of principles, the making those instincts prevalent, the conversion of the world. Is it not the chief disgrace in the world, not to be an unit; — not to be reckoned one character; — not to yield that peculiar fruit which each man was created to bear, but to be reckoned in the gross, in the hundred, or the thousand, of the party, the section, to which we belong; and our opinion predicted geographically, as the north, or the south? Not so, brothers and friends — please God, ours shall not be so. We will walk on our own feet; we will work with our own hands; we will speak our own minds. The study of letters shall be no longer a name for pity, for doubt, and for sensual indulgence. The dread of man and the love of man shall be a wall of defence and a wreath of joy around all. A nation of men will for the first time exist, because each believes himself inspired by the Divine Soul which also inspires all men.

Nathaniel Hawthorne · 1804-1864

Hawthorne contributed to literature a transcription of the mood, temper, and thought of seventeenth-century New England. More than any other writer he has made clear to modern readers the doctrines and ways of life of the American Puritan. But it is incorrect to assume that Hawthorne wrote from the Puritan point of view. His constant interest in the nature of sin and its effect on the individual may be a Puritan heritage, but the reader of *The Scarlet Letter* will find, readily enough, that the author's sympathies are with Hester Prynne rather than with her Puritan persecutors. Hawthorne condemns the narrowness and bigotry and harshness of the Puritan point of view. He brings to his work a transcendental faith in idealism and a romantic trust of Nature, concepts which were by no means essentially characteristic of Puritan life. His interest in sin, in the clash between the Puritan and Cavalier attitudes, is the interest of the psychologist rather than of the follower of Cromwell.

Yet it was into a little world of Puritan inheritance that Hawthorne was born, in Salem, Massachusetts, on July 4, 1804. He was descended from a line of seafaring Salemites who had lived in the town for some two hundred years. After his father's death, when Hawthorne was only four years of age, the boy was brought up by his mother in quiet seclusion, insulated even from the little world of Salem. As a youth he was a solitary figure. Even at Bowdoin College, from which he was graduated in 1825, he is reputed to have made but few friends and to have held himself fairly aloof from his classmates. Returning to Salem, Hawthorne set himself the task of writing short stories. For years he wrote and destroyed his writing, publishing little, but evolving a style and setting for himself a rather narrow field of interest which he made definitely his own. For two years he worked in the Boston Custom house; later he was given an appointment as surveyor in the Custom House at Salem. In 1842 he married Sophia Peabody. Some ten years later he purchased a residence in Concord, Wayside. The next year, however, Franklin Pierce, President of the United States and an old Bowdoin acquaintance, appointed the author and custom-house officer to the post of Consul at Liverpool, and at last Hawthorne was moved out of his little New England world. The four years at Liverpool were followed by three years of travel and residence in Italy.

Within a few years after his return to the United States, Hawthorne died on May 18, 1864, at Plymouth, New Hampshire.

Among the most important works of the writer may be listed: *Twice-Told Tales* (the first series issued in 1837, the second in 1842), collections of stories called "twice-told" because many of the tales had had earlier publication in one journal or another; *Mosses from an Old Manse* (1846); *The Scarlet Letter* (1850), a novel which deals with the problem of sin in Puritan life and society, and is generally conceded to be not only the writer's most important book but perhaps the greatest of American novels; *The House of Seven Gables* (1851); *The Blithedale Romance* (1852); and *The Marble Faun* (1860).

As a stylist, Hawthorne was a master of atmosphere. His figures move in and out of shadows, working out their fates in the gloom of primeval forests, in old houses, and in districts remote from society. As a conscious literary artist he was superior to any contemporary New England writer and, in this regard, was equalled in America only by Poe. His work is often marked by a gentle irony and a grim sort of humor. He was fond of expressing abstract moral problems concretely through the action of his characters, problems which resulted from departures from conventional codes and which had to do with characters who forgot their common human responsibilities through pride (as in *Ethan Brand*) or through scepticism (as in *Young Goodman Brown*). Hawthorne wrote frequently of people who were morbid and psychologically abnormal. And it was common practice with him to express his meaning through allegory. Thus the Maypole of Merrymount becomes much more than a maypole — a symbol for a whole manner of living — and the scarlet letter worn by Hester Prynne becomes a central figure in the novel. In the stories which follow, this tendency is obvious in the stony heart, harder even than the marble burnt in the kiln of Ethan Brand, and in the part played by Faith, the wife of Goodman Brown.

SUGGESTED REFERENCES: Edward Wagenknecht, *Nathaniel Hawthorne, Man and Writer* (1961); Terence Martin, *Nathaniel Hawthorne* (1965); A. N. Kaul, ed., *Hawthorne. A Collection of Critical Essays* (1966).

Short Stories of Hawthorne

The following stories should be read to secure an understanding and appreciation of Hawthorne's style, the Puritan background against which his mind functioned (often without sympathy for it), the ability of the author to create atmosphere, and the kind of atmosphere most natural to him. The curious reader will find numerous instances of the use of allegory.

YOUNG GOODMAN BROWN

Young Goodman Brown came forth at sunset into the street at Salem village; but put his head back, after crossing the threshold, to exchange a parting kiss with his young wife. And Faith, as the wife was aptly named, thrust her own pretty head into the street, letting the wind play with the pink ribbons of her cap while she called to Goodman Brown.

"Dearest heart," whispered she, softly and rather sadly, when her lips were close to his ear, "prithee put off your journey until sunrise and sleep in your own bed to-night. A lone woman is troubled with such dreams and such thoughts that she's afeard of herself sometimes. Pray tarry with me this night, dear husband, of all nights in the year."

"My love and my Faith," replied young Goodman Brown, "of all nights in the year, this one night must I tarry away from thee. My journey, as thou callest it, forth and back again, must needs be done 'twixt now and sunrise. What, my sweet wife, dost thou doubt me already, and we but three months married?"

"Then God bless you!" said Faith, with the pink ribbons; "and may you find all well when you come back."

"Amen!" cried Goodman Brown. "Say thy prayers, dear Faith, and go to bed at dusk, and no harm will come to thee."

So they parted; and the young man pursued his way until, being about to turn the corner by the meeting-house, he looked back and saw the head of Faith still peeping after him with a melancholy air, in spite of her pink ribbons.

"Poor little Faith!" thought he, for his heart smote him, "What a wretch am I to leave her on such an errand! She talks of dreams, too. Methought as she spoke there was trouble in her face, as if a dream had warned her what work is to be done to-night. But no, no; 'twould kill her to think it. Well, she's a blessed angel on earth; and after this one night I'll cling to her skirts and follow her to heaven."

With this excellent resolve for the future, Goodman Brown felt himself justified in making more haste on his present evil purpose. He had taken a dreary road, darkened by all the gloomiest trees of the forest, which barely stood aside to let the narrow path creep through, and closed immediately behind. It was all as lonely as could be; and there is this peculiarity in such a solitude, that the traveller knows not who may be concealed by the innumerable trunks and the thick boughs overhead; so that with lonely footsteps he may yet be passing through an unseen multitude.

"There may be a devilish Indian behind every tree," said Goodman Brown to himself; and he glanced fearfully behind him as he added, "What if the devil himself should be at my very elbow!"

His head being turned back, he passed a crook of the road, and, looking forward again, beheld the figure of a man, in grave and decent attire, seated at the foot of an old tree. He arose at Goodman Brown's approach and walked onward side by side with him.

"You are late, Goodman Brown," said he. "The clock of the Old South was striking as I came through Boston, and that is full fifteen minutes agone."

"Faith kept me back awhile," replied the young man, with a tremor in his voice, caused by the sudden appearance of his companion, though not wholly unexpected.

It was now deep dusk in the forest, and deepest in that part of it where these two were journeying. As nearly as could be discerned, the second traveller was about fifty years old, apparently in the same rank of life as Goodman Brown, and bearing a considerable resemblance to him, though perhaps more in expression than features. Still they might have been taken for father and son. And yet, though the elder person was as simply clad as the younger, and as simple in manner too, he had an indescribable air of one who knew the world, and who would not have felt abashed at the governor's dinner table or in King William's court, were it possible that his affairs should call him thither. But the only thing about him that could be fixed upon as remarkable was his staff, which bore the likeness of a great black snake, so curiously wrought that it might almost be seen to twist and wriggle itself like a living serpent. This, of course, must have been an ocular deception, assisted by the uncertain light.

"Come, Goodman Brown," cried his fellow-traveller, "this is a dull pace for the beginning of a journey. Take my staff, if you are so soon weary."

"Friend," said the other, exchanging his slow pace for a full stop, "having kept covenant by meeting thee here, it is my purpose now to return whence I came. I have scruples touching the matter thou wot'st of."

"Sayest thou so?" replied he of the serpent, smiling apart. "Let us walk on, nevertheless, reasoning as we go; and if I convince thee not thou shalt turn back. We are but a little way in the forest yet."

"Too far! too far!" exclaimed the goodman, unconsciously resuming his walk. "My father never went into the woods on such an errand, nor his father before him. We have been a race of honest men and good Christians since the days of the martyrs; and shall I be the first of the name of Brown that ever took this path and kept——"

"Such company, thou wouldst say," observed the elder person, interpreting his pause. "Well said, Goodman Brown! I have been as well acquainted with your family as with ever a one among the Puritans; and that's no trifle to say. I helped your grandfather, the constable, when he lashed the Quaker woman so smartly through the streets of Salem; and it was I that brought your father a pitch-pine knot, kindled at my own hearth, to set fire to an Indian village, in King Philip's war. They were my good friends, both; and many a pleasant walk have we had along this path, and returned merrily after midnight. I would fain be friends with you for their sake."

"If it be as thou sayest," replied Goodman Brown, "I marvel they never spoke of these matters; or, verily, I marvel not, seeing that the least rumor of the sort would have driven them from New England. We are a people of prayer, and good works to boot, and abide no such wickedness."

"Wickedness or not," said the traveller with the twisted staff, "I have a very general acquaintance here in New England. The deacons of many a church have drunk the communion wine with me; the selectmen of divers towns make me their chairman; and a majority of the Great and General Court are firm supporters of my interest. The governor and I, too—— But these are state secrets."

"Can this be so?" cried Goodman Brown, with a stare of amazement at his undisturbed companion. "Howbeit, I have nothing to do with the governor and council; they have their own ways, and are no rule for a simple husbandman like me.

But, were I to go on with thee, how should I meet the eye of that good old man, our minister, at Salem village? Oh, his voice would make me tremble both Sabbath day and lecture day."

Thus far the elder traveller had listened with due gravity; but now burst into a fit of irrepressible mirth, shaking himself so violently that his snake-like staff actually seemed to wriggle in sympathy. "Ha! ha! ha!" shouted he again and again; then composing himself, "Well, go on, Goodman Brown, go on; but, prithee, don't kill me with laughing."

"Well, then, to end the matter at once," said Goodman Brown, considerably nettled, "there is my wife, Faith. It would break her dear little heart; and I'd rather break my own."

"Nay, if that be the case," answered the other, "e'en go thy ways, Goodman Brown. I would not for twenty old women like the one hobbling before us that Faith should come to any harm."

As he spoke he pointed his staff at a female figure on the path, in whom Goodman Brown recognized a very pious and exemplary dame, who had taught him his catechism in youth, and was still his moral and spiritual adviser, jointly with the minister and Deacon Gookin.

"A marvel, truly, that Goody Cloyse should be so far in the wilderness at nightfall," said he. "But with your leave, friend, I shall take a cut through the woods until we have left this Christian woman behind. Being a stranger to you, she might ask whom I was consorting with and whither I was going."

"Be it so," said his fellow-traveller. "Betake you to the woods, and let me keep the path."

Accordingly the young man turned aside, but took care to watch his companion, who advanced softly along the road until he had come within a staff's length of the old dame. She, meanwhile, was making the best of her way, with singular speed for so aged a woman, and mumbling some indistinct words — a prayer, doubtless — as she went. The traveller put forth his staff and touched her withered neck with what seemed the serpent's tail.

"The devil!" screamed the pious old lady.

"Then Goody Cloyse knows her old friend?" observed the traveller, confronting her and leaning on his writhing stick.

"Ah, forsooth, and is it your worship indeed?" cried the good dame. "Yea, truly is it, and in the very image of my old gossip, Goodman Brown, the grandfather of the silly fellow that now is. But — would your worship believe it? — my broomstick hath strangely disappeared, stolen, as I suspect, by that unhanged witch, Goody Cory, and that, too, when I was all anointed with the juice of smallage, and cinquefoil, and wolf's bane ——"

"Mingled with fine wheat and the fat of a newborn babe," said the shape of old Goodman Brown.

"Ah, your worship knows the recipe," cried the old lady, cackling aloud. "So, as I was saying, being all ready for the meeting, and no horse to ride on, I made up my mind to foot it; for they tell me there is a nice young man to be taken into communion to-night. But now your good worship will lend me your arm, and we shall be there in a twinkling."

"That can hardly be," answered her friend. "I may not spare you my arm, Goody Cloyse; but here is my staff, if you will."

So saying, he threw it down at her feet, where, perhaps, it assumed life, being one of the rods which its owner had formerly lent to the Egyptian magi. Of this fact, however, Goodman Brown could not take cognizance. He had cast up his eyes in astonishment, and, looking down again, beheld neither Goody Cloyse nor the serpentine staff, but his fellow-traveller alone, who waited for him as calmly as if nothing had happened.

"That old woman taught me my catechism," said the young man; and there was a world of meaning in this simple comment.

They continued to walk onward, while the elder traveller exhorted his companion to make good speed and persevere in the path, discoursing so aptly that his arguments seemed rather to spring up in the bosom of his auditor than to be suggested by himself. As they went, he plucked a branch of maple to serve for a walking stick, and began to strip it of the twigs and little boughs, which were wet with evening dew. The moment his fingers touched them they became strangely withered and dried up as with a week's sunshine. Thus the pair proceeded, at a good free pace, until suddenly, in a gloomy hollow of the road, Goodman Brown sat himself down on the stump of a tree and refused to go any farther.

"Friend," said he, stubbornly, "my mind is made up. Not another step will I budge on this errand. What if a wretched old woman do choose to go to the devil when I thought she was going to heaven: is that any reason why I should quit my dear Faith and go after her?"

"You will think better of this by and by," said his acquaintance, composedly. "Sit here and rest yourself a while; and when you feel like moving again, there is my staff to help you along."

Without more words, he threw his companion the maple stick, and was as speedily out of sight as if he had vanished into the gloom. The young man sat a few moments by the roadside, applauding himself greatly, and thinking with how clear a conscience he should meet the minister in his morning walk, nor shrink from the eye of good old Deacon Gookin. And what calm sleep would be his that very night, which was to have been spent so wickedly, but so purely and sweetly now, in the arms of Faith! Amidst these pleasant and praiseworthy meditations, Goodman Brown heard the tramp of horses along the road, and deemed it advisable to conceal himself within the verge of the forest, conscious of the guilty purpose that had brought him thither, though now so happily turned from it.

On came the hoof tramps and the voices of the riders, two grave old voices, conversing soberly as they drew near. These mingled sounds appeared to pass along the road, within a few yards of the young man's hiding-place; but, owing doubtless to the depth of the gloom at that particular spot, neither the travellers nor their steeds were visible. Though their figures brushed the small boughs by the wayside, it could not be seen that they intercepted, even for a moment, the faint gleam from the strip of bright sky athwart which they must have passed. Goodman Brown alternately crouched and stood on tiptoe, pulling aside the branches and thrusting forth his head as far as he durst without discerning so much as a shadow. It vexed him the more, because he could have sworn, were such a thing possible, that he recognized the voices of the minister and Deacon Gookin, jogging along quietly, as they were wont to do, when bound to some ordination or ecclesiastical council. While yet within hearing, one of the riders stopped to pluck a switch.

"Of the two, reverend sir," said the voice like the deacon's, "I had rather miss an ordination dinner than to-night's meeting. They tell me that some of our community are to be here from Falmouth and beyond, and others from Connecticut and Rhode Island, besides several of the Indian powwows, who, after their fashion, know almost as much deviltry as the best of us. Moreover, there is a goodly young woman to be taken into communion."

"Mighty well, Deacon Gookin!" replied the solemn old tones of the minister. "Spur up, or we shall be late. Nothing can be done, you know, until I get on the ground."

The hoofs clattered again; and the voices, talking so strangely in the empty air, passed on through the forest, where no church had ever been gathered or solitary Christian prayed. Whither, then, could these holy men be journeying so deep into the heathen wilderness? Young Goodman Brown caught hold of a tree for support, being ready to sink down on the ground, faint and overburdened with the heavy sickness of his heart. He looked up to the sky, doubting whether there really was a heaven above him. Yet there was the blue arch, and the stars brightening in it.

"With heaven above and Faith below, I will yet stand firm against the devil!" cried Goodman Brown.

While he still gazed upward into the deep arch of the firmament and had lifted his hands to pray, a cloud, though no wind was stirring, hurried across the zenith and hid the brightening stars. The blue sky was still visible, except directly overhead, where this black mass of cloud was sweeping swiftly northward. Aloft in the air, as if from the depths of the cloud, came a confused and doubtful sound of voices. Once the listener fancied that he could distinguish the accents of townspeople of his own, men and women, both pious and ungodly, many of whom he had met at the communion table, and had seen others rioting at the tavern. The next moment, so indistinct were the sounds, he doubted whether he had heard aught but the murmur of the old forest, whispering without a wind. Then came a stronger swell of those familiar tones, heard daily in the sunshine at Salem village, but never until now from a cloud of night. There was one voice, of a young woman, uttering lamentations, yet with an uncertain sorrow, and entreating for some favor, which, perhaps, it would grieve her to obtain; and all the unseen multitude, both saints and sinners, seemed to encourage her onward.

"Faith!" shouted Goodman Brown, in a voice of agony and desperation; and the echoes of the forest mocked him, crying, "Faith! Faith!" as if bewildered wretches were seeking her all through the wilderness.

The cry of grief, rage, and terror was yet piercing the night, when the unhappy husband held his breath for a response. There was a scream, drowned immediately in a louder murmur of voices, fading into far-off laughter, as the dark cloud swept away, leaving the clear and silent sky above Goodman Brown. But something fluttered lightly down through the air and caught on the branch of a tree. The young man seized it, and beheld a pink ribbon.

"My Faith is gone!" cried he, after one stupefied moment. "There is no good on earth; and sin is but a name. Come, devil; for to thee is this world given."

And, maddened with despair, so that he laughed loud and long, did Goodman Brown grasp his staff and set forth again, at such a rate that he seemed to fly along the forest path rather than to walk or run. The road grew wilder and drearier and more faintly traced, and vanished at length, leaving him in the heart of the dark wilderness, still rushing onward with the instinct that guides mortal man to evil. The whole forest was peopled with frightful sounds — the creaking of the trees, the howling of wild beasts, and the yell of Indians; while sometimes the wind tolled like a distant church bell, and sometimes gave a broad roar around the traveller, as if all Nature were laughing him to scorn. But he was himself the chief horror of the scene, and shrank not from its other horrors.

"Ha! ha! ha!" roared Goodman Brown when the wind laughed at him. "Let us hear which will laugh loudest. Think not to frighten me with your deviltry. Come witch, come wizard, come Indian powwow, come devil himself, and here comes Goodman Brown. You may as well fear him as he fear you."

In truth, all through the haunted forest there could be nothing more frightful than the figure of Goodman Brown. On he flew among the black pines, brandishing his staff with frenzied gestures, now giving vent to an inspiration of horrid blasphemy, and now shouting forth such laughter as set all the echoes of the forest laughing like demons around him. The fiend in his own shape is less hideous than when he rages in the breast of man. Thus sped the demoniac on his course, until, quivering among the trees, he saw a red light before him, as when the felled trunks and branches of a clearing have been set on fire, and throw up their lurid blaze against the sky, at the hour of midnight. He paused, in a lull of the tempest that had driven him onward, and heard the swell of what seemed a hymn, rolling solemnly from a distance with the weight of many voices. He knew the tune; it was a familiar one in the choir of the village meeting-house. The verse died heavily away, and was lengthened by a chorus, not of human voices, but of all the sounds of the benighted wilderness pealing in awful harmony together. Goodman Brown cried out, and his cry was lost to his own ear by its unison with the cry of the desert.

In the interval of silence he stole forward until the light glared full upon his eyes. At one extremity of an open space, hemmed in by the dark wall of the forest, arose a rock, bearing some rude, natural resemblance either to an altar or a pulpit, and surrounded by four blazing pines, their tops aflame, their stems untouched, like candles at an evening meeting. The mass of foliage that had overgrown the summit of the rock was all on fire, blazing high into the night and fitfully illuminating the whole field. Each pendent twig and leafy festoon was in a blaze. As the red light arose and

fell, a numerous congregation alternately shone forth, then disappeared in shadow, and again grew, as it were, out of the darkness, peopling the heart of the solitary woods at once.

"A grave and dark-clad company," quoth Goodman Brown.

In truth they were such. Among them, quivering to and fro between gloom and splendor, appeared faces that would be seen next day at the council board of the province, and others which, Sabbath after Sabbath, looked devoutly heavenward, and benignantly over the crowded pews, from the holiest pulpits in the land. Some affirm that the lady of the governor was there. At least there were high dames well known to her, and wives of honored husbands, and widows, a great multitude, and ancient maidens, all of excellent repute, and fair young girls, who trembled lest their mothers should espy them. Either the sudden gleams of light flashing over the obscure field bedazzled Goodman Brown, or he recognized a score of the church members of Salem village famous for their especial sanctity. Good old Deacon Gookin had arrived, and waited at the skirts of that venerable saint, his revered pastor. But, irreverently consorting with these grave, reputable, and pious people, these elders of the church, these chaste dames and dewy virgins, there were men of dissolute lives and women of spotted fame, wretches given over to all mean and filthy vice, and suspected even of horrid crimes. It was strange to see that the good shrank not from the wicked, nor were the sinners abashed by the saints. Scattered also among their palefaced enemies were the Indian priests, or powwows, who had often scared their native forest with more hideous incantations than any known to English witchcraft.

"But where is Faith?" thought Goodman Brown; and, as hope came into his heart, he trembled.

Another verse of the hymn arose, a slow and mournful strain, such as the pious love, but joined to words which expressed all that our nature can conceive of sin, and darkly hinted at far more. Unfathomable to mere mortals is the lore of fiends. Verse after verse was sung; and still the chorus of the desert swelled between like the deepest tone of a mighty organ; and with the final peal of that dreadful anthem there came a sound, as if the roaring wind, the rushing streams, the howling beasts, and every other voice of the unconcerted wilderness were mingling and according with the voice of guilty man in homage to the prince of all. The four blazing pines threw up a loftier flame, and obscurely discovered shapes and visages of horror on the smoke wreaths above the impious assembly. At the same moment the fire on the rock shot redly forth and formed a glowing arch above its base, where now appeared a figure. With reverence be it spoken, the figure bore no slight similitude, both in garb and manner, to some grave divine of the New England churches.

"Bring forth the converts!" cried a voice that echoed through the field and rolled into the forest.

At the word, Goodman Brown stepped forth from the shadow of the trees and approached the congregation, with whom he felt a loathful brotherhood by the sympathy of all that was wicked in his heart. He could have well-nigh sworn that the shape of his own dead father beckoned him to advance, looking downward from a smoke wreath, while a woman, with dim features of despair, threw out her hand to warn him back. Was it his mother? But he had no power to retreat one step, nor to resist, even in thought, when the minister and good old Deacon Gookin seized his arms and led him to the blazing rock. Thither came also the slender form of a veiled female, led between Goody Cloyse, that pious teacher of the catechism, and Martha Carrier, who had received the devil's promise to be queen of hell. A rampant hag was she. And there stood the proselytes beneath the canopy of fire.

"Welcome, my children," said the dark figure, "to the communion of your race. Ye have found thus young your nature and your destiny. My children, look behind you!"

They turned; and flashing forth, as it were, in a sheet of flame, the fiend worshippers were seen; the smile of welcome gleamed darkly on every visage.

"There," resumed the sable form, "are all whom ye have reverenced from youth. Ye deemed them holier than yourselves, and shrank from your own sin, contrasting it with their lives of righteousness and prayerful aspirations heavenward. Yet here are they all in my worshipping assembly. This night it shall be granted you to know their secret deeds: how hoary-bearded elders of the church have whispered wanton words to the young maids of their households; how many a woman, eager for widows' weeds, has given her husband a drink at bedtime and let him sleep his last sleep in her bosom; how beardless youths have made haste to inherit their fathers' wealth; and how fair damsels — blush not, sweet ones — have dug little graves in the garden, and bidden me, the sole guest, to an infant's funeral. By the sympathy of your human hearts for sin ye shall scent out all the places — whether in church, bedchamber, street, field, or forest — where crime has been committed, and shall exult to behold the whole earth one stain of guilt, one mighty blood spot. Far more than this. It shall be yours to penetrate, in every bosom, the deep mystery of sin, the fountain of all wicked arts, and which inexhaustibly supplies more evil impulses than human power — than my power at its utmost — can make manifest in deeds. And now, my children, look upon each other."

They did so; and, by the blaze of the hell-kindled torches, the wretched man beheld his Faith, and the wife her husband, trembling before that unhallowed altar.

"Lo, there ye stand, my children," said the figure, in a deep and solemn tone, almost sad with its despairing awfulness, as if his once angelic nature could yet mourn for our miserable race. "Depending upon one another's hearts, ye had still hoped that virtue were not all a dream. Now are ye undeceived. Evil is the nature of mankind. Evil must be your only happiness. Welcome again, my children, to the communion of your race."

"Welcome," repeated the fiend worshippers, in one cry of despair and triumph.

And there they stood, the only pair, as it seemed, who were yet hesitating on the verge of wickedness in this dark world. A basin was hollowed, naturally, in the rock. Did it contain water, reddened by the lurid light? or was it blood? or, perchance, a liquid flame? Herein did the shape of evil dip his hand and prepare to lay the mark of baptism upon their foreheads, that they might be partakers of the mystery of sin, more conscious of the secret guilt of others, both in deed and thought, than they could now be of their own. The husband cast one look at his pale wife, and Faith at him. What polluted wretches would the next glance show them to each other, shuddering alike at what they disclosed and what they saw!

"Faith! Faith!" cried the husband, "look up to heaven, and resist the wicked one."

Whether Faith obeyed he knew not. Hardly had he spoken when he found himself amid calm night and solitude, listening to a roar of the wind which died heavily away through the forest. He staggered against the rock, and felt it chill and damp; while a hanging twig, that had been all on fire, besprinkled his cheek with the coldest dew.

The next morning young Goodman Brown came slowly into the street of Salem village, staring around him like a bewildered man. The good old minister was taking a walk along the graveyard to get an appetite for breakfast and meditate his sermon, and bestowed a blessing, as he passed, on Goodman Brown. He shrank from the venerable saint as if to avoid an anathema. Old Deacon Gookin was at domestic worship, and the holy words of his prayer were heard through the open window. "What God doth the wizard pray to?" quoth Goodman Brown. Goody Cloyse, that excellent old Christian, stood in the early sunshine at her own lattice, catechizing a little girl who had brought her a pint of morning's milk. Goodman Brown snatched away the child as from the grasp of the fiend himself. Turning the corner by the meeting-house, he spied the head of Faith, with the pink ribbons, gazing anxiously forth, and bursting into such joy at sight of him that she skipped along the street and almost kissed her husband before the whole village. But Goodman Brown looked sternly and sadly into her face, and passed on without a greeting.

Had Goodman Brown fallen asleep in the forest and only dreamed a wild dream of a witch-meeting?

Be it so if you will; but, alas! it was a dream of evil omen for young Goodman Brown. A stern, a sad, a darkly meditative, a distrustful, if not a desperate man did he become from the night of that fearful dream. On the Sabbath day, when the congregation were singing a holy psalm, he could not listen because an anthem of sin rushed loudly upon his ear and drowned all the blessed strain. When the minister spoke from the pulpit with power and fervid eloquence, and, with his hand on the open Bible, of the sacred truths of our religion, and of saint-like lives and triumphant deaths, and of future bliss or misery unutterable, then did Goodman Brown turn pale, dreading lest the roof should thunder down upon the gray blasphemer and his hearers. Often, awaking suddenly at midnight, he shrank from the bosom of Faith; and at morning or eventide, when the family knelt down at prayer, he scowled and muttered to himself, and gazed sternly at his wife, and turned away. And when he had lived long, and was borne to his grave a hoary corpse, followed by Faith, an aged woman, and children and grandchildren, a goodly procession, besides neighbors not a few, they carved no hopeful verse upon his tombstone, for his dying hour was gloom.

ETHAN BRAND

Bartram the lime-burner, a rough, heavy-looking man, begrimed with charcoal, sat watching his kiln, at nightfall, while his little son played at building houses with the scattered fragments of marble, when, on the hillside below them, they heard a roar of laughter, not mirthful, but slow, and even solemn, like a wind shaking the boughs of the forest.

"Father, what is that?" asked the little boy, leaving his play, and pressing betwixt his father's knees.

"Oh, some drunken man, I suppose," answered the lime-burner; "some merry fellow from the bar-room in the village, who dared not laugh loud enough within doors lest he should blow the roof of the house off. So here he is, shaking his jolly sides at the foot of Graylock."

"But, father," said the child, more sensitive than the obtuse, middle-aged clown, "he does not laugh like a man that is glad. So the noise frightens me!"

"Don't be a fool, child!" cried his father, gruffly. "You will never make a man, I do believe; there is too much of your mother in you. I have known the rustling of a leaf startle you. Hark! Here comes the merry fellow now. You shall see that there is no harm in him."

Bartram and his little son, while they were talking thus, sat watching the same lime-kiln that had been the scene of Ethan Brand's solitary and meditative life, before he began his search for the Unpardonable Sin. Many years, as we have seen, had now elapsed, since that portentous night when the IDEA was first developed. The kiln, however, on the mountain-side, stood unimpaired, and was in nothing changed since he had thrown his dark thoughts into the intense glow of its furnace, and melted them, as it were, into the one thought that took possession of his life. It was a rude, round, tower-like structure about twenty feet high, heavily built of rough stones, and with a hillock of earth heaped about the larger part of its circumference; so that the blocks and fragments of marble might be drawn by cart-loads, and thrown in at the top. There was an opening at the bottom of the tower, like an oven-mouth, but large enough to admit a man in a stooping posture, and provided with a massive iron door. With the smoke and jets of flame issuing from the chinks and crevices of this door, which seemed to give admittance into the hillside, it resembled nothing so much as the private entrance to the infernal regions, which the shepherds of the Delectable Mountains were accustomed to show to pilgrims.

There are many such lime-kilns in that tract of country, for the purpose of burning the white marble which composes a large part of the substance of the hills. Some of them, built years ago, and long deserted, with weeds growing in the vacant round of the interior, which is open to the sky, and grass and wild-flowers rooting themselves into the chinks of the stones, look already like relics of antiquity, and may yet be overspread with the lichens of centuries to come. Others, where the lime-burner still feeds his daily and night-long fire, afford points of interest to the wanderer among the hills, who seats himself on a log of wood or a fragment of marble, to hold a chat with the solitary man. It is a lonesome, and, when the character is inclined to thought, may be an intensely thoughtful occupation; as it proved in the case of Ethan Brand, who had mused to such strange purpose, in days gone by, while the fire in this very kiln was burning.

The man who now watched the fire was of a different order, and troubled himself with no thoughts save the very few that were requisite to his business. At frequent intervals, he flung back the clashing weight of the iron door, and, turning his face from the insufferable glare, thrust in huge logs of oak, or stirred the immense brands with a long pole. Within the furnace were seen the curling and riotous flames, and the burning marble, almost molten with the intensity of heat; while without, the reflection of the fire quivered on the dark intricacy of the surrounding forest, and showed in the foreground a bright and ruddy little picture of the hut, the spring beside its door, the athletic and coal-begrimed figure of the lime-burner, and the half-frightened child, shrinking into the protection of his father's shadow. And when again the iron door was closed, then reappeared the tender light of the half-full moon, which vainly strove to trace out the indistinct shapes of the neighboring mountains; and, in the upper sky, there was a flitting congregation of clouds, still faintly tinged with the rosy sunset, though thus far down into the valley the sunshine had vanished long and long ago.

The little boy now crept still closer to his father, as footsteps were heard ascending the hillside, and a human form thrust aside the bushes that clustered beneath the trees.

"Halloo! who is it?" cried the lime-burner, vexed at his son's timidity, yet half infected by it. "Come forward, and show yourself, like a man, or I'll fling this chunk of marble at your head!"

"You offer me a rough welcome," said a gloomy voice, as the unknown man drew nigh. "Yet I neither claim nor desire a kinder one, even at my own fireside."

To obtain a distincter view, Bartram threw open the iron door of the kiln, whence immediately issued a gush of fierce light, that smote full upon the stranger's face and figure. To a careless eye there appeared nothing very remarkable in his aspect, which was that of a man in a coarse, brown, country-made suit of clothes, tall and thin, with the staff and heavy shoes of a wayfarer. As he advanced, he fixed his eyes — which were very bright — intently upon the brightness of the furnace, as if he beheld, or expected to behold, some object worthy of note within it.

"Good evening, stranger," said the lime-burner; "whence come you, so late in the day?"

"I come from my search," answered the wayfarer; "for, at last, it is finished."

"Drunk! — or crazy!" muttered Bartram to himself. "I shall have trouble with the fellow. The sooner I drive him away, the better."

The little boy, all in a tremble, whispered to his father, and begged him to shut the door of the kiln, so that there might not be so much light; for that there was something in the man's face which he was afraid to look at, yet could not look away from. And, indeed, even the lime-burner's dull and torpid sense began to be impressed by an indescribable something in that thin, rugged, thoughtful visage, with the grizzled hair hanging wildly about it, and those deeply sunken eyes, which gleamed like fires within the entrance of a mysterious cavern. But, as he closed the door, the stranger turned towards him, and spoke in a quiet, familiar way, that made Bartram feel as if he were a sane and sensible man, after all.

"Your task draws to an end, I see," said he. "This marble has already been burning three days. A few hours more will convert the stone to lime."

"Why, who are you?" exclaimed the lime-burner. "You seem as well acquainted with my business as I am myself."

"And well I may be," said the stranger; "for I followed the same craft many a long year, and here, too, on this very spot. But you are a new-comer in these parts. Did you never hear of Ethan Brand?"

"The man that went in search of the Unpardonable Sin?" asked Bartram, with a laugh.

"The same," answered the stranger. "He has found what he sought, and therefore he comes back again."

"What! then you are Ethan Brand himself?" cried the lime-burner, in amazement. "I am a new-comer here, as you say, and they call it eighteen years since you left the foot of Graylock. But, I can tell you, the good folks still talk about Ethan Brand, in the village yonder, and what a strange errand took him away from his lime-kiln. Well, and so you have found the Unpardonable Sin?"

"Even so!" said the stranger, calmly.

"If the question is a fair one," proceeded Bartram, "where might it be?"

Ethan Brand laid his finger on his own heart. "Here!" replied he.

And then, without mirth in his countenance, but as if moved by an involuntary recognition of the infinite absurdity of seeking throughout the world for what was the closest of all things to himself, and looking into every heart, save his own, for what was hidden in no other breast, he broke into a laugh of scorn. It was the same slow, heavy laugh, that had almost appalled the lime-burner when it heralded the wayfarer's approach.

The solitary mountain-side was made dismal by it. Laughter, when out of place, mistimed, or bursting forth from a disordered state of feeling, may be the most terrible modulation of the human voice. The laughter of one asleep, even if it be a little child, — the madman's laugh, — the wild, screaming laugh of a born idiot, — are sounds that we sometimes tremble to hear, and would always willingly forget. Poets have imagined no utterance of fiends or hobgoblins so fearfully appropriate as a laugh. And even the obtuse lime-burner felt his nerves shaken, as this strange man looked inward at his own heart, and burst into laughter that rolled away into the night, and was indistinctly reverberated among the hills.

"Joe," said he to his little son, "scamper down to the tavern in the village, and tell the jolly fellows there that Ethan Brand has come back, and that he has found the Unpardonable Sin!"

The boy darted away on his errand, to which Ethan Brand made no objection, nor seemed hardly to notice it. He sat on a log of wood, looking steadfastly at the iron door of the kiln. When the child was out of sight, and his swift and light footsteps ceased to be heard treading first on the fallen leaves and then on the rocky mountain-path, the lime-burner began to regret his departure. He felt that the little fellow's presence had been a barrier between his guest and himself, and that he must now deal, heart to heart, with a man who, on his own confession, had committed the one only crime for which Heaven could afford no mercy. That crime, in its indistinct blackness, seemed to overshadow him. The lime-burner's own sins rose up within him, and made his memory riotous with a throng of evil shapes that asserted their kindred with the Master Sin, whatever it might be, which it was within the scope of man's corrupted nature to conceive and cherish. They were all of one family; they went to and fro between his breast and Ethan Brand's, and carried dark greetings from one to the other.

Then Bartram remembered the stories which had grown traditionary in reference to this strange man, who had come upon him like a shadow of the night, and was making himself at home in his old place, after so long absence that the dead people, dead and buried for years, would have had more right to be at home, in any familiar spot, than he. Ethan Brand, it was said, had conversed with Satan himself in the lurid blaze of this very kiln.

The legend had been matter of mirth heretofore, but looked grisly now. According to this tale, before Ethan Brand departed on his search, he had been accustomed to evoke a fiend from the hot furnace of the lime-kiln, night after night, in order to confer with him about the Unpardonable Sin; the man and the fiend each laboring to frame the image of some mode of guilt which could neither be atoned for nor forgiven. And, with the first gleam of light upon the mountain-top, the fiend crept in at the iron door, there to abide the intensest element of fire, until again summoned forth to share in the dreadful task of extending man's possible guilt beyond the scope of Heaven's else infinite mercy.

While the lime-burner was struggling with the horror of these thoughts, Ethan Brand rose from the log, and flung open the door of the kiln. The action was in such accordance with the idea in Bartram's mind, that he almost expected to see the Evil One issue forth, red-hot, from the raging furnace.

"Hold! hold!" cried he, with a tremulous attempt to laugh; for he was ashamed of his fears, although they overmastered him. "Don't, for mercy's sake, bring out your Devil now!"

"Man!" sternly replied Ethan Brand, "what need have I of the Devil? I have left him behind me, on my track. It is with such half-way sinners as you that he busies himself. Fear not, because I open the door. I do but act by old custom, and am going to trim your fire, like a lime-burner, as I was once."

He stirred the vast coals, thrust in more wood, and bent forward to gaze into the hollow prison-house of the fire, regardless of the fierce glow that reddened upon his face. The lime-burner sat watching him, and half suspected this strange guest of a purpose, if not to evoke a fiend, at least to plunge bodily into the flames, and thus vanish from the sight of man. Ethan Brand, however, drew quietly back, and closed the door of the kiln.

"I have looked," said he, "into many a human heart that was seven times hotter with sinful passions than yonder furnace is with fire. But I found not there what I sought. No, not the Unpardonable Sin!"

"What is the Unpardonable Sin?" asked the lime-burner; and then he shrank farther from his companion, trembling lest his question should be answered.

"It is a sin that grew within my own breast," replied Ethan Brand, standing erect, with a pride that distinguishes all enthusiasts of his stamp. "A sin that grew nowhere else! The sin of an intellect that triumphed over the sense of brotherhood with man and reverence for God, and sacrificed everything to its own mighty claims! The only sin that deserves a recompense of immortal agony! Freely, were it to do again, would I incur the guilt. Unshrinkingly I accept the retribution!"

"The man's head is turned," muttered the lime-burner to himself. "He may be a sinner like the rest of us, — nothing more likely, — but, I'll be sworn, he is a madman too."

Nevertheless, he felt uncomfortable at his situation, alone with Ethan Brand on the wild mountain-side, and was right glad to hear the rough murmur of tongues, and the footsteps of what seemed a pretty numerous party, stumbling over the stones and rustling through the underbrush. Soon appeared the whole lazy regiment that was wont to infest the village tavern, comprehending three or four individuals who had drunk flip beside the bar-room fire through all the winters, and smoked their pipes beneath the stoop through all the summers, since Ethan Brand's departure. Laughing boisterously, and mingling all their voices together in unceremonious talk, they now burst into the moonshine and narrow streaks of firelight that illuminated the open space before the lime-kiln. Bartram set the door ajar again, flooding the spot with light, that the whole company might get a fair view of Ethan Brand, and he of them.

There, among other old acquaintances, was a once ubiquitous man, now almost extinct, but whom we were formerly sure to encounter at the hotel of every thriving village throughout the country. It was the stage-agent. The present specimen of the genus was a wilted and smoke-dried man, wrinkled and red-nosed, in a smartly cut, brown, bob-tailed coat, with brass buttons, who, for a length of time unknown, had kept his desk and corner in the bar-room, and was still puffing what seemed to be the same cigar that he had lighted twenty years before. He had great fame as a dry joker, though, perhaps, less on account of any intrinsic humor than from a certain flavor of brandy-toddy and tobacco-smoke, which impregnated all his ideas and expressions, as well as his person. Another well-remembered though strangely altered face was that of Lawyer Giles, as people still called him in courtesy; an elderly ragamuffin, in his soiled shirt-sleeves and tow-cloth trousers. This poor fellow had been an attorney, in what he called his better days, a sharp practitioner, and in great vogue among the village litigants; but flip, and sling, and toddy, and cocktails, imbibed at all hours, morning, noon, and night, had caused him to slide from intellectual to various kinds and degrees of bodily labor, till at last, to adopt his own phrase, he slid into a soap-vat. In other words, Giles was now a soap-boiler, in a small way. He had come to be but the fragment of a human being, a part of one foot having been chopped off by an axe, and an entire hand torn away by the devilish grip of a steam-engine. Yet, though the corporeal hand was gone, a spiritual member remained; for, stretching forth the stump, Giles steadfastly averred that he felt an invisible thumb and fingers with as vivid a sensation as before the real ones were amputated. A maimed and miserable wretch he was; but one, nevertheless, whom the world could not trample on, and had no right to scorn, either in this or any previous stage of his misfortunes, since he had still kept up the courage and spirit of a man, asked nothing in charity, and with his one hand — and that the left one — fought a stern battle against want and hostile circumstances.

Among the throng, too, came another personage, who, with certain points of similarity to Lawyer Giles, had many more of difference. It was the village doctor; a man of some fifty years, whom, at an earlier period of his life, we introduced as paying a professional visit to Ethan Brand during the latter's supposed insanity. He was now a purple-visaged, rude, and brutal, yet half-gentlemanly figure, with something wild, ruined, and desperate in his talk, and in all the details of his gesture and manners. Brandy possessed this man like an evil spirit, and made him as surly and savage as a wild beast, and as miserable as a lost soul; but there was supposed to be in him such wonderful skill, such native gifts of healing, beyond any which medical science could impart, that society caught hold of him, and would not let him sink out of its reach. So, swaying to and fro upon his horse, and grumbling thick accents at the bedside, he visited all the sick-chambers for miles about among the mountain towns, and sometimes raised a dying man, as it were, by miracle, or quite as often, no doubt, sent his patient to a grave that was dug many a year too soon. The doctor had an everlasting pipe in his mouth, and, as somebody said, in allusion to his habit of swearing, it was always alight with hell-fire.

These three worthies pressed forward, and greeted Ethan Brand each after his own fashion, earnestly inviting him to partake of the contents of a certain black bottle, in which, as they averred, he would find something far better worth seeking for than the Unpardonable Sin. No mind, which has wrought itself by intense and solitary meditation into a high state of enthusiasm, can endure the kind of contact with low and vulgar modes of thought and feeling to which Ethan Brand was now subjected. It made him doubt — and, strange to say, it was a painful doubt — whether he had indeed found the Unpardonable Sin, and found it within himself. The whole question on which he had exhausted life, and more than life, looked like a delusion.

"Leave me," he said bitterly, "ye brute beasts, that have made yourselves so, shrivelling up your souls with fiery liquors! I have done with you. Years and years ago, I groped into your hearts, and found nothing there for my purpose. Get ye gone!"

"Why, you uncivil scoundrel," cried the fierce doctor, "is that the way you respond to the kindness of your best friends? Then let me tell you the truth. You have no more found the Unpardonable Sin than yonder boy Joe has. You are but a crazy fellow, — I told you so twenty years ago, — neither better nor worse than a crazy fellow, and the fit companion of old Humphrey, here!"

He pointed to an old man, shabbily dressed, with long white hair, thin visage, and unsteady eyes. For some years past this aged person had been wandering about among the hills, inquiring of all travelers whom he met for his daughter. The girl, it seemed, had gone off with a company of circus-performers; and occasionally tidings of her came to the village, and fine stories were told of her glittering appearance as she rode on horseback in the ring, or performed marvelous feats on the tight-rope.

The white-haired father now approached Ethan Brand, and gazed unsteadily into his face.

"They tell me you have been all over the earth," said he, wringing his hands with earnestness. "You must have seen my daughter, for she makes a grand figure in the world, and everybody goes to see her. Did she send any word to her old father, or say when she was coming back?"

Ethan Brand's eye quailed beneath the old man's. That daughter, from whom he so earnestly desired a word of greeting, was the Esther of our tale, the very girl whom, with such cold and remorseless purpose, Ethan Brand had made the subject of a psychological experiment, and wasted, absorbed, and perhaps annihilated her soul, in the process.

"Yes," murmured he, turning away from the hoary wanderer; "it is no delusion. There is an Unpardonable Sin!"

While these things were passing, a merry scene was going forward in the area of cheerful light, beside the spring and before the door of the hut. A number of the youth of the village, young men and girls, had hurried up the hillside, impelled by curiosity to see Ethan Brand, the hero of so many a legend familiar to their childhood. Finding nothing, however, very remarkable in his aspect, — nothing but a sunburnt wayfarer, in plain garb and dusty shoes, who sat looking into the fire as if he fancied pictures among the coals, — these young people speedily grew tired of observing him. As it happened, there was other amusement at hand. An old German Jew, traveling with a diorama on his back, was passing down the mountain-road towards the village just as the party turned aside from it, and, in hopes of eking out the profits of the day, the showman had kept them company to the lime-kiln.

"Come, old Dutchman," cried one of the young men, "let us see your pictures, if you can swear they are worth looking at!"

"Oh, yes, Captain," answered the Jew, — whether as a matter of courtesy or craft, he styled everybody Captain, — "I shall show you, indeed, some very superb pictures!"

So, placing his box in a proper position, he invited the young men and girls to look through the glass orifices of the machine, and proceeded to exhibit a series of the most outrageous scratchings and daubings, as specimens of the fine arts, that ever an itinerant showman had the face to impose upon his circle of spectators. The pictures were worn out, moreover, tattered, full of cracks and wrinkles, dingy with tobacco-smoke, and otherwise in a most pitiable condition. Some purported to be cities, public edifices, and ruined castles in Europe; others represented Napoleon's battles and Nelson's sea-fights; and in the midst of these would be seen a gigantic, brown, hairy hand, — which might have been mistaken for the Hand of Destiny, though, in truth, it was only the showman's, — pointing its forefinger to various scenes of the conflict, while its owner gave historical illustrations. When, with much merriment at its abominable deficiency of merit, the exhibition was concluded, the German bade little Joe put his head into the box. Viewed through the magnifying-glasses, the boy's round, rosy visage assumed the strangest imaginable aspect of an immense Titanic child, the mouth grinning broadly, and the eyes and every other feature overflowing with fun at the joke. Suddenly, however, that merry face turned pale, and its expression changed to horror, for this easily impressed and excitable child had become sensible that the eye of Ethan Brand was fixed upon him through the glass.

"You make the little man to be afraid, Captain," said the German Jew, turning up the dark and strong outline of his visage, from his stooping posture. "But look again, and, by chance, I shall cause you to see somewhat that is very fine, upon my word!"

Ethan Brand gazed into the box for an instant, and then starting back, looked fixedly at the German. What had he seen? Nothing, apparently; for a curious youth, who had peeped in almost at the same moment, beheld only a vacant space of canvas.

"I remember you now," muttered Ethan Brand to the showman.

"Ah, Captain," whispered the Jew of Nuremberg, with a dark smile, "I find it to be a heavy matter in my show-box, — this Unpardonable Sin! By my faith, Captain, it has wearied my shoulders, this long day, to carry it over the mountain."

"Peace," answered Ethan Brand, sternly, "or get thee into the furnace yonder!"

The Jew's exhibition had scarcely concluded, when a great, elderly dog — who seemed to be his own master, as no person in the company laid claim to him — saw fit to render himself the object of public notice. Hitherto, he had shown himself a very quiet, well-disposed old dog, going round from one to another, and, by way of being sociable, offering his rough head to be patted by any kindly hand that would take so much trouble. But now, all of a sudden, this grave and venerable quadruped, of his own mere motion, and without the slightest suggestion from anybody else, began to run round after his tail, which, to heighten the absurdity of the proceeding, was a great deal shorter than it should have been. Never was seen such headlong eagerness in pursuit of an object that could not possibly be attained; never was heard such a tremendous outbreak of growling, snarling, barking, and snapping, — as if one end of the ridiculous brute's body were at deadly and most unforgivable enmity with the other. Faster and faster, round about went the cur; and faster and still faster fled the unapproachable brevity of his tail; and louder and fiercer grew his yells of rage and animosity; until, utterly exhausted, and as far from the goal as ever, the foolish old dog ceased his performance as suddenly as he had begun it. The next moment he was as mild, quiet, sensible, and respectable in his deportment, as when he first scraped acquaintance with the company.

As may be supposed, the exhibition was greeted with universal laughter, clapping of hands, and shouts of encore, to which the canine performer responded by wagging all that there was to wag of his tail, but appeared totally unable to repeat his very successful effort to amuse the spectators.

Meanwhile, Ethan Brand had resumed his seat upon the log, and moved, it might be, by a perception of some remote analogy between his own case and that of this self-pursuing cur, he broke into the awful laugh, which, more than any other token, expressed the condition of his inward being. From that moment, the merriment of the party was at an end; they stood aghast, dreading lest the inauspicious sound should be reverberated around the horizon, and that mountain would thunder it to mountain, and so the horror be prolonged upon their ears. Then, whispering one to another that it was late, — that the moon was almost down, — that the August night was growing chill, — they hurried homewards, leaving the lime-burner and little Joe to deal as they might with their unwelcome guest. Save for these three human beings, the open space on the hillside was a solitude, set in a vast gloom of forest. Beyond that darksome verge, the firelight glimmered on the stately trunks and almost black foliage of pines, intermixed with the lighter verdure of sapling oaks, maples, and poplars, while here and there lay the gigantic corpses of dead trees, decaying on the leaf-strewn soil. And it seemed to little Joe — a timorous and imaginative child — that the silent forest was holding its breath until some fearful thing should happen.

Ethan Brand thrust more wood into the fire, and closed the door of the kiln; then looking over his shoulder at the lime-burner and his son, he bade, rather than advised, them to retire to rest.

"For myself, I cannot sleep," said he. "I have matters that it concerns me to meditate upon. I will watch the fire, as I used to do in the old time."

"And call the Devil out of the furnace to keep you company, I suppose," muttered Bartram, who had been making intimate acquaintance with the black bottle above mentioned. "But watch, if you like, and call as many devils as you like! For my part, I shall be all the better for a snooze. Come, Joe!"

As the boy followed his father into the hut, he looked back at the wayfarer, and the tears came into his eyes, for his tender spirit had an intuition of the bleak and terrible loneliness in which this man had enveloped himself.

When they had gone, Ethan Brand sat listening to the crackling of the kindled wood, and looking at the little spirts of fire that issued through the chinks of the door. These trifles, however, once so familiar, had but the slightest hold of his attention, while deep within his mind he was reviewing the gradual but marvelous change that had been wrought upon him by the search to which he had devoted himself. He remembered how the night dew had fallen upon him, — how the dark forest had whispered to him, — how the stars had gleamed upon him, — a simple and loving man, watching his fire in the years gone by, and ever musing as it burned. He remembered with what tenderness, with what love and sympathy for mankind, and what pity for human guilt and woe, he had first begun to contemplate those ideas which afterwards became the inspiration of his life; with what reverence he had then looked into the heart of man, viewing it as a temple originally divine, and, however desecrated, still to be held sacred by a brother; with what awful fear he had deprecated the success of his pursuit, and prayed that the Unpardonable Sin might never be revealed to him. Then ensued that vast intellectual development, which, in its progress, disturbed the counterpoise between his mind and heart. The Idea that possessed his life had operated as a means of education; it had gone on cultivating his powers to the highest point of which they were susceptible; it had raised him from the level of an unlettered laborer to stand on a star-lit eminence, whither the philosophers of the earth, laden with the lore of universities, might vainly strive to clamber after him. So much for the intellect! But where was the heart? That, indeed, had withered, — had contracted, — had hardened, — had perished! It had ceased to partake of the universal throb. He had lost his hold of the magnetic chain of humanity. He was no longer a brother-man, opening the chambers or the dungeons of our common nature by the key of holy sympathy, which gave him a right to share in all its secrets; he was now a cold observer, looking on mankind as the subject of his experiment, and, at length, converting man and woman to be his puppets, and pulling the wires that moved them to such degrees of crime as were demanded for his study.

Thus Ethan Brand became a fiend. He began to be so from the moment that his moral nature had ceased to keep the pace of improvement with his intellect. And now, as his highest effort and inevitable development, — as the bright and gorgeous flower, and rich, delicious fruit of his life's labor, — he had produced the Unpardonable Sin!

"What more have I to seek? what more to achieve?" said Ethan Brand to himself. "My task is done, and well done!"

Starting from the log with a certain alacrity in his gait and ascending the hillock of earth that was raised against the stone circumference of the lime-kiln, he thus reached the top of the structure. It was a space of perhaps ten feet across, from edge to edge, presenting a view of the upper surface of the immense mass of broken marble with which the kiln was heaped. All these innumerable blocks and fragments of marble were red-hot and vividly on fire, sending up great spouts of blue flame, which quivered aloft and danced madly, as within a magic circle, and sank and rose again, with continual and multitudinous activity. As the lonely man bent forward over this terrible body of fire, the blasting heat smote up against his person with a breath that, it might be supposed, would have scorched and shrivelled him up in a moment.

Ethan Brand stood erect, and raised his arms on high. The blue flames played upon his face, and imparted the wild and ghastly light which alone could have suited its expression; it was that of a fiend on the verge of plunging into his gulf of intensest torment.

"O Mother Earth," cried he, "who art no more my Mother, and into whose bosom this frame shall never be resolved! O mankind, whose brotherhood I have cast off, and trampled thy great heart beneath my feet! O stars of heaven, that shone on me of old, as if to light me onward and upward! — farewell all, and forever. Come, deadly element of Fire, — henceforth my familiar frame! Embrace me, as I do thee!"

That night the sound of a fearful peal of laughter rolled heavily through the sleep of the lime-burner and his little son; dim shapes of horror and anguish haunted their dreams, and seemed still present in the rude hovel, when they opened their eyes to the daylight.

"Up, boy, up!" cried the lime-burner, staring about him. "Thank Heaven, the night is gone, at last; and rather than pass such another, I would watch my lime-kiln, wide awake, for a twelvemonth. This Ethan Brand, with his humbug of an Unpardonable Sin, has done me no such mighty favor, in taking my place!"

He issued from the hut, followed by little Joe, who kept fast hold of his father's hand. The early sunshine was already pouring its gold upon the mountain-tops, and though the valleys were still in shadow, they smiled cheerfully in the promise of the bright day that was hastening onward. The village, completely shut in by hills, which swelled away gently about it, looked as if it had rested peacefully in the hollow of the great hand of Providence. Every dwelling was distinctly visible; the little spires of the two churches pointed upwards, and caught a fore-glimmering of brightness from the sun-gilt skies upon their gilded weathercocks. The tavern was astir, and the figure of the old, smoke-dried stage-agent, cigar in mouth, was seen beneath the stoop. Old Graylock was glorified with a golden cloud upon his head. Scattered likewise over the breasts of the surrounding mountains, there were heaps of hoary mist, in fantastic shapes, some of them far down into the valley, others high up towards the summits, and still others, of the same family of mist or cloud, hovering in the gold radiance of the upper atmosphere. Stepping from one to another of the clouds that rested on the hills, and thence to the loftier brotherhood that sailed in air, it seemed almost as if a mortal man might thus ascend into the heavenly regions. Earth was so mingled with sky that it was a day-dream to look at it.

To supply that charm of the familiar and homely, which Nature so readily adopts into a scene like this, the stagecoach was rattling down the mountain-road, and the driver sounded his horn, while Echo caught up the notes, and intertwined them into a rich and varied and elaborate harmony, of which the original performer could lay claim to little share. The great hills played a concert among themselves, each contributing a strain of airy sweetness.

Little Joe's face brightened at once.

"Dear father," cried he, skipping cheerily to and fro, "that strange man is gone, and the sky and the mountains all seem glad of it!"

"Yes," growled the lime-burner, with an oath, "but he has let the fire go down, and no thanks to

him if five hundred bushels of lime are not spoiled. If I catch the fellow hereabouts again, I shall feel like tossing him into the furnace!"

With his long pole in his hand, he ascended to the top of the kiln. After a moment's pause, he called to his son.

"Come up here, Joe!" said he.

So little Joe ran up the hillock, and stood by his father's side. The marble was all burnt into perfect, snow-white lime. But on its surface, in the midst of the circle, — snow-white too, and thoroughly converted into lime, — lay a human skeleton, in the attitude of a person who, after long toil, lies down to long repose. Within the ribs — strange to say — was the shape of a human heart.

"Was the fellow's heart made of marble?" cried Bartram, in some perplexity at this phenomenon. "At any rate, it is burnt into what looks like special good lime; and, taking all the bones together, my kiln is half a bushel the richer for him."

So saying, the rude lime-burner lifted his pole, and, letting it fall upon the skeleton, the relics of Ethan Brand were crumbled into fragments.

Alfred, Lord Tennyson · 1809–1892

The rapidly changing economic and social conditions in England during the first decades of the nineteenth century brought, as we have seen, a new emphasis to the writing of such men as Wordsworth and Coleridge, Byron, Shelley, and Keats. But these poets withdrew from the city, some even left England for Italy, and looked at the shifting political and industrial scene from afar. With Tennyson, whose best work was done twenty or thirty years after theirs, we come to a poet who could not avoid the issues raised by the new science in conflict with orthodox religion, the rising struggle between capital and labor, the politics of the time. In this sense, then, different as were the conditions of Victorian England from those of today, Tennyson may be called a modern poet.

Alfred Tennyson was born in Somersby, Lincolnshire, where his father was rector, on August 6, 1809. He received his education for a few years at Louth, nearby, and then passed under his father's tutelage before matriculating at Trinity College, Cambridge. Something of the tone of this early education may be inferred from his remark to the critic Edmund Gosse that his father would not let him leave home for Cambridge until he could repeat from memory, on successive days, all of the odes of Horace.

At twelve Tennyson had written an "epic" and at fourteen a poetic drama. It is natural, then, to find the poet at Cambridge winning a prize with his poem, *Timbuctoo*. His father's illness and death called the young poet home from the university before he had earned his degree, but not before he had been there long enough to make a close friend of Arthur Hallam with whom, some time later, he took an extensive journey through the Pyrenees and along the Rhine. The next year Hallam, who had become engaged to Tennyson's sister Emily, died. For the nine or ten years following Hallam's death, Tennyson lived quietly and in semi-retirement, suffering keenly the loss of his friend and assuming responsibility for the care of part of his family. Subsequent publication proved that the period had been well employed in writing.

The great year in Tennyson's life was 1850. At this time he was able to marry Emily Sellwood after an engagement which, because of his financial responsibilities and poor health, had extended over more than ten years. This same year he was made poet laureate to succeed Wordsworth and published *In Memoriam*, a tribute to his friend Arthur Hallam and perhaps the most significant of his poetic works.

It was not long before Tennyson was accepted throughout England as her leading poet. Twice offered a baronetcy, he declined; increased income made it possible for him to buy an estate, Farringford, on the Isle of Wight; he was honored with the degree of D.C.L. at Oxford and his college at Cambridge made him an Honorary Fellow; he prospered to the extent that he began the construction of a new home at Aldworth, near Haslemere. In 1884, through recognition accorded him by Gladstone, he was raised to the peerage, as Baron Tennyson of Aldworth and Farringford. When he died, October 6, 1892, at the age of eighty-three, he was buried with the pomp of a national ceremony in Westminster Abbey.

Tennyson's work ranged over a wide variety of interests and subjects and embraced several types of poetic composition. He was much given to revising and adding to his work so that in different editions a single poem or series — *The Idylls of the King* is an example — might differ greatly. Some of the more important publications are: *Poems by Two Brothers* (1827), written in collaboration with his brother Charles and interesting chiefly as an example of the poet's earlier work; *Poems* (1832–33), marking a great advance in technique and power and containing several of the more important pieces, such as *The Lotos Eaters; Poems* (1842), in two volumes — the first largely a revision of the earlier work, the second introducing such major examples of his poetry as *Ulysses* and *Locksley Hall; In Memoriam* (1850), a tribute to the memory of Arthur Hallam, made up of many separate poems written at diverse intervals over a period of many years and only loosely bound together into a whole; *Idylls of the King* (1859 and 1869, etc.), narrative poems based on the Arthurian legends and making a wide popular appeal to England; and *Locksley Hall Sixty Years After* (1886), which repudiated the Byronic mood of the earlier *Locksley Hall*. Toward the end of his life, Tennyson attempted a series of historical plays, perhaps the most lasting in value being *Becket* (1884).

Tennyson expressed the Victorian spirit. Here are the doubts and the beliefs of nineteenth-century England. Here is the new science conflicting with orthodox religion, and a sometimes stuffy and formal morality. Here, too, are the patriotism and the politics of Gladstone's time. Industry raises new problems of capital versus labor. It was Tennyson's effort to reconcile the conflicting attitudes, to bring peace where strife threatened. However, that there is much more in Tennyson than this concern with social questions is proved by the colorful record of the Round Table which he left us in the *Idylls*, by the challenge of *Ulysses*, the lyrical outbursts of the *Princess*, the fine defense of doubt in *In Memoriam*, the humor and characterization of the *Northern Farmer*, and the stirring action in such a ballad as that of *The Revenge*. Tennyson has a tendency to substitute emotion and sentiment for thought, to express a somewhat wilful optimism, and a forced delicacy which one feels is dictated by a smug Victorian society looking over his shoulder as he writes. His strength lies in a capacity to convey emotion, a rich use of imagery, a wide range — both as to subject and manner, and a real sense for music. Standing between the romanticism of the opening years of the century and the realism of its closing years, Tennyson nevertheless cast his die with the romantics.

SUGGESTED REFERENCES: Charles Tennyson, *Alfred Tennyson* (1949); J. H. Buckley, *Tennyson. The Growth of a Poet* (1960); Valeria Pitt, *Tennyson Laureate* (1962); P. F. Baum, *Tennyson Sixty Years After* (1963).

Morte d'Arthur [1]

In the *Idylls of the King*, of which this poem was eventually made a part, Tennyson exemplifies the romantic tendency to turn to a glorious past. To the past, however, Tennyson adds a nineteenth-century morality and religious spirit.

So all day long the noise of battle rolled
Among the mountains by the winter sea,
Until King Arthur's table, man by man,
Had fallen in Lyonness [2] about their lord,
King Arthur; then, because his wound was deep, 5
The bold Sir Bedivere uplifted him,
Sir Bedivere, the last of all his knights,
And bore him to a chapel nigh the field,
A broken chancel with a broken cross,
That stood on a dark strait of barren land. 10
On one side lay the Ocean and on one
Lay a great water, and the moon was full.
Then spake King Arthur to Sir Bedivere:
"The sequel of to-day unsolders all
The goodliest fellowship of famous knights 15
Whereof this world holds record. Such a sleep
They sleep — the men I loved. I think that we
Shall never more, at any future time,
Delight our souls with talk of knightly deeds,
Walking about the gardens and the halls 20
Of Camelot,[3] as in the days that were.
I perish by this people which I made, —
Tho' Merlin [4] sware that I should come again
To rule once more — but let what will be, be,
I am so deeply smitten thro' the helm 25
That without help I cannot last till morn.
Thou therefore take my brand Excalibur,
Which was my pride; for thou rememberest how
In those old days, one summer noon, an arm
Rose up from out the bosom of the lake, 30
Clothed in white samite,[5] mystic, wonderful,
Holding the sword — and how I rowed across
And took it, and have worn it, like a king;
And, wheresoever I am sung or told
In aftertime, this also shall be known. 35
But now delay not; take Excalibur,
And fling him far into the middle mere; [6]
Watch what thou seest, and lightly [7] bring me word."
To him replied the bold Sir Bedivere:
"It is not meet, Sir King, to leave thee thus, 40

Aidless, alone, and smitten thro' the helm.
A little thing may harm a wounded man.
Yet I thy hest will all perform at full,
Watch what I see, and lightly bring thee word."
So saying, from the ruined shrine he stept 45
And in the moon athwart the place of tombs,
Where lay the mighty bones of ancient men,
Old knights, and over them the sea-wind sang
Shrill, chill, with flakes of foam. He, stepping down
By zigzag paths, and juts of pointed rock, 50
Came on the shining levels of the lake.
There drew he forth the brand Excalibur,
And o'er him, drawing it, the winter moon,
Brightening the skirts of a long cloud, ran forth
And sparkled keen with frost against the hilt; 55
For all the haft twinkled with diamond sparks,
Myriads of topaz-lights, and jacinth [1] work
Of subtlest jewellery. He gazed so long
That both his eyes were dazzled, as he stood,
This way and that dividing the swift mind, 60
In act to throw; but at the last it seemed
Better to leave Excalibur concealed
There in the many-knotted waterflags,
That whistled stiff and dry about the marge.
So strode he back slow to the wounded king. 65
Then spake King Arthur to Sir Bedivere:
"Hast thou performed my mission which I gave?
What is it thou hast seen? or what hast heard?"
And answer made the bold Sir Bedivere:
"I heard the ripple washing in the reeds, 70
And the wild water lapping on the crag."
To whom replied King Arthur, faint and pale:
"Thou hast betrayed thy nature and thy name,
Not rendering true answer, as beseemed
Thy fealty, nor like a noble knight; 75
For surer sign had followed, either hand,
Or voice, or else a motion of the mere.
This is a shameful thing for men to lie.
Yet now, I charge thee, quickly go again
As thou art lief [2] and dear, and do the thing 80
I bade thee, watch, and lightly bring me word."
Then went Sir Bedivere the second time
Across the ridge, and paced beside the mere,
Counting the dewy pebbles, fixed in thought;
But when he saw the wonder of the hilt, 85
How curiously and strangely chased, he smote
His palms together, and he cried aloud:
"And if indeed I cast the brand away,
Surely a precious thing, one worthy note,
Should thus be lost forever from the earth, 90
Which might have pleased the eyes of many men.

---

[1] Tennyson's poem is based on **Malory xxi,** 5.
[2] Said to have been in Cornwall.
[3] Arthur's capital.
[4] Advisor to Arthur, a magician.
[5] silk.
[6] lake.
[7] quickly.

[1] zircon, a semi-valuable jewel.
[2] beloved.

What good should follow this, if this were done?
What harm, undone? deep harm to disobey,
Seeing obedience is the bond of rule.
Were it well to obey then, if a king demand   95
An act unprofitable, against himself?
The King is sick, and knows not what he does.
What record, or what relic of my lord
Should be to aftertime, but empty breath
And rumors of a doubt? but were this kept,   100
Stored in some treasure-house of mighty kings,
Some one might show it at a joust of arms,
Saying, 'King Arthur's sword, Excalibur,
Wrought by the lonely maiden of the lake;
Nine years she wrought it, sitting in the
    deeps   105
Upon the hidden bases of the hills.'
So might some old man speak in the aftertime
To all the people, winning reverence;
But now much honor and much fame were lost."

So spake he, clouded with his own conceit,[1]   110
And hid Excalibur the second time,
And so strode back slow to the wounded King.
Then spoke King Arthur, breathing heavily:
"What is it thou hast seen? or what hast heard?"
And answer made the bold Sir Bedivere: 115
"I heard the water lapping on the crag,
And the long ripple washing in the reeds."
To whom replied King Arthur, much in wrath:
"Ah, miserable and unkind, untrue,
Unknightly, traitor-hearted! Woe is me!   120
Authority forgets a dying king,
Laid widowed of the power in his eye
That bowed the will. I see thee what thou art,
For thou, the latest-left of all my knights,
In whom should meet the offices of all,   125
Thou wouldst betray me for the precious hilt;
Either from lust of gold, or like a girl
Valuing the giddy pleasure of the eyes.
Yet, for a man may fail in duty twice,
And the third time may prosper, get thee hence;
But, if thou spare to fling Excalibur,   131
I will arise and slay thee with my hands."
Then quickly rose Sir Bedivere, and ran,
And, leaping down the ridges lightly, plunged
Among the bulrush-beds, and clutched the
    sword,   135
And strongly wheeled and threw it. The great
    brand
Made lightnings in the splendor of the moon,
And flashing round and round, and whirled in an
    arch,
Shot like a streamer of the northern morn,
Seen where the moving isles[2] of winter shock   140

[1] fancy.
[2] i.e., icebergs.

By night, with noises of the northern sea.
So flashed and fell the brand Excalibur;
But ere he dipt the surface, rose an arm
Clothed in white samite, mystic, wonderful,
And caught him by the hilt, and brandished
    him   145
Three times, and drew him under in the mere.
And lightly went the other to the King.
Then spoke King Arthur, drawing thicker
    breath:
"Now see I by thine eyes that this is done.
Speak out; what is it thou hast heard, or seen?"   150
And answer made the bold Sir Bedivere:
"Sir King, I closed mine eyelids, lest the gems
Should blind my purpose, for I never saw,
Nor shall see, here or elsewhere, till I die,
Not tho' I live three lives of mortal men,   155
So great a miracle as yonder hilt.
Then with both hands I flung him, wheeling him;
But when I looked again, behold an arm,
Clothed in white samite, mystic, wonderful,
That caught him by the hilt, and brandished him
Three times, and drew him under in the mere."   161
And answer made King Arthur, breathing
    hard:
"My end draws nigh; 'tis time that I were gone.
Make broad thy shoulders to receive my weight,
And bear me to the margin; yet I fear   165
My wound hath taken cold, and I shall die."
So saying, from the pavement he half rose,
Slowly, with pain, reclining on his arm,
And looking wistfully with wide blue eyes
As in a picture. Him Sir Bedivere   170
Remorsefully regarded thro' his tears,
And would have spoken, but he found not words,
Then took with care, and kneeling on one knee,
O'er both his shoulders drew the languid hands,
And rising bore him thro' the place of tombs.   175
But, as he walked, King Arthur panted hard,
Like one that feels a nightmare on his bed
When all the house is mute. So sighed the King,
Muttering and murmuring at his ear, "Quick,
    quick!
I fear it is too late, and I shall die."   180
But the other swiftly strode from ridge to ridge,
Clothed with his breath, and looking, as he
    walked,
Larger than human on the frozen hills.
He heard the deep behind him, and a cry
Before. His own thought drove him like a goad.
Dry clashed his harness in the icy caves   186
And barren chasms, and all to left and right
The bare black cliff clanged round him, as he based
His feet on juts of slippery crag that rang
Sharp-smitten with the dint of armed heels —   190
And on a sudden, lo! the level lake,

And the long glories of the winter moon.
　Then saw they how there hove a dusky barge,
Dark as a funeral scarf from stem to stern,
Beneath them; and descending they were ware　195
That all the decks were dense with stately forms
Black-stoled, black-hooded, like a dream — by
　these
Three Queens with crowns of gold — and from
　them rose
A cry that shivered to the tingling stars,
And, as it were one voice, an agony　200
Of lamentation, like a wind, that shrills
All night in a waste land, where no one comes,
Or hath come, since the making of the world.
　Then murmured Arthur, "Place me in the
　barge,"
And to the barge they came.　There those three
　queens　205
Put forth their hands, and took the king, and wept.
But she, that rose the tallest of them all
And fairest, laid his head upon her lap,
And loosed the shattered casque, and chafed his
　hands,
And called him by his name, complaining loud,
And dropping bitter tears against his brow　211
Striped with dark blood; for all his face was white
And colorless, and like the withered moon
Smote by the fresh beam of the springing east;
And all his greaves and cuisses dashed with drops
Of onset; and the light and lustrous curls —　216
That made his forehead like a rising sun
High from the dais-throne — were parched with
　dust;
Or, clotted into points and hanging loose,
Mixed with the knightly growth that fringed his
　lips.　220
So like a shattered column lay the king;
Not like that Arthur who, with lance in rest,
From spur to plume a star of tournament,
Shot thro' the lists at Camelot, and charged
Before the eyes of ladies and of kings.　225
　Then loudly cried the bold Sir Bedivere:
"Ah! my Lord Arthur, whither shall I go?
Where shall I hide my forehead and my eyes?
For now I see the true old times are dead,
When every morning brought a noble chance,　230
And every chance brought out a noble knight.
Such times have been not since the light that led
The holy Elders with the gift of myrrh.
But now the whole ROUND TABLE is dissolved
Which was an image of the mighty world;　235
And I, the last, go forth companionless,
And the days darken round me, and the years,
Among new men, strange faces, other minds."
　And slowly answered Arthur from the barge:
"The old order changeth, yielding place to new,

And God fulfils himself in many ways,　241
Lest one good custom should corrupt the world.
Comfort thyself: what comfort is in me?
I have lived my life, and that which I have done
May He within himself make pure! but thou,　245
If thou shouldst never see my face again,
Pray for my soul.　More things are wrought by
　prayer
Than this world dreams of.　Wherefore, let thy
　voice
Rise like a fountain for me night and day.
For what are men better than sheep or goats　250
That nourish a blind life within the brain,
If, knowing God, they lift not hands of prayer
Both for themselves and those who call them
　friend?
For so the whole round earth is every way
Bound by gold chains about the feet of God.　255
But now farewell.　I am going a long way
With these thou seest — if indeed I go —
(For all my mind is clouded with a doubt)
To the island-valley of Avilion;
Where falls not hail, or rain, or any snow,　260
Nor ever wind blows loudly; but it lies
Deep-meadowed, happy, fair with orchard lawns
And bowery hollows crowned with summer sea,
Where I will heal me of my grievous wound."
　So said he, and the barge with oar and sail　265
Moved from the brink, like some full-breasted swan
That, fluting a wild carol ere her death,
Ruffles her pure cold plume, and takes the flood
With swarthy webs.　Long stood Sir Bedivere
Revolving many memories, till the hull　270
Looked one black dot against the verge of dawn,
And on the mere the wailing died away.

Ulysses

One of the greatest poems of Tennyson, indeed one
of the great poems in English literature, *Ulysses* is a
masterpiece of style.　Here is a classical subject —
Ulysses back at home after his adventures — treated
romantically.　In the first part of the poem, Tennyson
weaves together phrases and figures of speech from
many poets, classical and modern.　The "rainy Hyades"
is Virgilian, the "dim sea" Homeric; but the tone, the
spirit of courage, was one Tennyson believed necessary
for his nineteenth-century England.　The whole poem
deserves to be memorized as part of one's cultural equipment — particularly lines 10–32 and 56–70.　In this
poem Tennyson draws a lesson for the new world from
the old — the need to press on, unafraid, despite dis-
couragements and difficulties.　The form is that of the
dramatic monologue.

It little profits that an idle king,
By this still hearth, among these barren crags,

Matched with an aged wife, I mete and dole
Unequal laws unto a savage race,
That hoard, and sleep, and feed, and know not
me.   5
I cannot rest from travel; I will drink
Life to the lees. All times I have enjoyed
Greatly, have suffered greatly, both with those
That loved me, and alone; on shore, and when
Thro' scudding drifts the rainy Hyades[1]   10
Vext the dim sea. I am become a name;
For always roaming with a hungry heart
Much have I seen and known, — cities of men
And manners, climates, councils, governments,
Myself not least, but honored of them all, —   15
And drunk delight of battle with my peers,
Far on the ringing plains of windy Troy.
I am a part of all that I have met;
Yet all experience is an arch wherethro'
Gleams that untravelled world, whose margin
fades   20
For ever and for ever when I move.
How dull it is to pause, to make an end,
To rust unburnished, not to shine in use!
As tho' to breathe were life! Life piled on life
Were all too little, and of one to me   25
Little remains; but every hour is saved
From that eternal silence, something more,
A bringer of new things; and vile it were
For some three suns to store and hoard myself,
And this gray spirit yearning in desire   30
To follow knowledge, like a sinking star,
Beyond the utmost bound of human thought.

This is my son, mine own Telemachus,
To whom I leave the sceptre and the isle, —
Well-loved of me, discerning to fulfil   35
This labor, by slow prudence to make mild
A rugged people, and thro' soft degrees
Subdue them to the useful and the good.
Most blameless is he, centred in the sphere
Of common duties, decent not to fail   40
In offices of tenderness, and pay
Meet adoration to my household gods,
When I am gone. He works his work, I mine.

There lies the port; the vessel puffs her sail;
There gloom the dark, broad seas. My mariners,
Souls that have toiled, and wrought, and thought
with me, —   46
That ever with a frolic welcome took
The thunder and the sunshine, and opposed
Free hearts, free foreheads, — you and I are old;
Old age hath yet his honor and his toil.   50
Death closes all; but something ere the end,
Some work of noble note, may yet be done,
Not unbecoming men that strove with Gods.

[1] Stars in the constellation Taurus, supposed to
promise rain.

The lights begin to twinkle from the rocks;
The long day wanes; the slow moon climbs; the
deep
Moans round with many voices. Come, my   55
friends,
'Tis not too late to seek a newer world.
Push off, and sitting well in order smite
The sounding furrows; for my purpose holds
To sail beyond the sunset, and the baths   60
Of all the western stars, until I die.
It may be that the gulfs will wash us down;
It may be we shall touch the Happy Isles,
And see the great Achilles, whom we knew.
Tho' much is taken, much abides; and tho'   65
We are not now that strength which in old days
Moved earth and heaven, that which we are, we
are, —
One equal temper of heroic hearts,
Made weak by time and fate, but strong in will
To strive, to seek, to find, and not to yield.   70

Break, Break, Break

Break, break, break,
    On thy cold gray stones, O Sea!
And I would that my tongue could utter
    The thoughts that arise in me.

O well for the fisherman's boy,
    That he shouts with his sister at play!   5
O well for the sailor lad,
    That he sings in his boat on the bay!

And the stately ships go on
    To their haven under the hill;   10
But O for the touch of a vanished hand,
    And the sound of a voice that is still!

Break, break, break,
    At the foot of thy crags, O Sea!
But the tender grace of a day that is dead   15
    Will never come back to me.

Songs from *The Princess*

I

Sweet and low, sweet and low,
    Wind of the western sea,
Low, low, breathe and blow,
    Wind of the western sea!
Over the rolling waters go,   5
Come from the dying moon, and blow,
    Blow him again to me;
While my little one, while my pretty one, sleeps.

Sleep and rest, sleep and rest,
   Father will come to thee soon;   10
Rest, rest, on mother's breast,
   Father will come to thee soon;
Father will come to his babe in the nest,
Silver sails all out of the west
   Under the silver moon;   15
Sleep, my little one, sleep, my pretty one, sleep.

2

The splendor falls on castle walls
   And snowy summits old in story;
The long light shakes across the lakes,
   And the wild cataract leaps in glory.   20
Blow, bugle, blow, set the wild echoes flying,
Blow, bugle; answer, echoes, dying, dying, dying.

O, hark, O, hear! how thin and clear,
   And thinner, clearer, farther going!
O, sweet and far from cliff and scar   25
   The horns of Elfland faintly blowing!
Blow, let us hear the purple glens replying,
Blow, bugle; answer, echoes, dying, dying, dying.

O love, they die in yon rich sky,
   They faint on hill or field or river;   30
Our echoes roll from soul to soul,
   And grow for ever and for ever.
Blow, bugle, blow, set the wild echoes flying,
And answer, echoes, answer, dying, dying, dying.

3

Tears, idle tears, I know not what they mean,   35
Tears from the depth of some divine despair
Rise in the heart, and gather to the eyes,
In looking on the happy autumn-fields,
And thinking of the days that are no more.

Fresh as the first beam glittering on a sail,   40
That brings our friends up from the underworld,
Sad as the last which reddens over one
That sinks with all we love below the verge;
So sad, so fresh, the days that are no more.

Ah, sad and strange as in dark summer dawns   45
The earliest pipe of half-awakened birds
To dying ears, when unto dying eyes
The casement slowly grows a glimmering square;
So sad, so strange, the days that are no more.

Dear as remembered kisses after death,   50
And sweet as those by hopeless fancy feigned
On lips that are for others; deep as love,
Deep as first love, and wild with all regret;
O Death in Life, the days that are no more.

4

Home they brought her warrior dead;   55
   She nor swooned, nor uttered cry.
All her maidens, watching, said,
   "She must weep or she will die."

Then they praised him, soft and low,
   Called him worthy to be loved,   60
Truest friend and noblest foe;
   Yet she neither spoke nor moved.

Stole a maiden from her place,
   Lightly to the warrior stept,
Took the face-cloth from the face;   65
   Yet she neither moved nor wept.

Rose a nurse of ninety years,
   Set his child upon her knee —
Like summer tempest came her tears —
   "Sweet my child, I live for thee."   70

5

Ask me no more: the moon may draw the sea;
   The cloud may stoop from heaven and take the
      shape,
With fold to fold, of mountain or of cape;
But O too fond, when have I answered thee?
   Ask me no more.   75

Ask me no more: what answer should I give?
   I love not hollow cheek or faded eye:
Yet, O my friend, I will not have thee die!
Ask me no more, lest I should bid thee live;
   Ask me no more.   80

Ask me no more: thy fate and mine are sealed;
   I strove against the stream and all in vain:
Let the great river take me to the main.
No more, dear love, for at a touch I yield;
   Ask me no more.   85

6

Now sleeps the crimson petal, now the white;
Nor waves the cypress in the palace walk;
Nor winks the gold fin in the porphyry font.
The fire-fly wakens; waken thou with me.

Now droops the milkwhite peacock like a ghost,
And like a ghost she glimmers on to me.   91

Now lies the Earth all Danaë¹ to the stars,
And all thy heart lies open unto me.

¹ Danaë was visited in her tower by Zeus who took
the form of a shower of gold.

Now slides the silent meteor on, and leaves
A shining furrow, as thy thoughts in me.   95

Now folds the lily all her sweetness up,
And slips into the bosom of the lake.
So fold thyself, my dearest, thou, and slip
Into my bosom and be lost in me.

7

Come down, O maid, from yonder mountain
    height: 100
What pleasure lives in height (the shepherd sang)
In height and cold, the splendor of the hills?
But cease to move so near the heavens, and cease
To glide a sunbeam by the blasted pine,
To sit a star upon the sparkling spire;   105
And come, for Love is of the valley, come,
For Love is of the valley, come thou down
And find him; by the happy threshold, he,
Or hand in hand with Plenty in the maize,
Or red with spirted purple of the vats,   110
Or foxlike in the vine; nor cares to walk
With Death and Morning on the Silver Horns,
Nor wilt thou snare him in the white ravine
Nor find him dropt upon the firths of ice,
That huddling slant in furrow-cloven falls   115
To roll the torrent out of dusky doors.
But follow; let the torrent dance thee down
To find him in the valley; let the wild
Lean-headed Eagles yelp alone, and leave
The monstrous ledges there to slope, and spill   120
Their thousand wreaths of dangling water-smoke,
That like a broken purpose waste in air.
So waste not thou, but come; for all the vales
Await thee; azure pillars of the hearth
Arise to thee; the children call, and I   125
Thy shepherd pipe, and sweet is every sound,
Sweeter thy voice. but every sound is sweet;
Myriads of rivulets hurrying thro' the lawn,
The moan of doves in immemorial elms,
And murmuring of innumerable bees.   130

In Memoriam A. H. H.

Although *In Memoriam* was not published until
1850, Tennyson began writing short poems based on
his grief at the loss of a Cambridge friend, Arthur
Henry Hallam, soon after Hallam's death at Vienna
in 1833. These scattered poems were later brought
together into a whole which has been recognized as one
of the world's great elegies. Some of the shorter units
of the poem follow.

I

I held it truth, with him who sings
    To one clear harp in divers tones,

    That men may rise on stepping-stones
    Of their dead selves to higher things.

But who shall so forecast the years   5
    And find in loss a gain to match?
    Or reach a hand thro' time to catch
The far-off interest of tears?

Let Love clasp Grief lest both be drowned,
    Let darkness keep her raven gloss.   10
    Ah, sweeter to be drunk with loss,
To dance with Death, to beat the ground,

Than that the victor Hours should scorn
    The long result of love, and boast,
    "Behold the man that loved and lost,   15
But all he was is overworn."

2

Old yew, which graspest at the stones
    That name the underlying dead,
    Thy fibres net the dreamless head,
Thy roots are wrapt about the bones.   20

The seasons bring the flower again,
    And bring the firstling to the flock;
    And in the dusk of thee, the clock
Beats out the little lives of men.

O, not for thee the glow, the bloom,   25
    Who changest not in any gale,
    Nor branding summer suns avail
To touch thy thousand years of gloom:

And gazing on thee, sullen tree,
    Sick for thy stubborn hardihood,   30
    I seem to fail from out my blood
And grow incorporate into thee.

3

O Sorrow, cruel fellowship,
    O Priestess in the vaults of Death,
    O sweet and bitter in a breath,   35
What whispers from thy lying lip?

"The stars," she whispers, "blindly run;
    A web is woven across the sky;
    From out waste places comes a cry,
And murmurs from the dying sun;   40

"And all the phantom, Nature, stands —
    With all her music in her tone,
    A hollow echo of my own, —
A hollow form with empty hands."

And shall I take a thing so blind, 45
    Embrace her as my natural good;
    Or crush her, like a vice of blood,
Upon the threshold of the mind?

4

To Sleep I give my powers away;
    My will is bondsman to the dark;
    I sit within a helmless bark, 50
And with my heart I muse and say:

O heart, how fares it with thee now,
    That thou shouldst fail from thy desire,
    Who scarcely darest to inquire, 55
"What is it makes me beat so low?"

Something it is which thou hast lost,
    Some pleasure from thine early years.
    Break, thou deep vase of chilling tears,
That grief hath shaken into frost! 60

Such clouds of nameless trouble cross
    All night below the darkened eyes;
    With morning wakes the will, and cries,
"Thou shalt not be the fool of loss."

. . . .

27

I envy not in any moods 65
    The captive void of noble rage,
    The linnet born within the cage,
That never knew the summer woods;

I envy not the beast that takes
    His license in the field of time, 70
    Unfettered by the sense of crime,
To whom a conscience never wakes;

Nor, what may count itself as blest,
    The heart that never plighted troth
    But stagnates in the weeds of sloth; 75
Nor any want-begotten rest.

I hold it true, whate'er befall;
    I feel it, when I sorrow most;
    'Tis better to have loved and lost
Than never to have loved at all. 80

28

The time draws near the birth of Christ.[1]
    The moon is hid, the night is still;
    The Christmas bells from hill to hill
Answer each other in the mist.

Four voices of four hamlets round, 85
    From far and near, on mead and moor,

[1] First Christmas after the death of Hallam.

Swell out and fail, as if a door
Were shut between me and the sound;

Each voice four changes on the wind,
    That now dilate, and now decrease, 90
    Peace and goodwill, goodwill and peace,
Peace and goodwill, to all mankind.

This year I slept and woke with pain,
    I almost wished no more to wake,
    And that my hold on life would break 95
Before I heard those bells again;

But they my troubled spirit rule,
    For they controlled me when a boy;
    They bring me sorrow touched with joy,
The merry, merry bells of Yule. 100

29

With such compelling cause to grieve
    As daily vexes household peace,
    And chains regret to his decease,
How dare we keep our Christmas-eve;

Which brings no more a welcome guest 105
    To enrich the threshold of the night
    With showered largess of delight
In dance and song and game and jest?

Yet go, and while the holly boughs
    Entwine the cold baptismal font, 110
    Make one wreath more for Use and Wont,
That guard the portals of the house;

Old sisters of a day gone by,
    Gray nurses, loving nothing new —
    Why should they miss their yearly due 115
Before their time? They too will die.

30

With trembling fingers did we weave
    The holly round the Christmas hearth;
    A rainy cloud possessed the earth,
And sadly fell our Christmas-eve. 120

At our old pastimes in the hall
    We gamboled, making vain pretence
    Of gladness, with an awful sense
Of one mute Shadow watching all.

We paused: the winds were in the beech; 125
    We heard them sweep the winter land;
    And in a circle hand-in-hand
Sat silent, looking each at each.

Then echo-like our voices rang;
    We sung, tho' every eye was dim, 130

A merry song we sang with him
Last year; impetuously we sang.

We ceased; a gentler feeling crept
    Upon us: surely rest is meet.
    "They rest," we said, "their sleep is sweet,"
And silence followed, and we wept.   136

Our voices took a higher range;
    Once more we sang: "They do not die
    Nor lose their mortal sympathy,
Nor change to us, although they change;   140

"Rapt from the fickle and the frail
    With gathered power, yet the same,
    Pierces the keen seraphic flame
From orb to orb, from veil to veil."

Rise, happy morn, rise, holy morn,   145
    Draw forth the cheerful day from night:
    O Father, touch the east, and light
The light that shone when Hope was born.

. . . .

54

O, yet we trust that somehow good
    Will be the final goal of ill,   150
    To pangs of nature, sins of will,
Defects of doubt, and taints of blood;

That nothing walks with aimless feet;
    That not one life shall be destroy'd,
    Or cast as rubbish to the void,   155
When God hath made the pile complete;

That not a worm is cloven in vain;
    That not a moth with vain desire
    Is shrivel'd in a fruitless fire,
Or but subserves another's gain.   160

Behold, we know not anything;
    I can but trust that good shall fall
    At last — far off — at last, to all,
And every winter change to spring.

So runs my dream; but what am I?   165
    An infant crying in the night;
    An infant crying for the light,
And with no language but a cry.

55

The wish, that of the living whole
    No life may fail beyond the grave,   170
    Derives it not from what we have
The likest God within the soul?

Are God and Nature then at strife,
    That Nature lends such evil dreams?
    So careful of the type she seems,   175
So careless of the single life,

That I, considering everywhere
    Her secret meaning in her deeds,
    And finding that of fifty seeds
She often brings but one to bear,   180

I falter where I firmly trod,
    And falling with my weight of cares
    Upon the great world's altar-stairs
That slope thro' darkness up to God,

I stretch lame hands of faith, and grope,   185
    And gather dust and chaff, and call
    To what I feel is Lord of all,
And faintly trust the larger hope.

56

"So careful of the type?" but no.
    From scarped cliff and quarried stone   190
    She cries, "A thousand types are gone;
I care for nothing, all shall go.

"Thou makest thine appeal to me.
    I bring to life, I bring to death;
    The spirit does but mean the breath: 195
I know no more."   And he, shall he,

Man, her last work, who seem'd so fair,
    Such splendid purpose in his eyes,
    Who roll'd the psalm to wintry skies,
Who built him fanes of fruitless prayer,   200

Who trusted God was love indeed
    And love Creation's final law —
    Tho' Nature, red in tooth and claw
With ravine, shriek'd against his creed —

Who loved, who suffer'd countless ills,   205
    Who battled for the True, the Just,
    Be blown about the desert dust,
Or seal'd within the iron hills?

No more?   A monster then, a dream,
    A discord.   Dragons of the prime,   210
    That tare each other in their slime,
Were mellow music match'd with him.

O life as futile, then, as frail!
    O for thy voice to soothe and bless!
    What hope of answer, or redress?   215
Behind the veil, behind the veil.

. . . .

78

Again at Christmas did we weave
    The holly round the Christmas hearth;
    The silent snow possessed the earth,
And calmly fell our Christmas-eve.   220

The yule-clog sparkled keen with frost,
    No wing of wind the region swept,
    But over all things brooding slept
The quiet sense of something lost.

As in the winters left behind,   225
    Again our ancient games had place,
    The mimic picture's breathing grace,
And dance and song and hoodman-blind.

Who showed a token of distress?
    No single tear, no type of pain —   230
    O sorrow, then can sorrow wane?
O grief, can grief be changed to less?

O last regret, regret can die!
    No — mixt with all this mystic frame,
    Her deep relations are the same,   235
But with long use her tears are dry.

. . . .

96

You say, but with no touch of scorn,
    Sweet-hearted, you, whose light-blue eyes
    Are tender over drowning flies,
You tell me, doubt is Devil-born.   240

I know not: one indeed I knew
    In many a subtle question versed,
    Who touch'd a jarring lyre at first,
But ever strove to make it true;

Perplext in faith, but pure in deeds,   245
    At last he beat his music out.
    There lives more faith in honest doubt,
Believe me, than in half the creeds.

He fought his doubts and gather'd strength,
    He would not make his judgment blind,   250
    He faced the specters of the mind
And laid them; thus he came at length

To find a stronger faith his own,
    And Power was with him in the night,
    Which makes the darkness and the light,   255
And dwells not in the light alone,

But in the darkness and the cloud,
    As over Sinai's peaks of old,

While Israel made their gods of gold,
Altho' the trumpet blew so loud.   260

. . . .

104

The time draws near the birth of Christ;
    The moon is hid, the night is still;
    A single church below the hill
Is pealing, folded in the mist.

A single peal of bells below,   265
    That wakens at this hour of rest
    A single murmur in the breast,
That these are not the bells I know.

Like strangers' voices here they sound,
    In lands where not a memory strays,   270
    Nor landmark breathes of other days,
But all is new unhallow'd ground.

105

Tonight ungather'd let us leave
    This laurel, let this holly stand:
    We live within the stranger's land,   275
And strangely falls our Christmas-eve.

Our father's dust is left alone
    And silent under other snows:
    There in due time the woodbine blows,
The violet comes, but we are gone.   280

Nor more shall wayward grief abuse
    The genial hour with mask and mime;
    For change of place, like growth of time,
Has broke the bond of dying use.

Let cares that petty shadows cast,   285
    By which our lives are chiefly proved,
    A little spare the night I loved,
And hold it solemn to the past.

But let no footstep beat the floor,
    Nor bowl of wassail mantle warm;   290
    For who would keep an ancient form
Thro' which the spirit breathes no more?

Be neither song, nor game, nor feast;
    Nor harp be touch'd, nor flute be blown;
    No dance, no motion, save alone   295
What lightens in the lucid East

Of rising worlds by yonder wood.
    Long sleeps the summer in the seed;
    Run out your measured arcs, and lead
The closing cycle rich in good.   300

106

Ring out, wild bells, to the wild sky,
　　The flying cloud, the frosty light:
　　The year is dying in the night;
Ring out, wild bells, and let him die.

Ring out the old, ring in the new, 305
　　Ring, happy bells, across the snow:
　　The year is going, let him go;
Ring out the false, ring in the true.

Ring out the grief that saps the mind,
　　For those that here we see no more;　310
　　Ring out the feud of rich and poor,
Ring in redress to all mankind.

Ring out a slowly dying cause,
　　And ancient forms of party strife;
　　Ring in the nobler modes of life,　315
With sweeter manners, purer laws.

Ring out the want, the care, the sin,
　　The faithless coldness of the times;
　　Ring out, ring out my mournful rhymes,
But ring the fuller minstrel in.　320

Ring out false pride in place and blood,
　　The civic slander and the spite;
　　Ring in the love of truth and right,
Ring in the common love of good.

Ring out old shapes of foul disease;　325
　　Ring out the narrowing lust of gold;
　　Ring out the thousand wars of old,
Ring in the thousand years of peace.

Ring in the valiant man and free,
　　The larger heart, the kindlier hand;　330
　　Ring out the darkness of the land,
Ring in the Christ that is to be.

. . . .

118

Contemplate all this work of Time,
　　The giant laboring in his youth;
　　Nor dream of human love and truth,　335
As dying Nature's earth and lime;

But trust that those we call the dead
　　Are breathers of an ampler day
　　For ever nobler ends.　They say,
The solid earth whereon we tread　340

In tracts of fluent heat began,
　　And grew to seeming-random forms,

The seeming prey of cyclic storms,
Till at the last arose the man;

Who throve and branched from clime to clime,　345
　　The herald of a higher race,
　　And of himself in higher place,
If so he type [1] this work of time

Within himself, from more to more;
　　Or, crowned with attributes of woe　350
　　Like glories, move his course, and show
That life is not as idle ore,

But iron dug from central gloom,
　　And heated hot with burning fears,
　　And dipt in baths of hissing tears,　355
And battered with the shocks of doom

To shape and use.　Arise and fly
　　The reeling Faun, the sensual feast;
　　Move upward, working out the beast,
And let the ape and tiger die.　360

. . . .

The Brook

I come from haunts of coot and hern,
　　I make a sudden sally,
And sparkle out among the fern,
　　To bicker down a valley.

By thirty hills I hurry down,　5
　　Or slip between the ridges,
By twenty thorps, a little town,
　　And half a hundred bridges.

Till last by Philip's farm I flow
　　To join the brimming river,　10
For men may come and men may go,
　　But I go on for ever.

I chatter over stony ways,
　　In little sharps and trebles,
I bubble into eddying bays,　15
　　I babble on the pebbles.

With many a curve my banks I fret
　　By many a field and fallow,
And many a fairy foreland set
　　With willow-weed and mallow.　20

I chatter, chatter, as I flow
　　To join the brimming river,
For men may come and men may go,
　　But I go on for ever.

[1] Serve as a type for.

I wind about, and in and out, 25
  With here a blossom sailing,
And here and there a lusty trout,
  And here and there a grayling,

And here and there a foamy flake
  Upon me, as I travel 30
With many a silvery water-break
  Above the golden gravel,

And draw them all along, and flow
  To join the brimming river,
For men may come and men may go, 35
  But I go on for ever.

I steal by lawns and grassy plots,
  I slide by hazel covers;
I move the sweet forget-me-nots
  That grow for happy lovers. 40

I slip, I slide, I gloom, I glance,
  Among my skimming swallows;
I make the netted sunbeam dance
  Against my sandy shallows.

I murmur under moon and stars 45
  In brambly wildernesses;
I linger by my shingly bars,
  I loiter round my cresses;

And out again I curve and flow
  To join the brimming river, 50
For men may come and men may go,
  But I go on for ever.

The Higher Pantheism

Pantheism is the worship of objects in nature. The "higher" pantheism is that which identifies both nature and spirit, the finite and the infinite. Emerson's *Brahma* might be read in connection with this poem.

The sun, the moon, the stars, the seas, the hills
  and the plains, —
Are not these, O Soul, the Vision of Him who
  reigns?

Is not the Vision He, though He be not that which
  He seems?
Dreams are true while they last, and do we not live
  in dreams?

Earth, these solid stars, this weight of body and
  limb, 5
Are they not sign and symbol of thy division from
  Him?

Dark is the world to thee; thyself art the reason
  why,
For is He not all but thou, that hast power to feel
  "I am I"?

Glory about thee, without thee; and thou fulfillest
  thy doom,
Making Him broken gleams and a stifled splendor
  and gloom. 10

Speak to Him, thou, for He hears, and Spirit with
  Spirit can meet —
Closer is He than breathing, and nearer than hands
  and feet.

God is law, say the wise; O Soul, and let us rejoice,
For if He thunder by law the thunder is yet His
  voice.

Law is God, say some; no God at all, says the fool,
For all we have power to see is a straight staff bent
  in a pool; 16

And the ear of man cannot hear, and the eye of
  man cannot see;
But if we could see and hear, this Vision — were
  it not He?

The Revenge

A BALLAD OF THE FLEET

I

At Flores in the Azores Sir Richard Grenville lay,
And a pinnace, like a flutter'd bird, came flying
  from far away:
"Spanish ships of war at sea! we have sighted
  fifty-three!"
Then sware Lord Thomas Howard: "'Fore God I
  am no coward;
But I cannot meet them here, for my ships are out
  of gear, 5
And the half my men are sick. I must fly, but
  follow quick.
We are six ships of the line; can we fight with
  fifty-three?"

II

Then spake Sir Richard Grenville: "I know you
  are no coward;
You fly them for a moment to fight with them again.
But I've ninety men and more that are lying sick
  ashore. 10
I should count myself the coward if I left them, my
  Lord Howard,
To these Inquisition dogs and the devildoms of
  Spain."

III

So Lord Howard past away with five ships of war
    that day,
Till he melted like a cloud in the silent summer
    heaven;
But Sir Richard bore in hand all his sick men from
    the land   15
Very carefully and slow,
Men of Bideford in Devon,
And we laid them on the ballast down below;
For we brought them all aboard,
And they blest him in their pain, that they were
    not left to Spain,   20
To the thumbscrew and the stake, for the glory of
    the Lord.

IV

He had only a hundred seamen to work the ship
    and to fight,
And he sailed away from Flores till the Spaniard
    came in sight,
With his huge sea-castles heaving upon the weather
    bow.
"Shall we fight or shall we fly?   25
Good Sir Richard, tell us now,
For to fight is but to die!
There'll be little of us left by the time this sun be
    set."
And Sir Richard said again: "We be all good
    English men.
Let us bang these dogs of Seville, the children of
    the devil,   30
For I never turn'd my back upon Don or devil
    yet."

V

Sir Richard spoke and he laugh'd, and we roar'd
    a hurrah, and so
The little Revenge ran on sheer into the heart of
    the foe,
With her hundred fighters on deck, and her ninety
    sick below;
For half of their fleet to the right and half to the
    left were seen,   35
And the little Revenge ran on thro' the long sea-
    lane between.

VI

Thousands of their soldiers look'd down from their
    decks and laugh'd,
Thousands of their seamen made mock at the mad
    little craft
Running on and on, till delay'd
By their mountain-like San Philip that, of fifteen
    hundred tons,   40

And up-shadowing high above us with her yawn-
    ing tiers of guns,
Took the breath from our sails, and we stay'd.

VII

And while now the great San Philip hung above us
    like a cloud
Whence the thunderbolt will fall
Long and loud,   45
Four galleons drew away
From the Spanish fleet that day,
And two upon the larboard and two upon the
    starboard lay,
And the battle-thunder broke from them all.

VIII

But anon the great San Philip, she bethought her-
    self and went,   50
Having that within her womb that had left her ill
    content;
And the rest they came aboard us, and they fought
    us hand to hand,
For a dozen times they came with their pikes and
    musqueteers,
And a dozen times we shook 'em off as a dog that
    shakes his ears
When he leaps from the water to the land.   55

IX

And the sun went down, and the stars came out
    far over the summer sea,
But never a moment ceased the fight of the one
    and the fifty-three.
Ship after ship, the whole night long, their high-
    built galleons came,
Ship after ship, the whole night long, with her
    battle-thunder and flame;
Ship after ship, the whole night long, drew back
    with her dead and her shame.   60
For some were sunk and many were shatter'd,
    and so could fight us no more —
God of battles, was ever a battle like this in the
    world before?

X

For he said, "Fight on! fight on!"
Tho' his vessel was all but a wreck;
And it chanced that, when half of the short sum-
    mer night was gone,   65
With a grisly wound to be drest he had left the
    deck,
But a bullet struck him that was dressing it sud-
    denly dead,
And himself he was wounded again in the side and
    the head,
And he said, "Fight on! fight on!"

XI

And the night went down, and the sun smiled out
    far over the summer sea,   70
And the Spanish fleet with broken sides lay round
    us all in a ring;
But they dared not touch us again, for they fear'd
    that we still could sting,
So they watch'd what the end would be.
And we had not fought them in vain,
But in perilous plight were we,   75
Seeing forty of our poor hundred were slain,
And half of the rest of us maim'd for life
In the crash of the cannonades and the desperate
    strife;
And the sick men down in the hold were most of
    them stark and cold,
And the pikes were all broken or bent, and the
    powder was all of it spent;   80
And the masts and the rigging were lying over the
    side;
But Sir Richard cried in his English pride:
"We have fought such a fight for a day and a night
As may never be fought again!
We have won great glory, my men!   85
And a day less or more
At sea or ashore,
We die — does it matter when?
Sink me the ship, Master Gunner — sink her,
    split her in twain!
Fall into the hands of God, not into the hands of
    Spain!"   90

XII

And the gunner said, "Ay, ay," but the seamen
    made reply:
"We have children, we have wives,
And the Lord hath spared our lives.
We will make the Spaniard promise, if we yield,
    to let us go;
We shall live to fight again and to strike another
    blow."   95
And the lion there lay dying, and they yielded to
    the foe.

XIII

And the stately Spanish men to their flagship bore
    him then,
Where they laid him by the mast, old Sir Richard
    caught at last,
And they praised him to his face with their courtly
    foreign grace;
But he rose upon their decks, and he cried: 100
"I have fought for Queen and Faith like a valiant
    man and true;
I have only done my duty as a man is bound to do.

With a joyful spirit I Sir Richard Grenville die!"
And he fell upon their decks, and he died.

XIV

And they stared at the dead that had been so
    valiant and true,   105
And had holden the power and glory of Spain so
    cheap
That he dared her with one little ship and his
    English few;
Was he devil or man? He was devil for aught they
    knew,
But they sank his body with honor down into the
    deep,
And they mann'd the Revenge with a swarthier
    alien crew,   110
And away she sail'd with her loss and long'd for
    her own;
When a wind from the lands they had ruin'd
    awoke from sleep,
And the water began to heave and the weather to
    moan,
And or ever that evening ended a great gale blew,
And a wave like the wave that is raised by an
    earthquake grew,   115
Till it smote on their hulls and their sails and their
    masts and their flags,
And the whole sea plunged and fell on the shot-
    shatter'd navy of Spain,
And the little Revenge herself went down by the
    island crags
To be lost evermore in the main.

Crossing the Bar

Sunset and evening star,
    And one clear call for me!
And may there be no moaning of the bar,
    When I put out to sea,

But such a tide as moving seems asleep,   5
    Too full for sound and foam,
When that which drew from out the boundless deep
    Turns again home.

Twilight and evening bell,
    And after that the dark!   10
And may there be no sadness of farewell,
    When I embark;

For though from out our bourne of Time and
    Place
    The flood may bear me far,
I hope to see my Pilot face to face   15
    When I have crost the bar.

Robert Browning · 1812-1889

The life of Robert Browning disproves most convincingly the old belief that a poet is a rebel against society living an impoverished life in an attic. Rarely have poets lived more conventionally than Browning.

The poet was born May 7, 1812, in a suburb of London, Camberwell, into a home of comfort and cultivation. Browning's father held an important post in the Bank of England and enjoyed a good income. His parents' appreciation of literature and rare books, of music and art, of intelligent conversation, early influenced him. The father was indulgent and somewhat experimental in the education he gave young Robert; the boy had little formal schooling, but was urged to read widely and encouraged in special interests as they developed. In this way Browning became well informed on such subjects as the classics, musical composition, art, and philosophy. Boxing and riding were equally sponsored, for Robert was no weakling. For a brief period he attended lectures on Greek at London University.

Early in his development the young Robert had announced his intention of becoming a poet, and his father, who had always resented the routine of banking, agreed that his son should follow his natural bent. Part of this preparation for his life as a poet called for travel on the continent. In 1834 Browning visited Russia and Italy; in 1838 he paid another visit to Italy. In 1846 he married Elizabeth Barrett, who was herself a poet. As Miss Barrett's health demanded a more temperate climate the young couple made their home in Florence, a city which they left only on brief visits. After Mrs. Browning's death, fifteen years later, Browning lived chiefly in London but made several prolonged visits to Italy. His life was dignified, rich in friendships, without financial stress, and free from social or political rebellion.

A background so different from that of such poets as Burns and Wordsworth or Shelley and Keats naturally results in poetry of a different impress. Browning's enthusiasm as a poet appears to have been for people and for their responses to life at moments of great crises. He advances little that can be thought of as "a philosophy." He believed that as man had evolved physically from his primitive beginning it was both his privilege and his responsibility to advance spiritually to new capacities. How was this development to be fostered? By a recognition of the power of beauty and love:

> If you get simple beauty and naught else,
> You get about the best thing God invents.

And by a striving for the ideal:

> Ah, but a man's reach should exceed his grasp
> Or what's a heaven for?

Success does not lie so much in attainment as in a desire for something beyond; it is not accomplishment by which men are to be measured so much as by the goals which they set themselves. The important qualities in man are within him, the drive which urges him on to action, his concern for ideal progress. And, as in *Love Among the Ruins*, this progress is, we are told, most likely to be secured when we learn to exclude the "centuries of folly"

> With their triumphs and their glories and the rest

and understand that "Love is best." Browning, it will be seen, presents no panacea for the ills of society; he leaves progress and improvement within the will of the individual.

Though Browning has proved his ability to portray real life action in some of the *Cavalier Tunes* and in such a vivid bit as *How They Brought the Good News from Ghent to Aix*, and has, in several poems, established his sense of humor, he must be thought of primarily as a poet portraying human character. His most original contribution to literature is the "dramatic monologue," a form which, through the conversation of one character, reveals "a soul in action." Browning had the ability to fit the speech and thought appropriately to the character presented. *Andrea del Sarto* will stand as a good example of this type of the poet's writing. Many readers will agree with the estimate of Landor:

> Since Chaucer was alive and hale,
> No man hath walked along our roads with step
> So active, so inquiring eye, or tongue
> So varied in discourse.

Browning's romantic temper is not immediately discernible. His fidelity to human character, his analysis of the personality of the individual, and his concern for truth are certainly realistic rather than romantic tendencies. Browning had the quality of the realist, too, in that he found human beings and society exciting and manifested no desire to isolate himself from them. On the other hand the poet's penchant for the psychological and the subjective, as well as the terseness of his literary style, ally him with the more modern movement of expressionism. From this point of view he proves himself a forerunner of such writers as Virginia Woolf, James Joyce, and Hart Crane. But, on the whole, Browning differs from both the realist and these moderns in his optimism, in his insistence that "truth will triumph," in his reliance on faith rather than reason, and in his general idealistic outlook. And these doctrines are not only good Browning but good romanticism as well.

Some of the more important works are: *Pauline* (1833), a failure, of which not a copy was sold but which taught Browning much; *Paracelsus* (1835), which brought him definite recognition from the few who knew poetry; *Strafford* (1837), a play which ran four nights; *Sordello* (1840); *Bells and Pomegranates* (1841–46), a series of poems in pamphlet issues; *Pippa Passes* (1841); *Men and Women* (1855); *Dramatis Personæ* (1864); and *The Ring and the Book* (1868–69), a long poem of over 21,000 lines, generally conceded to be the poet's greatest accomplishment.

SUGGESTED REFERENCES: W. C. DeVane, *A Browning Handbook* (2nd ed., 1955); R. A. King, *The Bow and the Lyre. The Art of Robert Browning* (1957); G. K. Chesterton, *Robert Browning* (4th ed., 1961).

A Grammarian's Funeral

SHORTLY AFTER THE REVIVAL OF LEARNING
IN EUROPE

The poem reflects Browning's interest in the Renaissance. It is a faithful study of the spirit of Renaissance learning in Italy.

Let us begin and carry up this corpse,
  Singing together.
Leave we the common crofts,[1] the vulgar thorpes[2]
  Each in its tether
Sleeping safe on the bosom of the plain,   5
  Cared-for till cock-crow:
Look out if yonder be not day again
  Rimming the rock-row!
That's the appropriate country; there, man's
    thought,
  Rarer, intenser,   10

[1] A small field or farm.   [2] villages.

Self-gathered for an outbreak, as it ought,
  Chafes in the censer.
Leave we the unlettered plain its herd and crop;
  Seek we sepulture
On a tall mountain, citied to the top,   15
  Crowded with culture!
All the peaks soar, but one the rest excels;
  Clouds overcome it;
No! yonder sparkle is the citadel's
  Circling its summit.   20
Thither our path lies; wind we up the heights;
  Wait ye the warning?
Our low life was the level's and the night's;
  He's for the morning.
Step to a tune, square chest, erect each head,   25
  'Ware the beholders!
This is our master, famous, calm and dead,
  Borne on our shoulders.
Sleep, crop and herd! sleep, darkling thorpe and croft,
  Safe from the weather!   30

He, whom we convoy to his grave aloft,
    Singing together,
He was a man born with thy face and throat,
    Lyric Apollo!
Long he lived nameless: how should Spring take
    note   35
    Winter would follow?
Till lo, the little touch, and youth was gone!
    Cramped and diminished,
Moaned he, "New measures, other feet anon!
    My dance is finished"?   40
No, that's the world's way: (keep the mountain-
    side,
    Make for the city!)
He knew the signal, and stepped on with pride
    Over men's pity;
Left play for work, and grappled with the world 45
    Bent on escaping:
"What's in the scroll," quoth he, "thou keepest
    furled?
    Show me their shaping,
Theirs who most studied man, the bard and
    sage —
    Give!" — So, he gowned him,   50
Straight got by heart that book to its last page:
    Learnèd, we found him.
Yea, but we found him bald too, eyes like lead,
    Accents uncertain:
"Time to taste life," another would have said, 55
    "Up with the curtain!"
This man said rather, "Actual life comes next?
    Patience a moment!
Grant I have mastered learning's crabbèd text,
    Still there's the comment.   60
Let me know all! Prate not of most or least,
    Painful or easy!
Even to the crumbs I'd fain eat up the feast,
    Ay, nor feel queasy."
Oh, such a life as he resolved to live,   65
    When he had learned it,
When he had gathered all books had to give!
    Sooner, he spurned it.
Image the whole, then execute the parts —
    Fancy the fabric   70
Quite, ere you build, ere steel strike fire from
    quartz,
    Ere mortar dab brick!
(Here's the town-gate reached: there's the market-
    place
    Gaping before us.)
Yea, this in him was the peculiar grace   75
    (Hearten our chorus!)
That before living he'd learn how to live —
    No end to learning:
Earn the means first — God surely will contrive
    Use for our earning.   80

Others mistrust and say, "But time escapes:
    Live now or never!"
He said, "What's time? Leave Now for dogs and
    apes!
    Man has Forever."
Back to his book then: deeper drooped his head: 85
    Calculus [1] racked him:
Leaden before, his eyes grew dross of lead:
    Tussis [2] attacked him.
"Now, master, take a little rest!" — not he!
    (Caution redoubled,   90
Step two abreast, the way winds narrowly!)
    Not a whit troubled,
Back to his studies, fresher than at first,
    Fierce as a dragon
He (soul-hydroptic [3] with a sacred thirst) 95
    Sucked at the flagon.
Oh, if we draw a circle premature,
    Heedless of far gain,
Greedy for quick returns of profit, sure
    Bad is our bargain!   100
Was it not great? did not he throw on God,
    (He loves the burthen) —
God's task to make the heavenly period
    Perfect the earthen?
Did not he magnify the mind, show clear   105
    Just what it all meant?
He would not discount life, as fools do here,
    Paid by instalment.
He ventured neck or nothing — heaven's success
    Found, or earth's failure: 110
"Wilt thou trust death or not?" He answered
    "Yes!
    Hence with life's pale lure!"
That low man seeks a little thing to do,
    Sees it and does it:
This high man, with a great thing to pursue, 115
    Dies ere he knows it.
That low man goes on adding one to one,
    His hundred's soon hit:
This high man, aiming at a million,
    Misses an unit.   120
That, has the world here — should he need the next,
    Let the world mind him!
This, throws himself on God, and unperplexed
    Seeking shall find him.
So, with the throttling hands of death at strife, 125
    Ground he at grammar;
Still, through the rattle, parts of speech were rife;
    While he could stammer
He settled *Hoti's* [4] business — let it be! —
    Properly based *Oun* [4] —   130
Gave us the doctrine of the enclitic *De* [4]

[1] the stone, a disease.   [2] A cough.
[3] soul-thirsty.
[4] Greek particles: *that*, *therefore*, and *towards*.

Dead from the waist down.
Well, here's the platform, here's the proper place:
    Hail to your purlieus,
All ye highfliers of the feathered race,   135
    Swallows and curlews!
Here's the top-peak; the multitude below
    Live, for they can, there:
This man decided not to Live but Know —
    Bury this man there?   140
Here — here's his place, where meteors shoot,
    clouds form,
    Lightnings are loosened,
Stars come and go! Let joy break with the storm,
    Peace let the dew send!
Lofty designs must close in like effects: 145
    Loftily lying,
Leave him — still loftier than the world suspects,
    Living and dying.

Pippa's Song

The year's at the spring
And day's at the morn;
Morning's at seven;
The hillside's dew-pearled;
The lark's on the wing;   5
The snail's on the thorn:
God's in his heaven —
All's right with the world!

My Last Duchess

FERRARA

Ferrara, in northern Italy, was the home of the House of Este during the Renaissance. In *My Last Duchess* the Duke of Este is presented in a dramatic monologue speaking to the representative of a family seeking an alliance with the Duke through the marriage of their daughter. The Duke of Este amuses himself by relating to the negotiator the fate of his "last duchess."

That's my last Duchess painted on the wall,
Looking as if she were alive. I call
That piece a wonder, now: Frà Pandolf's [1] hands
Worked busily a day, and there she stands.
Will't please you sit and look at her? I said   5
"Frà Pandolf" by design, for never read
Strangers like you that pictured countenance,
The depth and passion of its earnest glance,
But to myself they turned (since none puts by
The curtain I have drawn for you, but I)   10
And seemed as they would ask me, if they durst,
How such a glance came there; so, not the first

[1] The name is fictitious.

Are you to turn and ask thus. Sir, 'twas not
Her husband's presence only, called that spot
Of joy into the Duchess' cheek: perhaps   15
Frà Pandolf chanced to say, "Her mantle laps
Over my lady's wrist too much," or "Paint
Must never hope to reproduce the faint
Half-flush that dies along her throat": such stuff
Was courtesy, she thought, and cause enough   20
For calling up that spot of joy. She had
A heart — how shall I say? — too soon made glad,
Too easily impressed; she liked whate'er
She looked on, and her looks went everywhere.
Sir, 'twas all one! My favor at her breast,   25
The dropping of the daylight in the West,
The bough of cherries some officious fool
Broke in the orchard for her, the white mule
She rode with round the terrace — all and each
Would draw from her alike the approving speech,
Or blush, at least. She thanked men, — good! but
    thanked
    31
Somehow — I know not how — as if she ranked
My gift of a nine-hundred-years-old name
With anybody's gift. Who'd stoop to blame
This sort of trifling? Even had you skill   35
In speech — (which I have not) — to make your will
Quite clear to such an one, and say, "Just this
Or that in you disgusts me; here you miss,
Or there exceed the mark" — and if she let
Herself be lessoned so, nor plainly set   40
Her wits to yours, forsooth, and made excuse,
— E'en then would be some stooping; and I choose
Never to stoop. Oh, sir, she smiled, no doubt,
Whene'er I passed her; but who passed without
Much the same smile? This grew; I gave com-
    mands;   45
Then all smiles stopped together. There she
    stands
As if alive. Will't please you rise? We'll meet
The company below, then. I repeat,
The Count your master's known munificence
Is ample warrant that no just pretense   50
Of mine for dowry will be disallowed;
Though his fair daughter's self, as I avowed
At starting, is my object. Nay, we'll go
Together down, sir. Notice Neptune, though,
Taming a sea-horse, thought a rarity,   55
Which Claus of Innsbruck cast in bronze for me!

Soliloquy of the Spanish Cloister

Gr-r-r — there go, my heart's abhorrence!
    Water your damned flower-pots, do!
If hate killed men, Brother Lawrence,
    God's blood, would not mine kill you!
What? your myrtle-bush wants trimming?   5

Oh, that rose has prior claims —
Needs its leaden vase filled brimming?
Hell dry you up with its flames!

At the meal we sit together:
Salve tibi! [1] I must hear   10
Wise talk of the kind of weather,
Sort of season, time of year:
Not a plenteous cork-crop: scarcely
Dare we hope oak-galls, I doubt:
What's the Latin name for "parsley"?   15
What's the Greek name for Swine's Snout?

Whew! We'll have our platter burnished,
Laid with care on our own shelf!
With a fire-new spoon we're furnished,
And a goblet for ourself,   20
Rinsed like something sacrificial
Ere 'tis fit to touch our chaps —
Marked with L for our initial!
(He-he! There his lily snaps!)

Saint, forsooth! While brown Dolores   25
Squats outside the Convent bank
With Sanchicha, telling stories,
Steeping tresses in the tank,
Blue-black, lustrous, thick like horsehairs,
— Can't I see his dead eye glow,   30
Bright as 'twere a Barbary corsair's?
(That is, if he'd let it show!)

When he finishes refection,[2]
Knife and fork he never lays
Cross-wise, to my recollection,   35
As do I, in Jesu's praise.
I the Trinity illustrate,
Drinking watered orange-pulp —
In three sips the Arian [3] frustrate;
While he drains his at one gulp.   40

Oh, those melons! If he's able
We're to have a feast! so nice!
One goes to the Abbot's table,
All of us get each a slice.
How go on your flowers? None double?   45
Not one fruit-sort can you spy?
Strange! — And I, too, at such trouble
Keep them close-nipped on the sly!

There's a great text in Galatians,
Once you trip on it, entails   50
Twenty-nine distinct damnations,
One sure, if another fails:

[1] Hail to thee.   [2] The meal.
[3] As Arian had denied the Trinity, his followers were
deemed heretics.

If I trip him just a-dying,
Sure of heaven as sure can be,
Spin him round and send him flying   55
Off to hell, a Manichee? [1]

Or, my scrofulous French novel
On gray paper with blunt type!
Simply glance at it, you grovel
Hand and foot in Belial's [2] gripe: 60
If I double down its pages
At the woeful sixteenth print,
When he gathers his greengages,
Ope a sieve and slip it in't?

Or, there's Satan! — one might venture   65
Pledge one's soul to him, yet leave
Such a flaw in the indenture
As he'd miss till, past retrieve,
Blasted lay that rose-acacia
We're so proud of! *Hy, Zy, Hine* ...   70
'St, there's Vespers! *Plena gratiâ,*
Ave, Virgo! [3] Gr-r-r — you swine!

The Lost Leader

In response to a query as to whether or not Browning
referred to Wordsworth in this poem, the poet wrote:
"DEAR MR. GROSART, — I have been asked the
question you now address me with, and as duly answered
it, I can't remember how many times; there is no sort
of objection to one more assurance or rather confession,
on my part, that I *did* in my hasty youth presume
to use the great and venerated personality of Wordsworth
as a sort of painter's model; one from which this
or the other particular feature may be selected and
turned to account; had I intended more, above all,
such a boldness as portraying the entire man, I should
not have talked about 'handfuls of silver and bits of
ribbon.' These never influenced the change of politics
in the great poet, whose defection, nevertheless, accompanied
as it was by a regular face-about of his special
party, was to my juvenile apprehension, and even
mature consideration, an event to deplore. But just
as in the tapestry on my wall I can recognize figures
which have *struck out* a fancy, on occasion, that though
truly enough thus derived, yet would be preposterous
as a copy, so, though I dare not deny the original of
my little poem, I altogether refuse to have it considered
as the 'very effigies' of such a moral and intellectual
superiority.   Faithfully yours,
                          "ROBERT BROWNING."

Just for a handful of silver he left us,
    Just for a riband to stick in his coat —
Found the one gift of which fortune bereft us,

[1] Follower of the Persian Manes, subscriber to a
dualistic doctrine not then popular with the Church.
[2] The devil's.   [3] Hail, Mary, full of grace!

Lost all the others she lets us devote;
They, with the gold to give, doled him out silver, 5
  So much was theirs who so little allowed:
How all our copper had gone for his service!
  Rags — were they purple, his heart had been
    proud!
We that had loved him so, followed him, honored
  him,
  Lived in his mild and magnificent eye, 10
Learned his great language, caught his clear ac-
  cents,
  Made him our pattern to live and to die!
Shakespeare was of us, Milton was for us,
  Burns, Shelley, were with us, — they watch
    from their graves!
He alone breaks from the van and the freemen, 15
  — He alone sinks to the rear and the slaves!
We shall march prospering, — not through his
  presence;
  Songs may inspirit us, — not from his lyre;
Deeds will be done, — while he boasts his quies-
  cence, 19
  Still bidding crouch whom the rest bade aspire:
Blot out his name, then, record one lost soul more,
  One task more declined, one more footpath un-
    trod,
One more devils'-triumph and sorrow for angels,
  One wrong more to man, one more insult to God!
Life's night begins: let him never come back to us!
  There would be doubt, hesitation and pain, 26
Forced praise on our part — the glimmer of twi-
  light,
  Never glad confident morning again!
Best fight on well, for we taught him — strike gal-
  lantly,
  Menace our heart ere we master his own; 30
Then let him receive the new knowledge and wait
  us,
  Pardoned in heaven, the first by the throne!

Meeting at Night

The gray sea and the long black land;
And the yellow half-moon large and low;
And the startled little waves that leap
In fiery ringlets from their sleep,
As I gain the cove with pushing prow, 5
And quench its speed i' the slushy sand.

Then a mile of warm sea-scented beach;
Three fields to cross till a farm appears;
A tap at the pane, a quick sharp scratch
And blue spurt of a lighted match, 10
And a voice less loud, through its joys and fears,
Than the two hearts beating each to each!

Parting at Morning

Round the cape of a sudden came the sea,
And the sun looked over the mountain's rim:
And straight was a path of gold for him,
And the need of a world of men for me.

Home-Thoughts, from Abroad

Oh, to be in England
Now that April's there,
And whoever wakes in England
Sees, some morning, unaware,
That the lowest boughs and the brush-wood sheaf
Round the elm-tree bole are in tiny leaf, 6
While the chaffinch sings on the orchard bough
In England — now!

And after April, when May follows, 9
And the whitethroat builds, and all the swallows!
Hark, where my blossomed pear-tree in the hedge
Leans to the field and scatters on the clover
Blossoms and dewdrops — at the bent spray's
  edge —
That's the wise thrush; he sings each song twice
  over,
Lest you should think he never could recapture 15
The first fine careless rapture!
And though the fields look rough with hoary dew,
All will be gay when noontide wakes anew
The buttercups, the little children's dower
  — Far brighter than this gaudy melon-flower! 20

Home-Thoughts, from the Sea

Nobly, nobly Cape Saint Vincent to the North-
  west died away;
Sunset ran, one glorious blood-red, reeking into
  Cadiz Bay;
Bluish 'mid the burning water, full in face Trafal-
  gar lay;
In the dimmest Northeast distance dawned Gi-
  braltar grand and gray;
"Here and here did England help me: how can I
  help England?" — say, 5
Whoso turns as I, this evening, turn to God to
  praise and pray,
While Jove's planet rises yonder, silent over Africa.

The Bishop Orders His Tomb at Saint Praxed's Church

Vanity, saith the preacher, vanity!
Draw round my bed: is Anselm keeping back?

Nephews — sons mine... ah God, I know not!
    Well —
She, men would have to be your mother once,
Old Gandolf envied me, so fair she was!   5
What's done is done, and she is dead beside,
Dead long ago, and I am Bishop since,
And as she died so must we die ourselves,
And thence ye may perceive the world's a dream.
Life, how and what is it? As here I lie   10
In this state-chamber, dying by degrees,
Hours and long hours in the dead night, I ask
"Do I live, am I dead?" Peace, peace seems all.
Saint Praxed's ever was the church for peace;
And so, about this tomb of mine. I fought   15
With tooth and nail to save my niche, ye know:
— Old Gandolf cozened [1] me, despite my care;
Shrewd was that snatch from out the corner South
He graced his carrion with, God curse the same!
Yet still my niche is not so cramped but thence   20
One sees the pulpit o' the epistle-side,
And somewhat of the choir, those silent seats,
And up into the aery dome where live
The angels, and a sunbeam's sure to lurk:
And I shall fill my slab of basalt there,   25
And 'neath my tabernacle take my rest,
With those nine columns round me, two and two,
The odd one at my feet where Anselm stands:
Peach-blossom marble all, the rare, the ripe
As fresh-poured red wine of a mighty pulse.   30
— Old Gandolf with his paltry onion-stone,[2]
Put me where I may look at him! True peach,
Rosy and flawless: how I earned the prize!
Draw close: that conflagration of my church
— What then? So much was saved if aught were
    missed!   35
My sons, ye would not be my death? Go dig
The white-grape vineyard where the oil-press
    stood,
Drop water gently till the surface sink,
And if ye find ... Ah God, I know not, I! ...
Bedded in store of rotten fig-leaves soft,   40
And corded up in a tight olive-frail,[3]
Some lump, ah God, of *lapis lazuli*,
Big as a Jew's head cut off at the nape,
Blue as a vein o'er the Madonna's breast ...
Sons, all have I bequeathed you, villas, all,   45
That brave Frascati villa with its bath,
So, let the blue lump poise between my knees,
Like God the Father's globe on both his hands
Ye worship in the Jesu Church so gay,
For Gandolf shall not choose but see and burst!   50
Swift as a weaver's shuttle fleet our years:
Man goeth to the grave, and where is he?

Did I say basalt for my slab, sons? Black —
'Twas ever antique-black I meant! How else
Shall ye contrast my frieze to come beneath?   55
The bas-relief in bronze ye promised me,
Those Pans and Nymphs ye wot of, and perchance
Some tripod, thyrsus,[1] with a vase or so,
The Savior at his sermon on the mount,
Saint Praxed in a glory, and one Pan   60
Ready to twitch the Nymph's last garment off,
And Moses with the tables ... but I know
Ye mark me not! What do they whisper thee,
Child of my bowels, Anselm? Ah, ye hope
To revel down my villas while I gasp   65
Bricked o'er with beggar's moldy travertine [2]
Which Gandolf from his tomb-top chuckles at!
Nay, boys, ye love me — all of jasper, then!
'Tis jasper ye stand pledged to, lest I grieve
My bath must needs be left behind, alas!   70
One block, pure green as a pistachio-nut,
There's plenty jasper somewhere in the world —
And have I not Saint Praxed's ear to pray
Horses for ye, and brown [3] Greek manuscripts,
And mistresses with great smooth marbly limbs?
— That's if ye carve my epitaph aright,   76
Choice Latin, picked phrase, Tully's [4] every word,
No gaudy ware like Gandolf's second line —
Tully, my masters? Ulpian [5] serves his need!
And then how I shall lie through centuries,   80
And hear the blessed mutter of the mass,
And see God made and eaten all day long,
And feel the steady candle-flame, and taste
Good strong thick stupefying incense-smoke!
For as I lie here, hours of the dead night,   85
Dying in state and by such slow degrees,
I fold my arms as if they clasped a crook,
And stretch my feet forth straight as stone can
    point,
And let the bedclothes, for a mortcloth, drop
Into great laps and folds of sculptor's work: 90
And as yon tapers dwindle, and strange thoughts
Grow, with a certain humming in my ears,
About the life before I lived this life,
And this life too, popes, cardinals and priests,
Saint Praxed at his sermon on the mount,   95
Your tall pale mother with her talking eyes,
And new-found agate urns as fresh as day,
And marble's language, Latin pure, discreet,
— Aha, ELUCESCEBAT [6] quoth our friend?
No Tully, said I, Ulpian at the best!   100
Evil and brief hath been my pilgrimage.

[1] A wand carried by the followers of Bacchus, a staff
bearing ivy and vine leaves and often crowned with a
pine cone.
[2] A cheap marble.   [3] old.   [4] Cicero's.
[5] A late Latin writer who died about 228 A.D.
[6] "began to shine."

[1] cheated.
[2] Comparatively, a cheaper marble.
[3] A basket.

All *lapis*, all, sons! Else I give the Pope
My villas! Will ye ever eat my heart?
Ever your eyes were as a lizard's quick,
They glitter like your mother's for my soul,   105
Or ye would heighten my impoverished frieze,
Piece out its starved design, and fill my vase
With grapes, and add a visor and a Term,[1]
And to the tripod ye would tie a lynx
That in his struggle throws the thyrsus down,   110
To comfort me on my entablature
Whereon I am to lie till I must ask
"Do I live, am I dead?" There, leave me, there!
For ye have stabbed me with ingratitude
To death — ye wish it — God, ye wish it! Stone —
Gritstone,[2] a-crumble! Clammy squares which
  sweat   116
As if the corpse they keep were oozing through —
And no more *lapis* to delight the world!
Well, go! I bless ye. Fewer tapers there,
But in a row: and, going, turn your backs   120
— Ay, like departing altar-ministrants,
And leave me in my church, the church for peace,
That I may watch at leisure if he leers —
Old Gandolf — at me, from his onion-stone,
As still he envied me, so fair she was!   125

Evelyn Hope

Beautiful Evelyn Hope is dead!
  Sit and watch by her side an hour.
That is her book-shelf, this her bed;
  She plucked that piece of geranium-flower,
Beginning to die too, in the glass;   5
  Little has yet been changed, I think:
The shutters are shut, no light may pass
  Save two long rays through the hinge's chink.

Sixteen years old when she died!
  Perhaps she had scarcely heard my name;   10
It was not her time to love; beside,
  Her life had many a hope and aim,
Duties enough and little cares,
  And now was quiet, now astir,
Till God's hand beckoned unawares, —   15
  And the sweet white brow is all of her.

Is it too late then, Evelyn Hope?
  What, your soul was pure and true,
The good stars met in your horoscope,
  Made you of spirit, fire and dew —   20
And, just because I was thrice as old
  And our paths in the world diverged so wide,
Each was naught to each, must I be told?
  We were fellow mortals, naught beside?

[1] Bust mounted on a pedestal.
[2] A cheap, soft stone.

No, indeed! for God above   25
  Is great to grant, as mighty to make,
And creates the love to reward the love:
  I claim you still, for my own love's sake!
Delayed it may be for more lives yet,
  Through worlds I shall traverse, not a few: 30
Much is to learn, much to forget
  Ere the time be come for taking you.

But the time will come, — at last it will,
  When, Evelyn Hope, what meant (I shall say)
In the lower earth, in the years long still,   35
  That body and soul so pure and gay?
Why your hair was amber, I shall divine,
  And your mouth of your own geranium's red —
And what you would do with me, in fine,
  In the new life come in the old one's stead.   40

I have lived (I shall say) so much since then,
  Given up myself so many times,
Gained me the gains of various men,
  Ransacked the ages, spoiled the climes;
Yet one thing, one, in my soul's full scope,   45
  Either I missed or itself missed me:
And I want and find you, Evelyn Hope!
  What is the issue? let us see!

I loved you, Evelyn, all the while!
  My heart seemed full as it could hold?   50
There was place and to spare for the frank young
  smile,
  And the red young mouth, and the hair's young
  gold.
So, hush, — I will give you this leaf to keep:
  See, I shut it inside the sweet cold hand!
There, that is our secret: go to sleep!   55
  You will wake, and remember, and understand.

Love Among the Ruins

Where the quiet-colored end of evening smiles,
  Miles and miles,
On the solitary pastures where our sheep
  Half-asleep
Tinkle homeward through the twilight, stray or
  stop   5
  As they crop —
Was the site once of a city great and gay,
  (So they say)
Of our country's very capital, its prince
  Ages since   10
Held his court in, gathered councils, wielding far
  Peace or war.

Now, — the country does not even boast a tree,
  As you see,

To distinguish slopes of verdure, certain rills 15
    From the hills
Intersect and give a name to, (else they run
    Into one,)
Where the domed and daring palace shot its spires
    Up like fires 20
O'er the hundred-gated circuit of a wall
    Bounding all,
Made of marble, men might march on nor be
    pressed,
    Twelve abreast.

And such plenty and perfection, see, of grass 25
    Never was!
Such a carpet as, this summer-time, o'erspreads
    And embeds
Every vestige of the city, guessed alone,
    Stock or stone — 30
Where a multitude of men breathed joy and woe
    Long ago;
Lust of glory pricked their hearts up, dread of
    shame
    Struck them tame;

And that glory and that shame alike, the gold 35
    Bought and sold.
Now, — the single little turret that remains
    On the plains,
By the caper [1] overrooted, by the gourd
    Overscored, 40
While the patching houseleek's head of blossom
    winks
    Through the chinks —
Marks the basement whence a tower in ancient
    time
    Sprang sublime,
And a burning ring, all round, the chariots traced
    As they raced, 46
And the monarch and his minions and his dames
    Viewed the games.

And I know, while thus the quiet-colored eve
    Smiles to leave 50
To their folding, all our many-tinkling fleece
    In such peace,
And the slopes and rills in undistinguished gray
    Melt away —
That a girl with eager eyes and yellow hair 55
    Waits me there
In the turret whence the charioteers caught soul
    For the goal,
When the king looked, where she looks now,
    breathless, dumb
    Till I come. 60

[1] A shrub, the buds of which are used as a condiment.

But he looked upon the city, every side,
    Far and wide,
All the mountains topped with temples, all the
    glades'
    Colonnades,
All the causeys,[1] bridges, aqueducts, — and then,
    All the men! 66
When I do come, she will speak not, she will stand,
    Either hand
On my shoulder, give her eyes the first embrace
    Of my face, 70
Ere we rush, ere we extinguish sight and speech
    Each on each.

In one year they sent a million fighters forth
    South and North,
And they built their gods a brazen pillar high 75
    As the sky,
Yet reserved a thousand chariots in full force —
    Gold, of course.
Oh heart! oh blood that freezes, blood that burns!
    Earth's returns 80
For whole centuries of folly, noise and sin!
    Shut them in,
With their triumphs and their glories and the rest!
    Love is best.

Fra Lippo Lippi

A fifteenth-century Florentine painter and monk, Fra Lippo Lippi, is here pictured caught by the watch as he tries to slip back to his room after a gay night. Browning drew frequently on Vasari's *Lives of the Painters* for the background of his poems.

I am poor brother Lippo, by your leave!
You need not clap your torches to my face.
Zooks, what's to blame? you think you see a monk!
What, 'tis past midnight, and you go the rounds,
And here you catch me at an alley's end 5
Where sportive ladies leave their doors ajar?
The Carmine's my cloister: hunt it up,
Do, — harry out, if you must show your zeal,
Whatever rat, there, haps on his wrong hole,
And nip each softling of a wee white mouse, 10
Weke, weke, that's crept to keep him company!
Aha, you know your betters! Then, you'll take
Your hand away that's fiddling on my throat,
And please to know me likewise. Who am I?
Why, one, sir, who is lodging with a friend 15
Three streets off — he's a certain . . . how d'ye call?
Master — a . . . Cosimo of the Medici,[2]

[1] causeways, highways.

[2] A great patron of art and ruler of Florence

I' the house that caps the corner. Boh! you were
    best!
Remember and tell me, the day you're hanged,
How you affected such a gullet's-gripe!   20
But you, sir, it concerns you that your knaves
Pick up a manner nor discredit you:
Zooks, are we pilchards,[1] that they sweep the streets
And count fair prize what comes into their net?
He's Judas to a tittle, that man is!   25
Just such a face! Why, sir, you make amends.
Lord, I'm not angry! Bid your hangdogs go
Drink out this quarter-florin to the health
Of the munificent House that harbors me
(And many more beside, lads! more beside!)   30
And all's come square again. I'd like his face —
His, elbowing on his comrade in the door
With the pike and lantern, — for the slave that
    holds
John Baptist's head a-dangle by the hair
With one hand ("Look you, now," as who should
    say)   35
And his weapon in the other, yet unwiped!
It's not your chance to have a bit of chalk,
A wood-coal or the like? or you should see!
Yes, I'm the painter, since you style me so.
What, brother Lippo's doings, up and down,   40
You know them and they take you? like enough!
I saw the proper twinkle in your eye —
'Tell you, I liked your looks at very first.
Let's sit and set things straight now, hip to haunch.
Here's spring come, and the nights one makes up
    bands   45
To roam the town and sing out carnival,
And I've been three weeks shut within my mew,[2]
A-painting for the great man, saints and saints
And saints again. I could not paint all night —
Ouf! I leaned out of window for fresh air.   50
There came a hurry of feet and little feet,
A sweep of lute-strings, laughs, and whifts of
    song, —
Flower o' the broom,
Take away love, and our earth is a tomb!
Flower o' the quince,   55
I let Lisa go, and what good in life since?
Flower o' the thyme — and so on. Round they went.
Scarce had they turned the corner when a titter
Like the skipping of rabbits by moonlight, — three
    slim shapes,
And a face that looked up . . . zooks, sir, flesh and
    blood,   60
That's all I'm made of! Into shreds it went,
Curtain and counterpane and coverlet,
All the bed-furniture — a dozen knots,
There was a ladder! Down I let myself,

[1] A variety of fish.
[2] A cage for birds.

Hands and feet, scrambling somehow, and so
    dropped,   65
And after them. I came up with the fun
Hard by Saint Laurence,[1] hail fellow, well met, —
Flower o' the rose,
If I've been merry, what matter who knows?
And so, as I was stealing back again,   70
To get to bed and have a bit of sleep
Ere I rise up to-morrow and go work
On Jerome knocking at his poor old breast
With his great round stone to subdue the flesh,
You snap me of the sudden. Ah, I see!   75
Though your eye twinkles still, you shake your
    head —
Mine's shaved — a monk, you say — the sting's
    in that!
If Master Cosimo announced himself,
Mum's the word naturally; but a monk!
Come, what am I a beast for? tell us, now!   80
I was a baby when my mother died
And father died and left me in the street.
I starved there, God knows how, a year or two
On fig-skins, melon-parings, rinds and shucks,
Refuse and rubbish. One fine frosty day,   85
My stomach being empty as your hat,
The wind doubled me up, and down I went.
Old Aunt Lapaccia trussed me[2] with one hand,
(Its fellow was a stinger as I knew)
And so along the wall, over the bridge,   90
By the straight cut to the convent. Six words
    there,
While I stood munching my first bread that month:
"So boy, you're minded," quoth the good fat
    father,
Wiping his own mouth, 'twas refection-time, —
"To quit this very miserable world?   95
Will you renounce" . . . "the mouthful of bread?"
    thought I;
By no means! Brief, they made a monk of me;
I did renounce the world, its pride and greed,
Palace, farm, villa, shop, and banking-house,
Trash, such as these poor devils of Medici   100
Have given their hearts to — all at eight years old.
Well, sir, I found in time, you may be sure,
'Twas not for nothing — the good bellyful,
The warm serge and the rope that goes all round,
And day-long blessed idleness beside!   105
"Let's see what the urchin's fit for" — that came
    next.
Not overmuch their way, I must confess.
Such a to-do! They tried me with their books;
Lord, they'd have taught me Latin in pure waste!
Flower o' the clove,   110
All the Latin I construe is "amo," I love!

[1] A church of that name.
[2] tied me up.

But, mind you, when a boy starves in the streets
Eight years together, as my fortune was,
Watching folk's faces to know who will fling
The bit of half-stripped grape-bunch he desires, 115
And who will curse or kick him for his pains, —
Which gentleman processional and fine,
Holding a candle to the Sacrament,
Will wink and let him lift a plate and catch
The droppings of the wax to sell again, 120
Or holla for the Eight [1] and have him whipped, —
How say I? — nay, which dog bites, which lets drop
His bone from the heap of offal in the street, —
Why, soul and sense of him grow sharp alike,
He learns the look of things, and none the less 125
For admonition from the hunger-pinch.
I had a store of such remarks, be sure,
Which, after I found leisure, turned to use.
I drew men's faces on my copy-books,
Scrawled them within the antiphonary's [2] marge,
Joined legs and arms to the long music-notes, 131
Found eyes and nose and chin for A's and B's,
And made a string of pictures of the world
Betwixt the ins and outs of verb and noun,
On the wall, the bench, the door. The monks
looked black. 135
"Nay," quoth the Prior, "turn him out, d'ye say?
In no wise. Lose a crow and catch a lark.
What if at last we get our man of parts,
We Carmelites, like those Camaldolese [3]
And Preaching Friars,[4] to do our church up fine 140
And put the front on it that ought to be!"
And hereupon he bade me daub away.
Thank you! my head being crammed, the walls a
blank,
Never was such prompt disemburdening.
First, every sort of monk, the black and white, 145
I drew them, fat and lean: then, folk at church,
From good old gossips waiting to confess
Their cribs of barrel-droppings, candle-ends, —
To the breathless fellow at the altar-foot,
Fresh from his murder, safe and sitting there 150
With the little children round him in a row
Of admiration, half for his beard and half
For that white anger of his victim's son
Shaking a fist at him with one fierce arm,
Signing himself with the other because of Christ
(Whose sad face on the cross sees only this 156
After the passion of a thousand years)
Till some poor girl, her apron o'er her head,
(Which the intense eyes looked through) came at
eve

On tiptoe, said a word, dropped in a loaf, 160
Her pair of earrings and a bunch of flowers
(The brute took growling), prayed, and so was gone.
I painted all, then cried "'Tis ask and have;
Choose, for more's ready!" — laid the ladder flat,
And showed my covered bit of cloister-wall. 165
The monks closed in a circle and praised loud
Till checked, taught what to see and not to see,
Being simple bodies, — "That's the very man!
Look at the boy who stoops to pat the dog!
That woman's like the Prior's niece who comes 170
To care about his asthma: it's the life!"
But there my triumph's straw-fire flared and
funked;
Their betters took their turn to see and say:
The Prior and the learned pulled a face
And stopped all that in no time. "How? what's
here? 175
Quite from the mark of painting, bless us all!
Faces, arms, legs, and bodies like the true
As much as pea and pea! it's devil's-game!
Your business is not to catch men with show,
With homage to the perishable clay, 180
But lift them over it, ignore it all,
Make them forget there's such a thing as flesh.
Your business is to paint the souls of men —
Man's soul, and it's a fire, smoke . . . no, it's not . . .
It's vapor done up like a new-born babe — 185
(In that shape when you die it leaves your mouth)
It's . . . well, what matters talking, it's the soul!
Give us no more of body than shows soul!
Here's Giotto,[1] with his Saint a-praising God,
That sets us praising, — why not stop with him?
Why put all thoughts of praise out of our head 191
With wonder at lines, colors, and what not?
Paint the soul, never mind the legs and arms!
Rub all out, try at it a second time.
Oh, that white smallish female with the breasts, 195
She's just my niece . . . Herodias,[2] I would say, —
Who went and danced and got men's heads cut off!
Have it all out!" Now, is this sense, I ask?
A fine way to paint soul, by painting body
So ill, the eye can't stop there, must go further 200
And can't fare worse! Thus, yellow does for white
When what you put for yellow's simply black,
And any sort of meaning looks intense
When all beside itself means and looks naught.
Why can't a painter lift each foot in turn, 205
Left foot and right foot, go a double step,
Make his flesh liker and his soul more like,
Both in their order? Take the prettiest face,
The Prior's niece . . . patron-saint — is it so pretty
You can't discover if it means hope, fear, 210

---

[1] The magistrates of Florence.
[2] The book of service for the Church. It contains the
responses sung by the choir.
[3] Monks of Camaldoli.
[4] The Dominicans.

[1] Giotto di Bordone (1266–1337), famous Italian
painter.
[2] See St. Matthew xiv, 3–12.

Sorrow or joy? won't beauty go with these?
Suppose I've made her eyes all right and blue,
Can't I take breath and try to add life's flash,
And then add soul and heighten them threefold?
Or say there's beauty with no soul at all —   215
(I never saw it — put the case the same —)
If you get simple beauty and naught else,
You get about the best thing God invents:
That's somewhat: and you'll find the soul you have
         missed,
Within yourself, when you return him thanks.   220
"Rub all out!"   Well, well, there's my life, in
         short,
And so the thing has gone on ever since.
I'm grown a man no doubt, I've broken bounds:
You should not take a fellow eight years old
And make him swear to never kiss the girls.   225
I'm my own master, paint now as I please —
Having a friend, you see, in the Corner-house!
Lord, it's fast holding by the rings in front —
Those great rings serve more purposes than just
To plant a flag in, or tie up a horse!   230
And yet the old schooling sticks, the old grave eyes
Are peeping o'er my shoulder as I work,
The heads shake still — "It's art's decline, my son!
You're not of the true painters, great and old;
Brother Angelico's [1] the man, you'll find;   235
Brother Lorenzo [2] stands his single peer:
Fag on at flesh, you'll never make the third!"
Flower o' the pine,
You keep your mistr . . . manners, and I'll stick to
         mine!
I'm not the third, then: bless us, they must know!
Don't you think they're the likeliest to know,   241
They with their Latin?   So, I swallow my rage,
Clench my teeth, suck my lips in tight, and paint
To please them — sometimes do and sometimes
         don't;
For, doing most, there's pretty sure to come   245
A turn, some warm eve finds me at my saints —
A laugh, a cry, the business of the world —
(*Flower o' the peach,*
Death for us all, and his own life for each!)
And my whole soul revolves, the cup runs over, 250
The world and life's too big to pass for a dream,
And I do these wild things in sheer despite,
And play the fooleries you catch me at,
In pure rage!   The old mill-horse, out at grass
After hard years, throws up his stiff heels so, 255
Although the miller does not preach to him
The only good of grass is to make chaff.
What would men have?   Do they like grass or no —
May they or mayn't they? all I want's the thing
Settled for ever one way.   As it is,   260

[1] Fra Angelico (1387–1455), a pious, spiritual painter.
[2] Fra Lorenzo, another religious painter.

You tell too many lies and hurt yourself:
You don't like what you only like too much,
You do like what, if given you at your word,
You find abundantly detestable.
For me, I think I speak as I was taught;   265
I always see the garden and God there
A-making man's wife: and, my lesson learned,
The value and significance of flesh,
I can't unlearn ten minutes afterwards.

You understand me: I'm a beast, I know.   270
But see, now — why, I see as certainly
As that the morning-star's about to shine,
What will hap some day.   We've a youngster here
Comes to our convent, studies what I do,
Slouches and stares and lets no atom drop: 275
His name is Guidi [1] — he'll not mind the monks —
They call him Hulking Tom, he lets them talk —
He picks my practice up — he'll paint apace,
I hope so — though I never live so long,
I know what's sure to follow.   You be judge!   280
You speak no Latin more than I, belike;
However, you're my man, you've seen the world
— The beauty and the wonder and the power,
The shapes of things, their colors, lights and shades,
Changes, surprises, — and God made it all!   285
— For what?   Do you feel thankful, ay or no,
For this fair town's face, yonder river's line,
The mountain round it and the sky above,
Much more the figures of man, woman, child,
These are the frame to?   What's it all about?   290
To be passed over, despised? or dwelt upon,
Wondered at? oh, this last of course! — you say.
But why not do as well as say, — paint these
Just as they are, careless what comes of it?
God's works — paint any one, and count it crime
To let a truth slip.   Don't object, "His works   296
Are here already; nature is complete:
Suppose you reproduce her — (which you can't)
There's no advantage! you must beat her, then."
For, don't you mark? we're made so that we love
First when we see them painted, things we have
         passed   301
Perhaps a hundred times nor cared to see;
And so they are better, painted — better to us,
Which is the same thing.   Art was given for that;
God uses us to help each other so,   305
Lending our minds out.   Have you noticed, now,
Your cullion's [2] hanging face?   A bit of chalk,
And trust me but you should, though!   How much
         more,
If I drew higher things with the same truth!
That were to take the Prior's pulpit-place,   310

[1] Tommaso Guidi, painter and monk, a predecessor
rather than the pupil of Fra Lippo.
[2] A crude fellow.

Interpret God to all of you! Oh, oh,
It makes me mad to see what men shall do
And we in our graves! This world's no blot for us,
Nor blank; it means intensely, and means good:
To find its meanings is my meat and drink.   315
"Ay, but you don't so instigate to prayer!"
Strikes in the Prior: "when your meaning's plain
It does not say to folk — remember matins,
Or, mind you fast next Friday!" Why, for this
What need of art at all? A skull and bones,   320
Two bits of stick nailed crosswise, or, what's best,
A bell to chime the hour with, does as well.
I painted a Saint Laurence six months since
At Prato,[1] splashed the fresco in fine style:
"How looks my painting, now the scaffold's
     down?"   325
I ask a brother: "Hugely," he returns —
"Already not one phiz of your three slaves
Who turn the Deacon[2] off his toasted side,
But's scratched and prodded to our heart's content,
The pious people have so eased their own   330
With coming to say prayers there in a rage:
We get on fast to see the bricks beneath.
Expect another job this time next year,
For pity and religion grow i' the crowd —
Your painting serves its purpose!" Hang the
     fools!   335

— That is — you'll not mistake an idle word
Spoke in a huff by a poor monk, God wot,
Tasting the air this spicy night which turns
The unaccustomed head like Chianti wine!
Oh, the church knows! don't misreport me, now!
It's natural a poor monk out of bounds   341
Should have his apt word to excuse himself:
And hearken how I plot to make amends.
I have bethought me: I shall paint a piece
... There's for you! Give me six months, then
     go, see   345
Something in Sant' Ambrogio's![3] Bless the nuns!
They want a cast o' my office.[4] I shall paint
God in the midst, Madonna and her babe,
Ringed by a bowery, flowery angel-brood,
Lilies and vestments and white faces, sweet   350
As puff on puff of grated orris-root
When ladies crowd to Church at midsummer.
And then i' the front, of course a saint or two —
Saint John, because he saves the Florentines,   354
Saint Ambrose, who puts down in black and white
The convent's friends and gives them a long day,

[1] Near Florence.
[2] St. Lawrence suffered death by being roasted on a gridiron.
[3] St. Ambrose's, a Florentine convent. Lippi painted *The Coronation of the Virgin* for the church.
[4] Some of my work.

And Job, I must have him there past mistake,
The man of Uz[1] (and Us without the z,
Painters who need his patience). Well, all these
Secured at their devotion, up shall come   360
Out of a corner when you least expect,
As one by a dark stair into a great light,
Music and talking, who but Lippo! I! —
Mazed, motionless, and moonstruck — I'm the
     man!
Back I shrink — what is this I see and hear?   365
I, caught up with my monk's-things by mistake,
My old serge gown and rope that goes all round.
I, in this presence, this pure company!
Where's a hole, where's a corner for escape?
Then steps a sweet angelic slip of a thing   370
Forward, puts out a soft palm — "Not so fast!"
— Addresses the celestial presence, "nay —
He made you and devised you, after all,
Though he's none of you! Could Saint John
     there draw —
His camel-hair make up a painting-brush?   375
We come to brother Lippo for all that,
Iste perfecit opus!"[2] So, all smile —
I shuffle sideways with my blushing face
Under the cover of a hundred wings
Thrown like a spread of kirtles when you're gay   380
And play hot cockles, all the doors being shut,
Till, wholly unexpected, in there pops
The hothead husband! Thus I scuttle off
To some safe bench behind, not letting go
The palm of her, the little lily thing   385
That spoke the good word for me in the nick,
Like the Prior's niece ... Saint Lucy, I would say.
And so all's saved for me, and for the church
A pretty picture gained. Go, six months hence!
Your hand, sir, and good-by: no lights, no lights!
The street's hushed, and I know my own way back,
Don't fear me! There's the gray beginning.
     Zooks!   392

Andrea Del Sarto[3]

CALLED "THE FAULTLESS PAINTER"

Another Florentine painter, Andrea del Sarto (died 1531), was in love with Lucrezia del Fede. To keep her happy, and to build her a house, del Sarto used funds given to him by Francis I of France for the purchase of paintings. Del Sarto was called "the Faultless Painter."

But do not let us quarrel any more,
No, my Lucrezia; bear with me for once:

[1] "There was a man in the land of Uz, whose name was Job." — Job i, 1.   [2] He did the work.
[3] Called *del Sarto* because his father was a tailor. (1486–1531).

Sit down and all shall happen as you wish.
You turn your face, but does it bring your heart?
I'll work then for your friend's friend, never fear, 5
Treat his own subject after his own way,
Fix his own time, accept too his own price,
And shut the money into this small hand
When next it takes mine.   Will it? tenderly?
Oh, I'll content him, — but to-morrow, Love!   10
I often am much wearier than you think,
This evening more than usual, and it seems
As if — forgive now — should you let me sit
Here by the window with your hand in mine
And look a half-hour forth on Fiesole,   15
Both of one mind, as married people use,
Quietly, quietly the evening through,
I might get up to-morrow to my work
Cheerful and fresh as ever.   Let us try.
To-morrow, how you shall be glad for this!   20
Your soft hand is a woman of itself,
And mine the man's bared breast she curls inside.
Don't count the time lost, neither; you must serve
For each of the five pictures we require:
It saves a model.   So! keep looking so —   25
My serpentining beauty, rounds on rounds!
— How could you ever prick those perfect ears,
Even to put the pearl there! oh, so sweet —
My face, my moon, my everybody's moon,
Which everybody looks on and calls his,   30
And, I suppose, is looked on by in turn,
While she looks — no one's: very dear, no less.
You smile? why, there's my picture ready made,
There's what we painters call our harmony!
A common grayness silvers everything, —   35
All in a twilight, you and I alike
— You, at the point of your first pride in me
(That's gone you know), — but I, at every point;
My youth, my hope, my art, being all toned down
To yonder sober pleasant Fiesole.[1]   40
There's the bell clinking from the chapel-top;
That length of convent-wall across the way
Holds the trees safer, huddled more inside;
The last monk leaves the garden; days decrease,
And autumn grows, autumn in everything.   45
Eh? the whole seems to fall into a shape
As if I saw alike my work and self
And all that I was born to be and do,
A twilight-piece.   Love, we are in God's hand.
How strange now looks the life he makes us lead; 50
So free we seem, so fettered fast we are!
I feel he laid the fetter: let it lie!
This chamber for example — turn your head —
All that's behind us!   You don't understand
Nor care to understand about my art,   55
But you can hear at least when people speak:
And that cartoon, the second from the door

[1] A suburb of Florence.

— It is the thing, Love! so such things should be —
Behold Madonna! — I am bold to say.
I can do with my pencil what I know,   60
What I see, what at bottom of my heart
I wish for, if I ever wish so deep —
Do easily, too — when I say, perfectly,
I do not boast, perhaps: yourself are judge,
Who listened to the Legate's talk last week,   65
And just as much they used to say in France.
At any rate 'tis easy, all of it!
No sketches first, no studies, that's long past:
I do what many dream of all their lives,
— Dream? strive to do, and agonize to do,   70
And fail in doing.   I could count twenty such
On twice your fingers, and not leave this town,
Who strive — you don't know how the others
     strive
To paint a little thing like that you smeared
Carelessly passing with your robes afloat, —   75
Yet do much less, so much less, Someone says,
(I know his name, no matter) — so much less!
Well, less is more, Lucrezia: I am judged.
There burns a truer light of God in them,
In their vexed beating stuffed and stopped-up
     brain,   80
Heart, or whate'er else, than goes on to prompt
This low-pulsed forthright craftsman's hand of
     mine.
Their works drop groundward, but themselves, I
     know,
Reach many a time a heaven that's shut to me,
Enter and take their place there sure enough,   85
Though they come back and cannot tell the world.
My works are nearer heaven, but I sit here.
The sudden blood of these men! at a word —
Praise them, it boils, or blame them, it boils too.
I, painting from myself and to myself,   90
Know what I do, am unmoved by men's blame
Or their praise either.   Somebody remarks
Morello's[1] outline there is wrongly traced,
His hue mistaken; what of that? or else,
Rightly traced and well ordered; what of that?   95
Speak as they please, what does the mountain care?
Ah, but a man's reach should exceed his grasp,
Or what's a heaven for?   All is silver-gray
Placid and perfect with my art: the worse!
I know both what I want and what might gain,   100
And yet how profitless to know, to sigh
"Had I been two, another and myself,
Our head would have o'erlooked the world!"
     No doubt.
Yonder's a work now, of that famous youth
The Urbinate[2] who died five years ago.   105

[1] One of the Apennines, near Florence.
[2] Raphael (1483–1520), born at Urbino.

('Tis copied, George Vasari [1] sent it me.)
Well, I can fancy how he did it all,
Pouring his soul, with kings and popes to see,
Reaching, that heaven might so replenish him,
Above and through his art — for it gives way; 110
That arm is wrongly put — and there again —
A fault to pardon in the drawing's lines,
Its body, so to speak: its soul is right,
He means right — that, a child may understand.
Still, what an arm! and I could alter it: 115
But all the play, the insight and the stretch —
Out of me, out of me! And wherefore out?
Had you enjoined them on me, given me soul,
We might have risen to Rafael, I and you!
Nay, Love, you did give all I asked, I think — 120
More than I merit, yes, by many times.
But had you — oh, with the same perfect brow,
And perfect eyes, and more than perfect mouth,
And the low voice my soul hears, as a bird
The fowler's pipe, and follows to the snare — 125
Had you, with these the same, but brought a mind!
Some women do so. Had the mouth there urged
"God and the glory! never care for gain.
The present by the future, what is that?
Live for fame, side by side with Agnolo! [2] 130
Rafael is waiting: up to God, all three!"
I might have done it for you. So it seems:
Perhaps not. All is as God overrules.
Besides, incentives come from the soul's self;
The rest avail not. Why do I need you? 135
What wife had Rafael, or has Agnolo?
In this world, who can do a thing, will not;
And who would do it, cannot, I perceive:
Yet the will's somewhat — somewhat, too, the
    power —
And thus we half-men struggle. At the end, 140
God, I conclude, compensates, punishes.
'Tis safer for me, if the award be strict,
That I am something underrated here,
Poor this long while, despised, to speak the truth.
I dared not, do you know, leave home all day, 145
For fear of chancing on the Paris lords.
The best is when they pass and look aside;
But they speak sometimes; I must bear it all.
Well may they speak! That Francis, [3] that first
    time,
And that long festal year at Fontainebleau! 150
I surely then could sometimes leave the ground,
Put on the glory, Rafael's daily wear,
In that humane great monarch's golden look, —
One finger in his beard or twisted curl

[1] Wrote *Lives of the Painters*, which Browning used
as the source for several of his poems.
[2] Michelangelo (1475–1564).
[3] Francis I of France. Andrea was employed by
King Francis for a period.

Over his mouth's good mark that made the smile,
One arm about my shoulder, round my neck, 156
The jingle of his gold chain in my ear,
I painting proudly with his breath on me,
All his court round him, seeing with his eyes,
Such frank French eyes, and such a fire of souls 160
Profuse, my hand kept plying by those hearts, —
And, best of all, this, this, this face beyond,
This in the background, waiting on my work,
To crown the issue with a last reward!
A good time, was it not, my kingly days? 165
And had you not grown restless . . . but I know —
'Tis done and past; 'twas right, my instinct said;
Too live the life grew, golden and not gray,
And I'm the weak-eyed bat no sun should tempt
Out of the grange whose four walls make his world.
How could it end in any other way? 171
You called me, and I came home to your heart.
The triumph was — to reach and stay there; since
I reached it ere the triumph, what is lost?
Let my hands frame your face in your hair's gold,
You beautiful Lucrezia that are mine! 176
"Rafael did this, Andrea painted that;
The Roman's is the better when you pray,
But still the other's Virgin was his wife" —
Men will excuse me. I am glad to judge 180
Both pictures in your presence; clearer grows
My better fortune, I resolve to think.
For, do you know, Lucrezia, as God lives,
Said one day Agnolo, his very self,
To Rafael . . . I have known it all these years . . . 185
(When the young man was flaming out his thoughts
Upon a palace-wall for Rome to see,
Too lifted up in heart because of it)
"Friend, there's a certain sorry little scrub
Goes up and down our Florence, none cares how,
Who, were he set to plan and execute 191
As you are, pricked on by your popes and kings,
Would bring the sweat into that brow of yours!"
To Rafael's! — And indeed the arm is wrong.
I hardly dare . . . yet, only you to see, 195
Give the chalk here — quick, thus the line should
    go!
Ay, but the soul! he's Rafael! rub it out!
Still, all I care for, if he spoke the truth,
(What he? why, who but Michel Agnolo?
Do you forget already words like those?) 200
If really there was such a chance, so lost, —
Is, whether you're — not grateful — but more
    pleased.
Well, let me think so. And you smile indeed!
This hour has been an hour! Another smile?
If you would sit thus by me every night 205
I should work better, do you comprehend?
I mean that I should earn more, give you more.
See, it is settled dusk now: there's a star;

Morello's gone, the watch-lights show the wall,
The cue-owls speak the name we call them by. 210
Come from the window, love, — come in, at last,
Inside the melancholy little house
We built to be so gay with. God is just.
King Francis may forgive me: oft at nights
When I look up from painting, eyes tired out, 215
The walls become illumined, brick from brick
Distinct, instead of mortar, fierce bright gold,
That gold of his I did cement them with!
Let us but love each other. Must you go?
That Cousin here again? he waits outside? 220
Must see you — you, and not with me? Those
      loans?
More gaming debts to pay? you smiled for that?
Well, let smiles buy me! have you more to spend?
While hand and eye and something of a heart
Are left me, work's my ware, and what's it worth?
I'll pay my fancy. Only let me sit 226
The gray remainder of the evening out,
Idle, you call it, and muse perfectly
How I could paint, were I but back in France,
One picture, just one more — the Virgin's face, 230
Not yours this time! I want you at my side
To hear them — that is, Michel Agnolo —
Judge all I do and tell you of its worth.
Will you? To-morrow, satisfy your friend.
I take the subjects for his corridor, 235
Finish the portrait out of hand — there, there,
And throw him in another thing or two
If he demurs; the whole should prove enough
To pay for this same Cousin's freak. Beside,
What's better and what's all I care about, 240
Get you the thirteen scudi [1] for the ruff!
Love, does that please you? Ah, but what does he,
The Cousin! what does he to please you more?

I am grown peaceful as old age to-night.
I regret little, I would change still less. 245
Since there my past life lies, why alter it?
The very wrong to Francis! — it is true
I took his coin, was tempted and complied,
And built this house and sinned, and all is said.
My father and my mother died of want. 250
Well, had I riches of my own? you see
How one gets rich! Let each one bear his lot.
They were born poor, lived poor, and poor they
      died:
And I have labored somewhat in my time
And not been paid profusely. Some good son 255
Paint my two hundred pictures — let him try!
No doubt, there's something strikes a balance.
      Yes,
You loved me quite enough, it seems to-night.
This must suffice me here. What would one have?

      [1] A scudo was worth something less than a dollar.

In heaven, perhaps, new chances, one more
      chance — 260
Four great walls in the New Jerusalem,
Meted on each side by the angel's reed,
For Leonard,[1] Rafael, Agnolo and me
To cover — the three first without a wife,
While I have mine! So — still they overcome 265
Because there's still Lucrezia, — as I choose.

      Again the Cousin's whistle! Go, my Love.

Prospice [2]

Fear death? — to feel the fog in my throat,
      The mist in my face,
When the snows begin, and the blasts denote
      I am nearing the place,
The power of the night, the press of the storm, 5
      The post of the foe;
Where he stands, the Arch Fear in a visible form,
      Yet the strong man must go:
For the journey is done and the summit attained,
      And the barriers fall, 10
Though a battle's to fight ere the guerdon be
      gained,
      The reward of it all.
I was ever a fighter, so — one fight more,
      The best and the last!
I would hate that death bandaged my eyes, and
      forbore, 15
      And bade me creep past.
No! let me taste the whole of it, fare like my peers
      The heroes of old,
Bear the brunt, in a minute pay life's glad arrears
      Of pain, darkness and cold. 20
For sudden the worst turns the best to the brave,
      The black minute's at end,
And the elements' rage, the fiend-voices that rave,
      Shall dwindle, shall blend,
Shall change, shall become first a peace out of pain,
      Then a light, then thy breast, 26
O thou soul of my soul! I shall clasp thee [3] again,
      And with God be the rest!

Epilogue to Asolando

At the midnight in the silence of the sleeptime,
      When you set your fancies free,
Will they pass to where — by death, fools think,
      imprisoned —

      [1] Leonardo da Vinci (1452–1519).
      [2] "Look forward."
      [3] Mrs. Browning had died a few months before this
was written.

Low he lies who once so loved you, whom you
    loved so,
      — Pity me? 5

Oh to love so, be so loved, yet so mistaken!
    What had I on earth to do
With the slothful, with the mawkish, the unmanly?
Like the aimless, helpless, hopeless, did I drivel
      — Being — who? 10

One who never turned his back but marched breast
    forward,
    Never doubted clouds would break,

Never dreamed, though right were worsted, wrong
    would triumph,
Held we fall to rise, are baffled to fight better,
    Sleep to wake. 15

No, at noonday in the bustle of man's worktime
    Greet the unseen with a cheer!
Bid him forward, breast and back as either should
    be,
"Strive and thrive!" cry "Speed, — fight on,
    fare ever
      There as here!" 20

THE
SYMBOLISTS

❧

I'll seek you where your shadows are.

MALLARMÉ

SYMBOLISM IN LITERATURE is really only a particular expression of the romantic spirit. What, in general, such romantics as Shelley and Keats had stood for, the symbolist writers stood for too; the difference is that this special romantic school advocated a narrower kind of romanticism, a special manner. The symbolists veiled their meaning with a specialized vocabulary and sought to make their impressions through a reliance on rhythms, tones, and colors. It was their effort to present the essence of an idea or a situation. They were, in this sense, romantics of indirection.

As a term in literary criticism, "symbolism" carries both a general and a specific meaning. Symbols, of course, have been used in art and in literature since men first etched their images and ideas on the walls of prehistoric caves. Employed in this popular sense, the term means little more than figurative expression; it is the language which speaks of "the green mantle of the standing pool" and characterizes the sons of Belial as "flown with insolence and wine." The sailor scanning the horizon for suggestion of the next day's weather may report that all is "calm"; but the poet, less bound by practical matters, finds that same evening "quiet as a nun." There is that in man which, once he has satisfied the needs of food and shelter, makes him reach out to an expression beyond practical, prosaic

811

statement. Symbolism of this variety is little more than a gauze curtain which the author lets down between his work and the reader, a curtain decorated with allegorical figures, with mystical symbols.

The name, "symbolism," came into importance with the rise of *"les symbolistes"* in France during the 1880's. Here only did symbolism take on the aspect of a school. Yet even in the time of the most important French symbolists, Baudelaire, Rimbaud, Villiers de l'Isle Adam, Verlaine, Régnier, Mallarmé, Huysmans, Maeterlinck, it is doubtful if more than two of them could have been made to subscribe to any one set of tenets. "If one should question symbolist poets separately," Adolphe Retté is quoted as saying, "one would receive as many different answers as individuals; symbolism has never meant similarity in method, but unity of ideals." Even Mallarmé, who was more generally looked upon as giving the movement voice, who spent his Tuesday evenings in a rocker talking to the literati of Paris visiting him, could hardly be called their spokesman.

Symbolism, like so many literary movements in France, was a revolt against a prevailing school — in this case against the Parnassians. As the Parnassians had themselves rebelled against the sentimentality of some romantics, the symbolists in turn took issue against the hard precision of their predecessors. For the impersonal realistic manner of the Parnassians, the symbolists substituted a faith in the personal and the associative. Where the earlier group had concerned itself with minute detail, a precise representation of nature, and was almost classical in its insistence on form rather than content, the later group interested itself in the enigma of life, exalted suggestion over precision, and was essentially romantic in its insistence on presenting the internal and emotional rather than the external and factual. Vagueness and possible unintelligibility, the symbolists believed, were not too great a price to pay if one could capture on paper the essence of a setting or a mood. And if they found life mysterious, strange, inexplicable, it was, they reasoned, only logical that they should present it as mysterious and strange rather than precise and definite. Rather than on the thing itself, then, they seized on the symbol of the thing; rather than use direction they proceeded indirectly. Their doctrine demanded that they call a flock of crows a "winged cemetery." Whatever amusement the reader may find in such indirection, he must admit that in bringing again to poetry, after the precision of the Parnassians, a sense of the ineffability of life, of the vagueness and elusiveness of human experience, the symbolists reawakened in French, and in English literature as well, a fine and genuine poetic sentiment.

Even French symbolism, then, is not to be confined within a formula. It meant different things in different years to different writers. One magazine could not suffice to interpret its doctrines; several were necessary. Each writer was a prism through which the light of life passed, throwing different colors into varying patterns. Even while knowing this to be true, we may try to be specific as to certain general interests and principles characterizing the group as a whole — if not always each individual.

Reliance on symbols. Not the thing itself in representation, but its inherent essence was the concern of the symbolists. "Do you know what symbolism is?" asks Jules Tellier. "The word is rather pompous, but the thing is very simple. To symbolize consists plainly, after one has found an image expressive of a state of the soul, in expressing not this state of the soul, but only the image that materializes it."

And so the symbolist proceeds indirectly. He scorns convention and triteness; he places emphasis on color and sound and rhythm. But always, more important than these and at the very heart of it all, is the substitution of a spiritual essence for the thing as a whole. Things equal to the same thing are, in the mathematics of the symbolist, still equal to each other. But with this difference — the formula by which one arrives at a literary equation is always concealed rather than revealed. X equals y and y equals z for him as for anyone else, but the symbolist will write always z and leave the reader to discover the x and the y by which he has arrived at the z. Or, to state it differently, the symbolist may be attracted by such a conventional item in nature as the dew on the rose. But he will by no means write "the dew on the rose." His process seems, rather, to go something like this: *dew* suggests *water, water* suggests *globule; rose* suggests *flower*, and *flower* suggests *orchid*. The phrase therefore becomes "the globuled orchid" and is for him that much better than the "dew on the rose" because it is unusual, remote, and because of the somewhat grotesque effect of *globuled* and the exotic suggestion carried by the word *orchid*. X and y have been concealed; z only remains. And naturally enough, when one has read a rather extended series of z substitutions the results are vague, suggestive rather than explicit, strange.[1] And strangeness, we have often been told, is one of the essential elements of poetry. With the symbolist it is almost the dominant element to be sought.

However, it must not be thought that this strangeness was to be secured by resort to chance. It was not a case of using *any* symbol. The artist was not so easily satisfied. The ultimate z must be inherently the essence of x, and serious study and reflection were necessary to hit upon an appropriate z. All the possibilities should be explored and that symbol or part selected which was vital, which afforded the proper *effect*, which gave the reader the mood and tone and harmony which the writer sought most clearly to create. And all this must be subordinate to *thought*, to the proper philosophical implication he might wish to lay down. It was as though writing in verse, for instance, he superimposed upon the pattern of his metrical plan and his rime-scheme a second pattern, suggestiveness, through a wisely chosen symbolism which paid proper regard to sound and image and idea. There was nothing facile about sincere symbolism; it might be argued, indeed, that the conscientious symbolist hedged himself about by more exacting and more meticulous prescriptions than writers of any other school.

It is both the weakness and the strength of symbolism that, like romanticism, it is intensely personal. The symbolist seizes upon his images not so much by logical as by associative processes — and what may be intuitive for Mallarmé may or may not be intuitive for John Jones. The manner of the symbolist is explained by Edmund Wilson as "an attempt by carefully studied means — a complicated association of ideas represented by a medley of metaphors — to communicate unique personal feelings." (See, for example, the last paragraph of Baudelaire's *Invitation to a Voyage*.) The essence of the thing is to be presented, the emotion which it arouses must somehow be put upon paper. But "straight" language is hardly capable of saying these things — and so the symbolist falls

---

[1] Examples from the work of Saint-Pol-Roux, as noted by Joseph Shipley, are "winged cemetery" (*for* a flock of crows), "romance for the nostrils" (*for* the scent of flowers), "leaves of living salad" (*for* frogs).

back on metaphors and makes from his metaphors symbols.   This unique personal aspect of symbolism is testified to by William Butler Yeats:

> He (the writer) has felt something in the depth of his mind and he wants to make it as visible and as powerful to our senses as possible.   He will use the most extravagant words or illustrations if they will suit his purpose.   Or he will invent a wild parable, and the more his mind is on fire or the more creative it is, the less will he look at the outer world or value it for its own sake.   It gives him metaphors and examples, and that is all.   He is even a little scornful of it, for it seems to him while the fit is on that the fire has gone out of it and left it but white ashes.   I cannot explain it, but I am certain that every high thing was invented in this way, between sleeping and waking, as it were, and that peering and peeping persons are but hawkers of stolen goods.   How else could their noses have grown so ravenous or their eyes so sharp?[1]

The symbolist, then, is concerned with presenting what he sees in the mirror of his mind rather than what exists in nature.   And even this mirrored reflection must be expressed figuratively, metaphorically, through symbols intuitively arrived at in an effort to seize upon spiritual essences.

Reliance on rhythm, musical effects and tones, and color.   The senses, Mallarmé and many of the French symbolists felt, must somehow be made to interpret the inner qualities.

> As long-drawn echoes heard far-off and dim
> Mingle to one deep sound and fade away;
> Vast as the night and brilliant as the day,
> Color and sound and perfume speak to him,

wrote Baudelaire in his *Correspondences.*

"The aim of the artist," says Cunliffe in writing of this aspect of Mallarmé's work, "is not so much to communicate his thoughts to others directly as to give them suggestions which will induce them to think and dream for themselves. . . . He (Mallarmé) professed to use in poetry a musical technique presenting simultaneously the principal idea, which is the melody, and the subsidiary ideas, which form the harmony."   Nitze and Dargan find that the symbolists held that "A poem must be an enigma for the vulgar, chamber-music for the initiated; further the chief Idea or Metaphor must be attended by numerous clustering minor images, which chime in with the central theme, and these analogies are, in his later work, crowded together with such compression as to break the molds of syntax and violate every principle of clearness."

Poetry, more especially symbolist poetry, was to this school of writers "a study in assonance."   But assonance in itself was too simple.   The poet was not only the musician seated at his organ-console with his stops before him; he was as well the artist playing his clavilux and the psychologist testing his audience with dainty phials of varied perfumes. And all these instruments he somehow managed to play at one time.   Rhythms and melodies and harmonies swept over the reader along with wide, sweeping arcs of pastel colors, and strange, exotic odors — the combination working mysteriously upon his senses

[1] From *Essays*, by W. B. Yeats.   By permission of The Macmillan Company, publishers.

in a way calculated to present the ethereal essence of the time or the mood invoked by the object rather than the object itself. Painting, music, literature — all of these were employed together to accomplish the purpose of the symbolist. (In this connection one should read Mallarmé's *L'Après-Midi d'un Faune*.)

Such subsidiary methods as these, added to the underlying symbolism of the work itself, necessarily resulted in writing which — at least to the unpracticed and uninitiated — deserves characterization as fantastic, exotic, extravagant. The effect of the symbolists, because of the rich medley of sense impressions upon which they rely, is that of a lost dream, a mystery faintly experienced.

> By unimagined Floridas I ran,
> Brilliant with flowers and panthers' eyes, and gay
> With barbarous hides and rainbows in whose span
> 'Neath far horizons glaucous cattle stray.
>
> *Rimbaud*

Naturalism and realism were abhorrent to them, for did not these literary moods pretend to present the thing itself and were they not, as symbolists, concerned beyond all else with the interpretation of the effect the *thing* makes on the mind, on the spirit? Read Mallarmé's *Sea-Wind*, Henri Bataille's *Memories*, Henri de Régnier's *The Stairway* — do these selections concern themselves with reality or with the impression reality makes on the mind?

"One's great objection to the symbolist school," writes André Gide, "is its lack of curiosity about life. With perhaps the single exception of Viélé-Griffin (and it is this that gives his verse so special a savor), all were pessimists, renunciants, resignationists, 'tired of the sad hospital' which the earth seemed to them — our 'monotonous and unmerited fatherland,' as Laforgue called it. Poetry had become to them a refuge, the only escape from the hideous realities; they threw themselves into it with a desperate fervor." [1]

The "School of Symbolism" rose to prominence and flourished in the 1880's and waned a decade or two later. But, as do most worth-while literary movements, it left a definite impress on literature. Symbolism did not die with Mallarmé. Writing for the past fifty or sixty years has been different because Rimbaud and Baudelaire and Régnier wrote as they did. William Butler Yeats, Maurice Maeterlinck, Amy Lowell, Carl Sandburg, T. S. Eliot, James Joyce, Paul Valéry, Henrik Ibsen, Marcel Proust, Thomas Wolfe — surely these figures prove in recent or contemporary fiction that French symbolism, while as a popular movement it came and went in a few years, has long colored the stream of European and American literature.

What has been said so far, the reliance on symbols, the effort to wed music to poetry and prose, the drawing upon the senses and the emotions rather than the intellect, the romantic outlook — all these suggest a certain nebulosity in symbolist writing. And the reader who first stumbles upon Mallarmé or Huysmans is likely to be bewildered. However, anyone who appreciates that life itself is more mysterious than any book will find a rich experience in going on these strange pilgrimages into the lands of music and color and exotic

[1] Quoted by Edmund Wilson in *Axel's Castle*, p. 257.

impressions. He will agree with André Fontainas who reduces all symbolistic effort to this sentence:

> The task of the symbolist artist is this: with full understanding, long study, and unflinching surety of his craft, to choose from the details and the whole of the object those aspects the balanced blending of which will correspond to the total effect desired, the expression sought, and will reconstruct, for the eyes, the heart, and the brain, a synthesis and a harmony that will most naturally hold the highest philosophical implications.[1]

[1] Quoted by Joseph T. Shipley in *The Literary Isms.*

The Bible

The two psalms which follow are evidence of the early use of symbolism in poetry. Here we find an elementary sort of symbolism, that which is really little more than an extended metaphor. In Psalm 23 God is envisioned as a shepherd, in Psalm 46 as a refuge. In this sense symbolism is common to poetry, early and late, in all lands. Literature has far to go and must become much more sophisticated before we shall come upon the involved symbolism of nineteenth-century France. But the basic principle of abstraction in terms of the concrete is the same whether in David or in Rimbaud.

The Book of Psalms is itself an anthology of old Hebrew verse, a collection which took the form we know today about the second century before Christ.

The Lord Is My Shepherd

The Lord is my shepherd; I shall not want.
He maketh me to lie down in green pastures:
He leadeth me beside the still waters.
He restoreth my soul:
He leadeth me in the paths of righteousness for
    his name's sake.   5
Yea, though I walk through the valley of the
    shadow of death,
I will fear no evil: for thou art with me;
Thy rod and thy staff they comfort me.
Thou preparest a table before me in the presence of
    mine enemies:
Thou anointest my head with oil; my cup runneth
    over.   10
Surely goodness and mercy shall follow me all the
    days of my life:
And I will dwell in the house of the Lord for ever.
                    (Psalm xxiii)

God Is Our Refuge

God is our refuge and strength,
A very present help in trouble.
Therefore will not we fear, though the earth be
    removed,

And though the mountains be carried into the
    midst of the sea;   4
Though the waters thereof roar and be troubled,
Though the mountains shake with the swelling
    thereof.
There is a river, the streams whereof shall make
    glad the city of God,
The holy place of the tabernacles of the most
    High.
God is in the midst of her; she shall not be moved:
God shall help her, and that right early.   10
The heathen raged, the kingdoms were moved:
He uttered his voice, the earth melted.
The Lord of hosts is with us;
The God of Jacob is our refuge.
Come, behold the works of the Lord,   15
What desolations he hath made in the earth.
He maketh wars to cease unto the end of the
    earth;
He breaketh the bow, and cutteth the spear in
    sunder;
He burneth the chariot in the fire.
"Be still, and know that I am God: 20
I will be exalted among the heathen,
I will be exalted in the earth."
The Lord of hosts is with us;
The God of Jacob is our refuge.
                    (Psalm xlvi)

John Donne · 1572–1631

John Donne, founder of the English "metaphysical" school of poetry, was brought up in the Catholic tradition. He entered Oxford in 1584, and later began to practice law in London. For a number of years he served as secretary to influential statesmen of his time and also participated in two expeditions to Spain and the Azores. In 1601, he broke with Catholicism and, fourteen years later, was ordained Anglican priest at the court of King James I. He was appointed divinity reader at Lincoln's Inn and for a while served as a chaplain to Lord Doncaster on his embassy to Germany. In 1621 he was made Dean of St. Paul's in London, an office he held until his death in 1631.

As a writer Donne was the first to break with the Petrarchan tradition which was then dominant in English poetry. He developed a new style which is best described as a blending of the intellectual with the emotional. In his best poetry, as T. S. Eliot observed, he achieves a "direct sensuous apprehension of thought, or a recreation of thought into feeling." Among seemingly incomparable images — like a falling star, a mandrake root, and the devil's foot — he finds some relationship. His method is to begin analytically, taking his subject apart piece by piece, and then to provide a synthesis in the final stanza or two.

Donne took his images from the practical world around him, from geography, alchemy and astronomy, thereby introducing the modern world of invention, discovery and scientific observation into a still medievalist scheme of poetic analogies. His images hardly ever strike us as poetic in themselves. A map has no obvious relation to the life of the emotions; and "gold to airy thinness beat" only by way of indirection can be made to denote the lovers' inseparable unity. By being linked with conventional themes of courtship, happy or unhappy love and woman's inconstancy, these extended metaphors gain a new dimension of meaning, a connotation that is alien to them in their natural context. The pair of twin compasses in "A Valediction: Forbidding Mourning," after all, can be made to illustrate the movement of the lovers' souls and thus adds to our knowledge of man's emotions.

The poetic technique of the "metaphysical" poets has been denounced by numerous critics in terms similar to those used by Samuel Johnson who spoke of "heterogeneous images" as being "yoked by violence together." Such a process, to Dr. Johnson as well as to the Romantic writers, seemed incompatible with the true spirit of poetry. Our century, however, has rediscovered Donne and his school along with the symbolist poets, whose poetry is distinguished by a similar contrast between subject-matter and meaning. The symbolists also resemble the "metaphysical" poets in their use of irony (Baudelaire) and in the intellectual complexity of their finished products (Mallarmé); Donne's and Mallarmé's poems are poetic puzzles entertaining the mind while at the same time stimulating the emotions.

SUGGESTED REFERENCES: Frank Kermode, ed., *Discussions of John Donne* (1962); J. B. Leishman, *The Monarch of Wit* (5th ed., 1962).

The Anniversary

All Kings, and all their favourites,
  All glory of honours, beauties, wits,
The Sun itself, which makes times, as they pass,
Is elder by a year, now, than it was
When thou and I first one another saw: 5
All other things to their destruction draw,
  Only our love hath no decay;
This, no to-morrow hath, nor yesterday,
Running it never runs from us away,
But truly keeps his first, last, everlasting day. 10

Two graves must hide thine and my corse,
  If one might, death were no divorce.
Alas, as well as other Princes, we,
(Who Prince enough in one another be,)
Must leave at last in death, these eyes, and ears, 15
Oft fed with true oaths, and with sweet salt tears;
  But souls where nothing dwells but love
(All other thoughts being inmates) then shall prove

This, or a love increasèd there above,
When bodies to their graves, souls from their graves
      remove.   20

    And then we shall be throughly blest,
    But we no more, than all the rest;
Here upon earth, we're Kings, and none but we
Can be such Kings, nor of such subjects be.
Who is so safe as we? where none can do   25
Treason to us, except one of us two.

    True and false fears let us refrain,
Let us love nobly, and live, and add again
Years and years unto years, till we attain
To write threescore: this is the second of our
      reign.   30

The Good-Morrow

I wonder by my troth, what thou and I
Did, till we lov'd? were we not wean'd till then?
But suck'd on country pleasures, childishly?
Or snorted we in the seven sleepers' den?
'Twas so; but this, all pleasures fancies be.   5
If ever any beauty I did see,
Which I desir'd, and got, 'twas but a dream of thee.

And now good-morrow to our waking souls,
Which watch not one another out of fear;
For love all love of other sights controls,   10
And makes one little room an everywhere.
Let sea-discoverers to new worlds have gone,
Let maps to other, worlds on worlds have shown,
Let us possess one world, each hath one, and is one.

My face in thine eye, thine in mine appears,   15
And true plain hearts do in the faces rest;
Where can we find two better hemispheres
Without sharp North, without declining West?
What ever dies, was not mixt equally;
If our two loves be one, or thou and I   20
Love so alike that none do slacken, none can die.

Song

Go, and catch a falling star,
    Get with child a mandrake root,
Tell me, where all past years are,
    Or who cleft the Devil's foot,
Teach me to hear Mermaids singing,   5
    Or to keep off envy's stinging,
      And find
      What wind
Serves to advance an honest mind.

If thou be'st born to strange sights,   10
    Things invisible to see,
Ride ten thousand days and nights,
    Till age snow white hairs on thee,
Thou, when thou return'st, wilt tell me
All strange wonders that befell thee,   15
      And swear
      No where
Lives a woman true, and fair.

If thou find'st one, let me know,
    Such a Pilgrimage were sweet;   20
Yet do not, I would not go,
    Though at next door we might meet,
Though she were true, when you met her,
And last, till you write your letter,
      Yet she   25
      Will be
False, ere I come, to two, or three.

The Sun Rising

Busy old fool, unruly Sun,
    Why dost thou thus,
Through windows, and through curtains call on
    us?
Must to thy motions lovers' seasons run?
    Saucy, pedantic wretch, go chide   5
    Late school-boys, and sour prentices,
Go tell Court-huntsmen, that the King will ride,
Call country ants to harvest offices;
Love, all alike, no season knows, nor clime,
Nor hours, days, months, which are the rags of
    time.   10

Thy beams so reverend, and strong
    Why shouldst thou think?
I could eclipse and cloud them with a wink,
But that I would not lose her sight so long:
    If her eyes have not blinded thine,   15
    Look, and to-morrow late, tell me,
Whether both th' Indias of spice and mine
Be where thou left'st them, or lie here with me.
Ask for those Kings whom thou saw'st yesterday,
And thou shalt hear, All here in one bed lay.   20

    She's all States, and all Princes, I,
    Nothing else is.
Princes do but play us; compar'd to this,
All honour's mimic; all wealth alchemy.
    Thou sun art half as happy as we,   25
    In that the world's contracted thus;
Thine age asks ease, and since thy duties be
To warm the world, that's done in warming us.
Shine here to us, and thou art everywhere;
This bed thy centre is, these walls, thy sphere.   30

Woman's Constancy

Now thou hast lov'd me one whole day,
To-morrow when thou leav'st, what wilt thou say?
Wilt thou then antedate some new made vow?
    Or say that now
We are not just those persons, which we were? 5
Or, that oaths made in reverential fear
Of Love, and his wrath, any may forswear?
Or, as true deaths true marriages untie,
So lovers' contracts, images of those,
Bind but till sleep, death's image, them unloose? 10
    Or, your own end to justify,
For having purpos'd change, and falsehood, you
Can have no way but falsehood to be true?
Vain lunatic, against these 'scapes I could
    Dispute, and conquer, if I would, 15
    Which I abstain to do,
For by to-morrow, I may think so too.

The Undertaking

I have done one braver thing
Than all the Worthies did;
And yet a braver thence doth spring,
Which is, to keep that hid.

It were but madness now to impart 5
The skill of specular stone,
When he, which can have learned the art
To cut it, can find none.

So, if I now should utter this,
Others — because no more 10
Such stuff to work upon there is —
Would love but as before.

But he who loveliness within
Hath found, all outward loathes,
For he who colour loves, and skin, 15
Loves but their oldest clothes.

If, as I have, you also do
Virtue in woman see,
And dare love that, and say so too,
And forget the He and She; 20

And if this love, though placed so,
From profane men you hide,
Which will no faith on this bestow,
Or, if they do, deride;

Then you have done a braver thing 25
Than all the Worthies did;

And yet a braver thence will spring,
Which is, to keep that hid.

The Canonization

For God's sake hold your tongue, and let me love;
  Or chide my palsy, or my gout,
My five grey hairs, or ruin'd fortune flout;
    With wealth your state, your mind with arts improve,
      Take you a course, get you a place, 5
      Observe his Honour, or his Grace,
Or the King's real, or his stamped face
  Contemplate; what you will, approve,
  So you will let me love.

Alas, alas, who's injur'd by my love? 10
  What merchant's ships have my sighs drown'd?
Who says my tears have overflow'd his ground?
    When did my colds a forward spring remove?
      When did the heats which my veins fill
      Add one more to the plaguy bill? 15
Soldiers find wars, and lawyers find out still
  Litigious men, which quarrels move,
  Though she and I do love.

Call us what you will, we are made such by love;
  Call her one, me another fly, 20
We're tapers too, and at our own cost die,
  And we in us find the Eagle and the Dove.
    The Phoenix riddle hath more wit
    By us; we two being one, are it.
So to one neutral thing both sexes fit, 25
  We die and rise the same, and prove
  Mysterious by this love.

We can die by it, if not live by love,
  And if unfit for tombs and hearse
Our legend be, it will be fit for verse; 30
  And if no piece of Chronicle we prove,
    We'll build in sonnets pretty rooms;
    As well a well-wrought urn becomes
The greatest ashes, as half-acre tombs,
  And by these hymns, all shall approve 35
  Us canonized for Love,

And thus invoke us: You whom reverend love
  Made one another's hermitage;
You, to whom love was peace, that now is rage;
  Who did the whole world's soul contract, and drove 40
    Into the glasses of your eyes
    (So made such mirrors, and such spies,
That they did all to you epitomize)
  Countries, Towns, Courts: beg from above
  A pattern of your love! 45

The Legacy

When I died last, and, Dear, I die
  As often as from thee I go,
  Though it be but an hour ago,
And Lovers' hours be full eternity,
I can remember yet, that I   5
  Something did say, and something did bestow;
Though I be dead, which sent me, I should be
Mine own executor and legacy.

I heard me say, Tell her anon,
  That my self (that is you, not I,)   10
  Did kill me, and when I felt me die,
I bid me send my heart, when I was gone;
But I alas could there find none,
  When I had ripp'd me, and search'd where hearts
            did lie;
It kill'd me again, that I who still was true,   15
In life, in my last Will should cozen you.

Yet I found something like a heart,
  But colours it, and corners had,
  It was not good, it was not bad,
It was entire to none, and few had part.   20
As good as could be made by art
  It seem'd; and therefore for our losses sad,
I meant to send this heart instead of mine,
But oh, no man could hold it, for 'twas thine.

A Valediction: Forbidding Mourning

As virtuous men pass mildly away,
  And whisper to their souls, to go,
Whilst some of their sad friends do say,
  The breath goes now, and some say, no:

So let us melt, and make no noise,   5
  No tear-floods, nor sigh-tempests move,
'Twere profanation of our joys
  To tell the laity our love.

Moving of th' earth brings harms and fears,
  Men reckon what it did and meant,   10
But trepidation of the spheres,
  Though greater far, is innocent.

Dull sublunary lovers' love
  (Whose soul is sense) cannot admit
Absence, because it doth remove   15
  Those things which elemented it.

But we by a love, so much refined,
  That our selves know not what it is,
Inter-assured of the mind,
  Care less, eyes, lips, and hands to miss.   20

Our two souls therefore, which are one,
  Though I must go, endure not yet
A breach, but an expansion,
  Like gold to airy thinness beat.

If they be two, they are two so   25
  As stiff twin compasses are two,
Thy soul, the fixed foot, makes no show
  To move, but doth, if th' other do.

And though it in the center sit,
  Yet when the other far doth roam,   30
It leans, and hearkens after it,
  And grows erect, as that comes home.

Such wilt thou be to me, who must
  Like th' other foot, obliquely run;
Thy firmness makes my circle just,   35
  And makes me end, where I begun.

Edgar Allan Poe · 1809–1849

Edgar Allan Poe, more than any other American writer, lived the sort of career which was once thought characteristic of a "genius." The background of his activity was a constantly shifting scene; even in the early years he did not long remain in any one environment. A writer of stories of mystery, he led a life of mystery.

Poe was born in Boston, January 19, 1809, to parents who were members of a troupe of actors which moved up and down the Atlantic seaboard from Maine to South Carolina and from South Carolina back to Maine. His father, David Poe, was of a Maryland family; his mother, Elizabeth Arnold, was an English actress. The father appears not to have been too practical, the mother doing most of the managing for her small family. When both his father and mother died in 1811, the orphaned Poe was adopted by a Mr. John Allan of Richmond, a tobacco merchant. With this adoption it seemed likely that life would become stable for Poe; Mr. Allan took the boy to England where for four years he attended an English school at Stoke-Newington. Upon his return to Richmond he was educated privately, then sent to the University of Virginia. When he had been there only one year, scrapes of a rather serious nature — particularly gambling debts — resulted in his removal by his foster-father. For a while the young man worked for Mr. Allan; then he ran away to Boston. Two years were spent in the United States Army, a few months more at West Point. While at the military academy, Poe learned that Mr. Allan had married a second time and, believing his own "prospects" weakened by this marriage, he managed to be expelled. He went to Baltimore to live with his father's sister, a Mrs. Clemm, and married his cousin, Virginia Clemm, a girl of thirteen. Soon his winning a hundred-dollar prize with the *Manuscript Found in a Bottle* called attention to his ability. A journalistic career opened to him. At one time or another he held various editorial positions: with the *Southern Literary Messenger*, the *Gentlemen's Magazine*, the *Evening Mirror*, the *Broadway Journal*. He was a clever editor and a trenchant critic. But every few years he changed his post, always planning for the day when he would edit a magazine of his own. The ill health of his wife Virginia, whose relation with him is symbolically presented in *Eleonora*, caused him serious worry. He died in Baltimore, October 7, 1849, in a hospital to which he had been taken after being found in a comatose condition, from liquor or drug, in the back room of a saloon then being used as a polling-booth. He had been on his way from Richmond to New York to start life anew, carrying with him a fairly large sum of money subscribed by Richmond friends toward his new venture.

The explanation of Poe's strange career is not simple. First the facts themselves are too often clouded. We know that Poe was given to drink, not as an habitual drunkard, but as one who periodically tried to escape from reality. We know, too, that his heredity and training were hardly stabilizing influences. Poe had to pay a high price for his unusual talent.

Poe's contribution to literature was three-fold: criticism, poetry, and short stories. His important published volumes include *Tamerlane and Other Poems* (1827); *Al Aaraaf* (1829); *Poems* (1831); *Tales of the Grotesque and Arabesque* (1839); and *The Raven and Other Poems* (1845). As a critic, Poe left a large body of writing, much of it ephemeral, but in at least two essays, *The Poetic Principle* and *The Philosophy of Composition*, and in a few book reviews, he set forth ideas which have proved of lasting significance. Two doctrines can be summarized here: his conviction that poetry is essentially the "rhythmical creation of beauty" and that, in the writing of tales, "a skillful literary artist," if wise, fashions "his thoughts to accommodate his incidents" and "having conceived, with deliberate care, a certain unique or single *effect* to be wrought out then invents such incidents . . . as may best aid him in establishing his preconceived effect." In these words Poe throws a clear light on his own literary practice.

Poe's poetry and prose have much in common. He did not care about normal human beings; he manifested little interest in character. He was blind to Nature and hated the commonplace. He insisted on technique and proved himself an artist in the artificial. He reworked a few situations: unearthly love and death, particularly the death of a beautiful woman. He confined himself rather narrowly to the field of the exotic, the "grotesque and arabesque." On the other hand no American poet, at least, has equaled Poe in his rhythmical, musical effects, in his capacity to create an exotic, supernal beauty, in his power to make the illogical and the impossible seem, for the moment, both logical and possible. And by developing the detective story he added to our literature a genre which has proved most popular.

Classifying Poe among the symbolists may strike some readers as an anachronism since the symbolist movement as such was not well under way until thirty or more years after Poe died. But Poe wrote in the mood of Mallarmé and Rimbaud; he was, by temper, akin to the French group. We have, of course, evidence for this in the regard with which the French symbolists esteemed the American writer, an esteem which they often expressed. But more conclusive than that is the poetry and prose of Poe himself. The symbolists exalted music, rhythm, assonance. So did Poe. Mallarmé and the rest placed unusual emphasis on color and emphasized form and technique. None more than Poe. The American writer's dictum that totality of effect should be the supreme goal of the writer might have been uttered by Huysmans. The spirit of the fantastic and the exotic in Verlaine, in Régnier, finds early parallel in a dozen poems and tales of Poe. Might not, for instance, Arthur Rimbaud have written *Ulalume* and Poe have sponsored the *Bateau Ivre?* Symbolism as a movement was of the 1880's; but symbolism as one of the tempers of man expressed in literature is as old as David the psalmist.

SUGGESTED REFERENCES: Vincent Buranelli, *Edgar Allan Poe* (1961); Edward Wagenknecht, *Edgar Allan Poe, The Man Behind the Legend* (1963); E. W. Parks, *Edgar Allan Poe as Literary Critic* (1964).

The City in the Sea

Lo! Death has reared himself a throne
In a strange city lying alone
Far down within the dim West,
Where the good and the bad and the worst and the
    best
Have gone to their eternal rest.   5
There shrines and palaces and towers
(Time-eaten towers that tremble not!)
Resemble nothing that is ours.
Around, by lifting winds forgot,
Resignedly beneath the sky   10
The melancholy waters lie.

No rays from the holy heaven come down
On the long night-time of that town;
But light from out the lurid sea
Streams up the turrets silently —   15
Gleams up the pinnacles far and free —
Up domes — up spires — up kingly halls —
Up fanes [1] — up Babylon-like walls —
Up shadowy long-forgotten bowers
Of sculptured ivy and stone flowers —   20
Up many and many a marvellous shrine
Whose wreathéd friezes intertwine
The viol, the violet, and the vine.
Resignedly beneath the sky
The melancholy waters lie.   25
So blend the turrets and shadows there
That all seem pendulous in air,
While from a proud tower in the town
Death looks gigantically down.

There open fanes and gaping graves   30
Yawn level with the luminous waves
But not the riches there that lie
In each idol's diamond eye —
Not the gaily-jewelled dead
Tempt the waters from their bed;   35

[1] temples.

For no ripples curl, alas!
Along that wilderness of glass —
No swellings tell that winds may be
Upon some far-off happier sea —
No heavings hint that winds have been   40
On seas less hideously serene.

But lo, a stir is in the air!
The wave — there is a movement there!
As if the towers had thrust aside,
In slightly sinking, the dull tide —   45
As if their tops had feebly given
A void within the filmy Heaven.
The waves have now a redder glow —
The hours are breathing faint and low —
And when, amid no earthly moans,   50
Down, down that town shall settle hence,
Hell, rising from a thousand thrones,
Shall do it reverence.

The Valley of Unrest

Once it smiled a silent dell
Where the people did not dwell;
They had gone unto the wars,
Trusting to the mild-eyed stars,
Nightly, from their azure towers,   5
To keep watch above the flowers,
In the midst of which all day
The red sunlight lazily lay.
Now each visitor shall confess
The sad valley's restlessness.   10
Nothing there is motionless —
Nothing save the airs that brood
Over the magic solitude.
Ah, by no wind are stirred those trees
That palpitate like the chill seas   15
Around the misty Hebrides! [1]
Ah, by no wind those clouds are driven
That rustle through the unquiet Heaven

[1] Islands west of Scotland.

Uneasily, from morn till even,
Over the violets there that lie   20
In myriad types of the human eye —
Over the lilies there that wave
And weep above a nameless grave!
They wave: — from out their fragrant tops
Eternal dews come down in drops,   25
They weep: — from off their delicate stems
Perennial tears descend in gems.

The Haunted Palace

In the greenest of our valleys
    By good angels tenanted,
Once a fair and stately palace —
    Radiant palace — reared its head.
In the monarch Thought's dominion —   5
    It stood there!
Never seraph spread a pinion
    Over fabric half so fair!

Banners yellow, glorious, golden,
    On its roof did float and flow,   10
(This — all this — was in the olden
    Time long ago,)
And every gentle air that dallied,
    In that sweet day,
Along the ramparts plumed and pallid,   15
    A wingéd odor went away.

Wanderers in that happy valley,
    Through two luminous windows, saw
Spirits moving musically,
    To a lute's well-tunéd law,   20
Round about a throne where, sitting,
    (Porphyrogene!)
In state his glory well befitting,
    The ruler of the realm was seen.

And all with pearl and ruby glowing   25
    Was the fair palace door,
Through which came flowing, flowing, flowing
    And sparkling evermore,
A troop of Echoes, whose sweet duty
    Was but to sing,   30
In voices of surpassing beauty,
    The wit and wisdom of their king.

But evil things, in robes of sorrow,
    Assailed the monarch's high estate.
(Ah, let us mourn! — for never morrow   35
    Shall dawn upon him desolate!)
And round about his home the glory
    That blushed and bloomed,
Is but a dim-remembered story
    Of the old time entombed.   40

And travellers, now, within that valley,
    Through the red-litten windows see
Vast forms, that move fantastically
    To a discordant melody,
While, like a ghastly rapid river,   45
    Through the pale door
A hideous throng rush out forever
    And laugh — but smile no more.

The Conqueror Worm

Lo! 'tis a gala night
    Within the lonesome latter years!
An angel throng, bewinged, bedight
    In veils, and drowned in tears,
Sit in a theatre, to see   5
    A play of hopes and fears,
While the orchestra breathes fitfully
    The music of the spheres.

Mimes, in the form of God on high,
    Mutter and mumble low,   10
And hither and thither fly —
    Mere puppets they, who come and go
At bidding of vast formless things
    That shift the scenery to and fro,
Flapping from out their Condor[1] wings   15
    Invisible Wo!

That motley drama — oh, be sure
    It shall not be forgot!
With its Phantom chased for evermore,
    By a crowd that seize it not,   20
Through a circle that ever returneth in
    To the self-same spot,
And much of Madness, and more of Sin,
    And Horror the soul of the plot.

But see, amid the mimic rout   25
    A crawling shape intrude!
A blood-red thing that writhes from out
    The scenic solitude!
It writhes! — it writhes! — with mortal pangs
    The mimes become its food,   30
And seraphs sob at vermin fangs
    In human gore imbued.

Out — out are the lights — out all!
    And, over each quivering form,
The curtain, a funeral pall,   35
    Comes down with the rush of a storm,
While the angels, all pallid and wan,
    Uprising, unveiling, affirm
That the play is the tragedy, "Man,"
    And its hero the Conqueror Worm.   40
    [1] A large vulture.

The Raven

Once upon a midnight dreary, while I pondered,
    weak and weary,
Over many a quaint and curious volume of for-
    gotten lore —
While I nodded, nearly napping, suddenly there
    came a tapping,
As of some one gently rapping, rapping at my
    chamber door.
"'Tis some visitor," I muttered, "tapping at my
    chamber door —   5
        Only this and nothing more."

Ah, distinctly I remember it was in the bleak
    December;
And each separate dying ember wrought its ghost
    upon the floor.
Eagerly I wished the morrow; — vainly I had
    sought to borrow
From my books surcease of sorrow — sorrow for
    the lost Lenore —   10
For the rare and radiant maiden whom the angels
    name Lenore —
        Nameless *here* for evermore.

And the silken, sad, uncertain rustling of each
    purple curtain
Thrilled me — filled me with fantastic terrors never
    felt before;
So that now, to still the beating of my heart, I
    stood repeating   15
"'Tis some visitor entreating entrance at my
    chamber door —
Some late visitor entreating entrance at my
    chamber door; —
        This it is and nothing more."

Presently my soul grew stronger; hestitating then
    no longer,
"Sir," said I, "or Madam, truly your forgiveness
    I implore;   20
But the fact is I was napping, and so gently you
    came rapping,
And so faintly you came tapping, tapping at my
    chamber door,
That I scarce was sure I heard you" — here I
    opened wide the door; —
        Darkness there and nothing more.

Deep into that darkness peering, long I stood there
    wondering, fearing,   25
Doubting, dreaming dreams no mortal ever dared
    to dream before;
But the silence was unbroken, and the stillness
    gave no token,

And the only word there spoken was the whispered
    word, "Lenore!"
This I whispered, and an echo murmured back the
    word "Lenore!"
        Merely this and nothing more.   30

Back into the chamber turning, all my soul within
    me burning,
Soon again I heard a tapping somewhat louder than
    before.
"Surely," said I, "surely that is something at my
    window lattice;
Let me see, then, what thereat is, and this mystery
    explore —
Let my heart be still a moment and this mystery
    explore; —   35
        'Tis the wind and nothing more!"

Open here I flung the shutter, when, with many a
    flirt and flutter
In there stepped a stately Raven of the saintly
    days of yore.
Not the least obeisance made he; not a minute
    stopped or stayed he;
But, with mien of lord or lady, perched above my
    chamber door —   40
Perched upon a bust of Pallas [1] just above my
    chamber door —
        Perched, and sat, and nothing more.

Then this ebony bird beguiling my sad fancy into
    smiling,
By the grave and stern decorum of the countenance
    it wore,
"Though thy crest be shorn and shaven, thou,"
    I said, "art sure no craven,   45
Ghastly grim and ancient Raven wandering from
    the Nightly shore —
Tell me what thy lordly name is on the Night's
    Plutonian shore!"
        Quoth the Raven, "Nevermore."

Much I marvelled this ungainly fowl to hear dis-
    course so plainly,
Though its answer little meaning — little rele-
    vancy bore;   50
For we cannot help agreeing that no living human
    being
Ever yet was blessed with seeing bird above his
    chamber door —
Bird or beast upon the sculptured bust above his
    chamber door,
        With such name as "Nevermore."

[1] Athena, goddess of wisdom.

But the Raven, sitting lonely on the placid bust,
    spoke only   55
That one word, as if his soul in that one word he
    did outpour.
Nothing farther then he uttered — not a feather
    then he fluttered —
Till I scarcely more than muttered, "Other friends
    have flown before —
On the morrow *he* will leave me, as my hopes have
    flown before."
        Then the bird said, "Nevermore." 60

Startled at the stillness broken by reply so aptly
    spoken,
"Doubtless," said I, "what it utters is its only
    stock and store
Caught from some unhappy master whom un-
    merciful Disaster
Followed fast and followed faster till his songs one
    burden bore —
Till the dirges of his Hope that melancholy burden
    bore   65
        Of 'Never — nevermore.'"

But the Raven still beguiling all my fancy into
    smiling,
Straight I wheeled a cushioned seat in front of bird
    and bust and door;
Then, upon the velvet sinking, I betook myself to
    linking
Fancy unto fancy, thinking what this ominous
    bird of yore — 70
What this grim, ungainly, ghastly, gaunt, and
    ominous bird of yore
        Meant in croaking "Nevermore."

This I sat engaged in guessing, but no syllable
    expressing
To the fowl whose fiery eyes now burned into my
    bosom's core;
This and more I sat divining, with my head at ease
    reclining 75
On the cushion's velvet lining that the lamp-light
    gloated o'er,
But whose velvet violet lining with the lamp-light
    gloating o'er,
    She shall press, ah, nevermore!

Then, methought, the air grew denser, perfumed
    from an unseen censer
Swung by Seraphim whose foot-falls tinkled on
    the tufted floor. 80
"Wretch," I cried, "thy God hath lent thee — by
    these angels he hath sent thee
Respite — respite and nepenthe [1] from thy me-
    mories of Lenore;

[1] A potion reputed to drive away pain and care.

Quaff, oh quaff this kind nepenthe and forget this
    lost Lenore!"
        Quoth the Raven, "Nevermore."

"Prophet!" said I, "thing of evil! — prophet still,
    if bird or devil! — 85
Whether Tempter sent, or whether tempest tossed
    thee here ashore,
Desolate yet all undaunted, on this desert land
    enchanted —
On this home by Horror haunted — tell me truly,
    I implore —
Is there — *is* there balm in Gilead? — tell me —
    tell me, I implore!"
        Quoth the Raven, "Nevermore." 90

"Prophet!" said I, "thing of evil! — prophet still,
    if bird or devil!
By that Heaven that bends above us — by that
    God we both adore —
Tell this soul with sorrow laden if, within the
    distant Aidenn,[1]
It shall clasp a sainted maiden whom the angels
    name Lenore —
Clasp a rare and radiant maiden whom the angels
    name Lenore." 95
        Quoth the Raven, "Nevermore."

"Be that word our sign of parting, bird or fiend!"
    I shrieked, upstarting —
"Get thee back into the tempest and the Night's
    Plutonian shore!
Leave no black plume as a token of that lie thy
    soul hath spoken!
Leave my loneliness unbroken! — quit the bust
    above my door! 100
Take thy beak from out my heart, and take thy
    form from off my door!"
        Quoth the Raven, "Nevermore."

And the Raven, never flitting, still is sitting, *still*
    is sitting
On the pallid bust of Pallas just above my chamber
    door;
And his eyes have all the seeming of a demon's that
    is dreaming, 105
And the lamp-light o'er him streaming throws his
    shadow on the floor;
And my soul from out that shadow that lies floating
    on the floor
        Shall be lifted — nevermore!

[1] A fanciful spelling for Eden; here used as "paradise."

Ulalume

The skies they were ashen and sober:
   The leaves they were crisped and sere —
   The leaves they were withering and sere;
It was night in the lonesome October
   Of my most immemorial year;   5
It was hard by the dim lake of Auber,
   In the misty mid region of Weir —
It was down by the dank tarn of Auber,
   In the ghoul-haunted woodland of Weir.

Here once, through an alley Titanic,   10
   Of cypress, I roamed with my Soul —
   Of cypress, with Psyche, my Soul.
These were days when my heart was volcanic
   As the scoriac[1] rivers that roll —
   As the lavas that restlessly roll   15
Their sulphurous currents down Yaanek
   In the ultimate climes of the pole —
That groan as they roll down Mount Yaanek
   In the realms of the boreal pole.

Our talk had been serious and sober,   20
   But our thoughts they were palsied and sere —
   Our memories were treacherous and sere —
For we knew not the month was October,
   And we marked not the night of the year —
   (Ah, night of all nights in the year!)   25
We noted not the dim lake of Auber —
   (Though once we had journeyed down here) —
Remembered not the dank tarn of Auber,
   Nor the ghoul-haunted woodland of Weir.

And now, as the night was senescent   30
   And star-dials pointed to morn —
   As the star-dials hinted of morn —
At the end of our path a liquescent
   And nebulous lustre was born,
Out of which a miraculous crescent   35
   Arose with a duplicate horn —
Astarte's[2] bediamonded crescent
   Distinct with its duplicate horn.

And I said — "She is warmer than Dian:
   She rolls through an ether of sighs —   40
   She revels in a region of sighs:
She has seen that the tears are not dry on
   These cheeks, where the worm never dies
And has come past the stars of the Lion[4]
   To point us the path to the skies —   45
   To the Lethean peace of the skies —

[1] lava-filled.
[2] The Phœnician Aphrodite, goddess of love.
[3] Diana, the moon goddess.
[4] The constellation of Leo.

Come up, in despite of the Lion,
   To shine on us with her bright eyes —
Come up through the lair of the Lion,
   With love in her luminous eyes."   50

But Psyche, uplifting her finger,
   Said — "Sadly this star I mistrust —
   Her pallor I strangely mistrust: —
Oh, hasten! — oh, let us not linger!
   Oh, fly! — let us fly! — for we must."   55
In terror she spoke, letting sink her
   Wings until they trailed in the dust —
In agony sobbed, letting sink her
   Plumes till they trailed in the dust —
   Till they sorrowfully trailed in the dust.   60

I replied — "This is nothing but dreaming:
   Let us on by this tremulous light!
   Let us bathe in this crystalline light!
Its Sibyllic[1] splendor is beaming
   With Hope and in Beauty to-night: —   65
   See! it flickers up the sky through the night!
Ah, we safely may trust to its gleaming,
   And be sure it will lead us aright —
We safely may trust to a gleaming
   That cannot but guide us aright,   70
   Since it flickers up to Heaven through the night."

Thus I pacified Psyche and kissed her,
   And tempted her out of her gloom —
   And conquered her scruples and gloom;
And we passed to the end of the vista,   75
   But were stopped by the door of a tomb —
   By the door of a legended tomb;
And I said — "What is written, sweet sister,
   On the door of this legended tomb?"
She replied — "Ulalume — Ulalume —   80
   'Tis the vault of thy lost Ulalume!"

Then my heart it grew ashen and sober
   As the leaves that were crisped and sere —
   As the leaves that were withering and sere,
And I cried — "It was surely October   85
   On *this* very night of last year
That I journeyed — I journeyed down here —
   That I brought a dread burden down here —
   On this night of all nights in the year,
   Ah, what demon has tempted me here?   90
Well I know, now, this dim lake of Auber —
   This misty mid region of Weir —
Well I know, now, this dank tarn of Auber,
   This ghoul-haunted woodland of Weir."

[1] The Sibyls were prophetesses. Poe is often more concerned with the *sound* than with the *meaning* of words. Here the word appears in the sense of *oracular*.

The Bells

1

Hear the sledges with the bells —
　　　Silver bells!
What a world of merriment their melody foretells!
　　How they tinkle, tinkle, tinkle,
　　　In the icy air of night!　　　5
　　While the stars that oversprinkle
　　All the heavens, seem to twinkle
　　　With a crystalline delight;
　　Keeping time, time, time,
　　　In a sort of Runic [1] rhyme,　　10
To the tintinnabulation that so musically wells
　　From the bells, bells, bells, bells,
　　　Bells, bells, bells —
From the jingling and the tinkling of the bells.

2

　　Hear the mellow wedding bells —　　15
　　　Golden Bells!
What a world of happiness their harmony foretells!
　　Through the balmy air of night
　　How they ring out their delight! —
　　From the molten-golden notes,　　20
　　　And all in tune,
　　What a liquid ditty floats
　　To the turtle-dove that listens, while she
　　　gloats
　　　On the moon!
　　Oh, from out the sounding cells,　　25
What a gush of euphony voluminously wells!
　　　How it swells!
　　　How it dwells
　　On the Future! — how it tells
　　Of the rapture that impels　　30
　　To the swinging and the ringing
　　Of the bells, bells, bells —
　　Of the bells, bells, bells, bells,
　　　Bells, bells, bells —
To the rhyming and the chiming of the bells!　35

3

　　Hear the loud alarum bells —
　　　Brazen bells!
What a tale of terror, now their turbulency tells!
　　In the startled ear of night
　　How they scream out their affright!　40
　　Too much horrified to speak,
　　They can only shriek, shriek,
　　　Out of tune,
In a clamorous appealing to the mercy of the fire,
In a mad expostulation with the deaf and frantic
　　　fire,
　　　　　45

[1] Primitive verse, often in the sense of obscure or
mystical.

　　Leaping higher, higher, higher,
　　With a desperate desire,
　　And a resolute endeavor
　　Now — now to sit, or never,
By the side of the pale-faced moon.　　50
　　Oh, the bells, bells, bells!
　　What a tale their terror tells
　　　Of Despair!
How they clang, and clash, and roar!
What a horror they outpour　　55
On the bosom of the palpitating air!
　　Yet the ear, it fully knows,
　　　By the twanging,
　　　And the clanging,
　　How the danger ebbs and flows;　　60
　　Yet the ear distinctly tells,
　　　In the jangling,
　　　And the wrangling,
　　How the danger sinks and swells,
By the sinking or the swelling in the anger of the
　　bells —
　　　　　65
　　　Of the bells —
　Of the bells, bells, bells, bells,
　　　Bells, bells, bells —
In the clamor and the clanging of the bells!

4

　　Hear the tolling of the bells —　　70
　　　Iron bells!
What a world of solemn thought their monody
　　compels!
　　In the silence of the night,
　　How we shiver with affright
　At the melancholy menace of their tone!
　For every sound that floats　　76
　From the rust within their throats
　　　Is a groan.
　And the people — ah, the people —
　They that dwell up in the steeple,　　80
　　　All alone,
　And who, tolling, tolling, tolling,
　　In that muffled monotone,
　Feel a glory in so rolling
　　On the human heart a stone —　　85
　They are neither man nor woman —
　They are neither brute nor human —
　　　They are Ghouls: —
　And their king it is who tolls: —
　And he rolls, rolls, rolls,
　　　Rolls　　90
　A pæan from the bells!
　And his merry bosom swells
　With the pæan of the bells!
　And he dances, and he yells;
　　Keeping time, time, time,　　95
　　In a sort of Runic rhyme,

To the pæan of the bells: —
　　Of the bells:
Keeping time, time, time
In a sort of Runic rhyme,
　　To the throbbing of the bells —
　　Of the bells, bells, bells —
To the sobbing of the bells: —
Keeping time, time, time,
　　As he knells, knells, knells,
In a happy Runic rhyme,
　　To the rolling of the bells —
　　Of the bells, bells, bells: —
　　To the tolling of the bells —
Of the bells, bells, bells, bells,
　　Bells, bells, bells —
To the moaning and the groaning of the bells.

Eldorado

Gaily bedight,
A gallant knight,
In sunshine and in shadow,
　　Had journeyed long,
　　Singing a song,
In search of Eldorado.

But he grew old —
This knight so bold —
And o'er his heart a shadow
　　Fell as he found
　　No spot of ground
That looked like Eldorado.

And, as his strength
Failed him at length,
He met a pilgrim shadow —
　　"Shadow," said he,
　　"Where can it be —
This land of Eldorado?"

"Over the Mountains
Of the Moon,
Down the Valley of the Shadow,
　　Ride, boldly ride,"
　　The shade replied, —
"If you seek for Eldorado."

The Masque of the Red Death

The "Red Death" had long devastated the
country. No pestilence had ever been so fatal, or
so hideous. Blood was its Avatar and its seal —
the redness and the horror of blood. There were
sharp pains, and sudden dizziness, and then profuse bleeding at the pores, with dissolution. The
scarlet stains upon the body and especially upon
the face of the victim, were the pest ban which
shut him out from the aid and from the sympathy
of his fellow-men. And the whole seizure, progress
and termination of the disease, were the incidents
of half an hour.

But the Prince Prospero was happy and dauntless and sagacious. When his dominions were half
depopulated, he summoned to his presence a
thousand hale and light-hearted friends from
among the knights and dames of his court, and
with these retired to the deep seclusion of one of his
castellated abbeys. This was an extensive and
magnificent structure, the creation of the prince's
own eccentric yet august taste. A strong and
lofty wall girdled it in. This wall had gates of
iron. The courtiers, having entered, brought
furnaces and massy hammers and welded the bolts.
They resolved to leave means neither of ingress or
egress to the sudden impulses of despair or of
frenzy from within. The abbey was amply pro-
visioned. With such precautions the courtiers
might bid defiance to contagion. The external
world could take care of itself. In the meantime
it was folly to grieve, or to think. The prince had
provided all the appliances of pleasure. There
were buffoons, there were improvisatori,[1] there
were ballet-dancers, there were musicians, there
was Beauty, there was wine. All these and security
were within. Without was the "Red Death."

It was toward the close of the fifth or sixth
month of his seclusion, and while the pestilence
raged most furiously abroad, that the Prince Prospero entertained his thousand friends at a masked
ball of the most unusual magnificence.

It was a voluptuous scene, that masquerade.
But first let me tell of the rooms in which it was
held. There were seven — an imperial suite. In
many palaces, however, such suites form a long and
straight vista, while the folding doors slide back
nearly to the walls on either hand, so that the view
of the whole extent is scarcely impeded. Here the
case was very different; as might have been expected from the duke's love of the *bizarre*. The
apartments were so irregularly disposed that the
vision embraced but little more than one at a time.
There was a sharp turn at every twenty or thirty
yards, and at each turn a novel effect. To the
right and left, in the middle of each wall, a tall and
narrow Gothic window looked out upon a closed
corridor which pursued the windings of the suite.
These windows were of stained glass whose color
varied in accordance with the prevailing hue of the

[1] Entertainers, particularly those who sang or recited
poetry which they *improvised* as they proceeded.

decorations of the chamber into which it opened. That at the eastern extremity was hung, for example, in blue — and vividly blue were its windows. The second chamber was purple in its ornaments and tapestries, and here the panes were purple. The third was green throughout, and so were the casements. The fourth was furnished and lighted with orange — the fifth with white — the sixth with violet. The seventh apartment was closely shrouded in black velvet tapestries that hung all over the ceiling and down the walls, falling in heavy folds upon a carpet of the same material and hue. But in this chamber only, the color of the windows failed to correspond with the decorations. The panes here were scarlet — a deep blood color. Now in no one of the seven apartments was there any lamp or candelabrum, amid the profusion of golden ornaments that lay scattered to and fro or depended from the roof. There was no light of any kind emanating from lamp or candle within the suite of chambers. But in the corridors that followed the suite, there stood, opposite to each window, a heavy tripod, bearing a brazier of fire that projected its rays through the tinted glass and so glaringly illumined the room. And thus were produced a multitude of gaudy and fantastic appearances. But in the western or black chamber the effect of the fire-light that streamed upon the dark hangings through the blood-tinted panes, was ghastly in the extreme, and produced so wild a look upon the countenances of those who entered, that there were few of the company bold enough to set foot within its precincts at all.

It was in this apartment, also, that there stood against the western wall, a gigantic clock of ebony. Its pendulum swung to and fro with a dull, heavy, monotonous clang; and when the minute-hand made the circuit of the face, and the hour was to be stricken, there came from the brazen lungs of the clock a sound which was clear and loud and deep and exceedingly musical, but of so peculiar a note and emphasis that, at each lapse of an hour, the musicians of the orchestra were constrained to pause, momentarily, in their performance, to hearken to the sound; and thus the waltzers perforce ceased their evolutions; and there was a brief disconcert of the whole gay company; and, while the chimes of the clock yet rang, it was observed that the giddiest grew pale, and the more aged and sedate passed their hands over their brows as if in confused reverie or meditation. But when the echoes had fully ceased, a light laughter at once pervaded the assembly; the musicians looked at each other and smiled as if at their own nervousness and folly, and made whispering vows, each

to the other, that the next chiming of the clock should produce in them no similar emotion; and then, after the lapse of sixty minutes, (which embrace three thousand and six hundred seconds of the Time that flies,) there came yet another chiming of the clock, and then were the same disconcert and tremulousness and meditation as before.

But, in spite of these things, it was a gay and magnificent revel. The tastes of the duke were peculiar. He had a fine eye for colors and effects. He disregarded the *decora* of mere fashion. His plans were bold and fiery, and his conceptions glowed with barbaric lustre. There are some who would have thought him mad. His followers felt that he was not. It was necessary to hear and see and touch him to be *sure* that he was not.

He had directed, in great part, the moveable embellishments of the seven chambers, upon occasion of this great *fête*; and it was his own guiding taste which had given character to the masqueraders. Be sure they were grotesque. There were much glare and glitter and piquancy and phantasm — much of what has been since seen in "Hernani." There were arabesque figures with unsuited limbs and appointments. There were delirious fancies such as the madman fashions. There was much of the beautiful, much of the wanton, much of the *bizarre*, something of the terrible, and not a little of that which might have excited disgust. To and fro in the seven chambers there stalked, in fact, a multitude of dreams. And these — the dreams — writhed in and about, taking hue from the rooms, and causing the wild music of the orchestra to seem as the echo of their steps. And, anon, there strikes the ebony clock which stands in the hall of the velvet. And then, for a moment, all is still, and all is silent save the voice of the clock. The dreams are stiff-frozen as they stand. But the echoes of the chime die away — they have endured but an instant — and a light, half-subdued laughter floats after them as they depart. And now again the music swells, and the dreams live, and writhe to and fro more merrily than ever, taking hue from the many-tinted windows through which stream the rays from the tripods. But to the chamber which lies most westwardly of the seven, there are now none of the maskers who venture; for the night is waning away; and there flows a ruddier light through the blood-colored panes; and the blackness of the sable drapery appals; and to him whose foot falls upon the sable carpet, there comes from the near clock of ebony a muffled peal more solemnly emphatic than any which reaches *their* ears who indulge in the more remote gaieties of the other apartments.

But these other apartments were densely crowded, and in them beat feverishly the heart of life. And the revel went whirlingly on, until at length there commenced the sounding of midnight upon the clock. And then the music ceased, as I have told; and the evolutions of the waltzers were quieted; and there was an uneasy cessation of all things as before. But now there were twelve strokes to be sounded by the bell of the clock; and thus it happened, perhaps, that more of thought crept, with more of time, into the meditations of the thoughtful among those who revelled. And thus, too, it happened, perhaps, that before the last echoes of the last chime had utterly sunk into silence, there were many individuals in the crowd who had found leisure to become aware of the presence of a masked figure which had arrested the attention of no single individual before. And the rumor of this new presence having spread itself whisperingly around, there arose at length from the whole company a buzz, or murmur, expressive of disapprobation and surprise — then, finally, of terror, of horror, and of disgust.

In an assembly of phantasms such as I have painted, it may well be supposed that no ordinary appearance could have excited such sensation. In truth the masquerade license of the night was nearly unlimited; but the figure in question had out-Heroded Herod, and gone beyond the bounds of even the prince's indefinite decorum. There are chords in the hearts of the most reckless which cannot be touched without emotion. Even with the utterly lost, to whom life and death are equally jests, there are matters of which no jest can be made. The whole company, indeed, seemed now deeply to feel that in the costume and bearing of the stranger neither wit nor propriety existed. The figure was tall and gaunt, and shrouded from head to foot in the habiliments of the grave. The mask which concealed the visage was made so nearly to resemble the countenance of a stiffened corpse that the closest scrutiny must have had difficulty in detecting the cheat. And yet all this might have been endured, if not approved, by the mad revellers around. But the mummer had gone so far as to assume the type of the Red Death. His vesture was dabbled in *blood* — and his broad brow, with all the features of the face, was besprinkled with the scarlet horror.

When the eyes of Prince Prospero fell upon this spectral image (which with a slow and solemn movement, as if more fully to sustain its *rôle*, stalked to and fro among the waltzers), he was seen to be convulsed, in the first moment with a strong shudder either of terror or distaste; but, in the next, his brow reddened with rage.

"Who dares?" he demanded hoarsely of the courtiers who stood near him — "who dares insult us with this blasphemous mockery? Seize him and unmask him — that we may know whom we have to hang at sunrise, from the battlements!"

It was in the eastern or blue chamber in which stood the Prince Prospero as he uttered these words. They rang throughout the seven rooms loudly and clearly — for the prince was a bold and robust man, and the music had become hushed at the waving of his hand.

It was in the blue room where stood the prince, with a group of pale courtiers by his side. At first, as he spoke, there was a slight rushing movement of this group in the direction of the intruder, who at the moment was also near at hand, and now, with deliberate and stately step, made closer approach to the speaker. But from a certain nameless awe with which the mad assumptions of the mummer had inspired the whole party, there were found none who put forth hand to seize him; so that, unimpeded, he passed within a yard of the prince's person; and, while the vast assembly, as if with one impulse, shrank from the centres of the rooms to the walls, he made his way uninterruptedly, but with the same solemn and measured step which had distinguished him from the first, through the blue chamber to the purple — through the purple to the green — through the green to the orange — through this again to the white — and even thence to the violet, ere a decided movement had been made to arrest him. It was then, however, that the Prince Prospero, maddening with rage and the shame of his own momentary cowardice, rushed hurriedly through the six chambers, while none followed him on account of a deadly terror that had seized upon all. He bore aloft a drawn dagger, and had approached, in rapid impetuosity, to within three or four feet of the retreating figure, when the latter, having attained the extremity of the velvet apartment, turned suddenly and confronted his pursuer. There was a sharp cry — and the dagger dropped gleaming upon the sable carpet, upon which, instantly afterwards, fell prostrate in death the Prince Prospero. Then, summoning the wild courage of despair, a throng of the revellers at once threw themselves into the black apartment, and, seizing the mummer, whose tall figure stood erect and motionless within the shadow of the ebony clock, gasped in unutterable horror at finding the grave-cerements and corpse-like mask which they handled with so violent a rudeness, untenanted by any tangible form.

And now was acknowledged the presence of the Red Death. He had come like a thief in the night.

And one by one dropped the revellers in the blood-bedewed halls of their revel, and died each in the despairing posture of his fall. And the life of the ebony clock went out with that of the last of the gay. And the flames of the tripods expired. And Darkness and Decay and the Red Death held illimitable dominion over all.

Eleonora

Sub conservatione formæ specificæ salva anima.[1]
Raymond Lully

I am come of a race noted for vigor of fancy and ardor of passion. Men have called me mad; but the question is not yet settled, whether madness is or is not the loftiest intelligence — whether much that is glorious — whether all that is profound — does not spring from disease of thought — from *moods* of mind exalted at the expense of the general intellect. They who dream by day are cognizant of many things which escape those who dream only by night. In their grey visions they obtain glimpses of eternity, and thrill, in awaking, to find that they have been upon the verge of the great secret. In snatches, they learn something of the wisdom which is of good, and more of the mere knowledge which is of evil. They penetrate, however, rudderless or compassless, into the vast ocean of the "light ineffable" and again, like the adventurers of the Nubian geographer, "*agressi sunt mare tenebrarum, quid in eo esset exploraturi.*"[2]

We will say, then, that I am mad. I grant, at least, that there are two distinct conditions of my mental existence — the condition of a lucid reason, not to be disputed, and belonging to the memory of events forming the first epoch of my life — and a condition of shadow and doubt, appertaining to the present, and to the recollection of what constitutes the second great era of my being. Therefore, what I shall tell of the earlier period, believe; and to what I may relate of the later time, give only such credit as may seem due; or doubt it altogether; or, if doubt it ye cannot, then play unto its riddle the Œdipus.[3]

She whom I loved in youth, and of whom I now pen calmly and distinctly these remembrances, was the sole daughter of the only sister of my mother long departed. Eleonora was the name of my cousin. We had always dwelled together, beneath a tropical sun, in the Valley of the Many-Colored Grass. No unguided footstep ever came upon that vale; for it lay far away up among a range of giant hills that hung beetling around about it, shutting out the sunlight from its sweetest recesses. No path was trodden in its vicinity; and, to reach our happy home, there was need of putting back, with force, the foliage of many thousands of forest trees, and of crushing to death the glories of many millions of fragrant flowers. Thus it was that we lived all alone, knowing nothing of the world without the valley, — I, and my cousin, and her mother.

From the dim regions beyond the mountains at the upper end of our encircled domain, there crept out a narrow and deep river, brighter than all save the eyes of Eleonora; and, winding stealthily about in mazy courses, it passed away; at length, through a shadowy gorge, among hills still dimmer than those whence it had issued. We called it the "River of Silence"; for there seemed to be a hushing influence in its flow. No murmur arose from its bed, and so gently it wandered along, that the pearly pebbles upon which we loved to gaze, far down within its bosom, stirred not at all, but lay in a motionless content, each in its own old station, shining on gloriously forever.

The margin of the river, and of the many dazzling rivulets that glided, through devious ways, into its channel, as well as the spaces that extended from the margins away down into the depths of the streams until they reached the bed of pebbles at the bottom, — these spots, not less than the whole surface of the valley, from the river to the mountains that girdled it in, were carpeted all by a soft green grass, thick, short, perfectly even, and vanilla-perfumed, but so besprinkled throughout with the yellow buttercup, the white daisy, the purple violet, and the ruby-red asphodel, that its exceeding beauty spoke to our hearts, in loud tones, of the love and of the glory of God.

And, here and there, in groves about this grass, like wildernesses of dreams, sprang up fantastic trees, whose tall slender stems stood not upright, but slanted gracefully towards the light that peered at noon-day into the centre of the valley. Their bark was speckled with the vivid alternate splendor of ebony and silver, and was smoother than all save the cheeks of Eleonora; so that but for the brilliant green of the huge leaves that spread from their summits in long tremulous lines, dallying with the Zephyrs, one might have fancied them giant serpents of Syria doing homage to their Sovereign the Sun.

Hand in hand about this valley, for fifteen years,

[1] "The soul is safe with the preservation of a specific form."
[2] "They advanced to the dark sea to explore the depths therein."
[3] This is an invitation to solve the riddle as did Œdipus that proposed by the Sphinx.

roamed I with Eleonora before Love entered within our hearts. It was one evening at the close of the third lustrum [1] of her life, and of the fourth of my own, that we sat, locked in each other's embrace, beneath the serpent-like trees, and looked down within the waters of the River of Silence at our images therein. We spoke no words during the rest of that sweet day; and our words even upon the morrow were tremulous and few. We had drawn the god Eros [2] from that wave, and now we felt that he had enkindled within us the fiery souls of our forefathers. The passions which had for centuries distinguished our race, came thronging with the fancies for which they had been equally noted, and together breathed a delirious bliss over the Valley of the Many-Colored Grass. A change fell upon all things. Strange brilliant flowers, star-shaped, burst out upon the trees where no flowers had been known before. The tints of the green carpet deepened; and when, one by one, the white daisies shrank away, there sprang up, in place of them, ten by ten of the ruby-red asphodel. And life arose in our paths; for the tall flamingo, hitherto unseen, with all gay glowing birds, flaunted his scarlet plumage before us. The golden and silver fish haunted the river, out of the bosom of which issued, little by little, a murmur that swelled, at length, into a lulling melody more divine than that of the harp of Æolus — sweeter than all save the voice of Eleonora. And now, too, a voluminous cloud, which we had long watched in the regions of Hesper, floated out thence, all gorgeous in crimson and gold, and settling in peace above us, sank, day by day, lower and lower, until its edges rested upon the tops of the mountains, turning all their dimness into magnificence, and shutting us up, as if forever, within a magic prison-house of grandeur and of glory.

The loveliness of Eleonora was that of the Seraphim; but she was a maiden artless and innocent as the brief life she had led among the flowers. No guile disguised the fervor of love which animated her heart, and she examined with me its inmost recesses as we walked together in the Valley of the Many-Colored Grass, and discoursed of the mighty changes which had lately taken place therein.

At length, having spoken one day, in tears, of the last sad change which must befall Humanity, she thenceforward dwelt only upon this one sorrowful theme, interweaving it into all our converse, as, in the songs of the bard of Schiraz,[3] the same

images are found occurring, again and again, in every impressive variation of phrase.

She had seen that the finger of Death was upon her bosom — that, like the ephemeron,[1] she had been made perfect in loveliness only to die; but the terrors of the grave, to her, lay solely in a consideration which she revealed to me, one evening at twilight, by the banks of the River of Silence. She grieved to think that, having entombed her in the Valley of the Many-Colored Grass, I would quit forever its happy recesses, transferring the love which now was so passionately her own to some maiden of the outer and every-day world. And, then and there, I threw myself hurriedly at the feet of Eleonora, and offered up a vow, to herself and to Heaven, that I would never bind myself in marriage to any daughter of Earth — that I would in no manner prove recreant to her dear memory, or to the memory of the devout affection with which she had blessed me. And I call the Mighty Ruler of the Universe to witness the pious solemnity of my vow. And the curse which I invoked of *Him* and of her, a saint in Helusion, should I prove traitorous to that promise, involved a penalty the exceeding great horror of which will not permit me to make record of it here. And the bright eyes of Eleonora grew brighter at my words; and she sighed as if a deadly burthen had been taken from her breast; and she trembled and very bitterly wept; but she made acceptance of the vow, (for what was she but a child?) and it made easy to her the bed of her death. And she said to me, not many days afterwards, tranquilly dying, that, because of what I had done for the comfort of her spirit, she would watch over me in that spirit when departed, and, if so it were permitted her, return to me visibly in the watches of the night; but, if this thing were, indeed, beyond the power of the souls in Paradise, that she would, at least, give me frequent indications of her presence; sighing upon me in the evening winds, or filling the air which I breathed with perfume from the censers of the angels. And, with these words upon her lips, she yielded up her innocent life, putting an end to the first epoch of my own.

Thus far I have faithfully said. But as I pass the barrier in Time's path formed by the death of my beloved, and proceed with the second era of my existence, I feel that a shadow gathers over my brain, and I mistrust the perfect sanity of the record. But let me on. — Years dragged themselves along heavily, and still I dwelled within the Valley of the Many-Colored Grass; — but a second change had come upon all things. The star-shaped

---

[1] A period of five years.
[2] God of love.
[3] A city in Persia which has had two famous poets: Sadi and Hafiz.

[1] A name for the May-fly; also applied to other short-lived beings.

flowers shrank into the stems of the trees, and appeared no more. The tints of the green carpet faded; and, one by one, the ruby-red asphodels withered away; and there sprang up, in place of them, ten by ten, dark eye-like violets that writhed uneasily and ere ever encumbered with dew. And Life departed from our paths; for the tall flamingo flaunted no longer his scarlet plumage before us, but flew sadly from the vale into the hills, with all the gay glowing birds that had arrived in his company. And the golden and silver fish swam down through the gorge at the lower end of our domain and bedecked the sweet river never again. And the lulling melody that had been softer than the wind-harp of Æolus and more divine than all save the voice of Eleonora, it died little by little away, in murmurs growing lower and lower, until the stream returned, at length, utterly, into the solemnity of its original silence. And then, lastly the voluminous cloud uprose, and, abandoning the tops of the mountains to the dimness of old, fell back into the regions of Hesper,[1] and took away all its manifold golden and gorgeous glories from the Valley of the Many-Colored Grass.

Yet the promises of Eleonora were not forgotten; for I heard the sounds of the swinging of the censers of the angels; and streams of a holy perfume floated ever and ever about the valley; and at lone hours, when my heart beat heavily, the winds that bathed my brow came unto me laden with soft sighs; and indistinct murmurs filled often the night air; and once — oh, but once only! I was awakened from a slumber like the slumber of death by the pressing of spiritual lips upon my own.

But the void within my heart refused, even thus, to be filled. I longed for the love which had before filled it to overflowing. At length the valley *pained* me through its memories of Eleonora, and I left it forever for the vanities and the turbulent triumphs of the world.

. . . .

I found myself within a strange city, where all things might have served to blot from recollection the sweet dreams I had dreamed so long in the Valley of the Many-Colored Grass. The pomps and pageantries of a stately court, and the mad clangor of arms, and the radiant loveliness of woman, bewildered and intoxicated my brain. But as yet my soul had proved true to its vows, and the indications of the presence of Eleonora were still given me in the silent hours of the night. Suddenly, these manifestations they ceased; and the world grew dark before mine eyes; and I stood aghast at the burning thoughts which possessed — at the terrible temptations which beset me; for there came from some far, far distant and unknown land, into the gay court of the king I served, a maiden to whose beauty my whole recreant heart yielded at once — at whose footstool I bowed down without a struggle, in the most ardent, in the most abject worship of love. What indeed was my passion for the young girl of the valley in comparison with the fervor, and the delirium, and the spirit-lifting ecstasy of adoration with which I poured out my whole soul in tears at the feet of the ethereal Ermengarde? — Oh bright was the seraph Ermengarde! and in that knowledge I had room for none other. — Oh divine was the angel Ermengarde! and as I looked down into the depths of her memorial eyes I thought only of them — and *of her.*

I wedded; — nor dreaded the curse I had invoked; and its bitterness was not visited upon me. And once — but once again in the silence of the night, there came through my lattice the soft sighs which had forsaken me; and they modelled themselves into familiar and sweet voice, saying:

"Sleep in peace! — for the Spirit of Love reigneth and ruleth, and, in taking to thy passionate heart her who is Ermengarde, thou art absolved, for reasons which shall be made known to thee in Heaven, of thy vows unto Eleonora."

[1] The evening star, king of the Western Land.

Charles Baudelaire · 1821-1867

Contemporaries, Poe and Baudelaire had much in common. Both men wrote of a strange, exotic world, both evinced a highly colorful prose style, and they both died, at forty-six, after having lived intense and unconventional lives.

Baudelaire was born in Paris, April 9, 1821, into a family of better than average financial and social standing. His father died when Charles was only six and his mother married Mr. Aupick, who rose to a generalship in the French army and to various ambassadorships at the courts of

Europe. Charles and his stepfather were by nature unsympathetic, with the result that the young man was estranged and began to spend his resources carelessly. To break up some of his associations in Paris, the parents sent young Baudelaire at twenty on a voyage to the Far East. His early writing was largely critical, but in 1857 he published his *Flowers of Evil*, a volume of verse so unconventional in its subject matter as to bring both the poet and his publisher to the attention of the courts. The book was temporarily suppressed. Much of Baudelaire's life was devoted to the careful, painstaking translation of the work of Poe. Among his contemporaries he claimed as friends such men as the painters Delacroix and Manet and the writers Gautier, Sainte-Beuve, and Flaubert. Never marrying, Baudelaire formed a twenty-year-long liaison with a mulatto, Jeanne Duval. Towards the close of his life, either as surcease from pain or from worldly care, the poet took to using opium.

Baudelaire's most important books are *The Flowers of Evil* and *The Spleen of Paris*. Both the poems and the prose manifest a desire to probe the depths of the human soul, with its concern for religion, death, and love. He was an aristocrat who sympathized rather than fraternized with the poor. He was convinced that the object of art was art rather than nature. Everything in his make-up rebelled at sentimentalism and sweetness. A romantic in his imagination and fancy, his romanticism was, nevertheless, held in check by his intellect. As a stylist he sought perfection of form, his work showing a meticulousness in metrical technique rarely equalled. If often he seemed to blaspheme, to seek deliberately to shock his reader, to seek out the sensual, it was because, in the words of Edna St. Vincent Millay, "he proposed to conquer ugliness by making beauty of it."

In seeking this beauty he relied greatly on tone and color, on words suggestive of sound and odor. Rhythm assumed unusual importance. Emotions and sensations were the stuff from which he spun his gossamer lines. He translated Poe not to borrow these qualities but because he found in the American an artist with his own ideals of the writer's art. And these qualities made Baudelaire, two decades later, the patron saint of the Symbolists. His technique and point of view justify our thinking of Baudelaire as one of the early "moderns."

SUGGESTED REFERENCES: Enid Starkie, *Charles Baudelaire* (2nd rev. ed., 1957); Pascal Pia, *Baudelaire* (1961); Henri Peyre, ed., *Baudelaire. A Collection of Critical Essays* (1962).

L'Invitation au Voyage [1]

There is a wonderful country, a country of Cockaigne, they say, which I dreamed of visiting with an old friend. It is a strange country, lost in the mists of our North, and one might call it the East of the West, the China of Europe, so freely does a warm and capricious fancy flourish there, and so patiently and persistently has that fancy illustrated it with a learned and delicate vegetation.

A real country of Cockaigne, where everything is beautiful, rich, quiet, honest; where order is the likeness and the mirror of luxury; where life is fat,

[1] Of the selections here given, the first two are translated by Arthur Symons, the next two by Joseph T. Shipley, the following seven by F. P. Sturm, and the last three by W. J. Robertson. They are taken from *Baudelaire, His Poetry and Prose*, edited by T. R. Smith, in The Modern Library, published by Random House.

and sweet to breathe; where disorder, tumult, and the unexpected are shut out; where happiness is wedded to silence; where even cooking is poetic, rich and highly flavored at once; where all, dear love, is made in your image.

You know that feverish sickness which comes over us in our cold miseries, that nostalgia of unknown lands, that anguish of curiosity? There is a country made in your image, where all is beautiful, rich, quiet and honest; where fancy has built and decorated a western China, where life is sweet to breathe, where happiness is wedded to silence. It is there that we should live, it is there that we should die!

Yes, it is there that we should breathe, dream, and lengthen out the hours by the infinity of sensations. A musician has written an "Invitation à la Valse": who will compose the "Invitation au Voyage" that we can offer to the beloved, to the chosen sister?

Yes, it is in this atmosphere that it would be good to live; far off, where slower hours contain more thoughts, where clocks strike happiness with a deeper and more significant solemnity.

On shining panels, or on gilded leather of a dark richness, slumbers the discreet life of pictures, deep, calm, and devout as the souls of the painters who created it. The sunsets which color so richly the walls of dining-room and drawing-room, are sifted through beautiful hangings or through tall wrought windows leaded into many panes. The pieces of furniture are large, curious, and fantastic, armed with locks and secrets like refined souls. Mirrors, metals, hangings, goldsmith's work and pottery, play for the eyes a mute and mysterious symphony; and from all things, from every corner, from the cracks of drawers and from the folds of hangings, exhales a singular odor, a "forget-me-not" of Sumatra, which is, as it were, the soul of the abode.

A real country of Cockaigne, I assure you, where all is beautiful, clean, and shining, like a clear conscience, like a bright array of kitchen crockery, like splendid jewellery of gold, like many-colored jewellery of silver! All the treasures of the world have found their way there, as to the house of a hard-working man who has put the whole world in his debt. Singular country, excelling others as Art excels Nature, where Nature is refashioned by dreams, where Nature is corrected, embellished, remoulded.

Let the alchemists of horticulture seek and seek again, let them set ever further and further back the limits to their happiness! Let them offer prizes of sixty and of a hundred thousand florins to whoever will solve their ambitious problems! For me, I have found my "black tulip" and my "blue dahlia!"

Incomparable flower, recaptured tulip, allegoric dahlia, it is there, is it not, in that beautiful country, so calm and so full of dreams, that you live and flourish? There would you not be framed within your own analogy, and would you not see yourself again, reflected, as the mystics say, in your own "correspondence"?

Dreams, dreams ever! and the more delicate and ambitious the soul, the further do dreams estrange it from possible things. Every man carries within himself his natural dose of opium, ceaselessly secreted and renewed, and, from birth to death, how many hours can we reckon of positive pleasure, or successful and decided action? Shall we ever live in, shall we ever pass into, that picture which my mind has painted, that picture made in your image?

These treasures, this furniture, this luxury, this order, these odors, these miraculous flowers, are you. You too are the great rivers and the quiet canals. The vast ships that drift down them, laden with riches, from whose decks comes the sound of the monotonous songs of laboring sailors, are my thoughts which slumber or rise and fall on your breast. You lead them softly towards the sea, which is the infinite, mirroring the depths of the sky in the crystal clearness of your soul; and when, weary of the surge and heavy with the spoils of the East, they return to the port of their birth, it is still my thoughts that come back enriched out of the infinite to you.

Anywhere Out of the World

Life is a hospital, in which every patient is possessed by the desire of changing his bed. One would prefer to suffer near the fire, and another is certain that he would get well if he were by the window.

It seems to me that I should always be happy if I were somewhere else, and this question of moving house is one that I am continually talking over with my soul.

"Tell me, my soul, poor chilly soul, what do you say to living in Lisbon? It must be very warm there, and you would bask merrily, like a lizard. It is by the sea; they say that it is built of marble, and that the people have such a horror of vegetation that they tear up all the trees. There is a country after your own soul; a country made up of light and mineral, and with liquid to reflect them."

My soul makes no answer.

"Since you love rest, and to see moving things, will you come and live in that heavenly land, Holland? Perhaps you would be happy in a country which you have so often admired in pictures. What do you say to Rotterdam, you who love forests of masts, and ships anchored at the doors of houses?"

My soul remains silent.

"Or perhaps Java seems to you more attractive? Well, there we shall find the mind of Europe married to tropical beauty."

Not a word. Can my soul be dead?

"Have you sunk then into so deep a stupor that only your own pain gives you pleasure? If that be so, let us go to the lands that are made in the likeness of Death. I know exactly the place for us, poor soul! We will book our passage to Torneo. We will go still further, to the last limits of the Baltic; and, if it be possible, further still from life; we will make our abode at the Pole. There the sun only grazes the earth, and the slow alternations of light and night put out variety and bring in the half of nothingness, monotony. There we can take great baths of darkness, while, from time to time, for our pleasure, the Aurora Borealis shall scatter its rosy sheaves before us, like reflections of fireworks in hell!"

At last my soul bursts into speech, and wisely she cries to me: "Anywhere, anywhere, out of the world!"

The Clock

The Chinese tell the time in the eyes of cats. One day a missionary, walking in the suburbs of Nanking, noticed that he had forgotten his watch, and asked a little boy what time it was.

The youngster of the heavenly Empire hesitated at first; then, carried away by his thought he answered: "I'll tell you." A few moments later he reappeared, bearing in his arms an immense cat, and looking, as they say, into the whites of its eyes, he announced without hesitation: "It's not quite noon." Which was the fact.

As for me, if I turn toward the fair feline, to her so aptly named, who is at once the honor of her sex, the pride of my heart and the fragrance of my mind, be it by night or by day, in the full light or in the opaque shadows, in the depths of her adorable eyes I always tell the time distinctly, always the same, a vast, a solemn hour, large as space, without division of minutes or of seconds, — an immovable hour which is not marked on the clocks, yet is slight as a sigh, is rapid as the lifting of a lash.

And if some intruder comes to disturb me while my glance rests upon that charming dial, if some rude and intolerant genie, some demon of the evil hour, comes to ask: "What are you looking at so carefully? What are you hunting for in the eyes of that being? Do you see the time there, mortal squanderer and do-nothing?" I shall answer, unhesitant: "Yes, I see the time, it is Eternity!"

Is not this, madame, a really worth-while madrigal, just as affected as yourself? Indeed, I have had so much pleasure in embroidering this pretentious gallantry, that I shall ask you for nothing in exchange.

The Plaything of the Poor

I should like to give you an idea for an innocent diversion. There are so few amusements that are not guilty ones!

When you go out in the morning for a stroll along the highways, fill your pockets with little penny contrivances — such as the straight merryandrew moved by a single thread, the blacksmiths who strike the anvil, the rider and his horse, with a whistle for a tail — and, along the taverns, at the foot of the trees, make presents of them to the unknown poor children whom you meet. You will see their eyes grow beyond all measure. At first, they will not dare to take; they will doubt their good fortune. Then their hands will eagerly seize the gift, and they will flee as do the cats who go far off to eat the bit you have given them, having learned to distrust man.

On a road, behind the rail of a great garden at the foot of which appeared the glitter of a beautiful mansion struck by the sun, stood a pretty, fresh child, clad in those country garments so full of affectation.

Luxury, freedom from care, and the habitual spectacle of wealth, make these children so pretty that one would think them formed of other paste than the sons of mediocrity or of poverty.

Beside him on the grass lay a splendid toy, fresh as its master, varnished, gilt, clad in a purple robe, covered with plumes and beads of glass. But the child was not occupied with his favored plaything, and this is what he was watching:

On the other side of the rail, on the road, among the thistles and the thorns, was another child, puny, dirty, fuliginous, one of those pariah-brats the beauty of which an impartial eye might discover if, as the eye of the connoisseur divines an ideal painting beneath the varnish of the coachmaker, it cleansed him of the repugnant patina of misery.

Across the symbolic bars which separate two worlds, the highway and the mansion, the poor child was showing the rich child his own toy, which the latter examined eagerly, as a rare and unknown object. Now, this toy, which the ragamuffin was provoking, tormenting, tossing in a grilled box, was a live rat! His parents, doubtless for economy, had taken the toy from life itself.

And the two children were laughing together fraternally, with teeth of equal *whiteness!*

Every Man His Chimæra

Beneath a broad grey sky, upon a vast and dusty plain devoid of grass, and where not even a nettle or a thistle was to be seen, I met several men who walked bowed down to the ground.

Each one carried upon his back an enormous Chimæra as heavy as a sack of flour or coal, or as the equipment of a Roman foot-soldier.

But the monstrous beast was not a dead weight, rather she enveloped and oppressed the men with

...er powerful and elastic muscles, and clawed with ...er two vast talons at the breast of her mount. ...Her fabulous head reposed upon the brow of the ...man like one of those horrible casques by which ...ncient warriors hoped to add to the terrors of the 5 ...nemy.

I questioned one of the men, asking him why ...they went so. He replied that he knew nothing, ...either he nor the others, but that evidently they ...vent somewhere, since they were urged on by an 10 ...nconquerable desire to walk.

Very curiously, none of the wayfarers seemed ...o be irritated by the ferocious beast hanging at ...is neck and cleaving to his back: one had said ...that he considered it as a part of himself. These 15 ...rave and weary faces bore witness to no despair. ...Beneath the splenetic cupola of the heavens, their ...eet trudging through the dust of an earth as ...esolate as the sky, they journeyed onwards with ...he resigned faces of men condemned to hope for 20 ...ver. So the train passed me and faded into the at...mosphere of the horizon at the place where the planet ...nveils herself to the curiosity of the human eye.

During several moments I obstinately endeav...red to comprehend this mystery; but irresistible 25 ...ndifference soon threw herself upon me, nor was I ...nore heavily dejected thereby than they by their ...rushing Chimæras.

The Sadness of the Moon

The Moon more indolently dreams to-night
Than a fair woman on her couch at rest,
Caressing, with a hand distraught and light,
Before she sleeps, the contour of her breast.

Upon her silken avalanche of down, 5
Dying she breathes a long and swooning sigh;
And watches the white visions past her flown,
Which rise like blossoms to the azure sky.

And when, at times, wrapped in her languor deep,
Earthward she lets a furtive tear-drop flow, 10
Some pious poet, enemy of sleep,

Takes in his hollow hand the tear of snow
Whence gleams of iris and of opal start,
And hides it from the Sun, deep in his heart.

Correspondences

In Nature's temple living pillars rise,
And words are murmured none have understood,
And man must wander through a tangled wood
Of symbols watching him with friendly eyes.

As long-drawn echoes heard far-off and dim 5
Mingle to one deep sound and fade away;
Vast as the night and brilliant as the day,
Color and sound and perfume speak to him.

Some perfumes are as fragrant as a child,
Sweet as the sound of hautboys, meadow-
green;
Others, corrupted, rich, exultant, wild, 11

Have all the expansion of things infinite:
As amber, incense, musk, and benzoin,
Which sing the sense's and the soul's delight.

The Flask

There are some powerful odors that can pass
Out of the stoppered flagon; even glass
To them is porous. Oft when some old box
Brought from the East is opened and the locks
And hinges creak and cry; or in a press 5
In some deserted house, where the sharp stress
Of odors old and dusty fills the brain;
An ancient flask is brought to light again,
And forth the ghosts of long-dead odors creep.
There, softly trembling in the shadows, sleep 10
A thousand thoughts, funereal chrysalides,
Phantoms of old the folding darkness hides,
Who make faint flutterings as their wings un
fold,
Rose-washed and azure-tinted, shot with gold.

A memory that brings languor flutters here: 15
The fainting eyelids droop, and giddy Fear
Thrusts with both hands the soul towards the pit
Where, like a Lazarus from his winding-sheet,
Arises from the gulf of sleep a ghost
Of an old passion, long since loved and lost. 20
So I, when vanished from man's memory
Deep in some dark and sombre chest I lie,
An empty flagon they have cast aside,
Broken and soiled, the dust upon my pride,
Will be your shroud, beloved pestilence! 25
The witness of your might and virulence,
Sweet poison mixed by angels; bitter cup
Of life and death my heart has drunken up!

The Seven Old Men

O swarming city, city full of dreams,
Where in full day the spectre walks and speaks;
Mighty colossus, in your narrow veins
My story flows as flows the rising sap.

One morn, disputing with my tired soul,   5
And like a hero stiffening all my nerves,
I trod a suburb shaken by the jar
Of rolling wheels, where the fog magnified
The houses either side of that sad street,
So they seemed like two wharves the ebbing flood
Leaves desolate by the river-side.   A mist,   11
Unclean and yellow, inundated space —
A scene that would have pleased an actor's soul.

Then suddenly an aged man, whose rags
Were yellow as the rainy sky, whose looks   15
Should have brought alms in floods upon his head,
Without the misery gleaming in his eye,
Appeared before me; and his pupils seemed
To have been washed with gall; the bitter frost
Sharpened his glance; and from his chin a beard   20
Sword-stiff and ragged, Judas-like stuck forth.
He was not bent but broken: his backbone
Made a so true right angle with his legs,
That, as he walked, the tapping stick which gave
The finish to the picture, made him seem   25
Like some infirm and stumbling quadruped
Or a three-legged Jew.   Through snow and mud
He walked with troubled and uncertain gait,
As though his sabots trod upon the dead,
Indifferent and hostile to the world.   30

His double followed him: tatters and stick
And back and eye and beard, all were the same;
Out of the same Hell, indistinguishable,
These centenarian twins, these spectres odd,
Trod the same pace toward some end unknown.   35
To what fell complot was I then exposed?
Humiliated by what evil chance?
For as the minutes one by one went by
Seven times I saw this sinister old man
Repeat his image there before my eyes!   40

Let him who smiles at my inquietude,
Who never trembled at a fear like mine,
Know that in their decrepitude's despite
These seven old hideous monsters had the mien
Of beings immortal.

                    Then, I thought, must I,   45
Undying, contemplate the awful eighth;
Inexorable, fatal, and ironic double;
Disgusting Phœnix, father of himself
And his own son?   In terror then I turned
My back upon the infernal band, and fled   50
To my own place, and closed my door; distraught
And like a drunkard who sees all things twice,
With feverish troubled spirit, chilly and sick,
Wounded by mystery and absurdity!
In vain my reason tried to cross the bar,   55

The whirling storm but drove her back again;
And my soul tossed, and tossed, an outworn wreck,
Mastless, upon a monstrous, shoreless sea.

The Death of the Poor

Death is consoler and Death brings to life;
   The end of all, the solitary hope;
We, drunk with Death's elixir, face the strife,
   Take heart, and mount till eve the weary slope.

Across the storm, the hoar-frost, and the snow,   5
   Death on our dark horizon pulses clear;
Death is the famous hostel we all know,
   Where we may rest and sleep and have good cheer.

Death is an angel whose magnetic palms
Bring dreams of ecstasy and slumberous calms   10
To smooth the beds of naked men and poor.

Death is the mystic granary of God;
The poor man's purse; his fatherland of yore;
The Gate that opens into heavens untrod!

A Landscape

I would, when I compose my solemn verse,
Sleep near the heaven as do astrologers,
Near the high bells, and with a dreaming mind
Hear their calm hymns blown to me on the wind.

Out of my tower, with chin upon my hands,   5
I'll watch the singing, babbling human bands;
And see clock-towers like spars against the sky,
And heavens that bring thoughts of eternity;

And softly, through the mist, will watch the birth
Of stars in heaven and lamplight on the earth;   10
The threads of smoke that rise above the town;
The moon that pours her pale enchantment down.

Seasons will pass till Autumn fades the rose;
And when comes Winter with his weary snows,
I'll shut the doors and window-casements tight,   15
And build my faery palace in the night.

Then I will dream of blue horizons deep;
Of gardens where the marble fountains weep;
Of kisses, and of ever-singing birds —
A sinless Idyll built of innocent words.   20

And Trouble, knocking at my window-pane
And at my closet door, shall knock in vain;
I will not heed him with his stealthy tread,
Nor from my reverie uplift my head;

For I will plunge deep in the pleasure still 25
Of summoning the spring-time with my will,
Drawing the sun out of my heart, and there
With burning thoughts making a summer air.

Exotic Fragrance

When, with closed eyes in the warm autumn night,
  I breathe the fragrance of thy bosom bare,
  My dream unfurls a clime of loveliest air,
Drenched in the fiery sun's unclouded light.

An indolent island dowered with heaven's delight,
  Trees singular and fruits of savor rare, 6
  Men having sinewy frames robust and spare,
And women whose clear eyes are wondrous bright.

Led by thy fragrance to those shores I hail
  A charmèd harbor thronged with mast and sail,
Still wearied with the quivering sea's unrest; 11

What time the scent of the green tamarinds
  That thrills the air and fills my swelling breast
Blends with the mariners' song and the sea-winds.

Music

Launch me, O music, whither on the soundless
      Sea my star gleams pale!
I beneath cloudy cope or rapt in boundless
      Æther set my sail;

With breast outblown, swollen by the wind that urges
      Swelling sheets, I scale 5
The summit of the wave whose vexed surges
      Night from me doth veil;

A laboring vessel's passions in my pulses
      Thrill the shuddering sense; 10
The wind that wafts, the tempest that convulses,
      O'er the gulf immense
Swing me. — Anon flat calm and clearer air
      Glass my soul's despair!

The Flawed Bell

Bitter and sweet it is, in winter night,
  Hard by the flickering fire that smokes, to list
While far-off memories rise in sad slow flight,
  With chimes that echo singing through the mist.

O blessèd be the bell whose vigorous throat, 5
  In spite of age alert, with strength unspent,
Utters religiously his faithful note,
  Like an old warrior watching near the tent!

My soul, alas! is flawed, and when despair
Would people with her songs the chill night-air 10
  Too oft they faint in hoarse enfeebled tones,

As when a wounded man forgotten moans
By the red pool, beneath a heap of dead,
And dying writhes in frenzy on his bed.

Henrik Ibsen · 1828-1906

A playwright for almost fifty years — the last five decades of the nineteenth century — Henrik Ibsen presented a consistent doctrine in a variety of literary styles. His drama was at times intensely poetic and mystic. In such a play as *Ghosts* he was thoroughly realistic. And in such later plays as *The Master Builder* and *When We Dead Awaken* Ibsen resorts to symbolism. Yet most of the plays, early or late, mystic or realistic, reiterate in one way or another his convictions that the individual must be permitted to live out his career fully, unhampered by family or society, and that love is so important an experience that interference with its full development is a major crime. Correlatives to these are Ibsen's belief that youth must not be denied, that idealism must be permitted its full flowering, that society, when it attempts to repress the strength and tendency of the individual, is an enemy of the people. Majority opinion was, Ibsen thought, always wrong. When he attacked Christianity, it was not Christianity as such which he attacked but its abuses and its hypocrisies.

After having written *Brand* (1866) and *Peer Gynt* (1867), two verse plays thoroughly Norwegian in character and spirit, Ibsen turned to realistic prose dramas such as *Pillars of Society* (1877),

A Doll's House (1879), *Ghosts* (1881), and *An Enemy of the People* (1882). Here he attacked the narrowness and rottenness of society in general; he advocated freedom and truth and espoused the cause of the individual. The emphasis on symbolism evident in his early verse plays is to be found again in the later dramas, *The Wild Duck* (1884), *The Master Builder* (1892), and *When We Dead Awaken* (1899). Actually there is hardly a play by Ibsen — not even the most realistic ones — that does not contain some symbolic elements.

Ibsen has made significant contributions to modern drama by introducing new techniques and by expressing ideas and raising problems that had not before been presented on the stage. However, most of these innovations have been superseded by more recent stage advances. His more permanent contributions are his understanding of the complexities and struggles of the individual in modern life and his concern with the universal conflicts between the individual and society, between reality and illusion, and between true and false idealism.

For one whose plays offer so wide a range, Ibsen led a surprisingly quiet and lonely life. He was born in Skien, Norway, on March 20, 1828, the son of a merchant whose death, when Henrik was only eight years old, left the family in impoverished circumstances. At fifteen the young man was apprenticed to a druggist but wrote poetry as a diversion to make his routine tolerable. At twenty-two Ibsen was in Christiania as a student, and almost immediately he began to write plays for the Christiania theatre. He soon attached himself to one playhouse or another in various capacities, serving now an apprenticeship in a field of his own choosing. He married Susanna Thoresen. When his career as a playwright was somewhat more assured and his request to the government for a pension had been refused, he left Norway for Italy. Soon he moved to Dresden and later to Munich where he lived for the next twenty-two years before returning to Christiania in 1891. He died in this latter city on May 28, 1906.

SUGGESTED REFERENCES: B. W. Downs, *A Study of Six Plays by Ibsen* (1950); G. W. Knight, *Henrik Ibsen* (1962); Rolf Fjelde, ed., *Ibsen. A Collection of Critical Essays* (1965).

The Master Builder

In *The Master Builder*, Ibsen is working with a theme that always attracted him — the destruction that comes from the pursuit of an ideal which allows no compromise. Uncompromising idealists Ibsen had shown before in such works as *Brand*, *An Enemy of the People*, *The Wild Duck*. Here it is the architect Solness whose consuming ambition to remain forever at the top of his profession becomes his downfall. In his consistent climb upwards he loses sight of human values and builds on the defeat and the resignations of others, among them his wife Aline, his old employee Brovik, the young draftsman Ragnar. Toward the end of the play, Solness, intent on climbing higher than ever before and encouraged by the young girl Hilda, mounts the scaffolding to place a wreath on the highest point of the new

house. Ragnar, representing the younger generation of builder which has been suppressed, does not believe that Solness will reach the top and expects him to turn. But Solness does not turn. In his impetuous climb into the fragile structure of success and greatness he goes too far and, finally, falls to his death.

The play is filled with personal references and autobiographical matters. It shows Ibsen's great concern with the place of the artist, here represented by the architect Solness, in relation to a younger generation, and the question of the artist achieving and holding supremacy in his art.

The text reprinted here is a slightly amended version by William Archer and Edmond Gosse (1893).

Characters

HALVARD SOLNESS, *Master Builder*

ALINE SOLNESS, *his wife*

DOCTOR HERDAL

KNUT BROVIK, *formerly an architect, now in Solness'*
employment

RAGNAR BROVIK, *his son, a draftsman*

KAIA FOSLI, *his niece, a bookkeeper*

MISS HILDA WANGEL

Some Women

A crowd in the street

The action takes place in and about the house of HALVARD SOLNESS.

ACT ONE

A plainly-furnished workroom in the house of
HALVARD SOLNESS. *Folding doors on the left lead
out to the hall. On the right is the door leading to
the inner rooms of the house. At the back is an open
door into the draftsmen's office. In front, on the left,
a desk with books, papers, and writing materials.
Farther back than the folding doors, a stove. In the
right-hand corner, a sofa, a table, and one or two
chairs. On the table a water-bottle and glass. A
smaller table, with a rocking-chair and armchair, in
front on the right. Lighted lamps with shades on
the table in the draftsmen's office, on the table in the
corner, and on the desk.*

In the draftsmen's office sit KNUT BROVIK *and
his son* RAGNAR, *occupied with plans and calculations. At the desk in the outer office stands* KAIA
FOSLI, *writing in the ledger.* KNUT BROVIK *is a
spare old man with white hair and beard. He wears
a rather threadbare but well-brushed black coat,
spectacles, and a somewhat discolored white neck-
cloth.* RAGNAR BROVIK *is a well-dressed, light-
haired man in his thirties, with a slight stoop.* KAIA
FOSLI *is a slightly-built girl, a little over twenty,
carefully dressed, and delicate-looking. She has a
green shade over her eyes. — All three go on working
for some time in silence.*

*Brovik (rises suddenly, as if in distress, from the
table; breathes heavily and laboriously as he comes
forward into the doorway).* No, I can't bear it
much longer!

Kaia (going up to him). You are feeling very ill
this evening, aren't you, uncle?

Brovik. Oh, I seem to get worse every day.

Ragnar (has risen and advances). You ought to
go home, father. Try to get a little sleep ——

Brovik (impatiently). Go to bed, I suppose?
Would you have me stifled outright?

Kaia. Then take a little walk.

Ragnar. Yes, do. I will come with you.

Brovik (with warmth). I will not go till he comes!
I am determined to have it out this evening with
— (*In a tone of suppressed bitterness.*) — with him
— with the chief.

Kaia (anxiously). Oh, no, uncle — do wait a
while before doing *that!*

Ragnar. Yes, better wait, father!

Brovik (draws his breath laboriously). Ha —
ha —! I haven't much time for waiting.

Kaia (listening). Hush! I hear him on the
stairs.

*(All three go back to their work. A short
silence.)*

*(*HALVARD SOLNESS *comes in through the hall door.
He is a man no longer young, but healthy and
vigorous, with close-cut curly hair, dark moustache, and dark, thick eyebrows. He wears a
grayish-green buttoned jacket with an upstanding
collar and broad lapels. On his head he wears
a soft gray felt hat, and he has one or two light
portfolios under his arm.)*

*Solness (near the door, points towards the drafts-
men's office, and asks in a whisper).* Are they gone?

Kaia (softly, shaking her head). No.

(She takes the shade off her eyes. SOLNESS
*crosses the room, throws his hat on a chair,
places the portfolios on the table by the
sofa, and approaches the desk again.
KAIA goes on writing without intermission, but seems nervous and uneasy.)*

Solness (aloud). What is that you are entering,
Miss Fosli?

Kaia (starts). Oh, it is only something that ——

Solness. Let me look at it, Miss Fosli. (*Bends
over her, pretends to be looking into the ledger, and
whispers.*) Kaia!

Kaia (softly, still writing). Well?

Solness. Why do you always take that shade off
when I come?

Kaia (as before). I look so ugly with it on.

Solness (smiling). Then you don't like to look
ugly, Kaia?

Kaia (half glancing up at him). Not for all the
world. Not in *your* eyes.

Solness (strokes her hair gently). Poor, poor little
Kaia ——

Kaia (bending her head). Hush — they can
hear you!

*(*SOLNESS *strolls across the room to the right,
turns and pauses at the door of the draftsmen's office.)*

Solness. Has anyone been here for me?

Ragnar (rising). Yes, the young couple who
want a villa built, out at Lövstrand.

Solness (growling). Oh, *those* two! *They* must
wait. I am not quite clear about the plans yet.

Ragnar (advancing, with some hesitation). They
were very anxious to have the drawings at once.

Solness (as before). Yes, of course — so they
all are.

Brovik (looks up). They say they are longing so
to get into a house of their own.

Solness. Yes, yes — we know all *that!* And so
they are content to take whatever is offered them.
They get a — a roof over their heads — an address
— but nothing to call a home. No, thank you!
In that case, let them apply to somebody else.
Tell them *that*, the next time they call.

Brovik (pushes his glasses up on his forehead and

looks in astonishment at him). To somebody else? Are you prepared to give up the commission?

Solness (*impatiently*). Yes, yes, yes, devil take it! If that is to be the way of it ——. Rather that, than build away at random. (*Vehemently.*) Besides, I know very little about these people as yet.

Brovik. The people are safe enough. Ragnar knows them. He is a friend of the family. Perfectly safe people.

Solness. Oh, safe — safe enough! That is not at all what I mean. Good lord — don't *you* understand me either? (*Angrily.*) I won't have anything to do with these strangers. They may apply to whom they please, so far as I am concerned.

Brovik (*rising*). Do you really mean that?

Solness (*sulkily*). Yes, I do. — For once in a way.

(*He comes forward.* BROVIK *exchanges a glance with* RAGNAR, *who makes a warning gesture. Then* BROVIK *comes into the front room.*)

Brovik. May I have a few words with you?

Solness. Certainly.

Brovik (*to* KAIA). Just go in there for a moment, Kaia.

Kaia (*uneasily*). Oh, but uncle ——

Brovik. Do as I say, child. And shut the door after you.

(KAIA *goes reluctantly into the draftsmen's office, glances anxiously and imploringly at* SOLNESS, *and shuts the door.*)

Brovik (*lowering his voice a little*). I don't want the poor children to know how ill I am.

Solness. Yes, you have been looking very poorly of late.

Brovik. It will soon be all over with me. My strength is ebbing — from day to day.

Solness. Won't you sit down?

Brovik. Thanks — may I?

Solness (*placing the armchair more conveniently*). Here — take this chair. — And now?

Brovik (*has seated himself with difficulty*). Well, you see, it's about Ragnar. That is what weighs most upon me. What is to become of him?

Solness. Of course your son will stay with me as long as ever he likes.

Brovik. But that is just what he does not like. He feels that he cannot stay here any longer.

Solness. Why, I should say he was very well off here. But if he wants more money, I should not mind ——

Brovik. No, no! It is not *that*. (*Impatiently.*) But sooner or later he, too, must have a chance of doing something on his own account.

Solness (*without looking at him*). Do you think that Ragnar has quite talent enough to stand alone?

Brovik. No, that is just the heartbreaking part of it — I have begun to have my doubts about the boy. For you have never said so much as — as one encouraging word about him. And yet I cannot but think there must be something in him — he *can't* be without talent.

Solness. Well, but he has learnt nothing — nothing thoroughly, I mean. Except, of course, to draw.

Brovik (*looks at him with covert hatred and says hoarsely*). *You* had learned little enough of the business when you were in my employment. But that did not prevent you from setting to work — (*Breathing with difficulty.*) — and pushing your way up, and taking the wind out of my sails — mine, and so many other people's.

Solness. Yes, you see — circumstances favored me.

Brovik. You are right there. Everything favored you. But then how can you have the heart to let me go to my grave — without having seen what Ragnar is fit for? And of course I am anxious to see them married, too — before I go.

Solness (*sharply*). Is it she who wishes it?

Brovik. Not Kaia so much as Ragnar — he talks about it every day. (*Appealingly.*) You must — you *must* help him to get some independent work now! I *must* see something that the lad has done. Do you hear?

Solness (*peevishly*). Hang it, man, you can't expect me to drag commissions down from the moon for him!

Brovik. He has the chance of a capital commission at this very moment. A big bit of work.

Solness (*uneasily, startled*). Has he?

Brovik. If *you* would give your consent.

Solness. What sort of work do you mean?

Brovik (*with some hesitation*). He can have the building of that villa out at Lövstrand.

Solness. That! Why, I am going to build that myself.

Brovik. Oh, *you* don't much care about doing it.

Solness (*flaring up*). Don't care! I! Who dares to say that?

Brovik. You said so yourself just now.

Solness. Oh, never mind what I *say*. — Would they give Ragnar the building of that villa?

Brovik. Yes. You see, he knows the family. And then — just for the fun of the thing — he has made drawings and estimates and so forth —

Solness. Are they pleased with the drawings? The people who will have to live in the house?

Brovik. Yes. If you would only look through them and approve of them ——

Solness. Then they would let Ragnar build their home for them?

Brovik. They were immensely pleased with his idea. They thought it exceedingly original, they said.

Solness. Oho! Original! Not the old-fashioned stuff that *I* am in the habit of turning out!

Brovik. It seemed to them *different.*

Solness (*with suppressed irritation*). So it was to see Ragnar that they came here — while I was out!

Brovik. They came to call upon you — and at the same time to ask whether you would mind retiring ——

Solness (*angrily*). Retire? I?

Brovik. In case you thought that Ragnar's drawings ——

Solness. I! Retire in favor of your son!

Brovik. Retire from the agreement, they meant.

Solness. Oh, it comes to the same thing. (*Laughs angrily.*) So that is it, is it? Halvard Solness is to see about retiring now! To make room for younger men! For the very youngest, perhaps! He must make room! Room! Room!

Brovik. Why, good heavens! there is surely room for more than one single man ——

Solness. Oh, there's not so *very* much room to spare either. But, be that as it may — I will never retire! I will never give way to anybody! Never of my own free will. Never in this world will I do *that!*

Brovik (*rises with difficulty*). Then I am to pass out of life without any certainty? Without a gleam of happiness? Without any faith or trust in Ragnar? Without having seen a single piece of work of his doing? Is that to be the way of it?

Solness (*turns half aside and mutters*). H'm — don't ask more just now.

Brovik. I must have an answer to this one question. Am I to pass out of life in such utter poverty?

Solness (*seems to struggle with himself; finally he says in a low but firm voice*). You must pass out of life as best you can.

Brovik. Then be it so. (*He goes up the room.*)

Solness (*following him, half in desperation*). Don't you understand that I *cannot* help it? I am what I am, and I cannot change my nature!

Brovik. No, no; I suppose you can't. (*Reels and supports himself against the sofa-table.*) May I have a glass of water?

Solness. By all means. (*Fills a glass and hands it to him.*)

Brovik. Thanks.

(*Drinks and puts the glass down again.* SOLNESS *goes up and opens the door of the draftsmen's office.*)

Solness. Ragnar — you must come and take your father home.

(RAGNAR *rises quickly. He and* KAIA *come into the workroom.*)

Ragnar. What is the matter, father?

Brovik. Give me your arm. Now let us go.

Ragnar. Very well. You had better put your things on too, Kaia.

Solness. Miss Fosli must stay — just for a moment. There is a letter I want written.

Brovik (*looks at* SOLNESS). Good-night. Sleep well — if you can.

Solness. Good-night.

(BROVIK *and* RAGNAR *go out by the hall door.* KAIA *goes to the desk.* SOLNESS *stands with bent head, to the right, by the armchair.*)

Kaia (*dubiously*). Is there any letter ——?

Solness (*curtly*). No, of course not. (*Looks sternly at her.*) Kaia!

Kaia (*anxiously, in a low voice*). Yes!

Solness (*points imperatively to a spot on the floor*). Come here! At once!

Kaia (*hesitatingly*). Yes.

Solness (*as before*). Nearer!

Kaia (*obeying*). What do you want with me?

Solness (*looks at her for a while*). Is it you I have to thank for all this?

Kaia. No, no, don't think that!

Solness. But confess now — you want to get married!

Kaia (*softly*). Ragnar and I have been engaged for four or five years, and so ——

Solness. And so you think it time there were an end of it. Isn't that so?

Kaia. Ragnar and Uncle say I *must.* So I suppose I shall have to give in.

Solness (*more gently*). Kaia, don't you really care a little bit for Ragnar, too?

Kaia. I cared very much for Ragnar once — before I came here to you.

Solness. But you don't now? Not in the least?

Kaia (*passionately, clasping her hands and holding them out towards him*). Oh, you know very well there is only *one* person I care for now! One, and one only, in all the world! I shall never care for anyone else.

Solness. Yes, you say that. And yet you go away from me — leave me alone here with everything on my hands.

Kaia. But could I not stay with you, even if Ragnar ——?

Solness (*repudiating the idea*). No, no, that is quite impossible. If Ragnar leaves me and starts work on his own account, then of course he will need you himself.

Kaia (wringing her hands). Oh, I feel as if I *could* not be separated from you! It's quite, quite impossible!

Solness. Then be sure you get those foolish notions out of Ragnar's head. Marry him as much as you please — (*Alters his tone.*) I mean — don't let him throw up his good situation with me. For then I can keep *you* too, my dear Kaia.

Kaia. Oh, yes, how lovely that would be, if it could only be managed!

Solness (clasps her head with his two hands and whispers). For I cannot get on without you, you see. I must have you with me every single day.

Kaia (in nervous exaltation). My God! My God!

Solness (kisses her hair). Kaia — Kaia!

Kaia (sinks down before him). Oh, how good you are to me! How unspeakably good you are!

Solness (vehemently). Get up! For goodness' sake get up! I think I hear someone!

(*He helps her to rise. She staggers over to the desk.*)

(MRS. SOLNESS *enters by the door on the right. She looks thin and wasted with grief, but shows traces of bygone beauty. Blond ringlets. Dressed with good taste, wholly in black. Speaks somewhat slowly and in a plaintive voice.*)

Mrs. Solness (in the doorway). Halvard!

Solness (turns). Oh, are you there, my dear ——?

Mrs. Solness (with a glance at KAIA). I am afraid I am disturbing you.

Solness. Not in the least. Miss Fosli has only a short letter to write.

Mrs. Solness. Yes, so I see.

Solness. What do you want with me, Aline?

Mrs. Solness. I merely wanted to tell you that Dr. Herdal is in the drawing-room. Won't you come and see him, Halvard?

Solness (looks suspiciously at her). H'm — is the doctor so very anxious to talk to me?

Mrs. Solness. Well, not exactly anxious. He really came to see me; but he would like to say how-do-you-do to you at the same time.

Solness (laughs to himself). Yes, I dare say. Well, you must ask him to wait a little.

Mrs. Solness. Then you will come in presently?

Solness. Perhaps I will. Presently, presently, dear. In a little while.

Mrs. Solness (glancing again at KAIA). Well now, don't forget, Halvard.

(*Withdraws and closes the door behind her.*)

Kaia (softly). Oh, dear, oh, dear — I am sure Mrs. Solness thinks ill of me in some way!

Solness. Oh, not in the least. Not more than usual, at any rate. But all the same, you had better go now, Kaia.

Kaia. Yes, yes, now I *must* go.

Solness (severely). And mind you get that matter settled for me. Do you hear?

Kaia. Oh, if it only depended on *me* ——

Solness. I *will* have it settled, I say! And tomorrow too — not a day later!

Kaia (terrified). If there's nothing else for it, I am quite willing to break off the engagement.

Solness (angrily). Break it off! Are you mad? Would you think of breaking it off?

Kaia (distracted). Yes, if necessary. For I *must* — I *must* stay here with you! I *can't* leave you! That is utterly — utterly impossible!

Solness (with a sudden outburst). But deuce take it — how about Ragnar then! It's Ragnar that I ——

Kaia (looks at him with terrified eyes). It is chiefly on Ragnar's account, that — that you ——?

Solness (collecting himself). No, no, of course not! You don't understand me either. (*Gently and softly.*) Of course it is *you* I want to keep — you above everything, Kaia. But for that very reason, you must prevent Ragnar, too, from throwing up his situation. There, there — now go home.

Kaia. Yes, yes — good-night, then.

Solness. Good-night. (*As she is going.*) Oh, stop a moment! Are Ragnar's drawings in there?

Kaia. I did not see him take them with him.

Solness. Then just go and find them for me. I might perhaps glance over them, after all.

Kaia (happy). Oh, yes, please do!

Solness. For your sake, Kaia dear. Now, let me have them at once, please.

(KAIA *hurries into the draftsmen's office, searches anxiously in the table-drawer, finds a portfolio, and brings it with her.*)

Kaia. Here are all the drawings.

Solness. Good. Put them down there on the table.

Kaia (putting down the portfolio). Good-night, then. (*Beseechingly.*) And please, please think kindly of me.

Solness. Oh, that I always do. Good-night, my dear little Kaia. (*Glances to the right.*) Go, go now!

(MRS. SOLNESS *and* DR. HERDAL *enter by the door on the right. He is a stoutish, elderly man, with a round, good-humored face, clean-shaven, with thin, light hair, and gold spectacles.*)

Mrs. Solness (still in the doorway). Halvard, I cannot keep the doctor any longer.

Solness. Well then, come in here.

Mrs. Solness (to KAIA, *who is turning down the desk-lamp).* Have you finished the letter already, Miss Fosli?

Kaia (*in confusion*). The letter ——?

Solness. Yes, it was quite a short one.

Mrs. Solness. It must have been very short.

Solness. You may go now, Miss Fosli. And please come in good time tomorrow morning.

Kaia. I will be sure to. Good-night, Mrs. Solness. (*She goes out by the hall door.*)

Mrs. Solness. She must be quite an acquisition to you, Halvard, this Miss Fosli.

Solness. Yes, indeed. She is useful in all sorts of ways.

Mrs. Solness. So it seems.

Dr. Herdal. Is she good at bookkeeping too?

Solness. Well — of course she has had a good deal of practice during these two years. And then she is so nice and willing to do whatever one asks of her.

Mrs. Solness. Yes, that must be very delightful ——

Solness. It is. Especially when one is not too much accustomed to that sort of thing.

Mrs. Solness (*in a tone of gentle remonstrance*). Can *you* say that, Halvard?

Solness. Oh, no, no, my dear Aline; I beg your pardon.

Mrs. Solness. There's no occasion. — Well then, Doctor, you will come back later on and have a cup of tea with us?

Dr. Herdal. I have only that one patient to see, and then I'll come back.

Mrs. Solness. Thank you.

(*She goes out by the door on the right.*)

Solness. Are you in a hurry, Doctor?

Dr. Herdal. No, not at all.

Solness. May I have a little chat with you?

Dr. Herdal. With the greatest of pleasure.

Solness. Then let us sit down. (*He motions the* DOCTOR *to take the rocking-chair and sits down himself in the armchair. Looks searchingly at him.*) Tell me — did you notice anything odd about Aline?

Dr. Herdal. Do you mean just now, when she was here?

Solness. Yes, in her manner to me. Did you notice anything?

Dr. Herdal (*smiling*). Well, I admit — one couldn't well avoid noticing that your wife — h'm ——

Solness. Well?

Dr. Herdal. — that your wife is not particularly fond of this Miss Fosli.

Solness. Is that all? I have noticed that myself.

Dr. Herdal. And I must say I am scarcely surprised at it.

Solness. At what?

Dr. Herdal. That she should not exactly approve of your seeing so much of another woman, all day and every day.

Solness. No, no, I suppose you are right there — and Aline too. But it's impossible to make any change.

Dr. Herdal. Could you not engage a clerk?

Solness. The first man that came to hand? No, thank you — that would never do for me.

Dr. Herdal. But now, if your wife ——? Suppose, with her delicate health, all this tries her too much?

Solness. Even then — I might almost say — it can make no difference. I *must* keep Kaia Fosli. No one else could fill her place.

Dr. Herdal. No one else?

Solness (*curtly*). No, no one.

Dr. Herdal (*drawing his chair closer*). Now listen to me, my dear Mr. Solness. May I ask you a question, quite between ourselves?

Solness. By all means.

Dr. Herdal. Women, you see — in certain matters, they have a deucedly keen intuition ——

Solness. They have, indeed. There is not the least doubt of that. But ——?

Dr. Herdal. Well, tell me now — if your wife can't endure this Kaia Fosli ——?

Solness. Well, what then?

Dr. Herdal. — may she not have just — just the least little bit of reason for this instinctive dislike?

Solness (*looks at him and rises*). Oho!

Dr. Herdal. Now don't be offended — but *hasn't* she?

Solness (*with curt decision*). No.

Dr. Herdal. No reason of any sort?

Solness. No other reason than her own suspicious nature.

Dr. Herdal. I know you have known a good many women in your time.

Solness. Yes, I have.

Dr. Herdal. And have been a good deal taken with some of them, too.

Solness. Oh, yes, I don't deny it.

Dr. Herdal. But as regards Miss Fosli, then? There is nothing of that sort in the case?

Solness. No; nothing at all — on *my* side.

Dr. Herdal. But on her side?

Solness. I don't think you have any right to ask that question, Doctor.

Dr. Herdal. Well, you know, we were discussing your wife's intuition.

Solness. So we were. And for that matter — (*Lowers his voice.*) — Aline's intuition, as you call it — in a certain sense, it has not been so far astray.

Dr. Herdal. Aha! there we have it!

Solness (*sits down*). Doctor Herdal — I am

going to tell you a strange story — if you care to listen to it.

Dr. Herdal. I like listening to strange stories.

Solness. Very well then. I dare say you recollect that I took Knut Brovik and his son into my employment — after the old man's business had gone to the dogs.

Dr. Herdal. Yes, so I have understood.

Solness. You see, they really are clever fellows, these two. Each of them has talent in his own way. But then the son took it into his head to get engaged; and the next thing, of course, was that he wanted to get married — and begin to build on his own account. That is the way with all these young people.

Dr. Herdal (laughing). Yes, they have a bad habit of wanting to marry.

Solness. Just so. But of course that did not suit *my* plans; for I needed Ragnar myself — and the old man too. He is exceedingly good at calculating bearing-strains and cubic contents — and all that sort of devilry, you know.

Dr. Herdal. Oh, yes, no doubt that's indispensable.

Solness. Yes, it is. But Ragnar was absolutely bent on setting to work for himself. He would hear of nothing else.

Dr. Herdal. But he has stayed with you all the same.

Solness. Yes, I'll tell you how that came about. One day this girl, Kaia Fosli, came to see them on some errand or other. She had never been here before. And when I saw how utterly infatuated they were with each other, the thought occurred to me: if I could only get her into the office here, then perhaps Ragnar too would stay where he is.

Dr. Herdal. That was not at all a bad idea.

Solness. Yes, but at the time I did not breathe a word of what was in my mind. I merely stood and looked at her — and kept on wishing intently that I could have her here. Then I talked to her a little, in a friendly way — about one thing and another. And then she went away.

Dr. Herdal. Well?

Solness. Well then, next day, pretty late in the evening, when old Brovik and Ragnar had gone home, she came here again, and behaved as if I had made an arrangement with her.

Dr. Herdal. An arrangement? What about?

Solness. About the very thing my mind had been fixed on. But I hadn't said one single word about it.

Dr. Herdal. That was most extraordinary.

Solness. Yes, was it not? And now she wanted to know what she was to do here — whether she could begin the very next morning, and so forth.

Dr. Herdal. Don't you think she did it in order to be with her sweetheart?

Solness. That was what occurred to me at first. But no, that was not it. She seemed to drift quite away from *him* — when once she had come here to me.

Dr. Herdal. She drifted over to you, then?

Solness. Yes, entirely. If I happen to look at her when her back is turned, I can tell that she feels it. She quivers and trembles the moment I come near her. What do you think of *that?*

Dr. Herdal. H'm — that's not very hard to explain.

Solness. Well, but what about the other thing? That she believed I had said to her what I had only wished and willed — silently — inwardly — to myself? What do you say to *that?* Can you explain that, Dr. Herdal?

Dr. Herdal. No, I won't undertake to do that.

Solness. I felt sure you would not; and so I have never cared to talk about it till now. — But it's a cursed nuisance to me in the long run, you understand. Here have I got to go on day after day pretending——. And it's a shame to treat her so, too, poor girl. *(Vehemently.)* But I *cannot* do anything else. For if *she* runs away from me — then Ragnar will be off too.

Dr. Herdal. And you have not told your wife the rights of the story?

Solness. No.

Dr. Herdal. Then why on earth don't you?

Solness (looks fixedly at him and says in a low voice). Because I seem to find a sort of — of salutary self-torture in allowing Aline to do me an injustice.

Dr. Herdal (shakes his head). I don't in the least understand what you mean.

Solness. Well, you see — it is like paying off a little bit of a huge, immeasurable debt ——

Dr. Herdal. To your wife?

Solness. Yes; and that always helps to relieve one's mind a little. One can breathe more freely for a while, you understand.

Dr. Herdal. No, goodness knows, I don't understand at all ——

Solness (breaking off, rises again). Well, well, well — then we won't talk any more about it. *(He saunters across the room, returns, and stops beside the table. Looks at the* DOCTOR *with a sly smile.)* I suppose you think you have drawn me out nicely now, Doctor?

Dr. Herdal (with some irritation). Drawn you out? Again I have not the faintest notion what you mean, Mr. Solness.

Solness. Oh, come, out with it; I have seen it quite clearly, you know.

Dr. Herdal. What have you seen?

Solness (in a low voice, slowly). That you have been quietly keeping an eye upon me.

Dr. Herdal. That *I* have! And why in all the world should I do *that?*

Solness. Because you think that I —— (*Passionately.*) Well, devil take it — you think the same of me as Aline does.

Dr. Herdal. And what does *she* think about you?

Solness (having recovered his self-control). She has begun to think that I am — that I am — ill.

Dr. Herdal. Ill! *You!* She has never hinted such a thing to me. Why, what can she think is the matter with you?

Solness (leans over the back of the chair and whispers). Aline has made up her mind that I am mad. *That* is what she thinks.

Dr. Herdal (rising). Why, my dear good fellow ——!

Solness. Yes, on my soul she does! I tell you it is so. And she has got you to think the same! Oh, I can assure you, Doctor, I see it in your face as clearly as possible. You don't take me in so easily, I can tell you.

Dr. Herdal (looks at him in amazement). Never, Mr. Solness — never has such a thought entered my mind.

Solness (with an incredulous smile). Really? Has it not?

Dr. Herdal. No, never! Nor your wife's mind either, I am convinced. I could almost swear to that.

Solness. Well, I wouldn't advise you to. For, in a certain sense, you see, perhaps — perhaps she is not so far wrong in thinking something of the kind.

Dr. Herdal. Come now, I really must say ——

Solness (interrupting, with a sweep of his hand). Well, well, my dear Doctor — don't let us discuss this any further. We had better agree to differ. (*Changes to a tone of quiet amusement.*) But look here now, Doctor — h'm ——

Dr. Herdal. Well?

Solness. Since you don't believe that I am — ill — and crazy — and mad, and so forth ——

Dr. Herdal. What then?

Solness. Then I dare say you fancy that I am an extremely happy man.

Dr. Herdal. Is *that* mere fancy?

Solness (laughs). No, no — of course not! Heaven forbid! Only think — to be Solness the master builder! Halvard Solness! What could be more delightful?

Dr. Herdal. Yes, I must say it seems to me you have had the luck on your side to an astounding degree.

Solness (suppresses a gloomy smile). So I have. I can't complain on *that* score.

Dr. Herdal. First of all that grim old robbers' castle was burnt down for you. And *that* was certainly a great piece of luck.

Solness (seriously). It was the home of Aline's family. Remember that.

Dr. Herdal. Yes, it must have been a great grief to *her.*

Solness. She has not got over it to this day — not in all these twelve or thirteen years.

Dr. Herdal. Ah, but what followed must have been the worst blow for her.

Solness. The one thing with the other.

Dr. Herdal. But you — yourself — *you* rose upon the ruins. You began as a poor boy from a country village — and now you are at the head of your profession. Ah, yes, Mr. Solness, you have undoubtedly had the luck on your side.

Solness (looking at him with embarrassment). Yes, but that is just what makes me so horribly afraid.

Dr. Herdal. Afraid? Because you have the luck on your side!

Solness. It terrifies me — terrifies me every hour of the day. For sooner or later the luck must turn, you see.

Dr. Herdal. Oh, nonsense! What should make the luck turn?

Solness (with firm assurance). The younger generation.

Dr. Herdal. Pooh! The younger generation! You are not laid on the shelf yet, I should hope. Oh, no — your position here is probably firmer now than it has ever been.

Solness. The luck *will* turn. I know it — I feel the day approaching. Someone or other will take it into his head to say: Give *me* a chance! And then all the rest will come clamoring after him, and shake their fists at me and shout: Make room — make room — make room! Yes, just you see, Doctor — presently the younger generation will come knocking at my door ——

Dr. Herdal (laughing). Well, and what if they do?

Solness. What if they do? Then there's an end of Halvard Solness.

(*There is a knock at the door on the left.*

Solness (starts). What's that? Didn't you hear something?

Dr. Herdal. Someone is knocking at the door.

Solness (loudly). Come in.

(HILDA WANGEL *enters by the hall door. She is of middle height, supple and delicately built; somewhat sunburnt. Dressed in a tourist costume, with skirt caught up for walking, a sailor's collar open at the throat, and a small sailor hat on her head. Knapsack on back, plaid shawl in strap, and alpenstock.)*

Hilda (goes straight up to SOLNESS, *her eyes sparkling with happiness).* Good-evening!

Solness (looks doubtfully at her). Good-evening ——

Hilda (laughs). I almost believe you don't recognize me!

Solness. No — I must admit that — just for the moment ——

Dr. Herdal (approaching). But *I* recognize you, my dear young lady ——

Hilda (pleased). Oh, is it you that ——

Dr. Herdal. Of course it is. *(To* SOLNESS.*)* We met at one of the mountain stations this summer. *(To* HILDA.*)* What became of the other ladies?

Hilda. Oh, *they* went westward.

Dr. Herdal. They didn't much like all the fun we used to have in the evenings.

Hilda. No, I believe they didn't.

Dr. Herdal (holds up his finger at her). And I am afraid it can't be denied that you flirted a little with us.

Hilda. Well, that was better fun than to sit there knitting stockings with all those old women.

Dr. Herdal (laughs). There I entirely agree with you!

Solness. Have you come to town this evening?

Hilda. Yes, I have just arrived.

Dr. Herdal. Quite alone, Miss Wangel?

Hilda. Oh, yes!

Solness. Wangel? Is your name Wangel?

Hilda (looks in amused surprise at him). Yes, of course it is.

Solness. Then you must be a daughter of the district doctor up at Lysanger?

Hilda (as before). Yes, who else's daughter should I be?

Solness. Oh, then I suppose we met up there, that summer when I was building a tower on the old church.

Hilda (more seriously). Yes, of course it was then we met.

Solness. Well, that is a long time ago.

Hilda (looks hard at him). It is exactly the ten years.

Solness. You must have been a mere child then, I should think.

Hilda (carelessly). Well, I was twelve or thirteen.

Dr. Herdal. Is this the first time you have ever been up to town, Miss Wangel?

Hilda. Yes, it is indeed.

Solness. And don't you know anyone here?

Hilda. Nobody but you. And of course, your wife.

Solness. So you know *her*, too?

Hilda. Only a little. We spent a few days together at the sanatorium.

Solness. Ah, up there?

Hilda. She said I might come and pay her a visit if ever I came up to town. *(Smiles.)* Not that that was necessary.

Solness. Odd that she should never have mentioned it.

*(*HILDA *puts her stick down by the stove, takes off the knapsack and lays it and the plaid on the sofa.* DR. HERDAL *offers to help her.* SOLNESS *stands and gazes at her.)*

Hilda (going towards him). Well, now I must ask you to let me stay the night here.

Solness. I am sure there will be no difficulty about that.

Hilda. For I have no other clothes than those I stand in, except a change of linen in my knapsack. And that has to go to the wash, for it's very dirty.

Solness. Oh, yes, that can be managed. Now I'll just let my wife know ——

Dr. Herdal. Meanwhile I will go and see my patient.

Solness. Yes, do; and come again later on.

Dr. Herdal (playfully, with a glance at HILDA*).* Oh, that I will, you may be very certain! *(Laughs.)* So your prediction has come true, Mr. Solness!

Solness. How so?

Dr. Herdal. The younger generation *did* come knocking at your door.

Solness (cheerfully). Yes, but in a very different way from what I meant.

Dr. Herdal. Very different, yes. That's undeniable.

(He goes out by the hall door. SOLNESS *opens the door on the right and speaks into the side room.)*

Solness. Aline! Will you come in here, please. Here is a friend of yours — Miss Wangel.

Mrs. Solness (appears in the doorway). Who do you say it is? *(Sees* HILDA.*)* Oh, is it *you*, Miss Wangel? *(Goes up to her and offers her hand.)* So you have come to town after all.

Solness. Miss Wangel has this moment arrived; and she would like to stay the night here.

Mrs. Solness. Here with us? Oh, yes, certainly.

Solness. Till she can get her things a little in order, you know.

Mrs. Solness. I will do the best I can for you. It's no more than my duty. I suppose your trunk is coming on later?

Hilda. I *have* no trunk.

Mrs. Solness. Well, it will be all right, I dare say. In the meantime, you must excuse my leaving you here with my husband, until I can get a room made a little comfortable for you.

Solness. Can we not give her one of the nurseries? *They* are all ready as it is.

Mrs. Solness. Oh, yes. There we have room and to spare. (*To* HILDA.) Sit down now, and rest a little.

(*She goes out to the right.* HILDA, *with her hands behind her back, strolls about the room and looks at various objects.* SOLNESS *stands in front, beside the table, also with his hands behind his back, and follows her with his eyes.*)

Hilda (*stops and looks at him*). Have you several nurseries?

Solness. There are three nurseries in the house.

Hilda. That's a lot. Then I suppose you have a great many children?

Solness. No. We have no child. But now *you* can be the child here, for the time being.

Hilda. For tonight, yes. I shall not cry. I mean to sleep as sound as a stone.

Solness. Yes, you must be very tired, I should think.

Hilda. Oh, no! But all the same —— It's so delicious to lie and dream.

Solness. Do you dream much of nights?

Hilda. Oh, yes! Almost always.

Solness. What do you dream about most?

Hilda. I shan't tell you tonight. Another time perhaps.

(*She again strolls about the room, stops at the desk, and turns over the books and papers a little.*)

Solness (*approaching*). Are you searching for anything?

Hilda. No, I am merely looking at all these things. (*Turns.*) Perhaps I mustn't?

Solness. Oh, by all means.

Hilda. Is it *you* that write in this great ledger?

Solness. No, it's my bookkeeper.

Hilda. Is it a woman?

Solness (*smiles*). Yes.

Hilda. One you employ here, in your office?

Solness. Yes.

Hilda. Is she married?

Solness. No, she is single.

Hilda. Oh, indeed!

Solness. But I believe she is soon going to be married.

Hilda. That's a good thing for *her.*

Solness. But not such a good thing for *me.* For then I shall have nobody to help me.

Hilda. Can't you get hold of someone else who will do just as well?

Solness. Perhaps *you* would stay here and — and write in the ledger?

Hilda (*measures him with a glance*). Yes, I dare say! No, thank you — nothing of that sort for me.

(*She again strolls across the room and sits down in the rocking-chair.* SOLNESS too goes to the table.)

Hilda (*continuing*). For there must surely be plenty of other things to be done here. (*Looks smilingly at him.*) Don't you think so, too?

Solness. Of course. First of all, I suppose, you want to make a round of the shops, and get yourself up in the height of fashion.

Hilda (*amused*). No, I think I shall let *that* alone!

Solness. Indeed?

Hilda. For you must know I have run through all my money.

Solness (*laughs*). Neither trunk nor money, then!

Hilda. Neither one nor the other. But never mind — it doesn't matter now.

Solness. Come now, I like you for *that.*

Hilda. Only for *that?*

Solness. For that among other things. (*Sits in the armchair.*) Is your father alive still?

Hilda. Yes, father's alive.

Solness. Perhaps you are thinking of studying here?

Hilda. No, that hadn't occurred to me.

Solness. But I suppose you will be staying for some time?

Hilda. That must depend upon circumstances.

(*She sits awhile rocking herself and looking at him, half seriously, half with a suppressed smile. Then she takes off her hat and puts it on the table in front of her.*)

Hilda. Mr. Solness!

Solness. Well?

Hilda. Have you a very bad memory?

Solness. A bad memory? No, not that I am aware of.

Hilda. Then have you nothing to say to me about what happened up there?

Solness (*in momentary surprise*). Up at Lysanger? (*Indifferently.*) Why, it was nothing much to talk about, it seems to me.

Hilda (*looks reproachfully at him*). How can you sit there and say such things?

Solness. Well, then, *you* talk to *me* about it.

Hilda. When the tower was finished, we had grand doings in the town.

Solness. Yes, I shall not easily forget that day.

Hilda (*smiles*). Will you not? That comes well from *you*.

Solness. Comes well?

Hilda. There was music in the churchyard — and many, many hundreds of people. We school-girls were dressed in white; and we all carried flags.

Solness. Ah, yes, those flags — I can tell you I remember *them!*

Hilda. Then you climbed right up the scaffolding, straight to the very top; and you had a great wreath with you; and you hung that wreath right away up on the weathervane.

Solness (*curtly interrupting*). I always did that in those days. It is an old custom.

Hilda. It was so wonderfully thrilling to stand below and look up at you. Fancy, if he should fall over! He — the master builder himself!

Solness (*as if to divert her from the subject*). Yes, yes, yes, that might very well have happened, too. For one of those white-frocked little devils — she went on in such a way, and screamed up at me so ——

Hilda (*sparkling with pleasure*). "Hurrah for Master Builder Solness!" Yes!

Solness. — and waved and flourished with her flag, so that I — so that it almost made me giddy to look at it.

Hilda (*in a lower voice, seriously*). That little devil — that was *I.*

Solness (*fixes his eyes steadily upon her*). I am sure of that now. It *must* have been you.

Hilda (*lively again*). Oh, it was so gloriously thrilling! I could not have believed there was a builder in the whole world that could build such a tremendously high tower. And then, that you yourself should stand at the very top of it, as large as life! And that you should not be the least bit dizzy! It was *that* above everything that made one — made one dizzy to think of.

Solness. How could you be so certain that I was not ——?

Hilda (*scouting the idea*). No, indeed! Oh, no! I knew that instinctively. For if you had been, you could never have stood up there and sung.

Solness (*looks at her in astonishment*). Sung? Did *I* sing?

Hilda. Yes, I should think you did.

Solness (*shakes his head*). I have never sung a note in my life.

Hilda. Yes, indeed, you sang then. It sounded like harps in the air.

Solness (*thoughtfully*). This is very strange — all this.

Hilda (*is silent awhile, looks at him and says in a low voice*). But then — it was after that — that the *real* thing happened.

Solness. The real thing?

Hilda (*sparkling with vivacity*). Yes, I surely don't need to remind you of *that?*

Solness. Oh, yes, do remind me a little of *that*, too.

Hilda. Don't you remember that a great dinner was given in your honor at the Club?

Solness. Yes, to be sure. It must have been the same afternoon, for I left the place next morning.

Hilda. And from the Club you were invited to come round to our house to supper.

Solness. Quite right, Miss Wangel. It is wonderful how all these trifles have impressed themselves on your mind.

Hilda. Trifles! I like that! Perhaps it was a trifle, too, that I was *alone* in the room when you came in?

Solness. Were you alone?

Hilda (*without answering him*). You didn't call me a little devil *then?*

Solness. No, I suppose I did not.

Hilda. You said I was lovely in my white dress, and that I looked like a little princess.

Solness. I have no doubt you did, Miss Wangel. — And besides — I was feeling so buoyant and free that day ——

Hilda. And then you said that when I grew up I should be *your* princess.

Solness (*laughing a little*). Dear, dear — did I say *that* too?

Hilda. Yes, you did. And when I asked how long I should have to wait, you said that you would come again in ten years — like a troll — and carry me off — to Spain or some such place. And you promised you would buy me a kingdom there.

Solness (*as before*). Yes, after a good dinner one doesn't haggle about the halfpence. But did I really *say* all that?

Hilda (*laughs to herself*). Yes. And you told me, too, what the kingdom was to be called.

Solness. Well, what was it?

Hilda. It was to be called the kingdom of Orangia, you said.

Solness. Well, that was an appetizing name.

Hilda. No, I didn't like it a bit; for it seemed as though you wanted to make game of me.

Solness. I am sure *that* cannot have been my intention.

Hilda. No, I should hope not — considering what you did next ——

Solness. What in the world did I do next?

Hilda. Well, that's the finishing touch, if you have forgotten *that* too. I should have thought no one could help remembering such a thing as that.

Solness. Yes, yes, just give me a hint, and then perhaps —— Well?

Hilda (looks fixedly at him). You came and kissed me, Mr. Solness.

Solness (open-mouthed, rising from his chair). I did!

Hilda. Yes, indeed you did. You took me in both your arms, and bent my head back, and kissed me — many times.

Solness. Now really, my dear Miss Wangel ——!

Hilda (rises). You surely cannot mean to deny it?

Solness. Yes, I do. I deny it altogether!

Hilda (looks scornfully at him). Oh, indeed!

(*She turns and goes slowly close up to the stove, where she remains standing motionless, her face averted from him, her hands behind her back. Short pause.*)

Solness (goes cautiously up behind her). Miss Wangel ——!

Hilda (is silent and does not move).

Solness. Don't stand there like a statue. You must have dreamt all this. (*Lays his hand on her arm.*) Now just listen ——

Hilda (makes an impatient movement with her arm).

Solness (as a thought flashes upon him). Or ——! Wait a moment! There is something under all this, you may depend!

Hilda (does not move).

Solness (in a low voice, but with emphasis). I must have *thought* all that. I must have *wished* it — have *willed* it — have *longed* to do it. And then —— May not that be the explanation?

Hilda (is still silent).

Solness (impatiently). Oh, very well, deuce take it all — then I *did* do it, I suppose.

Hilda (turns her head a little, but without looking at him). Then you admit it now?

Solness. Yes — whatever you like.

Hilda. You came and put your arms round me?

Solness. Oh, yes!

Hilda. And bent my head back?

Solness. Very far back.

Hilda. And kissed me?

Solness. Yes, I did.

Hilda. Many times?

Solness. As many as ever you like.

Hilda (turns quickly towards him and has once more the sparkling expression of gladness in her eyes). Well, you see, I got it out of you at last!

Solness (with a slight smile). Yes — just think of my forgetting such a thing as that.

Hilda (again a little sulky, retreats from him). Oh, you have kissed so many people in your time, I suppose.

Solness. No, you mustn't think *that* of me. (HILDA *seats herself in the armchair.* SOLNESS *stands and leans against the rocking-chair. Looks observantly at her.*) Miss Wangel!

Hilda. Yes!

Solness. How *was* it now? What came of all this — between us two?

Hilda. Why, nothing more came of it. You know that quite well. For then the other guests came in, and then — bah!

Solness. Quite so! The others came in. To think of my forgetting *that* too!

Hilda. Oh, you haven't really forgotten anything: you are only a little ashamed of it all. I am sure one doesn't forget things of that kind.

Solness. No, one would suppose not.

Hilda (lively again, looks at him). Perhaps you have even forgotten what day it was?

Solness. What day ——?

Hilda. Yes, on what day did you hang the wreath on the tower? Well? Tell me at once!

Solness. H'm — I confess I have forgotten the particular day. I only know it was ten years ago. Sometime in the autumn.

Hilda (nods her head slowly several times). It was ten years ago — on the nineteenth of September.

Solness. Yes, it must have been about that time. Fancy your remembering that too! (*Stops.*) But wait a moment ——! Yes — it's the nineteenth of September today.

Hilda. Yes, it is; and the ten years are gone. And you didn't come — as you had promised me.

Solness. Promised you? Threatened, I suppose you mean?

Hilda. I don't think there was any sort of threat in *that*.

Solness. Well, then a little bit of fun.

Hilda. Was *that* all you wanted? To make fun of me?

Solness. Well, or to have a little joke with you. Upon my soul, I don't recollect. But it must have been something of that kind; for you were a mere child then.

Hilda. Oh, perhaps I wasn't quite such a child either. Not such a mere chit as you imagine.

Solness (looks searchingly at her). Did you really and seriously expect me to come again?

Hilda (conceals a half-teasing smile). Yes, indeed! I did expect *that* of you.

Solness. That I should come back to your home, and take you away with me?

Hilda. Just like a troll — yes.

Solness. And make a princess of you?

Hilda. That's what you promised.

Solness. And give you a kingdom as well?

Hilda (*looks up at the ceiling*). Why not? Of course it need not have been an actual, everyday sort of kingdom.

Solness. But something else just as good?

Hilda. Yes, at least as good. (*Looks at him a moment.*) I thought, if you could build the highest church-towers in the world, you could surely manage to raise a kingdom of one sort or another as well.

Solness (*shakes his head*). I can't quite make you out, Miss Wangel.

Hilda. Can you not? To me it seems all so simple.

Solness. No, I can't make up my mind whether you mean all you say, or are simply having a joke with me.

Hilda (*smiles*). Making fun of you, perhaps? I, too?

Solness. Yes, exactly. Making fun — of both of us. (*Looks at her.*) Is it long since you found out that I was married?

Hilda. I have known it all along. Why do you ask me *that?*

Solness (*lightly*). Oh, well, it just occurred to me. (*Looks earnestly at her and says in a low voice.*) What have you come for?

Hilda. I want my kingdom. The time is up.

Solness (*laughs involuntarily*). What a girl you are!

Hilda (*gayly*). Out with my kingdom, Mr. Solness! (*Raps with her fingers.*) The kingdom on the table!

Solness (*pushing the rocking-chair nearer and sitting down*). Now, seriously speaking — what have you come for? What do you really want to do here?

Hilda. Oh, first of all, I want to go round and look at all the things that you have built.

Solness. That will give you plenty of exercise.

Hilda. Yes, I know you have built a tremendous lot.

Solness. I have indeed — especially of late years.

Hilda. Many church-towers among the rest? Immensely high ones?

Solness. No. I build no more church-towers now. Nor churches either.

Hilda. What *do* you build then?

Solness. Homes for human beings.

Hilda (*reflectively*). Couldn't you build a little — a little bit of a church-tower over these homes as well?

Solness (*starting*). What do you mean by *that?*

Hilda. I mean — something that points — points up into the free air. With the vane at a dizzy height.

Solness (*pondering a little*). Strange that you should say *that* — for that is just what I am most anxious to do.

Hilda (*impatiently*). Why don't you do it, then?

Solness (*shakes his head*). No, the people will not have it.

Hilda. Fancy their not wanting it!

Solness (*more lightly*). But now I am building a new home for myself — just opposite here.

Hilda. For yourself?

Solness. Yes. It is almost finished. And on that there is a tower.

Hilda. A high tower?

Solness. Yes.

Hilda. Very high?

Solness. No doubt people will say it is *too* high — too high for a dwelling-house.

Hilda. I'll go out and look at that tower the first thing tomorrow morning.

Solness (*sits resting his cheek on his hand and gazes at her*). Tell me, Miss Wangel — what is your name? Your Christian name, I mean?

Hilda. Why, Hilda, of course.

Solness (*as before*). Hilda? Indeed?

Hilda. Don't you remember *that?* You called me Hilda yourself — that day when you misbehaved.

Solness. Did I really?

Hilda. But then you said "*little* Hilda"; and I didn't like that.

Solness. Oh, you didn't like that, Miss Hilda?

Hilda. No, not at such a time as that. But — "Princess Hilda" — that will sound very well, I think.

Solness. Very well indeed. Princess Hilda of — of — what was to be the name of the kingdom?

Hilda. Pooh! I won't have anything to do with *that* stupid kingdom. I have set my heart upon quite a different one!

Solness (*has leaned back in the chair, still gazing at her*). Isn't it strange ——? The more I think of it now, the more it seems to me as though I had gone about all these years torturing myself with — h'm ——

Hilda. With what?

Solness. With the effort to recover something — some experience, which I seemed to have forgotten. But I never had the least inkling of what it could be.

Hilda. You should have tied a knot in your pocket-handkerchief, Mr. Solness.

Solness. In that case, I should simply have had to go racking my brains to discover what the knot could mean.

Hilda. Oh, yes, I suppose there are trolls of *that* kind in the world, too.

Solness (*rises slowly*). What a good thing it is that *you* have come to me now.

Hilda (*looks deeply into his eyes*). *Is* it a good thing!

Solness. For I have been so lonely here. I have been gazing so helplessly at it all. (*In a lower voice.*) I must tell you — I have begun to be so afraid — so terribly afraid of the younger generation.

Hilda (*with a little snort of contempt*). Pooh — is the younger generation a thing to be afraid of?

Solness. It is indeed. And that is why I have locked and barred myself in. (*Mysteriously.*) I tell you the younger generation will one day come and thunder at my door! They will break in upon me!

Hilda. Then I should say you ought to go out and open the door to the younger generation.

Solness. Open the door?

Hilda. Yes. Let them come in to you on friendly terms, as it were.

Solness. No, no, no! The younger generation — it means retribution, you see. It comes, as if under a new banner, heralding the turn of fortune.

Hilda (*rises, looks at him, and says with a quivering twitch of her lips*). Can *I* be of any use to you, Mr. Solness?

Solness. Yes, you can indeed! For you, too, come — under a new banner, it seems to me. Youth marshaled against youth ——!

(DR. HERDAL *comes in by the hall door.*)

Dr. Herdal. What — you and Miss Wangel here still?

Solness. Yes. We have had no end of things to talk about.

Hilda. Both old and new.

Dr. Herdal. Have you really?

Hilda. Oh, it has been the greatest fun! For Mr. Solness — he has such a miraculous memory. All the least little details he remembers instantly.

(MRS. SOLNESS *enters by the door on the right.*)

Mrs. Solness. Well, Miss Wangel, your room is quite ready for you now.

Hilda. Oh, how kind you are to me!

Solness (*to* MRS. SOLNESS). The nursery?

Mrs. Solness. Yes, the middle one. But first let us go in to supper.

Solness (*nods to* HILDA). Hilda shall sleep in the nursery, she shall.

Mrs. Solness (*looks at him*). Hilda?

Solness. Yes, Miss Wangel's name is Hilda. I knew her when she was a child.

Mrs. Solness. Did you really, Halvard? Well, shall we go? Supper is on the table.

(*She takes* DR. HERDAL'S *arm and goes out with him to the right.* HILDA *has meanwhile been collecting her traveling things.*)

Hilda (*softly and rapidly to* SOLNESS). Is it true what you said? Can I be of use to you?

Solness (*takes the things from her*). *You* are the very being I have needed most.

Hilda (*looks at him with happy, wondering eyes and clasps her hands*). But then, great heavens ——!

Solness (*eagerly*). What ——?

Hilda. Then I *have* my kingdom!

Solness (*involuntarily*). Hilda ——!

Hilda (*again with the quivering twitch of her lips*). Almost — I was going to say.

(*She goes out to the right;* SOLNESS *follows her.*)

CURTAIN

ACT TWO

A prettily furnished small drawing-room in SOL-NESS'S *house. In the back, a glass door leading out to the veranda and garden. The right-hand corner is cut off transversely by a large bay-window, in which are flower-stands. The left-hand corner is similarly cut off by a transverse wall, in which is a small door papered like the wall. On each side, an ordinary door. In front, on the right, a console table with a large mirror over it. Well-filled stands of plants and flowers. In front, on the left, a sofa with a table and chairs. Farther back, a bookcase. Well forward in the room, before the bay-window, a small table and some chairs. It is early in the day.*

SOLNESS *sits by the little table with* RAGNAR BROVIK'S *portfolio open in front of him. He is turning the drawings over and closely examining some of them.* MRS. SOLNESS *moves about noiselessly with a small watering-pot, attending to her flowers. She is dressed in black as before. Her hat, cloak, and parasol lie on a chair near the mirror. Unobserved by her,* SOLNESS *now and again follows her with his eyes. Neither of them speaks.*

(KAIA FOSLI *enters quietly by the door on the left.*)

Solness (*turns his head and says in an offhand tone of indifference*). Well, is that you?

Kaia. I merely wished to let you know that I have come.

Solness. Yes, yes, that's all right. Hasn't Ragnar come too?

Kaia. No, not yet. He had to wait a little while to see the doctor. But he is coming presently to hear ——

Solness. How is the old man today?

Kaia. Not well. He begs you to excuse him; he is obliged to keep his bed today.

Solness. Why, of course; by all means let him rest. But now, get to your work.

Kaia. Yes. (*Pauses at the door.*) Do you wish to speak to Ragnar when he comes?

Solness. No — I don't know that I have anything particular to say to him.

> (KAIA *goes out again to the left.* SOLNESS *remains seated, turning over the drawings.*)

Mrs. Solness (*over beside the plants*). I wonder if *he* isn't going to die now, as well?

Solness (*looks up at her*). As well as who?

Mrs. Solness (*without answering*). Yes, yes — depend upon it, Halvard, old Brovik is going to die too. You'll see that he will.

Solness. My dear Aline, shouldn't you go out for a little walk?

Mrs. Solness. Yes, I suppose I ought to.

> (*She continues to attend to the flowers.*)

Solness (*bending over the drawings*). Is she still asleep?

Mrs. Solness (*looking at him*). Is it Miss Wangel you are sitting there thinking about?

Solness (*indifferently*). I just happened to recollect her.

Mrs. Solness. Miss Wangel was up long ago.

Solness. Oh, was she?

Mrs. Solness. When I went in to see her, she was busy putting her things in order.

> (*She goes in front of the mirror and slowly begins to put on her hat.*)

Solness (*after a short pause*). So we have found a use for one of our nurseries after all, Aline.

Mrs. Solness. Yes, we have.

Solness. That seems to me better than to have them all standing empty.

Mrs. Solness. That emptiness is dreadful; you are right there.

Solness (*closes the portfolio, rises, and approaches her*). You will find that we shall get on far better after this, Aline. Things will be more comfortable. Life will be easier — especially for *you.*

Mrs. Solness (*looks at him*). After this?

Solness. Yes, believe me, Aline ——

Mrs. Solness. Do you mean — because *she* has come here?

Solness (*checking himself*). I mean, of course — when once we have moved into the new house.

Mrs. Solness (*takes her cloak*). Ah, do you think so, Halvard? Will it be better then?

Solness. I can't think otherwise. And surely you think so too?

Mrs. Solness. I think nothing at all about the new house.

Solness (*cast down*). It's hard for me to hear you say that; for you know it is mainly for your sake that I have built it. (*He offers to help her on with her cloak.*)

Mrs. Solness (*evades him*). The fact is, you do far too much for my sake.

Solness (*with a certain vehemence*). No, no, you really mustn't say that, Aline! I cannot bear to hear you say such things!

Mrs. Solness. Very well, then I won't say it Halvard.

Solness. But I stick to what *I* said. You'll see that things will be easier for you in the new place.

Mrs. Solness. Oh, heavens — easier for me ——!

Solness (*eagerly*). Yes, indeed they will! You may be quite sure of that! For you see — there will be so very, very much *there* that will remind you of your own home ——

Mrs. Solness. The home that used to be father's and mother's — and that was burnt to the ground ——

Solness (*in a low voice*). Yes, yes, my poor Aline. That was a terrible blow for you.

Mrs. Solness (*breaking out in lamentation*). You may build as much as ever you like, Halvard — you can never build up again a real home for *me!*

Solness (*crosses the room*). Well, in Heaven's name, let us talk no more about it then.

Mrs. Solness. We are not in the habit of talking about it. For you always put the thought away from you ——

Solness (*stops suddenly and looks at her*). Do I? And why should I do *that?* Put the thought away from me?

Mrs. Solness. Oh, yes, Halvard, I understand you very well. You are so anxious to spare me — and to find excuses for me too — as much as ever you can.

Solness (*with astonishment in his eyes*). *You!* Is it *you* — yourself, that you are talking about, Aline?

Mrs. Solness. Yes, who else should it be but myself?

Solness (*involuntarily to himself*). *That* too!

Mrs. Solness. As for the old house, I wouldn't mind so much about that. When once misfortune was in the air — why ——

Solness. Ah, you are right there. Misfortune will have its way — as the saying goes.

Mrs. Solness. But it's what came of the fire — the dreadful thing that followed ——! *That* is the thing! That, that, that!

Solness (*vehemently*). Don't think about that, Aline!

Mrs. Solness. Ah, that is exactly what I cannot

help thinking about. And now, at last, I must speak about it, too; for I don't seem able to bear it any longer. And then never to be able to forgive myself ——

Solness (*exclaiming*). Yourself ——!

Mrs. Solness. Yes, for I had duties on both sides — both towards you and towards the little ones. I ought to have hardened myself — not to have let the horror take such hold upon me — nor the grief for the burning of my home. (*Wrings her hands.*) Oh, Halvard, if I had only had the strength!

Solness (*softly, much moved, comes closer*). Aline — you must promise me never to think these thoughts any more. — Promise me that, dear!

Mrs. Solness. Oh, promise, promise! One can promise anything.

Solness (*clenches his hands and crosses the room*). Oh, but this is hopeless, hopeless! Never a ray of sunlight! Not so much as a gleam of brightness to light up our home!

Mrs. Solness. This is no home, Halvard.

Solness. Oh, no, you may well say that. (*Gloomily*). And God knows whether you are not right in saying that it will be no better for us in the new house, either.

Mrs. Solness. It will never be any better. Just as empty — just as desolate — there as here.

Solness (*vehemently*). Why in all the world have we built it then? Can you tell me that?

Mrs. Solness. No; you must answer that question for yourself.

Solness (*glances suspiciously at her*). What do you mean by *that*, Aline?

Mrs. Solness. What do I mean?

Solness. Yes, in the devil's name! You said it so strangely — as if you had some hidden meaning in it.

Mrs. Solness. No, indeed, I assure you ——

Solness (*comes closer*). Oh, come now — I know what I know. I have both my eyes and my ears about me, Aline — you may depend upon that!

Mrs. Solness. Why, what are you talking about? What is it?

Solness (*places himself in front of her*). Do you mean to say you don't find a kind of lurking, hidden meaning in the most innocent word I happen to say?

Mrs. Solness. *I*, do you say? *I* do that?

Solness (*laughs*). Ho-ho-ho! It's natural enough, Aline! When you have a sick man on your hands ——

Mrs. Solness (*anxiously*). Sick? Are you ill, Halvard?

Solness (*violently*). A half-mad man then! A crazy man! Call me what you will.

Mrs. Solness (*feels blindly for a chair and sits down*). Halvard — for God's sake ——

Solness. But you are wrong, both you and the Doctor. I am not in the state you imagine.

(*He walks up and down the room.* MRS. SOLNESS *follows him anxiously with her eyes. Finally he goes up to her.*)

Solness (*calmly*). In reality there is nothing whatever the matter with me.

Mrs. Solness. No, there isn't, is there? But then what is it that troubles you so?

Solness. Why *this*, that I often feel ready to sink under this terrible burden of debt ——

Mrs. Solness. Debt, do you say? But you owe no one anything, Halvard!

Solness (*softly, with emotion*). I owe a boundless debt to you — to you — to you, Aline.

Mrs. Solness (*rises slowly*). What is behind all this? You may just as well tell me at once.

Solness. But there *is* nothing behind it! I have never done you any wrong — not wittingly and willfully, at any rate. And yet — and yet it seems as though a crushing debt rested upon me and weighed me down.

Mrs. Solness. A debt to me?

Solness. Chiefly to you.

Mrs. Solness. Then you are — ill after all, Halvard.

Solness (*gloomily*). I suppose I must be — or not far from it. (*Looks towards the door to the right, which is opened at this moment.*) Ah! now it grows lighter.

(HILDA WANGEL *comes in. She has made some alteration in her dress and let down her skirt.*)

Hilda. Good morning, Mr. Solness!

Solness (*nods*). Slept well?

Hilda. Quite deliciously! Like a child in a cradle. Oh — I lay and stretched myself like — like a princess!

Solness (*smiles a little*). You were thoroughly comfortable then?

Hilda. I should think so.

Solness. And no doubt you dreamed, too.

Hilda. Yes, I did. But *that* was horrid.

Solness. Was it?

Hilda. Yes, for I dreamed I was falling over a frightfully high, sheer precipice. Do you never have that kind of dream?

Solness. Oh, yes — now and then ——

Hilda. It's tremendously thrilling — when you fall and fall ——

Solness. It seems to make one's blood run cold.

Hilda. Do you draw your legs up under you while you are falling?

Solness. Yes, as high as ever I can.

Hilda. So do I.

Mrs. Solness (*takes her parasol*). I must go into town now, Halvard. (*To* HILDA.) And I'll try to get one or two things that you may require.

Hilda (*making a motion to throw her arms round her neck*). Oh, you dear, sweet Mrs. Solness! You are really much too kind to me! Frightfully kind ——

Mrs. Solness (*deprecatingly, freeing herself*). Oh, not at all. It's only my duty, so I am very glad to do it.

Hilda (*offended, pouts*). But really, I think I am quite fit to be seen in the streets — now that I've put my dress to rights. Or do you think I am not?

Mrs. Solness. To tell you the truth, I think people would stare at you a little.

Hilda (*contemptuously*). Pooh! Is that all? That only amuses me.

Solness (*with suppressed ill-humor*). Yes, but people might take it into their heads that *you* were mad too, you see.

Hilda. Mad? Are there so many mad people here in town, then?

Solness (*points to his own forehead*). Here you see *one* at all events.

Hilda. You — Mr. Solness!

Mrs. Solness. Oh, don't talk like that, my dear Halvard!

Solness. Have you not noticed *that* yet?

Hilda. No, I certainly have not. (*Reflects and laughs a little.*) And yet — perhaps in one single thing.

Solness. Ah, do you hear *that*, Aline?

Mrs. Solness. What is that one single thing, Miss Wangel?

Hilda. No, I won't say.

Solness. Oh, yes, do!

Hilda. No, thank you — I am not so mad as that.

Mrs. Solness. When you and Miss Wangel are alone, I dare say she will tell you, Halvard.

Solness. Ah — you think she will?

Mrs. Solness. Oh, yes, certainly. For you have known her so well in the past. Ever since she was a child — you tell me.

(*She goes out by the door on the left.*)

Hilda (*after a little while*). Does your wife dislike me very much?

Solness. Did you think you noticed anything of the kind?

Hilda. Did you not notice it yourself?

Solness (*evasively*). Aline has become exceedingly shy with strangers of late years.

Hilda. Has she really?

Solness. But if only you could get to know her

thoroughly ——! Ah, she is so good — so kind — so excellent a creature ——

Hilda (*impatiently*). But if she is all that — what made her say that about her duty?

Solness. Her duty?

Hilda. She said that she would go out and buy something for me, because it was her *duty.* Oh, I can't bear that ugly, horrid word!

Solness. Why not?

Hilda. It sounds so cold, and sharp, and stinging. Duty — duty — duty. Don't you think so, too? Doesn't it seem to sting you?

Solness. H'm — haven't thought much about it.

Hilda. Yes, it does. And if she is so good — as you say she is — why should she talk in that way?

Solness. But, good Lord, what would you have had her say, then?

Hilda. She might have said she would do it because she had taken a tremendous fancy to me. She might have said something like that — something really warm and cordial, you understand.

Solness (*looks at her*). Is that how you would like to have it?

Hilda. Yes, precisely. (*She wanders about the room, stops at the bookcase and looks at the books.*) What a lot of books you have.

Solness. Yes, I have got together a good many.

Hilda. Do you read them all, too?

Solness. I used to try to. Do you read much?

Hilda. No, never! I have given it up. For it all seems so irrelevant.

Solness. That is just my feeling.

(HILDA *wanders about a little, stops at the small table, opens the portfolio, and turns over the contents.*)

Hilda. Are all these drawings yours?

Solness. No, they are drawn by a young man whom I employ to help me.

Hilda. Someone you have taught?

Solness. Oh, yes, no doubt he has learnt something from *me*, too.

Hilda (*sits down*). Then I suppose he is very clever. (*Looks at a drawing.*) Isn't he?

Solness. Oh, he might be worse. For *my* purpose ——

Hilda. Oh, yes — I'm sure he is frightfully clever.

Solness. Do you think you can see that in the drawings?

Hilda. Pooh — these scrawlings! But if he has been learning from *you* ——

Solness. Oh, so far as that goes — there are plenty of people here that have learnt from *me*, and have come to little enough for all that.

Hilda (*looks at him and shakes her head*). No,

I can't for the life of me understand how you can be so stupid.

Solness. Stupid? Do you think I am so very stupid?

Hilda. Yes, I do indeed. If you are content to go about here teaching all these people ——

Solness (with a slight start). Well, and why not?

Hilda (rises, half serious, half laughing). No indeed, Mr. Solness! What can be the good of that? No one but *you* should be allowed to build. You should stand quite alone — do it all yourself. Now you know it.

Solness (involuntarily). Hilda ——

Hilda. Well!

Solness. How in the world did *that* come into your head?

Hilda. Do you think I am so very far wrong then?

Solness. No, that's not what I mean. But now I'll tell you something.

Hilda. Well?

Solness. I keep on — incessantly — in silence and alone — brooding on that very thought.

Hilda. Yes, that seems to me perfectly natural.

Solness (looks somewhat searchingly at her). Perhaps you have noticed it already?

Hilda. No, indeed I haven't.

Solness. But just now — when you said you thought I was — off my balance? In one thing, you said ——

Hilda. Oh, I was thinking of something quite different.

Solness. What was it?

Hilda. I am not going to tell you.

Solness (crosses the room). Well, well — as you please. (*Stops at the bay-window.*) Come here, and I will show you something.

Hilda (approaching). What is it?

Solness. Do you see — over there in the garden ——?

Hilda. Yes?

Solness (points). Right above the great quarry ——?

Hilda. That new house, you mean?

Solness. The one that is being built, yes. Almost finished.

Hilda. It seems to have a very high tower.

Solness. The scaffolding is still up.

Hilda. Is that your new house?

Solness. Yes.

Hilda. The house you are soon going to move into?

Solness. Yes.

Hilda (looks at him). Are there nurseries in *that* house, too?

Solness. Three, as there are here.

Hilda. And no child.

Solness. And there never will be one.

Hilda (with a half-smile). Well, isn't it just as I said ——?

Solness. That ——?

Hilda. That you *are* a little — a little mad after all.

Solness. Was that what you were thinking of?

Hilda. Yes, of all the empty nurseries I slept in.

Solness (lowers his voice). We *have* had children — Aline and I.

Hilda (looks eagerly at him). Have you ——?

Solness. Two little boys. They were of the same age.

Hilda. Twins, then.

Solness. Yes, twins. It's eleven or twelve years ago now.

Hilda (cautiously). And so both of them ——? You have lost both the twins, then?

Solness (with quiet emotion). We kept them only about three weeks. Or scarcely so much. (*Bursts forth.*) Oh, Hilda, I can't tell you what a good thing it is for me that you have come! For now at last I have someone I can talk to!

Hilda. Can you not talk to — her, too?

Solness. Not about this. Not as I want to talk and must talk. (*Gloomily.*) And not about so many other things, either.

Hilda (in a subdued voice). Was that all you meant when you said you needed me?

Solness. That was mainly what I meant — at all events, yesterday. For today I am not so sure — (*Breaking off.*) Come here and let us sit down, Hilda. Sit there on the sofa — so that you can look into the garden. (HILDA *seats herself in the corner of the sofa.* SOLNESS *brings a chair closer.*) Should you like to hear about it?

Hilda. Yes, I shall love to sit and listen to you.

Solness (sits down). Then I will tell you all about it.

Hilda. Now I can see both the garden and you, Mr. Solness. So now, tell away! Begin!

Solness (points towards the bay-window). Out there on the rising ground — where you see the new house ——

Hilda. Yes?

Solness. Aline and I lived there in the first years of our married life. There was an old house up there that had belonged to her mother; and we inherited it, and the whole of the great garden with it.

Hilda. Was there a tower on *that* house, too?

Solness. No, nothing of the kind. From the outside it looked like a great, dark, ugly wooden box; but all the same, it was snug and comfortable enough inside.

Hilda. Then did you pull down the ramshackle old place?

Solness. No, it was burnt down.

Hilda. The whole of it?

Solness. Yes.

Hilda. Was that a great misfortune for you?

Solness. That depends on how you look at it. As a builder, the fire was the making of me ——

Hilda. Well, but ——?

Solness. It was just after the birth of the two little boys ——

Hilda. The poor little twins, yes.

Solness. They came into the world healthy and bonny. And they were growing too — you could see the difference from day to day.

Hilda. Little children do grow quickly at first.

Solness. It was the prettiest sight in the world to see Aline lying with the two of them in her arms. — But then came the night of the fire ——

Hilda (excitedly). What happened? Do tell me! Was anyone burnt?

Solness. No, not that. Everyone got safe and sound out of the house ——

Hilda. Well, and what then ——?

Solness. The fright had shaken Aline terribly. The alarm — the escape — the break-neck hurry — and then the ice-cold night air — for they had to be carried out just as they lay — both she and the little ones.

Hilda. Was it too much for them?

Solness. Oh, no, *they* stood it well enough. But Aline fell into a fever, and it affected her milk. She would insist on nursing them herself; because it was her duty, she said. And both our little boys, they — (*clenching his hands*) — they — oh!

Hilda. They did not get over *that*?

Solness. No, *that* they did not get over. *That* was how we lost them.

Hilda. It must have been terribly hard for you.

Solness. Hard enough for me; but ten times harder for Aline. (*Clenching his hands in suppressed fury.*) Oh, that such things should be allowed to happen here in the world! (*Shortly and firmly.*) From the day I lost them I had no heart for building churches.

Hilda. Did you not like the church-tower in our town?

Solness. I didn't like it. I know how free and happy I felt when that tower was finished.

Hilda. I know that, too.

Solness. And now I shall never — never build anything of that sort again! Neither churches nor church-towers.

Hilda (nods slowly). Nothing but houses for people to live in.

Solness. Homes for human beings, Hilda.

Hilda. But homes with high towers and pinnacles upon them.

Solness. If possible. (*Adopts a lighter tone.*) But, as I said before, that fire was the making of me — as a builder, I mean.

Hilda. Why don't you call yourself an architect, like the others?

Solness. I have not been systematically enough taught for that. Most of what I know I have found out for myself.

Hilda. But you succeeded all the same.

Solness. Yes, thanks to the fire. I laid out almost the whole of the garden in villa lots; and *there* I was able to build after my own heart. So I came to the front with a rush.

Hilda (looks keenly at him). You must surely be a very happy man, as matters stand with you.

Solness (gloomily). Happy? Do *you* say that, too — like all the rest of them?

Hilda. Yes, I should say you must be. If you could only cease thinking about the two little children ——

Solness (slowly). The two little children — they are not so easy to forget, Hilda.

Hilda (somewhat uncertainly). Do you still feel their loss so much — after all these years?

Solness (looks fixedly at her, without replying). A happy man you said ——

Hilda. Well, now, aren't you happy — in other respects?

Solness (continues to look at her). When I told you all this about the fire — h'm ——

Hilda. Well?

Solness. Was there not one special thought that you — that you seized upon?

Hilda (reflects in vain). No. What thought should *that* be?

Solness (with subdued emphasis). It was simply and solely by that fire that I was enabled to build homes for human beings. Cozy, comfortable, bright homes, where father and mother and the whole troop of children can live in safety and gladness, feeling what a happy thing it is to be alive in the world — and most of all to belong to each other — in great things and in small.

Hilda (ardently). Well, and is it not a great happiness for you to be able to build such beautiful homes?

Solness. The price, Hilda! The terrible price I had to pay for the opportunity!

Hilda. But can you *never* get over that?

Solness. No. That I might build homes for others, I had to forego — to forego for all time — the home that might have been my own. I mean a home for a troop of children — and for father and mother, too.

Hilda (*cautiously*). But *need* you have done that? For all time, you say?

Solness (*nods slowly*). *That* was the price of this happiness that people talk about. (*Breathes heavily.*) This happiness — h'm — this happiness was not to be bought any cheaper, Hilda.

Hilda (*as before*). But may it not come right even yet?

Solness. Never in this world — never. That is another consequence of the fire — and of Aline's illness afterwards.

Hilda (*looks at him with an indefinable expression*). And yet you build all these nurseries?

Solness (*seriously*). Have you never noticed, Hilda, how the impossible — how it seems to beckon and cry aloud to one?

Hilda (*reflecting*). The impossible? (*With animation.*) Yes, indeed! Is that how *you* feel too?

Solness. Yes, I do.

Hilda. Then there must be — a little of the troll in you too.

Solness. Why of the troll?

Hilda. What would *you* call it, then?

Solness (*rises*). Well, well, perhaps you are right. (*Vehemently.*) But how can I help turning into a troll, when this is how it always goes with me in everything — in everything!

Hilda. How do you mean?

Solness (*speaking low, with inward emotion*). Mark what I say to you, Hilda. All that I have succeeded in doing, building, creating — all the beauty, security, cheerful comfort — aye, and magnificence too — (*Clenches his hands.*) Oh, is it not terrible even to think of ——!

Hilda. What is so terrible?

Solness. That all this I have to make up for, to pay for — not in money, but in human happiness. And not with my own happiness only, but with other people's too. Yes, yes, do you see *that*, Hilda? That is the price which my position as an artist has cost me — and others. And every single day I have to look on while the price is paid for me anew. Over again, and over again — and over again forever!

Hilda (*rises and looks steadily at him*). Now I can see that you are thinking of — of *her*.

Solness. Yes, mainly of Aline. For Aline — *she*, too, had her vocation in life, just as much as I had mine. (*His voice quivers.*) But her vocation has had to be stunted, and crushed, and shattered — in order that mine might force its way to — to a sort of great victory. For you must know that Aline — she, too, had a talent for building.

Hilda. She! For building?

Solness (*shakes his head*). Not houses and tow-

ers, and spires — not such things as I work away at ——

Hilda. Well, but *what* then?

Solness (*softly, with emotion*). For building up the souls of little children, Hilda. For building up children's souls in perfect balance, and in noble and beautiful forms. For enabling them to soar up into erect and full-grown human souls. *That* was Aline's talent. And there it all lies now — unused and unusable forever — of no earthly service to anyone — just like the ruins left by a fire.

Hilda. Yes, but even if this were so ——?

Solness. It is so! It is so! I know it!

Hilda. Well, but in any case it is not *your* fault.

Solness (*fixes his eyes on her, and nods slowly*). Ah, *that* is the great, the terrible question. *That* is the doubt that is gnawing me — night and day.

Hilda. That?

Solness. Yes. Suppose the fault *was* mine — in a certain sense.

Hilda. Your fault! The fire!

Solness. All of it; the whole thing. And yet, perhaps — I may not have had anything to do with it.

Hilda (*looks at him with a troubled expression*). Oh, Mr. Solness — if you can talk like that, I am afraid you must be — ill, after all.

Solness. H'm — I don't think I shall ever be of quite sound mind on that point.

(RAGNAR BROVIK *cautiously opens the little door in the left-hand corner.* HILDA *comes forward.*)

Ragnar (*when he sees* HILDA). Oh, I beg pardon, Mr. Solness ——

(*He makes a movement to withdraw.*)

Solness. No, no, don't go. Let us get it over.

Ragnar. Oh, yes — if only we could.

Solness. I hear your father is no better.

Ragnar. Father is fast growing weaker — and therefore I beg and implore you to write a few kind words for me on one of the plans! Something for father to read before he ——

Solness (*vehemently*). I won't hear anything more about those drawings of yours!

Ragnar. Have you looked at them?

Solness. Yes — I have.

Ragnar. And they are good for nothing? And *I* am good for nothing, too?

Solness (*evasively*). Stay here with me, Ragnar. You shall have everything your own way. And then you can marry Kaia, and live at your ease — and happily too, who knows? Only don't think of building on your own account.

Ragnar. Well, well, then I must go home and tell father what you say — I promised I would. — *Is* this what I am to tell father — before he dies?

Solness (*with a groan*). Oh, tell him — tell him what you will, for me. Best to say nothing at all to him! (*With a sudden outburst.*) I *cannot* do anything else, Ragnar!

Ragnar. May I have the drawings to take with me?

Solness. Yes, take them — take them by all means! They are lying there on the table.

Ragnar (*goes to the table*). Thanks.

Hilda (*puts her hand on the portfolio*). No, no; leave them here.

Solness. Why?

Hilda. Because I want to look at them, too.

Solness. But you *have* been —— (*To* RAGNAR.) Well, leave them here, then.

Ragnar. Very well.

Solness. And go home at once to your father.

Ragnar. Yes, I suppose I must.

Solness (*as if in desperation*). Ragnar — you *must* not ask me to do what is beyond my power! Do you hear, Ragnar? You *must* not!

Ragnar. No, no. I beg your pardon ——

(*He bows and goes out by the corner door.* HILDA *goes over and sits down on a chair near the mirror.*)

Hilda (*looks angrily at* SOLNESS). That was a very ugly thing to do.

Solness. Do *you* think so, too?

Hilda. Yes, it was horribly ugly — and hard and bad and cruel as well.

Solness. Oh, you don't understand my position.

Hilda. No matter —— I say you ought not to be like that.

Solness. You said yourself, only just now, that no one but *I* ought to be allowed to build.

Hilda. I may say such things — but *you* must not.

Solness. I most of all, surely, who have paid so dear for my position.

Hilda. Oh, yes — with what you call domestic comfort — and that sort of thing.

Solness. And with my peace of soul into the bargain.

Hilda (*rising*). Peace of soul! (*With feeling.*) Yes, yes, you are right in that! Poor Mr. Solness — you fancy that ——

Solness (*with a quiet, chuckling laugh*). Just sit down again, Hilda, and I'll tell you something funny.

Hilda (*sits down; with intent interest*). Well?

Solness. It sounds such a ludicrous little thing; for, you see, the whole story turns upon nothing but a crack in a chimney.

Hilda. No more than that?

Solness. No, not to begin with.

(*He moves a chair nearer to* HILDA *and sits down.*)

Hilda (*impatiently, taps on her knee*). Well, now for the crack in the chimney!

Solness. I had noticed the split in the flue long, long before the fire. Every time I went up into the attic, I looked to see if it was still there.

Hilda. And it *was?*

Solness. Yes; for no one else knew about it.

Hilda. And you said nothing?

Solness. Nothing.

Hilda. And did not think of repairing the flue either?

Solness. Oh, yes, I thought about it — but never got any further. Every time I intended to set to work, it seemed just as if a hand held me back. Not today, I thought — tomorrow; and nothing ever came of it.

Hilda. But why did you keep putting it off like that?

Solness. Because I was revolving something in my mind. (*Slowly, and in a low voice.*) Through that little black crack in the chimney, I might, perhaps, force my way upwards — as a builder.

Hilda (*looking straight in front of her*). That must have been thrilling.

Solness. Almost irresistible — quite irresistible. For at that time it appeared to me a perfectly simple and straightforward matter. I would have had it happen in the wintertime — a little before midday. I was to be out driving Aline in the sleigh. The servants at home would have made huge fires in the stoves.

Hilda. For, of course, it was to be bitterly cold that day?

Solness. Rather biting, yes — and they would want Aline to find it thoroughly snug and warm when she came home.

Hilda. I suppose she is very chilly by nature?

Solness. She *is.* And as we drove home, we were to see the smoke.

Hilda. Only the smoke?

Solness. The smoke first. But when we came up to the garden gate, the whole of the old timber-box was to be a rolling mass of flames. — That is how I wanted it to be, you see.

Hilda. Oh, why, *why* couldn't it have happened so!

Solness. You may well say that, Hilda.

Hilda. Well, but now listen, Mr. Solness. Are you perfectly certain that the fire was caused by that little crack in the chimney?

Solness. No, on the contrary — I am perfectly certain that the crack in the chimney had nothing whatever to do with the fire.

Hilda. What!

Solness. It has been clearly ascertained that the

fire broke out in a clothes-cupboard — in a totally different part of the house.

Hilda. Then what is all this nonsense you are talking about the crack in the chimney!

Solness. May I go on talking to you a little, Hilda?

Hilda. Yes, if you'll only talk sensibly ——

Solness. I will try to.

(*He moves his chair nearer.*)

Hilda. Out with it, then, Mr. Solness.

Solness (*confidentially*). Don't you agree with me, Hilda, that there exist special, chosen people who have been endowed with the power and faculty of *desiring* a thing, *craving* for a thing, *willing* a thing — so persistently and so — so inexorably — that at last it *has* to happen? Don't you believe that?

Hilda (*with an indefinable expression in her eyes*). If that is so, we shall see, one of these days, whether *I* am one of the chosen.

Solness. It is not oneself *alone* that can do such great things. Oh, no — the helpers and the servers — they must do their part too, if it is to be of any good. But they never come of themselves. One has to call upon them very persistently — inwardly, you understand.

Hilda. What are these helpers and servers?

Solness. Oh, we can talk about that some other time. For the present, let us keep to this business of the fire.

Hilda. Don't you think that fire would have happened all the same — even without your wishing for it?

Solness. If the house had been old Knut Brovik's, it would never have burnt down so conveniently for *him*. I am sure of that; for he does not know how to call for the helpers — no, nor for the servers, either. (*Rises in unrest.*) So you see, Hilda — it is my fault, after all, that the lives of the two little boys had to be sacrificed. And do you think it is not my fault, too, that Aline has never been the woman she should and might have been — and that she most longed to be?

Hilda. Yes, but if it is all the work of those helpers and servers ——?

Solness. Who called for the helpers and servers? It was I! And they came and obeyed my will. (*In increasing excitement.*) *That* is what people call having the luck on your side; but I must tell you what this sort of luck feels like! It feels like a great raw place here on my breast. And the helpers and servers keep on flaying pieces of skin off other people in order to close *my* sore! — But still the sore is not healed — never, never! Oh, if you knew how it can sometimes gnaw and burn!

Hilda (*looks attentively at him*). You *are* ill, Mr. Solness. Very ill, I almost think.

Solness. Say *mad*; for that is what you mean.

Hilda. No, I don't think there is much amiss with your intellect.

Solness. With *what* then? Out with it!

Hilda. I wonder whether you were not sent into the world with a sickly conscience.

Solness. A sickly conscience? What devilry is that?

Hilda. I mean that your conscience is feeble — too delicately built, as it were — hasn't strength to take a grip of things — to lift and bear what is heavy.

Solness (*growls*). H'm! May I ask, then, what sort of a conscience one ought to have?

Hilda. I should like *your* conscience to be — to be thoroughly robust.

Solness. Indeed? Robust, eh? Is your own conscience robust, may I ask?

Hilda. Yes, I think it is. I have never noticed that it wasn't.

Solness. It has not been put very severely to the test, I should think.

Hilda (*with a quivering of the lips*). Oh, it was no such simple matter to leave father — I am so awfully fond of him.

Solness. Dear me! for a month or two ——

Hilda. I think I shall never go home again.

Solness. Never? Then why did you leave him?

Hilda (*half-seriously, half-banteringly*). Have you forgotten again that the ten years are up?

Solness. Oh, nonsense. Was anything wrong at home? Eh?

Hilda (*quite seriously*). It was this impulse within me that urged and goaded me to come — and lured and drew me on, as well.

Solness (*eagerly*). There we have it! There we have it, Hilda! There is a troll in you too, as in me. For it's the troll in one, you see — it is *that* that calls to the powers outside us. And then you *must* give in — whether you will or no.

Hilda. I almost think you are right, Mr. Solness.

Solness (*walks about the room*). Oh, there are devils innumerable abroad in the world, Hilda, that one never *sees*!

Hilda. Devils, too?

Solness (*stops*). Good devils and bad devils; light-haired devils and black-haired devils. If only you could always tell whether it is the light or dark ones that have got hold of you! (*Paces about.*) Ho-ho! Then it would be simple enough!

Hilda (*follows him with her eyes*). Or if one had a really vigorous, radiantly healthy conscience — so that one *dared* to do what one *would*.

Solness (*stops beside the console table*). I believe, now, that most people are just as puny creatures as I am in that respect.

Hilda. I shouldn't wonder.

Solness (leaning against the table). In the sagas —— Have you read any of the old sagas?

Hilda. Oh, yes! When I used to read books, I ——

Solness. In the sagas you read about vikings, who sailed to foreign lands, and plundered and burned and killed men ——

Hilda. And carried off women ——

Solness. —— and kept them in captivity ——

Hilda. —— took them home in their ships ——

Solness. —— and behaved to them like — like the very worst of trolls.

Hilda (looks straight before her, with a half-veiled look). I think *that* must have been thrilling.

Solness (with a short, deep laugh). To carry off women, eh?

Hilda. To *be* carried off.

Solness (looks at her a moment). Oh, indeed.

Hilda (as if breaking the thread of the conversation). But what made you speak of these vikings, Mr. Solness?

Solness. Why, *those* fellows must have had robust consciences, if you like! When they got home again, they could eat and drink, and be as happy as children. And the women, too! They often would not leave them on any account. Can you understand that, Hilda?

Hilda. Those women I can understand exceedingly well.

Solness. Oho! Perhaps you could do the same yourself?

Hilda. Why not?

Solness. Live — of your own free will — with a ruffian like that?

Hilda. If it was a ruffian I had come to love ——

Solness. *Could* you come to love a man like that?

Hilda. Good heavens, you know very well one can't choose whom one is going to love.

Solness (looks meditatively at her). Oh, no, I suppose it is the troll within one that's responsible for that.

Hilda (half-laughing). And all those blessèd devils, that *you* know so well — both the light-haired and the dark-haired ones.

Solness (quietly and warmly). Then I hope with all my heart that the devils will choose carefully for you, Hilda.

Hilda. For me they *have* chosen already — once and for all.

Solness (looks earnestly at her). Hilda — you are like a wild bird of the woods.

Hilda. Far from it. I don't hide myself away under the bushes.

Solness. No, no. There is rather something of the bird of prey in you.

Hilda. That is nearer it — perhaps. (*Very vehemently.*) And why not a bird of prey? Why should not *I* go a-hunting — I, as well as the rest? Carry off the prey I want — if only I can get my claws into it, and do with it as I will.

Solness. Hilda — do you know what you are?

Hilda. Yes, I suppose I am a strange sort of bird.

Solness. No. You are like a dawning day. When I look at you — I seem to be looking towards the sunrise.

Hilda. Tell me, Mr. Solness — are you certain that you have never called me to you? Inwardly, you know?

Solness (softly and slowly). I almost think I must have.

Hilda. What did you want with me?

Solness. You are the younger generation, Hilda.

Hilda (smiles). That younger generation that you are so afraid of?

Solness (nods slowly). And which, in my heart, I yearn towards so deeply.

> (HILDA *rises, goes to the little table, and fetches* RAGNAR BROVIK'S *portfolio.*)

Hilda (holds out the portfolio to him). We were talking of these drawings ——

Solness (shortly, waving them away). Put those things away! I have seen enough of them.

Hilda. Yes, but you have to write your approval on them.

Solness. Write my approval on them? Never!

Hilda. But the poor old man is lying at death's door! Can't you give him and his son this pleasure before they are parted? And perhaps he might get the commission to carry them out, too.

Solness. Yes, that is just what he would get. He has made sure of that — has my fine gentleman!

Hilda. Then, good heavens — if that is so — can't you tell the least little bit of a lie for once in a way?

Solness. A lie? (*Raging.*) Hilda — take those devil's drawings out of my sight!

Hilda (draws the portfolio a little nearer to herself). Well, well, well — don't bite me. — You talk of trolls — but I think you go on like a troll yourself. (*Looks around.*) Where do you keep your pen and ink?

Solness. There is nothing of the sort in here.

Hilda (goes towards the door). But in the office where that young lady is ——

Solness. Stay where you are, Hilda! — I ought to tell a lie, you say. Oh, yes, for the sake of his old father I might well do that — for in my time I have crushed him, trodden him under foot ——

Hilda. Him, too?

Solness. I needed room for myself. But this Ragnar — he must on no account be allowed to come to the front.

Hilda. Poor fellow, there is surely no fear of that. If he has nothing in him ——

Solness (comes closer, looks at her, and whispers). If Ragnar Brovik gets his chance, he will strike *me* to the earth. Crush me — as I crushed his father.

Hilda. Crush you? Has he the ability for that?

Solness. Yes, you may depend upon it *he* has the ability! He is the younger generation that stands ready to knock at my door — to make an end of Halvard Solness.

Hilda (looks at him with quiet reproach). And yet you would bar him out. Fie, Mr. Solness!

Solness. The fight I have been fighting has cost heart's blood enough. — And I am afraid, too, that the helpers and servers will not obey me any longer.

Hilda. Then you must go ahead without them. There is nothing else for it.

Solness. It is hopeless, Hilda. The luck is bound to turn. A little sooner or a little later. Retribution is inexorable.

Hilda (in distress, putting her hands over her ears). Don't talk like that! Do you want to kill me? To take from me what is more than my life?

Solness. And what is that?

Hilda. The longing to see you great. To see you, with a wreath in your hand, high, high up on a church-tower. (*Calm again.*) Come, out with your pencil now. You must have a pencil about you.

Solness (takes out his pocketbook). I have one here.

Hilda (lays the portfolio on the sofa-table). Very well. Now let us two sit down here, Mr. Solness. (SOLNESS *seats himself at the table.* HILDA *stands behind him, leaning over the back of the chair.*) And now we will write on the drawings. We must write very, very nicely and cordially — for this horrid Ruar — or whatever his name is.

Solness (writes a few words, turns his head, and looks at her). Tell me one thing, Hilda.

Hilda. Yes!

Solness. If you have been waiting for me all these ten years ——

Hilda. What then?

Solness. Why have you never written to me? Then I could have answered you.

Hilda (hastily). No, no, no! That was just what I did not want.

Solness. Why not?

Hilda. I was afraid the whole thing might fall to pieces. — But we were going to write on the drawings, Mr. Solness.

Solness. So we were.

Hilda (bends forward and looks over his shoulder while he writes). Mind now, kindly and cordially! Oh, how I hate — how I hate this Ruald ——

Solness (writing). Have you never really cared for anyone, Hilda?

Hilda (harshly). What do you say?

Solness. Have you never cared for anyone?

Hilda. For anyone else, I suppose you mean?

Solness (looks up at her). For anyone else, yes. Have you never? In all these ten years? Never?

Hilda. Oh, yes, now and then. When I was perfectly furious with you for not coming.

Solness. Then you did take an interest in other people, too?

Hilda. A little bit — for a week or so. Good heavens, Mr. Solness, you surely know how such things come about.

Solness. Hilda — what is it you have come for?

Hilda. Don't waste time talking. The poor old man might go and die in the meantime.

Solness. Answer me, Hilda. What do you want of me?

Hilda. I want my kingdom.

Solness. H'm ——

(*He gives a rapid glance towards the door on the left and then goes on writing on the drawings. At the same moment* MRS. SOLNESS *enters; she has some packages in her hand.*)

Mrs. Solness. Here are a few things I have got for you, Miss Wangel. The large parcels will be sent later on.

Hilda. Oh, how very, very kind of you!

Mrs. Solness. Only my simple duty. Nothing more than that.

Solness (reading over what he has written). Aline!

Mrs. Solness. Yes?

Solness. Did you notice whether the — the bookkeeper was out there?

Mrs. Solness. Yes, of course, *she* was there.

Solness (puts the drawings in the portfolio). H'm ——

Mrs. Solness. She was standing at the desk, as she always is — when *I* go through the room.

Solness (rises). Then I'll give this to her and tell her that ——

Hilda (takes the portfolio from him). Oh, no, let me have the pleasure of doing that! (*Goes to the door but turns.*) What is her name?

Solness. Her name is Miss Fosli.

Hilda. Pooh, that sounds so cold! Her Christian name, I mean.

Solness. Kaia — I believe.

Hilda (opens the door and calls out). Kaia, come

in here! Make haste! Mr. Solness wants to speak to you.

(KAIA FOSLI *appears at the door*.)

Kaia (*looking at him in alarm*). Here I am ——

Hilda (*handing her the portfolio*). See here, Kaia! You can take this home; Mr. Solness has written on them now.

Kaia. Oh, at last!

Solness. Give them to the old man as soon as you can.

Kaia. I will go straight home with them.

Solness. Yes, do. Now Ragnar will have a chance of building for himself.

Kaia. Oh, may he come and thank you for all ——?

Solness (*harshly*). I won't have any thanks! Tell him *that* from me.

Kaia. Yes, I will ——

Solness. And tell him at the same time that henceforward I do not require his services — nor yours either.

Kaia (*softly and quiveringly*). Not mine either?

Solness. You will have other things to think of now and to attend to; and that is a very good thing for you. Well, go home with the drawings now, Miss Fosli. At once! Do you hear?

Kaia (*as before*). Yes, Mr. Solness.
                                        (*She goes out.*)

Mrs. Solness. Heavens! what deceitful eyes she has.

Solness. She? That poor little creature?

Mrs. Solness. Oh — I can see what I can see, Halvard. —— Are you really dismissing them?

Solness. Yes.

Mrs. Solness. Her as well?

Solness. Was not that what you wished?

Mrs. Solness. But how can you get on without her ——? Oh well, no doubt you have someone else in reserve, Halvard.

Hilda (*playfully*). Well, *I* for one am not the person to stand at that desk.

Solness. Never mind, never mind — it will be all right, Aline. Now all you have to do is to think about moving into our new home — as quickly as you can. This evening we will hang up the wreath — (*Turns to* HILDA.) — right on the very pinnacle of the tower. What do you say to *that*, Miss Hilda?

Hilda (*looks at him with sparkling eyes*). It will be splendid to see you so high up once more.

Solness. Me!

Mrs. Solness. For Heaven's sake, Miss Wangel, don't imagine such a thing! My husband! — when he always gets so dizzy!

Hilda. He gets dizzy! No, I know quite well he does not!

Mrs. Solness. Oh, yes, indeed he does.

Hilda. But I have seen him with my own eyes right up at the top of a high church-tower!

Mrs. Solness. Yes, I hear people talk of that; but it is utterly impossible ——

Solness (*vehemently*). Impossible — impossible, yes! But there I stood all the same!

Mrs. Solness. Oh, how can you say so, Halvard? Why, you can't even bear to go out on the second-story balcony here. You have always been that.

Solness. You may perhaps see something different this evening.

Mrs. Solness (*in alarm*). No, no, no! Please God I shall never see that. I will write at once to the doctor — and I am sure he won't let you do it.

Solness. Why, Aline ——!

Mrs. Solness. Oh, you know you're ill, Halvard. This *proves* it! Oh, God — Oh, God!
                        (*She goes hastily out to the right.*)

Hilda (*looks intently at him*). Is it so, or is it not?

Solness. That I turn dizzy?

Hilda. That my master builder *dares* not — *cannot* — climb as high as he builds?

Solness. Is that the way you look at it?

Hilda. Yes.

Solness. I believe there is scarcely a corner in me that is safe from you.

Hilda (*looks towards the bay-window*). Up there, then. Right up there ——

Solness (*approaches her*). You might have the topmost room in the tower, Hilda — there you might live like a princess.

Hilda (*indefinably, between earnest and jest*.) Yes, that is what you promised me.

Solness. Did I really?

Hilda. Fie, Mr. Solness! You said I should be a princess and that you would give me a kingdom. And then you went and —— Well!

Solness (*cautiously*). Are you quite certain that this is not a dream — a fancy, that has fixed itself in your mind?

Hilda (*sharply*). Do you mean that you did not do it?

Solness. I scarcely know myself. (*More softly.*) But now I know *so much* for certain, that I ——

Hilda. That you ——? Say it at once!

Solness. —— that I *ought* to have done it.

Hilda (*exclaims with animation*). Don't tell me *you* can ever be dizzy!

Solness. This evening, then, we will hang up the wreath — Princess Hilda.

Hilda (with a bitter curve of the lips). Over your new home, yes.

Solness. Over the new house, which will never be a *home* for *me.*

(*He goes out through the garden door.*)

Hilda (looks straight in front of her with a far-away expression and whispers to herself. The only words audible are) —— frightfully thrilling ——

CURTAIN

ACT THREE

The large, broad veranda of SOLNESS'S *dwelling-house. Part of the house, with outer door leading to the veranda, is seen to the left. A railing along the veranda to the right. At the back, from the end of the veranda, a flight of steps leads down to the garden below. Tall old trees in the garden spread their branches over the veranda and towards the house. Far to the right, in among the trees, a glimpse is caught of the lower part of the new villa, with scaffold-ing round so much as is seen of the tower. In the background the garden is bounded by an old wooden fence. Outside the fence, a street with low, tumble-down cottages.*

Evening sky with sunlit clouds.

On the veranda, a garden bench stands along the wall of the house, and in front of the bench a long table. On the other side of the table, an armchair and some stools. All the furniture is of wickerwork.

MRS. SOLNESS, *wrapped in a large white crape shawl, sits resting in the armchair and gazes over to the right. Shortly after,* HILDA WANGEL *comes up the flight of steps from the garden. She is dressed as in the last act and wears her hat. She has in her bodice a little nosegay of small common flowers.*

Mrs. Solness (turning her head a little). Have you been round the garden, Miss Wangel?

Hilda. Yes, I have been taking a look at it.

Mrs. Solness. And found some flowers too, I see.

Hilda. Yes, indeed! There are such heaps of them in among the bushes.

Mrs. Solness. Are there really? Still? You see I scarcely ever go there.

Hilda (closer). What! Don't you take a run down into the garden every day, then?

Mrs. Solness (with a faint smile). I don't "run" anywhere, nowadays.

Hilda. Well, but do you not go down now and then to look at all the lovely things there?

Mrs. Solness. It has all become so strange to me. I am almost afraid to see it again.

Hilda. Your own garden!

Mrs. Solness. I don't feel that it is *mine* any longer.

Hilda. What do you mean ——?

Mrs. Solness. No, no, it is not —— not as it was in my mother's and father's time. They have taken away so much —— so much of the garden, Miss Wangel. Fancy —— they have parceled it out —— and built houses for strangers —— people that I don't know. And *they* can sit and look in upon me from their windows.

Hilda (with a bright expression). Mrs. Solness!

Mrs. Solness. Yes!

Hilda. May I stay here with you a little?

Mrs. Solness. Yes, by all means, if you care to.

(HILDA *moves a stool close to the armchair and sits down.*)

Hilda. Ah —— here one can sit and sun oneself like a cat.

Mrs. Solness (lays her hand softly on HILDA's *neck).* It is nice of you to be willing to sit with me. I thought you wanted to go in to my husband.

Hilda. What should I want with him?

Mrs. Solness. To help him, I thought.

Hilda. No, thank you. And besides, he is not in. He is over there with his workmen. But he looked so fierce that I did not dare to talk to him.

Mrs. Solness. He is so kind and gentle in reality.

Hilda. He!

Mrs. Solness. You do not really know him yet, Miss Wangel.

Hilda (looks affectionately at her). Are you pleased at the thought of moving over to the new house?

Mrs. Solness. I *ought* to be pleased; for it is what Halvard wants ——

Hilda. Oh, not just on that account, surely.

Mrs. Solness. Yes, yes, Miss Wangel; for it is only my duty to submit myself to *him.* But very often it is dreadfully difficult to force one's mind to obedience.

Hilda. Yes, that must be difficult indeed.

Mrs. Solness. I can tell you it is —— when one has so many faults as I have ——

Hilda. When one has gone through so much trouble as you have ——

Mrs. Solness. How do you know about that?

Hilda. Your husband told me.

Mrs. Solness. To me he very seldom mentions these things. —— Yes, I can tell you I have gone through more than enough trouble in my life, Miss Wangel.

Hilda (looks sympathetically at her and nods slowly). Poor Mrs. Solness. First of all there was the fire ——

Mrs. Solness (with a sigh). Yes, everything that was *mine* was burnt.

Hilda. And then came what was worse.

Mrs. Solness (looking inquiringly at her). Worse?

Hilda. The worst of all.

Mrs. Solness. What do you mean?

Hilda (softly). You lost the two little boys.

Mrs. Solness. Oh, yes, the boys. But, you see, *that* was a thing apart. That was a dispensation of Providence; and in such things one can only bow in submission — yes, and be thankful, too.

Hilda. Then you are so?

Mrs. Solness. Not always, I am sorry to say. I know well enough that it is my duty — but all the same I *cannot*.

Hilda. No, no, I think that is only natural.

Mrs. Solness. And often and often I have to remind myself that it was a righteous punishment for me ——

Hilda. Why?

Mrs. Solness. Because I had not fortitude enough in misfortune.

Hilda. But I don't see that ——

Mrs. Solness. Oh, no, no, Miss Wangel — do not talk to me any more about the two little boys. We ought to feel nothing but joy in thinking of *them;* for they are so happy — so happy now. No, it is the *small* losses in life that cut one to the heart — the loss of all that other people look upon as almost nothing.

Hilda (lays her arms on Mrs. Solness's *knees and looks up at her affectionately).* Dear Mrs. Solness — tell me what things you mean!

Mrs. Solness. As I say, only little things. All the old portraits were burnt on the walls. And all the old silk dresses were burnt, that had belonged to the family for generations and generations. And all mother's and grandmother's lace — that was burnt, too. And only think — the jewels, too! *(Sadly.)* And then all the dolls.

Hilda. The dolls?

Mrs. Solness (choking with tears). I had nine lovely dolls.

Hilda. And *they* were burnt too?

Mrs. Solness. All of them. Oh, it was hard — so hard for me.

Hilda. Had you put by all these dolls, then? Ever since you were little?

Mrs. Solness. I had not put them by. The dolls and I had gone on living together.

Hilda. After you were grown up?

Mrs. Solness. Yes, long after that.

Hilda. After you were married, too?

Mrs. Solness. Oh, yes, indeed. So long as he did not see it —— But they were all burnt up, poor things. No one thought of saving *them*. Oh, it is so miserable to think of. You mustn't laugh at me, Miss Wangel.

Hilda. I am not laughing in the least.

Mrs. Solness. For you see, in a certain sense, there was life in them, too. I carried them under my heart — like little unborn children.

(Dr. Herdal, *with his hat in his hand, comes out through the door and observes* Mrs. Solness *and* Hilda.)

Dr. Herdal. Well, Mrs. Solness, so you are sitting out here catching cold?

Mrs. Solness. I find it so pleasant and warm here today.

Dr. Herdal. Yes, yes. But is there anything going on here? I got a note from you.

Mrs. Solness (rises). Yes, there is something I must talk to you about.

Dr. Herdal. Very well; then perhaps we had better go in. *(To* Hilda.) Still in your mountain-eering dress, Miss Wangel?

Hilda (gaily, rising). Yes — in full uniform! But today I am not going climbing and breaking my neck. We two will stop quietly below and look on, Doctor.

Dr. Herdal. What are we to look on at?

Mrs. Solness (softly, in alarm, to Hilda). Hush, hush — for God's sake! He is coming! Try to get that idea out of his head. And let us be friends, Miss Wangel. Don't you think we can?

Hilda (throws her arms impetuously round Mrs. Solness's *neck).* Oh, if we only could!

Mrs. Solness (gently disengages herself). There, there, there! There he comes, Doctor. Let me have a word with you.

Dr. Herdal. Is it about *him?*

Mrs. Solness. Yes, to be sure it's about him. Do come in.

(*She and the* Doctor *enter the house. Next moment* Solness *comes up from the garden by the flight of steps. A serious look comes over* Hilda's *face.*)

Solness (glances at the house door, which is closed cautiously from within). Have you noticed, Hilda, that as soon as I come, she goes?

Hilda. I have noticed that as soon as you come, you *make* her go.

Solness. Perhaps so. But I cannot help it. *(Looks observantly at her.)* Are you cold, Hilda? I think you look cold.

Hilda. I have just come out of a tomb.

Solness. What do you mean by *that?*

Hilda. That I have got chilled through and through, Mr. Solness.

Solness (slowly). I believe I understand —

Hilda. What brings you up here just now?

Solness. I caught sight of you from over there.

Hilda. But then you must have seen her too?

Solness. I knew she would go at once if I came.

Hilda. Is it very painful for you that she should avoid you in this way?

Solness. In one sense, it's a relief as well.

Hilda. Not to have her before your eyes?

Solness. Yes.

Hilda. Not to be always seeing how heavily the loss of the little boys weighs upon her?

Solness. Yes. Chiefly that.

(HILDA *drifts across the veranda with her hands behind her back, stops at the railing, and looks out over the garden.*)

Solness (*after a short pause*). Did you have a long talk with her?

(HILDA *stands motionless and does not answer.*)

Solness. Did you have a long talk, I asked?

(HILDA *is silent as before.*)

Solness. What was she talking about, Hilda?

(HILDA *continues silent.*)

Solness. Poor Aline! I suppose it was about the little boys. (*A nervous shudder runs through* HILDA; *then she nods hurriedly once or twice.*) She will never get over it — never in this world. (*Approaches her.*) Now you are standing there again like a statue; just as you stood last night.

Hilda (*turns and looks at him, with great serious eyes*). I am going away.

Solness (*sharply*). Going away!

Hilda. Yes.

Solness. But I won't allow you to!

Hilda. What am I to do *here* now?

Solness. Simply to *be* here, Hilda!

Hilda (*measures him with a look*). Oh, thank you. You know it wouldn't end *there*.

Solness (*heedlessly*). So much the better!

Hilda (*vehemently*). I *cannot* do any harm to one whom I *know!* I can't take away anything that belongs to her.

Solness. Who wants you to do that?

Hilda (*continuing*). A stranger, yes! for that is quite a different thing! A person I have never set eyes on. But one that I have come into close contact with ——! Oh, no! Oh, no! Ugh!

Solness. Yes, but I never proposed you should.

Hilda. Oh, Mr. Solness, you know quite well what the end of it would be. And that is why I am going away.

Solness. And what is to become of *me* when you are gone? What shall I have to live for *then?* — After that?

Hilda (*with the indefinable look in her eyes*). It is surely not so hard for *you.* You have your duties to her. Live for those duties.

Solness. Too late. These powers — these — these ——

Hilda. —— devils ——

Solness. Yes, these devils! And the troll within me as well — they have drawn all the lifeblood out of her. (*Laughs in desperation.*) They did it for my *happiness!* Yes, yes! (*Sadly.*) And now she is dead — for my sake. And I am chained alive to a dead woman. (*In wild anguish.*) I — I who cannot live without joy in life!

HILDA *moves round the table and seats herself on the bench with her elbows on the table and her head supported by her hands.*)

Hilda (*sits and looks at him awhile.*) What will you build next?

Solness (*shakes his head*). I don't believe I shall build much more.

Hilda. Not those cozy, happy homes for mother and father and for the troop of children?

Solness. I wonder whether there will be any use for such homes in the coming time.

Hilda. Poor Mr. Solness! And you have gone all these ten years — and staked your whole life — on that alone.

Solness. Yes, you may well say so, Hilda.

Hilda (*with an outburst*). Oh, it all seems to me so foolish — so foolish!

Solness. All what?

Hilda. Not to be able to grasp at your own happiness — at your own life! Merely because someone you know happens to stand in the way!

Solness. One whom you have no right to set aside.

Hilda. I wonder whether one really has *not* the right! And yet, and yet —— Oh! if one could only sleep the whole thing away!

(*She lays her arms flat down on the table, rests the left side of her head on her hands, and shuts her eyes.*)

Solness (*turns the armchair and sits down at the table*). Had *you* a cozy, happy home — up there with your father, Hilda?

Hilda (*without stirring, answers as if half asleep*). I had only a cage.

Solness. And you are determined not to go back to it?

Hilda (*as before*). The wild bird never wants to go into the cage.

Solness. Rather range through the free air ——

Hilda (*still as before*). The bird of prey loves to range ——

Solness (*lets his eyes rest on her*). If only one had the viking-spirit in life ——

Hilda (*in her usual voice; opens her eyes but does not move.*) And the other thing? Say what *that* was!

Solness. A robust conscience.

(HILDA *sits erect on the bench, with animation. Her eyes have once more the sparkling expression of gladness.*)

Hilda (*nods to him*). *I* know what you are going to build next!

Solness. Then you know more than I do, Hilda.

Hilda. Yes, builders are such stupid people.

Solness. What is it to be then?

Hilda (*nods again*). The castle.

Solness. What castle?

Hilda. My castle, of course.

Solness. Do you want a castle now?

Hilda. Don't you owe me a kingdom, I should like to know?

Solness. You say I do.

Hilda. Well — you admit you owe me this kingdom. And you can't have a kingdom without a royal castle, I should think!

Solness (*more and more animated*). Yes, they usually go together.

Hilda. Good! Then build it for me! This moment!

Solness (*laughing*). Must you have that on the instant, too?

Hilda. Yes, to be sure! For the ten years are up now, and I am not going to wait any longer. So — out with the castle, Mr. Solness!

Solness. It's no light matter to owe *you* anything, Hilda.

Hilda. You should have thought of that before. It is too late now. So — (*Tapping the table.*) — the castle on the table! It is *my* castle! I will have it *at once!*

Solness (*more seriously, leans over towards her, with his arms on the table*). What sort of castle have you imagined, Hilda?

(*Her expression becomes more and more veiled. She seems gazing inwards at herself.*)

Hilda (*slowly*). My castle shall stand on a height — on a very great height — with a clear outlook on all sides, so that I can see far — far around.

Solness. And no doubt it is to have a high tower!

Hilda. A tremendously high tower. And at the very top of the tower there shall be a balcony. And I will stand out upon it ——

Solness (*involuntarily clutches at his forehead*). How can you like to stand at such a dizzy height ——?

Hilda. Yes, I will! Right up there will I stand and look down on the other people — on those that are building churches, and homes for mother and father and the troop of children. And *you* may come up and look on at it, too.

Solness (*in a low tone*). Is the builder to be allowed to come up beside the princess?

Hilda. If the builder *will.*

Solness (*more softly*). Then I think the builder will come.

Hilda (*nods*). The builder — he will come.

Solness. But he will never be able to build any more. Poor builder!

Hilda (*animated*). Oh, yes, he will! We two will set to work together. And then we will build the loveliest — the very loveliest — thing in all the world.

Solness (*intently*). Hilda — tell me what that is!

Hilda (*looks smilingly at him, shakes her head a little, pouts, and speaks as if to a child*). Builders — they are such very — very stupid people.

Solness. Yes, no doubt they are stupid. But now tell me what it is — the loveliest thing in the world — that we two are to build together.

Hilda (*is silent a little while, then says with an indefinable expression in her eyes*). Castles in the air.

Solness. Castles in the air?

Hilda (*nods*). Castles in the air, yes! Do you know what sort of thing a castle in the air is?

Solness. It is the loveliest thing in the world, you say.

Hilda (*rises with vehemence and makes a gesture of repulsion with her hand*). Yes, to be sure it is! Castles in the air — they are so easy to take refuge in. And so easy to build, too — (*Looks scornfully at him.*) — especially for the builders who have a — a dizzy conscience.

Solness (*rises*). After this day we two will build together, Hilda.

Hilda (*with a half-dubious smile*). A *real* castle in the air?

Solness. Yes. One with a firm foundation under it.

(RAGNAR BROVIK *comes out from the house. He is carrying a large, green wreath with flowers and silk ribbons.*)

Hilda (*with an outburst of pleasure.*) The wreath! Oh, that will be glorious!

Solness (*in surprise*). Have *you* brought the wreath, Ragnar?

Ragnar. I promised the foreman I would.

Solness (*relieved*). Ah, then I suppose your father is better?

Ragnar. No.

Solness. Was he not cheered by what I wrote?

Ragnar. It came too late.

Solness. Too late!

Ragnar. When she came with it he was unconscious. He had had a stroke.

Solness. Why, then, you must go home to him! You must attend to your father!

Ragnar. He does not need me any more.

Solness. But surely you ought to be with him.

Ragnar. *She* is sitting by his bed.

Solness (*rather uncertainly*). Kaia?

Ragnar (*looking darkly at him*). Yes — Kaia.

Solness. Go home, Ragnar — both to him and to her. Give *me* the wreath.

Ragnar (*suppresses a mocking smile*). You don't mean that you yourself ——?

Solness. I will take it down to them myself. (*Takes the wreath from him.*) And now you go home; we don't require you today.

Ragnar. I know you do not require me any more; but today I shall remain.

Solness. Well, remain then, since you are bent upon it.

Hilda (*at the railing*). Mr. Solness, I will stand here and look on at you.

Solness. At me!

Hilda. It will be fearfully thrilling.

Solness (*in a low tone*). We will talk about that presently, Hilda.

(*He goes down the flight of steps with the wreath and away through the garden.*)

Hilda (*looks after him, then turns to* RAGNAR). I think you might at least have thanked him.

Ragnar. Thanked him? Ought I to have thanked *him?*

Hilda. Yes, of course you ought!

Ragnar. I think it is rather *you* I ought to thank.

Hilda. How can you say such a thing?

Ragnar (*without answering her*). But I advise you to take care, Miss Wangel! For you don't know *him* rightly yet.

Hilda (*ardently*). Oh, no one knows him as I do!

Ragnar (*laughs in exasperation*). Thank him, when he has held me down year after year! When he made father disbelieve in me — made me disbelieve in myself! And all merely that he might ——!

Hilda (*as if divining something*). That he might ——? Tell me at once!

Ragnar. That he might keep her with him.

Hilda (*with a start towards him*). The girl at the desk?

Ragnar. Yes.

Hilda (*threateningly, clenching her hands*). That is not true! You are telling falsehoods about him!

Ragnar. I would not believe it either until today — when she said so herself.

Hilda (*as if beside herself*). *What* did she say? I *will* know! At once! at once!

Ragnar. She said that he had taken possession of her mind — her whole mind — centered all her thoughts upon himself alone. She says that she can never leave him — that she will remain here, where *he* is ——

Hilda (*with flashing eyes*). She will not be allowed to!

Ragnar (*as if feeling his way*). Who will not allow her?

Hilda (*rapidly*). *He* will not either!

Ragnar. Oh, no — I understand the whole thing now. After this, she would merely be — in the way.

Hilda. You understand nothing — since you can talk like that! No, *I* will tell you why he kept hold of her.

Ragnar. Well then, why?

Hilda. In order to keep hold of you.

Ragnar. Has he told you so?

Hilda. No, but it *is* so. It *must* be so! (*Wildly.*) I will — I *will* have it so!

Ragnar. And at the very moment when *you* came — he let her go.

Hilda. It was *you* — *you* that he let go! What do you suppose he cares about strange women like you?

Ragnar (*reflects*). Is it possible that all this time he has been afraid of me?

Hilda. He afraid! I would not be so conceited if I were you.

Ragnar. Oh, he must have seen long ago that I had something in me, too. Besides — cowardly — that is just what he is, you see.

Hilda. He! Oh, yes, I am likely to believe *that!*

Ragnar. In a certain sense he *is* cowardly — he, the great master builder. He is not afraid of robbing others of their life's happiness — as he has done both for my father and for me. But when it comes to climbing up a paltry bit of scaffolding — he will do anything rather than *that.*

Hilda. Oh, you should just have seen him high, high up — at the dizzy height where I once saw him.

Ragnar. Did you see that?

Hilda. Yes, indeed I did. How free and great he looked as he stood and fastened the wreath to the church vane!

Ragnar. I know that he ventured that, *once* in his life — one solitary time. It is a legend among us younger men. But no power on earth would induce him to do it again.

Hilda. Today he will do it again!

Ragnar (*scornfully*). Yes, I dare say!

Hilda. We shall see it!

Ragnar. That neither you nor I will see.

Hilda (*with uncontrollable vehemence*). I *will* see it! I *will* and I *must* see it!

Ragnar. But he will not do it. He simply dare not do it. For you see he cannot get over this infirmity — master builder though he be.

(MRS. SOLNESS *comes from the house
on to the veranda.*)

Mrs. Solness (*looks around*). Isn't he here? Where has he gone to?

Ragnar. Mr. Solness is down with the men.

Hilda. He took the wreath with him.

Mrs. Solness (*terrified*). Took the wreath with him! Oh, God! oh, God! Brovik — you must go down to him! Get him to come back here!

Ragnar. Shall I say you want to speak to him, Mrs. Solness?

Mrs. Solness. Oh, yes, do! — No, no — don't say that *I* want anything! You can say that somebody is here, and that he must come at once.

Ragnar. Good. I will do so, Mrs. Solness.

(*He goes down the flight of steps and away through the garden.*)

Mrs. Solness. Oh, Miss Wangel, you can't think how anxious I feel about him.

Hilda. Is there anything in this to be so terribly frightened about?

Mrs. Solness. Oh, yes; surely you can understand. Just think, if he were really to do it! If he should take it into his head to climb up the scaffolding!

Hilda (*eagerly*). Do you think he will?

Mrs. Solness. Oh, one can never tell what he might take into his head. I am afraid there is nothing he mightn't think of doing.

Hilda. Aha! Perhaps you too think that he is — well ——?

Mrs. Solness. Oh, I don't know what to think about him now. The doctor has been telling me all sorts of things; and putting it all together with several things I have heard him say ——

(DR. HERDAL *looks out at the door.*)

Dr. Herdal. Isn't he coming soon?

Mrs. Solness. Yes, I think so. I have sent for him at any rate.

Dr. Herdal (*advancing*). I am afraid you will have to go in, my dear lady ——

Mrs. Solness. Oh, no! Oh, no! I shall stay out here and wait for Halvard.

Dr. Herdal. But some ladies have just come to call on you ——

Mrs. Solness. Good heavens, *that* too! And just at this moment!

Dr. Herdal. They say they positively must see the ceremony.

Mrs. Solness. Well, well, I suppose I must go to them after all. It is my duty.

Hilda. Can't you ask the ladies to go away?

Mrs. Solness. No, that would never do. Now that they are here, it is my duty to see them. But you stay out here in the meantime — and receive him when he comes.

Dr. Herdal. And try to occupy his attention as long as possible ——

Mrs. Solness. Yes, do, dear Miss Wangel. Keep as firm hold of him as ever you can.

Hilda. Would it not be best for you to do that?

Mrs. Solness. Yes; God knows that is my duty. But when one has duties in so many directions ——

Dr. Herdal (*looks towards the garden*). There he is coming.

Mrs. Solness. And I have to go in!

Dr. Herdal (*to* HILDA). Don't say anything about *my* being here.

Hilda. Oh, no! I dare say I shall find something else to talk to Mr. Solness about.

Mrs. Solness. And be sure you keep firm hold of him. I believe *you* can do it best.

(MRS. SOLNESS *and* DR. HERDAL *go into the house.* HILDA *remains standing on the veranda.* SOLNESS *comes from the garden, up the flight of steps.*)

Solness. Somebody wants me, I hear.

Hilda. Yes; it is I, Mr. Solness.

Solness. Oh, is it you, Hilda? I was afraid it might be Aline or the Doctor.

Hilda. You are very easily frightened, it seems!

Solness. Do you think so?

Hilda. Yes; people say that you are afraid to climb about — on the scaffoldings, you know.

Solness. Well, that is quite a special thing.

Hilda. Then it is true that you are afraid to do it?

Solness. Yes, I am.

Hilda. Afraid of falling down and killing yourself?

Solness. No, not of that.

Hilda. Of what, then?

Solness. I am afraid of retribution, Hilda.

Hilda. Of retribution? (*Shakes her head.*) I don't understand that.

Solness. Sit down, and I will tell you something.

Hilda. Yes, do! At once!

(*She sits on a stool by the railing and looks expectantly at him.*)

Solness (*throws his hat on the table*). You know that I began by building churches.

Hilda (*nods*). I know that well.

Solness. For, you see, I came as a boy from a pious home in the country; and so it seemed to me that this church-building was the noblest task I could set myself.

Hilda. Yes, yes.

Solness. And I venture to say that I built those poor little churches with such honest and warm and heartfelt devotion that — that ——

Hilda. That ——? Well?

Solness. Well, that I think that he ought to have been pleased with me.

Hilda. He? What *he?*

Solness. He who was to have the churches, of course! He to whose honor and glory they were dedicated.

Hilda. Oh, indeed! But are you certain, then, that — that he was not — pleased with you?

Solness (scornfully). He pleased with *me!* How can you talk so, Hilda? He who gave the troll in me leave to lord it just as it pleased. He who bade them be at hand to serve me, both day and night — all these — all these ——

Hilda. Devils ——

Solness. Yes, of both kinds. Oh, no, he made me feel clearly enough that he was not pleased with me. (*Mysteriously.*) You see, that was really the reason why he made the old house burn down.

Hilda. Was that why?

Solness. Yes, don't you understand? He wanted to give me the chance of becoming an accomplished master in my own sphere — so that I might build all the more glorious churches for him. At first I did not understand what he was driving at; but all of a sudden it flashed upon me.

Hilda. When was that?

Solness. It was when I was building the church-tower up at Lysanger.

Hilda. I thought so.

Solness. For you see, Hilda — up there, amidst those new surroundings, I used to go about musing and pondering within myself. Then I saw plainly why he had taken my little children from me. It was that I should have nothing else to attach myself to. No such thing as love and happiness, you understand. I was to be only a master builder — nothing else. And all my life long I was to go on building for him. (*Laughs.*) But I can tell you nothing came of *that!*

Hilda. What did you do, then?

Solness. First of all, I searched and tried my own heart ——

Hilda. And then?

Solness. Then I did the *impossible* — I no less than *he.*

Hilda. The impossible?

Solness. I had never before been able to climb up to a great, free height. But that day I did it.

Hilda (leaping up). Yes, yes, you did!

Solness. And when I stood there, high over everything, and was hanging the wreath over the vane, I said to him: Hear me now, thou Mighty One! From this day forward I will be a free builder — I too, in my sphere — just as thou in thine. I will never more build churches for thee — only homes for human beings.

Hilda (with great sparkling eyes). That was the song that I heard through the air!

Solness. But afterwards his turn came.

Hilda. What do you mean by *that?*

Solness (looks despondently at her). Building homes for human beings — is not worth a rap, Hilda.

Hilda. Do you say *that* now?

Solness. Yes, for now I see it. Men have no use for these homes of theirs — to be happy in. And I should not have had any use for such a home, if I had had one. (*With a quiet, bitter laugh.*) See, that is the upshot of the whole affair, however far back I look. Nothing really built; nor anything sacrificed for the chance of building. Nothing, nothing! the whole is nothing!

Hilda. Then you will never build anything more?

Solness (with animation). On the contrary, I am just going to begin!

Hilda. What, then? What will you build? Tell me at once!

Solness. I believe there is only one possible dwelling-place for human happiness — and that is what I am going to build now.

Hilda (looks fixedly at him). Mr. Solness — you mean our castles in the air.

Solness. The castles in the air — yes.

Hilda. I am afraid you would turn dizzy before we got halfway up.

Solness. Not if I can mount hand in hand with you, Hilda.

Hilda (with an expression of suppressed resentment). Only with me? Will there be no others of the party?

Solness. Who else should there be?

Hilda. Oh — that girl — that Kaia at the desk. Poor thing — don't you want to take her with you too?

Solness. Oho! Was it about her that Aline was talking to you?

Hilda. Is it so — or is it not?

Solness (vehemently). I will not answer such a question. You must believe in me, wholly and entirely!

Hilda. All these ten years I have believed in you so utterly — so utterly.

Solness. You must go on believing in me!

Hilda. Then let me see you stand free and high up!

Solness (sadly). Oh, Hilda — it is not every day that I can do that.

Hilda (passionately). I will have you do it! I will have it! (*Imploringly.*) Just once more, Mr. Solness! Do the *impossible* once again!

Solness (*stands and looks deep into her eyes*). If I try it, Hilda, I will stand up there and talk to him as I did that time before.

Hilda (*in rising excitement*). What will you say to him?

Solness. I will say to him: Hear me, Mighty Lord — thou may'st judge me as seems best to thee. But hereafter I will build nothing but the loveliest thing in the world ——

Hilda (*carried away*). Yes — yes — yes!

Solness. —— build it together with a princess, whom I love ——

Hilda. Yes, tell him that! Tell him that!

Solness. Yes. And then I will say to him: Now I shall go down and throw my arms round her and kiss her ——

Hilda. —— many times! Say that!

Solness. —— many, many times, I will say.

Hilda. And then ——?

Solness. Then I will wave my hat — and come down to the earth — and do as I said to him.

Hilda (*with outstretched arms*). Now I see you again as I did when there was song in the air!

Solness (*looks at her with his head bowed*). How have you become what you are, Hilda?

Hilda. How have you made me what I am?

Solness (*shortly and firmly*). The princess shall have her castle.

Hilda (*jubilant, clapping her hands*). Oh, Mr. Solness ——! My lovely, lovely castle. Our castle in the air!

Solness. On a firm foundation.

> (*In the street a crowd of people has assembled, vaguely seen through the trees. Music of wind-instruments is heard far away behind the new house.*)

(MRS. SOLNESS, *with a fur collar round her neck,* DOCTOR HERDAL *with her white shawl on his arm, and some women come out on the veranda.* RAGNAR BROVIK *comes at the same time up from the garden.*)

Mrs. Solness (*to* RAGNAR). Are we to have music, too?

Ragnar. Yes. It's the band of the Masons' Union. (*To* SOLNESS.) The foreman asked me to tell you that he is ready now to go up with the wreath.

Solness (*takes his hat*). Good. I will go down to him myself.

Mrs. Solness (*anxiously*). What have you to do down there, Halvard?

Solness (*curtly*). I must be down below with the men.

Mrs. Solness. Yes, down below — only down below.

Solness. That is where I always stand — on everyday occasions.

> (*He goes down the flight of steps and away through the garden.*)

Mrs. Solness (*calls after him over the railing*). But do beg the man to be careful when he goes up! Promise me that, Halvard!

Dr. Herdal (*to* MRS. SOLNESS). Don't you see that I was right? He has given up all thought of that folly.

Mrs. Solness. Oh, what a relief! Twice workmen have fallen, and each time they were killed on the spot. (*Turns to* HILDA.) Thank you, Miss Wangel, for having kept such a firm hold upon him. I should never have been able to manage him.

Dr. Herdal (*playfully*). Yes, yes, Miss Wangel, you know how to keep firm hold on a man, when you give your mind to it.

> (MRS. SOLNESS *and* DR. HERDAL *go up to the women, who are standing nearer to the steps and looking over the garden.* HILDA *remains standing beside the railing in the foreground.* RAGNAR *goes up to her.*)

Ragnar (*with suppressed laughter, half whispering*). Miss Wangel — do you see all those young fellows down in the street?

Hilda. Yes.

Ragnar. They are my fellow students, come to look at the master.

Hilda. What do they want to look at *him* for?

Ragnar. They want to see how he daren't climb to the top of his own house.

Hilda. Oh, *that* is what those boys want, is it?

Ragnar (*spitefully and scornfully*). He has kept us down so long — now we are going to see *him* keep quietly down below himself.

Hilda. You will not see that — not this time.

Ragnar (*smiles*). Indeed! Then where shall we see him?

Hilda. High — high up by the vane! That is where you will see him!

Ragnar (*laughs*). Him! Oh, yes, I dare say!

Hilda. His *will* is to reach the top — so at the top you shall see him.

Ragnar. His *will*, yes; that I can easily believe. But he simply *cannot* do it. His head would swim round long, long before he got halfway. He would have to crawl down again on his hands and knees.

Dr. Herdal (*points across*). Look! There goes the foreman up the ladders.

Mrs. Solness. And of course he has the wreath to carry too. Oh, I do hope he will be careful!

Ragnar (*stares incredulously and shouts*). Why, but it's ——

Hilda (*breaking out in jubilation*). It is the master builder himself.

Mrs. Solness (*screams with terror*). Yes, it is Halvard! Oh, my great God——! Halvard! Halvard!

Dr. Herdal. Hush! Don't shout to him!

Mrs. Solness (*half beside herself*). I must go to him! I must get him to come down again!

Dr. Herdal (*holds her*). Don't move, any of you! Not a sound!

Hilda (*immovable, follows* SOLNESS *with her eyes*). He climbs and climbs. Higher and higher! Higher and higher! Look! Just look!

Ragnar (*breathless*). He *must* turn now. He can't possibly help it.

Hilda. He climbs and climbs. He will soon be at the top now.

Mrs. Solness. Oh, I shall die of terror. I cannot bear to see it.

Dr. Herdal. Then don't look up at him.

Hilda. There he is standing on the topmost planks. Right at the top!

Dr. Herdal. Nobody must move! Do you hear?

Hilda (*exulting, with quiet intensity*). At last! At last! Now I see him great and free again!

Ragnar (*almost voiceless*). But this is im——

Hilda. So I have seen him all through these ten years. How secure he stands! Frightfully thrilling all the same. Look at him! Now he is hanging the wreath round the vane!

Ragnar. I feel as if I were looking at something utterly impossible.

Hilda. Yes, it is the *impossible* that he is doing now! (*With the indefinable expression in her eyes.*) Can you see anyone else up there with him?

Ragnar. There is no one else.

Hilda. Yes, there is one he is striving with.

Ragnar. You are mistaken.

Hilda. Then do you hear no song in the air, either?

Ragnar. It must be the wind in the tree-tops.

Hilda. *I* hear a song — a mighty song! (*Shouts in wild jubilation and glee.*) Look, look! Now he is waving his hat! He is waving it to us down

here! Oh, wave, wave back to him! For now it is finished! (*Snatches the white shawl from the* DOCTOR, *waves it, and shouts up to* SOLNESS.) Hurrah for Master Builder Solness!

Dr. Herdal. Stop! Stop! For God's sake——!

(*The women on the veranda wave their pocket-handkerchiefs, and the shouts of "Hurrah" are taken up in the street below. Then they are suddenly silenced, and the crowd bursts out into a shriek of horror. A human body, with planks and fragments of wood, is vaguely perceived crashing down behind the trees.*)

Mrs. Solness and the women (*at the same time*). He is falling! He is falling!

(MRS. SOLNESS *totters, falls backwards, swooning, and is caught, amid cries and confusion, by the women. The crowd in the street breaks down the fence and storms into the garden. At the same time* DR. HERDAL, *too, rushes down thither. A short pause.*)

Hilda (*stares fixedly upwards and says, as if petrified*). My Master Builder.

Ragnar (*supports himself, trembling, against the railing*). He must be dashed to pieces — killed on the spot.

One of the Women (*while* MRS. SOLNESS *is carried into the house*). Run down for the doctor——

Ragnar. I can't stir a foot——

Another Woman. Then call to someone!

Ragnar (*tries to call out*). How is it? Is he alive?

A Voice (*below, in the garden*). Mr. Solness is dead!

Other Voices (*nearer*). The head is all crushed. — He fell right into the quarry.

Hilda (*turns to* RAGNAR *and says quietly*). I can't see him up there now.

Ragnar. This is terrible. So, after all, he could not do it.

Hilda (*as if in quiet spellbound triumph*). But he mounted right to the top. And I heard harps in the air. (*Waves her shawl in the air and shrieks with wild intensity.*) *My* — *my* Master Builder!

CURTAIN

Les Symbolistes

The following selections, in verse and prose, are taken from the work of members of the Symbolist Group in France. The characteristics and purposes of this group are set forth in the introductory essay on "The Symbolists." Never a large or popular movement, in the sense that classicism or realism were popular, symbolism is nevertheless important because of its effect on the literature of recent decades. (For references see page 883.)

Il Pleut Doucement sur la Ville

Tears fall within mine heart,
As rain upon the town:
Whence does this languor start,
Possessing all mine heart?

O sweet fall of the rain   5
Upon the earth and roof,
Unto an heart in pain,
O music of the rain.

Tears that have no reason
Fall in my sorry heart: 10
What, there was no treason?
This grief hath no reason.

Nay, the more desolate,
Because, I know not why,
(Neither for love nor hate)   15
Mine heart is desolate.

PAUL VERLAINE
(*Translated by Ernest Dowson*)

À Clymène

Mystical strains unheard,
A song without a word,
Dearest, because thine eyes,
Pale as the skies,

Because thy voice, remote   5
As the far clouds that float
Veiling for me the whole
Heaven of the soul,

Because the stately scent
Of thy swan's whiteness, blent   10
With the white lily's bloom
Of thy perfume,

Ah, because thy dear love,
The music breathed above
By angels halo-crowned,   15
Odor and sound,

Hath, in my subtle heart,
With some mysterious art
Transposed thy harmony,
So let it be.   20

PAUL VERLAINE
(*Translated by Arthur Symons*)

The Vase [1]

My heavy hammer sounded through the air,
I saw the river and the orchard trees,
The field, and the woods beyond, and the blue sky,
Then rose, then purple, with the setting sun.
Then I arose; happily tossed aside my day-long   5
    task,
Stiff with bending from the dawn to dusk
Before the block of marble I was hewing
Out of the rough, where my heavy hammer, falling
To the rhythm of the clear morning and the fair
    day,
Struck and resounded gladly through the air!   10

The vase was taking life in the fashioned stone.
Pure and graceful it arose, unformed
Still in its grace, and I stood by for days
With idle, restless hands, turning my head
To left, to right, following the slightest sound,   15
Yet did not polish its round nor raise the hammer.
The water flowed from the fountain as if taking
    breath.
In the silence, down the orchard branches, one by
    one,
I heard the fruit falling; I breathed the spent
    perfume

[1] From *Modern French Poetry*, an anthology compiled and translated by Joseph T. Shipley. (Greenberg, New York.)

Of distant flowers on the wind; at times I heard —
Or thought I heard — dim voices talking low,   21
And one day while I dreamed, though I did not
　　　sleep,
I culled across the meadow and the stream
The sound of flutes.

And once,   25
Between yellow and gold leaves of the woods
I saw the shining yellow limbs
Of a dancing faun;
And on another time
He came out of the woods and followed the road
And sat on a mound   31
And caught a butterfly on his horn.

Once, too,
A centaur swam the river;
The water rippled over his human skin and over his
　　　fur;   35
He took a few steps among the reeds,
Sniffed the air, whinnied, and was gone again;
The next morning the print of his heel
Was on the grass. . . .

Nude women   40
Went by; they carried baskets and sheaves;
They were far off, at the end of the plain.
One morning there were three at the fountain,
And one of them spoke to me.   She was nude.
She said: "Carve the stone,   45
Carve it as my form is graven on your fancy,
Make my clear face smile on the stone;
Hear the hours fly around you
Danced by my sisters in their twining round,
Interlaced,   50
Turning, singing, twining and untwined."

And I felt her warm kiss on my cheek.

Then the great orchard and the woods and plain
Shook with strange tumult, and the fountain flowed
More sparkling, and a laugh lay on its waters;   55
The three nymphs near three reeds held hands and
　　　danced;
The red fauns came in troops forth from the woods
And voices sang beyond the orchard trees
With flutes alert upon the tenuous air.

Earth sounded with the galloping of centaurs   60
To the sonorous deeps of the horizon,
And squatting there upon their quivering croups,
Holding bent staves and dark pot-bellied flasks,
Were hobbling satyrs stung by swarming bees,
And mane-spread mouths and purple lips were
　　　joined,
　　　　　　　　　　　　　　　　　　　　　65

And in immense and murmurous frenzied round
Light feet, or heavy hooves, croups, tunics, fleeces,
Turned passionately round me grave and calm,
Carving upon the curved sides of the vase
The whirlwind of the forces of all life.   70

From the perfume given off by ripened earth
A sweet intoxication filled my thoughts;
And in the odor of fruits and trampled grapes,
In the thud of hooves and the patter of flying heels,
In the wild scent of stallions and he-goats,   75
Under the wind of the round and the shrill of the
　　　laughter,
I carved on the marble all that was stirring there;
And amidst the warm flesh and the heated emana-
　　　tions,
Whinnying of muzzle or murmuring of lips,
I felt on my hands, in rough or loving contact,   80
The breathing of nostrils or the moist mouth's kiss.

Twilight came, and at last my head was lifted.

My drunkenness was dead with the task done;
And there at last on its base, from foot to handles,
The great vase stood upright in the stillness;   85
And carved in a spiral on the living stone
The scattered round (and in a far-off wind
Echo revived its tumult) of goats, and gods,
And sweet nude women turned, and prancing
　　　centaurs,
And adroit fauns; silently turned along the sides,
While alone forever in the gloomy night   91
I cursed the dawn and wept across the dark.

　　　　　　　　　　　　　　HENRI DE RÉGNIER

The Frenzied Ship[1]

As down the slow impassive streams I came,
No longer had I mariners as guides:
They had been targets for the Red-Skins' aim,
To painted posts were nailed their naked hides.

Careless of all the mercantile parade,   5
Trading in English cotton, Flemish grain,
I left my seamen and their broils, and made
Down the unchallenging waters to the main.

Last year I sailed, deaf as with childish fear,
Before the furious clackings of the brine: 10
The mightiest promontories with straining gear
Ne'er lived through hurly-burly more divine.

[1] Translated by Dorothy Martin and reprinted from
Sextette, published by The Scholartis Press, London,
England.

The storm has blessed my watches with its spume,
And cork-like I have danced for ten dark nights
Above the eternal body-rolling fume,   15
Nor missed the sorry blinking of the lights.

Sweeter the virid [1] water in my seams
Than luscious apple-flesh to childish hopes:
Spray, like blue wine, and vomit washed my beams
With quick snatch, fore and aft, at helm and ropes.

And long by the sweet lyric of the sea   21
Infused with stars, latescent,[2] was I bound,
Poring upon its verdurous blues where, free,
Float the pale ravished bodies of the drowned,

Where the slow-rhythmed ecstasies of day,   25
With sudden strain throughout the azure, move:
Headier than wine, vaster than music, they
Ferment the roseate bitterness of love.

I have seen lightnings riving heaven's face,
Surfs, currents, water-spouts; evening's soft gleam
And morning's noble as some dove-like race: 31
Seen, too, such things as few men even dream;

Seen low suns splashed with mystic infamy,
Illumining through clotted violet;
And heard the chorus of old tragedy   35
In the far breakers' wonder-wounded fret;

Conjured the seas' green depths, from whence arise
Slow kisses sparkling to the foam's far snow,
The alarms of blue and gold which phosphorus
        cries,
The unimagined stir of ocean's flow.   40

For long months I have sailed by coral rocks
Which cleft the swell to lines of plunging steers;
And pondered how their snarling muzzle mocks
At Ocean's pantings and the Virgin's tears.

By unimagined Floridas I ran,   45
Brilliant with flowers and panthers' eyes, and gay
With barbarous hides and rainbows in whose span
'Neath far horizons glaucous [3] cattle stray.

And I have seen great nets within whose paunch
Rotted Leviathans; seen fens dilate,   50
And distant waters into whirlpools launch;
Seen, in a lull, sea's cataractic spate; [4]

Glaciers and nacrous [5] waves, skies ember-show-
        ered,
Refulgent suns, grim wrecks in ocean's lees

[1] green.   [2] becoming obscure.
[3] sea-green.   [4] overflow.   [5] iridescent.

Where elephantine reptiles, bug-devoured,   55
Beguiled with evil scents contorted trees.

Could I have shown some child those dolphins gay,
Those singing fish, those carp of gold delight!
Foam-flowers have graced me as I gathered way,
And winds ineffable have winged my flight.   60

Charming each plunge with moans, at times the
        sea,
Worn martyr weary of the pilgrim's share,
Raised its pale-chaliced, ghostly flowers to me;
And I have lingered like a nun at prayer,

While land to me brought excrement and feud   65
Of wan-eyed sea-birds, peevishly distressed,
And while athwart my slender chains I viewed
The drowned sink down haphazardly to rest.

But I, forlorn wreck in the weeds' embrace,
Storm-hurled through ether far beyond all ken,   70
Whose sea-drunk carcass would have found no
        grace
In Monitors or Hanseatic men,

Petulant, free, streaming with crimson haze,
Who pierced the blushing sky-walls on which time
Had fondly lavished for a poet's praise   75
Sun-silvered fungi and sky-azured slime,

Who, darkly zoned by sea-horse retinue,
Rode on, crazed raft, with phosphorescence
        splashed,
When the bright archways of the vaulted blue
Before July's swift cudgellings had crashed,   80

Who, shuddering, sensed desire's recurring hurt,
Far off, in Maelstroms' or Behemoths' moans,
Eternal truant on the blue inert,
I long for Europe and her ancient stones.

In night's Ægean many an island star   85
Beckons from magic skies.   Within that sea
Of boundless void sleepest thou, exiled far,
O golden drift of wings, thou Might to be?

Much I have suffered.   The dawns lacerate,
Each moon is cruel, bitter each sun's sweep.   90
Slow, frenzied dreams from galling love dilate.
O that my keel might snap and plunge me deep!

Yet among Europe's waters I would see
The cold, dark pool 'neath evening's scented sky
Where, crouching low, a wistful child sets free   95
A boat as fragile as May butterfly.

Bathed in your languors, Ocean, I shall glide
No longer past the cotton-trader's bulk,
Nor challenge oriflammes' and pennons' pride,
Nor brave the glaring eyes of prison-hulk.   100

ARTHUR RIMBAUD

The Windows[1]

Tired of the almshouse drear, whose rank fumes
    crawl
Like incense up the curtains' tedious white
To where the cross sighs on the vacant wall,
The furtive inmate draws himself upright,

And, less to warm his gangrenes than to stare   5
Once more on sunlit stone, drags off to press
His bony features and white forelock where
The windows burn to each ray's bright caress.

His feverish lips, of the same ravenous hue
As when he went of old, an amorous swain,   10
To woo simplicity, greasily dew
In a long bitter kiss the gilded pane.

Rapt he remains, nor dose nor time recalls,
Nor bed enforced, nor fear of the last rite,
Nor cough; and when the glow of evening falls,   15
His eyes, upon horizons fraught with light,

See golden galleys in swan-like beauty sleep
On streams of perfume and of porphyry
Rocking their gleaming prows above a deep
Of heedlessness poignant with memory.   20

Thus, I, contemptuous of man's hardened heart
Spoiled by prosperity, glutted with food
For appetites alone, his chosen part
To gather precious ordures for his brood,

Quickly retreat to casements where we still   25
May turn aside from life; and there, reborn,
In windows where eternal dews distil,
Where pure and golden gleams the Infinite Morn,

I see myself transfigured!   And its beam
— Be the glass art or ecstasy — empowers   30
Me still to live and bear, gem-like, my dream
Up to the highest heaven where Beauty flowers.

But alas!   Earth constrains.   Nauseous, her stress
For ever lurks about my shelter's brink,
And the lewd vomitings of Foolishness   35
Even to the confines of the azure stink.

[1] Translated by Dorothy Martin and reprinted from
Sextette, published by The Scholartis Press, London,
England.

Yet may not I, I to whom sorrow clings,
Break through the crystal smirched by infamy,
And take far flight, on these poor, unfledged wings
— Chancing a fall throughout Eternity?   40

STÉPHANE MALLARMÉ

Sea-Wind

The flesh is sad, alas! and all the books are read.
Flight, only flight!   I feel that birds are wild to
    tread
The floor of unknown foam, and to attain the skies!
Nought, neither ancient gardens mirrored in the
    eyes,
Shall hold this heart that bathes in waters its de-
    light,   5
O nights! nor yet my waking lamp, whose lonely
    light
Shadows the vacant paper, whiteness profits best,
Nor the young wife who rocks her baby on her
    breast.
I will depart!   O steamer, swaying rope and spar,
Lift anchor for exotic lands that lie afar!   10
A weariness, outworn by cruel hopes, still clings
To the last farewell handkerchief's last beckonings!
And are not these, the masts inviting storms, not
    these
That an awakening wind bends over wrecking seas,
Lost, not a sail, a sail, a flowering isle, ere long?   15
But, O my heart, hear thou, hear thou, the sailors'
    song!

STÉPHANE MALLARMÉ
(Translated by Arthur Symons)

L'Après-Midi d'un Faune[1]

I would immortalize these nymphs: so bright
Their sunlit coloring, so airy light,
It floats like drowsy down.   Loved I a dream?
My doubts, born of oblivious darkness, seem
A subtle tracery of branches grown   5
The tree's true self — proving that I have known,
Thinking it love, the blushing of a rose.
But think.   These nymphs, their loveliness . . .
    suppose
They bodied forth your senses' fabulous thirst?
Illusion! which the blue eyes of the first,   10
As cold and chaste as is the weeping spring,
Beget: the other, sighing, passioning,
Is she the wind, warm in your fleece at noon?

[1] From Aldous Huxley's translation, in his Selected
Poems. By permission of Basil Blackwell, Oxford,
England.

No; through this quiet, when a weary swoon
Crushes and chokes the latest faint essay   15
Of morning, cool against the encroaching day,
There is no murmuring water, save the gush
Of my clear fluted notes; and in the hush
Blows never a wind, save that which through my
          reed
Puffs out before the rain of notes can speed   20
Upon the air, with that calm breath of art
That mounts the unwrinkled zenith visibly,
Where inspiration seeks its native sky.
You fringes of a calm Sicilian lake,
The sun's own mirror which I love to take,   25
Silent beneath your starry flowers, tell
How here I cut the hollow rushes, well
Tamed by my skill, when on the glaucous [1] *gold*
Of distant lawns about their fountain cold
A living whiteness stirs like a lazy wave;   30
And at the first slow notes my panpipes gave
These flocking swans, these naiads, rather, fly
Or dive.   Noon burns inert and tawny dry,
Nor marks how clean that Hymen [2] slipped away
From me who seek in song the real A.   35
Wake, then, to the first ardor and the sight,
O lonely faun, of the old fierce white light,
With, lilies, one of you for innocence.
Other than their lips' delicate pretense,
The light caress that quiets treacherous lovers,   40
My breast, I know not how to tell, discovers
The bitten print of some immortal's kiss.

But hush! a mystery so great as this
I dare not tell, save to my double reed,
Which, sharer of my every joy and need,   45
Dreams down its cadenced monologues that we
Falsely confuse the beauties that we see
With the bright palpable shapes our song creates:
My flute, as loud as passion modulates,
Purges the common dream of flank and breast   50
Seen through closed eyes and inwardly caressed,
Of every empty and monotonous line.

Bloom then, O Syrinx,[3] in thy flight malign,
A reed once more beside our trysting-lake.
Proud of my music, let me often make   55
A song of goddesses and see their rape
Profanely done on many a painted shape.
So when the grape's transparent juice I drain,
I quell regret for pleasures past and feign
A new real grape.   For holding towards the sky   60
The empty skin, I blow it tight and lie
Dream-drunk till evening, eyeing it.
                              Tell o'er

[1] sea-green.
[2] God of marriage, son of Apollo and a muse.
[3] An Arcadian nymph, changed into a reed from
which Pan made his pipes.

Remembered joys and plump the grape once more.
Between the reeds I saw their bodies gleam
Who cool no mortal fever in the stream   65
Crying to the woods the rage of their desires
And their bright hair went down in jeweled fire
Where crystal broke and dazzled shudderingly.
I check my swift pursuit: for see where lie,
Bruised, being twins in love, by languor sweet,   70
Two sleeping girls, clasped at my very feet.
I seize and run with them, nor part the pair,
Breaking this covert of frail petals, where
Roses drink scent of the sun and our light play
'Mid tumbled flowers shall match the death of day.   75
I love that virginal fury — ah, the wild
Thrill when a maiden body shrinks, defiled,
Shuddering like arctic light, from lips that sear
Its nakedness . . . the flesh in secret fear!
Contagiously through my linked pair it flies   80
Where innocence in either, struggling, dies,
Wet with fond tears or some less piteous dew.
Gay in the conquest of these fears, I grew
So rash that I must needs the sheaf divide
Of ruffled kisses heaven itself had tied.   85
For as I leaned to stifle in the hair
Of one my passionate laughter (taking care
With a stretched finger, that her innocence
Might stain with her companion's kindling sense
To touch the younger little one, who lay   90
Child-like unblushing) my ungrateful prey
Slips from me, freed by passion's sudden death
Nor heeds the frenzy of my sobbing breath.
Let it pass! others of their hair shall twist
A rope to drag me to those joys I missed.   95
See how the ripe pomegranates bursting red
To quench the thirst of the mumbling bees have
          bled;
So too our blood, kindled by some chance fire,
Flows for the swarming legions of desire.
At evening, when the woodland green turns gold
And ashen gray, 'mid the quenched leaves, be-
          hold!   101
Red Etna glows, by Venus visited,
Walking the lava with her snowy tread
Whene'er the flames in thunderous slumber die.
I hold the goddess!

                    Ah, sure penalty!   105

But the unthinking soul and body swoon
At last beneath the heavy hush of noon.
Forgetful let me lie where summer's drouth
Sifts fine the sand and then with gaping mouth
Dream planet-struck by the grape's round wine-
          red star.   110

Nymphs, I shall see the shade that now you are.
                              STÉPHANE MALLARMÉ

Memories [1]

Memories are rooms without a lock,
Empty rooms we no longer dare to enter,
For in them once old relatives have died.
We live in the house where there are these closed
    rooms,
We know that they are still there, that this one is
The blue room, that the rose. And so the house
Fills up with solitude, and we smile on.
When it wills, I gather up the passing memory,
And I say: "Go in there. I'll come to see you
    soon."
I know throughout my life it's waiting there
But sometimes I forget to go and see it.
There are so many thus in the old house.
They are resigned to our forgetfulness,
And if I do not come tonight, nor soon,
Ask of my heart no more than you ask of life . . .
I know they're sleeping there, behind the walls,
I therefore have no need to go to find them;
I can see their windows as I walk the road,
And it will be so until we die of them.
Yet sometimes I feel, amid the daily shadows,
An indeterminate shudder, and a cold
Whose hidden source I know not, and I pass . . .
Yet every time it is a mourning signal.
A tremor has secretly come to give us word
That a memory has gone forth, or has died . . .
It is not easy to tell which memory,
One is so old, one scarcely can remember . . .

And yet I feel dim eyelids close within me.

                HENRI BATAILLE

Vox Populi [2]

Grand review at the Champs-Elysées that day!
Twelve years have been suffered since that
vision. A summer sun shattered its long arrows of
gold against the roofs and domes of the ancient
capital. Thousands of panes reflected its dazzling
rays; the people, bathed in a powdery light,
thronged the streets to gaze at the army.

Sitting upon a high wooden stool before the
railing of the parvis of Notre Dame, his knees
folded under black rags, his hands joined under
the placard that legally sanctioned his blindness,
the centenarian beggar, patriarch of the Misery
of Paris — a mournful face of ashen tint, with skin

[1] From *Modern French Poetry*, an anthology compiled
and translated by Joseph T. Shipley. (Greenberg, New
York.)

[2] From *Pastels in Prose*, translated by Stuart Merrill.
By permission of Harper & Brothers, Publishers.

furrowed by wrinkles of the color of earth — lent
his shadowy presence to the *Te Deum* of the surrounding festival.

All these people, were they not his brethren?
The joyous passers-by, were they not his kin?
Were they not human, like him? Besides, that
guest of the sovereign portal was not entirely destitute: the State had recognized his right to be
blind.

Clothed with the title and respectability implied
in the official right to receive alms, enjoying, moreover, a voter's privilege, he was our equal — except
in light.

And that man, forgotten, as it were, among the
living, articulated from time to time a monotonous
plaint — evident syllabification of the profound
sighs of his whole lifetime:
"Have pity on the blind, if you please!"

Around him, beneath the powerful vibrations
fallen from the belfry — outside, yonder, beyond
the wall of his eyes — the trampling of cavalry,
the intermittent braying of trumpets, acclamations
mingled with salvoes of artillery from the *Invalides* with the proud shouts of command, the
rattle of steel, and the thunder of drums scanning
the interminable march of the passing infantry, a
rumor of glory reached him! His trained hearing
caught even the rustle of the floating standards
whose heavy fringes brushed against the cuirasses.
In the mind of the old captive of obscurity a
thousand flashes of sensation evoked visions fore-
known yet indistinct. A sort of divination informed him of what fevered the hearts and
thoughts of the city.

And the people, fascinated, as always, by the
prestige that comes from strokes of boldness and
fortune, clamored its prayer of the moment:
"Long live the Emperor!"

But during the lulls of the triumphal tempest a
lost voice arose in the direction of the mystic
railing. The old man, his neck thrown back
against the pillory of bars, rolling his dead eyeballs
towards the sky, forgotten by that people of which
he seemed alone to express the genuine prayer, the
prayer hidden under the hurrahs, the secret and
personal prayer, droned, like an augural interceder,
his now mysterious phrase:
"Have pity on the blind, if you please!"

Grand review at the Champs-Elysées that day!
Now ten years have flown since the sun of that
festival — same sounds, same voices, same smoke.
A sordine, however, tempered the tumult of the
public rejoicings. A shadow weighed on the eyes
of all. The ceremonial salvoes from the platform

of the Prytaneum were crossed this time by the distant growls of the batteries in our forts; and straining their ears, the people sought already to distinguish in the echoes the answer of the enemy's approaching cannon.

The Governor, borne by the ambling trot of his thoroughbred, passed, smiling upon all. The people, reassured by the confidence which an irreproachable demeanor always inspires, alternated with patriotic songs the military applause with which they honored the presence of the soldier.

But the syllables of the furious cheer of yore had been modified; the distracted people preferred the prayer of the moment:

"Long live the Republic!"

And yonder, in the direction of the sublime threshold, could still be distinguished the solitary voice of Lazarus. The sayer of the hidden thought of the people did not modify the rigidity of his fixed plaint. Sincere soul of the festival, uplifting his extinguished eyes to the sky, he cried out, during the silences, with the accent of one making a statement:

"Have pity on the blind, if you please!"

Grand review at the Champs-Elysées that day! Now nine months have been endured since that troubled sun. Oh! same rumors, same clashing of arms, same neighing of horses, more muffled, however, than the previous year, but yet noisy.

"Long live the Commune!" shouted the people to the passing wind.

And the voice of the secular Elect of Misfortune still repeated, yonder upon the sacred threshold, his refrain that connected the unique thought of the people. Raising his trembling head to the sky, he moaned in the shadow:

"Have pity on the blind, if you please!"

And two moons later, when, to the last vibrations of the tocsin, the generalissimo of the regular forces of the State reviewed his two hundred thousand guns, still smoking, alas! from the sad civil war, the terrified people shouted, while gazing upon the edifices flaming afar:

"Long live the Marshal!"

Yonder, in the direction of the pure enclosure, the immutable voice of the veteran of human misery mechanically repeated his dolorous and piteous observation:

"Have pity on the blind, if you please!"

And since then, from year to year, from review to review, from vociferations to vociferations, whatever might be the name thrown to the hazards of space by the cheering people, those who listen attentively to the sounds of the earth have always distinguished, above the revolutionary clamors and the warlike festivals that followed, the faraway Voice, the true Voice, the intimate Voice of the terrible symbolical beggar, of the incorruptible sentinel of the citizens' conscience, of him who restores integrally the occult prayer of the Crowd and expresses its sighs.

Inflexible Pontiff of fraternity, that authorized titulary of physical blindness, has never ceased, like an unconscious mediator, to invoke the divine charity upon his brethren in intelligence.

And when, intoxicated with fanfares, with peals of bells and with artillery, the people, dazed by the flattering uproar, endeavors vainly, under whatever syllables falsely enthusiastic, to hide from itself its veritable prayer, the beggar, groping through the sky, his arms uplifted, his face towards the heavy darkness, arises on the eternal threshold of the church, and seem, however, to carry beyond the stars, in tones more and more lamentable, which continues to cry his prophetic rectification:

"Have pity on the blind, if you please!"

VILLIERS DE L'ISLE-ADAM

Camaïeu in Red [1]

The room was hung with pink satin embossed with crimson sprays; the curtains fell amply from the windows, breaking their great folds of garnet velvet upon a purple-flowered carpet. On the walls were suspended *sanguines* [2] by Boucher, and platters of brass gemmed and inlaid with niello [3] by some artist of the Renaissance.

The divan, the arm-chairs, the chairs, were covered with stuffs similar to the hangings, with carnation fringes; and upon the mantle, surmounted by a glass that revealed an autumnal sky all empurpled by the setting sun and forests with leaves as red as wine, bloomed, in a vast stand, an enormous bouquet of carmine azaleas, of sage, of digitalis, and of amaranth.

The all-powerful goddess was buried in the cushions of the divan, rubbing her tawny tresses against the cherry-red satin, displaying her pink skirts, twirling her little morocco slipper at the end of her foot. She sighed affectedly, arose, stretched her arms, seized a large-bellied bottle, and poured out in a small glass, with slender stem

---

[1] From *Pastels in Prose*, translated by Stuart Merrill. By permission of Harper & Brothers, publishers.
[2] Drawings in red crayon.
[3] Black alloy inlaid on metalwork.

and wrought in the shape of a vise, a thread of reddish-brown port.

At that moment the sun inundated the boudoir with its red gleams, struck scintillating flashes from the spirals of the glass, caused the ambrosial liquor to sparkle like molten topazes, and, shattering its rays against the brass of the platters, lighted in it fulgurating [1] fires. It was a rutilant [2] confusion of flames against which stood out the features of the drinker, like those of the virgins of Cimabue and Angelico, whose heads are encircled with a nimbus of gold.

That fanfare of red stunned me; that gamut of furious intensity, of impossible violence, blinded me. I closed my eyes, and when I opened them once more, the dazzling tint had vanished, the sun had set!

Since that time the red boudoir and the drinker have disappeared; the magic blaze is extinguished.

In summer, however, when the nostalgia of red weighs more heavily upon me, I raise my head to the sun, and there, under its hot stings, impassible, with eyes obstinately closed, I see under the veil of my lids a red vapor; I recall my thoughts, and I see once more, for a minute, for a second, the disquieting fascination, the unforgotten enchantment.

                              JORIS-KARL HUYSMANS

In Autumn [3]

Since Maria has left me for another star — which one, Orion, Altaïr, or is it thou, green Venus? — I have always cherished solitude. How many long days have I passed alone with my cat! By *alone*, I mean with no material being; and my cat is a mystic companion, a spirit. I can therefore say that I have passed long days with my cat, and alone, with one of the last authors of the Latin decadence. For since the white creature is no more, strangely and singularly have I loved all that is summed up in that word: fall. Thus, of the year, my favorite season is the last languishing days of summer, that immediately precede autumn; and of the day, the hour that I choose for going forth is when the sun rests before sinking, with rays of yellow brass upon the gray walls, and of red brass upon the window-panes. In the same way the literature from which my spirit seeks a sad voluptuousness will be the agonizing poetry of the last moments of Rome, so long, however, as it in nowise betrays the rejuvenating approach of the Barbarians, and does not lisp the infantile Latin of the first Christian prose.

I was therefore reading one of those dear poems (whose scaling enamel has more charm for me than the carnation of youth), and had plunged a hand in the fur of the pure animal, when a barrel-organ began to sing languishingly and mournfully under my window. It played in the long walk of poplars, whose leaves seem to me yellow, even in summer, since Maria has passed there with tapers for the last time. The instrument of those that are sad, yes, truly: the piano scintillates, the violin opens light to the torn soul, but the barrel-organ, in the dusk of memory, has made me despairingly dream. Now that it was murmuring a joyously vulgar tune, that made the heart of the faubourgs grow merry, a superannuated and hackneyed tune, whence came it that its flourishes lured me to dreams and made me weep like a romantic ballad? I imbibed it slowly, and I refrained from throwing a penny out of the window, for fear of making a movement and of finding that the instrument was not singing of itself.

                              STÉPHANE MALLARMÉ

The Stairway [1]

At the foot of the stairway, under the sifted light of a window whose panes, in the shape of lozenges, are enchased in a network of lead, a fantastic beast, Dragon or Chimera, twists the coils of its tail and unclasps its sharp claws. With open jaws it seems to yawn with weariness or roar with rage. From its sinuous back, imbricated with scales, springs a sheaf of rare flowers that fall back to mirror themselves in the polished and swollen flanks of the monster. Reflections caress the carved wood, lustrously black and rigid as metal.

The stairway mounts, and plunges into warm shadow the torsion of its wrought balusters, which at every turn shine with a glossy sheen. Along the wall tapestries, in the softness of their deadened tints, unroll dreamy landscapes. They are bright and joyous hangings, but time has changed their colors. The pinks have whitened; the whites have become more eburnean and more creamy; the greens have been transmuted into blues, blues melting into shades more tender. And they offer sites of peace and repose a nature calm and artificial, a little chimerical, where one would fain lead one's vagrant thoughts through those scenes of joy and of happy siestas; parks whose alleys en-

---

[1] flashing.   [2] glittering.
[3] From *Pastels in Prose,* translated by Stuart Merrill. By permission of Harper & Brothers, publishers.

[1] From *Pastels in Prose,* translated by Stuart Merrill. By permission of Harper & Brothers, publishers.

circle lawns where the grass is represented by designs in arabesque; sheets of water bordered by vases and mythological statues, losing themselves under the blue shadow of the trees; basins into which drip overfull fountains. Cupids are at work gardening, wheeling flowers, digging parterres, letting harvests of roses overflow and fall from their childish arms. At the end of bluish avenues tranquil palaces rise in the fair horizontality of their lines; among the trees flutter multicolor paroquets. And I ascend, with my eyes full of the attenuated charm of these old things, discolored and soft as love — a love already ancient — that makes my heart beat as I push open the high door where run, underlining the woodwork, threads of gold. And in the room lightened by the shimmer of blue silks embroidered with light sprays, where fine curtains fall from the windows, indolently she is lying, stretched out on the divan, and lifts towards me the ineffable and languishing look of her eyes.

In the hollow of the stairway a round lantern hung from a silver chain. The light glintered along the balusters, and stole from step to step, fainter and fainter, leaving at the bottom the vagueness and mystery of a hole of shadows. And I descended slowly, with broken heart, carrying forever within me the memory of her cold looks and of her irremissible refusal.

The tapestries, whose colors were extinguished by the night, unrolled saddened landscapes; among the woods lost in darkness the multicolor paroquets were alone visible; the basins had disappeared; the hedges and grass made black spots in the design; the cupids, with feet on their spades, seemed to be digging a grave, and from their arms overflowed pale roses, so pale that they seemed like dead flowers; and the fantastic beast, Chimera or Dragon, was grinning wickedly, threatening and bellicose. In passing I took a flower, and the monster, twisting his tail, swelled his flanks as though to bark at my heels.

Through the dusk of the street, where were being lighted the swinging lanterns, a gust of wind passed, and the flower fell to pieces in my hand.

HENRI DE RÉGNIER

Butterflies [1]

Time tells the rosary of the sun.

In these hours colored like the treasure of the church, angel-cheeks soon to be devoured smile on the green branches of candelabra where dry-grass wags are calling. By the white bands of the light lowlands, where one slope is an idyll of Theocritus, one a bucolic of Virgil, come and go tunicked pilgrims, wreathed with a diadem that stubborn springs again, despite the puff of cloth whereby the peremptory hand, every twenty paces, effaces it. In an orchard milord Scarecrow over a desk is beating time to the cherrynotes played on a fife by a shepherd whose flock bleats under a lively flight of swallows knitting space. Meanwhile, before his threshold honeysuckle-decked, an old man come before his time sharpens the annual scythe, as if he were polishing a groundswell with the north wind.

Time tells the rosary of the sun.

SAINT-POL-ROUX

[1] From *Modern French Poetry*, an anthology compiled and translated by Joseph T. Shipley. (Greenberg, New York.)

References for

THE ROMANTIC MOOD

LITERATURE

Romanticism

LASCELLES ABERCROMBIE
Romanticism (1963)

MEYER HOWARD ABRAMS
The Mirror and The Lamp: Romantic Theory and The Critical Tradition (1953)

IRVING BABBITT
Rousseau and Romanticism (3rd ed., 1957)

JACQUES BARZUN
Classic, Romantic and Modern (1962)

JOSEPH W. BEACH
A Romantic View of Poetry (2nd ed., 1963)

ERNEST BERNBAUM
Guide Through the Romantic Movement (2nd ed., 1949)

C. M. BOWRA
The Romantic Imagination (1949)

DOUGLAS BUSH
Mythology and the Romantic Tradition in English Poetry (2nd ed., 1957)

R. F. GLECKNER and G. E. ENSCOE, eds.
Romanticism. Points of View (1962)

JOHN B. HALSTED, ed.
Romanticism. Problems of Definition, Explanation and Evaluation (1965)

F. L. LUCAS
The Decline and Fall of the Romantic Ideal (4th ed., 1963)

EMERY NEFF
A Revolution in European Poetry (1940)

EZRA POUND
The Spirit of Romance (1952)

MARIO PRAZ
The Romantic Agony (3rd ed., 1954)

HERBERT E. READ
The Sense of Glory (1930)

L. PEARSALL SMITH
"Four Romantic Words" in *Words and Idioms; Studies in the English Language* (1957)

Symbolism

MAURICE BEEBE, ed.
Literary Symbolism (1960)

ANGELO PHILIP BERTOCCI
From Symbolism to Baudelaire (1964)

C. M. BOWRA
The Heritage of Symbolism (3rd ed., 1959)

JOSEPH CHIARI
Symbolism from Poe to Mallarmé: The Growth of a Myth (1956)

KENNETH CORNELL
The Symbolist Movement (1951)

CHARLES FEIDELSON
Symbolism and American Literature (1953)

MARTIN FOSS
Symbol and Metaphor in Human Experience (1949)

SUSANNE K. LANGER
Philosophy in a New Key; A Study in the Symbolism of Reason, Rite and Art (6th ed., 1963)

MARCEL RAYMOND
From Baudelaire to Surrealism (1950)

A. N. WHITEHEAD
Symbolism, Its Meaning and Effect (2nd ed., 1959)

ART

In art, we do not distinguish between a symbolistic and a romantic style. In all ages, artists have created works that are more than imitations of nature, that present a symbolic treatment of abstract concepts. Various periods have favored allegorical representations, that is, human figures substituted for religious, moral, or philosophical ideas. While paintings on the whole remain in close touch with reality, insofar as they tend to produce an illusion of space, sculpture is more abstract, in being detached from its natural environment.

Historically speaking, the symbolist school of literature is coincident with the impressionistic movement in painting and music. It is only loosely connected with the various Romantic movements which precede it by more than half a century.

BOTTICELLI (1444–1510)
Birth of Venus
Adoration of the Magi

GIORGIONE (1477?–1511)
Stormy Landscape with Soldier and Gipsy
The Concert

TITIAN (1477–1576)
Alfonso d'Este and Laura Dianti
Lavinia Bearing a Salver of Fruit

RENI (1575–1642)
Venus and Cupid

883

RUBENS (1577–1640)
  La Ronda
  Helena Fourment and Son

WATTEAU (1684–1721)
  Fete d'Amour
  Embarkation for Cythera

BOUCHER (1703–1770)
  Girl with the Muff
  The Seasons: Winter

FRAGONARD (1732–1806)
  Love Letter
  Pursuit

GAINSBOROUGH (1727–1788)
  The Hon. Mrs. Graham
  Landscape with a Bridge

ROMNEY (1734–1802)
  Lady Hamilton as a Bacchante
  The Duchess of Gordon

LAWRENCE (1769–1830)
  The King of Rome
  Lady Robinson

TURNER (1775–1851)
  The Fighting Téméraire
  Meeting of the Waters

CONSTABLE (1776–1837)
  The Cornfield
  A View of Salisbury Cathedral

COROT (1796–1875)
  Spring
  Returning Home

THEODORE ROUSSEAU (1812–1867)
  Oaks

WATTS (1817–1904)
  Hope

INNESS (1825–1894)
  Delaware Valley
  Autumn

CHURCH (1826–1900)
  Cotopaxi

VEDDER (1836–1923)
  Questioner of the Sphinx

MUSIC

Although the classical composers adhered for the most part to the classical forms such as the sonata, some of them soon broke away in individual movements of compositions. They varied and elaborated the old forms, or else abandoned them entirely. These composers were the precursors of the romantic mood in music, a mood which stimulates the imagination and at the same time permits the greatest possible freedom of expression. One of the great romantic composers, Beethoven, when he was young, wrote sonatas and symphonies which show the influence of his distinguished predecessors, Haydn and Mozart, but he displayed a new spirit at work, in tone color, in structure, and in many lesser ways.

In music of the romantic mood themes are more emotional, and sometimes have definite non-musical ideas associated with them. Thus in Beethoven's Fifth Symphony the idea of Fate knocking at the door is frequently associated with the opening notes of the first movement. Names indicative of this shift away from pure music were given to compositions. A glance at the list of examples below is sufficient to indicate this. Much of classical music had an appeal chiefly to the intellect; most of romantic music plays to a large extent upon the emotions. Where a master is at work, as in the compositions of Beethoven, the listener is not always conscious of the way in which themes and their development work to create the most powerful emotional impact.

Beethoven may be regarded either as the last of the classicists or the first of the romanticists; there are numerous supporters for both viewpoints. In his early work, as has been said, he followed the rules more strictly; as he grew older he varied from them considerably, yet he seldom threw them out entirely. In his most romantic compositions there is still a profound feeling for form and structure and proportion. But the themes themselves, and their treatment in a manner which earlier musicians would have regarded as too unorthodox to bear listening to, mark him as a romantic. If we know Beethoven we have an understanding of what differentiates the classical from the romantic in music. He is, in a sense, the bridge between classicism and romanticism. Schumann and Wagner wrote music which is at times more purely melodic in its content and unrestrained in its form. Chopin is a romanticist who wrote music especially well suited to the piano; Schubert is the composer who had a talent for writing songs perfectly expressive of romanticism. Beethoven towers above them all because he wrote superbly in almost every available medium, and did so with incomparable skill. No one else displays so well the best romantic qualities controlled by a discipline learned in the classical school.

For pure romanticism, we may well examine the work of Brahms. Here we will find freedom of form, an emotional quality in themes, a more pronounced lyricism, richer and more varied orchestrations, and songs set to romantic poems which, romantic in their original version, have their romanticism intensified by the musical setting.

R. N. C.

COMPOSITIONS

MOZART (1756–1791)
Symphony No. 40 in G Minor, K. 550

The first two movements, especially, illustrate the use of essentially romantic musical material in a symphony in which the form is strictly classical.

Dies Iræ and the *Lacrymosa* from *The Requiem*

Here the words of the text permit the composer an expression which is not strictly classical; the words consciously dictate the nature of the music.

Concerto in D Minor for Piano and Orchestra, K. 466

This concerto is historically important because it is one of the first in which the piano is treated as a solo instrument rather than as just another voice in the orchestra. The form of the first and third movements is classical. The second movement (*Romanza*) has a gentle, melancholy tone which might be classified as romantic; the style of the movement is free — that is, not constructed on any of the formal patterns.

BACH (1685–1750)
O Pardon Me, My God from the *Passion of Our Lord According to St. Matthew*

Here, again, the words of the text play their part in removing the music from a strictly classical mood.

BEETHOVEN (1770–1827)
Sonata in A Major for Violin and Piano, Op. 47 ("Kreutzer")

The composer has written music now tender, now impassioned, — romantic music at its best. There is considerable reliance upon form, something he never neglected, though he was one of the chief modifiers of classical form.

Sonata in C Minor for Violin and Piano, Op. 30, No. 2

Less dramatic than the Kreutzer Sonata, but equally romantic.

Sonata in F Minor Op. 57 ("Appassionata")

Though the title is not the composer's, it clearly indicates the nature of the music, which is highly emotional and dramatic.

Symphony No. 5 in C Minor, Op. 67

This is perhaps Beethoven's most familiar and popular symphony. It has been examined, analyzed and discussed a thousand times. The opening notes of the symphony symbolized to the composer the idea of "Fate knocking at the door." One critic finds in the first movement a perfect musical expression of strife and conflict. The second is calm and thoughtful, the third is a characteristic Beethoven scherzo — his contribution to musical form which stands where normally we would find a minuet. The final movement, according to the same critic, represents the triumph of human will over hostile Fate and a malignant universe.

Symphony No. 9, Op. 125 ("Choral")

Beethoven's last symphony represents the magnification and ultimate refinement of all he sought after in the symphonic form, a vehicle for the expression of the most profound emotion. In the last movement, almost as if he despaired of achieving his end through instrumental means, he introduces voices, both solo and in chorus, singing the words of Schiller's "Ode to Joy."

BERLIOZ (1803–1869)
Symphonie Fantastique, Op. 14

Berlioz is the greatest figure in the French romantic movement. This symphony is a good sample of his orchestral work. It is autobiographic, composed in the midst of a mad passion for an English actress. Its subtitles (among them "A Ball," "March to the Scaffold," "Dreams of a Witches' Sabbath") not only portray the scenes but the emotions aroused when observing them.

BRAHMS (1833–1897)
Concerto No. 1 in D Minor for Piano and Orchestra

If Brahms is to be considered a typical romantic composer, we may regard the first movement as a splendid example of the reaction of a romantic to outside events. It was written when Brahms was suffering over an attempt at suicide by his friend and fellow-composer Schumann, and is interpreted as an expression of that suffering.

Quintet for Clarinet and Strings in B Minor, Op. 115 (2nd Movement)

One of his loveliest slow movements. The opening and closing sections have a note of resignation; the middle section uses a Hungarian theme, rhapsodic in character.

SCHUBERT (1797–1828)
Symphony No. 9 in C Major

Schubert possessed a gift for writing melodies which places him next to Mozart in that respect. This symphony, his last (sometimes called No. 7 or No. 10), is full of these melodies. Structurally it is inferior to the work of Beethoven, who was his contemporary; but it is always melodious and usually vigorous.

Song Cycles: "Die Schöne Müllerin"; "Die Winterreise"

These two cycles (of 20 and 24 songs respectively) written to the words of Wilhelm Müller tell of the Werther-like despair of young men whose love is not reciprocated. The individual songs capture the moods of happy reminiscence, gentle melancholy and utter despair. Man's relationship to and consolation in nature is a unifying theme in these masterpieces of the German Lied.

Quartet No. 6 in D Minor ("Death and the Maiden")

One of his finest chamber music works. The Andante is a poignantly beautiful set of variations on a melody taken from the song of the same name.

SCHUMANN (1810–1856)
Carnaval Op. 9 (for Piano Solo)

Schumann represents the school of composers upon whom the influence of literature in music was great. His father was a bookseller, and the boy did not neglect his opportunities to become acquainted with his wares. Hoffmann and Jean Paul (Richter) had an especially strong influence upon him, and much of his work reflects the fantastic element in their writings.
    There is a complicated "program" behind *Carnaval*, but is is best to listen to it merely as a series of delightfully romantic piano compositions.

Kreisleriana Op. 16 (for Piano Solo)

These are widely varied piano pieces, a sort of musical self-portrait. Like many romantic compositions, the title has its source in contemporary literature.

CHOPIN (1810–1849)
Nocturnes (for Piano Solo)

It has become trite to call Chopin the poet of the piano, but it is true. No one has written compositions so well suited to that instrument and most of his work could not be so effectively expressed on any other instrument. The Nocturnes are single-movement compositions, free in form, romantic in character, Chopin at his best.

WAGNER (1813–1883)
Love Duet from *Tristan und Isolde*

Immolation Scene from *Götterdämmerung*

In Wagner we find the full development of the characteristics of 19th-century German romanticism, adapted to the stage in a way that intensifies their effect. Wagner contributed a new form, the "Music Drama," in which the composer wrote the libretto, the music, dictated the stage setting and the action, and even designed a theatre of his own.
    These excerpts from two of Wagner's operas exemplify the way in which he wrote powerful emotional music for a given situation.

LISZT (1811–1886)
Les Préludes (Symphonic Poem No. 3)

Liszt was the first composer to write a symphonic poem — a continuous one-movement composition in which, unhampered by formal restrictions, he is able to let the form be moulded by the thought behind it. This composition is an imaginative interpretation of a poem by Lamartine.

SMETANA (1824–1884)
Die Moldau, No. 2 from the Symphonic Cycle *My Country* (Ma Vlast)

A composition which glorifies and depicts in music the chief river of the composer's native Bohemia. Nationalism is a romantic element in music as well as in literature.

Quartet in E Minor (Aus Meinem Leben)

This quartet is, as the title suggests, autobiographical in inspiration. During his latter years Smetana suffered from a malady one symptom of which was the illusion of a constantly sounding high note, hinted at in this quartet.

TSCHAIKOWSKY (1840–1893)
Symphony No. 6 in B Minor, Op. 74 ("Pathétique")

The composer himself wrote that this symphony is "penetrated by subjective sentiment." This is characteristic both of romanticism and of Tschaikowsky. Note especially the tragic feeling which pervades the final movement.

Romeo and Juliet — Overture

This is music which suggests on the one hand the enmity between the Montagues and the Capulets, and on the other the love of Romeo and Juliet, elaborated in sonata form. But the form is not so apparent as it would be in a classical composition; the emotional overtones of the music demand first attention.

Francesca da Rimini

The story is drawn from the fifth canto of Dante's "Inferno," and the music describes Hell, and the love of Paolo and Francesca.

RICHARD STRAUSS (1864–1949)
Ein Heldenleben (A Hero's Life)

Strauss was a disciple of Liszt whose symphonic poems (or tone poems) are like his master's in their imaginative interpretation of an idea or story. This one is characteristic. Some of it is over-dramatic and parts of it are tiresome, but the orchestration is magnificent. It is, as the title indicates, the musical representation of a hero's life.

SIBELIUS (1865–1957)
Swan of Tuonela

The musical setting of a legend from the Finnish epic "Kalevala." A note on the score sets forth the significance of the music: "Tuonela, the Kingdom of Death, the Hades of Finnish mythology, is surrounded by a broad river of black water and rapid current, in which the Swan of Tuonela glides in majestic fashion and sings."

THE

Realistic Temper

THE REALISTS

THE NATURALISTS

THE IMPRESSIONISTS

THE EXPRESSIONISTS

THE

Realistic Temper

THE REALISTS

THE NATURALISTS

THE IMPRESSIONISTS

THE EXPRESSIONISTS

THE

REALISTS

Were it not reasonable to prophesy that this exceeding great multitude of novel-writers and such like must, in a new generation, gradually do one of two things: either retire into the nurseries, and work for children, minors, and semi-fatuous persons of both sexes, or else, what were far better, sweep their novel-fabric into the dust-cart, and betake themselves with such faculty as they have to understand and record what is true, of which surely there is, and will forever be, a whole infinitude unknown to us of infinite importance to us? Poetry, it will more and more come to be understood, is nothing but higher knowledge; and the only genuine Romance (for grown persons), Reality.

CARLYLE

SINCE THE BEGINNING of man, realism has manifested itself in art. One writer by nature is conventional and holds that art may best find expression when governed by rules; him we designate the classicist. Another is equally convinced that it is the purpose of literature or painting to portray a better-than-known world — he wants to idealize; him we call the romantic. And a third, who alike scorns the formality of the classicist and the idealization of the romantic, who is prompted by a fervor for truth and believes that art must present reality; him we call the realist. And when a whole period, such as the first part of the eighteenth century in England, is under the influence of literary conventions, we have a "classical" period; when Coleridge, Shelley, Hugo idealize life we speak of a "romantic" movement; when Flaubert, Dostoevsky, Theodore Dreiser search deep into the souls of Emma Bovary, or Raskolnikoff, or Clyde Griffiths, we find ourselves in a "realistic" epoch.

These three attitudes toward art have existed in all ages. Man, as Emerson has pointed out, is a knot of roots. How much more is this true of the literature of man with its roots and tap-roots crossing, intertwining, striking deep into the ground and reaching up toward the surface, finding sustenance in soil and sun and rain each in its own way.

The realistic temper is older than Defoe and Fielding, even older than Homer. It is as old as the human race itself. It exists whenever man deliberately chooses to face facts, to let truth prevail, and confronts dreams with actuality.

Various qualities have, at different times and by different critics, been called essential to realism. Frequently its method is compared to that of photography. Again it is urged that realism is "concerned essentially with detail"; that it relies upon sense impressions. It is mere documentation; it is an interpretation of life based on facts; it is interested in the individual rather than the type; it presents social, economic, political doctrines; it has local color; it is "the truthful treatment of material"; it is "simple, natural, and honest"; it is "fidelity to life"; it is a "copying of actual facts"; it is a "deliberate choice of the common-place"; it is an intentional seeking out of "the unpleasant"; it subordinates action and incident to characters and motives; it is the literature of the proletariat; it is desirous of "widening the bounds of human sympathy."

As the temper and character of writers vary, so does the way in which they report life. Inheritance, environment, education, mood, physical condition — all these prevent any two men from seeing a mountain and a mouse with the same eyes. Chaucer writing his *Canterbury Tales* expresses reality largely through a faithfulness to character; Dostoevsky in *Crime and Punishment* or Thomas Mann in *The Magic Mountain* concern themselves with psychological reality. Émile Zola is interested in social reality. Realistic writers have in common an intent to think, feel, and to write straight of humanity, its backgrounds, its ambitions and failures, its problems and its emotions. Pleasure and pain, joy and regret, success and failure — as these are a part of life they are, equally, material for the realist. The realist is no stay-at-home. He lives in no ivory tower. He finds no dragons of romance, he explores no strange grottoes. He has, as William Dean Howells has said, a "talent that is robust enough to front the every-day world and catch the charm of its work-worn, care-worn, brave, kindly face...." He trains himself to but one end — to write down and interpret the life he finds.

It is not always easy to distinguish between romanticism and realism, for many authors have written realistically of material essentially romantic, and others romantically of material essentially realistic. But still it is possible to single out certain qualities which enter into realistic writing.

Realism seeks to present the truth. "The unforgivable sin," said O. E. Rölvaag, "is to write about life untruthfully." William Dean Howells is equally positive: "Realism is nothing more and nothing less than the truthful treatment of material." Perhaps the word *treatment* should be emphasized here. No writer, no matter how inexorable his purpose, can hope to present life in full and complete actuality. His art is a conscious treatment. A phonograph transcription of an actual dialogue would be less convincing by far than the same dialogue set down by a Henry James, since it is the function of the artist to present only the semblance of truth. The realist, like any artist, must select. Truth is the goal, then, but it is not the path.

The author who would write faithfully of life has certain definite demands placed upon him by his purpose. He must be accurate in description of background and setting; he must subordinate plot to character since plots are likely to be artificial things; he must bring his story not to a happy ending — as the romanticist is likely to do — but to a faithful ending, happy or unhappy. Realism does not, of course, demand that the writer set down only first-hand experiences, but it does require that he handle his material, imaginative or actual, in such a way as to give it the ring of truth. He must not pass off counterfeit metal. He must offer verisimilitude. He is not a reporter; he must present more than a collection of facts. A Sears-Roebuck catalogue bursts with facts; but it is not realism. Nor is it truth. The realist knows that facts are essential, but he knows too that his facts must be related, unified, must point in one common direction if truth is to be manifest.

This same reliance on the truth must prompt the realist's handling of emotion. There is no room for sentimentalism here. He need not, of course, be without emotion, but he must not be distracted by false or subsidiary emotions. If he be a true realist, such an artist will confine himself to the sensations, feelings, and passions appropriate to his characters rather than to himself. Falseness toward one's material whether it be in the direction of ugliness or beauty stands equally condemned before truth.

Indeed it is this introduction of the ugly and the morbid which most stands in the way of the acceptance of realism by some readers. It is not only arch-romantics who glibly declaim, "Yes, I know life is like that; but there is so much unhappiness around us that I do not see the necessity of introducing these sordid situations into literature." No authority has decreed that literature should deal only with the sweet, the beautiful. It is asking too much to expect the realist to cut corners and dodge fact to present only the ideal. "For a moment," says William Dean Howells, "it is charming to have the story end happily, but after one has lived a certain number of years, and read a certain number of novels, it is not the prosperous or adverse fortune of the characters that affects one, but the good or bad faith of the novelist in dealing with them."

To admit, however, that realism sometimes takes the reader through the back-yard, across the railroad tracks, and over back fences into tenements, is not the same thing as restricting realism to the unhappy phases of life. A quiet sunrise is as real as a hail storm which destroys the tenant farmer's crops. Realism does not play fair with itself when it turns over the log to look for crawling insect life. Shadows are found only where there is light. One may, at times, even indulge in romantic happiness and still be realistic — unless of course one prove such a misanthrope as to find living completely and perpetually despairing. Few writers, probably, so concern themselves with sordidness as Zola. Yet even Zola, in the midst of a description of a squalid Parisian tenement district where all is filth, disease, and hate, interrupts his description of a dyer's establishment, from which dirty water flows out into the street, to say,

> And, in order to get out, she [Gervaise] had to jump over a great puddle, which had trickled out of the dyer's. That day it was blue, the deep azure of a summer sky, which the little night-lamp of the concierge lit with stars.

In another passage, in *Germinal*, Zola describes a crowd reacting to Étienne's speech:

> Acclamations roared towards him from the depths of the forest. By now the moon lit up the whole clearing and picked out the isolated points in the sea of heads, far off into the dim recesses of the glades between the tall grey trunks. Here, in the icy winter night, was a whole people in a white heat of passion, with shining eyes and parted lips, famished men, women, and children let loose to pillage the wealth of ages, the wealth of which they had been dispossessed. They no longer felt cold, for these burning words had warmed them to the vitals. They were uplifted in a religious ecstasy, like the feverish hope of the early Christians expecting the coming reign of justice. Many obscure phrases had baffled them, they were far from understanding these technical and abstract arguments, but their very obscurity and abstract nature broadened still further the field of promises and carried them away into hallucinations. What a wonderful dream! To be the masters and suffer no more! To enjoy life at last!

The desire to present truth makes realistic writing at times appear to lack orderly arrangement of the parts. The realistic author does not unify the career of his characters artificially. It is, according to Henry James, the duty of the realist to catch "the strange irregular rhythm of life."

The realist seeks this truth through a faithful portrayal of character. His people are individuals. Incident grows from character; human motives dominate the action. Henry James tells us just what this relationship of character to action is:

> What is character but the determination of incident? What is incident but the illustration of character? What is either a picture or a novel that is *not* of character? What else do we seek in it and find in it? It is an incident for a woman to stand up with her hand resting on a table and look at you in a certain way; or if it be not an incident I think it will be hard to say what it is. At the same time it is an expression of character. . . . When a young man makes up his mind that he has not faith enough after all to enter the church as he intended, that is an incident, though you may not hurry to the end of the chapter to see whether perhaps he doesn't change his mind once more.

Realism, in short, substitutes men and women for the heroes and heroines of romance.

The classicist, certainly, concerned himself with people, but he focused his attention on one or two dominant traits of character — as drama, for instance, brings out the tragic "flaw." Romance, too, had its great fictitious personalities, but they were idealized. Heroic courage, great sacrifice, superhuman generosity made heroes, as cunning, selfishness, and cowardice made villains.

The realist moulds his characters quite differently from the classicist or the romantic. He is, for instance, almost as concerned with a minor gesture, a trivial incident, as the romantic could be with the winning of a battle. The realist, too, departs from the convention of telling the reader by direct analysis and at great length just what sort of person his heroine or hero is. That is too formal a method for the realist; he prefers to let his reader build up this impression cumulatively — a statement here, an incident there, and a reflection a few lines farther on. Moods and emotions, too, are made to reflect character, but they are likely to be suggested rather than bluntly stated.

With realism, too, has come the greater reliance on psychology. Perhaps it would be as true to say that with the development of psychology has come the greater emphasis on realism. "There are," said Henry James, "few things more exciting to me, in short, than a psychological reason." Wherever great writers have depicted human character truthfully, there has been, of course, psychological truth. However, in the last decades the rapid growth of our understanding of the mind has added a new emphasis to our interest in and understanding of character and action. For there is a realism of the mind and of the human spirit as well as a realism of the body.

Realism looks at life objectively. The realistic writer marshals his facts, he shows us character, he presents the background against which his people move — but as far as he can he restricts himself to the emotions of his people, forgetting his own prejudices and convictions. He must not manifest a great emotional sympathy with his hero; he must not confuse his own lot with that of his characters.

Try as he may to be objective, the fact remains that he must select some few people and some specific background. The choice he makes becomes a personal choice and, to that extent, reflects his individuality and his philosophy of life. Turgenev may write of the Russian serf objectively, but no one will make the mistake of thinking him indifferent to the welfare of the serf. The very material Turgenev selects to write about reflects his sympathy. Realism, judged on the basis of its impersonality, will appear at the opposite pole from romanticism, but it has never yet attained perfect objectivity. It does, however, eschew the idiosyncratic. It does try to discard personal bias. The realist must approach truth devoutly although knowing well that he will never see life as a complete whole and realizing, at the same time, that even if he could encompass all, both his art and his common sense would dictate that he be selective.

Realism attempts to represent life. Despite its effort to be objective and because of its desire to present truth and character, realism, perhaps more than any other manner of writing, gives significance to life. "The only reason for the existence of a novel," says Henry James, "is that it does attempt to represent life." Though the realist proceeds toward his end by the piling up of facts, by the method of documentation, no one becomes a writer simply by compiling a series of facts. "My own belief is that the writer with a notebook in his hand is always a bad writer," says Sherwood Anderson. And he is right. Some truth, some phase of life or of human character attracts an author; these he knows either through first-hand experience or through his imagination until he can see all elements fitting into a significant whole, until the important rise to the surface and the unimportant sink out of sight.

The realistic writer need but stretch out his hand, wherever he may be, to touch truth and actuality. Goldsmith found these qualities in a quiet English village, Sinclair Lewis in an American small town, Hemingway on the battlefield and in the *corridas*, Aldous Huxley in the drawing-room. George Eliot found significant reality in the life of a miser, Thomas Hardy in that of a furze-gatherer on Egdon Heath, and O. E. Rölvaag in that of a pioneer on the American plains. George Moore wrote of a servant girl, Theodore Dreiser of a hotel bell-boy, John Steinbeck of the itinerant worker. Samuel Butler found significant the boy growing up in the home of a dogmatic cleric, Somerset Maugham the life in cheap lodgings and in a London hospital, and Carl Sandburg the stockyards of Chicago. George Gissing interested himself in the life of a hackwriter in Grub Street, Robert Frost in the New England farmer, and Eugene O'Neill in the stoker at sea.

All these writers, and many others, find significance in the commonplace. They reveal, as Zona Gale finds all realistic novels do, "the infinitely familiar as infinitely strange." In touching life in all these varying social levels and in all these divergent geographical areas the authors use no camera, no notebook. Or if they do, they transmute what they find there, they elevate these commonplaces into art. Life, they know, is more than a chemical formula. In realism, unlike mathematics, the whole is *not* the sum of its parts. Until the facts broaden our understanding of life, until they increase our sympathies, realism is an empty husk. As romance gives us vicarious adventure, realism gives us vicarious experience in living. As naturalism gives us a chaotic world, realism introduces order and significance, not the artificially arranged order of the classicist, but order as life presents it.

The realistic writers leave to romance the picturing of the past and prophecy as to the future. Their concern is with men and women, emotions and moods, success and failure of life today. They study life in the coal-mine, in the village, on the farm, in politics, in business; their concern is with social conditions, with sex, with war. Any exact, truthful study of life, any accounting of experience demands a treatment of present conditions — the past is too remote, the future too uncertain. Again, if realism has a mission to make us know more fully the terms on which we meet life, then its greatest value is to be derived when it deals with the world in which we live.

Realism has its special technique as well as its particular set of interests, its method as well as its content.

Realism relies for much of its effect on the use of specific details. Of the various literary tempers only naturalism exceeds it on this count. Precision and accuracy are demanded in observation and diction. Details the romanticist would scorn as too insignificant or which he would refuse as too brash, the realist will accept if they but aid in a faithful building up of character or situation. "The immediate danger of the realist," Robert Louis Stevenson wrote, "is to sacrifice the beauty and significance of the whole to local dexterity, or, in the insane pursuit of completion, to immolate his readers under facts; . . . he comes in the last resort . . . to abjure all choice and . . . to communicate matter which is not worth learning." No doubt this is true — realists sin just as romanticists do. But the fault of the individual author need not be credited to the manner in which he writes. William Dean Howells knows as well as Stevenson that the realist can bury himself under facts and petty details. "When realism becomes false to itself," wrote Howells, "when it heaps up facts merely, and maps life instead of picturing it, realism will perish too."

In realistic writing details must be so harmonized, so blended, so pointed in a planned direction that they create in the reader the same impression which reality itself creates in the writer. They will, if handled by one who is more than a reporter, do even better than that since they will uncover a truth which we are only too likely to pass by. The artist will make us see the strange in the familiar, the great in the small, and the beautiful in the ugly. And while he is doing this he must be careful not to sentimentalize, not to distort. Realism is not limited to what may be seen by the eye; at its best it makes manifest to us truths of which we are aware only from within.

Facts are not useful until they are selected and arranged in accord with a literary, an artistic purpose, until in short a particular unity is given them. And this unity is an artistic one, and not that of nature itself. "The world of reality," writes Joseph Warren Beach, "is the world of newspapers and window displays, of self-starters and bumpy pavements, of telephone bills and telephone numbers scrawled on a pad. It is a world of irrelevant facts not yet got into order, unframed, unlighted, uninterpreted." It is the business of realism to arrange these facts.

In summing up, what has the realistic temper brought to literature?

First of all, it has helped to develop a new æsthetics. Instead of searching abroad for beauty, realism convinces us that it often lies disguised in the familiar and the commonplace. From it we learn that our daily walk may reveal human character, truth, suffering and accomplishment, pain and joy. We discover that a man striding across his front lawn pushing a mower may be as important in the eternal scheme of things as a Galahad searching distant countries for the Grail. From it we learn that it is only dulled senses which prevent our seeing beauty and truth; that habit is a husk which, torn aside, reveals strong, healthy grain.

With the advance of realism, literature has taken on a new vigor. It faces the workaday world instead of running from it. It knows that only when life is understood in *all* its aspects can something worthwhile be derived. Realism knows well that happiness secures its greatest endorsement from the presence of pain. The classicist subduing all to form, the romantic looking for surcease in escape, the symbolist reducing all to color and sound, the impressionist concerned with the fleeting moment — these and the other literary tempers see life only from a chosen vantage point and only partially. The realist climbs up to the mountain tops for perspective, not content until he has seen life from all points. He searches out actuality wherever he may find it. Because of his wide sympathy, he brings to literature a catholicity of interest. He looks anew at material used many times by his predecessors, but he also pioneers in new fields.

Geoffrey Chaucer · c. 1340–1400

Born into a family of vintners, Geoffrey Chaucer was as a boy employed at the court of Edward III in the service of Elizabeth, wife of the Duke of Clarence; before he was twenty he had been a soldier in France, taken prisoner, and ransomed. By 1368 he was an esquire of the king and only two years later, when about thirty years of age, he was sent abroad on a mission in the king's service. Shortly after this he left again for the Continent, this time for Italy under appointment as a commissioner, to arrange trade agreements with the city of Genoa. Later on in life he served the shire of Kent, his county, and his king in various capacities: as a comptroller of customs, as a diplomatic officer in France and Italy, as a justice of the peace, as a member of Parliament. In 1389 he was made clerk of the works under Richard II. Yet the public career which the poet followed brought not only quick success but also grueling disappointment. For some years he was highly successful, enjoying annuities and emoluments; then annuities were stopped and public positions reassigned as a new favorite gained influence at court. The record shows that on one occasion Chaucer was forced to seek official protection from his creditors. Shortly before he died another king of England, Henry IV, granted him a pension, perhaps as a result of the plaintive "complaint" to his empty purse:

> Me were as leef be layd upon my bere;
> For which unto your mercy thus I crye:
> Beth hevy ageyn, or elles mot I dye!

According to the inscription on his tomb in Westminster Abbey, Chaucer died on October 25, 1400. The corner in which he was buried is now called the Poet's Corner.

A busy career in public life did not hamper his literary activity. Chaucer's activities may be divided into two distinct periods, the "French" (during which he made translations and followed various French conventions) and the "Italian" (during which he came under the influence of Dante and Boccaccio and Petrarch). The two periods marked much more than an apprenticeship to writing since, during each, at least one or two of his best-known works appeared, but it was not until the poet threw off most of his imitative mannerisms and became more completely himself, as in *The Canterbury Tales*, that we feel the full power of his sympathy for people and catch a glimpse of his rich nature. His best-known work includes *The Book of the Duchesse, The House of Fame, The Parliament of Fowls, Troilus and Criseyde, The Legend of Good Women*, and, of course, *The Canterbury Tales*.

Chaucer has sometimes been called the father of English literature. In the sense that he was the greatest of the early poets, and still ranks along with Shakespeare and Milton, this is true. He has, however, too generally been credited with giving us our English language, much as we know it today, and thus with "fixing" our speech. Inasmuch as Chaucer wrote in an English dialect — the Midland — rather than in French or in Latin he only popularized a language until then not very commonly used for literary expression.

SUGGESTED REFERENCES: R. D. French, *A Chaucer Handbook* (new ed., 1955); D. W. Robertson, *A Preface to Chaucer* (new ed., 1962); E. J. Howard, *Geoffrey Chaucer* (1964).

The Canterbury Tales

Chaucer was by no means always a realist. His early work was mainly concerned with romantic stories of chivalry and love. Even many of the stories in the *Canterbury Tales* — that of the Knight, for instance — are dominantly romantic. But usually in the *Canterbury Tales* Chaucer turned to the people about him, those whom he saw in his daily life and, in the *Prologue*, gave us such a picture of medieval England as we find nowhere else. Here are portraits of actual people — the knight and his squire, the prioress and the monk and priests, the scholar, the parson, merchant, sailor, cook, the unforgettable Wife of Bath, in all twenty-nine pilgrims from various walks of life and from differing social levels. As the pilgrims advance along their route, this realistic quality is further heightened by the natural give and take of the talk of people on a journey; stories are interrupted with bickering and argument; the language they speak is that in common use; digression is now and then made to point out where the pilgrims are as the stories are being told and to give actual details of the journey. His long period of public service had taught Chaucer what human beings are like, with the result that we find his characters to be of lasting interest. Frequently the realism is relieved with humor. Over all his people he throws the light net of whimsy and irony, but seldom in such a way as to conceal the essential outlines of their real quality. The poet is more anxious to present people than to advance a philosophy, to describe the life about him than to criticize it. He constantly surprises with his range and the variety of his moods, at times pensive and serious, again gay and humorous. His work reflects an understanding both of people and of books. He knew three languages, Latin, French, and Italian; and he was acquainted with the science of his day — well enough acquainted to be sceptical of that pseudo-science, alchemy.

Chaucer's plan for *The Canterbury Tales* called for a series of a hundred and twenty or so tales. First, the pilgrims who are to tell the stories are introduced to the reader at the Tabard Inn in Southwark, a suburb of London. They are making a pilgrimage to a shrine at Canterbury, and each of them is to tell two stories on the way there and two more on the way back to Southwark. Harry Bailey, the host of the Tabard Inn, agrees not only to act as judge of the tales but also to serve a dinner to all the pilgrims at his inn upon their return. Unfortunately for us, however, Chaucer did not complete his plan; only twenty stories, and fragments of a few others, were actually finished.

The Prologue

Here bygynneth the Book of the Tales of Caunterbury

Whan that Aprille with his shoures soote [1]
The droghte of March hath perced to the roote,
And bathed every veyne in swich [2] licour
Of which vertu [3] engendred is the flour;
Whan Zephirus [4] eek [5] with his sweete breeth   5
Inspired hath in every holt and heeth
The tendre croppes, and the yonge sonne
Hath in the Ram his halve cours yronne, [6]
And smale foweles maken melodye,
That slepen al the nyght with open ye   10
(So priketh hem nature in hir corages [7]),
Thanne longen folk to goon on pilgrimages,
And palmeres for to seken straunge strondes,
To ferne [8] halwes, [9] kouthe [10] in sondry londes;
And specially from every shires ende   15
Of Engelond to Caunterbury they wende,
The hooly blisful martir [11] for to seke,
That hem hath holpen whan that they were seeke.

Bifil that in that seson on a day,
In Southwerk at the Tabard as I lay   20
Redy to wenden on my pilgrymage
To Caunterbury with ful devout corage,
At nyght was come into that hostelrye
Wel nyne and twenty in a compaignye,
Of sondry folk, by aventure yfalle   25
In felaweshipe, and pilgrimes were they alle,
That toward Caunterbury wolden ryde.
The chambres and the stables weren wyde,
And wel we weren esed [12] atte beste.
And shortly, whan the sonne was to reste,   30
So hadde I spoken with hem everichon
That I was of hir felaweshipe anon,
And made forward [13] erly for to ryse,

To take oure wey ther as I yow devyse.
But nathelees, whil I have tyme and space,   35
Er that I ferther in this tale pace,
Me thynketh it acordaunt to resoun
To telle yow al the condicioun
Of ech of hem, so as it semed me,
And whiche they weren, and of what degree,   40
And eek in what array that they were inne;
And at a knyght than wol I first bigynne.

A KNYGHT ther was, and that a worthy man,
That fro the tyme that he first bigan
To riden out, he loved chivalrie,   45
Trouthe and honor, fredom [1] and curteisie.
Ful worthy was he in his lordes werre,
And therto hadde he riden, no man ferre, [2]
As wel in cristendom as in hethenesse,
And evere honored for his worthynesse.   50
At Alisaundre he was whan it was wonne.
Ful ofte tyme he hadde the bord bigonne [3]
Aboven alle nacions in Pruce; [4]
In Lettow [5] hadde he reysed [6] and in Ruce,
No Cristen man so ofte of his degree.   55
In Gernade [7] at the seege eek hadde he be
Of Algezir, [8] and riden in Belmarye. [9]
At Lyeys [10] was he and at Satalye, [11]
Whan they were wonne; and in the Grete See
At many a noble armee hadde he be.   60
At mortal batailles hadde he been fiftene,
And foughten for oure feith at Tramyssene [12]
In lystes thries, and ay slayn his foo.
This ilke [13] worthy knyght hadde been also
Somtyme with the lord of Palatye [14]   65
Agayn another hethen in Turkye.
And everemoore he hadde a sovereyn prys; [15]
And though that he were worthy, he was wys,
And of his port as meeke as is a mayde.
He nevere yet no vileynye ne sayde   70

---

[1] sweet.   [2] such.   [3] quickening-power.
[4] The West Wind.   [5] also.   [6] run.
[7] heart or inclination.   [8] distant.
[9] shrines of saints.   [10] well-known.
[11] The shrine at Canterbury was dedicated to St. Thomas à Becket.
[12] entertained.   [13] covenant.

[1] liberality.   [2] farther.
[3] "begun the table"; i.e., sat at the head of the table.
[4] Prussia.   [5] Lithuania.
[6] made a military expedition.   [7] Granada.
[8] Algeciras.   [9] In northern Africa.
[10] Town in Armenia.   [11] In Asia Minor.
[12] In northern Africa.   [13] same.
[14] In Asia Minor.   [15] renown.

In al his lyf unto no maner wight.
He was a verray, parfit gentil knyght.
But, for to tellen yow of his array,
His hors were goode, but he was nat gay.
Of fustian he wered a gypon [1]   75
Al bismotered with his habergeon,[2]
For he was late ycome from his viage,
And wente for to doon his pilgrymage.

    With hym ther was his sone, a yong SQUIER,
A lovyere [3] and a lusty bacheler,[4]   80
With lokkes crulle [5] as they were leyd in presse.
Of twenty yeer of age he was, I gesse.
Of his stature he was of evene [6] lengthe,
And wonderly delyvere,[7] and of greet strengthe.
And he hadde been somtyme in chyvachie [8]   85
In Flaundres, in Artoys, and Pycardie,
And born hym weel, as of so litel space,
In hope to stonden in his lady grace.
Embrouded was he, as it were a meede
Al ful of fresshe floures, whyte and reede.   90
Syngynge he was, or floytynge,[9] al the day;
He was as fressh as is the month of May.
Short was his gowne, with sleves longe and wyde.
Wel koude he sitte on hors and faire ryde.
He koude songes make and wel endite,[10]   95
Juste and eek daunce, and weel purtreye and write,
So hoote he lovede that by nyghtertale [11]
He sleep namoore than dooth a nyghtyngale.
Curteis he was, lowely, and servysable,
And carf [12] biforn his fader at the table.   100

    A YEMAN hadde he and servantz namo [13]
At that tyme, for hym liste ride so;
And he was clad in cote and hood of grene.
A sheef of pecok arwes, bright and kene,
Under his belt he bar ful thriftily,   105
(Wel koude he dresse his takel [14] yemanly:
His arwes drouped noght with fetheres lowe)
And in his hand he baar a myghty bowe.
A not heed [15] hadde he, with a broun visage.
Of wodecraft wel koude [16] he al the usage.   110
Upon his arm he baar a gay bracer,[17]
And by his syde a swerd and a bokeler,
And on that oother syde a gay daggere
Harneised [18] wel and sharp as point of spere;
A Cristopher [19] on his brest of silver sheene.[20] 115
An horn he bar, the bawdryk [21] was of grene;

A forster [1] was he, soothly, as I gesse.

    Ther was also a Nonne, a PRIORESSE,
That of hir smylyng was ful symple and coy;
Hire gretteste ooth was but by Seinte Loy; [2]   120
And she was cleped madame Eglentyne.
Ful weel she soong the service dyvyne,
Entuned in hir nose ful semely,
And Frenssh she spak ful faire and fetisly,[3]
After the scole of Stratford atte Bowe,[4]   125
For Frenssh of Parys was to hire unknowe.
At mete wel ytaught was she with alle:
She leet no morsel from hir lippes falle,
Ne wette hir fyngres in hir sauce depe;
Wel koude she carie a morsel and wel kepe   130
That no drope ne fille upon hire brest.
In curteisie was set ful muchel hir lest [5]
Hir over-lippe wyped she so clene
That in hir coppe ther was no ferthyng [6] sene
Of grece, whan she dronken hadde hir draughte.
Ful semely after hir mete she raughte.[7]   136
And sikerly she was of greet desport,[8]
And ful plesaunt, and amyable of port,
And peyned hire to countrefete cheere [9]
Of court, and to been estatlich of manere,   140
And to ben holden digne [10] of reverence.
But, for to speken of hire conscience,
She was so charitable and so pitous
She wolde wepe, if that she saugh a mous
Kaught in a trappe, if it were deed or bledde.   145
Of smale houndes hadde she that she fedde
With rosted flessh, or milk and wastel-breed.[11]
But soore wepte she if oon of hem were deed,
Or if men smoot it with a yerde smerte; [12]
And al was conscience and tendre herte.   150
Ful semyly hir wympul pynched was;
Hir nose tretys,[13] hir eyen greye as glas,
Hir mouth ful smal, and therto softe and reed;
But sikerly she hadde a fair forheed;
It was almoost a spanne brood, I trowe;   155
For, hardily,[14] she was nat undergrowe.
Ful fetys [15] was hir cloke, as I was war.
Of smal coral aboute hire arm she bar
A peire [16] of bedes, gauded al with grene,
And theron heng a brooch of gold ful sheene,   160
On which ther was first write a crowned A,

---

[1] doublet.   [2] coat of mail.   [3] lover.
[4] A knight of low rank.   [5] curly.   [6] average.
[7] quick.   [8] military expeditions.
[9] playing the flute.   [10] compose.   [11] night-time.
[12] carved.   [13] no more.   [14] archery gear.
[15] cropped head.   [16] knew.
[17] arm-guard, used in shooting the bow.   [18] equipped.
[19] St. Christopher protected against accidents. The yeoman wore his image.
[20] bright.   [21] A belt to carry the horn.

[1] forester.
[2] St. Eligius. He refused to take an oath when required to do so by a king of France.
[3] elegantly.
[4] A monastery near London where an old dialect of France was spoken.
[5] delight.   [6] a small portion.   [7] reached.
[8] merriment.   [9] behavior.   [10] worthy.
[11] A cake-like bread.   [12] with a stick smartly.
[13] well-fashioned.   [14] scarcely.
[15] handsome.   [16] string.

And after *Amor vincit omnia.*[1]

Another NONNE with hire hadde she,
That was hir chapeleyne, and preestes thre.

A MONK ther was, a fair for the maistrie,[2] 165
An outridere,[3] that lovede venerie,[4]
A manly man, to been an abbot able.
Ful many a deyntee hors hadde he in stable,
And whan he rood, men myghte his brydel heere
Gynglen in a whistlynge wynd als cleere 170
And eek as loude as dooth the chapel belle.
Ther as this lord was kepere of the celle,
The reule of seint Maure or of seint Beneit,[5]
By cause that it was old and somdel streit[6]
This ilke Monk leet olde thynges pace, 175
And heeld after the newe world the space.
He yaf nat of that text a pulled[7] hen,
That seith that hunters ben nat hooly men,
Ne that a monk, when he is reccheleles,[8]
Is likned til a fissh that is waterlees,— 180
This is to seyn, a monk out of his cloystre.
But thilke text heeld he nat worth an oystre;
And I seyde his opinion was good.
What sholde he studie and make hymselven
wood,[9]
Upon a book in cloystre alwey to poure, 185
Or swynken[10] with his handes, and laboure,
As Austyn bit? How shal the world be served?
Lat Austyn have his swynk to hym reserved!
Therfore he was a prikasour[11] aright:
Grehoundes he hadde as swift as fowel in flight; 190
Of prikyng[12] and of huntyng for the hare
Was al his lust, for no cost wolde he spare.
I seigh his sleves purfiled[13] at the hond
With grys,[14] and that the fyneste of a lond;
And, for to festne his hood under his chyn, 195
He hadde of gold ywroght a ful curious pyn;
A love-knotte in the gretter ende ther was.
His heed was balled,[15] that shoon as any glas,
And eek his face, as he hadde been enoynt.
He was a lord ful fat and in good poynt;[16] 200
His eyen stepe,[17] and rollynge in his heed,
That stemed as a forneys of a leed;[18]
His bootes souple, his hors in greet estaat.
Now certeinly he was a fair prelaat;
He was nat pale as a forpyned[19] goost. 205
A fat swan loved he best of any roost.
His palfrey was as broun as is a berye.

A FRERE ther was, a wantowne and a merye,
A lymytour,[1] a ful solempne[2] man.
In alle the ordres foure[3] is noon that kan[4] 210
So muchel of daliaunce and fair langage.
He hadde maad ful many a mariage
Of yonge wommen at his owene cost.
Unto his ordre he was a noble post.[5]
Ful wel biloved and famulier was he 215
With frankeleyns[6] over al in his contree,
And eek with worthy wommen of the toun;
For he hadde power of confessioun,
As seyde hymself, moore than a curat,
For of his ordre he was licenciat. 220
Ful swetely herde he confessioun,
And plesaunt was his absolucioun:
He was an esy man to yeve[7] penaunce,
Ther as he wiste to have[8] a good pitaunce.
For unto a povre ordre for to yive 225
Is signe that a man is wel yshryve;
For if he yaf, he dorste make avaunt,[9]
He wiste that a man was repentaunt;
For many a man so hard is of his herte,
He may nat wepe, althogh hym soore smerte. 230
Therfore in stede of wepynge and preyeres
Men moote[10] yeve silver to the povre freres.
His typet[11] was ay farsed[12] ful of knyves
And pynnes, for to yeven faire wyves.
And certeinly he hadde a murye note: 235
Wel koude he synge and pleyen on a rote;[13]
Of yeddynges[14] he baar outrely the pris.[15]
His nekke whit was as the flour-de-lys;
Therto he strong was as a champioun.
He knew the tavernes wel in every toun 240
And everich hostiler and tappestere
Bet than a lazar[16] or a beggestere;[17]
For unto swich a worthy man as he
Acorded nat, as by his facultee,[18]
To have with sike lazars aqueyntaunce. 245
It is nat honest, it may nat avaunce,
For to deelen with no swich poraille,[19]
But al with riche and selleres of vitaille.
And over al, ther as[20] profit sholde arise,
Curteis he was and lowely of servyse. 250
Ther nas no man nowher so vertuous.
He was the beste beggere in his hous;

[1] Love conquers all.   [2] as for authority.
[3] one who rides out — an inspector.   [4] hunting.
[5] Saints Mauritius and Benedict were important figures in the Benedictine order.
[6] rigorous.   [7] plucked.   [8] careless.   [9] insane.
[10] work.   [11] a hard rider.   [12] riding.
[13] ornamented or trimmed.   [14] fur.   [15] bald.
[16] condition.   [17] bright.   [18] caldron.
[19] wasted away.

[1] A friar holding license to beg within certain limits.
[2] cheerful.
[3] The four were: Augustinian, Carmelite, Dominican, and Franciscan.
[4] knows.   [5] support.   [6] wealthy landowners.
[7] give.   [8] where he knew he should obtain.
[9] boast.   [10] one should.   [11] cape.   [12] stuffed.
[13] fiddle.   [14] songs.   [15] prize.   [16] leper.
[17] beggar-woman.
[18] It did not accord with his position.
[19] poor people.   [20] everywhere where.

For thogh a wydwe hadde noght a sho,
So plesaunt was his "*In principio*,"[1]
Yet wolde he have a ferthyng, er he wente. 255
His purchas[2] was wel bettre than his rente.[3]
And rage[4] he koude, as it were right a whelp.[5]
In love-dayes[6] ther koude he muchel help,
For ther he was nat lyk a cloysterer[7]
With a thredbare cope, as is a povre scoler, 260
But he was lyk a maister or a pope.
Of double worstede was his semycope,[8]
That rounded as a belle out of the presse.[9]
Somwhat he lipsed, for his wantownesse,
To make his Englissh sweete upon his tonge; 265
And in his harpyng, whan that he hadde songe,
His eyen twynkled in his heed aryght,
As doon the sterres in the frosty nyght.
This worthy lymytour was cleped Huberd.

A MARCHANT was ther with a forked berd, 270
In mottelee,[10] and hye on horse he sat;
Upon his heed a Flaundryssh bever hat,
His bootes clasped faire and fetisly.
His resons he spak ful solempnely,
Sownynge[11] alwey th' encrees of his wynnyng. 275
He wolde the see were kept for any thyng[12]
Bitwixe Middelburgh and Orewelle.[13]
Wel koude he in eschaunge sheeldes[14] selle.
This worthy man ful wel his wit bisette:[15]
Ther wiste no wight that he was in dette, 280
So estatly was he of his governaunce
With his bargaynes and with his chevyssaunce.[16]
For sothe he was a worthy man with alle,
But, sooth to seyn, I noot[17] how men hym calle.

A CLERK ther was of Oxenford also, 285
That unto logyk hadde longe ygo.
As leene was his hors as is a rake,
And he nas nat right fat, I undertake,
But looked holwe, and therto sobrely.
Ful thredbare was his overeste courtepy;[18] 290
For he hadde geten hym yet no benefice,
Ne was so worldly for to have office.
For hym was levere[19] have at his beddes heed
Twenty bookes, clad in blak or reed,
Of Aristotle and his philosophie, 295
Than robes riche, or fithele,[20] or gay sautrie.[21]

[1] John i, 1: "In the beginning was the word," etc.
[2] gifts acquired.   [3] income.   [4] romp.
[5] young dog.
[6] days set aside to arbitrate disputes.
[7] one who lives in a cloister.   [8] short cape.
[9] mould.   [10] cloth of motley color.
[11] relating to.   [12] at all costs.
[13] Ports in Holland and England. Orewelle is now Harwich.
[14] French crowns.   [15] used.   [16] dealing for profit.
[17] know not.   [18] short coat.   [19] rather.
[20] fiddle.   [21] A kind of harp.

But al be that he was a philosophre,
Yet hadde he but litel gold in cofre;
But al that he myghte of his freendes hente,[1]
On bookes and on lernynge he it spente, 300
And bisily gan for the soules preye
Of hem that yaf hym wherwith to scoleye.[2]
Of studie took he moost cure[3] and moost heede.
Noght o word spak he moore than was neede,
And that was seyd in forme and reverence, 305
And short and quyk and ful of hy sentence;[4]
Sownynge in moral vertu was his speche,
And gladly wolde he lerne and gladly teche.

A SERGEANT OF THE LAWE, war and wys,
That often hadde been at the Parvys,[5] 310
Ther was also, ful riche of excellence.
Discreet he was and of greet reverence —
He semed swich, his wordes weren so wise.
Justice he was ful often in assise,
By patente and by pleyn commissioun. 315
For his science and for his heigh renoun,
Of fees and robes hadde he many oon.
So greet a purchasour[6] was nowher noon:
Al was fee symple to hym in effect;[7]
His purchasyng myghte nat been infect.[8] 320
Nowher so bisy a man as he ther nas,
And yet he semed bisier than he was.
In termes hadde he caas and doomes[9] alle
That from the tyme of kyng William were falle.
Therto he koude endite, and make a thyng, 325
Ther koude no wight pynche at his writyng;
And every statut koude he pleyn by rote.
He rood but hoomly in a medlee cote,
Girt with a ceint[10] of silk, with barres smale;
Of his array telle I no lenger tale. 330

A FRANKELEYN[11] was in his compaignye.
Whit was his berd as is the dayesye;
Of his complexioun he was sangwyn.
Wel loved he by the morwe a sop in wyn;
To lyven in delit was evere his wone,[12] 335
For he was Epicurus owene sone,
That heeld opinioun that pleyn delit
Was verraily felicitee parfit.
An housholdere, and that a greet, was he;
Seint Julian[13] he was in his contree. 340
His breed, his ale, was alweys after oon,[14]
A bettre envyned[15] man was nowher noon.

[1] get.   [2] go to school.   [3] care.   [4] instruction.
[5] Porch at St. Paul's, a meeting place for lawyers.
[6] conveyancer.
[7] Chaucer says that he could make property appear to be held in fee simple no matter what restrictions might have been placed upon it.
[8] set aside.   [9] cases and judgments.   [10] girdle.
[11] wealthy landowner.   [12] custom.
[13] The patron saint of hospitality.
[14] equally good.   [15] stocked with wine.

Withoute bake mete [1] was nevere his hous
Of fissh and flessh, and that so plentevous,
It snewed in his hous of meter and drynke,   345
Of alle deyntees that men koude thynke.
After the sondry sesons of the yeer,
So chaunged he his mete and his soper.
Ful many a fat partrich hadde he in muwe,[2]
And many a breem and many a luce in stuwe.[3]   350
Wo was his cook but if his sauce were
Poynaunt and sharp, and redy al his geere.
His table dormant [4] in his halle alway
Stood redy covered al the longe day.
At sessiouns ther was he lord and sire;   355
Ful ofte tyme he was knyght of the shire.
An anlaas [5] and a gipser [6] al of silk
Heeng at his girdel, whit as morne milk.
A shirreve hadde he been, and a countour.[7]
Was nowher swich a worthy vavasour.[8]   360
    AN HABERDASSHERE and a CARPENTER,
A WEBBE, a DYERE, and a TAPYCER,[9] —
And they were clothed alle in o lyveree
Of a solempne and a greet fraternitee.[10]
Ful fressh and newe hir geere apiked [11] was;   365
Hir knyves were chaped [12] noght with bras
But al with silver; wroght ful clene and weel
Hire girdles and hir pouches everydeel.
Wel semed ech of hem a fair burgeys
To sitten in a yeldehalle on a deys.[13]   370
Everich, for the wisdom that he kan,
Was shaply for to been an alderman.
For catel [14] hadde they ynogh and rente,
And eek hir wyves wolde it wel assente;
And elles certeyn were they to blame.   375
It is ful fair to been ycleped "madame,"
And goon to vigilies [15] al bifore,
And have a mantel roialliche ybore.
    A COOK they hadde with hem for the nones
To boille the chiknes with the marybones,   380
And poudre-marchant tart [16] and galyngale.[17]
Wel koude he knowe a draughte of Londoun ale.
He koude rooste, and sethe,[18] and broille, and frye,
Maken mortreux,[19] and wel bake a pye.
But greet harm was it, as it thoughte me,   385
That on his shyne a mormal [20] hadde he.
For blankmanger,[21] that made he with the beste.
    A SHIPMAN was ther, wonynge [22] fer by weste;

For aught I woot, he was of Dertemouthe.
He rood upon a rouncy,[1] as he kouthe,[2]   390
In a gowne of faldyng [3] to the knee.
A daggere hangynge on a laas [4] hadde he
Aboute his nekke, under his arm adoun.
The hoote somer hadde maad his hewe al broun;
And certeinly he was a good felawe.   395
Ful many a draughte of wyn had he ydrawe
Fro Burdeux-ward, whil that the chapman [5] sleep.
Of nyce conscience took he no keep.
If that he faught, and hadde the hyer hond,
By water he sente hem hoom to every lond.   400
But of his craft to rekene wel his tydes,
His stremes,[6] and his daungers hym bisides,
His herberwe,[7] and his moone, his lodemenage,[8]
Ther nas noon swich from Hulle to Cartage.
Hardy he was and wys to undertake;   405
With many a tempest hadde his berd been shake.
He knew alle the havenes, as they were,
Fro Gootlond [9] to the cape of Fynystere,
And every cryke in Britaigne and in Spayne.
His barge ycleped was the Maudelayne.   410
    With us ther was a DOCTOUR OF PHISIK;
In al this world ne was ther noon hym lik,
To speke of phisik and of surgerye,
For he was grounded in astronomye.
He kepte his pacient a ful greet deel   415
In houres by his magyk natureel.
Wel koude he fortunen the ascendent
Of his ymages for his pacient.[10]
He knew the cause of everich maladye,
Were it of hoot, or coold, or moyste, or drye,   420
And where they engendred, and of what humour.[11]
He was a verray, parfit praktisour:
The cause yknowe, and of his harm the roote,
Anon he yaf the sike man his boote.[12]
Ful redy hadde he his apothecaries   425
To sende hym drogges and his letuaries,[13]
For ech of hem made oother for to wynne —
Hir frendshipe nas nat newe to bigynne.
Wel knew he the olde Esculapius,
And Deyscorides, and eek Rufus,   430
Olde Ypocras, Haly, and Galyen,
Serapion, Razis, and Avycen,
Averrois, Damascien, and Constantyn,

---

[1] cooked food.   [2] coop.   [3] fish-pond.
[4] permanent dining-table.   [5] dagger.   [6] purse.
[7] auditor.   [8] A rank below that of baron.
[9] upholsterer.   [10] guild.   [11] trimmed.
[12] The chape was a metal cap at the bottom of the sheath.
[13] dais.   [14] chattel or property.   [15] vigils.
[16] A pungent spice.   [17] A sweet spice.
[18] boil.   [19] A thick soup.   [20] sore.
[21] A dish like our creamed chicken.   [22] dwelling.

[1] nag.   [2] in the best way he could.
[3] coarse cloth.   [4] cord.   [5] trader.   [6] currents.
[7] harbors.   [8] pilotage fee.   [9] In the Baltic.
[10] The two lines assure us that he knew how to select hours astrologically favorable for making images with which to cure his patient.
[11] Qualities of the four elements (Air, Earth, Fire, and Water) and also of certain "humours." Health, according to the medical theory of the time, was dependent upon the proper balance among these qualities.
[12] remedy.   [13] syrups.

Bernard, and Gatesden, and Gilbertyn.[1]
Of his diete mesurable was he,   435
For it was of no superfluitee,
But of greet norissyng and digestible.
His studie was but litel on the Bible.
In sangwyn [2] and in pers [3] he clad was al,
Lyned with taffata and with sendal,[4]   440
And yet he was but esy of dispence,[5]
He kepte that he wan in pestilence.
For gold in phisik is a cordial,
Therefore he lovede gold in special.

    A good Wif was ther of biside Bathe,   445
But she was somdel [6] deef, and that was scathe.[7]
Of clooth-makyng she hadde swich an haunt,[8]
She passed hem of Ypres and of Gaunt.
In al the parisshe wif ne was ther noon
That to the offrynge bifore hire sholde goon;   450
And if ther dide, certeyn so wrooth was she,
That she was out of alle charitee.
Hir coverchiefs ful fyne weren of ground; [9]
I dorste swere they weyeden ten pound
That on a Sonday weren upon hir heed.   455
Hir hosen weren of fyn scarlet reed,
Ful streite yteyd, and shoes ful moyste and newe.
Boold was hir face, and fair, and reed of hewe.
She was a worthy womman al hir lyve:
Housbondes at chirche dore she hadde fyve,   460
Withouten [10] oother compaignye in youthe, —
But thereof nedeth nat to speke as nowthe.[11]
And thries hadde she been at Jerusalem;
She hadde passed many a straunge strem;
At Rome she hadde been, and at Boloigne,   465
In Galice at Seint Jame,[12] and at Coloigne.[13]
She koude muchel of wandrynge by the weye.
Gat-tothed [14] was she, soothly for to seye.
Upon an amblere [15] esily she sat,
Ywympled [16] wel, and on hir heed an hat   470
As brood as is a bokeler or a targe;[17]
A foot-mantel aboute hir hipes large,
And on hir feet a paire of spores [18] sharpe.
In felaweshipe wel koude she laughe and carpe.[19]
Of remedies of love she knew per chaunce,   475
For she koude of that art the olde daunce.[20]

    A good man was ther of religioun,
And was a povre Persoun [21] of a Toun,
But riche he was of hooly thoght and werk.
He was also a lerned man, a clerk,   480

---

[1] Medical authorities of the time.   [2] blood-red.
[3] sky-blue.   [4] A thin silk.   [5] expenditure.
[6] somewhat.   [7] a pity.   [8] skill.
[9] fine texture.   [10] without counting.   [11] right now.
[12] The shrine is at Campostella in Spain.
[13] Cologne.   [14] "snaggle-toothed."   [15] ambling nag.
[16] provided with a wimple, or pleated head covering.
[17] target.   [18] spurs.   [19] talk or chatter.
[20] the old game of love.   [21] parson.

That Cristes gospel trewely wolde preche;
His parisshens [1] devoutly wolde he teche.
Benygne he was, and wonder diligent,
And in adversitee ful pacient,
And swich he was ypreved ofte sithes.[2]   485
Ful looth were hym to cursen for his tithes,
But rather wolde he yeven, out of doute,
Unto his povre parisshens aboute
Of his offryng and eek of his substaunce.
He koude in litel thyng have suffisaunce.   490
Wyd was his parisshe, and houses fer asonder,
But he ne lefte nat, for reyn ne thonder,
In siknesse nor in meschief [3] to visite
The ferreste [4] in his parisshe, muche and lite,[5]
Upon his feet, and in his hand a staf.   495
This noble ensample to his sheep he yaf,
That first he wroghte, and afterward he taughte.
Out of the gospel he tho wordes caughte,
And this figure he added eek therto,
That if gold ruste, what shal iren do?   500
For if a preest be foul, on whom we truste,
No wonder is a lewed [6] man to ruste;
And shame it is, if a prest take keep,[7]
A shiten shepherde and a clene sheep.
Wel oghte a preest ensample for to yive,   505
By his clennesse, how that his sheep sholde lyve.
He sette nat his benefice to hyre
And leet [8] his sheep encombred in the myre
And ran to Londoun unto Seinte Poules
To seken hym a chaunterie [9] for soules,   510
Or with a bretherhed to been withholde; [10]
But dwelte at hoom, and kepte wel his folde,
So that the wolf ne made it nat myscarie;
He was a shepherde and noght a mercenarie.
And though he hooly were and vertuous,   515
He was to synful men nat despitous,
Ne of his speche daungerous ne digne,[11]
But in his techyng discreet and benygne.
To drawen folk to hevene by fairnesse,
By good ensample, this was his bisynesse.   520
But it were any persone obstinat,
What so he were, of heigh or lough estat,
Hym wolde he snybben [12] sharply for the nonys.
A bettre preest I trowe that nowher noon ys.
He waited after no pompe and reverence,   525
Ne maked him a spiced [13] conscience,
But Cristes loore and his apostles twelve
He taughte, but first he folwed it hymselve.

---

[1] parishioners.   [2] times.   [3] trouble.
[4] farthest.   [5] high and low, or rich and poor.
[6] ignorant.   [7] heed.   [8] left.
[9] Post of a priest who says masses.
[10] shut up with a brotherhood — as chaplain perhaps
for a guild.
[11] overbearing.   [12] "snub" or chide.
[13] scrupulous.

With hym ther was a PLOWMAN, was his brother,
That hadde ylad of dong ful many a fother;[1]   530
A trewe swynkere[2] and a good was he,
Lyvynge in pees and parfit charitee.
God loved he best with al his hoole herte
At alle tymes, thogh him gamed or smerte,[3]
And thanne his neighebor right as hymselve.   535
He wolde thresshe, and therto dyke and delve,
For Cristes sake, for every povre wight,
Withouten hire, if it lay in his myght.
His tithes payde he ful faire and wel,
Bothe of his propre swynk and his catel.[4]   540
In a tabard[5] he rood upon a mere.

Ther was also a REVE,[6] and a MILLERE,
A SOMNOUR,[7] and a PARDONER,[8] also,
A MAUNCIPLE,[9] and myself — ther were namo.
The MILLERE was a stout carl for the nones;   545
Ful byg he was of brawn, and eek of bones.
That proved wel, for over al ther he cam,[10]
At wrastlynge he wolde have alwey the ram.[11]
He was short-sholdred, brood, a thikke knarre;[12]
Ther was no dore that he nolde heve of harre,[13]
Or breke it at a rennyng with his heed.   551
His berd as any sowe or fox was reed,
And therto brood, as though it were a spade.
Upon the cop[14] right of his nose he hade
A werte, and theron stood a toft of herys,   555
Reed as the brustles of a sowes erys;
His nosethirles[15] blake were and wyde.
A swerd and bokeler bar he by his syde.
His mouth as greet was as a greet forneys.
He was a janglere and a goliardeys,[16]   560
And that was moost of synne and harlotries.
Wel koude he stelen corn and tollen thries;[17]
And yet he hadde a thombe of gold, pardee.
A whit cote and a blew hood wered he.
A baggepipe wel koude he blowe and sowne,   565
And therwithal he broghte us out of towne.

A gentil MAUNCIPLE was ther of a temple,
Of which achatours[18] myghte take exemple
For to be wise in byynge of vitaille;
For wheither that he payde or took by taille,[19]   570

[1] great quantity.   [2] worker.
[3] whether happy or in pain.
[4] his own work and his property.
[5] A loose frock.   [6] Steward of an estate.
[7] An officer whose duty it was to summon before the church courts those guilty of offenses.
[8] One who sells pardons or indulgences.
[9] A college purchasing officer or steward.
[10] for wherever he came.
[11] The ram offered as prize.   [12] sturdy fellow.
[13] hinge.   [14] tip.   [15] nostrils.
[16] noisy and scurrilous talker.
[17] take toll three times.   [18] buyers, caterers.
[19] charge account.

Algate he wayted so in his achaat[1]
That he was ay biforn and in good staat.
Now is nat that of God a ful fair grace
That swich a lewed[2] mannes wit shal pace
The wisdom of an heep of lerned men?   575
Of maistres hadde he mo than thries ten,
That weren of lawe expert and curious,
Of which ther were a duszeyne in that hous
Worthy to been stywardes of rente and lond
Of any lord that is in Engelond,   580
To make hym lyve by his propre good
In honour dettelees (but if he were wood),[3]
Or lyve as scarsly as hym list desire;
And able for to helpen al a shire
In any caas that myghte falle or happe;   585
And yet this Manciple sette hir aller cappe.[4]
The REVE was a sclendre colerik man.
His berd was shave as ny as ever he kan;
His heer was by his erys ful round yshorn;
His top was dokked lyk a preest biforn.[5]   590
Ful longe were his legges and ful lene,
Ylyk a staf, ther was no calf ysene.
Wel koude he kepe a gerner and a bynne;
Ther was noon auditour koude on him wynne.[6]
Wel wiste he by the droghte and by the reyn   595
The yeldynge of his seed and of his greyn.
His lordes sheep, his neet,[7] his dayerye,
His swyn, his hors, his stoor,[8] and his pultrye
Was hoolly in this Reves governyng,
And by his covenant yaf the rekenyng,   600
Syn that his lord was twenty yeer of age.
Ther koude no man brynge hym in arrerage.[9]
Ther nas baillif, ne hierde,[10] nor oother hyne,[11]
That he ne knew his sleighte and his covyne;[12]
They were adrad of hym as of the deeth.   605
His wonyng[13] was ful faire upon an heeth;
With grene trees yshadwed was his place.
He koude bettre than his lord purchace.
Ful riche he was astored[14] pryvely:
His lord wel koude he plesen subtilly,   610
To yeve and lene hym of his owene good,
And have a thank, and yet a cote and hood.
In youthe he hadde lerned a good myster;[15]
He was a wel good wrighte, a carpenter.
This Reve sat upon a ful good stot,[16]   615
That was al pomely[17] grey and highte Scot.
A long surcote of pers upon he hade,
And by his syde he baar a rusty blade.
Of Northfolk was this Reve of which I telle,
Biside a toun men clepen Baldeswelle.   620

[1] purchase.   [2] ignorant.   [3] unless he were crazy.
[4] made them all fools.   [5] in front.   [6] win over him.
[7] cattle.   [8] stock.   [9] catch him in debt.
[10] herdsman.   [11] farm worker.   [12] deceitfulness.
[13] dwelling.   [14] stored.   [15] trade.
[16] horse.   [17] dappled.

Tukked he was as is a frere aboute,
And evere he rood the hyndreste of oure route.

A SOMONOUR was ther with us in that place,
That hadde a fyr-reed cherubynnes face,
For saucefleem [1] he was, with eyen narwe.[2] 625
As hoot he was and lecherous as a sparwe,
With scalled [3] browes blake and piled [4] berd.
Of his visage children were aferd.
Ther nas quyk-silver, lytarge,[5] ne brymstoon,
Boras, ceruce,[6] ne oille of tartre noon; 630
Ne oynement that wolde clense and byte,
That hym myghte helpen of his whelkes [7] white,
Nor of the knobbes sittynge on his chekes.
Wel loved he garleek, oynons, and eek lekes,
And for to drynken strong wyn, reed as blood; 635
Thanne wolde he speke and crie as he were wood.[8]
And whan that he wel dronken hadde the wyn,
Thanne wolde he speke no word but Latyn.
A fewe termes hadde he, two or thre,
That he had lerned out of som decree — 640
No wonder is, he herde it al the day;
And eek ye knowen wel how that a jay
Kan clepen "Watte" [9] as wel as kan the pope.
But whoso koude in oother thyng hym grope,[10]
Thanne hadde he spent al his philosophie; 645
Ay "Questio quid iuris" [11] wolde he crie.
He was a gentil harlot [12] and a kynde;
A bettre felawe sholde men noght fynde.
He wolde suffre for a quart of wyn
A good felawe to have his concubyn 650
A twelf month, and excuse hym atte fulle;
Ful prively a fynch eek koude he pulle.[13]
And if he foond owher [14] a good felawe,
He wolde techen him to have noon awe
In swich caas of the ercedekenes curs,[15] 655
But if a mannes soule were in his purs;
For in his purs he sholde ypunysshed be.
"Purs is the ercedekenes helle," seyde he.
But wel I woot he lyed right in dede;
Of cursyng oghte ech gilty man him drede, 660
For curs wol slee right as assoillyng [16] savith,
And also war hym of a Significavit.[17]
In daunger [18] hadde he at his owene gise [19]
The yonge girles [20] of the diocise,

[1] pimpled.   [2] "narrow," close together.
[3] scabbed with scurf.   [4] thin.   [5] lead ointment.
[6] white lead.   [7] blotches.   [8] crazy.
[9] "Walter."   [10] test.
[11] "What's the law in the case?"   [12] rascal.
[13] he knew how to pluck a dupe, "to pull a finch."
[14] anywhere.
[15] Archdeacons had charge of church discipline.
The "curs" then is the condemnation of the Church.
[16] absolution.   [17] writ of excommunication.
[18] under his control.   [19] way.
[20] young people of both sexes.

And knew hir conseil, and was al hir reed.[1] 665
A gerland hadde he set upon his heed
As greet as it were for an ale-stake.[2]
A bokeleer hadde he maad hym of a cake.[3]

With hym ther rood a gentil PARDONER
Of Rouncivale,[4] his freend and his compeer, 670
That streight was comen fro the court of Rome.
Ful loude he soong "Com hider, love, to me!"
This Somonour bar to hym a stif burdoun;[5]
Was nevere trompe of half so greet a soun.
This Pardoner hadde heer as yelow as wex, 675
But smothe it heeng as dooth a strike of flex;
By ounces [6] henge his lokkes that he hadde,
And therwith he his shuldres overspradde;
But thynne it lay, by colpons [7] oon and oon.
But hood, for jolitee, wered he noon, 680
For it was trussed up in his walet.
Hym thoughte he rood al of the newe jet;[8]
Dischevelee, save his cappe, he rood al bare.
Swiche glarynge eyen hadde he as an hare.
A vernycle [9] hadde he sowed upon his cappe. 685
His walet lay biforn hym in his lappe,
Bretful [10] of pardoun, comen from Rome al hoot.
A voys he hadde as smal as hath a goot.
No berd hadde he, ne nevere sholde have;
As smothe it was as it were late shave. 690
I trowe he were a geldyng or a mare.
But of his craft, fro Berwyk into Ware,
Ne was ther swich another pardoner.
For in his male [11] he hadde a pilwe-beer,[12]
Which that he seyde was Oure Lady [13] veyl: 695
He seyde he hadde a gobet [14] of the seyl
That Seint Peter hadde, whan that he wente
Upon the see, til Jhesu Crist hym hente.
He hadde a croys of latoun [15] ful of stones,
And in a glas he hadde pigges bones. 700
But with thise relikes, whan that he fond
A povre person dwellynge upon lond,
Upon a day he gat hym moore moneye
Than that the person gat in monthes tweye;
And thus, with feyned flaterye and japes,[16] 705
He made the person and the peple his apes.
But trewely to tellen atte laste,
He was in chirche a noble ecclesiaste.
Wel koude he rede a lessoun or a storie,

[1] adviser.
[2] A pole to support the sign in front of an ale-house.
[3] flat loaf of bread.   [4] A London hospital.
[5] strong accompaniment.
[6] portions.   [7] shreds.   [8] fashion.
[9] A portrait of Christ. It represented that image of
Christ's face left upon the napkin with which St.
Veronica wiped Christ's face on the way to Calvary.
[10] brim-full.   [11] bag.   [12] pillowslip.
[13] The Virgin Mary.   [14] fragment.
[15] composition metal.   [16] tricks.

But alderbest [1] he song an offertorie; 710
For wel he wiste, whan that song was songe,
He moste preche and wel affile [2] his tonge
To wynne silver, as he ful wel koude;
Therefore he song the murierly [3] and loude.

Now have I toold you shortly, in a clause, 715
Th' estaat, th' array, the nombre, and eek the
  cause
Why that assembled was this compaignye
In Southwerk at this gentil hostelrye
That highte the Tabard, faste by the Belle.
But now is tyme to yow for to telle 720
How that we baren us that ilke nyght,
Whan we were in that hostelrie alyght,
And after wol I telle of our viage
And al the remenaunt of oure pilgrimage.
But first I pray yow, of youre curteisye, 725
That ye n'arette it nat my vileynye, [4]
Thogh that I pleynly speke in this mateere,
To telle yow hir wordes and hir cheere,
Ne thogh I speke hir wordes proprely.
For this ye knowen al so wel as I, 730
Whoso shal telle a tale after a man,
He moot reherce as ny as evere he kan
Everich a word, if it be in his charge,
Al speke he never so rudeliche and large, [5]
Or ellis he moot telle his tale untrewe, 735
Or feyne thyng, or fynde wordes newe.
He may nat spare, althogh he were his brother;
He moot as wel seye o word as another.
Crist spak hymself ful brode in hooly writ,
And wel ye woot no vileynye is it. 740
Eek Plato seith, whoso that kan hym rede,
The wordes moote be cosyn to the dede.
Also I prey yow to foryeve it me,
Al have I nat set folk in hir degree [6]
Heere in this tale, as that they sholde stonde. 745
My wit is short, ye may wel understonde.

Greet chiere made oure Hoost us everichon,
And to the soper sette he us anon.
He served us with vitaille at the beste;
Strong was the wyn, and wel to drynke us leste. [7]
A semely man OURE HOOSTE was withalle 751
For to han been a marchal in an halle.
A large man he was with eyen stepe [8] —
A fairer burgeys is ther noon in Chepe [9] —
Boold of his speche, and wys, and wel ytaught,
And of manhod hym lakkede right naught. 756
Eek therto he was right a myrie man,
And after soper pleyen he bigan,
And spak of myrthe amonges othere thynges,

Whan that we hadde maad our rekenynges, 760
And seyde thus: "Now, lordynges, trewely,
Ye been to me right welcome, hertely;
For by my trouthe, if that I shal nat lye,
I saugh nat this yeer so myrie a compaignye
Atones [1] in this herberwe [2] as is now. 765
Fayn wolde I doon yow myrthe, wiste I how.
And of a myrthe I am right now bythoght,
To doon yow ese, and it shal coste noght.

Ye goon to Caunterbury — God yow speede,
The blisful martir quite yow youre meede! [3] 770
And wel I woot, as ye goon by the weye,
Ye shapen yow to talen [4] and to pleye;
For trewely, confort ne myrthe is noon
To ride by the weye doumb as a stoon;
And therfore wol I maken yow disport, 775
As I seyde erst, [5] and doon yow som confort.
And if yow liketh alle by oon assent
For to stonden at my juggement,
And for to werken as I shal yow seye,
To-morwe, whan ye riden by the weye, 780
Now, by my fader soule that is deed,
But ye be myrie, I wol yeve yow myn heed!
Hoold up youre hondes, withouten moore speche."

Oure conseil was nat longe for to seche. [6]
Us thoughte it was noght worth to make it wys [7]
And graunted hym withouten moore avys, 786
And bad him seye his voirdit [8] as hym leste.
"Lordynges," quod he, "now herkneth for the
  beste;
But taak it nought, I prey yow, in desdeyn.
This is the poynt, to speken short and pleyn, 790
That ech of yow, to shorte with oure weye,
In this viage shal telle tales tweye
To Caunterbury-ward, I mene it so,
And homward he shal tellen othere two,
Of aventures that whilom han bifalle. 795
And which of yow that bereth hym best of alle,
That is to seyn, that telleth in this caas
Tales of best sentence and moost solaas, [9]
Shal have a soper at oure aller cost [10]
Heere in this place, sittynge by this post; 800
Whan that we come agayn fro Caunterbury.
And for to make yow the moore mury,
I wol myselven goodly with yow ryde,
Right at myn owene cost, and be youre gyde;
And whoso wole my juggement withseye [11] 805
Shal paye al that we spenden by the weye.

[1] at one time.   [2] shelter or inn.
[3] reward.   [4] tell tales.   [5] before.
[6] not long to seek — easily had.
[7] prudent; we did not think it worth while to deliberate about it.
[8] verdict.
[9] most thoughtful and most entertaining.
[10] at the cost of us all.   [11] dispute.

[1] best of all.   [2] smooth.   [3] more merrily.
[4] consider it not my rudeness.
[5] generally, in a wide sense.
[6] social rank.   [7] disposed.   [8] bright.
[9] Cheapside, a district in London.

And if ye vouche sauf that it be so,
Tel me anon, withouten wordes mo,[1]
And I wol erly shape me [2] therfore."

This thyng was graunted, and oure othes swore
With ful glad herte, and preyden hym also   811
That he wolde vouche sauf for to do so,
And that he wolde been oure governour,
And of our tales juge and reportour,
And sette a soper at a certeyn pris,   815
And we wol reuled been at his devys [3]
In heigh and lough; [4] and thus by oon assent
We been acorded to his juggement.
And therupon the wyn was fet [5] anon;
We dronken, and to reste wente echon,   820
Withouten any lenger taryynge.

Amorwe,[6] whan that day bigan to sprynge,
Up roos oure Hoost, and was oure aller cok,[7]
And gadrede us togidre alle in a flok,
And forth we riden a litel moore than paas [8]   825
Unto the wateryng of Seint Thomas;
And there oure Hoost bigan his hors areste
And seyde, "Lordynges, herkneth, if yow leste.
Ye woot youre foreward,[9] and I it yow recorde.[10]
If even-song and morwe-song accorde,   830
Lat se now who shal telle the firste tale.
As evere mote I drynke wyn or ale,
Whoso be rebel to my juggement
Shal paye for al that by the wey is spent.
Now draweth cut, er that we ferrer twynne;[11]   835
He which that hath the shorteste shal bigynne.
Sire Knyght," quod he, "my mayster and my lord,
Now draweth cut, for that is myn accord.
Cometh neer," quod he, "my lady Prioresse.
And ye, sire Clerk, lat be youre shamefastnesse,
Ne studieth noght; ley hond to, every man!"   841
Anon to drawen every wight bigan,
And shortly for to tellen as it was,
Were it by aventure, or sort, or cas,
The sothe is this, the cut fil to the Knyght,   845
Of which ful blithe and glad was every wyght,[12]
And telle he moste his tale, as was resoun,
By foreward and by composicioun,
As ye han herd; what nedeth wordes mo?
And whan this goode man saugh that it was so,
As he that wys was and obedient   851
To kepe his foreward by his free assent,
He seyde, "Syn I shal bigynne the game,
What, welcome be the cut, a Goddes name!
Now lat us ryde, and herkneth what I seye."   855
And with that word we ryden forth oure weye,

---

[1] more.   [2] make my plans.   [3] direction.
[4] in all things.   [5] fetched.   [6] on the morrow.
[7] "was the cock for all of us"; i.e., he woke us up.
[8] faster than a walk.   [9] promise or agreement.
[10] remind you of it.   [11] before we go farther.
[12] person.

And he bigan with right a myrie cheere
His tale anon, and seyde in this manere.

HERE ENDS THE PROLOGUE OF THIS BOOK AND
HERE BEGINS THE FIRST TALE, WHICH IS THE
KNIGHT'S TALE.

The Nun's Priest's Tale

*Heere bigynneth the Nonnes Preestes Tale of
the Cok and Hen, Chauntecleer and Pertelote.*

A povre wydwe,[1] somdeel stape [2] in age
Was whilom dwellyng in a narwe cotage,
Biside a grove, stondynge in a dale.
This wydwe, of which I telle yow my tale,
Syn thilke day that she was last a wyf,   5
In pacience ladde a ful symple lyf,
For litel was hir catel [3] and hir rente.
By housbondrie [4] of swich as God hire sente
She foond [5] hirself and eek hir doghtren two.
Thre large sowes hadde she, and namo,   10
Three keen,[6] and eek a sheep that highte Malle.
Ful sooty was hire bour and eek hir halle,
In which she eet ful many a sklendre meel.
Of poynaunt sauce hir neded never a deel.[7]
No deyntee morsel passed thurgh hir throte;   15
Hir diete was accordant to hir cote.
Repleccioun ne made hire nevere sik;
Attempree [8] diete was al hir phisik,
And exercise, and hertes suffisaunce.
The goute lette hire nothyng [9] for to daunce,   20
N'apoplexie shente [10] nat hir heed.
No wyn ne drank she, neither whit ne reed;
Hir bord was served moost with whit and blak,
Milk and broun breed, in which she foond no lak,
Seynd [11] bacoun, and somtyme an ey [12] or tweye;
For she was, as it were, a maner deye.[13]   26

A yeerd she hadde, enclosed al aboute
With stikkes, and a drye dych withoute,
In which she hadde a cok, hight Chauntecleer.
In al the land of crowyng nas his peer.   30
His voys was murier than the murie orgon
On messe-dayes that in the chirche gon.
Wel sikerer [14] was his crowyng in his logge
Than is a clokke or an abbey orlogge.[15]
By nature he knew ech ascencioun   35
Of the equynoxial in thilke toun;
For whan degrees fiftene [16] weren ascended,

---

[1] widow.   [2] advanced.
[3] property.   [4] economy.   [5] provided for.
[6] cows.   [7] not at all.   [8] temperate.
[9] did not prevent her.   [10] harmed.   [11] broiled.
[12] egg.   [13] dairywoman.   [14] more trustworthy.
[15] clock.   [16] each hour.

Thanne crew he, that it myghte nat been amended.
His coomb was redder than the fyn coral,
And batailled [1] as it were a castel wal;   40
His byle was blak, and as the jeet it shoon;
Lyk asure were his legges and his toon;
His nayles whitter than the lylye flour,
And lyk the burned gold was his colour.
This gentil cok hadde in his governaunce   45
Sevene hennes for to doon al his plesaunce,
Whiche were his sustres and his paramours,
And wonder lyk to hym, as of colours;
Of whiche the faireste hewed on hir throte
Was cleped faire damoysele Pertelote.   50
Curteys she was, discreet, and debonaire,
And compaignable, and bar hyrself so faire,
Syn thilke day that she was seven nyght oold,
That trewely she hath the herte in hoold
Of Chauntecleer, loken in every lith; [2]   55
He loved hire so that wel was hym therwith.
But swich a joye was it to here hem synge,
Whan that the brighte sonne gan to sprynge,
In sweete accord, "My lief is faren [3] in londe!"
For thilke tyme, as I have understonde,   60
Beestes and briddes koude speke and synge.

And so bifel that in a dawenynge,
As Chauntecleer among his wyves alle
Sat on his perche, that was in the halle,
And next hym sat this faire Pertelote,   65
This Chauntecleer gan gronen in his throte,
As man that in his dreem is drecched [4] soore.
And whan that Pertelote thus herde hym roore,
She was agast, and seyde, "Herte deere,
What eyleth yow, to grone in this manere?   70
Ye been a verray sleper; fy, for shame!"

And he answerde, and seyde thus: "Madame,
I pray yow that ye take it nat agrief.
By God, me mette [5] I was in swich meschief
Right now, that yet myn herte is soore afright.   75
Now God," quod he, "my swevene recche [6] aright,
And kepe my body out of foul prisoun!
Me mette how that I romed up and doun
Withinne our yeerd, wheer as I saugh a beest
Was lyk an hound, and wolde han maad areest   80
Upon my body, and wolde han had me deed.
His colour was bitwixe yelow and reed,
And tipped was his tayl and bothe his eeris
With blak, unlyk the remenant of his heeris;
His snowte smal, with glowynge eyen tweye.   85
Yet of his look for feere almoost I deye;
This caused me my gronyng, doutelees."

"Avoy!" [7] quod she, "fy on yow, hertelees!
Allas!" quod she, "for, by that God above,
Now han ye lost myn herte and al my love.   90

I kan nat love a coward, by my feith!
For certes, what so any womman seith,
We alle desiren, if it myghte bee,
To han housbondes hardy, wise, and free, [1]
And secree, and no nygard, ne no fool,   95
Ne hym that is agast of every tool,
Ne noon avauntour, [2] by that God above!
How dorste ye seyn, for shame, unto youre love
That any thyng myghte make yow aferd?
Have ye no mannes herte, and han a berd?   100
Allas! and konne ye been agast of swevenys?
Nothyng, God woot, but vanitee in sweven is.
Swevenes engendren of replecciouns, [3]
And ofte of fume [4] and of complecciouns, [5]
Whan humours been to habundant in a wight.   105
Certes this dreem, which ye han met tonyght,
Cometh of the greete superfluytee
Of youre rede colera, [6] pardee,
Which causeth folk to dreden in hir dremes
Of arwes, and of fyr with rede lemes, [7]   110
Of rede beestes, that they wol hem byte,
Of contek, [8] and of whelpes, grete and lyte;
Right as the humour of malencolie [9]
Causeth ful many a man in sleep to crie
For feere of blake beres, or boles [10] blake,   115
Or elles blake develes wole hem take.
Of othere humours koude I telle also
That werken many a man in sleep ful wo;
But I wol passe as lightly as I kan.

Lo Catoun, [11] which that was so wys a man,   120
Seyde he nat thus, 'Ne do no fors [12] of dremes?'
Now sire," quod she, "whan we flee fro the
bemes,
For Goddes love, as taak som laxatyf.
Up peril of my soule and of my lyf,
I conseille yow the beste, I wol nat lye,   125
That bothe of colere and of malencolye
Ye purge yow; and for ye shal nat tarie,
Though in this toun is noon apothecarie,
I shal myself to herbes techen yow
That shul been for youre hele and for youre prow; [13]
And in oure yeerd tho herbes shal I fynde   131
The whiche han of hire propretee by kynde [14]
To purge yow bynethe and eek above.
Foryet nat this, for Goddes owene love!
Ye been ful coleryk of compleccioun;   135
Ware the sonne in his ascencioun
Ne fynde yow nat repleet of humours hoote.
And if it do, I dar wel leye a grote,
That ye shul have a fevere terciane,
Or an agu, that may be youre bane.   140
A day or two ye shul have digestyves

---

[1] generous.   [2] boaster.   [3] over-eating.   [4] vapor.
[5] temperament.   [6] red bile.   [7] flames.   [8] contest.
[9] black bile.   [10] bulls.   [11] Dionysius Cato.
[12] take no account.   [13] profit.   [14] nature.

---

[1] indented.   [2] locked up in every limb.
[3] "My love is gone."   [4] troubled.
[5] I dreamed.   [6] expound my dream.   [7] fie!

Of wormes, er ye take youre laxatyves
Of lawriol,[1] centaure,[1] and fumetere,[1]
Or elles of ellebor,[2] that groweth there,
Of katapuce,[2] or of gaitrys beryis,[2]   145
Of herbe yve,[2] growyng in oure yeerd, ther mery
        is;
Pekke hem up right as they growe and ete hem yn.
Be myrie, housbonde, for youre fader kyn!
Dredeth no dreem, I kan sey yow namoore.''
        ''Madame,'' quod he, ''graunt mercy [3] of youre
                loore.   150
But nathelees, as touchyng daun Catoun,
That hath of wysdom swich a greet renoun,
Though that he bad no dremes for to drede,
By God, men may in olde bookes rede
Of many a man moore of auctorite   155
Than evere Caton was, so moot I thee,[4]
That al the revers seyn of this sentence,
And han wel founden by experience
That dremes been significaciouns
As wel of joye as of tribulaciouns   160
That folk enduren in this lif present.
Ther nedeth make of this noon argument;
The verray preeve sheweth it in dede.
        Oon of the gretteste auctour that men rede [5]
Seith thus; that whilom two felawes wente   165
On pilgrimage, in a ful good entente;
And happed so, they coomen in a toun
Wher as ther was swich congregacioun
Of peple, and eek so streit of herbergage, [6]
That they ne founde as muche as o cotage   170
In which they bothe myghte ylogged bee.
Wherfore they mosten of necessitee,
As for that nyght, departen compaignye;
And ech of hem gooth to his hostelrye,
And took his loggyng as it wolde falle.   175
That oon of hem was logged in a stalle,
Fer in a yeerd, with oxen of the plough;
That oother man was logged wel ynough,
As was his aventure or his fortune,
That us governeth alle as in commune.   180
        And so bifel that, longe er it were day,
This man mette [7] in his bed, ther as he lay,
How that his felawe gan upon hym calle,
And seyde, 'Allas! for in an oxes stalle
This nyght I shal be mordred ther I lye.   185
Now help me, deere brother, or I dye.
In alle haste com to me!' he sayde.

        [1] spurge-laurel, centaury, and fumitory.
        [2] hellebore, caper-spurge, buckthorn berries, ground
ivy.
        [3] best thanks.
        [4] as I may thrive.
        [5] Chaucer appears to have his stories indirectly from
Cicero.
        [6] so lacking in accommodation.   [7] dreamed.

This man out of his sleep for feere abrayde; [1]
But whan that he was wakened of his sleep,
He turned hym, and took of this no keep.[2]   190
Hym thoughte his dreem nas but a vanitee.
Thus twies in his slepyng dremed hee;
And atte thridde tyme yet his felawe
Cam, as hym thoughte, and seide, 'I am now
        slawe.[3]
Bihoold my bloody woundes depe and wyde!   195
Arys up erly in the morwe tyde,
And at the west gate of the toun,' quod he,
'A carte ful of dong ther shaltow se,
In which my body is hid ful prively;
Do thilke carte arresten boldely.   200
My gold caused my mordre, sooth to sayn.'
And tolde hym every point how he was slayn,
With a ful pitous face, pale of hewe.
And truste wel, his dreem he foond ful trewe,
For on the morwe, as soone as it was day,   205
To his felawes in he took the way;
And whan that he cam to this oxes stalle,
After his felawe he bigan to calle.
        The hostiler answerede hym anon,
And seyde, 'Sire, your felawe is agon.   210
As soone as day he wente out of the toun.'
        This man gan fallen in suspicioun,
Remembrynge on his dremes that he mette,
And forth he gooth — no lenger wolde he lette [4] —
Unto the west gate of the toun, and fond   215
A dong-carte, wente as it were to donge lond,
That was arrayed in that same wise
As ye han herd the dede man devyse.
And with an hardy herte he gan to crye
Vengeance and justice of this felonye.   220
'My felawe mordred is this same nyght,
And in this carte he lith gapyng upright.
I crye out on the ministres,' quod he,
'That sholden kepe and reulen this citee.
Harrow! allas! heere lith my felawe slayn!'   225
What sholde I moore unto this tale sayn?
The peple out sterte and caste the cart to grounde,
And in the myddel of the dong they founde
The dede man, that mordred was al newe.
        O blisful God, that art so just and trewe,   230
Lo, how that thou biwreyest [5] mordre alway!
Mordre wol out, that se we day by day.
Mordre is so wlatsom [6] and abhomynable
To God, that is so just and resonable,
That he ne wol nat suffre it heled [7] be,   235
Though it abyde a yeer, or two, or thre.
Mordre wol out, this my conclusioun.
And right anon, ministres of that toun

        [1] started up in fear.
        [2] ''took no care of this,'' ignored it.
        [3] slain.   [4] delay.   [5] revealest.
        [6] loathsome.   [7] concealed.

Han hent the carter and so soore hym pyned,[1]
And eek the hostiler so soore engyned,[2]   240
That they biknewe [3] hire wikkednesse anon,
And were anhanged by the nekke-bon.

Heere may men seen that dremes been to drede.
And certes in the same book I rede,
Right in the nexte chapitre after this —   245
I gabbe [4] nat, so have I joye or blis —
Two men that wolde han passed over see,
For certeyn cause, into a fer contree,
If that the wynd ne hadde been contrarie,
That made hem in a citee for to tarie   250
That stood ful myrie upon an haven-syde;
But on a day, agayn the even-tyde,
The wynd gan chaunge, and blew right as hem
        leste.
Jolif and glad they wente unto hir reste,
And casten hem ful erly for to saille.   255
But to that o man fil a greet mervaille:
That oon of hem, in slepyng as he lay,
Hym mette a wonder dreem agayn the day.
Hym thoughte a man stood by his beddes syde,
And hym comanded that he sholde abyde,   260
And seyde hym thus: 'If thou tomorwe wende,
Thow shalt be dreynt;[5] my tale is at an ende.'
He wook, and tolde his felawe what he mette,
And preyde hym his viage for to lette;[6]
As for that day, he preyde hym to byde.   265
His felawe, that lay by his beddes syde,
Gan for to laughe, and scorned him ful faste.
'No dreem,' quod he, 'may so myn herte agaste
That I wol lette for to do my thynges.
I sette nat a straw by thy dremynges,   270
For swevenes been but vanytees and japes.[7]
Men dreme alday of owles and of apes,
And eek of many a maze [8] therwithal;
Men dreme of thyng that nevere was ne shal.
But sith I see that thou wolt heere abyde,   275
And thus forslewthen [9] wilfully thy tyde,
God woot, it reweth me; and have good day!'
And thus he took his leve, and wente his way.
But er that he hadde half his cours yseyled,
Noot I nat why, ne what myschaunce it eyled,
But casuelly the shippes botme rente,   281
And ship and man under the water wente
In sighte of othere shippes it bisyde,
That with hem seyled at the same tyde.
And therfore, faire Pertelote so deere,   285
By swiche ensamples olde maistow [10] leere
That no man sholde been to recchelees
Of dremes; for I seye thee, doutelees,
That many a dreem ful soore is for to drede.

Lo, in the lyf of Seint Kenelm I rede,   290
That was Kenulphus sone, the noble kyng
Of Mercenrike,[1] how Kenelm mette a thyng.
A lite er he was mordred, on a day,
His mordre in his avysioun he say.
His norice [2] hym expowned every deel   295
His sweven, and bad hym for to kepe hym weel
For traisoun; but he nas but seven yeer oold,
And therfore litel tale hath he toold
Of any dreem, so hooly was his herte.
By God! I hadde levere than my sherte   300
That ye hadde rad his legende, as have I.
Dame Pertelote, I sey yow trewely,
Macrobeus,[3] that writ the avisioun
In Affrike of the worthy Cipioun,
Affermeth dremes, and seith that they been   305
Warnynge of thynges that men after seen.
And forthermoore, I pray yow, looketh wel
In the olde testament, of Daniel,
If he heeld dremes any vanitee.
Reed eek of Joseph, and ther shul ye see   310
Wher dremes be somtyme — I sey nat alle —
Warnynge of thynges that shul after falle.
Looke of Egipte the kyng, daun [4] Pharao,
His bakere and his butiller also,
Wher they ne felte noon effect in dremes.   315
Whoso wol seken actes of sondry remes [5]
May rede of dremes many a wonder thyng.
Lo Cresus, which that was of Lyde kyng,
Mette he nat that he sat upon a tree,
Which signified he sholde anhanged bee?   320
Lo heere Andromacha Ectores wyf,
That day that Ector sholde lese his lyf,
She dremed on the same nyght biforn
How that the lyf of Ector sholde be lorn,
If thilke day he wente into bataille.   325
She warned hym, but it myghte nat availle;
He wente for to fighte natheles,
But he was slayn anon of Achilles.
But thilke tale is al to longe to telle,
And eek it is ny day, I may nat dwelle.   330
Shortly I seye, as for conclusioun,
That I shal han of this avisioun [6]
Adversitee; and I seye forthermoor,
That I ne telle of laxatyves no stoor,[7]
For they been venymous, I woot it weel;   335
I hem diffye, I love hem never a deel!
Now let us speke of myrthe, and stynte [8] al this.
Madame Pertelote, so have I blis,
Of o thyng God hath sent me large grace;
For whan I se the beautee of youre face,   340
Ye been so scarlet reed aboute youre yen,

It maketh al my drede for to dyen;
For al so siker [1] as *In principio*,[2]
Mulier est hominis confusio, —
Madame, the sentence of this Latyn is,   345
'Womman is mannes joye and al his blis.'
For whan I feele a-nyght your softe syde,
Al be it that I may nat on yow ryde,
For that oure perche is maad so narwe, allas!
I am so ful of joye and of solas,   350
That I diffye bothe sweven and dreem?"
And with that word he fley doun fro the beem,
For it was day, and eke his hennes alle,
And with a chuk he gan hem for to calle,
For he hadde founde a corn, lay in the yerd.   355
Real [3] he was, he was namoore aferd.
He fethered Pertelote twenty tyme,
And trad hire eke as ofte, er it was pryme.
He looketh as it were a grym leoun,
And on his toos he rometh up and doun;   360
Hym deigned nat to sette his foot to grounde.
He chukketh, whan he hath a corn yfounde,
And to hym rennen thanne his wyves alle.
Thus roial, as a prince is in his halle,
Leve I this Chauntecleer in his pasture,   365
And after wol I telle his aventure.

     Whan that the month in which the world bigan,
That highte March, whan God first maked man,[4]
Was compleet, and passed were also,
Syn March bigan, thritty dayes and two,   370
Bifel that Chauntecleer in al his pryde,
His sevene wyves walkynge by his syde,
Caste up his eyen to the brighte sonne,
That in the signe of Taurus hadde yronne
Twenty degrees and oon, and somwhat moore,   375
And knew by kynde,[5] and by noon oother loore,
That it was pryme,[6] and crew with blisful stevene.[7]
"The sonne," he seyde, "is clomben up on hevene
Fourty degrees and oon, and moore ywis.
Madame Pertelote, my worldes blis,   380
Herkneth thise blisful briddes [8] how they synge,
And se the fresshe floures how they sprynge,
Ful is myn herte of revel and solas!"
But sodeynly hym fil a sorweful cas,
For evere the latter ende of joye is wo.   385
God woot that worldly joye is soone ago;
And if a rethor [9] koude faire endite,
He in a cronycle saufly myghte it write

As for a sovereyn notabilitee.
Now every wys man, lat him herkne me;   390
This storie is also trewe, I undertake,
As is the book of Launcelot de Lake,[1]
That wommen holde in ful greet reverence.
Now wol I torne agayn to my sentence.
     A col-fox,[2] ful of sly iniquitee,   395
That in the grove hadde woned [3] yeres three,
By heigh ymaginacioun forncast,[4]
The same nyght thurghout the hegges brast
Into the yerd ther Chauntecleer the faire
Was wont, and eek his wyves, to repaire;   400
And in a bed of wortes [5] stille he lay,
Til it was passed undren [6] of the day,
Waitynge his tyme on Chauntecleer to falle,
As gladly doon thise homycides alle
That in await liggen to mordre men.   405
O false mordrour, lurkynge in thy den!
O newe Scariot, newe Genylon,[7]
False dissymulour, o Greek Synon,[8]
That broghtest Troye al outrely to sorwe!
O Chauntecleer, acursed be that morwe   410
That thou into that yerd flaugh fro the bemes!
Thou were ful wel ywarned by thy dremes
That thilke day was perilous to thee;
But what that God forwoot moot nedes bee,
After the opinioun of certein clerkis.   415
Witnesse on hym that any parfit clerk is,
That in scole is greet altercacioun
In this mateere, and greet disputisoun,
And hath been of an hundred thousand men.
But I ne kan nat bulte it to the bren,[9]   420
As kan the hooly doctour Augustyn,
Or Boece,[10] or the Bisshop Bradwardyn,[11]
Wheither that Goddes worthy forwityng
Streyneth [12] me nedely for to doon a thyng, —
"Nedely" clepe I symple necessitee;   425
Or elles, if free choys be graunted me
To do that same thyng, or do it noght,
Though God forwoot it er that it was wroght;
Or if his wityng streyneth never a deel
But by necessitee condicioneel.   430
I wol nat han to do of swich mateere;
My tale is of a cok, as ye may heere,
That tok his conseil of his wyf, with sorwe,
To walken in the yerd upon that morwe
That he hadde met that dreem that I yow tolde.

[1] just so sure.
[2] Chantecleer confounds Pertelote with his learning:
starting off with the first line of the Gospel of St. John
he ends with "woman is the destruction of man" which
he translates in line 346 as something quite different.
[3] royal.
[4] Medieval thought held that the world was created
at the vernal equinox.   [5] nature.
[6] nine A.M.   [7] voice.   [8] birds.   [9] rhetorician.

[1] An Arthurian romance.
[2] fox with black (coal) markings.   [3] dwelt.
[4] premeditated.   [5] herbs.   [6] mid-morning.
[7] A traitor in the *Song of Roland*.
[8] He who convinced the Trojans that the Greek
horse should be taken into the city.
[9] "sift it to the bran," get to the bottom of it all.
[10] Boethius.   [11] English theologian.
[12] constrains or binds.

Wommennes conseils been ful ofte colde;[1]   436
Wommannes conseil broghte us first to wo,
And made Adam fro Paradys to go,
Ther as he was ful myrie and wel at ese.
But for I noot to whom it myght displese,   440
If I conseil of wommen wolde blame,
Passe over, for I seyde it in my game.
Rede auctours, where they trete of swich mateere,
And what they seyn of wommen ye may heere.
Thise been the cokkes wordes, and nat myne;   445
I kan noon harm of no womman divyne.

    Faire in the soond, to bathe hire myrily,
Lith Pertelote, and alle hire sustres by,
Agayn the sonne, and Chauntecleer so free
Soong murier than the mermayde in the see;   450
For Phisiologus[2] seith sikerly
How that they syngen wel and myrily.
And so bifel that, as he caste his ye
Among the wortes on a boterflye,
He was war of this fox, that lay ful lowe.   455
Nothyng ne liste hym thanne for to crowe,
But cride anon, "Cok! cok!" and up he sterte
As man that was affrayed in his herte.
For natureely a beest desireth flee
Fro his contrarie, if he may it see,   460
Though he never erst hadde seyn it with his ye.

    This Chauntecleer, whan he gan hym espye,
He wolde han fled, but that the fox anon
Seyde, "Gentil sire, allas! wher wol ye gon?
Be ye affrayed of me that am youre freend?   465
Now, certes, I were worse than a feend,
If I to yow wolde harm or vileynye!
I am nat come youre conseil for t'espye,
But trewely, the cause of my comynge
Was oonly for to herkne how that ye synge.   470
For trewely, ye have as myrie a stevene
As any aungel hath that is in hevene.
Therwith ye han in musyk moore feelynge
Than hadde Boece, or any that kan synge.
My lord youre fader — God his soule blesse! —
And eek youre mooder, of hire gentillesse,   476
Han in myn hous ybeen to my greet ese;
And certes, sire, ful fayn wolde I yow plese.
But for men speke of syngyng, I wol seye,
So moote I brouke[3] wel myne eyen tweye,   480
Save yow, I herde nevere man so synge
As dide youre fader in the morwenynge.
Certes, it was of herte, al that he song.
And for to make his voys the moore strong,
He wolde so peyne hym that with bothe his yen
He moste wynke, so loude he wolde cryen,   486
And stonden on his tiptoon therwithal,

¹ disastrous.
² An old Latin work presenting much spurious science
as to the nature of animals.
³ enjoy or use.

And strecche forth his nekke long and smal.
And eek he was of swich discrecioun
That ther nas no man in no regioun
That hym in song or wisedom myghte passe.   490
I have wel rad in 'Daun Burnel the Asse,'[1]
Among his vers, how that ther was a cok,
For that a preestes sone yaf hym a knok
Upon his leg whil he was yong and nyce,[2]   495
He made hym for to lese his benefice.
But certeyn, ther nys no comparisoun
Betwixe the wisedom and discrecioun
Of youre fader and of his subtiltee.
Now syngeth, sire, for seinte charitee;   500
Lat se, konne ye youre fader countrefete?"[3]
    This Chauntecleer his wynges gan to bete,
As man that koude his traysoun nat espie,
So was he ravysshed with his flaterie.
    Allas! ye lordes, many a fals flatour   505
Is in youre courtes, and many a losengeour,[4]
That plesen yow wel moore, by my feith,
Than he that soothfastnesse unto yow seith.
Redeth Ecclesiaste of flaterye;
Beth war, ye lordes, of hir trecherye.   510
    This Chauntecleer stood hye upon his toos,
Strecchynge his nekke, and heeld his eyen cloos,
And gan to crowe loude for the nones.[5]
And daun Russell the fox stirte up atones,[6]
And by the gargat[7] hente Chauntecleer,   515
And on his bak toward the wode hym beer,
For yet ne was ther no man that hym sewed.[8]
    O destinee, that mayst nat been eschewed!
Allas, that Chauntecleer fleigh fro the bemes!
Allas, his wyf ne roghte nat of dremes!   520
And on a Friday fil al this meschaunce.
O Venus, that art goddesse of plesaunce,
Syn that thy servant was this Chauntecleer,
And in thy servyce dide al his poweer,
Moore for delit than world to multiplye,   525
Why woldestow suffre hym on thy day to dye?
O Gaufred,[9] deere maister soverayn,
That whan thy worthy kyng Richard was slayn
With shot, compleynedest his deeth so soore,
Why ne hadde I now thy sentence and thy loore
The Friday for to chide, as diden ye?   531
For on a Friday, soothly, slayn was he.
Thanne wolde I shewe yow how that I koude
         pleyne[10]
For Chauntecleres drede and for his peyne.
    Certes, swich cry ne lamentacion,   535
Was nevere of ladyes maad whan Ylion

¹ A satirical poem.   ² foolish.
³ equal or imitate.   ⁴ flatterer.   ⁵ time being.
⁶ at once.   ⁷ throat.   ⁸ pursued.
⁹ Geoffrey, author of a treatise on poetry which
Chaucer quite evidently did not respect.
¹⁰ lament.

Was wonne, and Pirrus with his streite swerd,
Whan he hadde hent [1] kyng Priam by the berd,
And slayn hym, as seith us *Eneydos*,[2]
As maden alle the hennes in the clos,   540
Whan they had seyn of Chauntecleer the sighte.
But sovereynly dame Pertelote shrighte,
Ful louder than dide Hasdrubales wyf,
Whan that hir housbonde hadde lost his lyf,
And that the Romayns hadde brend Cartage.   545
She was so ful of torment and of rage
That wilfully into the fyr she sterte,
And brende hirselven with a stedefast herte.
  O woful hennes, right so criden ye,
As, whan that Nero brende the citee   550
Of Rome, cryden senatoures wyves
For that hir husbondes losten alle hir lyves;
Withouten gilt this Nero hath hem slayn.
Now wole I turne to my tale agayn.
  This sely [3] wydwe and eek hir doghtres two   555
Herden thise hennes crie and maken wo,
And out at dores stirten they anon,
And syen the fox toward the grove gon,
And bar upon his bak the cok away,
And cryden, "Out! harrow! and weylaway!   560
Ha! ha! the fox!" and after hym they ran,
And eek with staves many another man.
Ran Colle oure dogge, and Talbot, and Gerland,
And Malkyn, with a dystaf in hir hand;
Ran cow and calf, and eek the verray hogges,   565
So fered for the berkyng of the dogges
And shoutyng of the men and wommen eeke,
They ronne so hem thoughte hir herte breeke.
They yolleden as feendes doon in helle;
The dokes cryden as men wolde hem quelle; [4]   570
The gees for feere flowen over the trees;
Out of the hyve cam the swam of bees.
So hydous was the noyse, a, *benedicitee!*
Certes, he Jakke Straw [5] and his meynee
Ne made nevere shoutes half so shrille,   575
Whan that they wolden any Flemyng kille,
As thilke day was maad upon the fox.
Of bras they broghten bemes,[6] and of box,
Of horn, of boon, in whiche they blewe and powped,
And therwithal they skriked and they howped.   580
It seemed as that hevene sholde falle.
  Now, goode men, I prey yow herkneth alle:
Lo, how Fortune turneth sodeynly
The hope and pryde eek of hir enemy!
This cok, that lay upon the foxes bak,   585
In al his drede unto the fox he spak,
And seyde, "Sire, if that I were as ye,
Yet sholde I seyn, as wys [7] God helpe me,

'Turneth agayn, ye proude cherles alle!
A verray pestilence upon yow falle!   590
Now am I come unto the wodes syde;
Maugree [1] youre heed, the cok shal heere abyde.
I wol hym ete, in feith, and that anon!'"
  The fox answerde, "In feith, it shal be don."
And as he spak that word, al sodeynly   595
This cok brak from his mouth delyverly,[2]
And heighe upon a tree he fleigh anon.
And whan the fox saugh that the cok was gon,
  "Allas!" quod he, "O Chauntecleer, allas!
I have to yow," quod he, "ydoon trespas,   600
In as muche as I maked yow aferd
Whan I yow hente and broghte out of the yerd.
But, sire, I dide it in no wikke entente.
Com doun, and I shal telle yow what I mente;
I shal seye sooth to yow, God help me so!"   605
  "Nay thanne," quod he, "I shrewe [3] us bothe two.
And first I shrewe myself, bothe blood and bones,
If thou bigyle me ofter than ones.
Thou shalt namoore, thurgh thy flaterye,
Do me to synge and wynke with myn ye;   610
For he that wynketh, whan he sholde see,
Al wilfully, God lat him nevere thee!" [4]
  "Nay," quod the fox, "but God yeve hym meschaunce,
That is so undiscreet of governaunce
That jangleth [5] whan he sholde holde his pees."   615
  Lo, swich it is for to recchelees   616
And necligent, and truste on flaterye.
  But ye that holden this tale a folye,
As of a fox, or of a cok and hen,
Taketh the moralite, goode men.   620
For seint Paul seith that al that writen is,
To oure doctrine it is ywrite, ywis;
Taketh the fruyt, and lat the chaf be stille.
Now, goode God, if that it be thy wille,
As seith my lord, so make us alle goode men,   625
And brynge us to his heighe blisse! Amen.

Heere is ended the Nonnes Preestes Tale.

The Pardoner's Tale

THE PARDONER'S PROLOGUE

Heere Folweth the Prologe of the Pardoners Tale.

Radix malorum est Cupiditas.   Ad Thimotheum, 6°.

  "Lordynges," quod he, "in chirches whan I preche,
I peyne me to han an hauteyn speche,[6]

---

    [1] seized.   [2] Æneid.   [3] hapless.   [4] kill.
    [5] The revolt led by Straw had taken place only a few
years before Chaucer wrote.
    [6] trumpets.   [7] surely.

    [1] in spite of.   [2] quickly.
[3] curse.   [4] prosper.   [5] talketh.
[6] I take pains to use a proud manner of speaking.

And rynge it out as round as gooth a belle,
For I kan al by rote [1] that I telle.
My theme is alwey oon, and evere was —   5
Radix malorum est Cupiditas.[2]

First I pronounce whennes that I come,
And thanne my bulles shewe I, alle and some.
Oure lige lordes seel on my patente,[3]
That shewe I first, my body to warente,   10
That no man be so boold, ne preest ne clerk,
Me to destourbe of Cristes hooly werk.
And after that thanne telle I forth my tales;
Bulles of popes and of cardynales,
Of patriarkes and bishops I shewe,   15
And in Latyn I speke a wordes fewe,
To saffron with my predicacioun,[4]
And for to stire hem to devocioun.
Thanne shewe I forth my longe cristal stones,
Ycrammed ful of cloutes [5] and of bones, —   20
Relikes been they, as wenen [6] they echoon.
Thanne have I in latoun [7] a sholder-boon
Which that was of an hooly Jewes sheep.
'Goode men,' I seye, 'taak of my wordes keep,[8]
If that this boon be wasshe in any welle,   25
If cow, or calf, or sheep, or oxe swelle
That any worm hath ete, or worm ystonge,
Taak water of that welle and wassh his tonge,
And it is hool [9] anon; and forthermoore,
Of pokkes and of scabbe, and every soore   30
Shal every sheep be hool that of this welle
Drynketh a draughte.   Taak kep eek what I telle:
If that the good-man that the beestes oweth [10]
Wol every wyke,[11] er that the cok hym croweth,
Fastynge, drynken of this welle a draughte,   35
As thilke hooly Jew oure eldres taughte,
His beestes and his stoor shal multiplie.

And, sires, also it heeleth jalousie;
For though a man be falle in jalous rage,
Lat maken with this water his potage,   40
And nevere shal he moore his wyf mystriste,
Though he the soothe of hir defaute wiste,
Al had she taken prestes two or thre.
Heere is a miteyn eek, that ye may se.
He that his hand wol putte in this mitayn,   45
He shal have multipliyng of his grayn,
Whan he hath sowen, be it whete or otes,
So that he offre pens, or elles grotes.

Goode men and wommen, o thyng warne I yow:
If any wight be in this chirche now   50

That hath doon synne horrible, that he
Dar nat, for shame, of it yshryven [1] be,
Or any womman, be she yong or old,
That hath ymaad hir housbonde cokewold,
Swich folk shal have no power ne no grace   55
To offren to my relikes in this place.
And whoso fyndeth hym out of swich blame,
He wol come up and offre in Goddes name,
And I assoille [2] him by the auctoritee
Which that by bulle ygraunted was to me.'   60
By this gaude [3] have I wonne, yeer by yeer,
An hundred mark [4] sith I was pardoner.
I stonde lyk a clerk in my pulpet,
And whan the lewed [5] peple is doun yset,
I preche so as ye han herd bifoore,   65
And telle an hundred false japes moore.
Thanne peyne I me to strecche forth the nekke,
And est and west upon the peple I bekke,[6]
As dooth a dowve sittynge on a berne.
Myne handes and my tonge goon so yerne [7]   70
That is it joye to se my bisynesse.
Of avarice and of swich cursednesse
Is al my prechyng, for to make hem free
To yeven hir pens, and namely [8] unto me.
For myn entente is nat but for to wynne,   75
And nothyng for correccioun of synne.
I rekke nevere, whan that they been beryed,
Though that hir soules goon a-blakeberyed! [9]
For certes, many a predicacioun
Comth ofte tyme of yvel entencioun;   80
Som for plesance of folk and flaterye,
To been avaunced by ypocrisye,
And som for veyne glorie, and som for hate.
For whan I dar noon oother weyes debate,[10]
Thanne wol I stynge hym with my tonge smerte   85
In prechyng, so that he shal nat asterte [11]
To been defamed falsly, if that he
Hath trespased to my bretheren or to me.
For though I telle noght his propre name,
Men shal wel knowe that it is the same,   90
By signes, and by othere circumstances.
Thus quyte I folk that doon us displesances;
Thus spitte I out my venym under hewe
Of hoolynesse, to semen hooly and trewe.
But shortly myn entente I wol devyse: 95
I preche of no thyng but for coveityse.
Therfore my theme is yet, and evere was,
Radix malorum est Cupiditas.
Thus kan I preche agayn that same vice

---

[1] by memory.
[2] "For the love of money is the root of all evil,"
I Timothy vi, 10.
[3] Official document establishing his status in the
Church.
[4] to give color to my sermon.   [5] rags.
[6] as each supposes.   [7] A zinc and copper alloy.
[8] heed.   [9] whole or well.   [10] owneth.   [11] week.

[1] shrived; i.e., to receive confession.
[2] absolve.   [3] trick.
[4] In modern terms this would be something like the
salary of a United States senator or of the mayor of a
large city.
[5] ignorant.   [6] nod.   [7] fast.   [8] especially.
[9] go a-blackberrying.   [10] quarrel.   [11] escape.

Which that I use, and that is avarice.   100
But though myself be gilty in that synne,
Yet kan I maken oother folk to twynne [1]
From avarice, and soore to repente.
But that is nat my principal entente;
I preche nothyng but for coveitise.   105
Of this mateere it oghte ynogh suffise.

Thanne telle I hem ensamples many oon
Of olde stories longe tyme agoon.
For lewed peple loven tales olde;
Swiche thynges kan they wel reporte and holde.
What, trowe ye, that whiles I may preche,   111
And wynne gold and silver for I teche,
That I wol lyve in poverte wilfully?
Nay, nay, I thoghte it nevere, trewely!
For I wol preche and begge in sondry landes;   115
I wol nat do no labour with myne handes,
Ne make baskettes, and lyve therby,
By cause I wol nat beggen ydelly.
I wol noon of the apostles countrefete; [2]
I wol have moneie, wolle, chese, and whete,   120
Al were it yeven of the povereste page,
Or of the povereste wydwe in a village,
Al sholde hir children sterve for famyne.
Nay, I wol drynke licour of the vyne,
And have a joly wenche in every toun.   125
But herkneth, lordynges, in conclusioun:
Youre likyng is that I shal telle a tale.
Now have I dronke a draughte of corny ale,
By God, I hope I shal yow telle a thyng
That shal by reson been at youre likyng.   130
For though myself be a full vicious man,
A moral tale yet I yow telle kan,
Which I am wont to preche for to wynne.
Now hoold youre pees! my tale I wol bigynne."

THE PARDONER'S TALE

Heere Bigynneth the Pardoners Tale

In Flaundres whilom was a compaignye
Of yonge folk that haunteden [3] folye,
As riot, hasard, stywes,[4] and tavernes,
Where as with harpes, lutes, and gyternes,
They daunce and pleyen at dees bothe day and
    nyght,   5
And eten also and drynken over hir myght,
Thurgh which they doon the devel sacrifise
Withinne that develes temple, in cursed wise,
By superfluytee abhomynable.
Hir othes been so grete and so dampnable   10
That it is grisly for to heere hem swere.
Oure blissed Lordes body they totere,[5] —

[1] depart from.   [2] imitate.
[3] practised.   [4] brothels.
[5] rend. tear to pieces.

Hem thoughte that Jewes rente hym noght
    ynough;
And ech of hem at otheres synne lough.
And right anon thanne comen tombesteres [1]   15
Fetys [2] and smale, and yonge frutesteres,[3]
Syngeres with harpes, baudes, wafereres,[4]
Whiche been the verray develes officeres
To kyndle and blowe the fyr of lecherye,
That is annexed unto glotonye.   20
The hooly writ take I to my witnesse
That luxurie is in wyn and dronkenesse.

Lo, how that dronken Looth,[5] unkyndely,[6]
Lay by his doghtres two, unwityngly;
So dronke he was, he nyste what he wroghte.   25

Herodes, whoso wel the stories soghte,
Whan he of wyn was repleet at his feeste,
Right at his owene table he yaf his heeste [7]
To sleen the Baptist John, ful giltelees.

Senec [8] seith a good word doutelees;   30
He seith he kan no difference fynde
Bitwix a man that is out of his mynde
And a man which that is dronkelewe, [9]
But that woodnesse, yfallen in a shrewe,[10]
Persevereth lenger than dooth dronkenesse.   35
O glotonye, ful of cursednesse!
O cause first of oure confusioun!
O original of oure dampnacioun,
Til Crist hadde boght us with his blood agayn!
Lo, how deere, shortly for to sayn,   40
Aboght was thilke cursed vileynye!
Corrupt was al this world for glotonye.

Adam oure fader, and his wyf also,
Fro Paradys to labour and to wo
Were dryven for that vice, it is no drede.[11]   45
For whil that Adam fasted, as I rede,
He was in Paradys; and whan that he
Eet of the fruyt deffended [12] on the tree,
Anon he was out cast to wo and peyne.
O glotonye, on thee wel oghte us pleyne!   50
O, wiste a man how manye maladyes —
Folwen of excesse and of glotonyes,
He wolde been the moore mesurable
Of his diete, sittynge at his table.
Allas! the shorte throte, the tendre mouth,   55
Maketh that est and west and north and south,
In erthe, in eir, in water, men to swynke [13]
To gete a glotoun deyntee mete and drynke!
Of this matiere, o Paul, wel kanstow trete:
"Mete unto wombe, and wombe eek unto mete,   60

[1] dancing girls.   [2] well-shaped.
[3] girls selling fruit.   [4] confectioners.
[5] Lot. See Genesis xx, 30–38.   [6] unnaturally.
[7] command.   [8] Seneca.   [9] drunk.
[10] madness, when it comes to an evil man.
[11] assuredly, without doubt.
[12] forbidden.   [13] work.

Shal God destroyen bothe," as Paulus seith.[1]
Allas! a foul thyng is it, by me feith,
To seye this word, and fouler is the dede,
Whan man so drynketh of the white and rede
That of his throte he maketh his pryvee,   65
Thurgh thilke cursed superfluitee.
  The apostel wepyng seith ful pitously,
"Ther walken manye of whiche yow toold have
    I—
I seye it now wepyng, with pitous voys—
That they been enemys of Cristes croys,   70
Of whiche the ende is deeth, wombe is hir god!"[2]
O wombe! O bely! O stynkyng cod,[3]
Fulfilled of dong and of corrupcioun!
At either ende of thee foul is the soun.
How greet labour and cost is thee to fynde![4]   75
Thise cookes, how they stampe, and streyne, and
    grynde,
And turnen substaunce into accident,[5]
To fulfille al thy likerous talent![6]
Out of the harde bones knokke they
The mary,[7] for they caste noght awey   80
That may go thurgh the golet softe and swoote.
Of spicerie of leef, and bark, and roote
Shal been his sauce ymaked by delit,
To make hym yet a newer appetit.
But, certes, he that haunteth swiche delices   85
Is deed, whil that he lyveth in tho vices.
  A lecherous thyng is wyn, and dronkenesse
Is ful of stryvyng and of wrecchednesse.
O dronke man, disfigured is thy face,
Sour is thy breeth, foul artow to embrace,   90
And thurgh thy dronke nose semeth the soun
As though thou seydest ay "Sampsoun, Samp-
    soun!"
And yet, God woot, Sampsoun drank nevere no
    wyn.
Thou fallest as it were a styked swyn;[8]
Thy tonge is lost, and al thyn honeste cure;[9]   95
For dronkenesse is verray sepulture
Of mannes wit and his discrecioun.
In whom that drynke hath dominacioun
He kan no conseil kepe, it is no drede.[10]
Now kepe yow fro the white and fro the rede,   100

And namely[1] fro the white wyn of Lepe,[2]
That is to selle in Fysshstrete or in Chepe.[3]
This wyn of Spaigne crepeth subtilly
In othere wynes, growynge faste by,[4]
Of which ther ryseth swich fumositee.[5]   105
That whan a man hath dronken draughtes thre,
And weneth that he be at hoom in Chepe,
He is in Spaigne, right at the toune of Lepe,—
Nat at the Rochele, ne at Burdeux toun;   109
And thanne wol he seye "Sampsoun, Sampsoun!"
  But herkneth, lordynges, o word, I yow preye,
That alle the sovereyn actes, dar I seye,
Of victories in the Olde Testament,
Thurgh verray God, that is omnipotent,
Were doon in abstinence and in preyere.   115
Looketh the Bible, and ther ye may it leere.
  Looke, Attilla, the grete conquerour,
Deyde in his sleep, with shame and dishonour,
Bledynge ay at his nose in dronkenesse.
A capitayn sholde lyve in sobrenesse.   120
And over[6] al this, avyseth yow right wel
What was comaunded unto Lamuel[7]—
Nat Samuel, but Lamuel, seye I—
Redeth the Bible, and fynde it expresly
Of wyn-yevyng to hem that han justise.   125
Namoore of this, for it may wel suffise.
  And now that I have spoken of glotonye,
Now wol I yow deffenden hasardrye.[8]
Hasard is verray mooder of lesynges,[9]
And of deceite, and cursed forswerynges,   130
Blaspheme of Crist, manslaughtre, and wast also
Of catel[10] and of tyme; and forthermo,
It is repreeve[11] and contrarie of honour
For to ben holde a commune hasardour.
And ever the hyer he is of estaat,   135
The moore is he yholden desolaat.
If that a prynce useth hasardrye,
In alle governaunce and policye
He is, as by commune opinioun,
Yholde the lasse in reputacioun.   140
  Stilboun, that was a wys embassadour,
Was sent to Corynthe, in ful greet honour,
Fro Lacidomye, to make hire alliaunce.
And whan he cam, hym happede, par chaunce,
That alle the gretteste that were of that lond,   145

[1] "Meats for the belly, and the belly for meats: but
God shall destroy both it and them."   I Corinthians
vi, 13.
   [2] Philippians iii, 18–19.
   [3] bag; i.e., the stomach.   [4] provide for.
   [5] This refers to a medieval philosophical concept relating to essential substance and superficial appearance.
The food in its natural state is taken by the cook and
turned into something quite different in appearance
and taste.
   [6] gluttonous appetite.   [7] marrow.   [8] stuck pig.
   [9] care about honorable things.   [10] doubt.

   [1] specially.
   [2] A town in Andalusia, Spain.
   [3] Cheapside, a section in London.
   [4] The intent here is to warn against the mixing of
the wine of Spain with that of France — it "creepeth
subtilly."
   [5] fumes.   [6] furthermore.
   [7] "It is not for kings, O Lemuel, it is not for kings
to drink wine, nor for princes strong drink."   Proverbs
xxxi, 4.   [8] forbid gambling.
   [9] lying.   [10] property.   [11] shame.

Pleyynge atte hasard he hem fond.
For which, as soone as it myghte be,
He stal hym hoom agayn to his contree,
And seyde, "Ther wol I nat lese my name,
Ne I wol nat take on me so greet defame,   150
Yow for to allie unto none hasardours.
Sendeth othere wise embassadours;
For, by my trouthe, me were levere dye
Than I yow sholde to hasardours allye.
For ye, that been so glorious in honours,   155
Shul nat allyen yow with hasardours
As by my wyl, ne as by my tretee."
This wise philosophre, thus seyde hee.

    Looke eek that to the kyng Demetrius
The kyng of Parthes, as the book seith us,   160
Sente him a paire of dees of gold in scorn,
For he hadde used hasard ther-biforn;
For which he heeld his glorie or his renoun
At no value or reputacioun.
Lordes may fynden oother maner pley   165
Honest ynough to dryve the day awey.

    Now wol I speke of othes false and grete
A word or two, as olde bookes trete.
Gret sweryng is a thyng abhominable,
And fals sweryng is yet moore reprevable.   170
The heighe God forbad sweryng at al,
Witnesse on Mathew;[1] but in special
Of sweryng seith the hooly Jeremye,[2]
"Thou shalt swere sooth thyne othes, and nat lye,
And swere in doom, and eek in rightwisnesse";   175
But ydel sweryng is a cursednesse.
Bihoold and se that in the first table
Of heighe Goddes heestes[3] honurable,
Hou that the seconde[4] heeste of hym is this:
"Take nat my name in ydel or amys."   180
Lo, rather he forbedeth swich sweryng
Than homycide or many a cursed thyng;
I seye that, as by ordre, thus it stondeth;
This knoweth, that his heestes understondeth,
How that the seconde heeste of God is that.   185
And forther over, I wol thee telle al plat,[5]
That vengeance shal nat parten from his hous
That of his othes is to outrageous.
"By Goddes precious herte," and "By his nayles,"
And "By the blood of Crist that is in Hayles,[6]   190
Sevene is my chaunce, and thyn is cynk and
    treye!"[7]
"By Goddes armes, if thou falsly pleye,
This daggere shal thurghout thyn herte go!"

This fruyt cometh of the bicched bones[1] two,
Forsweryng, ire, falsenesse, homycide.   195
Now, for the love of Crist, that for us dyde,
Lete youre othes, bothe gret and smale.
But, sires, now wol I telle forth my tale.

    Thise riotoures thre of whiche I telle,
Longe erst er prime[2] rong of any belle,   200
Were set hem in a taverne for to drynke,
And as they sat, they herde a belle clynke
Biforn a cors, was caried to his grave.
That oon of hem gan callen to his knave:[3]
"Go bet,"[4] quod he, "and axe redily   205
What cors is this that passeth heer forby;
And looke that thou reporte his name weel."

    "Sire," quod this boy, "it nedeth never-a-deel;[5]
It was me toold er ye cam heer two houres.
He was, pardee, an old felawe of youres;   210
And sodeynly he was yslayn to-nyght,[6]
Fordronke,[7] as he sat on his bench upright.
Ther cam a privee theef, men clepeth Deeth,
That in this contree al the peple sleeth,
And with his spere he smoot his herte atwo,   215
And wente his wey withouten wordes mo.
He hath a thousand slayn this pestilence.
And, maister, er ye come in his presence,
Me thynketh that it were necessarie
For to be war of swich an adversarie.   220
Beth redy for to meete hym everemoore;
Thus taughte me my dame; I sey namoore."
"By seinte Marie!" seyde this taverner,
"The child seith sooth, for he hath slayn this yeer,
Henne[8] over a mile, withinne a greet village,   225
Bothe man and womman, child, and hyne,[9] and
    page;
I trowe his habitacioun be there.
To been avysed greet wysdom it were,
Er that he dide a man a dishonour."

    "Ye, Goddes armes!" quod this riotour,   230
"Is it swich peril with hym for to meete?
I shal hym seke by wey and eek by strete,
I make avow to Goddes digne bones!
Herkneth, felawes, we thre been al ones;
Lat ech of us holde up his hand til oother,   235
And ech of us bicomen otheres brother,
And we wol sleen this false traytour Deeth.
He shal be slayn, he that so manye sleeth,
By Goddes dignitee, er it be nyght!"

    Togidres han thise thre hir trouthes plight   240
To lyve and dyen ech of hem for oother,
As though he were his owene ybore brother.
And up they stirte, al dronken in this rage,
And forth they goon towardes that village

---

[1] Matthew v, 33–37.   [2] Jeremiah iv, 2.
[3] commandments.
[4] the third in the Protestant Bible.   [5] plainly.
[6] An abbey in this town in Gloucestershire was reputed to have a portion of Christ's blood as a relic.
[7] five and three.   The game is "hazard" — somewhat like craps.

[1] cursed dice.   [2] nine in the morning.
[3] servant.   [4] go quickly.
[5] not a bit necessary.   [6] last night.
[7] thoroughly drunk.   [8] hence.   [9] servant.

Of which the taverner hadde spoke biforn. 245
And many a grisly ooth thanne han they sworn,
And Cristes blessed body al torente [1] —
Deeth shal be deed, if that they may hym hente!

Whan they han goon nat fully half a mile,
Right as they wolde han troden over a stile, 250
An oold man and a povre with hem mette.
This olde man ful mekely hem grette, [2]
And seyde thus, "Now, lordes, God yow see!" [3]

The proudeste of thise riotoures three
Answerde agayn, "What, carl, [4] with sory grace!
Why artow al forwrapped [5] save thy face? 256
Why lyvestow [6] so longe in so greet age?"

This olde man gan looke in his visage,
And seyde thus, "For I ne kan nat fynde
A man, though that I walked into Ynde, 260
Neither in citee ne in no village,
That wolde chaunge his youthe for myn age;
And therfore moot I han myn age stille,
As longe tyme as it is Goddes wille.
Ne Deeth, allas! ne wol nat han my lyf. 265
Thus walke I, lyk a restelees kaityf, [7]
And on the ground, which is my moodres gate,
I knokke with my staf, bothe erly and late,
And seye 'Leeve mooder, leet me in!
Lo how I vanysshe, flessh, and blood, and skyn!
Allas! whan shul my bones been at reste? 271
Mooder, with yow wolde I chaunge my cheste
That in my chambre longe tyme hath be,
Ye, for an heyre clowt to wrappe in me!'
But yet to me she wol nat do that grace, 275
For which ful pale and welked [8] is my face.

But, sires, to yow it is no curteisye
To speken to an old man vileynye,
But he trespasse in word, or elles in dede.
In Hooly Writ ye may yourself wel rede: 280
'Agayns [9] an oold man, hoor upon his heed,
Ye sholde arise;' wherfore I yeve yow reed,
Ne dooth unto an oold man noon harm now,
Namoore than that ye wolde men did to yow
In age, if that ye so longe abyde. 285
And God be with yow, where ye go [10] or ryde!
I moot go thider as I have to go."

"Nay, olde cherl, by God, thou shalt nat so,"
Seyde this oother hasardour anon;
"Thou partest nat so lightly, by Seint John! 290
Thou spak right now of thilke traytour Deeth,
That in this contree alle oure freendes sleeth.
Have heer my trouthe, as thou art his espye, [11]
Telle where he is, or thou shalt it abye, [12]
By God, and by the hooly sacrement! 295
For soothly thou art oon of his assent

[1] tore apart.   [2] greeted.   [3] bless or protect.
[4] fellow.   [5] wrapped up.   [6] do you live.
[7] wretch.   [8] withered.   [9] before.
[10] walk.   [11] spy.   [12] pay for.

To sleen us yonge folk, thou false theef!"
"Now, sires," quod he, "if that ye be so leef
To fynde Deeth, turne up this croked wey,
For in that grove I lafte hym, by my fey, 300
Under a tree, and there he wole abyde;
Noght for youre boost he wole him no thyng hyde.
Se ye that ook? Right there ye shal hym fynde.
God save yow, that boghte agayn mankynde,
And yow amende!" Thus seyde this olde man; 305
And everich of thise riotoures ran
Til he cam to that tree, and ther they founde
Of floryns fyne of gold ycoyned rounde
Wel ny an eighte busshels, as hem thoughte.
No lenger thanne after Deeth they soughte, 310
But ech of hem so glad was of that sighte,
For that the floryns been so faire and brighte,
That doun they sette hem by this precious hoord.
The worste of hem, he spak the firste word.

"Bretheren," quod he, "taak kep what that I
    seye; 315
My wit is greet, though that I bourde [1] and pleye.
This tresor hath Fortune unto us yiven,
In myrthe and jolitee oure lyf to lyven,
And lightly as it comth, so wol we spende.
Ey! Goddes precious dignitee! who wende 320
To-day that we sholde han so fair a grace?
But myghte this gold be caried fro this place
Hoom to myn hous, or elles unto youres —
For wel ye woot that al this gold is oures —
Thanne were we in heigh felicitee. 325
But trewely, by daye it may nat bee.
Men wolde seyn that we were theves stronge,
And for oure owene tresor doon us honge. [2]
This tresor moste ycaried be by nyghte
As wisely and as slyly as it myghte. 330
Wherfore I rede that cut among us alle
Be drawe, and lat se wher the cut wol falle;
And he that hath the cut with herte blithe
Shal renne to the town, and that ful swithe, [3]
And brynge us breed and wyn ful prively. 335
And two of us shul kepen subtilly
This tresor wel; and if he wol nat tarie,
Whan it is nyght, we wol this tresor carie,
By oon assent, where as us thynketh best."
That oon of hem the cut broghte in his fest, 340
And bad hem drawe, and looke where it wol falle;
And it fil on the yongeste of hem alle,
And forth toward the toun he wente anon.
And also soone as that he was gon,
That oon of hem spak thus unto that oother: 345
"Thow knowest wel thou art my sworen brother;
Thy profit wol I telle thee anon.
Thou woost wel that oure felawe is agon,
And heere is gold, and that ful greet plentee,
That shal departed [4] been among us thre. 350

[1] jest.   [2] be hanged.   [3] quickly.   [4] shared.

But nathelees, if I kan shape it so
That it departed were among us two,
Hadde I nat doon a freendes torn to thee?"
    That oother answerde, "I noot hou that may be.
He woot wel that the gold is with us tweye;   355
What shal we doon?   What shal we to hym seye?"
    "Shal it be conseil?" [1] seyed the firste shrewe,[2]
"And I shal tellen in a wordes fewe
What we shal doon, and brynge it wel aboute."
    "I graunte," quod that oother, "out of doute,
That, by my trouthe, I wol thee nat biwreye."   361
    "Now," quod the firste, "thou woost wel we
        be tweye,
And two of us shul strenger be than oon.
Looke whan that he is set, that right anoon
Arys as though thou woldest with hym pleye,   365
And I shal ryve [3] hym thurgh the sydes tweye
Whil that thou strogelest with hym as in game,
And with thy daggere looke thou do the same;
And thanne shal al this gold departed be,
My deere freend, bitwixen me and thee.   370
Thanne may we bothe oure lustes all fulfille,
And pleye at dees right at oure owene wille."
And thus acorded been thise shrewes tweye
To sleen the thridde, as ye han herd me seye.
    This yongeste, which that wente to the toun,   375
Ful ofte in herte he rolleth up and doun
The beautee of thise floryns newe and brighte.
"O Lord!" quod he, "if so were that I myghte
Have al this tresor to myself allone,
Ther is no man that lyveth under the trone   380
Of God that sholde lyve so murye as I!"
And atte laste the feend, oure enemy,
Putte in his thought that he sholde poyson beye,
With which he myghte sleen his felawes tweye;
For-why the feend foond hym in swich lyvynge   385
That he hadde leve him to sorwe brynge.
For this was outrely his fulle entente,
To sleen hem bothe, and nevere to repente.
And forth he gooth, no lenger wolde he tarie,
Into the toun, unto a pothecarie,   390
And preyde hym that he hym wolde selle
Som poyson, that he myghte his rattes quelle; [4]
And eek ther was a polcat in his hawe,[5]
That, as he seyde, his capouns hadde yslawe,
And fayn he wolde wreke hym, if he myghte,   395
On vermyn that destroyed hym by nyghte.
    The pothecarie answerde, "And thou shalt have
A thyng that, also God my soule save,
In al this world ther is no creature,
That eten or dronken hath of this confiture   400
Noght but the montance [6] of a corn of whete,
That he ne shal his lif anon forlete;

[1] a secret.   [2] rogue.
[3] pierce.   [4] kill.
[5] yard.   [6] amount.

Ye, sterve [1] he shal, and that in lasse while
Than thou wolt goon a paas [2] nat but a mile,
This poysoun is so strong and violent."   405
    This cursed man hath in his hond yhent
This poysoun in a box, and sith he ran
Into the nexte strete unto a man,
And borwed hym large botelles thre;
And in the two his poyson poured he;   410
The thridde he kepte clene for his drynke.
For al the nyght he shoop hym for to swynke [3]
In cariynge of the gold out of that place.
And whan this riotour, with sory grace,
Hadde filled with wyn his grete botels thre,   415
To his felawes agayn repaireth he.
    What nedeth it to sermone of it moore?
For right as they hadde cast his deeth bifoore,
Right so they han hym slayn, and that anon.   419
And whan that this was doon, thus spak that oon:
"Now lat us sitte and drynke, and make us merie,
And afterward we wol his body berie."
And with that word it happed hym, par cas,[4]
To take the botel ther the poyson was,
And drank, and yaf his felawe drynke also,   425
For which anon they storven [5] bothe two.
    But certes, I suppose that Avycen [6]
Wroot nevere in no canon, ne in no fen,[7]
Mo wonder [8] signes of empoisonyng
Than hadde thise wrecches two, er hir endyng.   430
Thus ended been thise homycides two,
And eek the false empoysonere also.
    O cursed synne of alle cursednesse!
O traytours homycide, O wikkednesse!
O glotonye, luxurie, and hasardrye!   435
Thou blasphemour of Crist with vileynye
And othes grete, of usage and of pride!
Allas! mankynde, how may it bitide
That to thy creatour, which that the wroghte,
And with his precious herte-blood thee boghte,   440
Thou art so fals and so unkynde, allas?
    Now goode men, God foryeve yow youre trespas,
And ware yow fro [9] the synne of avarice!
Myn hooly pardoun may yow alle warice,[10]
So that ye offre nobles or sterlynes,[11]   445
Or elles silver broches, spoones, rynges.
Boweth youre heed under this hooly bulle!
Cometh up, ye wyves, offreth of youre wolle! [12]
Youre names I entre heer in my rolle anon;
Into the blisse of hevene shul ye gon.   450

[1] die.   [2] at a walk.   [3] he planned to work.
[4] by chance.   [5] died.
[6] A famous physician of the eleventh century.
[7] Avicenna had written a book on medicine and called his section divisions fen.
[8] wonderful.   [9] beware of.   [10] cure.
[11] nobles were gold coins, sterlings were silver.
[12] wool.

I yow assoille,[1] by myn heigh power,
Yow that wol offre, as clene and eek as cleer
As ye were born. — And lo, sires, thus I preche.
And Jhesu Crist, that is oure soules leche,[2]
So graunte yow his pardoun to receyve, 455
For that is best; I wol yow nat deceyve.
    But, Sires,[3] o word forgat I in my tale;
I have relikes and pardoun in my male,[4]
As faire as any man in Engelond,
Whiche were me yeven by the popes hond. 460
If any of yow wole, of devocion,
Offren, and han myn absolucion,
Com forth anon, and kneleth heere adoun,
And mekely receyveth my pardoun;
Or elles taketh pardoun as ye wende, 465
Al newe and fressh at every miles ende,
So that ye offren, alwey newe and newe,
Nobles or pens, whiche that be goode and trewe.
It is an honour to everich that is heer
That ye mowe have a suffisant pardoneer 470
T'assoille yow, in contree as ye ryde,
For aventures whiche that may bityde.
Paraventure ther may fallen oon or two
Doun of his hors, and breke his nekke atwo.
Looke which a seuretee is it to yow alle 475
That I am in youre felaweshipe yfalle,
That may assoille yow, bothe moore and lasse
Whan that the soule shal fro the body passe.
I rede that oure Hoost heere shal bigynne,
For he is moost envoluped in synne. 480
Com forth, sire Hoost, and offre first anon,
And thou shalt kisse the relikes everychon,
Ye, for a grote! Unbokele anon thy purs,
    "Nay, nay!" quod he, "thanne have I Cristes
    curs!
Lat be," quod he, "it shal nat be, so theech![5] 485
Thou woldest make me kisse thyn olde breech,[6]
And swere it were a relyk of a seint,"
    .   .   .   .
    This Pardoner answerde nat a word;
So wrooth he was, no word ne wold he seye. 495
    "Now," quod oure Hoost, "I wol no lenger pleye
With thee, ne with noon oother angry man."

[1] absolve.   [2] physician.
[3] The other pilgrims in the party.   [4] bag.
[5] as I hope to prosper.   [6] breeches.

But right anon the worthy Knyght bigan,
Whan that he saugh that al the peple lough,
"Namoore of this, for it is right ynough! 500
Sire Pardoner, be glad and myrie of cheere;
And ye, sire Hoost, that been to me so deere,
I prey yow that ye kisse the Pardoner.
And Pardoner, I prey thee, drawe thee neer,
And, as we diden, lat us laughe and pleye." 505
Anon they kiste, and ryden forth hir weye.

Heere is ended the Pardoners Tale.

The Complaint of Chaucer to His Purse

In medieval poetry a "complaint" is usually addressed to the poet's lady, begging her to have pity on him. Here Chaucer writes a parody of this type of poem by complaining to his empty purse.

To yow, my purse, and to noon other wight
Complayne I, for ye be my lady dere!
I am so sory, now that ye been lyght;
For certes, but ye make me hevy chere,
Me were as leef be layd upon my bere;[1] 5
For which unto your mercy thus I crye:
Beth hevy ageyn, or elles mot I dye!

Now voucheth sauf this day, or yt be nyght,
That I of yow the blisful soun may here,
Or see your colour lyk the sonne bryght, 10
That of yelownesse hadde never pere.
Ye be my lyf, ye be myn hertes stere,[2]
Quene of comfort and of good companye:
Beth hevy ageyn, or elles moote I dye!

Now purse, that ben to me my lyves lyght 15
And saveour, as doun in this world here,
Out of this toune helpe me thurgh your
    myght,
Syn that ye wole nat ben my tresorere;
For I am shave as nye[3] as any frere.
But yet I pray unto your curtesye: 20
Beth hevy agen, or elles moote I dye!

[1] bier.   [2] steersman.   [3] close.

Daniel Defoe · 1660–1731

From Chaucer to Defoe is a leap of three hundred years in the history of English literature and, strangely enough, we find our next realistic author writing at the height of the neo-classical period. Defoe's contemporaries were Swift and Pope, Addison and Steele, men who, on the whole, wrote with a classical restraint and polish almost foreign to the plain-spoken, factual-minded author of *Robinson Crusoe* and *Moll Flanders*.

Yet Defoe, like his neo-classical contemporaries, lived in a journalistic, political-minded England and, like them, joined in the campaigns of pamphlets and tracts on current problems. Like them, Defoe made frequent use of satire to criticize the political and social life of England under William III, Queen Anne, or George I. Where Addison wrote formal drama and kindly pictures of English society, and Pope wrote conventional and trenchant verse, Defoe made his literary reputation as the author of tough-fibered, realistic accounts of adventurers, thieves, and travelers. While his contemporaries were expressing themselves in language conventionally formal and polite (with the notable exception of some of Swift's work), Defoe used the vernacular and wrote of the bourgeois man and woman on the street, in prison, or on foreign soil.

Defoe, the son of James Foe, a butcher, was born in Cripplegate, a section of London, in 1660. Born into a family of Nonconformists, the young man was educated for the Presbyterian ministry. But Defoe never entered the ministry. He became a manufacturer of hosiery, a commission merchant dealing in foreign goods, and the owner of a tile factory. His failures in business were not so much a reflection on his business acumen as they were the result of his inability to keep out of political difficulty. His *Shortest Way with Dissenters*, a pamphlet satirically arguing for bitter persecution of his own religious group, was misunderstood both by his own people and by leaders of the Established Church. For this "seditious writing" Defoe was fined, imprisoned, and exposed in the public pillory on three separate days. While the people of London supported Defoe and made his time in the pillory an occasion for rallying to his support, his business was ruined and failure resulted.

It must be admitted that Defoe was no more successful in the field of politics than he was in business. As a young man he took part in Monmouth's rebellion in 1685 but luckily escaped punishment. In 1695, having attracted attention to himself through his writing — he sometimes signed his name Foe, sometimes Defoe — he was appointed a government accountant. In 1703 came his imprisonment for writing the *Shortest Way*. Though he was freed from prison through the interest of Robert Harley, Secretary of State, he could not long remain free from trouble. Defoe sold his pen to both sides of a controversy. Both the Tories and the Whigs received his support. At one time he served as a secret agent for the government, but even in this capacity he had dealings with the opposition. After spending a summer in secret hiding as the result of some political duplicity, Defoe died in Ropemaker's Alley, Moorfields, on April 24, 1731.

Defoe was one of the most prolific writers in English literature. The ephemeral quality of much of his argumentative and journalistic work makes it difficult to assign certain pieces clearly to him, but lists of his work run from three hundred to four hundred titles. It was not until fairly late in his life — 1719 when he was almost sixty years old — that Defoe hit upon the type of work which gave him his assured position in literary history. This later writing can be characterized as fiction realistic in presentation. He employed common language, he related small details of daily life, he made even such an unreal character as Robinson Crusoe live and breathe with reality for generations of future readers. The best known of his books were those published in his later years: *The Life and Strange Surprizing Adventures of Robinson Crusoe, of York, Mariner* (1719); *Memoirs of a Cavalier* (1720); *Piracies of the Famous Captain Singleton* (1720); *The Fortunes and Misfortunes of Moll Flanders* (1722); *A Journal of the Plague Year* (1722); and *Roxana* (1724).

SUGGESTED REFERENCES: James Sutherland, *Defoe* (1956); J. R. Moore, *Daniel Defoe, Citizen of the Modern World* (1958).

A True Relation of the Apparition of Mrs. Veal,

The Next Day After Her Death, to One Mrs. Bargrave, at Canterbury, the 8th of September, 1705.

The following "ghost story" probably relates a series of events currently much talked about. Defoe appears to have done no more than take the details, as recounted by acquaintances, and mold them into a narrative full of factual detail and with all the verisimilitude which characterizes his fiction. The events of the story are highly romantic; the *method* is that of realism. On reading the account one wonders whether or not these events actually happened. "The Preface" to the tale reflects Defoe's characteristic interest in moral teaching.

THE PREFACE

This relation is matter of fact, and attended with such circumstances as may induce any reasonable man to believe it. It was sent by a gentleman, a justice of peace at Maidstone, in Kent, and a very intelligent person, to his friend in London, as it is here worded; which discourse is attested by a very sober and understanding gentleman, who had it from his kinswoman, who lives in Canterbury, within a few doors of the house in which the within-named Mrs. Bargrave lived; and who he believes to be of so discerning a spirit, as not to be put upon by any fallacy, and who positively assured him that the whole matter as it is related and laid down is really true, and what she herself had in the same words, as near as may be, from Mrs. Bargrave's own mouth, who, she knows, had no reason to invent and publish such a story, or any design to forge and tell a lie, being a woman of much honesty and virtue, and her whole life a course, as it were, of piety. The use which we ought to make of it is to consider that there is a life to come after this, and a just God who will retribute to every one according to the deeds done in the body, and therefore to reflect upon our past course of life we have led in the world; that our time is short and uncertain; and that if we would escape the punishment of the ungodly and receive the reward of the righteous, which is the laying hold of eternal life, we ought, for the time to come to return to God by a speedy repentance, ceasing to do evil, and learning to do well; to seek after God early, if haply He may be found of us, and lead such lives for the future as may be well pleasing in His sight.

A RELATION, &c.

This thing is so rare in all its circumstances, and on so good authority, that my reading and conversation have not given me anything like it. It is fit to gratify the most ingenious and serious inquirer. Mrs. Bargrave is the person to whom Mrs. Veal appeared after her death; she is my intimate friend, and I can avouch for her reputation for these last fifteen or sixteen years, on my own knowledge; and I can confirm the good character she had from her youth to the time of my acquaintance; though since this relation she is calumniated by some people that are friends to the brother of Mrs. Veal who appeared, who think the relation of this appearance to be a reflection, and endeavor what they can to blast Mrs. Bargrave's reputation, and to laugh the story out of countenance. But by the circumstances thereof, and the cheerful disposition of Mrs. Bargrave, notwithstanding the ill-usage of a very wicked husband, there is not the least sign of dejection in her face; nor did I ever hear her let fall a desponding or murmuring expression; nay, not when actually under her husband's barbarity, which I have been witness to, and several other persons of undoubted reputation.

Now you must know Mrs. Veal [1] was a maiden gentlewoman of about thirty years of age, and for some years last past had been troubled with fits, which were perceived coming on her by her going off from her discourses very abruptly to some impertinence. She was maintained by an only brother, and kept his house in Dover. [2] She was a very pious woman, and her brother a very sober man, to all appearance; but now he does all he can to null or quash the story. Mrs. Veal was intimately acquainted with Mrs. Bargrave from her childhood. Mrs. Veal's circumstances were then mean; her father did not take care of his children as he ought, so that they were exposed to hardships; and Mrs. Bargrave in those days had as unkind a father, though she wanted neither for food nor clothing, whilst Mrs. Veal wanted for both, insomuch that she would often say, "Mrs. Bargrave, you are not only the best, but the only friend I have in the world; and no circumstance in life shall ever dissolve my friendship." They would often condole each other's adverse fortunes, and read together Drelincourt *Upon Death*, and other good books; and so, like two Christian friends, they comforted each other under their sorrow.

Some time after Mr. Veal's friends got him a place in the custom-house at Dover, which oc-

---

[1] "Mrs.," in Defoe's time was used for single as well as married women.

[2] Near Canterbury.

casioned Mrs. Veal, by little and little, to fall off from her intimacy with Mrs. Bargrave, though there never was any such thing as a quarrel; but an indifferency came on by degrees, till at last Mrs. Bargrave had not seen her in two years and a half; though about a twelve-month of the time Mrs. Bargrave had been absent from Dover, and this last half-year had been in Canterbury about two months of the time, dwelling in a house of her own.

In this house, on the 8th of September 1705, she was sitting alone, in the forenoon, thinking over her unfortunate life, and arguing herself into a due resignation to Providence, though her condition seemed hard. "And," said she, "I have been provided for hitherto, and doubt not but I shall be still; and am well satisfied that my afflictions shall end when it is most fit for me;" and then took up her sewing-work, which she had no sooner done but she hears a knocking at the door. She went to see who was there, and this proved to be Mrs. Veal, her old friend, who was in a riding-habit; at that moment of time the clock struck twelve at noon.

"Madam," says Mrs. Bargrave, "I am surprised to see you, you have been so long a stranger"; but told her she was glad to see her, and offered to salute her, which Mrs. Veal complied with, till their lips almost touched; and then Mrs. Veal drew her hand across her own eyes and said, "I am not very well," and so waived it. She told Mrs. Bargrave she was going a journey, and had a great mind to see her first. "But," says Mrs. Bargrave, "how came you to take a journey alone? I am amazed at it, because I know you have a good brother." "Oh," says Mrs. Veal, "I gave my brother the slip, and came away, because I had so great a desire to see you before I took my journey." So Mrs. Bargrave went in with her into another room within the first, and Mrs. Veal set her down in an elbow-chair, in which Mrs. Bargrave was sitting when she heard Mrs. Veal knock. Then says Mrs. Veal, "My dear friend, I am come to renew our old friendship again, and beg your pardon for my breach of it; and if you can forgive me, you are the best of women." "Oh," says Mrs. Bargrave, "do not mention such a thing. I have not had an uneasy thought about it; I can easily forgive it." "What did you think of me?" said Mrs. Veal. Says Mrs. Bargrave, "I thought you were like the rest of the world, and that prosperity had made you forget yourself and me." Then Mrs. Veal reminded Mrs. Bargrave of the many friendly offices she did in her former days, and much of the conversation they had with each other in the times of their adversity; what books they read, and what comfort in particular they received from Drelincourt's *Book of Death*,[1] which was the best, she said, on that subject ever written. She also mentioned Dr. Sherlock, the two Dutch books which were translated, written upon Death, and several others; but Drelincourt, she said, had the clearest notions of death and of the future state of any who had handled that subject. Then she asked Mrs. Bargrave whether she had Drelincourt. She said, "Yes." Says Mrs. Veal, "Fetch it." And so Mrs. Bargrave goes upstairs and brings it down. Says Mrs. Veal, "Dear Mrs. Bargrave, if the eyes of our faith were as open as the eyes of our body, we should see numbers of angels about us for our guard. The notions we have of heaven now are nothing like to what it is, as Drelincourt says. Therefore be comforted under your afflictions, and believe that the Almighty has a particular regard to you, and that your afflictions are marks of God's favor; and when they have done the business they are sent for, they shall be removed from you. And believe me, my dear friend, believe what I say to you, one minute of future happiness will infinitely reward you for all your sufferings; for I can never believe" (and claps her hands upon her knees with great earnestness, which indeed ran through most of her discourse) "that ever God will suffer you to spend all your days in this afflicted state; but be assured that your afflictions shall leave you, or you them, in a short time." She spake in that pathetical and heavenly manner that Mrs. Bargrave wept several times, she was so deeply affected with it.

Then Mrs. Veal mentioned Dr. Horneck's *Ascetic*, at the end of which he gives an account of the lives of the primitive Christians. Their pattern she recommended to our imitation, and said, "Their conversation was not like this of our age; for now," says she, "there is nothing but frothy, vain discourse, which is far different from theirs. Theirs was to edification, and to build one another up in faith; so that they were not as we are, nor are we as they were; but," said she, "we ought to do as they did. There was a hearty friendship among them; but where is it now to be found?" Says Mrs. Bargrave, "It is hard indeed to find a true friend in these days." Says Mrs. Veal, "Mr. Norris has a fine copy of verses, called *Friendship in Perfection*, which I wonderfully admire. Have you seen the book?" says Mrs. Veal. "No," says Mrs. Bargrave, "but I have the

[1] This "True Relation" of Defoe's was first published in Peter Drelincourt's *Christian's Defence against the Fear of Death* in 1706. Drelincourt, a Frenchman, was a Protestant clergyman. It has been suggested, probably inaccurately, that Defoe wrote the story to promote the sale of Drelincourt's volume.

verses of my own writing out." "Have you?" says Mrs. Veal; "then fetch them." Which she did from above-stairs, and offered them to Mrs. Veal to read, who refused, and waived the thing, saying holding down her head would make it ache; and then desired Mrs. Bargrave to read them to her, which she did. As they were admiring *Friendship*, Mrs. Veal said, "Dear Mrs. Bargrave, I shall love you for ever." In these verses there is twice used the word Elysian. "Ah!" says Mrs. Veal, "these poets have such names for heaven!" She would often draw her hand across her own eyes and say, "Mrs. Bargrave, do not you think I am mightily impaired by my fits?" "No," says Mrs. Bargrave, "I think you look as well as ever I knew you."

After all this discourse, which the apparition put in much finer words than Mrs. Bargrave said she could pretend to, and as much more than she can remember, for it cannot be thought that an hour and three-quarters' conversation could be retained, though the main of it she thinks she does, she said to Mrs. Bargrave she would have her write a letter to her brother, and tell him she would have him give rings to such and such, and that there was a purse of gold in her cabinet, and that she would have two broad pieces given to her cousin Watson.

Talking at this rate, Mrs. Bargrave thought that a fit was coming upon her, and so placed herself in a chair just before her knees, to keep her from falling to the ground, if her fits should occasion it (for the elbow-chair, she thought, would keep her from falling on either side); and to divert Mrs. Veal, as she thought, took hold of her gown-sleeve several times and commended it. Mrs. Veal told her it was a scoured silk, and newly made up. But for all this, Mrs. Veal persisted in her request, and told Mrs. Bargrave that she must not deny her, and she would have her tell her brother all their conversation when she had an opportunity. "Dear Mrs. Veal," said Mrs. Bargrave, "this seems so impertinent [1] that I cannot tell how to comply with it; and what a mortifying story will our conversation be to a young gentleman? Why," says Mrs. Bargrave, "it is much better, methinks, to do it yourself." "No," says Mrs. Veal, "though it seems impertinent to you now, you will see more reason for it hereafter." Mrs. Bargrave then, to satisfy her importunity, was going to fetch a pen and ink, but Mrs. Veal said, "Let it alone now, but do it when I am gone; but you must be sure to do it;" which was one of the last things she enjoined her at parting. So she promised her.

Then Mrs. Veal asked for Mrs. Bargrave's daughter. She said she was not at home, "But if you have a mind to see her," says Mrs. Bargrave,

"I'll send for her." "Do," says Mrs. Veal. On which she left her, and went to a neighbor's to see for her; and by the time Mrs. Bargrave was returning, Mrs. Veal was got without the door into the street, in the face of the beast-market, on a Saturday (which is market-day), and stood ready to part, as soon as Mrs. Bargrave came to her. She asked her why she was in such haste. She said she must be going, though perhaps she might not go her journey until Monday; [1] and told Mrs. Bargrave she hoped she should see her again at her cousin Watson's before she went whither she was going. Then she said she would take her leave of her, and walked from Mrs. Bargrave in her view, till a turning interrupted the sight of her, which was three-quarters after one in the afternoon.

Mrs. Veal died the 7th of September, at twelve o'clock at noon, of her fits, and had not above four hours' sense before death, in which time she received the sacrament. The next day after Mrs. Veal's appearing, being Sunday, Mrs. Bargrave was so mightily indisposed with a cold and a sore throat, that she could not go out that day; but on Monday morning she sent a person to Captain Watson's to know if Mrs. Veal was there. They wondered at Mrs. Bargrave's inquiry, and sent her word that she was not there, nor was expected. At this answer, Mrs. Bargrave told the maid she had certainly mistook the name or made some blunder. And though she was ill, she put on her hood, and went herself to Captain Watson's, though she knew none of the family, to see if Mrs. Veal was there or not. They said they wondered at her asking, for that she had not been in town; they were sure, if she had, she would have been there. Says Mrs. Bargrave, "I am sure she was with me on Saturday almost two hours." They said it was impossible; for they must have seen her, if she had. In comes Captain Watson while they are in dispute, and said that Mrs. Veal was certainly dead, and her escutcheons [2] were making. This strangely surprised Mrs. Bargrave, when she sent to the person immediately who had the care of them, and found it true. Then she related the whole story to Captain Watson's family, and what gown she had on, and how striped, and that Mrs. Veal told her it was scoured. Then Mrs. Watson cried out, "You have seen her indeed, for none knew but Mrs. Veal and myself that the gown was scoured." And Mrs. Watson owned that she described the gown exactly; "for," said she, "I helped her to make it up." This Mrs. Watson blazed all about the town, and avouched the demonstration of the truth of Mrs. Bargrave's seeing

[1] Foreign to the present discussion.

[1] The day of the actual burial.
[2] Signs displayed at the funeral.

Mrs. Veal's apparition; and Captain Watson carried two gentlemen immediately to Mrs. Bargrave's house to hear the relation from her own mouth. And when it spread so fast that gentlemen and persons of quality, the judicious and sceptical part of the world, flocked in upon her, it at last became such a task that she was forced to go out of the way; for they were in general extremely well satisfied of the truth of the thing, and plainly saw that Mrs. Bargrave was no hypochondriac, for she always appears with such a cheerful air and pleasing mien, that she has gained the favor and esteem of all the gentry, and it is thought a great favor if they can but get the relation from her own mouth. I should have told you before that Mrs. Veal told Mrs. Bargrave that her sister and brother-in-law were just come down from London to see her. Says Mrs. Bargrave, "How came you to order matters so strangely?" "It could not be helped," said Mrs. Veal. And her brother and sister did come to see her, and entered the town of Dover just as Mrs. Veal was expiring. Mrs. Bargrave asked her whether she would drink some tea. Says Mrs. Veal, "I do not care if I do; but I'll warrant you this mad fellow" (meaning Mrs. Bargrave's husband) "has broken all your trinkets." "But," says Mrs. Bargrave, "I'll get something to drink in for all that." But Mrs. Veal waived it, and said, "It is no matter; let it alone;" and so it passed.

All the time I sat with Mrs. Bargrave, which was some hours, she recollected fresh sayings of Mrs. Veal. And one material thing more she told Mrs. Bargrave — that old Mr. Breton allowed Mrs. Veal ten pounds a year, which was a secret, and unknown to Mrs. Bargrave till Mrs. Veal told it her. Mrs. Bargrave never varies in her story, which puzzles those who doubt of the truth or are unwilling to believe it. A servant in the neighbor's yard adjoining to Mrs. Bargrave's house heard her talking to somebody an hour of the time Mrs. Veal was with her. Mrs. Bargrave went out to her next neighbor's the very moment she parted with Mrs. Veal, and told her what ravishing conversation she had with an old friend, and told the whole of it. Drelincourt's *Book of Death* is, since this happened, bought up strangely. And it is to be observed that, notwithstanding all the trouble and fatigue Mrs. Bargrave has undergone upon this account, she never took the value of a farthing, nor suffered her daughter to take anything of anybody, and therefore can have no interest in telling the story.

But Mr. Veal does what he can to stifle the matter, and said he would see Mrs. Bargrave; but yet it is certain matter of fact that he has been at Captain Watson's since the death of his sister, and yet never went near Mrs. Bargrave; and some of his friends report her to be a liar, and that she knew of Mr. Breton's ten pounds a year. But the person who pretends to say so has the reputation of a notorious liar among persons whom I know to be of undoubted credit. Now, Mr. Veal is more of a gentleman than to say she lies, but says a bad husband has crazed her. But she needs only present herself and it will effectually confute that pretence. Mr. Veal says he asked his sister on her deathbed whether she had a mind to dispose of anything, and she said no. Now, the things which Mrs. Veal's apparition would have disposed of were so trifling, and nothing of justice aimed at in their disposal, that the design of it appears to me to be only in order to make Mrs. Bargrave so to demonstrate the truth of her appearance, as to satisfy the world of the reality thereof as to what she had seen and heard, and to secure her reputation among the reasonable and understanding part of mankind. And then again Mr. Veal owns that there was a purse of gold; but it was not found in her cabinet, but in a comb-box. This looks improbable; for that Mrs. Watson owned that Mrs. Veal was so very careful of the key of the cabinet that she would trust nobody with it; and if so, no doubt she would not trust her gold out of it. And Mrs. Veal's often drawing her hand over her eyes, and asking Mrs. Bargrave whether her fits had not impaired her, looks to me as if she did it on purpose to remind Mrs. Bargrave of her fits, to prepare her not to think it strange that she should put her upon writing to her brother to dispose of rings and gold, which looks so much like a dying person's request; and it took accordingly with Mrs. Bargrave, as the effects of her fits coming upon her; and was one of the many instances of her wonderful love to her and care of her that she should not be affrighted, which indeed appears in her whole management, particularly in her coming to her in the daytime, waiving the salutation, and when she was alone, and then the manner of her parting to prevent a second attempt to salute her.

Now, why Mr. Veal should think this relation a reflection, as it is plain he does by his endeavoring to stifle it, I cannot imagine, because the generality believe her to be a good spirit, her discourse was so heavenly. Her two great errands were to comfort Mrs. Bargrave in her affliction, and to ask her forgiveness for the breach of friendship, and with a pious discourse to encourage her. So that after all to suppose that Mrs. Bargrave could hatch such an invention as this from Friday noon to Saturday noon, supposing that she knew of Mrs. Veal's death the very first moment, without jumbling circumstances, and without any interest too, she must be more witty, fortunate, and wicked too than any indifferent person, I dare say, will allow. I asked Mrs. Bargrave several times if she was sure she felt the gown. She answered modestly, "If my senses are to be relied on, I am sure of it." I asked her if she heard a sound when she clapped her hands upon her knees. She said she did not remember she did, but said she appeared to be as much a substance as I did, who talked with her. "And I may," said she, "be as soon persuaded that your apparition is talking to me now as that I did not really see her; for I was under no manner of fear, and received her as a friend, and parted with her as such. I would not," says she, "give one farthing to make any one believe it; I have no interest in it. Nothing but trouble is entailed upon me for a long time, for aught I know; and had it not come to light by accident, it would never have been made public." But now she says she will make her own private use of it, and keep herself out of the way as much as she can; and so she has done since. She says she had a gentleman who came thirty miles to her to hear the relation, and that she had told it to a room full of people at a time. Several particular gentlemen have had the story from Mrs. Bargrave's own mouth.

This thing has very much affected me, and I am as well satisfied as I am of the best grounded matter of fact. And why we should dispute matter of fact because we cannot solve things of which we have no certain or demonstrative notions, seems strange to me. Mrs. Bargrave's authority and sincerity alone would have been undoubted in any other case.

Honoré de Balzac · 1799–1850

In reading Balzac we come to the period — the nineteenth century — when the realistic temper first became of major importance to literature. The romantic movement was then spending its force. Writers turned from their dreams of perfection and an unreal, ideal world to an interpretation of life about them. Although there were writers in all ages — such as Petronius in classical times, Chaucer in the fourteenth century, and Defoe in the neo-classical eighteenth century — who approached their times from the realistic point of view, it was not until about the middle of the nineteenth century that writers persistently attempted to look at life as it is. Balzac's artistic achievement and his popularity as a writer had much to do with this swing toward realism.

Few great writers have worked one literary vein so thoroughly as did Balzac. In more than a hundred novels and stories, in which he created over two thousand characters, he wrote of contemporary French society, its foibles and hypocrisies, its tragedies and its failures, its virtues and its vices. It was his purpose in the *Human Comedy* to write out fully life as he knew it — in business, in politics, in daily living. He studied his characters carefully and sought out their way of life in Paris and in the provinces, in the palace and in the hovel, in youth and in age. He wrote, perhaps as thoroughly as one man can write, the record of a civilization.

Of Balzac's shorter stories, the following may be selected for particular mention: *La Grande Bretèche*, a horror story based on jealousy suggestive of the manner of Poe; *The Unknown Masterpiece*, a study in the insanity of an artist; *A Seashore Drama*, a story of retribution visited upon a father who undertook to be both judge and executioner of his son; *An Episode under the Terror*, a portrayal of the working of conscience; *The Conscript*, a tale of mother love psychologically, or at least psychically, presented; and *A Passion in the Desert*, the story of the strange friendship which grew up between a panther and a Provençal soldier. Among his best-known novels are *Eugénie Grandet* (1833), and *Old Goriot* (1834).

The stories and novels which Balzac designated as parts of the *Human Comedy*, taken together as a group, create an impression of torrential force. Here are found not only many people from various levels of society but also a mass of fact and detail setting forth the life of the times. Balzac sometimes all but overpowers his reader with his data; yet always the record of actuality is illuminated by an understanding of human character. Unlike Flaubert who selected carefully, Balzac creates his effect through the presentation of vast numbers of characters. Where one was exact the other is forceful; where one chiseled his block of marble with fine tools, the other carved his figures from the rough granite of the mountain-sides. Other writers have left more impressive single masterpieces; few have left a greater whole. It is true that when the balance is finally struck, Balzac appears impressed by the unhappiness of the world, by its viciousness and its vice. Failure outweighs and outnumbers success.

Balzac's method is that of the realist, though he is never content with facts and details alone. Like any true realist he selects and relates his details. To a greater degree than most realists, he brings a considerable element of imagination to play upon his people and settings, with the result that some critics have found Balzac almost as much the romantic as the realist. At any rate Balzac proved himself a powerful influence on the writers who followed him.

Honoré de Balzac was born at Tours on May 20, 1799. His father's family was one of little social pretention, though the father ultimately rose to positions of some importance in the non-military branches of the French army. The young Honoré was educated in the grammar schools of Vendôme and Tours and by private tutors in Paris. He studied law and was admitted to practice, though after a year or so he gave up the law in order to write. His life was troubled by various ventures into business, ventures which invariably left him in debt. Like Walter Scott and Mark Twain he tried to recoup what he had lost in commerce through his writing. After a courtship of seventeen years he married Madame Hanska, a Russian-Polish woman of rank and society, in 1850. He died in the same year and was buried in the cemetery, the Père Lachaise in Paris, where he had laid away Old Goriot.

SUGGESTED REFERENCES: Samuel Rogers, *Balzac and the Novel* (1953); Philippe Bertault, *Balzac and the Human Comedy* (1963).

Old Goriot

Balzac's manner and method are illustrated in the opening pages of *Old Goriot* which follow. Here we catch a glimpse of a Balzacian interior, of a typical group of characters, and see something of the writer's method of handling details in support of characterization. Here, too, we catch glimpses of the author's tendency to project his own ideas, his own philosophy, into his story. Balzac is always ready with comment and the comment is usually significant. In these pages we meet such memorable characters as Goriot, Madame Vauquer, Rastignac, Vautrin, and the two Goriot daughters, Anastasie and Delphine. In later pages Balzac weaves together two stories: the relationship of father Goriot to his daughters and the experiences of Rastignac in the society of Paris. The fact that the father-and-daughters' story revolves about the same problem as that of King Lear and his daughters has been often pointed out. *Goriot* is one of the great novels of the *Human Comedy*.

The translation is by Ellen Marriage and is published in the Everyman's Library by E. P. Dutton & Co., Inc., New York.

Mme. Vauquer (*née* de Conflans) is an elderly person, who for the past forty years has kept a lodging-house in the Rue Neuve-Sainte-Geneviève, in the district that lies between the Latin Quarter and the Faubourg Saint-Marcel. Her house (known in the neighborhood as the *Maison Vauquer*) receives men and women, old and young, 30

and no word has ever been breathed against her respectable establishment; but, at the same time, it must be said that as a matter of fact no young woman has been under her roof for thirty years, 5 and that if a young man stays there for any length of time it is a sure sign that his allowance must be of the slenderest. In 1819, however, the time when this drama opens, there was an almost penniless young girl among Mme. Vauquer's board-10 ers.

That word drama has been somewhat discredited of late; it has been overworked and twisted to strange uses in these days of dolorous literature; but it must do service again here, not because this 15 story is dramatic in the restricted sense of the world, but because some tears may perhaps be shed *intra et extra muros* before it is over.

Will any one without the walls of Paris understand it? It is open to doubt. The only audience 20 who could appreciate the results of close observation, the careful reproduction of minute detail and local color, are dwellers between the heights of Montrouge and Montmartre, in a vale of crumbling stucco watered by streams of black mud, a vale of 25 sorrows which are real and of joys too often hollow; but this audience is so accustomed to terrible sensations, that only some unimaginable and wellnigh impossible woe could produce any lasting impression there. Now and again there are tragedies 30 so awful and so grand by reason of the complication of virtues and vices that bring them about, that egoism and selfishness are forced to pause and are moved to pity; but the impression that they receive is like a luscious fruit, soon consumed. Civilisation, like the car of Juggernaut, is scarcely stayed perceptibly in its progress by a heart less easy to break than the others that lie in its course; this also is broken, and Civilisation continues on her course triumphant. And you, too, will do the like; you who with this book in your white hand will sink back among the cushions of your arm-chair, and say to yourself, "Perhaps this may amuse me." You will read the story of Old Goriot's secret woes, and, dining thereafter with an unspoiled appetite, will lay the blame of your insensibility upon the writer, and accuse him of exaggeration, of writing romances. Ah! once for all, this drama is neither a fiction nor a romance! *All is true,* — so true, that every one can discern the elements of the tragedy in his own house, perhaps in his own heart.

The lodging-house is Mme. Vauquer's own property. It is still standing at the lower end of the Rue Neuve-Sainte-Geneviève, just where the road slopes so sharply down to the Rue de l'Arba-lète, that wheeled traffic seldom passes that way, because it is so stony and steep. This position is sufficient to account for the silence prevalent in the streets shut in between the dome of the Panthéon and the dome of the Val-de-Grâce, two conspicu-ous public buildings which give a yellowish tone to the landscape and darken the whole district that lies beneath the shadow of their leaden-hued cupolas.

In that district the pavements are clean and dry, there is neither mud nor water in the gutters, grass grows in the chinks of the walls. The most heed-less passer-by feels the depressing influences of a place where the sound of wheels creates a sensa-tion; there is a grim look about the houses, a sug-gestion of a jail about those high garden walls. A Parisian straying into a suburb apparently com-posed of lodging-houses and public institutions would see poverty and dulness, old age lying down to die, and joyous youth condemned to drudgery. It is the ugliest quarter of Paris, and, it may be added, the least known. But, before all things, the Rue Neuve-Sainte-Geneviève is like a bronze frame for a picture for which the mind cannot be too well prepared by the contemplation of sad hues and sober images. Even so, step by step the day-light decreases, and the cicerone's droning voice grows hollower as the traveller descends into the Catacombs. The comparison holds good! Who shall say which is more ghastly, the sight of the bleached skulls or of dried-up human hearts?

The front of the lodging-house is at right angles to the road, and looks out upon a little garden, so that you see the side of the house in section, as it were, from the Rue Neuve-Sainte-Geneviève. Beneath the wall of the house front there lies a channel, a fathom wide, paved with cobble-stones, and beside it runs a gravelled walk bordered by geraniums and oleanders and pomegranates set in great blue and white glazed earthenware pots. Access into the gravelled walk is afforded by a door, above which the words MAISON VAUQUER may be read, and beneath, in rather smaller letters, "*Lodgings for both sexes, etc.*"

During the day a glimpse into the garden is easily obtained through a wicket to which a bell is attached. On the opposite wall, at the further end of the gravelled walk, a green marble arch was painted once upon a time by a local artist, and in this semblance of a shrine a statue representing Cupid is installed; a Parisian Cupid, so blistered and disfigured that he looks like a candidate for one of the adjacent hospitals, and might suggest an allegory to lovers of symbolism. The half-obliterated inscription on the pedestal beneath determines the date of this work of art, for it bears witness to the widespread enthusiasm felt for Vol-taire on his return to Paris in 1777 —

"Whoe'er thou art, thy master see;
He is, or was, or ought to be."

At night the wicket gate is replaced by a solid door. The little garden is no wider than the front of the house; it is shut in between the wall of the street and the partition wall of the neighboring house. A mantle of ivy conceals the bricks and attracts the eyes of passers-by to an effect which is picturesque in Paris, for each of the walls is cov-ered with trellised vines that yield a scanty dusty crop of fruit, and furnish besides a subject of con-versation for Mme. Vauquer and her lodgers; every year the widow trembles for her vintage.

A straight path beneath the walls on either side of the garden leads to a clump of lime-trees at the further end of it; *line*-trees, as Mme. Vauquer per-sists in calling them, in spite of the fact that she was a de Conflans, and regardless of repeated cor-rections from her lodgers.

The central space between the walks is filled with artichokes and rows of pyramid fruit-trees, and surrounded by a border of lettuce, pot-herbs, and parsley. Under the lime-trees there are a few green-painted garden seats and a wooden table, and hither, during the dog-days, such of the lodgers as are rich enough to indulge in a cup of coffee come to take their pleasure, though it is hot enough to roast eggs even in the shade.

The house itself is three stories high, without counting the attics under the roof. It is built of rough stone, and covered with the yellowish stucco that gives a mean appearance to almost every house in Paris. There are five windows in each story in the front of the house; all the blinds visible through the small square panes are drawn up awry, so that the lines are all at cross purposes. At the side of the house there are but two windows on each floor, and the lowest of all are adorned with a heavy iron grating.

Behind the house a yard extends for some twenty feet, a space inhabited by a happy family of pigs, poultry, and rabbits; the wood-shed is situated on the further side, and on the wall between the wood-shed and the kitchen window hangs the meat-safe, just above the place where the sink discharges its greasy streams. The cook sweeps out the refuse out through a little door into the Rue Neuve-Sainte-Geneviève, and frequently cleanses the yard with copious supplies of water, under pain of pestilence.

The house might have been built on purpose for its present uses. Access is given by a French window to the first room on the ground floor, a sitting-room which looks out upon the street through the two barred windows already mentioned. Another door opens out of it into the dining-room, which is separated from the kitchen by the well of the staircase, the steps being constructed partly of wood, partly of tiles, which are colored and beeswaxed. Nothing can be more depressing than the sight of that sitting-room. The furniture is covered with horse hair woven in alternate dull and glossy stripes. There is a round table in the middle, with a purplish-red marble top, on which there stands, by way of ornament, the inevitable white china tea-service, covered with a half-effaced gilt network. The floor is sufficiently uneven, the wainscot rises to elbow height, and the rest of the wall space is decorated with a varnished paper, on which the principal scenes from *Télémaque* are depicted, the various classical personages being colored. The subject between the two windows is the banquet given by Calypso to the son of Ulysses, displayed thereon for the admiration of the boarders, and has furnished jokes these forty years to the young men who show themselves superior to their position by making fun of the dinners to which poverty condemns them. The hearth is always so clean and neat that it is evident that a fire is only kindled there on great occasions; the stone chimney-piece is adorned by a couple of vases filled with faded artificial flowers imprisoned under glass shades, on either side of a bluish marble clock in the very worst taste.

The first room exhales an odor for which there is no name in the language, and which should be called the *odeur de pension*. The damp atmosphere sends a chill through you as you breathe it; it has a stuffy, musty, and rancid quality; it permeates your clothing; after-dinner scents seem to be mingled in it with smells from the kitchen and scullery and the reek of a hospital. It might be possible to describe it if some one should discover a process by which to distil from the atmosphere all the nauseating elements with which it is charged by the catarrhal exhalations of every individual lodger, young or old. Yet, in spite of these stale horrors, the sitting-room is as charming and as delicately perfumed as a boudoir, when compared with the adjoining dining-room.

The panelled walls of that apartment were once painted some color, now a matter of conjecture, for the surface is incrusted with accumulated layers of grimy deposit, which cover it with fantastic outlines. A collection of dim-ribbed glass decanters, metal discs with a satin sheen on them, and piles of blue-edged earthenware plates of Touraine ware cover the sticky surfaces of the sideboards that line the room. In a corner stands a box containing a set of numbered pigeon-holes, in which the lodgers' table napkins, more or less soiled and stained with wine, are kept. Here you see that indestructible furniture never met with elsewhere, which finds its way into lodging-houses much as the wrecks of our civilisation drift into hospitals for incurables. You expect in such places as these to find the weather-house whence a Capuchin issues on wet days; you look to find the execrable engravings which spoil your appetite, framed every one in a black varnished frame, with a gilt beading round it; you know the sort of tortoise-shell clock-case, inlaid with brass; the green stove, the Argand lamps, covered with oil and dust, have met your eyes before. The oilcloth which covers the long table is so greasy that a waggish *externe* will write his name on the surface, using his thumb nail as a style. The chairs are broken-down invalids; the wretched little hempen mats slip away from under your feet without slipping away for good; and finally, the foot-warmers are miserable wrecks, hingeless, charred, broken away about the holes. It would be impossible to give an idea of the old, rotten, shaky, cranky, worm-eaten, halt, maimed, one-eyed, rickety, and ramshackle condition of the furniture without an exhaustive description, which would delay the progress of the story to an extent that impatient people would not pardon. The red tiles of the floor are full of depressions brought about by scouring and periodical renewings of color. In short, there is no illusory grace left to the poverty that reigns here; it is dire, parsimonious, concentrated, threadbare poverty; as yet it has not sunk into the mire, it is only splashed by it, and though not in rags as yet, its clothing is ready to drop to pieces.

This apartment is in all its glory at seven o'clock in the morning, when Mme. Vauquer's cat appears, announcing the near approach of his mistress, and jumps upon the sideboards to sniff at the milk in the bowls, each protected by a plate, while he purrs his morning greeting to the world. A moment later the widow shows her face; she is tricked out in a net cap attached to a false front set on awry, and shuffles into the room in her slipshod fashion. She is an oldish woman, with a bloated countenance, and a nose like a parrot's beak set in the middle of it; her fat little hands (she is as sleek as a church rat) and her shapeless, slouching figure are in keeping with the room that reeks of misfortune, where hope is reduced to speculate for the meanest stakes. Mme. Vauquer alone can breathe that tainted air without being disheartened by it. Her face is as fresh as a frosty morning in autumn; there are wrinkles about the eyes that vary in their expression from the set smile of a ballet-dancer to the dark, suspicious scowl of a discounter of bills; in short, she is at once the embodiment and interpretation of her lodging-house, as surely as her lodging-house implies the existence of its mistress. You can no more imagine the one without the other, than you can think of a jail without a turn-key. The unwholesome corpulence of the little woman is produced by the life she leads, just as typhus fever is bred in the tainted air of a hospital. The very knitted woollen petticoat that she wears beneath a skirt made of an old gown, with the wadding protruding through the rents in the material, is a sort of epitome of the sitting-room, the dining-room, and the little garden; it discovers the cook; it foreshadows the lodgers — the picture of the house is completed by the portrait of its mistress. Mme. Vauquer at the age of fifty is like all women who "have seen a deal of trouble." She has the glassy eyes and innocent air of a trafficker in flesh and blood, who will wax virtuously indignant to obtain a higher price for her services, but who is quite ready to betray a Georges or a Pichegru, if a Georges or a Pichegru were in hiding and still to be betrayed, or for any other expedient that may alleviate her lot. Still, "she is a good woman at bottom," said the lodgers, who believed that the widow was wholly dependent upon the money that they paid her, and sympathised when they heard her cough and groan like one of themselves. What had M. Vauquer been? The lady was never very explicit on this head. How had she

lost her money? "Through trouble," was her answer. He had treated her badly, had left her nothing but her eyes to cry over his cruelty, the house she lived in, and the privilege of pitying nobody, because, so she was wont to say, she herself had been through every possible misfortune.

Sylvie, the stout cook, hearing her mistress's shuffling footsteps, hastened to serve the lodgers' breakfasts. Beside those who lived in the house, Mme. Vauquer took boarders who came for their meals; but these *externes* usually only came to dinner, for which they paid thirty francs a month.

At the time when this story begins, the lodging-house contained seven inmates. The best rooms in the house were on the first story, Mme. Vauquer herself occupying the least important, while the rest were let to a Mme. Couture, the widow of a commissary-general in the service of the Republic. With her lived Victorine Taillefer, a schoolgirl, to whom she filled the place of mother. These two ladies paid eighteen hundred francs a year.

The two sets of rooms on the second floor were respectively occupied by an old man named Poiret and a man of forty or thereabouts, the wearer of a black wig and dyed whiskers, who gave out that he was a retired merchant, and was addressed as M. Vautrin. Two of the four rooms on the third floor were also let — one to an elderly spinster, a Mlle. Michonneau, and the other to a retired manufacturer of vermicelli, Italian paste and starch, who allowed the others to address him as "Old Goriot." The remaining rooms were allotted to various birds of passage, to impecunious students, who, like 'Old Goriot' and Mlle. Michonneau, could only muster forty-five francs a month to pay for their board and lodging. Mme. Vauquer had little desire for lodgers of this sort; they ate too much bread, and she only took them in default of better.

At that time one of the rooms was tenanted by a law student, a young man from the neighborhood of Angoulême, one of a large family who pinched and starved themselves to spare twelve hundred francs a year for him. Misfortune had accustomed Eugène de Rastignac, for that was his name, to work. He belonged to the number of young men who know as children that their parents' hopes are centred on them, and deliberately prepare themselves for a great career, subordinating their studies from the first to this end, carefully watching the indications of the course of events, calculating the probable turn that affairs will take, that they may be the first to profit by them. But for his observant curiosity, and the skill with which he managed to introduce himself into the salons of

Paris, this story would not have been colored by the tones of truth which it certainly owes to him, for they are entirely due to his penetrating sagacity and desire to fathom the mysteries of an appalling condition of things, which was concealed as carefully by the victim as by those who had brought it to pass.

Above the third story there was a garret where the linen was hung to dry, and a couple of attics. Christophe, the man-of-all-work, slept in one, and Sylvie, the stout cook, in the other. Beside the seven inmates thus enumerated, taking one year with another, some eight law or medical students dined in the house, as well as two or three regular comers who lived in the neighborhood. There were usually eighteen people at dinner, and there was room, if need be, for twenty at Mme. Vauquer's table; at breakfast, however, only the seven lodgers appeared. It was almost like a family party. Every one came down in dressing-gown and slippers, and the conversation usually turned on anything that had happened the evening before; comments on the dress or appearance of the dinner contingent were exchanged in friendly confidence.

These seven lodgers were Mme. Vauquer's spoiled children. Among them she distributed, with astronomical precision, the exact proportion of respect and attention due to the varying amounts they paid for their board. One single consideration influenced all these human beings thrown together by chance. The two second-floor lodgers only paid seventy-two francs a month. Such prices as these are confined to the Faubourg Saint-Marcel and the district between La Bourbe and the Salpêtrière; and, as might be expected, poverty, more or less apparent, weighed upon them all, Mme. Couture being the sole exception to the rule.

The dreary surroundings were reflected in the costumes of the inmates of the house; all were alike threadbare. The color of the men's coats was problematical; such shoes, in more fashionable quarters, are only to be seen lying in the gutter; the cuffs and collars were worn and frayed at the edges; every limp article of clothing looked like the ghost of its former self. The women's dresses were faded, old-fashioned, dyed and re-dyed; they wore gloves that were glazed with hard wear, much-mended lace, dingy ruffles, crumpled muslin fichus. So much for their clothing; but, for the most part, their frames were solid enough; their constitutions had weathered the storms of life; their cold, hard faces were worn like coins that have been withdrawn from circulation, but there were greedy teeth behind the withered lips. Dramas

brought to a close or still in progress are foreshadowed by the sight of such actors as these, not the dramas that are played before the footlights and against a background of painted canvas, but dumb dramas of life, frost-bound dramas that sear hearts like fire, dramas that do not end with the actors' lives.

Mlle. Michonneau, that elderly young lady, screened her weak eyes from the daylight by a soiled green silk shade with a rim of brass, an object fit to scare away the Angel of Pity himself. Her shawl, with its scanty, draggled fringe, might have covered a skeleton, so meagre and angular was the form beneath it. Yet she must have been pretty and shapely once. What corrosive had destroyed the feminine outlines? Was it trouble, or vice, or greed? Had she loved too well? Had she been a second-hand clothes dealer, a frequenter of the back-stairs of great houses, or had she been merely a courtesan? Was she expiating the flaunting triumphs of a youth overcrowded with pleasures by an old age in which she was shunned by every passer-by? Her vacant gaze sent a chill through you; her shrivelled face seemed like a menace. Her voice was like the shrill, thin note of the grasshopper sounding from the thicket when winter is at hand. She said that she had nursed an old gentleman, ill of catarrh of the bladder, and left to die by his children, who thought that he had nothing left. His bequest to her, a life annuity of a thousand francs, was periodically disputed by his heirs, who mingled slander with their persecutions. In spite of the ravages of conflicting passions, her face retained some traces of its former fairness and fineness of tissue, some vestiges of the physical charms of her youth still survived.

M. Poiret was a sort of automaton. He might be seen any day sailing like a grey shadow along the walks of the Jardin des Plantes, on his head a shabby cap, a cane with an old yellow ivory handle in the tips of his thin fingers; the outspread skirts of his threadbare overcoat failed to conceal his meagre figure; his breeches hung loosely on his shrunken limbs; the thin, blue-stockinged legs trembled like those of a drunken man; there was a notable breach of continuity between the dingy white waistcoat and crumpled shirt frills and the cravat twisted about a throat like a turkey gobbler's; altogether, his appearance set people wondering whether this outlandish ghost belonged to the audacious race of the sons of Japhet who flutter about on the Boulevard Italien. What kind of toil could have so shrivelled him? What devouring passions had darkened that bulbous countenance, which would have seemed outrageous as a caricature? What had he been? Well, perhaps he had been part of the machinery of justice, a clerk in the office to which the executioner sends in his accounts, — so much for providing black veils for parricides, so much for sawdust, so much for pulleys and cord for the knife. Or he might have been a receiver at the door of a public slaughter-house, or a sub-inspector of nuisances. Indeed, the man appeared to have been one of the beasts of burden in our great social mill; one of those Parisian Ratons whom their Bertrands do not even know by sight; a pivot in the obscure machinery that disposes of misery and things unclean; one of those men, in short, at sight of whom we are prompted to remark that, "After all, we cannot do without them."

Stately Paris ignores the existence of these faces bleached by moral or physical suffering; but, then, Paris is in truth an ocean that no line can plumb. You may survey its surface and describe it; but no matter what pains you take with your investigations and recognisances, no matter how numerous and painstaking the toilers in this sea, there will always be lonely and unexplored regions in its depths, caverns unknown, flowers and pearls and monsters of the deep overlooked or forgotten by the divers of literature. The Maison Vauquer is one of these curious monstrosities.

Two, however, of Mme. Vauquer's boarders formed a striking contrast to the rest. There was a sickly pallor, such as is often seen in anæmic girls, in Mlle. Victorine Taillefer's face; and her unvarying expression of sadness, like her embarrassed manner and pinched look, was in keeping with the general wretchedness of the establishment in the Rue Neuve-Sainte-Geneviève, which forms a background to this picture; but her face was young, there was youthfulness in her voice and elasticity in her movements. This young misfortune was not unlike a shrub, newly planted in an uncongenial soil, where its leaves have already begun to wither. The outlines of her figure, revealed by her dress of the simplest and cheapest materials, were also youthful. There was the same kind of charm about her too slender form, her faintly colored face and light-brown hair, that modern poets find in mediæval statuettes; and a sweet expression, a look of Christian resignation in the dark grey eyes. She was pretty by force of contrast; if she had been happy, she would have been charming. Happiness is the poetry of woman, as the toilette is her tinsel. If the delightful excitement of a ball had made the pale face glow with color; if the delights of a luxurious life had brought the color to the wan cheeks that were slightly hollowed already; if love had put light into the sad eyes, then Victorine might have ranked among the fairest; but

she lacked the two things which create woman a second time — pretty dresses and love-letters.

A book might have been made of her story. Her father was persuaded that he had sufficient reason for declining to acknowledge her, and allowed her a bare six hundred francs a year; he had further taken measures to disinherit his daughter, and had converted all his real estate into personalty, that he might leave it undivided to his son. Victorine's mother had died broken-hearted in Mme. Couture's house; and the latter, who was a near relation, had taken charge of the little orphan. Unluckily, the widow of the commissary-general to the armies of the Republic had nothing in the world but her jointure and her widow's pension, and some day she might be obliged to leave the helpless, inexperienced girl to the mercy of the world. The good soul, therefore, took Victorine to mass every Sunday, and to confession once a fortnight, thinking that, in any case, she would bring up her ward to be devout. She was right; religion offered a solution of the problem of the young girl's future. The poor child loved the father who refused to acknowledge her. Once every year she tried to see him to deliver her mother's message of forgiveness, but every year hitherto she had knocked at that door in vain; her father was inexorable. Her brother, her only means of communication, had not come to see her for four years, and had sent her no assistance; yet she prayed to God to unseal her father's eyes and to soften her brother's heart, and no accusations mingled with her prayers. Mme. Couture and Mme. Vauquer exhausted the vocabulary of abuse, and failed to find words that did justice to the banker's iniquitous conduct; but while they heaped execrations on the millionaire, Victorine's words were as gentle as the moan of the wounded dove, and affection found expression even in the cry drawn from her by pain.

Eugène de Rastignac was a thoroughly southern type; he had a fair complexion, blue eyes, black hair. In his figure, manner, and his whole bearing it was easy to see that he either came of a noble family, or that, from his earliest childhood, he had been gently bred. If he was careful of his wardrobe, only taking last year's clothes into daily wear, still upon occasion he could issue forth as a young man of fashion. Ordinarily he wore a shabby coat and waistcoat, the limp black cravat, untidily knotted, that students affect, trousers that matched the rest of his costume, and boots that had been re-soled.

Vautrin (the man of forty with the dyed whiskers) marked a transition stage between these two young people and the others. He was the kind of man that calls forth the remark: "He looks a jovial sort!" He had broad shoulders, a well-developed chest, muscular arms, and strong square-fisted hands; the joints of his fingers were covered with tufts of fiery red hair. His face was furrowed by premature wrinkles; there was a certain hardness about it in spite of his bland and insinuating manner. His bass voice was by no means unpleasant, and was in keeping with his boisterous laughter. He was always obliging, always in good spirits; if anything went wrong with one of the locks, he would soon unscrew it, take it to pieces, file it, oil and clean and set it in order, and put it back in its place again: "I am an old hand at it," he used to say. Not only so, he knew all about ships, the sea, France, foreign countries, men, business, law, great houses and prisons, — there was nothing that he did not know. If any one complained rather more than usual, he would offer his services at once. He had several times lent money to Mme. Vauquer, or to the boarders; but, somehow, those whom he obliged felt that they would sooner face death than fail to repay him; a certain resolute look, sometimes seen on his face, inspired fear of him, for all his appearance of easy good-nature. In the way he spat there was an imperturbable coolness which seemed to indicate that this was a man who would not stick at a crime to extricate himself from a false position. His eyes, like those of a pitiless judge, seemed to go to the very bottom of all questions, to read all natures, all feelings, and thoughts. His habit of life was very regular; he usually went out after breakfast, returning in time for dinner, and disappeared for the rest of the evening, letting himself in about midnight with a latch key, a privilege that Mme. Vauquer accorded to no other boarder. But then he was on very good terms with the widow; he used to call her "mamma," and put his arm round her waist, a piece of flattery perhaps not appreciated to the full! The worthy woman might imagine this to be an easy feat; but, as a matter of fact, no arm but Vautrin's was long enough to encircle her.

It was a characteristic trait of his generously to pay fifteen francs a month for the cup of coffee with a dash of brandy in it, which he took after dinner. Less superficial observers than young men engulfed by the whirlpool of Parisian life, or old men, who took no interest in anything that did not directly concern them, would not have stopped short at the vaguely unsatisfactory impression that Vautrin made upon them. He knew or guessed the concerns of every one about him; but none of them had been able to penetrate his thoughts, or to discover his occupation. He had deliberately made his apparent good-nature, his

unfailing readiness to oblige, and his high spirits into a barrier between himself and the rest of them, but not seldom he gave glimpses of appalling depths of character. He seemed to delight in scourging the upper classes of society with the lash of his tongue, to take pleasure in convicting it of inconsistency, in mocking at law and order with some grim jest worthy of Juvenal, as if some grudge against the social system rankled in him, as if there were some mystery carefully hidden away in his life.

Mlle. Taillefer felt attracted, perhaps unconsciously, by the strength of the one man, and the good looks of the other; her stolen glances and secret thoughts were divided between them; but neither of them seemed to take any notice of her, although some day a chance might alter her position, and she would be a wealthy heiress. For that matter, there was not a soul in the house who took any trouble to investigate the various chronicles of misfortunes, real or imaginary, related by the rest. Each one regarded the others with indifference, tempered by suspicion; it was a natural result of their relative positions. Practical assistance not one of them could give, this they all knew, and they had long since exhausted their stock of condolence over previous discussions of their grievances. They were in something the same position as an elderly couple who have nothing left to say to each other. The routine of existence kept them in contact, but they were parts of a mechanism which wanted oil. There was not one of them but would have passed a blind man begging in the street, not one that felt moved to pity by a tale of misfortune, not one who did not see in death the solution of the all-absorbing problem of misery which left them cold to the most terrible anguish in others.

The happiest of these hapless beings was certainly Mme. Vauquer, who reigned supreme over this hospital supported by voluntary contributions. For her, the little garden, which silence, and cold, and rain, and drought combined to make as dreary as an Asian *steppe*, was a pleasant shaded nook; the gaunt yellow house, the musty odors of a back shop had charms for her, and for her alone. Those cells belonged to her. She fed those convicts condemned to penal servitude for life, and her authority was recognised among them. Where else in Paris would they have found wholesome food in sufficient quantity at the prices she charged them, and rooms which they were at liberty to make, if not exactly elegant or comfortable, at any rate clean and healthy? If she had committed some flagrant act of injustice, the victim would have borne it in silence.

Such a gathering contained, as might have been expected, the elements out of which a complete society might be constructed. And, as in a school, as in the world itself, there was among the eighteen men and women who met round the dinner table a poor creature, despised by all the others, condemned to be the butt of all their jokes. At the beginning of Eugène de Rastignac's second twelvemonth, this figure suddenly started out into bold relief against the background of human forms and faces among which the law student was yet to live for another two years to come. This laughing-stock was the retired vermicelli-merchant, old Goriot, upon whose face a painter, like the historian, would have concentrated all the light in his picture.

How had it come about that the boarders regarded him with a half-malignant contempt? Why did they subject the oldest among their number to a kind of persecution, in which there was mingled some pity, but no respect for his misfortunes? Had he brought it upon himself by some eccentricity or absurdity, which is less easily forgiven or forgotten than more serious defects? The question strikes at the root of many a social injustice. Perhaps it is only human nature to inflict suffering on anything that will endure suffering, whether by reason of its genuine humility, or indifference, or sheer helplessness. Do we not, one and all, like to feel our strength even at the expense of some one or of something? The poorest sample of humanity, the street arab, will pull the bell handle at every street door in bitter weather, and scramble up to write his name on the unsullied marble of a monument.

In the year 1813, at the age of sixty-nine or thereabouts, "Old Goriot" had sold his business and retired — to Mme. Vauquer's boarding-house. When he first came there he had taken the rooms now occupied by Mme. Couture; he had paid twelve hundred francs a year like a man to whom five louis more or less was a mere trifle. For him Mme. Vauquer had made various improvements in the three rooms destined for his use, in consideration of a certain sum paid in advance, so it was said, for the miserable furniture, that is to say, for some yellow cotton curtains, a few chairs of stained wood covered with Utrecht velvet, several wretched colored prints in frames, and wall papers that a little suburban tavern would have disdained. Possibly it was the careless generosity with which old Goriot allowed himself to be overreached at this period of his life (they called him Monsieur Goriot very respectfully then) that gave Mme. Vauquer the meanest opinion of his business abilities; she looked on him as an imbecile where money was concerned.

Goriot had brought with him a considerable wardrobe, the gorgeous outfit of a retired tradesman who denies himself nothing. Mme. Vauquer's astonished eyes beheld no less than eighteen cambric-fronted shirts, the splendor of their fineness being enhanced by a pair of pins each bearing a large diamond, and connected by a short chain, an ornament which adorned the vermicelli maker's shirt front. He usually wore a coat of cornflower blue; his rotund and portly person was still further set off by a clean white waistcoat, and a gold chain and seals which dangled over that broad expanse. When his hostess accused him of being "a bit of a beau," he smiled with the vanity of a citizen whose foible is gratified. His cupboards (ormoires, as he called them in the popular dialect) were filled with a quantity of plate that he brought with him. The widow's eyes gleamed as she obligingly helped him to unpack the soup ladles, tablespoons, forks, cruet-stands, tureens, dishes, and breakfast services — all of silver, which were duly arranged upon the shelves, besides a few more or less handsome pieces of plate, all weighing no inconsiderable number of ounces; he could not bring himself to part with these gifts that reminded him of past domestic festivals.

"This was my wife's present to me on the first anniversary of our wedding day," he said to Mme. Vauquer, as he put away a little silver posset dish, with two turtle-doves billing on the cover. "Poor dear! she spent on it all the money she had saved before we married. Do you know, I would sooner scratch the earth with my nails for a living, madame, than part with that. But I shall be able to take my coffee out of it every morning for the rest of my days, thank the Lord! I am not to be pitied. There's not much fear of my starving for some time to come."

Finally, Mme. Vauquer's magpie's eye had discovered and read certain entries in the list of shareholders in the funds, and, after a rough calculation, was disposed to credit Goriot (worthy man) with something like ten thousand francs a year. From that day forward Mme. Vauquer (née de Conflans), who, as a matter of fact, had seen forty-eight summers, though she would only own to thirty-nine of them — Mme. Vauquer had her own ideas. Though Goriot's eyes seemed to have shrunk in their sockets, though they were weak and watery, owing to some glandular affection which compelled him to wipe them continually, she considered him to be a very gentlemanly and pleasant-looking man. Moreover, the widow saw favorable indications of character in the well-developed calves of his legs and in his square-shaped nose, indications still further borne out by the worthy man's full-moon countenance and look of stupid good-nature.

This, in all probability, was a strongly-built animal, whose brains mostly consisted in a capacity for affection. His hair, worn in *ailes de pigeon*, and duly powdered every morning by the barber from the École Polytechnique, described five points on his low forehead, and made an elegant setting to his face. Though his manners were somewhat boorish, he was always as neat as a new pin, and he took his snuff in a lordly way, like a man who knows that his snuff-box is always likely to be filled with maccaboy; so that when Mme. Vauquer lay down to rest on the day of M. Goriot's installation, her heart, like a larded partridge, sweltered before the fire of a burning desire to shake off the shroud of Vauquer and rise again as Goriot. She would marry again, sell her boarding-house, give her hand to this fine flower of citizenship, become a lady of consequence in the quarter, and ask for subscriptions for charitable purposes; she would make little Sunday excursions to Choisy, Soisy, Gentilly; she would have a box at the theatre when she liked, instead of waiting for the author's tickets that one of her boarders sometimes gave her, in July; the whole Eldorado of a little Parisian household rose up before Mme. Vauquer in her dreams. Nobody knew that she herself possessed forty thousand francs, accumulated *sou* by *sou*, that was her secret; surely as far as money was concerned she was a very tolerable match. "And in other respects, I am quite his equal," she said to herself, turning as if to assure herself of the charms of a form that the portly Sylvie found moulded in down feathers every morning.

For three months from that day Mme. Veuve Vauquer availed herself of the services of M. Goriot's coiffeur, and went to some expense over her toilette, expense justifiable on the ground that she owed it to herself and her establishment to pay some attention to appearances when such highly-respectable persons honored her house with their presence. She expended no small amount of ingenuity in a sort of weeding process of her lodgers, announcing her intention of receiving henceforward none but people who were in every way select. If a stranger presented himself, she let him know that M. Goriot, one of the best known and most highly-respected merchants in Paris, had singled out her boarding-house for a residence. She drew up a prospectus headed MAISON VAUQUER, in which it was asserted that hers was "*one of the oldest and most highly recommended boarding-houses in the Latin Quarter.*" "From the windows of the house," thus ran the prospectus, "there is a charming view of the Vallée des Gobelins (so there is — from the third floor), and a *beautiful* garden, *extending* down to *an avenue of lindens* at the further end." Mention was made of the bracing air of the place and its quiet situation.

It was this prospectus that attracted Mme. la Comtesse de l'Ambermesnil, a widow of six-and-thirty, who was awaiting the final settlement of her husband's affairs, and of another matter regarding a pension due to her as the wife of a general who had died "on the field of battle." On this Mme. Vauquer saw to her table, lighted a fire daily in the sitting-room for nearly six months, and kept the promise of her prospectus, even going to some expense to do so. And the Countess, on her side, addressed Mme. Vauquer as "my dear," and promised her two more boarders, the Baronne de Vaumerland and the widow of a colonel, the late Comte de Picquoisie, who were about to leave a boarding-house in the Marais, where the terms were higher than at the Maison Vauquer. Both these ladies, moreover, would be very well to do when the people at the War Office had come to an end of their formalities. "But Government departments are always so dilatory," the lady added.

After dinner the two widows went together up to Mme. Vauquer's room, and had a snug little chat over some cordial and various delicacies reserved for the mistress of the house. Mme. Vauquer's ideas as to Goriot were cordially approved by Mme. de l'Ambermesnil; it was a capital notion, which for that matter she had guessed from the very first; in her opinion the vermicelli maker was an excellent man.

"Ah! my dear lady, such a well-preserved man of his age, as sound as my eyesight — a man who might make a woman happy!" said the widow.

The good-natured Countess turned to the subject of Mme. Vauquer's dress, which was not in harmony with her projects. "You must put yourself on a war footing," said she.

After much serious consideration the two widows went shopping together — they purchased a hat adorned with ostrich feathers and a cap at the Palais Royal, and the Countess took her friend to the Magasin de la Petite Jeannette, where they chose a dress and a scarf. Thus equipped for the campaign, the widow looked exactly like the prize animal hung out for a sign above an à la mode beef shop; but she herself was so much pleased with the improvement, as she considered it, in her appearance, that she felt that she lay under some obligation to the Countess; and, though by no means open-handed, she begged that lady to accept a hat that cost twenty francs. The fact was that she needed the Countess's services on the delicate mission of sounding Goriot; the Countess must sing her praises in his ears. Mme.

de l'Ambermesnil lent herself very good-naturedly to this manœuvre, began her operations, and succeeded in obtaining a private interview; but the overtures that she made, with a view to securing him for herself, were received with embarrassment, not to say a repulse. She left him, revolted by his coarseness.

"My angel," said she to her dear friend, "you will make nothing of that man yonder. He is absurdly suspicious, and he is a mean curmudgeon, an idiot, a fool; you would never be happy with him."

After what had passed between M. Goriot and Mme. de l'Ambermesnil, the Countess would no longer live under the same roof. She left the next day, forgot to pay for six months' board, and left behind her her wardrobe, cast-off clothing to the value of five francs. Eagerly and persistently as Mme. Vauquer sought her quondam lodger, the Comtesse de l'Ambermesnil was never heard of again in Paris. The widow often talked of this deplorable business, and regretted her own too confiding disposition. As a matter of fact, she was as suspicious as a cat; but she was like many other people, who cannot trust their own kin and put themselves at the mercy of the next chance comer — an odd but common phenomenon, whose causes may readily be traced to the depths of the human heart.

Perhaps there are people who know that they have nothing more to look for from those with whom they live; they have shown the emptiness of their hearts to their housemates, and in their secret selves they are conscious that they are severely judged, and that they deserve to be judged severely; but still they feel an unconquerable craving for praises that they do not hear, or they are consumed by a desire to appear to possess, in the eyes of a new audience, the qualities which they have not, hoping to win the admiration or affection of strangers at the risk of forfeiting it again some day. Or, once more, there are other mercenary natures who never do a kindness to a friend or a relation simply because these have a claim upon them, while a service done to a stranger brings its reward to self-love. Such natures feel but little affection for those who are nearest to them; they keep their kindness for remoter circles of acquaintance, and show most to those who dwell on its utmost limits. Mme. Vauquer belonged to both these essentially mean, false, and execrable classes.

"If I had been here at the time," Vautrin would say at the end of the story, "I would have shown her up, and that misfortune would not have befallen you. I know that kind of phiz!"

Like all narrow natures, Mme. Vauquer was wont to confine her attention to events, and did not go very deeply into the causes that brought them about; she likewise preferred to throw the blame of her own mistakes on other people, so she chose to consider that the honest vermicelli maker was responsible for her misfortune. It had opened her eyes, so she said, with regard to him. As soon as she saw that her blandishments were in vain, and that her outlay on her toilette was money thrown away, she was not slow to discover the reason of his indifference. It became plain to her at once that there was *some other attraction*, to use her own expression. In short, it was evident that the hope she had so fondly cherished was a baseless delusion, and that she would "never make anything out of that man yonder," in the Countess's forcible phrase. The Countess seemed to have been a judge of character. Mme. Vauquer's aversion was naturally more energetic than her friendship, for her hatred was not in proportion to her love, but to her disappointed expectations. The human heart may find here and there a resting-place short of the highest height of affection, but we seldom stop in the steep, downward slope of hatred. Still, M. Goriot was a lodger, and the widow's wounded self-love could not vent itself in an explosion of wrath; like a monk harassed by the prior of his convent, she was forced to stifle her sighs of disappointment, and to gulp down her craving for revenge. Little minds find gratification for their feelings, benevolent or otherwise, by a constant exercise of petty ingenuity. The widow employed her woman's malice to devise a system of covert persecution. She began by a course of retrenchment — various luxuries which had found their way to the table appeared there no more.

"No more gherkins, no more anchovies; they have made a fool of me!" she said to Sylvie one morning, and they returned to the old bill of fare.

The thrifty frugality necessary to those who mean to make their way in the world had become an inveterate habit of life with M. Goriot. Soup, boiled beef, and a dish of vegetables had been, and always would be, the dinner he liked best, so Mme. Vauquer found it very difficult to annoy a boarder whose tastes were so simple. He was proof against her malice, and in desperation she spoke to him and of him slightingly before the other lodgers, who began to amuse themselves at his expense, and so gratified her desire for revenge.

Towards the end of the first year the widow's suspicions had reached such a pitch that she began to wonder how it was that a retired merchant with a secure income of seven or eight thousand livres, the owner of such magnificent plate and jewellery handsome enough for a kept mistress, should be living in her house. Why should he devote so small a proportion of his money to his expenses? Until the first year was nearly at an end, Goriot had dined out once or twice every week, but these occasions came less frequently, and at last he was scarcely absent from the dinner table twice a month. It was hardly to be expected that Mme. Vauquer should regard the increased regularity of her boarder's habits with complacency, when those little excursions of his had been so much to her interest. She attributed the change not so much to a gradual diminution of fortune as to a spiteful wish to annoy his hostess. It is one of the most detestable habits of a Lilliputian mind to credit other people with its own malignant pettiness.

Unluckily, towards the end of the second year, M. Goriot's conduct gave some color to the idle talk about him. He asked Mme. Vauquer to give him a room on the second floor, and to make a corresponding reduction in her charges. Apparently, such strict economy was called for, that he did without a fire all through the winter. Mme. Vauquer asked to be paid in advance, an arrangement to which M. Goriot consented, and thenceforward she spoke of him as "old Goriot."

What had brought about this decline and fall? Conjecture was keen, but investigation was difficult. Old Goriot was not communicative; in the sham countess's phrase, he was "a curmudgeon." Empty-headed people who babble about their own affairs because they have nothing else to occupy them, naturally conclude that if people say nothing of their doings it is because their doings will not bear being talked about; so the highly respectable merchant became a scoundrel, and the late beau was an old rogue. Opinion fluctuated. Sometimes, according to Vautrin, who came about this time to live in the Maison Vauquer, old Goriot was a man who went on Change and *dabbled* (to use the sufficiently expressive language of the Stock Exchange) in stocks and shares after he had ruined himself by heavy speculation. Sometimes it was held that he was one of those petty gamblers who nightly play for small stakes until they win a few francs. A theory that he was a detective in the employ of the Home Office found favor at one time, but Vautrin urged that "Goriot was not sharp enough for one of that sort." There were yet other solutions; old Goriot was a skinflint, a shark of a money-lender, a man who lived by selling lottery tickets. He was by turns all the most mysterious brood of vice and shame and misery; yet, however vile his life might be, the feel-

ing of repulsion which he aroused in others was not so strong that he must be banished from their society — he paid his way. Besides, Goriot had his uses, every one vented his spleen or sharpened his wit on him; he was pelted with jokes and belabored with hard words. The general consensus of opinion was in favor of a theory which seemed the most likely; this was Mme. Vauquer's view. According to her, the man so well preserved at his time of life, as sound as her eyesight, with whom a woman might be very happy, was a libertine who had strange tastes. These are the facts upon which Mme. Vauquer's slanders were based.

Early one morning, some few months after the departure of the unlucky Countess who had managed to live for six months at the widow's expense, Mme. Vauquer (not yet dressed) heard the rustle of a silk dress and a young woman's light footstep on the stair; some one was going to Goriot's room. He seemed to expect the visit, for his door stood ajar. The portly Sylvie presently came up to tell her mistress that a girl too pretty to be honest, "dressed like a goddess," and not a speck of mud on her laced cashmere boots, had glided in from the street like a snake, had found the kitchen, and asked for M. Goriot's room. Mme. Vauquer and the cook, listening, overheard several words affectionately spoken during the visit, which lasted for some time. When M. Goriot went downstairs with the lady, the stout Sylvie forthwith took her basket and followed the lover-like couple, under pretext of going to do her marketing.

"M. Goriot must be awfully rich, all the same, madame," she reported on her return, "to keep her in such style. Just imagine it! There was a splendid carriage waiting at the corner of the Place de l'Estrapade, and *she* got into it."

While they were at dinner that evening, Mme. Vauquer went to the window and drew the curtain, as the sun was shining into Goriot's eyes.

"You are beloved of fair ladies, M. Goriot — the sun seeks you out," she said, alluding to his visitor. "*Peste!* you have good taste; she was very pretty."

"That was my daughter," he said, with a kind of pride in his voice, and the rest chose to consider this as the fatuity of an old man who wishes to save appearances.

A month after this visit M. Goriot received another. The same daughter who had come to see him that morning came again after dinner, this time in evening dress. The boarders, in deep discussion in the dining-room, caught a glimpse of a lovely, fair-haired woman, slender, graceful, and much too distinguished-looking to be a daughter of old Goriot's.

"Two of them!" cried the portly Sylvie, who did not recognise the lady of the first visit.

A few days later, and another young lady — a tall, well-moulded brunette, with dark hair and bright eyes — came to ask for M. Goriot.

"Three of them!" said Sylvie.

Then the second daughter, who had first come in the morning to see her father, came shortly afterwards in the evening. She wore a ball dress, and came in a carriage.

"Four of them!" commented Mme. Vauquer and her plump handmaid. Sylvie saw not a trace of resemblance between this great lady and the girl in her simple morning dress who had entered her kitchen on the occasion of her first visit.

At that time Goriot was paying twelve hundred francs a year to his landlady, and Mme. Vauquer saw nothing out of the common in the fact that a rich man had four or five mistresses; nay, she thought it very knowing of him to pass them off as his daughters. She was not at all inclined to draw a hard-and-fast line, or to take umbrage at his sending for them to the Maison Vauquer; yet, inasmuch as these visits explained her boarder's indifference to her, she went so far (at the end of the second year) as to speak of him as an "ugly old wretch." When at length her boarder declined to nine hundred francs a year, she asked him very insolently what he took her house to be, after meeting one of these ladies on the stairs. Old Goriot answered that the lady was his eldest daughter.

"So you have two or three dozen daughters, have you?" said Mme. Vauquer sharply.

"I have only two," her boarder answered meekly, like a ruined man who is broken in to all the cruel usage of misfortune.

Nicolai Gogol · 1809-1852

The Russian temperament as expressed in literature is predominantly realistic. Various reasons can be found to explain this fact — racial, psychological, historical, geographical. But here we need look no further than the times in which Russian literature became known to the rest of the world — the hundred years between 1825 and 1925.

During these years Russia was in a turmoil. Young officers of the empire who had fought Napoleon took liberal ideas back to Russia. A new political philosophy stirred the people. Leaders began to argue for more honest and more open courts, for a greater generosity toward the serf, for more general education. Opposition to feudalism increased. Particularly were these leaders opposed to the arbitrary rule which had characterized Russian government. Radical changes were in the offing. In 1861 the serfs were given their freedom. But many minor revolutions were to take place before the Soviet Republic was proclaimed in 1917. It was against this background of political struggle and turbulence that Gogol, Turgenev, Dostoevsky, Tolstoy, and Gorki wrote.

Nicolai Vasilievich Gogol was born at Sorochintsky, in the Russian province of Poltava, on March 31, 1809. His family belonged to the Cossack gentry of the Ukraine. As a young man Gogol turned his attention to the stage, to a position in the civil service, to a professorship in history at the University of St. Petersburg, and failed in all three professions. During part of this time, however, he was writing short tales of Cossack life and it was in this activity that he found his success. In 1836 he took up his residence in Rome, a city he loved dearly and in which he continued to live — with journeys to Russia at times — until shortly before his death. In 1848 he went on a pilgrimage to the Holy Land in search of religious experience.

Gogol's most important volumes are *Evenings on a Farm* (1831), a collection of stories of Ukrainian life; *The Government Inspector* (1836), a comedy satirizing Russian bureaucracy; and *Dead Souls* (1842), a series of pictures of Russian life forming a sort of epic. It was during the early stages of the composition of *Dead Souls* that Gogol wrote to a friend: "If I ever complete this work in the manner I want to, what a colossal and original theme it will be! What a varied crowd of characters! The whole of Russia will appear in it! This will be the first product of mine that will preserve my name."

He was right in his prediction; he wrote a work which is considered by some critics as one of the literary masterpieces of the world.

Gogol has been hailed as the father both of the Russian novel and of Russian realism. What he did was to open up new vistas for realism and to remove certain taboos which had limited the Russian writers. "We are all descended from Gogol's *Cloak*," wrote one Russian. It may be said that Gogol wrote realistically of unreal people and events. And to his realism he adds a strongly imaginative quality, satire and irony, humor and, at times, even pathos.

SUGGESTED REFERENCES: Vladimir Nabokov, *Nikolai Gogol* (2nd ed., 1947); Janko Lavrin, *Nikolai Gogol* (new ed., 1962).

The Cloak

In the department of —— but it is better not to mention the department. The touchiest things in the world are departments, regiments, courts of justice, in a word, all branches of public service. Each individual nowadays thinks all society insulted in his person. Quite recently, a complaint was received from a district chief of police in which he plainly demonstrated that all the imperial institutions were going to the dogs, and that the Czar's sacred name was being taken in vain; and in proof he appended to the complaint a romance, in which the district chief of police is made to appear about once in every ten pages, and sometimes in a downright drunken condition. Therefore, in order to avoid all unpleasantness, it will be better to designate the department in question, as a certain department.

So, in a certain department there was a certain official — not a very notable one, it must be allowed — short of stature, somewhat pock-marked, red-haired, and mole-eyed, with a bald forehead, wrinkled cheeks, and a complexion of the kind known as sanguine. The St. Petersburg climate was responsible for this. As for his official rank — with us Russians the rank comes first — he was what is called a perpetual titular councillor, over which, as is well known, some writers make merry and crack their jokes, obeying the praiseworthy custom of attacking those who cannot bite back.

His family name was Bashmachkin. This name is evidently derived from bashmak (shoe); but, when, at what time, and in what manner, is not known. His father and grandfather, and all the Bashmachkins, always wore boots, which were re-soled two or three times a year. His name was Akaky Akakiyevich. It may strike the reader as rather singular and far-fetched; but he may rest assured that it was by no means far-fetched, and that the circumstances were such that it would have been impossible to give him any other.

This was how it came about.

Akaky Akakiyevich was born, if my memory fails me not, in the evening on the 23rd of March. His mother, the wife of a Government official, and a very fine woman, made all due arrangements for having the child baptised. She was lying on the bed opposite the door; on her right stood the god-father, Ivan Ivanovich Eroshkin, a most estimable man, who served as the head clerk of the senate; and the godmother, Arina Semyonovna Bielobrinsh-kova, the wife of an officer of the quarter, and a woman of rare virtues. They offered the mother her choice of three names, Mokiya, Sossiya, or that the child should be called after the martyr Khozdazat. "No," said the good woman, "all those names are poor." In order to please her, they opened the calendar at another place; three more names appeared, Triphily, Dula, and Varak-hasy. "This is awful," said the old woman. "What names! I truly never heard the like. I might have put up with Varadat or Varukh, but not Triphily and Varakhasy!" They turned to another page and found Pavsikakhy and Vakhtisy. "Now I see," said the old woman, "that it is plain-ly fate. And since such is the case, it will be better to name him after his father. His father's name was Akaky, so let his son's name be Akaky too." In this manner he became Akaky Akakiyevich. They christened the child, whereat he wept, and made a grimace, as though he foresaw that he was to be a titular councillor.

In this manner did it all come about. We have mentioned it in order that the reader might see for himself that it was a case of necessity, and that it was utterly impossible to give him any other name.

When and how he entered the department, and who appointed him, no one could remember. However much the directors and chiefs of all kinds were changed, he was always to be seen in the same place, the same attitude, the same occupation — always the letter-copying clerk — so that it was afterwards affirmed that he had been born in uniform with a bald head. No respect was shown him in the department. The porter not only did not rise from his seat when he passed, but never even glanced at him, any more than if a fly had flown through the reception-room. His superiors treated him in coolly despotic fashion. Some insignificant assistant to the head clerk would thrust a paper under his nose without so much as saying, "Copy," or, "Here's an interesting little case," or anything else agreeable, as is customary amongst well-bred officials. And he took it, looking only at the paper, and not observing who handed it to him, or whether he had the right to do so; simply took it, and set about copying it.

The young officials laughed at and made fun of him, so far as their official wit permitted; told in his presence various stories concocted about him, and about his landlady, an old woman of seventy; declared that she beat him; asked when the wedding was to be; and strewed bits of paper over his head, calling them snow. But Akaky Akakiyevich answered not a word, any more than if there had been no one there besides himself. It even had no effect upon his work. Amid all these annoyances he never made a single mistake in a letter. But if the joking became wholly unbearable, as when they jogged his head, and prevented his attending to his work, he would exclaim:

"Leave me alone! Why do you insult me?"

And there was something strange in the words and the voice in which they were uttered. There was in it something which moved to pity; so much so that one young man, a newcomer, who, taking pattern by the others, had permitted himself to make sport of Akaky, suddenly stopped short, as though all about him had undergone a transformation, and presented itself in a different aspect. Some unseen force repelled him from the comrades whose acquaintance he had made, on the supposition that they were decent, well-bred men. Long afterwards, in his gayest moments, there recurred to his mind the little official with the bald forehead, with his heart-rending words, "Leave me alone! Why do you insult me?" In these moving words, other words resounded — "I am thy brother." And the young man covered his face with his hand; and many a time afterwards, in the course of his life, shuddered at seeing how much inhumanity there is in man, how much savage coarseness is concealed beneath refined, cultured, worldly refinement, and even, O God! in that man whom the world acknowledges as honorable and upright.

It would be difficult to find another man who lived so entirely for his duties. It is not enough to say that Akaky labored with zeal; no, he labored with love. In his copying, he found a varied and agreeable employment. Enjoyment was written on his face; some letters were even favorites with him; and when he encountered these, he smiled, winked, and worked with his lips, till it seemed as though each letter might be read in his face, as his pen traced it. If his pay had been in proportion to his zeal, he would, perhaps, to his great surprise, have been made even a councillor of state. But he worked, as his companions, the wits, put it, like a horse in a mill.

However, it would be untrue to say that no attention was paid to him. One director being a kindly man, and desirous of rewarding him for his long service, ordered him to be given something more important than mere copying. So he was ordered to make a report of an already concluded affair, to another department; the duty consisting simply in changing the heading and altering a few words from the first to the third person. This caused him so much toil, that he broke into a perspiration, rubbed his forehead, and finally said, "No, give me rather something to copy." After that they let him copy on forever.

Outside this copying, it appeared that nothing existed for him. He gave no thought to his clothes. His uniform was not green, but a sort of rusty-meal color. The collar was low, so that his neck, in spite of the fact that it was not long, seemed inordinately so as it emerged from it, like the necks of the plaster cats which pedlars carry about on their heads. And something was always sticking to his uniform, either a bit of hay or some trifle. Moreover, he had a peculiar knack, as he walked along the street, of arriving beneath a window just as all sorts of rubbish was being flung out of it; hence he always bore about on his hat scraps of melon rinds, and other such articles. Never once in his life did he give heed to what was going on every day in the street; while it is well known that his young brother officials trained the range of their glances till they could see when any one's trouser-straps came undone upon the opposite sidewalk, which always brought a malicious smile to their faces. But Akaky Akakiyevich saw in all things the clean, even strokes of his written lines; and only when a horse thrust his nose, from some unknown quarter, over his shoulder, and sent a whole gust of wind down his neck from his nostrils, did he observe that he was not in the middle of a line, but in the middle of the street.

On reaching home, he sat down at once at the table, sipped his cabbage-soup up quickly, and swallowed a bit of beef with onions, never noticing their taste, and gulping down everything with flies and anything else which the Lord happened to send at the moment. When he saw that his stomach was beginning to swell, he rose from the table, and copied papers which he had brought home. If there happened to be none, he took copies for himself, for his own gratification, especially if the document was noteworthy, not on account of its style, but of its being addressed to some distinguished person.

Even at the hour when the grey St. Petersburg sky had quite disappeared, and all the official world had eaten or dined, each as he could, in accordance with the salary he received and his own fancy; when all were resting from the department jar of pens, running to and fro, for their own and other people's indispensable occupations, and from all the work that an uneasy man makes willingly for himself, rather than what is necessary; when officials hasten to dedicate to pleasure the time which is left to them, one bolder than the rest going to the theatre; another, into the street looking under the bonnets; another wasting his evening in compliments to some pretty girl, the star of a small official circle; another — and this is the common case of all — visiting his comrades on the third or fourth floor, in two small rooms with an ante-room or kitchen, and some pretensions to fashion, such as a lamp or some other trifle which has cost many a sacrifice of dinner or pleasure trip; in a word, at the hour when all officials disperse among the contracted quarters of their friends, to play whist, as they sip their tea from glasses with a kopek's worth of sugar, smoke long pipes, relate at time some bits of gossip which a Russian man can never, under any circumstances, refrain from, and when there is nothing else to talk of, repeat eternal anecdotes about the commandant to whom they had sent word that the tails of the horses on the Falconet Monument had been cut off; when all strive to divert themselves, Akaky Akakiyevich indulged in no kind of diversion. No one could even say that he had seen him at any kind of evening party. Having written to his heart's content, he lay down to sleep, smiling at the thought of the coming day — of what God might send him to copy on the morrow.

Thus flowed on the peaceful life of the man, who, with a salary of four hundred rubles, understood how to be content with his lot; and thus it would have continued to flow on, perhaps, to extreme old age, were it not that there are various ills strewn along the path of life for titular councillors as well as for private, actual, court, and every other species of councillor, even to those who never give any advice or take any themselves.

There exists in St. Petersburg a powerful foe of all who receive a salary of four hundred rubles a year, or thereabouts. This foe is no other than the Northern cold, although it is said to be very healthy. At nine o'clock in the morning, at the very hour when the streets are filled with men bound for the various official departments, it begins to bestow such powerful and piercing nips on all noses impartially, that the poor officials really do not know what to do with them. At an hour when the foreheads of even those who occupy exalted positions ache with the cold, and tears start to their eyes, the poor titular councillors are sometimes quite unprotected. Their only salvation lies in traversing as quickly as possible, in their thin little cloaks, five or six streets, and then warming their feet in the porter's room, and so thawing all their talents and qualifications for official service, which had become frozen on the way.

Akaky Akakiyevich had felt for some time that his back and shoulders were paining with peculiar poignancy, in spite of the fact that he tried to traverse the distance with all possible speed. He began finally to wonder whether the fault did not lie in his cloak. He examined it thoroughly at home, and discovered that in two places, namely, on the back and shoulders, it had become thin as gauze. The cloth was worn to such a degree that he could see through it, and the lining had fallen into pieces. You must know that Akaky Akakiyevich's cloak served as an object of ridicule to the officials. They even refused it the noble name of cloak, and called it a cape. In fact, it was of singular make, its collar diminishing year by year to serve to patch its other parts. The patching did not exhibit great skill on the part of the tailor, and was, in fact, baggy and ugly. Seeing how the matter stood, Akaky Akakiyevich decided that it would be necessary to take the cloak to Petrovich, the tailor, who lived somewhere on the fourth floor up a dark staircase, and who, in spite of his having but one eye and pock-marks all over his face, busied himself with considerable success in repairing the trousers and coats of officials and others; that is to say, when he was sober and not nursing some other scheme in his head.

It is not necessary to say much about this tailor, but as it is the custom to have the character of each personage in a novel clearly defined there is no help for it, so here is Petrovich the tailor. At first he was called only Grigory, and was some gentleman's serf. He commenced calling himself Petrovich from the time when he received his free papers, and further began to drink heavily on all holidays, at first on the great ones, and then on all church festivals without discrimination, wherever a cross stood in the calendar. On this point he was faithful to ancestral custom; and when quarrelling with his wife, he called her a low female and a German. As we have mentioned his wife, it will be necessary to say a word or two about her. Unfortunately, little is known of her beyond the fact that Petrovich had a wife, who wore a cap and a dress, but could not lay claim to beauty; at least, no one but the soldiers of the guard even looked under her cap when they met her.

Ascending the staircase which led to Petrovich's room — which staircase was all soaked with dishwater and reeked with the smell of spirits which affects the eyes, and is an inevitable adjunct to all dark stairways in St. Petersburg houses — ascending the stairs, Akaky Akakiyevich pondered how much Petrovich would ask, and mentally resolved not to give more than two rubles. The door was open, for the mistress, in cooking some fish, had raised such a smoke in the kitchen that not even the beetles were visible. Akaky Akakiyevich passed through the kitchen unperceived, even by the housewife, and at length reached a room where he beheld Petrovich seated on a large unpainted table, with his legs tucked under him like a Turkish pasha. His feet were bare, after the fashion of tailors as they sit at work; and the first thing which caught the eye was his thumb, with a deformed nail thick and strong as a turtle's shell. About Petrovich's neck hung a skein of silk and thread, and upon his knees lay some old garment. He had been trying unsuccessfully for three minutes to thread his needle, and was enraged at the darkness and even at the thread, growling in a low voice, "It won't go through, the barbarian! you pricked me, you rascal!"

Akaky Akakiyevich was vexed at arriving at the precise moment when Petrovich was angry. He liked to order something of Petrovich when he was a little downhearted, or, as his wife expressed it, "when he had settled himself with brandy, the one-eyed devil!" Under such circumstances Petrovich generally came down in his price very readily, and even bowed and returned thanks. Afterwards, to be sure, his wife would come, complaining that her husband had been drunk, and so had fixed the price too low; but, if only a ten-kopek piece were added then the matter would be settled. But now it appeared that Petrovich was in a sober condition, and therefore rough, taciturn, and inclined to demand, Satan only knows what price. Akaky Akakiyevich felt this, and would gladly have beat a retreat, but he was in for it. Petrovich screwed up his one eye very intently at him, and Akaky Akakiyevich involuntarily said, "How do you do, Petrovich?"

"I wish you a good morning, sir," said Petrovich, squinting at Akaky Akakiyevich's hands, to see what sort of booty he had brought.

"Ah! I — to you, Petrovich, this —" It must be known that Akaky Akakiyevich expressed himself chiefly by prepositions, adverbs, and scraps of phrases which had no meaning whatever. If the matter was a very difficult one, he had a habit of never completing his sentences, so that frequently, having begun a phrase with the words, "This, in fact, is quite —" he forgot to go on, thinking he had already finished it.

"What is it?" asked Petrovich, and with his one eye scanned Akaky Akakiyevich's whole uniform from the collar down to the cuffs, the back, the tails and the button-holes, all of which were well known to him, since they were his own handiwork. Such is the habit of tailors; it is the first thing they do on meeting one.

"But I, here, this — Petrovich — a cloak, cloth — here you see, everywhere, in different places, it is quite strong — it is a little dusty and looks old, but it is new, only here in one place it is a little — on the back, and here on one of the shoulders, it is a little worn, yes, here on this shoulder it is a little — do you see? That is all. And a little work —"

Petrovich took the cloak, spread it out, to begin with, on the table, looked at it hard, shook his head, reached out his hand to the window-sill for his snuff-box, adorned with the portrait of some general, though what general is unknown, for the place where the face should have been had been rubbed through by the finger and a square bit of paper had been pasted over it. Having taken a pinch of snuff, Petrovich held up the cloak, and inspected it against the light, and again shook his head. Then he turned it, lining upwards, and shook his head once more. After which he again lifted the general-adorned lid with its bit of pasted paper, and having stuffed his nose with snuff, closed and put away the snuff-box, and said finally, "No, it is impossible to mend it. It is a wretched garment!"

Akaky Akakiyevich's heart sank at these words. "Why is it impossible, Petrovich?" he said, almost in the pleading voice of a child. "All that ails it is, that it is worn on the shoulders. You must have some pieces ——"

"Yes, patches could be found, patches are easily found," said Petrovich, "but there's nothing to sew them to. The thing is completely rotten. If you put a needle to it — see, it will give way."

"Let it give way, and you can put on another patch at once."

"But there is nothing to put the patches on to. There's no use in strengthening it. It is too far gone. It's lucky that it's cloth, for, if the wind were to blow, it would fly away."

"Well, strengthen it again. How this, in fact ——"

"No," said Petrovich decisively, "there is nothing to be done with it. It's a thoroughly bad job. You'd better, when the cold winter weather comes on, make yourself some gaiters out of it, because stockings are not warm. The Germans invented them in order to make more money." Petrovich loved on all occasions to have a fling at the Germans. "But it is plain you must have a new cloak."

At the word "new" all grew dark before Akaky Akakiyevich's eyes, and everything in the room began to whirl round. The only thing he saw clearly was the general with the paper face on the lid of Petrovich's snuff-box. "A new one?" said he, as if still in a dream. "Why, I have no money for that."

"Yes, a new one," said Petrovich, with barbarous composure.

"Well, if it came to a new one, how — it ——"

"You mean how much would it cost?"

"Yes."

"Well, you would have to lay out a hundred and fifty or more," said Petrovich, and pursed up his lips significantly. He liked to produce powerful effects, liked to stun utterly and suddenly, and then to glance sideways to see what face the stunned person would put on the matter.

"A hundred and fifty rubles for a cloak!" shrieked poor Akaky Akakiyevich, perhaps for the first time in his life, for his voice had always been distinguished for softness.

"Yes, sir," said Petrovich, "for any kind of cloak. If you have a marten fur on the collar, or a silk-lined hood, it will mount up to two hundred."

"Petrovich, please," said Akaky Akakiyevich in a beseeching tone, not hearing, and not trying to hear, Petrovich's words, and disregarding all his "effects," "some repairs, in order that it may wear yet a little longer."

"No, it would only be a waste of time and money," said Petrovich. And Akaky Akakiyevich went away after these words, utterly discouraged. But Petrovich stood for some time after his departure, with significantly compressed lips, and without betaking himself to his work, satisfied that he would not be dropped, and an artistic tailor employed.

Akaky Akakiyevich went out into the street as if in a dream. "Such an affair!" he said to himself. "I did not think it had come to —" and then after a pause, he added, "Well, so it is! see what it has come to at last! and I never imagined that it ,was so!" Then followed a long silence, after which he exclaimed, "Well, so it is! see what already — nothing unexpected that — it would be nothing — what a strange circumstance!" So saying, instead of going home, he went in exactly the opposite direction without suspecting it. On the way, a chimney-sweep bumped up against him, and blackened his shoulder, and a whole hatful of rubbish landed on him from the top of a house which was building. He did not notice it, and only when he ran against a watchman, who, having planted his halberd beside him, was shaking some snuff from his box into his horny hand, did he recover himself a little, and that because the watchman said, "Why are you poking yourself into a man's very face? Haven't you the pavement?" This caused him to look about him, and turn towards home.

There only, he finally began to collect his thoughts, and to survey his position in its clear and actual light, and to argue with himself, sensibly and frankly, as with a reasonable friend, with whom one can discuss private and personal matters. "No," said Akaky Akakiyevich, "it is impossible to reason with Petrovich now. He is that — evidently, his wife has been beating him. I'd better go to him on Sunday morning. After Saturday night he will be a little cross-eyed and sleepy, for he will want to get drunk, and his wife won't give him any money, and at such a time, a ten-kopek piece in his hand will — he will become more fit to reason with, and then the cloak and that ——" Thus argued Akaky Akakiyevich with himself, regained his courage, and waited until the first Sunday, when, seeing from afar that Petrovich's wife had left the house, he went straight to him.

Petrovich's eye was indeed very much askew after Saturday. His head drooped, and he was very sleepy; but for all that, as soon as he knew what it was a question of, it seemed as though Satan jogged his memory. "Impossible," said he. "Please to order a new one." Thereupon Akaky Akakiyevich handed over the ten-kopek piece. "Thank you, sir. I will drink your good health," said Petrovich. "But as for the cloak, don't trouble yourself about it; it is good for nothing. I will make you a capital new one, so let us settle about it now."

Akaky Akakiyevich was still for mending it, but Petrovich would not hear of it, and said, "I shall certainly have to make you a new one, and you may depend upon it that I shall do my best. It may even be, as the fashion goes, that the collar can be fastened by silver hooks under a flap."

Then Akaky Akakiyevich saw that it was impossible to get along without a new cloak, and his spirit sank utterly. How, in fact, was it to be done? Where was the money to come from? He must have some new trousers, and pay a debt of long standing to the shoemaker for putting new tops to his old boots, and he must order three shirts from the seamstress, and a couple of pieces of linen. In short, all his money must be spent. And even if the director should be so kind as to order him to receive forty-five or even fifty rubles instead of forty, it would be a mere nothing, a mere drop in the ocean towards the funds necessary for a cloak, although he knew that Petrovich was often wrong-headed enough to blurt out some outrageous price, so that even his own wife could not refrain from exclaiming, "Have you lost your senses, you fool?" At one time he would not work at any price, and now it was quite likely that he had named a higher sum than the cloak would cost.

But although he knew that Petrovich would undertake to make a cloak for eighty rubles, still, where was he to get the eighty rubles from? He might possibly manage half. Yes, half might be procured, but where was the other half to come from? But the reader must first be told where the first half came from.

Akaky Akakiyevich had a habit of putting, for every ruble he spent, a groschen into a small box, fastened with lock and key, and with a slit in the top for the reception of money. At the end of every half-year he counted over the heap of coppers, and changed it for silver. This he had done for a long time, and in the course of years, the sum had mounted up to over forty rubles. Thus he had one half on hand. But where was he to find the other half? Where was he to get another forty rubles from? Akaky Akakiyevich thought and thought, and decided that it would be necessary to curtail his ordinary expenses, for the space of one year at least, to dispense with tea in the evening, to burn no candles, and, if there was anything which he must do, to go into his landlady's room, and work by her light. When he went into the street, he must walk as lightly as he could, and as cautiously, upon the stones, almost upon tiptoe, in order not to wear his heels down in too short a time. He must give the laundress as little to wash as possible; and, in order not to wear out his clothes, he must take them off as soon as he got home, and wear only his cotton dressing-gown, which had been long and carefully saved.

To tell the truth, it was a little hard for him at first to accustom himself to these deprivations. But he got used to them at length, after a fashion, and all went smoothly. He even got used to being hungry in the evening, but he made up for it by treating himself, so to say, in spirit, by bearing ever in mind the idea of his future cloak. From that time forth, his existence seemed to become, in some way, fuller, as if he were married, or as if some other man lived in him, as if, in fact, he were not alone, and some pleasant friend had consented to travel along life's path with him, the friend being no other than the cloak, with thick wadding and a strong lining incapable of wearing out. He became more lively, and even his character grew firmer, like that of a man who has made up his mind, and set himself a goal. From his face and gait, doubt and indecision, all hesitating and wavering disappeared of themselves. Fire gleamed in his eyes, and occasionally the boldest and most daring ideas flitted through his mind. Why not, for instance, have marten fur on the collar? The thought of this almost made him absent-minded. Once, in copying a letter, he nearly made a mistake, so that he exclaimed almost aloud, "Ugh!" and crossed himself. Once in the course of every month he had a conference with Petrovich ont he subject of the cloak, where it would be better to buy the cloth, and the color, and the price. He always returned home satisfied, though troubled, reflecting that the time would come at last when it could all be bought, and then the cloak made.

The affair progressed more briskly than he had expected. For beyond all his hopes, the director awarded neither forty nor forty-five rubles for Akaky Akakiyevich's share, but sixty. Whether he suspected that Akaky Akakiyevich needed a cloak, or whether it was merely chance, at all events, twenty extra rubles were by this means provided. This circumstance hastened matters. Two or three months more of hunger and Akaky Akakiyevich had accumulated about eighty rubles. His heart, generally so quiet, began to throb. On the first possible day, he went shopping in company with Petrovich. They bought some very good cloth, and at a reasonable rate too, for they had been considering the matter for six months, and rarely let a month pass without their visiting the shops to enquire prices. Petrovich himself said that no better cloth could be had. For lining, they selected a cotton stuff, but so firm and thick that Petrovich declared it to be better than silk, and even prettier and more glossy. They did not buy the marten fur, because it was, in fact, dear, but in its stead, they picked out the very best of cat-skin which could be found in the shop, and which might, indeed, be taken for marten at a distance.

Petrovich worked at the cloak two whole weeks, for there was a great deal of quilting; otherwise it would have been finished sooner. He charged twelve rubles for the job, it could not possibly have been done for less. It was all sewed with silk, in small, double seams, and Petrovich went over each seam afterwards with his own teeth, stamping in various patterns.

It was — it is difficult to say precisely on what day, but probably the most glorious one in Akaky Akakiyevich's life, when Petrovich at length brought home the cloak. He brought it in the morning, before the hour when it was necessary to start for the department. Never did a cloak arrive so exactly in the nick of time, for the severe cold had set in, and it seemed to threaten to increase. Petrovich brought the cloak himself as befits a good tailor. On his countenance was a significant expression, such as Akaky Akakiyevich had never beheld there. He seemed fully sensible that he had done no small deed, and crossed a gulf separating tailors who put in linings, and execute repairs, from those who make new things. He took the cloak out of the pocket-handkerchief in which he had brought it. The handkerchief was fresh from the laundress, and he put it in his pocket for use. Taking out the cloak, he gazed proudly at it, held it up with both hands, and flung it skilfully over the shoulders of Akaky Akakiyevich. Then he pulled it and fitted it down behind with his hand, and he draped it around Akaky Akakiyevich without buttoning it. Akaky Akakiyevich, like an experienced man, wished to try the sleeves. Petrovich helped him on with them, and it turned out that the sleeves were satisfactory also. In short, the cloak appeared to be perfect, and most seasonable. Petrovich did not neglect to observe that it was only because he lived in a narrow street, and had no signboard, and had known Akaky Akakiyevich so long, that he had made it so cheaply; but that if he had been in business on the Nevsky Prospect, he would have charged seventy-five rubles for the making alone. Akaky Akakiyevich did not care to argue this point with Petrovich. He paid him, thanked him, and set out at once in his new cloak for the department. Petrovich followed him, and pausing in the street, gazed long at the cloak in the distance, after which he went to one side expressly to run through a crooked alley, and emerge again into the street beyond to gaze once more upon the cloak from another point, namely, directly in front.

Meantime Akaky Akakiyevich went on in holiday mood. He was conscious every second of the time that he had a new cloak on his shoulders, and several times he laughed with internal satisfaction. In fact, there were two advantages; one was its warmth, the other its beauty. He saw nothing of the road, but suddenly found himself at the department. He took off his cloak in the ante-room, looked it over carefully, and confided it to the special care of the attendant. It is impossible to say precisely how it was that every one in the department knew at once that Akaky Akakiyevich had a new cloak, and that the "cape" no longer existed. All rushed at the same moment into the ante-room to inspect it. They congratulated him, and said pleasant things to him, so that he began at first to smile, and then to grow ashamed. When all surrounded him, and said that the new cloak must be "christened," and that he must at least give them all a party, Akaky Akakiyevich lost his head completely, and did not know where he stood, what to answer, or how to get out of it. He stood blushing all over for several minutes, trying to assure them with great simplicity that it was not a new cloak, that it was in fact the old "cape."

At length one of the officials, assistant to the head clerk, in order to show that he was not at all proud, and on good terms with his inferiors, said:

"So be it, only I will give the party instead of Akaky Akakiyevich; I invite you all to tea with me to-night. It just happens to be my name-day too."

The officials naturally at once offered the assistant clerk their congratulations, and accepted the invitation with pleasure. Akaky Akakiyevich would have declined; but all declared that it was discourteous, that it was simply a sin and a shame, and that he could not possibly refuse. Besides, the notion became pleasant to him when he recollected that he should thereby have a chance of wearing his new cloak in the evening also.

That whole day was truly a most triumphant festival for Akaky Akakiyevich. He returned home in the most happy frame of mind, took off his cloak, and hung it carefully on the wall, admiring afresh the cloth and the lining. Then he brought out his old, worn-out cloak, for comparison. He looked at it, and laughed, so vast was the difference. And long after dinner he laughed again when the condition of the "cape" recurred to his mind. He dined cheerfully, and after dinner wrote nothing, but took his ease for a while on the bed, until it got dark. Then he dressed himself leisurely, put on his cloak, and stepped out into the street.

Where the host lived, unfortunately we cannot say. Our memory begins to fail us badly. The houses and streets in St. Petersburg have become so mixed up in our head that it is very difficult to get anything out of it again in proper form. This much is certain, that the official lived in the best part of the city; and therefore it must have been anything but near to Akaky Akakiyevich's residence. Akaky Akakiyevich was first obliged to traverse a kind of wilderness of deserted, dimly-lighted streets. But in proportion as he approached the official's quarter of the city, the streets became more lively, more populous, and more brilliantly illuminated. Pedestrians began to appear; hand-somely dressed ladies were more frequently en-countered; the men had otter skin collars to their coats; shabby sleigh-men with their wooden, railed sledges stuck over with brass-headed nails, became rarer; whilst on the other hand, more and more drivers in red velvet caps, lacquered sledges and bear-skin coats began to appear, and carriages with rich hammer-cloths flew swiftly through the streets, their wheels scrunching the snow.

Akaky Akakiyevich gazed upon all this as upon a novel sight. He had not been in the streets during the evening for years. He halted out of curiosity before a shop-window, to look at a picture repre-senting a handsome woman, who had thrown off her shoe, thereby baring her whole foot in a very pretty way; whilst behind her the head of a man with whiskers and a handsome moustache peeped through the doorway of another room. Akaky Akakiyevich shook his head, and laughed, and then went on his way. Why did he laugh? Either because he had met with a thing utterly unknown, but for which every one cherishes, nevertheless, some sort of feeling, or else he thought, like many officials, "Well, those French! What is to be said? If they do go in for anything of that sort, why ——" But possibly he did not think at all.

Akaky Akakiyevich at length reached the house in which the head clerk's assistant lodged. He lived in fine style. The staircase was lit by a lamp, his apartment being on the second floor. On en-tering the vestibule, Akaky Akakiyevich beheld a whole row of goloshes on the floor. Among them, in the centre of the room, stood a samovar, hum-ming and emitting clouds of steam. On the walls hung all sorts of coats and cloaks, among which there were even some with beaver collars, or velvet facings. Beyond, the buzz of conversation was audible, and became clear and loud, when the servant came out with a trayful of empty glasses, cream-jugs, and sugar-bowls. It was evident that the officials had arrived long before, and had al-ready finished their first glass of tea.

Akaky Akakiyevich, having hung up his own cloak, entered the inner room. Before him all at once appeared lights, officials, pipes, and card-tables, and he was bewildered by a sound of rapid conversation rising from all the tables, and the noise of moving chairs. He halted very awk-wardly in the middle of the room, wondering what he ought to do. But they had seen him. They re-ceived him with a shout, and all thronged at once into the ante-room, and there took another look at his cloak. Akaky Akakiyevich, although some-what confused, was frank-hearted, and could not refrain from rejoicing when he saw how they praised his cloak. Then, of course, they all dropped him and his cloak, and returned, as was proper, to the tables set out for whist.

All this, the noise, the talk, and the throng of people, was rather overwhelming to Akaky Akaki-yevich. He simply did not know where he stood, or where to put his hands, his feet, and his whole body. Finally he sat down by the players, looked at the cards, gazed at the face of one and another, and after a while began to gape, and to feel that it was wearisome, the more so, as the hour was al-ready long past when he usually went to bed. He wanted to take leave of the host, but they would not let him go, saying that he must not fail to drink a glass of champagne, in honor of his new garment. In the course of an hour, supper, con-sisting of vegetable salad, cold veal, pastry, con-fectioner's pies, and champagne, was served. They made Akaky Akakiyevich drink two glasses of champagne, after which he felt things grow livelier.

Still, he could not forget that it was twelve o'-clock, and that he should have been at home long ago. In order that the host might not think of some excuse for detaining him, he stole out of the room quickly, sought out, in the ante-room, his cloak, which, to his sorrow, he found lying on the floor, brushed it, picked off every speck upon it, put it on his shoulders, and descended the stairs to the street.

In the street all was still bright. Some petty shops, those permanent clubs of servants and all sorts of folks, were open. Others were shut, but, nevertheless, showed a streak of light the whole length of the door-crack, indicating that they were not yet free of company, and that probably some domestics, male and female, were finishing their stories and conversations, whilst leaving their mas-ters in complete ignorance as to their whereabouts. Akaky Akakiyevich went on in a happy frame of mind. He even started to run, without knowing why, after some lady, who flew past like a flash of lightning. But he stopped short, and went on very quietly as before, wondering why he had quickened his pace. Soon there spread before him those deserted streets which are not cheerful in the daytime, to say nothing of the evening. Now they were even more dim and lonely. The lanterns began to grow rarer; oil, evidently, had been less liberally supplied. Then came wooden houses and fences. Not a soul anywhere; only the snow sparkled in the streets, and mournfully veiled the low-roofed cabins with their closed shutters. He approached the spot where the street crossed a vast square with houses barely visible on its farther side, a square which seemed a fearful desert.

Afar, a tiny spark glimmered from some watchman's-box, which seemed to stand on the edge of the world. Akaky Akakiyevich's cheerfulness diminished at this point in a marked degree. He entered the square, not without an involuntary sensation of fear, as though his heart warned him of some evil. He glanced back, and on both sides it was like a sea about him. "No, it is better not to look," he thought, and went on, closing his eyes. When he opened them, to see whether he was near the end of the square, he suddenly beheld, standing just before his very nose, some bearded individuals, of precisely what sort he could not make out. All grew dark before his eyes, and his heart throbbed.

"Of course, the cloak is mine!" said one of them in a loud voice, seizing hold of his collar. Akaky Akakiyevich was about to shout "Help!" when the second man thrust a fist, about the size of an official's head, at his very mouth, muttering, "Just you dare to scream!"

Akaky Akakiyevich felt them strip off his cloak, and give him a kick. He fell headlong upon the snow, and felt no more.

In a few minutes he recovered consciousness, and rose to his feet, but no one was there. He felt that it was cold in the square, and that his cloak was gone. He began to shout, but his voice did not appear to reach the outskirts of the square. In despair, but without ceasing to shout, he started at a run across the square, straight towards the watch-box, beside which stood the watchman, leaning on his halberd, and apparently curious to know what kind of a customer was running towards him shouting. Akaky Akakiyevich ran up to him, and began in a sobbing voice to shout that he was asleep, and attended to nothing, and did not see when a man was robbed. The watchman replied that he had seen two men stop him in the middle of the square, but supposed that they were friends of his, and that, instead of scolding vainly, he had better go to the police on the morrow, so that they might make a search for whoever had stolen the cloak.

Akaky Akakiyevich ran home and arrived in a state of complete disorder, his hair which grew very thinly upon his temples and the back of his head all tousled, his body, arms, and legs covered with snow. The old woman who was mistress of his lodgings, on hearing a terrible knocking sprang hastily from her bed, and, with only one shoe on, ran to open the door, pressing the sleeve of her chemise to her bosom out of modesty. But when she had opened it, she fell back on beholding Akaky Akakiyevich in such a condition. When he told her about the affair, she clasped her hands, and said that he must go straight to the district chief of police, for his subordinate would turn up his nose, promise well, and drop the matter there. The very best thing to do, therefore, would be to go to the district chief, whom she knew, because Finnish Anna, her former cook, was now nurse at his house. She often saw him passing the house, and he was at church every Sunday, praying, but at the same time gazing cheerfully at everybody; so that he must be a good man, judging from all appearances. Having listened to this opinion, Akaky Akakiyevich betook himself sadly to his room. And how he spent the night there, any one who can put himself in another's place may readily imagine.

Early in the morning, he presented himself at the district chief's, but was told the official was asleep. He went again at ten and was again informed that he was asleep. At eleven, and they said, "The superintendent is not at home." At dinner time, and the clerks in the ante-room would not admit him on any terms, and insisted upon knowing his business. So that at last, for once in his life, Akaky Akakiyevich felt an inclination to show some spirit, and said curtly that he must see the chief in person, that they ought not to presume to refuse him entrance, that he came from the department of justice, and that when he complained of them, they would see.

The clerks dared make no reply to this, and one of them went to call the chief, who listened to the strange story of the theft of the coat. Instead of directing his attention to the principal points of the matter, he began to question Akaky Akakiyevich. Why was he going home so late? Was he in the habit of doing so, or had he been to some disorderly house? So that Akaky Akakiyevich got thoroughly confused, and left him, without knowing whether the affair of his cloak was in proper train or not.

All that day, for the first time in his life, he never went near the department. The next day he made his appearance, very pale, and in his old cape, which had become even more shabby. The news of the robbery of the cloak touched many, although there were some officials present who never lost an opportunity, even such a one as the present, of ridiculing Akaky Akakiyevich. They decided to make a collection for him on the spot, but the officials had already spent a great deal in subscribing for the director's portrait, and for some book, at the suggestion of the head of that division.

who was a friend of the author; and so the sum was trifling.

One of them, moved by pity, resolved to help Akaky Akakiyevich with some good advice, at least, and told him that he ought not to go to the police, for although it might happen that a police-officer, wishing to win the approval of his superiors, might hunt up the cloak by some means, still, his cloak would remain in the possession of the police if he did not offer legal proof that it belonged to him. The best thing for him, therefore, would be to apply to a certain prominent personage; since this prominent personage, by entering into relation with the proper persons, could greatly expedite the matter.

As there was nothing else to be done, Akaky Akakiyevich decided to go to the prominent personage. What was the exact official position of the prominent personage, remains unknown to this day. The reader must know that the prominent personage had but recently become a prominent personage, having up to that time been only an insignificant person. Moreover, his present position was not considered prominent in comparison with others still more so. But there is always a circle of people to whom what is insignificant in the eyes of others, is important enough. Moreover, he strove to increase his importance by sundry devices. For instance, he managed to have the inferior officials meet him on the staircase when he entered upon his service; no one was to presume to come directly to him, but the strictest etiquette must be observed; the collegiate recorder must make a report to the government secretary, the government secretary to the titular councillor, or whatever other man was proper, and all business must come before him in this manner. In Holy Russia, all is thus contaminated with the love of imitation; every man imitates and copies his superior. They even say that a certain titular councillor, when promoted to the head of some small separate office, immediately partitioned off a private room for himself, called it the audience chamber, and posted at the door a lackey with red collar and braid, who grasped the handle of the door, and opened to all comers, though the audience chamber would hardly hold an ordinary writing table.

The manners and customs of the prominent personage were grand and imposing, but rather exaggerated. The main foundation of his system was strictness. "Strictness, strictness, and always strictness!" he generally said; and at the last word he looked significantly into the face of the person to whom he spoke. But there was no necessity for this, for the halfscore of subordinates, who formed the entire force of the office, were properly afraid. On catching sight of him afar off, they left their work, and waited, drawn up in line, until he had passed through the room. His ordinary converse with his inferiors smacked of sternness, and consisted chiefly of three phrases: "How dare you?" "Do you know whom you are speaking to?" "Do you realize who is standing before you?"

Otherwise he was a very kind-hearted man, good to his comrades, and ready to oblige. But the rank of general threw him completely off his balance. On receiving any one of that rank, he became confused, lost his way, as it were, and never knew what to do. If he chanced to be amongst his equals, he was still a very nice kind of man, a very good fellow in many respects, and not stupid, but the very moment that he found himself in the society of people but one rank lower than himself, he became silent. And his situation aroused sympathy, the more so, as he felt himself that he might have been making an incomparably better use of his time. In his eyes, there was sometimes visible a desire to join some interesting conversation or group, but he was kept back by the thought, "Would it not be a very great condescension on his part? Would it not be familiar? And would he not thereby lose his importance?" And in consequence of such reflections, he always remained in the same dumb state, uttering from time to time a few monosyllabic sounds, and thereby earning the name of the most wearisome of men.

To this prominent personage Akaky Akakiyevich presented himself, and this at the most unfavorable time for himself, though opportune for the prominent personage. The prominent personage was in his cabinet, conversing very gaily with an old acquaintance and companion of his childhood, whom he had not seen for several years, and who had just arrived, when it was announced to him that a person named Bashmachkin had come. He asked abruptly, "Who is he?" — "Some official," he was informed. "Ah, he can wait! This is no time for him to call," said the important man. It must be remarked here that the important man lied outrageously. He had said all he had to say to his friend long before, and the conversation had been interspersed for some time with very long pauses, during which they merely slapped each other on the leg, and said, "You think so, Ivan Abramovich!" "Just so, Stepan Varlamovich!" Nevertheless, he ordered that the official should be kept waiting, in order to show his friend, a man who had not been in the service for a long time, but had lived at home in the country, how long officials had to wait in his ante-room.

At length, having talked himself completely out, and more than that, having had his fill of pauses, and smoked a cigar in a very comfortable arm-chair with reclining back, he suddenly seemed to recollect, and said to the secretary, who stood by the door with papers of reports, "So it seems that there is an official waiting to see me. Tell him that he may come in." On perceiving Akaky Akakiye-vich's modest mien and his worn uniform, he turned abruptly to him, and said, "What do you want?" in a curt hard voice, which he had prac-tised in his room in private, and before the looking-glass, for a whole week before being raised to his present rank.

Akaky Akakiyevich, who was already imbued with a due amount of fear, became somewhat con-fused, and as well as his tongue would permit, ex-plained, with a rather more frequent addition than usual of the word "that," that his cloak was quite new, and had been stolen in the most inhuman manner; that he had applied to him, in order that he might, in some way, by his intermediation — that he might enter into correspondence with the chief of police, and find the cloak.

For some inexplicable reason, this conduct seemed familiar to the prominent personage.

"What, my dear sir!" he said abruptly, "are you not acquainted with etiquette? To whom have you come? Don't you know how such mat-ters are managed? You should first have pre-sented a petition to the office. It would have gone to the head of the department, then to the chief of the division, then it would have been handed over to the secretary, and the secretary would have given it to me."

"But, your excellency," said Akaky Akakiye-vich, trying to collect his small handful of wits, and conscious at the same time that he was perspiring terribly, "I, your excellency, presumed to trouble you because secretaries — are an untrustworthy race."

"What, what, what!" said the important per-sonage. "Where did you get such courage? Where did you get such ideas? What impudence towards their chiefs and superiors has spread among the young generation!" The prominent personage apparently had not observed that Akaky Akakiyevich was already in the neighborhood of fifty. If he could be called a young man, it must have been in comparison with some one who was seventy. "Do you know to whom you are speak-ing? Do you realize who is standing before you? Do you realise it? Do you realise it, I ask you!" Then he stamped his foot, and raised his voice to such a pitch that it would have frightened even a different man from Akaky Akakiyevich.

Akaky Akakiyevich's senses failed him. He staggered, trembled in every limb, and, if the por-ters had not run in to support him, would have fallen to the floor. They carried him out insen-sible. But the prominent personage, gratified that the effect should have surpassed his expec-tations, and quite intoxicated with the thought that his word could even deprive a man of his senses, glanced sideways at his friend in order to see how he looked upon this, and perceived, not without satisfaction, that his friend was in a most uneasy frame of mind, and even beginning on his part to feel a trifle frightened.

Akaky Akakiyevich could not remember how he descended the stairs, and got into the street. He felt neither his hands nor feet. Never in his life had he been so rated by any high official, let alone a strange one. He went staggering on through the snow-storm, which was blowing in the streets, with his mouth wide open. The wind, in St. Petersburg fashion, darted upon him from all quarters, and down every cross-street. In a twinkling it had blown a quinsy into his throat, and he reached home unable to utter a word. His throat was swollen, and he lay down on his bed. So powerful is sometimes a good scolding!

The next day a violent fever developed. Thanks to the generous assistance of the St. Peters-burg climate, the malady progressed more rapidly than could have been expected, and when the doc-tor arrived, he found, on feeling the sick man's pulse, that there was nothing to be done, except to prescribe a poultice, so that the patient might not be left entirely without the beneficent aid of medi-cine. But at the same time, he predicted his end in thirty-six hours. After this he turned to the landlady, and said, "And as for you, don't waste your time on him. Order his pine coffin now, for an oak one will be too expensive for him."

Did Akaky Akakiyevich hear these fatal words? And if he heard them, did they produce any over-whelming effect upon him? Did he lament the bitterness of his life? — We know not, for he con-tinued in a delirious condition. Visions inces-santly appeared to him, each stranger than the other. Now he saw Petrovich, and ordered him to make a cloak, with some traps for robbers, who seemed to him to be always under the bed; and he cried every moment to the landlady to pull one of them from under his coverlet. Then he inquired why his old mantle hung before him when he had a new cloak. Next he fancied that he was standing before the prominent person, listening to a thorough setting-down and saying, "Forgive me, your ex-cellency!" but at last he began to curse, uttering the most horrible words, so that his aged landlady crossed herself, never in her life having heard anything of the kind from him, and more so, as these words followed directly after the words "your excellency." Later on he talked utter nonsense, of which nothing could be made, all that was evident being that these incoherent words and thoughts hovered ever about one thing, his cloak.

At length poor Akaky Akakiyevich breathed his last. They sealed up neither his room nor his effects, because, in the first place, there were no heirs, and, in the second, there was very little to inherit beyond a bundle of goose-quills, a quire of white official paper, three pairs of socks, two or three buttons which had burst off his trousers, and the mantle already known to the reader. To whom all this fell, God knows. I confess that the person who told me this tale took no interest in the matter. They carried Akaky Akakiyevich out, and buried him.

And St. Petersburg was left without Akaky Akakiyevich, as though he had never lived there. A being disappeared, who was protected by none, dear to none, interesting to none, and who never even attracted to himself the attention of those students of human nature who omit no opportunity of thrusting a pin through a common fly and examining it under the microscope. A being who bore meekly the jibes of the department, and went to his grave without having done one unusual deed, but to whom, nevertheless, at the close of his life, appeared a bright visitant in the form of a cloak, which momentarily cheered his poor life, and upon him, thereafter, an intolerable misfortune descended, just as it descends upon the heads of the mighty of this world!

Several days after his death, the porter was sent from the department to his lodgings, with an order for him to present himself there immediately, the chief commanding it. But the porter had to return unsuccessful, with the answer that he could not come; and to the question, "Why?" replied, "Well, because he is dead! he was buried four days ago." In this manner did they hear of Akaky Akakiyevich's death at the department. And the next day a new official sat in his place, with a handwriting by no means so upright, but more inclined and slanting.

But who could have imagined that this was not really the end of Akaky Akakiyevich, that he was destined to raise a commotion after death, as if in compensation for his utterly insignificant life? But so it happened, and our poor story unexpectedly gains a fantastic ending.

A rumor suddenly spread through St. Petersburg, that a dead man had taken to appearing on the Kalinkin Bridge, and its vicinity, at night in the form of an official seeking a stolen cloak, and that, under the pretext of its being the stolen cloak, he dragged, without regard to rank or calling, every one's cloak from his shoulders, be it cat-skin, beaver, fox, bear, sable, in a word, every sort of fur and skin which men adopted for their covering. One of the department officials saw the dead man with his own eyes, and immediately recognised in him Akaky Akakiyevich. This, however, inspired him with such terror, that he ran off with all his might, and therefore did not scan the dead man closely, but only saw how the latter threatened him from afar with his finger. Constant complaints poured in from all quarters, that the backs and shoulders, not only of titular but even of court councillors, were exposed to the danger of a cold, on account of the frequent dragging off of their cloaks.

Arrangements were made by the police to catch the corpse, alive or dead, at any cost, and punish him as an example to others, in the most severe manner. In this they nearly succeeded, for a watchman, on guard in Kirinshkin Lane, caught the corpse by the collar on the very scene of his evil deeds, when attempting to pull off the frieze cloak of a retired musician. Having seized him by the collar, he summoned, with a shout, two of his comrades, whom he enjoined to hold him fast, while he himself felt for a moment in his boot, in order to draw out his snuff-box, and refresh his frozen nose. But the snuff was of a sort which even a corpse could not endure. The watchman having closed his right nostril with his finger, had no sooner succeeded in holding half a handful up to the left, than the corpse sneezed so violently that he completely filled the eyes of all three. While they raised their hands to wipe them, the dead man vanished completely, so that they positively did not know whether they had actually had him in their grip at all. Thereafter the watchmen conceived such a terror of dead men that they were afraid even to seize the living, and only screamed from a distance. "Hey, there! go your way!" So the dead official began to appear even beyond the Kalinkin Bridge, causing no little terror to all timid people.

But we have totally neglected that certain prominent personage who may really be considered as the cause of the fantastic turn taken by this true history. First of all, justice compels us to say, that after the departure of poor, annihilated Akaky Akakiyevich, he felt something like remorse. Suffering was unpleasant to him, for his heart was accessible to many good impulses, in spite of the fact that his rank often prevented his showing his true self. As soon as his friend had left his cabinet, he began to think about poor Akaky Akakiyevich. And from that day forth, poor Akaky Akakiyevich, who could not bear up under an official reprimand, recurred to his mind almost every day. The thought troubled him to such an extent, that a week later he even resolved to send an official to him, to learn whether he really could assist him. And when it was reported to him that Akaky Akakiyevich had died suddenly of fever, he was startled, hearkened to the reproaches of his conscience, and was out of sorts for the whole day.

Wishing to divert his mind in some way and drive away the disagreeable impression, he set out that evening for one of his friends' houses, where he found quite a large party assembled. What was better, nearly every one was of the same rank as himself, so that he need not feel in the least constrained. This had a marvellous effect upon his mental state. He grew expansive, made himself agreeable in conversation, in short, he passed a delightful evening. After supper he drank a couple of glasses of champagne — not a bad recipe for cheerfulness, as every one knows. The champagne inclined him to various adventures, and he determined not to return home, but to go and see a certain well-known lady, of German extraction, Karolina Ivanovna, a lady, it appears, with whom he was on a very friendly footing.

It must be mentioned that the prominent personage was no longer a young man, but a good husband and respected father of a family. Two sons, one of whom was already in the service, and a good-looking, sixteen-year-old daughter, with a slightly arched but pretty little nose, came every morning to kiss his hand and say, "*Bon jour*, papa." His wife, a still fresh and good-looking woman, first gave him her hand to kiss, and then, reversing the procedure, kissed his. But the prominent personage, though perfectly satisfied in his domestic relations, considered it stylish to have a friend in another quarter of the city. This friend was scarcely prettier or younger than his wife; but there are such puzzles in the world, and it is not our place to judge them. So the important personage descended the stairs, stepped into his sledge, said to the coachman, "To Karolina Ivanovna's," and, wrapping himself luxuriously in his warm cloak, found himself in that delightful frame of mind than which a Russian can conceive nothing better, namely, when you think of nothing yourself, yet when the thoughts creep into your mind of their own accord, each more agreeable than the other, giving you no trouble either to drive them away, or seek them. Fully satisfied, he recalled all the gay features of the evening just passed and all the

mots which had made the little circle laugh. Many of them he repeated in a low voice, and found them quite as funny as before; so it is not surprising that he should laugh heartily at them. Occasionally, however, he was interrupted by gusts of wind, which, coming suddenly, God knows whence or why, cut his face, drove masses of snow into it, filled out his cloak-collar like a sail, or suddenly blew it over his head with supernatural force, and thus caused him constant trouble to disentangle himself.

Suddenly the important personage felt some one clutch him firmly by the collar. Turning round, he perceived a man of short stature, in an old, worn uniform, and recognised, not without terror, Akaky Akakiyevich. The official's face was white as snow, and looked just like a corpse's. But the horror of the important personage transcended all bounds when he saw the dead man's mouth open, and heard it utter the following remarks, while it breathed upon him the terrible odor of the grave: "Ah, here you are at last! I have you, that — by the collar! I need your cloak. You took no trouble about mine, but reprimanded me. So now give up your own."

The pallid prominent personage almost died of fright. Brave as he was in the office and in the presence of inferiors generally, and although, at the sight of his manly form and appearance, every one said, "Ugh! how much character he has!" at this crisis, he, like many possessed of an heroic exterior, experienced such terror, that, not without cause, he began to fear an attack of illness. He flung his cloak hastily from his shoulders and shouted to his coachman in an unnatural voice, "Home at full speed!" The coachman, hearing the tone which is generally employed at critical moments, and even accompanied by something much more tangible, drew his head down between his shoulders in case of an emergency, flourished his whip, and flew on like an arrow. In a little more than six minutes the prominent personage was at the entrance of his own house. Pale, thoroughly scared, and cloakless, he went home instead of to Karolina Ivanovna's, reached his room somehow or other, and passed the night in the direst distress; so that the next morning over their tea, his daughter said, "You are very pale to-day, papa." But papa remained silent, and said not a word to any one of what had happened to him, where he had been, or where he had intended to go.

This occurrence made a deep impression upon him. He even began to say, "How dare you? Do you realise who is standing before you?" less frequently to the under-officials, and, if he did utter the words, it was only after first having learned the bearings of the matter. But the most noteworthy point was, that from that day forward the apparition of the dead official ceased to be seen. Evidently the prominent personage's cloak just fitted his shoulders. At all events, no more instances of his dragging cloaks from people's shoulders were heard of. But many active and solicitous persons could by no means reassure themselves, and asserted that the dead official still showed himself in distant parts of the city.

In fact, one watchman in Kolomen saw with his own eyes the apparition come from behind a house. But the watchman was not a strong man, so he was afraid to arrest him, and followed him in the dark, until, at length, the apparition looked round, paused, and inquired, "What do you want?" at the same time showing such a fist as is never seen on living men. The watchman said, "Nothing," and turned back instantly. But the apparition was much too tall, wore huge moustaches, and, directing its steps apparently towards the Obukhov Bridge, disappeared in the darkness of the night.

Ivan Turgenev · 1818–1883

Ivan Sergeyevich Turgenev ranks with Gogol, Tolstoy, and Dostoevsky among the great short story writers and novelists of nineteenth-century Russia. Like the other three, Turgenev wrote of social and political conditions in Russia, of the position of the serf, of the injustices of the bureaucracy, of the early revolutionary rumblings which, a few decades later, resulted in the overthrow of the Tsarist régime. Like them, he wrote realistically. But Turgenev's writing is distinguishable from the work of these others on two counts: his life in Berlin and Paris kept him somewhat remote from the actual scene he portrayed. Furthermore, his realism is somewhat more poetic, more lyrical, than that of the other three. Living in western Europe rather than in Russia, Turgenev saw his work accepted by Europeans at a time when the popularity of other Russian writers was largely restricted to their native country. Turgenev lays emphasis on atmosphere, on simplicity of style, is somewhat more insistent than the other three on the values of landscape and setting. He selected his language, he used a more purified diction than Gogol and the others. He portrayed, perhaps as completely as it can be portrayed by one man, the soul of the Russian of his century.

Turgenev, born at Oryol, in Russia, on October 28, 1818, was educated in Moscow, St. Petersburg, and Berlin. For a short period the novelist served as a government official, but gave this up, to the disgust of his mother, to follow the more precarious life of an author. Because of the liberalism of some of his early work, he was restricted to residence on his own estate for a period of several years. Shortly after this exile within his own country, Turgenev took up life abroad, in Berlin and Paris. In the latter city he became the friend of Flaubert.

Of Turgenev's many novels and stories perhaps the best known to readers outside of Russia are: *A Sportsman's Sketches* (1852), an early collection of short stories much concerned with the life of the serf; and the novels *On the Eve* (1860), *Fathers and Sons* (1862), *Smoke* (1867), and *Virgin Soil* (1877). Turgenev also wrote poems and plays.

SUGGESTED REFERENCES: Avrahm Yarmolinsky, *Turgenev: The Man, His Art, and His Age* (2nd ed., 1959); Richard Freeborn, *Turgenev: The Novelist's Novelist* (1960).

Mumu

Mumu illustrates several of Turgenev's more prominent qualities: his sympathy with the serf, his exposition of the cruelty of the nobles, his power to arouse pity. The story is reprinted from the book, *The Torrents of Spring*, as translated by Constance Garnett; by permission of the Macmillan Company.

In one of the outlying streets of Moscow, in a grey house with white columns and a balcony, warped all askew, there was once living a lady, a widow, surrounded by a numerous household of serfs. Her sons were in the government service at Petersburg; her daughters were married; she went out very little, and in solitude lived through the last years of her miserly and dreary old age. Her day, a joyless and gloomy day, had long been over; but the evening of her life was blacker than night.

Of all her servants, the most remarkable personage was the porter, Gerasim, a man full twelve inches over the normal height, of heroic build, and deaf and dumb from his birth. The lady, his owner, had brought him up from the village where he lived alone in a little hut, apart from his brothers, and was reckoned about the most punctual of her peasants in the payment of the seignorial dues. Endowed with extraordinary strength, he did the work of four men; work flew apace under his hands, and it was a pleasant sight to see him when he was ploughing, while, with his huge palms pressing hard upon the plough, he seemed alone, unaided by his poor horse, to cleave the yielding bosom of the earth, or when, about St. Peter's Day, he plied his scythe with a furious energy that might have mown a young birch copse up by the roots, or swiftly and untiringly wielded a flail over two yards long; while the hard oblong muscles of his shoulders rose and fell like a lever. His perpetual silence lent a solemn dignity to his unwearying labor. He was a splendid peasant, and, except for his affliction, any girl would have been glad to marry him. . . . But now they had taken Gerasim to Moscow, bought him boots, had him made a full-skirted coat for summer, a sheepskin for winter, put into his hand a broom and a spade, and appointed him porter.

At first he intensely disliked his new mode of life. From his childhood he had been used to field labor, to village life. Shut off by his affliction from the society of men, he had grown up, dumb and mighty, as a tree grows on a fruitful soil. When he was transported to the town, he could not understand what was being done with him; he was miserable and stupefied, with the stupefaction of some strong young bull, taken straight from the meadow, where the rich grass stood up to his belly, taken and put in the truck of a railway train, and there, while smoke and sparks and gusts of steam puff out upon the sturdy beast, he is whirled onwards, whirled along with loud roar and whistle, whither — God knows!

What Gerasim had to do in his new duties seemed a mere trifle to him after his hard toil as a peasant; in half-an-hour, all his work was done, and he would once more stand stock-still in the middle of the courtyard, staring open-mouthed at all the passers-by, as though trying to wrest from them the explanation of his perplexing position; or he would suddenly go off into some corner, and flinging a long way off the broom or the spade,

throw himself on his face on the ground, and lie for hours together without stirring, like a caged beast. But man gets used to anything, and Gerasim got used at last to living in town. He had little work to do; his whole duty consisted in keeping the courtyard clean, bringing in a barrel of water twice a day, splitting and dragging in wood for the kitchen and the house, keeping out strangers, and watching at night. And it must be said he did his duty zealously. In his courtyard there was never a shaving lying about, never a speck of dust; if sometimes, in the muddy season, the wretched nag, put under his charge for fetching water, got stuck in the road, he would simply give it a shove with his shoulder, and set not only the cart but the horse itself moving. If he set to chopping wood, the axe fairly rang like glass, and chips and chunks flew in all directions. And as for strangers, after he had one night caught two thieves and knocked their heads together — knocked them so that there was not the slightest need to take them to the police-station afterwards — every one in the neighborhood began to feel a great respect for him; even those who came in the day-time, by no means robbers, but simply unknown persons, at the sight of the terrible porter, waved and shouted to him as though he could hear their shouts. With all the rest of the servants, Gerasim was on terms, hardly friendly — they were afraid of him — but familiar; he regarded them as his fellows. They explained themselves to him by signs, and he understood them, and exactly carried out all orders, but knew his own rights too, and soon no one dared to take his seat at the table. Gerasim was altogether of a strict and serious temper, he liked order in everything; even the cocks did not dare to fight in his presence, or woe betide them! directly he caught sight of them, he would seize them by the legs, swing them ten times round in the air like a wheel, and throw them in different directions. There were geese, too, kept in the yard; but the goose, as is well known, is a dignified and reasonable bird; Gerasim felt a respect for them, looked after them, and fed them; he was himself not unlike a gander of the steppes. He was assigned a little garret over the kitchen; he arranged it himself to his own liking, made a bedstead in it of oak boards on four stumps of wood for legs — a truly Titanic bedstead; one might have put a ton or two on it — it would not have bent under the load; under the bed was a solid chest; in a corner stood a little table of the same strong kind, and near the table a three-legged stool, so solid and squat that Gerasim himself would sometimes pick it up and drop it again with a smile of delight. The garret was locked up by means of a padlock that looked like a kalatch or basket-shaped loaf, only black; the key of this padlock Gerasim always carried about him in his girdle. He did not like people to come to his garret.

So passed a year, at the end of which a little incident befell Gerasim.

The old lady, in whose service he lived as porter, adhered in everything to the ancient ways, and kept a large number of servants. In her house were not only laundresses, sempstresses, carpenters, tailors and tailoresses, there was even a harness-maker — he was reckoned as a veterinary surgeon, too — and a doctor for the servants; there was a household doctor for the mistress; there was, lastly, a shoemaker, by name Kapiton Klimov, a sad drunkard. Klimov regarded himself as an injured creature, whose merits were unappreciated, a culti-vated man from Petersburg, who ought not to be living in Moscow without occupation — in the wilds, so to speak; and if he drank, as he himself expressed it emphatically, with a blow on his chest, it was sorrow drove him to it. So one day his mistress had a conversation about him with her head steward, Gavrila, a man whom, judging solely from his little yellow eyes and nose like a duck's beak, fate itself, it seemed, had marked out as a person in authority. The lady expressed her regret at the corruption of the morals of Kapiton, who had, only the evening before, been picked up somewhere in the street.

"Now, Gavrila," she observed, all of a sudden, "now, if we were to marry him, what do you think, perhaps he would be steadier?"

"Why not marry him, indeed, 'm? He could be married, 'm," answered Gavrila, "and it would be a very good thing, to be sure, 'm."

"Yes; only who is to marry him?"

"Ay, 'm. But that's at your pleasure, 'm. He may, any way, so to say, be wanted for something; he can't be turned adrift altogether."

"I fancy he likes Tatiana."

Gavrila was on the point of making some reply, but he shut his lips tightly.

"Yes!... let him marry Tatiana," the lady de-cided, taking a pinch of snuff complacently. "Do you hear?"

"Yes, 'm," Gavrila articulated, and he withdrew.

Returning to his own room (it was in a little lodge, and was almost filled up with metal-bound trunks), Gavrila first sent his wife away, and then sat down at the window and pondered. His mistress's unexpected arrangement had clearly put him in a difficulty. At last he got up and sent to call Kapiton. Kapiton made his appearance. ... But before reporting their conversation to the reader, we consider it not out of place to relate in few words who was this Tatiana, whom it was to be Kapiton's lot to marry, and why the great lady's order had disturbed the steward.

Tatiana, one of the laundresses referred to above (as a trained and skilful laundress she was in charge of the fine linen only), was a woman of twenty-eight, thin, fair-haired, with moles on her left cheek. Moles on the left cheek are regarded as of evil omen in Russia — a token of unhappy life.... Tatiana could not boast of her good luck. From her earliest youth she had been badly treated; she had done the work of two, and had never known affection; she had been poorly clothed and had re-ceived the smallest wages. Relations she had practically none; an uncle she had once had, a butler, left behind in the country as useless, and other uncles of hers were peasants — that was all. At one time she had passed for a beauty, but her good looks were very soon over. In disposition she was very meek, or, rather, scared; towards herself, she felt perfect indifference; of others, she stood in mortal dread; she thought of nothing but how to get her work done in good time, never talked to any one, and trembled at the very name of her mistress, though the latter scarcely knew her by sight. When Gerasim was brought from the country, she was ready to die with fear on seeing his huge figure, tried all she could to avoid meeting him, even dropped her eyelids when some-times she chanced to run past him, hurrying from the house to the laundry. Gerasim at first paid no special attention to her, then he used to smile when she came his way, then he began even to stare admiringly at her, and at last he never took his eyes off her. She took his fancy, whether by the mild expression of her face or the timidity of her movements, who can tell? So one day she was stealing across the yard, with a starched dressing-jacket of her mistress's carefully poised on her outspread fingers ... some one suddenly grasped her vigorously by the elbow; she turned round and fairly screamed; behind her stood Gerasim. With a foolish smile, making inarticulate caressing grunts, he held out to her a gingerbread cock with gold tinsel on his tail and wings. She was about to refuse it, but he thrust it forcibly into her hand, shook his head, walked away, and turning round, once more grunted something very affectionately to her. From that day forward he gave her no peace; wherever she went, he was on the spot at once, coming to meet her, smiling, grunting, waving his hands; all at once he would pull a ribbon out of the bosom of his smock and put it in her hand, or would sweep the dust out of her way. The poor girl simply did not know how to behave or what to do. Soon the whole household knew of the dumb porter's wiles; jeers, jokes, sly hints were showered upon Tatiana. At Gerasim, however, it was not every one who would dare to scoff; he did not like jokes; indeed, in his presence, she, too, was left in peace. Whether she liked it or not, the girl found herself to be under his protection. Like all deaf-mutes, he was very suspicious, and very readily perceived when they were laughing at him or at her. One day, at dinner, the wardrobe-keeper, Tatiana's superior, fell to nagging, as it is called, at her, and brought the poor thing to such a state that she did not know where to look, and was almost crying with vexation. Gerasim got up all of a sudden, stretched out his gigantic hand, laid it on the wardrobe-maid's head, and looked into her face with such grim ferocity that her head positively flopped upon the table. Every one was still. Gerasim took up his spoon again and went on with his cabbage-soup. "Look at him, the dumb devil, the wood-demon!" they all muttered in undertones, while the wardrobe-maid got up and went out into the maids' room. Another time, noticing that Kapiton — the same Kapiton who was the subject of the conversation reported above — was gossiping somewhat too attentively with Tatiana, Gerasim beckoned him to him, led him into the cartshed, and taking up a shaft that was standing in a corner by one end, lightly, but most significantly, menaced him with it. Since then no one addressed a word to Tatiana. And all this cost him nothing. It is true the wardrobe-maid, as soon as she reached the maids' room, promptly fell into a fainting-fit, and behaved altogether so skilfully that Gerasim's rough action reached his mistress's knowledge the same day. But the capricious old lady only laughed, and several times, to the great offence of the wardrobe-maid, forced her to repeat "how he bent your head down with his heavy hand," and next day she sent Gerasim a rouble. She looked on him with favor as a strong and faithful watchman. Gerasim stood in considerable awe of her, but, all the same, he had hopes of her favor, and was preparing to go to her with a petition for leave to marry Tatiana. He was only waiting for a new coat, promised him by the steward, to present a proper appearance before his mistress, when this same mistress suddenly took it into her head to marry Tatiana to Kapiton.

The reader will now readily understand the perturbation of mind that overtook the steward Gavrila after his conversation with his mistress. "My lady," he thought, as he sat at the window, "favors Gerasim, to be sure" — (Gavrila was well aware of this, and that was why he himself looked on him with an indulgent eye) — "still he is a speechless creature. I could not, indeed, put it before the mistress that Gerasim's courting Tatiana. But, after all, it's true enough; he's a queer sort of husband. But on the other hand, that devil, God forgive me, has only got to find out they're marrying Tatiana to Kapiton, he'll smash up everything in the house, 'pon my soul! There's no reasoning with him; why, he's such a devil, God forgive my sins, there's no getting over him nohow ... 'pon my soul!"

Kapiton's entrance broke the thread of Gavrila's reflections. The dissipated shoemaker came in, his hands behind him, and lounging carelessly against a projecting angle of the wall, near the door, crossed his right foot in front of his left, and tossed his head, as much as to say, "What do you want?"

Gavrila looked at Kapiton, and drummed with his fingers on the windowframe. Kapiton merely screwed up his leaden eyes a little, but he did not look down, he even grinned slightly, and passed his hand over his whitish locks which were sticking up in all directions. "Well, here I am. What is it?"

"You're a pretty fellow," said Gavrila, and paused. "A pretty fellow you are, there's no denying!"

Kapiton only twitched his little shoulders. "Are you any better, pray?" he thought to himself.

"Just look at yourself, now, look at yourself," Gavrila went on reproachfully; "now, what ever do you look like?"

Kapiton serenely surveyed his shabby tattered coat, and his patched trousers, and with special attention stared at his burst boots, especially the one on the tip-toe of which his right foot so gracefully poised, and he fixed his eyes again on the steward.

"Well?"

"Well?" repeated Gavrila. "Well? And then you say well? You look like old Nick himself, God forgive my saying so, that's what you look like."

Kapiton blinked rapidly.

"Go on abusing me, go on, if you like, Gavrila Andreitch," he thought to himself again.

"Here you've been drunk again," Gavrila began, "drunk again, haven't you? Eh? Come, answer me!"

"Owing to the weakness of my health, I have exposed myself to spirituous beverages, certainly," replied Kapiton.

"Owing to the weakness of your health! ... They let you off too easy, that's what it is; and you've been apprenticed in Petersburg. ... Much you learned in your apprenticeship! You simply eat your bread in idleness."

"In that matter, Gavrila Andreitch, there is one to judge me, the Lord God Himself, and no one else. He also knows what manner of man I be in this world, and whether I eat my bread in idleness. And as concerning your contention regarding drunkenness, in that matter, too, I am not to blame, but rather a friend; he led me into temptation, but was diplomatic and got away, while I..."

"While you were left, like a goose, in the street. Ah, you're a dissolute fellow! But that's not the point," the steward went on. "I've something to tell you. Our lady..." here he paused a minute, "it's our lady's pleasure that you should be married. Do you hear? She imagines you may be steadier when you're married. Do you understand?"

"To be sure I do."

"Well, then. For my part I think it would be better to give you a good hiding. But there — it's her business. Well? are you agreeable?"

Kapiton grinned.

"Matrimony is an excellent thing for any one, Gavrila Andreitch; and, as far as I am concerned, I shall be quite agreeable."

"Very well, then," replied Gavrila, while he reflected to himself: "There's no denying the man expresses himself very properly. Only there's one thing," he pursued aloud: "the wife our lady's picked out for you is an unlucky choice."

"Why, who is she, permit me to inquire?"

"Tatiana."

"Tatiana?"

And Kapiton opened his eyes, and moved a little away from the wall.

"Well, what are you in such a taking for?... Isn't she to your taste, hey?"

"Not to my taste, do you say, Gavrila Andreitch! She's right enough, a hardworking steady girl.... But you know very well yourself, Gavrila Andreitch, why that fellow, that wild man of the woods, that monster of the steppes, he's after her, you know...."

"I know, mate, I know all about it," the butler cut him short in a tone of annoyance: "but there, you see..."

"But upon my soul, Gavrila Andreitch! why, he'll kill me, by God, he will, he'll crush me like some fly; why, he's got a fist — why, you kindly look yourself what a fist he's got; why, he's simply got a fist like Minin Pozharsky's. You see he's deaf, he beats and does not hear how he's beating! He swings his great fists, as if he's asleep. And there's no possibility of pacifying him; and for why? Why, because, as you know yourself, Gavrila Andreitch, he's deaf, and what's more, has

no more wit than the heel of my foot. Why, he's a sort of beast, a heathen idol, Gavrila Andreitch, and worse... a block of wood; what have I done that I should have to suffer from him now? Sure it is, it's all over with me now; I've knocked about, I've had enough to put up with, I've been battered like an earthenware pot, but still I'm a man, after all, and not a worthless pot."

"I know, I know, don't go talking away...."

"Lord, my God!" the shoemaker continued warmly, "when is the end? when, O Lord! A poor wretch I am, a poor wretch whose sufferings are endless! What a life, what a life mine's been, come to think of it! In my young days, I was beaten by a German I was 'prentice to; in the prime of life beaten by my own countrymen, and last of all, in ripe years, see what I have been brought to...."

"Ugh, you flabby soul!" said Gavrila Andreitch. "Why do you make so many words about it?"

"Why, do you say, Gavrila Andreitch? It's not a beating I'm afraid of, Gavrila Andreitch. A gentleman may chastise me in private, but give me a civil word before folks, and I'm a man still; but see now, whom I've to do with...."

"Come, get along," Gavrila interposed impatiently. Kapiton turned away and staggered off.

"But, if it were not for him," the steward shouted after him, "you would consent for your part?"

"I signify my acquiescence," retorted Kapiton as he disappeared.

His fine language did not desert him, even in the most trying positions.

The steward walked several times up and down the room.

"Well, call Tatiana now," he said at last.

A few instants later, Tatiana had come up almost noiselessly, and was standing in the doorway.

"What are your orders, Gavrila Andreitch?" she said in a soft voice.

The steward looked at her intently.

"Well, Taniusha," he said, "would you like to be married? Our lady has chosen a husband for you."

"Yes, Gavrila Andreitch. And whom has she deigned to name as a husband for me?" she added falteringly.

"Kapiton, the shoemaker."

"Yes, sir."

"He's a feather-brained fellow, that's certain. But it's just for that the mistress reckons upon you."

"Yes, sir."

"There's one difficulty... you know the deaf

man, Gerasim, he's courting you, you see. How
did you come to bewitch such a bear? But you
see, he'll kill you, very like, he's such a bear...."

"He'll kill me, Gavrila Andreitch, he'll kill me,
and no mistake."

"Kill you.... Well, we shall see about that.
What do you mean by saying he'll kill you? Has
he any right to kill you? Tell me yourself."

"I don't know, Gavrila Andreitch, about his
having any right or not."

"What a woman! why, you've made him no
promise, I suppose...."

"What are you pleased to ask of me?"

The steward was silent for a little, thinking,
"You're a meek soul!" "Well, that's right," he
said aloud; "we'll have another talk with you later;
now you can go, Taniusha; I see you're not unruly,
certainly."

Tatiana turned, steadied herself a little against
the doorpost, and went away.

"And, perhaps, our lady will forget all about
this wedding by to-morrow," thought the steward;
"and here am I worrying myself for nothing! As
for that insolent fellow, we must tie him down, if
it comes to that, we must let the police know..."
"Ustinya Fyedorovna!" he shouted in a loud voice
to his wife, "heat the samovar, my good soul...."
All that day Tatiana hardly went out of the laundry. At first she had started crying, then she
wiped away her tears, and set to work as before.
Kapiton stayed till late at night at the ginshop
with a friend of his, a man of gloomy appearance,
to whom he related in detail how he used to live
in Petersburg with a gentleman, who would have
been all right, except he was a bit too strict, and
he had a slight weakness besides, he was too fond
of drink; and, as to the fair sex, he didn't stick
at anything. His gloomy companion merely said
yes; but when Kapiton announced at last that, in
a certain event, he would have to lay hands on
himself to-morrow, his gloomy companion remarked that it was bedtime. And they parted in
surly silence.

Meanwhile, the steward's anticipations were not
fulfilled. The old lady was so much taken up
with the idea of Kapiton's wedding, that even in
the night she talked of nothing else to one of her
companions, who was kept in her house solely to
entertain her in case of sleeplessness, and, like a
night cabman, slept in the day. When Gavrila
came to her after morning tea with his report, her
first question was: "And how about our wedding —
is it getting on all right?" He replied, of course,
that it was getting on first rate, and that Kapiton
would appear before her to pay his reverence to
her that day. The old lady was not quite well;

she did not give much time to business. The
steward went back to his own room, and called a
council. The matter certainly called for serious
consideration. Tatiana would make no difficulty,
of course; but Kapiton had declared in the hearing
of all that he had but one head to lose, not two or
three.... Gerasim turned rapid sullen looks on
every one, would not budge from the steps of the
maids' quarters, and seemed to guess that some
mischief was being hatched against him. They
met together. Among them was an old sideboard
waiter, nicknamed Uncle Tail, to whom every one
looked respectfully for counsel, though all they
got out of him was, "Here's a pretty pass! to be
sure, to be sure, to be sure!" As a preliminary
measure of security, to provide against contin-
gencies, they locked Kapiton up in the lumber-
room where the filter was kept; then considered
the question with the gravest deliberation. It
would, to be sure, be easy to have recourse to force.
But Heaven save us! there would be an uproar,
the mistress would be put out — it would be awful!
What should they do? They thought and thought,
and at last thought out a solution. It had many
a time been observed that Gerasim could not bear
drunkards.... As he sat at the gates, he would
always turn away with disgust when some one
passed by intoxicated, with unsteady steps and
his cap on one side of his ear. They resolved that
Tatiana should be instructed to pretend to be
tipsy, and should pass by Gerasim staggering and
reeling about. The poor girl refused for a long
while to agree to this, but they persuaded her at
last; she saw, too, that it was the only possible
way of getting rid of her adorer. She went out.
Kapiton was released from the lumber-room; for,
after all, he had an interest in the affair. Gerasim
was sitting on the curb-stone at the gates, scraping
the ground with a spade.... From behind every
corner, from behind every window-blind, the others
were watching him.... The trick succeeded beyond
all expectations. On seeing Tatiana, at first, he
nodded as usual, making caressing, inarticulate
sounds; then he looked carefully at her, dropped
his spade, jumped up, went up to her, brought his
face close to her face.... In her fright she staggered more than ever, and shut her eyes.... He
took her by the arm, whirled her right across the
yard, and going into the room where the council
had been sitting, pushed her straight at Kapiton.
Tatiana fairly swooned away.... Gerasim stood,
looked at her, waved his hand, laughed, and went
off, stepping heavily, to his garret.... For the next
twenty-four hours, he did not come out of it. The
postillion Antipka said afterwards that he saw
Gerasim through a crack in the wall, sitting on his

bedstead, his face in his hand. From time to time he uttered soft regular sounds; he was wailing a dirge, that is, swaying backwards and forwards with his eyes shut, and shaking his head as drivers or bargemen do when they chant their melancholy songs. Antipka could not bear it, and he came away from the crack. When Gerasim came out of the garret next day, no particular change could be observed in him. He only seemed, as it were, more morose, and took not the slightest notice of Tatiana or Kapiton. The same evening, they both had to appear before their mistress with geese under their arms, and in a week's time they were married. Even on the day of the wedding Gerasim showed no change of any sort in his behavior. Only, he came back from the river without water, he had somehow broken the barrel on the road; and at night, in the stable, he washed and rubbed down his horse so vigorously, that it swayed like a blade of grass in the wind, and staggered from one leg to the other under his fists of iron.

All this had taken place in the spring. Another year passed by, during which Kapiton became a hopeless drunkard, and as being absolutely of no use for anything, was sent away with the store waggons to a distant village with his wife. On the day of his departure, he put a very good face on it at first, and declared that he would always be at home, send him where they would, even to the other end of the world; but later on he lost heart, began grumbling that he was being taken to uneducated people, and collapsed so completely at last that he could not even put his own hat on. Some charitable soul stuck it on his forehead, set the peak straight in front, and thrust it on with a slap from above. When everything was quite ready, and the peasants already held the reins in their hands, and were only waiting for the words "With God's blessing!" to start, Gerasim came out of his garret, went up to Tatiana, and gave her as a parting present a red cotton handkerchief he had bought for her a year ago. Tatiana, who had up to that instant borne all the revolting details of her life with great indifference, could not control herself upon that; she burst into tears, and as she took her seat in the cart, she kissed Gerasim three times like a good Christian. He meant to accompany her as far as the town-barrier, and did walk beside her cart for a while, but he stopped suddenly at the Crimean ford, waved his hand, and walked away along the riverside.

It was getting towards evening. He walked slowly, watching the water. All of a sudden he fancied something was floundering in the mud close to the bank. He stooped over, and saw a little white-and-black puppy, who, in spite of all its efforts, could not get out of the water; it was struggling, slipping back, and trembling all over its thin wet little body. Gerasim looked at the unlucky little dog, picked it up with one hand, put it into the bosom of his coat, and hurried with long steps homewards. He went into his garret, put the rescued puppy on his bed, covered it with his thick overcoat, ran first to the stable for straw, and then to the kitchen for a cup of milk. Carefully folding back the overcoat, and spreading out the straw, he set the milk on the bedstead. The poor little puppy was not more than three weeks old, its eyes were only just open — one eye still seemed rather larger than the other; it did not know how to lap out of a cup, and did nothing but shiver and blink. Gerasim took hold of its head softly with two fingers, and dipped its little nose into the milk. The pup suddenly began lapping greedily, sniffing, shaking itself, and choking. Gerasim watched and watched it, and all at once he laughed outright. ... All night long he was waiting on it, keeping it covered, and rubbing it dry. He fell asleep himself at last, and slept quietly and happily by its side.

No mother could have looked after her baby as Gerasim looked after his little nursling. At first, she — for the pup turned out to be a bitch — was very weak, feeble, and ugly, but by degrees she grew stronger and improved in looks, and thanks to the unflagging care of her preserver, in eight months' time she was transformed into a very pretty dog of the spaniel breed, with long ears, a bushy spiral tail, and large expressive eyes. She was devotedly attached to Gerasim, and was never a yard from his side; she always followed him about wagging her tail. He had even given her a name — the dumb know that their inarticulate noises call the attention of others. He called her Mumu. All the servants in the house liked her, and called her Mumu, too. She was very intelligent, she was friendly with every one, but was only fond of Gerasim. Gerasim, on his side, loved her passionately, and he did not like it when other people stroked her; whether he was afraid for her, or jealous — God knows! She used to wake him in the morning, pulling at his coat; she used to take the reins in her mouth, and bring him up the old horse that carried the water, with whom she was on very friendly terms. With a face of great importance, she used to go with him to the river; she used to watch his brooms and spades, and never allowed any one to go into his garret. He cut a little hole in his door on purpose for her, and she seemed to feel that only in Gerasim's garret she was completely mistress and at home; and directly she went in, she used to jump with a satisfied air upon the bed. At night she did not sleep at all, but she never barked without sufficient cause, like some stupid house-dog, who, sitting on its hind-legs, blinking, with its nose in the air, barks simply from dulness, at the stars, usually three times in succession. No! Mumu's delicate little voice was never raised without good reason; either some stranger was passing close to the fence, or there was some suspicious sound or rustle somewhere.... In fact, she was an excellent watchdog. It is true that there was another dog in the yard, a tawny old dog with brown spots, called Wolf, but he was never, even at night, let off the chain; and, indeed, he was so decrepit that he did not even wish for freedom. He used to lie curled up in his kennel, and only rarely uttered a sleepy, almost noiseless bark, which broke off at once, as though he were himself aware of its uselessness. Mumu never went into the mistress's house; and when Gerasim carried wood into the rooms, she always stayed behind, impatiently waiting for him at the steps, pricking up her ears and turning her head to right and to left at the slightest creak of the door....

So passed another year. Gerasim went on performing his duties as house-porter, and was very well content with his lot, when suddenly an unexpected incident occurred.... One fine summer day the old lady was walking up and down the drawing-room with her dependants. She was in high spirits; she laughed and made jokes. Her servile companions laughed and joked too, but they did not feel particularly mirthful; the household did not much like it, when their mistress was in a lively mood, for, to begin with, she expected from every one prompt and complete participation in her merriment, and was furious if any one showed a face that did not beam with delight, and secondly, these outbursts never lasted long with her, and were usually followed by a sour and gloomy mood. That day she had got up in a lucky hour; at cards she took the four knaves, which means the fulfilment of one's wishes (she used to try her fortune on the cards every morning), and her tea struck her as particularly delicious, for which her maid was rewarded by words of praise, and by twopence in money. With a sweet smile on her wrinkled lips, the lady walked about the drawing-room and went up to the window. A flower-garden had been laid out before the window, and in the very middle bed, under a rose-bush, lay Mumu busily gnawing a bone. The lady caught sight of her.

"Mercy on us!" she cried suddenly; "what dog is that?"

The companion, addressed by the old lady, hesitated, poor thing, in that wretched state of uneasiness which is common in any person in a dependent position who doesn't know very well what significance to give to the exclamation of a superior.

"I d...d...don't know," she faltered: "I fancy it's the dumb man's dog."

"Mercy!" the lady cut her short: "but it's a charming little dog! order it to be brought in. Has he had it long? How is it I've never seen it before?... Order it to be brought in."

The companion flew at once into the hall.

"Boy, boy!" she shouted: "bring Mumu in at once! She's in the flower-garden."

"Her name's Mumu then," observed the lady: "a very nice name."

"Oh, very, indeed!" chimed in the companion. "Make haste, Stepan!"

Stepan, a sturdily-built young fellow, whose duties were those of a footman, rushed head-long into the flower-garden, and tried to capture Mumu, but she cleverly slipped from his fingers, and with her tail in the air, fled full speed to Gerasim, who was at that instant in the kitchen, knocking out and cleaning a barrel, turning it upside down in his hands like a child's drum. Stepan ran after her, and tried to catch her just at her master's feet; but the sensible dog would not let a stranger touch her, and with a bound, she got away. Gerasim looked on with a smile at all this ado; at last, Stepan got up, much amazed, and hurriedly explained to him by signs that the mistress wanted the dog brought in to her. Gerasim was a little astonished; he called Mumu, however, picked her up, and handed her over to Stepan. Stepan carried her into the drawing-room, and put her down on the parquette floor. The old lady began calling the dog to her in a coaxing voice. Mumu, who had never in her life been in such magnificent apartments, was very much frightened, and made a rush for the door, but, being driven back by the obsequious Stepan, she began trembling, and huddled close up against the wall.

"Mumu, Mumu, come to me, come to your mistress," said the lady; "come, silly thing... don't be afraid."

"Come, Mumu, come to the mistress," repeated the companions. "Come along!"

But Mumu looked round her uneasily, and did not stir.

"Bring her something to eat," said the old lady. "How stupid she is! she won't come to her mistress. What's she afraid of?"

"She's not used to your honor yet," ventured one of the companions in a timid and conciliatory voice.

Stepan brought in a saucer of milk, and set it down before Mumu, but Mumu would not even sniff at the milk, and still shivered, and looked round as before.

"Ah, what a silly you are!" said the lady, and going up to her, she stooped down, and was about to stroke her, but Mumu turned her head abruptly, and showed her teeth. The lady hurriedly drew back her hand....

A momentary silence followed. Mumu gave a faint whine, as though she would complain and apologise.... The old lady moved back, scowling. The dog's sudden movement had frightened her.

"Ah!" shrieked all the companions at once, "she's not bitten you, has she? Heaven forbid! (Mumu had never bitten any one in her life.) Ah! ah!"

"Take her away," said the old lady in a changed voice. "Wretched little dog! What a spiteful creature!"

And, turning round deliberately, she went towards her boudoir. Her companions looked timidly at one another, and were about to follow her, but she stopped, stared coldly at them, and said, "What's that for, pray? I've not called you," and went out.

The companions waved their hands to Stepan in despair. He picked up Mumu, and flung her promptly outside the door, just at Gerasim's feet, and half-an-hour later a profound stillness reigned in the house, and the old lady sat on her sofa looking blacker than a thunder-cloud.

What trifles, if you think of it, will sometimes disturb any one!

Till evening the lady was out of humor; she did not talk to any one, did not play cards, and passed a bad night. She fancied the eau-de-Cologne they gave her was not the same as she usually had, and that her pillow smelt of soap, and she made the wardrobe-maid smell all the bed linen — in fact she was very upset and cross altogether. Next morning she ordered Gavrila to be summoned an hour earlier than usual.

"Tell me, please," she began, directly the latter, not without some inward trepidation, crossed the threshold of her boudoir, "what dog was that barking all night in our yard? It wouldn't let me sleep!"

"A dog, 'm ... what dog, 'm ... may be, the dumb man's dog, 'm," he brought out in a rather unsteady voice.

"I don't know whether it was the dumb man's or whose, but it wouldn't let me sleep. And I wonder what we have such a lot of dogs for! I wish to know. We have a yard dog, haven't we?"

"Oh yes, 'm, we have, 'm. Wolf, 'm."

"Well, why more, what do we want more dogs for? It's simply introducing disorder. There's

no one in control in the house — that's what it is. And what does the dumb man want with a dog? Who gave him leave to keep dogs in my yard? Yesterday I went to the window, and there it was lying in the flower-garden; it had dragged in some nastiness it was gnawing, and my roses are planted there...."

The lady ceased.

"Let her be gone from to-day ... do you hear?"

"Yes, 'm."

"To-day. Now go. I will send for you later for the report."

Gavrila went away.

As he went through the drawing-room, the steward by way of maintaining order moved a bell from one table to another; he stealthily blew his duck-like nose in the hall, and went into the outer-hall. In the outer-hall, on a locker was Stepan asleep in the attitude of a slain warrior in a battalion picture, his bare legs thrust out below the coat which served him for a blanket. The steward gave him a shove, and whispered some instructions to him, to which Stepan responded with something between a yawn and a laugh. The steward went away, and Stepan got up, put on his coat and his boots, went out and stood on the steps. Five minutes had not passed before Gerasim made his appearance with a huge bundle of hewn logs on his back, accompanied by the inseparable Mumu. (The lady had given orders that her bedroom and boudoir should be heated at times even in the summer.) Gerasim turned sideways before the door, shoved it open with his shoulder, and staggered into the house with his load. Mumu, as usual, stayed behind to wait for him. Then Stepan, seizing his chance, suddenly pounced on her, like a kite on a chicken, held her down to the ground, gathered her up in his arms, and without even putting on his cap, ran out of the yard with her, got into the first fly he met, and galloped off to a market-place. There he soon found a purchaser, to whom he sold her for a shilling, on condition that he would keep her for at least a week tied up; then he returned at once. But before he got home, he got off the fly, and going right round the yard, jumped over the fence into the yard from a back street. He was afraid to go in at the gate for fear of meeting Gerasim.

His anxiety was unnecessary, however; Gerasim was no longer in the yard. On coming out of the house he had at once missed Mumu. He never remembered her failing to wait for his return, and began running up and down, looking for her, and calling her in his own way.... He rushed up to his garret, up to the hay-loft, ran out into the street, this way and that.... She was lost! He turned to the other serfs, with the most despairing signs, questioned them about her, pointing to her height from the ground, describing her with his hands.... Some of them really did not know what had become of Mumu, and merely shook their heads; others did know, and smiled to him for all response, while the steward assumed an important air, and began scolding the coachmen. Then Gerasim ran right away out of the yard.

It was dark by the time he came back. From his worn-out look, his unsteady walk, and his dusty clothes, it might be surmised that he had been running over half Moscow. He stood still opposite the windows of the mistress' house, took a searching look at the steps where a group of house-serfs were crowded together, turned away, and uttered once more his inarticulate "Mumu." Mumu did not answer. He went away. Every one looked after him, but no one smiled or said a word, and the inquisitive postillion Antipka reported next morning in the kitchen that the dumb man had been groaning all night.

All the next day Gerasim did not show himself, so that they were obliged to send the coachman Potap for water instead of him, at which the coachman Potap was anything but pleased. The lady asked Gavrila if her orders had been carried out. Gavrila replied that they had. The next morning Gerasim came out of his garret, and went about his work. He came in to his dinner, ate it, and went out again, without a greeting to any one. His face, which had always been lifeless, as with all deaf-mutes, seemed now to be turned to stone. After dinner he went out of the yard again, but not for long; he came back, and went straight up to the hay-loft. Night came on, a clear moonlight night. Gerasim lay breathing heavily, and incessantly turning from side to side. Suddenly he felt something pull at the skirt of his coat. He started, but did not raise his head, and even shut his eyes tighter. But again there was a pull, stronger than before; he jumped up... before him, with an end of string round her neck, was Mumu, twisting and turning. A prolonged cry of delight broke from his speechless breast; he caught up Mumu, and hugged her tight in his arms, she licked his nose and eyes, and beard and moustache, all in one instant.... He stood a little, thought a minute, crept cautiously down from the hay-loft, looked round, and having satisfied himself that no one could see him, made his way successfully to his garret. Gerasim had guessed before that his dog had not got lost by her own doing, that she must have been taken away by the mistress' orders; the servants had explained to him by signs that his

Mumu had snapped at her, and he determined to take his own measures. First he fed Mumu with a bit of bread, fondled her, and put her to bed, then he fell to meditating, and spent the whole night long in meditating how he could best conceal her. At last he decided to leave her all day in the garret, and only to come in now and then to see her, and to take her out at night. The hole in the door he stopped up effectually with his old overcoat, and almost before it was light he was already in the yard, as though nothing had happened, even — innocent guile! — the same expression of melancholy on his face. It did not even occur to the poor deaf man that Mumu would betray herself by her whining; in reality, every one in the house was soon aware that the dumb man's dog had come back, and was locked up in his garret, but from sympathy with him and with her, and partly, perhaps, from dread of him, they did not let him know that they had found out his secret. The steward scratched his head, and gave a despairing wave of his hand, as much as to say, "Well, well, God have mercy on him! If only it doesn't come to the mistress' ears!"

But the dumb man had never shown such energy as on that day; he cleaned and scraped the whole courtyard, pulled up every single weed with his own hand, tugged up every stake in the fence of the flower-garden, to satisfy himself that they were strong enough, and unaided drove them in again; in fact, he toiled and labored so that even the old lady noticed his zeal. Twice in the course of the day Gerasim went stealthily in to see his prisoner; when night came on, he lay down to sleep with her in the garret, not in the hay-loft, and only at two o'clock in the night he went out to take her a turn in the fresh air. After walking about the courtyard a good while with her, he was just turning back, when suddenly a rustle was heard behind the fence on the side of the back street. Mumu pricked up her ears, growled — went up to the fence, sniffed, and gave vent to a loud shrill bark. Some drunkard had thought fit to take refuge under the fence for the night. At that very time the old lady had just fallen asleep after a prolonged fit of "nervous agitation"; these fits of agitation always overtook her after too hearty a supper. The sudden bark waked her up: her heart palpitated, and she felt faint. "Girls, girls!" she moaned. "Girls!" The terrified maids ran into her bedroom. "Oh, oh, I am dying!" she said, flinging her arms about in her agitation. "Again, that dog again!... Oh, send for the doctor. They mean to be the death of me.... The dog, the dog again! Oh!" And she let her head fall back, which always signified a swoon. They rushed for the doctor, that is, for the household physician, Hariton. This doctor, whose whole qualification consisted in wearing soft-soled boots, knew how to feel the pulse delicately. He used to sleep fourteen hours out of the twenty-four, but the rest of the time he was always sighing, and continually dosing the old lady with cherrybay drops. This doctor ran up at once, fumigated the room with burnt feathers, and when the old lady opened her eyes, promptly offered her a wineglass of the hallowed drops on a silver tray. The old lady took them, but began again at once in a tearful voice complaining of the dog, of Gavrila, and of her fate, declaring that she was a poor old woman, and that every one had forsaken her, no one pitied her, everyone wished her dead. Meanwhile the luckless Mumu had gone on barking, while Gerasim tried in vain to call her away from the fence. "There ... there ... again," groaned the old lady, and once more she turned up the whites of her eyes. The doctor whispered to a maid, she rushed into the outer-hall, and shook Stepan, he ran to wake Gavrila, Gavrila in a fury ordered the whole household to get up.

Gerasim turned round, saw lights and shadows moving in the windows, and with an instinct of coming trouble in his heart, put Mumu under his arm, ran into his garret, and locked himself in. A few minutes later five men were banging at his door, but feeling the resistance of the bolt, they stopped. Gavrila ran up in a fearful state of mind, and ordered them all to wait there and watch till morning. Then he flew off himself to the maids' quarter, and through an old companion, Liubov Liubimovna, with whose assistance he used to steal tea, sugar, and other groceries and to falsify the accounts, sent word to the mistress that the dog had unhappily run back from somewhere, but that to-morrow she should be killed, and would the mistress be so gracious as not to be angry and to overlook it. The old lady would probably not have been so soon appeased, but the doctor had in his haste given her fully forty drops instead of twelve. The strong dose of narcotic acted; in a quarter of an hour the old lady was in a sound and peaceful sleep; while Gerasim was lying with a white face on his bed, holding Mumu's mouth tightly shut.

Next morning the lady woke up rather late. Gavrila was waiting till she should be awake, to give the order for a final assault on Gerasim's stronghold, while he prepared himself to face a fearful storm. But the storm did not come off. The old lady lay in bed and sent for the eldest of her dependent companions.

"Liubov Liubimovna," she began in a subdued weak voice — she was fond of playing the part of an oppressed and forsaken victim; needless to say, every one in the house was made extremely uncomfortable at such times — "Liubov Liubimovna, you see my position; go, my love to Gavrila Andreitch, and talk to him a little. Can he really prize some wretched cur above the repose — the very life — of his mistress? I could not bear to think so," she added, with an expression of deep feeling. "Go, my love; be so good as to go to Gavrila Andreitch for me."

Liubov Liubimovna went to Gavrila's room. What conversation passed between them is not known, but a short time after, a whole crowd of people was moving across the yard in the direction of Gerasim's garret. Gavrila walked in front, holding his cap on with his hand, though there was no wind. The footmen and cooks were close behind him; Uncle Tail was looking out of a window, giving instructions, that is to say, simply waving his hands. At the rear there was a crowd of small boys skipping and hopping along; half of them were outsiders who had run up. On the narrow staircase leading to the garret sat one guard; at the door were standing two more with sticks. They began to mount the stairs, which they entirely blocked up. Gavrila went up to the door, knocked with his fist, shouting, "Open the door!"

A stifled bark was audible, but there was no answer.

"Open the door, I tell you," he repeated.

"But, Gavrila Andreitch," Stepan observed from below, "he's deaf, you know — he doesn't hear."

They all laughed.

"What are we to do?" Gavrila rejoined from above.

"Why, there's a hole there in the door," answered Stepan, "so you shake the stick in there."

Gavrila bent down.

"He's stuffed it up with a coat or something."

"Well, you just push the coat in."

At this moment a smothered bark was heard again.

"See, see — she speaks for herself," was remarked in the crowd, and again they laughed.

Gavrila scratched his ear.

"No, mate," he responded at last, "you can poke the coat in yourself, if you like."

"All right, let me."

And Stepan scrambled up, took the stick, pushed in the coat, and began waving the stick about in the opening, saying, "Come out, come out!" as he did so. He was still waving the stick, when suddenly the door of the garret was flung open; all the crowd flew pell-mell down the stairs instantly, Gavrila first of all. Uncle Tail locked the window.

"Come, come, come," shouted Gavrila from the yard, "mind what you're about."

Gerasim stood without stirring in his doorway. The crowd gathered at the foot of the stairs. Gerasim, with his arms akimbo, looked down at all these poor creatures in German coats; in his red peasant's shirt he looked like a giant before them. Gavrila took a step forward.

"Mind, mate," said he, "don't be insolent."

And he began to explain to him by signs that the mistress insisted on having his dog; that he must hand it over at once, or it would be the worse for him.

Gerasim looked at him, pointed to the dog, made a motion with his hand round his neck, as though he were pulling a noose tight, and glanced with a face of inquiry at the steward.

"Yes, yes," the latter assented, nodding; "yes, just so."

Gerasim dropped his eyes, then all of a sudden roused himself and pointed to Mumu, who was all the while standing beside him, innocently wagging her tail and pricking up her ears inquisitively. Then he repeated the strangling action round his neck and significantly struck himself on the breast, as though announcing he would take upon himself the task of killing Mumu.

"But you'll deceive us," Gavrila waved back in response.

Gerasim looked at him, smiled scornfully, struck himself again on the breast, and slammed-to the door.

They all looked at one another in silence.

"What does that mean?" Gavrila began. "He's locked himself in."

"Let him be, Gavrila Andreitch," Stepan advised; "he'll do it if he's promised. He's like that, you know.... If he makes a promise, it's a certain thing. He's not like us others in that. The truth's the truth with him. Yes, indeed."

"Yes," they all repeated, nodding their heads, "yes — that's so — yes."

Uncle Tail opened his window, and he too said, "Yes."

"Well, may be, we shall see," responded Gavrila; "any way, we won't take off the guard. Here you, Eroshka!" he added, addressing a poor fellow in a yellow nankeen coat, who considered himself to be a gardener, "what have you to do? Take a stick and sit here, and if anything happens, run to me at once!"

Eroshka took a stick, and sat down on the bottom stair. The crowd dispersed, all except a few inquisitive small boys, while Gavrila went home and sent word through Liubov Liubimovna to the mistress, that everything had been done, while he sent a postillion for a policeman in case of need. The old lady tied a knot in her handkerchief, sprinkled some eau-de-Cologne on it, sniffed at it, and rubbed her temples with it, drank some tea, and, being still under the influence of the cherrybay drops, fell asleep again.

An hour after all this hubbub the garret door opened, and Gerasim showed himself. He had on his best coat; he was leading Mumu by a string. Eroshka moved aside and let him pass. Gerasim went to the gates. All the small boys in the yard stared at him in silence. He did not even turn round; he only put his cap on in the street. Gavrila sent the same Eroshka to follow him and keep watch on him as a spy. Eroshka, seeing from a distance that he had gone into a cookshop with his dog, waited for him to come out again.

Gerasim was well known at the cookshop, and his signs were understood. He asked for cabbage soup with meat in it, and sat down with his arms on the table. Mumu stood beside his chair, looking calmly at him with her intelligent eyes. Her coat was glossy; one could see she had just been combed down. They brought Gerasim the soup. He crumbled some bread into it, cut the meat up small, and put the plate on the ground. Mumu began eating in her usual refined way, her little muzzle daintily held so as scarcely to touch her food. Gerasim gazed a long while at her; two big tears suddenly rolled from his eyes; one fell on the dog's brow, the other into the soup. He shaded his face with his hand. Mumu ate up half the plateful, and came away from it, licking her lips. Gerasim got up, paid for the soup, and went out, followed by the rather perplexed glances of the waiter. Eroshka, seeing Gerasim, hid round a corner, and letting him get in front, followed him again.

Gerasim walked without haste, still holding Mumu by a string. When he got to the corner of the street, he stood still as though reflecting, and suddenly set off with rapid steps to the Crimean Ford. On the way he went into the yard of a house, where a lodge was being built, and carried away two bricks under his arm. At the Crimean Ford, he turned along the bank, went to a place where there were two little rowing-boats fastened to stakes (he had noticed them there before), and jumped into one of them with Mumu. A lame old man came out of a shed in the corner of a kitchen-garden and shouted after him; but Gerasim only nodded, and began rowing so vigorously, though against stream, that in an instant he had darted two hundred yards away. The old man stood for a while, scratched his back first with the left and then with the right hand, and went back hobbling to the shed.

Gerasim rowed on and on. Moscow was soon left behind. Meadows stretched each side of the bank, market gardens, fields, and copses; peasants' huts began to make their appearance. There was the fragrance of the country. He threw down his oars, bent his head down to Mumu, who was sitting facing him on a dry cross seat — the bottom of the boat was full of water — and stayed motionless, his mighty hands clasped upon her back, while the boat was gradually carried back by the current towards the town. At last Gerasim drew himself up hurriedly, with a sort of sick anger in his face, he tied up the bricks he had taken with string, made a running noose, put it round Mumu's neck, lifted her up over the river, and for the last time looked at her . . . she watched him confidingly and without any fear, faintly wagging her tail. He turned away, frowned, and wrung his hands. . . . Gerasim heard nothing, neither the quick shrill whine of Mumu as she fell, nor the heavy splash of the water; for him the noisiest day was soundless and silent as even the stillest night is not silent to us. When he opened his eyes again, little wavelets were hurrying over the river, chasing one another; as before they broke against the boat's side, and only far away behind wide circles moved widening to the bank.

Directly Gerasim had vanished from Eroshka's sight, the latter returned home and reported what he had seen.

"Well, then," observed Stepan, "he'll drown her. Now we can feel easy about it. If he once promises a thing. . . ."

No one saw Gerasim during the day. He did not have dinner at home. Evening came on; they were all gathered together to supper, except him.

"What a strange creature that Gerasim is!" piped a fat laundrymaid; "fancy, upsetting himself like that over a dog. . . . Upon my word!"

"But Gerasim has been here," Stepan cried all at once, scraping up his porridge with a spoon.

"How? when?"

"Why, a couple of hours ago. Yes, indeed! I ran against him at the gate; he was going out again from here; he was coming out of the yard. I tried to ask him about his dog, but he wasn't in the best of humors, I could see. Well, he gave me a shove; I suppose he only meant to put me out of his way, as if he'd say, 'Let me go, do!' but he fetched me such a crack on my neck, so seriously, that — oh! oh!" And Stepan, who could not help

laughing, shrugged up and rubbed the back of his head. "Yes," he added; "he has got a fist; it's something like a fist, there's no denying that!"

They all laughed at Stepan, and after supper they separated to go to bed.

Meanwhile, at that very time, a gigantic figure with a bag on his shoulders and a stick in his hand was eagerly and persistently stepping out along the T—— highroad. It was Gerasim. He was hurrying on without looking round; hurrying homewards, to his own village, to his own country. After drowning poor Mumu, he had run back to his garret, hurriedly packed a few things together in an old horsecloth, tied it up in a bundle, tossed it on his shoulder, and so was ready. He had noticed the road carefully when he was brought to Moscow; the village his mistress had taken him from lay only about twenty miles off the highroad. He walked along it with a sort of invincible purpose, a desperate and at the same time joyous determination. He walked, his shoulders thrown back and his chest expanded; his eyes were fixed greedily straight before him. He hastened as though his old mother were waiting for him at home, as though she were calling him to her after long wanderings in strange parts, among strangers. The summer night, that was just drawing in, was still and warm; on one side, where the sun had set, the horizon was still light and faintly flushed with the last glow of the vanished day; on the other side a blue-grey twilight had already risen up. The night was coming up from that quarter. Quails were in hundreds around; corncrakes were calling to one another in the thickets. . . . Gerasim could not hear them; he could not hear the delicate night-whispering of the trees, by which his strong legs carried him, but he smelt the familiar scent of the ripening rye, which was wafted from the dark fields; he felt the wind, flying to meet him — the wind from home — beat caressingly upon his face, and play with his hair and his beard. He saw before him the whitening road homewards, straight as an arrow. He saw in the sky stars innumerable, lighting up his way, and stepped out, strong and bold as a lion, so that when the rising sun shed its moist rosy light upon the still fresh and unwearied traveller, already thirty miles lay between him and Moscow.

In a couple of days he was at home, in his little hut, to the great astonishment of the soldier's wife who had been put in there. After praying before the holy pictures, he set off at once to the village elder. The village elder was at first surprised; but the hay-cutting had just begun; Gerasim was a first-rate mower, and they put a scythe into his hand on the spot, and he went to mow in his old way, mowing so that the peasants were fairly astounded as they watched his wide sweeping strokes and the heaps he raked together. . . .

In Moscow the day after Gerasim's flight they missed him. They went to his garret, rummaged about in it, and spoke to Gavrila. He came, looked, shrugged his shoulders, and decided that the dumb man had either run away or had drowned himself with his stupid dog. They gave information to the police, and informed the lady. The old lady was furious, burst into tears, gave orders that he was to be found whatever happened, declared she had never ordered the dog to be destroyed, and, in fact, gave Gavrila such a rating that he could do nothing all day but shake his head and murmur, "Well!" until Uncle Tail checked him at last, sympathetically echoing "We-ell!" At last the news came from the country of Gerasim's being there. The old lady was somewhat pacified; at first she issued a mandate for

him to be brought back without delay to Moscow; afterwards, however, she declared that such an ungrateful creature was absolutely of no use to her. Soon after this she died herself; and her heirs had no thought to spare for Gerasim; they let their mother's other servants redeem their freedom on payment of an annual rent.

And Gerasim is living still, a lonely man in his lonely hut; he is strong and healthy as before, and does the work of four men as before, and as before is serious and steady. But his neighbors have observed that ever since his return from Moscow he has quite given up the society of women; he will not even look at them, and does not keep even a single dog. "It's his good luck, though," the peasants reason; "that he can get on without female folk; and as for a dog — what need has he of a dog? you wouldn't get a thief to go into his yard for any money!" Such is the fame of the dumb man's Titanic strength.

Walt Whitman · 1819–1892

Born in 1819, Whitman was at his full power as a writer during those years when the frontiers of the United States were disappearing, when democracy was undergoing its supreme test in the Civil War, when agriculture and village life were giving way to the development of great industries and the growth of large cities, and when the confined religious thought of the early settlers was breaking down before the greater freedom of Unitarian doctrine and the transcendentalism of Emerson and Thoreau. Whitman, more than any other American writer of this time, interprets the United States in the light of this new spirit.

Walt Whitman was born on Long Island, which in his writings he called by the Indian name of Paumanok. His father, Walter Whitman, was a farmer-carpenter-contractor. When the young Walter was four or five years old, the family moved to Brooklyn where the boy was educated in the public schools until he was twelve years of age.

"Walt" — he chose the shortened form to distinguish him from Walter the father — derived his education from three major sources: wide reading, travel in the United States, and an intimate association with people. To accomplish the first he familiarized himself with the Greek classics, with Dante, Cervantes, Shakespeare, Goethe, Rousseau, Carlyle, the Bible, and read fairly extensively in Hindu thought. The ideas of Emerson and Thoreau — two contemporaries who befriended him — were current in the atmosphere he breathed. Whitman attended concerts, the opera, the theatre, and public lectures. He gained his first-hand knowledge of the States and of their people through travel and intimate association with people in various callings. In 1849 he undertook an extended trip which carried him slowly and leisurely — at times working his way as a journeyman printer — through the northern states, the South, and about the Mississippi, Ohio, and southern Canada. His work in New York for years took him across the river on the Brooklyn ferries, trips on which he found perpetual delight in the pilots of the boats and the life of the river. He made countless trips through the city, up Broadway and down, riding with bus drivers and learning their ideas and manner of living. For some two or three years, of the ten he resided in Washington, he worked as a war-nurse in the hospitals, helping and comforting the soldiers of the North and South alike. And always Whitman went about not as an outsider studying a life which was novel to him but as a participant and friend. The poet's life was not, however, entirely spent in reading, travel, and meeting people. He earned his living in various ways: as printer, as carpenter in his father's business, as editor of two Brooklyn papers, the *Eagle* and the *Freeman*, and as a government clerk in Washington offices. In 1873, perhaps as a consequence of his work in the Washington hospitals, Whitman suffered a paralytic stroke and was forced to leave the capital and his clerkship. He went to Camden, New Jersey, where he continued to reside until his death, after a second stroke, March 26, 1892.

Now recognized as one of the greatest American writers — along with Poe, Emerson, Melville, and Hawthorne — Whitman was slow in finding a reading public. True, Emerson and Thoreau early recognized him as an original genius. William Michael Rossetti edited a selection of his poetry which brought him sympathetic readers in England. John Addington Symonds and Robert Louis Stevenson commended him abroad. But almost everything about Whitman's verse — its concern with the physical, its strange verse form, its "barbaric yawp," its glorification of the commonplace — threw his American readers into consternation. "This is not poetry; this is obscenity" was the popular verdict. He was discharged from a government post in Washington as the author of an "indecent" volume of poems, a fact which prompted Douglas O'Connor to write a defence of Whitman called "The Good Gray Poet."

Both the thought and expression of *Leaves of Grass* were strange to Whitman's contemporaries. The volume may be thought of as a trilogy celebrating the human body, democracy, and religion. Certain ideas recur in Whitman's poetry: the life of the body is good; real satisfaction comes in a complete accord with nature; the material and the spiritual are one and exist each in the other; we must forget convention and live in the spirit; life is progress toward perfection; immortality is the lesson we find in all about us; evolution is a means toward divinity; democracy, strong, vivid, physical democracy, is the hope of the world; sex is wholesome, not a thing to be concealed or to cause shame; industry is good; a man must be an individual and be self-reliant; it is the mission of the United States to carry democracy to the world at large. He taught comradeship, the need for contentment, good cheer, optimism, and trust in the future of both man and society.

With conventional poetry Whitman was well acquainted, but the poet of Paumanok believed that the United States, a new country putting in practice new political ideals, needed a new literary manner to express these ideals and convictions. This new manner, he felt, was his responsibility to develop. He set himself carefully to write and revise until he had purged himself of stock "poetic touches" and had evolved a form which he thought characteristic of this new nation. This handmade manner was what we call free-verse, a chant depending on rhythm rather than rime. He built what he called a "recitative."

To this free form, Whitman added other qualities. His long lists, "catalogues," of items — cities, rivers, historical events — are highly suggestive. He developed an almost Homeric capacity for the epithet: "the splendid silent sun," "pent-up aching rivers," "still, nodding night," "vast and well-veiled death." To a tendency to disregard grammar, Whitman added a love of foreign words and phrases: "Allons," "Camerado," and the rest. Whitman has been called egotistic, but much of the use of the first personal pronoun may not seem so to one who understands Whitman's intent. It was one of the poet's purposes to show the possibility of democracy, of the dignity of man, by portraying an "archetypal microcosm," a common man who embraces all the qualities of all men. Whitman pointed out that what he said of himself could be said of mankind, that he was, he knew, no more and no less than others.

Whitman is here classified as a realist. His lack of constraint, his idealism, his preoccupation with death, his insistence on the divinity in nature are distinctly romantic overtones. On the other hand, Whitman's concern with the world of his time, his praise of the human body and his sensual passages, his frank vocabulary, his reliance on the itemized catalogue of facts — these are qualities we associate with the realistic temper.

The following poems are reprinted from *Leaves of Grass*, by Walt Whitman, copyright, 1924, by Doubleday, Doran and Company, Inc.

SUGGESTED REFERENCES: G. W. Allen, *Walt Whitman as Man, Poet, and Legend* (1961); J. E. Miller, *Walt Whitman* (1962); R. H. Pearce, ed., *Whitman. A Collection of Critical Essays* (1962).

One's-self I Sing

One's-self I sing, a simple separate person,
Yet utter the word Democratic, the word En-
Masse.

Of physiology from top to toe I sing,
Not physiognomy alone nor brain alone is worthy
for the Muse, I say the Form complete is
worthier far,
The Female equally with the Male I sing.   5

Of Life immense in passion, pulse, and power,
Cheerful, for freest action form'd under the laws
divine,
The Modern Man I sing.

On Journeys Through the States

On journeys through the States we start,
(Ay through the world, urged by these songs,
Sailing henceforth to every land, to every sea,)
We willing learners of all, teachers of all, and lovers
of all.

We have watch'd the seasons dispensing themselves and passing on,   5
And have said, Why should not a man or woman
do as much as the seasons, and effuse as
much?

We dwell a while in every city and town,
We pass through Kanada, the North-east, the
vast valley of the Mississippi, and the
Southern States,
We confer on equal terms with each of the States,
We make trial of ourselves and invite men and
women to hear,   10
We say to ourselves, Remember, fear not, be
candid, promulge the body and the soul,
Dwell a while and pass on, be copious, temperate,
chaste, magnetic,
And what you effuse may then return as the sea-
sons return,
And may be just as much as the seasons.

The Song of the Open Road

In this poem Whitman chants a song of comradeship
and physical well-being. The thought is characteristically romantic, the manner realistic. The optimism,
the sheer joy in vagabondage, the spiritual values inherent in nature, the conviction of the dignity of the
common man are ideas familiar in romanticism. Yet
the manner of expression evident in the frank diction
and in the catalogue of details, in stanza three for instance, are common realistic qualities.

1

Afoot and light-hearted I take to the open road,
Healthy, free, the world before me,
The long brown path before me leading wherever I
choose.

Henceforth I ask not good-fortune, I myself am
good-fortune,
Henceforth I whimper no more, postpone no more,
need nothing,   5
Done with indoor complaints, libraries, querulous
criticisms,
Strong and content I travel the open road.

The earth, that is sufficient,
I do not want the constellations any nearer,
I know they are very well where they are,   10
I know they suffice for those who belong to them.
(Still here I carry my old delicious burdens,
I carry them, men and women, I carry them with
me wherever I go,
I swear it is impossible for me to get rid of them,
I am fill'd with them, and I will fill them in return.)

2

You road I enter upon and look around, I believe
you are not all that is here,   16
I believe that much unseen is also here.

Here the profound lesson of reception, nor preference nor denial,
The black, with his woolly head, the felon, the
diseas'd, the illiterate person, are not
denied;
The birth, the hasting after the physician, the beggar's tramp, the drunkard's stagger, the
laughing party of mechanics,   20
The escaped youth, the rich person's carriage, the
fop, the eloping couple,
The early market-man, the hearse, the moving of
furniture into the town, the return back
from the town,
They pass, I also pass, anything passes, none can
be interdicted,
None but are accepted, none but shall be dear to
me.

3

You air that serves me with breath to speak! 25
You objects that call from diffusion my meanings
and give them shape!
You light that wraps me and all things in delicate
equable showers!
You paths worn in the irregular hollows by the
roadsides!
I believe you are latent with unseen existences,
you are so dear to me.

You flagg'd walks of the cities! you strong curbs
at the edges!
You ferries! you planks and posts of wharves! you 30
timber-lined sides! you distant ships!
You rows of houses! you window-pierc'd façades!
you roofs!
You porches and entrances! you copings and iron
guards!
You windows whose transparent shells might expose so much!
You doors and ascending steps! you arches! 35
You gray stones of interminable pavements! you
trodden crossings!
From all that has touch'd you I believe you have
imparted to yourselves, and now would impart the same secretly to me,
From the living and the dead you have peopled your
impassive surfaces, and the spirits thereof would be evident and amicable with me.

4

The earth expanding right hand and left hand,
The picture alive, every part in its best light, 40
The music falling in where it is wanted, and stop-
ping where it is not wanted,
The cheerful voice of the public road, the gay fresh
sentiment of the road.

O highway I travel, do you say to me *Do not leave
me?*
Do you say *Venture not — if you leave me you are
lost?*
Do you say *I am already prepared, I am well-
beaten and undenied, adhere to me?* 45

O public road, I say back I am not afraid to leave
you, yet I love you,
You express me better than I can express myself,
You shall be more to me than my poem.
I think heroic deeds were all conceiv'd in the open
air, and all free poems also,
I think I could stop here myself and do miracles, 49
I think whatever I shall meet on the road I shall
like, and whoever beholds me shall like me,
I think whoever I see must be happy.

5

From this hour I ordain myself loos'd of limits and
imaginary lines,
Going where I list, my own master total and absolute,
Listening to others, considering well what they
say,
Pausing, searching, receiving, contemplating, 55
Gently, but with undeniable will, divesting myself
of the holds that would hold me.

I inhale great draughts of space,
The east and the west are mine, and the north and
the south are mine.

I am larger, better than I thought, 60
I did not know I held so much goodness.

All seems beautiful to me,
I can repeat over to men and women You have
done such good to me I would do the same
to you,
I will recruit for myself and you as I go,
I will scatter myself among men and women as I
go, 65
I will toss a new gladness and roughness among
them,
Whoever denies me it shall not trouble me,
Whoever accepts me he or she shall be blessed and
shall bless me.

6

Now if a thousand perfect men were to appear it
would not amaze me,
Now if a thousand beautiful forms of women appear'd it would not astonish me. 70

Now I see the secret of the making of the best persons,
It is to grow in the open air and to eat and sleep
with the earth.

Here a great personal deed has room,
(Such a deed seizes upon the hearts of the whole
race of men,
Its effusion of strength and will overwhelms law
and mocks all authority and all argument
against it.) 75

Here is the test of wisdom,
Wisdom is not finally tested in schools,
Wisdom cannot be pass'd from one having it to
another not having it,
Wisdom is of the soul, is not susceptible of proof,
is its own proof,

Applies to all stages and objects and qualities and
  is content,   80
Is the certainty of the reality and immortality of
  things, and the excellence of things;
Something there is in the float of the sight of things
  that provokes it out of the soul.

Now I re-examine philosophies and religions,
They may prove well in lecture-rooms, yet not
  prove at all under the spacious clouds and
  along the landscape and flowing currents.

Here is realization,   85
Here is a man tallied — he realizes here what he
  has in him,
The past, the future, majesty, love — if they are
  vacant of you, you are vacant of them.

Only the kernel of every object nourishes;
Where is he who tears off the husks for you and
  me?
Where is he that undoes stratagems and envelopes
  for you and me?   90

Here is adhesiveness, it is not previously fashion'd, it is apropos;
Do you know what it is as you pass to be loved by
  strangers?
Do you know the talk of those turning eyeballs?

7

Here is the efflux [1] of the soul,
The efflux of the soul comes from within through
  embower'd gates, ever provoking questions,
These yearnings why are they? these thoughts in
  the darkness why are they?   96
Why are there men and women that while they
  are nigh me the sunlight expands my blood?
Why when they leave me do my pennants of joy
  sink flat and lank?
Why are there trees I never walk under but large
  and melodious thoughts descend upon me?
(I think they hang there winter and summer on
  those trees and always drop fruit as I pass;)
What is it I interchange so suddenly with strangers?   101
What with some driver as I ride on the seat by his
  side?
What with some fisherman drawing his seine by
  the shore as I walk by and pause?
What gives me to be free to a woman's and man's
  good-will? what gives them to be free to
  mine?

  [1] A flowing forth.

8

The efflux of the soul is happiness, here is happiness,   105
I think it pervades the open air, waiting at all
  times,
Now it flows unto us, we are rightly charged.

Here rises the fluid and attaching character,
The fluid and attaching character is the freshness
  and sweetness of man and woman,
(The herbs of the morning sprout no fresher and
  sweeter every day out of the roots of themselves, than it sprouts fresh and sweet continually out of itself.)   110
Toward the fluid and attaching character exudes
  the sweat of the love of young and old,
From it falls distill'd the charm that mocks beauty
  and attainments,
Toward it heaves the shuddering longing ache of
  contact.

9

Allons! [1] whoever you are come travel with me!
Traveling with me you find what never tires.   115

The earth never tires,
The earth is rude, silent, incomprehensible at first,
  Nature is rude and incomprehensible at
  first,
Be not discouraged, keep on, there are divine
  things well envelop'd,
I swear to you there are divine things more beautiful than words can tell.
Allons! we must not stop here,   120
However sweet these laid-up stores, however convenient this dwelling we cannot remain
  here,
However shelter'd this port and however calm
  these waters we must not anchor here,
However welcome the hospitality that surrounds
  us we are permitted to receive it but a little
  while.

10

Allons! the inducements shall be greater,
We will sail pathless and wild seas,   125
We will go where winds blow, waves dash, and the
  Yankee clipper speeds by under full sail.

Allons! with power, liberty, the earth, the elements,
Health, defiance, gayety, self-esteem, curiosity;
Allons! from all formules!
From your formules, O bat-eyed and materialistic
  priests.   130

  [1] Let us go!

The stale cadaver blocks up the passage — the burial waits no longer.

Allons! yet take warning!
He traveling with me needs the best blood, thews, endurance,
None may come to the trial till he or she bring courage and health,
Come not here if you have already spent the best of yourself,   135
Only those may come who come in sweet and determin'd bodies,
No diseas'd person, no rum-drinker or venereal taint is permitted here.

(I and mine do not convince by arguments, similes, rhymes,
We convince by our presence.)

11

Listen! I will be honest with you,   140
I do not offer the old smooth prizes, but offer rough new prizes,
These are the days that must happen to you:
You shall not heap up what is call'd riches,
You shall scatter with lavish hand all that you earn or achieve,
You but arrive at the city to which you were destin'd, you hardly settle yourself to satisfaction before you are call'd by an irresistible call to depart,   145
You shall be treated to the ironical smiles and mockings of those who remain behind you,
What beckonings of love you receive you shall only answer with passionate kisses of parting,
You shall not allow the hold of those who spread their reach'd hands toward you.

12

Allons! after the great Companions, and to belong to them!
They too are on the road — they are the swift and majestic men — they are the greatest women,   150
Enjoyers of calms of seas and storms of seas,
Sailors of many a ship, walkers of many a mile of land,
Habitués of many distant countries, habitués of far-distant dwellings,
Trusters of men and women, observers of cities, solitary toilers,
Pausers and contemplators of tufts, blossoms, shells of the shore,   155
Dancers at wedding-dances, kissers of brides, tender helpers of children, bearers of children,

Soldiers of revolts, standers by gaping graves, lowerers-down of coffins,
Journeyers over consecutive seasons, over the years, the curious years each emerging from that which preceded it,
Journeyers as with companions, namely their own diverse phases,
Forth-steppers from the latent unrealized baby-days,   160
Journeyers gayly with their own youth, journeyers with their bearded and well-grain'd manhood,
Journeyers with their womanhood, ample, unsurpass'd, content,
Journeyers with their own sublime old age of manhood or womanhood,
Old age, calm, expanded, broad with the haughty breadth of the universe,
Old age, flowing free with the delicious near-by freedom of death.   165

13

Allons! to that which is endless as it was beginningless,
To undergo much, tramps of days, rests of nights,
To merge all in the travel they tend to, and the days and nights they tend to,
Again to merge them in the start of superior journeys,
To see nothing anywhere but what you may reach it and pass it,   170
To conceive no time, however distant, but what you may reach it and pass it,
To look up or down no road but it stretches and waits for you, however long but it stretches and waits for you,
To see no being, not God's or any, but you also go thither.
To see no possession but you may possess it, enjoying all without labor or purchase, abstracting the feast yet not abstracting one particle of it,
To take the best of the farmer's farm and the rich man's elegant villa, and the chaste blessings of the well-married couple, and the fruits of orchards and flowers of gardens,   175
To take to your use out of the compact cities as you pass through,
To carry buildings and streets with you afterward wherever you go,
To gather the minds of men out of their brains as you encounter them, to gather the love out of their hearts,
To take your lovers on the road with you, for all that you leave them behind you,

To know the universe itself as a road, as many
    roads, as roads for traveling souls.   180

All parts away for the progress of souls,
All religion, all solid things, arts, governments
    — all that was or is apparent upon this
    globe or any globe, falls into niches and cor-
    ners before the procession of souls along
    the grand roads of the universe.

Of the progress of the souls of men and women
    along the grand roads of the universe, all
    other progress is the needed emblem and
    sustenance.
Forever alive, forever forward,
Stately, solemn, sad, withdrawn, baffled, mad,
    turbulent, feeble, dissatisfied,   185
Desperate, proud, fond, sick, accepted by men,
    rejected by men,
They go! they go! I know that they go, but I
    know not where they go,
But I know that they go toward the best — toward
    something great.

Whoever you are, come forth! or man or woman
    come forth!
You must not stay sleeping and dallying there in
    the house, though you built it, or though it
    has been built for you.   190

Out of the dark confinement! out from behind the
    screen!
It is useless to protest, I know all and expose it.

Behold through you as bad as the rest,
Through the laughter, dancing, dining, supping, of
    people,
Inside of dresses and ornaments, inside of those
    wash'd and trimm'd faces,   195
Behold a secret silent loathing and despair.

No husband, no wife, no friend, trusted to hear the
    confession,
Another self, a duplicate of every one, skulking and
    hiding it goes,
Formless and wordless through the streets of the
    cities, polite and bland in the parlors,
In the cars of railroads, in steamboats, in the pub-
    lic assembly,   200
Home to the houses of men and women, at the
    table, in the bedroom, everywhere,
Smartly attired, countenance smiling, form up-
    right, death under the breast-bones, hell
    under the skull-bones,
Under the broadcloth and gloves, under the ribbons
    and artificial flowers,

Keeping fair with the customs, speaking not a
    syllable of itself,
Speaking of any thing else but never of itself.   205

14

Allons! through struggles and wars!
The goal that was named cannot be counter-
    manded.
Have the past struggles succeeded?
What has succeeded? yourself? your nation?
    Nature?
Now understand me well — it is provided in the
    essence of things that from any fruition of
    success, no matter what, shall come forth
    something to make a greater struggle
    necessary.   210

My call is the call of battle, I nourish active re-
    bellion,
He going with me must go well arm'd,
He going with me goes often with spare diet,
    poverty, angry enemies, desertions.

15

Allons! the road is before us!
It is safe — I have tried it — my own feet have
    tried it well — be not detain'd!   215
Let the paper remain on the desk unwritten, and
    the book on the shelf unopen'd!
Let the tools remain in the workshop! let the
    money remain unearn'd!
Let the school stand! mind not the cry of the
    teacher!
Let the preacher preach in his pulpit! let the lawyer
    plead in the court, and the judge expound
    the law.

Camerado, I give you my hand!   220
I give you my love more precious than money,
I give you myself before preaching or law;
Will you give me yourself? will you come travel
    with me?
Shall we stick by each other as long as we live?

Crossing Brooklyn Ferry

This poem presents several phases of characteristic
Whitman doctrine. Here is an expression of his joy
in comradeship, his sense of beauty in the American
industrial scene, his conviction of the close relationship
which exists between the physical and the spiritual.
The student first making the acquaintance of Whitman need not be repelled by the constant use of "I";
with Whitman the personal pronoun may refer to the
poet as an individual or to Whitman the unit of manhood speaking for all mankind (see stanzas 3 and 5).

The following excerpt from Whitman's prose pages
— *Specimen Days* — explains the background from
which this poem was written:

"Living in Brooklyn or New York city from this
time forward, my life, then, and still more the following
years, was curiously identified with Fulton ferry, already becoming the greatest of its sort in the world for
general importance, volume, variety, rapidity, and
picturesqueness. Almost daily, later ('50 to '60), I
cross'd on the boats, often up in the pilot-houses where
I could get a full sweep, absorbing shows, accompani-
ments, surroundings. What oceanic currents, eddies,
underneath — the great tides of humanity also, with
ever-shifting movements! Indeed, I have always had
a passion for ferries; to me they afford inimitable,
streaming, never-failing, living poems. The river and
bay scenery, all about New York island, any time of a
fine day — the hurrying, splashing sea-tides — the
changing panorama of steamers, all sizes, often a string
of big ones outward bound to distant ports — the
myriads of white sail'd schooners, sloops, skiffs, and
the marvellously beautiful yachts — the majestic
Sound boats as they rounded the Battery and came
along towards 5, afternoon, eastward bound — the
prospect off towards Staten Island, or down the
Narrows, or the other way up the Hudson — what refreshment of spirit such sights and experiences gave
me years ago (and many a time since)! My old pilot
friends, the Balsirs, Johnny Cole, Ira Smith, William
White, and my young ferry friend, Tom Gere — how
well I remember them all!"

1

Flood-tide below me! I see you face to face!
Clouds of the west — sun there half an hour high
    — I see you also face to face.

Crowds of men and women attired in the usual
    costumes, how curious you are to me!
On the ferry-boats the hundreds and hundreds
    that cross, returning home, are more curious
    to me than you suppose,
And you that shall cross from shore to shore years
    hence are more to me, and more in my medi-
    tations, than you might suppose.   5

2

The impalpable sustenance of me from all things
    at all hours of the day,
The simple, compact, well-join'd scheme, myself
    disintegrated, every one disintegrated yet
    part of the scheme,
The similitudes of the past and those of the future,
The glories strung like beads on my smallest sights
    and hearings, on the walk in the street and
    the passage over the river,
The current rushing so swiftly and swimming with
    me far away,   10

The others that are to follow me, the ties between
    me and them,
The certainty of others, the life, love, sight, hearing
    of others.

Others will enter the gates of the ferry and cross
    from shore to shore,
Others will watch the run of the flood-tide,
Others will see the shipping of Manhattan north
    and west, and the heights of Brooklyn to the
    south and east,   15
Others will see the islands large and small;
Fifty years hence, others will see them as they
    cross, the sun half an hour high,
A hundred years hence, or ever so many hundred
    years hence, others will see them,
Will enjoy the sunset, the pouring-in of the flood-
    tide, the falling-back to the sea of the ebb-
    tide.

3

It avails not, time nor place — distance avails not,
I am with you, you men and women of a generation,
    or ever so many generations hence,   21
Just as you feel when you look on the river and sky,
    so I felt,
Just as any of you is one of a living crowd, I was
    one of a crowd,
Just as you are refresh'd by the gladness of the
    river and the bright flow, I was refresh'd,
Just as you stand and lean on the rail, yet hurry
    with the swift current, I stood yet was
    hurried,   25
Just as you look on the numberless masts of ships
    and the thick-stemm'd pipes of steamboats,
    I look'd.

I too many and many a time cross'd the river of
    old,
Watched the Twelfth-month sea-gulls, saw them
    high in the air floating with motionless
    wings, oscillating their bodies,
Saw how the glistening yellow lit up parts of their
    bodies and left the rest in strong shadow,
Saw the slow-wheeling circles and the gradual
    edging toward the south,   30
Saw the reflection of the summer sky in the water,
Had my eyes dazzled by the shimmering track of
    beams,
Look'd at the fine centrifugal spokes of light round
    the shape of my head in the sunlit water,
Look'd on the haze on the hills southward and
    south-westward,
Look'd on the vapor as it flew in fleeces tinged with
    violet,   35

Look'd toward the lower bay to notice the vessels
    arriving,
Saw their approach, saw aboard those that were
    near me,
Saw the white sails of schooners and sloops, saw
    the ships at anchor,
The sailors at work in the rigging or out astride the
    spars,
The round masts, the swinging motion of the hulls,
    the slender serpentine pennants,   40
The large and small steamers in motion, the pilots
    in their pilot-houses,
The white wake left by the passage, the quick
    tremulous whirl of the wheels.
The flags of all nations, the falling of them at sun-
    set,
The scallop-edged waves in the twilight, the ladled
    cups, the frolicsome crests and glistening,
The stretch afar growing dimmer and dimmer, the
    gray walls of the granite storehouses by the
    docks,   45
On the river the shadowy group, the big steam-tug
    closely flank'd on each side by the barges,
    the hay-boat, the belated lighter,
On the neighboring shore the fires from the foundry
    chimneys burning high and glaringly into
    the night,
Casting their flicker of black contrasted with wild
    red and yellow light over the tops of houses,
    and down into the clefts of streets.

4

These and all else were to me the same as they are
    to you,
I loved well those cities, loved well the stately and
    rapid river,   50
The men and women I saw were all near to me,
Others the same — others who look back on me
    because I look'd forward to them,
(The time will come, though I stop here to-day
    and to-night.)

5

What is it then between us?
What is the count of the scores or hundreds of
    years between us?   55

Whatever it is, it avails not — distance avails not,
    and place avails not,
I too lived, Brooklyn of ample hills was mine,
I too walk'd the streets of Manhattan island, and
    bathed in the waters around it,
I too felt the curious abrupt questionings stir with-
    in me,
In the day among crowds of people sometimes they
    came upon me,   60

In my walks home late at night or as I lay in my
    bed they came upon me,
I too had been struck from the float forever held in
    solution,
I too had receiv'd identity by my body,
That I was I knew was of my body, and what I
    should be I knew I should be of my body.

6

It is not upon you alone the dark patches fall,   65
The dark threw its patches down upon me also,
The best I had done seem'd to me blank and sus-
    picious,
My great thoughts as I supposed them, were they
    not in reality meagre?
Nor is it you alone who know what it is to be evil,
I am he who knew what it was to be evil,   70
I too knitted the old knot of contrariety,
Blabb'd, blush'd, resented, lied, stole, grudg'd,
Had guile, anger, lust, hot wishes I dared not speak,
Was wayward, vain, greedy, shallow, sly, cowardly,
    malignant,
The wolf, the snake, the hog, not wanting in me,   75
The cheating look, the frivolous word, the adulter-
    ous wish, not wanting,
Refusals, hates, postponements, meanness, laziness,
    none of these wanting,
Was one with the rest, the days and haps of the
    rest,
Was call'd by my nighest name by clear loud
    voices of young men as they saw me ap-
    proaching or passing,
Felt their arms on my neck as I stood, or the neg-
    ligent leaning of their flesh against me as I
    sat,   80
Saw many I loved in the street or ferry-boat or
    public assembly, yet never told them a word,
Lived the same life with the rest, the same old
    laughing, gnawing, sleeping,
Play'd the part that still looks back on the actor or
    actress,
The same old rôle, the rôle that is what we make it,
    as great as we like,
Or as small as we like, or both great and small.

7

Closer yet I approach you,   86
What thought you have of me now, I had as much
    of you — I laid in my stores in advance,
I consider'd long and seriously of you before you
    were born.
Who was to know what should come home to me?
Who knows but I am enjoying this?   90
Who knows, for all the distance, but I am as good
    as looking at you now, for all you cannot
    see me?

8

Ah, what can ever be more stately and admirable
to me than mast-hemm'd Manhattan?
River and sunset and scallop-edg'd waves of flood-
tide?
The sea-gulls oscillating their bodies, the hay-boat
in the twilight, and the belated lighter?

What gods can exceed these that clasp me by
the hand, and with voices I love call me
promptly and loudly by my nighest name
as I approach?   95

What is more subtle than this which ties me to the
woman or man that looks in my face?
Which fuses me into you now, and pours my meaning into you?

We understand then do we not?
What I promis'd without mentioning it, have you
not accepted?
What the study could not teach — what the preaching could not accomplish is accomplish'd,
is it not?   100

9

Flow on, river! flow with the flood-tide, and ebb
with the ebb-tide!
Frolic on, crested and scallop-edg'd waves!
Gorgeous clouds of the sunset! drench with your
splendor me, or the men and women generations after me!
Cross from shore to shore, countless crowds of passengers!
Stand up, tall masts of Mannahatta! stand up,
beautiful hills of Brooklyn!   105
Throb, baffled and curious brain! throw out questions and answers!
Suspend here and everywhere, eternal float of solution!
Gaze, loving and thirsting eyes, in the house or
street or public assembly!
Sound out, voices of young men! loudly and musically call me by my nighest name!
Live, old life! play the part that looks back on the
actor or actress!   110
Play the old rôle, the rôle that is great or small according as one makes it!
Consider, you who peruse me, whether I may not
in unknown ways be looking upon you;
Be firm, rail over the river, to support those who
lean idly, yet haste with the hasting current;
Fly on, sea-birds! fly sideways, or wheel in large
circles high in the air;

Receive the summer sky, you water, and faithfully
hold it till all downcast eyes have time to
take it from you!   115
Diverge, fine spokes of light, from the shape of my
head, or any one's head, in the sunlit water!
Come on, ships from the lower bay! pass up or
down, white-sail'd schooners, sloops, light-
ers!
Flaunt away, flags of all nations! be duly lower'd at
sunset!
Burn high your fires, foundry chimneys! cast black
shadows at nightfall! cast red and yellow
light over the tops of the houses!
Appearances, now or henceforth, indicate what you
are,   120
You necessary film, continue to envelop the soul,
About my body for me, and your body for you, be
hung our divinest aromas,
Thrive, cities — bring your freight, bring your
shows, ample and sufficient rivers,
Expand, being than which none else is perhaps
more spiritual,
Keep your places, objects than which none else is
more lasting.   125

You have waited, you always wait, you dumb,
beautiful ministers,
We receive you with free sense at last, and are insatiate henceforward,
Not you any more shall be able to foil us, or withhold yourselves from us,
We use you, and do not cast you aside — we plant
you permanently within us,
We fathom you not — we love you — there is perfection in you also,   130
You furnish your parts toward eternity,
Great or small, you furnish your parts toward the
soul.

I Hear America Singing

I hear America singing, the varied carols I hear,
Those of mechanics, each one singing his as it
should be blithe and strong,
The carpenter singing his as he measures his plank
or beam,
The mason singing his as he makes ready for work,
or leaves off work,
The boatman singing what belongs to him in his
boat, the deckhand singing on the steam-
boat deck,   5
The shoemaker singing as he sits on his bench, the
hatter singing as he stands,
The wood-cutter's song, the ploughboy's on his
way in the morning, or at noon intermission
or at sundown,

The delicious singing of the mother, or of the
 young wife at work, or of the girl sewing or
 washing,
Each singing what belongs to him or her and to
 none else,
The day what belongs to the day — at night the
 party of young fellows, robust, friendly, 10
Singing with open mouths their strong melodious
 songs.

Pioneers! O Pioneers!

One of Whitman's most constant themes was democracy. He held high ambitions for the United
States and its republican form of government. This
poem, written at the close of the Civil War, expresses
renewed conviction in America and her people. A
further intent of the poet is clear when one reads this
passage from *Specimen Days*:

"Lying by one rainy day in Missouri to rest after quite
a long exploration — first trying a big volume I found
there of 'Milton, Young, Gray, Beattie and Collins,'
but giving it up for a bad job — enjoying however for
awhile, as often before, the reading of Walter Scott's
poems, 'Lay of the Last Minstrel,' 'Marmion,' and so
on — I stopp'd and laid down the book, and ponder'd
the thought of a poetry that should in due time express
and supply the teeming region I was in the midst of,
and have briefly touch'd upon. One's mind needs but
a moment's deliberation anywhere in the United States
to see clearly enough that all the prevalent book and
library poets, either as imported from Great Britain,
or follow'd and *doppel-gang'd* here, are foreign to our
States, copiously as they are read by us all. But to
fully understand not only how absolutely in opposition
to our times and lands, and how little and cramp'd,
and what anachronisms and absurdities many of their
pages are, for American purposes, one must dwell or
travel awhile in Missouri, Kansas and Colorado, and
get rapport with their people and country.
Will the day ever come — no matter how long de-
ferr'd — when those models and lay-figures from the
British islands — and even the precious traditions of
the classics — will be reminiscences, studies only?
The pure breath, primitiveness, boundless prodigality
and amplitude, strange mixture of delicacy and power,
of continence, of real and ideal, and of all original and
first-class elements, of these prairies, the Rocky Mountains, and of the Mississippi and Missouri rivers —
will they ever appear in, and in some sort form a standard for our poetry and art?"

Come my tan-faced children,
Follow well in order, get your weapons ready,
Have you your pistols? have you your sharp-edged
 axes?
 Pioneers! O pioneers!

For we cannot tarry here, 5
We must march my darlings, we must bear the
 brunt of danger,
We the youthful sinewy races, all the rest on us
 depend,
 Pioneers! O pioneers!

O you youths, Western youths,
So impatient, full of action, full of manly pride and
 friendship, 10
Plain I see you Western youths, see you tramping
 with the foremost,
 Pioneers! O pioneers!

Have the elder races halted?
Do they droop and end their lesson, wearied over
 there beyond the sea?
We take up the task eternal, and the burden and
 the lesson, 15
 Pioneers! O Pioneers!

All the past we leave behind,
We debouch upon a newer mightier world, varied
 world,
Fresh and strong the world we seize, world of labor
 and the march,
 Pioneers! O pioneers! 20

We detachments steady throwing,
Down the edges, through the passes, up the moun-
 tain steep,
Conquering, holding, daring, venturing as we go
 the unknown ways,
 Pioneers! O pioneers!

We primeval forests felling, 25
We the rivers stemming, vexing we and piercing
 deep the mines within,
We the surface broad surveying, we the virgin soil
 upheaving,
 Pioneers! O pioneers!

Colorado men are we,
From the peaks gigantic, from the great sierras
 and the high plateaus, 30
From the mine and from the gully, from the hunt-
 ing trail we come,
 Pioneers! O pioneers!

From Nebraska, from Arkansas,
Central inland race are we, from Missouri, with
 the continental blood intervein'd,
All the hands of comrades clasping, all the South-
 ern, all the Northern, 35
 Pioneers! O pioneers!

O resistless restless race!
O beloved race in all!   O my breast aches with
 tender love for all!
O I mourn and yet exult, I am rapt with love for
 all,
 Pioneers!   O pioneers!   40

Raise the mighty mother mistress,
Waving high the delicate mistress, over all the
 starry mistress (bend your heads all),
Raise the fang'd and warlike mistress, stern, im-
 passive, weapon'd mistress,
 Pioneers! O pioneers!

See my children, resolute children,   45
By those swarms upon our rear we must never
 yield or falter,
Ages back in ghostly millions frowning there be-
 hind us urging,
 Pioneers!   O pioneers!

On and on the compact ranks,
With accessions ever waiting, with the places of
 the dead quickly fill'd,   50
Through the battle, through defeat, moving yet
 and never stopping,
 Pioneers!   O pioneers!

O to die advancing on!
Are there some of us to droop and die? has the hour
 come?
Then upon the march we fittest die, soon and sure
 the gap is fill'd,   55
 Pioneers!   O pioneers!

All the pulses of the world,
Falling in they beat for us, with the Western move-
 ment beat,
Holding single or together, steady moving to the
 front, all for us,
 Pioneers!   O pioneers!   60

Life's involv'd and varied pageants,
All the forms and shows, all the workmen at their
 work,
All the seamen and the landsmen, all the masters
 with their slaves,
 Pioneers!   O pioneers!

All the hapless silent lovers,   65
All the prisoners in the prisons, all the righteous
 and the wicked,
All the joyous, all the sorrowing, all the living, all
 the dying,
 Pioneers!   O pioneers!

I too with my soul and body,
We, a curious trio, picking, wandering on our
 way,   70
Through these shores amid the shadows, with the
 apparitions pressing,
 Pioneers!   O pioneers!

Lo, the darting bowling orb!
Lo, the brother orbs around, all the clustering suns
 and planets,
All the dazzling days, all the mystic nights with
 dreams,   75
 Pioneers!   O pioneers!

These are of us, they are with us,
All for primal needed work, while the followers
 there in embryo wait behind,
We to-day's procession heading, we the route for
 travel clearing,
 Pioneers!   O pioneers!   80

O you daughters of the West!
O you young and elder daughters!   O you mothers
 and you wives!
Never must you be divided, in our ranks you move
 united,
 Pioneers!   O pioneers!

Minstrels latent on the prairies!   85
(Shrouded bards of other lands, you may rest, you
 have done your work),
Soon I hear you coming warbling, soon you rise
 and tramp amid us,
 Pioneers!   O pioneers!

Not for delectations sweet,
Not the cushion and the slipper, not the peaceful
 and the studious,   90
Not the riches safe and palling, not for us the tame
 enjoyment,
 Pioneers!   O pioneers!

Do the feasters gluttonous feast?
Do the corpulent sleepers sleep?   Have they
 lock'd and bolted doors?
Still be ours the diet hard, and the blanket on the
 ground,   95
 Pioneers!   O pioneers!

Has the night descended?
Was the road of late so toilsome? did we stop dis-
 couraged nodding on our way?
Yet a passing hour I yield you in your tracks to
 pause oblivious,
 Pioneers!   O pioneers!   100

Till with sound of trumpet,
Far, far off the daybreak call — hark! how loud
    and clear I hear it wind,
Swift! to the head of the army! — swift! spring to
    your places,
    Pioneers! O pioneers!

O Captain! My Captain!

O Captain! My Captain! and the poem which follows
it are both tributes to Abraham Lincoln, the first a
dirge in a conventional verse form unusual with Whitman, the second in the free-verse form normally employed by the poet. The student who finds himself
skeptical of Whitman's poetic method may well ask
himself which of these two poems is the more effective.

O Captain! my Captain! our fearful trip is done,
The ship has weather'd every rack, the prize we
    sought is won,
The port is near, the bells I hear, the people all
    exulting,
While follow eyes the steady keel, the vessel grim
    and daring;
    But O heart! heart! heart!   5
      O the bleeding drops of red,
        Where on the deck my Captain lies,
          Fallen cold and dead.

O Captain! my Captain! rise up and hear the bells;
Rise up — for you the flag is flung — for you the
    bugle trills,   10
For you bouquets and ribbon'd wreaths — for you
    the shores a-crowding,
For you they call, the swaying mass, their eager
    faces turning;
    Here Captain! dear father!
      This arm beneath your head!
      It is some dream that on the deck,   15
        You've fallen cold and dead.

My Captain does not answer, his lips are pale and
    still,
My father does not feel my arm, he has no pulse
    nor will,
The ship is anchor'd safe and sound, its voyage
    closed and done,
From fearful trip the victor ship comes in with
    object won;   20
    Exult O shores, and ring O bells!
      But I with mournful tread,
      Walk the deck my Captain lies,
        Fallen cold and dead.

When Lilacs Last in the Dooryard Bloom'd

The British poet Swinburne termed *When Lilacs
Last in the Dooryard Bloom'd* "the most sonorous
anthem ever chanted in the church of the world." In
this poem Lincoln's funeral cortège moves across the
country against the background of America. The
poet takes the occasion to glorify death, "cool-enfolding
death," and does so in one of his most impassioned
lyrical outbursts. Notable, too, is the symbolism of the
poem, a symbolism which revolves about the star, the
thrush, and the cloud.

1

When lilacs last in the dooryard bloom'd,
And the great star early droop'd in the western
    sky in the night,
I mourn'd, and yet shall mourn with ever-returning
    spring

Ever-returning spring, trinity sure to me you
    bring,
Lilac blooming perennial and drooping star in the
    west,   5
And thought of him I love.

2

O powerful western fallen star!
O shades of night — O moody, tearful night!
O great star disappear'd — O the black murk that
    hides the star!
O cruel hands that hold me powerless — O helpless
    soul of me!   10
O harsh surrounding cloud that will not free my
    soul.

3

In the dooryard fronting an old farm-house near
    the white-wash'd palings,
Stands the lilac-bush, tall-growing with heart-
    shaped leaves of rich green,
With many a pointed blossom rising delicate, with
    the perfume strong I love,
With every leaf a miracle — and from this bush
    in the dooryard,   15
With delicate-color'd blossoms and heart-shaped
    leaves of rich green,
A sprig with its flower I break.

4

In the swamp in secluded recesses,
A shy and hidden bird is warbling a song.

Solitary the thrush, 20
The hermit withdrawn to himself, avoiding the
    settlements,
Sings by himself a song.

Song of the bleeding throat,
Death's outlet song of life (for well dear brother I
    know,
If thou was not granted to sing thou would'st
    surely die). 25

5

Over the breast of the spring, the land, amid cities,
Amid lanes and through old woods, where lately
    the violets peep'd from the ground, spotting
    the gray débris,
Amid the grass in the fields each side of the lanes,
    passing the endless grass;
Passing the yellow-spear'd wheat, every grain
    from its shroud in the dark-brown fields
    uprisen,
Passing the apple-tree blows of white and pink
    in the orchards, 30
Carrying a corpse to where it shall rest in the grave,
Night and day journeys a coffin.

6

Coffin that passes through lanes and streets,
Through day and night with the great cloud dark-
    ening the land,
With the pomp of the inloop'd flags with the cities
    draped in black, 35
With the show of the States themselves as of crape-
    veil'd women standing,
With processions long and winding and the flam-
    beaus of the night,
With the countless torches lit, with the silent sea
    of faces and the unbared heads,
With the waiting depot, the arriving coffin, and
    the somber faces,
With dirges through the night, with the thousand
    voices rising strong and solemn, 40
With all the mournful voices of the dirges pour'd
    around the coffin,
The dim-lit churches and the shuddering organs —
    where amid these you journey,
With the tolling tolling bells' perpetual clang,
Here, coffin that slowly passes,
I give you my sprig of lilac. 45

7

(Nor for you, for one alone,
Blossoms and branches green to coffins all I bring.
For fresh as the morning, thus would I carol a
    song to you O sane and sacred death.
All over bouquets of roses,

O death, I cover you over with roses and early
    lilies,
But mostly and now the lilac that blooms the first, 50
Copious I break, I break the sprigs from the bushes.
With loaded arms I come, pouring for you,
For you and the coffins of all of you O death.)

8

O western orb sailing the heaven, 55
Now I know what you must have meant as a
    month since I walk'd,
As I walk'd in silence the transparent shadowy
    night,
As I saw you had something to tell as you bent to
    me night after night,
As you droop'd from the sky low down as if to my
    side (while the other stars all look'd on),
As we wander'd together the solemn night (for
    something I know not what kept me from
    sleep), 60
As the night advanced, and I saw on the rim of the
    west how full you were of woe,
As I stood on the rising ground in the breeze in the
    cold transparent night,
As I watch'd where you pass'd and was lost in the
    netherward black of the night,
As my soul in its trouble dissatisfied sank, as where
    you sad orb,
Concluded, dropt in the night, and was gone. 65

9

Sing on there in the swamp,
O singer bashful and tender, I hear your notes, I
    hear your call,
I hear, I come presently, I understand you,
But a moment I linger, for the lustrous star has
    detain'd me,
The star my departing comrade holds and detains
    me. 70

10

O how shall I warble myself for the dead one there
    I loved?
And how shall I deck my song for the large sweet
    soul that has gone?
And what shall my perfume be for the grave of
    him I love?

Sea-winds blown from east and west,
Blown from the Eastern sea and blown from the
    Western sea till there on the Prairies meet-
    ing: 75
These and with these and the breath of my chant
I'll perfume the grave of him I love.

11

O what shall I hang on the chamber walls?
And what shall the pictures be that I hang on the
    walls,
To adorn the burial-house of him I love?   80

Pictures of growing spring and farms and homes,
With the Fourth-month eve at sundown, and the
    gray smoke lucid and bright,
With floods of the yellow gold of the gorgeous,
    indolent, sinking sun, burning, expanding
    the air,
With the fresh sweet herbage under foot, and the
    pale green leaves of the trees prolific,
In the distance the flowing glaze, the breast of the
    river, with a wind-dapple here and there; 85
With ranging hills on the banks, with many a line
    against the sky and shadows;
And the city at hand with dwellings so dense, and
    stacks of chimneys,
And all the scenes of life and the workshops, and
    the workmen homeward returning.

12

Lo, body and soul — this land,
My own Manhattan with spires, and the sparkling
    and hurrying tides, and the ships,   90
The varied and ample land, the South and the
    North in the light — Ohio's shores and
    flashing Missouri,
And ever the far-spreading prairies cover'd with
    grass and corn.

Lo, the most excellent sun so calm and haughty,
The violet and purple morn with just-felt breezes,
The gentle soft-born measureless light,   95
The miracle spreading bathing all, the fulfill'd
    noon,
The coming eve delicious, the welcome night and
    the stars,
Over my cities shining all, enveloping man and
    land.

13

Sing on, sing on you gray-brown bird,
Sing from the swamps, the recesses, pour your
    chant from the bushes;   100
Limitless out of the dusk, out of the cedars and
    pines.

Sing on dearest brother, warble your reedy song,
Loud human song, with voice of uttermost woe.

O liquid and free and tender!
O wild and loose to my soul — O wondrous singer!

You only I hear — yet the star holds me (but will
    soon depart),   106
Yet the lilac with mastering odor holds me.

14

Now while I sat in the day and look'd forth,
In the close of the day with its light and the fields
    of spring, and the farmers preparing their
    crops,
In the large unconscious scenery of my land with
    its lakes and forests,   110
In the heavenly aërial beauty (after the perturb'd
    winds and the storms),
Under the arching heavens of the afternoon swift
    passing, and the voices of children and
    women.
The many-moving sea-tides, and I saw the ships
    how they sail'd,
And the summer approaching with richness, and
    the fields all busy with labor,
And the infinite separate houses, how they all
    went on, each with its meals and minutia of
    daily usages;   115
And the streets how their throbbings throbb'd, and
    the cities pent — lo, then and there,
Falling upon them all and among them all, envelop-
    ing me with the rest,
Appear'd the cloud, appear'd the long black trail;
And I knew death, its thought, and the sacred
    knowledge of death.

Then with the knowledge of death as walking one
    side of me,   120
And the thought of death close-walking the other
    side of me,
And I in the middle as with companions, and as
    holding the hands of companions,
I fled forth to the hiding receiving night that talks
    not,
Down to the shores of the water, the path by the
    swamp in the dimness,
To the solemn shadowy cedars and ghostly pines
    so still.   125
And the singer so shy to the rest receiv'd me,
The gray-brown bird I know receiv'd us comrades
    three,
And he sang the carol of death, and a verse for
    him I love.

From deep secluded recesses,
From the fragrant cedars and the ghostly pines so
    still,   130
Came the carol of the bird.
And the charm of the carol rapt me,
As I held as if by their hands my comrades in the
    night;

And the voice of my spirit tallied the song of the
bird.

Come lovely and soothing death, 135
Undulate round the world, serenely arriving, arriving,
In the day, in the night, to all, to each,
Sooner or later delicate Death.

Prais'd be the fathomless universe,
For life and joy, and for objects and knowledge
curious, 140
And for love, sweet love — but praise! praise! praise!
For the sure-enwinding arms of cool-enfolding death.

Dark mother always gliding near with soft feet,
Have none chanted for thee a chant of fullest welcome?
Then I chant it for thee, I glorify thee above all, 145
I bring thee a song that when thou must indeed come,
come unfalteringly.

Approach strong Deliveress,
When it is so, when thou hast taken them, I joyously
sing the dead,
Lost in the loving floating ocean of thee,
Laved in the flood of thy bliss O death. 150

From me to thee glad serenades,
Dances for thee I propose saluting thee, adornments
and feastings for thee,
And the sights of the open landscape and the high-
spread sky are fitting,
And life and the fields, and the huge and thoughtful
night.

The night in silence under many a star, 155
The ocean shore and the husky whispering wave
whose voice I know,
And the soul turning to thee O vast and well-veil'd
death,
And the body gratefully nestling close to thee.

Over the tree-tops I float thee a song,
Over the rising and sinking waves, over the myriad
fields and the prairies wide, 160
Over the dense-pack'd cities all and the teeming
wharves and ways,
I float this carol with joy, with joy to thee O death!

15

To the tally of my soul.
Loud and strong kept up the gray-brown bird,
With pure, deliberate notes spreading filling the
night. 165

Loud in the pines and cedars dim,
Clear in the freshness moist and the swamp-per-
fume,
And I with my comrades there in the night.

While my sight that was bound in my eyes un-
closed,
As to long panoramas of visions. 170
And I saw askant the armies,
I saw as in noiseless dreams hundreds of battle-
flags,
Borne through the smoke of the battles and pierc'd
with missiles I saw them,
And carried hither and yon through the smoke, and
torn and bloody,
And at last but a few shreds left on the staffs, (and
all in silence,) 175
And the staffs all splinter'd and broken.

I saw battle-corpses, myriads of them,
And the white skeletons of young men, I saw them,
I saw the debris and debris of all the slain soldiers
of the war,
But I saw they were not as was thought, 180
They themselves were fully at rest, they suffer'd
not,
The living remain'd and suffer'd, the mother
suffer'd,
And the wife and the child and the musing comrade
suffer'd,
And the armies that remain'd suffer'd.

16

Passing the visions, passing the night, 185
Passing, unloosing the hold of my comrades' hands,
Passing the song of the hermit bird and the tallying
song of my soul,
Victorious song, death's outlet song, yet varying
ever-altering song,
As low and wailing, yet clear the notes, rising and
falling, flooding the night,
Sadly sinking and fainting, as warning and warning,
and yet again bursting with joy, 190
Covering the earth and filling the spread of the
heaven,
As that powerful psalm in the night I heard from
recesses,
Passing, I leave thee lilac with heart-shaped leaves,
I leave thee there in the door-yard, blooming,
returning with spring.

I cease from my song for thee, 195
From my gaze on thee in the west, fronting the
west, communing with thee,
O comrade lustrous with silver face in the night.

Yet each to keep and all, retrievements out of the
night,
The song, the wondrous chant of the gray-brown
bird,
And the tallying chant, the echo arous'd in my soul,

With the lustrous and drooping star with the
    countenance full of woe,   201
With the holders holding my hand nearing the call
    of the bird,
Comrades mine and I in the midst, and their
    memory ever to keep, for the dead I loved
    so well,
For the sweetest, wisest soul of all my days and
    lands — and this for his dear sake,
Lilac and star and bird twined with the chant of
    my soul,   205
There in the fragrant pines and the cedars dusk
    and dim.

Come Up from the Fields Father

Come up from the fields father, here's a letter
    from our Pete,
And come to the front door mother, here's a letter
    from thy dear son.

Lo, 'tis autumn,
Lo, where the trees, deeper green, yellower and
    redder,
Cool and sweeten Ohio's villages with leaves
    fluttering in the moderate wind,   5
Where apples ripe in the orchards hang and grapes
    on the trellis'd vines,
(Smell you the smell of the grapes on the vines?
Smell you the buckwheat where the bees were
    lately buzzing?)

Above all, lo, the sky so calm, so transparent after
    the rain, and with wondrous clouds,
Below too, all calm, all vital and beautiful, and
    the farm prospers well.   10

Down in the fields all prospers well,
But now from the fields come father, come at the
    daughter's call,
And come to the entry mother, to the front door
    come right away.

Fast as she can she hurries, something ominous,
    her steps trembling,
She does not tarry to smooth her hair nor adjust
    her cap.   15

Open the envelope quickly,
O this is not our son's writing, yet his name is
    sign'd,
O a strange hand writes for our dear son, O stricken
    mother's soul!
All swims before her eyes, flashes with black, she
    catches the main words only,

Sentences broken, *gunshot wound in the breast,*
    cavalry skirmish, taken to hospital,   20
At present low, but will soon be better.

Ah now the single figure to me,
Amid all teeming and wealthy Ohio with all its
    cities and farms,
Sickly white in the face and dull in the head, very
    faint,
By the jamb of a door leans.   25
Grieve not so, dear mother, (the just-grown daughter
    speaks through her sobs,
The little sisters huddle around speechless and
    dismay'd,)
See, dearest mother, the letter says Pete will soon be
    better.

Alas poor boy, he will never be better, (nor may-be
    needs to be better, that brave and simple
    soul,)
While they stand at home at the door he is dead
    already,   30
The only son is dead.

But the mother needs to be better,
She with thin form presently drest in black,
By day her meals untouch'd, then at night fitfully
    sleeping, often waking,
In the midnight waking, weeping, longing with
    one deep longing,   35
O that she might withdraw unnoticed, silent from
    life escape and withdraw,
To follow, to seek, to be with her dear dead son.

To a Locomotive in Winter

Thee for my recitative,[1]
Thee in the driving storm even as now, the snow,
    the winter-day declining,
Thee in thy panoply, thy measur'd dual throbbing
    and thy beat convulsive,
Thy black cylindric body, golden brass and silvery
    steel,
Thy ponderous side-bars, parallel and connecting
    rods, gyrating, shuttling at thy sides,   5
Thy metrical, now swelling pant and roar, now
    tapering in the distance,
Thy great protruding head-light fix'd in front,
Thy long, pale, floating vapor-pennants, tinged
    with delicate purple,
The dense and murky clouds out-belching from
    thy smoke-stack,

[1] A word frequently used by Whitman to characterize
the chant-like quality of his verse.

Thy knitted frame, thy springs and valves, the
    tremulous twinkle of thy wheels,   10
Thy train of cars behind, obedient, merrily follow-
    ing,
Through gale or calm, now swift, now slack, yet
    steadily careering;
Type of the modern — emblem of motion and
    power — pulse of the continent,
For once come serve the Muse and merge in verse,
    even as here I see thee,
With storm and buffeting gusts of wind and
    falling snow,   15
By day thy warning ringing bell to sound its notes,
By night thy silent signal lamps to swing.

Fierce-throated beauty!
Roll through my chant with all thy lawless music
    thy swinging lamps at night,
Thy madly-whistled laughter, echoing, rumbling
    like an earthquake, rousing all,   20
Law of thyself complete, thine own track firmly
    holding,
(No sweetness debonair of tearful harp or glib
    piano thine,)
Thy trills of shrieks by rocks and hills return'd,
Launch'd o'er the prairies wide, across the
    lakes,
To the free skies unpent and glad and strong.   25

Fyodor Dostoevsky · 1821–1881

Fyodor Mikhaylovitch Dostoevsky, the son of a hospital physician, was born at Moscow, October 30, 1821. Educated in the School of Military Engineers in St. Petersburg and commissioned in the army, Dostoevsky gave up his military career to devote his life to writing. As a young man he associated himself with a group of liberals to discuss socialism and political reform for Russia, an activity which brought him into such disfavor with the state that, along with others, he was sentenced to death but at the last moment was granted a reprieve and sentenced to exile in Siberia. In 1859 he returned to society and his civil rights were restored. Dostoevsky's life was almost a constant struggle with poverty, illness, and reversals. Even his first marriage — he was married twice — was most unhappy. The moment of his greatest fame came when in 1880, a few months before his death, he was requested to give the chief address at the dedication of a Pushkin memorial in Moscow, an oration which brought him at last full recognition from his compatriots.

Dostoevsky's most important novels include: *Poor Folk* (1846), *The House of the Dead* (1861), *The Insulted and Injured* (1861), *Crime and Punishment* (1866), *The Idiot* (1868), *The Possessed* (1871), and *The Brothers Karamazov* (1880). His writing is marked by a powerful imagination, psychological interest, keen dramatic sense, and the realistic portrayal of life and characters. It reveals the achievements of "a realist in the higher sense of the word" who, in Dostoevsky's own words, depicts "all the depths of the human soul." He is constantly concerned with problems of evil, with the morbidly psychological. Like other novelists he asks, "What is life?" but more than most writers he goes on to raise the further question, "And why all this suffering?" His lack of restraint, his attitude toward the evil he feels is inherent, and his concern with the spiritual aspects of man's life mark him as typically Russian, but his particular treatment of the situations he creates in his novels distinguish him from his other famous countrymen, Tolstoy, Gogol, and Chekhov. Dostoevsky himself has proved a major influence on later European writers.

SUGGESTED REFERENCES: Avrahm Yarmolinsky, *Dostoevsky: His Life and Art* (2nd ed., 1957); E. J. Simmons, *Dostoevsky. The Making of a Novelist* (new ed., 1962); Temira Pachmuss, *F. M. Dostoevsky: Dualism and Synthesis of the Human Soul* (1963); Edward Wasiolek, *Dostoevsky, The Major Fiction* (1964).

Crime and Punishment

The story of *Crime and Punishment* springs from one incident — Raskolnikoff's murder of a wealthy old woman. Inherently a decent man, Raskolnikoff, depressed and hungry, convinced that he is superior and that his superiority justifies his action, murders ostensibly for money but then neglects to take any of the wealth. The following pages, from the opening chapters, describe the crime and the psychological revulsion which follows.

THE CRIME

Luckily for him, everything went well again at the gates. At that very moment, as though expressly for his benefit, a huge waggon of hay had just driven in at the gate, completely screening him as he passed under the gateway, and the waggon had scarcely had time to drive through into the yard, before he had slipped in a flash to the right. On the other side of the waggon he could hear shouting and quarrelling; but no one noticed him and no one met him. Many windows looking into that huge quadrangular yard were open at that moment, but he did not raise his head — he had not the strength to. The staircase leading to the old woman's room was close by, just on the right of the gateway. He was already on the stairs....

Drawing a breath, pressing his hand against his throbbing heart, and once more feeling for the axe and setting it straight, he began softly and cautiously ascending the stairs, listening every minute. But the stairs, too, were quite deserted; all the doors were shut; he met no one. One flat indeed on the first floor was wide open and painters were at work in it, but they did not glance at him. He stood still, thought a minute and went on. "Of course it would be better if they had not been here, but ... it's two storeys above them."

And here was the fourth storey, here was the door, here was the flat opposite, the empty one. The flat underneath the old woman's was apparently empty also; the visiting card nailed on the door had been torn off — they had gone away! ... He was out of breath. For one instant the thought floated through his mind "Shall I go back?" But he made no answer and began listening at the old woman's door, a dead silence. Then he listened again on the staircase, listened long and intently ... then looked about him for the last time, pulled himself together, drew himself up, and once more tried the axe in the noose. "Am I very pale?" he wondered. "Am I not evidently agitated? She is mistrustful.... Had I better wait a little longer ... till my heart leaves off thumping?"

But his heart did not leave off. On the contrary, as though to spite him, it throbbed more and more violently. He could stand it no longer, he slowly put out his hand to the bell and rang. Half a minute later he rang again, more loudly.

No answer. To go on ringing was useless and out of place. The old woman was, of course, at home, but she was suspicious and alone. He had some knowledge of her habits ... and once more he put his ear to the door. Either his senses were peculiarly keen (which it is difficult to suppose), or the sound was really very distinct. Anyway, he suddenly heard something like the cautious touch of a hand on the lock and the rustle of a skirt at the very door. Some one was standing stealthily close to the lock and just as he was doing on the outside was secretly listening within, and seemed to have her ear to the door.... He moved a little on purpose and muttered something aloud that he might not have the appearance of hiding, then rang a third time, but quietly, soberly and without impatience. Recalling it afterwards, that moment stood out in his mind vividly, distinctly, for ever; he could not make out how he had had such cunning, for his mind was as it were clouded at moments and he was almost unconscious of his body.... An instant later he heard the latch unfastened.

The door was as before opened a tiny crack, and again two sharp and suspicious eyes stared at him out of the darkness. Then Raskolnikov lost his head and nearly made a great mistake.

Fearing the old woman would be frightened by their being alone, and not hoping that the sight of him would disarm her suspicions, he took hold of the door and drew it towards him to prevent the old woman from attempting to shut it again. Seeing this she did not pull the door back, but she did not let go the handle so that he almost dragged her out with it on to the stairs. Seeing that she was standing in the doorway not allowing him to pass, he advanced straight upon her. She stepped back in alarm, tried to say something, but seemed unable to speak and stared with open eyes at him.

"Good evening, Alyona Ivanovna," he began, trying to speak easily, but his voice would not obey him, it broke and shook. "I have come ... I have brought something ... but we'd better come in ... to the light...."

And leaving her, he passed straight into the room uninvited. The old woman ran after him; her tongue was unloosed.

"Good heavens! What is it? Who is it? What do you want?"

"Why, Alyona Ivanovna, you know me ...

Raskolnikov . . . here, I brought you the pledge [1] I promised the other day . . ." and he held out the pledge.

The old woman glanced for a moment at the pledge, but at once stared in the eyes of her uninvited visitor. She looked intently, maliciously and mistrustfully. A minute passed; he even fancied something like a sneer in her eyes, as though she had already guessed everything. He felt that he was losing his head, that he was almost frightened, so frightened that if she were to look like that and not say a word for another half minute, he thought he would have run away from her.

"Why do you look at me as though you did not know me?" he said suddenly, also with malice. "Take it if you like, if not I'll go elsewhere, I am in a hurry."

He had not even thought of saying this, but it was suddenly said of itself. The old woman recovered herself, and her visitor's resolute tone evidently restored her confidence.

"But why, my good sir, all of a minute. . . . What is it?" she asked, looking at the pledge.

"The silver cigarette case; I spoke of it last time, you know."

She held out her hand.

"But how pale you are, to be sure . . . and your hands are trembling too? Have you been bathing, or what?"

"Fever," he answered abruptly. "You can't help getting pale . . . if you've nothing to eat," he added, with difficulty articulating the words.

His strength was failing him again. But his answer sounded like the truth; the old woman took the pledge.

"What is it?" she asked once more, scanning Raskolnikov intently and weighing the pledge in her hand.

"A thing . . . cigarette case. . . . Silver. . . . Look at it."

"It does not seem somehow like silver. . . . How he has wrapped it up!"

Trying to untie the string and turning to the window, to the light (all her windows were shut, in spite of the stifling heat), she left him altogether for some seconds and stood with her back to him. He unbuttoned his coat and freed the axe from the noose, but did not yet take it out altogether, simply holding it in his right hand under the coat. His hands were fearfully weak, he felt them every moment growing more numb and more wooden.

[1] An article to be pawned. In this instance it was a piece of metal between boards, securely wrapped, to resemble a cigarette case.

He was afraid he would let the axe slip and fall. . . . A sudden giddiness came over him.

"But what has he tied it up like this for?" the old woman cried with vexation and moved towards him.

He had not a minute more to lose. He pulled the axe quite out, swung it with both arms, scarcely conscious of himself, and almost without effort, almost mechanically, brought the blunt side down on her head. He seemed not to use his own strength in this. But as soon as he had once brought the axe down, his strength returned to him.

The old woman was as always bareheaded. Her thin, light hair, streaked with grey, thickly smeared with grease, was plaited in a rat's tail and fastened by a broken horn comb which stood out on the nape of her neck. As she was so short, the blow fell on the very top of her skull. She cried out, but very faintly, and suddenly sank all of a heap on the floor, raising her hands to her head. In one hand she still held "the pledge." Then he dealt her another and another blow with the blunt side and on the same spot. The blood gushed as from an overturned glass, the body fell back. He stepped back, let it fall, and at once bent over her face; she was dead. Her eyes seemed to be starting out of their sockets, the brow and the whole face were drawn and contorted convulsively.

He laid the axe on the ground near the dead body and felt at once in her pocket (trying to avoid the streaming body) — the same right hand pocket from which she had taken the key on his last visit. He was in full possession of his faculties, free from confusion or giddiness, but his hands were still trembling. He remembered afterwards that he had been particularly collected and careful, trying all the time not to get smeared with blood. . . . He pulled out the keys at once, they were all, as before, in one bunch on a steel ring. He ran at once into the bedroom with them. It was a very small room with a whole shrine of holy images. Against the other wall stood a big bed, very clean and covered with a silk patchwork wadded quilt. Against a third wall was a chest of drawers. Strange to say, so soon as he began to fit the keys into the chest, so soon as he heard their jingling, a convulsive shudder passed over him. He suddenly felt tempted again to give it all up and go away. But that was only for an instant; it was too late to go back. He positively smiled at himself, when suddenly another terrifying idea occurred to his mind. He suddenly fancied that the old woman might be still alive and might recover her senses. Leaving the keys in the chest, he ran back to the body, snatched up the axe and lifted it once more over the old woman, but did not bring it down.

There was no doubt that she was dead. Bending down and examining her again more closely, he saw clearly that the skull was broken and even battered in on one side. He was about to feel it with his finger, but drew back his hand, and indeed it was evident without that. Meanwhile there was a perfect pool of blood. All at once he noticed a string on her neck; he tugged at it, but the string was strong and did not snap and besides, it was soaked with blood. He tried to pull it out from the front of the dress, but something held it and prevented its coming. In his impatience he raised the axe again to cut the string from above on the body, but did not dare, and with difficulty, smearing his hand and the axe in the blood, after two minutes' hurried effort, he cut the string and took it off without touching the body with the axe; he was not mistaken — it was a purse. On the string were two crosses, one of Cyprus wood and one of copper, and an image in silver filigree, and with them a small greasy chamois leather purse with a steel rim and ring. The purse was stuffed very full; Raskolnikov thrust it in his pocket without looking at it, flung the crosses on the old woman's body and rushed back into the bedroom, this time taking the axe with him.

He was in terrible haste; he snatched the keys, and began trying them again. But he was un-successful. They would not fit in the locks. It was not so much that his hands were shaking, but that he kept making mistakes; though he saw for instance that a key was not the right one and would not fit, still he tried to put it in. Suddenly he re-membered and realised that the big key with the deep notches, which was hanging there with the small keys, could not possibly belong to the chest of drawers (on his last visit this had struck him), but to some strong box, and that everything per-haps was hidden in that box. He left the chest of drawers, and at once felt under the bedstead, know-ing that old women usually keep boxes under their beds. And so it was; there was a good-sized box under the bed, at least a yard in length, with an arched lid covered with red leather and studded with steel nails. The notched key fitted at once and unlocked it. At the top, under a white sheet, was a coat of red brocade lined with hareskin; under it was a silk dress, then a shawl, and it seemed as though there was nothing below but clothes. The first thing he did was to wipe his blood-stained hands on the red brocade. "It's red, and on red blood will be less noticeable," the thought passed through his mind; then he, suddenly came to him-self. "Good God, am I going out of my senses?" he thought with terror.

But no sooner did he touch the clothes than a gold watch slipped from under the fur coat. He made haste to turn them all over. There turned out to be various articles made of gold among the clothes — probably all pledges, unredeemed or waiting to be redeemed — bracelets, chains, ear-rings, pins and such things. Some were in cases, others simply wrapped in newspaper, carefully and exactly folded, and tied round with tape. Without any delay, he began filling up the pockets of his trousers and overcoat without examining or undoing the parcels and cases; but he had not time to take many....

He suddenly heard steps in the room where the old woman lay. He stopped short and was still as death. But all was quiet, so it must have been his fancy. All at once he heard distinctly a faint cry, as though some one had uttered a low broken moan. Then again dead silence for a minute or two. He sat squatting on his heels by the box and waited holding his breath. Suddenly he jumped up, seized the axe and ran out of the bedroom.

In the middle of the room stood Lizaveta with a big bundle in her arms. She was gazing in stupe-faction at her murdered sister, white as a sheet and seeming not to have the strength to cry out. Seeing him run out of the bedroom, she began faintly quivering all over, like a leaf, a shudder ran down her face; she lifted her hand, opened her mouth, but still did not scream. She began slowly backing away from him into the corner, staring intently, persistently at him, but still uttered no sound, as though she could not get breath to scream. He rushed at her with the axe; her mouth twitched piteously, as one sees babies' mouths, when they begin to be frightened, stare intently at what frightens them and are on the point of scream-ing. And this hapless Lizaveta was so simple and had been so thoroughly crushed and scared that she did not even raise a hand to guard her face, though that was the most necessary and natural action at the moment, for the axe was raised over her face. She only put up her empty left hand, but not to her face, slowly holding it out before her as though motioning him away. The axe fell with the sharp edge just on the skull and split at one blow all the top of the head. She fell heavily at once. Raskolnikov completely lost his head, snatched up her bundle, dropped it again and ran into the entry.

Fear gained more and more mastery over him, especially after this second, quite unexpected murder. He longed to run away from the place as fast as possible. And if at that moment he had been capable of seeing and reasoning more cor-rectly, if he had been able to realise all the difficul-ties of his position, the hopelessness, the hideousness and the absurdity of it, if he could have understood how many obstacles and, perhaps, crimes he had still to overcome or to commit, to get out of that place and to make his way home, it is very possible that he would have flung up everything, and would have gone to give himself up, and not from fear, but from simple horror and loathing of what he had done. The feeling of loathing especially surged up within him and grew stronger every minute. He would not now have gone to the box or even into the room for anything in the world.

But a sort of blankness, even dreaminess had begun by degrees to take possession of him; at moments he forgot himself, or rather forgot what was of importance and caught at trifles. Glancing, however, into the kitchen and seeing a bucket half full of water on a bench, he bethought him of washing his hands and the axe. His hands were sticky with blood. He dropped the axe with the blade in the water, snatched a piece of soap that lay in a broken saucer on the window, and began washing his hands in the bucket. When they were clean, he took out the axe, washed the blade and spent a long time, about three minutes, washing the wood where there were spots of blood, rubbing them with soap. Then he wiped it all with some linen that was hanging to dry on a line in the kitchen and then he was a long while attentively examining the axe at the window. There was no trace left on it, only the wood was still damp. He carefully hung the axe in the noose under his coat. Then as far as was possible, in the dim light in the kitchen, he looked over his overcoat, his trousers and his boots. At the first glance there seemed to be nothing but stains on the boots. He wetted the rag and rubbed the boots. But he knew he was not looking thoroughly, that there might be something quite noticeable that he was overlooking. He stood in the middle of the room, lost in thought. Dark agonising ideas rose in his mind — the idea that he was mad and that at that moment he was incapable of reasoning, of protecting himself, that he ought perhaps to be doing something utterly different from what he was now doing. "Good God!" he muttered, "I must fly, fly," and he rushed into the entry. But here a shock of terror awaited him such as he had never known before.

He stood and gazed and could not believe his eyes: the door, the outer door from the stairs, at which he had not long before waited and rung, was standing unfastened and at least six inches open. No lock, no bolt, all the time, all that time! The old woman had not shut it after him perhaps as a precaution. But, good God! Why, he had

seen Lizaveta afterwards! And how could he, how could he have failed to reflect that she must have come in somehow! She could not have come through the wall!

He dashed to the door and fastened the latch.

"But no, the wrong thing again! I must get away, get away...."

He unfastened the latch, opened the door and began listening on the staircase.

He listened a long time. Somewhere far away, it might be in the gateway, two voices were loudly and shrilly shouting, quarrelling and scolding. "What are they about?" He waited patiently. At last all was still, as though suddenly cut off; they had separated. He was meaning to go out, but suddenly, on the floor below, a door was noisily opened and some one began going downstairs humming a tune. "How is it they all make such a noise!" flashed through his mind. Once more he closed the door and waited. At last all was still, not a soul stirring. He was just taking a step towards the stairs when he heard fresh footsteps.

The steps sounded very far off, at the very bottom of the stairs, but he remembered quite clearly and distinctly that from the first sound he began for some reason to suspect that this was some one coming *there*, to the fourth floor, to the old woman. Why? Were the sounds somehow peculiar, significant? The steps were heavy, even and unhurried. Now *he* had passed the first floor, now he was mounting higher, it was growing more and more distinct! He could hear his heavy breathing. And now the third storey had been reached. Coming here! And it seemed to him all at once that he was turned to stone, that it was like a dream in which one is being pursued, nearly caught and will be killed, and is rooted to the spot and cannot even move one's arms.

At last when the unknown was mounting to the fourth floor, he suddenly started, and succeeded in slipping neatly and quickly back into the flat and closing the door behind him. Then he took the hook and softly, noiselessly, fixed it in the catch. Instinct helped him. When he had done this, he crouched holding his breath, by the door. The unknown visitor was by now also at the door. They were now standing opposite one another, as he had just before been standing with the old woman, when the door divided them and he was listening.

The visitor panted several times. "He must be a big, fat man," thought Raskolnikov, squeezing the axe in his hand. It seemed like a dream indeed. The visitor took hold of the bell and rang loudly.

As soon as the tin bell tinkled, Raskolnikov

seemed to be aware of something moving in the room. For some seconds he listened quite seriously. The unknown rang again, waited and suddenly tugged violently and impatiently at the handle of the door. Raskolnikov gazed in horror at the hook shaking in its fastening, and in blank terror expected every minute that the fastening would be pulled out. It certainly did seem possible, so violently was he shaking it. He was tempted to hold the fastening, but *he* might be aware of it. A giddiness came over him again. "I shall fall down!" flashed through his mind, but the unknown began to speak and he recovered himself at once.

"What's up? Are they asleep or murdered? D-damn them!" he bawled in a thick voice, "Hey, Alyona Ivanovna, old witch! Lizaveta Ivanovna, hey, my beauty! open the door! Oh, damn them! Are they asleep or what?"

And again, enraged, he tugged with all his might a dozen times at the bell. He must certainly be a man of authority and an intimate acquaintance.

At this moment light hurried steps were heard not far off, on the stairs. Some one else was approaching. Raskolnikov had not heard them at first.

"You don't say there's no one at home," the new-comer cried in a cheerful, ringing voice, addressing the first visitor who still went on pulling the bell. "Good evening, Koch."

"From his voice he must be quite young," thought Raskolnikov.

"Who the devil can tell? I've almost broken the lock," answered Koch. "But how do you come to know me?"

"Why! The day before yesterday I beat you three times running at billiards at Gambrinus'."

"Oh!"

"So they are not at home? That's queer? It's awfully stupid though. Where could the old woman have gone? I've come on business."

"Yes; and I have business with her, too."

"Well, what can we do? Go back, I suppose. Aie — aie! And I was hoping to get some money!" cried the young man.

"We must give it up, of course, but what did she fix this time for? The old witch fixed the time for me to come herself. It's out of my way. And where the devil she can have got to, I can't make out. She sits here from year's end to year's end, the old hag; her legs are bad and yet here all of a sudden she is out for a walk!"

"Hadn't we better ask the porter?"

"What?"

"Where she's gone and when she'll be back."

"Hm.... Damn it all!... We might ask....

But you know she never does go anywhere."

And he once more tugged at the door-handle.

"Damn it all. There's nothing to be done, we must go!"

"Stay!" cried the young man suddenly. "Do you see how the door shakes if you pull it?"

"Well?"

"That shows it's not locked, but fastened with the hook! Do you hear how the hook clanks?"

"Well?"

"Why, don't you see? That proves that one of them is at home. If they were all out, they would have locked the door from outside with the key and not with the hook from inside. There, do you hear how the hook is clanking? To fasten the hook on the inside they must be at home, don't you see. So there they are sitting inside and don't open the door!"

"Well! And so they must be!" cried Koch, astonished. "What are they about in there!" And he began furiously shaking the door.

"Stay!" cried the young man again. "Don't pull at it! There must be something wrong.... Here, you've been ringing and pulling at the door and still they don't open! So either they've both fainted or..."

"What?"

"I tell you what. Let's go and fetch the porter, let him wake them up."

"All right."

Both were going down.

"Stay. You stop here while I run down for the porter."

"What for?"

"Well, you'd better."

"All right."

"I'm studying the law, you see! It's evident, e-vi-dent there's something wrong here!" the young man cried hotly, and he ran downstairs.

Koch remained. Once more he softly touched the bell, which gave one tinkle, then gently, as though reflecting and looking about him, began touching the door-handle, pulling it and letting it go to make sure once more that it was only fastened by the hook. Then puffing and panting he bent down and began looking at the keyhole; but the key was in the lock on the inside and so nothing could be seen.

Raskolnikov stood keeping tight hold of the axe. He was in a sort of delirium. He was even making ready to fight when they should come in. While they were knocking and talking together, the idea several times occurred to him to end it all at once and shout to them through the door. Now and then he was tempted to swear at them, to jeer at them, while they could not open the door! "Only make haste!" was the thought that flashed through his mind.

"But what the devil is he about?..." Time was passing, one minute, and another — no one came. Koch began to be restless.

"What the devil?" he cried suddenly and in impatience deserting his sentry duty, he, too, went down, hurrying and thumping with his heavy boots on the stairs. The steps died away.

"Good heavens! What am I to do?"

Raskolnikov unfastened the hook, opened the door — there was no sound. Abruptly, without any thought at all, he went out, closing the door as thoroughly as he could, and went downstairs.

He had gone down three flights when he suddenly heard a loud noise below — where could he go! There was nowhere to hide. He was just going back to the flat.

"Hey there! Catch the brute!"

Somebody dashed out of a flat below, shouting, and rather fell than ran down the stairs, bawling at the top of his voice.

"Mitka! Mitka! Mitka! Mitka! Mitka! Blast him!"

The shout ended in a shriek; the last sounds came from the yard; all was still. But at the same instant several men talking loud and fast began noisily mounting the stairs. There were three or four of them. He distinguished the ringing voice of the young man. "They!"

Filled with despair he went straight to meet them, feeling "Come what must!" If they stopped him — all was lost; if they let him pass — all was lost too; they would remember him. They were approaching; they were only a flight from him — and suddenly deliverance! A few steps from him on the right, there was an empty flat with the door wide open, the flat on the second floor where the painters had been at work, and which, as though for his benefit, they had just left. It was they, no doubt, who had just run down, shouting. The floor had only just been painted, in the middle of the room stood a pail and a broken pot with paint and brushes. In one instant he had whisked in at the open door and hidden behind the wall, and only in the nick of time; they had already reached the landing. Then they turned and went on up to the fourth floor, talking loudly. He waited, went out on tiptoe and ran down the stairs.

No one was on the stairs, nor in the gateway. He passed quickly through the gateway and turned to the left in the street.

He knew, he knew perfectly well that at that moment they were at the flat, that they were greatly astonished at finding it unlocked, as the door had just been fastened, that by now they were looking at the bodies, that before another minute had passed they would guess and completely realise that the murderer had just been there, and had succeeded in hiding somewhere, slipping by them and escaping. They would guess most likely that he had been in the empty flat, while they were going upstairs. And meanwhile he dared not quicken his pace much, though the next turning was still nearly a hundred yards away. "Should he slip through some gateway and wait somewhere in an unknown street? No, hopeless! Should he fling away the axe? Should he take a cab? Hopeless, hopeless!"

At last he reached the turning. He turned down it more dead than alive. Here he was halfway to safety, and here understood it; it was less risky because there was a great crowd of people, and he was lost in it like a grain of sand. But all he had suffered had so weakened him that he could scarcely move. Perspiration ran down him in drops, his neck was all wet. "My word, he has been going it!" some one shouted at him when he came out on the canal bank.

He was only dimly conscious of himself now, and the farther he went the worse it was. He remembered however, that on coming out on to the canal bank, he was alarmed at finding few people there and so being more conspicuous, and he had thought of turning back. Though he was almost falling from fatigue, he went a long way round so as to get home from quite a different direction.

He was not fully conscious when he passed through the gateway of his house! he was already on the staircase before he recollected the axe. And yet he had a very grave problem before him, to put it back and to escape observation as far as possible in doing so. He was of course incapable of reflecting that it might perhaps be far better not to restore the axe at all, but to drop it later on in somebody's yard. But it all happened fortunately, the door of the porter's room was closed but not locked, so that it seemed most likely that the porter was at home. But he had so completely lost all power of reflection that he walked straight to the door and opened it. If the porter had asked him "What do you want?" he would perhaps have simply handed him the axe. But again the porter was not at home, and he succeeded in putting the axe back under the bench and even covering it with the chunk of wood as before. He met no one, not a soul, afterwards on the way to his room; the landlady's door was shut. When he was in his room, he flung himself on the sofa just as he was — he did not sleep, but sank into blank forgetfulness. If any one had come into his room then, he would have jumped up at once and screamed. Scraps and shreds of thoughts were simply swarming in his brain, but he could not catch at one, he could not rest on one, in spite of all his efforts. . . .

So he lay a very long while. Now and then he seemed to wake up, and at such moments he noticed that it was far into the night, but it did not occur to him to get up. At last he noticed that it was beginning to get light. He was lying on his back, still dazed from his recent oblivion. Fearful, despairing cries rose shrilly from the street, sounds which he heard every night, indeed, under his window after two o'clock. They woke him up now.

"Ah! the drunken men are coming out of the taverns," he thought, "it's past two o'clock," and at once he leaped up, as though some one had pulled him from the sofa.

"What! Past two o'clock!"

He sat down on the sofa — and instantly recollected everything! All at once, in one flash, he recollected everything.

For the first moment he thought he was going mad. A dreadful chill came over him; but the chill was from the fever that had begun long before in his sleep. Now he was suddenly taken with violent shivering, so that his teeth chattered and all his limbs were shaking. He opened the door and began listening; everything in the house was asleep. With amazement he gazed at himself and everything in the room around him, wondering how he could have come in the night before without fastening the door, and have flung himself on the sofa without undressing, without even taking his hat off. It had fallen off and was lying on the floor near his pillow.

"If any one had come in, what would he have thought? That I'm drunk but . . ."

He rushed to the window. There was light enough, and he began hurriedly looking himself all over from head to foot, all his clothes; were there no traces? But there was no doing it like that; shivering with cold, he began taking off everything and looking over again. He turned everything over to the last threads and rags, and mistrusting himself, went through his search three times.

But there seemed to be nothing, no trace, except in one place, where some thick drops of congealed blood were clinging to the frayed edge of his trousers. He picked up a big claspknife and cut off the frayed thread. There seemed to be nothing more.

Suddenly he remembered that the purse and the things he had taken out of the old woman's box were still in his pockets! He had not thought till then of taking them out and hiding them! He had not even thought of them while he was examining his clothes! What next? Instantly he rushed to take them out, and fling them on the table. When he had pulled out everything, and turned the pocket inside out to be sure there was nothing left, he carried the whole heap to the corner. The paper had come off the bottom of the wall and hung there in tatters. He began stuffing all the things into the hole under the paper: "They're in! All out of sight, and the purse too!" he thought gleefully, getting up and gazing blankly at the hole, which bulged out more than ever. Suddenly he shuddered all over with horror; "My God!" he whispered in despair: "what's the matter with me? Is that hidden? Is that the way to hide things?"

He had not reckoned on having trinkets to hide. He had only thought of money, and so had not prepared a hiding-place.

"But now, now, what am I glad of?" he thought. "Is that hiding things? My reason's deserting me — simply!"

He sat down on the sofa in exhaustion and was at once shaken by another unbearable fit of shivering. Mechanically he drew from a chair beside him his old student's winter coat, which was still warm though almost in rags, covered himself up with it and once more sank into drowsiness and delirium. He lost consciousness.

Not more than five minutes had passed when he jumped up a second time, and at once pounced in a frenzy on his clothes again.

"How could I go to sleep again with nothing done? Yes, yes; I have not taken the loop off the armhole! I forgot it, forgot a thing like that! Such a piece of evidence!"

He pulled off the noose, hurriedly cut it to pieces and threw the bits among his linen under the pillow.

"Pieces of torn linen couldn't rouse suspicion, whatever happened; I think not, I think not, any way!" he repeated, standing in the middle of the room, and with painful concentration he fell to gazing about him again, at the floor and everywhere, trying to make sure he had not forgotten anything. The conviction that all his faculties, even memory, and the simplest power of reflection were failing him, began to be an insufferable torture.

"Surely it isn't beginning already! Surely it isn't my punishment coming upon me? It is!"

The frayed rags he had cut off his trousers were actually lying on the floor in the middle of the room, where any one coming in would see them!

"What is the matter with me!" he cried again, like one distraught.

Then a strange idea entered his head; that, perhaps, all his clothes were covered with blood, that, perhaps, there were a great many stains, but that he did not see them, did not notice them because his perceptions were failing, were going to pieces... his reason was clouded.... Suddenly he remembered that there had been blood on the purse too. "Ah! Then there must be blood on the pocket too, for I put the wet purse in my pocket!"

In a flash he had turned the pocket inside out and, yes! — there were traces, stains on the lining of the pocket!

"So my reason has not quite deserted me, so I still have some sense and memory, since I guessed it of myself," he thought triumphantly, with a deep sigh of relief: "It's simply the weakness of fever, a moment's delirium," and he tore the whole lining out of the left pocket of his trousers. At that instant the sunlight fell on his left boot; on the sock which poked out from the boot, he fancied there were traces! He flung off his boots: "traces indeed! The tip of the sock was soaked with blood"; he must have unwarily stepped into that pool.... "But what am I to do with this now? Where am I to put the sock and rags and pocket?"

He gathered them all up in his hands and stood in the middle of the room.

"In the stove? But they would ransack the stove first of all. Burn them? But what can I burn them with? There are no matches even. No, better go out and throw it all away somewhere. Yes, better throw it away," he repeated, sitting down on the sofa again, "and at once, this minute, without lingering..."

But his head sank on the pillow instead. Again the unbearable icy shivering came over him; again he drew his coat over him.

Leo Tolstoy · 1828-1910

Count Leo Tolstoy, novelist and social philosopher, was born on the family estate, Yasnaya Polyana, in the Russian province of Tula. He knew comfort and ease and enjoyed such advantages as in Russia went with membership in a family of the ruling class. Educated by private tutors and at the university of Kazan, Tolstoy grew to maturity during a period when Russia was feeling the urge toward a new social order. After a very active life, a mystical "conversion" occurred, and he adopted the ways and dress of the peasant, turning frequently to such manual labor as shoemaking. Losing faith in the right of an individual to enjoy the advantages of wealth, he turned over all his property to his wife, but continued to live in the environment which his wealth had made possible. His later years, however, became embittered, and he left his home, accompanied by his daughter.

The author of several novels, an important drama or two, many short stories, and criticism, Tolstoy is best known as the author of *War and Peace* (1869), *Anna Karenina* (1877), the *Kreutzer Sonata* (1890), *Resurrection* (1899), and an essay, *What is Art?* (1898), which developed the thesis that good art is moral art.

Tolstoy was a realistic writer. He was concerned with psychological and moral values, and his purpose was to describe the inner consciousness of his characters. On large canvases, against the background of contemporary Russian society and of peasant life, he drew his characters with great skill. Interwoven into the main action of his novels and shorter stories are scenes of infinite detail — in *Anna Karenina*, for instance, a spring planting, a horse-race, the protracted dying of a man wasting away with disease, a ball, the interior of army barracks. Tolstoy is a master of analysis. So deep is his understanding of human motives and emotions that he has been called a "psychological eavesdropper."

Tolstoy emphasizes the conflict within man between the promptings of reason and the desire for natural, spontaneous action unhampered by convention or social standards. His characters are divided between those seeking a natural Rousseauism and those trying to live by an inner desire for restraint and moderation. Tolstoy detested the artificiality of the educated and wealthy and he distrusted the ignorance of the peasant, but he once said that if one class was to teach the other then society should sit at the footstool of the laborer since, on the whole, more would be learned that way.

His most common themes are the prejudices and convictions of human beings, their pettiness and their greatness, their behavior in the face of death and their search for God. In the last years of his life, after the time of his conversion, Tolstoy preached certain specific doctrines: non-resistance, belief in a god of abstract goodness rather than a personal deity, the necessity for man to avoid greed and hate, the evil of property.

SUGGESTED REFERENCES: Ernest J. Simmons, *Leo Tolstoy* (2nd ed. 1960); Theodore Redpath, *Tolstoy* (1960).

Anna Karenina

Any critical reader making a list of the ten great novels of the world is compelled to include *Anna Karenina*. This is a two-fold story: one branch of the narrative tells of the illicit love of Anna and Vronsky and of the disaster and tragedy which result; the second branch recounts the experiences of Levin — who is Tolstoy himself — in a quieter life on a Russian farm and incorporates the author's theories of agriculture and of the relations of men of wealth with the peasant. The first is a story of the passion of love, of the circles of Russian urban society, of man's vanity and ambition; the second is a story of the country and the family, of the seasons the hunt and the harvest, of man's search for peace.

In the selections which follow, the second and third relate to the plot of tragic love, the first and the fourth to the theme of rural peace.

FARMING IN OLD RUSSIA

In the early days after his return from Moscow, whenever Levin shuddered and grew red, remembering the disgrace of his rejection, he said to himself: "This was just how I used to shudder and blush, thinking myself utterly lost, when I was plucked [1] in physics and did not get my remove; and how I thought myself utterly ruined after I had mismanaged that affair of my sister's that was intrusted to me. And yet, now that years have passed, I recall it and wonder that it could distress me so much. It will be the same thing too with this trouble. Time will go by and I shall not mind about this [2] either."

But three months had passed and he had not left off minding about it; and it was as painful for him to think of it as it had been those first days. He could not be at peace because after dreaming so long of family life, and feeling himself so ripe for it, he was still not married, and was further than ever from marriage. He was painfully conscious himself, as were all about him, that at his years it is not well for man to be alone. He remembered

[1] failed.
[2] Levin's proposal of marriage has been refused by Kitty, the Princess Shtcherbatsky, who, however, marries him later on in the novel.

how before starting for Moscow he had once said to his cowman Nikolay, a simple-hearted peasant, whom he liked talking to: "Well, Nikolay! I mean to get married," and how Nikolay had promptly answered, as of a matter on which there could be no possible doubt: "And high time too, Konstantin Dmitrievitch." But marriage had now become further off than ever. The place was taken, and whenever he tried to imagine any of the girls he knew in that place, he felt that it was utterly impossible. Moreover, the recollection of the rejection and the part he had played in the affair tortured him with shame. However often he told himself that he was in no wise to blame in it, that recollection, like other humiliating reminiscences of a similar kind, made him twinge and blush. There had been in his past, as in every man's, actions, recognized by him as bad, for which his conscience ought to have tormented him; but the memory of these evil actions was far from causing him so much suffering as those trivial but humiliating reminiscences. These wounds never healed. And with these memories was now ranged his rejection and the pitiful position in which he must have appeared to others that evening. But time and work did their part. Bitter memories were more and more covered up by the incidents — paltry in his eyes, but really important — of his country life. Every week he thought less often of Kitty. He was impatiently looking forward to the news that she was married, or just going to be married, hoping that such news would, like having a tooth out, completely cure him.

Meanwhile spring came on, beautiful and kindly, without the delays and treacheries of spring — one of those rare springs in which plants, beasts, and man rejoice alike. This lovely spring roused Levin still more, and strengthened him in his resolution of renouncing all his past and building up his lonely life firmly and independently. Though many of the plans with which he had returned to the country had not been carried out, still his most important resolution — that of purity — had been kept by him. He was free from that shame, which had usually harassed him after a fall; and he could look every one straight in the face. In February he had received a letter from Marya Nikolaevna telling him that his brother Nikolay's health was getting worse, but that he would not take advice, and in consequence of this letter Levin went to Moscow to his brother's, and succeeded in persuading him to see a doctor and to go to a watering-place abroad. He succeeded so well in persuading his brother, and in lending him money for the journey without irritating him, that he was satisfied with himself in that matter. In addition to his farming, which called for special attention in spring, in addition to reading, Levin had begun that winter a work on agriculture, the plan of which turned on taking into account the character of the laborer on the land as one of the unalterable data of the question, like the climate and the soil, and consequently deducing all the principles of scientific culture, not simply from the data of soil and climate, but from the data of soil, climate, and a certain unalterable character of the laborer. Thus, in spite of his solitude, or in consequence of his solitude, his life was exceedingly full. Only rarely he suffered from an unsatisfied desire to communicate his stray ideas to some one besides Agafea Mihalovna. With her indeed he not unfrequently fell into discussions upon physics, the theory of agriculture, and especially philosophy; philosophy was Agafea Mihalovna's favorite subject.

Spring was slow in unfolding. For the last few weeks it had been steadily fine frosty weather. In the daytime it thawed in the sun, but at night there were even seven degrees of frost. There was such a frozen surface on the snow that they drove the wagons anywhere off the roads. Easter came in the snow. Then all of a sudden, on Easter Monday, a warm wind sprang up, storm-clouds swooped down, and for three days and three nights the warm, driving rain fell in streams. On Thursday the wind dropped, and a thick gray fog brooded over the land as though hiding the mysteries of the transformations that were being wrought in nature. Behind the fog there was the flowing of water, the cracking and floating of ice, the swift rush of turbid, foaming torrents; and on the following Monday, in the evening, the fog parted, the storm-clouds split up into little curling crests of cloud, the sky cleared, and the real spring had come. In the morning the sun rose brilliant and quickly wore away the thin layer of ice that covered the water, and all the warm air was quivering with the steam that rose up from the quickened earth. The old grass looked greener, and the young grass thrust up its tiny blades; the buds of the guelder-rose and of the currant and the sticky birch-buds were swollen with sap, and an exploring bee was humming about the golden blossoms that studded the willow. Larks trilled unseen above the velvety green fields and the ice-covered stubble-land; peewits wailed over the low lands and marshes flooded by the pools; cranes and wild geese flew high across the sky uttering their spring calls. The cattle, bald in patches where the new hair had not grown yet, lowed in the pastures; the bow-legged lambs frisked round their bleating mothers. Nimble children ran about the drying paths, covered with the prints of bare feet. There was a merry chatter of peasant women over their linen at the pond, and the ring of axes in the yard, where the peasants were repairing ploughs and harrows. The real spring had come.

Levin put on his big boots, and, for the first time, a cloth jacket, instead of his fur cloak, and went out to look after his farm, stepping over streams of water that flashed in the sunshine and dazzled his eyes, and treading one minute on ice and the next into sticky mud.

Spring is the time of plans and projects. And, as he came out into the farmyard, Levin, like a tree in spring that knows not what form will be taken by the young shoots and twigs imprisoned in its swelling buds, hardly knew what undertakings he was going to begin upon now in the farm-work that was so dear to him. But he felt that he was full of the most splendid plans and projects. First of all he went to the cattle. The cows had been let out into their paddock, and their smooth sides were already shining with their new, sleek, spring coats; they basked in the sunshine and lowed to go to the meadow. Levin gazed admiringly at the cows he knew so intimately to the minutest detail of their condition, and gave orders for them to be driven out into the meadow, and the calves to be let into the paddock. The herdsman ran gaily to get ready for the meadow. The cowherd girls, picking up their petticoats, ran splashing through the mud with bare legs, still white, not yet brown from the sun, waving brushwood in their hands, chasing the calves that frolicked in the mirth of spring.

After admiring the young ones of that year, who were particularly fine — the early calves were the size of a peasant's cow, and Pava's daughter, at three months old, was as big as a yearling — Levin gave orders for a trough to be brought out and for them to be fed in the paddock. But it appeared that as the paddock had not been used during the winter, the hurdles made in the autumn for it were broken. He sent for the carpenter, who, according to his orders, ought to have been at work at the thrashing-machine. But it appeared that the carpenter was repairing the harrows, which ought to have been repaired before Lent. This was very annoying to Levin. It was annoying to come upon that everlasting slovenliness in the farm-work against which he had been striving with all his might for so many years. The hurdles, as he ascertained, being not wanted in winter, had been carried to the cart horses' stable, and there broken, as they were of light construction, only meant for folding calves. Moreover, it was apparent also that the harrows and all the agricultural implements, which he had directed to be looked over and repaired in the winter, for which very purpose he had hired three carpenters, had not been put into repair, and the harrows were being repaired when they ought to have been harrowing the field. Levin sent for his bailiff, but immediately went off himself to look for him. The bailiff, beaming all over, like every one that day, in a sheepskin bordered with astrachan, came out of the barn, twisting a bit of straw in his hands.

"Why isn't the carpenter at the thrashing-machine?"

"Oh, I meant to tell you yesterday, the harrows want repairing. Here it's time they got to work in the fields."

"But what were they doing in the winter, then?"

"But what did you want the carpenter for?"

"Where are the hurdles for the calves' paddock?"

"I ordered them to be got ready. What would you have with those peasants!" said the bailiff, with a wave of his hand.

"It's not those peasants but this bailiff!" said Levin, getting angry. "Why, what do I keep you for?" he cried. But, bethinking himself that this would not help matters, he stopped short in the middle of a sentence, and merely sighed. "Well, what do you say? Can sowing begin?" he asked, after a pause.

"Behind Turkin to-morrow or next day they might begin."

"And the clover?"

"I've sent Vassily and Mishka; they're sowing. Only I don't know if they'll manage to get through; it's so slushy."

"How many acres?"

"About fifteen."

"Why not sow all?" cried Levin.

That they were only sowing the clover on fifteen acres, not in all the forty-five, was still more annoying to him. Clover, as he knew, both from books and from his own experience, never did well except when it was sown as early as possible, almost in the snow. And yet Levin could never get this done.

"There's no one to send. What would you have with such a set of peasants? Three haven't turned up. And there's Semyon..."

"Well, you should have taken some men from the thatching."

"And so I have, as it is."

"Where are the peasants, then?"

"Five are making *compôte*" (which meant compost), "four are shifting the oats for fear of a touch of mildew, Konstantin Dmitrievitch."

Levin knew very well that "a touch of mildew" meant that his English seed oats were already ruined. Again they had not done as he had ordered.

"Why, but I told you during Lent to put in pipes," he cried.

"Don't put yourself out; we shall get it all done in time."

Levin waved his hand angrily, went into the granary to glance at the oats, and then to the stable. The oats were not yet spoiled. But the peasants were carrying the oats in spades when they might simply let them slide down into the lower granary; and arranging for this to be done, and taking two workmen from there for sowing clover, Levin got over his vexation with the bailiff. Indeed, it was such a lovely day that one could not be angry.

"Ignat!" he called to the coachman, who, with his sleeves tucked up, was washing the carriage wheels, "saddle me..."

"Which, sir?"

"Well, let it be Kolpik."

"Yes, sir."

While they were saddling his horse, Levin again called up the bailiff, who was hanging about in sight, to make it up with him, and began talking to him about the spring operations before them, and his plans for the farm.

The wagons were to begin carting manure earlier, so as to get all done before the early mowing. And the ploughing of the further land to go on without a break so as to let it ripen lying fallow. And the mowing to be all done by hired labor, not on half-profits. The bailiff listened attentively, and obviously made an effort to approve of his employer's projects. But still he had that look Levin knew so well that always irritated him, a look of hopelessness and despondency. That look said: "That's all very well, but as God wills."

Nothing mortified Levin so much as that tone. But it was the tone common to all the bailiffs he had ever had. They had all taken up that attitude to his plans, and so now he was not angered by it, but mortified, and felt all the more roused to struggle against this, as it seemed, elemental force continually ranged against him, for which he could find no other expression than "as God wills."

"If we can manage it, Konstantin Dmitrievitch,' said the bailiff.

"Why ever shouldn't you manage it?"

"We positively must have another fifteen laborers. And they don't turn up. There were some here to-day asking seventy roubles for the summer."

Levin was silent. Again he was brought face to face with that opposing force. He knew that however much they tried, they could not hire more than forty — thirty-seven perhaps or thirty-eight — laborers for a reasonable sum. Some forty had been taken on, and there were no more. But still he could not help struggling against it.

"Send to Sury, to Tchefirovka; if they don't come we must look for them."

"Oh, I'll send, to be sure," said Vassily Fedorovitch despondently. "But there are the horses too, they're not good for much."

"We'll get some more. I know, of course," Levin added laughing, "you always want to do with as little and as poor quality as possible; but this year I'm not going to let you have things your own way. I'll see to everything myself."

"Why, I don't think you take much rest as it is. It cheers us up to work under the master's eye . . ."

"So they're sowing clover behind the Birch Dale? I'll go and have a look at them," he said, getting on to the little bay cob, Kolpik, who was led up by the coachman.

"You can't get across the streams, Konstantin Dmitrievitch," the coachman shouted.

"All right, I'll go by the forest."

And Levin rode through the slush of the farm-yard to the gate and out into the open country, his good little horse, after his long inactivity, stepping out gallantly, snorting over the pools, and asking, as it were, for guidance. If Levin had felt happy before in the cattle-pens and farmyard, he felt happier yet in the open country. Swaying rhythmically with the ambling paces of his good little cob, drinking in the warm yet fresh scent of the snow and the air, as he rode through his forest over the crumbling, wasted snow, still left in parts, and covered with dissolving tracks, he rejoiced over every tree, with the moss reviving on its bark and the buds swelling on its shoots. When he came out of the forest, in the immense plain before him, his grass fields stretched in an unbroken carpet of green, without one bare place or swamp, only spotted here and there in the hollows with patches of melting snow. He was not put out of temper even by the sight of the peasants' horses and colts trampling down his young grass (he told a peasant

he met to drive them out), nor by the sarcastic and stupid reply of the peasant Ipat, whom he met on the way, and asked, "Well, Ipat, shall we soon be sowing?" "We must get the ploughing done first, Konstantin Dmitrievitch," answered Ipat. The further he rode, the happier he became, and plans for the land rose to his mind each better than the last; to plant all his fields with hedges along the southern borders, so that the snow should not lie under them; to divide them up into six fields of arable and three of pasture and hay; to build a cattle-yard at the further end of the estate, and to dig a pond and to construct movable pens for the cattle as a means of manuring the land. And then eight hundred acres of wheat, three hundred of potatoes, and four hundred of clover, and not one acre exhausted.

Absorbed in such dreams, carefully keeping his horse by the hedges, so as not to trample his young crops, he rode up to the laborers who had been sent to sow clover. A cart with the seed in it was standing, not at the edge, but in the middle of the crop, and the winter-corn had been torn up by the wheels and trampled by the horse. Both the laborers were sitting in the hedge, probably smoking a pipe together. The earth in the cart, with which the seed was mixed, was not crushed to powder, but crusted together or adhering in clods. Seeing the master, the laborer, Vassily, went towards the cart, while Mishka set to work sowing. This was not as it should be, but with the laborers Levin seldom lost his temper. When Vassily came up, Levin told him to lead the horse to the hedge.

"It's all right, sir, it'll spring up again," responded Vassily.

"Please don't argue," said Levin, "but do as you're told."

"Yes, sir," answered Vassily, and he took the horse's head. "What a sowing, Konstantin Dmitrievitch," he said, hesitating; "first rate. Only it's a work to get about! You drag a ton of earth on your shoes."

"Why is it you have earth that's not sifted?" said Levin.

"Well, we crumble it up," answered Vassily, taking up some seed and rolling the earth in his palms.

Vassily was not to blame for their having filled up his cart with unsifted earth, but still it was annoying.

Levin had more than once already tried a way he knew for stifling his anger, and turning all that seemed dark right again, and he tried that way now. He watched how Mishka strode along, swinging the huge clods of earth that clung to each foot; and getting off his horse, he took the sieve from Vassily and started sowing himself.

"Where did you stop?"

Vassily pointed to the mark with his foot, and Levin went forward as best he could, scattering the seed on the land. Walking was as difficult as on a bog, and by the time Levin had ended the row he was in a great heat, and he stopped and gave up the sieve to Vassily.

"Well, master, when summer's here, mind you don't scold me for these rows," said Vassily.

"Eh?" said Levin cheerily, already feeling the effect of his method.

"Why, you'll see in the summer-time. It'll look different. Look you where I sowed last spring. How I did work at it! I do my best, Konstantin Dmitrievitch, d'ye see, as I would for my own father. I don't like bad work myself, nor would I let another man do it. What's good for the master's good for us too. To look out yonder now," said Vassily, pointing, "it does one's heart good."

"It's a lovely spring, Vassily."

"Why, it's a spring such as the old men don't remember the like of. I was up home; an old man up there has sown wheat too, about an acre of it. He was saying you wouldn't know it from rye."

"Have you been sowing wheat long?"

"Why, sir, it was you taught us the year before last. You gave me two measures. We sold about eight bushels and sowed a rood."

"Well, mind you crumble up the clods," said Levin, going towards his horse, "and keep an eye on Mishka. And if there's a good crop you shall have half a rouble for every acre."

"Humbly thankful. We are very well content, sir, as it is."

Levin got on his horse and rode towards the field where was last year's clover, and the one which was ploughed ready for the spring corn.

The crop of clover coming up in the stubble was magnificent. It had survived everything, and stood up vividly green through the broken stalks of last year's wheat. The horse sank in up to the pasterns, and he drew each hoof with a sucking sound out of the half-thawed ground. Over the ploughland riding was utterly impossible; the horse could only keep a foothold where there was ice, and in the thawing furrows he sank deep in at each step. The ploughland was in splendid condition; in a couple of days it would be fit for harrowing and sowing. Everything was capital, everything was cheering. Levin rode back across the streams, hoping the water would have gone down. And he did in fact get across, and startled two ducks. "There must be snipe too," he thought, and just as he reached the turning homewards he met the forest keeper, who confirmed his theory about the snipe.

Levin went home at a trot, so as to have time to eat his dinner and get his gun ready for the evening.

THE STEEPLECHASE

The horses who had run in the last race were being led home, steaming and exhausted, by the stable-boys, and one after another the fresh horses for the coming race made their appearance, for the most part English racers, wearing horsecloths, and looking with their drawn-up bellies like strange, huge birds. On the right was led in Frou-Frou, lean and beautiful, lifting up her elastic, rather long pasterns, as though moved by springs. Not far from her they were taking the rug off the lop-eared Gladiator. The strong, exquisite, perfectly correct lines of the stallion, with his superb hindquarters and excessively short pasterns almost over his hoofs, attracted Vronsky's attention in spite of himself. He would have gone up to his mare, but he was again detained by an acquaintance.

"Oh, there's Karenina!" said the acquaintance with whom he was chatting. "He's looking for his wife, and she's in the middle of the pavilion. Didn't you see her?"

"No," answered Vronsky, and without even glancing round towards the pavilion where his friend was pointing out Madame Karenina, he went up to his mare.

Vronsky had not had time to look at the saddle, about which he had to give some direction, when the competitors were summoned to the pavilion to receive their numbers and places in the row at starting. Seventeen officers, looking serious and severe, many with pale faces, met together in the pavilion and drew the numbers. Vronsky drew the number seven. The cry was heard: "Mount!"

Feeling that with the others riding in the race, he was the center upon which all eyes were fastened, Vronsky walked up to his mare in that state of nervous tension in which he usually became deliberate and composed in his movements. Cord, in honor of the races, had put on his best clothes, a black coat buttoned up, a stiffly starched collar, which propped up his cheeks, a round black hat, and top-boots. He was calm and dignified as ever, and was with his own hands holding Frou-Frou by both reins, standing straight in front of her. Frou-Frou was still trembling as though in a fever. Her eye, full of fire, glanced sideways at Vronsky. Vronsky slipped his finger under the saddle-girth. The mare glanced aslant at him, drew up her lip, and twitched her ear. The Englishman puckered up his lips, intending to indicate a smile that any one should verify his saddling.

"Get up; you won't feel so excited."

Vronsky looked round for the last time at his rivals. He knew that he would not see them during the race. Two were already riding forward to the point from which they were to start. Galtsin, a friend of Vronsky's and one of his more formidable rivals, was moving round a bay horse that would not let him mount. A little light hussar in tight riding-breeches rode off at a gallop, crouched up like a cat on the saddle, in imitation of English jockeys. Prince Kuzovlev sat with a white face on his thoroughbred mare from the Grabovsky stud, while an English groom led her by the bridle. Vronsky and all his comrades knew Kuzovlev and his peculiarity of "weak nerves" and terrible vanity. They knew that he was afraid of everything, afraid of riding a spirited horse. But now, just because it was terrible, because people broke their necks, and there was a doctor standing at each obstacle, and an ambulance with a cross on it, and a sister of mercy, he had made up his mind to take part in the race. Their eyes met, and Vronsky gave him a friendly and encouraging nod. Only one he did not see, his chief rival, Mahotin on Gladiator.

"Don't be in a hurry," said Cord to Vronsky, "and remember one thing: don't hold her in at the fences, and don't urge her on; let her go as she likes."

"All right, all right," said Vronsky, taking the reins.

"If you can, lead the race; but don't lose heart till the last minute, even if you're behind."

Before the mare had time to move, Vronsky stepped with an agile, vigorous movement into the steel-toothed stirrup, and lightly and firmly seated himself on the creaking leather of the saddle. Getting his right foot in the stirrup, he smoothed the double reins, as he always did, between his fingers, and Cord let go.

As though she did not know which foot to put first, Frou-Frou started, dragging at the reins with her long neck, and as though she were on springs, shaking her rider from side to side. Cord quickened his step, following him. The excited mare, trying to shake off her rider first on one side and then the other, pulled at the reins, and Vronsky tried in vain with voice and hand to soothe her.

They were just reaching the dammed-up stream on their way to the starting-point. Several of the riders were in front and several behind, when suddenly Vronsky heard the sound of a horse galloping in the mud behind him, and he was overtaken by Mahotin on his white-legged, lop-eared Gladiator. Mahotin smiled, showing his long teeth, but Vronsky looked angrily at him. He did not like him, and regarded him now as his most formidable rival. He was angry with him for galloping past and exciting his mare. Frou-Frou started into a gallop, her left foot forward, made two bounds, and fretting at the tightened reins, passed into a jolting trot, bumping her rider up and down. Cord too scowled, and followed Vronsky almost at a trot.

There were seventeen officers in all riding in this race. The race-course was a large three-mile ring of the form of an ellipse in front of the pavilion. On this course nine obstacles had been arranged: the stream, a big and solid barrier five feet high, just before the pavilion, a dry ditch, a ditch full of water, a precipitous slope, an Irish barricade (one of the most difficult obstacles, consisting of a mound fenced with brushwood, beyond which was a ditch out of sight for the horses, so that the horse had to clear both obstacles or might be killed); then two more ditches filled with water, and one dry one; and the end of the race was just facing the pavilion. But the race began not in the ring, but two hundred yards away from it, and in that part of the course was the first obstacle, a dammed-up stream, seven feet in breadth, which the racers could leap or wade through as they preferred.

Three times they were ranged ready to start, but each time some horse thrust itself out of line, and they had to begin again. The umpire who was starting them, Colonel Sestrin, was beginning to lose his temper, when at last for the fourth time he shouted "Away!" and the racers started.

Every eye, every opera-glass, was turned on the brightly colored group of riders at the moment they were in line to start.

"They're off! They're starting!" was heard on all sides after the hush of expectation.

And little groups and solitary figures among the public began running from place to place to get a better view. In the very first minute the close group of horsemen drew out, and it could be seen that they were approaching the stream in twos and threes and one behind another. To the spectators it seemed as though they had all started simultaneously, but to the racers there were seconds of difference that had great value to them.

Frou-Frou, excited and over-nervous, had lost the first moment, and several horses had started before her, but before reaching the stream, Vronsky, who was holding in the mare with all his force as she tugged at the bridle, easily overtook three, and there were left in front of him Mahotin's chestnut Gladiator, whose hind-quarters were moving lightly and rhythmically up and down exactly in front of Vronsky, and in front of all, the dainty mare Diana bearing Kuzovlev more dead than alive.

For the first instant Vronsky was not master either of himself or his mare. Up to the first obstacle, the stream, he could not guide the motions of his mare.

Gladiator and Diana came up to it together and almost at the same instant; simultaneously they rose above the stream and flew across to the other side; Frou-Frou darted after them, as if flying; but at the very moment when Vronsky felt himself in the air, he suddenly saw almost under his mare's hoofs Kuzovlev, who was floundering with Diana on the further side of the stream. (Kuzovlev had let go the reins as he took the leap, and the mare had sent him flying over her head.) Those details Vronsky learned later; at the moment all he saw was that just under him, where Frou-Frou must alight, Diana's legs or head might be in the way. But Frou-Frou drew up her legs and back in the very act of leaping, like a falling cat, and, clearing the other mare, alighted beyond her.

"O the darling!" thought Vronsky.

After crossing the stream Vronsky had complete control of his mare, and began holding her in, intending to cross the great barrier behind Mahotin, and to try to overtake him in the clear ground of about five hundred yards that followed it.

The great barrier stood just in front of the imperial pavilion. The Tsar and the whole court and crowds of people were all gazing at them — at him, and Mahotin a length ahead of him, as they drew near the "devil," as the solid barrier was called. Vronsky was aware of those eyes fastened upon him from all sides, but he saw nothing except the ears and neck of his own mare, the ground racing to meet him, and the back and white legs of Gladiator beating time swiftly before him, and keeping always the same distance ahead. Gladiator rose, with no sound of knocking against anything. With a wave of his short tail he disappeared from Vronsky's sight.

"Bravo!" cried a voice.

At the same instant, under Vronsky's eyes, right before him flashed the palings of the barrier. Without the slightest change in her action his mare flew over it; the palings vanished, and he heard only a crash behind him. The mare, excited by Gladiator's keeping ahead, had risen too soon before the barrier, and grazed it with her hind hoofs. But her pace never changed, and Vronsky, feeling a spatter of mud in his face, realized that he was once more the same distance from Gladiator. Once more he perceived in front of him the same back and short tail, and again the same

swiftly moving white legs that got no further away.

At the very moment when Vronsky thought that now was the time to overtake Mahotin, Frou-Frou herself, understanding his thoughts, without any incitement on his part, gained ground considerably, and began getting alongside of Mahotin on the most favorable side, close to the inner cord. Mahotin would not let her pass that side. Vronsky had hardly formed the thought that he could perhaps pass on the outer side, when Frou-Frou shifted her pace and began overtaking him on the other side. Frou-Frou's shoulder, beginning by now to be dark with sweat, was even with Gladiator's back. For a few lengths they moved evenly. But before the obstacle they were approaching, Vronsky began working at the reins, anxious to avoid having to take the outer circle, and swiftly passed Mahotin just upon the declivity. He caught a glimpse of his mud-stained face as he flashed by. He even fancied that he smiled. Vronsky passed Mahotin, but he was immediately aware of him close upon him, and he never ceased hearing the even-thudding hoofs and the rapid and still quite fresh breathing of Gladiator.

The next two obstacles, the watercourse and the barrier, were easily crossed, but Vronsky began to hear the snorting and thud of Gladiator closer upon him. He urged on his mare, and to his delight felt that she easily quickened her pace, and the thud of Gladiator's hoofs was again heard at the same distance away.

Vronsky was at the head of the race, just as he wanted to be and as Cord had advised, and now he felt sure of being the winner. His excitement, his delight, and his tenderness for Frou-Frou grew keener and keener. He longed to look round again, but he did not dare do this, and tried to be cool and not to urge on his mare, so to keep the same reserve of force in her as he felt that Gladiator still kept. There remained only one obstacle, the most difficult; if he could cross it ahead of the others, he would come in first. He was flying towards the Irish barricade, Frou-Frou and he both together saw the barricade in the distance, and both the man and the mare had a moment's hesitation. He saw the uncertainty in the mare's ears and lifted the whip, but at the same time felt that his fears were groundless; the mare knew what was wanted. She quickened her pace and rose smoothly, just as he had fancied she would, and as she left the ground gave herself up to the force of her rush, which carried her far beyond the ditch; and with the same rhythm, without effort, with the same leg forward, Frou-Frou fell back into her pace again.

"Bravo, Vronsky!" he heard shouts from a knot of men — he knew they were his friends in the regiment — who were standing at the obstacle. He could not fail to recognize Yashvin's voice though he did not see him.

"O my sweet!" he said inwardly to Frou-Frou, as he listened for what was happening behind. "He's cleared it!" he thought, catching the thud of Gladiator's hoofs behind him. There remained only the last ditch, filled with water and five feet wide. Vronsky did not even look at it, but anxious to get in a long way first began sawing away at the reins, lifting the mare's head and letting it go in time with her paces. He felt that the mare was at her very last reserve of strength; not her neck and shoulders merely were wet, but the sweat was standing in drops on her mane, her head, her sharp ears, and her breath came in short, sharp gasps. But he knew that she had strength left more than enough for the remaining five hundred yards. It was only from feeling himself nearer the ground and from the peculiar smoothness of his motion that Vronsky knew how greatly the mare had quickened her pace. She flew over the ditch as though not noticing it. She flew over it like a bird; but at the same instant Vronsky, to his horror, felt that he had failed to keep up with the mare's pace, that he had, he did not know how, made a fearful, unpardonable mistake, in recovering his seat in the saddle. All at once his position had shifted and he knew that something awful had happened. He could not yet make out what had happened, when the white legs of a chestnut horse flashed by close to him, and Mahotin passed at a swift gallop. Vronsky was touching the ground with one foot, and his mare was sinking on that foot. He just had time to free his leg when she fell on one side, gasping painfully, and, making vain efforts to rise with her delicate, soaking neck, she fluttered on the ground at his feet like a shot bird. The clumsy movement made by Vronsky had broken her back. But that he only knew much later. At that moment he knew only that Mahotin had flown swiftly by, while he stood staggering alone on the muddy, motionless ground, and Frou-Frou lay gasping before him, bending her head back and gazing at him with her exquisite eyes. Still unable to realize what had happened, Vronsky tugged at his mare's reins. Again she struggled all over like a fish, and her shoulders setting the saddle heaving, she rose on her front legs but unable to lift her back, she quivered all over and again fell on her side. With a face hideous with passion, his lower jaw trembling, and his cheeks white, Vronsky kicked her with his heel in the stomach and again fell to tugging at the rein.

She did not stir, but thrusting her nose into the ground, she simply gazed at her master with her speaking eyes.

"A — a — a!" groaned Vronsky, clutching at his head. "Ah! what have I done!" he cried. "The race lost! And my fault! shameful, unpardonable! And the poor darling, ruined mare! Ah! what have I done!"

A crowd of men, a doctor and his assistant, the officers of his regiment, ran up to him. To his misery he felt that he was whole and unhurt. The mare had broken her back, and it was decided to shoot her. Vronsky could not answer questions, could not speak to any one. He turned, and without picking up his cap that had fallen off, walked away from the race-course, not knowing where he was going. He felt utterly wretched. For the first time in his life he knew the bitterest sort of misfortune, misfortune beyond remedy, and caused by his own fault.

Yashvin overtook him with his cap, and led him home, and half an hour later Vronsky had regained his self-possession. But the memory of that race remained for long in his heart, the cruelest and bitterest memory of his life.

ANNA VISITS HER SON

One of Anna's objects in coming back to Russia had been to see her son. From the day she left Italy the thought of it had never ceased to agitate her. And as she got nearer to Petersburg, the delight and importance of this meeting grew ever greater in her imagination. She did not even put to herself the question how to arrange it. It seemed to her natural and simple to see her son when she should be in the same town with him. But on her arrival in Petersburg she was suddenly made distinctly aware of her present position in society, and she grasped the fact that to arrange this meeting was no easy matter.

She had now been two days in Petersburg. The thought of her son never left her for a single instant, but she had not yet seen him. To go straight to the house, where she might meet Alexey Alexandrovitch,[1] that she felt she had no right to do. She might be refused admittance and insulted. To write and so enter into relations with her husband — that it made her miserable to think of doing; she could only be at peace when she did not think of her husband. To get a glimpse of her son out walking, finding out where and when he went out, was not enough for her; she had so looked forward to this meeting, she had so much she must say to

[1] Her husband. Anna is now living with Vronsky.

him, she so longed to embrace him, to kiss him. Seryozha's old nurse might be a help to her and show her what to do. But the nurse was not now living in Alexey Alexandrovitch's house. In this uncertainty, and in efforts to find the nurse, two days had slipped by.

Hearing of the close intimacy between Alexey Alexandrovitch and Countess Lidia Ivanovna, Anna decided on the third day to write to her a letter, which cost her great pains, and in which she intentionally said that permission to see her son must depend on her husband's generosity. She knew that if the letter were shown to her husband, he would keep up his character of magnanimity, and would not refuse her request.

The commissionaire who took the letter had brought her back the most cruel and unexpected answer, that there was no answer. She had never felt so humiliated as at the moment when, sending for the commissionaire, she heard from him the exact account of how he had waited, and how afterwards he had been told there was no answer. Anna felt humiliated, insulted, but she saw that from her point of view Countess Lidia Ivanovna was right. Her suffering was the more poignant that she had to bear it in solitude. She could not and would not share it with Vronsky. She knew that to him, although he was the primary cause of her distress, the question of her seeing her son would seem a matter of very little consequence. She knew that he would never be capable of understanding all the depth of her suffering, that for his cool tone at any allusion to it she would begin to hate him. And she dreaded that more than anything in the world, and so she hid from him everything that related to her son. Spending the whole day at home she considered ways of seeing her son, and had reached a decision to write to her husband. She was just composing this letter when she was handed the letter from Lidia Ivanovna. The countess's silence had subdued and depressed her, but the letter, all that she read between the lines in it, so exasperated her, this malice was so revolting beside her passionate, legitimate tenderness for her son, that she turned against other people and left off blaming herself.

"This coldness — this pretense of feeling!" she said to herself. "They must needs insult me and torture the child, and I am to submit to it! Not on any consideration! She is worse than I am. I don't lie, anyway." And she decided on the spot that next day, Seryozha's birthday, she would go straight to her husband's house, bribe or deceive the servants, but at any cost see her son and overturn the hideous deception with which they were encompassing the unhappy child.

She went to a toy-shop, bought toys and thought over a plan of action. She would go early in the morning at eight o'clock, when Alexey Alexandrovitch would be certain not to be up. She would have money in her hand to give the hall-porter and the footman, so that they should let her in, and not raising her veil, she would say that she had come from Seryozha's godfather to congratulate him, and that she had been charged to leave the toys at his bedside. She had prepared everything but the words she should say to her son. Often as she had dreamed of it, she could never think of anything.

The next day, at eight o'clock in the morning, Anna got out of a hired sledge and rang at the front entrance of her former home.

"Run and see what's wanted. Some lady," said Kapitonitch, who, not yet dressed, in his overcoat and goloshes, had peeped out of the window and seen a lady in a veil standing close up to the door. His assistant, a lad Anna did not know, had no sooner opened the door to her than she came in, and pulling a three-rouble note out of her muff put it hurriedly into his hand.

"Seryozha — Sergey Alexeitch," she said, and was going on. Scrutinizing the note, the porter's assistant stopped her at the second glass-door.

"Whom do you want?" he asked.

She did not hear his words and made no answer.

Noticing the embarrassment of the unknown lady, Kapitonitch went out to her, opened the second door for her, and asked her what she was pleased to want.

"From Prince Skorodumov for Sergey Alexeitch," she said.

"His honor's not up yet," said the porter, looking at her attentively.

Anna had not anticipated that the absolutely unchanged hall of the house where she had lived for nine years would so greatly affect her. Memories sweet and painful rose one after another in her heart, and for a moment she forgot what she was here for.

"Would you kindly wait?" said Kapitonitch, taking off her fur cloak.

As he took off the cloak, Kapitonitch glanced at her face, recognized her, and made her a low bow in silence.

"Please walk in, your excellency," he said to her.

She tried to say something, but her voice refused to utter any sound; with a guilty and imploring glance at the old man she went with light, swift steps up the stairs. Bent double, and his goloshes catching in the steps, Kapitonitch ran after her, trying to overtake her.

"The tutor's there; maybe he's not dressed. I'll let him know."

Anna still mounted the familiar staircase, not understanding what the old man was saying.

"This way, to the left, if you please. Excuse its not being tidy. His honor's in the old parlor now," the hall-porter said, panting. "Excuse me, wait a little, your excellency; I'll just see," he said, and overtaking her, he opened the high door and disappeared behind it. Anna stood still waiting. "He's only just awake," said the hall-porter, coming out. And at the very instant the porter said this, Anna caught the sound of a childish yawn. From the sound of this yawn alone she knew her son and seemed to see him living before her eyes.

"Let me in; go away!" she said, and went in through the high doorway. On the right of the door stood a bed, and sitting up in the bed was the boy. His little body bent forward with his night-shirt unbuttoned, he was stretching and still yawning. The instant his lips came together they curved into a blissfully sleepy smile, and with that smile he slowly and deliciously rolled back again.

"Seryozha!" she whispered, going noiselessly up to him.

When she was parted from him, and all this latter time when she had been feeling a fresh rush of love for him, she had pictured him as he was at four years old, when she had loved him most of all. Now he was not even the same as when she had left him; he was still further from the four-year-old baby, more grown and thinner. How thin his face was, how short his hair was! What long hands! How he had changed since she left him! But it was he with his head, his lips, his soft neck and broad little shoulders.

"Seryozha!" she repeated just in the child's ear.

He raised himself again on his elbow, turned his tangled head from side to side as though looking for something, and opened his eyes. Slowly and inquiringly he looked for several seconds at his mother standing motionless before him, then all at once he smiled a blissful smile, and shutting his eyes, rolled not backwards but towards her into her arms.

"Seryozha! my darling boy!" she said, breathing hard and putting her arms round his plump little body. "Mother!" he said, wriggling about in her arms so as to touch her hands with different parts of him.

Smiling sleepily still with closed eyes, he flung his fat little arms round her shoulders, rolled towards her, with the delicious sleepy warmth and fragrance that is only found in children, and began rubbing his face against her neck and shoulders.

"I know," he said, opening his eyes; "it's my birthday to-day. I knew you'd come. I'll get up directly."

And saying that he dropped asleep.

Anna looked at him hungrily; she saw how he had grown and changed in her absence. She knew, and did not know, the bare legs so long now, that were thrust out below the quilt, those short-cropped curls on his neck in which she had so often kissed him. She touched all this and could say nothing; tears choked her.

"What are you crying for, mother?" he said, waking completely up. "Mother, what are you crying for?" he cried in a tearful voice.

"I won't cry . . . I'm crying for joy. It's so long since I've seen you. I won't, I won't," she said, gulping down her tears and turning away. "Come, it's time for you to dress now," she added, after a pause, and, never letting go his hands, she sat down by his bedside on the chair, where his clothes were put ready for him.

"How do you dress without me? How . . ." she tried to begin talking simply and cheerfully, but she could not, and again she turned away.

"I don't have a cold bath, papa didn't order it. And you've not seen Vassily Lukitch? He'll come in soon. Why, you're sitting on my clothes!"

And Seryozha went off into a peal of laughter. She looked at him and smiled.

"Mother, darling, sweet one!" he shouted, flinging himself on her again and hugging her. It was as though only now, on seeing her smile, he fully grasped what had happened.

"I don't want that on," he said, taking off her hat. And as it were, seeing her afresh without her hat, he fell to kissing her again.

"But what did you think about me? You didn't think I was dead?"

"I never believed it."

"You didn't believe it, my sweet?"

"I knew, I knew!" he repeated his favorite phrase, and snatching the hand that was stroking his hair, he pressed the open palm to his mouth and kissed it.

Meanwhile Vassily Lukitch had not at first understood who this lady was, and had learned from their conversation that it was no other person than the mother who had left her husband, and whom he had not seen, as he had entered the house after her departure. He was in doubt whether to go in or not, or whether to communicate with Alexey Alexandrovitch. Reflecting finally that his duty was to get Seryozha up at the hour fixed, and that it was therefore not his business to consider who was there, the mother or any one else, but simply to do his duty, he finished dressing, went to the door and opened it.

But the embraces of the mother and child, the sound of their voices, and what they were saying, made him change his mind.

He shook his head, and with a sigh he closed the door. "I'll wait another ten minutes," he said to himself, clearing his throat and wiping away tears.

Among the servants of the household there was intense excitement all this time. All had heard that their mistress had come, and that Kapitonitch had let her in, and that she was even now in the nursery, and that their master always went in person to the nursery at nine o'clock, and every one fully comprehended that it was impossible for the husband and wife to meet, and that they must prevent it. Korney, the valet, going down to the hall-porter's room, asked who had let her in, and how it was he had done so, and ascertaining that Kapitonitch had admitted her and shown her up, he gave the old man a talking-to. The hall-porter was doggedly silent, but when Korney told him he ought to be sent away, Kapitonitch darted up to him, and waving his hands in Korney's face, began:

"Oh yes, to be sure you'd not have let her in! After ten years' service, and never a word but of kindness, and there you'd up and say, 'Be off, go along, get away with you!' Oh yes, you're a shrewd one at politics, I dare say! You don't need to be taught how to swindle the master, and to filch fur coats!"

"Soldier!" said Korney contemptuously, and he turned to the nurse who was coming in. "Here, what do you think, Marya Efimovna: he let her in without a word to any one," Korney said, addressing her. "Alexey Alexandrovitch will be down immediately — and go into the nursery!"

"A pretty business, a pretty business!" said the nurse. "You, Korney Vassilievitch, you'd best keep him some way or other, the master, while I'll run and get her away somehow. A pretty business!"

When the nurse went into the nursery, Seryozha was telling his mother how he and Nadinka had had a fall in sledging downhill, and had turned over three times. She was listening to the sound of his voice, watching his face and the play of expression on it, touching his hand, but she did not follow what he was saying. She must go, she must leave him — this was the only thing she was thinking and feeling. She heard the steps of Vassily Lukitch coming up to the door and coughing; she heard, too, the steps of the nurse as she came near; but she sat like one turned to stone, incapable of beginning to speak or to get up.

"Mistress, darling!" began the nurse, going up to Anna and kissing her hands and shoulders. "God has brought joy indeed to our boy on his birthday. You aren't changed one bit."

"Oh, nurse dear, I didn't know you were in the house," said Anna, rousing herself for a moment.

"I'm not living here, I'm living with my daughter. I came for the birthday, Anna Arkadyevna, darling!"

The nurse suddenly burst into tears, and began kissing her hand again.

Seryozha, with radiant eyes and smiles, holding his mother by one hand and his nurse by the other, pattered on the rug with his fat little bare feet. The tenderness shown by his beloved nurse to his mother threw him into an ecstasy.

"Mother! She often comes to see me, and when she comes . . ." he was beginning, but he stopped, noticing that the nurse was saying something in a whisper to his mother, and that in his mother's face there was a look of dread and something like shame, which was so strangely unbecoming to her.

She went up to him.

"My sweet!" she said.

She could not say good-bye, but the expression on her face said it, and he understood. "Darling, darling Kootik!" she used the name by which she had called him when he was little, "you won't forget me? You . . ." but she could not say more.

How often afterwards she thought of words she might have said. But now she did not know how to say it, and could say nothing. But Seryozha knew all she wanted to say to him. He understood that she was unhappy and loved him. He understood even what the nurse had whispered. He had caught the words "always at nine o'clock," and he knew that this was said of his father, and that his father and mother could not meet. That he understood, but one thing he could not understand — why there should be a look of dread and shame in her face? . . . She was not in fault, but she was afraid of him and ashamed of something. He would have liked to put a question that would have set at rest this doubt, but he did not dare; he saw that she was miserable, and he felt for her. Silently he pressed close to her and whispered, "Don't go yet. He won't come just yet."

The mother held him away from her to see what he was thinking, what to say to him, and in his frightened face she read not only that he was speaking of his father, but, as it were, asking her what he ought to think about his father.

"Seryozha, my darling," she said, "love him; he's better and kinder than I am, and I have done him wrong. When you grow up you will judge."

"There's no one better than you!..." he cried in despair through his tears, and, clutching her by the shoulders, he began squeezing her with all his force to him, his arms trembling with the strain.

"My sweet, my little one!" said Anna, and she cried as weakly and childishly as he.

At that moment the door opened. Vassily Lukitch came in.

At the other door there was the sound of steps, and the nurse in a scared whisper said, "He's coming," and gave Anna her hat.

Seryozha sank onto the bed and sobbed, hiding his face in his hands. Anna removed his hands, once more kissed his wet face, and with rapid steps went to the door. Alexey Alexandrovitch walked in, meeting her. Seeing her, he stopped short and bowed his head.

Although she had just said he was better and kinder than she, in the rapid glance she flung at him, taking in his whole figure in all its details, feelings of repulsion and hatred for him and jealousy over her soon took possession of her. With a swift gesture she put down her veil, and, quickening her pace, almost ran out of the room.

She had not time to undo, and so carried back with her, the parcel of toys she had chosen the day before in a toy-shop with such love and sorrow.

LEVIN FINDS HIS FAITH

Ever since, by his beloved brother's deathbed, Levin had first glanced into the questions of life and death in the light of these new convictions, as he called them, which had during the period from his twentieth to his thirty-fourth year imperceptibly replaced his childish and youthful beliefs — he had been stricken with horror, not so much of death, as of life, without any knowledge of whence, and why, and how, and what it was. The physical organization, its decay, the indestructibility of matter, the law of the conservation of energy, evolution, were the words which usurped the place of his old belief. These words and the ideas associated with them were very well for intellectual purposes. But for life they yielded nothing, and Levin felt suddenly like a man who has changed his warm fur cloak for a muslin garment, and going for the first time into the frost is immediately convinced, not by reason, but by his whole nature that he is as good as naked, and that he must infallibly perish miserably.

From that moment, though he did not distinctly face it, and still went on living as before, Levin had never lost this sense of terror at his lack of knowledge.

He vaguely felt, too, that what he called his new convictions were not merely lack of knowledge, but that they were part of a whole order of ideas, in which no knowledge of what he needed was possible.

At first, marriage, with the new joys and duties bound up with it, had completely crowded out these thoughts. But of late, while he was staying in Moscow after his wife's confinement, with nothing to do, the question that clamored for solution had more and more often, more and more insistently, haunted Levin's mind.

The question was summed up for him thus: "If I do not accept the answers Christianity gives to the problems of my life, what answers do I accept?" And in the whole arsenal of his convictions, so far from finding any satisfactory answers, he was utterly unable to find anything at all like an answer.

He was in the position of a man seeking food in toy-shops and tool-shops.

Instinctively, unconsciously, with every book, with every conversation, with every man he met, he was on the lookout for light on these questions and their solution.

What puzzled and distracted him above everything was that the majority of men of his age and circle had, like him, exchanged their old beliefs for the same convictions, and yet saw nothing to lament in this, and were perfectly satisfied and serene. So that, apart from the principal question, Levin was tortured by other questions too. Were these people sincere? he asked himself, or were they playing a part? or was it that they understood the answers science gave to these problems in some different, clearer sense than he did? And he assiduously studied both these men's opinions and the books which treated of these scientific explanations.

One fact he had found out since these questions had engrossed his mind, was that he had been quite wrong in supposing from the recollections of the circle of his young days at college, that religion had outlived its day, and that it was now practically non-existent. All the people nearest to him who were good in their lives were believers. The old prince, and Lvov, whom he liked so much, and Sergey Ivanovitch, and all the women believed, and his wife believed as simply as he had believed in his earliest childhood, and ninety-nine hundredths of the Russian people, all the working-people for whose life he felt the deepest respect, believed.

Another fact of which he became convinced, after reading many scientific books, was that the men who shared his views had no other construction to put on them, and that they gave no explanation of the questions which he felt he could not live without answering, but simply ignored their existence and attempted to explain other questions of no possible interest to him, such as the evolution of organisms, the materialistic theory of consciousness, etc.

Moreover, during his wife's confinement, something had happened that seemed extraordinary to him. He, an unbeliever, had fallen into praying, and at the moment he prayed, he believed. But that moment had passed, and he could not make his state of mind at that moment fit into the rest of his life.

He could not admit that at that moment he knew the truth, and that now he was wrong; for as soon as he began thinking calmly about it, it all fell to pieces. He could not admit that he was mistaken then, for his spiritual condition then was precious to him, and to admit that it was a proof of weakness would have been to desecrate those moments. He was miserably divided against himself, and strained all his spiritual forces to the utmost to escape from this condition.

These doubts fretted and harassed him, growing weaker or stronger from time to time, but never leaving him. He read and thought, and the more he read and the more he thought, the further he felt from the aim he was pursuing.

Of late in Moscow and in the country, since he had become convinced that he would find no solution in the materialists, he had read and re-read thoroughly Plato, Spinoza, Kant, Schelling, Hegel, and Schopenhauer, the philosophers who gave a non-materialistic explanation of life.

Their ideas seemed to him fruitful when he was reading or was himself seeking arguments to refute other theories, especially those of the materialists; but as soon as he began to read or sought for himself a solution of problems, the same thing always happened. As long as he followed the fixed definition of obscure words such as *spirit, will, freedom, essence,* purposely letting himself go into the snare of words the philosophers set for him, he seemed to comprehend something. But he had only to forget the artificial train of reasoning, and to turn from life itself to what had satisfied him while thinking in accordance with the fixed definitions, and all this artificial edifice fell to pieces at once like a house of cards, and it became clear that the edifice had been built up out of those transposed words, apart from anything in life more important than reason.

At one time, reading Schopenhauer, he put in place of his *will* the word *love,* and for a couple of days this new philosophy charmed him, till he removed a little away from it. But then, when he

turned from life itself to glance at it again, it fell away too, and proved to be the same muslin garment with no warmth in it.

His brother Sergey Ivanovitch advised him to read the theological works of Homiakov. Levin read the second volume of Homiakov's works, and in spite of the elegant, epigrammatic, argumentative style which at first repelled him, he was impressed by the doctrine of the church he found in them. He was struck at first by the idea that the apprehension of divine truths had not been vouchsafed to man, but to a corporation of men bound together by love — to the church. What delighted him was the thought how much easier it was to believe in a still existing living church, embracing all the beliefs of men, and having God at its head, and therefore holy and infallible, and from it to accept the faith in God, in the creation, the fall, the redemption, than to begin with God, a mysterious, far-away God, the creation, etc. But afterwards, on reading a Catholic writer's history of the church, and then a Greek orthodox writer's history of the church, and seeing that the two churches, in their very conception infallible, each deny the authority of the other, Homiakov's doctrine of the church lost all its charm for him, and this edifice crumbled into dust like the philosophers' edifices.

All that spring he was not himself, and went through fearful moments of horror.

"Without knowing what I am and why I am here, life's impossible; and that I can't know, and so I can't live," Levin said to himself.

"In infinite time, in infinite matter, in infinite space, is formed a bubble-organism, and that bubble lasts a while and bursts, and that bubble is Me."

It was an agonizing error, but it was the sole logical result of ages of human thought in that direction.

This was the ultimate belief on which all the systems elaborated by human thought in almost all their ramifications rested. It was the prevalent conviction, and of all other explanations Levin had unconsciously, not knowing when or how, chosen it, as any way the clearest, and made it his own.

But it was not merely a falsehood, it was the cruel jeer of some wicked power, some evil, hateful power, to whom one could not submit.

He must escape from this power. And the means of escape every man had in his own hands. He had but to cut short this dependence on evil. And there was one means — death.

And Levin, a happy father and husband, in perfect health, was several times so near suicide that he hid the cord that he might not be tempted to hang himself, and was afraid to go out with his gun for fear of shooting himself.

But Levin did not shoot himself, and did not hang himself; he went on living.

When Levin thought what he was and what he was living for, he could find no answer to the questions and was reduced to despair, but he left off questioning himself about it. It seemed as though he knew both what he was and for what he was living, for he acted and lived resolutely and without hesitation. Indeed, in these latter days he was far more decided and unhesitating in life than he had ever been.

When he went back to the country at the beginning of June, he went back also to his usual pursuits. The management of the estate, his relations with the peasants and the neighbors, the care of his household, the management of his sister's and brother's property, of which he had the direction, his relations with his wife and kindred, the care of his child, and the new bee-keeping hobby he had taken up that spring, filled all his time.

These things occupied him now, not because he justified them to himself by any sort of general principles, as he had done in former days; on the contrary, disappointed by the failure of his former efforts for the general welfare, and too much occupied with his own thought and the mass of business with which he was burdened from all sides, he had completely given up thinking of the general good, and he busied himself with all this work simply because it seemed to him that he must do what he was doing — that he could not do otherwise. In former days — almost from childhood, and increasingly up to full manhood — when he had tried to do anything that would be good for all, for humanity, for Russia, for the whole village, he had noticed that the idea of it had been pleasant, but the work itself had always been incoherent, that then he had never had a full conviction of its absolute necessity, and that the work that had begun by seeming so great, had grown less and less, till it vanished into nothing. But now, since his marriage, when he had begun to confine himself more and more to living for himself, though he experienced no delight at all at the thought of the work he was doing, he felt a complete conviction of its necessity, saw that it succeeded far better than in old days, and that it kept on growing more and more.

Now, involuntarily it seemed, he cut more and more deeply into the soil like a plough, so that he could not be drawn out without turning aside the furrow.

To live the same family life as his father and fore-fathers — that is, in the same condition of culture — and to bring up his children in the same, was incontestably necessary. It was as necessary as dining when one was hungry. And to do this, just as it was necessary to cook dinner, it was necessary to keep the mechanism of agriculture at Pokrovskoe going so as to yield an income. Just as incontestably as it was necessary to repay a debt was it necessary to keep the property in such a condition that his son, when he received it as a heritage, would say "thank you" to his father as Levin had said "thank you" to his grandfather for all he built and planted. And to do this it was necessary to look after the land himself, not to let it, and to breed cattle, manure the fields, and plant timber.

It was impossible not to look after the affairs of Sergey Ivanovitch, of his sister, of the peasants who came to him for advice and were accustomed to do so — as impossible as to fling down a child one is carrying in one's arms. It was necessary to look after the comfort of his sister-in-law and her children, and of his wife and baby, and it was impossible not to spend with them at least a short time each day.

And all this, together with shooting and his new bee-keeping, filled up the whole of Levin's life, which had no meaning at all for him, when he began to think.

But besides knowing thoroughly what he had to do, Levin knew just in the same way *how* he had to do it all, and what was more important than the rest.

He knew he must hire laborers as cheaply as possible; but to hire men under bond, paying them in advance at less than the current rate of wages, was what he must not do, even though it was very profitable. Selling straw to the peasants in times of scarcity of provender was what he might do, even though he felt sorry for them; but the tavern and the pothouse must be put down, though they were a source of income. Felling timber must be punished as severely as possible, but he could not exact forfeits for cattle being driven onto his fields; and though it annoyed the keeper and made the peasants not afraid to graze their cattle on his land, he could not keep their cattle as a punishment.

To Pyotr, who was paying a money-lender ten per cent a month, he must lend a sum of money to set him free. But he could not let off peasants who did not pay their rent, nor let them fall into arrears. It was impossible to overlook the bailiff's not having mown the meadows and letting the hay spoil; and it was equally impossible to mow those acres where a young copse had been planted. It was impossible to excuse a laborer who had gone home in the busy season because his father was dying, however sorry he might feel for him, and he must subtract from his pay those costly months of idleness. But it was impossible not to allow monthly rations to the old servants who were of no use for anything.

Levin knew that when he got home he must first of all go to his wife, who was unwell, and that the peasants who had been waiting for three hours to see him could wait a little longer. He knew too that, regardless of all the pleasure he felt in taking a swarm, he must forego that pleasure, and leave the old man to see to the bees alone, while he talked to the peasants who had come after him to the bee-house.

Whether he were acting rightly or wrongly he did not know, and far from trying to prove that he was, nowadays he avoided all thought or talk about it.

Reasoning had brought him to doubt, and prevented him from seeing what he ought to do and what he ought not. When he did not think, but simply lived, he was continually aware of the presence of an infallible judge in his soul, determining which of two possible courses of action was the better and which was the worse, and as soon as he did not act rightly, he was at once aware of it.

So he lived, not knowing and not seeing any chance of knowing what he was and what he was living for, and harassed at this lack of knowledge to such a point that he was afraid of suicide, and yet firmly laying down his own individual definite path in life.

The day on which Sergey Ivanovitch came to Pokrovskoe was one of Levin's most painful days. It was the very busiest working-time, when all the peasantry show an extraordinary intensity of self-sacrifice in labor, such as is esteemed in any other conditions of life, and would be highly esteemed if the men who showed these qualities themselves thought highly of them, and if it were not repeated every year, and if the results of this intense labor were not so simple.

To reap and bind the rye and oats and to carry it, to mow the meadows, turn over the fallows, thrash the seed and sow the winter corn — all this seems so simple and ordinary; but to succeed in getting through it all every one in the village, from the old man to the young child, must toil incessantly for three or four weeks, three times as hard as usual, living on rye-beer, onions, and black bread, thrashing and carrying the sheaves at night, and not giving more than two or three hours in the twenty-four to sleep. And every year this is done all over Russia.

Having lived the greater part of his life in the country and in the closest relations with the peasants, Levin always felt in this busy time that he was infected by this general quickening of energy in the people.

In the early morning he rode over to the first sowing of the rye, and to the oats, which were being carried to the stacks, and returning home at the time his wife and sister-in-law were getting up, he drank coffee with them and walked to the farm, where a new thrashing-machine was to be set working to get ready the seed-corn.

He was standing in the cool granary, still fragrant with the leaves of the hazel branches interlaced on the freshly peeled aspen beams of the new thatch roof. He gazed through the open door in which the dry bitter dust of the thrashing whirled and played, at the grass of the thrashing-floor in the sunlight and the fresh straw that had been brought in from the barn, then at the speckly-headed, white-breasted swallows that flew chirping in under the roof and, fluttering their wings, settled in the crevices of the doorway, then at the peasants bustling in the dark, dusty barn, and he thought strange thoughts.

"Why is it all being done?" he thought. "Why am I standing here, making them work? What are they all so busy for, trying to show their zeal before me? What is that old Matrona, my old friend, toiling for? (I doctored her, when the beam fell on her in the fire)" he thought, looking at a thin old woman who was raking up the grain, moving painfully with her bare, sun-blackened feet over the uneven, rough floor. "Then she recovered, but to-day or to-morrow or in ten years she won't; they'll bury her, and nothing will be left either of her or of that smart girl in the red jacket, who with that skilful, soft action shakes the ears out of their husks. They'll bury her and this piebald horse, and very soon too," he thought, gazing at the heavily moving, panting horse that kept walking up the wheel that turned under him. "And they will bury her and Fyodor the thrasher with his curly beard full of chaff and his shirt torn on his white shoulders — they will bury him. He's untying the sheaves, and giving orders, and shouting to the women, and quickly setting straight the strap on the moving wheel. And what's more, it's not them alone — me they'll bury too, and nothing will be left. What for?"

He thought this, and at the same time looked at his watch to reckon how much they thrashed in an hour. He wanted to know this so as to judge by it the task to set for the day.

"It'll soon be one, and they're only beginning the third sheaf," thought Levin. He went up to the man that was feeding the machine, and shouting over the roar of the machine he told him to put it in more slowly. "You put in too much at a time, Fyodor. Do you see — it gets choked, that's why it isn't getting on. Do it evenly."

Fyodor, black with the dust that clung to his moist face, shouted something in response, but still went on doing it as Levin did not want him to.

Levin, going up to the machine, moved Fyodor aside, and began feeding the corn in himself. Working on till the peasants' dinner-hour, which was not long in coming, he went out of the barn with Fyodor and fell into talk with him, stopping beside a neat yellow sheaf of rye laid on the thrashing-floor for seed.

Fyodor came from a village at some distance from the one in which Levin had once allotted land to his coöperative association. Now it had been let to a former house-porter.

Levin talked to Fyodor about this land and asked whether Platon, a well-to-do peasant of good character belonging to the same village, would not take the land for the coming year.

"It's a high rent; it wouldn't pay Platon, Konstantin Dmitrievitch," answered the peasant, picking the ears off his sweat-drenched shirt.

"But how does Kirillov make it pay?"

"Mituh!" (so the peasant called the house-porter, in a tone of contempt), "you may be sure he'll make it pay, Konstantin Dmitrievitch! He'll get his share, however he has to squeeze to get it! He's no mercy on a Christian. But Uncle Fokanitch" (so he called the old peasant Platon), "do you suppose he'd flay the skin off a man? Where there's debt, he'll let any one off. And he'll not wring the last penny out. He's a man too."

"But why will he let any one off?"

"Oh, well, of course, folks are different. One man lives for his own wants and nothing else, like Mituh, he only thinks of filling his belly, but Fokanitch, is a righteous man. He lives for his soul. He does not forget God."

"How thinks of God? How does he live for his soul?" Levin almost shouted.

"Why, to be sure, in truth, in God's way. Folks are different. Take you now, you wouldn't wrong a man...."

"Yes, yes, good-bye!" said Levin, breathless with excitement, and turning round he took his stick and walked quickly away towards home. At the peasant's words that Fokanitch lived for his soul, in truth, in God's way, undefined but significant ideas seemed to burst out as though they had been locked up, and all striving towards one goal, they thronged whirling through his head, blinding him with their light.

Levin strode along the highroad, absorbed not so much in his thoughts (he could not yet disentangle them) as in his spiritual condition, unlike anything he had experienced before.

The words uttered by the peasant had acted on his soul like an electric shock, suddenly transforming and combining into a single whole the whole swarm of disjointed impotent, separate thoughts that incessantly occupied his mind. These thoughts had unconsciously been in his mind even when he was talking about the land.

He was aware of something new in his soul, and joyfully tested this new thing, not yet knowing what it was.

"Not living for his own wants, but for God? For what God? And could one say anything more senseless than what he said? He said that one must not live for one's own wants, that is, that one must not live for what we understand, what we are attracted by, what we desire, but must live for something incomprehensible, for God, whom no one can understand nor even define. What of it? Didn't I understand those senseless words of Fyodor's? And understanding them, did I doubt of their truth? Did I think them stupid, obscure, inexact? No, I understood him, and exactly as he understands the words. I understood them more fully and clearly than I understand anything in life, and never in my life have I doubted nor can I doubt about it. And not only I, but every one, the whole world understands nothing fully but this, and about this only they have no doubt and are always agreed.

"And I looked out for miracles, complained that I did not see a miracle which would convince me. A material miracle would have persuaded me. And here is a miracle, the sole miracle possible, continually existing, surrounding me on all sides, and I never noticed it!

"Fyodor says that Kirillov lives for his belly. That's comprehensible and rational. All of us as rational beings can't do anything else but live for our belly. And all of a sudden the same Fyodor says that one mustn't live for one's belly, but must live for truth, for God, and at a hint I understand him! And I and millions of men, men who lived ages ago and men living now — peasants, the poor in spirit and the learned, who have thought and written about it, in their obscure words saying the same thing — we are all agreed about this one thing: what we must live for and what is good. I and all men have only one firm, incontestable, clear knowledge, and that knowledge cannot be explained by the reason — it is outside it, and has no causes and can have no effects.

"If goodness has causes, it is not goodness; if it

has effects, a reward, it is not goodness either. So goodness is outside the chain of cause and effect.

"And yet I know it, and we all know it.

"What could be a greater miracle than that?

"Can I have found the solution of it all? can my sufferings be over?" thought Levin, striding along the dusty road, not noticing the heat nor his weariness, and experiencing a sense of relief from prolonged suffering. This feeling was so delicious that it seemed to him incredible. He was breathless with emotion and incapable of going farther; he turned off the road into the forest and lay down in the shade of an aspen on the uncut grass. He took his hat off his hot head and lay propped on his elbow in the lush, feathery, woodland grass.

"Yes, I must make it clear to myself and understand," he thought, looking intently at the untrampled grass before him, and following the movements of a green beetle, advancing along a blade of couch-grass and lifting up in its progress a leaf of goat-weed. "What have I discovered?" he asked himself, bending aside the leaf of goat-weed out of the beetle's way and twisting another blade of grass above for the beetle to cross over onto it. "What is it makes me glad? What have I discovered?

"I have discovered nothing. I have only found out what I knew. I understand the force that in the past gave me life, and now too gives me life. I have been set free from falsity, I have found the Master.

"Of old I used to say that in my body, that in the body of this grass and of this beetle (there, she didn't care for the grass, she's opened her wings and flown away), there was going on a transformation of matter in accordance with physical, chemical, and physiological laws. And in all of us, as well as in the aspens and the clouds and the misty patches, there was a process of evolution. Evolution from what? into what? — Eternal evolution and struggle. . . . As though there could be any sort of tendency and struggle in the eternal! And I was astonished that in spite of the utmost effort of thought along that road I could not discover the meaning of life, the meaning of my impulses and yearnings. Now I say that I know the meaning of my life: 'To live for God, for my soul.' And this meaning, in spite of its clearness, is mysterious and marvelous. Such, indeed, is the meaning of everything existing. Yes, pride," he said to himself, turning over on his stomach and beginning to tie a noose of blades of grass, trying not to break them.

"And not merely pride of intellect, but dulness of intellect. And most of all, the deceitfulness; yes, the deceitfulness of intellect. The cheating knavishness of intellect, that's it," he said to himself.

And he briefly went through, mentally, the whole course of his ideas during the last two years, the beginning of which was the clear confronting of death at the sight of his dear brother hopelessly ill.

Then, for the first time, grasping that for every man, and himself too, there was nothing in store but suffering, death, and forgetfulness, he had made up his mind that life was impossible like that, and that he must either interpret life so that it would not present itself to him as the evil jest of some devil, or shoot himself.

But he had not done either, but had gone on living, thinking, and feeling, and had even at that very time married, and had had many joys and had been happy, when he was not thinking of the meaning of his life.

What did this mean? It meant that he had been living rightly, but thinking wrongly.

He had lived (without being aware of it) on those spiritual truths that he had sucked in with his mother's milk, but he had thought, not merely without recognition of these truths, but studiously ignoring them.

Now it was clear to him that he could only live by virtue of the beliefs in which he had been brought up.

"What should I have been, and how should I have spent my life, if I had not had these beliefs, if I had not known that I must live for God and not for my own desires? I should have robbed and lied and killed. Nothing of what makes the chief happiness of my life would have existed for me." And with the utmost stretch of imagination he could not conceive the brutal creature he would have been himself, if he had not known what he was living for.

"I looked for an answer to my question. And thought could not give an answer to my question — it is incommensurable with my question. The answer has been given me by life itself, in my knowledge of what is right and what is wrong. And that knowledge I did not arrive at in any way, it was given to me as to all men, *given*, because I could not have got it from anywhere.

"Where could I have got it? By reason could I have arrived at knowing that I must love my neighbor and not oppress him? I was told that in my childhood, and I believed it gladly, for they told me what was already in my soul. But who discovered it? Not reason. Reason discovered the struggle for existence, and the law that requires us to oppress all who hinder the satisfaction of our desires. That is the deduction of reason. But loving one's neighbor reason could never discover, because it's irrational."

And Levin remembered a scene he had lately witnessed between Dolly and her children. The children, left to themselves, had begun cooking raspberries over the candles and squirting milk into each other's mouths with a syringe. Their mother, catching them at these pranks, began reminding them in Levin's presence of the trouble their mischief gave to the grown-up people, and that this trouble was all for their sake, and that if they smashed the cups they would have nothing to drink their tea out of, and that if they wasted the milk, they would have nothing to eat, and die of hunger.

And Levin had been struck by the passive, weary incredulity with which the children heard what their mother said to them. They were simply annoyed that their amusing play had been interrupted, and did not believe a word of what their mother was saying. They could not believe it indeed, for they could not take in the immensity of all they habitually enjoyed, and so could not conceive that what they were destroying was the very thing they lived by.

"That all comes of itself," they thought, "and there's nothing interesting or important about it because it has always been so, and always will be so. And it's all always the same. We've no need to think about that, it's all ready. But we want to invent something of our own, and new. So we thought of putting raspberries in a cup, and cooking them over a candle, and squirting milk straight into each other's mouths. That's fun, and something new, and not a bit worse than drinking out of cups."

"Isn't it just the same that we do, that I did, searching by the aid of reason for the significance of the forces of nature and the meaning of the life of man?" he thought.

"And don't all the theories of philosophy do the same, trying by the path of thought, which is strange and not natural to man, to bring him to a knowledge of what he has known long ago, and knows so certainly that he could not live at all without it? Isn't it distinctly to be seen in the development of each philosopher's theory, that he knows what is the chief significance of life beforehand, just as positively as the peasant Fyodor, and not a bit more clearly than he, and is simply trying by a dubious intellectual path to come back to what every one knows?

"Now then, leave the children to themselves to get things alone and make their crockery, get the milk from the cows, and so on. Would they be naughty then? Why, they'd die of hunger! Well, then, leave us with our passions and thoughts, without any idea of the one God, of the Creator, or without any idea of what is right, without any idea of moral evil.

"Just try and build up anything without those ideas!

"We only try and destroy them, because we're spiritually provided for. Exactly like the children!

"Whence have I that joyful knowledge, shared with the peasant, that alone gives peace to my soul? Whence did I get it?

"Brought up with an idea of God, a Christian, my whole life filled with the spiritual blessings Christianity has given me, full of them, and living on these blessings, like the children I did not understand them, and destroy, that is try to destroy, what I live by. And as soon as an important moment of life comes, like the children when they are cold and hungry, I turn to Him, and even less than the children when their mother scolds them for their childish mischief, do I feel that my childish efforts at wanton madness are reckoned against me.

"Yes, what I know, I know not by reason, but it has been given to me, revealed to me, and I know it with my heart, by faith in the chief thing taught by the church.

"The church! the church!" Levin repeated to himself. He turned over on the other side, and leaning on his elbow, fell to gazing into the distance at a herd of cattle crossing over to the river.

"But can I believe in all the church teaches?" he thought, trying himself, and thinking of everything that could destroy his present peace of mind. Intentionally he recalled all those doctrines of the church which had always seemed most strange and had always been a stumbling-block to him.

"The Creation? But how did I explain existence? By existence? By nothing? The devil and sin. But how do I explain evil? . . . The atonement? . . .

"But I know nothing, nothing, and I can know nothing but what has been told to me and all men."

And it seemed to him that there was not a single article of faith of the church which could destroy the chief thing — faith in God, in goodness, as the one goal of man's destiny.

Under every article of faith of the church could be put the faith in the service of truth instead of one's desires. And each doctrine did not simply leave that faith unshaken, each doctrine seemed essential to complete that great miracle, continually manifest upon earth, that made it possible for each man and millions of different sorts of men, wise men and imbeciles, old men and children — all men, peasants, Lvov, Kitty, beggars and kings to understand perfectly the same one thing, and to build up thereby that life of the soul which alone is worth living, and which alone is precious to us.

Lying on his back, he gazed up now into the high, cloudless sky. "Do I not know that that is infinite space, and that it is not a round arch? But, however I screw up my eyes and strain my sight, I cannot see it not round and not bounded, and in spite of my knowing about infinite space, I am incontestably right when I see a solid blue dome, and more right that when I strain my eyes to see beyond it."

Levin ceased thinking, and only, as it were, listened to mysterious voices that seemed talking joyfully and earnestly within him.

"Can this be faith?" he thought, afraid to believe in his happiness. "My God, I thank Thee!" he said, gulping down his sobs, and with both hands brushing away the tears that filled his eyes.

Anton Chekhov · 1860-1904

Anton Chekhov was born in Taganrog (Russia) in 1860. A descendant of serfs growing up in extreme poverty, he had to contribute, at an early age, to the family income. In 1879 he went to Moscow to study medicine. There he became interested in social problems and began to work on the improvement of living conditions among the people of Russia. He visited the island of Sakhalin, the official concentration camp of the time, and undertook to describe the hardships under which the prisoners suffered. In years that followed, Chekhov donated books to the Taganrog library and made plans for a People's Palace, a kind of popular information center to be opened in Moscow.

Chekhov became first known as a writer of humorous stories and as a contributor to various magazines. His stories are realistic in character; in many of them the description of scenes in nature forms a major part of the story. The dramatic quality we find in Maupassant is lacking here; instead, Chekhov's stories reflect a mood or describe the complexities of the development of an intimate relation between sensitive people. Chekhov wants to deal with the simple things in life, especially those tinged with a hue of melancholy. He has an aversion for the strong and the happy, preferring the dreamer to the man of action. The particular form of the short story invented by him has served as a model for many of the great writers of the next generation, among them James Joyce and Katherine Mansfield.

Chekhov's plays, chief among which are *The Sea Gull* (1896), *Three Sisters* (1901), *Uncle Vanya* (1899), and *The Cherry Orchard* (1904), are dramas of frustration; they do not revolve around actions or brave decisions but are extended images of emotional reactions to a chain of spiritually significant events. They are not concerned with heroes, all characters being alike protagonist-reflectors of the general atmosphere which is mirrored in their individual minds. Chekhov does not present the moments of rationalized effort or courageous action; he chooses the moments of reflection, when the characters are visibly overcome by the impact of their destiny. There is little determinism in the psychology of his characters, who are rarely changed by the circumstances and do not actually communicate with each other. Although Chekhov depicts social situations, he avoids highly dramatic dialogues. The scenes do not develop into a climax or into a cathartic moment of recognition. The author is concerned only with the emotions themselves and the constant shifting of their outward appearance from laughter to tears.

As the emotions reproduced in Chekhov's plays are transitional, so are the social values of the generation he brings on stage. The pre-revolutionary age with its socialistic tendencies we find embodied in Peter Trofimov who in *The Cherry Orchard* defends the new concept of social justice and equality. Chekhov's sympathy, however, is with the landowners as well as with the idlers and the revolutionary prophets of the new age. This sympathy accounts for difficulties in the interpretation of the play. Chekhov himself was firmly convinced that with *The Cherry Orchard* he had written a comedy, while Stanislavsky, co-director of the Moscow Art Theater where it was to be performed, maintained that in it "too many tears are shed," and for no obvious reason.

The cherry orchard which Chekhov has chosen as the main symbol of the play is a symbolic object in which are reflected the divergent attitudes of all the characters: Madame Ranevskaya loves it for its beauty and for the sake of the tradition with which it has been intimately connected; to Trofimov it represents the garden (social utopia, paradise) which belongs to the whole of the Russian people, while Lopahin is concerned only with its material value, that is, as an object of financial speculation. Chekhov's play reflects the spiritual and social situation of a transitional age in which Russia awakened to become a modern and Europeanized country, an age also in which tradition was cut off from its base and the Lopahins were bereft of their economic gains.

At the time of writing *The Cherry Orchard* Chekhov was seriously ill. Only a few months after the first performance of the play, which took place at the Moscow Art Theater in 1904, he died of consumption.

SUGGESTED REFERENCES: Avrahm Yarmolinsky, ed., *The Portable Chekhov* (1947); David Magarshack, *Chekhov, the Dramatist* (1952); W. H. Bruford, *Anton Chekhov* (1957).

The Schoolmistress[1]

At half-past eight they drove out of the town.

The highroad was dry, a lovely April sun was shining warmly, but the snow was still lying in the ditches and in the woods. Winter, dark, long, and spiteful, was hardly over; spring had come all of a sudden. But neither the warmth nor the languid transparent woods, warmed by the breath of spring, nor the black flocks of birds flying over the huge puddles that were like lakes, nor the marvelous fathomless sky, into which it seemed one would have gone away so joyfully, presented anything new or interesting to Marya Vassilyevna who was sitting in the cart. For thirteen years she had been schoolmistress, and there was no reckoning how many times during all those years she had been to the town for her salary; and whether it was spring as now, or a rainy autumn evening, or winter, it was all the same to her, and she always — invariably — longed for one thing only, to get to the end of her journey as quickly as could be.

She felt as though she had been living in that part of the country for ages and ages, for a hundred years, and it seemed to her that she knew every stone, every tree on the road from the town to her school. Her past was here, her present was here, and she could imagine no other future than the school, the road to the town and back again, and again the school and again the road. . . .

She had got out of the habit of thinking of her past before she became a schoolmistress, and had almost forgotten it. She had once had a father and mother; they had lived in Moscow in a big flat near the Red Gate, but of all that life there was left in her memory only something vague and fluid like a dream. Her father had died when she was ten years old, and her mother had died soon after. . . . She had a brother, an officer; at first they used to write to each other, then her brother had given up answering her letters, he had got out of the way of writing. Of her old belongings, all that was left was a photograph of her mother, but it had grown dim from the dampness of the school, and now nothing could be seen but the hair and the eyebrows.

When they had driven a couple of miles, old Semyon, who was driving, turned round and said:

"They have caught a government clerk in the town. They have taken him away. The story is that with some Germans he killed Alexeyev, the Mayor, in Moscow."

"Who told you that?"

"They were reading it in the paper, in Ivan Ionov's tavern."

And again they were silent for a long time. Marya Vassilyevna thought of her school, of the examination that was coming soon, and of the girl and four boys she was sending up for it. And just as she was thinking about the examination, she was overtaken by a neighboring landowner called Hanov in a carriage with four horses, the very man who had been examiner in her school the year before. When he came up to her he recognized her and bowed.

"Good-morning," he said to her. "You are driving home, I suppose."

This Hanov, a man of forty with a listless expression and a face that showed signs of wear, was

[1] From Anton Chekhov, *The Schoolmistress and Other Stories*, translated by Constance Garnett; copyright, 1921, by The Macmillan Company, and reprinted with the permission of The Macmillan Company and of Chatto and Windus Ltd.

beginning to look old, but was still handsome and admired by women. He lived in his big homestead alone, and was not in the service; and people used to say of him that he did nothing at home but walk up and down the room whistling, or play chess with his old footman. People said, too, that he drank heavily. And indeed at the examination the year before the very papers he brought with him smelt of wine and scent. He had been dressed all in new clothes on that occasion, and Marya Vassilyevna thought him very attractive, and all the while she sat beside him she had felt embarrassed. She was accustomed to see frigid and sensible examiners at the school, while this one did not remember a single prayer, or know what to ask questions about, and was exceedingly courteous and delicate, giving nothing but the highest marks.

"I am going to visit Bakvist," he went on, addressing Marya Vassilyevna, "but I am told he is not at home."

They turned off the highroad into a by-road to the village, Hanov leading the way and Semyon following. The four horses moved at a walking pace, with effort dragging the heavy carriage through the mud. Semyon tacked from side to side, keeping to the edge of the road, at one time through a snow-drift, at another through a pool, often jumping out of the cart and helping the horse. Marya Vassilyevna was still thinking about the school, wondering whether the arithmetic questions at the examination would be difficult or easy. And she felt annoyed with the Zemstvo board at which she had found no one the day before. How unbusiness-like! Here she had been asking them for the last two years to dismiss the watchman, who did nothing, was rude to her, and hit the schoolboys; but no one paid any attention. It was hard to find the president at the office, and when one did find him he would say with tears in his eyes that he hadn't a moment to spare; the inspector visited the school at most once in three years, and knew nothing whatever about his work, as he had been in the Excise Duties Department, and had received the post of school inspector through influence. The School Council met very rarely, and there was no knowing where it met; the school guardian was an almost illiterate peasant, the head of a tanning business, unintelligent, rude, and a great friend of the watchman's — and goodness knows to whom she could appeal with complaints or inquiries. . . .

"He really is handsome," she thought, glancing at Hanov.

The road grew worse and worse. . . . They drove into the wood. Here there was no room to turn around, the wheels sank deeply in, water splashed and gurgled through them, and sharp twigs struck them in the face.

"What a road!" said Hanov, and he laughed.

The schoolmistress looked at him and could not understand why this queer man lived here. What could his money, his interesting appearance, his refined bearing do for him here, in this mud, in this God-forsaken, dreary place? He got no special advantages out of life, and here, like Semyon, was driving at a jog-trot on an appalling road and enduring the same discomforts. Why live here if one could live in Petersburg or abroad? And one would have thought it would be nothing for a rich man like him to make a good road instead of this bad one, to avoid enduring this misery and seeing the despair on the faces of his coachman and Semyon; but he only laughed, and apparently did not mind, and wanted no better life. He was kind, soft, naïve, and he did not understand this coarse life, just as at the examination he did not know the prayers. He subscribed nothing to the schools but globes, and genuinely regarded himself as a useful person and a prominent worker in the cause of popular education. And what use were his globes here?

"Hold on, Vassilyevna!" said Semyon.

The cart lurched violently and was on the point of upsetting; something heavy rolled on to Marya Vassilyevna's feet — it was her parcel of purchases. There was a steep ascent uphill through the clay; here in the winding ditches rivulets were gurgling. The water seemed to have gnawed away the road; and how could one get along here! The horses breathed hard. Hanov got out of his carriage and walked at the side of the road in his long overcoat. He was hot.

"What a road!" he said, and laughed again. "It would soon smash up one's carriage."

"Nobody obliges you to drive about in such weather," said Semyon surlily. "You should stay at home."

"I am dull at home, grandfather. I don't like staying at home."

Beside old Semyon he looked graceful and vigorous, but yet in his walk there was something just perceptible which betrayed in him a being already touched by decay, weak, and on the road to ruin. And all at once there was a whiff of spirits in the wood. Marya Vassilyevna was filled with dread and pity for this man going to his ruin for no visible cause or reason, and it came into her mind that if she had been his wife or sister she would have devoted her whole life to saving him from ruin. His wife! Life was so ordered that here he was living in his great house alone, and she was living in a God-forsaken village alone, and yet for some reason the mere thought that he and she might be close to one another and equals seemed impossible and absurd. In reality, life was arranged and human relations were complicated so utterly beyond all understanding that when one thought about it one felt uncanny and one's heart sank.

"And it is beyond all understanding," she thought, "why God gives beauty, this graciousness, and sad, sweet eyes to weak, unlucky, useless people — why they are so charming."

"Here we must turn off to the right," said Hanov, getting into his carriage. "Good-by! I wish you all things good!"

And again she thought of her pupils, of the examination, of the watchman, of the School Council; and when the wind brought the sound of the retreating carriage these thoughts were mingled with others. She longed to think of beautiful eyes, of love, of the happiness which would never be. . . .

His wife? It was cold in the morning, there was no one to heat the stove, the watchman disappeared; the children came in as soon as it was light, bringing in snow and mud and making a noise: it was all so inconvenient, so comfortless. Her abode consisted of one little room and the kitchen close by. Her head ached every day after her work, and after dinner she had heart-burn. She had to collect money from the school-children for wood and for the watchman, and to give it to the school guardian, and then to entreat him — that overfed, insolent peasant — for God's sake to send her wood. And at night she dreamed of examinations, peasants, snowdrifts. And this life was making her grow old and coarse, making her ugly, angular, and awkward, as though she were made of lead. She was always afraid, and she would get up from her seat and not venture to sit down in the presence of a member of the Zemstvo or the school guardian. And she used formal, deferential expressions when she spoke of any one of them. And no one thought her attractive, and life was passing drearily, without affection, without friendly sympathy, without interesting acquaintances. How awful it would have been in her position if she had fallen in love!

"Hold on, Vassilyevna!"

Again a sharp ascent uphill. . . .

She had become a schoolmistress from necessity, without feeling any vocation for it; and she had never thought of a vocation, of serving the cause of enlightenment; and it always seemed to her that what was most important in her work was not the children, nor enlightenment, but the examinations. And what time had she for thinking of vocation, of serving the cause of enlightenment? Teachers, badly paid doctors, and their assistants, with their

terribly hard work, have not even the comfort of thinking that they are serving an idea or the people, as their heads are always stuffed with thoughts of their daily bread, of wood for the fire, of bad roads, of illnesses. It is a hard-working, an uninteresting life, and only silent, patient cart-horses like Marya Vassilyevna could put up with it for long; the lively, nervous, impressionable people who talked about a vocation and serving the idea were soon weary of it and gave up the work.

Semyon kept picking out the driest and shortest way, first by a meadow, then by the backs of the village huts; but in one place the peasants would not let them pass, in another it was the priest's land and they could not cross it, in another Ivan Ionov had bought a plot from the landowner and had dug a ditch round it. They kept having to turn back.

They reached Nizhneye Gorodistche. Near the tavern on the dung-strewn earth, where the snow was still lying, there stood wagons that had brought great bottles of crude sulphuric acid. There were a great many people in the tavern, all drivers, and there was a smell of vodka, tobacco, and sheepskins. There was a loud noise of conversation and the banging of the swing-door. Through the wall, without ceasing for a moment, came the sound of a concertina being played in the shop. Marya Vassilyevna sat down and drank some tea, while at the next table peasants were drinking vodka and beer, perspiring from the tea they had just swallowed and the stifling fumes of the tavern.

"I say, Kuzma!" voices kept shouting in confusion. "What there!" "The Lord bless us!" "Ivan Dementyitch, I can tell you that!" "Look out, old man!"

A little pock-marked man with a black beard, who was quite drunk, was suddenly surprised by something and began using bad language.

"What are you swearing at, you there?" Semyon, who was sitting some way off, responded angrily. "Don't you see the young lady?"

"The young lady!" someone mimicked in another corner.

"Swinish crow!"

"We meant nothing . . ." said the little man in confusion. "I beg your pardon. We pay with our money and the young lady with hers. Good-morning!"

"Good-morning," answered the schoolmistress.

"And we thank you most feelingly."

Marya Vassilyevna drank her tea with satisfaction, and she, too, began turning red like the peasants, and fell to thinking again about firewood, about the watchman. . . .

"Stay, old man," she heard from the next table,

"it's the schoolmistress from Vyazovye. . . . We know her; she's a good young lady."

"She's all right!"

The swing-door was continually banging, some coming in, others going out. Marya Vassilyevna sat on, thinking all the time of the same things, while the concertina went on playing and playing. The patches of sunshine had been on the floor, then they passed to the counter, to the wall, and disappeared altogether; so by the sun it was past midday. The peasants at the next table were getting ready to go. The little man, somewhat unsteadily, went up to Marya Vassilyevna and held out his hand to her; following his example, the others shook hands, too, at parting, and went out one after another, and the swing-door squeaked and slammed nine times.

"Vassilyevna, get ready," Semyon called to her.

They set off. And again they went at a walking pace.

"A little while back they were building a school here in their Nizhneye Gorodistche," said Semyon, turning around. "It was a wicked thing that was done!"

"Why, what?"

"They say the president put a thousand in his pocket, and the school guardian another thousand in his, and the teacher five hundred."

"The whole school only cost a thousand. It's wrong to slander people, grandfather. That's all nonsense."

"I don't know, . . . I only tell you what folks say."

But it was clear that Semyon did not believe the schoolmistress. The peasants did not believe her. They always thought she received too large a salary, twenty-one roubles a month (five would have been enough), and that of the money that she collected from the children for the firewood and the watchman the greater part she kept for herself. The guardian thought the same as the peasants, and he himself made a profit off the firewood and received payments from the peasants for being a guardian — without the knowledge of the authorities.

The forest, thank God! was behind them, and now it would be flat, open ground all the way to Vyazovye, and there was not far to go now. They had to cross the river and then the railway line, and then Vyazovye was in sight.

"Where are you driving?" Marya Vassilyevna asked Semyon. "Take the road to the right to the bridge."

"Why, we can go this way as well. It's not deep enough to matter."

"Mind you don't drown the horse."

"What?"

"Look, Hanov is driving to the bridge," said Marya Vassilyevna, seeing the four horses far away to the right. "It is he, I think."

"It is. So he didn't find Bakvist at home. What a pigheaded fellow he is. Lord have mercy upon us! He's driven over there, and what for? It's fully two miles nearer this way."

They reached the river. In the summer it was a little stream easily crossed by wading. It usually dried up in August, but now, after the spring floods, it was a river forty feet in breadth, rapid, muddy, and cold; on the bank and right up to the water there were fresh tracks of wheels, so it had been crossed here.

"Go on!" shouted Semyon angrily and anxiously, tugging violently at the reins and jerking his elbows as a bird does its wings. "Go on!"

The horse went on into the water up to his belly and stopped, but at once went on again with an effort, and Marya Vassilyevna was aware of a keen chilliness in her feet.

"Go on!" she, too, shouted, getting up. "Go on!"

They got out on the bank.

"Nice mess it is, Lord have mercy upon us!" muttered Semyon, setting straight the harness. "It's a perfect plague with this Zemstvo. . . ."

Her shoes and goloshes were full of water, the lower part of her dress and of her coat and one sleeve were wet and dripping: the sugar and flour had got wet, and that was worst of all, and Marya Vassilyevna could only clasp her hands in despair and say:

"Oh, Semyon, Semyon! How tiresome you are, really! . . ."

The barrier was down at the railway crossing. A train was coming out of the station. Marya Vassilyevna stood at the crossing waiting till it should pass, and shivering all over with cold. Vyazovye was in sight now, and the school with the green roof, and the church with its crosses flashing in the evening sun: and the station windows flashed too, and a pink smoke rose from the engine . . . and it seemed to her that everything was trembling with cold.

Here was the train; the windows reflected the gleaming light like the crosses on the church: it made her eyes ache to look at them. On the little platform between two first-class carriages a lady was standing, and Marya Vassilyevna glanced at her as she passed. Her mother! What a resemblance! Her mother had had just such luxuriant hair, just such a brow and bend of the head. And with amazing distinctness, for the first time in those thirteen years, there rose before her mind a vivid picture of her mother, her father, her brother, their flat in Moscow, the aquarium with little fish, everything to the tiniest detail; she heard the sound of the piano, her father's voice; she felt as she had been then, young, good-looking, well-dressed, in a bright warm room among her own people. A feeling of joy and happiness suddenly came over her, she pressed her hands to her temples in an ecstasy, and called softly, beseechingly:

"Mother!"

And she began crying, she did not know why. Just at that instant Hanov drove up with his team of four horses, and seeing him she imagined happiness such as she had never had, and smiled and nodded to him as an equal and a friend, and it

seemed to her that her happiness, her triumph, was glowing in the sky and on all sides, in the windows and on the trees. Her father and mother had never died, she had never been a schoolmistress, it was a long, tedious, strange dream, and now she had awakened. . . .

"Vassilyevna, get in!"

And at once it all vanished. The barrier was slowly raised. Marya Vassilyevna, shivering and numb with cold, got into the cart. The carriage with the four horses crossed the railway line; Semyon followed it. The signalman took off his cap.

"And here is Vyazovye. Here we are."

The Cherry Orchard[1]

A Comedy in Four Acts

Characters

LYUBOV ANDREYEVNA RANEVSKAYA, *a landowner*
ANYA, *her daughter, seventeen years old*
VARYA, *her adopted daughter, twenty-two years old*
LEONID ANDREYEVICH GAYEV, *her brother*
YERMOLAY ALEXEYEVICH LOPAHIN, *a merchant*
PYOTR (PETYA) SERGEYEVICH TROFIMOV, *a student*
BORIS BORISOVICH SIMEONOV-PISHCHIK, *a landowner*
CHARLOTTA IVANOVNA, *a governess*

SEMYON YEPIHODOV, *a clerk*
DUNYASHA, *a parlormaid*
FIRS, *a footman, eighty-seven years old*
YASHA, *a young footman*
TRAMP
STATION-MASTER
POST-OFFICE CLERK
GUESTS, SERVANTS

The action takes place on MME. RANEVSKAYA'S *estate.*

ACT ONE

A room which has always been called the nursery. One of the doors leads into ANYA'S *room. Dawn, sun rises during the scene. May, the cherry trees in flower, but it is cold in the garden with the frost of early morning. Windows closed. Enter* DUNYASHA *with a candle, and* LOPAHIN *with a book in his hand.*

Lopahin. The train's in, thank God. What time is it?

Dunyasha. Nearly two. (*Puts out the candle.*) It's almost daylight.

Lopahin. That train was certainly late! Two hours at least. (*Yawns and stretches.*) A fine fool I've been. Came here on purpose to meet them at the station, sat down in this chair and promptly fell asleep. So stupid; you might have waked me. . . .

[1] Printed with permission of the translator, Irina Skariatina. The translation was made for Eva Le Gallienne's production of the play.

Dunyasha. I thought you'd gone. (*Listens.*) There! I believe they're coming!

Lopahin (*also listens*). No, what with the luggage and one thing and another . . . (*Pause*) Lyubov Andreyevna has been abroad five years; I wonder what she's like now. . . . She's a splendid woman, a good-natured, simple woman. I remember when I was a lad of fifteen, my poor father . . . he used to keep a little store here in the village in those days . . . we were here in the yard, I forget what we'd come about . . . he hit me in the face with his fist and made my nose bleed. He'd been drinking. Lyubov Andreyevna, I can see her now . . . she was still very young and very thin . . . led me to the wash-bowl, here in this very room . . . the nursery. She said, "Don't cry, little peasant, it'll be all right in time for your wedding day . . . (*Pause*) Little peasant . . . my father was a peasant, it's true, but here I am in a white waistcoat and yellow shoes, like a pig in clover. I've plenty of money, I'm a rich man. . . . But when you come right down to it, a peasant is always a peasant. (*Turns over the leaves of the book.*) I've been trying to read this book ... can't understand a word of it ... fell asleep over it ... (*Pause*)

Dunyasha. The dogs didn't sleep all night, they felt their masters were coming.

Lopahin. Why, Dunyasha, why are you so ... ?

Dunyasha. My hands are shaking. I think I'm going to faint.

Lopahin. You're too soft, Dunyasha. You're dressed like a lady, and look at your hair. That's not right. One should know one's place.

(*Enter* YEPIHODOV *with a nosegay; he wears highly-polished squeaking top boots. He drops the nose-gay as he comes in.*)

Yepihodov (*picking up the nosegay*). Here. The gardener sent this, says you're to put it in the dining-room. (*Gives* DUNYASHA *the nosegay.*)

Lopahin. And bring me some kvass.

Dunyasha. Very well. (*Goes out.*)

Yepihodov. There's a frost this morning — three degrees — though the cherries are all in bloom. I cannot condone our climate. (*Sighs.*) I cannot. Our climate is incapable of suitable co-operation. Yermolay Alexeyevich, permit me to call your attention to a further fact: the other day I purchased myself a pair of boots, and I dare to assure you, they squeak, so that it's really impossible.

Lopahin. Leave me alone! Don't bother me.

Yepihodov. Every day some misfortune befalls me. I don't complain; I'm used to it; I even take it with a smile.

(DUNYASHA *comes in, hands* LOPAHIN *the kvass.*)

Yepihodov. I am going. (*Stumbles against a chair, which falls over.*) There! (*Triumphantly*) There, you see, again. Pardon my insistence, but misfortune ... it's positively remarkable.

(*Goes out.*)

Dunyasha. Do you know, Yermolay Alexeyevich, I must tell you, Yepihodov has proposed to me.

Lopahin. Ah!

Dunyasha. I'm sure I don't know ... he's a quiet fellow, but sometimes when he begins talking, it doesn't make sense. It's all very fine — makes you want to cry — but there's no understanding it. I kind of like him though, and he loves me to distraction. He's an unlucky man ... every day something happens to him. They tease him about it ... Twenty-Two Misfortunes, he's called.

Lopahin (*listening*). There! I do believe they're coming.

Dunyasha. They *are* coming! What's the matter with me? I'm cold all over!

Lopahin. They really are coming. Let's go and meet them. Will she know me? It's five years since I saw her.

Dunyasha (*in a flutter*). I'm going to faint. ... I know I am ...

(*There is a sound of two carriages driving up to the house.* LOPAHIN *and* DUN-YASHA *go out quickly. The stage is left empty. A noise is heard from the adjoining rooms.* FIRS, *who has driven to meet* LYUBOV ANDREYEVNA, *crosses the stage hurriedly, leaning on a stick. He is wearing old-fashioned livery and a high hat. He says something to himself but the words are indistinguishable. The noise behind the scenes goes on increasing. A voice: "Come, let's go in here." En-ter* LYUBOV ANDREYEVNA, ANYA *and* CHARLOTTA IVANOVNA, *with a pet dog on a chain, all in traveling dresses;* VARYA, *in an out-door coat with a kerchief over her head.* GAYEV, SIMEONOV-PISHCHIK, LOPAHIN, DUNYASHA *with bag and parasol, servants with other articles. All walk across the room.*)

Anya. Let's come in here. Do you remember this room, Mamma?

Lyubov (*joyfully, through her tears*). The nursery!

Varya. How cold it is! My hands are frozen! (*To* LYUBOV ANDREYEVNA) Your rooms are just the same, Mamma, the white one and the lavender.

Lyubov. My dear old nursery! My lovely room! I used to sleep here when I was a child ... (*Cries.*) and here I am, like a child again! (*Kisses her brother and* VARYA, *and then her brother again.*) Varya's just the same as ever, like a nun. And I recognized Dunyasha. (*Kisses* DUNYASHA.)

Gayev. The train was two hours late. What do you think of that? What a way to do things!

Charlotta (*to* PISHCHIK). My dog eats nuts, too.

Pishchik (*wonderingly*). Just imagine!

(*They all go out, except* ANYA *and* DUN-YASHA.)

Dunyasha. We've been expecting you for hours. (*Takes* ANYA'S *hat and coat.*)

Anya. Four nights I haven't slept on the train ... and now I'm frozen ...

Dunyasha. You left us in Lent; there was snow and frost, and now. ... My darling! (*Laughs and kisses her.*) I *have* missed you, my treasure, my joy! But I must tell you ... I can't put it off another minute ...

Anya (wearily). What now?

Dunyasha. The book-keeper, Yepihodov, proposed to me, just after Easter.

Anya. There you go, always the same thing . . . *(Straightening her hair)* I've lost all my hairpins . . .   *(She is staggering from exhaustion.)*

Dunyasha. Really, I don't know what to think. He loves me — he does love me so!

Anya (looking towards her door, tenderly). My own room, my windows, just as though I'd never been away. I'm home! Tomorrow morning I shall get up and run into the garden. Oh, if I could get some sleep. I didn't close my eyes the whole journey — I was so anxious and worried.

Dunyasha. Mr. Trofimov came the day before yesterday.

Anya (joyfully). Petya!

Dunyasha. He's asleep in the bath-house. He has settled in there. He said he was afraid of being in the way. *(Looks at her watch.)* I should have waked him, but Miss Varya told me not to. "Don't you wake him," says she.

(Enter VARYA with a bunch of keys at her waist.)

Varya. Dunyasha, coffee and be quick . . . Mamochka's asking for coffee.

Dunyasha. This minute.   *(Goes out.)*

Varya. Well, thank God you've come. You're home again. *(Fondling her.)* My pretty one's come home again.

Anya. Oh, what I've been through!

Varya. I can imagine.

Anya. When we left it was Holy Week, it was cold then, and all the way Charlotta would talk and show off her tricks. What did you want to burden me with Charlotta for?

Varya. You couldn't have traveled all alone, darling — at seventeen!

Anya. We got to Paris, it was cold there — snowing. My French is dreadful. Mamma lived on the fifth floor, I went up to her, and there were all kinds of French people, ladies, an old priest with a book. The place was full of smoke, and so uncomfortable. Suddenly I felt so sorry for Mamma — I put my arms round her and hugged her and wouldn't let her go. . . . Then Mamma made such a fuss over me, and she kept crying . . .

Varya (through tears). Don't talk about it . . . don't . . .

Anya. She had sold her villa at Mentone, she had nothing left, nothing. I hadn't a kopek left either, we only just had enough to get here. And Mamma wouldn't understand! When we had dinner at the stations, she always ordered the most expensive things, and gave the waiters a whole ruble. Charlotta's just the same. Yasha insisted

on having everything we had — it's simply awful. You know Yasha's Mamma's footman now, we brought him here with us.

Varya. Yes, I've seen the little wretch.

Anya. Well, tell me — have you paid the arrears on the mortgage?

Varya. What with?

Anya. Oh, God!

Varya. In August they'll put the place up for sale.

Anya. My God!

(LOPAHIN *peeps in at the door and moos like a cow.*)

Lopahin. Moo-oo. *(Disappears.)*

Varya (weeping). There — that's what I could do to him!   *(Shakes her fist.)*

Anya (embracing VARYA, softly). Varya, has he proposed to you? (VARYA *shakes her head.*) But he loves you. Why can't you make up your minds? What are you waiting for?

Varya. Oh, nothing will ever come of it. He's too busy, has no time for me . . . takes no notice of me. Somehow . . . it's hard for me to see him. They all talk about our getting married — they all congratulate me — and all the time, there's really nothing in it — it's just a dream. *(In another tone)* You have a new brooch like a bumble-bee.

Anya (mournfully). Mamma bought it. *(She goes into her own room, and speaks gaily like a child.)* And you know, in Paris I went up in a balloon.

Varya. My little one's home, my baby's home again!

(DUNYASHA *returns with the coffee-pot.*)

Varya (stands at the door of ANYA'S *room).* All day long, darling, as I go about the house, I keep dreaming. If only we could marry you to a rich man, I should feel more at peace. Then I would go off by myself on a pilgrimage to Kiev, to Moscow . . . I would spend my life going from one holy place to another . . . I'd go on and on . . . how blessed that would be!

Anya. The birds are singing in the garden. What time is it?

Varya. Must be nearly three. Time you were asleep, darling. *(Goes into* ANYA'S *room.)* How blessed that would be!

(YASHA *enters with a rug and a traveling bag. He crosses the stage, delicately.*)

Yasha. May one come in here, pray?

Dunyasha. Yasha! I didn't know you! How you've changed abroad!

Yasha. Hm-m . . . and who are you?

Dunyasha. When you went away I was that

high — Dunyasha — Fyodor's daughter ... don't you remember?

Yasha. Hm! a little peach!

(*He looks round and then embraces her. She shrieks and drops a saucer.* YASHA *goes out quickly.*)

Varya (*in the doorway, in a tone of vexation*). What's going on here?

Dunyasha (*through tears*). I've broken a saucer.

Varya. Well, that's good luck.

Anya (*comes out of her room*). We should warn Mamma Petya's here.

Varya. I left orders not to wake him.

Anya (*thoughtfully*). Six years ago Father died. A month later brother Grisha was drowned in the river ... such a pretty little boy he was — only seven. It was more than Mamma could bear, so she went away, went away without looking back ... (*Shudders.*) How well I understand her, if she only knew. (*Pause.*) And Petya Trofimov was Grisha's tutor, he may bring it all back to her.

(*Enter* FIRS *wearing a frock-coat and a white waist-coat. He goes up to the coffee-pot anxiously.*)

Firs. The mistress will be served here. (*Puts on white gloves.*) Is the coffee ready? (*Sternly, to* DUNYASHA.) Ech, you! Where's the cream?

Dunyasha. Ach, my God! (*Goes out quickly.*)

Firs. Ech, you good-for-nothing! (*Fusses round the coffee-pot, muttering to himself.*) Home from Paris. And the old master used to go to Paris too ... horses all the way. (*He laughs.*)

Varya. Firs, what are you muttering about?

Firs. What is your wish? (*Joyfully*) My lady has come home, and I have lived to see it! Now I can die. (*Weeps with joy.*)

(*Enter* LYUBOV ANDREYEVNA, GAYEV, LOPAHIN *and* SIMEONOV-PISHCHIK. *The latter is in a short-waisted, full coat of fine cloth, and full trousers.* GAYEV, *as he comes in, makes a gesture with his arms and body, as though he were playing billiards.*)

Lyubov. Let's see, how does it go? Carom off the red!

Gayev. That's it — in off the white! Once upon a time, sister, you and I used to sleep in this very room, and now I'm fifty-one, strange as it may seem.

Lopahin. Yes, time flies.

Gayev. Who?

Lopahin. Time, I say, flies.

Gayev. Pooh! what a smell of patchouli!

Anya. I'm going to bed. Good-night, Mamma. (*Kisses her mother.*)

Lyubov. My precious child! (*Kisses her hands.*) Are you happy to be home? I can't believe it's true.

Anya. Good-night, Uncle.

Gayev (*kissing her face and hands*). God bless you, how like your mother you are! (*To his sister*) At her age, Lyuba, you were just like her.

(ANYA *shakes hands with* LOPAHIN *and* PISHCHIK, *then goes out, shutting the door after her.*)

Lyubov. She's very tired.

Pishchik. Well, it's a long journey.

Varya (*to* LOPAHIN *and* PISHCHIK). How about it, gentlemen? It's nearly three o'clock — time you were going.

Lyubov (*laughs*). You're just the same as ever, Varya. (*Draws her to her and kisses her.*) I'll drink my coffee and then we'll all say good-night. (FIRS *puts a cushion under her feet.*) Thank you, my friend. I can't live without coffee. I drink it day and night. Thanks, (*Kisses him.*) you sweet little old man.

Varya. I'd better see if all the things have been brought in. (*She goes out.*)

Lyubov. Can it really be me sitting here? (*She laughs.*) I feel like dancing and clapping my hands. And yet in a second, I could be fast asleep. God knows I love my country, I love it tenderly; I couldn't look out of the window in the train, I kept crying so. (*Through tears*) However, I must drink my coffee. Thank you, Firs, thank you, dear old man. I'm so happy that you're still alive.

Firs. Day before yesterday.

Gayev. He's grown very deaf.

Lopahin. I must go in a minute. I'm leaving for Kharkov at five o'clock. So tiresome. I'd like to go on looking at you; I'd like to go on talking ... you're just as magnificent as ever.

Pishchik (*breathing heavily*). She's even better-looking ... dressed in the latest Paris fashion ... (*Hums*) "I'd give up my four-wheeled wagon, With its horses ..." ... all for her!

Lopahin. Your brother, Leonid Andreyevich, calls me a vulgar profiteer. But what do I care ... let him talk. I only want you to believe in me as you used to. I want you to look at me with those beautiful eyes full of tenderness, as you used to in the old days. Dear God! to think my father was a serf of your father's and your grandfather's, but you, you yourself, did so much for me once ... so much .... that I forget all about that; I love you as though you were my sister — even more than that.

Lyubov. I can't sit still, I simply can't ... (*Jumps up and walks about in violent agitation.*) It's too much happiness ... laugh at me, I know I'm silly! My own little book-case! My little table!

Gayev. Nurse died while you were away.

Lyubov. Yes, God rest her soul; they wrote me about it.

Gayev. And Anastasy is dead, Pyotr Kossoy has left me and has gone into town to work for the sheriff. (*Takes a box of caramels out of his pocket and sucks one.*)

Pishchik. My little daughter Dashenka sends her regards.

Lopahin. I want to tell you something pleasant and cheering. (*Glances at his watch.*) I'm leaving directly, there's not much time to talk. Well, I can put it in a couple of words. As you already know, your cherry orchard is to be sold to pay your debts. The sale is to be on the twenty-second of August; but don't you worry, my dear lady, you may sleep in peace; there is a way out. This is my plan! I beg your attention! Your estate is only twenty miles from the town; the railway runs close by it; and if the cherry orchard and the land along the river bank were cut up into building lots and then let on lease for summer bungalows, you would make an income of at least 25,000 rubles a year out of it.

Gayev. Forgive me . . . that's just nonsense.

Lyubov. I don't quite understand you, Yermolay Alexeyevich.

Lopahin. You will get a rent of at least 10 rubles a year per acre, and if you announce it now, I'll bet you what you like there won't be one square foot of ground vacant by the autumn; all the lots will be taken. In fact you're saved . . . congratulations! The site is perfect — by that deep river . . . only, of course it must be cleared . . . all the old buildings, for instance, must be demolished, even this house, which is quite worthless . . . and of course, the cherry orchard must be cut down.

Lyubov. Cut down! My dear fellow, forgive me, but you don't know what you're talking about. If there's one thing interesting — remarkable indeed — in the whole province, it's just our cherry orchard.

Lopahin. The only remarkable thing about this orchard is that it's a very large one. There's a crop of cherries every alternate year, and nothing's ever done with them; no one buys them.

Gayev. This orchard is mentioned in the Encyclopedia.

Lopahin (*glancing at his watch*). If we can't think of a solution, if we don't decide on something, on the twenty-second of August this cherry orchard and the entire estate will be sold at auction. Make up your minds — it's the only way out — I swear it!

Firs. In the old days, forty or fifty years ago, the cherries would be dried, soaked, pickled, and made into jam too, and frequently . . .

Gayev. Be quiet, Firs.

Firs. And frequently the preserved cherries would be sent in cart-loads to Moscow and to Kharkov. They made money then! And the preserved cherries in those days were soft and juicy, sweet and fragrant . . . they knew the recipe then . . .

Lyubov. And where is the recipe now?

Firs. Forgotten. Nobody remembers it.

Pishchik (*to* Lyubov). And how about Paris? Did you eat frogs there?

Lyubov. I ate crocodiles.

Pishchik. Just imagine!

Lopahin. There used to be only landowners and peasants in the country, but now these summer residents have appeared on the scene . . . All the towns, even the small ones, are surrounded by these bungalows; and there's no doubt that in another twenty years they'll be everywhere. At present the summer visitor only drinks tea on his porch, but maybe he'll take to working his bit of land too, and then your cherry orchard would become happy, rich and prosperous. . . .

Gayev. What nonsense!

(*Enter* Varya *and* Yasha.)

Varya. There are two telegrams for you, Mamochka — (*Takes out keys and opens an old-fashioned book-case with a loud crack.*) Here they are.

Lyubov. From Paris. (*Tears the telegrams without reading them.*) I'm through with Paris.

Gayev. Do you know, Lyuba, how old this book-case is? Last week I pulled out the bottom drawer and there I found the date branded in it. The book-case was made exactly a hundred years ago. Think of that! We might have celebrated its jubilee. True, it's an inanimate object, but nevertheless, a book-case . . .

Pishchik (*amazed*). A hundred years! Just imagine!

Gayev. Yes, (*Tapping it*) that's something . . . Dear, honored book-case, hail to thee who, for more than a hundred years, hast served the pure ideals of truth and justice! Thy silent call to fruitful labor has never weakened in all those hundred years, maintaining (*Weeps.*), through succeeding generations of mankind, courage and faith in a better future, and fostering in us ideals of good and social consciousness . . . (*A pause*)

Lopahin. Yes . . .

Lyubov. You're just the same as ever, Leonid.

Gayev (*a little embarrassed*). Carom off the right, into the pocket . . .

Lopahin (*looks at his watch*). Well, it's time I was off . . .

Yasha (*handing* LYUBOV ANDREYEVNA *medicine*). Maybe you'll take your pills now.

Pishchik. One shouldn't take medicines, my dearest lady, they do neither harm nor good ... give them here, honored lady — (*Takes the pill-box, pours the pills into his hand, blows on them, puts them in his mouth, and drinks off some kvass.*) There!

Lyubov (*in alarm*). You must be out of your mind!

Pishchik. I've taken all the pills.

Lopahin. The old glutton!   (*They all laugh.*)

Firs. Stayed with us in Easter week — ate half a pail of cucumbers ...   (*Mutters.*)

Lyubov. What's he talking about?

Varya. He's taken to muttering like that for the last three years — we're used to it.

Yasha. His declining years!

(CHARLOTTA IVANOVNA, *very thin, tightly laced, dressed in white, with a lorgnette at her waist, walks across the stage.*)

Lopahin. Forgive me, Charlotta Ivanovna, I've not had time to greet you. (*Tries to kiss her hand.*)

Charlotta (*pulling away her hand*). If I let you kiss my hand, you'll be wanting to kiss my elbow and then my shoulder.

Lopahin. I've no luck today. (*They all laugh.*) Charlotta Ivanovna, show us a trick.

Charlotta. Quite unnecessary. I wish to sleep.
(*She goes out.*)

Lopahin. In three weeks we'll meet again. (*Kisses* LYUBOV ANDREYEVNA's *hand.*) Good-by till then. I must go. (*To* GAYEV) Good-by. (*He kisses* PISHCHIK.) Good-by. (*Gives his hand to* VARYA, *then to* FIRS *and* YASHA.) I don't want to go. (*To* LYUBOV) If you think over my plan for the bungalows and make up your mind, let me know; I'll get you a loan of 50,000 rubles. Think it over seriously.

Varya (*angrily*). Well, do go, for goodness' sake!

Lopahin. I'm going, I'm going. (*He goes out.*)

Gayev. Vulgar fellow! I beg pardon though ... Varya's going to marry him, he's Varya's young man.

Varya. Don't talk nonsense, Uncle.

Lyubov. Well, Varya, I shall be delighted. He's a good man.

Pishchik. Yes, one must admit, he's a most worthy man. And my Dashenka ... also says that ... she says ... various things. (*Snores; but at once wakes up.*) But never mind about that. Honored lady, could you oblige me ... with a loan of 240 rubles ... to pay the interest on my mortgage tomorrow ... ?

Varya (*dismayed*). We haven't any, we haven't!

Lyubov. I really haven't any money.

Pishchik. It'll turn up. (*Laughs.*) I never lose hope, I thought everything was over, I was a ruined man, when lo and behold! the railway passed through my land ... and I was paid for it ... and something else will turn up again, if not today, then tomorrow ... Dashenka will win two hundred thousand ... she's got a lottery ticket.

Lyubov. We've finished our coffee, now let's go to bed.

Firs (*brushes* GAYEV *reprovingly*). You've got the wrong trousers on again. What am I to do with you?

Varya (*softly*). Anya's asleep. (*Softly opens the window.*) Now that the sun's coming up it's not a bit cold. Look, Mamochka, how beautiful the trees are! and the starlings are singing!

Gayev (*opens the other window*). The orchard is all white. You've not forgotten, Lyuba? That's the long avenue that runs straight, straight as an arrow, do you remember how it shines on a moonlight night? You've not forgotten?

Lyubov (*looking out of the window into the garden*). Oh, my childhood, my innocence! I used to sleep in this nursery — look out into the orchard, happiness waked with me every morning, the orchard was just the same then ... nothing has changed. (*She laughs with happiness.*) All, all white! Oh, my orchard! After the dark, stormy autumn and the cold winter, you are young again, and full of happiness, the heavenly angels have never left you.... If I could only escape from this burden that weighs on my heart, if I could forget the past!

Gayev. Yes, and the orchard will be sold to pay our debts, strange as it may seem ...

Lyubov. Look! There is our dear mother walking in the orchard ... all in white ... (*She laughs with delight.*) It is she!

Gayev. Where?

Varya. Oh, please! For God's sake, Mamochka!

Lyubov. There isn't anyone, I just imagined it. To the right, by the path to the arbor, there's a little white tree, bending, like a woman ...

(*Enter* TROFIMOV, *wearing a shabby student's uniform and spectacles.*)
What an amazing orchard! White masses of blossom, a blue sky ...

Trofimov. Lyubov Andreyevna! (*She looks round at him.*) I just want to pay my respects to you, then leave you at once. (*Kisses her hand warmly.*) I was told to wait until morning, but I hadn't the patience ...

(LYUBOV ANDREYEVNA *looks at him in perplexity.*)

Varya (through her tears). This is Petya Trofimov.

Trofimov. Petya Trofimov, who was your Grisha's tutor . . . Can I have changed so much?

(LYUBOV *embraces him and weeps quietly.*)

Gayev. There, there, Lyuba.

Varya (crying). I told you, Petya, to wait until tomorrow.

Lyubov. My Grisha . . . my little boy . . . Grisha — my son!

Varya. What can one do, Mamochka, it's God's will.

Trofimov (softly through his tears). There . . . there.

Lyubov (weeping quietly). My little boy was lost . . . drowned. What for? What for, dear Petya? (*More quietly*) Anya's asleep in there, and here I am talking loudly . . . making all this noise . . . but, Petya? Why have you grown so ugly? Why have you grown so old?

Trofimov. In the train a peasant woman called me a moth-eaten gentleman.

Lyubov. You were quite a boy then, just a young student, and now your hair's thin — and you've got on glasses! Is it possible you're still a student? (*She goes towards the door.*)

Trofimov. I'll most likely be an eternal student.

Lyubov (kisses her brother, then VARYA). Now, go to bed . . . you look older too, Leonid.

Pishchik (goes to her). Yes, it's time we were asleep. Och, my gout! I'm staying the night. Lyubov Andreyevna, my dear soul, if you could . . . tomorrow morning . . . 240 rubles.

Gayev. There he goes again . . . the same old story.

Pishchik. 240 rubles . . . to pay the interest on my mortgage . . .

Lyubov. My darling man, I have no money.

Pishchik. I'll give it back, my dear . . . it's a trifling sum.

Lyubov. All right, Leonid will give it to you. Go on, give it to him, Leonid.

Gayev. Me give it to him! My pockets are sealed!

Lyubov. It can't be helped. Give it to him! He needs it. He'll pay it back.

(LYUBOV, TROFIMOV, PISHCHIK *and* FIRS *go out.* GAYEV, VARYA *and* YASHA *remain.*)

Gayev. Sister hasn't got out of the habit of flinging away her money. (*To* YASHA) Get away, my good fellow, you smell of the barnyard.

Yasha (with a grin). And you, Leonid Andreyevich, are just the same as ever.

Gayev. Who? (*To* VARYA) What did he say?

Varya (to YASHA). Your mother's come from the village; she's been sitting in the servants' room since yesterday, waiting to see you.

Yasha. Ach! that old nuisance!

Varya. For shame!

Yasha. As if I needed her! She could have come tomorrow. (*Goes out.*)

Varya. Mamochka's just the same as ever; she hasn't changed a bit. If she had her own way she'd give away everything.

Gayev. Yes . . . (*Pause*) If a great many remedies are suggested for some disease, it means that the disease is incurable; I keep thinking and racking my brains; I have many remedies, a great many, and that really amounts to none. We might come in for a legacy from somebody; we might marry our Anya to a very rich man; or we might go to Yaroslavl and try our luck with our aunt, the Countess. Auntie's very, very rich, you know . . .

Varya (weeping). If only God would help us!

Gayev. Stop bawling. Aunt's very rich, but she doesn't like us. In the first place, sister married a lawyer instead of a nobleman . . . (ANYA *appears in the doorway.*) Married a man who was beneath her and her behavior was anything but virtuous. She's good, kind, sweet, and I love her, but however one allows for extenuating circumstances, there's no denying that she's an immoral woman. One feels it in her slightest gesture.

Varya (in a whisper). Anya's in the doorway.

Gayev. Who? (*Pause*) Most extraordinary! I've got something in my right eye — I can't see out of it . . . And on Thursday, when I was in the district court . . .

Varya. Why aren't you asleep, Anya?

Anya. I can't get to sleep, I can't.

Gayev. My little pet! (*He kisses* ANYA's *face and hands.*) My child! (*Weeps.*) You are not my niece, you're my angel! You're everything to me. Believe me, believe . . .

Anya. I believe you, Uncle. Everyone loves you and respects you . . . but, dear Uncle, you should be silent . . . simply be silent. What were you saying just now about my mother? Your own sister? What made you say that?

Gayev. Yes, yes . . . (*Puts her hand over his face.*) Really, that was awful! God help me! Only today I made a speech to the book-case . . . so stupid! And only when I had finished, I understood how stupid it was.

Varya. It's true, Uncle. You ought to keep quiet. Just don't talk, that's all.

Anya. If you could only keep silent, it would make things easier for you too.

Gayev. I'll be silent. (*Kisses* ANYA's *and* VARYA's *hands.*) Quite silent. Only this is about business. On Thursday I was in the district court; well, there was a large party of us there, and we began talking of one thing and another, and this and that, and do you know, I believe it will be possible to raise a loan on an I O U to pay the arrears on the mortgage.

Varya. If only the Lord would help us!

Gayev. On Tuesday I'll go and talk of it again. (*To* VARYA) Stop bawling. (*To* ANYA) Your Mamma will talk to Lopahin, and he of course will not refuse her . . . and as soon as you're rested, you'll go to Yaroslavl to the Countess your great-aunt. So we'll all set to work from three directions at once, and the whole business is as good as settled. We shall pay off the arrears — I'm convinced of it (*Puts a caramel in his mouth.*) I swear on my honor, I swear by anything you like, the estate shan't be sold. (*Excitedly*) By my own happiness I swear it! Here's my hand on it, you can call me a cheat and a scoundrel if I let it come to an auction! With all my soul I swear it!

Anya (quite happy again). How good you are, Uncle, and how clever! (*She embraces her uncle.*) Now I'm at peace, quite at peace, I'm happy.

(*Enter* FIRS.)

Firs (reproachfully). Leonid Andreyevich, have you no fear of God? When are you going to bed?

Gayev. Directly, directly. Go away, Firs, I'll . . . yes, I will undress myself. Now, children, bye-bye. We'll go into details tomorrow, but now go to sleep. (*Kisses* ANYA *and* VARYA.) I am a man of the 'eighties; they don't appreciate that period nowadays. Nevertheless, during the course of my life I have suffered not a little for my convictions. It's not for nothing that the peasant loves me; one should know the peasant; one should know from which . . .

Anya. There you go again, Uncle.

Varya. Uncle dear, be quiet.

Firs (angrily). Leonid Andreyevich!

Gayev. I'm coming, I'm coming! Go to bed! Potted the shot — clean as a whistle — a beauty! (*He goes out,* FIRS *hobbling after him.*)

Anya. I feel easier now, I don't want to go to Yaroslavl — I don't like my great-aunt, but still, I feel easier, thanks to Uncle. (*She sits down.*)

Varya. We must get some sleep. I'm going now. While you were away something unpleasant happened. In the old servants' quarters there are only the old servants, as you know. They began letting all sorts of tramps in to spend the night. . . . I didn't say anything. Then I heard they'd been spreading a report that I gave them nothing but dried peas to eat — out of meanness, you know . . . and it was all Yevstigney's doing. . . . All right, I thought, if that's how it is, I thought, wait a bit.

I sent for Yevstigney . . . (*Yawns.*) He comes. . . . "How's this, Yevstigney?" I said, "you could be such a fool as to" . . . (*Looking at* ANYA) Anichka! (*A pause*) She's asleep. (*Puts her arm around* ANYA.) Come to your little bed . . . Come . . . (*Leads her.*) My darling has fallen asleep . . . Come along! (*They go. Far away beyond the orchard a shepherd plays on a pipe.* TROFIMOV *crosses the stage and, seeing* VARYA *and* ANYA, *stands still.*) Sh! She's asleep . . . asleep. . . . Come, my own.

Anya (softly, half-asleep). I'm so tired. All those bells . . . Uncle . . . dear . . . Mamma and Uncle . . .

Varya. Come, my own, come along.

(*They go into* ANYA's *room.*)

Trofimov (tenderly, with emotion). My sunshine, my spring!

CURTAIN

ACT TWO

The open country. An old, dilapidated little chapel, long abandoned; near it there is a well, large slabs that had evidently once been tombstones, and an old bench. The road to the Gayev estate is visible. To one side there are poplars looming darkly: there the cherry orchard begins. In the distance, a row of telegraph poles, and far off on the horizon there is the faint outline of a large city which can be seen only in fine, clear weather. It is near sunset. CHARLOTTA, YASHA *and* DUNYASHA *are sitting on the bench.* YEPIHODOV *is standing near, playing something mournful on a guitar.* CHARLOTTA *wears an old forage-cap. She has taken a gun from her shoulder and is tightening the buckle on the strap.*

Charlotta (musingly). I haven't a real passport, and I don't know how old I am. But I always feel that I must be very young. When I was a little girl, my father and mother used to travel about to fairs and give performances — very good ones. And I used to jump the salto mortale, and all sorts of other things. And when Papa and Mamma died, a German lady adopted me and had me educated. So far so good. And I grew up and became a governess, but where I come from and who I am, I don't know. . . . Who were my parents? Perhaps they weren't even married . . . I don't know . . . (*Takes a cucumber out of her pocket and eats it.*) I don't know anything. (*Pause*) One wants so much to talk, and there isn't anyone to talk to . . . I haven't anybody.

Yepihodov (plays on the guitar and sings). "What do I care for the noisy world, What do I care for friend or foe . . ." How pleasant it is to play the mandolin.

Dunyasha. That's a guitar, not a mandolin.
(*Looks in a hand-mirror and powders herself.*)

Yepihodov. To a man mad with love it's a mandolin. (*Sings.*) "Were her heart but aglow with love's mutual flame . . ."

(YASHA *joins in.*)

Charlotta. How abominably these people sing. Phoo! Like jackals!

Dunyasha (to YASHA). How wonderful, though, to visit foreign lands!

Yasha. Ah, yes, I cannot but agree with you there.   (*He yawns and lights a cigar.*)

Yepihodov. That's understandable. In foreign lands, everything has long since reached its full completion.

Yasha. Of course, that's obvious.

Yepihodov. I'm a cultivated man, I read all kinds of remarkable books, yet I can never decide which path of life I am impelled to follow — should I live, or should I shoot myself, speaking precisely. Nevertheless, I always carry a revolver . . . here it is . . .   (*Shows revolver.*)

Charlotta. I've had enough. I'm going. (*Puts gun over her shoulder.*) You, Yepihodov, are a very clever man, and very terrifying; all the women must be wild about you. Br-r-r! (*Starts to go.*) These clever men are all so stupid; there's no one for me to talk to . . . always alone, alone, I haven't anybody . . . and who I am, and why I am, nobody knows.   (*She goes out slowly.*)

Yepihodov. Speaking personally, not touching upon other subjects, I am forced to the conclusion that fate behaves mercilessly to me, as a storm to a little boat. If I am incorrect in this supposition, then why, for example, did I wake up this morning, and look around, and there on my chest was a spider of fearful magnitude . . . like this . . . ? Again, I take up a jug of kvass to quench my thirst, and in it there is something highly indecent in the nature of a cockroach. (*A pause*) Have you read Buckle? (*Pause*) I am desirous of troubling you, Dunyasha, with a couple of words.

Dunyasha. Well, speak.

Yepihodov. I should be desirous to speak with you alone.   (*Sighs.*)

Dunyasha (*embarrassed*). Very well — only first bring me my little cape. You'll find it by the cupboard. It's rather damp here.

Yepihodov. Certainly, madam; I will fetch it, madam. Now I know what I must do with my revolver. (*Takes guitar and goes off playing on it.*)

Yasha. Twenty-Two Misfortunes! Between ourselves, he's a fool.   (*He yawns.*)

Dunyasha. Pray God he doesn't shoot himself! (*Pause*) I've become so nervous, I'm always in a flutter. I was quite a little girl when I was taken into the master's house, I've grown quite unused to the simple life, and my hands are white — as white as a lady's. I've become so refined. I'm such a delicate, sensitive creature, I'm afraid of everything. I'm so frightened; and if you deceive me, Yasha, I don't know what will happen to my nerves.

Yasha (*kisses her*). You're a peach! Of course, a nice girl should never forget herself; what I dislike more than anything is a girl who is flighty in her behavior.

Dunyasha. I'm passionately in love with you, Yasha; you're a man of culture — you can give your opinion about anything.

Yasha (*yawns*). Yes, my girl, that's so. Now in my opinion, it's like this: if a girl loves anyone, it means she has no morals. (*Pause*) It's pleasant smoking a cigar in the open air. (*Listen.*) Someone's coming this way . . . it's them! (DUNYASHA *embraces him impulsively.*) You go home, as though you'd been to the river to bathe; go by the little path, or else they'll meet you and suspect me of having made an appointment with you here. That I can't endure.

Dunyasha (*coughing softly*). The cigar's made my head ache.

(*She goes off. Enter* LYUBOV ANDREYEVNA, GAYEV *and* LOPAHIN.)

Lopahin. You must make up your mind once and for all — there's no time to lose. It's quite a simple question, you know. Will you allow your land to be built on or not? Answer one word, yes or no; only one word!

Lyubov. Who's smoking such abominable cigars here?   (*Sits down.*)

Gayev. Now the railway line has been brought near it's made things very convenient. (*Sits down.*) We went over and lunched in town, and here we are back again. Carom off the white . . . I feel like going in and playing just one game.

Lyubov. You have plenty of time.

Lopahin. Only one word! (*Imploringly*) Do give me an answer!

Gayev (*yawning*). Who?

Lyubov (*looks in her purse*). Yesterday this purse was nearly full, and now it's almost empty. My poor Varya tries to economize; she feeds us all on milk soup; in the kitchen the old people get nothing but dried peas to eat, while I squander my money like a fool — (*She drops the purse, scattering gold pieces.*) There . . . you see . . .

Yasha. Allow me — I'll pick them up at once.
(*He picks up the money.*)

Lyubov. There's a good boy, Yasha. And why did I go to lunch in town? Your nasty little restaurant, with its music and the tablecloth smelling of soap . . . Why drink so much, Leonid? Why eat so much? Why talk so much? Today you talked a great deal again, and all so pointlessly — about the 'seventies, about the decadents! And to whom? To the waiters! Talking to waiters about decadents!

Gayev (waving his hand). I'm incorrigible; that's evident. (*Irritably, to* YASHA) Why do you keep fidgeting about in front of us?

Yasha (laughs). It's funny — it's your voice — it always makes me laugh . . .

Gayev. Either he or I . . .

Lyubov. Get along — go away, Yasha.

Yasha (giving LYUBOV *her purse).* I'm going — directly (*Hardly able to suppress his laughter*), this minute.   (*He goes.*)

Lopahin. That rich man, Deriganov, wants to buy your estate. They say he's coming to the sale himself.

Lyubov. Where did you hear that?

Lopahin. That's what they say in town.

Gayev. Our aunt from Yaroslavl has promised to send help; but when and how much she will send, no one knows.

Lopahin. How much will she send? A hundred thousand? two hundred?

Lyubov. Oh, well, ten or fifteen thousand; and we must be thankful to get that.

Lopahin. Forgive me, but such frivolous people as you are — so strange and unbusinesslike — I never met in all my life. One tells you in plain language your estate is going to be sold, and you behave as if you didn't understand it.

Lyubov. What are we to do? Tell us what to do.

Lopahin. I do tell you, every day; every day I say the same thing! The cherry orchard and the land must be leased to build bungalows, and as soon as possible — immediately. The auction's right on top of us. Please understand! For God's sake make up your mind — then you could raise as much money as you like, and you're saved.

Lyubov. Bungalows — summer visitors — forgive me, but it's all so cheap and vulgar.

Gayev. I absolutely agree with you.

Lopahin. I shall either sob or scream or have a fit! I can't stand it! You're driving me mad! (*To* GAYEV) You're an old woman!

Gayev. Who?

Lopahin. An old woman!   (*Gets up to go.*)

Lyubov (in dismay). No, don't go! Please stay, I beg you. Perhaps we shall think of something.

Lopahin. What is there to think of?

Lyubov. Don't go, I entreat you. With you here it's more cheerful anyway. (*Pause*) I keep expecting something, as if the house were going to fall about our ears.

Gayev (in profound thought). Potted the white — it fails — a kiss . . .

Lyubov. We have been great sinners . . .

Lopahin. What sins have you to repent of?

Gayev (puts a caramel in his mouth). They say I've eaten up my property in caramels! (*Laughs.*)

Lyubov. Oh my sins! I've frittered my money away recklessly, like a lunatic. I married a man who did nothing but get into debt. My husband died of champagne, he drank horribly. And then, in my grief, I loved another man, I lived with him. And immediately, that was my first punishment, inexorably the blow fell here in the river, my little boy was drowned . . . and I went abroad, went away forever . . . never to come back, never to see this river again. . . . I closed my eyes and fled, distracted . . . but *he* followed me, pitiless, brutal. I bought a villa near Mentone, because he fell ill there; and for three years, day and night, I knew neither peace nor rest. Ill as he was, he tormented me — and my soul grew parched and withered. Then last year, when the villa was sold to pay the debts — I went to Paris, and there he robbed me, abandoned me, went to live with another woman. I tried to poison myself — so stupid, so shameful — and then suddenly I felt irresistibly drawn back to Russia — back to my own country — to my little girl. (*Through tears*) Lord, oh Lord! Be merciful, forgive me my sins — don't punish me any more! (*Takes a telegram out of her purse.*) This came today from Paris — he begs me to forgive him, implores me to take him back . . . (*Tears up the telegram.*) Don't I hear music somewhere? (*Listens.*)

Gayev. That's our famous Jewish orchestra, you remember? Four violins, a flute and a double bass.

Lyubov. Does that still exist? We ought to send for them some evening and give a dance.

Lopahin (listens). I don't hear anything. (*Hums softly.*) "For money a German will Frenchify a Russian." I saw a wonderful play at the theater yesterday — very funny.

Lyubov. There was probably nothing funny about it. You shouldn't look at plays, you should look at yourselves more often. How drab your lives are — how full of unnecessary talk!

Lopahin. That's true; come to think of it we do live like fools. (*Pause*) My father was a peasant, an idiot; he understood nothing, never taught me anything, all he did was beat me when he was drunk, and always with a stick. Basically, I'm just the same kind of dumb idiot. I never learned anything — I write so that I feel ashamed before people, like a pig.

Lyubov. You should get married, my friend.

Lopahin. Yes . . . that's true.

Lyubov. To our Varya, she's a good girl.

Lopahin. Yes.

Lyubov. She's a nice, simple girl, she's busy all day long; but the main thing is, she loves you. Besides, you've liked her for a long time now.

Lopahin. Well, why not? She's a good girl.

(*Pause*)

Gayev. I've been offered a place in the bank — 6,000 rubles a year — have you heard?

Lyubov. That would never do for you. You'd better stay here.

(*Enter* FIRS *with overcoat.*)

Firs. Put this on, sir, it's damp.

Gayev (*putting it on*). You bother me, old fellow.

Firs. Never mind about that. This morning you went out without leaving word.

(*Looks him over.*)

Lyubov. How old you look, Firs!

Firs. What is your wish?

Lopahin. She said, how old you look!

Firs. I've had a long life; they were arranging my wedding before your Papa was born. (*Laughs.*) I was already head footman when the Emancipation came. I wouldn't consent to be set free then; I stayed on with the old master . . . (*Pause*) I remember they were all very happy, but why they were happy, they didn't know themselves.

Lopahin. The good old days! There was flogging, anyway!

Firs (*not hearing*). To be sure. The peasants knew their masters, and the masters knew their peasants; but now everything's all broken up, there's no making it out.

Gayev. Be quiet, Firs. I must go to town tomorrow. They've promised to introduce me to a general who might let us have a loan.

Lopahin. Nothing will come of that. You won't even be able to pay the interest, make no mistake about that.

Lyubov. He's raving, there is no such general.

(*Enter* TROFIMOV, ANYA *and* VARYA.)

Gayev. Here come the girls.

Anya. There's Mamma . . .

Lyubov (*tenderly*). Come here, come along, my darlings. (*Embraces* ANYA *and* VARYA.) If you only knew how I love you both! Sit beside me — there, like that.

Lopahin. Our eternal student is always with the young ladies.

Trofimov. That's not your business.

Lopahin. He'll soon be fifty, and he's still a student!

Trofimov. Stop your silly jokes.

Lopahin. What are you so cross about, you funny fellow?

Trofimov. Oh, leave me alone . . .

Lopahin (*laughs*). Allow me to ask you, what's your real opinion of me?

Trofimov. My real opinion of you, Yermolay Alexeyevich, is that you are a rich man who will soon be a millionaire. Well, just as in the economy of nature a wild beast is necessary, who devours everything that comes in his way, so you too have your uses. (*They all laugh.*)

Varya. Better tell us something about the planets, Petya.

Lyubov. No, let's go on with yesterday's conversation.

Trofimov. What was it about?

Gayev. About the pride of man.

Trofimov. Yesterday we talked a long time, but we came to no conclusion. In pride, as you understand it, there is something mystical. Perhaps you're right, from your personal point of view. But if one discusses it in the abstract, simply and without prejudice, then what kind of pride can there be, since man is physiologically so imperfect, since in the great majority of cases he is coarse, unintelligent and profoundly unhappy? One should stop admiring oneself — one should work, and nothing else.

Gayev. One must die, in any case.

Trofimov. Who knows? and what does it mean — to die? Perhaps man has a hundred senses, and at his death only the five we know will perish, while the other ninety-five remain alive.

Lyubov. How clever you are, Petya!

Lopahin. Fearfully clever!

Trofimov. Humanity advances, perfecting its powers. Everything that is unattainable now will one day become familiar and comprehensible; only we must work, helping with all our strength those who seek the truth. Here among us in Russia such workers are still very few. The great majority of the intelligentsia, as far as I can see, seeks nothing, does nothing, is totally unfit for work of any kind. They call themselves the intelligentsia — yet they patronize their servants, treat the peasants like animals, don't bother to study, never read anything serious, do absolutely nothing at all — only talk about science, and understand very little about the arts. They are all solemn, have severe faces, they all philosophize and talk of weighty matters, and in the meanwhile the vast majority of us, ninety-nine out of a hundred, live like savages. The slightest thing and — wham! a punch in the jaw, and a string of curses! We eat disgustingly, sleep in dirt and stuffiness, bed-bugs everywhere — stench and damp and moral filth. And obviously the only purpose of all this fine talk of ours is to divert our attention from the realities.

Kindly show me where to find the public nurseries we've heard so much about, and the libraries. We read about them in novels, but in reality they don't exist; there is nothing but dirt, vulgarity and Asiatic fatalism. I don't like very serious faces — I'm afraid of them — I'm afraid of serious conversations. We'd far better be silent.

Lopahin. Do you know, I get up at five o'clock in the morning, and I work from morning to night; and I've money, my own and other people's, always passing through my hands, and I see what humanity is really like. You've only to start doing anything to see how few honest, decent people there are. Sometimes when I lie awake at night, I think "Oh, Lord, thou hast given us immense forests, boundless plains, the widest horizons, and living in such surroundings, we ourselves ought really to be giants."

Lyubov. Now you want giants! They're only good in fairy tales; otherwise they're frightening.

(YEPIHODOV *crosses in the background playing on the guitar.*)

(*Dreamily*) There goes Yepihodov.

Anya (*dreamily*). There goes Yepihodov.

Gayev. Messieurs, 'Dames, the sun has set.

Trofimov. Yes.

Gayev (*not loud, but as if declaiming*). Oh, nature, divine nature, thou shinest with eternal radiance, beautiful and indifferent! Thou, whom we call our mother, thou dost unite within thee life and death! Thou givest life, and dost destroy!

Varya (*pleadingly*). Uncle!

Anya. Uncle, you're at it again.

Trofimov. You'd much better be caroming off the red.

Gayev. I'm silent, I'm silent . . .

(*They all sit plunged in thought. Perfect stillness. The only thing audible is the muttering of* FIRS. *Suddenly there is a sound in the distance — as it were from the sky — the sound of a breaking harp-string, mournfully dying away.*)

Lyubov. What is that?

Lopahin. I don't know. Somewhere far away, in the pits, a bucket's broken loose and fallen; but somewhere very far away.

Gayev. Or it might be some sort of bird, perhaps a heron.

Trofimov. Or an owl . . .

Lyubov (*shudders*). It's uncanny, somehow.

(*Pause*)

Firs. Before the calamity the same thing happened — the owl screeched, and the samovar hissed all the time.

Gayev. Before what calamity?

Firs. Before the Emancipation. (*Pause*)

Lyubov. Come, my friends, let's be going. It's getting dark. (*To* ANYA) You have tears in your eyes. What is it, my little one? (*Embraces her.*)

Anya. I don't know, Mamma; it's nothing.

Trofimov. Somebody's coming.

(*A* TRAMP *appears in a shabby white forage-cap and an overcoat. He is slightly drunk.*)

Tramp. Allow me to inquire, may I cut through this way to the station?

Gayev. You may. Just follow that road.

Tramp. My heartfelt thanks. (*He coughs.*) The weather is beautiful. (*Declaims.*) "My brother, my suffering brother . . . Go to the Volga! Whose groans do you hear?" (*To* VARYA) Mademoiselle, vouchsafe a hungry Russian 30 kopecks . . .

(VARYA *utters a shriek of alarm.*)

Lopahin (*Angrily*). If you have to behave so outrageously, you might at least . . .

Lyubov (*hurriedly*). Here, take this. (*Looks in her purse.*) There isn't any silver . . . Never mind, here's a gold coin.

Tramp. My heartfelt thanks.

(*He goes off. Laughter.*)

Varya (*frightened*). I'm going home — I'm going . . . Oh, Mamochka, at home the servants have nothing to eat, and you gave him a gold coin!

Lyubov. What are you to do with me? I'm such a fool. When we get home, I'll give you everything I have. Yermolay Alexeyevich, you'll lend me some more . . .

Lopahin. Of course.

Lyubov. Come, Messieurs, 'Dames, it's time to be going. Oh! Varya, we've arranged the marriage for you. Congratulations!

Varya (*through tears*). Really, Mamma, that's not a joking matter.

Lopahin. "Ochmelia, get thee to a nunnery . . ."

Gayev. And do you know, my hands are trembling, because I haven't played billiards for so long.

Lopahin. "Ochmelia, O nymph, in your prayers, remember me!"

Lyubov. Let's go, it's almost supper-time.

Varya. He frightened me! My heart's pounding.

Lopahin. Let me remind you, ladies and gentlemen, on the twenty-second of August the cherry orchard will be put up for sale. Think about that! Think about it!

(*They all go off except* TROFIMOV *and* ANYA.)

Anya (*laughs*). I'm grateful to that awful man . . . he frightened Varya and so we're alone.

Trofimov. Varya's afraid we shall fall in love with each other. She hasn't left us alone for days.

She's so narrow-minded, she can't grasp that we're above love. To eliminate the petty and transitory, which prevent us from being free and happy — that is the end and the meaning of our life. Forward! We go forward irresistibly, towards the bright star that shines in the distance. Forward! Do not fall behind, friends!

Anya (*claps her hands*). How well you speak! (*Pause*) It's divine here today.

Trofimov. Yes, the weather's wonderful.

Anya. What have you done to me, Petya? Why do I not love the cherry orchard as I used to? I loved it so tenderly. It seemed to me there was no spot on earth lovelier than our orchard.

Trofimov. All Russia is our orchard. Our land is vast and beautiful — there are many beautiful places in it. (*Pause*) Think of it, Anya, your grandfather, your great-grandfather and all your ancestors were slave-owners — the owners of living souls — and from every cherry in the orchard, from every leaf, from every trunk there are human creatures looking at you. Don't you hear their voices? Oh, it's terrifying! Your orchard is a fearful thing, and when in the evening or at night one passes through the orchard, the old bark on the trees gleams faintly in the dusk, and the old cherry trees seem to be dreaming of centuries gone by, and haunted by ghastly visions. Yes, what can one say? We're at least two hundred years behind, we've really gained nothing yet — we have no definite relation to the past, we only philosophize, complain of nostalgia, or drink vodka. It's all so clear — in order to live in the present, we should first expiate our past, finish with it — and we can expiate it only through suffering, only through extraordinary, unceasing labor. Remember that, Anya.

Anya. The house in which we live has long ceased to be our own, and I shall leave it, I give you my word.

Trofimov. If you have the keys, fling them into the well and go away. Be free as the wind.

Anya. How beautifully you said that!

Trofimov. Believe me, Anya, believe me! I'm not yet thirty, I'm young, I'm still a student — but I've already suffered so much. In winter I'm hungry, sick, harassed, poor as a beggar, pursued and hunted by fate. And still my soul, always, every moment of the day and night, is filled with nebulous visions . . . a vision of happiness, Anya . . . already I can see it!

Anya (*pensively*). The moon is rising.

(*YEPIHODOV is heard playing the same mournful song on the guitar. The moon rises. Somewhere near the poplars*

VARYA is looking for ANYA *and calling* "Anya, where are you?")

Trofimov. Yes, the moon is rising. (*Pause*) Here is happiness, here it comes, it's coming nearer and nearer, I can already hear its footsteps. And if we never see it, if we may never know it, what does it matter? Others will see it after us!

(VARYA's *voice:* "Anya! Where are you?")

Trofimov. That Varya again! (*Angrily*) It's revolting!

Anya. Never mind, let's go down to the river. It's lovely there.

Trofimov. Yes, let's go. (*They go.*)

(VARYA's *voice:* "Anya! Anya!")

CURTAIN

ACT THREE

A drawing-room divided by an arch from a larger drawing-room. Chandelier burning. The Jewish orchestra is heard playing in the ante-room. In the larger drawing-room they are dancing the "Grand Rond." PISHCHIK calls, "Promenade à une paire." Enter the drawing-room in couples: PISHCHIK and CHARLOTTA, TROFIMOV and LYUBOV, ANYA and the POST-OFFICE CLERK, VARYA and the STATION-MASTER. VARYA is quietly weeping and wiping away her tears as she dances. DUNYASHA is in the last couple. PISHCHIK shouts: "Grand rond, balancez" and "Les cavaliers à genoux et remerciez vos dames." FIRS in a swallow-tail coat brings in seltzer water on a tray.

Pishchik. I'm a full-blooded man; I've already had two strokes. Dancing's hard work for me; but as they say, "If you can't bark with the pack, you can at least wag your tail." Still, I'm as strong as a horse. My late lamented father, who would have his joke, God rest his soul, used to say this about our origin: that the ancient stock of the Simeonov-Pishchiks was derived from the very horse that Caligula made a member of the Senate. But the trouble is — I have no money. A hungry dog believes in nothing but meat; it's the same with me — I believe in nothing but money.

Trofimov. You know, there's something about you which does remind one of a horse.

Pishchik. Well, what about it? A horse is a fine animal — one can sell a horse.

(*Sound of billiards being played in an adjoining room.* VARYA *appears in the archway.*)

Trofimov (*teasing her*). Madame Lopahina! Madame Lopahina!

Varya (*angrily*). Moth-eaten gentleman!

Trofimov. Yes, I am a moth-eaten gentleman and I'm proud of it.

Varya (bitterly). Here we've hired musicians! What shall we pay them with? *(She goes out.)*

Trofimov (to PISHCHIK). If the energy you have devoted during your lifetime to searching for money to pay your interest had gone into something else, you might in the end have turned the world upside down.

Pishchik. Nietzsche, a philosopher, brilliant and illustrious, a man of colossal intellect, says in his works that it is permissible to forge bank-notes.

Trofimov. Have you read Nietzsche?

Pishchik. What next? Dashenka told me . . . and now I've got to the point where forging bank-notes is about the only way out . . . The day after tomorrow I have to pay 310 rubles — I already have 130 . . . *(He feels in his pockets. In alarm)* The money's gone! I've lost my money! *(Through tears)* Where's my money? *(Joyfully)* Here it is! Inside the lining. . . . I'm sweating all over . . .

(Enter LYUBOV and CHARLOTTA.)

Lyubov (hums the "Lezginka"). Why is Leonid so long? What can he be doing in town? Dunyasha, offer the musicians some tea.

Trofimov. The auction hasn't taken place, most likely.

Lyubov. It's the wrong time to have the orchestra, and the wrong time to give a dance. Well, never mind. *(Sits down and hums softly.)*

Charlotta (gives PISHCHIK a pack of cards). Here is a pack of cards. Think of any card you like.

Pishchik. I've thought of one.

Charlotta. Shuffle the pack now. That's right. Give it here, my dear Mr. Pishchik. Eins, zwei, drei! Now look — it's in your pocket.

Pishchik (taking the card out of his pocket). The eight of spades! Perfectly right! Just imagine!

Charlotta (holding pack of cards in her hands — to TROFIMOV). Tell me quickly, which is the top card.

Trofimov. Well, let's see — the queen of spades.

Charlotta. It is! *(To PISHCHIK)* Now which is the top card?

Pishchik. The ace of hearts.

Charlotta. It is! *(She claps her hands and the pack of cards disappears.)* Ah, what lovely weather it is today! *(A mysterious feminine voice which seems to come out of the floor answers her: "Oh, yes, it's magnificent weather, Madam.")* You are my perfect ideal. *(The voice: "And I greatly admire you too, Madam.")*

The Station-master (applauding). The lady ventriloquist — bravo!

Pishchik. Just imagine! Enchanting Charlotta Ivanovna, I'm simply in love with you.

Charlotta. In love? Are you capable of love? Guter Mensch, aber schlechter Musikant!

Trofimov (clapping PISHCHIK on the shoulder). You old horse, you!

Charlotta. I beg attention! One more trick! *(Takes a traveling rug from a chair.)* Here is a very good plaid; I want to sell it. *(Shaking it out)* Does anyone want to buy it?

Pishchik. Just imagine!

Charlotta. Eins, zwei, drei!

(Behind the rug stands ANYA. She makes a curtsy, runs to her mother, embraces her, and runs back into the larger room, amidst general enthusiasm.)

Lyubov (applauds). Bravo! Bravo!

Charlotta. Now again! Eins, zwei, drei!

(Behind the rug stands VARYA bowing.)

Pishchik. Just imagine!

Charlotta. That's the end.

(Throws the plaid at PISHCHIK, makes a curtsy, runs into the larger drawing-room.)

Pishchik. Mischievous little creature! Just imagine! *(Goes out.)*

Lyubov. And still Leonid doesn't come. What is he doing in town so long? Everything must be over by now. Either the estate is sold, or the auction hasn't taken place. Why keep us so long in suspense?

Varya (trying to console her). Uncle's bought it, I feel sure of that.

Trofimov (ironically). Oh, yes!

Varya. Great-aunt sent him an authorization to buy it in her name, and to transfer the debt. She's doing it for Anya's sake. I'm sure with God's help, Uncle has bought it.

Lyubov. My aunt in Yaroslavl sent fifteen thousand to buy the estate in her name, she doesn't trust us — but that's not even enough to pay off the interest. *(Hides her face in her hands.)* Today my fate will be decided — my fate!

Trofimov (teasing VARYA). Madame Lopahina!

Varya (angrily). Eternal student! Twice already you've been expelled from the University.

Lyubov. What are you so angry about, Varya? He's teasing you about Lopahin. Well, what of that? If you want to marry Lopahin, do. He's a good man, and interesting; if you don't want to, don't. Nobody's compelling you, my pet!

Varya. Frankly, Mamma, I take this thing seriously; he's a good man and I like him.

Lyubov. All right then, marry him! I can't see what you're waiting for.

Varya. But Mamma. I can't propose to him myself! For the last two years everyone's been talking to me about him — talking! But he either keeps silent, or else makes a joke. I understand; he's growing rich, he's absorbed in business — he has no time for me. If I had money, were it ever so little, if I had only 100 rubles, I'd throw everything up and go far away — I'd go into a nunnery.

Trofimov. How blessed . . . !

Varya. A student ought to have some sense. (*Softly, with tears in her voice*) How ugly you've grown, Petya! How old you look! (*To* LYUBOV) But I can't live without work, Mamochka; I must keep busy every minute.

(*Enter* YASHA.)

Yasha (*hardly restraining his laughter*). Yepihodov has broken a billiard cue! (*He goes out.*)

Varya. Why is Yepihodov here? Who allowed him to play billiards? I don't understand these people! (*She goes out.*)

Lyubov. Don't tease her, Petya. She's unhappy enough without that.

Trofimov. She's so officious — always meddling in other people's business. All summer long she's given Anya and me no peace. She's afraid of a love-affair between us. What business is it of hers? Besides, I've given no grounds for it — I'm not interested in such banalities. We are above love.

Lyubov. And I suppose I'm beneath love? (*Very uneasily*) What can be keeping Leonid? If I only knew whether the estate has been sold or not. Such a calamity seems so incredible that I don't know what to think — I feel lost . . . I could scream . . . I could do something stupid . . . save me, Petya, tell me something, talk to me!

Trofimov. Whether the estate is sold today or not makes no difference. That's all done with long ago — there's no turning back, the path is overgrown. Calm yourself, dear Lyubov Andreyevna. You mustn't deceive yourself. For once in your life you must face the truth.

Lyubov. What truth? You can still see the truth, but I seem to have lost my sight — I see nothing. You settle every great problem so boldly, but tell me, my dear boy, isn't it because you're young — because you haven't yet understood one of your problems through suffering? You look ahead fearlessly, but isn't it that you don't see and don't expect anything dreadful, because life is still hidden from your young eyes? You're bolder, more honest, more profound than we are, but think, be just a little magnanimous — have some compassion; after all, I was born here, my father and mother lived here, my grandfather lived here, and I love this house. I can't conceive of life without the cherry orchard, and if it really must be sold, then sell me with the orchard. (*Embraces* TROFIMOV, *kisses him on the forehead.*) My son was

drowned here (*Weeps.*) — pity me, my dear, kind fellow!

Trofimov. You know, I sympathize with all my heart.

Lyubov. But that should have been said differently, so differently! (*Takes out her handkerchief — a telegram falls on the floor.*) My heart is so heavy today — you can't imagine! My soul quivers at every sound — I'm trembling all over. But I can't go away; I'm afraid of quiet and solitude. Don't judge me, Petya. . . . I love you as though you were one of us, I would gladly let you marry Anya — I swear I would — only, my dear boy, you must study — you must take your degree — you do nothing — you let yourself be tossed by fate from place to place — it's so strange. It is, isn't it? And you should do something with your beard, to make it grow somehow! (*She laughs.*) You're so funny!

Trofimov (*picks up the telegram*). I've no wish to be a beauty.

Lyubov. That's a telegram from Paris. I get one every day. One yesterday and one today. That ferocious creature is ill again — he's in trouble again. He begs forgiveness, entreats me to go to him, and really I ought to go to Paris to be near him. You look shocked, Petya; but what is there to do, my dear boy? What am I to do? He's ill, he's alone and unhappy, and who is to look after him, who is to keep him from doing the wrong thing, who is to give him his medicine on time? And why hide it or be silent — I love him! Isn't that clear? I love him — love him! He's a millstone round my neck — he'll drag me to the bottom, but I love that stone — I can't live without it. (*Presses* TROFIMOV'S *hand.*) Don't think badly of me, Petya — and don't say anything, don't say . . .

Trofimov (*through his tears*). For God's sake forgive me my frankness; but after all, he robbed you!

Lyubov. No, no, no, you mustn't say such things! (*Covers her ears.*)

Trofimov. He's no good! You're the only one who doesn't know it. He's mean — worthless — beneath contempt!

Lyubov. You are twenty-six or twenty-seven years old, but you're still a school-boy.

Trofimov. Possibly.

Lyubov. You should be a man at your age. You should understand what love means — and you ought to be in love yourself. You ought to fall in love! (*Angrily*) Yes, yes! And it's not purity in you, you're simply a prude, a comic fool, a freak!

Trofimov. What is she saying?

Lyubov. "I am above love!" You're not above love, but simply, as our Firs says, you're a good-for-nothing. At your age not to have a mistress!

Trofimov. This is awful! What is she saying! (*He goes rapidly into the larger drawing-room, clutching his head.*) It's awful — I can't stand it — I'm going! All is over between us! (*He goes.*)

Lyubov (*shouts after him*). Petya! Wait a minute! You funny creature, I was joking. Petya! (*There is a sound of somebody running quickly downstairs and suddenly falling with a crash.* ANYA *and* VARYA *scream. But there is a sound of laughter at once.*)

LYUBOV. What's the matter? What's happened?

(ANYA *runs in.*)

Anya. Petya's fallen downstairs!

(*She runs out again.*)

Lyubov. What a funny creature that Petya is! (*The musicians begin to play a waltz — they all dance.* TROFIMOV, ANYA, VARYA *and* LYUBOV *come in from the ante-room.*)

Lyubov. Petya, Petya, you pure in heart! Please forgive me. Let's have a dance. (*Dances with* PETYA. ANYA *and* VARYA *dance.* FIRS *comes in, puts his stick down by the door.* YASHA *comes in.*)

Yasha. Well, Grandpa, what's the matter with you?

Firs. I don't feel well. In the old days we had generals, barons and admirals dancing at our balls, and now we have to send for the Post-Office clerk and the Station-master, and even they are none too willing to come. Why do I feel so weak? The late master, the grandfather, used to give us all sealing-wax when we were ill. I've been taking sealing-wax every day for twenty years or more. Perhaps that's what's kept me alive.

Yasha. You bore me, Grampa. (*Yawns.*) It's time you kicked the bucket.

Firs. Ach, you good-for-nothing. (*Mutters.*) (TROFIMOV *and* LYUBOV *dance into the drawing-room.*)

Lyubov. Merci. I'll sit down for a little while. I'm tired.

(*Enter* ANYA *excitedly.*)

Anya. A man was saying in the kitchen just now that the cherry orchard had been sold.

Lyubov. Sold! To whom?

Anya. He didn't say. He's gone away.

(*She dances off with* TROFIMOV.)

Yasha. There was an old man gossiping there — a stranger.

Firs. Leonid Andreyevich isn't here yet, he hasn't come back. He has on his light overcoat, demi-saison; you'll see, he'll catch cold. Ach, foolish young things!

Lyubov. I shall die — I shall die! Go, Yasha, find out to whom it has been sold.

Yasha. But the old man left long ago.

(*He laughs.*)

Lyubov. What are you laughing at? What are you so pleased about?

Yasha. Yepihodov is so funny. A silly fellow, Twenty-Two Misfortunes!

Lyubov. Firs, if they sell the estate, where will you go?

Firs. Where you bid me, there I'll go.

Lyubov. Why do you look like that? Are you ill? You ought to be in bed.

Firs (*ironically*). Yes! Me go to bed, and who's to serve here? Who's to supervise things? I'm the only one in the whole house.

Yasha (*to* LYUBOV). Lyubov Andreyevna, permit me to make a request of you: if you go back to Paris, take me with you, I implore you. It's positively impossible for me to stay here. Whatever they may say, you can see for yourself, it's an uncivilized country, the people have no morals, and then the boredom! The food in the kitchen's revolting, and Firs wanders about muttering all sorts of inappropriate remarks. Take me with you — please do!

(PISHCHIK *enters.*)

Pishchik. Allow me to ask you for a waltz, most beautiful lady. (LYUBOV *goes with him.*) Enchanting lady, you really must let me have 180 rubles. (*They dance.*) Only one hundred and eighty rubles. (*They pass into the larger room.*)

(YASHA *stands humming softly. In the larger drawing-room a figure in a gray top hat and check trousers gesticulates and jumps about; shouts:* "Bravo, Charlotta Ivanovna!" DUNYASHA *enters.*)

Dunyasha (*stopping to powder her face*). My young mistress has ordered me to dance. There are too many gentlemen and not enough ladies, but dancing make me dizzy, my heart begins to flutter. Firs, the Post-Office clerk said something to me just now that quite took my breath away.

Firs. What did he say?

Dunyasha. He said I was like a flower.

Yasha (*yawns*). What ignorance!

(*He goes out.*)

Dunyasha. Like a flower! I'm such a delicate creature. I simply adore romantic speeches.

Firs. Your head's being turned.

(*Enter* YEPIHODOV.)

Yepihodov. You do not desire to see me, Dunyasha . . . as though I were some sort of an insect.

(*Sighs.*)

Dunyasha. What do you wish?

Yepihodov. Undoubtedly you may be right. (*Sighs.*) But of course, if one looks at it from that point of view, you have, if I allow myself so to express myself, forgive me my frankness, completely reduced me to this state of mind. I know my fate. Every day some misfortune befalls me, and I have long ago grown accustomed to it, so that I look upon my fate with a smile. You gave me your word, and though I . . .

Dunyasha. Let's have a talk later, I beg you. But now leave me in peace; for I am lost in reverie.

Yepihodov. I have a misfortune every day; and if I may allow myself so to express myself, I merely smile at it, I even laugh.

(VARYA *enters.*)

Varya. Are you still here, Yepihodov? What a disrespectful creature you are really! Go along, Dunyasha. (*To* YEPIHODOV) Either you're playing billiards and breaking the cues, or you're wandering about the drawing-room as though you were a guest.

Yepihodov. You really cannot, if I allow myself so to express myself, demand compensation from me.

Varya. I'm not demanding compensation; I'm just speaking to you. You merely wander from place to place, and don't do your work. We keep you as book-keeper, but Heaven knows what for.

Yepihodov (*offended*). Whether I work or whether I walk, whether I eat or whether I play billiards, is a matter to be discussed only by persons of understanding and of mature judgment.

Varya. You dare say that to me — you dare! You mean to say I've no understanding? Get out of here at once, this minute!

Yepihodov (*intimidated*). I beg you to express yourself with delicacy.

Varya (*beside herself*). Out you go this minute! Get out! (YEPIHODOV *goes towards the door,* VARYA *following him.*) Twenty-Two Misfortunes! Take yourself off — don't let me set eyes on you again.

(YEPIHODOV's *voice from behind the door:* "I shall lodge a complaint against you!")

Varya. You're coming back, are you? (*She snatches up the stick* FIRS *has put down near the door.*) Well, come on then . . . come on . . . I'll show you . . . Take that!

(*She swings the stick at the very moment that* LOPAHIN *comes in.*)

Lopahin. Very much obliged to you.

Varya. I beg your pardon.

Lopahin. Not at all. I humbly thank you for your kind reception.

Varya. Don't mention it. (*Softly*) I didn't hurt you, did I?

Lopahin. Oh, no, not at all. There's an enormous bump coming up, though.

(*Voices from the inner room:* "Lopahin has come, Lopahin!")

Pishchik (*comes in*). What's this I see and hear? (*Kisses* LOPAHIN.) There's a little whiff of cognac about you, my dear soul — and we've been celebrating here, too.

(*Enter* LYUBOV.)

Lyubov. Is that you, Yermolay Alexeyevich? Why have you been so long? Where's Leonid?

Lopahin. Leonid Andreyevich arrived with me. He's coming.

Lyubov. Well, but what . . . ? Well . . . did the sale take place? Tell me, speak!

Lopahin. The sale was over at four o'clock. We missed the train — had to wait till half-past nine. Ugh! I feel a little dizzy.

(*Enter* GAYEV. *In his right hand he has purchases, with his left he is wiping away his tears.*)

Lyubov. Well, Leonid, what news? Quickly, for God's sake!

Gayev (*doesn't answer — simply waves his hand. To* FIRS, *weeping*). Here, take these; anchovies, Kerch herrings. . . . I've eaten nothing all day. What I've been through! I'm terribly tired. Firs, help me change my clothes.   (*They go out.*)

Pishchik. How about the sale? Tell us what happened.

Lyubov. Is the cherry orchard sold?

Lopahin. It is sold.

Lyubov. Who bought it?

Lopahin. I bought it. (*Pause.* LYUBOV *is crushed; she would fall down, if she were not near an armchair and table.* VARYA *takes the keys from her waistband, flings them on the floor in the middle of the drawing-room and goes out.*) I have bought it. Wait a bit, ladies and gentlemen, pray, my head's not quite clear — I can't talk. (*Laughs.*) We got to the auction and there was Deriganov. Leonid Andreyevich had only fifteen thousand and Deriganov bid thirty thousand besides the arrears, straight off. I saw how the land lay; I bid against him — bid forty thousand. He bid forty-five thousand. I bid fifty-five. And it went on, he adding five thousand and I adding ten. Well . . . so it ended. I bid ninety and it was knocked down to me. Now the cherry orchard's mine — mine! (*Bursts out into laughter.*) Lord, God, the cherry orchard's mine! Tell me that I'm drunk — out of my mind — that it's all a dream. (*Stamps his feet.*) Don't laugh at me! If my father and my grandfather could rise from their graves and see all that has happened — how their Yermolay, who used to run about barefoot in winter, how that very Yermolay has bought the finest estate in the world — I have bought the estate where my father and grandfather were serfs, where they weren't even allowed to enter the kitchen — I'm asleep — I'm dreaming — it's all my fancy — it's the work of your imagination, plunged in the darkness of ignorance! (*Picks up the keys, smiling.*) She threw away the keys — wants to show she's no longer the mistress here. (*Jingles the keys.*) Well, what of it? Hey, musicians! Play! I want to hear you! Come, all of you, and look how Yermolay Lopahin will take the ax to the cherry orchard and fell the trees to the ground. We will build summer houses on it, and our grandsons and great-grandsons will see a new life springing here. Music! Play up!

(*Music begins to play.* LYUBOV *has sunk into a chair and is weeping bitterly.*)

(*Reproachfully*) Why, why didn't you listen to me? My dear friend, my poor friend, you can't bring it back now. (*With tears*) Oh, if only this were over, if only our unhappy disjointed lives might somehow soon be changed.

Pishchik (*taking him by the arm; in a low voice*). She's crying. Let us go into the other room. Let her be alone. Come.

(*Takes him by the arm and leads him into the larger drawing-room.*)

Lopahin. What's that? Musicians, play up! All must be as I wish it. (*Ironically*) Here comes the new master, the owner of the cherry orchard. (*He accidentally tips over a little table, almost upsetting the candelabra.*) I can pay for everything!

(*Goes out with* PISHCHIK.)

(LYUBOV, *all alone on the stage, sits huddled up, weeping bitterly. Music plays softly.* ANYA *and* TROFIMOV *come in quickly.* ANYA *goes to her mother and falls on her knees before her.* TROFIMOV *stands in the doorway.*)

Anya. Mamma, Mamma, you're crying! Dear, kind, good Mamma, my precious, I love you, I bless you. The cherry orchard is sold, it's gone, that's true, that's true. But don't cry, Mamma, life is still before you, you still have your good, pure heart. Let us go, let us go, darling, away from here. We will plant a new orchard, even finer than this one. You will see it, you will understand, and joy will sink into your soul like the sun at evening, and you will smile, Mamma. Come, darling, let us go.

CURTAIN

ACT FOUR

Setting same as in Act I. No curtains or pictures — only a little furniture, piled up as if for sale. A sense of desolation. Packed trunks, traveling bags, etc. near the outside door. Door left open — one can hear the voices of VARYA *and* ANYA *calling.* LOPAHIN *stands waiting.* YASHA *holds a tray with glasses full of champagne.* YEPIHODOV, *in the entrance hall, is tying up a box. In the background behind the scene a hum of talk from the peasants who have come to say good-by. Voice of* GAYEV: "Thanks, brothers, thank you."

Yasha. The peasants have come to say good-by. In my opinion, Yermolay Alexeyevich, the peasants are kind people, but they just don't know anything.

(*The hum of talk dies away. Enter* LYUBOV *and* GAYEV; *she is pale, her face twitches, she is unable to speak.*)

Gayev. You gave them your purse, Lyuba. That won't do — that won't do!

Lyubov. I couldn't help it — I couldn't.

(*Both go out.*)

Lopahin (*calls after them*). Please, I beg of you, a little glass at parting. I didn't think of bringing any from town and at the station I could only find this one bottle. Please — won't you? (*Pause*) What's the matter? Don't you want any? If I'd known, I wouldn't have bought it. Well, then I won't drink any either. (YASHA *carefully sets the tray down.*) Here, Yasha, at least you have a glass.

Yasha. To the travelers — may they be happy! (*Drinks.*) This champagne isn't the real thing I can assure you.

Lopahin. Eight rubles a bottle. (*Pause*) It's damnably cold here.

Yasha. They didn't start the fires today — it wasn't worth it, since we're leaving. (*Laughs.*)

Lopahin. What's the matter with you?

Yasha. I'm just pleased.

Lopahin. It's October, yet it's as still and sunny as though it were summer. Good weather for building. (*Looks at his watch. Says in the doorway:*) Bear in mind, ladies and gentlemen, the train goes in forty-seven minutes, so you ought to start for the station in twenty minutes. Better hurry up!

(TROFIMOV, *in an overcoat, comes in.*)

Trofimov. It must be time to start. The horses are ready. The devil only knows what's become of my galoshes; they're lost. (*In the doorway*) Anya! My galoshes are gone — I couldn't find them.

Lopahin. I must go to Kharkov — I'm going in the same train with you. I'll spend the winter in Kharkov. I've been hanging round here wasting my time with you — going mad with nothing to do. I can't live without work — I don't know what to do with my hands — they flap about as if they didn't belong to me.

Trofimov. Well, we'll soon be gone, then you can go on with your profitable labors again.

Lopahin. Have a little glass.

Trofimov. No, I won't, thanks.

Lopahin. So you're going to Moscow now?

Trofimov. Yes. I'll go with them as far as the town, and tomorrow I shall go on to Moscow.

Lopahin. I bet the professors aren't giving any lectures — they're waiting for your arrival.

Trofimov. That's none of your business.

Lopahin. Exactly how many years have you been at the university?

Trofimov. Can't you think of something newer than that? That's stale and flat. We shall probably never see each other again, so allow me to give you a piece of advice at parting; don't gesticulate so much with your hands — get out of the habit. And another thing; building bungalows, figuring that summer residents will eventually become independent farmers, figuring like that is just another form of gesticulation . . . After all, I'm fond of you; you have fine delicate fingers, like an artist, you have a fine, delicate soul.

Lopahin (*embraces him*). Good-by, my dear fellow. Thank you for everything. Let me give you some money for the journey if you need it.

Trofimov. What for? I don't need it.

Lopahin. But you haven't any.

Trofimov. Yes, I have, thank you. I got some money for a translation — here it is in my pocket — but where can my galoshes be?

Varya (*from the next room*). Here! take the disgusting things.

(*Flings a pair of galoshes onto the stage.*)

Trofimov. What are you so cross about, Varya? Hm . . . and these are not my galoshes.

Lopahin. I sowed twenty-five hundred acres of poppies in the spring, and now I've cleared forty thousand profit; and when my poppies were in bloom — what a picture! So, as I say, I made forty thousand; that means I'm offering you a loan because I can afford it. Why turn up your nose at it? I'm a peasant — I speak bluntly.

Trofimov. Your father was a peasant, mine was a druggist — that proves absolutely nothing whatever. (LOPAHIN *takes out his pocket-book.*) Stop it — stop that! If you were to offer me two hundred thousand I wouldn't take it — I'm a free man, and everything that all of you, rich and poor alike, prize so highly and hold so dear hasn't the slightest power over me — it's like so much fluff, floating in the air. I can get on without you, I can pass by you, I'm strong and proud. Humanity is advancing towards the highest truth, the highest happiness which is possible on earth, and I am in the front ranks.

Lopahin. Will you get there?

Trofimov. I shall get there. (*Pause*) I shall get there, or I shall show others the way to get there.

(*In the distance is heard the stroke of an ax on a tree.*)

Lopahin. Well, good-by, my dear fellow, it's time to be off. We may turn up our noses at one another, but life goes on all the while. When I'm working hard, without resting, my spirit grows lighter, and it seems to me that I too know why I exist. But how many people are there in Russia, my dear fellow, who exist nobody knows what for? Well, it doesn't matter. That's not what makes the world go round. They say Leonid Andreyevich has taken a situation in the bank — 6,000 rubles a year. Only, of course, he won't stick to it — he's too lazy.

Anya (*in the doorway*). Mamma begs you not to start chopping down the orchard until she's gone.

Trofimov. How can people be so tactless!

(*He goes out.*)

Lopahin. I'll see to it — at once! Of all the . . .

(*Goes out after him.*)

Anya. Has Firs been taken to the hospital?

Yasha. I told them this morning. They must have taken him.

Anya (*to* YEPIHODOV, *who passes across the room*). Yepihodov, find out, please, if Firs has been taken to the hospital.

Yasha (*offended*). I told Yegor this morning — why ask a dozen times?

Yepihodov. The aged Firs, in my conclusive opinion, is beyond repair. It's time he was gathered to his forefathers — and I can only envy him. (*He puts a trunk down on a cardboard hat-box and crushes it.*) There now — of course! I might have known it.

Yasha. Twenty-Two Misfortunes!

Varya (*through the door*). Has Firs been taken to the hospital?

Anya. Yes.

Varya. Then why wasn't the note for the doctor taken too?

Anya. Oh! Then we must send it after them.

(*Goes out.*)

Varya (*from the next room*). Where's Yasha? Tell him his mother's come and wants to say good-by.

Yasha (*waves his hand*). She makes me lose all patience.

Dunyasha (*who has been busy with luggage, etc.*)

You might just give me one little look, Yasha. You're going away — you're deserting me —

(*Weeps and throws herself on his neck.*)

Yasha. What's there to cry about? (*Drinks champagne.*) In six days I shall be in Paris again. Tomorrow we shall get into the express train and roll away — that's the last you'll see of us. . . . I can scarcely believe it — Vive la France! It doesn't suit me here — I just can't live here — that's all there is to it. I've had enough of the ignorance here — more than enough. (*Drinks champagne.*) What's there to cry about? Behave yourself properly — then you won't cry.

Dunyasha (*powders her face, looking in a pocket mirror*). Do send me a letter from Paris. You know how I loved you, Yasha, how I loved you! I'm a tender creature, Yasha.

Yasha. Look out! They're coming!

(*Busies himself about the trunks.*)

(*Enter* LYUBOV, GAYEV, ANYA *and* CHARLOTTA.)

Gayev. We ought to be off. There's not much time now. (*He looks at* YASHA.) What a smell of herring!

Lyubov. In about ten minutes we should be getting into the carriages. (*Looks about the room.*) Good-by, old house, dear old home of our fathers. Winter will pass, spring will come, you will no longer be here, they will have torn you down. How much these walls have seen! (*Kisses* ANYA.) My treasure, how radiant you look! Your eyes are sparkling like diamonds. Are you glad, very glad?

Anya. Very glad. A new life is beginning, Mamma.

Gayev. Well, after all, everything is all right now. Before the cherry orchard was sold, we were all worried and wretched; but afterwards, when once the question was settled conclusively, irrevocably, we all calmed down, and even felt quite cheerful. I'm a bank clerk now — a financier — carom off the red! And you, Lyuba, in spite of everything, are looking better, there's no doubt of that.

Lyubov. Yes, my nerves are better, that's true. (DUNYASHA *hands her her hat and coat.*) I'm sleeping well. Carry out my things, Yasha, it's time. (*To* ANYA) My little girl, we shall soon see each other again. I'm going to Paris — I'll live there on the money your Yaroslavl auntie sent us to buy the estate with — long live Auntie! But that money won't last long.

Anya. You'll come back soon — soon, Mamma, won't you? Meanwhile I'll study, I'll pass my examination at the high school, and then I'll go to work and be able to help you. We'll read all kinds of books together, Mamma, won't we? We'll read in the autumn evenings, we'll read lots of books, and a new wonderful world will open out before us. Mamma, come back soon.

Lyubov. I shall come back, my precious treasure.

(*Embraces her.*)

(*Enter* LOPAHIN. CHARLOTTA *softly hums a song.*)

Gayev. Charlotta's happy. She's singing.

Charlotta (*picks up a bundle like a swaddled baby*). Bye-bye, my baby. (*A baby is heard crying* "Ooah! Ooah!") Hush, hush, my pretty boy! ("Ooah! Ooah!") Poor little thing! (*Throws the bundle back.*) You must please find me a situation — I can't go on like this.

Lopahin. We'll find you one, Charlotta Ivanovna, don't worry.

Gayev. Everyone's leaving us. Varya's going away. We've suddenly become of no use.

Charlotta. There's no place for me to live in town — I must go away. (*Hums.*) What care I . . .

(*Enter* PISHCHIK.)

Lopahin. The freak of nature!

Pishchik (*gasping*). Oh . . . let me get my breath . . . I am in agony . . . my most honored . . . give me some water . . .

Gayev. Wants some money, I suppose. Your humble servant . . . I'll go out of the way of temptation. (*Goes out.*)

Pishchik. It's a long while since I've been to see you, lovely lady. (*To* LOPAHIN) You are here . . . glad to see you . . . a man of colossal intellect . . . here . . . take . . . (*Gives* LOPAHIN *money.*) 400 rubles — so I still owe you 840.

Lopahin (*in amazement*). I must be dreaming — where did you get it?

Pishchik. Wait a bit . . . I'm hot . . . most extraordinary occurrence! Some Englishmen came along and found in my land some sort of white clay. (*To* LYUBOV) And 400 for you . . . most lovely . . . most wonderful . . . (*Gives her the money.*) The rest later. (*Sips water.*) A young man in the train was telling me just now that a great philosopher reommends jumping off roof-tops. "Jump!" says he; "the whole crux of the problem lies in that." Just imagine!

Lopahin. What Englishmen?

Pishchik. I've given them the right to dig the clay for twenty-four years . . . and now, forgive me, I can't stay . . . I must be dashing on . . . I'm going to Znoikov . . . to Kardamanov . . . I'm in debt all round . . . (*Drinks water.*) To your very good health . . . I'll come back on Thursday . . .

Lyubov. We're just off to the town; and tomorrow I leave for abroad.

Pishchik (*in agitation*). What? Why to the

town? ... That's why ... I see ... the furniture
... the suitcases ... never mind! (*Through his
tears*) Never mind ... Men of colossal intellect,
these Englishmen ... never mind ... be happy.
God will help you ... Never mind ... Everything
in this world must have an end. (*Kisses* LYUBOV's
hand.) If the rumor reaches you that my end has
come, remember this old horse, and say: "Once
upon a time there lived in the world a man ...
Simeonov-Pishchik ... God rest his soul...." 10
Glorious weather ... Yes .... (*Goes out in violent
agitation but at once returns and says in the doorway:*)
My daughter Dashenka sends her regards to you.
                                          (*He goes out.*)

Lyubov. Now we can go — I leave with two 15
cares in my heart — the first is leaving Firs ill.
(*Glancing at her watch*) We still have five minutes.

Anya. Mamma, Firs has already been taken to
the hospital. Yasha sent him this morning.

Lyubov. My other anxiety is Varya. She's used 20
to getting up early and working; and now, without
work, she'll be like a fish out of water. She has
grown thin and pale, and can't stop crying, poor
little thing. (*Pause*) You are well aware, Yermolay
Alexeyevich, I dreamed of marrying her to you. 25
(*Whispers to* ANYA *and motions to* CHARLOTTA —
they both go out.) She loves you. She suits you. I
don't know — I don't know why it is you seem
deliberately to avoid each other; I can't understand it. 30

Lopahin. To tell you the truth, I don't understand it myself. It is strange. If there's still time,
I'm ready now — at once. Let's settle it straight
off, and be done with it! But without you, I feel
I'll never be able to propose. 35

Lyubov. That's splendid — after all, it will only
take a minute. I'll call her at once.

Lopahin. And there's champagne all ready too.
(*Looks at the glasses.*) Empty! Somebody's drunk
it all — (YASHA *coughs.*) That's what you might 40
call lapping it up.

Lyubov. We'll go out. Yasha, *allez!* I'll call
her. (*At the door*) Varya! leave everything and
come here. Come along! (*Goes out with* YASHA.)

Lopahin (*looking at his watch*). Yes ... (*Pause*) 45
        (*Behind the door, smothered laughter and
        whispering; at last, enter* VARYA.)

Varya (*looking over the things*). How strange — I
can't find it ...

Lopahin. What are you looking for? 50

Varya. ... packed it myself ... don't remember ...   (*Pause*)

Lopahin. Where are you going now, Varya?

Varya. I? To the Ragulins. I've arranged to
take charge of their house — as housekeeper. 55

Lopahin. That's in Yashnevo — about seventy

miles away. (*Pause*) Well — life in this house is
ended!

Varya (*looking among the things*). Where is it?
Perhaps I put it in the little trunk. Yes, life in
this house is ended ... there will be no more of it. 5

Lopahin. And I'm just off to Kharkov — by
this next train. I've a lot of business there. I'm
leaving Yepihodov here — I've taken him on.

Varya. Oh?

Lopahin. Last year at this time it was snowing, 10
if you remember, but now it's fine and sunny. It's
cold, though — three degrees of frost.

Varya. I didn't look. (*Pause*) And besides, our
thermometer's broken.   (*Pause*)
        (*Voice from the yard:* "Yermolay Al-
        exeyevich!")

Lopahin (*eagerly, as though he had been waiting
for the call*). This minute!   (*Goes out quickly.*)
        (VARYA *sitting on the floor lays her head on
        the little trunk and sobs quietly.* LYUBOV
        comes in cautiously.)

Lyubov. Well? (*Pause*) We must be going.

Varya. Yes, it's time, Mamochka. I'll be able
to get to the Ragulins' today — if only you don't
miss the train.

Lyubov (*in the doorway*). Anya, put your things
on.

(*Enter* ANYA, GAYEV, CHARLOTTA. *Servants come
        in.* YEPIHODOV *bustles about the luggage.*)

Lyubov. Now we can start on our journey.

Anya (*joyfully*). On our journey!

Gayev. My friends, my dear, my precious
friends, leaving this house forever, can I be silent?
Can I refrain from giving utterance at leave-taking
to those emotions which now flood all my being?

Anya. Uncle!

Varya. Uncle, Uncle, don't.

Gayev (*forlornly*). Carom and into the pocket
... I'll be silent ...

(*Enter* TROFIMOV *and* LOPAHIN.)

Trofimov. Well, ladies and gentlemen, it's time
to go.

Lopahin. Yepihodov, my coat.

Lyubov. I'll sit down just a minute. It seems
as though I've never seen before what the walls
in this house were like, the ceilings — and now I
look at them hungrily, with such tender love.

Gayev. I remember when I was six years old sitting on that window sill on Whitsunday, watching
my father going to church.

Lyubov. Have all the things been taken?

Lopahin. I think so. (*Putting on overcoat*) You,
Yepihodov, see that everything's in order.

Yepihodov (*in a husky voice*). You needn't worry,
Yermolay Alexeyevich.

Lopahin. What kind of voice is that?

Yepihodov. I just had a drink of water. I must have swallowed something.

Yasha. What ignorance!

Lyubov. We're going, and not a soul will be left here.

Lopahin. Not till the spring.

(VARYA *pulls an umbrella out of a bundle, as though about to hit someone with it.* LOPAHIN *makes a gesture as though alarmed.*)

Lopahin. Now, now, I didn't mean anything!

Trofimov. Ladies and gentlemen, let's get into the carriage — it's time. The train will be in directly.

Varya. Petya, here they are — your galoshes — by that trunk. And what dirty old things they are!

Trofimov (*puts on galoshes*). Let's go, friends.

Gayev (*greatly upset, afraid of weeping*). The train — the station! Ah!

Lyubov. Let us go.

Lopahin. Are we all here? No one in there? (*Through the door*) There are some things stored there — better lock up. Let us go.

Anya. Good-by, home. Good-by to the old life!

Trofimov. Welcome to the new life!

(*He goes out with* ANYA. VARYA *looks round the room and goes out slowly.* YASHA *and* CHARLOTTA *with her pet dog go out.*)

Lopahin. And so, until the spring. Come friends, till our next meeting.

(LYUBOV *and* GAYEV *remain alone. As though they had been waiting for this, they throw themselves on each other's necks, and break into subdued, smothered sobbing, afraid of being overheard.*)

Gayev. My sister! My sister!

Lyubov. Oh, my orchard — my sweet, my beau- tiful orchard! My life, my youth, my happiness, — good-by, good-by!

(*Voice of* ANYA *calling gaily:* "Mamma!")

(*Voice of* TROFIMOV *gaily:* "Ah-oo!")

Lyubov. One last look at the walls, at the windows. Our poor mother loved to walk about this room.

Gayev. My sister, my sister!

(*Voice of* ANYA: "Mamma!")

(*Voice of* TROFIMOV: "Ah-oo!")

Lyubov. We're coming.

(*They go out.*)

(*The stage is empty, sound of doors being locked, of carriages driving away. Then silence. In the stillness there is the dull stroke of an ax on a tree, clanging with a mournful, lonely sound. Footsteps are heard.* FIRS *appears in the doorway on the right. He is dressed as usual in a jacket and white waistcoat, but with slippers on his feet. He is ill. He goes to the door and tries the handle.*)

Firs. It's locked! They've gone ... (*Sits down on sofa.*) Why, they've forgotten me. ... Never mind ... I'll sit here a bit. ... I'll be bound Leonid Andreyevich hasn't put his fur coat on — he's gone off in his light overcoat. (*Sighs anxiously.*) I didn't look after him ... ah, these young people ... (*Mutters something that can't be distinguished.*) Life has gone by as though I had never lived. (*Lies down.*) I'll lie down a bit ... there's no strength in you, nothing left you, all gone. Ech, you good-for-nothing! (*Lies motionless.*)

(*A sound is heard that seems to come from the sky, like a breaking harp-string, dying away mournfully. All is still again. Nothing is heard but the strokes of the ax against a tree far away in the orchard.*)

CURTAIN

Luigi Pirandello · 1867–1936

Luigi Pirandello, the Italian novelist and playwright, was born in Agrigento, (Sicily) in 1867. His parents were financially well off and thus able to have their son study at the University of Rome. In the course of an academic dispute, however, the young student of philology was advised to leave Rome; he therefore continued his studies at the University of Bonn in Germany. At Bonn Pirandello wrote a dissertation on his native dialect and taught Italian language and literature. In Germany he also became familiar with German idealistic philosophy and the methods of abstract thinking which, later on, he was to employ in composing his "plays of the intellect." In 1891 he returned to Rome where, for some time, he taught Italian literature at a girls' college.

Between 1891 and 1904, Pirandello published his first novel, *The Outcast*, and a number of short stories, a genre in which his literary master, Giovanni Verga, had excelled. In 1904, a second novel, *The Late Mattia Pascal*, appeared, in which all the elements of his mature art were contained. With this novel Pirandello introduced into Italian literature the Grottesco, a genre which is mainly concerned with the mask of human character and with the exposition of the instincts hidden behind that mask. The theme of *The Late Mattia Pascal* is that of a man who, renouncing his former identity, dies for the world but lives on under a different name, a stranger among his old friends and his relatives. From the beginning, Pirandello was determined to tear off man's social mask and to show how the psychological mechanism conditioning man's behavior operates.

Six years later, having been urged to dramatize some of his short stories, he published *The Trap*, the first of a series of plays dealing with the somber aspects of daily life. Among his early plays are many one-act adaptations from the stories, most of them realistic — either comic or tragic. But soon Pirandello began to work on several problem plays trying to develop a new form of anti-realistic drama, the Naked Mask (*Maschera Nuda*) as he called it. Best known among his mature plays are *Six Characters in Search of an Author* (1921) and *Henry IV* (1922), both of which have been performed in many countries and widely acclaimed as representative works of a truly modern theatre. With his reputation as a playwright established, he was awarded the Nobel Prize for literature in 1934. The last two years of his life he spent in Hollywood where he prepared the filmscript of *Six Characters in Search of an Author*. He died in 1936, soon after his return from the United States.

Most of Pirandello's literary biographers have undertaken a classification of his plays under various general headings. Domenico Vittorini, for instance, has divided them into "plays in the wake of naturalism, drama of being and seeming, social plays, drama of womanhood and plays of art and life." Another critic, Lander MacClintock, has instead worked out four basic concepts underlying Pirandello's art: the power of the subconscious to doubt the validity of the accepted moral code, the contrast of flux and fixity in life, the multiplicity of the ego, and the relativity of truth. The titles of certain of Pirandello's plays illustrate the concepts enumerated by Professor MacClintock: *The Fool's Cap* (1917), *Tonight We Improvise* (1930), *Two in One* (1920), and *It's True — If You Think It Is* (1917).

In his preface to one of the editions of *Six Characters in Search of an Author*, Pirandello has made it clear that as an artist he is mainly concerned with the complexities of life and form. Form, he maintains, is frozen life; it is a suspension of movement and organic development. In order to show what character really means (character: a repetition, by habit, of certain actions), he designs live marionettes and analyzes their mechanical actions. Pirandello's art, however, is neither symbolic nor allegorical; it reproduces automatisms of character which are explained from a purely psychological point of view and which do not leave room for a higher level of meaning. Character turns out to be an illusion, an invention of the world around us; and the same is true also for the world as we see it and for truth — our way of seeing it. Pirandello's is a theatre of relativity, a pessimistic version of Shaw's social utopianism of the stage. For Pirandello, as for his characters, self-recognition is always painful. If man wants to survive, he has to keep up his illusions about himself and his fellow-beings. As two forms of the discrepancy between reality and appearance, the comic and the tragic are no longer opposed; they are distinguished only by tone and not by material. Pirandello's plays are too abstract to cause delight or pity; they must be grasped by the intellect.

The one-act play we have selected here can conveniently be called realistic in style, although it contains elements of Pirandello's later more abstract art. In it, character is exposed, but not developed. The action progresses by leaps in a dialectical movement from absolute to relative and from ideal to real. Here we see embodied the idea of contrast developed in Pirandello's essay on *L'Umorismo* ("Humor"), an investigation of the comic, or tragic, discrepancy between what is and what appears to be.

SUGGESTED REFERENCES: Lander MacClintock, *The Age of Pirandello* (1951); Walter Starkie, *Luigi Pirandello* (1965).

The Jar [1]

The Jar (1917) is sheer comedy. The action is centered on the fragility of the jar, that is, the fragility of Don Lolò's sense of justice. His insistence on a fair application of the law is in contrast to his fierce and unrestrained temper. In the end, Lolò is bound to destroy the jar and the mask of his character. Behind Don Lolò's subtlety is shown the superman's hidden craving for power and supremacy over his fellow-beings.

Characters

DON LOLÒ ZIRAFA, *a Sicilian farmer* (*don*, "*mister*")
ZI' DIMA LICASI, *a tinker* (*zi' for zio*, "*uncle*")
SCIMÈ, *a lawyer*
'MPARI PÈ, *boss farmer to Don Lolò* ('*mpari for compare*, "*godfather*")
TARARÀ, *an olive shaker*
FILLICÒ, *another olive shaker*
'GNA TANA, *an olive gatherer* ('*gna for signora*)
TRISUZZA, *another olive gatherer*
CARMINELLA, *a third olive gatherer*
A DRIVER (*of mules*)
NOCIARELLO, *a country lad*

A grass-grown yard in front of DON LOLÒ's farmhouse on the crest of a hill.

Left, the façade of the farmhouse, a rustic building, of two stories; in the middle, a door, red, but somewhat weatherbeaten; above the door a window opening on a little balcony; windows upstairs and down, the lower ones fitted with iron gratings. Right, an olive tree, huge, of great age, its trunk gnarled and twisted. A stone settee has been built in around the trunk, completely encircling it. Beyond the olive tree the yard drops off down the steep hill, showing the end of a rough mountain road. Rear, the tops of olive trees, following the descending slope.

It is October.

As the curtain rises 'MPARI PÈ *is seated on the stone seat under the olive tree.*

A rustic folk song. Peasant women, olive gatherers, are singing as they climb the hill along the road, right. Their baskets are heaped high with olives. Two of the women have their baskets on their heads. The other is carrying hers in her arms.

As 'MPARI PÈ *hears the song, he rises, leaps up on the settee to see better, and then calls:*

'mpari Pè. Oh! Oooh! Hey you old pumps without pistons! And you there, drip nose! Look what you're doing, name of Satan! You're losing your load! (*The women come on stage up over the road, right.* NOCIARELLO *is with them. They have ceased their song.*)

[1] Translated from the Italian by Arthur Livingston. From *The One-Act Plays of Luigi Pirandello.* Copyright, 1928, by E. P. Dutton & Co., Inc.

Trisuzza. What's stuck in your gullet, 'mpari Pè?

La 'gna Tana. Lord bless us, if he isn't learning to curse and swear as bad as the boss!

Carminella. Even a tree would learn to curse, just standing around this place!

'mpari Pè. You don't have to spread your olives all over the road, do you?

Trisuzza. My olives? On the road? Not a one! Not a one did I drop!

'mpari Pè. Lord, pity you, if don Lolò had been at the window and seen what you were doing!

La 'gna Tana. Let him sit at the window till his bottom aches! When a woman earns her day's pay, she isn't afraid of anyone.

'mpari Pè. Why didn't you look where you were going? Singing there with your nose in the air!

Carminella. A woman can't even sing around here?

La 'gna Tana. Nosireesir! All you can do is curse and swear! He and the boss must be trying for a prize, to see which can spit the dirtiest words.

Trisuzza. Why the good Lord hasn't struck this house with lightning is more than I know!

'mpari Pè. Hey, you old hens, stop your cackling, and get rid of your loads! What do you think you're paid for, screeching and gabbing?

Carminella. What, another trip, today?

'mpari Pè. Leave it to you, and every day would be Saturday, so's you could knock off at noon! There's time aplenty for two more trips. Shake your squeaky bones, and get back to work! (*He shoos the women, with* NOCIARELLO, *around the corner of the house, left. The women begin to sing again "a dispetto."*)

'mpari Pè (*turns and calls up toward the balcony*). Hey, don Lolò.

Don Lolò (*inside*). Who wants me this time!

'mpari Pè. The mules have come, with the manure!

(DON LOLÒ *storms out of the house. He is a powerful man, about forty, with shifting, suspicious eyes. He is in a temper most of the time. On his head a broad-brimmed straw hat that shows signs of wear; in his ears, two rings, gold. He is in his shirt sleeves, the cuffs rolled up to his elbows. The shirt of rough, checker-board flannel, purple and white, is open in front so as to show the hair on his chest.*)

Don Lolò. The mules? At this time of day? Where are they? Which way did you steer them?

'mpari Pè. Don't lose your temper! There they are, over there! The driver wants to know where he is to unload.

Don Lolò. Unload, hey? So he wants to unload? And without my seeing what kind of stuff he has brought! And just now I can't. I'm busy with my lawyer!

'mpari Pè. And how about moving the big jar?

Don Lolò (*surveying him from head to foot*). Say, tell me: who's running this shebang, you or me . . . ?

'mpari Pè. Oh, I meant . . .

Don Lolò. Don't mean anything! Your job is to do what I tell you! Don't mean anything! Now I should like to know why in hell I should be talking to the lawyer about the jar? . . .

'mpari Pè. Well, you don't know how worried I am. That's a brand new jar. And it's standing there right in the open, in the press room. (*He points, left, toward the house.*) Take my advice, don Lolò, stand it somewhere else!

Don Lolò. No! I've told you a hundred times — no! It stands where it is, and no one is going to lay a finger on it!

'mpari Pè. But right by the door, with women and youngsters running in and out . . . !

Don Lolò. Blood of Jehosophat! You're bound to have me crazy about that jar?

'mpari Pè. Well, so long as you don't mind if it's broken!

Don Lolò. God, here I am busy with a lawyer! And I don't want to bother with anything else! Where do you expect me to stand the jar? In the storeroom, no! There isn't any room there, till I get the old hogshead out! And now, I haven't got time, I haven't got time! (*The mule driver comes in, right.*)

Driver. Well, how about it? Where do I dump that manure? It will be dark in no time!

Don Lolò. And now it's you! Saints Rhubarb and Calomel strain your eyes out — you and your mules with you! Is this the time of day to come?

Driver. I got here as soon as I could!

Don Lolò. Well, you can't sell me any cats in a bag. I see what I pay for! And you spread it around the pasture as I tell you and where I tell you. And today — it's too late!

Driver. You don't say? Want to hear some news, don Lolò? I dump my load right behind that wall, the first place I come to. Then I go home.

Don Lolò. Now I'd just like to see you do it!

Driver. Well you watch, and I'll show you something! (*He starts away in a rage.*)

'mpari Pè (*restraining him*). Oh, come now, why all the fuss?

Don Lolò. Let him go — let him try it!

Driver. Is he the only one who has a right to get mad? I can get as mad as he can! What a man to work for! Every trip, a fight!

Don Lolò. Say, sonny, if you know anybody that wants an argument with me — look . . . (*he draws from his pocket a little red book*) — they've got this to reckon with! Know what this is? Prayer-book, perhaps you think, for some of the women folks to go to church with! Well sir, I'll tell you what it is — look, "C-i-v-i-l C-o-d-e" — "The Civil Code." My lawyer gave it to me — he's paying me a visit, you know. And I've learned how to use it, this little book; and no one, not even God Almighty, is going to play any tricks on me after this. It's all here — every thing foreseen, case by case . . . Besides, I hire my lawyer by the year! . . .

'mpari Pè. Here he is now! (SCIMÈ, *the lawyer, appears in the farmhouse door, an old straw hat on his head, a newspaper open in his hands.*)

Scimè. What's up now, don Lolò?

Don Lolò. Look, signor Scimè, this salamander here comes around at sundown with a load of manure for the pasture, and instead of excusing himself . . .

Driver (*trying to get in a word to the lawyer*). I told him I couldn't get here any sooner . . .

Don Lolò. . . . why, he threatens me . . .

Driver. No such thing! . . .

Don Lolò. . . . threatens to dump it down behind the wall . . .

Driver. . . . because you said . . .

Don Lolò. . . . said what? I said I wanted it spread over the pasture in piles all of the same size!

Driver. Give us a rest! Why doesn't he come along then? There's still two hours of sun, signor Scimè. Fact is, if you want to know the truth, fact is, he wants to paw the stuff over with his hands, saving your presence, turd by turd! You don't know him!

Don Lolò. Say, who hires this lawyer, you or me? Don't listen to him, signor Scimè! Just walk along down the road there, same as you always do, and you'll find a nice cool place under the mulberry to read your paper in. I'll be down before long, and we'll go on with that matter of the jar. (*To the* DRIVER) And you, come along with me! How many mules did you bring? (*He starts away with the* DRIVER, *right.*)

Driver. We agreed on twelve! Twelve I brought! (*They disappear behind the farmhouse.*)

Scimè (raising his hands in despair and shaking them toward the point where DON LOLÒ *has disappeared).* Whew, whew, whew! This rural blessedness is too much for me! I get away from here tomorrow morning, headed for some nice quiet city! That man! He's driving me crazy!

'*mpari Pè.* He drives everybody crazy! And what an idea you had to go and give him that little red book! Before that, whenever anything went against the grain he used to say: "Hitch up the old gray mule!" ...

Scimè. Yes, to ride into town and bother me with God knows what! That's why I gave him the little red book. I thought he would work off steam trying to decide the law for himself — it would give me a chance to breathe! What devil ever put it into my head to come out here to spend a week? The doctor, you see, thought I ought to take a little vacation in the country — rest, air! The minute this fellow found out about it — well, he would have it that I should come here. I say yes, finally, but on condition that we do no talking about business. And what does he do? For five days past he's been after me day and night talking about a jar ... what jar, in the name of God?

'*mpari Pè.* Oh, I know — the big jar, for the olive oil! It came in last week from the factory in Santo Stefano di Camestra. That's where they make them. Oooo! A beauty, big round as this, and high as this — fat, fat as a Mother Superior in a convent. But what's up? Dispute with the factory people there?

Scimè. Dispute? The devil's to pay! They charged him twenty-five for it, and he says he expected a bigger one!

'*mpari Pè (amazed).* A bigger one!

Scimè. Five days, five days of it! *(He starts down the road).* But tomorrow, tomorrow morning, before the chickens are up — I'm off! *(He disappears down the road. From far away across the field, behind the scenes, the cadenced call of the tinker, ZI' DIMA LICASI: "Old plates to mend," "Old cups to mend," "Old jars to mend." Down the path from behind the farmhouse come* TARARÀ *and* FILLICÒ, *the one with a ladder on his shoulders, the other with two bamboo rods in his hand.)*

'*mpari Pè (as they appear).* How's this? Stopped work already?

Fillicò. The boss told us to come in, as he went by with the mules ...

'*mpari Pè.* ... told you you could go home?

Tararà. Not him! He said we should wait here to help with some job or other in the storeooom.

Fillicò. Help get out the old hogshead!

'*mpari Pè.* Good for him! Glad he took my advice for once in his life! Come along, Tararà! *(He*

starts away, left, but from behind the farmhouse, with empty baskets, come* TRISUZZA, LA 'GNA TANA *and* CARMINELLA.)*

La 'gna Tana (at sight of the two helpers). What? Aren't you going to shake any more down for us?

'*mpari Pè.* Knocking off, for today.

Trisuzza. If you don't shake them down, how are we going to pick them up?

'*mpari Pè.* Brains! Brains! ... Wait till the boss gets back, and he'll tell you!

Carminella. We just sit here, our hands in our laps?

'*mpari Pè.* What do I know about it? You might start picking over, in the barn.

La 'gna Tana. Me? Without orders from the boss? I won't do anything!

'*mpari Pè.* Well, send someone and get the orders. *(He goes off, right, with* TARARÀ *and* FILLICÒ.)*

Carminella. You go, Nociarello.

La 'gna Tana. And tell him just what I say: the men have finished shaking, and the women want to know what they've got to do next ...

Trisuzza. ... and whether he wants us to begin picking over — you tell him just what I say!

Nociarello (to CARMINELLA*).* I'll tell him just what you say. *(To* TRISUZZA*)* I'll tell him just what you say, I will.

Carminella. Run, shoo! *(*NOCIARELLO *runs off full speed, by the path, right. From the left, thunderstruck, frightened, in evident dismay — they show this state of mind by gestures of arms and hands — come first* FILLICÒ, *then* TARARÀ, *and then* 'MPARI PÈ.)*

Fillicò. Holy Virgin, Holy Virgin, help us!

Tararà. I wish I was somewhere else!

'*mpari Pè.* What did I tell him! What did I tell him! Serves him right!

The Women (together, crowding around). What's the matter? What is it? What has happened?

'*mpari Pè.* The jar! The new jar!

Tararà (with a gesture). Like you would with a knife!

The Women (together). The jar? Oh! Holy Mother help us!

Fillicò. In two, you know — clean as a whistle!

La 'gna Tana. How did it happen?

Trisuzza. No one touched it!

Carminella. Don Lolò will say things no woman should hear!

Trisuzza. He'll run wild!

Fillicò. This is no place for me! I'll leave my pay envelope and go look for another job!

Tararà. You're crazy! Then he'll blame us, and there'll be no getting it out of his head! No, everybody stays here. *(To* 'MPARI PÈ*)* You go and call him. Or rather, no! Call him from here! Just give him a call!

'mpari Pè (getting up on the seat around the tree). Well, I'll try! *(He calls several times, using his hands for a megaphone.)* Don Lolò-ò-ò. Don Lolò-ò-ò-ò! No use. He doesn't hear. He's swearing along there behind the mules! Don Lolò-ò-ò-ò! No, better to go down and get him!

Tararà. But, in the name of God, don't let him get the idea we . . .

'mpari Pè. Don't worry! How could I blame you, honestly! *(He runs off, top speed, along the path.)*

Tararà. And us people, we stand together, whatever he says, whatever he does — we all say the same thing: the jar broke all by itself!

La 'gna Tana. 'Twouldn't be the first time such a thing happened!

Trisuzza. Everybody knows that: new jars always break by themselves!

Fillicò. Because — you know how it is — oftentimes when they bake them in the furnace — a spark — you know — gets caught in the clay — and then, all of a sudden — crack! . . .

Carminella. Just so! The way a gun goes off! *(Crossing herself)* The Lord deliver us! *(From within, right, the voices of* DON LOLÒ *and* 'MPARI PÈ)

Don Lolò's Voice. I'm going to find out who did it, if I go to hell for it.

'mpari Pè's Voice. But no one did it — I can swear!

Trisuzza. He's coming!

La 'gna Tana (crossing herself). Lord, help us! *(*DON LOLÒ *comes down the path, followed by* 'MPARI PÈ *and* NOCIARELLO. *He rushes first up to* TARARÀ, *then up to* FILLICÒ, *seizing them by their shirtfronts and shaking them.)*

Don Lolò. Was it you? Was it you? One of you it must have been, and you'll foot the bill, so help me God!

Tararà and Fillicò (together, meanwhile trying to tear loose). Me? You're crazy! Let me go! Off me, those hands! I swear to God!

The Others (all together, 'MPARI PÈ *joining in).* It broke by itself! It broke by itself! Nobody's fault! We found it broken! I told you so, over and over again!

Don Lolò (at his wits' end, insisting now at one, now at another). Crazy, me crazy? Of course, all innocent little lambs! It broke by itself! Is that so! It broke by itself! Well, you'll all chip in, that's what you'll do! Each his share! Go and get it and bring it here! *(*'MPARI PÈ, TARARÀ, FILLICÒ, *hurry off to get the jar.)* We'll have a look at it, in broad daylight! And if there's any sign of a

kick, or a bump — I take you fools by the throat and choke the price out of you! You'll all chip in, that's what you'll do — men and women alike!

The Women (all together). Us? We will, eh? Us? What did we have to do with it? Never even looked at the thing!

Don Lolò. But you too were going in and out of the press-room!

Trisuzza. Yeah, and we broke the jar, brushing it with our skirts, this way! *(She gathers her skirt up in one hand and, to make fun of him, pretends to whip him across the legs with it. The three men return from the left, bringing in the big broken jar.)*

La 'gna Tana. What a pity! Look at the poor thing!

Don Lolò (raising his arms in despair, as though he were mourning for some dead relative). The new one! Twenty-five gone up in smoke! And where do I put the new crop of oil? And what a beauty! Spite, or else plain deviltry! Twenty-five just thrown away! And there was a crop this year! What'll I do? What'll I do?

Tararà. No, no! Look!

Fillicò. It can be mended!

'mpari Pè. Only a piece off!

Tararà. Just one piece!

Fillicò. A clean break!

Tararà. May have been cracked when it came!

Don Lolò. Cracked, hell! It rang like a bell!

'mpari Pè. That's right! I tried it myself.

Fillicò. The right mender could make it good as new, so's you couldn't even see the crack!

Tararà. Zi' Dima Licasi! He can do it! And he must be in the neighborhood! I heard him calling!

La 'gna Tana. A fine workman, that — brains! He has a cement that, once it's set, you couldn't break it with a hammer! Run, Nociarello! He's somewhere near here! Oh, there he is, down by Mosca's fence! Run and tell him to come here at once. *(*NOCIARELLO *goes off, left, on the dead run.)*

Don Lolò (shouting). Will you all shut up? I can't hear myself think! Licasi and his cement be damned! That jar is gone!

'mpari Pè. Well, I told you so, I told you so!

Don Lolò (too angry to enunciate). What did you tell me, belly of a jackass! What did you tell me! Weren't you saying she broke by herself? Well, suppose I'd have kept it with the Body of Christ . . . wouldn't she have broken just the same?

Tararà (to 'MPARI PÈ). You talk too much!

Don Lolò. That fool would damn a man's soul!

Fillicò. You'll see, you'll see! You can have it fixed good as new, for a few cents! And you know, a mended jar lasts longer than a brand new one!

Don Lolò. And, damn it, damn it, I have those

mules on my hands, half way up the hill! (*To* 'MPARI Pè) What are you doing here, standing around staring like an idiot! Get to work! Get to work! Run up there and see what he's doing! ('MPARI Pè *runs up the path.*) Ah! Oh! Uh! (*Wiping his forehead*) Zi' Dima! Blast zi' Dima! This is a matter for the lawyer! If she broke by herself — well, there must have been something wrong with her! But she rang, though, she rang, like a bell! And I took her for all right! I signed the receipt my own self! Twenty-five lost, twenty-five! Kiss it goodbye, that money! (Zi' DIMA LICASI *comes in down the path, left, followed by* NOCI-ARELLO.)

Fillicò. Oh, zi' Dima, zi' Dima!

Tararà (*whispering to* DON LOLÒ). Notice, he never talks!

La 'gna Tana (*whispering to* DON LOLÒ, *mysteriously*). He never talks, never a word!

Don Lolò. Don't talk, eh? (*To* ZI' DIMA) No words, and no manners, eh? No manners! Don't you ever say howdydo, when you come to a man's house?

Zi' Dima Licasi. What do you want, my work or my manners? It's my work that earns my living! Tell me what you want done, and I do it!

Don Lolò. So you can talk, when you want to sass people! Haven't you got eyes in your head? Can't you see what I want done?

Fillicò. Mend her up, this jar! You know, zi' Dima, some of your cement!

Don Lolò. They say it does wonders! Make it yourself! (ZI' DIMA LICASI *looks at him sullenly, and makes no answer.*) Show us some of your cement.

Tararà (*whispering to* DON LOLÒ). You won't get anywhere with him in that tone of voice!

La 'gna Tana. He never let's nobody see it!

Don Lolò. What is the damn mud anyway — dust from the throne of God Almighty? (*To* ZI' DIMA LICASI.) Well, tell me whether you can fix the damn thing.

Zi' Dima Licasi (*setting his tool box on the ground, and taking out a little bundle wrapped in a dirty blue handkerchief*). What's all the hurry, hey? Give me a chance to look at it! (*He sits flat on the ground, unrolls the handkerchief, slowly, cautiously. All crane their necks for a glimpse of the wonderful cement.*)

La 'gna Tana (*whispering to Don Lolò*). It's the cement!

Don Lolò. Looks to me more like vomit! (*Eventually* ZI' DIMA LICASI *gets the handkerchief unwound, and produces from it a pair of eyeglasses, the bows and the nose-piece broken and replaced with string.*)

Everybody (*laughing*). Eyeglasses! Who'd have thought? Is that his famous cement? Looks more like a halter for a donkey!

Zi' Dima Licasi (*very deliberately wiping the glasses with a corner of the dirty handkerchief, examining them carefully, and finally adjusting them to his nose. Then, just as deliberately, he examines the jar*). I can fix it.

Don Lolò. Oyez, Oyez! Boom-m-m! His Honor pronounces sentence! But I tell you one thing, I don't take any stock in that cement of yours! We'll have rivets, clinched on the inside! (ZI' DIMA LICASI *looks up at him. Then he takes off the glasses, wraps them up in the handkerchief again, puts the handkerchief in the tool box, and the tool box on his shoulder, and starts away.*) Say, what's the idea? Where are you going?

Zi' Dima Licasi. About my business!

Don Lolò. Pig or Holy Ghost, you treat them all alike!

Fillicò (*trying to pacify* ZI' DIMA LICASI). Oh say now, zi' Dima, don't mind him!

Tararà (*taking him on the other side*). Just do as he says, what's the difference?

Don Lolò. Who does he think he is, the Father of his country? Scab on a pig's hide, can't you see I've got to put oil in her? Well, it soaks through, the oil does. Split a mile long — and just a little cement? It's got to have rivets — rivets as well as cement? Who's paying for this job?

Zi' Dima Licasi. They're all like that! Just like them all! No brains! No brains! Pitcher, bowl, cup, mug, no matter how big, no matter how little, always rivets! False teeth in an old woman's face to tell the world: "I'm busted, and they fixed me up!" I offer a good job, and nobody wants it! They won't let a man do a clean job the way it ought to be done! (*He walks up to* DON LOLÒ.) Listen to me, if this jar don't ring like new when I get through — just with cement . . .

Don Lolò. I said no! I said no! Think I'm going to argue with that man? (*To* TARARÀ) One good thing — you say he doesn't talk much! (*To* ZI' DIMA LICASI) No use preaching to me! If they all want rivets, it's a sign that rivets is what they want. . . .

Zi' Dima Licasi. No it isn't! It's a sign they don't know anything!

La 'gna Tana. I know I don't know anything, but I like rivets too, zi' Dima!

Trisuzza. 'Course there ought to be rivets — they hold better!

Zi' Dima Licasi. But they make holes! Can't you see they make holes! Each pair of rivets, two holes: twenty pairs, forty holes! But with just cement . . .

Don Lolò. Balsam, what a head! Find me a mule as balky as that! Holes, very well! Holes! Holes is what I want, holes with rivets in them! And I'm paying here! (*To the women*) You, now, off to the barn, and start picking over! (*To the men*) And you, you go into the storeroom, and help get out the old hogshead. Lively now! (*He pushes them off toward the farmhouse.*)

Zi' Dima Licasi. Hold on there — not so fast!

Don Lolò. Oh, we'll see about the money when you get through — you don't waste any more of my time!

Zi' Dima Licasi. And you leave me here alone? Someone's got to hold up the broken piece. That's a big jar!

Don Lolò. Yes — hey there, Tararà — you help him! Fillicò, you come with me! (*He goes out with* FILLICÒ. *The women, with* NOCIARELLO, *have already disappeared.* ZI' DIMA LICASI *sets to work at once, in bad humor, however. He takes a bit and stock from his tool box and begins making the holes for the rivets, first in the jar, then in the broken fragment. As he works* TARARÀ *engages him in conversation.*)

Tararà. Lucky it's no worse than it is. I don't see how we got off so easy! I thought my time had come! Don't let that man spoil your breakfast, zi' Dima. He wants rivets? Give him rivets! Twenty, thirty? (ZI' DIMA LICASI *looks up at him.*) More than that? Thirty-five? (ZI' DIMA LICASI *looks up at him.*) How many, you think?

Zi' Dima Licasi. See this bit I'm working with? Every time I make it go round? Ruh-ruh-ruh-ruh! Every sound is a grind at my heart!

Tararà. Is it true what they say — that you got your mixture for your cement in a dream?

Zi' Dima Licasi (*without stopping*). Yes, I dreamt it!

Tararà. Who was it came to you, in a dream?

Zi' Dima Licasi. My father!

Tararà. Oh, your father! So he came to you in a dream, and told you how to mix it?

Zi' Dima Licasi. Puddenhead!

Tararà. Me? Why?

Zi' Dima Licasi. Know who my father was?

Tararà. No, who was he?

Zi' Dima Licasi. The Devil that's going to get you!

Tararà. So the Devil was your father! And who was your mother?

Zi' Dima Licasi. The pitch all you know-nothings are going to boil in!

Tararà. Black pitch!

Zi' Dima Licasi. White pitch! The Old Man showed me how to make it white! You'll see how it works, when he begins to stew you, down there in Hell! There, however, you'll find it black! Bring your two fingers together and you never get them loose again! If I stick your upper lip to your nose, you stay Zulu the rest of your life!

Tararà. You get it on *your* fingers, and it doesn't seem to hurt *you!*

Zi' Dima Licasi. Puddenhead! Whoever heard of a dog biting his own master! (*He tosses the bit-stock aside and rises to his feet.*) Come here now! You just hold this up! (*He makes* TARARÀ *support the broken piece, while he draws a tin can from his tool box, opens it, and takes out a pinch of cement with his thumb and finger, holding it up.*) Look at this? Cement, eh? Just ordinary cement! Well, you watch! (*He spreads the cement over the broken edge of the jar, then on the edges of the fragment*). Three or four pinches like this — just the least little! Don't let it fall! Now I get inside. . . .

Tararà. Oh, from the inside you work!

Zi' Dima Licasi. How else, puddenhead? If you're going to clinch the rivets, you have to do it on the inside, don't you? Wait a minute! (*He rummages around in his tool box.*) Wire, I need, and pincers! (*He finds what he wants, and gets inside the jar.*) You now, just wait till I get comfortable here . . . here we are . . . now just raise that piece, and fit it in — just a little higher, just a little higher — even all round? . . . easy now . . . oh, there . . . there we are . . . now hold her there, hold her! (TARARÀ *does as he is told, and* ZI' DIMA LICASI *is hidden within the jar. Shortly after, sticking his head out of the mouth of the jar*) Now pull, damn you, pull! Not a rivet in her! Awh, pull, use your muscle! There you see? Could you move it? Could you move it? Not the fraction of an inch! Well, you couldn't stir it with ten pairs of oxen, either. Go! Go and tell your boss!

Tararà. All right, zi' Dima, but are you sure you can get out now?

Zi' Dima Licasi. Never had any trouble getting out before!

Tararà. But this jar . . . I don't know — the mouth seems to be a little tight for a man your size. Try, and let's see! ('MPARI PÈ *comes back up the road, right.*)

'mpari Pè. What's that? Stuck? Stuck in the jar?

Tararà (*to* ZI' DIMA LICASI, *in the jar*). Not so hard! Wait, let me tip it!

'mpari Pè. One arm at a time now! Your arm! . . .

Tararà. No, your arm, your arm!

Zi' Dima Licasi. What the devil! How's this? Can't I squeeze through there?

'mpari Pè. So small at the mouth, a jar that size?

Tararà (*laughing*). It would be a joke if he couldn't get out, now that he's got it all fixed.

Zi' Dima Licasi. What are you laughing at, blood of Satan! Give me a hand! (*He leaps furiously up at the mouth of the jar.*)

'mpari Pè. Wait, that doesn't do any good! Let's try tipping it over!

Zi' Dima Licasi. No, that's worse! I stick here, at the shoulders!

Tararà. It's a fact! You have a little too much shoulder on one side!

Zi' Dima Licasi. Me, too much? You said yourself the jar was too narrow at the mouth!

'mpari Pè. And now what are we going to do about it?

Tararà. This, now, is something to talk about! Hah, hah (*laughing, and running toward the farmhouse, calling*). Hey, Fillicò, 'gna Tana! Hey Trisuzza, Carminella, hey! Come quick! Zi' Dima is stuck in the jar! He can't get out! (FILLICÒ, LA 'GNA TANA, TRISUZZA, CARMINELLA, *and* NOCIARELLO *come running on, right.*)

All of Them (*together*). Stuck in the jar? He is? Hah! Hah! How did it happen? He can't get out?

Zi' Dima Licasi (*raising his voice over the hubbub, and snarling like an angry cat*). Hey, get me out of here! My hammer there, in the tool-box!

'mpari Pè. Hammer nothing! Are you crazy? Think you're going to break that jar, now you've just got it mended? The boss must tell you to do that, himself!

Fillicò. Here he comes now! (DON LOLÒ *comes running on, right.*)

The Women (*telling the glad tidings, running to meet him*). Stuck in the jar! Stuck in the jar! He can't get out!

Don Lolò. In the jar?

Zi' Dima Licasi (*at the same time*). Help! Help! Help!

Don Lolò. How can I help you, dunce of an old rat, if you didn't have brains enough to measure the hump on your back (*general laughter*), before you went and stuck yourself in there!

La 'gna Tana. Look what a fix he's in, poor zi' Dima!

Fillicò. The funniest damn thing you ever saw in your life!

Don Lolò. Wait, man, wait! Not so fast! Try one arm first!

'mpari Pè. No use! We've tried that, and every other way!

Zi' Dima Licasi (*getting one arm out at last, while the others pull on it*). Ouch! Ouch! Don't! Don't! You're pulling me in two!

Don Lolò. Don't get excited — just one more pull!

Zi' Dima Licasi (*tearing loose*). No, let me alone! Let me alone!

Don Lolò. Well, what can I do then?

Zi' Dima Licasi. Just hand me that hammer! . . .

Don Lolò. What, break it? After you've just mended it?

Zi' Dima Licasi. Think I'm going to stay in here?

Don Lolò. Well, we've got to see what we can do about it!

Zi' Dima Licasi. See, hell! I'm going to get out of here, see or no see!

The Women (*in chorus*). He's right! You can't keep him in there! We've got to break it!

Don Lolò. Did you ever see the like of this! Just a moment now, just a moment now, while I look in the little red book . . . this is something new! This case never came up before! (*To* NOCIARELLO) Here, boy, you run. . . . No, it's better if you go, Fillicò (*Pointing toward the path, right*) Down there, under the mulberry — the lawyer! And tell him to come here, quick! (*As* FILLICÒ *goes off, right, he turns to* ZI' DIMA LICASI *who is still struggling inside the jar.*) Quiet, in there, you! (*To the others*) Keep him quiet, will you! First it breaks by itself, and now. . . . That's no jar — that's some contraption of the Devil! (*To* ZI' DIMA LICASI, *who is still making a noise*) Easy, there, I tell you! Don't you dare break that jar!

Zi' Dima Licasi. Either you break it, or I tip it over myself and roll it against one of those trees, if I break my neck doing it! Get me out! Get me out!

Don Lolò. The lawyer will be here in just a jiffy. He'll settle the rights and wrongs of this case! I stick to my claims on the jar, and I begin by doing my duty! All the people bear witness — I pay you a ten spot, a fair price for your job! (*He draws from a pocket a large leather pocketbook, tied around with twine, and takes from it a ten lira bill.*)

Zi' Dima Licasi. I won't take it! I want to get out!

Don Lolò. You'll get out when the lawyer says you can! Meantime, I pay you! (*He lifts the bill, conspicuously, in one hand and lets it down inside the jar. Up the path, right, comes the lawyer,* SCIMÈ, *laughing, followed by* FILLICÒ, *also laughing.*)

Don Lolò (*observing his good humor*). What's there to laugh about? Of course, it's no concern of yours! The jar is mine!

Scimè (*holding his sides, while the others join in his mirth*). But do you think . . . do you think you can . . . can keep him in . . . in there . . . in there just because you . . . you don't . . . don't want to lose your jar?

Don Lolò. You think it all falls on me? I stand the loss, I do, as well as be made a fool of?

Scimè. You don't want to go to jail for kidnapping, do you? That's kidnapping!

Don Lolò. Kidnapping? Who's doing the kidnapping? He kidnapped himself! I'll prove it! (*To* Zi' DIMA LICASI) Who is keeping you in there? Come out of that jar! Come out of that jar!

Zi' Dima Licasi. You get me out, if you can see a way to do it!

Don Lolò. Oh, excuse me, it's not my job to get you out! You went in of your own accord! Come out, I say!

Scimè. Ladies and gentlemen, may I have the floor?

Tararà. Speak! Let's hear the lawyer! What's the law in the case?

Scimè. There are two points involved, gentlemen of the jury, and the two contestants must govern themselves accordingly! (*He first addresses* DON LOLÒ.) You, on the one hand, don Lolò, are bound to liberate the man, Licasi! . . .

Don Lolò (speaking up). I am? I am? And how, by breaking the jar?

Scimè. Wait, let me finish! On the other hand — God's sake, let me finish, won't you? — you've got to — otherwise, kidnapping, kidnapping! (*Now to* Zi' DIMA LICASI) On the other hand, you, zi' Dima Licasi, must answer for the damage you have caused by getting inside the jar without considering whether you would be able to get out! . . .

Zi' Dima Licasi. But, if you please, signor Scimè, I didn't pay any attention to that. I've been at this trade for years. I have mended a million jars, always from inside, to clinch the rivets, as you have to do. I never wasn't able to get out before. It's for him then to go and talk with the man who made this damn jar with such a small mouth! No fault of mine!

Don Lolò. But that hump on your back — did the man who made the jar make the hump on your back, just to keep you from getting out? If I sue on grounds of the narrow mouth, signor Scimè, the minute he comes in with that hump, the judge begins to laugh — and I'm left with the costs! . . .

Zi' Dima Licasi. That isn't so! I've had this hump many a year, I'd have you know, and this is the first jar I couldn't get out of! From the others, as easy as through the door of my house! . . .

Scimè. That doesn't excuse you, zi' Dima Licasi. You were bound to take the measure before you got in, to see whether you could get out . . .

Don Lolò. . . . so he's got to pay me for the jar!

Zi' Dima Licasi. . . . Pay for your grandmother!

Scimè. Not so fast, now! Not so fast! . . . Pay for it as new?

Don Lolò. Of course, new! Why not?

Scimè. It was broken, man!

Zi' Dima Licasi. And I fixed it!

Don Lolò. You fixed it! You fixed it! And you said yourself — as good as new! But if I break it again to get you out, I won't be able to mend it again, and I lose the whole jar, signor Scimè!

Scimè. That's why I said — zi' Dima Licasi must stand his share of the loss! Let me do the talking, will you?

Don Lolò. Talk! Talk!

Scimè. My dear zi' Dima, take your choice: either your cement was good for something or else it wasn't . . .

Don Lolò (delighted, addressing the crowd, confidentially). Just listen to that! Oh I tell you, when he starts that way, you can't fool him! Some lawyer! . . . We've got him in a fix! . . .

Scimè. If your cement was good for nothing — well, in that case you're guilty of making false pretenses, like any other swindler. But if, on the other hand, it's good for something, why then, the jar, mended as it is, must have a certain value! What value? I leave it to you! How high would you put it?

Zi' Dima Licasi. With me inside? (*General laughter*)

Scimè. No joking — the way it is!

Zi' Dima Licasi. I'll tell you what! If Don Lolò had let me fix it the way I wanted to, with just cement, in the first place, I wouldn't have had to get inside, because I could have done it from out there; and in the second place, the jar would have been as good as new, and would have been worth every cent he paid for it. But all patched up the way it is, with all those holes for those rivets, it's worth just about as much as my old woman's tin dishpan! It isn't worth a penny more than a third of what it cost!

Don Lolò. A third? A third?

Scimè (quickly to DON LOLÒ, *pretending to be parrying a blow).* A third, he said! Sh-h-h you, let him talk! A third? How much would a third be?

Don Lolò. It cost twenty-five: a third, eight thirty-three . . .

Zi' Dima Licasi. Less, perhaps! More, not a bit!

Scimè. We take you at your word — you pay Don Lolò eight thirty-three!

Zi' Dima Licasi. To him! Me? I pay him eight thirty-three? . . .

Scimè. . . . so that he will break the jar and let you out! You pay the actual value you set on the jar yourself?

Don Lolò. Smooth as oil!

Zi' Dima Licasi. Me pay? Me pay? You've gone crazy, signor Scimè! The worms are going to get me, right in here! Say you, Tararà, my pipe, there in the toolbox!

Tararà (obeying). This one?

Zi' Dima Licasi. Thanks, and now a light! (TARARÀ *strikes a match and lights the pipe.*) Thanks, and a good day to everybody! (*He disappears inside the jar, his pipe smoking.*)

Don Lolò (dumbfounded). And now what's to be done about it, if he won't come out?

Scimè (scratching his head, laughing). Yes, to tell the truth, so long as he was anxious to get out, we could do something; but now, with him refusing to come out. . . .

Don Lolò (going up to the jar and calling to ZI' DIMA LICASI). Well, what's your idea? Going to stay there the rest of your life?

Zi' Dima Licasi (putting his head out). More comfortable here than in my own house! Cool, cool as a cucumber! (*He disappears again, the smoke rising from the jar.*)

Don Lolò (angry at the general laughter). And you jackasses, shut up! You all bear witness that it's him that's refusing to come out, in order not to pay what he owes me, while I offer to break the jar! (*With an idea, to the lawyer*) Couldn't I sue him for rent?

Scimè (laughing). 'Course you could! But you have to have a constable to evict him first!

Don Lolò. But as long as he is in there I can't use the jar!

Zi' Dima Licasi (appearing at the mouth of the jar). You're wrong! I'm not in here of choice. Let me out, and I go away, skidoo! But if it's money out of me, you're dreaming, man, you're dreaming! I don't budge!

Don Lolò (seizing the jar by the edge of the mouth and shaking it furiously). You don't budge, eh? You don't budge!

Zi' Dima Licasi (at the opening). You see — it's my cement! There aren't any rivets!

Don Lolò. Well, then, who did the harm, pickpocket, me or you? And you think I'm going to pay?

Scimè (dragging him away by an arm). Don't do that! You make it worse! Let him spend a night in there, and you'll see that by morning he'll be glad enough to come out! When we get him in that state of mind, you . . . well, eight thirty-three or nothing! . . . So now, we go away, and leave him to stew in his own juice! (*He drags* DON LOLÒ *off toward the farmhouse.*)

Zi' Dima Licasi (at the mouth of the jar). Say, don Lolò!

Scimè (to DON LOLÒ, *without stopping).* Don't pay any attention! Come along, come along!

Zi' Dima Licasi (before they get into the house). Good night, Scimè — but see what I got! (*He holds up the ten lira bill; then as the two disappear, to the others.*) The rest of us, we celebrate — a housewarming for my new mansion! Say Tararà, take this, and down at Mosca's — wine, bread, fried fish, *peperoni!* And we celebrate!

All of Them (clapping and cheering, as TARARÀ *runs away to buy the things).* Good for zi' Dima! We celebrate! What fun!

Fillicò. Couldn't have better weather. Look at that moon! Just coming up! (*Pointing to the left*) It's as bright as day!

Zi' Dima Licasi. Oh-ay, I can't see the moon, I can't see the moon! I want to see the moon! Roll me over that way a little, so's I can see the moon! But be easy! (*All take a hand and roll the jar over toward the path, right.*) Easy, easy! There we are! And I can see the moon! Oh what a moon! Bright as the sun! How about a little music? Who sings the first song?

La 'gna Tana. You, Trisuzza!

Trisuzza. No, I couldn't! Carminella!

Zi' Dima Licasi. Well, we all sing! You, Fillicò, out with your harmonica! And we all join in! The women folks will dance a little! Hey, there, you old cows, shake a leg there! (FILLICÒ *produces his harmonica and begins a tune; the others join hands and begin to dance, confusedly, round and round the jar,* ZI' DIMA LICASI *shouting to mark time. Shortly, the door of the farm house swings open, and* DON LOLÒ *rushes out in a fury.*)

Don Lolò. What's this, blood of Satan, where do you think you are, in a bawdy house? Here, you lousy old camel, put this in your pipe and smoke it! (*He gives the jar a violent kick, and it goes rolling down the hill, amid the cries of the company. The jar is heard to crash against a tree.*)

La 'gna Tana (screaming). You killed him!

Fillicò (looking down the hill). No, there he is! He's crawling out! Didn't hurt him! (*The company claps and cheers.*)

Everybody. Three cheers for Zi' Dima Licasi! Hurrah! Hurrah! Hurrah! (*As* ZI' DIMA LICASI *appears up the hill, they lift him to their shoulders and carry him off in triumph, left.*)

Zi' Dima Licasi. I win, I win, I win!

CURTAIN.

Thomas Mann · 1875-1955

Thomas Mann was born in Lübeck, Germany, on June 6, 1875. His father was a senator of the city and twice its mayor; his mother, the daughter of a German planter, was born in Brazil. Mann's enthusiasm for writing and for the world of ideas was indicated by his participating, as a boy at school, in the publication of a youthful magazine called the "Journal of Art, Literature, and Philosophy" — an early alliance with three subjects which have consistently enriched his writing. The death of his father resulted in the young man's moving with his mother to Munich where he took up work in the office of a fire-insurance firm and later became an editorial assistant on the staff of the magazine *Simplicissimus*. The publication of *Buddenbrooks* (1901), the detailed account of the history of a family in the Hanseatic city of Lübeck, established his literary reputation. *Death in Venice* (1912) and *The Magic Mountain* (1924) gave additional proof of his creative ability. Mann received world-wide recognition when he was awarded the Nobel Prize in literature in 1929. Not in sympathy with Nazi Germany, he lived after 1933 in Switzerland and the United States, of which country he became a citizen. He decided to spend the years of his old age in his native Europe, and he died in Zurich at the age of eighty.

Mann is not a facile writer. Following the practice of many great authors of the past, he would work and live with a piece of writing for years. *The Magic Mountain*, for instance, was the product of ten years of labor. So was his great trilogy concerned with the Biblical story of Joseph and his brothers and entitled *Joseph and his Brothers* (1933-44). Later important novels were *Doctor Faustus* (1948) and *The Holy Sinner* (1951). His shorter stories were collected in 1936 under the title of *Stories of Three Decades*, a volume of interest also for the brief preface written by the author himself in defense of his literary work. In 1947 appeared a collection of Mann's essays, *Essays of Three Decades*, which manifests his philosophical and artistic predilection for Schopenhauer, Nietzsche, Wagner, and Freud.

Mann's writings are the product of a slow and careful process of imaginative investigations into various phenomena of life and art. Mainly interested in the psychology of his characters, Mann nevertheless thinks it necessary to record even the minutest exterior facts. Such accuracy in observation binds his characters to the society which is their environment. As in *Buddenbrooks*, they are often heroes in the great German tradition of the "Bildungsroman" — a form of the novel preoccupied with the development, throughout youth and early manhood, of a character representative of certain definite traits in his age, his country, or his class. One aspect of social life gained particular importance for the German author: the position of the artist and how it is reflected in his art. Particularly in his late novel, *Doctor Faustus*, Mann dealt with the problems arising from the artist's gradual isolation from contemporary society. He was never content with a superficial description of human experiences without trying to explain their origin in the character's psychological constitution. At an early age, he became interested in Sigmund Freud's science of psychoanalysis, and ever after he devoted much effort to tracing subconscious processes: the rise of artistic genius, for instance, man's predisposition toward mental disease, and their mysterious interrelation. His characters, for all the individual and hidden life they are shown to possess, are likely to be surrounded by symbolic objects or are themselves representative of basic mental concepts or abstract philosophies. They have not only private but also universal significance. To intensify the psychological, Mann, in his laters years, had recourse to myth — Biblical myth in *Joseph and his Brothers*, Indian myth in *The Transposed Heads*, Christian myth in *The Holy Sinner*. Yet he came to look at these from an ironical, detached and enlightened modern point of view. Just as his early works show the influence of Tolstoy and the works of the middle period that of the Bible, in his later years he developed a sense for the eccentric humor of Cervantes' *Don Quixote*.

Mann's work has branched out over the years until it presents an image of the world, an artistic microcosm. Writers of his stature and scope can be found at only rare moments of history. Goethe and Tolstoy are two examples of artists living in that real Utopia created and constantly re-created by Thomas Mann.

SUGGESTED REFERENCES: Charles Neider, ed., *The Stature of Thomas Mann* (1947); Erich Heller, *The Ironic German. A Study of Thomas Mann* (1958); Henry Hatfield, *Thomas Mann: An Introduction to His Fiction* (rev. ed., 1962).

The Infant Prodigy [1]

In his preface to the American edition of *Stories of Three Decades*, Thomas Mann describes three of his tales as "wearing the impress of much melancholy and ironic reflection on the subject of art and the artist; his isolation and equivocal position in the world of reality, considered socially and physically and as a result of his double bond with nature and spirit." "The Infant Prodigy" (1903) deals with just this problem.

It is a fairy tale with several levels of meaning. Mann points out the peculiarly exalted position of both nobleman and artist, a position based on tradition in one case, and on genius in the other. The prodigy, who stands for the species "artist" in general, seems to identify art with artificiality. His performance is that of a showman. Yet he is aware of a basic distinction between the two modes of expression; he feels himself to be superior to the vulgar mass, the audience, which has to be impressed by means incompatible with the truly artistic spirit. The art critic alone, watching both the prodigy and the audience, sees through the mechanism of the superficially reciprocal communication; he recognizes the prematurity of the artist's claim to mastery.

Thomas Mann treats his subject ironically, and yet with genuine sympathy for the exceptional position of the artist in the modern world; for he knows that only the greatest of artists can afford to be simple and remain "themselves."

The infant prodigy entered. The hall became quiet.

It became quiet and then the audience began to clap, because somewhere at the side a leader of mobs, a born organizer, clapped first. The audience had heard nothing yet, but they applauded; for a mighty publicity organization had heralded the prodigy and people were already hypnotized, whether they knew it or not.

The prodigy came from behind a splendid screen embroidered with Empire garlands and great conventionalized flowers, and climbed nimbly up the steps to the platform, diving into the applause as into a bath; a little chilly and shivering, but yet as though into a friendly element. He advanced to

[1] Reprinted from *Stories of Three Decades* by Thomas Mann, by permission of Alfred A. Knopf, Inc. Copyright 1936 by Alfred A. Knopf, Inc.

the edge of the platform and smiled as though he were about to be photographed; he made a shy, charming gesture of greeting, like a little girl.

He was dressed entirely in white silk, which the audience found enchanting. The little white jacket was fancifully cut, with a sash underneath it, and even his shoes were made of white silk. But against the white socks his bare little legs stood out quite brown; for he was a Greek boy.

He was called Bibi Saccellaphylaccas. And such indeed was his name. No one knew what Bibi was the pet name for, nobody but the impresario, and he regarded it as a trade secret. Bibi had smooth black hair reaching to his shoulders; it was parted on the side and fastened back from the narrow domed forehead by a little silk bow. His was the most harmless childish countenance in the world, with an unfinished nose and guileless mouth. The area beneath his pitch-black mouselike eyes was already a little tired and visibly lined. He looked as though he were nine years old but was really eight and given out for seven. It was hard to tell whether to believe this or not. Probably everybody knew better and still believed it, as happens about so many things. The average man thinks that a little falseness goes with beauty. Where should we get any excitement out of our daily life if we were not willing to pretend a bit? And the average man is quite right, in his average brains!

The prodigy kept on bowing until the applause died down, then he went up to the grand piano, and the audience cast a last look at its programmes. First came a *Marche solonnelle*, then a *Rêverie*, and then *Le Hibou et les moineaux* — all by Bibi Saccellaphylaccas. The whole programme was by him, they were all his compositions. He could not score them, of course, but he had them all in his extraordinary little head and they possessed real artistic significance, or so it said, seriously and objectively, in the programme. The programme sounded as though the impresario had wrested these concessions from his critical nature after a hard struggle.

The prodigy sat down upon the revolving stool and felt with his feet for the pedals, which were raised by means of a clever device so that Bibi could reach them. It was Bibi's own piano, he took it everywhere with him. It rested upon wooden trestles and its polish was somewhat marred by the constant transportation — but all that only made things more interesting.

Bibi put his silk-shod feet on the pedals; then he made an artful little face, looked straight ahead of him, and lifted his right hand. It was a brown, childish little hand; but the wrist was strong and unlike a child's, with well-developed bones.

Bibi made his face for the audience because he was aware that he had to entertain them a little. But he had his own private enjoyment in the thing too, an enjoyment which he could never convey to anybody. It was that prickling delight, that secret shudder of bliss, which ran through him every time he sat at an open piano — it would always be with him. And here was the keyboard again, these seven black and white octaves, among which he had so often lost himself in abysmal and thrilling adventures — and yet it always looked as clean and untouched as a newly washed blackboard. This was the realm of music that lay before him. It lay spread out like an inviting ocean, where he might plunge in and blissfully swim, where he might let himself be borne and carried away, where he might go under in night and storm, yet keep the mastery: control, ordain — he held his right hand poised in the air.

A breathless stillness reigned in the room — the tense moment before the first note came. . . . How would it begin? It began so. And Bibi, with his index finger, fetched the first note out of the piano, a quite unexpectedly powerful first note in the middle register, like a trumpet blast. Others followed, an introduction developed — the audience relaxed.

The concert was held in the palatial hall of a fashionable first-class hotel. The walls were covered with mirrors framed in gilded arabesques, between frescoes of the rosy and fleshly school. Ornamental columns supported a ceiling that displayed a whole universe of electric bulbs, in clusters darting a brilliance far brighter than day and filling the whole space with thin, vibrating golden light. Not a seat was unoccupied, people were standing in the side aisles and at the back. The front seats cost twelve marks; for the impresario believed that anything worth having was worth paying for. And they were occupied by the best society, for it was in the upper classes, of course, that the greatest enthusiasm was felt. There were even some children, with their legs hanging down demurely from their chairs and their shining eyes staring at their gifted little white-clad contemporary.

Down in front on the left side sat the prodigy's mother, an extremely obese woman with a powdered double chin and a feather on her head. Beside her was the impresario, a man of oriental appearance with large gold buttons on his conspicuous cuffs. The princess was in the middle of the front row — a wrinkled, shrivelled little old princess but still a patron of the arts, especially everything full of sensibility. She sat in a deep, velvet-upholstered arm-chair, and a Persian carpet was spread before her feet. She held her hands folded over her grey striped-silk breast, put her head on one side, and presented a picture of elegant composure as she sat looking up at the performing prodigy. Next her sat her lady-in-waiting, in a green striped-silk gown. Being only a lady-in-waiting she had to sit up very straight in her chair.

Bibi ended in a grand climax. With what power this wee manikin belaboured the keyboard! The audience could scarcely trust its ears. The march theme, an infectious, swinging tune, broke out once more, fully harmonized, bold and showy; with every note Bibi flung himself back from the waist as though he were marching in a triumphal procession. He ended *fortissimo*, bent over, slipped sideways off the stool, and stood with a smile awaiting the applause.

And the applause burst forth, unanimously, enthusiastically; the child made his demure little maidenly curtsy and people in the front seat thought: "Look what slim little hips he has! Clap, clap! Hurrah, bravo, little chap, Saccophylax or whatever your name is! Wait, let me take off my gloves — what a little devil of a chap he is!"

Bibi had to come out three times from behind the screen before they would stop. Some late-comers entered the hall and moved about looking for seats. Then the concert continued. Bibi's *Rêverie* murmured its numbers, consisting almost entirely of arpeggios, above which a bar of melody rose now and then, weak-winged. Then came *Le Hibou et les moineaux*. This piece was brilliantly successful, it made a strong impression; it was an effective childhood fantasy, remarkably well envisaged. The bass represented the owl, sitting morosely rolling his filmy eyes; while in the treble the impudent, half-frightened sparrows chirped. Bibi received an ovation when he finished, he was called out four times. A hotel page with shiny buttons carried up three great laurel wreaths onto the stage and proffered them from one side while Bibi nodded and expressed his thanks. Even the princess shared in the applause, daintily and noiselessly pressing her palms together.

Ah, the knowing little creature understood how to make people clap! He stopped behind the screen, they had to wait for him; lingered a little on the steps of the platform, admired the long streamers on the wreaths — although actually such things bored him stiff by now. He bowed with the utmost charm, he gave the audience plenty of time to rave itself out, because applause is valuable and must not be cut short. "*Le Hibou* is my drawing card," he thought — this expression he had learned from the impresario. "Now I will play the fantasy, it is a lot better than *Le Hibou*, of course, especially the C-sharp passage. But you idiots dote on the *Hibou*, though it is the first and the silliest thing I wrote." He continued to bow and smile.

Next came a *Méditation* and then an *Étude* — the programme was quite comprehensive. The *Méditation* was very like the *Rêverie* — which was nothing against it — and the *Étude* displayed all of Bibi's virtuosity, which naturally fell a little short of his inventiveness. And then the *Fantaisie*. This was his favourite; he varied it a little each time, giving himself free rein and sometimes surprising even himself, on good evenings, by his own inventiveness.

He sat and played, so little, so white and shining, against the great black grand piano, elect and alone, above that confused sea of faces, above the heavy, insensitive mass soul, upon which he was labouring to work with his individual, differentiated soul. His lock of soft black hair with the white silk bow had fallen over his forehead, his trained and bony little wrists pounded away, the muscles stood out visibly on his brown childish cheeks.

Sitting there he sometimes had moments of oblivion and solitude, when the gaze of his strange little mouselike eyes with the big rings beneath them would lose itself and stare through the painted stage into space that was peopled with strange vague life. Then out of the corner of his eye he would give a quick look back into the hall and be once more with his audience.

"Joy and pain, the heights and the depths — that is my *Fantaisie*," he thought lovingly. "Listen, here is the C-sharp passage." He lingered over the approach, wondering if they would notice anything. But no, of course not, how should they? And he cast his eyes up prettily at the ceiling so that at least they might have something to look at.

All these people sat there in their regular rows, looking at the prodigy and thinking all sorts of things in their regular brains. An old gentleman with a white beard, a seal ring on his finger and a bulbous swelling on his bald spot, a growth if you like, was thinking to himself: "Really, one ought to be ashamed." He had never got any further

than "Ah, thou dearest Augustin" on the piano, and here he sat now, a grey old man, looking on while this little hop-o'-my-thumb performed miracles. Yes, yes, it is a gift of God, we must remember that. God grants His gifts, or He withholds them, and there is no shame in being an ordinary man. Like with the Christ Child. — Before a child one may kneel without feeling ashamed. Strange that thoughts like these should be so satisfying — he would even say so sweet, if it was not too silly for a tough old man like him to use the word. That was how he felt, anyhow.

Art . . . the business man with the parrot-nose was thinking. "Yes, it adds something cheerful to life, a little good white silk and a little tumty-ti-titum. Really he does not play so badly. Fully fifty seats, twelve marks apiece, that makes six hundred marks — and everything else besides. Take off the rent of the hall, the lighting and the programmes, you must have fully a thousand marks profit. That is worth while."

That was Chopin he was just playing, thought the piano-teacher, a lady with a pointed nose; she was of an age when the understanding sharpens as the hopes decay. "But not very original — I will say that afterwards, it sounds well. And his hand position is entirely amateur. One must be able to lay a coin on the back of the hand — I would use a ruler on him."

Then there was a young girl, at that self-conscious and chlorotic time of life when the most ineffable ideas come into the mind. She was thinking to herself: "What is it he is playing? It is expressive of passion, yet he is a child. If he kissed me it would be as though my little brother kissed me — no kiss at all. Is there such a thing as passion all by itself, without any earthly object, a sort of child's-play of passion? What nonsense! If I were to say such things aloud they would just be at me with some more codliver oil. Such is life."

An officer was leaning against a column. He looked on at Bibi's success and thought: "Yes, you are something and I am something, each in his own way." So he clapped his heels together and paid to the prodigy the respect which he felt to be due to all the powers that be.

Then there was a critic, an elderly man in a shiny black coat and turned-up trousers splashed with mud. He sat in his free seat and thought: "Look at him, this young beggar of a Bibi. As an individual he has still to develop, but as a type he is already quite complete, the artist *par excellence*. He has in himself all the artist's exaltation and his utter worthlessness, his charlatanry and his sacred fire, his burning contempt and his secret raptures. Of course I can't write all that, it is too good. Of course, I should have been an artist myself if I had not seen through the whole business so clearly."

Then the prodigy stopped playing and a perfect storm arose in the hall. He had to come out again and again from behind his screen. The man with the shiny buttons carried up more wreaths: four laurel wreaths, a lyre made of violets, a bouquet of roses. He had not arms enough to convey all these tributes, the impresario himself mounted the stage to help him. He hung a laurel wreath round Bibi's neck, he tenderly stroked the black hair — and suddenly as though overcome he bent down and gave the prodigy a kiss, a resounding kiss, square on the mouth. And then the storm became a hurricane. That kiss ran through the room like an electric shock, it went direct to peoples' marrow and made them shiver down their backs. They were carried away by a helpless compulsion of sheer noise. Loud shouts mingled with the hysterical clapping of hands. Some of Bibi's commonplace little friends down there waved their handkerchiefs. But the critic thought: "Of course that kiss had to come — it's a good old gag. Yes, good Lord, if only one did not see through everything quite so clearly —"

And so the concert drew to a close. It began at half past seven and finished at half past eight. The platform was laden with wreaths and two little pots of flowers stood on the lamp-stands of the piano. Bibi played as his last number his *Rhapsodie grecque*, which turned into the Greek national hymn at the end. His fellow-countrymen in the audience would gladly have sung it with him if the company had not been so august. They made up for it with a powerful noise and hullabaloo, a hot-blooded national demonstration. And the aging critic was thinking: "Yes, the hymn had to come too. They have to exploit every vein — publicity cannot afford to neglect any means to its end. I think I'll criticize that as inartistic. But perhaps I am wrong, perhaps that is the most artistic thing of all. What is the artist? A jack-in-the-box. Criticism is on a higher plane. But I can't say that." And away he went in his muddy trousers.

After being called out nine or ten times the prodigy did not come any more from behind the screen but went to his mother and the impresario down in the hall. The audience stood about among the chairs and applauded and pressed forward to see Bibi close at hand. Some of them wanted to see the princess too. Two dense circles formed, one round the prodigy, the other round the princess, and you could actually not tell which of them was receiving more homage. But the court lady was commanded to go over to Bibi; she smoothed down his silk jacket a bit to make it look suitable for a court function, led him by the arm to the princess, and solemnly indicated to him that he was to kiss the royal hand. "How do you do it, child?" asked the princess. "Does it come into your head of itself when you sit down?" "*Oui, madame*," answered Bibi. To himself he thought: "Oh, what a stupid old princess!" Then he turned round shyly and uncourtier-like and went back to his family.

Outside in the cloak-room there was a crowd. People held up their numbers and received with open arms furs, shawls, and galoshes. Somewhere among her acquaintances the piano-teacher stood making her critique. "He is not very original," she said audibly and looked about her.

In front of one of the great mirrors an elegant young lady was being arrayed in her evening cloak and fur shoes by her brothers, two lieutenants. She was exquisitely beautiful, with her steel-blue eyes and her clean-cut, well-bred face. A really noble dame. When she was ready she stood waiting for her brothers. "Don't stand so long in front of the glass, Adolf," she said softly to one of them, who could not tear himself away from the sight of his simple, good-looking young features. But Lieutenant Adolf thinks: What cheek! He would button his overcoat in front of the glass, just the same. Then they went out on the street where the arc-lights gleamed cloudily through the white mist. Lieutenant Adolf struck up a little nigger-dance on the frozen snow to keep warm, with his hands in his slanting overcoat pockets and his collar turned up.

A girl with untidy hair and swinging arms, accompanied by a gloomy-faced youth, came out just behind them. A child! she thought. A charming child. But in there he was an awe-inspiring ... and aloud in a toneless voice she said: "We are all infant prodigies, we artists."

"Well, bless my soul!" thought the old gentleman who had never got further than Augustin on the piano, and whose boil was now concealed by a top hat. "What does all that mean? She sounds very oracular." But the gloomy youth understood. He nodded his head slowly.

Then they were silent and the untidy-haired girl gazed after the brothers and sister. She rather despised them, but she looked after them until they had turned the corner.

The Magic Mountain [1]

The Magic Mountain recounts the thoughts and experiences of Hans Castorp, a young engineer from Hamburg, at a sanitarium in the Swiss Alps. Castorp has gone to the retreat to visit a cousin who is there recuperating from tuberculosis, but, finding that he is himself infected, turns the three weeks' visit into a seven years' sojourn. Before reading the following pages the reader should know the following facts: Hans has tired of a convalescence which restricts him to the balcony off his room and to the short walks in the vicinity of the hotel. He has secretly and against the doctor's orders purchased skis and extended his movements into the hills near by. He is determined to make a long excursion.

It is well to understand the significance of Castorp's experience in the snowstorm, as described in the following episode. While being retained in the sanitarium, Hans has been repeatedly subjected to philosophical discussions carried on between two of the other patients, Naphta and Settembrini. For him they represented two contrary philosophies of life. Naphta's is a religious attitude; he believes in the religious calling of the human soul. Its mystic reunion with the divine can only be the result of man's complete submission to Fate. In Castorp's experience, Fate is represented by the snowstorm — and Naphta's decision would be to resign to it. Settembrini argues the humanist's point of view. He is a believer in progress, a rebel who detests the superstitions cherished by religious dogmatists. His comments relating to the patients and the medical staff of the sanitarium, for instance, are biting, ironical, and somewhat malignant — in short, they are enlightened.

In the snowstorm Hans Castorp faces an important and grave decision. It is a practical decision which corresponds, however, to a similar, theoretical one which would approve of Naphta's or Settembrini's doctrines. The two possibilities, between which a choice has to be made, are: either to succumb to the onslaught of nature or to overcome the lethargy and exhaustion and find the way back to society. In a hallucinatory dream Castorp observes the happy and enlightened society, as it still pays homage to the primitive gods. Waking up from the dream, he understands that in the future he must neither rely on the facile and shallow creed of Settembrini nor on the passive religious quietism of Naphta. Instead, he must take a middle position between life (the active) and death (the passive), the two "counter-positions" which he is to reconcile with the help of goodness and love. Having undergone such spiritual purgation, symbolized by his escape from the catastrophe, Castorp returns to the sanitarium. At the end of the novel he is back in society experiencing the horrors of the First World War.

[1] The translation of *The Magic Mountain* is by H. T. Lowe-Porter. The passage used here is reprinted by permission of and special arrangement with Alfred A. Knopf, Inc.

SNOW

In a word, Hans Castorp was valorous up here — if by valor we mean not mere dull matter-of-factness in the face of nature, but conscious submission to her, the fear of death cast out by irre-5 sistible oneness. Yes, in his narrow, hypercivilized breast, Hans Castorp cherished a feeling of kinship with the elements, connected with the new sense of superiority he had lately felt at sight of the silly people on their little sleds; it had made him feel 10 that a profounder, more spacious, less luxurious solitude than that afforded by his balcony chair would be beyond all price. He had sat there and looked abroad, at those mist-wreathed summits, at the carnival of snow, and blushed to be gaping 15 thus from the breastwork of material well-being. This motive, and no momentary fad — no, nor yet any native love of bodily exertion — was what impelled him to learn the use of skis. If it was uncanny up there in the magnificence of the moun-20 tains, in the deathly silence of the snows — and uncanny it assuredly was, to our son of civilization — this was equally true, that in these months and years he had already drunk deep of the uncanny, in spirit and in sense. Even a colloquy with 25 Naphta and Settembrini, was not precisely the canniest thing in the world, it too led one on into uncharted and perilous regions. So if we can speak of Hans Castorp's feeling of kinship with the wild powers of the winter heights, it is in this sense, that 30 despite his pious awe he felt these scenes to be a fitting theatre for the issue of his involved thoughts, a fitting stage for one to make who, scarcely knowing how, found it had devolved upon him to take stock of himself, in reference to the rank and status 35 of the *Homo Dei*.

No one was here to blow a warning to the rash one — unless, indeed, Herr Settembrini, with his farewell shout at Hans Castorp's disappearing back, had been that man. But possessed by val-40 orous desire, our youth had given the call no heed — as little as he had the steps behind him on a certain carnival night. "*Eh, Ingegnere, un po' di ragione, sa!*" [1] "Yes, yes, pedagogic Satana, with your *ragione* [2] and your *ribellione*," [3] he 45 thought. "But I'm rather fond of you. You are a wind-bag and a hand-organ man, to be sure. But you mean well, you mean much better, and more to my mind, than that knife-edged little Jesuit and Terrorist, apologist of the Inquisition 50 and the knout, with his round eye-glasses — though he is nearly always right when you and he come to grips over my paltry soul, like God and the Devil in the mediæval legends."

[1] "Eh, engineer, a little reason, you know!"
[2] reason.   [3] rebellion.

He struggled, one day, powdered in snow to the waist, up a succession of snow-shrouded terraces, up and up, he knew not whither. Nowhither, perhaps; these upper regions blended with a sky no less misty-white than they, and where the two came together, it was hard to tell. No summit, no ridge was visible, it was a haze and a nothing, toward which Hans Castorp strove; while behind him the world, the inhabited valley, fell away swiftly from view, and no sound mounted to his ears. In a twinkling he was as solitary, he was as lost, as heart could wish, his loneliness was profound enough to awake the fear which is the first stage of valor. "*Præterit figura huius mundi*," he said to himself, quoting Naphta, in a Latin hardly humanistic in spirit. He stopped and looked about. On all sides there was nothing to see, beyond small single flakes of snow, which came out of a white sky and sank to rest on the white earth. The silence about him refused to say aught to his spirit. His gaze was lost in the blind white void, he felt his heart pulse from the effort of the climb — that muscular organ whose animal-like shape and contracting motion he had watched, with a feeling of sacrilege, in the x-ray laboratory. A naïve reverence filled him for that organ of his, for the pulsating human heart, up here alone in the icy void, alone with its question and its riddle.

On he pressed; higher and higher toward the sky. Walking, he thrust the end of his stick in the snow and watched the blue light follow it out of the hole it made. That he liked; and stood for long at a time to test the little optical phenomenon. It was a strange, subtle color, this greenish-blue; color of the heights and deeps, ice-clear, yet holding shadow in its depths, mysteriously exquisite. It reminded him of the color of certain eyes, whose shape and glance had spelled his destiny; eyes to which Herr Settembrini, from his humanistic height, had referred with contempt as "Tartar slits" and "wolf's eyes" — eyes seen long ago and then found again, the eyes of Pribislav Hippe and Clavdia Chauchat.[1] "With pleasure," he said aloud, in the profound stillness. "But don't break it — *c'est à visser, tu sais.*"[2] And his spirit heard behind him words of warning in a mellifluous tongue.

A wood loomed, misty, far off to the right. He turned that way, to the end of having some goal before his eyes, instead of sheer white transcendence; and made toward it with a dash, not remarking an intervening depression of the ground. He could not have seen it, in fact; everything swam before his eyes in the white mist, obliterating all contours. When he perceived it, he gave himself to the decline, unable to measure its steepness with his eye.

The grove that had attracted him lay the other side of the gully into which he had unintentionally steered. The trough, covered with fluffy snow, fell away on the side next the mountains, as he observed when he pursued it a little distance. It went downhill, the steep sides grew higher, this fold of the earth's surface seemed like a narrow passage leading into the mountain. Then the points of his skis turned up again, there began an incline, soon there were no more side walls; Hans Castorp's trackless course ran once more uphill along the mountain-side.

He saw the pine grove behind and below him, on his right, turned again toward it, and with a quick descent reached the laden trees; they stood in a wedge-shaped group, a vanguard thrust out from the mist-screened forests above. He rested beneath their boughs, and smoked a cigarette. The unnatural stillness, the monstrous solitude, still oppressed his spirit; yet he felt proud to have conquered them, brave in the pride of having measured to the height of surroundings such as these.

It was three in the afternoon. He had set out soon after luncheon, with the idea of cutting part of the long rest-cure, and tea as well, in order to be back before dark. He had brought some chocolate in his breeches pocket, and a small flask of wine; and told himself exultantly that he had still several hours to revel in all this grandeur.

The position of the sun was hard to recognize, veiled as it was in haze. Behind him, at the mouth of the valley, above that part of the mountains that was shut off from view, the clouds and mist seemed to thicken and move forward. They looked like snow — more snow — as though there were pressing demand for it! Like a good hard storm. Indeed, the little soundless flakes were coming down more quickly as he stood.

Hans Castorp put out his arm and let some of them come to rest on his sleeve; he viewed them with the knowing eye of the nature-lover. They looked mere shapeless morsels; but he had more than once had their like under his good lens, and was aware of the exquisite precision of form displayed by these little jewels, insignia, orders, agraffes[1] — no jeweller, however skilled, could do finer, more minute work. Yes, he thought, there was a difference, after all, between this light, soft, white powder he trod with his skis, that weighed down the trees, and covered the open spaces, a difference between it and the sand on the beaches at home, to which he had likened it. For this

---

[1] It is with Clavdia that Hans falls in love.

[2] "It should be twisted, you know."

[1] clasps.

powder was not made of tiny grains of stone; but of myriads of tiniest drops of water, which in freezing had darted together in symmetrical variation — parts, then, of the same anorganic substance which was the source of protoplasm, of plant life, of the human body. And among these myriads of enchanting little stars, in their hidden splendor that was too small for man's naked eye to see, there was not one like unto another; an endless inventiveness governed the development and unthinkable differentiation of one and the same basic scheme, the equilateral, equiangled hexagon. Yet each, in itself — this was the uncanny, the antiorganic, the life-denying character of them all — each of them was absolutely symmetrical, icily regular in form. They were too regular, as substance adapted to life never was to this degree — the living principle shuddered at this perfect precision, found it deathly, the very marrow of death — Hans Castorp felt he understood now the reason why the builders of antiquity purposely and secretly introduced minute variation from absolute symmetry in their columnar structures.

He pushed off again, shuffling through the deep snow on his flexible runners, along the edge of the wood, down the slope, up again, at random, to his heart's content, about and into this lifeless land. Its empty, rolling spaces, its dried vegetation of single dwarf firs sticking up through the snow, bore a striking resemblance to a scene on the dunes. Hans Castorp nodded as he stood and fixed the likeness in his mind. Even his burning face, his trembling limbs, the peculiar and half-intoxicated mingled sensations of excitement and fatigue were pleasurable, reminding him as they did of that familiar feeling induced by the sea air, which could sting one like whips, and yet was so laden with sleepy essences. He rejoiced in his freedom of motion, his feet were like wings. He was bound to no path, none lay behind him to take him back whence he had come. At first there had been posts, staves set up as guides through the snow — but he had soon cut free from their tutelage, which recalled the coastguard with his horn, and seemed inconsistent with the attitude he had taken up toward the wild.

He pressed on, turning right and left among rocky, snow-clad elevations, and came behind them on an incline, then a level spot, then on the mountains themselves — how alluring and accessible seemed their softly covered gorges and defiles! His blood leaped at the strong allurement of the distance and the height, the ever profounder solitude. At risk of a late return he pressed on, deeper into the wild silence, the monstrous and the menacing, despite that gathering darkness was sinking down over the region like a veil, and heightening his inner apprehension until it presently passed into actual fear. It was this fear which first made him conscious that he had deliberately set out to lose his way and the direction in which valley and settlement lay — and had been as successful as heart could wish. Yet he knew that if he were to turn in his tracks and go downhill, he would reach the valley bottom — even if at some distance from the Berghof — and that sooner than he had planned. He would come home too early, not have made full use of his time. On the other hand, if he were overtaken unawares by the storm, he would probably in any case not find his way home. But however genuine his fear of the elements, he refused to take premature flight; his being scarcely the sportsman's attitude, who only meddles with the elements so long as he knows himself their master, takes all precautions, and prudently yields when he must — whereas what went on in Hans Castorp's soul can only be described by the one word challenge. It was perhaps a blameworthy, presumptuous attitude, even united to such genuine awe. Yet this much is clear, to any human understanding: that when a young man has lived years long in the way this one had, something may gather — may accumulate, as our engineer might put it — in the depths of his soul, until one day it suddenly discharges itself, with a primitive exclamation of disgust, a mental "Oh, go to the devil!" a repudiation of all caution whatsoever, in short with a challenge. So on he went, in his seven-league slippers, glided down this slope too and pressed up the incline beyond, where stood a wooden hut that might be a hayrick or shepherd's shelter, its roof weighted with flat stones. On past this to the nearest mountain ridge, bristling with forest, behind whose back the giant peaks towered upward in the mist. The wall before him, studded with single groups of trees, was steep, but looked as though one might wind to the right and get round it by climbing a little way up the slope. Once on the other side, he could see what lay beyond. Accordingly Hans Castorp set out on this tour of investigation, which began by descending from the meadow with the hut into another and rather deep gully that dropped off from right to left.

He had just begun to mount again when the expected happened, and the storm burst, the storm that had threatened so long. Or may one say "threatened" of the action of blind, nonsentient forces, which have no purpose to destroy us — that would be comforting by comparison — but are merely horribly indifferent to our fate should we become involved with them? "Hullo!"

Hans Castorp thought, and stood still, as the first blast whirled through the densely falling snow and caught him. "That's a gentle zephyr — tells you what's coming." And truly this wind was savage. The air was in reality frightfully cold, probably some degrees below zero; but so long as it remained dry and still one almost found it balmy. It was when a wind came up that the cold began to cut into the flesh; and in a wind like the one that blew now, of which that first gust had been a forerunner, the furs were not bought that could protect the limbs from its icy rigors. And Hans Castorp wore no fur, only a woollen waistcoat, which he had found quite enough, or even, with the faintest gleam of sunshine, a burden. But the wind was at his back, a little sidewise; there was small inducement to turn and receive it in the face; so the mad youth, letting that fact reinforce the fundamental challenge of his attitude, pressed on among the single tree-trunks, and tried to outflank the mountain he had attacked.

It was no joke. There was almost nothing to be seen for swimming snow-flakes, that seemed without falling to fill the air to suffocation by their whirling dance. The icy gusts made his ears burn painfully, his limbs felt half paralysed, his hands were so numb he hardly knew if they held the staff. The snow blew inside his collar and melted down his back. It drifted on his shoulders and right side; he thought he should freeze as he stood into a snow-man, with his staff stiff in his hands. And all this under relatively favoring circumstances; for let him turn his face to the storm and his situation would be still worse. Getting home would be no easy task — the harder, the longer he put it off.

At last he stopped, gave an angry shrug, and turned his skis the other way. Then the wind he faced took his breath on the spot, so that he was forced to go through the awkward process of turning round again to get it back, and collect his resolution to advance in the teeth of his ruthless foe. With bent head and cautious breathing he managed to get under way; but even thus forewarned, the slowness of his progress and the difficulty of seeing and breathing dismayed him. Every few minutes he had to stop, first to get his breath in the lee of the wind, and then because he saw next to nothing in the blinding whiteness, and moving as he did with head down, had to take care not to run against trees, or be flung headlong by unevennesses in the ground. Hosts of flakes flew into his face, melted there, and he anguished with the cold of them. They flew into his mouth, and died away with a weak, watery taste; flew against his eyelids so that he winked, overflowed his eyes and made seeing as difficult as it was now almost

impossible for other reasons: namely, the dazzling effect of all that whiteness, and the veiling of his field of vision, so that his sense of sight was almost put out of action. It was nothingness, white, whirling nothingness, into which he looked when he forced himself to do so. Only at intervals did ghostly-seeming forms from the world of reality loom up before him: a stunted fir, a group of pines, even the pale silhouette of the hay-hut he had lately passed.

He left it behind, and sought his way back over the slope on which it stood. But there was no path. To keep direction, relatively speaking, into his own valley would be a question far more of luck than management; for while he could see his hand before his face, he could not see the ends of his skis. And even with better visibility, the host of difficulties must have combined to hinder his progress: the snow in his face, his adversary the storm, which hampered his breathing, made him fight both to take a breath and to exhale it, and constantly forced him to turn his head away to gasp. How could anyone — either Hans Castorp or another and much stronger than he — make head? He stopped, he blinked his lashes free of water drops, knocked off the snow that like a coat of mail was sheathing his body in front — and it struck him that progress, under the circumstances, was more than anyone could expect.

And yet Hans Castorp did progress. That is to say, he moved on. But whether in the right direction, whether it might not have been better to stand still, remained to be seen. Theoretically the chances were against it; and in practice he soon began to suspect something was wrong. This was not familiar ground beneath his feet, not the easy slope he had gained on mounting with such difficulty from the ravine, which had of course to be retraversed. The level distance was too short, he was already mounting again. It was plain that the storm, which came from the south-west, from the mouth of the valley, had with its violence driven him from his course. He had been exhausting himself, all this time, with a false start. Blindly, enveloped in white, whirling night, he labored deeper and deeper into this grim and callous sphere.

"No, you don't," said he, suddenly, between his teeth, and halted. The words were not emotional, yet he felt for a second as though his heart had been clutched by an icy hand; it winced, and then knocked rapidly against his ribs, as it had the time Rhadamanthus found the moist cavity. Pathos in the grand manner was not in place, he knew, in one who had chosen defiance as his rôle, and was indebted to himself alone for all his present plight. "Not bad," he said, and discovered that his facial muscles were not his to command, that he could not express in his face any of his soul's emotions, for that it was stiff with cold. "What next? Down this slope; follow your nose home, I suppose, and keep your face to the wind — though that is a good deal easier said than done," he went on, panting with his efforts, yet actually speaking half aloud, as he tried to move on again: "but something has to happen, I can't sit down and wait, I should simply be buried in six-sided crystalline symmetricality, and Settembrini, when he came with his little horn to find me, would see me squatting here with a snow-cap over one ear." He realized that he was talking to himself, and not too sensibly — for which he took himself to task, and then continued on purpose, though his lips were so stiff he could not shape the labials, and so did without them, as he had on a certain other occasion that came to his mind. "Keep quiet, and get along with you out of here," he admonished himself, adding: "You seem to be wool-gathering, not quite right in your head, and that looks bad for you."

But this he only said with his reason — to some extent detached from the rest of him, though after all nearly concerned. As for his natural part, it felt only too much inclined to yield to the confusion which laid hold upon him with his growing fatigue. He even remarked this tendency and took thought to comment upon it. "Here," said he, "we have the typical reaction of a man who loses himself in the mountains in a snowstorm and never finds his way home." He gasped out other fragments of the same thought as he went, though he avoided giving it more specific expression. "Whoever hears about it afterwards, imagines it as horrible; but he forgets that disease — and the state I am in is, in a way of speaking, disease — so adjusts its man that it and he can come to terms; there are sensory appeasements, short circuits, a merciful narcosis — yes, oh yes, yes. But one must fight against them, after all, for they are two-faced, they are in the highest degree equivocal, everything depends upon the point of view. If you are not meant to get home, they are a benefaction, they are merciful; but if you mean to get home, they become sinister. I believe I still do. Certainly I don't intend — in this heart of mine so stormily beating it doesn't appeal to me in the least — to let myself be snowed under by this idiotically symmetrical crystallometry."

In truth, he was already affected, and his struggle against oncoming sensory confusion was feverish and abnormal. He should have been more alarmed on discovering that he had already declined from the level course — this time apparently on the other slope. For he had pushed off with the wind coming slantwise at him, which was ill-advised, though more convenient for the moment. "Never mind," he thought, "I'll get my direction again down below." Which he did, or thought he did — or, truth to tell, scarcely even thought so; worst of all, began to be indifferent whether he had done or no. Such was the effect of an insidious double attack, which he but weakly combated. Fatigue and excitement combined were a familiar state to our young man — whose acclimatization, as we know, still consisted in getting used to not getting used; and both fatigue and excitement were now present in such strength as to make impossible any thought of asserting his reason against them. He felt as often after a colloquy with Settembrini and Naphta, only to a far greater degree: dazed and tipsy, giddy, a-tremble with excitement. This was probably why he began to color his lack of resistance to the stealing narcosis with half-maudlin references to the latest-aired complex of theories. Despite his scornful repudiation of the idea that he might lie down and be covered up with hexagonal symmetricality, something within him maundered on, sense or no sense: told him that the feeling of duty which bade him fight against insidious sensory appeasements was a purely ethical reaction, representing the sordid bourgeois view of life, irreligion, Philistinism; while the desire, nay, craving, to lie down and rest, whispered him in the guise of a comparison between this storm and a sandstorm on the desert, before which the Arab flings himself down and draws his burnous over his head. Only his lack of a burnous, the unfeasibility of drawing his woollen waistcoat over his head, prevented him from following suit — this although he was no longer a child, and pretty well aware of the conditions under which a man freezes to death.

There had been a rather steep declivity, then level ground, then again an ascent, a stiff one. This was not necessarily wrong; one must of course, on the way to the valley, traverse rising ground at times. The wind had turned capriciously round, for it was now at Hans Castorp's back, and that, taken by itself, was a blessing. Owing, perhaps, to the storm, or the soft whiteness of the incline before him, dim in the whirling air, drawing him toward it, he bent as he walked. Only a little further — supposing one were to give way to the temptation, and his temptation was great; it was so strong that it quite lived up to the many descriptions he had read of the "typical danger-state." It asserted itself, it refused to be classified with the general order of things, it insisted on being an exception, its very exigence challenged comparison — yet at the same time it never disguised its origin or aura, never denied that it was, so to speak, garbed in Spanish black, with snow-white, fluted ruff, and stood for ideas and fundamental conceptions that were characteristically gloomy, strongly Jesuitical and anti-human, for the rack-and-knout discipline which was the particular horror of Herr Settembrini, though he never opposed it without making himself ridiculous, like a hand-organ man for ever grinding out *"ragione"* to the same old tune.

And yet Hans Castorp did hold himself upright and resist his craving to lie down. He could see nothing, but he struggled, he came forward. Whether to the purpose or not, he could not tell; but he did his part, and moved on despite the weight the cold more and more laid upon his limbs. The present slope was too steep to ascend directly, so he slanted a little, and went on thus awhile without much heed whither. Even to lift his stiffened lids to peer before him was so great and so nearly useless an effort as to offer him small incentive. He merely caught glimpses: here clumps of pines that merged together; there a ditch or stream, a black line marked out between overhanging banks of snow. Now, for a change, he was going downhill, with the wind in his face, when, at some distance before him, and seeming to hang in the driving wind and mist, he saw the faint outline of a human habitation.

Ah, sweet and blessed sight! Verily he had done well, to march stoutly on despite all obstacles, until now human dwellings appeared, in sign that the inhabited valley was at hand. Perhaps there were even human beings, perhaps he might enter and abide the end of the storm under shelter, then get directions, or a guide if the dark should have fallen. He held toward this chimerical goal, that often quite vanished in mist, and took an exhausting climb against the wind before it was reached; finally drew near it — to discover, with what staggering astonishment and horror may be imagined, that it was only the hay-hut with the weighted roof, to which, after all his striving, by all his devious paths, he had come back.

That was the very devil. Hans Castorp gave vent to several heart-felt curses — of which his lips were too stiff to pronounce the labials. He examined the hut, to get his bearings, and came to the conclusion that he had approached it from the same direction as before — namely, from the rear; and therefore, what he had accomplished for the past hour — as he reckoned it — had been sheer waste of time and effort. But there it was, just as the books said. You went in a circle, gave

yourself endless trouble under the delusion that you were accomplishing something, and all the time you were simply describing some great silly arc that would turn back to where it had its beginning, like the riddling year itself. You wandered about, without getting home. Hans Castorp recognized the traditional phenomenon with a certain grim satisfaction — and even slapped his thigh in astonishment at this punctual general law fulfilling itself in his particular case.

The lonely hut was barred, the door locked fast, no entrance possible. But Hans Castorp decided to stop for the present. The projecting roof gave the illusion of shelter, and the hut itself, on the side turned toward the mountains, afforded, he found, some little protection against the storm. He leaned his shoulder against the rough-hewn timber, since his long skis prevented him from leaning his back. And so he stood, obliquely to the wall, having thrust his staff in the snow; hands in pockets, his collar turned up as high as it would go, bracing himself on his outside leg, and leaning his dizzy head against the wood, his eyes closed, but opening them every now and then to look down his shoulder and across the gully to where the high mountain wall palely appeared and disappeared in mist.

His situation was comparatively comfortable. "I can stick it like this all night, if I have to," he thought, "if I change legs from time to time, lie on the other side, so to speak, and move about a bit between whiles, as of course I must. I'm rather stiff, naturally, but the effort I made has accumulated some inner warmth, so after all it was not quite in vain, that I have come round all this way. Come round — not coming round — that's the regular expression they use, of people drowned or frozen to death. — I suppose I used it because I am not quite so clear in the head as I might be. But it is a good thing I can stick it out here; for this frantic nuisance of a snow-storm can carry on until morning without a qualm, and if it only keeps up until dark it will be quite bad enough, for in the dark the danger of going round and round and *not* coming round is as great as in a storm. It must be toward evening already, about six o'clock, I should say, after all the time I wasted on my circular tour. Let's see, how late is it?" He felt for his watch; his numbed fingers could scarcely find and draw it from his pocket. Here it was, his gold hunting-watch, with his monogram on the lid, ticking faithfully away in this lonely waste, like Hans Castorp's own heart, that touching human heart that beat in the organic warmth of his interior man.

It was half past four. But deuce take it, it had

been nearly so much before the storm burst. Was it possible his whole bewildered circuit had lasted scarcely a quarter of an hour? "'Coming round' makes time seem long," he noted. "And when you *don't* 'come round' — does it seem longer? But the fact remains that at five or half past it will be regularly dark. Will the storm hold up in time to keep me from running in circles again? Suppose I take a sip of port — it might strengthen me."

He had brought with him a bottle of that amateurish drink, simply because it was always kept ready in flat bottles at the Berghof, for excursions — though not, of course, excursions like this unlawful escapade. It was not meant for people who went out in the snow and got lost and nightbound in the mountains. Had his senses been less befogged, he must have said to himself that if he were bent on getting home, it was almost the worst thing he could have done. He did say so, after he had drunk several swallows, for they took effect at once, and it was an effect much like that of the Kulmbacher beer on the evening of his arrival at the Berghof, when he had angered Settembrini by his ungoverned prattle anent fish-sauces and the like — Herr Ludovico, the pedagogue, the same who held madmen to their senses when they would give themselves rein. Hans Castorp heard through thin air the mellifluous sound of his horn; the orator and schoolmaster was nearing by forced marches, to rescue his troublesome nursling, life's delicate child, from his present desperate pass and lead him home. — All which was of course sheer rubbish, due to the Kulmbacher he had so foolishly drunk. For of course Herr Settembrini had no horn, how could he have? He had a handorgan, propped by a sort of wooden leg against the pavement, and as he played a sprightly air, he flung his humanistic eyes up to the people in the houses. And furthermore he knew nothing whatever of what had happened, as he no longer lived in House Berghof, but with Lukaçek the tailor, in his little attic room with the water-bottle, above Naphta's silken cell. Moreover, he would have nor right nor reason to interfere — no more than upon that carnival night on which Hans Castorp had found himself in a position quite as mad and bad as this one, when he gave the ailing Clavdia Chauchat back *son crayon* — his, Pribislav Hippe's, pencil. What position was that? What position could it be but the horizontal, literally and not metaphorically the position of all long-termers up here? Was he himself not used to lie long hours out of doors, in snow and frost, by night as well as day? And he was making ready to sink down when the idea seized him, took him as it were by

the collar and fetched him up standing, that all this nonsense he was uttering was still inspired by the Kulmbacher beer and the impersonal, quite typical and traditional longing to lie down and sleep, of which he had always heard, and which would by quibbling and sophistry now betray him.

"That was the wrong way to go to work," he acknowledged to himself. "The port was not at all the right thing; just the few sips of it have made my head so heavy I cannot hold it up, and my thoughts are all just confused, stupid quibbling with words. I can't depend on them — not only the first thought that comes into my head, but even the second one, the correction which my reason tries to make upon the first — more's the pity. '*Son crayon!*' That means her pencil, not his pencil, in this case; you only say *son* because *crayon* is masculine. The rest is just a pretty feeble play on words. Imagine stopping to talk about that when there is a much more important fact; namely, that my left leg, which I am using as a support, reminds me of the wooden leg on Settembrini's hand-organ, that he keeps jolting over the pavement with his knee, to get up close to the window and hold out his velvet hat for the girl up there to throw something into. And at the same time, I seem to be pulled, as though with hands, to lie down in the snow. The only thing to do is to move about. I must pay for the Kulmbacher, and limber up my wooden leg."

He pushed himself away from the wall with his shoulder. But one single pace forward, and the wind sliced at him like a scythe, and drove him back to the shelter of the wall. It was unquestionably the position indicated for the time; he might change it by turning his left shoulder to the wall and propping himself on the right leg, with sundry shakings of the left, to restore the circulation as much as might be. "Who leaves the house in weather like this?" he said. "Moderate activity is all right; but not too much craving for adventure, no coying with the bride of the storm. Quiet, quiet — if the head be heavy, let it droop. The wall is good, a certain warmth seems to come from the logs — probably the feeling is entirely subjective. — Ah, the trees, the trees! Oh, living climate of the living — how sweet it smells!"

It was a park. It lay beneath the terrace on which he seemed to stand — a spreading park of luxuriant green shade-trees, elms, planes, beeches, oaks, birches, all in the dappled light and shade of their fresh, full, shimmering foliage, and gently rustling tips. They breathed a deliciously moist, balsamic breath into the air. A warm shower passed over them, but the rain was sunlit. One could see high up in the sky the whole air filled with the bright ripple of raindrops. How lovely it was! Oh, breath of the homeland, oh, fragrance and abundance of the plain, so long foregone! The air was full of bird song — dainty, sweet, blithe fluting, piping, twittering, cooing, trilling, warbling, though not a single little creature could be seen. Hans Castorp smiled, breathing gratitude. But still more beauties were preparing. A rainbow flung its arc slanting across the scene, most bright and perfect, a sheer delight, all its rich, glossy, banded colors moistly shimmering down into the thick, lustrous green. It was like music, like the sound of harps commingled with flutes and violins. The blue and the violet were transcendent. And they descended and magically blended, were transmuted and re-unfolded more lovely than at first. Once, some years before, our young Hans Castorp had been privileged to hear a world-famous Italian tenor, from whose throat had gushed a glorious stream to witch the world with gracious art. The singer took a high note, exquisitely; then held it, while the passionate harmony swelled, unfolded, glowed from moment to moment with new radiance. Unsuspected veils dropped from before it one by one; the last one sank away, revealing what must surely be the ultimate tonal purity — yet no, for still another fell, and then a well-nigh incredible third and last, shaking into the air such an extravagance of tear-glistening splendor, that confused murmurs of protest rose from the audience, as though it could bear no more; and our young friend found that he was sobbing. — So now with the scene before him, constantly transformed and transfigured as it was before his eyes. The bright, rainy veil fell away; behind it stretched the sea, a southern sea of deep, deepest blue shot with silver lights, and a beautiful bay, on one side mistily open, on the other enclosed by mountains whose outline paled away into blue space. In the middle distance lay islands, where palms rose tall and small white houses gleamed among cypress groves. Ah, it was all too much, too blest for sinful mortals, that glory of light, that deep purity of the sky, that sunny freshness on the water! Such a scene Hans Castorp had never beheld, nor anything like it. On his holidays he had barely sipped at the south, the sea for him meant the colorless, tempestuous northern tides, to which he clung with inarticulate, childish love. Of the Mediterranean, Naples, Sicily, he knew nothing. And yet — he remembered. Yes, strangely enough, that was recognition which so moved him. "Yes, yes, its very image," he was crying out, as though in his heart he had always cherished a picture of this spacious, sunny bliss. Always — and that always went far,

far, unthinkably far back, as far as the open sea there on the left where it ran out to the violet sky bent down to meet it.

The sky-line was high, the distance seemed to mount to Hans Castorp's view, looking down as he did from his elevation on the spreading gulf beneath. The mountains held it embraced, their tree-clad foot-hills running down to the sea; they reached in half-circle from the middle distance to the point where he sat, and beyond. This was a mountainous littoral, at one point of which he was crouching upon a sun-warmed stone terrace, while before him the ground, descending among undergrowth, by moss-covered rocky steps, ran down to a level shore, where the reedy shingle formed little blue-dyed bays, minute archipelagoes and harbors. And all the sunny region, these open coastal heights and laughing rocky basins, even the sea itself out to the islands, where boats plied to and fro, was peopled far and wide. On every hand human beings, children of sun and sea, were stirring or sitting. Beautiful young human creatures, so blithe, so good and gay, so pleasing to see — at sight of them Hans Castorp's whole heart opened in a responsive love, keen almost to pain.

Youths were at work with horses, running hand on halter alongside their whinnying, head-tossing charges; pulling the refractory ones on a long rein, or else, seated bareback, striking the flanks of their mounts with naked heels, to drive them into the sea. The muscles of the riders' backs played beneath the sun-bronzed skin, and their voices were enchanting beyond words as they shouted to each other or to their animals. A little bay ran deep into the coast line, mirroring the shore as does a mountain lake; about it girls were dancing. One of them sat with her back toward him, so that her neck, and the hair drawn to a knot above it smote him with loveliness. She sat with her feet in a depression of the rock, and played on a shepherd's pipe, her eyes roving above the stops to her companions, as in long, wide garments, smiling, with outstretched arms, alone, or in pairs swaying gently toward each other, they moved in the paces of the dance. Behind the flute-player — she too was white-clad, and her back was long and slender, laterally rounded by the movement of her arms — other maidens were sitting, or standing entwined to watch the dance, and quietly talking. Beyond them still, young men were practising archery. Lovely and pleasant it was to see the older ones show the younger, curly-locked novices, how to span the bow and take aim; draw with them, and laughing support them staggering back from the push of the arrow as it leaped from the bow. Others were fishing, lying prone on a jut of rock, waggling one leg in the air, holding the line out over the water, approaching their heads in talk. Others sat straining forward to fling the bait far out. A ship, with mast and yards, lying high out of the tide, was being eased, shoved, and steadied into the sea. Children played and exulted among the breaking waves. A young female, lying out-stretched, drawing with one hand her flowered robe high between her breasts, reached with the other in the air after a twig bearing fruit and leaves, which a second, a slender-hipped creature, erect at her head, was playfully withholding. Young folk were sitting in nooks of the rocks, or hesitating at the water's edge, with crossed arms clutching either shoulder, as they tested the chill with their toes. Pairs strolled along the beach, close and confiding, at the maiden's ear the lips of the youth. Shaggy-haired goats leaped from ledge to ledge of the rocks, while the young goatherd, wearing perched on his brown curls a little hat with the brim turned up behind, stood watching them from a height, one hand on his hip, the other hold-ing the long staff on which he leaned.

"Oh, lovely, lovely," Hans Castorp breathed. "How joyous and winning they are, how fresh and healthy, happy and clever they look! It is not alone the outward form, they seem to be wise and gentle through and through. That is what makes me in love with them, the spirit that speaks out of them, the sense, I might almost say, in which they live and play together." By which he meant the friendliness, the mutual courteous regard these children of the sun showed to each other, a calm, reciprocal reverence veiled in smiles, manifested almost imperceptibly, and yet possessing them all by the power of sense association and ingrained idea. A dignity, even a gravity, was held, as it were, in solution in their lightest mood, perceptible only as an ineffable spiritual influence, a high seriousness without austerity, a reasoned goodness conditioning every act. All this, indeed, was not without its ceremonial side. A young mother, in a brown robe loose at the shoulder, sat on a rounded mossy stone and suckled her child, saluted by all who passed with a characteristic gesture which seemed to comprehend all that lay implicit in their general bearing. The young men, as they ap-proached, lightly and formally crossed their arms on their breasts, and smilingly bowed; the maidens shaped the suggestion of a curtsy, as the wor-shipper does when he passes the high altar, at the same time nodding repeatedly, blithely and heartily. This mixture of formal homage with lively friendliness, and the slow, mild mien of the mother as well, where she sat pressing her breast with her forefinger to ease the flow of milk to her babe, glancing up from it to acknowledge with a smile the reverence paid her — this sight thrilled Hans Castorp's heart with something very close akin to ecstasy. He could not get his fill of look-ing, yet asked himself in concern whether he had a right, whether it was not perhaps punishable, for him, an outsider, to be a party to the sunshine and gracious loveliness of all these happy folk. He felt common, clumsy-booted. It seemed un-scrupulous.

A lovely boy, with full hair drawn sideways across his brow and falling on his temples, sat directly beneath him, apart from his companions, with arms folded on his breast — not sadly, not ill-naturedly, quite tranquilly on one side. This lad looked up, turned his gaze upward and looked at him, Hans Castorp, and his eyes went between the watcher and the scenes upon the strand, watching his watching, to and fro. But suddenly he looked past Hans Castorp into space, and that smile, common to them all, of polite and brotherly regard, disappeared in a moment from his lovely, purely cut, half-childish face. His brows did not darken, but in his gaze there came a solemnity that looked as though carven out of stone, inexpressive, unfathomable, a deathlike reserve, which gave the scarcely reassured Hans Castorp a thorough fright, not unaccompanied by a vague apprehension of its meaning.

He too looked in the same direction. Behind him rose towering columns, built of cylindrical blocks without bases, in the joinings of which moss had grown. They formed the façade of a temple gate, on whose foundations he was sitting, at the top of a double flight of steps with space between. Heavy of heart he rose, and, descending the stair on one side, passed through the high gate below, and along a flagged street, which soon brought him before other propylæa. He passed through these as well, and now stood facing the temple that lay before him, massy, weathered to a grey-green tone, on a foundation reached by a steep flight of steps. The broad brow of the temple rested on the capitals of powerful, almost stunted columns, tapering toward the top — sometimes a fluted block had been shoved out of line and projected a little in profile. Painfully, helping himself on with his hands, and sighing for the growing oppression of his heart, Hans Castorp mounted the high steps and gained the grove of columns. It was very deep, he moved in it as among the trunks in a forest of beeches by the pale northern sea. He purposely avoided the centre, yet for all that slanted back again, and presently stood before a group of statuary, two female figures carved in stone, on a high base: mother and daughter, it seemed; one of them sitting, older than the other, more dignified, right goddesslike and mild, yet with mourning brows above the lightless empty eye-sockets; clad in a flowing tunic and a mantle of many folds, her matronly brow with its waves of hair covered with a veil. The other figure stood in the protecting embrace of the first, with round, youthful face, and arms and hands wound and hidden in the folds of the mantle.

Hans Castorp stood looking at the group, and from some dark cause his laden heart grew heavier still, and more oppressed with its weight of dread and anguish. Scarcely daring to venture, but following an inner compulsion, he passed behind the statuary, and through the double row of columns beyond. The bronze door of the sanctuary stood open, and the poor soul's knees all but gave way beneath him at the sight within. Two grey old women, witchlike, with hanging breasts and dugs of fingerlength, were busy there, between flaming braziers, most horribly. They were dismembering a child. In dreadful silence they tore it apart with their bare hands — Hans Castorp saw the bright hair blood-smeared — and cracked the tender bones between their jaws, their dreadful lips dripped blood. An icy coldness held him. He would have covered his eyes and fled, but could not. They at their gory business had already seen him, they shook their reeking fists and uttered curses — soundlessly, most vilely, with the last obscenity, and in the dialect of Hans Castorp's native Hamburg. It made him sick, sick as never before. He tried desperately to escape; knocked into a column with his shoulder — and found himself, with the sound of that dreadful whispered brawling still in his ears, still wrapped in the cold horror of it, lying by his hut, in the snow, leaning against one arm, with his head upon it, his legs in their skis stretched out before him.

It was no true awakening. He blinked his relief at being free from those execrable hags, but was not very clear, nor even greatly concerned, whether this was a hay-hut, or the column of a temple, against which he lay; and after a fashion continued to dream, no longer in pictures, but in thoughts hardly less involved and fantastic.

"I felt it was a dream, all along," he rambled. "A lovely and horrible dream. I knew all the time that I was making it myself — the park with the trees, the delicious moisture in the air, and all the rest, both dreadful and dear. In a way, I knew it all beforehand. But how is it a man can know all that and call it up to bring him bliss and terror both at once? Where did I get the beautiful bay with the islands, where the temple precincts, whither the eyes of that charming boy pointed me,

as he stood there alone? Now I know that it is not out of our single souls we dream. We dream anonymously and communally, if each after his fashion. The great soul of which we are a part may dream through us, in our manner of dreaming, its own secret dreams, of its youth, its hope, its joy and peace — and its blood-sacrifice. Here I lie at my column and still feel in my body the actual remnant of my dream — the icy horror of the human sacrifice, but also the joy that had filled my heart to its very depths, born of the happiness and brave bearing of those human creatures in white. It is meet and proper, I hereby declare that I have a prescriptive right to lie here and dream these dreams. For in my life up here I have known reason and recklessness. I have wandered lost with Settembrini and Naphta in high and mortal places. I know all of man. I have known mankind's flesh and blood. I gave back to the ailing Clavdia Chauchat Pribislav Hippe's lead-pencil. But he who knows the body, life, knows death. And that is not all; it is, pedagogically speaking, only the beginning. One must have the other half of the story, the other side. For all interest in disease and death is only another expression of interest in life, as is proven by the humanistic faculty of medicine, that addresses life and its ails always so politely in Latin, and is only a division of the great and pressing concern which, in all sympathy, I now name by its name: the human being, the delicate child of life, man, his state and standing in the universe. I understand no little about him, I have learned much from 'those up here,' I have been driven up from the valley, so that the breath almost left my poor body. Yet now from the base of my column I have no meagre view. I have dreamed of man's state, of his courteous and enlightened social state; behind which, in the temple, the horrible blood-sacrifice was consummated. Were they, those children of the sun, so sweetly courteous to each other, in silent recognition of that horror? It would be a fine and right conclusion they drew. I will hold to them, in my soul, I will hold with them and not with Naphta, neither with Settembrini. They are both talkers; the one luxurious and spiteful, the other for ever blowing on his penny pipe of reason, even vainly imagining he can bring the mad to their senses. It is all Philistinism and morality, most certainly it is irreligious. Nor am I for little Naphta either, or his religion, that is only a *guazzabuglio* [1] of God and the Devil, good and evil, to the end that the individual soul shall plump into it head first, for the sake of mystic immersion in the universal. Pedagogues both!

[1] hodgepodge.

Their quarrels and counter-positions are just a *guazzabuglio* too, and a confused noise of battle, which need trouble nobody who keeps a little clear in his head and pious in his heart. Their aristocratic question! Disease, health! Spirit, nature! Are those contradictions? I ask, are they problems? No, they are no problems, neither is the problem of their aristocracy. The recklessness of death is in life, it would not be life without it — and in the centre is the position of the *Homo Dei*,[1] between recklessness and reason, as his state is between mystic community and windy individualism. I, from my column, perceive all this. In this state he must live gallantly, associate in friendly reverence with himself, for only he is aristocratic, and the counter-positions are not at all. Man is the lord of counter-positions, they can be only through him, and thus he is more aristocratic than they. More so than death, too aristocratic for death — that is the freedom of his mind. More aristocratic than life, too aristocratic for life, and that is the piety in his heart. There is both rhyme and reason in what I say, I have made a dream poem of humanity. I will cling to it. I will be good. I will let death have no mastery over my thoughts. For therein lies goodness and love of humankind, and in nothing else. Death is a great power. One takes off one's hat before him, and goes weavingly on tiptoe. He wears the stately ruff of the departed and we do him honor in solemn black. Reason stands simple before him, for reason is only virtue, while death is release, immensity, abandon, desire. Desire, says my dream. Lust, not love. Death and love — no, I cannot make a poem of them, they don't go together. Love stands opposed to death. It is love, not reason, that is stronger than death. Only love, not reason, gives sweet thoughts. And from love and sweetness alone can form come: form and civilization, friendly, enlightened, beautiful human intercourse — always in silent recognition of the blood-sacrifice. Ah, yes, it is well and truly dreamed. I have taken stock. I will remember. I will keep faith with death in my heart, yet well remember that faith with death and the dead is evil, is hostile to humankind, so soon as we give it power over thought and action. *For the sake of goodness and love, man shall let death have no sovereignty over his thoughts.* — And with this — I awake. For I have dreamed it out to the end, I have come to my goal. Long, long have I sought after this word, in the place where Hippe appeared to me, in my loggia, everywhere. Deep into the snow mountains my search has led me. Now I have it fast. My dream has given it me,

[1] Man of God.

in utter clearness, that I may know it for ever. Yes, I am in simple raptures, my body is warm, my heart beats high and knows why. It beats not solely on physical grounds, as fingernails grow on a corpse; but humanly, on grounds of my joyful spirits. My dream world was a draught, better than port or ale, it streams through my veins like love and life, I tear myself from my dream and sleep, knowing as I do, perfectly well, that they are highly dangerous to my young life. Up, up! Open your eyes! These are your limbs, your legs here in the snow! Pull yourself together, and up! Look — fair weather!"

The bonds held fast that kept his limbs involved. He had a hard struggle to free himself — but the inner compulsion proved stronger. With a jerk he raised himself on his elbows, briskly drew up his knees, shoved, rolled, wrestled to his feet; stamped with his skis in the snow, flung his arms about his ribs and worked his shoulders violently, all the while casting strained, alert glances about him and above, where now a pale blue sky showed itself between grey-bluish clouds, and these presently drew away to discover a thin sickle of a moon. Early twilight reigned: no snow-fall, no storm. The wall of the opposite mountain, with its shaggy, tree-clad ridge, stretched out before him, plain and peaceful. Shadow lay on half its height, but the upper half was bathed in palest rosy light. How were things in the world? Was it morning? Had he, despite what the books said, lain all night in the snow and not frozen? Not a member was frost-bitten, nothing snapped when he stamped, shook and struck himself, as he did vigorously, all the time seeking to establish the facts of his situation. Ears, toes, finger-tips, were of course numb, but not more so than they had often been at night in his loggia. He could take his watch from his pocket — it was still going, it had not stopped, as it did if he forgot to wind it. It said not yet five — was in fact considerably earlier, twelve, thirteen minutes. Preposterous! Could it be he had lain here in the snow only ten minutes or so, while all these scenes of horror and delight and those presumptuous thoughts had spun themselves in his brain, and the hexagonal hurly vanished as it came? If that were true, then he must be grateful for his good fortune; that is, from the point of view of a safe home-coming. For twice such a turn had come, in his dream and fantasy, as had made him start up — once from horror, and again for rapture. It seemed, indeed, that life meant well by her lone-wandering delicate child.

Be all that as it might, and whether it was morning or afternoon — there could in fact be no doubt that it was still late afternoon — in any case, there was nothing in the circumstances or in his own condition to prevent his going home, which he accordingly did: descending in a fine sweep, as the crow flies, to the valley, where, as he reached it, lights were showing, though his way had been well enough lighted by reflection from the snow. He came down the Brehmenbühl, along the edge of the forest, and was in the Dorf by half past five. He left his skis at the grocer's, rested a little in Herr Settembrini's attic cell, and told him how the storm had overtaken him in the mountains.

The horrified humanist scolded him roundly, and straightway lighted his spirit-kettle to brew coffee for the exhausted one — the strength of which did not prevent Hans Castorp from falling asleep as he sat.

An hour later the highly civilized atmosphere of the Berghof caressed him. He ate enormously at dinner. What he had dreamed was already fading from his mind. What he had thought — even that selfsame evening it was no longer so clear as it had been at first.

Ernest Hemingway · 1899-1961

Ernest Hemingway was born at Oak Park, Illinois, July 21, 1899. The son of a physician practicing in this Chicago suburb, Hemingway was educated in the public schools of the city, where he early gained considerable repute as a football player and a boxer. A portion of his boyhood was spent in northern Michigan, a period recorded somewhat fully in his volume of sketches and stories *In Our Time* (1925).

When Hemingway was about fifteen years old, he ran away from home, and at seventeen he was working as a reporter on the *Kansas City Star*. Before the United States entered World War I, Hemingway drove an ambulance in France, an activity he gave up to enlist as a soldier in the Italian army. Serving at the front, he was wounded, decorated by the Italian government; he then "spent most of the time," according to his own statement, "in hospitals." Returning to the United States after the war, Hemingway found his way to Canada where he was a reporter on the *Toronto Star*. Soon he was back in Europe chronicling the events of the Greek revolution for Canadian readers and, later on, in Paris as a correspondent for the Hearst papers. This period is described in his collection of sketches, *A Moveable Feast*, published posthumously (1964). During the Spanish revolution, Hemingway reported the civil war for American newspapers and subsequently used his experiences as a background for his novel, *For Whom the Bell Tolls* (1940). In his later life, Hemingway maintained an estate in Cuba, a place in Florida, and a home in Ketchum, Idaho. He died on July 2, 1961, of a self-inflicted shotgun wound.

An enthusiastic athlete, hunter, and fisherman — the *Neomerinthe hemingwayi* is a species of rose fish named after him — Hemingway led an active life, hunting big game in Africa, frequenting bullfights in Madrid, working as a war correspondent in Greece and Spain. The nervous action which marked his life distinguishes his literary style. He wrote of the outdoors, of fishing and hunting, of bullfights and war. Indeed, some readers, such as J. B. Priestley who speaks of the author's "swaggering masculinity," protest against this constant activity and find it a pose. Hemingway wrote of "primitive" people in a manner characteristically brutal and straightforward. His characters move through violence. He wrote frequently of love, but in a manner referred to as "hardboiled." His modernism is shown in his realistic, sometimes naturalistic, treatment of subjects which, in the hands of other writers, would likely be turned into romantic stories of adventure. His frank diction, his refusal to end stories happily, his keen regard for the specific detail — these are, however, essentially realistic qualities.

Besides the volumes mentioned above, the author's best known books are *The Sun Also Rises* (1926), *A Farewell to Arms* (1929), *Across the River and into the Trees* (1950), and *The Old Man and the Sea* (1952), for which he received the Nobel Prize for Literature in 1954, and his collections of short stories, *Men Without Women* (1927) and *The Fifth Column and the First Forty-Nine* (1938).

SUGGESTED REFERENCES: John Atkins, *The Art of Ernest Hemingway. His Work and Personality* (rev. ed., 1962); R. P. Weeks, ed., *Hemingway. A Collection of Critical Essays* (1962); C. H. Baker, *Hemingway: The Writer as Artist* (3rd rev. ed., 1963).

The Undefeated [1]

Manual Garcia climbed the stairs to Don Miguel Retana's office. He set down his suitcase and knocked on the door. There was no answer. Manuel, standing in the hallway, felt there was some one in the room. He felt it through the door.

"Retana," he said, listening.

There was no answer.

He's there, all right, Manuel thought.

"Retana," he said and banged the door.

"Who's there?" said some one in the office.

"Me, Manolo," Manuel said.

"What do you want?" asked the voice.

"I want to work," Manuel said.

Something in the door clicked several times and it swung open. Manuel went in, carrying his suit-case.

A little man sat behind a desk at the far side of the room. Over his head was a bull's head, stuffed by a Madrid taxidermist; on the walls were framed photographs and bull-fight posters.

The little man sat looking at Manuel.

"I thought they'd killed you," he said.

Manuel knocked with his knuckles on the desk. The little man sat looking at him across the desk.

"How many corridas [2] you had this year?" Retana asked.

"One," he answered.

"Just that one?" the little man asked.

"That's all."

"I read about it in the papers," Retana said. He leaned back in the chair and looked at Manuel.

Manuel looked up at the stuffed bull. He had seen it often before. He felt a certain family interest in it. It had killed his brother, the promising one, about nine years ago. Manuel remembered the day. There was a brass plate on the oak shield the bull's head was mounted on. Manuel could not read it, but he imagined it was in memory of his brother. Well, he had been a good kid.

The plate said: "The Bull 'Mariposa' of the Duke of Veragua, which accepted 9 varas [3] for 7 caballos, [1] and caused the death of Antonio Garcia, Novillero, April 27, 1909."

Retana saw him looking at the stuffed bull's head.

"The lot the Duke sent me for Sunday will make a scandal," he said. "They're all bad in the legs. What do they say about them at the Café?"

"I don't know," Manuel said. "I just got in."

"Yes," Retana said. "You still have your bag."

He looked at Manuel, leaning back behind the big desk.

"Sit down," he said. "Take off your cap."

Manuel sat down; his cap off, his face was changed. He looked pale, and his coleta [2] pinned forward on his head, so that it would not show under the cap, gave him a strange look.

"You don't look well," Retana said.

"I just got out of the hospital," Manuel said.

"I heard they'd cut your leg off," Retana said.

"No," said Manuel. "It got all right."

Retana leaned forward across the desk and pushed a wooden box of cigarettes toward Manuel.

"Have a cigarette," he said.

"Thanks."

Manuel lit it.

"Smoke?" he said, offering the match to Retana.

"No," Retana waved his hand, "I never smoke."

Retana watched him smoking.

"Why don't you get a job and go to work?" he said.

"I don't want to work," Manuel said. "I am a bull-fighter."

"There aren't any bull-fighters any more," Retana said.

"I'm a bull-fighter," Manuel said.

"Yes, while you're in there," Retana said.

Manuel laughed.

Retana sat, saying nothing and looking at Manuel.

"I'll put you in a nocturnal if you want," Retana offered.

"When?" Manuel asked.

[1] From *Men Without Women*, by Ernest Hemingway. Reprinted by permission of Charles Scribner's Sons.
[2] bullfights.
[3] A pointed shaft used to infuriate the bull.

[1] horses.
[2] A braided pigtail — mark of the bullfighter.

"To-morrow night."

"I don't like to substitute for anybody," Manuel said. That was the way they all got killed. That was the way Salvador got killed. He tapped with his knuckles on the table.

"It's all I've got," Retana said.

"Why don't you put me on next week?" Manuel suggested.

"You wouldn't draw," Retana said. "All they want is Litri and Rubito and La Torre. Those kids are good."

"They'd come to see me get it," Manuel said, hopefully.

"No, they wouldn't. They don't know who you are any more."

"I've got a lot of stuff," Manuel said.

"I'm offering to put you on to-morrow night," Retana said. "You can work with young Hernandez and kill two novillos [1] after the Charlots."

"Whose novillos?" Manuel asked.

"I don't know. Whatever stuff they've got in the corrals. What the veterinaries won't pass in the daytime."

"I don't like to substitute," Manuel said.

"You can take it or leave it," Retana said. He leaned forward over the papers. He was no longer interested. The appeal that Manuel had made to him for a moment when he thought of the old days was gone. He would like to get him to substitute for Larita because he could get him cheaply. He could get others cheaply too. He would like to help him though. Still he had given him the chance. It was up to him.

"How much do I get?" Manuel asked. He was still playing with the idea of refusing. But he knew he could not refuse.

"Two hundred and fifty pesetas," [2] Retana said. He had thought of five hundred, but when he opened his mouth it said two hundred and fifty.

"You pay Villalta seven thousand," Manuel said.

"You're not Villalta," Retana said.

"I know it," Manuel said.

"He draws it, Manolo," Retana said in explanation.

"Sure," said Manuel. He stood up. "Give me three hundred, Retana."

"All right," Retana agreed. He reached in the drawer for a paper.

"Can I have fifty now?" Manuel asked.

"Sure," said Retana. He took a fifty-peseta note out of his pocket-book and laid it, spread out flat, on the table.

Manuel picked it up and put it in his pocket.

"What about a cuadrilla?" [1] he asked.

"There's the boys that always work for me nights," Retana said. "They're all right."

"How about picadors?" [2] Manuel asked.

"They're not much," Retana admitted.

"I've got to have one good pic," [3] Manuel said.

"Get him then," Retana said. "Go and get him."

"Not out of this," Manuel said. "I'm not paying for any cuadrilla out of sixty duros." [4]

Retana said nothing but looked at Manuel across the big desk.

"You know I've got to have one good pic," Manuel said.

Retana said nothing but looked at Manuel from a long way off.

"It isn't right," Manuel said.

Retana was still considering him, leaning back in his chair, considering him from a long way away.

"There're the regular pics," he offered.

"I know," Manuel said. "I know your regular pics."

Retana did not smile. Manuel knew it was over.

"All I want is an even break," Manuel said reasonably. "When I go out there I want to be able to call my shots on the bull. It only takes one good picador."

He was talking to a man who was no longer listening.

"If you want something extra," Retana said, "go and get it. There will be a regular cuadrilla out there. Bring as many of your own pics as you want. The charlotada is over by 10.30."

"All right," Manuel said. "If that's the way you feel about it."

"That's the way," Retana said.

"I'll see you to-morrow night," Manuel said.

"I'll be out there," Retana said.

Manuel picked up his suitcase and went out.

"Shut the door," Retana called.

Manuel looked back. Retana was sitting forward looking at some papers. Manuel pulled the door tight until it clicked.

He went down the stairs and out of the door into the hot brightness of the street. It was very hot in the street and the light on the white buildings was sudden and hard on the eyes. He walked

[1] Bulls not eligible for a formal bullfight.

[2] About twenty cents.

[1] assistant.

[2] An assistant to the matador who "pics" the bull from on horseback.

[3] picador.

[4] A five-peseta coin.

down the shady side of the steep street toward the Puerta del Sol. The shade felt solid and cool as running water. The heat came suddenly as he crossed the intersecting streets. Manuel saw no one he knew in all the people he passed.

Just before the Puerto del Sol he turned into a café.

It was quiet in the café. There were a few men sitting at tables against the wall. At one table four men played cards. Most of the men sat against the wall smoking, empty coffee-cups and liqueur-glasses before them on the tables. Manuel went through the long room to a small room in back. A man sat at a table in the corner asleep. Manuel sat down at one of the tables.

A waiter came in and stood beside Manuel's table.

"Have you seen Zurito?" Manuel asked him.

"He was in before lunch," the waiter answered. "He won't be back before five o'clock."

"Bring me some coffee and milk and a shot of the ordinary," Manuel said.

The waiter came back into the room carrying a tray with a big coffee-glass and a liqueur-glass on it. In his left hand he held a bottle of brandy. He swung these down to the table and a boy who had followed him poured coffee and milk into the glass from two shiny, spouted pots with long handles.

Manuel took off his cap and the waiter noticed his pigtail pinned forward on his head. He winked at the coffee-boy as he poured out the brandy into the little glass beside Manuel's coffee. The coffee-boy looked at Manuel's pale face curiously.

"You fighting here?" asked the waiter, corking up the bottle.

"Yes," Manuel said. "To-morrow."

The waiter stood there, holding the bottle on one hip.

"You in the Charlie Chaplins?" he asked.

The coffee-boy looked away, embarrassed.

"No. In the ordinary."

"I thought they were going to have Chaves and Hernandez," the waiter said.

"No. Me and another."

"Who? Chaves or Hernandez?"

"Hernandez, I think."

"What's the matter with Chaves?"

"He got hurt."

"Where did you hear that?"

"Retana."

"Hey, Looie," the waiter called to the next room, "Chaves got cogida."[1]

Manuel had taken the wrapper off the lumps of sugar and dropped them into his coffee. He

[1] Tossed by a bull.

stirred it and drank it down, sweet, hot, and warming in his empty stomach. He drank off the brandy.

"Give me another shot of that," he said to the waiter.

The waiter uncorked the bottle and poured the glass full, slopping another drink into the saucer. Another waiter had come up in front of the table. The coffee-boy was gone.

"Is Chaves hurt bad?" the second waiter asked Manuel.

"I don't know," Manuel said, "Retana didn't say."

"A hell of a lot he cares," the tall waiter said. Manuel had not seen him before. He must have just come up.

"If you stand in with Retana in this town, you're a made man," the tall waiter said. "If you aren't in with him, you might just as well go out and shoot yourself."

"You said it," the other waiter who had come in said. "You said it then."

"You're right I said it," said the tall waiter. "I know what I'm talking about when I talk about that bird."

"Look what he's done for Villalta," the first waiter said.

"And that ain't all," the tall waiter said. "Look what he's done for Marcial Lalanda. Look what he's done for Nacional."

"You said it, kid," agreed the short waiter.

Manuel looked at them, standing talking in front of his table. He had drunk his second brandy. They had forgotten about him. They were not interested in him.

"Look at that bunch of camels," the tall waiter went on. "Did you ever see this Nacional II?"

"I seen him last Sunday didn't I?" the original waiter said.

"He's a giraffe," the short waiter said.

"What did I tell you?" the tall waiter said. "Those are Retana's boys."

"Say, give me another shot of that," Manuel said. He had poured the brandy the waiter had slopped over in the saucer into his glass and drank it while they were talking.

The original waiter poured his glass full mechanically, and the three of them went out of the room talking.

In the far corner the man was still asleep, snoring slightly on the intaking breath, his head back against the wall.

Manuel drank his brandy. He felt sleepy himself. It was too hot to go out into the town. Besides there was nothing to do. He wanted to see Zurito. He would go to sleep while he waited.

He kicked his suitcase under the table to be sure it was there. Perhaps it would be better to put it back under the seat, against the wall. He leaned down and shoved it under. Then he leaned forward on the table and went to sleep.

When he woke there was some one sitting across the table from him. It was a big man with a heavy brown face like an Indian. He had been sitting there some time. He had waved the waiter away and sat reading the paper and occasionally looking down at Manuel, asleep, his head on the table. He read the paper laboriously, forming the words with his lips as he read. When it tired him he looked at Manuel. He sat heavily in the chair, his black Cordoba hat tipped forward.

Manuel sat up and looked at him.

"Hello, Zurito," he said.

"Hello, kid," the big man said.

"I've been asleep." Manuel rubbed his forehead with the back of his fist.

"I thought maybe you were."

"How's everything?"

"Good. How is everything with you?"

"Not so good."

They were both silent. Zurito, the picador, looked at Manuel's white face. Manuel looked down at the picador's enormous hands folding the paper to put away in his pocket.

"I got a favor to ask you, Manos," Manuel said.

Manosduros was Zurito's nickname. He never heard it without thinking of his huge hands. He put them forward on the table self-consciously.

"Let's have a drink," he said.

"Sure," said Manuel.

The waiter came and went and came again. He went out of the room looking back at the two men at the table.

"What's the matter, Manolo?" Zurito set down his glass.

"Would you pic two bulls for me to-morrow night?" Manuel asked, looking up at Zurito across the table.

"No," said Zurito. "I'm not pic-ing."

Manuel looked down at his glass. He had expected that answer; now he had it. Well, he had it.

"I'm sorry, Manolo, but I'm not pic-ing." Zurito looked at his hands.

"That's all right," Manuel said.

"I'm too old," Zurito said.

"I just asked you," Manuel said.

"Is it the nocturnal to-morrow?"

"That's it. I figured if I had just one good pic, I could get away with it."

"How much are you getting?"

"Three hundred pesetas."

"I get more than that for pic-ing."

"I know," said Manuel. "I didn't have any right to ask you."

"What do you keep on doing it for?" Zurito asked. "Why don't you cut off your coleta, Manolo?"

"I don't know," Manuel said.

"You're pretty near as old as I am," Zurito said.

"I don't know," Manuel said. "I got to do it. If I can fix it so that I get an even break, that's all I want. I got to stick with it, Manos."

"No, you don't."

"Yes, I do. I've tried keeping away from it."

"I know how you feel. But it isn't right. You ought to get out and stay out."

"I can't do it. Besides, I've been going good lately."

Zurito looked at his face.

"You've been in the hospital."

"But I was going great when I got hurt."

Zurito said nothing. He tipped the cognac out of his saucer into his glass.

"The papers said they never saw a better faena,"[1] Manuel said.

Zurito looked at him.

"You know when I get going I'm good," Manuel said.

"You're too old," the picador said.

"No," said Manuel. "You're ten years older than I am."

"With me it's different."

"I'm not too old," Manuel said.

They sat silent, Manuel watching the picador's face.

"I was going great till I got hurt," Manuel offered.

"You ought to have seen me, Manos," Manuel said, reproachfully.

"I don't want to see you," Zurito said. "It makes me nervous."

"You haven't seen me lately."

"I've seen you plenty."

Zurito looked at Manuel, avoiding his eyes.

"You ought to quit it, Manolo."

"I can't," Manuel said. "I'm going good now, I tell you."

Zurito leaned forward, his hands on the table.

"Listen. I'll pic for you and if you don't go big to-morrow night, you'll quit. See? Will you do that?"

"Sure."

Zurito leaned back, relieved.

"You got to quit," he said. "No monkey business. You got to cut the coleta."

[1] Loosely, "performance."

(continued on page 1067)

The Realistic Temper

FIRST GROUP: REALISM AND NATURALISM

REALISTIC ART like realistic literature is by no means confined to a definite period of history. Whatever art seeks faithfully to reproduce life and the human character is called realistic. Realism in art is distinguished from classicism by its renunciation of rigid outline and symmetrical structure (cf. *Dr. Tulp's Anatomy Lesson*) and from romanticism by its concern with reality rather than with ideas or myths (*Los Borrachos*). It is centered in man and his personality and concerned with the man-made universe. Realism, humanistic in its modern form, sprang up in the humanistic age of the Renaissance and is closely connected with the development of the concepts of democracy and human rights.

Nineteenth-century realism was mainly concerned with the world of craftsmen, laborers or peasants (*Man with the Hoe, The Fog Warning, The Haymakers*) and with the faithful photographic reproduction of natural scenes (*Turning the Stake Boat, The Stag's Thicket*). This is not true, however, for the earlier realists. These were frequently employed by kings and princes (*Las Meniñas*), or had for patrons noblemen (*Nicolo da Uzzano*), merchants (*Georg Gisze*), guilds and distinguished citizens (*Jean Arnolfini*). In the commissioned portraits, the person depicted was often surrounded by the emblems of his profession (the coins and scales in the *Portrait of Georg Gisze*). At the same time, other realistic painters invented idyllic and picturesque scenes of low life (*Los Borrachos*).

Naturalism is not, as is often maintained, a mere continuation and intensification of realism — an even greater concern with material details, that is, — but is distinguished from it by its emphasis on man's environment over man's proper existence (*The Haymakers*). The naturalistic painters like to reproduce landscapes, and impressionism (see Second Group) arises in reaction to their manner of painting. A similar relation can be established between realism and expressionism (see Second Group): where the realists are content with showing the portrait, the physiognomy of an individual, in which its character may or may not be inscribed, the expressionists attempt to reveal what is behind the face, which for them is only a mask or the frozen image of the living soul. Being less concerned with the chronology of modern art (i.e., the sequence of realism, naturalism, impressionism, expressionism) we suggest for discussion the following equation: naturalism is to impressionism what realism is to expressionism.

Plate 31   PORTRAIT OF GEORG GISZE   *Holbein*

Plate 32   THE ESCAPED COW   *Dupré*

Plate 33   MAN WITH THE HOE   *Millet*

Plate 34   ÆSOP   *Velasquez*

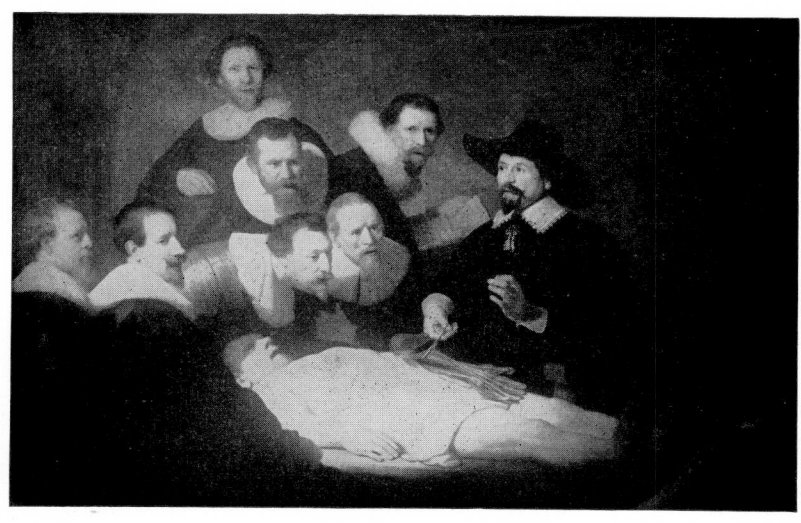

Plate 35   DR. TULP'S ANATOMY LESSON   *Rembrandt*

Plate 36   THE FOG WARNING   Homer

Plate 37   JEAN ARNOLFINI AND HIS WIFE   Van Eyck

Plate 38   LAS MENIÑAS   *Velasquez*

Plate 39   TURNING THE STAKE BOAT   *Eakins*

Plate 40   THE STAG'S THICKET   *Courbet*

Plate 41   THE HAYMAKERS   *Bastien-Lepage*

Plate 42   LOS BORRACHOS (THE TOPERS)   *Velasquez*

Plate 43   NICCOLÒ DA UZZANO   *Donatello*

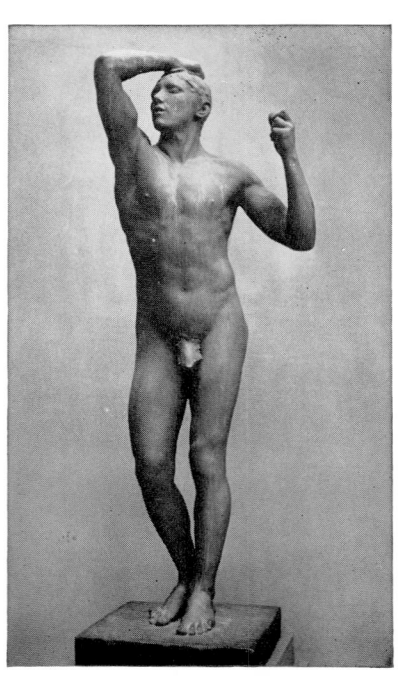

Plate 44   AGE OF BRONZE   *Rodin*

"I won't have to quit, Manuel said. "You watch me. I've got the st."

Zurito stood up. He retired from arguing.

"You got to quit," he said. "I'll cut your coleta myself."

"No, you won't," Man said. "You won't have a chance."

Zurito called the waiter

"Come on," said Zurit "Come on up to the house."

Manuel reached under seat for his suitcase. He was happy. He kn Zurito would pic for him. He was the best p or living. It was all simple now.

"Come on up to the h and we'll eat," Zurito said.

Manuel stood in the o de caballos waiting for the Charlie Chaplins be over. Zurito stood beside him. Where the od it was dark. The high door that led int e bull-ring was shut. Above them they hear shout, then another shout of laughter. 1 there was silence. Manuel liked the smell the stables about the patio de caballos. It lt good in the dark. There was another roa m the arena and then applause, prolonged ap se, going on and on.

"You ever seen the llows?" Zurito asked, big and looming beside uel in the dark.

"No," Manuel said.

"They're pretty fu" Zurito said. He smiled to himself in th k.

The high, double, -fitting door into the bull-ring swung open Manuel saw the ring in the hard light of the a hts, the plaza, dark all the way around, rising; around the edge of the ring were running and ng two men dressed like tramps, followed by d in the uniform of a hotel bellboy who st and picked up hats and canes thrown do to the sand and tossed them back up into th ness.

The electric light n in the patio.

"I'll climb onto o those ponies while you collect the kids," Zur d.

Behind them came ngle of the mules, coming out to go into th a and be hitched onto the dead bull.

The members of adrilla, who had been watching the burles om the runway between the barrera 1 and the came walking back and stood in a group ta under the electric light in the patio. A go ing lad in a silver-and-orange suit came up anuel and smiled.

"I'm Hernandez, id and put out his hand.

Manuel shook it.

1 Fence surroundin ullfight arena or ring.

"They're regular elephants we've got to-night," the boy said cheerfully.

"They're big ones with horns," Manuel agreed.

"You drew the worst lot," the boy said.

"That's all right," Manuel said. "The bigger they are, the more meat for the poor."

"Where did you get that one?" Hernandez grinned.

"That's an old one," Manuel said. "You line up your cuadrilla, so I can see what I've got."

"You've got some good kids," Hernandez said. He was very cheerful. He had been on twice before in nocturnals and was beginning to get a following in Madrid. He was happy the fight would start in a few minutes.

"Where are the pics?" Manuel asked.

"They're back in the corrals fighting about who gets the beautiful horses," Hernandez grinned.

The mules came through the gate in a rush, the whips snapping, bells jangling and the young bull ploughing a furrow of sand.

They formed up for the paseo 1 as soon as the bull had gone through.

Manuel and Hernandez stood in front. The youths of the cuadrillas were behind, their heavy capes furled over their arms. In back, the four picadors, mounted, holding their steel-tipped push-poles erect in the half-dark of the corral.

"It's a wonder Retana wouldn't give us enough light to see the horses by," one picador said.

"He knows we'll be happier if we don't get too good a look at these skins," 2 another pic answered.

"This thing I'm on barely keeps me off the ground," the first picador said.

"Well, they're horses."

"Sure, they're horses."

They talked, sitting their gaunt horses in the dark.

Zurito said nothing. He had the only steady horse of the lot. He had tried him, wheeling him in the corrals, and he responded to the bit and the spurs. He had taken the bandage off his right eye and cut the strings where they had tied his ears tight shut at the base. He was a good, solid horse, solid on his legs. That was all he needed. He intended to ride him all through the corrida. He had already, since he had mounted, sitting in the half-dark in the big, quilted saddle, waiting for the paseo, pic-ed through the whole corrida in his mind. The other picadors went on talking on both sides of him. He did not hear them.

The two matadors stood together in front of

1 Formal entry.
2 Low-grade horses.

their three peones,[1] their capes furled over their left arms in the same fashion. Manuel was thinking about the three lads in back of him. They were all three Madrilenos, like Hernandez, boys about nineteen. One of them, a gypsy, serious, aloof, and dark-faced, he liked the look of. He turned.

"What's your name, kid?" he asked the gypsy.

"Fuentes," the gypsy said.

"That's a good name," Manuel said.

The gypsy smiled, showing his teeth.

"You take the bull and give him a little run when he comes out," Manuel said.

"All right," the gypsy said. His face was serious. He began to think about just what he would do.

"Here she goes," Manuel said to Hernandez.

"All right. We'll go."

Heads up, swinging with the music, their right arms swinging free, they stepped out, crossing the sanded arena under the arc-lights, the cuadrillas opening out behind, the picadors riding after; behind came the bull-ring servants and the jingling mules. The crowd applauded Hernandez as they marched across the arena. Arrogant, swinging, they looked straight ahead as they marched.

They bowed before the president, and the procession broke up into its component parts. The bull-fighters went over to the barrera and changed their heavy mantles for the light fighting capes. The mules went out. The picadors galloped jerkily around the ring, and two rode out the gate they had come in by. The servants swept the sand smooth.

Manuel drank a glass of water poured for him by one of Retana's deputies, who was acting as his manager and sword-handler. Hernandez came over from speaking with his own manager.

"You got a good hand, kid," Manuel complimented him.

"They like me," Hernandez said happily.

"How did the paseo go?" Manuel asked Retana's man.

"Like a wedding," said the handler. "Fine. You came out like Joselito and Belmonte."

Zurito rode by, a bulky equestrian statue. He wheeled his horse and faced him toward the toril[2] on the far side of the ring where the bull would come out. It was strange under the arc-light. He pic-ed in the hot afternoon sun for big money. He didn't like this arc-light business. He wished they would get started.

Manuel went up to him.

"Pic him, Manos," he said. "Cut him down to size for me."

[1] A fighter who works on foot, assistant to a matador.
[2] Enclosure from which the bull enters the ring.

"I'll pic him, ki'" Zurito spat on the sand. "I'll make him jum out of the ring."

"Lean on him, Mos," Manuel said.

"I'll lean on him Zurito said. "What's holding it up?"

"He's coming no' Manuel said.

Zurito sat there, feet in the box-stirrups, his great legs in the buk in-covered armor gripping the horse, the reins his left hand, the long pic held in his right h, his broad hat well down over his eyes to sha hem from the lights, watching the distant door the toril. His horse's ears quivered. Zurito p d him with his left hand.

The red door of toril swung back and for a moment Zurito look into the empty passageway far across the arena. hen the bull came out in a rush, skidding on his legs as he came out under the lights, then cha in a gallop, moving softly in a fast gallop, sile cept as he woofed through wide nostrils as he ged, glad to be free after the dark pen.

In the first row o ts, slightly bored, leaning forward to write on cement wall in front of his knees, the substitut llfight critic of El Heraldo scribbled: "Campag , Negro, 42, came out at 90 miles an hour wi enty of gas——"

Manuel, leaning st the barrera, watching the bull, waved his and the gypsy ran out, trailing his cape. ull, in full gallop, pivoted and charged the cap head down, his tail rising. The gypsy moved in zag, and as he passed, the bull caught sight of and abandoned the cape to charge the man. gyp sprinted and vaulted the red fence of the era as the bull struck it with his horns. H ed into it twice with his horns, banging into ood blindly.

The critic of El He lit a cigarette and tossed the match at the bu n wrote in his note-book, "large and with eno orns to satisfy the cash customers, Campag owed a tendency to cut into the terrane[1] of ll-fighters."

Manuel stepped o he hard sand as the bull banged into the fenc t of the corner of his eye he saw Zurito sittin white horse close to the barrera, about a qu of the way around the ring to the left. M held the cape close in front of him, a fold h hand, and shouted at the bull. "Huh! !" The bull turned, seemed to brace aga fence as he charged in a scramble, driving ie cape as Manuel sidestepped, pivoted on els with the charge of the bull, and swung ape just ahead of the horns. At the end wing he was facing the bull again and held be in the same position close in front of his b d pivoted again as the

[1] "terrain" or territo

bull recharged. Each ti as he swung, the crowd shouted.

Four times he swung w the bull, lifting the cape so it billowed full, an ch time bringing the bull around to charge agai Then, at the end of the fifth swing, he held t cape against his hip and pivoted, so the cape ing out like a ballet dancer's skirt and wound bull around himself like a belt, to step clear, ving the bull facing Zurito on the white hors ome up and planted firm, the horse facing the l, its ears forward, its lips nervous, Zurito, his over his eyes, leaning forward, the long pole sti g out before and behind in a sharp angle u his right arm, held half-way down, the triang iron point facing the bull.

El Heraldo's second-str critic, drawing on his cigarette, his eyes on the , wrote: "the veteran Manolo designed a series acceptable veronicas,[1] ending in a very Belmon recorte[2] that earned applause from the regula nd we entered the tercio of the cavalry."

Zurito sat his horse, n ring the distance between the bull and the en the pic. As he looked, the bull gathered hims ogether and charged, his eyes on the horse's t. As he lowered his head to hook, Zurito su he point of the pic in the swelling hump of scle above the bull's shoulder, leaned all his ght on the shaft, and with his left hand pull e white horse into the air, front hoofs pawing, swung him to the right as he pushed the bull r and through so the horns passed safely un horse's belly and the horse came down, quiv the bull's tail brushing his chest as he charged cape Hernandez offered him.

Hernandez ran side, taking the bull out and away with the cap ward the other picador. He fixed him with a of the cape, squarely facing the horse and nd stepped back. As the bull saw the hors harged. The picador's lance slid along his b nd as the shock of the charge lifted the hor e picador was already half-way out of the le, lifting his right leg clear as he missed wi lance and falling to the left side to keep the between him and the bull. The horse, li nd gored, crashed over with the bull driving him, the picador gave a shove with his boo inst the horse and lay clear, waiting to be and hauled away and put on his feet.

Manuel let the b ve into the fallen horse; he was in no hurry, icador was safe; besides, it did a picador li good to worry. He'd

[1] Gestures with the
[2] A movement whi s the bull quickly.

stay on longer next time. Lousy pics! He looked across the sand at Zurito a little way out from the barrera, his horse rigid, waiting.

"Huh!" he called to the bull, "Tomar!"[1] holding the cape in both hands so it would catch his eye. The bull detached himself from the horse and charged the cape, and Manuel, running sideways and holding the cape spread wide, stopped, swung on his heels, and brought the bull sharply around facing Zurito.

"Campagnero accepted a pair of varas for the death of one rosinante, with Hernandez and Manolo at the quites,"[2] *El Heraldo's* critic wrote. "He pressed on the iron and clearly showed he was no horse-lover. The veteran Zurito resurrected some of his old stuff with the pike-pole, notably the suerte [3]——"

"Olé! Olé!" the man sitting beside him shouted. The shout was lost in the roar of the crowd, and he slapped the critic on the back. The critic looked up to see Zurito, directly below him, leaning far out over his horse, the length of the pic rising in a sharp angle under his armpit, holding the pic almost by the point, bearing down with all his weight, holding the bull off, the bull pushing and driving to get at the horse, and Zurito, far out, on top of him, holding him, holding him, and slowly pivoting the horse against the pressure, so that at last he was clear. Zurito felt the moment when the horse was clear and the bull could come past, and relaxed the absolute steel lock of his resistance, and the triangular steel point of the pic ripped in the bull's hump of shoulder muscle as he tore loose to find Hernandez's cape before his muzzle. He charged blindly into the cape and the boy took him out into the open arena.

Zurito sat patting his horse and looking at the bull charging the cape that Hernandez swung for him out under the bright light while the crowd shouted.

"You see that one?" he said to Manuel.

"It was a wonder," Manuel said.

"I got him that time," Zurito said. "Look at him now."

At the conclusion of a closely turned pass of the cape the bull slid to his knees. He was up at once, but far out across the sand Manuel and Zurito saw the shine of the pumping flow of blood, smooth against the black of the bull's shoulder.

"I got him that time," Zurito said.

"He's a good bull," Manuel said.

[1] "Take!"
[2] "taking away" — movements by which the fighters "take away" the bull from a fellow fighter in trouble.
[3] A conventional movement in a fight.

"If they gave me another shot at him, I'd kill him," Zurito said.

"They'll change the thirds on us," Manuel said.

"Look at him now," Zurito said.

"I got to go over there," Manuel said, and started on a run for the other side of the ring, where the monos[1] were leading a horse out by the bridle toward the bull, whacking him on the legs with rods and all, in a procession, trying to get him toward the bull, who stood, dropping his head, pawing, unable to make up his mind to charge.

Zurito, sitting his horse, walking him toward the scene, not missing any detail, scowled.

Finally the bull charged, the horse leaders ran for the barrera, the picador hit too far back, and the bull got under the horse, lifted him, threw him onto his back.

Zurito watched. The monos, in their red shirts, running out to drag the picador clear. The picador, now on his feet, swearing and flopping his arms. Manuel and Hernandez standing ready with their capes. And the bull, the great, black bull, with a horse on his back, hooves dangling, the bridle caught in the horns. Black bull with a horse on his back, staggering short-legged, then arching his neck and lifting, thrusting, charging to slide the horse off, horse sliding down. Then the bull into a lunging charge at the cape Manuel spread for him.

The bull was slower now, Manuel felt. He was bleeding badly. There was a sheen of blood all down his flank.

Manuel offered him the cape again. There he came, eyes open, ugly, watching the cape. Manuel stepped to the side and raised his arms, tightening the cape ahead of the bull for the veronica.

Now he was facing the bull. Yes, his head was going down a little. He was carrying it lower. That was Zurito.

Manuel flopped the cape; there he comes; he side-stepped and swung in another veronica. He's shooting awfully accurately, he thought. He's had enough fight, so he's watching now. He's hunting now. Got his eye on me. But I always give him the cape.

He shook the cape at the bull; there he comes; he side-stepped. Awful close that time. I don't want to work that close to him.

The edge of the cape was wet with blood where it had swept along the bull's back as he went by.

All right, here's the last one.

Manuel, facing the bull, having turned with him each charge, offered the cape with his two hands. The bull looked at him. Eyes watching, horns straight forward, the bull looked at him, watching.

[1] servants.

"Huh!" Manuel said, "Toro!"[1] and leaning back, swung the ſe forward. Here he comes. He side-stepped, ſng the cape in back of him, and pivoted, so the bull followed a swirl of cape and then was left ſh nothing, fixed by the pass, dominated by the ſe. Manuel swung the cape under his muzzle ſ one hand, to show the bull was fixed, and walſ away.

There was no aſuse.

Manuel walked ſss the sand toward the barrera, while Zurito ſde out of the ring. The trumpet had blown ſhange the act to the planting of the banderillos ſe Manuel had been working with the bull. He ſ not consciously noticed it. The monos were ſding canvas over the two dead horses and spſling sawdust around them.

Manuel came uſ the barrera for a drink of water. Retana's ſ handed him the heavy porous jug.

Fuentes, the tallſsy, was standing holding a pair of banderillos,ſlding them together, slim, red sticks, fish-hoſoints out. He looked at Manuel.

"Go on out therſ Manuel said.

The gypsy trottſt. Manuel set down the jug and watched. ſ wiped his face with his handkerchief.

The critic of *El Hſo* reached for the bottle of warm champagne tſood between his feet, took a drink, and finisheſ paragraph.

"—— the aged Nſo rated no applause for a vulgar series of lanſith the cape and we entered the third of tſings."

Alone in the centſ the ring the bull stood, still fixed. Fuentſll, flat-backed, walking toward him arrogaſhis arms spread out, the two slim, red sticks,ſn each hand, held by the fingers, points straiſrward. Fuentes walked forward. Back of hſd to one side was a peon with a cape. The ſoked at him and was no longer fixed.

His eyes watchedſtes, now standing still. Now he leaned baſlling to him. Fuentes twitched the two baſos and the light on the steel points caught tſl's eye.

His tail went up aſcharged.

He came straight,ſs on the man. Fuentes stood still, leaning bſhe banderillos pointing forward. As the buſered his head to hook, Fuentes leaned backſhis arms came together and rose, his two haſuching, the banderillos two descending red ſand leaning forward drove the points intoſull's shoulder, leaning

[1] bull.

[2] Long, sharp-pointeſ used to pierce the bull's hide.

far in over the bull's horns apivoting on the two upright sticks, his legs tig together, his body curving to one side to let tbull pass.

"Olé!" from the crowd.

The bull was hooking ily, jumping like a trout, all four feet off the grd. The red shaft of the banderillos tossed as hmped.

Manuel standing at the tera, noticed that he hooked always to the righ

"Tell him to drop the neair on the right," he said to the kid who starter run out to Fuentes with the new banderillos.

A heavy hand fell on shoulder. It was Zurito.

"How do you feel, kid?: asked.

Manuel was watching t'ull.

Zurito leaned forward or barrera, leaning the weight of his body on his ;. Manuel turned to him.

"You're going good," 7o said.

Manuel shook his headle had nothing to do now until the next thirdThe gypsy was very good with the banderillosne bull would come to him in the next third in gchape. He was a good bull. It had all been eap to now. The final stuff with the sword wasne worried over. He did not really worry. H not even think about it. But standing thereiad a heavy sense of apprehension. He lookut at the bull, planning his faena, his work the red cloth that was to reduce the bull, to mim manageable.

The gypsy was wallout toward the bull again, walking heel-andnsultingly, like a ballroom dancer, the redts of the banderillos twitching with his wallhe bull watched him, not fixed now, huntinl, but waiting to get close enough so he cot sure of getting him, getting the horns into

As Fuentes walkedard the bull charged. Fuentes ran across thrter of a circle as the bull charged and, as hed running backward, stopped, swung forwose on his toes, arms straight out, and sue banderillos straight down into the tight ohig shoulder muscles as the bull missed him.

The crowd were wiut it.

"That kid won't s this night stuff long," Retana's man said too.

"He's good," Zuri.

"Watch him now.'

They watched.

Fuentes was standth his back against the barrera. Two of thrilla were back of him, with their capes rei flop over the fence to distract the bull.

1 A bullfight is divie three "acts."

The bull, with his tongue out, his barrel heaving, was watching the gypsy. He thought he had him now. Back against the red planks. Only a short charge away. The bull watched him.

The gypsy bent back, drew back his arms, the banderillos pointing at the bull. He called to the bull, stamped one foot. The bull was suspicious. He wanted the man. No more barbs in the shoulder.

Fuentes walked a little closer to the bull. Bent back. Called again. Somebody in the crowd shouted a warning.

"He's too damn close," Zurito said.

"Watch him," Retana's man said.

Leaning back, inciting the bull with the banderillos, Fuentes jumped, both feet off the ground. As he jumped the bull's tail rose and he charged. Fuentes came down on his toes, arms straight out, whole body arching forward, and drove the shafts straight down as he swung his body clear of the right horn.

The bull crashed into the barrera where the flopping capes had attracted his eye as he lost the man.

The gypsy came running along the barrera toward Manuel, taking the applause of the crowd. His vest was ripped where he had not quite cleared the point of the horn. He was happy about it, showing it to the spectators. He made the tour of the ring. Zurito saw him go by, smiling, pointing at his vest. He smiled.

Somebody else was planting the last pair of banderillos. Nobody was paying any attention.

Retana's man tucked a baton inside the red cloth of a muleta,1 folded the cloth over it, and handed it over the barrera to Manuel. He reached in the leather sword-case, took out a sword, and holding it by its leather scabbard, reached it over the fence to Manuel. Manuel pulled the blade out by the red hilt and the scabbard fell limp.

He looked at Zurito. The big man saw he was sweating.

"Now you get him, kid," Zurito said.

Manuel nodded.

"He's in good shape," Zurito said.

"Just like you want him," Retana's man assured him.

Manuel nodded.

The trumpeter, up under the roof, blew for the final act, and Manuel walked across the arena toward where, up in the dark boxes, the president must be.

In the front row of seats the substitute bullfight critic of El Heraldo took a long drink of the warm

1 Cloth on stick used to defend the fighter and to control the bull.

champagne. He had decided it was not worth while to write a running story and would write up the corrida back in the office. What the hell was it anyway? Only a nocturnal. If he missed anything he would get it out of the morning papers. He took another drink of the champagne. He had a date at Maxim's at twelve. Who were these bullfighters anyway? Kids and bums. A bunch of bums. He put his pad of paper in his pocket and looked over toward Manuel, standing very much alone in the ring, gesturing with his hat in a salute toward a box he could not see high up in the dark plaza. Out in the ring the bull stood quiet, looking at nothing.

"I dedicate this bull to you, Mr. President, and to the public of Madrid, the most intelligent and generous of the world," was what Manuel was saying. It was a formula. He said it all. It was a little long for nocturnal use.

He bowed at the dark, straightened, tossed his hat over his shoulder, and, carrying the muleta in his left hand and the sword in his right, walked out toward the bull.

Manuel walked toward the bull. The bull looked at him; his eyes were quick. Manuel noticed the way the banderillos hung down on his left shoulder and the steady sheen of blood from Zurito's pic-ing. He noticed the way the bull's feet were. As he walked forward, holding the muleta in his left hand and the sword in his right, he watched the bull's feet. The bull could not charge without gathering his feet together. Now he stood square on them, dully.

Manuel walked toward him, watching his feet. This was all right. He could do this. He must work to get the bull's head down, so he could go in past the horns and kill him. He did not think about the sword, not about killing the bull. He thought about one thing at a time. The coming things oppressed him, though. Walking forward, watching the bull's feet, he saw successively his eyes, his wet muzzle, and the wide, forward-pointing spread of his horns. The bull had light circles about his eyes. His eyes watched Manuel. He felt he was going to get this little one with the white face.

Standing still now and spreading the red cloth of the muleta with the sword, pricking the point into the cloth so that the sword, now held in his left hand, spread the red flannel like the jib of a boat, Manuel noticed the points of the bull's horns. One of them was splintered from banging against the barrera. The other was sharp as a porcupine quill. Manuel noticed while spreading the muleta that the white base of the horn was stained red. While he noticed these things he did not lose sight

of the bull's feet. The bull watched Manuel steadily.

He's on the defensive now, Manuel thought. He's reserving himself. I've got to bring him out of that and get his head down. Always get his head down. Zurito had his head down once, but he's come back. He'll bleed when I start him going and that will bring it down.

Holding the muleta, with the sword in his left hand widening it in front of him, he called to the bull.

The bull looked at him.

He leaned back insultingly and shook the wide-spread flannel.

The bull saw the muleta. It was a bright scarlet under the arc-light. The bull's legs tightened.

Here he comes. Whoosh! Manuel turned as the bull came and raised the muleta so that it passed over the bull's horns and swept down his broad back from head to tail. The bull had gone clean up in the air with the charge. Manuel had not moved.

At the end of the pass the bull turned like a cat coming around a corner and faced Manuel.

He was on the offensive again. His heaviness was gone. Manuel noticed the fresh blood shining down the black shoulder and dripping down the bull's leg. He drew the sword out of the muleta and held it in his right hand. The muleta held low down in his left hand, leaning toward the left, he called to the bull. The bull's legs tightened, his eyes on the muleta. Here he comes, Manuel thought. Yuh!

He swung with the charge, sweeping the muleta ahead of the bull, his feet firm, the sword following the curve, a point of light under the arcs.

The bull recharged as the pase natural [1] finished and Manuel raised the muleta for a pase de pecho. Firmly planted, the bull came by his chest under the raised muleta. Manuel leaned his head back to avoid the clattering banderillo shafts. The hot, black bull body touched his chest as it passed.

Too damn close, Manuel thought. Zurito, leaning on the barrera, said rapidly to the gypsy, who trotted out toward Manuel with a cape. Zurito pulled his hat down and looked out across the arena at Manuel.

Manuel was facing the bull again, the muleta held low and to the left. The bull's head was down as he watched the muleta.

"If it was Belmonte doing that stuff, they'd go crazy," Retana's man said.

Zurito said nothing. He was watching Manuel out in the centre of the arena.

[1] A technical movement made with the cape.

"Where did the boss digs fellow up?" Retana's man asked.

"Out of the hospital," Zu said.

"That's where he's going in quick," Retana's man said.

Zurito turned on him.

"Knock on that," he sa pointing to the barrera.

"I was just kidding, ma Retana's man said.

"Knock on the wood."

Retana's man leaned ford and knocked three times on the barrera.

"Watch the faena," Zur said.

Out in the centre of the g, under the lights, Manuel was kneeling, fac the bull, and as he raised the muleta in both ds the bull charged, tail up.

Manuel swung his body r and, as the bull recharged, brought around muleta in a half-circle that pulled the bull is knees.

"Why, that one's a grea ll-fighter," Retana's man said.

"No, he's not," said Zu

Manuel stood up and muleta in his left hand, the sword in his :, acknowledged the applause from the dark p

The bull had humped elf up from his knees and stood waiting, his h ung low.

Zurito spoke to two ie other lads of the cuadrilla and they ran out and back of Manuel with their capes. There re four men back of him now. Hernandez bllowed him since he first came out with the leta. Fuentes stood watching, his cape held nst his body, tall, in repose, watching lazy-e Now the two came up. Hernandez motio hem to stand one at each side. Manuel sto ne, facing the bull.

Manuel waved back men with the capes. Stepping back cautiou hey saw his face was white and sweating.

Didn't they know e to keep back? Did they want to catch th's eye with the capes after he was fixed and'? He had enough to worry about without ind of thing.

The bull was stan his four feet square, looking at the muleta. nuel furled the muleta in his left hand. The eyes watched it. His body was heavy on h. He carried his head low, but not too low.

Manuel lifted the at him. The bull did not move. Only his vatched.

He's all lead, Man ught. He's all square. He's framed right. ake it.

He thought in bu terms. Sometimes he had a thought and articular piece of slang would not come in mind and he could not

realize the thought. His instincts and his knowledge worked automatically, and his brain worked slowly and in words. He knew all about bulls. He did not have to think about them. He just did the right thing. His eyes noted things and his body performed the necessary measures without thought. If he thought about it, he would be gone.

Now, facing the bull, he was conscious of many things at the same time. There were the horns, the one splintered, the other smoothly sharp, the need to profile himself toward the left horn, lance himself short and straight, lower the muleta so the bull would follow it, and, going in over the horns, put the sword all the way into a little spot about as big as a five-peseta piece straight in back of the neck, between the sharp pitch of the bull's shoulders. He must do all this and must then come out from between the horns. He was conscious he must do all this, but his only thought was in words: "Corto y derecho."

"Corto y derecho," he thought, furling the muleta. Short and straight. Corto y derecho, he drew the sword out of the muleta, profiled on the splintered left horn, dropped the muleta across his body, so his right hand with the sword on the level with his eye made the sign of the cross, and, rising on his toes, sighted along the dipping blade of the sword at the spot high up between the bull's shoulders.

Corto y derecho he lanced himself on the bull.

There was a shock, and he felt himself go up in the air. He pushed on the sword as he went up and over, and it flew out of his hand. He hit the ground and the bull was on him. Manuel, lying on the ground, kicked at the bull's muzzle with his slippered feet. Kicking, kicking, the bull after him, missing him in his excitement, bumping him with his head, driving the horns into the sand. Kicking like a man keeping a ball in the air, Manuel kept the bull from getting a clean thrust at him.

Manuel felt the wind on his back from the capes flopping at the bull, and then the bull was gone, gone over him in a rush. Dark, as his belly went over. Not even stepped on.

Manuel stood up and picked up the muleta. Fuentes handed him the sword. It was bent where it had struck the shoulder-blade. Manuel straightened it on his knee and ran toward the bull, standing now beside one of the dead horses. As he ran, his jacket flopped where it had been ripped under his armpit.

"Get him out of there," Manuel shouted to the gypsy. The bull had smelled the blood of the dead horse and ripped into the canvas-cover with his horns. He charged Fuentes's cape, with the canvas hanging from his splintered horn, and the crowd laughed. Out in the ring, he tossed his head to rid himself of the canvas. Hernandez, running up from behind him, grabbed the end of the canvas and neatly lifted it off the horn.

The bull followed it in a half-charge and stopped still. He was on the defensive again. Manuel was walking toward him with the sword and muleta. Manuel swung the muleta before him. The bull would not charge.

Manuel profiled toward the bull, sighting along the dipping blade of the sword. The bull was motionless, seemingly dead on his feet, incapable of another charge.

Manuel rose to his toes, sighting along the steel, and charged.

Again there was the shock and he felt himself being borne back in a rush, to strike hard on the sand. There was no chance of kicking this time. The bull was on top of him. Manuel lay as though dead, his head on his arms, and the bull bumped him. Bumped his back, bumped his face in the sand. He felt the horn go into the sand between his folded arms. The bull hit him in the small of the back. His face drove into the sand. The horn drove through one of his sleeves and the bull ripped it off. Manuel was tossed clear and the bull followed the capes.

Manuel got up, found the sword and muleta, tried the point of the sword with his thumb, and then ran toward the barrera for a new sword.

Retana's man handed him the sword over the edge of the barrera.

"Wipe off your face," he said.

Manuel, running again toward the bull, wiped his bloody face with his handkerchief. He had not seen Zurito. Where was Zurito?

The cuadrilla had stepped away from the bull and waited with their capes. The bull stood, heavy and dull again after the action.

Manuel walked toward him with the muleta. He stopped and shook it. The bull did not respond. He passed it right and left, left and right before the bull's muzzle. The bull's eyes watched it and turned with the swing, but he would not charge. He was waiting for Manuel.

Manuel was worried. There was nothing to do but go in. Corto y derecho. He profiled close to the bull, crossed the muleta in front of his body and charged. As he pushed in the sword, he jerked his body to the left to clear the horn. The bull passed him and the sword shot up in the air, twinkling under the arc-lights, to fall red-hilted on the sand.

Manuel ran over and picked it up. It was bent and he straightened it over his knee.

As he came run— toward the bull, fixed again now, he passed Handez standing with his cape.

"He's all bone,—e boy said encouragingly.

Manuel nod—ecping his face. He put the bloody handkerch—n his pocket.

There was the b— He was close to the barrera now. Damn hi— Maybe he was all bone. Maybe there wa— any place for the sword to go in. The hell the—sn't! He'd show them.

He tried a pass—n the muleta and the bull did not move. Man—hopped the muleta back and forth in front of t—ull. Nothing doing.

He furled the m—a, drew the sword out, profiled and drove in—he bull. He felt the sword buckle as he shov—in, leaning his weight on it, and then it shot—in the air, end-over-ending into the crowd. —uel had jerked clear as the sword jumped.

The first cushio—rown down out of the dark missed him. Th—e hit him in the face, his bloody face looki—n—the crowd. They were coming down fast—potting the sand. Somebody threw an em—hampagne-bottle from close range. It hit Ma—on the foot. He stood there watching the dark—re the things were coming from. Then som—g whished through the air and struck by hi—Manuel leaned over and picked it up. It —is sword. He straightened it over his knee an—tured with it to the crowd.

"Thank you," h—l. "Thank you."

Oh, the dirty b—s! Dirty bastards! Oh, the lousy, dirty ba—! He kicked into a cushion as he ran.

There was the l— The same as ever. All right, you dirty, lo—astard!

Manuel passed t—leta in front of the bull's black muzzle.

Nothing doing.

You won't! All—. He stepped close and jammed the sharp—of the muleta into the bull's damp muzzle—

The bull was on—s he jumped back, and as he tripped on a cu—he felt the horn go into him, into his side. —rabbed the horn with his two hands and rod—ward, holding tight onto the place. The bu—d him and he was clear. He lay still. It —l right. The bull was gone.

He got up coughi—feeling broken and gone. The dirty bastards!

"Give me the sw—he shouted. "Give me the stuff."

Fuentes came up—e muleta and the sword.

Hernandez put hi—around him.

"Go on to the infi— man," he said. "Don't be a damn fool."

"Get away from me," Manuel said. "Get to hell away from me."

He twisted free. Hernandez shrugged his shoulders. Manuel ran toward the bull.

There was the bull standing, heavy, firmly planted.

All right, you bastard! Manuel drew the sword out of the muleta, sighted with the same movement, and flung himself onto the bull. He felt the sword go in all the way. Right up to the guard. Four fingers and his thumb into the bull. The blood was hot on his knuckles and he was on top of the bull.

The bull lurched with him as he lay on, and seemed to sink; then he was standing clear. He looked at the bull going down slowly over on his side, then suddenly four feet in the air.

Then he gestured at the crowd, his hand warm from the bull blood.

All right, you bastards! He wanted to say something, but he started to cough. It was hot and choking. He looked down for the muleta. He must go over and salute the president. President hell! He was sitting down looking at something. It was the bull. His four feet up. Thick tongue out. Things crawling around on his belly and under his legs. Crawling where the hair was thin. Dead bull. To hell with the bull! To hell with them all! He started to get to his feet and commenced to cough. He sat down again, coughing. Somebody came and pushed him up.

They carried him across the ring to the infirmary, running with him across the sand, standing blocked at the gate as the mules came in, then around under the dark passageway, men grunting as they took him up the runway, and then laid him down.

The doctor and two men in white were waiting for him. They laid him on the table. They were cutting away his shirt. Manuel felt tired. His whole chest felt scalded inside. He started to cough and they held something to his mouth. Everybody was very busy.

There was an electric light in his eyes. He shut his eyes.

He heard some one coming very heavily up the stairs. Then he did not hear it. Then he heard a noise far off. That was the crowd. Well, somebody would have to kill the other bull. They had

cut away all his shirt. The doctor smiled at him. There was Retana.

"Hello, Retana!" Manuel said. He could not hear his voice.

Retana smiled at him and said something. Manuel could not hear it.

Zurito stood beside the table, bending over where the doctor was working. He was in his picador clothes, without his hat.

Zurito said something to him. Manuel could not hear it.

Zurito was speaking to Retana. One of the men in white smiled and handed Retana a pair of scissors. Retana gave them to Zurito. Zurito said something to Manuel. He could not hear it.

To hell with this operating-table! He'd been on plenty of operating-tables before. He was not going to die. There would be a priest if he was going to die.

Zurito was saying something to him. Holding up the scissors.

That was it. They were going to cut off his coleta. They were going to cut off his pigtail.

Manuel sat up on the operating-table. The doctor stepped back, angry. Some one grabbed him and held him.

"You couldn't do a thing like that, Manos," he said.

He heard suddenly, clearly, Zurito's voice.

"That's all right," Zurito said. "I don't do it. I was joking."

"I was going good," Manuel said. "I didn't have any luck. That was all."

Manuel lay back. They had put something over his face. It was all familiar. He inhaled deeply. He felt very tired. He was very, very tired. They took the thing away from his face.

"I was going good," Manuel said weakly. "I was going great."

Retana looked at Zurito and started for the door.

"I'll stay here with him," Zurito said.

Retana shrugged his shoulders.

Manuel opened his eyes and looked at Zurito.

"Wasn't I going good, Manos?" he asked, for confirmation.

"Sure," said Zurito. "You were going great."

The doctor's assistant put the cone over Manuel's face and he inhaled deeply. Zurito stood awkwardly, watching.

William Faulkner · 189-1962

Born in Mississippi in 1897, Faulkner grew up in the little universitown of Oxford which later he was to transform into fabulous Jefferson, capital of fictitious Yapatawpha County. At the age of twenty, Faulkner joined the Canadian, and later the Brit, Royal Air Force. After his return to Oxford, he took several courses offered by his native versity, but did not obtain an academic degree. In the years following, Faulkner became a clerk New York bookstore and for a while lived in New Orleans, where he worked for a local newspapod made the acquaintance of the famous novelist Sherwood Anderson. He returned to his h town where he devoted himself to his writings. On a few occasions, he went to Hollywoodwork on film scripts. In 1950 he received the Nobel Prize for Literature, an international recogm of his work as a novelist and writer of short stories. Lectures in France and Japan followed, aor one year, from 1957 to 1958, Faulkner was connected with the University of Virginia as ter-in-residence. Having surpassed in critical esteem Hemingway, Lewis, Steinbeck, and Wolfe is now regarded, in his own country and abroad, as the most important American novelis the twentieth century. He died on July 6, 1962, in Oxford.

Faulkner began as a poet. Two collections of his poetry were publil in the late twenties and early thirties; neither has established his reputation as a writer of lyrictry. He did not succeed in expressing genuine feelings or emotions. Faulkner's poems do notape traditionalism; they tend to be commonplace. His critics have insisted that his prose stylderived from Elizabethan poetry. In saying this, they intend to emphasize that it has thelent baroque quality of Elizabethan dramatic blank verse rather than the sweet and soothcadence of Elizabethan lyric poetry.

William Faulkner distinguished himself only as a writer of novels anort stories. Best known among his novels are *The Sound and the Fury* (1929), *As I Lay Dyi*930), *Sanctuary* (1931), *Light in August* (1932), *Absalom, Absalom* (1936), *The Wild Palms* b), *Intruder in the Dust* (1948), and *A Fable* (1954). His last work, *The Reivers* (1962), showeat Faulkner's delight in experimenting had in no way diminished. Two collections of short sb, *These Thirteen* (1931) and *Doctor Martino* (1934), have been included in *Collected Stories illiam Faulkner* (1950). His only dramatic composition, *Requiem for a Nun*, appeared in 1951.

Faulkner's prose writing can be, and has been, considered under a va of aspects. It is somewhat difficult to present a unified picture of its merits and demerits oestablish a reliable and generally acknowledged critical canon. In the early thirties, for instawhen Faulkner's work was first discussed in some of the little magazines, critics like Aubreyrke contended that his talent for writing humorous fiction would assure him a place beside Markin in American literary history. Many of his short stories seem to have grown out of the Southeidition of the humorous tall tale. In one of them, "The Spotted Horses," we encounter a numf characters related in spirit to and descending from David Crockett and his clan. At the same Faulkner's pessimistic attitude toward life and his misanthropy have been fully discussed by thmanists as well as the Marxists. What he thought of the Negro and of his position in modociety (in this respect Faulkner was a conservative, and not an abolitionist), his alleged priism, coupled with his indulgence in portraying scenes of decadence, crime and horror, becam issue of fierce attacks against him both as man and as artist. Critics frequently maintain that lner's technique — the deliberate distortion of time sequences and the historical process of actne use of suspense and the withholding of vital information from the reader — unnecessarily is the latter's mental capacity and credulity.

Faulkner is not a master logician. His grammar is sometimes faulty;entences are involved and inflated; his works are overcharged with emotion. Faulkner has jtbeen accused of overwriting; of his style it has been said that it is halfway between that of Dostoevsky and that of Hollywood script-writers. Critics are particularly fond of bringing home their point by analyzing a six-page sentence in "The Bear," one of the more popular of Faulkner's stories.

Faulkner himself never undertook to refute the charges raised against him and his work. He kept aloof from such controversy and continued writing in the manner he found suitable to his artistic purpose. In a preface written for the Modern Library edition of *Sanctuary* he frankly admitted that in writing this novel he wanted to cater to the public and earn cheap money. Over the years, he published a great many stories in popular magazines such as the *Saturday Evening Post, Collier's* and *Life*. The question remains open whether or not these stories fall short of the artistic standards set by Faulkner's full-length novels.

But neither the economic nor any other of the extra-artistic aspects will, in the long run, bear upon a discussion of the artistic quality of Faulkner's work. Once having decided to create a saga of his own — a family or tribal history rather than a myth — he invented one after the other a host of characters typical of this historical growth and subsequent decadence of the South. Together, they form a closed society of white farmers, of "poor white trash," of Negroes and aboriginal Indians. The human drama in Faulkner's novels is thus built on the model of the actual, historical drama extending over the last century and a quarter. Each story and each novel contributes to the construction of the whole, which is Yoknapatawpha County and its inhabitants. The reader's ingenuity is taxed in that he has to discover the place assigned to the individual segments in the vast structure. There are many points of intersection between Now and Then, Here and There; and often they are barely visible or even carefully screened.

On the whole, Faulkner's work is — or at least appears to be — fatalistic in outlook. Critics have complained that in it the possibility of choice is excluded, that Fate lurks behind the actions, as death lurks behind a hospital full of incurable invalids (Malraux). We certainly should be aware of such trends in many of the novels, but we may venture to explain that the fatalism is not accidental but, on the contrary, essential to the conception of Faulkner's fictitious universe. The use of the time element is especially appropriate to this discussion; it helps to bring about the static and deterministic quality of novels like *The Sound and the Fury* and *As I Lay Dying*. French critics — chief among them Jean Paul Sartre, André Malraux, and Albert Camus — have pointed out that there is no future contained in Faulkner's time scheme. Not only Faulkner's idiots and morons play with the concept of past and present, but so do the fully responsible grown-ups and even the educated among his characters. Myth, we all know, is timeless and working toward abstraction; Faulkner's tribal saga re-introduces time by limiting it to a continuous past.

This is one of the reasons we discuss Faulkner here as a realistic writer of fiction; for the society he creates is neither Utopian nor, in the proper sense of the word, mythical. It is an image of the living society of the South which has been given, however, a more definite historical and moral significance. In *The Portable Faulkner*, Malcolm Cowley has attempted to arrange Faulkner's stories and various sections from his novels in a pattern to establish a chronology of events, dating from the settling of Yoknapatawpha County through the Civil War down to our own days. Faulkner himself has supplied a brief outline of his principal characters, but his biographies are hymns and eulogies rather than accurate character sketches.

SUGGESTED REFERENCES: Malcolm Cowley, ed., *The Portable Faulkner* (1946); F. J. Hoffman, *William Faulkner* (1961); Irving Howe, *William Faulkner, A Critical Study* (2nd rev. ed., 1962); Lawrance Thompson, *William Faulkner. An Introduction and Interpretation* (1963); E. L. Volpe, *A Reader's Guide to William Faulkner* (1964).

A Name for the City [1]

The story here reproduced in full length, *A Name for the City*, was written by Faulkner for the Centennial issue of *Harper's Magazine*, published in October, 1950, and was later published in substantially the same form as part of Act One of *Requiem for a Nun*.

It is concerned with the origin of the name, Jefferson, which is given to Yoknapatawpha County's capital. What Faulkner calls a story, may be referred to as an anecdote; to it is added the author's comment which attempts to place the events related in the mythical context of Faulkner's other works. This means that the comment is not necessarily relevant only to the one story it refers to. In Faulkner's fictitious universe the action does not progress linearly, but may best be compared to a fan in that the chronology may be distorted or weighty matter included by way of parenthesis. Faulkner employs a technique of exploring the Before and After of a situation — the *was*, the *would be* and the *was to be* — and furnishing ample detail irrelevant to a full understanding of its meaning. Only in passing he introduces direct speech (dialogue), and even then he does so only for the sake of reproducing a character's idiom, and not in order to intensify and dramatize the somewhat epic flow of the narration. In becoming distinct individuals, Faulkner's characters speak his own, personal language. Only once in a while the author attempts a reproduction of interior monologues, using material developed in a character's brain, e.g. "Which was manifest nonsense, a physical impossibility either in lock or horse," only to fall back upon the narrator's superior, because omniscient, voice, e.g. ". . . especially as while they were still trying to unravel it. . . ."

The narrator is fond of startling metaphorical extensions such as: "They had simply sealed . . . him into their civic crisis as the desperate and defenseless oyster immobilizes its atom of inevictable grit." His is the language of poetry, somewhat out-of-the-way in this epic context. *A Name for the City* may be called a chapter from the mythical history of the American mind; and that is why Pettigrew, the post rider, in the end emerges as the hero of the story, as the conscience, that is, and as a personification of the United States. His legendary reputation constitutes the myth which underlies the historical narration, and the anecdote is saved only by way of an anticlimax with which the story ends: Pettigrew is bribed and will no longer consider playing the informer.

In reading *A Name for the City* one should keep well in mind the aspect under which the story may be seen: the myth of the American mind as it is juxtaposed to the fun to be had from the slyness of the American frontiersman. Thus the realism of many of Faulkner's stories may be defined as the interplay of myth and anecdote.

"Experience," Uncle Gavin said, "is not in the senses, but in the heart. I cite you the world travelers, the tense and furious circumnavigators: first, three years, then one year, then three months and then one month and then ninety hours and now — or am I wrong? — thirty hours, and who knows but what perhaps at this very instant somebody with still more money, for whom somebody has invented a still faster machine, has just departed to do it in three hours, leaving behind him, embalmed in cosmos-flung television to beat among the very stars themselves, his immortal epitaph: 'Goodbye, Ma, and may the best man win.' I cite you blind Homer, unable to quit the Athenian stone he sat on without a child to lead him, yet plumbed and charted the ultimate frontiers of passion and defeat and glory and ambition and hope and fear." And as he — Uncle Gavin — grew older, he began to spend more and more of his time trying to prove this to me. I mean, he used to tell me the old tales about Jefferson and the county in order to explain something I had seen, or that he and I had seen together; now he began to tell them for their own sake, as though he himself had been there a hundred or a hundred and fifty years ago; he, the middle-aging country lawyer in the second half of the twentieth century, was the *I was* and *I did* and *I saw* of a time when some of the progenitors of America still lived and breathed, and General Andrew Jackson's political star had not even risen yet, and even old Issetibbeha, the Chickasaw King, still existed in the memories of living men. Which was where this one came from about the ancient clumsy monster of a homemade iron lock which came all the long way overland by horseback from Carolina to Mississippi, and not only named a town but even created it.

Jefferson was not even Jefferson then. It was not even a town. It was a Chickasaw agency trading-post: a store, a tavern, a jail or calaboose, a half-dozen log cabins set in a disorderly huddle in the middle of the wilderness domain which Ikkemotubbe, old Issetibbeha's successor, was ceding to the white men for land — peace, escape, whatever he and his people called it — in what was to be Oklahoma territory. There was no church, no school, least of all, a courthouse. Because although they probably knew from the first that they wanted, needed, would some day have a church and a school, it would be almost a quarter of a century before they would discover suddenly that they not only had to have a courthouse, but they had to have it quick. They had something to put in it of course, as a kind of nest egg; even the simple dispossession of Indians begot in time a minuscule of archive and record, not to mention the normal

litter of man's ramshackle confederation against
environment — that time and that wilderness. In
this case, it was a meager, fading, dog-eared, uncor-
related, at times illiterate sheaf of land grants and
patents and transfers and deeds, and tax- and
militia-rolls, and bills of sale for slaves, and count-
ing-house lists of exchange rates and spurious currency, and liens and mortgages, and rewards for
escaped or stolen Negroes and other livestock, and
diary-like annotations of births and marriages and
deaths and public hangings and land auctions, ac-
cumulating slowly in a sort of iron pirate's chest
in the back room of the post-office-trading-post-
store, until one day twenty-five years later when,
because of a jail break compounded by the ancient
monster Carolina lock, the box was removed to a
small leanto room like a wood- or a tool-shed built
two days ago against one outside wall of the
mortised-log, mud-chinked shakedown jail; by
which fortuity was born the Yoknapatawpha
County courthouse, the box containing the records
not moved from any place but simply to one, removed from the trading-post back room not for any
reason inherent in either the back room or the box,
but on the contrary since the box was not only in
nobody's way in the back room, it was even missed
when gone since it had served as another seat or
stool among the powder- and whiskey-kegs and
firkins of salt and lard and molasses about the stove
on winter nights, and was moved at all for the simple reason that the settlement (overnight it was a
town without having been a village; one day in
about a hundred years it would wake frantically
from its communal slumber in a rash of Rotary and
Lions Clubs and Chambers of Commerce and City
Beautifuls: a furious beating of hollow drums toward nowhere, but simply to sound louder than the
next tiny human clotting to its north or south or
east or west, dubbing itself city as Napoleon
dubbed himself emperor, and defending the expedient by padding its census-rolls — a fever, a
delirium in which it would confound forever seething with motion and motion with progress) found
itself faced with a problem — or rather, under the
Damocles sword of a dilemma — from which
nothing could save it except the consecration or
ordination or whatever you call it, of a courthouse.

Even the jailbreak was fortuity: a gang — three
or four — of Natchez Trace bandits (twenty-five
years later legend would begin to affirm, and a hundred years later would still be affirming, that two
of the bandits were the Harpes themselves, Big
Harpe anyway, since the circumstances, the
method, of the breakout left behind like a smell, an
odor, a kind of Gargantuan and bizarre playfulness

at once humorous and terrifying, as if the settlement had fallen, blundered, into the notice or range
of an idle and whimsical giant. Which — that they
were the Harpes — was impossible, since the
Harpes and even the last of Mason's ruffians were
dead or scattered by this time, and the robbers
would have had to belong to Murrell's organization
— if they needed to belong to any at all other than
the simple fraternity of rapine) captured by chance
by a band of militia and brought in to the settlement jail because it was the nearest. Or a chance
band of militia rather, since the presence of the
band was a third fortuity, it having been part of
a general muster at the settlement two days ago for
a Fourth of July barbecue, which by the next day
had boiled down into one drunken brawling which
rendered even the last hardy survivors vulnerable
enough for the residents of the settlement to eject
them, this particular band having been carried,
still comatose, in one of the evicting wagons, to a
swamp four miles away known as Hurricane Bottoms, where they made camp to regain their
strength or anyway their legs, and where the
bandits, on their way across country to their hide-
out after their last exploit on the Trace, stumbled
onto the campfire. And here report varied, divided; some said that the sergeant in command of
the militia recognized one of the bandits as a de-
serter from his corps, others said that one of the
bandits recognized in the sergeant a former follower
of his, the bandit's, trade. Anyway, on the following morning all of them, captors and prisoners,
returned to the settlement in a group, some said in
confederation now seeking more drink, others said
that the captors brought their prizes back to the
settlement in revenge for their eviction because
these were frontier, pioneer, times, when — as
Uncle Gavin said — personal liberty and freedom
were almost a physical condition like fire or flood,
and no community was going to interfere with any
mere amoralist so long as he practiced somewhere
else, and the settlement, being neither on the Trace
nor the river but lying about midway between,
wanted no part of the underworld of either.

But, like it or no, they had some of it now. They
put the bandits into the jail, which until now had
had no lock at all, its clients so far being amateurs
— local brawlers and drunkards and runaway
slaves — for whom a single wooden bar in slots
across the outside of the door like on a corncrib, had
sufficed. But they had now what might be four —
three — Dillingers or Jesse Jameses of the time,
with rewards on their heads. So they locked the
jail this time. They did it right. They bored an
auger hole through the door and another through
the jamb and passed a length of heavy chain

through them, and sent a messenger at a run back to the post-office-store to fetch the old Carolina lock from the latest Nashville mail-pouch — the lock, the iron monster weighing almost fifteen pounds, with a key almost as long as a bayonet, not just the only lock in that part of the country, but the oldest lock in that cranny of the United States, brought there by one of the three men who were what was to be Yoknapatawpha County's coeval pioneers and settlers, leaving in it the three oldest names — Alexander Holston, who came as half groom and half bodyguard to Doctor Samuel Habersham, and half nurse and half tutor to the doctor's eight-year-old motherless son, the three of them riding horseback across Tennessee from the Cumberland Gap along with Louis Grenier, the Huguenot younger son who brought the first slaves into the country and was granted the first big land patent and so became the first cotton planter; while Doctor Habersham, with his worn black bag of pills and knives and his brawny taciturn bodyguard and his half orphan child, became the settlement itself (for a time, before it was named, the settlement was known as Doctor Habersham's, then Habersham's, then simply Habersham; a hundred years later, during a schism between two ladies' clubs over the naming of the streets in order to get free mail delivery, a movement was started, first, to change the name back to Habersham; then failing that, to divide the town in two and call one half of it Habersham after the old pioneer doctor and founder) — friend of old Issetibbeha, the Chickasaw chief (the motherless Habersham boy, now a man of twenty-five, married one of Issetibbeha's granddaughters and in the thirties emigrated to Oklahoma with his wife's dispossessed people), first unofficial, then official Chickasaw agent until he resigned in a letter of furious denunciation addressed to the President of the United States himself; and — his charge and pupil a man now — Alexander Holston became the settlement's first publican, establishing the tavern still known as the Holston House, the original log walls and puncheon floors and hand-mortised joints of which are still buried somewhere beneath the modern pressed glass and brick veneer and neon tubes.

The lock was his: fifteen pounds of useless iron lugged a thousand miles through a desert of precipice and swamp, of flood and drought and wild beasts and wild Indians and wilder white men, displacing that fifteen pounds better given to food or seed to plant food or even powder to defend with, to become a fixture, a kind of landmark, in the bar of a wilderness ordinary, locking and securing nothing, because there was nothing behind the heavy bars and shutters needing further locking and securing, not even a paper weight because the only papers in the Holston House were the twisted spills in an old powder horn above the mantel for lighting tobacco; always a little in the way, since it had constantly to be moved: from bar to shelf to mantel then back to bar again until they finally thought about putting it on the bimonthly mail-pouch; familiar, known, presently the oldest unchanged thing in the settlement, older than the people since Issetibbeha and Doctor Habersham were dead, and Alexander Holston was an old man crippled with arthritis, and Louis Grenier had a settlement of his own on his own vast plantation now, half of which was not even in Yoknapatawpha County, and the settlement rarely saw him; older than the town, since there were new names in it now even when the old blood ran in them, and you no longer shot a bear or deer or wild turkey simply by standing for a while in your kitchen door, not to mention the pouch of mail — letters and even newspapers — which came from Nashville every two weeks by a special horseman who did nothing else and was paid a salary for it by the federal government; and that was the second phase of the monster Carolina lock's transubstantiation into the Yoknapatawpha County courthouse.

The pouch didn't always reach the settlement every two weeks, nor even always every month. But sooner or later it did, and everybody knew it would, because it — the cowhide saddlebag not even large enough to hold a full change of clothing, containing three or four letters and half that many badly-printed one- and two-page newspapers already three or four months out of date and usually half and sometimes wholly wrong or misinformed to begin with — was the United States, the power and the will to liberty, owing allegiance to no man, bringing even into that still almost pathless wilderness the thin peremptory voice of the nation which had wrenched its freedom from one of the most powerful peoples on earth and then again within the same lifespan successfully defended it; so peremptory and audible that the man who carried the pouch on the galloping horse didn't even carry any arms except a tin horn, traversing month after month, blatantly, flagrantly, almost contemptuously, a region where for no more than the boots on his feet, men would murder a traveler and gut him like a bear or deer or fish and fill the cavity with rocks and sink the evidence in the nearest water; not even deigning to pass quietly where other men, even though armed and in parties, tried to move secretly or at least without uproar, but instead announcing his solitary advent as far ahead of himself as the ring of the horn would carry. So it was not long before Alexander Holston's lock had moved to the mail-pouch. Not that the pouch needed one, having come already the three hundred miles from Nashville without a lock. (It had been projected at first that the lock remain on the pouch constantly. That is, not just while the pouch was in the settlement, but while it was on the horse between Nashville and the settlement too. The rider refused, succinctly, in three words, one of which was printable. His reason was the lock's weight. They pointed out to him that this would not hold water, since not only — the rider was a frail irascible little man weighing less than a hundred pounds — would the fifteen pounds of lock even then fail to bring his weight up to that of a normal adult male, the added weight of the lock would merely match that of the pistols which his employer, the United States government, believed he carried and even paid him for having done so, the rider's reply to this being succinct too though not so glib: that the lock weighed fifteen pounds either at the back door of the store in the settlement, or at that of the post office in Nashville. But since Nashville and the settlement were three hundred miles apart, by the time the horse had carried it from one to the other, the lock weighed fifteen pounds times three hundred miles, or forty-five hundred pounds. Which was manifest nonsense, a physical impossibility either in lock or horse. Yet indubitably fifteen pounds times three hundred miles was forty-five hundred something, either pounds or miles — especially as while they were still trying to unravel it, the rider repeated his first three succinct — two unprintable — words.)

So less than ever would the pouch need a lock in the back room of the trading-post, surrounded and enclosed once more by civilization, where its very intactness, its presence to receive a lock, proved its lack of that need during the three hundred miles of rapine-haunted Trace; needing a lock as little as it was equipped to receive one, since it had been necessary to slit the leather with a knife just under each jaw of the opening and insert the lock's iron mandible through the two slits and clash it home, so that any other hand with a similar knife could have cut the whole lock from the pouch as easily as it had been clasped onto it. So the old lock was not even a symbol of security: it was a gesture of salutation, of free men to free men, of civilization to civilization across not just the three hundred miles of wilderness to Nashville, but the fifteen hundred to Washington: of respect without servility, allegiance without abasement to the government which they had helped to found and had accepted with pride but still as free men, still free to withdraw from it at any moment when the two of

them found themselves no longer compatible, the old lock meeting the pouch each time on its arrival, to clasp it in iron and inviolable symbolism, while old Alec Holston, childless bachelor, grew a little older and grayer, a little more arthritic in flesh and temper too, a little stiffer and more rigid in bone and pride too, since the lock was still his, he had merely lent it, and so in a sense he was the grandfather in the settlement of the inviolability not just of government mail, but of a free government of free men too, so long as the government remembered to let men live free, not under it but beside it.

That was the lock; they put it on the jail. They did it quickly, not even waiting until a messenger could have got back from the Holston House with old Alec's permission to remove it from the mail-pouch or use it for the new purpose. Not that he would have objected on principle nor refused his permission except by simple instinct; that is, he would probably have been the first to suggest the lock if he had known in time or thought of it first, but he would have refused at once if he thought the thing was contemplated without consulting him. Which everybody in the settlement knew, though this was not at all why they didn't wait for the messenger. In fact, no messenger had ever been sent to old Alec; they didn't have time to send one, let alone wait until he got back; they didn't want the lock to keep the bandits in, since (as was later proved) the old lock would have been no more obstacle for the bandits to pass than the customary wooden bar; they didn't need the lock to protect the settlement from the bandits, but to protect the bandits from the settlement. Because the prisoners had barely reached the settlement when it developed that there was a faction bent on lynching them at once, out of hand, without preliminary — a small but determined gang which tried to wrest the prisoners from their captors while the militia was still trying to find someone to surrender them to, and would have succeeded except for a man named Compson, who came to the settlement a few years ago with a race horse, which he swapped to Ikkemotubbe, Issetibbeha's successor in the chiefship, for a square mile of what was to be the most valuable land in the future town of Jefferson, who, legend said, drew a pistol and held the ravishers at bay until the bandits could be got into the jail and the auger holes bored and someone sent to fetch old Alec Holston's lock. Because there were indeed new names and faces too in the settlement now — faces so new as to have (to the older residents) no discernible antecedents other than mammalinity, nor past other than the simple years which had scored them; and names so new as to have no discernible (nor discoverable either) antecedents or past at all, as though they had been invented yesterday, report dividing again: to the effect that there were more people in the settlement that day than the militia sergeant whom one or all of the bandits might recognize.

So Compson locked the jail, and a courier with the two best horses in the settlement — one to ride and one to lead — cut through the woods to the Trace to ride the hundred-odd miles to Natchez with the news of the capture and authority to dicker for the reward; and that evening in the Holston House kitchen was held the settlement's first municipal meeting, prototype not only of the town council after the settlement would be a town, but of the chamber of commerce when it would begin to proclaim itself a city, with Compson presiding, not old Alec, who was quite old now, grim, taciturn, sitting even on a hot July night before a smoldering log in his vast chimney, his back even turned to the table (he was not interested in the deliberation; the prisoners were his already since his lock held them; whatever the conference decided would have to be submitted to him for ratification anyway before anyone could touch his lock to open it) around which the progenitors of the Jefferson city fathers sat in what was almost a council of war, not only discussing the collecting of the reward, but the keeping and defending of it. Because there were two factions of opposition now: not only the lynching party, but the militia band too, who now claimed that as prizes the prisoners still belonged to their original captors; that they — the militia — had merely surrendered the prisoners' custody but had relinquished nothing of any reward: on the prospect of which, the militia band had got more whiskey from the trading-post-store and had built a tremendous bonfire in front of the jail, around which they and the lynching party had now confederated in a wassail or conference of their own. Or so they thought. Because the truth was that Compson, in the name of the public peace and welfare, had made formal demand on Doctor Peabody, old Doctor Habersham's successor, and the three of them — Compson, Peabody, and the post trader, Ratcliffe — added the laudanum to the keg of whiskey and sent it as a gift from the settlement to the astonished militia sergeant, and returned to the Holston House kitchen to wait until the last of the uproar died; then the law-and-order party made a rapid sortie and gathered up all the comatose opposition, lynchers and captors too, and dumped them all into the jail with the prisoners and locked the door again and went home to bed — until the next morning, when the first arrivals were met by a scene resembling an outdoor stage setting: which was how the legend of the mad Harpes

started: a thing not just fantastical but incomprehensible, not just whimsical but a little terrifying (though at least it was bloodless, which would have contented neither Harpe): not just the lock gone from the door nor even just the door gone from the jail, but the entire wall gone, the mud-chinked, axe-mortised logs unjointed neatly and quietly in the darkness and stacked as neatly to one side, leaving the jail open to the world like a stage on which the late insurgents still lay sprawled and various in deathlike slumber, the whole settlement gathered now to watch Compson trying to kick at least one of them awake, until one of the Holston slaves — the cook's husband, the waiter-groom-hostler — ran into the crowd shouting, "Whar de lock, whar de lock, old Boss say whar de lock."

It was gone (as were three horses belonging to three of the lynching faction). They couldn't even find the heavy door and the chain, and at first they were almost betrayed into believing that the bandits had had to take the door in order to steal the chain and lock, catching themselves back from the very brink of this wanton accusation of rationality. But the lock was gone; nor did it take the settlement long to realize that it was not the escaped bandits and the aborted reward, but the lock, and not a simple situation which faced them, but a problem which threatened, the slave departing back to the Holston House at a dead run and then reappearing at the dead run almost before the door, the walls, had had time to hide him, engulf and then eject him again, darting through the crowd and up to Compson himself now, saying, "Old Boss say fetch de lock" — not send the lock, but bring the lock. So Compson and his lieutenants (and this was where the mail rider began to appear, or rather, to emerge — the fragile wisp of a man ageless, hairless, and toothless, who looked too frail even to approach a horse, let alone ride one six hundred miles every two weeks, yet who did so, and not only that but had wind enough left not only to announce and precede but even follow his passing with the jeering musical triumph of the horn: a contempt for possible — probable — despoilers matched only by that for the official dross of which he might be despoiled, and which agreed to remain in civilized bounds only so long as the despoiler had the taste to refrain) repaired to the kitchen where old Alec still sat before his smoldering log, his back still to the room, and still not turning it this time either.

And that was all. He ordered the immediate return of his lock. It was not even an ultimatum, it was a simple instruction, a decree, impersonal, the mail rider now well into the fringe of the group, saying nothing and missing nothing, like a weightless desiccated or fossil bird, not a vulture of course nor even quite a hawk, but say a pterodactyl chick arrested just out of the egg ten glaciers ago and so old in simple infancy as to be worn and weary ancestor of all subsequent life. They pointed out to old Alec that the only reason the lock could be missing was that the bandits had not had time or been able to cut it out of the door, and that even three fleeing madmen on stolen horses would not carry a six-foot oak door very far, and that a party of Ikkemotubbe's young men were even now trailing the horses westward toward the river and that without doubt the lock would be found at any moment, probably under the first bush at the edge of the settlement: knowing better, knowing that there was no limit to the fantastic and the terrifying and the bizarre, of which the men were capable who already, just to escape from a log jail, had quietly removed one entire wall and stacked it in neat piecemeal at the roadside, and that not they nor old Alec neither would ever see his lock again.

Nor did they; the rest of that afternoon and all the next day too, while old Alec still smoked his pipe in front of his smoldering log, the settlement's sheepish and raging elders hunted for it, with (by now: the next afternoon) Ikkemotubbe's Chickasaws helping too, or anyway present, watching: the wild men, the wilderness's tameless evictant children looking only the more wild and homeless for the white man's denim and butternut and felt and straw which they wore, standing or squatting or following, grave, attentive, and interested, while the white men sweated and cursed among the bordering thickets of their punily-clawed foothold; and always the rider, Pettigrew, ubiquitous, everywhere, not helping search himself and never in anyone's way, but always present, inscrutable, saturnine, missing nothing: until at last toward sundown Compson crashed savagely out of the last bramble-brake and flung the sweat from his face with a full-armed sweep sufficient to repudiate a throne, and said,

"All right, God damn it, we'll pay him for it." Because they had already considered that last gambit; they had already realized its seriousness from the very fact that Peabody had tried to make a joke about it which everyone knew that even Peabody did not think humorous:

"Yes — and quick too, before he has time to advise with Pettigrew and price it by the pound."

"By the pound?" Compson said.

"Pettigrew just weighed it by the three hundred miles from Nashville. Old Alec might start from Carolina. That's fifteen thousand pounds."

"Oh," Compson said. So he blew in his men by means of a foxhorn which one of the Indians wore on a thong around his neck, though even then they paused for one last quick conference; again it was Peabody who stopped them.

"Who'll pay for it?" he said. "It would be just like him to want a dollar a pound for it, even if by Pettigrew's scale he had found it in the ashes of his fireplace." They — Compson anyway — had probably already thought of that; that, as much as Pettigrew's presence, was probably why he was trying to rush them into old Alec's presence with the offer so quickly that none would have the face to renege on a pro rata share. But Peabody had torn it now. Compson looked about at them, sweating, grimly enraged.

"That means Peabody will probably pay one dollar," he said. "Who pays the other fourteen? Me?" Then Ratcliffe, the trader, the store's proprietor, solved it — a solution so simple, so limitless in retroaction, that they didn't even wonder why nobody had thought of it before; which not only solved the problem but abolished it; and not just that one, but all problems, from now on into perpetuity, opening to their vision like the rending of a veil, like a glorious prophesy, the vast splendid limitless panorama of America: that land of boundless opportunity, that bourne, created not by nor of the people, but for the people, as was the heavenly manna of old, with no return demand on man save the chewing and swallowing since out of its own matchless Allgood it would create, produce, train, support, and perpetuate a race of laborers dedicated to the single purpose of picking the manna up and putting it into his lax hand or even between his jaws — illimitable, vast, without beginning or end, not even a trade or a craft but a beneficence as are sunlight and rain and air, inalienable and immutable.

"Put it on the Book," Ratcliffe said — the Book: not a ledger, but *the* ledger, since it was probably the only thing of its kind between Nashville and Natchez, unless there might happen to be a similar one a few miles south at the first Chocktaw agency at Yalo Busha — a ruled, paper-backed copybook such as might have come out of a schoolroom, in which accrued, with the United States as debtor, in Mohataha's name (the Chickasaw matriarch, Ikkemotubbe's mother and old Issetibbeha's sister, who — she could write her name, or anyway make something with a pen or pencil which was agreed to be, or at least accepted to be, a valid signature — signed all the conveyances as her son's kingdom passed to the white people, regularizing it in law anyway) the crawling tedious list of calico and gunpowder, whiskey and salt and snuff and denim pants and osseous candy drawn from

Ratcliffe's shelves by her descendants and subjects and Negro slaves.

That was all the settlement had to do: add the lock to the list, the account. It wouldn't even matter at what price they entered it. They could have priced it on Pettigrew's scale of fifteen pounds times the distance not just to Carolina but to Washington itself, and nobody would ever notice it probably; they could have charged the United States with seventeen thousand five hundred dollars' worth of the fossilized and indestructible candy, and none would ever read the entry. So it was solved, done, finished, ended. They didn't even have to discuss it. They didn't even think about it any more, unless perhaps here and there to marvel (a little speculatively probably) at their own moderation, since they wanted nothing — least of all, to escape any just blame — but a fair and decent adjustment of the lock. They went back to where old Alec still sat with his pipe in front of his dim hearth. Only they had overestimated him; he didn't want any money at all, he wanted his lock. Whereupon what little remained of Compson's patience went too.

"Your lock's gone," he told old Alec harshly. "You'll take fifteen dollars for it," he said, his voice already fading, because even that rage could recognize impasse when it saw it. Nevertheless, the rage, the impotence, the sweating, the *too much* — whatever it was — forced the voice on for one word more: "Or —" before it stopped for good and allowed Peabody to fill the gap:

"Or else?" Peabody said, and not to old Alec, but to Compson. "Or else what?" Then Ratcliffe saved that too.

"Wait," he said. "Uncle Alec's going to take fifty dollars for his lock. A guarantee of fifty dollars. He'll give us the name of the blacksmith back in Cal'lina that made it for him, and we'll send back there and have a new one made. Going and coming and all'll cost about fifty dollars. We'll give Uncle Alec the fifty dollars to hold as a guarantee. Then when the new lock comes, he'll give us back the money. All right, Uncle Alec?"

And that could have been all of it. It probably would have been, except for Pettigrew. It was not that they had forgotten him, or even assimilated him. They had simply sealed — healed him off (so they thought) — him into their civic crisis as the desperate and defenseless oyster immobilizes its atom of inevictable grit. Nobody had seen him move; yet he now stood in the center of them where Compson and Ratcliffe and Peabody faced old Alec in the chair. You might have said that he had oozed there, except for that adamantine quality which might (in emergency) become invisible but

never insubstantial and never in this world fluid; he spoke in a voice bland, reasonable, and impersonal, then stood there being looked at, frail and child-sized, impermeable as diamond and manifest with portent, bringing into that backwoods room a thousand miles deep in pathless wilderness, the whole vast incalculable weight of federality, not just representing the government nor even himself just the government; for that moment at least, he was the United States.

"Uncle Alec hasn't lost any lock," he said. "That was Uncle Sam."

After a moment someone said, "What?"

"That's right," Pettigrew said. "Whoever put that lock of Holston's on that mail bag either made a voluntary gift to the United States, and the same law covers the United States government that covers minor children: you can give something to them, but you can't take it back; or he or they done something else."

They looked at him. Again after a while somebody said something; it was Ratcliffe. "What else?" Ratcliffe said. Pettigrew answered, still bland, impersonal, heartless, and glib:

"Committed a violation of Act of Congress as especially made and provided for the defacement of government property, penalty of five thousand dollars or not less than one year in a federal jail or both. For whoever cut them two slits in the bag to put the lock in, Act of Congress as especially made and provided for the injury or destruction of government property, penalty of ten thousand dollars or not less than five years in a federal jail or both." He did not move even yet; he simply spoke directly to old Alec: "I reckon you're going to have supper here same as usual sooner or later or more or less."

"Wait," Ratcliffe said. He turned to Compson. "Is that true?"

"What the hell difference does it make whether it's true or not?" Compson said. "What do you think he's going to do as soon as he gets to Nashville?" He said violently to Pettigrew: "You were supposed to leave for Nashville yesterday. What were you hanging around here for?"

"Nothing to go to Nashville for," Pettigrew said. "You don't want any mail. You ain't got anything to lock it up with."

"So we ain't," Ratcliffe said. "So we'll let the United States find the United States' lock." This time Pettigrew looked at no one. He wasn't even speaking to anyone, any more than old Alec had been when he decreed the return of his lock:

"Act of Congress as made and provided for the unauthorized removal and/or use or willful or felonious use or misuse or loss of government

property, penalty the value of the article plus five
hundred to ten thousand dollars or thirty days to
twenty years in a federal jail or both. They may
even make a new one when they read where you
have charged a Post Office Department lock to the
Bureau of Indian Affairs." He moved; now he was
speaking to old Alec again: "I'm going out to my
horse. When this meeting is over and you get back
to cooking, you can send your nigger for me."

Then he was gone. After a while Ratcliffe said,
"What do you reckon he aims to get out of this?
A reward?" But that was wrong; they all knew
better than that.

"He's already getting what he wants," Compson
said, and cursed again. "Confusion. Just
damned confusion." But that was wrong too; they
all knew that too, though it was Peabody who
said it:

"No. Not confusion. A man who will ride six
hundred miles through this country every two
weeks, with nothing for protection but a foxhorn,
ain't really interested in confusion any more than
he is in money." So they didn't know yet what
was in Pettigrew's mind. But they knew what he
would do. That is, they knew that they did not
know at all, either what he would do, or how, or
when, and that there was nothing whatever that
they could do about it until they discovered why.
And they saw now that they had no possible means
to discover that; they realized now that they had
known him for three years now, during which,
fragile and inviolable and undeviable and preceded
for a mile or more by the strong sweet ringing of
the horn, on his strong and tireless horse he would
complete the bi-monthly trip from Nashville to the
settlement and for the next three or four days
would live among them, yet that they knew nothing
whatever about him, and even now knew only that
they dared not, simply dared not, take any chance,
sitting for a while longer in the darkening room
while old Alec still smoked, his back still squarely
turned to them and their quandary too; then dis-
persing to their own cabins for the evening meal —
with what appetite they could bring to it, since
presently they had drifted back through the summer darkness when by ordinary they would have
been already in bed, to the back room of Ratcliffe's
store now, to sit again while Ratcliffe recapitulated
in his mixture of bewilderment and alarm (and
something else which they recognized was respect
as they realized that he — Ratcliffe — was unshak-
ably convinced that Pettigrew's aim was money;
that Pettigrew had invented or evolved a scheme
so richly rewarding that he — Ratcliffe — had not
only been unable to forestall him and do it first, he
— Ratcliffe — couldn't even guess what it was

after he had been given a hint) until Compson interrupted him.

"Hell," Compson said. "Everybody knows
what's wrong with him. It's ethics. He's a
damned moralist."

"Ethics?" Peabody said. He sounded almost
startled. He said quickly: "That's bad. How can
we corrupt an ethical man?"

"Who wants to corrupt him?" Compson said.
"All we want him to do is stay on that damned
horse and blow whatever extra wind he's got into
that damned horn."

But Peabody was not even listening. He said,
"Ethics," almost dreamily. He said, "Wait."
They watched him. He said suddenly to Ratcliffe: "I've heard it somewhere. If anybody here
knows it, it'll be you. What's his name?"

"His name?" Ratcliff said. "Pettigrew's? Oh.
His Christian name." Ratcliffe told him. "Why?"

"Nothing," Peabody said. "I'm going home.
Anybody else coming?" He spoke directly to nobody and said and would say no more, but that
was enough: a straw perhaps, but at least a straw;
enough anyway for the others to watch and say
nothing either as Compson got up too and said to
Ratcliffe, "You coming?" and the three of them
walked away together, beyond earshot then beyond
sight too. Then Compson said, "All right. What?"

"It may not work," Peabody said. "But you
two will have to back me up. When I speak for the
whole settlement, you and Ratcliffe will have to
make it stick. Will you?"

Compson cursed. "But at least tell us a little of
what we're going to guarantee." So Peabody told
them, some of it, and the next morning entered the
stall in the Holston House stable where Pettigrew
was grooming his ugly hammer-headed iron-
muscled horse.

"We decided not to charge that lock to old
Mohataha, after all," Peabody said. "That so?"
Pettigrew said. "Nobody in Washington would
ever catch it. Certainly not the ones that can
read."

"We're going to pay for it ourselves," Peabody
said. "In fact, we're going to do a little more.
We've got to repair that jail wall anyhow; we've got
to build one wall anyway. So by building three
more, we will have another room. We got to build
one anyway, so that don't count. So by building
an extra three-wall room, we will have another
four-wall house. That will be the courthouse."
Pettigrew had been hissing gently between his
teeth at each stroke of the brush, like a professional Irish groom. Now he stopped, the brush
and his hand arrested in midstroke, and turned his
head a little.

"Courthouse?"

"We're going to have a town," Peabody said. "We already got a church — that's Whitfield's cabin. And we're going to build a school too, soon as we get around to it. But we're going to build the courthouse today; we've already got something to put in it to make it a courthouse: that iron box that's been in Ratcliffe's way in the store for the last ten years. Then we'll have a town. We've already even named her."

Now Pettigrew stood up, very slowly. They looked at one another. After a moment Pettigrew said, "So?"

"Ratcliffe says your name's Jefferson," Peabody said.

"That's right," Pettigrew said. "Thomas Jefferson Pettigrew. I'm from old Ferginny."

"Any kin?" Peabody said.

"No," Pettigrew said. "My ma named me for him, so I would have some of his luck."

"Luck?" Peabody said.

Pettigrew didn't smile. "That's right. She didn't mean luck. She never had any schooling. She didn't know the word she wanted to say."

"Have you had it?" Peabody said. Nor did Pettigrew smile now. "I'm sorry," Peabody said. "Try to forget it." He said: "We decided to name her Jefferson." Now Pettigrew didn't seem to breathe even. He just stood there, small, frail, less than boy-size, childless and bachelor, incorrigibly kinless and tieless, looking at Peabody. Then he breathed, and raising the brush, he turned back to the horse and for an instant Peabody thought he was going back to the grooming. But instead of making the stroke, he laid the hand and the brush against the horse's flank and stood for a moment, his face turned away and his head bent a little. Then he raised his head and turned his face back toward Peabody.

"You could call that lock 'axle grease' on that Indian account," he said.

"Fifty dollars worth of axle grease?" Peabody said.

"To grease the wagons for Oklahoma," Pettigrew said.

"So we could," Peabody said. "Only her name's Jefferson now. We can't forget that any more now."

THE

NATURALISTS

❧

*As you can see, our only mistake in all this is that we accept only nature,
and that we are not willing to correct what is by what should be.*

ÉMILE ZOLA

NATURALISM IS REALISM *plus*. As a term in literary criticism, "naturalism" was in use in the 1850's; as denoting a definite school in writing the term did not, however, assume importance until the late seventies or the early eighties in France when Émile Zola and his coterie deliberately adopted it.

At that time naturalistic tendencies were in the air. The development of science in the eighteenth century, the political reform which came with the French Revolution, the writing of Balzac and perhaps particularly of Stendhal, the *Madame Bovary* of Flaubert, the enthusiasm for detailed pictures of historical epochs manifested by the brothers Goncourt, the emphasis Hippolyte Taine placed on the social backgrounds of literature — all these influences helped to stimulate the scientific, social, factual study of man in relation to his environment. Taine had written: "It is not my intention to comment or moralize ... only to investigate, to expose, to lay all before you. ..." And again: "Vice and virtue are products like sugar and vitriol." And it soon became the avowed purpose of French naturalism to study the chemistry of man, the effect of heredity and of environment on human beings in a contemporary society. A new interest in science was introduced into literature. And this enthusiasm for the scientific study of man was augmented greatly by Zola's interpretation of Claude Bernard's *Introduction à l'Etude de la médecine experimentale.* Bernard was a physician who had written of the scientific method of medicine. Zola, stirred by the volume, decided that the method of the scientist should become the method of the writer. In *The Experimental Novel* he paraphrased Bernard's method and applied his ideas to literature. By 1879 Zola had created a furor with his *L'Assommoir* (*The Dram-Shop*). About him gathered such young writers as Maupassant and Huysmans who, under his leadership, in 1880 issued a volume of stories, *Les Soirées de Médan,* a collection which has been called a "Zolaist manifesto." So ascendant was this spirit in literature as to make at least one critic refer to the 1880's as the period of "la littérature brutale." And yet, only a few years later, in 1891, the *Echo de Paris* was able to conduct a questionnaire among writers and critics as to the fate of naturalism and inform its readers of a waning interest.

Nevertheless, literature had not "done with naturalism." What had passed were the first excesses of the manner; what remained was a greater willingness to face the truth, a greater concern with people of the lower social scale, an increased interest in the study of heredity and environment, a sterner view of nature, and a freedom of expression which scorned "literary" diction. Writers had found that science could not, after all, save the world of literature; but they had found as well that the scientific approach could go far toward evoking a clearer interpretation of life. Like the realists, the naturalists sought truth and shunned sentimentality, expressed concern with a contemporary society, and built their novels on a solid foundation of observed fact. Like realism, naturalism moves slowly, subordinating plot to milieu and the individual to the society in which he moves.

In four aspects, at least, naturalism extends the usual boundaries of realism. *First*, the outlook on life of the naturalists is more deterministic, more mechanistic than that of the realists. Man is an animal, motivated largely by the same forces which prompt the activities of the beasts of the field. He is the plaything of a callous nature. He is helpless against fate. His body is almost, if not fully, as important as his mind. *Second*, man, to the naturalist, is subject to scientific investigation. He is a case study. *Third*, the naturalist studies and writes often with the intention of bringing about social reform. "What is this man's environment?" the naturalist asks. "To what extent is that man the product of the mining district in which he lives?" Or "What factors in the heredity of Nana sent her out to walk the streets of Paris?" And since it is the betterment of man's condition which so largely motivates the naturalist, it is only to be expected that most frequently he draws his characters from the humble ranks of life. *Fourth*, the naturalist, approaching life and humankind from his analytical and scientific point of view, manifests the scientist's tolerant conviction as to the worthwhileness of all things for study. No manner of living, no social stratum, no individual is without significance.

Naturalism interprets life from the deterministic point of view. Man is not a free agent; he is the subject of a dominant and arbitrary nature, both psychically and physically. Whatever man does he does mechanistically, because of the commands of an impersonal nature beyond him. The naturalist sets for himself the task of analyzing these responses, of building up laws. As the physician recognizes disease by a diagnosis of symptoms, the naturalist accounts for man's conduct by a study of man in relation to the society in which he lives. The conduct of man, the naturalist believes, can be studied and reported upon with the precision of the chemist or the physicist evolving laws in his laboratory. Such an attitude quite naturally precludes the intervention of any supernatural agency in the activities of mankind.

To the naturalist, man is a pygmy in a world of chaotic forces. What we may say or think makes little difference. Whether man's situation is dictated by harsh natural law, environment, heredity, the society in which he lives, the chemistry of his body or mind, inscrutable Fate, a cruel deity, or just his own ignorance, the naturalist knows that humanity is at the mercy of forces, sometimes friendly, sometimes inimical. He knows, too, that rarely can man do anything about it.

Naturalism spurns idealism. Committed as this literary manner is to materialism, to the deterministic concept of life, it rarely recognizes any spiritual quality in man. "The duty of naturalism," wrote Lafcadio Hearn, "was to destroy idealism — to paint life as it is — to depict precisely what idealism seeks to conceal." Were he truly objective, truly scientific, the naturalist would be neither pessimistic nor optimistic in his outlook on the world about him. He would neither shut his eyes to the idealistic nor yet lay emphasis upon it. But his objectivity rarely goes this far. By disposition he is pretty well convinced that the sordid outweighs the glamorous in life. His work is "unashamed and unabridged." It is not strange, then, that often he arrives at the position announced by Maupassant in *Sur l'Eau:*

> Happy are those who do not perceive with unutterable disgust that nothing changes and that all is weariness. . . . How is it that the world audience has not yet called out "Curtain," has not yet demanded the next act, with other beings than mankind, other manners, other pleasures, other plants, other planets, other inventions, other adventures?

And yet the naturalistic manner is not dismissed simply by labeling it as bitter, pessimistic. Every walk we take into our tenement areas, our factory regions, our rural districts, shows us men and women slaves of themselves and of their environment. So long as life is contaminated, muddied by filth, misery, cruelty, the naturalist will focus on these aspects. He must not use rose-colored spectacles. Objective and scientific as he may try to be, there is something in his temperament which makes him, while humanity struggles and suffers, throw in his art for an understanding of the suppressed. His science and his objectivity, no matter how fervently he may proclaim them, are not equal to the task of glossing over injustice and human misery.

Naturalism manifests a strong social purpose. This does not mean, however, that the naturalistic temper is to be confused with the attitude of the reformer. "These are the conditions in which labor lives," says the writer, but he does not go on to say, as the strictly sociological novelist probably would say, "and this is what should be done about it." His concern is with social facts and principles, "laws," rather than with remedies. The naturalist is content to awaken interest, to stimulate sympathy, to arouse concern. But he does not preach. He "places" his novel or story in a factory, a tenement district, a farm area, and by the facts he marshals makes clear the life people are obliged to lead under this set of conditions. He takes a problem or situation connected with drink, or sex, or marriage, or labor, and sets forth, through a case study of an individual or a family, the conditions surrounding this problem in society. Zola set the pattern here, and his books offer perhaps the most obvious examples of this tendency. Each of the volumes in the Rougon-Macquart series can be reduced to some one social problem: thus *L'Assommoir* is a study of the effects of liquor, *Germinal* of labor, *Nana* of sex, *La Terre* of the farm. In this latter book, Zola does not hesitate to introduce long pages of economics and social discussion. He even reads into his record tracts and documents of social theory. In fact, all of Zola's twenty novels may be said to fit together into a general study of the interplay of heredity and environment as it works out in the lives of a family. "Indeed our great study is just there," he wrote, "in the reciprocal effect of society on the individual, and the individual on society." And again: "We are looking for the causes of social evil; we study the anatomy of classes and individuals to explain the derangements which are produced in society and in man."

Thus it might be said that in the naturalistic novel society becomes the antagonist. Society takes over the role played by Fate in classical tragedy. Humanity, limited from the past by its particular inheritance and circumscribed in the present by the environment in which it moves, is as restricted, as bound in its personal freedom, as was Prometheus to his rock.

Naturalism, in brief, is the expression in literature of that artistic temperament which leans to an extreme realism, which looks upon life as largely the result of the interplay of mechanistic forces on the individual and which studies, with a more or less scientific impartiality, the role played by man in society, interpreting that role largely as the sum total of man's environment and inherited characteristics. It is catholic enough to include any or all the activities of the individual, though by nature it is likely to reserve its sympathy for those human beings who are downtrodden and mistreated by their society.

Émile Zola · 1840-1902

The decade of the 1880's was a period of literary change. In England, Tennyson and Browning were writing verse dominantly romantic but with differences which set them off from such other romantics as Wordsworth and Byron; in France, it was the decade of the symbolists Mallarmé and Huysmans and the naturalistic Zola; in Russia, Tolstoy was expressing his social convictions through the temper of realism. It was a period of shifting emphases, varying moods, and changing attitudes.

Émile Zola was born in Paris, April 2, 1840. His father was of Italian-Greek parentage, his mother French. Most of Zola's boyhood was spent in the provinces, his early education, such as it was, being obtained at Aix. At the age of eighteen Zola returned to Paris, thrown pretty much on his own resources and forced to eke out a scant living as best he could. It was during these years that the author of *L'Assommoir* gained such first-hand experience as he had with the poor of Paris.

Eventually Zola secured a post as clerk in a bookstore, but his early writing brought him the opposition of the government censorship and he was forced to give up his clerkship. Not long after this Zola fixed on his life purpose — to write an extensive and thorough record of a family, a record which would show how that family worked out its fate on various levels of society. This plan developed into the famous Rougon-Macquart series embracing twenty novels, the first volume of which was published in 1871 and the last in 1893. In 1898 Zola undertook the defence of Captain Dreyfus, who had been cashiered from the army and sent to Devil's Island. It was a long and serious struggle, one which does great credit to Zola as a humanitarian, and though it resulted in Zola's voluntary exile to England, Dreyfus was eventually vindicated, his rank restored, and Zola was recognized as the hero of the whole "affair."

Zola's writing embraced three fields: criticism, short stories, and the novel. In criticism his most important contribution is his long essay on *The Experimental Novel* in which he develops his theory that fiction is the *scientific* study of society and individuals. Perhaps his most famous short story is *The Attack on the Mill*.

But Zola's reputation is most firmly based on the twenty novels of the Rougon-Macquart series, each of which may be thought of as a study in some one social problem even as the whole was, at least in Zola's mind, a study of the problem of heredity. Of the twenty novels, five stand out most prominently: *L'Assommoir* (1878), a study of alcoholism; *Nana* (1880), a study of sex; *Germinal* (1885), based on the problem of labor in the coal-mines; *La Terre* (1888), which portrays the economics and way of living of the French peasant; and *Le Débâcle* (1892), a study of failing imperialism.

Naturalism in literature found its most ardent advocate in Zola. His writing presents a profusion of details and scenes against broad backgrounds sometimes so all-inclusive as to make his novels ponderous. He incorporates documents and records sights, sounds, odors, language of the work-a-day world. He uses a diction shot through with slang and vulgar words in common usage. His work, however, has resulted in an extension of the vocabulary of fiction. At the same time, Zola is able to write vital and dramatic episodes and proves his ability as a literary artist.

The stuff from which Zola wove his naturalistic novels was found in the contemporary social structure of France. He sat, like a physician, with a finger on the pulse of society. In *The Experimental Novel* he develops at length the thesis that the writer must approach his material as the scientist approaches his, analyzing and experimenting:

"Now," writes Zola, "science enters the domain of us novelists, who are today the analyzers of man, in his individual and social relations. We are continuing, by our observations and experiments, the work of the physiologist, who has continued that of the physicist and chemist. . . . In one word we should operate on the characters, the passions, on the human and social data, in the same way that the chemist and physicist operate on inanimate beings, and as the physiologist operates on living beings."

SUGGESTED REFERENCES: Angus Wilson, *Émile Zola* (1952), F. W. J. Hemmings, *Émile Zola* (1953); Marc Bernard, *Zola* (1960).

L'Assommoir [1]

The pages which follow from *L'Assommoir* (sometimes translated *The Dramshop*) present an incident which occurs near the beginning of the novel. Gervaise, the heroine of the narrative, has just been deserted by Lantier, the father of her two children. In the public laundry where the women of the locality resort to do their washing, a sister of the girl for whom Lantier deserted Gervaise gibes at her and Gervaise promptly fights back. In its vividness and coarseness the scene is characteristically Zolaesque, though from it we gather no suggestion of Zola's real social conscience.

THE FIGHT IN THE LAUNDRY

It was an immense shed, with large light windows, and a flat ceiling, showing the beams supported on cast-iron pillars. Pale rays of light passed freely through the hot steam, which remained suspended like a milky fog. Smoke arose from certain corners, spreading about and covering the recesses with a bluish veil. A heavy moisture hung around, impregnated with a soapy odor, a damp insipid smell, continuous though at moments overpowered by the more potent fumes of the chemicals. Along the washing-places, on either side of the central alley, were rows of women, with bare arms and necks, and skirts tucked up, showing colored stockings and heavy lace-up shoes. They were beating furiously, laughing, leaning back to call out a word in the midst of the din, or stooping over their tubs, all of them brutal, ungainly, foul of speech, and soaked as though by a shower, with their flesh red and reeking. Around them, beneath them, was a great flow of water, steaming pailfuls carried about and emptied at one

[1] Reprinted from *L'Assommoir*, by Émile Zola, and translated by Havelock Ellis. By permission of and special arrangement with Alfred A. Knopf, Inc., authorized publishers.

shoot, high up, taps of cold water turned on and discharging their contents, the splashings caused by the beetles, the drippings from the rinsed clothes, the pools in which the women trod trickling away in streamlets over the sloping flagstones; and, in the midst of the cries, of the cadenced blows, of the murmuring noise of rain, of that storm-like clamor dying away beneath the saturated ceiling, the engine on the right, all white with steam, puffed and snorted unceasingly, the dancing trepidation of its flywheel seeming to regulate the magnitude of the uproar.

Gervaise passed slowly along the alley, looking to the right and left. She carried her bundle of clothes on her arm, with one hip higher than the other, and limping more than usual, in the passing, backwards and forwards, of the other women who jostled against her.

"This way, my dear!" cried Madame Boche, in her loud voice. Then, when the young woman had joined her, at the very end on the left, the doorkeeper, who was furiously rubbing a sock, began to talk incessantly, without leaving off her work. "Put your things there, I've kept your place. Oh! I shan't be long over what I've got. Boche scarcely dirties his things at all. And you, you won't be long either, will you? Your bundle's quite a little one. Before twelve o'clock we shall have finished, and we can go off to lunch. I used to send my things to a laundress in the Rue Poulet, but she destroyed everything with her chlorine and her brushes; so now I do the washing myself. It's so much saved; it only costs the soap. I say, you should have put those shirts to soak. Those little rascals of children, on my word! one would think their bodies were covered with soot."

Gervaise, having undone her bundle, was spreading out the little ones' shirts, and as Madame Boche advised her to take a pailful of lye, she answered,

'Oh, no! warm water will do. I'm used to it.''

She had sorted the clothes, and put the few colored things on one side. Then, after filling her tub with four pailfuls of cold water taken from the tap behind her, she dipped in the pile of linen, and, tucking up her skirt, drawing it tight between her legs, she got into a kind of upright box, the sides of which reached nearly to her waist.

"You're used to it, eh?" repeated Madame Boche. "You were a washerwoman in your native place, weren't you, my dear?"

Gervaise, with her sleeves turned up, displaying her fine fair arms, still young, and scarcely reddened at the elbows, commenced getting the dirt out of her linen. She had spread a chemise over the narrow plank of the washing place, whitened and eaten away by the wear and tear of the water; she rubbed it over with soap, turned it, and rubbed it on the other side. Before answering, she seized her beetle and began to beat, shouting out her sentences, and punctuating them with rough and regular blows.

"Yes, yes, a washerwoman — When I was ten — That's twelve years ago — We used to go to the river — It smelt nicer there than it does here — You should have seen, there was a nook under the trees, with clear running water — You know, at Plassans[1] — Don't you know Plassans? — It's near Marseilles."

"How she goes at it!" exclaimed Madame Boche, amazed at the strength of her blows. "What a wench it is! She'd flatten out a piece of iron with her little lady-like arms."

The conversation continued in a very high tone. At times, the doorkeeper, not catching what was said, was obliged to lean forward. All the linen was beaten, and with a will! Gervaise plunged it into the tub again, and then took it out once more, each article separately, to rub it over with soap a second time and brush it. With one hand she held the article firmly on to the plank; with the other, which grasped the short couch-grass brush, she extracted from the linen a dirty lather, which fell in long drips. Then, in the slight noise caused by the brush, the two women drew together, and conversed in a more intimate way.

"No, we're not married," resumed Gervaise. "I don't hide it. Lantier isn't so nice for anyone to care to be his wife. Ah! if it wasn't for the children! I was fourteen and he eighteen years old when we had our first; the other came four years later. It happened as it always does, you know. I wasn't happy at home. Old Macquart, for a yes or a no, would give me no end of kicks behind; so I preferred to keep away from him.

[1] The city of Aix.

We might have been married, but — I forget why — our parents wouldn't consent."

She shook her hands, which were growing red in the white suds. "The water's awfully hard in Paris," said she.

Madame Boche was now washing only very slowly. She kept leaving off, making her work last as long as she could, so as to remain there, to listen to that story, which her curiosity had been hankering to know for a fortnight past. Her mouth was half open in the midst of her big, fat face; her eyes, which were almost at the top of her head, were gleaming. She was thinking, with the satisfaction of having guessed right.

"That's it, the little one gossips too much. There's been a row."

Then, she observed out loud, "He isn't nice, then?"

"Don't mention it!" replied Gervaise. "He used to behave very well in the country; but, since we've been in Paris, he's been unbearable. I must tell you that his mother died last year and left him some money — about seventeen hundred francs. He would come to Paris, so, as old Macquart was for ever knocking me about without warning, I consented to come away with him. We made the journey with the two children. He was to set me up as a laundress, and work himself at his trade of a hatter. We should have been very happy; but, you see, Lantier's ambitious and a spendthrift, a fellow who only thinks of amusing himself. In short, he's not worth much. On arriving, we went to the Hôtel Montmartre, in the Rue Montmartre. And then there were dinners, and cabs, and the theatre; a watch for himself and a silk dress for me, for he's not unkind when he's got the money. You understand, he went in for everything, and so well that at the end of two months we were cleaned out. It was then that we came to live at the Hôtel Boncoeur, and that this horrible life began."

She interrupted herself. A lump had suddenly risen in her throat, and she could scarcely restrain her tears. She had finished brushing the things.

"I must go and fetch my hot water," she murmured.

But Madame Boche, greatly disappointed at this break-off in the disclosures, called to the washhouse boy, who was passing,

"My little Charles, kindly get madame a pail of hot water; she's in a hurry."

The boy took the pail and brought it back filled. Gervaise paid him; it was a sou the pailful. She poured the hot water into the tub, and soaped the things a last time with her hands, leaning over them in a mass of steam, which deposited small beads of grey vapor in her light hair.

"Here, put some soda in, I've got some by me," said the concierge, obligingly.

And she emptied into Gervaise's tub what remained of a bag of soda which she had brought with her. She also offered her some of the chemical water, but the young woman declined it; it was only good for grease and wine stains.

"I think he's rather a loose fellow," resumed Madame Boche, returning to Lantier, but without naming him.

Gervaise, bent almost double, her hands all shrivelled, and thrust in amongst the clothes, merely tossed her head.

"Yes, yes," continued the other, "I've noticed several little things —" But she suddenly interrupted herself, as Gervaise jumped up, with a pale face, and staring wildly at her. Then she exclaimed, "Oh, no! I don't know anything! He likes to laugh a bit, I think, that's all. For instance, you know the two girls who lodge at my place, Adèle and Virginie. Well, he larks about with 'em, but it doesn't go any further, I'm sure."

The young woman standing before her, her face covered with perspiration, the water dripping from her arms, continued to stare at her with a fixed and penetrating look. Then the concierge got excited, giving herself a blow on the chest, and pledging her word of honor, she cried,

"I know nothing, I mean it when I say so!"

Then, calming herself, she added in a gentle voice, as if speaking to a person on whom loud protestations would have no effect, "I think he has a frank look about the eyes. He'll marry you, my dear, I'm sure of it!"

Gervaise passed her wet hand over her forehead. She drew another article of clothing from the water, as she again tossed her head. For a while they both remained silent. Peacefulness prevailed around them; eleven o'clock was striking. Half the women, resting one leg on the edges of their tubs, and with open bottles of wine at their feet, were eating sausages between slices of bread. Only the women who had families, and had come there just to wash their little bundles of clothes, hurried over their work as they kept glancing up at the clock which hung above the office. A few beetle strokes were still heard at intervals, in the midst of quiet laughter and conversations, which were drowned in the noise of a glutinous movement of jaws; whilst the steam-engine, ever at work, without truce or repose, seemed to raise its vibrating, snorting voice, until it filled the immense building. But not one of the women noticed it: it was as it were the very breathing of the wash-house — a scorching breath which accumulated, beneath the beams of the ceiling, the mist that incessantly floated about. The heat was becoming unbearable. Rays of sunshine entered through the tall windows on the left, transforming the smoking vapors into opaque masses of a pale pink and bluish grey tint; and, as complaints arose, the boy Charles went from one window to the other and lowered some coarse blinds; then he crossed to the other side, the shady one, and opened some of the casements. His movements were greeted with acclamations. There was a general clapping of hands, a boisterous gaiety passed over all. Then the last beetles were laid down. The women, with their mouths full, now only made gestures with the open knives that they held in their hands. The silence became so general that one could hear, at regular intervals, the grating of the stoker's shovel at the further end, as he scooped up the coal and threw it into the furnace.

Gervaise was washing her colored things in the hot water thick with lather, which she had kept for the purpose. When she had finished, she drew a trestle towards her and hung across it all the different articles, the drippings from which made bluish puddles on the floor; and then she commenced rinsing. Behind her, the cold water tap was set running into a vast tub fixed to the ground, and across which were two wooden bars whereon to lay the clothes. High up in the air were two other bars for the things to finish dripping on.

"We're almost finished, and it's not a pity," said Madame Boche. "I'll wait and help you wring all that."

"Oh! it's not worth while; I'm much obliged though," replied the young woman, who was kneading with her hands and sousing the colored things in some clean water. "If I'd any sheets, it would be another thing."

But she had, however, to accept the concierge's assistance. They were wringing between them, one at each end, a woollen skirt of a washed-out chestnut color, from which dribbled a yellowish water, when Madame Boche exclaimed:

"Why, there's tall Virginie! What has she come here to wash, when all her wardrobe that isn't on her would go into a pocket handkerchief?"

Gervaise quickly raised her head. Virginie was a girl of her own age, taller than she was, dark and pretty in spite of her face being rather long. She had on an old black dress with flounces, and a red ribbon round her neck; and her hair was done up carefully, the chignon being enclosed in a blue silk net. She stood an instant, in the middle of the central alley, screwing up her eyes as though seeking someone; then, when she caught sight of

Gervaise, she passed close to her, erect, insolent, and with a swinging gait, and took a place in the same row, five tubs away from her.

"There's a freak for you!" continued Madame Boche in a lower tone of voice. "She never even washes a pair of cuffs. Ah! she's a regular slut, I can tell you! A needlewoman who doesn't even sew the buttons on her boots! It's the same with her sister, the burnisher, that trollop Adèle, who's away from the workshop two days out of three! They know neither their father nor their mother, and they live no one knows how; and if one cared to talk — What's that she's rubbing there? Eh? it's a petticoat! Isn't it in a filthy state? It must have seen some fine goings-on, that petticoat!"

Madame Boche was evidently trying to make herself agreeable to Gervaise. The truth was she often took a cup of coffee with Adèle and Virginie, when the girls had any money. Gervaise did not answer, but hurried over her work with feverish hands. She had just prepared her blue in a little tub that stood on three legs. She dipped in the linen things, and shook them an instant at the bottom of the colored water, the reflection of which had a pinky tinge; and, after wringing them lightly, she spread them out on the wooden bars, up above. During the time she was occupied with this work, she made a point of turning her back on Virginie. But she heard her chuckles; she could feel her sidelong glances. Virginie appeared only to have come here to provoke her. At one moment, Gervaise having turned round, they both stared into each other's faces.

"Leave her alone," murmured Madame Boche. "You're not going to pull each other's hair out, I hope. When I tell you there's nothing! It isn't her, there!"

At this moment, as the young woman was hanging up the last article of clothing, there was a sound of laughter at the door of the wash-house.

"Here are two brats who want their mamma!" cried Charles.

All the women leant forward. Gervaise recognized Claude and Etienne. As soon as they caught sight of her, they ran to her through the puddles, the heels of their unlaced shoes resounding on the flagstones. Claude, the eldest, held his little brother by the hand. The women, as they passed them, uttered little exclamations of affection as they noticed their frightened, though smiling, faces. And they stood there, in front of their mother, without letting go of each other's hands, and holding their fair heads erect.

"Has papa sent you?" asked Gervaise.

But as she stooped to tie the laces of Etienne's shoes, she saw the key of their room on one of Claude's fingers, with the brass number hanging from it.

"Why, you've brought the key!" said she, greatly surprised. "What's that for?"

The child, seeing the key, which he had forgotten, on his finger, appeared to recollect, and exclaimed in his clear voice:

"Papa's gone."

"He's gone to buy the lunch, and told you to come here to fetch me?"

Claude looked at his brother, hesitated, no longer recollecting. Then he resumed all in a breath: "Papa's gone. He jumped off the bed, he put all the things in the box, he carried the box down to a cab. He's gone."

Gervaise, who was squatting down, slowly rose to her feet, her face ghastly pale. She put her hands to her cheeks and temples, as though she felt her head was breaking; and she could find only these words, which she repeated twenty times in the same tone of voice:

"Ah! good heavens! — ah! good heavens! — ah! good heavens!"

Madame Boche, however, also questioned the child, quite delighted at the chance of hearing the whole story.

"Come, child, you must tell us just what happened. It was he who locked the door and who told you to bring the key, wasn't it?" And, lowering her voice, she whispered in Claude's ear: "Was there a lady in the cab?"

The child again got confused. Then he recommenced his story in a triumphant manner: "He jumped off the bed, he put all the things in the box. He's gone."

Then, when Madame Boche let him go, he drew his brother in front of the tap, and they amused themselves by turning on the water. Gervaise was unable to cry. She was choking, leaning back against her tub, her face still buried in her hands. Slight shivering fits seized her. At times a deep sigh escaped her, whilst she thrust her fists firmer into her eyes, as though to bury herself in the darkness of her abandonment. It was a gloomy abyss to the bottom of which she seemed to fall.

"Come, my dear, pull yourself together!" murmured Madame Boche.

"If you only knew! if you only knew!" said she at length very faintly. "He sent me this morning to pawn my shawl and my shifts to pay for that cab."

And she burst out crying. The recollection of her errand at the pawn-place, fixing in her mind one of the events of the morning, had given an outlet to the sobs which were choking her. That errand was an abomination — the great grief in her despair. The tears ran down on to her chin, which her hands had already wetted, without her even thinking of taking a handkerchief.

"Be reasonable, do be quiet, everyone's looking at you," Madame Boche, who hovered round her, kept repeating. "How can you worry yourself so much on account of a man? You loved him, then, all the same, did you, my poor darling? A little while ago you were saying all sorts of things against him; and now you're crying for him, and almost breaking your heart. Dear me, how silly we all are!"

Then she became quite maternal.

"A pretty little woman like you! can it be possible? One may tell you everything now, I suppose. Well! you recollect when I passed under your window, I already had my suspicions. Just fancy, last night, when Adèle came home, I heard a man's footsteps with hers. So I thought I would see who it was. I looked up the staircase. The fellow was already on the second landing; but I certainly recognized M. Lantier's overcoat. Boche, who was on the watch this morning, saw him coolly come down. It was with Adèle, you understand. Virginie has a gentleman now to whom she goes twice a week. Only it's highly improper all the same, for they've only one room and an alcove, and I can't very well say where Virginie managed to sleep."

She interrupted herself an instant, turned round, and then resumed, subduing her loud voice:

"She's laughing at seeing you cry, that heartless thing over there. I'd stake my life that her washing's all a pretence. She's packed off the other two, and she's come here so as to tell them how you take it."

Gervaise removed her hands from her face and looked. When she beheld Virginie in front of her, amidst three or four women, speaking low and staring at her, she was seized with a mad rage. She thrust out her arms, turned right round as she felt on the ground, trembling in every limb, then walked a few steps, and noticing a bucket full of water, she seized it with both hands and threw the contents with all her might.

"Get out, you bitch!" yelled tall Virginie.

She had stepped back, and her boots alone got wet. The other women, who for some minutes past had all been greatly upset by Gervaise's tears, jostled each other in their anxiety to see the fight. Some, who were finishing their lunch, got on the tops of their tubs. Others hastened forward, their hands smothered with soap. A ring was formed.

"Ah! the bitch!" repeated tall Virginie. "What's the matter with her? she's mad!"

Gervaise, standing on the defensive, her chin thrust out, her features convulsed, said nothing, not having yet acquired the Paris gift of the gab. The other continued:

"Get out! It's tired of wallowing about in the country; it wasn't twelve years old when it let the soldiers make free with it; it's left its leg behind in its native place. The leg fell off; it was rotting away."

The lookers-on burst out laughing. Virginie, seeing her success, advanced a couple of steps, drawing herself up to her full height, and yelling louder than ever:

"Here! come a bit nearer, just to see how I'll settle you! Don't you come annoying us here. Do I even know her, the hussy? If she'd wetted me, I'd have pretty soon turned up her skirts, as you'd have seen. Let her just say what I've ever done to her. Speak, you vixen; what's been done to you?"

"Don't talk so much," stammered Gervaise. "You know well enough. Someone saw my husband last night. And shut up, because if you don't I'll most certainly strangle you."

"Her husband! Ah! that's a good joke, that is! Madame's husband! as if one with such a carcass had husbands! It isn't my fault if he's chucked you up. You don't suppose I've stolen him. I'm ready to be searched. I'll tell you why he's gone: you were infecting the man! He was too nice for you. Did he have his collar on, though? Who's found madame's husband? A reward is offered."

The laughter burst forth again. Gervaise contented herself with continually murmuring in an almost low tone of voice:

"You know well enough, you know well enough. It's your sister, I'll strangle her — your sister."

"Yes, go and try it on with my sister," resumed Virginie sneeringly. "Ah! it's my sister! That's very likely. My sister looks a trifle different to you; but what's that to me? Can't one come and wash one's clothes in peace now? Just dry up, d'ye hear, because I've had enough of it!"

But it was she who returned to the attack, after giving five or six strokes with her beetle, intoxicated by the insults she had been giving utterance to, and worked up into a passion. She left off and recommenced again, speaking in this way three times:

"Well, yes! it's my sister. There now, does that satisfy you? They adore each other. You should just see them bill and coo! And he's left you with your bastards. Those pretty kids with their snotty faces! One of 'em's by a gendarme, isn't he? and you had three others made away with because you didn't want to have to pay for extra luggage on your journey. It's your Lantier who told us that. Ah! he's been telling some fine things; he'd had enough of you!"

"You dirty jade! you dirty jade! you dirty jade!" yelled Gervaise, beside herself, and again seized with a furious trembling. She turned round, looking once more about the ground; and only observing the little tub, she seized hold of it by the legs, and flung the whole of the blue water at Virginie's face.

"The cow! she's spoilt my dress!" cried the latter, whose shoulder was sopping wet and whose left hand was dyed blue. "Wait a minute, you dirty whore!"

In her turn she seized a bucket, and emptied it over the young woman. Then a formidable battle began. They both ran along the rows of tubs, seized hold of the pails that were full, and returned to dash the contents at each other's heads. And each deluge was accompanied by a volley of words. Gervaise herself answered now:

"There! dirty beast! You got it that time. It'll help to cool you."

"Ah! the carrion! That's for your filth. Wash yourself for once in your life."

"Yes, yes, I'll take the shine out of you, you lanky strumpet!"

"Another one! Rinse your teeth, make yourself smart for your watch tonight at the corner of the Rue Belhomme."

They ended by filling the buckets at the taps. And as they waited while these filled, they continued their foul language. The first pailfuls, badly aimed, scarcely touched them; but they soon got the range. It was Virginie who first received one full in the face; the water entered at the neck of her dress, ran down her back and bosom, and flowed out under her petticoats. She was still quite giddy with the shock, when a second one caught her sideways, giving her a sharp blow on the left ear and soaking her chignon, which unrolled like a ball of string. Gervaise was first hit in the legs; the water filled her shoes and rebounded as high as her thighs; two other pailfuls inundated her hips. Soon, however, it became no longer possible to count the hits. They were both of them dripping from their heads to their heels, the bodies of their dresses were sticking to their shoulders, their skirts clung to their loins, and they appeared thinner, stiffer, and shivering, as the water dropped on all sides as it does off umbrellas during a heavy shower.

"They look jolly funny!" said the hoarse voice of one of the women.

Every one in the wash-house was highly amused. A good space was left to the combatants, as nobody cared to get splashed. Applause and jokes circu-lated in the midst of the sluice-like noise of the buckets emptied in rapid succession. On the floor the puddles were running one into another, and the two women were wading in them up to their ankles. Virginie, however, who had been meditating a treacherous move, suddenly seized hold of a pail of boiling lye, which one of her neighbors had left there, and threw it. The same cry arose from all. Every one thought Gervaise was scalded; but only her left foot had been slightly touched. And, exasperated by the pain, she seized a bucket, without troubling herself to fill it this time, and threw it with all her might at the legs of Virginie, who fell to the ground. All the women spoke together.

"She's broken one of her limbs!"

"Well, the other tried to cook her!"

"She's right, after all, the fair one, if her man's been taken from her!"

Madame Boche held up her arms to heaven, uttering all sorts of exclamations. She had prudently retreated out of the way between two tubs; and the children, Claude and Etienne, crying, choking, terrified, clung to her dress, with the continuous cry of "Mamma! mamma!" broken by their sobs. When she saw Virginie fall she hastened forward, and tried to pull Gervaise away by her skirt, repeating the while:

"Come now, go home! be reasonable. On my word, it's quite upset me. Never was such a butchery seen before."

But she had to draw back and seek refuge again between the two tubs, with the children. Virginie had just flown at Gervaise's throat. She squeezed her round the neck, trying to strangle her. The latter freed herself with a violent jerk, and in her turn hung on to the tail of the other's chignon, as though she was trying to pull her head off. The battle was silently resumed, without a cry, without an insult. They did not seize each other round the body, they attacked each other's faces with open hands and clawing fingers, pinching, scratching whatever they caught hold of. The tall, dark girl's red ribbon and blue silk hair net were torn off. The body of her dress, giving way at the neck, displayed a large portion of her shoulder; whilst the blonde, half stripped, a sleeve gone from her loose white jacket without her knowing how, had a rent in her underlinen, which exposed to view the naked line of her waist. Shreds of stuff flew in all directions. It was from Gervaise that the first blood was drawn, three long scratches from the mouth to the chin; and she sought to protect her eyes, shutting them at every grab the other made for fear of having them torn out. No blood showed on Virginie as yet. Gervaise aimed at her ears, maddened at not being able to reach them. At length she succeeded in seizing hold of one of the earrings — an imitation pear in yellow glass — when she pulled and slit the ear, and the blood flowed.

"They're killing each other! Separate them, the vixens!" exclaimed several voices.

The other women had drawn nearer. They formed themselves into two camps. Some excited the combatants in the same way as the mob urge on snarling curs, while the others, more nervous and trembling, turned away their heads, having had enough of it, and kept repeating that they were sure they would be ill; and a general battle was on the point of taking place. The combatants styled each other heartless and good for nothing; bare arms were thrust out — three slaps were heard. Madame Boche, meanwhile, was trying to discover the wash-house boy.

"Charles! Charles! Wherever has he got to?" And she found him in the front rank, looking on with his arms folded. He was a big fellow, with an enormous neck. He was laughing and enjoying the sight of the bits of skin which the two women displayed. The little blonde was as plump as a quail. It would be fine if her chemise slit up.

"Why!" murmured he, winking his eye, "she's got a strawberry mark under the arm."

"What! you're there!" cried Madame Boche, as she caught sight of him. "Just come and help us separate them. You can easily separate them, you can!"

"Oh, no! thank you, not if I know it," said he, coolly. "To get my eye scratched like I did the other day, I suppose! I'm not here for that sort of thing; I should have too much work if I was. Don't be afraid, a little bleeding does 'em good; it'll soften 'em."

The doorkeeper then talked of fetching the police; but the mistress of the wash-house, the delicate young woman with the sore eyes, would not allow her to do this. She kept saying:

"No, no, I won't; it'll compromise my establishment."

The struggle on the ground continued. All on a sudden, Virginie raised herself up on her knees. She had just got hold of a beetle and brandished it on high. She had a rattling in her throat, and, in an altered voice, she exclaimed:

"Here's something that'll settle you! Get your dirty linen ready!"

Gervaise quickly thrust out her hand, and also seized a beetle, and held it up like a club; and she too spoke in a choking voice:

"Ah! you want to wash. Let me get hold of your skin that I may beat it into dish-cloths!"

For a moment they remained there, on their knees, menacing each other. Their hair all over their faces, their breasts heaving, muddy, swelling with rage, they watched one another, as they waited and took breath. Gervaise gave the first blow. Her beetle glided off Virginie's shoulder, and she at once threw herself on one side to avoid the latter's beetle, which grazed her hip. Then, warming to their work, they struck at each other like washerwomen beating clothes, roughly and in time. Whenever there was a hit, the sound was deadened, so that one might have thought it a blow in a tub full of water. The other women around them no longer laughed. Several had gone off, saying that it quite upset them; those who remained stretched out their necks, their eyes lighted up with a gleam of cruelty, admiring the pluck displayed. Madame Boche had led Claude and Etienne away, and one could hear at the other end of the building the sound of their sobs, mingled with the sonorous shocks of the two beetles. But Gervaise suddenly yelled. Virginie had caught her a whack with all her might on her bare arm, just above the elbow. A large red mark appeared, the flesh at once began to swell. Then she threw herself upon Virginie, and everyone thought she was going to beat her to death.

"Enough! enough!" was cried on all sides.

Her face bore such a terrible expression, that no one dared approach her. Her strength seemed to have increased tenfold. She seized Virginie round the waist, bent her down and pressed her face against the flagstones; then, in spite of her struggles, she tore her skirts sheer off her. When she came to her drawers she thrust her hand into the opening and gave it a tear which exposed her naked thighs and buttocks. Raising her beetle, she commenced beating as she used to beat at Plassans, on the banks of the Viorne, when her mistress washed the clothes of the garrison. The wood seemed to yield to the flesh with a damp sound. At each whack a red weal marked the white skin.

"Oh, oh!" murmured the boy Charles, opening his eyes to their full extent and gloating over the sight.

Laughter again burst forth from the lookers-on, but soon the cry, "Enough! enough!" recommenced. Gervaise heard not, neither did she tire. She examined her work, bent over it, anxious not to leave a dry place. She wanted to see the whole of that skin beaten, covered with contusions. And she talked, seized with a ferocious gaiety, recalling a washerwoman's song:

"Bang! bang! Margot at her tub — Bang! bang! beating rub-a-dub — Bang! bang! tries to wash her heart — Bang! bang! black with grief to part —"

And then she resumed: "That's for you, that's for your sister, that's for Lantier. When you next see them, you can give them that. Attention! I'm going to begin again. That's for Lantier, that's for your sister, that's for you. Bang! bang! Margot at her tub — Bang! bang! beating rub-a-dub —"

The others were obliged to drag Virginie from her. The tall dark girl, her face bathed in tears and purple with shame, picked up her things and hastened away. She was vanquished. Gervaise slipped on the sleeve of her jacket again, and fastened up her petticoats. Her arm pained her a good deal, and she asked Madame Boche to place her bundle of clothes on her shoulder. The concierge referred to the battle, spoke of her emotions, and talked of examining the young woman's person, just to see.

"You may, perhaps, have something broken. I heard a tremendous blow."

But Gervaise wanted to go home. She made no reply to the pitying remarks and the noisy ovation of the other women who surrounded her, erect in their aprons. When she was laden she gained the door, where the children awaited her.

"Two hours, that makes two sous," said the mistress of the wash-house, already back at her post in the glazed closet.

Why two sous? She no longer understood that she was asked to pay for her place there. Then she gave the two sous; and, limping very much beneath the weight of the wet clothes on her shoulder, the water dripping from off her, her elbow black and blue, her cheek covered with blood, she went off, dragging Claude and Etienne with her bare arms, whilst they trotted along on either side of her, still trembling, and their faces besmeared with their tears.

Behind her, the wash-house resumed its great sluice-like noise. The women had eaten their bread and drunk their wine, and they beat harder than ever, their faces brightened up, enlivened by the set-to between Gervaise and Virginie. Along the rows of tubs arms were again working furiously, whilst angular, puppet-like profiles, with bent backs and distorted shoulders, kept jerking violently forward as though on hinges. The conversations continued along the different alleys. The voices, the laughter and the indecent remarks mingled with the gurgling sound of the water. The taps were running, the buckets overflowing, and there was quite a little river beneath the washing-places. It was the busiest moment of the afternoon, the pounding of the clothes with the beetles. The vapors floating about the immense building assumed a reddish hue, only broken here and there by orbs of sunshine, golden balls that found admittance through the holes in the blinds. One breathed a stifling, luke-warm atmosphere, charged with soapy odors. All on a sudden the place became filled with a white vapor. The enormous lid of the copper full of boiling lye was rising mechanically on a central toothed rod, and the gaping hole in the midst of the brickwork exhaled volumes of steam savoring of potash. Close by, the wringing machine was in motion. Bundles of wet clothes, inserted between the cast-iron cylinders, yielded forth their water at one turn of the wheel of the panting, smoking machine, which quite shook the building with the continuous working of its arms of steel.

When Gervaise turned into the entry of the Hôtel Boncoeur, her tears again mastered her. It was a dark, narrow passage, with a gutter for the dirty water running alongside the wall; and the stench which she again encountered there caused her to think of the fortnight she had passed in the place with Lantier — a fortnight of misery and quarrels, the recollection of which was now a bitter regret. It seemed to bring her abandonment home to her.

Maxim Gorki · 1868–1936

At the age of nine Maxim Gorki was thrown upon his own resources. His father had died four years before, his mother had married again, and his grandfather, in whose hands he had been left, was unable to help him. Soon after began Gorki's years of wandering, working at this job and at that — as a cobbler, a ship's cook, a baker, a gardener, a railway porter. When he was nineteen years old he shot himself, but the bullet wound proved not to be fatal and he was spared, as he once said, to devote himself to the apple-business. During these years of struggle, Gorki met three men who took a large part in moulding his career: the chief cook on a river steamer who impressed on the boy the necessity for reading extensively; a lawyer who encouraged the young man and let him catch a glimpse of intellectual life; and the writer Korolenko who insisted that Gorki seriously study to improve his literary style.

Gorki was born in Nizhni-Novgorod on March 14, 1868. His real name was Alexei Maximovich Peshkov, but when he published his first story, in 1892, he took for himself the name of "Gorki," "the bitter one," in reference to his years of starvation. In 1897 he published his first volume of short stories. It brought him immediate popularity. His understanding of the underprivileged in Russian society made his writing particularly acceptable to the working people of whose life he wrote; his sympathy with social reform and revolution brought him to the attention of ruling Russian society — and of the police. In 1907 he left Russia for Capri. Subsequent years were spent in Italy and Russia. After the Russian revolution he proved himself the friend of intellectuals before the Bolshevik tribunal. He died in Moscow, on June 18, 1936.

Maxim Gorki wrote short stories, plays, novels, and autobiographical reminiscences. His greatest literary reputation, however, lies in the field of the short story. He wrote of rogues and rascals and outcasts whom he had known well in his maturing years. He transcribed Russian life and scenery. He pointed up, without didacticism, the need for social reform. His naturalisic stories are something more than a mere turning of the knife in the wounds of Russian society; at times they present in almost lyrical expression the beauties of Russian nature and landscape — rivers, fields, and villages. His peasants live in squalor and poverty, but they know goodness as well as meanness, generosity as well as degradation.

SUGGESTED REFERENCES: Richard Hare, *Maxim Gorky: Romantic Realist and Conservative Revolutionary* (1962); Dan Levin, *Stormy Petrel: The Life and Work of Maxim Gorky* (1965).

Chums

Chums illustrates the bleak Russian life of the downtrodden. Here is the method of naturalism — its interest in the underprivileged, its deterministic outlook, its frail heroes. It is a story told in plain-spoken language. The reader feels the chill in the spring air of Russia. Jig-Leg the cripple and Hopeful who is dying of tuberculosis, the shaggy horse to be sold for her hide — surely this is misery enough. And yet Gorki is not blind to poetic values: "The white stems of birches, silvered by the moon, stood out like wax candles against a dark background of oaks, elms, and brushwood."

The story is reprinted from *A Book of Short Stories* by Maxim Gorki, translated by Avrahm Yarmolinsky, with the permission of the publishers, Henry Holt and Company, Inc.

One of them was called Jig-Leg, the other Hopeful, and both were thieves by trade.

They lived on the outskirts of the city, in a suburb that straggled queerly along a ravine, in one of the dilapidated shanties built of clay and half-rotten wood, which looked like heaps of rubbish that had been thrown down into the 25 ravine. The pals did their thieving in the near-by villages, for in the city it was difficult to steal, and

in the suburb the neighbors had nothing worth taking.

Both of them were cautious and modest: having nabbed a piece of linen, a coat, or an ax, a piece of 5 harness, a shirt, or a hen, for a long time they would keep away from the village where they had made their haul. But in spite of this prudent way of working, the suburban peasants knew them well, and threatened on occasion to beat the lives out 10 of them. The occasion, however, did not present itself to the peasants, and the bones of the two friends remained whole, although they had been hearing these threats for full six years.

Jig-Leg was a man of forty, tall, somewhat bent, 15 lean and muscular. He walked with his head bowed, his long arms crossed behind his back, with a long leisurely stride, and as he moved along, he kept glancing restlessly and anxiously from side to side with his sharp, puckered-up eyes. He 20 wore his hair clipped short and shaved his beard; his thick, grayish, military mustaches covered his mouth, lending his face a bristling, dour look. His left leg must have been dislocated or broken, and it mended in such a way that it was longer than 25 the right one. When he lifted it in walking, it jumped up in the air and jerked sideways. This peculiarity of his gait earned him his nickname.

Hopeful was about five years older than his comrade; he was shorter, and broader in the shoulders. But he had a persistent, hollow cough, and his knobby face was covered with a large black beard, streaked with gray, which did not hide his sickly, yellow complexion. He had large, black eyes, which looked at everything with a guilty and amiable expression. As he walked, he would press his thick lips together in the shape of a heart, and he whistled softly a sad, monotonous melody, always the same. His shoulders were covered by a short garment made of motley rags, something resembling a wadded pea-jacket; Jig-Leg wore a long, gray kaftan, with a belt.

Hopeful was by birth a peasant, his comrade was the son of a sexton, and had at one time been a footman and a marker. They were always together, and the peasants, seeing them, would say: "There are the chums again!... Watch out."

The chums would tramp along some country road, keeping a sharp look-out, and avoiding people. Hopeful coughed and whistled his tune; his comrade's leg jigged in the air, as though trying to wrench itself loose and dash away from its master's dangerous path. Or else they lay on the edge of a forest, in the rye, or in a gully, and quietly discussed how to steal something in order to eat.

. . . .

In winter even the wolves, who are better adapted to the struggle for life than the two friends, have a hard time of it. Lean, hungry, and vicious, they stalk the roads, and though people kill them, these same people are afraid of them: they have claws and fangs for self-defense, and, above all, their hearts are softened by nothing. This last point is very important, for, in order to be victorious in the struggle for existence, man must have either keen intelligence or the heart of a beast.

In winter the chums were hard put to it. Often both of them went into the streets in the evening and begged, trying not to be noticed by the police. They rarely succeeded in stealing anything; it was inconvenient to go into the country because it was cold, and because one left traces in the snow; besides, it was useless to visit the villages when everything there was locked up and snowbound. In winter the comrades lost much strength fighting hunger, and perhaps no one awaited spring as eagerly as they did.

And then, at last, spring would come! The pals, exhausted and ailing, crawled out of their ravine, and gazed joyfully at the fields, where, every day, the snow thawed more rapidly, brown patches began to appear, the puddles shone like mirrors, and streams babbled gaily. The sun lavished upon the earth its disinterested caresses, and both friends warmed themselves in its rays, figuring out how soon the earth would get dry and at last it would be possible to "do business" in the villages. Often Hopeful, who suffered from insomnia, would wake his friend in the early morning, and would announce joyfully:

"Hey! Get up! The rooks have come!"

"They have?"

"Honest. You hear them cawing?"

Leaving their shanty, they would watch eagerly for a long time how the black messengers of spring were weaving new nests and repairing old ones, filling the air with their loud, anxious chatter.

"Now it's the larks' turn," Hopeful would say, and set about mending his old, half-rotten bird-net.

The larks would come. The comrades would go into the fields, set up the net on a brown patch, and racing through the wet, muddy field, would drive into the net the hungry birds, exhausted by their long flight and looking for food on the moist earth that had just been released from the snow. Having caught the birds, they would sell them for five and ten kopecks apiece. Then nettles appeared. They picked them and took them to the marketplace to sell them to the women who traded in greens. Almost every spring day brought them something new, some additional, if small, earnings. They knew how to take advantage of everything: pussy-willows, sorrel, mushrooms, strawberries — nothing escaped them. The soldiers would come out for rifle practice. When the shooting was over the friends would dig in the earthworks looking for bullets, which they would afterwards sell at twelve kopecks a pound. All these odd jobs, although they prevented the friends from dying of hunger, very rarely gave them a chance to relish the sense of having eaten their fill, the pleasant feeling of a full stomach busily digesting the food it held.

. . . .

One day in April, when the trees were only beginning to bud, when the woods were enveloped in a bluish haze, and on the brown, rich, sun-flooded fields the grass was just starting to show, the friends were walking on the highroad, smoking cheap cigarettes that they themselves had rolled, and engaged in talk.

"Your cough is getting harder," Jig-Leg calmly warned his comrade.

"I don't give a damn! The sun will warm me, and I'll be myself again."

"H'm! Maybe you ought to go to the hospital."

"Nonsense! What do I need a hospital for? If I have to die, I'll die anyway!"

"True enough."

They were walking along through a birch grove, and the trees cast upon them the patterned shadows of their delicate branches. Sparrows hopped on the road, chirping gaily.

"You don't walk as well as you used to," observed Jig-Leg, after a pause.

"It's because I have a choky feeling," explained Hopeful. "These days the air is thick and rich, and it's hard for me to swallow it."

And, stopping short, he had a coughing-fit.

Jig-Leg stood by, smoked away, and looked at him uncertainly. Hopeful shook with coughing and rubbed his chest with his hands. His face turned blue.

"It clears my lungs, anyway!" he said, when he had stopped coughing.

And they went further, scaring away the sparrows.

"Now we are on the way to Mukhina," said Jig-Leg, tossing away the cigarette-butt and spitting. "We'll go round it the back way: maybe we'll be able to pick up something. Then across the Sivtsova woods we'll make for Kuznechikha. ... From there we'll turn off to Markovka, and then we'll strike out for home."

"That will make a good thirty versts,"[1] said Hopeful.

"If only we get something out of it!"

To the left of the road there was a forest that looked dark and forbidding; among the naked branches there was not a single green patch to cheer the eye. A small horse with a shaggy, matted coat and woefully fallen-in flanks was straying along the edge of the wood. Its ribs were as prominent as the hoops of a barrel. The friends halted again and for a long time watched it slowly putting one foot after the other, lowering its muzzle toward the ground, getting hold of the faded grass-blades with its lips and carefully munching them with its worn-down yellow teeth.

"She's gotten thin, too," observed Hopeful.

"Whoa-whoa!" cried Jig-Leg coaxingly.

The horse looked at him, and shaking its head, bent it earthwards again.

"She doesn't like you," Hopeful interpreted the horse's tired movement.

"Come on. If we turn her over to the Tartars ... they might give us some seven rubles for her," said Jig-Leg pensively.

"No, they won't! What good would she be to them?"

"What about the hide?"

"The hide? Will they give all that for the hide? They won't give more than three for it."

[1] A verst is about two thirds of a mile.

"Still ..."

"But look at that hide. It's not a hide, it's an old rag."

Jig-Leg looked at his comrade, and, after a pause, said:

"Well?"

"There might be trouble..." Hopeful said, doubtfully.

"Why?"

"We'd leave tracks.... The earth is damp.... They could see where we'd gone."

"We could put bast shoes on her feet."

"If you like."

"Come along! Let's drive into the wood and wait in the ravine until dark. At night we'll take her out and drive her to the Tartars. It's not far — only three versts."

"Well," Hopeful nodded, "let's go. A bird in the hand, you know ... But what if ... ?"

"Nothing will happen," said Jig-Leg confidently.

They left the road, and glancing about them, walked toward the wood. The horse looked at them, snorted, waved its tail, and again began to crop the faded grass.

. . . .

At the bottom of the deep ravine in the wood it was dark, damp, and quiet. The murmur of a stream was wafted through the stillness, sad and monotonous, like a lament. Naked branches of hazel, snowball trees, and honeysuckle were hanging down the steep sides of the ravine; here and there roots, washed out by spring freshets, were helplessly sticking out of the ground. The forest was still dead; the evening twilight added to the lifeless monotony of its hues and the mournful stillness that lurked in it filled it with the gloomy, solemn peace of a cemetery.

For a long time the chums had been sitting in the damp and silent dusk, under a clump of aspens which had slid down to the bottom of the ravine together with a huge mass of earth. A small fire burned brightly before them, and, warming their hands over it, they fed it twigs, from time to time, taking care that the flame should burn evenly and not smoke. The horse stood not far off. They had wrapped its muzzle with a sleeve torn from Hopeful's rags, and had tied it by the bridle to the trunk of a tree.

Hopeful, crouching by the fire, looked pensively into it and whistled his tune; his comrade, having cut a bunch of osier-twigs, was weaving a basket out of them, and, busy with his task, he was silent.

The melancholy sound of the stream and the low whistle of the luckless man blended together and floated piteously on the stillness of the evening and the forest; sometimes the twigs crackled in the fire, crackled and hissed, as if they were sighing out of pity for the two men whose life was more painful than their own death in the flames.

"Are we starting out soon?" asked Hopeful.

"It's too early. Wait till it gets quite dark, and then we'll start," said Jig-Leg, without lifting his head from his work.

Hopeful sighed and began to cough.

"Chilly, eh?" asked his comrade, after a long pause.

"No.... I'm not quite right."

"So?" and Jig-Leg shook his head.

"My heart bothers me."

"Sick, eh?"

"I suppose so... and maybe it's something else."

Jig-Leg said:

"See here!... Don't think!"

"What about?"

"Oh, about everything."

"You see —" Hopeful suddenly grew animated — "I can't help thinking. I look at her —" he pointed to the horse — "I look at her and it comes home to me. I too used to have one like that.... She's not much to look at, but on a farm, she's worth everything. At one time I had a pair of them.... I worked hard in those days."

"What did you get out of it?" asked Jig-Leg. "I don't like this streak in you. Once you tune up, you don't stop playing. And what's the good of it?"

Hopeful silently threw a handful of twigs, broken up small, into the fire, and watched the sparks fly upward and go out in the damp air. He kept on blinking, and shadows ran across his face. Then he turned his head in the direction of the horse and looked at it for a long time.

The horse was standing motionless, as though rooted in the earth; her head, disfigured by the cloth, was dropping dejectedly.

"We must look at things more simply," Jig-Leg said, sternly and impressively. "Our life is like this — a day and a night, and twenty-fours hours are gone! If there is food — good; if not — squeal a bit, and then stop, it doesn't get you anywhere. ... But you, once you start, you never stop. It's disgusting to listen to. It's because you're sick, that's why."

"It must be sickness," Hopeful agreed meekly, but after a pause he added, "And maybe because my heart is soft."

"And your heart is soft because of sickness," declared Jig-Leg categorically.

He bit off a twig, waved it, cut the air with a swish, and said sternly:

"I'm all right, and I don't act up that way."

The horse shifted from one leg to another; a twig creaked; some earth plumped into the stream with a splash that brought a new note into its soft melody; then from somewhere two little birds started up and flew along the ravine, screeching uneasily. Hopeful followed them with his eyes and spoke quietly:

"What birds are those? If they are starlings they have no business in the woods. They must be waxwings...."

"And maybe they're cross-bills," said Jig-Leg.

"It's too early for cross-bills, and besides, cross-bills like evergreens. They have no business here. They're sure to be waxwings."

"Who cares?"

"You're right!" agreed Hopeful, and for some reason drew a deep sigh.

Jig-Leg was working rapidly; he had already woven the bottom of the basket, and he was deftly making the sides. He cut the twigs with a knife, bit them through with his teeth, bent and wattled them with quick movements of his fingers, and wheezed from time to time, bristling his mustaches.

Hopeful looked at him and at the horse, petrified in its dejected post, at the sky, already almost dark, yet starless.

"The peasant will look for the horse," he suddenly spoke up in a strange voice, "and it won't be there — he'll look here, and there — no horse!"

Hopeful spread his arms wide. There was a foolish look on his face, and his eyes blinked rapidly as though he were looking at a bright light that had suddenly flared up before him.

"What are you driving at?" asked Jig-Leg sternly.

"I was reminded of something..." said Hopeful guiltily.

"What is it?"

"Well, it's this way.... They stole a horse... from a neighbor of mine... Mikhaila was his name... he was a tall fellow... pock-marked...."

"Well?"

"Well, it was stolen. It was grazing in the pasture, and then it was gone. So when he, Mikhaila that is, understood that he had lost his horse, he threw himself on the ground, and he howled! Brother, how he howled!... And he plumped down as though he had broken his legs...."

"Well?"

"Well... he carried on like that for a long time."

"What's that to you?"

At this sharp question, Hopeful moved away from his comrade and answered timidly:

"Nothing.... I just happened to think of it. Because without a horse, a peasant is done for."

"Let me tell you something," began Jig-Leg sternly, looking pointblank at Hopeful, "give it up! This kind of talk gets you nowhere, understand? Your neighbor, Mikhaila! It's not your affair."

"But it's a pity," Hopeful objected, shrugging his shoulders.

"A pity! Does anybody pity us?"

"That's true."

"Well, then, shut up! We'll soon have to go."

"Soon?"

"Yes."

Hopeful edged toward the fire, poked it with a stick, and looking out of the corner of his eye at Jig-Leg, who was again absorbed in his work, he said in a soft, beseeching tone:

"Hadn't we better let that horse go?"

"You have a mean nature!" exclaimed Jig-Leg, aggrieved.

"But honest," said Hopeful softly and persuasively. "Think of it, it's dangerous! We'll have to drag her along for a distance of four or five versts. . . . And what if the Tartars don't take her? Then what!"

"That's my business."

"As you please. But it would be better to let her go. She can go and roam about. Look what an old nag she is!"

Jig-Leg held his peace, but his fingers moved faster than ever.

"What are we going to get for her?" Hopeful drawled, softly but stubbornly. "And this the best time. It will be dark soon. If we go along the ravine we'll come out at Dubenka, and there we may pick up something worth while."

Hopeful's monotonous murmur, blending with the babble of the stream, floated down the ravine, and irritated the industrious Jig-Leg.

He was silent, his teeth clenched, and because of his excitement the osier-twigs snapped under his fingers.

"The women are bleaching their linen at this time."

The horse sighed audibly and grew restive. Wrapped in the darkness, it looked uglier and more pitiable than ever. Jig-Leg looked at it and spat into the fire.

"And the poultry is at large now . . . there are geese in the puddles. . . ."

"How long will it take you to dry up, you devil!" Jig-Leg asked savagely.

"It's God's truth. . . . Don't be angry at me, Stepan. To the devil with her. Really!"

"Did you have any grub today?" cried Jig-Leg.

"No," answered Hopeful, abashed and frightened by his comrade's shout.

"Then, deuce take you, you may starve here, for all I care."

Hopeful looked at him silently, while he, collecting the osier-twigs into a heap, tied them up into a sheaf, and snorted angrily. The fire threw a reflection on his whiskered face, and it looked red and angry.

Hopeful turned away and heaved a deep sigh.

"Look here, I don't care, do as you please," said Jig-Leg angrily, in a hoarse voice. "But let me tell you this," he went on, "if you go on that way, I'm no company for you! All right, it's enough. I know you, that's what . . ."

"You're a queer fellow. . . ."

"Not another word."

Hopeful shrank together and coughed; then when his fit of coughing was over, he said, breathing heavily:

"Why do I insist? Because it's dangerous."

"All right!" Jig-Leg shouted angrily.

He picked up the twigs, threw them on his shoulder, took the unfinished basket under his arm, and rose to his feet.

Hopeful also rose, looked at his comrade, and quietly went over to the horse.

"Whoa! Christ be with you! Don't be afraid!" his hollow voice resounded through the ravine.

"Whoa! Whoa! Stop! Well — go now — go along. There you are, you fool!"

Jig-Leg watched his comrade fussing over the horse, unwinding the rag from its muzzle, and the thief's mustache twitched.

"Let's go," he said, moving forwards.

"Let's," Hopeful agreed.

And, forcing their way through the bushes, they went silently along the ravine in the darkness which filled it to the brim.

The horse followed them.

Presently behind them they heard a splash which broke the murmur of the stream.

"The fool! She slipped into the stream," said Hopeful.

Jig-Leg snorted angrily, but said nothing.

In the darkness and the morose silence of the ravine, resounded the gentle cracking of twigs; the sound floated from the spot where the red heap of embers shone on the ground like a monstrous eye, malicious and mocking.

The moon rose.

Its transparent radiance filled the ravine with a smoky gloom; there were shadows everywhere, making the forest all the denser, and the silence fuller and more severe. The white stems of birches, silvered by the moon, stood out like wax candles against the dark background of oaks, elms, and brushwood.

The chums walked along the bottom of the ravine in silence. It was hard going; sometimes their feet slipped, or sank deep in the mud. Hopeful frequently breathed fast, and a whistling, wheezing, rattling sound came from his chest, as though a large clock that had not been cleaned for a long time were hidden there. Jig-Leg walked ahead; the shadow of his tall, straight figure fell upon Hopeful.

"Going, are we?" he broke out, in a hurt, petulant tone. "Where to? What are we looking for? Eh?"

Hopeful sighed, and said nothing.

"And these nights are shorter than a sparrow's beak. It will be dawn before we get to the village. ... And how are we walking? Like ladies... taking a stroll."

"I don't feel well, brother," said Hope quietly.

"Don't feel well!" exclaimed Jig-Leg ironically. "And why?"

"I have trouble breathing," replied the sick thief.

"Breathing? Why do you have trouble breathing?"

"It's the sickness, I suppose."

"You're wrong! It's your foolishness."

Jig-Leg halted, turned his face to his comrade, and wagging his finger under his nose, added:

"It's because of your foolishness that you have trouble breathing. Yes.... Yes! Understand?"

Hopeful bowed his head low and said guiltily: "You're right!"

He wanted to add something, but a fit of coughing seized him. He clasped a tree-trunk with his trembling hands, and coughed for a long time, stamping about on one spot, tossing his head, opening his mouth wide.

Jig-Leg looked attentively at his face, which stood out haggard, earthy, and greenish in the moonlight.

"You'll wake up all the wood-sprites," he said at last in a surly tone.

And when Hopeful had done coughing, and, throwing back his head, breathed freely, he spoke peremptorily:

"Take a rest. Let's sit down."

They sat down on the damp earth in the shadow of the bushes. Jig-Leg rolled a cigarette, lit it, looked at the glow of it, and began slowly:

"If we had something to eat at home... we could go back...."

"That's true," Hopeful nodded.

Jig-Leg looked at him out of the corner of his eye and continued:

"But since there's nothing at home, we must go on."

"So we must," sighed Hopeful.

"Although we've nowhere to go, because no good will come of it. And the main reason is, we're foolish. What fools we are!"

Jig-Leg's dry voice cut through the air, and must have greatly disturbed Hopeful: he kept writhing on the ground, sighing, and making strange rumbling sounds.

"And I'm so damn hungry," Jig-Leg concluded his reproachful speech.

Hopeful resolutely rose to his feet.

"What's the matter?" asked Jig-Leg.

"Let's go!"

"Why so lively all of a sudden?"

"Let's go!"

"All right —" Jig-Leg rose too — "only it's no use...."

"What will happen will happen!" and Hopeful waved his hand.

"So you've plucked up courage again?"

"What? Here you've been nagging and nagging me, and scolding and scolding me.... Oh, Lord!"

"Then why do you act foolishly?"

"Why?"

"Yes."

"Well, don't you see, I felt so sorry."

"For whom? For what?"

"For whom? For that peasant, I suppose."

"Peasant?" drawled Jig-Leg. "That's an idea to chew on! You've a heart of gold, but no brains. What's the peasant to you? Understand? Why, he'd nab you and crack you under his nail like a flea! That's the time for you to be sorry for him! Go and show him what a fool you are, and in return for your pity he'll torture you seven ways at once. He'll wind your guts round his wrist, and pull your veins out, an inch an hour. ... And you talk of... pity! You'd better pray God that they do you in without any 'pity,' at one blow, and make an end of it! Oh, you! To the devil with you! Pity... faugh!"

He was indignant, this Jig-Leg.

His cutting voice, full of irony and contempt for his comrade, resounded through the wood, and the branches of the bushes waved with a gentle rustle, as if confirming his stern, just words.

Hopeful, crushed by these reproaches, was walking slowly, his legs trembling, his hands in the sleeves of his jacket, and his head bent low over his chest.

"Wait!" he said at last. "Never mind. I'll be all right. We'll get to the village.... I'll go, I'll go all alone.... You needn't come at all.... I'll nab the first thing that comes to hand.... Then we'll make for home! We'll get there and I'll lie down! I'm feeling bad."

He spoke almost inaudibly, gasping for breath,

with a rattling and gurgling in his chest. Jig-Leg looked at him suspiciously, stopped, and was about to say something, but waved his arm, and without a word walked on again.

For a long time they walked in silence.

Near-by cocks were crowing; a dog howled; then the melancholy sound of the watchman's bell floated towards them from a distant village church, and was swallowed by the silence of the forest. A large bird, like a big black spot, rushed into the murky moonlight, and in the ravine the sweep of wings made an eerie sound.

"It must be a crow, or a rook," observed Jig-Leg.

"Listen," said Hopeful, lowering himself heavily to the ground, "You go, I'll stay here.... I can't go on.... I'm choking.... I'm dizzy."

"Well, that's a fine thing!" said Jig-Leg crossly. "You really can't go on?"

"I can't."

"Congratulations. Faugh!"

"I'm so weak."

"Of course; we've been walking since morning on an empty stomach."

"No, it's not that.... I'm done for ... look how the blood gushes!"

And Hopeful raised his hand to Jig-Leg's face, all smeared with something dark. The other looked askance at the hand and, lowering his voice, asked:

"What are we going to do?"

"You go ahead.... I'll stay here.... Maybe if I rest, I'll feel better."

"Where can I go? Suppose I go to the village and say there's a man in the woods who's taken sick?"

"Look out.... They'll beat you up."

"True enough. Just give them the chance."

Hopeful lay on his back, coughing a hollow cough, and spitting out whole gobs of blood.

"Is it still coming?" asked Jig-Leg, standing over him, but looking aside.

"It's flowing fast," said Hopeful, almost inaudibly, and was seized with another fit of coughing.

Jig-Leg swore loudly and cynically.

"If only we could call someone!"

"Whom?" asked Hopeful, his voice like a dismal echo.

"Maybe you could get up ... and walk ... slowly? ..."

"No chance...."

Jig-Leg sat beside his comrade's head, and clasping his own knees with his hands began to look into his face. Hopeful's chest rose convulsively with a hollow rattle, his eyes sank into his head, his lips gaped strangely and seemed to cling to his teeth. From the left corner of his mouth a dark living stream was trickling down his cheek.

"Still flowing?" asked Jig-Leg quietly, and in the tone of his question there was something akin to respect.

Hopeful's face quivered.

"Flowing," came a weak rattle.

Jig-Leg leaned his head on his knees and was silent.

Above them was the wall of the ravine, deeply furrowed by the spring freshets. From the top of it a shaggy row of moonlit trees looked down into the ravine. The other side of the ravine, which sloped more gently, was overgrown with shrubs; here and there above their dark mass rose the gray stems of aspens, and on their naked branches rooks' nests were clearly visible.... The ravine, flooded by moonlight, was like a tedious dream, lacking the colors of life; and the gentle murmur of the stream emphasized its lifelessness and brought out the melancholy silence.

"I am dying," said Hopeful, in a hardly audible whisper, and then immediately afterwards repeated in a loud, clear voice: "I am dying, Stepan!"

Jig-Leg shuddered, squirmed, snorted, and raising his head from his knees spoke in an awkward, gentle voice, as if he were afraid of creating a disturbance:

"Oh, it's not that bad ... don't be afraid.... It's nothing.... Maybe it's just ... It's nothing, brother!"

"Lord Jesus Christ!" Hopeful sighed heavily.

"It's nothing," whispered Jig-Leg, bending over his face. "Just stick it for a little while ... maybe it will pass over!"

Hopeful began to cough again; there was a new sound in his chest: it was as though a wet rag were slapping against his ribs. Jig-Leg was looking at him and was silently bristling his mustaches. When the coughing-fit was over, Hopeful began to pant loudly and jerkily, as though he were running with all his might. He went on breathing that way for a long time. Then he said:

"Forgive me, Stepan ... if anything I ... about that horse, you know.... Forgive me, brother!"

"You forgive me!" interrupted Jig-Leg, and after a pause, added:

"And I ... where shall I go now? What will I do?"

"It's all right.... May the Lor ..." He broke off in the middle of the word, and was silent.

Then he began to make a rattling sound ... he stretched out his legs ... one of them jerked sideways.

Jig-Leg looked at him without blinking. Minutes passed that were as long as hours.

Then Hopeful lifted his head, but at once it fell helplessly back onto the ground.

"What is it, brother?" Jig-Leg bent over him. But he did not answer, he lay quiet and motionless.

For a while Jig-Leg sat at his comrade's side. Then he rose, took off his cap, crossed himself, and slowly went on his way along the ravine. His face was drawn, his eyebrows and mustaches bristled, and he strode firmly as though he were striking the earth with his feet, as though he were trying to hurt it.

It was already daybreak. The sky was gray and harsh; a sullen silence reigned in the ravine; only the stream was talking monotonously and tediously.

But suddenly there was a noise — a clump of earth must have rolled down to the bottom of the ravine. A rook awoke, and with a cry of alarm, flew off. Then a titmouse piped. In the damp chill air of the ravine sounds did not last long; they arose and immediately died away. . . .

THE

IMPRESSIONISTS

> *. . . to project upon that wide field of the artist's vision — which hangs there ever in place like the white sheet suspended for the figures of a child's magic-lantern — a more fantastic and more moveable shadow.*

HENRY JAMES

IMPRESSIONISM IS ONE of the more vaguely understood of the literary tempers. In its simplest sense, impressionistic literature is writing which records chiefly the artist's *impressions* of a scene, a character, an incident. It makes its appeal largely through the senses by its concern with feeling, with emotion. Narrative and plot are subordinated to mood, and effect becomes all-important. If a narrative in this temper appears inconsecutive or vague in outline, and if we find difficulty in tracing the causal relationships between events, it is because impressionism as a temper employs a logic different from that used in more conventional writing. For an external relationship between people or events it substitutes the internal relationship evoked in the mind of the writer; for an objective cause-and-effect relationship it substitutes a subjective, personal ideology.

The essence of impressionism, thus understood, *is perhaps its emphasis on the revelation of the moment.* It is an instantaneous exposure, but an exposure on a special sort of film which records moods and colors and atmosphere even as it strains out the objective reality of the setting or person photographed. The negative shown to the reader carries more of the mind of the writer than of the external world. The impressionist believes that we need less imitation of nature; he holds that what we rather need is an interpretation of human nature. Accordingly, while he draws on the facts and details of nature, he selects them according to the mood, the attitude, the tonal value which he personally finds in the scene. He neither spurns one type of detail nor seeks another; rather he seizes upon what, for him, is the essence of the moment, and accordingly we may have, indeed do have, strange juxta-positions of the beautiful and the ugly. The details presented are not selected for their lulling qualities (as in some forms of romance) or their shocking qualities (as sometimes seems the case in naturalism); they are selected because, at least to the writer, they some-how present the essential spirit of the setting or incident portrayed. For impressionism shows us what we see as colored by the mind and mood of the artist. This is obvious, for instance, in the beginning of Conrad's *Lagoon*:

> The forests, sombre and dull, stood motionless and silent on each side of the broad stream. At the foot of big, towering trees, trunkless nipa palms rose from the mud of the bank, in bunches of leaves enormous and heavy, that hung unstirring over the brown swirl of eddies. In the stillness of the air every tree, every leaf, every bough, every tendril of creeper and every petal of minute blossoms seemed to have been bewitched into an immobility perfect and final. . . . And the white man's canoe, advancing upstream in the short-lived disturb-ance of its own making, seemed to enter the portals of a land from which the very memory of motion had forever departed.

Impressionism manifests a strong regard for color and tonal effects — for atmosphere. The French writer, Pierre Loti, characterizes his memoirs as "composed of incongruous details, minute observations, colors, shapes, scents, and sounds." Thus he shows how much the impressionists are indebted to painting. Monet saw a landscape not as we see it, but broken down into numerous particles of light and shadow. It was thus mirrored in his mind; and by applying dabs and splashes of color to his canvas he reproduced the over-all impression. The finished painting has to be looked at from a pre-determined point of view, from the same distance from which the artist had originally perceived the object. If this is done, the painted landscape will appear to us as it did to Monet.

Following this technique, impressionistic writers learned to seek out the essence of a char-acter or a situation by describing their personal impression of it. Though at first glance their writings seem incoherent or muddled to us, in the end they bring about the desired effect by properly reproducing the impression of the scene described. Three things writers learned from the impressionistic painters: (1) to break a scene or a situation into small parts and relate them to the whole anew, what Herbert Read called "holding the prism up to nature"; (2) to know that a truer impression of actuality may often be secured by an emphasis upon salient features and an omission of details unrelated to the particular effect or mood to be created; and (3) a conviction that writing need not restrict itself to presenting a character or a scene or an episode as they *know* it but that they may present their ma-terial as they *see*, or *feel*, it at a particular moment and under particular conditions.

Thus interpreted, impressionism is in no sense an easy, slipshod play of the fancy; rather it calls for a highly imaginative mind, demands study of feelings, and relies on the intellect as well as the emotions. It produces emotion in the reader or spectator by a careful, analyti-cal, and intellectual effort on the part of the writer or painter. By his magic the impression-ist introduces us to a fresh beauty in a familiar world.

Impressionistic writing is directed toward presenting emotions, feelings, individual attitudes. A true impressionist is, more than likely, a true poet. He deals in moods. He captures the fleeting moment. He proceeds by indirection in that he suggests rather than states. His stock in trade is sensations. "In fact," says Brunetière,

> ... it is only sensation that can speak to the senses; sounds to the ears, colors to the eyes. It would then be necessary for every thought or sentiment that one wishes to express, to find a sensation exactly corresponding, and of various sensations that do correspond, to select one that will appeal to all the world, an old experience, or at least the outlines, if I may use the expression, of an experience easy to fill in.

The reproduction of sensation is very close to the heart of impressionism. Cézanne labored for years that he might put down in color and form the sensations aroused in him by a landscape. Motivations are to the impressionist of less interest than this portrayal of sensation. Impressionism is realism with a special emphasis; only those elements and details are selected which serve to build up the dominant sensation and to communicate the desired impression.

Since emotions and sensations are evanescent and fleeting, a thing of the moment, the impressionist is greatly concerned to get down on paper such momentary revelations. "Lord Jim," thrown into momentary consternation, deserts his ship; but Conrad is not content with the act itself; we are carefully shown the sensations he experiences; we are prepared for them by pages of accounting, and they are explained for us afterward at great length. As light itself, the shadow on a hayrick, the sun on a wall, in any given moment received the attention of the French impressionistic painters, so the flight of Lord Jim and the sensation of a wife who learns that her husband is a coward (as in Henry James' *The Liar*) are developed with care, no significant detail excluded, no irrelevant detail admitted.

In the Preface to *The Nigger of the Narcissus* Joseph Conrad sets forth his convictions on the question of affecting the reader through the emotions:

> Fiction — if it at all aspires to be art — appeals to temperament. And in truth it must be, like painting, like music, like all art, the appeal of one temperament to all the other innumerable temperaments whose subtle and resistless power endows passing events with their true meaning, and creates the moral, the emotional atmosphere of the place and time. Such an appeal to be effective must be an impression conveyed through the senses; and, in fact, it cannot be made in any other way, because temperament, whether individual or collective, is not amenable to persuasion. All art, therefore, appeals primarily to the senses, and the artistic aim when expressing itself in written words must also make its appeal through the senses, if its high desire is to reach the secret spring of responsive emotions.

The common conventions of structure and orderly arrangement of parts are frequently violated to build up a particular impression. Impressionism frequently introduces a technique of its own. As the writer wishes to present a single mood or emotion, he subordinates plot-structure to this mood; as what happens in the story is less important than the recreating of the sensation, suspense in narrative is relatively unimportant. Atmosphere and feelings and colors and tonal quality take precedence over the old standards of unity and coherence, or it would be more accurate to say that unity and coherence are still respected but are directed toward a different end.

As the French impressionistic painters broke masses up into details, so the impressionistic writer will break up his story into episodes and accounts which may violate chronology but which, nevertheless, are logical from the impressionistic point of view. The story-teller has long allowed himself the privilege of rearranging episodes from life in such a way as to build up a climax and a dénouement. "Very well," says the impressionist, "I do the same. The only difference is that I make a still different arrangement, since I care little for suspense and care much for building up my own particular response."

This inconsecutiveness springs from the conviction which impressionists generally hold, that life in its transiency is important. The flashes reveal the whole. A bolt of lightning tells a far different story from an arc-light. Change, the impressionist knows, is a law of life. A tree, a stone wall is never to be seen twice exactly alike. The sun is different from hour to hour and day to day; clouds adjust themselves every moment to alter the landscape. And with people, with society, this same flitting quality persists. The impressionist is intrigued by it. He tries to put these fleeting moods and sensations and passions on paper.

The impressionist is an interpreter of life. His concern is truth. He speaks through the language of the emotions and of sensation, and his speech is full of color and tonal words so that he may somehow reproduce for us the quality of a moment of actuality by an appeal to our senses.

The Bible

While in general the particular technique of impressionism is a development of the last few decades, the mood is one frequently found in passages of ancient as well as modern writing. Wherever we find writing which modifies actualities of the external world and presents the external scene from the subjective point of view of the author, we have work which is at least partially impressionistic.

Many of the Psalms, perhaps most, are impressionistic in mood since they are a pouring out of religious feeling and the expression of a momentary emotion. They are essentially responses to an inner stimulus toward piety. The mind of the poet is an individual mind, the thought expressed is personal.

What Is Man?

O Lord our Lord,
How excellent is thy name in all the earth!
Who hast set thy glory above the heavens.
Out of the mouth of babes and sucklings hast thou
    ordained strength
Because of thine enemies,   5
That thou mightest still the enemy and the
    avenger.
When I consider thy heavens, the work of thy
    fingers,
The moon and the stars, which thou hast ordained;
What is man, that thou art mindful of him?

And the son of man, that thou visitest him?   10
For thou hast made him a little lower than the
    angels,
And hast crowned him with glory and honor.
Thou madest him to have dominion over the works
    of thy hands;
Thou hast put all things under his feet:
All sheep and oxen,   15
Yea, and the beasts of the field;
The fowl of the air, and the fish of the sea,
And whatsoever passeth through the paths of the
    seas.
O Lord our Lord,
How excellent is thy name in all the earth!   20
              (Psalm viii)

The Voice of the Lord

Give unto the Lord, O ye mighty,
Give unto the Lord glory and strength.
Give unto the Lord the glory due unto his name;
Worship the Lord in the beauty of holiness.
The voice of the Lord is upon the waters: 5
The God of glory thundereth,
The Lord is upon many waters.
The voice of the Lord is powerful;
The voice of the Lord is full of majesty.
The voice of the Lord breaketh the cedars;   10
Yea, the Lord breaketh the cedars of Lebanon.[1]
He maketh them also to skip like a calf;
Lebanon and Sirion[2] like a young unicorn.
The voice of the Lord divideth the flames of fire.
The voice of the Lord shaketh the wilderness;   15
The Lord shaketh the wilderness of Kadesh.
The voice of the Lord maketh the hinds to calve,
And discovereth the forests:
And in his temple doth every one speak of his glory.
The Lord sitteth upon the flood;   20
Yea, the Lord sitteth King for ever.
The Lord will give strength unto his people;
The Lord will bless his people with peace.
                                   (Psalm xxix)

How Amiable Are Thy Tabernacles

How amiable are thy tabernacles,
O Lord of hosts!

[1] A mountain.   [2] Mount Hermon.

My soul longeth, yea, even fainteth for the courts
        of the Lord;
My heart and my flesh crieth out for the living God.
Yea, the sparrow hath found a house,   5
And the swallow a nest for herself, where she may
        lay her young,
Even thine altars, O Lord of hosts,
My King, and my God.
Blessed are they that dwell in thy house:
They will be still praising thee.   10
Blessed is the man whose strength is in thee;
In whose heart are the ways of them.
Who passing through the valley of Baca[1] make it a
        well;
The rain also filleth the pools.
They go from strength to strength,   15
Every one of them in Zion appeareth before God.
O Lord God of hosts, hear my prayer:
Give ear, O God of Jacob.
Behold, O God our shield,
And look upon the face of thine anointed.   20
For a day in thy courts is better than a thousand.
I had rather be a doorkeeper in the house of my
        God,
Than to dwell in the tents of wickedness.
For the Lord God is a sun and shield:
The Lord will give grace and glory: 25
No good thing will he withhold from them that
        walk uprightly.
O Lord of hosts,
Blessed is the man that trusteth in thee.
                                   (Psalm lxxxiv)

[1] A valley of misery.

Henry James · 1843–1916

Where realists like Balzac and Turgenev have made us accustomed to a realism which takes us to city streets, tenements, and farms, Henry James prefers the drawing-room and shows us the conduct and manner of thinking of the urbane and privileged few. Most characteristically, perhaps, he portrays the touring American against the backdrop of European tradition and culture, in Venice, in Paris, in London.

The literary manner which James perfected for himself — and it was developed only after long and careful study, particularly of such French writers as Flaubert, Balzac, and Daudet — is marked by intensive psychological analysis. He showed a greater interest in character than in action, and usually subordinated character to a social situation. In his stories subtle talk and intelligent dialogue are of major significance. This is to say that Henry James is, by temper, an impressionist. His concern is with the *quality* of a setting or a character rather than with external appearances. Attitudes and emotions are more important than action or plot. For James the revelation of a moment is an index to a character's whole life. His effort is to present the essence of an act rather than the act itself. His intent is to interpret nature rather than to imitate it.

The son of a philosopher and clergyman, the young James early knew the calm and culture which may accompany wealth. Much of his education was obtained in private schools and from tutors, in America and in Europe, and from extensive travel and residence abroad. At nineteen he entered the Harvard Law School. Law, however, held only temporary attraction for James. In a few years he was back in Europe, spending most of his time in England where, about 1880, he settled permanently except for occasional visits to the Continent and to America. His later years he devoted to writing, to the London "season," to art and travel. In 1915 he became a British subject.

The contribution of James to literature took three forms: the novel, the short story, and critical writing. Some of his best-known stories are *The Real Thing*, *The Altar of the Dead*, *The Turn of the Screw*, and *The Liar*. His most popular novels include *Daisy Miller* (1878), *Portrait of a Lady* (1881), *The Bostonians* (1886), *What Maisie Knew* (1897), and *The Ambassadors* (1903).

SUGGESTED REFERENCES: Leon Edel, *Henry James* (3 vols., 1953–1963) and ed., *Henry James. A Collection of Critical Essays* (1963); B. R. McElderly Jr., *Henry James* (1965).

The Liar[1]

The Liar, which follows, illustrates the Jamesian manner: it presents impressions of people who move in London society; it presents a social problem; it offers an interpretation rather than a transcription of life; it is concerned with the quality of a situation rather than with plot.

The train was half an hour late and the drive ₁₀ from the station longer than he had supposed, so that when he reached the house its inmates had dispersed to dress for dinner and he was conducted straight to his room. The curtains were drawn in this asylum, the candles lighted, the fire bright, ₁₅ and when the servant had quickly put out his clothes the comfortable little place might have been one of the minor instruments in a big orchestra — seemed to promise a pleasant house, a various party, talk, acquaintances, affinities, to ₂₀ say nothing of very good cheer. He was too occupied with his profession often to pay country visits, but he had heard people who had more time for them speak of establishments where "they do you very well." He foresaw that the proprietors ₂₅ of Stayes would do him very well. In his bedroom on such occasions he always looked first at the books on the shelf and the prints on the walls; these things would give in a sort the social, the conversational value of his hosts. Though he ₃₀ had but little time to devote to them on this occasion a cursory inspection assured him that if the literature, as usual, was mainly American and humorous the art consisted neither of the water-color studies of the children nor of "goody" en- ₃₅ gravings. The walls were adorned with old-fashioned lithographs, mostly portraits of country gentlemen with high collars and riding-gloves: this suggested — and it was encouraging — that the tradition of portraiture was held in esteem. There ₅ was the customary novel of Mr. Le Fanu for the bedside, the ideal reading in a country house for the hours after midnight. Oliver Lyon could scarcely forbear beginning it while he buttoned his shirt.

Perhaps that is why he had not only found every one assembled in the hall when he went down, but saw from the way the move to dinner was instantly made that they had been waiting for him. There was no delay to introduce him to a lady, for he went out unimportant and in a group of unmated men. The men, straggling behind, sidled and edged as usual at the door of the dining-room, and the *dénouement* of this little comedy was that he ₂₀ came to his place last of all. This made him suppose himself in a sufficiently distinguished company, for if he had been humiliated — which he was not — he couldn't have consoled himself with the reflexion that such a fate was natural to an obscure and struggling young artist. He could no longer think of himself as notably young, alas, and if his position wasn't so brilliant as it ought to be he could no longer justify it by calling it a struggle. He was appreciably "known" and was ₃₀ now apparently in a society of the known if not of the knowing. This idea added to the curiosity with which he looked up and down the long table as he settled himself in his place.

It was a numerous party — five-and-twenty ₃₅ people; rather an odd occasion to have proposed to him, as he thought. He wouldn't be surrounded by the quiet that ministers to good work; however, it had never interfered with his work to

[1] *The Liar* is reprinted from *Novels and Tales*, by Henry James, copyright, 1889, with the permission of the publishers, Charles Scribner's Sons.

feel the human scene enclose it as a ring. And though he didn't know this, it was never quiet at Stayes. When he was working well he found himself in that happy state — the happiest of all for an artist — in which things in general interweave with his particular web and make it thicker and stronger and more many-colored. Moreover there was an exhilaration (he had felt it before) in the rapid change of scene — the jump, in the dusk of the afternoon, from foggy London and his familiar studio to a centre of festivity in the middle of Hertfordshire and a drama half-acted, a drama of pretty women and noted men and wonderful orchids in silver jars. He observed as a not unimportant fact that one of the pretty women was beside him: a gentleman sat on his other hand. But he appraised his neighbors little as yet: he was busy with the question of Sir David, whom he had never seen and about whom he naturally was curious.

Evidently, however, Sir David was not at dinner, a circumstance sufficiently explained by the other circumstance forming our friend's principal knowledge of him — his being ninety years of age. Oliver Lyon had looked forward with pleasure to painting a picked nonagenarian, so that though the old man's absence from table was something of a disappointment — it was an opportunity the less to observe him before going to work — it seemed a sign that he was rather a sacred and perhaps therefore an impressive relic. Lyon looked at his son with the greater interest — wondered if the glazed bloom of such a cheek had been transmitted from Sir David. That would be jolly to paint in the old man — the withered ruddiness of a winter apple, especially if the eye should be still alive and the white hair carry out the frosty look. Arthur Ashmore's hair had a midsummer glow, but Lyon was glad his call had been for the great rather than the small bearer of the name, in spite of his never having seen the one and of the other's being seated there before him now in the very highest relief of impersonal hospitality.

Arthur Ashmore was a fresh-colored thick-necked English gentleman, but he was just not a subject; he might have been a farmer and he might have been a banker; you could scarcely paint him in character. His wife didn't make up the amount; she was a large bright negative woman who had the same air as her husband of being somehow tremendously new; an appearance as of fresh varnish — Lyon could scarcely tell whether it came from her complexion or from her clothes — so that one felt she ought to sit in a gilt frame and be dealt with by reference to a catalogue or a price-list. It was as if she were already rather

a bad though expensive portrait, knocked off by an eminent hand, and Lyon had no wish to copy that work. The pretty woman on his right was engaged with her neighbor, while the gentleman on his other side looked detached and desperate, so that he had time to lose himself in his favorite diversion of watching face after face. This amusement gave him the greatest pleasure he knew, and he often thought it a mercy the human mask did interest him and that it had such a need, frequently even in spite of itself, to testify, since he was to make his living by reproducing it. Even if Arthur Ashmore wouldn't be inspiring to paint (a certain anxiety rose in him lest, should he make a hit with her father-in-law, Mrs. Arthur should take it into her head that he had now proved himself worthy to handle her husband); even if he had looked a little less like a page — fine as to print and margin — without punctuation, he would still be a refreshing iridescent surface. But the gentleman four persons off — what was he? Would he be a subject, or was his face only the legible door-plate of his identity, burnished with punctual washing and shaving — the least thing that was decent you might know him by?

This face arrested Oliver Lyon, striking him at first as very handsome. The gentleman might still be called young, and his features were regular: he had a plentiful fair moustache that curled up at the ends, a brilliant gallant almost adventurous air, together with a big shining breastpin in the middle of his shirt. He appeared a fine satisfied soul, and Lyon perceived that wherever he rested his friendly eye there fell an influence as pleasant as the September sun — as if he could make grapes and pears or even human affection ripen by looking at them. What was odd in him was a certain mixture of the correct and the extravagant: as if he were an adventurer imitating a gentleman with rare perfection, or a gentleman who had taken a fancy to go about with hidden arms. He might have been a dethroned prince or the war-correspondent of a newspaper: he represented both enterprise and tradition, good manners and bad taste. Lyon at length fell into conversation with the lady beside him — they dispensed, as he had had to dispense at dinner-parties before, with an introduction — by asking who this personage might be.

"Oh Colonel Capadose, don't you know?" Lyon didn't know and asked for further information. His neighbor had a sociable manner and evidently was accustomed to quick transitions; she turned from her other interlocutor with the promptness of a good cook who lifts the cover of the next saucepan. "He has been a great deal in India

— isn't he rather celebrated?" she put it. Lyon confessed he had never heard of him, and she went on: "Well, perhaps he isn't; but he says he is, and if you think it that's just the same, isn't it?"

"If *you* think it?"

"I mean if he thinks it — that's just as good, I suppose."

"Do you mean if he thinks he has done things he hasn't?"

"Oh dear no; because I never really know the difference between what people say —! He's exceedingly clever and amusing — quite the cleverest person in the house, unless indeed you're more so. But that I can't tell yet, can I? I only know about the people I know; I think that's celebrity enough!"

"Enough for them?"

"Oh I see you're clever. Enough for me! But I've heard of you," the lady went on. "I know your pictures; I admire them. But I don't think you look like them."

"They're mostly portraits," Lyon said, "and what I usually try for is not my own resemblance."

"I see what you mean. But they've much more color. Don't you suppose Vandyke's things tell a lot about him? And now you're going to do some one here?"

"I've been invited to do Sir David. I'm rather disappointed at not seeing him this evening."

"Oh he goes to bed at some unnatural hour — eight o'clock, after porridge and milk. You know he's rather an old mummy."

"An old mummy?" Oliver Lyon repeated.

"I mean he wears half a dozen waistcoats and sits by the fire. He's always cold."

"I've never seen him and never seen any portrait or photograph of him," Lyon said. "I'm surprised at his never having had anything done — at their waiting all these years."

"Ah that's because he was afraid, you know; it was his pet superstition. He was sure that if anything were done he would die directly afterwards. He has only consented to-day."

"He's ready to die then?"

"Oh now he's so old he doesn't care."

"Well, I hope I shan't kill him," said Lyon. "It was rather unnatural of his son to send for me."

"Oh they've nothing to gain — everything is theirs already!" his companion rejoined, as if she took this speech quite literally. Her talkativeness was systematic — she fraternised as seriously as she might have played whist. "They do as they like — they fill the house with people — they have *carte blanche*."

"I see — but there's still the 'title.'"

"Yes, but what's the tuppenny title?"

Our artist broke into laughter at this, whereat his companion stared. Before he had recovered himself she was scouring the plain with her other neighbor. The gentleman on his left at last risked an observation as if it had been a move at chess, exciting in Lyon however a comparative wantonness. This personage played his part with difficulty: he uttered a remark as a lady fires a pistol, looking the other way. To catch the ball Lyon had to bend his ear, and this movement led to his observing a handsome creature who was seated on the same side, beyond his interlocutor. Her profile was presented to him and at first he was only struck with its beauty; then it produced an impression still more agreeable — a sense of undimmed remembrance and intimate association. He had not recognised her on the instant only because he had so little expected to see her there; he had not seen her anywhere for so long, and no news of her now ever came to him. She was often in his thoughts, but she had passed out of his life. He thought of her twice a week; that may be called often, even for fidelity, when it has been kept up a dozen years. The moment after he recognised her he felt how true it was that only she could carry that head, the most charming head in the world and of which there could never be a replica. She was leaning forward a little; she remained in profile, slightly turned to some further neighbor. She was listening, but her eyes moved, and after a moment Lyon followed their direction. They rested on the gentleman who had been described to him as Colonel Capadose — rested, he made out, as with an habitual visible complacency. This was not strange, for the Colonel was unmistakeably formed to attract the sympathetic gaze of woman; but Lyon felt it as the source of an ache that she could let *him* look at her so long without giving him a glance. There was nothing between them to-day and he had no rights, but she must have known he was coming — it was of course no such tremendous event, but she couldn't have been staying in the house without some echo of it — and it wasn't natural this should absolutely fail to affect her.

She was looking at Colonel Capadose as if she had been in love with him — an odd business for the proudest, most reserved of women. But doubtless it was all right if her husband was satisfied: he had heard indefinitely, years before, that she was married, and he took for granted — as he had not heard — the presence of the happy man on whom she had conferred what she had refused to a poor art-student at Munich. Colonel Capadose seemed aware of nothing, and this fact, incongruously enough, rather annoyed Lyon than pleased him. Suddenly the lady moved her head showing her full face to our hero. He was so prepared with a greeting that he instantly smiled, as a shaken jug overflows; but she made no response, turned away again and sank back in her chair. All her face said in that instant was "You see I'm as handsome as ever." To which he mentally subjoined: "Yes, and as much good as ever it does me!" He asked the young man beside him if he knew who that beautiful being was — the fourth person beyond him. The young man leaned forward, considered and then said: "I think she's Mrs. Capadose."

"Do you mean his wife — that fellow's?" And Lyon indicated the subject of the information given him by his other neighbor.

"Oh is *he* Mr. Capadose?" said the young man, to whom it appeared to mean little. He admitted his ignorance of these values and explained it by saying that there were so many people and he had come but the day before. What was definite to our friend was that Mrs. Capadose was in love with her husband — so that he wished more than ever he might have married her.

"She's very fond and true," he found himself saying three minutes later, with a small ironic ring, to the lady on his right. He added that he meant Mrs. Capadose.

"Ah you know her then?"

"I knew her once upon a time — when I was living abroad."

"Why then were you asking me about her husband?"

"Precisely for that reason." Lyon was clear. "She married after that — I didn't even know her present name."

"How then do you know it now?"

"This gentleman has just told me — he appears to know."

"I didn't know he knew anything," said the lady with a crook that took him in.

"I don't think he knows anything but that."

"Then you've found out for yourself that she's — what do you call it? — tender and true? What do you mean by that?"

"Ah you mustn't question me — I want to put things to *you*," Lyon said. "How do you all like her here?"

"You ask too much! I can only speak for myself. I think she's hard."

"That's only because she's honest and straightforward."

"Do you mean I like people in proportion as they deceive?"

"I think we all do, so long as we don't find them out," Lyon said. "And then there's something in her face — a sort of nobleness of the Roman type, in spite of her having such English eyes. In fact she's English down to the ground; but her complexion, her low forehead and that beautiful close little wave in her dark hair make her look like a transfigured Trasteverina."

"Yes, and she always sticks pins and daggers into her head, to bring out that effect. I must say I like her husband better: he *gives* so much."

"Well, when I knew her there was no comparison that could injure her," Lyon richly sighed. "She was altogether the most delightful thing in Munich."

"In Munich?"

"Her people lived there; they weren't rich — in pursuit of economy in fact, and Munich was very cheap. Her father was the younger son of some noble house; he had married a second time and had a lot of little mouths to feed. She was the child of the first wife and didn't like her stepmother, but she was charming to her little brothers and sisters. I once made a sketch of her as Werther's Charlotte[1] cutting bread and butter while the children clustered round her. All the artists in the place were in love with her, but she wouldn't look at 'the likes' of us. She was too proud — I grant you that, but not stuck up nor young-ladyish, only perfectly simple and frank about it. She used to remind me of Thackeray's Ethel Newcome.[2] She told me she must marry well: it was the one thing she could do for her family. I suppose you'd say she *has* married well."

"She told *you?*" smiled Lyon's neighbor.

"Oh of course I proposed to her too. But she evidently thinks so herself!" he added. "I mean that it's no mistake."

When the ladies left the table the host as usual bade the gentlemen draw together, so that Lyon found himself opposite to Colonel Capadose. The conversation was mainly about the "run," for it had apparently been a great day in the hunting-field. Most of the men had a comment or an anecdote, several had many; but the Colonel's pleasant voice was the most audible in the chorus. It was a bright and fresh but masculine organ, just such a voice as, to Lyon's sense, such a "fine man" ought to have had. It appeared from his allusions that he was a very straight rider, which was also very much what Lyon would have expected. Not that he swaggered, for his points were all quietly and casually made; but they had all to do with some dangerous experiment or close shave. Lyon noted after a little that the attention paid by the company to the Colonel's remarks was not in direct proportion to the interest they

[1] In Goethe's *Sorrows of Werther*.
[2] In *The Newcomes*.

seemed to offer; the result of which was that the speaker, who noticed that *he* at least was listening, began to treat him as his particular auditor and to fix his eyes on him as he talked. Lyon had nothing to do but to look sympathetic and assent — the narrator building on the tribute so rendered. A neighboring squire had had an accident; he had come a cropper in an awkward place — just at the finish — with consequences that looked grave. He had struck his head; he remained insensible up to the last accounts: there had evidently been concussion of the brain. There was some exchange of views as to his recovery, how soon it would take place or whether it would take place at all; which led the Colonel to confide to our artist across the table that *he* shouldn't despair of a fellow even if he didn't come round for weeks — for weeks and weeks and weeks — for months, almost for years. He leaned forward (Lyon leaned forward to listen) and mentioned that he knew from personal experience how little limit there really was to the time a fellah might lie like a stone without being the worse for it. It had happened to him in Ireland years before; he had been pitched out of a dogcart, had turned a sheer somersault and landed on his head. They had thought he was dead, but he wasn't; they had carried him first to the nearest cabin, where he lay for some days with the pigs, and then to an inn in a neighboring town — it was a near thing they hadn't put him underground. He had been completely insensible — without a ray of recognition of any human thing — for three whole months; hadn't had a glimmer of consciousness of any blessed thing. It had been touch and go to that degree that they couldn't come near him, couldn't feed him, could scarcely look at him. Then one day he had opened his eyes — as fit as a flea!

"I give you my honor it had done me good — it rested my brain." He conveyed, though without excessive emphasis, that with an intelligence so active as his these periods of repose were providential. Lyon was struck by his story, but wanted to ask if he hadn't shammed a little; not in relating it, only in keeping so quiet. He hesitated however, in time, to betray a doubt — he was so impressed with the tone in which Colonel Capadose pronounced it the turn of a hair that they hadn't buried him alive. That had happened to a friend of his in India — a fellow who was supposed to have died of jungle-fever and whom they clapped into a coffin. He was going on to recite the further fate of this unfortunate gentleman when Mr. Ashmore said a word and everyone rose for the move to the drawing-room. Lyon noticed that by this time no one was heeding his new friend's

prodigies. These two came round on either side of the table and met while their companions hung back for each other.

"And do you mean your comrade was literally buried alive?" asked Lyon in some suspense.

The Colonel looked at him as with the thread of the conversation already lost. Then his face brightened — and when it brightened it was doubly handsome. "Upon my soul he was shoved into the ground!"

"And left there?"

"Left there till I came and hauled him out."

"*You* came?"

"I dreamed about him — it's the most extraordinary story: I heard him calling to me in the night. I took on myself to dig him up. You know there are people in India — a kind of beastly race, the ghouls — who violate graves. I had a sort of presentiment that they would get at him first. I rode straight, I can tell you; and, by Jove, a couple of them had just broken ground! Crack — crack from a couple of barrels, and they showed me their heels as you may believe. Would you credit that I took him out myself? The air brought him round and he was none the worse. He has got his pension — he came home the other day. He'd do anything for me," the narrator added.

"He called to you in the night?" said Lyon, much thrilled.

"That's the interesting point. Now *what was it?* It wasn't his ghost, because he wasn't dead. It wasn't himself, because he couldn't. It was some confounded brain-wave or other! You see India's a strange country — there's an element of the mysterious: the air's full of things you can't explain."

They passed out of the dining-room, and this master of anecdote, who went among the first, was separated from his newest victim; but a minute later, before they reached the drawing-room, he had come back. "Ashmore tells me who you are. Of course I've often heard of you. I'm very glad to make your acquaintance. My wife used to know you."

"I'm glad she remembers me. I recognised her at dinner and was afraid she didn't."

"Ah I dare say she was ashamed," said the Colonel with genial ease.

"Ashamed of me?" Lyon replied in the same key.

"Wasn't there something about a picture? Yes; you painted her portrait."

"Many times," Lyon said; "and she may very well have been ashamed of what I made of her."

"Well, *I* wasn't, my dear sir; it was the sight of that picture, which you were so good as to present to her, that made me first fall in love with her."

Our friend lived over again for a few seconds a lost felicity. "Do you mean one with the children — cutting bread and butter?"

"Bread and butter? Bless me, no — vine-leaves and a leopard-skin. A regular Bacchante."

"Ah yes," said Lyon; "I remember. It was the first decent portrait I painted. I should be curious to see it to-day."

"Don't ask her to show it to you — she'll feel it awkward," the Colonel went on.

"Awkward?" — our artist wondered.

"We parted with it — in the most disinterested manner," the other laughed. "An old friend of my wife's — her family had known him intimately when they lived in Germany — took the most extraordinary fancy to it: the Grand Duke of Silberstadt-Schreckenstein, don't you know? He came out to Bombay while we were there and he spotted your picture (you know he's one of the greatest collectors in Europe) and made such eyes at it that, upon my word — it happened to be his birthday — she told him he might have it to get rid of him. He was perfectly enchanted — but we miss the picture."

"It's very good of you," Lyon said. "If it's in a great collection — a work of my incompetent youth — I'm infinitely honored."

"Oh he keeps it in one of his castles; I don't know which — you know he has so many. He sent us, before he left India — to return the compliment — a magnificent old vase."

"That was more than the thing was worth," Lyon modestly urged.

Colonel Capadose gave no heed to this observation; his thoughts now seemed elsewhere. After a moment, however, he said: "If you'll come and see us in town she'll show you the vase." And as they passed into the drawing-room he gave his fellow visitor a friendly propulsion. "Go and speak to her; there she is. She'll be delighted."

Oliver Lyon took but a few steps into the wide saloon; he stood there a moment looking at the bright composition of the lamplit group of fair women, the single figures, the great setting of white and gold, the panels of old damask, in the center of each of which was a single celebrated picture. There was a subdued lustre in the scene and an air as of the shining trains of dresses tumbled over the carpet. At the furthest end of the room sat Mrs. Capadose, rather isolated; she was on a small sofa with an empty place beside her. Lyon couldn't flatter himself she had been keeping it for him; her failure to take up his shy signal at table contradicted this, but his desire to join her was too strong. Moreover he had her husband's sanction; so he crossed the room, step-ping over the tails of gowns, and stood before her with his appeal. "I hope you don't mean to repudiate me."

She looked up at him with frank delight. "I'm so glad to see you. I was charmed when I heard you were coming."

"I tried to get a smile from you at dinner — but I couldn't," Lyon returned.

"I didn't see — I didn't understand. Besides, I hate smirking and telegraphing. Also I'm very shy — you won't have forgotten that. Now we can communicate comfortably." And she made a better place for him on her sofa. He sat down and they had a talk that smote old chords in him; the sense of what he had loved her for came back to him, as well as not a little of the actual effect of that cause. She was still the least spoiled beauty he had ever seen, with an absence of the "wanton" or of any insinuating art that resembled an omitted faculty: she affected him at moments as some fine creature from an asylum — a surprising deaf-mute or one of the operative blind. Her noble pagan head gave her privileges that she neglected, and when people were admiring her brow she was wondering if there were a good fire in her bedroom, or at the very most in theirs. She was simple, kind and good; inexpressive but not inhuman, not stupid. Now and again she dropped something, some small fruit of discrimination, that might have come from a mind, have been an impression at first hand. She had no imagination and only the simpler feelings, but several of these had grown up to full size. Lyon talked of the old days in Munich, reminded her of incidents, pleasures and pains, asked her about her father and the others; and she spoke in return of her being so impressed with his own fame, his brilliant position in the world, that she hadn't felt sure he would notice her or that his mute appeal at table was meant for her. This was plainly a perfectly truthful speech — she was incapable of any other — and he was affected by such humility on the part of a woman whose grand line was unique. Her father was dead; one of her brothers was in the navy and the other on a ranch in America; two of her sisters were married and the youngest just coming out and very pretty. She didn't mention her stepmother. She questioned him on his own story, and he described it mainly as his not having married.

"Oh you ought to," she answered. "It's the best thing."

"I like that — from you!"

"Why not from me? I'm very happy."

"That's just why I can't be," he returned. "It's cruel of you to praise your state. But I've had the pleasure of making the acquaintance of your husband. We had a good bit of talk in the other room."

"You must know him better — you must know him really well," said Mrs. Capadose.

"I'm sure that the further you go the more you find. But he makes a fine show too."

She rested her good grey eyes on this recovered "backer." "Don't you think he's handsome?"

"Handsome and clever and entertaining. You see I'm generous."

"Yes; you must know him well," Mrs. Capadose repeated.

"He has seen a great deal of life," said her companion.

"Ah we've been in so many situations. You must see my little girl. She's nine years old — she's too beautiful."

Lyon rose fully to the occasion. "You must bring her to my studio some day — I should like to paint her."

"Oh don't speak of that," said Mrs. Capadose. "It reminds me of something so distressing."

"I hope you don't mean of when *you* used to sit to me — though that may well have bored you."

"It's not what you did — it's what we've done. It's a confession I must make — it's a weight on my mind! I mean on the subject of the lovely picture you gave me — it used to be so much admired. When you come to see me in London — and I count on your doing that very soon — I shall see you looking all round. I can't tell you I keep it in my own room because I love it so, for the simple reason ——" It fairly pulled her up.

"Because you can't tell wicked lies," said Lyon.

"No, I can't. So before you ask for it ——"

"Oh I know you parted with it — the blow has already fallen," Lyon interrupted.

"Ah then you've heard? I was sure you would! But do you know what we got for it? Two hundred pounds."

"You might have got much more," the artist smiled.

"That seemed a great deal at the time. We were in want of the money — it was a good while ago, when we first married. Our means were very small then, but fortunately that has changed rather for the better. We had the chance; it really seemed a big sum, and I'm afraid we jumped at it. My husband had expectations which have partly come into effect, so that now we do well enough. But meanwhile the picture went."

"Fortunately the original remained. But do you mean that two hundred was the value of the vase?" Lyon asked.

"Of the vase?"

"The beautiful old Indian vase — the Grand Duke's offering."

"The Grand Duke?"

"What's his name? — Silberstadt-Schreckenstein. Your husband mentioned the transaction."

"Oh my husband!" said Mrs. Capadose; and Lyon now saw her change color.

Not to add to her embarrassment, but to clear up the ambiguity, which he perceived the next moment he had better have left alone, he went on: "He tells me it's now in his collection."

"In the Grand Duke's? Ah you know its reputation? I believe it contains treasures." She was bewildered, but she recovered herself, and Lyon made the mental reflexion that for some reason which would seem good when he knew it the husband and the wife had prepared different versions of the same incident. It was true that he didn't exactly see Everina Brant preparing a version; that wasn't her line of old, and indeed there was no such subterfuge in her eyes to-day. At any rate they both had the matter too much on their conscience. He changed the subject — said Mrs. Capadose must really bring the little girl. He sat with her some time longer and imagined — perhaps too freely — her equilibrium slightly impaired, as if she were annoyed at their having been even for a moment at cross-purposes. This didn't prevent his saying to her at the last, just as the ladies began to gather themselves for bed: "You seem much impressed, from what you say, with my renown and my prosperity, and you are so good as greatly to exaggerate them. Would you have married me if you had known I was destined to success?"

"I did know it."

"*I* didn't, then!"

"You were too modest."

"You didn't think so when I proposed to you."

"Well, if I had married you I couldn't have married *him* — and he's so awfully nice," Mrs. Capadose said. Lyon knew this was her faith — he had learned that at dinner — but it vexed him a little to hear her proclaim it. The gentleman designated by the pronoun came up, amid the prolonged handshaking for good-night, and Mrs. Capadose remarked to her husband as she turned away, "He wants to paint Amy."

"Ah she's a charming child, a most interesting little creature," the Colonel said to Lyon. "She does the most remarkable things."

Mrs. Capadose stopped in the rustling procession that followed the hostess out of the room. "Don't tell him, please don't," she said.

"Don't tell him what?"

"Why, what she does. Let him find out for himself." And she passed on.

"She thinks I swagger about the child — that I bore people," said the Colonel. "I hope you smoke." He appeared ten minutes later in the smoking-room, brilliantly equipped in a suit of crimson foulard covered with little white spots. He gratified Lyon's eye, made him feel that the modern age has its splendor too and its opportunities for costume. If his wife was an antique he was a fine specimen of the period of color: he might have passed for a Venetian of the sixteenth century. They were a remarkable couple, Lyon thought, and as he looked at the Colonel standing in bright erectness before the chimney-piece and emitting great smoke-puffs he didn't wonder Everina couldn't regret she hadn't married *him*. All the men collected at Stayes were not smokers and some of them had gone to bed. Colonel Capadose remarked that there probably would be a smallish muster, they had had such a hard day's work. That was the worst of a hunting-house — the men were so sleepy after dinner; it was a great sell for the ladies, even for those who hunted themselves, women being so tough that they never showed it. But most fellows revived under the stimulating influences of the smoking-room, and some of them, in this confidence, would turn up yet. Some of the grounds of their confidence — not all — might have been seen in a cluster of glasses and bottles on a table near the fire, which made the great salver and its contents twinkle sociably. The others lurked as yet in various improper corners of the minds of the most loquacious. Lyon was alone with Colonel Capadose for some moments before their companions, in varied eccentricities of uniform, straggled in, and he felt how little loss of vital tissues this wonderful man had to repair.

They talked about the house, Lyon having noticed an oddity of construction in the smoking-room; and the Colonel explained that it consisted of two distinct parts, one of very great antiquity. They were two complete houses in short, the old and the new, each of great extent and each very fine in its way. The two formed together an enormous structure — Lyon must make a point of going all over it. The modern piece had been erected by the old man when he bought the property; oh yes, he had bought it forty years before — it hadn't been in the family: there hadn't been any particular family for it to be in. He had had the good taste not to spoil the original house — he had not touched it beyond what was just necessary for joining it on. It was very curious indeed — a most irregular rambling mysterious pile, where they now and then discovered a walled-up room

or a secret staircase. To his mind it was deadly depressing, however; even the modern additions, splendid as they were, failed to make it cheerful. There was some story of how a skeleton had been found years before, during some repairs, under a stone slab of the floor of one of the passages; but the family were rather shy of its being talked about. The place they were in was of course in the old part, which contained after all some of the best rooms: he had an idea it had been the primitive kitchen, half-modernized at some intermediate period.

"My room is in the old part too then — I'm very glad," Lyon said. "It's very comfortable and contains all the latest conveniences, but I observed the depth of the recess of the door and the evident antiquity of the corridor and staircase — the first short one — after I came out. That panelled corridor is admirable; it looks as if it stretched away, in its brown dimness (the lamps didn't seem to me to make much impression on it) for half a mile."

"Oh don't go to the end of it!" the Colonel warningly smiled.

"Does it lead to the haunted room?" Lyon asked.

His companion looked at him a moment. "Ah you know about that?"

"No, I don't speak from knowledge, only from hope. I've never had any luck — I've never stayed in a spooky house. The places I go to are always as safe as Charing Cross. I want to see — whatever there is, the regular thing. *Is* there a ghost here?"

"Of course there is — a rattling good one."

"And have you seen him?"

"Oh don't ask me what *I've* seen — I should tax your credulity. I don't like to talk of these things. But there are two or three as bad — that is, as good! — rooms as you'll find anywhere."

"Do you mean in my corridor?" Lyon asked.

"I believe the worst is at the far end. But you'd be ill-advised to sleep there."

"Ill-advised?"

"Until you've finished your job. You'll get letters of importance the next morning and take the 10.20."

"Do you mean I shall invent a pretext for running away?"

"Unless you're braver than almost any one has ever been. They don't often put people to sleep there, but sometimes the house is so crowded that they have to. The same thing always happens — ill-concealed agitation at the breakfast-table and letters of the greatest importance. Of course it's a bachelor's room, and my wife and I are at the other end of the house. But we saw the comedy three days ago — the day after we got here. A young fellow had been put there — I forget his name — the house was so full; and the usual consequence followed. Letters at breakfast — an awfully queer face — an urgent call to town — so sorry his visit was cut short. Ashmore and his wife looked at each other and off the poor devil went."

"Ah that wouldn't suit me; I must do my job," said Lyon. "But do they mind your speaking of it? Some people who've a good ghost are very proud of it, you know."

What answer Colonel Capadose was on the point of making to this query our hero was not to learn, for at that moment their host had walked into the room accompanied by three or four of their fellow guests. Lyon was conscious that he was partly answered by the Colonel's not going on with the subject. This on the other hand was rendered natural by the fact that one of the gentlemen appealed to him for an opinion on a point under discussion, something to do with the everlasting history of the day's run. To Lyon himself Mr. Ashmore began to talk, expressing his regret for the delay of this pleasure. The topic that suggested itself was naturally that most closely connected with the motive of the artist's visit. The latter observed that it was a great disadvantage to him not to have had some preliminary acquaintance with Sir David — in most cases he found this so important. But the present sitter was so far advanced in life that there was doubtless no time to lose. "Oh I can tell you all about him," said Mr. Ashmore; and for half an hour he told him a good deal. It was very interesting as well as a little extravagant, and Lyon felt sure he was a fine old boy to have endeared himself so to a son who was evidently not a gusher. At last he got up — he said he must go to bed if he wished to be fresh for his work in the morning. To which his host replied "Then you must take your candle; the lights are out; past this hour I don't keep my servants up."

In a moment Lyon had his glimmering taper in hand, and as he was leaving the room — he didn't disturb the others with a good-night, they were absorbed in the lemon-squeezer and the soda-water cork — he remembered other occasions on which he had made his way to bed alone through a darkened country-house: such occasions had not been rare, for he was almost always the first to leave the smoking-room. If he hadn't stayed at places of markedly evil repute he had, none the less — having too much imagination — sometimes found the great black halls and staircases rather "creepy": there had been often a sinister effect for his nerves in the sound of his tread through the long passages or the way the winter moon peeped into tall windows on landings. It occurred to him that if houses without supernatural pretensions could look so wicked at night the old corridors of Stayes would certainly give him a sensation. He didn't know whether the proprietors were sensitive; very often, as he had said to Colonel Capadose, people enjoyed the impeachment. What determined him to speak despite the risk was a need that had suddenly come to him to measure the Colonel's accuracy. As he had his hand on the door he said to his host: "I hope I shan't meet any ghosts."

"Any ghosts?"

"You ought to have some — in this fine old part."

"We do our best, but they're difficult to raise," said Mr. Ashmore. "I don't think they like the hot-water pipes."

"They remind them too much of their own climate? But haven't you a haunted room — at the end of my passage?"

"Oh there are stories — we try to keep them up."

"I should like very much to sleep there," Lyon said.

"Well you can move there to-morrow if you like."

"Perhaps I had better wait," Lyon smiled "till I've done my work." But he was to have presently the slightly humiliated sense of having been "arch" about nothing.

"Very good; but you won't work there, you know. My father will sit to you in his own apartments."

"Oh it isn't that; it's the fear of running away — like that gentleman three days ago."

"Three days ago? What gentleman?" Mr. Ashmore asked.

"The one who got urgent letters at breakfast and fled by the 10.20. Did he stand more than one night?"

"I don't know what you're talking about" — the son of Stayes was sturdy and blank. "There was no such gentleman — three days ago."

"Ah so much the better," said Lyon, nodding good-night and departing. He took his course, as he remembered it, with his wavering candle, and, though he encountered a great many gruesome objects, safely reached the passage out of which his room opened. In the complete darkness it seemed to stretch away still further, but he followed it, for the curiosity of the thing, to the end. He passed several doors with the name of the room painted up, but found nothing else. He was tempted to try the last door, to look into the room his friend had incriminated; but he felt this would be indiscreet, that gentleman's warrant was some-how a document of too many flourishes. There might be apparitions or other uncanny things and there mightn't; but there was surely nothing in the house so odd as Colonel Capadose.

II

Lyon found Sir David Ashmore a beautiful subject as well as the serenest and blandest of sitters. Moreover he was a very informing old man, tremendously puckered but not in the least dim; and he wore exactly the furred dressing-gown his portrayer would have chosen. He was proud of his age but ashamed of his infirmities, which however he greatly exaggerated and which didn't prevent his submitting to the brush as bravely as he might have to the salutary surgical knife. He sat there with the firm eyes and set smile of "Well, do your worst!" He demolished the legend of his having feared the operation would be fatal, giving an explanation which pleased our friend much better. He held that a gentleman should be painted but once in his life — that it was eager and fatuous to be hung up all over the place. That was good for women, who made a pretty wall-pattern; but the male face didn't lend itself to decorative repe-tition. The proper time for the likeness was at the last, when the whole man was there, when you got the sum of his experience. Lyon couldn't reply, as he would have done in many a case, that this was not a real synthesis — you had to allow so for leakage; since there had been no crack in Sir David's crystallisation. He spoke of his portrait as a plain map of the country, to be con-sulted by his children in a case of uncertainty. A proper map could be drawn up only when the country had been travelled. He gave Lyon his mornings, till luncheon, and they talked of many things, not neglecting, as a stimulus to gossip, the company at Stayes. Now that he didn't "go out," as he said, he saw much less of the people in his house — processions that came and went, that he knew nothing about and that he liked to hear Lyon describe. The artist sketched with a fine point and didn't caricature, and it usually befell that when Sir David didn't know the sons and daughters he had known the fathers and mothers. He was one of those terrible old persons who keep the book of antecedents. But in the case of the Capadose family, at whom they arrived by an easy stage, his knowledge embraced two, or even three, gen-erations. General Capadose was an old crony, and he remembered his father before him. The Gen-eral was rather a smart soldier, but in private life of too speculative a turn — always sneaking into

the City to put his money into some rotten thing. He had married a girl who brought him something — and with it half a dozen children. He scarcely knew what had become of the rest of them, except that one was in the Church and had found prefer-ment — wasn't he Dean of Rockingham? Clem-ent, the fellow who was at Stayes, had apparently some gift for arms; he had served in the East and married a pretty girl. He had been at Eton with Arthur and used then to come to Stayes in his holidays. Lately, back in England, he had turned up with his wife again; that was before he — the old man — had been put to grass. He was a taking dog but had a monstrous foible.

"A monstrous foible?" Lyon echoed.

"He pulls the long bow — the longest that ever was."

Lyon's brush stopped short, while he repeated, for somehow the words both startled him and brought light: "'The longest that ever was'?"

"You're very lucky not to have had to catch him."

Lyon debated. "Well, I think I *have* rather caught him. He revels in the miraculous."

"Oh it isn't always the miraculous. He'll lie about the time of day, about the name of his hatter. It's quite disinterested."

"Well, it's very base," Lyon declared, feeling rather sick for what Everina Brant had done with herself.

"Oh it's an extraordinary trouble to take," said the old man, "but this fellow isn't in himself at all base. There's no harm in him and no bad intention; he doesn't steal nor cheat nor gamble nor drink; he's very kind — he sticks to his wife, is fond of his children. He simply can't give you a straight answer."

"Then everything he told me last night, I now see, was tarred with that brush: he delivered him-self of a series of the steepest statements. They stuck when I tried to swallow them, yet I never thought of so simple an explanation."

"No doubt he was in the vein," Sir David went on. "It's a natural peculiarity — as you might limp or stutter or be left-handed. I believe it comes and goes with changes of the wind. My son tells me that his friends quite allow for it and don't pin him down — for the sake of his wife, whom every one likes."

"Oh his wife — his wife!" Lyon murmured, painting fast.

"I dare say she's used to it."

"Never in the world, Sir David. How can she be used to it?"

"Why, my dear sir, when a woman's fond —! And don't they mostly rather handle that instrument themselves? They're connoisseurs in the business," Sir David cackled with a harmless old-time cynicism. "They've a sympathy for a fellow performer."

Lyon wondered; he had no ground for denying that Mrs. Capadose was attached to her husband. But after a little he rejoined: "Oh not this one! I knew her years ago — before her marriage; knew her well and admired her. She was as clear as a bell."

"I like her very much," Sir David said, "but I've seen her back him up."

Lyon considered his host a moment not in the light of a sitter. "Are you very sure?"

The old man grinned and brought out: "My dear sir, you're in love with her."

"Very likely. God knows I used to be!"

"She must help him out — she can't expose him."

"She can hold her tongue," Lyon returned.

"Well, before you probably she will."

"That's what I'm curious to see." And he added privately: "Mercy on us, what he must have made of her!" He kept this reflexion to himself, for he considered that he had sufficiently betrayed his state of mind with regard to Mrs. Capadose. None the less it occupied him now immensely, the question of how such a woman would arrange herself in such a position. He watched her with an interest deeply quickened when he mingled with the company; he had had his own troubles in life, but had rarely been so anxious about anything as about this question of what the loyalty of a wife and the infection of an example would have made of a perfectly candid mind. Oh he would answer for it that whatever other women might be prone to do she, of old, had stuck to the truth as a bather who can't swim sticks to shallow water. Even if she hadn't been too simple for deviations she would have been too proud, and if she hadn't had too much conscience would have had too little eagerness. The lie was the last thing she would have endured or condoned — the particular thing she wouldn't have forgiven. Did she sit in torment while her husband gave the rein, or was she now too so perverse that she thought it a fine thing to be striking at the expense — Lyon would have been ready to say — of one's decency? It would have taken a wondrous alchemy — working backwards, as it were — to produce this latter result. Besides these alternatives — that she suffered misery in silence and that she was so much in love that her husband's exorbitance seemed to her but an added richness, a proof of life and talent — there was still the possibility that she hadn't found him out, that she took his

false coinage at his own valuation. A little reflexion rendered this hypothesis untenable; it was too evident that the account he gave of things must repeatedly have contradicted her own knowledge. Within an hour or two of his meeting them Lyon had seen her confronted with that perfectly gratuitous invention about the profit they had made of his early picture. Even then indeed she had not, so far as he could see, smarted, and — but for the present he could only stare at the mystery!

Even if it hadn't been interfused, through his uneradicated interest in Mrs. Capadose, with an element of suspense, the question would still have been attaching and worrying; since, truly, he hadn't painted portraits so many years without becoming curious of queer cases. His attention was limited for the moment to the opportunity the following three days might yield, as the Colonel and his wife were going on to another house. It fixed itself largely of course upon the Colonel too — the fellow was *so* queer a case. Moreover it had to go on very quickly. Lyon was at once too discreet and too fond of his own intimate inductions to ask other people how they answered his conundrum — too afraid also of exposing the woman he once had loved. It was probable indeed that light would come to him from the talk of their companions; the Colonel's idiosyncrasy, both as it affected his own situation and as it affected his wife, would be a familiar theme in any house in which he was in the habit of staying. Lyon hadn't observed in the circles in which he visited any marked abstention from comment on the singularities of their members. It interfered with his progress that the Colonel hunted all day, while he plied his brushes and chatted with Sir David; but a Sunday intervened and that partly made it up. Mrs. Capadose fortunately didn't hunt and, his work done, was not inaccessible. He took a couple of good walks with her — she was fond of good walks — and beguiled her at tea into a friendly nook in the hall. Regard her as he might he couldn't make out to himself that she was consumed by a hidden shame; the sense of being married to a man whose word had no worth was not, in her spirit, so far as he could guess, the canker within the rose. Her mind appeared to have nothing on it but its own placid frankness, and when he sounded her eyes — with the long plummet he occasionally permitted himself to use — they had no uncomfortable consciousness. He talked to her again and still again of the dear old days — reminded her of things he hadn't had (before this reunion) any sense of himself remembering. Then he spoke to her of her husband, praised his appearance, his talent for conversation, professed to have felt a quick friendship for him and asked, with an amount of "cheek" for which he almost blushed, what manner of man he was. "What manner?" she echoed. "Dear me, how can one describe one's husband? I like him very much."

"Ah you've insisted on that to me already!" Lyon growled to exaggeration.

"Then why do you ask me again?" She added in a moment, as if she were so happy that she could afford to take pity on him: "He's everything that's good and true and kind. He's a soldier and a gentleman and a dear! He hasn't a fault. And he has great, great ability."

"Yes, he strikes one as having great, great ability. But of course I can't think him a dear."

"I don't care what you think him!" Everina laughed, looking still handsomer in the act than he had ever seen her. She was either utterly brazen or of a contrition quite impenetrable, and he had little prospect of extorting from her what he somehow so longed for — some avowal that she had after all better have married a man who was not a by-word for the most contemptible, the least heroic of vices. Hadn't she seen, hadn't she felt, the smile, the cold faded smile of complete depreciation, go round when her husband perjured himself to some particularly characteristic blackness? How could a woman of her quality live with that day after day, year after year, except by her quality's altering? But he would believe in the alteration only when he should have heard *her* lie. He was held by his riddle and yet impatient of it, he asked himself all kinds of questions. Didn't she lie, after all, when she let *his* lies pass without turning a hair? Wasn't her life a perpetual complicity, and didn't she aid and abet him by the simple fact that she wasn't disgusted with him? Then again perhaps she *was* disgusted and it was the mere desperation of her pride that had given her an inscrutable mask. Perhaps she protested in private, passionately; perhaps every night, in their own apartments, after the day's low exhibition, she had things out with him in a manner known only to the pair themselves. But if such scenes were of no avail and he took no more trouble to cure himself, how could she regard him, and after so many years of marriage too, with the perfectly artless complacency that Lyon had surprised in her in the course of the first day's dinner? If our friend hadn't been in love with her he would surely have taken the Colonel's delinquencies less to heart. As the case stood they fairly turned to the tragical for him, even while he was sharply aware of how merely "his funny way" they were

to others — and of how funny his, Oliver Lyon's, own way of regarding them would have seemed to every one.

The observation of these three days showed him that if Capadose was an abundant he was not a malignant liar and that his fine faculty exercised itself mainly on subjects of small direct importance. "He's the liar platonic," he said to himself; "he's disinterested, as Sir David said, he doesn't operate with a hope of gain or with a desire to injure. It's art for art — he's prompted by some love of beauty. He has an inner vision of what might have been, of what ought to be, and he helps on the good cause by the simple substitution of a shade. He lays on color, as it were, and what less do I do myself?" His disorder had a wide range, but a family likeness ran through all its forms, which consisted mainly of their singular futility. It was this that made them an affliction; they encumbered the field of conversation, took up valuable space, turned it into the desert of a perpetual shimmering mirage. For the falsehood uttered under stress a convenient place can usually be found, as for a person who presents himself with an author's order at the first night of a play. But the mere luxurious lie is the gentleman without a voucher or a ticket who accommodates himself with a stool in the passage.

Of one possible charge Lyon acquitted his successful rival; it had puzzled him that, irrepressible as he was, he had never got into a mess in the Service. But it was to be made out that he drew the line at the Service — over that august institution he never flapped his wings. Moreover, for all the personal pretension in his talk it rarely came, oddly enough, to swagger about his military exploits. He had a passion for the chase, he had followed it in far countries, and some of his finest flowers were reminiscences of what he had prodigiously done and miraculously escaped when off by himself. The more by himself he had been of course the bigger the commemorative nosegay bloomed. A new acquaintance always received from him, in honor of their meeting, one of the most striking of these tributes — that generalization Lyon very promptly made. And the extraordinary man had inconsistencies and unexpected lapses — lapses into the very commonplace of the credible. Lyon recognized what Sir David had told him, that he flourished and drooped by an incalculable law and would sometimes keep the truce of God for a month at a time. The muse of improvization breathed on him at her pleasure and appeared sometimes quite to avert her face. He would neglect the finest openings and then set sail with everything against him. As a general thing he affirmed the impossible rather than denied the certain, though this too had lively exceptions. Very often, when it was loud enough — for he liked a noise about him — he joined in the reprobation that cast him out, he allowed he was trying it on and that one didn't know what had happened to one till one *had* tried. Still, he never completely retracted nor retreated — he dived and came up in another place. Lyon guessed him capable on occasion of defending his position with violence, though only when it was very bad. Then he might easily be dangerous — then he would hit out and not care whom he touched. Such moments as those would test his wife's philosophy — Lyon would have liked to see her there. In the smoking-room and elsewhere the company, so far as it was composed of his familiars, had an hilarious protest always at hand; but among the men who had known him long his big brush was an old story, so old that they had ceased to talk about it, and Lyon didn't care, as I have said, to bring to a point those impatiences that might have resembled his own.

The oddest thing of all was that neither surprise nor familiarity prevented the Colonel's being liked; his largest appeals even to proved satiety passed for an overflow of life and high spirits — almost of simple good looks. If he was fond of treating his gallantry with a flourish he was none the less unmistakeably gallant. He was a first-rate rider and shot, in spite of his fund of anecdote illustrating these accomplishments: in short he was very nearly as clever and brave, and his adventures and observations had been very nearly as numerous and wonderful, as the list he unrolled. His best quality however remained that indiscriminate sociability which took interest and favor for granted and about which he bragged least. It made him cheap, it made him even in a manner vulgar; but it was so contagious that his listener was more or less on his side as against the probabilities. It was a private reflexion of Oliver Lyon's that he not only was mendacious but made any charmed converser feel as much so by the very action of the charm — of a certain guilty submission of which no intention of ridicule could yet purge you. In the evening, at dinner and afterwards, our friend, better placed for observation than the first night, watched his wife's face to see if some faint shade or spasm never passed over it. But she continued to show nothing, and the wonder was that when he spoke she almost always listened. That was her pride: she wished not to be even suspected of not facing the music. Lyon had none the less an importunate vision of a veiled figure coming the next day in the dusk to certain

places to repair the Colonel's ravages, as the relatives of kleptomaniacs punctually call at the shops that have suffered from their depredations.

"I must apologise; or course it wasn't true; I hope no harm is done; it's only his incorrigible —" oh to hear that woman's voice in that deep abasement! Lyon had no harsh design, no conscious wish to practise on her sensibility or her loyalty; but he did say to himself that he should have liked to bring her round, liked to see her *show* him that a vision of the dignity of not being married to a mountebank sometimes haunted her dreams. He even imagined the hour when, with a burning face, she might ask *him* not to take the question up. Then he should be almost consoled — he would be magnanimous.

He finished his picture and took his departure, after having worked in a glow of interest which made him believe in his success, until he found he had pleased every one, especially Mr. and Mrs. Ashmore, when he began to be sceptical. The party at any rate changed: Colonel and Mrs. Capadose went their way. He was able to say to himself however that his parting with Everina wasn't so much an end as a beginning, and he called on her soon after his return to town. She had told him the hours she was at home — she seemed to like him. If she liked him why hadn't she married him, or at any rate why wasn't she sorry she hadn't? If she was sorry she concealed it too well. The point he made of some visible contrition in her on this head may strike the reader as extravagant, but something must be allowed so disappointed a man. He didn't ask much after all; not that she should love him to-day or that she should allow him to tell her that he loved her, but only that she should give him some sign she didn't feel her choice as *all* gain. Instead of this, for the present, she contented herself with exhibiting her small daughter to him. The child was beautiful and had the prettiest eyes of innocence he had ever seen: which didn't prevent his wondering if she told horrid fibs. This idea much occupied and rather darkly amused him — the picture of the anxiety with which her mother would watch as she grew older for symptoms of the paternal strain. That was a pleasant care for such a woman as Everina Brant! Did she lie to the child herself about her father — was that necessary when she pressed her daughter to her bosom to cover up his tracks? Did he control himself before the little girl — so that she mightn't hear him say things she knew to be other than his account of them? Lyon scarcely thought that probable: his genius would be ever too strong for him, and the only guard for Amy would be in her being too simple for criticism.

One couldn't judge yet — she was too young to show. If she should grow up clever sne would be sure to tread in his steps — a delightful improvement in her mother's situation! Her little face was not shifty, but neither was her father's big one; so that proved nothing.

Lyon reminded his friends more than once of their promise that Amy should sit to him, and it was now only a question of his own leisure. The desire grew in him to paint the Colonel also — an operation from which he promised himself a rich private satisfaction. He would draw him out, he would set him up in that totality about which he had talked with Sir David, and none but the initiated would know. They, however, would rank the picture high, and it would be indeed six rows deep — a masterpiece of fine characterisation, of legitimate treachery. He had dreamed for years of some work that should show the master of the deeper vision as well as the mere reporter of the items, and here at last was his subject. It was a pity it wasn't better, but that wasn't *his* fault. It was his impression that already no one "drew" the Colonel in the social sense more effectively than he, and he did this not only by instinct but on a plan. There were moments when he almost winced at the success of his plan — the poor gentleman went so terribly far. He would pull up some day, look at his critic between the eyes and guess he was being played upon — which would lead to his wife's guessing it also. Not that Lyon cared much for that however, so long as she failed to suppose — and she couldn't divine it — that *she* was a part of his joke. He formed such a habit now of going to see her of a Sunday afternoon that he was angry when she went out of town. This occurred often, as the couple were great visitors and the Colonel was always looking for sport, which he liked best when it could be had at the expense of others. Lyon would have supposed the general gregarious life, the constant presence of a gaping "gallery," particularly little to her taste, for it was naturally in country-houses that her husband came out strongest. To let him go off without her, not to see him expose himself — that ought properly to have been her relief and her nearest approach to a luxury. She mentioned to her friend in fact that she preferred staying at home, but she didn't say it was because in other people's houses she was on the rack: the reason she gave was that she liked so to be with the child. It wasn't perhaps criminal to deal in such "whoppers," but it was damned vulgar: poor Lyon was delighted when he arrived at that formula. Certainly some day too he would cross the line — he would practise the fraud to which his talked "rot"

had the same relation as the experiments of the forger have to the signed cheque. And in the meantime, yes, he was vulgar, in spite of his facility, his impunity, his so remarkably fine person. Twice, by exception, toward the end of the winter, when he left town for a few days' hunting, his wife remained at home. Lyon hadn't yet reached the point of asking himself if the wish not to miss two of his visits might have had something to do with this course. That enquiry would perhaps have been more in place later, when he began to paint her daughter and she made a rule of coming with her. But it wasn't in her to give the wrong name, to affect motives, and Lyon could see she had the maternal passion in spite of the bad blood in the little girl's veins.

She came inveterately, though Lyon multiplied the sittings: Amy was never entrusted to the governess or the maid. He had knocked off poor old Sir David in ten days, but the simple face of the child held him and worried him and gave him endless work. He asked for sitting after sitting, and it might have struck a solicitous spectator that he was wearing the little girl out. He knew better, however, and Mrs. Capadose also knew: they were present together at the long intermissions he gave her, when she left her pose and roamed about the great studio, amusing herself with its curiosities, playing with the old draperies and costumes, having unlimited leave to handle. Then her mother and their so patient friend — much more patient than her piano-mistress — sat and talked; he laid aside his brushes and leaned back in his chair; he always gave her tea. What Mrs. Capadose couldn't suspect was the rate at which, during these weeks, he neglected other orders: women have no faculty of imagination with regard to a man's work beyond a vague idea that it doesn't matter. Lyon in fact put off everything and made high celebrities wait. There were half-hours of silence, when he plied his brushes, during which he was mainly conscious that Everina was sitting there. She easily fell into that if he didn't insist on talking, and she wasn't embarrassed nor bored by any lapse of communication. Sometimes she took up a book — there were plenty of them about; sometimes, a little way off in her chair, she watched his progress — though without in the least advising or correcting — as if she cared for every stroke that was to contribute to his result. These strokes were occasionally a little wild; he was thinking so much more of his heart than of his hand. He wasn't more embarrassed than she, but he was more agitated: it was as if in the sittings (for the child too was admirably quiet) something had beautifully settled itself between them or had already

grown — a tacit confidence, an inexpressible
secret. He at least felt it that way, but he after
all couldn't be sure she did. What he wanted her
to do for him was very little; it wasn't even to
allow that she was unhappy. She would satisfy
him by letting him know even by some quite silent
sign that she could imagine her happiness with him
— well, more unqualified. Perhaps indeed — his
presumption went so far — that was what she did
mean by contentedly sitting there.

III

At last he broached the question of painting the
Colonel: it was now very late in the season — there
would be little time before the common dispersal.
He said they must make the most of it; the great
thing was to begin; then in the autumn, with the
resumption of their London life, they could go forward. Mrs. Capadose objected to this that she
really couldn't consent to accept another present
of such value. Lyon had sacrificed to her the portrait of herself of old — he knew what they had
had the indelicacy to do with it. Now he had
offered her this wondrous memorial of the child
— wondrous it would evidently be when he should
be able to bring it to a finish; a precious possession that, this time, they would cherish forever.
But his generosity and their indiscretion must stop
there — they couldn't be so tremendously "beholden" to him. They couldn't order the picture,
which of course he would understand without her
explaining: it was a luxury beyond their reach,
since they knew the great prices he received. Besides, what had they ever done — what above all
had *she* ever done, that he should overload them
with benefits? No, he was too dreadfully good;
it was really impossible that Clement should sit.
Lyon listened to her without protest, without in-
terruption, while he bent forward at his work; and
at last returned: "Well, if you won't take it why
not let him sit just for my own pleasure and
profit? Let it be a favor, a service I ask of him.
All the generosity and charity will so be on your
side. It will do me a lot of good to paint him and
the picture will remain in my hands."

"How will it do you a lot of good?" Mrs. Capadose asked.

"Why he's such a rare model — such an interesting subject. He has such an expressive face.
It will teach me no end of things."

"Expressive of what?" said Mrs. Capadose.

"Why of his inner man."

"And you want to paint his inner man?"

"Of course I do. That's what a great portrait
gives you, and with a splendid comment on it

thrown in for the money. I shall make the
Colonel's a great one. It will put me up high.
So you see my request is eminently interested."

"How can you be higher than you are?"

"Oh I'm an insatiable climber. So don't stand
in my way," said Lyon.

"Well, everything in him is very noble," Mrs.
Capadose gravely contended.

"Ah trust me to bring everything out!" Lyon
returned, feeling a little ashamed of himself.

Mrs. Capadose, before she went, humored him
to the point of saying that her husband would
probably comply with his invitation; but she
added: "Nothing would induce me to let you pry
into *me* that way!"

"Oh you," her friend laughed — "I could do
you in the dark!"

The Colonel shortly afterwards placed his leisure
at the painter's disposal and by the end of July
had paid him several visits. Lyon was disappointed neither in the quality of his sitter nor in
the degree to which he himself rose to the occasion; he felt really confident of producing what he
had conceived. He was in the spirit of it, charmed
with his motive and deeply interested in his problem. The only point that troubled him was the
idea that when he should send his picture to the
Academy he shouldn't be able to inscribe it in the
catalogue under the simple rubric to which all
propriety pointed. He couldn't in short send in
the title as "The Liar" — more was the pity.
However, this little mattered, for he had now determined to stamp that sense on it as legibly — and
to the meanest intelligence — as it was stamped
for his own vision on the living face. As he saw
nothing else in the Colonel to-day, so he gave himself up to the joy of "rendering" nothing else.
How he did it he couldn't have told you, but he felt
a miracle of method freshly revealed to him every
time he sat down to work. It was in the eyes and
it was in the mouth, it was in every line of the
face and every fact of the attitude, in the indenta-
tion of the chin, in the way the hair was planted,
the moustache was twisted, the smile came and
went, the breath rose and fell. It was in the way
he looked out at a bamboozled world in short
— the way he would look out forever. There
were half a dozen portraits in Europe that Lyon
rated as supreme; he thought of them always as
immortal things, for they were as perfectly preserved as they were consummately painted. It
was to this small exemplary group that he aspired
to attach the canvas on which he was now engaged. One of the productions that helped to
compose it was the magnificent Moroni of the
National Gallery — the young tailor in the white

jacket at his board with his shears. The Colonel was not a tailor, nor was Moroni's model, unlike many tailors, a liar; the very man, body and soul, should bloom into life under his hand with just that assurance of no loss of a drop of the liquor. The Colonel, as it turned out, liked to sit, and liked to talk while sitting: which was very fortunate, as his talk was half the inspiration of his artist. Lyon applied without mercy his own gift of provocation; he couldn't possibly have been in a better relation to him for the purpose. He encouraged, beguiled, excited him, manifested an unfathomable credulity, and his own sole lapses were when the Colonel failed, as he called it, to "act." He had his intermissions, his hours of sterility, and then Lyon knew that the picture also drooped. The higher his companion soared, the more he circled and sang in the blue, the better he felt himself paint; he only couldn't make the flights and the evolutions last. He lashed his victim on when he flagged; his one difficulty was his fear again that his game might be suspected. The Colonel, however, was easily beguiled; he basked and expanded in the fine steady light of the painter's attention. In this way the picture grew very fast, astonishingly faster, in spite of its so much greater "importance," than the simple-faced little girl's. By the fifth of August it was pretty well finished: that was the date of the last sitting the Colonel was for the present able to give — he was leaving town the next day with his wife. Lyon was amply content — he saw his way so clear: he should be able to do at leisure the little that remained, in respect to which his friend's attendance would be a minor matter. As there was no hurry, in any case, he would let the thing stand over till his own return to London, in November, when he should come back to it with a fresh eye. On the Colonel's asking him if Everina might have a sight of it next day, should she find a minute — this being so greatly her desire — Lyon begged as a special favor that she would wait: what he had yet to do was small in amount, but it would make all the difference. This was the repetition of a proposal Mrs. Capadose had made on the occasion of his last visit to her, and he had then recommended her not coming till he should be himself better pleased. He had really never been, at a corresponding stage, better pleased; and he blushed a little for his subtlety.

By the fifth of August the weather was very warm, and on that day, while the Colonel sat at his usual free practice Lyon opened for the sake of ventilation a little subsidiary door which led directly from his studio into the garden and sometimes served as an entrance and an exit for models and for visitors of the humbler sort, and as a passage for canvases, frames, packing-boxes and other professional gear. The main entrance was through the house and his own apartments, and this approach had the charming effect of admitting you first to a high gallery, from which a winding staircase, happily disposed, dropped to the wide decorated encumbered room. The view of this room beneath them, with all its artistic ingenuities and the objects of value that Lyon had collected, never failed to elicit exclamations of delight from persons stepping into the gallery. The way from the garden was plainer and at once more practicable and more private. Lyon's domain, in Saint John's Wood, was not vast, but when the door stood open of a summer's day it offered a glimpse of flowers and trees, there was a sweetness in the air and you heard the birds. On this particular morning the side-door had been found convenient by an unannounced visitor, a youngish woman who stood in the room before the Colonel was aware of her, but whom he was then the first to see. She was very quiet — she looked from one of the men to the other. "Oh dear, here's another!" Lyon exclaimed as soon as his eyes rested on her. She belonged in fact to the somewhat importunate class of the model in search of employment, and she explained that she had ventured to come straight in, that way, because very often when she went to call upon gentlemen the servants played her tricks, turned her off and wouldn't take in her name.

"But how did you get into the garden?" Lyon asked.

"The gate was open, sir — the servants' gate. The butcher's cart was there."

"The butcher ought to have closed it," said Lyon.

"Then you don't require me, sir?" the lady continued.

Lyon continued to paint; he had given her a sharp look at first, but now his eyes were only for his work. The Colonel, however, examined her with interest. She was a person of whom you could scarcely say whether being young she looked old or old looked young; she had at any rate clearly rounded several of the corners of life; she had a face that was rosy, yet that failed to suggest freshness. She was nevertheless rather pretty and even looked as if at one time she might have sat for the complexion. She wore a hat with many feathers, a dress with many bugles, long black gloves encircled with silver bracelets, and very bad shoes. There was something about her not exactly of the governess out of place nor completely of the actress seeking an engagement, but that savored

(continued on page 1131)

ILLUSTRATIONS

The Realistic Temper

SECOND GROUP: IMPRESSIONISM AND EXPRESSIONISM

THE FIRST six plates are impressionistic in mood. The paintings are characterized by vagueness of line (*Boulevard des Italiens at Night*), by an emphasis on color and tone rather than on outline (*The Dancer*), by their reflection of atmosphere or mood rather than by their reproduction of situation (*The Poplars*). As one looks at the Rodin sculpture, he is aware of the desire of the sculptor to express sensation and fleeting movement, to reveal what cannot be shown by accurate description. In all these works, impression and suggestion have replaced observation and statement. The impressionists, and even more so the pointillists (*La Grande Jatte*), strive to make reality appear as a conglomerate of sensations, while both classicists and realists stress the firmness of design and the interdependence of parts in the objects reproduced. Impressionistic art is landscape art, and only superficially concerned with the human body.

With the final ten illustrations, we turn to the expressionistic temper. Here we find the artist bent on representing rather than reproducing nature or his own sensation. Into these paintings (*Landscape with Cypresses, Mahana no Atua*) and sculptures (*Blossoming*) the artists have projected their own emotions, thus modifying external objects in a way to make them images of the mind. This process of subjective transformation is frequently correlated with a tendency toward abstraction. The formal structure of the objects selected for pictorial representation appears distorted or manneristic, because the artist wants to superimpose his own personality upon nature. He can do so, however, only by developing a style radically opposed to naturalistic imitation. In Cezanne's landscapes, for instance, the natural forms are transformed into geometrical planes. In Picasso's cubistic pictures the planes have altogether lost their identity with the objects of which they are representations (*Guernica*). In Van Gogh's landscapes the trees and the sky are stylized into curved and conical, jagged forms. Henry Moore's figures, finally, grow out of the material without ever fully emerging from it (*Reclining Figure*).

In surrealism, the visionary, the subconscious — the world of dreams and nightmares — is transferred to the canvas. Klee's *Twittering Machine* is a product of the fancy, with a name that has little bearing on the formal content of the picture. All these manners or styles (the cubistic, expressionistic, and surrealistic) are here grouped together under the name of expressionism. Their common origin can be traced to the reaction against the art of the impressionists.

Plate 45　　THE POPLARS　　*Monet*

Plate 46　　LE MOULIN DE LA GALETTE　　*Renoir*

Plate 47   THE DANCER   *Dégas*

Plate 48   BOULEVARD DES ITALIENS AT NIGHT   *Pissarro*

Plate 49   LA GRANDE JATTE   *Seurat*

Plate 50   THE DANAÏD   *Rodin*

Plate 51   LANDSCAPE WITH CYPRESSES   *Van Gogh*

Plate 52   LA CASCADE   *Rousseau*

Plate 53   MAHANA NO ATUA   *Gauguin*

Plate 54   LANDSCAPE   *Cezanne*

Plate 56

THE TWITTERING MACHINE

Klee

Plate 55

THE GREEN VIOLINIST

Chagall

Plate 57   GUERNICA   *Picasso*

SCENE FROM "THE HAIRY APE"   *Throckmorton*

Plate 58   SCENE FROM "THE HAIRY APE"   *Throckmorton*

Plate 59   BLOSSOMING   *Lipchitz*

Plate 60   RECLINING FIGURE, 1936   *Moore*

of a precarious profession, perhaps even of a blighted career. She was perceptibly soiled and tarnished, and after she had been in the room a few moments the air, or at any rate the nostril, became acquainted with a vague alcoholic waft. She was unpractised in the *h*, and when Lyon at last thanked her and said he didn't want her — he was doing nothing for which she could be useful — she replied in rather a wounded manner: "Well, you know you *'ave* 'ad me!"

"I don't remember you," Lyon protested.

"Well, I dare say the people who saw your pictures do! I haven't much time, but I thought I'd look in."

"I'm much obliged to you."

"If ever you should require me and just send me a postcard —"

"I never send postcards," said Lyon.

"Oh well, I should value a private letter! Anything to Miss Geraldine, Mortimer Terrace Mews, Notting 'ill —"

"Very good; I'll remember," said Lyon.

Miss Geraldine lingered. "I thought I'd just stop on the chance."

"I'm afraid I can't hold out hopes, I'm so busy with portraits," Lyon continued.

"Yes; I see you are. I wish I was in the gentleman's place."

"I'm afraid in that case it wouldn't look like the gentleman," the Colonel sociably laughed.

"Oh of course it couldn't compare — it wouldn't be so 'andsome! But I do hate them portraits!" Miss Geraldine declared. "It's so much bread out of our mouths."

"Well, there are many who can't paint them," Lyon suggested for comfort.

"Oh I've sat to the very first — and only to the first! There's many couldn't do anything without me."

"I'm glad you're in such demand." Lyon's amusement had turned to impatience and he added that he wouldn't detain her — he would send for her in case of need.

"Very well; remember it's the Mews — more's the pity! You don't sit so well as *us!*" Miss Geraldine pursued, looking at the Colonel. "If *you* should require me, sir —"

"You put him out; you embarrass him," said Lyon.

"Embarrass him, oh gracious!" the visitor cried with a laugh that diffused a fragrance. "Perhaps *you* send postcards, eh?" she went on to the Colonel; but she retreated with a wavering step. She passed out into the garden as she had come.

"How very dreadful — she's drunk!" said Lyon. He was painting hard, but looked up, checking himself: Miss Geraldine, in the open doorway, had thrust in her head again.

"Yes, I do hate it — that sort of thing!" she cried with an explosion of mirth which confirmed Lyon's charge. On which she disappeared.

"What sort of thing — what does she mean?" the Colonel asked.

"Oh my painting you when I might be painting her."

"And have you ever painted her?"

"Never in the world; I've never seen her. She's quite mistaken."

The Colonel just waited; then he remarked: "She was very pretty — ten years ago."

"I dare say, but she's quite ruined. For me the least 'drop too much' spoils them; I shouldn't care for her at all."

"My dear fellow, she's not a model," the Colonel laughed.

"To-day, no doubt, she's not worthy of the name; but she has done her time."

"*Jamais de la vie!* That's all a pretext."

"A pretext?" Lyon pricked up his ears — he wondered what now would come.

"She didn't want you — she wanted *me.*"

"I noticed she paid you some attention. What then does she want of you?"

"Oh to do me an ill turn. She hates me — lots of women do. She's watching me — she follows me."

Lyon leaned back in his chair — without a single grain of faith. He was all the more delighted with what he heard and with the Colonel's bright and candid manner. The story had shot up and bloomed, from the dropped seed, on the spot. "My dear Colonel!" he murmured with friendly interest and commiseration.

"I was vexed when she came in — but I wasn't upset," his sitter continued.

"You concealed it very well if you were."

"Ah when one has been through what I have! To-day, however, I confess I was half-prepared. I've noticed her hanging about — she knows my movements. She was near my house this morning — she must have followed me."

"But who is she then — with such charming 'cheek'?"

"Yes, she has plenty of cheek," said the Colonel; "but as you observed she was primed. Still, she carried it off as a cool hand. Oh she's a bad 'un! She isn't a model and never was; no doubt she has known some of those women and picked up their form. She had hold of a friend of mine ten years ago — a young jackanapes who might have been left to be plucked but whom I was obliged to take an interest in for family reasons. It's a long story

— I had really forgotten all about it. She's thirty-seven if she's a day. I was able to make a diversion and let him get off — after which I sent her about her business. She knew it was me she had to thank. She has never forgiven me — I think she's off her head. Her name isn't Geraldine at all and I doubt very much if that's her address."

"Ah what *is* her name?" Lyon was all participation. He had always noted that when once his friend was launched there was no danger in asking; the more you asked the more abundantly you were served.

"It's Pearson — Harriet Pearson; but she used to call herself Grenadine — wasn't that a rum notion? Grenadine — Geraldine — the jump was easy." Lyon was charmed with this flow of facility, and his interlocutor went on: "I hadn't thought of her for years — I had quite lost sight of her. I don't know what her idea is, but practically she's harmless. As I came in I thought I saw her a little way up the road. She must have found out I come here and have arrived before me. I dare say — or rather I'm sure — she's waiting for me there now."

"Hadn't you better have protection?" Lyon asked with amusement.

"The best protection's five shillings — I'm willing to go to that length. Unless indeed she has a bottle of vitriol. But they only throw vitriol on the fellows who have 'undone' them, and I never undid her — I told her the first time I saw her that it wouldn't do. Oh if she's there we'll walk a little way together and talk it over, and, as I say, I'll go as far as five shillings."

"Well," said Lyon, "I'll contribute another five." He felt this little to pay for what he was getting.

That entertainment was interrupted, however, for the time, by the Colonel's departure. Lyon hoped for some sequel to match — a report, by note, of the next scene in the drama as his friend had met it, but this genius apparently didn't operate with the pen. At any rate he left town without writing — they had taken a tryst for three months later. Oliver Lyon always passed the holidays in the same way; during the first weeks he paid a visit to his elder brother, the happy possessor, in the south of England, of a rambling old house with formal gardens, in which he delighted, and then he went abroad — usually to Italy or Spain. This year he carried out his custom after taking a last look at his all but finished work and feeling as nearly pleased with it as decency permitted, the translation of the idea by the hand appearing always to him at the best a pitiful compromise. One yellow afternoon in the country, as he smoked his pipe on one of the old terraces, he

was taken with a fancy for another look at what he had lately done, and with that in particular of doing two or three things more to it: he had been much haunted with this unrest while he lounged there. The provocation was not to be resisted, and though he was at any rate so soon to be back in London he was unable to brook delay. Five minutes with his view of the Colonel would be enough — it would clear up questions that hummed in his brain; so that the next morning, to give himself this luxury, he took the train for town. He sent no word in advance; he would lunch at his club and probably return into Sussex by the 5.45.

In Saint John's Wood the tide of human life flows at no time very fast, and in the first days of September Lyon found mere desolation in the straight sunny roads where the little plastered garden-walls, with their incommunicative doors, looked feebly Oriental. There was definite stillness in his own house, to which he admitted himself by his pass-key, it being a matter of conscience with him sometimes to take his servants unawares. The good woman set in authority over them and who cumulated the functions of cook and housekeeper was, however, quickly summoned by his step, and — as he cultivated frankness of intercourse with his domestics — received him without the confusion of surprise. He reassured her as to any other effect of unpreparedness — he had come up but for a few hours and should be busy in the studio. She announced that he was just in time to see a lady and a gentleman who were there at the moment — they had arrived five minutes before. She had told them he was absent but they said it was all right; they only wanted to look at a picture and would be very careful of everything. "I hope it's all right, sir," this informant concluded. "The gentleman says he's a sitter and he gave me his name — rather an odd name; I think it's military. The lady's a very fine lady, sir; at any rate there they are."

"Oh it's all right" — Lyon read the identity of his visitors. The good woman couldn't know, having when he was at home so little to do with the comings and goings; his man, who showed people in and out, had accompanied him to the country. He was a good deal surprised at the advent of Mrs. Capadose, who knew how little he wished her to see the portrait unfinished, but it was a familiar truth to him that she was a woman of a high spirit. Besides, perhaps the lady wasn't Everina; the Colonel might well have brought some inquisitive friend, a person who perhaps wanted a portrait of *her* husband. What were they doing in town, in any case, at that moment? Lyon made his way to the studio with a certain curiosity; he

wondered vaguely what his friends were "up to."
He laid his hand upon the curtain draping the door
of communication, the door opening upon the gallery constructed for relief at the time the studio was
added to the house; but with his motion to slide
the tapestry on its rings arrested in the act. A
singular startling sound reached him from the room
beneath; it had the appearance of a passionate
wail, or perhaps rather a smothered shriek, accompanied by a violent burst of tears. Oliver Lyon
listened intently and then passed in to the balcony,
which was covered with an old thick Moorish rug.
His step was noiseless without his trying to keep it
so, and after that first instant he found himself
profiting irresistibly by the accident of his not
having attracted the attention of the two persons
in the studio, who were some twenty feet below
him. They were in truth so deeply and strangely
engaged that their unconsciousness of observation
was explained. The scene that took place before
Lyon's eyes was more extraordinary than any he
had ever felt free to overlook. Delicacy and the
failure to understand kept him at first from inter-
fering — what he saw was a woman who had
thrown herself in a flood of tears on her companion's bosom; after which surprise and discretion
gave way to a force that made him step back behind the curtain. This same force, further — the
force of a *need* to know — caused him to avail
himself for better observation of a crevice formed
by his gathering together the two halves of his
swinging tapestry. He was perfectly aware of
what he was about — he was for the moment an
eavesdropper and a spy; but he was also aware
that something irregular, as to which his confidence
had been trifled with, was on foot, and that he was
as much concerned with the reasons of it as he
might be little concerned with the taken form.
His observation, his reflexions, accomplished themselves in a flash.

His visitors were in the middle of the room; Mrs.
Capadose clung to her husband, weeping; she
sobbed as if her heart would break. Her distress
was horrible to Oliver Lyon, but his astonishment
was greater than his horror when he heard the
Colonel respond to it by the vehement imprecation
"Damn him, damn him, damn him!" What in
the world had happened? why was she sobbing and
whom was he damning? What had happened,
Lyon saw the next instant, was that the Colonel
had finally rummaged out the canvas before which
he had been sitting — he knew the corner where
the artist usually placed it, out of the way and its
face to the wall — and had set it up for his wife
on an empty easel. She had looked at it a few
moments and then — apparently — what she

saw in it had produced an explosion of dismay and
resentment. She was too overcome, and the
Colonel too busy holding her and re-expressing his
wrath, to look round or look up. The scene was so
unexpected to Lyon that all impulse failed in him
on the spot for a proof of the triumph of his hand
— of a tremendous hit: he could only wonder what
on earth was the matter. The idea of the triumph
was yet to come. He could see his projected figure,
however, from where he stood; he was startled
with its look of life — he hadn't supposed the
force of the thing could so prevail. Mrs. Capadose
flung herself away from her husband — she dropped
into the nearest chair, leaned against a table,
buried her face in her arms. The sound of her woe
diminished, but she shuddered there as if overwhelmed with anguish and shame. Her husband
stood a moment glaring at the picture, then went
to her, bent over her, took hold of her again,
soothed her. "What is it, darling — what the
devil is it?"

Lyon fairly drank in her answer. "It's cruel
— oh it's too cruel!"

"Damn him, damn him, damn him!" the Colonel
repeated.

"It's all there — it's all there!" Mrs. Capadose
went on.

"Hang it, what's all there?"

"Everything there oughtn't to be — everything
he has seen. It's too dreadful!"

"Everything he has seen? Why, ain't I a good-
looking fellow? I'll be bound to say he has made
me handsome."

Mrs. Capadose had sprung up again; she had
darted another glance at the painted betrayal.
"Handsome? Hideous, hideous! Not that
— never, never!"

"Not *what*, in heaven's name?" the Colonel
almost shouted. Lyon could see his flushed bewildered face.

"What he has made of you — what you know!
He knows — he has seen. Everyone will, everyone
know and see. Fancy that thing in the Academy!"

"You're going wild, darling; but if you hate it so
it needn't go," the poor branded man declared.

"Ah he'll send it — it's so good! Come away
— come away!" Mrs. Capadose wailed, seizing
her husband.

"It's so good?" the victim cried.

"Come away — come away," she only repeated,
and she turned toward the staircase that ascended
to the gallery.

"Not that way — not through the house in the
state you're in," Lyon heard her companion object.
"This way — we can pass," he added; and he drew
his wife to the small door that opened into the gar-

den. It was bolted, but he pushed the bolt and opened the door. She passed out quickly, but he stood there looking back into the room. "Wait for me a moment!" he cried out to her; and with an excited stride he re-entered the studio. He came up to the picture again — again he covered it with his baffled glare. "Damn him — damn him — damn him!" he broke out once more. Yet it wasn't clear to Lyon whether this malediction had for object the guilty original or the guilty painter. The Colonel turned away and moved about as if looking for something; Lyon for the moment wondered at his intention; saying to himself the next, however, below his breath: "He's going to do it a harm!" His first impulse was to raise a preventive cry, but he paused with the sound of Everina Brant's sobs still in his ears. The Colonel found what he was looking for — found it among some odds and ends on a small table and strode back with it to the easel. At one and the same moment Lyon recognized the object seized as a small Eastern dagger and saw that he had plunged it into the canvas. Animated as with a sudden fury and exercising a rare vigor of hand, he dragged the instrument down — Lyon knew it to have no very fine edge — making a long and abominable gash. Then he plucked it out and dashed it again several times into the face of the likeness, exactly as if he were stabbing a human victim: it had the most portentous effect — that of some act of prefigured or rehearsed suicide. In a few seconds more the Colonel had tossed the dagger away — he looked at it in this motion as for the sight of blood — and hurried out of the place with a bang of the door.

The strangest part of all was — as will doubtless appear — that Oliver Lyon lifted neither voice nor hand to save his picture. The point is that he didn't feel as if he were losing it or didn't care if he were, so much more was he conscious of gaining a certitude. His old friend *was* ashamed of her husband, and he had made her so, and he had scored a great success, even at the sacrifice of his precious labor. The revelation so excited him — as indeed the whole scene did — that when he came down the steps after the Colonel had gone he trembled with his happy agitation; he was dizzy and had to sit down a moment. The portrait had a dozen jagged wounds — the Colonel literally had hacked himself to death. Lyon left it there where it grimaced, never touched it, scarcely looked at it; he only walked up and down his studio with a sense of such achieved success as nothing finished and framed, varnished and delivered and paid for had ever given him. At the end of this time his good woman came to offer him luncheon; there was a passage under the staircase from the offices.

"Ah the lady and gentleman have gone, sir? I didn't hear them."

"Yes; they went by the garden."

But she had stopped, staring at the picture on the easel. "Gracious, how you 'ave served it, sir!"

Lyon imitated the Colonel. "Yes, I cut it up — in a fit of disgust."

"Mercy, after all your trouble! Because they weren't pleased, sir?"

"Yes; they weren't pleased."

"Well, they must be very grand! Blest if I would!"

"Have it chopped up; it will do to light fires," Lyon magnificently said.

He returned to the country by the 3.30 and a few days later passed over to France. There was something he found himself looking for during these two months on the Continent; he had an expectation — he could hardly have said of what; of some characteristic sign or other on the Colonel's part. Wouldn't he write, wouldn't he explain, wouldn't he take for granted Lyon had discovered the way he had indeed been "served" and hold it only decent to show some form of pity for his mystification? Would he plead guilty or would he repudiate suspicion? The latter course would be difficult, would really put his genius to the test, in view of the ready and responsible witness who had admitted the visitors the day of the ravage and would establish the connexion between their presence and that perpetration. Would the Colonel proffer some apology or some amends, or would any word from him be only a further expression of that exasperated wonder which our friend had seen his wife so suddenly and so fatally communicate? He would have either to take oath that he hadn't touched the picture or to admit that he had, and in either case would be at costs for a difficult version. Lyon was impatient for this probably remarkable story, and as no letter came was disappointed at the failure of the exhibition. His impatience however was much greater in respect to Mrs. Capadose's inevitable share in the report, if report there was to be; for certainly that would be the real test, would show how far she would go for her husband on the one side or for himself on the other. He could scarcely wait to see what line she would take — whether she would simply adopt the Colonel's, whatever it might be. It would have met his impatience most to draw her out without waiting, to get an idea in advance. He wrote to her, to this end, from Venice, in the tone of their established friendship, asking for news, telling her of his movements, hoping for their reunion in London and not saying a word about the picture. Day followed day, after the time, and he received no answer; on which he reflected that she couldn't trust herself to write — was still too deeply ruffled, too disconcerted, by his "betrayal." Her husband had espoused her resentment and she had espoused the action he had taken in consequence of it; the rupture was therefore complete and everything at an end. Lyon was frankly rueful over this prospect, at the same time that he thought it deplorable such charming people should have put themselves so grossly in the wrong. He was at last cheered, though little further enlightened, by the arrival of a letter, brief but breathing good humor and hinting neither at a grievance nor at a bad conscience. The most interesting part of it to him was the postscript, which ran as follows: "I have a confession to make to you. We were in town for a couple of days, early in September, and I took the occasion to defy your authority: this was very bad of me but I couldn't help it. I made Clement take me to your studio — I wanted so dreadfully to see what you had done with him, your wishes to the contrary notwithstanding. We made your servants let us in and I took a good look at the picture. It is really wonderful!" "Wonderful" was noncommittal, but at least with this letter there was no rupture.

The third day after his return was a Sunday, so that he could go and ask Mrs. Capadose for luncheon. She had given him in the spring a general invitation to do so and he had several times profited by it. These had been the occasions, before his sittings, when he saw the Colonel most familiarly. Directly after the meal his host disappeared (went out, as he said, to call on *his* women) and the second half-hour was the best, even when there were other people. Now, in the first days of December, Lyon had the luck to find the pair alone, without even Amy, who appeared but little in public. They were in the drawing-room, waiting for the repast to be announced, and as soon as he came in the Colonel broke out: "My dear fellow, I'm delighted to see you! I'm so keen to begin again."

"Oh do go on; it's so beautiful," Mrs. Capadose said as she gave him her hand.

Lyon looked from one to the other; he didn't know what he had expected, but he hadn't expected this. "Ah then you think I've got something?"

"You've got everything." And Mrs. Capadose smiled from her golden-brown eyes.

"She wrote you of our little crime?" her husband asked. "She dragged me there — I had to go." Lyon wondered for a moment whether he meant by their little crime the assault on the canvas; but his friend's next words made this impossible. "You

know I like to sit — you want me animated, and it leaves me so to wag my tongue. And just now I've time."

"You must remember how near I had got to the end," Lyon returned.

"So you had. More's the pity. I should like you to begin again."

"My dear fellow, I shall have to begin again!" laughed the painter with his eyes on Mrs. Capadose. She didn't meet them — she had got up to ring for luncheon. "The picture has been smashed," Lyon continued.

"Smashed? Ah what did you do that for?" cried Everina, standing there before him in all her clear rich beauty. Now that she did look at him she was impenetrable.

"I didn't — I found it so — with a dozen holes punched in it!"

"I say!" cried the Colonel — "what a jolly shame!"

Lyon took him in with a wide smile. "I hope *you* didn't go for it?"

"Is it done for?" the Colonel earnestly asked. He was as brightly true as his wife and looked simply as if Lyon's question couldn't be serious. "For the love of sitting to you? My dear fellow, if I had thought of it I would!"

"Nor you either?" the painter demanded of Mrs. Capadose.

Before she had time to reply her husband had seized her arm as if a lurid light had come to him. "I say, my dear, that woman — that woman!"

"That woman?" Mrs Capadose repeated; and Lyon too wondered what woman he meant.

"Don't you remember when we came out, she was at the door — or a little way from it? I spoke to you of her — I told you about her. Geraldine — Grenadine — the one who burst in that day," he explained to Lyon. "We saw her hanging about — I called Everina's attention to her."

"Do you mean she got at my picture?"

"Ah yes, I remember," said Mrs. Capadose with a vague recovery.

"She burst in again — she had learned the way — she was waiting for her chance," the Colonel continued. "Ah the horrid little brute!"

Lyon looked down; he felt himself coloring. This was what he had been waiting for — the day the Colonel should wantonly sacrifice some innocent person. And could his wife be a party to that final atrocity? He had reminded himself repeatedly during the previous weeks that when her husband perpetrated his misdeed she had already quitted the room; but he had argued none the less — it was a virtual certainty — that he had on rejoining her at once mentioned his misdeed. He was in the flush of performance; and even if he hadn't reported what he had done she would have guessed it. Lyon didn't for an instant believe poor Miss Geraldine to have been hovering about his door, nor had the account given by the Colonel the summer before of his relations with this lady affected him as in the least convincing. Lyon had never seen her till the day she planted herself in his studio, but he knew her and classified her as if he had made her. He was acquainted with the London model in all her feminine varieties — in every phase of her development and every step of her decay. When he entered his house that September morning just after the arrival of his two friends there had been no symptoms whatever, up and down the road, of Miss Geraldine's reappearance. That fact had been fixed in his mind by his recollecting the vacancy of the prospect when his cook told him that a lady and a gentleman were in his studio: he had wondered there was neither carriage nor cab at his door. Then he had reflected that they would have come by the underground railway; he was near the Marlborough Road station and he knew the Colonel, repeating his pilgrimage so often, habitually made use of that convenience. "How in the world did she get in?" He addressed the question to his companions indifferently.

"Let us go down to luncheon," said Mrs. Capadose, passing out of the room.

"We went by the garden — without troubling your servant — I wanted to show my wife." Lyon followed his hostess with her husband, and the Colonel stopped him at the top of the stairs. "My dear fellow, I *can't* have been guilty of the folly of not fastening the door?"

"I'm sure I don't know, Colonel," Lyon said as they went down. "It was a very determined hand that did the deed — in the spirit of a perfect wild-cat."

"Well, she *is* a wild-cat — confound her! That's why I wanted to get him away from her."

"But I don't understand her motive."

"Well, she's practically off her head — and she hates me. That was her motive."

"But she doesn't hate me, my dear fellow!" Lyon amusedly urged.

"She hated the picture — don't you remember she said so? The more portraits, the less employment for such as her."

"Yes; but if she's not really the model she pretends to be, how can that hurt her?" Lyon asked.

The question baffled the Colonel an instant — but only an instant. "Ah she's so bad she goes it blind. She doesn't know where she is."

They passed into the dining-room, where Mrs.

Capadose was taking her place. "It's too low, it's too horrid!" she said. "You see the fates are against you. Providence won't let you be so disinterested — throwing off masterpieces for nothing."

"Did *you* see the woman?" Lyon put to her with something like a sternness he couldn't mitigate.

She seemed not to feel it, or not to heed it if she did. "There was a person, not far from your door, whom Clement called my attention to. He told me something about her, but we were going the other way."

"And do you think she did it?"

"How can I tell? If she did she was mad, poor wretch."

"I should like very much to get hold of her," said Lyon. This was a false plea for the truth: he had no desire for any further conversation with Miss Geraldine. He had exposed his friends to his own view, but without wish to expose them to others, and least of all to themselves.

"Oh depend upon it she'll never show again. You're all right *now!*" the Colonel guaranteed.

"But I remember her address — Mortimer Terrace Mews, Notting Hill."

"Oh that's pure humbug. There isn't any such place."

"Lord, what a practised deceiver!" said Lyon.

"Is there any one else you suspect?" his host went on.

"Not a creature."

"And what do your servants say?"

"They say it wasn't *them*, and I reply that I never said it was. That's about the substance of our interviews."

"And when did they discover the havoc?"

"They never discovered it at all. I noticed it first — when I came back."

"Well, she could easily have stepped in," said the subject of Miss Geraldine's pursuit. "Don't you remember how she turned up that day like the clown in the ring?"

"Yes, yes; she could have done the job in three seconds, except that the picture wasn't out."

"Ah my dear fellow," the Colonel groaned, "don't utterly curse me! — but of course I dragged it out."

"You didn't put it *back?*" Lyon tragically cried.

"Ah Clement, Clement, didn't I tell you to?" Mrs. Capadose reproachfully wailed.

The Colonel almost howled for compunction; he covered his face with his hands. His wife's words were for Lyon the finishing touch; they made his whole vision crumble — his theory that she had secretly kept herself true. Even to her old lover she wouldn't be so! He was sick; he couldn't eat; he knew how strange he must have looked. He attempted some platitude about spilled milk and the folly of crying over it — he tried to turn the talk to other things. But it was a horrid effort and he wondered how it pressed upon *them*. He wondered all sorts of things: whether they guessed he disbelieved them — that he had seen them of course they would never guess; whether they had arranged their story in advance or it was only an inspiration of the moment; whether she had resisted, protested, when the Colonel proposed it to her, and then had been borne down by him; whether in short she didn't loathe herself as she sat there. The cruelty, the cowardice of fastening their unholy act upon the wretched woman struck him as monstrous — no less monstrous indeed than the levity that could make them run the risk of her giving them, in her righteous indignation, the lie. Of course that risk could only exculpate her and not inculpate them — the probabilities protected them so perfectly; and what the Colonel counted on — what he would have counted upon the day he delivered himself, after first seeing her, at the studio, if he had thought about the matter at all and not spoken from the pure spontaneity of his genius — was simply that Miss Geraldine must have vanished forever into her native unknown. Lyon wanted so much to cut loose, in his disgust, that when after a little Mrs. Capadose said to him, "But can nothing be done, can't the picture be repaired? You know they do such wonders in that way now," he only made answer: "I don't know, I don't care, it's all over, *n'en parlons plus!*" Her hypocrisy revolted him. And yet by way of plucking off the last veil of her shame he broke out to her again, shortly afterwards: "And you *did* like it, really?" To which she returned, looking him straight in his face, without a blush, a pallor, an evasion: "Oh *cher grand maître*, I loved it!" Truly her husband had trained her well. After that Lyon said no more, and his companions forbore temporarily to insist, like people of tact and sympathy aware that the odious accident had made him sore.

When they quitted the table the Colonel went away without coming upstairs; but Lyon returned to the drawing-room with his hostess, remarking to her however on the way that he could remain but a moment. He spent that moment — it prolonged itself a little — standing with her before the chimney-piece. She neither sat down nor asked him to; her manner betrayed some purpose of going out. Yes, her husband had trained her

well; yet Lyon dreamed for a moment that now he was alone with her she would perhaps break down, retract, apologise, confide, say to him: "My dear old friend, forgive this hideous comedy — you understand!" And then how he would have loved her and pitied her, guarded her, helped her always! If she weren't ready to do something of that sort why had she treated him so as a dear old friend; why had she let him for months suppose certain things — or almost; why had she come to his studio day after day to sit near him on the pretext of her child's portrait, as if she liked to think what might have been? Why had she come so near a tacit confession if she wasn't willing to go an inch further? And she wasn't willing — she wasn't; he could see that as he lingered there. She moved about the room a little, rearranging two or three objects on the tables, but she did nothing more. Suddenly he said to her: "Which way was she going when you came out?"

"She — the woman we saw?"

"Yes, your husband's strange friend. It's a clue worth following." He didn't want to scare or to shake her; he only wanted to communicate the impulse that would make her say: "Ah spare me — and spare *him!* There was no such person."

Instead of this Everina replied: "She was going away from us — she crossed the road. We were coming toward the station."

"And did she appear to recognise the Colonel — did she look round?"

"Yes; she looked round, but I didn't notice much. A hansom came along and we got into it. It wasn't till then that Clement told me who she was: I remember he said that she was there for no good. I suppose we ought to have gone back."

"Yes; you'd have saved the picture."

For a moment she said nothing; then she smiled. "For you, *cher maître*, I'm very sorry. But you must remember I possess the original!"

At this he turned away. "Well, I must go," he said; and he left her without any other farewell and made his way out of the house. As he went slowly up the street the sense came back to him of that first glimpse of her he had had at Stayes — of how he had seen her gaze across the table at her husband. He stopped at the corner, looking vaguely up and down. He would never go back — he couldn't. Nor should he ever sound her abyss. He believed in her absolute straightness where she and her affairs alone might be concerned, but she was still in love with the man of her choice, and since she couldn't redeem him she would adopt and protect him. So he had trained her.

Joseph Conrad · 1857-1924

Anyone who likes stories of adventure in out-of-the-way corners of the world, tales of men struggling with wind, rain, and fire, at sea and on land, will be eager to read Joseph Conrad. In twenty volumes of narrative the author carries the reader to Java and the Malay Peninsula, to the Celebes, the Mediterranean, to South America, up strange rivers and to palm-dotted tropical islands. On these expeditions the reader accompanies rugged men, some "good," some "bad," in their struggles against nature and man, sharing their adventures, feeling their emotions of hate and fear and love and jealousy. The world presented in these stories of Conrad, however, is not that of common romance; the tales are colored by Conrad's questioning mind, his irony, and his melancholic uncertainty as to the significance of life. The reader of Conrad shares two adventures — that of the body and that of the human spirit. He learns that physical failure may be turned into spiritual success, that all judgments are relative, and that men may raise themselves above normal standards by their power of mind and their strength of will.

Conrad's literary style — like that of James Joyce — has caused much discussion. The reader who makes a first acquaintance with Conrad through *Lord Jim* or *Chance*, for instance, is likely to be uncertain whether he is in the world of the present or of the past, whether he is participating in action or listening to a narrative of previous events, whether he is in the external world or within the mind of a character. Few writers have so blended the subjective with the objective. But a second reading or further experience with Conrad dispels most of these difficulties; the reader finds the romantic blended with the realistic, the external with the internal. Conrad is a literary impressionist. He reveals his story gradually. One character contributes a portion of the narrative, a second or perhaps a third lets us see the scene or the action from another angle. We are given a bit of a setting, several apparently unrelated incidents, snatches of conversation, and urged to co-operate with the author in fitting them together until the whole assumes unity and a cumulative force. With Conrad actual details are not enough. The facts are accompanied by sense impressions, by notes indicating their emotional and psychological significance. In the end we find that we have not only witnessed the action but have actually participated in it.

Joseph Conrad was born, December 3, 1857, in the Polish Ukraine. His father, a member of the gentry and an author in his own right, was obliged to leave home because of his part in a political intrigue. The young Conrad — whose Polish name was Teodor Józef Konrad Korzeniowski — spent his boyhood in Cracow. His early enthusiasm for Marryat and Cooper fixed his attention on the sea, with the result that when he was sixteen or seventeen years of age he found his way to the Marseilles docks and sailed on a French ship. Subsequent voyages took him about the Mediterranean and to South America. At twenty-one he arrived in England, studied the language, earned his "papers," and, rated as third mate, left for Sydney on a British ship. In 1886 he passed his examination as a master mariner and became a British citizen. He married an English woman, Jessie George. After sixteen years in the British merchant service, Conrad retired to live at Bedford and in various places in Kent. His later years were spent in quiet seclusion, writing in what was for him a foreign language — English.

From the author's many volumes it is difficult to point to a few titles as those of Conrad's "best" work. Perhaps, however, the reader to whom Conrad is little known will most quickly familiarize himself with the author's mood and manner by choosing among: *Almayer's Folly* (1895), *The Nigger of the Narcissus* (1897), *Lord Jim* (1900), *Youth and Other Stories* (1902), *Typhoon* (1902), *Nostromo* (1904), *Chance* (1913), and *The Shadow Line* (1917).

SUGGESTED REFERENCES: A. J. Guerard, *Conrad the Novelist* (1958); Adam Gillon, *The Eternal Solitary: A Study of Joseph Conrad* (1960); Leo Gurko, *Joseph Conrad: Giant in Exile* (1962).

The Lagoon

The Lagoon, which follows, is one of the author's earliest short stories, perhaps somewhat sentimental, and characteristic in its impressionistic manner, its tropical setting, its concern with a human passion, as well as in its unity secured through atmosphere.

The story is taken from *Tales of Unrest*, by Joseph Conrad, copyright, 1898, 1920, by Doubleday, Doran and Company, Inc.

The white man, leaning with both arms over the roof of the little house in the stern of the boat, said to the steersman ——

"We will pass the night in Arsat's clearing. It is late."

The Malay only grunted, and went on looking fixedly at the river. The white man rested his chin on his crossed arms and gazed at the wake of the boat. At the end of the straight avenue of forests cut by the intense glitter of the river, the sun appeared unclouded and dazzling, poised low over the water that shone smoothly like a band of metal. The forests, sombre and dull, stood motionless and silent on each side of the broad stream. At the foot of big, towering trees, trunkless nipa palms rose from the mud of the bank, in bunches of leaves enormous and heavy, that hung unstirring over the brown swirl of eddies. In the stillness of the air every tree, every leaf, every bough, every tendril of creeper and every petal of minute blossoms seemed to have been bewitched into an immobility perfect and final. Nothing moved on the river but the eight paddles that rose flashing regularly, dipped together with a single splash; while the steersman swept right and left with a periodic and sudden flourish of his blade describing a glinting semicircle above his head. The churned-up water frothed alongside with a confused murmur. And the white man's canoe, advancing upstream in the short-lived disturbance of its own making, seemed to enter the portals of a land from which the very memory of motion had forever departed.

The white man, turning his back upon the setting sun, looked along the empty and broad expanse of the sea-reach. For the last three miles of its course the wandering, hesitating river, as if enticed irresistibly by the freedom of an open horizon, flows straight into the sea, flows straight to the east — to the east that harbors both light and darkness. Astern of the boat the repeated call of some bird, a cry discordant and feeble, skipped along over the smooth water and lost itself, before it could reach the other shore, in the breathless silence of the world.

The steersman dug his paddle into the stream, and held hard with stiffened arms, his body thrown forward. The water gurgled aloud; and suddenly the long straight reach seemed to pivot on its centre, the forests swung in a semicircle, and the slanting beams of sunset touched the broadside of the canoe with a fiery glow, throwing slender and distorted shadows of its crew upon the streaked glitter of the river. The white man turned to look ahead. The course of the boat had been altered at right-angles to the stream, and the carved dragon-head of its prow was pointing now at a gap in the fringing bushes of the bank. It glided through, brushing the overhanging twigs, and disappeared from the river like some slim and amphibious creature leaving the water for its lair in the forests.

The narrow creek was like a ditch: tortuous, fabulously deep; filled with gloom under the thin strip of pure and shining blue of the heaven. Immense trees soared up, invisible behind the festooned draperies of creepers. Here and there, near the glistening blackness of the water, a twisted root of some tall tree showed amongst the tracery of small ferns, black and dull, writhing and motionless, like an arrested snake. The short words of the paddlers reverberated loudly between the thick and sombre walls of vegetation. Darkness oozed out from between the trees, through the tangled maze of the creepers, from behind the great fantastic and unstirring leaves; the darkness, mysterious and invincible; the darkness scented and poisonous of impenetrable forests.

The men poled in the shoaling water. The creek broadened, opening out into a wide sweep of a stagnant lagoon. The forests receded from the marshy bank, leaving a level strip of bright green, reedy grass to frame the reflected blueness of the sky. A fleecy pink cloud drifted high above, trailing the delicate coloring of its image under the floating leaves and the silvery blossoms of the lotus. A little house, perched on high piles, appeared black in the distance. Near it, two tall nibong palms, that seemed to have come out of the forests in the background, leaned slightly over the ragged roof, with a suggestion of sad tenderness and care in the droop of their leafy and soaring heads.

The steersman, pointing with his paddle, said, "Arsat is there. I see his canoe fast between the piles."

The polers ran along the sides of the boat glancing over their shoulders at the end of the day's journey. They would have preferred to spend the night somewhere else than on this lagoon of weird aspect and ghostly reputation. Moreover, they disliked Arsat, first as a stranger, and also because he who repairs a ruined house, and dwells in it, proclaims that he is not afraid to live amongst the spirits that haunt the places abandoned by mankind. Such a man can disturb the course of fate by glances or words; while his familiar ghosts are not easy to propitiate by casual wayfarers upon whom they long to wreak the malice of their human master. White men care not for such things, being unbelievers and in league with the Father of Evil, who leads them unharmed through the invisible dangers of this world. To the warnings of the righteous they oppose an offensive pretence of disbelief. What is there to be done?

So they thought, throwing their weight on the end of their long poles. The big canoe glided on swiftly, noiselessly, and smoothly, towards Arsat's clearing, till, in a great rattling of poles thrown down, and the loud murmurs of "Allah be praised!" it came with a gentle knock against the crooked piles below the house.

The boatmen with uplifted faces shouted discordantly, "Arsat! O Arsat!" Nobody came. The white man began to climb the rude ladder giving access to the bamboo platform before the house. The juragan [1] of the boat said sulkily, "We will cook in the sampan, and sleep on the water."

"Pass my blankets and the basket," said the white man, curtly.

He knelt on the edge of the platform to receive the bundle. Then the boat shoved off, and the white man, standing up, confronted Arsat, who had come out through the low door of his hut. He was a man young, powerful, with broad chest and muscular arms. He had nothing on but his sarong. His head was bare. His big, soft eyes stared eagerly at the white man, but his voice and demeanor were composed as he asked, without any words of greeting ——

"Have you medicine, Tuan?"

"No," said the visitor in a startled tone. "No. Why? Is there sickness in the house?"

"Enter and see," replied Arsat, in the same calm manner, and turning short round passed again through the small doorway. The white man, dropping his bundles, followed.

In the dim light of the dwelling he made out on a couch of bamboos a woman stretched on her back under a broad sheet of red cotton cloth. She lay still, as if dead; but her big eyes, wide open, glittered in the gloom, staring upwards at the slender rafters, motionless and unseeing. She was in a high fever, and evidently unconscious. Her cheeks were sunk slightly, her lips were partly open, and on the young face there was the ominous

[1] Leader of the native crew.

and fixed expression — the absorbed, contemplating expression of the unconscious who are going to die. The two men stood looking down at her in silence.

"Has she been long ill?" asked the traveller.

"I have not slept for five nights," answered the Malay, in a deliberate tone. "At first she heard voices calling her from the water and struggled against me who held her. But since the sun of to-day rose she hears nothing — she hears not me. She sees nothing. She sees not me — me!"

He remained silent for a minute. then asked softly —

"Tuan, will she die?"

"I fear so," said the white man, sorrowfully. He had known Arsat years ago, in a far country in times of trouble and danger, when no friendship is to be despised. And since his Malay friend had come unexpectedly to dwell in the hut on the lagoon with a strange woman, he had slept many times there, in his journeys up and down the river. He liked the man who knew how to keep faith in council and how to fight without fear by the side of his white friend. He liked him — not so much perhaps as a man likes his favorite dog — but still he liked him well enough to help and ask no questions, to think sometimes vaguely and hazily in the midst of his own pursuits, about the lonely man and the long-haired woman with audacious face and triumphant eyes, who lived together hidden by the forests — alone and feared.

The white man came out of the hut in time to see the enormous conflagration of sunset put out by the swift and stealthy shadows that, rising like a black and impalpable vapor above the tree-tops, spread over the heaven, extinguishing the crimson glow of floating clouds and the red brilliance of departing daylight. In a few moments all the stars came out above the intense blackness of the earth and the great lagoon gleaming suddenly with reflected lights resembled an oval patch of night sky flung down into the hopeless and abysmal night of the wilderness. The white man had some supper out of the basket, then collecting a few sticks that lay about the platform, made up a small fire, not for warmth, but for the sake of the smoke, which would keep off the mosquitoes. He wrapped himself in the blankets and sat with his back against the reed wall of the house, smoking thoughtfully.

Arsat came through the doorway with noiseless steps and squatted down by the fire. The white man moved his outstretched legs a little.

"She breathes," said Arsat in a low voice, anticipating the expected question. "She breathes and burns as if with a great fire. She speaks not; she hears not — and burns!"

He paused for a moment, then asked in a quiet, incurious tone ——

"Tuan . . . will she die?"

The white man moved his shoulders uneasily and muttered in a hesitating manner ——

"If such is her fate."

"No, Tuan," said Arsat, calmly. "If such is my fate. I hear, I see, I wait. I remember . . . Tuan, do you remember the old days? Do you remember my brother?"

"Yes," said the white man. The Malay rose suddenly and went in. The other, sitting still outside, could hear the voice in the hut. Arsat said: "Hear me! Speak!" His words were succeeded by a complete silence. "O Diamelen!" he cried, suddenly. After that cry there was a deep sigh. Arsat came out and sank down again in his old place.

They sat in silence before the fire. There was no sound within the house, there was no sound near them; but far away on the lagoon they could hear the voices of the boatmen ringing fitful and distinct on the calm water. The fire in the bows of the sampan shone faintly in the distance with a hazy red glow. Then it died out. The voices ceased. The land and the water slept invisible, unstirring and mute. It was as though there had been nothing left in the world but the glitter of stars streaming, ceaseless and vain, through the black stillness of the night.

The white man gazed straight before him into the darkness with wide-open eyes. The fear and fascination, the inspiration and the wonder of death — of death near, unavoidable, and unseen, soothed the unrest of his race and stirred the most indistinct, the most intimate of his thoughts. The ever-ready suspicion of evil, the gnawing suspicion that lurks in our hearts, flowed out into the stillness round him — into the stillness profound and dumb, and made it appear untrustworthy and infamous, like the placid and impenetrable mask of an unjustifiable violence. In that fleeting and powerful disturbance of his being the earth enfolded in the starlight peace became a shadowy country of inhuman strife, a battle-field of phantoms terrible and charming, august or ignoble, struggling ardently for the possession of our helpless hearts. An unquiet and mysterious country of inextinguishable desires and fears.

A plaintive murmur rose in the night; a murmur saddening and startling, as if the great solitudes of surrounding woods had tried to whisper into his ear the wisdom of their immense and lofty indifference. Sounds hesitating and vague floated in the air round him, shaped themselves slowly into words; and at last flowed on gently in a murmuring stream of soft and monotonous sentences. He stirred like a man waking up and changed his position slightly. Arsat, motionless and shadowy, sitting with bowed head under the stars, was speaking in a low and dreamy tone —

" . . . for where can we lay down the heaviness of our trouble but in a friend's heart? A man must speak of war and of love. You, Tuan, know what war is, and you have seen me in time of danger seek death as other men seek life! A writing may be lost; a lie may be written; but what the eyes has seen is truth and remains in the mind!"

"I remember," said the white man, quietly. Arsat went on with mournful composure —

"Therefore I shall speak to you of love. Speak in the night. Speak before both night and love are gone — and the eye of day looks upon my sorrow and my shame; upon my blackened face; upon my burnt-up heart."

A sigh, short and faint, marked an almost imperceptible pause, and then his words flowed on, without a stir, without a gesture.

"After the time of trouble and war was over and you went away from my country in the pursuit of your desires, which we, men of the islands, cannot understand, I and my brother became again, as we had been before, the sword-bearers of the Ruler. You know we were men of family, belonging to a ruling race, and more fit than any to carry on our right shoulder the emblem of power. And in the time of prosperity Si Dendring showed us favor, as we, in time of sorrow, had showed to him the faithfulness of our courage. It was a time of peace. A time of deer-hunts and cock-fights; of idle talks and foolish squabbles between men whose bellies are full and weapons are rusty. But the sower watched the young rice-shoots grow up without fear, and the traders came and went, departed lean and returned fat into the river of peace. They brought news, too. Brought lies and truth mixed together, so that no man knew when to rejoice and when to be sorry. We heard from them about you also. They had seen you here and had seen you there. And I was glad to hear, for I remembered the stirring times, and I always remember you, Tuan, till the time came when my eyes could see nothing in the past, because they had looked upon the one who is dying there — in the house."

He stopped to exclaim in an intense whisper, "O Mara bahia! O Calamity!" then went on speaking a little louder:

"There's no worse enemy and no better friend than a brother, Tuan, for one brother knows another, and in perfect knowledge is strength for good or evil. I loved my brother. I went to him and told him that I could see nothing but one face, hear nothing but one voice. He told me: 'Open your heart so that she can see what is in it — and wait. Patience is wisdom. Inchi Midah may die or our Ruler may throw off his fear of a woman!' ... I waited! ... You remember the lady with the veiled face, Tuan, and the fear of our Ruler before her cunning and temper. And if she wanted her servant, what could I do? But I fed the hunger of my heart on short glances and stealthy words. I loitered on the path to the bath-houses in the daytime, and when the sun had fallen behind the forest I crept along the jasmine hedges of the women's courtyard. Unseeing, we spoke to one another through the scent of flowers, through the veil of leaves, through the blades of long grass that stood still before our lips; so great was our prudence, so faint was the murmur of our great longing. The time passed swiftly ... and there were whispers amongst women — and our enemies watched — my brother was gloomy, and I began to think of killing and of a fierce death. . . . We are of a people who take what we want — like you whites. There is a time when a man should forget loyalty and respect. Might and authority are given to rulers, but to all men is given love and strength and courage. My brother said, 'You shall take her from their midst. We are two who are like one.' And I answered, 'Let it be soon, for I find no warmth in sunlight that does not shine upon her.' Our time came when the Ruler and all the great people went to the mouth of the river to fish by torchlight. There were hundreds of boats, and on the white sand, between the water and the forests, dwellings of leaves were built for the households of the Rajahs. The smoke of cooking-fires was like a blue mist of the evening, and many voices rang in it joyfully. While they were making the boats ready to beat up the fish, my brother came to me and said, 'To-night!' I looked to my weapons, and when the time came our canoe took its place in the circle of boats carrying the torches. The lights blazed on the water, but behind the boats there was darkness. When the shouting began and the excitement made them like mad we dropped out. The water swallowed our fire, and we floated back to the shore that was dark with only here and there the glimmer of embers. We could hear the talk of slave-girls amongst the sheds. Then we found a place deserted and silent. We waited there. She came. She came running along the shore, rapid and leaving no trace, like a leaf driven by the wind into the sea. My brother said gloomily, 'Go and take her; carry her into our boat.' I lifted her in my arms. She panted. Her heart was beating against my breast. I said, 'I take you from those

people. You came to the cry of my heart, but my arms take you into my boat against the will of the great!' 'It is right,' said my brother. 'We are men who take what we want and can hold it against many. We should have taken her in daylight.' I said, 'Let us be off'; for since she was in my boat I began to think of our Ruler's many men. 'Yes. Let us be off,' said my brother. 'We are cast out and this boat is our country now — and the sea is our refuge.' He lingered with his foot on the shore, and I entreated him to hasten, for I remembered the strokes of her heart against my breast and thought that two men cannot withstand a hundred. We left, paddling downstream close to the bank; and as we passed by the creek where they were fishing, the great shouting had ceased, but the murmur of voices was loud like the humming of insects flying at noonday. The boats floated, clustered together, in the red light of torches, under a black roof of smoke; and men talked of their sport. Men that boasted, and praised, and jeered — men that would have been our friends in the morning, but on that night were already our enemies. We paddled swiftly past. We had no more friends in the country of our birth. She sat in the middle of the canoe with covered face; silent as she is now; unseeing as she is now — and I had no regret at what I was leaving because I could hear her breathing close to me — as I can hear her now."

He paused, listened with his ear turned to the doorway, then shook his head and went on:

"My brother wanted to shout the cry of challenge — one cry only — to let the people know we were freeborn robbers who trusted our arms and the great sea. And again I begged him in the name of our love to be silent. Could I not hear her breathing close to me? I knew the pursuit would come quick enough. My brother loved me. He dipped his paddle without a splash. He only said, 'There is half a man in you now — the other half is in that woman. I can wait. When you are a whole man again, you will come back with me here to shout defiance. We are sons of the same mother.' I made no answer. All my strength and all my spirit were in my hands that held the paddle — for I longed to be with her in a safe place beyond the reach of men's anger and of women's spite. My love was so great, that I thought it could guide me to a country where death was unknown, if I could only escape from Inchi Midah's fury and from our Ruler's sword. We paddled with haste, breathing through our teeth. The blades bit deep into the smooth water. We passed out of the river; we flew in clear channels amongst the shallows. We skirted the black coast; we skirted the sand beaches where the sea speaks in whispers to the land; and the gleam of white sand flashed back past our boat, so swiftly she ran upon the water. We spoke not. Only once I said, 'Sleep, Diamelen, for soon you may want all your strength.' I heard the sweetness of her voice, but I never turned my head. The sun rose and still we went on. Water fell from my face like rain from a cloud. We flew in the light and heat. I never looked back, but I knew that my brother's eyes, behind me, were looking steadily ahead, for the boat went as straight as a bushman's dart, when it leaves the end of the sumpitan. There was no better paddler, no better steersman than my brother. Many times, together, we had won races in that canoe. But we never had put out our strength as we did then — then, when for the last time we paddled together! There was no braver or stronger man in our country than my brother. I could not spare the strength to turn my head and look at him, but every moment I heard the hiss of his breath getting louder behind me. Still he did not speak. The sun was high. The heat clung to my back like a flame of fire. My ribs were ready to burst, but I could no longer get enough air into my chest. And then I felt I must cry out with my last breath, 'Let us rest!'... 'Good!' he answered; and his voice was firm. He was strong. He was brave. He knew not fear and no fatigue... My brother!"

A murmur powerful and gentle, a murmur vast and faint; the murmur of trembling leaves, of stirring boughs, ran through the tangled depths of the forests, ran over the starry smoothness of the lagoon, and the water between the piles lapped the slimy timber once with a sudden splash. A breath of warm air touched the two men's faces and passed on with a mournful sound — a breath loud and short like an uneasy sigh of the dreaming earth.

Arsat went on in an even, low voice.

"We ran our canoe on the white beach of a little bay close to a long tongue of land that seemed to bar our road; a long wooded cape going far into the sea. My brother knew that place. Beyond the cape a river has its entrance, and through the jungle of that land there is a narrow path. We made a fire and cooked rice. Then we lay down to sleep on the soft sand in the shade of our canoe, while she watched. No sooner had I closed my eyes than I heard her cry of alarm. We leaped up. The sun was halfway down the sky already, and coming in sight in the opening of the bay we saw a prau manned by many paddlers. We knew it at once; it was one of our Rajah's praus. They were watching the shore, and saw us. They beat the gong, and turned the head of the prau into the bay. I felt my heart become weak within my breast. Diamelen sat on the sand and covered her face. There was no escape by sea. My brother laughed. He had the gun you had given him, Tuan, before you went away, but there was only a handful of powder. He spoke to me quickly: 'Run with her along the path. I shall keep them back, for they have no firearms, and landing in the face of a man with a gun is certain death for some. Run with her. On the other side of that wood there is a fisherman's house — and a canoe. When I have fired all the shots I will follow. I am a great runner, and before they can come up we shall be gone. I will hold out as long as I can, for she is but a woman — that can neither run nor fight, but she has your heart in her weak hands.' He dropped behind the canoe. The prau was coming. She and I ran, and as we rushed along the path I heard shots. My brother fired — once — twice — and the booming of the gong ceased. There was silence behind us. That neck of land is narrow. Before I heard my brother fire the third shot I saw the shelving shore, and I saw the water again; the mouth of a broad river. We crossed a grassy glade. We ran down to the water. I saw a low hut above the black mud, and a small canoe hauled up. I heard another shot behind me. I thought, 'That is his last charge.' We rushed down to the canoe; a man came running from the hut, but I leaped on him, and we rolled together in the mud. Then I got up, and he lay still at my feet. I don't know whether I had killed him or not. I and Diamelen pushed the canoe afloat. I heard yells behind me, and I saw my brother run across the glade. Many men were bounding after him, I took her in my arms and threw her into the boat, then leaped in myself. When I looked back I saw that my brother had fallen. He fell and was up again, but the men were closing around him. He shouted, 'I am coming!' The men were close to him. I looked. Many men. Then I looked at her. Tuan, I pushed the canoe! I pushed it into deep water. She was kneeling forward looking at me, and I said, 'Take your paddle,' while I struck the water with mine. Tuan, I heard him cry. I heard him cry my name twice; and I heard voices shouting, 'Kill! Strike!' I never turned back. I heard him calling my name again with a great shriek, as when life is going out together with the voice — and I never turned my head. My own name!... My brother! Three times he called — but I was not afraid of life. Was she not there in that canoe? And could I not with her find a country where death is forgotten — where death is unknown!"

The white man sat up. Arsat rose and stood, indistinct and silent figure above the dying embers of the fire. Over the lagoon a mist drifting and low had crept, erasing slowly the glittering images of the stars. And now a great expanse of white vapor covered the land: it flowed cold and gray in the darkness, eddied in noiseless whirls round the tree-trunks and about the platform of the house, which seemed to float upon a restless and impalpable illusion of a sea. Only far away the tops of the trees stood outlined on the twinkle of heaven, like a sombre and forbidding shore — a coast deceptive, pitiless and black.

Arsat's voice vibrated loudly in the profound peace.

"I had her there! I had her! To get her I would have faced all mankind. But I had her — and ——"

His words went out ringing into the empty distances. He paused, and seemed to listen to them dying away very far — beyond help and beyond recall. Then he said quietly —

"Tuan, I loved my brother."

A breath of wind made him shiver. High above his head, high above the silent sea of mist the drooping leaves of the palms rattled together with a mournful and expiring sound. The white man stretched his legs. His chin rested on his chest, and he murmured sadly without lifting his head —

"We all love our brothers."

Arsat burst out with an intense whispering violence —

"What did I care who died? I wanted peace in my own heart."

He seemed to hear a stir in the house — listened — then stepped in noiselessly. The white man stood up. A breeze was coming in fitful puffs. The stars shone paler as if they had retreated into the frozen depths of immense space. After a chill gust of wind there were a few seconds of perfect calm and absolute silence. Then from behind the black and wavy line of the forests a column of golden light shot up into the heavens and spread over the semicircle of the eastern horizon. The sun had risen. The mist lifted, broke into drifting patches, vanished into thin flying wreaths; and the unveiled lagoon lay, polished and black, in the heavy shadows at the foot of the wall of trees. A white eagle rose over it with a slanting and ponderous flight, reached the clear sunshine and appeared dazzlingly brilliant for a moment, then soaring higher, became a dark and motionless speck before it vanished into the blue as if it had left the earth forever. The white man, standing gazing upwards before the doorway, heard in the hut a confused and broken murmur of distracted words ending with a loud groan. Suddenly Arsat stumbled out with outstretched hands, shivered, and stood still for some time with fixed eyes. Then he said —

"She burns no more."

Before his face the sun showed its edge above the tree-tops rising steadily. The breeze freshened; a great brilliance burst upon the lagoon, sparkled on the rippling water. The forests came out of the clear shadows of the morning, became distinct, as if they had rushed nearer — to stop short in a great stir of leaves, of nodding boughs, of swaying branches. In the merciless sunshine the whisper of unconscious life grew louder, speaking in an incomprehensible voice round the dumb darkness of that human sorrow. Arsat's eyes wandered slowly, then stared at the rising sun.

"I can see nothing," he said half aloud to himself.

"There is nothing," said the white man, moving to the edge of the platform and waving his hand to his boat. A shout came faintly over the lagoon and the sampan began to glide towards the abode of the friend of ghosts.

"If you want to come with me, I will wait all the morning," said the white man, looking away upon the water.

"No, Tuan," said Arsat, softly. "I shall not eat or sleep in this house, but I must first see my road. Now I can see nothing — see nothing! There is no light and no peace in the world; but there is death — death for many. We are sons of the same mother — and I left him in the midst of enemies; but I am going back now."

He drew a long breath and went on in a dreamy tone:

"In a little while I shall see clear enough to strike — to strike. But she has died, and . . . now . . . darkness."

He flung his arms wide open, let them fall along his body, then stood still with unmoved face and stony eyes, staring at the sun. The white man got down into his canoe. The polers ran smartly along the sides of the boat, looking over their shoulders at the beginning of a weary journey. High in the stern, his head muffled up in white rags, the juragan sat moody, letting his paddle trail in the water. The white man, leaning with both arms over the grass roof of the little cabin, looked back at the shining ripple of the boat's wake. Before the sampan passed out of the lagoon into the creek he lifted his eyes. Arsat had not moved. He stood lonely in the searching sunshine; and he looked beyond the great light of a cloudless day into the darkness of a world of illusions.

Paul Claudel · 1868–1955

Paul Claudel was born in 1868 in a small village in northern France which subsequently provided the setting for several of his plays. He went to school in Paris, associating with many promising students of literature such as Leon Daudet and Marcel Schwob. He was the last survivor of the generation of great French writers that included André Gide, Paul Valéry, and Charles Péguy.

Since his parents had abandoned the tenets of the Catholic Church, their son was not brought up in its tradition. In December, 1886, two events — the death of his grandfather and the boy's discovery of Arthur Rimbaud's poetry — combined to make him suddenly aware of a religious craving to be gratified only by joining the Church. Many years afterwards, Claudel published a detailed report of his conversion and his struggle for a new and lasting faith. One can trace this spiritual development in the poet's early plays. The first versions of *La Tête d'or* and *La Ville* still manifest a pessimistic and somber attitude toward life, an attitude which appears to have radically changed in subsequent versions.

After graduation from a political academy at the age of twenty-five, Claudel entered the diplomatic service and was appointed French consul in New York and later in Boston. In 1894 he was transferred to China where he remained, with interruptions, until 1908. It is no wonder then that the East became for him not only a second home but a spiritual obsession. In his book *Connaissance de l'est* (*The East I Know*) Claudel describes the loneliness and beauty of the strange Oriental country and its influence on his art and thought. The years preceding World War I he spent as a French consul in Czechoslovakia and Germany. In 1914 he returned to France and later in the same year was assigned to the French embassy in Rome. In 1917 he was chosen to represent his government first in Rio de Janeiro, then in Copenhagen, and later in Tokyo, where he witnessed the terrible earthquake of 1923 which devastated large parts of the main island. In 1927 Claudel returned to the United States, this time as ambassador to Washington, and stayed here until 1931 when he went back to Europe, soon retiring from his diplomatic career. In his last years he divided his time between Paris and a small monastery town in northern France. He died in Paris in 1955.

It was many years before Claudel's fellow-poets and countrymen came to recognize him as one of the outstanding writers of his time. Not until 1912 was any play of his performed; it was *L'Annonce faite à Marie* (*Tidings Brought to Mary*), a revised version of an earlier play called *La Jeune fille Violaine*. And it was not until 1947 that Claudel was made a member of the Acadèmie Française, that illustrious body of French thinkers and artists. François Mauriac, another great Catholic writer, received the new member into the Académie.

Although considered to be an outsider and the least French of all French poets, Claudel was in close contact with many of his contemporaries. As a young man, together with Gide, Valéry, Wilde, and Yeats, he attended the famous Tuesday evening receptions in the house of Stéphane Mallarmé, the master of symbolist poetry. Over a period of approximately twenty years he exchanged letters with Gide, and it is well known that he acted as a kind of spiritual confessor to numerous famous writers finding their way back to Catholicism. He helped to convert Charles Péguy, Francis Jammes, and Jacques Rivière; with Gide, however, he did not succeed. Gide's frankness in admitting flaws in his moral disposition and his refusal to omit certain offending passages from his novels frequently strained their otherwise amicable relationship.

Claudel's work consists of a large number of plays, poems, dialogues, and theoretical treatises. Chief among the plays, besides those already mentioned, are *L'Echange*, *Partage de midi*, *Le Pain dur*, *Le Père humilié*, and *Le Soulier de satin* (*The Satin Slipper*). Best known among numerous collections of his poetry are *Cinq grands odes* and *Corona Benignitatis Anni Dei*, the latter a companion for the Church Year of saints' days, seasons, and holidays. Of his prose works *The East I Know* has been mentioned. Of equal importance are *Art poétique* (*Poetic Art*), a metaphysical study of the essence of poetry, and *Positions et propositions,* a collection of brief essays on various religious and artistic subjects.

Claudel's reception in America has never been enthusiastic. Several of his plays, notably *L'Annonce faite à Marie,* have been translated into English and performed on Broadway, but American critics have shown little interest in them and have never undertaken an intelligent and fair discussion of Claudel's achievement as a poet of the theater.

Most critics call Claudel a mystic — and that is as far as they will go in interpreting the specific character of his poetry. As a playwright, Claudel was profoundly influenced by Æschylus, whose dramatic trilogy he translated into his native tongue, and yet neither of his plays possesses the tragic quality inherent in Greek drama. What happens in Claudel's plays can be related in a few words. While in Sartre's plays, for example, the action centers on one or a series of existential decisions, in Claudel's drama the decision is already understood in the beginning and only the temptation, a negative decision, is shown. His plays minimize the time element and insist upon a static hierarchy of universal religious values. They are written in verse distinguished by its sonorous and deeply musical quality. It is not the conventional blank verse, nor rhymed verse, which constitutes the rhythmic pattern of a play like *The Satin Slipper;* the unit of the Claudelian verse is the natural rhythm, that is, the duration of a breath. This relationship between physiology and poetry is only one of many pervading Claudel's artistic universe. The natural and the supernatural, the poetic and the religious are other forms of the same analogical relationship which he defends in his perceptive although somewhat obscure book, *Poetic Art.*

Claudel's style has been called impressionistic because his plays do not progress logically or dialectically as he develops the dramatic theme and the tragic conflict; they are rather musical compositions based on religious themes dogmatically preconceived in the poet's mind. There are only few scenes of pure action; most scenes serve to convey impressions or to reproduce monologues or dialogues suffused with rich and abundant imagery. Claudel aims at building up a religious mood in his audience and at transforming his plays into rituals similar to the medieval Mystery Plays. Claudel's playwriting technique is resourceful and suggestive. He introduced many of the features now common on the modern stage: improvised stage-settings, the use of narrators and commentators, and the rapid shifting of a multiplicity of scenes.

SUGGESTED REFERENCES: Mary Ryan, *Introduction to Paul Claudel* (1951); Wallace Fowlie, *Paul Claudel* (1957).

The Satin Slipper [1]

Claudel's poetic work culminates in *The Satin Slipper* or *The Worst is Not the Surest.* Like most of Claudel's plays, this one is neither a tragedy nor a comedy proper; the author simply calls it a Spanish Action in Four Days, a title referring to the Spanish tragedy of the Golden Age with its four Jornadas.

The play, with its fifty-two scenes of which this Action is composed, was written between 1919 and 1924; it was first performed in 1943 during the days of the Nazi occupation, when Jean-Louis Barrault produced it in the Comedie Française. As one critic put it, the French audience took *The Satin Slipper* for a sym-

bolic manifestation of their spirit of independence and their resistance movement. This is one but certainly not the only interpretation possible. Claudel, writing it more than twenty years earlier, had stated that "the argument is that all things minister to a Divine Purpose and so to one another, be it events or personalities. Even the falterings of circumstance and the patterns of personality, sin, and falsehood are made to serve truth and justice, and above all, salvation in the long run." Elaborating this concept, he invented a rich, grandiose spectacle, an action which takes place in the wide realm of sixteenth-century Spain and its colonies, an empire on which the sun never sets.

Claudel's stage directions suggest that the universe of *The Satin Slipper* is assembled from a large number of more or less fragmentary scenes; it resembles a mosaic. The scenes vary in length and mood; they are

[1] From *The Satin Slipper* or *The Worst Is Not the Surest* by Paul Claudel, translated by the Rev. John O'Connor, published by Sheed and Ward, New York and London.

now lyrical and lofty, now brutal, abstract, or humorous. Seven scenes (II, V, VII, VIII, XI, XII, XIV) from the First Day of the Action have been selected as representative of the work as a whole and its poetic structure. The First Day presents a fairly coherent action in striking the keynote of the whole play: the profound and religious love of Rodrigo and Prouheze never to be consummated on earth.

The following summaries of all fourteen scenes of the First Day have been prepared by the translator:

SCENE I: A Jesuit, dying abandoned on a plundered ship, prays for his brother Rodrigo, the hero of the action, that, since he has refused the directest way to God, he may find the selfsame by whatever winding road his own will may build unto itself; and that his sinful love, bereft of consummation may avail to draw him from self and love of self until he attain to selflessness.

SCENE II: Pelagio, husband of Prouheze (Dona Maravilla) manifests himself as a man of rigid principle just garnished with humanity. Balthazar, consciously very human but strong in military honour, accepts the charge of escorting Dona Prouheze, mildly suggesting his unfitness to take charge of any pretty lady, save in the capacity of husband.

SCENE III: Don Camillo, the villain, discloses a determination to win Prouheze, guessing that she is but lightly attached to her husband. She dallies with him just enough to implicate the whole tragic developments of the drama.

SCENE IV: Dona Isabel makes with Don Luis the secret assignation which leads to the wounding of Rodrigo much later on.

SCENE V: Don Balthazar is setting off in escort to Dona Prouheze, who reveals that she has written to Rodrigo. Account of her passion for him, her forced and loveless marriage of reverential fear with Pelagio. They both look up at the statue of Our Lady, and Prouheze takes off one shoe, which, standing on her mule, she places in the image's hands: "that when I would go headlong into evil it may be with halting foot."

SCENE VI: The Spanish King at Belem, discussing with his Chancellor the need of a strong hand in the new realm of America, asks for a suggestion. The Chancellor suggests Don Rodrigo. With some demur the King accepts and commands him to be brought.

SCENE VII: Rodrigo, avoiding the pursuivants of the King, is resting towards evening, and discussing with his Chinese servant his love of Prouheze; he is interrupted by musket-fire in a distant wood and rushes to the rescue of Saint James, whose image, he thinks, is being set upon by brigands.

SCENE VIII: Jobarbara the negress servant of Prouheze, is distraught from severe vigilance by a Neapolitan Sergeant who has fooled her out of her most precious possessions. The Sergeant mentions that he is rescuing Dona Musica from Don Pelagio's matrimonial disposition of her.

SCENE IX: Dona Isabel (of Scene IV) sees her lover killed by Rodrigo in defence of Saint James' image from the sham attack she had arranged with Don Luis. Rodrigo, badly wounded by Don Luis, borrows a carriage from Isabel's brother and goes off to be nursed in his mother's castle.

SCENE X: Musica and Prouheze, at the fortress inn, discuss their lovers fancifully, but Prouheze's intensity caps the scene.

SCENE XI: The negress is spell-binding to bring back the Sergeant. The Chinese servant of Rodrigo comes instead, looking for the money of which she has cheated him. She tells him Dona Maravilla is within the fortress — he tells her of Rodrigo's mischance and his present lodging, and how Prouheze must be got to him. A band of knights is seeking Musica and he has told them she is quartered at this inn. So they are going to attack next evening, and then the negress must get Prouheze to leave under cover of the tumult.

SCENE XII: Prouheze escapes with great difficulty. Her Guardian Angel looks on, marking and suggesting.

SCENE XIII: Balthazar confesses that he has connived at the escape of Prouheze. He is planning a sham defence for a reason visible in ——

SCENE XIV: The Chinaman confesses to Balthazar his responsibility for the attack. The old soldier grimly makes him share his risks, which now are turning into certainties of sudden death. Supper is served. The attackers ask for Musica. Balthazar compels the Chinaman to sing for them. On the sea a boat sails by with negress, Sergeant and Musica. Balthazar falls across the table shot dead.

In the remaining Days of the Action, Claudel describes Rodrigo's departure for the Americas after he has been defeated by Camillo, who is to marry Prouheze, and his adventures there. The author designs a picture of strange tropical regions belonging to or bordering on the Spanish Empire. Many years later Rodrigo is shown returning to Mogador and meeting Prouheze; but once more she refuses to leave the fortress and Don Camillo, her husband. She gives her child, Dona Sevensword, into Rodrigo's keeping. This child is destined to carry on her task while Rodrigo himself falls into disgrace and dies, forgotten and mutilated, a captive of his enemies. As he dies, he receives word that Dona Sevensword has safely reached the ship of Don Juan d'Austria, the King's illegitimate son and the future hero of Lepanto.

SCENE II

DON PELAGIO, DON BALTHAZAR

The front of a nobleman's house in Spain. First hour of the morning. The garden full of orange trees. A little blue terra-cotta fountain under the trees.

Don Pelagio. Don Balthazar, there are two roads going away from this house.

And one, if one could gauge it at a glance, through many towns and villages

Rising, falling, like a neglected skein on a rope-maker's trestle, bears from here straight to the sea, not far from a certain hostelry I know hidden among great trees.

That is the way a knight at arms escorts Dona Prouheze. Yes, I wish that by him Dona Prouheze be taken from my sight.

Meanwhile, by another road among the broom and climbing among the scattered rocks, I will yield to the call come to me from that white spot up there,

This letter from the widow in the mountain,

This letter from my cousin in my hand.

As to Maravilla my lady, there is nothing for it but to watch well the sealine towards the East, in which those sails appear which have to bring her and me to our governorship in Africa.

Don Balthazar. Eh what, señor, going away so soon?

The home of your childhood, after so many months on savage soil, what! leave it again?

Don Pelagio. True, it is the only spot in the world where I feel understood and taken for granted.

Here I used to seek refuge in silence whilst I was His Majesty's dreadful judge, extirpator of robbers and rebels.

A judge is not beloved.

But I found straight away that there was no greater charity than to kill off malefactors.

What days I have spent here, with no company from morning till night but my old gardener,

These orange trees which I watered with my own hands, and that little nanny-goat which was not afraid of me!

Yes, she used to butt me in play and come and eat vine leaves from my hand.

Don Balthazar. And now here is Dona Maravilla who is more to you than the little nanny-goat.

Don Pelagio. Take care of her, Don Balthazar, on this journey. I entrust her to your honour.

Don Balthazar. What, it is to me you want to entrust Dona Prouheze?

Don Pelagio. Why not? Have you not told me yourself that your duties are calling you to Catalonia? It will not much lengthen your road.

Don Balthazar. I beg you to excuse me. Is there no other knight to whom you can entrust this charge?

Don Pelagio. Not one other.

Don Balthazar. Don Camillo, for instance, your ensign and lieutenant over there, who is going to set off at once?

Don Pelagio (dourly). He will go alone.

Don Balthazar. And cannot you let Dona Prouheze wait for you here?

Don Pelagio. I shall not have time to come back.

Don Balthazar. What imperious duty calls you?

Don Pelagio. My cousin, Dona Viriana, who is dying and no man by her,

No money in the proud and lowly dwelling, hardly bread, add to that six daughters to marry off — and the eldest only a little short of twenty.

Don Balthazar. Isn't it she we used to call Dona Musica? — I lived round there while I was raising the levies for Flanders —

On account of that guitar which she never let go and never played on,

And those big, wide, trustful eyes on you, ready to take in wonder,

And those teeth, like blanched almonds, biting the red lip; and her laughter!

Don Pelagio. Why haven't you married her?

Don Balthazar. I am leaner than an old wolf.

Don Pelagio. And all the money that you earn goes to your brother, the head of the house, down in Flanders?

Don Balthazar. There is no better house between the Escaut and the Meuse.

Don Pelagio. I undertake Musica and I give you charge of Prouheze.

Don Balthazar. Like yourself indeed, señor, despite my age I feel better suited to be a pretty woman's husband than her guardian.

Don Pelagio. Neither she nor you, noble friend, I am sure, has anything to dread in these few days' companionship.

And, besides, you will always find my wise servant with her; beware of black Jobarbara!

No better guarded is a peach-tree growing right through a prickly pear.

Then, your sojourn will not be long: in a short time I shall have put everything to rights.

Don Balthazar. And married the six girls?

Don Pelagio. For each of them already I have chosen two husbands, and the order has gone forth summoning my gallants. But who would dare to resist Pelagio, the terrible judge?

They'll only have to choose; else I have chosen for them. The cloister gapes for them.

The Aragonese is no surer of his market when he lands on the place of barter with six new mares. There they are all together quietly in the shade of a big chestnut —

And they do not see the buyer passing from one to the other with delicacy and understanding, hiding the bit behind his back.

Don Balthazar (*with a huge sigh*). Farewell, Musica!

Don Pelagio. And while I have a little time left I will finish explaining you the situation on the African coast. The Sultan Muley . . .

(*They withdraw.*)

SCENE V

DONA PROUHEZE, DON BALTHAZAR

Same as Scene II. Evening. A whole caravan ready to set out. Mules, luggage, arms, saddle horses, etc.

Don Balthazar. Madam, since it has pleased your consort, by a sudden inspiration, to entrust to me the ordering of your deeply respected Lady-ship,

I have thought it necessary, before setting out, to make known to you the clauses which should guide our intercourse.

Dona Prouheze. I listen to you with submission.

Don Balthazar. Oh, I wish this were the retreat from Breda over again! Yes indeed, sooner than order a handsome woman about,

I would lead a disbanded troop of starving mercenaries across a land of brushwood towards a horizon of gallows!

Dona Prouheze. Don't be broken-hearted, señor, and give me that paper which I see ready in your hand.

Don Balthazar. Read it, I beg you, and be so good as to put your signature at the mark which I have made.

I have felt quite comfortable since I set down my orders so, upon that paper. That is what we shall have to obey from this time on, myself the first.

You will find everything clearly indicated, the stages, the hours of departure and of meals

And those moments, too, when it shall be free to you to converse with me, for I know that women cannot be condemned to silence.

Then I shall tell you about my campaigns, the beginnings of my family, the customs of Flanders, my country.

Dona Prouheze. But I, shall I not have leave to put in a word occasionally?

Don Balthazar. Siren, I have already given you too much hearing.

Dona Prouheze. Is it so unpleasant to think that for some days my fate and my life will not be less to you than your own!

And that in such close companionship you will indeed feel every moment that I have you for sole defender!

Don Balthazar. I swear it! They shall not snatch you from my hands.

Dona Prouheze. Why should I try to run away, since you are guiding me to the very place where I wanted to go?

Don Balthazar. And which I refused: it is your consort who commands me!

Dona Prouheze. If you had refused me, then I should have set off alone. Yes indeed, I should have found a way.

Don Balthazar. Dona Maravilla, I am sorry to hear your father's daughter speak like this.

Dona Prouheze. Was he a man often crossed in his plans?

Don Balthazar. No, poor count! Ah, what a friend I have lost. I still feel that sword-thrust he gave me through the body, one carnival morn-ing. That is how our brotherhood began.

I seem to see him again when I look at your eyes, you were in them then.

Dona Prouheze. It would be better for me not to tell you that I have sent that letter.

Don Balthazar. A letter to whom?

Dona Prouheze. To Don Rodrigo; yes, telling him to come and find me in that very inn where you are going to convey me.

Don Balthazar. Have you really done this fool-ish thing?

Dona Prouheze. If I had not profited by that amazing opportunity — the gipsy who was making straight for Avila, where I know that knight is living —

Would it not have been a sin, as the Italians say?

Don Balthazar. Don't be profane and please don't look at me like that, I beg you. Are you not ashamed of your behaviour and have you no fear of Don Pelagio? What would he do if he came to know of it?

Dona Prouheze. No doubt he would kill me without any hurry, and after taking time for con-sideration, as he does in everything.

Don Balthazar. Have you no fear of God?

Dona Prouheze. I swear that I do not want to do evil; that is why I have told you all. Oh, it was hard to open you my heart; I fear that you have understood nothing,

Save my real regard for you. So much the

worse! Now it is you who are responsible and bound to defend me.

Don Balthazar. You must help me, Prouheze.

Dona Prouheze. Ah, that would be too easy! I am not watching my chance, I am waiting for it to come to me.

And I have loyally warned you, the campaign is opening.

You are my defender. All that I can do to escape from you and to get back to Rodrigo,

I give you warning, I will do it.

Don Balthazar. Do you want this detestable thing to come about?

Dona Prouheze. Foreseeing is not wishing, and you see that I so mistrust my liberty that I have put it into your hands.

Don Balthazar. Do you love your husband not at all?

Dona Prouheze. I love him.

Don Balthazar. Would you forsake him just now when the King himself forgets him,

Would you leave him all alone on that wild coast in the midst of infidels,

Without troops, without money, without any kind of security?

Dona Prouheze. Ah! That hurts me more than all the rest. Yes, the thought of so betraying Africa and our charge,

And the honour of my husband's name — I know that he cannot do without me —

Those poor children whom I mother instead of those I have not had of God, those women being nursed, those few and poor retainers who have given themselves to us; to forsake all that —

I confess that the thought of it makes me blench.

Don Balthazar. Then what is calling you to this knight?

Dona Prouheze. His voice.

Don Balthazar. You have known him only a few days.

Dona Prouheze. His voice! I am for ever hearing it.

Don Balthazar. And what does it say to you?

Dona Prouheze. Ah, if you want to stop me from going to him,

Then tie me up; do not leave me this cruel freedom!

Put me in a deep dungeon behind iron bars!

But what prison could hold me in, when even that of my body threatens to break asunder!

Ah me, it is but too solid, and when my master calls me it is more than enough to hold in most obstinately this soul which is his.

My soul which he calls for and which belongs to him!

Don Balthazar. Soul and body too?

Dona Prouheze. Why do you speak of this body when 'tis that which is my enemy and keeps me from darting in one flight straight to Rodrigo?

Don Balthazar. And, in Rodrigo's eyes, is this body only — your prison?

Dona Prouheze. Nay, it is but the spoil of war to cast at the feet of the beloved!

Don Balthazar. You would give it him, then, if you could?

Dona Prouheze. What is there of mine that does not belong to him? I would give him all the world if I could!

Don Balthazar. Be off! Go to him!

Dona Prouheze. Señor, I have already told you that I have put myself no longer in my own ward but in yours.

Don Balthazar. Don Pelagio alone is your warden.

Dona Prouheze. Speak! Tell him all.

Don Balthazar. Ah, why was I so quick to pledge you my word?

Dona Prouheze. What! Are you not touched by the trust I have placed in you? Come, force me to confess that there are things that I could not tell except to you alone.

Don Balthazar. After all I have only obeyed Don Pelagio.

Dona Prouheze. Ah, how well you are going to guard me, and how I like you! I have nothing more to do, I leave it all to you,

And even now I am planning in my mind a thousand tricks to get away from you!

Don Balthazar. There is another guardian who will help me and from whom you will not escape so easily.

Dona Prouheze. Who, señor?

Don Balthazar. The angel that God has set over you since the day when you were a little innocent child.

Dona Prouheze. An angel against the demons! And to defend me against men I must have a tower like friend Balthazar,

The Tower and the Sword riding along in one and that handsome gold beard which marks him out at any distance!

Don Balthazar. You are still French.

Dona Prouheze. Just as you are still Flemish. Isn't it pretty, my little Franche-Comté accent? That's not true! But all these people had great need of us to teach them how to be the real Spanish stuff — they so little know how to set about it!

Don Balthazar. How was it that your husband married you, he already old and you so young?

Dona Prouheze. Doubtless I fitted in with those parts of his nature most severely kept up and most secretly cherished.

So that when I went with my father to Madrid, where the business of his province called him,

Those two grand señors were not long in coming to an agreement,

That I should fall in love with Don Pelagio as soon as he was presented — love him above all things and for all the days of my life as the law and obligation is between husband and wife.

Don Balthazar. At least you cannot doubt that he fulfils his part of the contract.

Dona Prouheze. If he loves me I was not deaf to hear him tell me so.

Yes, however low he had spoken it — one word — my ear was fine enough to take it in.

I was not deaf to hear the word my heart was listening for.

Very often I thought I caught it in those eyes, whose gaze altered as soon as my own tried to search it.

I interpreted that hand, which lay for one second upon my own.

Alas, I know I am no use to him; what I do I am never certain that he approves;

I have not even been able to give him a son.

Or perhaps what he feels towards me, I try sometimes to believe,

Is a thing so sacred that it must waste its sweetness on the desert air; it must not be disturbed by putting into words:

Yes, he let me hear something of the kind once in his queer wry manner.

Or maybe he is so proud that, to make me love him, he scorns to appeal to anything short of the truth.

I see him so little, and I am so cowed by him!

And yet for a long while I did not think that I could be anywhere except in his shadow.

You see yourself that it is he who takes leave of me today, and not I who wanted to leave him.

Nearly all day he leaves me alone, and just like him is this dark forsaken house here, so poor, so proud.

With this murdering sun outside and this delicious fragrance all within!

Yes, one might say that his mother had left him like this in a strict religious order, and had just gone away,

A great lady, unspeakably noble, whom you would hardly dare to look at.

Don Balthazar. His mother died giving him life.

Dona Prouheze (*pointing to the statue above the gate*). Perhaps that is the mother of whom I speak.

(DON BALTHAZAR *gravely takes off his hat. Both look at the Virgin's statue in silence.*)

Dona Prouheze (*as if seized with an inspiration*).

Don Balthazar, would you do me the favour to hold my mule?

(DON BALTHAZAR *holds the mule's head and* DONA PROUHEZE *climbs up on the saddle; taking off her shoe she puts the satin thing between the hands of the Virgin.*)

Dona Prouheze. Virgin, patron and mother of this house, protectress and surety of this man whose heart lies open to you more than to me, and companion of his long loneliness.

If not for my sake then at least for his, since this bond between him and me has not been my doing but your intervening will:

Keep me from being to this house whose door you guard, O mighty extern, a cause of corruption:

Keep me from being false to this name which you have given me to bear, and from ceasing to be honourable in the eyes of them that love me.

I cannot say that I understand this man whom you picked out for me, but you I understand, who are his mother and mine.

See, while there is yet time, holding my heart in one hand and my shoe in the other,

I give myself over to you! Virgin mother, I give you my shoe, Virgin mother, keep in your hand my luckless little foot!

I warn you that presently I shall see you no longer and that I am about to set everything going against you!

But when I try to rush on evil let it be with limping foot! The barrier that you have set up,

When I want to cross it, be it with a crippled wing!

I have done so much as I could; keep you my poor little shoe,

Keep it against your heart, tremendous Mother of mine!

SCENE VII

DON RODRIGO, THE CHINESE SERVANT

The Castilian desert. A spot among the low shrubs from which is seen a vast expanse. Romantic mountains in the distance. An evening of crystalline clearness. DON RODRIGO and the CHINESE SERVANT are stretched upon a sloping bluff at the foot of which their horses are grazing unbridled, and they are scanning the horizon.

Don Rodrigo. Our horsemen have disappeared.

The Chinese Servant. They are down there in the little pinewood making their horses lie down; one of them is white and shows up all the rest.

Don Rodrigo. Tonight we will give them the slip.

The Chinese Servant. It isn't us they are looking

for. We are on the highroad from Galicia to Sara-
gossa. Isn't this the way St. James goes every
year, on his feast —

Solemnly to call on Our Lady of the Pillar. (It
is today, you see that star threading its way?)

Don Rodrigo. Are they pilgrims going to join
the procession?

The Chinese Servant. Pilgrims — I have seen
arms by the gleam of that phosphorescent blob —

Pilgrims not very wary of showing themselves
too soon.

Don Rodrigo. Very good, very good, this business is none of ours.

The Chinese Servant. Still, I am keeping an eye
on that little wood of old firs.

Don Rodrigo. And I am keeping an eye on you,
my dear Isidore.

The Chinese Servant. Oh! don't be afraid that I
shall make off —

So long as you respect our agreement and don't
make me spend the night near any running water,
well or spring.

Don Rodrigo. Are you so afraid that I shall
baptize you by stealth?

The Chinese Servant. And why should I give
you thus for nothing the right to make me Christian
and to go to heaven with the decoration that I
provide? And to make up for other plans that
are less pure,

You must first do a little service to my lord your
servant.

Don Rodrigo. That I go with you where a certain black hand is beckoning you?

The Chinese Servant. Near by a white hand is
beckoning to you.

Don Rodrigo. It is nothing base that I want.

The Chinese Servant. Do you call gold a base
thing?

Don Rodrigo. It is a soul in pain that I am
helping.

The Chinese Servant. And I my own which is in
bondage.

Don Rodrigo. Imprisoned at the bottom of a
purse?

The Chinese Servant. Everything that is mine
is me.

Don Rodrigo. Do you grumble because I want
to help you?

The Chinese Servant. Master, may it humbly
please your Worship to take it that I have no confidence in your Worship.

Yes, I would much like to be in other hands
than yours; why have I put myself there?

Don Rodrigo. 'Tis I that am in yours.

The Chinese Servant. We have captured each
other, and there is no way of getting unstuck.

Ah, I was wrong to make you that promise in
haste, in the excitement of my disposition!

When all is said and done, what is that water
which you want to spill on my head, and why are
you so set upon it? What do you get by it, presuming that things are as you say,

And as for this spiritual change you speak of, do
you think it will be comfortable? Who would enjoy his kidneys shifting about? My soul is easy
as it is, and I don't much care for others to peep
into it and mess it about to their fancy.

Don Rodrigo. If you go back upon your word
'tis ill, 'twill be revenged upon you.

The Chinese Servant (with a sigh). All right,
have it your own way. I give up that gold over
there and you give up that parti-coloured idol!

Don Rodrigo. You are wrong, Isidore. I say
again that my only anxiety is the help I owe to this
soul in peril.

The Chinese Servant. And you don't want me
to be frightened when I hear a man talk like that!

Poor Isidore! What a master have you drawn
in the lottery of fate! Into what hands have you
fallen by the disagreement between the light and
heavy elements of your matter?

You once took me to the comedy at Madrid, but
I never saw anything like it there. Hail, saviour
of other men's wives!

Pull yourself together, señor, make your heart
lesser; open yourself to my soothing reasonable
words, let them sink into your sick mind like music.

What is this woman you are in love with, please?
Outside that mouth painted as with a brush, those
eyes more beautiful than if they were balls of
glass, those limbs exactly knitted and fitted,

But within, the vexation of demons, the worm,
the fire, the vampire fastened on your substance!
The matter of man, which has entirely withdrawn
from him and thus remains no more than a limp
and shrivelled shape, like the carcase of a cricket.
Oh horror!

Am I not in the retinue of your Lordship? How
often have I not begged It to think of the salvation
of Its own soul and mine?

In a hundred years what will be that hundred
pounds of female flesh with which your soul is
amalgamated? —

A little filth and dust and bone.

Don Rodrigo. At present she's alive.

The Chinese Servant. And I will warrant that in
a former existence that she-devil made you sign a
paper and the promise of carnal commerce!

If you wish, I will undertake to reason with this
unbecoming creature, and make her give back by
torment and physical entreaty your pre-natal note
of hand.

Don Rodrigo. You amaze me, Isidore. Holy Church does not recognize life in any soul anterior to its birth.

The Chinese Servant (hurt). Still, I have studied all the books that you gave me and I could recite them from end to end. Brother Leo pretends that I know as much of them as he does.

Don Rodrigo. From those things which are behind me and hunting me,

And from those things which are in front of me, a white spot on the sea between the dark trees,

I feel I cannot get away.

The Chinese Servant. What is it that is behind you?

Don Rodrigo. The gallop of horses pursuing me, the command of the King upon his throne, choosing me out of all men to give me half the world,

That half which from all time has been unknown and lost, like an infant in its swathing bands,

That share of the world, all fresh and new like a star that has risen upon me out of the deep and the dark.

And there'll be no need for me to struggle for a footing there and carve myself a tiny province in that land —

I have her whole and entire when still fresh and dewy, she gives herself for ever to my impress and my kiss.

The Chinese Servant. And what is in front of you?

Don Rodrigo. A flashing point off there, like the vision of death. Is it a waving handkerchief? Is it a wall smitten by the noon-day sun?

The Chinese Servant. I know, it is down there that there is a certain black monster to whom in the cheerfulness of my soul, because even a sage is not exempt from incertitude, and as it were by a slip, if I may say so, *quasi in lubrico,*

I so far forgot myself as to lend money. (*He wrings his hands and rolls his eyes.*)

Don Rodrigo. Not without interest, I am sure. I know your kind of generosity.

The Chinese Servant. What, is it not virtue to give there and then to those who ask?

And how can one tell what is virtue except that it brings immediately its own reward.

Don Rodrigo. Go on, we will get back your money since you are set on getting it only from your negress.

Devil knows what deal you have been wangling!

And I will baptize you and be quit of you; you can go back to China.

The Chinese Servant. It is my dearest wish, 'tis time that I bore fruit among the heathen. For what good is the new wine, save for the innkeeper to put it into old bottles? What good the bushel,

save to measure those pearls which we are commanded to cast before swine,

Instead of storing up therein the futile glimmer of our personal wick?

Don Rodrigo. You use the scriptures like a Lutheran grocer.

The Chinese Servant. Only bring me back to Barcelona.

Don Rodrigo. Isn't it there that you implored me not to go?

The Chinese Servant. If I cannot hold you off from this madness, at least I may as well profit by it.

Don Rodrigo. Madness anyone would call it, but I am madly right!

The Chinese Servant. Is it right to want to save a soul by drowning it?

Don Rodrigo. There is one thing that just now I alone can bring her.

The Chinese Servant. And what is this unique thing?

Don Rodrigo. Joy!

The Chinese Servant. Have you not made me read fifty times over that for you, a Christian, it is sacrifice that saves?

Don Rodrigo. Joy alone is the mother of sacrifice.

The Chinese Servant. What joy?

Don Rodrigo. The vision of the joy she gives me.

The Chinese Servant. Call you joy the torment of desire?

Don Rodrigo. It is not desire that she has read upon my lips. It is recognition.

The Chinese Servant. Recognition? Tell me even the colour of her eyes.

Don Rodrigo. I do not know. Ah, I admire her so much that I have forgotten to look at her!

The Chinese Servant. Excellent! I have seen big ugly blue eyes!

Don Rodrigo. It is not her eyes, it is her whole self that is my star!

Long ago on the Caribbean Sea, when at the first hour of morning I came out of my stifling box to take the watch,

When for an instant I was shown that queenly star, that resplendent gem all alone in the diadem of clear-browed heaven,

Ah, it was the same sudden thrill, the same wild unmeasured joy!

No man can live without admiration. There is within us the soul which shudders at ourselves,

There is this prison of which we tire, there are those eyes which have a right to see to the end, there is a heart which craves to be filled!

Too soon I found in the firmament nothing but this accustomed leaden flame,

The dim, secure ship-lantern, the seaman's sorry guide over the inappeasable waters.

But now there is quite another star for me, that point of light in the live sands of the night,

Someone human like myself, whose presence and whose countenance, beyond the ugliness and misery of this world, are compatible with a state of bliss alone.

The Chinese Servant. A treat for every sense.

Don Rodrigo. The senses! I liken them to the camp followers that come after the army

To plunder the dead and batten on the captured towns.

I will not so easily accept this ransom paid by the body for the soul which has gone thence;

Or that there is anything in her which I cease to crave.

But I am saying ill; I will not slander these senses which God has made.

For they are not base acolytes; they are our servants ranging the whole world through

Till they find at last Beauty, before whose face we are so glad to disappear.

All that we ask of her is that we evermore have only to open our eyes to see her again.

The Chinese Servant. Nothing else really? It was not worth putting ourselves about. I fear that our conversation is not of very much profit to this lady.

Don Rodrigo. Is it nothing that I have found her out, who was so well hidden?

The Chinese Servant. Plague take that storm which cast us on the coast of Africa and that fever which kept us there!

Don Rodrigo. It was her face that I saw when I woke again.

Say, do you think that I recognize her without her knowing?

The Chinese Servant. You would have to know all that happened before our birth. Just then I saw nothing; yes, I remember well that I had not yet come to the use of eyesight:

So that nothing occurred to disturb my preparation of the butterfly Isidore.

Don Rodrigo. Drop your pre-natal life, save that in the thought of Him who made us we were in some queer way together.

The Chinese Servant. Truly, truly! We were already together, all three.

Don Rodrigo. Already was she the single boundary of this heart which brooks none.

The Chinese Servant. Already, my dear godfather, you were thinking of giving me her for godmother.

Don Rodrigo. Already she held this joy which is mine by right and which I am on the way to ask her to give back.

Already she looked upon me with that face which destroys death.

For what is it that they call dying except ceasing to be needful? When has she been able to do without me? When shall I cease to be that, which lacking, she could not have been herself?

You ask what joy she brings me? Ah, if you knew the words that she says to me while I am sleeping,

Those words which she does not know she is saying, which I have but to shut my eyes to hear!

The Chinese Servant. Words that shut your eyes and shut my mouth.

Don Rodrigo. Those words which poison death, those words which stop the heart and say time shall be no more.

The Chinese Servant. It is no more! Look, already one of those stars of yours which are no longer any use, look at it going

Away and across the skiey page, making a great scrape of fire.

Don Rodrigo. How I love these millions getting on together! There is no soul so broken that the sight of this immeasurable concert does not wake to thin melody!

Lo, while the earth, like a wounded man that is out of the fight, is drawing solemn breath,

The peopled heavens without any discompose, as if bent upon a sum, all thronging to their mysterious task!

The Chinese Servant. In the middle the three stars, the staff of that huge pilgrim who visits the two hemispheres by turns,

What you call Saint James's Staff.

Don Rodrigo (*in a half whisper and as if to himself*). "Look, beloved! All that is thine, and 'tis I who will give it thee."

The Chinese Servant. Queer light, those million drops of milk!

Don Rodrigo. Below there, under the leaves, it shines upon a woman who weeps for joy and is kissing her bare shoulder.

The Chinese Servant. What means that shoulder, I pray you, Mr. Saviour of souls?

Don Rodrigo. That too is a part of those things which I shall not possess in this life.

Did I say it was her soul alone I loved? It is her whole self.

And I know that her soul is immortal, but the body is not less so.

And the two together make the seed which is destined to flower in another garden.

The Chinese Servant. A shoulder which is part of a soul, and all that together is a flower — poor Isidore, do you understand? Oh, my head, my head!

Don Rodrigo. Ah, Isidore! If you but knew how I love her and long for her!

The Chinese Servant. Now I understand you, and you are not talking Chinese any more.

Don Rodrigo. And do you think that her body alone could enkindle in mine such longing?

What I love in her is not at all what can be dissolved and escape me and be far away, and some time cease to love me; it is what causes herself to be herself and brings forth life to my kisses and not death!

If I teach her that she was not born to die, if I ask of her her immortality, that star in the deeps of her which she is without knowing,

Ah, how could she refuse me?

It is not what in her is troubled and mingled and unsure that I ask of her, not what is inert and neutral and perishable,

It is the naked essence, the pure life,

It is that love as strong as me, burning under my longing like a great naked flame, like laughter in my face!

Ah, if she gave it me (I am failing, and night is coming on my eyes)

If she gave it me (and she must not give it me), It is not her beloved body that would ever content me!

Never, save through each other, should we contrive to get rid of death,

Just as violet melting into orange sets free pure red.

The Chinese Servant. Tse gu! Tse gu! Tse gu! We know what hides under those fine words.

Don Rodrigo. I know that this union of my being with hers is impossible in this life, and I will have no other.

Only the star that is herself

Can slake this dreadful thirst of mine.

The Chinese Servant. Why then are we presently making for Barcelona?

Don Rodrigo. Did I never tell you that I have received a letter from her?

The Chinese Servant. Things are clearing up bit by bit.

Don Rodrigo (reciting as if he were reading). "Come, I shall be at X . . . I am setting out for Africa. There is much to reproach you with."

A gipsy woman brought me this paper. I set off, yielding to your importunity, while the King's people were on my track.

The Chinese Servant. Oh yes, it's me! Blame me, I pray you! The business of my soul and my purse — that is all you had at heart!

Don Rodrigo. It was all weighed in the same scale. The drop of water gathering.

And all Spain to me like a table tilted.

The Chinese Servant. Ah, that black image over there and that money of mine. Oh! Oh!

Oh, that purse I gave her in the impetuosity of my intestinal emotion!

I did hope that under that exotic bosom it would swell slowly, melodiously, like a fruit!

Don Rodrigo. "Reproach" said she — How wrong I was! Yes, I shall hear nothing from her but reproach.

I must not go on existing. I must be given to understand those things which kill her love for me.

The Chinese Servant. I on my side can provide some.

Don Rodrigo. I shall have to see that she is quite right and that I approve! I must hear her pass sentence on this heart which beats for her alone!

I thirst for those devastating words! More! More! I am hungry for this nothingness that she wants to plant in me.

For I know that it is only in the absolute void of all things that I shall meet her.

Is it because I am handsome or noble or virtuous that I want her to love me? Or have I other reason than this desperate need I have of her soul?

Or when I think of her do I ask nothing of her but that sudden sacred transport of her heart towards me? Does not her whole self then disappear, yes, even those matchless eyes?

I want to confront her as witness of this separation between us so wide, that the other one, caused by that man who took her before me, is only the painted semblance.

This abyss going down to the roots of nature,

To be bridged without motive or merit by the act of faith alone that we are to make in each other, that oath in the eternal —

I know that she cannot be mine save by her free self-giving.

The Chinese Servant. Nothing is got for nothing except that precious elixir, caked at the bottom of the tiny phial, which liquefies at the blessing of Our Lady of Compassion.

And look you, the drops that escape from it take fire as soon as they touch our gross air.

Don Rodrigo. It is not Our Lady that you have in mind, but that Chinese idol on a lotus which you found and which you cannot take your eyes from.

The Chinese Servant. One single drop of perfume is more precious than a great deal of spilt water.

Don Rodrigo. Do you say that of your own or where did you get it?

The Chinese Servant. When I shut my eyes on a night like this, many things come back to my thoughts from no one knows where.

I hear a deep sound like that of a brazen gong,
and that is bound up with an idea of the wilderness
and great sun and a nameless town behind battle-
mented walls.

I see a canal mirroring the crescent moon, and
can hear an unseen boat rustle in the reeds.

Don Rodrigo. Still you were very small as yet,
you told me, when you left China, after the Jesuits
by purchase had saved you from death.

The Chinese Servant. From death of body and
of soul, thanks be to the heaven above! —

Whose starry substance I see like a stream of
molten ore gaining

On this bridge which the Earth makes between
the two Houses of the Night.

Don Rodrigo (raising himself on his elbows).
Just so! What's this? Away down in the west I
see coming on in good order a number of little
lights.

The Chinese Servant. And away down in the
east, on the crest of that hill, appears another
procession.

Don Rodrigo. It is James, who, every year on
his feast day, comes over to call on the Mother
of his God.

The Chinese Servant. And she, mother-wise,
goes a third of the way to meet him.

As has been solemnly stipulated before notary
after long disputes.

Don Rodrigo. Look! I see the little lights in
the west scattering; all is quenched! Nay it is the
red flash of muskets! Hark! there are cries!

The Chinese Servant. I am afraid it may be our
pilgrims of just now, those whom we saw hiding
behind the pine wood.

Don Rodrigo. Do you think they are making
for Saint James?

The Chinese Servant. Doubtless they are heretics
or Moors and the statue is all solid silver.

Don Rodrigo (starting up). My sword! To the
help of our lord Saint James!

The Chinese Servant (also standing up). And
when we have rescued him from the miscreants
we will not give him back without a goodly ransom.
(*They go out.*)

SCENE VIII

The Negress Jobarbara, the Neapolitan
Sergeant

The inn at X . . . on the seashore.

The Negress (rushing at the sergeant shrieking).
Oh you cheat! I must kill you. Fie! Shame!
Shame! Tell me what you've done with my nice
bingle-bangle you took o' me?

The sergeant. How do you do, ma'am!

The Negress. Bad man, I couldn't forget you in
a hurry.

The Sergeant. And I don't want to listen to you.
(*He takes his nose in two fingers of his right hand,
with the left arm imitating Punch's big stick.*)

The Negress (panting for breath). In gold, I gave
you, my nice bracelet all of gold — I gave you, it
was worth more than two hundred pistoles!

And there was a hand hanging on it, and a
guitar, and a key, and a guava, and a halfpenny,
and a little fish, and twenty other nice things, and
they all bring luck together.

But take care, I've prayed over it, yes, I've sung
over it, I've danced over it and I've drowned it in
the blood of a black hen!

So that it is all right for me, but him that takes
it from me goes sick, he croaks!

The Sergeant. I am glad to be rid of it.

The Negress. What, is it true you sold it, you
mongrel?

The Sergeant. Didn't you give it to me?

The Negress. I had lent it to you; you said it
would bring you luck, villain!

In a certain job you had to do in hell!

And after that you left here by a crack in the
wall, pulling up your leg

Like lizards, scorpions, crickets, daddy-longlegs,
and the other dusty animals.

The Sergeant. Tell me, the captain that is setting
off for India, the first thing he does, isn't it to go
to the banker, who gets him arms and foodstuff,

Money to pay his soldiers and his sailors?

The next year he comes back with ten bags of
gold.

The Negress. But you haven't brought back one.

The Sergeant. I haven't brought back one bag?
And it won't be nice if I give you a big piece of
green and red silk, enough to make fifteen handkerchiefs, and a gold necklace that will go four
times round your neck?

And a gold bracelet? And another gold bracelet? And ditto another gold bracelet and over and
above that another three, four, five gold bracelets?

The Negress (examining him all over). Where
have you put all that?

The Sergeant. Where have I put all that? Why,
where he put your mammy —

After hiding behind a clump of banana trees he
got her, as all the women of the village were stack-
ing the grain by moonlight, that brave Portingale
of Portugal, when he took her to Brazil to teach her
good manners and the taste of sugar cane, nothing
to beat it

If he had not had that happy thought, instead

of being today that respectable matron, the oracle of the Judge's house,

All dressed up in a bit of paper and your hair done up in palm oil,

You'd still be dancing like a ninny on the banks of the river Zaire, trying to snap the moon in your teeth.

The Negress (*dazed*). Matron ... moonlight ... cane-oil ... you make my head swim. Now I do not know where I was — (*with a screech*) — I was at the money you took, you thief!

The Sergeant. The money I took? And isn't it much better than money, this star that I have been to the mountain to pick with my fingers?

This firefly that I caught in my hand and put in a little cage,

Just when he was trying to embrace a jasmine flower with the cockles of his heart?

The Negress. You are talking of that poor girl you brought with you the other day —

Both of you hidden at the bottom of that cart-load of rushes?

The Sergeant. Now the boat is ready — this evening, if the wind is too,

We weigh for the Latin shore.

The Negress. And what about the bracelet you took and the chain you have to give me instead?

The Sergeant. Follow them! Stick close to me! What is to keep you from going with us?

The Negress. What do you want to do with that poor girl?

The Sergeant. I have promised to give her the King of Naples — why not? That's a brain-wave that I got all of a sudden; I am sure there is a King at Naples!

I told her that the King of Naples had seen her in a dream, ah, what a scrumptious young man I made up for her — double-quick — him sending me to rummage the world to find her.

I am to know her by the sign of a dove-shaped mark under the shoulder.

The Negress. And had she really that sign?

The Sergeant (*hitting one hand with the other*). There is the queer thing; she had! She told me so, but she would never let me see it.

The Negress. What is her name?

The Sergeant. They call her Dona Musica on account of a guitar which fortunately she never plays. Her real name is Dona Delicia.

The Negress. Didn't anyone see her go?

The Sergeant. They wanted to marry her by force to a big specimen of an ugly cattle drover, all dressed in leather, a solemn mug come down to them from the Goths!

The poor little sweetheart said that she wanted to go into a neighbouring convent to pray for light

and guidance, and we set off to pray for light and guidance, both on the same horse.

The Negress. Were you followed?

The Sergeant. They won't catch us. (*He wets his finger and holds it up.*) Already I feel the first puffs of this blessed wind from Castile; soon it will take our fairy barque away.

The Negress. What are you going to do with the poor girl?

The Sergeant. Do you think that I am going to hurt her? It would be like a pastry-cook eating his own tarts.

I fade away at her feet with respect and tender feeling!

I blow on her to remove the dust! I sprinkle a little water on her with the end of my fingers! I polish her every morning with a feather-mop of the down of the humming bird!

Mother, keep your eye on that road that goes twisting away there,

As far as that mountain that looks like a lion crouching,

Till there is a sign of that thing that makes me sick to think of,

A certain cloud of dust with the flash of arms and stirrups!

— Ah, what a fine trade mine is! It never brings me so much wages that I wouldn't like some more.

The Negress. The rope will be your salary, you big ugly blackguard.

The Sergeant. Never a rope for me! I retreat in good order! I shut my eyes and suddenly you cannot tell me from a pomegranate stump.

Cheer up, darling girls! Your love, the golden Sergeant, is still here to find you, at the bottom of those holes where you are mouldering, with a fishing rod.

When your little innocent hearts begin to swell, when your souls sigh daintily at the sound of the unknown beloved down there,

When you feel that you are like those seeds that nature has provided with down and feathers to fly away on the breath of April,

Then I turn up on your window-sill, flapping my wings and painted all yellow.

SCENE XI

THE NEGRESS and afterwards THE CHINAMAN

Near the inn. A region of fantastic rocks and white sand. The negress naked, dancing and whirling in the moonlight.

The Negress. Hurrah, lovely mammy made me black and shiny.

I'm the little fish of night, the little tom-tom twirling, I'm the pot bobbing, bouncing in the cold, cold water, bustling, boiling. (*She rises starkly on tiptoe.*)

Sing hi to you, daddy mammy crocodile,
Sing hee to you, daddy hippo potam horse.
— while the river turn to me, while all the forest turn to me, while all the villages turn, turn, turn, to me, while all the boats turn to me,
Because the hole I make, because the boil I make,
Because the knot I make in the water bubbling, troubling,
I've water to wash me, oil to smoothe me, grass to rub me down!
I'm not black, I shine like lookin'-glass, I buck like pig, I duck like fish, I roll like little cannon!
Hi! Hi! Hi!
Here I am, here I am,
Come, come, come, come, little Mister Italian!
Yes, yes, yes, yes, my little yellow canary,
I put a halfpenny in your pocket.
All that kept you from loving me I killed; I broke it with the blood of a cut chicken!
I need only turn about, turn about; come to me, you cannot go against me.
(*Enter* THE CHINAMAN.)
All the threads that tie me to you I roll 'em up, wind 'em on me like on a reel. You come, I come to you, I bring you near, twisting round about like a little cannon, turning like a rope on the windlass that drags the anchor from among the roots.
Hi! Hi! Hi! Hi! Here! Here! Here! Here!
(*She falls, quite done, into the arms of the* CHINA-MAN, *who catches her from behind. She rolls a white eye, then screeching bounces away and wraps herself in her clothes.*)

The Chinaman. Beardless creature, vain for thee to plaster on thy black hide this parti-coloured integument; I can pierce thee to the soul.

The Negress. Hey!

The Chinaman. I see your heart quite smothered by the dug, like a clot of blackness shedding an evil ray.

The Negress. Hi!

The Chinaman. I see your liver, like an anvil which the demons use to forge untruth, and the two lungs above, like frightful bellows.

The Negress. Ho!

The Chinaman. I see your guts, like a bag of reptiles letting off their pestilential and balsamic vapour.

The Negress. And what more do you see?

The Chinaman (*gnashing his teeth*). I see my money all cluttered up on each side of the spinal column, like the grain in a head of maize!

And I am going to get it back on the spot. (*He draws his knife.*)

The Negress (*screaming*). Stop, stop, ducky dear, if you kill me I shan't be able to show you the devil.

The Chinaman. You promised me before, and that's how you got that money out of me.

The Negress. Never again shall your master set eyes on Dona Prouheze.

The Chinaman. Unclean alligator! Musky child of mud and fat worm of low tide!
We will take up this conversation adulteriously, I warrant you.

The Negress. Dona Maravilla is in this stronghold and Don Balthazar is defending her, and Don Pelagio is coming back tomorrow, or day after, and he is taking away Dona Maravilla, to Africa. Don Rodrigo will never see her again. Tra-la-la! He will never see her again, tra-la-la.

The Chinaman. Listen, Señor Rodrigo has been cut up and knocked over while, sword in hand, he was desperately defending James against the robbers.

The Negress. What James?

The Chinaman. Saint James in silver. We have brought him here (I mean Rodrigo) into the castle of my lady his mother, which is four leagues from this inn.

The Negress. Sweet Mother!

The Chinaman. Tell her he is going to croak, tell her he wants to see her; tell her to come and meet him soon, and be hanged to good form.
As for me, since my exhortations, together with my profound groanings, have not contrived to give him back his bodily substance,
There is nothing left for me but to withdraw in silence, having planted him in the middle of his vomit, giving modesty a free hand.
As for thee I will not let thee go until thou hast shown me the devil.

The Negress. And why are you so set on seeing the accursed?

The Chinaman. The handsomer dealings I have on that side the more precious will my soul be in the eyes of those who want to water me.

The Negress. But how do you expect Dona Prouheze to leave this inn, which is guarded on every side?

The Chinaman. Listen, this morning I met a band of knights.
They were looking for a lady called Musica, whom a certain blackguard from Naples has carried off.

The Negress. Musica? Heavens!

The Chinaman. You know her?

The Negress. Go on.

The Chinaman. Very soon, by force and threats, they wrung from me the confession that the said Musica is at this seaside inn full of dreadful pirates.

The Negress. But that's not true.

The Chinaman. I know; what does it matter? Tomorrow evening they attack Balthazar and his men.

The Negress. But they'll find nothing at all.

The Chinaman. They will at least find a certain witch whom I have described,

Who is the most dangerous accomplice of the thief with the velvet eyes.

The Negress. I won't go back to the inn.

The Chinaman. Then I will kill you on the spot.

The Negress. Dona Prouheze is there, and will know how to settle everything.

The Chinaman. Tell her to get away with you under cover of the tumult.

The Negress. How so?

The Chinaman. A hundred yards from the inn, down there behind the prickly pears, I will wait for her, with my groom and with horses for her and you.

SCENE XII

The Guardian Angel, Dona Prouheze

A deep ravine surrounding the inn, full of briars, creepers and shrubs intertangled. On the brink the Guardian Angel *in costume of the period, sword at side.*

The Guardian Angel. See her, making her way right through the tangled thorns and creepers, slipping, scrambling, recovering, with knees and nails trying to scale that steep ascent! Ah, what that desperate heart can hold!

Who says the angels cannot weep?

Am I not a creature like her? Are God's creatures not bound together by any bond?

What they call suffering — does that go on in a world apart, shut out from all the rest? Does it escape an Angel's vision? Is suffering a pleasant thing to countenance for one who has charge even of its object?

Is it quite separate from that love and justice whose ministers we are? What use were it to be a Guardian Angel if we did not understand it?

One who sees good in its fulness — only he fully understands what evil is. *They* know not wath they do.

And should I have been chosen to guard her, without a secret kinship with her?

— At last! She has, in spite of all, come to the end of those briars and charitable thorns that try to hold her back. Here she is, showing on the brink of the ditch.

(Dona Prouheze *comes out of the ditch. She is in man's clothes, all torn, her hands and face disfigured.*)

Yes, thou art beautiful, poor child, with that disordered hair, that unseemly costume.

Those cheeks dabbled in blood and clay, and that look, which hurts me, in thine eyes, of resolution and madness!

Ah, thou dost me honour and I am pleased to show my little sister thus. If only there were none to see us!

Dona Prouheze (*looking round her, dazed*). I am alone.

The Guardian Angel. She says she is alone.

Dona Prouheze. I am free.

The Guardian Angel. Ah me!

Dona Prouheze. Nothing has kept me back.

The Guardian Angel. We wanted no other prison for you but honour.

Dona Prouheze. I should have been better guarded. I have been loyal. I gave full warning to Don Balthazar.

The Guardian Angel. He is going to pay for thy escape with his life.

Dona Prouheze. Rodrigo is going to die.

The Guardian Angel. There is yet time to lose his soul.

Dona Prouheze. Rodrigo is going to die.

The Guardian Angel. He lives.

Dona Prouheze. He lives, someone tells me he still lives! There is still time to give him the sight of me and so keep him from dying.

The Guardian Angel. 'Tis not Prouheze's love that will keep him from dying.

Dona Prouheze. At least I can die with him.

The Guardian Angel. Hark how glibly she speaks of putting away that soul which does not belong to her — which has cost so much to make and to redeem!

Dona Prouheze. There is no one but Rodrigo in the world.

The Guardian Angel. Try then to go to him.

(*She falls fainting on the ground.*)

Dona Prouheze (*panting*). Oh, this effort has been too much for me! I am dying! I thought I should never manage to get out of that horrible ditch!

The Guardian Angel (*setting his foot on her heart*). It would be easy for me to keep thee here if I would.

Dona Prouheze (*very low*). Rodrigo is calling me.

The Guardian Angel. Bring him that heart, then, on which my foot is planted.

Dona Prouheze (*as before*). I must.

The Guardian Angel (*removing his foot*). See where thou art going to lead me.

Dona Prouheze (*in a low voice*). Up, Prouheze.

(She gets up, staggering.)

The Guardian Angel. I am looking on our God.

Dona Prouheze. Rodrigo!

The Guardian Angel. Ah me, I hear another voice in the fire, saying: "Prouheze."

Dona Prouheze. How far the way is to that bush yonder!

The Guardian Angel. It was still longer up to Calvary.

Dona Prouheze. Rodrigo, I am thine.

The Guardian Angel. Thou art his? Is it thou that shalt fulfil him with thine outlawed body?

Dona Prouheze. I know I am his treasure.

The Guardian Angel. One cannot get this idea out of her silly little head.

Dona Prouheze (stepping out). March!

The Guardian Angel (stepping at her side). March!

Dona Prouheze (taking a few tottering steps). Rodrigo, I am thine! Thou seest how I have broken this bitter bond!

Rodrigo, I am thine! Rodrigo, I come to thee!

The Guardian Angel. And I — I am coming With thee.

(Exeunt.)

SCENE XIV

Don Balthazar, Alferes, The Chinaman, A Sergeant, Soldiers, Servants

Same place.

A Soldier (bringing in The Chinaman*).* Here is the fellow.

Don Balthazar. Good day, Master Chinaman. I am sorry to hear the news that you bring from Don Rodrigo.

The Chinaman. There is nothing in this to do with Don Rodrigo.

Don Balthazar. Were not you his servant?

The Chinaman. I am the man whom Providence has put near him, to give him the chance to save his soul.

Don Balthazar. How's that?

The Chinaman. If he procures me holy baptism will it not be an immense joy to heaven, to whom a Chinese catechized

Gives more honour than ninety-nine Spaniards who persevere?

Don Balthazar. No doubt.

The Chinaman. Such merit, which depends on me alone to earn for him when I like,

Is worth much care and sedulity on his part. I will not give up my soul to him so easily and for a song.

So that, properly speaking, he is rather my servant than I his.

Don Balthazar. Still it seems to me, my son, that you do him very good service.

But that is not the question just now; and since you speak of song, why, just all I want is to know if you can sing.

The Chinaman. What, sing?

Don Balthazar. Why, yes. *(He lilts coaxingly.)* Tra-la-la! Sing, what? I have no guitar. But you need only take this plate and beat time with a knife, whatever you like. Something pretty!

The Chinaman (shaking all over). And you don't want to know what I was doing last night talking to that negress of the devil?

Don Balthazar. My only desire in the world is is to hear your sweet voice.

The Chinaman (falling on his knees). Señor, spare me, I will tell you all!

Don Balthazar (to Alferes*).* There is nothing that frightens people more than things they don't understand.

(To The Chinaman*).* Come along!

"A song that rises to the lips
Is like a swelling honey-drop
That overflows the heart."

The Chinaman. The truth is that, prowling round the castle in the interest of Don Rodrigo,

I blundered on to a party of knights-at-arms who asked me if I had heard tell of a certain Dona Musica.

Don Balthazar. Musica, did you say?

The Chinaman. They told me that you knew her —

Of a certain Dona Musica, who may have gone away with an Italian sergeant and whom they are looking for.

Then it was that I had the idea of pointing out to them this castle as filled with pirates so that I could myself, under cover of the attack and the noise,

Carry off the persons that you are guarding.

Don Balthazar. You would do better not to talk of Musica, and to sing as I asked you. *(He draws his sword.)*

The Chinaman. Mercy, señor!

(Enter a Sergeant.*)*

Sergeant. Señor, there is at the gate a man who, without removing his hat and in very curt terms, demands that we forthwith let him look for Dona Musica whom we are guarding in this place.

Don Balthazar. Tell him, without removing your hat and in very curt terms, that we are keeping our music to ourselves.

The Chinaman. You see I did not lie.

Don Balthazar. Dona Musica will never be so

well guarded, wherever she is, as Dona Prouheze shall be by me today.

The Chinaman. I see! You think that we are all secretly agreed and that it is Dona Prouheze we are after. Oh! Oh!

Don Balthazar. Oh! Oh!
"I dreamt I was in heaven
And woke up in your arms."
(*He pricks* THE CHINAMAN, *who gets up screeching.*)
On, I pray you, carry on.
(*Enter* SERVANTS *carrying covered dishes of everything needed for supper.*)

Don Balthazar. What is that?

The Servants. Your supper, which we have brought you hither as you commanded.

Don Balthazar. Good! We can take it easy here eating in the shade, while those gentlemen will see about making a show for us.

Alferes. You will be very uncomfortable. All the shots they fire through this door will be for you.

Don Balthazar. Not at all; it is the Chinaman that will get them. Look you, Chinaman, if your friends fire 'tis you they will kill.

The Chinaman. I am not afraid of anything at all. So long as I am not baptized a bullet cannot hurt me.

Don Balthazar. Meanwhile look at this table covered for us with the finest fruits of land and sea,
Sweet stuff and salt stuff; these shells, blue like the night; this fine pink trout under its silver skin, like an eatable nymph; this scarlet crayfish;
This honeycomb; these pellucid grapes; these over-ripe figs a-bursting; these peaches like globes of nectar —
(*Enter a* SOLDIER.)

Soldier. Captain, there is a group of armed men making for the gate with a ladder and axes. What must we do?

Don Balthazar. Why, let them come on. I have given my orders.
(*Exit* SOLDIER.)
Where was I? — these peaches like globes of nectar — (*Above the gate appears a man in black cloak and great plumed felt hat, taking aim at* DON BALTHAZAR *with a carbine.* DON BALTHAZAR *flings a peach at him, hits him full in the face — he tumbles down.*) — this ham ready carved; this wine of delicious bouquet in a glittering decanter; this pasty like a sepulchre of meats embalmed with powerful spices to rise again in the stomach with a glow of well-being.
The earth could not get together for us on this table-cloth anything more pleasant.
Let us look it over for the last time, for we shall never again taste any of that, my comrade.
(*Violent knocking at the door.*)

Don Balthazar. What do you want?

Voice outside. We want Dona Musica.

Don Balthazar. You want music? Sing, Chinaman.

The Chinaman. I cannot sing.

Don Balthazar (*threatening him*). Sing, I tell you.

The Chinaman (*singing*).
If a man should hear me sing
He would think me very gay
I am like the little bird
Singing with his death on him.

Voice outside. We want Dona Musica.

Don Balthazar. No use, she has just set sail for Barbary. Sing, Chinaman; that'll cheer them up.

The Chinaman (*singing*).
I took ship in a little shell
To go to Barbaree-ee
To try to find the hair of a frog
Because there's none in Spain.

Voice outside. If you don't open we are going to fire.

Don Balthazar. Sing, Chinaman.

The Chinaman (*singing*).
I went into the meadows
To ask the violet
If there was anything could stop
The bitter pain of love.
She answered me . . .
(*Through a split in the door a musket barrel is seen to come which swivels right and left.*)

The Chinaman (*jumping right and left to avoid the musket*). And what she said was this . . .
And what she said was this.

Don Balthazar. Well, well, what did she say?
(*On the sea at the back of the scene a boat appears with a red sail on which are* MUSICA, *the* NEGRESS *and the* NEAPOLITAN SERGEANT. *The musket withdraws.*)

The Negress (*singing in a sharp voice*).
That for the pain of love
There never was no salve.

The Chinaman (*looking towards the sea*). Heavens, what do I see?

Don Balthazar. What do you see?

The Chinaman. Look yourself.

Don Balthazar (*singing*). Don't look at me!
They are looking at us
To see if you are looking at me.
(*Hatchet blows on the door.*)

A Soldier. Captain, captain, must we fire?

Don Balthazar. Not till I order. What do you see, Chinaman?

The Chinaman. I see a boat putting out to sea And in it there is that negress of calamity with her yellow devil. But look yourself.

Don Balthazar. It is too tiring to look round.

The Chinaman. Señor, make away, those people are getting ready to fire.

Don Balthazar. No.

   (The barrel of the musket again passes 5 *through the hole in the door, aiming at* DON BALTHAZAR. *The boat has disappeared.)*

The voice of MUSICA *(unseen).*

          A tear! a tear!   10
   A tear from the brim of your eyes!
   A tear from your lovely eyes.

Don Balthazar. Ah, what a charming voice! I have never heard anything so beautiful.

The Voice (supported by those of the NEGRESS *and the* SERGEANT *in parts)*

   . . . it runs down your face
   It falls to the deep of your heart,
   To the deep deep heart, if falls!

   (Shots. DON BALTHAZAR *falls dead face downwards among the fruit, holding the table in his arms.)*

The Voice (farther away and farther). A tear! a tear!
   A tear from the brim of your eyes!
   A tear from the bottom of the sea!

END OF FIRST DAY

Katherine Mansfield · 1888–1923

Katherine Mansfield (Kathleen Beauchamp) was born in Wellington, New Zealand, October 14, 1888. Her father, Sir Harold Beauchamp, was a banker. When thirteen years of age she went to England for her education. At Queen's College, London, she edited the college magazine. For a long time she wrote short stories without finding a publisher and was obliged to support herself, since she did not wish to live in New Zealand, by playing minor parts in a traveling opera company. Soon her health broke and she went to Germany for rest. From this experience developed a series of short stories, *In a German Pension*, which were published in a British magazine called the *New Age* when Miss Mansfield was twenty-three years old. In 1913 she married John Middleton Murry with whom, for a short time, she edited *Rhythm*. From 1915 to her death eight years later Miss Mansfield suffered poor health, going from one resort or sanitarium to another in search of recovery. Pleurisy developed into tuberculosis. She died at Avon, near Fontainebleau, January 9, 1923. The inscription marking her burial place reads: "Out of this nettle, danger, we pluck this flower, safety."

Katherine Mansfield had two of the qualities that make a great writer: a desire to say something significant and to say it significantly. She was a perfectionist, completing many more stories in her mind than she ever placed on paper. Chekhov, the Russian story-writer, was her chosen master. Always dissatisfied with her work, she once remarked of her stories: "There is not one that I dare to show to God." Most of Miss Mansfield's reputation rests upon four volumes of stories and one book of verse: *Bliss* (1920), *The Garden Party* (1922), *The Dove's Nest* (1923), *The Little Girl* (1924), and *Poems* (1923).

SUGGESTED REFERENCES: Sylvia Berkman, *Katherine Mansfield* (1951); S. R. Daly, *Katherine Mansfield* (1965).

The Voyage [1]

In *The Voyage* Miss Mansfield never tells us that the subject of her story is a little girl who has lost her mother and is going to live with her grandparents. She uses the method of the impressionist, showing us the parting, the trip, and the arrival, and leaving it to us to find our own emotions invoked by the simple and artful narrative. Charged with pathos, the whole story scarcely carries a single expression of pity.

The Picton boat was due to leave at half-past eleven. It was a beautiful night, mild, starry, only when they got out of the cab and started to walk down the Old Wharf that jutted out into the harbor, a faint wind blowing off the water ruffled under Fenella's hat, and she put up her hand to keep it

[1] From *The Garden Party and Other Stories*, by Katherine Mansfield, by permission of and special arrangement with Alfred A. Knopf, Inc., authorized publishers.

on. It was dark on the Old Wharf, very dark; the wool sheds, the cattle trucks, the cranes standing up so high, the little squat railway engine, all seemed carved out of solid darkness. Here and there on a rounded woodpile, that was like the stalk of a huge black mushroom, there hung a lantern, but it seemed afraid to unfurl its timid, quivering light in all that blackness; it burned softly, as if for itself.

Fenella's father pushed on with quick, nervous strides. Beside him her grandma bustled along in her crackling black ulster; they went so fast that she had now and again to give an undignified little skip to keep up with them. As well as her luggage strapped into a neat sausage, Fenella carried clasped to her her grandma's umbrella, and the handle, which was a swan's head, kept giving her shoulder a sharp little peck as if it too wanted her to hurry.... Men, their caps pulled down, their collars turned up, swung by; a few women all muffled scurried along; and one tiny boy, only his little black arms and legs showing out of a white woolly shawl, was jerked along angrily between his father and mother; he looked like a baby fly that had fallen into the cream.

Then suddenly, so suddenly that Fenella and her grandma both leapt, there sounded from behind the largest wool shed, that had a trail of smoke hanging over it, *Mia-oo-oo-O-O!*

"First whistle," said her father briefly, and at that moment they came in sight of the Picton boat. Lying beside the dark wharf, all strung, all beaded with round golden lights, the Picton boat looked as if she was more ready to sail among stars than out into the cold sea. People pressed along the gangway. First went her grandma, then her father, then Fenella. There was a high step down on to the deck, and an old sailor in a jersey standing by gave her his dry, hard hand. They were there; they stepped out of the way of the hurrying people, and standing under a little iron stairway that led to the upper deck they began to say good-bye.

"There, mother, there's your luggage!" said Fenella's father, giving grandma another strapped-up sausage.

"Thank you, Frank."

"And you've got your cabin tickets safe?"

"Yes, dear."

"And your other tickets?"

Grandma felt for them inside her glove and showed him the tips.

"That's right."

He sounded stern, but Fenella, eagerly watching him, saw that he looked tired and sad. *Mia-oo-oo-O-O!* The second whistle blared just above

their heads, and a voice like a cry shouted, "Any more for the gangway?"

"You'll give my love to father," Fenella saw her father's lips say. And her grandma, very agitated, answered, "Of course I will, dear. Go now. You'll be left. Go now, Frank. Go now."

"It's all right, mother. I've got another three minutes." To her surprise Fenella saw her father take off his hat. He clasped grandma in his arms and pressed her to him. "God bless you, mother!" she heard him say.

And grandma put her hand, with the black thread glove that was worn through on her ring finger, against his cheek, and she sobbed, "God bless you, my own brave son."

This was so awful that Fenella quickly turned her back on them, swallowed once, twice, and frowned terribly at a little green star on a mast head. But she had to turn round again; her father was going.

"Good-bye, Fenella. Be a good girl." His cold, wet moustache brushed her cheek. But Fenella caught hold of the lapels of his coat.

"How long am I going to stay?" she whispered anxiously. He wouldn't look at her. He shook her off gently, and gently said, "We'll see about that. Here! Where's your hand?" He pressed something into her palm. "Here's a shilling in case you should need it."

A shilling! She must be going away forever! "Father!" cried Fenella. But he was gone. He was the last off the ship. The sailors put their shoulders to the gangway. A huge coil of dark rope went flying through the air and fell "thump" on the wharf. A bell rang; a whistle shrilled. Silently the dark wharf began to slip, to slide, to edge away from them. Now there was a rush of water between. Fenella strained to see with all her might. "Was that father turning round? — or waving? — or standing alone? — or walking off by himself?" The strip of water grew broader, darker. Now the Picton boat began to swing round steady, pointing out to sea. It was no good looking any longer. There was nothing to be seen but a few lights, the face of the town clock hanging in the air, and more lights, little patches of them, on the dark hills.

The freshening wind tugged at Fenella's skirts; she went back to her grandma. To her relief grandma seemed no longer sad. She had put the two sausages of luggage one on top of the other, and she was sitting on them, her hands folded, her head a little on one side. There was an intent, bright look on her face. Then Fenella saw that her lips were moving and guessed that she was praying. But the old woman gave her a bright nod as if to say the prayer was nearly over. She unclasped her hands, sighed, clasped them again, bent forward, and at last gave herself a soft shake.

"And now, child," she said, fingering the bow of her bonnet-strings, "I think we ought to see about our cabins. Keep close to me, and mind you don't slip."

"Yes, grandma!"

"And be careful the umbrellas aren't caught in the stair rail. I saw a beautiful umbrella broken in half like that on my way over."

"Yes, grandma."

Dark figures of men lounged against the rails. In the glow of their pipes a nose shone out, or the peak of a cap, or a pair of surprised-looking eyebrows. Fenella glanced up. High in the air, a little figure, his hands thrust in his short jacket pockets, stood staring out to sea. The ship rocked ever so little, and she thought the stars rocked too. And now a pale steward in a linen coat, holding a tray high in the palm of his hand, stepped out of a lighted doorway and skimmed past them. They went through that doorway. Carefully over the high brass-bound step on to the rubber mat and then down such a terribly steep flight of stairs that grandma had to put both feet on each step, and Fenella clutched the clammy brass rail and forgot all about the swan-necked umbrella.

At the bottom grandma stopped: Fenella was rather afraid she was going to pray again. But no, it was only to get out the cabin tickets. They were in the saloon. It was glaring bright and stifling; the air smelled of paint and burnt chop-bones and india rubber. Fenella wished her grandma would go on, but the old woman was not to be hurried. An immense basket of ham sandwiches caught her eye. She went up to them and touched the top one delicately with her finger.

"How much are the sandwiches?" she asked.

"Tuppence!" bawled a rude steward, slamming down a knife and fork.

"Twopence *each?*" she asked.

"That's right," said the steward, and he winked at his companion.

Grandma made a small, astonished face. Then she whispered primly to Fenella. "What wickedness!" And they sailed out at the further door and along a passage that had cabins on either side. Such a very nice stewardess came to meet them. She was dressed all in blue, and her collar and cuffs were fastened with large brass buttons. She seemed to know grandma well.

"Well, Mrs. Crane," said she, unlocking their washstand. "We've got you back again. It's not often you give yourself a cabin."

"No," said grandma. "But this time my dear son's thoughtfulness —"

"I hope —" began the stewardess. Then she turned round and took a long mournful look at grandma's blackness and at Fenella's black coat and skirt, black blouse, and hat with a crape rose.

Grandma nodded. "It was God's will," said she.

The stewardess shut her lips and, taking a deep breath, she seemed to expand.

"What I always say is," she said, as though it was her own discovery, "sooner or later each of us has to go, and that's a certingty." She paused. "Now, can I bring you anything, Mrs. Crane? A cup of tea? I know it's no good offering you a little something to keep the cold out."

Grandma shook her head. "Nothing, thank you. We've got a few wine biscuits, and Fenella has a very nice banana."

"Then I'll give you a look later on," said the stewardess, and she went out, shutting the door.

What a very small cabin it was! It was like being shut up in a box with grandma. The dark round eye above the washstand gleamed at them dully. Fenella felt shy. She stood against the door, still clasping her luggage and the umbrella. Were they going to get undressed in here? Already her grandma had taken off her bonnet, and, rolling up the strings, she fixed each with a pin to the lining before she hung the bonnet up. Her white hair shone like silk; the little bun at the back was covered with a black net. Fenella hardly ever saw her grandma with her head uncovered; she looked strange.

"I shall put on the woollen fascinator your dear mother crocheted for me," said grandma, and, unstrapping the sausage, she took it out and wound it round her head; the fringe of grey bobbles danced at her eyebrows as she smiled tenderly and mournfully at Fenella. Then she undid her bodice, and something under that, and something else underneath that. Then there seemed a short, sharp tussle, and grandma flushed faintly. Snip! Snap! She had undone her stays. She breathed a sigh of relief, and sitting on the plush couch, she slowly and carefully pulled off her elastic-sided boots and stood them side by side.

By the time Fenella had taken off her coat and skirt and put on her flannel dressing-gown grandma was quite ready.

"Must I take off my boots, grandma? They're lace."

Grandma gave them a moment's deep consideration. "You'd feel a great deal more comfortable if you did, child," said she. She kissed Fenella. "Don't forget to say your prayers. Our dear Lord is with us when we are at sea even more than when we are on dry land. And because I am an experienced traveller," said grandma briskly, "I shall take the upper berth."

"But, grandma, however will you get up there?"

Three little spider-like steps were all Fenella saw. The old woman gave a small silent laugh before she mounted them nimbly, and she peered over the high bunk at the astonished Fenella.

"You didn't think your grandma could do that, did you?" said she. And as she sank back Fenella heard her light laugh again.

The hard square of brown soap would not lather, and the water in the bottle was like a kind of blue jelly. How hard it was, too, to turn down those stiff sheets; you simply had to tear your way in. If everything had been different, Fenella might have got the giggles.... At last she was inside, and while she lay there panting, there sounded from above a long, soft whispering, as though some one was gently, gently rustling among tissue paper to find something. It was grandma saying her prayers....

A long time passed. Then the stewardess came in; she trod softly and leaned her hand on grandma's bunk.

"We're just entering the Straits," she said. "Oh!"

"It's a fine night, but we're rather empty. We may pitch a little."

And indeed at that moment the Picton boat rose and rose and hung in the air just long enough to give a shiver before she swung down again, and there was the sound of heavy water slapping against her sides. Fenella remembered she had left that swan-necked umbrella standing up on the little couch. If it fell over, would it break? But grandma remembered too, at the same time.

"I wonder if you'd mind, stewardess, laying down my umbrella," she whispered.

"Not at all, Mrs. Crane." And the stewardess, coming back to grandma, breathed, "Your little granddaughter's in such a beautiful sleep."

"God be praised for that!" said grandma.

"Poor little motherless mite!" said the stewardess. And grandma was still telling the stewardess all about what happened when Fenella fell asleep.

But she hadn't been asleep long enough to dream before she woke up again to see something waving in the air above her head. What was it? What could it be? It was a small grey foot. Now another joined it. They seemed to be feeling about for something; there came a sigh.

"I'm awake, grandma," said Fenella.

"Oh, dear, am I near the ladder?" asked grandma. "I thought it was this end."

"No, grandma, it's the other. I'll put your foot on it. Are we there?" asked Fenella.

"In the harbor," said grandma. "We must get up, child. You'd better have a biscuit to steady yourself before you move."

But Fenella had hopped out of her bunk. The lamp was still burning, but night was over, and it was cold. Peering through that round eye, she could see far off some rocks. Now they were scattered over with foam; now a gull flipped by; and now there came a long piece of real land.

"It's land, grandma," said Fenella, wonderingly, as though they had been at sea for weeks together. She hugged herself; she stood on one leg and rubbed it with the toes of the other foot; she was trembling. Oh, it had all been so sad lately. Was it going to change? But all her grandma said was, "Make haste, child. I should leave your nice banana for the stewardess as you haven't eaten it." And Fenella put on her black clothes again, and a button sprang off one of her gloves and rolled to where she couldn't reach it. They went up on deck.

But if it had been cold in the cabin, on deck it was like ice. The sun was not up yet, but the stars were dim, and the cold pale sky was the same color as the cold pale sea. On the land a white mist rose and fell. Now they could see quite plainly dark bush. Even the shapes of the umbrella ferns showed, and those strange silvery withered trees that are like skeletons.... Now they could see the landing-stage and some little houses, pale too, clustered together, like shells on the lid of a box. The other passengers tramped up and down, but more slowly than they had the night before, and they looked gloomy.

And now the landing-stage came out to meet them. Slowly it swam towards the Picton boat, and a man holding a coil of rope, and a cart with a small drooping horse and another man sitting on the step, came too.

"It's Mr. Penreddy, Fenella, come for us," said grandma. She sounded pleased. Her white waxen cheeks were blue with cold, her chin trembled, and she had to keep wiping her eyes and her little pink nose.

"You've got my ——"

"Yes, grandma." Fenella showed it to her.

The rope came flying through the air, and "smack" it fell on to the deck. The gangway was lowered. Again Fenella followed her grandma on to the wharf over to the little cart, and a moment later they were bowling away. The hooves of the little horse drummed over the wooden piles, then sank softly into the sandy road. Not a soul was to be seen; there was not even a feather of smoke. The mist rose and fell, and the sea still sounded asleep as slowly it turned on the beach.

"I seen Mr. Crane yestiddy," said Mr. Penreddy. "He looked himself then. Missus knocked him up a batch of scones last week."

And now the little horse pulled up before one of the shell-like houses. They got down. Fenella put her hand on the gate, and the big, trembling dewdrops soaked through her glove-tips. Up a little path of round white pebbles they went, with drenched sleeping flowers on either side. Grandma's delicate white picotees [1] were so heavy with dew that they were fallen, but their sweet smell was part of the cold morning. The blinds were down in the little house; they mounted the steps on to the veranda. A pair of old bluchers was on one side of the door, and a large red watering-can on the other.

"Tut! tut! Your grandpa," said grandma. She turned the handle. Not a sound. She called, "Walter!" And immediately a deep voice that sounded half stifled called back, "Is that you, Mary?"

"Wait, dear," said grandma. "Go in there." She pushed Fenella gently into a small dusky sitting-room.

On the table a white cat, that had been folded

[1] A variety of carnation.

up like a camel, rose, stretched itself, yawned, and then sprang on to the tips of its toes. Fenella buried one cold little hand in the white, warm fur, and smiled timidly while she stroked and listened to grandma's gentle voice and the rolling tones of grandpa.

A door creaked. "Come in, dear." The old woman beckoned, Fenella followed. There, lying to one side of an immense bed, lay grandpa. Just his head with a white tuft, and his rosy face and long silver beard showed over the quilt. He was like a very old wide-awake bird.

"Well, my girl!" said grandpa. "Give us a kiss!" Fenella kissed him. "Ugh!" said grandpa. "Her little nose is as cold as a button. What's that she's holding? Her grandma's umbrella?"

Fenella smiled again, and crooked the swan neck over the bed rail. Above the bed there was a big text in a deep-black frame:

Lost! One Golden Hour
Set with Sixty Diamond Minutes.
No Reward Is Offered
For It Is Gone For Ever!

"Yer grandma painted that," said grandpa. And he ruffled his white tuft and looked at Fenella so merrily she almost thought he winked at her.

THE

EXPRESSIONISTS

&

I have not tried to reproduce Nature:
I have represented it.

CÉZANNE

IT WAS DURING the second decade of the twentieth century that expressionism became a definitely recognized manner in literature. However, even before the turn of the century Strindberg had foreshadowed this new temper in *To Damascus*, the first part of which was written in 1897–98, and had carried the manner further in *The Ghost Sonata*, published in 1909. If in painting it was in France that expressionism (post-impressionism) found its most ardent advocates, in literature it was Germany that took the lead in expressionism.

Without giving a formal definition of expressionism, let us attempt to offer an explanation of the major tenets of this literary manner.

Expressionism is, first and foremost, subjective. The expressionist's personal consciousness takes on a greater importance than any objective setting or character or action which may come under his observation. Instead of trying to communicate ideas, to give a direct sig-

1167

nificance to the life about him, he admits only the importance of the responses his inner awareness makes to the stimulus from without. He is, in fact, an expressionist simply because he gives expression to his inner vision, his feeling, his emotion, his inner spirit, his intuition; he is an expressionist by virtue of the fact that he *expresses* instead of imitating.

Expressionism reverses the process employed in impressionism. In impressionism the literary inspiration moves from the outside to the center (the mind of the writer); in expressionism the movement is from the mind of the writer to the outside world. A landscape by Monet is an actual landscape. One may visit the place and recognize it, even though it presents a setting at a particular moment and under a particular mood. A landscape by Rousseau, however, is less a portrayal of the actual setting observed than of Rousseau's inner vision of that landscape. The impressionist still represents what he sees; the expressionist starts with actuality but portrays the associations and reactions which arise in his mind. For instance, James Joyce in *Ulysses* expresses the external world as it passes through the inner consciousness of Leopold Bloom. In this way expressionism gives form to subjective associations. The expressionist transcribes his inner visions (in Picasso's term — "apparitions"), his emotions, before a scene or an incident; his pen is subject to the dictation of his "soul"; he indites perceptions, writes down implications, gives rein to his feelings, and allows himself to be driven by his intuitions. He is — or should be — a sensitive spirit; and his work is, for the reader, removed from the practical world by just the degree to which this sensitivity is increased. He expresses with immediacy and directness the associations and emotions called up in his own mind by the thing or the action or the idea before him. In this sense the expressionist tends to be realistic in presenting his own reactions and emotions and romantic in his attitude toward the external world.

Should it be objected that it is the writer's function to communicate ideas and not distort the objective world by presenting an esoteric and personal reaction, the only possible reply is "Why so? How do you know?" Literature has changed its course on many previous occasions Must one more change be ruled out? We have never demanded that the musician give us back only what he sees and hears in external nature. We expect, we even demand, that the musician give us melodies and images, and through them the emotions which only he has heard, and seen, and felt, which have aroused responses in his soul only. Why, then, must the poet, the painter, the architect reflect only external form? Why should not they be allowed the privilege of setting forth their individual vision, of painting form as they see it inwardly, of arranging words to reflect their personal attitude, their individualistic response?

Expressionism discards imitation. Surface reality is, the modernist holds, a shallow thing. He finds his enthusiasm in trying for inner reality, for what may be thought of as the *essence* of an object or an idea. A sunflower is not simply a sunflower; in the mind or emotion of an expressionistic painter it may be a yellow glare. A bridge is not a structure of iron and steel to Hart Crane but a something uniting, binding together civilizations or peoples or ideas. A jungle may not be merely trees and ferns and fronds to a Rousseau so much as a color or a mood or a design. The essence, the expressionist believes, may be as significant to paint or to write about as those qualities which are apparent to the eyes. He is not so much concerned with presenting appearances as with expressing essential and hidden qualities.

"This all," says Sheldon Cheney, "might be put in a nutshell — the beliefs of the modernists tend to one conclusion: *Things not imitable can be revealed, expressed, presented in another form.*"

Expressionism sets for itself the purpose of presenting the abstract and the typical; it is fourth-dimensional; it is mystical. As has already been said, the expressionistic painter or writer takes little more than his point of departure from the external object; his concern from then on is with the essence, the inner quality. Thus the painter does not portray concretely mother and child but maternity; not simply a nude but fecundity; not individual blades of grass but greenness; not a Christ on the cross but sorrow; not merely peasants eating potatoes but degradation and poverty; not simply form and outline but effect and sensation.

In their effort to portray the world of reality behind the world of appearances the expressionists are, after all, subscribing to a very real, a very sincere, and a very ancient conception; they are calling attention to the conviction that behind the externalities, behind what William James called "the furniture of earth and choir of heaven," is a world of etherealities and impermanence which is, after all, the only permanence. It is the introduction of this new dimension which gives a new perspective to the work of the expressionistic writers. Since the new point of view is intensely individualistic and subjective, and the new concern is with internal qualities rather than external appearances, the reader finds difficulty in adjusting himself to the manner. Expressionism appears to him distorted, strange, like nothing he knows in nature. He has difficulty in explaining to himself the refraction of life which is presented to him with new angles, like the portion of a stick which is immersed in water.

Just how this abstract, fourth-dimensional, and mystical element is introduced may perhaps best be shown by quoting a statement of M. Zervos [1] regarding Picasso's method of composition:

> The moments of creation with Picasso are dominated by anguish. This anguish Picasso analyzed for me recently. His only wish has been desperately to be himself; in fact, he acts according to suggestions which come to him from beyond his own limits. He sees descending upon him a superior order of exigencies, he has a very clear impression that something compels him imperiously to empty his spirit of all that he only just discovered, even before he has been able to control it, so that he can admit other suggestions. Hence his torturing doubts. But this anguish is not a misfortune for Picasso. It is just this which enables him to break down all his barriers, leaving the field of the possible free to him, and opening up to him the perspectives of the unknown.

[1] From *Cahiers d'Art*, quoted by Herbert Read in *Art Now* (1948).

Being largely intuitional, expressionistic writing leans heavily on psychoanalysis. This statement should certainly not be construed to mean that authors using the expressionistic manner are students of psychology. However, our discussion of the nature of expressionism — its strong subjective quality, its reliance on the ego of the author, its esoteric and mystical character — makes clear at once the part psychoanalysis plays in this new writing. Freud and Jung, if not fathers, are at least godfathers of expressionism. His regard for the subconscious, his concern with sensation, his effort to set forth his emotions, his pains to create a new world according to his secret desires make the expressionistic writer an interesting study for the psychoanalyst.

Expressionism makes ample use of symbols. It moves by indirection; it starts from reality but presents only reflections of this reality as they are revealed in the mind of the author through a sort of poetic vision. Indeed it might almost be said that expressionism is little more than realism hiding itself behind an abstraction, an abstraction often symbolized in some concrete image. Suggestion and implication being so vital a part of expressionistic writing, the author naturally relies largely on symbols. What is Hart Crane's *The Bridge* except an expanded piece of symbolism? And T. S. Eliot's *Waste Land?* And Joyce's *Ulysses* is a symbolic representation of man, a symbol enriched by its allusion to Homer and its implication that as man was then the object of forces playing upon him from without so is he now the object of forces playing upon him from within.

Expressionism in its concern with the inherent essence or quality of an object in nature as the mind of the artist conceives it — man, hill, animal — is not calculated to portray external appearances but very definitely calculated to present inner meanings. These intrinsic qualities are abstractions, and abstractions do not lend themselves completely to the methods of poetry or the novel or drama. How, then, is the literary artist to put them down on paper? His answer is the use of symbolic figures.

In general, expressionistic writers seem to despair of life; society, government, industry, religion, man himself, are presented as in a chaotic state. This impression of chaos is, at least partially, inherent in the subjective quality of expressionism. When every writer disregards external nature and primarily insists on presenting his individual reaction to the life about him, it is not strange if the reader gains an impression of a lack of order or synthesis. James Joyce presents life in Dublin as chaotic; John Dos Passos finds life in New York pitiful; Kafka illustrates the corruption of consciousness; and the world to T. S. Eliot is a Waste Land. Expressionism holds a mirror up to nature, but the mirror being uneven gives back reflections strangely distorted; the image it reflects is deformed.

It is because of this disillusionment with the world about them, then, that the expressionists would create for us a new world. They found life as they knew it not exactly the sort which should be reproduced or perpetuated in art or literature. "The chief task of art," wrote

Kasimir Edschmid, a leading spokesman for German expressionism, "is to penetrate the world before our eyes, to seek out its intrinsic essence, and create it anew." And Gauguin has written: "It is said that God put a piece of clay into His hand and created all that you know. The artist, in his turn, if he wishes to create a really divine work, must not imitate nature, but use the elements of nature to create a new element." The expressionistic writer looks out on an old world but expresses it in a new way — searches for what he believes to be the essence and then, as C. Lewis Hind said of Matisse, "he approaches a fresh canvas as if there were no past in art, as if he were the first artist who ever painted."

These purposes of the expressionist manifest themselves through an unconventional literary technique. Structure, in the usual sense, these writers ignore in the conviction that new purposes call for a new manner. In an effort to secure immediacy of communication they resort to suggestion, to implication, even to a rearrangement of words calculated by their strange juxtapositions to convey emotional reactions. Antithesis is frequent; the beautiful and the ugly are found next to each other:

> The moon has lost her memory.
> A washed-out smallpox cracks her face —

James Joyce once told Max Eastman that the demand he made upon his reader was that he should devote his whole life to reading his works. The esoteric quality, the distortion of form and diction, the personal psychology presented, the concern with the abstract — all these, though consciously sought for, are natural barriers between the writer and the average reader.

However, for those who are attracted by expressionism an enrichening experience is in store. To them is opened up a new realm of thought and emotion; to them, for the first time, may be revealed a synthesis in the spirit of man through the putting down on paper of psychological reactions which are within the subjective experience of all; to them comes the revelation of a new beauty, the stimulation of a new kind of communication between human beings.

James Joyce · 1882–1941

The twentieth-century writer who has influenced English literary form and style most is, no doubt, James Joyce. His work includes an early collection of poetry (*Chamber Music*, 1907), conventional in technique and light in content; a play (*Exiles*, 1918); a collection of short stories (*Dubliners*, 1914); and three full-length novels, *A Portrait of the Artist as a Young Man* (1916), *Ulysses* (1922), and *Finnegan's Wake* (1939).

James Joyce was born in Dublin on February 2, 1882. In school, he received Jesuit training. After earning a degree at the University of Dublin, he studied medicine in Paris for a while. His first novel, *A Portrait of the Artist as a Young Man*, carries the story of his life up to 1902. Here he speaks of the realization of his desire to become an artist. Dedalus, the "fabulous artificer" of Greek mythology, is the pseudonym under which Joyce travels in both novels, the *Portrait* and *Ulysses*. As he grew older, Joyce lived his art: not content with being a renegade from dogmatic religion, he left his native Ireland to become a citizen of Europe and the world:

> When the soul of a man is born in this country, there are nets flung at it to hold it back from flight. You talk to me of nationality, language, religion. I shall try to fly by those nets. I will not serve that in which I no longer believe, whether it call itself my home, my fatherland or my church: and I will try to express myself in some mode of life or art as freely as I can and as wholly as I can, using for my defence the only arms I allow myself to use, silence, exile and cunning.

Going into exile, Joyce became a restless wanderer, living now in Trieste, now in Paris and in Zürich, where death came to the almost blind writer in 1941. His books shared the exile of their author. *A Portrait of the Artist as a Young Man* was burned by the Irish publisher who had accepted it for publication and, like *Ulysses*, is still banned from Joyce's native country. *Ulysses* was admitted to this country in 1927, after charges of obscenity and impropriety raised against it had been dismissed.

Joyce worked on his books with all the "cunning" a literary craftsman of his calibre possesses. Not content with psychologically describing a realistic situation, Joyce makes use of various devices in creating "the uncreated conscience of his race." This "uncreated conscience" is the myth to which he returns by having his native city of Dublin assume universal symbolic significance. *Ulysses* knows only one scene, and that is Dublin, but this scene is related to the Homeric world and its heroes.

In order to recreate the myth he wants to use, Joyce has to dispense with and abstract from the personal and individual. He does so by introducing the *interior monologue:* the action is described by the characters as they see themselves and record their reactions. We see the facts of life and man's experience only through their eyes. The individual is lost in the maze of associations which emerge from its unconscious. The language itself broadens out into more and more universal significance. Words are telescoped and only a few, often trivial, symbolic objects keep us in touch with what we call the action of the novel.

Joyce's ideal of beauty in art is sublime and elevated. Flashes of insight reveal a pattern or a coherent phase of that floating, rhythmically moving whole which is *Ulysses*. Joyce calls them *epiphanies*, events of minor importance which yet serve to convey the essence of a thing or a state of mind. Joyce's characters are not heroes. They are mock-heroes, ironically perverted by their own thoughts which hardly ever extend beyond the obscene and the banal. But these characters are all waiting for a sudden transformation into the mythical.

Joyce is not just an experimenter with form; far from that, he feels himself to be in the great tradition of myth-makers. His myths include the whole of life: they are the reality of our world as it appears on our subconscious eye. The imitators of Joyce have misjudged and abused his art and his craft. They play only with the fragments of his artistic universe which, it has to be admitted, is of too vast a conception to be fully intelligible to even the most erudite and prophetic among modern minds.

SUGGESTED REFERENCES: Richard Ellman, *James Joyce* (1959); Harry Levin, *James Joyce, A Critical Introduction* (rev. ed., 1960); S. L. Goldberg, *James Joyce* (1962).

Ulysses

Joyce's novel *Ulysses* is confined to the events of one day, June 16, 1904, as they relate to a host of characters, the most important of which are Stephen Dedalus (representing Ulysses' son, Telemachus), Leopold Bloom, a Jewish advertising solicitor (Ulysses), and his wife Marion-Molly, a singer (Penelope). Patterned on Homer's *Odyssey*, the book is divided into episodes planned so as to parallel the Greek epic. The Interment of Patrick Dignam, for instance, takes up the Hades episode in Book XI of Homer's work.

Reference to the contents of that book is made in several ways. We have direct allusions to classical gods, mythical characters (fidus Achates, Moira, Athos), indirect references to such characters as Sisyphus and Tantalus, prominent mythical figures who are significantly punished in Hades (wheelwright, shoulder to the wheel, Tantalus glasses), and finally, proverbial debunking of words which denote states of existence in death and things related to the dead (dead nuts, trenchant, overdose, cakes for the dead, coroner's ears — referring to the judgment and re-assignment of the deceased souls to their various habitats in Hades).

Also it should be noted that the whole novel is concerned with the Father-Son relationship between Bloom and Dedalus. It is a spiritual relationship, a substitute to Bloom for the physical relationship which ended with the death of Bloom's little son, Rudi. Joyce relates Bloom's quest for another Rudi. The situation is further complicated by Molly's infatuation for the music teacher, Blazes Boylan, who briefly figures in this chapter.

Symbols abound and some of them recur frequently in the novel. For instance, the piece of soap in Bloom's hip pocket occupies his thoughts over and over again. This repetition is one of the reasons why Joyce's *Ulysses* gives the impression of being a static rather than a dynamic work.

Yet the texture of the writing is far from static. In the chapter which follows, local and contemporary allusions rapidly alternate with passages of reverie and stream of consciousness, giving a sense of perpetual shift and motion from the outer to the inner world.

THE INTERMENT OF PATRICK DIGNAM[1]

Martin Cunningham, First, poked his silk-hatted head into the creaking carriage and, entering deftly, seated himself. Mr. Power stepped in after him, curving his height with care.

— Come on, Simon.

— After you, Mr. Bloom said.

Mr. Dedalus covered himself quickly and got in, saying:

— Yes, yes.

— Are we all here now? Martin Cunningham asked. Come along, Bloom.

Mr. Bloom entered and sat in the vacant place. He pulled the door to after him and slammed it tight till it shut tight. He passed an arm through the armstrap and looked seriously from the open carriage window at the lowered blinds of the avenue. One dragged aside: an old woman peeping. Nose whiteflattened against the pane. Thanking her stars she was passed over. Extraordinary the interest they take in a corpse. Glad

[1] Reprinted by permission of Random House, Inc.

to see us go we give them such trouble coming Job seems to suit them. Huggermugger in corners Slop about in slipper-slappers for fear he'd wake. Then getting it ready. Laying it out. Molly and Mrs. Fleming making the bed. Pull it more to your side. Our windingsheet. Never know who will touch you dead. Wash and shampoo. I believe they clip the nails and the hair. Keep a bit in an envelope. Grow all the same after. Unclean job.

All waited. Nothing was said. Stowing in the wreaths probably. I am sitting on something hard. Ah, that soap in my hip pocket. Better shift it out of that. Wait for an opportunity.

All waited. Then wheels were heard from in front turning: then nearer: then horses' hoofs. A jolt. Their carriage began to move, creaking and swaying. Other hoofs and creaking wheels started behind. The blinds of the avenue passed and number nine with its craped knocker, door ajar. At walking pace.

They waited still, their knees jogging, till they had turned and were passing along the tramtracks. Tritonville road. Quicker. The wheels rattled rolling over the cobbled causeway and the crazy glasses shook rattling in the door frames.

— What way is he taking us? Mr. Power asked through both windows.

— Irishtown, Martin Cunningham said. Ringsend. Brunswick street.

Mr. Dedalus nodded, looking out.

— That's a fine old custom, he said. I am glad to see it has not died out.

All watched awhile through their windows caps and hats lifted by passers. Respect. The carriage swerved from the tramtrack to the smoother road past Watery lane. Mr. Bloom at gaze saw a lithe young man, clad in mourning, a wide hat.

— There's a friend of yours gone by, Dedalus, he said.

— Who is that?

— Your son and heir.

— Where is he? Mr. Dedalus said, stretching over, across.

The carriage, passing the open drains and mounds of ripped-up roadway before the tenement houses, lurched round the corner and, swerving back to the tramtrack, rolled on noisily with chattering wheels. Mr. Dedalus fell back, saying:

— Was that Mulligan cad with him? His *fidus Achates*?

— No, Mr. Bloom said. He was alone.

— Down with his aunt Sally, I suppose, Mr. Dedalus said, the Goulding faction, the drunken little costdrawer and Crissie, papa's little lump of dung, the wise child that knows her own father.

Mr. Bloom smiled joylessly on Ringsend road. Wallace Bros. the bottleworks. Dodder bridge.

Richie Goulding and the legal bag. Goulding, Collis and Ward he calls the firm. His jokes are getting a bit damp. Great card he was. Waltzing in Stamer street with Ignatius Gallaher on a Sunday morning, the landlady's two hats pinned on his head. Out on the rampage allnight. Beginning to tell on him now: that backache of his, I fear. Wife ironing his back. Thinks he'll cure it with pills. All breadcrumbs they are. About six hundred per cent profit.

— He's in with a lowdown crowd, Mr. Dedalus snarled. That Mulligan is a contaminated bloody double-dyed ruffian by all accounts. His name stinks all over Dublin. But with the help of God and His blessed mother I'll make it my business to write a letter one of those days to his mother or his aunt or whatever she is that will open her eyes as wide as a gate. I'll tickle his catastrophe, believe you me.

He cried above the clatter of the wheels.

— I won't have her bastard of a nephew ruin my son. A counterjumper's son. Selling tapes in my cousin, Peter Paul M'Swiney's. Not likely.

He ceased. Mr. Bloom glanced from his angry moustache to Mr. Power's mild face and Martin Cunningham's eyes and beard, gravely shaking. Noisy selfwilled man. Full of his son. He is right. Something to hand on. If little Rudy had lived. See him grow up. Hear his voice in the house. Walking beside Molly in an Eton suit. My son. Me in his eyes. Strange feeling it would be. From me. Just a chance. Must have been that morning in Raymond terrace she was at the window, watching the two dogs at it by the wall of the cease to do evil. And the sergeant grinning up. She had that cream gown on with the rip she never stitched. Give us a touch, Poldy. God, I'm dying for it. How life begins.

Got big then. Had to refuse the Greystones concert. My son inside her. I could have helped him on in life. I could. Make him independent. Learn German too.

— Are we late? Mr. Power asked.

— Ten minutes, Martin Cunningham said, looking at his watch.

Molly. Milly. Same thing watered down. Her tomboy oaths. O jumping Jupiter! Ye gods and little fishes! Still, she's a dear girl. Soon be a woman. Mullingar. Dearest Papli. Young student. Yes, yes: a woman too. Life. Life.

The carriage heeled over and back, their four trunks swaying.

— Corny might have given us a more commodious yoke, Mr. Power said.

— He might, Mr. Dedalus said, if he hadn't that squint troubling him. Do you follow me?

He closed his left eye. Martin Cunningham began to brush away crustcrumbs from under his thighs.

— What is this, he said, in the name of God? Crumbs?

— Someone seems to have been making a picnic party here lately, Mr. Power said.

All raised their thighs, eyed with disfavor the mildewed buttonless leather of the seats. Mr. Dedalus, twisting his nose, frowned downward and said:

— Unless I'm greatly mistaken. What do you think, Martin?

— It struck me too, Martin Cunningham said.

Mr. Bloom set his thigh down. Glad I took that bath. Feel my feet quite clean. But I wish Mrs. Fleming had darned these socks better.

Mr. Dedalus sighed resignedly.

— After all, he said, it's the most natural thing in the world.

— Did Tom Kernan turn up? Martin Cunningham asked, twirling the peak of his beard gently.

— Yes, Mr. Bloom answered. He's behind with Ned Lambert and Hynes.

— And Corny Kelleher himself? Mr. Power asked.

— At the cemetery, Martin Cunningham said.

— I met M'Coy this morning, Mr. Bloom said. He said he'd try to come.

The carriage halted short.

— What's wrong?

— We're stopped.

— Where are we?

Mr. Bloom put his head out of the window.

— The grand canal, he said.

Gas works. Whooping cough they say it cures. Good job Milly never got it. Poor children! Doubles them up black and blue in convulsions. Shame really. Got off lightly with illness compared. Only measles. Flaxseed tea. Scarlatina influenza epidemics. Canvassing for death. Don't miss this chance. God's home over there. Poor old Athos! Be good to Athos, Leopold, is my last wish. Thy will be done. We obey them in the grave. A dying scrawl. He took it to heart, pined away. Quiet brute. Old men's dogs usually are.

A raindrop spat on his hat. He drew back and saw an instant of shower spray dots over the grey flags. Apart. Curious. Like through a colander. I thought it would. My boots were creaking I remember now.

— The weather is changing, he said quietly.

— A pity it did not keep up fine, Martin Cunningham said.

— Wanted for the country, Mr. Power said. There's the sun again coming out.

Mr. Dedalus peering through his glasses towards the veiled sun, hurled a mute curse at the sky.

— It's as uncertain as a child's bottom, he said.

— We're off again.

The carriage turned again its stiff wheels and their trunks swayed gently. Martin Cunningham twirled more quickly the peak of his beard.

— Tom Kernan was immense last night, he said. And Paddy Leonard taking him off to his face.

— O draw him out, Martin, Mr. Power said eagerly. Wait till you hear him, Simon, on Ben Dollard's singing of *The Croppy Boy*.

— Immense, Martin Cunningham said pompously. *His singing of that simple ballad, Martin, is the most trenchant rendering I ever heard in the whole course of my experience.*

— Trenchant, Mr. Power said laughing. He's dead nuts on that. And the retrospective arrangement.

— Did you read Dan Dawson's speech? Martin Cunningham asked.

— I did not then, Mr. Dedalus said. Where is it?

— In the paper this morning.

Mr. Bloom took the paper from his inside pocket. That book I must change for her.

— No, no, Mr. Dedalus said quickly. Later on, please.

Mr. Bloom's glance travelled down the edge of the paper, scanning the deaths. Callan, Coleman, Dignam, Fawcett, Lowry, Naumann, Peake, what Peake is that? is it the chap was in Crosbie and Alleyne's? no, Sexton, Urbright. Inked characters fast fading on the frayed breaking paper. Thanks to the Little Flower. Sadly missed. To the inexpressible grief of his. Aged 88 after a long and tedious illness. Month's mind Quinlan. On whose soul Sweet Jesus have mercy.

It is now a month since dear Henry fled
To his home up above in the sky
While his family weeps and mourns his loss
Hoping some day to meet him on high.

I tore up the envelope? Yes. Where did I put her letter after I read it in the bath? He patted his waistcoat pocket. There all right. Dear Henry fled. Before my patience are exhausted.

National school. Meade's yard. The hazard. Only two there now. Nodding. Full as a tick. Too much bone in their skulls. The other trotting round with a fare. An hour ago I was passing there. The jarvies raised their hats.

A pointsman's back straightened itself upright suddenly against a tramway standard by Mr. Bloom's window. Couldn't they invent something automatic so that the wheel itself much handier? Well but that fellow would lose his job then? Well but then another fellow would get a job making the new invention?

Antient concert rooms. Nothing on there. A man in a buff suit with a crape armlet. Not much grief there. Quarter mourning. People in law, perhaps.

They went past the bleak pulpit of Saint Mark's, under the railway bridge, past the Queen's theatre: in silence. Hoardings. Eugene Stratton. Mrs. Bandman Palmer. Could I go to see *Leah* tonight, I wonder. I said I. Or the *Lily of Killarney?* Elster Grimes Opera company. Big powerful change. Wet bright bills for next week. *Fun on the Bristol.* Martin Cunningham could work a pass for the Gaiety. Have to stand a drink or two. As broad as it's long.

He's coming in the afternoon. Her songs.

Plasto's. Sir Philip Crampton's memorial fountain bust. Who was he?

— How do you do? Martin Cunningham said, raising his palm to his brow in salute.

— He doesn't see us, Mr. Power said. Yes, he does. How do you do?

— Who? Mr. Dedalus asked.

— Blazes Boylan, Mr. Power said. There he is airing his quiff. Just that moment I was thinking.

Mr. Dedalus bent across to salute. From the door of the Red Bank the white disc of a straw hat flashed reply: passed.

Mr. Bloom reviewed the nails of his left hand, then those of his right hand. The nails, yes. Is there anything more in him that they she sees? Fascination. Worst man in Dublin. That keeps him alive. They sometimes feel what a person is. Instinct. But a type like that. My nails. I am just looking at them: well pared. And after: thinking alone. Body getting a bit softy. I would notice that from remembering. What causes that I suppose the skin can't contract quickly enough when the flesh falls off. But the shape is there. The shape is there still. Shoulders. Hips. Plump. Night of the dance dressing. Shift stuck between the cheeks behind.

He clasped his hands between his knees and, satisfied, sent his vacant glance over their faces.

Mr. Power asked:

— How is the concert tour getting on, Bloom?

— O very well, Mr. Bloom said. I hear great accounts of it. It's a good idea, you see ...

— Are you going yourself?

— Well no, Mr. Bloom said. In point of fact I

have to go down to the county Clare on some private business. You see the idea is to tour the chief towns. What you lose on one you can make up on the other.

— Quite so, Martin Cunningham said. Mary Anderson is up there now.

— Have you good artists?

— Louis Werner is touring her, Mr. Bloom said. O yes, we'll have all topnobbers. J. C. Doyle and John MacCormack I hope and. The best, in fact.

— *And Madame*, Mr. Power said, smiling. Last but not least.

Mr. Bloom unclasped his hands in a gesture of soft politeness and clasped them. Smith O'Brien. Someone has laid a bunch of flowers there. Woman. Must be his deathday. For many happy returns. The carriage wheeling by Farrell's statue united noiselessly their unresisting knees.

Oot: a dullgarbed old man from the curbstone tendered his wares, his mouth opening: oot.

— Four bootlaces for a penny.

Wonder why he was struck off the rolls. Had his office in Hume street. Same house as Molly's namesake. Tweedy, crown solicitor for Waterford. Has that silk hat ever since. Relics of old decency. Mourning too. Terrible comedown, poor wretch! Kicked about like snuff at a wake. O'Callaghan on his last legs.

And *Madame*. Twenty past eleven. Up. Mrs. Fleming is in to clean. Doing her hair, humming: *voglio e non vorrei*. No: *vorrei e non*. Looking at the tips of her hairs to see if they are split. *Mi trema un poco il*. Beautiful on that *tre* her voice is: weeping tone. A thrush. A throstle. There is a word throstle that expressed that.

His eyes passed lightly over Mr. Power's goodlooking face. Greyish over the ears. *Madame:* smiling. I smiled back. A smile goes a long way. Only politeness perhaps. Nice fellow. Who knows is that true about the woman he keeps? Not pleasant for the wife. Yet they say, who was it told me, there is no carnal. You would imagine that would get played out pretty quick. Yes, it was Crofton met him one evening bringing her a pound of rump steak. What is this she was? Barmaid in Jury's. Or the Moira, was it?

They passed under the hugecloaked Liberator's form.

Martin Cunningham nudged Mr. Power.

— Of the tribe of Reuben, he said.

A tall blackbearded figure, bent on a stick, stumping round the corner of Elvery's elephant house showed them a curved hand open on his spine.

— In all his pristine beauty, Mr. Power said.

Mr. Dedalus looked after the stumping figure and said mildly:

— The devil break the hasp of your back!

Mr. Power, collapsing in laughter, shaded his face from the window as the carriage passed Gray's statue.

— We have all been there, Martin Cunningham said broadly.

His eyes met Mr. Bloom's eyes. He caressed his beard adding:

— Well, nearly all of us.

Mr. Bloom began to speak with sudden eagerness to his companions' faces.

— That's an awfully good one that's going the rounds about Reuben J. and the son.

— About the boatman? Mr. Power asked.

— Yes. Isn't it awfully good?

— What is that? Mr. Dedalus asked. I didn't hear it.

— There was a girl in the case, Mr. Bloom began, and he determined to send him to the isle of Man out of harm's way but when they were both....

— What? Mr. Dedalus asked. That confirmed bloody hobbledehoy is it?

— Yes, Mr. Bloom said. They were both on the way to the boat and he tried to drown...

— Drown Barabbas! Mr. Dedalus cried. I wish to Christ he did!

Mr. Power sent a long laugh down his shaded nostrils.

— No, Mr. Bloom said, the son himself...

Martin Cunningham thwarted his speech rudely.

— Reuben J. and the son were piking it down the quay next the river on their way to the isle of Man boat and the young chiseller suddenly got loose and over the wall with him into the Liffey.

— For God' sake! Mr. Dedalus exclaimed in fright. Is he dead?

— Dead! Martin Cunningham cried. Not he! A boatman got a pole and fished him out by the slack of the breeches and he was landed up to the father on the quay. More dead than alive. Half the town was there.

— Yes, Mr. Bloom said. But the funny part is...

— And Reuben J., Martin Cunningham said, gave the boatman a florin for saving his son's life.

A stifled sigh came from under Mr. Power's hand.

— O, he did, Martin Cunningham affirmed. Like a hero. A silver florin.

— Isn't it awfully good? Mr. Bloom said eagerly.

— One and eightpence too much, Mr. Dedalus said drily.

Mr. Power's choked laugh burst quietly in the carriage.

Nelson's pillar.

— Eight plums a penny! Eight for a penny!

— We had better look a little serious, Martin Cunningham said.

Mr. Dedalus sighed.

— And then indeed, he said, poor little Paddy wouldn't grudge us a laugh. Many a good one he told himself.

— The Lord forgive me! Mr. Power said, wiping his wet eyes with his fingers. Poor Paddy! I little thought a week ago when I saw him last and he was in his usual health that I'd be driving after him like this. He's gone from us.

— As decent a little man as ever wore a hat, Mr. Dedalus said. He went very suddenly.

— Breakdown, Martin Cunningham said. Heart. He tapped his chest sadly.

Blazing face: redhot. Too much John Barleycorn. Cure for a red nose. Drink like the devil till it turns adelite. A lot of money he spent coloring it.

Mr. Power gazed at the passing houses with rueful apprehension.

— He had a sudden death, poor fellow, he said.

— The best death, Mr. Bloom said.

Their wide open eyes looked at him.

— No suffering, he said. A moment and all is over. Like dying in sleep. No-one spoke.

Dead side of the street this. Dull business by day, land agents, temperance hotel, Falconer's railway guide, civil service college, Gill's, catholic club, the industrious blind. Why? Some reason. Sun or wind. At night too. Chummies and slaveys. Under the patronage of the late Father Mathew. Foundation stone for Parnell. Breakdown. Heart.

White horses with white frontlet plumes came round the Rotunda corner, galloping. A tiny coffin flashed by. In a hurry to bury. A mourning coach. Unmarried. Black for the married. Piebald for bachelors. Dun for a nun.

— Sad, Martin Cunningham said. A child.

A dwarf's face mauve and wrinkled like little Rudy's was. Dwarf's body, weak as putty, in a whitelined deal box. Burial friendly society pays. Penny a week for a sod of turf. Our. Little. Beggar. Baby. Meant nothing. Mistake of nature. If it's healthy it's from the mother. If not the man. Better luck next time.

— Poor little thing, Mr. Dedalus said. It's well out of it.

The carriage climbed more slowly the hill of Rutland square. Rattle his bones. Over the stones. Only a pauper. Nobody owns.

— In the midst of life, Martin Cunningham said.

— But the worst of all, Mr. Power said, is the man who takes his own life.

Martin Cunningham drew out his watch briskly, coughed and put it back.

— The greatest disgrace to have in the family, Mr. Power added.

— Temporary insanity, of course, Martin Cunningham said decisively. We must take a charitable view of it.

— They say a man who does it is a coward, Mr. Dedalus said.

— It is not for us to judge, Martin Cunningham said.

Mr. Bloom, about to speak, closed his lips again. Martin Cunningham's large eyes. Looking away now. Sympathetic human man he is. Intelligent. Like Shakespeare's face. Always a good word to say. They have no mercy on that here or infanticide. Refuse christian burial. They used to drive a stake of wood through his heart in the grave. As if it wasn't broken already. Yet sometimes they repent too late. Found in the riverbed clutching rushes. He looked at me. And that awful drunkard of a wife of his. Setting up house for her time after time and then pawning the furniture on him every Saturday almost. Leading him the life of the damned. Wear the heart out of a stone, that. Monday morning start afresh. Shoulder to the wheel. Lord, she must have looked a sight that night, Dedalus told me he was in there. Drunk about the place and capering with Martin's umbrella:

— *And they call me the jewel of Asia,*
Of Asia,
The geisha.

He looked away from me. He knows. Rattle his bones.

That afternoon of the inquest. The redlabelled bottle on the table. The room in the hotel with hunting pictures. Stuffy it was. Sunlight through the slats of the Venetian blinds. The coroner's ears, big and hairy. Boots giving evidence. Thought he was asleep first. Then saw like yellow streaks on his face. Had slipped down to the foot of the bed. Verdict: overdose. Death by misadventure. The letter. For my son Leopold.

No more pain. Wake no more. Nobody owns.

The carriage rattled swiftly along Blessington street. Over the stones.

— We are going the pace, I think, Martin Cunningham said.

— God grant he doesn't upset us on the road, Mr. Power said.

— I hope not, Martin Cunningham said. That

will be a great race tomorrow in Germany. The Gordon Bennett.

— Yes, by Jove, Mr. Dedalus said. That will be worth seeing, faith.

As they turned into Berkeley street a street organ near the Basin sent over and after them a rollicking rattling song of the halls. Has anybody here seen Kelly? Kay ee double ell wy. Dead march from *Saul*. He's as bad as old Antonio. He left me on my ownio. Pirouette! The *Mater Misericordiae*. Eccles street. My house down there. Big place. Ward for incurables there. Very encouraging. Our Lady's Hospice for the dying. Dead-house handy underneath. Where old Mrs. Riordan died. They look terrible the women. Her feeding cup and rubbing her mouth with the spoon. Then the screen round her bed for her to die. Nice young student that was dressed that bite the bee gave me. He's gone over to the lying-in hospital they told me. From one extreme to the other.

The carriage galloped round a corner: stopped.

— What's wrong now?

A divided drove of branded cattle passed the windows, lowing, slouching by on padded hoofs, whisking their tails slowly on their clotted bony croups. Outside them and through them ran raddled sheep bleating their fear.

— Emigrants, Mr. Power said.

— Huuuh! the drover's voice cried, his switch sounding on their flanks. Huuuh! Out of that!

Thursday of course. Tomorrow is killing day. Springers. Cuffe sold them about twenty-seven quid each. For Liverpool probably. Roast beef for old England. They buy up all the juicy ones. And then the fifth quarter is lost: all that raw stuff, hide, hair, horns. Comes to a big thing in a year. Dead meat trade. Byproducts of the slaughterhouses for tanneries, soap, margarine. Wonder if that dodge works now getting dicky meat off the train at Clonsilla.

The carriage moved on through the drove.

— I can't make out why the corporation doesn't run a tram-line from the parkgate to the quays, Mr. Bloom said. All those animals could be taken in trucks down to the boats.

— Instead of blocking up the thoroughfare, Martin Cunningham said. Quite right. They ought to.

— Yes, Mr. Bloom said, and another thing I often thought is to have municipal funeral trams like they have in Milan, you know. Run the line out to the cemetery gates and have special trams, hearse and carriage and all. Don't you see what I mean?

— O that be damned for a story, Mr. Dedalus said. Pullman car and saloon diningroom.

— A poor lookout for Corny, Mr. Power added.

— Why? Mr. Bloom asked, turning to Mr. Dedalus. Wouldn't it be more decent than galloping two abreast?

— Well, there's something in that, Mr. Dedalus granted.

— And, Martin Cunningham said, we wouldn't have scenes like that when the hearse capsized round Dunphy's and upset the coffin on to the road.

— That was terrible, Mr. Power's shocked face said, and the corpse fell about the road. Terrible!

First round Dunphy's, Mr. Dedalus said, nodding. Gordon Bennett cup.

— Praises be to God! Martin Cunningham said piously.

Bom! Upset. A coffin bumped out on to the road. Burst open. Paddy Dignam shot out and rolling over stiff in the dust in a brown habit too large for him. Red face: grey now. Mouth fallen open. Asking what's up now. Quite right to close it. Looks horrid open. Then the insides decompose quickly. Much better to close up all the orifices. Yes, also. With wax. The sphincter loose. Seal up all.

— Dunphy's, Mr. Power announced as the carriage turned right.

Dunphy's corner. Mourning coaches drawn up drowning their grief. A pause by the wayside. Tiptop position for a pub. Expect we'll pull up here on the way back to drink his health. Pass round the consolation. Elixir of life.

But suppose now it did happen. Would he bleed if a nail say cut him in the knocking about? He would and he wouldn't, I suppose. Depends on where. The circulation stops. Still some might ooze out of an artery. It would be better to bury them in red: a dark red.

In silence they drove along Phibsborough road. An empty hearse trotted by, coming from the cemetery: looks relieved.

Crossguns bridge: the royal canal.

Water rushed roaring through the sluices. A man stood on his dropping barge between clamps of turf. On the towpath by the lock a slack-tethered horse. Aboard of the *Bugabu*.

Their eyes watched him. On the slow weedy waterway he had floated on his raft coastward over Ireland drawn by a haulage rope past beds of reeds, over slime, mudchoked bottles, carrion dogs. Athlone, Mullingar, Moyvalley, I could make a walking tour to see Milly by the canal. Or cycle down. Hire some old crock, safety. Wren had one the other day at the auction but a lady's.

Developing waterways. James M'Cann's hobby to row me o'er the ferry. Cheaper transit. By easy stages. Houseboats. Camping out. Also hearses. To heaven by water. Perhaps I will without writing. Come as a surprise, Leixlip, Clonsilla. Dropping down, lock by lock to Dublin. With turf from the midland bogs. Salute. He lifted his brown straw hat, saluting Paddy Dignam.

They drove on past Brian Boroimhe house. Near it now.

— I wonder how is our friend Fogarty getting on, Mr. Power said.

— Better ask Tom Kernan, Mr. Dedalus said.

— How is that? Martin Cunningham said. Left him weeping I suppose.

— Though lost to sight, Mr. Dedalus said, to memory dear.

The carriage steered left for Finglas road.

The stonecutter's yard on the right. Last lap. Crowded on the spit of land silent shapes appeared, white, sorrowful, holding out calm hands, knelt in grief, pointing. Fragments of shapes, hewn. In white silence: appealing. The best obtainable. Thos. H. Dennany, monumental builder and sculptor.

Passed.

On the curbstone before Jimmy Geary the sexton's an old tramp sat, grumbling, emptying the dirt and stones out of his huge dustbrown yawning boot. After life's journey.

Gloomy gardens then went by, one by one: gloomy houses.

Mr. Power pointed.

— That is where Childs was murdered, he said. The last house.

— So it is, Mr. Dedalus said. A gruesome case. Seymour Bushe got him off. Murdered his brother. Or so they said.

— The crown had no evidence, Mr. Power said.

— Only circumstantial, Martin Cunningham said. That's the maxim of the law. Better for ninety-nine guilty to escape than for one innocent person to be wrongfully condemned.

They looked. Murderer's ground. It passed darkly. Shuttered, tenantless, unweeded garden. Whole place gone to hell. Wrongfully condemned. Murder. The murderer's image in the eye of the murdered. They love reading about it. Man's head found in a garden. Her clothing consisted of. How she met her death. Recent outrage. The weapon used. Murderer is still at large. Clues. A shoelace. The body to be exhumed. Murder will out.

Cramped in this carriage. She mightn't like me to come that way without letting her know.

Must be careful about women. Catch them once with their pants down. Never forgive you after. Fifteen.

The high railings of Prospects rippled past their gaze. Dark poplars, rare white forms. Forms more frequent, white shapes thronged amid the trees, white forms and fragments streaming by mutely, sustaining vain gestures on the air.

The felly harshed against the curbstone: stopped. Martin Cunningham put out his arm and, wrenching back the handle, shoved the door open with his knee. He stepped out. Mr. Power and Mr. Dedalus followed.

Change that soap now. Mr. Bloom's hand unbuttoned his hip pocket swiftly and transferred the paperstuck soap to his inner handkerchief pocket. He stepped out of the carriage, replacing the newspaper his other hand still held.

Paltry funeral: coach and three carriages. It's all the same. Pallbearers, gold reins, requiem mass, firing a volley. Pomp of death. Beyond the hind carriage a hawker stood by his barrow of cakes and fruit. Simnel cakes those are, stuck together: cakes for the dead. Dogbiscuits. Who ate them? Mourners coming out.

He followed his companions. Mr. Kernan and Ned Lambert followed, Hynes walking after them. Corny Kelleher stood by the opened hearse and took out the two wreaths. He handed one to the boy.

Where is that child's funeral disappeared to?

A team of horses passed from Finglas with toiling plodding tread, dragging through the funereal silence a creaking wagon on which lay a granite block. The waggoner marching at their head saluted.

Coffin now. Got here before us, dead as he is. Horse looking round at it with his plume skeowways. Dull eye: collar tight on his neck, pressing on a bloodvessel or something. Do they know what they cart out here every day? Must be twenty or thirty funerals every day. Then Mount Jerome for the protestants. Funerals all over the world everywhere every minute. Shovelling them under by the cartload doublequick. Thousands every hour. Too many in the world.

Mourners came out through the gates: woman and a girl. Leanjawed harpy, hard woman at a bargain, her bonnet awry. Girl's face stained with dirt and tears, holding the woman's arm looking up at her for a sign to cry. Fish's face, bloodless and livid.

The mutes shouldered the coffin and bore it in through the gates. So much dead weight. Felt heavier myself stepping out of that bath. First the stiff: then the friends of the stiff. Corny

Kelleher and the boy followed with their wreaths. Who is that beside them? Ah, the brother-in-law.

All walked after.

Martin Cunningham whispered:

— I was in mortal agony with you talking of suicide before Bloom.

— What? Mr. Power whispered. How so?

— His father poisoned himself, Martin Cunningham whispered. Had the Queen's hotel in Ennis. You heard him say he was going to Clare. Anniversary.

— O God! Mr. Power whispered. First I heard of it. Poisoned himself!

He glanced behind him to where a face with dark thinking eyes followed towards the cardinal's mausoleum. Speaking.

— Was he insured? Mr. Bloom asked.

— I believe so, Mr. Kernan answered, but the policy was heavily mortgaged. Martin is trying to get the youngster into Artane.

— How many children did he leave?

— Five. Ned Lambert says he'll try to get one of the girls into Todd's.

— A sad case, Mr. Bloom said gently. Five young children.

— A great blow to the poor wife, Mr. Kernan added.

— Indeed yes, Mr. Bloom agreed.

Has the laugh at him now.

He looked down at the boots he had blacked and polished. She had outlived him, lost her husband. More dead for her than for me. One must outlive the other. Wise men say. There are more women than men in the world. Condole with her. Your terrible loss. I hope you'll soon follow him. For Hindu widows only. She would marry another. Him? No. Yet who knows after? Widowhood not the thing since the old queen died. Drawn on a guncarriage. Victorian and Albert. Frogmore memorial mourning. But in the end she put a few violets in her bonnet. Vain in her heart of hearts. All for a shadow. Consort not even a king. Her son was the substance. Something new to hope for not like the past she wanted back, waiting. It never comes. One must go first: alone under the ground: and lie no more in her warm bed.

— How are you, Simon? Ned Lambert said softly, clasping hands. Haven't seen you for a month of Sundays.

— Never better. How are all in Cork's own town?

— I was down there for the Cork park races on Easter Monday, Ned Lambert said. Same old six and eightpence. Stopped with Dick Tivy.

— And how is Dick, the solid man?

— Nothing between himself and heaven, Ned Lambert answered.

— By the holy Paul! Mr. Dedalus said in subdued wonder. Dick Tivy bald?

— Martin is going to get up a whip for the youngsters, Ned Lambert said, pointing ahead. A few bob a skull. Just to keep them going till the insurance is cleared up.

— Yes, yes, Mr. Dedalus said dubiously. Is that the eldest boy in front?

— Yes, Ned Lambert said, with the wife's brother. John Henry Menton is behind. He put down his name for a quid.

— I'll engage he did, Mr. Dedalus said. I often told poor Paddy he ought to mind that job. John Henry is not the worst in the world.

— How did he lose it? Ned Lambert asked. Liquor, what?

— Many a good man's fault, Mr. Dedalus said with a sigh.

They halted about the door of the mortuary chapel. Mr. Bloom stood behind the boy with the wreath, looking down at his sleek combed hair and the slender furrowed neck inside his brand-new collar. Poor boy! Was he there when the father? Both unconscious. Lighten up at the last moment and recognize for the last time. All he might have done. I owe three shillings to O'Grady. Would he understand? The mutes bore the coffin into the chapel. Which end is his head?

After a moment he followed the others in, blinking in the screened light. The coffin lay on its bier before the chancel four tall yellow candles at its corners. Always in front of us. Corny Kelleher, laying a wreath at each fore corner, beckoned to the boy to kneel. The mourners knelt here and there in praying desks. Mr. Bloom stood behind near the font and, when all had knelt dropped carefully his unfolded newspaper from his pocket and knelt his right knee upon it. He fitted his black hat gently on his left knee and, holding its brim, bent over piously....

The priest closed his book and went off, followed by the server. Corny Kelleher opened the sidedoors and the grave diggers came in, hoisted the coffin again, carried it out and shoved it on their cart. Corny Kelleher gave one wreath to the boy and one to the brother-in-law. All followed them out of the sidedoors into the mild grey air. Mr. Bloom came last, folding his paper again into his pocket. He gazed gravely at the ground till the coffincart wheeled off to the left. The metal wheels ground the gravel with a sharp grating cry and the pack of blunt boots followed the barrow along a lane of sepulchres.

The ree the ra the ree the ra the roo. Lord. I mustn't lilt here.

— The O'Connell circle, Mr. Dedalus said about him.

Mr. Power's soft eyes went up to the apex of the lofty cone.

— He's at rest, he said, in the middle of his people, old Dan O'. But his heart is buried in Rome. How many broken hearts are buried here, Simon!

— Her grave is over there, Jack, Mr. Dedalus said. I'll soon be stretched beside her. Let Him take me whenever He likes.

Breaking down, he began to weep to himself quietly, stumbling a little in his walk. Mr. Power took his arm.

— She's better where she is, he said kindly.

— I suppose so, Mr. Dedalus said with a weak gasp. I suppose she is in heaven if there is a heaven.

Corny Kelleher stepped aside from his rank and allowed the mourners to plod by.

— Sad occasions, Mr. Kernan began politely.

Mr. Bloom closed his eyes and sadly twice bowed his head.

— The others are putting on their hats, Mr. Kernan said. I suppose we can do so too. We are the last. This cemetery is a treacherous place.

They covered their heads.

— The reverend gentleman read the service too quickly, don't you think? Mr. Kernan said with reproof.

Mr. Bloom nodded gravely, looking in the quick bloodshot eyes. Secret eyes, secret searching eyes. Mason, I think: not sure. Beside him again. We are the last. In the same boat. Hope he'll say something else.

Mr. Kernan added:

— The service of the Irish church, used in Mount Jerome, is simpler, more impressive, I must say.

Mr. Bloom gave prudent assent. The language of course was another thing.

Mr. Kernan said with solemnity:

— *I am the resurrection and the life*. That touches a man's inmost heart.

— It does, Mr. Bloom said.

Your heart perhaps but what price the fellow in the six feet by two with his toes to the daisies? No touching that. Seat of the affections. Broken heart. A pump after all, pumping thousands of gallons of blood every day. One fine day it gets bunged up and there you are. Lots of them lying around here: lungs, hearts, livers. Old rusty pumps: damn the thing else. The resurrection and the life. Once you are dead you are dead. That last day idea. Knocking them all up out of

their graves. Come forth, Lazarus! And he came fifth and lost the job. Get up! Last day! Then every fellow mousing around for his liver and his lights and the rest of his traps. Find damn all of himself that morning. Pennyweight of powder in a skull. Twelve grammes one pennyweight. Troy measure.

Corny Kelleher fell into step at their side.

— Everything went off A I, he said. What?

He looked on them from his drawling eye. Policeman's shoulders. With your tooraloom tooraloom.

— As it should be, Mr. Kernan said.

— What? Eh? Corny Kelleher said.

Mr. Kernan assured him.

— Who is that chap behind with Tom Kernan? John Henry Menton asked. I know his face.

Ned Lambert glanced back.

— Bloom, he said, Madam Marion Tweedy that was, is, I mean, the soprano. She's his wife.

— O, to be sure, John Henry Menton said. I haven't seen her for some time. She was a fine-looking woman. I danced with her, wait, fifteen seventeen golden years ago, at Mat Dillon's, in Roundtown. And a good armful she was.

He looked behind through the others.

— What is he? he asked. What does he do? Wasn't he in the stationery line? I fell foul of him one evening, I remember, at bowls.

Ned Lambert smiled.

— Yes, he was, he said, in Wisdom Hely's. A traveller for blottingpaper.

— In God's name, John Henry Menton said, what did she marry a coon like that for? She had plenty of game in her then.

— Has still, Ned Lambert said. He does some canvassing for ads.

John Henry Menton's large eyes stared ahead.

The barrow turned into a side lane. A portly man, ambushed among the grasses, raised his hat in homage. The gravediggers touched their caps.

— John O'Connell, Mr. Power said, pleased. He never forgets a friend.

Mr. O'Connell shook all their hands in silence. Mr. Dedalus said:

— I am come to pay you another visit.

— My dear Simon, the caretaker answered in a low voice. I don't want your custom at all.

Saluting Ned Lambert and John Henry Menton he walked on at Martin Cunningham's side, puzzling two keys at his back.

— Did you hear that one, he asked them, about Mulcahy from the Coombe?

— I did not, Martin Cunningham said.

They bent their silk hats in concert and Hynes inclined his ear. The caretaker hung his thumbs

in the loops of his gold watch chain and spoke in a
discreet tone to their vacant smiles.

— They tell the story, he said, that two drunks
came out here one foggy evening to look for the
grave of a friend of theirs. They asked for Mulcahy from the Coombe and were told where he was
buried. After traipsing about in the fog they
found the grave, sure enough. One of the drunks
spelt out the name: Terence Mulcahy. The other
drunk was blinking up at a statue of our Savior
the widow had got put up.

The caretaker blinked up at one of the sepulchres they passed. He resumed:

— And, after blinking up at the sacred figure,
Not a bloody bit like the man, says he. *That's not
Mulcahy,* says he, *whoever done it.*

Rewarded by smiles he fell back and spoke with
Corny Kelleher, accepting the dockets given him,
turning them over and scanning them as he walked.

— That's all done with a purpose, Martin Cunningham explained to Hynes.

— I know, Hynes said, I know that.

— To cheer a fellow up, Martin Cunningham
said. It's pure goodheartedness: damn the thing
else.

Mr. Bloom admired the caretaker's prosperous
bulk. All want to be on good terms with him.
Decent fellow, John O'Connell, real good sort.
Keys: like Keyes's ad: no fear of anyone getting out,
no passout checks. *Habeas corpus.* I must see
about that ad after the funeral. Did I write Balls-
bridge on the envelope I took to cover when she
disturbed me writing to Martha? Hope it's not
chucked in the dead letter office. Be the better of
a shave. Grey sprouting beard. That's the first
sign when the hairs come out grey and temper
getting cross. Silver threads among the grey.
Fancy being his wife. Wonder how he had the
gumption to propose to any girl. Come out and
live in the graveyard. Dangle that before her.
It might thrill her first. Courting death . . .
Shades of night hovering here with all the dead
stretched about. The shadows of the tombs when
churchyards yawn and Daniel O'Connell must be a
descendant I suppose who is this used to say he was
a queer breedy man great catholic all the same like
a big giant in the dark. Will o' the wisp. Gas of
graves. Want to keep her mind off it to conceive
at all. Women especially are so touchy. Tell
her a ghost story in bed to make her sleep. Have
you ever seen a ghost? Well, I have. It was pitch-
dark night. The clock was on the stroke of twelve.
Still they'd kiss all right if properly keyed up.
Whores in Turkish graveyards. Learn anything
if taken young. You might pick up a young
widow here. Men like that. Love among the

tombstones. Romeo. Spice of pleasure. In the
midst of death we are in life. Both ends meet.
Tantalising for the poor dead. Smell of grilled
beefsteaks to the starving gnawing their vitals.
Desire to grig people. Molly wanting to do it at
the window. Eight children he has anyway.

He has seen a fair share go under in his time,
lying around him field after field. Holy fields.
More room if they buried them standing. Sitting
or kneeling you couldn't. Standing? His head
might come up some day above ground in a land-
slip with his hand pointing. All honeycombed
the ground must be: oblong cells. And very neat
he keeps it too, trim grass and edgings. His garden
Major Gamble calls Mount Jerome. Well so it is.
Ought to be flowers of sleep. Chinese cemeteries
with giant poppies growing produce the best opium
Mastiansky told me. The Botanic Gardens are
just over there. It's the blood sinking in the earth
gives new life. Same idea those jews they said
killed the christian boy. Every man his price.
Well preserved fat corpse gentlemen, epicure, invaluable for fruit garden. A bargain. By carcass
of William Wilkinson, auditor and accountant,
lately deceased, three pounds thirteen and six.
With thanks.

I daresay the soil would be quite fat with corpse
manure, bones, flesh, nails, charnelhouses. Dreadful. Turning green and pink, decomposing. Rot
quick in damp earth. The lean old ones tougher.
Then a kind of a tallowy kind of a cheesy. Then
begin to get black, treacle oozing out of them.
Then dried up. Deathmoths. Of course the cells
or whatever they are go on living. Changing
about. Live for ever practically. Nothing to feed
on feed on themselves.

But they must breed a devil of a lot of maggots.
Soil must be simply swirling with them. Your
head it simply swurls. Those pretty little seaside
gurls. He looks cheerful enough over it. Gives
him a sense of power seeing all the others go under
first. Wonder how he looks at life. Cracking his
jokes too: warms the cockles of his heart. The
one about the bulletin. Spurgeon went to heaven
4 A.M. this morning. 11 P.M. (closing time). Not
arrived yet. Peter. The dead themselves the
men anyhow would like to hear an odd joke or
the women to know what's in fashion. A juicy
pear or ladies' punch, hot, strong and sweet. Keep
out of the damp. You must laugh sometimes so
better do it that way. Gravediggers in *Hamlet.*
Shows the profound knowledge of the human heart.
Daren't joke about the dead for two years at
least. *De mortuis nil nisi prius.* Go out of
mourning first. Hard to imagine his funeral.
Seems a sort of a joke. Read your own obituary

notice they say you live longer. Gives you second wind. New lease of life.

— How many have you for tomorrow? the caretaker asked.

— Two, Corny Kelleher said. Half ten and eleven.

The caretaker put the papers in this pocket. The barrow had ceased to trundle. The mourners split and moved to each side of the hole, stepping with care round the graves. The gravediggers bore the coffin and set its nose on the brink, looping the bands round it.

Burying him. We come to bury Caesar. His ides of March or June. He doesn't know who is here nor care.

Now who is that lankylooking galoot over there in the macintosh? Now who is he I'd like to know? Now, I'd give a trifle to know who he is. Always someone turns up you never dreamt of. A fellow could live on his lonesome all his life. Yes, he could. Still he'd have to get someone to sod him after he died though he could dig his own grave. We all do. Only man buries. No ants too. First thing strikes anybody. Bury the dead. Say Robinson Crusoe was true to life. Well then Friday buried him. Every Friday buries a Thursday if you come to look at it.

O, poor Robinson Crusoe,
How could you possibly do so?

Poor Dignam! His last lie on the earth in his box. When you think of them all it does seem a waste of wood. All gnawed through. They could invent a handsome bier with a kind of panel sliding let it down that way. Ay but they might object to be buried out of another fellow's. They're so particular. Lay me in my native earth. Bit of clay from the holy land. Only a mother and deadborn child ever buried in the one coffin. I see what it means. I see. To protect him as long as possible even in the earth. The Irishman's house is his coffin. Embalming in catacombs, mummies, the same idea.

Mr. Bloom stood far back, his hat in his hand, counting the bared heads. Twelve. I'm thirteen. No. The chap in the macintosh is thirteen. Death's number. Where the deuce did he pop out of? He wasn't in the chapel, that I'll swear. Silly superstition that about thirteen.

Nice soft tweed Ned Lambert has in that suit. Tinge of purple. I had one like that when we lived in Lombard street west. Dressy fellow he was once. Used to change three suits in the day. Must get that grey suit of mine turned by Mesias. Hello. It's dyed. His wife I forgot he's not married or his landlady ought to have picked out those threads for him.

The coffin dived out of sight, eased down by the men straddled on the gravetrestles. They struggled up and out: and all uncovered. Twenty.

Pause.

If we were all suddenly somebody else.

Far away a donkey brayed. Rain. No such ass. Never see a dead one, they say. Shame of death. They hide. Also poor papa went away.

Gentle sweet air blew round the bared heads in a whisper. Whisper. The boy by the gravehead held his wreath with both hands staring quietly in the black open space. Mr. Bloom moved behind the portly kindly caretaker. Well cut frockcoat. Weighing them up perhaps to see which will go next. Well it is a long rest. Feel no more. It's the moment you feel. Must be damned unpleasant. Can't believe it at first. Mistake must be: someone else. Try the house opposite. Wait, I wanted to I haven't yet. Then darkened deathchamber. Light they want. Whispering around you. Would you like to see a priest? Then rambling and wandering. Delirium all you hid all your life. The death struggle. His sleep is not natural. Press his lower eyelid. Watching is his nose pointed is his jaw sinking are the soles of his feet yellow. Pull the pillow away and finish it off on the floor since he's doomed. Devil in that picture of sinner's death showing him a woman. Dying to embrace her in his shirt. Last act of *Lucia. Shall I nevermore behold thee?* Bam! expires. Gone at last. People talk about you a bit: forget you. Don't forget to pray for him. Remember him in your prayers. Even Parnell. Ivy day dying out. Then they follow: dropping into a hole one after the other.

We are praying now for the repose of his soul. Hoping you're well and not in hell. Nice change of air. Out of the fryingpan of life into the fire of purgatory.

Does he ever think of the hole waiting for himself? They say you do when you shiver in the sun. Someone walking over it. Callboy's warning. Near you. Mine over there towards Finglas, the plot I bought. Mamma poor mamma, and little Rudy.

The gravediggers took up their spades and flung heavy clods of clay in on the coffin. Mr. Bloom turned his face. And if he was alive all the time? Whew! By Jingo, that would be awful! No, no: he is dead, of course. Of course he is dead. Monday he died. They ought to have some law to pierce the heart and make sure or an electric clock or a telephone in the coffin and some kind of a canvas airhole. Flag of distress. Three days.

Rather long to keep them in summer. Just as well to get shut of them as soon as you are sure there's no.

The clay fell softer. Begin to be forgotten. Out of sight, out of mind.

The caretaker moved away a few paces and put on his hat. Had enough of it. The mourners took heart of grace, one by one, covering themselves without show. Mr. Bloom put on his hat and saw the portly figure make its way deftly through the maze of graves. Quietly, sure of his ground, he traversed the dismal fields.

Hynes jotting down something in his notebook. Ah, the names. But he knows them all. No: coming to me.

— I am just taking the names, Hynes said below his breath. What is your christian name? I'm not sure.

— L, Mr. Bloom said. Leopold. And you might put down M'Coy's name too. He asked me to.

— Charley, Hynes said writing. I know. He was on the *Freeman* once.

So he was before he got the job in the morgue under Louis Byrne. Good idea a postmortem for doctors. Find out what they imagine they know. He died on a Tuesday. Got the run. Levanted with the cash of a few ads. Charley, you're my darling. That was why he asked me to. O well, does no harm. I saw to that, M'Coy. Thanks, old chap: much obliged. Leave him under an obligation: costs nothing.

— And tell us, Hynes said, do you know that fellow in the, fellow was over there in the...

He looked around.

— Macintosh. Yes, I saw him, Mr. Bloom said. Where is he now?

— Macintosh, Hynes said, scribbling. I don't know who he is. Is that his name?

He moved away, looking about him.

— No, Mr. Bloom began, turning and stopping. I say, Hynes!

Didn't hear. What? Where has he disappeared to? Not a sign. Well of all the. Has anybody here seen? Kay ee double ell. Become invisible. Good Lord, what became of him?

A seventh gravedigger came beside Mr. Bloom to take up an idle spade.

— O, excuse me!

He stepped aside nimbly.

Clay, brown, damp, began to be seen in the hole. It rose. Nearly over. A mound of damp clods rose more, rose, and the gravediggers rested their spades. All uncovered again for a few instants. The boy propped his wreath against a corner: the brother-in-law his on a lump. The gravediggers put on their caps and carried their earthy spades towards the barrow. Then knocked the blades lightly on the turf: clean. One bent to pluck from the haft a long tuft of grass. One, leaving his mates, walked slowly on with shouldered weapon, its blade blueglancing. Silently at the gravehead another coiled the coffinband. His navelcord. The brother-in-law, turning away, placed something in his free hand. Thanks in silence. Sorry, sir: trouble. Headshake. I know that. For yourselves just.

The mourners moved away slowly, without aim, by devious paths, staying awhile to read a name on a tomb.

— Let us go round by the chief's grave, Hynes said. We have time.

— Let us, Mr. Power said.

They turned to the right, following their slow thoughts. With awe Mr. Power's blank voice spoke:

— Some say he is not in that grave at all. That the coffin was filled with stones. That one day he will come again.

Hynes shook his head.

— Parnell will never come again, he said. He's there, all that was mortal of him. Peace to his ashes.

Mr. Bloom walked unheeded along his grove by saddened angels, crosses, broken pillars, family vaults, stone hopes praying with upcast eyes, old Ireland's hearts and hands. More sensible to spend the money on some charity for the living. Pray for the repose of the soul of. Does anybody really? Plant him and have done with him. Like down a coalshoot. Then lump them together to save time. All souls' day. Twenty-seventh I'll be at his grave. Ten shillings for the gardener. He keeps it free of weeds. Old man himself. Bent down double with his shears clipping. Near death's door. Who passed away. Who departed this life. As if they did it of their own accord. Got the shove, all of them. Who kicked the bucket. More interesting if they told you what they were. So and so, wheelwright. I travelled for cork lino. I paid five shillings in the pound. Or a woman's with her saucepan. I cooked good Irish stew. Eulogy in a country churchyard it ought to be that poem of whose is it Wordsworth or Thomas Campbell. Entered into rest the protestants put it. Old Dr. Murren's. The great physician called him home. Well it's God's acre for them. Nice country residence. Newly plastered and painted. Ideal spot to have a quiet smoke and read the *Church Times*. Marriage ads they never try to beautify. Rusty wreaths hung on knobs, garlands of bronze-foil. Better value that for the money. Still, the flowers are more poetical. The other gets rather tiresome, never withering. Expresses nothing. Immortelles.

A bird sat tamely perched on a poplar branch. Like stuffed. Like the wedding present alderman Hooper gave us. Hu! Not a budge out of him. Knows there are no catapults to let fly at him. Dead animal even sadder. Silly-Milly burying the little dead bird in the kitchen matchbox, a daisychain and bits of broken chainies on the grave.

The Sacred Heart that is: showing it. Heart on his sleeve. Ought to be sideways and red it should be painted like a real heart. Ireland was dedicated to it or whatever that. Seems anything but pleased. Why this infliction? Would birds come then and peck like the boy with the basket of fruit but he said no because they ought to have been afraid of the boy. Apollo that was.

How many! All these here once walked round Dublin. Faithful departed. As you are now so once were we.

Besides how could you remember everybody? Eyes, walk, voice. Well, the voice, yes: gramophone. Have a gramophone in every grave or keep it in the house. After dinner on a Sunday. Put on poor old greatgrandfather Kraahraark! Hellohellohello amawfullyglad kraark awfullygladaseeragain hellohello amarawf kopthsth. Remind you of the voice like the photograph reminds you of the face. Otherwise you couldn't remember the face after fifteen years, say. For instance who? For instance some fellow that died when I was in Wisdom Hely's.

Rtststr! A rattle of pebbles. Wait. Stop.

He looked down intently into a stone crypt. Some animal. Wait. There he goes.

An obese grey rat toddled along the side of the crypt, moving the pebbles. An old stager: greatgrandfather: he knows the ropes. The grey alive crushed itself in under the plinth, wriggled itself in under it. Good hidingplace for treasure.

Who lives there? Are laid the remains of Robert Emery. Robert Emmet was buried here by torchlight, wasn't he? Making his rounds.

Tail gone now.

One of those chaps would make short work of a fellow. Pick the bones clean no matter who it was. Ordinary meat for them. A corpse is meat gone bad. Well and what's cheese? Corpse of milk. I read in that *Voyages in China* that the Chinese say a white man smells like a corpse. Cremation better. Priests dead against it. Devilling for the other firm. Wholesale burners and Dutch oven dealers. Time of the plague. Quicklime fever pits to eat them. Lethal chamber. Ashes to ashes. Or bury at sea. Where is that Parsee tower of silence?

Eaten by birds. Earth, fire, water. Drowning they say is the pleasantest. See your whole life in a flash. But being brought back to life no. Can't bury in the air however. Out of a flying machine. Wonder does the news go about whenever a fresh one is let down. Underground communication. We learned that from them. Wouldn't be surprised. Regular square feed for them. Flies come before he's well dead. Got wind of Dignam. They wouldn't care about the smell of it. Saltwhite crumbling mush of corpse: smell, taste like raw white turnips.

The gates glimmered in front: still open. Back to the world again. Enough of this place. Brings you a bit nearer every time. Last time I was here was Mrs. Sinico's funeral. Poor papa too. The love that kills. And even scraping up the earth at night with a lantern like that case I read of to get at fresh buried females or even putrefied with running gravesores. Give you the creeps after a bit. I will appear to you after death. You will see my ghost after death. My ghost will haunt you after death. There is another world after death named hell. I do not like that other world she wrote. No more do I. Plenty to see and hear and feel yet. Feel live warm beings near you. Let them sleep in their maggoty beds. They are not going to get me this innings. Warm beds: warm fullblooded life.

Martin Cunningham emerged from a sidepath, talking gravely.

Solicitor, I think, I know his face. Menton. John Henry, solicitor, commissioner for oaths and affidavits. Dignam used to be in his office. Mat Dillon's long ago. Jolly Mat convicial evenings. Cold fowl, cigars, the Tantalus glasses. Heart of gold really. Yes, Menton. Got his rag out that evening on the bowling green because I sailed inside him. Pure fluke of mine: the bias. Why he took such a rooted dislike to me. Hate at first sight. Molly and Floey Dillon linked under the lilactree, laughing. Fellow always like that, mortified if women are by.

Got a dinge in the side of his hat. Carriage probably.

— Excuse me, sir, Mr. Bloom said beside them. They stopped.

— Your hat is a little crushed, Mr. Bloom said, pointing.

John Henry Menton stared at him for an instant without moving.

— There, Martin Cunningham helped, pointing also.

John Henry Menton took off his hat, bulged out the dinge and smoothed the nap with care on his coatsleeve. He clapped the hat on his head again.

— It's all right now, Martin Cunningham said. John Henry Menton jerked his head down in acknowledgment.

— Thank you, he said shortly.

They walked on towards the gates. Mr. Bloom, chapfallen, drew behind a few paces so as not to overhear. Martin laying down the law. Martin could wind a sappyhead like that round his little finger without his seeing it.

Oyster eyes. Never mind. Be sorry after perhaps when it dawns on him. Get the pull over him 5 that way.

Thank you. How grand we are this morning.

Franz Kafka : 1883–1924

Franz Kafka was born in Prague on July 3, 1883. Although determined early in life that nothing should prevent him from accomplishing his art, he completed his studies of law at the German University of Prague, where he received his doctorate in jurisprudence. Looking for a job that would occupy him during only part of the day, he accepted a position with one of the semi-official insurance companies in his native city. There he worked for years, until poor health made it necessary for him to enter a sanitarium.

In his youth, Kafka's relations with his parents were of a peculiar nature. In more than one respect, he felt embarrassed and impeded in his physical and intellectual growth by his father's vitality and the authority he exercised upon his children. An unrelieved feeling of guilt, stemming from this feeling of oppression, is clearly perceptible in many of Kafka's works. In a recently published letter to his father — which was held by his mother and never delivered to him — Kafka tries to account for his psychological constitution resulting from such a precarious relationship.

Max Brod states in his biography that in life Kafka displayed much sense of humor and a charm which endeared him to his friends and colleagues. It was into his works that Kafka poured all his unhappiness, pessimism, doubt and despair. Born a Jew, with but few — and those only casual — connections with orthodox religion, Kafka gradually came to an understanding of the essence of Judaism, both orthodox and enlightened. His works are often a dialectical expression of his attitude toward the various aspects of religious belief and of the absolute incompatibility of God with man.

Kafka's sensitiveness and general emotional disposition were the cause of his failure to tie himself permanently to the objects of his love. His excessive conscientiousness and his lack of decision prevented him from marrying a girl from Berlin to whom, over a period of approximately five years, he had been twice engaged. Kafka was always afraid of making decisions; Fate had to make them for him. His lungs were badly affected, and after repeated hemorrhages, he developed a tuberculosis of the larynx. After a stay in a sanitarium and later in a clinic near Vienna, Kafka died on June 3, 1924, less than forty-two years old.

All during his life, Kafka had been opposed to the publication of his works — and it is only due to the efforts of Max Brod who broke his promise not to publish the literary heritage of his friend that we now possess Kafka's three full-length novels, *The Trial*, *The Castle*, and *America*. Only three volumes of short stories, which contain the well-known "The Metamorphosis," "In the Penal Colony," and "The Judgment," were published in his lifetime. Much of his work, however, is irretrievably lost. The diaries in their present form, for instance, contain entries made over a period of a few years only. The rest was destroyed by the author himself. Of Kafka's letters, only his correspondence with Milena, one of the women to whom he was devoted, has been published so far.

Kafka's style of writing is expressionistic; although he shows particular fondness for the description of details, his plots revolve about one basic spiritual situation, which is the sudden metamorphosis of individual characters and their attempt to explain that alienation. Kafka's heroes, whose names are thinly veiled pseudonyms of his own — K, Karl Rossmann, Garta — struggle with the unknown. They try to understand an order of existence which is alien to them and which they will never comprehend.

The action unfolds as the protagonist himself sees it; its scenes are not real, but resemble dreams and visions. This accounts for the sudden transitions and transpositions as well as for the co-existence, in space and time, of various levels of action. Kafka's writings tend to become allegories of the mind, but many of them are more flexible and assume symbolic character. They symbolize the anxiety and the frustration of the generation between the two world wars.

SUGGESTED REFERENCES: Charles Neider, *The Frozen Sea: A Study of Franz Kafka* (1948); Ronald Gray, ed., *Franz Kafka. A Collection of Critical Essays* (1962); Heinz Politzer, *Franz Kafka, Parable and Paradox* (1962).

In the following two stories is described, symbolically, the position of the artist in society. The stories are ironical in so far as the voluntary detachment of the artist — in this case, the trapeze and hunger artists — goes hand in hand with the loss of interest in his performance among the public. "First Sorrow" excludes the public altogether and only relates the artist's deliberate exile on the trapeze. It shows how this deliberation is transformed into an urge which ends in reflection and sorrow. Thus, the exceptional role of the artist in the world (his severance from it) becomes mere eccentricity (the double trapeze). Reflection and sorrow, however, are of a special kind. The artist has to be treated like a child by the manager who is afraid of losing this sensational attraction.

"A Hunger Artist" is more serious in its approach to the problem. Here the artist's genius is seen to be destructive rather than productive. For him, to hunger is a *must*, and no longer an art, as the public is made to believe. It is only his personal realization of despair which, for the sake of publicity, has to be portioned out in forty-day periods by the manager. Quite content with being left alone — and yet still hungering for attention — the artist dies of hunger, himself the only one aware of the genuineness and the achievement of his art. His cage is emptied, and a panther, the symbol of life in the raw, substituted for the artist.

First Sorrow [1]

A trapeze artist — this art, practiced high in the vaulted domes of the great variety theaters, is admittedly one of the most difficult humanity can achieve — had so arranged his life that, as long as he kept working in the same building, he never came down from his trapeze by night or day, at

[1] This story and "A Hunger Artist" are reprinted from Franz Kafka, *The Penal Colony*, copyright 1948, by permission of Schocken Books, Inc.

first only from a desire to perfect his skill, but later because custom was too strong for him. All his needs, very modest needs at that, were supplied by relays of attendants who watched from below and sent up and hauled down again in specially constructed containers whatever he required. This way of living caused no particular inconvenience to the theatrical people, except that, when other turns were on the stage, his being still up aloft, which could not be dissembled, proved somewhat distracting, as also the fact that, although at such times he mostly kept very still, he drew a stray glance here and there from the public. Yet the management overlooked this, because he was an extraordinary and unique artist. And of course they recognized that this mode of life was no mere prank, and that only in this way could he really keep himself in constant practice and his art at the pitch of its perfection.

Besides, it was quite healthful up there, and when in the warmer seasons of the year the side windows all round the dome of the theater were thrown open and sun and fresh air came pouring irresistibly into the dusky vault, it was even beautiful. True, his social life was somewhat limited, only sometimes a fellow acrobat swarmed up the ladder to him, and then they both sat on the trapeze, leaning left and right against the supporting ropes, and chatted, or builders' workmen repairing the roof exchanged a few words with him through an open window, or the fireman, inspecting the emergency lighting in the top gallery, called over to him something that sounded respectful but could hardly be made out. Otherwise nothing disturbed his seclusion; occasionally, perhaps, some theater hand straying through the empty theater of an afternoon gazed thoughtfully up into the great height of the roof, almost beyond eyeshot, where the trapeze artist, unaware that he was being observed, practiced his art or rested.

The trapeze artist could have gone on living peacefully like that, had it not been for the inevitable journeys from place to place, which he found extremely trying. Of course his manager saw to it that his sufferings were not prolonged one moment more than necessary; for town travel, racing automobiles were used, which whirled him, by night if possible or in the earliest hours of the morning, through the empty streets at breakneck speed, too slow all the same for the trapeze artist's impatience; for railway journeys, a whole compartment was reserved, in which the trapeze artist, as a possible though wretched alternative to his usual way of living, could pass the time up on the luggage rack; in the next town on their circuit, long before he arrived, the trapeze was already slung up in the theater and all the doors leading to the stage were flung wide open, all corridors kept free — yet the manager never knew a happy moment until the trapeze artist set his foot on the rope ladder and in a twinkling, at long last, hung aloft on his trapeze.

Despite so many journeys having been successfully arranged by the manager, each new one embarrassed him again, for the journeys, apart from everything else, got on the nerves of the artist a great deal.

Once when they were again traveling together, the trapeze artist lying on the luggage rack dreaming, the manager leaning back in the opposite window seat reading a book, the trapeze artist addressed his companion in a low voice. The manager was immediately all attention. The trapeze artist, biting his lips, said that he must always in future have two trapezes for his performance instead of only one, two trapezes opposite each other. The manager at once agreed. But the trapeze artist, as if to show that the manager's consent counted for as little as his refusal, said that never again would he perform on only one trapeze, in no circumstances whatever. The very idea that it might happen at all seemed to make him shudder. The manager, watchfully feeling his way, once more emphasized his entire agreement, two trapezes were better than one, besides it would be an advantage to have a second bar, more variety could be introduced into the performance. At that the trapeze artist suddenly burst into tears. Deeply distressed, the manager sprang to his feet and asked what was the matter, then getting no answer climbed up on the seat and caressed him, cheek to cheek, so that his own face was bedabbled by the trapeze artist's tears. Yet it took much questioning and soothing endearment until the trapeze artist sobbed: "Only the one bar in my hands — how can I go on living!" That made it somewhat easier for the manager to comfort him; he promised to wire from the very next station for a second trapeze to be installed in the first town on their circuit; reproached himself for having let the artist work so long on only one trapeze, and thanked and praised him warmly for having at last brought the mistake to his notice. And so he succeeded in reassuring the trapeze artist, little by little, and was able to go back to his corner. But he himself was far from reassured, with deep uneasiness he kept glancing secretly at the trapeze artist over the top of his book. Once such ideas began to torment him, would they ever quite leave him alone? Would they not rather increase in urgency? Would they not threaten his very existence? And indeed the manager believed he could see, during the apparently peaceful sleep which had succeeded the fit of tears, the first furrows of care engraving themselves upon the trapeze artist's smooth, childlike forehead.

A Hunger Artist

During these last decades the interest in professional fasting has markedly diminished. It used to pay very well to stage such great performances under one's own management, but today that is quite impossible. We live in a different world now. At one time the whole town took a lively interest in the hunger artist; from day to day of his fast the excitement mounted; everybody wanted to see him at least once a day; there were people who bought season tickets for the last few days and sat from morning till night in front of his small barred cage; even in the nighttime there were visiting hours, when the whole effect was heightened by torch flares; on fine days the cage was set out in the open air, and then it was the children's special treat to see the hunger artist; for their elders he was often just a joke that happened to be in fashion, but the children stood openmouthed, holding each other's hands for greater security, marveling at him as he sat there pallid in black tights, with his ribs sticking out so prominently, not even on a seat but down among straw on the ground, sometimes giving a courteous nod, answering questions with a constrained smile, or perhaps stretching an arm through the bars so that one might feel how thin it was, and then again withdrawing deep into himself, paying no attention to anyone or anything, not even to the all-important striking of the clock that was the only piece of furniture in his cage, but merely staring into vacancy with half-shut eyes, now and then taking a sip from a tiny glass of water to moisten his lips.

Besides casual onlookers there were also relays of permanent watchers selected by the public, usually butchers, strangely enough, and it was their task to watch the hunger artist day and night, three of them at a time, in case he should have some secret recourse to nourishment. This was nothing but a formality, instituted to reassure the masses, for the initiates knew well enough that during his fast the artist would never in any circumstances, not even under forcible compulsion, swallow the smallest morsel of food; the honor of his profession forbade it. Not every watcher, of course, was capable of understanding this, there were often groups of night watchers who were very lax in carrying out their duties and deliberately huddled together in a retired corner to play cards with great absorption, obviously intending to give the hunger artist the chance of a little refreshment, which they supposed he could draw from some private hoard. Nothing annoyed the artist more than such watchers; they made him miserable; they made his fast seem unendurable; sometimes he mastered his feebleness sufficiently to sing during their watch for as long as he could keep going, to show them how unjust their suspicions were. But that was of little use; they only wondered at his cleverness in being able to fill his mouth even while singing. Much more to his taste were the watchers who sat close up to the bars, who were not content with the dim night lighting of the hall but focused him in the full glare of the electric pocket torch given them by the impresario. The harsh light did not trouble him at all, in any case he could never sleep properly, and he could always drowse a little, whatever the light, at any hour, even when the hall was thronged with noisy onlookers. He was quite happy at the prospect of spending a sleepless night with such watchers; he was ready to exchange jokes with them, to tell them stories out of his nomadic life, anything at all to keep them awake and demonstrate to them again that he had no eatables in his cage and that he was fasting as not one of them could fast. But his happiest moment was when the morning came and an enormous breakfast was brought them, at his expense, on which they flung themselves with the keen appetite of healthy men after a weary night of wakefulness. Of course there were people who argued that this breakfast was an unfair attempt to bribe the watchers, but that was going rather too far, and when they were invited to take on a night's vigil without a breakfast, merely for the sake of the cause, they made themselves scarce, although they stuck stubbornly to their suspicions.

Such suspicions, anyhow, were a necessary accompaniment to the profession of fasting. No one could possibly watch the hunger artist continuously, day and night, and so no one could produce first-hand evidence that the fast had really been rigorous and continuous; only the artist himself could know that, he was therefore bound to be the sole completely satisfied spectator of his own fast. Yet for other reasons he was never satisfied; it was not perhaps mere fasting that had brought him to such skeleton thinness that many people had regretfully to keep away from his exhibitions, because the sight of him was too much for them, perhaps it was dissatisfaction with himself that had worn him down. For he alone knew, what no other initiate knew, how easy it was to fast. It was the easiest thing in the world. He made no secret of this, yet people did not believe him, at the best they set him down as modest, most of them, however, thought he was out for publicity or else was some kind of cheat who found it easy to fast because he had discovered a way of making it easy, and then had the impudence to admit the fact, more or less. He had to put up with all that, and in the course of time had got used to it, but his inner dissatisfaction always rankled, and never yet, after any term of fasting — this must be granted to his credit — had he left the cage of his own free will. The longest period of fasting was fixed by his impresario at forty days, beyond that term he was not allowed to go, not even in great cities, and there was good reason for it, too. Experience had proved that for about forty days the interest of the public could be stimulated by a steadily increasing pressure of advertisement, but after that the town began to lose interest, sympathetic support began notably to fall off; there were of course local variations as between one town and another or one country and another, but as a general rule forty days marked the limit. So on the fortieth day the flower-bedecked cage was opened, enthusiastic spectators filled the hall, a military band played, two doctors entered the cage to measure the results of the fast, which were announced through a megaphone, and finally two young ladies appeared, blissful at having been selected for the honor, to help the hunger artist down the few steps leading to a small table on which was spread a carefully chosen invalid repast. And at this very moment the artist always turned stubborn. True, he would entrust his bony arms to the outstretched helping hands of the ladies bending over him, but stand up he would not. Why stop fasting at this particular moment, after forty days of it? He had held out for a long time, an illimitably long time; why stop now, when he was in his best fasting form, or rather, not yet quite in his best fasting form? Why should he be cheated of the fame he would get for fasting longer, for being not only the record hunger artist of all time, which presumably he was already, but for beating his own record by a performance beyond human imagination, since he felt that there were no limits to his capacity for fasting? His public pretended to admire him so much, why should it have so little patience with him; if he could endure fasting longer, why shouldn't the public endure it? Besides, he was tired, he was comfortable sitting in the straw, and now he was supposed to lift himself to his full height and go down to a meal the very thought of which gave him a nausea that only the presence of the ladies kept him from betraying, and even that with an effort. And he looked up into the eyes of the ladies who were apparently so friendly and in reality so cruel, and shook his head, which felt too heavy on its strengthless neck. But then there happened yet again what always happened. The impresario came forward, without a word — for the band made speech impossible — lifted his arms in the air above the artist, as if inviting Heaven to look down upon its creature here in the straw, this suffering martyr, which indeed he was, although in quite another sense; grasped him round the emaciated waist, with exaggerated caution, so that the frail condition he was in might be appreciated; and committed him to the care of the blenching ladies, not without secretly giving him a shaking so that his legs and body tottered and swayed. The artist now submitted completely; his head lolled on his breast as if it had landed there by chance; his body was hollowed out; his legs in a spasm of self-preservation clung close to each other at the knees, yet scraped on the ground as if it were not really solid ground, as if they were only trying to find solid ground; and the whole weight of his body, a featherweight after all, relapsed onto one of the ladies, who, looking round for help and panting a little — this post of honor was not at all what she had expected it to be — first stretched her neck as far as she could to keep her face at least free from contact with the artist, then finding this impossible, and her more fortunate companion not coming to her aid but merely holding extended on her own trembling hand the little bunch of knuckle-bones that was the artist's, to the great delight of the spectators burst into tears and had to be replaced by an attendant who had long been stationed in readiness. Then came the food, a little of which the impresario managed to get between the artist's lips, while he sat in a kind of half-fainting trance, to the accompaniment of cheerful patter designed to distract the public's attention from the artist's condition; after that, a toast was drunk to the public, supposedly prompted by a whisper from the artist in the impresario's ear; the band confirmed it with a mighty flourish, the spectators melted away, and no one had any cause to be dissatisfied with the proceedings, no one except the hunger artist himself, he only, as always.

So he lived for many years, with small regular intervals of recuperation, in visible glory, honored by the world, yet in spite of that troubled in spirit, and all the more troubled because no one would take his trouble seriously. What comfort could he possibly need? What more could he possibly wish for? And if some good-natured person, feeling sorry for him, tried to console him by pointing out that his melancholy was probably caused by fasting, it could happen, especially when he had been fasting for some time, that he reacted with an outburst of fury and to the general alarm began to shake the bars of his cage like a wild animal. Yet the impresario had a way of punishing these outbreaks which he rather enjoyed putting into operation. He would apologize publicly for the artist's behavior, which was only to be excused, he admitted, because of the irritability caused by fasting; a condition hardly to be understood by well-fed people; then by natural transition he went on to mention the artist's equally incomprehensible boast that he could fast for much longer than he was doing; he praised the high ambition, the good will, the great self-denial undoubtedly implicit in such a statement; and then quite simply countered it by bringing out photographs, which were also on sale to the public, showing the artist on the fortieth day of a fast lying in bed almost dead from exhaustion. This perversion of the truth, familiar to the artist though it was, always unnerved him afresh and proved too much for him. What was a consequence of the premature ending of his fast was here presented as the cause of it! To fight against this lack of understanding, against a whole world of non-understanding, was impossible. Time and again in good faith he stood by the bars listening to the impresario, but as soon as the photographs appeared he always let go and sank with a groan back on to his straw, and the reassured public could once more come close and gaze at him.

A few years later when the witnesses of such scenes called them to mind, they often failed to understand themselves at all. For meanwhile the aforementioned change in public interest had set in; it seemed to happen almost overnight; there may have been profound causes for it, but who was going to bother about that; at any rate the pampered hunger artist suddenly found himself deserted one fine day by the amusement seekers, who went streaming past him to other more favored attractions. For the last time the impresario hurried him over half Europe to discover whether the old interest might still survive here and there; all in vain; everywhere, as if by secret agreement, a positive revulsion from professional fasting was in evidence. Of course it could not really have sprung up so suddenly as all that, and many premonitory symptoms which had not been sufficiently remarked or suppressed during the rush and glitter of success now came retrospectively to mind, but it was now too late to take any countermeasures. Fasting would surely come into fashion again at some future date, yet that was no comfort for those living in the present. What, then, was the hunger artist to do? He had been applauded by thousands in his time and could hardly come down to showing himself in a street booth at village fairs, and as for adopting another profession, he was not only too old for that but too fanatically devoted to fasting. So he took leave of the impresario, his partner in an unparalleled career, and hired himself to a large circus; in order to spare his own feelings he avoided reading the conditions of his contract.

A large circus with its enormous traffic in replacing and recruiting men, animals and apparatus can always find a use for people at any time, even for a hunger artist, provided of course that he does not ask too much, and in this particular case anyhow it was not only the artist who was taken on but his famous and long-known name as well, indeed considering the peculiar nature of his performance, which was not impaired by advancing age, it could not be objected that here was an artist past his prime, no longer at the height of his professional skill, seeking a refuge in some quiet corner of a circus, on the contrary, the hunger artist averred that he could fast as well as ever, which was entirely credible, he even alleged that if he were allowed to fast as he liked, and this was at once promised him without more ado, he could astound the world by establishing a record never yet achieved, a statement which certainly provoked a smile among the other professionals, since it left out of account the change in public opinion, which the hunger artist in his zeal conveniently forgot.

He had not, however, actually lost his sense of the real situation and took it as a matter of course that he and his cage should be stationed, not in the middle of the ring as a main attraction, but outside, near the animal cages, on a site that was after all easily accessible. Large and gaily painted placards made a frame for the cage and announced what was to be seen inside it. When the public came thronging out in the intervals to see the animals, they could hardly avoid passing the hunger artist's cage and stopping there for a moment, perhaps they might even have stayed longer had not those pressing behind them in the narrow gangway, who did not understand why they should be held up on their way towards the excitements of the menagerie, made it impossible for anyone to stand gazing quietly for any length of time. And that was the reason why the hunger artist, who had of course been looking forward to these visiting hours as the main achievement of his life, began instead to shrink from them. At first he could hardly wait for the intervals; it was exhilarating to watch the crowds come streaming his way, until only too soon — not even the most obstinate self-deception, clung to almost consciously, could hold out against the fact — the conviction was borne in upon him that these people, most of them, to judge from their actions, again and again, without exception, were all on their way to the menagerie. And the first sight of them from the distance remained the best. For when they reached his cage he was at once deafened by the storm of shouting and abuse that arose from the two contending factions, which renewed themselves continuously, of those who wanted to stop and stare at him — he soon began to dislike them more than the others — not out of real interest but only out of obstinate self-assertiveness, and those who wanted to go straight on to the animals. When the first great rush was past, the stragglers came along, and these, whom nothing could have prevented from stopping to look at him as long as they had breath, raced past with long strides, hardly even glancing at him, in their haste to get to the menagerie in time. And all too rarely did it happen that he had a stroke of luck, when some father of a family fetched up before him with his children, pointed a finger at the hunger artist and explained at length what the phenomenon meant, telling stories of earlier years when he himself had watched similar but much more thrilling performances, and the children, still rather uncomprehending, since neither inside nor outside school had they been sufficiently prepared for this lesson — what did they care about fasting? — yet showed by the brightness of their intent eyes that new and better times might be coming. Perhaps, said the hunger artist to himself many a time, things would be a little better if his cage were set not quite so near the menagerie. That made it too easy for people to make their choice, to say nothing of what he suffered from the stench of the menagerie, the animals' restlessness by night, the carrying past of raw lumps of flesh for the beasts of prey, the roaring at feeding times, which depressed him continually. But he did not dare to lodge a complaint with the management; after all, he had the animals to thank for the troops of people who passed his cage, among whom there might always be one here and there to take an interest in him, and who could tell where they might seclude him if he called attention to his existence and thereby to the fact that, strictly speaking, he was only an impediment on the way to the menagerie.

A small impediment, to be sure, one that grew steadily less. People grew familiar with the strange idea that they could be expected, in times like these, to take an interest in a hunger artist, and with this familiarity the verdict went out against him. He might fast as much as he could, and he did so; but nothing could save him now, people passed him by. Just try to explain to anyone the art of fasting! Anyone who has no feeling for it cannot be made to understand it. The fine placards grew dirty and illegible, they were torn down; the little notice board telling the number of fast days achieved, which at first was changed carefully every day, had long stayed at the same figure, for after the first few weeks even this small task seemed pointless to the staff; and so the artist simply fasted on and on, as he had once dreamed of doing, and it was no trouble to him, just as he had always foretold, but no one counted the days, no one, not even the artist himself, knew what records he was already breaking, and his heart grew heavy. And when once in a time some leisurely passer-by stopped, made merry over the old figure on the board and spoke of swindling, that was in its way the stupidest lie ever invented by indifference and inborn malice, since it was not the hunger artist who was cheating, he was working honestly, but the world was cheating him of his reward.

Many more days went by, however, and that too came to an end. An overseer's eye fell on the cage one day and he asked the attendants why this perfectly good stage should be left standing there unused with dirty straw inside it; nobody knew, until one man, helped out by the notice board, remem-bered about the hunger artist. They poked into the straw with sticks and found him in it. "Are you still fasting?" asked the overseer, "when on earth do you mean to stop?" "Forgive me, everybody," whispered the hunger artist; only the overseer, who had his ear to the bars, understood him. "Of course," said the overseer, and tapped his forehead with a finger to let the attendants know what state the man was in, "we forgive you." "I always wanted you to admire my fasting," said the hunger artist. "We do admire it," said the overseer, affably. "But you shouldn't admire it," said the hunger artist. "Well then we don't admire it," said the overseer, "but why shouldn't we admire it?" "Because I have to fast, I can't help it," said the hunger artist. "What a fellow you are," said the overseer, "and why can't you help it?" "Because," said the hunger artist, lifting his head a little and speaking, with his lips pursed, as if for a kiss, right into the overseer's ear, so that no syllable might be lost, "because I couldn't find the food I liked. If I had found it, believe me, I should have made no fuss and stuffed myself like you or anyone else." These were his last words, but in his dimming eyes remained the firm though no longer proud persuasion that he was still continuing to fast.

"Well, clear this out now!" said the overseer, and they buried the hunger artist, straw and all. Into the cage they put a young panther. Even the most insensitive felt it refreshing to see this wild creature leaping around the cage that had so long been dreary. The panther was all right. The food he liked was brought him without hesitation by the attendants; he seemed not even to miss his freedom; his noble body, furnished almost to the bursting point with all that it needed, seemed to carry freedom around with it too; somewhere in his jaws it seemed to lurk; and the joy of life streamed with such ardent passion from his throat that for the onlookers it was not easy to stand the shock of it. But they braced themselves, crowded round the cage, and did not want ever to move away.

Eugene O'Neill · 1888-1953

Generally considered America's greatest dramatist, Eugene Gladstone O'Neill came naturally by his interest in the theater. He was born in a New York hotel at the corner of 43rd Street and Broadway — in the heart of the theatrical district — on October 16, 1888. His father, an able actor of the time, toured America for some years with a company playing *The Count of Monte Cristo*, and the young Eugene traveled with the company. Later on O'Neill was sent to Catholic schools, to

Betts Academy at Stamford, Connecticut, and finally went to Princeton. Then followed years of roughing it, of gaining first-hand experience with life, of coming to know people, their habits of thought, their manner of living — particularly those people whom conventional society looks upon with suspicion.

In December, 1912, O'Neill's health broke. He was threatened with tuberculosis and was forced to enter a sanitarium. These months of seclusion and rest gave O'Neill time to take stock of himself, his experience, and his interests. He read widely, particularly the work of Strindberg. For a while he wrote verses and many one-act plays. One or two full-length plays which he submitted to managers were returned unread, one manager saying that "plays by actors' sons are never good." In 1914 appeared the first volume of plays — *Thirst and Other One-Act Plays*. The next year (1914–1915) the writer spent at Harvard as a member of Professor Baker's "47 Workshop," studying to perfect his technique. After that he joined a young group of amateurs, the "Provincetown Players," who were the first to produce one of his plays, *Bound East for Cardiff.*

Three of his early dramas, *Beyond the Horizon* (1920), *Anna Christie* (1922), and *Strange Interlude* (1928), won Pulitzer Prizes. In 1936 he was awarded the much coveted Nobel Prize. Other notable plays by O'Neill are: *Emperor Jones* (1920), *The Hairy Ape* (1922), *Desire Under the Elms* (1924), *Marco Millions* (1928), *The Great God Brown* (1926), *Dynamo* (1929), *Mourning Becomes Electra* (1931), *Ah, Wilderness* (1933), and *The Iceman Cometh* (1946). Ill health prevented O'Neill from writing a cycle of nine plays. *A Touch of the Poet* (1957) and the unfinished *More Stately Mansions* (1964), which belong to this cycle, were first produced by the Royal Dramatic Theater in Stockholm. In the same theater, *Long Day's Journey into Night* (1955) had its world premiere two years after O'Neill's death. In this autobiographical play, which combines in one action most of the important themes O'Neill had touched upon in his earlier works and was written "in tears and blood", O'Neill became the haunted hero of his own tragic life.

O'Neill brought into the American theater a strength and a vitality which had not been characteristic of the earlier American drama. He made new and interesting use of established devices and techniques of the theater of the past. In addition, he showed a great deal of versatility and real interest in experimentation. It is for these advances in techniques, his insight into the soul of modern man, and his versatility and originality of expression that O'Neill may be considered one of the important playwrights of the first half of the twentieth century.

SUGGESTED REFERENCES: E. A. Engel, *The Haunted Heroes of Eugene O'Neill* (1953); Oscar Cargill, ed., *O'Neill and His Plays: Four Decades of Criticism* (1961); Arthur and Barbara Gelb, *Eugene O'Neill* (1962).

The Hairy Ape [1]

A Comedy of Ancient and Modern Life in Eight Scenes

The Hairy Ape, characterized by the language of realism, expresses a desire for a life not attainable. As in several of O'Neill's plays, we are told that a trust of the intellect may be dangerous. Yank may well be a symbol of civilization, itself as yet only half-emergent from primitivism, just as the play as a whole would seem to assess the values of society. Is progress desirable? Are machines or capitalism or labor to rule? The drama is a tragedy of "belonging"; Yank, accosted by the policeman, pleads guilty: "I was born, see? Sure, dat's de charge . . . I was born, get me!"

The play is expressionistic in intent and technique. The emphasis on geometric design in the forecastle scene, the "brazen metallic quality" of the chorus-like dialogue in the stoke-hole, the mechanical movements of the "gaudy marionettes" in the church-parade on Fifth Avenue, the voices in the jail, the rhythm of stoking in the bowels of the liner — these are devices used by O'Neill to project the inner strivings and longings of man caught in the confusion of the modern world.

[1] Reprinted by permission of Random House, Inc.

Characters

ROBERT SMITH, "YANK"
PADDY
LONG
MILDRED DOUGLAS   5
HER AUNT
SECOND ENGINEER
A GUARD
A SECRETARY OF AN ORGANIZATION
STOKERS, LADIES, GENTLEMEN, ETC.   10

Scenes

SCENE I: The firemen's forecastle of an ocean liner
— an hour after sailing from New York.

SCENE II: Section of promenade deck, two days   15
out — morning.

SCENE III: The stokehole.   A few minutes later.

SCENE IV: Same as Scene I.   Half an hour later.

SCENE V: Fifth Avenue, New York.   Three weeks   20
later.

SCENE VI: An island near the city.   The next
night.

SCENE VII: In the city.   About a month later.

SCENE VIII: In the city.   Twilight of the next day.   25

SCENE ONE

SCENE: *The firemen's forecastle of a transatlantic
liner an hour after sailing from New York for the
voyage across.   Tiers of narrow, steel bunks, three*   30
*deep, on all sides.   An entrance in rear.   Benches
on the floor before the bunks.   The room is crowded
with men, shouting, cursing, laughing, singing
— a confused, inchoate uproar swelling into a sort
of unity, a meaning — the bewildered, furious,*   35
*baffled defiance of a beast in a cage.   Nearly all
the men are drunk.   Many bottles are passed
from hand to hand.   All are dressed in dungaree
pants, heavy ugly shoes.   Some wear singlets,
but the majority are stripped to the waist.*   40

*The treatment of this scene, or of any other
scene in the play, should by no means be naturalistic.   The effect sought after is a cramped space
in the bowels of a ship, imprisoned by white steel.
The lines of bunks, the uprights supporting them,*   45
*cross each other like the steel framework of a cage.
The ceiling crushes down upon the men's heads.
They cannot stand upright.   This accentuates
the natural stooping posture which shoveling coal
and the resultant overdevelopment of back and*   50
*shoulder muscles have given them.   The men
themselves should resemble those pictures in which
the appearance of Neanderthal Man* [1] *is guessed
at.   All are hairy-chested, with long arms of
tremendous power, and low, receding brows above*   55

[1] Primitive man of ancient cave-dwelling epoch.

*their small, fierce, resentful eyes.   All the civilized
white races are represented, but except for the
slight differentiation in color of hair, skin, eyes,
all these men are alike.*

The curtain rises on a tumult of sound. YANK
*is seated in the foreground.   He seems broader,
fiercer, more truculent, more powerful, more sure
of himself than the rest.   They respect his superior
strength — the grudging respect of fear.   Then,
too, he represents to them a self-expression, the
very last word in what they are, their most highly
developed individual.*

Voices.
    Gif me trink dere, you!
    'Ave a wet!
    Salute!
    Gesundheit!
    Skoal!
    Drunk as a lord, God stiffen you!
    Here's how!
    Luck!
    Pass back that bottle, damn you!
    Pourin' it down his neck!
    Ho, Froggy!   Where the devil have you been?
    La Touraine.
    I hit him smash in yaw, py Gott!
    Jenkins — the First — he's a rotten swine ——
    And the coppers nabbed him — and I run ——
    I like peer better.   It don't pig head gif you.
    A slut, I'm sayin'!   She robbed me aslape ——
    To hell with 'em all!
    You're a bloody liar!
    Say dot again!
        (*Commotion.   Two men about to fight are
            pulled apart.*)
    No scrappin' now!
    Tonight ——
    See who's the best man!
    Bloody Dutchman!
    Tonight on the for'ard square.
    I'll bet on Dutchy.
    He packa da wallop, I tella you!
    Shut up, Wop!
    No fightin', maties.   We're all chums, ain't we?
        (*A voice starts bawling a song.*)
    "Beer, beer, glorious beer!
    Fill yourselves right up to here."

YANK (*for the first time seeming to take notice of
the uproar about him, turns around threateningly
— in a tone of contemptuous authority*).   Choke off
dat noise!   Where d'yuh get dat beer stuff?   Beer,
hell!   Beer's for goils — and Dutchmen.   Me for
somep'n wit a kick to it!   Gimme a drink, one of
youse guys.   (*Several bottles are eagerly offered.
He takes a tremendous gulp at one of them; then,*

keeping the bottle in his hand, glares belligerently at the owner, who hastens to acquiesce in this robbery by saying:) All righto, Yank. Keep it and have another. (YANK *contemptuously turns his back on the crowd again. For a second there is an embarrassed silence. Then* ——)

Voices.

We must be passing the Hook.

She's beginning to roll to it.

Six days in hell — and then Southampton.

Py Yesus, I vish somepody take my first vatch for me!

Gittin' seasick, Square-head?

Drink up and forget it!

What's in your bottle?

Gin.

Dot's nigger trink.

Absinthe? It's doped. You'll go off your chump, Froggy!

Cochon! [1]

Whisky, that's the ticket!

Where's Paddy?

Going asleep.

Sing us that whisky song, Paddy.

(They all turn to an old, wizened Irishman who is dozing, very drunk, on the benches forward. His face is extremely monkey-like with all the sad, patient pathos of that animal in his small eyes.)

Singa da song, Caruso Pat!

He's gettin' old. The drink is too much for him.

He's too drunk.

Paddy (blinking about him, starts to his feet resentfully, swaying, holding on to the edge of a bunk). I'm never too drunk to sing. 'Tis only when I'm dead to the world I'd be wishful to sing at all. *(With a sort of sad contempt.)* "Whisky Johnny," ye want? A chanty, ye want? Now that's a queer wish from the ugly like of you, God help you. But no mather. *(He starts to sing in a thin, nasal, doleful tone):*

Oh, whisky is the life of man!
　　　　　(They all join in on this.)
Whisky! O Johnny!
Oh, whisky is the life of man!
Whisky for my Johnny! *(Again chorus.)*
Oh, whisky drove my old man mad!
Whisky! O Johnny!
Oh, whisky drove my old man mad!
Whisky for my Johnny!

Yank (again turning around scornfully). Aw hell! Nix on dat old sailing ship stuff! All dat bull's

[1] French word for *pig.*

dead, see? And you're dead, too, yuh damned old Harp, on'y yuh don't know it. Take it easy, see. Give us a rest. Nix on de loud noise. *(With a cynical grin.)* Can't youse see I'm tryin' to t'ink?

All (repeating the word after him as one with the same cynical amused mockery). Think! *(The chorused word has a brazen metallic quality as if their throats were phonograph horns. It is followed by a general uproar of hard, barking laughter.)*

Voices.

Don't be cracking your head wit ut, Yank.

You gat headache, py yingo!

One thing about it — it rhymes with drink!

Ha, ha, ha!

Drink, don't think!

Drink, don't think!

Drink, don't think!

(A whole chorus of voices has taken up this refrain, stamping on the floor, pounding on the benches with fists.)

Yank (taking a gulp from his bottle — good-naturedly). Aw right. Can de noise. I got yuh de foist time. *(The uproar subsides. A very drunken sentimental tenor begins to sing):*

"Far away in Canada,
　　Far across the sea,
　　There's a lass who fondly waits
　　　　Making a home for me ——"

Yank (fiercely contemptuous). Shut up, yuh lousy boob! Where d'yuh get dat tripe? Home? Home, hell! I'll make a home for yuh! I'll knock yuh dead. Home! T'hell wit home! Where d'yuh get dat tripe? Dis is home, see? What d'yuh want wit home? *(Proudly.)* I runned away from mine when I was a kid. On'y too glad to beat it, dat was me. Home was lickings for me, dat's all. But yuh can bet your shoit no one ain't never licked me since! Wanter try it, any of youse? Huh! I guess not. *(In a more placated but still contemptuous tone.)* Goils waitin' for yuh, huh? Aw, hell! Dat's all tripe. Dey don't wait for no one. Dey'd double-cross yuh for a nickel. Dey're all taits, get me? Treat 'em rough, dat's me. To hell wit 'em. Tarts, dat's what, de whole bunch of 'em.

Long (very drunk, jumps on a bench excitedly, gesticulating with a bottle in his hand). Listen 'ere, Comrades. Yank 'ere is right. 'E says this 'ere stinkin' ship is our 'ome. And 'e says as 'ome is 'ell. And 'e's right! This is 'ell. We lives in 'ell, Comrades — and right enough we'll die in it. *(Raging.)* And who's ter blame, I arsks yer? We ain't. We wasn't born this rotten way. All men is born free and ekal. That's in the bleedin'

Bible, maties. But what d'they care for the Bible
— them lazy, bloated swine what travels first
cabin? Them's the ones. They dragged us down
'til we're on'y wage slaves in the bowels of a
bloody ship, sweatin', burnin' up, eatin' coal dust!
Hit's them's ter blame — the damned Capitalist
clarss! (*There had been a gradual murmur of contemptuous resentment rising among the men until
now he is interrupted by a storm of catcalls, hisses,
boos, hard laughter.*)
    Voices.

> Turn it off!
> Shut up!
> Sit down!
> Closa da face!
> Tamn fool! (*Etc.*)

Yank (*standing up and glaring at* LONG). Sit
down before I knock yuh down! (LONG *makes
haste to efface himself.* YANK *goes on contemptuously.*) De Bible, huh? De Cap'tlist class, huh?
Aw nix on dat Salvation Army-Socialist bull.
Git a soapbox! Hire a hall! Come and be saved,
huh? Jerk us to Jesus, huh? Aw g'wan! I've
listened to lots of guys like you, see. Yuh're all
wrong. Wanter know what I t'ink? Yuh ain't
no good for no one. Yuh're de bunk. Yuh ain't
got no noive, get me? Yuh're yellow, dat's what.
Yellow, dat's you. Say! What's dem slobs in de
foist cabin got to do wit us? We're better men
dan dey are, ain't we? Sure! One of us guys
could clean up de whole mob wit one mit. Put
one of 'em down here for one watch in de stokehole,
what'd happen? Dey'd carry him off on a stretcher.
Dem boids don't amount to nothin'. Dey're just
baggage. Who makes dis old tub run? Ain't it
us guys? Well den, we belong, don't we? We
belong and dey don't. Dat's all. (*A loud chorus
of approval.* YANK *goes on.*) As for dis bein' hell
— aw, nuts! Yuh lost your noive, dat's what.
Dis is a man's job, get me? It belongs. It runs
dis tub. No stiffs need apply. But yuh're a stiff,
see? Yuh're yellow, dat's you.
    Voices (*with a great hard pride in them*).

> Righto!
> A man's job!
> Talk is cheap, Long.
> He never could hold up his end.
> Divil take him!
> Yank's right. We make it go.
> Py Gott, Yank say right ting!
> We don't need no one cryin' over us.
> Makin' speeches.
> Throw him out!
> Yellow!
> Chuck him overboard!
> I'll break his jaw for him!

(*They crowd around* LONG *threateningly.*)
    Yank (*half good-natured again — contemptuously*).
Aw, take it easy. Leave him alone. He ain't
woith a punch. Drink up. Here's how, whoever
owns dis. (*He takes a long swallow from his bottle.
All drink with him. In a flash all is hilarious
amiability again, back-slapping, loud talk, etc.*)
    Paddy (*who has been sitting in a blinking, melan-
choly daze — suddenly cries out in a voice full of
old sorrow*). We belong to this, you're saying?
We make the ship to go, you're saying? Yerra [1]
then, that Almighty God have pity on us! (*His
voice runs into the wail of a keen, he rocks back and
forth on his bench. The men stare at him, startled
and impressed in spite of themselves.*) Oh, to be
back in the fine days of my youth, ochone! [2] Oh,
there was fine beautiful ships them days — clippers
wid tall masts touching the sky — fine strong men
in them — men that was sons of the sea as if 'twas
the mother that bore them. Oh, the clean skins
of them, and the clear eyes, the straight backs and
full chests of them! Brave men they was, and
bold men surely! We'd be sailing out, bound down
round the Horn maybe. We'd be making sail in
the dawn, with a fair breeze, singing a chanty song
wid no care to it. And astern the land would be
sinking low and dying out, but we'd give it no heed
but a laugh, and never a look behind. For the
day that was, was enough, for we was free men
— and I'm thinking 'tis only slaves do be giving
heed to the day that's gone or the day to come
— until they're old like me. (*With a sort of
religious exaltation.*) Oh, to be scudding south
again wid the power of the Trade Wind driving her
on steady through the nights and the days! Full
sail on her! Nights and days! Nights when the
foam of the wake would be flaming wid fire, when
the sky'd be blazing and winking wid stars. Or
the full of the moon maybe. Then you'd see her
driving through the gray night, her sails stretching
aloft all silver and white, not a sound on the deck,
the lot of us dreaming dreams, till you'd believe
'twas no real ship at all you was on but a ghost
ship like the *Flying Dutchman* they say does be
roaming the seas forevermore widout touching a
port. And there was the days, too. A warm sun
on the clean decks. Sun warming the blood of
you, and wind over the miles of shiny green ocean
like strong drink to your lungs. Work — aye,
hard work — but who'd mind that at all? Sure,
you worked under the sky and 'twas work wid
skill and daring to it. And wid the day done, in
the dog watch, smoking me pipe at ease, the look-
out would be raising land maybe, and we'd see the
mountains of South Americy wid the red fire of

---

[1] An exclamation of surprise.   [2] alas.

the setting sun painting their white tops and the clouds floating by them! (*His tone of exaltation ceases. He goes on mournfully.*) Yerra, what's the use of talking? 'Tis a dead man's whisper. (*To* YANK *resentfully.*) 'Twas them days men belonged to ships, not now. 'Twas them days a ship was part of the sea, and a man was part of a ship, and the sea joined all together and made it one. (*Scornfully.*) Is it one wid this you'd be, Yank — black smoke from the funnels smudging the sea, smudging the decks — the bloody engines pounding and throbbing and shaking — wid divil a sight of sun or a breath of clean air — choking our lungs wid coal dust — breaking our backs and hearts in the hell of the stokehole — feeding the bloody furnace — feeding our lives along wid the coal, I'm thinking — caged in by steel from a sight of the sky like bloody apes in the Zoo! (*With a harsh laugh.*) Ho-ho, divil mend you! Is it to belong to that you're wishing? Is it a flesh and blood wheel of the engines you'd be?

Yank (*who has been listening with a contemptuous sneer, barks out the answer*). Sure ting! Dat's me. What about it?

Paddy (*as if to himself — with great sorrow*). Me time is past due. That a great wave wid sun in the heart of it may sweep me over the side sometime I'd be dreaming of the days that's gone!

Yank. Aw, yuh crazy Mick! (*He springs to his feet and advances on Paddy threateningly — then stops, fighting some queer struggle within himself — lets his hands fall to his sides — contemptuously.*) Aw, take it easy. Yuh're aw right, at dat. Yuh're bugs, dat's all — nutty as a cuckoo. All dat tripe yuh been pullin' — Aw, dat's all right. On'y it's dead, get me? Yuh don't belong no more, see. Yuh don't get de stuff. Yuh're too old. (*Disgustedly.*) But aw say, come up for air onct in a while, can't yuh? See what's happened since yuh croaked. (*He suddenly bursts forth vehemently, growing more and more excited.*) Say! Sure! Sure I meant it! What de hell — Say, lemme talk! Hey! Hey, you old Harp! Hey, youse guys! Say, listen to me — wait a moment — I gotta talk, see. I belong and he don't. He's dead but I'm livin'. Listen to me! Sure I'm part of de engines! Why de hell not! Dey move, don't dey? Dey're speed, ain't dey? Dey smash trou, don't dey? Twenty-five knots a hour! Dat's goin' some! Dat's new stuff! Dat belongs! But him, he's too old. He gets dizzy. Say, listen. All dat crazy tripe about nights and days; all dat crazy tripe about stars and moons; all dat crazy tripe about suns and winds, fresh air and de rest of it — Aw hell, dat's all a dope dream! Hittin' de pipe of de past, dat's what he's doin'. He's old

and don't belong no more. But me, I'm young! I'm in de pink! I move wit it! It, get me! I mean de ting dat's de guts of all dis. It ploughs trou all de tripe he's been sayin'. It blows dat up! It knocks dat dead! It slams dat offen de face of de oith! It, get me! De engines and de coal and de smoke and all de rest of it! He can't breathe and swallow coal dust, but I kin, see? Dat's fresh air for me! Dat's food for me! I'm new, get me? Hell in de stokehole? Sure! It takes a man to work in hell. Hell, sure, dat's my fav'rite climate. I eat it up! I git fat on it! It's me makes it hot! It's me makes it roar! It's me makes it move! Sure, on'y for me everyting stops. It all goes dead, get me? De noise and smoke and all de engines movin' de woild, dey stop. Dere ain't nothing' no more! Dat's what I'm sayin'. Everyting else dat makes de woild move, somep'n makes it move. It can't move witout somep'n else, see? Den yuh get down to me. I'm at de bottom, get me! Dere ain't nothin' foither. I'm de end! I'm de start! I start somep'n and de woild moves! It — dat's me! — de new dat's moiderin' de old! I'm de ting in coal dat makes it boin; I'm steam and oil for de engines; I'm de ting in noise dat makes yuh hear it; I'm smoke and express trains and steamers and factory whistles; I'm de ting in gold dat makes money! And I'm what makes iron into steel! Steel, dat stands for de whole ting! And I'm steel — steel — steel! I'm de muscles in steel, de punch behind it! (*As he says this he pounds with his fist against the steel bunks. All the men, roused to a pitch of frenzied self-glorification by his speech, do likewise. There is a deafening metallic roar, through which* YANK'S *voice can be heard bellowing.*) Slaves, hell! We run de whole woiks. All de rich guys dat tink dey're somep'n, dey ain't nothin'! Dey don't belong. But us guys, we're in de move, we're at de bottom, de whole ting is us! (PADDY *from the start of* YANK'S *speech has been taking one gulp after another from his bottle, at first frightenedly, as if he were afraid to listen, then desperately, as if to drown his senses, but finally has achieved complete indifferent, even amused, drunkenness.* YANK *sees his lips moving. He quells the uproar with a shout.*) Hey, youse guys, take it easy! Wait a moment! De nutty Harp is sayin' somep'n.

Paddy (*is heard now — throws his head back with a mocking burst of laughter*). Ho-ho-ho-ho-ho ——

Yank (*drawing back his fist, with a snarl*). Aw! Look out who yuh're givin' the bark!

Paddy (*begins to sing the "Miller of Dee" with enormous good nature*).

"I care for nobody, no, not I,
    And nobody cares for me."

Yank (good-natured himself in a flash, interrupts PADDY *with a slap on the bare back like a report).* Dat's de stuff! Now yuh're gettin' wise to somep'n. Care for nobody, dat's de dope! To hell wit 'em all! And nix on nobody else carin'. I kin care for myself, get me! *(Eight bells sound, muffled, vibrating through the steel walls as if some enormous brazen gong were imbedded in the heart of the ship. All the men jump up mechanically, file through the door silently close upon each other's heels in what is very like a prisoners' lockstep.* YANK *slaps* PADDY *on the back.)* Our watch, yuh old Harp! *(Mockingly.)* Come on down in hell. Eat up de coal dust. Drink in de heat. It's it, see! Act like yuh liked it, yuh better — or croak yuhself.

Paddy (with jovial defiance). To the divil wid it! I'll not report this watch. Let thim log me and be damned. I'm no slave the like of you. I'll be sittin' here at me ease, and drinking, and thinking, and dreaming dreams.

Yank (contemptuously). Tinkin' and dreamin', what'll that get yuh? What's tinkin' got to do wit it? We move, don't we? Speed, ain't it? Fog, dat's all you stand for. But we drive trou dat, don't we? We split dat up and smash trou — twenty-five knots a hour! *(Turns his back on* PADDY *scornfully.)* Aw, yuh make me sick! Yuh don't belong! *(He strides out the door in rear.* PADDY *hums to himself, blinking drowsily.)*

CURTAIN

SCENE TWO

SCENE: *Two days out. A section of the promenade deck.* MILDRED DOUGLAS *and her aunt are discovered reclining in deck chairs. The former is a girl of twenty, slender, delicate, with a pale, pretty face marred by a self-conscious expression of disdainful superiority. She looks fretful, nervous and discontented, bored by her own anemia. Her aunt is a pompous and proud — and fat — old lady. She is a type even to the point of a double chin and lorgnettes. She is dressed pretentiously, as if afraid her face alone would never indicate her position in life.* MILDRED *is dressed all in white.*

The impression to be conveyed by this scene is one of the beautiful, vivid life of the sea all about — sunshine on the deck in a great flood, the fresh sea wind blowing across it. In the midst of this, these two incongruous, artificial figures, inert and disharmonious, the elder like a gray lump of dough touched up with rouge, the younger looking as if the vitality of her stock had been sapped before she was conceived, so that she is the expression not of its life energy but merely of the artificialities that energy had won for itself in the spending.

Mildred (looking up with affected dreaminess). How the black smoke swirls back against the sky! Is it not beautiful?

Aunt (without looking up). I dislike smoke of any kind.

Mildred. My great-grandmother smoked a pipe — a clay pipe.

Aunt (ruffling). Vulgar!

Mildred. She was too distant a relative to be vulgar. Time mellows pipes.

Aunt (pretending boredom but irritated). Did the sociology you took up at college teach you that — to play the ghoul on every possible occasion, excavating old bones? Why not let your great-grandmother rest in her grave?

Mildred (dreamily). With her pipe beside her — puffing in Paradise.

Aunt (with spite). Yes, you are a natural born ghoul. You are even getting to look like one, my dear.

Mildred (in a passionless tone). I detest you, Aunt. *(Looking at her critically.)* Do you know what you remind me of? Of a cold pork pudding against a background of linoleum tablecloth in the kitchen of a — but the possibilities are wearisome.
(She closes her eyes.)

Aunt (with a bitter laugh). Merci for your candor. But since I am and must be your chaperon — in appearance — at least — let us patch up some sort of armed truce. For my part you are quite free to indulge any pose of eccentricity that beguiles you — as long as you observe the amenities ——

Mildred (drawling). The inanities?

Aunt (going on as if she hadn't heard). After exhausting the morbid thrills of social service work on New York's East Side — how they must have hated you, by the way, the poor that you made so much poorer in their own eyes! — you are now bent on making your slumming international. Well, I hope Whitechapel will provide the needed nerve tonic. Do not ask me to chaperon you there, however. I told your father I would not. I loathe deformity. We will hire an army of detectives and you may investigate everything — they allow you to see.

Mildred (protesting with a trace of genuine earnestness). Please do not mock at my attempts to discover how the other half lives. Give me credit for some sort of groping sincerity in that at least. I would like to help them. I would like to be of some use in the world. Is it my fault I don't know how? I would like to be sincere, to touch life somewhere. *(With weary bitterness.)* But I'm afraid I have neither the vitality nor integrity. All that was burnt out in our stock before I was born. Grandfather's blast furnaces, flaming to the sky, melting steel, making millions — then father keeping those home fires burning, making more millions — and little me at the tailend of it all. I'm a waste product in the Bessemer process — like the millions. Or rather, I inherit the acquired trait of the by-product, wealth, but none of the energy, none of the strength of the steel that made it. I am sired by gold and damned by it, as they say at the race track — damned in more ways than one. (*She laughs mirthlessly.*)

Aunt (*unimpressed — superciliously*). You seem to be going in for sincerity today. It isn't becoming to you, really — except as an obvious pose. Be as artificial as you are, I advise. There's a sort of sincerity in that, you know. And, after all, you must confess you like that better.

Mildred (*again affected and bored*). Yes, I suppose I do. Pardon me for my outburst. When a leopard complains of its spots, it must sound rather grotesque. (*In a mocking tone.*) Purr, little leopard. Purr, scratch, tear, kill, gorge yourself and be happy — only stay in the jungle where your spots are camouflage. In a cage they make you conspicuous.

Aunt. I don't know what you are talking about.

Mildred. It would be rude to talk about anything to you. Let's just talk. (*She looks at her wrist watch.*) Well, thank goodness, it's about time for them to come for me. That ought to give me a new thrill, Aunt.

Aunt (*affectedly troubled*). You don't mean to say you're really going? The dirt — the heat must be frightful ——

Mildred. Grandfather started as a puddler. I should have inherited an immunity to heat that would make a salamander shiver. It will be fun to put it to the test.

Aunt. But don't you have to have the captain's — or someone's — permission to visit the stokehole?

Mildred (*with a triumphant smile*). I have it — both his and the chief engineer's. Oh, they didn't want to at first, in spite of my social service credentials. They didn't seem a bit anxious that I should investigate how the other half lives and works on a ship. So I had to tell them that my father, the president of Nazareth Steel, chairman of the board of directors of this line, had told me it would be all right.

Aunt. He didn't.

Mildred. How naïve age makes one! But I said he did, Aunt. I even said he had given me a letter to them — which I had lost. And they were afraid to take the chance that I might be lying. (*Excitedly.*) So it's ho! for the stokehole. The second

engineer is to escort me. (*Looking at her watch again.*) It's time. And here he comes, I think.

(*The* SECOND ENGINEER *enters. He is a husky, fine-looking man of thirty-five or so. He stops before the two and tips his cap, visibly embarrassed and ill-at-ease.*)

Second Engineer. Miss Douglas?

Mildred. Yes. (*Throwing off her rugs and getting to her feet.*) Are we all ready to start?

Second Engineer. In just a second, ma'am. I'm waiting for the Fourth. He's coming along.

Mildred (*with a scornful smile*). You don't care to shoulder this responsibility alone, is that it?

Second Engineer (*forcing a smile*). Two are better than one. (*Disturbed by her eyes, glances out to sea — blurts out.*) A fine day we're having.

Mildred. Is it?

Second Engineer. A nice warm breeze ——

Mildred. It feels cold to me.

Second Engineer. But it's hot enough in the sun ——

Mildred. Not hot enough for me. I don't like Nature. I was never athletic.

Second Engineer (*forcing a smile*). Well, you'll find it hot enough where you're going.

Mildred. Do you mean hell?

Second Engineer (*flabbergasted, decides to laugh*). Ho-ho! No, I mean the stokehole.

Mildred. My grandfather was a puddler. He played with boiling steel.

Second Engineer (*all at sea — uneasily*). Is that so? Hum, you'll excuse me, ma'am, but are you intending to wear that dress?

Mildred. Why not?

Second Engineer. You'll likely rub against oil and dirt. It can't be helped.

Mildred. It doesn't matter. I have lots of white dresses.

Second Engineer. I have an old coat you might throw over ——

Mildred. I have fifty dresses like this. I will throw this one into the sea when I come back. That ought to wash it clean, don't you think?

Second Engineer (*doggedly*). There's ladders to climb down that are none too clean — and dark alleyways ——

Mildred. I will wear this very dress and none other.

Second Engineer. No offense meant. It's none of my business. I was only warning you ——

Mildred. Warning? That sounds thrilling.

Second Engineer (*looking down the deck — with a sigh of relief*). There's the Fourth now. He's waiting for us. If you'll come ——

Mildred. Go on. I'll follow you. (*He goes.*

MILDRED *turns a mocking smile on her aunt.*) An oaf — but a handsome, virile oaf.

Aunt (scornfully). Poser!

Mildred. Take care. He said there were dark alleyways ——

Aunt (in the same tone). Poser!

Mildred (biting her lips angrily). You are right. But would that my millions were not so anemically chaste!

Aunt. Yes, for a fresh pose I have no doubt you would drag the name of Douglas in the gutter!

Mildred. From which it sprang. Good-by, Aunt. Don't pray too hard that I may fall into the fiery furnace.

Aunt. Poser!

Mildred (viciously). Old hag! (*She slaps her aunt insultingly across the face and walks off, laughing gaily.*)

Aunt (screams after her). I said poser!

CURTAIN

SCENE THREE

SCENE: *The stokehole. In the rear, the dimly-outlined bulks of the furnaces and boilers. High overhead one hanging electric bulb sheds just enough light through the murky air laden with coal dust to pile up masses of shadows everywhere. A line of men, stripped to the waist, is before the furnace doors. They bend over, looking neither to right nor left, handling their shovels as if they were part of their bodies, with a strange, awkward, swinging rhythm. They use the shovels to throw open the furnace doors. Then from these fiery round holes in the black a flood of terrific light and heat pours full upon the men who are outlined in silhouette in the crouching, inhuman attitudes of chained gorillas. The men shovel with a rhythmic motion, swinging as on a pivot from the coal which lies in heaps on the floor behind to hurl it into the flaming mouths before them. There is a tumult of noise — the brazen clang of the furnace doors as they are flung open or slammed shut, the grating, teeth-gritting grind of steel against steel, of crunching coal. This clash of sounds stuns one's ears with its rending dissonance. But there is order in it, rhythm, a mechanical regulated recurrence, a tempo. And rising above all, making the air hum with the quiver of liberated energy, the roar of leaping flames in the furnaces, the monotonous throbbing beat of the engines.*

As the curtain rises, the furnace doors are shut. The men are taking a breathing spell. One or two are arranging the coal behind them, pulling it into more accessible heaps. The others can be dimly made out leaning on their shovels in relaxed attitudes of exhaustion.

Paddy (from somewhere in the line — plaintively). Yerra, will this divil's own watch nivir end? Me back is broke. I'm destroyed entirely.

Yank (from the center of the line — with exuberant scorn). Aw, yuh make me sick! Lie down and croak, why don't yuh? Always beefin', dat's you! Say, dis is a cinch! Dis was made for me! It's my meat, get me! (*A whistle is blown — a thin, shrill note from somewhere overhead in the darkness. YANK curses without resentment.*) Dere's de damn engineer crackin' de whip. He tinks we're loafin'.

Paddy (vindictively). God stiffen him!

Yank (in an exultant tone of command). Come on, youse guys! Git into de game! She's gittin' hungry! Pile some grub in her. Trow it into her belly! Come on now, all of youse! Open her up! (*At this last all the men, who have followed his movements of getting into position, throw open their furnace doors with a deafening clang. The fiery light floods over their shoulders as they bend round for the coal. Rivulets of sooty sweat have traced maps on their backs. The enlarged muscles form bunches of high light and shadow.*)

Yank (chanting a count as he shovels without seeming effort). One — two — tree —— (*His voice rising exultantly in the joy of battle.*) Dat's de stuff! Let her have it! All togedder now! Sling it into her! Let her ride! Shoot de piece now! Call de toin on her! Drive her into it! Feel her move! Watch her smoke! Speed, dat's her middle name! Give her coal, youse guys! Coal, dat's her booze! Drink it up, baby! Let's see yuh sprint! Dig in and gain a lap! Dere she go-o-es. (*This last in the chanting formula of the gallery gods at the six-day bike race. He slams his furnace door shut. The others do likewise with as much unison as their wearied bodies will permit. The effect is of one fiery eye after another being blotted out with a series of accompanying bangs.*)

Paddy (groaning). Me back is broke. I'm bate out — bate — (*There is a pause. Then the inexorable whistle sounds again from the dim regions above the electric light. There is a growl of cursing rage from all sides.*)

Yank (shaking his fist upward — contemptuously). Take it easy dere, you! Who d'yuh tinks runnin' dis game, me or you? When I git ready, we move. Not before! When I git ready, get me!

Voices (approvingly).

That's the stuff!

Yank tal him, py golly!

Yank ain't afeerd.

Goot poy, Yank!

Give him hell!
Tell 'im 'e's a bloody swine!
Bloody slave-driver!

Yank (*contemptuously*). He ain't got no noive. He's yellow, get me? All de engineers is yellow. Dey got streaks a mile wide. Aw, to hell with him! Let's move, youse guys. We had a rest. Come on, she needs it! Give her pep! It ain't for him. Him and his whistle, dey don't belong. But we belong, see! We gotter feed de baby! Come on! (*He turns and flings his furnace door open. They all follow his lead. At this instant the* SECOND *and* FOURTH ENGINEERS *enter from the darkness on the left with* MILDRED *between them. She starts, turns paler, her pose is crumbling, she shivers with fright in spite of the blazing heat, but forces herself to leave the* ENGINEERS *and take a few steps near the men. She is right behind* YANK. *All this happens quickly while the men have their backs turned.*)

Yank. Come on, youse guys! (*He is turning to get coal when the whistle sounds again in a peremptory, irritating note. This drives* YANK *into a sudden fury. While the other men have turned full around and stopped dumbfounded by the spectacle of* MILDRED *standing there in her white dress,* YANK *does not turn far enough to see her. Besides, his head is thrown back, he blinks upward through the murk trying to find the owner of the whistle, he brandishes his shovel murderously over his head in one hand, pounding on his chest, gorilla-like, with the other, shouting.*) Toin off dat whistle! Come down outa dere, yuh yellow, brass-buttoned, Belfast bum, yuh! Come down and I'll knock yer brains out! Yuh lousy, stinkin', yellow mut of a Catholic-moiderin' bastard! Come down and I'll moider yuh! Pullin' dat whistle on me, huh? I'll show yuh! I'll crash yer skull in! I'll drive yer teet' down yer troat! I'll slam yer nose trou de back of yer head! I'll cut yer guts out for a nickel, yuh lousy boob, yuh dirty, crummy, muck-eatin' son of a —— (*Suddenly he becomes conscious of all the other men staring at something directly behind his back. He whirls defensively with a snarling, murderous growl, crouching to spring, his lips drawn back over his teeth, his small eyes gleaming ferociously. He sees* MILDRED, *like a white apparition in the full light from the open furnace doors. He glares into her eyes, turned to stone. As for her, during his speech she has listened, paralyzed with horror, terror, her whole personality crushed, beaten in, collapsed, by the terrific impact of this unknown, abysmal brutality, naked and shameless. As she looks at his gorilla face, as his eyes bore into hers, she utters a low, choking cry and shrinks away from him, putting both hands up before her eyes to shut out the sight of his face, to protect her own. This startles* YANK *to a re-*

action. His mouth falls open, his eyes grow bewildered.)

Mildred (*about to faint — to the* ENGINEERS, *who now have her one by each arm — whimperingly*). Take me away! Oh, the filthy beast! (*She faints. They carry her quickly back, disappearing in the darkness at the left, rear. An iron door clangs shut. Rage and bewildered fury rush back on* YANK. *He feels himself insulted in some unknown fashion in the very heart of his pride. He roars.*) God damn yuh! (*And hurls his shovel after them at the door which has just closed. It hits the steel bulkhead with a clang and falls clattering on the steel floor. From overhead the whistle sounds again in a long, angry, insistent command.*)

CURTAIN

SCENE FOUR

SCENE: *The firemen's forecastle.* YANK'S *watch has just come off duty and had dinner. Their faces and bodies shine from a soap and water scrubbing but around their eyes, where a hasty dousing does not touch, the coal dust sticks like black make-up, giving them a queer, sinister expression.* YANK *has not washed either face or body. He stands out in contrast to them, a blackened, brooding figure. He is seated forward on a bench in the exact attitude of Rodin's "The Thinker." The others, most of them smoking pipes, are staring at* YANK *half-apprehensively, as if fearing an outburst; half-amusedly, as if they saw a joke somewhere that tickled them.*

Voices. He ain't ate nothin'.
    Py golly, a fallar gat to gat grub in him.
    Divil a lie.
    Yank feeda da fire, no feeda da face.
    Ha-ha.
    He ain't even washed hisself.
    He's forgot.
    Hey, Yank, you forgot to wash.

Yank (*sullenly*). Forgot nothin'! To hell wit washin'.

Voices. It'll stick to you.
    It'll get under your skin.
    Give yer the bleedin' itch, that's wot.
    It makes spots on you — like a leopard.
    Like a piebald nigger, you mean.
    Better wash up, Yank.
    You sleep better.
    Wash up, Yank.
    Wash up! Wash up!

Yank (*resentfully*). Aw say, youse guys. Lemme alone. Can't youse see I'm tryin' to tink?

All (*repeating the word after him as one with cynical mockery*). Think! (*The word has a brazen, metallic quality as if their throats were phonograph horns. It is followed by a chorus of hard, barking laughter.*)

Yank (*springing to his feet and glaring at them belligerently*). Yes, tink! Tink, dat's what I said! What about it? (*They are silent, puzzled by his sudden resentment at what used to be one of his jokes. Yank sits down again in the same attitude of "The Thinker."*)

Voices. Leave him alone.
    He's got a grouch on.
    Why wouldn't he?

Paddy (*with a wink at the others*). Sure I know what's the matther. 'Tis aisy to see. He's fallen in love, I'm telling you.

All (*repeating the word after him as one with cynical mockery*). Love! (*The word has a brazen, metallic quality as if their throats were phonograph horns. It is followed by a chorus of hard, barking laughter.*)

Yank (*with a contemptuous snort*). Love, hell! Hate, dat's what. I've fallen in hate, get me?

Paddy (*philosophically*). 'Twould take a wise man to tell one from the other. (*With a bitter, ironical scorn, increasing as he goes on.*) But I'm telling you it's love that's in it. Sure what else but love for us poor bastes in the stokehole would be bringing a fine lady, dressed like a white quane, down a mile of ladders and steps to be havin' a look at us? (*A growl of anger goes up from all sides.*)

Long (*jumping on a bench — hecticly*). Hinsultin' us! Hinsultin' us, the bloody cow! And them bloody engineers! What right 'as they got to be exhibitin' us 's if we was bleedin' monkeys in a menagerie? Did we sign for hinsults to our dignity as 'onest workers? Is that in the ship's articles? You kin bloody well bet it ain't! But I knows why they done it. I arsked a deck steward 'o she was and 'e told me. 'Er old man's a bleedin' millionaire, a bloody Capitalist! 'E's got enuf bloody gold to sink this bleedin' ship! 'E makes arf the bloody steel in the world! 'E owns this bloody boat! And you and me, Comrades, we're 'is slaves! And the skipper and mates and engineers, they're 'is slaves! And she's 'is bloody daughter and we're all 'er slaves, too! And she gives 'er orders as 'ow she wants to see the bloody animals below decks and down they takes 'er! (*There is a roar of rage from all sides.*)

Yank (*blinking at him bewilderedly*). Say! Wait a moment! Is all dat straight goods?

Long. Straight as string! The bleedin' steward as waits on 'em, 'e told me about 'er. And what're we goin' ter do, I arsks yer? 'Ave we got ter swaller 'er hinsults like dogs? It ain't in the ship's articles. I tell yer we got a case. We kin go to law ——

Yank (*with abysmal contempt*). Hell! Law!

All (*repeating the word after him as one with cynical mockery*). Law! (*The word has a brazen metallic quality as if their throats were phonograph horns. It is followed by a chorus of hard, barking laughter.*)

Long (*feeling the ground slipping from under his feet — desperately*). As voters and citizens we kin force the bloody governments ——

Yank (*with abysmal contempt*). Hell! Governments!

All (*repeating the word after him as one with cynical mockery*). Governments! (*The word has a brazen metallic quality as if their throats were phonograph horns. It is followed by a chorus of hard, barking laughter.*)

Long (*hysterically*). We're free and equal in the sight of God ——

Yank (*with abysmal contempt*). Hell! God!

All (*repeating the word after him as one with cynical mockery*). God! (*The word has a brazen metallic quality as if their throats were phonograph horns. It is followed by a chorus of hard, barking laughter.*)

Yank (*witheringly*). Aw, join de Salvation Army!

All. Sit down! Shut up! Damn fool! Sea-lawyer! (Long *slinks back out of sight.*)

Paddy (*continuing the trend of his thoughts as if he had never been interrupted — bitterly*). And there she was standing behind us, and the Second pointing at us like a man you'd hear in a circus would be saying: In this cage is a queerer kind of baboon than ever you'd find in darkest Africy. We roast them in their own sweat — and be damned if you won't hear some of thim saying they like it! (*He glances scornfully at* Yank.)

Yank (*with a bewildered uncertain growl*). Aw!

Paddy. And there was Yank roarin' curses and turning round wid his shovel to brain her — and she looked at him, and him at her ——

Yank (*slowly*). She was all white. I tought she was a ghost. Sure.

Paddy (*with heavy, biting sarcasm*). 'Twas love at first sight, divil a doubt of it! If you'd seen the endearin' look on her pale mug when she shriveled away with her hands over her eyes to shut out the sight of him! Sure, 'twas as if she'd seen a great hairy ape escaped from the Zoo!

Yank (*stung — with a growl of rage*). Aw!

Paddy. And the loving way Yank heaved his shovel at the skull of her, only she was out the door! (*A grin breaking over his face.*) 'Twas touching, I'm telling you! It put the touch of home, swate home in the stokehole.

    (*There is a roar of laughter from all.*)

Yank (*glaring at* PADDY *menacingly*). Aw, choke dat off, see!

Paddy (*not heeding him — to the others*). And her grabbin' at the Second's arm for protection. (*With a grotesque imitation of a woman's voice.*) Kiss me, Engineer dear, for it's dark down here and me old man's in Wall Street making money! Hug me tight, darlin', for I'm afeerd in the dark and me mother's on deck makin' eyes at the skipper! (*Another roar of laughter.*)

Yank (*threateningly*). Say! What yuh tryin' to do, kid me, yuh old Harp?

Paddy. Divil a bit! Ain't I wishin' myself you'd brained her?

Yank (*fiercely*). I'll brain her! I'll brain her yet, wait 'n' see! (*Coming over to* PADDY *slowly.*) Say, is dat what she called me — a hairy ape?

Paddy. She looked it at you if she didn't say the word itself.

Yank (*grinning horribly*). Hairy ape, huh? Sure! Dat's de way she looked at me, aw right. Hairy ape! So dat's me, huh? (*Bursting into rage — as if she were still in front of him.*) Yuh skinny tart! Yuh white-faced bum, yuh! I'll show yuh who's a ape! (*Turning to the others, bewilderment seizing him again.*) Say, youse guys. I was bawlin' him out for pullin' de whistle on us. You heard me. And den I seen youse lookin' at somep'n and I tought he'd sneaked down to come up in back of me, and I hopped round to knock him dead wit de shovel. And dere she was wit de light on her! Christ, yuh coulda pushed me over with a finger! I was scared, get me? Sure! I tought she was a ghost, see? She was all in white like dey wrap around stiffs. You seen her. Kin yuh blame me? She didn't belong, dat's what. And den when I come to and seen it was a real skoit and seen de way she was lookin' at me — like Paddy said — Christ, I was sore, get me? I don't stand for dat stuff from nobody. And I flung de shovel — on'y she'd beat it. (*Furiously.*) I wished it'd banged her! I wished it'd knocked her block off!

Long. And be 'anged for murder or 'lectrocuted? She ain't bleedin' well worth it.

Yank. I don't give a damn what! I'd be square wit her, wouldn't I? Tink I wanter let her put somep'n over on me? Tink I'm goin' to let her git away wit dat stuff? Yuh don't know me! No one ain't never put nothin' over on me and got away wit it, see! — not dat kind of stuff — no guy and no skoit neither! I'll fix her! Maybe she'll come down again —

Voice. No chance, Yank. You scared her out of a year's growth.

Yank. I scared her? Why de hell should I scare her? Who de hell is she? Ain't she de same as me? Hairy ape, huh? (*With his old confident bravado.*) I'll show her I'm better'n her, if she on'y knew it. I belong and she don't, see! I move and she's dead! Twenty-five knots a hour, dat's me! Dat carries her but I make dat. She's on'y baggage. Sure! (*Again bewilderedly.*) But, Christ, she was funny lookin'! Did yuh pipe her hands? White and skinny. Yuh could see de bones through 'em. And her mush, dat was dead white, too. And her eyes, dey was like dey'd seen a ghost. Me, dat was! Sure! Hairy ape! Ghost, huh? Look at dat arm! (*He extends his right arm, swelling out the great muscles.*) I coulda took her wid dat, wit' just my little finger even, and broke her in two. (*Again bewilderedly.*) Say, who is dat skoit, huh? What is she? What's she come from? Who made her? Who give her de noive to look at me like dat? Dis ting's got my goat right. I don't get her. She's new to me. What does a skoit like her mean, huh? She don't belong, get me! I can't see her. (*With growing anger.*) But one ting I'm wise to, aw right, aw right! Youse all kin bet your shoits I'll git even wit her. I'll show her if she tinks she — She grinds de organ and I'm on de string, huh? I'll fix her! Let her come down again and I'll fling her in de furnace! She'll move den! She won't shiver at nothin', den! Speed, dat'll be her! She'll belong den! (*He grins horribly.*)

Paddy. She'll never come. She's had her bellyful, I'm telling you. She'll be in bed now, I'm thinking, wid ten doctors and nurses feedin' her salts to clean the fear out of her.

Yank (*enraged*). Yuh tink I made her sick, too, do yuh? Just lookin' at me, huh? Hairy ape, huh? (*In a frenzy of rage.*) I'll fix her! I'll tell her where to git off! She'll git down on her knees and take it back or I'll bust de face offen her! (*Shaking one fist upward and beating on his chest with the other.*) I'll find yuh! I'm comin', d'yuh hear? I'll fix yuh, God damn yuh! (*He makes a rush for the door.*)

Voices. Stop him!
He'll get shot!
He'll murder her!
Trip him up!
Hold him!
He's gone crazy!
Gott, he's strong!
Hold him down!
Look out for a kick!
Pin his arms!

(*They have all piled on him and, after a fierce struggle, by sheer weight of numbers have borne him to the floor just inside the door.*)

Paddy (*who has remained detached*). Kape him down till he's cooled off. (*Scornfully.*) Yerra, Yank, you're a great fool. Is it payin' attention at all you are to the like of that skinny sow widout one drop of rale blood in her?

Yank (*frenziedly, from the bottom of the heap*). She done me doit! She done me doit, didn't she? I'll git square wit her! I'll get her some way! Git offen me, youse guys! Lemme up! I'll show her who's a ape!

CURTAIN

SCENE FIVE

SCENE: *Three weeks later. A corner of Fifth Avenue in the Fifties on a fine Sunday morning. A general atmosphere of clean, well-tidied, wide street; a flood of mellow, tempered sunshine; gentle, genteel breezes. In the rear, the show windows of two shops, a jewelry establishment on the corner, a furrier's next to it. Here the adornments of extreme wealth are tantalizingly displayed. The jeweler's window is gaudy with glittering diamonds, emeralds, rubies, pearls, etc., fashioned in ornate tiaras, crowns, necklaces, collars, etc. From each piece hangs an enormous tag from which a dollar sign and numerals in intermittent electric lights wink out the incredible prices. The same in the furrier's. Rich furs of all varieties hang there bathed in a downpour of artificial light. The general effect is of a background of magnificence cheapened and made grotesque by commercialism, a background in tawdry disharmony with the clear light and sunshine on the street itself.*

Up the side street YANK *and* LONG *come swaggering.* LONG *is dressed in shore clothes, wears a black Windsor tie, cloth cap.* YANK *is in his dirty dungarees. A fireman's cap with black peak is cocked defiantly on the side of his head. He has not shaved for days and around his fierce, resentful eyes — as around those of* LONG *to a lesser degree — the black smudge of coal dust still sticks like make-up. They hesitate and stand together at the corner, swaggering, looking about them with a forced, defiant contempt.*

Long (*indicating it all with an oratorical gesture*). Well, 'ere we are. Fif' Avenoo. This 'ere's their bleedin' private lane, as yer might say. (*Bitterly.*) We're trespassers 'ere. Proletarians keep orf the grass!

Yank (*dully*). I don't see no grass, yuh boob. (*Staring at the sidewalk.*) Clean, ain't it? Yuh could eat a fried egg offen it. The white wings got some job sweepin' dis up. (*Looking up and down the avenue — surlily.*) Where's all de white-collar stiffs yuh said was here — and de skoits — her kind?

Long. In church, blarst 'em! Arskin' Jesus to give 'em more money.

Yank. Choich, huh? I useter go to choich onct — sure — when I was a kid. Me old man and woman, dey made me. Dey never went demselves, dough. Always got too big a head on Sunday mornin', dat was dem. (*With a grin.*) Dey was scrappers for fair, bot' of dem. On Satiday nights when dey bot' got a skinful dey could put up a bout oughter been staged at de Garden. When dey got trough dere wasn't a chair or table wit a leg under it. Or else dey bot' jumped on me for somep'n. Dat was where I loined to take punishment. (*With a grin and a swagger.*) I'm a chip offen de old block, get me?

Long. Did yer old man follow the sea?

Yank. Naw. Worked along shore. I runned away when me old lady croaked wit de tremens. I helped at truckin' and in de market. Den I shipped in de stokehole. Sure. Dat belongs. De rest was nothin'. (*Looking around him.*) I ain't never seen dis before. De Brooklyn waterfront, dat was where I was dragged up. (*Taking a deep breath.*) Dis ain't so bad at dat, huh?

Long. Not bad? Well, we pays for it wiv our bloody sweat, if yer wants to know!

Yank (*with sudden angry disgust*). Aw, hell! I don't see no one, see — like her. All dis gives me a pain. It don't belong. Say, ain't dere a back room around dis dump? Let's go shoot a ball. All dis is too clean and quiet and dolled-up, get me? It gives me a pain.

Long. Wait and yer'll bloody well see ——

Yank. I don't wait for no one. I keep on de move. Say, what yuh drag me up here for, anyway? Tryin' to kid me, yuh simp, yuh?

Long. Yer wants to get back at 'er, don't yer? That's what yer been sayin' every bloomin' hour since she hinsulted yer.

Yank (*vehemently*). Sure ting I do! Didn't I try to get even wit her in Southampton? Didn't I sneak on de dock and wait for her by de gangplank? I was goin' to spit in her pale mug, see! Sure, right in her pop-eyes! Dat woulda made me even, see? But no chanct. Dere was a whole army of plainclothes bulls around. Dey spotted me and gimme de bum's rush. I never seen her. But I'll git square wit her yet, you watch! (*Furiously.*) De lousy tart! She tinks she kin get away with moider — but not wit me! I'll fix her! I'll tink of a way!

Long (*as disgusted as he dares to be*). Ain't that why I brought yer up 'ere — to show yer? Yer been lookin' at this 'ere 'ole affair wrong. Yer been actin' an' talkin' 's if it was all a bleedin' personal matter between yer and that bloody cow. I wants to convince yer she was on'y a representative of 'er clarss. I wants to awaken yer bloody clarss consciousness. Then yer'll see it's 'er clarss yer've got to fight, not 'er alone. There's a 'ole mob of 'em like 'er, Gawd blind 'em!

Yank (spitting on his hands — belligerently). De more de merrier when I gits started. Bring on de gang!

Long. Yer'll see 'em in arf a mo', when that church lets out. (*He turns and sees the window display in the two stores for the first time.*) Blimey! Look at that, will yer? (*They both walk back and stand looking in the jeweler's.* LONG *flies into a fury.*) Just look at this 'ere bloomin' mess! Just look at it! Look at the bleedin' prices on 'em — more'n our 'ole bloody stokehole makes in ten voyages sweatin' in 'ell! And they — 'er and 'er bloody clarss — buys 'em for toys to dangle on 'em! One of these 'ere would buy scoff for a starvin' family for a year!

Yank. Aw, cut de sob stuff! T' hell wit de starvin' family! Yuh'll be passin' de hat to me next. (*With naïve admiration.*) Say, dem tings is pretty, huh? Bet yuh dey'd hock for a piece of change aw right. (*Then turning away, bored.*) But, aw hell, what good are dey? Let 'er have 'em. Dey don't belong no more'n she does. (*With a gesture of sweeping the jewelers into oblivion.*) All dat don't count, get me?

Long (who has moved to the furrier's — indignantly). And I s'pose this 'ere don't count neither — skins of poor, 'armless animals slaughtered so as 'er and 'ers can keep their bleedin' noses warm!

Yank (who has been staring at something inside — with queer excitement). Take a slant at dat! Give it de once-over! Monkey fur — two t'ousand bucks! (*Bewilderedly.*) Is dat straight goods — monkey fur? What de hell ——?

Long (bitterly). It's straight enuf. (*With grim humor.*) They wouldn't bloody well pay that for a 'airy ape's skin — no, nor for the 'ole livin' ape with all 'is 'ead, and body, and soul thrown in!

Yank (clenching his fists, his face growing pale with rage as if the skin in the window were a personal insult). Trowin' it up in my face! Christ! I'll fix her!

Long (excitedly). Church is out. 'Ere they come, the bleedin' swine. (*After a glance at* YANK'S *lowering face — uneasily.*) Easy goes, Comrade. Keep yer bloomin' temper. Remember force defeats itself. It ain't our weapon. We must impress our demands through peaceful means — the votes of the on-marching proletarians of the bloody world!

Yank (with abysmal contempt). **Votes,** hell! Votes is a joke, see. Votes for women! **Let dem do it!**

Long (still more uneasily). Calm, now. Treat 'em wiv the proper contempt. Observe the bleedin' parasites but 'old yer 'orses.

Yank (angrily). Git away from me! Yuh're yellow, dat's what. Force, dat's me! De punch, dat's me every time, see! (*The crowd from church enter from the right, sauntering slowly and affectedly, their heads held stiffly up, looking neither to right nor left, talking in toneless, simpering voices. The women are rouged, calcimined, dyed, overdressed to the nth degree. The men are in Prince Alberts, high hats, spats, canes, etc. A procession of gaudy marionettes, yet with something of the relentless horror of Frankenstein monsters in their detached, mechanical unawareness.*)

Voices.
Dear Doctor Caiaphas! He is so sincere!
What was the sermon? I dozed off.
About the radicals, my dear — and the false
doctrines that are being preached.
We must organize a hundred per cent American bazaar.
And let everyone contribute one one-hundredth
per cent of their income tax.
What an original idea!
We can devote the proceeds to rehabilitating
the veil of the temple.
But that has been done so many times.

Yank (glaring from one to the other of them — with an insulting snort of scorn). Huh! Huh! (*Without seeming to see him, they make wide detours to avoid the spot where he stands in the middle of the sidewalk.*)

Long (frightenedly). Keep yer bloomin' mouth shut, I tells yer.

Yank (viciously). G'wan! Tell it to Sweeney! (*He swaggers away and deliberately lurches into a top-hatted gentleman, then glares at him pugnaciously.*) Say, who d'yuh tink yuh're bumpin'? Tink yuh own de oith?

Gentleman (coldly and affectedly). I beg your pardon.

(*He has not looked at* YANK *and passes on without a glance, leaving him bewildered.*)

Long (rushing up and grabbing YANK'S *arm).* 'Ere! Come away! This wasn't what I meant. Yer'll 'ave the bloody coppers down on us.

Yank (savagely — giving him a push that sends him sprawling). G'wan!

Long (picks himself up — hysterically). I'll pop

orf then. This ain't what I meant. And whatever 'appens, yer can't blame me. (*He slinks off left.*)

Yank. T' hell wit youse! (*He approaches a lady — with a vicious grin and a smirking wink.*) Hello, Kiddo. How's every little ting? Got anyting on for tonight? I know an old boiler down to de docks we kin crawl into. (*The lady stalks by without a look, without a change of pace.* YANK *turns to others — insultingly.*) Holy smokes, what a mug! Go hide yuhself before de horses shy at yuh. Gee, pipe de heine on dat one! Say, youse, yuh look like de stoin of a ferryboat. Paint and powder! All dolled up to kill! Yuh look like stiffs laid out for de boneyard! Aw, g'wan, de lot of youse! Yuh give me de eye-ache. Yuh don't belong, get me! Look at me, why don't youse dare? I belong, dat's me! (*Pointing to a skyscraper across the street which is in process of construction — with bravado.*) See dat building goin' up dere? See de steel work? Steel, dat's me! Youse guys live on it and tink yuh're somep'n. But I'm *in* it, see! I'm de hoistin' engine dat makes it go up! I'm it — de inside and bottom of it! Sure! I'm steel and steam and smoke and de rest of it! It moves — speed — twenty-five stories up — and me at de top and bottom — movin'! Youse simps don't move. Yuh're on'y dolls I winds up to see 'm spin. Yuh're de garbage, get me — de leavins — de ashes we dump over de side! Now, what 'a' yuh gotta say? (*But as they seem neither to see nor hear him, he flies into a fury.*) Bums! Pigs! Tarts! Bitches! (*He turns in a rage on the men, bumping viciously into them but not jarring them the least bit. Rather it is he who recoils after each collision. He keeps growling.*) Git off de oith! G'wan, yuh bum! Look where yuh're goin', can't yuh? Git outa here! Fight, why don't yuh? Put up yer mits! Don't be a dog! Fight or I'll knock yuh dead! (*But, without seeming to see him, they all answer with mechanical affected politeness.*) I beg your pardon. (*Then at a cry from one of the women, they all scurry to the furrier's window.*)

The Woman (*ecstatically, with a gasp of delight*). Monkey fur! (*The whole crowd of men and women chorus after her in the same tone of affected delight.*) Monkey fur!

Yank (*with a jerk of his head back on his shoulders, as if he had received a punch full in the face — raging*). I see yuh, all in white! I see yuh, yuh white-faced tart, yuh! Hairy ape, huh? I'll hairy ape yuh! (*He bends down and grips at the street curbing as if to pluck it out and hurl it. Foiled in this, snarling with passion, he leaps to the lamp-post on the corner and tries to pull it up for a club. Just at that moment a bus is heard rumbling up. A fat, high-hatted, spatted gentleman runs out from the side*

street. *He calls out plaintively.*) Bus! Bus! Stop there! (*And runs full tilt into the bending, straining* YANK, *who is bowled off his balance.*)

Yank (*seeing a fight — with a roar of joy as he springs to his feet*). At last! Bus, huh! I'll bust yuh! (*He lets drive a terrific swing, his fist landing full on the fat gentleman's face. But the gentleman stands unmoved as if nothing had happened.*)

Gentleman. I beg your pardon. (*Then irritably.*) You have made me lose my bus. (*He claps his hands and begins to scream.*) Officer! Officer! (*Many police whistles shrill out on the instant and a whole platoon of policemen rush in on* YANK *from all sides. He tries to fight but is clubbed to the pavement and fallen upon. The crowd at the window have not moved or noticed this disturbance. The clanging gong of the patrol wagon approaches with a clamoring din.*)

CURTAIN

SCENE SIX

SCENE: *Night of the following day. A row of cells in the prison on Blackwell's island. The cells extend back diagonally from right front to left rear. They do not stop, but disappear in the dark background as if they ran on, numberless, into infinity. One electric bulb from the low ceiling of the narrow corridor sheds its light through the heavy steel bars of the cell at the extreme front and reveals part of the interior.* YANK *can be seen within, crouched on the edge of his cot in the attitude of Rodin's "The Thinker." His face is spotted with black and blue bruises. A blood-stained bandage is wrapped around his head.*

Yank (*suddenly starting as if awakening from a dream, reaches out and shakes the bars — aloud to himself, wonderingly*). Steel. Dis is de Zoo, huh? (*A burst of hard, barking laughter comes from the unseen occupants of the cells, runs back down the tier, and abruptly ceases.*)

Voices (*mockingly*).
   The Zoo? That's a new name for this coop — a damn good name!
   Steel, eh? You said a mouthful. This is the old iron house.
   Who is that boob talkin'?
   He's the bloke they brung in out of his head.
   The bulls had beat him up fierce.

Yank (*dully*). I musta been dreamin'. I tought I was in a cage at de Zoo — but de apes don't talk, do dey?

Voices (*with mocking laughter*).
   You're in a cage aw right.
   A coop!

A pen!

A sty!

A kennel! (*Hard laughter — a pause.*)

Say, guy! Who are you? No, never mind lying. What are you?

Yes, tell us your sad story. What's your game?

What did they jug yuh for?

Yank (*dully*). I was a fireman — stokin' on de liners. (*Then with sudden rage, rattling his cell bars.*) I'm a hairy ape, get me? And I'll bust youse all in de jaw if yuh don't lay off kiddin' me.

Voices.

Huh! You're a hard boiled duck, ain't you!

When you spit, it bounces! (*Laughter.*)

Aw, can it. He's a regular guy. Ain't you?

What did he say he was — a ape?

Yank (*defiantly*). Sure ting! Ain't dat what youse all are — apes? (*A silence. Then a furious rattling of bars from down the corridor.*)

A Voice (*thick with rage*). I'll show yuh who's a ape, yuh bum!

Voices. Ssshh! Nix!

Can de noise!

Piano!

You'll have the guard down on us!

Yank (*scornfully*). De guard? Yuh mean de keeper, don't yuh?

(*Angry exclamations from all the cells.*)

Voice (*placatingly*). Aw, don't pay no attention to him. He's off his nut from the beatin'-up he got. Say, you guy! We're waitin' to hear what they landed you for — or ain't yuh tellin'?

Yank. Sure, I'll tell youse. Sure! Why de hell not? On'y — youse won't get me. Nobody gets me but me, see? I started to tell de Judge and all he says was: "Toity days to tink it over." Tink it over! Christ, dat's all I been doin' for weeks! (*After a pause.*) I was tryin' to git even wit someone, see? — someone dat done me doit.

Voices (*cynically*).

De old stuff, I bet. Your goil, huh?

Give yuh the double-cross, huh?

That's them every time!

Did yuh beat up de odder guy?

Yank (*disgustedly*). Aw, yuh're all wrong! Sure dere was a skoit in it — but not what youse mean, not dat old tripe. Dis was a new kind of skoit. She was dolled up all in white — in de stokehole. I tought she was a ghost. Sure. (*A pause.*)

Voices (*whispering*). Gee, he's still nutty.

Let him rave. It's fun listenin'.

Yank (*unheeding — groping in his thoughts*). Her hands — dey was skinny and white like dey wasn't real but painted on somep'n. Dere was a million miles from me to her — twenty-five knots a hour. She was like some dead ting de cat brung in. Sure, dat's what. She didn't belong. She belonged in de window of a toy store, or on de top of a garbage can, see! Sure! (*He breaks out angrily.*) But would yuh believe it, she had de noive to do me doit. She lamped me like she was seein' somep'n broke loose from de menagerie. Christ, yuh'd oughter seen her eyes! (*He rattles the bars of his cell furiously.*) But I'll get back at her yet, you watch! And if I can't find her I'll take it out on de gang she runs wit. I'm wise to where dey hangs out now. I'll show her who belongs! I'll show her who's in de move and who ain't. You watch my smoke!

Voices (*serious and joking*). Dat's de talkin'!

Take her for all she's got!

What was this dame, anyway? Who was she, eh?

Yank. I dunno. First cabin stiff. Her old man's a millionaire, dey says — name of Douglas.

Voices.

Douglas? That's the president of the Steel Trust, I bet.

Sure. I seen his mug in de papers.

He's filthy with dough.

Voice. Hey, feller, take a tip from me. If you want to get back at that dame, you better join the Wobblies. You'll get some action then.

Yank. Wobblies? What de hell's dat?

Voice. Ain't you ever heard of the I.W.W.?

Yank. Naw. What is it?

Voice. A gang of blokes — a tough gang. I been readin' about 'em today in the paper. The guard give me the *Sunday Times.* There's a long spiel about 'em. It's from a speech made in the Senate by a guy named Senator Queen. (*He is in the cell next to* YANK'S. *There is a rustling of paper.*) Wait'll I see if I got light enough and I'll read you. Listen. (*He reads.*) "There is a menace existing in this country today which threatens the vitals of our fair Republic — as foul a menace against the very life-blood of the American Eagle as was the foul conspiracy of Catiline against the eagles of ancient Rome!"

Voice (*disgustedly*). Aw, hell! Tell him to salt de tail of dat eagle!

Voice (*reading*). "I refer to that devil's brew of rascals, jailbirds, murderers and cutthroats who libel all honest working men by calling themselves the Industrial Workers of the World; but in the light of their nefarious plots, I call them the Industrious *Wreckers* of the World!"

Yank (*with vengeful satisfaction*). Wreckers, dat's de right dope! Dat belongs! Me for dem!

Voice. Ssshh! (*Reading.*) "This fiendish organization is a foul ulcer on the fair body of our Democracy ——"

Voice. Democracy, hell! Give him the boid, fellers — the raspberry! (*They do.*)

Voice. Ssshh! (*Reading.*) "Like Cato I say to this Senate, the I.W.W. must be destroyed! For they represent an ever-present dagger pointed at the heart of the greatest nation the world has ever known, where all men are born free and equal, with equal opportunities to all, where the Founding Fathers have guaranteed to each one happiness, where Truth, Honor, Liberty, Justice, and the Brotherhood of Man are a religion absorbed with one's mother's milk, taught at our father's knee, sealed, signed, and stamped upon in the glorious Constitution of these United States!" (*A perfect storm of hisses, catcalls, boos, and hard laughter.*)

Voices (*scornfully*). Hurrah for de Fort' of July!
Pass de hat!
Liberty!
Justice!
Honor!
Opportunity!
Brotherhood!

All (*with abysmal scorn*). Aw, hell!

Voice. Give that Queen Senator guy the bark! All togedder now — one — two — tree —— (*A terrific chorus of barking and yapping.*)

Guard (*from a distance*). Quiet there, youse — or I'll git the hose. (*The noise subsides.*)

Yank (*with growling rage*). I'd like to catch dat senator guy alone for a second. I'd loin him some trute!

Voice. Ssshh! Here's where he gits down to cases on the Wobblies. (*Reads.*) "They plot with fire in one hand and dynamite in the other. They stop not before murder to gain their ends, nor at the outraging of defenseless womanhood. They would tear down society, put the lowest scum in the seats of the mighty, turn Almighty God's revealed plan for the world topsy-turvy, and make of our sweet and lovely civilization a shambles, a desolation where man, God's masterpiece, would soon degenerate back to the ape!"

Voice (*to* YANK). Hey, you guy. There's your ape stuff again.

Yank (*with a growl of fury*). I got him. So dey blow up tings, do dey? Dey turn tings round, do dey? Hey, lend me dat paper, will yuh?

Voice. Sure. Give it to him. On'y keep it to yourself, see. We don't wanter listen to no more of that slop.

Voice. Here you are. Hide it under your mattress.

Yank (*reaching out*). Tanks. I can't read much but I kin manage. (*He sits, the paper in the hand at*

his side, in the attitude of Rodin's "The Thinker." A pause. Several snores from down the corridor. Suddenly YANK jumps to his feet with a furious groan as if some appalling thought had crashed on him — bewilderedly.*) Sure — her old man — president of de Steel Trust — makes half de steel in de world — steel — where I tought I belonged — drivin' trou — movin' — in dat — to make *her* — and cage me in for her to spit on! Christ. (*He shakes the bars of his cell door till the whole tier trembles. Irritated, protesting exclamatioms from those awakened or trying to get to sleep.*) He made dis — dis cage! Steel! *It* don't belong, dat's what! Cages, cells, locks, bolts, bars — dat's what it means! — holdin' me down wit him at de top! But I'll drive trou! Fire, dat melts it! I'll be fire — under de heap — fire dat never goes out — hot as hell — breakin' out in de night — (*While he has been saying this last he has shaken his cell door to a clanging accompaniment. As he comes to the "breakin' out" he seizes one bar with both hands and, putting his two feet up against the others so that his position is parallel to the floor like a monkey's, he gives a great wrench backwards. The bar bends like a licorice stick under his tremendous strength. Just at this moment the* PRISON GUARD *rushes in, dragging a hose behind him.*)

Guard (*angrily*). I'll loin youse bums to wake me up! (*Sees* YANK.) Hello, it's you, huh? Got the D.T.'s, hey? Well, I'll cure 'em. I'll drown your snakes for yuh! (*Noticing the bar.*) Hell, look at dat bar bended! On'y a bug is strong enough for dat!

Yank (*glaring at him*). Or a hairy ape, yuh big yellow bum! Look out! Here I come! (*He grabs another bar.*)

Guard (*scared now — yelling off left*). Toin de hose on, Ben! — full pressure! And call de others — and a straitjacket! (*The curtain is falling. As it hides* YANK *from view, there is a splattering smash as the stream of water hits the steel of* YANK'S *cell.*)

CURTAIN

SCENE SEVEN

SCENE: *Nearly a month later. An I.W.W. local near the waterfront, showing the interior of a front room on the ground floor, and the street outside. Moonlight on the narrow street, buildings massed in black shadow. The interior of the room, which is general assembly room, office, and reading room, resembles some dingy settlement boys' club. A desk and high stool are in one corner. A table with papers, stacks of pamphlets, chairs about it, is at center. The whole is decidedly cheap, banal, commonplace and unmysterious as a room could well be. The* SECRETARY *is perched on the stool making entries in a large ledger. An eye shade casts his face into shadows. Eight or ten men, longshoremen, iron workers, and the like are grouped about the table. Two are playing checkers. One is writing a letter. Most of them are smoking pipes. A big signboard is on the wall at the rear,* "Industrial Workers of the World — Local No. 57."

Yank (comes down the street outside. He is dressed as in Scene Five. He moves cautiously, mysteriously. He comes to a point opposite the door; tiptoes softly up to it, listens, is impressed by the silence within, knocks carefully, as if he were guessing at the password to some secret rite. Listens. No answer. Knocks again a bit louder. No answer. Knocks impatiently, much louder).

Secretary (turning around on his stool). What the hell is that — someone knocking? *(Shouts.)* Come in, why don't you? *(All the men in the room look up.* YANK *opens the door slowly, gingerly, as if afraid of an ambush. He looks around for secret doors, mystery, is taken aback by the commonplaceness of the room and the men in it, thinks he may have gotten in the wrong place, then sees the signboard on the wall and is reassured.)*

Yank (blurts out). Hello.

Men (reservedly). Hello.

Yank (more easily). I tought I'd bumped into de wrong dump.

Secretary (scrutinizing him carefully). Maybe you have. Are you a member?

Yank. Naw, not yet. Dat's what I come for — to join.

Secretary. That's easy. What's your job — longshore?

Yank. Naw. Fireman — stoker on de liners.

Secretary (with satisfaction). Welcome to our city. Glad to know you people are waking up at last. We haven't got many members in your line.

Yank. Naw. Dey're all dead to de woild.

Secretary. Well, you can help to wake 'em. What's your name? I'll make out your card.

Yank (confused). Name? Lemme tink.

Secretary (sharply). Don't you know your own name?

Yank. Sure; but I been just Yank for so long — Bob, dat's it — Bob Smith.

Secretary (writing). Robert Smith. *(Fills out the rest of card.)* Here you are. Cost you half a dollar.

Yank. Is dat all — four bits? Dat's easy.

(Gives the SECRETARY *the money.)*

Secretary (throwing it in drawer). Thanks. Well, make yourself at home. No introductions needed. There's literature on the table. Take some of those pamphlets with you to distribute aboard ship. They may bring results. Sow the seed, only go about it right. Don't get caught and fired. We got plenty out of work. What we need is men who can hold their jobs — and work for us at the same time.

Yank. Sure. *(But he still stands, embarrassed and uneasy.)*

Secretary (looking at him — curiously). What did you knock for? Think we had a coon in uniform to open doors?

Yank. Naw. I tought it was locked — and dat yuh'd wanter give me the once-over trou a peephole or somep'n to see if I was right.

Secretary (alert and suspicious but with an easy laugh). Think we were running a crap game? That door is never locked. What put that in your nut?

Yank (with a knowing grin, convinced that this is all camouflage, a part of the secrecy). Dis burg is full of bulls, ain't it?

Secretary (sharply). What have the cops got to do with us? We're breaking no laws.

Yank (with a knowing wink). Sure. Youse wouldn't for woilds. Sure. I'm wise to dat.

Secretary. You seem to be wise to a lot of stuff none of us knows about.

Yank (with another wink). Aw, dat's aw right, see. *(Then made a bit resentful by the suspicious glances from all sides.)* Aw, can it! Youse needn't put me trou de toid degree. Can't youse see I belong? Sure! I'm reg'lar. I'll stick, get me? I'll shoot de woiks for youse. Dat's why I wanted to join in.

Secretary (breezily, feeling him out). That's the right spirit. Only are you sure you understand what you've joined? It's all plain and aboveboard; still, some guys get a wrong slant on us. *(Sharply.)* What's your notion of the purpose of the I.W.W.?

Yank. Aw, I know all about it.

Secretary (sarcastically). Well, give us some of your valuable information.

Yank (cunningly). I know enough not to speak outa my toin. *(Then resentfully again.)* Aw, say! I'm reg'lar. I'm wise to de game. I know yuh got to watch your step wit a stranger. For all youse know, I might be a plain-clothes dick, or somep'n, dat's what yuh're tinkin', huh? Aw. forget it! I belong, see? Ask any guy down to de docks if I don't.

Secretary. Who said you didn't?

Yank. After I'm 'nitiated, I'll show yuh.

Secretary (astounded). Initiated? There's no initiation.

Yank (*disappointed*). Ain't there no password — no grip nor nothin'?

Secretary. What'd you think this is — the Elks — or the Black Hand?

Yank. De Elks, hell! De Black Hand, dey're a lot of yellow backstickin' Ginees. Naw. Dis is a man's gang, ain't it?

Secretary. You said it! That's why we stand on our two feet in the open. We got no secrets.

Yank (*surprised but admiringly*). Yuh mean to say yuh always run wide open — like dis?

Secretary. Exactly.

Yank. Den yuh sure got your noive wit youse!

Secretary (*sharply*). Just what was it made you want to join us? Come out with that straight.

Yank. Yuh call me? Well, I got noive, too! Here's my hand. Yuh wanter blow tings up, don't yuh? Well, dat's me! I belong!

Secretary (*with pretended carelessness*). You mean change the unequal conditions of society by legitimate direct action — or with dynamite?

Yank. Dynamite! Blow it offen de oith — steel — all de cages — all de factories, steamers, buildings, jails — de Steel Trust and all dat makes it go.

Secretary. So — that's your idea, eh? And did you have any special job in that line you wanted to propose to us? (*He makes a sign to the men, who get up cautiously one by one and group behind* YANK.)

Yank (*boldly*). Sure, I'll come out wit it. I'll show youse I'm one of de gang. Dere's dat millionaire guy, Douglas ——

Secretary. President of the Steel Trust, you mean? Do you want to assassinate him?

Yank. Naw, dat don't get yuh nothin'. I mean blow up de factory, de woiks, where he makes de steel. Dat's what I'm after — to blow up de steel, knock all de steel in de woild up to de moon. Dat'll fix tings! (*Eagerly, with a touch of bravado.*) I'll do it by me lonesome! I'll show yuh! Tell me where his woiks is, how to git there, all de dope. Gimme de stuff, de old butter — and watch me do de rest! Watch de smoke and see it move! I don't give a damn if dey nab me — long as it's done! I'll soive life for it — and give 'em de laugh! (*Half to himself.*) And I'll write her a letter and tell her de hairy ape done it. Dat'll square tings.

Secretary (*stepping away from* YANK). Very interesting. (*He gives a signal. The men, huskies all, throw themselves on* YANK *and before he knows it they have his legs and arms pinioned. But he is too flabbergasted to make a struggle, anyway. They feel him over for weapons.*)

Man. No gat, no knife. Shall we give him what's what and put the boots to him?

Secretary. No. He isn't worth the trouble we'd get into. He's too stupid. (*He comes closer and laughs mockingly in* YANK's *face.*) Ho-ho! By God, this is the biggest joke they've put up on us yet. Hey, you Joke! Who sent you — Burns or Pinkerton? No, by God, you're such a bonehead I'll bet you're in the Secret Service! Well, you dirty spy, you rotten agent provocator, you can go back and tell whatever skunk is paying you blood-money for betraying your brothers that he's wasting his coin. You couldn't catch a cold. And tell him that all he'll ever get on us, or ever has got, is just his own sneaking plots that he's framed up to put us in jail. We are what our manifesto says we are, neither more nor less — and we'll give him a copy of that any time he calls. And as for you —— (*He glares scornfully at* YANK, *who is sunk in an oblivious stupor.*) Oh, hell, what's the use of talking? You're a brainless ape.

YANK (*aroused by the word to fierce but futile struggles*). What's dat, yuh Sheeny bum, yuh!

Secretary. Throw him out, boys. (*In spite of his struggle, this is done with gusto and éclat. Propelled by several parting kicks,* YANK *lands sprawling in the middle of the narrow cobbled street. With a growl he starts to get up and storm the closed door, but stops bewildered by the confusion in his brain, pathetically impotent. He sits there, brooding, in as near to the attitude of Rodin's "Thinker" as he can get in his position.*)

Yank (*bitterly*). So dem boids don't tink I belong, neider. Aw, to hell wit 'em! Dey're in de wrong pew — de same old bull — soapboxes and Salvation Army — no guts! Cut out an hour offen de job a day and make me happy! Gimme a dollar more a day and make me happy! Tree square a day, and cauliflowers in de front yard — ekal rights — a woman and kids — a lousy vote — and I'm all fixed for Jesus, huh? Aw, hell! What does dat get yuh? Dis ting's in your inside, but it ain't your belly. Feedin' your face — sinkers and coffee — dat don't touch it. It's way down — at de bottom. Yuh can't grab it, and yuh can't stop it. It moves, and everything moves. It stops and de whole woild stops. Dat's me now — I don't tick, see? — I'm a busted Ingersoll, dat's what. Steel was me, and I owned de woild. Now I ain't steel, and de woild owns me. Aw, hell! I can't see — it's all dark, get me? It's all wrong! (*He turns a bitter mocking face up like an ape gibbering at the moon.*) Say, youse up dere, Man in de Moon, yuh look so wise, gimme de answer, huh? Slip me de inside dope, de information right from de stable — where do I get off at, huh?

A Policeman (*who has come up the street in time to hear this last — with grim humor*). You'll get off at the station, you boob, if you don't get up out of that and keep movin'.

Yank (*looking up at him — with a hard, bitter laugh*). Sure! Lock me up! Put me in a cage! Dat's de on'y answer yuh know. G'wan, lock me up!

Policeman. What you been doin'?

Yank. Enuf to gimme life for! I was born, see? Sure, dat's de charge. Write it in de blotter. I was born, get me!

Policeman (*jocosely*). God pity your old woman! (*Then matter-of-fact.*) But I've no time for kidding. You're soused. I'd run you in but it's too long a walk to the station. Come on now, get up, or I'll fan your ears with this club. Beat it now!

(*He hauls* YANK *to his feet.*)

Yank (*in a vague mocking tone*). Say, where do I go from here?

Policeman (*giving him a push — with a grin, indifferently*). Go to hell.

CURTAIN

SCENE EIGHT

SCENE: *Twilight of the next day. The monkey house at the Zoo. One spot of clear gray light falls on the front of one cage so that the interior can be seen. The other cages are vague, shrouded in shadow from which chatterings pitched in a conversational tone can be heard. On the one cage a sign from which the word "gorilla" stands out. The gigantic animal himself is seen squatting on his haunches on a bench in much the same attitude as Rodin's "Thinker." YANK enters from the left. Immediately a chorus of angry chattering and screeching breaks out. The gorilla turns his eyes but makes no sound or move.*

Yank (*with a hard, bitter laugh*). Welcome to your city, huh? Hail, hail, de gang's all here! (*At the sound of his voice the chattering dies away into an attentive silence. YANK walks up to the gorilla's cage and, leaning over the railing, stares in at its occupant, who stares back at him, silent and motionless. There is a pause of dead stillness. Then YANK begins to talk in a friendly confidential tone, half-mockingly, but with a deep undercurrent of sympathy.*) Say, yuh're some hard-lookin' guy, ain't yuh? I seen lots of tough nuts dat de gang called gorillas, but yuh're de foist real one I ever seen. Some chest yuh got, and shoulders, and dem arms and mits! I bet yuh got a punch in eider fist dat'd knock 'em all silly! (*This with genuine admiration. The gorilla, as if he understood, stands upright, swelling out his chest and pounding on it with his fist. YANK grins sympathetically.*) Sure, I get yuh. Yuh challenge de whole woild, huh? Yuh got what I was sayin' even if yuh muffed de woids. (*Then bitterness creeping in.*) And why wouldn't yuh get me? Ain't we both members of de same club — de Hairy Apes? (*They stare at each other — a pause — then YANK goes on slowly and bitterly.*) So yuh're what she seen when she looked at me, de white-faced tart! I was you to her, get me? On'y outa de cage — broke out — free to moider her, see? Sure! Dat's what she tought. She wasn't wise dat I was in a cage, too — worser'n yours — sure — a damn sight — 'cause you got some chanct to bust loose — but me —— (*He grows confused.*) Aw, hell! It's all wrong, ain't it? (*A pause.*) I s'pose yuh wanter know what I'm doin' here, huh? I been warmin' a bench down to de Battery — ever since last night. Sure. I seen de sun come up. Dat was pretty, too — all red and pink and green. I was lookin' at de skyscrapers — steel — and all de ships comin' in, sailin' out, all over de oith — and dey was steel, too. De sun was warm, dey wasn't no clouds, and dere was a breeze blowin'. Sure, it was great stuff. I got it aw right — what Paddy said about dat bein' de right dope — on'y I couldn't get *in* it, see? I couldn't belong in dat. It was over my head. And I kept tinkin' — and den I beat it up here to see what youse was like. And I waited till dey was all gone to git yuh alone. Say, how d'yuh feel sittin' in dat pen all de time, havin' to stand for 'em comin' and starin' at yuh — de white-faced, skinny tarts and de boobs what marry 'em — makin' fun of yuh, laughin' at yuh, gittin' scared of yuh — damn 'em! (*He pounds on the rail with his fist. The gorilla rattles the bars of his cage and snarls. All the other monkeys set up an angry chattering in the darkness. YANK goes on excitedly.*) Sure! Dat's de way it hits me, too. On'y yuh're lucky, see? Yuh don't belong wit 'em and yuh know it. But me, I belong wit 'em — but I don't, see? Dey don't belong wit me, dat's what. Get me? Tinkin' is hard —— (*He passes one hand across his forehead with a painful gesture. The gorilla growls impatiently. YANK goes on gropingly.*) It's dis way, what I'm drivin' at. Youse can sit and dope dream in de past, green woods, de jungle and de rest of it. Den yuh belong and dey don't. Den yuh kin laugh at 'em, see? Yuh're de champ of de woild. But me — I ain't got no past to tink in, nor nothin' dat's comin', on'y what's now — and dat don't belong. Sure, you're de best off! Yuh can't tink, can yuh? Yuh can't talk neider. But I kin make a bluff at talkin' and tinkin' — a'most git away wit it — a'most! — and dat's where de joker comes in. (*He laughs.*) I ain't on oith and I ain't in heaven, get me? I'm in de middle tryin' to separate 'em, takin' all de woist punches from bot' of 'em. Maybe dat's what dey call hell, huh? But you, yuh're at de bottom. You belong! Sure! Yuh're de on'y one in de woild dat does, yuh lucky stiff! (*The gorilla growls proudly.*) And dat's why dey gotter put yuh in a cage, see? (*The gorilla roars angrily.*) Sure! Yuh get me. It beats it when you try to tink it or talk it — it's way down — deep — behind — you 'n' me we feel it. Sure! Bot' members of dis club! (*He laughs — then in a savage tone.*) What de hell! T' hell wit it! A little action, dat's our meat! Dat belongs! Knock 'em down and keep bustin' 'em till dey croaks yuh wit a gat — wit steel! Sure! Are yuh game? Dey've looked at youse, ain't dey — in a cage? Wanter get even? Wanter wind up like a sport 'stead of croakin' slow in dere? (*The gorilla roars an emphatic affirmative.* YANK *goes on with a sort of furious exaltation.*) Sure! Yuh're reg'lar! Yuh'll stick to de finish! Me 'n' you, huh? — bot' members of this club! We'll put up one last star bout dat'll knock 'em offen deir seats! Dey'll have to make de cages stronger after we're trou! (*The gorilla is straining at his bars, growling, hopping from one foot to the other.* YANK *takes a jimmy from under his coat and forces the lock on the cage door. He throws this open.*) Pardon from de governor! Step out and shake hands! I'll take yuh for a walk down Fif' Avenoo. We'll knock 'em offen de oith and croak wit de band playin'. Come on, Brother. (*The gorilla scrambles gingerly out of his cage. Goes to* YANK *and stands looking at*

him. YANK *keeps his mocking tone — holds out his hand.*) Shake — de secret grip of our order. (*Something, the tone of mockery, perhaps, suddenly enrages the animal. With a spring he wraps his huge arms around* YANK *in a murderous hug. There is a crackling snap of crushed ribs — a gasping cry, still mocking, from* YANK.) Hey, I didn't say kiss me! (*The gorilla lets the crushed body slip to the floor; stands over it uncertainly, considering; then picks it up, throws it in the cage, shuts the door, and shuffles off menacingly into the darkness at left. A great uproar of frightened chattering and whimpering comes from the other cages. Then* YANK *moves, groaning, opening his eyes, and there is silence. He mutters painfully.*) Say — dey oughter match him — wit Zybszko. He got me, aw right. I'm trou. Even him didn't tink I belonged. (*Then, with sudden passionate despair.*) Christ, where do I get off at? Where do I fit in? (*Checking himself as suddenly.*) Aw, what de hell! No squawkin', see! No quittin', get me! Croak wit your boots on! (*He grabs hold of the bars of the cage and hauls himself painfully to his feet — looks around him bewilderedly — forces a mocking laugh.*) In de cage, huh? (*In the strident tones of a circus barker.*) Ladies and gents, step forward and take a slant at de one and only — (*His voice weakened*) — one and original — Hairy Ape from de wilds of —— (*He slips in a heap on the floor and dies. The monkeys set up a chattering, whimpering wail. And, perhaps, the Hairy Ape at last belongs.*)

CURTAIN

T. S. Eliot · 1888–1965

The published work of T. S. Eliot — criticism, drama, and poetry — in bulk hardly equals the longer novels of Thackeray or Thomas Wolfe. *The Waste Land*, Eliot's best-known poem, runs to less than five hundred lines. Yet Eliot, with James Joyce, shares the distinction of being among the most discussed and also among the most influential modern writers in the English language. There are two main reasons for Eliot's prominence among his contemporaries: he early developed a manner of writing, original in its recourse to poetic stylization. Then, by putting into his poetry a pessimistic outlook upon our modern culture and civilization he made himself the mouthpiece of a generation disappointed by the historical degeneration of human existence.

Among Eliot's most important works are his poems, collected under the titles of *Prufrock and Other Observations* (1917), *The Waste Land* (1922), *Ash Wednesday* (1930) and *Four Quartets* (1943). He published seven plays, one of which, *Murder in the Cathedral*, was written for the Canterbury Festival in 1935, while the others, from the very beginning, enjoyed commercial success on European stages and in New York. Eliot's *Essays Ancient and Modern* (1936), a series of papers in literary criticism, became the basis of many of the more recent systems of criticism. However, even before his death in 1965 both his poetry and critical doctrines came under attack by a new group of less traditionalistic writers.

Eliot's poetry is expressionistic in that it is highly stylized and in that it presents a general human, mostly psychological situation rather than a detailed description of individual experiences. In his early writings Eliot made frequent use of the stream-of-consciousness technique; by using associative processes of the mind, he expressed the subconscious thoughts of his characters (Sweeney, Prufrock). In his later, more religious poetry, however, he abandoned this manner altogether and instead abstracted his characters even from their own mental environment by placing them in a cosmic or religio-mythical setting. In his early poem, *The Hollow Men* (1925), one recognizes a certain elation and a compact style which remind one of the prophetic or apocalyptic books of the Bible.

To emphasize the feeling of strangeness and alienation, Eliot even introduced allusions to non-existing situations or quotations from little-known literatures. His symbols are partly private and communicable only by the context in which they occur. His unity of style is frequently disrupted by quotations, in translation or in the original, from the Bible, the Greek playwrights, Dante, Shakespeare and his contemporaries, or the French Symbolist school of poetry. By contrasting unity of mood with diversity of expression, Eliot creates startling effects and holds his reader's attention.

SUGGESTED REFERENCES: F. O. Matthiessen, *The Achievement of T. S. Eliot* (2nd ed., 1947); Northrop Frye, *T. S. Eliot* (1963); Hugh Kenner, ed., *T. S. Eliot. A Collection of Critical Essays* (1965).

Sweeney Among the Nightingales

Apeneck Sweeney spreads his knees
Letting his arms hang down to laugh,
The zebra stripes along his jaw
Swelling to maculate giraffe.

The circles of the stormy moon   5
Slike westward toward the River Plate,
Death and the Raven drift above
And Sweeney guards the horned gate.

Gloomy Orion and the Dog
Are veiled; and hushed the shrunken seas;   10
The person in the Spanish cape
Tries to sit on Sweeney's knees

Slips and pulls the table cloth
Overturns a coffee-cup,
Reorganised upon the floor   15
She yawns and draws a stocking up;

The silent man in mocha brown
Sprawls at the window-sill and gapes;
The waiter brings in oranges
Bananas figs and hothouse grapes;   20

The silent vertebrate in brown
Contracts and concentrates, withdraws;
Rachel *née* Rabinovitch
Tears at the grapes with murderous paws;

She and the lady in the cape   25
Are suspect, thought to be in league;
Therefore the man with heavy eyes
Declines the gambit, shows fatigue,

Leaves the room and reappears
Outside the window, leaning in,   30
Branches of wistaria
Circumscribe a golden grin;

The host with someone indistinct
Converses at the door apart,
The nightingales are singing near   35
The Convent of the Sacred Heart,

And sang within the bloody wood
When Agamemnon cried aloud,
And let their liquid siftings fall
To stain the stiff dishonored shroud.   40

Rhapsody on a Windy Night

Twelve o'clock.
Along the reaches of the street
Held in a lunar synthesis,
Whispering lunar incantations
Dissolve the floors of memory   5

And all its clear relations,
Its divisions and precisions,
Every street lamp that I pass
Beats like a fatalistic drum,
And through the spaces of the dark   10
Midnight shakes the memory
As a madman shakes a dead geranium.

Half-past one,
The street-lamp sputtered,
The street-lamp muttered,   15
The street-lamp said, "Regard that woman
Who hesitates toward you in the light of the door
Which opens on her like a grin.
And see the border of her dress
Is torn and stained with sand,   20
And you see the corner of her eye
Twists like a crooked pin."

The memory throws up high and dry
A crowd of twisted things;
A twisted branch upon the beach   25
Eaten smooth, and polished
As if the world gave up
The secret of its skeleton,
Stiff and white.
A broken spring in a factory yard,   30
Rust that clings to the form that the strength has
        left
Hard and curled and ready to snap.

Half-past two,
The street-lamp said,
"Remark the cat which flattens itself in the
        gutter,   35
Slips out its tongue
And devours a morsel of rancid butter."
So the hand of the child, automatic,
Slipped out and pocketed a toy that was running
        along the quay.
I could see nothing behind that child's eye. 40
I have seen eyes in the street
Trying to peer through lighted shutters,
And a crab one afternoon in a pool,
An old crab with barnacles on his back,
Gripped the end of a stick which I held him.   45

Half-past three,
The lamp sputtered,
The lamp muttered in the dark.
The lamp hummed:
"Regard the moon,   50
La lune ne garde aucune rancune,
She winks a feeble eye,
She smiles into corners.
She smooths the hair of the grass.

The moon has lost her memory.   55
A washed-out smallpox cracks her face,
Her hand twists a paper rose,
That smells of dust and eau de Cologne,
She is alone
With all the old nocturnal smells   60
That cross and cross across her brain."
The reminiscence comes
Of sunless dry geraniums
And dust in crevices,
Smells of chestnuts in the streets,   65
And female smells in shuttered rooms,
And cigarettes in corridors
And cocktail smells in bars.

The lamp said,
"Four o'clock,   70
Here is the number on the door.
Memory!
You have the key,
The little lamp spreads a ring on the stair,
Mount.   75
The bed is open; the tooth-brush hangs on the wall,
Put your shoes at the door, sleep, prepare for life."

The last twist of the knife.

The Hollow Men

A Penny for the Old Guy

I

We are the hollow men
We are the stuffed men
Leaning together
Headpiece filled with straw. Alas!
Our dried voices, when   5
We whisper together
Are quiet and meaningless
As wind in dry grass
Or rats' feet over broken glass
In our dry cellar   10

Shape without form, shade without color,
Paralysed force, gesture without motion;

Those who have crossed
With direct eyes, to death's other Kingdom
Remember us — if at all — not as lost   15
Violent souls, but only
As the hollow men
The stuffed men.

II

Eyes I dare not meet in dreams
In death's dream kingdom   20

These do not appear:
There, the eyes are
Sunlight on a broken column
There, in a tree swinging
And voices are   25
In the wind's singing
More distant and more solemn
Than a fading star.

Let me be no nearer
In death's dream kingdom   30
Let me also wear
Such deliberate disguises
Rat's coat, crowskin, crossed staves
In a field
Behaving as the wind behaves   35
No nearer —

Not that final meeting
In the twilight kingdom

III

This is the dead land
This is cactus land   40
Here the stone images
Are raised, here they receive
The supplication of a dead man's hand
Under the twinkle of a fading star.

Is it like this   45
In death's other kingdom
Waking alone
At the hour when we are
Trembling with tenderness
Lips that would kiss   50
Form prayers to broken stone.

IV

The eyes are not here
There are no eyes here
In this valley of dying stars
In this hollow valley   55
This broken jaw of our lost kingdoms

In this last of meeting places
We grope together
And avoid speech
Gathered on this beach of the tumid river   60

Sightless, unless
The eyes reappear
As the perpetual star
Multifoliate rose
Of death's twilight kingdom   65
The hope only
Of empty men.

V

Here we go round the prickly pear
Prickly pear prickly pear
Here we go round the prickly pear   70
At five o'clock in the morning.

Between the idea
And the reality
Between the motion
And the act   75
Falls the Shadow

                              For Thine is the Kingdom

Between the conception
And the creation
Between the emotion   80
And the response
Falls the Shadow

                                    Life is very long

Between the desire
And the spasm   85
Between the potency
And the existence
Between the essence
And the descent
Falls the Shadow   90

                              For Thine is the Kingdom

For Thine is
Life is
For Thine is the

This is the way the world ends   95
This is the way the world ends
This is the way the world ends
Not with a bang but a whimper.

THE REALISTIC TEMPER

LITERATURE

Realism and Naturalism

ERICH AUERBACH
  Mimesis, trans. by W. R. Trask (1953)
G. J. BECKER, ed.
  Documents of Modern Literary Realism (1963)
GEORGE BOAS, ed.
  Courbet and the Naturalistic Movement (1938)
EDMOND and JULES DE GONCOURT
  The Goncourt Journals, 1851–1870, ed. and trans. by
    Lewis Galantière (new ed., 1958)
GRANT C. KNIGHT
  The Critical Period in American Literature (1951)
HARRY LEVIN
  The Gates of Horn. A Study of Five French Realists
    .. (1963)
GYORGY LUKACS
  *Studies in European Realism; A Sociological Survey
    of the Writings of Balzac, Stendhal, Zola, Tolstoy,
    Gorki and Others*, trans. by Edith Bone (1950)
  *Realism in Our Time; Literature and the Class
    Struggle*, trans. by John and Necke Mander (1964)
J. W. MARRIOTT
  "The Drift Towards Naturalism" and "Naturalism
    on the Stage," in *Modern Drama* (1934), 60–86
V. L. PARRINGTON
  *The Beginnings of Critical Realism in America,
    1860–1920*, Vol. III of *Main Currents in American
    Thought* (2nd ed., 1958)
PHILIP RAHV
  Image and Idea (2nd ed., 1957)
STEPHEN SPENDER
  The New Realism; A Discussion (1939)
"A Symposium on Realism," arranged by Harry Levin,
  Comparative Literature, III (Summer, 1951), 193–285
LIONEL TRILLING
  The Liberal Imagination (2nd ed., 1953)
CHARLES CHILD WALCUTT
  American Literary Naturalism, A Divided Stream
    (1956)
BERHARD WEINBERG
  French Realism; The Critical Reaction (1937)

Impressionism

PIERRE DE BACOURT AND JOHN W. CUNLIFFE
  French Literature During the Last Half Century (1923)
JOSEPH WARREN BEACH
  The Twentieth Century Novel (1932)
NORMAN FOERSTER
  "Impressionism," *Toward Standards*, II (1930),
    42–74
B. J. GIBBS
  "Impressionism as a Literary Movement," *Modern
    Language Journal*, XXXVI (1952), 175–183
HENRY JAMES
  The Art of the Novel (new ed., 1960)
JOSEPH T. SHIPLEY
  The Literary Isms (1931)

Expressionism

ANNA BALAKIAN
  Literary Origins of Surrealism (1947)
SELDON CHENEY
  Expressionism in Art (1934)
ISAAC GOLDBERG
  The Drama of Transition (1922)
LUDWIG LEWISOHN
  Expressionism in America (1932)
HERBERT E. READ
  Surrealism (1936)
WALTER HERBERT SOKEL
  *The Writer in Extremis: Expressionism in Twentieth
    Century German Literature* (1959)

ART

Realism and Naturalism

PERUGINO (1446–1524)
  Portrait of a Youth
  St. Jerome in the Wilderness

GIOVANNI BELLINI (c. 1430–1516)
Mary Magdalene
Portrait of a Condottiere

ANTONELLO DA MESSINA (fl. 1465–1493)
Madonna and Child
Il Condottiere

HOLBEIN (1497–1543)
Sir Brian Tuke
Portrait of Erasmus

MORONI (1525?–1578)
A Gentleman in Adoration before the Madonna

VELASQUEZ (1599–1660)
Pope Innocent X

REMBRANDT (1606–1669)
Syndics of the Cloth Hall
The Carpenter's Household

NICHOLAES MAES (1632–1693)
Portrait of a Man
An Old Woman Dozing over a Book

HOGARTH (1697–1764)
The Rake's Progress: The Levee
The Rake's Progress: The Gaming House

MILLET (1814–1875)
The Sower
The Gleaners

COURBET (1819–1877)
Funeral at Ornans

BASTIEN-LEPAGE (1848–1934)
Jeanne d'Arc

HOMER (1836–1910)
The Gale
The Lookout: All's Well

SARGENT (1856–1925)
James Whitcomb Riley

Egyptian (IV Dynasty)
Kaaper (Sheikh-el-Beled)

Hellenistic Period
Menelaos and Patroklos

Roman
Terra Cotta Head

DONATELLO (1386–1466)
David
St. John the Baptist

ANTONIO ROSSELLINO (1427–1478)
Young St. John the Baptist

ANDREA DELLA ROBBIA (1435–1525)
Bust of a Child

DA MAJANO (1442–1497)
Bust of Pietro Mellini

MICHELANGELO (1475–1564)
Drunken Bacchus

HOUDON (1741–1828)
Busts of Washington and Mirabeau

HUNTINGTON (1876–)
Jeanne d'Arc

Impressionism

FRANS HALS (1580?–1666)
The Laughing Cavalier
Portrait of a Man

PISSARO (1830–1903)
Landscape in Sunshine
Côte des Boeufs

DEGAS (1834–1917)
Le Foyer de la Danse
Café, Boulevard Montmartre

MONET (1840–1926)
Grand Canal, Venice
Houses of Parliament

SISLEY (1840–1899)
Snow at Louveciennes

RENOIR (1841–1919)
Luncheon of the Boating Party

CHILDE HASSAM (1859–1935)
Church at Old Lyme

RODIN (1840–1917)
Balzac
The Kiss

Expressionism

EL GRECO (1548–1625)
Burial of the Count of Orgaz
View of Toledo

WILLIAM BLAKE (1757–1827)
When the Morning Stars Sang Together
The Piper

CÉZANNE (1839–1906)
Mont St. Victoire
Self Portrait

GAUGUIN (1848–1903)
Flowers

VAN GOGH (1853–1890)
Landscape with Cypresses
La Berceuse

MATISSE (1869–1954)
Flowers
Odalisque aux Bras Levés

PICASSO (1881–)
Le Corsage Jaune
Les Demoiselles d'Avignon

Music

The music of the realistic temper is more readily detected than is the music of some of the other manners. Musicians call it "program music"; it is not music for music's sake, but music which paints a picture or tells a story, either directly or by suggestion.

Naturalism is not a word which we encounter much in music; its associations are more definitely literary. If we define it as "realism which goes beyond realism," we still have difficulty in pinning it down in music.

Debussy is usually thought of as the leading impressionistic composer. He and the group which worked at the same time or followed him, were not so much concerned with telling a story or with emotional expression of sentiment as they were with delicate suggestions of tone color, with *tone* as *tone*, much as the impressionists in painting were preoccupied with *light* as *light*. Where others depicted, Debussy suggested. In his music he creates incomparable pictures; he is especially successful in representing in magnificent tone color such things as the sea. He uses the instruments of his orchestra as another artist would use his brushes, and the melodies and harmonies which they play are like the colors of the artist's palette. He makes extensive use of a scale (whole-tone scale) which helps him create his atmospheric effects, and abandons form, as his predecessors knew it, entirely.

Ravel, another composer frequently called an impressionist, is less truly one than Debussy, for the reason that his music is less "misty" or "atmospheric." He based many compositions on writers like Mallarmé, Verlaine, Verhaeren, Henri de Régnier, and other French symbolists, but his work is so much firmer and clearer in outline than Debussy's that he is less truly representative of impressionism in music.

The word "expressionism" is associated with a school of German painters who stated that it was their belief that "the painter should attempt a direct expression of his emotions, or a direct reproduction of forms that have shaped themselves within his mind." In their painting they discarded all the rules, and it was natural that they should claim kinship with a composer who did the same thing.

If we ask what made the group select Schönberg as their musician, we are led to believe that it is in his abandonment of traditional rules and styles that he has qualified. Upon this quality rests our ability to recognize examples of the music of expressionism. Schönberg founded a new twelve-tone scale with no leading or tonic note and no internal relationship; this has been used in much modern music and produces what is known as the atonal style. The set of piano pieces listed below is representative of the scale and the way in which he used it.

COMPOSITIONS

RICHARD STRAUSS (1864–1949)

Symphonia Domestica, Op. 53
Themes represent Husband, Wife, and Child, who play their part in telling the story of a day in the life of a family.

MOUSSORGSKY (1839–1881)

Pictures at an Exhibition
Musical reproductions of some paintings by a friend of the composer. Particularly realistic are the descriptions of conversation between two Jews and the chattering of women at a market. Other sections, "The Old Castle" and "Catacombs," have an almost impressionistic quality.

The Nursery
The songs of this composer, which are the height of musical realism, are characteristic of him. These are in English translations which are not entirely happy, but they enable the hearer to grasp the realistic details with ease.

DEBUSSY (1862–1918)

La Mer
Nocturnes
Préludes pour Piano

These three compositions represent especially well the composer's impressionistic technique.

RAVEL (1875–1937)

Jeux d'Eau
This composition, with its novel effects, should be played with Debussy's, to illustrate the difference in their impressionistic styles.

FALLA (1876–1946)

Nights in the Gardens of Spain
Evocations of the atmosphere of the old palaces of Granada in the moonlight with musical ornaments suggesting the fountains of the old Moorish courts and of gypsies dancing and singing in the distance. This piece for piano and orchestra is an excellent example of the impressionistic facet of the modern Spanish composer.

SCHÖNBERG (1874–1951)

Piano Pieces, Op. 11, 25

SUPPLEMENTARY BIBLIOGRAPHY

CHRONOLOGICAL TABLE OF AUTHORS

GUIDE TO THE TYPES OF LITERATURE

INDEX

Students will find the following books useful as general reading in the fields of literature, art, and music.

LITERATURE

DRAMA

Bentley, Eric. *The Life of the Drama.* New York: Atheneum, 1964.

Brooks, Cleanth, and Robert B. Heilman. *Understanding Drama.* Third edition. New York: Holt, Rinehart and Winston, 1963.

Brustein, Robert Sanford. *The Theatre of Revolt.* Boston: Little, Brown, 1964.

Cheney, Sheldon. *The Theater, Three Thousand Years of Drama, Acting, and Stagecraft.* Revised edition. New York: McKay, 1963.

Esslin, Martin. *The Theatre of the Absurd.* Garden City, N.Y.: Doubleday, 1961.

Fergusson, Francis. *The Idea of a Theater.* Garden City, N.Y.: Doubleday, 1953.

Gassner, John. *Masters of the Drama.* Third edition. New York: Dover Publications, 1954.

POETRY

Adams, Hazard. *The Contexts of Poetry.* Boston: Little, Brown, 1963.

Brooks, Cleanth, and Robert Penn Warren. *Understanding Poetry.* Third edition. New York: Holt, Rinehart and Winston, 1960.

Deutsch, Babette. *Poetry in Our Time.* Second edition. New York: Holt, Rinehart and Winston, 1963.

Eastman, Max. *Enjoyment of Poetry.* New edition. New York: Charles Scribner's Sons, 1951.

Hillyer, Robert. *In Pursuit of Poetry.* New York: McGraw-Hill, 1960.

Korg, Jacob. *An Introduction to Poetry.* New York: Holt, Rinehart and Winston, 1963.

FICTION

Beach, Joseph Warren. *The Twentieth Century Novel; Studies in Techniques.* New York: The Century Company, 1932.

Brooks, Cleanth, and Robert Penn Warren. *Understanding Fiction.* Second edition. New York: Appleton-Century-Crofts, 1959.

Ker, W. P. *Epic and Romance.* New edition. New York: The Macmillan Company, 1957.

Lubbock, Percy. *The Craft of Fiction.* New edition. New York: Peter Smith, 1957.

Muir, Edwin. *The Structure of the Novel.* Second edition. New York: Harcourt, Brace and Company, 1960.

Sale, Roger, ed. *Discussions of the Novel.* Boston: D. C. Heath and Company, 1960.

Stanton, Robert. *An Introduction to Fiction.* New York: Holt, Rinehart and Winston, 1965.

CRITICISM

Ellmann, Richard, and Charles Feidelson, eds. *The Modern Tradition: Backgrounds of Modern Literature.* New York: Oxford University Press, 1965.

Friedrich, W. P., and D. H. Malone. *Outline of Comparative Literature. From Dante Alighieri to Eugene O'Neill.* Chapel Hill: University of North Carolina Press, 1954.

Frye, Northrop. *Anatomy of Criticism.* Princeton: Princeton University Press, 1963.

Schorer, Mark, *et al. Criticism; The Foundations of Modern Literary Judgment.* Revised edition. New York: Harcourt, Brace and Company, 1958.

Schreiber, S. M. *An Introduction to Literary Criticism.* Oxford: Pergamon Press, 1965.

Smith, James Harry, and Edd Winfield Parks, eds. *The Great Critics; An Anthology of Literary Criticism.* Revised edition. New York: W. W. Norton and Company, 1951.

Stallknecht, Newton P., and Horst Frenz, eds. *Comparative Literature. Method and Perspective.* Chapel Hill: University of North Carolina Press, 1961.

Wellek, René, and Austin Warren. *Theory of Literature.* Third edition. New York: Harcourt, Brace and Company, 1963.

Wellek, René. *Concepts of Criticism.* New Haven: Yale University Press, 1963.

——. *History of Modern Criticism.* Four vols. New Haven: Yale University Press, 1955–1965.

Wimsatt, William K., and Cleanth Brooks. *Literary Criticism, A Short History.* Second edition. New York: Knopf, 1959.

REFERENCE BOOKS

Abrams, M. H. *A Glossary of Literary Terms.* New York: Holt, Rinehart and Winston, 1964.

Deutsch, Babette. *Poetry Handbook; A Dictionary of Terms.* New edition. New York: Funk and Wagnalls, 1962.

Hartnoll, Phyllis, ed. *The Oxford Companion to the Theatre.* Third edition. New York: Oxford University Press, 1964.

Preminger, Alex, ed. *Encyclopedia of Poetry and Poetics.* Princeton: Princeton University Press, 1965.

Shipley, Joseph T., ed. *Dictionary of World Literature.* New revised edition. New York: Philosophical Library, 1953.

Smith, Horatio, ed. *Columbia Dictionary of Modern European Literature.* New York: Columbia University Press, 1947.

Steinberg, S. H., ed. *Cassel's Encyclopedia of World Literature.* Two vols. New York: Funk and Wagnalls, 1954.

Thrall, W. F., Addison Hibbard, and Hugh Holman. *A Handbook to Literature.* Revised edition. New York: The Odyssey Press, 1960.

ART

Bazin, Germain. *The Loom of Art*. New York: Simon and Schuster, 1962.

Braun-Vogelstein, Julie. *Art. The Image of the West*. New York: Pantheon, 1952.

Cheney, Sheldon. *A Primer of Modern Art*. Thirteenth edition. New York: Tudor Publishing Company, 1958.

Dewey, John. *Art as Experience*. New York: Minton, Balch and Company, 1934.

Gardner, Helen. *Art Through the Ages*. Fourth revised edition. New York: Harcourt, Brace and Company, 1959.

Giedion, Sigfried. *Space, Time and Architecture*. Third edition. Cambridge: Harvard University Press, 1954.

Malraux, André. *The Voices of Silence*. Garden City, N.Y.: Doubleday, 1953.

Ortega y Gasset, José. *The Dehumanization of Art and Other Writings on Art and Culture*. Trans. by W. R. Trask. Garden City, N.Y.: Doubleday, 1956.

Panofsky, Erwin. *Meaning in the Visual Arts*. Garden City, N.Y.: Doubleday, 1955.

Read, Herbert. *Art Now; An Introduction to the Theory of Modern Painting and Sculpture*. New York: Pitman Publishing Corporation, 1948.

——. *The Philosophy of Modern Art*. Cleveland: The World Publishing Company, 1955.

Taylor, Frances Henry. *Fifty Centuries of Art*. New York: Harper and Brothers, 1954.

Worringer, Wilhelm. *Abstraction and Empathy*. Trans. by Michael Bullock. New York: International Universities Press, 1953.

MUSIC

Apel, Willi. *Harvard Dictionary of Music*. Cambridge: Harvard University Press, 1946.

Blom, Eric, ed. *Grove's Dictionary of Music and Musicians*. Fifth edition. New York: The Macmillan Company, 1961.

Boyden, David Dodge. *An Introduction to Music*. New York: Knopf, 1956.

Brandt, William E. *The Way of Music*. Boston: Allyn and Bacon, 1963.

Brockway, Wallace, and Herbert Weinstock. *Men of Music*. Revised edition. New York: Simon and Schuster, 1950.

Cannon, B. C., A. H. Johnson, and W. G. Waite. *The Art of Music*. New York: Thomas Y. Crowell, 1960.

Copland, Aaron. *What to Listen for in Music*. Revised edition. New York: McGraw-Hill, 1957.

Ferguson, D. N. *A History of Musical Thought*. Third edition. New York: Appleton-Century-Crofts, 1959.

Hughes, Rupert, and Deems Taylor, eds. *Music Lover's Encyclopedia*. Revised edition. Garden City, N.Y.: Garden City Books, 1954.

Machlis, Joseph. *The Enjoyment of Music*. Revised edition. New York: W. W. Norton and Company, 1963.

Portnoy, Julius. *Music in the Life of Man*. New York: Holt, Rinehart and Winston, 1963.

Robertson, Alec, and Denis Stevens, eds. *The Pelican History of Music*. Baltimore: Penguin Books, 1962.

Sachs, Curt. *Our Musical Heritage*. Second edition. New York: Prentice-Hall, 1955.

Scholes, Percy, ed. *The Oxford Companion to Music*. New York: Oxford University Press, 1950.

Ulrich, Homer. *A History of Music and Musical Style*. New York: Harcourt, Brace and World, 1963.

INTERRELATION OF THE ARTS

Barzun, Jacques, ed. *Pleasures of Music*. New York: The Viking Press, 1951.

Brown, Calvin S. *Music and Literature; A Comparison of the Arts*. Athens, Georgia: The University of Georgia Press, 1948.

Edman, Irvin. *Arts and the Man*. New York: W. W. Norton and Company, 1939.

Fleming, William. *Arts and Ideas*. Revised edition. New York: Holt, Rinehart and Winston, 1963.

Hatzfeld, Helmut. *Literature Through Art; A New Approach to French Literature*. New York: Oxford University Press, 1952.

Hauser, Arnold. *The Social History of Art*. Trans. by Stanley Godman. New York: Knopf, 1953.

Lang, Paul Henry. *Music in Western Civilization*. New York: W. W. Norton and Company, 1941.

Munro, Thomas. *The Arts and Their Interrelations*. New York: Liberal Arts Press, 1949.

Sachs, Curt. *The Commonwealth of Art*. New York: W. W. Norton and Company, 1946.

Sypher, Wylie. *Rococo to Cubism in Art and Literature*. New York: Vintage Books, 1960.

Thimme, Diether, and William H. Heist, eds. *An Introduction to Literature and the Fine Arts*. Lansing: Michigan State University Press, 1950.

Weber, Eugene, ed. *Paths to the Present. Aspects of European Thought from Romanticism to Existentialism*. New York: Dodd, Mead and Company, 1962.

CHRONOLOGICAL TABLE OF AUTHORS

	Nationality	Classification	Page
HOMER (*c. ninth century* B.C.)	GREEK	CLASSICISM	11
The *Iliad*, Books I, XVIII — The *Odyssey*, Books VI, IX, XXI			
ÆSCHYLUS (525–456 B.C.)	GREEK	CLASSICISM	70
Agamemnon			
SOPHOCLES (496–406 B.C.)	GREEK	CLASSICISM	92
Antigone			
EURIPIDES (484–406 B.C.)	GREEK	CLASSICISM	110
Medea			
ARISTOPHANES (445–385 B.C.)	GREEK	CLASSICISM	130
The Frogs			
PLATO (427–347 B.C.)	GREEK	CLASSICISM	156
Dialogues: The Apology			
ARISTOTLE (384–322 B.C.)	GREEK	CLASSICISM	169
The Nature of Tragedy			
THEOCRITUS (*c.* 270 B.C.)	GREEK	CLASSICISM	175
Epigrams — Daphnis and Menalcas — At the Festival of Adonis — The Cyclops in Love			
LUCRETIUS (98–55 B.C.)	ROMAN	CLASSICISM	180
On the Nature of Things: Proem; Substance Is Eternal; The Soul Is Mortal; Folly of the Fear of Death; The Origin of Life; Origin of Mankind; Beginnings of Civilization			
VIRGIL (70–19 B.C.)	ROMAN	CLASSICISM	191
The *Æneid*, Books II, IV, VI			
HORACE (65–8 B.C.)	ROMAN	CLASSICISM	224
Alphius — To Lycè — The Reconciliation — Contentment — The Bore — My Prayers with This I Used to Charge			
OVID (43 B.C.–17 A.D.)	ROMAN	ROMANTICISM	404
From the *Metamorphoses:* Apollo and Daphne — Alpheus and Arethusa — Orpheus and Eurydice — Narcissus — The Rape of Proserpine — From *Heroides:* Dido to Æneas			
MARCUS AURELIUS (121–180 A.D.)	ROMAN	CLASSICISM	233
Meditations			
LUCIAN (*c.* 120–*c.* 180)	GREEK	CLASSICISM	240
Dialogues of the Dead: Dialogue X: Charon and Hermes. *Dialogues of the Gods:* Dialogue XX: The Judgment of Paris. Sale of Creeds			

	Nationality	Classification	Page
APULEIUS (c. 160)	ROMAN	ROMANTICISM	413
From *The Golden Ass:* The Robbers; Cupid and Psyche			
From the BEOWULF (*seventh century*)	ENGLISH	ROMANTICISM	427
AUCASSIN AND NICOLETE (*twelfth century*)	FRENCH	ROMANTICISM	453
From THE NIBELUNGENLIED (c. 1200)	GERMAN	ROMANTICISM	442
How Gunther Won Brunhild — How Sigfrid Was Slain			
DANTE (1265–1321)	ITALIAN	ROMANTICISM	473
From *The Divine Comedy:* Hell (Cantos I–II–III–IV–V); Purgatory (Cantos I–II–III–IV); Paradise (Cantos XXXI–XXXII–XXXIII)			
BOCCACCIO (1313–1375)	ITALIAN	ROMANTICISM	493
From *The Decameron:* Introduction; Simona and Pasquino; Federigo's Falcon; Patient Griselda			
CHAUCER (c. 1340–1400)	ENGLISH	REALISM	895
From *The Canterbury Tales:* The Prologue; The Nun's Priest's Tale; The Pardoner's Tale — The Complaint of Chaucer to His Purse			
RABELAIS (1494–1553)	FRENCH	ROMANTICISM	511
From *Gargantua:* The Author's Prologue; The Study of Gargantua — Old Plan; The Study of Gargantua — New Plan; Great Strife and Debate; How a Monk of Sevillé Saved the Abbey; How Pantagruel Persuadeth Panurge to Take Counsel of a Fool			
MONTAIGNE (1533–1592)	FRENCH	CLASSICISM	250
The Author to the Reader — That We Taste Nothing Pure — Of Commerce With Books — Of the Inconvenience of Greatness			
CERVANTES (1547–1616)	SPANISH	ROMANTICISM	522
From *Don Quixote:* The Quality and Way of Living of Don Quixote; Of Don Quixote's First Sally; Don Quixote Is Dubbed a Knight; The Adventure of the Windmills			
SPENSER (1554–1598)	ENGLISH	ROMANTICISM	534
A Letter of the Authors — From *The Faerie Queene:* Legend of the Knight of the Red Crosse			
SHAKESPEARE (1564–1616)	ENGLISH	ROMANTICISM	549
Songs fro them Plays — *Sonnets* — King Lear			
JONSON (1573–1637)	ENGLISH	CLASSICISM	257
Hymn to Diana — Song: To Celia — To Celia — To the Memory of My Beloved Master, William Shakespeare — A Song — Her Triumph			

	Nationality	Classification	Page

DONNE (1573–1631) — ENGLISH — SYMBOLISM — 817

The Anniversary — The Good-Morrow — Song — The Sun Rising — Woman's Constancy — The Undertaking — The Canonization — The Legacy — A Valediction: Forbidding Mourning

MILTON (1608–1674) — ENGLISH — CLASSICISM — 260

L'Allegro — Il Penseroso — Lycidas — *Sonnets* — Paradise Lost (Books I and II)

MOLIÈRE (1622–1673) — FRENCH — CLASSICISM — 287

The Misanthrope

RACINE (1639–1699) — FRENCH — CLASSICISM — 309

Phædra

DEFOE (1660–1731) — ENGLISH — REALISM — 920

A True Relation of the Apparition of Mrs. Veal

SWIFT (1667–1745) — ENGLISH — CLASSICISM — 328

From *Gulliver's Travels:* A Voyage to Laputa

POPE (1688–1744) — ENGLISH — CLASSICISM — 349

An Essay on Criticism — The Rape of the Lock

VOLTAIRE (1694–1778) — FRENCH — CLASSICISM — 366

Selections from *Candide*

ROUSSEAU (1712–1778) — FRENCH — ROMANTICISM — 596

A Discourse on the Origin of Inequality — From *Confessions:* The Stolen Ribbon; A Day's Excursion; Life at Les Charmettes; Rousseau's Opera Is Presented

GOETHE (1749–1832) — GERMAN — ROMANTICISM — 613

From *Faust:* Prologue in Heaven; Faust — Part I

BURNS (1759–1796) — ENGLISH — ROMANTICISM — 643

To a Mouse — Tam o' Shanter — Green Grow the Rashes, O — Of A' the Airts — Auld Lang Syne — John Anderson My Jo — Willie Brewed a Peck o' Maut — Ye Flowery Banks — A Red, Red Rose — Scots, Wha Hae — Highland Mary — Is There for Honest Poverty — O, Wert Thou in the Cauld Blast — Mary Morison

WORDSWORTH (1770–1850) — ENGLISH — ROMANTICISM — 652

Expostulation and Reply — The Tables Turned — Lines Composed Above Tintern Abbey — My Heart Leaps Up — To the Cuckoo — *Sonnets* — The Solitary Reaper — I Wandered Lonely as a Cloud — Ode to Duty — Ode on Intimations of Immortality — Preface to Lyrical Ballads

	Nationality	Classification	Page

COLERIDGE (1772–1834) — ENGLISH — ROMANTICISM — 670
Kubla Khan — Christabel — From *Biographia Literaria:*
Chapters XVII and XVIII

BYRON (1788–1824) — ENGLISH — ROMANTICISM — 685
Maid of Athens, Ere We Part — Sonnet on Chillon —
She Walks in Beauty — When We Two Parted — From
Childe Harold: Solitude; Rome — and the Vanity of Hu-
man Wishes — So We'll Go No More A-Roving — From
Don Juan: The Lake Poets — and Others; The Isles of
Greece

SHELLEY (1792–1822) — ENGLISH — ROMANTICISM — 700
Hymn to Intellectual Beauty — Ode to the West Wind
— To a Skylark — Ozymandias — Mutability — Adonais — To —— From *Prometheus Unbound:* The Future
of Society; The Ability of Man; The Goal Reached

KEATS (1795–1821) — ENGLISH — ROMANTICISM — 714
On First Looking into Chapman's Homer — Proem
(from *Endymion*) — When I Have Fears that I May Cease
to Be — Robin Hood — Lines on the Mermaid Tavern
— The Eve of St. Agnes — Ode on a Grecian Urn — Ode
to a Nightingale — La Belle Dame Sans Merci — Fame
— Lamia — Sonnet

HEINE (1797–1856) — GERMAN — ROMANTICISM — 732
The Mountain Echo — The Grenadiers — Whene'er I
Look Into Thine Eyes — A Pine Tree Stands So Lonely
— I Do Not Know Why This Confronts Me — Oh Lovely
Fishermaiden — The Yellow Moon Has Risen — Child,
You Are Like a Flower — Life in This World — Where
Is Now Your Precious Darling? — Doctrine — Night
Has Come

BALZAC (1799–1850) — FRENCH — REALISM — 925
Selection from *Old Goriot*

HUGO (1802–1885) — FRENCH — ROMANTICISM — 735
From *Les Misérables:* The Escape Through the Sewers

EMERSON (1803–1882) — AMERICAN — ROMANTICISM — 750
Written in Naples — Written at Rome — The Rhodora
— Each and All — The Sphinx — Musketaquid —
Days — Brahma — The American Scholar

HAWTHORNE (1804–1864) — AMERICAN — ROMANTICISM — 764
Young Goodman Brown — Ethan Brand

GOGOL (1809–1852) — RUSSIAN — REALISM — 937
The Cloak

	Nationality	Classification	Page
POE (1809–1849) The City in the Sea — The Valley of Unrest — The Haunted Palace — The Conqueror Worm — The Raven — Ulalume — The Bells — Eldorado — The Masque of the Red Death — Eleonora	AMERICAN	SYMBOLISM	820
TENNYSON (1809–1892) Morte d'Arthur — Ulysses — Break, Break, Break — Songs (from *The Princess*) — From *In Memoriam A.H.H.* — The Brook — The Higher Pantheism — The Revenge, A Ballad of the Fleet — Crossing the Bar	ENGLISH	ROMANTICISM	778
BROWNING (1812–1889) A Grammarian's Funeral — Pippa's Song — My Last Duchess — Soliloquy of the Spanish Cloister — The Lost Leader — Meeting at Night — Parting at Morning — Home-Thoughts, from Abroad — Home-Thoughts, from the Sea — The Bishop Orders His Tomb at Saint Praxed's Church — Evelyn Hope — Love Among the Ruins — Fra Lippo Lippi — Andrea Del Sarto — Prospice — Epilogue to *Asolando*	ENGLISH	ROMANTICISM	793
TURGENEV (1818–1883) Mumu	RUSSIAN	REALISM	951
WHITMAN (1819–1892) One's-self I Sing — On Journeys Through the States — The Song of the Open Road — Crossing Brooklyn Ferry — I Hear America Singing — Pioneers! O Pioneers! — O Captain! My Captain! — When Lilacs Last in the Dooryard Bloom'd — Come Up from the Fields Father — To a Locomotive in Winter	AMERICAN	REALISM	964
BAUDELAIRE (1821–1867) L'Invitation au Voyage — Anywhere Out of the World — The Clock — The Plaything of the Poor — Every Man His Chimæra — The Sadness of the Moon — Correspondences — The Flask — The Seven Old Men — The Death of the Poor — A Landscape — Exotic Fragrance — Music — The Flawed Bell	FRENCH	SYMBOLISM	833
DOSTOEVSKY (1821–1881) From *Crime and Punishment:* The Crime	RUSSIAN	REALISM	981
IBSEN (1828–1906) The Master Builder	NORWEGIAN	SYMBOLISM	839
TOLSTOY (1828–1910) From *Anna Karenina:* Farming in Old Russia; The Steeplechase; Anna Visits Her Son; Levin Finds His Faith	RUSSIAN	REALISM	989
ZOLA (1840–1902) From *L'Assommoir:* The Fight in the Laundry	FRENCH	NATURALISM	1091

	Nationality	Classification	Page
"Les Symbolistes"	FRENCH	SYMBOLISM	874
Paul Verlaine, Il Pleut Doucement sur la Ville — *Paul Verlaine*, À Clymène — *Henri de Régnier*, The Vase — *Arthur Rimbaud*, The Frenzied Ship — *Stéphane Mallarmé*, The Windows — *Stéphane Mallarmé*, Sea-Wind — *Stéphane Mallarmé*, L'Après-Midi d'un Faune — *Henri Bataille*, Memories — *Villiers de l'Isle-Adam*, Vox Populi — *Joris-Karl Huysmans*, Camaïeu in Red — *Stéphane Mallarmé*, In Autumn — *Henri de Régnier*, The Stairway — *Saint-Pol-Roux*, Butterflies			
James (1843–1916)	AMERICAN	IMPRESSIONISM	1113
The Liar			
Conrad (1857–1924)	ENGLISH	IMPRESSIONISM	1138
The Lagoon			
Chekhov (1860–1904)	RUSSIAN	REALISM	1008
The Schoolmistress — The Cherry Orchard			
Pirandello (1867–1936)	ITALIAN	REALISM	1034
The Jar			
Gorki (1868–1936)	RUSSIAN	NATURALISM	1099
Chums			
Claudel (1868–1955)	FRENCH	IMPRESSIONISM	1145
Selections from *The Satin Slipper*			
Mann (1875–1955)	GERMAN	REALISM	1045
The Infant Prodigy — From *The Magic Mountain:* Snow			
Joyce (1882–1941)	IRISH	EXPRESSIONISM	1171
From *Ulysses:* The Interment of Patrick Dignam			
Kafka (1883–1924)	CZECH	EXPRESSIONISM	1186
First Sorrow — A Hunger Artist			
Mansfield (1888–1923)	ENGLISH	IMPRESSIONISM	1162
The Voyage			
O'Neill (1888–1953)	AMERICAN	EXPRESSIONISM	1192
The Hairy Ape			
Eliot (1888–1965)	AMERICAN	EXPRESSIONISM	1212
Sweeney Among the Nightingales — Rhapsody on a Windy Night — The Hollow Men			
Faulkner (1897–1962)	AMERICAN	REALISM	1076
A Name for the City			
Hemingway (1899–1961)	AMERICAN	REALISM	1061
The Undefeated			

GUIDE TO THE TYPES OF LITERATURE

The Address

EMERSON
The American Scholar 756

Autobiography

ROUSSEAU
From *Confessions:*
The Stolen Ribbon 604
A Day's Excursion 606
Life at Les Charmettes . . . 608
Rousseau's Opera Is Presented . . 610

The Ballad

ENGLISH POPULAR BALLADS
Edward 466
Lord Thomas and Fair Annet . . . 467
Lamkin 468
The Twa Corbies 470
Sir Patrick Spence 470
The Dæmon Lover 470
Robin Hood's Death and Burial . . 471
Bonny Barbara Allan 472

TENNYSON
The Revenge, A Ballad of the Fleet . 790

Drama

ÆSCHYLUS
Agamemnon 71

SOPHOCLES
Antigone 93

EURIPIDES
Medea 111

ARISTOPHANES
The Frogs 131

MOLIÈRE
The Misanthrope 288

JEAN RACINE
Phædra 310

SHAKESPEARE
King Lear 555

GOETHE
From *Faust:*
Prologue in Heaven 614
Faust — Part I 615

IBSEN
The Master Builder 840

CHEKHOV
The Cherry Orchard 1013

PIRANDELLO
The Jar 1036

CLAUDEL
From *The Satin Slipper* . . . 1146

O'NEILL
The Hairy Ape 1193

Dramatic Monologue

TENNYSON
Ulysses 782

BROWNING
A Grammarian's Funeral . . . 794
My Last Duchess 796
Soliloquy of the Spanish Cloister . 796
The Bishop Orders His Tomb at Saint
Praxed's Church 798
Fra Lippo Lippi 801
Andrea Del Sarto 805

The Epic

HOMER
The *Iliad*, Books I, XVIII 12
The *Odyssey*, Books VI, IX, XXI . . 33

VIRGIL
The *Æneid*, Books II, IV, VI . . . 191

MILTON
Paradise Lost (Books I and II) . . 268

From the BEOWULF 427

From THE NIBELUNGENLIED

How Gunther Won Brunhild 443
How Sigfrid Was Slain 448

DANTE
From *The Divine Comedy:*
Hell (Cantos I–II–III–IV–V) . . . 474
Purgatory (Cantos I–II–III–IV) . . 482
Paradise (Cantos XXXI–XXXII–XXXIII) 488

SPENSER
From *The Faerie Queene:*
Legend of the Knight of the Red Crosse 537

The Mock Epic

BYRON
From *Don Juan:*
The Lake Poets — and Others . . . 696
The Isles of Greece 698

Epigrams

THEOCRITUS
For a Herdsman's Offering 175
For a Picture 175

Essays

PLATO
Dialogues:
The Apology 157

MARCUS AURELIUS
Meditations 234

MONTAIGNE
The Author to the Reader 251
That We Taste Nothing Pure . . . 252
Of Commerce With Books 253
Of the Inconvenience of Greatness . 255

ROUSSEAU
A Discourse on the Origin of Inequality . 597

Literary Criticism

ARISTOTLE
The Nature of Tragedy 169

WORDSWORTH
Preface to Lyrical Ballads 660

COLERIDGE
From *Biographia Literaria:*
Chapters XVII and XVIII 679

Lyric Poetry

HORACE
The Reconciliation 226

JONSON
Hymn to Diana 258
Song: To Celia 258
To Celia 258
To the Memory of My Beloved Master, William Shakespeare 258
A Song 259
Her Triumph 259

MILTON
Sonnets:
On His Being Arrived to the Age of Twenty-Three 267
On His Blindness 267
On Shakespeare 267

SHAKESPEARE
Songs from the Plays:
When icicles hang by the wall . . . 551
Who is Silvia? 551
Under the greenwood tree . . . 551
Blow, blow, thou winter wind! . . 551
O Mistress mine, where are you roaming? 551
Take, O, take those lips away . . . 551
Hark, hark! the lark 551
Fear no more the heat o' the sun . . 552
Full fathom five thy father lies . . 552
Sonnets:
When I consider everything that grows 552
Shall I compare thee to a summer's day? 552
As an unperfect actor on the stage . . 552
When in disgrace with fortune and men's eyes 553
When to the sessions of sweet silent thought 553
If thou survive my well-contented day . 553
O, how much more doth beauty beauteous seem 553
Not marble, nor the gilded monuments 553
When I have seen by Time's fell hand defaced 553
Since brass, nor stone, nor earth, nor boundless sea 554

That time of year thou mayst in me behold 554
How like a winter hath my absence been 554
To me, fair friend, you never can be old 554
When in the chronicle of wasted time . 554
Not mine own fears, nor the prophetic soul 554
O, never say that I was false of heart . 554
Let me not to the marriage of true minds 555
My mistress' eyes are nothing like the sun 555

BURNS
To a Mouse 644
Tam o' Shanter 645
Green Grow the Rashes, O . . . 647
Of A' the Airts 648
Auld Lang Syne 648
John Anderson My Jo 649
Willie Brewed a Peck o' Maut . . 649
Ye Flowery Banks 649
A Red, Red Rose 649
Scots, Wha Hae 650
Highland Mary 650
Is There for Honest Poverty . . . 650
O, Wert Thou in the Cauld Blast . . 651
Mary Morison 651

WORDSWORTH
Expostulation and Reply 653
The Tables Turned 653
My Heart Leaps Up 656
To the Cuckoo 656
Sonnets:
Composed Upon Westminster Bridge . 656
It Is a Beauteous Evening, Calm and Free 656
London, 1802 656
The World Is Too Much With Us . 657
The Solitary Reaper 657
I Wandered Lonely as a Cloud . . 657

BYRON
Maid of Athens, Ere We Part . . . 686
Sonnet on Chillon 686
She Walks in Beauty 687
When We Two Parted 687
From Childe Harold:
Solitude 687
Rome — and the Vanity of Human Wishes 690
So We'll Go No More A-Roving . . 696

SHELLEY
Hymn to Intellectual Beauty . . . 701
Ozymandias 704
Mutability 705

Adonais 705
To —— 712

KEATS
On First Looking into Chapman's Homer . 715
Proem (from Endymion) 715
When I Have Fears that I May Cease to Be 716
Robin Hood 716
Lines on the Mermaid Tavern . . . 717
The Eve of St. Agnes 717
La Belle Dame Sans Merci . . . 724
Fame 724
Sonnet 732

HEINE
The Mountain Echo 733
The Grenadiers 733
Whene'er I Look into Thine Eyes . . 733
A Pine Tree Stands So Lonely . . . 733
I Do Not Know Why This Confronts Me . 734
Oh Lovely Fishermaiden 734
The Yellow Moon Has Risen . . . 734
Child, You Are Like a Flower . . . 734
Life in This World 734
Where Is Now Your Precious Darling? . 734
Doctrine 735
Night Has Come 735

EMERSON
Written in Naples 752
Written at Rome 752
The Rhodora 752
Each and All 753
The Sphinx 753
Musketaquid 755
Days 755
Brahma 756

TENNYSON
Break, Break, Break 783
Songs (from The Princess) 783
The Brook 789
Crossing the Bar 792

BROWNING
Pippa's Song 796
The Lost Leader 797
Meeting at Night 798
Parting at Morning 798
Home-Thoughts, from Abroad . . . 798
Home-Thoughts, from the Sea . . . 798
Evelyn Hope 800
Love Among the Ruins 800
Prospice 808
Epilogue to Asolando 808

THE BIBLE

The Lord Is My Shepherd (Psalm xxiii) . . 816
God Is Our Refuge (Psalm xlvi) . . . 816
What Is Man? (Psalm viii) 1117
The Voice of the Lord (Psalm xxix) . . 1117
How Amiable Are Thy Tabernacles (Psalm
  lxxxiv) 1118

DONNE

The Anniversary 817
The Good-Morrow 818
Song 818
The Sun Rising 818
Woman's Constancy 819
The Undertaking 819
The Canonization 819
The Legacy 820
A Valediction: Forbidding Mourning . . 820

POE

The City in the Sea 822
The Valley of Unrest 822
The Haunted Palace 823
The Conqueror Worm 823
The Raven 824
Ulalume 826
The Bells 827
Eldorado 828

BAUDELAIRE

The Sadness of the Moon 837
Correspondences 837
The Flask 837
The Seven Old Men 837
The Death of the Poor 838
A Landscape 838
Exotic Fragrance 839
Music 839
The Flawed Bell 839

"LES SYMBOLISTES"

Paul Verlaine, Il Pleut Doucement sur la
  Ville 874
Paul Verlaine, À Clymène 874
Henri de Régnier, The Vase 874
Arthur Rimbaud, The Frenzied Ship . . 875
Stéphane Mallarmé, The Windows . . . 877
Stéphane Mallarmé, Sea-Wind . . . 877
Stéphane Mallarmé, L'Après-Midi d'un
  Faune 877
Henri Bataille, Memories 879

WHITMAN

One's-self I Sing 966
On Journeys Through the States . . . 966

The Song of the Open Road 966
Crossing Brooklyn Ferry 970
I Hear America Singing 973
Pioneers! O Pioneers! 974
O Captain! My Captain! 976
When Lilacs Last in the Dooryard Bloom'd 976
Come Up from the Fields Father . . . 980
To a Locomotive in Winter 980

ELIOT

Sweeney Among the Nightingales . . . 1213
Rhapsody on a Windy Night 1213
The Hollow Men 1214

The Ode

WORDSWORTH

Ode to Duty 657
Ode on Intimations of Immortality . . 658

SHELLEY

Ode to the West Wind 702
To a Skylark 703

KEATS

Ode on a Grecian Urn 722
Ode to a Nightingale 723

CHAUCER

The Complaint of Chaucer to His Purse . 919

Pastorals

THEOCRITUS

Daphnis and Menalcas 175
The Cyclops in Love 178

MILTON

L'Allegro 261
Il Penseroso 263
Lycidas 265

Philosophic Verse

LUCRETIUS

On the Nature of Things:
  Proem 181
  Substance Is Eternal 183
  The Soul Is Mortal 184
  Folly of the Fear of Death . . . 185
  The Origin of Life 187
  Origin of Mankind 188
  Beginnings of Civilization . . . 189

WORDSWORTH
Lines Composed Above Tintern Abbey . 654

SHELLEY
From *Prometheus Unbound:*
The Future of Society 712
The Ability of Man 713
The Goal Reached 714

TENNYSON
From *In Memoriam A.H.H.* 785
The Higher Pantheism 790

Poetic Narrative

OVID
Apollo and Daphne 404
Alpheus and Arethusa 406
Orpheus and Eurydice 407
Narcissus 408
The Rape of Proserpine 409
Dido to Æneas 410

COLERIDGE
Kubla Khan 671
Christabel 672

KEATS
Lamia 724

CHAUCER
From *The Canterbury Tales:*
The Prologue 897
The Nun's Priest's Tale 906
The Pardoner's Tale 912

Prose Narrative

THE BIBLE
The Creation of the World (Genesis) . . 55
The Story of Joseph and His Brethren
(Genesis) 56
The Giving of the Law (Exodus) . . 61
The Story of Samson (Judges) . . 61
Ruth (Ruth) 64
The Sermon on the Mount (Matthew) . 67

APULEIUS
From *The Golden Ass:*
The Robbers 413
Cupid and Psyche 419

BOCCACCIO
From *The Decameron:*
Introduction 494
Simona and Pasquino 502
Federigo's Falcon 503
Patient Griselda 506

HUGO
From *Les Misérables:*
The Escape Through the Sewers . . 736

HAWTHORNE
Young Goodman Brown 765
Ethan Brand 771

POE
The Masque of the Red Death . . . 828
Eleonora 831

BAUDELAIRE
L'Invitation au Voyage 834
Anywhere Out of the World . . . 835
The Clock 836
The Plaything of the Poor . . . 836
Every Man His Chimæra 836

"LES SYMBOLISTES"
Villiers de l'Isle-Adam, Vox Populi . 879
Joris-Karl Huysmans, Camaïeu in Red . 880
Stéphane Mallarmé, In Autumn . . 881
Henri de Régnier, The Stairway . . 881
Saint-Pol-Roux, Butterflies . . . 882

DEFOE
A True Relation of the Apparition of Mrs.
Veal 921

BALZAC
Selection from *Old Goriot* 926

GOGOL
The Cloak 938

TURGENEV
Mumu 951

DOSTOEVSKY
From *Crime and Punishment:*
The Crime 982

TOLSTOY
From *Anna Karenina:*
Farming in Old Russia 990
The Steeplechase 994

Anna Visits Her Son 997
Levin Finds His Faith 1001

CHEKHOV
The Schoolmistress 1009

MANN
The Infant Prodigy 1046
From *The Magic Mountain:*
Snow 1050

HEMINGWAY
The Undefeated 1062

FAULKNER
A Name for the City 1078

ZOLA
From *L'Assommoir:*
The Fight in the Laundry 1092

GORKI
Chums 1100

JAMES
The Liar 1114

CONRAD
The Lagoon 1139

MANSFIELD
The Voyage 1162

JOYCE
From *Ulysses:*
The Interment of Patrick Dignam . . 1173

KAFKA
First Sorrow 1187
A Hunger Artist 1188

The Romance

AUCASSIN AND NICOLETE 453

TENNYSON
Morte d'Arthur 780

Satire

THEOCRITUS
At the Festival of Adonis. 177

HORACE
Alphius 225
To Lycè 226
Contentment 227
The Bore 229
My Prayers With This I Used to Charge . 231

LUCIAN
Dialogues of the Dead:
Dialogue X — Charon and Hermes . . 240
Dialogues of the Gods:
Dialogue XX — The Judgment of Paris 242
Sale of Creeds 245

SWIFT
From *Gulliver's Travels:*
A Voyage to Laputa 329

POPE
An Essay on Criticism 350
The Rape of the Lock 357

VOLTAIRE
Selections from *Candide* 367

RABELAIS
From *Gargantua:*
The Author's Prologue . . . 511
The Study of Gargantua — Old Plan . 513
The Study of Gargantua — New Plan . 514
Great Strife and Debate 517
How a Monk of Sevillé Saved the Abbey 518
How Pantagruel Persuadeth Panurge to
Take Counsel of a Fool 520

CERVANTES
From *Don Quixote:*
The Quality and Way of Living of Don
Quixote 523
Of Don Quixote's First Sally . . . 525
Don Quixote is Dubbed a Knight . . 528
The Adventure of the Windmills . . 531

The Sermon

THE BIBLE
The Giving of the Law (Exodus) . . 61
The Sermon on the Mount (Matthew) . 67

INDEX

OF AUTHORS, TITLES, AND FIRST LINES OF POETRY

Author's names are printed in capitals and small capitals; the titles of both poetry and
prose selections, in italic type; and the first lines of the poetry selections, in roman type.

A Clymène, 874
A general silence fell; and all gave ear, 192
A gentle Knight was pricking on the plaine, 538
A povre wydwe, somdeel stape in age, 906
A thing of beauty is a joy for ever, 715
Ability of Man, The, 713–714
Adonais, 705–712
Adventure of the Windmills, The, 531–534
Aeneid, The (selections), 191–224
AESCHYLUS, 70–92
Afoot and light-hearted I take to the open road, 966
After such words and tears, he flung free rein, 212
Agamemnon, 71–92
"Ah, what can ail thee, Knight-at-arms," 724
All Kings, and all their favourites, 817
Alone in Rome. Why, Rome is lonely too, 752
Alpheus and Arethusa, 406–407
Alphius, 225–226
American Scholar, The, 756–764
And now what cause, 189
Andrea Del Sarto, 805–808
Anna Karenina (selections), 990–1008
Anna Visits Her Son, 997–1001
Anniversary, The, 817–818
Antigone, 93–109
Anywhere Out of the World, 835–836
Apeneck Sweeney spreads his knees, 1213
Apollo and Daphne, 404–406
Apology, The, 157–168
APULEIUS, 413–427
ARISTOPHANES, 130–156
ARISTOTLE, 169–175
As an unperfect actor on the stage, 552
As down the slow impassive streams I came, 875
As I was walking all alone, 470
As virtuous men pass mildly away, 820
Ask me no more: the moon may draw the sea, 784
At Flores in the Azores Sir Richard Grenville lay, 790
At sad slow pace across the vale, 733
At the Festival of Adonis, 177–178
At the midnight in the silence of the sleeptime, 808
Aucassin and Nicolete, 453–466
Auld Lang Syne, 648
Author to the Reader, The, 251–252
Author's Prologue, The (from *Gargantua*), 511–513

Ballads, English Popular, 466–472
BALZAC, HONORÉ DE, 925–937
BATAILLE, HENRI, 879
BAUDELAIRE, CHARLES, 833–839
Beat on the drum and blow the fife, 735
Beautiful Evelyn Hope is dead! 800
Because I was content with these poor fields, 755
Beginnings of Civilization, 189–191
Behold her, single in the field, 657
Bells, The, 827–828
Beowulf (selection), 427–442
Bible, The (selections), 54–70, 816, 1112–1113
Biographia Literaria (selections), 679–685
Bishop Orders His Tomb at Saint Praxed's Church, The, 798–800

Bitter and sweet it is, in winter night, 839
Blow, blow, thou winter wind! 551
Bob Southey! You're a poet — Poet-laureate, 696
BOCCACCIO, GIOVANNI, 493–510
Bonny Barbara Allan, 472
Bore, The, 229–231
Brahma, 756
Break, Break, Break, 783
Bright star, would I were steadfast as thou art, 732
Brook, The, 789–790
BROWNING, ROBERT, 793–809
BURNS, ROBERT, 643–651
Busy old fool, unruly Sun, 818
But anxious cares the pensive nymph opprest, 363
But do not let us quarrel any more, 805
But mortal man, 188
Butterflies, 882
By this the Northerne wagoner had set, 544
BYRON, LORD (GEORGE GORDON), 685–700

Camaïeu in Red, 880–881
Candide (selections), 367–384
Canonization, The, 819
Canterbury Tales, The (selections), 896–919
CERVANTES, 522–534
CHAUCER, GEOFFREY, 895–919
CHEKHOV, ANTON, 1008–1034
Cherry Orchard, The, 1013–1034
Child, You Are Like a Flower, 734
Childe Harold (selections), 687–696
Christabel, 672–679
Chums, 1100–1108
City in the Sea, The, 822
CLAUDEL, PAUL, 1145–1162
Cloak, The, 938–951
Clock, The, 836
Close by those meads, for ever crowned with flowers, 361
COLERIDGE, SAMUEL TAYLOR, 670–685
Come down, O maid, from yonder mountain height, 785
Come, my Celia, let us prove, 258
Come my tan-faced children, 974
Come Up from the Fields Father, 980
Come up from the fields father, here's a letter from our Pete, 980
Complaint of Chaucer to His Purse, The, 919
Composed Upon Westminster Bridge, 656
Confessions (selections), 604–612
Conqueror Worm, The, 823
CONRAD, JOSEPH, 1138–1144
Contentment, 227–229
Correspondences, 837
Creation of the World, The, 55–56
Crime and Punishment (selection), 982–989
Crime, The, 982–989
Crossing Brooklyn Ferry, 970
Crossing the Bar, 792
Cupid and Psyche, 419–427
Cyclops in Love, The, 178–180

Daemon Lover, The, 470–471

DANTE ALIGHIERI, 473-492
Daphnis and Menalcas, 175-177
Daughters of Time, the hypocritic Days, 755
Day's Excursion, A, 606-608
Days, 755
Death is consoler and Death brings to life, 838
Death of the Poor, The, 838
Decameron, The (selections), 494-510
DEFOE, DANIEL, 920-925
Dialogues of the Dead (selection), 240-242
Dialogues of the Gods (selection), 242-244
Dido to Aeneas, 410-412
Discourse on the Origin of Inequality, A, 597-604
Divine Comedy, The (selection), 474-492
Doctrine, 735
Don Juan (selections), 696-700
Don Quixote (selections), 523-534
Don Quixote Is Dubbed a Knight, 528-531
DONNE, JOHN, 817-820
DOSTOEVSKY, FYODOR, 981-989
Drink to me only with thine eyes, 258

Each and All, 753
Each matin bell, the Baron saith, 676
Earth has not anything to show more fair, 656
Edward, 466-467
Eldorado, 828
Eleonora, 831-833
ELIOT, T. S., 1212-1215
EMERSON, RALPH WALDO, 750-764
Endymion (proem from), 715-716
English Popular Ballads, 466-472
Epigram: For a Herdsman's Offering, 175
Epigram: For a Picture, 175
Epilogue to Asolando, 808-809
Escape Through the Sewers, The, 736-750
Essay on Criticism, An, 350-357
Eternal Spirit of the chainless Mind! 686
Ethan Brand, 771-778
EURIPIDES, 110-130
Eve of St. Agnes, The, 717-722
Evelyn Hope, 800
Every Man His Chimaera, 836-837
Exotic Fragrance, 839
Expostulation and Reply, 653

Faerie Queene, The (selection), 537-549
Fame, 724
Fame, like a wayward Girl, will still be coy, 724
Farming in Old Russia, 990-994
FAULKNER, WILLIAM, 1076-1086
Faust (selection), 614-643
Fear death? — to feel the fog in my throat, 808
Fear no more the heat o' the sun, 552
Federigo's Falcon, 503-506
Fight in the Laundry, The, 1092-1099
First Part of the Tragedy (Faust), 615-643
First Sorrow, 1187-1188
Five years have passed; five summers, with the length,
    654
Flask, The, 837
Flawed Bell, The, 839
Flood-tide below me! I see you face to face! 971
Folly of the Fear of Death, 185-187
For auld lang syne, my dear, 648
For God's sake hold your tongue, and let me love, 819
Fra Lippo Lippi, 801-805
Frenzied Ship, The, 875-877
Frogs, The, 131-156
Full fathom five thy father lies, 552
Future of Society, The, 712-713

Gaily bedight, 828
Gargantua (selection), 511-522
Give unto the Lord, O ye mighty, 1113
Giving of the Law, The, 61
Go, and catch a falling star, 818
Goal Reached, The, 714
God Is Our Refuge, 816
God is our refuge and strength, 816
GOETHE, JOHANN WOLFGANG VON, 613-643
GOGOL, NICOLAI, 937-951
Golden Ass, The (selection), 413-427
Good-Morrow, The, 818
GORKI, MAXIM, 1099-1108
Grammarian's Funeral, A, 794-796
Great Strife and Debate, 517-518
Green Grow the Rashes, O, 647-648
Grenadiers, The, 733
Gr-r-r — there go, my heart's abhorrence! 796
Gulliver's Travels (selection), 329-348

Hail to thee, blithe Spirit! 703
Hairy Ape, The, 1193-1212
Happy the man, in busy schemes unskilled, 225
Hark, hark! the lark at heaven's gate sings, 551
Haunted Palace, The, 823
HAWTHORNE, NATHANIEL, 764-778
Hear the sledges with the bells, 827
HEINE, HEINRICH, 732-735
Hell (selection), 474-481
HEMINGWAY, ERNEST, 1061-1075
Hence, loathèd Melancholy, 261
Hence, vain deluding Joys, 263
Her Triumph, 259-260
Heroides (selection), 410-412
High on a throne of royal state, which far, 276
Higher Pantheism, The, 790
Highland Mary, 650
Hollow Men, The, 1214-1215
Home they brought her warrior dead, 784
Home-Thoughts, from Abroad, 798
Home-Thoughts, from the Sea, 798
HOMER, 11-54
HORACE, 224-232
How a Monk of Sevillé Saved the Abbey, 518-520
How Amiable Are Thy Tabernacles, 1113
How Gunther Won Brunhild, 443-448
How like a winter hath my absence been, 554
*How Pantagruel Persuadeth Panurge to Take Counsel of
    a Fool*, 520-522
How Sigfrid Was Slain, 448-452
How soon hath Time, the subtle thief of youth, 267
HUGO, VICTOR, 735-750
Hunger Artist, A, 1188-1192
HUYSMANS, JORIS-KARL, 880-881
Hymn to Diana, 258
Hymn to Intellectual Beauty, 701-702

I am poor brother Lippo, by your leave! 801
I come from haunts of coot and hern, 789
I Do Not Know Why This Confronts Me, 734
I have done one braver thing, 819
I Hear America Singing, 973-974
I hear America singing, the varied carols I hear, 973
I held it truth, with him who sings, 785
I met a traveller from an antique land, 704
I Wandered Lonely as a Cloud, 657
I weep for Adonais — he is dead! 706
I wonder by my troth, what thou and I, 818
I would immortalize these nymphs: so bright, 877

I would, when I compose my solemn verse, 838
IBSEN, HENRIK, 839–873
If the red slayer think he slays, 756
If thou survive my well-contented day, 553
Il Penseroso, 263–265
Il Pleut Doucement sur la Ville, 874
Iliad, The (selections), 12–33
In Autumn, 881
In May, when sea-winds pierced our solitudes, 752
In Memoriam A. H. H. (selections), 785–789
In Nature's temple living pillars rise, 837
In the beginning, earth gave forth, around, 187
In the greenest of our valleys, 823
In Xanadu did Kubla Khan, 672
Infant Prodigy, The, 1046–1049
Interment of Patrick Dignam, The, 1173–1186
Introduction (from The Decameron), 494–502
Is There for Honest Poverty, 650–651
Isles of Greece, The, 698–700
It chanced that I, the other day, 229
It's Lamkin was a mason good, 468
It Is a Beauteous Evening, Calm and Free, 656
It little profits that an idle king, 782
It was in and about the Martinmas time, 472

JAMES, HENRY, 1113–1137
Jar, The, 1036–1044
John Anderson My Jo, 649
John Anderson my jo, John, 649
JONSON, BEN, 257–259
Joseph and His Brethren, The Story of, 56–61
JOYCE, JAMES, 1171–1186
Judgment of Paris, The, 242–244
Just for a handful of silver he left us, 797

KAFKA, FRANZ, 1186–1192
KEATS, JOHN, 714–732
King Lear, The Tragedy of, 555–595
Kubla Khan, 671–672

L'Allegro, 261–263
L'Après-Midi d'un Faune, 877–878
L'Assommoir (selection), 1092–1099
L'Invitation au Voyage, 834–835
L'Isle-Adam, Villiers de, 879–880
La Belle Dame Sans Merci, 724
Lagoon, The, 1139–1144
Lake Leman woos me with its crystal face, 687
Lake Poets — and Others, The, 696–697
Lamia, 724–732
Lamkin, 468–470
Landscape, A, 838–839
Launch me, O music, whither on the soundless, 839
Learn then what MORALS Critics ought to show, 355
Legacy, The, 820
Legend of the Knight of the Red Crosse, 537–549
Les Misérables (selection), 736–750
LES SYMBOLISTES, 874–882
Let me not to the marriage of true minds, 555
Let us begin and carry up this corpse, 794
Letter of the Authors, A, 535–537
Levin Finds His Faith, 1001–1008
Liar, The, 1114–1137
Life at Les Charmettes, 608–610
Life in This World, 734
Life in this world is a muddled existence, 734
Lines Composed Above Tintern Abbey, 654–655
Lines on the Mermaid Tavern, 717
Little thinks, in the field, yon red-cloaked clown, 753
Lo! Death has reared himself a throne, 822
Lo! I, the man whose Muse whylome did maske, 537

Lo! 'tis a gala night, 823
London, 1802, 656
Lord Is My Shepherd, The, 816
Lord Thomas and Fair Annet, 467–468
"Lordynges," quod he, "in chirches whan I preche," 920
Lost Leader, The, 797–798
Love Among the Ruins, 800–801
Love in a hut, with water and a crust, 729
LUCIAN, 240–250
LUCRETIUS, 180–191
Lycidas, 265–267

Magic Mountain, The (selection), 1050–1061
Maid of Athens, Ere We Part, 686
MALLARMÉ, STÉPHANE, 877–878, 881
Man, oh, not men! a chain of linkèd thought, 713
MANN, THOMAS, 1045–1061
MANSFIELD, KATHERINE, 1162–1166
MARCUS AURELIUS (ANTONINUS), 233–239
Mary Morison, 651
Masque of the Red Death, The, 828–831
Master Builder, The, 840–873
Medea, 111–130
Meditations, 234–239
Meeting at Night, 798
Memories, 879
Memories are rooms without a lock, 879
Metamorphoses, The (selections), 404–410
MILTON, JOHN, 260–286
Milton! thou shouldst be living at this hour, 656
Misanthrope, The, 288–309
MOLIÈRE, 287–309
MONTAIGNE, MICHAEL EYQUEM DE, 250–257
Morte d'Arthur, 780–782
Mother of Rome, delight of Gods and men, 181
Mountain Echo, The, 733
Much have I traveled in the realms of gold, 715
Mumu, 951–964
Music, 839
Musketaquid, 755
Mutability, 705
My heart aches, and a drowsy numbness pains, 723
My Heart Leaps Up, 656
My heart leaps up when I behold, 656
My heavy hammer sounded through the air, 874
My Last Duchess, 796
My mistress' eyes are nothing like the sun, 555
My Prayers with This I Used to Charge, 231–233
Mystical strains unheard, 874

Name for the City, A, 1078–1086
Narcissus, 408–409
Nature of Tragedy, The, 169–175
Nibelungenlied, The (selections), 442–452
Night Has Come, 735
Night has come with silent footsteps, 735
No! those days are gone away, 716
Nobly, nobly Cape Saint Vincent to the Northwest
  died away, 798
Not marble, nor the gilded monuments, 553
Not mine own fears, nor the prophetic soul, 554
Not with more glories, in th' ethereal plain, 359
Now come: that thou mayst able to be to know, 184
Now felt the Queen the sharp, slow-gathering pangs, 202
Now sleeps the crimson petal, now the white, 784
Now thou hast lov'd me one whole day, 819
Nun's Priest's Tale, The, 906–912

O blithe New-comer! I have heard, 656
O Captain! My Captain! 976

O Captain! my Captain! our fearful trip is done, 976
O do not wanton with those eyes, 259
O, how much more doth beauty beauteous seem, 553
O Lord our Lord, 1112
O Mary, at thy window be! 651
O Mistress mine, where are you roaming? 551
O, my luve is like a red, red rose, 649
O, never say that I was false of heart, 554
O swarming city, city full of dreams, 837
O, Wert Thou in the Cauld Blast, 651
"O where have you been, my long, long love," 470
O wild West Wind, thou breath of Autumn's being, 702
Ode on a Grecian Urn, 722–723
Ode on Intimations of Immortality, 658–660
Ode to a Nightingale, 723–724
Ode to Duty, 657–658
Ode to the West Wind, 702–703
Odyssey, The (selections), 33–54
Of A' the Airts, 648
Of a' the airts the wind can blaw, 648
Of all the causes which conspire to blind, 352
Of Commerce with Books, 253–255
Of Don Quixote's First Sally, 525–528
Of Man's first disobedience, and the fruit, 268
Of the Inconvenience of Greatness, 255–257
Oh Love! no habitant of earth thou art, 690
Oh Lovely Fishermaiden, 734
Oh, to be in England, 798
Old Goriot (selection), 926–937
O'NEILL, EUGENE, 1192–1212
On First Looking into Chapman's Homer, 715
On His Being Arrived to the Age of Twenty-Three, 267
On His Blindness, 267
On Journeys Through the States, 966
On journeys through the States we start, 966
On Shakespeare, 267–268
On the Nature of Things (selections), 181–191
Once it smiled a silent dell, 822
Once upon a midnight dreary, while I pondered, weak
    and weary, 824
One word is too often profaned, 712
One's-self I Sing, 966
One's-self I sing, a simple separate person, 966
Origin of Life, The, 187–188
Origin of Mankind, 188–189
Orpheus and Eurydice, 407–408
OVID (PUBLIUS OVIDIUS NASO), 404–412
Ozymandias, 704

Paradise (selection), 488–492
Paradise Lost (selection), 268–286
Pardoner's Tale, The, 912–919
Parting at Morning, 798
Patient Griselda, 506–510
Phaedra, 310–328
Pine Tree Stands So Lonely, A, 733–734
Pioneers! O Pioneers! 974–976
Pippa's Song, 796
PIRANDELLO, LUIGI, 1034–1044
PLATO, 156–168
Plaything of the Poor, The, 836
POE, EDGAR ALLAN, 820–833
POPE, ALEXANDER, 349–366
Preface to Lyrical Ballads, 660–670
Proem (from *Endymion*), 715–716
Proem (from *On the Nature of Things*), 181–183
Prologue (from *Beowulf*), 428–442
Prologue, The (Chaucer), 897–906
Prologue in Heaven, 614–615
Prometheus Unbound (selections), 712–714

Prospice, 808
Purgatory (selection), 482–488

Quality and Way of Living of Don Quixote, The, 523–525
Queen and Huntress, chaste and fair, 258

RABELAIS, FRANÇOIS, 511–522
RACINE, JEAN, 309–328
Rape of Proserpine, The, 409–410
Rape of the Lock, The, 357–366
Raven, The, 824–825
Reconciliation, The, 226
Red, Red Rose, A, 649–650
RÉGNIER, HENRI DE, 874–875, 881–882
Revenge, The, 790–792
Rhapsody on a Windy Night, 1213–1214
Rhodora, The, 752–753
RIMBAUD, ARTHUR, 875–877
Robbers, The, 413–419
Robin Hood, 716–717
Robin Hood's Death and Burial, 471–472
Rome — and the Vanity of Human Wishes, 690–696
Round the cape of a sudden came the sea, 798
ROUSSEAU, JEAN JACQUES, 596–612
Rousseau's Opera Is Presented at Court, 610–612
Ruth, 64–67

Sadness of the Moon, The, 837
St. Agnes' Eve — Ah, bitter chill it was! 717
SAINT-POL-ROUX, 882
Sale of Creeds, 245–250
Samson, The Story of, 61–64
Satin Slipper, The (selections), 1046–1062
Schoolmistress, The, 1009–1013
Scots, Wha Hae, 650
Scots, wha hae wi' Wallace bled, 650
Sea-Wind, 877
See the chariot at hand here of love, 259
Sermon on the Mount, The, 67–70
Seven Old Men, The, 837–838
SHAKESPEARE, WILLIAM, 549–595
Shall I compare thee to a summer's day? 552
She said: the pitying audience melt in tears, 365
She Walks in Beauty, 687
She walks in beauty, like the night, 687
SHELLEY, PERCY BYSSHE, 700–714
Simona and Pasquino, 502–503
Since brass, nor stone, nor earth, nor boundless sea, 554
Sir Patrick Spence, 470
Snow, 1050–1061
So all day long the noise of battle rolled, 780
So We'll Go No More A-Roving, 696
Soliloquy of the Spanish Cloister, 796–797
Solitary Reaper, The, 657
Solitude, 687–690
Song (Donne), 818
Song, A (Jonson), 259
Song of the Open Road, The, 966–970
Song: To Celia, 258
Songs from the Plays (Shakespeare), 551–552
Songs from The Princess, 783–785
Sonnet (Keats), 732
Sonnet on Chillon, 686–687
Sonnets (Shakespeare), 552–555
SOPHOCLES, 92–109
Soul is Mortal, The, 184–185
Souls of Poets dead and gone, 717
SPENSER, EDMUND, 534–549
Sphinx, The, 753–755
Stairway, The, 881–882

Steeplechase, The, 994–997
Stern Daughter of the Voice of God! 657
Stolen Ribbon, The, 604–606
Study of Gargantua — Old Plan, The, 513–514
Study of Gargantua — New Plan, The, 514–517
Substance is Eternal, 183–184
Sun Rising, The, 818
Sunset and evening star, 792
Sweeney Among the Nightingales, 1213
Sweet and low, sweet and low, 783
SWIFT, JONATHAN, 328–348

Tables Turned, The, 653–654
Take, O, take those lips away, 551
Tam o' Shanter, 645–647
Tears fall within mine heart, 874
Tears, idle tears, I know not what they mean, 784
Tell me, Maecenas, if you can, 227
TENNYSON, ALFRED, LORD, 778–792
That time of year thou mayst in me behold, 554
That We Taste Nothing Pure, 252–253
That's my last Duchess painted on the wall, 796
The awful shadow of some unseen Power, 701
The flesh is sad, alas! and all the books are read, 877
The flower that smiles to-day, 705
The gray sea and the long black land, 798
The king sits in Dumferling toune, 470
The Lord is my shepherd; I shall not want, 816
The Moon more indolently dreams to-night, 837
The skies they were ashen and sober, 826
The Sphinx is drowsy, 753
The splendor falls on castle walls, 784
The sun, the moon, the stars, the seas, the hills and the plains, 790
The world is too much with us; late and soon, 657
The year's at the spring, 796
Thee for my recitative, 980
THEOCRITUS, 175–180
There are some powerful odors that can pass, 837
There was a time when meadow, grove, and stream, 658
Therefore death to us, 185
This is the day, which down the void abysm, 714
This terror, then, this darkness of the mind, 183
Thou still unravished bride of quietness, 722
Though your drink were the Tanais, chillest of rivers, 226
Thus, usually, when *he* was asked to sing, 698
Tired of the almshouse drear, whose rank fumes crawl, 877
'Tis hard to say, if greater want of skill, 350
'Tis the middle of night by the castle clock, 672
To ———, 712
To a Locomotive in Winter, 980–981
To a Mouse, 644–645
To a Skylark, 703–704
To Celia, 258
To draw no envy, Shakespeare, on thy name, 258
To Lycè, 226
To me, fair friend, you never can be old, 554
To the Cuckoo, 656
To the Memory of My Beloved Master, William Shakespeare, 258–259
To yow, my purse, and to noon other wight, 919
TOLSTOY, LEO, 989–1008
True Relation of the Apparition of Mrs. Veal, A, 921–925
TURGENEV, IVAN, 951–964
Twa Corbies, The, 470
Twelve o'clock, 1213
Two grenadiers travell'd tow'rds France one day, 733

Ulalume, 826
Ulysses (Joyce) (selection), 1172–1186
Ulysses (Tennyson), 782–783
Undefeated, The, 1062–1075
Under the greenwood tree, 551
Undertaking, The, 819
Up! up! my friend, and quit your books, 653
Upon a time, before the faery broods, 725

Valediction, A: Forbidding Mourning, 820
Valley of Unrest, The, 822–823
Vanity, saith the preacher, vanity! 798
Vase, The, 874–875
VERLAINE, PAUL, 874
VIRGIL, 191–224
Voice of the Lord, The, 1113
VOLTAIRE, 366–384
Vox Populi, 879–880
Voyage, The, 1162–1166
Voyage to Laputa, A (selections), 329–348

We are na fou, we're nae that fou, 649
We are the hollow men, 1214
We are what we are made; each following day, 752
Wee, sleekit, cowrin, tim'rous beastie, 644
Whan that Aprille with his shoures soote, 897
What dire offence from amorous causes springs, 358
What Is Man? 1112
What needs my Shakespeare for his honored bones, 267
When chapman billies leave the street, 645
When I consider everything that grows, 552
When I consider how my light is spent, 267
When I died last, and, Dear, I die, 820
When I Have Fears that I May Cease to Be, 716
When I have seen by Time's fell hand defaced, 553
When icicles hang by the wall, 551
When in disgrace with fortune and men's eyes, 553
When in the chronicle of wasted time, 554
When Lilacs Last in the Dooryard Bloom'd, 976–980
When Robin Hood and Little John, 471
When to the sessions of sweet silent thought, 553
When We Two Parted, 687
When, with closed eyes in the warm autumn night, 830
Whene'er I Look Into Thine Eyes, 733
Where Is Now Your Precious Darling? 734
Where the quiet-colored end of evening smiles, 800
Whilst I was dear and thou were kind, 226
WHITMAN, WALT, 964–981
Who is Silvia? what is she, 551
"Why dois your brand sae drap wi bluid, Edward, Edward," 466
"Why, William, on that old gray stone," 653
Willie Brewed a Peck o' Maut, 649
Windows, The, 877
Woman's Constancy, 819
WORDSWORTH, WILLIAM, 652–670
World is Too Much With Us, The, 657
Written at Rome, 752
Written in Naples, 752

Ye banks and braes and streams around, 650
Ye Flowery Banks, 649
Ye flowery banks o' bonie Doon, 649
Yellow Moon Has Risen, The, 734
Yet once more, O ye Laurels, and once more, 265
Young Goodman Brown, 765–771

ZOLA, ÉMILE, 1091–1099